D0147033

FIFTH EDITION

Cognitive Neuroscience

The Biology of the Mind

MICHAEL S. GAZZANIGA
University of California, Santa Barbara

RICHARD B. IVRY
University of California, Berkeley

GEORGE R. MANGUN
University of California, Davis

With special appreciation for the Fifth Edition to Rebecca A. Gazzaniga, MD

W. W. NORTON & COMPANY
NEW YORK · LONDON

W. W. Norton & Company has been independent since its founding in 1923, when William Warder Norton and Mary D. Herter Norton first published lectures delivered at the People's Institute, the adult education division of New York City's Cooper Union. The firm soon expanded its program beyond the Institute, publishing books by celebrated academics from America and abroad. By midcentury, the two major pillars of Norton's publishing program—trade books and college texts—were firmly established. In the 1950s, the Norton family transferred control of the company to its employees, and today—with a staff of four hundred and a comparable number of trade, college, and professional titles published each year—W. W. Norton & Company stands as the largest and oldest publishing house owned wholly by its employees.

Printed in Canada

Editor: Sheri Snavely

Senior Developmental Editor: Andrew Sobel

Senior Associate Managing Editor, College: Carla L. Talmadge

Assistant Editor: Eve Sanoussi

Managing Editor, College: Marian Johnson

Managing Editor, College Digital Media: Kim Yi

Associate Director of Production, College: Benjamin Reynolds

Media Editor: Kaitlin Coats

Associate Media Editor: Victoria Reuter

Media Project Editor: Danielle Belfiore

Media Editorial Assistant: Allison Smith

Ebook Production Manager: Danielle Lehmann

Marketing Manager, Psychology: Ashley Sherwood

Designer: Juan Paolo Francisco

Director of College Permissions: Megan Schindel

College Permissions Specialist: Bethany Salminen

Photo Editor: Trish Marx

Composition: MPS North America LLC

Illustrations: Quade Paul, Echo Medical Media LLC

Manufacturing: Transcontinental Interglobe—Beauceville, Quebec

Permission to use copyrighted material is included in the back matter.

Library of Congress Cataloging-in-Publication Data

Names: Gazzaniga, Michael S., author. | Ivry, Richard B., author. | Mangun, G. R. (George Ronald), 1956- author.
Title: Cognitive neuroscience : the biology of the mind / Michael S. Gazzaniga, University of California, Santa Barbara, Richard B. Ivry, University of California, Berkeley, George R. Mangun, University of California, Davis ; with special appreciation for the fifth edition to Rebecca A. Gazzaniga, M.D.
Description: Fifth edition. | New York : W.W. Norton & Company, 2019. | Includes bibliographical references and index.
Identifiers: LCCN 2018039129 | **ISBN 9780393603170 (hardcover)**
Subjects: LCSH: Cognitive neuroscience.
Classification: LCC QP360.5 .G39 2019 | DDC 612.8/233—dc23 LC record available at https://lccn.loc.gov/2018039129

W. W. Norton & Company, Inc., 500 Fifth Avenue, New York, NY 10110
wwnorton.com
W. W. Norton & Company Ltd., 15 Carlisle Street, London W1D 3BS

1 2 3 4 5 6 7 8 9 0

For Lilly, Emmy, Garth, Dante, Rebecca, and Leonardo

M.S.G.

For Henry and Sam

R.B.I.

For Nicholas and Alexander

G.R.M.

About the Authors

Michael S. Gazzaniga is the director of the Sage Center for the Study of the Mind at the University of California, Santa Barbara. He received a PhD from the California Institute of Technology in 1964, where he worked with Roger Sperry and had primary responsibility for initiating human split-brain research. He has carried out extensive studies on both subhuman primate and human behavior and cognition. He established the Program in Cognitive Neuroscience at Cornell Medical School, the Center for Cognitive Neuroscience at Dartmouth College, and the Center for Neuroscience at UC Davis. He is the founding editor of the *Journal of Cognitive Neuroscience* and also a founder of the Cognitive Neuroscience Society. For 20 years he directed the Summer Institute in Cognitive Neuroscience, and he serves as editor in chief of the major reference text *The Cognitive Neurosciences.* He was a member of the President's Council on Bioethics from 2001 to 2009. He is a member of the American Academy of Arts and Sciences, the National Academy of Medicine, and the National Academy of Sciences.

Richard B. Ivry is a professor of psychology and neuroscience at the University of California, Berkeley. He received his PhD from the University of Oregon in 1986, working with Steven Keele on a series of studies that helped bring the methods of cognitive neuroscience into the domain of motor control. His research program focuses on human performance, asking how cortical and subcortical networks in the brain select, initiate, and control movements. At Berkeley, he was the director of the Institute of Cognitive and Brain Sciences for 10 years and a founding member of the Helen Wills Neuroscience Institute. After serving as an associate editor for the *Journal of Cognitive Neuroscience* for 13 years, he is now a senior editor at *eLife*. His research accomplishments have been recognized with numerous awards, including the Troland Award from the National Academy of Sciences and the William James Fellow Award for lifetime achievement from the Association for Psychological Science.

George R. Mangun is a professor of psychology and neurology at the University of California, Davis. He received his PhD in neuroscience from the University of California, San Diego, in 1987, training with Steven A. Hillyard in human cognitive electrophysiology. His research investigates brain attention mechanisms using multimodal brain imaging. He founded and directed the Center for Cognitive Neuroscience at Duke University, and the Center for Mind and Brain at UC Davis, where he also served as dean of social sciences. He served as editor of the journal *Cognitive Brain Research*, was a member (with Gazzaniga) of the founding committee of the Cognitive Neuroscience Society, and is an associate editor of the *Journal of Cognitive Neuroscience.* He is a fellow of the Association for Psychological Science, and of the American Association for the Advancement of Science.

Brief Contents

Preface

Welcome to the Fifth Edition! When cognitive neuroscience emerged in the late 1970s, it remained to be seen whether this new field would have "legs." Today, the answer is clear: the field has blossomed in spectacular fashion. Cognitive neuroscience is well represented at all research universities, providing researchers and graduate students with the tools and opportunities to develop the interdisciplinary research programs that are the mainstay of the field. Multiple journals, some designed to cover the entire field, and others specialized for particular methodologies or research themes, have been launched to provide venues to report the latest findings. The number of papers increases at an exponential rate. The Cognitive Neuroscience Society has also flourished and just celebrated its 25th year.

The fundamental challenge we faced in laying the groundwork for our early editions was to determine the basic principles that make cognitive neuroscience distinct from physiological psychology, neuroscience, cognitive psychology, and neuropsychology. It is now obvious that cognitive neuroscience overlaps with, and synthesizes, these disciplinary approaches as researchers aim to understand the neural bases of cognition. In addition, cognitive neuroscience increasingly informs and is informed by disciplines outside the mind–brain sciences, such as systems science and physics, as exemplified by our new Chapter 14: "The Consciousness Problem."

As in previous editions of this book, we continue to seek a balance between psychological theory, with its focus on the mind, and the neuropsychological and neuroscientific evidence about the brain that informs this theory. We make liberal use of patient case studies to illustrate essential points and observations that provide keys to understanding the architecture of cognition, rather than providing an exhaustive description of brain disorders. In every section, we strive to include the most current information and theoretical views, supported by evidence from the cutting-edge technologies that are such a driving force in cognitive neuroscience. In contrast to purely cognitive or neuropsychological approaches, this text emphasizes the convergence of evidence that is a crucial aspect of any science, particularly studies of higher mental function. To complete the story, we also provide examples of research that uses computational techniques.

Teaching students to think and ask questions like cognitive neuroscientists is a major goal of our text. As cognitive neuroscientists, we examine mind–brain relationships using a wide range of techniques, such as functional and structural brain imaging, neurophysiological recording in animals, human EEG and MEG recording, brain stimulation methods, and analysis of syndromes resulting from brain damage. We highlight the strengths and weaknesses of these methods to demonstrate how these techniques must be used in a complementary manner.

We want our readers to learn what questions to ask, how to choose the tools and design experiments to answer these questions, and how to evaluate and interpret the results of those experiments. Despite the stunning progress of the neurosciences, the brain remains a great mystery, with each insight inspiring new questions. For this reason, we have not used a declarative style of writing throughout the book. Instead, we tend to present results that can be interpreted in more than one way, helping the reader to recognize that alternative interpretations are possible.

Since the first edition, there have been many major technological, methodological, and theoretical developments. There has been an explosion of brain-imaging studies; indeed, thousands of functional imaging studies are published each year. New technologies used for noninvasive brain stimulation, magnetic resonance spectroscopy, electrocorticography, and optogenetics have been added to the arsenal of the cognitive neuroscientist. Fascinating links to genetics, comparative anatomy, computation, and robotics have emerged. Parsing all of these studies and deciding which ones should be included has been a major challenge for us. We firmly believe that technology is a cornerstone of scientific advancement. Thus we have felt it essential to capture the cutting-edge trends in the field, while keeping in mind that this is an undergraduate survey text.

The first four editions provide compelling evidence that our efforts have led to a highly useful text for undergraduates taking their first course in cognitive neuroscience, as well as a concise reference volume for graduate students and researchers. Over 500 colleges and universities worldwide have adopted the text. Moreover, instructors tell us that in addition to our interdisciplinary approach, they like that our book has a strong narrative voice and offers a manageable number of chapters to teach in a one-semester survey course.

With every revised edition including this one, we have had to do some pruning and considerable updating to stay current with all of the developments in the field of cognitive neuroscience. We thought it essential to include new methods and, correspondingly, new insights that these tools have provided into the function of the brain, while being selective in the description of specific experimental results. The following table lists the major changes for each chapter.

Chapter	Changes in the Fifth Edition
1. A Brief History of Cognitive Neuroscience	Expanded discussion of the theoretical leap made by the early Greeks that enabled scientific endeavors. Added discussion of monism versus dualism and the mind–brain problem.
2. Structure and Function of the Nervous System	Added discussion of specific neurotransmitters. Added discussion of neural circuits, networks, and systems. Expanded discussion of the cortex from the viewpoint of functional subtypes. Added discussion of neurogenesis throughout the life span.
3. Methods of Cognitive Neuroscience	Updated discussion of direct and indirect stimulation methods used to probe brain function and as a tool for rehabilitation. Expanded discussion of electrocorticography. Added discussion of new methods to analyze fMRI data, including measures of connectivity. Added section on magnetic resonance spectroscopy.
4. Hemispheric Specialization	Expanded discussion of the problem of cross-cuing when evaluating the performance of split-brain patients. Added discussion of differing patterns of functional connectivity in the right and left hemispheres. Added discussion of atypical patterns of hemispheric lateralization. Expanded section on modularity.
5. Sensation and Perception	Added section on olfaction, tears, and sexual arousal. Added review of new concepts regarding gustatory maps in the cortex. Expanded section on perceptual and cortical reorganization after sensory loss. Added section on cochlear implants.
6. Object Recognition	Added section on decoding the perceptual content of dreams. Added discussion of deep neural networks as a model of the hierarchical organization of visual processing. Added section on feedback mechanisms in object recognition. Expanded section on category specificity.
7. Attention	Expanded discussion of neural oscillations and neural synchrony and attention. Updated discussion of pulvinar contributions to attentional modulation and control.
8. Action	Expanded discussion of the recovery from stroke. Updated with latest findings in research on brain–machine interface systems. Updated discussion of deep brain stimulation and Parkinson's disease. Added discussion of the contributions of the cortex and subcortex to skilled motor movement.

Chapter	Changes in the Fifth Edition
9. Memory	Added brief section on dementias. Added discussion of the contribution of corticobasal ganglia loops to procedural memory. Expanded discussion of priming and amnesia. Updated discussion of frontal cortex activity and memory formation. Added brief section on learning while sleeping. Updated discussion of an unexpected finding concerning the cellular mechanisms of memory storage.
10. Emotion	Added section on the hypothalamic-pituitary-adrenal axis. Added discussion of theoretical disagreements between researchers of human emotion and nonhuman animal emotion. Added brief discussion of the role of the periaqueductal gray in emotion. Updated discussion of emotion and decision making.
11. Language	Added brief description of connectome-based lesion-symptom mapping for aphasic patients. Added section on feedback control and speech production. Updated discussion of language evolution in primates. Added investigation of how the brain represents semantic information.
12. Cognitive Control	Added section on cognitive control issues associated with neuropsychiatric disorders. Expanded discussion of decision making and reward signals in the brain. Added section on brain training to improve cognitive control.
13. Social Cognition	Added brief section on the development of social cognition. Added brief discussion of social isolation. Updated section on autism spectrum disorder. Updated discussion of the default network and social cognition. Added section on embodiment and visual body illusions, and body integrity identity disorder.
14. The Consciousness Problem	Added section on levels of arousal. Added section on the layered architecture of complex systems. Added discussion of sentience versus the content of conscious experience. Added discussion of the principle of complementarity in physics and how it may apply to the mind–brain problem.

Inspired by feedback from our adopters, we have also made the text even more user-friendly and focused on the takeaway points. Some ways in which we have made the Fifth Edition more accessible include the following:

- Each chapter now begins with a series of "Big Questions" to frame the key themes of the chapter.
- The introductory stories have been trimmed, and many of them feature patient case studies to engage students.
- "Anatomical Orientation" figures open Chapters 4 through 14 to highlight the brain anatomy that will be addressed in the pages that follow.
- Major section headings have been numbered for easy assigning. Each section ends with a set of bulleted "Take-Home Messages."
- Figure captions have been made more concise and more focused on the central teaching point.
- Two new types of boxes ("Lessons from the Clinic" and "Hot Science") feature clinical and research examples in cognitive neuroscience.

As with each edition, this book is the result of a dynamic yet laborious interactive effort among the three of us, along with extensive discussions with our colleagues, our students, and our reviewers. The product has benefited immeasurably from these interactions. Of course, we are ready to modify and improve any and all of our work. In our earlier editions, we asked readers to contact us with suggestions and questions, and we do so again. We live in an age where interaction is swift and easy. We are to be found as follows: gazzaniga@ucsb.edu; mangun@ucdavis.edu; ivry@berkeley.edu.

Good reading and learning!

Acknowledgments

Once again, we are indebted to a number of people. First and foremost we would like to thank Rebecca A. Gazzaniga, MD, for her extensive and savvy editing of the Fifth Edition. She mastered every chapter, with an eye to making sure that the story was clear and engaging. We could not have completed this edition without her superb scholarship and editing skills.

The Fifth Edition also benefited from the advice of various specialists in the field of cognitive neuroscience. Karolina Lampert at the University of Pennsylvania assisted us with the study of emotion. Carolyn Parkinson at UCLA helped update our chapter on social cognition. Nikkie Marinsek from UC Santa Barbara did the same for the topic of lateralization. Geoff Woodman from Vanderbilt University and Sabine Kastner from Princeton provided valuable advice on attention. Arne Ekstrom, Charan Ranganath, Brian Wilgen, and Andy Yonelinas from UC Davis; Ken Paller from Northwestern University; Nancy A. Dennis from Pennsylvania State University; and Michael Miller from UC Santa Barbara provided numerous insights about memory. Ellen F. Lau from the University of Maryland, Gina Kuperberg from Tufts University and Massachusetts General Hospital, Alexander Huth and Jack Gallant from UC Berkeley, David Corina from UC Davis, and Jeffrey Binder from the Medical College of Wisconsin advised us on mechanisms of language and semantic representation. For answering miscellaneous questions that cropped up in the methods chapter, we tip our hats to Scott Grafton from UC Santa Barbara and Danielle Bassett from the University of Pennsylvania. For the perception and object recognition chapters, David Somers from Boston University, as well as Jack Gallant (again!) and Kevin Weiner from UC Berkeley, gave useful advice and supplied us with beautiful graphics.

We are also especially grateful to Tamara Y. Swaab, PhD (UC Davis), for the language chapter in this and prior editions; Michael B. Miller, PhD (UC Santa Barbara), for contributions to the chapter on hemispheric lateralization; and Stephanie Cacioppo, PhD (University of Chicago), for contributions to the chapter on emotion.

For work on the previous editions that continues to play an active part in this new edition, we thank again Megan Steven (Dartmouth College), Jeff Hutsler (University of Nevada, Reno), and Leah Krubitzer (UC Davis) for evolutionary perspectives; Jennifer Beer (University of Texas at Austin) for insights on social cognition; and Liz Phelps (New York University) for her work on emotion. Tim Justus (Pitzer College) is to be thanked for sharing his advice and wisdom, and for helping along the way. Also Jason Mitchell, PhD (Harvard University), for contributions to the social cognition chapter. We thank Frank Forney for his art in the previous editions, and Echo Medical Media for the new art in the fourth and fifth editions. We also thank our many colleagues who provided original artwork or scientific figures. We would also like to thank our readers Annik Carson and Mette Clausen-Bruun, who took the time to point out typos in our previous edition; to anatomist Carlos Avendaño, who alerted us to some anatomical errors; and to Sophie van Roijen, who suggested the very good idea of adding an index of abbreviations.

Several instructors took time from their busy schedules to review our previous edition and make suggestions for the Fifth Edition. We thank the following:

Maxwell Bertolero, *University of California, Berkeley*
Flavia Cardini, *Anglia Ruskin University*
Joshua Carlson, *Northern Michigan University*
Tim Curran, *University of Colorado, Boulder*
Mark D'Esposito, *University of California, Berkeley*
Karin H. James, *Indiana University*
Mark Kohler, *University of South Australia*
Bruno Laeng, *University of Oslo, Norway*
Karolina M. Lempert, *University of Pennsylvania*
Carolyn Parkinson, *University of California, Los Angeles*
David Somers, *Boston University*
Weiwei Zhang, *University of California, Riverside*

In addition, we are indebted to many scientists and personal friends. Writing a textbook is a major commitment of time, intellect, and affect! Those who helped significantly are noted below. Some reviewed our words and critiqued our thoughts. Others allowed us to interview them. To all those listed here who reviewed past and present editions or media, we owe our deep gratitude and thanks.

Eyal Aharoni, *Georgia State University*
David G. Amaral, *University of California, Davis*
Franklin R. Amthor, *University of Alabama, Birmingham*

Michael Anderson, *University of Cambridge*
Adam Aron, *University of California, San Diego*
Ignacio Badiola, *University of Pennsylvania*
David Badre, *Brown University*
Juliana Baldo, *VA Medical Center, Martinez, California*
Gary Banker, *Oregon Health Sciences University*
Horace Barlow, *University of Cambridge*
Danielle Bassett, *University of Pennsylvania*
Kathleen Baynes, *University of California, Davis*
N. P. Bechtereva, *Russian Academy of Sciences*
Mark Beeman, *Northwestern University*
Jennifer Beer, *University of Texas at Austin*
Marlene Behrmann, *Carnegie Mellon University*
Maxwell Bertolero, *University of California, Berkeley*
Jeffrey Binder, *Medical College of Wisconsin*
Robert S. Blumenfeld, *California State Polytechnic University, Pomona*
Elizabeth Brannon, *University of Pennsylvania*
Rainer Breitling, *University of Manchester*
Silvia Bunge, *University of California, Berkeley*
Stephanie Cacioppo, *University of Chicago*
Flavia Cardini, *Anglia Ruskin University*
Joshua Carlson, *Northern Michigan University*
Valerie Clark, *University of California, Davis*
Clay Clayworth, *University of California, Berkeley*
Asher Cohen, *Hebrew University*
Jonathan Cohen, *Princeton University*
Roshan Cools, *Radboud University, Nijmegen*
J. M. Coquery, *Université des Sciences et Technologies de Lille*
Michael Corballis, *University of Auckland*
Paul Corballis, *University of Auckland*
David Corina, *University of California, Davis*
Tim Curran, *University of Colorado, Boulder*
Clayton Curtis, *New York University*
Anders Dale, *University of California, San Diego*
Antonio Damasio, *University of Southern California*
Hanna Damasio, *University of Southern California*
Lila Davachi, *New York University*
Daniel C. Dennett, *Tufts University*
Nancy A. Dennis, *Pennsylvania State University*
Michel Desmurget, *Centre de Neuroscience Cognitive*
Mark D'Esposito, *University of California, Berkeley*
Joern Diedrichsen, *University of Western Ontario*
Nina Dronkers, *University of California, Davis*
Arne Ekstrom, *University of California, Davis*
Paul Eling, *Radboud University, Nijmegen*
Russell Epstein, *University of Pennsylvania*
Martha Farah, *University of Pennsylvania*
Harlan Fichtenholtz, *Keene State College*
Peter T. Fox, *University of Texas*
Karl Friston, *University College London*
Rusty Gage, *Salk Institute*
Jack Gallant, *University of California, Berkeley*
Vittorio Gallese, *University of Parma, Italy*
Isabel Gauthier, *Vanderbilt University*
Christian Gerlach, *University of Southern Denmark*
Robbin Gibb, *University of Lethbridge*
Gail Goodman, *University of California, Davis*
Elizabeth Gould, *Princeton University*
Jay E. Gould, *University of West Florida*
Scott Grafton, *University of California, Santa Barbara*
Charlie Gross, *Princeton University*
Nouchine Hadjikhani, *Massachusetts General Hospital*
Peter Hagoort, *Max Planck Institute for Psycholinguistics*
Todd Handy, *University of British Columbia*
Jasmeet Pannu Hayes, *Boston University*
Eliot Hazeltine, *University of Iowa*
Hans-Jochen Heinze, *University of Magdeburg*
Arturo Hernandez, *University of Houston*
Laura Hieber Adery, *Vanderbilt University*
Steven A. Hillyard, *University of California, San Diego*
Hermann Hinrichs, *University of Magdeburg*
Jens-Max Hopf, *University of Magdeburg*
Joseph Hopfinger, *University of North Carolina, Chapel Hill*
Richard Howard, *National University of Singapore*
Drew Hudson, *University of California, Berkeley*
Jeffrey Hutsler, *University of Nevada, Reno*
Alexander Huth, *University of Texas at Austin*
Akira Ishiguchi, *Ochanomizu University*
Lucy Jacobs, *University of California, Berkeley*
Karin H. James, *Indiana University*
Amishi Jha, *University of Miami*
Cindy Jordan, *Michigan State University*
Tim Justus, *Pitzer College*
Nancy Kanwisher, *Massachusetts Institute of Technology*
Sabine Kastner, *Princeton University*
Larry Katz, *Harvard University*
Steven Keele, *University of Oregon*
Leon Kenemans, *University of Utrecht*
Steve Kennerley, *University College London*
Alan Kingstone, *University of British Columbia*
Robert T. Knight, *University of California, Berkeley*
Mark Kohler, *University of South Australia*
Talia Konkle, *Harvard University*
Stephen M. Kosslyn, *Harvard University*
Neal Kroll, *University of California, Davis*
Leah Krubitzer, *University of California, Davis*
Gina Kuperberg, *Tufts University and Massachusetts General Hospital*
Marta Kutas, *University of California, San Diego*
Bruno Laeng, *University of Oslo, Norway*

Ayelet Landau, *Hebrew University*
Ellen F. Lau, *University of Maryland*
Joseph E. Le Doux, *New York University*
Karolina M. Lempert, *University of Pennsylvania*
Matt Lieberman, *University of California, Los Angeles*
Steven J. Luck, *University of California, Davis*
Jennifer Mangels, *Baruch College*
Nikki Marinsek, *University of California, Santa Barbara*
Chad Marsolek, *University of Minnesota*
Nancy Martin, *University of California, Davis*
James L. McClelland, *Stanford University*
Michael B. Miller, *University of California, Santa Barbara*
Teresa Mitchell, *University of Massachusetts*
Ryan Morehead, *Harvard University*
Amy Needham, *Vanderbilt University*
Kevin Ochsner, *Columbia University*
Ken A. Paller, *Northwestern University*
Galina V. Paramei, *Liverpool Hope University*
Carolyn Parkinson, *University of California, Los Angeles*
Steven E. Petersen, *Washington University in St. Louis*
Liz Phelps, *New York University*
Steven Pinker, *Harvard University*
Lara Polse, *University of California, San Diego*
Michael I. Posner, *University of Oregon*
David Presti, *University of California, Berkeley*
Robert Rafal, *University of Delaware*
Marcus Raichle, *Washington University School of Medicine*
Charan Ranganath, *University of California, Davis*
Patricia Reuter-Lorenz, *University of Michigan*
Jesse Rissman, *University of California, Los Angeles*
Leah Roesch, *Emory University*
Matthew Rushworth, *University of Oxford*
Kim Russo, *University of California, Davis*
Alexander Sack, *Maastricht University*
Mikko E. Sams, *Aalto University*
Donatella Scabini, *University of California, Berkeley*
Daniel Schacter, *Harvard University*
Ariel Schoenfeld, *University of Magdeburg*
Michael Scholz, *University of Magdeburg*
Art Shimamura, *University of California, Berkeley*
Michael Silver, *University of California, Berkeley*
Michael Silverman, *Simon Fraser University*
Noam Sobel, *Weizmann Institute of Science*
David Somers, *Boston University*
Allen W. Song, *Duke University*
Larry Squire, *University of California, San Diego*
Alit Stark-Inbar, *University of California, Berkeley*
Michael Starks, *3DTV Corporation*
Megan Steven, *Dartmouth College*
Tamara Y. Swaab, *University of California, Davis*
Thomas M. Talavage, *Purdue University*
Keiji Tanaka, *Riken Institute*
Michael Tarr, *Carnegie Mellon University*
Jordan Taylor, *Princeton University*
Sharon L. Thompson-Schill, *University of Pennsylvania*
Roger Tootell, *Massachusetts General Hospital*
Carrie Trutt, *Duke University*
Endel Tulving, *Rotman Research Institute, Baycrest Center*
Kevin Weiner, *University of California, Berkeley*
C. Mark Wessinger, *University of Nevada, Reno*
Megan Wheeler, *Eric Schmidt Foundation*
Susanne Wiking, *University of Tromsø*
Kevin Wilson, *Gettysburg College*
Brian Wiltgen, *University of California, Davis*
Ginger Withers, *Whitman College*
Marty G. Woldorff, *Duke University*
Geoff Woodman, *Vanderbilt University*
Andrew Yonelinas, *University of California, Davis*
Weiwei Zhang, *University of California, Riverside*

Often we forget to thank the many participants in the research work that we discuss, some of whom have generously given hundreds of hours of their time. Without their contributions, cognitive neuroscience would not be where it is today.

Finally, we would like to thank the outstanding editorial and production team at W. W. Norton: Sheri Snavely, Andrew Sobel, Carla Talmadge, Ben Reynolds, Kaitlin Coats, Tori Reuter, Eve Sanoussi, Allison Smith, and Stephanie Hiebert, whose sharp eyes and wise counsel have helped us produce this exciting new edition of our textbook.

Contents

PART I Background and Methods

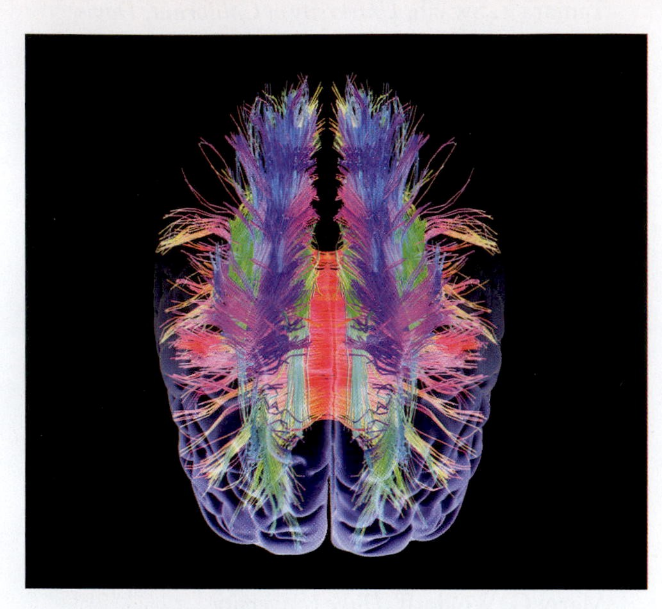

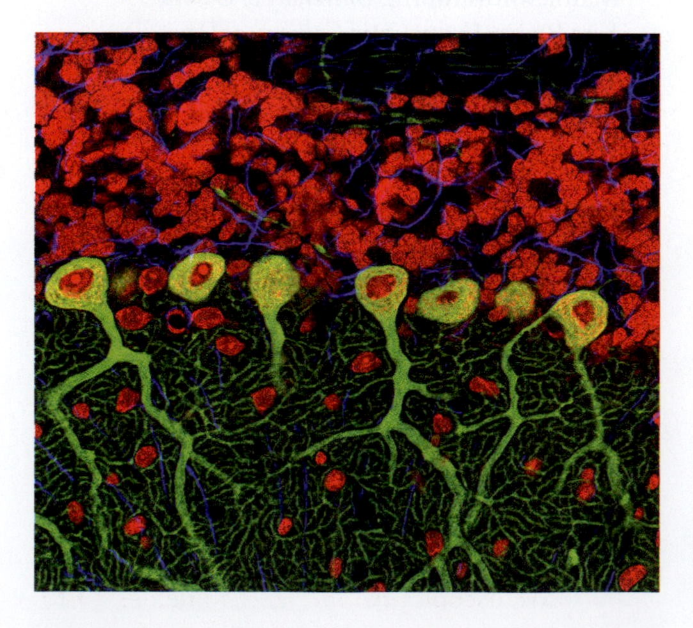

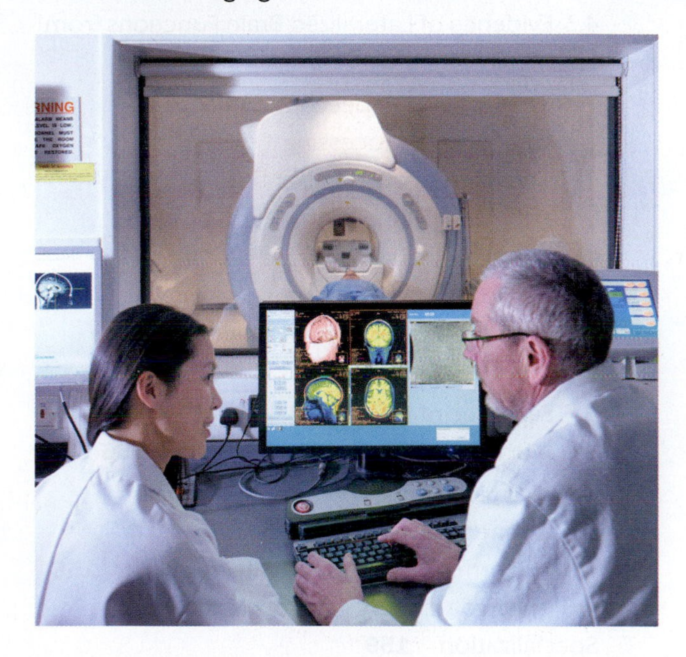

PART II Core Processes

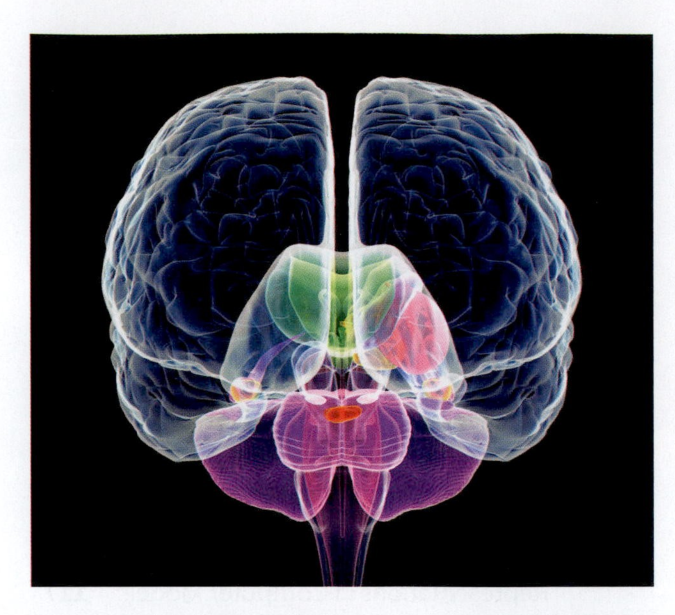

PART III Control Processes

FIFTH EDITION

Cognitive Neuroscience

The Biology of the Mind

In science it often happens that scientists say, "You know that's a really good argument; my position is mistaken," and then they actually change their minds and you never hear that old view from them again. They really do it. It doesn't happen as often as it should, because scientists are human and change is sometimes painful. But it happens every day. I cannot recall the last time something like that happened in politics or religion.

Carl Sagan, 1987

A Brief History of Cognitive Neuroscience

CHAPTER

1

ANNE GREEN WALKED to the gallows in the castle yard of Oxford, England, in 1650, about to be executed for a crime she had not committed: murdering her stillborn child. No doubt she felt scared, angry, and frustrated, and many thoughts raced through her head. However, "I am about to play a role in the founding of clinical neurology and neuroanatomy"—though accurate—certainly was not one of them. She proclaimed her innocence to the crowd, a psalm was read, and she was hanged. She hung there for a full half hour before she was taken down, pronounced dead, and placed in a coffin provided by Drs. Thomas Willis and William Petty. This was when her luck began to improve. Willis and Petty were physicians and had been given permission from King Charles I to dissect, for medical research, the bodies of any criminals killed within 21 miles of Oxford. So, instead of being buried, Green's body was carried to their office.

An autopsy, however, was not what took place. As if in a scene from Edgar Allan Poe, the coffin began to emit a grumbling sound. Green was alive! The doctors poured spirits in her mouth and rubbed a feather on her neck to make her cough. They rubbed her hands and feet for several minutes, bled 5 ounces of blood, swabbed her neck wounds with turpentine, and cared for her through the night. The next morning, feeling more chipper, she asked for a beer. Five days later, she was out of bed and eating normally (Molnar, 2004; Zimmer, 2004).

After her ordeal, the authorities wanted to hang Green again. But Willis and Petty fought in her defense, arguing that her baby had been stillborn and its death was not her fault. They declared that divine providence had stepped in and provided her miraculous escape from death, thus proving her innocence. Their arguments prevailed. Green was set free and went on to marry and have three more children.

This miraculous incident was well publicized in England (**Figure 1.1**). Thomas Willis (**Figure 1.2**) owed much to Anne Green and the fame brought to him by the events of her resurrection. With it came money he desperately needed and the

BIG Questions

- Why were the ancient Greeks important to science?
- What historical evidence suggested that the brain's activities produce the mind?
- What can we learn about the mind and brain from modern research methods?

FIGURE 1.1
An artistic rendition of the miraculous resurrection of Anne Green in 1650.

prestige to publish his work and disseminate his ideas, and he had some good ones. Willis became one of the best-known doctors of his time: He coined the term *neurology*, and he was the first anatomist to link specific brain damage—that is, changes in brain structure—to specific behavioral deficits and to theorize how the brain transfers information. He drew these conclusions after treating patients throughout their lives and autopsying them after their deaths.

With his colleague and friend Christopher Wren (the architect who designed St. Paul's Cathedral in London), Willis created drawings of the human brain that remained the most accurate representations for 200 years (**Figure 1.3**). He also coined names for numerous brain regions (**Table 1.1**; Molnar, 2004; Zimmer, 2004). In short, Willis set in motion the ideas and knowledge base that took hundreds of years to develop into what we know today as the field of cognitive neuroscience.

FIGURE 1.2
Thomas Willis (1621–1675), a founder of clinical neuroscience.

In this chapter we discuss some of the scientists and physicians who have made important contributions to this field. You will discover the origins of cognitive neuroscience and how it has developed into what it is today: a discipline geared toward understanding how the brain works, how brain structure and function affect behavior, and ultimately how the brain enables the mind.

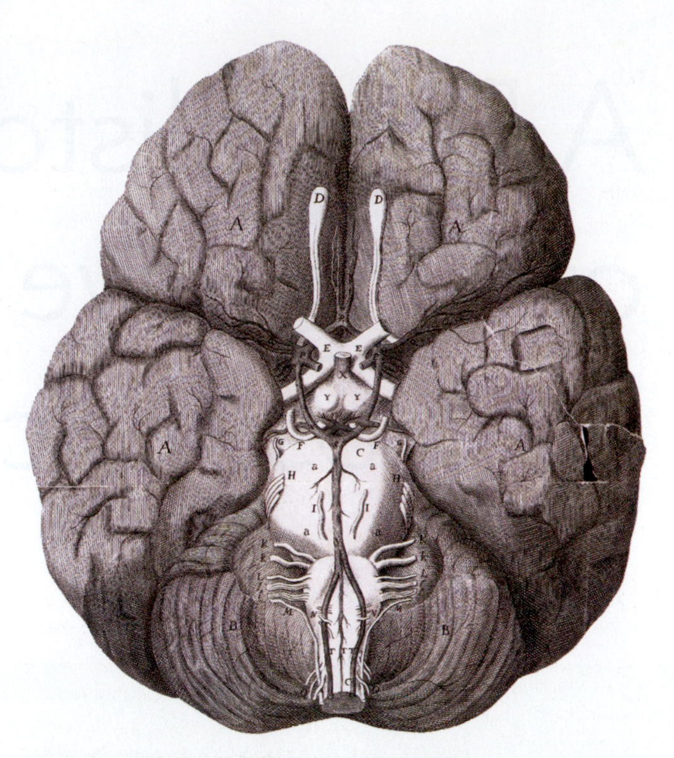

FIGURE 1.3 The human brain (ventral view) drawn by Christopher Wren.
Wren made drawings for Thomas Willis's *Anatomy of the Brain and Nerves*. The circle of dark vessels in the very center of the drawing was named the circle of Willis by one of Willis's students, Richard Lower.

1.1 A Historical Perspective

The scientific field of **cognitive neuroscience** received its name in the late 1970s in the back seat of a New York City taxi. One of us (M.S.G.) was riding with the great cognitive psychologist George A. Miller on the way to a dinner meeting at the Algonquin Hotel. The dinner was being held for scientists from Rockefeller and Cornell universities, who were joining forces to study how the brain enables the mind—a subject in need of a name. Out of that taxi ride came the term *cognitive neuroscience*—from *cognition*, or the process of knowing (i.e., what arises from awareness, perception, and reasoning), and *neuroscience* (the study of how the nervous system is organized and functions). This seemed the perfect term to describe the question of understanding how the functions of the physical brain can yield the thoughts, ideas, and beliefs of a seemingly intangible mind. And so the term took hold in the scientific community.

When considering the miraculous properties of brain function, bear in mind that Mother Nature built our brains through the process of evolution by natural selection. Unlike computers, our brains were designed not by a team of rational engineers, but through trial and error, and they are made of living cells, not inert substances.

TABLE 1.1 A Selection of Terms Coined by Thomas Willis

Term	Definition
Anterior commissure	Axonal fibers connecting the middle and inferior temporal gyri of the left and right hemispheres.
Cerebellar peduncles	Axonal fibers connecting the cerebellum and brainstem.
Claustrum	A thin sheath of gray matter located between two brain areas: the external capsule and the putamen.
Corpus striatum	A part of the basal ganglia consisting of the caudate nucleus and the lenticular nucleus.
Inferior olives	The part of the brainstem that modulates cerebellar processing.
Internal capsule	White matter pathways conveying information from the thalamus to the cortex.
Medullary pyramids	A part of the medulla that consists of corticospinal fibers.
Neurology	The study of the nervous system and its disorders.
Optic thalamus	The portion of the thalamus relating to visual processing.
Spinal accessory nerve	The 11th cranial nerve, which innervates the head and shoulders.
Stria terminalis	The white matter pathway that sends information from the amygdala to the basal forebrain.
Striatum	Gray matter structure of the basal ganglia.
Vagus nerve	The 10th cranial nerve, which, among other functions, has visceral motor control of the heart.

We must keep both these things in mind when we try to understand the brain's architecture and function.

Life first appeared on our 4.5-billion-year-old Earth approximately 3.8 billion years ago, but human brains, in their present form, have been around for only about 100,000 years, a mere drop in the bucket. The primate brain appeared between 34 million and 23 million years ago, during the Oligocene epoch. It evolved into the progressively larger brains of the great apes in the Miocene epoch between roughly 23 million and 7 million years ago. The human lineage diverged from the last common ancestor that we shared with the chimpanzee somewhere in the range of 5 million to 7 million years ago. Since that divergence, our brains have evolved into the present human brain, capable of all sorts of wondrous feats.

Throughout this book, we will be reminding you to take the evolutionary perspective: Why might this behavior have been selected for? How could it have promoted survival and reproduction? WWHGD? (What would a hunter-gatherer do?) The evolutionary perspective often helps us to ask more informed questions and provides insight into how and why the brain functions as it does.

During most of our history, life was given over to the practical matter of survival. Nonetheless, the brain mechanisms that enable us to generate theories about the characteristics of human nature thrived inside the heads of ancient humans. As civilization developed, our ancestors began to spend time looking for causes of and constructing complex theories about the motives of fellow humans. But in these early societies, people thought of the natural world just as they thought of themselves—having thoughts, desires, and emotions.

It was the ancient Greeks who made the theoretical leap to the view that we are separate from the world we occupy. This delineation allowed them to conceive of the natural world as an object, an "it" that could be studied objectively—that is, scientifically. Egyptologist Henri Frankfort called this leap "breath-taking": "These men proceeded, with preposterous boldness on an entirely unproved assumption. They held that the universe is an intelligible whole. In other words, they presumed that a single order underlies the chaos of our perceptions and, furthermore, that we are able to comprehend that order" (Frankfort et al., 1977). The pre-Socratic Greek philosopher Thales, presaging modern cognitive neuroscience, rejected supernatural explanations of phenomena and proclaimed that every event had a natural cause. But on the subject of cognition, the early Greeks were limited in what they could say: They did not have the methodology to systematically explore the brain and the thoughts it produces (the mind) through experimentation.

Over the past 2,500 years, there has been an underlying tension between two ideas concerning the brain and the conscious mind. Thales represents one perspective, which posits that the flesh-and-blood brain produces thoughts—a stance known as *monism*. René Descartes (**Figure 1.4**), the 17th-century French philosopher, mathematician, and scientist, is known for the other. He believed that the body (including the brain) had material properties and worked like a machine, whereas the mind was nonmaterial and thus did not follow the laws of nature (i.e., Newton's laws of physics). Even so,

FIGURE 1.4
René Descartes (1596–1650). Portrait by Frans Hals.

he thought that the two interacted: The mind could influence the body and, through "the passions," the body could influence the mind. He had a difficult time figuring out where this interaction occurred but decided it must have been inside a single brain structure (i.e., not one found bilaterally), and the pineal gland was all that he could find that fit this description, so he settled on it. Descartes's stance that the mind appears from elsewhere and is not the result of the machinations of the brain is known as *dualism*.

Cognitive neuroscience takes Thales's monistic perspective that the conscious mind is a product of the brain's physical activity and not separate from it. We will see that evidence for this view initially came from studying patients with brain lesions, and later from scientific investigations.

The modern tradition of observing, manipulating, and measuring became the norm in the 19th century as scientists started to determine how the brain gets its jobs done. To understand how biological systems work, we must make an observation, ask why it came about, form a hypothesis, design and perform an experiment that will either support or refute that hypothesis, and, finally, draw a conclusion. Then, ideally, a different researcher reads our work, replicates the experiment, and obtains the same findings. If not, then the topic needs to be revisited. This approach is known as the *scientific method*, and it is the only way that a topic can move along on sure footing. And in the case of cognitive neuroscience, there is no end of rich phenomena to study.

1.2 The Brain Story

Imagine that you are given a problem to solve. A hunk of biological tissue is known to think, remember, attend, solve problems, tell jokes, want sex, join clubs, write novels, exhibit bias, feel guilty, and do a zillion other things. You are supposed to figure out how it works. You might start by looking at the big picture and asking yourself a couple of questions. "Hmm, does the blob work as a unit, with each part contributing to a whole? Or is the blob full of individual processing parts, each carrying out specific functions, so the result is something that looks like it is acting as a whole unit?" From a distance, the city of New York (another type of blob) appears as an integrated whole, but it is actually composed of millions of individual processors—that is, people. Perhaps people, in turn, are made of smaller, more specialized units.

This central issue—whether the mind is enabled by the whole brain working in concert or by specialized parts of the brain working at least partly independently—is what fuels much of modern research in cognitive neuroscience. As we will see, the dominant view has changed back and forth over the years, and it continues to change today.

FIGURE 1.5 Franz Joseph Gall (1758–1828), one of the founders of phrenology.

Thomas Willis foreshadowed cognitive neuroscience with the notion that isolated brain damage (biology) could affect behavior (psychology), but his insights slipped from view. It took another century for Willis's ideas to resurface. They were expanded upon by a young Austrian physician and neuroanatomist, Franz Joseph Gall (**Figure 1.5**). After studying numerous patients, Gall became convinced that the brain was the organ of the mind and that innate faculties were localized in specific regions of the cerebral cortex. He thought that the brain was organized around some 35 or more specific functions, ranging from cognitive basics such as language and color perception to more ephemeral capacities such as affection and a moral sense, and that each was supported by specific brain regions. These ideas were well received, and Gall took his theory on the road, lecturing throughout Europe.

Gall and his disciple, Johann Spurzheim, hypothesized that if a person used one of the faculties with greater frequency than the others, the part of the brain representing that function would grow (Gall & Spurzheim, 1810–1819). This increase in local brain size would cause a bump in the overlying skull. Logically, then, Gall and his colleagues believed that a careful analysis of the skull could go a long way in describing the personality of the person inside the skull. Gall called this technique *anatomical personology*. The idea that character could be divined through palpating the skull was dubbed **phrenology** by Spurzheim and, as you may well imagine, soon fell into the hands of charlatans (**Figure 1.6**). Some employers even required job applicants to have their skulls "read" before they were hired.

Gall, apparently, was not politically astute. When asked to read the skull of Napoleon Bonaparte, he did not ascribe to it the noble characteristics that the future emperor was sure he possessed. When Gall later applied to the Academy of Sciences of Paris, Napoleon decided that phrenology needed closer scrutiny and ordered the academy to obtain some scientific evidence of its validity. Although Gall was a physician and neuroanatomist, he was not a scientist. He observed correlations and sought only to confirm, not disprove, them. The academy asked physiologist Marie-Jean-Pierre Flourens (**Figure 1.7**) to see whether he could come up with any concrete findings that could back up this theory.

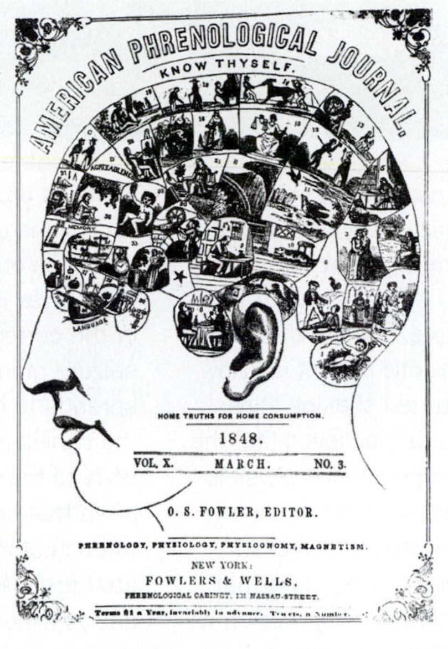

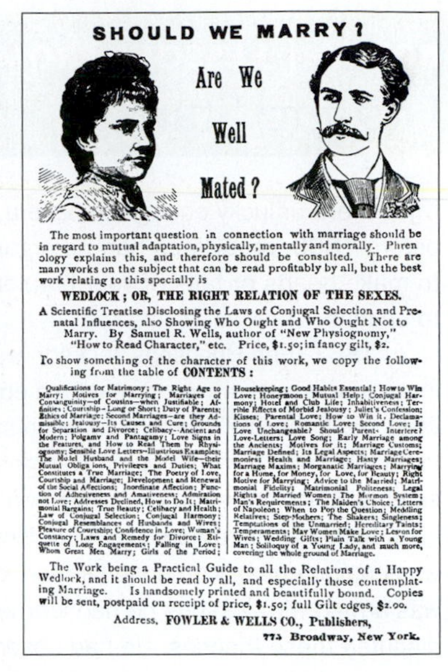

SHOULD WE MARRY?

Are We Well Mated?

The most important question in connection with marriage should be in regard to mutual adaptation, physically, mentally and morally. Phrenology explains this, and therefore should be consulted. There are many works on the subject that can be read profitably by all, but the best work relating to this specially is

WEDLOCK; OR, THE RIGHT RELATION OF THE SEXES.

A Scientific Treatise Disclosing the Laws of Conjugal Selection and Prenatal Influences, also Showing Who Ought and Who Ought Not to Marry. By Samuel R. Wells, author of "New Physiognomy," "How to Read Character," etc. Price, $1.50; in fancy gilt, $2.

To show something of the character of this work, we copy the following from the table of **CONTENTS**:

Qualifications for Matrimony; The Right Age to Marry; Motives for Marrying; Marriages of Consanguinity—of Cousins—when Justifiable; Affinities; Courtship—Long or Short; Duty of Parents; Ethics of Marriage; Second Marriages—are they Admissible; Jealousy—Its Causes and Cure; Grounds for Separation and Divorce; Celibacy—Ancient and Modern; Polgamy and Pantagamy; Love Signs in the Features, and How to Read Them by Physiognomy; Sensible Love Letters—Illustrious Examples; The Model Husband and the Model Wife—their Mutual Obligations, Privileges and Duties; What Constitutes a True Marriage; The Poetry of Love, Courtship and Marriage; Development and Renewal of the Social Affections; Inordinate Affection; Function of Adhesiveness and Amativeness; Admiration not Love; Addresses Declined, How to Do It; Matrimonial Bargains; True Beauty; Celibacy and Health; Law of Conjugal Selection; Conjugal Harmony; Conjugal Resemblances of Husbands and Wives; Pleasure of Courtship; Confidence in Love; Woman's Constancy; Laws and Remedy for Divorce; Etiquette of Long Engagements; Falling in Love; Whom Great Men Marry; Girls of the Period; Housekeeping; Good Habits Essential; How to Win Love; Honeymoon; Mutual Help; Conjugal Harmony; Hotel and Club Life; Inhabitiveness; Terrible Effects of Morbid Jealousy; Juliet's Confession; Kisses; Parental Love; How to Win it, Declamations of Love; Romantic Love; Second Love; Is Love Unchangeable? Should Parents Interfere? Love-Letters; Love Song; Early Marriage among the Ancients; Motives for it; Marriage Customs; Marriage Defined; Its Legal Aspects; Marriage Ceremonies; Health and Marriage; Hasty Marriages; Marriage Maxims; Morganatic Marriages; Marrying for a Home, for Money, for Love, for Beauty; Right Motive for Marrying; Advice to the Married; Matrimonial Fidelity; Matrimonial Politeness; Legal Rights of Married Women; The Mormon System; Man's Requirements; The Maiden's Choice; Letters of Napoleon; When to Pop the Question; Meddling Relatives; Step-Mothers; The Shakers; Singleness; Temptations of the Unmarried; Hereditary Taints; Temperaments; May Women Make Love; Lesson for Wives; Wedding Gifts; Plain Talk with a Young Man; Soliloquy of a Young Lady, and much more, covering the whole ground of Marriage.

The Work being a Practical Guide to all the Relations of a Happy Wedlock, and it should be read by all, and especially those contemplating Marriage. Is handsomely printed and beautifully bound. Copies will be sent, postpaid on receipt of price, $1.50; full Gilt edges, $2.00.

Address, **FOWLER & WELLS CO., Publishers,**
775 Broadway, New York.

a b c

FIGURE 1.6 Phrenology goes mainstream.
(a) An analysis of Presidents Washington, Jackson, Taylor, and McKinley by Jessie A. Fowler, from the *Phrenological Journal*, June 1898. **(b)** The phrenological map of personal characteristics on the skull, from the *American Phrenological Journal*, March 1848. **(c)** Fowler & Wells Co. publication on marriage compatibility based on phrenology, 1888.

Flourens set to work. He destroyed parts of the brains of pigeons and rabbits and observed what happened. He was the first to show that, indeed, certain parts of the brain were responsible for certain functions. For instance, when he removed the cerebral hemispheres, the animal no longer had perception, motor ability, and judgment. Without the cerebellum, the animals became uncoordinated and lost their equilibrium. He could not, however, find any areas for advanced abilities such as memory or cognition, and he concluded that these were more diffusely scattered throughout the brain.

Flourens developed the notion that the whole brain participated in behavior—a view later known as the **aggregate field theory**. In 1824 Flourens wrote, "All sensations, all perceptions, and all volitions occupy the same seat in these (cerebral) organs. The faculty of sensation, percept and volition is then essentially one faculty." The theory of localized brain functions, known as localizationism, fell out of favor.

a b

FIGURE 1.7
(a) Marie-Jean-Pierre Flourens (1794–1867), who supported the idea later termed the *aggregate field theory*. **(b)** The posture of a pigeon deprived of its cerebral hemispheres, as described by Flourens.

That state of affairs didn't last long, however. New evidence started trickling in from across Europe, and the pendulum slowly swung back to the localizationist view. In 1836 a neurologist from Montpellier, Marc Dax, provided one of the first bits. He sent a report to the French Academy of Sciences about three patients, noting that each had similar speech disturbances and similar left-hemisphere lesions found at autopsy. At the time, a report from the provinces got short shrift in Paris, and it would be another 30 years before anyone took much notice of this observation that speech could be disrupted by a specific lesion in the left hemisphere.

Meanwhile, in England, the neurologist John Hughlings Jackson (**Figure 1.8**) began to publish his observations on the behavior of persons with brain damage. A key feature of Jackson's

FIGURE 1.8
John Hughlings Jackson (1835–1911), an English neurologist who was one of the first to recognize the localizationist view.

BOX 1.1 | LESSONS FROM THE CLINIC

Fits and Starts

If you were unlucky enough to have a neurological ailment before 1860, physicians had no organized way of thinking to make heads or tails of your problem. But that was about to change.

In 1867 John Hughlings Jackson wrote, "One of the most important questions we can ask an epileptic patient is, 'How does the fit begin?'" Before Jackson started shaking things up in the world of neurology, it was generally believed that the cerebral cortex was not excitable, and experimental physiologists had been convinced by Pierre Flourens that the cortex was equipotential, with no localized functions. But Jackson was armed with lessons he had learned from the clinic that disputed these theories. He had observed the progression of some of his patients' seizures and found consistent patterns to them: "I think the mode of beginning makes a great difference as to the march of the fit. When the fit begins in the face, the convulsion involving the arm may go down the limb. . . . When the fit begins in the leg, the convulsion marches up; when the leg is affected after the arm, the convulsion marches down the leg" (J. H. Jackson, 1868).

These observations led to Jackson's many conclusions: The cortex is excitable; seizures begin in a localized region of the cortex, and that particular region defines where the seizure manifests in the body; excitability of the cortex spreads to neighboring regions of the brain and, because the convulsion gradually progresses from one part of the body to the part immediately adjacent, the regions in the brain that correspond to the body parts must also be next to each other. From his clinical observations, Jackson created the conceptual framework for clinical neurophysiology and provided a systematic way to go about diagnosing diseases of the nervous system (York & Steinberg, 2006), which were later backed by experimentation. Throughout this book, we will follow in Jackson's footsteps and provide observations from clinical practice that must be taken into account when forming hypotheses about brain function.

writings was the incorporation of suggestions for experiments to test his observations. He noticed, for example, that during the start of their seizures, some epileptic patients moved in such characteristic ways that the seizure appeared to be stimulating a set map of the body in the brain; that is, the abnormal firings of neurons in the brain produced clonic and tonic jerks in muscles that progressed in the same orderly pattern from one body part to another. This phenomenon led Jackson to propose a *topographic* organization in the cerebral cortex: A map of the body was represented across a particular cortical area, where one part would represent the foot, another the lower leg, and so on (see **Box 1.1**). As we will see, this proposal was verified over a half century later by Wilder Penfield.

Although Jackson was also the first to observe that lesions on the right side of the brain affect visuospatial processes more than do lesions on the left side, he did not maintain that specific parts of the right side of the brain were solely committed to this important human cognitive function. Being an observant clinical neurologist, Jackson noticed that it was rare for a patient to lose a function completely. For example, most people who lost their capacity to speak following a cerebral stroke could still say some words. Patients unable to move their hands voluntarily to specific places on their bodies could still easily scratch those places if they itched. When Jackson made these observations, he concluded that many regions of the brain contribute to a given behavior.

Back in Paris, the well-known and respected physician Paul Broca (**Figure 1.9a**) published, in 1861, the results of his autopsy on a patient who had been nicknamed Tan (his real name was Leborgne)—perhaps the most

a

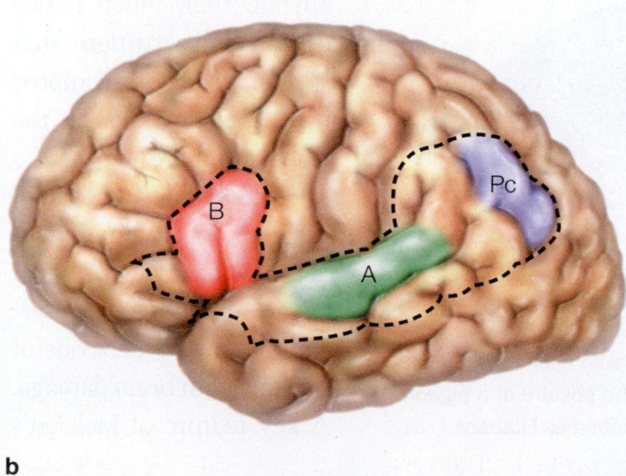

b

FIGURE 1.9
(a) Paul Broca (1824–1880). **(b)** The connections between the speech centers, from Carl Wernicke's 1876 article on aphasia. A = Wernicke's sensory speech center; B = Broca's area for speech; Pc = Wernicke's area concerned with language comprehension and meaning.

famous neurological case in history. Tan had developed aphasia: He could understand language, but "tan" was the only word he could utter. Broca found that Tan had a syphilitic lesion in his left-hemisphere inferior frontal lobe. This region is now called *Broca's area.* The impact of this finding was huge. Here was a specific aspect of language that was impaired by a specific lesion. Soon Broca had a series of such patients.

This theme was picked up by the German neurologist Carl Wernicke. In 1876 Wernicke reported on a stroke victim who (unlike Broca's patient) could talk quite freely but made little sense when he spoke. Wernicke's patient also could not understand spoken or written language. He had a lesion in a more posterior region of the left hemisphere, an area in and around where the temporal and parietal lobes meet, now referred to as *Wernicke's area* (**Figure 1.9b**).

Today, differences in how the brain responds to focal disease are well known (H. Damasio et al., 2004; Wise, 2003), but over 100 years ago Broca's and Wernicke's discoveries were earth-shattering. (Note that people had largely forgotten Willis's observations that isolated brain damage could affect behavior. Throughout the history of brain science, an unfortunate and oft-repeated trend is that we fail to consider crucial observations made by our predecessors.) With the discoveries of Broca and Wernicke, attention was again paid to this startling point: Focal brain damage causes specific behavioral deficits.

As is so often the case, the study of humans leads to questions for those who work on animal models. Shortly after Broca's discovery, the German physiologists Gustav Fritsch and Eduard Hitzig electrically stimulated discrete parts of a dog brain and observed that this stimulation produced characteristic movements in the dog. This discovery led neuroanatomists to more closely analyze the cerebral cortex and its cellular organization; they wanted support for their ideas about the importance of local regions. Because these regions performed different functions, it followed that they ought to look different at the cellular level.

Going by this logic, German neuroanatomists began to analyze the brain by using microscopic methods to view the cell types in different brain regions. Perhaps the most famous of the group was Korbinian Brodmann, who analyzed the cellular organization of the cortex and characterized 52 distinct regions (**Figure 1.10**). He published his cortical maps in 1909.

Brodmann used tissue stains, such as the one developed by the German neuropathologist Franz Nissl, that permitted him to visualize the different cell types in different brain regions. How cells differ between brain regions is called **cytoarchitectonics**, or *cellular architecture.* Soon, many now famous anatomists—including Oskar Vogt, Vladimir Betz, Theodor Meynert, Constantin von Economo, Gerhardt von Bonin, and Percival Bailey—contributed to this work, and several

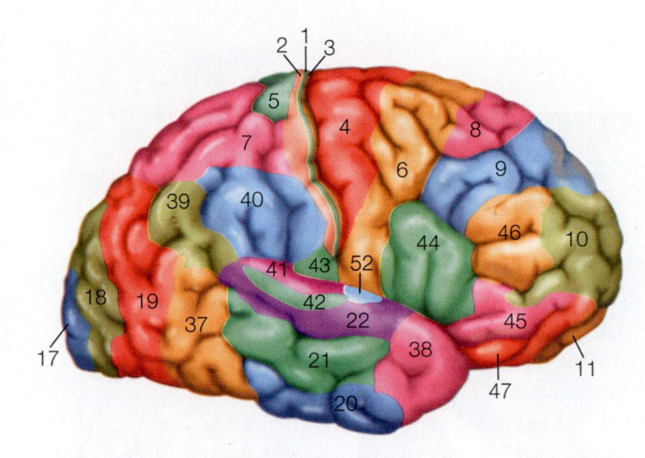

FIGURE 1.10 Brodmann's areas.
Sampling of the 52 distinct areas described by Brodmann on the basis of cell structure and arrangement.

subdivided the cortex even further than Brodmann had. To a large extent, these investigators discovered that various cytoarchitectonically described brain areas do indeed represent functionally distinct brain regions.

Despite all of this groundbreaking work in cytoarchitectonics, the truly huge revolution in our understanding of the nervous system was taking place elsewhere. In Italy and Spain, an intense struggle was going on between two brilliant neuroanatomists. Oddly, it was the work of one that led to the insights of the other. Camillo Golgi (**Figure 1.11**), an Italian physician, developed one of the most famous cell stains in the history of the world: the silver method for staining neurons—*la reazione nera,* "the black reaction"—which impregnated individual neurons with silver chromate. This stain permits visualization of individual neurons in their entirety.

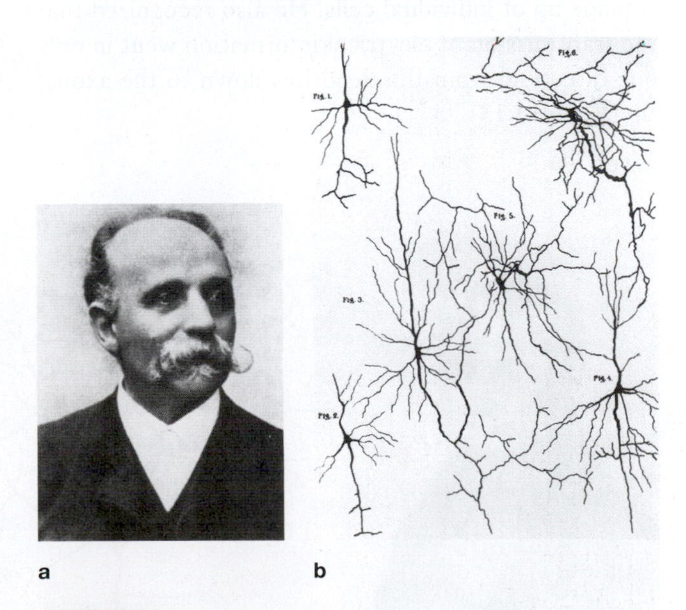

FIGURE 1.11
(a) Camillo Golgi (1843–1926), cowinner of the 1906 Nobel Prize in Physiology or Medicine. **(b)** Golgi's drawings of different types of ganglion cells in dog and cat.

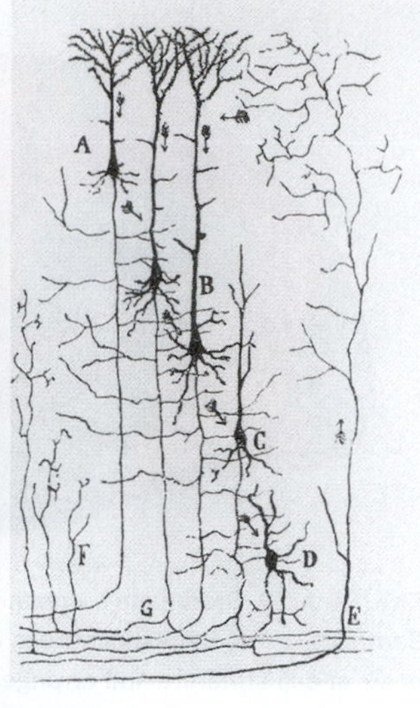

a b

FIGURE 1.12
(a) Santiago Ramón y Cajal (1852–1934), cowinner of the 1906 Nobel Prize in Physiology or Medicine. (b) Ramón y Cajal's drawing of the afferent inflow to the mammalian cortex.

Using Golgi's method, the Spanish pathologist Santiago Ramón y Cajal (**Figure 1.12**) went on to find that, contrary to the view of Golgi and others, neurons were discrete entities. Golgi had believed that the whole brain was a **syncytium**, a continuous mass of tissue that shares a common cytoplasm. Ramón y Cajal, who some call the father of modern neuroscience, was the first to identify the unitary nature of neurons and to articulate what came to be known as the **neuron doctrine**, the concept that the nervous system is made up of individual cells. He also recognized that the transmission of electrical information went in only one direction, from the dendrites down to the axonal tip (**Figure 1.13**).

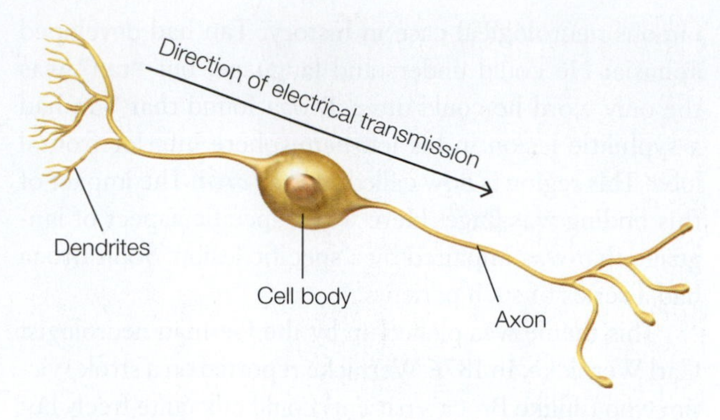

FIGURE 1.13
A bipolar retinal cell, illustrating the dendrites and axon of the neuron.

Many gifted scientists were involved in the early history of the neuron doctrine (Shepherd, 1991). For example, Jan Evangelista Purkinje (**Figure 1.14**), a Czech physiologist, described the first nerve cell in the nervous system in 1837. The German physician and physicist Hermann von Helmholtz (**Figure 1.15**) figured out that electrical current in the cell was not a by-product of cellular activity, but rather the medium that was actually carrying information along the axon of a nerve cell. He was also the first to suggest that invertebrates would be good models for studying vertebrate brain mechanisms. British physiologist Sir Charles Sherrington vigorously pursued the neuron's behavior and coined the term *synapse* to describe the junction between two neurons. With Golgi, Ramón y Cajal, and these other bright minds, the neuron doctrine was born—a discovery whose importance was highlighted by two Nobel Prizes in Physiology or Medicine: the 1906 prize shared by Golgi and Ramón y Cajal, and the 1932 prize awarded to Sherrington along with his colleague Edgar Adrian.

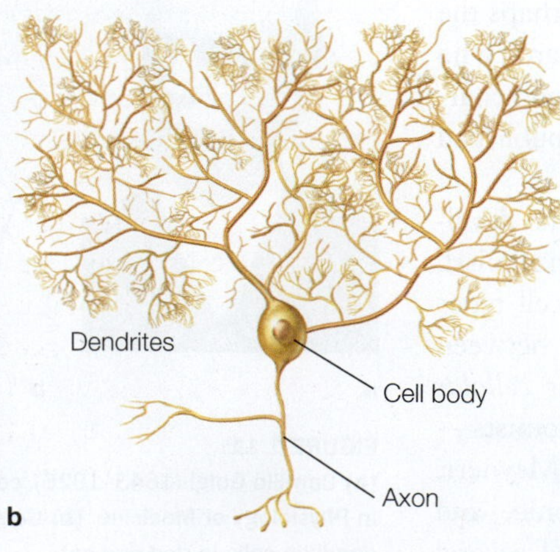

a b

FIGURE 1.14
(a) Jan Evangelista Purkinje (1787–1869), who described the first nerve cell in the nervous system. (b) A Purkinje cell of the cerebellum.

a

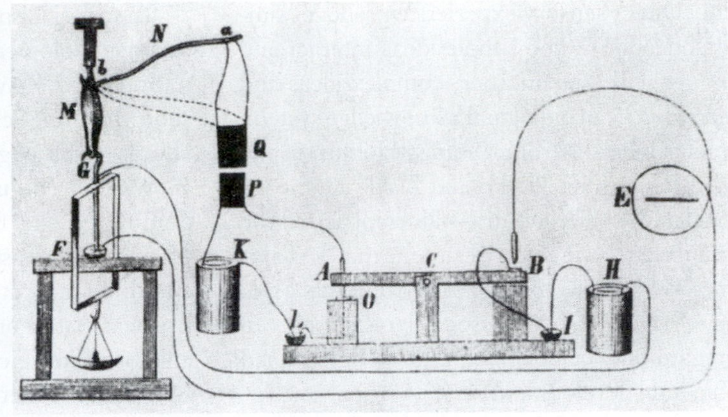

b

FIGURE 1.15
(a) Hermann Ludwig von Helmholtz (1821–1894). (b) Helmholtz's apparatus for measuring the velocity of neuronal conduction.

As the 20th century progressed, the localizationist views were mediated by those who saw that, even though particular neuronal locations might serve independent functions, the network of these locations and the interactions between them are what yield the integrated, holistic behavior that humans exhibit. Once again, this neglected idea had previously been discussed nearly a century earlier, this time by the French biologist Claude Bernard, who wrote in 1865,

> If it is possible to dissect all the parts of the body, to isolate them in order to study them in their structure, form and connections it is not the same in life, where all parts cooperate at the same time in a common aim. An organ does not live on its own, one could often say it did not exist anatomically, as the boundary established is sometimes purely arbitrary. What lives, what exists, is the whole, and if one studies all the parts of any mechanisms separately, one does not know the way they work. (Bernard, 1865/1957, quoted in Finger, 1994, p. 57)

Thus, scientists have come to believe that the knowledge of the parts (the neurons and brain structures) must be understood in conjunction with the whole (i.e., what the parts make when they come together: the mind). Next we explore the history of research on the mind.

1.3 The Psychological Story

Physicians were the early pioneers studying how the brain worked. In 1868 a Dutch ophthalmologist, Franciscus Donders, was the first to propose the now common method of using differences in reaction times to infer differences in cognitive processing (Donders, 1868/1969). He suggested that the difference between the amount of time it took to react to a light and the amount of time needed to react to a particular color of light was the amount of time required for the process of identifying a color. Psychologists began to use this approach, claiming that they could study the mind by measuring behavior, and experimental psychology was born.

Before the start of experimental psychological science, the mind had been the province of philosophers who wondered about the nature of knowledge and how we come to know things. The philosophers had two main positions: **rationalism** and **empiricism**. Rationalism grew out of the Enlightenment period and held that all knowledge could be gained through the use of reason alone: Truth was intellectual, not sensory. Through thinking, then, rationalists would determine true beliefs and would reject beliefs that, although perhaps comforting, were unsupportable and even superstitious. Among intellectuals and scientists, rationalism replaced religion and became the only way to think about the world. In particular, this view, in one form or another, was supported by René Descartes, Baruch Spinoza, and Gottfried Leibniz.

Although rationalism is frequently equated with logical thinking, the two are not identical. Rationalism considers such issues as the meaning of life, whereas logic does not. Logic relies simply on inductive reasoning, statistics, probabilities, and the like. It does not concern itself with personal mental states like happiness, self-interest, and public good. Each person weighs these issues differently, and as a consequence, a rational decision is more problematic than a simple logical decision.

Empiricism, by contrast, is the idea that all knowledge comes from sensory experience, that the brain begins life as a blank slate. Direct sensory experience produces simple ideas and concepts. When simple ideas interact and become *associated* with one another, complex ideas and concepts are created in an individual's knowledge system. The British philosophers—from Thomas Hobbes in the 17th century, through John Locke and David Hume, to John Stuart Mill in the 19th century—all emphasized the role of experience. It is no surprise, then, that a major school of experimental psychology arose from this associationist view. Psychological associationists believed that the aggregate of a person's experience determined the course of mental development.

One of the first scientists to study **associationism** was the German psychologist Hermann Ebbinghaus, who, in the late 1800s, decided that complex processes like memory could be measured and analyzed. He took his lead from the great psychophysicists Gustav Fechner and Ernst Heinrich Weber, who were hard at work relating the physical properties of things such as light and sound to the psychological experiences that they produce in the observer. These measurements were rigorous and reproducible. Ebbinghaus was one of the first to understand that mental processes that are more internal, such as memory, also could be measured (see Chapter 9).

Even more influential to the shaping of the associationist view was a 1911 monograph by the American psychologist Edward Thorndike (**Figure 1.16**). In it, he described his observations that a response that was followed by a reward would be stamped into the organism as a habitual response. If no reward followed a response, the response would disappear. Thus, rewards provided a mechanism for establishing a more adaptive response.

Associationism became the psychological explanation for behavior, and soon the American behavioral psychologist John B. Watson (**Figure 1.17**) dominated the field. He proposed that psychology could be objective only if it was based on observable behavior. He rejected Ebbinghaus's methods and declared that all talk of mental processes, which cannot be publicly observed, should be avoided. These ideas evolved into the methodological stance of **behaviorism.**

FIGURE 1.16
Edward L. Thorndike (1874–1949).

Behaviorism became committed to an idea, widely popularized by Watson, that he could turn any baby into an adult that could do anything from tightrope walking to neurosurgery. Learning was the key, he proclaimed, and everybody had the same neural equipment on which learning could build. Appealing to the American sense of equality, American psychology was giddy with this idea of the brain as a *blank slate* upon which to build through learning and experience. Though disciples of the blank slate and behaviorism were well-intentioned, a behaviorist–associationist bias had crept in, and every prominent psychology department in the country was run by people who held this view. Behaviorism persisted despite the already well-established position—first articulated by Descartes, Leibniz, Immanuel Kant, Charles Darwin, and others—that complexity is built into the human organism. Sensory

a

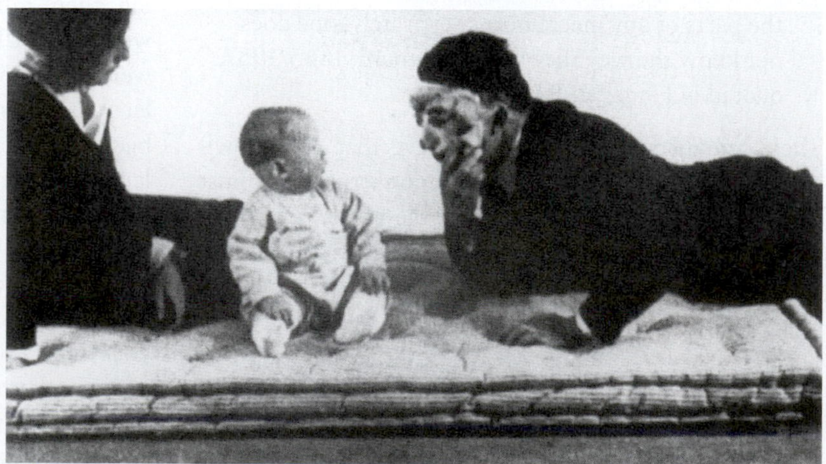

b

FIGURE 1.17
(a) John B. Watson (1878–1958). (b) Watson and "Little Albert," the focus of study in one of Watson's fear-conditioning experiments.

information is merely data on which preexisting mental structures act. This idea, which dominates psychology today, was blithely asserted in that golden age, and later forgotten or ignored.

Psychologists in Britain and Canada did not share the behaviorist bias, however, and Montreal became a hot spot for new ideas on how biology shapes cognition and behavior. In 1928 Wilder Penfield (**Figure 1.18**), an American who had studied neuropathology with Sherrington at Oxford, became that city's first neurosurgeon. In collaboration with Herbert Jasper, Penfield invented the **Montreal procedure** for treating epilepsy, in which he surgically destroyed the neurons in the brain that produced the seizures. To determine which cells to destroy, he stimulated various parts of the brain with electrical probes and observed the results on the patients—who were awake, lying on the operating table under local anesthesia only. From these observations, he was able to create maps of the sensory and motor cortices in the brain (Penfield & Jasper, 1954), confirming the topographic predictions of John Hughlings Jackson from over half a century earlier.

Penfield was joined by a Nova Scotian psychologist, Donald Hebb (**Figure 1.19**), to study the effects of brain surgery and injury on the functioning of the brain. Hebb became convinced that the workings of the brain explained behavior, and that the psychology and biology of an organism could not be separated. Although this idea—which has kept popping up, only to be swept under the carpet again and again, over the past few hundred years—is well accepted now, Hebb was a maverick at the time.

In 1949 he published a book, *The Organization of Behavior: A Neuropsychological Theory*, that rocked the psychological world. In it he postulated that learning had a biological basis. The well-known neuroscience mantra "cells that fire together, wire together" is a distillation of his proposal that neurons can combine together into a single processing unit, and that the connection patterns of these units make up the ever-changing algorithms that determine the brain's response to a stimulus. He pointed out that the brain is active all the time, not just when stimulated by an impulse, and that inputs from the outside can only modify the ongoing activity. Hebb's theory was subsequently used in the design of artificial neural networks.

Hebb's British graduate student Brenda Milner (**Figure 1.20**) continued the behavioral studies on Penfield's patients, both before and after their surgery. When postsurgical patients began to complain about mild memory loss, Milner became interested and was the first to provide anatomical and physiological proof that there are multiple memory systems. Brenda Milner is one of the earliest in a long line of influential women in the field.

The true end of the dominance of behaviorism and stimulus–response psychology in the United States did not come until the late 1950s, when psychologists began to think in terms of cognition, not just behavior. George Miller (**Figure 1.21**), who had been a confirmed behaviorist, had a change of heart in the 1950s. In 1951 he had written an influential book entitled *Language and Communication* and noted in the preface, "The bias is behavioristic." Eleven years later, in 1962, he wrote another book, called *Psychology, the Science of Mental Life*—a title signaling a complete rejection of the idea that psychology should study only behavior.

Upon reflection, Miller determined that the exact date of his rejection of behaviorism and his cognitive awakening was September 11, 1956, during the second Symposium on Information Theory, held at the Massachusetts Institute of Technology (MIT). That year had been a rich one for several disciplines. In computer science, Allen Newell and Herbert Simon successfully introduced Information Processing Language I, a powerful program that simulated the proof of logic theorems.

FIGURE 1.18
Wilder Penfield (1891–1976).

FIGURE 1.19
Donald O. Hebb (1904–1985).

FIGURE 1.20
Brenda Milner (1918–).

FIGURE 1.21
George A. Miller (1920–2012).

The computer guru John von Neumann wrote the Silliman lectures on neural organization, in which he considered the possibility that the brain's computational activities were similar to a massively parallel computer. A famous meeting on artificial intelligence was held at Dartmouth College, where Marvin Minsky, Claude Shannon (known as the father of information theory), and many others were in attendance.

Big things were also happening in psychology. Signal detection and computer techniques, developed in World War II to help the U.S. Department of Defense detect submarines, were now being applied by psychologists James Tanner and John Swets to study perception. In 1956 Miller published his classic and entertaining paper "The Magical Number Seven, Plus-or-Minus Two," in which he described an experiment revealing a limit to the amount of information we can keep in short-term memory: about seven items. Miller concluded that the brain, among other things, is an information processor and, breaking the bonds of behaviorism, he realized that the contents of the mind could be studied, setting into motion the "cognitive revolution."

That same year, Miller also came across a preliminary version of the linguist Noam Chomsky's ideas on syntactic theories (**Figure 1.22**; for a review, see Chomsky, 2006). In an article titled "Three Models for the Description of Language," Chomsky showed how the sequential predictability of speech follows from adherence to grammatical, not probabilistic, rules. For example, while children are exposed to only a finite set of word orders, they can come up with a sentence and word order that they have never heard before. They did not assemble that new sentence using associations made from previous exposure to word orders. Chomsky's deep message, which Miller gleaned, was that learning theory—that is, associationism, then heavily championed by the behaviorist B. F. Skinner—could *in no way* explain how children learned language. The complexity of language was built into the brain, and it ran on rules and principles that transcended all people and all languages. It was innate and it was universal.

Thus, on September 11, 1956, after a year of great development and theory shifting, Miller realized that, although behaviorism had important theories to offer, it could not explain all learning. He then set out with Chomsky to understand the psychological implications of Chomsky's theories by using psychological testing methods, and the field of cognitive psychology was born. Miller's ultimate goal was to understand how the brain works as an integrated whole—to understand the workings of the brain *and* the conscious mind it produces. Many followed his mission, and a few years later a new field was born: cognitive neuroscience.

FIGURE 1.22 Noam Chomsky (1928–).

FIGURE 1.23 Patricia Goldman-Rakic (1937–2003).

What has come to be a hallmark of cognitive neuroscience is that it is made up of an *insalata mista* ("mixed salad") of different disciplines. Miller had stuck his nose into the worlds of linguistics and computer science and had come out with revelations for psychology and neuroscience. In the same vein, in the 1970s Patricia Goldman-Rakic (**Figure 1.23**) put together a multidisciplinary team of people working in biochemistry, anatomy, electrophysiology, pharmacology, and behavior. She was curious about one of Brenda Milner's memory systems, working memory, and chose to ignore the behaviorists' claim that the higher cognitive function of the prefrontal cortex could not be studied. As a result, she produced the first description of the circuitry of the prefrontal cortex and how it relates to working memory (Goldman-Rakic, 1987).

Later, Goldman-Rakic discovered that individual cells in the prefrontal cortex are dedicated to specific memory tasks, such as remembering a face or a voice. She also performed the first studies on the influence of dopamine on the prefrontal cortex. Her findings caused a phase shift in the understanding of many mental illnesses—including schizophrenia, which previously had been thought to be the result of bad parenting.

1.4 The Instruments of Neuroscience

Changes in electrical impulses, fluctuations in blood flow, and shifts in utilization of oxygen and glucose are the driving forces of the brain's business. They are also the parameters that are measured and analyzed in the various methods used to study how mental activities are supported by brain functions. The advances in technology and the invention of these methods have provided cognitive neuroscientists the tools to study how the brain enables the mind. Without these instruments, the discoveries made in the past 30 years would not have been possible. In this section we provide a brief history of the people, ideas, and inventions behind some of the noninvasive techniques used in cognitive neuroscience. Many of these methods are discussed in greater detail in Chapter 3.

Electroencephalography

In 1875, shortly after Hermann von Helmholtz figured out that it was actually an electrical impulse wave that carried messages along the axon of a nerve, British physician Richard Caton used a galvanometer to measure continuous spontaneous electrical activity from the cerebral cortex and skull surface of live dogs and apes. A fancier version, the "string galvanometer," designed by a Dutch physician, Willem Einthoven, was able to make photographic recordings of the electrical activity. Using this apparatus, the German psychiatrist Hans Berger published a paper describing recordings of a human brain's electrical currents in 1929. He named the type of recording an electroencephalogram. The method for making the recordings, electroencephalography, remained the sole technique for noninvasive brain study for a number of years.

Measuring Blood Flow in the Brain

Angelo Mosso, a 19th-century Italian physiologist, was interested in blood flow in the brain and studied patients who had skull defects as a result of neurosurgery. He recorded pulsations as blood flowed around and through the cortex in these patients (**Figure 1.24**) and noticed that the pulsations of the brain increased locally during mental activities such as mathematical calculations. He inferred that blood flow followed function.

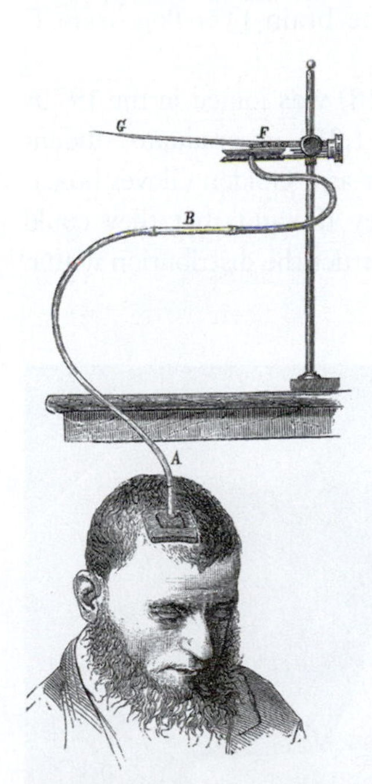

FIGURE 1.24
Angelo Mosso's experimental setup was used to measure pulsations of the brain at the site of a skull defect.

These observations slipped from view and were not pursued until 1928, when the neurophysiologist and physician John Fulton presented the case of patient Walter K., who was evaluated for a vascular malformation that resided above his visual cortex (**Figure 1.25**). The patient mentioned that he heard a noise at the back of his head that increased when he used his eyes but not his other senses. This noise was a bruit, the sound that blood makes when it rushes through a narrowing of its channel. Fulton concluded that blood flow to the visual cortex varied with the attention paid to surrounding objects.

Another 20 years slipped by before Seymour Kety (**Figure 1.26**), a young physician at the University of Pennsylvania, realized that if you could perfuse arterial blood with an inert gas, such as nitrous oxide, then the gas would circulate through the brain and be absorbed independently of the brain's metabolic activity. Its accumulation would depend only on measurable physical parameters such as diffusion, solubility, and perfusion.

With this idea in mind, he developed a method to measure the blood flow and metabolism of the human brain as a whole and, using more drastic methods in animals (they were decapitated, and their brains then removed and analyzed), was able to measure the blood flow to specific regions of the brain (Landau et al., 1955). His animal studies provided evidence that blood flow was related directly to brain function. Kety's method and results were used in developing positron emission tomography (described later in this section), which uses radioactive tracers rather than an inert gas.

Computerized Axial Tomography

Although blood flow was of interest to those studying brain function, having good anatomical images that could pinpoint the location of tumors was motivating other developments in instrumentation. Investigators needed to be able to obtain three-dimensional views of the inside of the human body. In the 1930s, the Italian radiologist Alessandro Vallebona developed tomographic

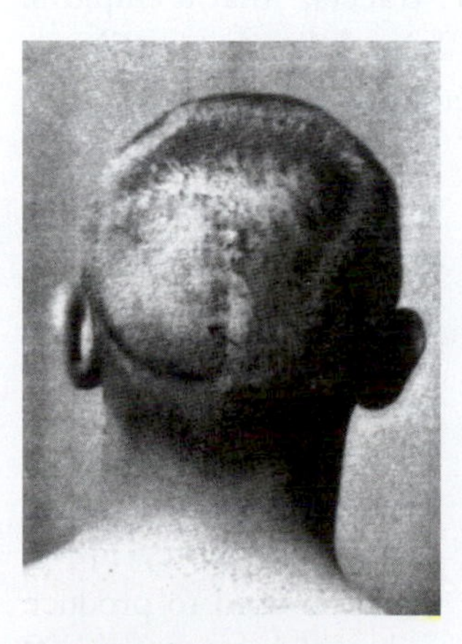

FIGURE 1.25
Walter K.'s head, showing the skull defect over the occipital cortex.

FIGURE 1.26
Seymour S. Kety (1915–2000).

radiography, a technique in which a series of transverse sections are taken. Improving on these initial attempts, UCLA neurologist William Oldendorf (1961) wrote an article providing the first description of the basic concept that was later used in computerized tomography (CT), in which a series of transverse X-rays could be reconstructed into a three-dimensional picture.

Oldendorf's concept was revolutionary, but he could not find any manufacturers willing to capitalize on his idea. It took insight and cash, which were provided by four lads from Liverpool, the company EMI, and Godfrey Newbold Hounsfield, a computer engineer who worked at the Central Research Laboratories of EMI, Ltd. EMI was an electronics firm that also owned Capitol Records and the Beatles' recording contract. Hounsfield, using mathematical techniques and multiple two-dimensional X-rays to reconstruct a three-dimensional image, developed his first scanner, and as the story goes, EMI, flush with cash from the Beatles' success, footed the bill. Hounsfield performed the first computerized axial tomography (CAT) scan in 1972. (Note that the terms *computerized tomography*, or CT, and *computerized axial tomography*, CAT, are equivalent.)

Positron Emission Tomography and Radioactive Tracers

While CAT was great for revealing anatomical detail, it revealed little about function. Researchers at Washington University, however, used CAT as the basis for developing positron emission tomography (PET), a noninvasive sectioning technique that could provide information about function. Observations and research by a huge number of people over many years have been incorporated into what ultimately is today's PET.

The development of PET is interwoven with that of the radioactive isotopes, or "tracers," that it employs. In 1934 the French scientist Irène Joliot-Curie (**Figure 1.27**) and her husband, Frédéric Joliot-Curie, discovered that some originally nonradioactive nuclides emitted penetrating radiation after being irradiated. This observation led Ernest O. Lawrence (the inventor of the cyclotron) and his colleagues at UC Berkeley to realize that the cyclotron could be used to produce radioactive substances. If radioactive forms of oxygen, nitrogen, or carbon could be produced, then they could be injected into the blood circulation and would become incorporated into biologically active molecules. These molecules would concentrate in an organ, where the radioactivity would begin to decay. The concentration of the tracers could then be measured over time, allowing inferences about metabolism.

FIGURE 1.27
Irène Joliot-Curie (1897–1956).

In 1950, Gordon Brownell at Harvard University realized that positron decay (of a radioactive tracer) was associated with two gamma particles being emitted 180° apart. This handy discovery made possible the design and construction of a simple positron scanner with a pair of sodium iodide detectors. The machine was scanning patients for brain tumors in a matter of months (Sweet & Brownell, 1953). In 1959 David E. Kuhl, a radiology resident at the University of Pennsylvania who had been dabbling with radiation since high school (did his parents know?), and Roy Edwards, an engineer, combined tomography with gamma-emitting radioisotopes and obtained the first emission tomographic image.

The problem with most radioactive isotopes of nitrogen, oxygen, carbon, and fluorine is that their half-lives are measured in minutes. Anyone who was going to use them had to have their own cyclotron and be ready to roll as the isotopes were created. It happened that Washington University had both a cyclotron that produced radioactive oxygen-15 (^{15}O) and two researchers, Michel Ter-Pogossian and William Powers, who were interested in using it. They found that when injected into the bloodstream, ^{15}O-labeled water could be used to measure blood flow in the brain (Ter-Pogossian & Powers, 1958).

Ter-Pogossian (**Figure 1.28**) was joined in the 1970s by Michael Phelps (**Figure 1.29**), a graduate student who had started out his career as a Golden Gloves boxer. Excited about X-ray CT, they thought that they could adapt the technique to reconstruct the distribution within

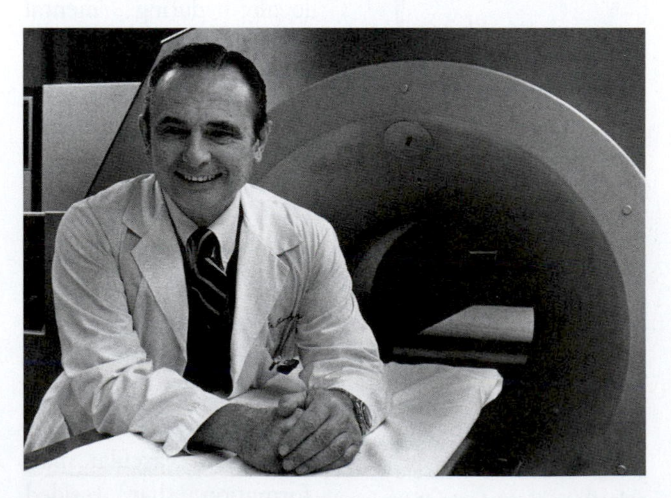

FIGURE 1.28
Michel M. Ter-Pogossian (1925–1996).

FIGURE 1.29
Michael E. Phelps (1939–).

an organ of a short-lived "physiological" radionuclide from its emissions. They designed and constructed the first positron emission tomograph and dubbed the method PETT (positron emission transaxial tomography; Ter-Pogossian et al., 1975), which later was shortened to PET.

Another metabolically important molecule in the brain is glucose. Under the direction of Joanna Fowler and Al Wolf, using Brookhaven National Laboratory's powerful cyclotron, ^{18}F-labeled 2-fluorodeoxy-D-glucose (2FDG) was created (Ido et al., 1978). Fluorine-18 has a half-life that is amenable to use in PET imaging and can give precise values of energy metabolism in the brain. The first work using PET to look for neural correlates of human behavior began when Phelps and Kuhl got together. Using 2FDG, they established a method for imaging the tissue consumption of glucose. Phelps, in a leap of insight, invented the block detector, a device that eventually increased spatial resolution of PET from 3 cm to 3 mm.

Magnetic Resonance Imaging

Magnetic resonance imaging (MRI) is based on the principle of nuclear magnetic resonance, which was first described and measured by the physicist Isidor Rabi in 1938. Discoveries made independently in 1946 by physicists Felix Bloch at Harvard University and Edward Purcell at Stanford University expanded the understanding of nuclear magnetic resonance to liquids and solids. For example, the protons in a water molecule line up like little bar magnets when placed in a magnetic field. If the equilibrium of these protons is disturbed by being zapped with radio frequency pulses, then a measurable voltage is induced in a receiver coil. The voltage changes over time as a function of the proton's environment. Analysis of the voltages can yield information about the examined tissue.

While on sabbatical in 1971, the chemist Paul Lauterbur (**Figure 1.30**) was thinking grand thoughts as he ate a fast-food hamburger. He scribbled his ideas on a nearby napkin, and from these humble beginnings he developed the theoretical model that led to the invention of the first magnetic resonance imaging scanner, located at SUNY Stony Brook (Lauterbur, 1973). It was another 20 years, however, before MRI was used to investigate brain function.

In the early 1990s, researchers at Massachusetts General Hospital demonstrated that after contrast material was injected into the bloodstream, changes in the blood volume of a human brain, produced by physiological manipulation of blood flow, could be measured using MRI (Belliveau et al., 1990). Not only were excellent anatomical images produced, but they could be linked to physiology that was germane to brain function. Lauterbur ultimately won the 2003 Nobel Prize in Physiology or Medicine for developing the theory behind MRI, though his first attempt at publishing his findings had been rejected by the journal *Nature*. He later quipped, "You could write the entire history of science in the last 50 years in terms of papers rejected by *Science* or *Nature*" (Wade, 2003).

FIGURE 1.30
Paul Lauterbur (1929–2007).

Functional Magnetic Resonance Imaging

When PET was introduced, the conventional wisdom was that increased blood flow to differentially active parts of the brain was driven by the brain's need for more oxygen. An increase in oxygen delivery permitted more glucose to be metabolized, and thus more energy would be available for performing the task. Although this idea sounded reasonable, few data were available to back it up. In fact, if this proposal were true, then increases in blood flow induced by functional demands should be similar to the increase in oxygen consumption. This would mean that the ratio of oxygenated to deoxygenated hemoglobin should stay constant. PET data, however, did not back up the hypothesis (Raichle, 2008).

Instead, Peter Fox and Marc Raichle, at Washington University, found that although functional activity induced increases in blood flow, there was no corresponding increase in oxygen consumption (Fox & Raichle, 1986). In addition, more glucose was being used than would be predicted from the amount of oxygen consumed (Fox et al., 1988). What was up with that? Raichle (2008) relates that, oddly enough, a random scribble written in the margin of Michael Faraday's lab notes in 1845 (Faraday, 1933) provided the hint that led to the solution of this puzzle. It was Linus Pauling and Charles Coryell who somehow happened upon this clue.

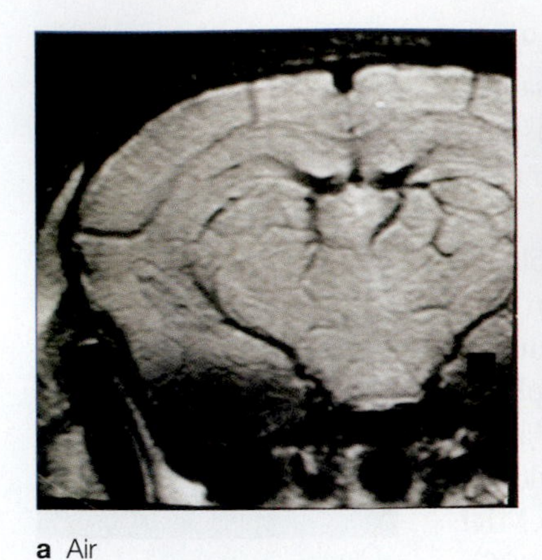

a Air

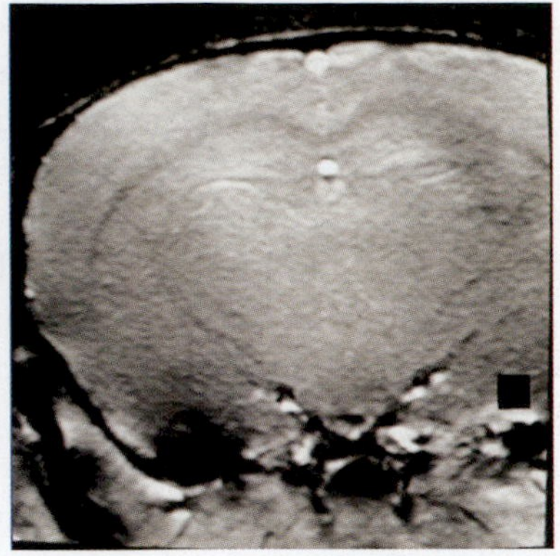

b O_2

FIGURE 1.31
Images of a mouse brain under varying oxygen conditions: (a) air; (b) O_2.

Faraday had noted that dried blood was not magnetic, and in the margin of his notes he had written that he must try fluid blood. He was puzzled because hemoglobin contains iron, a typically magnetic element. Ninety years later, Pauling and Coryell (1936), after reading Faraday's notes, became curious too. They found that, indeed, oxygenated and deoxygenated hemoglobin behave very differently in a magnetic field. Deoxygenated hemoglobin is weakly magnetic because of the exposed iron in the hemoglobin molecule.

Years later, Keith Thulborn remembered and capitalized on this property described by Pauling and Coryell, realizing that it was feasible to measure the state of oxygenation in vivo (Thulborn et al., 1982). Seiji Ogawa (1990) and his colleagues at AT&T Bell Laboratories tried manipulating oxygen levels by administering 100% oxygen alternated with room air (21% oxygen) to human subjects who were undergoing MRI. They discovered that on room air, the structure of the venous system was visible because of the contrast provided by the deoxygenated hemoglobin that was present. On 100% O_2, however, the venous system completely disappeared (**Figure 1.31**). Thus, contrast depended on the blood oxygen level. BOLD (blood oxygen level–dependent) contrast was born.

This technique led to the development of functional magnetic resonance imaging (fMRI). Functional MRI does not use ionizing radiation, it combines beautifully detailed images of the body with physiology related to brain function, and it is sensitive. Ken Kwong (a nuclear medicine physicist at Mass General) and his colleagues published the first human fMRI scans in 1992 (**Figure 1.32**). With all of these advantages, it did not take long for MRI and fMRI to be adopted by the research community, resulting in explosive growth of functional brain imaging.

Machines are useful only if you know what to do with them and what their limitations are. Raichle understood the potential of these new scanning methods, but he also realized that some basic problems had to be solved. If generalized information about brain function and anatomy were to be obtained, then the scans from different individuals performing the same tasks under the same circumstances had to be comparable. Achieving comparable results was proving difficult, however, since no two brains are precisely the same size and shape. Furthermore, early data were a mishmash of results that varied in anatomical location from person to person. Eric Reiman, a psychiatrist working with Raichle, suggested that averaging blood flow across subjects might solve this problem. The results of this approach were unambiguous, and the landmark paper that followed (Fox et al., 1988) presented the first integrated approach for the design, execution, and interpretation of functional brain images.

What really can be learned about the brain and the behavior of a human when a person is lying prone in a scanner? Cognitive psychologists Michael Posner, Steve Petersen, and Gordon Shulman, at Washington University, had developed innovative experimental paradigms including the cognitive subtraction method (first proposed by Franciscus Donders) for use while scanning with PET. The methodology was soon applied to fMRI. This joining together of cognitive psychology's experimental methods with brain imaging was the beginning of human functional brain mapping. Throughout this book, we will draw from the wealth of brain-imaging data that has been amassed in the last 40 years in our quest to learn about how the brain enables the mind.

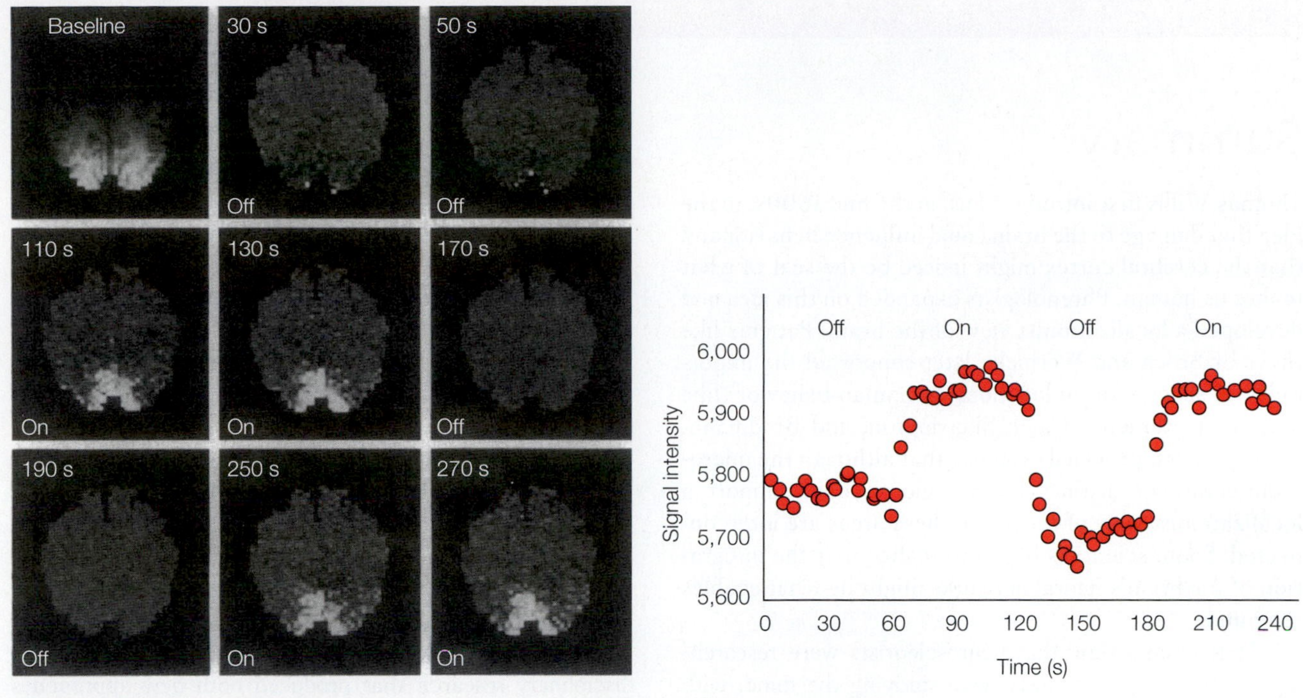

a fMRI images

b MRI visual cortex response

FIGURE 1.32 The first set of images from fMRI done on humans.
(a) Activation of the V1 region of visual cortex. (b) MRI visual cortex response. Signal intensity increases for a region of interest within the visual cortex when a light is off and then switched on. When the light is then turned off again, an undershoot in signal intensity occurs, consistent with known physiological oxygenation and pH changes.

1.5 The Book in Your Hands

Our goals in this book are to introduce you to the big questions and discussions in cognitive neuroscience and to teach you how to think, ask questions, and approach those questions like a cognitive neuroscientist. In the next chapter we introduce the biological foundations of the brain by presenting an overview of its cellular mechanisms and neuroanatomy. In Chapter 3 we discuss the methods that are available to us for observing mind–brain relationships, and we introduce how scientists go about interpreting and questioning those observations. Building on this foundation, in Chapters 4 through 11 we launch into the core processes of cognition: hemispheric specialization, sensation and perception, object recognition, attention, the control of action, learning and memory, emotion, and language, devoting a chapter to each. These are followed by chapters on cognitive control, social cognition, and consciousness.

Each chapter begins with a story that illustrates and introduces the chapter's main topic. Beginning with Chapter 4, the story is followed by an anatomical orientation highlighting the portions of the brain that we know are involved in these processes. Next, the heart of the chapter focuses on a discussion of the cognitive process and what is known about how it functions, followed by a summary and suggestions for further reading for those whose curiosity has been aroused.

Summary

Thomas Willis first introduced us, in the mid 1600s, to the idea that damage to the brain could influence behavior and that the cerebral cortex might indeed be the seat of what makes us human. Phrenologists expanded on this idea and developed a localizationist view of the brain. Patients like those of Broca and Wernicke later supported the importance of specific brain locations on human behavior (like language). Ramón y Cajal, Sherrington, and Brodmann, among others, provided evidence that although the microarchitecture of distinct brain regions could support a localizationist view of the brain, these areas are interconnected. Soon, scientists began to realize that the integration of the brain's neural networks might be what enables the mind.

At the same time that neuroscientists were researching the brain, psychologists were studying the mind, with its thoughts, beliefs, intentions, and so forth. Out of the philosophical theory of empiricism came the idea of associationism: that any response followed by a reward would be maintained, and that these associations were the basis of how the mind learned. Associationism was the prevailing theory for many years, until Hebb emphasized the biological basis of learning, and Chomsky and Miller realized that associationism couldn't explain all learning or all actions of the mind.

Neuroscientists and psychologists both reached the conclusion that there is more to the brain than just the sum of its parts, that the brain must enable the mind—but how? The term *cognitive neuroscience* was coined in the late 1970s because the fields of neuroscience and psychology were once again coming together. Neuroscience was in need of the theories of the psychology of the mind, and psychology was ready for a greater understanding of the working of the brain. The resulting marriage is cognitive neuroscience.

The last half of the 20th century saw a blossoming of interdisciplinary research that produced both new approaches and new technologies resulting in noninvasive methods for imaging brain structure, metabolism, and function.

So, welcome to cognitive neuroscience! It doesn't matter what your background is; there's a place for you here.

Key Terms

aggregate field theory (p. 7)
associationism (p. 12)
behaviorism (p. 12)
cognitive neuroscience (p. 4)
cytoarchitectonics (p. 9)
empiricism (p. 11)
Montreal procedure (p. 13)
neuron doctrine (p. 10)
phrenology (p. 6)
rationalism (p. 11)
syncytium (p. 10)

Think About It

1. Can we study how the mind works without studying the brain?
2. Will modern brain-imaging experiments become the new phrenology?
3. How do you think the brain might be studied in the future?
4. Why do good ideas and theories occasionally get lost over the passage of time? How do they often get rediscovered?

Suggested Reading

Finger, S. (1994). *Origins of neuroscience.* New York: Oxford University Press.

Frankfort, H., Frankfort, H. A., Wilson, J. A., & Jacobsen, T. (1977). *The intellectual adventure of ancient man: An essay of speculative thought in the ancient Near East* (first Phoenix ed.). Chicago: University of Chicago Press.

Kass-Simon, G., & Farnes, P. (1990). *Women of science: Righting the record.* Bloomington: Indiana University Press.

Lindzey, G. (Ed.). (1936). *History of psychology in autobiography* (Vol. 3). Worcester, MA: Clark University Press.

Miller, G. (2003). The cognitive revolution: A historical perspective. *Trends in Cognitive Sciences, 7,* 141–144.

Raichle, M. E. (1998). Behind the scenes of functional brain imaging: A historical and physiological perspective. *Proceedings of the National Academy of Sciences, USA, 95,* 765–772.

Shepherd, G. M. (1991). *Foundations of the neuron doctrine.* New York: Oxford University Press.

Zimmer, C. (2004). *Soul made flesh: The discovery of the brain—and how it changed the world.* New York: Free Press.

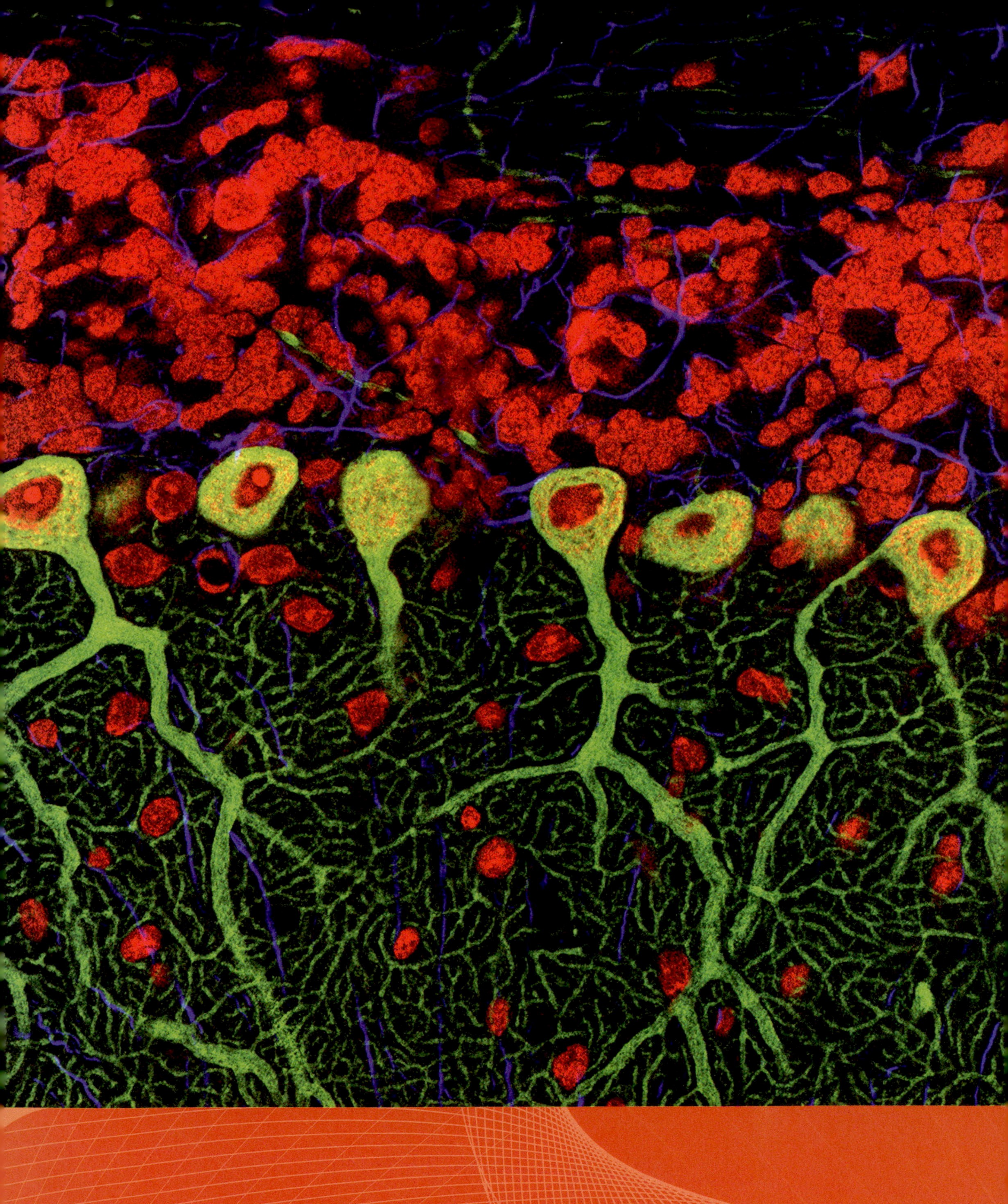

You shake my nerves and you rattle my brain.

Jerry Lee Lewis

Structure and Function of the Nervous System

CHAPTER

2

ONE DAY IN 1963, neuroscientist Jose Delgado coolly stood in a bullring in Córdoba, Spain, facing a charging bull. He did not sport the Spanish matador's typical gear of toreador pants, jacket, and sword, however. Instead, he stepped into the ring in slacks and a pullover sweater—and, for effect, a matador's cape—while holding a small electronic device in his hand. He was about to see if it worked.

The bull turned and charged, but Delgado stood his ground, his finger on the device's button. Then he pushed it. The bull skidded to a stop, standing a few feet before the scientist (**Figure 2.1**). The now placid bull stood there looking at Delgado, who gazed back, smiling. This otherwise ordinary bull had one odd feature that gave Delgado confidence: a surgically implanted electric stimulator in its caudate nucleus. The device in Delgado's hand was a radio transmitter that he had built to activate the stimulator. By stimulating the bull's caudate nucleus, Delgado had turned off its aggression.

What motivated Delgado's unusual scientific experiment? Years before, Delgado had been horrified by the increasingly popular frontal lobotomy surgical procedure that destroyed brain tissue—and along with it, its function—in order to treat mental disorders. He was interested in finding a more conservative approach to treating these disorders through electrical stimulation. Using his knowledge of the electrical properties of neurons, neuroanatomy, and brain function, Delgado designed the first remote-controlled neural implants ever to be used. Exceedingly controversial at the time, they were the forerunners of the now common intracranial devices that are used for stimulating the brain to treat disorders such as Parkinson's disease, chronic pain, neuromuscular dysfunction, and other maladies.

Delgado understood that the nervous system uses electrochemical signaling for communication. He also understood that inside the brain, neurons and their long-distance projections (axons) form intricate wiring patterns. An electrical signal

BIG Questions

- What are the elementary building blocks of the brain?
- How is information coded and transmitted in the brain?
- What are the organizing principles of the brain?
- What does the brain's structure tell us about its function and the behaviors it supports?

FIGURE 2.1 Jose Delgado halting a charging bull by remote control.

initiated at one location can travel to another location to trigger the contraction of a muscle, or the initiation or cessation of a behavior. This knowledge is the foundation on which all theories of neuronal signaling are built.

Our goal as cognitive neuroscientists is to figure out what the 89 billion neurons of the human brain do and how their collective action enables us to walk, talk, and imagine the unimaginable. We can approach the biological system that is the brain from several levels of analysis: from atomic, molecular, and cellular levels upward to circuit, network, system, and cognitive levels, and finally, to the highest levels, involving the interactions of humans with each other—our familial, societal, and cultural lives.

Since all theories of how the brain enables the mind must ultimately mesh with the actual nuts and bolts of the nervous system, and what it can and cannot do, we need to understand the basics of neurons. We must appreciate the structure and function of neurons on the individual level, as well as when they are strung together into the circuits, networks, and systems that form the brain and the nervous system as a whole. Thus, for us, it is important to understand the basic physiology of neurons and the anatomy of the nervous system. In this chapter we review the principles of brain structure that support cognition. In chapters that follow, we look at what results from the activity within and among specific brain circuits, networks, and systems (e.g., perception, cognition, emotion, and action).

2.1 The Cells of the Nervous System

The nervous system is composed of two main classes of cells: neurons and glial cells. **Neurons** are the basic signaling units that transmit information throughout the nervous system. As Santiago Ramón y Cajal and others of his time deduced, neurons take in information, make a "decision" about it following some relatively simple rules, and then, by changes in their activity levels, pass the signal along to other neurons or muscles. Neurons vary in their form, location, and interconnectivity within the nervous system (**Figure 2.2**), and these variations are closely related to their functions. **Glial cells** serve various functions in the nervous system, providing structural support and electrical insulation to neurons and modulating neuronal activity. We begin with a quick look at glial cells, after which we will turn our focus back to neurons.

Glial Cells

There are roughly as many glial cells in the brain as there are neurons. The central nervous system has three main types of glial cells: astrocytes, microglial cells, and oligodendrocytes (**Figure 2.3**). *Astrocytes* are large glial cells with round or radially symmetrical forms; they surround neurons and are in close contact with the brain's vasculature. An astrocyte makes contact with blood vessels at specializations called end feet, which permit the astrocyte to transport ions across the vascular wall.

The astrocytes create a barrier, called the **blood–brain barrier (BBB)**, between the tissues of the central nervous system and the blood. The BBB restricts the diffusion of microscopic objects (such as most bacteria) and large hydrophilic molecules in the blood from entering the neural tissue, but it allows the diffusion of small hydrophobic molecules, such as oxygen, carbon dioxide, and hormones. Many drugs and certain neuroactive agents, including dopamine and norepinephrine, when placed in the blood, cannot cross the BBB. Thus, it plays a vital role in protecting the central nervous system from blood-borne agents such as chemical compounds and also pathogens.

Evidence gathered over the past decade suggests that astrocytes also have an active role in brain function. In vitro studies indicate that they respond to and release neurotransmitters and other neuroactive substances that affect neuronal activity and modulate synaptic strength. In vivo studies found that when astrocyte activity is blocked, neuronal activity increases, supporting the notion that neuronal activity is moderated by astrocyte activity (Schummers et al., 2008). It is hypothesized that

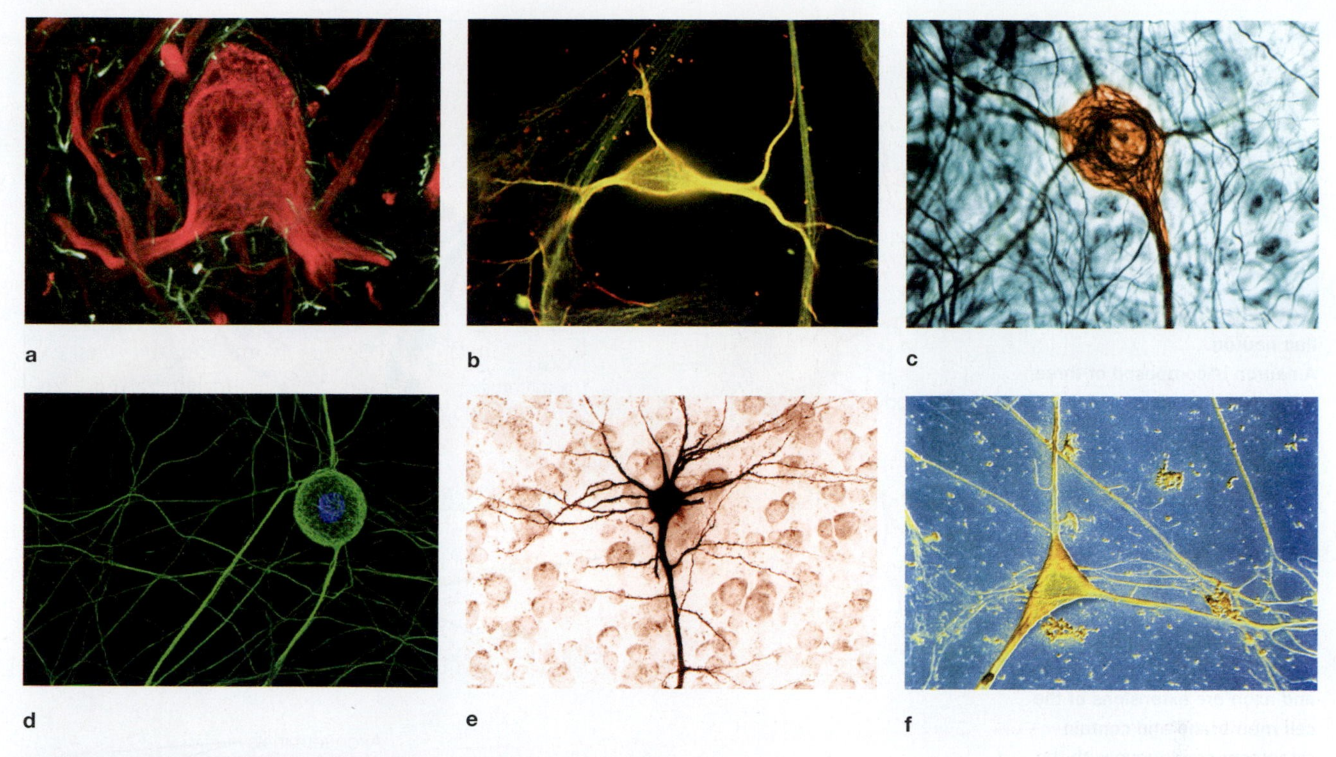

FIGURE 2.2 Mammalian neurons show enormous anatomical variety.
(a) Neuron (red) from the vestibular area of the brain. Glial cells are the thin, lighter structures (confocal light micrograph). **(b)** Hippocampal neuron (yellow; fluorescent micrograph). **(c)** Neuron (brown) in mouse dorsal root ganglion of the spinal cord (transmission electron micrograph). **(d)** Neuron in cell culture from dorsal root ganglia of an embryonic rat (fluorescent micrograph). **(e)** Pyramidal neuron from the brain. **(f)** Multipolar neuron cell body from human cerebral cortex (scanning electron micrograph).

astrocytes either directly or indirectly regulate the reuptake of neurotransmitters.

Glial cells also form the fatty substance called **myelin** in the nervous system. In the central nervous system, *oligodendrocytes* form myelin; in the peripheral nervous system, *Schwann cells* carry out this task (Figure 2.3). Both glial cell types create myelin by wrapping their cell membranes around the axon in a concentric manner during development and maturation. The cytoplasm in that portion of the glial cell is squeezed out, leaving layers of the lipid bilayer of the glial cell sheathing the membrane. Myelin is a good electrical insulator, preventing loss of electrical current across the cell membrane. It increases the speed and distance that information can travel along a neuron.

Microglial cells, which are small and irregularly shaped (Figure 2.3), are phagocytes that devour and remove damaged cells. Unlike many cells in the central nervous system, microglial cells can proliferate even in adults (as do other glial cells).

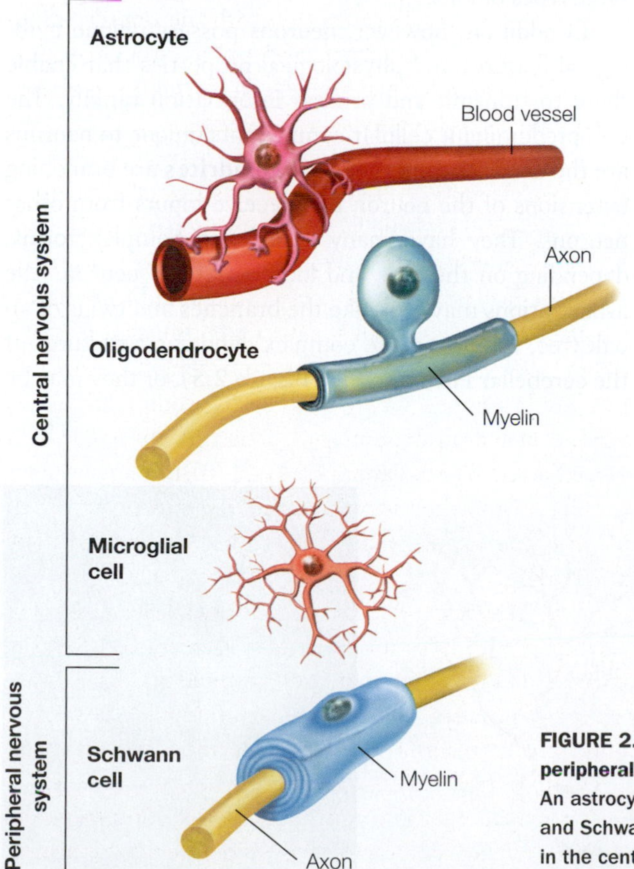

FIGURE 2.3 Various types of glial cells in the mammalian central and peripheral nervous systems.
An astrocyte is shown with end feet attached to a blood vessel. Oligodendrocytes and Schwann cells produce myelin around the axons of neurons (oligodendrocytes in the central nervous system, Schwann cells in the peripheral nervous system). Microglial cells dispose of damaged cells.

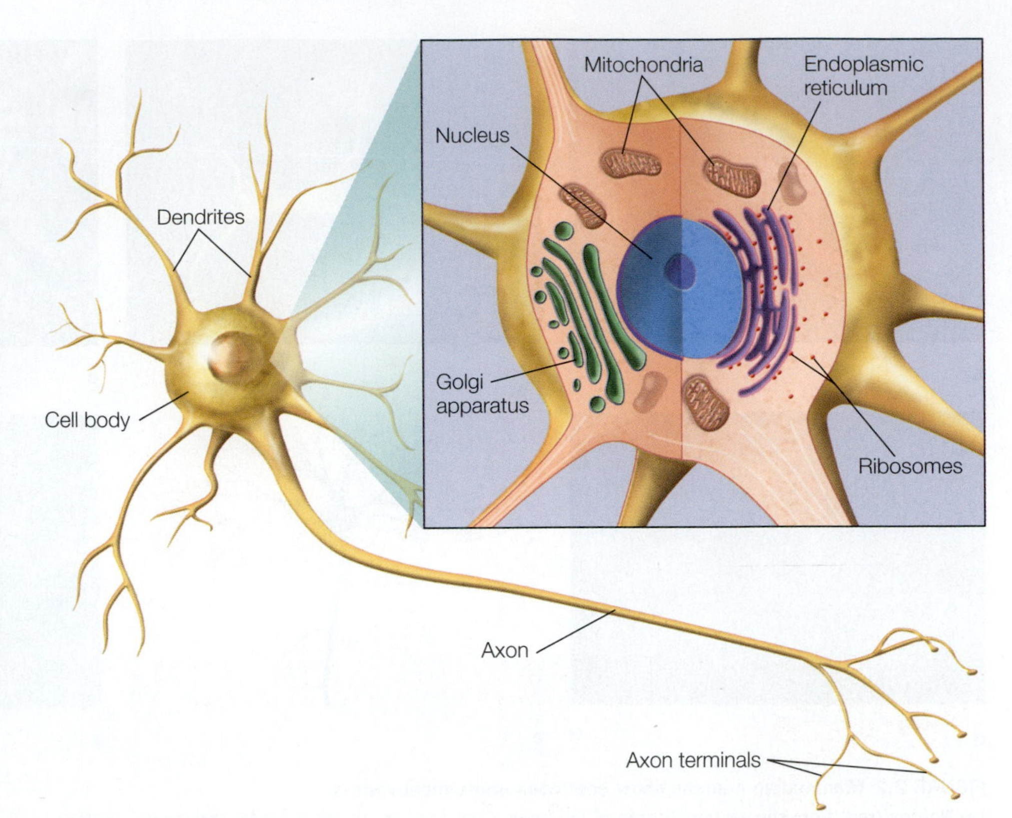

FIGURE 2.4 Idealized mammalian neuron.
A neuron is composed of three main parts: a cell body, dendrites, and an axon. The cell body contains the cellular machinery for the production of proteins and other macromolecules. Like other cells, the neuron contains a nucleus, endoplasmic reticulum, ribosomes, mitochondria, Golgi apparatus, and other intracellular organelles (inset). The dendrites and axon are extensions of the cell membrane and contain cytoplasm continuous with the cytoplasm inside the cell body.

Neurons

The standard cellular components found in almost all eukaryotic cells are also found in neurons (as well as in glial cells). A cell membrane encases the cell body (in neurons, it is sometimes called the **soma**; Greek for "body"), which contains the metabolic machinery that maintains the neuron: nucleus, endoplasmic reticulum, cytoskeleton, mitochondria, Golgi apparatus, and other common intracellular organelles (**Figure 2.4**). These structures are suspended in cytoplasm, the salty intracellular fluid that is made up of a combination of ions (molecules or atoms that have either a positive or negative electrical charge)—predominantly ions of potassium, sodium, chloride, and calcium—as well as molecules such as proteins. The neuron itself, like any other cell, sits in a bath of salty extracellular fluid, which is made up of a mixture of the same types of ions.

In addition, however, neurons possess unique cytological features and physiological properties that enable them to transmit and process information rapidly. The two predominant cellular components unique to neurons are the dendrites and the axon. **Dendrites** are branching extensions of the neuron that receive inputs from other neurons. They have many varied and complex forms, depending on the type and location of the neuron. The arborizations may look like the branches and twigs of an oak tree, as seen in the complex dendritic structures of the cerebellar Purkinje cells (**Figure 2.5**), or they may be

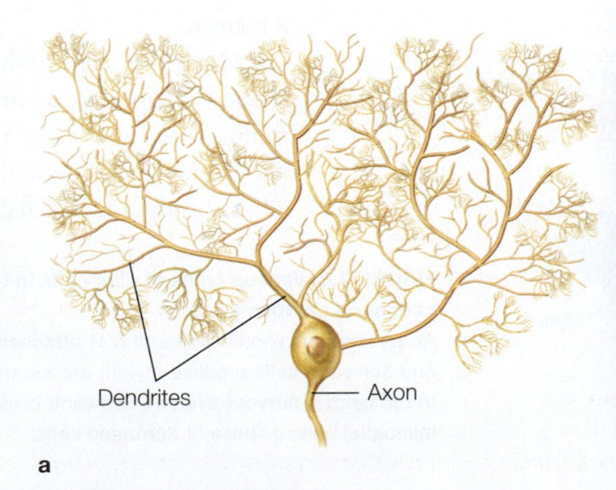

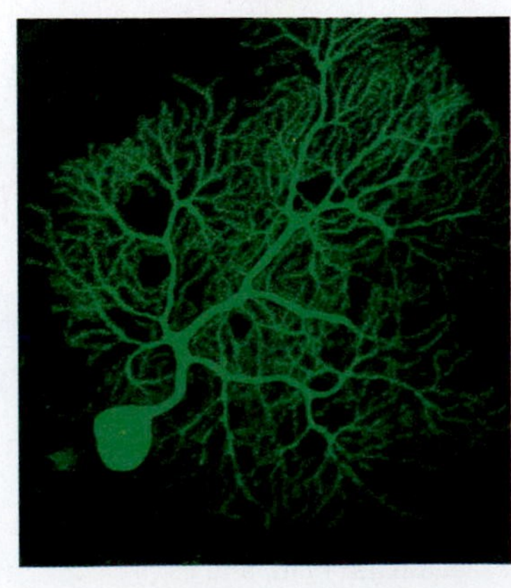

FIGURE 2.5 Soma and dendritic tree of a Purkinje cell from the cerebellum.
The Purkinje cells are arrayed in rows in the cerebellum. Each one has a large dendritic tree that is wider in one direction than the other. (**a**) Drawing of Purkinje cell as viewed in a cross section through a cerebellar folium. (**b**) Confocal micrograph of a Purkinje cell from mouse cerebellum. The cell is visualized using fluorescence methods.

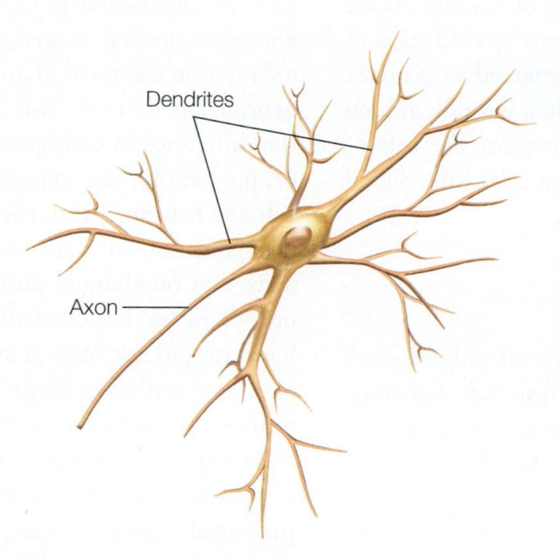

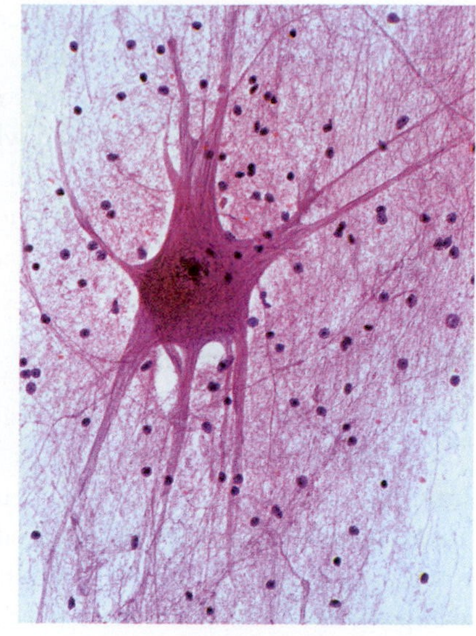

FIGURE 2.6 Spinal motor neuron.
(a) Neurons located in the ventral horn of the spinal cord send their axons out the ventral root to make synapses on muscle fibers. **(b)** A spinal cord motor neuron stained with cresyl echt violet stain.

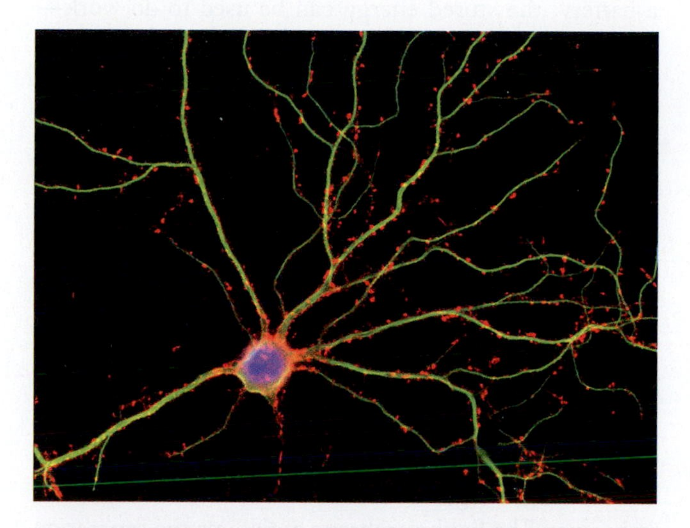

FIGURE 2.7 Dendritic spines on cultured rat hippocampal neurons. This neuron has been triple stained to reveal the cell body (blue), dendrites (green), and spines (red).

much simpler, such as the dendrites in spinal motor neurons (**Figure 2.6**). Most dendrites also have specialized processes called **spines**, little knobs attached by small necks to the surface of the dendrites, where the dendrites receive inputs from other neurons (**Figure 2.7**).

The **axon** is a single process that extends from the cell body. This structure represents the output side of the neuron. Electrical signals travel along the length of the axon to its end, the axon terminals, where the neuron transmits the signal to other neurons or other targets. Transmission occurs at the **synapse**, a specialized structure where two neurons come into close contact so that chemical or electrical signals can be passed from one cell to the next. Some axons branch to form **axon collaterals** that can transmit signals to more than one cell (**Figure 2.8**).

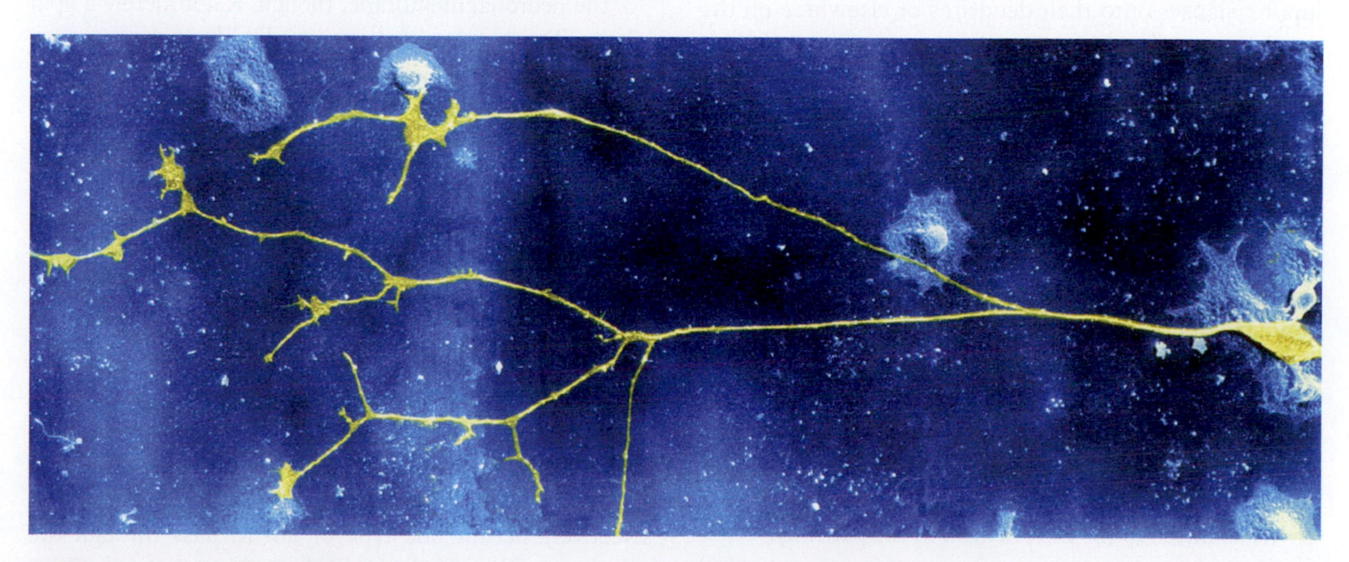

FIGURE 2.8 Axons can take different forms.
A neuron (far right) and its axon collaterals (left half of image) are shown stained in yellow. The cell body (at far right) gives rise to an axon, which branches, forming collaterals that can make contact with many different neurons.

Many axons are wrapped in layers of myelin. Along the length of the axons, there are evenly spaced gaps in the myelin; these gaps are commonly referred to as nodes of Ranvier (see Figure 2.12). Later, when we look at how signals move down an axon, we will explore the role of myelin and the nodes of Ranvier in accelerating signal transmission.

Neuronal Signaling

Neurons receive, evaluate, and transmit information. These processes are referred to as *neuronal signaling*. Information that is received by the neuron at its input synapses passes through the cell body and then, via the axon, to output synapses on the axon terminals. At these output synapses, information is transferred across synapses from one neuron to the next neuron; or to nonneuronal cells such as those in muscles or glands; or to other targets, such as blood vessels.

Within a neuron, information moves from input synapses to output synapses through changes in the electrical state of the neuron caused by the flow of electrical currents within the neuron and across its neuronal membrane. *Between* neurons, information transfer across synapses is typically mediated chemically by neurotransmitters (signaling molecules); these synapses are called *chemical synapses*. At *electrical synapses*, however, signals between neurons travel via transsynaptic electrical currents. Regarding information flow, neurons are referred to as either presynaptic or postsynaptic in relation to any particular synapse. *Most neurons are both presynaptic and postsynaptic:* They are **presynaptic** when their axon's output synapses make connections onto other neurons or targets, and they are **postsynaptic** when other neurons make a connection at input synapses onto their dendrites or elsewhere on the receiving neuron.

THE MEMBRANE POTENTIAL The process of signaling has several stages. Let's return to Delgado's bull, whose neurons process information in the same way ours do. The bull is snorting about in the dirt, head down, when suddenly a sound wave—produced by Delgado entering the ring—courses down its auditory canal and hits the tympanic membrane (eardrum). The resultant stimulation of the auditory receptor cells (auditory hair cells) generates neuronal signals that are transmitted via the auditory pathways to the brain. At each stage of this ascending auditory pathway, neurons receive inputs on their dendrites that typically cause them to generate signals that are transmitted to the next neuron in the pathway.

How does the neuron generate these signals, and what are these signals? To answer these questions, we have to understand several things about neurons. First, energy is needed to generate the signals. Second, this energy is in the form of an electrical potential across the neuronal membrane. This electrical potential is defined as the difference in voltage across the neuronal membrane or, put simply, the voltage inside the neuron versus outside the neuron. Third, these two voltages depend on the concentrations of potassium, sodium, and chloride ions, as well as on charged protein molecules both inside and outside of the cell. Fourth, when a neuron is in its resting state and not actively signaling, the inside of a neuron is more negatively charged than the outside. The voltage difference across the neuronal membrane in the resting state is typically about −70 millivolts (mV) inside, which is known as the *resting potential* or **resting membrane potential**. This electrical-potential difference means that the neuron has at its disposal a kind of battery; and like a battery, the stored energy can be used to do work—signaling work (**Figure 2.9**).

How does the neuron generate and maintain this resting potential, and how does it use it for signaling? To answer these questions about function, we first need to examine the structures in the neuron that are involved in signaling. The bulk of the *neuronal membrane* is a bilayer of fatty lipid molecules that separates the cytoplasm from the extracellular milieu. Because the membrane is composed of lipids, it does not dissolve in the watery environments found inside and outside of the neuron, and it blocks the flow of water-soluble substances between the inside and the outside. It prevents ions, proteins, and other water-soluble molecules from moving across it. To understand neuronal signaling, we must focus on ions. This point is important: The lipid membrane maintains the separation of intracellular and extracellular ions and electrical charge that ultimately permits neuronal communication.

The neuronal membrane, though, is not merely a lipid bilayer. The membrane is peppered with transmembrane proteins, some of which serve as conduits for ions to move across the membrane (Figure 2.9, inset). These proteins are of two main types: ion channels and ion pumps. **Ion channels**, as we will see, are proteins with a pore through the center, and they allow certain ions to flow down their electrochemical and concentration gradients. **Ion pumps** use energy to actively transport ions across the membrane against their concentration gradients—that is, from regions of low concentration to regions of higher concentration.

Ion channels. The transmembrane passageways created by ion channels are formed from the three-dimensional structure of these proteins. These hydrophilic channels selectively permit one type of ion to pass through the membrane. The ion channels of concern to us—the ones found in neurons—are selective for sodium, potassium,

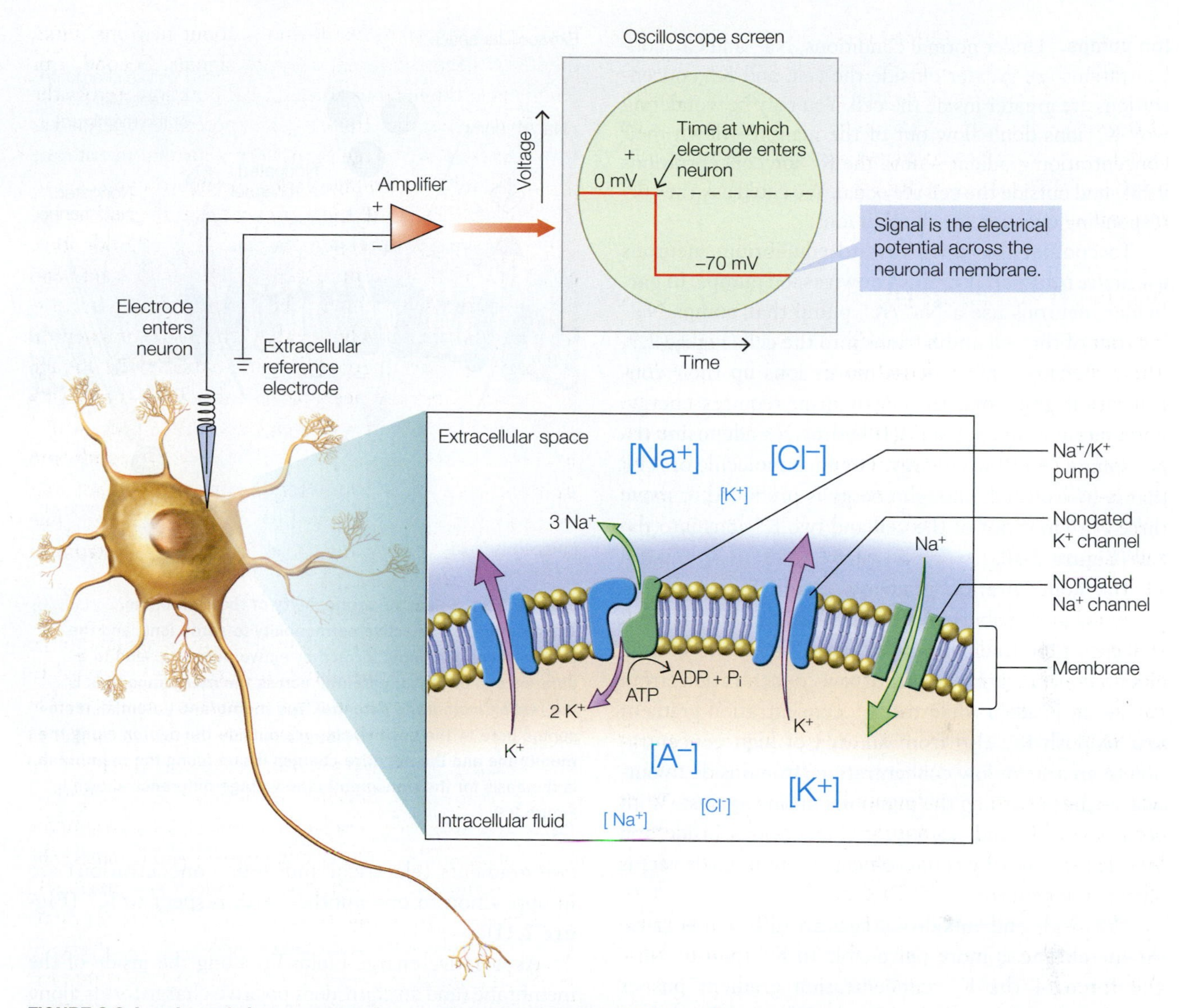

FIGURE 2.9 Ion channels in a segment of neuronal membrane and measuring resting membrane potential.
Idealized neuron (left), shown with an intracellular recording electrode penetrating the neuron. The electrode measures the difference between the voltage inside versus outside the neuron, and this difference is amplified and displayed on an oscilloscope screen (top). The oscilloscope screen shows voltage over time. Before the electrode enters the neuron, the voltage difference between the electrode and the extracellular reference electrode is zero, but when the electrode is pushed into the neuron, the difference becomes −70 mV, which is the resting membrane potential. The resting membrane potential arises from the asymmetrical distribution of ions of sodium (Na^+), potassium (K^+), and chloride (Cl^-), as well as of charged protein molecules (A^-), across the neuron's cell membrane (inset).

calcium, or chloride ions (Na^+, K^+, Ca^{2+}, and Cl^-, respectively; Figure 2.9, inset). The extent to which a particular ion can cross the membrane through a given ion channel is referred to as its **permeability**. This characteristic of ion channels gives the neuronal membrane the attribute of *selective permeability*. (Selective permeability is actually a property of all cells in the body; as part of cellular homeostasis, it enables cells to maintain internal chemical stability.) The neuronal membrane is more permeable to K^+ than to Na^+ (or other) ions—a property that contributes to the resting membrane potential, as we will learn shortly. The membrane permeability to K^+ is larger because there are many more K^+-selective channels than any other type of ion channel.

Unlike most cells in the body, neurons are excitable, meaning that their membrane permeability can change (because the membranes have ion channels that are capable of changing their permeability for a particular ion). Such proteins are called *gated ion channels*. They open or close in response to changes in nearby transmembrane voltage, or to chemical or physical stimuli. In contrast, ion channels that are unregulated, and hence always allow the associated ion to pass through, are known as *nongated ion channels*.

Ion pumps. Under normal conditions, Na^+ and Cl^- concentrations are greater outside the cell, and K^+ concentrations are greater inside the cell. You may be wondering why K^+ ions don't flow out of the neuron—down their concentration gradient—until the K^+ ion concentrations inside and outside the cell are equal. We could ask the corresponding question for all other ions.

To combat this drive toward equilibrium, neurons use *active transport* proteins known as ion pumps. In particular, neurons use a Na^+/K^+ pump that pumps Na^+ ions out of the cell and K^+ ions into the cell (Figure 2.9, inset). Because this process moves ions up their concentration gradients, the mechanism requires energy. Each pump is an enzyme that hydrolyzes adenosine triphosphate (ATP) for energy. For each molecule of ATP that is hydrolyzed, enough energy is produced to move three Na^+ ions out of the cell and two K^+ ions into the cell (**Figure 2.10**).

The concentration gradients create forces due to the unequal distribution of ions. The force of the Na^+ concentration gradient acts to push Na^+ from an area of high concentration to one of low concentration (from outside to inside), while the K^+ concentration gradient acts to push K^+ also from an area of high concentration to an area of low concentration (from inside to outside)—the very thing the pump is working against. With both positively and negatively charged ions inside and outside the cell, why is the voltage different inside versus outside the neuron?

The inside and outside voltages are different because the membrane is more permeable to K^+ than to Na^+. The force of the K^+ concentration gradient pushes some K^+ out of the cell, leaving the inside of the neuron slightly more negative than the outside. This difference creates another force, an **electrical gradient**, because each K^+ ion carries one unit of positive charge out of the neuron as it moves across the membrane. These two gradients (electrical and ionic concentration) are in opposition to one another with respect to K^+ (**Figure 2.11**).

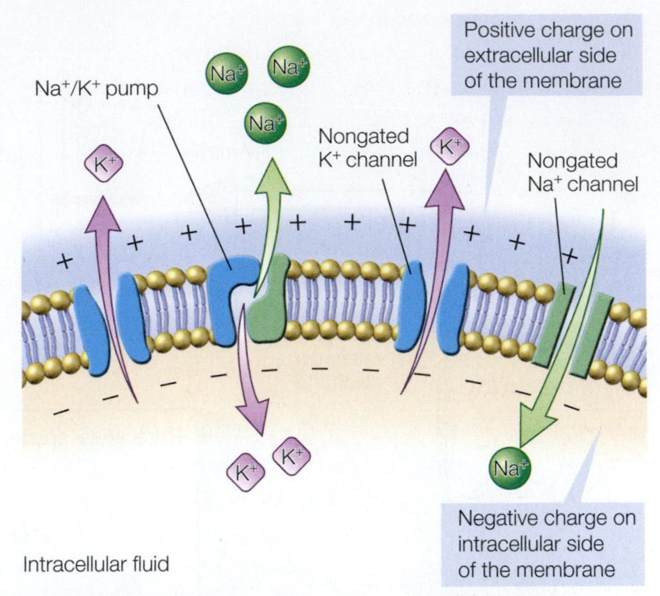

FIGURE 2.11 Selective permeability of the membrane. The membrane's selective permeability to some ions, and the concentration gradients formed by active pumping, lead to a difference in electrical potential across the membrane; this is the *resting membrane potential*. The membrane potential, represented here by the positive charges outside the neuron along the membrane and the negative charges inside along the membrane, is the basis for the transmembrane voltage difference shown in Figure 2.9.

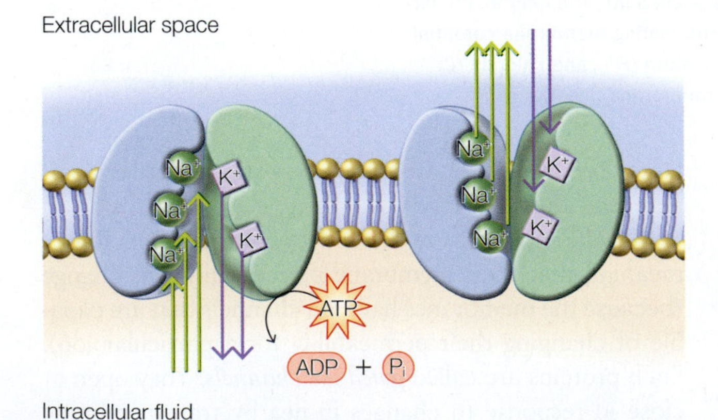

FIGURE 2.10 Ion pumps transport ions across the membrane. The Na^+/K^+ pump preserves the cell's resting potential by maintaining a larger concentration of K^+ inside the cell and Na^+ outside the cell. The pump uses ATP as energy.

As negative charge builds up along the inside of the membrane (and an equivalent positive charge forms along the extracellular side), the positively charged K^+ ions outside of the cell are drawn electrically back into the neuron through the same ion channels that are allowing K^+ ions to leave the cell by diffusion. Eventually, the force of the concentration gradient pushing K^+ out through the K^+ channels is equal to the force of the electrical gradient driving K^+ in. When that happens, the opposing forces are said to reach *electrochemical equilibrium*. The difference in charge thus produced across the membrane is the resting membrane potential, that –70 mV difference. The value for the resting membrane potential of any cell can be calculated by using knowledge from electrochemistry, provided that the concentrations of ions inside and outside the neuron are known.

THE ACTION POTENTIAL We now understand the basis of the energy source that neurons can use for signaling. Next we want to learn how this energy can be used to transmit information within a neuron, from its dendrites, which receive inputs from other neurons, to its axon terminals, where it signals to the next neuron(s) in the chain. The process begins when synapses on a neuron's dendrites receive a signal (e.g., a neurotransmitter binding to a receptor), resulting in the opening of ion channels in the dendrite, which causes ionic currents to flow. For excitatory synaptic inputs, *excitatory postsynaptic potentials (EPSPs)* occur in the dendrite, and ionic currents flow through the volume of the neuron's cell body. If these currents happen to be strong enough to reach distant axon terminals, then the process of neuronal signaling is complete. In the vast majority of cases, however, the distance from dendrites to axon terminals is too great for the EPSP to have any effect. Why?

The small electrical current produced by the EPSP is passively conducted through the cytoplasm of the dendrite, cell body, and axon. Passive current conduction is called **electrotonic conduction** or *decremental conduction:* "decremental" because it diminishes with distance from its origin—the synapse on the dendrites, in this case. The maximum distance a passive current will flow in a neuron is only about 1 mm. In most neurons, a millimeter is too short to effectively conduct electrical signals, although sometimes, like in a structure such as the retina, a millimeter is sufficient to permit neuron-to-neuron communication via decremental conduction. Most of the time, however, the reduction in signal intensity with decremental conduction means that long-distance communication within a neuron from dendrite to axon terminal will fail (your toes would be in trouble, for example, because they are about 1 meter from the spinal cord and close to 2 meters from the brain). How does the neuron solve this problem of decremental conduction and the need to conduct signals over long distances?

Neurons evolved a clever mechanism to regenerate and pass along the signal received at synapses on the dendrite: the **action potential**. It works something like 19th-century firefighters in a bucket brigade. An action potential is a rapid depolarization and repolarization of a small region of the membrane on the neuron's output via its axon caused by the opening and closing of ion channels.

An action potential is a different process from the EPSP and the ionic currents involved in decremental conduction. The action potential doesn't decrement after only 1 mm. Action potentials enable signals to travel for meters with no loss in signal strength, because they continually regenerate the signal at each patch of membrane on the axon. This is one reason why giraffes and blue whales can have neurons whose axon terminals may be many meters from their dendrites.

The action potential is able to regenerate itself because of the presence of **voltage-gated ion channels** located in the neuronal membrane (**Figure 2.12a**, inset). The densest concentration of ion channels is found at the

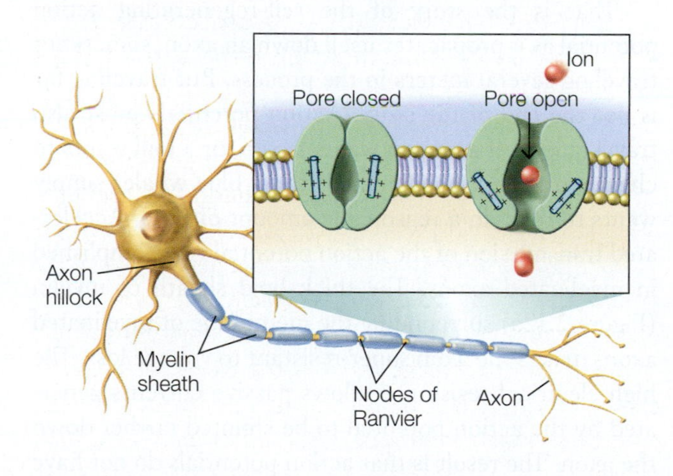

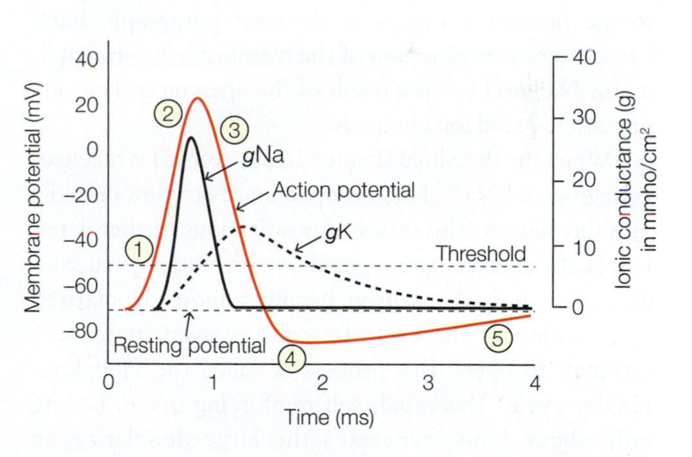

FIGURE 2.12 The neuronal action potential, voltage-gated ion channels, and changes in channel conductance.

(a) An idealized neuron with myelinated axon and axon terminals. Voltage-gated ion channels located in the spike-triggering zone at the axon hillock and along the extent of the axon at the nodes of Ranvier open and close rapidly, changing their conductance to specific ions (e.g., Na^+), altering the membrane potential and resulting in the action potential (inset). **(b)** The relative time course of changes in membrane voltage during an action potential, and the underlying causative changes in membrane conductance to Na^+ (gNa) and K^+ (gK). The initial depolarizing phase of the action potential (red line) is mediated by increased Na^+ conductance (black line), and the later repolarizing, descending phase of the action potential is mediated by an increase in K^+ conductance (dashed line) that occurs when the K^+ channels open. The Na^+ channels have closed during the last part of the action potential, when repolarization by the K^+ current is taking place. The action potential undershoots the resting membrane potential at the point where the membrane becomes more negative than the resting membrane potential.

spike-triggering zone in the **axon hillock**, a specialized region of the neuronal soma where the axon emerges. As its name denotes, the spike-triggering zone initiates the action potential. (The term *spike* is shorthand for an action potential because it represents a rapid change and a peak in the depolarization of the membrane potential, and it actually looks like a spike when viewed as a recording displayed on an oscilloscope or computer screen.) Ion channels are also found along the axon. In myelinated axons, voltage-gated ion channels along the axon's length are restricted to the **nodes of Ranvier**. Named after the French histologist and anatomist Louis-Antoine Ranvier, who first described them, they are regular intervals along the axon where gaps in myelination occur (Figure 2.12a).

How does the spike-triggering zone initiate an action potential? The passive electrical currents that are generated following EPSPs on multiple distant dendrites sum together at the axon hillock. This current flows across the neuronal membrane in the spike-triggering zone, depolarizing the membrane. If the depolarization is strong enough, meaning that the membrane moves from its resting potential of about –70 mV to a less negative value of approximately –55 mV, then an action potential is triggered. We refer to this **depolarized** membrane potential value as the **threshold** for initiating an action potential. **Figure 2.12b** illustrates an idealized action potential. The numbered circles in the figure correspond to the numbered events in the next paragraph. Each event alters a small region of the membrane's permeability for Na^+ and K^+ as a result of the opening and closing of voltage-gated ion channels.

When the threshold (Figure 2.12b, event 1) is reached, voltage-gated Na^+ channels open and Na^+ flows rapidly into the neuron. This influx of positive ions further depolarizes the neuron, opening additional voltage-gated Na^+ channels; thus, the neuron becomes more depolarized (2), continuing the cycle by causing even more Na^+ channels to open. This process is called the Hodgkin–Huxley cycle. This rapid, self-reinforcing cycle, lasting only about 1 ms, generates the large depolarization that is the first portion of the action potential. Next, the voltage-gated K^+ channels open, allowing K^+ to flow out of the neuron down its concentration gradient. This outward flow of positive ions begins to shift the membrane potential back toward its resting potential (3). The opening of the K^+ channels outlasts the closing of the Na^+ channels, causing a second repolarizing phase of the action potential; this repolarization drives the membrane potential toward the equilibrium potential of K^+, which is even more negative than the resting potential. The **equilibrium potential** is the membrane potential at which there is no net flux of a given ion. As a result, the membrane is temporarily **hyperpolarized:** At about –80 mV, the membrane potential is more negative than both the resting membrane potential and the threshold required for triggering an action potential (4). Hyperpolarization causes the K^+ channels to close, in response to which the membrane potential gradually returns to its resting state (5).

During this transient hyperpolarization state, the voltage-gated Na^+ channels are unable to open, and no other action potential can be generated. This is known as the *absolute refractory period*. It is followed by the *relative refractory period*, during which the neuron can generate action potentials, but only with larger-than-normal depolarizing currents. The entire **refractory period** lasts only a couple of milliseconds and has two consequences. One is that the neuron's speed for generating action potentials is limited to about 200 action potentials per second. The other is that the passive current that flows from the action potential cannot reopen the ion-gated channels that generated it. The passive current, however, does flow down the axon with enough strength to depolarize the membrane a bit farther on, where the ion channels are not in a refractory state, opening voltage-gated channels in this next portion of the membrane. The result is that the action potential moves down the axon in one direction only—from the axon hillock toward the axon terminal.

That is the story of the self-regenerating action potential as it propagates itself down an axon, sometimes traveling several meters in the process. But traveling far is not the end of the story. Action potentials must also travel quickly if a person wants to run, or a bull wants to charge, or a very large animal (think blue whale) simply wants to react in a reasonable amount of time. Accelerated transmission of the action potential is accomplished in myelinated axons. The thick lipid sheath of myelin (Figure 2.12a) surrounding the membrane of myelinated axons makes the axon super-resistant to voltage loss. The high electrical resistance allows passive currents generated by the action potential to be shunted farther down the axon. The result is that action potentials do not have to be generated as often, and they can be spread out along the axon at wider intervals.

Indeed, action potentials in myelinated axons need occur only at the nodes of Ranvier, where myelination is interrupted. As a result, the action potential appears to jump down the axon at great speed, from one node of Ranvier to the next. We call this **saltatory conduction** (the term is derived from the Latin word *saltare*, meaning "to jump or leap"). The importance of myelin for efficient neuronal conduction is notable when it is damaged or lost, which is what happens in multiple sclerosis (MS).

There is one more interesting tidbit concerning action potentials: Because they always have the same amplitude, they are said to be *all-or-none* phenomena. Since one action potential has the same amplitude as any other, the strength of the action potential does not communicate anything about the strength of the stimulus that initiated it. The intensity of a stimulus (e.g., a sensory signal) is communicated by the *rate of firing* of the action potentials: More intense stimuli elicit higher action-potential firing rates.

NEURAL OSCILLATIONS So far, we have presented an idealized situation: A neuron is sitting in a resting state, awaiting inputs that might cause it to experience EPSPs and action potentials at the axon hillock that move down the axon to transmit signals. But most neurons actually fire at a continuous baseline rate. This rate is different in different types of neurons, and it can be the result of either intrinsic properties of the neuron itself or activity in small neural circuits or larger neural networks. These neuronal oscillations are important for understanding some of the signals we can receive from electrodes placed in an intact brain or on the surface of the scalp. Because postsynaptic potentials like EPSPs can be recorded from populations of neurons, they are another measure of neuronal activity in addition to recordings of action potentials. In Chapter 3 we describe how these postsynaptic potentials, and not the action potentials, are the sources of electrical signals that can be recorded from the cortical surface or scalp in humans and animals using electroencephalography.

TAKE-HOME MESSAGES

- Glial cells form myelin around the axons of neurons. Myelin enables the rapid transmission of action potentials down an axon and increases the distance over which transmission can occur.
- Neurons communicate with other neurons and cells at specialized structures called synapses, where chemical and electrical signals can be conveyed between neurons.
- The electrical gradient across a neuron's membrane results from the asymmetrical distribution of ions. The electrical difference across the membrane is the basis of the resting potential, the voltage difference across the neuronal membrane during rest (i.e., not during any phase of the action potential).
- Ion channels, formed by transmembrane proteins, can be either passive (always open) or gated (open only in the presence of electrical, chemical, or physical stimuli).
- Synaptic inputs result in postsynaptic potentials, and current to flow in the postsynaptic neuron.
- Postsynaptic currents can depolarize the axon hillock region, generating an action potential.
- Action potentials are all-or-none phenomena: The amplitude of the action potential does not depend on the size of the triggering depolarization, as long as that depolarization reaches the threshold for initiating the action potential.
- Nodes of Ranvier are the spaces between sheaths of myelin where voltage-gated Na^+ and K^+ channels are located and action potentials occur.
- Postsynaptic potentials lead to action potentials but also can be measured from large populations of neurons by electrodes located some distance away, such as the scalp, as when the oscillatory signals in an electroencephalogram (EEG) are being recorded.

2.2 Synaptic Transmission

Neurons communicate with other neurons, with muscles, or with glands at synapses, and the transfer of a signal from the axon terminal of one neuron to the next neuron is called *synaptic transmission*. There are two major kinds of synapses—chemical and electrical—each using very different mechanisms for synaptic transmission.

Chemical Transmission

Most neurons send a signal to the cell across the synapse by releasing chemical neurotransmitters into the **synaptic cleft**, the gap between neurons at the synapse. The general mechanism is as follows: The arrival of the action potential at the axon terminal leads to depolarization of the terminal membrane, causing voltage-gated Ca^{2+} channels to open. The opening of these channels triggers small **vesicles** containing neurotransmitter to fuse with the membrane at the synapse and release the transmitter into the synaptic cleft. Different neurons produce and release different neurotransmitters, and some may release more than one type at a time, in what is called co-transmission. The transmitter diffuses across the cleft and, on reaching the postsynaptic membrane, binds with specific receptors embedded in it (**Figure 2.13**).

There are two types of postsynaptic receptors: ligand-gated ion channels where neurotransmitter binding directly gates (opens) the ion channel, and G protein–coupled receptors (GPCRs) where biochemical signals indirectly cause the gating of ion channels; G proteins are those that bind the guanine nucleotides GDP and GTP (guanosine di- and triphosphate) and act as molecular switches in cells. Specific neurotransmitters bind to each type of postsynaptic receptor. In ligand-gated ion channels, binding induces a conformational change in the receptor. The change in shape opens an ion channel, resulting in an influx of ions

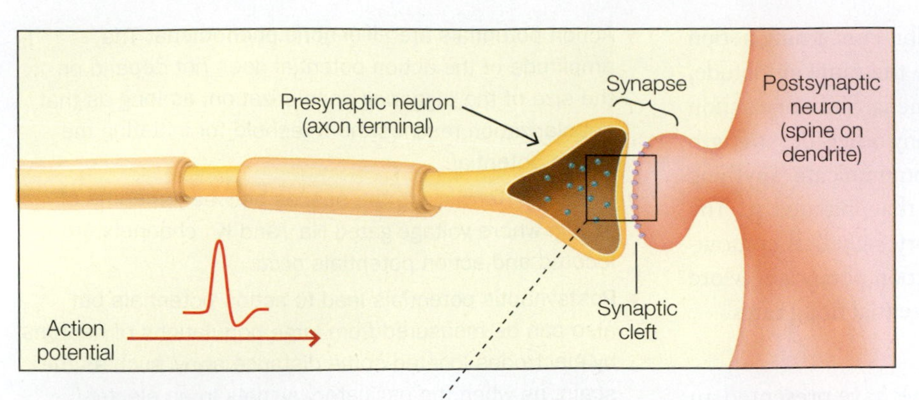

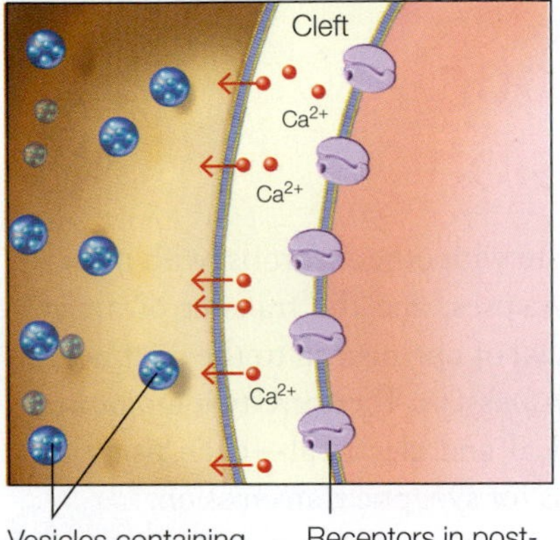

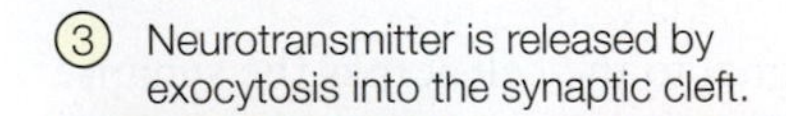

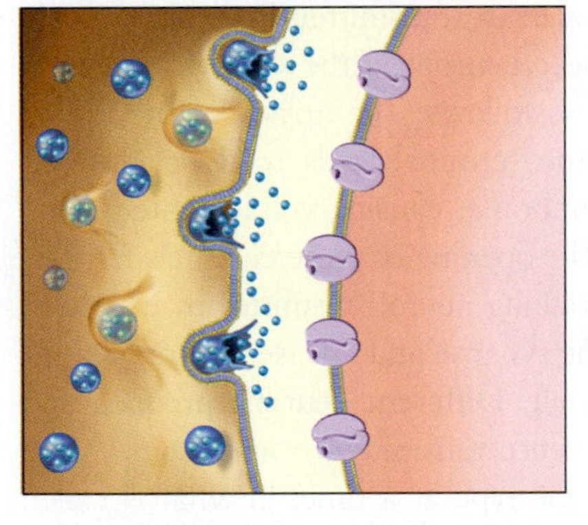

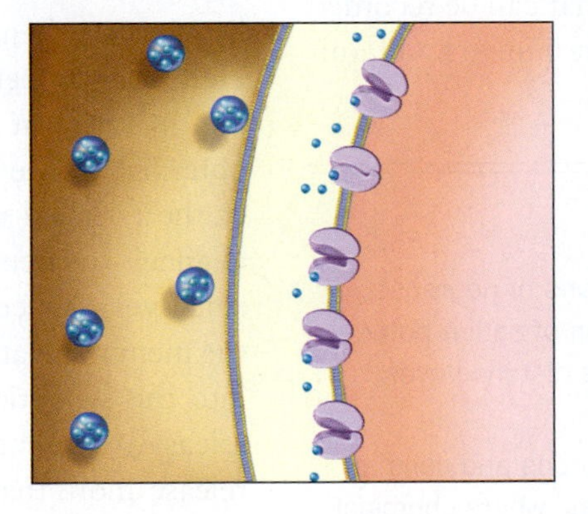

FIGURE 2.13 Neurotransmitter release at the synapse, into the synaptic cleft. The synapse consists of various specializations where the presynaptic and postsynaptic membranes are close together. When the action potential invades the axon terminals, it causes voltage-gated Ca^{2+} channels to open (1), triggering vesicles to bind to the presynaptic membrane (2). Neurotransmitter is released into the synaptic cleft by exocytosis and diffuses across the cleft (3). Binding of the neurotransmitter to receptor molecules in the postsynaptic membrane completes the process of transmission (4).

leading to either depolarization (excitation) or hyperpolarization (inhibition) of the postsynaptic cell (**Figure 2.14**). Hyperpolarization of the postsynaptic neuron produces an inhibitory postsynaptic potential (IPSP).

Excitatory and inhibitory neurons are also capable of modulating functions through the GPCRs. There are over 1,000 different GPCRs, giving us an idea of the complexity of the system. The particular GPCRs that are present depend on the neuron and where it is located. Each type of GPCR is activated by a specific signaling molecule, which could be a neurotransmitter, a neuropeptide (a small protein-like molecule secreted by neurons or glial cells), or a neurosteroid, among other possible signals.

When a signaling molecule specifically binds to its GPCR, the conformational change activates a G protein within the cell, which in turn activates or regulates a specific target protein, typically an enzyme, which produces a diffusible molecule of some sort called a *second messenger*. The second messenger, in turn, triggers a biochemical cascade of reactions. While directly gated channels mediate fast signaling, measured in milliseconds, GPCR-mediated signaling is slower, occurring over hundreds of milliseconds or even seconds and producing longer-lasting modulatory changes to the functional state. For example, the neurotransmitter epinephrine binds to a particular GPCR. Once bound, a G protein is activated that seeks

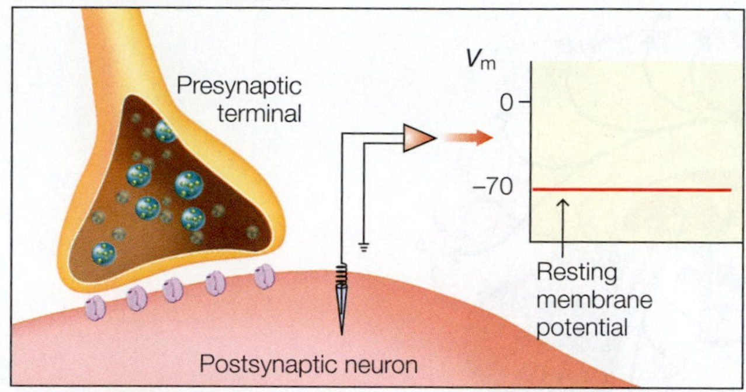

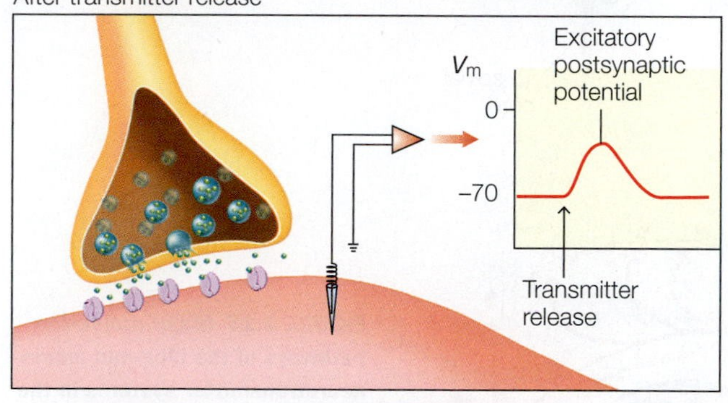

FIGURE 2.14 Neurotransmitter leading to a postsynaptic potential. The binding of neurotransmitter to the postsynaptic membrane receptors changes the membrane potential (V_m). These postsynaptic potentials can be either excitatory (depolarizing the membrane), as shown here, or inhibitory (hyperpolarizing the membrane).

out the protein adenylate cyclase and activates it. Activated adenylate cyclase turns ATP into cAMP (cyclic adenosine monophosphate), which acts as a second messenger of information instructing the postsynaptic neuron.

NEUROTRANSMITTERS While you may have heard of a few of the classic **neurotransmitters**, more than 100 have been identified. What makes a molecule a neurotransmitter?

- It is synthesized by and localized within the presynaptic neuron, and stored in the presynaptic terminal before release.
- It is released by the presynaptic neuron when action potentials depolarize the terminal (mediated primarily by Ca^{2+}).
- The postsynaptic neuron contains receptors specific for it.
- When artificially applied to a postsynaptic cell, it elicits the same response that stimulating the presynaptic neuron would.

Biochemical classification of neurotransmitters. Some neurotransmitters are amino acids: aspartate, gamma-aminobutyric acid (GABA), glutamate, and glycine. Another category of neurotransmitters, called *biogenic amines*, includes dopamine, norepinephrine, and epinephrine (these three are known as the catecholamines), serotonin (5-hydroxytryptamine), and histamine. Acetylcholine (ACh) is a well-studied neurotransmitter that is in its own biochemical class. Another large group of neurotransmitters consists of slightly larger molecules, the *neuropeptides*, which are made up of strings of amino acids. More than 100 neuropeptides are active in the mammalian brain, and they are divided into five groups:

1. *Tachykinins* (brain-gut peptides, which are peptides secreted by endocrine cells and enteric neurons in the GI tract and also neurons in the central nervous system). This group includes substance P, which affects vasoconstriction and is a spinal neurotransmitter involved in pain.
2. *Neurohypophyseal hormones.* Oxytocin and vasopressin are in this group. The former is involved in mammary functions and has been tagged the "love hormone" for its role in pair bonding and maternal behaviors; the latter is an antidiuretic hormone.
3. *Hypothalamic releasing hormones.* This group includes corticotropin-releasing hormone, involved in the stress response; somatostatin, an inhibitor of growth hormone; and gonadotropin-releasing hormone, involved with the development, growth, and functioning of the body's reproductive processes.
4. *Opioid peptides.* This group is named for its similarity to opiate drugs, and these peptides bind to opiate receptors. It includes the endorphins and enkephalins.
5. *Other neuropeptides.* This group includes peptides that do not fit neatly into another category, such as insulins, secretins (e.g., glucagon), and gastrins.

Some neurons produce only one type of neurotransmitter, but others produce multiple kinds. Neurons that do produce particular neurotransmitters sometimes form distinct systems, such as the cholinergic system, the noradrenergic system, the dopaminergic system, and the serotonergic system. When a neurotransmitter system is activated, large areas of the brain can be affected (**Figure 2.15**). Neurons that produce more than one type of transmitter may release them together or separately, depending on the conditions of stimulation. For example, the rate of stimulation by the action potential can induce the release of a specific neurotransmitter.

Functional classification of neurotransmitters. As mentioned earlier, the effect of a neurotransmitter on the postsynaptic neuron is determined by the postsynaptic receptor's properties rather than by the transmitter itself. A particular neurotransmitter may have more than one type of postsynaptic receptor to which it binds, mediating different responses. Thus, the same neurotransmitter released from the same presynaptic neuron onto two different postsynaptic cells might cause one to increase

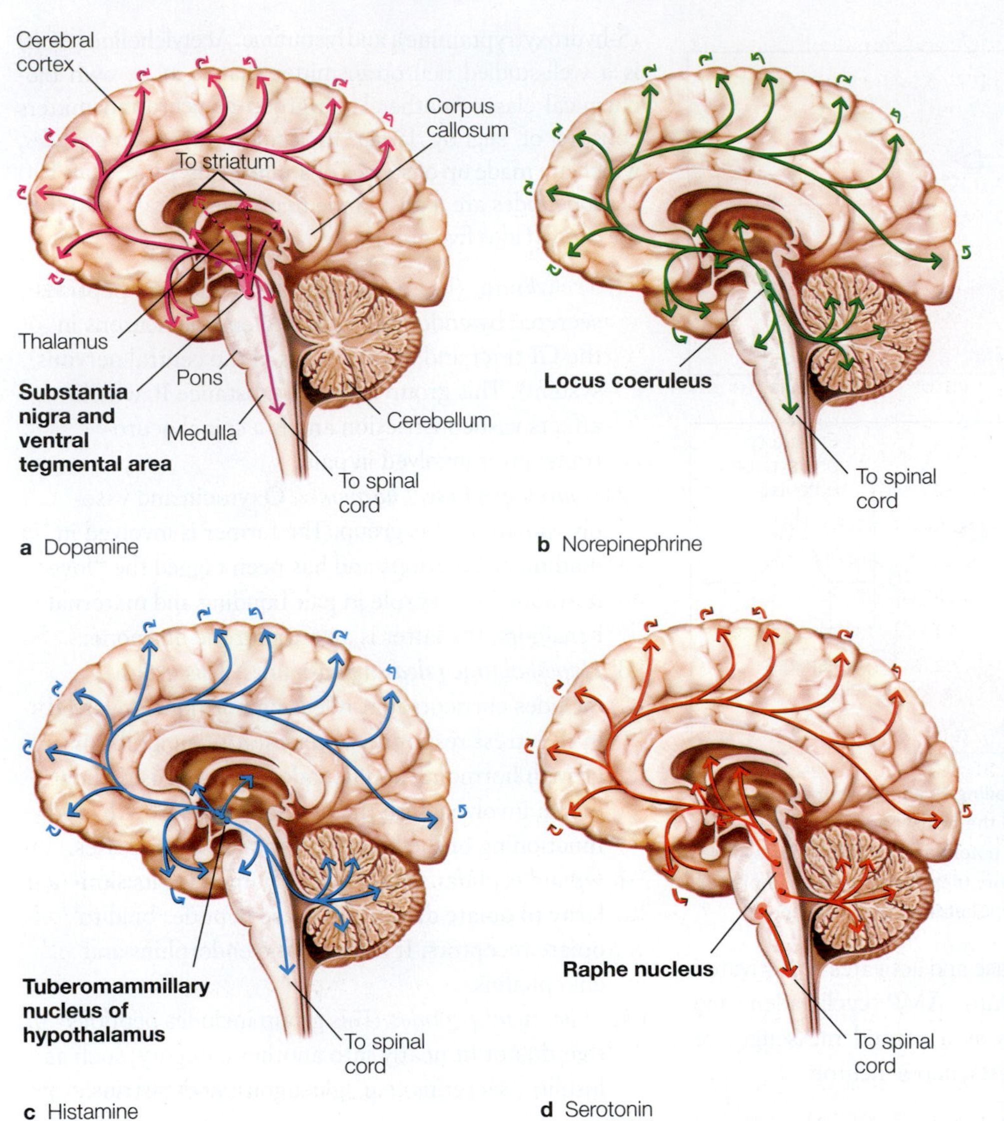

FIGURE 2.15 Major projection pathways of the biogenic amine neurotransmitter systems in the human brain. Shown are the projections of the dopamine (a), norepinephrine (b), histamine (c), and serotonin (d) systems using the neurotransmitters. The views are midsagittal cuts through the human brain, showing the medial surface of the right hemisphere; the frontal pole is at left. In each image, the primary source of the biogenic amine is in bold type.

firing and the other to decrease firing, depending on the receptors to which the transmitter binds.

The effects also depend on the concentration of the transmitter; the type, number, and density of the receptors; whether, when, and which co-neurotransmitters are also released; and the long-range connections of the neuron. For example, if different co-transmitters are released—one binding to a directly gated receptor with fast signaling and the other to a GPCR with slower signaling—they may produce opposite actions, and their overall combined effect may produce many possible outcomes, even complementary effects. Nevertheless, neurotransmitters can be classified not only biochemically, but also by the *typical effect* that they induce in the postsynaptic neuron.

Neurotransmitters that usually have an excitatory effect include ACh, the catecholamines, glutamate, histamine, serotonin, and some of the neuropeptides. Neurotransmitters that are typically inhibitory include GABA, glycine, and some of the neuropeptides. Some neurotransmitters act directly to excite or inhibit a postsynaptic neuron, but other neurotransmitters act only in concert with other factors. These are sometimes referred to as *conditional neurotransmitters* because their action is conditioned on the presence of another transmitter in the synaptic cleft or activity in the neural circuit. These types of mechanisms permit the nervous system to achieve complex modulations of information processing by modulating neurotransmission.

Some common neurotransmitters and their functions. The primary players in the balancing act between excitation and inhibition are glutamate and GABA. *Glutamate* is released by the pyramidal cells of the cortex, the most common cortical neurons. As a result, glutamate is the most prevalent neurotransmitter and is found in most of the fast excitatory synapses in the brain and spinal cord. A few different types of receptors bind glutamate, and some of these are found in modifiable synapses (i.e., ones that can change in strength) involved in learning and memory. Too much glutamate (excitation) can be toxic and cause cell death and has been implicated in stroke, epilepsy, and neurodegenerative diseases such as Alzheimer's and Parkinson's.

GABA is the second most prevalent neurotransmitter and is synthesized from glutamate. It is found in most of the fast inhibitory synapses across the brain. As with glutamate, there is more than one type of GABA receptor, but the most common one opens Cl^- channels to allow an influx of negatively charged ions into the cell, negatively shifting (hyperpolarizing) the membrane potential and, in essence, inhibiting the neuron by making it much less likely to fire. GABA's role in information processing is varied and complex and is actively being researched.

Over the past few years, several populations of neurons that researchers believed released only glutamate, acetylcholine, dopamine, or histamine have also been found to release GABA (reviewed in Tritsch et al., 2016). For example, although glutamate and GABA have opposing functions, their co-release has recently been documented from individual CNS axons (in the ventral tegmental area and entopeduncular nucleus). Defects in the GABA system may be local or affect the entire CNS. Decreased levels of GABA (decreased inhibition) can result in seizures, as well as increases in emotional reactivity, heart rate, blood pressure, food and water intake, sweating, insulin secretion, gastric acid, and colonic motility. Too much GABA can lead to coma.

Acetylcholine (ACh) is present in the synapses between neurons and between neurons and muscles (neuromuscular junctions), where it has an excitatory effect and activates muscles. In the brain, ACh acts as a neurotransmitter and a neuromodulator and supports cognitive function. It binds to two main types of receptors, nicotinic and muscarinic, that have different properties and mechanisms. There are muscle-type and neuronal-type *nicotinic ACh receptors*; the latter type are located in the autonomic ganglia of the sympathetic and parasympathetic nervous systems (discussed later in this chapter). Nicotine also binds to these receptors and imitates the actions of ACh—hence their name. *Muscarinic ACh receptors* are found in both the central nervous system and in the heart, lungs, upper gastrointestinal tract, and sweat glands. Some ACh receptors have inhibitory effects; others have excitatory effects. In the CNS, the drug nicotine binds to nicotinic acetylcholine receptors to increase arousal, sustain attention, enhance learning and memory, and increase REM sleep.

Many plants and animals produce toxins and venoms that affect ACh levels. For example, botulinum toxin suppresses the release of ACh at the neuromuscular junction, causing flaccid paralysis. Because of this property, Botox, a commercial product containing minuscule amounts of botulinum toxin, is used to relax the muscles in multiple disorders characterized by overactive muscle activity, such as post-stroke spasticity. It is also used for cosmetic purposes, because a small injection into subcutaneous muscles results in reduced wrinkling of the overlying skin in areas such as around the eyes. The plant toxin curare has a different mechanism. It binds to the nicotinic ACh receptor, also decreasing ACh levels, and causing muscle weakness and, in sufficient doses, flaccid paralysis of the diaphragm and death. Some toxins and venoms inhibit the action of the ACh breakdown enzyme acetylcholinesterase (AChE), leading to excess ACh at the neuromuscular junction and resulting in continuous activation of muscles, causing rigid paralysis. In this case, death can be caused by hyperactivity and rigidity of the muscles needed for breathing.

The primary sites of *dopamine* production are the adrenal glands and a few small areas of the brain. Brain areas with significant dopaminergic innervation include the striatum, substantia nigra, and hypothalamus. So far, five different types of dopamine receptors have been identified (with hints of two more), labeled from D_1 to D_5, all of which are G protein–coupled receptors, exerting their effects on postsynaptic neurons via the second-messenger mechanism. There are several dopaminergic pathways, each sprouting from one of the small brain areas where it is produced and each involved in particular functions, including cognitive and motor control, motivation, arousal, reinforcement, and reward, among others. Parkinson's disease, schizophrenia, attention deficit hyperactivity disorder, and addiction are associated with deficits in dopamine systems.

Serotonin in the brain is released largely by the neurons of the raphe nuclei, located in the brainstem. Axons from the raphe nuclei neurons extend to most parts of the central nervous system, forming a neurotransmitter system. Serotonin receptors—both ligand-gated ion channels and GPCRs—are found on the cell membrane of neurons and other cell types that mediate both excitatory and inhibitory neurotransmission. Serotonergic pathways are involved in the regulation of mood, temperature, appetite, behavior, muscle contraction, sleep, and the cardiovascular and endocrine systems. Serotonin also has effects on learning and memory. Drugs such as the selective serotonin reuptake inhibitors (SSRIs), used to treat clinical depression, act on the raphe nuclei and their targets in the brain.

Norepinephrine (NE), also known as *noradrenaline*, is the sympathetic nervous system's go-to neurotransmitter. It is produced and used by neurons with cell bodies in the locus coeruleus (LC), an area of the brain involved with physiological responses to stress and located in one of the brainstem's structures, the pons. These neurons have extensive projections to the cortex, cerebellum, and spinal cord. Activity in the LC is low during sleep, runs at a baseline level during awake periods, steps up the action when presented with an attention-drawing stimulus, and strongly activates when potential danger is sensed.

Outside the brain, NE is released by the adrenal glands. There are two types of receptors for NE: alpha (α_1 and α_2) and beta (β_1, β_2, and β_3), both of which are GPCRs. Alpha-2 receptors tend to have inhibitory effects, while alpha-1 and the beta receptors tend to have excitatory effects. NE mediates the fight-or-flight response. Its general effect is to prepare the body and its organs for action. It increases arousal, alertness, and vigilance; focuses attention; and enhances memory formation. Along with these effects come increased anxiety and restlessness. The body responds to NE with increased heart rate, blood pressure, and blood flow to skeletal muscles, and decreased blood flow to the gastrointestinal system. It also increases the availability of stored glucose for energy.

Neurosteroids are steroids synthesized in the brain. Only in the last 40 years have researchers found evidence that the brain can synthesize steroids. There are many different neurosteroids, some inhibitory and some excitatory; they can modulate the binding of various neurotransmitters on both directly and indirectly gated receptors and also directly activate GPCRs (reviewed in Do Rego et al., 2009). Neurosteroids are involved with the control of various neurobiological processes, including cognition, stress, anxiety, depression, aggressiveness, body temperature, blood pressure, locomotion, feeding behavior, and sexual behavior.

For example, *estradiol* is a hormone derived from cholesterol (like other steroid hormones) and is produced primarily in the ovaries of women and the testes of men. The brain, however, also has the molecules and enzymes necessary for the conversion of cholesterol into steroids such as estradiol (as well as progesterone and testosterone), and it has specific receptors for each of these neurosteroids and for peripherally produced steroid hormones. Estradiol is a neuroprotective factor, and recent discoveries indicate that neural estrogen receptors coordinate multiple signaling mechanisms that protect the brain from neurodegenerative diseases, affective disorders, and cognitive decline (reviewed in Arevalo et al., 2015).

Inactivation of neurotransmitters after release. Following the release of neurotransmitter into the synaptic cleft and its binding with the postsynaptic membrane receptors, the remaining transmitter must be removed to prevent further excitatory or inhibitory signal transduction. This removal can be accomplished by active reuptake of the substance back into the presynaptic terminal, by enzymatic breakdown of the transmitter in the synaptic cleft, or merely by diffusion of the neurotransmitter away from the region of the synapse or site of action (e.g., in the case of hormones that act on target cells distant from the synaptic terminals).

Neurotransmitters that are removed from the synaptic cleft by reuptake mechanisms include the biogenic amines (dopamine, norepinephrine, epinephrine, histamine, and serotonin). The reuptake mechanism is mediated by active transporters, which are transmembrane proteins that pump the neurotransmitter back across the presynaptic membrane.

An example of a neurotransmitter that is eliminated from the synaptic cleft by enzymatic action is ACh. The enzyme AChE, located in the synaptic cleft, breaks down ACh after it has acted on the postsynaptic membrane. In fact, special AChE stains (chemicals that bind to AChE) can be used to label AChE on muscle cells, thus revealing where motor neurons innervate the muscle.

To monitor the level of neurotransmitter in the synaptic cleft, presynaptic neurons have autoreceptors. These autoreceptors are located on the presynaptic terminal and bind with the released neurotransmitter, enabling the presynaptic neuron to regulate the synthesis and release of the transmitter.

Electrical Transmission

Some neurons communicate via electrical synapses, which are very different from chemical synapses. In electrical synapses, no synaptic cleft separates the neurons. Instead, the neuronal membranes touch at specializations called *gap junctions*, and the cytoplasms of the two neurons are essentially continuous. These gap junction channels create pores connecting the cytoplasms of the two neurons (**Figure 2.16**). As a result, the two neurons are *isopotential* (i.e., they have the same electrical potential), meaning that electrical changes in one are reflected instantaneously in the other. Following the principles of electrotonic conduction, however, the passive currents that flow between the

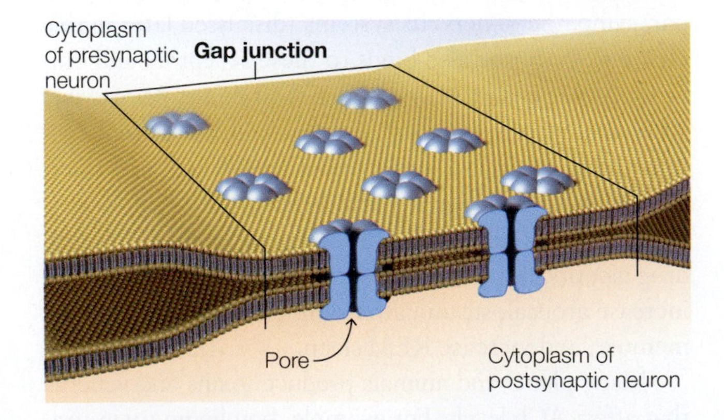

FIGURE 2.16 Electrical synapse between two neurons. Electrical synapses are formed by gap junctions, places where multiple transmembrane proteins in the pre- and postsynaptic neurons connect to create pathways that connect the cytoplasms of the two neurons.

neurons when one of them is depolarized (or hyperpolarized) decrease and are therefore smaller in the postsynaptic neuron than in the presynaptic neuron. Under most circumstances, the communication is bidirectional; however, so-called rectifying synapses limit current flow in one direction, as is typical in chemical synapses.

Electrical synapses are useful when information must be conducted rapidly, such as in the escape reflex of some invertebrates. Groups of neurons with these synapses can activate muscles quickly to get the animal out of harm's way. For example, the well-known tail flip reflex of crayfishes involves powerful rectifying electrical synapses. Electrical synapses are also useful when groups of neurons should operate synchronously, as with some hypothalamic neurosecretory neurons. Electrical synapses also have some limitations: They are much less plastic than chemical synapses, and they cannot amplify a signal (whereas an action potential that triggers a chemical synapse could cause a large release of neurotransmitter, thus amplifying the signal).

TAKE-HOME MESSAGES

- Synapses are the locations where one neuron can transfer information to another neuron or a specialized nonneuronal cell. They are found on dendrites and at axon terminals but can also be found on the neuronal cell body.
- Chemical transmission results in the release of neurotransmitters from the presynaptic neuron and the binding of those neurotransmitters on the postsynaptic neuron, which in turn causes excitatory or inhibitory postsynaptic potentials (EPSPs or IPSPs), depending on the properties of the postsynaptic receptor.
- Neurotransmitters must be removed from the receptor after binding. This removal can be accomplished by active reuptake back into the presynaptic terminal, enzymatic breakdown of the transmitter in the synaptic cleft, or diffusion of the neurotransmitter away from the region of the synapse.
- Electrical synapses are different from chemical synapses because they operate by passing current directly from one neuron (presynaptic) to another neuron (postsynaptic) via specialized channels in gap junctions that connect the cytoplasm of one cell directly to the other.

2.3 Overview of Nervous System Structure

Until now, we have been talking about only one or two neurons at a time. This approach is useful in understanding how neurons transmit information, but it is only one part of how the nervous system and the brain function. Neural communication depends on patterns of connectivity in the nervous system, the neural "highways" along which information travels from one place to another. Identifying patterns of connectivity in the nervous system is tricky because most neurons are not wired together in simple, serial circuits. Instead, neurons are extensively connected in both serial and parallel circuits.

A single cortical neuron is likely to be innervated by (i.e., receive inputs from) a large number of neurons: A typical cortical neuron has between 1,000 and 5,000 synapses, while a Purkinje neuron in the cerebellum may have up to 200,000 synapses. The axons from these input neurons can originate in widely distributed regions. Thus, there is tremendous convergence in the nervous system, but also divergence, in which a single neuron can project to multiple target neurons in different regions.

Localized interconnected neurons form what is known as a **microcircuit**. They process specific kinds of information and can accomplish sophisticated tasks such as processing sensory information, generating movements, and mediating learning and memory. For example, microcircuits in the retina of the eye process information from small regions of visual space. The patterns of light entering the eye strike photoreceptors, and the information from adjacent photoreceptors is processed through the microcircuitry of the retina to encode spatial information. This encoding permits a much smaller number of retinal ganglion cells to transmit the coded information down the optic nerve.

Although most axons are short projections from neighboring cortical cells, some are quite long, originating in one region of the brain and projecting to another at some distance. For example, the ganglion cells of the retina project via the optic nerve to the lateral geniculate nucleus of the thalamus, and the lateral geniculate neurons project via the optic radiations to primary visual cortex. Axons from neurons in the cortex may reach distant targets by descending below the cortical sheath into the white matter, traveling through long fiber tracts, and then entering another region of cortex, subcortical nucleus, or spinal layer to synapse on another neuron.

These long-distance connections between various brain regions connect to form more complex **neural networks**, which are *macro*circuits that are made up of multiple embedded microcircuits. Neural networks support more complex analyses, integrating information processing from many microcircuits. Connections between two cortical regions are referred to as *corticocortical* connections, following the convention that the first part of the term identifies the source and the second part identifies the target.

Inputs that originate in subcortical structures such as the thalamus would be referred to as *thalamocortical* connections; the reverse are *corticothalamic* or, more generally, *corticofugal* projections (projections extending from more central structures, like cortex, outward toward the peripheral nervous system).

Ultimately, neural networks are organized into neural systems. So, for example, the microcircuits of the retina, the lateral geniculate nucleus of the thalamus, and the patches of visual cortex are organized to create neural networks such as the thalamocortical network. This progression ultimately leads to the organization of the visual system as a whole, with its numerous cortical areas and subcortical components. (We will discuss the organization of the visual system in detail in Chapter 5.) In the next section we go on a brief anatomical tour of the brain. Early in each of Chapters 4 through 14, a section highlights the anatomy most relevant to the cognitive functions discussed in that chapter. The anatomy presented here and in the coming chapters will help you see which structures of the brain are related to which of its functions.

The two main divisions of the nervous system are the **central nervous system (CNS)**, consisting of the brain and spinal cord, and the **peripheral nervous system (PNS)**, consisting of the nerves (bundles of axons and glial cells) and ganglia (clumps of nerve cell bodies) outside of the CNS (**Figure 2.17**). The CNS can be thought of as the command-and-control center of the nervous system. The PNS represents a courier network that delivers sensory information to the CNS and carries motor commands from the CNS to the muscles. These activities are accomplished through two subsystems: the *somatic motor system* that controls the voluntary muscles of the body, and the *autonomic motor system* that controls the automated visceral functions. Before we concentrate on the CNS, a word about the autonomic nervous system.

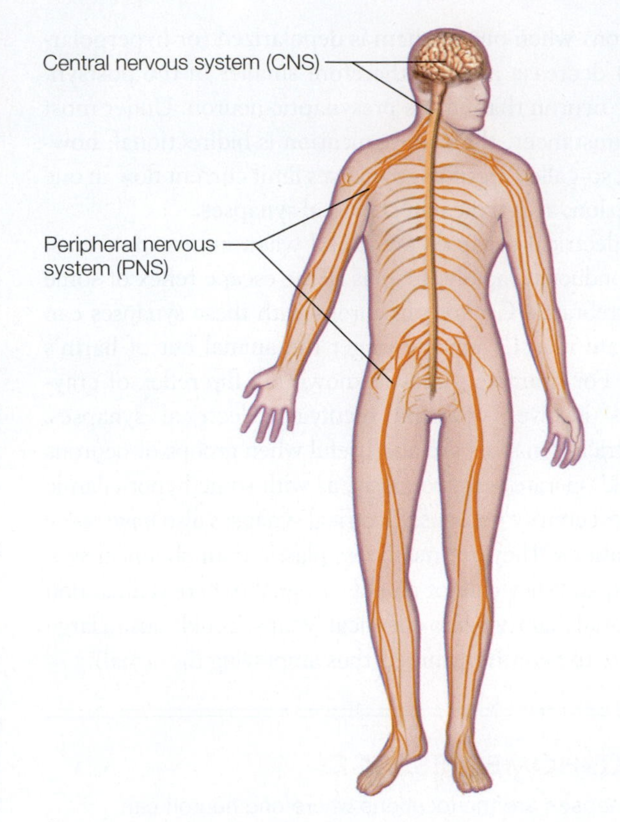

FIGURE 2.17 The peripheral and central nervous systems of the human body.
The nervous system is generally divided into two main parts. The central nervous system (CNS) includes the brain and spinal cord. The peripheral nervous system (PNS), comprising the sensory and motor nerves and associated nerve cell ganglia (groups of neuronal cell bodies), is located outside the central nervous system.

The Autonomic Nervous System

The **autonomic nervous system** (also called the *autonomic motor system* or *visceral motor system*) is involved in controlling the involuntary action of smooth muscles, the heart, and various glands. It also has two subdivisions: the *sympathetic* and *parasympathetic* branches (**Figure 2.18**). In general, the sympathetic system uses the neurotransmitter norepinephrine, and the parasympathetic system uses acetylcholine as its transmitter. The two systems frequently operate antagonistically. For example, activation of the sympathetic system increases heart rate, diverts blood from the digestive tract to the somatic musculature, and prepares the body for action (fight or flight) by stimulating the adrenal glands to release adrenaline. In contrast, activation of the parasympathetic system slows heart rate, stimulates digestion, and in general helps the body with functions germane to maintaining itself (rest and digest).

In the autonomic system, a great deal of specialization takes place that is beyond the scope of this chapter. Still, understanding that the autonomic system is involved in a variety of reflex and involuntary behaviors (mostly below the level of consciousness) is useful for interpreting information presented later in the book. In Chapter 10, on emotion, we will discuss arousal of the autonomic nervous system and how changes in a number of psychophysiological measures tap into emotion-related changes in the autonomic nervous system. For example, changes in skin conductance are related to sweat gland activity, and sweat glands are under the control of the autonomic nervous system.

In the rest of this chapter we focus on the CNS in order to lay the groundwork for the studies of cognition

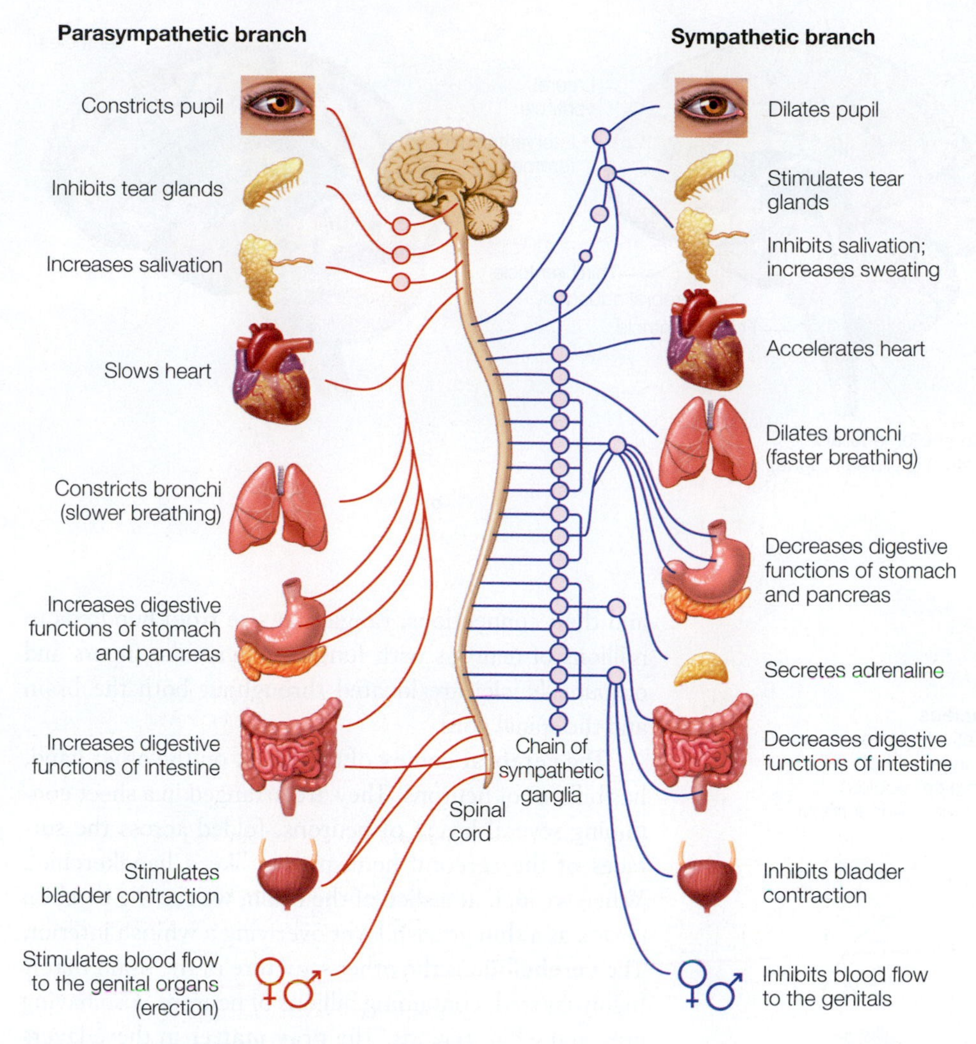

FIGURE 2.18 **Organization of the autonomic nervous system.**

presented throughout the rest of the book. When we talk about brain anatomy, we will use standard terminology to locate parts of the brain in three-dimensional space (see **Box 2.1**).

The Central Nervous System

The CNS is made up of the brain and spinal cord, and each is covered with three protective membranes, the *meninges*. The outer membrane is the thick dura mater; the middle is the arachnoid mater; and the inner and most delicate is the pia mater, which firmly adheres to the surface of the brain. Between the arachnoid membrane and the pia mater is the subarachnoid space, which is filled with *cerebrospinal fluid (CSF)*, as are the brain's ventricles, cisterns, and sulci, along with the central canal of the spinal cord. The brain actually floats in the CSF, which offsets the pressure and damage that would be present if it were merely sitting and scraping on the base of the skull. CSF also reduces shock to the brain and spinal cord during rapid accelerations or decelerations, such as when we fall, ride roller coasters, or are struck on the head.

Within the brain are four large interconnected cavities called **ventricles** (**Figure 2.19**). The largest are the two lateral ventricles in the cerebrum, which are connected to the more caudal third ventricle in the brain's midline and the fourth ventricle in the brainstem below the cerebellum. The walls of the ventricles contain a system of specialized cells and capillaries, the *choroid plexus*, which produces CSF from blood plasma. The CSF circulates through the ventricles and on to either the subarachnoid space surrounding the brain or the spinal canal. It is reabsorbed in the brain by the *arachnoid villi*, protrusions into the venous system in the sagittal sinus.

In the CNS, neurons are bunched together in various ways (**Figure 2.20**). Two of the most common organizational clusters are the **nucleus** and the **layer**. A nucleus is a relatively compact arrangement of nerve cell bodies

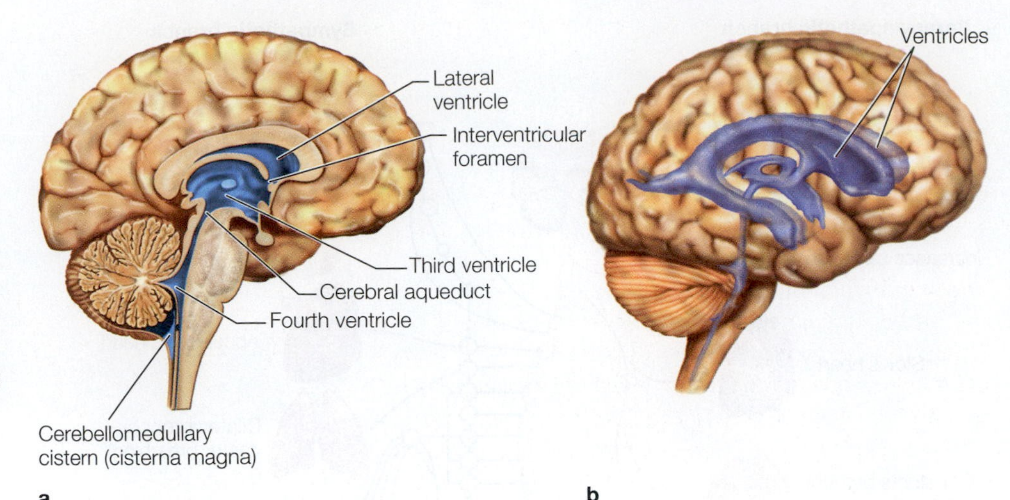

FIGURE 2.19 Ventricles of the human brain.
(a) Midsagittal section, showing the medial surface of the left hemisphere. **(b)** Transparent brain, showing the ventricular system in 3-D view.

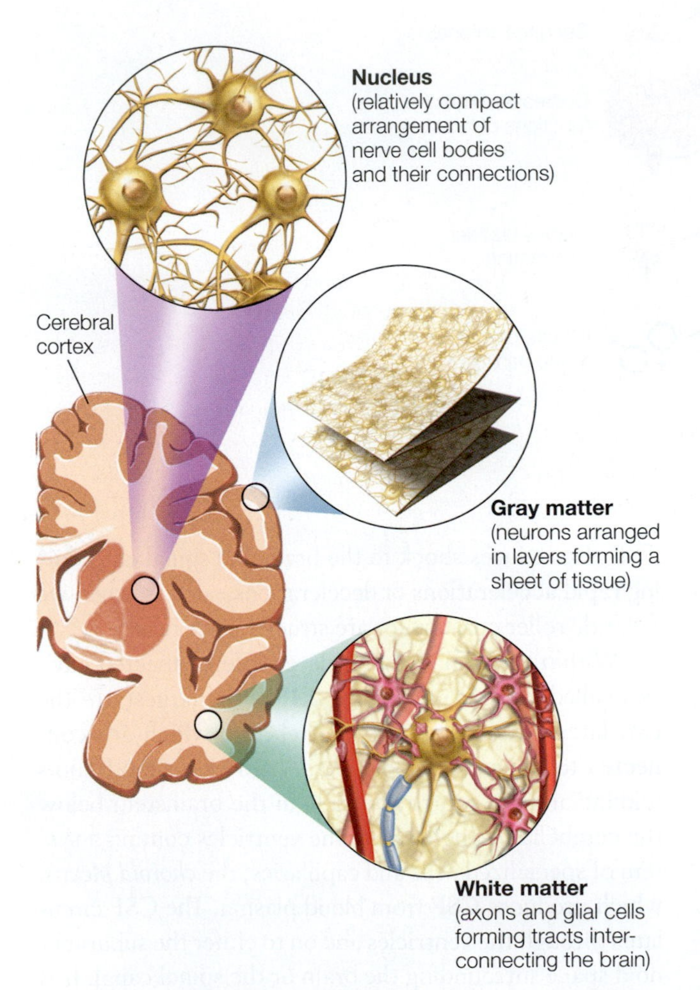

FIGURE 2.20 Organization of neurons in the CNS.
In the CNS, neurons can be organized in clumps called nuclei (top—not to be confused with the nucleus inside each neuron), which are most commonly found in subcortical and spinal structures, or sheets called layers (middle), which are most commonly found in the cortex. The cell bodies of glial cells are located in the white matter (bottom—e.g., oligodendrocytes), and in the cortex.

and their connections, ranging in size from hundreds to millions of neurons with functionally similar inputs and outputs. Nuclei are located throughout both the brain and the spinal cord.

The **cerebral cortex** of the brain, on the other hand, has billions of neurons. They are arranged in a sheet containing several layers of neurons, folded across the surfaces of the cerebral hemispheres like a handkerchief. When we look at a slice of the brain, we see the cerebral cortex as a thin grayish layer overlying a whitish interior. The **cerebellum** is the other structure of the brain that is highly layered, containing billions of neurons, also having gray and white regions. The **gray matter** in these layers is composed of neuronal cell bodies, whereas the **white matter** consists of axons and glial cells.

Much like nerves in the PNS, the axons forming the white matter are grouped together in **tracts** that run from one cortical region to another within a hemisphere (*association tracts*), or that run to and from the cerebral cortex to the deeper subcortical structures and the spinal cord (*projection tracts*). Finally, axons may project from one cerebral hemisphere to the other in bundles that are called **commissures.** The largest of these interhemispheric projections is the main commissure crossing between the hemispheres, the **corpus callosum.**

Blood Supply and the Brain

The brain needs energy and oxygen, which it extracts from blood. Approximately 20% of the blood flowing from the heart is pumped to the brain. A constant flow of blood is necessary because the brain has no way of storing glucose or extracting energy without oxygen. If the flow of oxygenated blood to the brain is disrupted for even a few minutes, unconsciousness and death can result.

BOX 2.1 | THE COGNITIVE NEUROSCIENTIST'S TOOLKIT

Navigating the Brain

For anatomists, the head is merely an appendage of the body, so the terms used to describe the orientation of the head and its brain are in relation to the body. Confusion arises because of differences in how the head and body are arranged in animals that walk on four legs versus humans, who are upright. Let's first picture the body of the cutest kind of dog, an Australian shepherd, looking off to the left of the page (**Figure 2.21a**). The front end is the *rostral* end, meaning "nose." The opposite end is the *caudal* end, the "tail." Along the dog's back is the *dorsal* surface, just as the dorsal fin is on the back of a shark. The bottom surface along the dog's belly is the *ventral* surface.

We can use the same coordinates to describe the dog's nervous system (**Figure 2.21b**). The part of the brain toward the front is the rostral end (toward the frontal lobes); the posterior end is the caudal end (toward the occipital lobe). Along the top of the dog's head is the dorsal surface, and the bottom surface of the brain is the ventral surface.

We humans are atypical animals because we stand upright and therefore tilt our heads forward in order to be parallel with the ground. Thus, the dorsal surfaces of the human body and brain are at right angles to each other (**Figure 2.22**). In humans, we also use the terms *superior* to refer to the dorsal surface of the brain and *inferior* to refer to the ventral surface of the brain. Similarly, the terms *anterior* and *posterior* are used to refer to the front (rostral) and back (caudal) ends of the brain, respectively (Figure 2.22b). When we consider the spinal cord, the coordinate systems align with the body axis. Thus, in the spinal cord *rostral* means "toward the brain," just as it does in the dog.

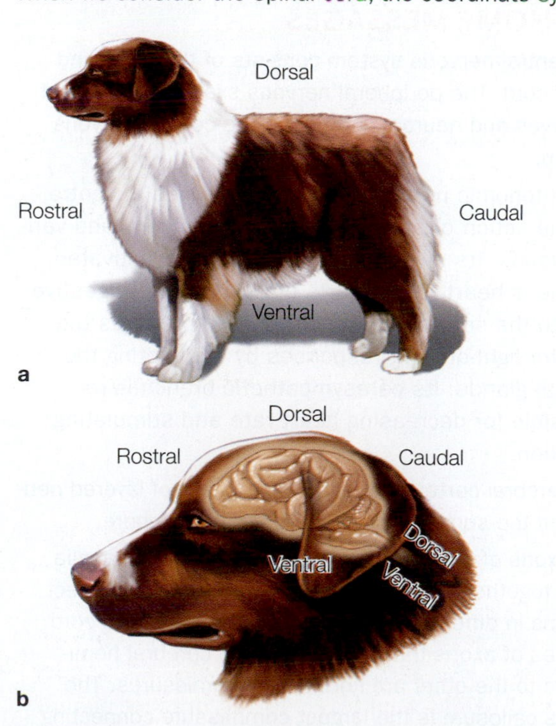

FIGURE 2.21 A dog brain in relation to the body.

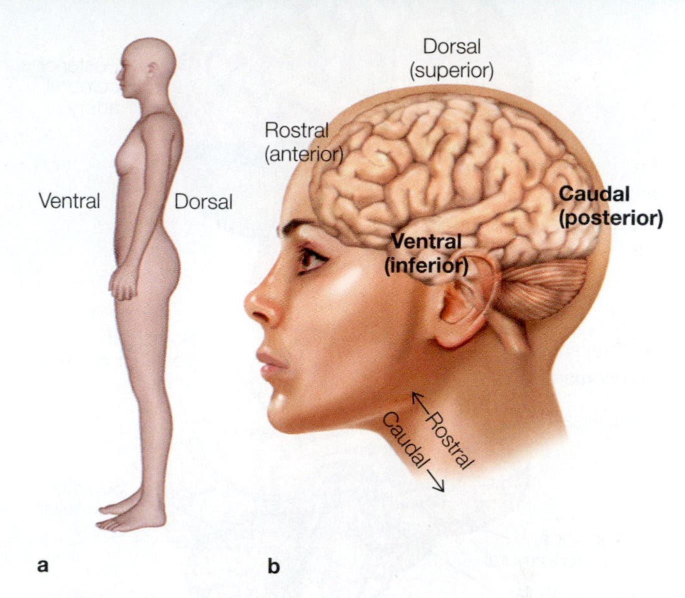

FIGURE 2.22 Navigating the human brain.

Throughout this book, pictures of brain slices are usually in one of three planes (**Figure 2.23**). If we slice the brain from nose to tail, we get a *sagittal* section. When we slice directly through the middle, we get a *midsagittal* or *medial* section. If we slice off to the side, we get a *lateral sagittal* section. If we slice perpendicular to a midsagittal section, separating the front of the brain from the back, we get a *coronal* section. When we slice in a plane that separates dorsal from ventral, we get a section that is described as *axial*, *transverse*, or *horizontal*.

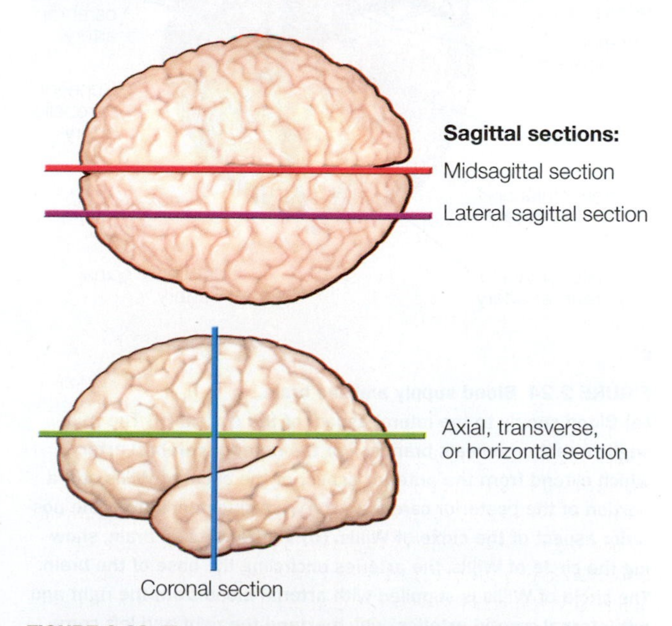

FIGURE 2.23 Three types of orthogonal planes through the brain.

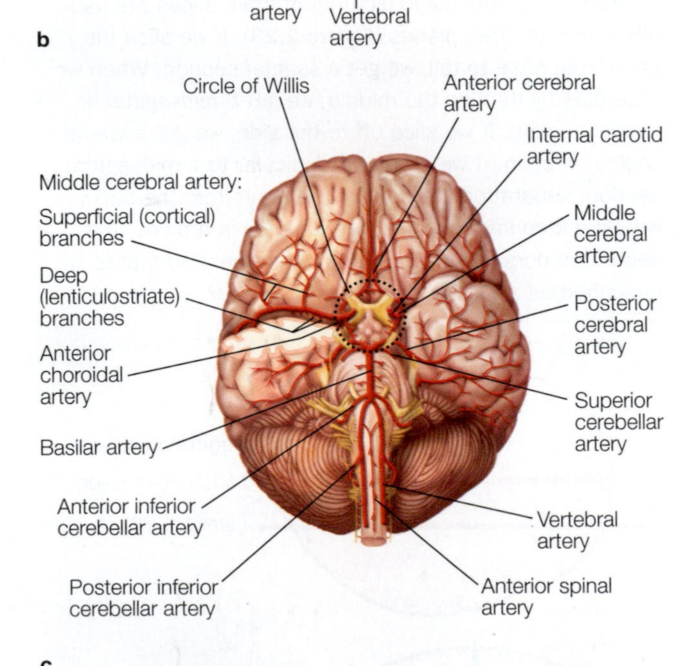

FIGURE 2.24 Blood supply and the brain.
(a) Blood supply to the lateral aspect of the cortex. (b) The midsagittal section reveals branches of the anterior cerebral artery, which extend from the anterior aspect of the circle of Willis and a portion of the posterior cerebral artery, which extends from the posterior aspect of the circle of Willis. (c) Ventral view of brain, showing the circle of Willis, the arteries encircling the base of the brain. The circle of Willis is supplied with arterial blood from the right and left internal carotid arteries, which extend the right and left common carotid artery and the basilar artery formed by the right and left vertebral arteries, which are branches of the subclavian artery.

Two sets of arteries bring blood to the brain: the vertebral arteries, which supply blood to the caudal portion of the brain, and the internal carotid arteries, which supply blood to wider brain regions (**Figure 2.24**). Although the major arteries sometimes join together and then separate again, little mixing of blood occurs between the rostral and caudal arterial supplies or between the right and left sides of the rostral portion of the brain. As a safety measure, in the event of a blockage or ischemic attack, the circulatory system can reroute blood to reduce the probability of a disruption in blood supply; in practice, however, this rerouting of the blood supply is relatively poor.

Blood flow in the brain is tightly coupled with metabolic demand of the local neurons. Hence, increases in neuronal activity lead to a coupled increase in regional cerebral blood flow. The primary purpose of increased blood flow is not to increase the delivery of oxygen and glucose to the active tissue, but rather to hasten removal of the resultant metabolic by-products of the increased neuronal activity. The precise mechanisms for altering blood flow, however, remain hotly debated. These local changes in blood flow permit regional cerebral blood flow to be used as a measure of local changes in neuronal activity, serving as the basis for some types of functional neuroimaging, such as positron emission tomography and functional magnetic resonance imaging.

TAKE-HOME MESSAGES

- The central nervous system consists of the brain and spinal cord. The peripheral nervous system consists of all nerves and neurons outside of the central nervous system.
- The autonomic nervous system is involved in controlling the action of smooth muscles, the heart, and various glands. Its sympathetic branch, when activated, increases heart rate, diverts blood from the digestive tract to the somatic musculature, and prepares the body for fight-or-flight responses by stimulating the adrenal glands. Its parasympathetic branch is responsible for decreasing heart rate and stimulating digestion.
- The cerebral cortex is a continuous sheet of layered neurons on the surface of each cerebral hemisphere.
- The axons of cortical neurons and subcortical ganglia travel together in white matter tracts that interconnect neurons in different parts of the brain and spinal cord. Bundles of axons that cross from one cerebral hemisphere to the other are known as commissures. The corpus callosum is the largest commissure connecting the two hemispheres of the brain.

2.4 A Guided Tour of the Brain

When we see a brain, the cerebral cortex, the outer layer, is most prominent. Yet the cerebral cortex is just the frosting on the cake; it's the last thing to develop from an evolutionary, as well as an embryological, point of view. Deep within, at the base of the brain, are structures that are found in most vertebrates and have been evolving for hundreds of millions of years. These parts of the brain control our most basic survival functions, such as breathing, heart rate, and temperature. In contrast, the prefrontal cortex, which is found only in mammals, is the evolutionarily youngest part of the brain. Damage to the prefrontal cortex may not be immediately fatal, but it will likely affect such things as our ability to make decisions and to control our social behavior. We begin our tour of the CNS with a brief look at the spinal cord, and we will work our way up to the cortex.

The Spinal Cord

The spinal cord takes in sensory information from the body's peripheral sensory receptors, relays it to the brain, and conducts the outgoing motor signals from the brain to the muscles. In addition, each level (segment) of the spinal cord has monosynaptic reflex pathways that involve synapses only in the spinal cord itself, and not in the brain. For example, a tap by your doctor on your patellar tendon at the knee sends a sensory signal to the spinal cord that, via interneurons, directly stimulates motor neurons to fire action potentials leading to muscle contraction and the resultant brief knee jerk. This is an example of a monosynaptic reflex arc (**Figure 2.25**). Most neural circuits, however, process information through more than a single synapse.

The spinal cord runs from the brainstem at about the first spinal vertebra to its termination in the *cauda equina* (meaning "horse's tail"). It is enclosed in the bony *vertebral column*—a stack of separate bones, the *vertebrae*, that extend from the base of the skull to the fused vertebrae at the *coccyx* (tailbone). The vertebral column is divided into sections: cervical, thoracic, lumbar, sacral, and coccygeal. The spinal cord is similarly divided (excluding the coccygeal region, since we no longer have tails) into 31 segments. Each segment has a right and a left *spinal nerve* that enters and exits from the vertebral column through openings called *foramina* (singular *foramen*). Each spinal nerve has both sensory and motor axons: the afferent neuron carries sensory input through the dorsal root into the spinal cord, and the efferent neuron carries motor output through the ventral root away from the spinal cord.

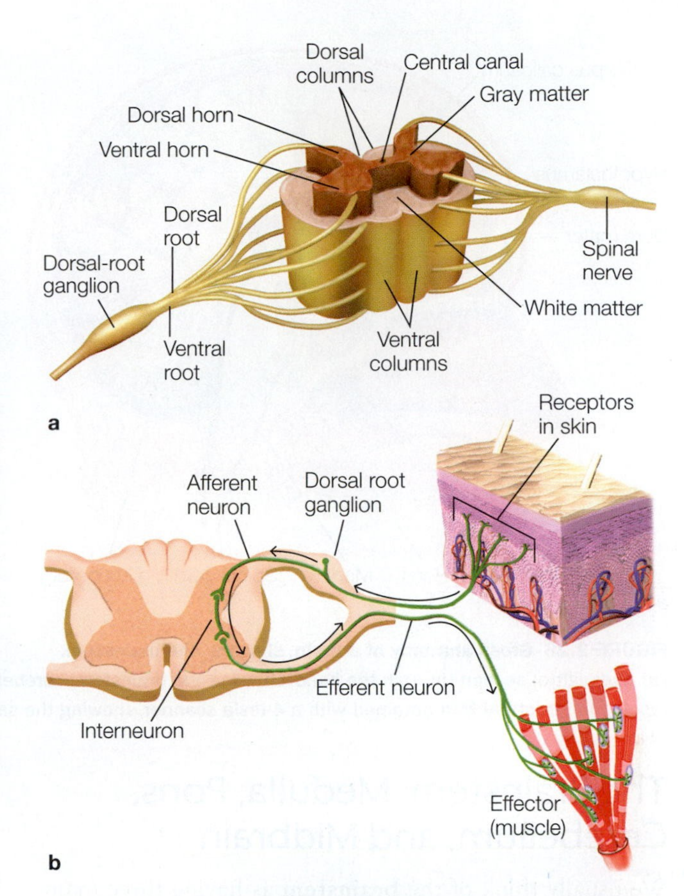

FIGURE 2.25 Gross anatomy of the spinal cord and reflex arc. This cross-sectional 3-D representation of the spinal cord **(a)** shows the central butterfly-shaped gray matter (which contains neuronal cell bodies) and the surrounding white matter axon tracts (which convey information down the spinal cord from the brain to the peripheral neurons and up the spinal cord from peripheral receptors to the brain). The cell bodies of peripheral sensory inputs reside in the dorsal-root ganglion and project their axons into the central nervous system via the dorsal root. The ventral horn of the spinal cord houses motor neurons that project their axons out the ventral roots to innervate peripheral muscles. The dorsal and ventral roots fuse to form peripheral nerves. The interneurons directly connect the afferent sensory nerves to the efferent motor nerves, forming a neural circuit that mediates spinal cord reflexes such as the knee jerk **(b)**.

As the cross section of the spinal cord in Figure 2.25 shows, the peripheral region is made up of white matter tracts. The more centrally located gray matter, consisting of neuronal cell bodies, resembles a butterfly with two separate sections, or "horns": the *dorsal horn* and the *ventral horn*. The ventral horn contains the large motor neurons that project to muscles. The dorsal horn contains sensory neurons and interneurons. The interneurons project to motor neurons on the same (*ipsilateral*) and opposite (*contralateral*) sides of the spinal cord to aid in the coordination of limb movements. They also form local circuits between ipsilateral sensory and motor nerves that mediate spinal reflexes. The gray matter surrounds the *central canal*, which is an anatomical extension of the ventricles in the brain and contains cerebrospinal fluid.

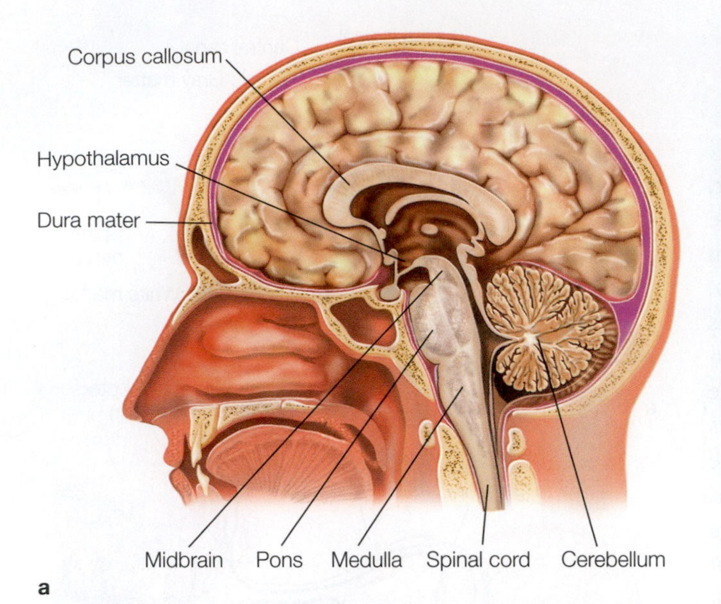

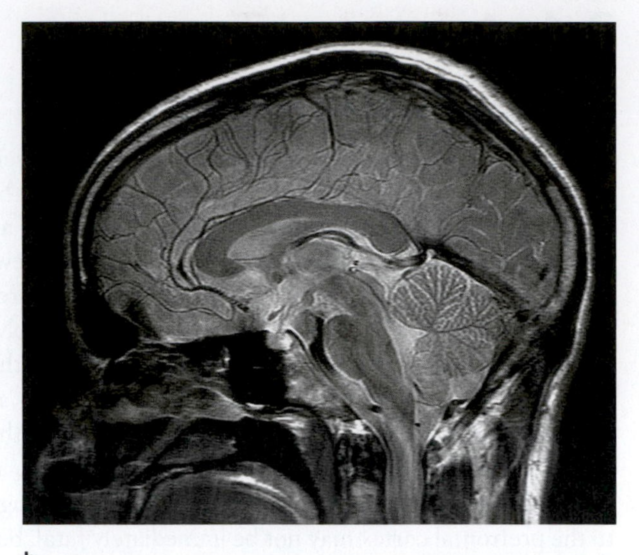

FIGURE 2.26 Gross anatomy of a brain, showing the brainstem.
(a) Midsagittal section through the head, showing the brainstem, cerebellum, and spinal cord. (b) High-resolution structural MRI obtained with a 4-tesla scanner, showing the same plane of section as in (a).

The Brainstem: Medulla, Pons, Cerebellum, and Midbrain

We usually think of the **brainstem** as having three main parts: the medulla (myelencephalon), the pons and cerebellum (metencephalon), and the midbrain (mesencephalon). These three sections form the central nervous system between the spinal cord and the diencephalon. The brainstem contains groups of motor and sensory nuclei, nuclei of widespread modulatory neurotransmitter systems, and white matter tracts of ascending sensory information and descending motor signals. Though it is rather small compared to the vast bulk of the forebrain (**Figure 2.26**), the brainstem plays a starring role: Damage to the brainstem is life-threatening, largely because brainstem nuclei control respiration and global states of consciousness such as sleep and wakefulness.

The medulla, pons, and cerebellum make up the hindbrain, which we look at next.

MEDULLA The brainstem's most caudal portion is the **medulla**, which is continuous with the spinal cord (**Figure 2.27**). The medulla is essential for life. It houses the cell bodies of many of the 12 cranial nerves, providing sensory and motor innervations to the face, neck, abdomen, and throat (including taste), as well as the motor nuclei that innervate the heart. The medulla controls vital functions such as respiration, heart rate, and arousal.

All of the ascending somatosensory information entering from the spinal cord passes through the medulla via two bilateral nuclear groups, the *gracile* and *cuneate nuclei*.

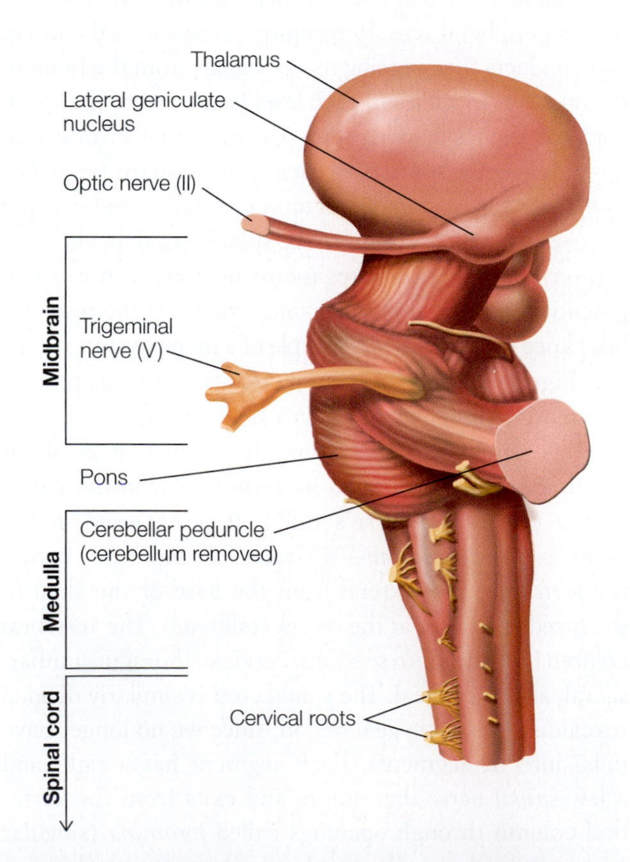

FIGURE 2.27 Lateral view of the brainstem, showing the thalamus, pons, medulla, midbrain, and spinal cord.
In this left lateral view of the brainstem, the top is the anterior portion of the brain, and the spinal cord is toward the bottom. The cerebellum is removed in this drawing.

These projection systems continue through the brainstem to synapse in the thalamus en route to the somatosensory cortex. Another interesting feature of the medulla is that the corticospinal motor axons, tightly packed in a pyramid-shaped bundle (called the *pyramidal tract*), cross here to form the *pyramidal decussation*. Thus, the motor neurons originating in the right hemisphere cross to control muscles on the left side of the body, and vice versa.

Functionally, the medulla is a relay station for sensory and motor information between the body and brain; it is the crossroads for most of the body's motor fibers; it controls several autonomic functions, including the essential reflexes that determine respiration, heart rate, blood pressure, and digestive and vomiting responses.

PONS The **pons**, Latin for "bridge," is so named because it is the main connection between the brain and the cerebellum. Sitting anterior to the medulla, the pons is made up of a vast system of fiber tracts interspersed with nuclei (Figure 2.27). Many of the cranial nerves synapse in the pons, including the sensory and motor nuclei from the face and mouth, and the visuomotor nuclei controlling some of the extraocular muscles. Thus, the pons is important for some eye movements, as well as movements of the face and mouth. In addition, some auditory information is channeled through another pontine structure, the superior olive.

This level of the brainstem contains a large portion of the reticular formation, a set of interconnected nuclei located throughout the brainstem that modulate arousal and pain, and that have various other functions, including cardiovascular control. The reticular formation has three columns of nuclei: the *raphe nuclei*, where the brain's serotonin is synthesized; the *parvocellular reticular nuclei*, which regulate exhalation; and the *gigantocellular nuclei*, which help to regulate cardiovascular functions. Interestingly, the pons is also responsible for generating rapid eye movement (REM) sleep.

CEREBELLUM The cerebellum (literally, "small cerebrum" or "little brain") clings to the brainstem at the level of the pons (Figure 2.26a). It is—perhaps surprisingly, given its size—home to most of the brain's neurons, estimated at 69 billion of the 89 billion neurons we have. Visually, the surface of the cerebellum appears to be covered with thinly spaced, parallel grooves, but in reality it is a continuous layer of tightly folded neural tissue (like an accordion). It forms the roof of the fourth ventricle and sits on the cerebellar *peduncles* (meaning "feet"), which are massive input and output fiber tracts of the cerebellum (Figure 2.27). The cerebellum has several gross subdivisions, including the cerebellar cortex, four pairs of deep nuclei (**Figure 2.28**), and the internal

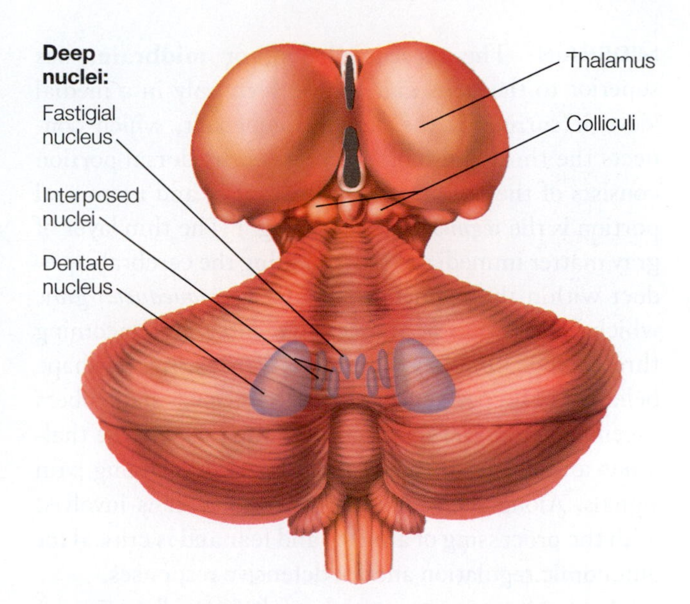

FIGURE 2.28 Gross anatomy of the cerebellum.
In this view, the top is toward the anterior of the brain, and the spinal cord is toward the bottom (not shown). This dorsal view of the cerebellum shows the underlying deep nuclei in a see-through projection—the fastigial nucleus, the dentate nucleus, and the interposed nuclei, which are made up of two fused nuclei: the emboliform and globose nuclei.

white matter. In this way, the cerebellum resembles the forebrain's cerebral hemispheres.

Most of the fibers arriving at the cerebellum project to the cerebellar cortex, conveying information about motor outputs and sensory inputs describing body position. Inputs from vestibular projections involved in balance, as well as auditory and visual inputs, also project to the cerebellum from the brainstem. The output from the cerebellum originates in the deep nuclei. Ascending outputs travel to the thalamus and then to the motor and premotor cortex. Other outputs project to nuclei of the brainstem, where they impinge on descending projections to the spinal cord.

The cerebellum is critical for maintaining posture, walking, and performing coordinated movements. It does not directly control movements; instead, it integrates information about the body, such as its size and speed, with motor commands. Then it modifies motor outflow to effect smooth, coordinated movements. The cerebellum is the reason why Yo-Yo Ma can play the cello and the Harlem Globetrotters can dunk a ball with such panache. If your cerebellum is damaged, your movements will be uncoordinated and halting, and you may not be able to maintain balance. In Chapter 8 we look more closely at the cerebellum's role in motor control. In the 1990s, it was discovered that the cerebellum is involved with more than motor functions. It has been implicated in aspects of cognitive processing including language, attention, learning, and mental imagery.

MIDBRAIN The mesencephalon, or **midbrain**, lies superior to the pons and can be seen only in a medial view. It surrounds the cerebral aqueduct, which connects the third and fourth ventricles. Its dorsal portion consists of the *tectum* (meaning "roof"), and its ventral portion is the *tegmentum* ("covering"). The thin layer of gray matter immediately surrounding the cerebral aqueduct within the tegmentum is the *periaqueductal gray*, which hosts a hub of activity that integrates incoming threatening stimuli and outputs processing to shape behavior. The periaqueductal gray receives pain fibers ascending from the spinal cord on their way to the thalamus and is key to the modulation of descending pain signals. Along with multiple other roles, it is involved with the processing of anxiety and fear and is critical for autonomic regulation and for defensive responses.

Large fiber tracts course through the midbrain's ventral regions from the forebrain to the spinal cord, cerebellum, and other parts of the brainstem. The midbrain also contains some of the cranial nerve ganglia and two other important structures: the superior and inferior colliculi (**Figure 2.29**). The *superior colliculus* plays a role in perceiving objects in the periphery and orienting our gaze directly toward them, bringing them into sharper view. The *inferior colliculus* is used for locating and orienting toward auditory stimuli. Another structure, the *red nucleus*, is involved in certain aspects of motor coordination. It helps a baby crawl or coordinates the swing of your arms as you walk. Much of the midbrain is occupied by the mesencephalic reticular formation, a rostral continuation of the pontine and medullary reticular formation, which contains nuclei that have neurotransmitters like norepinephrine and serotonin, touched on earlier.

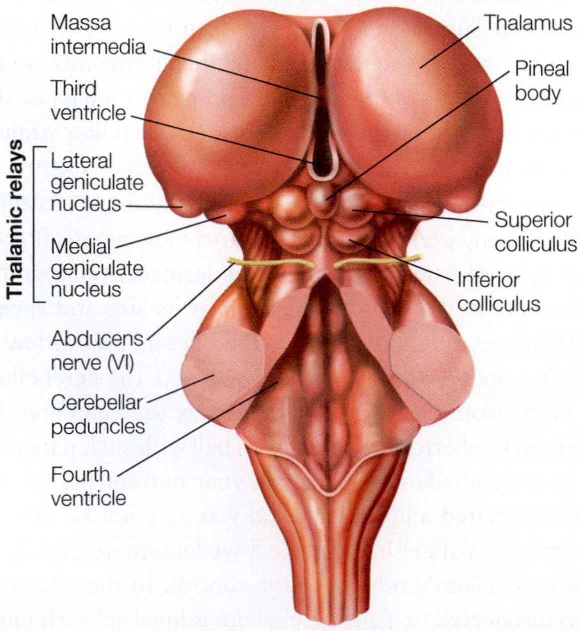

FIGURE 2.29 Anatomy of the midbrain.
The dorsal surface of the brainstem is shown with the cerebral cortex and cerebellum removed.

The Diencephalon: Thalamus and Hypothalamus

After leaving the brainstem, we arrive at the diencephalon, which is made up of the thalamus and hypothalamus. These subcortical structures are composed of groups of nuclei with interconnections to widespread brain areas.

THALAMUS Almost exactly in the center of the brain and perched on top of the brainstem (at the anterior end; Figure 2.27), the **thalamus** is the larger of the diencephalon structures. The thalamus is divided into two parts—one in the right hemisphere and one in the left—that straddle the third ventricle. In most people, the two parts are connected by a bridge of gray matter called the *massa intermedia* (Figure 2.29). Above the thalamus are the fornix and corpus callosum; beside it is the *internal capsule*, containing ascending and descending axons running between the cerebral cortex and the medulla and spinal cord.

The thalamus has been referred to as the "gateway to the cortex" because, except for some olfactory inputs, all of the sensory modalities make synaptic relays in the thalamus before continuing to the primary cortical sensory receiving areas (**Figure 2.30**). The thalamus also receives inputs from the basal ganglia, cerebellum, neocortex, and

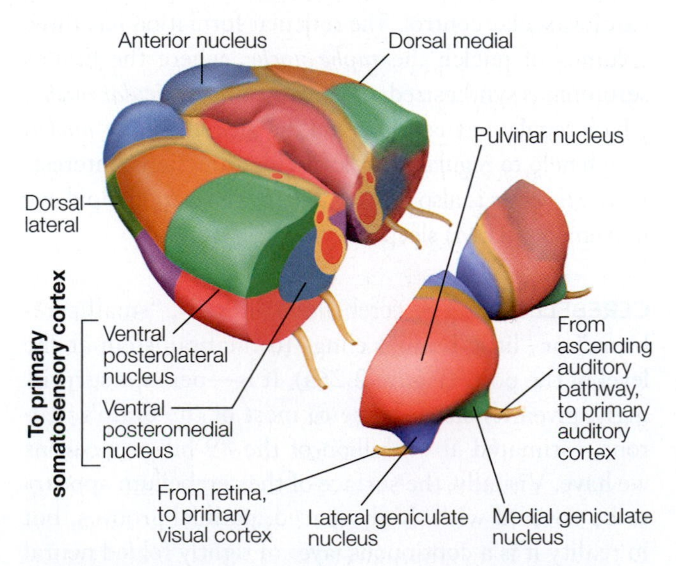

FIGURE 2.30 The thalamus, showing inputs and outputs and major subdivisions.
The various subdivisions of the thalamus serve different sensory systems and participate in various cortical–subcortical circuits. The posterior portion of the thalamus (lower right) is cut away in cross section and separated from the rest of the thalamus to reveal the internal organization of the thalamic nuclei (on the left).

medial temporal lobe, and sends projections back to these structures to create circuits involved in many different functions. Thus, the thalamus, a veritable Grand Central Station of the brain, is considered a relay center where neurons from one part of the nervous system synapse on neurons that travel to another region.

The thalamus is divided into several nuclei that act as specific relays for incoming sensory information. The *lateral geniculate nucleus* receives information from the ganglion cells of the retina and sends axons to the primary visual cortex. Similarly, the *medial geniculate nucleus* receives information from the inner ear, via other brainstem nuclei in the ascending auditory pathway, and sends axons to the primary auditory cortex. Somatosensory information projects via the *ventral posterior (medial and lateral) nuclei of the thalamus* to the primary somatosensory cortex. Sensory relay nuclei of the thalamus not only project axons to the cortex, but also receive heavy descending projections back from the same cortical area that they contact. Located at the posterior pole of the thalamus is the *pulvinar nucleus*, which is involved in attention and in integrative functions involving multiple cortical areas.

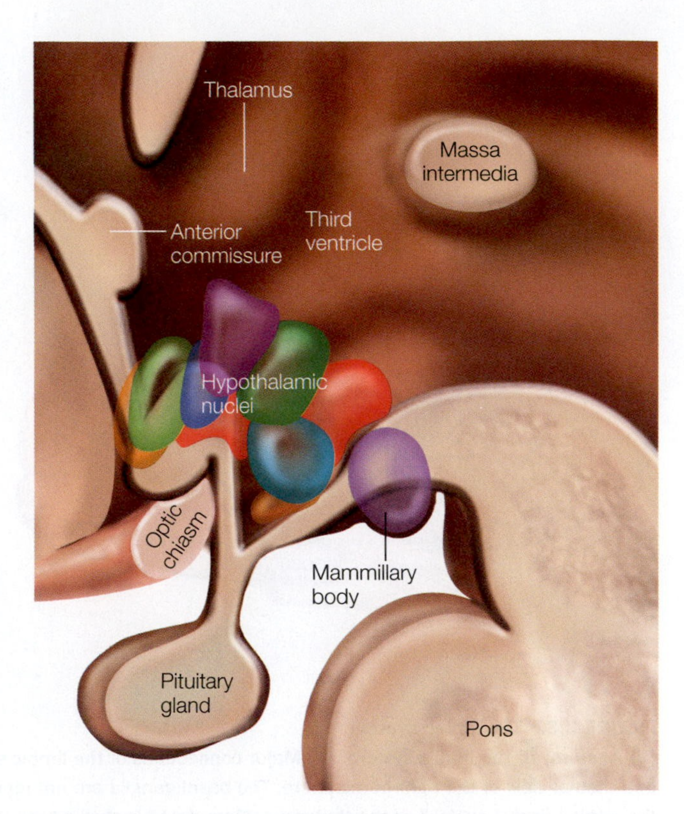

FIGURE 2.31 Midsagittal view of the hypothalamus. Various nuclear groups are shown diagrammatically. The hypothalamus is the floor of the third ventricle and, as the name suggests, sits below the thalamus. Anterior is to the left in this drawing.

HYPOTHALAMUS The main link between the nervous system and the endocrine system is the **hypothalamus**, which is the chief site for hormone production and control. Easily located, the hypothalamus lies on the floor of the third ventricle (Figure 2.26a). The two bumps seen on the ventral surface of the brain, the *mammillary bodies*, belong to the small collection of nuclei and fiber tracts contained in the hypothalamus (**Figure 2.31**). The hypothalamus receives inputs from limbic system structures and other brain areas. One of its jobs is to control circadian rhythms (light–dark cycles) with inputs from the mesencephalic reticular formation, amygdala, and retina. Extending from the hypothalamus are major projections to the prefrontal cortex, amygdala, spinal cord, and pituitary gland. The pituitary gland is attached to the base of the hypothalamus.

The hypothalamus controls the functions necessary for maintaining the normal state of the body (homeostasis): basal temperature and metabolic rate, glucose and electrolyte levels, hormonal state, sexual phase, circadian cycles, and immunoregulation. It sends out signals that drive behavior to alleviate such feelings as thirst, hunger, and fatigue. It accomplishes much of this work through the endocrine system via control of the **pituitary gland**.

The hypothalamus produces hormones, as well as factors that regulate hormone production in other parts of the brain. For example, hypothalamic neurons send axonal projections to the *median eminence*, an area bordering the pituitary gland that releases regulatory hormones into the circulatory system of the anterior pituitary gland. These in turn trigger (or inhibit) the release of a variety of hormones from the anterior pituitary into the bloodstream, such as growth hormone, thyroid-stimulating hormone, adrenocorticotropic hormone, and the gonadotropic hormones.

Hypothalamic neurons in the anteromedial region, including the *supraoptic nucleus* and *paraventricular nuclei*, send axonal projections into the posterior pituitary gland. There they stimulate the gland to release the hormones vasopressin and oxytocin into the blood to regulate water retention in the kidneys, milk production, and uterine contractility, among other functions. Circulating peptide hormones in the bloodstream can also act on distant sites and influence a wide range of behaviors, from the fight-or-flight response to maternal bonding. The hypothalamus can itself be stimulated by hormones circulating in the blood that were produced in other regions of the body.

The Telencephalon: Cerebrum

Toward the front of and evolutionarily newer than the diencephalon, the telencephalon develops into the cerebrum, which includes most of the limbic system's structures, the basal ganglia, the olfactory bulb, and, covering it all, the cerebral cortex, which we will explore in detail

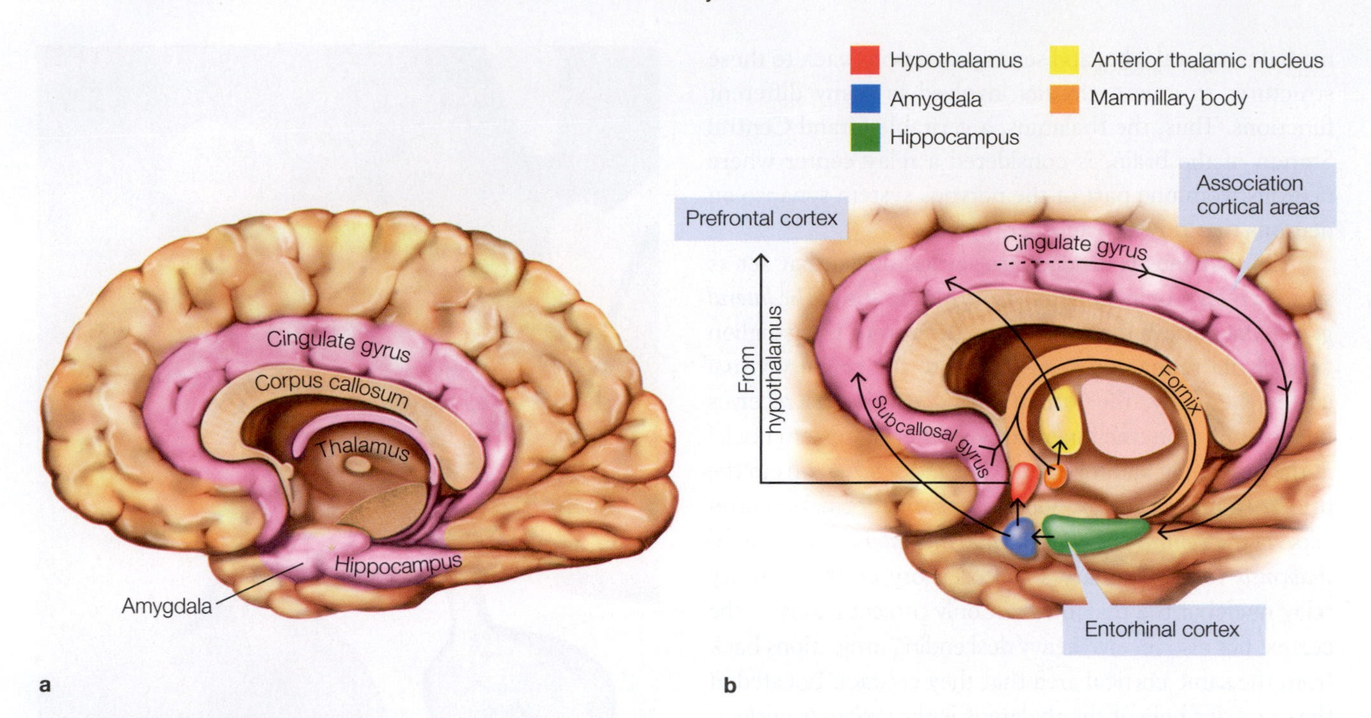

FIGURE 2.32 The limbic system.
(a) Anatomy of the limbic system. (b) Major connections of the limbic system, shown diagrammatically in a medial view of the right hemisphere. The basal ganglia are not represented in this figure, nor is the medial dorsal nucleus of the thalamus. More detail is shown here than needs to be committed to memory, but this figure provides a reference that will come in handy in later chapters.

in Section 2.5. We now look at the first two of these regions more closely.

LIMBIC SYSTEM In the 17th century, Thomas Willis observed that the brainstem appeared to sport a cortical border encircling it. He named it the *cerebri limbus* (in Latin, *limbus* means "border"). The classical limbic lobe (**Figure 2.32**) is made up of the *cingulate gyrus* (a band of cerebral cortex that extends above the corpus callosum in the anterior–posterior direction and spans both the frontal and parietal lobes), the hypothalamus, the anterior thalamic nuclei, and the **hippocampus**, an area located on the ventromedial aspect of the temporal lobe.

In the 1930s, James Papez (pronounced "payps") first suggested the idea that these structures were organized into a system for emotional behavior, which led to use of the term *Papez circuit*. It was named the **limbic system** by Paul MacLean in 1952 when he suggested including the **amygdala**, a group of neurons anterior to the hippocampus, along with the orbitofrontal cortex and parts of the basal ganglia (Figure 2.32). Sometimes the medial dorsal nucleus of the thalamus is also included. Some formulations make a distinction between limbic and paralimbic structure, as we describe later in the chapter (see Figure 2.39).

The structures included in the limbic system are tightly interconnected with many distinct circuits and share the characteristic that they are the most capable of plasticity in the cortex. They also share behavioral specializations that neuropsychologist M.-Marsel Mesulam (2000) has summarized into five categories: binding scattered information concerning recent events and experiences, which supports memory; focusing emotion and motivational states (drives such as thirst, hunger, libido) on extrapersonal events and mental content; linking autonomic, hormonal, and immunological states with mental activity; coordinating affiliative behaviors; and perceiving taste, smell, and pain. The limbic system is described in more detail in Chapter 10.

BASAL GANGLIA The **basal ganglia** are a collection of nuclei bilaterally located deep in the brain beneath the anterior portion of the lateral ventricles, near the thalamus (**Figure 2.33**). These subcortical nuclei—the *caudate nucleus*, *putamen*, *globus pallidus*, *subthalamic nucleus*, and *substantia nigra*—are extensively interconnected. The caudate nucleus together with the putamen is known as the *striatum*. The basal ganglia receive inputs from sensory and motor areas, and the striatum receives extensive feedback projections from the thalamus.

A comprehensive understanding of how these deep brain nuclei function remains elusive. They are involved in a variety of crucial brain functions including action selection, action gating, motor preparation, timing, fatigue, and task switching (Cameron et al., 2009). Notably, the basal ganglia have many dopamine receptors. The dopamine signal appears to represent the *error* between predicted

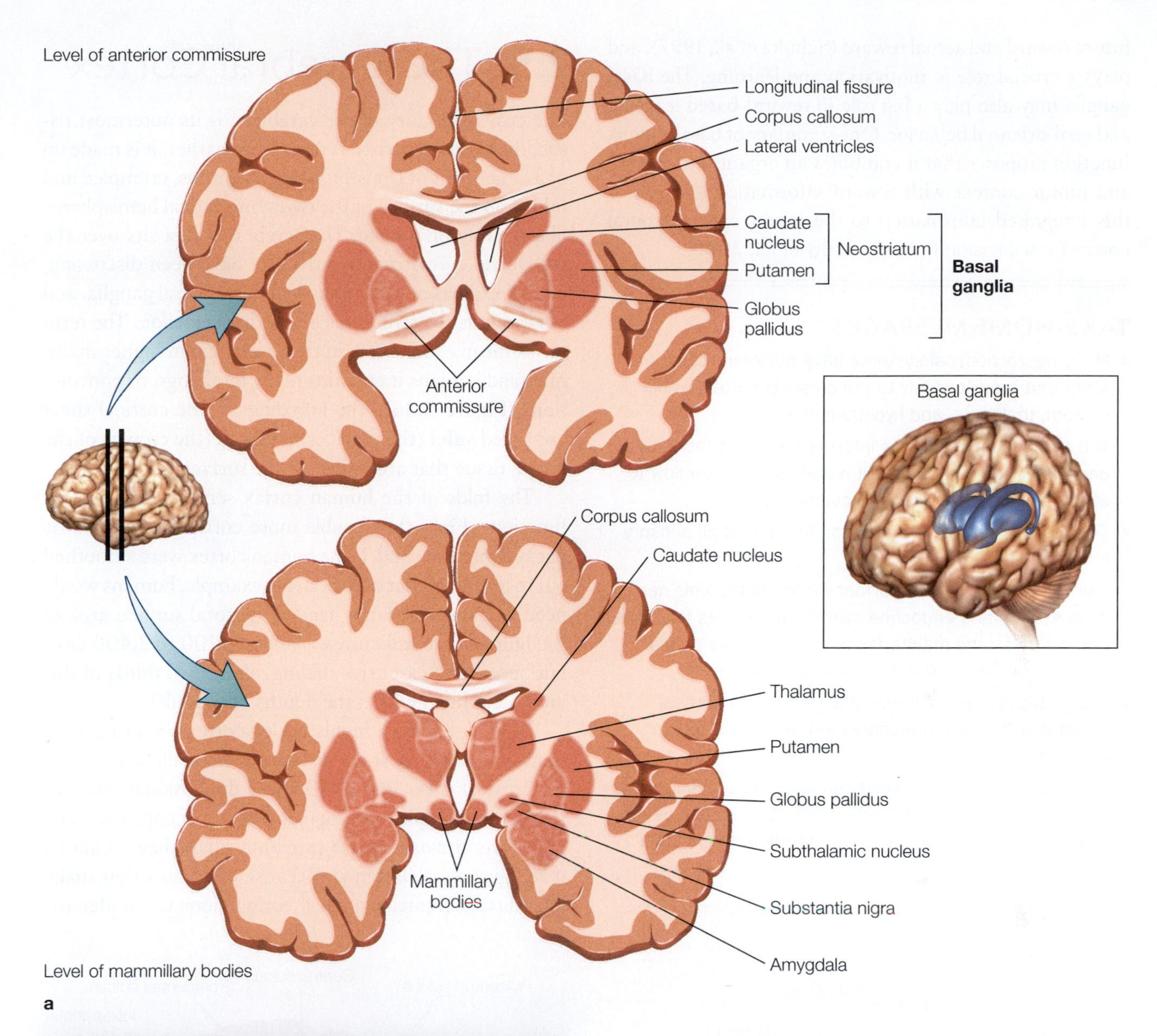

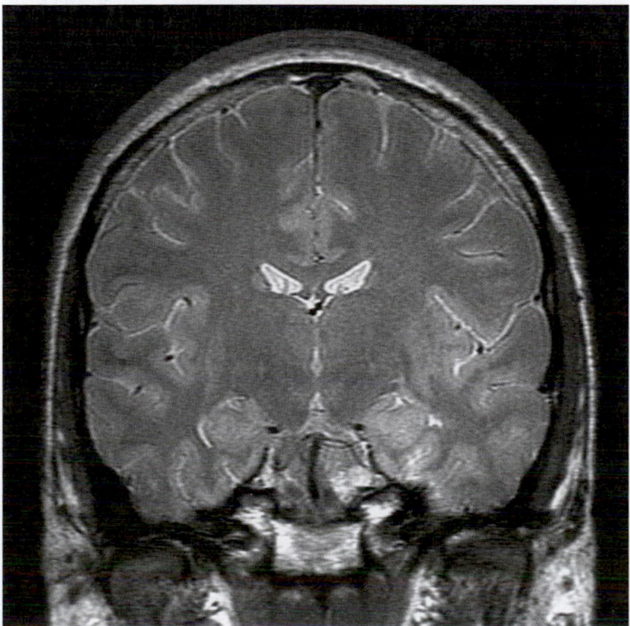

FIGURE 2.33 Coronal and transparent views of the brain showing the basal ganglia.
(a) Cross sections through the brain at two anterior–posterior levels (as indicated), showing the basal ganglia. **Inset:** A transparent brain with the basal ganglia in blue. **(b)** Corresponding high-resolution, structural MRI (4-tesla scanner) taken at approximately the same level as the more posterior drawing in (a). This image also shows the brainstem, as well as the skull and scalp, which are not shown in (a).

future reward and actual reward (Schultz et al., 1997), and plays a crucial role in motivation and learning. The basal ganglia may also play a big role in reward-based learning and goal-oriented behavior. One summary of basal ganglia function proposes that it combines an organism's sensory and motor context with reward information and passes this integrated information to the motor and prefrontal cortex for a decision (Chakravarthy et al., 2009).

TAKE-HOME MESSAGES

- Many neurochemical systems have nuclei in the brainstem that project widely to the cerebral cortex, limbic system, thalamus, and hypothalamus.
- The cerebellum integrates information about the body and motor commands, and it modifies motor outflow to effect smooth, coordinated movements.
- The thalamus is the relay station for almost all sensory information.
- The hypothalamus is important for the autonomic nervous system and endocrine system. It controls functions necessary for the maintenance of homeostasis. It is also involved in control of the pituitary gland.
- The limbic system includes subcortical and cortical structures that are interconnected and play a role in emotion.
- The basal ganglia are involved in a variety of crucial brain functions, including action selection, action gating, reward-based learning, motor preparation, timing, task switching, and more.

2.5 The Cerebral Cortex

The crowning glory of the cerebrum is its outermost tissue, the cerebral cortex. As described earlier, it is made up of a large sheet of (mostly) layered neurons, crumpled and folded on the surface of the two symmetrical hemispheres like frosting on a cake. The cerebral cortex sits over the top of the core structures that we have been discussing, including parts of the limbic system and basal ganglia, and it surrounds the structures of the diencephalon. The term *cortex* means "bark," as in tree bark, and in higher mammals and humans it contains many infoldings, or convolutions (**Figure 2.34**). The infoldings of the cortical sheet are called **sulci** (the crevices) and **gyri** (the crowns of the folded tissue that are visible on the surface).

The folds of the human cortex serve two important functions. First, they enable more cortical surface to be packed into the skull. If the human cortex were smoothed out to resemble that of the rat, for example, humans would need to have very large heads. The total surface area of the human cerebral cortex is about 2,200 to 2,400 cm^2, but because of extensive folding, about two thirds of this area is confined within the depths of the sulci.

Second, having a highly folded cortex brings neurons that are located at some distance from each other along the cortical sheet into closer three-dimensional relationships; for example, the opposing layers of cortex in each gyrus are in closer linear proximity than they would be if the gyri were flattened. Because the axons that make long-distance corticocortical connections run under the

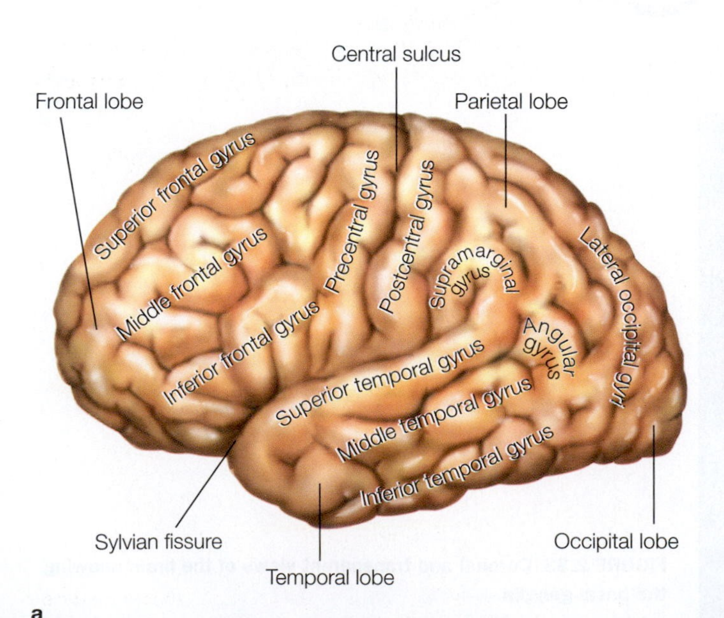

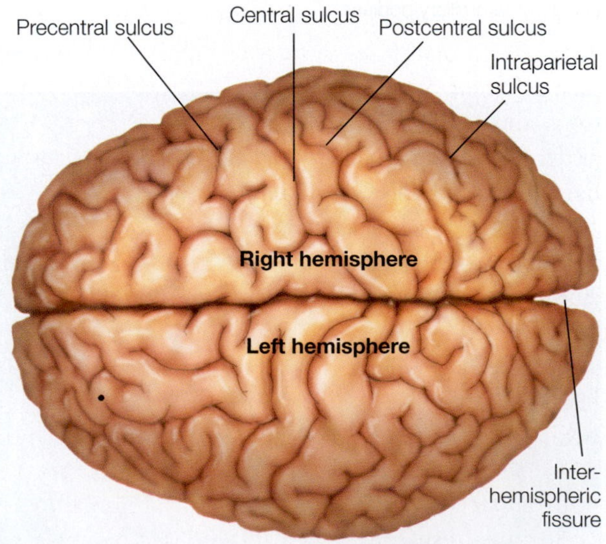

FIGURE 2.34 The cerebral cortex.
Lateral view of the left hemisphere (a) and dorsal view of the human brain (b). The major features of the cortex include the four cortical lobes and various key gyri. Gyri are separated by sulci and result from the folding of the cerebral cortex that occurs during development of the nervous system.

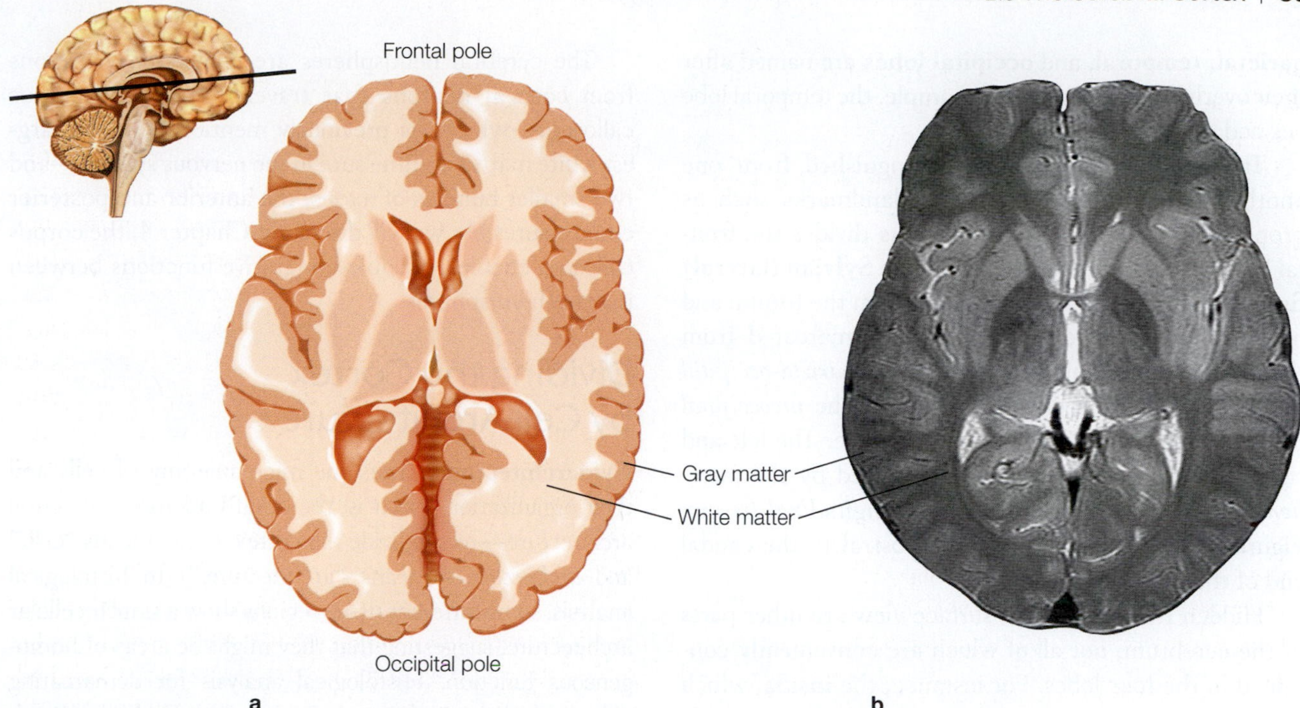

FIGURE 2.35 Cerebral cortex and white matter tracts.
(a) Horizontal section through the cerebral hemispheres at the level indicated at upper left. White matter is composed of myelinated axons, and gray matter is composed primarily of neurons. This diagram shows that the gray matter on the surface of the cerebral hemispheres forms a continuous sheet that is heavily folded. **(b)** High-resolution structural MRI in a similar plane of section in a living human. This T2 image was obtained on a 4-tesla scanner. Note that the imaging technique used for T2 images makes the white matter appear darker than the gray matter.

cortex through the white matter and do not follow the foldings of the cortical surface in their paths to distant cortical areas, they can project directly to the neurons brought closer together by folding.

The cortex ranges from 1.5 to 4.5 mm in thickness, but in most regions it is approximately 3 mm thick. It contains the cell bodies of neurons, their dendrites, and some of their axons. In addition, the cortex includes axons and axon terminals of neurons projecting to the cortex from other brain regions, such as the subcortical thalamus. The cortex also contains blood vessels.

Because the cerebral cortex has such a high density of cell bodies, it appears grayish in relation to underlying regions that are composed primarily of the axons that connect the neurons of the cerebral cortex to other locations in the brain. These underlying regions appear slightly paler or even white because of their lipid myelin sheaths (**Figure 2.35a**). As described earlier, this is the reason anatomists coined the terms *gray matter* and *white matter* when referring to areas of cell bodies and axon tracts, respectively. Yet no well-defined anatomical boundaries are visible in the wrinkled cortex. As a result, it can be divided up on the basis of its surface features, its microscopic architecture, or its functional features. We will explore all three of these divisional schemes.

Dividing the Cortex by Surface Features

The cerebral cortex can be divided by the gross anatomical features of the cortical surface. The cortex of each hemisphere has four main divisions, or lobes, that are best seen in a lateral view (**Figure 2.36**). The **frontal,**

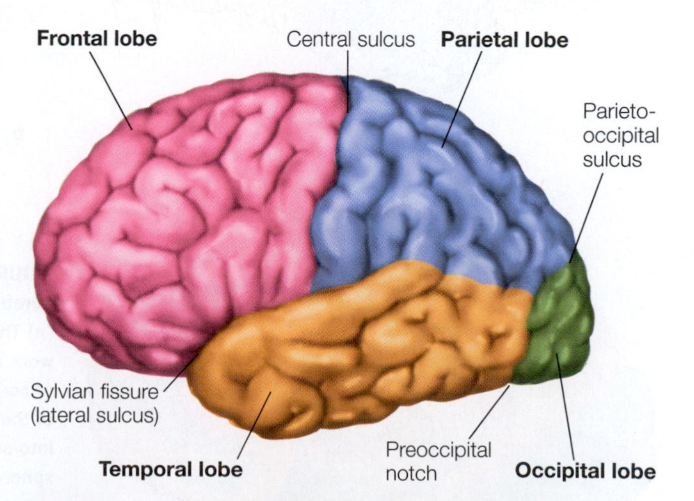

FIGURE 2.36 The four lobes of the cerebral cortex.
This lateral view of the left hemisphere shows the four major lobes of the brain, along with some of the major landmarks that separate them.

parietal, **temporal**, and **occipital lobes** are named after their overlying skull bones; for example, the temporal lobe lies underneath the temporal bone.

The lobes can usually be distinguished from one another by prominent anatomical landmarks such as pronounced sulci. The **central sulcus** divides the frontal lobe from the parietal lobe, and the **Sylvian (lateral) fissure** separates the temporal lobe from the frontal and parietal lobes. The occipital lobe is demarcated from the parietal and temporal lobes by the *parieto-occipital sulcus* on the brain's dorsal surface and the *preoccipital notch* located on the ventrolateral surface. The left and right cerebral hemispheres are separated by the *interhemispheric fissure* (also called the *longitudinal fissure*; Figure 2.34b) that runs from the rostral to the caudal end of the forebrain.

Hidden from the lateral surface view are other parts of the cerebrum, not all of which are conveniently contained in the four lobes. For instance, the **insula**, which is located between the temporal and frontal lobes, is, as its name implies, an island of folded cortex hidden deep in the lateral sulcus. Large enough that it could be considered another lobe, the insula is divided into the larger anterior insula and smaller posterior insula.

The cerebral hemispheres are connected via axons from cortical neurons that travel through the corpus callosum—which, as previously mentioned, is the largest white matter commissure in the nervous system—and two smaller bundles of axons, the anterior and posterior commissures. As we will discuss in Chapter 4, the corpus callosum enables valuable integrative functions between the two hemispheres.

Dividing the Cortex by Cell Architecture

Cytoarchitectonics uses the microanatomy of cells and their organization—that is, the brain's microscopic neural architecture—to subdivide the cortex. (*Cyto-* means "cell," and *architectonics* means "architecture.") In histological analysis, some different tissue regions show a similar cellular architecture, suggesting that they might be areas of homogeneous function. Histological analysis for demarcating different brain areas began in earnest with Korbinian Brodmann at the beginning of the 20th century. He identified approximately 52 regions of the cerebral cortex. These areas were categorized and numbered according to differences in cellular morphology and organization (**Figure 2.37**).

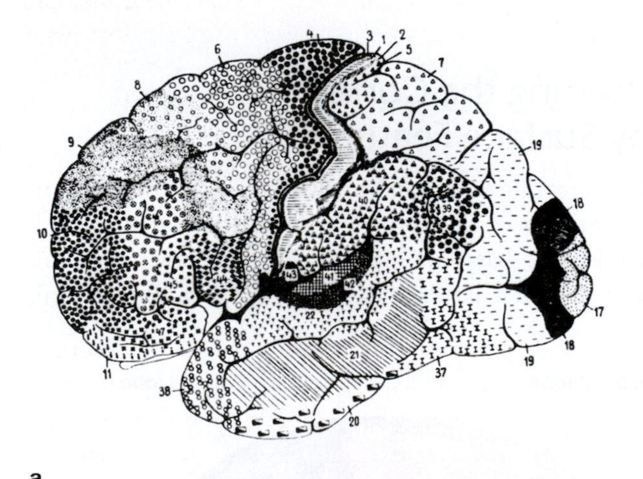

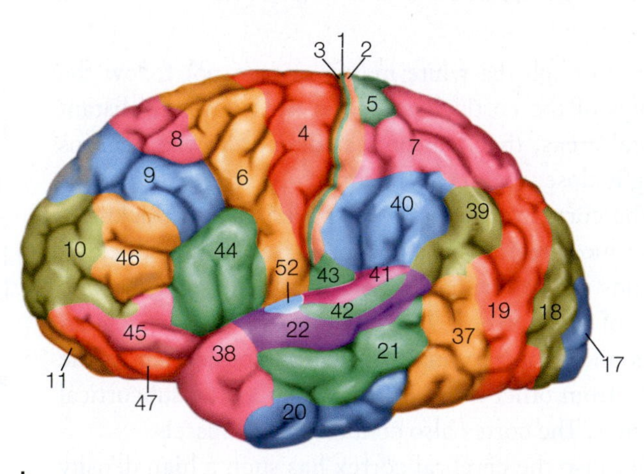

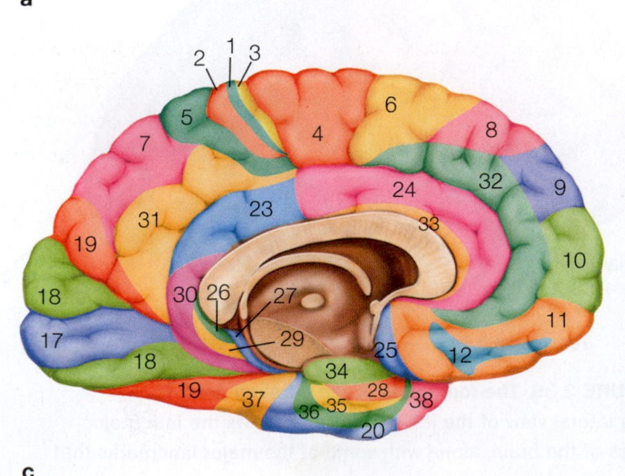

FIGURE 2.37 Cytoarchitectonic subdivisions of the cerebral cortex.
(a) The original cytoarchitectonic map from Brodmann's work around the start of the 20th century. Different regions of cortex have been demarcated by histological examination of the cellular microanatomy. Brodmann divided the cortex into about 52 areas. **(b)** Lateral view of the right hemisphere, showing Brodmann's areas color-coded. Over the years, the map has been modified, and the standard version no longer includes some areas. **(c)** Medial view of the left hemisphere, showing Brodmann's areas. Most of the areas are roughly symmetrical in the two hemispheres.

Other anatomists further subdivided the cortex into almost 200 cytoarchitectonically defined areas. A combination of cytoarchitectonic and functional descriptions of the cortex is probably the most effective way of dividing the cerebral cortex into meaningful units. In the sections that follow, we use Brodmann's numbering system and anatomical names to describe the cerebral cortex.

The Brodmann system often seems unsystematic. Indeed, the numbering has more to do with the order in which Brodmann sampled a region than with any meaningful relation between areas. Nonetheless, in some regions the numbering system roughly corresponds with the relations between areas that carry out similar functions, such as the association of vision with Brodmann areas 17, 18, and 19. Unfortunately, the nomenclature of the cortex (and indeed the nervous system) is not fully standardized. Hence, a region might be referred to by its Brodmann name, a cytoarchitectonic name, a gross anatomical name, or a functional name.

As an example, let's consider the first area in the cortex to receive visual inputs from the thalamus: the primary sensory cortex for vision. Its Brodmann name is area 17 (or Brodmann area 17—i.e., BA17); a cytoarchitectonic name for it is *striate cortex* (owing to the highly visible stripe of myelin in cross sections of this cortex, known as the *stria of Gennari*); its gross anatomical name is *calcarine cortex* (the cortex surrounding the calcarine fissure in humans); and its functional name is *primary visual cortex*, which also got the name *area V1* (for "visual area 1") from studies of the visual systems of monkeys.

We chose primary visual cortex as our example here because all these different names refer to the same cortical area. Unfortunately, for much of the cortex, this is not the case; that is, different nomenclatures often do not refer to precisely the same area with a one-to-one mapping. For example, BA18 of the visual system is not fully synonymous with V2 (for "visual area 2").

Using Brodmann's map and nomenclature has its limitations. If you are studying a particular brain using modern imaging tools, you cannot know whether its cellular anatomy precisely corresponds to what Brodmann found in the brain that he examined and used to determine his map. Thus, you use the brain's topography (e.g., 5 mm anterior to the central sulcus), not its microanatomy, to make comparisons. This approach can lead to inaccuracies in any conclusions drawn, because of individual differences in microanatomy, which can be known only by dissection and histology. That said, advances in imaging are providing improved resolution for examining microanatomy in living humans. How far we can push this in the future is, in part, up to you!

Using different microscopic anatomical criteria, it is also possible to subdivide the cerebral cortex according to the general patterns of the cortical layers (**Figure 2.38a and b**). Ninety percent of the cortex is composed of **neocortex**, *cortex that contains six cortical layers or that passed through a developmental stage involving six cortical layers.* Neocortex includes areas like primary sensory and motor cortex and association cortex (areas not obviously primary sensory or motor). *Mesocortex* is a term for the so-called paralimbic region, which includes the cingulate gyrus, parahippocampal gyrus, insular cortex, entorhinal cortex, and orbitofrontal cortex. With three to six layers, mesocortex is interposed between neocortex and allocortex, acting as a transition layer between them. The evolutionarily oldest *allocortex* typically has only one to four layers of neurons and includes the hippocampal complex (sometimes referred to as *archicortex*) and primary olfactory cortex (sometimes referred to as *paleocortex*).

The cortical layers in the neocortex are numbered I through VI, with layer I being the most superficial. The neurons of each layer are typically similar within a layer but different between layers. For instance, neocortical layer IV is packed with stellate neurons, and layer V consists of predominantly pyramidal neurons (**Figure 2.38c**). The deeper layers, V and VI, mature earlier during gestation and project primarily to targets outside the cortex. Layer IV is typically the input layer, receiving information from the thalamus, as well as information from other, more distant cortical areas. Layer V, on the other hand, is typically considered an output layer that sends information from the cortex back to the thalamus, facilitating feedback. The superficial layers mature last and primarily project to targets within the cortex. It has been suggested that the superficial layers and the connections they form within the cortex participate in the higher cognitive functions.

The neurons in any one sheet, while interwoven with the other neurons in the same layer, are also lined up with the neurons in the sheets above and below them, forming columns of neurons running perpendicular to the sheets. These columns are known as *minicolumns* or *microcolumns*. These columns are not just an anatomical nicety. The neurons within a column synapse with those from the layers above and below them, forming an elemental circuit, and appear to function as a unit. Neuronal columns are the fundamental processing unit within the cerebral cortex, and bundles of microcolumns assembled together, dubbed *cortical columns*, create functional units in the cortex.

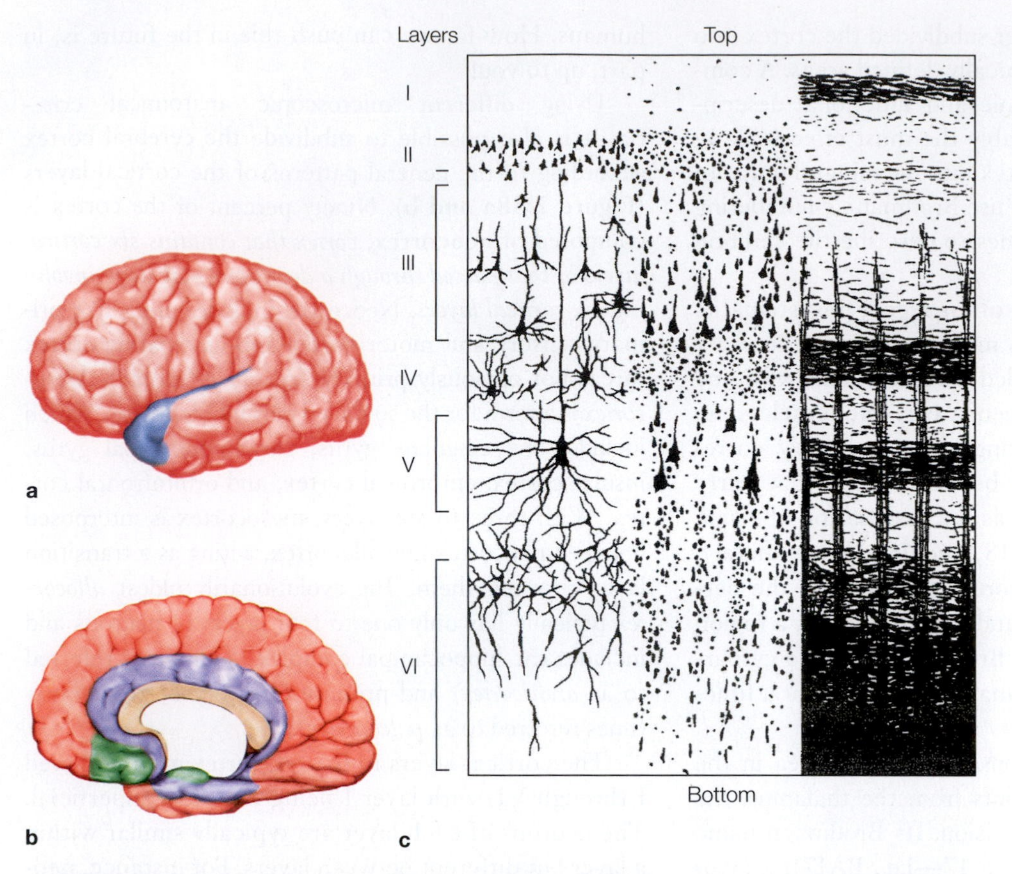

FIGURE 2.38 Cerebral cortex, color-coded to show the regional differences in cortical layering that specify different types of cortex.
(a) Lateral surface of the left hemisphere. **(b)** Medial surface of the right hemisphere. Neocortex is shown in red, mesocortex in blue, and allocortex in green. **(c)** Idealized cross section of neocortex, showing a variety of cell types and the patterns produced by three different types of staining techniques. On the left, the Golgi preparation is apparent: Only a few neurons are stained, but each is completely visualized. In the middle, we see primarily cell bodies from the Nissl stain. On the right, we see the fiber tracts in a Weigert stain, which selectively stains myelin.

Dividing the Cortex by Function

The lobes of the cerebral cortex have a variety of functional roles in neural processing. Sometimes we get lucky and can relate the gross anatomical subdivisions of the cerebral cortex to fairly specific functions, as with the precentral gyrus where the primary motor cortex resides, or the face recognition area of the fusiform gyrus. More typically, however, cognitive brain systems are composed of networks whose component parts are located in different lobes of the cortex. In addition, most functions in the brain—whether sensory, motor, or cognitive—rely on both cortical and subcortical components. Nevertheless, the cortex has generally been subdivided into five principal functional subtypes: primary sensory areas, primary motor areas, unimodal association areas, multimodal (heteromodal) association areas, and paralimbic and limbic areas (**Figure 2.39**; reviewed in Mesulam, 2000).

The primary visual, auditory, somatosensory, and motor regions are highly differentiated cytoarchitectonically and also, of course, functionally. A greater portion of the cerebral cortex is given over to what are classically known as association areas that integrate processing. They may be unimodal areas (meaning that they process one type of information—e.g., motor information or visual information) or multimodal (integrating more than one type). The rest of this section provides a beginner's guide to the functional anatomy of the cortex. The detailed functional anatomy of the brain will be revealed in the next twelve chapters. We will start with primary motor and sensory areas and their unimodal association areas.

THE FRONTAL LOBE: MOTOR CORTEX The frontal lobe has two main functional subdivisions: the prefrontal cortex (a higher-order association area that we will discuss later in this section) and the motor cortex

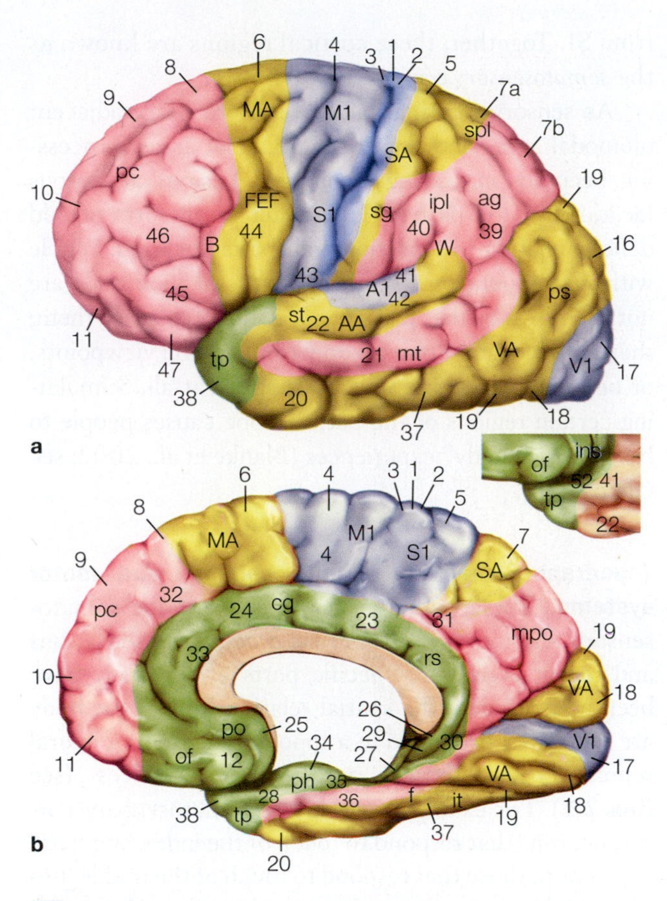

Primary sensory areas (S1, V1, A1) and motor areas (M1)

Unimodal association areas:
AA = auditory association cortex; f = fusiform gyrus;
FEF = frontal eye fields; it = inferior temporal gyrus;
MA = motor association cortex; ps = peristriate cortex;
SA = somatosensory association cortex;
sg = supramarginal gyrus; spl = superior parietal lobule;
st = superior temporal gyrus; VA = visual association cortex

Multimodal association areas:
ag = angular gyrus; B = Broca's area; ipl = inferior parietal lobule; mpo = medial parieto-occipital area; mt = middle temporal gyrus; pc = prefrontal cortex; W = Wernicke's area

Paralimbic areas: cg = cingulate cortex; ins = insula;
of = orbitofrontal region; ph = parahippocampal region;
po = parolfactory area; rs = retrosplenial area;
tp = temporopolar cortex

FIGURE 2.39 Functional areas in relationship to Brodmann's map of the human brain.
Unimodal association areas process one type of information. Multimodal association areas integrate more than one type of information. Core limbic structures, such as amygdala, are not shown. (a) Lateral view of the left hemisphere. (b) Midsagittal view of the right hemisphere. The small image shows the insula, not seen in the other views.

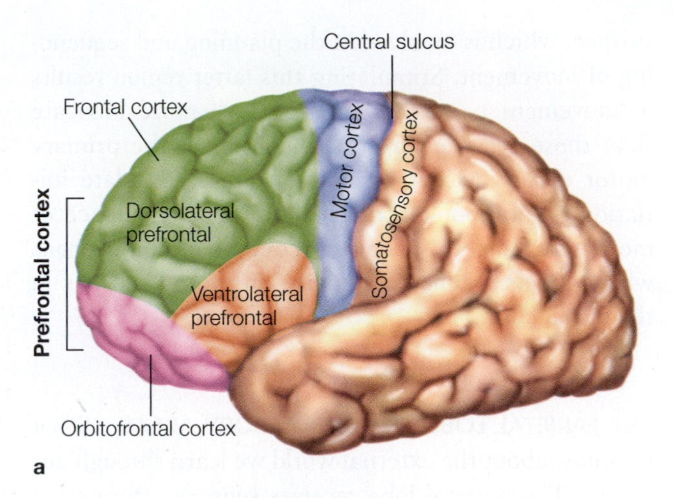

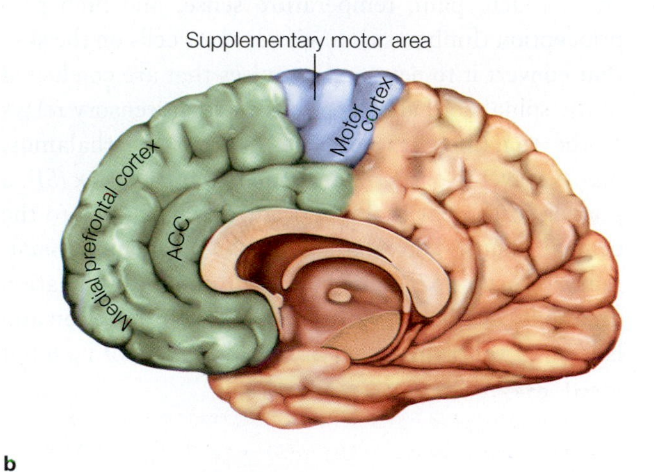

FIGURE 2.40 Cortical divisions of the frontal lobe.
(a) The frontal lobe contains both motor and higher-order association areas. For example, the prefrontal cortex is involved in executive functions, memory, decision making, and other processes.
(b) Midsagittal section of the brain, showing the medial prefrontal regions, which include the anterior cingulate cortex (ACC). Also visible is the supplementary motor area.

(**Figure 2.40**). The motor cortex sits in front of the central sulcus, beginning in the depths of the sulcus and extending anteriorly. The primary motor cortex corresponds to BA4. It includes the anterior bank of the central sulcus and much of the precentral gyrus (the prefix *pre-* in neuroanatomy means "in front of"). It receives input from the cerebellum and basal ganglia via the thalamus and the premotor area. It is mainly responsible for generating neural signals that control movement. The output layer of primary motor cortex contains the largest neurons in the cerebral cortex: the pyramidal neurons known as *Betz's cells*. They reach 60 to 80 micrometers (μm) in diameter at the cell body, and some of them send axons several feet long down the spinal cord.

Anterior to the primary motor cortex are two motor association areas of cortex located within BA6: the *premotor cortex* on the lateral surface of the hemisphere, which contributes to motor control, and the *supplementary motor cortex*, which lies dorsal to the premotor area and extends around to the hemisphere's medial surface, which is involved in the planning and sequencing of movement. Stimulating this latter region results in movement patterns that are much more intricate than those resulting from stimulation of the primary motor cortex. Motor association areas modulate initiation, inhibition, planning, and sensory guidance of motor movements, and they contain motor neurons whose axons extend to synapse on motor neurons in the spinal cord.

THE PARIETAL LOBE: SOMATOSENSORY AREAS What we know about the external world we learn through our senses. The parietal lobe receives sensory information about touch, pain, temperature sense, and limb proprioception (limb position) via receptor cells on the skin that convert it to neuronal impulses that are conducted to the spinal cord and then to the somatosensory relays of the thalamus (**Figure 2.41**). From the thalamus, inputs travel to the *primary somatosensory cortex (S1)*, a portion of the parietal lobe immediately caudal to the central sulcus. The next stop is the *secondary somatosensory cortex (S2)*, which is a unimodal association area that continues to process sensory information and is located ventrally to S1; S2 receives most of its input from S1. Together, these cortical regions are known as the *somatosensory cortex*.

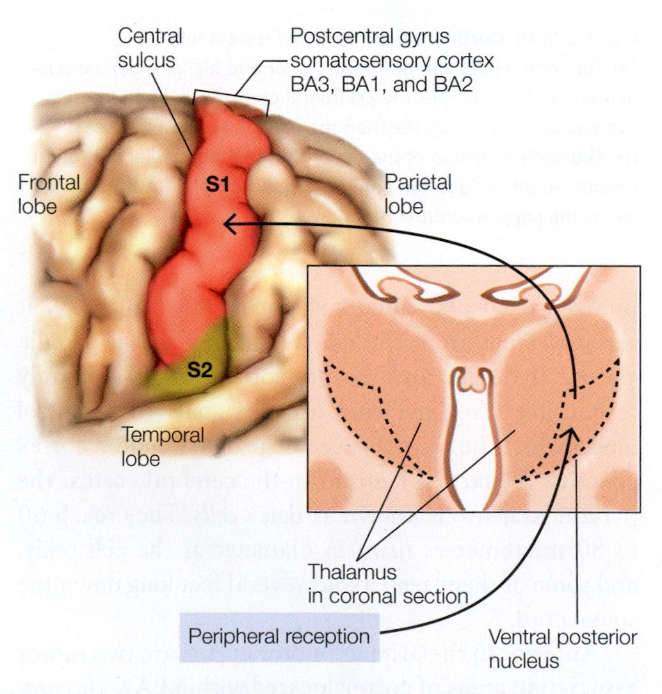

FIGURE 2.41 The somatosensory cortex, located in the postcentral gyrus.
Inputs from peripheral receptors project via the thalamus (shown in cross section) to the primary somatosensory cortex (S1). Secondary somatosensory cortex (S2) is also shown.

As sensory information moves from S1 to adjacent unimodal areas and then to multimodal areas, processing becomes increasingly complex. Lesions at various locations in the parietal lobe result in all sorts of odd deficits relating to sensation and spatial location: People with such lesions may think that parts of their body are not their own or that parts of space don't exist for them; they may recognize objects only from certain viewpoints, or be unable to locate objects in space at all. Stimulating certain regions of the parietal lobe causes people to have "out-of-body" experiences (Blanke et al., 2002; see Chapter 13).

Topographic mapping of the sensory and motor systems. The specific cortical regions of the somatosensory and motor cortices that process the sensations and motor control of specific parts of the body have been mapped out. The spatial relationships of the body are fairly well preserved in a topographic map of neural representations draped across these cortices (see **Box 2.2**). For example, within the somatosensory cortex, neurons that respond to touch of the index finger are adjacent to those that respond to touch of the middle finger, which are also next to neurons that respond to touch of the ring finger. Similarly, the hand area as a whole is adjacent to the lower arm area, which is near the upper arm, and so forth. There are discontinuities, however. For example, the genital region's representation is just below that of the feet.

This mapping of specific parts of the body to specific areas of the somatosensory cortex is known as **somatotopy**, resulting in somatotopic maps in the cortical areas. These maps are not set in stone, however, and do not necessarily have distinct borders. For example, the amount of cortical representation of a body part can decrease when that part is incapacitated and not used for extended periods, or it can increase with concentrated use. Loss of a limb can result in increased cortical representation of body parts represented adjacent to the representation of the lost limb. Topographic maps are a common feature of the nervous system (see Chapter 5).

THE OCCIPITAL LOBE: VISUAL PROCESSING AREAS The business of the occipital lobe is vision. Visual information from the outside world is processed by multiple layers of cells in the retina and transmitted via the optic nerve to the lateral geniculate nucleus of the thalamus, and from there to V1—a pathway often referred to as the *retinogeniculostriate* or primary visual pathway

BOX 2.2 | LESSONS FROM THE CLINIC

Cortical Topography

From the pattern of muscle spasms that progress across the body during a seizure, John Hughlings Jackson, whom we met in the previous chapter, inferred that the cortical hemispheres contain an orderly, maplike representation of the body. Sixty years later, neurosurgeon Wilder Penfield and physiologist/neurologist Herbert Jasper (Jasper & Penfield, 1954), at the Montreal Neurological Institute, were able to directly stimulate the cortex of their patients undergoing brain surgery, and in doing so, they found evidence for Jackson's inference. Because there are no pain receptors in the central nervous system, brain surgery can be performed while patients are awake and able to verbally describe their subjective experiences. Penfield and Jasper, during the same procedure in which they were removing damaged brain tissue, systematically explored the effects of small levels of electrical current applied to the cortical surface.

They found a topographic correspondence between cortical regions and body surface with respect to somatosensory and motor processes. This correspondence is represented in **Figure 2.42** by drawings of body parts being overlaid on drawings of coronal sections of the motor and somatosensory cortices. The resulting map of the body's surface on the cortex is sometimes called a *homunculus,* because it is an organized representation of the body across a given cortical area.

Note that there is an indirect relation between the actual size of a body part and its cortical representation: Body parts that have behaviorally relevant sensors or require fine motor movement have more cortical space dedicated to them on the sensory and motor maps. For example, areas within the motor homunculus that activate muscles in the fingers, mouth, and tongue are much larger than would be expected if the representation was proportional, indicating that large areas of cortex are involved in the fine coordination required when we manipulate objects or speak. Other animals also have topographically ordered sensory and motor representations. For example, rats have large areas dedicated to whisker sensations.

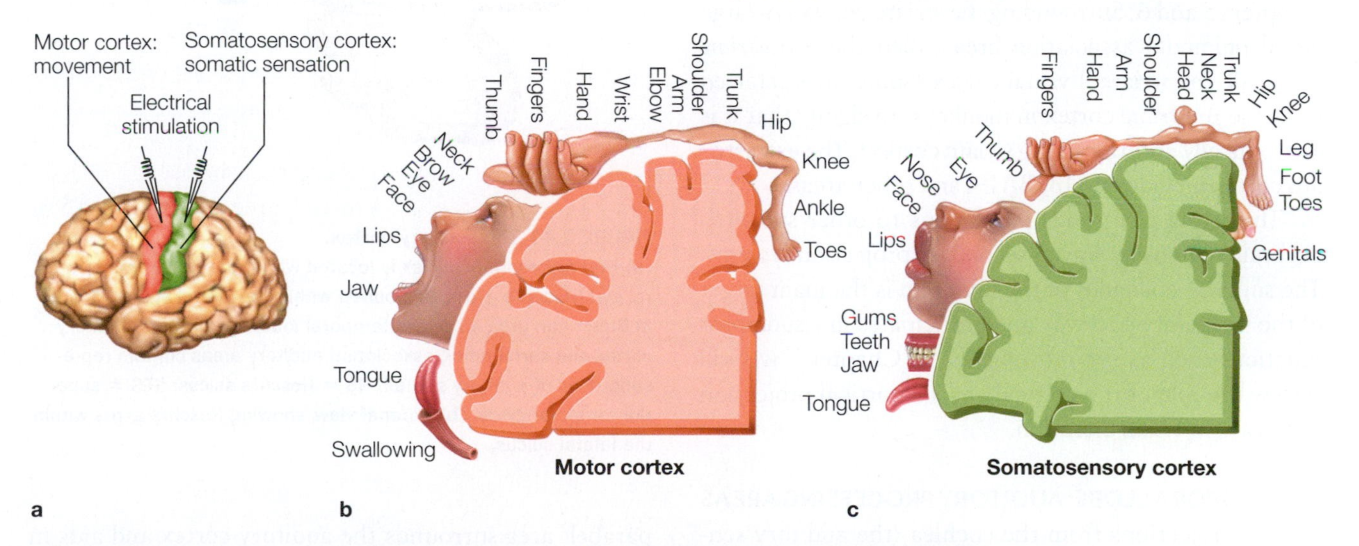

FIGURE 2.42 Topographic correspondence between cortical regions and body surface with respect to somatosensory and motor processes.
The two coronal sections, showing motor cortex (b) and somatosensory cortex (c), correspond to the colored regions highlighted in the lateral view of the whole brain (a). Only the left hemisphere is shown and the coronal sections are shown as viewed from a posterior viewpoint.

(**Figure 2.43**). The primary visual cortex is where the cerebral cortex begins to process visual information. As mentioned earlier, this area is also known as *striate cortex*, *V1* (for "visual area 1"), or *BA17*.

In humans, the primary visual cortex is on the medial surface of the cerebral hemispheres, extending only slightly onto the posterior hemispheric pole. Thus, most of the primary visual cortex is effectively hidden from view, between the two hemispheres. The cortex in this area has six layers and begins the cortical coding of visual features like luminance, spatial frequency, orientation, and motion—features that we will take up in detail in

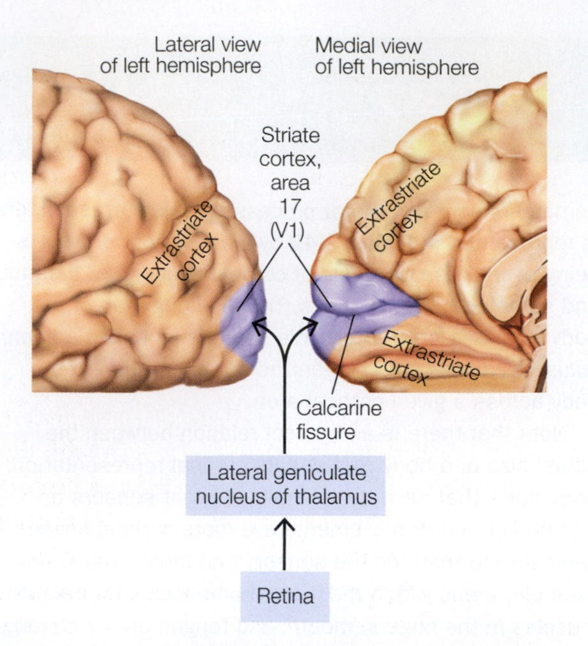

FIGURE 2.43 The visual cortex, located in the occipital lobe. Brodmann area 17—also called the *primary visual cortex*, visual area 1 (V1), and striate cortex—is located at the occipital pole and extends onto the medial surface of the hemisphere, where it is largely buried within the calcarine fissure.

Chapters 5 and 6. Surrounding the striate cortex is a large visual unimodal association area called the *extrastriate* ("outside the striate") visual cortex (sometimes referred to as the *prestriate* cortex in monkeys, to signify that it is anatomically anterior to the striate cortex). The extrastriate cortex includes BA18, BA19, and other areas.

The retina also sends projections to other subcortical brain regions by way of secondary projection systems. The superior colliculus of the midbrain is the main target of the secondary pathway and participates in visuomotor functions such as eye movements. In Chapter 7 we will review the role of the cortical and subcortical projection pathways in visual attention.

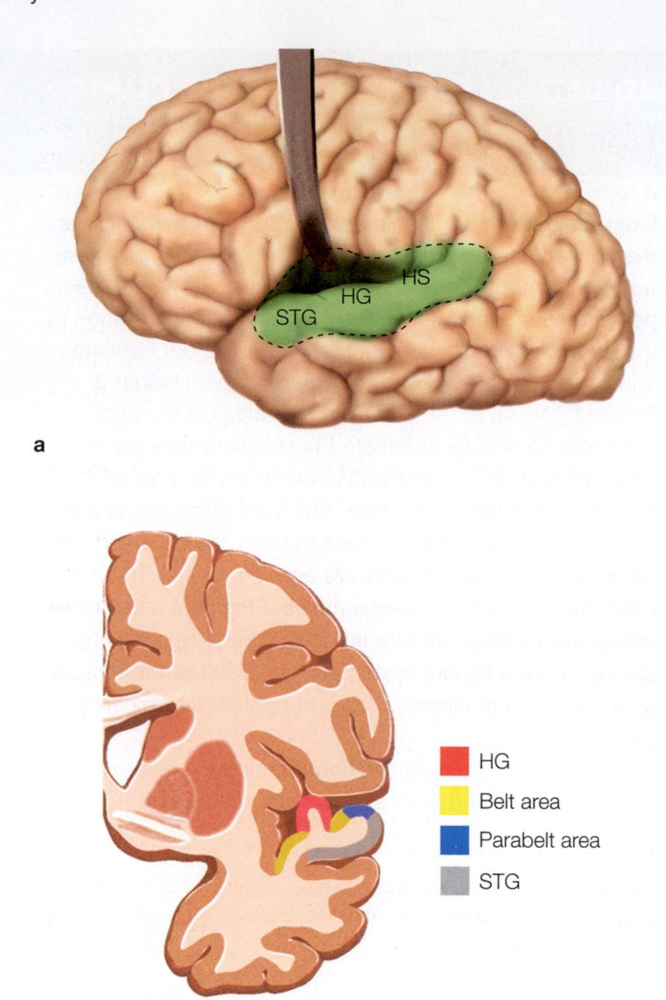

FIGURE 2.44 The auditory cortex.
(a) Primary auditory cortex is located within the transverse temporal gyri (Heschl's gyrus, HG) buried within the lateral sulcus located in Brodmann area 41 of the temporal lobe. The primary auditory cortex and surrounding association auditory areas contain representations of auditory stimuli. HS = Heschl's sulcus; STG = superior temporal gyrus. **(b)** Coronal view, showing Heschl's gyrus within the lateral sulcus.

THE TEMPORAL LOBE: AUDITORY PROCESSING AREAS

Neural projections from the cochlea (the auditory sensory organ in the inner ear) proceed through the subcortical relays to the medial geniculate nucleus of the thalamus and then to the primary auditory cortex. The primary auditory cortex lies in the superior temporal gyrus of the temporal lobe and extends into the lateral sulcus, where the transverse temporal gyri, which make up a region known as *Heschl's gyrus* that roughly corresponds with Brodmann area 41, are buried (**Figure 2.44a**). Previously, the auditory cortex was subdivided into primary auditory cortex (A1), secondary auditory cortex (A2), and other association areas. These are now referred to, respectively, as the core (BA41), belt (BA42), and parabelt areas (**Figure 2.44b**). The parabelt area surrounds the auditory cortex and aids in the perception of auditory inputs; when this area is stimulated, sensations of sound are produced in humans.

The auditory cortex has a tonotopic organization, meaning that the physical layout of the neurons is based on the frequency of sound. Neurons in the auditory cortex that respond best to low frequencies are at one end, and those that respond to high frequencies are at the other. The macroanatomy, microanatomy, and tonotopic pattern vary substantially across individuals. While sound localization appears to be processed in the brainstem, processing in the auditory cortex is likely essential for performing more complex functions, such as sound identification. Its role in hearing remains unclear and under investigation.

ASSOCIATION CORTEX If someone were to make you angry, would you have the "knee-jerk" reaction of punching that person? As mentioned earlier, the knee jerk is a result of a monosynaptic, stimulus–response reflex arc that leaves cortical processing out of the loop (Figure 2.25). Most of our neurons, however, feed through a series of cortical synapses before the behavioral response occurs. These synapses provide integrative and modular processing in association areas, the outcomes of which are our cognition—including memory, attention, planning, and so forth—and our behavior, which might or might not be a punch.

As mentioned earlier, a good portion of the neocortex that is neither primary sensory cortex nor primary motor cortex has traditionally been termed **association cortex**. Each primary sensory area is linked to its own unimodal association area that receives and processes information from only that sense. For example, though the primary visual cortex is necessary for normal vision, neither it nor the extrastriate cortex is the sole locus of visual perception. Regions of visual association cortex in the parietal and temporal lobes process information from the primary visual cortex about color, simple boundaries, and contours to enable recognition of these features as, for example, a face. Moreover, visual association cortex can be activated during mental imagery when we call up a visual memory, even in the absence of visual stimulation.

Unimodal areas are not connected to each other, protecting the sensory reliability of experiences and delaying cross contamination from other senses (Mesulam, 2000). While unimodal areas can encode and store perceptional information, and while they can identify whether sensory features are the same—say, comparing two faces—without information from other modalities, they don't have the ability to tie that perception to any other experience. Thus, within a unimodal area the face remains generic; it can't be recognized as a specific person, and no name is attached to it. Those tasks require more input, and to get it, processing moves on to multimodal cortex.

Multimodal association cortex contains cells that may be activated by more than one sensory modality. It receives and integrates inputs from many cortical areas. For example, inputs of the various qualities of a particular stimulus (e.g., the pitch, loudness, and timbre of a voice) are integrated with other sensory inputs—such as vision, along with memory, attention, emotion, and so forth—to produce our experience of the world. Multimodal areas are also responsible for all of our high-end human abilities, such as language, abstract thinking, and designing a Maserati.

THE FRONTAL LOBE REVISITED: PREFRONTAL CORTEX The more anterior region of the frontal lobe, the **prefrontal cortex**, is the last to develop and is the evolutionarily youngest region of the brain. It is proportionately larger in humans compared to other primates. Its main regions are the dorsolateral prefrontal cortex, the ventrolateral prefrontal cortex, the orbitofrontal cortex (Figure 2.40a), and the medial prefrontal regions, including the anterior cingulate cortex (Figure 2.40b).

The prefrontal cortex takes part in the more complex aspects of planning, organizing, controlling, and executing behavior—tasks that require the integration of information over time. Because of its facility with these tasks, the frontal lobe is often said to be the center of cognitive control, frequently referred to as *executive function*. People with frontal lobe lesions often have difficulty reaching a goal. They may know the steps that are necessary to attain it but just can't figure out how to put them together. Another problem associated with frontal lobe lesions is a lack of motivation to initiate action, to modulate it, or to stop it once it is happening. The frontal lobes also are involved in social functioning, so inappropriate social behavior often accompanies frontal lobe lesions.

PARALIMBIC AREAS The paralimbic areas form a belt around the basal and medial aspects of the cerebral hemispheres and don't reside in a single lobe. They can be subdivided into the olfactocentric and hippocampocentric formations. The former includes the temporal pole, insula, and posterior orbitofrontal cortex; the latter includes the parahippocampal cortex, the retrosplenial area, the cingulate gyrus, and the subcallosal regions. The paralimbic areas lie intermediate between the limbic areas and the cortex, and they are major players linking visceral and emotional states with cognition. Processing in these areas provides critical information about the relevance of a stimulus for behavior, rather than just its physical characteristics, which are provided by the sensory areas. This information affects various aspects of behavior reviewed in our earlier discussion of the limbic system.

LIMBIC AREAS While most of the structures in the limbic system are subcortical, the limbic areas of cortex lie on the ventral and medial surfaces of the cerebral hemispheres and include the amygdala, the piriform cortex, the septal area, the substantia innominata, and the hippocampal formation. These areas have the greatest number of reciprocal interconnections with the hypothalamus. Like the paralimbic areas, the limbic areas are major contributors to behavior via the roles they play in processing emotion, arousal, motivation, and memory.

TAKE-HOME MESSAGES

- Gyri are the protruding areas seen on the surface of the cortex; sulci, or fissures, are the infolded regions of cortex. The brain's major sulci divide the brain into the frontal, parietal, temporal, and occipital lobes.
- Brodmann divided the brain into distinct regions based on the underlying structure and organization of the cells they comprise.
- The cortex can also be divided into functional regions that include primary motor and sensory cortices, unimodal and multimodal association areas, and paralimbic and limbic areas.
- Topography is the principle that the anatomical organization of the body is reflected in the cortical representation of the body, in both the sensory cortex and the motor cortex.
- Multimodal association cortices are the regions of cortex that lie outside the sensory-specific and motor cortical regions, and they receive and integrate input from multiple sensory modalities.

2.6 Connecting the Brain's Components into Systems

Systems scientists will tell you that in order to figure out how complex systems, including our brain, process information, we need to grasp their organizational architecture. To do this, we need to remember that the brain and its architecture are a product of evolution. Throughout the 20th century, the "big brain theory"—the idea that humans are more intelligent because we have a proportionately larger brain for our body size than the other great apes have—garnered quite a few fans. In 2009, Suzana Herculano-Houzel and her coworkers refined this theory when they used a new technique to more accurately count neuron numbers (Azevedo et al., 2009; Herculano-Houzel, 2009). They found that the ratio of neuron number to brain size is about the same for all primates, including humans.

The advantage we have over other primates is that our brains are larger in absolute volume and weight; therefore, we have more neurons. The advantage that primates have over other species of mammals, such as rats, cetaceans, and elephants, is that primate brains use space more economically: Primates have more neurons per unit volume of brain than other mammals have. Rodents may have more brain volume per body weight, and elephants and cetaceans may have larger brains overall, but primates get more neurons per cubic inch. While the exact neuron counts for cetaceans and elephants aren't in, there is evidence, as Herculano-Houzel argues, that humans have more total neurons in our brains than any other species, suggesting that the absolute neuron number may contribute to humans' enhanced abilities.

In addition to neuron number, other aspects of brain structure might affect cognitive ability. For example, denser neuronal connectivity could affect computational power. While one might expect that more neurons would be accompanied by more connections per neuron, this is not what happens. Just consider if human brains were fully connected—that is, if each neuron were connected to every other one: Our brains would have to be 20 km in diameter (D. D. Clark & Sokoloff, 1999) and would require so much energy that all our time (and then some) would be spent eating. With such vast distances for axons to travel across the brain, the processing speed would be extremely slow, creating an uncoordinated body and a rather dull-witted person.

Instead, certain laws govern connectivity as brains increase in size (Striedter, 2005). As the brain increases in size, long-distance connectivity decreases. The number of neurons that an average neuron connects to actually does not change with increasing brain size. By maintaining absolute connectivity, not proportional connectivity, large brains became less interconnected. There's no need to worry about this, because evolution came up with two clever solutions:

- *Minimizing connection lengths.* Short connections keep processing localized, with the result that the connection costs are less. That is, shorter axons take up less space; less energy is required for building, maintenance, and transmission; and signaling is faster over shorter distances. From an evolutionary perspective, this organization set the stage for local networks to divide up and specialize, forming multiple clusters of independent processing units, called *modules.*
- *Retaining a small number of very long connections between distant sites.* Primate brains in general and human brains in particular have developed what is known as "small-world" architecture, an organizational structure that is common to many complex systems, including human social relations. It combines many short, fast local connections with a few long-distance connections to communicate the results of local processing. It also has the advantage that fewer steps connect any two processing units. This design allows

both a high degree of local efficiency and, at the same time, quick communication to the global network.

The big picture is that as the number of neurons increases, the connectivity pattern changes, resulting in anatomical and functional changes. We will explore the modular brain and small-world architecture in more detail in Chapter 4.

As we have seen in the primary sensory areas and their adjacent association areas, localized regions of processing are highly intraconnected to compute specialized functions. For coordinating complex behaviors, however, communication extends between more distant regions, forming a larger-scale neural network. For instance, Broca's and Wernicke's areas, each performing separate specialized functions for language, must communicate with each other for us to be able to both produce and understand language. These two areas are densely interconnected via a bundle of nerve fibers, the *arcuate fasciculus*. The cost of large-scale communication networks is offset by reducing connections between modules that specialize in unrelated cognitive functions. For example, when you are in flight mode, your legs don't need fast direct connections to Broca's and Wernicke's areas, but they do need them to the motor cortex.

Structural connectivity networks have been identified in a variety of ways. Anatomists beginning as early as the 16th century dissected human cadaver brains and teased out the white matter fiber tracts connecting regions of the brain. In addition, work on animals helped to identify the projection pathways of major brain systems. In animals, researchers injected dyes that could be taken up by neurons and transported via the plasma of the axon to the cell bodies or axon terminals, revealing either the brain regions a structure projected to, or the regions it received projections from. After a specified amount of time had elapsed, the investigators sacrificed the animal and dissected its brain to find the final location of the dye.

Through hundreds of such studies, connections between brain areas were mapped and cataloged. In the last 20 years, researchers have developed noninvasive techniques such as diffusion-based magnetic resonance imaging combined with computer algorithms to trace white matter tracts. These methods, which we will discuss in the next chapter, have enabled us to begin locating the structural connections and functional relationships between distant regions that make up neural systems in living human and animal brains.

Besides the predominantly left-hemisphere language network, other large-scale neural networks include the right-hemisphere spatial attention network with connections among the posterior parietal cortex, the frontal eye fields, and the cingulate gyrus; the face/object network with lateral temporal and temporopolar connections; the cognitive control network with lateral prefrontal, orbitofrontal, and posterior parietal cortical connections; and the default network with links connecting the posterior cingulate cortex, the medial prefrontal cortex, the angular gyrus, and their subnetworks. These functional networks are currently being identified by functional MRI, which we will also talk more about in the next chapter.

TAKE-HOME MESSAGES

- Although the human brain is about three times larger than the chimpanzee brain, the absolute number of connections per neuron is the same.
- As primate brains increased in size, their overall connectivity patterns changed, resulting in anatomical and functional changes.
- A network with small-world architecture allows both a high degree of local efficient processing and, at the same time, quick communication to distant circuits.

2.7 Development of the Nervous System

Thus far, we have been discussing the neuroanatomy of the developed adult brain. In humans and many other species, the fetal brain is well developed and shows cortical layers, neuronal connectivity, and myelination; in short, the fetal brain is already extremely complex, although by no means completely developed. This section provides an introduction to development, with special attention to development of the cerebral cortex.

Overview of Early Development

Fertilization of the egg is followed by a series of events that lead to the formation of a multicellular blastula, which has already begun to specialize. The blastula contains three main cell lines that, after a few days, form three layers: the *ectoderm* (outer layer) that will form the nervous system and the outer skin, lens of the eye, inner ear, and hair; the *mesoderm* (middle layer) that will form the skeletal system and voluntary muscle; and the *endoderm* (inner layer) that will form the gut and digestive organs. The early processes

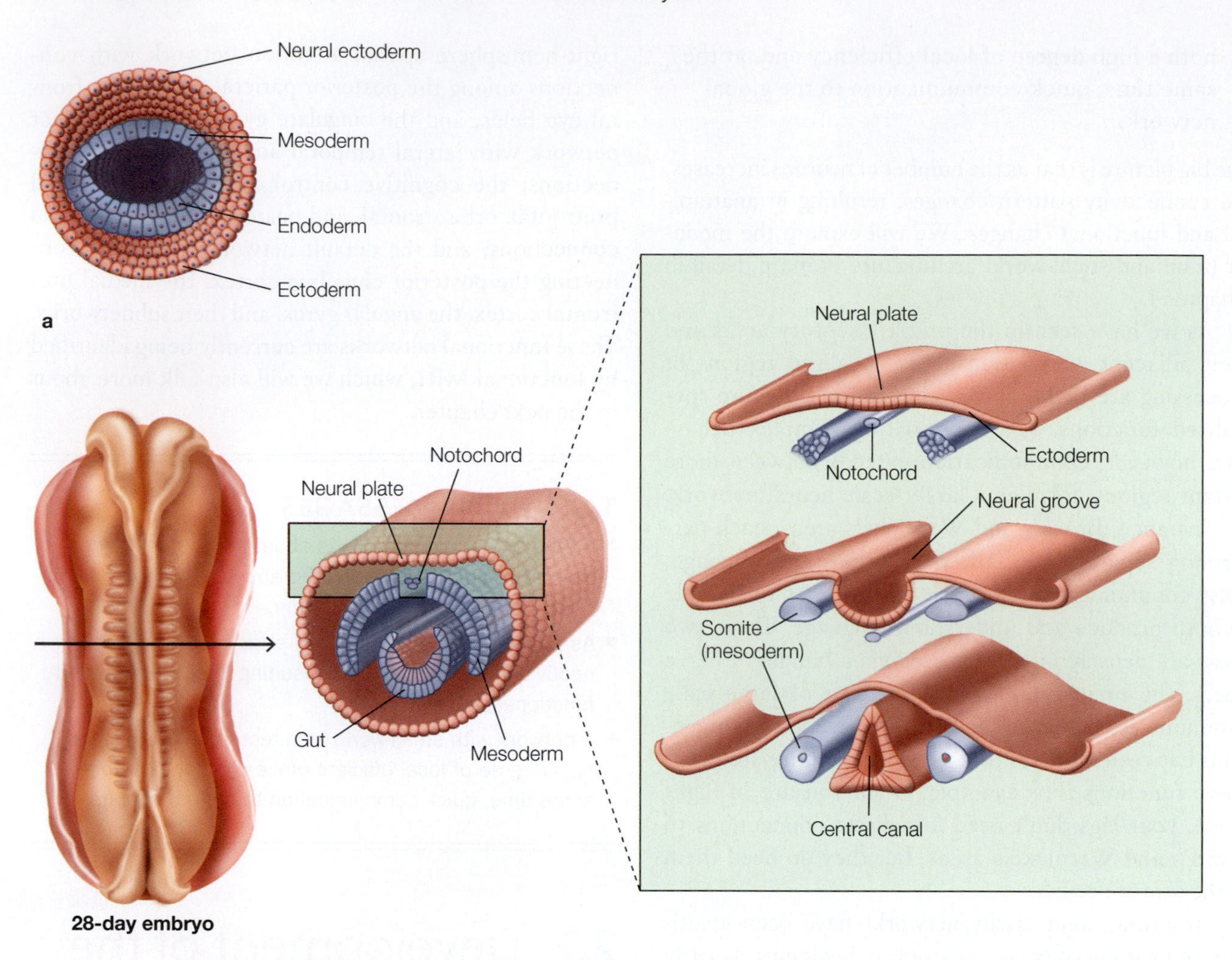

FIGURE 2.45 Development of the vertebrate nervous system.
Cross sections through the blastula and embryo at various developmental stages during the first 21 days of life. (a) Early in embryogenesis, the multicellular blastula contains cells destined to form various body tissues. (b) Migration and specialization of different cell lines leads to formation of the primitive nervous system around the neural groove and, after it fuses, the neural tube (not shown) on the dorsal surface of the embryo. The brain is located at the anterior end of the embryo and is not shown in these more posterior sections, which are taken at the level of the spinal cord.

that go into forming the nervous system are called *neurulation* (**Figure 2.45**). During this stage, the ectodermal cells on the dorsal surface form the neural plate.

As the nervous system continues to develop, the cells at the lateral borders of the neural plate push upward. (Imagine joining the long sides of a rectangular piece of dough to form a tube.) This movement causes the more central cells of the neural plate to invaginate, or dip inward, to form the *neural groove*. As the groove deepens, the cells pushing up at the border of the neural fold region eventually meet and fuse, forming the *neural tube* that runs anteriorly and posteriorly along the embryo. The adjacent nonneural ectoderm then reunites to seal the neural tube within an ectodermal covering that surrounds the embryo.

At both ends of the neural tube are openings (the anterior and the posterior neuropores) that close on about the 23rd to 26th day of gestation. When the anterior neuropore is sealed, this cavity forms the primitive brain, consisting of three spaces, or ventricles. If the neuropores do not close correctly, neural tube defects such as anencephaly (absence of a major portion of the brain and skull) or spina bifida (incomplete formation of some of the vertebrae) may result. From this stage on, the brain's gross features are formed by growth and flexion (bending) of the neural tube's anterior portions (**Figure 2.46**). The result is a cerebral cortex that envelops the subcortical and brainstem structures. The final three-dimensional relations of the brain's structures are the product of continued cortical enlargement and folding.

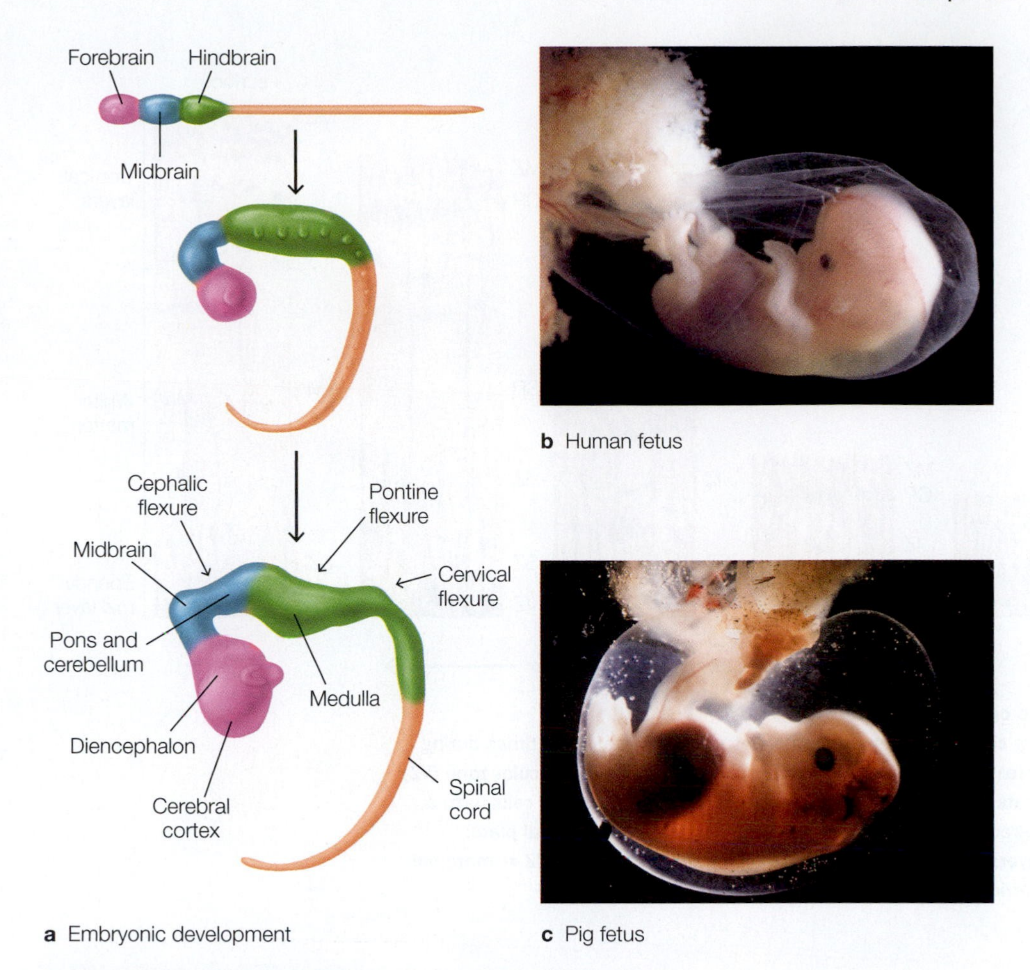

FIGURE 2.46 Early stages of embryonic development in mammals.
(a) Developing embryo. The embryo goes through a series of folds, or flexures, during development. These alterations in the gross structure of the nervous system give rise to the compact organization of the adult brain and brainstem in which the cerebral cortex overlies the diencephalon and midbrain within the human skull. There is significant similarity between the gross features of the developing fetuses of mammals, as comparison of a human fetus (b) and a pig fetus (c) shows.

The posterior portion of the neural tube differentiates into a series of repeated segments that form the spinal cord.

In primates, almost the full complement of neurons is generated prenatally during the middle third of gestation. The entire adult pattern of gross and cellular neural anatomical features is present at birth, and very few neurons are generated after birth (but see the end of this section, "Birth of New Neurons Throughout Life"). Although axonal myelination continues for some period postnatally (e.g., until adulthood in the human frontal lobe), the newborn has a well-developed cortex that includes the cortical layers and areas characterized in adults. For instance, BA17 (the primary visual cortex) can be distinguished from the motor cortex by cytoarchitectonic analysis of its neuronal makeup at the time of birth.

NEURAL PROLIFERATION AND MIGRATION OF CORTICAL CELLS The neurons that form the brain arise from a layer of precursor cells in *proliferative zones* located adjacent to the ventricles of the developing brain. The cortical neurons arise from the *subventricular zone*, and those that form other parts of the brain arise from precursor cells in the *ventricular zone*. **Figure 2.47** shows a cross section through the cortex and the precursor cell layers at various times during gestation. The cells that form the cortex will be the focus of this discussion. The *precursor cells* are undifferentiated cells from which all cortical cells (including neuronal subtypes and glial cells) arise through cell division and differentiation. For the first 5 to 6 weeks of gestation, the cells in the subventricular zone divide in a symmetrical fashion. The result is exponential growth in the number of precursor cells.

At the end of 6 weeks, when there is a stockpile of precursor cells, asymmetrical division begins. After every cell division, one of the two cells formed becomes a migratory cell destined to be part of another layer; the other cell remains in the subventricular zone, where it continues to divide asymmetrically. Later in gestation,

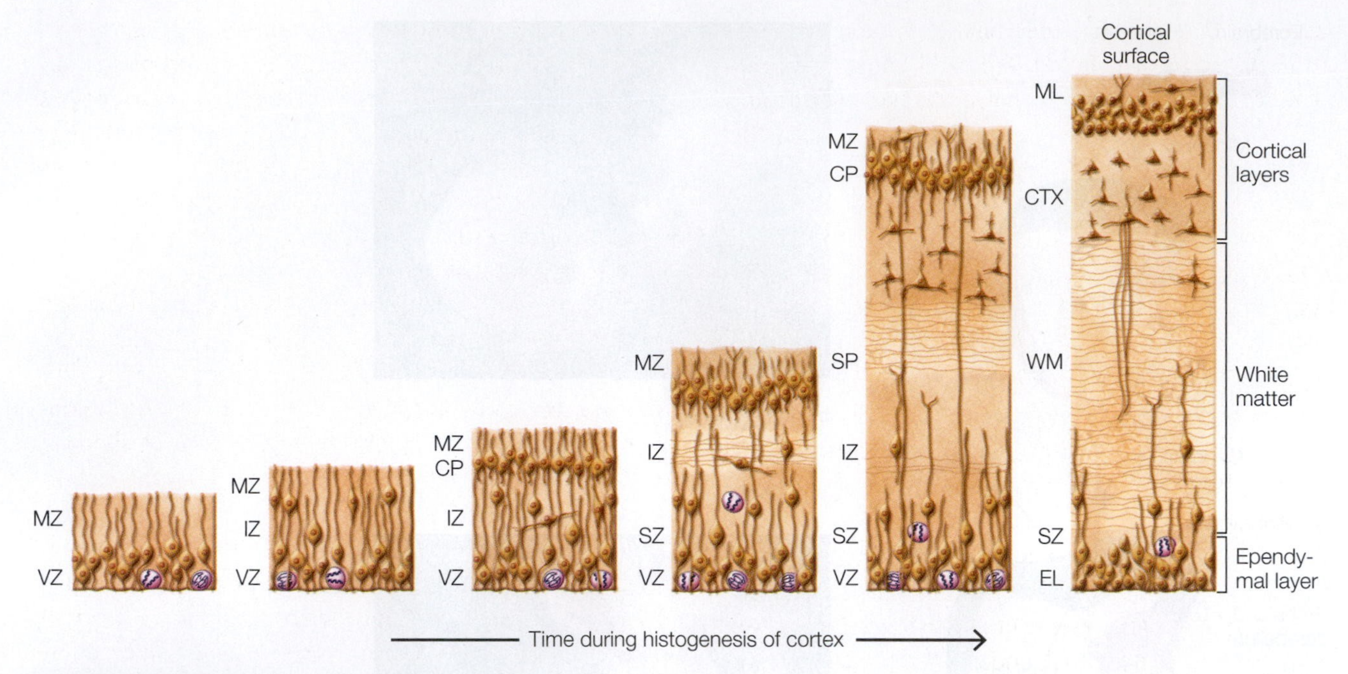

FIGURE 2.47 Histogenesis of the cerebral cortex.
Cross-sectional views of developing cerebral cortex from early (left) through late (right) times during histogenesis. The mammalian cortex develops from the inside out as cells in the ventricular zone (VZ) divide, and some of the cells migrate to the appropriate layer in the cortex. Radial glial cells form a superhighway along which the migrating cells travel en route to the cortex. CP = cortical plate; CTX = cortex; EL = ependymal layer; IZ = intermediate zone; ML = molecular layer; MZ = marginal zone; SP = subplate; SZ = subventricular zone; WM = white matter.

the proportion of migratory cells increases until a laminar (i.e., layered) cortex made up of the migratory cells is formed. This cortex has a foundational epithelial layer that becomes the cell lining of the ventricles and is known as the *ependymal cell layer.*

The migratory cells travel outward from the subventricular zone by moving along peculiar cells known as radial glial cells, which stretch from the subventricular zone to the surface of the developing cortex. The work of radial glial cells does not end with development. These cells are transformed into astrocytes in the adult brain, helping to form part of the blood–brain barrier.

As the first migrating neurons approach the surface of the developing cortex—a point known as the *cortical plate*—they stop short of the surface. Neurons that migrate later pass beyond the termination point of the initial neurons and end up in more superficial positions—positions nearer the outer cortical surface. Thus, it is said that the cortex is built from the inside out, because the first neurons to migrate lie in the deepest cortical layers, whereas the last to migrate move farthest out toward the cortical surface.

NEURONAL DETERMINATION AND DIFFERENTIATION

The cortex is made up of many different types of neurons organized in a laminar fashion. Layer IV, for example, contains large pyramidal cells, layer III is populated primarily by stellate cells, and so on. You may be wondering how that population of virtually identical precursor cells gives rise to the variety of neurons and glial cells in the adult cortex. What determines the type of neuron that a migrating cell is fated to become?

The answer lies in the timing of neurogenesis. Experimental manipulation of developing cells has shown that the differentiated cell type is not hardwired into the code of each developing neuron. Neurons that are experimentally prevented from migrating, by being exposed to high-energy X-rays, eventually form cell types and patterns of connectivity that would be expected from neurons created at the same gestational stage. Even though the thwarted neurons might remain in the ventricular zone, they display interconnections with other neurons that would be normal if they had migrated to the cortical layers normally.

The timeline of cortical neurogenesis differs across cortical cytoarchitectonic areas, but the inside-out pattern is the same for all cortical areas. Because the timeline of cortical neurogenesis determines the ultimate pattern of cortical lamination, anything that affects the genesis of cortical neurons will lead to an ill-constructed cortex. A good example of how neuronal migration can be disrupted in humans is *fetal alcohol syndrome.* In cases of chronic maternal alcohol abuse, neuronal migration is severely disrupted and results in a disordered cortex, leading to a plethora of cognitive, emotional, and physical disabilities.

The Baby Brain: Ready to Rock 'n' Roll?

A host of behavioral changes takes place during the first months and years of life. What accompanying neurobiological changes enable these developments? Even if we assume that neuronal proliferation continues, we know that at birth, the human brain has a fairly full complement of neurons, and these are organized to form a human nervous system that is normal, even if not complete in all details. Which details are incomplete, and what is known about the time course of brain maturation?

Although the brain nearly quadruples in size from birth to adulthood, the change is not due to an increase in neuron number. A substantial amount of that growth comes from **synaptogenesis** (the formation of synapses) and the growth of dendritic trees. Synapses in the brain begin to form long before birth—before week 27 in humans (counting from conception)—but they do not reach peak density until after birth, during the first 15 months of life. Synaptogenesis is more pronounced early in the deeper cortical layers and occurs later in more superficial layers, following the pattern of neurogenesis described earlier.

At roughly the same time that synaptogenesis is occurring, neurons of the brain are increasing the size of their dendritic arborizations, extending their axons, and undergoing myelination. Synaptogenesis is followed by **synapse elimination** (sometimes called *pruning*), which continues for more than a decade. Synapse elimination is a means by which the nervous system fine-tunes neuronal connectivity, presumably eliminating the interconnections between neurons that are redundant, unused, or do not remain functional.

Use it or lose it! The person you become is shaped by the growth and elimination of synapses, which in turn are shaped by the world you're exposed to and the experiences you have. A specific example of synaptic pruning comes from primary visual cortex (BA17): Initially, there is overlap between the projections of the two eyes onto neurons in BA17. After synapse elimination, the cortical inputs from the two eyes within BA17 are nearly completely segregated. The axon terminals relaying information from each eye form a series of equally spaced patches (called *ocular dominance columns*), and each patch receives inputs from predominantly one eye.

One of the central hypotheses about the process of human synaptogenesis and synapse elimination is that the time course of these events differs in different cortical regions. The data suggest that in humans, synaptogenesis and synapse elimination peak earlier in sensory (and motor) cortex than in association cortex. By contrast, in the brain development of other primates, synaptogenesis and pruning appear to occur at the same rates across different cortical regions. Differences in methodology, however, must be resolved before these interspecies variations will be wholly accepted. Nonetheless, compelling evidence suggests that different regions of the human brain reach maturity at different times.

The increase in brain volume that occurs postnatally is also a result of both myelination and the proliferation of glial cells. White matter volume increases linearly with age across cortical regions (Giedd et al., 1999). In contrast, gray matter volume increases nonlinearly, showing a preadolescent increase followed by a postadolescent decrease. In addition, the time courses of gray matter increase and decrease are not the same across different cortical regions. In general, these data support the idea that postnatal developmental changes in the human cerebral cortex may not occur with the same time course across all cortical regions (see also Shaw et al., 2006).

Birth of New Neurons Throughout Life

One principle about the human brain that once dominated in the neuroscience community was the idea that the adult brain produces no new neurons. This view was held despite a variety of claims of neurogenesis in the brain in histological studies dating as far back as the time of Ramón y Cajal. In the last couple of decades, however, studies using an array of modern neuroanatomical techniques have challenged this belief.

Neurogenesis in adult mammals has now been well established in two brain regions: the hippocampus and the olfactory bulb. Neurogenesis in the hippocampus is particularly noteworthy because it plays a key role in learning and memory. In rodents, studies have shown that stem cells in a region of the hippocampus known as the dentate gyrus produce new neurons in the adult, and these can migrate into regions of the hippocampus where similar neurons are already functioning. It is important to know that these new neurons can form dendrites and send out axons along pathways expected of neurons in this region of the hippocampus, and they can also show signs of normal synaptic activity. These findings are particularly interesting because the number of new neurons correlates positively with learning or enriched experience (more social contact or challenges in the physical environment) and negatively with stress (e.g., living in an overcrowded environment). Moreover, the number of newborn neurons is related to hippocampal-dependent memory (Shors, 2004).

Other investigators have found that these new neurons become integrated into functional networks of neurons and participate in behavioral and cognitive functions in the same way that those generated during development do (Ramirez-Amaya et al., 2006). Future work will be required to establish whether adult neurogenesis occurs more broadly in the mammalian brain or is restricted to the olfactory bulb and hippocampus.

What about the adult human brain? Does neurogenesis also occur in mature humans? In a fascinating line of research, a team of scientists from California and Sweden (Eriksson et al., 1998) explored this question in a group of terminally ill cancer patients. As part of a diagnostic procedure related to their treatment, the patients were given BrdU, a synthetic form of thymidine used as a label to identify neurogenesis. The purpose was to assess the extent to which the tumors in the cancer patients were proliferating; tumor cells that were dividing would also take up BrdU, and this label could be used to quantify the progress of the disease.

Neurons undergoing mitotic division during neurogenesis in these patients also took up BrdU, which could be observed in postmortem histological examinations of their brains. The postmortem tissue was immunostained to identify neuron-specific cell surface markers. The scientists found cells labeled with BrdU in the subventricular zone of the caudate nucleus and in the granular cell layer of the dentate gyrus of the hippocampus (**Figure 2.48**). By staining the tissue to identify neuronal markers, the researchers showed that the BrdU-labeled cells were neurons (**Figure 2.49**). These findings demonstrate that new neurons are produced in the adult human brain, and that our brains renew themselves throughout life to an extent not previously thought possible.

These exciting results hold great promise for the future of neuroscience. Research is under way to investigate the functionality of new neurons in the adult brain and to determine whether such neuronal growth can be facilitated to ameliorate brain damage or the effects of diseases such as Alzheimer's.

TAKE-HOME MESSAGES

- Neuronal proliferation is the process of cell division in the developing embryo and fetus. It is responsible for populating the nervous system with neurons.
- Neurons and glial cells are formed from precursor cells. After mitosis, these cells migrate along the radial glial cells to the developing cortex. The type of cell that is made (e.g., a stellate or pyramidal cell) appears to be based on when the cell is born (genesis) rather than when it begins to migrate.
- Synaptogenesis is the birth of new synapses; neurogenesis is the birth of new neurons.
- A belief once strongly held by most neuroscientists was that the adult brain produces no new neurons. We now know that this is not the case; new neurons form throughout life in certain brain regions.

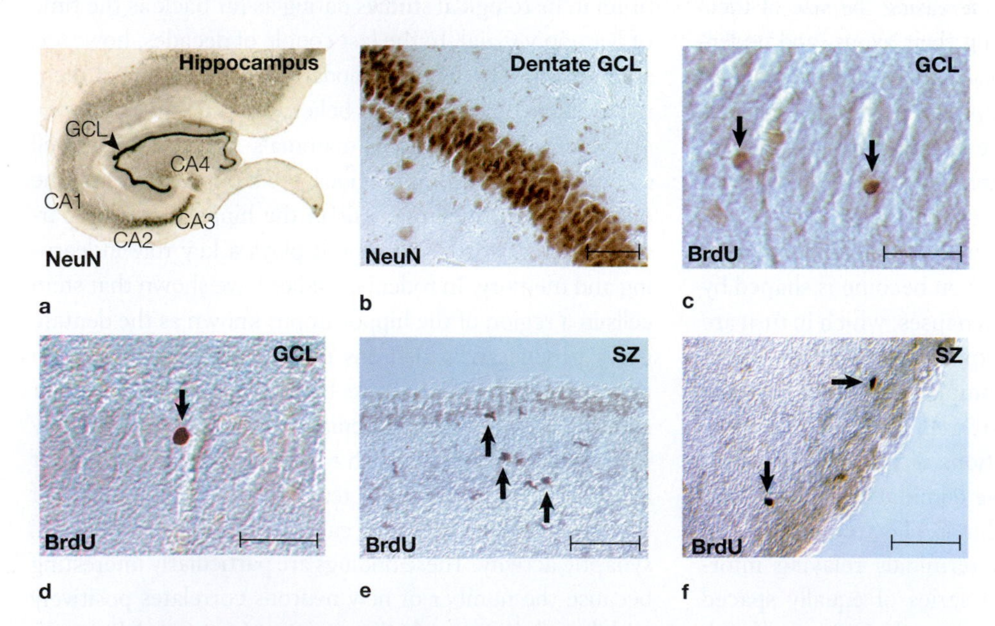

FIGURE 2.48 Newly born neurons in adult human brain tissue.
(a) The hippocampus of the adult human brain, stained for a neuronal marker (NeuN). **(b)** The dentate gyrus granule cell layer (GCL) in a NeuN-stained section. **(c)** BrdU-labeled nuclei (arrows) in the granule cell layer of the dentate gyrus. **(d)** BrdU-labeled cells (arrow) in the granule cell layer of the dentate gyrus. **(e)** BrdU-stained cells (arrows) adjacent to the ependymal lining in the subventricular zone (SZ) of the human caudate nucleus. These neurons have elongated nuclei resembling the migrating cells that typically are found in the rat subventricular zone. **(f)** BrdU-stained cells (arrows) with round to elongated nuclei in the subventricular zone of the human caudate nucleus. Scale bars throughout = 50 μm.

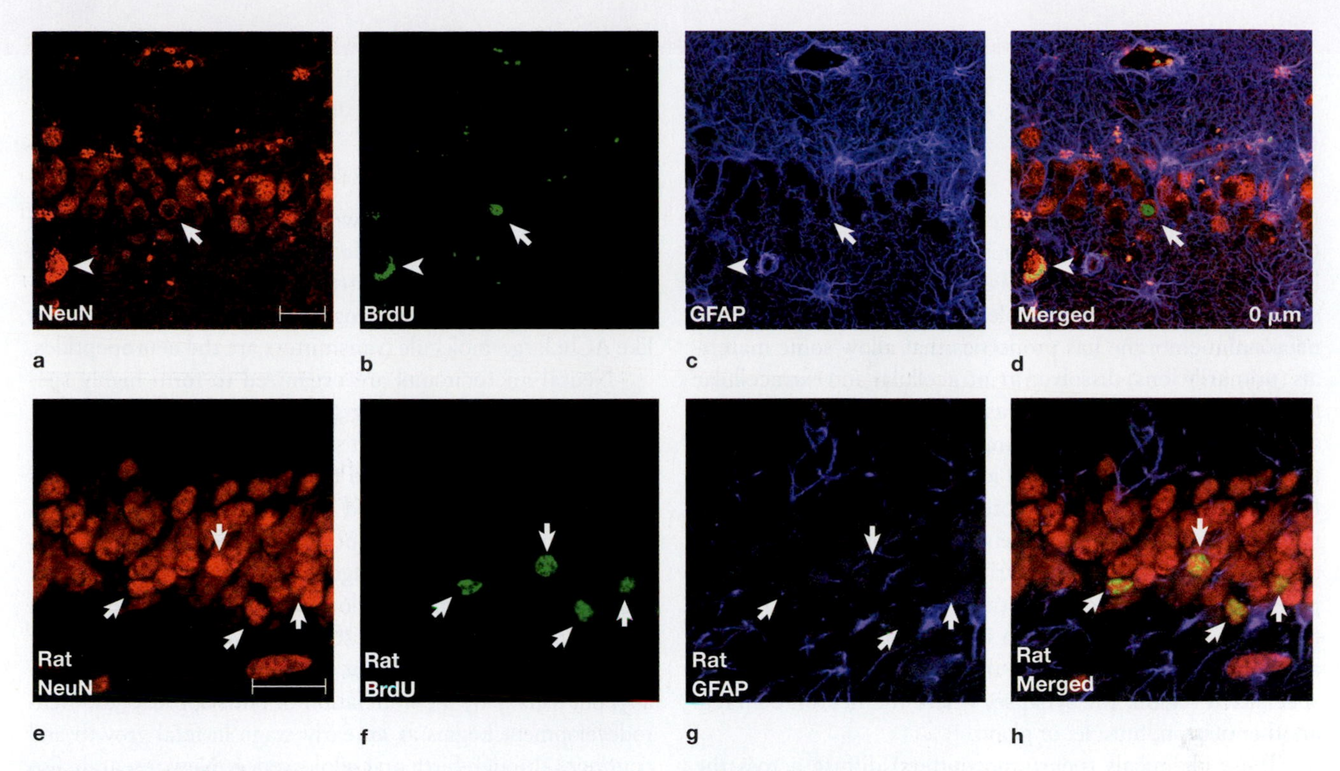

FIGURE 2.49 The birth of new neurons in the dentate gyrus of the adult human (a–d) compared to those in the adult rat (e–h).

New neurons show simultaneous labeling for different stains. **(a)** A neuron is labeled for NeuN, a neuronal marker. **(b)** The same cell is labeled with BrdU, indicating that it is newly born (full arrow). (Note that the lone arrowheads in (a) through (d) are pointing to neurons that are fluorescing red or green, owing to nonspecific staining; i.e., these are not newly born neurons.) **(c)** This same cell is not stained by glial fibrillary acidic protein (GFAP), indicating that it is not an astrocyte. **(d)** The three stained sections are merged in this image, which shows that a BrdU-labeled cell could specifically coexpress NeuN without expressing GFAP. Panels **(e)** through **(h)** show the similarity of the BrdU-labeled neurons in rat dentate gyrus. Note: The scale bar is equal to 25 μm for both sets of images, so the magnification is greater in (e) through (h) than in (a) through (d).

Summary

In the brain and the rest of the nervous system, nerve cells (neurons) provide the mechanism for information processing. Neurons receive and process sensory inputs, plan and organize motor acts, and enable human thought. At rest, the neuronal membrane has properties that allow some materials (primarily ions) dissolved in intracellular and extracellular fluids to pass through more easily than others. In addition, active transport processes pump ions across the membrane to separate different species of ions, thereby setting the stage for differences in electrical potential inside and outside the neuron. These electrical differences are a form of energy that can be used to generate electrical currents that, via action potentials, can travel great distances down axons away from the neuron's cell body. When the action potential reaches an axon terminal, it prompts the release of chemicals at a specialized region, the synapse, where the neuron contacts another neuron, muscle, or gland.

These chemicals (neurotransmitters) diffuse across the synaptic cleft between the neurons and contact receptor molecules in the next (postsynaptic) neuron. This chemical transmission of signals leads to the generation of currents in the postsynaptic neuron and the continuation of the signal through the system of neurons that make up a neural circuit. Ion channels are the specialized mediators of neuronal membrane potential. They are large transmembrane proteins that create pores through the membrane. Transmembrane proteins also form receptors on postsynaptic neurons. These are the receptors that bind with neurotransmitters, leading to changes in the membrane potential. Neurotransmitters come in a large variety of forms. Small-molecule transmitters include amino acids, biogenic amines, and substances like ACh; large-molecule transmitters are the neuropeptides.

Neural microcircuits are organized to form highly specific interconnections among groups of neurons at different levels of processing to support specific neural functions. Brain areas are also interconnected to form higher-level networks and systems that are involved in complex behaviors such as motor control, visual perception, and cognitive processes that include memory, language, and attention. Functions of the nervous system might be localized within discrete regions that contain a few or many subdivisions, identifiable either anatomically (microscopic or gross anatomy) or functionally, but usually by a combination of both approaches. Neurodevelopment begins at an early stage in fetal growth and continues through birth and adolescence. New research also suggests that new neurons and new synapses form throughout life, allowing, at least in part, for cortical plasticity. In terms of evolution, the oldest parts of the brain, which make up the brainstem structures, control our most basic survival functions, such as breathing, heart rate, and temperature, and our survival drives, such as thirst, hunger, and libido. The more rostral structures evolved more recently and mediate more complex behaviors. The most rostral and youngest structure, the prefrontal cortex, is found only in mammals.

Key Terms

action potential (p. 31)
amygdala (p. 50)
association cortex (p. 61)
autonomic nervous system (p. 40)
axon (p. 27)
axon collaterals (p. 27)
axon hillock (p. 32)
basal ganglia (p. 50)
blood–brain barrier (BBB) (p. 24)
brainstem (p. 46)
central nervous system (CNS) (p. 40)
central sulcus (p. 54)
cerebellum (p. 42)
cerebral cortex (p. 42)
commissure (p. 42)
corpus callosum (p. 42)
cytoarchitectonics (p. 54)
dendrites (p. 26)
depolarization (p. 32)
electrical gradient (p. 30)
electrotonic conduction (p. 31)
equilibrium potential (p. 32)
frontal lobe (p. 53)
glial cell (p. 24)
gray matter (p. 42)
gyrus (p. 52)
hippocampus (p. 50)
hyperpolarization (p. 32)
hypothalamus (p. 49)
insula (p. 54)
ion channel (p. 28)
ion pump (p. 28)
layer (p. 41)
limbic system (p. 50)
medulla (p. 46)
microcircuit (p. 39)
midbrain (p. 48)
myelin (p. 25)
neocortex (p. 55)
neural network (p. 39)
neuron (p. 24)
neurotransmitter (p. 35)
node of Ranvier (p. 32)
nucleus (p. 41)
occipital lobe (p. 54)
parietal lobe (p. 54)
peripheral nervous system (PNS) (p. 40)
permeability (p. 29)
pituitary gland (p. 49)
pons (p. 47)
postsynaptic (p. 28)
prefrontal cortex (p. 61)
presynaptic (p. 28)

refractory period (p. 32)
resting membrane potential (p. 28)
saltatory conduction (p. 32)
soma (p. 26)
somatotopy (p. 58)
spike-triggering zone (p. 32)
spine (p. 27)
sulcus (p. 52)
Sylvian (lateral) fissure (p. 54)
synapse (p. 27)
synapse elimination (p. 67)
synaptic cleft (p. 33)
synaptogenesis (p. 67)
temporal lobe (p. 54)
thalamus (p. 48)
threshold (p. 32)
tract (p. 42)
ventricle (p. 41)
vesicle (p. 33)
voltage-gated ion channel (p. 31)
white matter (p. 42)

Think About It

1. If action potentials are all or none, how does the nervous system code differences in sensory stimulus amplitudes?
2. What property (or properties) of ion channels makes them selective to only one ion, such as K^+, and not another, such as Na^+? Is it the size of the channel, other factors, or a combination?
3. Given that synaptic currents produce electrotonic potentials that are decremental, how do inputs located distantly on a neuron's dendrites have any influence on the firing of the cell?
4. What would be the consequence for the activity of a postsynaptic neuron if reuptake or degradation systems for neurotransmitters were damaged?
5. What are glial cells, and what functions do they perform?
6. Which region of the cerebral cortex has increased in size the most across species during evolution? What function does this brain region carry out in humans that is absent or reduced in animals?
7. How do the factors of brain size, neuron number, and connectivity contribute to human cognitive capacity?
8. What brain areas have been associated with the creation of new neurons, and what functions are they thought to perform?

Suggested Reading

Aimone, J. B., Deng, W., & Gage, F. H. (2010). Adult neurogenesis: Integrating theories and separating functions. *Trends in Cognitive Sciences, 14*(7), 325–337. [Epub, May 12]

Bullock, T. H., Bennett, M. V., Johnston, D., Josephson, R., Marder, E., & Fields, R. D. (2005). The neuron doctrine, redux. *Science, 310*, 791. doi:10.1126/science.1114394

Häusser, M. (2000). The Hodgkin–Huxley theory of the action potential. *Nature Reviews Neuroscience, 3*, 1165.

Mesulam, M.-M. (2000). Behavioral neuroanatomy: Large-scale networks, association cortex, frontal syndromes, the limbic system, and hemispheric specialization. In M.-M. Mesulam (Ed.), *Principles of behavioral and cognitive neurology* (pp. 1–34). New York: Oxford University Press.

Shepherd, G. M. (1988). *Neurobiology* (2nd ed.). New York: Oxford University Press.

Shors, T. J. (2004). Memory traces of trace memories: Neurogenesis, synaptogenesis and awareness. *Trends in Neurosciences, 27*, 250–256.

Sterling, P., & Laughlin, S. (2015). *Principles of neural design*. Cambridge, MA: MIT Press.

Striedter, G. (2005). *Principles of brain evolution* (pp. 217–253). Sunderland, MA: Sinauer.

Though this be madness, yet there is method in't.

William Shakespeare

Methods of Cognitive Neuroscience

CHAPTER

3

IN THE YEAR 2010, *Halobacterium halobium* and *Chlamydomonas reinhardtii* made it to prime time as integral parts of optogenetics, the journal *Nature's* "Method of the Year." Scientists hailed these microscopic creatures for their potential to treat a wide range of neurological and psychiatric conditions: anxiety disorder, depression, and Parkinson's disease, to name just a few. How did a bacterium that hangs out in warm brackish waters and an alga more commonly known as pond scum reach such heights?

Their story begins early in the 1970s. Two curious biochemists, Dieter Oesterhelt and Walther Stoeckenius (1971), wanted to understand why, when removed from its salty environment, *Halobacterium* broke up into fragments, one of which took on an unusual purple hue. They found that the purple color was due to the interaction of retinal (a form of vitamin A) and a protein produced by a set of "opsin genes," creating a light-sensitive protein that they dubbed bacteriorhodopsin.

This particular pairing surprised the researchers. Previously, the only other place anyone had observed the combined form of retinal and an opsin protein was in the mammalian eye, where it serves as the chemical basis for vision. In *Halobacterium*, however, bacteriorhodopsin functions as an ion pump, converting light energy into metabolic energy as it transfers ions across the cell membrane. Other members of this protein family were identified over the next 25 years, including channelrhodopsin from the green alga *C. reinhardtii* (G. Nagel et al., 2002).

Thirty years after the discovery of bacteriorhodopsin, Gero Miesenböck realized that the light-sensitive properties of microbial rhodopsins might fulfill a longtime dream of neuroscientists. Francis Crick, a codiscoverer of the structure of DNA, had turned his attention to the brain later in his career, and at the top of his neuroscience wish list was a method to selectively switch neurons on and off with great temporal precision. This tool would enable

BIG Questions

- Why is cognitive neuroscience an interdisciplinary field?
- How do the various methods used in cognitive neuroscience research differ in terms of their spatial and temporal resolution?
- How do these differences impact the kinds of insights that can be drawn?
- Which methods rely on drawing inferences from patterns of correlation, and which methods allow manipulations to test causal hypotheses?

researchers to directly probe how neurons functionally relate to each other and control behavior. Crick suggested that light, precisely delivered in timed pulses, might somehow serve as the switch (Crick, 1999). To this end, Miesenböck inserted the genes for microbial rhodopsins into neurons. When the genes expressed themselves as photosensitive proteins, the targeted cells became light responsive (Zemelman et al., 2002). Expose the cell to light and voilà! the neuron would fire.

Miesenböck's initial compound proved to have limitations, but a few years later, two graduate students at Stanford, Karl Deisseroth and Ed Boyden, focused on a different protein, channelrhodopsin-2 (ChR-2). Using Miesenböck's technique, they inserted the gene for ChR-2 into a neuron. Once the ChR-2 gene was inside the neurons and the protein constructed, Deisseroth and Boyden performed the critical test: They projected a light beam onto the cells. Immediately, the targeted cells began to respond. By pulsing the light, the researchers were able to precisely control the neuronal activity. Each pulse of light stimulated the production of an action potential, and when the pulse stopped, the neuron shut down (Boyden et al., 2005). Francis Crick had his switch.

The story of optogenetics captures the essential features of the most fundamental tool for all scientists: the *scientific method*. Beginning with an observation of a phenomenon, a scientist devises an explanatory hypothesis. Of course, generating the hypothesis is not the unique province of scientists; the drive to explain things seems to be a fundamental feature of the human mind. However, the scientist does not stop with the hypothesis, but rather uses a hypothesis to generate predictions and designs experiments to test the predictions, with the results producing new phenomena that allow the cycle to repeat itself. This basic approach—observation, hypothesis, prediction, experimental test—is at the heart of all of the methods that we discuss in this chapter.

Scientists like to make clear that the scientific method entails an interesting asymmetry. Experimental results can disprove a hypothesis, providing evidence that a prevailing idea needs modification: As the Nobel laureate physicist Richard Feynman once quipped, "Exceptions prove that the rule is wrong" (Feynman, 1998). Results, however, cannot prove that a hypothesis is true; they can only provide evidence that it *may* be true, because there are always alternative hypotheses to consider. With this process of observation, hypothesis formation, and experimentation, the scientific method allows our understanding of the world to progress.

The field of cognitive neuroscience emerged in part because of the invention of new methods. In this chapter we discuss a broad range of methods, describing how each one works and what kind of information we can obtain with it, as well as what its limitations are. It is also important to keep in mind the interdisciplinary nature of cognitive neuroscience, and to understand how scientists have cleverly integrated paradigms across fields and methodologies. To highlight this essential feature of cognitive neuroscience, the chapter concludes with examples of this integration.

3.1 Cognitive Psychology and Behavioral Methods

Cognitive psychology is the study of mental activity as an information-processing problem. Cognitive psychologists seek to identify the internal processing—the acquisition, storage, and use of information—that underlies observable behavior. A basic assumption of cognitive psychology is that we do not directly perceive and act in the world. Rather, our perceptions, thoughts, and actions depend on internal transformations or computations of information obtained by our sense organs. Our ability to comprehend that information, to recognize it as something that we have experienced before and to choose an appropriate response, depends on a complex interplay of processes.

Cognitive psychologists design experiments to test hypotheses about mental operations by adjusting what goes into the brain and then seeing what comes out. Put more simply, we input information into the brain, something secret happens to it, and out comes our behavior. Cognitive psychologists are detectives trying to figure out what those secrets are.

For example, input the following text to your brain and let's see what comes out:

> ocacdrngi ot a sehrerearc ta macbriegd ineyurvtis, ti edost'n rttaem ni awth rreod eht tlteser ni a rwdo rea, eht ylon pirmtoatn gihtn si atth het rifts nda satl ttelre eb ta het ghitr clepa. eht srte anc eb a otlta sesm dan ouy anc itlls arde ti owtuthi moprbel. ihst si cebusea eth nuamh nidm sedo otn arde yrvee telrte yb stifle, tub eth rdow sa a lohew.

Not much, eh? Now take another shot at it:

> Aoccdrnig to a rseheearcr at Cmabrigde Uinervtisy, it deosn't mttaer in waht oredr the ltteers in a wrod are, the olny iprmoatnt tihng is taht the frist and lsat ltteer be at the rghit pclae. The rset can be a total mses and you can sitll raed it wouthit porbelm. Tihs is bcuseae the huamn mnid deos not raed ervey lteter by istlef, but the wrod as a wlohe.

Oddly enough, it is surprisingly easy to read the second passage. As long as the first and last letters of each word are in the correct position, we can accurately infer the word, especially when the surrounding context helps generate expectations. Simple demonstrations like this one help us discern the content of mental representations, and thus help us gain insight into how the brain manipulates information. In summary, two key concepts underlie the cognitive approach:

1. Information processing depends on mental representations.
2. These mental representations undergo internal transformations.

Mental Representations

We usually take for granted the idea that information processing depends on mental representations. Consider the concept "ball." Are you thinking of an image, a linguistic description, or a mathematical formula? Each instance is an alternative form of representing the "circular" or "spherical" concept and depends on our visual system, our auditory system, our ability to comprehend the spatial arrangement of a curved drawing, our ability to comprehend language, or our ability to comprehend geometric and algebraic relations. Context helps dictate which representational format is most useful. For example, if we want to show that the ball rolls down a hill, a pictorial representation is likely to be much more useful than an algebraic formula—unless you're taking a physics final, where you would likely be better off with the formula.

A letter-matching task, first introduced by Michael Posner (1986) at the University of Oregon, provides a powerful demonstration that, even with simple stimuli, the mind derives multiple representations (**Figure 3.1**). In each trial, the participant sees two letters presented simultaneously. The participant's task is to evaluate whether both letters are vowels, both are consonants, or one is a vowel and one is a consonant. The participant presses one button if the letters are from the same category and another button if they are from different categories.

One version of this experiment includes five conditions. In the physical-identity condition, the two letters are the same. In the phonetic-identity condition, the two letters have the same identity, but one letter is a capital

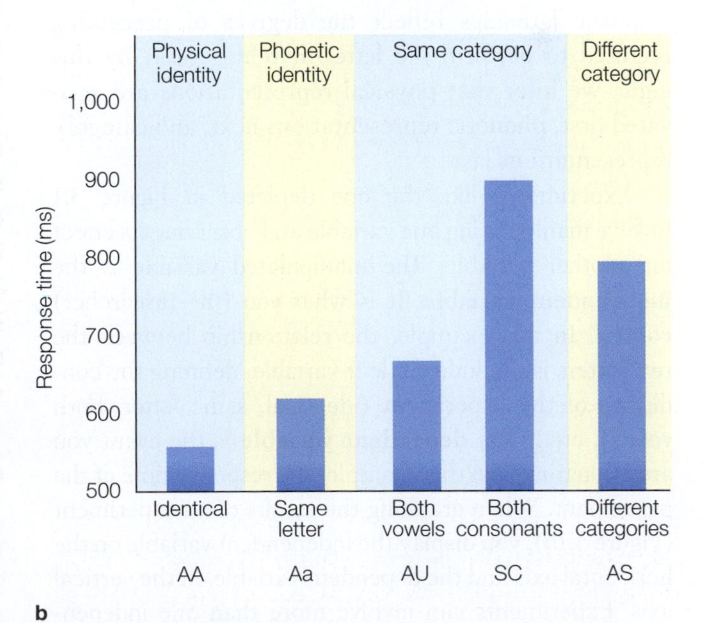

FIGURE 3.1 Letter-matching task.
(a) Participants press one of two buttons to indicate whether or not the letters belong to the same category. (b) The relationship between the two letters is plotted on the *x*-axis. This relationship is the independent variable, the variable that the experimenter is manipulating. Reaction time is plotted on the *y*-axis. It is the dependent variable, the variable that the experimenter is measuring.

and the other is lowercase. There are two same-category conditions, in which the two letters fall into the same category: In one, both letters are vowels; in the other, both letters are consonants. Finally, in the different-category condition, the two letters are from different categories and can be either of the same type size or of different sizes.

Note that the first four conditions—physical identity, phonetic identity, and the two same-category conditions—require the "same" response: On all three types of trials, the correct response is that the two letters are from the same category. Nonetheless, as Figure 3.1b shows, response latencies differ significantly. Participants respond fastest to the physical-identity condition, next fastest to the phonetic-identity condition, and slowest to the same-category condition, especially when the two letters are both consonants.

The results of Posner's experiment suggest that we derive multiple representations of stimuli. We base one representation on the physical aspects of the stimulus. In this experiment, the representation is visually derived from the shape presented on the screen. A second representation corresponds to the letter's identity. This representation reflects the fact that many stimuli can correspond to the same letter. For example, we can recognize that *A*, *a*, and **a** all represent the same letter. A third level of abstraction represents the category to which a letter belongs. At this level, the letters *A* and *E* activate our internal representation of the category "vowel." Posner maintains that different response latencies reflect the degrees of processing required to perform the letter-matching task. By this logic, we infer that physical representations are activated first, phonetic representations next, and category representations last.

Experiments like the one depicted in Figure 3.1 involve manipulating one variable and observing its effect on another variable. The manipulated variable is the **independent variable**. It is what you (the researcher) control. In this example, the relationship between the two letters is the independent variable, defining the conditions of the experiment (identical, same letter, both vowels, etc.). The **dependent variable** is the event you are evaluating—in this example, the response time of the participant. When graphing the results of an experiment (Figure 3.1b), you display the independent variable on the horizontal axis and the dependent variable on the vertical axis. Experiments can involve more than one independent and dependent variable.

As you may have experienced personally, experiments generally elicit as many questions as answers. Why do participants take longer to judge that two letters are consonants than they do to judge that two letters are vowels? Would the same advantage for identical stimuli exist for spoken letters? What if one letter were seen and the other were heard? We can address these questions by introducing new independent variables—for example, we could compare visual and auditory stimuli to see whether the physical-identity advantage also holds in audition. Cognitive psychologists address questions like these and then devise methods for inferring the mind's machinery from observable behaviors.

Internal Transformations

The second critical notion of cognitive psychology is that our mental representations undergo internal transformations. This is obvious when we consider how sensory signals connect with stored information in memory. For example, a whiff of garlic may transport you to your grandmother's house or to a back alley in Palermo, Italy. In this instance, your brain has somehow transformed an olfactory sensation such that it calls up a memory.

Taking action often requires that we translate perceptual representations into action representations in order to achieve a goal. For example, you see and smell garlic bread on the table at dinner. Your brain transforms these sensations into perceptual representations and, by processing them, enables you to decide on a course of action and to carry it out—to pick up the bread and place it in your mouth. Take note, though, that information processing is not simply a sequential process from sensation to perception to memory to action. Memory may alter how we perceive something. You may see a dog and, remembering a beloved childhood pet, perceive it as cute and reach out to pet it. However, if a dog bit you in the past, you may instead perceive it as dangerous and draw back in fear. The manner in which information is processed is also subject to attentional constraints. Did you register that last sentence, or did all the talk about garlic shift your attention to dinner plans? Cognitive psychology is all about how we manipulate representations.

CHARACTERIZING TRANSFORMATIONAL OPERATIONS

Suppose you arrive at the grocery store and discover that you forgot to bring your shopping list. You know you need coffee and milk, the main reasons you came, but what else? As you cruise the aisles, scanning the shelves, you hope something will prompt your memory. Is the peanut butter gone? How many eggs are left?

As we have just learned, the fundamental goal of cognitive psychology is to identify the different mental operations or transformations that are required to perform tasks such as this. Memory retrieval tasks draw on a number of cognitive capabilities.

Saul Sternberg (1975) introduced an experimental task that bears some similarity to the problem faced by an absentminded shopper. In Sternberg's task, however, the job is not recalling items stored in memory, but rather comparing sensory information with representations that are active in memory. In each trial, the participant sees a set of letters to memorize (**Figure 3.2a**). The memory set could consist of one, two, or four letters. Then he sees a single letter and must decide whether this letter was part of the memorized set. He presses one button to indicate that the target was part of the memory set ("yes" response) and a second button to indicate that the target was not part of the set ("no" response). Once again, the primary dependent variable is reaction time.

Sternberg postulated that, to respond on this task, the participant must engage in four primary mental operations:

1. *Encoding.* The participant must identify the visible target.
2. *Comparing.* The participant must compare the mental representation of the target with the representations of the items in memory.
3. *Deciding.* The participant must decide whether the target matches one of the memorized items.
4. *Responding.* The participant must respond appropriately for the decision made in Step 3.

By postulating a set of mental operations, we can devise experiments to explore how participants carry them out.

A basic question for Sternberg was how to characterize the efficiency of recognition memory. Assuming that our brains actively represent all items in the memory set, the recognition process might work in one of two ways: A highly efficient system might simultaneously compare a representation of the target with all of the items in the memory set. Or, the recognition process might be able to handle only a limited amount of information at any point in time. For example, the system might require comparison of the target to each item in memory in succession.

Sternberg realized that the reaction time data could distinguish between these two alternatives. If the comparison process can be simultaneous for all items—a *parallel* process—then reaction time should be independent of the number of items in the memory set. But if the comparison process operates in a sequential, or *serial*, manner, then reaction time should slow down as the memory set becomes larger, because more time is required to compare an item against a large memory list than a small memory list. Sternberg's results convincingly supported the serial hypothesis. In fact, reaction time increased in a constant, or linear, manner with set size, and the functions for the "yes" and "no" trials were essentially identical (**Figure 3.2b**).

Although memory comparison appears to be a serial process, much of the activity in our mind operates in parallel. A classic demonstration of parallel processing is the word superiority effect (Reicher, 1969). In this experiment, participants briefly see a stimulus and then decide which of two target letters (e.g., *A* or *E*) they saw. The stimulus is a set of letters that can be a word, a nonsense string, or a string in which every letter is an *X* except for

a

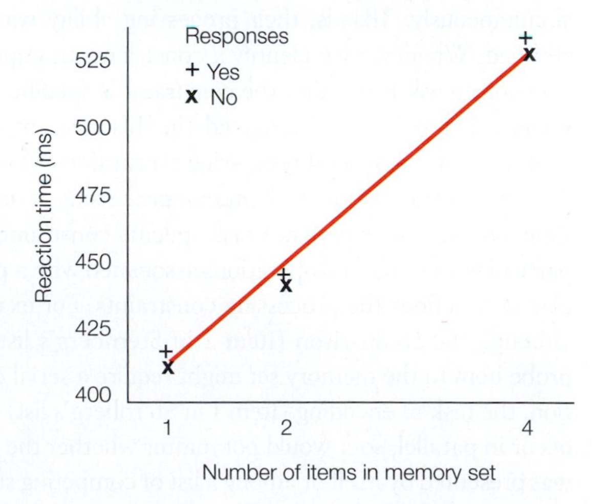

b

FIGURE 3.2 Memory comparison task.
(a) The participant is presented with a set of one, two, or four letters and asked to memorize them. After a delay, a single probe letter appears, and the participant indicates whether that letter was a member of the memory set. (b) Reaction time increases with set size, indicating that the target letter must be compared with the memory set sequentially rather than in parallel.

Does the stimulus contain an *A* or an *E*?

Condition	Stimulus	Accuracy
Word	RACK	90%
Nonsense string	KARC	80%
Xs	XAXX	80%

FIGURE 3.3 Word superiority effect.
Participants are more accurate in identifying the target vowel when it is embedded in a word. This result suggests that letter and word levels of representation are activated in parallel.

the target letter (**Figure 3.3**). Because the critical question centers on whether context affects performance, presentation times are brief and errors will occur.

The phrase *word superiority effect* refers to the fact that participants are most accurate in identifying the target letter when the stimulus is a word. As we saw earlier, this finding suggests that we do not need to identify all the letters of a word before we recognize the word. Rather, when reading a list of words, we activate representations corresponding to the individual letters and to the entire word in parallel for each item. Parallel processing facilitates our performance because both representations can provide information as to whether the target letter is present.

Constraints on Information Processing

In the experiment in Figure 3.2, participants were not able to compare the target item to all items in the memory set simultaneously. That is, their processing ability was constrained. Whenever we identify a constraint, an important question to ask is whether the constraint is specific to the system that is being investigated (in this case, memory) or if it is a more general processing constraint. People can do only a certain amount of internal processing at any one time, but we also experience task-specific constraints. The particular set of mental operations associated with a particular task defines the processing constraints. For example, although the comparison (Item 2 in Sternberg's list) of a probe item to the memory set might require a serial operation, the task of encoding (Item 1 in Sternberg's list) might occur in parallel, so it would not matter whether the probe was presented by itself or among a list of competing stimuli.

Exploring the limitations in task performance is a central concern for cognitive psychologists. Consider a simple color-naming task—devised in the early 1930s by J. R. Stroop, an aspiring doctoral student (1935; for a review, see MacLeod, 1991)—that has become one of the most widely employed tasks in all of cognitive psychology and

Color matches word	Color without word	Color doesn't match word
RED	XXXXX	GREEN
GREEN	XXXXX	BLUE
RED	XXXXX	RED
BLUE	XXXXX	BLUE
BLUE	XXXXX	GREEN
GREEN	XXXXX	RED
BLUE	XXXXX	GREEN
RED	XXXXX	BLUE

FIGURE 3.4 Stroop task.
Time yourself as you work through each column, naming the color of the ink of each stimulus as fast as possible. Assuming you do not squint to blur the words, it should be easy to read the first and second columns but quite difficult to read the third.

that we will refer to again in this book. The Stroop task involves presenting the participant with a list of words and then asking her to name the color of each word as fast as possible. As **Figure 3.4** illustrates, this task is much easier when the words match the ink colors.

The Stroop effect powerfully demonstrates the multiplicity of mental representations. The stimuli in this task appear to activate at least two separable representations. One representation corresponds to the color of each stimulus; it is what allows the participant to perform the task. The second representation corresponds to the color concept associated with each word. Participants are slower to name the colors when the ink color and words are mismatched, indicating that the second representation is activated even though it is irrelevant to the task. Indeed, the activation of a representation based on the word rather than the color of the word appears to be automatic.

The Stroop effect persists even after thousands of practice trials, because skilled readers have years of practice in analyzing letter strings for their symbolic meaning. However, we can reduce the interference from the words by requiring a key press rather than a vocal response. Thus, the word-based representations are closely linked to the vocal response system and have little effect when the responses are produced manually.

TAKE-HOME MESSAGES

- Cognitive psychology focuses on understanding how the brain represents and manipulates objects or ideas.
- Fundamental goals of cognitive psychology include identifying the mental operations that are required to perform cognitive tasks and exploring the limitations in task performance.

3.2 Studying the Damaged Brain

In the previous section we provided a sampling of the behavioral methods that cognitive psychologists use to build models of how the mind represents and processes information. Much of this work is based on research with the psychologist's favorite laboratory animal, the college student. Cognitive psychologists assume that fundamental principles of cognition can be learned from this limited population but also recognize the importance of testing other populations. Developmental studies provide insight into the emergence of our cognitive capabilities, and studies of older populations help us understand the changes in cognition that occur as we age. Additional important research is showing how variables such as gender and socioeconomic status can impact cognition.

A core method in cognitive neuroscience involves testing a unique population—people who have suffered brain damage. This approach is very important from a clinical perspective: To help design and evaluate rehabilitation programs, clinical neuropsychologists employ tests to characterize the patient's problems and capabilities. There is also a long research legacy involving patients with neurological disorders. Indeed, as we saw in Chapter 1, recognition that the brain gave rise to the mind came about through the observation of changes resulting from brain damage. We will see many examples in this textbook of how inferences can be drawn about the function of the normal brain from studies of the disturbed brain. We first begin with a basic overview of the major natural causes of brain dysfunction.

Causes of Neurological Dysfunction

Nature has sought to ensure that the brain remains healthy. Structurally, the skull provides a thick, protective encasement, engendering phrases like "hardheaded" and "thick as a brick." The distribution of arteries is extensive, ensuring an adequate blood supply. Even so, the brain is subject to many disorders, and their rapid treatment is frequently essential to reduce the possibility of chronic, debilitating problems or death. Here we discuss some of the more common types of disorders.

VASCULAR DISORDERS As with all other tissue, neurons need a steady supply of oxygen and glucose. These substances are essential for the cells to produce energy, fire action potentials, and make transmitters for neuronal communication. The brain, however, is an energy hog. It uses 20% of all the oxygen we breathe—an extraordinary amount, considering that it accounts for only 2% of the total body mass. What's more, a continuous supply of oxygen is essential: Loss of oxygen for as little as 10 minutes can result in neuronal death.

Cerebral vascular accidents, or strokes, occur when there is a sudden disruption of the blood flow to the brain. The most frequent cause of stroke is occlusion of the normal passage of blood by a foreign substance. Over years, atherosclerosis, the buildup of fatty tissue, occurs in the arteries. If this tissue breaks free, becoming an embolus, the bloodstream will carry it off. An embolus that enters the cranium may easily pass through the large carotid or vertebral arteries. As the arteries reach the end of their distribution, however, they decrease in diameter, finally dividing into capillaries. Eventually, the embolus becomes stuck, blocking the flow of blood and depriving all downstream tissue of oxygen and glucose. Within a short time, this tissue will become dysfunctional, and if the blood flow remains insufficient, an infarct (a small localized area of dead tissue) results (**Figure 3.5a**).

Other types of cerebral vascular disorders can lead to ischemia (inadequate blood supply). A sudden drop in blood pressure—resulting from shock or massive bleeding, for example—may prevent blood from reaching the brain. A sudden rise in blood pressure can cause an aneurysm, a weak spot or distention in a blood vessel, to rupture and hemorrhage (**Figure 3.5b**).

The vascular system is fairly consistent between individuals; thus, stroke of a particular artery typically leads to destruction of tissue in a consistent anatomical location. For example, occlusion of the posterior cerebral artery invariably results in deficits of visual perception. The location, as well as the extent of the vascular disruption, will affect the short- and long-term consequences of the stroke. A person may lose consciousness and die within minutes. In such cases, the infarct is usually near the brainstem. When the infarct is cortical, the initial symptoms may be striking, such as sudden loss of speech and comprehension, or subtle, such as a mild headache or a clumsy feeling using the hands. The severity of the initial symptoms can predict chronic problems, especially in a domain such as motor function. In other domains, such as language, acute symptoms may resolve within a few days.

TUMORS A *tumor*, or *neoplasm*, is a mass of tissue that grows abnormally and has no physiological function. Brain tumors are relatively common; most originate in glial cells and other supporting white matter tissues. Tumors also can develop from gray matter or neurons, but these are much less common, particularly in adults. Tumors are benign when they do not recur after removal

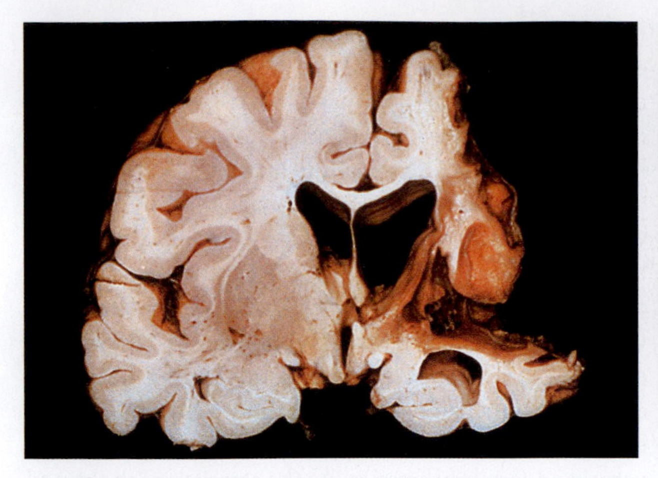

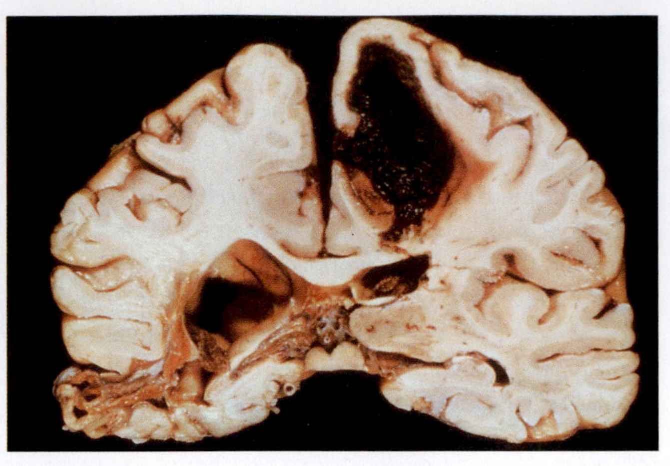

a b

FIGURE 3.5 Vascular disorders of the brain.
(a) Strokes occur when blood flow to the brain is disrupted. This brain is from a person who had an occlusion of the middle cerebral artery. The person survived the stroke. After death, a postmortem analysis showed that almost all of the tissue supplied by this artery had died and been absorbed.
(b) This coronal brain section is from a person who died following a cerebral hemorrhage. The hemorrhage destroyed the dorsomedial region of the left hemisphere. The effects of a cerebral vascular accident 2 years before death can be seen in the temporal region of the right hemisphere.

and tend to remain in the area of their germination (although they can become quite large). Malignant (cancerous) tumors, often distributed over several different areas, are likely to recur after removal. With a brain tumor, the first concern is its location, not whether it is benign or malignant. Concern is greatest when the tumor threatens critical neural structures.

DEGENERATIVE AND INFECTIOUS DISORDERS Many neurological disorders result from progressive disease. **Table 3.1** lists some of the more prominent degenerative and infectious disorders. Here we focus on the etiology and clinical diagnosis of **degenerative disorders.** In later chapters we will explore the cognitive problems associated with some of them. Degenerative disorders have been associated with both genetic aberrations and environmental agents. A prime example of a genetic degenerative disorder is Huntington's disease. The genetic link in other degenerative disorders, such as Parkinson's disease and Alzheimer's disease, is weaker. Investigators suspect that environmental factors are important, perhaps in combination with genetic predispositions.

Today, diagnosis of degenerative disorders is usually confirmed by MRI scans. We can see the primary pathology resulting from Huntington's disease or Parkinson's disease in the basal ganglia, a subcortical structure that figures prominently in the motor pathways (see Chapter 8). In contrast, the pathology seen in Alzheimer's disease is associated with marked atrophy of the cerebral cortex (**Figure 3.6**).

TABLE 3.1 Prominent Degenerative and Infectious Disorders of the Central Nervous System

Disorder	Type	Most Common Pathology
Alzheimer's disease	Degenerative	Tangles and plaques in limbic and temporoparietal cortex
Parkinson's disease	Degenerative	Loss of dopaminergic neurons
Huntington's disease	Degenerative	Atrophy of interneurons in caudate and putamen nuclei of basal ganglia
Pick's disease	Degenerative	Frontotemporal atrophy
Progressive supranuclear palsy (PSP)	Degenerative	Atrophy of brainstem, including colliculus
Multiple sclerosis (MS)	Possibly infectious	Demyelination, especially of fibers near ventricles
AIDS dementia	Viral infection	Diffuse white matter lesions
Herpes simplex	Viral infection	Destruction of neurons in temporal and limbic regions
Korsakoff's syndrome	Nutritional deficiency	Destruction of neurons in diencephalon and temporal lobes

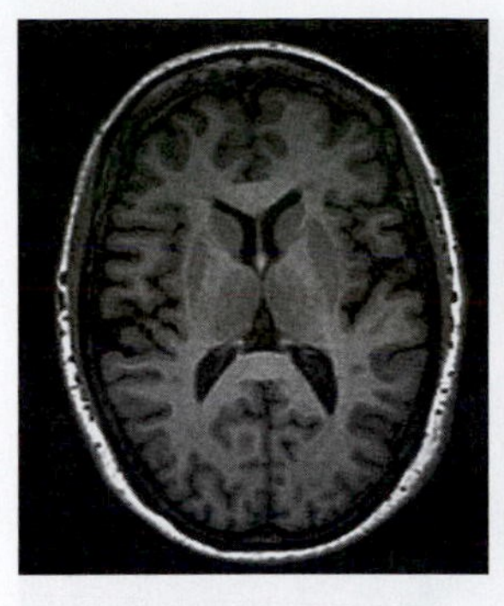

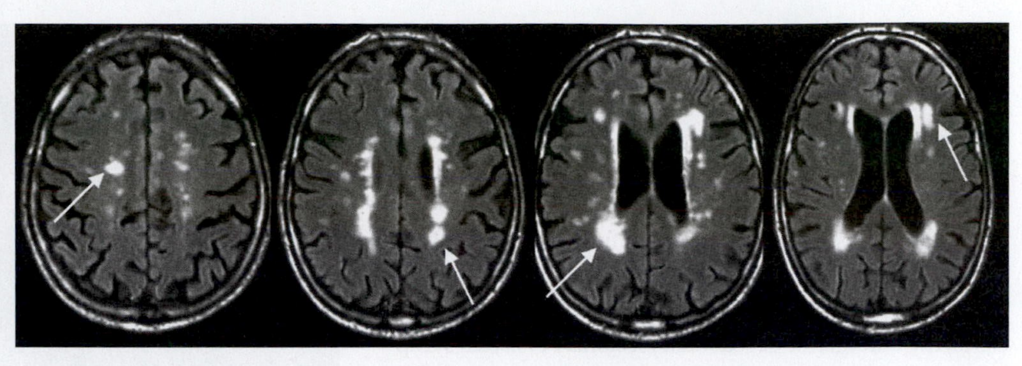

a b

FIGURE 3.6 Degenerative disorders of the brain.
(a) Normal brain of a 60-year-old male. **(b)** Axial slices at four sections of the brain in a 79-year-old male with Alzheimer's disease. Arrows show growth of white matter lesions.

Viruses can also cause progressive neurological disorders. The human immunodeficiency virus (HIV) that causes acquired immunodeficiency syndrome (AIDS) has a tendency to lodge in subcortical regions of the brain, producing diffuse lesions of the white matter by destroying axonal fibers resulting in dementia. The herpes simplex virus, on the other hand, destroys neurons in cortical and limbic structures if it migrates to the brain. Some researchers also suspect viral infection in multiple sclerosis, although evidence for such a link is indirect, coming from epidemiological studies. For example, the incidence of multiple sclerosis is highest in temperate climates. Some isolated tropical islands never had any residents that developed multiple sclerosis until they had visitors from other regions.

TRAUMATIC BRAIN INJURY The most common brain affliction that lands patients in a neurology ward is **traumatic brain injury (TBI)**. In a given year in the United States, there are about 2.5 million adult TBI incidents and another half million incidents involving children (Centers for Disease Control and Prevention, 2014). Common causes of head injuries are car accidents, falls, contact sports, bullet or shrapnel wounds, and bomb blasts. While the damage may be at the site of the blow, it can also occur at distant locations because of the reactive forces that arise as the brain moves within and against the skull. The inside surface of the skull is markedly jagged above the eye sockets; as **Figure 3.7** shows, this rough surface can produce extensive tearing

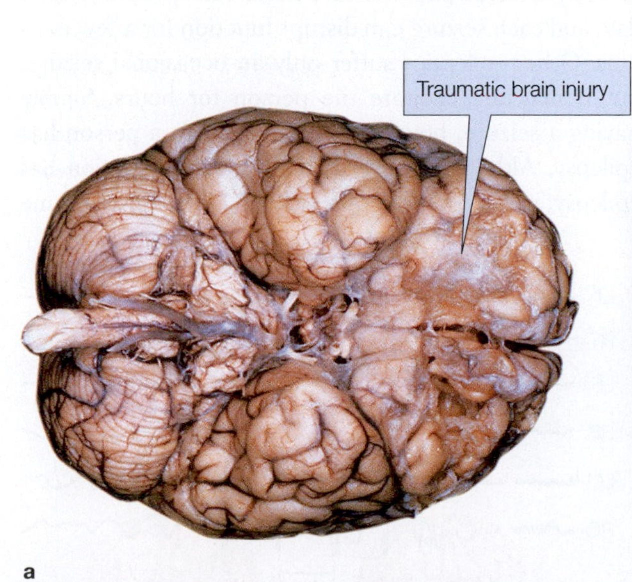

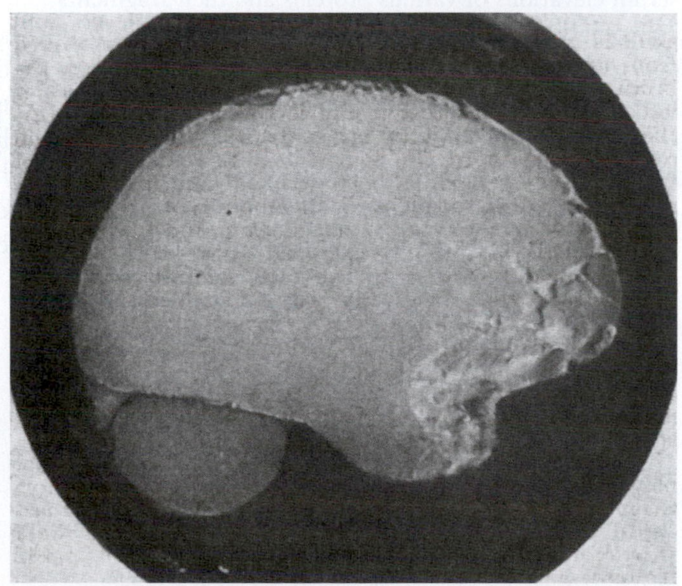

a b

FIGURE 3.7 Traumatic brain injury.
(a) Ventral view of the brain of a 54-year-old man who sustained a severe head injury 24 years before death. Tissue damage is evident in the orbitofrontal regions and was associated with intellectual deterioration after the injury. **(b)** The susceptibility of the orbitofrontal region to trauma was made clear by A. Holbourn of Oxford, who in 1943 filled a skull with gelatin and then violently rotated the skull. Although most of the brain retains its smooth appearance, the orbitofrontal region has been chewed up.

of brain tissue in the orbitofrontal region. In addition, accelerative forces created by the impact can cause extensive shearing of dendritic arbors, even if the neuronal somata survive the injury.

One consequence of the primary lesion from a TBI is edema (swelling) around the lesion. Limited space within the skull causes an increase in the intracranial pressure, in turn reducing the perfusion pressure and flow of blood throughout the brain, resulting in ischemia and, in some cases, the emergence of secondary lesions. Persistent symptoms and recent data indicate that even mild TBI (mTBI), or "concussion," may lead to chronic neurodegenerative consequences. For example, using diffusion tensor imaging (discussed later in the chapter), researchers have shown that professional boxers exhibit sustained damage in white matter tracts (Chappell et al., 2006; **Figure 3.8**). Similarly, repeated concussions suffered by football and soccer players may cause changes in neural connectivity that produce chronic cognitive problems (Shi et al., 2009).

The axons are particularly vulnerable to the mechanical forces that affect the brain during these injuries and subsequent disruptions, and diffuse axonal injury (DAI) is common in TBI. The twisting, buckling, or distortion of the white matter that occurs with an injury disrupts the axonal cytoskeleton and thus also axonal transport. Originally thought to be limited to moderate and severe TBI, more recent evidence indicates that DAI may be the main pathology involved with mTBI, even without focal lesions and subsequent edema. Physicians have begun to use serum elevations of various proteins and their fragments as biomarkers to detect the severity of axonal injury in concussions and to predict who will have persistent neurocognitive dysfunction (see V. E. Johnson et al., 2016).

EPILEPSY Epilepsy is a condition characterized by excessive and abnormally patterned activity in the brain. The cardinal symptom is a seizure, a transient loss of consciousness. The extent of other disturbances varies. Some epileptics shake violently and lose their balance. For others, seizures may be perceptible only to the most attentive friends and family. Electroencephalography (EEG) can confirm seizure activity. During a seizure, large-amplitude oscillations of the brain's electrical current mark the EEG profile (**Figure 3.9**).

The frequency of seizures is highly variable. The most severely affected patients have hundreds of seizures each day, and each seizure can disrupt function for a few minutes. Other epileptics suffer only an occasional seizure, but it may incapacitate the person for hours. Simply having a seizure, however, does not mean a person has epilepsy. Although 0.5% of the general population has epilepsy, about 5% of people will have a seizure at some

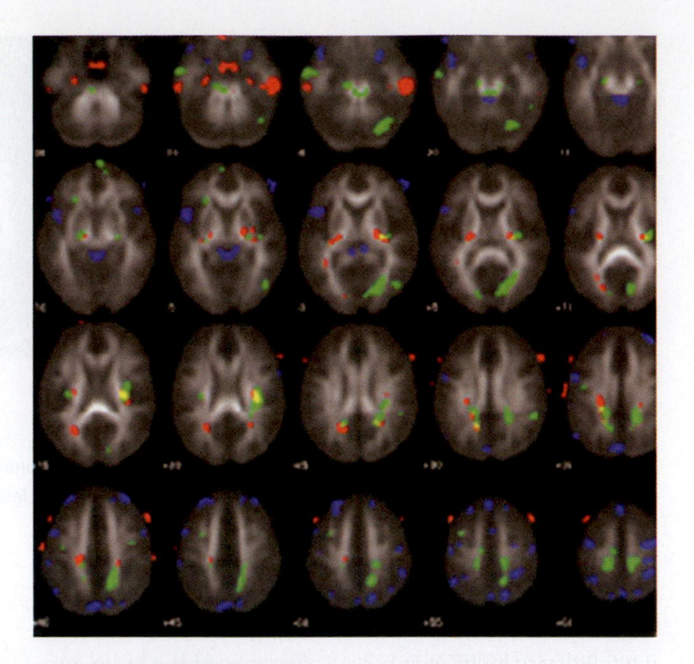

FIGURE 3.8 Sports-related TBI.
Colored regions indicate white matter tracts that are abnormal in the brains of professional boxers.

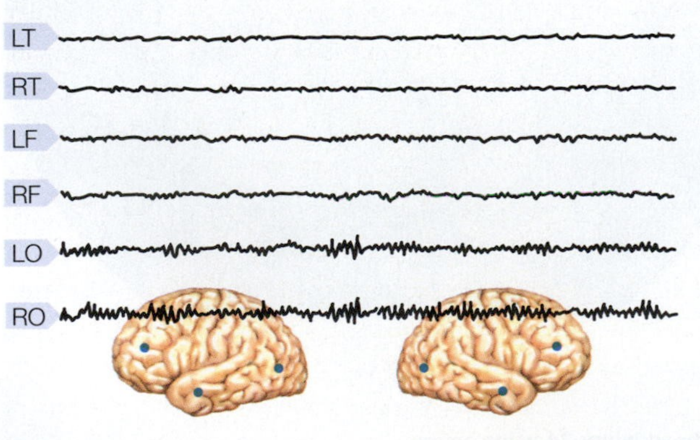

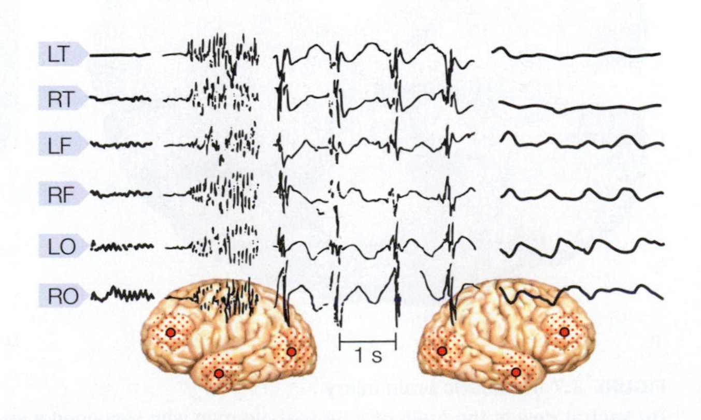

FIGURE 3.9 Electrical activity in a normal (a) and an epileptic (b) brain.
Electroencephalographic recordings from six electrodes, positioned over the temporal (T), frontal (F), and occipital (O) cortex on both the left (L) and the right (R) sides. (a) Activity during normal cerebral activity. (b) Activity during a grand mal seizure.

BOX 3.1 | THE COGNITIVE NEUROSCIENTIST'S TOOLKIT

Single and Double Dissociations

When a lesion to brain area *X* impairs the ability of a patient to do task *A* but not task *B*, then we can say that brain area *X* and task *A* are *associated*, whereas brain area *X* and task *B* are *dissociated*. We call this a **single dissociation**. For example, damage to Broca's area in the left hemisphere impairs a person's ability to speak fluently, but it does not impair comprehension.

From this observation, we could infer that tasks *A* and *B* use different brain areas. But, armed with only a single dissociation, we would be jumping to conclusions. We could make other inferences instead: Perhaps both tasks need area *X*, but task *B* does not require as many resources from area *X* as task *A* does, or damaging area *X* has a greater effect on task *A* than on task *B*. Or perhaps both tasks require area *Y*, but task *A* requires both areas *X* and *Y*. Single dissociations have unavoidable problems. We may assume that two tasks are equally sensitive to differences between the two brain areas, but that is often not the case. One task may be more demanding, require more concentration or finer motor skills, or draw more resources from a common processing area.

Double dissociations avoid these problems. A double dissociation occurs when damage to area *X* impairs the ability to do task *A* but not task *B*, and damage to area *Y* impairs the ability to do task *B* but not task *A*. The two areas have complementary processing. So, amending the example of Broca's area, we can add another piece of information to turn it into a double dissociation: Damage to Wernicke's area impairs comprehension but not the ability to speak fluently.

A double dissociation identifies whether two cognitive functions are independent of each other—something that a single association cannot do. Double dissociations can also be sought when comparing groups, where Group 1 is impaired on task *X* (but not task *Y*) and Group 2 is impaired on task *Y* (but not task *X*). The researcher can compare the performances of the two groups to each other or, more commonly, compare the patient groups to a control group that shows no impairment on either task. With a double dissociation, it is no longer reasonable to argue that a difference in performance results merely from the unequal sensitivity of the two tasks. Double dissociations offer the strongest neuropsychological evidence that a patient or patient group has a selective deficit in a certain cognitive operation.

---

point during life, usually triggered by an acute event such as trauma, exposure to toxic chemicals, or high fever.

Studying Brain–Behavior Relationships Following Neural Disruption

The logic of studying participants with brain lesions is straightforward. If a neural structure contributes to a task, then a structure that is dysfunctional through either surgical intervention or natural causes should impair performance of that task. Lesion studies have provided key insights into the relationship between brain and behavior. Observing the effects of brain injury has led to the development of fundamental concepts, such as the left hemisphere's dominant role in language and the dependence of visual functions on posterior cortical regions.

Historically, limited information about the extent and location of brain lesions in humans hampered the study of participants with neurological dysfunction. However, since the advent of neuroimaging methods such as computerized tomography (CT) and magnetic resonance imaging (MRI), we can precisely localize brain injury in vivo. In addition, cognitive psychology has provided the tools for making sophisticated analyses of the behavioral deficits. Early work focused on localizing complex tasks such as language, vision, executive control, and motor programming. Since then, the cognitive revolution has shaken things up. We know that these complex tasks require integrated processing of component operations that involve many different regions of the brain. By testing patients with brain injuries, researchers have been able to link these operations to specific brain structures and to make inferences about the component operations that underlie normal cognitive performance.

Lesion studies rest on the assumption that brain injury is eliminative—that brain injury disturbs or eliminates the processing ability of the affected structure. Consider this example: Suppose that damage to brain area *X* results in impaired performance on task *A*. One conclusion is that area *X* contributes to the processing required for task *A*. For example, if task *A* is reading, we might conclude that area *X* is critical for reading. From cognitive psychology, however, we know that a complex task like reading has many component operations: We must perceive fonts, letters and letter strings must activate representations of their corresponding meanings, and syntactic operations must link individual words into a coherent stream. If we test only reading ability, we will not know which component operation or operations are impaired when there are lesions to area *X* (see **Box 3.1**).

What the cognitive neuropsychologist wants to do is design tasks that will test specific hypotheses about brain–function relationships. If a reading problem stems from a general perceptual problem, then we should see comparable deficits on a range of tests of visual perception. If the problem reflects a loss of semantic knowledge, then the deficit should be limited to tasks that require some form of object identification or recognition.

Associating neural structures with specific processing operations calls for appropriate *control conditions*. The most basic control is to compare the performance of a patient or group of patients with that of healthy participants. We might take poorer performance by the patients as evidence that the affected brain regions are involved in the task. Thus, if a group of patients with lesions in the frontal cortex showed impairment on our reading task, we might suppose that this region of the brain was critical for reading.

Keep in mind, however, that brain injury can produce widespread changes in cognitive abilities. Besides having trouble reading, the frontal lobe patient might also demonstrate impairment on other tasks, such as problem solving, memory, or motor planning. The challenge for the cognitive neuroscientist is to determine whether the observed behavioral problem results from damage to a particular mental operation or is secondary to a more general disturbance. For example, many patients are depressed after a neurological disturbance such as a stroke, and depression affects performance on a wide range of tasks.

Surgical interventions for treating neurological disorders have provided a unique opportunity to investigate the link between brain and behavior. The best example comes from research involving patients who have undergone surgical treatment for the control of intractable epilepsy. Surgeons document the extent of tissue removal, enabling researchers to investigate correlations between lesion site and cognitive deficits. We must exercise caution, however, in attributing cognitive deficits to surgically induced lesions. Since seizures spread beyond the epileptogenic tissue, structurally intact tissue may be dysfunctional because of the chronic effects of epilepsy.

Historically, an important paradigm for cognitive neuroscience involved the study of patients who had the fibers of the corpus callosum severed. In these patients, the two hemispheres are disconnected—in a procedure referred to as a *callosotomy* operation or, more informally, the *split-brain* procedure. Although this procedure has always been uncommon and, in fact, is rarely performed now because alternative procedures have been developed, extensive study of a small set of split-brain patients has provided insights into the roles of the two hemispheres on a wide range of cognitive tasks. We discuss these studies more extensively in Chapter 4.

The lesion method also has a long tradition in research involving laboratory animals, in large part because the experimenter can control the location and extent of the lesion. Over the years, surgical and chemical lesioning techniques have been refined, allowing for even greater precision. For example, 1-methyl-4-phenyl-1,2,3,6-tetrahydropyridine (MPTP) is a neurochemical agent that destroys dopaminergic cells in the substantia nigra, producing an animal version of Parkinson's disease (see Chapter 8). Other chemicals have reversible effects, allowing researchers to produce a transient disruption in neural function. When the drug wears off, function gradually returns.

The appeal of reversible lesions or control lesioning of animals is that each animal can serve as its own control. You can compare performance during the "lesion" and "nonlesion" periods. We will discuss this work further when we address pharmacological methods. Bear in mind, however, the limitations to using animals as models for human brain function. Although humans and many animals have some similar brain structures and functions, there are some notable differences.

In both human and animal studies, the lesion approach itself has limitations. For naturally occurring lesions associated with strokes or tumors, considerable variability exists among patients. Moreover, it is not always easy to analyze the function of a missing part by looking at the operation of the remaining system. You don't have to be an auto mechanic to understand that cutting the spark plug wires or the gas line will cause an automobile to stop running, but this does not mean that spark plug wires and the gas line have the same function; rather, removing either one of these parts has similar functional consequences.

Similarly, a lesion may alter the function of neural regions that connect to it, either because the damage deprives the regions of normal neural input or because synaptic connections fail, resulting in no output. New methods using fMRI data to construct connectivity maps, which we discuss later in this chapter, are helping to identify the extent of the changes that occur after damage to a restricted part of the brain.

Lesions may also result in the development of compensatory processes. For example, when surgical lesions deprive monkeys of sensory feedback to one arm, the monkeys stop using the limb. However, if they later lose the sensory feedback to the other arm, the animals begin to use both limbs (Taub & Berman, 1968). The monkeys prefer to use a limb that has normal sensation, but the second surgery shows that they could indeed use the compromised limb.

TAKE-HOME MESSAGES

- Researchers study patients with neurological disorders or brain lesions to examine structure–function relationships. Double dissociations are better evidence than single dissociations that damage to a particular brain region may result in a selective deficit of a certain cognitive operation.
- Traumatic brain injuries are the most common cause of brain lesions. Even when the injuries are mild, they can have chronic neurodegenerative consequences.
- Impairments in a particular cognitive process do not mean that the damaged part of the brain "performs" that process. Brain lesions can disrupt processing in intact brain structures or disrupt brain networks on a larger scale.

3.3 Methods to Perturb Neural Function

We can glean many insights from careful observations of people with neurological disorders, but as we will see throughout this book, such methods are, in essence, correlational. This concern points to the need for methods that can produce transient disruption in brain function.

Pharmacology

The release of neurotransmitters at neuronal synapses and the resultant responses are critical for information transfer from one neuron to the next. Though protected by the blood–brain barrier (BBB), the brain is not a locked compartment. Many different drugs, known as psychoactive drugs (e.g., caffeine, alcohol, and cocaine, as well as the pharmaceutical drugs used to treat depression and anxiety), can disturb these interactions, resulting in changes in cognitive function. **Pharmacological studies** may involve the administration of *agonist* drugs, those that have a similar structure to a neurotransmitter and mimic its action, or *antagonist* drugs, those that bind to receptors and block or dampen neurotransmission.

For the researcher studying the impacts of pharmaceuticals on human populations, there are "native" groups to study, given the prevalence of drug use in our culture. For example, in Chapter 12 we examine studies of cognitive impairments associated with chronic cocaine abuse. Researchers also administer drugs in a controlled environment to monitor the effects of the agent on cognitive function. For instance, the neurotransmitter dopamine is a key ingredient in reward-seeking behavior.

One study looked at the effect of dopamine on decision making when a potential monetary reward or loss was involved. One group of participants received the drug haloperidol, a dopamine receptor antagonist; another received the receptor agonist L-dopa, the metabolic precursor of dopamine (though dopamine itself is unable to cross the BBB, L-dopa can and is then converted to dopamine). Individuals of each group performed a learning task with several trials. In each trial, the participant saw two symbols on a computer screen. Each symbol was associated with a certain unknown probability of gain or no gain, loss or no loss, or no gain or loss. For instance, a squiggle stood an 80% chance of winning a British pound and a 20% chance of winning nothing, but a figure eight stood an 80% chance of losing a pound and a 20% chance of no loss, and a circular arrow resulted in no win or loss. The participants had to choose one of the symbols in each trial, with the goal of maximizing their payoff (Pessiglione et al., 2006; **Figure 3.10**). On gain trials, the L-dopa-treated group won more money than the haloperidol-treated group, whereas on loss trials, the groups did not differ. These results are consistent with the hypothesis that dopamine has a selective effect on reward-driven learning.

A major drawback of studies using drugs injected into the bloodstream is the lack of specificity. Because the entire body and brain are awash in the drug, it is unknown how much of it actually reaches the site of interest in the brain. In addition, the potential impact of the drug on other sites in the body and the dilution effect confound data analysis. In some animal studies, direct injection of a study drug to specific brain regions helps obviate this problem. For example, Judith Schweimer examined the brain mechanisms involved in deciding how much effort an individual should expend to gain a reward (Schweimer & Hauber, 2006). For instance, do you stay on the couch and watch a favorite TV show or get dressed up to go out to a party and perhaps make a new friend?

Earlier work showed (a) that rats depleted of dopamine are unwilling to make effortful responses that are highly rewarding (Schweimer et al., 2005) and (b) that the anterior cingulate cortex (ACC), a part of the prefrontal cortex, is important for evaluating the cost versus benefit of performing an action (Rushworth et al., 2004). Knowing that there are two types of dopamine receptors in the ACC, called D_1 and D_2, Schweimer wondered which was involved. In one group of rats, she injected a drug into the ACC that blocked the D_1 receptor; in another, she

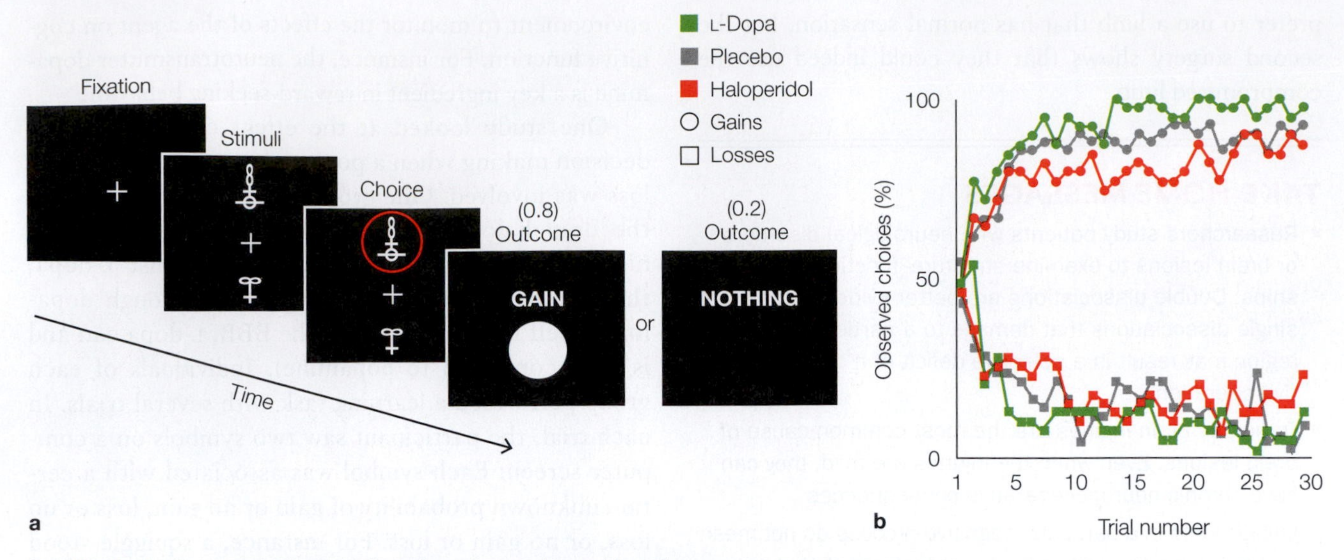

FIGURE 3.10 Pharmacological manipulation of reward-based learning.
(a) Participants chose the upper or lower of two abstract visual stimuli and observed the outcome. The selected stimulus, circled in red, is associated with an 80% chance of winning 1 pound and a 20% chance of winning nothing. The probabilities are different for other stimuli. **(b)** Learning functions showing the probability of selecting stimuli associated with gains (circles) or avoiding stimuli associated with losses (squares) as a function of the number of times each stimulus was presented. Participants given L-dopa (green), a dopamine agonist, were faster in learning to choose stimuli associated with gains, compared to participants given a placebo (gray). Participants given haloperidol (red), a dopamine antagonist, were slower in learning to choose the gain stimuli. The drugs did not affect how quickly participants learned to avoid the stimuli associated with a loss.

injected a D_2 antagonist. The group whose D_1 receptors were blocked turned out to act like couch potatoes, but the rats with blocked D_2 receptors were willing to make the effort to pursue the high reward. This double dissociation indicates that dopamine input to the D_1 receptors within the ACC is critical for effort-based decision making.

Genetic Manipulations

The start of the 21st century witnessed the climax of one of the great scientific challenges: the mapping of the human genome. Scientists now possess a complete record of the genetic sequence contained in our chromosomes, yet we have only begun to understand how these genes code for the structure and function of the nervous system. In essence, we now have a map containing the secrets to many treasures: What causes people to grow old? Why do some people have great difficulty recognizing faces? What dictates whether embryonic tissue will become a skin cell or a brain cell? Deciphering this map is an imposing task that will take years of intensive study.

Genetic disorders are manifest in all aspects of life, including brain function. As noted earlier, disorders such as Huntington's disease are clearly heritable. By analyzing individuals' genetic codes, scientists can predict whether the children of individuals carrying the Huntington's disease gene will develop this debilitating disorder. Moreover, by identifying the genetic locus of this disorder, scientists hope to devise techniques to alter the aberrant genes by modifying them or preventing their expression.

In a similar way, scientists have sought to understand other aspects of normal and abnormal brain function through the study of genetics. Behavioral geneticists have long known that many aspects of cognitive function are heritable. For example, selective breeding of rats for spatial-learning performance allowed researchers to develop "maze-bright" and "maze-dull" strains. Rats that quickly learn to navigate mazes are likely to have offspring with similar abilities, even if foster parent rats that are slow to navigate the same mazes raise them.

Such correlations are also observed across a range of human behaviors, including spatial reasoning, reading speed, and even preferences in watching television (Plomin et al., 1990). However, we should not conclude from this finding that our intelligence or behavior is genetically determined. Maze-bright rats perform quite poorly if raised in an impoverished environment. The truth surely reflects complex interactions between the environment and genetics (see **Box 3.2**).

To explore the genetic component in this equation by studying the functional role of many genes, researchers have concentrated on two species that reproduce quickly: the fruit fly and the mouse. A key methodology is to develop genetically altered animals using a *knockout procedure*. The term *knockout* comes from the fact that scientists manipulate a specific gene (or set of genes)

BOX 3.2 | LESSONS FROM THE CLINIC

Brain Size → PTSD, or PTSD → Brain Size?

People who have experienced a traumatic event and later suffer from chronic posttraumatic stress disorder (PTSD) have smaller hippocampi than do individuals without PTSD (Bremner et al., 1997; M. B. Stein et al., 1997). We have also learned from animal studies that exposure to prolonged stress, and the resulting increase in glucocorticoid steroids, can cause atrophy in the hippocampus (Sapolsky et al., 1990). Can we conclude this chain of events: traumatic event → acute stress → PTSD (chronic stress) → reduced hippocampal volume?

The issue of causation is important to consider in any discussion of scientific observation. In elementary statistics courses, we learn to be wary about inferring causation from correlation, but the temptation can be strong. The tendency to infer causation from correlation can be especially great when we are comparing the contribution of nature and nurture to brain and behavior, or when we hold a bias in one direction over another.

It is also important to consider that the causal story may run in the opposite direction. In this case, it could be that individuals with smaller hippocampi, perhaps because of genetic variation, are more vulnerable to the effects of stress, and thus at higher risk for developing PTSD: reduced hippocampal volume → traumatic event → acute stress → PTSD. What study design could distinguish between the two hypotheses—one that emphasizes environmental factors (e.g., PTSD, via chronic stress, causes reduction in size of the hippocampus) and one that emphasizes genetic factors (e.g., individuals with small hippocampi are at greater risk for developing PTSD)?

A favorite approach of behavioral geneticists in exploring questions like these is to study identical twins. Mark Gilbertson and his colleagues at the Veterans Affairs Medical Center in Manchester, New Hampshire (2002), studied a cohort of 40 pairs of identical twins. Within each twin pair, one member had experienced severe trauma during a tour of duty in Vietnam, and the other had not. Thus, each high-stress participant had a very well-matched control: an identical twin brother.

Although all of the active-duty participants had experienced severe trauma during their time in Vietnam (one of the inclusion criteria for the study), not all of these individuals had developed PTSD. Thus, the experimenters could look at various factors associated with the onset of PTSD in a group of individuals with similar environmental experiences. Consistent with previous studies, anatomical MRIs showed that people with PTSD had smaller hippocampi than did unrelated individuals without PTSD—but so did their twin brothers, even though they did not have PTSD and did not report having experienced unusual trauma in their lifetime. Moreover, the severity of the PTSD correlated negatively with the size of the hippocampus in both the patient with PTSD (**Figure 3.11a**) and the matched twin control (**Figure 3.11b**). Thus, the researchers concluded that small hippocampal size was a risk factor for developing PTSD and that PTSD alone did not cause the decreased hippocampal size.

This study serves as an example of the need for caution: Experimenters must be careful when making causal inferences based on correlational data. The study also provides an excellent example of how scientists are studying interactions between genes and the environment in influencing behavior and brain structure.

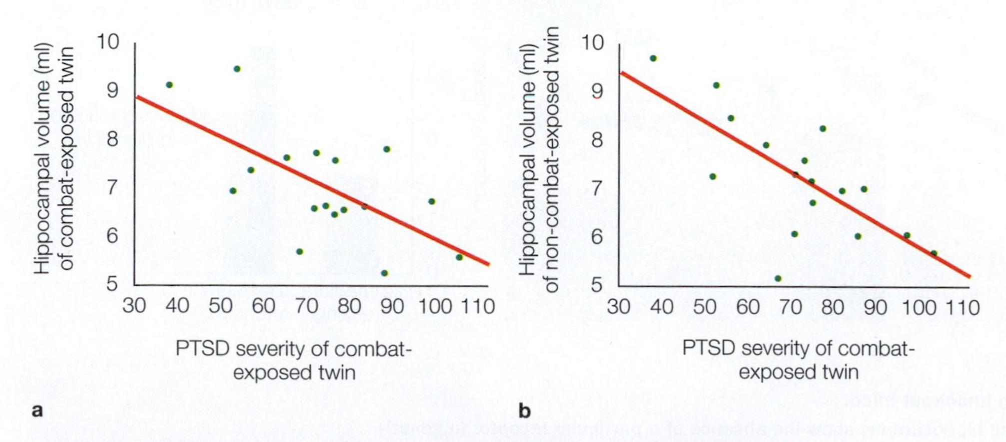

FIGURE 3.11 Exploring the relationship between PTSD and hippocampal size.
Scatter plots illustrate the relationship of symptom severity in combat veterans with PTSD to their own hippocampal volumes (a) and to the hippocampal volumes of their identical twin brothers who had not seen combat (b). Symptom severity represents the total score received on the Clinician-Administered PTSD Scale (CAPS).

such that it does not express itself. They can then study the knockout strains to explore the consequences of this change. For example, *weaver* mice are a knockout strain in which Purkinje cells, the prominent cell type in the cerebellum, fail to develop. As their name implies, these mice exhibit coordination problems.

At a more focal level, researchers use knockout procedures to create strains that lack a single type of postsynaptic receptor in specific brain regions, while leaving other types of receptors intact. Susumu Tonegawa at the Massachusetts Institute of Technology and his colleagues developed a mouse strain in which *N*-methyl-D-aspartate (NMDA) receptors were absent in cells within a subregion of the hippocampus (M. A. Wilson & Tonegawa, 1997; also see Chapter 9). Mice lacking these receptors exhibited poor learning on a variety of memory tasks, providing a novel approach for linking memory with its molecular substrate (**Figure 3.12**). In a sense, this approach constitutes a lesion method, but at a microscopic level.

Neurogenetic research is not limited to identifying the role of each gene individually. Complex brain function and behavior arise from interactions between many genes and the environment. Our increasingly sophisticated genetic tools will put scientists in a better position to detect polygenic influences on brain function and behavior.

Invasive Stimulation Methods

Given the risks associated with neurosurgery, researchers reserve invasive methods for studies in animals and for patients with neurological problems that require surgical intervention. Direct neural stimulation involves the placement of electrodes on or into the brain. As with all stimulation methods, the procedure is reversible in that testing can be done with stimulation on or stimulation off. This within-participant comparison provides a unique opportunity to investigate the link between brain and behavior.

In humans, direct stimulation of the cerebral cortex is used primarily during surgery to treat neurological disorders. Prior to any incisions, the surgeon stimulates parts of the cortex to determine the function of tissue surrounding lesions or seizure foci in order not to damage or remove vital areas. The best example of direct stimulation comes from research involving patients who are undergoing surgical treatment for the control of intractable epilepsy.

DEEP BRAIN STIMULATION Another invasive approach is **deep brain stimulation (DBS)**, a procedure in which surgeons implant electrodes in specific brain regions for an extended period to modulate neuronal activity. The most common application of this method is as a treatment for Parkinson's disease, a movement disorder resulting from basal ganglia dysfunction. The standard treatment for this disease is medication, yet the efficacy of the drug can change over time and may produce debilitating side effects. In such cases, neurosurgeons can implant electrodes in the subcortex, usually the subthalamic nucleus of the basal ganglia (thus giving rise to the term *deep* brain stimulation; **Figure 3.13**), and the electrodes deliver continuous electrical stimulation to the area.

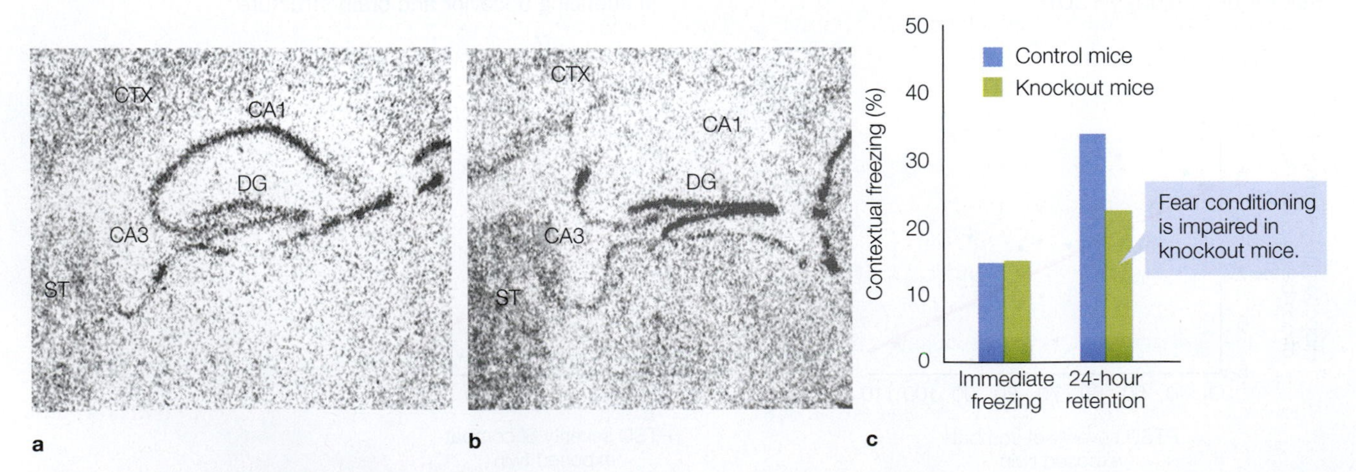

FIGURE 3.12 Fear conditioning in knockout mice.
(a, b) These brain slices through the hippocampus show the absence of a particular receptor in genetically altered mice. CTX = cortex; DG = dentate gyrus; ST = striatum. Cells containing the gene associated with the receptor are stained in black, but these cells are absent in the CA1 region of the slice from the knockout mouse **(b)**. **(c)** Fear conditioning is impaired in knockout mice. After receiving a shock, the mice freeze. When normal mice are placed in the same context 24 hours later, they show strong learning by the large increase in the percentage of freezing responses. This increase is reduced in the knockout mice.

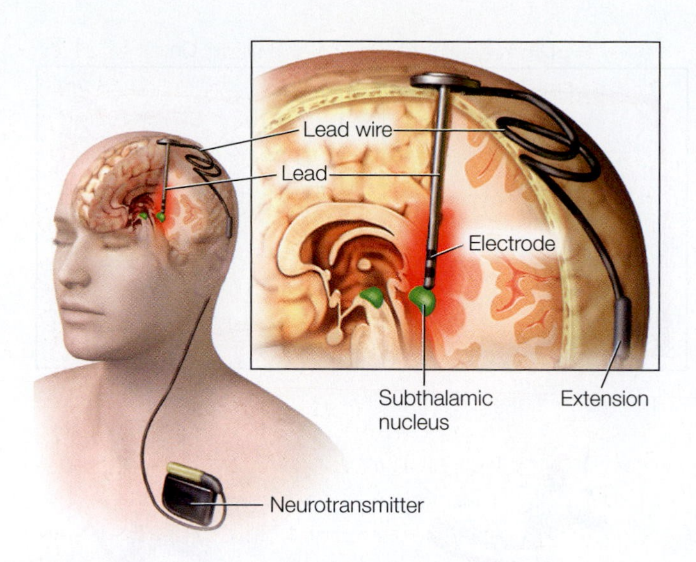

FIGURE 3.13 Deep brain stimulation for treatment of Parkinson's disease.
A battery-powered neurostimulator is surgically implanted beneath the skin of the chest. It sends electrical pulses through a wire that extends subcutaneously along the neck to the skull, where a small hole is drilled. The wire passes through the hole to an electrode placed in the subthalamic nucleus of the basal ganglia. The electrical pulses interfere with neuronal activity at the target site.

Although the exact mechanism of the benefits remains controversial, DBS produces dramatic and sustained improvements in the motor function of patients (Hamani et al., 2006; Krack et al., 1998), even though the progression of the disease itself is not halted. The success of DBS for Parkinson's disease has led researchers to explore the efficacy of DBS in treating a wide range of neurological and psychiatric disorders including coma, posttraumatic stress disorder, and obsessive-compulsive disorder, with various cortical and subcortical regions candidates for stimulation.

OPTOGENETICS As described at the beginning of the chapter, **optogenetics** has provided a reliable switch to activate neurons using *viral transduction*. Here, researchers attach a specific piece of DNA to a neutral virus and allow the virus to infect targeted cells with the DNA. Those cells construct proteins from the DNA instructions; for example, with the gene for ChR-2, the cells will construct light-sensitive ion channels. The locations where the tailored virus is injected are quite specific, limited to either a small region of the brain or certain types of neurons or receptors.

In one of the initial studies, scientists inserted the ChR-2 gene into the part of a mouse's brain that contains the motor neurons controlling its whiskers. Once the light-sensitive ion channels were constructed and a tiny optical fiber was inserted in the same region, the neurons were ready to rock 'n' roll: When a blue light was pulsed, the animal moved its whiskers (Aravanis et al., 2007). It is important to note that the infected neurons continue to perform their normal function. For example, the neurons also fired when the animal moved its whiskers while exploring its environment. This natural firing requires a voltage change across the cell membrane (see Chapter 2); with optogenetics, the ion channels open and close in response to a specific wavelength of light.

Optogenetic techniques are versatile (for a video on optogenetics, see http://spie.org/x48167.xml?ArticleID=x48167), especially with the discovery of many new opsins, including ones that respond to different colors of visible light and to infrared light. Infrared light is advantageous because it penetrates tissue and thus may eliminate the need for implanting optical fibers to deliver the light pulse. Using optogenetic methods to turn cells on and off in many parts of the brain, researchers can manipulate behavior. This method has the twin advantages of having high neuronal (or receptor) specificity, as well as high temporal resolution.

Optogenetic methods also have potential as an intervention for clinicians to modulate neuronal activity. A demonstration comes from a study in which optogenetic methods were able to reduce anxiety in mice (Tye et al., 2011). After light-sensitive neurons were created in the amygdalae of the mice (see Chapter 10), a flash of light was sufficient to motivate the mice to move away from the wall of their home cage and boldly step out into the center (**Figure 3.14**).

While there are currently no human applications, researchers are using this method to explore treatments for Parkinson's symptoms in a mouse model of the disease. Early work here suggests that the most effective treatments may result not from the stimulation of specific cells, but rather from the way in which stimulation changes the interactions between different types of cells (Kravitz et al., 2010). This finding underscores the idea that many diseases of the nervous system disrupt the flow of information.

Noninvasive Stimulation Methods

Researchers have devised numerous methods to modulate neural function noninvasively by imposing electrical or magnetic fields on the scalp that create changes in the electrical fields at the cortical surface. These noninvasive methods have been widely used to alter neural function in the normal brain and, with increasing popularity, as a tool for therapeutic purposes.

TRANSCRANIAL MAGNETIC STIMULATION **Transcranial magnetic stimulation (TMS)** produces relatively focal stimulation of the human brain noninvasively. The TMS device consists of a tightly wrapped wire coil encased in an insulated sheath and connected to powerful

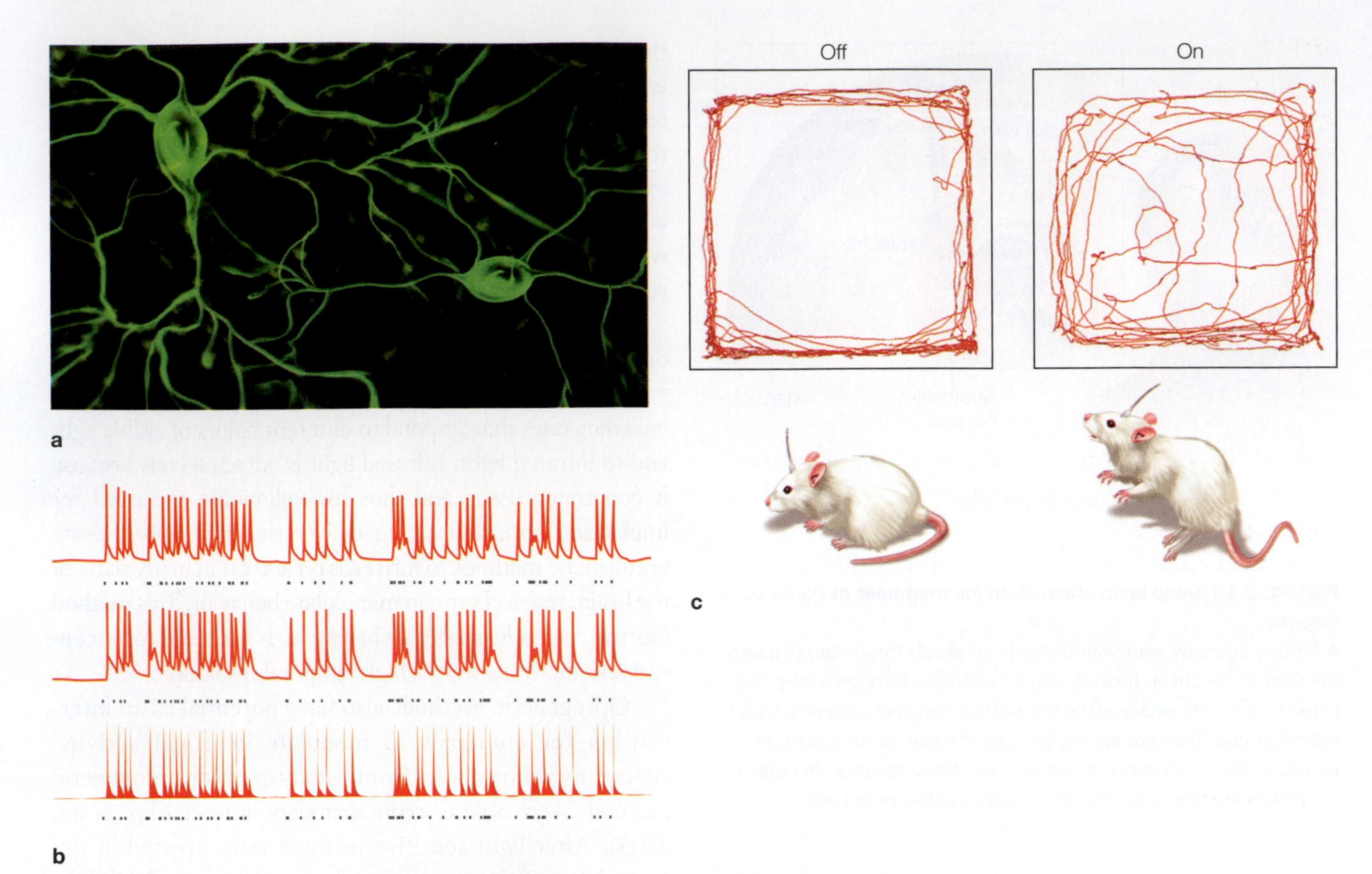

FIGURE 3.14 Optogenetic control of neuronal activity.
(a) Hippocampal neuron that has been genetically modified to express channelrhodopsin-2, a protein that forms light-gated ion channels. (b) Activity in three neurons when exposed to a blue light. The small gray dashes below each neuron indicate when the light was turned on (same stimulus for all three neurons). The firing pattern of the cells is tightly coupled to the light, indicating that the experimenter can control the activity of the cells. (c) Behavioral changes resulting from optogenetic stimulation of cells in a subregion of the amygdala. When placed in an open, rectangular arena, mice generally stay close to the walls (left). With amygdala activation, the mice become less fearful, venturing out into the open part of the arena (right).

electrical capacitors (**Figure 3.15a**). Triggering the capacitors sends a large electrical current through the coil and, as with all electrical currents, generates a magnetic field. The magnetic field propagates through the layers of the scalp and skull, reaching the cortical surface below the coil and altering the electrical activity in the neurons; with a modest level of stimulation, the neurons briefly fire. The exact mechanism causing the neuronal discharge is not well understood. Perhaps the current leads to the generation of action potentials in the soma; alternatively, the current may directly stimulate axons.

The area of neural activation depends on the shape and positioning of the TMS coil. For example, when the coil is over the hand area of the motor cortex, stimulation activates the muscles of the wrist and fingers. The sensation can be rather bizarre: The hand visibly twitches, yet the participant is aware that the movement is involuntary! For most areas of the cortex, however, the TMS pulse produces no directly observable effect. Rather, experimental protocols employ a control condition against which to compare performance during TMS.

There are numerous such protocols, or ways in which stimulation can be manipulated. Researchers can administer TMS pulses at various intensities, timings (single, repetitive, continuous), and frequencies. They can do this "online" (while the participant performs a task) or "offline" (using protocols in which the consequences

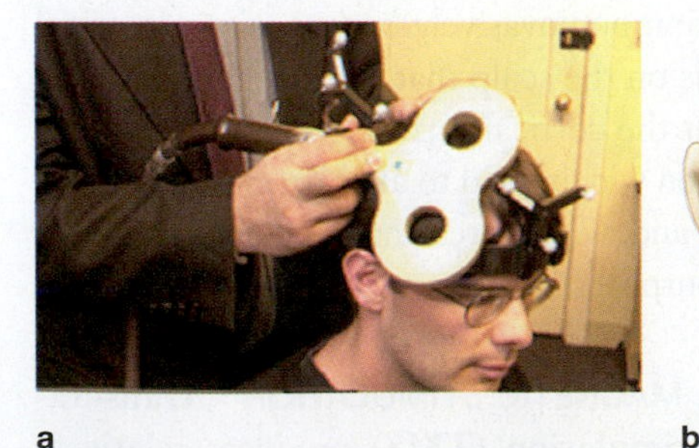

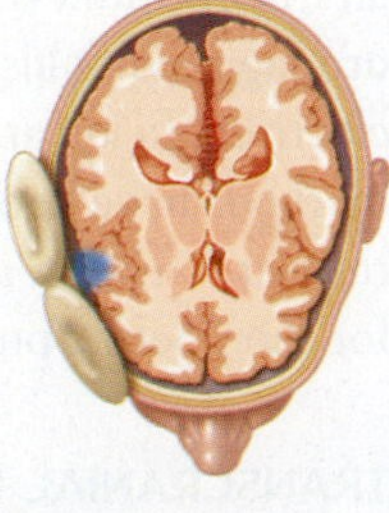

FIGURE 3.15 Transcranial magnetic stimulation.
(a) The TMS coil is held by the experimenter against the participant's head. (b) The TMS pulse directly alters neural activity in a spherical area of approximately 1 cm^3 (represented here with blue coloring).

of TMS are known to last well beyond the duration of the stimulation itself). Researchers find offline protocols especially appealing because the participant's task performance is affected only by the neural consequences of the stimulation, and not by discomfort or other sensations from the procedure itself.

Depending on the protocol, the effects of stimulation may either inhibit or enhance neural activity. For example, in *repetitive TMS (rTMS)*, the researcher applies bursts of TMS pulses over several minutes. At a low frequency (1 cycle per second, or 1 Hz) applied over 10 to 15 minutes, this procedure has the effect of depressing cortical excitability. At higher frequencies, such as 10 Hz, excitability increases. Another offline protocol, *continuous theta burst stimulation (cTBS)*, applies very-high-frequency stimulation for 40 seconds (600 pulses). Interestingly, this short period of stimulation depresses activity in the targeted cortical region for 45 to 60 minutes.

TMS has become a valuable research tool in cognitive neuroscience because of its ability to induce "virtual lesions" (Pascual-Leone et al., 1999). By stimulating the brain, the experimenter is disrupting normal activity in a selected region of the cortex. Similar to the logic behind lesion studies, researchers use the behavioral consequences of the stimulation to shed light on the normal function of the disrupted tissue. This method is appealing because the technique, when properly conducted, is safe and noninvasive, producing only a relatively brief alteration in neural activity and allowing comparisons between stimulated and nonstimulated conditions in the same individual. Such comparison is not possible with brain-injured patients.

Using the virtual-lesion approach, participants are usually not aware of any stimulation effects. For example, stimulation over visual cortex (**Figure 3.16**) interferes with a person's ability to identify a letter (Corthout et al., 1999). The synchronized discharge of the underlying visual neurons interferes with their normal operation. To plot the time course of processing, the experimenter manipulates the timing between the onset of the TMS pulse and the onset of the stimulus (e.g., presentation of a letter). In the letter identification task, the person will err only if the stimulation occurs between 70 and 130 milliseconds (ms) after presentation of the letter. If TMS is given before this interval, the neurons have time to recover; if given after this interval, the visual neurons have already responded to the stimulus.

As with all methods, TMS has its limitations. With currently available coils, the area of primary activation has about a 1-cm radius and thus can activate only relatively superficial areas (**Figure 3.15b**). New techniques to allow stimulation of deeper structures, perhaps by combining the effects of multiple coils, are being developed. Moreover, while the effects of stimulation are maximal directly underneath the coil, there are

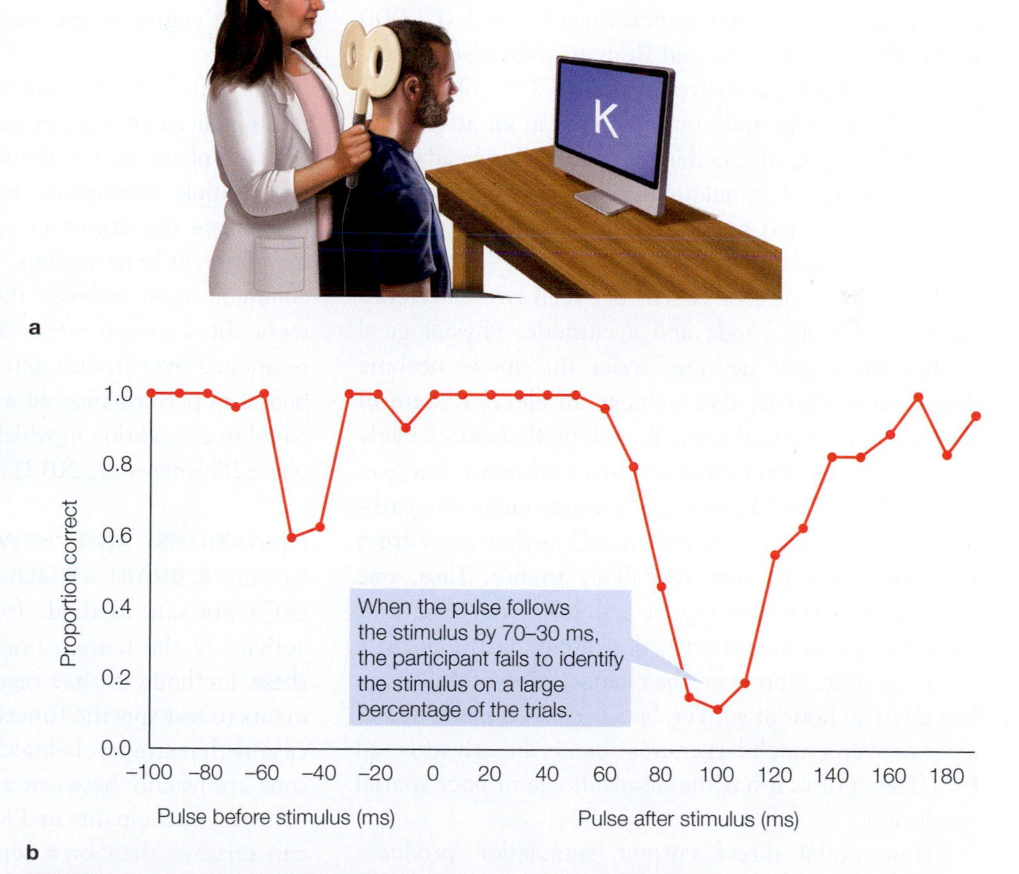

FIGURE 3.16 Transcranial magnetic stimulation over the occipital lobe. **(a) The center of the coil is positioned over the occipital lobe to disrupt visual processing. The participant attempts to name letters that are briefly presented on the screen. A TMS pulse is applied on some trials, either just before or just after the letter. (b) The independent variable is the time between the TMS pulse and letter presentation. Visual perception is markedly disrupted when the pulse occurs 70 to 130 ms after the letter, because of the disruption of neural activity in the visual cortex. There is also a drop in performance if the pulse comes before the letter. This is likely an artifact that is due to the participant blinking in response to the sound of the TMS pulse.**

secondary effects on connected cortical areas, further limiting its spatial resolution.

As with many research tools, the needs of clinical medicine originally drove the development of TMS. Direct stimulation of the motor cortex provides a relatively simple way to assess the integrity of motor pathways, because about 20 ms after stimulation we can detect muscle activity in the periphery. Repetitive TMS has also begun to be used as a treatment for unipolar depression in cases that have not benefited from medication or therapy. Physicians are considering its use as a treatment for a wide range of other conditions, including hallucinations, drug craving, neurological diseases such as Parkinson's disease, and stuttering. Rehabilitation studies are also testing the use of rTMS for patients with disorders of motor or language function (Rossi et al., 2009).

Researchers are constantly looking for new ways to noninvasively stimulate the brain. **Transcranial direct current stimulation (tDCS)** is a brain stimulation procedure that delivers a constant, low current to the brain via electrodes placed on the scalp. The essence of this method has been around in some form for the last 2,000 years. The early Greeks and Romans used electric torpedo fish, which can deliver from 8 to 220 volts of DC electricity, to stun and numb patients in an attempt to alleviate the pain of childbirth and migraine headaches. Today's electrical stimulation uses a much smaller current (1–4 mV) that feels like a tingling or itchy feeling when it is turned on or off.

In tDCS, a current is sent between two electrodes on the scalp: an anode and a cathode. Physiological studies show that neurons under the anode become depolarized; that is, they achieve an elevated state of excitability, close to threshold, making them more likely to initiate an action potential when a stimulus or movement occurs (see Chapter 2). Neurons under the cathode become hyperpolarized: Pushed farther away from threshold, they become less likely to fire. Thus, one advantage of tDCS is that it can selectively excite or inhibit targeted neural areas depending on the polarity of the current. Moreover, the changes in excitability can last up to an hour or so. Yet, because tDCS alters neural activity over a much larger area than is directly affected by a TMS pulse, it has the disadvantage of poor spatial resolution.

Transcranial direct current stimulation produces changes in a wide range of sensory, motor, and cognitive tasks, sometimes within a single experimental session. Anodal tDCS generally leads to improvements in performance, perhaps because the neurons are in a more excitable state. Cathodal stimulation may hinder performance, akin to TMS, although the effects of cathodal stimulation are generally less consistent. Patients with various neurological conditions, such as stroke or chronic pain, can benefit from tDCS. Though the immediate physiological effects are short-lived, lasting for perhaps an hour beyond the stimulation phase, repeated application of tDCS can prolong the duration of the benefit from minutes to weeks (Boggio et al., 2007).

TRANSCRANIAL ALTERNATING CURRENT STIMULATION **Transcranial alternating current stimulation (tACS)** is a newer procedure in which the electrical current oscillates rather than remaining constant as in tDCS. The experimenter controls the rate of tACS oscillation, providing another tool to modulate brain function. This added level of control is especially appealing because research has shown that different frequencies of brain oscillations are associated with different cognitive functions (Başar et al., 2001; Engel et al., 2001). With tACS, the experimenter can induce oscillations at specific frequencies, providing a unique opportunity to causally link brain oscillations of a specific frequency range to cognitive processes (C. S. Herrmann et al., 2013).

As with TMS, the direction and the duration of the tACS-induced effects can vary with the frequency, intensity, and phase of the stimulation. Simultaneously applying multiple stimulators enables the experimenter to manipulate the degree of synchronization in activity of two different brain regions, with the intent of enhancing communication between the areas. For example, when researchers applied 6-Hz tACS in phase over electrodes positioned over frontal and parietal regions, they found boosts to performance on a working memory task compared to a condition in which the stimulators were out of phase (Polanía et al., 2012).

LIMITATIONS AND NEW DIRECTIONS IN NONINVASIVE BRAIN STIMULATION TMS, tDCS, and tACS are safe methods for transiently disrupting the activity of the human brain. An appealing feature of these methods is that researchers can design experiments to test specific functional hypotheses. Unlike the case with neuropsychological studies in which comparisons are usually between a patient group and matched controls, participants in TMS, tDCS, and tACS studies can serve as their own controls because the effects of these stimulation procedures are transient.

In terms of limitations, tDCS, tACS, and to a lesser extent TMS all have poor spatial resolution, limiting the ability to make strong inferences concerning mind–brain relationships. In addition, although these techniques offer great promise, to date the results have been somewhat inconsistent. The reasons for this inconsistency are the subject of intensive study. Many variables can influence the strength of the electrical field at the cortex induced by stimulation applied to the scalp, such as the thickness of the skull and layers of the meninges. Individuals may also vary in their sensitivity to electrical stimulation because of their unique physiology and neurochemistry. We need a better understanding of how differences in anatomy and neurochemistry produce differences in sensitivity and responsiveness to brain stimulation.

TRANSCRANIAL STATIC MAGNETIC STIMULATION AND TRANSCRANIAL FOCUSED ULTRASOUND **Transcranial static magnetic stimulation (tSMS)** uses strong magnets to create magnetic fields that, as with TMS, perturb electrical activity and thus temporarily alter cortical function. The technique is inexpensive and does not require a skilled operator. Nor does it produce some of the side effects associated with other stimulation techniques, such as the itching or tingling of tDCS or the occasional headaches of TMS. Indeed, real and sham stimulation conditions are indistinguishable to the participant.

Another emerging method, one that promises improved spatial resolution and the ability to target deeper structures, is **transcranial focused ultrasound (tFUS)**. It involves the generation of a low-intensity, low-frequency ultrasound signal. This signal increases the activity of voltage-gated sodium and calcium channels, thus triggering action potentials. Early work with this method has shown that tFUS can produce focal effects limited to a 5-mm area.

TAKE-HOME MESSAGES

- Brain function can be perturbed by drugs, genetic manipulations, and magnetic or electrical stimulation. In most cases, these methods allow the same participants to be tested in both "on" and "off" states, enabling within-participant comparisons of performance.
- Genetic manipulations have played a major role in neuroscience studies using animal models. Knockout technology enables scientists to explore the consequences of the lack of expression of a specific gene in order to determine its role in behavior. Optogenetic methods provide the experimenter with the ability to control neuronal activity in targeted cells.
- Noninvasive stimulation methods perturb neural activity in healthy and neurologically impaired humans. By varying the stimulation protocols, we can enhance or suppress neural activity in targeted regions.

3.4 Structural Analysis of the Brain

We now turn to the methods used to analyze brain structure. Structural methods take advantage of the differences in physical properties that different tissues possess. For instance, the most noticeable thing in an X-ray is that bones appear starkly white and the surrounding structures vary in intensity from black to white. The density of biological material varies, and the absorption of X-ray radiation correlates with tissue density. In this section we introduce methods that exploit these properties to image different structural properties of the brain.

Visualizing the Gross Anatomy of the Brain

Computerized tomography (CT or **CAT)** scanning was the first method to offer an in vivo look at the human brain. In concept, this method was an extension of X-rays, an imaging technology developed at the start of the 20th century. While conventional X-rays compress three-dimensional objects into two dimensions, in a CT scan a computer constructs the 3-D perspective from a series of thin-sliced 2-D images. This method, introduced commercially in the 1970s, was an extremely important tool in the early days of cognitive neuroscience. It enabled researchers to pinpoint with considerable precision the locus of pathology following neurological insult and to characterize lesion–behavior relationships.

Although CT scanning continues to be an extremely important medical procedure for clinical purposes, **magnetic resonance imaging (MRI)** is now the preferred method for whole-brain imaging because it provides images of much higher resolution. MRI exploits the magnetic properties of atoms that make up organic tissue. One such atom that is pervasive in the brain, and indeed in all organic tissue, is hydrogen. The proton in a hydrogen atom is in constant motion, spinning about its principal axis. This motion creates a tiny magnetic field. In their normal state, the protons in a tissue are randomly oriented, unaffected by the Earth's weak magnetic field. An MRI system creates a powerful magnetic field within the scanner environment. This field, measured in tesla (T) units, typically ranges from 0.5 to 3 T in hospital scanners—orders of magnitude more powerful than the 0.00005-T strength of the Earth's magnetic field.

When someone is in the MRI scanner, a significant proportion of that person's protons become oriented parallel to the machine's strong magnetic field (**Figure 3.17a**). Radio waves then pass through the magnetized regions,

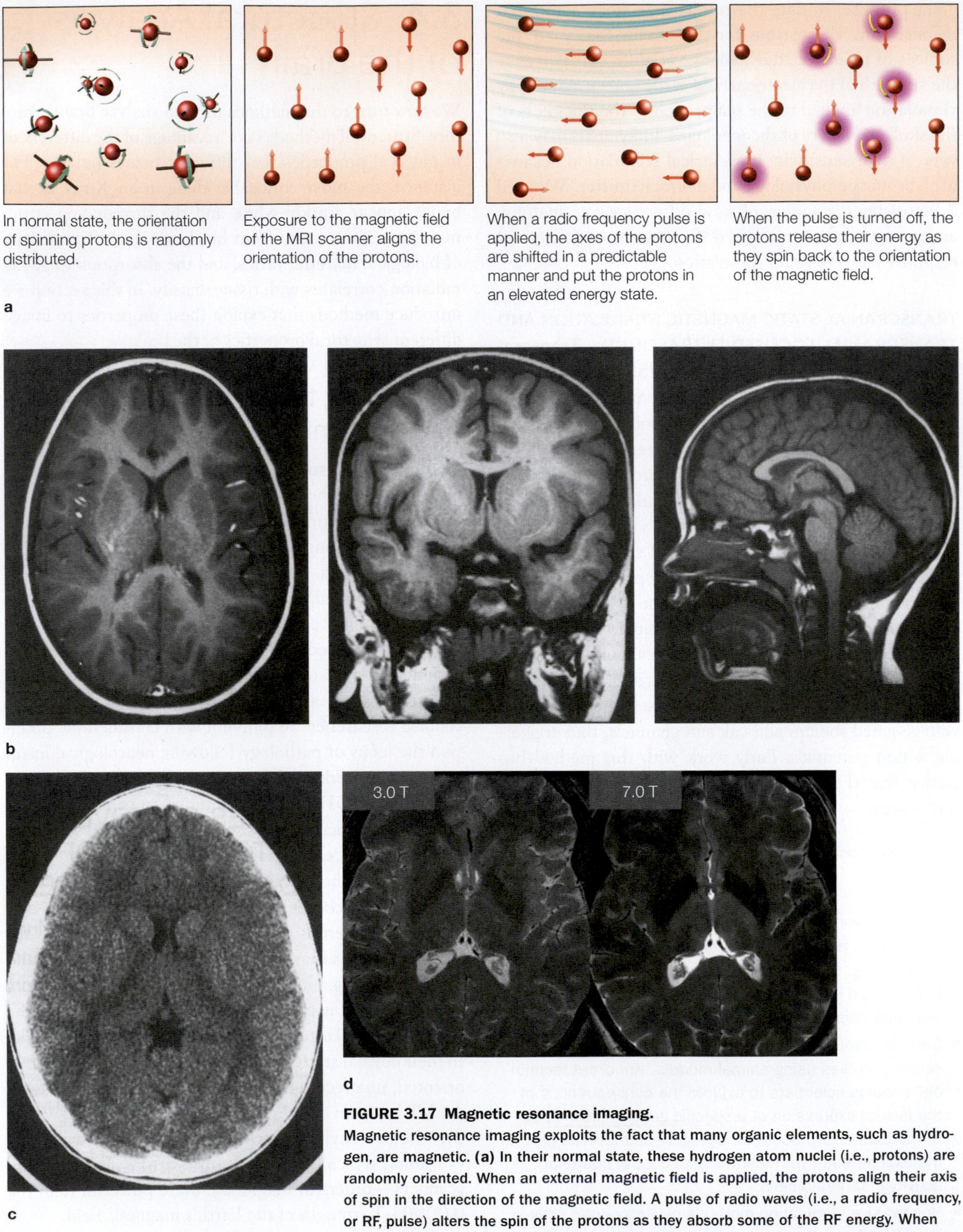

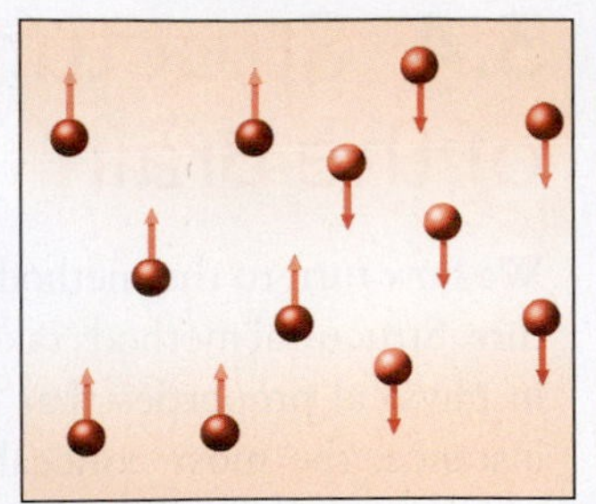
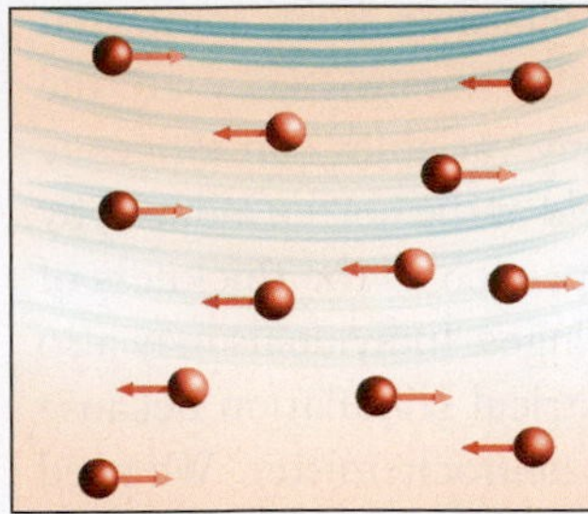
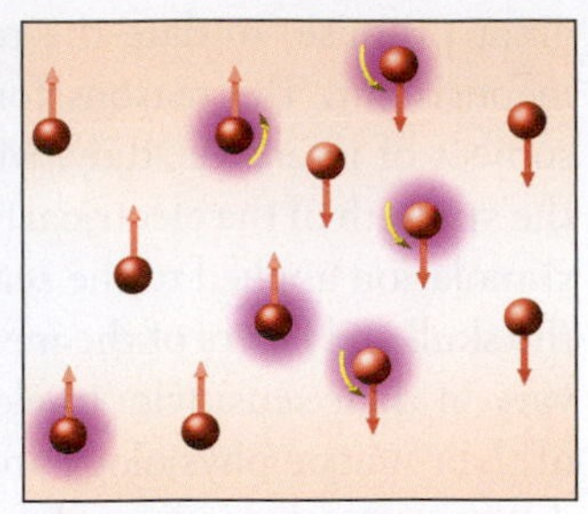

In normal state, the orientation of spinning protons is randomly distributed.

Exposure to the magnetic field of the MRI scanner aligns the orientation of the protons.

When a radio frequency pulse is applied, the axes of the protons are shifted in a predictable manner and put the protons in an elevated energy state.

When the pulse is turned off, the protons release their energy as they spin back to the orientation of the magnetic field.

a

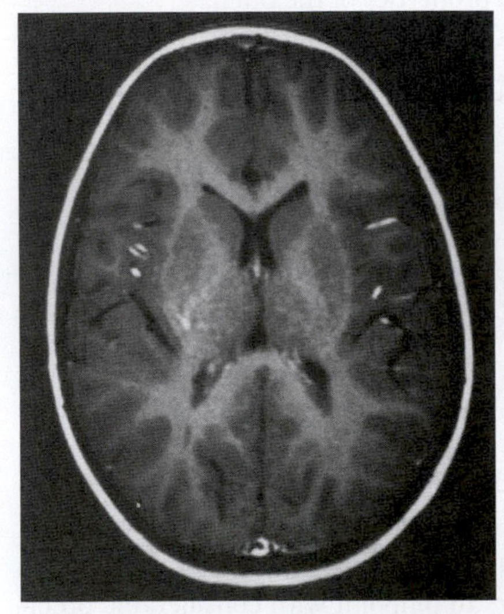
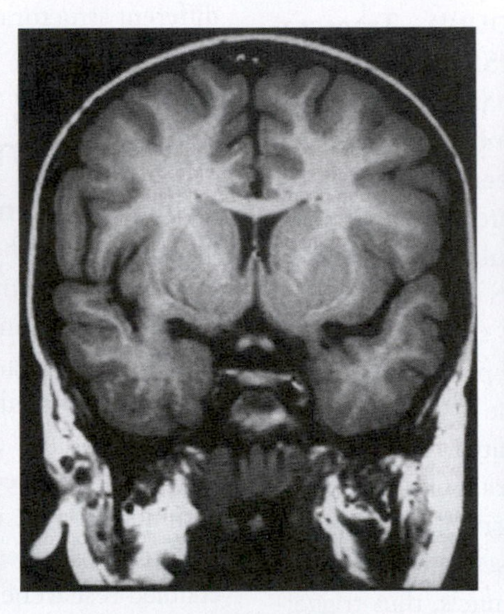
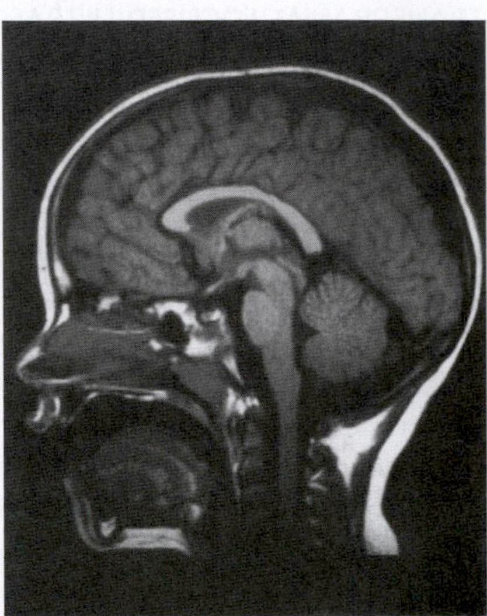

b

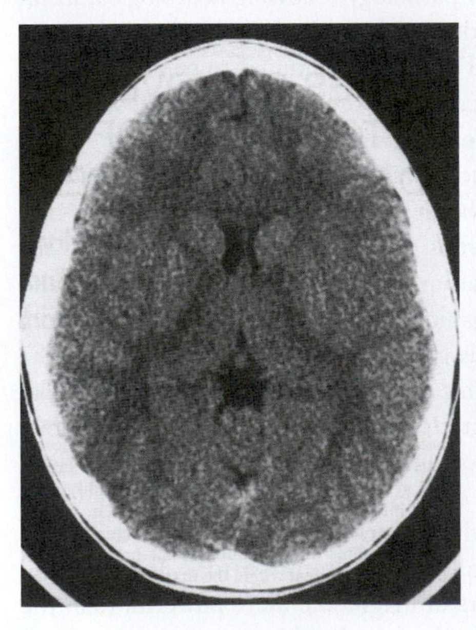

c

d

FIGURE 3.17 Magnetic resonance imaging.
Magnetic resonance imaging exploits the fact that many organic elements, such as hydrogen, are magnetic. **(a)** In their normal state, these hydrogen atom nuclei (i.e., protons) are randomly oriented. When an external magnetic field is applied, the protons align their axis of spin in the direction of the magnetic field. A pulse of radio waves (i.e., a radio frequency, or RF, pulse) alters the spin of the protons as they absorb some of the RF energy. When the RF pulse is turned off, the protons emit their own RF energy, which is detected by the MRI machine. The density of hydrogen atoms is different in white and gray matter, making it easy to visualize these regions. **(b)** Transverse, coronal, and sagittal MRI images. **(c)** Comparing this CT image to the transverse slice on the left in part (b) reveals the finer resolution offered by MRI. Both images show approximately the same level of the brain. **(d)** Resolution and clarity differences between 3.0-T and 7.0-T MRI images.

and as the protons absorb the energy in these waves, their orientation is perturbed in a predictable direction. Turning off the radio waves causes the absorbed energy to dissipate and the protons to rebound toward the orientation of the magnetic field. This synchronized rebound produces energy signals that detectors surrounding the head of the participant pick up. By systematically measuring the signals throughout the three-dimensional volume of the head, an MRI system can construct an image based on the distribution of the protons and other magnetic agents in the tissue. The distribution of water throughout the brain largely determines the hydrogen proton distribution, enabling MRI to clearly distinguish the brain's gray matter, white matter, and ventricles.

MRI scans (**Figure 3.17b**) provide a much clearer image of the brain than is possible with CT scans (**Figure 3.17c**). The reason for the improvement is that the density of protons is much greater in gray matter than in white matter. With MRI, it is easy to see the individual sulci and gyri of the cerebral cortex. A sagittal section at the midline reveals the impressive size of the corpus callosum. Standard MRI scans can resolve structures that are much smaller than 1 mm, enabling elegant views of small, subcortical structures such as the mammillary bodies or superior colliculus.

Even better spatial resolution is possible with more powerful scanners, and a few research centers now have 7-T MRI (**Figure 3.17d**). Almost ready for prime time, at least for research purposes, is a $270 million 11.75-T scanner, the INUMAC (Imaging of Neuro Disease Using High Field MR and Contrastophores) at the NeuroSpin center outside Paris. Its magnet weighs 132 tons! With a resolution of 0.1 mm, this system will allow visualization of the cortical layers.

Visualizing the Structural Connectivity of the Brain

A variant of traditional MRI is **diffusion tensor imaging (DTI)**. Used to study the anatomical structure of the axon tracts that form the brain's white matter, this method offers information about anatomical connectivity between regions. DTI takes advantage of the fact that all living tissue contains water molecules that are in continuous random motion (otherwise known as diffusion or Brownian motion). DTI is performed with an MRI scanner that measures the density and the motion of these water molecules and, taking into account the known diffusion characteristics of water, determines the boundaries that restrict water movement throughout the brain (Behrens et al., 2003).

Free diffusion of water is *isotropic*; that is, it occurs equally in all directions. In an anisotropic material, one that is directionally dependent, water molecules do not diffuse at the same speed in all directions. In the brain, anisotropy is greatest in axons because the myelin sheath creates a nearly pure lipid (fat) boundary. This boundary limits the directional flow of the water molecules to a much greater degree in white matter than in gray matter or cerebrospinal fluid. Specifically, water is much more likely to move in a direction parallel to the axons.

By introducing two large pulses to the magnetic field, MRI signals become sensitive to the diffusion of water. The first pulse determines the initial position of the protons carried by water. The second pulse, introduced after a short delay, provides a second image; presumably, each proton has moved during the delay, and the DTI procedure estimates the diffusion of the protons. To do this in a complex 3-D material such as the brain requires computation of a diffusion tensor, an array of numbers that estimate the diffusion from each point in the material. Mathematical procedures create 3-D models of variation in the flow direction (DaSilva et al., 2003). Because the flow of water is constrained by the axons, the resulting image reveals the major white matter tracts (**Figure 3.18**).

TAKE-HOME MESSAGES

- Computerized tomography (CT or CAT) and magnetic resonance imaging (MRI) provide 3-D images of the brain.
- The spatial resolution of MRI is superior to CT.
- Diffusion tensor imaging (DTI), performed with an MRI scanner, measures white matter pathways in the brain and provides information about anatomical connectivity between regions.

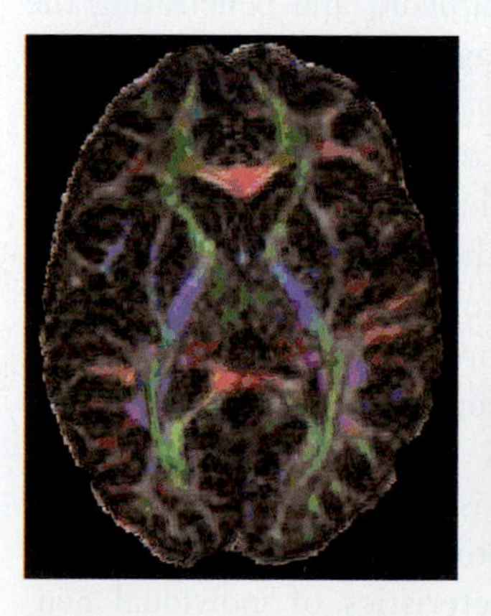

a

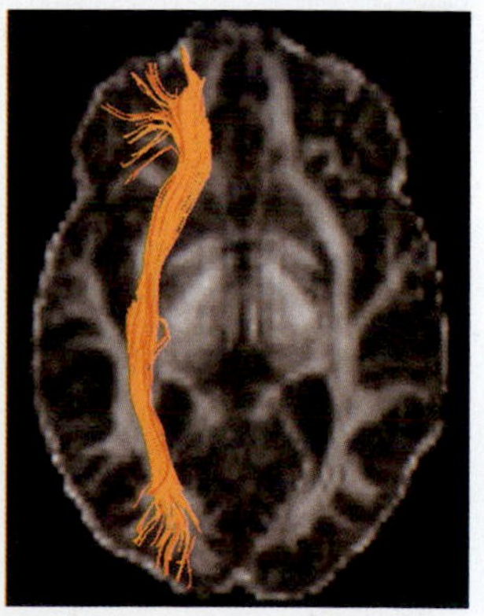

b

FIGURE 3.18 Diffusion tensor imaging.
(a) This axial slice of a human brain reveals the directionality and connectivity of the white matter. The colors correspond to the principal directions of the white matter tracts in each region. **(b)** DTI data can be analyzed to trace white matter connections in the brain. The tracts shown here form the inferior fronto-occipital fasciculus, which, as the name suggests, connects the visual cortex to the frontal lobe.

3.5 Methods to Measure Neural Activity

The fundamental building block of communication within the nervous system is the activity of neurons. This essential fact has inspired neuroscientists to develop many methods to measure these physiological events. Some methods isolate the activity of single neurons, while others measure the activity of groups of neurons, asking how their firing patterns interact with one another. We open with a brief discussion of the invasive methods to measure neuronal activity and then turn to the blossoming number of noninvasive methods used to study neural activity.

Single-Cell Neurophysiology in Animals

The development of methods for **single-cell recording** was perhaps the most important technological advance in the history of neuroscience. By measuring the action potentials produced by individual neurons in living animals, researchers could begin to uncover how the brain responds to sensory information, produces movement, and changes with learning.

To make a single-cell recording, a neurophysiologist inserts a thin electrode through a surgical opening in the skull into the cortex or deeper brain structures. When the electrode is near a neuronal membrane, changes in electrical activity can be measured (see Chapter 2). Although the surest way to guarantee that the electrode records the activity of a single cell is to record intracellularly, this technique is difficult, and penetrating the membrane frequently damages the cell. Thus, researchers typically place the electrode on the outside of the neuron to make single-cell recordings. There is no guarantee, however, that the changes in electrical potential at the electrode tip reflect the activity of a single neuron. More likely, the tip will record the activity of a small set of neurons. Computer algorithms can differentiate this pooled activity into the contributions from individual neurons.

The neurophysiologist is interested in what causes change in the synaptic activity of a neuron. To determine the response characteristics of individual neurons, their activity is correlated with a given stimulus pattern (input) or behavior (output). The primary goal of single-cell-recording experiments is to determine which experimental manipulations produce a consistent change in the response rate of an isolated cell. For instance, does the cell increase its firing rate when the animal moves its arm? If so, is this change specific to movements in a particular direction? Does the firing rate for that movement depend on the outcome of the action (e.g., reaching for a food morsel or reaching to scratch an itch)? Equally interesting, what makes the cell decrease its response rate?

Since neurons are constantly firing even in the absence of stimulation or movement, the researcher measures these changes against a backdrop of activity, and this baseline activity varies widely from one brain area to another. For example, some cells within the basal ganglia have spontaneous firing rates of over 100 spikes per second, whereas cells in another basal ganglia region have a baseline rate of only 1 spike per second. Further confounding the analysis of the experimental measurements, these spontaneous firing levels fluctuate.

Neuroscientists have made single-cell recordings from most regions of the brain across a wide range of nonhuman species. For sensory neurons, the researcher might manipulate the input by changing the type of stimulus presented to the animal. For motor neurons, the researcher might make output recordings as the animal performs a task or moves about. Some significant advances in neurophysiology have come about as researchers have probed higher brain centers to examine changes in cellular activity related to goals, emotions, and rewards.

Researchers often obtain single-cell recordings from a cluster of neurons in a targeted area of interest. For example, to study visual function the researcher inserts the electrode into a cortical region containing cells that respond to visual stimulation (**Figure 3.19a**). Because the activity of a single neuron is quite variable, it is important to record the activity from many trials in which a given stimulus is presented (**Figure 3.19b**). The data are represented in what is called a *raster plot*, where each row represents a single trial and the action potentials are marked as ticks. To give a sense of the average response of the neuron over the course of a trial, the researcher sums the data and presents it as a bar graph called a *peristimulus histogram*. A histogram allows scientists to visualize the rate and timing of neuronal spike discharges in relation to an external stimulus or event.

A single cell is not responsive to all visual stimuli. A number of stimulus parameters might correlate with the variation in the cell's firing rate; examples include the shape of the stimulus, its color, and whether it is moving (see Chapter 5). An important factor is the location of the stimulus. As Figure 3.19a shows, all visually sensitive cells respond to stimuli in only a limited region of space. This region of space is that cell's **receptive field**. The figure shows a neuron that responds to stimuli presented in the upper right portion of the visible field. For other neurons, the stimulus may have to be in the lower right.

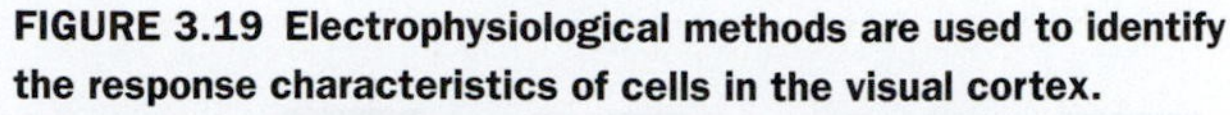

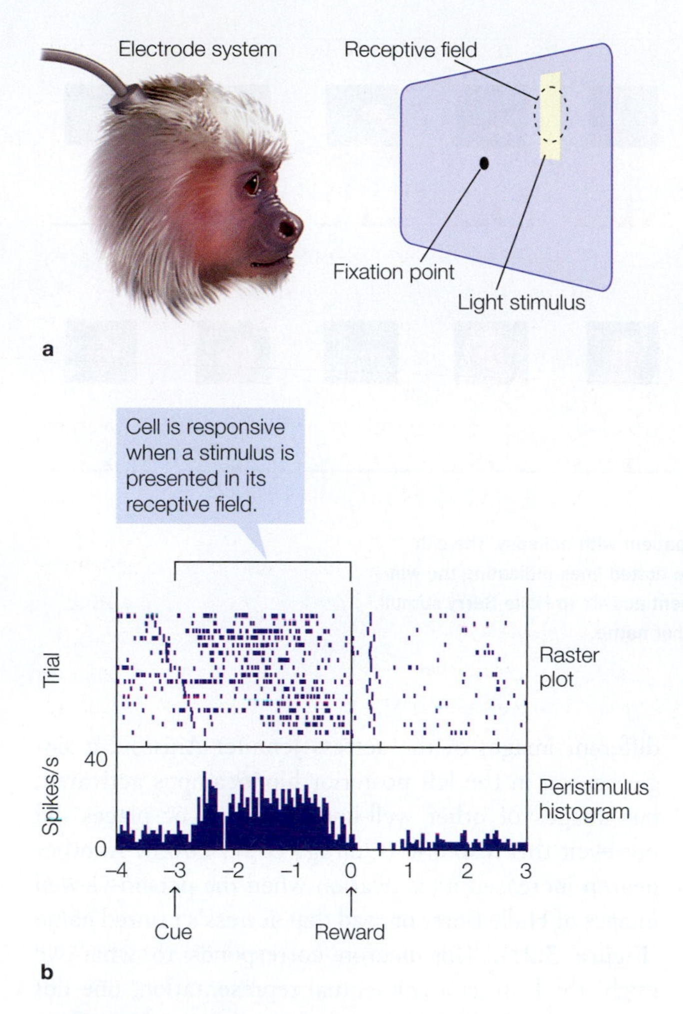

FIGURE 3.19 Electrophysiological methods are used to identify the response characteristics of cells in the visual cortex. (a) An electrode is attached to a neuron in the optical cortex. While the activity of a single cell is monitored, the monkey is required to maintain fixation, and stimuli are presented at various positions in its field of view. The yellow region indicates the region of space that activated a particular cell. This region is the cell's receptive field. (b) A raster plot shows action potentials as a function of time. Each line of a raster plot represents a single trial, and the action potentials are marked as ticks in a row. In this example, the trials are when the light was presented in the cell's receptive field. The graph includes data from before the start of the trial, providing a picture of the baseline firing rate of the neuron. It then shows changes in firing rate as the stimulus is presented and the animal responds. To give a sense of the average response of the neuron over the course of a trial, the data are summed and presented as a peristimulus histogram below.

Neighboring cells have at least partially overlapping receptive fields. As you traverse a region of visually responsive cells, there is an orderly relation between the receptive-field properties of these cells and the external world. Neurons represent external space in a continuous manner across the cortical surface: Neighboring cells have receptive fields of neighboring regions of external space. As such, cells form a topographic representation—an orderly mapping between an external dimension, such as spatial location, and the neural representation of that dimension. In vision, we refer to topographic representations as **retinotopic maps.** Cell activity within a retinotopic map correlates with the location of the stimulus (**Figure 3.20**).

With the advent of the single-cell method, neuroscientists hoped they would finally solve the mysteries of brain function. All they needed was a catalog of contributions by different cells. Yet it soon became clear that the aggregate behavior of neurons might be more than just the sum of its parts. Researchers realized that they might better understand the function of an area by identifying correlations in the firing patterns of groups of neurons rather than identifying the response properties of each individual neuron. This idea inspired single-cell physiologists to develop new techniques that enabled them to record many neurons simultaneously: **multiunit recording.**

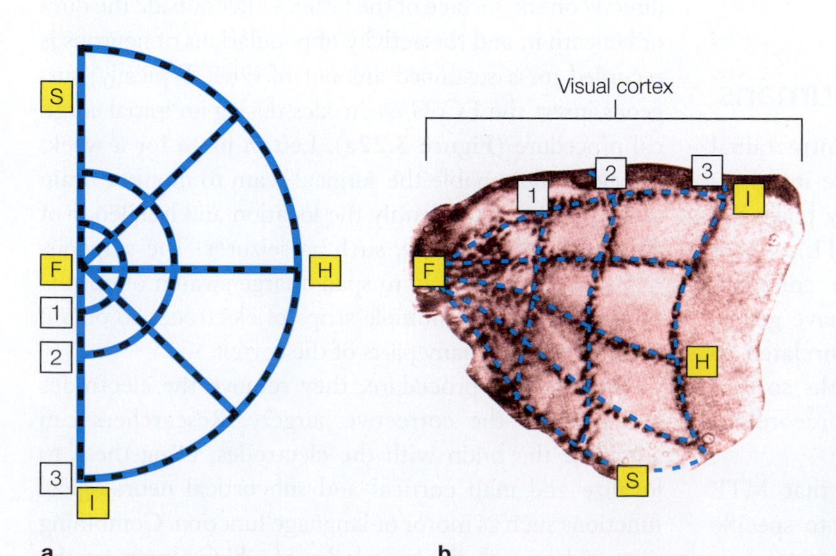

FIGURE 3.20 Topographic maps of the visual cortex. In the visual cortex the receptive fields of the cells define a retinotopic map. While viewing the stimulus (a), a monkey was injected with a radioactive agent. (b) Metabolically active cells in the visual cortex absorb the agent, revealing how the topography of the retina is preserved across the striate cortex.

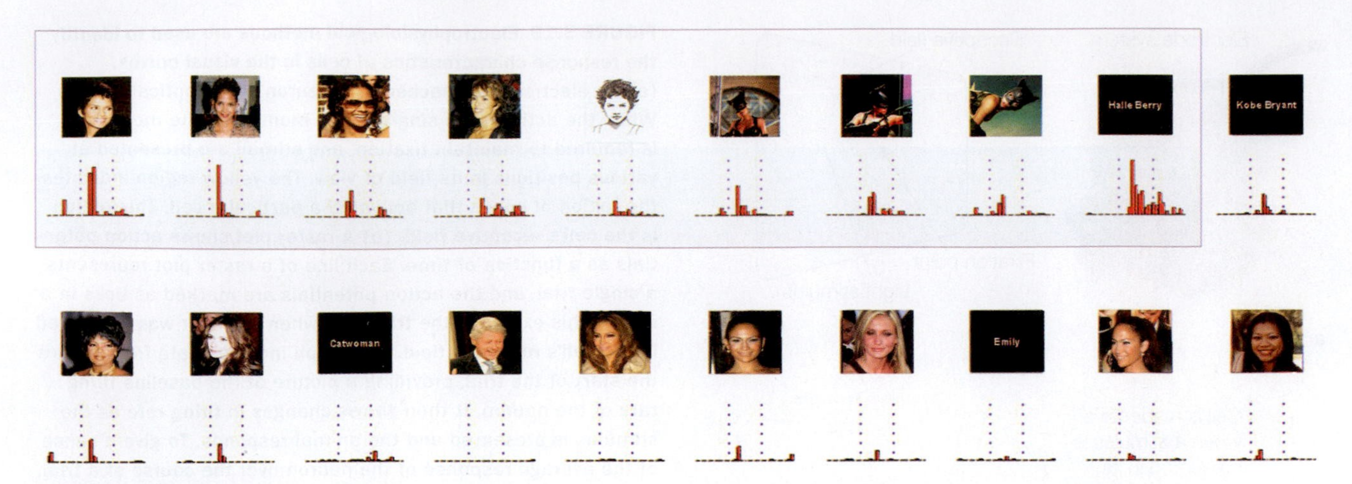

FIGURE 3.21 The Halle Berry neuron?
Recordings were made from a single neuron in the hippocampus of a patient with epilepsy. The cell activity in response to each picture is shown in the histograms, with the dotted lines indicating the window within which the stimulus was presented. This cell showed prominent activity to Halle Berry stimuli, including photos of the actress, photos of her as Catwoman, and even her name.

A pioneering study using this approach revealed how the rat hippocampus represents spatial information (M. A. Wilson & McNaughton, 1994). By looking at the pattern of activity from simultaneous recordings taken from about 150 cells, the researchers showed how the rat coded both a space and its own experience in traversing that space. Today, it is common to record from over 400 cells simultaneously (Lebedev & Nicolelis, 2006). As we will see in Chapter 8, researchers use multiunit recordings from motor areas of the brain to enable animals to control artificial limbs just by thinking about movement. This dramatic medical advance may change the way we design rehabilitation programs for paraplegics. For example, we can obtain multiunit recordings while people think about actions they would like to perform, and computers can analyze this information to control robotic or artificial limbs.

Invasive Neurophysiology in Humans

As mentioned earlier, surgeons may insert intracranial electrodes to localize an abnormality before its surgical resection. For epilepsy, surgeons usually place the electrodes in the medial temporal lobe (MTL), where the focus of generalized seizures is most common. Many patients with implanted electrodes have generously volunteered for research purposes unrelated to their surgery, engaging in experimental tasks so that researchers can obtain neurophysiological recordings in humans.

Itzhak Fried and his colleagues found that MTL neurons in humans can respond selectively to specific familiar images. For instance, when one patient saw different images of the actress Jennifer Aniston, a single neuron in the left posterior hippocampus activated, but images of other well-known people or places did not elicit this response (Quiroga et al., 2005). Another neuron increased its activation when the person viewed images of Halle Berry or read that actress's printed name (**Figure 3.21**). This neuron corresponds to what we might think of as a conceptual representation, one not tied to a particular sensory modality (e.g., vision). Consistent with this idea, cells like these also activate when the person imagines Jennifer Aniston or Halle Berry or thinks about movies these actresses have performed in (Cerf et al., 2010).

A different invasive neurophysiological method used to study the human brain is **electrocorticography (ECoG)**. In this procedure a grid or strip of electrodes is placed directly on the surface of the brain, either outside the dura or beneath it, and the activity of populations of neurons is recorded for a sustained amount of time. Typically, surgeons insert the ECoG electrodes during an initial surgical procedure (**Figure 3.22a**). Left in place for a week, the electrodes enable the surgical team to monitor brain activity in order to identify the location and frequency of abnormal brain activity, such as seizures. The surgeons may place a single grid to span a large swatch of cortex, or they may insert multiple strips of electrodes to obtain recordings from many parts of the cortex.

In a second procedure, they remove the electrodes and perform the corrective surgery. Researchers can stimulate the brain with the electrodes, using them to localize and map cortical and subcortical neurological functions such as motor or language function. Combining seizure data with the knowledge of which structures the

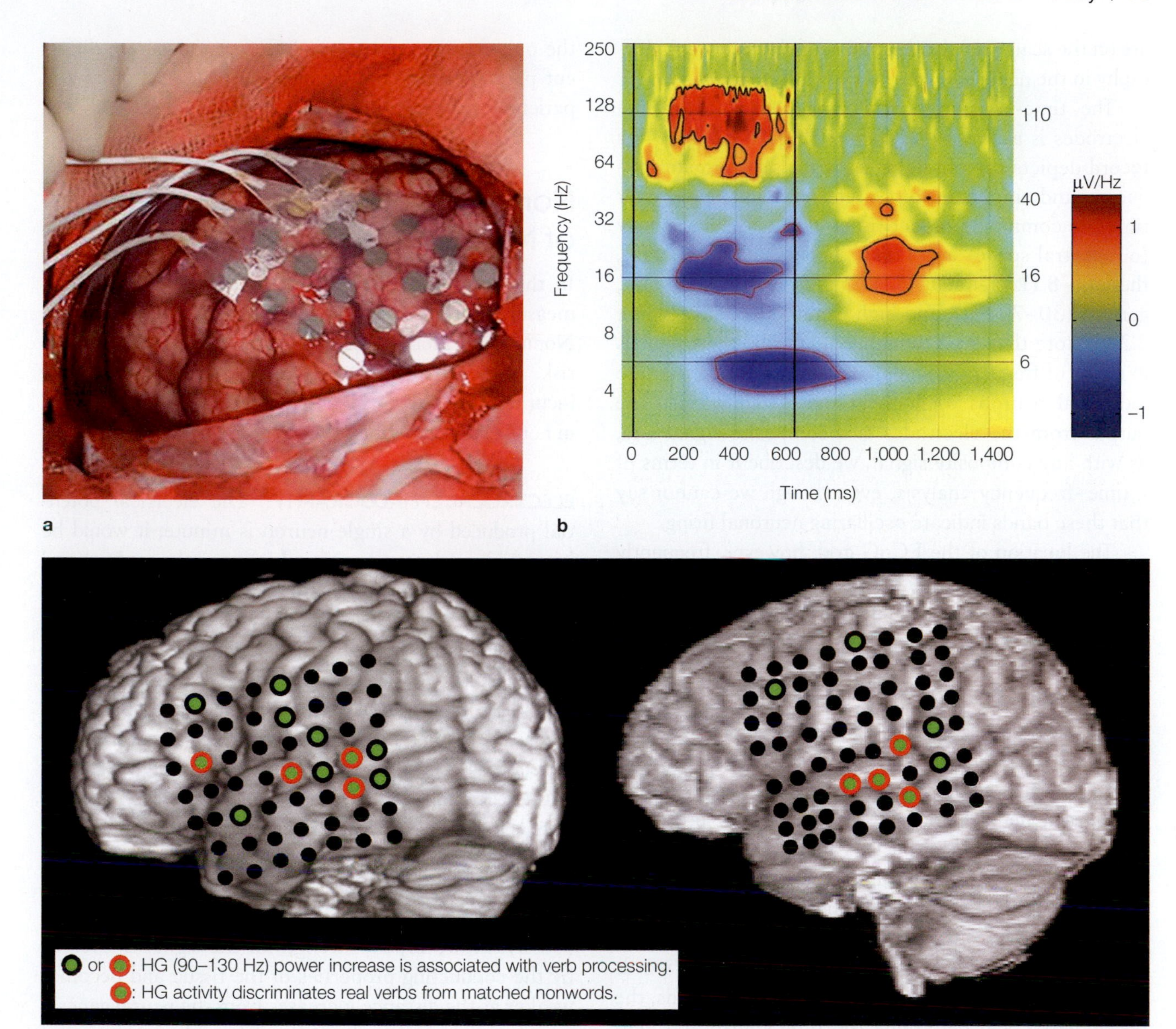

FIGURE 3.22 Structural MRI renderings with electrode locations for four study participants, and ECoG response from one electrode.

(a) Implant procedure for ECoG. **(b)** Event related time–frequency plot. The verb was presented at time 0. Verb onset (0 ms) and offset (637 ms) are marked by solid black vertical lines. Color represents power (as indicated by the bar on the right, where blue is the lowest activity and red the highest) of a particular frequency at various times both before and after the stimulus was presented. Note the initial strong HG (~110 Hz) power increase (red) and beta (~16 Hz) power decrease (blue), followed by very late beta increase. **(c)** These structural MRI images indicate the position of the electrode grid on four patients. Electrodes that exhibited an increase in high gamma (HG) "power," or activity, following the presentation of verbs are shown in green. Red circles indicate electrodes where HG activity was also observed when the verb condition was compared to acoustically matched nonwords. Verb processing is distributed across cortical areas in the superior temporal cortex and frontal lobe.

surgery will affect enables the surgeon to make a risk–benefit profile.

Because the implants are in place for a week, there is time to conduct studies in which the person performs experimental tasks. Unlike those in single-cell neurophysiology, ECoG electrodes are quite large, meaning that the method is always based on measurement of the activity of populations of neurons. Nevertheless, the spatial and temporal resolution of ECoG is excellent because the electrodes sit directly on the brain, resulting in minimal attenuation or distortion; in other words, ECoG produces a level of clarity that is not possible when the electrodes are on the scalp (see the discussion of electroencephalography in the next section).

The time-varying record of the signals from the electrodes is an *electrocorticogram* (**Figure 3.22b**). This record depicts the physiological signals in terms of frequency and amplitude (often referred to as *power*) over time. A common practice is to divide the frequency (or spectral space) into bands such as delta (1–4 Hz), theta (4–8 Hz), alpha (7.5–12.5 Hz), beta (13–30 Hz), gamma (30–70 Hz), and high gamma (>70 Hz; Figure 3.24). Note that even though we describe these signals in terms of frequency bands, we cannot assume that the individual neurons oscillate at these frequencies. The output from the electrodes is a composite signal and, as with any composite signal, we describe it in terms of a time–frequency analysis, even though we cannot say that these bands indicate oscillating neuronal firing.

The location of the ECoG grid, however, frequently dictates the experimental question in ECoG studies. For example, Robert Knight and his colleagues (Canolty et al., 2007) studied patients who had ECoG grids that spanned temporal and frontal regions of the left hemisphere (**Figure 3.22c**). They monitored the electrical response when these people processed words. By examining the signal changes across several frequency bands, the researchers could depict the successive recruitment of different neural regions 100 ms after they presented the stimulus. The signal for very high-frequency components of the ECoG signal (high-gamma range) increased over the temporal cortex. Later they observed an activity change over the frontal cortex.

By comparing trials in which the stimuli were words and trials in which the stimuli were nonsense sounds, the researchers could determine the time course and neural regions involved in distinguishing speech from nonspeech. With multiple grids implanted, researchers have the opportunity to compare ECoG activity from different parts of the brain simultaneously (e.g., frontal and parietal regions).

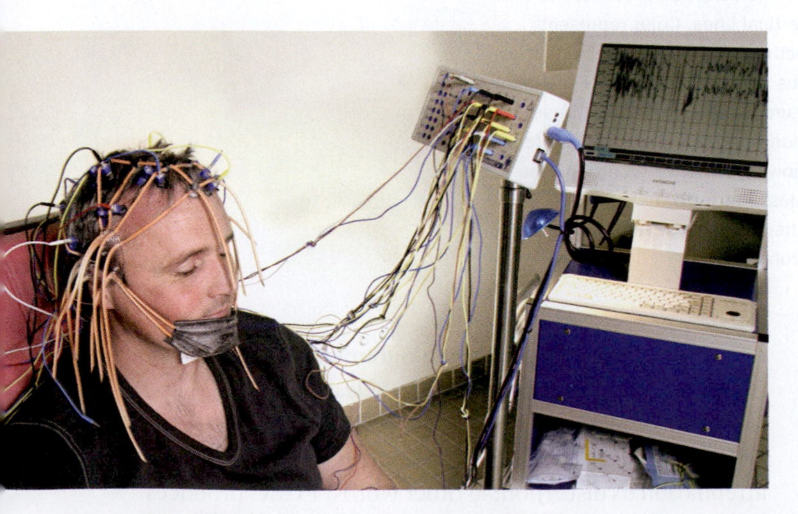

FIGURE 3.23 Person wired up for an EEG study.

Noninvasive Electrical Recording of Neural Activity

In this section we turn to methods that noninvasively measure electrical signals arising from neural activity. Noninvasive methods are much more common, lower-risk, and less expensive than invasive methods, and they incur few side effects. Healthy individuals can participate in noninvasive experiments.

ELECTROENCEPHALOGRAPHY The electrical potential produced by a single neuron is minute; it would be impossible to detect that signal from an electrode placed on the scalp. When populations of neurons are active, they generate a much larger composite electrical signal. While we can measure these population signals with great fidelity via ECoG electrodes, we can also measure them noninvasively by using electrodes placed on the scalp, a method known as **electroencephalography (EEG)**. These surface electrodes, usually 20 to 256 of them embedded in an elastic cap (**Figure 3.23**), record signals from the cortex (and subcortex).

We can record the electrical potential at the scalp because the tissues of the brain, skull, and scalp passively conduct the electrical currents produced by synaptic activity. However, the strength of the signal is affected by the conducting properties of the tissue and becomes weaker as the distance increases from the neural generators to the recording electrodes. Thus, the resolution of EEG signals is considerably weaker than that obtained with ECoG. Of course, the biggest advantage of EEG is that it does not require brain surgery, making it a very popular tool for obtaining physiological signals with superb temporal resolution.

Many years of research have shown that the power in these bands is an excellent indicator of the state of the brain (and person!). For example, an increase in alpha power is associated with reduced states of attention; an increase in theta power is associated with engagement in a cognitively demanding task. Because we have come to understand that predictable EEG signatures are associated with different behavioral states, electroencephalography has many important clinical applications. In deep sleep, for example, slow, high-amplitude oscillations characterize the EEG, presumably resulting from rhythmic changes in the activity states of large groups of neurons (**Figure 3.24**). In other phases of sleep and in various wakeful states, the pattern changes, but always in

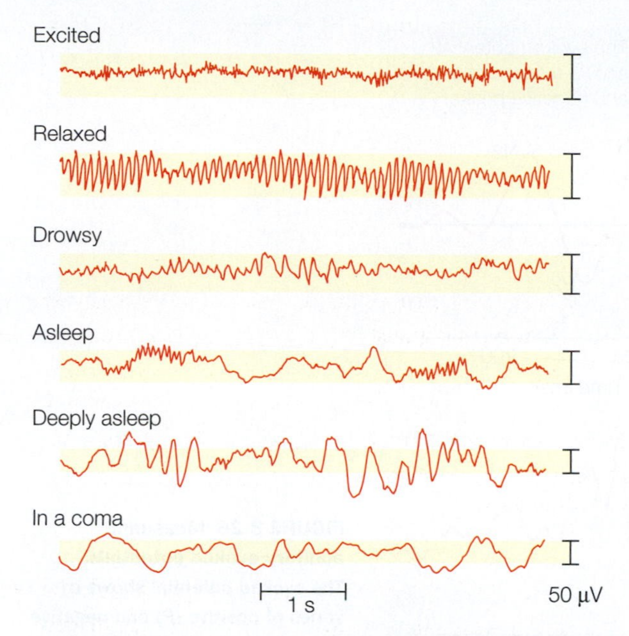

FIGURE 3.24 EEG profiles obtained during various states of consciousness.
Recorded from the scalp, the electrical potential exhibits a waveform with time on the *x*-axis and voltage on the *y*-axis. Over time, the waveform oscillates between a positive and negative voltage. Very slow oscillations dominate in deep sleep, or what is called the delta wave. When awake, the oscillations occur much faster when the person is relaxed (alpha) or reflect a combination of many components when the person is excited.

a predictable manner. Because normal EEG patterns are consistent among individuals, we can detect abnormalities in brain function from EEG recordings. For example, EEG provides valuable information in the assessment and treatment of epilepsy (Figure 3.9b) and sleep disorders.

EVENT-RELATED POTENTIALS The data collected with an EEG system can also be used to examine how a particular task modulates brain activity. This method requires extracting the response evoked by an external event, such as the onset of a stimulus or a movement, from the global EEG signal. To do this, we align EEG traces from a series of trials relative to the event and then average them. This alignment eliminates variations in the brain's electrical activity unrelated to the events of interest. The evoked response, or **event-related potential (ERP)**, is a tiny signal embedded in the ongoing EEG triggered by the stimulus or movement. By averaging the traces, investigators can extract this signal, which reflects neural activity specifically related to the sensory, motor, or cognitive event that evoked it—hence the name (**Figure 3.25**).

ERP graphs show the average of EEG waves time-locked to specific events. We name a component of the waveform according to its polarity, *N* for negative and *P* for positive, and the time the wave appeared after stimulus onset. Thus, a wave tagged N100 is a negative wave that appeared about 100 ms after a stimulus. Unfortunately, there are some idiosyncrasies in the literature. Some researchers label components to reflect their order of appearance. Thus, N1 can refer to the first negative peak (as in Figure 3.26). Also be careful when looking at the wave polarity, because some researchers plot negative in the upward direction and others in the downward direction.

Many components of the ERP have been associated with specific psychological processes. Components observed in the first 50 to 100 ms are strongly linked to sensory processing, making them an important tool for clinicians evaluating the integrity of sensory pathways. Attentional states can modulate ERPs that appear 100 ms after stimulus presentation. Two early ones, the N100 and P100, are associated with selective attention. An unexpected stimulus, even if task-irrelevant (e.g., a G tone in a series of C tones while the person is watching a silent movie), elicits an N200 ERP, the so-called mismatch negativity component. When the instruction is

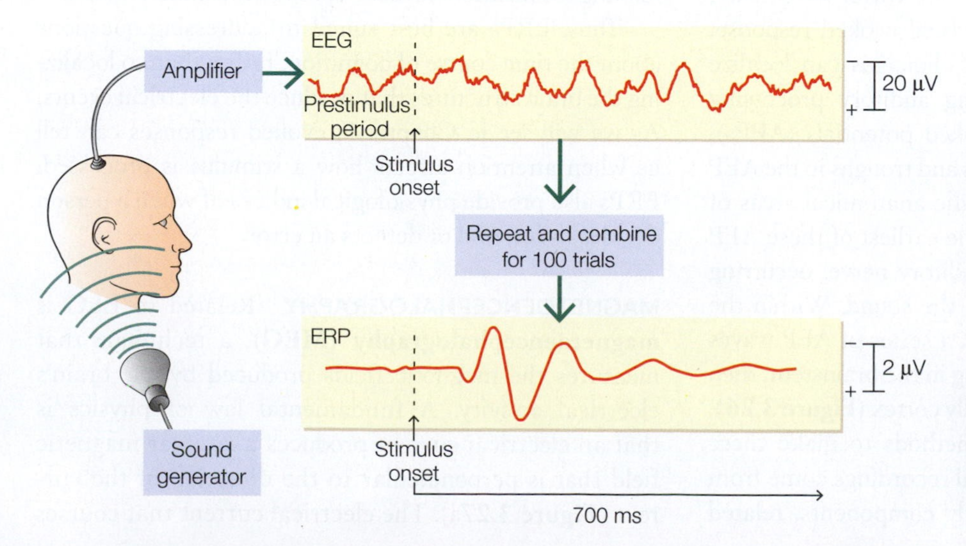

FIGURE 3.25 Recording an ERP.
The relatively small electrical responses to specific events can be observed only if the EEG traces are averaged over a series of trials. The large background oscillations of the EEG trace make it impossible to detect the evoked response to the sensory stimulus from a single trial. Averaging across tens or hundreds of trials, however, removes the background EEG, leaving the ERP. Time is plotted on the *x*-axis and voltage on the *y*-axis. Note the difference in scale between the EEG and ERP waveforms.

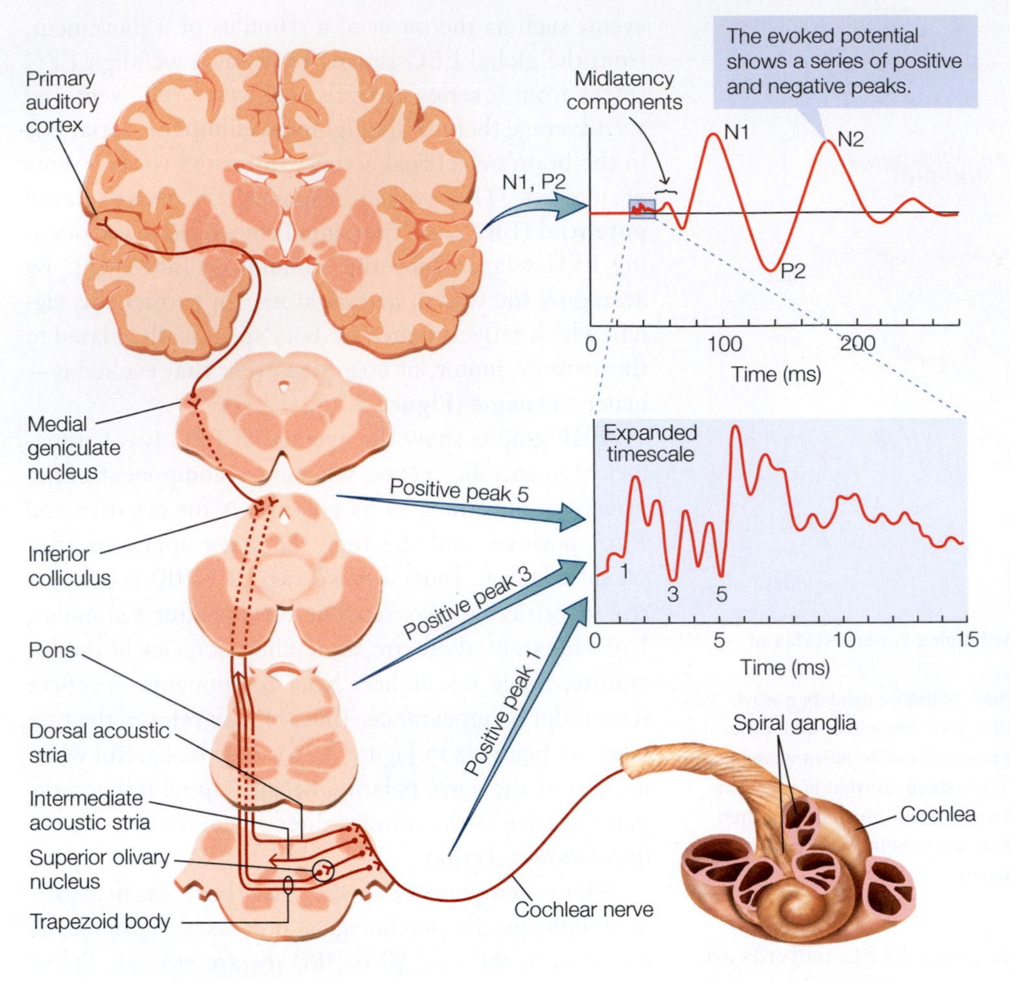

FIGURE 3.26 Measuring auditory evoked potentials. The evoked potential shows a series of positive (P) and negative (N) peaks at predictable points in time. Here components are labeled to reflect their order of appearance, and N1 refers to the first negative peak. In this AEP, the early peaks are invariant and have been linked to neural activity in specific brain structures. Later peaks are task dependent, and localization of their source has been a subject of much investigation and debate.

to attend to a particular stimulus (e.g., C notes, but not G notes), the appearance of the target elicits a P300 in the participant's EEG, especially if the target stimulus is relatively rare.

ERPs also provide an important tool for clinicians. For example, the visual evoked potential can be useful in diagnosing multiple sclerosis, a disorder that leads to demyelination. When demyelination occurs in the optic nerve, the electrical signal does not travel as quickly, delaying the early peaks of the visual evoked response. Similarly, in the auditory system clinicians can localize tumors compressing or damaging auditory processing areas by the use of auditory evoked potentials (AEPs), because characteristic wave peaks and troughs in the AEP arise from neural activity in specific anatomical areas of the ascending auditory system. The earliest of these AEP waves indicates activity in the auditory nerve, occurring within just a few milliseconds of the sound. Within the first 20 to 30 ms after the sound, a series of AEP waves indicates, in sequence, neural firing in the brainstem, then midbrain, then thalamus, and finally cortex (**Figure 3.26**).

Note that we use indirect methods to make these localizations; that is, the electrical recordings come from the surface of the scalp. For early components, related to the transmission of signals along sensory pathways, we infer the neural generators from the findings of other studies that use direct recording techniques and from the amount of time required for neuronal signals to travel. This approach is not possible when researchers look at evoked responses generated by cortical structures. The auditory cortex relays its message to many cortical areas, which all contribute to the measured evoked response, making localization of these components much harder.

Thus, ERPs are best suited to addressing questions about the time course of cognition, rather than to localizing the brain structures that produce the electrical events. As we will see in Chapter 7, evoked responses can tell us when attention affects how a stimulus is processed. ERPs also provide physiological indices of when a person decides to respond or detects an error.

MAGNETOENCEPHALOGRAPHY Related to EEG is **magnetoencephalography (MEG)**, a technique that measures the magnetic fields produced by the brain's electrical activity. A fundamental law of physics is that an electrical current produces a circular magnetic field that is perpendicular to the direction of the current (**Figure 3.27a**). The electrical current that courses

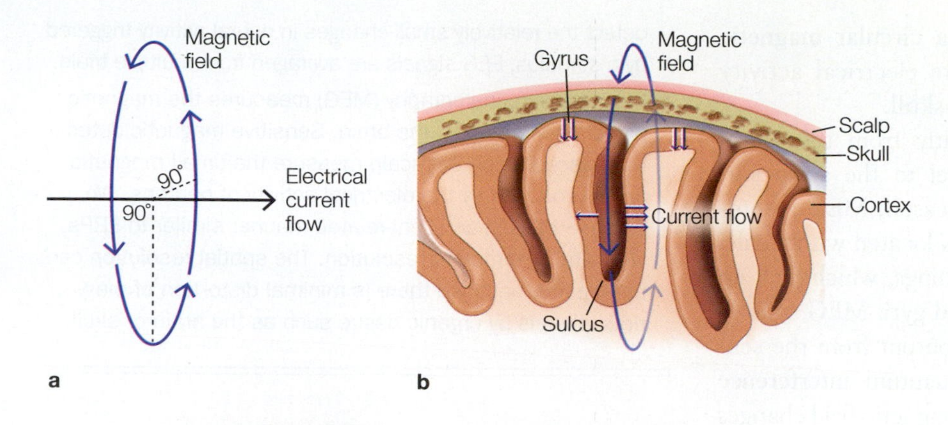

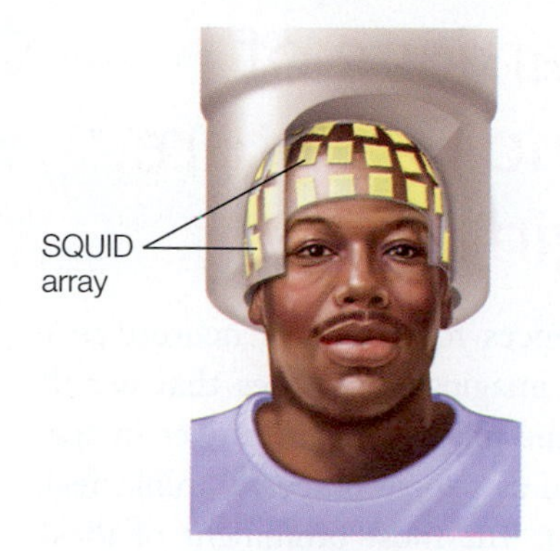

c Subject undergoing MEG procedure

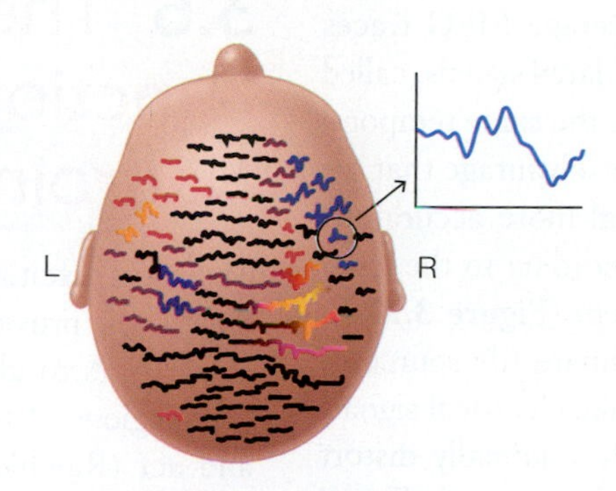

d MEG analysis of a response to a tone

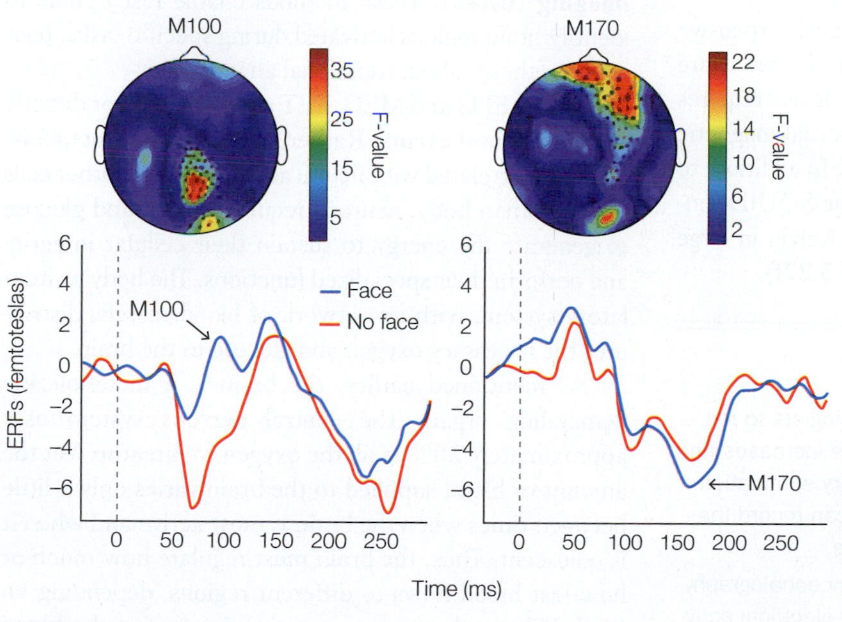

e Face vs. no face

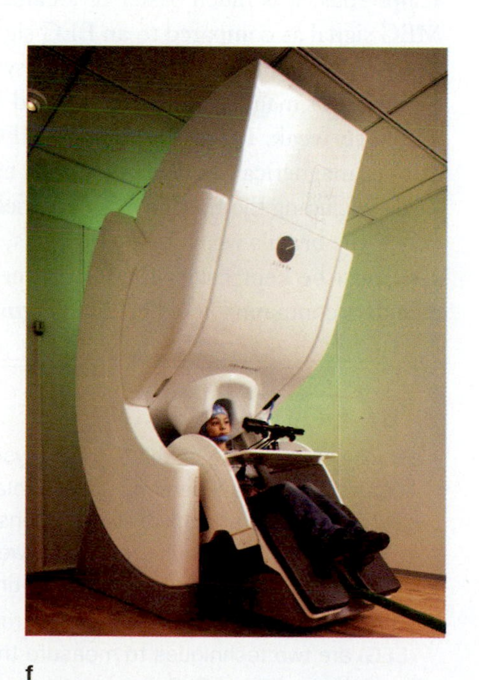

f

FIGURE 3.27 Magnetoencephalography as a noninvasive presurgical mapping procedure.
(a) Electrical current produces a magnetic field perpendicular to the flow of that current. (b) A magnetic field is generated by intracellular currents in apical dendrites. Those that run parallel to the scalp surface are most easily measured and tend to be in the cortical sulci. (c) MEG sensor helmet. (d) Plot of ERFs (produced by repeated tactile stimulation of the finger) for all sensors arranged topographically according to their position in the helmet. (e) Time course (bottom) and cortical distribution (top) of ERFs when people view faces or scrambled images. Faces produce a positive deflection of the ERF over posterior cortex at 100 ms and a large negative deflection over frontal cortex at 170 ms. (f) The MEG system.

through a neuron also produces a circular magnetic field. Thus, MEG devices measure electrical activity that is parallel to the surface of the skull.

This signal comes predominantly from the apical dendrites that are oriented parallel to the scalp surface in the cortical sulci. For this reason, MEG recordings come mainly from the neurons located within sulci (**Figure 3.27b**), unlike EEG recordings, which pick up voltage changes from both sulci and gyri. MEG sensors are arrayed in a helmet, with the output from the sensors linked to superconducting quantum interference devices (SQUIDs) that record the magnetic field changes (**Figure 3.27c**).

As with EEG, we record and average MEG traces over a series of trials to obtain event-related signals, called *event-related fields (ERFs)*. ERFs have the same temporal resolution as ERPs, but they have the advantage that we can estimate the source of the signal more accurately. ERFs are plotted topographically according to the location of the sensor that generated them (**Figure 3.27d**), and topoplots can be created to estimate the source of the MEG signal (**Figure 3.27e**). Unlike electrical signals detected by EEG, MEG signals only minimally distort magnetic fields as they pass through the brain, skull, and scalp. Thus, it is much easier to localize the source of a MEG signal as compared to an EEG signal.

MEG's major limitation is that the system is expensive because the magnetic fields generated by the brain are extremely weak. To be effective, the MEG device requires a room magnetically shielded from all external magnetic fields, including the Earth's magnetic field. In addition, to detect the brain's weak magnetic fields, the SQUID sensors must be kept colder than 4 degrees Kelvin in large cylinders containing liquid helium (**Figure 3.27f**).

TAKE-HOME MESSAGES

- Single-cell recording enables neurophysiologists to record from individual neurons and correlate increases and decreases in neuronal activity with sensory stimulation or behavior. With multiunit recording, we can record the activity of many neurons at the same time.
- Electrocorticography (ECoG) and electroencephalography (EEG) are two techniques to measure the electrical activity of the brain. In ECoG, the electrodes sit directly on the brain; in EEG, the electrodes are on the scalp. These methods can measure endogenous changes in electrical activity, as well as changes triggered by specific events (e.g., stimuli or movements). Although the resolution of ECoG signals is much greater than that of EEG, it is used only in people undergoing neurosurgery.
- An event-related potential (ERP) is a change in electrical activity that is time-locked to specific events, such as the presentation of a stimulus or the onset of a response. To detect the relatively small changes in neural activity triggered by a stimulus, EEG signals are averaged from multiple trials.
- Magnetoencephalography (MEG) measures the magnetic signals generated by the brain. Sensitive magnetic detectors placed along the scalp measure the small magnetic fields produced by the electrical activity of neurons. We can use MEG in an event-related manner similar to ERPs, with similar temporal resolution. The spatial resolution can be superior because there is minimal distortion of magnetic signals by organic tissue such as the brain or skull.

3.6 The Marriage of Function and Structure: Neuroimaging

The most exciting advances for cognitive neuroscience have been provided by imaging techniques that enable researchers to identify the physiological changes in specific regions of the brain as people perceive, think, feel, and act (Raichle, 1994). The most prominent of these neuroimaging methods are **positron emission tomography (PET)** and **functional magnetic resonance imaging (fMRI)**. These methods enable researchers to identify brain regions activated during specific tasks, testing hypotheses about functional anatomy.

Unlike EEG and MEG, PET and fMRI do not directly measure neural events. Rather, they measure metabolic changes correlated with neural activity. Like all other cells of the human body, neurons require oxygen and glucose to generate the energy to sustain their cellular integrity and perform their specialized functions. The body's circulatory system, with its network of blood vessels, distributes the necessary oxygen and glucose to the brain.

As mentioned earlier, the brain is a metabolically demanding organ. The central nervous system uses approximately 20% of all the oxygen we breathe. Yet the amount of blood supplied to the brain varies only a little between times when the brain is most active and when it is quiescent. Thus, the brain must regulate how much or how fast blood flows to different regions, depending on need. When a brain area is active, increasing the blood flow to that region provides it with more oxygen and glucose at the expense of other parts of the brain. PET and fMRI can detect this change in blood flow, known as a **hemodynamic response**.

When considering these methods for recording neural activity, keep in mind that they are essentially correlational. In order to make causal inferences, we combine them with other methods, which we will discuss toward the end of the chapter.

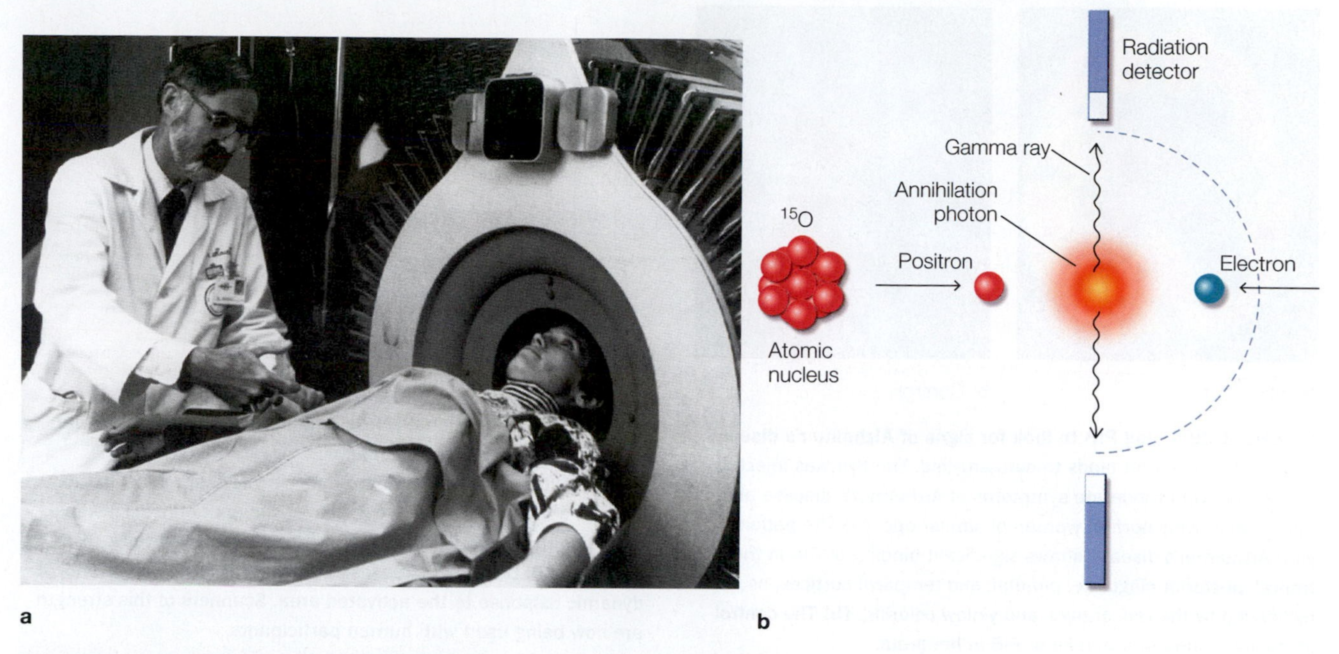

FIGURE 3.28 Positron emission tomography.
(a) PET scanning enables the measurement of metabolic activity in the human brain. (b) In the most common form of PET, water labeled with radioactive oxygen, ^{15}O, is injected into the participant. As positrons break off from this unstable isotope, they collide with electrons. A by-product of this collision is the generation of two gamma rays, or photons, that move in opposite directions. The PET scanner measures these photons and calculates their source. Regions of the brain that are most active will increase their demand for oxygen; hence, active regions will have a stronger PET signal.

Positron Emission Tomography

PET activation studies use radioactive-labeled compounds to measure local variations in cerebral blood flow that correlate with mental activity (**Figure 3.28**). The radiologist injects a radioactive substance, or tracer, into the bloodstream, which distributes it throughout the brain in step with its metabolic needs; the more active neural areas have a higher metabolic demand and thus receive more tracer. The PET scanner monitors the radiation emitted by the tracer.

A common tracer isotope used in PET studies is oxygen-15 (^{15}O), an unstable isotope with a half-life of 122 seconds. While a participant is engaged in a cognitive task, the researcher injects this isotope, in the form of water ($H_2{}^{15}O$), into that person's bloodstream. The ^{15}O nuclei rapidly decay, each one emitting a positron. The collision of a positron with an electron creates two photons, or gamma rays. The two photons move in opposite directions at the speed of light, passing unimpeded through brain tissue, skull, and scalp. The PET scanner—essentially a gamma ray detector—determines where the collision took place.

Although all areas of the body use some of the radioactive oxygen, the fundamental assumption of PET is that there is increased blood flow to the brain regions that have heightened neural activity. Thus, PET activation studies measure relative activity, not absolute metabolic activity. In a typical PET experiment, the researcher administers the tracer at least twice: during a control condition and during one or more experimental conditions. The results are usually reported as a change in **regional cerebral blood flow (rCBF)** between the control and experimental conditions.

PET scanners are capable of resolving metabolic activity to regions, or **voxels**, of approximately 5 to 10 mm^3. (Think of a voxel as a tiny cube, the three-dimensional analogue of a pixel.) Although this volume includes only thousands of neurons, it is sufficient to identify cortical and subcortical areas of enhanced activity. It can even show functional variation within a given cortical area.

Recognizing that PET scanners can measure any radioactive agent, researchers have sought to develop specialized molecules that might serve as biomarkers of particular neurological disorders and pathologies. Historically, Alzheimer's disease depended on a clinical diagnosis (and was frequently misdiagnosed) because only a postmortem analysis of brain tissue could confirm the presence of the disease's defining beta-amyloid plaques and neurofibrillary tangles. A leading hypothesis for the cause of Alzheimer's is that the production of amyloid, a ubiquitous protein in tissue, goes awry and leads to the characteristic plaques, though there

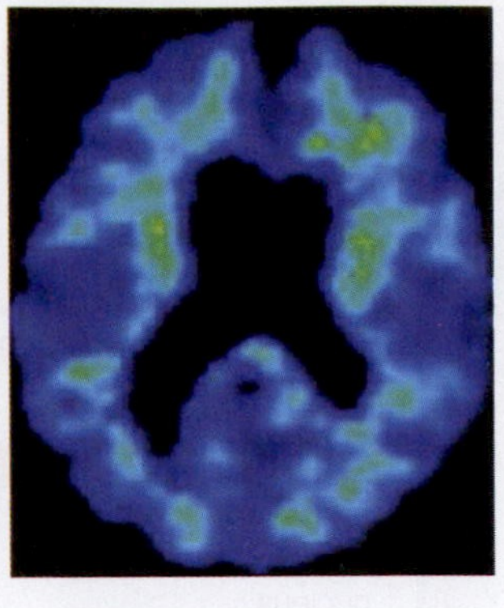

a Alzheimer's

b Control

FIGURE 3.29 Using PiB to look for signs of Alzheimer's disease. PiB is a PET dye that binds to beta-amyloid. The dye was injected into a man with moderate symptoms of Alzheimer's disease and into a cognitively normal woman of similar age. (a) The patient with Alzheimer's disease shows significant binding of PiB in the frontal, posterior cingulate, parietal, and temporal cortices, as evidenced by the red, orange, and yellow coloring. (b) The control participant shows no uptake of PiB in her brain.

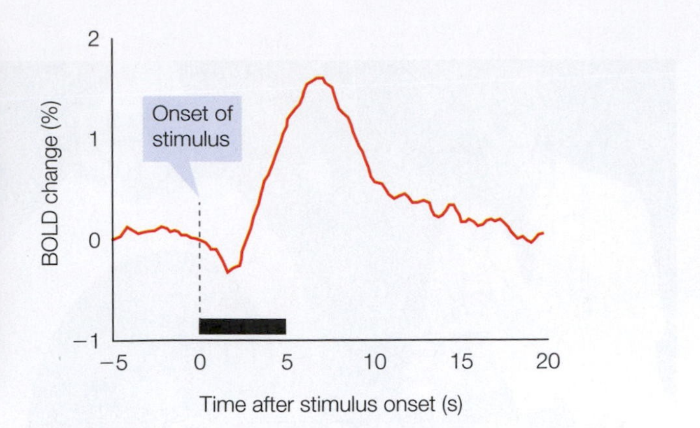

FIGURE 3.30 Functional MRI signal observed from cat visual cortex with a 4.7-tesla scanner.
The black bar indicates the duration of a visual stimulus. Initially there is a dip in the blood oxygen level–dependent (BOLD) signal, reflecting the depletion of oxygen from the activated cells. Over time, the BOLD signal increases, reflecting the increased hemodynamic response to the activated area. Scanners of this strength are now being used with human participants.

is recent evidence against this hypothesis (Drachman, 2014; Freiherr et al., 2013).

Motivated by a desire to diagnose and monitor Alzheimer's in living individuals, Chester Mathis and William Klunk at the University of Pittsburgh set out to find a radioactive compound that would specifically label beta-amyloid. After testing hundreds of compounds, they identified a protein-specific, ^{11}C-labeled dye they could use as a PET tracer, which they called PiB, or Pittsburgh Compound B (Klunk et al., 2004). (Carbon-11 has a half-life of 20 minutes.) PiB binds to beta-amyloid (**Figure 3.29**), providing physicians with an in vivo assay of the presence of this biomarker.

PET scans can now measure beta-amyloid plaques, thus adding a new tool for diagnosing Alzheimer's. What's more, physicians can screen asymptomatic patients and those with very early stages of cognitive impairment to predict their likelihood of developing Alzheimer's. Being able to diagnose the disease definitively improves patient treatment and decreases the substantial risk of misdiagnosis. It also allows scientists to develop new experimental drugs designed either to disrupt the pathological development of plaques or to treat the symptoms of Alzheimer's.

Functional Magnetic Resonance Imaging

As with PET, fMRI exploits the fact that local blood flow increases in active parts of the brain. The procedure is essentially identical to the one used in traditional MRI. Radio waves cause the protons in hydrogen atoms to oscillate, and a detector measures local energy fields emitted as the protons return to the orientation of the magnetic field created by the MRI scanner. With fMRI, however, the magnetic properties of the deoxygenated form of hemoglobin, deoxyhemoglobin, are the focus of the imaging. Deoxygenated hemoglobin is paramagnetic (i.e., weakly magnetic in the presence of a magnetic field), whereas oxygenated hemoglobin is not. The fMRI detectors measure the ratio of oxygenated to deoxygenated hemoglobin; this value is referred to as the **blood oxygen level–dependent (BOLD)** effect.

Intuitively, one might expect the proportion of deoxygenated hemoglobin to be greater in the area surrounding active brain tissue, given the intensive metabolic costs associated with neural function. Results from fMRI, however, generally report an *increase* in the ratio of oxygenated to deoxygenated hemoglobin. This change occurs because as a region of the brain becomes active, the amount of blood directed to that area increases. The neural tissue is unable to absorb all of the excess oxygen. Functional MRI studies measure the time course of this process. Although neural events occur on a timescale measured in milliseconds, changes in blood flow occur much more slowly. In **Figure 3.30**, note that following the presentation of a stimulus (in this case, a visual stimulus), an increase in the BOLD response is observed after a few seconds, peaking 6 to 10 seconds later. Thus, with fMRI we can obtain an indirect measure of neuronal activity by measuring changes in the oxygen concentration in the blood.

Functional MRI offers several advantages over PET. MRI scanners are much less expensive and easier to maintain, and fMRI uses no radioactive tracers, so it does not incur the additional costs, hassles, and hazards associated

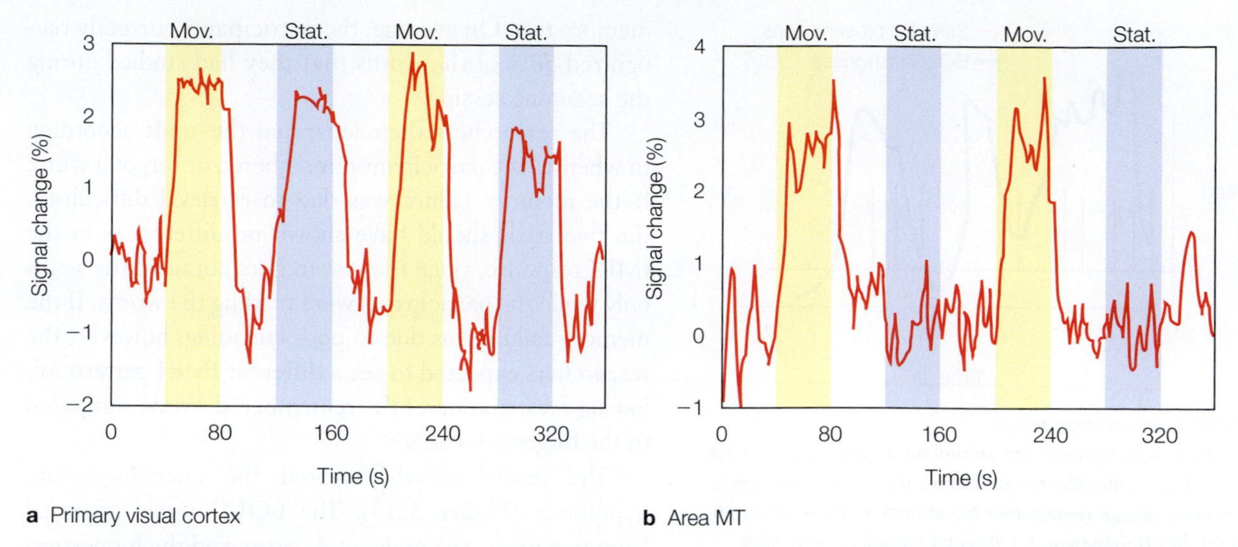

FIGURE 3.31 Block design.
Functional MRI measures time-dependent fluctuations in oxygenation with good spatial resolution. The participant in this experiment viewed a field of randomly positioned white dots on a black background. The dots would either remain stationary (Stat.) or move along the radial axis (Mov.). The 40-second intervals of stimulation (shaded background) alternated with 40-second intervals during which the screen was blank (white background). (a) Measurements from primary visual cortex (V1) showed consistent increases during the stimulation intervals compared to the blank intervals. (b) In area MT, a visual region associated with motion perception (see Chapter 5), the increase was observed only when the dots were moving.

with handling these materials. Because fMRI does not require the injection of radioactive tracers, researchers can test the same individual repeatedly, either in a single session or over multiple sessions. Thus, it becomes possible to perform a complete statistical analysis on the data from a single participant. In addition, the images from fMRI data have better spatial resolution than is possible with PET. For these reasons, fMRI has led to revolutionary changes in cognitive neuroscience, with scanners commonplace now at research universities and articles using this method filling up the pages of neuroscience journals.

BLOCK DESIGN VERSUS EVENT-RELATED DESIGN

Functional MRI and PET differ in their temporal resolution, which has ramifications for study designs. PET imaging requires sufficient time for detecting enough radiation to create images of adequate quality. The participant must engage continuously in a single given experimental task for at least 40 seconds, and metabolic activity is averaged over this interval. Because of this time requirement, researchers must use block design experiments with PET.

In a **block design** experiment (**Figure 3.31**), the researcher integrates the recorded neural activity over a "block" of time during which the participant performs multiple trials of the same type. For example, during some blocks of 40 seconds, the participant might view static dots, whereas in other 40-second blocks, the dots are moving about in a random fashion. The comparison can be either between the two stimulus conditions, or between these conditions and a control condition in which there is no visual stimulation. Because of the extended time requirement, the specificity of correlating activation patterns with a specific cognitive process suffers.

Functional MRI studies can use either a block design, in which the experimenter compares the neural activations between experimental and control scanning phases, or an **event-related design** (**Figure 3.32**). As in ERP studies, the term *event-related* refers to the fact that, across experimental trials, the BOLD response links to specific events, such as the presentation of a stimulus or the onset of a movement. Although metabolic changes to any single event are likely to be hard to detect among background fluctuations in the brain's hemodynamic response, we can obtain a clear signal by averaging over repetitions of these events. Because of the extended time course of the hemodynamic response, the BOLD responses to successive trials will overlap (Figure 3.32). However, sophisticated statistical methods can be used to determine the contribution of each event to the measured BOLD response.

Event-related fMRI improves the experimental design because the researcher presents the experimental and control trials randomly. This approach helps ensure that the participants are in a similar attentional state

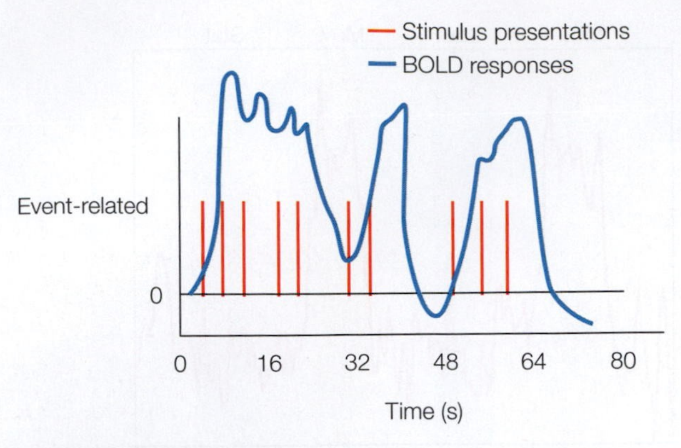

FIGURE 3.32 Event-related design.
Unlike a block design, in which the stimuli for a given condition are clustered into blocks and the activity across the block is averaged, the event-related design randomizes the stimuli for different conditions, and the BOLD response to particular stimuli or responses can be extracted from the signal data. The measured BOLD response will include contributions from many different trials. Statistical methods are then used to extract the contribution related to each event.

during both types of trials, increasing the likelihood that the observed differences reflect the hypothesized processing demands rather than more generic factors, such as a change in overall arousal. Although a block design experiment is better able to detect small effects, researchers can use a greater range of experimental setups with event-related design; indeed, they can study some questions only by using event-related fMRI.

A powerful feature of event-related fMRI is that the experimenter can choose to combine the data from completed scans in many different ways. For example, consider memory failure. Most of us have had the frustrating experience of meeting someone at a party and then, just 2 minutes later, not remembering the person's name. Did this happen because we failed to listen carefully during the original introduction, so the information never really entered memory? Or did the information enter our memory stores but then, after 2 minutes of distraction, we lost the ability to access it? The former would constitute a problem with memory encoding; the latter would reflect a problem with memory retrieval. Distinguishing between these two possibilities has been difficult, as evidenced by the thousands of articles on this topic that have appeared in cognitive psychology journals over the past 100 years.

Anthony Wagner and his colleagues used event-related fMRI to take a fresh look at the question of memory encoding versus retrieval (A. D. Wagner et al., 1998). They obtained fMRI scans while participants were studying a list of words, where one word appeared every 2 seconds. About 20 minutes after the scanning session ended, they gave the participants a recognition memory test. On average, the participants correctly recognized 88% of the words that they had studied during the scanning session.

The researchers then separated the trials according to whether the participant remembered or forgot a word. If the memory failure was due to retrieval difficulties, the two trials should have shown no differences in the fMRI response, since the researchers obtained the scans only while the participants were reading the words. If the memory failure was due to poor encoding, however, the researchers expected to see a different fMRI pattern following presentation of the remembered words compared to the forgotten words.

The results clearly favored the encoding-failure hypothesis (**Figure 3.33**). The BOLD signal recorded from two areas, the prefrontal cortex and the hippocampus, was stronger following presentation of the remembered words. (As we will see in Chapter 9, these two areas of the brain play a critical role in memory formation.) Block design is a poor choice for a study like this, because with that method the signal is averaged over all the events within each scanning phase.

The massive amounts of data generated in fMRI studies have motivated researchers to develop sophisticated analysis tools—tools that go beyond simply comparing an experimental and control condition to ask whether patterns of activity contain information about cognitive states. One such method is **multivoxel pattern analysis (MVPA)**, a pattern classification algorithm in which the researcher identifies the distributed patterns of neural activity consistently present for a particular event, task, stimulus, and so forth. These activation patterns can provide information about the functional role not just of brain areas, but of networks within and beyond them (see Section 3.7).

Arielle Tambini and Lila Davachi (2013) used MVPA to ask whether consolidation continues in the hippocampus after something is learned. They first identified BOLD patterns across hippocampal voxels during encoding. Then they asked whether these same patterns persisted during periods of rest, when the participants did not receive stimulation. To test for the specificity of the content of memory, they asked the participants to perform two different encoding tasks—one in which they examined photos of faces, and another in which they examined photos of objects.

The MVPA analysis revealed activation patterns during rest to be similar to those observed during encoding. Furthermore, the patterns were different for the faces and object photos. Thus, the researchers could predict from the brain activity which type of stimulus the participant was "thinking" about during the rest periods. Even more impressive, when tested on a subsequent memory test,

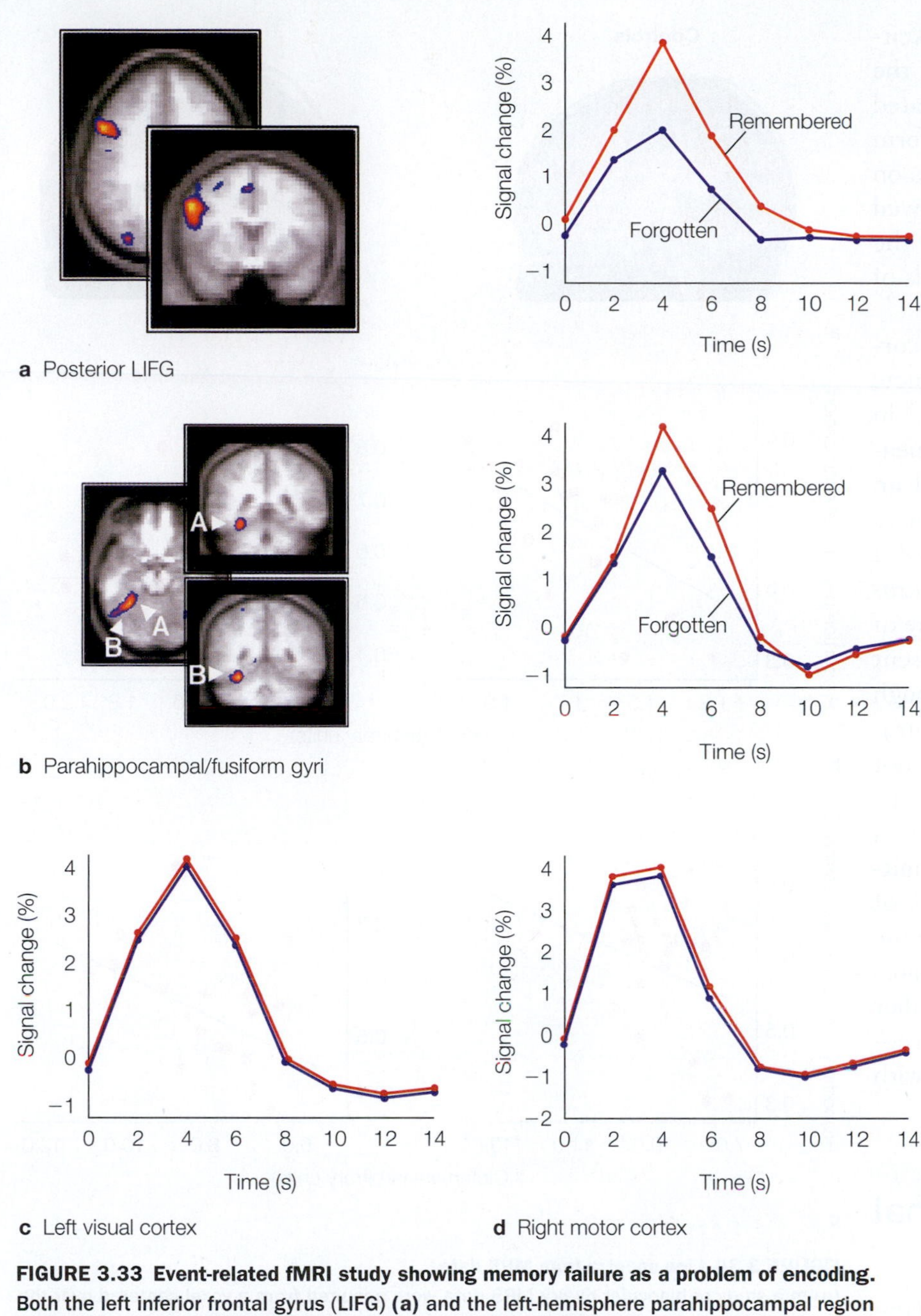

FIGURE 3.33 Event-related fMRI study showing memory failure as a problem of encoding. Both the left inferior frontal gyrus (LIFG) **(a)** and the left-hemisphere parahippocampal region **(b)** exhibit greater activity during encoding for words that were subsequently remembered compared to those that were forgotten. (A = parahippocampal region; B = fusiform gyrus.) Activity over the left visual cortex **(c)** and right motor cortex **(d)** was identical following words that subsequently were either remembered or forgotten. These results demonstrate that the memory effect is specific to the frontal and hippocampal regions.

the remembered items were the ones that had shown the strongest patterns during encoding and persistent activity in the post-encoding rest period.

MAGNETIC RESONANCE SPECTROSCOPY We can also use the MRI machine to measure other properties of brain tissue. One method, **magnetic resonance spectroscopy (MRS)**, offers a tool to obtain, in vivo, information about the chemical composition of tissues (as opposed to the anatomical information obtained from standard, structural MRIs). We can do this because molecules have unique proton compositions that behave differently in a magnetic field. From the MRS data, researchers can estimate the concentration of different neurochemicals in one brain area or the same neurotransmitter in multiple areas. They can also ask how these concentrations change during or after a person performs a task, similar to how they use fMRI research to measure task-dependent changes in the BOLD response. Because the signals for the neurotransmitters are quite weak, MRS scans require using large voxels and scanning times of about 10 minutes for each voxel.

The neurotransmitter gamma-aminobutyric acid (GABA) has been the focus of many MRS studies. One reason for its popularity is methodological: The signature of GABA is in a stable part of the MRS spectrum. The other is that it is also functional: GABA is the most prevalent inhibitory neurotransmitter in the cortex and has been linked to many psychiatric disorders. For example, one hypothesis suggests that an imbalance between excitatory and inhibitory neurotransmission is a central feature of the neurobiology of autism, and animal studies suggest that the imbalance is a result of disruptions in GABA pathways.

To explore this hypothesis, Caroline Robertson and her colleagues (2016) employed a visual perception task in which the two eyes compete for control of perception. **Binocular rivalry** is a phenomenon that occurs when one image is presented to one eye and a different image to the other. We initially perceive one image and then, after a few seconds, our perception switches to the other image—and back and forth they go. The neural inputs to each eye appear to vie for dominance, presumably entailing a competition between excitatory and inhibitory processes in the visual cortex. Robertson demonstrated that individuals with autism perform differently from control participants on this task. The autistic individuals showed a slower rate of switching between the two images, as well as longer periods of mixed perception.

To examine the neurochemical correlates of this behavioral difference, the researchers focused on a voxel in the occipital lobe, using MRS to measure concentrations of GABA and an excitatory neurotransmitter, glutamate (**Figure 3.34**). The controls showed a correlation between GABA concentrations in the visual cortex and the rate of switching. This relationship was absent in the autistic individuals, even though they had the same average concentration of GABA. The researchers did not find this difference between the groups for glutamate. These findings point to a possible link between a neurotransmitter and certain behavioral features of autism. Interestingly, it may not be the amount of the transmitter that is abnormal in autistic individuals, but rather how that transmitter is used (e.g., receptor sensitivity) or how it interacts with other transmitters.

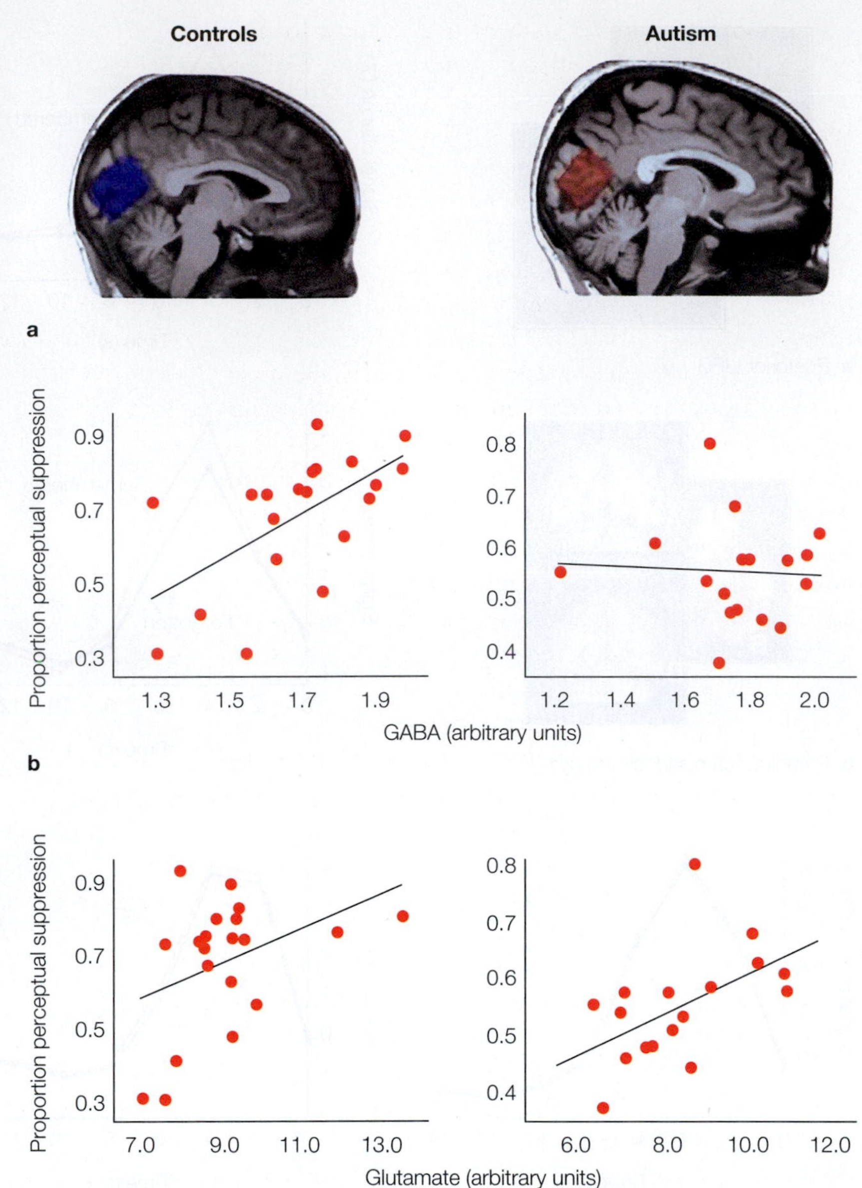

FIGURE 3.34 Line spectra from MRS data.
(a) In a study of binocular rivalry, MRS data were acquired from a voxel centered over the visual cortex. The analysis focused on two neurotransmitters: GABA and glutamate. In the control individuals, GABA (b) and glutamate (c) levels strongly predicted the strength of perceptual suppression during binocular rivalry, the proportion of each trial spent viewing a dominant percept. In the individuals with autism, however, this relationship was observed only with glutamate. The lack of correlation between perception and GABA levels may be related to the lower switching rates in this group.

Limitations of Functional Imaging Techniques

It is important to understand the limitations of imaging techniques such as PET and fMRI. First, PET and fMRI have poor temporal resolution compared with single-cell recordings or ERPs. PET is constrained by the decay rate of the radioactive agent (on the order of minutes), and fMRI is dependent on the hemodynamic changes that underlie the BOLD response (on the order of seconds). A complete picture of the physiology and anatomy of cognition usually requires integrating results obtained in ERP studies with those obtained in fMRI studies.

Second, to relate function and structure, it is necessary to be able to map the data obtained with functional imaging methods such as fMRI or PET onto corresponding structural MRI scans. The structural scans can be a slice, a computerized 3-D image of the entire cortical surface, or an inflated cortical surface to better reflect the distance between areas in cortical space. These methods work because brains, in general, all have the same components. Just like fingerprints, however, no two brains are the same. They vary in overall size, in the size and location of gyri, in the size of individual regions, in shape, and in connectivity. This variation presents a problem for comparisons of the functional imaging data across individuals.

One solution is to use mathematical methods to align individual brain images within a common space, building on the assumption that points deep in the cerebral hemispheres have a predictable relationship to the horizontal planes running through the anterior and posterior commissures, two large white matter tracts connecting the two cerebral hemispheres. In 1988, Jean Talairach and Pierre Tournoux published a standardized, three-dimensional, proportional grid system to identify and measure brain components despite their variability. Using the postmortem brain of a 60-year-old French woman, they divided the brain into thousands of voxels with dimensions in the millimeter range. Each voxel was given a 3-D *Talairach coordinate* in relation to the anterior commissure, on the x (left or right), y (anterior or posterior), and z (superior or inferior) axes. By using these standard anatomical landmarks, researchers can take structural MRI scans and morph them onto standard Talairach space as a way to combine information across individuals. A limitation with this approach, though, is that to fit brains to the standardized atlas, we must warp the images to fit the standard template.

Functional imaging signals are also quite variable. To improve a signal, researchers apply data averaging procedures, smoothing the BOLD signals across neighboring voxels. The assumption is that this activation should be similar in neighboring voxels and that at least some of the variation is noise. However, it may well be that discontinuities arise because in one individual, neighboring voxels come from cortical regions that are on opposite sides of a sulcus. Thus, there is a cost to these smoothing techniques, especially when we analyze the data from different individuals with different anatomies.

A third difficulty arises on interpretation of the data from a PET or fMRI study. The data sets from an imaging study are massive, presenting challenging statistical problems. Choosing the proper significance threshold is important. Too high, and you may miss regions that are significant; too low, and you risk including random activations. Functional imaging studies frequently use what are termed "corrected" significance levels, implying that the statistical criteria have been adjusted to account for the many comparisons involved in the analysis.

Fourth, even with proper statistical procedures, comparisons between different experimental conditions are likely to produce many differences. This should be no surprise, given what we know about the distributed nature of brain function. For example, asking someone to generate a verb associated with a noun (experimental task) likely requires many more cognitive operations than just saying the noun (control task). Thus it is difficult to make inferences about each area's functional contribution from neuroimaging data. We have to remember that correlation does not imply causation. In addition, neuronal input, not output, is the primary driver of the BOLD signal (Logothetis et al., 2001); therefore, an area showing increased activation may be downstream from brain areas that provide the critical computations.

TAKE-HOME MESSAGES

- Positron emission tomography (PET) measures metabolic activity in the brain by monitoring the distribution of a decaying radioactive tracer. A popular tracer for cognitive studies is ^{15}O because the distribution of oxygen increases in neural regions that are active. Researchers can design tracers to target particular types of tissue. The PiB tracer was designed to bind to beta-amyloid, providing an in vivo assay of an important biomarker for Alzheimer's disease.
- In functional magnetic resonance imaging (fMRI), the MRI scanner is configured to measure changes in the oxygen content of the blood (hemodynamic response). We assume these changes correlate with local changes in neural activity.
- In magnetic resonance spectroscopy (MRS), the MRI scanner is configured to target specific metabolites, providing a tool to measure the concentration of neurotransmitters.
- Compared to methods that measure electrical signals, PET and fMRI have poor temporal resolution, averaging metabolic signals over seconds or even minutes. However, we can use them simultaneously to obtain images of the entire brain with reasonable spatial resolution.

3.7 Connectivity Maps

Functional imaging methods have provided cognitive neuroscientists with an amazing tool for functional localization. By carefully selecting experimental and control conditions, researchers can investigate the neural regions involved in almost any cognitive task. Just consider something as fundamental as face perception, a task we will examine in detail in Chapter 6. Not only can we study the brain areas activated during face perception, but we can also make more subtle distinctions, asking which parts of the brain are active when we look at the faces of celebrities, or loved ones, or people from other racial groups. The results from these studies capture the public imagination: Barely a week goes by without an article appearing in the newspaper stating something like, "Scientists have found the part of the brain associated with romantic love!"

What we miss in such oversimplifications is the appreciation that brain regions do not work in isolation, but rather as part of a vastly complex, interconnected network. To understand how the brain supports any cognitive process, we need tools that can illuminate these patterns of connectivity. Over the past decade,

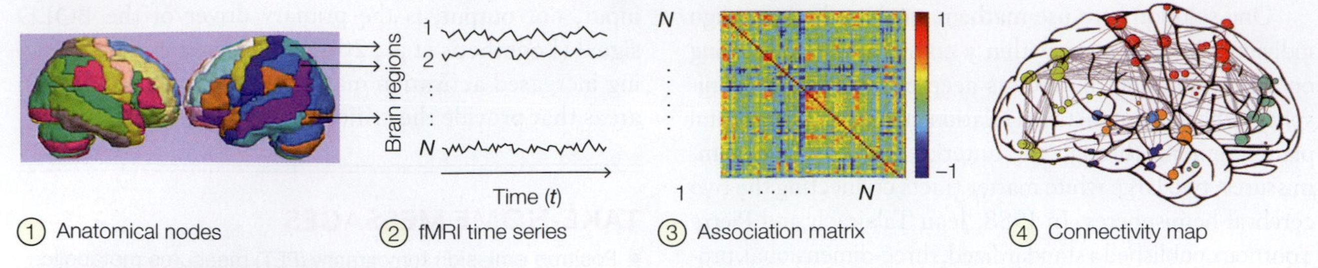

FIGURE 3.35 Constructing a human brain network.
A brain network can be constructed with either structural or functional imaging data. (1) Data from imaging methods such as anatomical MRI or fMRI are divided into nodes. With EEG and MEG, the sensors can serve as the nodes. (2) The correlations between all possible pairs of nodes are measured, and (3) an association matrix is generated to visualize the pairwise associations between the nodes. These correlations can be plotted to form a connectivity map, or connectome (4). The connectivity map shown here was constructed from a different fMRI data set than was used to construct the association matrix pictured in Step 3. Links are plotted between node pairs that exhibit significant functional correlations (i.e., connectivity). The size of each node indicates its number of links. Each of the colors, which highlight functional networks within the map, indicates the lobe of the brain that a node occupies.

considerable effort has gone into developing such tools, and this work has yielded different ways to describe **connectivity maps**. These maps, sometimes referred to as **connectomes**, are visualizations of structural or functional connections within the brain.

A brain network can be constructed from either structural or functional imaging data. Its construction requires four steps, as depicted in **Figure 3.35**:

1. Define the network nodes. Data from structural imaging methods such as anatomical MRI or fMRI are divided into nodes, visualized in a parcellation map. With EEG and MEG, the sensors can serve as the nodes.
2. Measure the correlation between all possible pairs of nodes, using the dependent variable of interest—for example, fractional anisotropy (a measure of diffusion) for DTI, or BOLD response for fMRI.
3. Generate an association matrix by compiling all pairwise associations between the nodes.
4. Visualize the correlations in a connectivity map. One way to create these maps is to depict brain regions as *nodes* of a network and indicate connections as *edges* between them. The geometric relationships of the nodes and edges define the network and provide a visualization of brain organization.

We can construct connectivity maps at many scales. On the micro scale, a node could be a single neuron. For instance, the only entire network of cellular neural connections that researchers have described is in the nematode worm *Caenorhabditis elegans*. The worm's very limited nervous system enabled them to construct a connectivity map in which each node is a neuron, and to identify all of the connections. On the scale of the human brain, the nodes and edges typically represent anatomically or functionally defined units. For instance, the nodes might be clusters of voxels and the edges a representation of nodes that show correlated patterns of activation. In this manner, researchers can differentiate between nodes that act as hubs, sharing links with many neighboring nodes, and nodes that act as connectors, providing links to more distant clusters. Connectivity maps can also depict the relative strength, or weighting, of the edges.

Because neuroscientists can construct connectivity maps by using the data obtained from just about any neuroimaging method, such maps provide a valuable way to compare results from experiments using different methods (Bullmore & Bassett, 2011). For instance, connectomes based on anatomical measures, such as DTI, can be compared with connectomes based on functional measures, such as fMRI. Connectomes also provide ways to visualize the organizational properties of neural networks. For instance, three studies employing vastly different data sets to produce graphical models reported similar associations between general intelligence and connectivity measures of brain network efficiency (Bassett et al., 2009; Y. Li et al. 2009; van den Heuvel et al., 2009).

Functional MRI data are especially useful for constructing connectivity maps because fMRI can efficiently collect data from across the entire brain for relatively long periods. A simple way to examine functional connectivity is to look at the correlation across time between any two voxels or clusters of voxels. We can correlate the BOLD time series for the pair of voxels to define how "connected" the two areas are: A high correlation, either positive or negative, means high connectivity. There are different ways of looking for distributed patterns of activation. For instance, we can look across the entire cortex and define for each region the areas that show the highest connectivity. Alternatively, we can do a more focused *region of interest (ROI)* analysis using a particular voxel as the seed, comparing its BOLD response with all the other voxels.

As you might imagine, connectivity analyses can quickly become a huge computational and statistical problem. Given that a whole-brain fMRI scan contains over 200,000 voxels, a full map involving just pairwise comparisons would require 40 billion correlations for each time point! To make things more tractable, we employ smoothing procedures to create a smaller set of larger voxels—a reasonable procedure, given that activity in neighboring voxels is usually highly correlated.

Perhaps the biggest growth industry in cognitive neuroscience over the past decade has been the use of *resting-state fMRI (rs-fMRI)* to study functional connectivity. As the name implies, the fMRI data for this procedure are collected while the participants are at rest, having been given this instruction: "Keep your eyes open and just relax." You might imagine that the connectivity maps would vary greatly from one individual to another. "Just relax" might lead to very different cognitive states across individuals: One person might plan the dinner menu for the evening, another might daydream about a recent trip to Hawaii, and a third might wonder how possibly to relax while lying in a narrow tube that is emitting strange sounds! Hundreds of studies, however, have shown that resting-state data, obtained from as little as 6 minutes of scanning, produce highly reliable connectivity maps revealing what one could call the intrinsic functional connectivity of the human brain.

In one large-scale study, researchers collected rs-fMRI data from 1,000 individuals (Yeo et al., 2011). Depending on the criteria used to define a unique network, they found they could capture the activity patterns across 1,175 voxels with 7 to 17 networks (**Figure 3.36**). This pattern is highly reliable: The same picture emerged not only when the 1,000 individuals were separated into

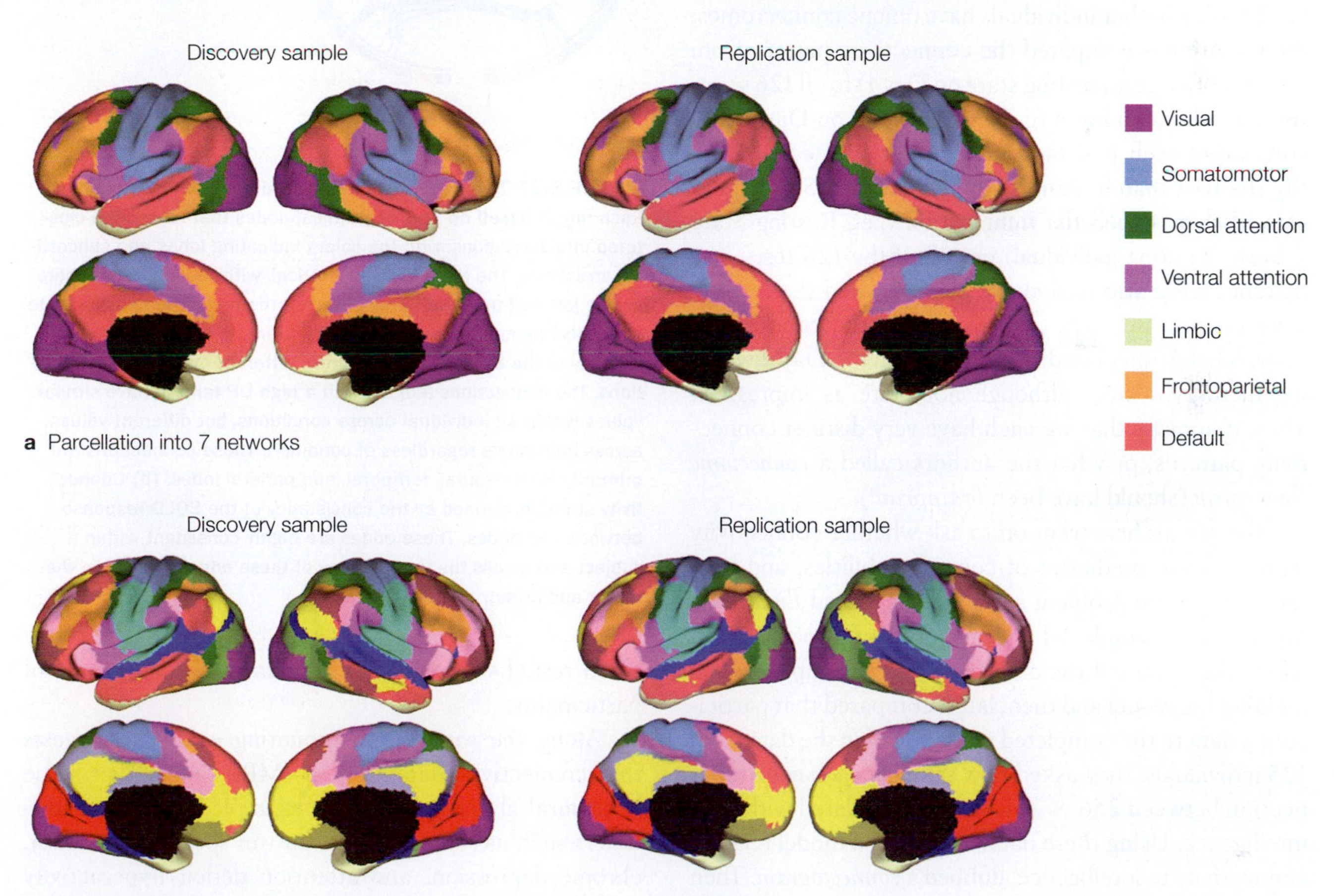

FIGURE 3.36 Network cortical parcellation.
(a) Seven main networks were identified from 500 discovery participants. These networks' functional names (see the legend), commonly used in neuroimaging, are not meant to correspond exactly to the functions they indicate. In the "default" ("mind-wandering") network, BOLD is especially prominent at rest and decreases when the participant is engaged in a task. Scans of the same seven networks, based on a replication sample of 500 scans, demonstrate how consistent this measure is. (b) An alternative parcellation shows 17 networks from the 500 discovery participants. The 17-network replication sample.

two groups of 500 brains each, but also when much smaller samples were used. These networks are also manifest in studies using experimental tasks (active-state scans), although the strength of a network depends on the task. For example, a medial network is most active in tasks that require self-reflection, whereas a frontoparietal network is active in tasks that require active monitoring of the environment.

The evidence shows that brain networks are consistent across individuals. What about within an individual? Will the correlation patterns observed in one session correspond to those observed in a different session? And if so, can we use this information to predict differences between individuals? Emily Finn and her colleagues at Yale University (2015) obtained resting-state scans and active-state scans (during working memory, motor, language, and emotion tasks) from 126 individuals on two different days and created connectomes for each condition for each individual.

To ask whether individuals have unique connectomes, the researchers compared the connectivity pattern from one condition (e.g., resting state on Day 1) to all 126 scans from another condition (e.g., resting state on Day 2). By correlating each pair of connectomes, they could identify the best match. Amazingly, for Resting State 1, the algorithm produced the right match (i.e., Resting State 2 from the same individual) on 117 of the 126 tests. The matches were also well above chance when the resting-state connectome was used to predict the connectivity maps for the other conditions (e.g., with the Day 2 working memory scans), although not quite as impressive. Thus, it appears that we each have very distinct connectivity patterns, or what the authors called a *connectome fingerprint* (should have been *brainprint*!).

The researchers went on to ask whether connectivity patterns were predictive of cognitive abilities, and here they focused on problem-solving skills, called *fluid intelligence*. They employed a leave-one-out procedure, in which they omitted the data from one participant when building the model and then, later, compared that participant's data to the completed model. Taking the data from 125 individuals, they asked how strongly each edge (connection between 256 × 256 voxels) correlated with fluid intelligence. Using these data, they built a model relating connectivity to intelligence, dubbed a *connectogram*. Then they fed the connectivity pattern for the 126th person into the model, generating a prediction of that person's intelligence. They repeated this procedure for each of the 126 individuals. One individual's connectogram is shown in **Figure 3.37**. The researchers were able to make good predictions of general intelligence using either the whole-brain connectome or just the connections within the frontoparietal network. The model was also successful

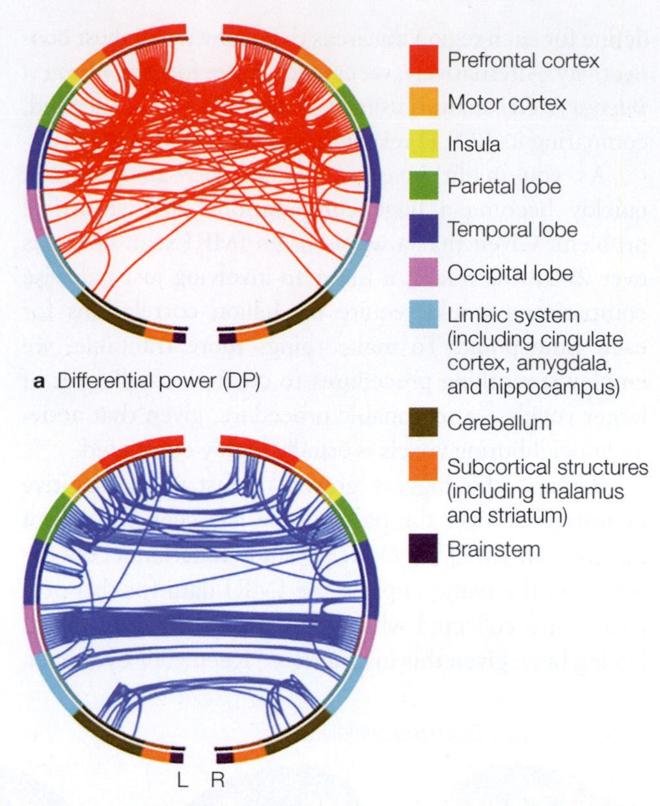

FIGURE 3.37 Two ways to derive individual connectograms. Each ring is based on 268 anatomical nodes that have been clustered into 10 regions, with the colors indicating lobes and subcortical structures. The rings are symmetrical, with the left hemisphere on the left and the right hemisphere on the right. The lines indicate edges (connections). **(a)** Connectivity strength, defined by the consistency of the BOLD response across different experimental conditions. The connections (edges) with a high DP tend to have similar values within an individual across conditions, but different values across individuals regardless of condition. These connections are primarily in the frontal, temporal, and parietal lobes. **(b)** Connectivity strength, defined by the consistency of the BOLD response between two nodes. These edges are highly consistent within a subject and across the group. Many of these edges are within the motor and primary visual networks.

when tested with rs-fMRI data from a new sample of participants.

Along the same lines, mounting evidence suggests that connectivity data from rs-fMRI can predict some behavioral abnormalities. For example, psychiatric disorders such as schizophrenia, autism spectrum disorder, chronic depression, and attention deficit hyperactivity disorder (ADHD) are associated with abnormalities in rs-fMRI connectivity profiles (Fornito & Bullmore, 2010). In studies designed to describe the emergence, timing, and development of functional connections, as well as to look for early biomarkers that might predict developmental disorders (Thomason et al., 2013), researchers have used rs-fMRI on fetal brains in utero. Amazingly, clear patterns of connectivity can be measured in the fetus by

Week 25. The stage is thus set for future work to ask how these patterns might be affected by prenatal events such as infections, stress, and alcohol or drug use.

There is also considerable interest in using connectivity analyses both to predict learning and to examine how brain activity changes with learning. Networks can be analyzed to ask how connectivity patterns change with learning, whether over the short term (minutes) or over longer time periods (years). One method used here is *dynamic network analysis*, employed in a study designed to reveal how networks reconfigure when people learn a new skill and to explore individual differences in our capacity to learn (Basset et al., 2015). The researchers identified changes in functional connectivity between brain regions over the course of learning a motor task, and they then showed how those changes related to differences in the rate at which people learned the skill.

On Day 1 of the experiment, participants underwent two scans: a resting-state scan, and a pretraining active-state scan in which they practiced six 10-element sequences of keyboard presses. Over the next 6 weeks, the participants were required to practice the sequences on their own computers at home 5 days each week, but the amount of practice varied for specific sequences. Two sequences were practiced only once in each of the 30 sessions, two were repeated 10 times each session, and two were practiced 75 times each session. Participants repeated the scanning procedure (rest and active) after 2 weeks (early in training), 4 weeks (midpoint), and 6 weeks (late; **Figure 3.38**). As expected, over the 6 weeks the participants became much faster at producing the sequences, especially those they practiced most frequently.

To look for changes in functional connectivity, the researchers collapsed 200,000 voxels into 120 regions of interest. Data from the active-state scans showed high activity in motor and visual areas across the four scanning sessions—a result that is not surprising, given the task. With practice, however, the activity between these two regions became less correlated. One interpretation is that with practice, the production of sequential movements became less dependent on visual input. This decrease varied across individuals, with some individuals developing more motor autonomy than others.

Increasing autonomy, however, did not predict individual differences in learning rate. Rather, it was changes in connectivity between regions of the frontal lobe and anterior cingulate that predicted learning speed: Faster learning was associated with faster reduction in the correlation between these two areas; that is, participants whose cognitive control system disengaged soonest learned fastest (see Chapter 12). It may be that cognitive

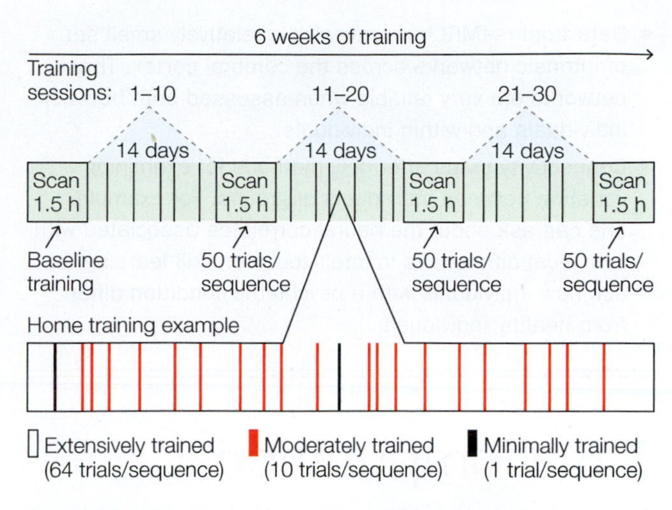

FIGURE 3.38 Training schedule for measuring learning. Participants underwent a resting-state scan and an active-state scan before training, and then again every 2 weeks for the following 6 weeks.

assistance provided by these regions can facilitate learning early on, but once performance becomes more automatic, communication between these regions is no longer essential and may even slow learning.

In a follow-up study using these data, the researchers asked whether they could predict individual differences in learning rates from the rs-fMRI data (Mattar et al., in press). They hypothesized that individuals would learn a motor task more swiftly if their motor systems were more flexible and "primed" for autonomy, as indicated by fewer connections between their motor and visual systems when at rest. Indeed, individuals who had relatively weak connections between the early visual areas and the premotor area at rest learned faster. The researchers suggest that fewer such connections correspond to motor systems with a propensity to "liberate" movement selection from stimulus-driven to internally driven mechanisms.

Connectivity studies have enabled cognitive neuroscientists to creatively exploit the massive data sets produced in fMRI studies. Network analyses provide a picture complementary to the one obtained in studies that focus on characterizing activity patterns within specific regions. Together, these functional imaging approaches have greatly advanced our understanding of the specialized functions of various brain areas and of how they operate in networks to support cognition.

TAKE-HOME MESSAGES

- Connectivity maps capture correlated patterns of activity between different brain regions. Researchers derive these maps from fMRI data obtained during both a resting-state scan (while engaged in no task) and an active-state scan (while performing a task).

- Data from rs-fMRI have revealed a relatively small set of intrinsic networks across the cerebral cortex. These networks are very reliable when assessed both between individuals and within individuals.
- Connectivity maps offer new methods for examining variation between individuals or groups. For example, one can ask about the neural correlates associated with individual differences in intelligence or skill learning, or ask how individuals with a psychiatric condition differ from healthy individuals.

3.8 Computational Neuroscience

Creating computer models to simulate postulated brain processes is a research method that complements the other methods discussed in this chapter. A **simulation** is an imitation, a reproduction of behavior in an alternative medium. The simulated cognitive processes are commonly referred to as *artificial intelligence (AI)*—artificial in the sense that they are artifacts, or human creations, and intelligent in that the computers perform complex functions. Computational neuroscientists design simulations to mimic behavior and the cognitive processes supporting that behavior. By observing the behavior, researchers can assess how well it matches behavior produced by a real mind.

For the computer to succeed, however, the modeler must specify how the computer represents and processes the information within its program. To this end, the modeler must generate concrete hypotheses regarding the "mental" operations needed for the machine. Computer simulations thus provide a useful tool for testing theories of cognition. The successes and failures of various models yield valuable insights into the strengths and weaknesses of a theory.

Computer models are useful because we can analyze them in detail. This does not mean that a computer's operation is always completely predictable, or that the programmer knows the outcome of a simulation in advance. Computer simulations can incorporate random events or be so complex that the outcome resists any analytic prediction. However, we must understand at a meaningful level how the computer processes the information. Computer simulations are especially helpful to cognitive neuroscientists in recognizing problems that the brain must solve to produce coherent behavior.

Braitenberg (1984) provided elegant examples of how modeling brings insight to information processing. Imagine observing the two creatures shown in **Figure 3.39** as they move about a minimalist world consisting of a single heat source, such as a sun. From the outside, the creatures look identical: They both have two sensors and four

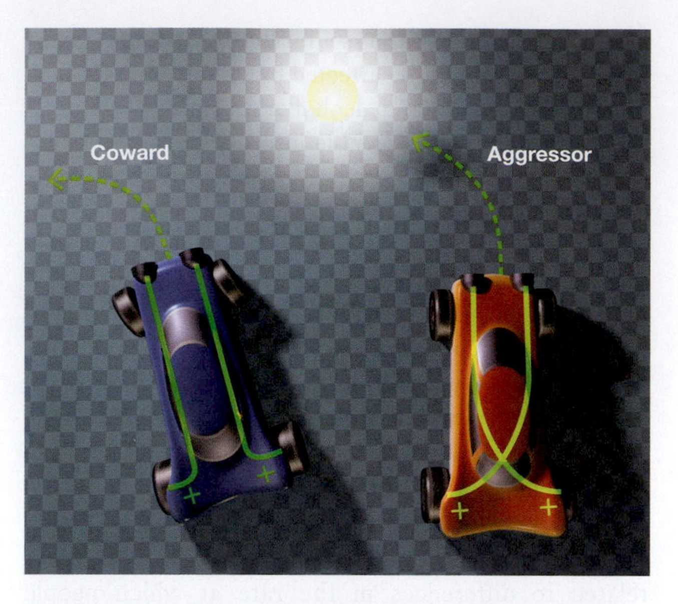

FIGURE 3.39 Behavioral differences due to different circuitry. Two very simple vehicles, each equipped with two sensors that excite motors on the rear wheels. The wheel linked to the sensor closest to the "sun" will turn faster than the other wheel, thus causing the vehicle to turn. Simply changing the wiring scheme from uncrossed (left) to crossed (right) radically alters the behavior of the vehicles. The "coward" will always avoid the sun, whereas the "aggressor" will relentlessly pursue it.

wheels. Despite this similarity, their behavior is distinct: One creature moves away from the sun, and the other homes in on it. Why the difference? As outsiders with no access to the internal operations of these creatures, we might conjecture that they have had different experiences, so the same input activates different representations. Perhaps one had a sunburn at an early age and fears the sun, and maybe the other likes the warmth.

As a look inside the creatures reveals, however, their behavioral differences depend on how they are wired. Uncrossed connections make the creature on the left turn away from the sun; crossed connections force the creature on the right to orient toward the sun. Thus, the two creatures' behavioral differences arise from a slight variation in how sensory information maps onto motor processes.

These creatures are exceedingly simple and inflexible in their actions. At best, they offer only the crudest model of how an invertebrate might move in response to a phototropic sensor. The point of Braitenberg's example is not to model a behavior; rather, it represents how a single computational change—from crossed to uncrossed wiring—can yield a major behavioral change. When interpreting such a behavioral difference, we might postulate extensive internal operations and representations. When we look inside Braitenberg's models, however, we see that there is no difference in how the two models process information, but only a difference in their patterns of connectivity.

Representations in Computer Models

Computer models differ widely in their representations. Symbolic models include, as we might expect, units that represent symbolic entities. A model for object recognition might have units that represent visual features like corners or volumetric shapes. An alternative architecture that figures prominently in cognitive neuroscience is the **neural network**. In neural networks, information processing is distributed over units whose inputs and outputs represent specific features. For example, they may indicate whether a stimulus contains a visual feature, such as a vertical or a horizontal line.

Models can be powerful tools for solving complex problems. Simulations cover the gamut of cognitive processes, including perception, memory, language, and motor control. One of the most appealing aspects of neural networks is that the architecture resembles the nervous system, at least superficially. Similar to the way neural structures depend on the activity of many neurons, in these models many units process information. The contribution of any single unit may be small in relation to the system's total output, but the aggregate action of all the units generates complex behaviors. In addition, the computations occur in parallel, and the activation levels of the units in the network can update in a relatively continuous and simultaneous manner.

Recent work in neural networks has sparked a new revolution in artificial intelligence. The impetus comes from the research of Geoffrey Hinton and his colleagues who have developed *deep learning* models, networks composed of many layers (see Chapter 14). The representational diversity and complexity that emerge from multiple layers allow these networks to recognize complex patterns such as speech sounds or individual faces. The principles of deep learning models have led to recent barriers being broken in AI: Computers are now proving to be nearly unbeatable at games such as chess, Go, and poker, and to be able to drive, well, driverless cars. In essence, these networks have shown that, if exposed to lots of varied input, learning algorithms distributed over many small processing elements can learn optimal solutions much more efficiently than can systems with hardwired input–output relationships.

Computational models can vary widely in the level of explanation they seek to provide. Some models simulate behavior at the systems level, seeking to show how a network of interconnected processing units generates cognitive operations, such as motion perception or skilled movements. In other cases, the simulations operate at a cellular or even molecular level. For example, investigations concerning how variation in transmitter uptake is a function of dendrite geometry use neural network models (Volfovsky et al., 1999). The question under investigation dictates the amount of detail to incorporate into the model. Many problems are difficult to evaluate without simulations—both experimentally, because the available experimental methods are insufficient, and mathematically, because the solutions become too complicated, given the many interactions of the processing elements.

An appealing aspect of neural network models, especially for people interested in cognitive neuroscience, is that with "lesion" techniques, we can demonstrate how a model's performance changes with altered parts. Unlike strictly serial computer models that collapse if a circuit is broken, neural network models degrade gracefully: The model may continue to perform appropriately after removing some units, because each unit plays only a small part in the processing. Artificial lesioning is thus a fascinating way to test a model's validity. You begin by constructing a model to see whether it adequately simulates normal behavior. Then you add "lesions" to see whether the breakdown in the model's performance resembles the behavioral deficits observed in neurological patients.

Models Lead to Testable Predictions

The contribution of computer modeling usually goes beyond assessing whether a model succeeds in mimicking a cognitive process. Models can generate novel predictions that we can test with real brains. An example of the predictive power of computer modeling comes from the work of Szabolcs Kali of the Hungarian Academy of Sciences and Peter Dayan at University College London (Kali & Dayan, 2004). They designed computer models to ask questions about how people store and retrieve information in memory relating to specific events—what is called *episodic memory* (see Chapter 9).

Observations from the neurosciences suggest that the *formation* of episodic memories depends critically on the hippocampus and adjacent areas of the medial temporal lobe, whereas the *storage* of such memories involves the neocortex. Kali and Dayan used a computer model to explore a specific question: How is access to stored memories maintained in a system where the neocortical connections are ever changing? (See the discussion on cortical plasticity in Chapter 5.) Does the maintenance of memories over time require the reactivation of hippocampal–neocortical connections, or can neocortical representations remain stable despite fluctuations and modifications over time?

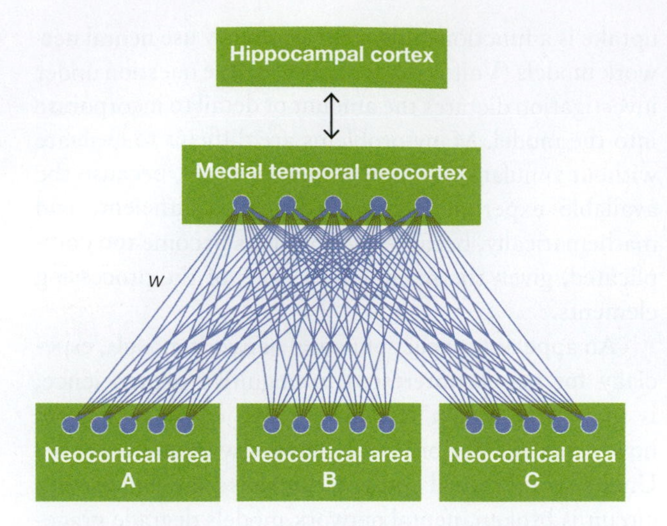

FIGURE 3.40 Computational model of episodic memory. "Neurons" (●) in neocortical areas A, B, and C are connected in a bidirectional manner to "neurons" in the medial temporal neocortex, which is itself connected bidirectionally to the hippocampus. Areas A, B, and C represent highly processed inputs (e.g., inputs from visual, auditory, or tactile domains). As the model learns, it extracts categories, trends, and correlations from the statistics of the inputs (or patterns of activations) and converts these to weights (*w*) that correspond to the strengths of the connections. Before learning, the weights might be equal or set to random values. With learning, the weights adjust to reflect correlations between the processing units.

Kali and Dayan based the model's architecture on anatomical facts about patterns of connectivity between the hippocampus and neocortex (**Figure 3.40**), and they trained it on a set of patterns that represented distinct episodic memories. For example, one pattern of activation might correspond to the first time you visited the Pacific Ocean, and another pattern to the lecture in which you first learned about the Stroop effect. Once the model mastered the memory set by showing that it could correctly recall a full episode when given only partial information, Kali and Dayan tested it on a consolidation task: If cortical units continued to follow their initial learning rules, could old memories remain after the hippocampus was disconnected from the cortex? In essence, this was a test of whether lesions to the hippocampus would disrupt long-term episodic memory.

The results indicated that after the hippocampus was disconnected from the cortex, episodic memory became quite impaired. Thus, the model predicts that hippocampal *reactivation* is necessary for maintaining even well-consolidated episodic memories. In the model, this maintenance process requires a mechanism that keeps hippocampal and neocortical representations in register with one another, even as the neocortex undergoes subtle changes associated with daily learning.

Researchers initiated this modeling project because studies on people with lesions of the hippocampus had failed to provide a clear answer about the role of this structure in memory consolidation. This model, based on known principles of neuroanatomy and neurophysiology, could test specific hypotheses concerning one type of memory, episodic memory, and could direct future research. The goal here was not to make a model that had perfect memory consolidation, but rather to ask how human memory works.

The contribution of computer simulations continues to grow in the cognitive neurosciences. The trend in the field is for modeling work to be more constrained by neuroscience. Researchers will replace generic processing units with elements that embody the biophysics of the brain. In a reciprocal manner, computer simulations provide a useful way to develop theory, which may then aid researchers in designing experiments and interpreting results.

TAKE-HOME MESSAGES

- We can use computer models to simulate neural networks in order to ask questions about cognitive processes and generate predictions that can be tested in future research.
- Models can be "lesioned" to test whether the resulting change in performance resembles the behavioral deficits observed in neurological patients. Lesioning thus provides a tool to assess whether the model accurately simulates a particular cognitive process or domain and, more important, to shed light on the credibility of the model.

3.9 Converging Methods

As we have seen throughout these early chapters, cognitive neuroscience is an interdisciplinary field that draws on ideas and methodologies from cognitive psychology, neurology, the neurosciences, and computer science. Optogenetics is a prime example of how the paradigms and methods from different disciplines have coalesced into a startling new methodology for cognitive neuroscientists and, perhaps soon, for clinicians. The great strength of cognitive neuroscience lies in the ways that diverse methodologies are integrated.

Many examples of converging methods will be evident as you make your way through this book. For example, other methodologies frequently guide the interpretation of results from neuroimaging studies. Single-cell-recording studies of primates can guide the identification of regions of interest in an fMRI study of humans. We can use imaging studies to isolate a component operation linked to a particular brain region by observing the performance of patients with injuries to that area.

We can also use imaging studies to generate hypotheses that we can test with alternative methodologies. A striking example of this approach comes from work asking how people identify objects through touch. An fMRI study on this problem revealed an unexpected result: Even when participants kept their eyes closed, tactile object recognition led to pronounced activation of the visual cortex (Deibert et al., 1999; **Figure 3.41a**). One possible reason for visual cortex activation is that the participants identified the objects through touch and then generated visual images of them. Alternatively, the participants might have constructed visual images during tactile exploration and then used the images to identify the objects.

Pitting these hypotheses against one another, a follow-up study used transcranial magnetic stimulation (TMS; Zangaladze et al., 1999). TMS over the visual cortex impaired tactile object recognition, but only when the TMS pulses occurred 180 ms after the hand touched the object; earlier or later stimulation had no effect (**Figure 3.41b**). These results indicate that the visual representations generated during tactile exploration were essential for inferring object shape from touch. These studies demonstrate how the combination of fMRI and TMS enables investigators to test causal accounts of neural function, as well as to make inferences about the time course of processing. Obtaining converging evidence from various methodologies allows the strongest conclusions possible.

Building on advances in unraveling the human genome, cognitive neuroscientists are employing genetic approaches in their work, frequently combining these data with imaging and behavioral methods. This approach is widely employed in studies of psychiatric conditions known to have a genetic basis, such as schizophrenia. Daniel Weinberger and his colleagues at the National Institutes of Health have proposed that the efficacy of antipsychotic medications in treating schizophrenia varies with the expression of a particular gene, called a *polymorphism* (Bertolino et al., 2004; Weickert et al., 2004). Specifically, individuals with schizophrenia who have one variant of a gene linked to the release of dopamine in prefrontal cortex show improved performance on tasks requiring working memory and correlated changes in prefrontal activity when given an antipsychotic drug. In contrast, those with a different variant of the gene do not respond to the drugs.

Applying the logic underlying these clinical studies, we can ask how genetic differences within the normal population relate to individual variations in brain function and behavior. A common polymorphism in the human brain relates to the gene that codes for monoamine oxidase A (MAOA). Using a large sample of healthy individuals,

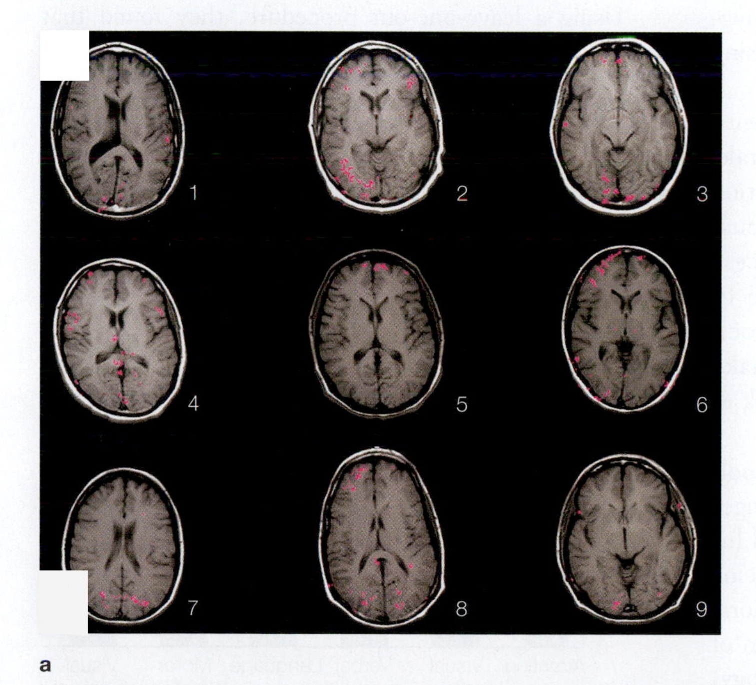

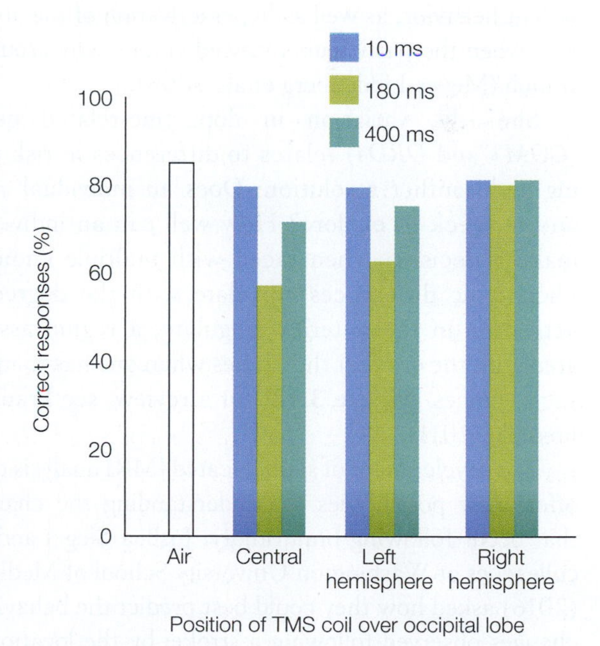

FIGURE 3.41 Combined use of fMRI and TMS to demonstrate the role of the visual cortex in tactile perception.
(a) Functional MRI showing areas of activation in 9 participants during tactile exploration with the eyes closed. All of the participants show some activation in striate and extrastriate cortex. **(b)** Accuracy in judging the orientation of a tactile stimulus that is vibrated against the right index finger. Performance is disrupted when the pulse is applied 180 ms after stimulus onset, but only when the coil is positioned over the left occipital lobe or at a midline point between the left and right sides of the occipital lobe.

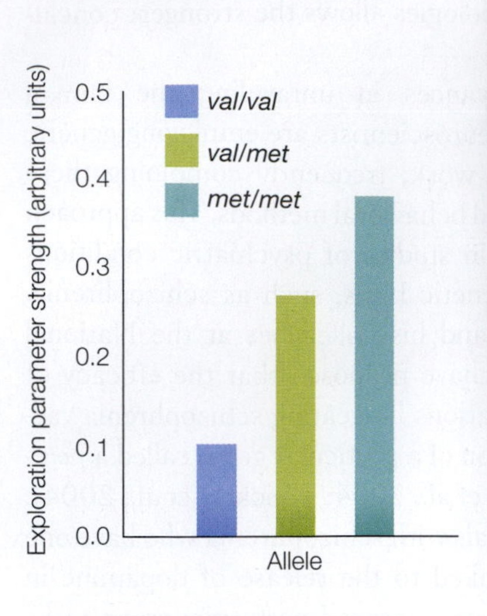

a *COMT* gene–dose effects

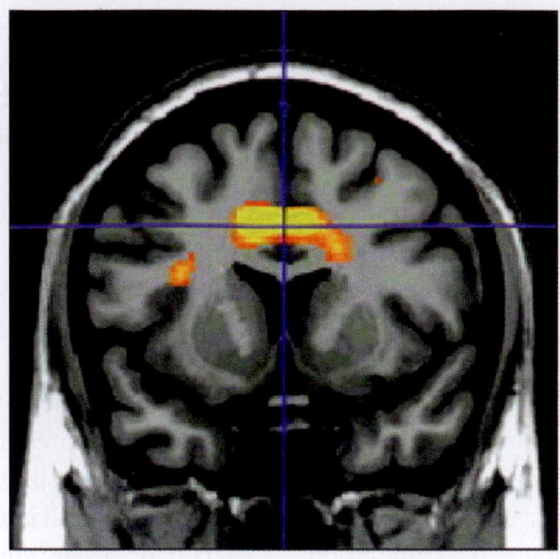

b Activation differences correlated with different alleles of the *DRD4* gene

FIGURE 3.42 Genetic effects on decision making.
(a) Participants were divided into three groups determined by a genetic analysis of the *COMT* gene: *val/val*, *val/met*, and *met/met*. They performed a decision-making task, and a model was used to estimate how likely they were to explore new but uncertain choices. Those with the *met/met* allele were more likely to explore, compared to those with the *val/val* allele. (b) Allele differences in the *DRD4* gene influenced the level of conflict-related activity in the anterior cingulate cortex (yellow-orange highlighting).

Weinberger's group found that the low-expression variant was associated with an increased tendency toward violent behavior, as well as hyperactivation of the amygdala when the participants viewed emotionally arousing stimuli (Meyer-Lindenberg et al., 2006).

Similarly, variation in dopamine-related genes (*COMT* and *DRD4*) relates to differences in risk taking and conflict resolution: Does an individual stick out her neck to explore? How well can an individual make a decision when faced with multiple choices? Phenotypic differences correlate with the degree of activation in the anterior cingulate, a region associated with the conflict that arises when one has to make such choices (**Figure 3.42**; for a review, see Frank & Fossella, 2011).

The development of sophisticated fMRI analysis tools offers new possibilities for understanding the changes that occur following brain injury. Joshua Siegel and his colleagues at Washington University School of Medicine (2016) asked how they could best predict the behavioral changes observed following a stroke: by the location of the lesion (the classic approach of behavioral neurology) or by changes in functional connectivity? For a sample of 132 stroke patients with lesions in various regions, they obtained anatomical MRI scans to measure lesion topography; rs-fMRI scans to measure their resting functional connectivity; and behavior measures in six domains (attention, visual memory, verbal memory, language, motor function, and visual function) to access neurological impairment.

Using a leave-one-out procedure, they found that lesion location was the best predictor of motor and visual function, but connectivity was a better predictor of memory function (**Figure 3.43**). The researchers were able to predict attention and language function equally well by either method. Memory may be a more distributed process than motor control or visual perception, and thus patterns of connectivity may be more important than the

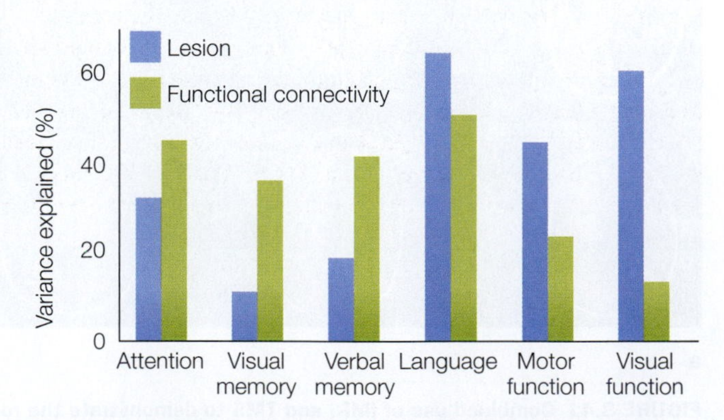

FIGURE 3.43 The accuracy of lesion-deficit and functional-connectivity-deficit models varies by domain.
The bar graph shows the percentage of variance in the six behavioral domains. In the motor and visual domains, the location of the lesion is a better predictor of the deficit, whereas functional connectivity is the better predictor in the memory domain.

integrity of specific areas. Other studies have indicated that the benefits of cognitive rehabilitation programs are greatest in patients who have intact hubs.

We can also explore these questions in healthy individuals, using TMS to transiently perturb brain activity. Caterina Gratton and colleagues (2013) measured resting-state functional connectivity before and after theta-burst rTMS. In one session, the researcher applied TMS to the left dorsolateral prefrontal cortex, a key node of the frontoparietal attention network (FPAN). In the other session, she applied TMS over the left primary somatosensory cortex (S1), a region that is not part of the FPAN. As **Figure 3.44** shows, TMS increased connectivity across the brain: Give it a jolt and things perk up! Nevertheless, the increase in connectivity was much larger when the stimulation was to the FPN network. Note that this study also makes the point that TMS applied to a specified location can induce broad changes across the brain. An integrative perspective is always important to maintain when studying something as complex as the brain.

TAKE-HOME MESSAGES

- We can gain powerful insights into the structural and functional underpinnings of cognitive behavior from experiments that combine methods.
- Combining methods may enable progress from correlational observations to experimental approaches that provide inferential tests of causation.

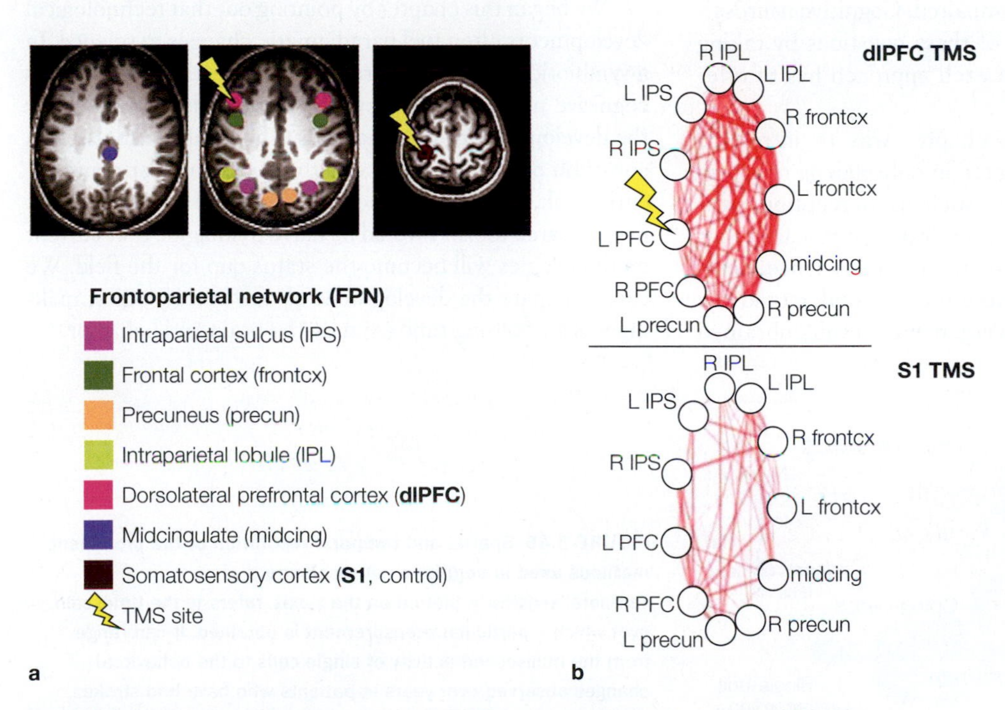

FIGURE 3.44 Connectivity changes to left dlPFC and somatosensory cortex with TMS.
(a) Cognitive control networks and TMS stimulation sites. Connectivity measurements were made before and after TMS to the left dlPFC (a region in the FPN) and to the left somatosensory cortex (S1) as a control location. Lightning bolts indicate where TMS was targeted. (b) Connectivity changes after TMS to the left dlPFC and left S1. Red lines indicate increased connectivity after TMS, and thicker, darker lines indicate greater magnitude of change. After TMS, there is a generalized increase in connectivity across the brain, which is much larger when the control network location (dlPFC) is stimulated than when S1 is.

Summary

Two goals guided our overview of cognitive neuroscience methods in this chapter. The first was to provide a sense of how various methodologies have come together to form the interdisciplinary field of cognitive neuroscience (**Figure 3.45**). Practitioners of the neurosciences, cognitive psychology, and neurology differ in the tools they use and, often, in the questions they seek to answer. The neurologist may request a CT scan of an aging boxer to determine whether the patient's confusional state is a symptom of atrophy of the frontal lobes. The neuroscientist may want a blood sample from the patient to search for metabolic markers indicating a reduction in a transmitter system. The cognitive psychologist may design a reaction time experiment to test whether a component operation of decision making is selectively impaired. Cognitive neuroscience endeavors to answer all of these questions by taking advantage of the insights that each approach has to offer and using them together.

The second goal of this chapter was to introduce methods that we will encounter in subsequent chapters focusing on content domains such as perception, language, and memory. Each chapter draws on research that uses the diverse methods of cognitive neuroscience, demonstrating how we employ these tools to understand the brain and behavior. The convergence of results obtained by using different methodologies frequently offers the most complete theories. A single method often cannot bring about a complete understanding of the complex processes of cognition.

We have reviewed many methods, but the review is incomplete. New methodologies for investigating the relation of the brain and behavior spring to life each year. Technological change is also a driving force in our understanding of the human mind. Our current imaging tools are constantly being refined. Each year, equipment that is more sensitive is available to measure the electrophysiological signals of the brain or the metabolic correlates of neural activity. The mathematical tools for analyzing these data are also increasingly more sophisticated.

We began this chapter by pointing out that technological developments often fuel paradigmatic changes in science. In a symbiotic way, the maturation of a scientific field such as cognitive neuroscience provides a tremendous impetus for the development of new methods. The available tools often constrain our ability to answer the questions that neuroscientists ask, but such questions promote the development of new research tools. It would be naive to imagine that current methodologies will become the status quo for the field. We can anticipate the development of new technologies, making this an exciting time to study the brain and behavior.

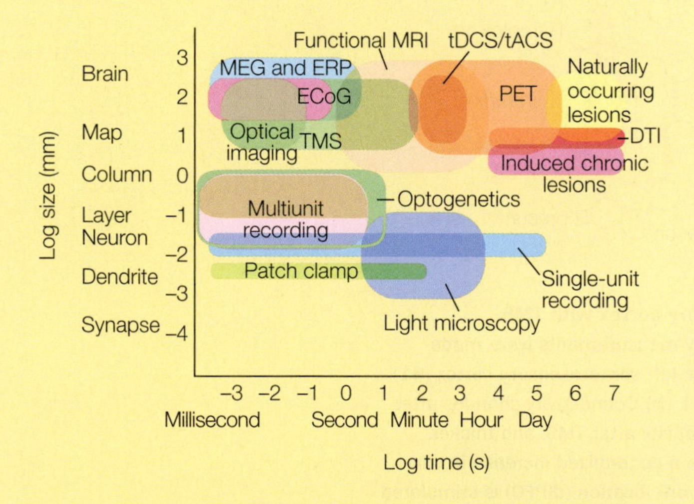

FIGURE 3.45 Spatial and temporal resolution of the prominent methods used in cognitive neuroscience.
Temporal sensitivity, plotted on the *x*-axis, refers to the timescale over which a particular measurement is obtained. It can range from the millisecond activity of single cells to the behavioral changes observed over years in patients who have had strokes. Spatial sensitivity, plotted on the *y*-axis, refers to the localization capability of the methods. For example, real-time changes in the membrane potential of isolated dendritic regions can be detected with patch clamps, providing excellent temporal and spatial resolution. In contrast, naturally occurring lesions damage large regions of the cortex and are detectable with MRI.

Key Terms

binocular rivalry (p. 109)
block design (p. 107)
blood oxygen level–dependent (BOLD) (p. 106)
cerebral vascular accident (p. 79)
cognitive psychology (p. 74)
computerized tomography (CT, CAT) (p. 93)
connectivity map (connectome) (p. 112)
deep brain stimulation (DBS) (p. 88)
degenerative disorder (p. 80)
dependent variable (p. 76)
diffusion tensor imaging (DTI) (p. 95)
double dissociation (p. 83)
electrocorticography (ECoG) (p. 98)
electroencephalography (EEG) (p. 100)
event-related design (p. 107)

event-related potential (ERP) (p. 101)
functional magnetic resonance imaging (fMRI) (p. 104)
hemodynamic response (p. 104)
independent variable (p. 76)
magnetic resonance imaging (MRI) (p. 93)
magnetic resonance spectroscopy (MRS) (p. 109)
magnetoencephalography (MEG) (p. 102)
multiunit recording (p. 97)
multivoxel pattern analysis (MVPA) (p. 108)
neural network (p. 117)
optogenetics (p. 89)
pharmacological study (p. 85)
positron emission tomography (PET) (p. 104)
receptive field (p. 96)
regional cerebral blood flow (rCBF) (p. 105)
retinotopic map (p. 97)
simulation (p. 116)
single-cell recording (p. 96)
single dissociation (p. 83)
transcranial alternating current stimulation (tACS) (p. 92)
transcranial direct current stimulation (tDCS) (p. 92)
transcranial focused ultrasound (tFUS) (p. 93)
transcranial magnetic stimulation (TMS) (p. 89)
transcranial static magnetic stimulation (tSMS) (p. 93)
traumatic brain injury (TBI) (p. 81)
voxel (p. 105)

Think About It

1. To a large extent, progress in all scientific fields depends on the development of new technologies and methodologies. What technological and methodological developments have advanced the field of cognitive neuroscience?
2. Cognitive neuroscience is an interdisciplinary field that incorporates aspects of neuroanatomy, neurophysiology, neurology, and cognitive psychology. What do you consider the core feature of each discipline that allows it to contribute to cognitive neuroscience? What are the limits of each discipline in addressing questions related to the brain and mind?
3. In recent years, functional magnetic resonance imaging (fMRI) has taken the field of cognitive neuroscience by storm. The first studies with this method were reported in the early 1990s; now hundreds of papers are published each month. Provide at least three reasons why this method is so popular. Discuss some of the technical and inferential limitations associated with this method (*inferential*, meaning limitations in the kinds of questions the method can answer). Finally, propose an fMRI experiment you would conduct if you were interested in identifying the neural differences between people who like scary movies and those who don't. Be sure to clearly state the different conditions of the experiment.
4. Research studies show that people who performed poorly on spatial reasoning tasks have reduced volume in the parietal lobe. Discuss why caution is advised in assuming that poor reasoning is caused by the smaller size of the parietal lobe. To provide a stronger test of causality, outline an experiment that involves a training program, describing your conditions, experimental manipulation, outcome measures, and predictions.
5. Consider how you might study a problem such as color perception by using the multidisciplinary techniques of cognitive neuroscience. Predict the questions that you might ask about this topic, and outline the types of studies that cognitive psychologists, neurophysiologists, and neurologists might consider.

Suggested Reading

Frank, M. J., & Fossella, J. A. (2011). Neurogenetics and pharmacology of learning, motivation and cognition. *Neuropsychopharmacology*, *36*, 133–152.

Hillyard, S. A. (1993). Electrical and magnetic brain recordings: Contributions to cognitive neuroscience. *Current Opinion in Neurobiology*, *3*, 710–717.

Huang, Y. Z., Lu, M. K., Antal, A., Classen, J., Nitsche, M., Ziemann, U., et al. (2017). Plasticity induced by non-invasive transcranial brain stimulation: A position paper. *Clinical Neurophysiology*, *128*, 2318–2329.

Lopes da Silva, F. (2013). EEG and MEG: Relevance to neuroscience. *Neuron*, *80*, 1112–1128.

Mori, S. (2007). *Introduction to diffusion tensor imaging.* New York: Elsevier.

Poldrack, R. A., Mumford, J. A., and Nichols, T. E. (2011). *Handbook of functional MRI data analysis.* Cambridge: Cambridge University Press.

Rapp, B. (2001). *The handbook of cognitive neuropsychology: What deficits reveal about the human mind.* Philadelphia: Psychology Press.

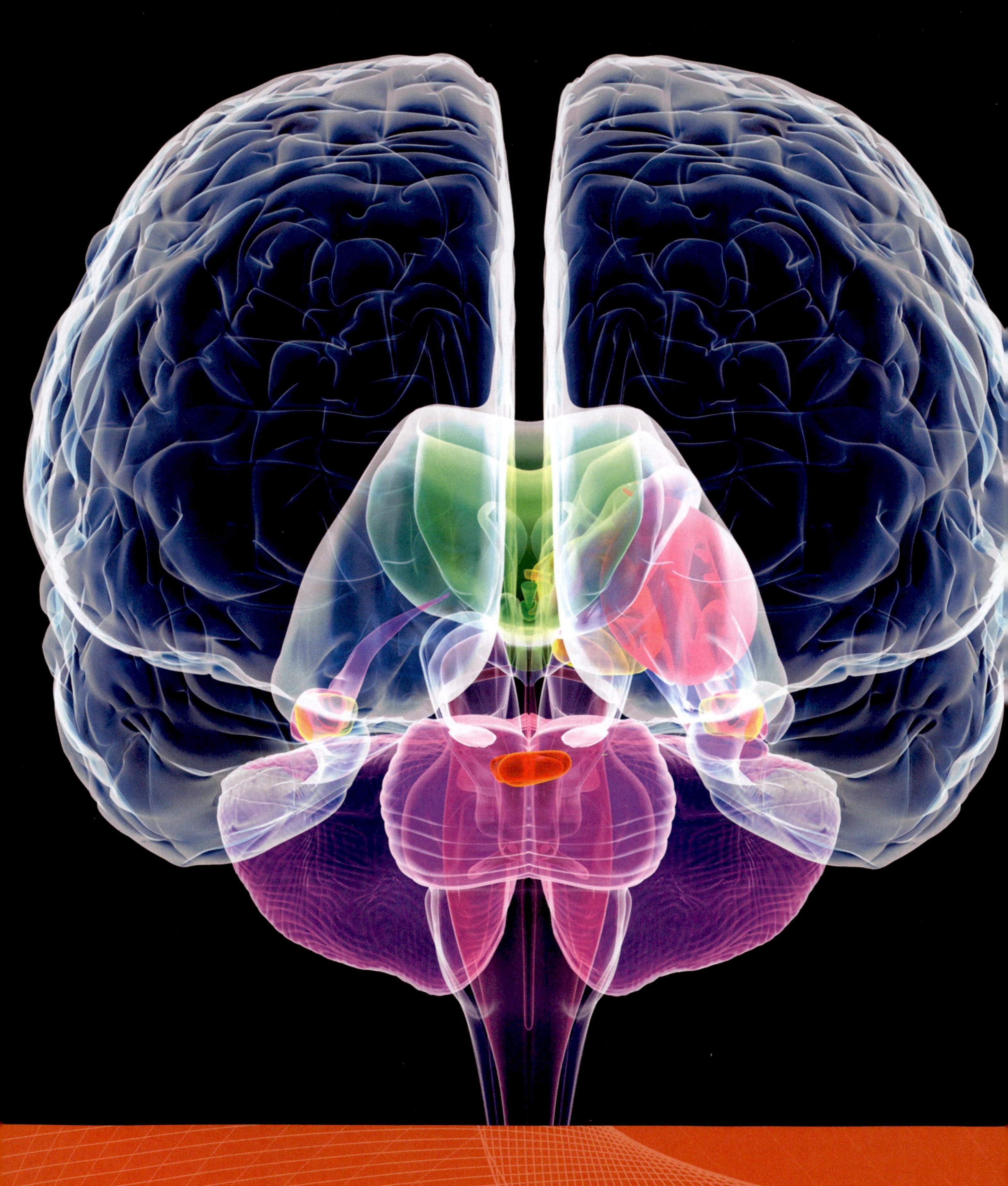

Practically everybody in New York has half a mind to write a book, and does.

Groucho Marx

CHAPTER

4

Hemispheric Specialization

IT WAS 1961, and for the previous ten years, W.J., a charismatic war veteran, had been suffering two grand mal seizures a week. Although he appeared perfectly normal otherwise, each seizure upended his life and required a full day of recovery. He was willing to try anything that might improve his situation.

After critically reviewing the medical literature, neurosurgery resident Joseph Bogen suggested a rarely performed procedure: severing the corpus callosum, the tract of nerves connecting the right and left cerebral hemispheres. Twenty years earlier, a series of patients in Rochester, New York, had undergone the surgery. None had reported ill side effects, and all had shown improvement in seizure control (Akelaitis, 1941).

Reassuringly, psychological studies done before and after the patients' surgeries revealed no differences in their brain function or behavior. Yet a concern lingered: Studies on cats, monkeys, and chimps that had undergone this surgery had found that it resulted in dramatically altered brain function. Nonetheless, W.J. chose to risk the procedure. The surgery was a great success: W.J. noticed no odd side effects; his temperament, intellect, and delightful personality remained unchanged; and his seizures were completely resolved. W.J. felt better than he had felt in years (Gazzaniga et al., 1962).

It was puzzling that humans seemed to suffer no effects from severing the two hemispheres when other animals did. To help solve this mystery, W.J., ever the gentleman, submitted to hours of tests both before and after the surgery. Taking advantage of the fact that information from the right visual field is processed solely in the left hemisphere (and vice versa), one of this book's authors (M.S.G.) devised a way to communicate with each hemisphere separately, a method that had not been tried on the previous patients.

It was expected that W.J. would be able to name items presented to his right visual field because the brain's speech center is located in the left hemisphere. A picture of a spoon was flashed to W.J.'s right visual field; when asked if he had

BIG Questions

- Do the differences in the anatomy of the two hemispheres explain their functional differences?
- Why do split-brain patients generally feel unified and no different after surgery, even though their two hemispheres no longer communicate with each other?
- Do separated hemispheres each have their own sense of self?
- Which half of the brain decides what gets done and when?

ANATOMICAL ORIENTATION

Hemispheres of the Brain

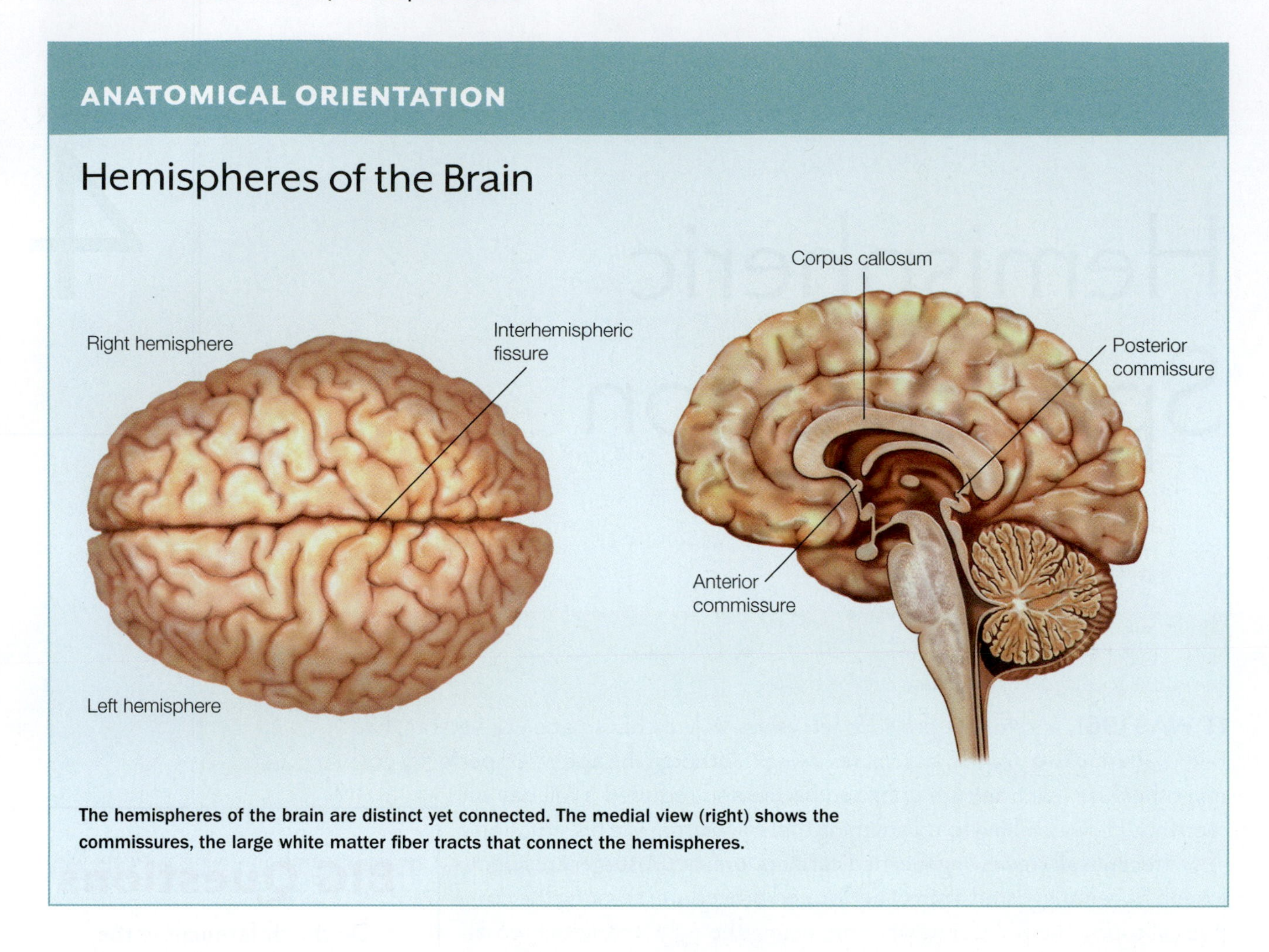

The hemispheres of the brain are distinct yet connected. The medial view (right) shows the commissures, the large white matter fiber tracts that connect the hemispheres.

seen anything, he said "spoon," as predicted. Because no abnormalities had been found in the Rochester patients, the corpus callosum was thought to be unnecessary for interhemispheric integration of information in humans. If so, W.J. should also have been able to say what was flashed to his left visual field and processed in his right hemisphere. It was time for the critical test. A picture was flashed to his left visual field, and W.J. was again asked, "Did you see anything?" He firmly replied, "No, I didn't see anything."

W.J. exuded such confidence in his declaration that it seemed as if he must have gone blind in his left visual field. Had he? To test this, the investigators allowed W.J. to respond by using a Morse code key with his left hand (the right hemisphere controls the left hand) rather than verbally. When a light was flashed to his left visual field (hence, the right hemisphere), he pressed the key with his left hand, yet he stated (his left hemisphere talking) that he saw nothing.

More tests resulted in more remarkable findings: W.J.'s right hemisphere could do things that his left could not do, and vice versa. For example, before surgery W.J. could write dictated sentences and carry out any kind of command, such as making a fist, with his right hand (controlled by the left hemisphere). After surgery, though, his right hand could not arrange four red and white blocks to match a simple pattern, yet his left hand (controlled by the right hemisphere) was a wiz at this type of test. When W.J.'s right hand attempted to arrange the blocks, his left hand kept trying to intervene. W.J. had to sit on his left hand so that the right hand could at least try!

Next, both hands were allowed to arrange the blocks. This experiment was the beginning of the idea that "Mind Left" can have one view of the world, its own desires and aspirations, and "Mind Right" can have another. As soon as Mind Right, working through W.J.'s left hand, began to arrange the blocks correctly, Mind Left would undo the good work. The hands were in competition! The specializations of each hemisphere were different, and growing out of that difference were the behaviors of each half of the brain. These results raised all sorts of questions and gave birth to the field of human split-brain research.

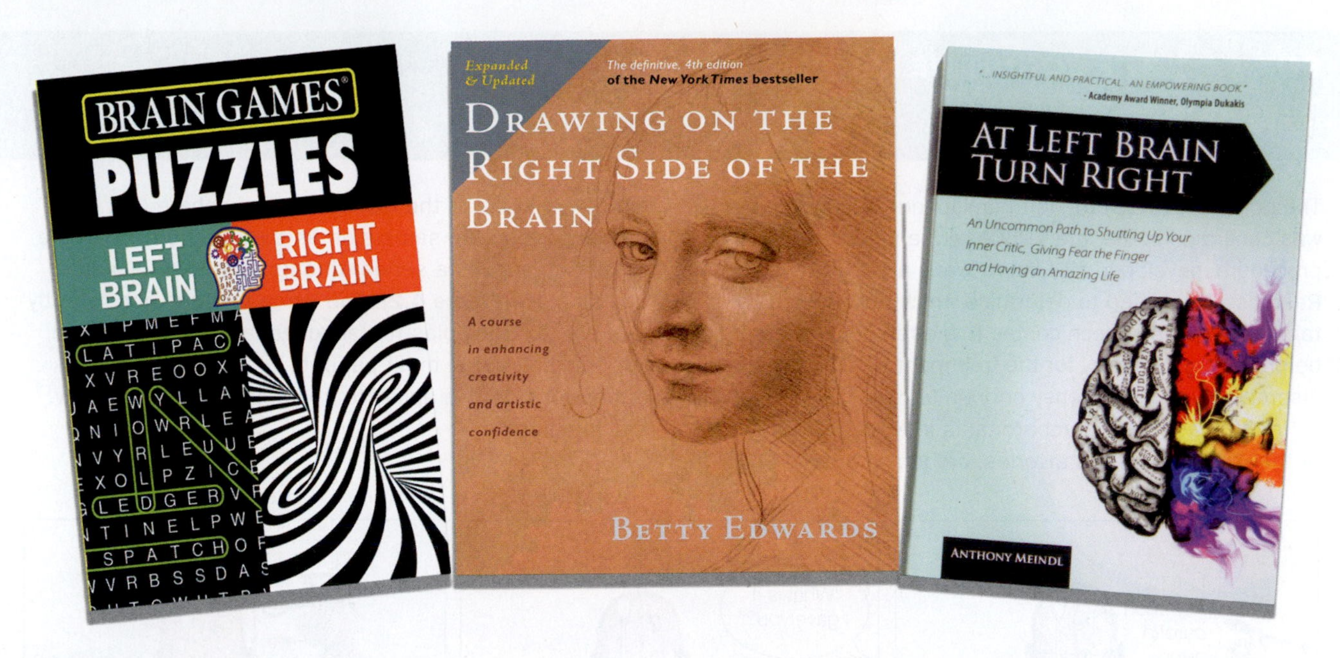

FIGURE 4.1
These books perpetuate the common but naively simplified idea that the "left brain" is logical and analytical, while the "right brain" is creative and intuitive.

In this chapter we examine the processing differences between the right and left cerebral hemispheres. Using data from studies of both split-brain patients and patients with unilateral focal brain lesions, we underscore the crucial role played by lateralized processes in cognition. This research and recent computational investigations of lateralization and specialization have advanced the field far beyond the simplistic interpretations by the popular press that the "left brain" is analytical and the "right brain" is creative (**Figure 4.1**). We also examine the type of neural architecture that results in specialized circuits, and the possible reasons why lateralized functions evolved. We begin by looking first at the structure and function of the two halves and their interconnections.

4.1 Anatomical Correlates of Hemispheric Specialization

For centuries, the effects of unilateral brain damage have revealed major functional differences between the two hemispheres. The most dramatic and most studied has been the effect of left-hemisphere damage on language functions (see **Box 4.1**). PET and fMRI neuroimaging studies have further confirmed that language processing is preferentially biased to the left hemisphere (Binder & Price, 2001).

In the last 60 years, research involving patients who have had their cerebral hemispheres disconnected for medical reasons has also produced dramatic effects, including, most shockingly, two separately conscious hemispheres within a single brain! This finding has ramifications that we will discuss in Chapter 14 on consciousness, but in this chapter we will focus on the processing differences currently known between the two hemispheres. To begin with, we need to get a handle on the macroscopic and microscopic differences between the two hemispheres, the anatomy of the fiber tracts that connect the two hemispheres, and how those differences in anatomy may contribute to any functional differences between the two hemispheres.

Macroscopic Anatomical Asymmetries

The major lobes (occipital, parietal, temporal, and frontal; see Figure 2.36 in Chapter 2) appear, at least superficially, to be symmetrical, and each half of the cerebral cortex of the human brain has approximately the same size and surface area. The two hemispheres are offset, however. The right protrudes in front, and the left protrudes in back. The right is chubbier (actually has more volume) in the frontal region, and the left is larger posteriorly, in the occipital region, frequently nudging the right hemisphere off center and bending the

BOX 4.1 | THE COGNITIVE NEUROSCIENTIST'S TOOLKIT

The Wada Test

The dominant role of the left hemisphere in language was confirmed in the late 1950s by the **Wada test**. This procedure, developed by Juhn A. Wada and Theodore Rasmussen, is used to determine which hemisphere contains the brain's speech center. It is often administered before elective surgery for the treatment of neurological disorders, such as epilepsy or brain tumors.

In the Wada test, amobarbital is injected into one of the patient's carotid arteries, producing a rapid and brief anesthesia of the ipsilateral hemisphere (i.e., the hemisphere on the same side as the injection). Then the patient undergoes a series of tests related to language and memory (**Figure 4.2**). The Wada test has consistently revealed a strong bias for language lateralization to the left hemisphere: In most patients, when the injection is to the left side, the ability to speak is disrupted for several minutes.

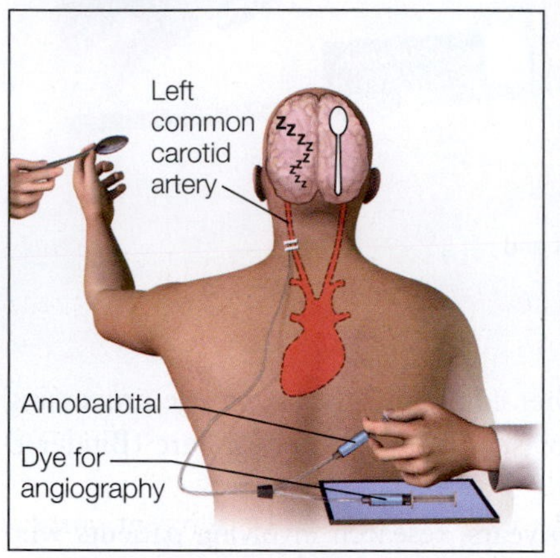

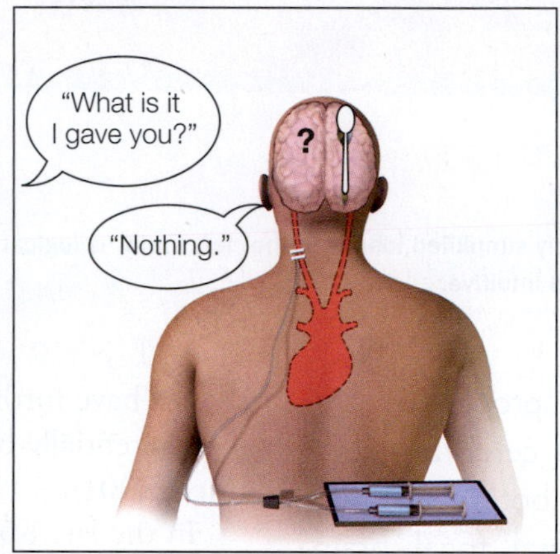

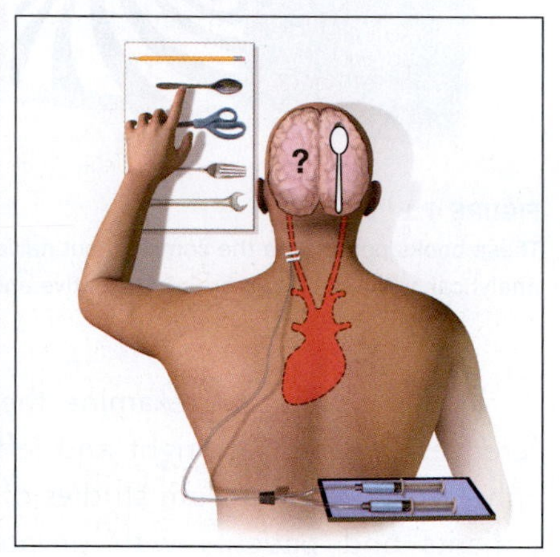

FIGURE 4.2 Methods used in amobarbital testing.
(a) After angiography, amobarbital is administered to the left hemisphere, anesthetizing the language and speech systems. A spoon is placed in the left hand, and the right hemisphere takes note. **(b)** When the left hemisphere regains consciousness, the participant is asked what was placed in his left hand, and he responds, "Nothing." **(c)** Showing the patient a board with a variety of objects pinned to it reveals that the patient can easily point to the appropriate object, because the right hemisphere directs the left hand during the match-to-sample task.

longitudinal fissure between the two hemispheres to the right (**Figure 4.3**).

Anatomists of the 19th century observed that the **Sylvian fissure** (also called the *lateral fissure*)—the large sulcus that defines the superior border of the temporal lobe—has a more prominent upward curl in the right hemisphere than it does in the left hemisphere, where it is relatively flat. This difference in the shape of the Sylvian fissure between the two cerebral hemispheres is directly related to subsequent reports of size differences in adjacent cortical regions buried within the fissure.

At Harvard Medical School in the 1960s, Norman Geschwind examined brains obtained postmortem from 100 people known to be right-handed (Geschwind & Levitsky, 1968). After slicing through the lateral fissure, Geschwind measured the temporal lobe's surface area and discovered that the **planum temporale**, the cortical area at the center of Wernicke's area (involved with the understanding of written and spoken language), was larger in the left hemisphere—a pattern found in 65% of the brains. Of the remaining brains, 11% had a larger surface area in the right hemisphere, and 24% had no asymmetry. The asymmetry in this region of the temporal lobe may extend to subcortical structures connected to these areas. For example, portions of the thalamus (the lateral posterior nucleus) also tend to be larger on the left.

Because these temporal lobe asymmetries seem to be a characteristic of the normally lateralized brain, other investigators have explored whether the asymmetry is absent in individuals with developmental language

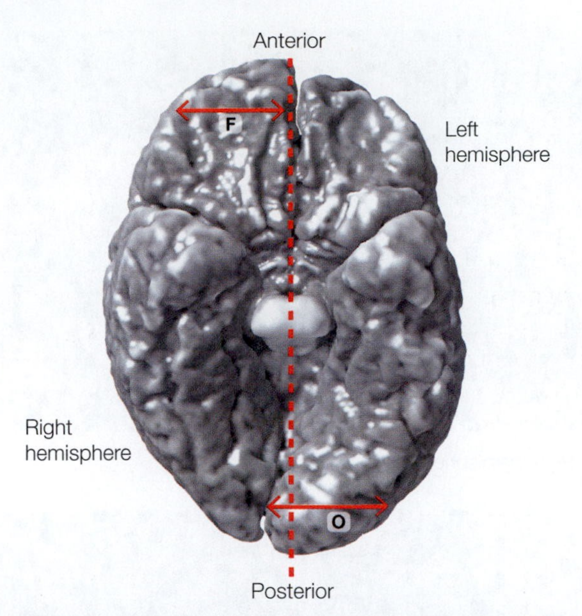

FIGURE 4.3 Anatomical asymmetries between the two cerebral hemispheres.
View of the inferior surface of the brain. (Note that the left hemisphere appears on the right side of the image.) In this computer-generated reconstruction, the anatomical asymmetries have been exaggerated. F = frontal lobe; O = occipital lobe.

disorders. Interestingly, MRI studies reveal that the area of the planum temporale is approximately symmetrical in children with dyslexia—a clue that their language difficulties may stem from the lack of a specialized left hemisphere.

A recent study examined the surface area of the planum temporale in children who hadn't yet learned how to read. Children with no family history of dyslexia exhibited the usual leftward asymmetry in planum temporale surface area, but children with a family history of dyslexia had more symmetrical planum temporale surface areas. This finding suggests that the atypical language areas observed in people with dyslexia precede their learning how to read (Vanderauwera et al., 2016).

In addition, a study examining white matter tracts in children with dyslexia found that several of the white matter pathways in dyslexic children had greater rightward asymmetry (i.e., white matter tracts that are usually left-lateralized were more symmetrical, and white matter tracts that are usually symmetrical were more right-lateralized), and that these rightward shifts of lateralization were predictive of the children's reading deficits (Zhao et al., 2016).

The asymmetry of the planum temporale is one of the few examples in which an anatomical index is correlated with a well-defined **functional asymmetry**. The complex functions of language comprehension presumably require more cortical surface. Some questions remain, however, concerning both the validity and the explanatory power of this asymmetry. First, although the left-hemisphere planum temporale is larger in 65% of right-handers, functional measures indicate that 96% of right-handers show left-hemisphere language dominance. Second, there is a suggestion that the apparent asymmetries in the planum temporale result from the techniques and criteria used to identify this region. When three-dimensional imaging techniques—techniques that take into account asymmetries in curvature patterns of the lateral fissures—are applied, hemispheric asymmetries become negligible. Whether or not this view is correct, the anatomical basis for left-hemisphere dominance in language may not be fully reflected in gross morphology. We also need to examine the neural circuits within these cortical locations.

Microscopic Anatomical Asymmetries

By studying the cellular basis of hemispheric specialization, we seek to understand whether differences in neural circuits between the hemispheres might underlie functional asymmetries in tasks such as language. Perhaps specific organizational characteristics of local neural networks—such as the number of synaptic connections—are responsible for the unique functions of different cortical areas. In addition, regions of the brain with greater volume may contain more minicolumns and their connections (Casanova & Tillquist, 2008; see Chapter 2, "Dividing the Cortex by Cell Architecture"). A promising approach has been to look for specializations in cortical circuitry within **homotopic areas** of the cerebral hemispheres (i.e., areas in corresponding locations in the two hemispheres) that are known to be functionally asymmetrical—and what better place to look than in the language area?

Differences have been found in the cortical microcircuitry between the two hemispheres in both anterior (Broca's) and posterior (Wernicke's) language-associated cortex. We leave the discussion of the function of these areas to Chapter 11; here, we are concerned with merely their structural differences.

As we learned in Chapter 2 (Section 2.5), the cortex is a layered sheet of tightly spaced columns of cells, each comprising a circuit of neurons that is repeated over and over across the cortical surface. From studies of visual cortex, we know that cells in an individual column act together to encode relatively small features of the visual world. Individual columns connect with adjacent and distant columns to form ensembles of neurons that can encode more complex features.

In language-associated regions, several types of micro-level asymmetries between the hemispheres have been identified. Some of these asymmetries occur at the level of the individual neurons that make up a single cortical column. For instance, neurons in the left and right hemispheres have different distributions of dendritic branch orders, where "order" indicates the generation of a branch offshoot: First-order branches shoot off from the cell body, second-order branches shoot off from first-order branches, and so on. In humans, neurons in the left hemisphere have more high-order dendritic branching than do neurons in homotopic regions of the right hemisphere, which have more low-order dendritic branching (Scheibel et al., 1985). If you compare dendritic branching to the branching of a tree, a left-hemisphere neuron would be more similar to an elm tree, which has few large limbs but extensive higher-order branching, and a right-hemisphere neuron would be more similar to a pine tree, which has many first- and second-order branches but very few high-order branches.

Other asymmetries are found in the relationships between adjacent neuronal columns: Within Wernicke's area in the left hemisphere, for example, columns are spaced farther apart, possibly to accommodate additional connectional fibers between the columns. Asymmetries also are found in larger ensembles of more distant cortical columns (Hutsler & Galuske, 2003). Individual cells within a column of the left primary auditory cortex have a tangential dendritic spread that accommodates the greater distance between cell columns, but secondary auditory areas that show the same increase in distance between the columns do not have longer dendrites in the left hemisphere. The cells in these columns contact fewer adjacent cell columns than do those in the right hemisphere.

Additional structural differences have been documented in both anterior and posterior language cortex. These asymmetries include cell size differences between the hemispheres, such as those shown in **Figure 4.4**, and may suggest a greater long-range connectivity in the language-associated regions of the left hemisphere. Asymmetries in connectivity between the two hemispheres have been demonstrated directly by tracing the neuronal connections within posterior language-associated regions using dyes that diffuse through postmortem tissue. Such dyes show a patchy pattern of connectivity within these regions of each hemisphere, but within the left hemisphere these patches are spaced farther apart than in the right hemisphere (Galuske et al., 2000).

What is the functional significance of these various asymmetries within cortical circuitry, and how might these changes specifically alter information processing in the language-dominant hemisphere? Most interpretations of these findings have focused on the relationship between adjacent neurons and adjacent columns, highlighting the fact that differences in both columnar spacing and dendritic tree size would cause cells in the left hemisphere to connect to fewer neurons. This structural specialization might underlie more elaborate and less redundant patterns of connectivity, which in turn might give rise to better separation between local processing streams. In addition, further refinement of this type could be driving the larger distance between patches in the left hemisphere, since this larger spacing might also imply more refined connections.

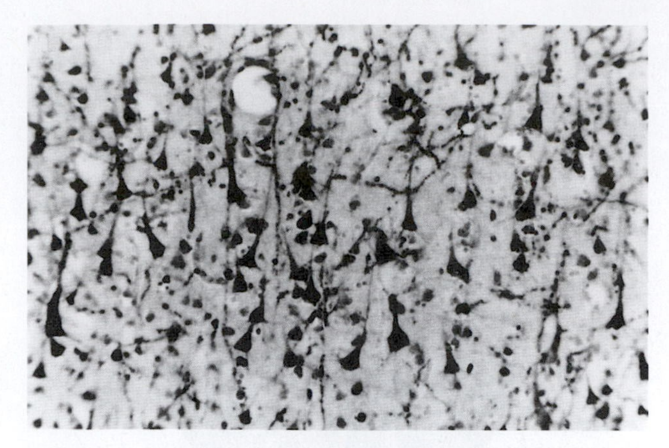

a Right hemisphere

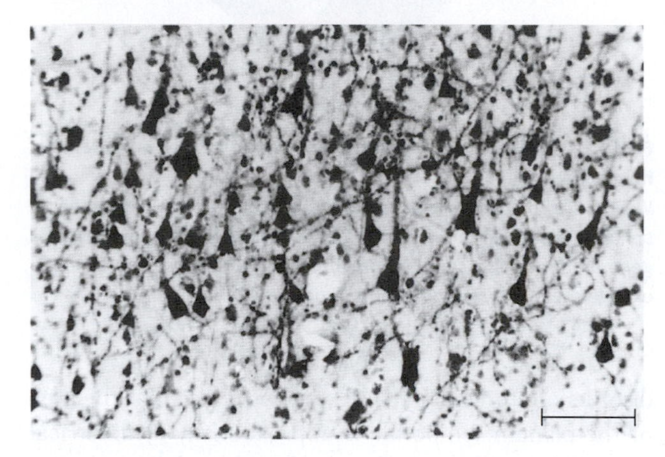

b Left hemisphere

FIGURE 4.4 Layer III pyramidal cell asymmetry.
Visual examination reveals a subtle difference in the sizes of the largest subgroups of layer III pyramidal cells (Nissl-stained): in the right hemisphere (a), they are smaller than in the left hemisphere (b). Scale bar = 50 μm.

A thorough understanding of the anatomy and physiology of language-associated cortices could shed considerable light on the cortical mechanisms that facilitate linguistic analysis and production, which we will discuss in Chapter 11. Because cortical areas have a basic underlying organization, documenting cortical locations involved in certain functions should distinguish, in terms of form and variety, between the neural structures common to all regions and the structures critical for a region to carry out particular cognitive functions.

These questions hold importance not only for the greater understanding of species-specific adaptations such as language, but also for understanding how evolution may build functional specialization into the framework of cortical organization. There are also implications for developmental problems such as dyslexia and autism. For instance, minicolumns in individuals with autism are smaller but more numerous. If these anatomical changes occur early in the developing brain, then they will result in altered corticocortical connections and information processing (Casanova et al., 2002, 2006).

Anatomy of Communication: The Corpus Callosum and the Commissures

The left and right cerebral hemispheres are connected by the largest white matter structure in the brain (the **corpus callosum**) and two much smaller fiber tracts (the anterior and posterior **commissures**). The corpus callosum is made up of approximately 250 million axonal fibers that cross from one side of the brain to the other, facilitating interhemispheric communication. It is located beneath the cortex and runs along the longitudinal fissure. The corpus callosum is divided on a macroscopic level into the anterior portion, called the *genu*; the middle portion, known as the *body*; and the posterior portion, called the **splenium** (**Figure 4.5**).

The neuronal fiber sizes vary across the corpus callosum: Smaller fibers (about 0.4 μm) are located anteriorly, fitfully grading to larger fibers (5 μm) located more posteriorly (Aboitiz et al., 1992). The prefrontal and temporoparietal visual areas are connected by the small-diameter, slow-conducting fibers, and the large fibers connect sensorimotor cortices in each hemisphere (Lamantia & Rakic, 1990). As with many parts of the brain, the fiber tracts in the corpus callosum maintain a topographic organization (Zarei et al., 2006).

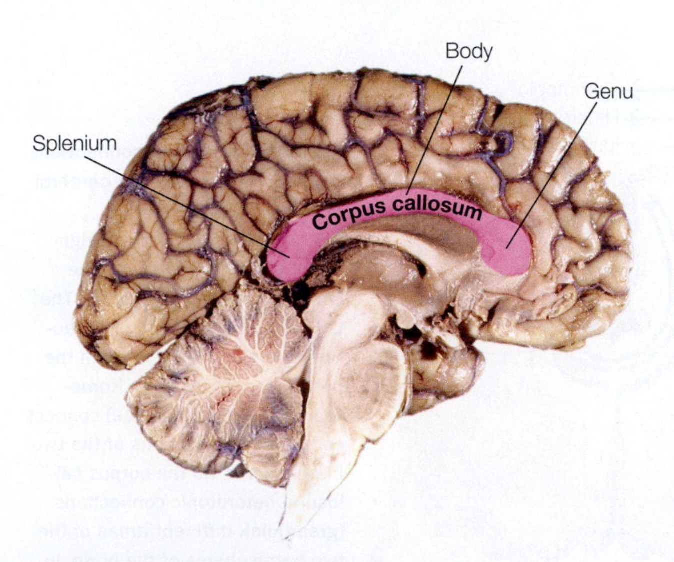

FIGURE 4.5 The corpus callosum.
A sagittal view of the left hemisphere of a postmortem brain. The corpus callosum is the dense fiber tract located below the folds of the cortex. It is divided into three regions: the genu (anterior), body (middle), and splenium (posterior).

By using the MRI technique known as diffusion tensor imaging (DTI; see Chapter 3), researchers have traced the white fiber tracts from one hemisphere across the corpus callosum to the other hemisphere. The results indicate that the corpus callosum can be partitioned into vertical segments carrying **homotopic connections** (those that go to a corresponding region in the other hemisphere) and **heterotopic connections** (those that travel to a different region in the other hemisphere; Hofer & Frahm, 2006).

As illustrated in **Figure 4.6**, the corpus callosum contains fibers that project into the prefrontal, premotor, primary motor, primary sensory, parietal, occipital, and temporal areas. Almost all of the visual information processed in the parietal, occipital, and temporal cortices is transferred to the opposite hemisphere via the posterior third of the corpus callosum, whereas premotor and supplementary motor information is transferred across a large section of the middle third of the corpus callosum.

Many of the callosal projections link homotopic areas (**Figure 4.7**). For example, regions in the left prefrontal cortex project to homotopic regions in the right prefrontal cortex. Although this pattern holds for most areas of the association cortex, it is not always seen in primary cortex. Callosal projections connecting the two halves of the primary visual cortex link only those areas that represent the most eccentric regions of space; and in both the primary motor and the somatosensory cortices, homotopic callosal projections are sparse (Innocenti et al., 1995).

Callosal fibers also connect **heterotopic areas**, regions with different locations in the two hemispheres. These projections generally mirror the ones found within a hemisphere. For instance, a prefrontal area sending projections to premotor areas in the same hemisphere is also likely to send projections to the analogous premotor area in the contralateral hemisphere. Yet heterotopic projections are usually less extensive than ipsilateral projections.

The **anterior commissure** is a much smaller band of fibers connecting the two hemispheres. It is about one-tenth the size of the corpus callosum, is found inferior to the anterior portion of the corpus callosum, and primarily connects certain regions of the temporal lobes,

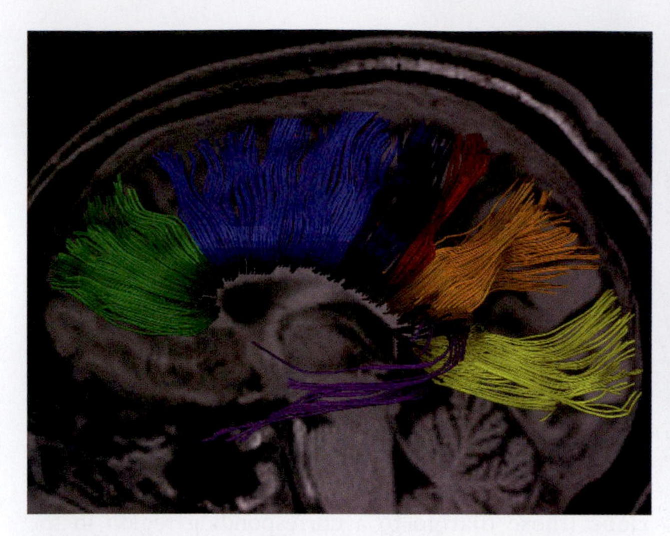

a

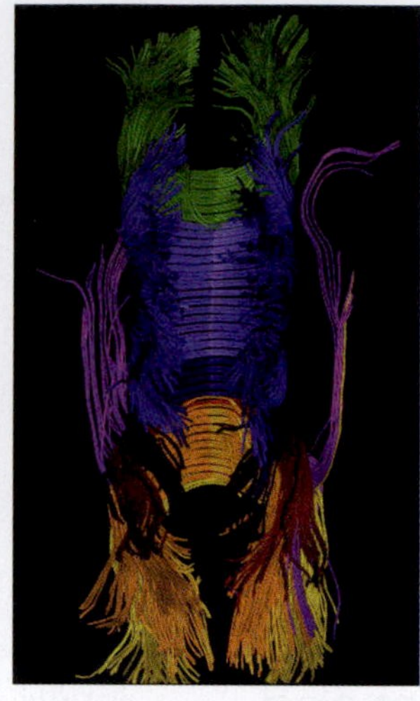

b

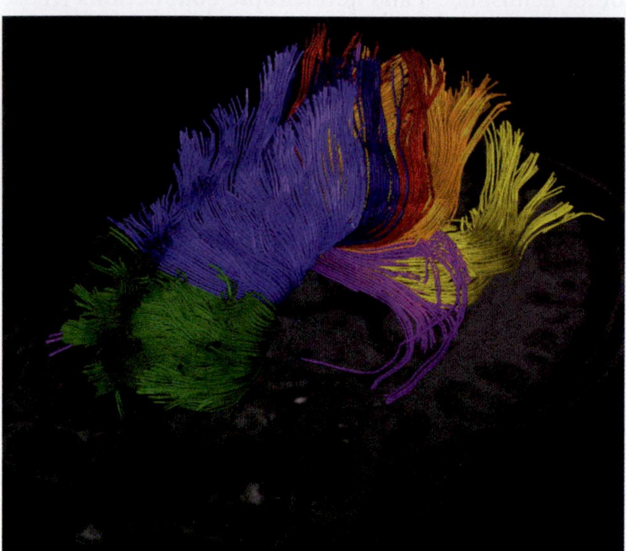

c

FIGURE 4.6 3-D reconstruction of transcallosal fiber tracts placed on anatomical reference images. Callosal fiber bundles projecting into the prefrontal lobe (coded in green), premotor and supplementary motor areas (light blue), primary motor cortex (dark blue), primary somatosensory cortex (red), parietal lobe (orange), occipital lobe (yellow), and temporal lobe (violet). **(a)** Sagittal view. **(b)** Top view. **(c)** Oblique view.

Homotopic
Heterotopic
Ipsilateral
Corpus callosum
Corpus callosum
Plane of section in (b) (roughly premotor area)

a b

FIGURE 4.7 Tracing connections between and within the cerebral cortices.
(a) Midsagittal view of the right cerebral hemisphere, with the corpus callosum labeled. **(b)** The caudal surface of a coronal section of brain roughly through the premotor cortical area. Homotopic callosal fibers (blue) connect corresponding sections of the two hemispheres via the corpus callosum; heterotopic connections (green) link different areas of the two hemispheres of the brain. In primates, both types of contralateral connections (blue and green), as well as ipsilateral connections (red), start and finish at the same layer of neocortex.

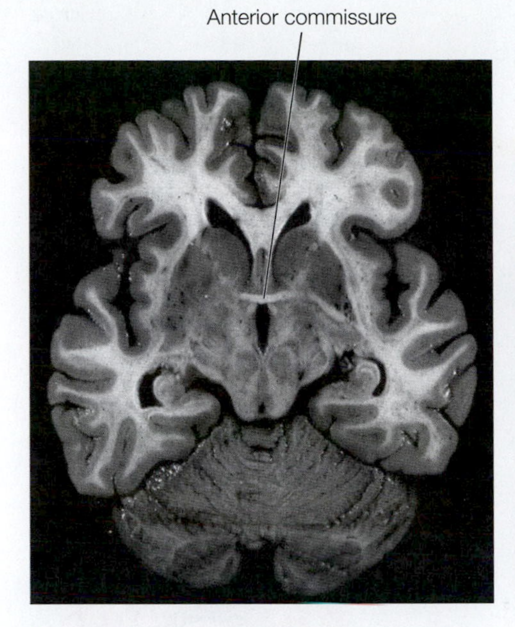

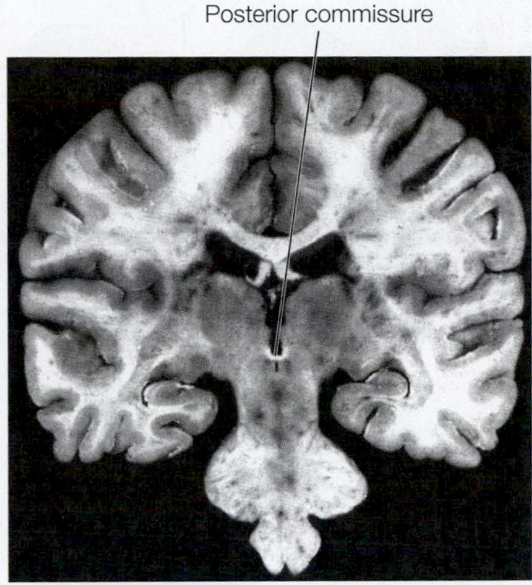

FIGURE 4.8 The commissures. (a) Obliquely cut (about 45° from horizontal) transverse section at the level of the anterior commissure. **(b)** Coronal section at the level of the posterior commissure.

including the two amygdalae (**Figure 4.8a**). It also contains decussating fibers from the olfactory tract and is part of the neospinothalamic tract for pain. Even smaller is the **posterior commissure**, which also carries some interhemispheric fibers. It is above the cerebral aqueduct at the junction of the third ventricle (**Figure 4.8b**). The posterior commissure contains fibers that contribute to the pupillary light reflex.

Function of the Corpus Callosum

Functionally, the corpus callosum is the primary communication highway between the two cerebral hemispheres. Researchers are interested in exactly what is being communicated and how. Several functional roles have been proposed for callosal connections. For instance, some researchers point out that in the visual association cortex, receptive fields can span both visual fields. Communication across the callosum enables information from both visual fields to contribute to the activity of these cells. Indeed, the callosal connections could play a role in synchronizing oscillatory activity in cortical neurons as an object passes through these receptive fields (**Figure 4.9**). In this view, callosal connections facilitate processing by pooling diverse inputs.

Other researchers view callosal function as predominantly inhibitory. If the callosal fibers are inhibitory, they provide a means for each hemisphere to compete for control of current processing. For example, multiple movements might be activated, all geared to a common goal; later processing would select one of these candidate movements (see Chapter 8). Inhibitory connections across the corpus callosum might be one contributor to this selection process.

In young developing animals, including humans, callosal projections are diffuse and more evenly distributed across the cortical surface. In adults, however, callosal connections are a scaled-down version of what is found in immature individuals. For example, cats and monkeys lose approximately 70% of their callosal axons during development; some of these transient projections are between portions of the primary sensory cortex that, in adults, are not connected by the callosum. Yet this loss of axons does not produce cell death in each cortical hemisphere.

The reason axon loss doesn't equate to cell loss in both hemispheres is that a single cell body can send out more than one axon terminal: one to cortical areas on the same side of the brain, and one to the other side of the brain. Thus, loss of a callosal axon may well leave its cell body—with its secondary collateral connection to the ipsilateral hemisphere—alive and well, just like pruning a bifurcating peach tree branch leaves the branch thriving. The refinement of connections is a hallmark of callosal development, just as such refinement characterizes intrahemispheric development.

As with the cerebral hemispheres, researchers have investigated functional correlates of anatomical differences in the corpus callosum. Usually, investigators measure gross aspects like the cross-sectional area or shape of the callosum. Variations in these measures are linked to gender, handedness, mental retardation, autism, and schizophrenia. Interpretation of these data, however, is complicated by methodological

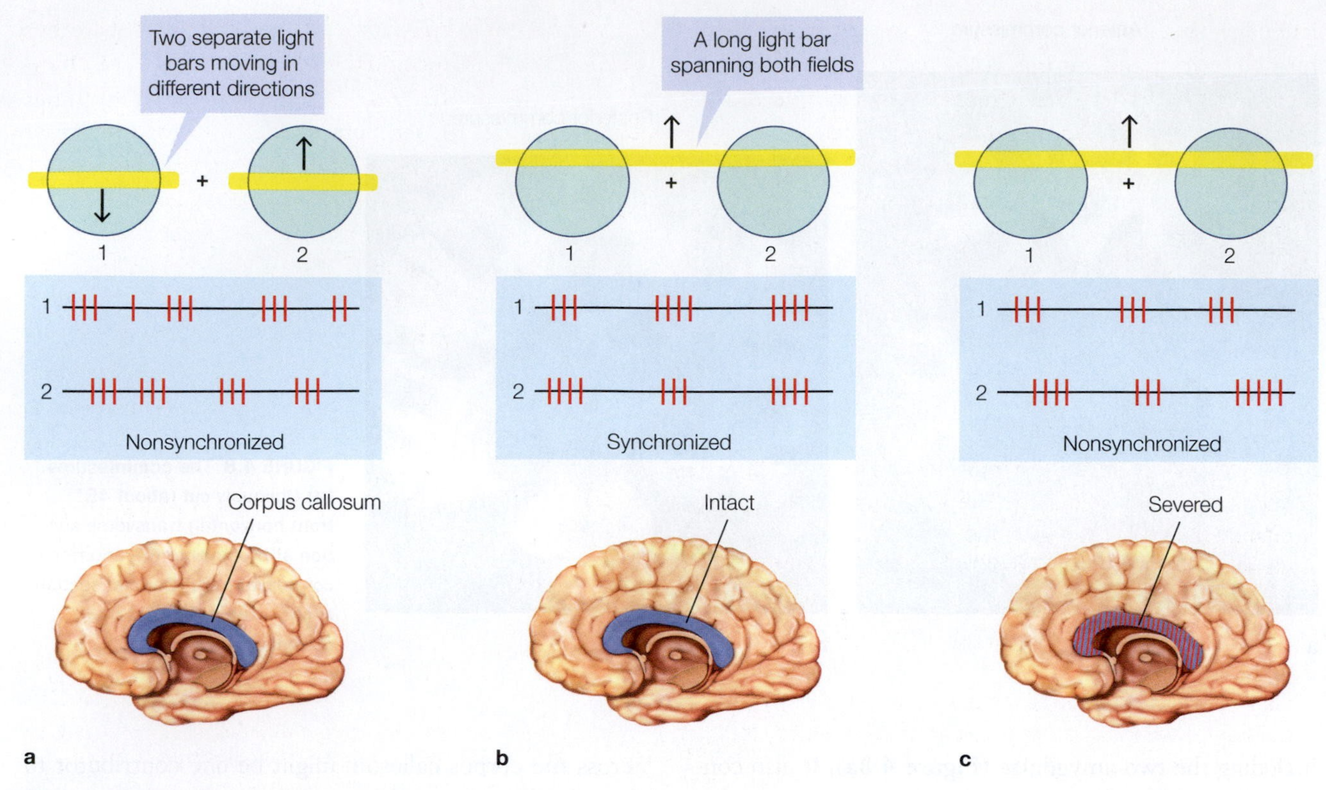

FIGURE 4.9 Synchrony in cortical neurons.
(a) When receptive fields (1 and 2) on either side of fixation are stimulated by two separate light bars moving in different directions (as indicated by the arrows), the firing rates of the two cells are not correlated. **(b)** In animals with an intact corpus callosum, cells with spatially separate receptive fields fire synchronously when they are stimulated by a common object, such as a long light bar spanning both fields. **(c)** In animals whose corpus callosum has been severed, synchrony is rarely observed.

disagreements and contradictory results. The underlying logic of measuring the corpus callosum's cross-sectional area relies on the relation of area to structural organization. Callosal size could be related to the number and diameter of axons, the proportion of myelinated axons, the thickness of myelin sheaths, and measures of nonneural structures such as the size of blood vessels or the volume of extracellular space, with resultant functional differences.

Differences in corpus callosum size may also be attributed to differences in brain size. For example, the corpus callosum is generally larger in men than in women, but men also have larger brains in general. It is unclear whether sex-based differences in corpus callosum size persist after brain volume is taken into account. Some researchers find that some portions of the corpus callosum are actually larger in women than in men relative to brain size (Ardekani et al., 2013), but other studies find no sex-based differences in corpus callosum size. A recent study attempted to determine whether corpus callosum size is affected by gender or merely by total brain size: The study's participants were women with relatively large brains and men with relatively small brains. When the male and female brains were matched for total brain volume, no significant differences were found in corpus callosum size (Luders et al., 2014).

There may be sex-based differences in the shape of the corpus callosum, however. Studies looking at the parasagittal size and asymmetry of the corpus callosum have found an increased rightward callosal asymmetry in males compared to females (Luders et al., 2006). That is, a larger chunk of the callosum bulges off to the right side in males. It may be that the side of the hemispheric fence where the major part of the callosum sits is the important factor. Thus, this sexually dimorphic organization of the corpus callosum (more on the right than on the left in males) may involve not just the corpus callosum, but also asymmetrical hemispheric development, as reflected in the distribution of parasagittal callosal fibers (Chura et al., 2010).

This view is consistent with the Geschwind–Galaburda theory of development, which states that high levels of fetal testosterone slow the development of the posterior parts of the left hemisphere, which could in turn account for the observed patterns of accelerated language development in females, the enhanced performance in males during visuospatial tasks, and the increased rate of left-handedness in males. Indeed, the research by Linda Chura and her colleagues found that with increasing levels of fetal testosterone, there was a significantly increasing rightward asymmetry (e.g., right > left) of a posterior subsection of the callosum, called the isthmus, that projects mainly to parietal and superior temporal areas.

TAKE-HOME MESSAGES

- The planum temporale encompasses Wernicke's area and is involved in language. The asymmetry of the planum temporale is one of the few examples in which an anatomical index is correlated with a well-defined functional asymmetry.
- In the language-associated regions, micro-level asymmetries between the hemispheres have been identified, including different distributions of dendritic branch orders, different distances between adjacent neuronal columns, cell size differences, and asymmetries in connectivity.
- The two halves of the cerebral cortex are connected primarily by the corpus callosum, which is the largest fiber system in the brain. Two smaller bands of fibers, the anterior and posterior commissures, also connect the two hemispheres.
- The corpus callosum has both homotopic and heterotopic connections. Homotopic fibers connect the corresponding regions of each hemisphere (e.g., V1 on the right to V1 on the left), whereas heterotopic fibers connect different areas (e.g., V1 on the right to V2 on the left).

4.2 Splitting the Brain: Cortical Disconnection

Because the corpus callosum is the primary means of communication between the two cerebral hemispheres, we learn a great deal when we sever the callosal fibers. This approach was successfully used in the pioneering animal studies of Ronald Myers and Roger Sperry at the California Institute of Technology. They developed a series of animal experiments to assess whether the corpus callosum is crucial for unified cortical function. First, they trained cats to choose a "plus" stimulus versus a "circle" stimulus randomly alternated between two doors. When a cat chose correctly, it was rewarded with food. Myers and Sperry made the startling discovery that when the corpus callosum and anterior commissure were sectioned, such visual discriminations learned by one hemisphere did not transfer to the other hemisphere. Further studies done on monkeys and chimpanzees showed that visual and tactile information that was lateralized to one hemisphere did not transfer to the opposite hemisphere, thus corroborating the results from cats.

This important research laid the groundwork for comparable human studies initiated by Sperry and one of the authors of this book (M.S.G.; Sperry et al., 1969). Unlike the case with lesion studies, no cortical tissue is destroyed in patients who have undergone split-brain surgery; the surgery simply eliminates the connections between the two hemispheres. With split-brain patients, functional inferences are not based on how behavior changes after a cortical area is eliminated. Rather, it becomes possible to see how each hemisphere operates in relative isolation.

The Surgery in Humans

Corpus callosotomy, or split-brain surgery, is used to treat intractable epilepsy when other forms of treatment, such as medication, have failed. This procedure was first performed in 1940 by a Rochester, New York, surgeon, William van Wagenen. One of Van Wagenen's patients, who had a history of severe epileptic seizures, improved after developing a tumor in his corpus callosum (Van Wagenen & Herren, 1940). Since epileptic seizures are the result of abnormal electrical discharges that zip across the brain, the improvement in this patient gave Van Wagenen the idea that severing the patient's corpus callosum might block the seizure-causing electrical impulses from traveling between hemispheres. The epileptogenic activity would then be held in check, and a generalized seizure would be prevented.

The idea was radical, particularly when so little was really understood about brain function. The surgery itself was also painstaking, especially without today's microsurgical techniques, because only a thin wall of cells separates the ventricles from the corpus callosum. With the limited treatment options available at the time, however, Van Wagenen had desperate patients who cried out for desperate measures. One great fear loomed: What would be the side effect—a split personality with two minds fighting for control over one body?

To everyone's relief, the surgery was a great success. Remarkably, the patients appeared and felt completely normal. The seizures typically subsided immediately, even in patients who, before the operation, experienced up to 15 seizures per day. Eighty percent of the patients enjoyed a 60% to 70% decrease in seizure activity, and some were free of seizures altogether (Akelaitis, 1941). Everyone was happy, yet puzzled. Twenty of the surgeries were performed without any discernible psychological side effects: no changes to psyche, personality, intellect, sensory processing, or motor coordination. Andrew Akelaitis, the psychologist who tested these patients, concluded,

> The observations that some of these patients were able to perform highly complex synchronous bilateral activities as piano-playing, typewriting by means of the touch system and dancing postoperatively suggests strongly that commissural pathways other than the corpus callosum are being utilized. (Akelaitis, 1943, p. 259)

Methodological Considerations in Studying Split-Brain Patients

The main method of testing the perceptual and cognitive functions of each hemisphere has changed little over the past 50 years. Researchers use primarily visual stimulation, not only because of the preeminent status of this modality for humans, but also because the visual system is more strictly lateralized than are other sensory modalities, such as the auditory and olfactory systems.

The ability to communicate solely to one hemisphere is based on the anatomy of the optic nerve. Look at an object directly in front of you. Information from the right side of your visual field hits the left side of the retina in both eyes, and information from the left side hits the right side of the retina. The visual field information stays separated as it travels up the optic nerve of each eye. At the optic chiasm, the optic nerve divides in half, and the fibers that carry the visual information from the medial portion of each retina cross and project to the visual cortex of the opposite hemisphere, while the fibers that carry visual information from the lateral portion of the retina continue on to the visual cortex of the ipsilateral hemisphere (**Figure 4.10**).

Thus, all the information from the left half of the visual field ends up in the right hemisphere, and all from the right half in the left hemisphere. If all communication were severed between the two halves of the cerebral cortex, then information presented solely to the right visual field would be processed in the left hemisphere only, and information presented to the left visual field would be processed solely in the right hemisphere, and neither would have access to the other.

In tests of split-brain patients, experimenters restrict the visual stimulus to a single hemisphere by quickly flashing the stimulus in one visual field or the other (**Figure 4.11**) while the patient fixates on a point in space directly in front of the eyes. The brevity of stimulation is necessary to prevent eye movements, which would redirect the information into the unwanted hemisphere. Eye movements take roughly 200 ms, so if the stimulus is presented for a briefer period of time, the experimenter can be confident that the stimulus was lateralized. More recent image stabilization tools—tools that move in correspondence with the participant's eye movements—allow a more prolonged, naturalistic form of stimulation. This technological development has opened the way for new discoveries in the neurological and psychological aspects of hemispheric disconnection.

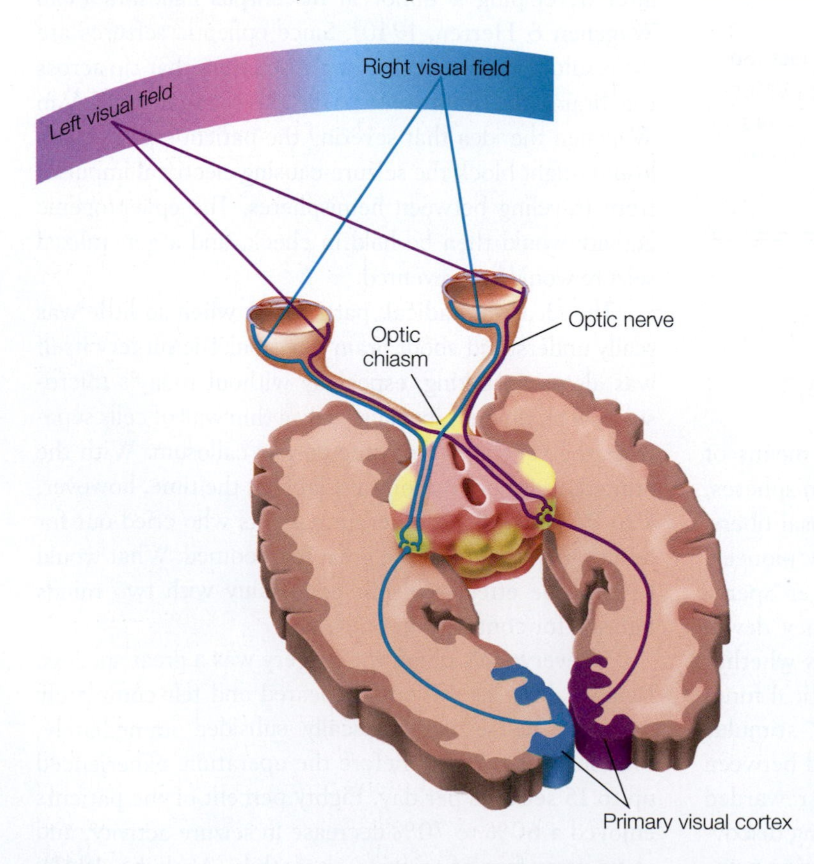

FIGURE 4.10 The optic nerve and its pathway to the primary visual cortex.

A number of methodological issues arise in evaluations of the performance of split-brain patients. First, bear in mind that these patients were not neurologically normal before their callosotomy; they all had chronic epilepsy, and their multiple seizures may have caused neurological damage. Therefore, it is reasonable to ask whether they provide an appropriate barometer of normal hemispheric function after the operation. There is no easy answer to this question. Some split-brain patients do display abnormal performance on neuropsychological assessments, and some

FIGURE 4.11 Restricting visual stimuli to one hemisphere. The split-brain patient reports through the speaking hemisphere only the items flashed to the right half of the screen and denies seeing left-field stimuli or recognizing objects presented to the left hand. Nevertheless, the left hand correctly retrieves objects presented in the left visual field, about which the patient verbally denies knowing anything.

may be profoundly mentally impaired. In other patients, however, the cognitive impairments are negligible; these are the patients who have been studied in closest detail.

Second, it is important to consider whether the transcortical connections were completely sectioned, or whether some fibers remained intact. At the time of the original California operations, reviewing surgical notes was the only way to determine the completeness of the surgical sections. Since then, however, MRI (**Figure 4.12**), diffusion tensor imaging, and electrical brain-mapping techniques have provided a more accurate representation of the extent of surgical sections.

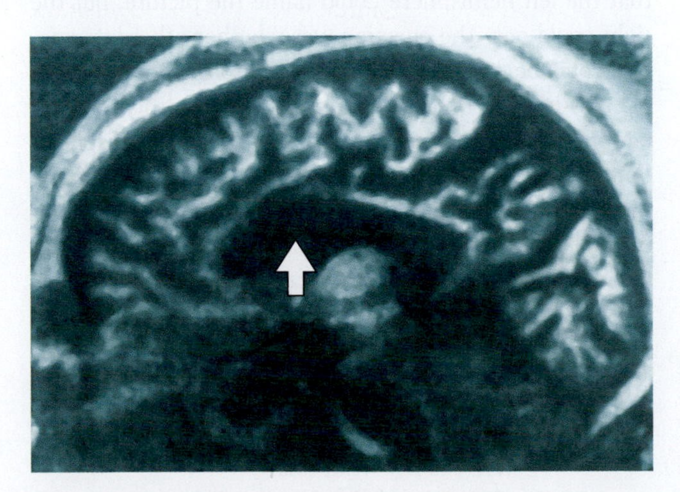

FIGURE 4.12 A complete corpus callosotomy. This MRI shows a sagittal view of a brain in which the corpus callosum has been entirely sectioned. The arrow indicates the region of resection.

In fact, data from some older studies had to be reinterpreted when some intact fibers were identified in the patients in question. Accurate documentation of a callosal section is crucial for learning about the organization of the cerebral commissure.

Third, experiments must be meticulously designed to eliminate the possibility of cross-cuing, which occurs when one hemisphere initiates a behavior that the other hemisphere detects externally, giving it a cue about the answer to a test. Eliminating cross-cuing can be highly challenging or even impossible, depending on the design (S. E. Seymour et al., 1994). To avoid cross-cuing situations, it is important to understand what continues to be shared between the hemispheres after callosotomy.

We will learn more about this later in the chapter, but here it is important to note that while the right hemisphere controls the left half of the body and the left hemisphere controls the right half of the body, both hemispheres can guide the proximal muscles of the ipsilateral side of the body, such as the upper arms, and gross movements of the hands and legs, but not the distal muscles (those farthest from the center of the body), which include the muscles that perform fine motor movements (Gazzaniga et al., 1962; Volpe et al., 1982), such as pressing a buzzer or pointing. Thus, the left hemisphere controls the fine motor movements of the right hand but can also make more generalized movements of the left arm's proximal muscles, which may give the right hemisphere cues for predicting answers.

While cross-cuing behavior is sometimes readily observable, such as one hand nudging the other, it can also be very subtle. For example, an eye movement or a facial muscle contraction initiated by one hemisphere (because some of the facial musculature is innervated bilaterally) can cue the other hemisphere to the answer. Barely discernible reaction time differences can indicate that cross-cuing has occurred. Cross-cuing is not intentional on the part of the patient; it is an unconscious attempt to meet the challenges of the test.

Functional Consequences of the Split-Brain Procedure

The results of testing done on the split-brain patient W.J., as described at the beginning of this chapter, contradicted earlier reports on the effects of the callosotomy procedure. For instance, Akelaitis (1941) had found no significant neurological and psychological effects after the callosum was sectioned. Careful testing with W.J. and other patients, however, revealed that, indeed, visual information presented to one half of the brain was not available to the other half.

The same principle applied to touch. Patients were able to name and describe objects placed in the right hand but not objects presented in the left hand. Sensory information restricted to one hemisphere was also not available to accurately guide movements with the ipsilateral hand. For example, when a picture of a hand portraying the "OK" sign was presented to the left hemisphere, the patient was able to make the gesture with the right hand, which is controlled by the left half of the brain. The patient was unable to make the same gesture with the left hand, however, in which the fine motor movements are normally controlled by the right hemisphere.

From a cognitive point of view, these initial studies confirmed long-standing neurological knowledge about the nature of the two cerebral hemispheres, which had been obtained earlier from patients with unilateral hemispheric lesions: The left hemisphere is dominant for language, speech, and major problem solving. Its verbal IQ and problem-solving capacity (including mathematical tasks, geometric problems, and hypothesis formation) remain intact after callosotomy (Gazzaniga, 1985). Isolating half the brain, cutting its acreage by 50%, causes no major changes in cognitive function—nor do the patients notice any change in their abilities. The right hemisphere is impoverished in its ability to perform cognitive tasks, but it appears specialized for visuospatial tasks such as drawing cubes and other three-dimensional patterns.

Split-brain patients cannot name or describe visual and tactile stimuli presented to the right hemisphere, because the sensory information is disconnected from the dominant left (speech) hemisphere. This does not mean that *knowledge* about the stimuli is absent in the right hemisphere, however. Nonverbal response techniques are required to demonstrate the competence of the right hemisphere. For example, the left hand can be used to point to named objects or to demonstrate the function of depicted objects presented in the left visual field, which travel to the right hemisphere.

SPLIT-BRAIN EVIDENCE FOR CALLOSAL FUNCTION SPECIFICITY We have seen that when the corpus callosum is fully sectioned, little or no perceptual or cognitive interaction occurs between the hemispheres. Surgeons sometimes perform the split-brain procedure in stages, however, restricting the initial operation to the anterior or posterior half of the callosum. The remaining fibers are sectioned in a second operation only if the seizures continue to persist.

This two-stage procedure offers a unique glimpse into what the anterior and posterior callosal regions transfer between the cerebral hemispheres. For example, when the splenium, the posterior area of the callosum that interconnects the occipital lobe, is spared, visual information is transferred normally between the two cerebral hemispheres

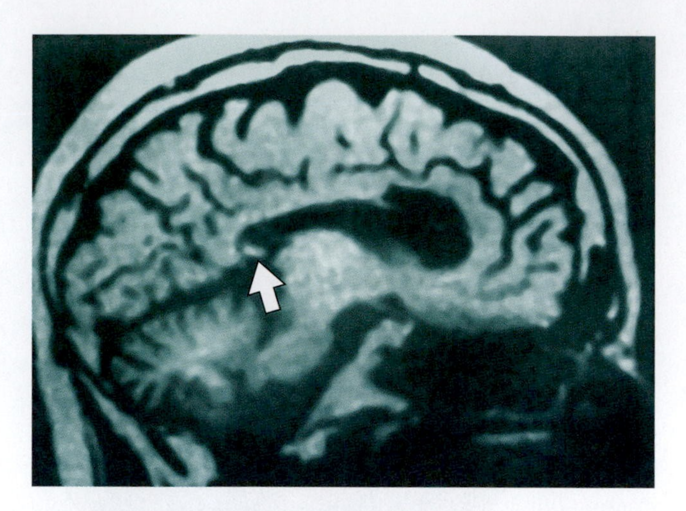

FIGURE 4.13 An incomplete corpus callosotomy. This MRI shows that the splenium (*arrow*) was spared in the split-brain procedure performed on this patient. As a result, visual information could still be transferred between the cerebral hemispheres.

(**Figure 4.13**). In these instances, pattern, color, and linguistic information presented anywhere in either visual field can be matched with information presented to the other half of the brain. The patients, however, show no evidence of interhemispheric transfer of tactile information from touched objects. Tactile information turns out to be transferred by fibers in a region just anterior to the splenium, still located in the posterior half of the callosum.

When the posterior half of the callosum is sectioned, transfer of visual, tactile, and auditory sensory information is severely disrupted, but the remaining intact anterior region of the callosum is still able to transfer higher-order information. For example, one patient (J.W.) was tested soon after this surgery. The first test, flashing a simple picture to either hemisphere, resulted in the expected finding that the left hemisphere could name the picture, but the right could not. The question was whether other information could be transferred anteriorly, resulting in some type of cross-integration of information. To make this determination, a different stimulus was flashed to each hemisphere. For example, the left hemisphere saw the word "sun," and the right hemisphere saw a black-and-white drawing of a traffic light. J.W. was asked, "What did you see?" The following conversation ensued (Gazzaniga, 2015, p. 242):

M.S.G.: What did you see?

J.W.: The word *sun* on the right and a picture of something on the left. I don't know what it is but I can't say it. I wanna but I can't. I don't know what it is.

M.S.G.: What does it have to do with?

J.W.: I can't tell you that either. It was the word *sun* on the right and a picture of something on the left . . . I can't think of what it is. I can see it right in my eyes and I can't say it.

M.S.G.: Does it have to do with airplanes?
J.W.: No.
M.S.G.: Does it have to do with cars?
J.W.: Yeah (nodding his head). I think so . . . it's a tool or something . . . I dunno what it is and I can't say it. It's terrible.
M.S.G.: . . . are colors involved in it?
J.W.: Yeah, red, yellow . . . traffic light?
M.S.G.: You got it.

Two months after surgery, J.W. was playing this "20 questions" type of game with himself. This time the word "knight" was flashed to the right hemisphere. He had the following dialogue with himself: "I have a picture in mind but can't say it. Two fighters in a ring. Ancient and wearing uniforms and helmets . . . on horses . . . trying to knock each other off . . . Knights?" (Sidtis et al., 1981). The word that his right hemisphere had seen (but his left hemisphere had not) elicited higher-order associations in the right hemisphere. Close examination revealed that the left hemisphere was receiving higher-order cues about the stimulus without having access to the sensory information about the stimulus itself (**Figure 4.14**). In short, the anterior part of the callosum transfers semantic information about the stimulus but not the stimulus itself (Sidtis et al., 1981). After the anterior callosal region was sectioned in this patient, this capacity was lost.

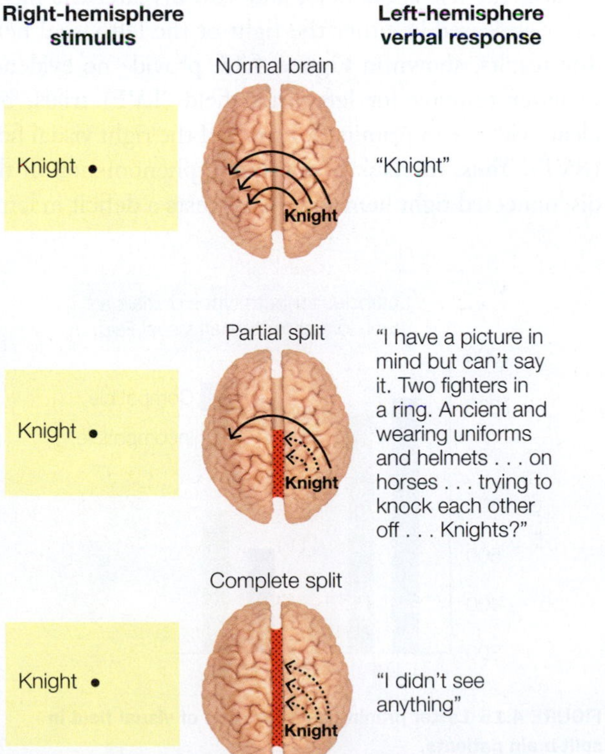

Occasionally, part of the callosum was inadvertently spared during surgery. In most cases this fact was not fully appreciated until many years after the surgery was done, when newer scanning technologies made detecting these remaining fibers possible. Older findings had to be reevaluated and often reinterpreted in light of the updated existence of callosal connections.

FIGURE 4.14 Location of callosal resection determines what information is transferred between hemispheres.
Schematic representation of split-brain patient J.W.'s naming ability for objects in the left visual field at each operative stage.

TAKE-HOME MESSAGES

- The anatomy of the optic nerve allows visual information to be presented uniquely to one hemisphere or the other in split-brain patients.
- Methodological issues that arise in evaluating the performance of split-brain patients include identifying prior neurological damage, accurately evaluating the extent of the sectioning, and paying meticulous attention to experimental design in order to eliminate the possibility of cross-cuing between the hemispheres.
- The splenium is the most posterior portion of the corpus callosum. When the posterior half of the callosum is sectioned in humans, the transfer of visual, tactile, and auditory sensory information is severely disrupted.
- The anterior part of the callosum is involved in the transfer of higher-order semantic information.

4.3 Evidence of Lateralized Brain Functions from Split-Brain Patients

As we saw in Chapter 1, the history of **cerebral specialization**—the notion that different regions of the brain have specific functions—began with Franz Joseph Gall in the early 1800s. Although it fell repeatedly in and out of fashion, this idea could not be discounted, because so many clinical findings, especially in patients who had suffered strokes, provided unassailable evidence that it was so. Over the last 50 years, studies done with split-brain patients have demonstrated that some of the brain's processing is lateralized.

In this section we review findings from split-brain patients, from patients with unilateral lesions, and from research participants with normal brains. The most prominent lateralized function in the human brain is the left hemisphere's capacity for language and speech, which we examine first. We also look at the lateralization of visuospatial processing, attention and perception, information processing, and how we interpret the world around us.

Language and Speech

When attempting to understand the neural bases of language, it is useful to distinguish between grammatical and lexical functions. The grammar–lexicon distinction is different from the more traditional syntax–semantics distinction commonly invoked to improve understanding of the differential effects of brain lesions on language processes (see Chapter 11). *Grammar* is the rule-based system that humans have for ordering words to facilitate communication. For example, in English the typical order of a sentence is subject (noun)–action (verb)–object (noun). The *lexicon* is the mind's dictionary, where words are associated with specific meanings. The word *dog* is associated with a dog, but so is *Hund*, *kutya*, or *cane*, depending on the language you speak.

The grammar–lexicon distinction takes into account factors such as memory, because with memory, word strings as idioms can be learned by rote. For example, "How are you?" or "*Comment allez-vous?*" is most likely a single lexical entry. Although the lexicon cannot possibly encompass the infinite number of unique phrases and sentences that humans can generate—such as the one you are now reading—memory does play a role in many short phrases. When uttered, such word strings do not reflect an underlying interaction of syntax and semantic systems; they are, instead, essentially an entry from the lexicon.

This grammar–lexicon distinction is more apparent when you are learning a new language. You often learn stock phrases that you speak as a unit rather than struggling with the grammar. It might therefore be predicted that some brain areas ought to be wholly responsible for grammar, whereas the lexicon's location ought to be more elusive, since it reflects learned information and, thus, is part of the brain's general memory and knowledge systems. The grammar system, then, ought to be discrete and hence localizable, whereas the lexicon should be distributed and hence more difficult to damage completely.

Language and speech are rarely present in both hemispheres; they are in either one or the other. While the separated left hemisphere normally comprehends all aspects of language, the right hemisphere does have linguistic capabilities, although they are uncommon. Indeed, out of dozens of split-brain patients who have been carefully examined, only six showed clear evidence of residual linguistic functions in the right hemisphere. And even in these patients, the extent of right-hemisphere language functions is severely limited and restricted to the lexical aspects of comprehension.

Interestingly, the left and right lexicons of these special patients can be nearly equal in their capacity, but they are organized quite differently. For example, both hemispheres show a phenomenon called the *word superiority effect* (see Chapter 3). Normal English readers are better able to identify letters (e.g., *L*) in the context of real English words (e.g., *belt*) than when the same letters appear in pseudowords (e.g., *kelt*) or nonsense letter strings (e.g., *ktle*). Because pseudowords and nonwords do not have lexical entries, letters occurring in such strings do not receive the additional processing benefit bestowed on words. Thus, the word superiority effect emerges.

While patients with right-hemisphere language exhibit a visual lexicon, the two hemispheres might access this lexicon in different ways. To test this possibility, investigators used a letter-priming task. Participants were asked to indicate whether a briefly flashed uppercase letter was an *H* or a *T*. On each trial, the uppercase letter was preceded by a lowercase letter that was either an *h* or a *t*. Normally, participants are significantly faster, or primed, when an uppercase *H* is preceded by a lowercase *h* than when it is preceded by a lowercase *t*.

The difference between response latency on compatible (*h*–*H*) versus incompatible (*t*–*H*) trials is taken to be a measure of letter priming. J.W., a split-brain participant, performed a lateralized version of this task in which the prime was displayed for 100 ms to either the right or the left visual field, and 400 ms later the target letter appeared in either the right or the left visual field. The results, shown in **Figure 4.15**, provide no evidence of letter priming for left visual field (LVF) trials, but clear evidence of priming for trials of the right visual field (RVF). Thus, the lack of a priming phenomenon in the disconnected right hemisphere suggests a deficit in letter

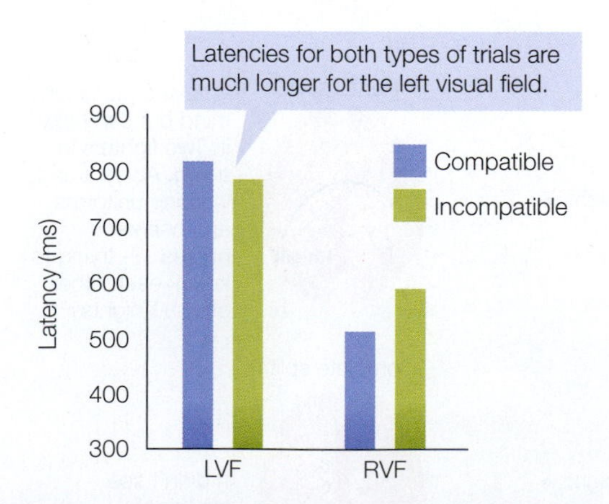

FIGURE 4.15 Letter priming as a function of visual field in split-brain patients.
The graph shows the response latencies for compatible and incompatible pairs of letters in the left and right visual fields (LVF and RVF, respectively). The latencies for both types of trials are much longer for the LVF (right hemisphere).

recognition, prohibiting access to parallel processing mechanisms. J.W. exhibited a variety of other deficiencies in right-hemisphere function as well. For example, he was unable to judge whether one word was superordinate to another (e.g., *furniture* and *chair*), or whether two words were antonyms (e.g., *love* and *hate*).

In sum, there appear to be two lexicons, one in each hemisphere. The right hemisphere's lexicon seems organized differently from the left hemisphere's lexicon, and these lexicons are accessed in different ways. These observations are consistent with the view that lexicons reflect learning processes and, as such, are more widely distributed in the cerebral cortex. It has long been held that in the general population, the lexicon appears to be in the left hemisphere. More recent evidence from functional imaging studies, however, suggests a broader role for the right hemisphere in language processing, although the precise nature of that role remains to be defined (Price, 2012; Vigneau et al., 2011).

Some theorists have suggested that the language ability of the left hemisphere gives it a superior ability to perform higher cognitive functions like making inferences and solving mathematics problems. Split-brain patients who have an extensive right-hemisphere lexicon, however, do not show any attendant increase in their right hemisphere's ability to perform these tasks (Gazzaniga & Smylie, 1984).

In contrast, generative syntax is present in only one hemisphere. Generative syntax means that by following rules of grammar, we can combine words to create an unlimited number of meanings. Although the right hemisphere of some patients clearly has a lexicon, it performs erratically on other aspects of language, such as understanding verbs, pluralizations, the possessive, and active–passive differences. In these patients, the right hemisphere also fails to use word order to disambiguate stimuli for correct meaning. For instance, the meaning of the phrase "The dog chases the cat" cannot be differentiated from the meaning of "The cat chases the dog."

Yet the right hemisphere in these cases can indicate when a sentence ends with a semantically odd word. "The dog chases cat the" would be flagged as wrong. What's more, right hemispheres with language capacities can make grammar judgments. For some peculiar reason, although they cannot use syntax to disambiguate stimuli, they can judge that one set of utterances is grammatical while another set is not. This startling finding suggests that patterns of speech are learned by rote. Yet, recognizing the pattern of acceptable utterances does not mean that a neural system can use this information to understand word strings.

A hallmark of most split-brain patients is that their speech is produced in the left hemisphere and not the right. This observation, along with amobarbital studies (see Wada & Rasmussen, 1960) and functional imaging studies, confirms that the left hemisphere is the dominant hemisphere for speech production in most (96%) of us. Nonetheless, in a handful of documented cases, split-brain patients can produce speech from both the left and the right hemispheres. Although speech is restricted to the left hemisphere following callosotomy, in this handful of patients the capacity to make one-word utterances from the disconnected right hemisphere has emerged over time.

This intriguing development raises the question of whether information is somehow transferring to the dominant hemisphere for speech output or whether the right hemisphere itself is capable of developing speech production. Results from extensive testing supported the latter hypothesis. For example, the patients were able to name an object presented in the left field (say, a spoon) and in the right field (a cow) but were not able to judge whether the two objects were the same. Or, when words like *father* were presented such that the fixation point fell between the *t* and the *h*, the patients said either "fat" or "her," depending on which hemisphere controlled speech production. These findings illustrate that extraordinary plasticity changes can occur, sometimes appearing as late as 10 years after callosotomy. In one patient, in fact, the right hemisphere had no speech production capability for approximately 13 years before it "spoke."

Finally, note that although most language capabilities are left-lateralized, the processing of the emotional content of language appears to be right-lateralized. It is well known that patients with damage to certain regions of the left hemisphere have language comprehension difficulties. Speech, however, can communicate emotional information beyond the meanings and structures of the words. A statement such as "John, come here," can be interpreted in different ways if it is said in an angry tone, a fearful tone, a seductive tone, or a surprised tone.

This nonlinguistic, emotional component of speech is called *emotional prosody*. One patient with left-hemisphere damage reportedly has difficulty comprehending words but shows little deficit in interpreting the meaning of emotional prosody (A. M. Barrett et al., 1999). At the same time, several patients with damage to the temporoparietal lobe in the right hemisphere have been shown to comprehend the meaning of language perfectly but have difficulty interpreting phrases when emotional prosody plays a role (Heilman et al., 1975). This double dissociation between language and emotional prosody in the comprehension of meaning suggests that the right hemisphere is specialized for comprehending emotional expressions of speech.

Visuospatial Processing

Early testing of W.J. made it clear that the two hemispheres have different visuospatial capabilities. As **Figure 4.16** shows, the isolated right hemisphere is frequently superior on neuropsychological tests such as the block design task, a subtest of the Wechsler Adult Intelligence Scale. In this simple task of arranging red and white blocks to match a given pattern, the left hemisphere of a split-brain patient performs poorly, while the right hemisphere easily completes the task. However, continued research has proved this functional asymmetry to be inconsistent. In some patients, performance is impaired with either hand; in others, the left hemisphere is quite adept at this task.

Further research suggested that perhaps a component of this task is lateralized, rather than the whole task, which has proved to be the case. Additional testing has shown that patients who demonstrate a right-hemisphere superiority for the block design task exhibit no asymmetry on the perceptual aspects of the task (contrary to what you may have predicted). If a picture of the block design pattern is lateralized, either hemisphere can easily find the match from a series of pictures. Since each hand is sufficiently dexterous, the crucial link must be in the mapping of the sensory message onto the capable motor system.

The right hemisphere is also specialized for efficiently detecting upright faces and discriminating among similar faces (Gazzaniga & Smylie, 1983). The left hemisphere is not good at distinguishing among similar faces, but it is able to distinguish among dissimilar ones when it can tag the feature differences with words (*blonde* versus *brunette*, *big nose* versus *button nose*). As for the task of recognizing familiar faces in general, the right hemisphere outperforms the left hemisphere (**Figure 4.17**; Turk et al., 2002).

FIGURE 4.16 The block design test.
The pattern in red on the white card is the shape that the patient is trying to create with the blocks given to him. **(a)** With his right hand (left hemisphere), he is unable to duplicate the pattern. **(b)** With his left hand (right hemisphere), he is able to perform the task correctly.

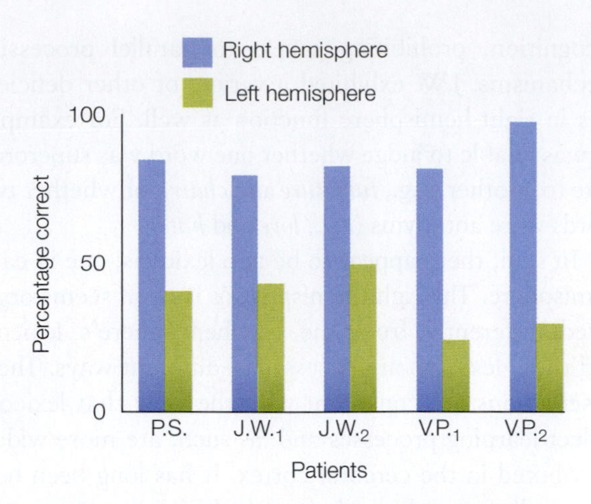

FIGURE 4.17 The right hemisphere is better at recognizing familiar faces.
Data from three split-brain patients show that the right hemisphere is more accurate than the left in recognizing familiar faces.

What about that most familiar of faces, one's own? In one study, software was used to morph the face of one split-brain patient, J.W., in 10% increments, into that of a familiar other, Mike (**Figure 4.18a**). The faces were flashed randomly to J.W.'s separated hemispheres. Then the hemisphere that saw the face was asked, in the first condition, "Is that you?" and, in another condition, "Is that Mike?" A double dissociation was found (**Figure 4.18b**). The left hemisphere was biased toward recognizing one's own face, while the right hemisphere had a recognition bias for familiar others (Turk et al., 2002).

Both hemispheres can generate spontaneous facial expressions, but you need your left hemisphere to produce voluntary facial expressions. Indeed, people appear to have two neural systems for controlling facial expressions (**Figure 4.19**; Gazzaniga & Smylie, 1990). The left hemisphere sends its messages directly to the contralateral facial nucleus via cranial nerve VII, which in turn innervates the right facial muscles. At the same time, it also sends a command over the corpus callosum to the right half of the brain. The right hemisphere sends the message down to the left facial nucleus, which in turn innervates the left half of the face.

The result is that a person can make a symmetrical voluntary facial response, such as a smile or frown. In a

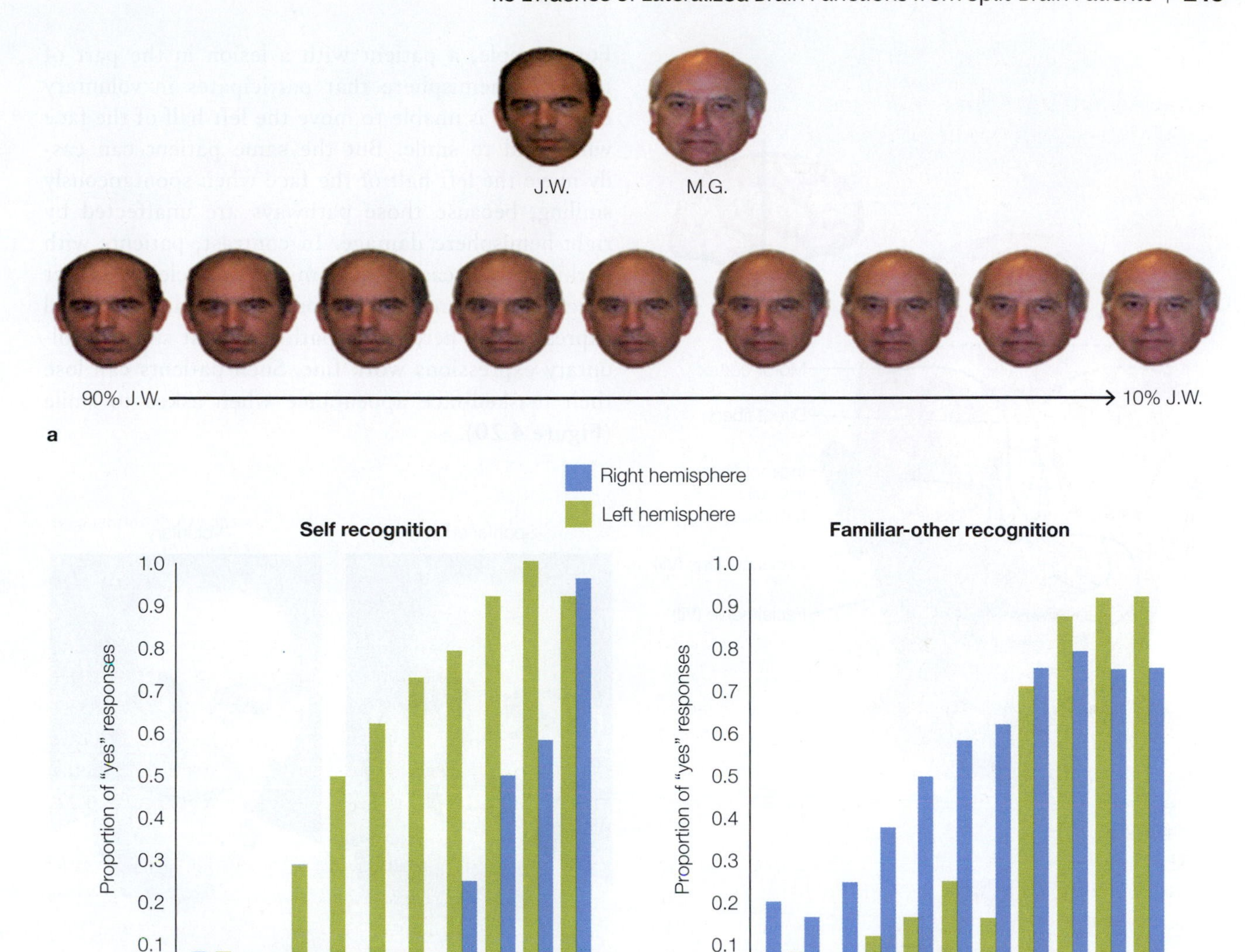

FIGURE 4.18 Is it Mike or me?
(a) The far-left image in the series contains 10% M.G. (Mike) and 90% J.W. The succeeding images change in 10% increments, ending with 90% M.G. and 10% J.W. on the far right. The two original photographs of M.G. and J.W. pictured above and these nine morphed images were presented to each hemisphere randomly. **(b)** The left hemisphere is better at recognizing the self, and the right hemisphere is better at recognizing a familiar other. The proportion of "yes" responses to recognition judgments is plotted on the *y*-axis as a function of the percentage of the individual contained in the image and the cerebral hemisphere to which the image was presented.

split-brain patient, however, when the left hemisphere is given the command to smile, the lower-right side of the face responds first, while the left side responds about 180 ms later. Why does the left side respond at all? Most likely the signal is rerouted through secondary ipsilateral pathways that connect to both facial nuclei, which then eventually send the signal over to the left-side facial muscles.

Unlike voluntary expressions, which only the left hemisphere can trigger, spontaneous expressions can be managed by either half of the brain. When either half triggers a spontaneous response, the pathways that activate the brainstem nuclei are signaled through another pathway—one that does not course through the cortex. Each hemisphere sends signals straight down through the midbrain and out to the brainstem nuclei, which then signal the facial muscles.

Clinical neurologists know of the distinction between these two ways of controlling facial muscles.

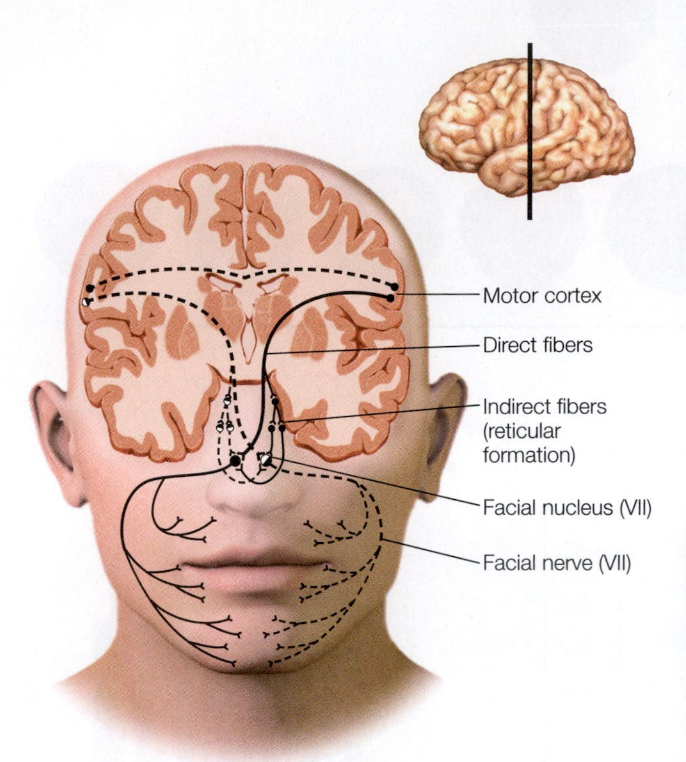

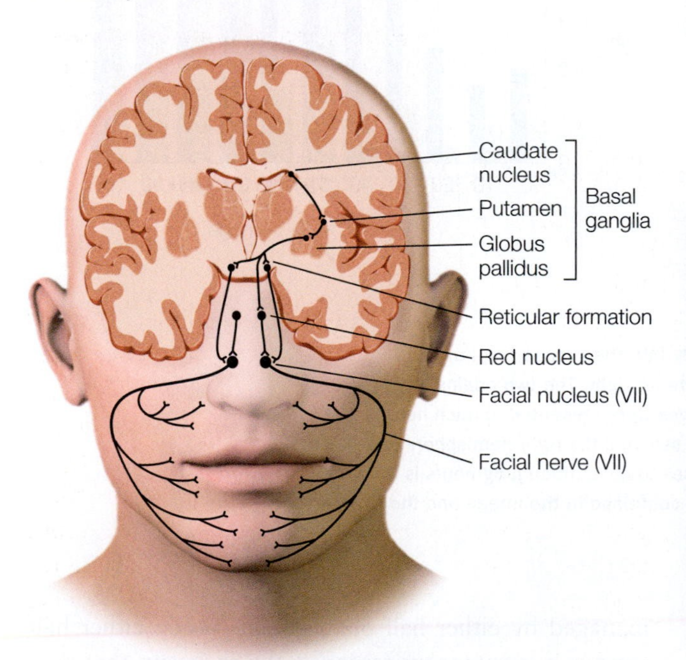

FIGURE 4.19 The neural pathways that control voluntary and spontaneous facial expression are different.
(a) Voluntary expressions that can signal intention have their own cortical networks in humans. **(b)** The neural networks for spontaneous expressions involve older brain circuits and appear to be the same as those in chimpanzees. Inset: The location of the section that has been overlaid on each face.

For example, a patient with a lesion in the part of the right hemisphere that participates in voluntary expressions is unable to move the left half of the face when told to smile. But the same patient can easily move the left half of the face when spontaneously smiling, because those pathways are unaffected by right-hemisphere damage. In contrast, patients with Parkinson's disease, whose midbrain nuclei no longer function, are unable to produce spontaneous facial expressions, whereas the pathways that support voluntary expressions work fine. Such patients can lose their masked-face appearance when asked to smile (**Figure 4.20**).

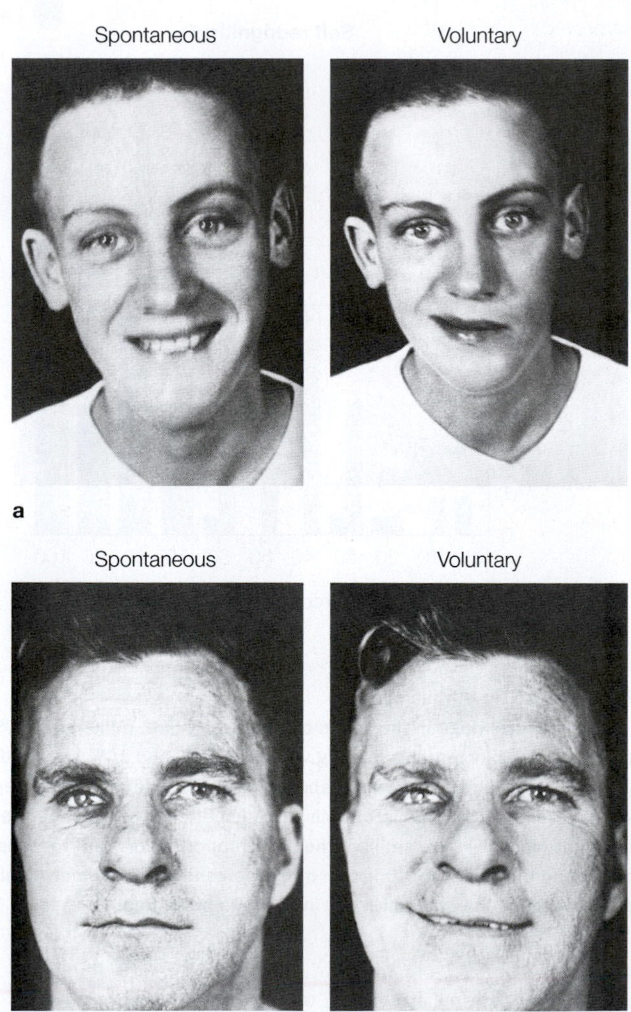

FIGURE 4.20 Facial expressions of two kinds of patients.
(a) This patient suffered brain damage to the right hemisphere. The lesion did not interfere with spontaneous expression (left) but did interfere with voluntary expression (right). **(b)** This Parkinson's disease patient has a typical masked face (left). Because the disease involves the part of the brain that controls spontaneous facial expression, the faces of these patients, when they are told to smile (right), light up because the other pathway is still intact.

The Interactions of Attention and Perception

The attentional and perceptual abilities of split-brain patients have been extensively explored. After cortical disconnection, perceptual information is not shared between the two cerebral hemispheres. Sometimes the supporting cognitive processes of attentional mechanisms, however, do interact. Some forms of attention are integrated at the subcortical level, and other forms act independently in the separated hemispheres.

We noted earlier that split-brain patients cannot integrate visual information between the two visual fields. When visual information is lateralized to either the left or the right disconnected hemisphere, the unstimulated hemisphere cannot use the information for perceptual analysis. The same is true for certain types of somatosensory information presented to each hand. Although touching any part of the body is noted by either hemisphere, patterned somatosensory information is lateralized. Thus, when holding an object in the left hand, a split-brain patient is unable to find an identical object with the right hand.

Some investigators argue that higher-order perceptual information is integrated by way of subcortical structures, but others have not replicated these results. For example, split-brain patients sometimes drew pictures that combined word information presented to the two hemispheres. When "ten" was flashed to one hemisphere and "clock" was flashed to the other, the patient drew a clock set at 10. This outcome initially seemed to imply that subcortical transfer of higher-order information was taking place between the hemispheres, yet a couple of problems plagued this notion. Visual feedback increased the incidence of the integration phenomenon, and in about 25% of the left-hand drawings, only the word presented to the right hemisphere was drawn. If information were being integrated subcortically, neither of these things should have happened.

This is the time to think about external cuing, and to keep in mind that each hemisphere can control the proximal arm muscles on the ipsilateral side of the body. A second experiment was designed to see whether higher-order information was being transferred and integrated subcortically or peripherally (**Figure 4.21**; Kingstone & Gazzaniga, 1995).

Conceptually ambiguous word pairs such as "hot dog" were presented to a split-brain patient—one word shown to each hemisphere. During the first 60 trials, only the patient's left hand drew the response, and on the following 60 trials the right hand did the drawing. The patient never drew the emergent object (e.g., a frankfurter) with either hand, and if the words were combined, they were always depicted literally (e.g., a dog panting in the heat). In addition, as in the previous experiment, the left hand sometimes drew word information presented to the left hemisphere to the exclusion of the word information presented to the right hemisphere, yet the reverse did not happen: Word information presented to the right hemisphere was never drawn by the right hand to the exclusion of left-hemisphere word information. These results suggest that the left hemisphere tends to dominate the right hemisphere in such tasks and frequently overrides the right hemisphere's control of the left hand.

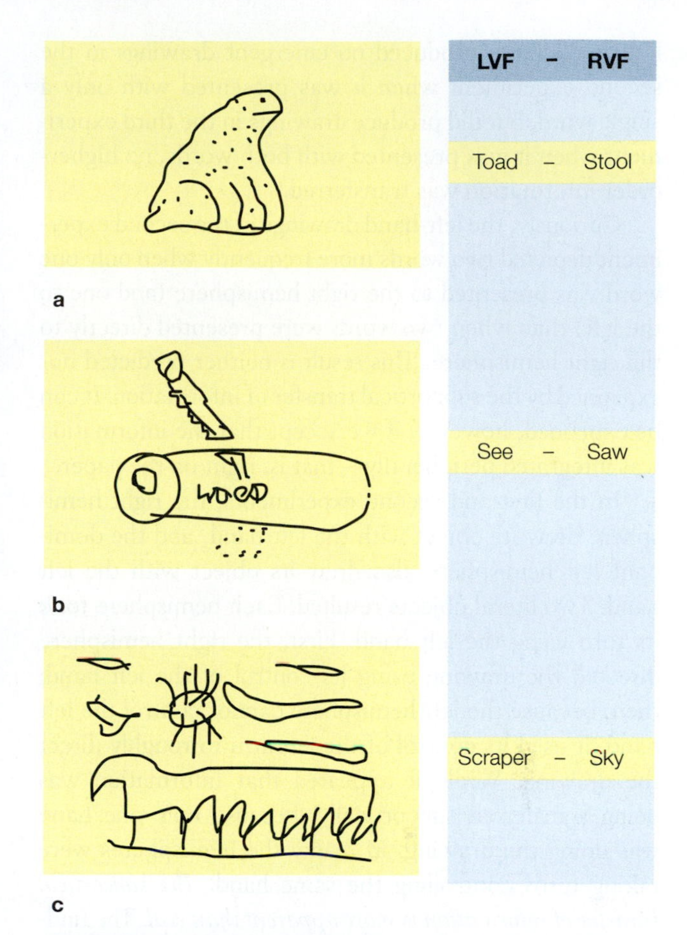

FIGURE 4.21 Pictures drawn by split-brain participant J.W.'s left hand in response to stimuli presented to the left and right visual fields (LVF and RVF).
(a) Drawing of the LVF word "Toad" (presented to the visual field ipsilateral to the drawing hand). **(b)** Drawing of the RVF word "Saw" (contralateral to the drawing hand). **(c)** Drawing combining both the words "Scraper" and "Sky" (ipsilateral + contralateral).

In a third experiment, both words were flashed to either hemisphere to see whether either hemisphere would integrate the information and produce a drawing of an emergent object. This time, when both words were flashed to the left hemisphere, the patient drew the emergent object, yet when both words were flashed to the right hemisphere, a literal depiction of just a single word was usually drawn. These results suggest that because the left hemisphere produced no emergent drawings in the second experiment when it was presented with only a single word, but did produce drawings in the third experiment when it was presented with both words, no higher-order information was transferred.

Curiously, the left-hand drawings in the second experiment depicted two words more frequently when only one word was presented to the right hemisphere (and one to the left) than when two words were presented directly to the right hemisphere. This result is neither predicted nor explained by the subcortical transfer of information. It can be explained, however, if we accept that the information was integrated peripherally—that is, right on the paper.

In the first and second experiments, the right hemisphere drew its object with the left hand, and the dominant left hemisphere also drew its object with the left hand. Two literal objects resulted. Each hemisphere took its turn using the left hand: First, the right hemisphere directed the drawing using its control of the left hand; then, because the left hemisphere cannot control the left hand, it used its control of the left arm to roughly direct the drawing. While it appeared that information was being transferred subcortically, because only one hand was doing the drawing, in reality the hemispheres were taking turns controlling the same hand. *The subcortical transfer of information is more apparent than real.* The finding that the right hemisphere drew only one of the two words presented to it in the third experiment also suggests that it has limited integrative capacity for cognitive tasks.

We have seen that *object identification* seems to occur in isolation in each hemisphere of split-brain patients. In other studies, evidence suggests that crude information concerning *spatial locations* can be integrated between the hemispheres. In one set of experiments, the patient fixated on a central point located between two four-point grids, one in each visual field (Holtzman, 1984).

In a given trial, one of the positions on one of the grids was highlighted for 500 ms. Thus, information was sent to either the left hemisphere or the right hemisphere, depending on which grid was illuminated. In one example the upper-left point of the grid in the LVF was highlighted (**Figure 4.22a**). This information was registered in the right hemisphere of the participant. After 1 second, a tone sounded and the participant was asked to move his eyes to the highlighted point *within* the visual field containing the highlighted stimulus. The results were as expected. Information from the LVF that went to the right hemisphere guided eye movement back to the same location where the light had flashed.

In the second condition the participant was required to move his eyes to the corresponding point on the grid in the visual field opposite the field containing the highlighted stimulus (**Figure 4.22b**). Being able to do this

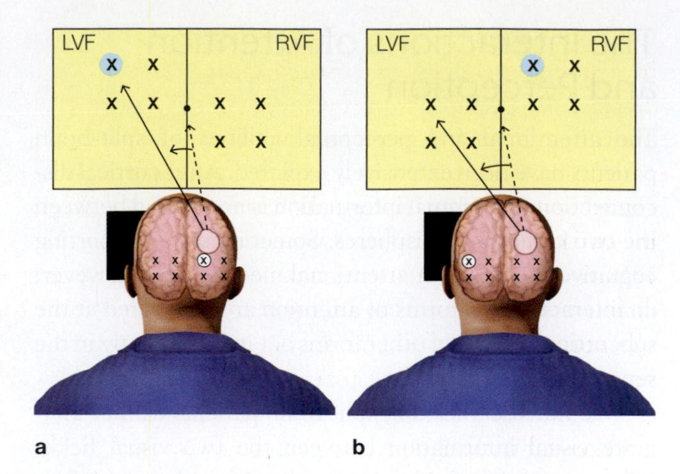

FIGURE 4.22 Cross-integration of spatial information.
(a) On within-field trials, the eye moved to the stimulus that was surrounded by the probe. (b) On between-field trials, the eye moved to the corresponding stimulus in the other hemifield.

would mean that information about the location of the stimulus was entering the left hemisphere from the RVF and guiding the participant's eye movement to the corresponding location in the right-hemisphere-controlled LVF. Split-brain participants performed this task easily. So, some type of spatial information was being transferred and integrated between the two hemispheres, enabling attention to be transferred to either visual field. The ability remained intact even when the grid was randomly positioned in the test field.

These results raised a question: Are the attentional processes associated with spatial information affected by cortical disconnection? Surprisingly (as we will see in Chapter 7), split-brain patients can use either hemisphere to direct attention to positions in the LVF or the RVF. This conclusion was based on studies using a modified version of the spatial cuing task. In this task, participants respond as quickly as possible upon detecting a target that appears at one of several possible locations. The target is preceded by a cue, either at the target location (a valid cue) or at another location (an invalid cue). Responses are faster on valid trials, indicating spatial orienting to the cued location. In split-brain patients, as with normal participants, a cue to direct attention to a particular point in the visual field was honored no matter which half of the brain was presented with the critical stimulus (Holtzman et al., 1981). These results suggest that the two hemispheres rely on a common orienting system to maintain a single focus of attention.

The discovery that spatial attention can be directed with ease to either visual field raised the question of whether each separate cognitive system in the split-brain patient, if instructed to do so, could independently and simultaneously direct attention to a part of its own visual field. Can the right hemisphere direct attention to a point in the LVF while the left hemisphere attends to a point in the RVF? Normal participants cannot divide their attention in this way, but perhaps the split-brain operation frees the two hemispheres from this constraint. As it turns out, the answer is no. The integrated spatial attention system remains intact following cortical disconnection (Reuter-Lorenz & Fendrich, 1990). *Thus, as in neurologically intact observers, the attention system of split-brain patients is unifocal.* They, like normal individuals, are unable to prepare simultaneously for events taking place in two spatially disparate locations.

The dramatic effects on perception and cognition of disconnecting the cerebral hemispheres initially suggested that each hemisphere has its own attentional resources (Kinsbourne, 1982). If that model were true, then the cognitive operations of one hemisphere, no matter what the difficulty, would have little influence on the cognitive activities of the other. The left hemisphere could be solving a differential equation while the right hemisphere was planning for the coming weekend. The alternative view is that the brain has limited resources to manage such processes: If most of our resources are being applied to solving math problems, then fewer resources are available for planning the weekend's activities. This phenomenon has been studied extensively, and all of the results have supported the latter model: Our central resources are limited.

ATTENTIONAL RESOURCES ARE SHARED The concept that attentional resources are limited should be distinguished from limitations in processing that are a result of other properties of the sensory systems. Even though the overall resources that a brain commits to a task appear constant, the method of deploying them can vary depending on the task. For example, the time needed to detect a complex object, such as a black circle among gray circles and black squares, increases as more items are added to the display. Normal control participants require an additional 70 ms to detect the target when two extra items are added to the display, and another 70 ms for each additional pair of items. In split-brain patients, when the items are equally distributed across the midline of the visual field (so that each visual field contains half the objects—i.e., a bilateral array), as opposed to all being in one visual field, the increase in reaction time to added stimuli is cut almost in half (**Figure 4.23**; Luck et al., 1989).

Two half brains working separately can do the job in half the time that one whole brain can. Division of cognitive resources improved performance; separation of the hemispheres seems to have turned a unified perceptual system into two simpler perceptual systems that, because

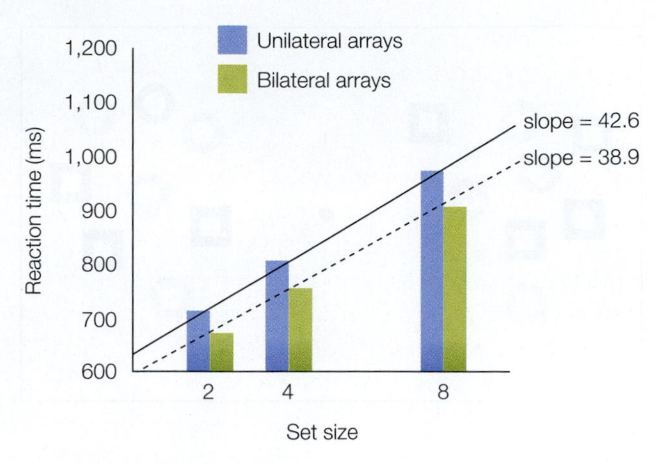

a Control patients

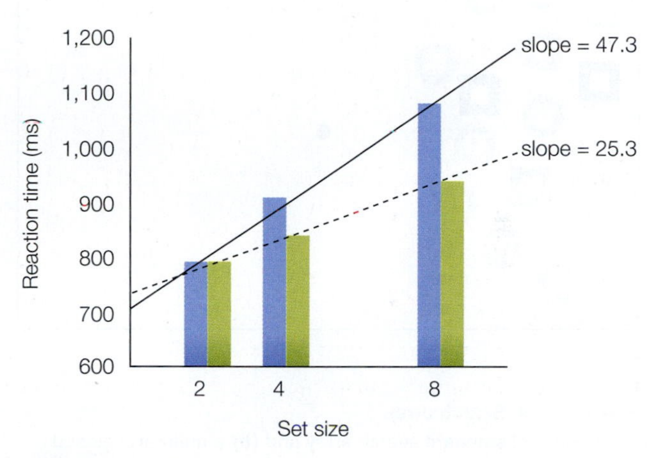

b Split-brain patients

FIGURE 4.23 Division of cognitive resources in split-brain patients improved visual search performance.
As more items are added to a set, the increase in reaction time of control patients remains constant (a). But for split-brain patients (b), the increase in reaction time for bilateral arrays is only half as fast as when all objects are confined to one side.

they are unable to communicate, don't "interfere" with each other. The large perceptual problem, which the normal brain faces, is broken down into smaller problems that a half brain can solve when each hemisphere perceives only half the problem. It appears as if the patient's total information-processing capacity has increased so that it is superior to that of normal participants. How can this be, if resources remain constant? This conundrum forces us to consider where resources are applied in a perceptual–motor task.

It appears that each hemisphere employs a different strategy to examine the contents of its visual field. The left hemisphere adopts a helpful cognitive strategy in solving the problem, whereas the right hemisphere does not possess those extra cognitive skills. This phenomenon was shown in a different experiment. Here, the task was to find a black circle in a field of equally numbered black squares

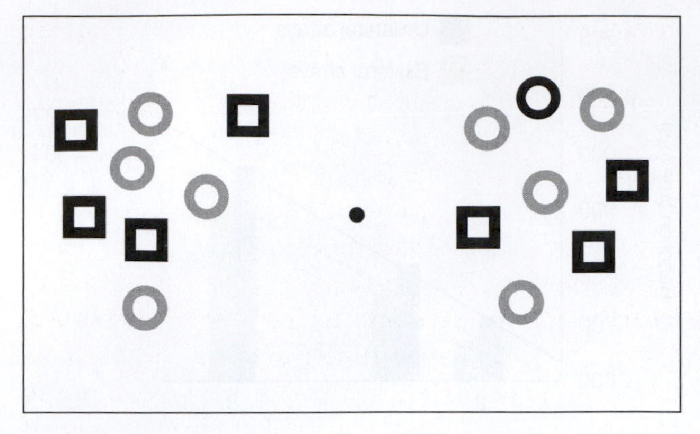

a

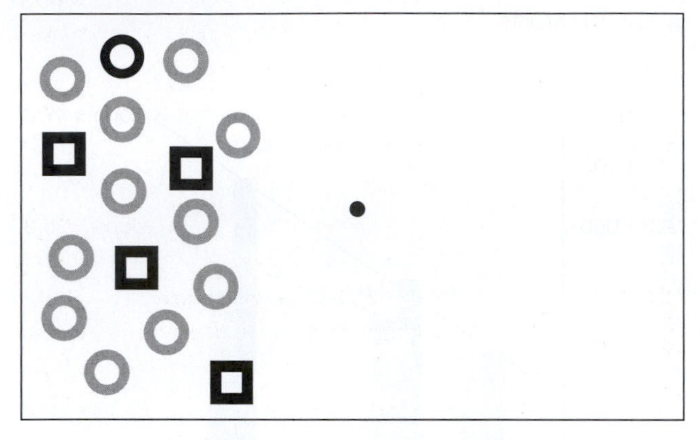

b

FIGURE 4.24 Search array.
(a) A bilateral standard search array and **(b)** a unilateral guided search array for a black-circle target, where a clue is given: There are fewer black squares than gray circles, in a ratio of about 2:5. The "smart" approach to complete the task faster is to use the clue and concentrate on the black figures. In two out of three split-brain patients, the left hemisphere used the clue, which decreased its reaction time in the guided trials, but the right hemisphere did not.

and gray circles (**Figure 4.24**). Randomly interspersed through the trials were "guided" trials, where the patient was given a clue: There were fewer black squares than gray circles, in a ratio of about 2:5. A cognitive or "smart" approach would be to use the clue and concentrate on color (black versus gray) instead of on shape (circle versus square), which should enable faster completion of the task.

In two out of three split-brain patients, the left, dominant hemisphere used the clue, which decreased its reaction time in the guided trials, but the right hemisphere did not (Kingstone et al., 1995). In control groups, 70% of people have a faster reaction time in guided trials and use the "smart" strategy. This result indicates that not all people use guided search, but when they do, it's the left hemisphere doing the work. This apparent discrepancy supports other evidence that multiple mechanisms of attention operate at different stages of visual search processing, from early to late, some of which might be shared across the disconnected hemispheres and others of which might be independent. *Thus, each hemisphere uses the available resources, but at different stages of processing.*

What's more, using a "smart strategy" does not mean the left hemisphere is always better at orienting attention. It depends on the job. For instance, the right hemisphere, superior in processing upright faces, automatically shifts attention to where a face is looking, but the left hemisphere does not have the same response to gaze direction (Kingstone et al., 2000).

When thinking about neural resources and their limitations, people often consider the mechanisms that are being engaged while performing voluntary processing. For example, what is happening as you try to rub your stomach, pat your head, and do a calculus problem at the same time? Searching a visual scene, however, calls upon processes that may well be automatic, built-in properties of the visual system itself. Indeed, the hemispheres interact quite differently in how they control reflex and voluntary attentional processes. It appears that reflexive automatic attention orienting is independent in the two hemispheres, as the right hemisphere's automatic shifting of attention to gaze direction indicates. Voluntary attention orienting, however, is a horse of a different color. Here, it appears, the hemispheres are competing, and the left has more say (Kingstone et al., 1995). That these systems are distinct is reflected in the discovery that splitting brains has a different effect on the processes.

GLOBAL AND LOCAL PROCESSING What does the picture in **Figure 4.25** show? A house, right? Now describe it more fully. You might note its architectural style, and you might point out the detailing on the front

FIGURE 4.25 Global and local representations.
We represent information at multiple scales. At its most global scale, this drawing is of a house. On a local scale, we can also recognize and focus on the component parts of the house.

door, the double-hung windows running across the front façade, and the shingled roof. Your description of the picture will have been hierarchical. The house can be classified by multiple facets: Its shape and attributes indicate it is a house. But it is also a specific house, with a specific configuration of doors, windows, and materials. This description is hierarchical in that the finer (local) levels of description are embedded in the higher (global) levels. The shape of the house evolves from the configuration of its component parts—an idea that will be developed in Chapter 6.

David Navon (1977) of the University of Haifa introduced a model task for studying **hierarchical structure.** He created stimuli that could be identified on two different levels, as the example in **Figure 4.26** illustrates. At each level, the stimulus contains an identifiable letter. The critical feature is that the letter defined by the global shape is composed of smaller letters (the local shape). In Figure 4.26a, for example, the global *H* is composed of local *F*'s.

Navon was interested in how we perceive hierarchical stimuli. He initially found that the perceptual system first extracted the global shape. The time required to identify the global letter was independent of the identity of the constituent elements, but when it came to identifying the small letters, reaction time was slowed if the global shape was incongruent with the local shapes. Subsequent research qualified these conclusions. Global precedence does depend on object size and the number of local elements. Perhaps different processing systems are used for representing local and global information.

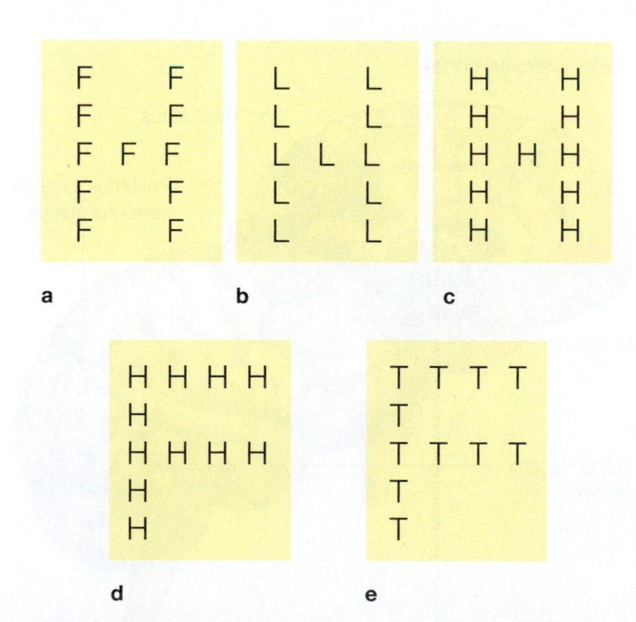

FIGURE 4.26 Local and global stimuli used to investigate hierarchical representation.
Each stimulus is composed of a series of identical letters whose global arrangement forms a larger letter. The participants' task is to indicate whether the stimulus contains an *H* or an *L*. When the stimulus set included competing targets at the two levels (**b**), the participants were instructed to respond either to local targets only or to global targets only. Neither target is present in (**e**).

Lynn Robertson and her colleagues found evidence that supports this hypothesis by studying patients with unilateral brain lesions (L. C. Robertson et al., 1988). When testing such patients, the usual method is to compare the performance of patients who have right-hemisphere lesions against those who have corresponding left-hemisphere lesions. An appealing feature of this approach is that there is no need to lateralize the stimuli to one side or the other; laterality effects are assumed to arise because of the unilateral lesions. For example, if lesions to the left hemisphere result in more disruption in reading tasks, then the deficit is attributed to the hemisphere's specialization in reading processes.

To properly interpret these types of studies, it is necessary to carry out double dissociations (see Chapter 3) to determine whether similar lesions to the opposite hemisphere produce a similar deficit. For instance, it has been demonstrated consistently that lesions in the left hemisphere can produce deficits in language functions (such as speaking and reading) that are not seen in patients with comparable lesions to the right hemisphere. Similarly, lesions to the right hemisphere can disrupt spatial orientation, such as the ability to accurately locate visually presented items. Comparable lesions to the left hemisphere do not cause corresponding spatial deficits.

Robertson presented patients who had a lesion in either the left or the right hemisphere with local and global stimuli in the center of view (the critical laterality factor was whether the lesion was in the left or right hemisphere). Patients with left-side lesions were slow to identify *local* targets, and patients with right-side lesions were slow with *global* targets, demonstrating that the left hemisphere is more adept at representing local information and the right hemisphere is better with global information.

In another study, patients who had recently had a stroke in either the right or the left hemisphere were shown a hierarchical stimulus and asked to reproduce it from memory (Delis et al., 1986). Drawings from patients with left-hemisphere lesions faithfully followed the contour, but without any hint of local elements. In contrast, patients with right-hemisphere lesions produced only local elements (**Figure 4.27**). Note that this pattern was consistent whether the stimuli were linguistic or nonlinguistic; hence, the representational deficits were not restricted to certain stimuli. Note also that, because of the plasticity of the brain, such stark differences might dissipate and not be seen months after the stroke.

Keep in mind that both hemispheres can abstract either level of representation, but they differ in how *efficiently* local and global information are represented. The right is better at the big picture, and the left is more detail oriented.

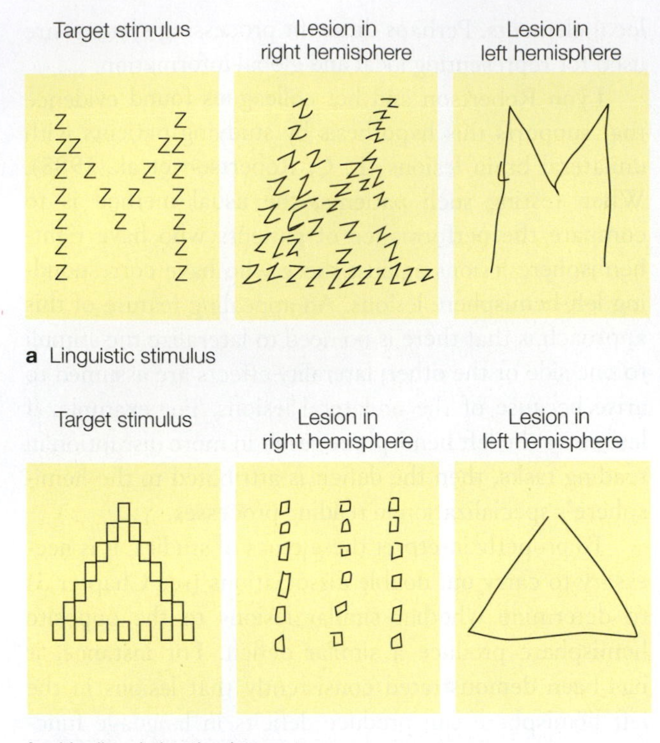

FIGURE 4.27 Extreme failures of hierarchical processing following brain damage.
Two patients were asked to draw the two elements shown in the left column of each panel. The patient with right-hemisphere damage was quite accurate in producing the local element—the *Z* in (a) or the square in (b)—but failed to arrange these elements into the correct global configuration. The patient with left-hemisphere damage drew the overall shapes—the *M* in (a) or the triangle in (b)—but left out all of the local elements. Note that for each patient, the drawings were quite consistent for both linguistic (a) and nonlinguistic (b) stimuli, suggesting a task-independent representational deficit.

Thus, patients with left-hemisphere lesions are able to analyze the local structure of a hierarchical stimulus, but they must rely on an intact right hemisphere, which is less efficient at abstracting local information. Further support for this idea comes from studies of local and global stimuli with split-brain patients (L. C. Robertson et al., 1993). Here, too, patients generally identify targets at either level, regardless of the side of presentation. As with normal participants and patients with unilateral lesions, however, split-brain patients are faster at identifying local targets presented to the RVF (the left hemisphere) and global targets presented to the LVF (the right hemisphere).

Theory of Mind

The term *theory of mind* refers to our ability to understand that other individuals have thoughts, beliefs, and desires. In terms of laterality, theory of mind is an interesting case. You might expect theory of mind to be another hemispheric specialization, lateralized to the left hemisphere like language is, given its dependency on reasoning. Much of the prevailing research on theory of mind, however, suggests that if it is lateralized at all, it is lateralized to the right hemisphere.

Many neuroimaging studies show a network of regions in both hemispheres engaged in theory-of-mind tasks, including the medial portion of the prefrontal cortex (PFC), the posterior portion of the superior temporal sulcus (STS), the precuneus, and the amygdala–temporopolar cortex (**Figure 4.28**). Rebecca Saxe and her colleagues (2009), however, have used a version of the false-belief task (see Chapter 13) in several fMRI studies to demonstrate that the critical component of the theory of mind—the attribution of beliefs to another person—is localized to the temporal–parietal junction in the right hemisphere.

This finding may sound merely interesting to you, but to split-brain researchers it was shocking. Think about it for a second. If this information about the beliefs of others is housed in the right hemisphere, and if, in split-brain patients, it isn't transferred to the speaking, left hemisphere, wouldn't you expect these patients to suffer a disruption in social and moral reasoning? Yet they don't. Split-brain patients act like everyone else. Do these findings also suggest that the recursive nature of thinking about the beliefs of another person is lateralized to the right hemisphere?

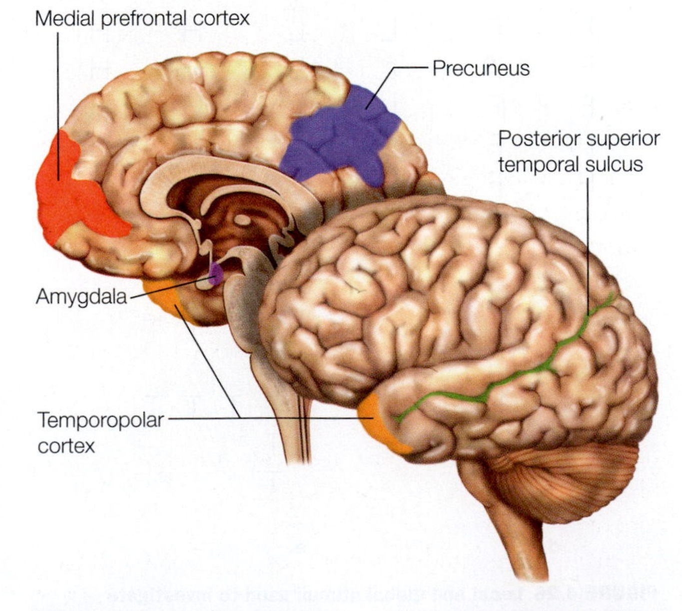

FIGURE 4.28 Theory-of-mind tasks activate a network of regions bilaterally.
These include the medial prefrontal cortex, posterior superior temporal sulcus, precuneus (hidden in the medial longitudinal fissure in the parietal lobe), and the amygdala–temporopolar cortex. The attribution of beliefs is located in the right hemisphere's temporal–parietal junction.

A split-brain study by University of California professor Michael Miller and his colleagues may provide some insight into these questions (M. B. Miller et al., 2010). Miller's team tested three full-callosotomy patients and three partial-callosotomy patients on a moral reasoning task that depended on the ability to attribute beliefs to another person (the same task used by Saxe and colleagues, which produced activations in the right hemisphere).

The task involved hearing a scenario in which the actions of an agent conflicted with the beliefs of the agent. Here's an example: Grace works in a chemical plant, and she is fixing coffee for her friend. She adds a white powder to her friend's coffee, believing that the white powder is sugar. The white powder was mislabeled, however, and is actually quite toxic. Her friend drinks the coffee and dies. After hearing the scenario, the participant is asked this question: Was it morally acceptable for Grace to give the coffee to her friend? Participants with an intact corpus callosum typically say it was morally acceptable to give her friend the coffee, because they think Grace believed that the white powder was sugar and intended no harm. That is, they realize that Grace had a false belief.

If the special mechanisms that attribute belief are lateralized to the right hemisphere, then the speaking left hemisphere of the split-brain patients should be cut off from those mechanisms. Split-brain patients would thus respond in a way that relies on the outcome of the actions (the friend's death) and is not based on the beliefs of the actors. Children younger than age 4 typically respond in this way (because they do not yet have a fully developed theory of mind). Indeed, Miller and colleagues found that all of the split-brain patients responded that Grace's action was morally unacceptable.

This intriguing result leaves open a question: If the left hemispheres of split-brain patients are cut off from this important theory-of-mind mechanism, why don't these patients act like severely autistic individuals, who are unable to comprehend the thinking and beliefs of other people? Some scientists have suggested that the specialized mechanism observed in the right hemisphere may be used for the fast, automatic processing of belief attributions, and that slower, more deliberate reasoning mechanisms of the left hemisphere could perform the same function, given time for deliberation.

In fact, Miller and colleagues observed that patients in the moral reasoning study were often uncomfortable after hearing themselves utter their initial judgments. They would offer spontaneous rationalizations for responding in a particular way. For example, in another scenario a waitress *knowingly* served sesame seeds to somebody who she believed was highly allergic to them. The outcome, however, was harmless, because the person was not allergic. The split-brain patient judged the waitress's action to be morally acceptable. Some moments later, however, he appeared to rationalize his response by saying, "Sesame seeds are tiny little things. They don't hurt nobody." According to the automatic-versus-deliberate-response hypothesis, the patient had to square his initial response, which did not benefit from information about the belief state of the waitress, with what he rationally and consciously knew was permissible in the world.

There is another interpretation of what could be occurring here, however. When the left hemisphere gives its answer vocally, the right hemisphere hears the judgment for the first time, just as the experimenter does. The right hemisphere's emotional reaction to the judgment may be the same as what the experimenter feels: surprise and dismay. These emotions, produced subcortically, are felt by both hemispheres. Now the left hemisphere experiences an unexpected negative emotional response. What does it do? It has to explain it away. This brings us to a discussion of the left hemisphere's interpreter mechanism.

TAKE-HOME MESSAGES

- The right hemisphere is specialized for detecting upright faces, discriminating among similar faces, and recognizing the faces of familiar others. The left hemisphere is better at recognizing one's own face.
- Only the left hemisphere can trigger voluntary facial expressions, but both hemispheres can trigger involuntary expressions.
- Some forms of attention are integrated at the subcortical level, and other forms act independently in the separated hemispheres. Split-brain patients can use either hemisphere to direct attention to positions in either the left or the right visual field.
- The right hemisphere has limited integrative capacity for cognitive tasks.
- Functional MRI studies show that the critical component of theory of mind—the attribution of beliefs to another person—is localized to the temporal–parietal junction in the right hemisphere.

4.4 The Interpreter

A hallmark of human intelligence is our ability to make causal interpretations about the world around us. We make these interpretations on a moment-to-moment basis, usually without realizing it. Imagine going to a movie on a sunny afternoon. Before entering the theater, you notice that the street and parking lot are dry, and only a few clouds are in the sky. When the movie is over and you walk back outside, however, the sky is gray and the ground is very wet. What do you instantly assume? You probably assume that it rained while you were watching the movie. Even though you did not witness the rain and nobody told you it had rained, you base that causal inference on the evidence of the wet ground and gray skies. This ability to make inferences is a critical component of our intellect, enabling us to formulate hypotheses and predictions about the events and actions in our lives, to create a continuous sensible narrative about our place in the world, and to interpret reasons for the behavior of others.

After a callosotomy, the verbal intelligence and problem-solving skills of a split-brain patient remain relatively intact. There may be minor deficits, including in free recall ability, but for the most part, intelligence remains unchanged. An intact intelligence, however, is true only for the speaking left hemisphere; in the right hemisphere intellectual abilities and problem-solving skills are seriously impoverished. A large part of the right hemisphere's impoverishment can be attributed to the finding that causal inferences and interpretations appear to be a specialized ability of the left hemisphere. So, it is not that the right hemisphere has lost these abilities, but rather that it never had them at all. One of the authors of this book (M.S.G.) has referred to this unique specialization of the left hemisphere as the **interpreter**.

The interpreter has revealed itself in many classic experiments over the years. A typical observation occurs when the speaking left hemisphere offers some kind of rationalization to explain actions that were initiated by the right hemisphere but were spurred on by a motivation unknown to the left hemisphere. For example, when the split-brain patient P.S. was given a command to stand up in a way that only the right hemisphere could view, P.S. stood up. When the experimenter asked him why he was standing, P.S.'s speaking left hemisphere immediately came up with a plausible explanation: "Oh, I felt like getting a Coke." If his corpus callosum had been intact, then P.S. would have responded that he stood up because that was the instruction he had received. One constant finding throughout the testing of split-brain patients is that the left hemisphere *never* admits ignorance about the behavior of the right hemisphere. It *always* makes up a story to fit the behavior.

The interpreter makes itself manifest in a number of ways. Sometimes it interprets the actions initiated by the right hemisphere, as in the example just described, and sometimes it interprets the moods caused by the experiences of the right hemisphere. Emotional states appear to transfer between the hemispheres subcortically, so severing the corpus callosum does not prevent the emotional state of the right hemisphere from being transferred to the left hemisphere, even though all of the perceptions and experiences leading up to that emotional state are still isolated.

Author M.S.G. reported on a case in which he showed some negatively arousing stimuli to the right hemisphere alone. The patient denied seeing anything, but at the same time she was visibly upset. Her left hemisphere felt the autonomic response to the emotional stimulus but had no idea what had caused it. When asked what the matter was, her left hemisphere responded that the experimenter was upsetting her. In this case, the left hemisphere felt the valence of the emotion but was unable to explain the actual cause of it, so the interpreter constructed a theory from the available information.

Probably the most notable example of the interpreter at work is an experiment done by M.S.G. and Joseph LeDoux using a simultaneous concept task (Gazzaniga & LeDoux, 1978). A split-brain patient was shown two pictures, one exclusively to the left hemisphere and one exclusively to the right. Then he was asked to choose, from an array of pictures placed in full view in front of him, those that were associated with pictures lateralized to the left and right sides of the brain (**Figure 4.29**).

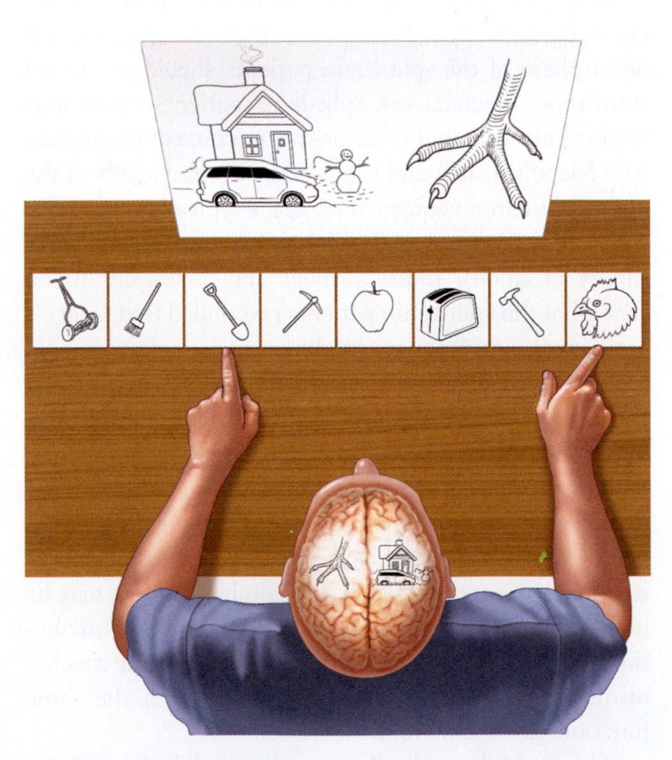

FIGURE 4.29 The interpreter at work.
The left hemisphere of split-brain patient P.S. was shown a chicken claw, and his right hemisphere was shown a snow scene. When P.S. was asked to point to a picture associated with the image he had just seen, his right hand (guided by his left hemisphere) pointed to the chicken, and his left hand pointed to the shovel. When asked why he had pointed to those things, he replied, "Oh, that's simple. The chicken claw goes with the chicken, and you need a shovel to clean out the chicken shed."

In one example of this kind of test, a picture of a chicken claw was flashed to the left hemisphere and a picture of a snow scene to the right hemisphere. Of the array of pictures placed in front of the participant, the obviously correct association is a chicken for the chicken claw and a shovel for the snow scene. Patient P.S. responded by choosing the shovel with the left hand and the chicken with the right. When asked why he chose these items, he (his left hemisphere) replied, "Oh, that's simple. The chicken claw goes with the chicken, and you need a shovel to clean out the chicken shed."

Remember that the left hemisphere has no knowledge about the snow scene or why he picked the shovel. The left hemisphere, having seen the left hand's response, has to interpret that response in a context consistent with what it knows. What it knows is that there is a chicken, and his left hand is pointing to a shovel. It does not have a clue about a snow scene. What is the first sensible explanation it can come up with? Ah—the chicken shed is full of chicken manure that must be cleaned out.

The interpreter can affect a variety of cognitive processes. For example, it may be a major contributor to the distortion of memories. In a study by Elizabeth Phelps and M.S.G., split-brain patients were asked to examine a series of pictures that depicted an everyday story line, such as a man getting out of bed and getting ready for work (Phelps & Gazzaniga, 1992). During a recognition test, the patients were shown an intermingled series of photos that included the previously studied pictures, new pictures unrelated to the story line, and new pictures that were closely related to the story line (**Figure 4.30**).

The left hemisphere falsely recognized the new pictures related to the story, while the right hemisphere rarely made that mistake. Both hemispheres were equally good at recognizing the previously studied pictures and rejecting new unrelated pictures. The right hemisphere, however, was more accurate at weeding out the new related pictures. Because of the left hemisphere's tendency to infer that events must have occurred because they fit with the general schema it has created (the overall gist of the story), it falsely recognized new related photos.

The left hemisphere also tends to make more semantic inferences than the right hemisphere makes. In one study, split-brain patients were briefly shown pairs of words in either the LVF or the RVF and had to infer the relationship between the items (Gazzaniga and Smylie, 1984). For example, in one trial the word "pan" and the

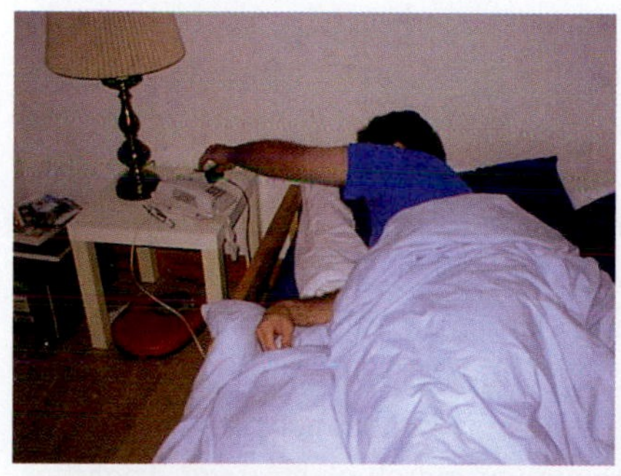

a A story in pictures

b Distractor picture (not related to story) **c** Distractor picture (related to story)

FIGURE 4.30 Left-hemisphere superiority in interpretation and inference affects memory performance. Split-brain patients first examined a series of pictures **(a)** that told the story of a man getting up in the morning and getting ready to go to work. A recognition test was done a while later, testing each hemisphere separately. In this test the patients were shown a stack of pictures that included the original pictures along with other, distractor pictures, some of which had no relation to the story **(b)** and others that could have been part of the story but weren't **(c)**.

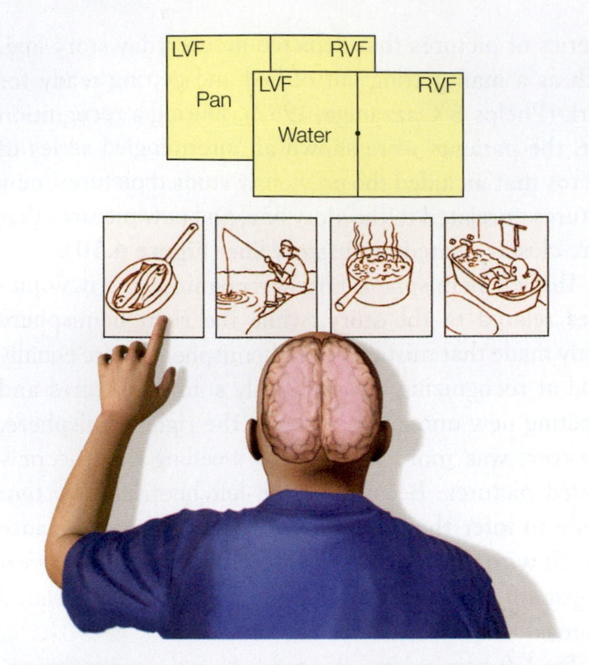

FIGURE 4.31 The right hemisphere is unable to infer causality. The capacity of the right hemisphere to make inferences is extremely limited. In this test, two words are presented in serial order, and the right hemisphere (left hand) is simply required to point to a picture that best depicts what happens when the words are causally related. The left hemisphere finds this sort of task trivial, but the right cannot perform the task.

word "water" were briefly presented to the left hemisphere (**Figure 4.31**). The participant was then shown four pictures—for example, pictures of food frying in a pan, a person fishing, water boiling in a pan, and a person bathing—and asked to point to the picture that represented the combination of the pair of words presented earlier. The words "person" and "fish" would combine to form a person fishing, and "pan" and "water" would combine to form boiling water.

After presenting these stimuli separately to each hemisphere, researchers found that the left hemisphere performed significantly better than the right hemisphere in the two split-brain patients that were tested. Patient J.W.'s left hemisphere answered 15 of 16 questions correctly, while his right hemisphere correctly answered only 7 of 16. Similarly, patient V.P.'s left hemisphere answered 16 of 16 questions correctly, while her right hemisphere correctly answered 9 of 16.

The left hemisphere's edge in this task is not due to a better memory or a better lexicon. Follow-up tests demonstrated that both the left and right hemispheres could equally remember the word pairs and explain the inferred concepts (such as fishing or boiling water). Instead, this experiment suggests that the left hemisphere is better at making inferences about semantic relationships and cause and effect.

George Wolford and colleagues at Dartmouth College also demonstrated this phenomenon by using a probability-guessing paradigm (Wolford et al., 2000). Participants were presented with a simple task of trying to guess which of two events would happen next. Each event had a different probability of occurrence (e.g., a red stimulus might appear 75% of the time and a green one 25% of the time), but the order of occurrence of the events was entirely random.

There are two possible strategies for responding in this task: *matching* and *maximizing.* In the red–green example, frequency matching involves guessing red 75% of the time and guessing green 25% of the time. Because the order of occurrence is random, this strategy is likely to result in a great number of errors. The second strategy, maximizing, involves simply guessing red every time. This approach ensures an accuracy rate of 75% because red appears 75% of the time. Animals such as rats and goldfish maximize. Humans match. The result is that nonhuman animals perform better than humans in this task. Humans' use of this suboptimal strategy has been attributed to our propensity to try to find patterns in sequences of events, even when we are told that the sequences are random. In Las Vegas casinos, the house maximizes; you don't. We all know how that ends up.

Wolford and colleagues tested each hemisphere of split-brain patients using the probability-guessing paradigm. They found that the left hemisphere used the frequency-matching strategy, whereas the right hemisphere maximized. When patients with unilateral damage to the left or right hemisphere were tested on the probability-guessing paradigm, the findings indicated that damage to the left hemisphere resulted in use of the maximizing strategy, whereas damage to the right hemisphere resulted in use of the suboptimal frequency-matching strategy. Together, these findings suggest that the right hemisphere outperformed the left hemisphere because the right hemisphere approached the task in the simplest possible manner, with no attempt to form complicated hypotheses about the task. The left hemisphere, on the other hand, engaged in the human tendency to find order in chaos.

The left hemisphere persists in forming hypotheses about the sequence of events, even in the face of evidence that no pattern exists. Although this tendency to search for causal relationships has many potential benefits, it can lead to suboptimal behavior when there is no simple causal relationship. Some common errors in decision making are consistent with the notion that we are prone to search for and posit causal relationships, even when the evidence is insufficient or random. You might think you caught the touchdown pass because you were wearing your old red socks, but that is not the case. They are not lucky socks. This search for causal explanations appears to be a left-hemisphere activity and is the hallmark of the interpreter.

Systematic changes in reasoning are also seen in patients with unilateral brain injuries, depending on whether the right or left hemisphere is damaged. In general, patients with damage to their left frontal lobes are worse at inferring relationships between things that are actually related, compared to patients with damage to their right frontal lobes, but the two groups perform similarly when it comes to rejecting items that are not related (Ferstl et al., 2002; Goel et al., 2007). This result suggests that, compared to the right frontal cortex, the left frontal cortex is better equipped for detecting relationships and making inferences.

In some cases the relationships between items cannot be determined. For example, if you are told that Kim is older than William and Kim is older than Stephen, you cannot logically infer that Stephen is older than William. When a relationship cannot logically be inferred, patients with right frontal lesions tend to make inferences anyway and, in turn, make more errors than patients with left frontal lesions do (Goel et al., 2007). These results are consistent with the studies of split-brain patients that we discussed earlier. The left hemisphere excels at making inferences, but it may make excessive inferences when it is unchecked by the right hemisphere, possibly leading to errors.

Note, however, that the right hemisphere is not devoid of causal reasoning. Matt Roser and colleagues (2005) discovered that while judgments of *causal inference* are best when the information is presented in the RVF to the left hemisphere, judgments of *causal perception* are better when the information is presented in the LVF. In one experiment, Roser had both control and split-brain participants watch a scenario in which two switches are pressed, either alone or together. When switch A is pressed, a light goes on; when B is pressed, it does not go on; when both are pressed, again the light comes on. When asked what caused the light to come on, only the left hemisphere could make the *inference* that it was switch A.

In a separate test, Roser had the same participants look at films of two balls interacting. Either one ball hit the second and the second ball moved; one hit the second and there was a time gap before the second ball moved; or one came close, but there was a space gap and the second one moved. The participant was asked whether one ball caused the other to move. In this case, the right hemisphere could determine the causal nature of the collision. These results suggest that the right hemisphere is more adept at detecting that one object is influencing another object in both time and space—computations essential for causal perception.

To perceive objects in the environment as unified, the visual system must often extrapolate from incomplete information about contours and boundaries. Paul Corballis and colleagues (1999) used stimuli containing illusory contours to reveal that the right hemisphere can perceptually process some things better than the left can. Both the left and right hemispheres perceived a fat shape in the top image of **Figure 4.32a** and a skinny shape in the bottom image, but only the right hemisphere could perceive the same shapes in the figures of amodal completion (**Figure 4.32b**). Corballis called this ability of the right hemisphere the "right-hemisphere interpreter."

The unique specialization of the left hemisphere—the interpreter—allows the mind to seek explanations for internal and external events in order to produce appropriate response behaviors. For the interpreter, facts are helpful but not necessary. It has to explain whatever is at hand and may have to ad-lib; the first explanation that makes sense will do.

As the interpreter searches for causes and effects, it tries to create order from the chaos of inputs that bombard it all day long. It takes whatever information it gets, both from the brain and from the environment, and weaves it into a story that makes sense. If some sort of brain malfunction sends it odd information, the

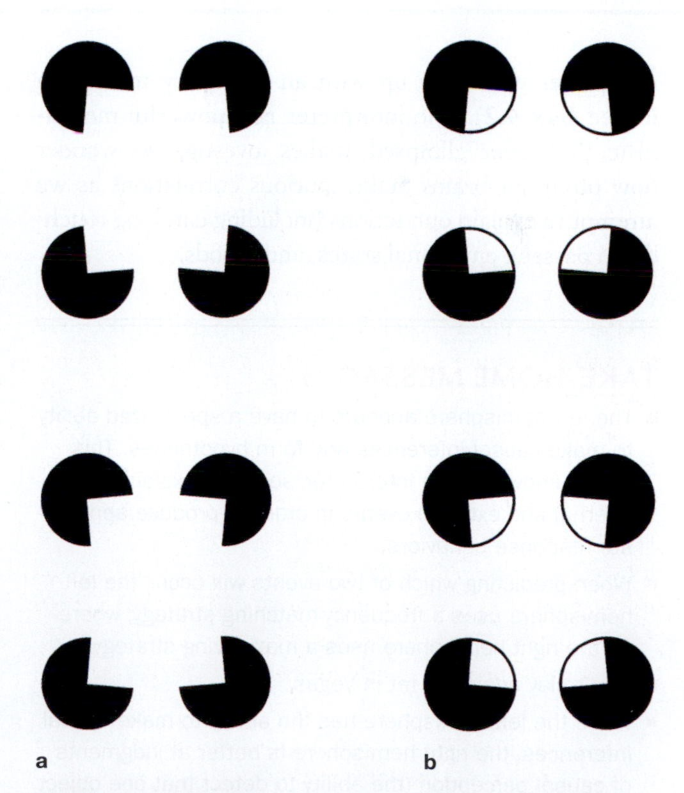

FIGURE 4.32 The right hemisphere can process some things better than the left.
Either hemisphere can decide whether the illusory shapes in the left column **(a)** are "fat" or "thin"; if outlines are added **(b)**, then only the right hemisphere can still tell the difference. The right hemisphere is able to perceive the whole when only a part is visible, known as amodal completion.

BOX 4.2 | LESSONS FROM THE CLINIC

The Maine Idea

Reduplicative paramnesia is a rare but illustrative syndrome in which the patient has a delusional belief that a place has been duplicated, or exists in two different locations at the same time, or has been moved to a different location. The syndrome is usually associated with an acquired brain injury such as a stroke, intracerebral hemorrhage, or tumor. One of the authors of this book (M.S.G.) interviewed a woman with this syndrome in his office at New York Hospital. She was intelligent and calmly read the *New York Times* while waiting for the appointment. The interview went like this (Gazzaniga, 2011):

M.S.G.: So, where are you?

Patient: I am in Freeport, Maine. I know you don't believe it. Dr. Posner told me this morning when he came to see me that I was in Memorial Sloan Kettering Hospital and that when the residents come on rounds to say that to them. Well, that is fine, but I know I am in my house on Main Street in Freeport, Maine!

M.S.G.: Well, if you are in Freeport and in your house, how come there are elevators outside the door here?

Patient: Doctor, do you know how much it cost me to have those put in?

This patient's left-hemisphere interpreter tried to make sense of what she knew and felt and did. Because of her lesion, the part of the brain that represents locality was sending out an erroneous message about her location. The interpreter is only as good as the information it receives, and in this instance it was getting a wacky piece of information. Yet the interpreter's function is to make sense of the input it receives. It has to explain that wacky input. It still has to field questions and make sense of other incoming information—information that to the interpreter is self-evident. The result? A lot of imaginative stories.

interpreter will come up with an odd story to explain it (see **Box 4.2**). The interpreter is a powerful mechanism that, once glimpsed, makes investigators wonder how often our brains make spurious correlations as we attempt to explain our actions (including catching touchdown passes), emotional states, and moods.

TAKE-HOME MESSAGES

- The left hemisphere appears to have a specialized ability to make causal inferences and form hypotheses. This ability, known as the interpreter, seeks to explain both internal and external events in order to produce appropriate response behaviors.
- When predicting which of two events will occur, the left hemisphere uses a frequency-matching strategy, whereas the right hemisphere uses a maximizing strategy.
- Don't play against a rat in Vegas.
- While the left hemisphere has the ability to make causal inferences, the right hemisphere is better at judgments of causal perception (the ability to detect that one object is influencing another object in both time and space).
- The right hemisphere's ability to extrapolate a unified picture of the environment from incomplete perceptual information about contours and boundaries is called the "right-hemisphere interpreter."

4.5 Evidence of Lateralized Brain Functions from the Normal and Malfunctioning Brain

Researchers have also designed clever experiments to test the differential processing of the two hemispheres in people with intact brains. In the visual domain, comparisons are made between presentations of stimuli to the left or right visual field. Although this procedure ensures that information will be projected initially to the contralateral hemisphere, the potential for rapid transcortical transfer is high. Even so, consistent differences are observed, depending on which visual hemifield is stimulated. For example, participants are more adept at recognizing whether a briefly presented string of letters forms a word when the stimulus is shown in the RVF than they are when it is presented in the LVF. Such results have led to hypotheses that transfer of information between the hemispheres is of limited functional utility, or that the information becomes degraded during transfer. Thus, we conclude that performance is dominated by the contralateral hemisphere with peripheral visual input.

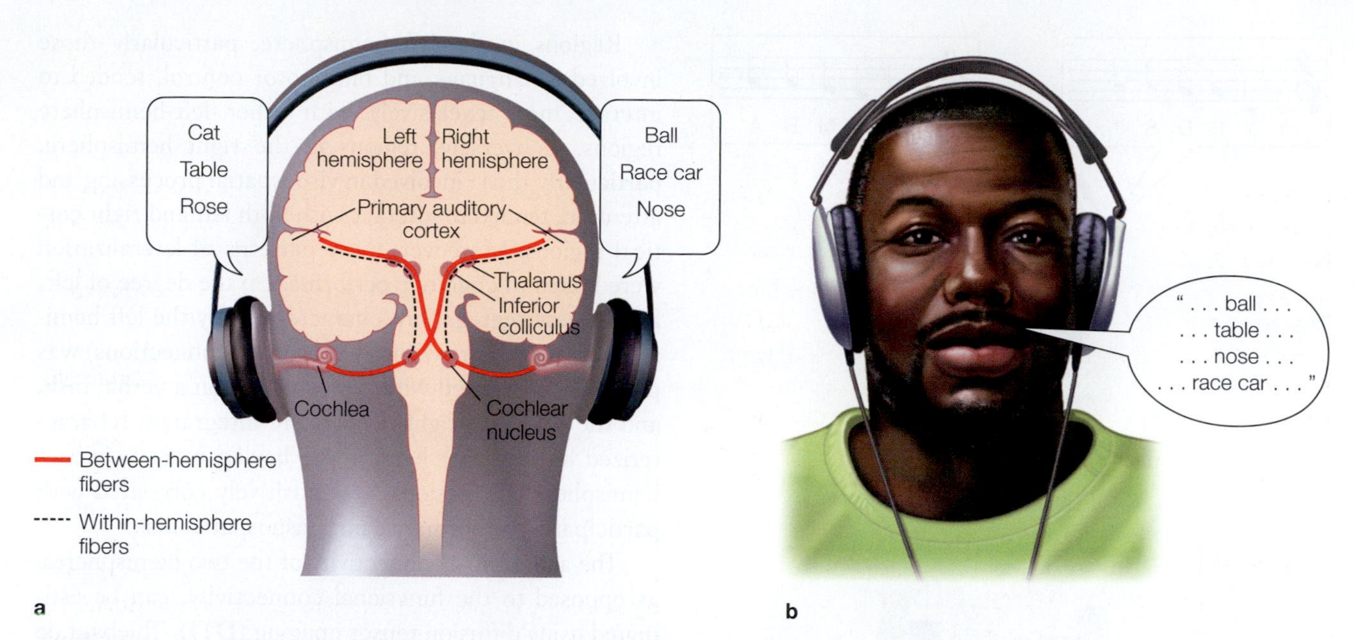

FIGURE 4.33 The dichotic listening task.
The dichotic listening task is used to compare hemispheric specialization in auditory perception. (a) Competing messages are presented, one to the left ear and one to the right ear. Auditory information is projected bilaterally. Although most of the ascending fibers from the cochlear nucleus project to the contralateral thalamus, some fibers ascend on the ipsilateral side. Participants are asked either to report the stimuli (b) or to judge whether a probe stimulus was part of the dichotic message. Comparisons focus on whether the participant heard the reported information in the right or left ear, with the assumption that the predominant processing occurred in the contralateral hemisphere. With linguistic stimuli, participants are more accurate in reporting the information presented to the right ear.

Studies of auditory perception similarly attempt to isolate the input to one hemisphere. As in vision work, the stimuli can be presented monaurally—that is, restricted to one ear. Because auditory pathways are not as strictly lateralized as visual pathways (see Figure 5.18 in Chapter 5), however, an alternative methodology for isolating the input is the **dichotic listening task** shown in **Figure 4.33**. In this task, two competing messages are presented simultaneously, one to each ear, and the participant tries to report both messages. The ipsilateral projections from each ear presumably are suppressed when a message comes over the contralateral pathway from the other ear.

In a typical study, participants heard a series of dichotically presented words. When asked to repeat as many words as possible, participants consistently produced words that had been presented to the right ear—an effect dubbed the *right-ear advantage*. Results like these mesh well with expectations that the left hemisphere is dominant for language.

The demonstration of visual and auditory performance asymmetries with lateralized stimuli generated great excitement among psychologists. Here at last were simple methods for learning about hemispheric specialization in neurologically healthy people (see Kimura, 1973). It is not surprising that thousands of laterality studies on healthy participants have been conducted, using almost every imaginable stimulus manipulation.

The limitations of this kind of laterality research should be kept in mind, however (Efron, 1990):

- The effects are small and inconsistent, perhaps because healthy people have two functioning hemispheres connected by an intact corpus callosum that transfers information quite rapidly.
- There is a bias in the scientific review process toward publishing papers that find significant differences over papers that report no differences. It is much more exciting to report asymmetries in the way we remember lateralized pictures of faces than to report that effects are similar for RVF and LVF presentations.
- Interpretation is problematic. What can be inferred from an observed asymmetry in performance with lateralized stimuli? In the preceding examples, the advantages of the RVF and the right ear were assumed to reflect that these inputs had better access to the language processes of the left hemisphere. Perhaps, however, people are just better at identifying information in the RVF or in the right ear.

To rule out this last possibility, investigators must identify tasks that produce an advantage for the left ear or left visual field. For example, scientists discovered that people

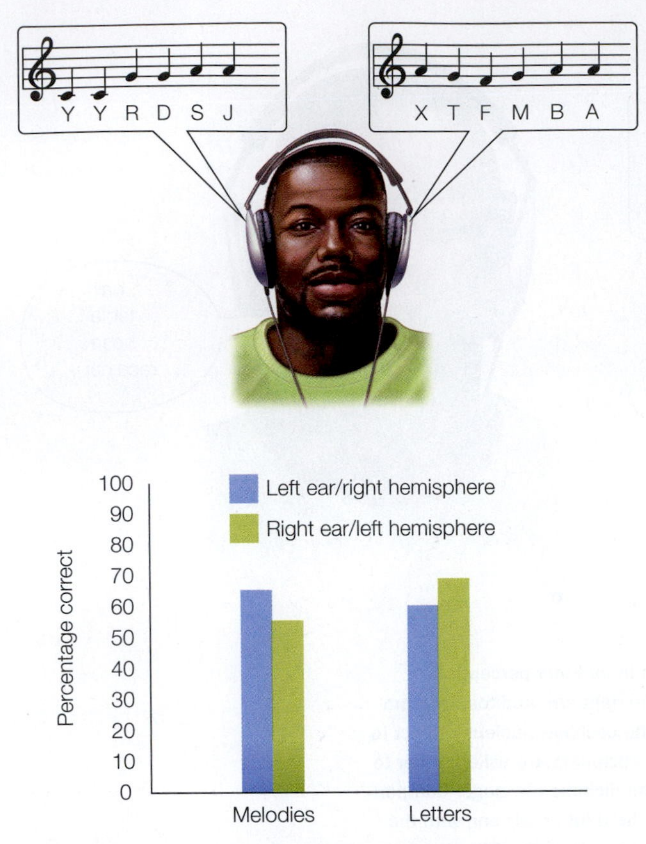

FIGURE 4.34 A right-ear advantage is not found on all tasks. Participants listened to a dichotic message in which each ear was presented with a series of letters sung to short melodies. When given a recognition memory test, participants were more accurate on the letters task for stimuli heard in the right ear. In contrast, a left-ear advantage was observed when the participants were tested on the melodies.

are better at recognizing the left-ear member of dichotic melody pairs; indeed, a double dissociation happens when participants are presented with dichotic pairs of sung melodies (Bartholomeus, 1974). We find a right-ear advantage for the song's words but a left-ear advantage for its melodies (**Figure 4.34**).

Mapping Functional and Anatomical Connectivity

Researchers can also use fMRI techniques to explore hemispheric differences in healthy individuals. In one study, Gotts and colleagues (2013) used fMRI to investigate hemispheric differences in functional connectivity—that is, the connections between brain regions that tend to have similar neural activity and presumably have similar functions. On measuring the functional connectivity of brain regions within the same hemisphere and between the two hemispheres, they found that the left and right hemispheres had different patterns of functional connectivity.

Regions in the left hemisphere, particularly those involved in language and fine motor control, tended to interact more exclusively with other left-hemisphere regions. Conversely, regions in the right hemisphere, particularly those involved in visuospatial processing and attention, tended to interact with both left and right cortical regions. Moreover, these patterns of lateralization were linked to cognitive performance; the degree of left-hemisphere segregation (characterized by the left hemisphere having more within-hemisphere connections) was positively correlated with performance on a verbal task, and the degree of right-hemisphere integration (characterized by the right hemisphere having more between-hemisphere connections) was positively correlated with participants' performance on a visuospatial task.

The anatomical connectivity of the two hemispheres, as opposed to the functional connectivity, can be estimated using diffusion tensor imaging (DTI). Thiebaut de Schotten and colleagues (2011) used DTI to measure the size of white matter tracts running between participants' parietal and frontal cortices, and they found that one white matter bundle was larger in the right hemisphere than in the left. Moreover, they found that the degree to which this white matter bundle was bigger in a participant's right hemisphere (versus the left) predicted performance on different attentional tasks.

In the first task, participants had to detect targets that appeared in their right or left visual fields. Participants with larger rightward white matter asymmetries could detect targets in the LVF faster. In the second task, participants were asked to indicate where the midpoint of a horizontal line was. This task is commonly given to stroke patients who ignore one side of space. Patients who neglect the left side of space tend to draw the midpoint toward the rightmost part of the line, since they ignore the left part of the line, and vice versa. Interestingly, the researchers found that participants with larger rightward white matter asymmetries drew the midpoint farther toward the left on the line. These results suggest that the rightward lateralization of this white matter tract is associated with an attentional bias toward the left side of space, which results in a "pseudoneglect" effect in healthy participants toward the right side of space.

Abnormal Hemispheric Lateralization

Emerging evidence suggests that certain brain disorders may be linked to abnormal patterns of hemispheric lateralization. Schizophrenic patients, for example, may have *reduced* hemispheric asymmetry (reviewed in Oertel-Knöchel & Linden, 2011). Schizophrenic patients are more likely than controls to be left-handed or ambidextrous, and they have a reduced right-ear advantage in dichotic listening tasks. The brain anatomy of schizophrenic patients also reflects a reduction in the normal pattern of hemispheric asymmetry. They tend to have a reduced or reversed asymmetry of the planum temporale, and they tend to lack the normal "tilt" of the brain's midline produced by bulges in the posterior left hemisphere and anterior right hemisphere.

Autism is also associated with abnormal hemispheric asymmetry. People with autism appear to have a rightward shift in lateralization. For example, language areas that are normally left-lateralized are more symmetrical in autistic individuals (Eyler et al., 2012). In one study, researchers found that many functional brain networks, including networks for vision, audition, motor control, executive function, language, and attention, had rightward shifts of asymmetry in children with autism. That is, networks that are normally left-lateralized were more bilateral in autistic children, and networks that are normally bilateral were more right-lateralized in autistic children (Cardinale et al., 2013).

There is also evidence that people with autism have altered structural and functional connectivity. Neurotypical individuals tend to have more long-range, global connections in the right hemisphere and more short-range, local connections in the left hemisphere, but this asymmetry is reduced in individuals with autism (Carper et al., 2016). In addition, the corpus callosum of someone with autism tends to be smaller than that of someone without autism (T. W. Frazier et al., 2012; Prigge et al., 2013), and people born without a corpus callosum are more likely to display autistic traits than the general population is (Lau et al., 2013; Paul et al., 2014). These observations are congruent with the disconnection theory of autism, which suggests that autism is associated with a deficiency of long-range connections, which in turn leads to less global processing and more local processing.

It's important to note that it is unclear whether the abnormal hemispheric asymmetries observed in these disorders are a cause or an effect. That is, we do not know whether abnormal hemispheric asymmetry causes the symptoms that are characteristic of these disorders, or whether the abnormal asymmetry is the consequence of dysfunctional cortex or some other factor responsible for the disorders' symptoms.

One disorder that is more directly tied to abnormal hemispheric connectivity is agenesis of the corpus callosum (ACC). ACC is a congenital disorder in which the corpus callosum partially or completely fails to form, thus creating a "natural split brain." Cognitive outcomes of children with ACC are highly variable. In general, these children tend to have IQ scores below average, but most fall within the normal range, and some are even above average. Compared to healthy children, children with ACC tend to have poorer visuomotor skills, impaired visual and spatial processing, slower processing speeds, impaired language skills, and trouble sustaining attention.

TAKE-HOME MESSAGES

- Neurologically healthy participants exhibit a right-ear advantage when performing the dichotic listening task. When listening to songs, however, while there is a right-ear advantage for the song's words, there is a left-ear advantage for its melodies.
- While the left hemisphere tends to have more within-hemisphere functional connectivity and to interact almost exclusively with other regions of the left hemisphere, the right hemisphere has more balanced within-hemisphere and cross-hemisphere connectivity and tends to interact with both left and right cortical regions.
- Certain brain disorders, such as schizophrenia and autism, appear to have abnormal patterns of hemispheric lateralization.

4.6 The Evolutionary Basis of Hemispheric Specialization

So far in this chapter, we have reviewed general principles of hemispheric specialization in humans. Humans, of course, have evolutionary ancestors, so we might expect to find examples of lateralized functions in other animals. Indeed, this is the case. We begin this section looking at such evidence in other animals, and we then discuss aspects of the brain's organization that allow specialized brain functions to exist. Next we consider whether each hemisphere has become specialized to the point that each can truly be said to have its own processing style. Finally, we turn to the question of whether there is a causal relationship between the predominance of right-handedness and the left hemisphere's specialization for language.

Hemispheric Specialization in Nonhumans

Because of the central role of language in hemispheric specialization, laterality research has focused primarily on humans. But the evolutionary pressures that underlie hemispheric specialization—the need for unified action, rapid communication, and reduced costs associated with interhemispheric processing—would also be potentially advantageous to other species. It is now clear that hemispheric specialization is not a uniquely human feature (Bradshaw & Rogers, 1993) and is present in all vertebrate classes (reviewed by Vallortigara et al., 2011). Evidence is beginning to indicate left–right asymmetries in invertebrates as well (reviewed by Frasnelli et al., 2012). For example, fruit flies, octopuses, bees, spiders, crabs, and snails all exhibit some asymmetries in behavior, among which are asymmetries in olfaction, preferential leg use, memory storage, and turning direction.

In birds, almost all of the optic fibers cross at the optic chiasm, ensuring that all of the visual input from each eye projects solely to the contralateral hemisphere. The lack of crossed and uncrossed fibers probably reflects the fact that there is little overlap in the visual fields of birds, owing to the lateral placement of the eyes (**Figure 4.35**). Moreover, birds lack a corpus callosum, so communication between the visual systems within each hemisphere is limited, and functional asymmetries might result.

Several asymmetries are known in birds. Chickens and pigeons are better at categorizing stimuli viewed by the right eye and left hemisphere than by the left eye and right hemisphere. You may wonder what is meant when a chicken categorizes stimuli. Here is one such category: edible or not? Chickens are more proficient in discriminating food from nonfood items when stimuli are presented to the right eye, whereas the right hemisphere (left eye) is more adept when they are trained to respond to unique properties like color, size, and shape, or when the task requires them to learn the exact location of a food source.

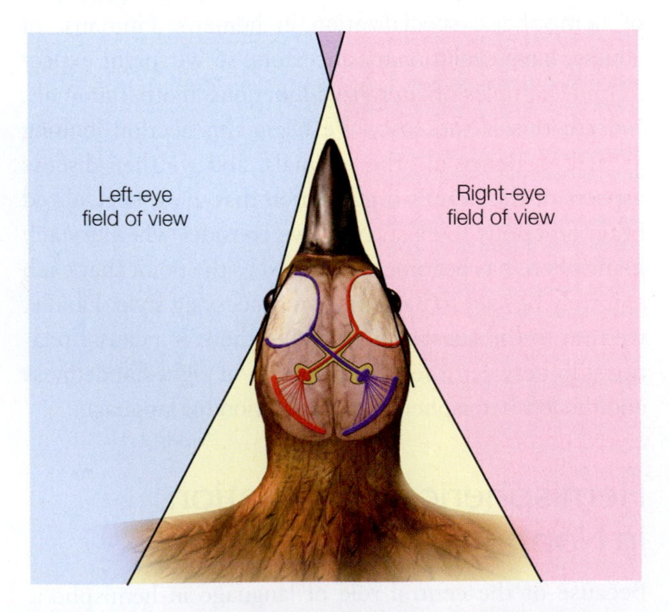

FIGURE 4.35 Visual pathways in birds are completely crossed. This organization indicates that there is little overlap in the regions of space seen by each eye, and thus the visual input to the left hemisphere is independent of the visual input to the right hemisphere. This anatomical segregation would be expected to favor the emergence of hemispheric asymmetries.

Almost all birds have a communication system: They caw, tweet, and chirp to scare away enemies, mark territory, and lure mates. In many species, the mechanisms of song production depend on structures in the left hemisphere. Fernando Nottebohm of Rockefeller University discovered that sectioning the hypoglossal nerve of the canary's left hemisphere, which innervates the tongue, severely disrupted song production (Nottebohm, 1980). In contrast, right-hemisphere lesions had little effect. A similar effect can be found in other bird species, although in some species lesions to either hemisphere can interfere with song production.

Just as humans show **handedness**, favoring either the left or right hand, dogs and cats both show "pawedness." But males and females demonstrate opposite preferences: Males favor their left paws, while females favor their right paws (Quaranta et al., 2004; Wells & Millsopp, 2009). Parrots and cockatoos also show asymmetries when it comes to manipulating food and objects with their feet, which they are quite adept at. Their "footedness" proportions are similar to handedness in humans (L. J. Harris, 1989; L. J. Rogers & Workman, 1993).

Nonhuman primates also show differences in hemispheric structure and perhaps function. Old World monkeys and apes have lateral fissures that slope upward in the right hemisphere, similar to the asymmetry found in humans. Behaviorally, monkeys exhibit lateralized behavior when performing complex tasks, using their right hand when extracting food from containers (Meguerditchian & Vauclair, 2006; Spinozzi et al., 1998). Until recently, it was thought that great apes do not commonly show a predominance of right-handedness, but larger samples, including a meta-analysis of 1,524 great apes, report a 3:1 ratio of right-handedness to left-handedness for chimps, using more fine-tuned behaviors such as throwing and pulling food out of a tube (Hopkins, 2006).

There does seem to be a link between handedness and brain asymmetries in chimpanzees. Right-handed chimps have a leftward bias in cortical gyrification, which was observed to be absent in non-right-handed animals (Hopkins, Cantalupe, et al., 2007). The right-handed chimps also showed a higher neuronal density of layer II/III cells on the left side in the primary motor cortex (Sherwood et al., 2007). Great apes and baboons also appear to use the right hand and arm when making communicative gestures (Hopkins, 2006; Meguerditchian et al., 2010, 2011). We will discuss handedness in communication further in Chapter 11, as it suggests the possibility that gestural communication was a forerunner of language.

Perceptual studies provide provocative indications of asymmetrical functions in nonhuman primates as well. Like humans, rhesus monkeys are better at tactile discriminations of shape when using the left hand. Even more impressive is that split-brain monkeys and split-brain humans have similar hemispheric interactions in visual perception tasks. For example, in a face recognition task, monkeys, like humans, have a right-hemisphere advantage; in a line orientation task, monkeys share a left-hemisphere advantage with humans.

The visual system of monkeys, however, transfers visual information across an intact anterior commissure, whereas there is no transfer of visual information across the human anterior commissure. In addition, left-hemisphere lesions in the Japanese macaque can impair the animal's ability to comprehend the vocalizations of conspecifics. Unlike the effects on some aphasic patients, however, this deficit is mild and transient. There is also evidence from split-brain monkeys that, unlike the case with humans, the left hemisphere is better at spatial judgments. This observation is tantalizing, because it is consistent with the idea that the evolution of language in the left hemisphere in humans has resulted in the loss of some visuospatial abilities from the left hemisphere.

In summary, like humans, nonhuman species exhibit differences in the function of the two hemispheres. The question remains, How should we interpret these findings? Does the left hemisphere, which specializes in birdsong and human language, reflect a common evolutionary antecedent? If so, this adaptation has an ancient history, because humans and birds have not shared a common ancestor since before the dinosaurs. Perhaps, however, the hemispheric specialization that occurs in many species instead reflects a general design principle of the brain.

The Brain's Modular Architecture

In general terms, hemispheric specialization must have been influenced and constrained by callosal evolution. We might predict that the appearance of new cortical areas would have required more connections across the callosum. However, our best evidence currently suggests that lateralization might have been facilitated by a *lack* of callosal connections. The resultant isolation would have promoted divergence among the functional capabilities of homotopic regions, resulting in cerebral specializations.

A first step toward understanding why a lack of connections may have caused specializations is to look at the organizing principles of the brain. In Chapter 2 we briefly touched on the idea that certain "wiring laws" apply to the evolutionary development of the large human brain (Striedter, 2005). We saw that as the brain grew larger, the proportional connectivity decreased, thus changing the internal structure and resulting in a decrease in overall connectivity.

The wiring plan that evolved, which has a high degree of local efficiency, yet fast communication with the global network, is known as "small-world" architecture (**Figure 4.36**; Watts & Strogatz, 1998). This architecture ensures that only a few steps are needed to connect any two randomly selected elements. It is characterized by many short connections between components, and only a few long-distance connections between "hubs" that serve as shortcuts between distant sites. This type of wiring results in faster signaling and lower energy requirements, and it gives the overall system greater tolerance in the event of failure of individual components or connections. Gray matter networks have been shown to have small-world topology and relatively low wiring costs (Bassett et al., 2010).

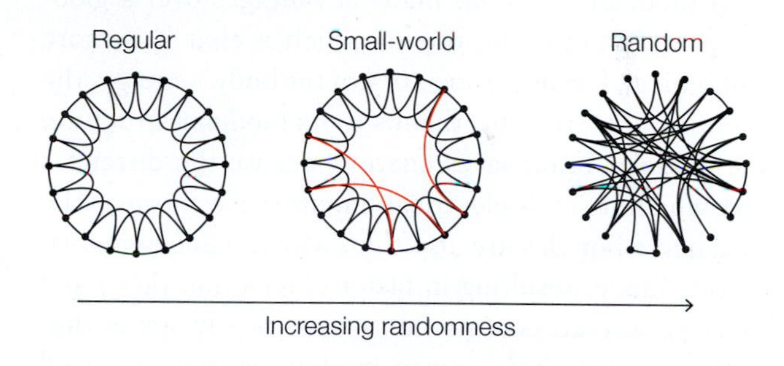

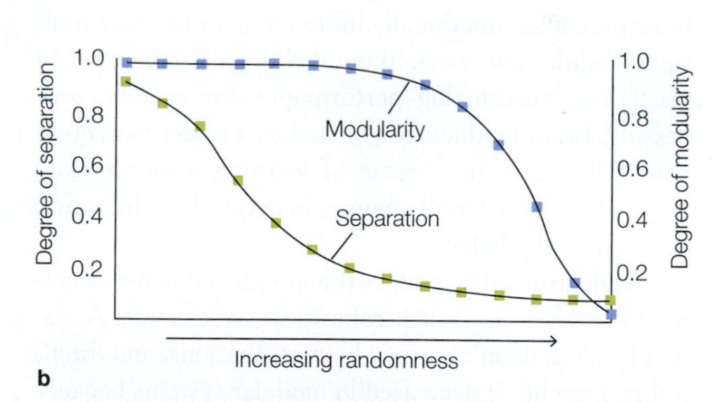

FIGURE 4.36 Small-world architecture.
(a) Large, sparsely interconnected networks can be linked in a variety of ways. In the regular network (left), each node is regularly interconnected with its neighbor nodes only. The small-world network (center) is regularly interconnected with its neighbors and has a few shortcuts (shown in red) between distant nodes. The network on the right has random interconnections. **(b)** A regular but sparsely interconnected network has a high degree of modularity but is highly separated, requiring more "wire" and more time for information to pass between distant nodes. A randomly interconnected network has short connection distances (low separation) but has lost its modularity. A small-world architecture has both a high degree of modularity and short connection distances. Adapted from Striedter (2005).

Multiple studies have shown that the human brain is organized into **modules** of functionally interconnected regions (Meunier et al., 2010). Modules are independent, local, specialized networks (or circuits) that can perform unique functions and can adapt or evolve to external demands. The brain's modules are made up of elements (neurons) that are more highly connected to one another than to elements in other modular networks. The general concept of modularity is that the components of a system can be categorized according to their functions (Bassett & Gazzaniga, 2011), and the most convincing evidence for a modular brain has always come from neurology and neuropsychology clinics. Patients who have suffered localized damage to specific cortical regions of their brains have impairments of some specific cognitive abilities or have lost those abilities because the network of neurons responsible for those abilities no longer functions, but other abilities remain intact.

A modular brain has many advantages over a globally functioning brain, one of which is that it is more economical. Despite using 20% of the body's energy, the brain is fairly efficient, thanks to its modular structure. The modular brain saves energy because the distances over which it sends electrical impulses are shorter. The local nerve bundles are also thin, which reduces electrical resistance, resulting in faster conduction times and lower energy costs. Another source of savings is that only regions within a given module or network need to be active to perform specific processing. Modular brains are also functionally more efficient because multiple modules can work in parallel. Local networks can specialize, maximizing performance for specific processing. Brain modularity also makes it easier to acquire new skills; over the course of learning a motor skill, researchers have found changes in network architecture (Bassett et al., 2015).

Modularity both reduces the interdependence of networks and increases their robustness to stressors. A system is *robust* if isn't harmed by perturbations, and *fragile* if it is. Fragility is decreased in modular systems because knocking out a local network—or even multiple local networks—doesn't knock out the entire system. What's more, a modular system facilitates behavioral adaptation (Kirschner & Gerhart, 1998), because each network can both function and change its function without affecting the rest of the system. This ability to adapt to changes enables modular networks to improve their function when faced with challenges from the environment—that is, to evolve. Systems that improve with perturbations have been called *antifragile* (Taleb, 2014).

By reducing constraints on change, the principle of modularity forms the structural basis on which subsystems can evolve and adapt (G. P. Wagner et al., 2007) in a highly variable environment, and this may be their most important advantage. Because one module at a time can change or duplicate, the system as a whole isn't at risk of losing other well-adapted modules, and well-functioning aspects of the system aren't threatened by further evolution.

This robustness (or even antifragility) to changing conditions confers a major advantage on any system evolving by competitive selection. Human brains are not the only modular brains; modular brains are found throughout the animal world, from worms to flies to cats. Nor are brains the only body system that is modular. Gene regulation networks, protein–protein interaction networks, and metabolic networks are modular too (Sporns & Betzel, 2016). Going beyond the body, even human social networks are modular.

If modular systems are so common, how did they evolve? While there are several hypotheses, research indicates that modularity is most likely caused by multiple forces acting to different degrees, depending on the context (G. P. Wagner et al., 2007). Since it is not practical to watch modularity evolve in biological systems themselves, computer simulations with evolutionary dynamics are the common research tool, and the question of how modular neural circuitry evolved in the brain hooked computer scientist Hod Lipson and his colleagues.

Their first idea was that modularity would spontaneously arise in a changing environment, grounded in the notion that modular systems would adapt better and thus would survive better in such an environment. Yet a changing environment was not sufficient to produce modularity (Lipson et al., 2002). A few years later they decided to test out Striedter's untested "wiring laws" hypothesis: the idea that modularity evolved as a by-product when selection was based on maximizing performance and minimizing wiring costs (Clune et al., 2013).

They ran two separate simulations of 25,000 generations of evolution, each in a changing and unchanging environment. They programmed a direct selection pressure into the first simulation to maximize performance alone; they then programmed the second simulation to both maximize performance *and* minimize connection costs. The connection costs of any kind of network include the cost of manufacturing, constructing, and maintaining the connections; the cost of transmitting energy along them; and the cost of signal delays. The shorter the connections are and the fewer their number, the cheaper the network is to build and ultimately maintain (Ahn et al., 2006; B. L. Chen et al., 2006; Cherniak et al., 2004). Short connections also mean a faster network, a definite plus when trying to survive in a competitive environment full of predators.

In the first simulation, where performance was the only criterion, modules did not appear. But in the second, when wiring cost minimization was added, modules immediately popped up both in changing and unchanging environments. Not only were the networks with maximized performance *and* minimized connection costs cheaper, but they also performed better and evolved much quicker in markedly fewer generations than did the networks programmed only to maximize performance. These simulation experiments strongly suggest that networks that are significantly more modular and that evolve more quickly result when selection pressure exists for both performance and cost.

Taking the idea that modularity forms the structural basis on which subsystems can adapt and evolve a step further, hemispheric specialization suggests that cerebral asymmetries in this modular organization must also have adaptive value. Therefore, cerebral asymmetries should not be proposed lightly, and investigators must be sure they are real. For instance, early neuroimaging studies during the 1990s led to a popular model of the organization of memory in the brain suggesting that episodic encoding was predominantly a left-hemisphere function and that episodic retrieval was predominantly a right-hemisphere function (the model was called HERA, for hemispheric encoding/retrieval asymmetry).

When this model was tested directly with split-brain patients, however, it turned out that each hemisphere was equally efficient at encoding and retrieval (M. B. Miller et al., 2002). This study showed that apparent asymmetries in memory encoding were not a memory system asymmetry, but could be traced to the stimuli being encoded. Verbal material was preferentially processed in the participants' left hemisphere, and facial material was preferentially processed in the right—a pattern somewhat reminiscent of the chickens' and pigeons' lateralized object discrimination.

Hemispheric Specialization: A Dichotomy in Function or Stylishly Different?

Laterality researchers continually grapple with appropriate ways to describe asymmetries in the function of the two hemispheres (M. Allen, 1983; Bradshaw & Nettleton, 1981; Bryden, 1982). While early hypotheses fixed on the stimuli's properties and the tasks employed, a more recent approach is to look for differences in *processing style*. This concept suggests that the two hemispheres process information in complementary ways, dividing the workload of processing a stimulus by tackling it differently. From this perspective, the left hemisphere has been described as analytic and sequential, and the right hemisphere is viewed as holistic and parallel.

Hemispheric specializations may emerge because certain tasks benefit from one processing style or another. Language, for example, is seen as sequential: We hear speech as a continuous stream that requires rapid dissection and analysis of its component parts. Spatial representations, in contrast, call for not just perceiving the component parts, but seeing them as a coherent whole. The finding that the right hemisphere is more efficient at global processing is consistent with this idea.

Although this analytic–holistic dichotomy has intuitive appeal, it is difficult to know whether a particular cognitive task would benefit more from analytic or holistic processing. In many cases, the theoretical interpretation disintegrates into a circular re-description of results. For example, a right-ear advantage exists in the perception of consonants, but no asymmetry is found for vowels; consonants require the sequential, analytic processors of the left hemisphere, and vowel perception entails a more holistic form of processing. Here we have redefined the requirements of processing vowels and consonants according to our theoretical framework, rather than using the data to establish and modify that theoretical framework.

With verbal–spatial and analytic–holistic hypotheses, we assume that a single fundamental dichotomy can characterize the differences in function between the two hemispheres. The appeal of "dichotomania" is one of parsimony: The simplest account of hemispheric specialization rests on a single difference. Current dichotomies, however, all have their limitations.

It is also reasonable to suppose that a fundamental dichotomy between the two hemispheres is a fiction. Hemispheric asymmetries have been observed in many task domains: language, motor control, attention, and object recognition. Perhaps specializations are specific to particular task domains and are the consequences of more primitive hemispheric specializations. There need not be a causal connection between hemispheric specialization in motor control (e.g., why people are right- or left-handed) and hemispheric differences in representing language or visuospatial information. Maybe the commonality across task domains is their evolution: As the two hemispheres became segregated, they shared an impetus for the evolution of systems that were non-identical.

Asymmetry in how information is processed, represented, and used may be a more efficient and flexible design principle than redundancy across the hemispheres. With a growing demand for cortical space, perhaps the forces of natural selection began to modify one hemisphere but not the other while conserving the redundancy of the life-maintaining subcortex, keeping it more robust in the face of injury. Because the corpus callosum exchanges information between the hemispheres, mutational events could occur in one lateralized cortical area while leaving the contralateral hemisphere intact, thus continuing to provide the previous cortical function to the entire cognitive system. In short, asymmetrical development allowed for no-cost extensions; cortical capacity could expand by reducing redundancy and extending its space for new cortical zones.

Support for this idea is provided by the fascinating work of Ralf Galuske and colleagues, which has revealed that differences in the neuronal organization of the left and right Brodmann area 22 are related to the processing of auditory signals associated with human speech (Galuske et al., 2000; Gazzaniga, 2000). The left is specialized for word detection and generation; the right is specialized for melody, pitch, and intensity, which are properties of all auditory communication, from bird tweets to monkey calls.

The idea of asymmetrical processing also underscores an important point in modern conceptualizations of hemispheric specialization—namely, that the two hemispheres may work in concert to perform a task, even though their contributions may vary widely. There is no need to suppose that some sort of master director decides which hemisphere is needed for a task. While language is predominantly the domain of the left hemisphere, the right hemisphere may also contribute, although the types of representations it derives may not be efficient or capable of certain tasks. In addition, the left hemisphere does not defer to the right hemisphere on visuospatial tasks, but rather processes this information in a different way.

Seeing the brain organized like this, we begin to realize that much of what we learn from clinical tests of hemispheric specialization tells us less about the computations performed by each hemisphere, and more about the tasks themselves. This point is also evident in split-brain research. With the notable exception of speech production, each hemisphere has some competence in every cognitive domain.

Is There a Connection Between Handedness and Left-Hemisphere Language Dominance?

With all this talk of laterality, your left hemisphere no doubt is searching for a causal relationship between the predominance of right-handedness and the left hemisphere's specialization for language. Join the club. Many researchers have tried to establish a causal relationship between the two by pointing out that the dominant role of the left hemisphere in language strongly correlates with handedness. About 96% of right-handers are left-hemisphere dominant for speech. A majority of left-handers (60%), however, are also left-hemisphere dominant for speech (Risse et al., 1997). The fact that left-handers constitute only 7% to 8% of the total population means that 93% of humans, regardless of which hand is dominant, have a left-hemisphere specialization for language.

Some theorists point to the need for a single motor center as the critical factor. Although there may be benefits to perceiving information in parallel (since the input can be asymmetrical), our response to these stimuli must consist of a unified output. Imagine if your left hemisphere could choose one course of action while your right hemisphere opted for another. What would happen when one hemisphere commanded half your body to sit, and the other hemisphere told the other half to vacuum? Our brains may have two halves, but we have only one body. By localizing action planning in a single hemisphere, the brain achieves unification.

One hypothesis is that the left hemisphere is specialized for the planning and production of sequential movements. Speech certainly depends on such movements. Our ability to produce speech is the result of many evolutionary changes that include the shape of the vocal tract and articulatory apparatus. These adaptations make it possible for us to communicate, and to do so at phenomenally high rates (think of auctioneers). The official record is 637 words per minute, set in the late 1980s on the British television show *Motormouth*. Such competence requires exquisite control of the sequential gestures of the vocal cords, jaw, tongue, and other articulators.

The left hemisphere has also been linked to sequential movements in domains that are not involved with speech. For example, left-hemisphere lesions are more likely to cause apraxia, a deficit in motor planning in which the ability to produce coherent actions is lost, even though the muscles work properly and the person understands and wants to perform an action (see Chapter 8). In addition, oral movements have left-hemisphere dominance, whether the movements create speech or nonverbal facial gestures.

Evidence suggests that facial gestures are more pronounced on the right side of the face, and that the right facial muscles are activated more quickly than the corresponding muscles on the left. Time-lapse photography reveals that smiles light up the right side of the face first. Hence, the left hemisphere may have a specialized role in the control of sequential actions, and this role may underlie hemispheric asymmetries in both language and motor functions.

Some have theorized that the recursive processing capabilities used by the speech center are available to other left-hemisphere functions, including control of the right hand. With bipedalism, the hands became free to operate independently. This ability is unlike that of our quadruped friends, whose forelimbs and hind limbs are used primarily for locomotion. Here, symmetry is vital for the animal to move in a linear trajectory. If the limbs on one side of the body were longer or stronger than those on the other side, an animal would move in a circle. As our ancestors adopted an upright posture, however, they no longer had to use their hands to move symmetrically.

The generative and recursive aspects of an emerging communication system also could have been applied to the way hands manipulated objects, and the lateralization of these properties would have favored the right hand. The favoring of one hand over another would be most evident in tool use. Although nonhuman primates and birds can fashion primitive tools to gain access to foods that are out of reach or encased in hard shells, humans manufacture tools generatively: We design tools to solve an immediate problem, and we also can recombine the parts to create new tools. The wheel, an efficient component of devices for transportation, can be used to extract energy from a flowing river or record information in a compact, easily accessible format. Handedness, then, is most apparent in our use of tools. As an example, right-handers differ only slightly in their ability to use either hand to block balls thrown at them. But when they are asked to catch or throw the balls, the dominant hand has a clear advantage.

Or, the situation could have been reversed: The left hemisphere's dominance in language may be a consequence of an existing specialization in motor control. The asymmetrical use of hands to perform complex actions, including those associated with tool use, may have promoted the development of language. From comparative studies of language, we believe that most sentence forms convey actions; infants issue commands such as "come" or "eat" before they start using adjectives (e.g., "hungry"). If the right hand was being used for many of these actions, there may have been a selective pressure for the left hemisphere to be more proficient in establishing these symbolic representations.

Remember, though, that correlation is not causation. It is also possible (and your left hemisphere is just going to have to get over it) that the mechanisms producing hemispheric specialization in language and motor performance are unrelated. The correlation between these two cardinal signs of hemispheric asymmetry is not perfect. Not only do a small percentage of right-handers exhibit either right-hemisphere language or bilateral language, but in at least half of the left-handed population, the left hemisphere is dominant for language.

These differences may reflect the fact that handedness is affected at least partly by environmental factors. Children may be encouraged to use one hand instead of the other, perhaps because of cultural biases or parental pressure. Or handedness and language dominance may be driven by genetic factors. One model states that one gene has two alleles: The *D* (as in the Latin *dexter*) allele specifies right-handedness, and the *C* allele leaves the handedness to chance. In this model, 100% of *DD* homozygous individuals are right-handed, 75% of the heterozygotes (*CD*) are right-handed, and 50% of *CC* homozygous individuals are right-handed (McManus, 1999).

Marian Annett proposed another model, in which handedness exists on a spectrum and the alleles control cerebral dominance rather than handedness (Annett, 2002). In her model, right-handedness implies left-hemisphere dominance. Her two alleles are the "right shift" allele (RS^{+}) and an ambivalent allele that has no directional shift (RS^{-}). Homozygous $RS^{+/+}$ individuals would be strongly right-handed; heterozygous individuals ($RS^{+/-}$) would be less strongly right-handed; and the handedness of homozygous $RS^{-/-}$ individuals would be up to chance on a spectrum from right- to left-handed, where some would be ambidextrous. Although genes may play a role in handedness or other asymmetries, no genes for handedness have been identified.

TAKE-HOME MESSAGES

- "Small-world" architecture combines a high degree of local efficiency and fast communication with global networks.
- Modules are specialized and frequently localized networks of neurons that serve a specific function. A modular system is adaptable.
- Modular neural networks appear to evolve when both maximized performance and minimized network costs are selected for.
- Hypotheses about hemispheric asymmetries may emphasize asymmetries in function or asymmetries in how the same stimulus is processed—that is, processing style.
- The two hemispheres may work in concert to perform a task, even though their contributions may vary.

Summary

Research on laterality has provided extensive insights into the organization of the human brain. Surgical disconnection of the cerebral hemispheres has produced an extraordinary opportunity to study how perceptual and cognitive processes are distributed and coordinated within the cerebral cortex. Visual perceptual information, for example, remains strictly lateralized to one hemisphere following callosal section. Tactile-patterned information also remains lateralized, but attentional mechanisms are not divided by separation of the two hemispheres. Taken together, the evidence indicates that cortical disconnection produces two independent sensory information-processing systems that call upon a common attentional resource system in the carrying out of perceptual tasks.

Split-brain studies also have revealed the complex mosaic of mental processes that contribute to human cognition. The two hemispheres do not represent information in an identical manner, as evidenced by the fact that each hemisphere has developed its own set of specialized capacities. In the vast majority of individuals, the left hemisphere is clearly dominant for language and speech and seems to possess a uniquely human capacity to interpret behavior, moods, and emotional reactions, and to construct theories about the relationship between perceived events and feelings. Right-hemisphere superiority, on the other hand, can be seen in tasks such as facial recognition and attentional monitoring and, surprisingly, in understanding the intentions of others. Both hemispheres are likely to be involved in the performance of any complex task, but each contributes in its specialized manner.

Complementary studies on patients with focal brain lesions and on normal participants tested with lateralized stimuli have underscored not only the presence, but the importance, of lateralized processes for cognitive and perceptual tasks. Recent work has moved laterality research toward a more computational account of hemispheric specialization, seeking to explicate the mechanisms underlying many lateralized perceptual phenomena. These theoretical advances have moved the field away from the popular interpretations of cognitive style and have refocused researchers on understanding the computational differences and specializations of cortical regions in the two hemispheres.

Key Terms

anterior commissure (p. 131)
cerebral specialization (p. 139)
commissures (p. 131)
corpus callosum (p. 131)
dichotic listening task (p. 157)
functional asymmetry (p. 129)
handedness (p. 160)
heterotopic areas (p. 131)
heterotopic connections (p. 131)
hierarchical structure (p. 149)
homotopic areas (p. 129)
homotopic connections (p. 131)
interpreter (p. 152)
modules (p. 162)
planum temporale (p. 128)
posterior commissure (p. 133)
splenium (p. 131)
Sylvian fissure (p. 128)
Wada test (p. 128)

Think About It

1. What have we learned from over 50 years of split-brain research? What are some of the questions that remain to be answered?
2. What are the strengths of testing patients who have suffered brain lesions? Are there any shortcomings to this research approach? If so, what are they? What are some of the ethical considerations?
3. Why are double dissociations diagnostic of cerebral specializations? What pitfalls exist if a conclusion is based on a single dissociation?
4. Why do you think the human brain evolved cognitive systems that are represented asymmetrically between the cerebral hemispheres? What are the advantages of asymmetrical processing? What are some possible disadvantages?

Suggested Reading

Brown, H., & Kosslyn, S. (1993). Cerebral lateralization. *Current Opinion in Neurobiology, 3*, 183–186.

Gazzaniga, M. S. (2000). Cerebral specialization and interhemispheric communication: Does the corpus callosum enable the human condition? *Brain, 123*, 1293–1326.

Gazzaniga, M. S. (2005). Forty-five years of split-brain research and still going strong. *Nature Reviews Neuroscience, 6*, 653–659.

Gazzaniga, M. S. (2015). *Tales from both sides of the brain.* New York: Harper Collins.

Hellige, J. B. (1993). *Hemispheric asymmetry: What's right and what's left.* Cambridge, MA: Harvard University Press.

Hutsler, J., & Galuske, R. A. (2003). Hemispheric asymmetries in cerebral cortical networks. *Trends in Neuroscience, 26*, 429–435.

Vallortigara, G., Chiandetti, C., & Sovrano, V. A. (2011). Brain asymmetry (animal). *Wiley Interdisciplinary Reviews: Cognitive Science, 2*(2), 146–157.

Monet is only an eye, but my God, what an eye!

Cézanne

CHAPTER

5

Sensation and Perception

IN HOSPITALS ACROSS THE COUNTRY, Neurology Grand Rounds is a weekly event. Staff neurologists, internists, and residents gather to review the most puzzling and unusual cases being treated on the ward. One morning in 1987, the chief of neurology at a hospital in Portland, Oregon, presented such a case. He was not puzzled about what had caused his patient's problem. That was clear: The patient, P.T., had suffered a cerebral vascular accident, commonly known as a stroke. In fact, he had sustained two strokes. The first, suffered 6 years previously, had been a left-hemisphere stroke, and over time, the patient had shown a nearly complete recovery. However, P.T. had recently incurred a second stroke, and the CT scan showed that the damage this time was in the right hemisphere. This finding was consistent with the patient's initial left-sided weakness.

The unusual aspect of P.T.'s case was the collection of perceptual symptoms he continued to experience 4 months later. As he tried to resume the daily routines required on his small family farm, P.T. had difficulty recognizing familiar places and objects. While working on a stretch of fence, for example, he might look out over the hills and suddenly realize that the landscape looked unfamiliar. It was hard for him to pick out individual dairy cows—a matter of concern, lest he attempt to milk a bull!

Disturbing as this was, it was not the worst of his problems. Most troubling of all, he no longer recognized the people around him, including his wife. He had no trouble seeing her and could even accurately describe her actions, but when it came to identifying her, he was at a complete loss. She was completely unrecognizable to him! He knew that her parts—body, legs, arms, and head—formed a person, but P.T. failed to see these parts as belonging to a specific individual. This deficit was not limited to P.T.'s wife; he had the same problem with other members of his family and friends from his small town, a place he had lived for 66 years.

BIG Questions

- How is information in the world, carried by light, sound, smell, taste, and touch, translated into neuronal signals by our sense organs?
- How do these sensory signals result in our rich perceptual experiences?
- How might neural plasticity in sensory cortex manifest itself?

A striking feature of P.T.'s impairment was that his inability to recognize objects and people was limited to the visual modality. As soon as his wife spoke, he recognized her. Indeed, he claimed that, on hearing her voice, the visual percept of her would "fall into place." The shape in front of him would suddenly morph into his wife. In a similar fashion, he could recognize specific objects by touching, smelling, or tasting them.

The overarching reason why you are sitting here reading this book today is that you had ancestors who successfully survived their environment and reproduced. One reason they were able to do this was their ability to sense and perceive things that could be threatening to their survival and then act on those perceptions. While this seems obvious, it is important to recognize that most of these perceptions and behavioral responses never reach our conscious awareness, and that those that do are not exact replicas of the stimulus. This latter phenomenon becomes more evident when we are presented with optical illusions.

In this chapter we begin with an overview of sensation and perception and then turn to a description of what we know about the anatomy and function of the individual senses. Next we tackle the issue of how information from our different sensory systems is integrated to produce a coherent representation of the world. We end by discussing atypical cases of sensory experience, such as those of individuals who are deprived of a sensory system (e.g., are blind) or have an atypical blending of the senses (e.g., experience synesthesia). As we will see, experience imposes a strong constraint on our perception of the world.

5.1 Senses, Sensation, and Perception

Perception begins when a stimulus from the environment, such as sound, light, or touch, stimulates one of the sense organs, such as the ear, eye, or skin. The sense organ transduces the input into neuronal activity, which then goes to the brain for processing. *Sensation* is this initial activation of the nervous system, the translation of information about the environment into patterns of neural activity. The mental representation of that original stimulus, whether it accurately reflects the stimulus or not, is called a *percept*. Thus, perception is the process of constructing the percept.

Our *senses* are our physiological capacities to provide input from the environment to our neurological system. Hence, our sense of sight is our capacity to capture light waves on the retina, convert them into electrical signals, and ship them on for further processing. We tend to give most of the credit for our survival to our sense of sight, but it does not operate alone. For instance, the classic "we don't have eyes in the back of our head" problem means we can't see the bear sneaking up behind us. Instead, the rustling of branches or the snap of a twig warns us. We do not see particularly well in the dark either, resulting in many a stubbed toe. And though the milk may look fine, one sniff tells us to dump it.

In normal perception, all of the senses are critical. Effectively and safely driving a car down a busy highway requires the successful integration of sight, touch, hearing, and perhaps even smell (quit riding the brakes!). Enjoying a meal also involves the interplay of the senses. We cannot enjoy food intensely without smelling its aroma. The sense of touch gives us an appreciation for the texture of the food: the creamy smoothness of whipped cream or the satisfying crunch of an apple. Even visual cues enhance our gustatory experience: A plate of bright green broccoli is more enticing than a cluster of limp, gray florets.

Common Processing Across the Senses

Before dealing with each sense individually, let's look at the anatomical and processing features that the sensory systems have in common. Each system begins with some sort of anatomical structure for collecting, filtering, and amplifying information from the environment. For instance, the outer ear, ear canal, and inner ear concentrate and amplify sound. In vision, eye movements regulate where we look, the size of the pupil adjusts to filter the light, and the cornea and lens serve to focus the light, much as a camera lens does.

Each system has specialized receptor cells that transduce the environmental stimulus, such as sound waves, light waves, or chemicals, into neuronal signals. These signals are then passed along specific sensory nerve pathways: The olfactory signals travel via the olfactory nerve, visual signals via the optic nerve, auditory signals via the cochlear nerve, taste via the facial and glossopharyngeal nerves, facial sensation via the trigeminal nerve, and sensation for the rest of the body via the sensory nerves that synapse in the dorsal roots of the spinal cord.

These nerves terminate either monosynaptically or disynaptically (i.e., with either one synapse or two) in different parts of the thalamus. From the thalamus, neural

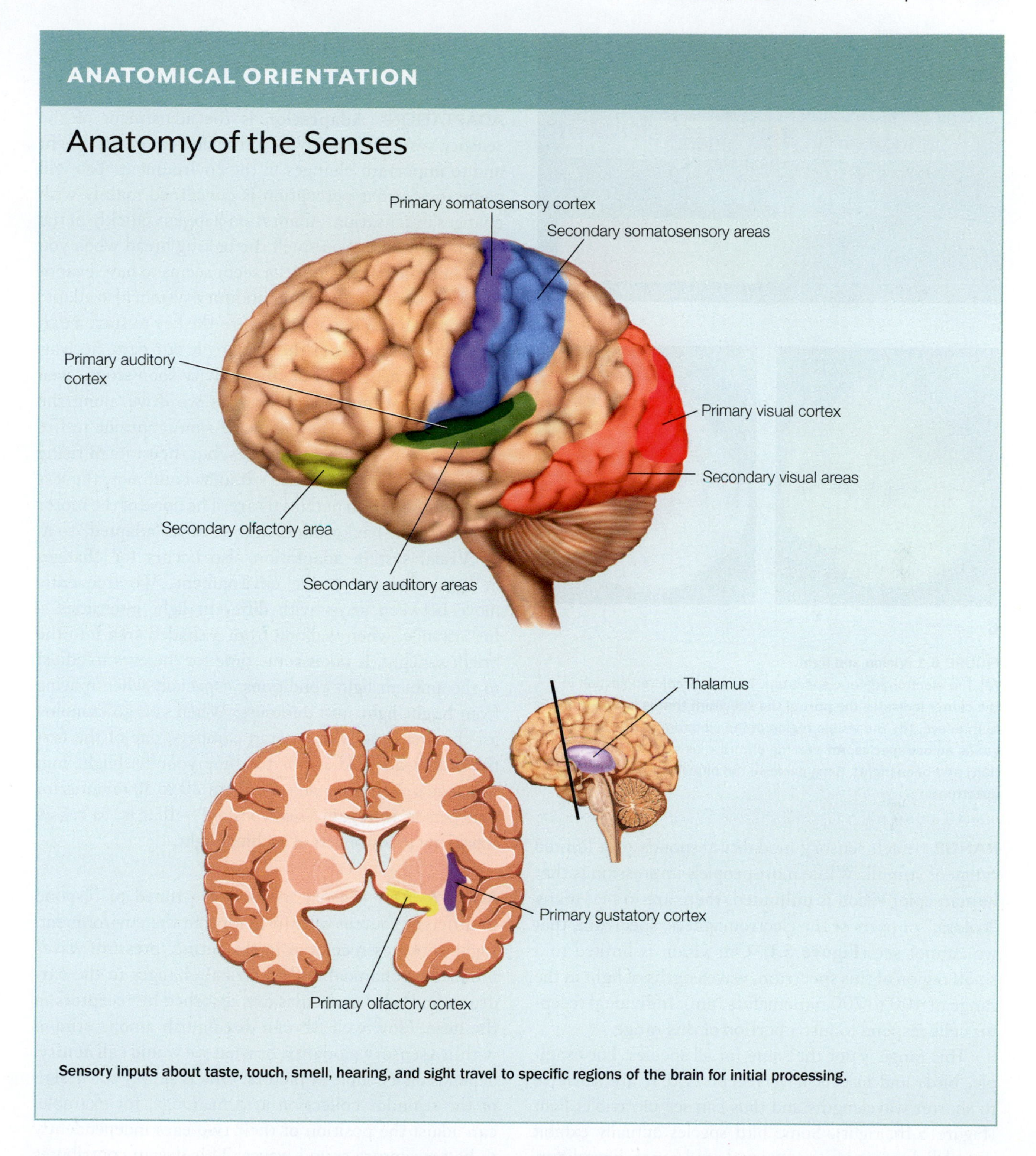

Sensory inputs about taste, touch, smell, hearing, and sight travel to specific regions of the brain for initial processing.

connections from each of these pathways travel first to what are known as primary sensory regions of the cortex, and then to secondary sensory areas (see the "Anatomical Orientation" box above). The olfactory nerve is a bit of a rogue. It is the shortest cranial nerve and follows a different course. It terminates in the olfactory bulb, and axons extend directly from there to the primary and secondary olfactory cortices without going through the brainstem or the thalamus.

Sensory Receptors

Across the senses, receptor cells share a few general properties. Receptor cells are limited in the range of stimuli they respond to, and as part of this limitation, their capability to transmit information has only a certain degree of precision. Receptor cells do not become active until the stimulus exceeds a minimum intensity level. Moreover, they are not inflexible, but rather adapt as the environment changes.

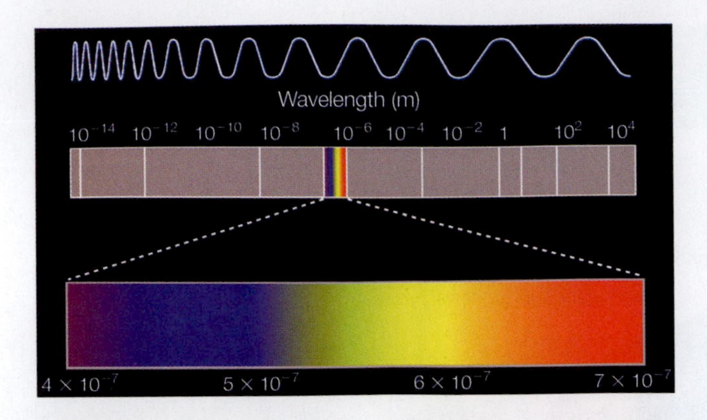

a

b

FIGURE 5.1 Vision and light.
(a) The electromagnetic spectrum. The small, colored section in the center indicates the part of the spectrum that is visible to the human eye. **(b)** The visible region of the electromagnetic spectrum varies across species. An evening primrose as seen by humans (left) and bees (right). Bees perceive the ultraviolet part of the spectrum.

RANGE Each sensory modality responds to a limited range of stimuli. While most people's impression is that human color vision is unlimited, there are in fact many "colors," or parts of the electromagnetic spectrum, that we cannot see (**Figure 5.1**). Our vision is limited to a small region of this spectrum, wavelengths of light in the range of 400 to 700 nanometers (nm). Individual receptor cells respond to just a portion of this range.

This range is not the same for all species. For example, birds and insects have receptors that are sensitive to shorter wavelengths and thus can see ultraviolet light (Figure 5.1b, right). Some bird species actually exhibit sexual dichromatism (i.e., the male and female have different coloration) that is not visible to humans. Audition has similar range differences. We are reminded of this when we blow a dog whistle (which was invented by Francis Galton, Charles Darwin's cousin): We immediately have the dog's attention, but we cannot hear the high-pitched sound ourselves. Dogs can hear sound-wave frequencies of up to about 60 kilohertz (kHz), whereas humans hear sounds only below about 20 kHz. Although a dog has better night vision than we do, we see more colors. As limited as our receptor cells may be, we do respond to a wide range of stimulus intensities.

ADAPTATION **Adaptation** is the adjustment of the sensory system's sensitivity to the current environment and to important changes in the environment. You will come to see that perception is concerned mainly with changes in sensation. Adaptation happens quickly in the olfactory system: You smell the baking bread when you walk into the bakery, but the scent seems to have evaporated just seconds later. Our auditory system also adapts rather rapidly. When we first turn the key to start a car, the sound waves from the motor hit our ears, activating sensory neurons. But this activity soon stops, even though the stimulus continues as we drive along the highway. More precisely, some neurons continue to fire as long as the stimulus continues, but their rate of firing slows down. The longer the stimulus continues, the less frequent the action potentials are: The noise of the motor drops into the background, and we have "adapted" to it.

Visual system adaptation also occurs for changes in light intensity in the environment. We frequently move between areas with different light intensities—for instance, when walking from a shaded area into the bright sunlight. It takes some time for the eyes to adjust to the ambient light conditions, especially when moving from bright light into darkness. When you go camping for the first time with veteran campers, one of the first things you are told is not to shine your flashlight into someone's eyes. It would take about 20 to 30 minutes for that person to regain "night vision"—that is, to regain sensitivity to low levels of ambient light.

ACUITY Our sensory systems are tuned to respond to different sources of information in the environment. Light activates receptors in the retina, pressure waves produce mechanical and electrical changes in the eardrum, and odor molecules are absorbed by receptors in the nose. How well we can distinguish among stimuli within a sensory modality, or what we would call **acuity**, depends on a couple of factors. One is simply the design of the stimulus collection system. Dogs, for example, can adjust the position of their two ears independently to better capture sound waves. This design contributes to their ability to hear sounds that are up to four times farther away than humans are capable of hearing.

Another factor is the number and distribution of the receptors. For instance, for touch we have many more receptors on our fingers than we do on our back; thus, we can discern stimuli better with our fingers. Our visual acuity is better than that of most animals, but not better than an eagle's. Our acuity is best in the center of the visual field, because the central region of the retina, the *fovea*, is packed with photoreceptors. The farther away from the fovea, the fewer the receptors. The same is true for the eagle, but the eagle has two foveae.

Having high-resolution acuity in a restricted part of space rather than across the entire visual field may be more efficient, but it comes at a cost. We have to move our eyes frequently in order to focus on different parts of the visual scene. These rapid eye movements are called **saccades**, and they occur about three to four times a second. Researchers can easily measure saccades, which have provided an interesting window to the phenomenon of attention, an issue we will take up in Chapter 7.

In general, if a sensory system devotes more receptors to certain types of information, there is a corresponding increase in cortical representation of that information. For example, although the human fovea occupies only about 1% of the retina's acreage, it is densely packed with photoreceptors, and the representation of foveal information takes up more than 50% of the visual cortex. Similarly, our cortical representation of the hands is much larger than that of the trunk, despite the difference in physical size of these two parts of the body (see Figure 2.42).

One puzzling caveat to keep in mind, though, is that many creatures carry out exquisite perception without a cortex. So, what is our cortex doing with all of this sensory information? The expanded sensory capabilities in humans, and in mammals in general, probably did not evolve to support better sensation per se; rather, they enable that information to support flexible behavior, because of greatly increased memory capacity and pathways linking that information to our action and attention systems.

SENSORY STIMULI SHARE AN UNCERTAIN FATE The sensed physical stimulus is transduced into neuronal activity by the receptors and sent through subcortical and cortical regions of the brain to be processed. Sometimes a stimulus may produce subjective sensory awareness. When that happens, the stimulus is not the only factor contributing to the experience; each level of processing—including attention, memory, and emotion systems—contributes as well. Even with all of this activity going on, most sensory stimulation never reaches the level of consciousness. No doubt if you close your eyes right now, you will not be able to describe everything that is in front of you, even though it has all been recorded on your retina. Try it. Shut your eyes and think: What's on my desk, or outside my window?

Connective Similarities

People typically think of sensory processing as working in one direction—that is, as information moving from the sense organs to the brain. Neural activity, however, is really a two-way street: At all levels of the sensory pathways, neural connections go in both directions. This feature is especially pronounced at the interface between the subcortex and cortex. Sensory signals from the visual, auditory, somatosensory, and gustatory (taste) systems all synapse within the thalamus before projecting onto specific regions within the cortex.

Exactly what is going on in the thalamus is unclear, but it appears to be more than just a relay station. Not only are there projections from thalamic nuclei to the cortex, but the thalamic nuclei are interconnected, providing an opportunity for **multisensory integration**, a topic we turn to later in the chapter. The thalamus also receives descending, or feedback, connections from primary sensory regions of the cortex, as well as other areas of the cortex, such as the frontal lobe. These connections appear to provide a way for the cortex to control, to some degree, the flow of information from the sensory systems.

Now that we have a general idea of what is similar about the anatomy of the various sensory systems and processing of sensory stimuli, let's take a closer look at the individual sensory systems. We will start with the least studied sense, olfaction, and progress toward the most studied of the senses, vision.

TAKE-HOME MESSAGES

- Senses are physiological systems that translate information about the environment and the body into neuronal signals. Thus, they enable the nervous system to process information about the world and to act in response to that information.
- Each sense has specific receptors that are activated by specific types of stimuli. The output from these receptors eventually collects in dedicated sensory nerves, or bundles of axons, that transmit information to the central nervous system.
- Sensory systems are especially sensitive to changes in the environment.

5.2 Olfaction

We have the greatest awareness of our senses of sight, sound, taste, and touch. Yet the more primitive sense of *olfaction* is especially essential for our survival. The ability to smell is essential for terrestrial mammals, helping them to recognize foods that are nutritious and safe. While olfaction may have evolved primarily as a mechanism for evaluating whether a potential food is edible, it now serves other important roles as well—for instance, detecting hazards such as fire or airborne toxins.

Olfaction also plays an important role in social communication: Pheromones are excreted or secreted chemicals that trigger a social response in another individual of the same species when perceived by the olfactory system. Pheromones have been well documented in some insects, reptiles, and mammals, and they also appear to factor into human social interactions. For example, odors generated by women appear to vary across the menstrual cycle, and we are all familiar with the strong smells generated by people coming back from a long run. The physiological responses to such smells may be triggered by pheromones (Wallrabenstein et al., 2015). Before we discuss the functions of olfaction, let's review the neural pathways of the brain that respond to odors.

Neural Pathways of Olfaction

Smell is the sensory experience that results from the transduction of odor molecules, or **odorants**, into neuronal signals sent to the olfactory cortex. These molecules enter the nasal cavity during the course of normal breathing or when we sniff. They will also flow into the nose passively, because air pressure in the nasal cavity is typically lower than in the outside environment, creating a pressure gradient. Odorants can also enter the system through the mouth (e.g., during consumption of food), and from there travel back up into the nasal cavity.

The human sense of smell uses the input from odor receptors embedded in the mucous membrane of the roof of the nasal cavity, the *olfactory epithelium*, to discriminate among odorants. How the activation of olfactory receptors leads to signals that will result in the perception of specific odors remains unclear. One popular hypothesis is that olfaction arises from the overall pattern of activity induced when odorants attach to odor receptors. There are tens of thousands of odorants and over a thousand types of receptors; most receptors respond to only a limited number of odorants, though a single odorant can bind to more than one type of receptor.

Another hypothesis is that the molecular vibrations of groups of odorant molecules contribute to odor recognition (Franco et al., 2011; Turin, 1996). This model predicts that odorants with similar vibrational spectra should elicit similar olfactory responses, and it explains why similarly shaped molecules with dissimilar vibrations have very different fragrances. For example, alcohols and thiols have almost exactly the same structure, but alcohols have a fragrance of, well, alcohol, while thiols smell like rotten eggs.

Figure 5.2 details the olfactory pathway. The olfactory receptors are called *bipolar neurons* because appendages extend from opposite sides of their cell bodies. When an odorant triggers one of these receptors, whether by shape or vibration, it sends a signal to the **glomeruli**, the neurons in the olfactory bulbs. Tremendous convergence and divergence take place in the olfactory bulbs. One bipolar neuron may activate over 8,000 glomeruli, and each glomerulus, in turn, receives input from up to 750 receptors. The axons from the glomeruli then exit laterally from the olfactory bulb, forming the olfactory nerve. Their destination is the **primary olfactory cortex**, or *pyriform cortex*, located at the ventral junction of the frontal and temporal cortices.

The olfactory pathway to the brain is unique in two ways. First, most of the axons of the olfactory nerve project to the ipsilateral cortex. Only a small number cross over to innervate the contralateral hemisphere. Second, unlike the other sensory nerves, the olfactory nerve arrives at the primary olfactory cortex without passing through the thalamus. The primary olfactory cortex projects to a secondary olfactory area within the *orbitofrontal cortex*, and it makes connections with other brain regions

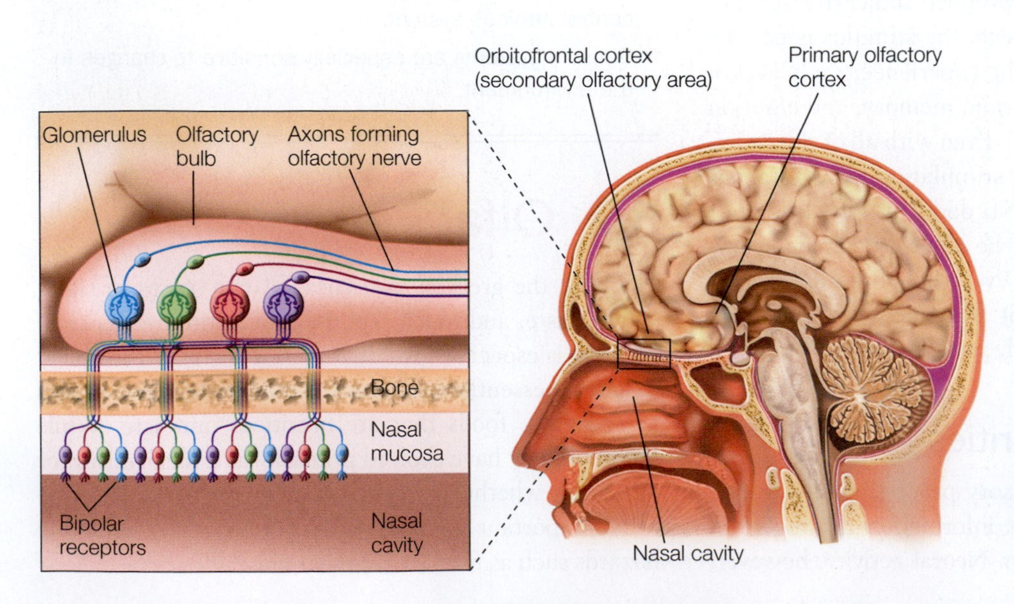

FIGURE 5.2 Olfaction. The olfactory receptors lie within the nasal cavity, where they interact directly with odorants. The receptors then send information to the glomeruli in the olfactory bulb, the axons of which form the olfactory nerve that relays information to the primary olfactory cortex. The orbitofrontal cortex is a secondary olfactory processing area.

as well, including the thalamus, hypothalamus, hippocampus, and amygdala. With these wide-ranging connections, odor cues appear to influence autonomic behavior, attention, memory, and emotions, as we all know from experience.

The Role of Sniffing

Olfaction has historically gotten short shrift from cognitive neuroscientists. This neglect reflects, in part, our failure to appreciate the importance of olfaction in people's lives: We have handed the sniffing crown over to bloodhounds and their ilk. In addition, some thorny technical challenges must be overcome to apply tools such as functional MRI to studying the human olfactory system. First is the problem of delivering odors to a participant in a controlled manner (**Figure 5.3a**). Nonmagnetic systems must be constructed to allow the odorized air to be directed to the nostrils while a participant is in the fMRI magnet. Second, it is hard to determine when an odor is no longer present. The molecules that carry the odor can linger in the air for a long time. Third, although some odors overwhelm our senses, most are quite subtle, requiring exploration through the act of sniffing to detect and identify. Whereas it is almost impossible to ignore a sound, we can exert considerable control over the intensity of our olfactory experience.

Noam Sobel of the Weizmann Institute in Israel developed methods to overcome these challenges, conducting neuroimaging studies of olfaction that revealed an intimate relationship between smelling and sniffing (Mainland & Sobel, 2006; Sobel et al., 1998). Participants were scanned while being exposed to either nonodorized, clean air or one of two chemicals: vanillin or decanoic acid. The former has a fragrance like vanilla; the latter, like crayons. The odor-absent and odor-present conditions alternated every 40 seconds. Throughout the scanning session, the instruction "Sniff and respond; is there an odor?" was presented every 8 seconds. Using this method, the researchers sought to identify areas in which brain activity was correlated with sniffing versus smelling (**Figure 5.3b**).

Surprisingly, smelling failed to produce consistent activation in the primary olfactory cortex. Instead, the presence of the odor produced a consistent increase in the fMRI response in lateral parts of the orbitofrontal cortex, a region typically thought to be a secondary olfactory area. Activity in the primary olfactory cortex was closely linked to the rate of sniffing. Each time the participant took a sniff, the fMRI signal increased regardless of whether the odor was present. These puzzling results suggested that the primary olfactory cortex might be more a part of the motor system for olfaction.

Upon further study, however, the lack of activation in the primary olfactory cortex became clear. Neurophysiological studies of the primary olfactory cortex in the rat had shown that these neurons habituate (adapt) quickly. It was suggested that the reason the primary olfactory cortex lacks a smell-related response is that the hemodynamic response measured by fMRI exhibits a similar habituation. To test this idea, Sobel's group modeled the fMRI signal by assuming that a sharp increase in activation would be followed by an extended drop after the presentation of an odor—an elegant example of how single-cell results can be used to interpret imaging data. When analyzed in this manner, the hemodynamic response in the primary olfactory cortex was found to be related to both smelling and sniffing.

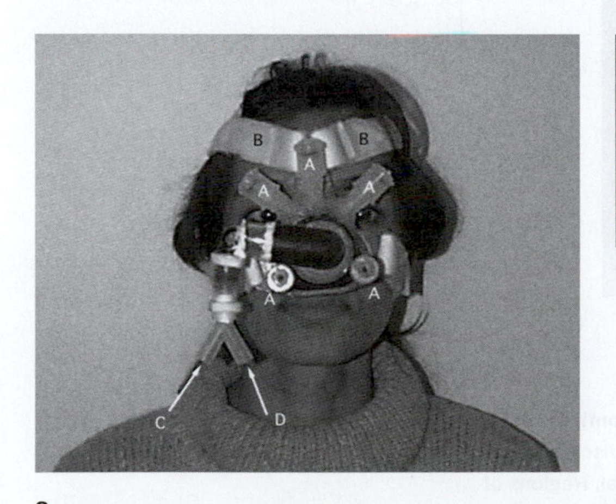

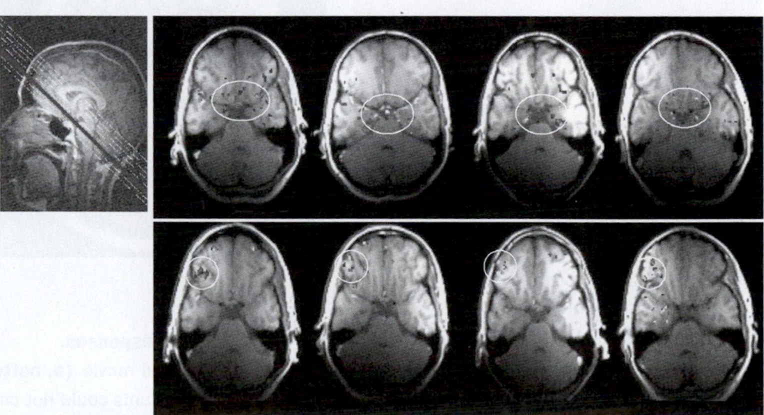

FIGURE 5.3 Sniffing and smelling.
(a) This special device was constructed to deliver controlled odors during fMRI scanning.
(b, top) Regions activated during sniffing. The circled region includes the primary olfactory cortex and a posteromedial region of the orbitofrontal cortex. **(b, bottom)** Regions more active during sniffing when an odor was present compared to when the odor was absent.

These results suggest that the role of the primary olfactory cortex might be essential for detecting a change in the external odor and that the secondary olfactory cortex plays a critical role in identifying the odor itself. Each sniff represents an active sampling of the olfactory environment, and the primary olfactory cortex plays a critical role in determining whether a new odor is present.

The Nose Knows

Many species have the capability to shed tears as a way to combat a foreign body in the eye or to lubricate the eye. But unique to humans is the ability to shed tears as an emotional expression—to cry. From an evolutionary standpoint, Darwin proposed that expressive behaviors such as crying and blushing are initially adaptive because they regulate the behavior of others, even if they may eventually take on more generalized roles as emotional signals. Crying certainly elicits an empathetic response, but via what stimulus? Is it just the visual image of a person in distress—or might it be a more primitive sensory signal?

Sobel and his colleagues wondered whether emotional tearing in humans provided a chemical signal of distress (Gelstein et al., 2011). To study this hypothesis, they collected real tears from "donor women" who cried while watching a sad movie, and then they had male participants sniff either the tears or an odorless saline solution (**Figure 5.4a**). The men could not distinguish between the two solutions, indicating that emotional tears do not have a discernible odor.

Nevertheless, the solutions had differential effects on the men's behavior and brain activity. First, in a behavioral experiment, the men were asked to rate pictures of women's faces in terms of sexual attraction. Interestingly, 17 out of 24 men rated the women as less sexually attractive when sniffing the tears compared to when they were sniffing the saline solution. Then, in an fMRI experiment, the men watched short film clips while sniffing either the tears or the saline solution. In two areas of the brain associated with sexual arousal (the hypothalamus and fusiform gyrus) the BOLD response to emotionally evocative clips was lower after the men had been exposed to the tears (**Figure 5.4b**).

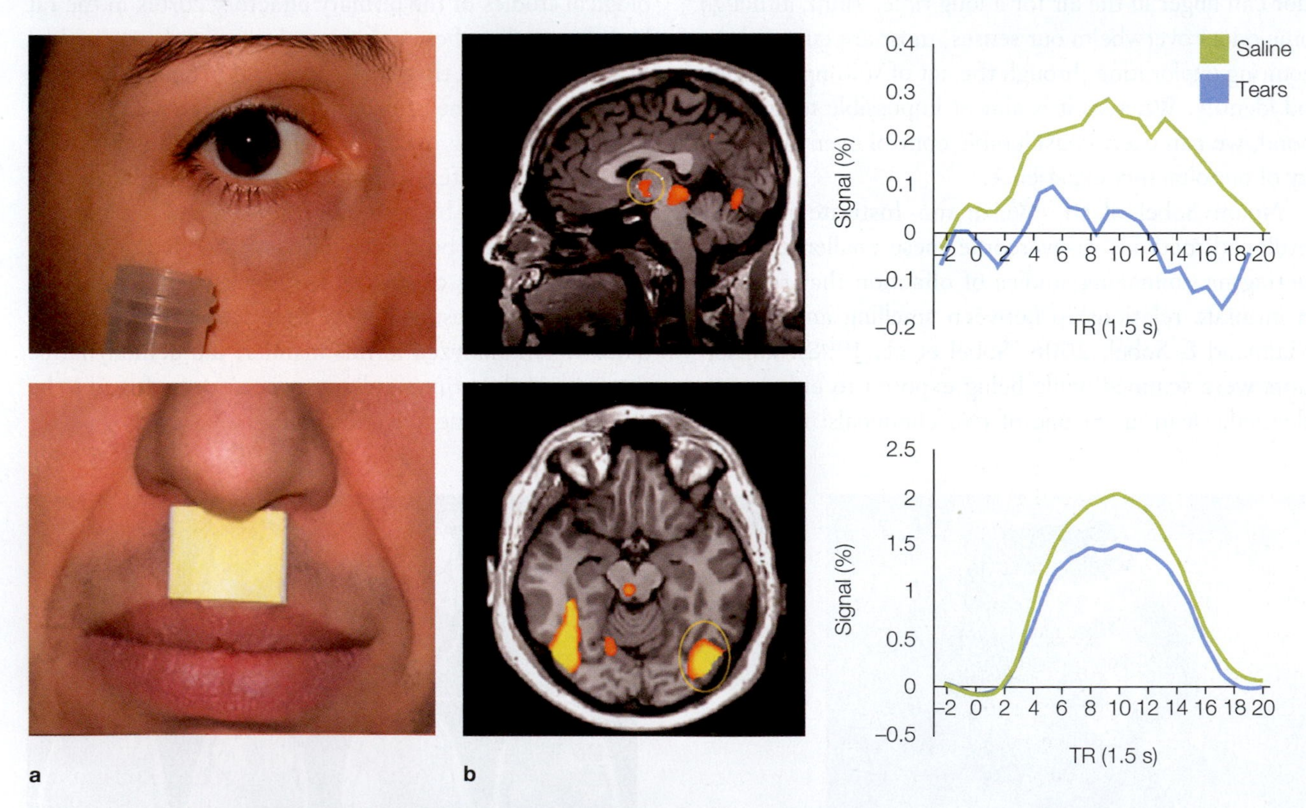

FIGURE 5.4 Chemical signals in emotional tears affect sexual responses.
(a, top) Tears were collected from "donors" while they watched a sad movie. **(a, bottom)** Participants sniffed either tears or saline (control) while doing tasks. The participants could not consciously discriminate between the two odors. **(b)** Typical BOLD response associated with sexual arousal. Regions of interest were the hypothalamus, circled in the sagittal MRI image, and the left fusiform gyrus, circled in the horizontal image (left-right reversed). The BOLD response to watching an emotionally arousing movie was much lower in these regions when the participants were sniffing tears compared to sniffing saline. The graphs show the average activity time course from 16 men within the regions of interest. TR is a standard unit in fMRI research and stands for *repetition time*, the time between each sample of the brain data. In this study, TR = 1,500 ms, so each tick represents 1.5 seconds, with 0 being the onset of the short film clip.

These researchers hypothesize that tears modulate social and sexual interactions with others by decreasing sexual arousal, physiological arousal, testosterone level, and brain activity. While these findings open up a Pandora's box of questions, they suggest that olfaction may play a broader role in chemosensation—one that goes beyond the detection and recognition of odors.

TAKE-HOME MESSAGES

- Signal transduction of odors begins when the odorant attaches to receptors in the olfactory epithelium. The signal is then sent to the olfactory bulb through the olfactory nerve, which projects to the primary olfactory cortex. Signals are also relayed to the orbitofrontal cortex, a secondary olfactory processing area.
- The primary olfactory cortex is important for detecting a change in external odor, and the secondary olfactory cortex is important for identifying the smell itself.

5.3 Gustation

The sense of taste depends greatly on the sense of smell. Indeed, the two senses are often grouped together because they both begin with a chemical stimulus. Since these two senses interpret the environment by discriminating between different chemicals, they are referred to as the **chemical senses**.

Neural Pathways of Gustation

Gustation begins with the tongue. Strewn across the surface of the tongue in specific locations are different types of *papillae*, the little bumps you can feel on the surface. Papillae serve multiple functions. Some are concerned with gustation, some with sensation, and some with the secretion of lingual lipase, an enzyme that helps break down fats. Whereas the papillae in the anterior region of the tongue contain just a few *taste buds*, the papillae found near the back of the tongue have hundreds to thousands of taste buds (**Figure 5.5a**). Taste buds are also found in the cheeks and in parts of the roof of the mouth. *Taste pores* are the conduits that lead from the surface of the tongue to the taste buds, and each taste bud contains many *taste receptor cells* (**Figure 5.5b**).

There are five basic tastes: salty, sour, bitter, sweet, and *umami*—the savory taste you experience when you eat steak or other protein-rich substances. Each taste cell is responsive to only one of these tastes. Contrary to what was previously believed, there is no map of the tongue that corresponds to different tastes. All five tastes are present across the tongue.

Sensory transduction in the gustatory system begins when a food molecule, or **tastant**, stimulates a taste receptor cell *and* causes it to depolarize. Each of the basic taste sensations has a different form of chemical signal transduction. For example, the experience of a salty taste begins when the salt molecule (NaCl) breaks down into Na^+ and Cl^- ions, and the Na^+ ion is absorbed by a taste receptor cell, leading the cell to depolarize. Other taste transduction pathways, such as those for sweet carbohydrate tastants, are more complex, involving receptor binding that does not lead directly to depolarization. Rather, the presence of certain tastants initiates a cascade of chemical "messengers" that eventually leads to cellular depolarization.

Synapsing with the taste receptor cells in the taste buds are bipolar neurons. Their axons form the chorda tympani nerve, which joins with other fibers to form the 7th cranial nerve, the facial nerve. This nerve projects to the gustatory nucleus, located in the rostral region of the *nucleus of the solitary tract* in the brainstem (**Figure 5.5c**). Meanwhile, the caudal region of the solitary tract nucleus receives sensory neurons from the gastrointestinal tract. The integration of information at this level can provide a rapid reaction. For example, you might gag if you taste something that is "off," a strong signal that the food should be avoided.

The next synapse in the gustatory system is on the *ventral posterior medial nucleus* (VPM) of the thalamus. Axons from the VPM synapse in the **primary gustatory cortex** (Figure 5.5c), a region in the *insula* and *operculum*, two structures at the intersection of the temporal and frontal lobes. The primary gustatory cortex is connected to secondary processing areas of the orbitofrontal cortex, providing an anatomical basis for the integration of tastes and smells. Though there are only five types of taste cells, we are capable of experiencing a complex range of tastes. This ability must result from the integration of information in areas like the orbitofrontal cortex.

The tongue does more than just taste. Some papillae contain nociceptive receptors, a type of pain receptor. These are activated by irritants such as capsaicin (contained in chili peppers), carbon dioxide (carbonated drinks), and acetic acid (vinegar). The output from these receptors follows a different path, joining the 5th cranial nerve, the trigeminal nerve. This nerve not only carries pain information, but also signals position and temperature. You are well aware of the reflex response to activation by these irritants if you have ever eaten a hot chili: salivation, tearing, vasodilation (the red face), nasal secretion, bronchospasm (coughing), and

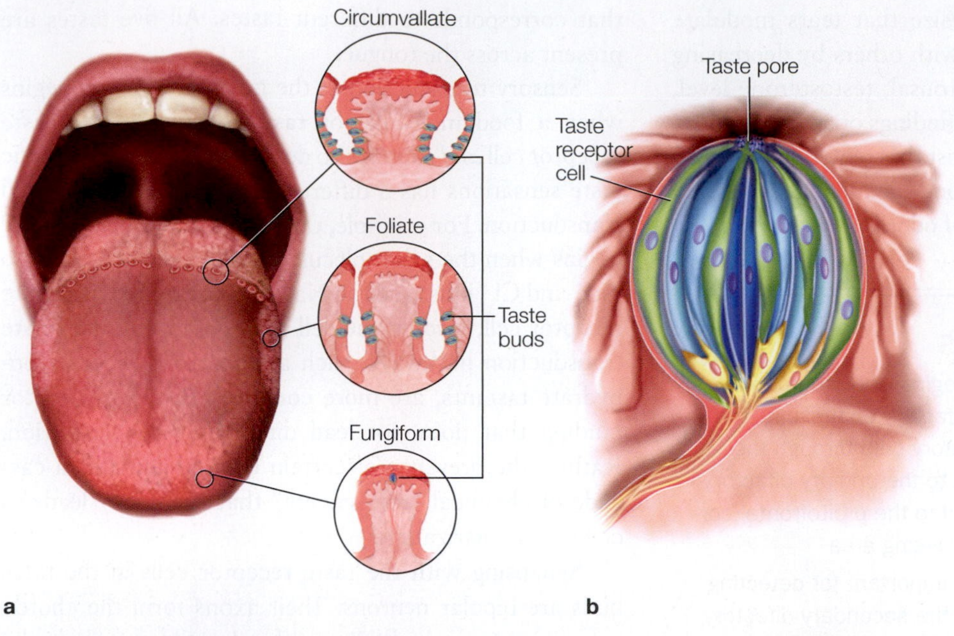

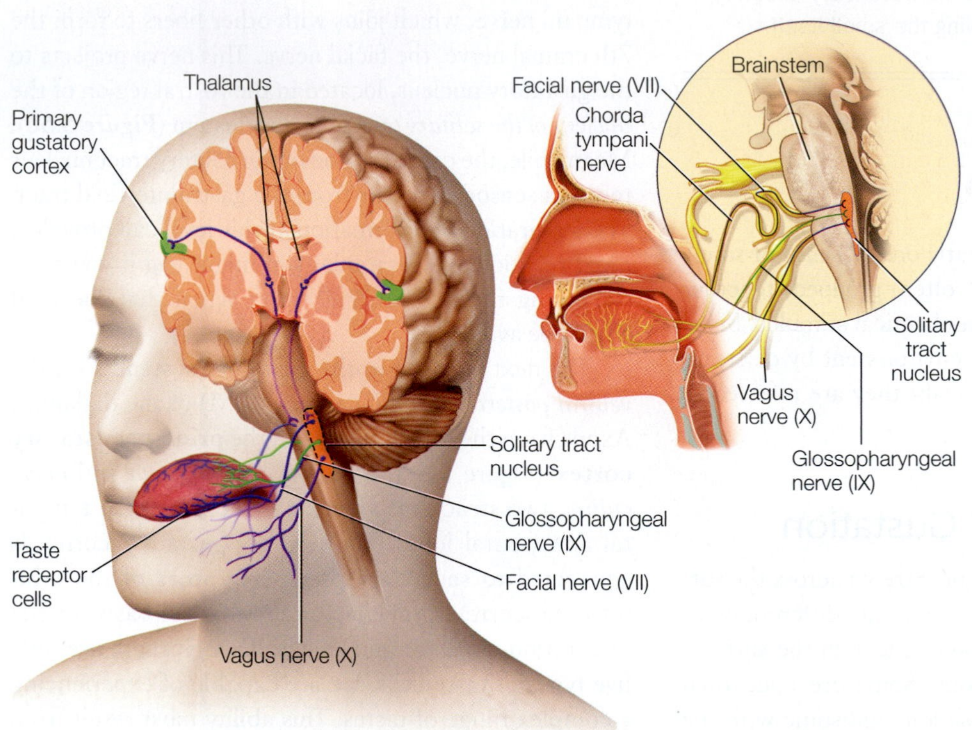

FIGURE 5.5 The gustatory transduction pathway.
(a) Three different types of taste papillae span the surface of the tongue. Taste buds are located on the papillae. While *circumvallate papillae* can contain thousands of taste buds and *foliate papillae* can contain hundreds, *fungiform papillae* contain only one or a few. (b) Taste pores on the surface of the tongue open into the taste bud, which contains taste receptor cells. (c) The chorda tympani nerve, formed by the axons from the taste cells, joins with the facial nerve as it enters the skull and passes through the middle ear to synapse in the nucleus of the solitary tract in the brainstem, as do the sensory nerves from the GI tract via the vagus nerve. The taste pathway projects to the ventral posterior medial nucleus of the thalamus, and information is then relayed to the gustatory area in the insula cortex.

decreased respiration. All of these responses are meant to dilute that irritant and get it out of your system as quickly as possible.

Gustatory Processing

Taste perception varies from person to person because the number and types of papillae and taste buds vary considerably between individuals. People with large numbers of taste buds are known as supertasters. They taste things more intensely, especially bitterness, and they tend not to like bitter foods such as coffee, beer, grapefruit, and arugula. Supertasters also tend to feel more pain from tongue irritants. You can spot the two ends of the tasting spectrum at the dining table: One is pouring on the salsa or drinking grapefruit juice while the other is cringing. Interestingly, women generally have more taste buds than men (Bartoshuk et al., 1994).

The basic tastes give the brain information about the types of food that are being consumed, and their essential role is to activate the appropriate behavioral actions: consume or reject. The sensation of umami tells the body that protein-rich food is being ingested, sweet tastes indicate carbohydrate intake, and salty tastes give us information that is important for the balance between minerals or electrolytes and water. The tastes of bitter and sour likely developed as warning signals. Many toxic plants taste bitter, and a strong bitter taste can induce vomiting. Other evidence suggesting that bitterness is a warning signal is the fact that we can detect bitter substances 1,000 times better than, say, salty substances. Therefore, a significantly smaller amount of bitter tastant will yield a taste response, so that toxic bitter substances can be quickly avoided. Similarly, but to a lesser extent, a sour taste indicates spoiled food (e.g., sour milk) or unripe fruits.

Gustotopic Maps

As we discussed in Chapter 2, the somatosensory, auditory, and visual cortices contain topographic maps, spatially organized representations of some property of the environment or body. Recent studies in the mouse indicate that the gustatory cortex may contain a gustotopic map. Xiaoke Chen and colleagues (2011) examined the activity of neurons in response to various taste stimulants (**Figure 5.6a**). Using extracellular recording methods, they first recorded signals from neurons in the thalamus and found that the neurons were taste specific, showing restricted responses to sweet, bitter, sour, salty, or umami (**Figure 5.6b**). The researchers then injected an anterograde tracer into taste-specific regions of the thalamus to see how these neurons projected to gustatory cortex in the insula (**Figure 5.6c**). The results showed that the clustering by taste type was maintained in the cortex. Clusters were clearly

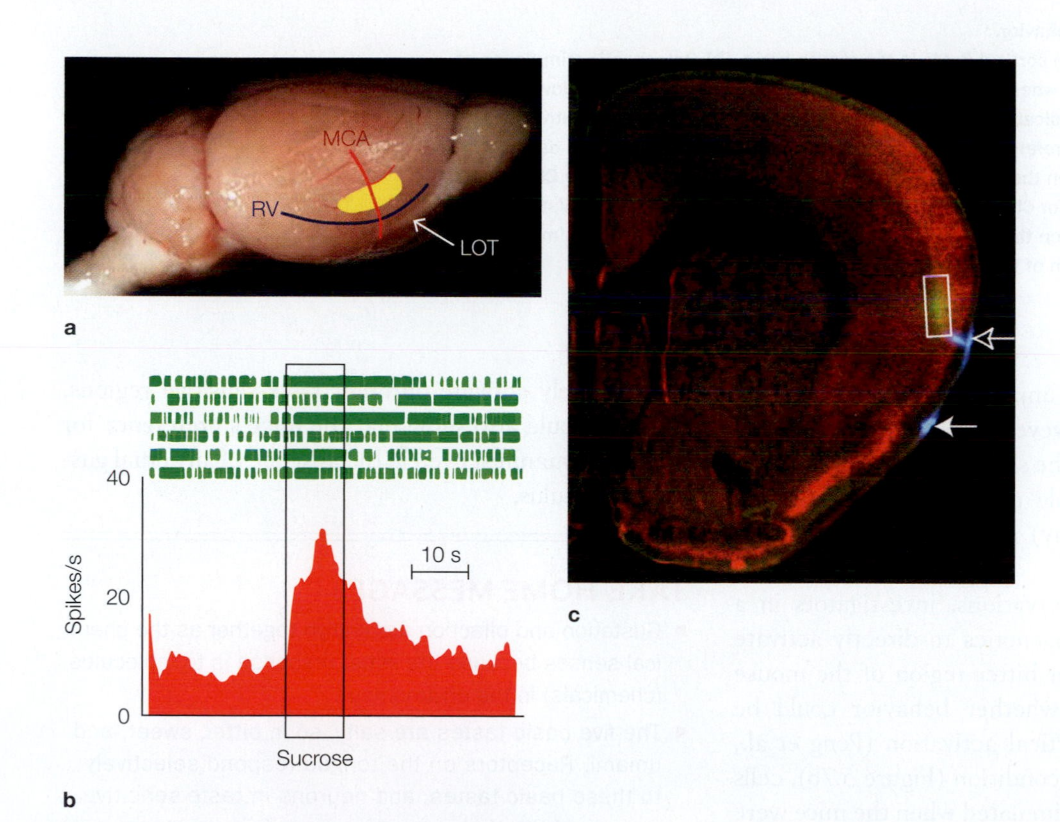

FIGURE 5.6 Imaging the gustatory cortex in the mouse insula. **(a)** Mouse brain. The gustatory cortex is in yellow, with two main blood vessels identified as anatomical landmarks: middle cerebral artery (MCA), and rhinal vein (RV). The lateral olfactory tract (LOT) is the white structure. **(b)** Extracellular recordings of a sweet-sensitive thalamic taste neuron's response to sucrose; the box indicates when the sugar was given. **(c)** After taste neurons were identified, they were injected with an anterograde tracer. The white box indicates the labeled tissue location in gustatory cortex of the thalamocortical projections. For localization, both the intersection between the RV and MCA (solid arrow) and 1 mm above the intersection (hollow arrow) were injected with dye.

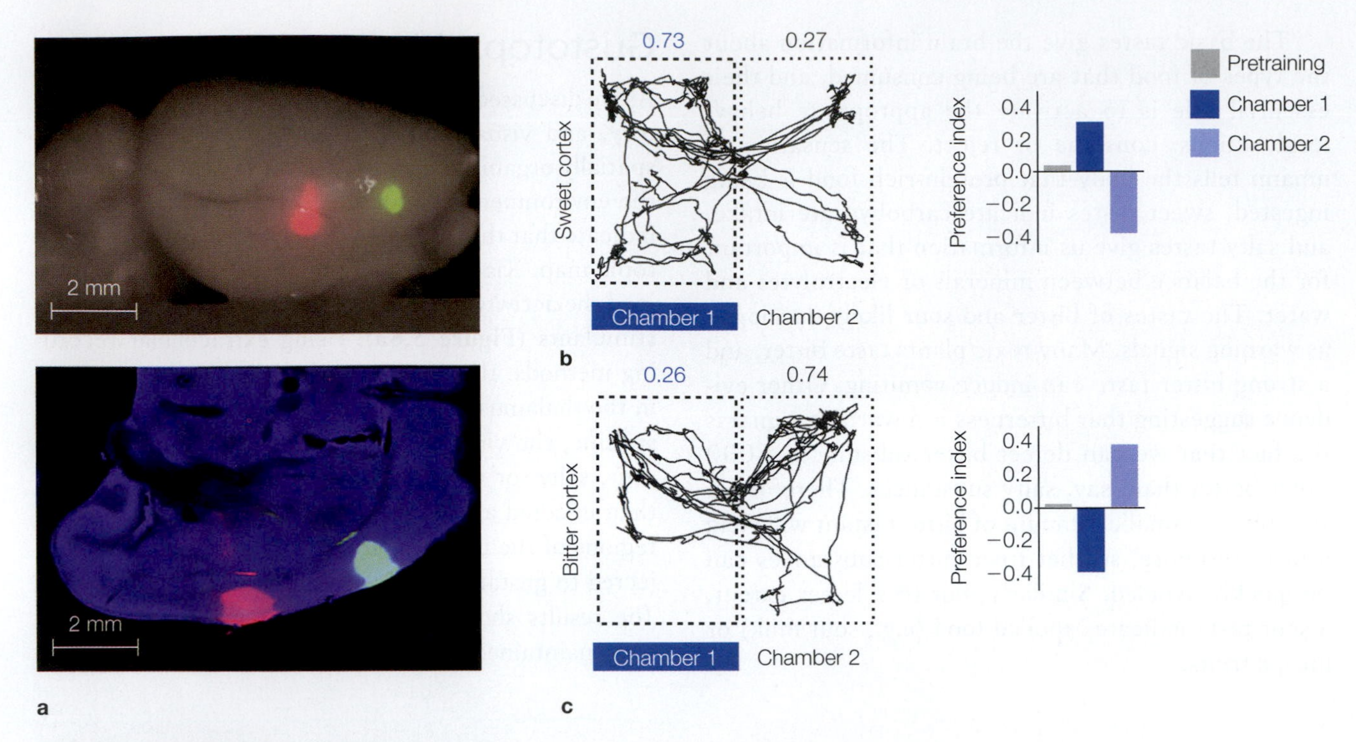

FIGURE 5.7 Linking taste to behavior.
(a) Sweet (green) and bitter (red) cortical fields in the mouse brain. **(b)** Optogenetic stimulation of the sweet cortical field occurred when the mice were in Chamber 1. Then they were allowed to roam between the two chambers to indicate their preference. Shown at left are a representative mouse's ramblings during the 5-minute preference period, with the percentage of time spent in each chamber shown on top. In the bar graph on the right, positive numbers indicate a preference for Chamber 1 and negative numbers a preference for Chamber 2. **(c)** In this condition, optogenetic stimulation in the bitter cortical field was given when the mice were in Chamber 1. The ramblings of this mouse are opposite to that elicited by stimulation of the sweet cortical field.

evident for bitter, sweet, umami, and salty. They did not find one for sour, however. The absence of a sour cluster may indicate that the signal about acidic stimuli is distributed over multiple pathways (including, for example, the pain pathway) rather than restricted to a single region.

Building on these observations, investigators in a follow-up study used optogenetics to directly activate cells in either the sweet or bitter region of the mouse gustatory cortex to see whether behavior could be manipulated by direct cortical activation (Peng et al., 2015; **Figure 5.7**). In one condition (Figure 5.7b), cells in the sweet region were stimulated when the mice were placed in the left side of a two-arm maze (Chamber 1). After this conditioning period, the mice were free to roam between the two chambers. The mice showed a strong preference to visit Chamber 1. In the other condition (Figure 5.7c), the same procedure was applied, but with the stimulation now targeted at the bitter region. In the free roaming period, the mice now preferred the right-hand chamber (Chamber 2). Thus, not only could the experimenters exploit the gustotopic map to selectively activate different taste-sensitive regions, but they could also show that the mice's preference for sweet was manifest even in the absence of an actual gustatory stimulus.

TAKE-HOME MESSAGES

- Gustation and olfaction are known together as the chemical senses because the initial response is to molecules (chemicals) in the environment.
- The five basic tastes are salty, sour, bitter, sweet, and umami. Receptors on the tongue respond selectively to these basic tastes, and neurons in taste-sensitive regions of the thalamus show specificity to these tastes.
- A gustotopic map has recently been identified in the primary gustatory cortex of the mouse brain, with considerable segregation of areas responsive to the five basic tastes. The perception of more complex tastes arises from the combination of these fundamental tastes, perhaps in the secondary gustatory cortex within the orbitofrontal cortex.

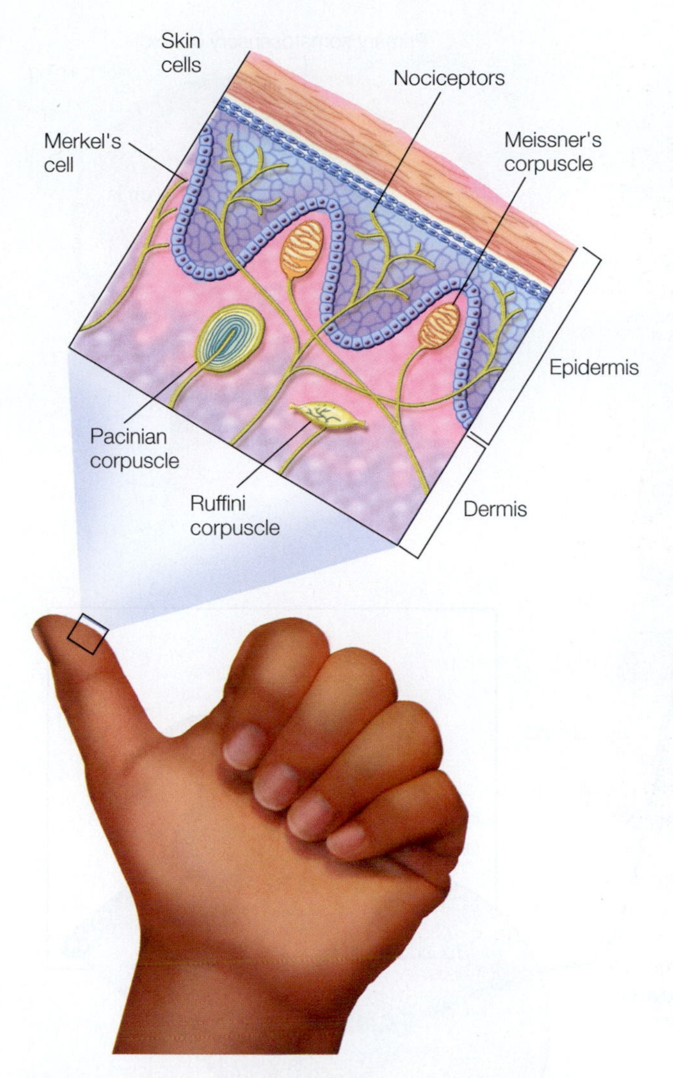

FIGURE 5.8 Somatosensory receptors underneath the skin. Merkel's cells detect regular touch; Meissner's corpuscles, light touch; Pacinian corpuscles, deep pressure; Ruffini corpuscles, temperature. Nociceptors (also known as free nerve endings) detect pain.

5.4 Somatosensation

Somatosensory perception is the perception of all mechanical stimuli that affect the body, including the interpretation of signals that indicate the position of our limbs and the position of our head, as well as our senses of temperature, pressure, touch, and pain. Perhaps to a greater degree than with our other sensory systems, the somatosensory system includes an intricate array of specialized receptors and vast projections to many regions of the central nervous system.

Neural Pathways of Somatosensation

Somatosensory receptors lie under the skin (**Figure 5.8**) and at the musculoskeletal junctions. Touch is signaled by specialized receptors in the skin, including *Meissner's corpuscles*, *Merkel's cells*, *Pacinian corpuscles*, and *Ruffini corpuscles*. These receptors differ in how quickly they adapt and in their sensitivity to various types of touch, such as deep pressure or vibration.

Pain is signaled by **nociceptors**, the least differentiated of the skin's sensory receptors. Nociceptors come in three flavors: thermal receptors that respond to heat or cold, mechanical receptors that respond to heavy mechanical stimulation, and multimodal receptors that respond to a wide range of noxious stimuli, including heat, mechanical insults, and chemicals. The experience of pain is often the result of chemicals, such as histamine, that the body releases in response to injury. Nociceptors are located on the skin, below the skin, and in muscles and joints.

Afferent pain neurons may be either myelinated or unmyelinated. The myelinated fibers quickly conduct information about pain. Activation of these cells usually produces immediate action. For example, when you touch a hot stove, the myelinated nociceptors can trigger a response that will cause you to quickly lift your hand, possibly even before you are aware of the temperature. The unmyelinated fibers are responsible for the duller, longer-lasting pain that follows the initial burn and reminds you to care for the damaged skin.

Specialized nerve cells provide information about the body's position, or what is called **proprioception** (from *proprius*, Latin for "own," and *-ception*, "receptor"; thus, a receptor for the self). Proprioception enables the sensory and motor systems to represent information about the state of the muscles and limbs. Proprioceptive cues, for example, signal when a muscle is stretched and can be used to monitor whether that movement is due to an external force or to our own actions (see Chapter 8).

Somatosensory receptors have their cell bodies in the dorsal-root ganglia (or equivalent cranial-nerve ganglia). The somatosensory receptors enter the spinal cord via the dorsal root (**Figure 5.9**). Some synapse on motor neurons in the spinal cord to form reflex arcs. Others synapse on neurons that send axons up the dorsal column of the spinal cord to the medulla. From here, information crosses over to the ventral posterior nucleus of the thalamus and then travels to the cerebral cortex. As in audition and vision (covered in Sections 5.5 and 5.6), the primary peripheral projections to the brain are cross-wired; that is, information from one side of the body is represented primarily in the opposite, or contralateral, hemisphere. In addition to the cortical projections, proprioceptive and somatosensory information is projected to many subcortical structures, such as the cerebellum.

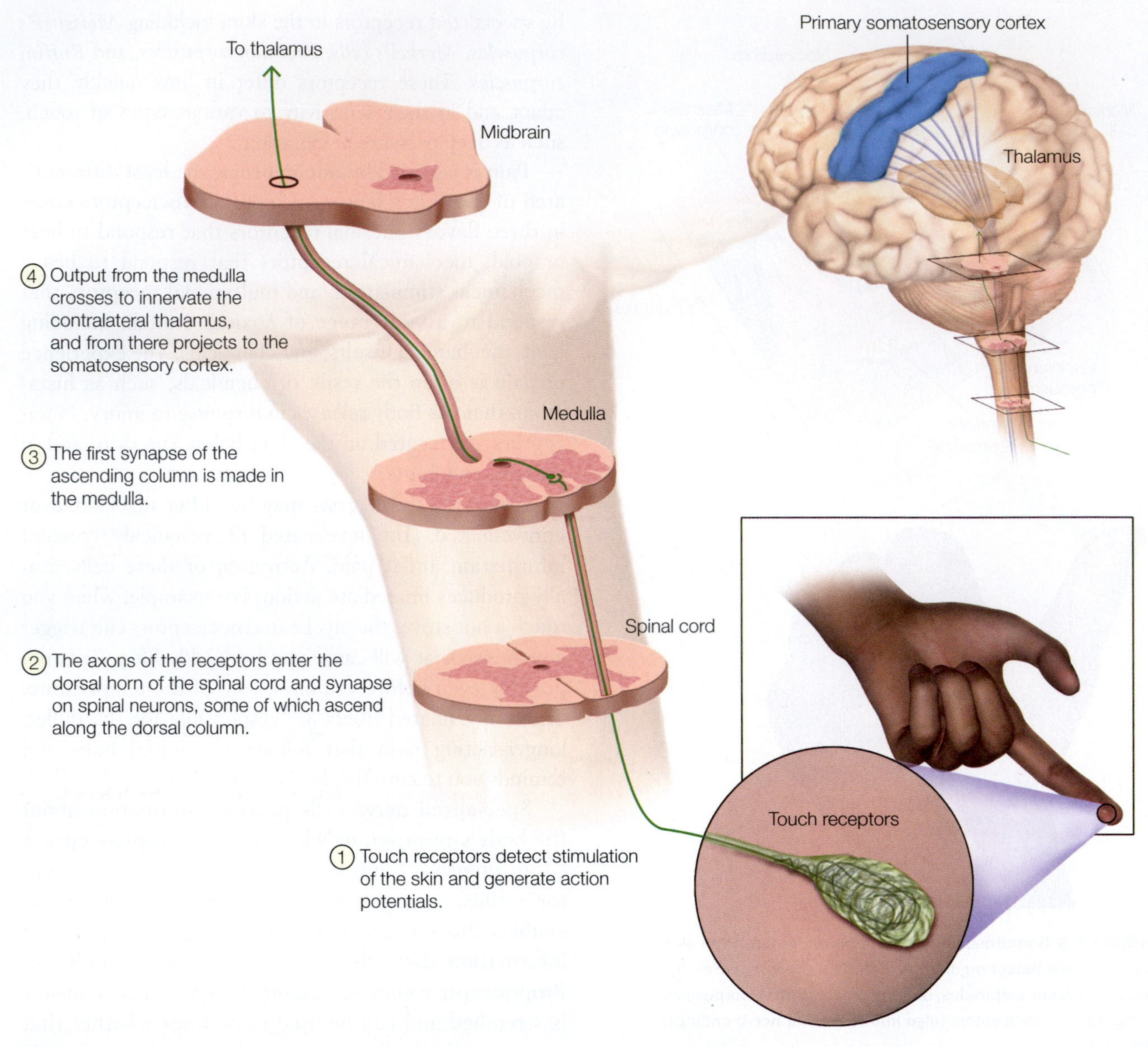

FIGURE 5.9 From skin to cortex, the primary pathway of the somatosensory system.

Somatosensory Processing

The initial cortical receiving area is called the **primary somatosensory cortex**, or **S1** (**Figure 5.10a**), which includes Brodmann areas 1, 2, and 3. S1 contains a somatotopic representation of the body, called the *sensory homunculus* (**Figure 5.10b**). As noted in the earlier discussion of acuity, the relative amount of cortical representation in the sensory homunculus corresponds to the relative importance of somatosensory information for that part of the body. The large representation of the hands is essential, given the great precision we need in using our fingers to manipulate objects and explore surfaces. When blindfolded, we can readily identify an object placed in our hands, but we would have great difficulty identifying an object rolled across our back.

Somatotopic maps show considerable variation across species. In each species, the body parts that are the most important for sensing the outside world through touch are the ones that have the largest cortical representation. A great deal of the spider monkey's cortex is devoted to its tail, which it uses to explore objects that might be edible foods or to grab on to tree limbs. The rat, on the other hand, uses its whiskers to explore the world, so a vast portion of the rat somatosensory cortex is devoted to representing information obtained from the whiskers (**Figure 5.11**).

The **secondary somatosensory cortex (S2)** builds more complex representations. From touch, for example, S2 neurons may code information about object texture and size. Interestingly, because of projections across the

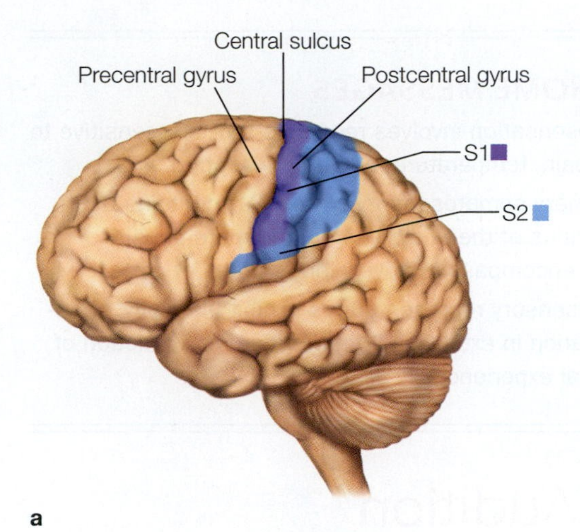

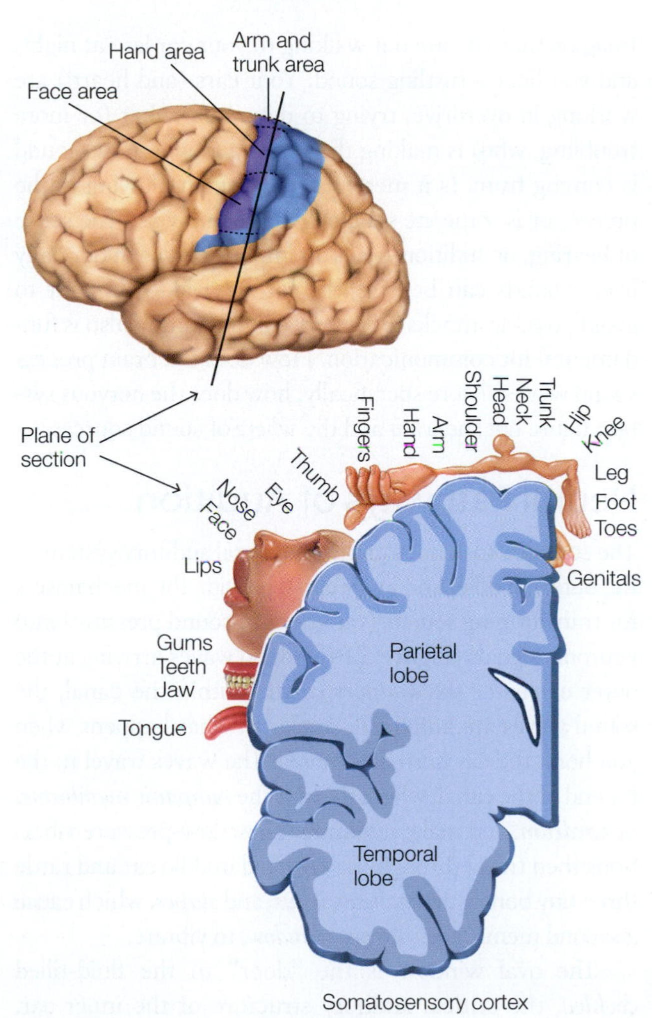

FIGURE 5.10
(a) The primary somatosensory cortex (S1) lies in the postcentral gyrus, the most anterior portion of the parietal lobe. The secondary somatosensory cortex (S2) is ventral to S1. (b) The somatosensory homunculus, as seen along the lateral surface and in greater detail in the coronal section. Note that the body parts with the larger cortical representations are most sensitive to touch.

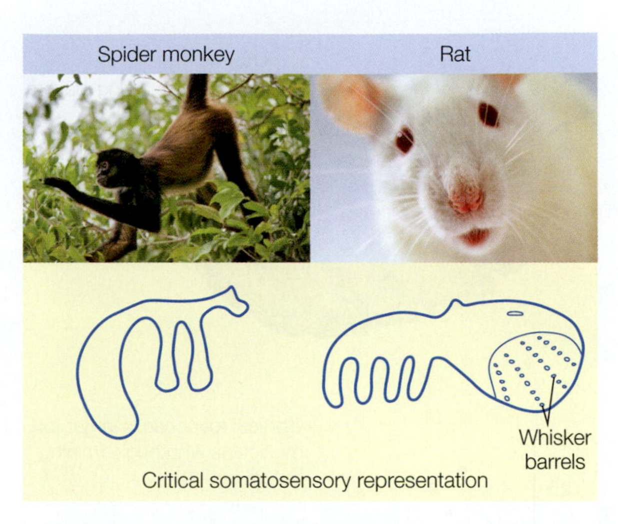

FIGURE 5.11 Variation in the organization of somatosensory cortex reflects behavioral differences across species. **The cortical area representing the tail of the spider monkey is large because this animal uses its tail to explore the environment, as well as for support. The rat explores the world with its whiskers; clusters of neurons form whisker barrels in the rat somatosensory cortex.**

corpus callosum, S2 in each hemisphere receives information from both the left and the right sides of the body. Thus, when we manipulate an object with both hands, an integrated representation of the somatosensory information can be built up in S2.

Plasticity in the Somatosensory Cortex

Looking at the somatotopic maps may make you wonder just how much of that map is set in stone. If you worked at the post office for many years sorting mail, would you see changes in parts of the visual cortex that discriminate numbers? Or, if you were a professional violinist, would your motor cortex be any bigger than that of a person who has never picked up a bow? We will discuss cortical reorganization more extensively near the end of the chapter (Section 5.9); here, we will look at whether changes in experience within the normal range—say, due to training and practice—can result in changes in the organization of the adult human brain.

Thomas Elbert and his colleagues at the University of Konstanz, Germany, used magnetoencephalography (MEG) to investigate the somatosensory representations of the hand area in violin players (Elbert et al., 1995). They found that the responses in the musicians' right hemisphere, which controls the left-hand fingers that manipulate the violin strings, were stronger

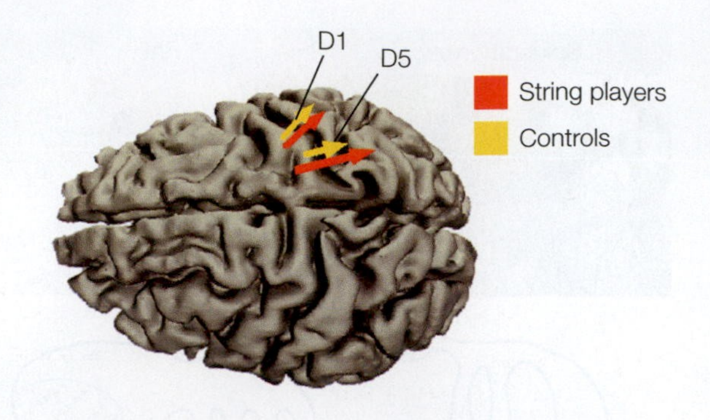

a

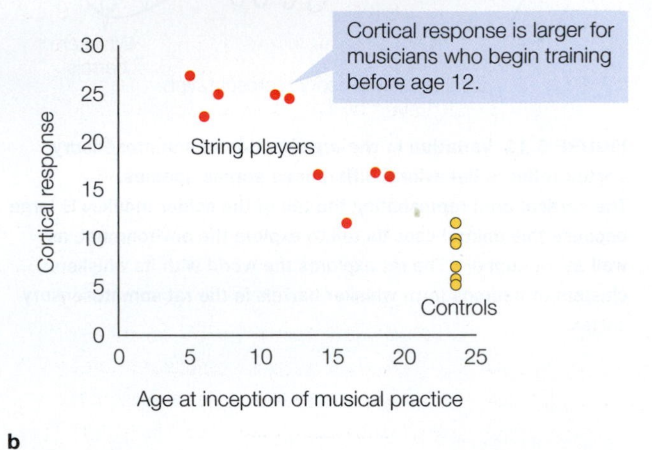

b

FIGURE 5.12 Increase in cortical representation of the fingers in musicians who play string instruments.
(a) Source of MEG activity for controls (yellow) and musicians (red) following stimulation of the thumb (Digit 1, D1) and fifth finger (D5). The length of each arrow indicates the extent of the responsive region. **(b)** The size of the cortical response, plotted as a function of the age at which the musicians begin training. Responses were larger for those who began training before the age of 12 years; controls are shown in the lower-right corner of the graph.

than those observed in nonmusicians (**Figure 5.12**). What's more, they observed that the enhancement of the response was correlated with the age at which the players began their musical training: The effect was especially pronounced in musicians who started their training at a young age. These findings suggest that violin players have a larger cortical area dedicated to representing the sensations from the fingers of the left hand, presumably because of their altered left-hand experience.

The realization that plasticity is alive and well in the brain has fueled hopes that stroke victims who have damaged cortex with resultant loss of limb function may be able to structurally reorganize their cortex and regain function. How this process might be encouraged is actively being pursued, as we will discuss further in Section 5.9. (See **Box 5.1** for other applications associated with somatosensory plasticity.)

TAKE-HOME MESSAGES

- Somatosensation involves receptors that are sensitive to touch, pain, temperature, and proprioception.
- The primary somatosensory cortex (S1) contains a homunculus of the body, wherein the more sensitive regions encompass relatively larger areas of cortex.
- Somatosensory representations exhibit plasticity, showing variation in extent and organization as a function of individual experience.

5.5 Audition

Imagine that you are out walking to your car late at night, and you hear a rustling sound. Your ears (and heart!) are working in overdrive, trying to determine what (or more troubling, who) is making the sound and where the sound is coming from. Is it merely a tree branch blowing in the breeze, or is someone sneaking up behind you? The sense of hearing, or audition, plays an important role in our daily lives. Sounds can be essential for survival—we want to avoid possible attacks and injury—but audition also is fundamental for communication. How does the brain process sound waves? More specifically, how does the nervous system figure out the *what* and the *where* of sound sources?

Neural Pathways of Audition

The complex structures of the peripheral auditory system—the outer, middle, and inner ear—provide the mechanisms for transforming sounds (variations in sound pressure) into neuronal signals (**Figure 5.14**). Sound waves arriving at the outer ear enter the *auditory canal*. Within the canal, the sound waves are amplified, similar to what happens when you honk the car horn in a tunnel. The waves travel to the far end of the canal, where they hit the *tympanic membrane*, or *eardrum*, and make it vibrate. These low-pressure vibrations then travel through the air-filled middle ear and rattle three tiny bones, the *malleus*, *incus*, and *stapes*, which cause a second membrane, the *oval window*, to vibrate.

The oval window is the "door" to the fluid-filled *cochlea*, the critical auditory structure of the inner ear. Within the cochlea are tiny *hair cells* located along the inner surface of the *basilar membrane*. The hair cells are the sensory receptors of the auditory system. Hair cells are composed of tiny filaments known as *stereocilia* that float in the fluid. The vibrations at the oval window produce tiny waves in the fluid that move the basilar membrane, deflecting the stereocilia.

The location of a hair cell on the basilar membrane determines its *frequency tuning*, the sound frequency that it responds to. This is because the thickness, and thus

BOX 5.1 | LESSONS FROM THE CLINIC

The Invisible Hand

V.Q., an intelligent 17-year-old, had his left arm amputated 2½ inches above the elbow. Four weeks later, V. S. Ramachandran pulled out a Q-tip to test V.Q.'s sensation. While V.Q. kept his eyes closed, Ramachandran used a Q-tip to touch various spots on V.Q.'s body, and V.Q. reported what he felt. When touched in one place on the left side of his face, V.Q. reported simultaneously feeling the touch there and a tingling in his missing left thumb; when touched in another spot on his face, he felt tingling in his missing index finger. Ramachandran was able to plot "receptive fields" for each finger on a specific part of the face (**Figure 5.13**). A second finger map was found on the left upper arm just above the amputation. Once again, specific spots produced simultaneous sensations on the arm and in the phantom hand. Stimuli anywhere else on V.Q.'s body were never mislocalized. When the tests were repeated several weeks later, the new maps were unchanged (Ramachandran et al., 1992).

At the time of V.Q.'s examination, it was widely accepted dogma that the adult mammalian brain was relatively stable, but Ramachandran was prepared to call that idea into question. Look again at the cortical somatosensory map in Figure 5.10b. What body part is represented next to the fingers and hand? Since the face area and arm area are next to the hand area, Ramachandran reasoned that a cortical rearrangement was taking place. Feelings of sensation in missing limbs are the well-known phenomenon of *phantom limb sensation*. The sensation in the missing limb is produced by touching a body part that has appropriated the missing limb's old acreage in the cortex.

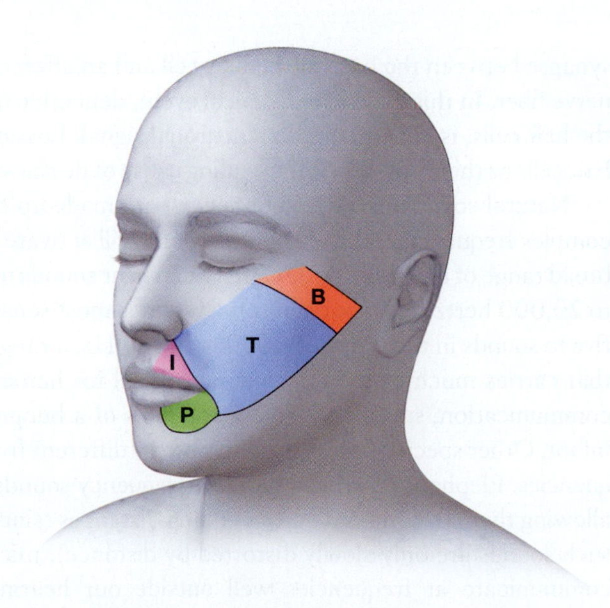

FIGURE 5.13 Perceived sensation of a phantom, amputated hand following stimulation of the face.
A Q-tip was used to lightly brush different parts of the face. The letters indicate the location of the patient's perceptual experience on the phantom limb: B = ball of the thumb; I = index finger; P = pinky finger; T = thumb.

Bioengineers designing prosthetic limbs for amputees like V.Q. have generally focused on the motor side of the equation, enabling individuals to move about on artificial legs or use a grasping device to pick up an object. Minimal attention has been given to sensory considerations. Can what we know about cortical reorganization and neuroplasticity help us make an artificial limb feel as if it is actually a part of the body and not just a piece of equipment?

One important insight here is that we can easily be fooled into misidentifying an inanimate object as part of our body. In the rubber hand illusion, for example, a rubber limb is placed in a biologically plausible position on a table in full view of the participant, while the real limb is blocked from her view (see www.youtube.com/watch?v=TCQbygjGORU). When a brush is moved over the participant's hand while she watches the same motion being applied to the rubber hand, a radical transformation will occur within a few minutes: The participant will come to "feel" that the rubber hand is her own. If blindfolded and asked to point to her hand, she will point to the rubber hand rather than her own. Even more dramatically, if the experimenter suddenly reaches out and hits the rubber hand with a hammer, the participant is likely to scream.

Researchers in Stockholm wondered whether they could bypass the peripheral stimulation and directly activate S1 to produce a similar feeling of ownership (K. L. Collins et al., 2017). They were able to perform a variation of the rubber hand illusion on two patients undergoing ECoG monitoring in preparation for epilepsy surgery: Instead of stroking the hand of each patient, the researchers electrically stimulated the hand area of S1 while the patient viewed the rubber hand being stroked. Indeed, the patients experienced the sensation of illusory ownership of the rubber hand when the electrical stimulation was synchronized with the brushing motion on the rubber hand. Asynchronous stimulation, however, did not produce the illusion.

These findings suggest that the brain can integrate visual input and direct stimulation of the somatosensory cortex to create the multisensory illusion of ownership of an artificial limb. Furthermore, this research provides a conceptual step toward creating a prosthesis for V.Q. (and others like him) that feels like it is part of the body.

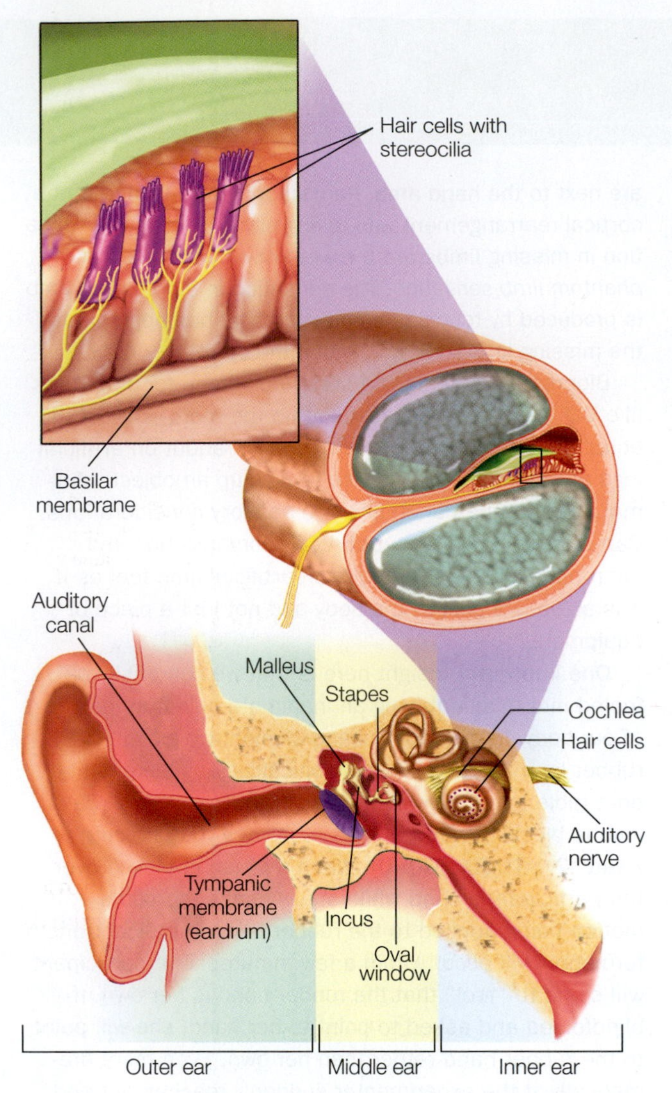

FIGURE 5.14 The peripheral auditory system.
The cochlea is the critical structure of the inner ear, and its hair cells are the primary sensory receptors for sound.

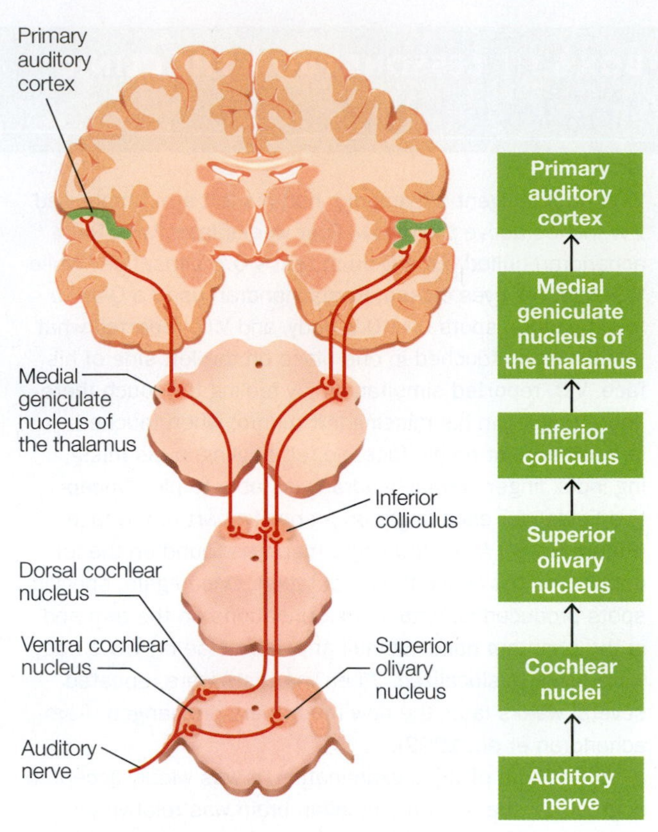

FIGURE 5.15 The central auditory system.
Output from the auditory nerve projects to the cochlear nuclei in the brainstem. Ascending fibers reach the auditory cortex after synapses in the inferior colliculus and medial geniculate nucleus.

stiffness, of the basilar membrane varies along its length from the oval window to the apex of the cochlea, constraining how the membrane will move in response to the fluid waves. Near the oval window, the membrane is thick and stiff. Hair cells attached here can respond to high-frequency vibrations in the waves. At the other end, the apex of the cochlea, the membrane is thinner and less stiff. Hair cells attached here will respond only to low frequencies. This spatial arrangement of the sound receptors is known as *tonotopy*, and the arrangement of the hair cells along the cochlear canal forms a **tonotopic map**. Thus, even at this early stage of the auditory system, information about the sound source can be discerned.

The hair cells act as *mechanoreceptors*. When deflected by the membrane, mechanically gated ion channels open in the hair cells, allowing positively charged ions of potassium and calcium to flow into the cell. If the cell is sufficiently depolarized, it will release transmitter into a synapse between the base of the hair cell and an afferent nerve fiber. In this way, a mechanical event, deflection of the hair cells, is converted into a neuronal signal. Loss of hair cells or their function is the leading cause of deafness.

Natural sounds like music or speech are made up of complex frequencies. Thus, a natural sound will activate a broad range of hair cells. Although we can hear sounds up to 20,000 hertz (Hz), our auditory system is most sensitive to sounds in the range of 1,000 to 4,000 Hz, a range that carries much of the information critical for human communication, such as speech or the cries of a hungry infant. Other species have sensitivity to very different frequencies. Elephants can hear very low-frequency sounds, allowing them to communicate over long distances (since such sounds are only slowly distorted by distance); mice communicate at frequencies well outside our hearing system. These species-specific differences likely reflect evolutionary pressures that arose from the capabilities of different animals to produce sounds. Our speech apparatus has evolved to produce changes in sound frequencies in the range of our highest sensitivity.

The central auditory system contains several synapses between the hair cells and the cortex (**Figure 5.15**). The **cochlear nerve**, also called the auditory nerve, projects

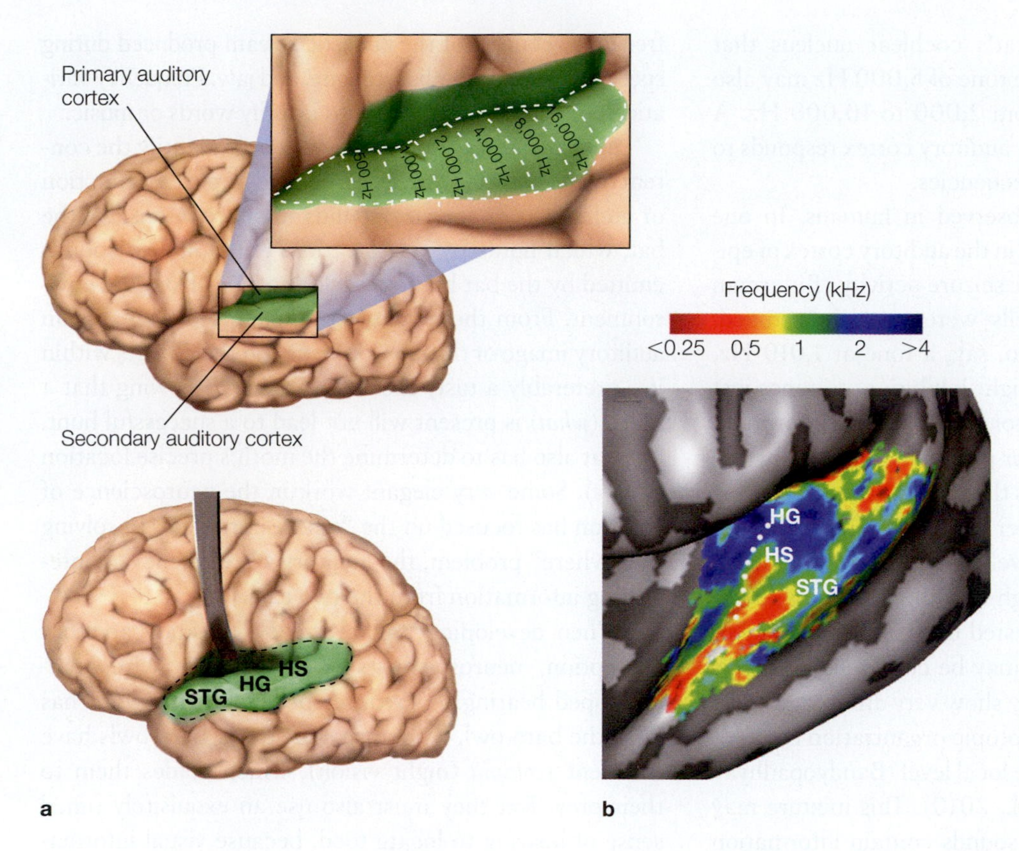

FIGURE 5.16 The auditory cortex and tonotopic map. (a) The primary auditory cortex is located in the superior portion of the temporal lobe (left and right hemispheres), with the majority of the region buried in the lateral sulcus on the transverse temporal gyrus (Heschl's gyrus, HG) and extending onto the superior temporal gyrus (STG). HS = Heschl's sulcus. (b) Left-hemisphere tonotopic map. The colored scale represents sensitivity to frequencies ranging from low (red) to high (blue). The white, dotted line indicates the location of Heschl's gyrus.

to the **cochlear nuclei** in the medulla. Axons from the cochlear nuclei travel up to the pons and split to innervate the left and right **olivary nucleus**, providing the first point within the auditory pathways where information is shared from both ears. Axons from the cochlear and olivary nuclei project to the **inferior colliculus**, higher up in the midbrain. At this stage, the auditory signals can access motor structures; for example, motor neurons in the colliculus can orient the head toward a sound. From the midbrain, auditory information ascends to the *medial geniculate nucleus (MGN)* of the thalamus, which in turn projects to the **primary auditory cortex (A1)** in the superior part of the temporal lobe.

Auditory Cortex

Neurons throughout the auditory pathway continue to have frequency tuning and maintain their tonotopic arrangement as they travel up to the cortex. Cells in the rostral part of A1 tend to be responsive to low-frequency sounds; cells in the caudal part of A1 are more responsive to high-frequency sounds. The high-resolution pictures provided by high-field 7-tesla (7-T) fMRI provide exquisite pictures of tonotopic maps in humans, evident not only in A1 but also in secondary auditory areas of the cortex (**Figure 5.16**).

As **Figure 5.17** shows, the tuning curves for auditory cells can be quite broad. The finding that individual cells do not give precise frequency information but provide only coarse coding may seem puzzling, because animals can differentiate between very small differences in sound frequencies. Interestingly, the tuning of individual neurons becomes sharper as we move through the auditory

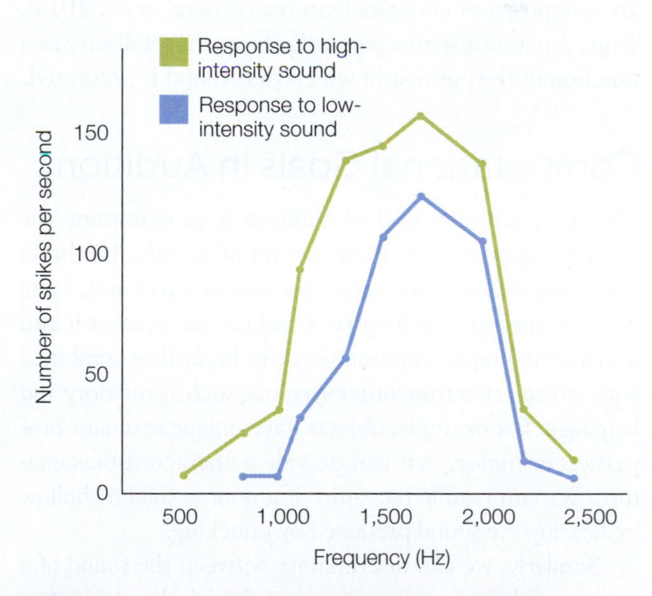

FIGURE 5.17 Frequency-dependent receptive fields for a cell in the auditory nerve of the squirrel monkey. This cell is maximally sensitive to a sound of 1,600 Hz, and the firing rate falls off rapidly for either lower- or higher-frequency sounds. The cell is also sensitive to intensity differences, showing stronger responses to louder sounds. Other cells in the auditory nerve would show tuning for different frequencies.

system. A neuron in the cat's cochlear nucleus that responds maximally to a pure tone of 5,000 Hz may also respond to tones ranging from 2,000 to 10,000 Hz. A comparable neuron in the cat auditory cortex responds to a much narrower range of frequencies.

The same principle is observed in humans. In one study, electrodes were placed in the auditory cortex of epileptic patients to monitor for seizure activity (Bitterman et al., 2008). Individual cells were exquisitely tuned, showing a strong response to, say, a tone at 1,010 Hz, but no response, or even a slight inhibition, to tones just 20 Hz different. This fine resolution is essential for making precise discriminations for perceiving sounds, including speech. Indeed, it appears that human auditory tuning is sharper than that of all other species except the bat.

While A1 is, at a gross level, tonotopically organized, more recent studies using high-resolution imaging methods in the mouse have suggested that, at a finer level of resolution, the organization may be quite messy. At this level, adjacent cells frequently show very different tuning. Thus, there is large-scale tonotopic organization but considerable heterogeneity at the local level (Bandyopadhyay et al., 2010; Rothschild et al., 2010). This mixture may reflect the fact that natural sounds contain information across a broad range of frequencies; the local organization may have arisen from experience with these sounds. Similarly, while topographic maps are usually generated by presenting pure tones (i.e., stimuli at a single frequency), the BOLD response in most auditory voxels observed with fMRI is quite different when the stimuli are composed of complex features (Moerel et al., 2013). Thus, the response to a particular frequency will vary as a function of the context in which that sound is presented.

Computational Goals in Audition

The computational goal of audition is to determine the identity (*what*) and location (*where*) of sounds. The brain must take the auditory signal (the sound wave) and, using acoustic cues such as frequency and timbre, convert it into a perceptual representation that can be further combined with information from other systems, such as memory and language. For example, objects have unique resonant properties, or *timbre*, that can provide a characteristic signature. We can readily recognize if a door is solid or hollow by hearing the sound produced by knocking.

Similarly, we can discriminate between the sound of a banjo and that of a guitar. Yet even though the two instruments produce different sounds, we are still able to identify a "G" from both as the same note. This is because the notes share the same base frequency. In a similar way, we can produce our range of speech sounds by varying the resonant properties of the vocal tract. We can also change the frequency content of the acoustic stream produced during speech by moving our lips, tongue, and jaw. Frequency variation is essential for a listener to identify words or music.

Auditory perception does not merely identify the content of an acoustic stimulus. A second important function of audition is to localize sounds in space. Consider the bat, which hunts by echolocation. High-pitched sounds emitted by the bat bounce back as echoes from the environment. From these echoes, the bat's brain creates an auditory image of the environment and the objects within it—preferably a tasty moth. But merely knowing that a moth (*what*) is present will not lead to a successful hunt. The bat also has to determine the moth's precise location (*where*). Some very elegant work in the neuroscience of audition has focused on the "where" problem. In solving the "where" problem, the auditory system relies on integrating information from the two ears.

When developing animal models to study auditory perception, neuroscientists select animals with well-developed hearing. A favorite species for this work has been the barn owl, a nocturnal creature. Barn owls have excellent *scotopia* (night vision), which guides them to their prey. But they must also use an exquisitely tuned sense of hearing to locate food, because visual information can be unreliable at night. The low levels of illumination provided by the moon and stars fluctuate with the lunar cycle and clouds. Sound, such as the patter of a mouse scurrying across a field, offers a more reliable stimulus. Indeed, barn owls have little trouble finding prey in a completely dark laboratory.

Barn owls rely on two cues to localize sounds: the difference in when a sound reaches each of the two ears (the **interaural time**) and the difference in the sound's intensity at the two ears. Both cues exist because the arriving sound is not identical at both ears. Unless the sound source is directly parallel to the head's orientation, the sound will reach one ear before the other. Moreover, because the intensity of a sound wave attenuates over time, the magnitude of the signal also differs at each ear. These time and intensity differences are minuscule. For example, if the stimulus is located at a 45° angle to the line of sight, the interaural time difference will be approximately 1/10,000 of a second.

The intensity differences resulting from sound attenuation are even smaller. However, these small differences are amplified by a unique asymmetry of owl anatomy: The left ear is higher than eye level and points downward, and the right ear is lower than eye level and points upward (**Figure 5.18**). Because of this asymmetry, sounds coming from below are louder in the left ear than the right. Humans do not have this asymmetry, but the complex structure of the human outer ear, or pinna, amplifies the intensity difference between sounds heard at the two ears.

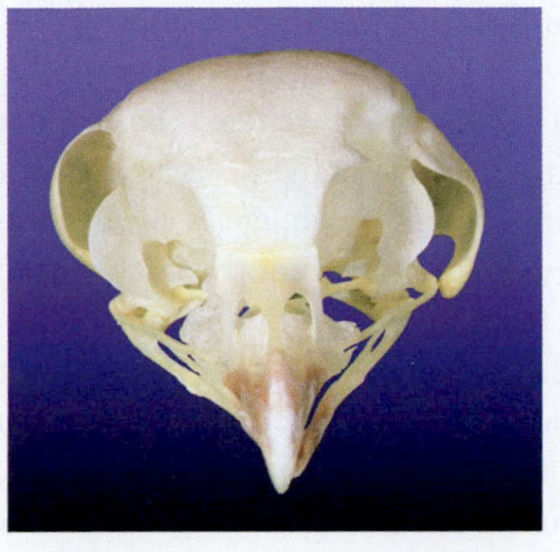

a b

FIGURE 5.18 Owl ears!
(a) The tufts that we see on many species of owls, such as the great horned owl pictured here, are just feathers, not ears. (b) The owl's ears are hidden among the feathers and are not symmetrically placed.

Interaural time and intensity differences provide independent cues for sound localization. One mechanism for computing time differences involves *coincidence detectors* (M. Konishi, 1993). To be activated, these neurons must simultaneously receive input from each ear (**Figure 5.19**). In computer science terms, these neurons act as AND operators. An input from either ear alone or in succession is not sufficient; the neurons will fire only if an input arrives at the same time from both ears. The position of the activated coincidence detector can provide a representation of the horizontal position of the sound source. Variation in interaural intensity provides additional information about the sound source. Here, the critical input is the influence of the stimulus on the neuron's firing rate: The stronger the input signal, the more strongly the cell fires. Neurons sum the combined intensity signals from both ears to pinpoint the vertical position of the source.

In Konishi's model, sound localization is solved at the level of the brainstem in the barn owl. Interestingly, humans with anencephaly (the absence of cerebral cortex due to genetic or developmental causes) or hydranencephaly (very minimal cerebral cortex, often the result of fetal trauma or disease) have relatively preserved hearing, at least in terms of their ability to judge if two sounds

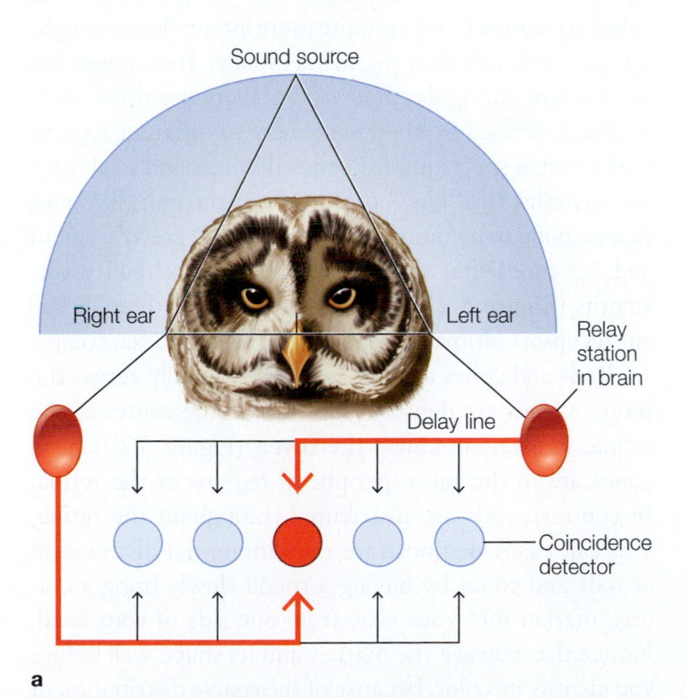

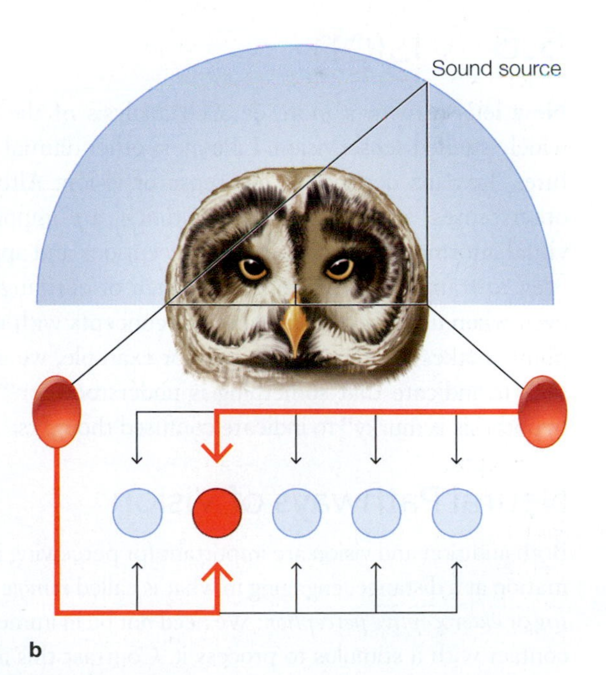

FIGURE 5.19 Slight asymmetries in the arrival times at the two ears can be used to locate the lateral position of a stimulus.
(a) When the sound source is directly in front of the owl, the stimulus reaches the two ears at the same time. As activation is transmitted across the delay lines, the coincidence detector representing the central location is activated simultaneously from both ears. (b) When the sound source is located to the owl's left, the sound reaches the left ear first. Now a coincidence detector offset to the opposite side receives simultaneous activation from the two ears.

are the same or different or determine their location (Merker, 2007).

Of course, hearing involves much more than determining the location of a sound. Cortical processing is likely essential for performing more complex functions, such as sound identification or the conversion of auditory information into action. The owl does not want to attack the source of every sound it hears; it must decide whether the sound is generated by potential prey. The owl needs a more detailed analysis of the sound frequencies to determine whether a stimulus results from the movement of a mouse or a deer.

TAKE-HOME MESSAGES

- Signal transduction from sound wave to neuronal signal begins at the eardrums. Sound waves disturb the hair cells. This mechanical input is transformed into neural output at the cochlea Auditory information is then conveyed to the inferior colliculus and cochlear nucleus in the brainstem before projecting to the medial geniculate nucleus of the thalamus and on to the primary auditory cortex.
- Neurons throughout the auditory pathway maintain their tonotopic arrangement as they travel up to the cortex, but the organization is complicated by the fact that natural sounds are composed of complex frequency patterns.
- Audition requires solving a number of computational problems to determine the location and identity of a sound.

5.6 Vision

Now let's turn to a more detailed analysis of the most widely studied sense: vision. Like most other diurnal creatures, humans depend on our sense of vision. Although other senses, such as hearing and touch, are important, visual information dominates our perceptions and appears even to frame the way we think. Much of our language, even when used to describe abstract concepts with metaphors, makes reference to vision. For example, we say "I see" to indicate that something is understood, or "Your hypothesis is murky" to indicate confused thoughts.

Neural Pathways of Vision

Both audition and vision are important for perceiving information at a distance, engaging in what is called *remote sensing* or *exteroceptive perception*: We need not be in immediate contact with a stimulus to process it. Contrast this ability with the sense of touch, for which we must have direct contact with the stimulus. The advantages of remote sensing are obvious. An organism surely can avoid a predator better when it can detect the predator at a distance. It is probably too late to flee once a shark has sunk its teeth into you, no matter how fast your neural response is to the pain.

PHOTORECEPTORS Visual information is contained in the light reflected from objects. To perceive objects, we need sensory detectors that respond to the reflected light. As light passes through the lens of the eye, the image is inverted and focused to project onto the **retina**, the back surface of the eyeball (**Figure 5.20**). The retina is only about 0.5 mm thick, but it is made up of densely packed layers of neurons. The deepest layers are composed of millions of **photoreceptors** that contain *photopigments*, protein molecules that are sensitive to light. When exposed to light, the photopigments become unstable and split apart. Unlike most neurons, the retina's photoreceptors do not fire action potentials. Instead, the decomposition of the photopigments alters the membrane potential of the photoreceptors, and the resulting chemical changes trigger action potentials in downstream neurons. Thus, these photoreceptors transduce an external stimulus, light, into an internal neuronal signal that the brain can interpret.

The photoreceptors consist of rods and cones. **Rods** contain the photopigment *rhodopsin*, which is destabilized by low levels of light. Rods are most useful at night, when light energy is reduced. Rods also respond to bright light, but the pigment quickly becomes depleted and the rods cease to function until it is replenished. Because this replenishment takes several minutes, they are of little use during the day.

Cones contain a different type of photopigment, called *photopsin*. Cones require more intense levels of light but can replenish their pigments rapidly. Thus, cones are most active during daytime vision. There are three types of cones, defined by their sensitivity to different regions of the visible spectrum: (a) cones that respond to shorter wavelengths, the "blue" part of the spectrum; (b) cones that respond to medium wavelengths, the "green" region; and (c) cones that respond to the longer "red" wavelengths (**Figure 5.21**). The activity of these three different receptors ultimately leads to our ability to see color.

Rods and cones are not distributed equally across the retina. Cones are densely packed near the center of the retina, in a region called the **fovea** (Figure 5.20). Few cones are in the more peripheral regions of the retina. In contrast, rods are distributed throughout the retina. You can easily demonstrate the differential distribution of rods and cones by having a friend slowly bring a colored marker into your view from one side of your head. Notice that you see the marker and its shape well before you identify its color, because of the sparse distribution of cones in the retina's peripheral regions.

FROM THE RETINA TO THE CENTRAL NERVOUS SYSTEM The rods and cones are connected to bipolar neurons that synapse with the **ganglion cells**, the output layer of the retina. The axons of these cells form

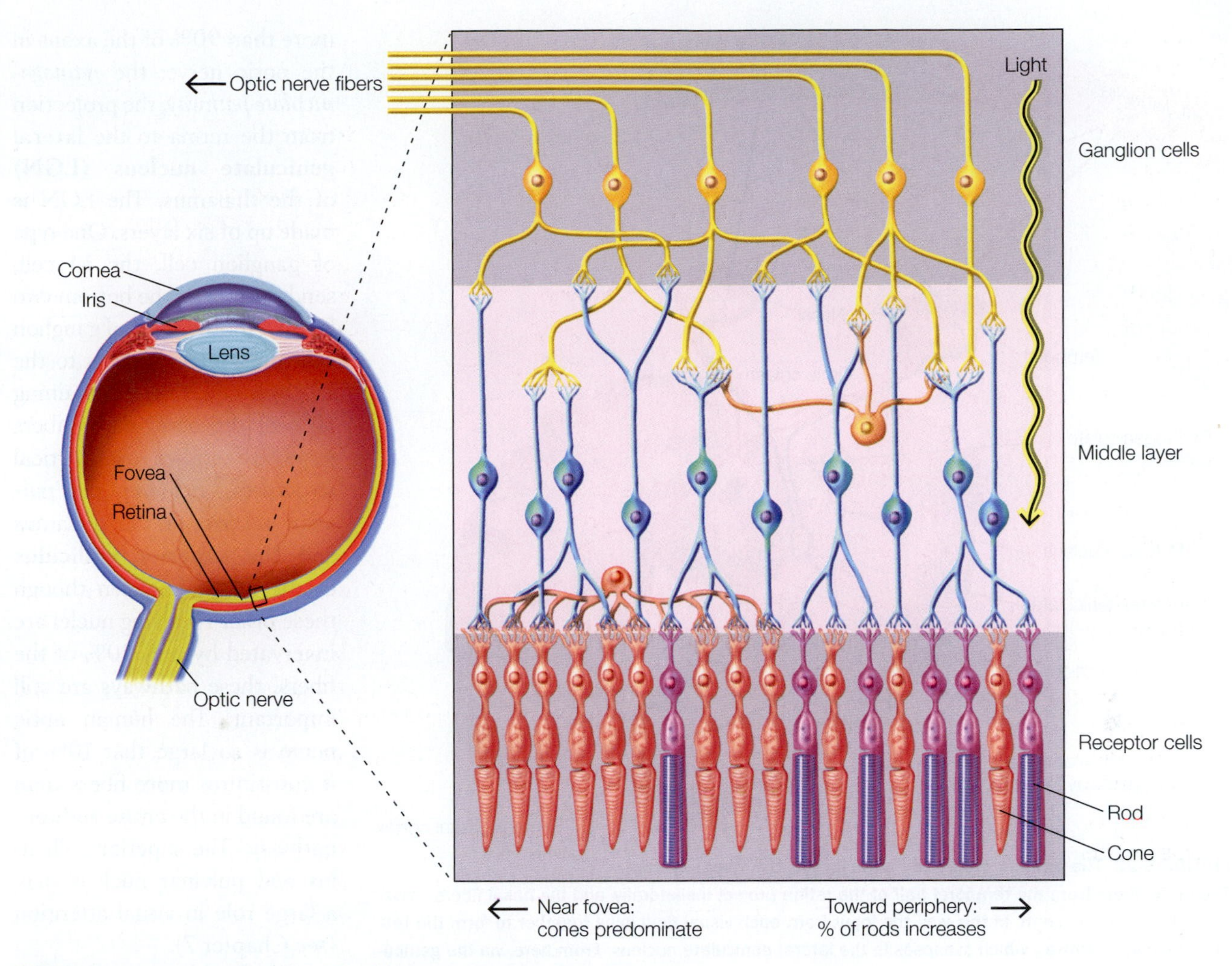

FIGURE 5.20 Anatomy of the eye and retina.
Light enters through the cornea and activates the receptor cells of the retina located along the rear surface. There are two types of receptor cells: rods and cones. The output of the receptor cells is processed in the middle layer of the retina and then relayed to the central nervous system via the optic nerve, the axons of the ganglion cells.

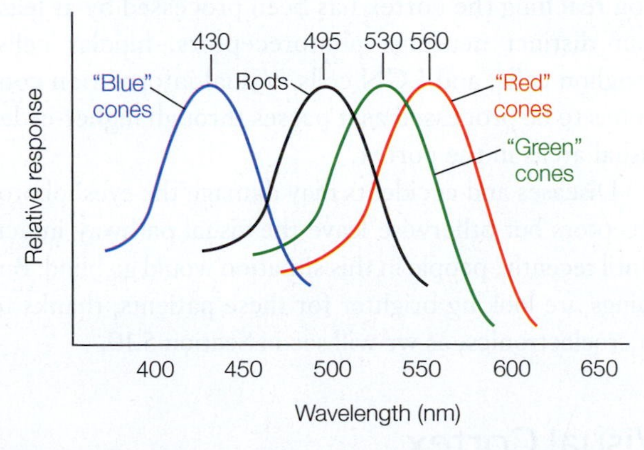

FIGURE 5.21 Spectral sensitivity functions for rods and the three types of cones.
The short-wavelength ("blue") cones are maximally responsive to light with a wavelength of 430 nm. The peak sensitivities of the medium-wavelength ("green") and long-wavelength ("red") cones are shifted to longer wavelengths. White light, such as daylight, activates all three cone receptors because it contains all wavelengths.

a bundle, the *optic nerve*, that transmits information to the central nervous system. Before any information is shipped down the optic nerve, however, extensive processing occurs within the retina, where an elaborate convergence of information takes place. Indeed, though humans have an estimated 260 million photoreceptors, we have only 2 million ganglion cells to telegraph information from the retina. By summing their outputs, the rods can activate a ganglion cell even in low-light situations. For cones, however, the story is different: Each ganglion cell is innervated by only a few cones. These few receptors provide much more detailed information from a smaller region of space, ultimately providing a sharper image. The compression of information, as with the auditory system, suggests that higher-level visual centers should be efficient processors to unravel this information and recover the details of the visual world.

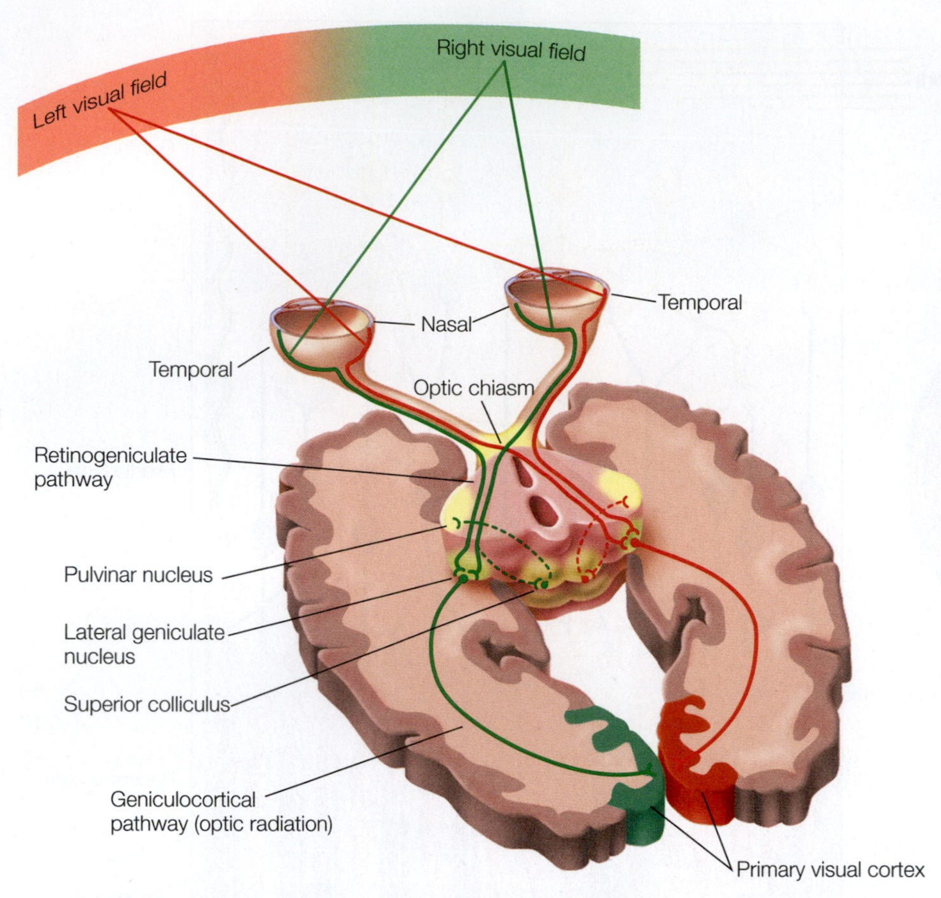

FIGURE 5.22 The primary projection pathways of the visual system.
The optic fibers from the temporal half of the retina project ipsilaterally, and the nasal fibers cross over at the optic chiasm. In this way, the input from each visual field joins together to form the retinogeniculate pathway, which synapses in the lateral geniculate nucleus. From here, via the geniculocortical pathway, the fibers project to the primary visual cortex. A small percentage of visual fibers of the optic nerve terminate in the superior colliculus and pulvinar nucleus (dashed lines).

Figure 5.22 diagrams how visual information is conveyed from the eyes to the central nervous system. Because of the retina's curvature, objects in the left visual field stimulate the nasal hemi-retina of the left eye and the lateral hemi-retina of the right eye. In the same fashion, objects from the right field stimulate the nasal hemi-retina of the right eye and the lateral hemi-retina of the left eye. As we discussed in Chapter 4, each optic nerve splits into two parts before entering the brain: The temporal (lateral) branch continues to traverse along the ipsilateral side. The nasal (medial) branch crosses over to project to the contralateral side; this crossover place is called the *optic chiasm*. Given the eye's optics, the crossover of nasal fibers ensures that visual information from each side of external space will project to contralateral brain structures. That is, information from the right visual field will be processed by the left sides of both retinas and shuttled on to the left hemisphere, and vice versa for information from the left visual field.

Each optic nerve divides into several pathways that differ with respect to where they terminate in the subcortex. Figure 5.22 focuses on the pathway that contains more than 90% of the axons in the optic nerve: the *retinogeniculate pathway*, the projection from the retina to the **lateral geniculate nucleus (LGN)** of the thalamus. The LGN is made up of six layers. One type of ganglion cell, the M cell, sends output to the bottom two layers. Another type of ganglion cell, the P cell, projects to the top four layers. The remaining 10% of the optic nerve fibers innervate other subcortical structures, including the *pulvinar nucleus* of the thalamus and the **superior colliculus** of the midbrain. Even though these other receiving nuclei are innervated by only 10% of the fibers, these pathways are still important. The human optic nerve is so large that 10% of it constitutes more fibers than are found in the entire auditory pathway. The superior colliculus and pulvinar nucleus play a large role in visual attention (see Chapter 7).

The final projection to the visual cortex is via the *geniculocortical pathway*. This bundle of axons exits the LGN and ascends to the cortex, and almost all of the fibers terminate in the **primary visual cortex (V1)** of the occipital lobe. Thus, visual information reaching the cortex has been processed by at least four distinct neurons: photoreceptors, bipolar cells, ganglion cells, and LGN cells. Visual information continues to be processed as it passes through higher-order visual areas in the cortex.

Diseases and accidents may damage the eyes' photoreceptors but otherwise leave the visual pathway intact. Until recently, people in this situation would go blind. But things are looking brighter for these patients, thanks to microelectronics, as we will see in Section 5.10.

Visual Cortex

Just as the auditory system determines the *what* and *where* of sounds, so the visual system identifies the *what* and *where* of objects. We will look first at characteristics of visual neurons, and then at the anatomical and functional organization of the visual cortex.

VISUAL NEURONS Because of the optics of the eye, light reflecting off objects in the environment strikes the eye in an orderly manner. Light reflected off an object located to the right of someone's gaze will activate photoreceptors on the medial, or nasal, side of the right retina and the lateral, or temporal, side of the left retina. Neurons in the visual system keep track of where objects are located in space by responding only when a stimulus is presented in a specific region of space, defined as the **receptive field** of the neuron. For example, a cell in the left visual cortex may respond to a bar of light, but only if that bar is presented in a specific region of space (e.g., the upper right visual field; see Figure 3.19).

Moreover, as with the somatosensory and auditory systems, the receptive fields of visual cells within neural regions such as the LGN or V1 form an orderly mapping between an external dimension (in this case, spatial location) and the neural representation of that dimension. In vision, these topographic representations are referred to as **retinotopic maps.** A full retinotopic map contains a representation of the entire contralateral hemifield (e.g., the left-hemisphere V1 contains a full representation of the right side of external visual space).

In pioneering neurophysiological experiments conducted in the 1950s, Stephen Kuffler elegantly described the receptive-field organization of ganglion cells in the cat retina. This work was then extended by David Hubel and Torsten Wiesel (1977), who set out to characterize computational principles for processing within the visual system. Although they had little difficulty identifying individual cortical cells, the cells in the primary visual cortex, despite many attempts, failed to respond to the small black or white circles that Kuffler had used to map the receptive fields of individual ganglion cells.

Hubel and Wiesel's breakthrough came somewhat serendipitously. They had created dark stimuli by marking spots on a glass slide. Although these dark spots also failed to elicit robust responses from V1 cells, the researchers noticed a burst of activity as they moved the edge of the glass across the space that fell within the cell's receptive field. Eventually, it became clear that V1 neurons are fussy: They respond to edges, and mainly to edges having a particular orientation.

After much experimentation, Hubel and Wiesel deduced how inputs from the LGN produce the "on–off" edge detectors of V1 neurons. The receptive fields of cells in the LGN are circular, responding vigorously whenever a stimulus spans a cell's "on" region but not its "off" region (**Figure 5.23a**). These circular receptive fields combine to

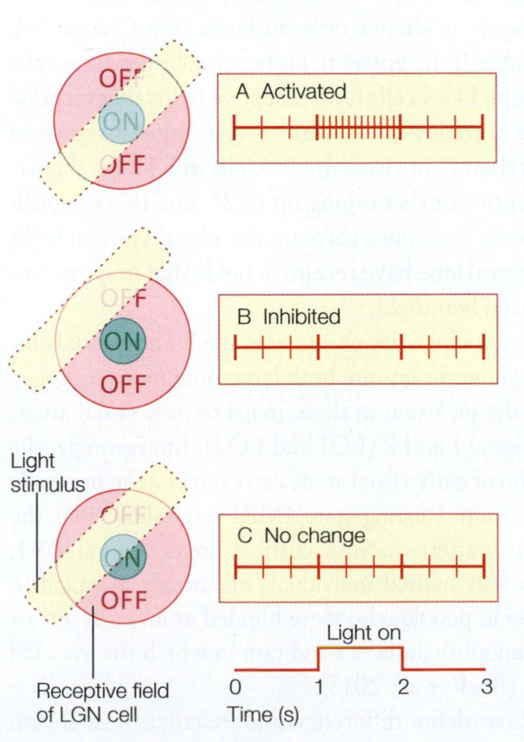

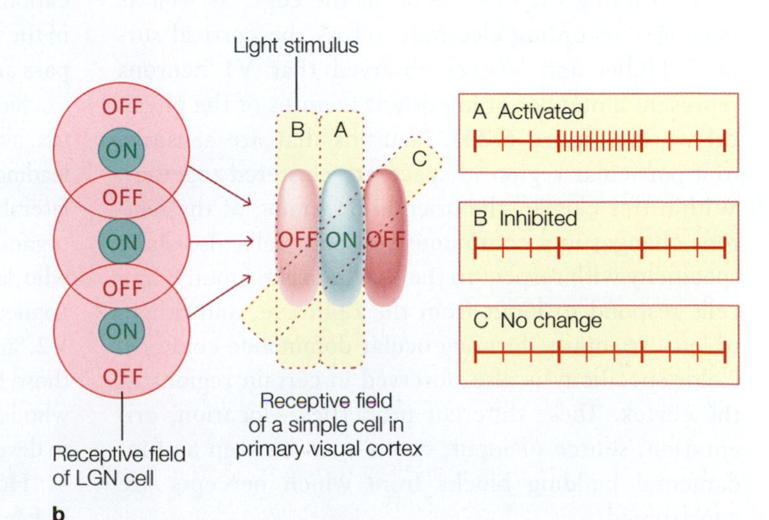

FIGURE 5.23 Characteristic response of LGN cells.
(a) Cells in the lateral geniculate nucleus (LGN) have concentric receptive fields with either an on-center, off-surround organization or an off-center, on-surround organization. The on-center, off-surround cell shown here fires rapidly when the light encompasses the center region (A) and is inhibited when the light is positioned over the surround (B). A stimulus that spans both the center and the surround produces little change in activity (C). Thus, LGN cells are ideal for signaling changes in illumination, such as those that arise from stimulus edges. **(b)** Simple cells in the primary visual cortex can be formed by the linking of outputs from concentric LGN cells with adjacent receptive fields. In addition to signaling the presence of an edge, simple V1 cells are selective for orientation. The simple cell illustrated here is either excited or inhibited by an edge that follows its preferred orientation. It shows no change in activity if the edge does not have the preferred orientation.

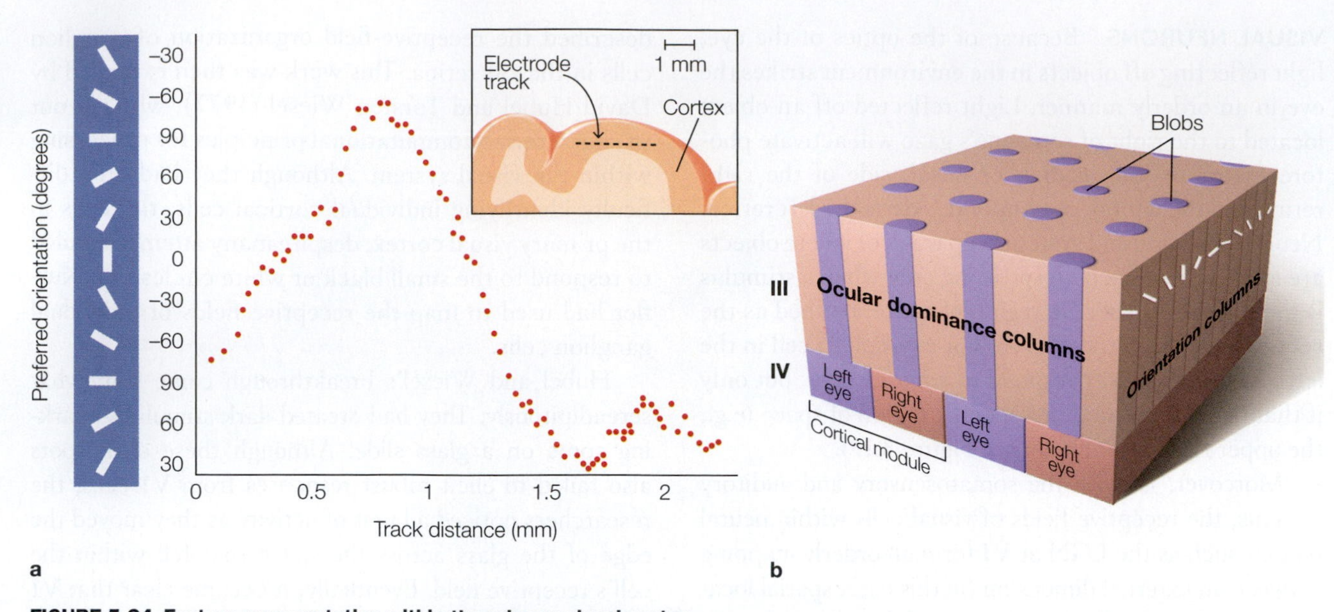

FIGURE 5.24 Feature representation within the primary visual cortex. **(a) As a recording electrode is moved along the cortex, the preferred orientation of the cells continuously varies and is plotted as a function of the location of the electrode. (b) The orientation columns are crossed with ocular dominance columns to form a cortical module. Within a module, the cells have similar receptive fields (location sensitivity), but they vary in input source (left or right eye) and sensitivity to orientation, color, and size.**

form oriented receptive fields in V1 neurons (**Figure 5.23b**). Now, when the cell is active, the signal indicates not only the position of the stimulus (e.g., within its receptive field), but also the orientation of the edge of the stimulus. For example, the cell shown in Figure 5.23b responds vigorously to a vertical stimulus that spans its "on" region, is inhibited if that stimulus spans its "off" region, and shows no change when the stimulus is at a different orientation. These observations clarify a fundamental principle of perception: The nervous system is interested in change. We recognize an elephant not by the homogeneous gray surface of its body, but by the contrast of the gray edge of its shape against the background.

By varying the orientation of the edge, as well as moving a recording electrode across the cortical surface, Hubel and Wiesel observed that V1 neurons represent a number of important features of the physical world (**Figure 5.24**). Neurons that are sensitive to a particular region in space are clustered together. Within this cluster, the orientation tuning of the neurons changes in a continuous manner. Cells also show specificity with respect to the source of the input: Some cells respond to input from the right eye, and others to left-eye inputs, forming ocular dominance columns. Color specificity is also observed in certain regions of the cortex. These different properties—location, orientation, source of input, color—can be seen as fundamental building blocks from which percepts are constructed.

VISUAL AREAS **Figure 5.25** provides an overview of some of the main visual areas in the brain of a macaque monkey. The optimal stimulus becomes more complex as information moves through the system: Cells in the retina and LGN respond best to small spots of light, while cells in V1 are sensitive to edges. Farther up the system, in areas like V4 and TE, the optimal stimulus becomes much more complex, such as shapes or even faces (see Chapter 6). Correspondingly, receptive fields become larger across the visual system. LGN cells have receptive fields that respond only if the stimulus falls within a very limited region of space, less than 1° of visual angle. Cells in V1 have slightly larger receptive fields ranging up to 2°, and this magnification process continues through the visual system: Cells in the temporal lobe have receptive fields that may encompass an entire hemifield.

Similar principles are observed in the human visual cortex, although our brains are both larger and more complex, leading to the inclusion in these maps of new visual areas, lateral occipital 1 and 2 (LO1 and LO2). Interestingly, the organization of early visual areas can even be seen in people who lack vision. Resting-state fMRI data show that the connectivity patterns across cortical areas spanning V1, V2, and V3 in sighted individuals are nearly identical to those found in people who were blinded at an early age or who have anophthalmia, a condition in which the eyes fail to develop (Bock et al., 2015).

How do we define different visual areas like those shown in Figure 5.25? In some cases, anatomical differences can

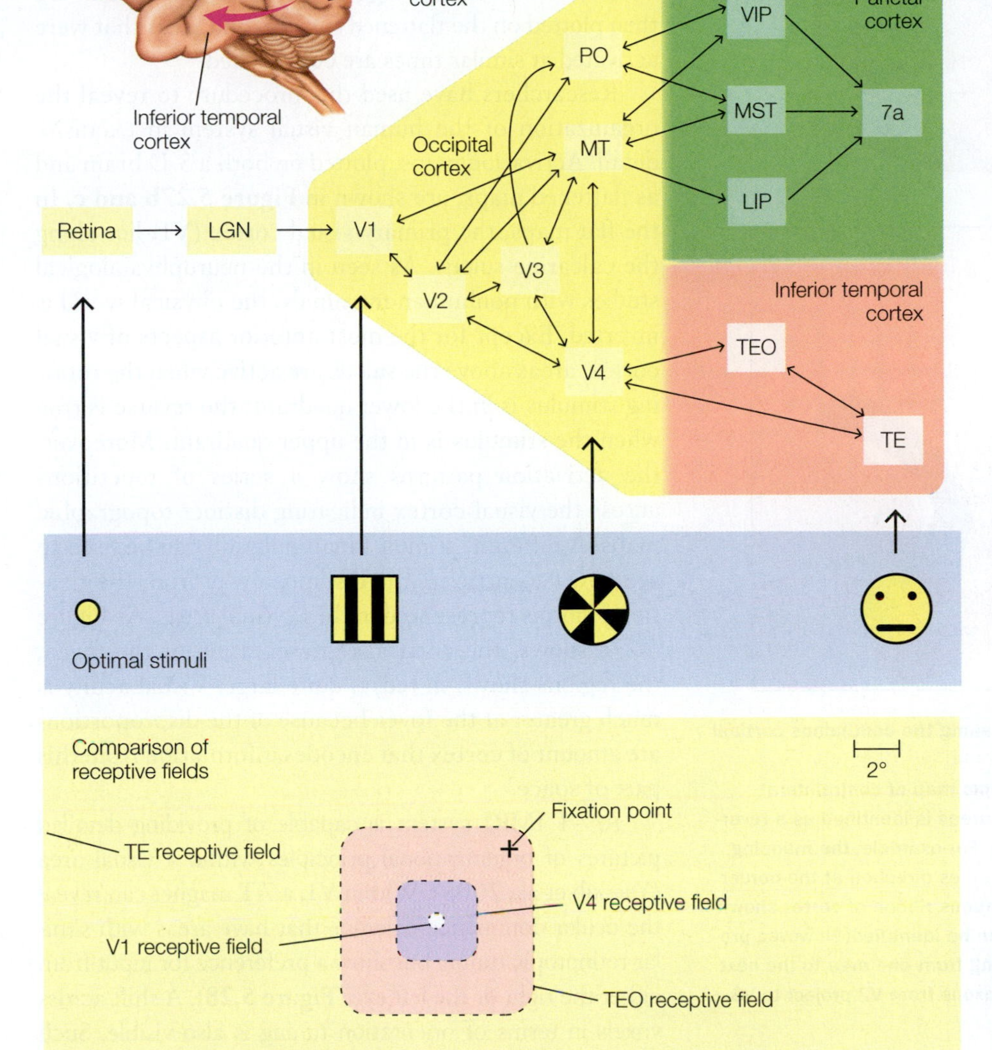

FIGURE 5.25 Prominent cortical visual areas and the pattern of connectivity in the macaque brain.
Whereas cortical processing begins in V1, the projections form two major processing streams, one along a dorsal pathway (green) and the other along a ventral pathway (pink; see Chapter 6). The stimulus required to produce optimal activation of a cell becomes more complex along the ventral stream. The labels for the areas reflect a combination of physiological (e.g., V1) and anatomical (e.g., LIP) terms.

be identified. For example, Brodmann's cytoarchitectonic method identified a clear division between primary and secondary visual cortex (see Chapter 2). However, the multiple areas shown in Figure 5.25 are defined physiologically, with the basic criterion being that each area delineates a retinotopic map. The boundaries between anatomically adjacent visual areas are determined by topographic reversals.

To understand this, consider the following analogy: Imagine a clothing store where the pants and blouses are all in the same row. Within each section, the items are ordered by size. Suppose the pants start with size S and end with XL. We could just repeat that progression with the blouses. But if instead we reverse the order for the blouses, so that they start with XL and end with S, the XL shopper finds her pants and blouses adjacent to each other. The S shopper still has to travel from one end of the pants to the other end of the blouses to find her sizes. But if jackets follow the blouses, we can reverse the order again, now having the S blouses adjacent to the S jackets.

This economy of organization has been adopted by nature. **Figure 5.26** shows a cross section of the visual cortex, where each visual area has its own retinotopic map and borders are defined by such reversals. As one area projects to another, spatial information is preserved by these multiple retinotopic maps, at least in early visual areas (those involved in the initial processing of visual information). Over 30 distinct **cortical visual areas** have been identified in the monkey, and the evidence indicates that humans have even more.

Following the conventions adopted in single-cell studies in monkeys, the visual areas are numbered in increasing order, where the primary visual cortex (V1) is most posterior and the secondary visual areas (V2, V3/VP, V4) more anterior. Although we use names such as V1, V2, V3, and V4, this numbering scheme should not be taken to mean that the synapses proceed sequentially from one area to the next. In fact, since originally described, V3 has been divided into two separate visual areas: V3 and VP. The lines connecting these **extrastriate visual areas** demonstrate extensive convergence and divergence across visual areas. In addition, connections between many areas are reciprocal; areas frequently receive input from an area to which they project.

Vision scientists have developed sophisticated fMRI techniques to study the organization of human visual

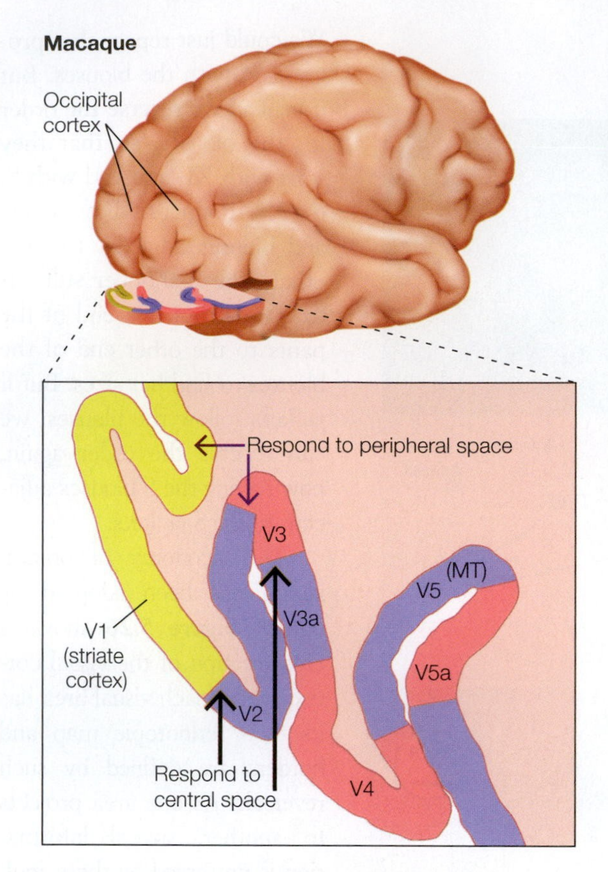

FIGURE 5.26 Multiple visual areas along the continuous cortical surface.
Each visual area contains a retinotopic map of contralateral space, and the border between two areas is identified as a reversal in the retinotopic representation. For example, the mapping from peripheral to central space reverses direction at the border of two visual areas. Along the continuous ribbon of cortex shown here, seven different visual areas can be identified. However, processing is not restricted to proceeding from one area to the next in a sequential order. For example, axons from V2 project to V3, V4, and V5/MT.

cortex. In these studies a stimulus is systematically moved across the visual field. For example, a wedge-shaped checkerboard pattern is slowly rotated about the center of view (**Figure 5.27a**). In this way, the BOLD response for areas representing the superior quadrant will be activated at a different time than for areas representing the inferior quadrant—and in fact, the representation of the entire visual field can be continuously tracked. To compare areas that respond to foveal stimulation and those that respond to peripheral stimulation, researchers use a dilating and contracting ring stimulus. By combining these different stimuli, they can measure the cortical representation of external space.

The convoluted nature of the human visual cortex would make deciphering the results from such an experiment difficult if the data were plotted on the anatomical maps found in a brain atlas. To avoid this problem, vision scientists prefer to work with flat maps of the brain. High-resolution anatomical MRI scans are obtained, and computer algorithms transform the folded, cortical surface into a two-dimensional map by tracing the gray matter. The activation signals from the fMRI study are then plotted on the flattened surface, and areas that were activated at similar times are color-coded.

Researchers have used this procedure to reveal the organization of the human visual system in exquisite detail. Activation maps, plotted on both a 3-D brain and as flattened maps, are shown in **Figure 5.27b and c**. In the flat maps, the primary visual cortex (V1) lies along the calcarine sulcus. As seen in the neurophysiological studies with nonhuman mammals, the physical world is inverted. Except for the most anterior aspects of visual cortex, areas above the sulcus are active when the rotating stimulus is in the lower quadrant; the reverse is true when the stimulus is in the upper quadrant. Moreover, the activation patterns show a series of repetitions across the visual cortex indicating distinct topographic maps. A different stimulus manipulation can be used to see how eccentricity, the distance away from the fixation point, is represented in these visual areas. As Figure 5.27c shows, the cortical representation of the fovea, the regions shown in red, is quite large. Visual acuity is much greater at the fovea because of the disproportionate amount of cortex that encodes information from this part of space.

A 7-T fMRI system is capable of providing detailed pictures of organizational principles within a visual area (Yacoub et al., 2008). Within V1, a 7-T magnet can reveal the ocular dominance columns that have areas with similar retinotopic tuning but show a preference for input from either the right or the left eye (**Figure 5.28**). A shift across voxels in terms of orientation tuning is also visible. Such specificity is striking when we keep in mind that the activation within a voxel reflects the contributions of millions of neurons. Orientation tuning does not mean that all of these neurons have similar orientation preferences. Rather, it means that the relative contribution of orientation-selective neurons varies across voxels. Some voxels have a stronger contribution from vertically oriented cells; others, a stronger contribution from horizontally oriented cells.

FUNCTIONAL ORGANIZATION OF THE VISUAL CORTICAL AREAS Why has the primate brain evolved so many visual areas? One possibility is that visual processing is *hierarchical*. Each area, representing the stimulus in a unique way, successively elaborates on the representation derived by processing in earlier areas. As we have seen, some cells in the primary visual cortex calculate edges. Other cells in the secondary visual areas use the information to represent corners and edge terminations. In turn, higher-order visual neurons integrate

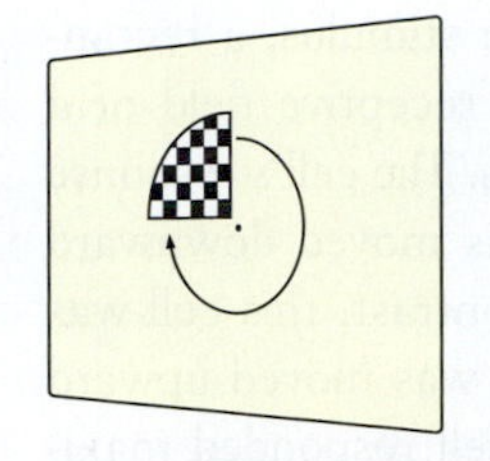
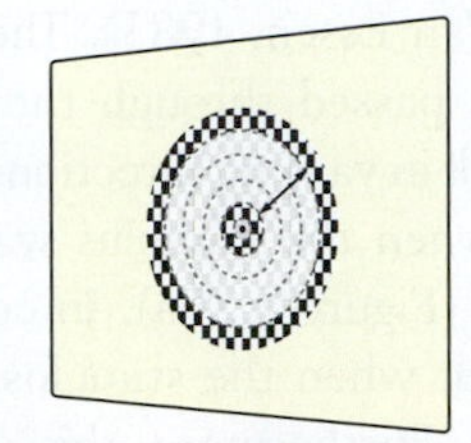

a

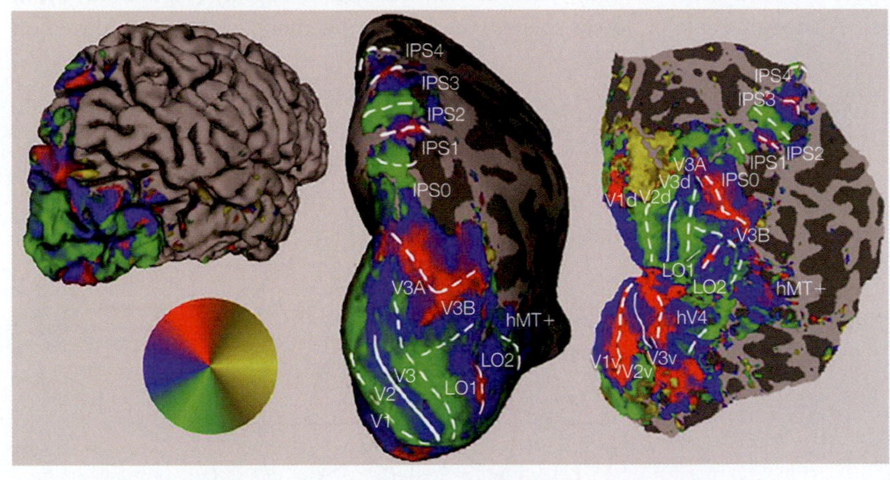

b

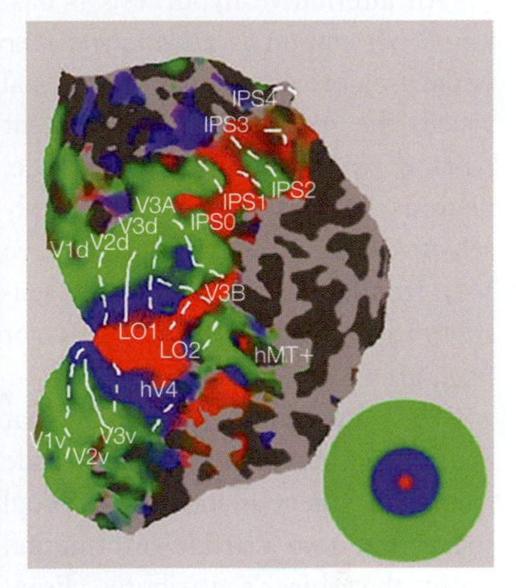

c

FIGURE 5.27 Mapping visual fields with functional magnetic resonance imaging (fMRI). **(a)** The participant views a rotating circular wedge while fMRI scans are obtained. The wedge passes from one visual quadrant to the next, and the BOLD response in visual cortex is measured continuously to map out how the regions of activation change in a corresponding manner. **(b)** Retinotopic maps in the human brain identified with fMRI, showing representations in the right hemisphere of the angular position of a stimulus; the color wheel indicates stimulus position. The data are shown on a 3-D MRI reconstruction (left), inflated brain (center), and flat map (right). Five hemifield maps are seen along the medial bank of the intraparietal sulcus (IPS). **(c)** The same data are plotted on a flat map with colors indicating stimulus position from fovea to periphery. The boundaries between visual cortical areas in (b) and (c) are defined by the reversals in the retinotopic maps. Maps courtesy of David Somers.

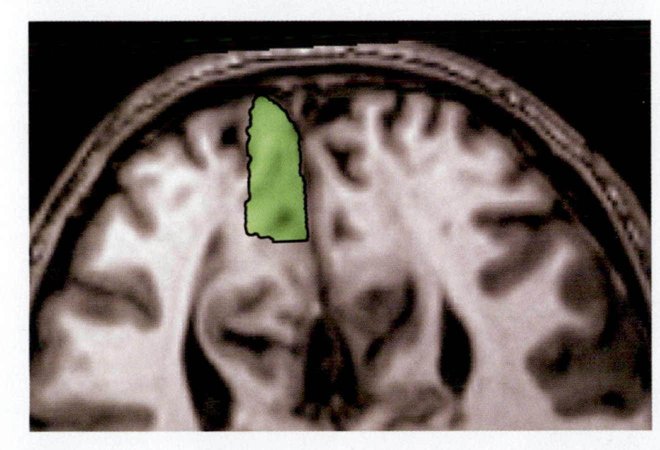

a

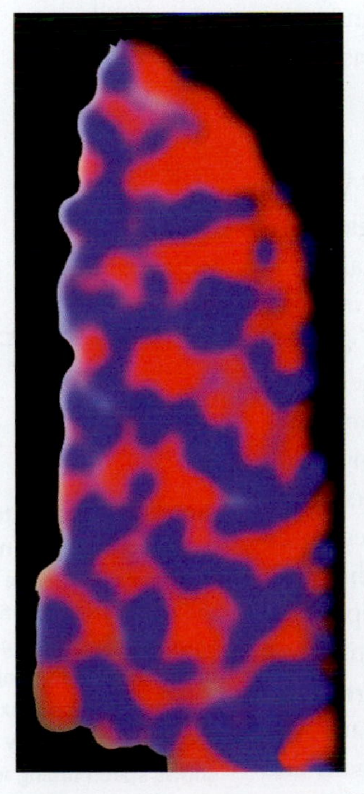

b

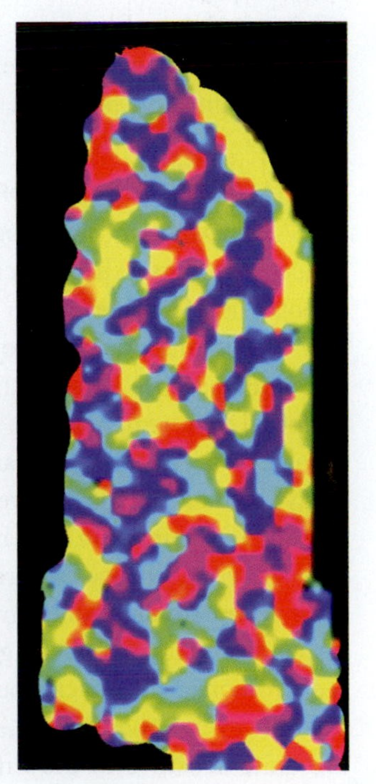

c

FIGURE 5.28 High field resolution of human visual cortex. **(a)** Selected region of interest (ROI) in the primary visual cortex targeted with a 7-T fMRI scanner. **(b)** At this resolution, it is possible to image ocular dominance columns. Here, red indicates areas that were active when the stimulus was presented to the right eye, and blue, areas that were active when the stimulus was presented to the left eye. **(c)** Orientation map in the ROI. Colors indicate preferences for bars presented at different angles.

information to represent shapes. Successive elaboration culminates in formatting the representation of the stimulus so that it matches (or doesn't match) information in memory. An interesting idea, but there is a problem. As Figure 5.25 shows, there is no simple hierarchy; rather, extensive patterns of convergence and divergence result in multiple pathways.

An alternative hypothesis is based on the idea that visual perception is an *analytic process.* Although each visual area provides a map of external space, the maps represent different *types* of information. For instance, neurons in some areas are highly sensitive to color variation (e.g., area V4). In other areas, neurons are sensitive to movement but not to color (e.g., area MT).

This hypothesis suggests that neurons within an area not only code where an object is located in visual space, but also provide information about the object's attributes. From this perspective, visual perception can be considered to entail a divide-and-conquer strategy. Instead of all visual areas containing representations of all attributes of an object, each visual area provides its own limited analysis. Processing is distributed and specialized. As signals advance through the visual system, different areas elaborate on the initial information in V1 and begin to integrate this information across dimensions to form recognizable percepts.

SPECIALIZED FUNCTION OF VISUAL AREAS Extensive physiological evidence supports the specialization hypothesis. Consider cells in **area MT** (sometimes referred to as V5), so named because it lies in the *m*iddle *t*emporal lobe region of the macaque monkey, a species used in many physiology studies. Single-cell recordings reveal that neurons in this region do not show specificity regarding the color of the stimulus; for example, they respond similarly to either a green or a red circle on a white background.

However, these MT neurons are quite sensitive to movement and direction, as **Figure 5.29** shows (Maunsell & Van Essen, 1983). The stimulus, a rectangular bar, was passed through the receptive field of a specific MT cell in varying directions. The cell's response was greatest when the stimulus was moved downward and to the left (Figure 5.29a). In contrast, this cell was essentially silent when the stimulus was moved upward or to the right. Furthermore, this cell responded maximally when the bar was moved rapidly (Figure 5.29b); at lower speeds, the bar's movement in the same direction

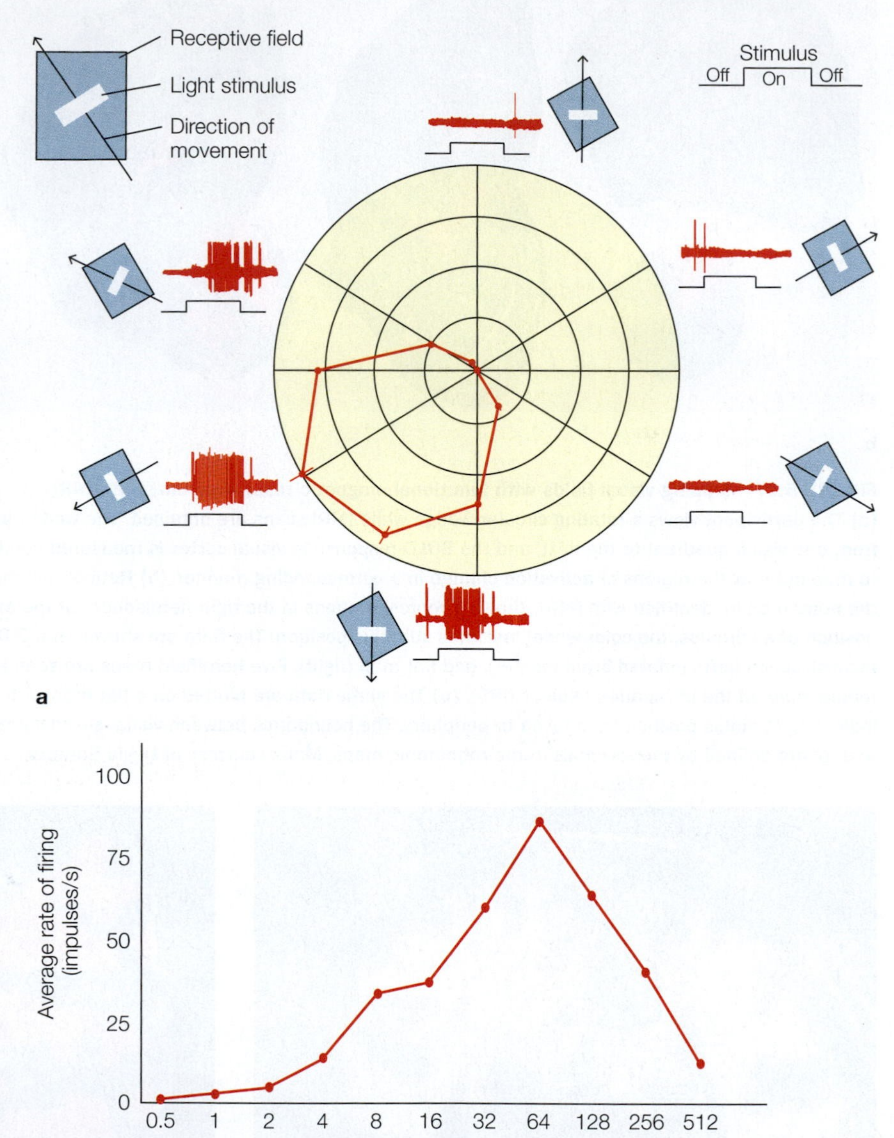

FIGURE 5.29 Direction and speed tuning of a neuron from area MT.
(a) A rectangle was moved through the receptive field of this cell in various directions. The red traces beside the stimulus cartoons indicate the responses of the cell to these stimuli. In the polar graph, the firing rates are plotted; the angular direction of each point indicates the stimulus direction, and the distance from the center indicates the firing rate as a percentage of the maximum firing rate. The polygon formed when the points are connected indicates that the cell was maximally responsive to stimuli that moved down and to the left; the cell responded minimally when the stimulus moved in the opposite direction. **(b)** This graph shows speed tuning for an MT cell. In all conditions, the motion was in the optimal direction. This cell responded most vigorously when the stimulus moved at a speed of 64° per second.

failed to raise the response rate above baseline. Thus, the activity of the macaque's MT neuron was correlated with three attributes. First, the cell was active only when the stimulus fell within its receptive field. Second, the cell's response was greatest when the stimulus moved in a certain direction. Third, the cell's activity was modulated by the speed of motion; different MT neurons respond to different speeds.

Neuroimaging methods have enabled researchers to describe similar specializations in the human brain. In a pioneering study, Semir Zeki of University College London and his colleagues at London's Hammersmith Hospital used PET imaging to identify areas that were involved in processing color or motion information (Barbur et al., 1993). They used subtractive logic by factoring out the activation in a control condition from the activation in an experimental condition. In the color experiment (**Figure 5.30a**), participants passively viewed a collage of either colored rectangles or achromatic rectangles. In the motion experiment (**Figure 5.30b**), participants viewed either a field of small black or white squares that moved or a field of squares that were stationary.

FIGURE 5.30 Stimuli used in a PET experiment to identify regions involved in color and motion perception.
(a) In the color experiment, the stimuli were composed of an arrangement of rectangles that were either shades of gray (control) or various colors (experimental, shown here). **(b)** For the motion experiment, a random pattern of black and white regions was either stationary (control) or moving (experimental).

The results of these studies provided clear evidence that the two tasks activated distinct brain regions. After subtracting activation during viewing of the achromatic collage, investigators found numerous residual foci of activation when participants viewed the colored collage. These foci were bilateral and located in the most anterior and inferior regions of the occipital lobe (**Figure 5.31a**). Although the spatial resolution of PET is coarse, these areas were determined to be in front of the striate (V1) and prestriate (V2) cortex, labeled human **area V4** by Zeki and colleagues.

In contrast, after the appropriate subtraction in the motion experiment, the residual foci were bilateral but located near the junction of the temporal, parietal, and occipital cortices (**Figure 5.31b**). These foci

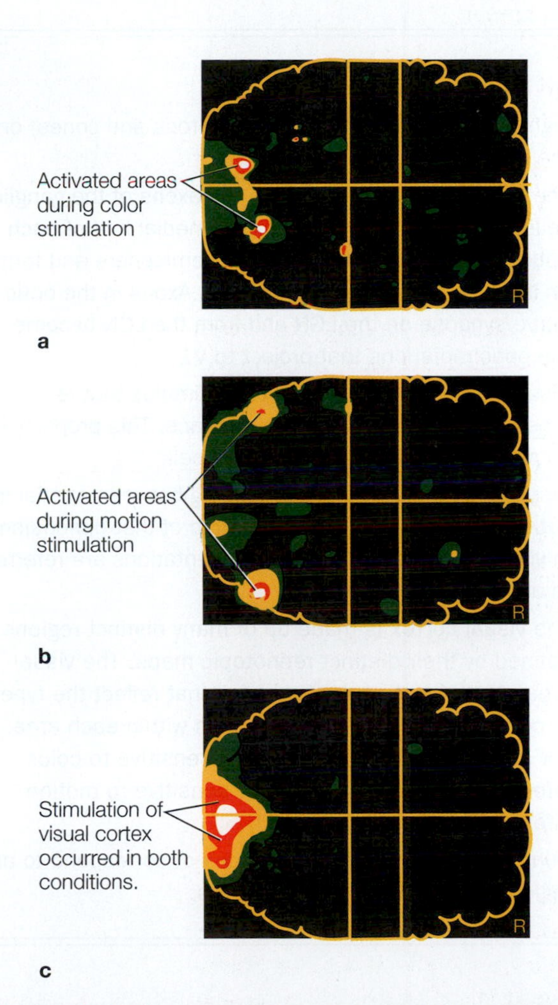

FIGURE 5.31 Regions of activation when the control conditions were subtracted from the experimental conditions in the experiment illustrated in Figure 5.30.
(a) In the color condition, the prominent activation was medial, in an area corresponding to human V4. **(b)** In the motion condition, the activation was more lateral, including human MT (also referred to as V5). The foci also differed along the dorsoventral axis: The slice showing MT is superior to that showing V4. **(c)** Both stimuli produced significant activation in the primary visual cortex, when compared to a control condition in which there was no visual stimulation.

were more superior and much more lateral than the color foci, and are referred to as area V5. Note that researchers frequently refer to area V5 as *human* area MT, even though the area is not in the temporal lobe in the human brain. Of course, with PET data we cannot be sure that the foci of activation really consist of just one visual area.

A comparison of Figures 5.26 and 5.31 reveals striking between-species differences in the relative position of the color and motion areas. For example, the human MT is on the lateral surface of the brain, whereas the monkey MT is more medial. Such differences exist because the surface area of the human brain is substantially larger than the monkey's, and this expansion required additional folding of the continuous cortical sheet over the course of evolutionary time.

TAKE-HOME MESSAGES

- Light activates the photoreceptors (rods and cones) on the retina.
- The optic nerve is formed from the axons of the ganglion cells. The axons that make up the medial half of each optic nerve cross to the opposite hemisphere and form an intersection at the optic chiasm. Axons in the optic nerve synapse on the LGN and from the LGN become the optic radiations that project to V1.
- Visual neurons respond only to a stimulus that is presented in a specific region of space. This property is known as the receptive field of the cell.
- Visual cells form an orderly mapping between spatial location and the neural representation of that dimension. In vision, these topographic representations are referred to as retinotopic maps.
- The visual cortex is made up of many distinct regions defined by their distinct retinotopic maps. The visual areas have functional differences that reflect the types of computations performed by cells within each area. For instance, cells in area V4 are sensitive to color information, and cells in V5 are sensitive to motion information.
- Humans have visual areas that do not correspond to any region in our close primate relatives.

5.7 From Sensation to Perception

In Chapter 6 we will explore the question of how our sensory experiences are turned into percepts—how we take the information from our sensory systems and use it to recognize objects and scenes. Here we briefly discuss the relationship between sensation and perception using vision, describing experiments that ask how activation in early sensory areas relates to our perceptual experience. For example, is activation in early visual cortex sufficient to support perception? Or does that information have to be relayed to higher visual areas in order for us to recognize the presence of a stimulus?

We saw in the previous section that certain elementary features are represented in early sensory areas, usually with some form of topographic organization. Cells in auditory cortex are tuned to specific frequency bands; cells in visual cortex represent properties such as orientation, color, and motion. The information represented in primary sensory areas is refined and integrated as we move into secondary sensory areas. An important question is: At what stage of processing does this sensory stimulation become a percept, something we experience phenomenally?

Where Are Percepts Formed?

One way to study this question is to "trick" our sensory processing systems with stimuli that cause us to form percepts that do not correspond to the true stimuli in the environment—that is, to perceive illusions. By following the processing of such stimuli using fMRI, we can attempt to determine where in the processing stream the signals become derailed. For instance, if we look at a colored disk that changes color every second from red to green, we have no problem seeing the two colors in succession. If the same display flips between the two colors 25 times per second (i.e., at 25 Hz), however, the percept is of a fused color—a constant, yellowish white disk (the additive effects of red and green light). This phenomenon is known as flicker fusion. At what stage in the visual system does our perception break down, failing to keep up with the flickering stimulus? Does the breakdown occur early in processing within the subcortical structures, or later, in one of the cortical visual areas?

Using a flickering stimulus, Sheng He and colleagues tested participants while observing the changes in visual cortex (Jiang et al., 2007). In **Figure 5.32**, compare the fMRI BOLD responses for visual areas V1, V4, and VO during a 5-Hz full-contrast flicker condition (perceptually two colors), a 30-Hz full-contrast flicker condition (perceptually one fused color), and a control condition, which was a 5-Hz subthreshold contrast condition (perceptually indistinguishable from the 30-Hz flicker).

Subcortical processing and several of the lower cortical processing areas, V1 and V4, were able to distinguish among the 5-Hz flicker, the 30-Hz flicker, and

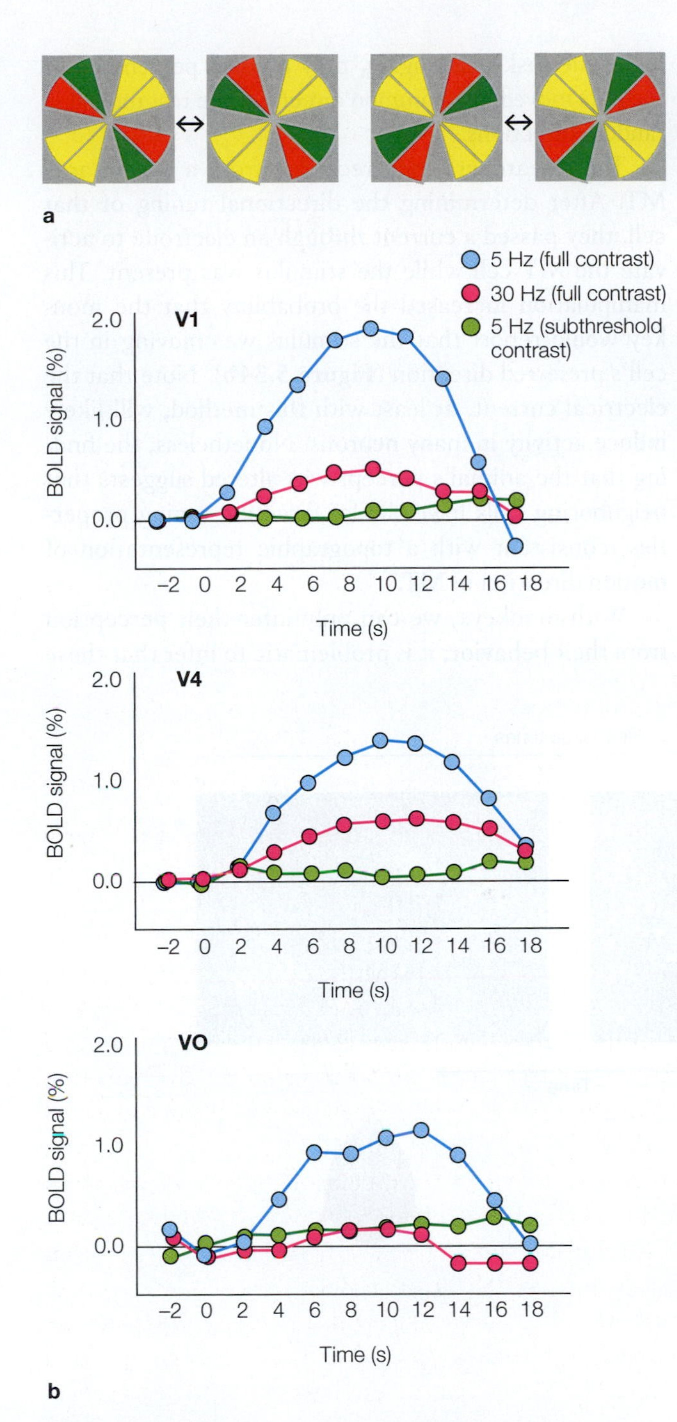

FIGURE 5.32 Imaging the neural correlates of perception. (a) Flickering pinwheel stimulus for studying limits of temporal resolution. The left and right stimuli alternated at different rates or contrast. (b) BOLD response to the flickering stimuli in three visual areas: V1, V4, and VO. The activation profile in VO matched the participants' perceptual experience because the color changes in the stimulus were invisible at the high 30-Hz rate or when the contrast was below threshold. In contrast, the activation profiles in V1 and V4 were correlated with the actual stimulus when the contrast was above threshold.

the 5-Hz nonflickering control. In contrast, the BOLD response within VO, a visual area just adjacent to V4, did not differentiate between the high-flicker stimulus and the static control stimulus (Figure 5.32). We can conclude that the illusion—a yellowish object that is not flickering—is formed in this higher visual area (known variously as either VO or V8), indicating that although the information is sensed accurately at earlier stages within the visual stream, conscious perception, at least of color, is more closely linked to higher-area activity.

A related study used fMRI to detect the neural fingerprints of unconscious "perception" (Haynes & Rees, 2005). Participants were shown a stimulus under one of two conditions: either for a 20th of a second, or for a 30th of a second but preceded and followed by a mask of crosshatched lines. The participants were to decide which of two ways the stimulus was oriented. In the first condition people responded with a high degree of accuracy, but in the second condition performance dropped to chance levels. Nonetheless, by using a sophisticated pattern recognition algorithm on the fMRI data from the second condition, the researchers were able to show that activity in V1 could distinguish which stimulus had been presented—an effect that was lost in V2 and V3.

As the preceding examples indicate, our primary sensory regions provide a representation that is closely linked to the physical stimulus, and our perceptual experience depends more on activity in secondary and association sensory regions. Note, though, that the examples base this argument on the fact that the absence of a perceptual experience was matched by the absence of detectable activity in secondary regions.

We can also consider the flip side of the coin and ask which brain regions show activation patterns that *are* correlated with illusory percepts. Stare at the Enigma pattern in **Figure 5.33**. After a few seconds, you should begin to see scintillating motion within the blue

FIGURE 5.33 The Enigma pattern: a visual illusion. When viewing the Enigma pattern, we perceive illusory motion. Viewing the pattern is accompanied by activation in area MT.

circles—an illusion created by their opposed orientation to the radial black and white lines. Both PET and fMRI have been used to show that viewing displays like the Enigma pattern does indeed lead to pronounced activity in V5, the visual area sensitive to motion. This activation is selective: Activity in V1 does not increase during illusory motion. (To try out more fascinating illusions, go to www.michaelbach.de/ot.)

An even stronger case for the hypothesis that perception is more closely linked to secondary sensory areas would require evidence showing that activity in these areas can be sufficient, and even predictive, of perception. Michael Shadlen and his colleagues (Ditterich et al., 2003) used a reverse engineering strategy to manipulate activation patterns in sensory cortex to test this idea. They trained monkeys to watch a screen with moving dots and then to move their eyes to indicate the perceived direction of a patch of dots (**Figure 5.34a**). To make the task challenging, only a small percentage of the dots moved in a common direction; the rest moved in random directions.

The researchers then recorded from a cell in area MT. After determining the directional tuning of that cell, they passed a current through an electrode to activate the MT cell while the stimulus was present. This manipulation increased the probability that the monkey would report that the stimulus was moving in the cell's preferred direction (**Figure 5.34b**). Note that the electrical current, at least with this method, will likely induce activity in many neurons. Nonetheless, the finding that the animal's percept was altered suggests that neighboring cells have similar direction-tuning properties, consistent with a topographic representation of motion direction in MT.

With monkeys, we can only infer their perception from their behavior; it is problematic to infer that these

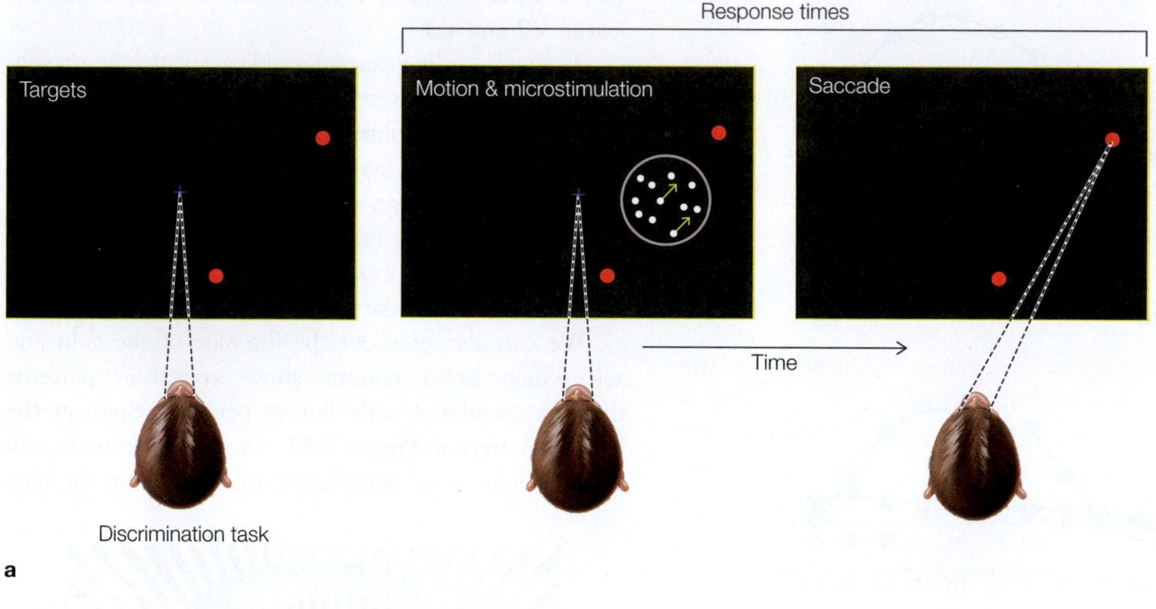

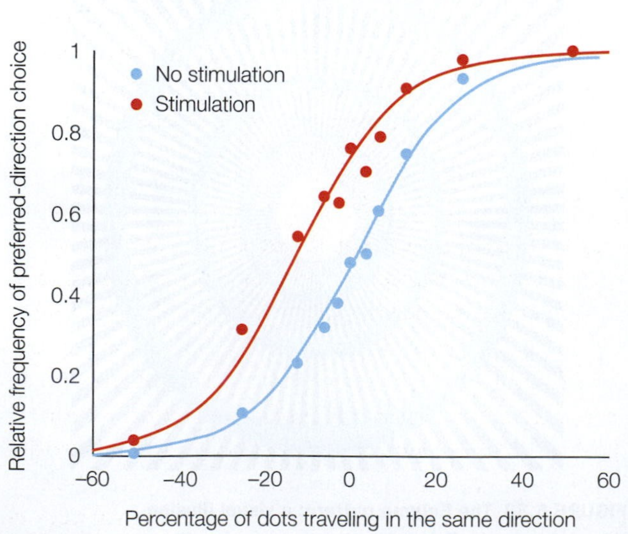

FIGURE 5.34 Activation of MT neurons influences the perceived direction of motion.
(a) Trial sequence. Two red dots indicate possible directions of motion (up and to the right, or downward). In 50% of the trials, electrical stimulation was briefly applied in area MT when the stimulus was presented. The stimulation was directed at neurons with a known preferred direction. After the stimulus, the monkey looked at one of the two red dots to indicate the perceived direction of motion. **(b)** When the stimulus was present, the monkey was more likely to respond that the direction of motion was in the preferred direction of the electrically stimulated cells. The *x*-axis represents the strength of the motion signal, indicating the percentage of dots traveling in the same direction. Zero percent signifies random motion, negative values signify motion opposite to the cell's preferred direction, and positive values signify motion in the cell's preferred direction.

percepts correspond to conscious experience. Similar stimulation methods have been used on rare occasions in humans during surgical procedures. In one such procedure (Murphey et al., 2008), electrodes were positioned along the ventral regions of visual cortex that include at least two areas known to be involved with color processing: the posterior center in the lingual gyrus of the occipital lobe (V4) and the anterior center in the medial fusiform gyrus of the temporal lobe (V4a).

When used as recording devices, electrodes in either area responded in a selective manner to chromatic stimuli. For example, the activity at one location was stronger in response to one color as compared to another color. Even more interesting is what happened when the electrodes were used as stimulating devices. In the anterior color region, stimulation led to the patient's reporting seeing a colored, amorphous shape. Moreover, the color of the illusion was similar to the preferred color for that site. Thus, in this higher visual area, there was a close correspondence between the perception of a color when it was elicited by a visual stimulus and its perception when the cortex was electrically stimulated.

FIGURE 5.35 People with achromatopsia see the world as devoid of color.
Because color differences are usually correlated with brightness differences, the objects in a scene might be distinguishable and appear as different shades of gray. This image shows how the world might look to a person with hemiachromatopsia. Most people who are affected have some residual color perception, although they cannot distinguish subtle color variations.

Deficits in Visual Perception

Before the advent of neuroimaging, much of what we learned about processing in the human brain came from the study of patients with lesions, including those with disorders of perception. In 1888, Louis Verrey (cited in Zeki, 1993a) described a patient who, after suffering a stroke, had lost the ability to perceive colors in her right visual field. Verrey reported that while the patient had problems with acuity within restricted portions of this right visual field, the color deficit was uniform and complete. After his patient's death, Verrey performed an autopsy. What he found led him to conclude that there was a "centre for the chromatic sense" (Zeki, 1993a) in the human brain, which he located in the lingual and fusiform gyri. We can guess that this patient's world looked similar to what **Figure 5.35** shows: On one side of space the world was multicolored; on the other it was a montage of grays.

DEFICITS IN COLOR PERCEPTION: ACHROMATOPSIA

When we speak of someone who is color-blind, we are usually describing a person who has inherited a gene that produces an abnormality in the photoreceptor system. *Dichromats*, people with only two photopigments, can be classified as red–green color-blind if they are missing the photopigment sensitive to either medium or long wavelengths, or blue–yellow color-blind if they are missing the short-wavelength photopigment. *Anomalous trichromats*, in contrast, have all three photopigments, but one of the pigments exhibits abnormal sensitivity. The incidence of these genetic disorders is high in males: about 8% of the population. The incidence in females is less than 1%.

Much rarer are disorders of color perception that arise from disturbances of the central nervous system. These disorders are called **achromatopsia** (from the prefix *a-*, "without," and the stem *chroma*, "hue"). J. C. Meadows of the National Hospital for Neurology and Neurosurgery in London described one such patient as follows:

> Everything looked black or grey [like the left side of Figure 5.35]. He had difficulty distinguishing British postage stamps of different value, which look alike, but are of different colors. He was a keen gardener, but found that he pruned live rather than dead vines. He had difficulty distinguishing certain foods on his plate where color was the distinguishing mark. (Meadows, 1974, p. 629)

Although lesions producing achromatopsia are typically relatively large, the pathology consistently tends to encompass V4 and the region anterior to V4. Individuals with these disorders are able to see and recognize objects; color is not a necessary cue for shape perception. Indeed, the subtlety of color perception is underscored when we consider that some people do not notice the change from black and white to color when Dorothy lands in Oz in the movie *The Wizard of Oz*. Nonetheless, when lost forever, the ability to detect this subtlety is sorely missed.

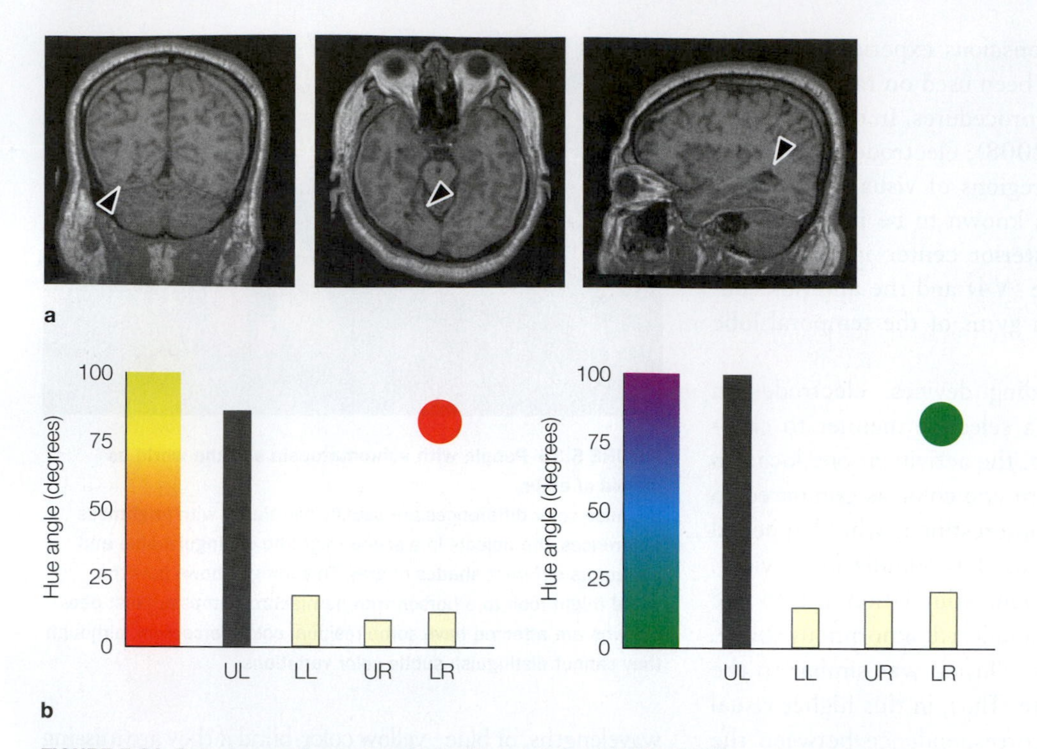

FIGURE 5.36 Color perception in a patient with a unilateral lesion of V4.
(a) MRI scans showing a small lesion (arrowheads) encompassing V4 in the right hemisphere. (b) Color perception thresholds in each visual quadrant (UL = upper left; LL = lower left; UR = upper right; LR = lower right). The patient was severely impaired on the hue-matching task when the test color was presented to the upper-left visual field. The *y*-axis indicates the color required to detect a difference between a patch shown in each visual quadrant and the target color shown at the fovea. The target color was red for the results shown on the left and green for the results shown on the right. *Hue angle* refers to the color wheel and is the number of degrees between the actual color and the first color recognized as a different hue.

Despite their relatively good visual recognition, achromatopsia patients are likely to have some impairments in their ability to perceive shape, given that color-sensitive neurons show tuning for other properties as well, such as orientation. Consider a case study of a patient who suffered a stroke resulting in a small lesion near the temporo-occipital border in the *right* hemisphere. The damage was centered in area V4 and anterior parts of the visual cortex (**Figure 5.36a**; Gallant et al., 2000).

To assess the patient's achromatopsia, a hue-matching experiment was performed in which a sample color was presented at the fovea, followed by a test color in one of the four quadrants of space. The patient's task was to judge whether the two colors were the same. Regardless of the sample hue, the patient was severely impaired on the hue-matching task when the test color was presented in the *upper left* visual field (**Figure 5.36b**). The fact that the deficit was found only in the upper *contralesional* visual field is consistent with previous reports of achromatopsia.

The next order of business was to examine shape perception. Would the patient show similar deficits in shape perception in the same quadrant? If so, what types of shape perception tasks would reveal the impairment? To answer these questions, a variety of tasks were administered. The stimuli are shown in **Figure 5.37.** On the basic visual discriminations of contrast, orientation, and motion (Figure 5.37a-c), the patient's performance was similar in all four quadrants and comparable to the performance of control participants. He showed impairment on tests of higher-order shape perception, however (Figure 5.37d, e); and again, this impairment was restricted to the upper-left quadrant. For these tasks, shape assessment requires combining information from neurons that might detect simple properties such as line orientation. For example, the orientation of the line separating the two semicircles (Figure 5.37d) is defined only by the combination of the lengths of the individual stripes and their offset.

Characterizing area V4 as a "color" area is too simplistic. This area is part of secondary visual areas devoted to shape perception. Color can provide an important cue about an object's shape. V4 may be invaluable for using color information as one cue to define the boundaries separating the objects that form our visual environment.

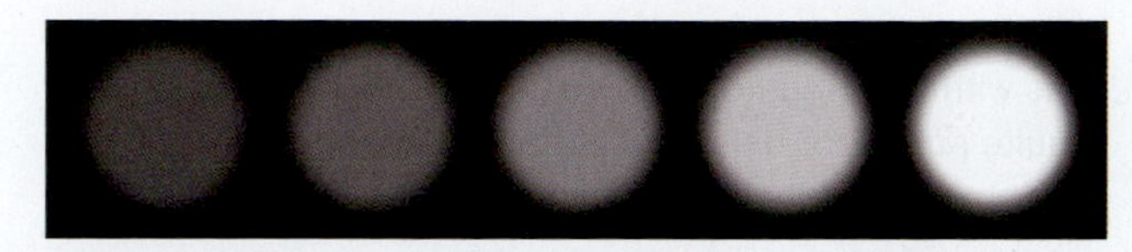

a Luminance

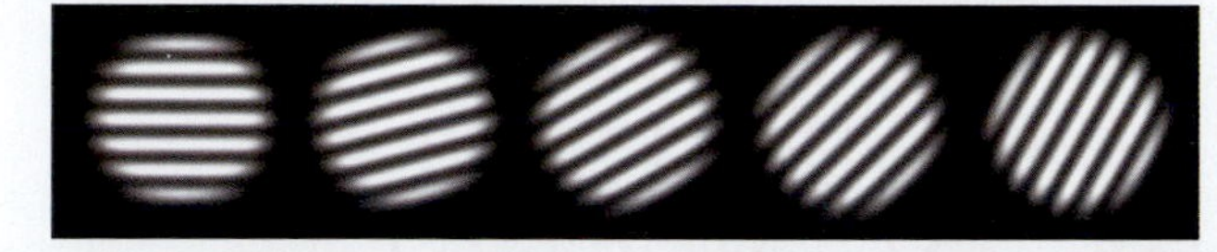

b Orientation

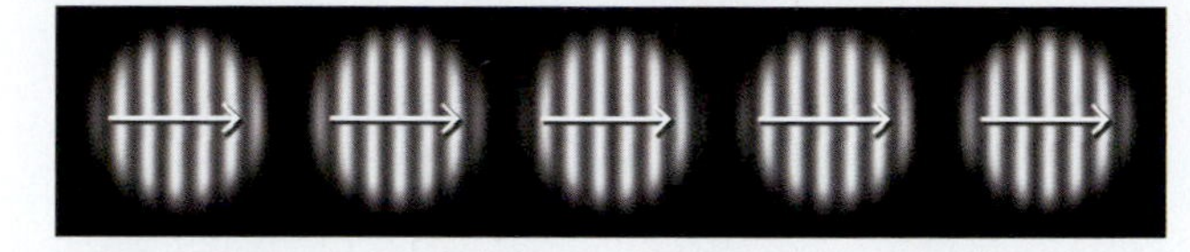

c Motion

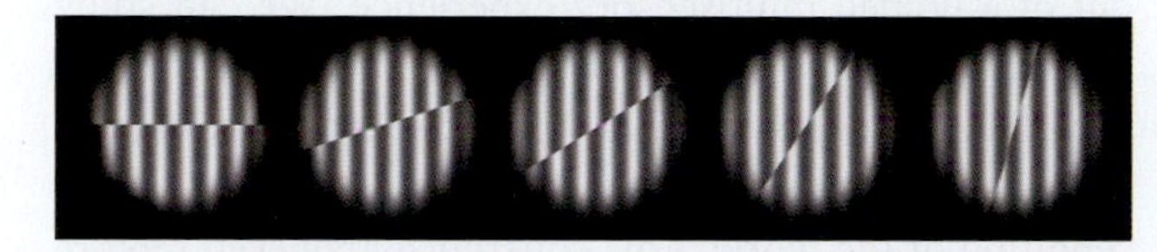

d Illusory contours

e Complex shapes

FIGURE 5.37 Tests of form perception.
Stimuli used to assess form perception in the patient with damage to area V4 illustrated in Figure 5.36. On basic tests of luminance (a), orientation (b), and motion (c), the patient's perceptual threshold was similar in all four quadrants. Thresholds for illusory contours (d) and complex shapes (e) were elevated in the upper-left quadrant.

Revisiting patient P.T. Let's return to patient P.T. from the beginning of the chapter. Recall that he had difficulty recognizing familiar places and objects. Further examination revealed some puzzling features of his perceptual deficits. He was shown the two paintings pictured in **Figure 5.38** and was asked to describe them. With the Monet he looked puzzled, declaring that he saw no definable forms, just an abstract blend of colors and shapes, similar to the deficits he experienced at home. Yet when he was shown the Picasso, he readily identified the figure in the painting as a woman or young girl.

This dissociation is compelling, for most people would readily agree that the Monet is more realistic. While Monet painted gradual changes in contrast and color, Picasso painted the parts of his work as separate units, with sharp contrasts in brightness and vivid colors. P.T.'s neurologist thought P.T.'s deficit was one of color perception, which accounted for one of the primary differences between the paintings. In the Monet painting, gradual variations in color demarcate the facial regions and separate them from the background landscape. A deficit in color perception provided a parsimonious account of the patient's problems in recognizing faces and landscapes: The rolling green hills of an Oregon farm can blur into a homogeneous mass if fine variations in color cannot be discerned. In a similar way, each face has its characteristic coloration.

DEFICITS IN MOTION PERCEPTION: AKINETOPSIA

In 1983, researchers at the Max Planck Institute in Munich reported the striking case of patient M.P., who had incurred a selective loss of motion perception, or **akinetopsia** (Zihl et al., 1983). M.P.'s perception was

a

b

FIGURE 5.38 Two portraits.
(a) Detail from *Luncheon on the Grass*, painted in the 1860s by the French impressionist Claude Monet. (b) Pablo Picasso's *Weeping Woman*, painted in 1937 during his cubist period. © 2008 Estate of Pablo Picasso/Artists Right Society (ARS), New York.

akin to viewing the world as a series of snapshots. Rather than seeing things move continuously in space, she saw moving objects appear in one position and then another. When pouring a cup of tea, she saw the liquid frozen in the air, failed to notice the tea rising in her cup, and was surprised when it overflowed. The loss of motion perception also made M.P. hesitant about crossing the street. As she noted, "When I'm looking at the car first, it seems far away. But then, when I want to cross the road, suddenly the car is very near" (Zihl et al., 1983, p. 315).

CT scans of M.P. revealed large, bilateral lesions involving the temporoparietal cortices, including posterior and lateral portions of the middle temporal gyrus. These lesions roughly corresponded to areas that participate in motion perception. Furthermore, the lesions were lateral and superior to human V4, including the area identified as V5, the human equivalent of area MT. With unilateral lesions of V5, motion perception deficits are much more subtle (Plant et al., 1993). Motion, by definition, is a dynamic percept, one that typically unfolds over an extended period of time. With longer viewing times, signals from early visual areas in the impaired hemisphere have an opportunity to reach secondary visual areas in the unimpaired hemisphere.

Still, the application of transcranial magnetic stimulation (TMS; see Chapter 3) over human V5 of one hemisphere can produce transient deficits in motion perception. In one such experiment, participants were asked to judge whether a stimulus moved up or down (Stevens et al., 2009). To make the task demanding, the displays consisted of a patch of dots, only some of which moved in the target direction; the rest moved in random directions. Moreover, the target was preceded and followed by "masking" stimuli in which all of the dots moved in random directions. Thus, the stimulus direction was visible during only a brief (100-ms) window. TMS was applied over either V5 or a control region, the motor cortex. Performance of the motion task was disrupted when the stimulation was applied over V5, creating a transient form of akinetopsia.

TAKE-HOME MESSAGES

- Our percepts are more closely related to activity in higher visual areas than to activity in the primary visual cortex.
- Lesions to areas in and around human V4 can result in achromatopsia, the inability to perceive color, and deficits in shape perception. Color is one attribute that facilitates the perception of shape.
- *Akinetopsia* refers to impairments in the ability to process motion. The impairment can be very dramatic if V5 is damaged in both the left and right hemispheres. As with many neurological conditions, the deficit can be quite subtle for unilateral lesions.

5.8 Multimodal Perception: I See What You're Sayin'

Each of our senses gives us unique information about the world we live in. Color is a visual experience; pitch is uniquely auditory. Even though the information provided by each sense is distinct, the resulting representation of the surrounding world is not one of disjointed sensations, but of a unified multisensory experience. We can study our sensory systems in isolation, but perception is really a synthetic process—one in which the organism uses all available information to converge on a coherent representation of the world. This coherence may even require that our perceptual system distort or modify the actual sensory input.

A particularly powerful demonstration of this distortion comes from the world of speech perception. Most people think of speech as an inherently auditory process: We decipher the sounds of language to identify phonemes, combining them into words, sentences, and phrases (see Chapter 11). However, the sounds we hear can be influenced by visual cues. This is made clear in a compelling illusion, the McGurk effect, in which the perception of speech—what you believe that you "hear"—is influenced by the lip movements that your eyes see. For example, when listening to a person say "fa" but watching a video of someone saying "ba," the percept clearly goes with the visual signal. (See a compelling example of this visual–auditory illusion at www.youtube.com/watch?v=G-lN8vWm3m0.)

Illusions work because they take advantage of correlations that are generally present between the senses in day-to-day life. The gestures of a speaker's lips normally conform to the sounds we hear. It is only through the illusion that the processing can be teased apart and we realize that information from different sensory systems has been integrated in our brain.

How Does Multimodal Processing Happen?

How does the brain integrate information from the different senses to form a coherent percept? An older view was that some senses dominated others. In particular, vision was thought to dominate all of the other senses. An alternative is that, in combining input from multiple sensory systems about a particular external property (e.g., the location of a sound or touch), the brain gives greater weight to the signals assumed to be the most reliable. In this view, visual capture occurs because the brain usually judges visual information to be the most reliable and thus gives it the most weight.

In the McGurk example, the visual input may be deemed more reliable because /b/ sounds always require that the lips come together, whereas the lips remain apart when articulating /f/ sounds. The weighting idea captures the idea that the system is flexible, with the context leading to changes in how information is weighed. When walking in the woods at dusk, we give more emphasis to somatosensory and auditory information as we step gingerly to avoid roots or listen carefully for breaking twigs that might signal that we've wandered off the path. In this case, the ambient light, or lack of it, favors the other senses.

The usual cast of questions pops up when we explore how the processing from different senses is integrated: Where is information from different sensory systems integrated in the brain? Is it early or late in processing? What pathways are involved?

Where Does Multimodal Processing Happen?

As discussed in Chapter 2, brain regions containing neurons that respond to more than one sense are described as multisensory or multimodal. Multisensory integration (N. P. Holmes & Spence, 2005) occurs at many different regions in the brain, both subcortically and cortically. Let's look at some of the studies that have explored this question.

In animal studies, neurophysiological methods have been especially useful: Once an electrode has been placed in a targeted brain region, the animal can be presented with a range of stimuli to see whether, and by what, the region is activated. For instance, when exploring visual responses, the researcher might vary the position of the stimulus, its color, or its movement. To evaluate multisensory processing, the researcher can present stimuli along different sensory channels, asking not only whether the cell responds to more than one sense, but also about the relationship between the responses to stimuli from different senses.

One well-studied multimodal site is the superior colliculus, the subcortical midbrain region involved with eye movements. The superior colliculus contains orderly topographic maps of the environment in visual, auditory, and even tactile domains. Many cells in the superior colliculus show multisensory properties, being activated by inputs from more than one sensory modality. These neurons combine and integrate information from different sensory channels. In fact, the response of the cell is stronger when there are inputs from multiple senses compared to when the input comes from a single modality (B. E. Stein et al., 2004).

Such enhanced responses are most effective when a unimodal stimulus fails to produce a response on its own. In this way the combination of weak, even subthreshold, unimodal signals can be detected and cause participants to orient toward the stimulus. Multisensory signals are treated by the brain as more reliable than signals from a single sensory channel. A rustling sound in the grass could indicate the presence of a snake or just the rising evening breeze. But if that sound is combined with a glimmer of animal movement, you can bet the brain will generate a fast-response eye movement to verify the presence of a snake.

Integration effects require that *the different stimuli be coincident in both space and time*. For example, if a flash of light, a visual event, is spatially and temporally synchronous with two beeps, the resulting multisensory response will be enhanced; in fact, participants perceive the light as having flashed twice (Shams, 2000). In this illusion, known as auditory driving, the stimulation of one sense (audition) appears to affect judgment about a property typically associated with a different sense (vision). Specifically, the auditory beeps create a context of two events, a feature that the brain then applies to the light, creating a coherent percept. If, however, the sound originates from a different location than the light, or is not temporally synchronized with the light, then the response of the collicular cell will be lower than if either stimulus were presented alone. Such effects again demonstrate how the brain weights information in terms of its reliability. In the natural world, we have learned that visual and auditory cues are usually closely synchronized; for example, we know that a distant visual event, such as a flash of lightning, will be followed by a crack of thunder.

Multisensory activity is also observed in many cortical regions. The superior temporal sulcus (STS) is known to have connections both coming from and going to the various sensory cortices. Neurophysiologists have identified cells in the STS of monkeys that respond to visual, auditory, and somatosensory stimuli (K. Hikosaka et al., 1988). Functional MRI has also been used to identify multisensory areas of the human cortex. For example, the STS in the left hemisphere is active when people are actively engaged in lip-reading (something that we unconsciously use during normal

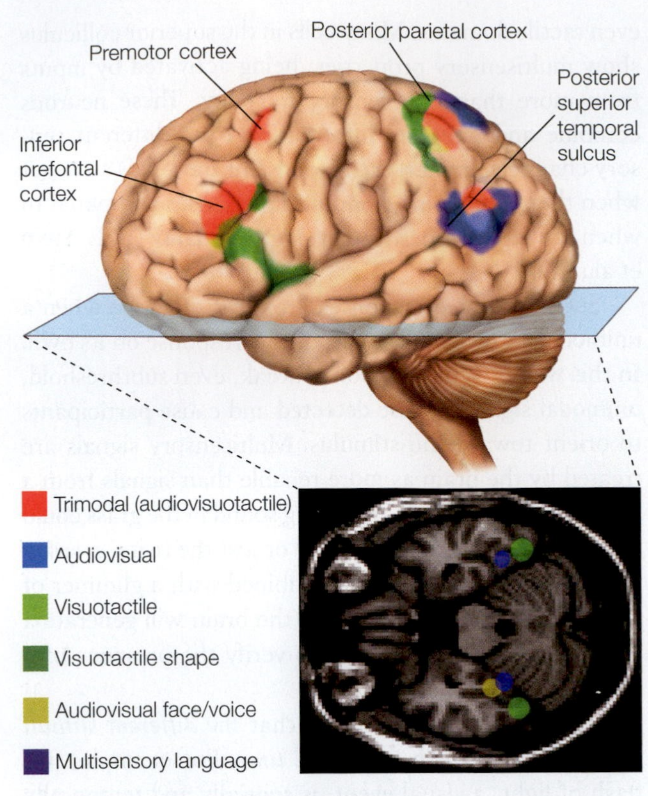

FIGURE 5.39 Multisensory regions of the cerebral cortex. Areas of the left hemisphere that show increased BOLD response when comparing responses to unisensory and multisensory stimulation. A similar picture is evident in the right hemisphere.

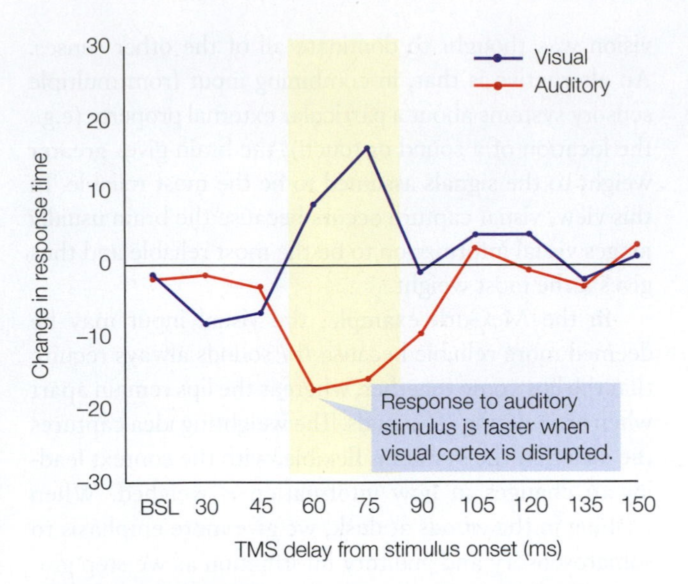

FIGURE 5.40 Interactions of visual and auditory information. Response time to an auditory stimulus is faster when the visual cortex is disrupted. Participants responded as quickly as possible to a visual or auditory stimulus. A single TMS pulse was applied over the occipital lobe at varying delays after stimulus onset (*x*-axis). The *y*-axis shows the change in response time for the different conditions. Responses to the visual stimulus were slower (positive numbers) in the shaded area, presumably because the TMS pulse made it harder to perceive the stimulus. Interestingly, responses to auditory stimuli were faster (negative numbers) during this same period. BSL = baseline before TMS.

speech comprehension), but not when the sounds are mismatched to the lip movements (Calvert et al., 1997).

Other brain regions showing similar sensory integration effects include various regions of the parietal and frontal lobes, as well as the hippocampus (**Figure 5.39**). With careful study, we can even see multisensory effects in areas that are traditionally thought to be sensory specific. For example, the very early visual component of the ERP wave is enhanced when the visual stimulus is presented close in space to a corresponding tactile stimulus (Kennett et al., 2001).

Vincenzo Romei and his colleagues at the University of Geneva (2007) have sought to understand how early sensory areas might interact to support multisensory integration. Participants in one of their studies were required to press a button as soon as they detected a stimulus. The stimulus could be a light, a sound, or both. To disrupt visual processing, the researchers applied a TMS pulse over the visual cortex just after the stimulus onset. As expected, the response to the visual stimulus was slower on trials in which the TMS pulse was applied compared to trials without TMS. But surprisingly, the response to the auditory stimulus was faster after TMS over the visual cortex (**Figure 5.40**).

Why might disruption of the visual cortex improve a person's ability to detect a sound? One possibility is that the two sensory systems are in competition with each other. Thus, TMS of the visual cortex handicaps a competitor of the auditory cortex. Alternatively, neurons in visual cortex that are activated by the TMS pulse might produce signals that are sent to the auditory cortex (as part of a multisensory processing pathway), and in this way enhance auditory cortex activity and produce faster responses to the sounds.

Romei came up with a clever way to evaluate these two hypotheses by looking at the reverse situation, asking whether an auditory stimulus could enhance visual perception. When TMS is applied over visual cortex, people report seeing phosphenes—illusory flashes of light. Romei first determined the intensity level of TMS required to produce phosphenes for each person. He then randomly stimulated the participants at a level that was a bit below the threshold in one of two conditions: alone or concurrently with an auditory stimulus. At this subthreshold level, the participants perceived phosphenes when the auditory stimulus was present, but not when the TMS pulse was presented alone. This finding supports the hypothesis that auditory and visual stimuli can enhance perception in the other sensory modality.

Errors in Multimodal Processing: Synesthesia

J.W. experiences the world differently from most people. He tastes words. The word *exactly*, for example, tastes like yogurt, and the word *accept* tastes like eggs. Most conversations are pleasant tasting, but when J.W. is tending bar, he cringes whenever Derek, a frequent customer, shows up. For J.W., the word *Derek* tastes of earwax!

This phenomenon, in which the senses are mixed, is known as **synesthesia** (from the Greek *syn-*, "union" or "together," and *aesthesis*, "sensation"). Synesthesia is characterized by an idiosyncratic union between (or within) sensory modalities. Tasting words is an extremely rare form of synesthesia. More common are synesthesias in which people hear words or music as colors, or see achromatic lettering (as in books or newspapers) as colored.

The frequency of synesthesia is hard to know, given that many individuals are unaware that their multisensory percepts are odd: Estimates range from as low as one in 2,000 to as high as one in 200. Synesthesia tends to recur in families, indicating that at least some forms have a genetic basis (Baron-Cohen et al., 1996; Smilek et al., 2005). If you think you may experience some form of synesthesia, you can find out by taking the tests at the Synesthesia Battery website (www.synesthete.org).

Colored-grapheme synesthesia, in which black or white letters or digits are perceived in assorted colors, is the most common and best-studied form of synesthesia. A synesthete might report "seeing" the letter *A* as red, the letter *B* as blue, and so forth for the entire set of characters (**Figure 5.41**). The appearance of color is a feature of many forms of synesthesia. In colored hearing, colors are experienced for spoken words or for sounds like musical notes. Colored touch and colored smell have also been reported. Much less common are synesthetic experiences that involve other senses. J.W. experiences taste with words; other rare cases have been reported in which touching an object induces specific tastes.

FIGURE 5.41 Colored-grapheme synesthesia.
This artistic rendition of the color-letter and color-number associations for one individual with synesthesia.

The associations are idiosyncratic for each synesthete. One person might see the letter *B* as red; another person might see it as green. Although the synesthetic associations are not consistent across individuals, they are consistent over time for an individual. A synesthete who reports the letter *B* as red when tested the first time in the lab will have the same percept if retested a few months later.

Given that synesthesia is such a personal experience, researchers have had to come up with clever methods to verify and explore this unique phenomenon. One approach with colored-grapheme synesthesia is to create modified versions of the Stroop task. As described in Chapter 3 (see Figure 3.4), the Stroop task requires a person to name the color of written words. For instance, if the word *green* is written in red ink, the participant is supposed to say "red."

In the synesthetic variant of the Stroop task with a colored-grapheme synesthete, the stimuli are letters, and the key manipulation is whether the colors of the letters are congruent or incongruent to the individual's synesthetic palette. For the example in Figure 5.41, when the letter *A* is presented in red, the physical color and synesthetic color are congruent. However, if the *A* is presented in green, the physical and synesthetic colors are incongruent. Synesthetes are faster to name the color of the letter when the physical color matches the synesthetic color for that letter (Mattingley et al., 2001). People without synesthesia, of course, do not show this effect. To them, any color–letter pairing is equally acceptable.

Synesthesia is generally believed to be the result of aberrant cross-activation of one cortical area by another. However, whether it is caused by extra structural connections between sensory regions that are not present in nonsynesthetes, or is the result of functional differences such as less inhibition of normal connections creating hypersensitive activity, is a matter of debate. Pursuing the notion that synesthesia results from hyperactive sensory systems, researchers in one study investigated whether a core property of synesthesia was enhanced perceptual processing (Banissy et al., 2009). That is, if you are a colored-grapheme synesthete, are you better at color discrimination than someone who is not?

The investigators compared the tactile and color sensitivity of four groups: individuals with color synesthesia, individuals with touch synesthesia, those who experienced both touch and color synesthesia, and controls with no form of synesthesia. They found that within the domains where individuals experience synesthesia, their sensory abilities are enhanced: Compared to controls, colored-grapheme synesthetes are better at color discrimination (even if not with letters), and touch synesthetes are better at tactile discrimination tasks.

Neuroimaging studies indicate that the multisensory experience of synesthesia arises and is manifest at various stages along the visual pathway. Jeffrey Gray at King's College in London performed an fMRI study with a group of individuals who had colored-hearing synesthesia (Nunn et al., 2002). When listening to words, these individuals reported seeing specific colors; when listening to tones, they had no visual experience. Compared to control participants, the synesthetes showed increased activation in regions around V4 (similar to what we have seen in other studies of illusory color perception) and in the STS (one of the brain regions associated with multimodal perception).

One puzzle, however, was that synesthetes' activation profiles for real colors (e.g., a letter printed in blue ink) and synesthetic colors (e.g., an achromatic letter that a synesthete saw as blue) overlapped very little. Achromatic stimuli that elicited synesthetic percepts instead produced broader activation of visual cortex compared to the responses that the same achromatic stimuli produced in nonsynesthetes.

Jean-Michel Hupé and his colleagues (2011) performed a more detailed fMRI study. Using colored stimuli, they identified regions of interest (ROIs) on an individual basis. Surprisingly, when perceiving synesthetic colors, the synesthetes did not show activation increases in the ROIs, or in fact in V4. The researchers also looked for structural differences between the synesthetes and controls. While measures of white and gray matter volume in color regions of the visual cortex were similar in the two groups, the synesthetes showed more white matter in the retrosplenial cortex, an area not typically associated with color processing. These results suggest that the abnormal mixing of visual dimensions may be distributed, rather than localized in the visual cortex.

Other researchers have looked for anatomical markers of synesthesia. Using diffusion tensor imaging (DTI), Romke Rouw and Steven Scholte (2007) at the University of Amsterdam showed that colored-grapheme synesthetes have greater anisotropic diffusion, a marker of larger white matter tracts, in the right inferior temporal cortex, the left parietal cortex, and bilaterally in the frontal cortex (red regions in **Figure 5.42**). Moreover, the researchers found that individual differences in the amount of connectivity in the inferior temporal cortex differentiated subtypes of synesthetes. Participants who saw color in the outside world (known as "projectors") had greater connectivity in the inferior temporal cortex compared with those who saw color in their "mind's eye" only (known as "associators"). Needless to say, no consensus has been reached on any neural basis for this phenomenon.

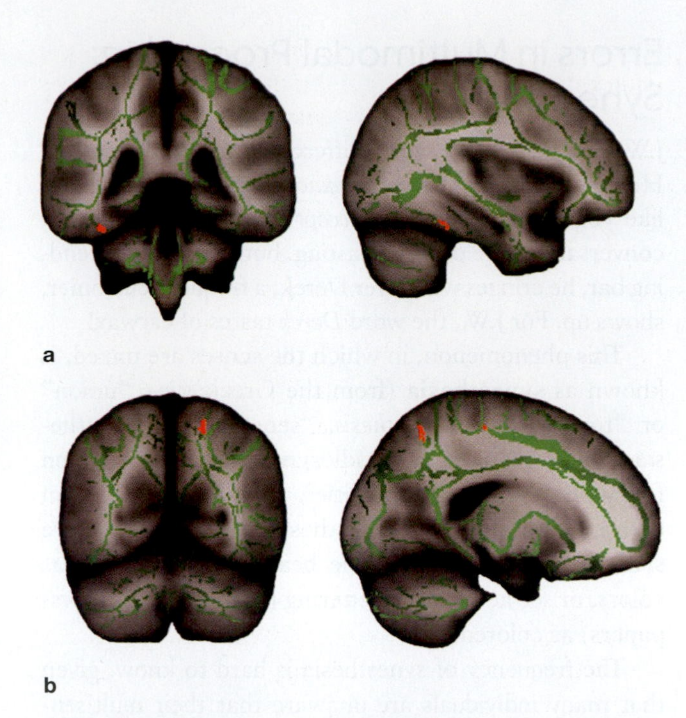

FIGURE 5.42 Stronger white matter connectivity in synesthetes. Green indicates white matter tracts identified with DTI in all participants. Red regions in the right inferior temporal cortex **(a)** and left parietal cortex **(b)** show areas where the fractional anisotropy value is higher in synesthetes compared to controls.

TAKE-HOME MESSAGES

- Some areas of the brain, such as the superior colliculus and superior temporal sulcus, process information from more than one sensory modality, integrating the multimodal information to increase perceptual sensitivity and accuracy.
- People with synesthesia experience a mixing of the senses—for example, colored hearing, colored graphemes, or colored taste.
- Synesthesia is associated with both abnormal activation patterns in functional imaging studies and abnormal patterns of connectivity in structural imaging studies.

5.9 Perceptual Reorganization

In 1949, Donald Hebb bucked the assumption that the brain was unchangeable after the early formative years. He suggested a theoretical framework for how functional reorganization, or what neuroscientists refer to as

cortical plasticity, might occur in the brain through the remodeling of neuronal connections. Since then, more people have been looking for and observing brain plasticity in action. For example, Michael Merzenich (Merzenich & Jenkins, 1995; Merzenich et al., 1988) at UC San Francisco and Jon Kaas (1995) at Vanderbilt University discovered that experience could alter the size and shape of cortical sensory and motor maps in adult monkeys.

After the researchers severed (deafferented) the nerve fibers from a monkey's finger to its spinal cord, the relevant part of its cortex no longer responded at first when that finger was touched; however, that cortical area soon became active again: It began to respond to stimulation of the finger adjacent to the amputated finger. The surrounding cortical area had filled in and taken over the silent area. The researchers found similar changes when a particular finger was given extended sensory stimulation: It gained a little more acreage on the cortical map. This functional plasticity suggests that the adult cortex is a dynamic place where remarkable changes can still happen. In this section we take a look at changes in perceptual organization that can occur.

Development of Sensory Systems

Just as the prenatal brain develops on a time clock, so do the sensory systems. Primary sensory areas exhibit experience-induced plasticity during defined windows of early life, known as critical periods. The brain requires external inputs during these periods to establish an optimal neural representation of the surrounding environment. For example, at birth the visual system needs input from the environment to properly develop the thalamic connections to cortical layer IV of the primary visual cortex.

Again it was Hubel and Wiesel (1970, 1977) who first showed this in cats and monkeys. They sutured one eye shut during the first few weeks after a kitten was born (or the first few months after a monkey was born) and found that the cats and monkeys failed to develop normal ocular dominance columns in the primary visual cortex. Instead, the input to layer IV was limited to the seeing eye, and the cortical representation of this eye took over most of the sutured eye's cortex. This change was permanent. When the sutures were removed after a few weeks, no cortical changes occurred, no rewiring took place, and the animals remained blind for life in that eye. When the researchers sutured one eye in an adult animal for even longer periods of time, however, the effect was minimal when the sutures were removed.

Human infants have also demonstrated the importance of critical time periods for the input of visual stimuli. For example, babies who have limited or no visual input from an eye because of a cataract must have the cataract removed in the first few weeks of life to gain vision in that eye. If the cataract is removed after the critical period, the child will not regain sight in that eye, whereas in an adult, a cataract formed later in life can be present for years and yet sight will be regained after its removal. Or consider infants born with strabismus (a misalignment of the eyes): If left unchecked beyond the critical period, this condition will result in abnormal development of the visual cortex and functional blindness in one eye. Recent research has found that cellular mechanisms can trigger, mediate, slow, and reopen critical windows (Werker & Hensch, 2015).

Both circuit maturation and experience are also important in speech perception. Initially, development of the auditory cortex relies on genetically controlled intrinsic factors, but the refinement of cortical connections relies on feedback from auditory stimulation—that is, exposure to spoken language. Auditory stimulation or deprivation can significantly impact the development of cortical infrastructure and associated behavioral abilities. Congenitally deaf infants have a high risk for permanent language impairment, but hearing aids or cochlear implants implanted at an early enough age can enable many individuals to develop spoken language perception and production skills close to those of the hearing population.

Perceptual Reorganization Secondary to Early Sensory Loss

What happens in the brain when it doesn't receive input from one sensory system? Is the brain hardwired, resulting in large swaths of the cerebral cortex remaining nonfunctional? Or does the brain reorganize—and if so, does this reorganization occur in a systematic manner?

Blindness or highly impaired vision affects about 3% of the U.S. population. Some of these individuals are born without vision—a condition known as congenital blindness. Blindness at birth is generally caused by congenital defects of the eye, such as anophthalmia, microphthalmia, coloboma (a hole in one of the eye's structures, such as the retina), cataract, retinal dystrophies, infantile glaucoma, or cloudy cornea. Blindness may also result from some perinatal insults, such as eye infections contracted from viral or bacterial infections of the birth canal (herpes, gonorrhea, or chlamydia), or cortical deficits from oxygen deprivation during birth.

Other individuals lose their sight at some point during life, usually from degenerative diseases such as macular degeneration, diabetic retinopathy, or cataracts. The great majority of these conditions are problems within the eye—that is, in the peripheral sense organ. Extensive experiments have been conducted with highly visually impaired individuals, as well as nonhuman species, to explore plasticity within the sensory systems and how it changes as a function of the time at which the sensory loss occurs.

The results from an early PET study revealed a remarkable degree of functional reorganization in the visual cortex of congenitally blind individuals (Sadato et al., 1996). The participants in this study either had normal vision or were congenitally blind. They were scanned under two experimental conditions. In one condition, they were simply required to sweep their fingers back and forth over a rough surface covered with dots. In the second condition, they were given tactile discrimination tasks such as deciding whether two grooves in the surface were the same or different. Blood flow in the visual cortex during each of these tasks was compared to that during a control condition in which the participants were scanned while keeping their hands still.

Amazingly, the two groups experienced opposite changes in activation in the visual cortex. For the sighted participants, a significant *drop* in activation was found in the primary visual cortex during the tactile discrimination tasks. Visual tasks were accompanied by analogous decreases in the auditory or somatosensory cortex. Therefore, as attention was directed to one modality, activation (as measured by blood flow) decreased in other sensory systems. In blind participants, however, activation in the primary visual cortex *increased* during discrimination tasks, but only when they were actively using the tactile information. Interestingly, a second group of participants, who had become blind early in childhood (before their fifth year), also showed the same recruitment of visual cortex when performing the tactile discrimination task. Subsequent work has shown similar results in a task of great practical value to the blind: reading Braille (Sadato et al., 1998). Blind individuals show increased activation of the primary and secondary visual cortices during Braille reading.

The recruitment of "visual areas" in blind individuals is not limited to somatosensory stimuli. Using fMRI, Marina Bedny and her colleagues (2015) examined the hemodynamic response to a range of sounds both in blind individuals and in sighted individuals who were blindfolded. For the sighted individuals, these auditory stimuli resulted in a decrease in the BOLD response—an effect that was pronounced in different secondary visual areas (**Figure 5.43**). In contrast, the BOLD response tended to increase in the blind participants. Interestingly, the increase here was limited to lateral and medial occipital regions. Moreover, the magnitude of the BOLD response varied for different classes of stimuli, with the effect most pronounced when the

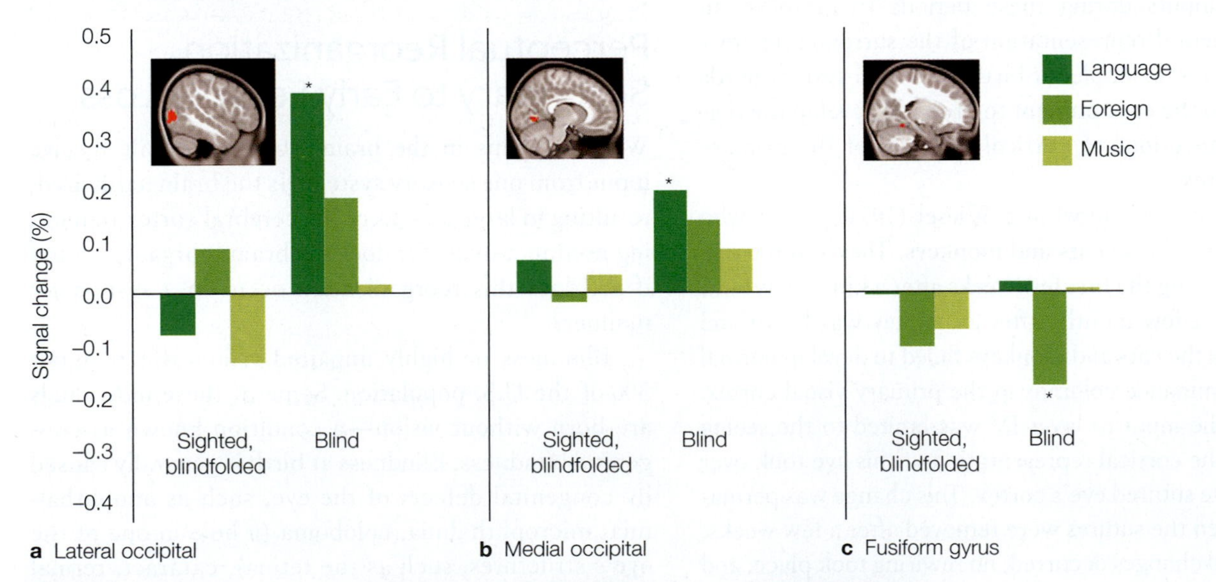

FIGURE 5.43 BOLD response of left occipital regions to language and to nonlinguistic sounds. In secondary visual areas—lateral occipital (a) and medial occipital (b)—the BOLD responses to an English-language story, a foreign-language story, and music were higher in blind individuals compared to blindfolded sighted individuals, although the effect was modest for music. This difference was not seen in the more ventral fusiform gyrus (c). Asterisks indicate when a particular condition is significantly different from the rest.

blind participants were listening to stories and minimal when the participants listened to music. Further analysis of these data suggests that the response to spoken language was not related to the participant's ability to use Braille.

The same lab then asked a more subtle question: Does the auditory recruitment of "visual areas" in blind individuals have some similarity to how the area responded to visual information in those with sight (Bedny et al., 2010)? Focusing on the medial temporal area MT/MST, which shows high sensitivity to visual motion in sighted individuals, they found that blind individuals showed a strong response in this area to dynamic auditory stimuli (i.e., auditory motion), such as the sound of footsteps. This effect was not observed in the sighted individuals: Here the BOLD response remained flat or even dropped when the auditory stimuli were presented.

However, in subsequent work using more sophisticated fMRI analyses, Lukas Strnad and his colleagues (2013) found that, even in sighted individuals, MT/MST contains information about dynamic auditory stimuli. These researchers performed multivoxel pattern analysis (MVPA), a method in which the pattern of activity across the voxels is used to classify the stimuli. As in the earlier study, only blind individuals showed an overall increase in the BOLD response in MT/MST to auditory motion. The interesting new finding was that with MVPA, information about the different auditory motion conditions could be observed in MT/MST (and not early visual cortex) in both blind and sighted individuals. These results suggest that neurons in MT/MST may be specialized in some way that makes them sensitive to dynamic information, regardless of whether that information is conveyed visually or through another modality.

Cortical reorganization appears to be a general phenomenon. Deaf individuals show activation to tactile and visual stimuli across Heschl's gyrus (Karns et al., 2012). One account of these large-scale changes in cortical representation is called *cross-modal plasticity*. When a sensory system is absent, inputs from a different sensory system may expand in terms of their cortical recruitment. This reorganization may be facilitated by connectivity patterns that exist between different sensory areas—a hypothesis that could also account for why an area such as MT/MST is sensitive to auditory motion information even in sighted individuals.

Consistent with the idea that the cortical representation of intact sensory systems is enhanced because of cross-modal plasticity, deaf individuals have been shown to have enhanced visual perception. This effect was evident in one study in which the participants (deaf signers, deaf nonsigners, and hearing signers) had to make a difficult discrimination at the center of vision and then detect a peripheral target among distractors. Deaf adults were significantly better at this task than sighted adults (Dye, Hauser, et al., 2009). A similar heightened visual acuity has been reported in deaf individuals for detecting visual motion (Shiell et al., 2014). This behavioral advantage was correlated with an increase in the volume of the right planum temporale, the region typically associated with auditory perception (Shiell et al., 2016).

Alternatively, the extensive plasticity observed when a sensory system is absent need not indicate that a region typically associated with one sensory system has now been taken over by a different sensory system. Instead, the recruitment of an area appears to be multimodal: In the congenitally blind, "visual areas" are recruited during tactile and auditory tasks; in the deaf, "auditory areas" are recruited during tactile and visual tasks. Bedny (2017) has raised the interesting hypothesis that reorganization within areas deprived of their natural input is best understood as an expansion of areas typically associated with more complex processing rather than linked to any particular sensory system.

Cortical Reorganization Over Shorter Time Spans

Much of the work on cortical reorganization has focused on individuals who have complete loss of one sensory system, usually audition or vision. The degree of reorganization in these populations is age dependent. For example, the BOLD response in MT/MST to auditory motion is much greater in individuals who were born without vision than in individuals who became blind during childhood. These studies are of great importance for understanding perception in individuals with sensory disabilities. A limitation here, at least for understanding the mechanisms and constraints on reorganization, is that the work is cross-sectional: The studies compare different groups of individuals at different time points, in terms either of age or of time elapsed since they incurred the sensory loss.

An alternative approach is to employ experimental manipulations that block or alter sensory information for a limited amount of time. Alvaro Pascual-Leone and his colleagues at Harvard Medical School (Merabet et al., 2008) studied cortical plasticity when *sighted* volunteers were deprived of visual information for 1 week. All of the study participants received intensive Braille training for

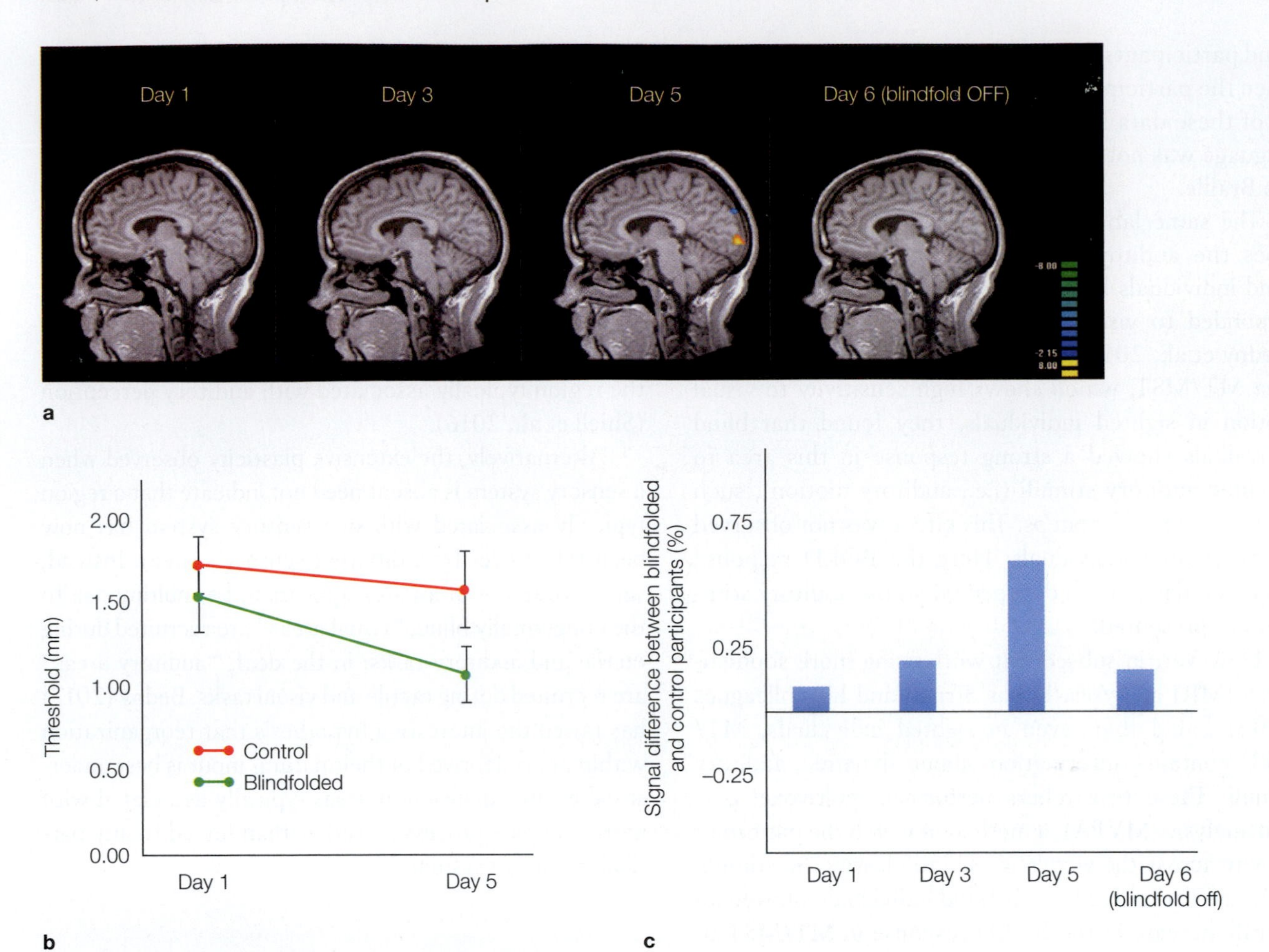

FIGURE 5.44 Perceptual and neural changes resulting from extended visual deprivation in sighted individuals.
(a) Functional MRI activation during tactile exploration. By Day 5, the blindfolded group showed greater activation than the controls in the occipital cortex. This effect disappeared after the blindfold was removed. (b) Performance on tactile acuity after 1 or 5 days of practice. Lower values correspond to better perceptual acuity. (c) Difference in occipital activation between blindfolded and control participants across days.

5 days (**Figure 5.44**). In one group, the participants were blindfolded for the entire week; participants in the control group did the same training but were not required to wear blindfolds.

At the end of training, the blindfolded participants were better at reading Braille, and their sensory advantage was also evident on other tactile discrimination tasks. Furthermore, at the end of training the blindfolded participants showed a BOLD response in visual cortex during tactile stimulation and disruptions in Braille reading when rTMS was applied over the visual cortex. Interestingly, these effects were relatively short-lived: Just one day after removing the blindfolds, the activation in visual cortex during tactile stimulation had disappeared (Figure 5.44a, c).

Paring down the time frame to an even shorter interval, another group of researchers examined the behavioral and neural consequences of altering somatosensory processing using a manipulation in which they glued together the index and middle fingers (Digits 2 and 3) of the participants' dominant hand (Kolasinski et al., 2016). After just 24 hours, the cortical representation of the fingers had altered. The most striking change was a shift in the cortical position of the ring finger away from the middle finger (**Figure 5.45**).

Paralleling these neural changes, the participants' tactile acuity also changed. The participants now were more accurate in judging the order in which tactile stimuli were applied to the middle and ring fingers, consistent with the idea that a consequence of the gluing was to make the representation of these two fingers more distinct. On the other hand (no pun intended), the participants had more difficulty judging the order of stimuli applied to the ring and pinky finger. These studies show that plastic changes occur over relatively short time frames.

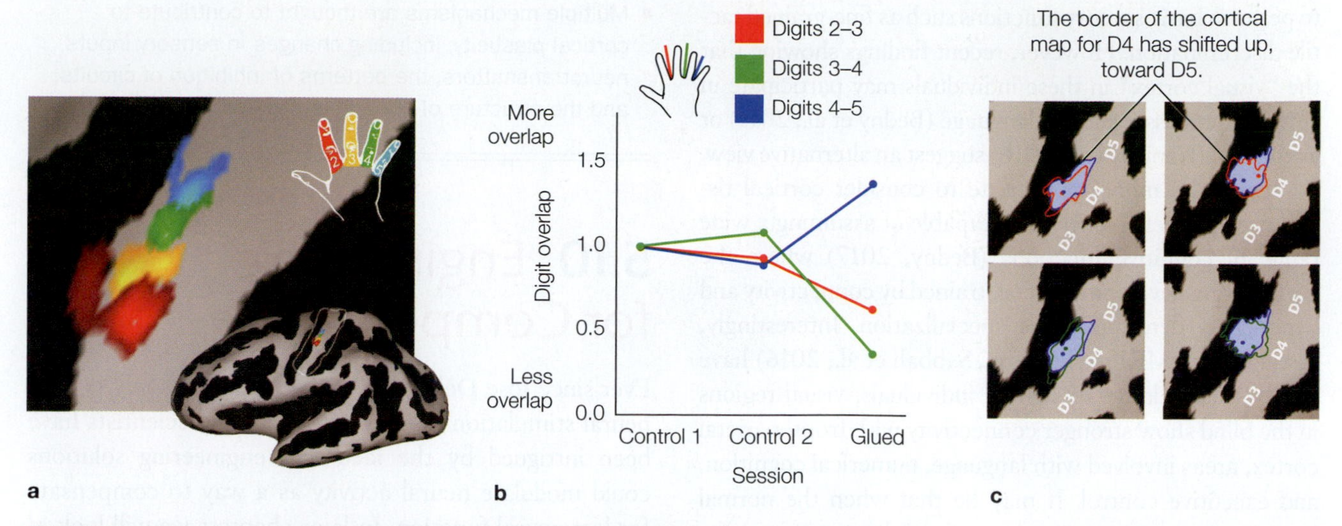

FIGURE 5.45 Rapid experience-dependent remapping in human S1.
(a) High-resolution 7-T fMRI shows digit representation in somatosensory cortex. Finger color on the hand corresponds to the color of the finger's mapped representation. Mapping of the four digits in S1 is seen on the whole brain (bottom right). The larger panel is a zoomed view of S1, nicely showing the tidy organization of the finger's mapping. **(b)** A summary of how cortical overlap shifted with gluing. The researchers normalized all values to 1 from an initial scan (Control 1). They then examined whether the cortical mapping changed after the Control 2 (unglued) or Glued conditions. After gluing, there was a significant decrease in cortical overlap of Digits 3 and 4 (D3 and D4) and an increase in overlap between D4 and D5. That is, the cortical map for D4 moved away from that of D3 and toward D5. **(c)** Pattern of shift in the cortical representation of D4 in two participants. Contours show the extent of D4 representation, with the dark-blue line indicating the border during the post-gluing scan. The red and green lines indicate the border during two separate control trials.

Mechanisms of Cortical Reorganization

The physiological mechanisms driving plasticity at the cellular level have been studied primarily in nonhuman animal models. The results suggest a cascade of effects operating across different timescales. In the short term, rapid changes probably reflect the unveiling of weak connections that already exist in the cortex, and immediate effects are likely to be the result of a sudden reduction in inhibition that normally suppresses inputs from neighboring regions.

Reorganization in the motor cortex has been found to depend on the level of gamma-aminobutyric acid (GABA), the principal inhibitory neurotransmitter (Ziemann et al., 2001). When GABA levels are high, activity in individual cortical neurons is relatively stable. If GABA levels are lower, the neurons respond to a wider range of stimuli. For example, a neuron that responds to the touch of one finger will respond to the touch of other fingers if GABA is blocked. Interestingly, temporary deafferentation of the hand (by blocking blood flow to it) leads to a lowering of GABA levels in the brain. These data suggest that short-term plasticity may be controlled by a release of tonic inhibition on synaptic input (thalamic or intracortical) from remote sources.

Changes in cortical mapping over a period of days probably involve changes in the efficacy of existing circuitry. After loss of normal somatosensory input (e.g., through amputation or peripheral nerve section), cortical neurons that previously responded to that input might undergo "denervation hypersensitivity." That is, the strength of the responses to any remaining weak excitatory input could be upregulated; remapping might well depend on such modulations of synaptic efficacy.

Strengthening of synapses is enhanced in the motor cortex by the neurotransmitters norepinephrine, dopamine, and acetylcholine; it is decreased in the presence of drugs that block the receptors for these transmitters (Meintzschel & Ziemann, 2005). These changes are similar to the forms of long-term potentiation and depression in the hippocampus that are thought to underlie the formation of spatial and episodic memories that we will discuss in Chapter 9. Finally, some evidence in animals suggests that the growth of intracortical axonal connections and even sprouting of new axons might contribute to very slow changes in cortical plasticity.

At a functional level, one theory has been that cortical areas continue to follow basic principles after sensory deprivation. For example, the finding that visual cortex is recruited during Braille reading in people who are congenitally blind has been taken to suggest that this area continues to perform basic sensory functions such as fine-grained tactile discrimination. However, recent findings showing that the "visual cortex" in these individuals may participate in complex processes such as language (Bedny et al., 2011) or arithmetic (Kanjlia et al., 2016) suggest an alternative view.

It may be more appropriate to consider cortical tissue as cognitively pluripotent, capable of assuming a wide range of cognitive functions (Bedny, 2017) where the input during development, constrained by connectivity and experience, determines the specialization. Interestingly, resting-state fMRI studies (e.g., Sabbah et al., 2016) have shown that, relative to sighted individuals, visual regions in the blind show stronger connectivity with frontoparietal cortex, areas involved with language, numerical cognition, and executive control. It may be that when the normal input is absent, these "sensory areas" become part of a broader network for more general cognitive functions.

TAKE-HOME MESSAGES

- Brain regions typically associated with a particular sensory system become reorganized in individuals who lack that sensory system. For example, regions usually involved in visual processing become responsive to auditory and tactile stimuli in blind individuals.
- These neural changes are frequently associated with behavioral changes. For example, deaf individuals show greater sensitivity than hearing individuals in detecting peripheral visual stimuli.
- Cortical reorganization could reflect cross-area plasticity, a reorganization in the processing of information for spared sensory inputs, or recruitment of the deprived areas for more integrative processing.
- Multiple mechanisms are thought to contribute to cortical plasticity, including changes in sensory inputs, neurotransmitters, the patterns of inhibition of circuits, and the structure of cortical layers and connections.

5.10 Engineering for Compensation

Ever since Jose Delgado stopped a bull in its tracks with neural stimulation (see Chapter 2), neuroscientists have been intrigued by the idea that engineering solutions could modulate neural activity as a way to compensate for lost neural function. In later chapters we will look at a number of recent developments in the field of neuroprosthetics, the use of invasive and noninvasive tools to exploit and control neural activity. Here we describe two procedures that have been developed to boost sensory processing. Knowing that sensation involves the translation of external signals into neuronal activity, neuroscientists and engineers have teamed up to create devices that can serve this function when our natural sensors have been lost.

Cochlear Implants

Cochlear implants are designed to help people with severe hearing problems for whom a typical hearing aid does not help. Permanent hearing loss is usually the result of damage or loss of the hair cells in the cochlea, often due to aging or frequent exposure to loud noise. Hearing aids facilitate hearing by amplifying the signals carried by sound waves and thus increasing the intensity of the stimulus arriving at the sensory transducers in the ear. Such amplification works only if an adequate number of hair cells are still functioning. In contrast, cochlear implants bypass the damaged portions of these transducers, directly stimulating the auditory nerve.

The cochlear implant system begins with an external processor, usually worn behind the ear. This processor contains a tiny microphone that converts sound waves into electrical signals (**Figure 5.46**). By means of sophisticated algorithms

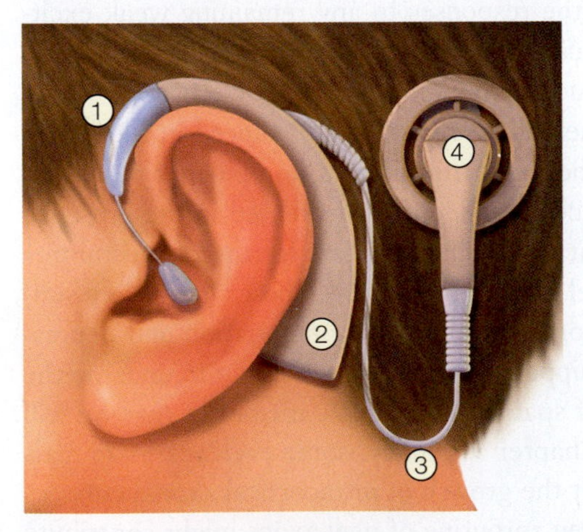

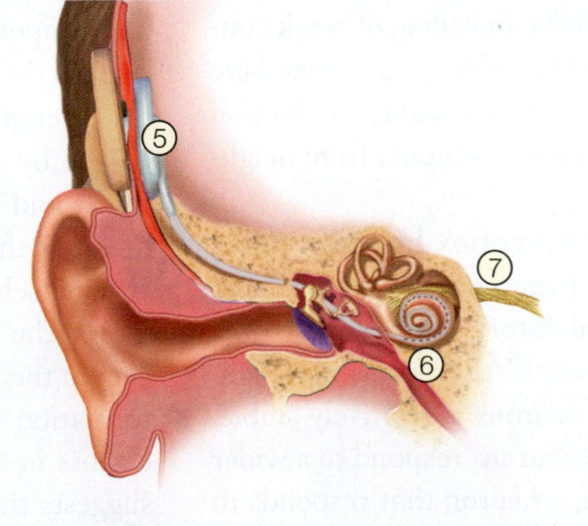

FIGURE 5.46 Cochlear implant.
Sound is picked up by a small microphone (1) located behind the ear and converted into an electrical signal. An external processor (2) converts the signals into complex digital representations of the sound, which travel by wire (3) to an external transmitter (4), which transmits them as radio waves to the internal processor (5). Here they are reconverted to electrical signals that travel by wire (6) to the cochlea, where 22 electrodes are placed. The electrodes stimulate the auditory nerve (7).

BOX 5.2 | HOT SCIENCE

Not-So-Blind Mice

A completely different approach to retinal implants, currently being developed in rodent models, uses optogenetic techniques. Recall that with optogenetics, cells are made to express light-sensitive receptors. Typically, these cells are located in the brain and thus require the implant of a light-emitting device. However, this same idea can be exploited to modify cells in the retina, using the natural light in the environment as the light source.

This approach has been tested in mice that have been genetically modified in two ways (Gaub et al., 2015). The first modification causes the mice to develop degeneration of the photoreceptors in the retina, similar to the effect of the disease retinitis pigmentosa. The second modification uses optogenetics to cause the mice to express light-sensitive receptors in bipolar cells. In normal animals, these cells integrate the output of the photoreceptors to drive ganglion cells; they are not directly responsive to light. The genetic mutants, when exposed to light, show typical mouse-like behavior, such as trying to move to darker places—a behavioral response that indicates they're seeing light. Physiological recordings verify that the ganglion cells show a high sensitivity to light. Although it's still in its infancy, this technique using the eye's functioning hardware is extremely promising as a treatment for a host of diseases in which the transduction of light into nerve signals is compromised.

based on years of research into the physics of sound and the physiology of the cochlea, these signals are converted into complex digital representations of the sound. The software can be tailored to filter out irrelevant sounds or adjusted to match the listener's personal preferences. The digital representation is then transmitted as radio waves through the skin to an internal processor, where it is reconverted to an electrical output that can activate up to 22 electrodes, each designed to produce signals corresponding to different sound frequencies. These electrodes electrically stimulate the cochlear nerve. The resulting patterns lack, to some degree, the richness of natural sound. Nonetheless, given the plasticity of the brain, people with cochlear implants find tremendous improvements in their hearing. Voices may not have the richness we are accustomed to, but normal conversations are now possible.

As of 2012 in the United States, where the Food and Drug Administration (FDA) has approved cochlear implants for people older than 12 months of age, the procedure had been done in roughly 58,000 adults and 38,000 children. Current efforts are aimed at determining whether this approach can also be used to treat children who are completely or severely deaf at birth because of malformations of middle-ear structures, prenatal infections (usually with cytomegalovirus), or genetically linked lack of hair cells in the cochlea. In Australia, cochlear implants have been used in infants younger than 12 months of age for several years.

A review of outcomes on speech perception, language, and speech production compared 403 children with congenital, bilateral, severe to profound hearing loss who had received cochlear implants at ages ranging from 6 months to 6 years. The findings demonstrated that those who received the implant before 12 months of age had superior communication outcomes, and that a greater percentage of children from this age group later demonstrated language outcomes within the normal range (Dettman et al., 2016).

Retinal Implants

Retinal implants are designed for patients who are blind because of degenerative diseases that affect the photoreceptors, resulting in progressive vision loss. Even when the visual loss is very advanced, many cells in the retina remain intact. In recognition of this fact, researchers have developed two basic types of retinal implants: the *subretinal implant*, which exploits the remaining photoreceptors, and the *epiretinal implant*, which bypasses the photoreceptor cells and directly stimulates the ganglion neurons of the retina. (See **Box 5.2** for still another approach.) At present, both systems have produced, at best, modest improvements in function.

We will focus on the epiretinal implant because it has been approved by the FDA for clinical use. The implant, driven by an external video camera worn on a pair of glasses, sits on top of the retina above the layers of nerves (**Figure 5.47**). The output of the camera is digitized into electrical pulses that are wirelessly transmitted to the

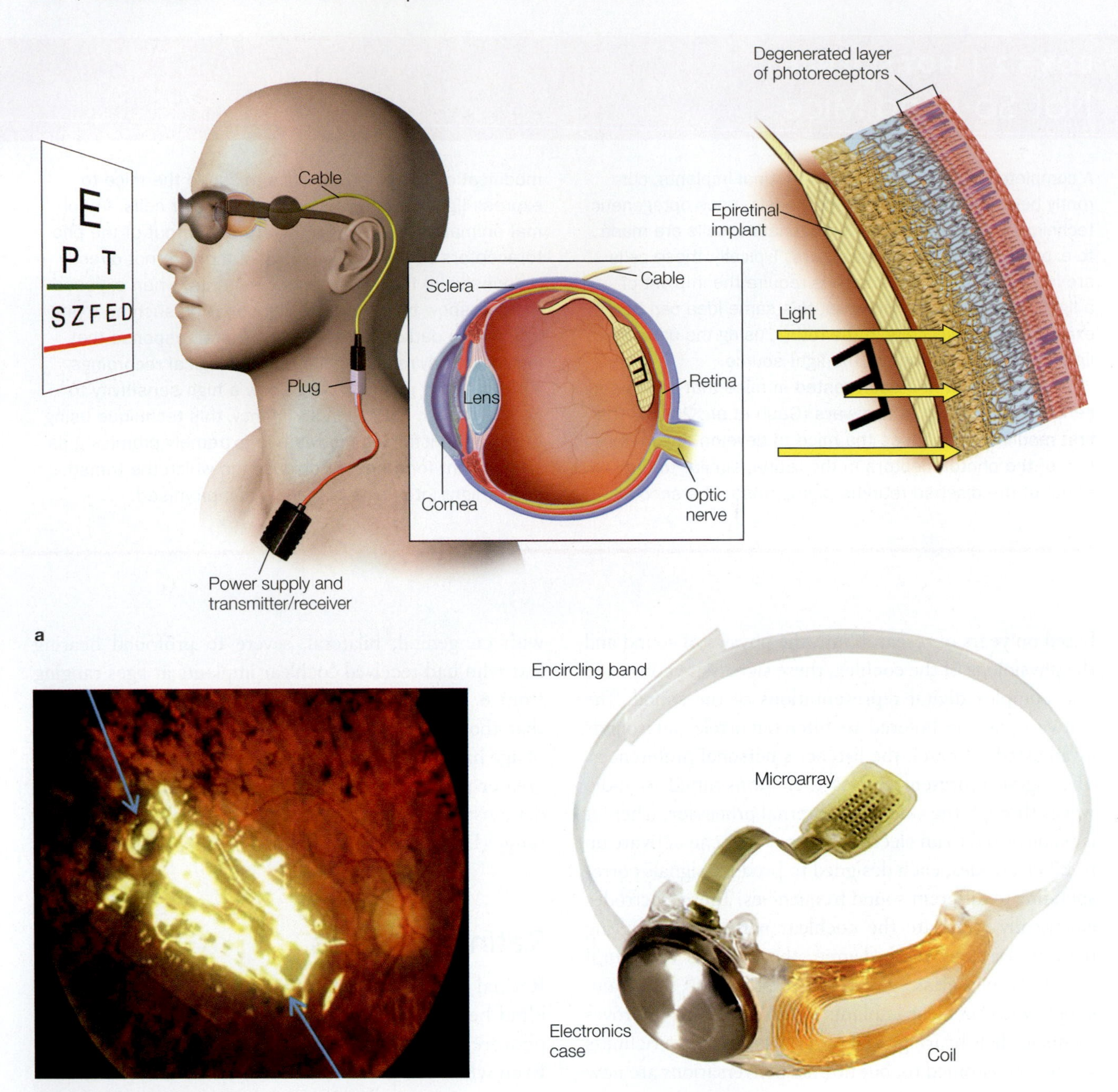

FIGURE 5.47 The epiretinal implant system.
(a) Drawing of an epiretinal implant in place. (b) An Argos II subretinal implant placed epiretinally over the macular region. The round faint-white area on the right is the optic disk. (c) Implanted portion showing the electrode microarray, the band that encircles the orbit of the eye, the electronics case, and the internal (receiver) coil.

implant. The pulses activate a bank of tiny electrodes, each of which covers an area equivalent to hundreds of photoreceptors. The output of the electrodes directly stimulates the retinal ganglion cells, resulting in the transmission of signals along the optic nerve (see Figure 5.20). In this manner, the electrodes mimic the effect of how patterns of light activate different regions of the retina.

The crude resolution of the video camera, at least in comparison to the human retina, accounts for the limited restorative effects of the epiretinal implant. To date, the system has been capable of restoring light sensitivity and low visual acuity (20/1262). With practice, users have been able to identify household objects, detect motion, and regain mobility—an early step in the right direction for those who have been blind for years.

TAKE-HOME MESSAGES

- A common cause of vision and hearing loss is the loss of sensory receptors: photoreceptors in the retina, and hair cells in the cochlea.
- Cochlear implants bypass the transduction of sounds into electrical signals by producing an electrical output that stimulates the auditory nerve. The benefits of cochlear implants can take some time to become optimal, likely because the brain has to learn to interpret the modified auditory input.
- A range of methods are being developed to create artificial systems that can replace the loss of photoreceptors. These may involve implants to serve as prosthetic photoreceptors or optogenetic manipulations to make spared neurons light sensitive.

Summary

Our senses translate information about the environment and our body into neuronal signals from which the brain generates perceptions that enable us to build a representation of the world. The five basic sensory systems are olfaction, gustation, somatosensation, audition, and vision. Each sense has specialized receptors that are activated by specific types of stimuli. Gustation and olfaction are known as the chemical senses because their initial response is to molecules (chemicals) in the environment. The somatosensory system has mechanical receptors to detect changes in touch, muscle length, and joint position, as well as nociceptors that respond to temperature and noxious stimuli. The hair cells in the cochlea act as mechanoreceptors in the auditory system. In the visual system, the photoreceptors in the retina (the rods and cones) contain pigments that are sensitive to light.

Within each sense, specialized mechanisms have evolved to solve computational problems to facilitate our ability to perceive the world, recognizing important properties that are essential for our survival. Gustation enables us to recognize the content of food—or be wary of something that might make us sick. Somatosensation helps us recognize things that might be dangerous (e.g., heat from a fire) or movements that might be injurious. Audition and vision enable us to recognize things at a distance, greatly enhancing the range of our perceptual experience.

The gustatory, somatosensory, auditory, and visual cortices contain topographic maps, spatially organized representations of some property of the environment or body. These are known as gustotopic maps in the gustatory system, somatotopic maps in the somatosensory system, tonotopic maps in the auditory system, and retinotopic maps in the visual system. The body parts that have the largest cortical representation on somatotopic maps are those that are most important to that species. Within each sensory system, there is a considerable degree of specialization and elaboration. For example, even in the absence of color or motion perception, we may still be able to recognize shapes.

The five senses work not in isolation, but rather in concert to construct a rich interpretation of the world. It is this integration that underlies much of human cognition and enables us to survive, and indeed thrive, in a multisensory world.

Key Terms

achromatopsia (p. 203)
acuity (p. 172)
adaptation (p. 172)
akinetopsia (p. 205)
area MT (p. 198)
area V4 (p. 199)
chemical senses (p. 177)
cochlear nerve (p. 186)
cochlear nuclei (p. 187)
cones (p. 190)
cortical plasticity (p. 211)
cortical visual areas (p. 195)
extrastriate visual areas (p. 195)
fovea (p. 190)
ganglion cells (p. 190)
glomeruli (p. 174)
inferior colliculus (p. 187)
interaural time (p. 188)
lateral geniculate nucleus (LGN) (p. 192)
multisensory integration (p. 173)
nociceptors (p. 181)
odorant (p. 174)
olivary nucleus (p. 187)
photoreceptors (p. 190)
primary auditory cortex (A1) (p. 187)
primary gustatory cortex (p. 177)
primary olfactory cortex (p. 174)
primary somatosensory cortex (S1) (p. 182)
primary visual cortex (V1) (p. 192)
proprioception (p. 181)
receptive field (p. 193)
retina (p. 190)
retinotopic map (p. 193)
rods (p. 190)
saccades (p. 173)
secondary somatosensory cortex (S2) (p. 182)
superior colliculus (p. 192)
synesthesia (p. 209)
tastant (p. 177)
tonotopic map (p. 186)

Think About It

1. Compare and contrast the functional organization of the visual and auditory systems. What computational problems must each system solve, and how are these solutions achieved in the nervous system?
2. A person arrives at the hospital in a confused state and appears to have some impairment in visual perception. As the attending neurologist, you suspect that the person has had a stroke. How would you go about examining the patient to determine the level in the visual pathways where damage has occurred? Emphasize the behavioral tests you would administer, but feel free to make predictions about what you expect to see on MRI scans.
3. Define the physiological concepts of *receptive field* and *visual area*. How is the receptive field of a cell established? How are the boundaries between visual areas identified by researchers using either single-cell-recording methods or fMRI?
4. This chapter focused mainly on salient visual properties such as color, shape, and motion. In looking around the environment, do you think these properties seem to reflect the most important cues for a highly skilled visual creature? What other sources of information might an adaptive visual system exploit?
5. How might abnormalities in multisensory processing (e.g., synesthesia) be important for understanding how and why information becomes integrated across different sensory channels? Similarly, given the plasticity of the brain, does it even make sense to talk about a "visual system" or an "auditory system"?

Suggested Reading

Bedny, M. (2017). Evidence from blindness for a cognitively pluripotent cortex. *Trends in Cognitive Sciences*, *21*(9), 637–648.

Driver, J., & Noesselt, T. (2008). Multisensory interplay reveals crossmodal influences on "sensory-specific" brain regions, neural responses, and judgments. *Neuron*, *57*, 11–23.

Grill-Spector, K., & Malach, R. (2004). The human visual cortex. *Annual Review of Neuroscience*, *27*, 649–677.

Palmer, S. E. (1999). *Vision science: Photons to phenomenology*. Cambridge, MA: MIT Press.

Ward, J. (2013). Synesthesia. *Annual Review of Psychology*, *64*, 49–75.

Yeshurun, Y., & Sobel, N. (2010). An odor is not worth a thousand words: From multidimensional odors to unidimensional odor objects. *Annual Review of Psychology*, *61*, 219–241.

I never forget a face—but I'm going to make an exception in your case.

Groucho Marx

CHAPTER

6

Object Recognition

WHILE STILL IN HIS 30S, G.S. suffered a stroke and nearly died. Although he eventually recovered most of his cognitive functions, G.S. continued to complain about one severe problem: He could not recognize objects.

His sensory abilities were intact, his language function was normal, and he had no problems with coordination. Most striking, he had no loss of visual acuity. He could easily judge which of two lines was longer and describe the color and general shape of objects. Nonetheless, when shown household objects such as a candle or a salad bowl, he was unable to name them, even though he could describe the candle as long and thin, and the salad bowl as curved and brown.

G.S.'s deficit did not reflect an inability to retrieve verbal labels of objects. When asked to name a round, wooden object in which lettuce, tomatoes, and cucumbers are mixed, he responded with "salad bowl." He could also identify objects by using other senses, such as touch or smell. For example, after visually examining a candle, he reported that it was a "long object." Upon touching it, he labeled it a "crayon"; after smelling it, he corrected himself and responded with "candle." Thus, his deficit was modality specific, confined to his visual system.

G.S. had even more difficulty recognizing objects in photographs. When shown and asked to name a picture of a combination lock, he initially failed to respond, looking at the picture with a puzzled expression. When prodded, he noted the round shape. Interestingly, while viewing the picture, he kept twirling his fingers, pantomiming the actions of opening a combination lock. When asked about this, he said it was a nervous habit. Further prompted by experimenters to provide more details or to make a guess, G.S. said the picture was of a telephone (he was referring to a rotary dial telephone, which was commonly used at the time). He remained adamant about this, even after he was informed that it was not a picture of a telephone. Finally, the experimenter asked him whether the object in the picture was a telephone, a lock, or a clock. By this time, convinced it was not a telephone, he responded with

BIG Questions

- What processes lead to the recognition of a coherent object?
- How is information about objects organized in the brain?
- Does the brain recognize all types of objects using the same processes? Is there something special about recognizing faces?

"clock." Then, after a look at his fingers, he proudly announced, "It's a lock, a combination lock."

G.S.'s actions were telling. Even though his eyes and optic nerve functioned normally, he could not recognize an object that he was looking at. In other words, sensory information was entering his visual system normally, and information about the components of an object in his visual field was being processed. He could differentiate and identify colors, lines, and shapes. He knew the names of objects and what they were for, so his memory was fine. In addition, when viewing the image of a lock, G.S.'s choice of a telephone was not random. He had perceived the numeric markings around the lock's circumference, a feature found on rotary-dial telephones.

G.S.'s finger twirling indicated that he knew more about the object in the picture than his erroneous statement that it was a telephone suggested. In the end, his hand motion gave him the answer—G.S. had let his fingers do the talking. Although his visual system perceived the parts, and he understood the function of the object he was looking at, G.S. could not put all of that information together to recognize the object. G.S. had a type of visual agnosia.

In the previous chapter we saw how visual signals arising from objects and scenes in the external world are analyzed as edges, shapes, and colors. In this chapter we explore how the brain combines these low-level inputs into high-level, coherent percepts. As we will see, the act of perceiving also touches on memory: To recognize a photograph of your mother requires a correspondence between the current percept and an internal representation of previously viewed images of your mother.

We begin this chapter with a discussion of some of the computational problems that the object recognition system has to solve and how they relate to the cortical real estate involved in object recognition. Then we address the question of how neuronal activity encodes perceptual information, turning to an exciting literature in which researchers put object recognition theories to the test by trying to predict what a person is viewing simply by looking at patterns of neuronal activity or correlates of this activity—the 21st-century version of mind reading. With these foundations in hand, we delve into the fascinating world of category-specific recognition problems and their implications for models of object recognition. We conclude the chapter by considering what the deficits of patients with special types of agnosia tell us about perception.

6.1 Computational Problems in Object Recognition

When thinking about object recognition, there are four major concepts to keep in mind.

1. *Use terms precisely.* At a fundamental level, cases like that of patient G.S. force researchers to be precise when using terms like *perceive* or *recognize*. G.S. could see the pictures, yet he failed to perceive or recognize them. Distinctions like these constitute a core issue in cognitive neuroscience, highlighting the limitations of the language used in everyday descriptions of thinking. Such distinctions are relevant in this chapter, and they will reappear when we turn to problems of attention and memory in Chapters 7 and 9.
2. *Object perception is unified.* Although our sensory systems use a divide-and-conquer strategy (as we saw in Chapter 5), our perception of objects is unified. Features like color and motion are processed along distinct neural pathways. Perception, however, requires more than simply perceiving the features of objects. For instance, when gazing at the northern coastline of San Francisco (**Figure 6.1**), we do not see just blurs of color floating among a sea of various shapes. Instead, our percepts are of the deep-blue water of the bay, the peaked towers of the Golden Gate Bridge, and the silver skyscrapers of the city.
3. *Perceptual capabilities are enormously flexible and robust.* The city vista looks the same whether we view it with both eyes or with only the left or the right eye. Changing our position on a San Francisco hillside may reveal the expanse of Golden Gate Park or present a view in which a building occludes most of the park, yet despite this variation in sensory input, we readily recognize that we are looking at the same city. Indeed, the percept remains stable even if we stand on our head and the retinal image is inverted.
4. *The product of perception is intimately interwoven with memory.* Object recognition is more than linking features to form a coherent whole; that whole triggers memories. Those of us who have spent many hours roaming the hills around San Francisco Bay recognize that the pictures in Figure 6.1 were taken from the Marin headlands just north of the city. Even if you have never been to San Francisco, when you look at these pictures, there is interplay between perception and memory. Indeed, part of memory retrieval is recognizing that things belong to certain categories. For the traveler arriving from Australia, the first view

a

b

FIGURE 6.1 Our view of the world depends on our vantage point. These two photographs are of the same scene, but taken from two different positions and under two different conditions. Each vantage point reveals new views of the scene, including objects that were obscured from the other vantage point. Moreover, the colors change, depending on the time of day and weather. Despite this variability, we easily recognize that both photographs are of the Golden Gate Bridge, with San Francisco in the distance.

of San Francisco is likely to evoke comparisons to Sydney; for the first-time tourist from Kansas, the vista may be so unusual that she recognizes it as such: a place unlike any other that she has seen.

Object constancy refers to our amazing ability to recognize an object in countless situations. **Figure 6.2a** shows four drawings of an automobile that have little in common with respect to sensory information reaching the eye. Yet we have no problem identifying the object in each picture as a car, and discerning that all four cars are the same model. The visual information emanating from an object varies as a function of three factors: viewing position, illumination conditions, and context.

1. *Viewing position.* Sensory information depends highly on your viewpoint, which changes not only as you view an object from different angles, but also when the object itself moves and thus changes its orientation relative to you. When your dog rolls over, or you call him to fetch a treat, your interpretation of the object (the dog) remains the same despite the radical changes in the visual information hitting your retina and the projection of that information to the brain.

The human perceptual system is adept at separating changes caused by shifts in viewpoint from changes intrinsic to an object itself. Many visual illusions exploit this ability, taking advantage of the fact that the brain uses its experience to make assumptions about a visual scene. For example, the Ames room illusion produces bizarre distortions in our perception of size (**Figure 6.3**). Because we assume that the room is rectangular with a flat ceiling, we perceive the distance to the back wall and the height of the room to be constants. Even when we are informed that the back wall and ceiling are slanted, creating a trapezoidal room, the illusion persists. The perceptual

a

b

FIGURE 6.2 Object constancy.
(a) The image on the retina is vastly different for each of these four drawings of a car. (b) Other sources of variation in sensory input include shadows and occlusion (where one object is in front of another). Despite this sensory variability, we rapidly recognize the objects and can judge whether pictures depict the same object or different objects.

a

b

FIGURE 6.3 Ames room.
(a) When we view people in an Ames room, our visual system assumes that the walls are parallel, the floor is flat, and the "squares" on the floor actually are square. Given these viewpoint assumptions, we experience the illusion that the people are of different sizes. (b) The structural design of the Ames room.

system automatically uses many sensory cues and past knowledge to maintain object constancy.

2. *Illumination.* While the visible parts of an object may differ depending on how light hits it and where shadows are cast (**Figure 6.2b**), recognition is largely insensitive to changes in illumination. A dog in the sun and a dog in the shade both register as a dog.
3. *Context.* Objects are rarely seen in isolation. People see objects surrounded by other objects and against varied backgrounds. Yet we have no trouble separating a dog from other objects on a crowded city street, even when the dog is partially obstructed by pedestrians, trees, and hydrants. Our perceptual system quickly partitions the scene into components.

Object recognition must accommodate these three sources of variability. But the system also has to recognize that changes in perceived shape may reflect actual changes in the object. Object recognition must be both general enough to support object constancy and specific enough to pick out slight differences between members of a category or class.

TAKE-HOME MESSAGES

- Sensation, perception, and recognition are distinct phenomena.
- Object constancy is the ability to recognize objects in countless situations, despite variation in the physical stimulus.

6.2 Multiple Pathways for Visual Perception

The pathways carrying visual information from the retina to the first few synapses in the cortex clearly segregate into multiple processing streams. Much of the information goes to the primary visual cortex, also called V1 or striate cortex (Chapter 5; see Figures 5.23 and 5.26), located in the occipital lobe.

Output from V1 is contained primarily in two major fiber bundles, or *fasciculi*, which carry visual information to regions of the parietal and temporal cortex (seen in the "Anatomical Orientation" box on p. 227) that are involved in visual object recognition. **Figure 6.4** shows that the *superior longitudinal fasciculus* takes a dorsal path from the striate cortex and other visual areas, terminating mostly in the posterior regions of the parietal lobe. The *inferior longitudinal fasciculus* follows a ventral route from the occipital striate cortex into the temporal lobe. These two pathways are referred to as the **ventral (occipitotemporal) stream** and the **dorsal (occipitoparietal) stream.**

This anatomical separation of information-carrying fibers from the visual cortex to two separate regions of the brain raises some questions. What are the different properties of processing within the ventral and dorsal streams? How do they differ in their representation of the visual input? How does processing within these two streams interact to support object perception?

ANATOMICAL ORIENTATION

Anatomy of Object Recognition

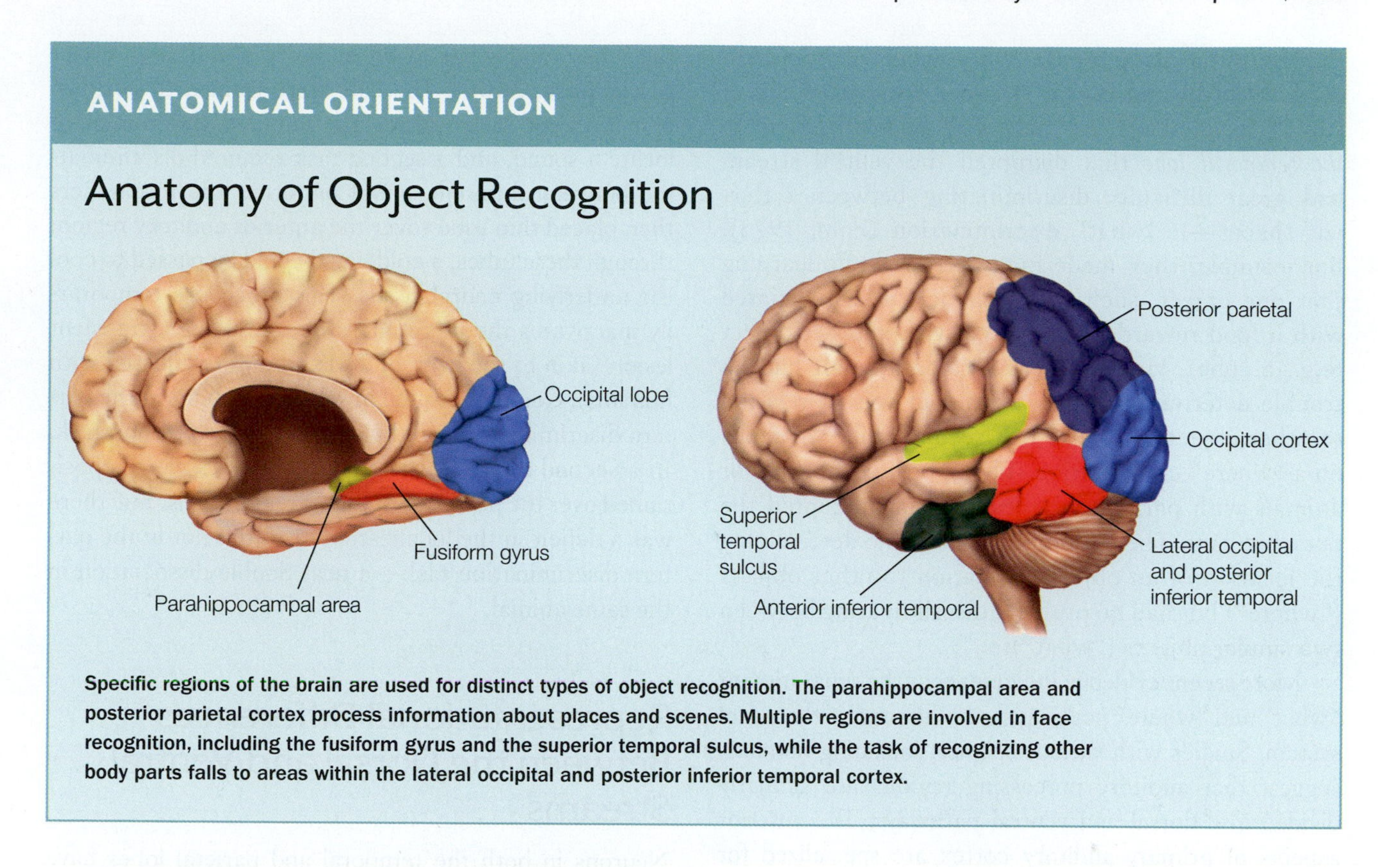

Specific regions of the brain are used for distinct types of object recognition. The parahippocampal area and posterior parietal cortex process information about places and scenes. Multiple regions are involved in face recognition, including the fusiform gyrus and the superior temporal sulcus, while the task of recognizing other body parts falls to areas within the lateral occipital and posterior inferior temporal cortex.

The "What" and "Where" Pathways

To address the first of these questions, Leslie Ungerleider and Mortimer Mishkin at the National Institutes of Health (1982) proposed that processing along these two pathways is designed to extract fundamentally different types of information. They hypothesized that the *ventral stream* is specialized for *object perception and recognition*—for determining *what* we're looking at. The *dorsal stream* is specialized for *spatial perception*—for determining *where* an object is—and for analyzing the spatial configuration between different objects in a scene. "What" and "where" are the two basic questions to be answered in visual perception. To respond appropriately, we must (a) recognize what we're looking at and (b) know where it is.

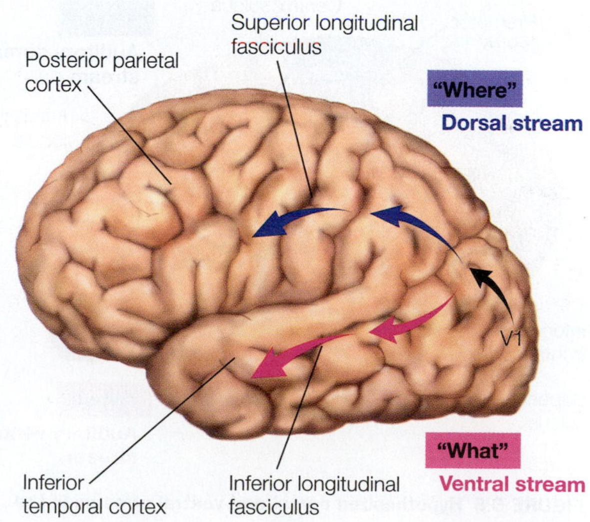

a

b

FIGURE 6.4 The major object recognition pathways.
(a) The longitudinal fasciculus, shown here in shades of purple. (b) The ventral "what" pathway terminates in the inferior temporal cortex, and the dorsal "where" pathway terminates in the posterior parietal cortex.

The initial data for the what–where dissociation of the ventral and dorsal streams came from lesion studies in monkeys. Animals with *bilateral lesions to the temporal lobe* that disrupted the ventral stream had great difficulty discriminating between different shapes—a "what" discrimination (Pohl, 1973). For example, they made many errors while learning that one object, such as a cylinder, was associated with a food reward when paired with another object (e.g., a cube). However, these same animals had no trouble determining where an object was in relation to other objects, because this second ability depends on a "where" computation. The opposite was true for animals with parietal lobe lesions that disrupted the dorsal stream. These animals had trouble determining the location of an object in relation to other objects ("where") but had no problem discriminating between two similar objects ("what").

More recent evidence indicates that the separation of "what" and "where" pathways is not limited to the visual system. Studies with various species, including humans, suggest that auditory processing regions are similarly divided into dorsal and ventral pathways. The anterior aspects of primary auditory cortex are specialized for auditory-pattern processing (what is the sound?) and belong to the ventral pathway, and posterior regions are specialized for identifying the spatial location of a sound (where is it coming from?) and make up part of the dorsal pathway (**Figure 6.5**).

One particularly clever experiment demonstrated this functional specialization by asking cats to identify the where and what of an auditory stimulus (Lomber & Malhotra, 2008). The cats were trained to perform two different tasks: One task required the animal to locate a sound, and a second task required discriminating between different sound patterns. The researchers then placed thin tubes over the anterior auditory region; through these tubes, a cold liquid could be passed to cool the underlying neural tissue. This procedure temporarily inactivates the targeted tissue, providing a transient lesion (akin to the logic of TMS studies conducted with humans). Cooling resulted in selective deficits in the pattern discrimination task but not in the localization task. In a second phase of the study, the tubes were repositioned over the posterior auditory region. This time there was a deficit in the localization task, but not in the pattern discrimination task—a neat double dissociation in the same animal.

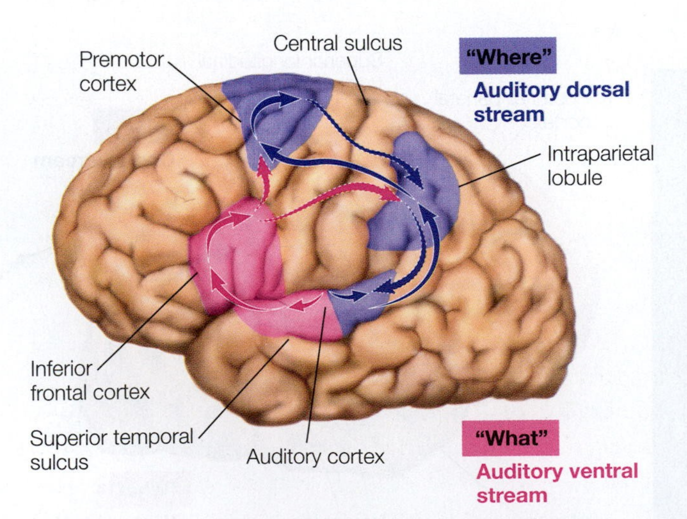

FIGURE 6.5 Hypothesized dorsal and ventral streams in the auditory pathway.
Neurons in the dorsal stream (blue) may preferentially analyze space and motion, whereas those in the ventral stream (pink) may be preferentially involved in auditory-object processing. Note that anterior auditory cortex is part of the ventral stream, and posterior auditory cortex is part of the dorsal stream.

Representational Differences Between the Dorsal and Ventral Streams

Neurons in both the temporal and parietal lobes have large receptive fields, but the physiological properties of the neurons within each lobe are quite distinct. Dorsal-stream neurons in the parietal lobe may respond similarly to many different stimuli (Robinson et al., 1978). For example, a parietal neuron recorded in a fully conscious monkey might be activated when a stimulus such as a spot of light is restricted to a small region of space or when the stimulus is a large object that encompasses much of the hemifield.

Although 40% of these neurons have receptive fields near the central region of vision (the fovea), the remaining cells have receptive fields that exclude the foveal region. These eccentrically tuned cells are ideally suited for detecting the presence and location of a stimulus, especially one that has just entered the field of view. Recall that, when we examined subcortical visual processing in Chapter 5, we suggested a similar role for the superior colliculus, which also plays an important role in visual attention (discussed in Chapter 7).

The response of neurons in the ventral stream of the temporal lobe is quite different (Ito et al., 1995). The receptive fields for these neurons *always encompass the fovea*, and most of these neurons can be activated by a stimulus that falls within either the left or the right visual field. The disproportionate representation of central vision appears to be ideal for a system devoted to object recognition. We usually look directly at things we wish to identify, thereby taking advantage of the greater acuity of foveal vision.

Cells within the visual areas of the temporal lobe have a diverse pattern of selectivity (Desimone, 1991). In the posterior region, earlier in processing, cells show a preference for relatively simple features such as edges. Others, farther along in the processing stream, have a preference for much more complex features, such as human body parts, apples, flowers, or snakes. Recordings from one such cell, located in the inferior temporal (IT) cortex, are shown in **Figure 6.6** (Desimone et al., 1984). This cell is most highly activated by the human hand. The first five images in the figure show the response of the cell to various views of a hand. Activity is high regardless of the hand's orientation and is only slightly reduced when the hand is considerably smaller. The sixth image, of a mitten, shows that the response diminishes if the same shape lacks defining fingers.

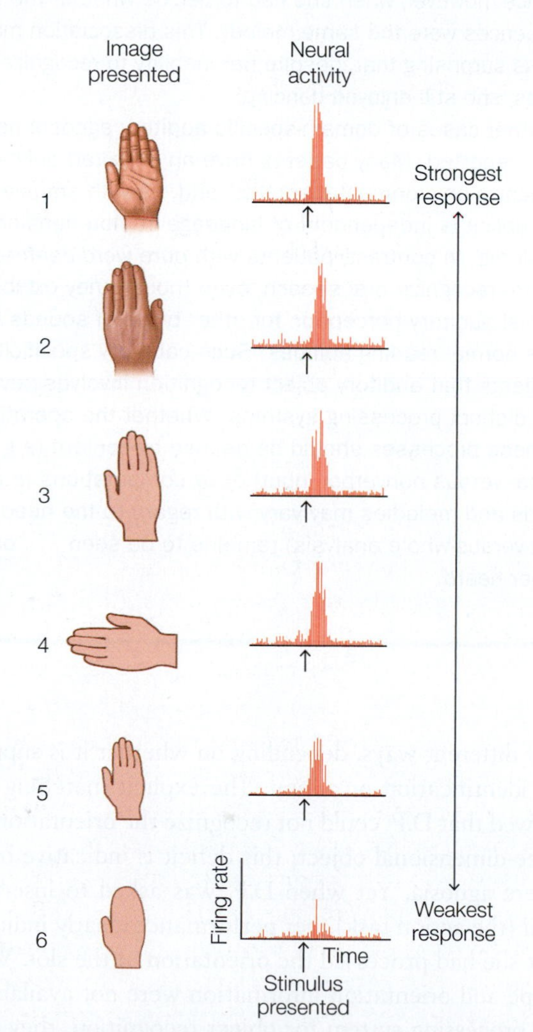

FIGURE 6.6 Single-cell recordings from a neuron in the inferior temporal cortex.
Neurons in the IT cortex rarely respond to simple stimuli such as lines or spots of light. Rather, they respond to more complex objects, such as hands. This cell responded weakly to image 6, which did not include the defining fingers.

Perception for Identification Versus Perception for Action

Patient studies offer more support for a dissociation of "what" and "where" processing. As we will see in Chapter 7, the parietal cortex is central to spatial attention. Lesions of this lobe can also produce severe disturbances in the ability to represent the world's spatial layout and the spatial relations of objects within it.

More revealing have been functional dissociations in the performance of patients with **agnosia**, an inability to process sensory information even though the sense organs and memory are not defective. The term *agnosia* was coined by Sigmund Freud, who derived it from the Greek *a-* ("without") and *gnosis* ("knowledge"). To be agnosic means to experience a failure of knowledge or recognition of objects, persons, shapes, sounds, or smells. When the disorder is limited to the visual modality, as with G.S., the syndrome is referred to as a **visual agnosia**, a deficit in recognizing objects even when the processes for analyzing basic properties such as shape, color, and motion are relatively intact.

Similarly, people can have an auditory agnosia, perhaps manifested as an inability to recognize music despite normal hearing (see **Box 6.1**), or agnosias limited to olfaction or somatosensation. The term *agnosia* is usually used in a modality-specific manner; if the problem is multimodal, it becomes hard to determine whether it is a perceptual problem per se, or more of a memory problem.

Mel Goodale and David Milner at the University of Western Ontario (1992) described a fascinating pattern of behavior in patient D.F., a 34-year-old woman who had suffered carbon monoxide intoxication from a leaky propane gas heater, resulting in a severe visual agnosia. When asked to name household items, she made errors such as labeling a cup an "ashtray" or a fork a "knife." She usually gave crude descriptions of a displayed object; for example, a screwdriver was "long, black, and thin." Picture recognition was even more disrupted. When shown drawings of common objects, D.F. could not identify a single one.

D.F.'s deficit could not be attributed to *anomia*, a problem with naming objects, because whenever an object was placed in her hand, she identified it. Sensory testing indicated that D.F.'s agnosia could not be attributed to a loss of visual acuity: She could detect small, gray targets displayed against a black background. Although her ability to discriminate small differences in hue was abnormal, she correctly identified primary colors.

Most relevant to our discussion is the dissociation of D.F.'s performance on two tasks, both designed to assess her ability to perceive the orientation of a three-dimensional object. For these tasks, D.F. was asked to

BOX 6.1 | LESSONS FROM THE CLINIC

The Day the Music Died

Other sensory modalities besides visual perception contribute to object recognition. Distinctive odors enable us to identify thyme and basil. Using touch, we can differentiate between cheap polyester and a fine silk. We depend on sounds, both natural (a baby's cry) and human-made (a siren), to cue our actions. Failures of object recognition have been documented in these other sensory modalities.

As with visual agnosia, a patient has to meet two criteria to be labeled agnosic. First, a deficit in object recognition cannot be secondary to a problem with perceptual processes. For example, to be classified as having auditory agnosia, patients must perform within normal limits on tests of tone detection; that is, the loudness of the tone presented to the patient for detection must fall within a normal range. Second, the deficit in recognizing objects must be restricted to a single modality. For example, a patient who cannot identify environmental sounds such as the ones made by flowing water or jet engines must be able to recognize a picture of a waterfall or an airplane.

C.N., a 35-year-old nurse, was diagnosed with a left middle cerebral artery aneurysm that required surgery (Peretz et al., 1994). Postoperatively, she immediately complained that her perception of music was deranged. *Amusia*, or impairment in music abilities, was verified by tests. For example, she could not recognize melodies taken from her personal record collection, nor could she recall the names of 140 popular tunes, including the Canadian national anthem.

C.N.'s deficit could not be attributed to a problem with long-term memory. She also failed when asked to decide whether two melodies were the same or different. Evidence that the problem was selective to auditory perception was provided by her excellent ability to identify these same songs when shown the lyrics. Similarly, when given the title of a musical piece such as *The Four Seasons*, C.N. responded that the composer was Vivaldi and could even recall when she had first heard the piece.

Just as interesting as C.N.'s amusia was her absence of problems with other auditory recognition tests. C.N. was able to comprehend and produce speech and to identify environmental sounds such as animal cries, transportation noises, and human voices. Even within the musical domain, C.N. did not have a generalized problem with all aspects of music comprehension. She could detect tones, and she performed as well as normal participants when asked to judge whether two-tone sequences had the same rhythm. Her performance fell to a level of near chance, however, when she had to decide whether the two sequences were the same melody. This dissociation makes it less surprising that, despite her inability to recognize songs, she still enjoyed dancing!

Other cases of domain-specific auditory agnosia have been reported. Many patients have an impaired ability to recognize environmental sounds, and, as with amusia, this deficit is independent of language comprehension problems. In contrast, patients with *pure word deafness* cannot recognize oral speech, even though they exhibit normal auditory perception for other types of sounds and have normal reading abilities. Such category specificity suggests that auditory object recognition involves several distinct processing systems. Whether the operation of these processes should be defined by content (e.g., verbal versus nonverbal input) or by computations (e.g., words and melodies may vary with regard to the need for part-versus-whole analysis) remains to be seen . . . or rather heard.

---

view a circular block into which a slot had been cut. The orientation of the slot could be varied by rotating the block. In the explicit matching task, D.F. was given a card and asked simply to orient her hand so that the card would fit into the slot. D.F. failed miserably, for example, orienting the card vertically even when the slot was horizontal (**Figure 6.7a**). When asked to insert the card into the slot, however, D.F. quickly reached forward and inserted the card (**Figure 6.7b**). Her performance on this visuomotor task did not depend on tactile feedback that would result when the card contacted the slot; her hand was properly oriented even before she reached the block.

D.F.'s performance can be understood if we consider how orientation information might be used in very different ways, depending on whether it is supporting identification or action. The explicit matching task showed that D.F. could not recognize the orientation of a three-dimensional object; this deficit is indicative of her severe agnosia. Yet when D.F. was asked to insert the card (the action task), her performance clearly indicated that she had processed the orientation of the slot. While shape and orientation information were not available to the processing system for object recognition, they were available for the visuomotor task.

The "what" system is essential for determining the identity of an object. If the object is familiar, people will recognize it as such; if it is novel, we may compare the percept to stored representations of similarly shaped

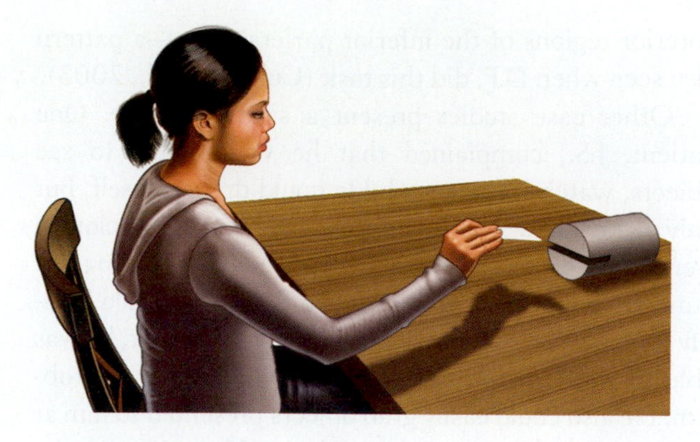

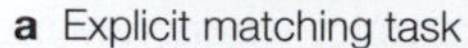

FIGURE 6.7 Dissociation between perception linked to awareness and perception linked to action.
(a) The patient performed poorly in the explicit matching task when asked only to match the orientation of the card to that of the slot. (b) In the action task, the patient was instructed to insert the card into the slot. Here, she produced the correct action without hesitation.

objects. The "where" system appears to be essential for more than determining the locations of different objects; it is also critical for *guiding interactions with these objects*.

D.F.'s performance is an example of how information accessible to action systems can be dissociated from information accessible to knowledge and consciousness. Indeed, Goodale and Milner argued that the dichotomy should be between "what" and "how," to emphasize that the dorsal visual system provides a strong input to motor systems to compute how a movement should be produced. Consider what happens when you grab a glass of water to drink. Your visual system has factored in where the glass is in relation to your eyes, your head, the table, and the path required to move the water glass directly to your mouth.

Goodale, Milner, and their colleagues later tested D.F. in many studies to explore the neural correlates of this striking dissociation between vision for recognition and vision for action (Goodale & Milner, 2004). Structural MRI scans showed that the carbon monoxide poisoning had resulted in bilateral atrophy that was especially pronounced in the ventral stream, including the **lateral occipital cortex (LOC)** (T. W. James et al., 2003; **Figure 6.8**). These regions are consistently activated in healthy individuals when engaged in object recognition tasks. In contrast, when these individuals are shown the same objects but now asked to grasp them, the activation shifts to more

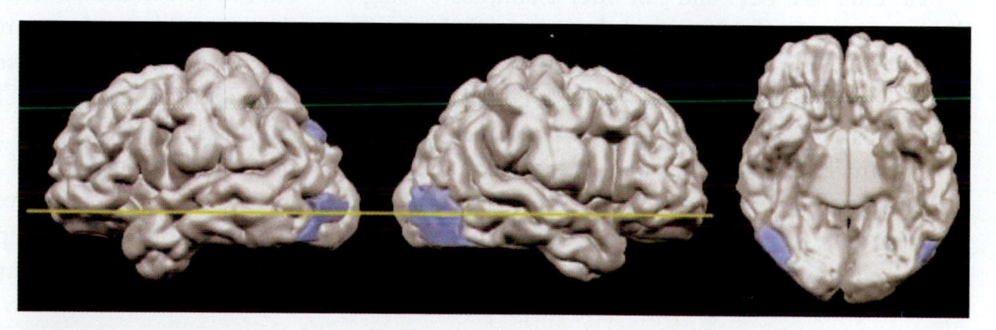

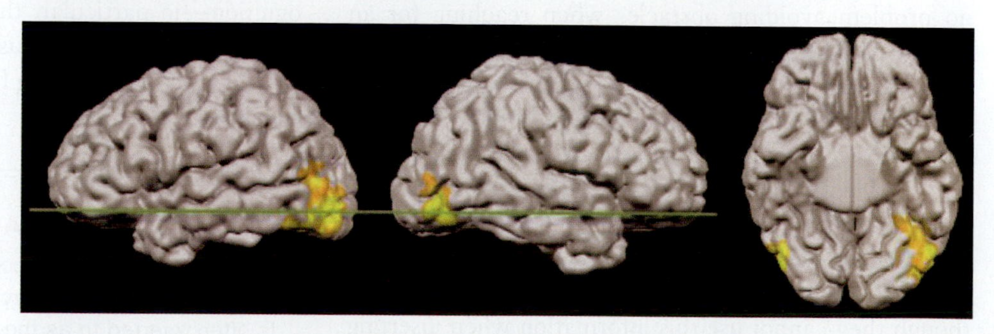

FIGURE 6.8 Ventral-stream lesions compared with the functionally defined lateral occipital cortex in healthy participants.
(a) Reconstruction of D.F.'s brain lesion. Lateral views of the left and right hemispheres are shown, as is a ventral view of the underside of the brain (the parietal lesion is not seen in this view). (b) The highlighted regions indicate activation in the lateral occipital cortex (LOC) of neurologically healthy individuals when they are recognizing objects.

anterior regions of the inferior parietal lobe—a pattern also seen when D.F. did this task (Culham et al., 2003).

Other case studies present a similar picture. One patient, J.S., complained that he was unable to see objects, watch TV, or read. He could dress himself, but only if he knew beforehand exactly where his clothes were located. What's more, he was unable to recognize familiar people by their faces, even though he could identify them by their voices. Oddly enough, however, he was able to walk around the neighborhood without a problem. He also could easily grab objects presented to him at different locations, even though he could not identify the objects (Karnath et al., 2009).

J.S. was examined with tests similar to those used in the studies of D.F. When shown an object, J.S. performed poorly in describing its size, but he could readily adjust his grip to match the object's size and pick it up. Or, if shown two flat and irregular shapes, J.S. found it very challenging to say whether they were the same or different, yet he could easily modify his hand shape to pick up each object. As with D.F., J.S. displayed a compelling dissociation in his abilities for object identification, even though his actions indicated that he "perceived" in exquisite detail the shape and orientation of the objects. MRI scans of J.S.'s brain revealed damage limited to the medial aspect of the ventral occipitotemporal cortex (OTC).

Patients like D.F. and J.S. offer examples of single dissociations. Each shows a selective (and dramatic) impairment in using vision to recognize objects while remaining proficient in using vision to perform actions. The opposite dissociation can also be found in the clinical literature: Patients with **optic ataxia** can recognize objects, yet they cannot use visual information to guide their actions. For instance, when someone with optic ataxia reaches for an object, she doesn't move directly toward it; rather, she gropes about like a person trying to find a light switch in the dark. Although D.F. had no problem avoiding obstacles when reaching for an object, patients with optic ataxia fail to take obstacles into account as they reach for something (Schindler et al., 2004).

Their eye movements present a similar loss of spatial knowledge. Saccades may be directed inappropriately and fail to bring the object within the fovea. When tested on the slot task used with D.F. (Figure 6.7), these patients can report the orientation of a visual slot, even though they cannot use this information when inserting an object into the slot. In accord with what researchers expect on the basis of dorsal–ventral dichotomy, optic ataxia is associated with lesions of the parietal cortex.

Although these examples are dramatic demonstrations of functional separation of "what" and "where" processing, do not forget that this evidence comes from the study of patients with rare disorders. It is also important to see whether similar principles hold in healthy brains. Lior Shmuelof and Ehud Zohary (2006) designed a study to compare activity patterns in the dorsal and ventral streams in normal participants. The participants viewed video clips of various objects that were being manipulated by a hand. The objects were presented in either the left or right visual field, and the hand approached the object from the opposite visual field. Activation of the dorsal parietal region was driven by the position of the hand. For example, when viewing a right hand reaching for an object in the left visual field, the activation was stronger in the left parietal region. In contrast, activation in ventral OTC was correlated with the position of the object. In a second experiment, the participants were asked either to identify the object or to judge how many fingers were used to grasp the object. Here again, ventral activation was stronger for the object identification task, but dorsal activation was stronger for the finger judgment task.

In sum, the what–where or what–how dichotomy offers a functional account of two computational goals of higher visual processing. This distinction is best viewed as heuristic rather than absolute. The dorsal and ventral streams are not isolated from one another, but rather communicate extensively. Processing within the parietal lobe, the termination of the "where" pathway, serves many purposes. We have focused here on its guiding of action; in Chapter 7 we will see that the parietal lobe also plays a critical role in *selective attention*, the enhancement of processing at some locations instead of others. Moreover, spatial information can be useful for solving "what" problems. For example, depth cues help segregate a complex scene into its component objects.

The rest of this chapter concentrates on object recognition—in particular, the visual system's assortment of strategies that make use of both dorsal-stream and ventral-stream processing for perceiving and recognizing the world.

TAKE-HOME MESSAGES

- The ventral stream, or occipitotemporal pathway, is specialized for object perception and recognition. This is often referred to as the "what" pathway. It focuses on vision for *recognition*.
- The dorsal stream, or occipitoparietal pathway, is specialized for spatial perception and is often referred to as the "where" (or "how") pathway. It focuses on vision for *action*.

- Neurons in the parietal lobe have large, nonselective receptive fields that include cells representing both the fovea and the periphery. Neurons in the temporal lobe have large receptive fields that are much more selective and always represent foveal information.
- Patients with selective lesions of the ventral pathway may have severe problems in consciously identifying objects, yet they can use the visual information to guide coordinated movement. Thus we see that visual information is used for a variety of purposes.
- Patients with optic ataxia can recognize objects but cannot use visual information to guide action. Optic ataxia is associated with lesions of the parietal cortex.

6.3 Seeing Shapes and Perceiving Objects

Object perception depends primarily on an analysis of the shape of a visual stimulus, though cues such as color, texture, and motion certainly also contribute to normal perception. For example, when people look at the surf breaking on the shore, their acuity is not sufficient to see grains of sand, and the water is essentially amorphous, lacking any definable shape. Yet the textures of the sand's surface and the water's edge, and their differences in color, enable us to distinguish between the two regions. The water's motion is important too.

Nevertheless, even if surface features like texture and color are absent or applied inappropriately, recognition is minimally affected: We can readily identify the elephant, apple, and human form in **Figure 6.9**, even though they are shown as blue and green geometric shapes, striped onyx, and a marble statue, respectively. Here, object recognition is derived from a perceptual ability to match an analysis of shape and form to an object, regardless of color, texture, or motion cues. How is a shape represented internally? What enables us to recognize differences between a triangle and a square, or between a chimp and a person?

Shape Encoding

In the previous chapter we introduced the idea that recognition may involve hierarchical representations in which each successive stage adds complexity. Simple features such as lines can be combined into edges, corners, and intersections, which—as processing continues up the hierarchy—are grouped into parts, and the parts grouped into objects. People recognize a pentagon because it contains five line segments of equal length, joined together to form five corners that define an enclosed region (**Figure 6.10**). The same five line segments can define other objects, such as a pyramid. With the pyramid, however, there are only four points of intersection, not five, and the lines define a more complicated shape that implies it is three-dimensional. The pentagon and the pyramid might activate similar representations at the lowest levels of the hierarchy, yet the combinations of these features into a shape produce distinct representations at higher levels of the processing hierarchy.

One way to investigate how we encode shapes is to identify areas of the brain that are active when we

FIGURE 6.9 Analyzing shape and form.
Despite the irregularities in how these objects are depicted, most people have little problem recognizing them. We may never have seen blue and green elephants or striped apples, but our object recognition system can still discern the essential features that identify these objects as elephants and apples.

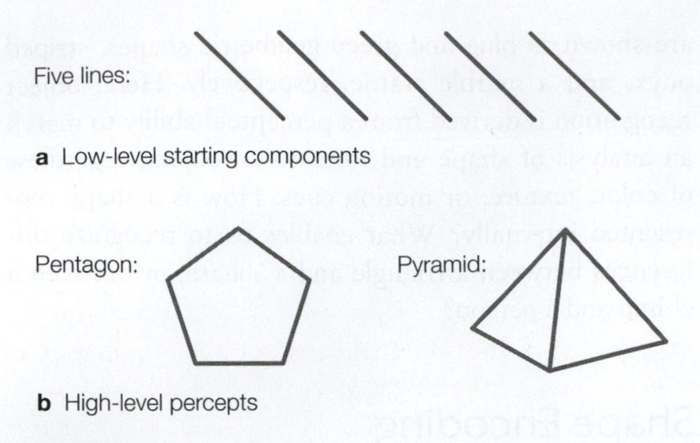

FIGURE 6.10
Basic elements and the different objects they can form.
The same basic components (five lines) can form different items (e.g., a pentagon or a pyramid), depending on their arrangement. Although the low-level components (a) are the same, the high-level percepts (b) are distinct.

compare contours that form a recognizable shape versus contours that are just squiggles. How do activity patterns in the brain change when a shape is familiar? This question emphasizes the idea that perception involves a connection between sensation and memory (recall our four guiding principles of object recognition).

Researchers explored this question in a PET study designed to isolate the specific mental operations used when people viewed familiar shapes, novel shapes, or stimuli formed by scrambling the shapes to generate random drawings (Kanwisher et al., 1997). All three types of stimuli should engage the early stages of visual perception, or what is called *feature extraction* (**Figure 6.11a**). To identify areas involved in object perception, a comparison can be made between responses to novel objects and responses to scrambled stimuli—as well as between responses to familiar objects and responses to scrambled stimuli—under the assumption that scrambled stimuli do not define objects per se. The memory retrieval contribution should be most evident when we are viewing novel or familiar objects.

Viewing both novel and familiar stimuli led to increases in regional cerebral blood flow bilaterally in lateral occipital cortex (LOC; **Figure 6.11b**) compared to viewing scrambled drawings without a recognizable shape. Since this study, many others have shown that the LOC is critical for shape and object recognition. Interestingly, no differences were found between the novel and familiar stimuli in the posterior cortical regions. At least within these areas, recognizing that something is familiar may be as taxing as recognizing that something is unfamiliar.

When we view an object such as a dog, whether it's a real dog, a drawing of a dog, a statue of a dog, or an outline of a dog made of flashing lights, we recognize it as a dog. This insensitivity to the specific visual cues that define an object is known as *cue invariance*.

Research has shown that, for the LOC, shape seems to be the most salient property of the stimulus. In one fMRI study, participants viewed stimuli in which shapes were defined either by luminance cues or by motion cues.

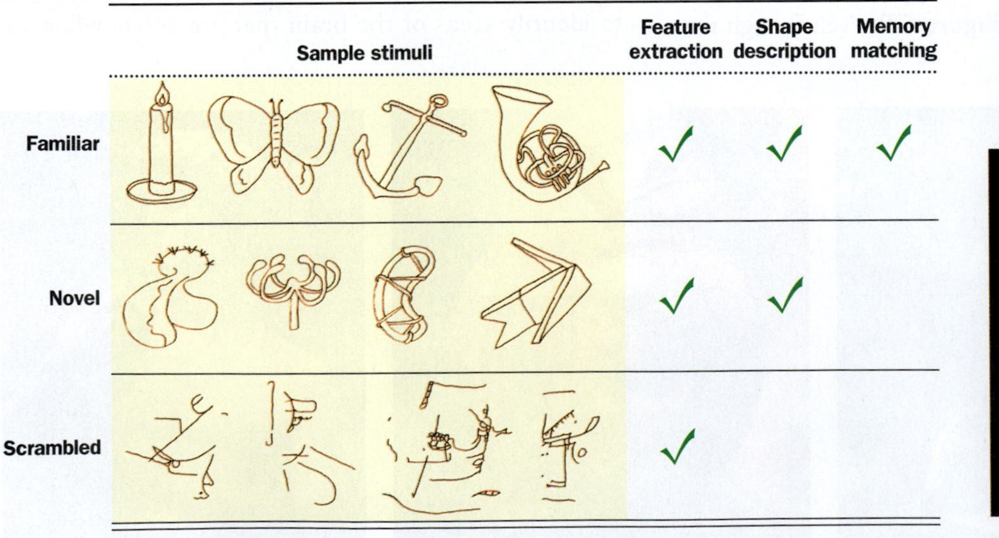

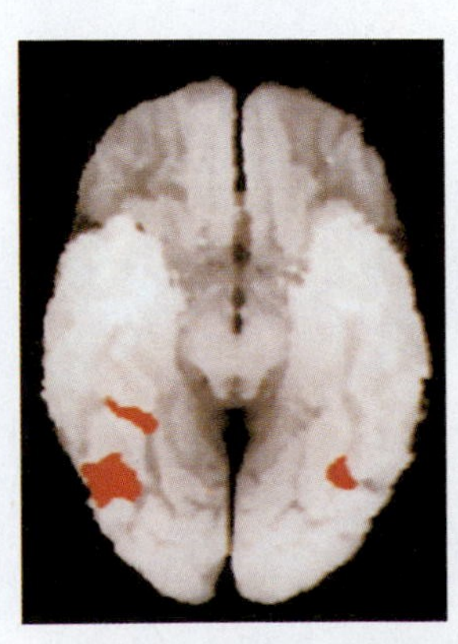

FIGURE 6.11 Component analysis of object recognition.
(a) Stimuli for the three conditions and the mental operations required in each condition. Novel objects are hypothesized to engage processes involved in perception even when verbal labels do not exist.
(b) When familiar and novel objects were viewed, activation was greater in the occipitotemporal cortex, shown here in a horizontal slice, than when scrambled stimuli with no recognizable object shape were viewed.

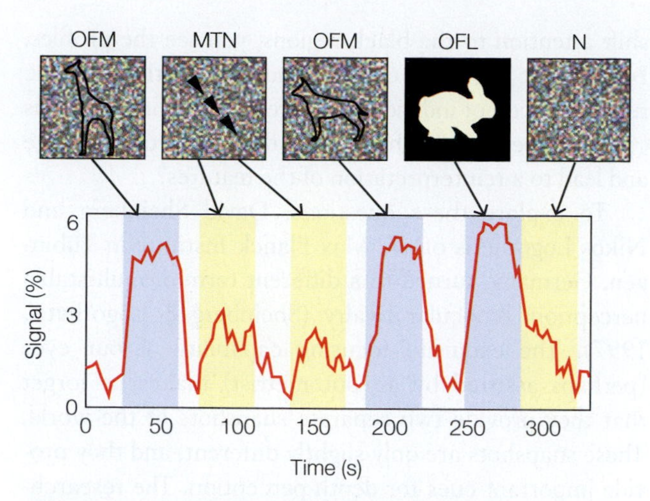

FIGURE 6.12 The BOLD response in lateral occipital cortex responds to shape even if object boundaries are not physically presented.
In an fMRI study using a block design, observers passively viewed four types of stimuli. There were two types of control stimuli without objects: one in which there was complete random motion of all the dots (N), and a second that had coherent motion of all the dots (MTN). The other two types of stimuli both depicted objects: either objects defined from luminance (OFL), which were silhouetted against a dark background, or objects defined from motion (OFM), which were coherently moving dots silhouetted against a background of dots moving in random directions. In this last case, the shape of the object became visible at the boundaries where the two types of motion met, producing the outline of the object. The BOLD response in the LOC increased in the OFL and OFM conditions.

When compared to control stimuli with similar sensory properties, the LOC response was also similar, regardless of whether the shape was defined by the juxtaposition of light against dark or the juxtaposition of coherently moving and randomly moving dots (Grill-Spector et al., 2001; **Figure 6.12**). Thus, the LOC can support the perception of an elephant shape even when the elephant is blue and green, or an apple shape even when the apple is made of onyx and striped.

The functional specification of the LOC for shape perception is evident even in 6-month-old babies (Emberson et al., 2017). As you might imagine, it would be quite a challenge to get infants to sit still in the fMRI scanner. An alternative method involves **functional near-infrared spectroscopy (fNIRS)**, which employs a lightweight system that looks similar to an EEG cap and can be comfortably placed on the infant's head. This system includes a source to generate infrared light, which takes advantage of the fact that infrared light can project through the scalp and skull. The absorption of the light differs for oxygenated and deoxygenated blood, and thus, as with fMRI, sensors of the fNIRS system are used to measure changes in hemodynamic activity. The system works best when targeting cortical tissue such as the LOC, which is close to the skull.

The researchers also made use of the finding, from various imaging studies, that when a stimulus is repeated, the BOLD response is lower in the second presentation compared to the first. This **repetition suppression (RS) effect** is hypothesized to indicate increased neural efficiency: The neural response to the stimulus is more efficient and perhaps faster when the pattern has been recently activated.

Not only do researchers have to give special consideration to the type of imaging methodology when working with infants, but they also have to come up with age-appropriate tasks. To study shape perception, the researchers created two sets of visual stimuli: one in which the stimuli varied in shape and color while texture was held constant, and another in which the stimuli varied in texture and color while shape was held constant (Emberson et al., 2017). In this way, color was a relevant feature for both sets, but only shape or texture was relevant in their respective conditions.

Taking advantage of the RS effect, the researchers focused on how the fNIRS response changed when certain features were repeated (**Figure 6.13a**). When a

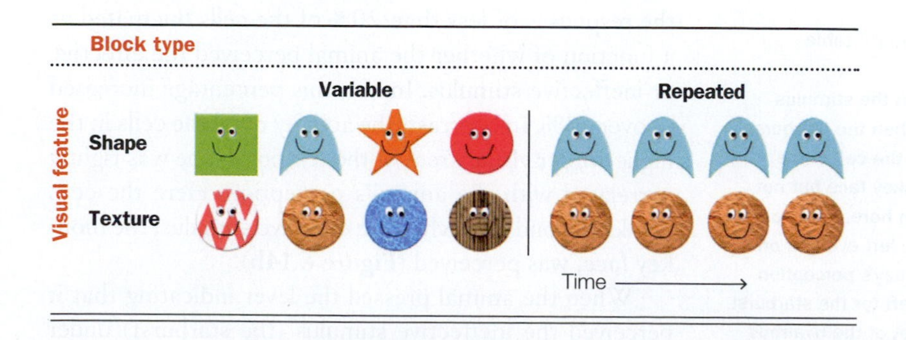

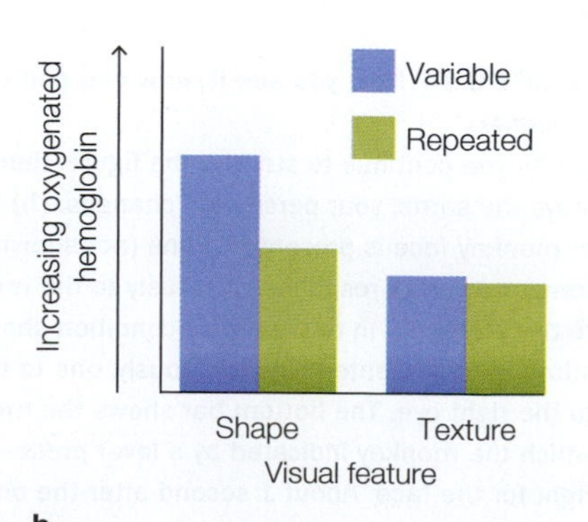

FIGURE 6.13 Specificity for shape identification in the LOC is evident by 6 months of age.
(a) Examples of stimuli. Within a block of trials, one dimension (either shape or texture) varied, and the other was held constant. (b) When a single shape was repeated eight times, the hemodynamic response in LOC decreased, as compared to when the shape varied with the texture repeated. This repetition suppression effect indicates that the LOC is selectively sensitive to shape.

shape was repeated, the hemodynamic response from the LOC decreased compared to when different shapes were shown. In contrast, there was no difference between conditions in which texture was repeated or varied (**Figure 6.13b**), providing evidence that the infant LOC is sensitive to shape but not to other visual features.

From Shapes to Objects

What does **Figure 6.14a** show? If you are like most people, you initially saw a vase. With continued viewing, the vase changes to the profiles of two people facing each other, and then back to the vase, and on and on, in an example of *multistable perception*. How are multistable percepts resolved in the brain? The stimulus information does not change at the points of transition from one percept to the other, but the interpretation of the pictorial cues does. When staring at the white region, you see the vase. If you shift attention to the black regions, you see the profiles. But here we run into a chicken-and-egg question. Did the representation of individual features change first and thus cause the percept to change? Or did the percept change and lead to a reinterpretation of the features?

To explore these questions, David Sheinberg and Nikos Logothetis of the Max Planck Institute in Tübingen, Germany, turned to a different form of multistable perception: binocular rivalry (Sheinberg & Logothetis, 1997). The exquisite focusing capability of our eyes (perhaps assisted by an optometrist) makes us forget that they provide two separate snapshots of the world. These snapshots are only slightly different, and they provide important cues for depth perception. The researchers made special glasses that present radically different images to each eye and have a shutter that can alternately block the input to one eye and then the other at very rapid rates. When humans don these glasses, they do not see two things in one location. As with the ambiguous vase–face profiles picture, only one object or the other is seen at any single point in time, although at transitions there is sometimes a period of fuzziness in which neither object is clearly perceived.

The researchers fitted monkeys with the glasses and presented them with radically different inputs to the two eyes, either separately or simultaneously. The monkeys were trained to press one of two levers to indicate which object was being perceived. To make sure the animals were not responding randomly, the researchers included non-rivalrous trials in which only one of the objects was presented. They then recorded from single cells in various areas of the visual cortex. Within each area they tested two objects, only one of which was effective in driving the cell. In this way the activity of the cell could be correlated with the animal's perceptual experience.

The researchers found that activity in early visual areas was closely linked to the stimulus, while activity in higher areas (IT cortex) was linked to the percept. In V1, the responses of less than 20% of the cells fluctuated as a function of whether the animal perceived the effective or ineffective stimulus. In V4, this percentage increased to over 33%. In contrast, the activity of all the cells in the higher-order visual areas of the temporal lobe was tightly correlated with the animal's perception. Here the cells would respond only when the effective stimulus, the monkey face, was perceived (**Figure 6.14b**).

When the animal pressed the lever indicating that it perceived the ineffective stimulus (the starburst) under rivalrous conditions, the cells were essentially silent. In both V4 and the temporal lobe, the cell activity changed in advance of the animal's response, indicating that the percept had changed. Thus, even when the stimulus did not change, an increase in activity was observed before

a

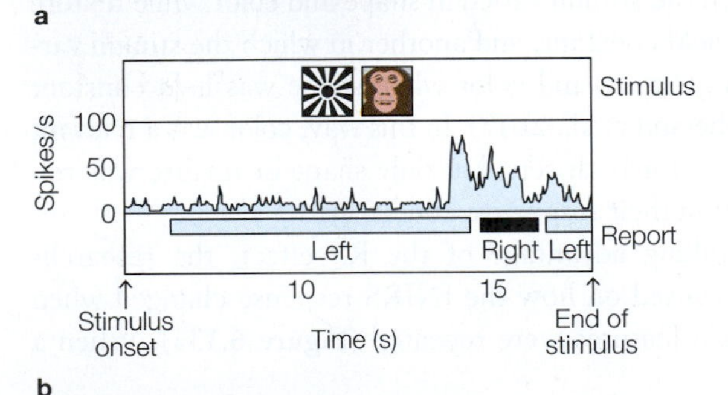

b

FIGURE 6.14 Now you see it, now you don't: multistable percepts.
(a) As you continue to stare at the figure, though the stimulus stays the same, your perception changes. **(b)** When the starburst or monkey face is presented alone (not shown), the cell in the temporal cortex responds vigorously to the monkey face but not to the starburst. In the rivalrous condition shown here, the two stimuli are presented simultaneously, one to the left eye and one to the right eye. The bottom bar shows the monkey's perception, which the monkey indicated by a lever press—left for the starburst, right for the face. About 1 second after the onset of the rivalrous stimulus, the animal perceives the starburst; the cell is silent during this period. About 7 seconds later, the cell shows a large increase in activity and, correspondingly, the monkey indicates that its perception has changed to the monkey face shortly thereafter. Then, 2 seconds later, the percept flips back to the starburst and the cell's activity is again reduced.

the transition from a perception of the ineffective stimulus to a perception of the effective stimulus.

These results suggest a competition during the early stages of cortical processing between the two possible "what" percepts in the ventral pathway. The activity of the cells in V1 and in V4 can be thought of as perceptual hypotheses, with the patterns across an ensemble of cells reflecting the strengths of the different hypotheses. Interactions between these cells ensure that, by the time the information reaches the inferior temporal lobe, one of these hypotheses has coalesced into a stable percept. Reflecting the properties of the real world, the brain is not fooled into believing that two objects exist at the same place at the same time.

Grandmother Cells and Ensemble Coding

How do we recognize specific objects? For example, what enables us to distinguish between a coyote and a dog, a peach and a nectarine, or the orchid *Dracula simia* and a monkey face (**Figure 6.15**)? Are there individual cells that respond only to specific integrated percepts, or does perception of an object depend on the firing of a collection or ensemble of cells? In the latter case, this would mean that when you see a peach, a group of neurons that code for different features of the peach might become active, with some subset of them also active when you see a nectarine.

FIGURE 6.15 Monkey orchid (*Dracula simia*). The flower of this species of orchid looks remarkably like a monkey's face.

The finding that cells in the IT cortex selectively respond to complex stimuli (e.g., objects, places, body parts, or faces; Figure 6.6) is consistent with hierarchical theories of object perception. According to these theories, cells in the initial areas of the visual cortex code elementary features such as line orientation and color. The outputs from these cells are combined to form detectors sensitive to higher-order features such as corners or intersections—an idea consistent with the findings of Hubel and Wiesel (see Chapter 5). The process continues as each successive stage codes more complex combinations (**Figure 6.16**). The type of neuron that can recognize a complex object has been called a **gnostic unit**, referring to the idea that the cell (or cells) signals the presence of a known stimulus—an object, a place, or an animal that has been encountered in the past.

It is tempting to conclude that the cell represented by the recordings in Figure 6.6 signals the presence of a hand, independent of viewpoint. Other cells in the IT cortex respond preferentially to complex stimuli, such as jagged contours or fuzzy textures. The latter might be useful for a monkey, to help it identify that an object has a fur-covered surface and therefore might be the backside of another member of its group.

Even more intriguing, researchers discovered cells in the IT gyrus and the floor of the superior temporal sulcus (STS) that are selectively activated by faces. In a tongue-in-cheek manner, they coined the term *grandmother cell* to convey the notion that people's brains might have a gnostic unit that becomes excited only when their grandmother comes into view. Other gnostic units would be specialized to recognize, for example, a blue Volkswagen or the Golden Gate Bridge.

Itzhak Fried and his colleagues at UCLA explored this question by making single-cell recordings in human participants (Quiroga et al., 2005). These participants all had epilepsy, and in preparation for a surgical procedure to alleviate their symptoms, electrodes were surgically implanted in the temporal lobe. In the study, they were shown a wide range of pictures, including animals, objects, landmarks, and individuals. The investigators' first observation was that, in general, it was difficult to make these cells respond. Even when the stimuli were individually tailored to each participant on the basis of an interview to determine that person's visual history, the temporal lobe cells were generally inactive.

Nonetheless, there were exceptions. Most notable, these exceptions revealed an extraordinary degree of stimulus specificity. Recall Figure 3.21, which shows the response of one temporal lobe neuron that was selectively activated in response to photographs of the actress Halle Berry. Ms. Berry could be wearing sunglasses, sporting a dramatically different haircut, or even in costume as

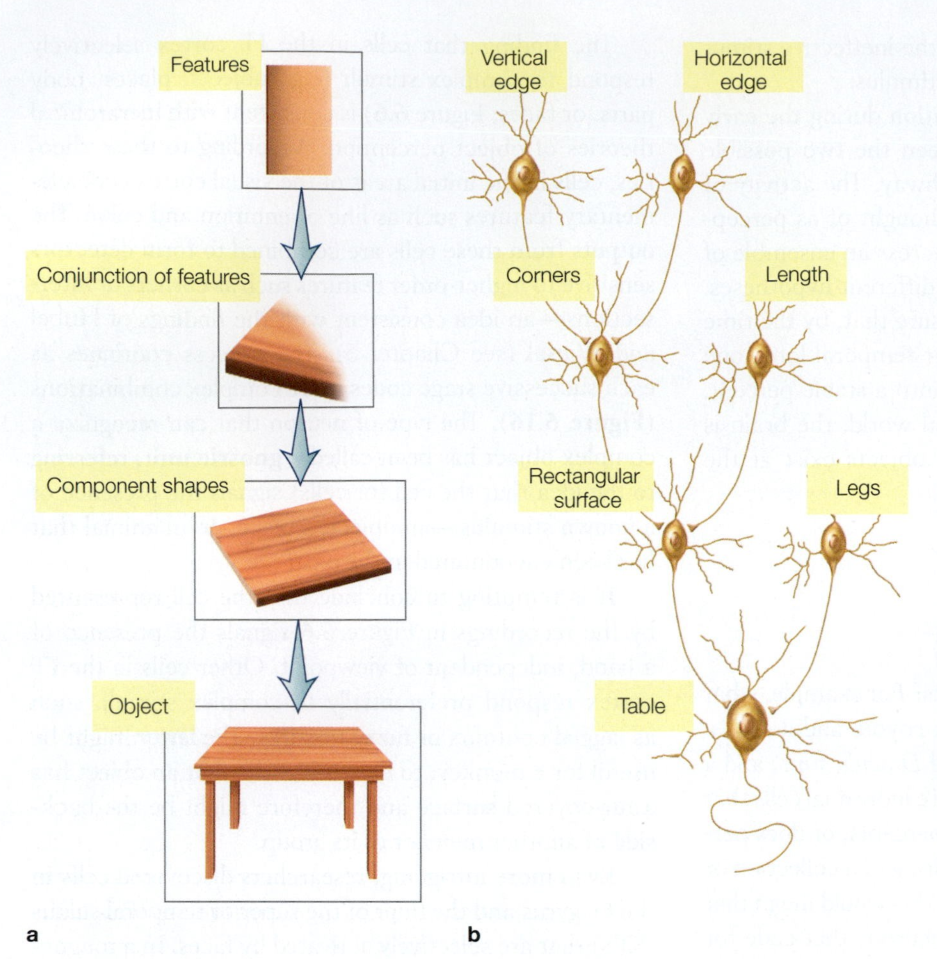

FIGURE 6.16 The hierarchical coding hypothesis.
Elementary features are combined to create objects that can be recognized by gnostic units. At the first level of the hierarchy depicted are edge detectors, which operate similarly to the simple cells discussed in Chapter 5. These feature units combine to form corner detectors, which in turn combine to form cells that respond to even more complex stimuli, such as surfaces. **(a)** Hypothesized computational stages for hierarchical coding. **(b)** Cartoon of neuronal implementation of the computational stages illustrated in (a).

Catwoman—in all cases, this particular neuron was activated. Other actresses or famous people failed to activate the neuron.

Although it is tempting to conclude that cells like these are gnostic units, it is important to keep in mind the limitations of such experiments. First, aside from the infinite number of possible stimuli, the recordings are performed on only a small subset of neurons. This cell potentially could be activated by a broader set of stimuli, and many other neurons might respond in a similar manner. Second, the results also suggest that these gnostic-like units are not really "perceptual." The same cell was also activated when the words "Halle Berry" were presented. This observation takes the wind out of the argument that this is a grandmother cell, at least in the original sense of the idea. Rather, the cell may represent the concept of "Halle Berry," or even represent the name Halle Berry, a name that is likely recalled from memory for any of the stimuli relevant to the actress.

One alternative to the grandmother-cell hypothesis is that object recognition results from activation across complex feature detectors (**Figure 6.17**). Granny, then, is recognized when some of these higher-order neurons are activated. Some of the cells may respond to her shape, others to the color of her hair, and still others to the features of her face. According to this ensemble hypothesis, recognition is due not to one unit but to the collective activation of many units. Ensemble theories readily account for why we can recognize similarities between objects (say, a tiger and a lion) and may confuse one visually similar object with another: Both objects activate many of the same neurons. Losing some units might degrade our ability to recognize an object, but the remaining units might suffice. Ensemble theories also account for our ability to recognize novel objects. Novel objects bear a similarity to familiar things, and our percepts result from activating units that represent their features.

The results of single-cell studies of temporal lobe neurons are in accord with ensemble theories of object recognition. Although it is striking that some cells are selective for complex objects, the selectivity is almost always relative, not absolute. The cells in the IT cortex prefer certain stimuli to others, but they are also activated by visually similar stimuli. The cell represented in Figure 6.6, for instance, increases its activity when presented with a mitten-like stimulus. No cells respond to a particular individual's hand; the hand-selective cell responds equally to just about any hand. In contrast, as people's perceptual abilities demonstrate, we make much finer discriminations.

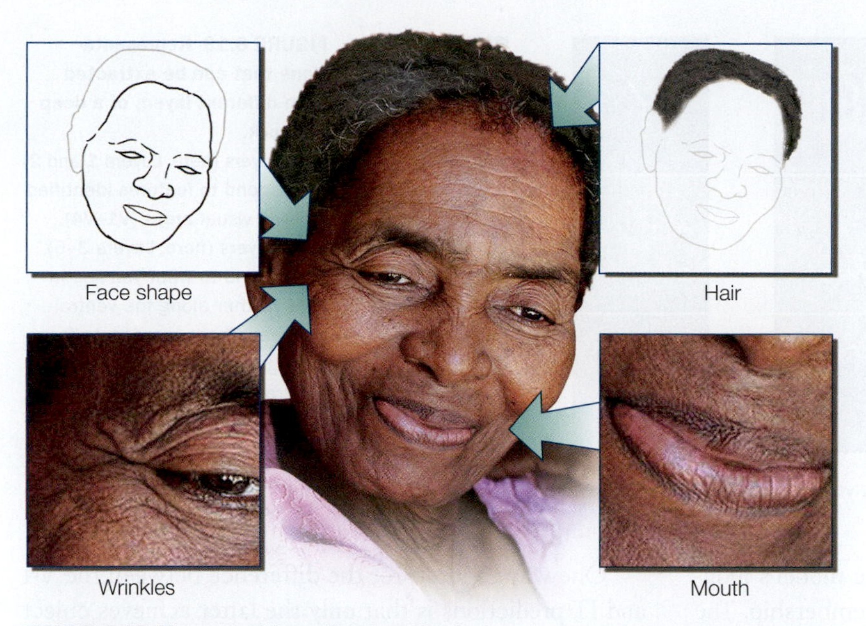

FIGURE 6.17 The ensemble coding hypothesis.
Objects are defined by the simultaneous activation of a set of defining properties. "Granny" is recognized here by the co-occurrence of her wrinkles, face shape, hair color, and so on.

Exploiting the Computational Power of Neural Networks

How are perceptual systems organized to make sense of the complex information that is constantly bombarding our sense organs? One suggestion is that a layered architecture with extensive connectivity and subject to some simple learning principles is optimal for learning about the rich structure of the environment. Although this conjecture has been debated at a theoretical level for a long time, recent advances in artificial intelligence research have enabled researchers to put the idea to the test, comparing simulations derived in deep learning networks (see Chapter 3) with data from neurophysiological experiments.

At the input layer of these networks, the representation may be somewhat akin to information in the environment; for example, a visual recognition network might have an input layer that corresponds to the pixels in an image. At the output layer, the representation might correspond to a decision; for example, is there a face in the image and if so, whose? The middle layers, or what are called the hidden layers, entail additional processing steps in which the information is recombined and reweighted according to different processing rules (**Figure 6.18**).

How this comes about depends on the algorithms used to train the system. In some cases, error signals might be created by comparing the output of the network with the correct answer and then using this information to modify the connections—for example, by weakening connections that are active when errors are made. In other cases, the training rules might be based on simple network properties, such as level of activity (e.g., making active connections stronger).

The key insight to be drawn from research with deep learning networks is that these systems are remarkably efficient at extracting statistical regularities or creating representations that can solve complex problems (**Figure 6.19**). Deep learning networks have surpassed human abilities in games such as Go and Texas Hold'em poker, and they are becoming highly proficient in some of our most exquisite perceptual abilities, such as judging whether a face is familiar.

To explore whether our visual system is organized in a similar manner, Jim DiCarlo and his colleagues at MIT (Yamins et al., 2014) constructed a hierarchical model with a layered architecture of the ventral pathway to solve a fundamental perceptual problem: determining the category of a visual stimulus. To train the network, the model was presented with 5,760 pictures that included objects from eight different categories (animals, boats, cars, chairs, faces, fruits, planes, and tables). This training would be analogous to a baby's continued exposure to different visual scenes.

Each image was then propagated through a four-layered network in which the processing at each stage incorporated computational principles derived from neurophysiological and computational studies. At the V1 stage, activation reflected the integration of luminance information from a small set of pixels. Higher stages combined the output from lower stages, with the output from

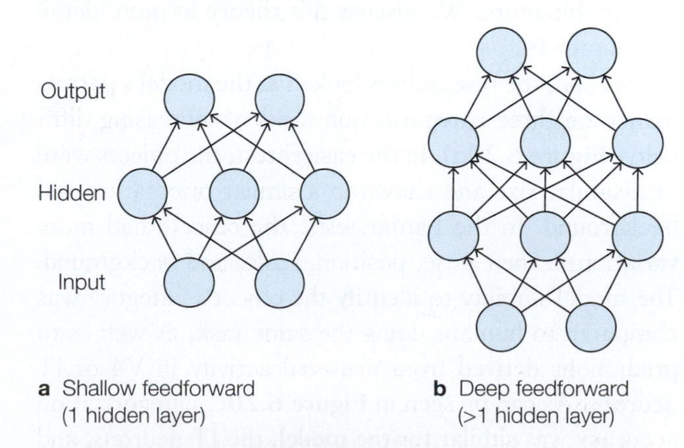

FIGURE 6.18 Layered feedforward networks.
(a) A shallow feedforward network has no hidden layers or one hidden layer. (b) A deep feedforward network has more than one hidden layer. The use of multilayered networks has been a major breakthrough in machine learning and neuroscience, allowing systems to solve complex problems.

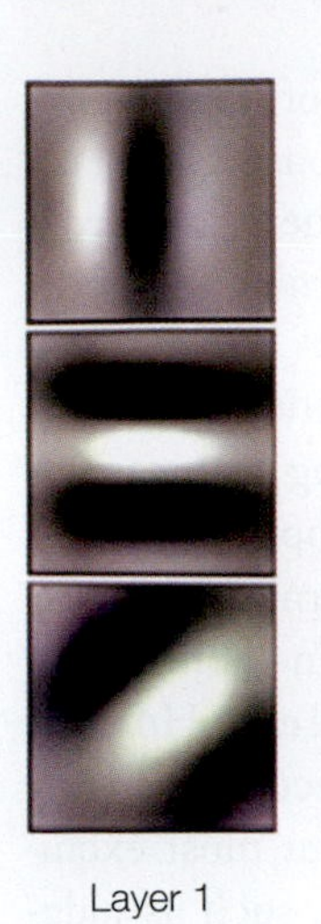

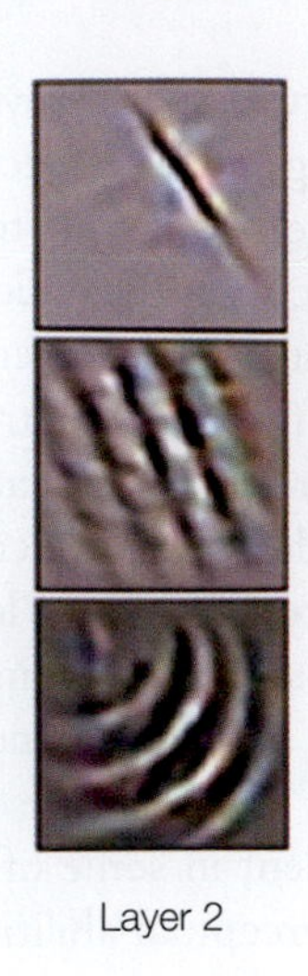

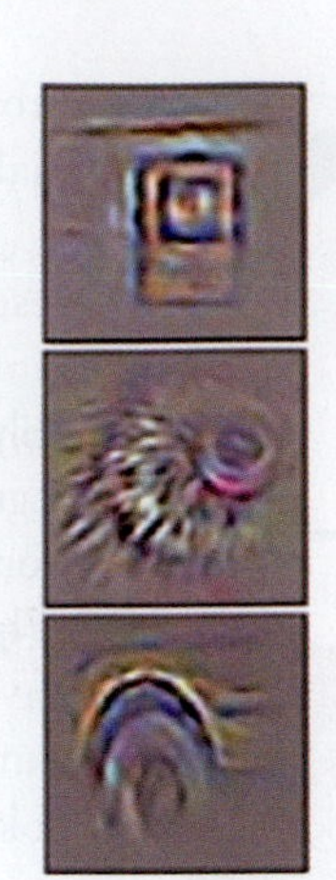

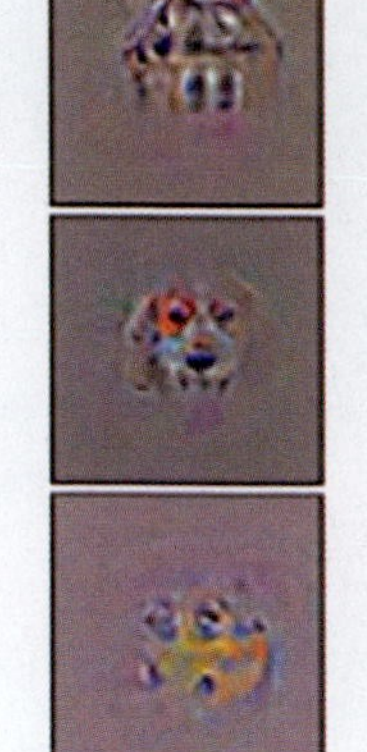

FIGURE 6.19 Representations that can be extracted from different layers of a deep network.
Early layers (here, Layers 1 and 2) correspond to features identified in early visual areas (V1–V4). Later layers (here, Layers 3–5) correspond to what you see in cells further along the ventral pathway. These representations emerge naturally when networks are trained to recognize objects.

the final stage used as a prediction of the model's judgment of the depicted object's category membership. The connections within each layer and between layers were refined according to how well the prediction matched the true answer; for example, if the prediction was wrong, active connections were weakened.

DiCarlo and his team provided two tests of the model. First, they asked how well the output from different layers in the model compared to neuronal activity at different levels of the ventral pathway. In particular, they showed the same pictures to monkeys while recording from cells in V4 and IT cortex. Interestingly, the output from the third layer of the network correlated strongly with the activity patterns in V4, whereas the output from the fourth layer correlated with activity patterns in the IT cortex. Even though the model entails radical simplifications of the complex interactions that underlie actual neuronal activity, there was a strong correspondence between the artificial and biological systems, providing support for the idea that the biological brain has a layered architecture. We discuss this theory in more detail in Chapter 14.

Second, the researchers looked at the model's performance on three categorization tasks of increasing difficulty (**Figure 6.20a**). In the easiest test, the objects were of a similar size and shown in a similar orientation and background. In the harder tests, the objects had more variation in their pose, position, scale, and background. The model's ability to identify the object's category was compared to humans doing the same task, as well as to predictions derived from neuronal activity in V4 or IT neurons. As can be seen in **Figure 6.20c**, categorization accuracy was similar for the model, the IT neurons, and the human observers. Moreover, as one would expect from what we have learned, V4 activity did a reasonably good job in predicting category membership for the easy task, but its performance dropped dramatically on the harder tasks.

One way to interpret the difference between the V4 and IT predictions is that only the latter achieves object constancy, identifying category membership independent of the actual stimulus. Humans are quite adept in maintaining object constancy—by definition, this is one form of categorization—and a simple, multilayered model with fairly simple processing rules was nearly as good as the human observers. We can well imagine that with more complexity and better learning algorithms, these complex networks might soon surpass human ability to rapidly scan through complex scenes. The airport security officer scanning X-ray images of your luggage is likely to be replaced by artificial intelligence.

Top-Down Effects on Object Recognition

Up to this point, we have emphasized a bottom-up perspective on processing within the visual system, showing how a multilayered system can combine features into more complex representations. This model appears to nicely capture the flow of information along the ventral pathway. However, it is also important to recognize that information processing is not a one-way, bottom-up street. For example, at Thanksgiving your sister may ask you to pass the potatoes. Your visual system does not meticulously inspect each food platter on the cluttered table to decide whether it contains the desired item. It can readily eliminate unlikely candidates, such as the turkey platter, and focus on the platters that contain a food with a color or consistency associated with potatoes.

One model of top-down effects emphasizes that input from the frontal cortex can influence processing along the ventral pathway. In this view, inputs from early visual areas are projected to the frontal lobe. Given their low position in the hierarchy, these representations are quite crude, perhaps just a blurry map of the distribution of

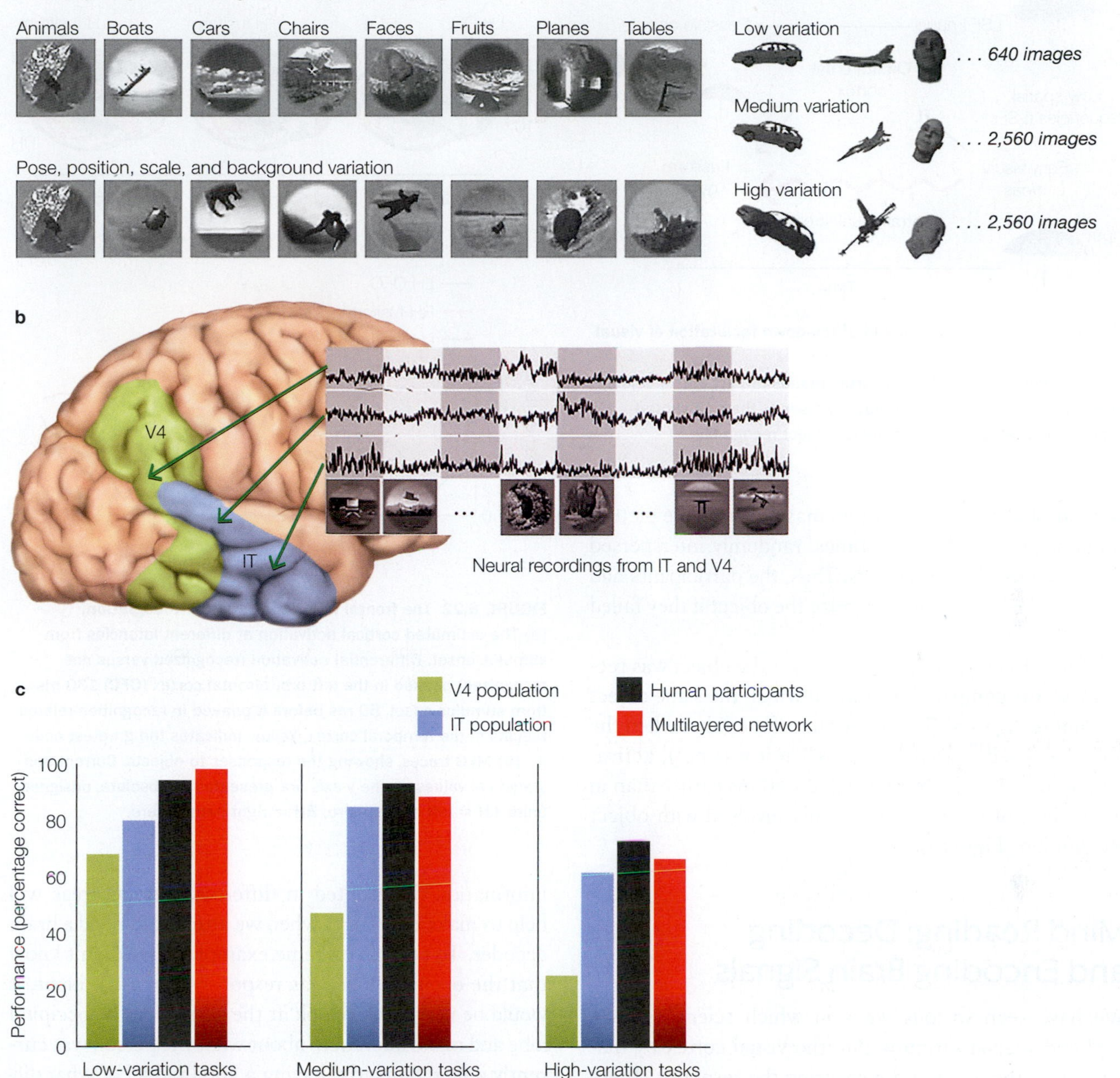

FIGURE 6.20 Performance results on an object categorization test.
(a) Test images were of eight object categories at three levels of object view variation. (b) Chronically implanted microelectrode arrays recorded the responses of neurons in V4 and IT cortex to about 6,000 images. (c) Neuronal responses from V4 (light-green bars), IT cortex (blue bars), and multilayered network models (red bars) were collected on the same image set and used to train classifiers from which population performance accuracy was evaluated. (The *y*-axis represents the percentage correct in an eight-way categorization, so chance performance would be 12.5%.) The responses of the human participants (black bars) were collected via psychophysics experiments.

objects in the scene—and even here, there may not be clear separation of the parts. The frontal lobe generates predictions about what the scene is, using this early scene analysis and knowledge of the current context. These top-down predictions can then be compared with the bottom-up analysis occurring along the ventral pathway of the temporal cortex, making for faster object recognition by limiting the field of possibilities (**Figure 6.21**).

To test this model, Moshe Bar and his colleagues had volunteers perform a visual recognition task while undergoing magnetoencephalography (MEG), a method with exquisite temporal resolution and reasonable spatial resolution. They were interested in comparing the time course of activation in frontal regions to that in recognition-related regions within the temporal cortex. The volunteers were very briefly shown pictures of

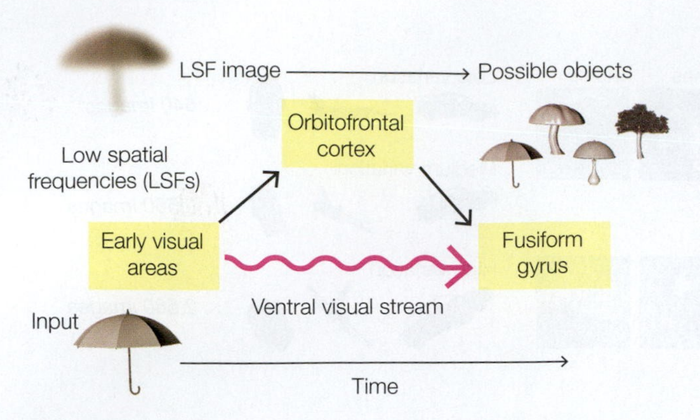

FIGURE 6.21 A proposed model of top-down facilitation of visual recognition.
In this model, the orbitofrontal cortex makes predictions of objects from partially analyzed visual input and sends them to ventral-stream processing areas to facilitate object recognition.

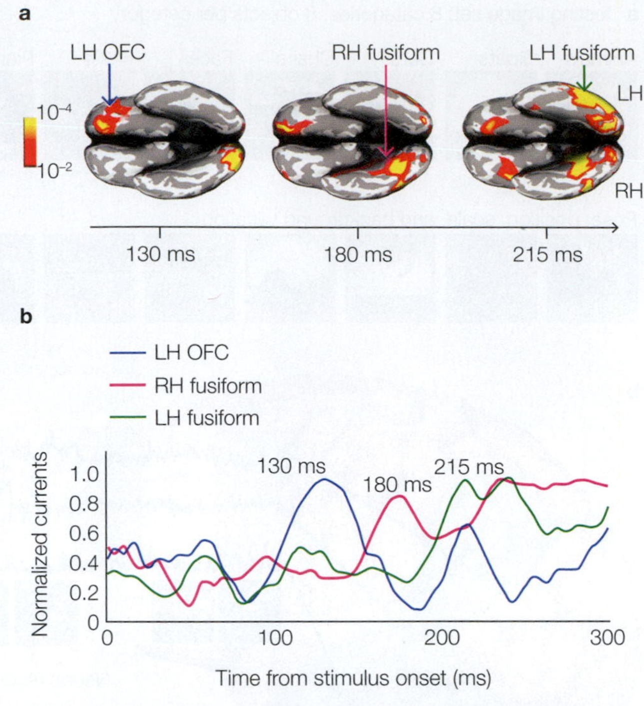

FIGURE 6.22 The frontal lobe aids in object recognition.
(a) The estimated cortical activation at different latencies from stimulus onset. Differential activation (recognized versus not recognized) peaked in the left orbitofrontal cortex (OFC) 130 ms from stimulus onset, 50 ms before it peaked in recognition-related regions in the temporal cortex. Yellow indicates the greatest activity. (b) MEG traces, showing the responses to objects. Current and statistical values on the *y*-axis are presented in absolute, unsigned units. LH = left hemisphere; RH = right hemisphere.

familiar objects flanked by two masks. The same picture could be presented several times, randomly interspersed with pictures of other objects. Thus, the participants had several opportunities to recognize the object if they failed on earlier brief glimpses.

The MEG response on trials when the object was recognized was compared to trials in which the same object was not recognized. The researchers found that when the object was recognized (versus when it was not), activation occurred in the frontal regions 50 ms earlier than in the regions of the temporal cortex involved with object recognition (**Figure 6.22**).

Mind Reading: Decoding and Encoding Brain Signals

We have seen various ways in which scientists have explored specialization within the visual cortex by manipulating the input and measuring the response. These observations have led investigators to realize that it should, at least in principle, be possible to analyze the system in the opposite direction (**Figure 6.23**). That is, we should be able to look at someone's brain activity and infer what the person is currently seeing (or has recently seen, assuming our measurements are delayed)—a form of mind reading. This idea is referred to as *decoding*: The brain activity provides the coded message, and the challenge is to decipher it and infer what is being represented.

A consideration of the computational challenges of decoding raises two key issues. One is that our ability to decode mental states is limited by our models of how the brain *encodes* information—that is, how information is represented in different cells or regions of the brain. Developing good hypotheses about the types of information represented in different cortical areas will help us make inferences when we attempt to build a brain decoder. To take an extreme example, if we didn't know that the occipital lobe was responsive to visual input, it would be very hard to look at the activity in the occipital lobe and make inferences about what the person was currently doing. Similarly, having a good model of what different regions represent—for example, that a high level of activity in V5 is correlated with motion perception—can be a powerful constraint on the predictions we make of what the person is seeing.

The second issue is technical: Our ability to decode will be limited by the resolution of our measurement system. With EEG, we have excellent temporal resolution but poor spatial resolution, both because electrical signals disperse and because we have a limited number of sensors. Spatial resolution is better with fMRI, but here temporal resolution is quite crude. Mind reading is not all that useful if the person has to maintain the same thought for, say, 10 or 20 seconds before we get a good read on her thoughts. Perception is a rapid, fluid process. A good mind-reading system should be able to operate at similar speeds.

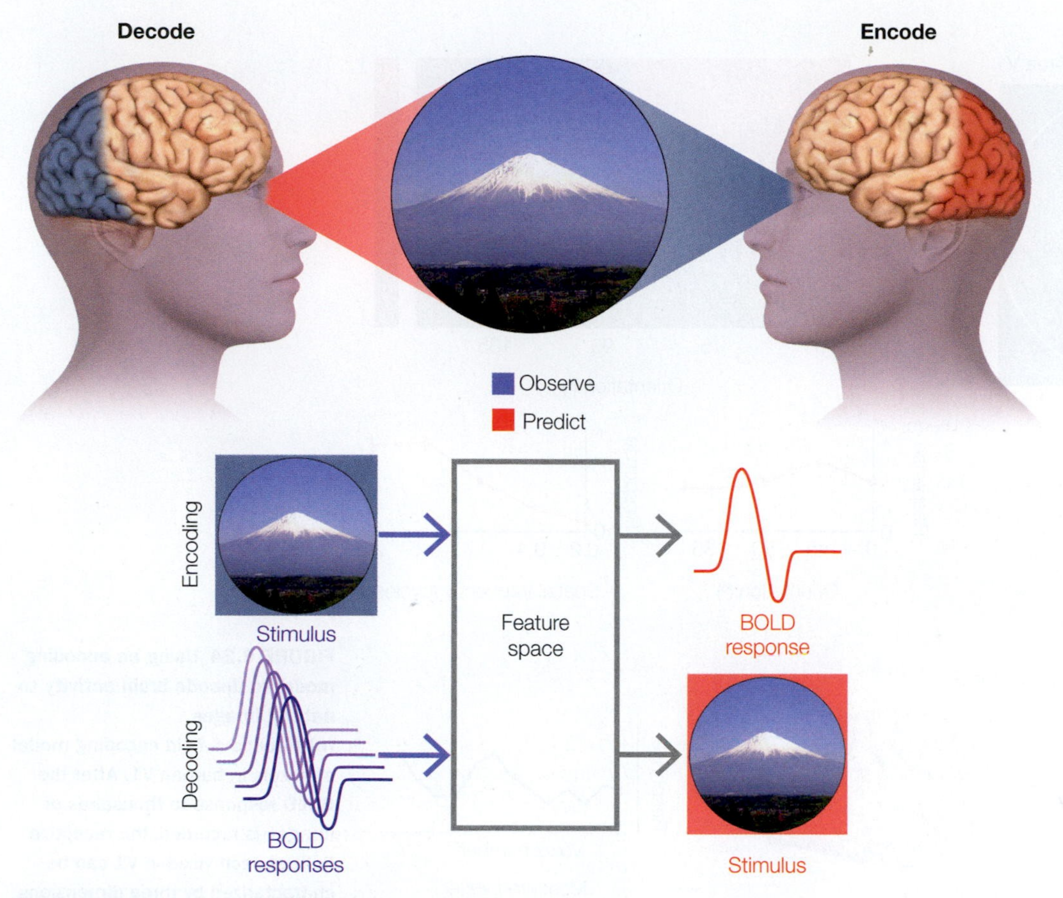

FIGURE 6.23 Encoding and decoding neural activity.
Encoding refers to the problem of how stimulus features are represented in neural activity. The image is processed by the sensory system, and the scientist wants to predict the resulting BOLD activity. *Decoding* (or mind reading) refers to the problem of predicting the stimulus that is being viewed when a particular brain state is observed. In fMRI decoding, the BOLD activity is used to predict the stimulus being observed by the participant. Successful encoding and decoding require having an accurate hypothesis of how information is represented in the brain (feature space).

How do we build a complex encoding model that operates at the level of the voxel or EEG electrode? One approach is to start with an educated guess. For example, in the visual system we could start by characterizing voxels in early visual processing areas that have tuning properties similar to what is seen with individual neurons—things like edges, orientation, and size. Keep in mind that each voxel contains hundreds of thousands, if not millions, of neurons, and that the neurons within one voxel will have different tuning profiles (e.g., for line orientation, some will be tuned for horizontal, vertical, or some other angle). Fortunately, having the same tuning profiles isn't essential. The essential thing is that voxels show detectable differences in their aggregate responses along these dimensions. That is, one voxel might contain more neurons that are tuned to horizontal lines, while another voxel has more neurons tuned to vertical lines.

Jack Gallant and his colleagues at UC Berkeley set out to build an encoding model based on these ideas (Kay et al., 2008). Recognizing the challenge of characterizing individual voxels, they opted against the standard experimental procedure of testing 15 to 20 naive participants for an hour each. Instead, they had two highly motivated people (i.e., two of the authors of the paper) lie in the MRI scanner for many hours, looking repeatedly at a set of 1,750 natural images. To further improve the spatial resolution, the BOLD response was recorded only in areas V1, V2, and V3. From this large data set, the researchers constructed the "receptive field" of each voxel (**Figure 6.24**).

They were then ready for the critical test. The participants were shown a set of 120 new images—images that had not been used to construct the encoding model. The BOLD response in each voxel was measured for each of the 120 images. From these hemodynamic signals, the decoder was asked to reconstruct the image. To test the accuracy of the decoded prediction, the researchers compared the predicted image to the actual image. They also quantified the results by determining the best match between the predicted image and the full set of 120 novel images.

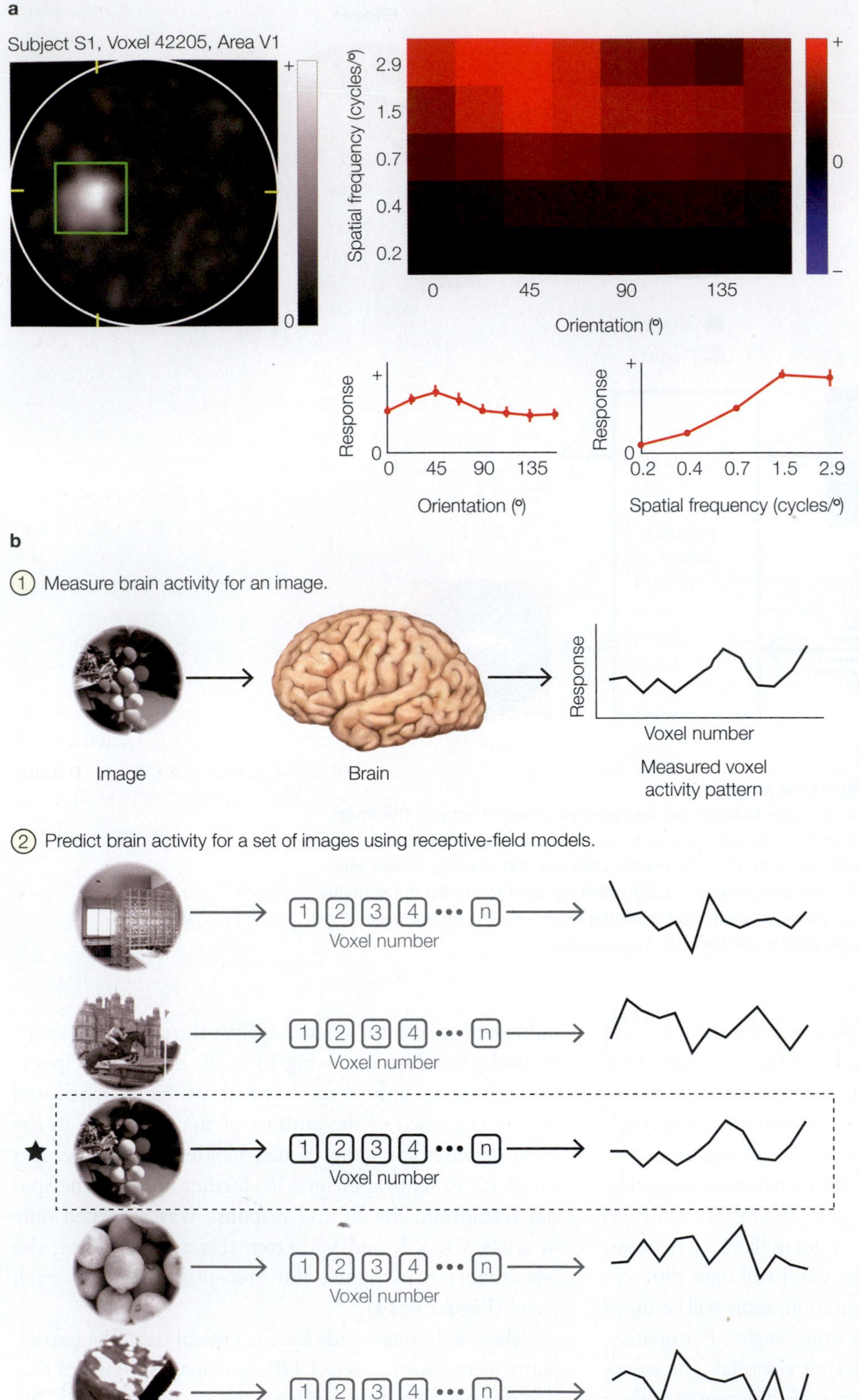

FIGURE 6.24 Using an encoding model to decode brain activity to natural images. **(a)** Receptive-field encoding model of voxels in human V1. After the BOLD response to thousands of images is recorded, the receptive field of each voxel in V1 can be characterized by three dimensions: location, orientation, and size. Note that each voxel reflects the activity of millions of neurons, but over the population, there remains some tuning for these dimensions. The heat map on the right side shows the relative response strength for one voxel to stimuli of different sizes (or, technically, spatial frequencies) and orientations. The resulting tuning functions are shown below the heat map. This process is repeated for each voxel to create the full encoding model. **(b)** Mind reading by decoding fMRI activity to visual images. (1) An image is presented to the participant, and the BOLD response is measured at each voxel. (2) The predicted BOLD response across the set of voxels is calculated for each image in the set. (3) The observed BOLD response from Step 1 is compared to all of the predicted BOLD responses, and the image with the best match is identified. If the match involves the same stimulus as the one shown, then the encoder is successful on that trial (as shown here).

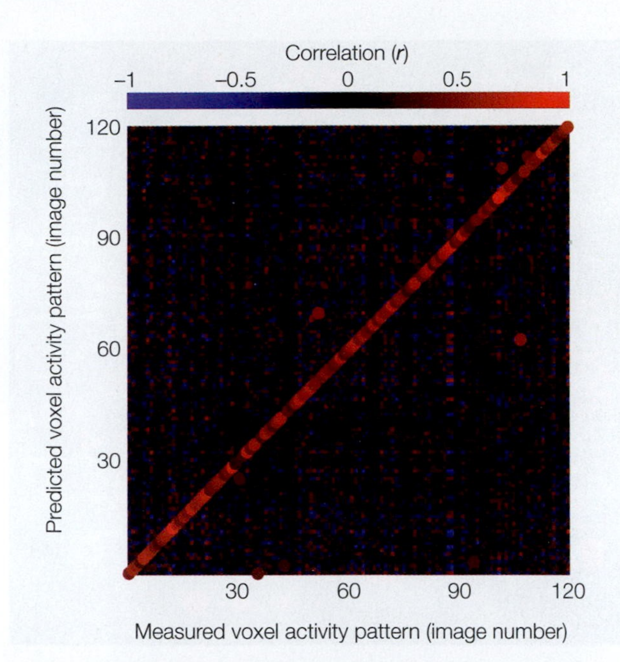

FIGURE 6.25 Accuracy of the brain decoder. Rather than just choosing the best match, the correlation coefficient can be calculated between the measured BOLD response for each image and the predicted BOLD response. For the 120 images, the best predictors almost always matched the actual stimulus, as indicated by the bright colors along the major diagonal.

The results were stunning (**Figure 6.25**). For one of the participants, the decoding model was accurate in picking the exact match for 92% of the stimuli. For the other, the decoder was accurate for 72% of the stimuli. If the decoder were acting randomly, an exact match would be expected for only 8% of the stimuli. As the Gallant research team likes to say, the experiment was similar to a magician performing a card trick: "Pick a card (or picture) from the deck, show me the BOLD response to that picture, and I'll tell you what picture you are looking at." No sleight of hand involved here—just good clean fMRI data.

As impressive as this preliminary study might be, we should remain skeptical that it constitutes real mind reading. The stimulation conditions were still highly artificial, owing to the successive presentation of a set of static images. Moreover, the encoding model was quite limited, restricted to representations of relatively simple visual features. An alternative coding scheme should build on our knowledge of how information is represented in higher-order visual areas, areas that are sensitive to more complex properties, such as places and faces. The encoding model here could be based on more than the physical properties of a stimulus. It could also incorporate semantic properties, such as "Does the stimulus contain a fruit?" or "Is a person present?"

To build a more comprehensive model, Gallant's lab combined two representational schemes. For early visual areas like V1, they used a model based on the receptive-field properties (as in Figure 6.24a). For higher visual areas, each voxel was modeled in terms of semantic properties whereby the BOLD response was based on the presence or absence of different features (**Figure 6.26**). In this way, the researchers sought to develop a general model that could be tested with an infinite set of stimuli, akin to the task that our visual system faces.

To develop the model, the stimuli were drawn from 6 million natural images, randomly selected from the Internet. This hybrid decoder was accurate in providing appropriate matches (**Figure 6.27**). It also proved informative in revealing the limitations of models that use only physical properties or only semantic properties (Huth et al., 2016). For example, when the physical model is used exclusively, it does well with information from the early visual areas but poorly with information from the higher visual areas. On the other hand, when the semantic model is used alone, it does well with the higher-order information but not as well with information from the early visual areas. When the two models are combined, the reconstructions (Figure 6.27b), although not completely accurate, reveal the essence of the image and are more accurate than either model alone.

The next step in this research was to add action to the encoding model. After all, the world and our visual experience are full of things that move. Because action is fast and fMRI is slow, the researchers had to give their encoding model the feature of motion, which is central to many regions of the brain. The test participants returned to the MRI scanner, this time to watch movie clips (Nishimoto et al., 2011).

Reams of data were collected and used to build an elaborate encoding model. Then it was time for the decoding test. The participants watched new movies, and the decoder was used to generate continuous predictions. You can see the results at http://www.youtube.com/user/gallantlabucb. While it is mind-boggling to see the match between the actual, fast-paced movie and the predicted movie, based solely on the (sluggish) fMRI data, it is also informative to consider the obvious mismatches between the two. These mismatches (feedback!) help guide researchers as they construct the next generation of encoding–decoding models.

One of the current goals of decoding research is to ask whether these methods can be used to decipher mental activity in the absence of actual sensory input, the ultimate challenge for mind reading. This would seem possible, given that fMRI activation patterns are similar whether people perceive objects or imagine them, even if the level of activity is much stronger in the former condition (e.g., Reddy et al., 2010). "Similar," though, is a relatively superficial criterion, observed in terms of similar global patterns of activation. A much more challenging problem is to determine whether activation patterns during imagery have sufficient information to predict specific percepts.

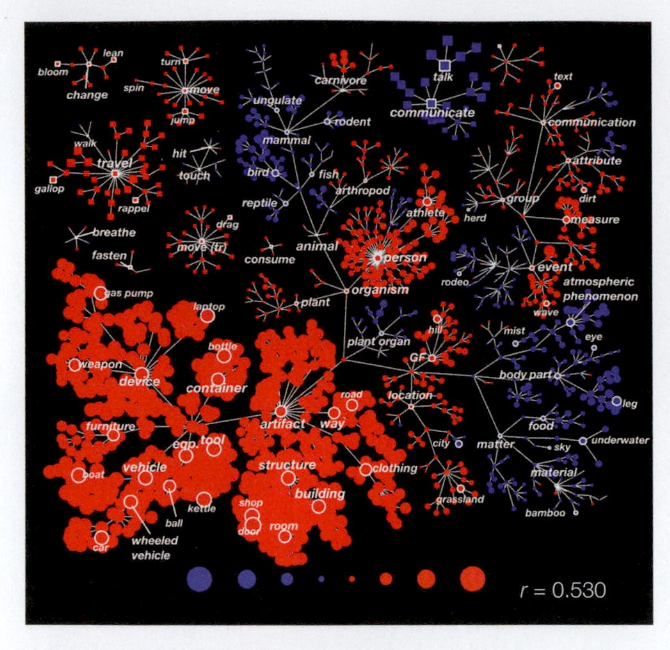

a Voxel AV-8592 (left parahippocampus)

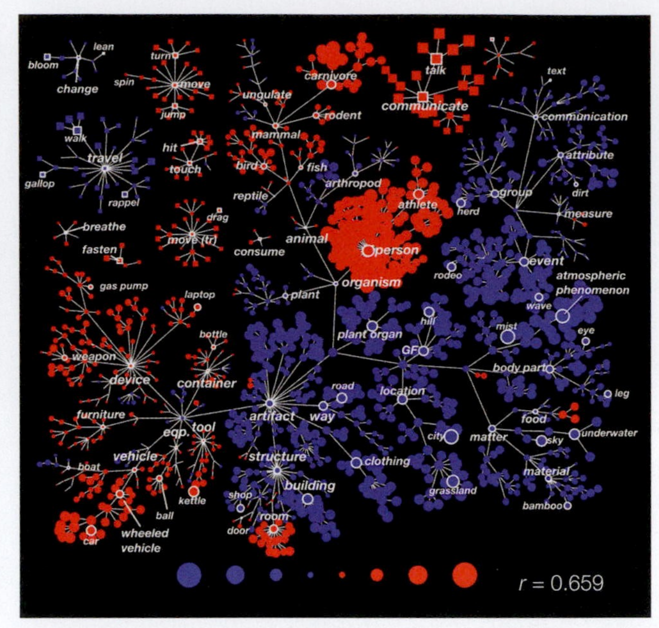

b Voxel AV-19987 (right precuneus)

FIGURE 6.26 Semantic representation of two voxels.
Rather than using basic features such as size and orientation, the encoding model for voxels in higher-order visual areas incorporates semantic properties. The colors indicate the contribution of each feature to the BOLD response: Red indicates that the feature produced a greater-than-average BOLD response; blue indicates that the feature produced a less-than-average BOLD response. The size of each circle indicates the strength of that effect. The parahippocampal voxel (a) is most activated when the scene contains artifacts such as tools and containers; the precuneus voxel (b) is most activated when the scene contains communicative carnivores.

a Original images

b Reconstructions

FIGURE 6.27 Visual images using a hybrid encoding model.
(a) Representative natural images (out of a nearly infinite set) that were presented to the model.
(b) The reconstructed images, based on a hybrid model of multivoxel responses across multiple visual areas. The model was developed by measurement of the BOLD response to a limited set of stimuli.

In one study of imagery, an encoding model was first created from representations limited to early-visual-area activities, with voxels sensitive to features such as retinotopic location, spatial frequency, and orientation (Naselaris et al., 2015). To generate this model, BOLD responses were obtained while the participants passively viewed 1,536 works of art. The researchers then asked the participants either to view or to imagine one of five paintings. As expected, the model was extremely accurate in identifying, from fMRI data, which of the five images the person was perceiving. But it also performed well above chance in decoding the imagined images. That is, it was possible to predict what the participant was thinking about, even in the absence of any sensory input!

This type of work opens up possibilities to tackle one of the great mysteries of the mind: the nature of dreams. As we've all experienced, it is very hard to describe the content of dreams, especially since we have to undergo a radical change in the state of consciousness (i.e., wake up!) to provide these reports. But a good decoder would avoid this problem.

As a first step in this direction, Tomoyasu Horikawa and colleagues (2013) built a decoder based on their participants' BOLD responses to images viewed when awake. Then, while the participants napped, simultaneous EEG and fMRI data were collected. The EEG data were used to indicate when the participants were in early-onset sleep Stage 1 or 2. At these points in time, the participants were awakened and asked to report their current dream (**Figure 6.28a**). Dream reports from sleep-onset awakenings share the features of dream frequency, length, and content with dream reports from REM sleep awakenings (Oudiette et al., 2012). Reports were taken during the sleep-onset period because it enabled the researchers to gather many observations during repeated awakenings. The dream reports were then compared to predictions generated from the BOLD activity just before the person was awakened. Focusing on a limited set of options (objects, scenes, people), the decoding model was successful in identifying the contents of the dreams (**Figure 6.28b**).

While mind reading raises some thorny ethical problems (see **Box 6.2**), it also has pressing clinical applications. For example, mind reading has the potential to provide a new method of communication for people who have severe neurological conditions and are unable to speak, as we will explore in Chapter 14. And we will see in Chapter 8 that for individuals who are paralyzed or have lost the use of a limb, decoders can be used to control machines via so-called brain–machine interfaces.

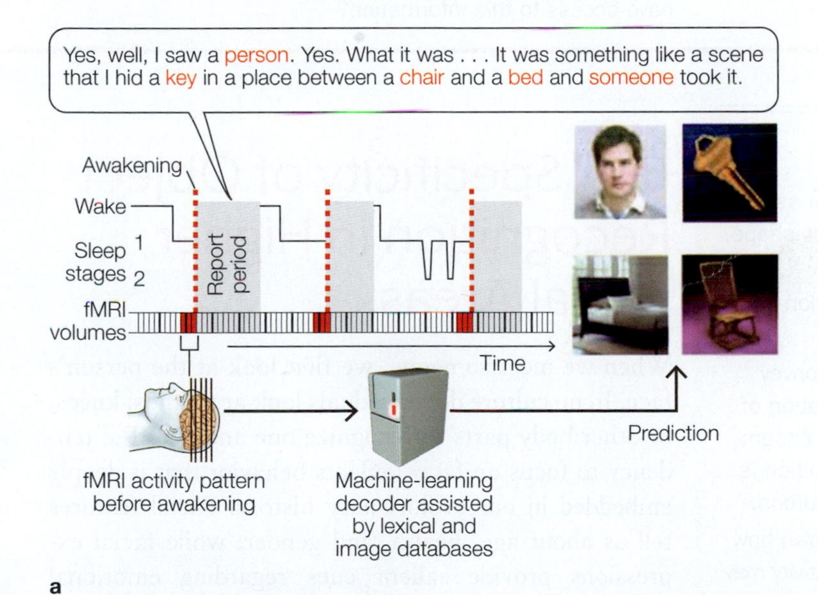

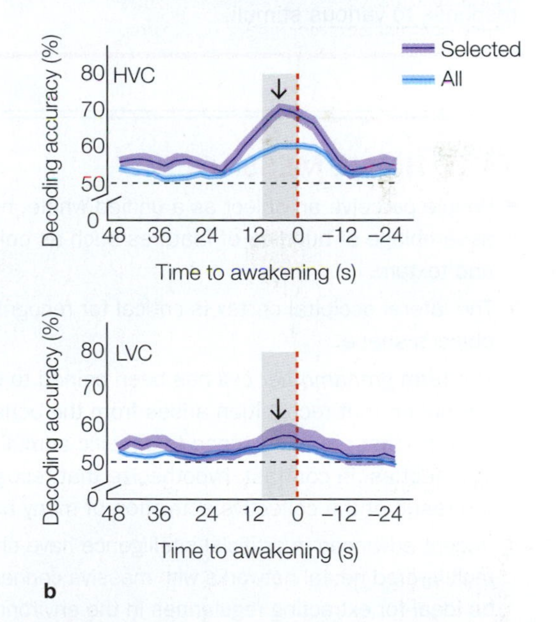

FIGURE 6.28 Decoding dreams.
(a) Experimental setup. As participants slept, fMRI and EEG data were acquired. Participants were awakened during sleep Stage 1 or 2 (red dashed line), and they immediately reported the visual activity they had experienced just before awakening. The fMRI data acquired immediately before awakening were used as the input for main decoding analyses. Words that described visual objects or scenes (red letters) were extracted. Then, machine-learning decoders trained on fMRI responses to natural images were used to predict the visual contents of the dream. (b) Accuracy in decoding the content of dream reports, relative to the moment of awakening, with the gray region highlighting the last 9 seconds of sleep. Higher visual cortex (HVC) includes lateral occipital cortex, as well as the fusiform face area and parahippocampal place area (two regions we will discuss in the next section); lower visual cortex (LVC) includes V1, V2, and V3. "All" indicates the decoding performance on a test set including all of the data, whereas the "Selected" set is limited to the items that were reported most frequently.

BOX 6.2 | HOT SCIENCE

A Wild and Crazy Future for Mind Reading

Mind-reading methods provide a powerful tool for testing theories of perception, where researchers ask whether signals such as the BOLD response can be used to predict what a person is looking at or even imagining. Ongoing research has also demonstrated the extent to which neuroimaging methods can be used to develop functional maps of much more abstract domains of thought. Networks that are engaged when people are making social judgments, deliberating moral dilemmas, or having religious experiences have been identified. Other work has sought to characterize brain activity in atypical populations, such as the response of psychopaths to movies that depict violent behavior. Work in these areas has led to the development of brain maps of moral reasoning, judgment, deception, and emotions.

We can envision that, with sophisticated models, the pattern of activity across these maps might reveal an individual's preferences, attitudes, or thoughts. Mind reading with these goals sounds like the plot of a bad movie—and certainly these ideas, if realized, are brimming with ethical issues. At the core of these concerns is the scenario under which a person's thoughts could be accurately determined from examination of the activity in that person's brain in response to various stimuli.

What standard would be required to determine that the mind-reading signals were reliable (Illes & Racine, 2005)? Surely we would not want to apply the $p = .05$ convention that is used in many scientific studies; for example, if we were to use mind-reading methods to determine psychopathic tendencies, we would not accept a misdiagnosis in one out of 20 cases. In addition, we would have to keep in mind that mind reading is inherently correlational.

Assuming, however, that such determinations could be made and would be accurate, the issue remains that people believe their thoughts are private and confidential. So, what do we need to consider if it becomes possible to decode people's thoughts without their consent or against their will? Are there circumstances in which private thoughts should be made public? For example, should a person's thoughts be admissible in court, just as DNA evidence now can be? Should a jury have access to the thoughts of child molesters, murder defendants, or terrorists—or even witnesses—to determine whether they are telling the truth or have a false memory? Should interviewers have access to the thoughts of applicants for jobs that involve children or for police or other security work? And who else should have access to this information?

TAKE-HOME MESSAGES

- People perceive an object as a unified whole, not as an assemblage of bundles of features such as color, shape, and texture.
- The lateral occipital cortex is critical for recognition of an object's shape.
- The term *grandmother cell* has been coined to convey the notion that recognition arises from the activation of neurons that are finely tuned to specific stimuli. Ensemble theories, in contrast, hypothesize that recognition is the result of the collective activation of many neurons.
- Recent advances in artificial intelligence have shown how multilayered neural networks with massive connectivity may be ideal for extracting regularities in the environment—a key computation for recognition and categorization.
- Object recognition, especially of ambiguous stimuli, appears to be enhanced by top-down processes, including information provided from the frontal cortex based on a fast but crude analysis of the visual input.
- Encoding models are used to predict the physiological response, such as the BOLD response, to a stimulus. Decoding models are used in the reverse manner, predicting the stimulus (or mental state) from a physiological response such as the BOLD activity across a set of voxels.

6.4 Specificity of Object Recognition in Higher Visual Areas

When we meet someone, we first look at the person's face. In no culture do individuals look at thumbs, knees, or other body parts to recognize one another. The tendency to focus on faces reflects behavior that is deeply embedded in our evolutionary history. Facial features tell us about age, health, and gender, while facial expressions provide salient cues regarding emotional states, helping us to discriminate between pleasure and displeasure, friendship and antagonism, agreement and confusion.

The face, and particularly the eyes, of another person can provide significant clues about what is important in his environment. Looking at someone's lips when she is speaking helps us to understand words more than we may realize. These observations, combined with neuropsychological reports of patients who had difficulty recognizing faces, led researchers to search for the neural mechanisms underlying face perception.

Is Face Processing Special?

It seems reasonable to suppose that our brains have a general-purpose system for recognizing all sorts of visual inputs, with faces constituting just one important class of problems to solve. However, the evidence suggests otherwise. Multiple studies argue that face perception does not use the same processing mechanisms as those used in object recognition, but instead depends on a specialized network of brain regions.

To investigate whether face recognition and other forms of object perception use distinct processing systems, we should consider whether there are particular regions of the brain or specialized cells that respond to faces separately from those that respond to other types of stimuli. If so, we should ask whether the systems are functionally and operationally independent. The logic of this query is essentially the same as that underlying the idea of double dissociations (see Chapter 3). Finally, we should ask whether the two systems process information in a different way. Let's see what evidence we have to answer these questions.

Do the processes of face recognition and nonfacial object recognition involve physically distinct mechanisms? Although clinical evidence showed that people could have what appeared to be selective problems in face perception, more compelling evidence of specialized face perception mechanisms comes from neurophysiological studies with nonhuman primates. In one study (Baylis et al., 1985), recordings were made from cells in the superior temporal sulcus (STS) of a monkey while the animal was presented with stimuli like those in **Figure 6.29a**.

Five of these stimuli (A–E) were faces: four of other monkeys, and one of a human (one of the experimenters). The other five stimuli (F–J) ranged in complexity

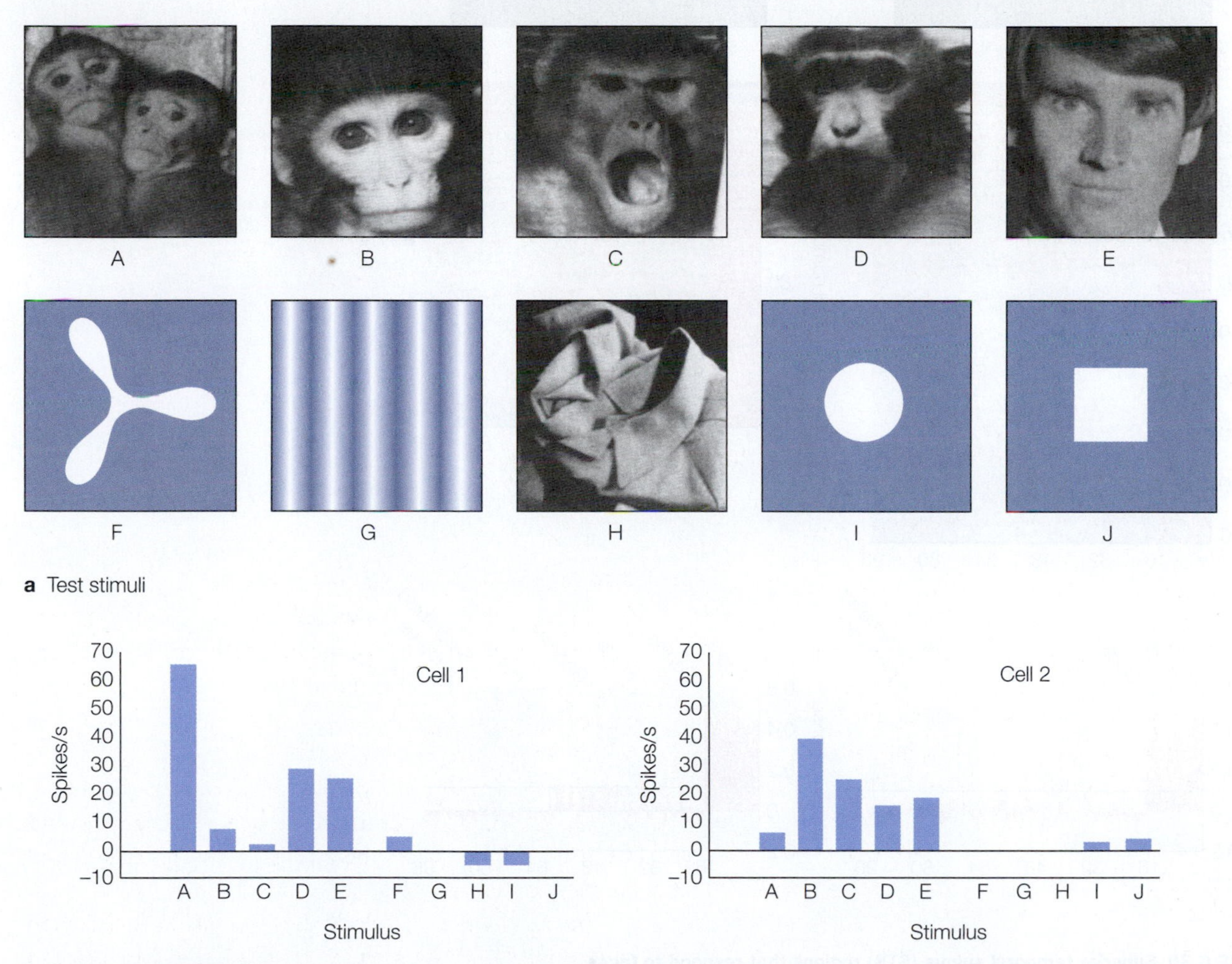

FIGURE 6.29 Identifying face cells in the superior temporal sulcus of the macaque monkey. The 10 stimuli (A–J) in part (a) produced the responses plotted in part (b) for two cells. Both cells responded vigorously to many of the facial stimuli. Either there was no change in activity when the animal looked at the objects, or, in some cases, the cells were actually inhibited relative to baseline. The firing-rate data are plotted as a change from baseline activity for that cell when no stimulus was presented.

but included the most prominent features in the facial stimuli. For example, the grating (image G) reflected the symmetry of faces, and the circle (image I) was similar to eyes. **Figure 6.29b** shows two cells that responded selectively to the five facial stimuli. These cells did not change their firing rate to the nonfacial stimuli, and for two of the stimuli, the response of cell 1 actually decreased to some of the nonfacial stimuli.

A subsequent study dramatically demonstrated the degree of this specificity by combining two neurophysiological methods in a novel manner. Monkeys were first placed in an fMRI scanner and shown pictures of faces or objects. As expected, sectors of the STS showed greater activation to the face stimuli (Tsao et al., 2006; **Figure 6.30a**).

The researchers then went on to record from individual neurons, using the imaging results to position

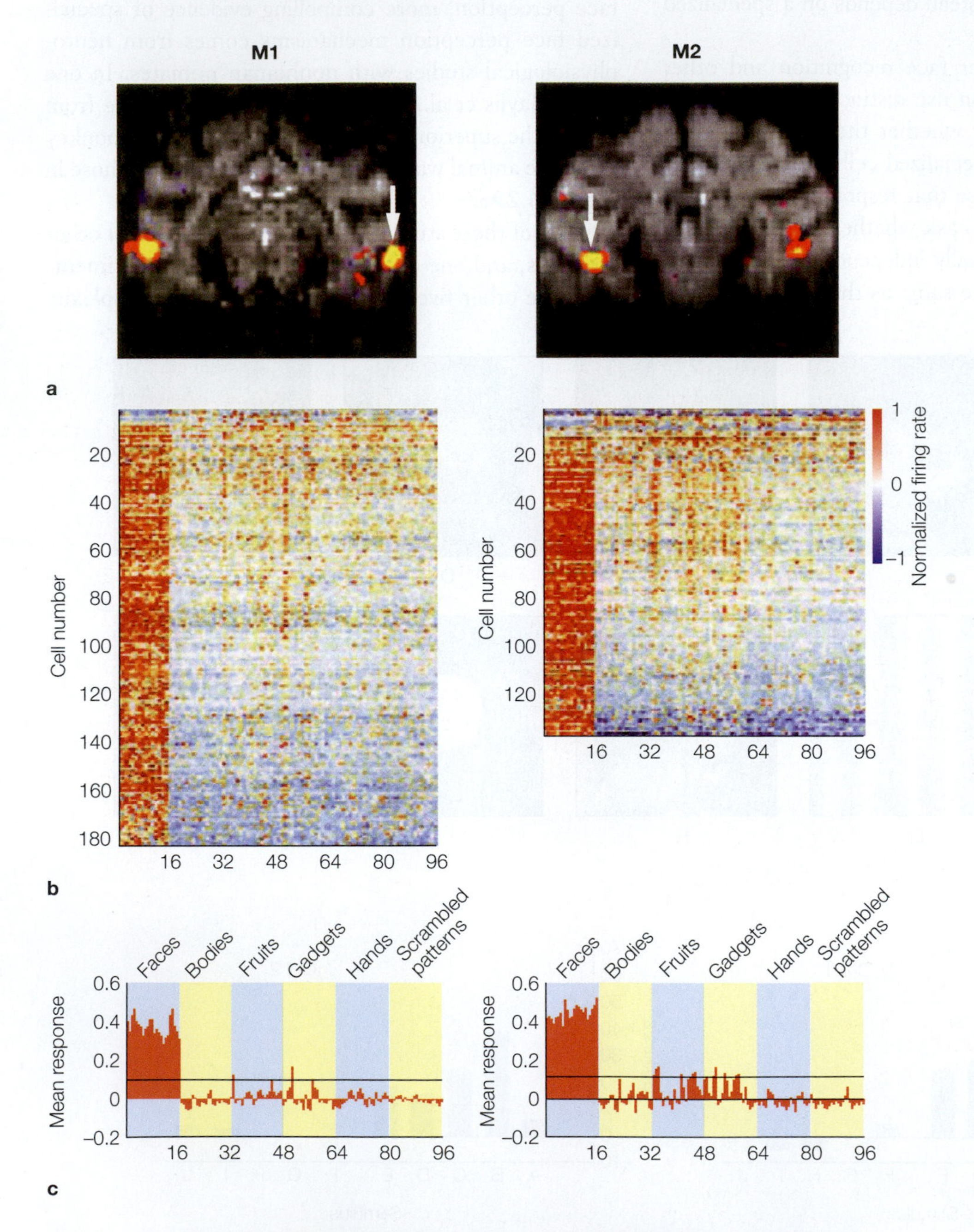

FIGURE 6.30 Superior temporal sulcus (STS) regions that respond to faces.
(a) Functional MRI activations during face perception in two macaque monkeys (M1 and M2). The white arrows indicate where subsequent neurophysiological recording was done (left STS in M1 and right STS in M2). **(b)** The activity of each of the cells recorded in the STS of M1 (182 cells) and M2 (138 cells) that responded to visual stimuli (face, bodies, fruits, gadgets, hands, or scrambled patterns). In these graphs, each row corresponds to a different cell, and each column corresponds to a different image, grouped by categories. **(c)** The average response size for each of the image categories across all cells. These cells were highly selective for face stimuli.

the electrodes within one of the face-sensitive subregions. In that subregion, 97% of the neurons exhibited a strong preference for faces, showing strong responses to any face-containing stimulus and minimal responses to a wide range of other stimuli, such as body parts, food, or objects (**Figure 6.30b, c**). These regions in macaque monkeys, which have been shown to be specialized for processing faces and have a high concentration of face-selective cells, are called *face patches*. These data provide one of the most dramatic examples of stimulus specificity within a restricted part of the visual system.

Functional MRI has also been used in many studies to explore how faces are perceived in the human brain. As in the monkey study just described, we can compare conditions in which the participants view different classes of stimuli, using either block or event-related designs. These studies consistently reveal a network of areas in which the BOLD response is strongest to face stimuli. The most prominent of these is along the ventral surface of the temporal lobe in the fusiform gyrus (**Figure 6.31**), leading researchers to refer to this region as the **fusiform face area** or **FFA**, a term that combines anatomy and function.

The FFA is not the only region in humans that shows a strong BOLD response to faces relative to other visual stimuli. Consistent with primate studies, face regions have been identified in other parts of the temporal lobe, including the STS. Furthermore, fMRI has shown that different face-sensitive regions are specialized for processing certain types of information that can be gleaned from faces.

For example, the more ventral face pathway is sensitive to static, invariant features of facial structure (e.g., eye spacing), information important for facial identification. In contrast, face-selective regions in the right STS respond to movement information (Pitcher et al., 2011), such as the direction of people's gaze, their emotional expressions, and their mouth movements. This distinction can be observed even when the faces are presented so quickly that people fail to perceive them consciously (Jiang & He, 2006). The BOLD response still shows an increase in FFA activity, independent of whether the faces depicted strong emotional expressions, while the

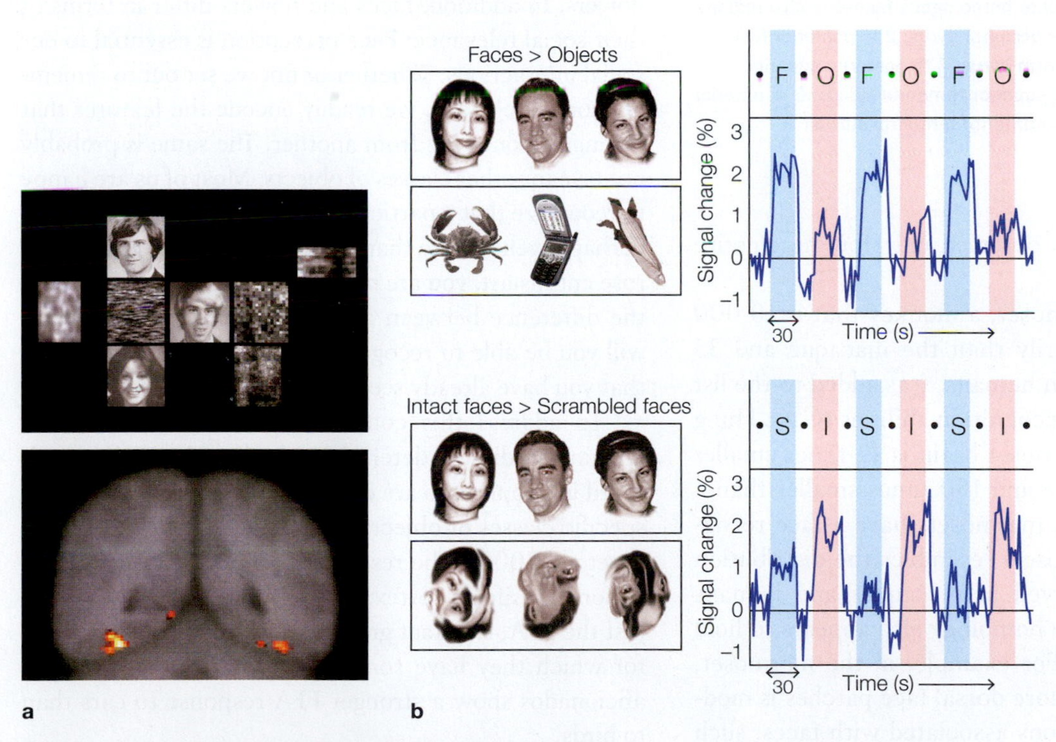

FIGURE 6.31 Isolating neural regions during face perception.
(a) Bilateral activation in the fusiform gyrus was observed with fMRI when participants viewed collages of faces and random patterns, as compared with collages of only random patterns. Note that, according to neuroradiological conventions, the right hemisphere is on the left. **(b)** In another fMRI study, participants viewed alternating blocks of stimuli. In one scanning run (top), the stimuli alternated between faces (F) and objects (O); in another run (bottom), they alternated between intact (I) and scrambled (S) faces. The right column shows the BOLD signal in the fusiform face area during the scanning run for the various stimuli. In each interval, the stimuli were drawn from the different sets, and these stimuli were separated by short intervals of fixation only. The BOLD signal was much stronger during intervals in which faces (versus objects) or intact faces (versus scrambled faces) were presented.

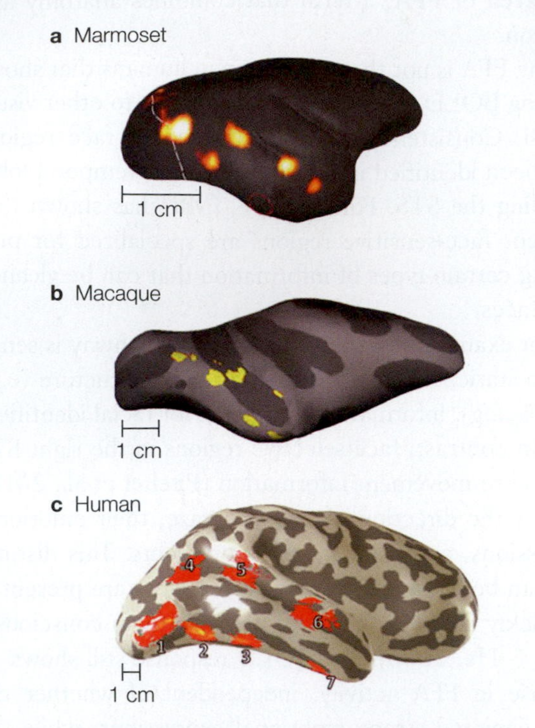

FIGURE 6.32 The evolution of face-processing networks. Cortical surface of a marmoset **(a)**, a macaque **(b)**, and a human **(c)**. Yellow to red colors indicate homologous face-selective regions for each species. 1 = inferior occipital gyrus; 2 = posterior fusiform gyrus; 3 = medial fusiform gyrus; 4 = posterior superior temporal sulcus; 5 = middle superior temporal sulcus; 6 = anterior superior temporal sulcus; 7 = anterior temporal sulcus.

response in the STS is observed only for the emotive faces.

Recently, the marmoset, a monkey that is 10,000 years older evolutionarily than the macaque and 35 million years older than humans, was added to the list of primates with face recognition abilities (C. C. Hung et al., 2015). The marmoset brain is 12 times smaller than that of a macaque and 180 times smaller than a human brain. Even so, marmosets have a face recognition network that closely resembles the distribution of face patches observed in macaques and humans (**Figure 6.32**), and the homology also appears to hold at a functional level. For example, in the marmoset, neural activity in the more dorsal face patches is modulated by natural motions associated with faces, such as movements of the mouth or eyes, whereas the more ventral face regions are sensitive to static properties of faces (Weiner & Grill-Spector, 2015).

Electrophysiological methods also reveal a neural signature of face perception in humans. Faces elicit a large negative evoked response in the EEG signal approximately 170 ms after stimulus onset, or what is known as the N170 response. A similar negative deflection is found for other classes of objects, such as cars, birds, and furniture, but the magnitude of the response is much larger for human faces (Carmel & Bentin, 2002; **Figure 6.33**). Interestingly, the stimuli need not be pictures of real human faces. The N170 response is also elicited when people view faces of apes and when the facial stimuli are crude, schematic line drawings (Sagiv & Bentin, 2001).

Although face stimuli are very good at producing activation in the FFA in humans, it is important to consider alternative hypotheses. One idea is that this region is recruited when people have to make fine perceptual discriminations among highly familiar stimuli. Advocates of this hypothesis point out that imaging studies comparing face and object recognition usually entail an important, if underemphasized, confound: *the level of expertise*.

Consider a comparison of faces and flowers. Although neurologically healthy individuals are all experts in perceiving faces, the same is not true when it comes to perceiving flowers. Unless you are a botanist or an avid gardener, you are unlikely to be an expert in recognizing flowers. In addition, faces and flowers differ in terms of their social relevance: Face perception is essential to our social interactions. Whether or not we set out to remember someone's face, we readily encode the features that distinguish one face from another. The same is probably not true for other classes of objects. Most of us are happy to recognize that a particular picture is of a pretty flower, perhaps even to note that it is a rose. But unless you are a rose enthusiast, you are not likely to recognize or encode the difference between a Dazzler and a Garibaldi, nor will you be able to recognize a particular individual rose that you have already seen.

To address this confound, researchers have used imaging studies to determine whether the FFA is activated in people who are experts at discriminating within specific classes of objects, such as cars or birds (Gauthier et al., 2000). The results are somewhat mixed. Activation in fusiform cortex, which is made up of more than just the FFA, is in fact greater when people view objects for which they have some expertise. For example, car aficionados show a stronger FFA response to cars than to birds.

What's more, if participants are trained to make fine discriminations between novel objects, the fusiform response increases as expertise develops (Gauthier et al., 1999). However, the categorization of objects by experts activates a much broader region of ventral OTC, extending well beyond the FFA (Grill-Spector et al., 2004; Rhodes et al., 2004). It appears that, even when

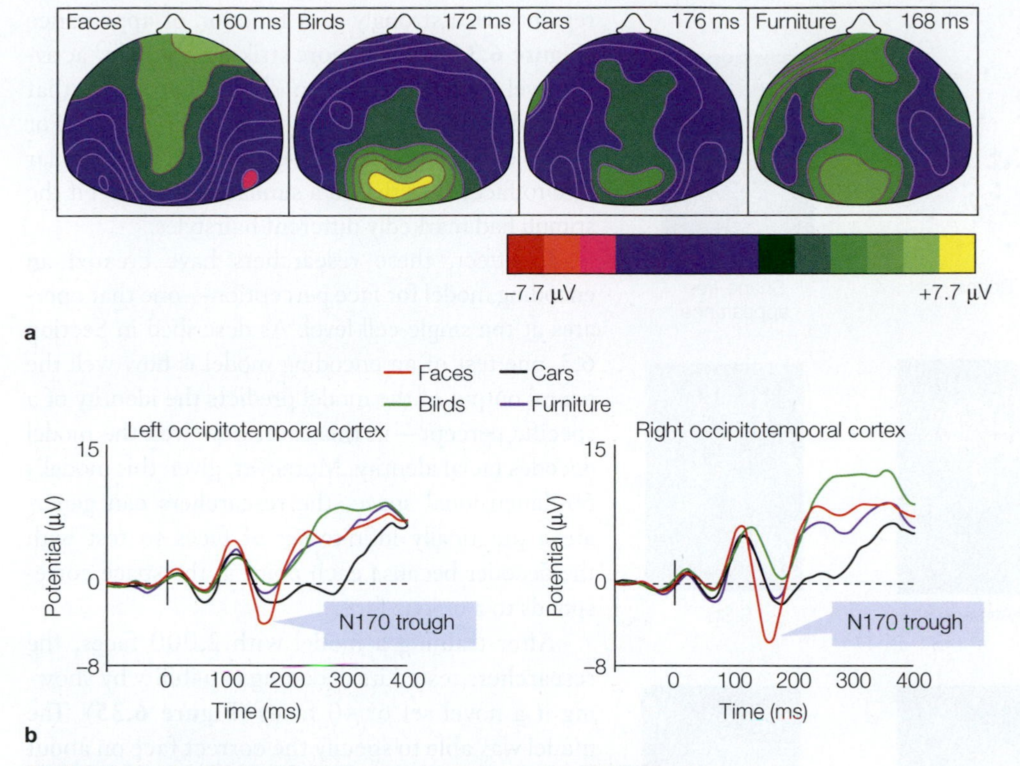

FIGURE 6.33 Electrophysiological response to faces: the N170 response.
(a) Participants viewed pictures of faces, birds, cars, and furniture and were instructed to press a button whenever they saw a picture of a car. (b) Electrodes placed over occipitotemporal cortex produced these event-related potentials. Note that the negative-going deflection in the waveform around 170 ms is much larger for the face stimuli compared to the other categories.

expertise effects are considered, there remains a strong bias for facial stimuli within more restricted regions such as the FFA.

Diving Deeply Into Facial Perception

In a landmark study, Le Chang and Doris Tsao (2017) at the California Institute of Technology claimed to have broken the code for face perception, at least in terms of how neurons represent information that supports our amazing ability to discriminate between faces and recognize individuals. To do so, they first took a set of 200 faces, chosen at random with the assumption that this selection process ensured a representative space that could characterize just about any face. (It is noteworthy that they used human faces here, rather than monkey faces.)

By marking 58 key points on each face (**Figure 6.34a**), they could then use algorithms to generate the data set's mathematically average face. They were also able to determine how different each face was from the average face and from other faces. The researchers used statistical measures to analyze this complex multidimensional space, asking whether certain dimensions best captured the similarities and differences between faces. Two prominent dimensions emerged: variation in shape (**Figure 6.34b**) and variation in appearance (**Figure 6.34c**). The researchers identified 25 unique parameters that captured variation on the shape dimension (e.g., width, height, roundness), and another 25 that captured variation on the appearance dimension (e.g., openness of eyes, hairstyle). With these tools, each of the 200 initial faces could be assigned a unique position in this 50-dimensional space.

The researchers then turned to neurophysiology to ask whether these statistically derived dimensions were biologically relevant. First they used fMRI to identify face-sensitive areas in the inferior temporal cortex of the macaque. Then they employed single-cell-recording methods to characterize the tuning profiles of neurons in lateral (LAT) and anterior (ANT) face areas within the IT cortex. Not surprisingly, the cells responded vigorously to the facial stimuli, with many showing little responsiveness to other classes of stimuli.

The results showed not only that the shape and appearance dimensions were critical in describing the tuning properties of the cells, but also that the two areas had differential specializations. The activity level of cells in the LAT region varied strongly as a function of the shape; in contrast, the activity level of cells in the ANT

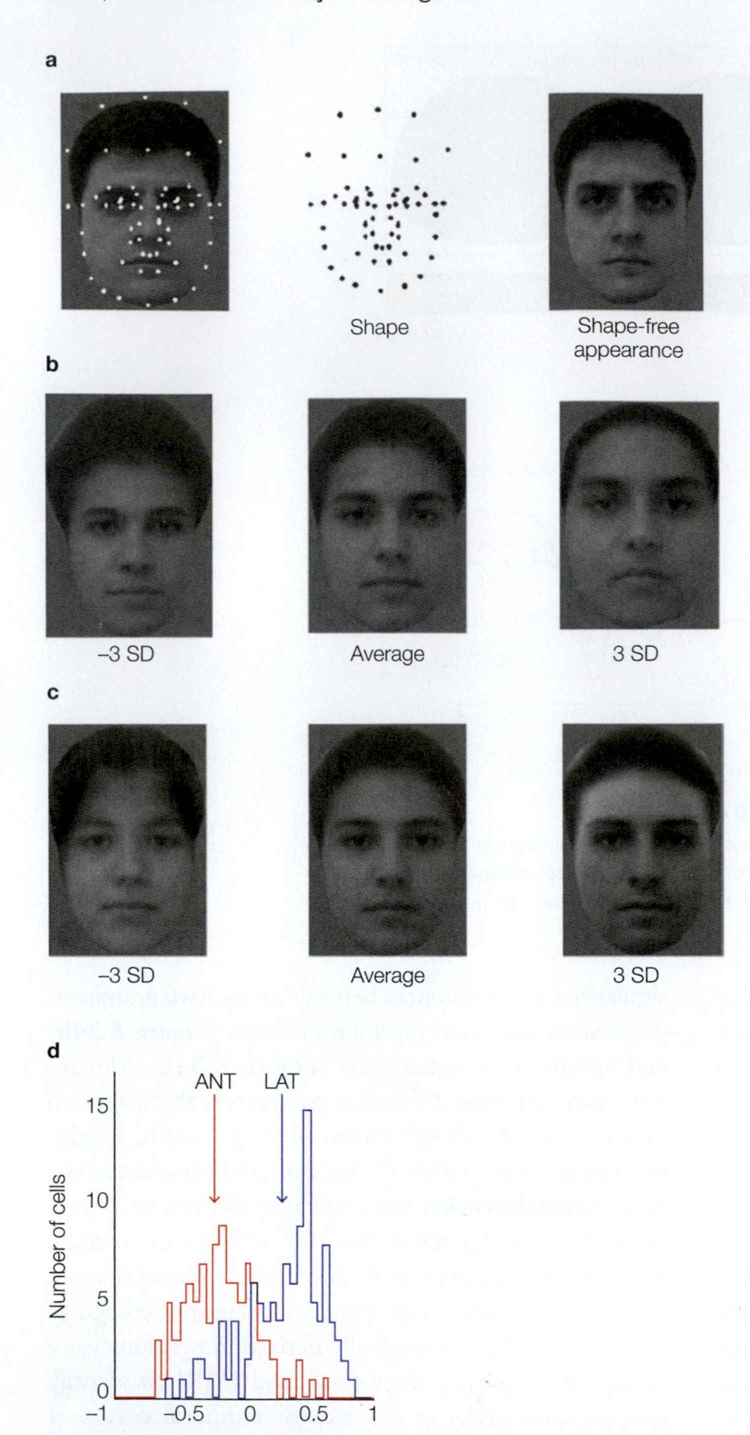

FIGURE 6.34 Discovering facial feature encoding.
(a) Dots were labeled on 200 facial images (left). The dot positions carried shape information about each facial image (middle). The landmarks were smoothly morphed to match the average landmark positions in the 200 faces, generating an image that carried shape-free appearance information about each face (right). **(b)** A face varying in shape across shape dimensions ranging from −3 standard deviations (SD) from the average to +3 standard deviations. The feature dimensions remain constant. **(c)** A face varying in the feature dimensions, with the shape remaining constant. **(d)** The number of cells in each area tested that were tuned to shape or appearance features. The lateral (LAT) face area cells (blue) within the IT cortex are tuned primarily to shape, whereas the anterior (ANT) face area cells (red) are tuned to appearance. The arrows indicate the population averages.

region varied strongly as a function of appearance (**Figure 6.34d**). Even more striking, the cells' activity level varied little when shown two faces that differed markedly on the irrelevant dimension. For example, a shape-responsive cell fired at a similar rate to faces that shared a similar shape, even if the stimuli had markedly different hairstyles.

In effect, these researchers have created an encoding model for face perception—one that operates at the single-cell level. As described in Section 6.3, one test of an encoding model is how well the neural output of the model predicts the identity of a specific percept—in this case, how well the model decodes facial identity. Moreover, given this model's 50-dimensional space, the researchers can generate a practically infinite set of faces to test with the decoder because each point in the space corresponds to a unique face.

After training a model with 2,000 faces, the researchers tested its decoding capability by showing it a novel set of 40 faces (**Figure 6.35**). The model was able to specify the correct face on about 50% of the trials using just the neural predictions from either face patch. Similar to what the physiological analysis had shown, accuracy remained high for LAT neurons if the model used only shape information and high for ANT neurons if the model used only appearance information. Other analyses showed that decoding accuracy remained high even if the stimuli varied in terms of viewing position or orientation, achieving a form of object constancy.

This pioneering study raises a number of interesting questions for future study. First, can this approach also be applied to understanding object recognition more generally, or are shape and appearance features specifically essential for face perception? Second, because activity was broadly distributed across the face-sensitive cells for all of the faces, it is more consistent with ensemble-coding models than with grandmother-cell models. Does this rule out the latter model? Or may the grandmother-cell model still apply further along the processing stream, perhaps when we have to give her a name?

Does the Visual System Contain Other Category-Specific Systems?

The finding that marmosets have a face recognition network similar to that of humans pushes the evolutionary origins of such a network back at least

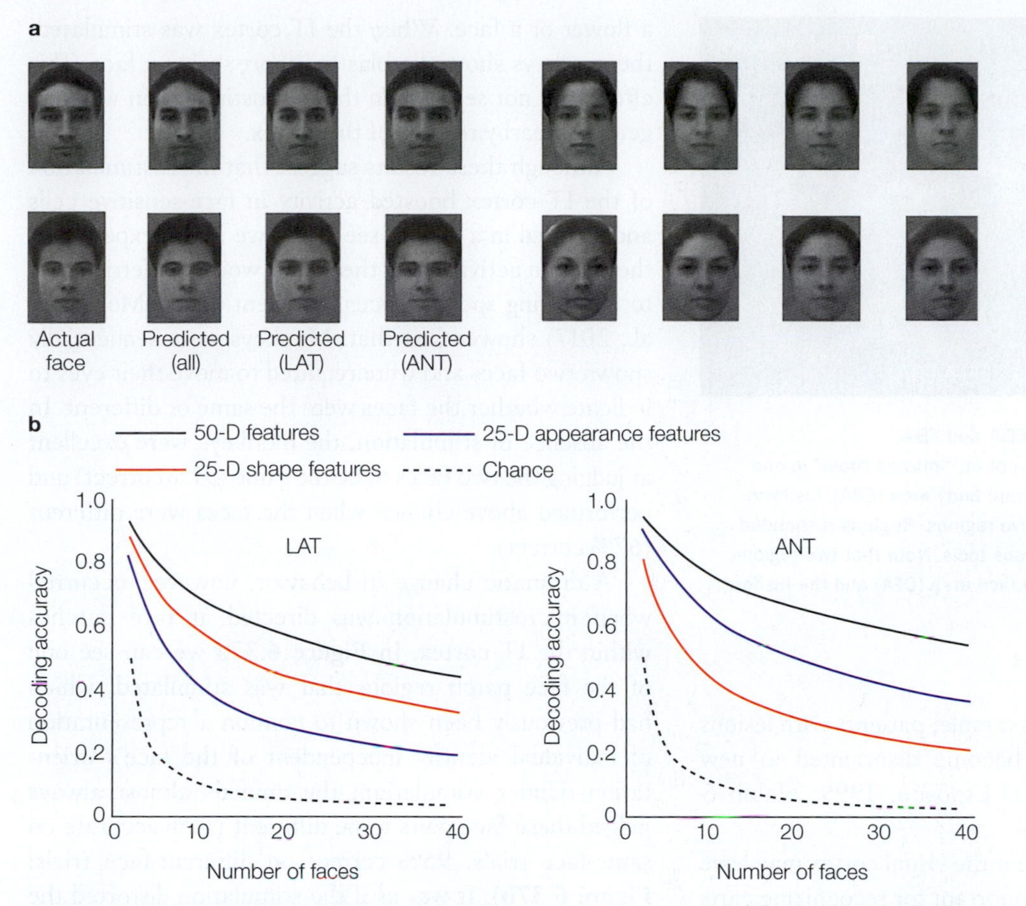

FIGURE 6.35 Decoding faces from neuronal output.
(a) Facial images reconstructed from the output of 200 cells. For comparison, the actual face is shown first, followed by what was predicted from combined data from both sites, predicted from just lateral (LAT) data, and predicted from just anterior (ANT) data. (b) Analysis showed the accuracy of the decoder using cells in LAT face area (left) or cells in ANT face area (right). Within each area, the decoder was based on activity related to shape features (red), appearance features (blue), or both (black), relative to chance (dotted). In LAT, decoding based on shape is more accurate; in ANT, decoding based on appearance is more accurate.

to the common ancestor of New World and Old World primates—that is, about 50 million years ago. One hypothesis is that evolutionary pressures led to the development of a specialized system for face perception. If so, a natural question would be whether additional specialized systems exist for other biologically important classes of stimuli.

In their investigations of the FFA, Russell Epstein and Nancy Kanwisher (1998) used a large set of control stimuli that were not faces. When they analyzed the results, they were struck by a serendipitous finding: One region of the ventral pathway, the parahippocampus, was consistently engaged when the control stimuli contained pictures of scenes such as landscapes. This region was not activated by face stimuli or by pictures of individual objects. Subsequent experiments confirmed this pattern, leading to the name **parahippocampal place area**, or **PPA**. The BOLD response in this region was especially pronounced when people were required to make judgments about spatial properties or relations (e.g., "Is this an image of an outdoor or indoor scene?" or "Is the house at the base of the mountain?").

Reasonable evolutionary arguments can be made concerning why the brain might have dedicated regions devoted to recognizing faces or places, or to distinguishing animate objects (living things that move on their own) from inanimate objects (living things that don't move on their own), or living things from nonliving things, but not to making other types of distinctions. Individuals who could distinguish one type of apple from another would be unlikely to have a strong adaptive advantage (although being able to perceive color differences that cue whether a particular piece of fruit is ripe would be important). Our ancestors who could remember where to find the ripe fruit, however, would have had a great advantage over their more forgetful peers. Clinical evidence supports the idea that there are regions dedicated

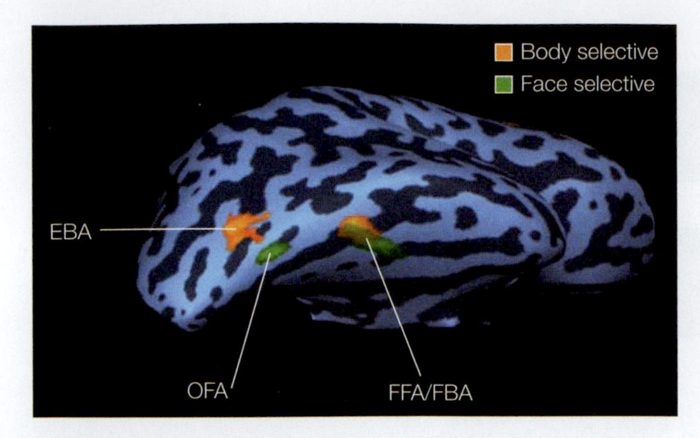

FIGURE 6.36 Locations of the EBA and FBA.
Right-hemisphere cortical surface of an "inflated brain" in one individual identifying the extrastriate body area (EBA), fusiform body area (FBA), and face-sensitive regions. Regions responded selectively to bodies or faces versus tools. Note that two regions responded to faces: the occipital face area (OFA) and the fusiform face area (FFA).

to recognizing places. For example, patients with lesions to the parahippocampus become disoriented in new environments (Aguirre & D'Esposito, 1999; Habib & Sirigu, 1987).

Other studies suggest that the visual cortex may have a region that is especially important for recognizing parts of the body (Downing et al., 2001; **Figure 6.36**). This area, at the border of the occipital and temporal cortices, is referred to as the **extrastriate body area (EBA)**. Another region, adjacent to and partially overlapping the FFA, shows a similar preference for body parts and has been called the **fusiform body area (FBA)** (Schwarzlose et al., 2005).

Testing Causality

Recording methods, either by single-cell physiology in the monkey or by fMRI and EEG recordings in people, are correlational in nature. Tests of causality generally require that the system be perturbed. For example, strokes can be considered a dramatic perturbation of normal brain function. More subtle methods involve transient perturbations. For example, when performing neurophysiological experiments in monkeys, the experimenter can make recordings to identify regions in which the cells show face-specific responses and then use the same electrodes to stimulate the brain (although the stimulation is generally at a level that activates many neurons).

Hossein Esteky and colleagues at the Shahid Beheshti University in Tehran used microstimulation to test the causal contribution of the IT cortex to face perception (Afraz et al., 2006). The monkeys were shown fuzzy images, and they had to judge whether the image included a flower or a face. When the IT cortex was stimulated, the monkeys showed a bias to report seeing a face. This effect was not seen when the microstimulation was targeted at nearby regions of the cortex.

Although these results suggest that microstimulation of the IT cortex boosted activity in face-sensitive cells and resulted in a bias to see faces, we might expect that the random activation of these cells would be detrimental to identifying specific faces. A recent study (Moeller et al., 2017) showed just that. Monkeys were sequentially shown two faces and were required to move their eyes to indicate whether the faces were the same or different. In the absence of stimulation, the monkeys were excellent at judging the two faces to be the same (91% correct) and performed above chance when the faces were different (67% correct).

A dramatic change in behavior, however, occurred when microstimulation was directed at face patches within the IT cortex. In **Figure 6.37a** we can see one of the face patch regions that was stimulated, which had previously been shown to contain a representation of individual identity independent of the face's orientation. Under stimulation, the animals almost always judged these face pairs to be different (14% accurate on same-face trials; 95% correct on different-face trials; **Figure 6.37b**). It was as if the stimulation distorted the face representations.

Stimulation methods have also been employed during neurosurgical procedures in which electrodes are implanted in a patient's brain to determine the origin of epileptic activity. Josef Parvizi and his colleagues at Stanford University (2012) described one such patient who had electrodes in the vicinity of the fusiform gyrus. When the electrode was used to stimulate the brain, the patient reported, "You just turned into somebody else. Your face metamorphosed." He went on to add, "You almost looked like somebody I'd seen before, but somebody different. That was a trip. . . . It's almost like the shape of your face, your features, drooped." (You can watch his reaction at http://www.popsci.com/science/article/2012-10/targeted-brain-stimulation-warps-perception-faces-melting-them-someone-else-video.)

Oddly, these face illusions don't require that the patient be looking at a face (Schalk et al., 2017). When shown a picture of a box while receiving stimulation in the fusiform area, one patient reported, "Just for the very first second . . . I saw an eye, an eye, and a mouth" (**Figure 6.38**). Such illusions were not observed when the stimulation was delivered through an electrode positioned in another part of the visual cortex.

The preceding studies provide examples of single dissociations: Face perception was altered following stimulation in face-sensitive areas but not following stimulation

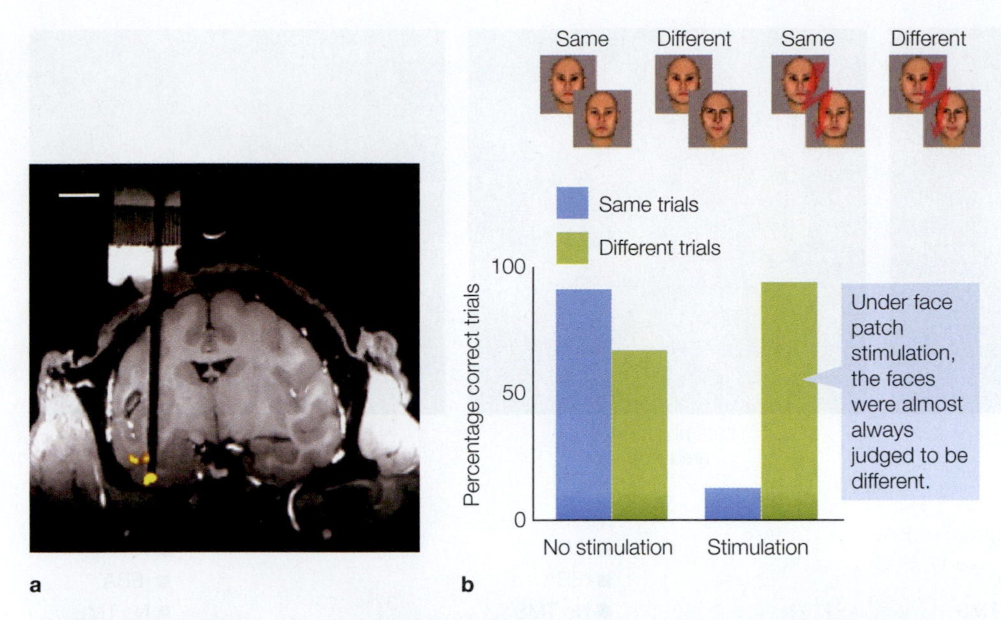

FIGURE 6.37 Perturbing the function of face patches in the IT cortex with microstimulation. **(a)** Coronal MRI slice showing one face patch region (yellow) that was stimulated in a monkey. The stimulating electrode is seen as the dark bar on the left. This face patch is the most anterior face patch and showed significant activation for faces versus objects. **(b)** Results for trials in which Cue 1 and Cue 2 were of the same identity (blue) or of different identities (light green), grouped according to whether stimulation was applied (right) or not applied (left). When the face patch was stimulated, the monkey's performance decreased on same-identity trials and increased on different-identity trials.

in other areas. As discussed in Chapter 3, double dissociations provide much stronger evidence.

Brad Duchaine and his colleagues used transcranial magnetic stimulation (TMS) to provide one such test. They disrupted activity in three different regions that had been shown to exhibit category specificity (Pitcher et al., 2009). The study participants performed a series of discrimination tasks that involved judgments about faces, bodies, and objects. In separate blocks of trials, the TMS coil was positioned over the right occipital face area (rOFA), the right extrastriate body area (rEBA), and the right lateral occipital area (rLO; **Figure 6.39a**). (The FFA was not used, because it is inaccessible to TMS.)

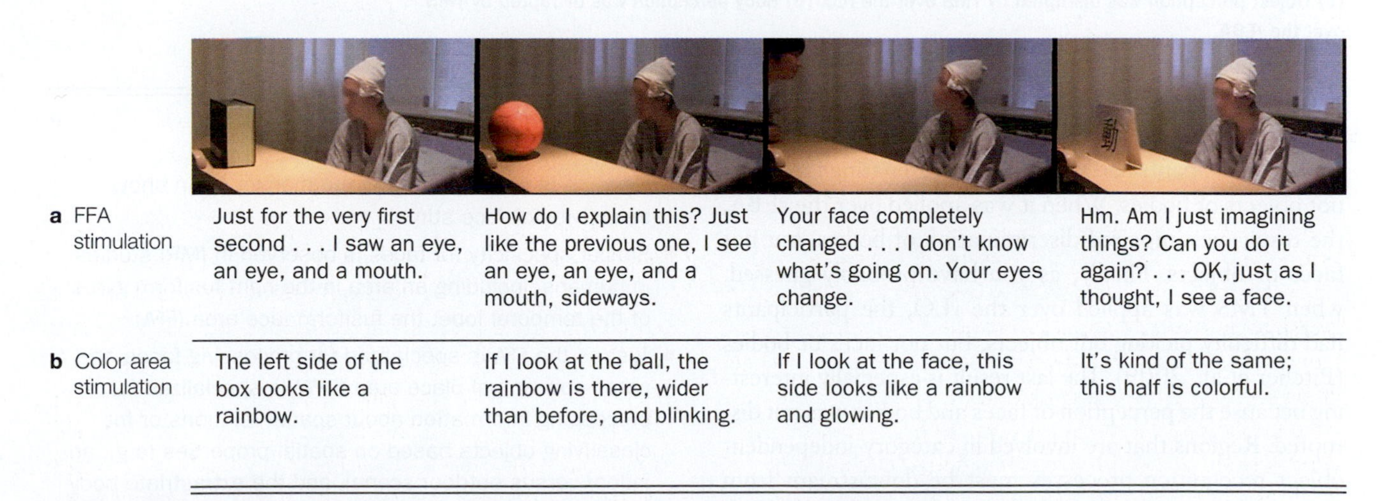

FIGURE 6.38 Patient's descriptions of various objects during electrical stimulation of the FFA and the color area.
The patient was shown a box, a ball, the experimenter's face, and a kanji character. In all cases, when the fusiform face area (FFA) was stimulated at the same time, the patient saw a face illusion **(a)**, but when the color region (V4; see Chapter 5) was stimulated, he saw multiple colors **(b)**.

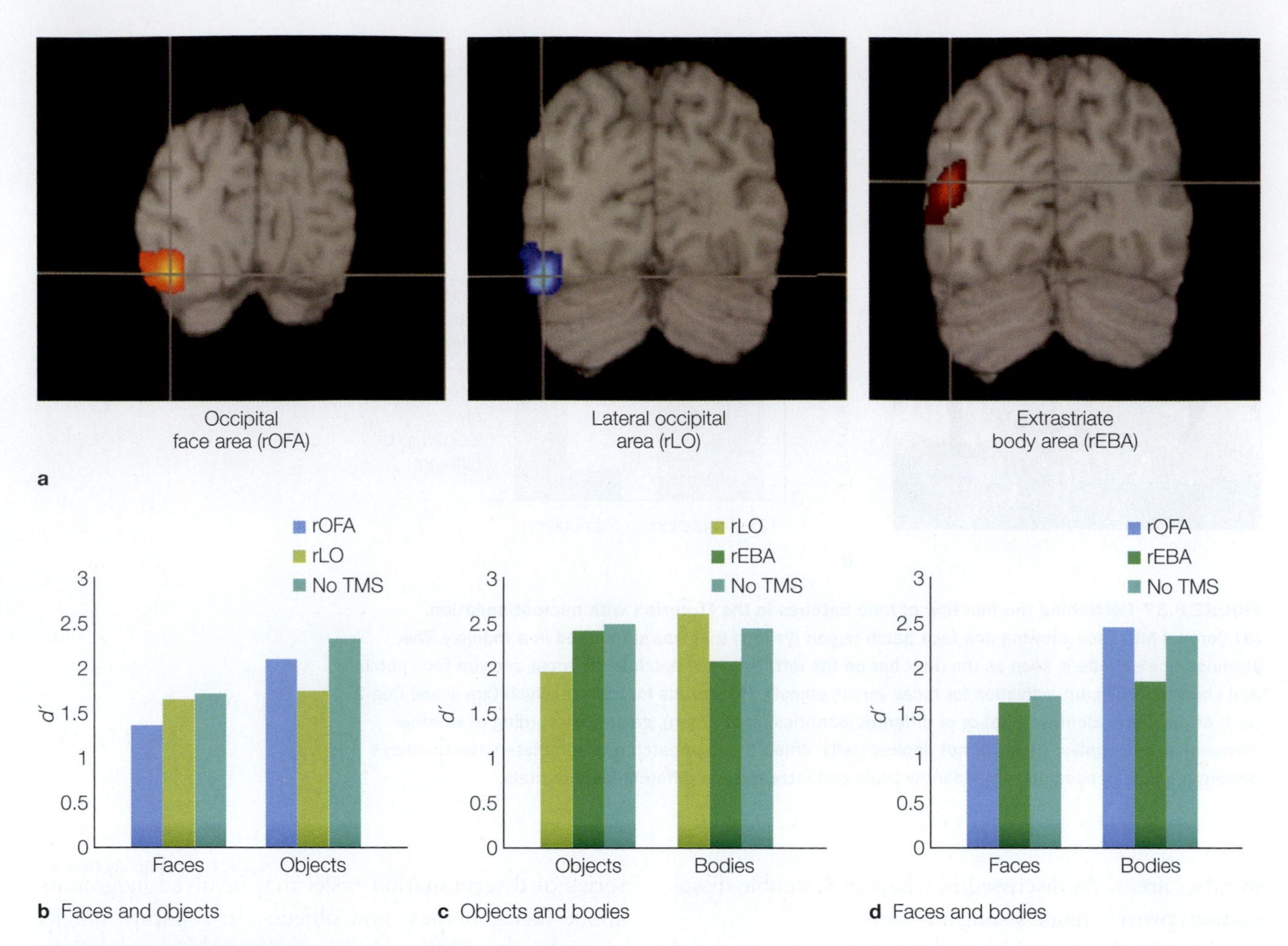

FIGURE 6.39 Triple dissociation of faces, bodies, and objects.
(a) TMS target sites based on fMRI studies identifying regions in the right hemisphere that are sensitive to faces (the right occipital face area, rOFA), objects (the right lateral occipital area, rLO), and bodies (the right extrastriate body area, rEBA). (b–d) In each panel, performance on two tasks was compared when TMS was applied in separate blocks to two of the stimulation sites, as well as in a control condition (no TMS). The dependent variable in each graph is *d'*, a measure of perceptual performance (high values = better performance). (b) Face performance was disrupted by TMS over the rOFA. (c) Object perception was disrupted by TMS over the rLO. (d) Body perception was disrupted by TMS over the rEBA.

The results showed a neat triple dissociation (**Figure 6.39b–d**). When TMS was applied over the rOFA, participants had problems discriminating faces, but not objects or bodies. When it was applied over the rEBA, the result was impaired discrimination of bodies, but not faces or objects. Finally, as you have probably guessed, when TMS was applied over the rLO, the participants had difficulty picking out objects, but not faces or bodies (Pitcher et al., 2009). The last result is especially interesting because the perception of faces and bodies was not disrupted. Regions that are involved in category-independent object recognition processes must be downstream from the rLO. We will return to the topic of disrupted face recognition in Section 6.6, after we explore deficits in object recognition in the next section.

TAKE-HOME MESSAGES

- Neurons in various areas of the monkey brain show selectivity for face stimuli.
- Similar specificity for faces is observed in fMRI studies in humans, including an area in the right fusiform gyrus of the temporal lobe: the fusiform face area (FFA).
- Just as the FFA is specialized for processing faces, the parahippocampal place area (PPA) is specialized for processing information about spatial relations or for classifying objects based on spatial properties (e.g., an indoor versus outdoor scene), and the extrastriate body area (EBA) and the fusiform body area (FBA) have been identified as more active when body parts are viewed.

6.5 Failures in Object Recognition

Patients with visual agnosia have provided a window into the processes that underlie object recognition. By analyzing the subtypes of visual agnosia and their associated deficits, we can draw inferences about the processes that lead to object recognition. Those inferences can help cognitive neuroscientists develop detailed models of these processes. Although the term *visual agnosia* (like many neuropsychological labels) has been applied to a number of distinct disorders associated with different neural deficits, patients with visual agnosia generally have difficulty recognizing objects that are presented visually or require the use of visually based representations. The key word is *visual*; these patients' deficit is restricted to the visual domain. Recognition through other sensory modalities, such as touch or audition, is typically just fine.

Subtypes of Visual Agnosia

The current literature broadly distinguishes among three major subtypes of visual agnosia: apperceptive, integrative, and associative. This division roughly reflects the idea that object recognition problems can arise at different levels of processing. Keep in mind, though, that specifying subtypes can be a messy business, because the pathology is frequently extensive and because a complex process such as object recognition, by its nature, involves a number of interacting component processes. Diagnostic categories are useful for clinical purposes but generally have limited utility when these neurological disorders are used to build models of brain function. With that caveat in mind, let's look at each of these forms of agnosia in turn.

APPERCEPTIVE VISUAL AGNOSIA In people with **apperceptive visual agnosia**, the recognition problem is one of developing a coherent percept: The basic components are there, but they can't be assembled. It's somewhat like going to Legoland but instead of seeing buildings, cars, and monsters, seeing only piles of Lego bricks. Elementary visual functions such as acuity, color vision, and brightness discrimination remain intact, and the patient may perform normally on shape discrimination tasks when the shapes are presented from perspectives that make salient the most important features. The object recognition problems become especially evident when a patient is asked to identify objects on the basis of limited stimulus information—for example, when the object is shown as a line drawing or seen from an unusual perspective.

The Unusual Views Object Test, developed by neuropsychologist Elizabeth Warrington, is one way to examine this type of impairment in object recognition. Participants are shown two photographs of an object, each from a distinct view (**Figure 6.40a**). In one photograph the object is oriented in a standard or prototypical view (e.g., a cat viewed from the front); in the other it is depicted from an unusual or atypical view (e.g., a rear view, without the cat's face or feet showing). People with apperceptive agnosia, especially those with right-hemisphere lesions, can name the objects when seen in the prototypical orientation but have difficulty identifying objects seen in unusual orientations. Moreover, these patients are unable to report that the two views show the same object.

This impairment can be understood in light of our earlier discussion of object constancy. Our perceptual systems can readily extract critical features from an infinite set of percepts to identify objects. Certain vantage points are better than others, but the brain overcomes variability in the sensory inputs to recognize their similarities and differences. This ability to achieve object constancy is compromised in patients with apperceptive agnosia. Although these patients can recognize objects, their ability to do so diminishes when the perceptual input is limited (as with shadows; **Figure 6.40b**) or does not include the most salient features (as with atypical views).

INTEGRATIVE VISUAL AGNOSIA People with **integrative visual agnosia**, a subtype of apperceptive visual agnosia, perceive the parts of an object but are unable to integrate them into a coherent whole. At Legoland they may see walls and doors and windows, but not a house. In a case study, one patient's object recognition problems became apparent when he was asked to identify objects that overlapped one another (G. W. Humphreys & Riddoch, 1987; G. W. Humphreys et al., 1994).

Either he was at a loss to describe what he saw, or he would build a percept in a step-by-step manner. Rather than perceive an object at a glance, the patient relied on recognizing salient features or parts. To recognize a dog, for example, he would perceive each of the legs and the characteristic shape of the body and head, and then use these part representations to identify the whole object. Such a strategy runs into problems when objects overlap, because the observer must not only identify the parts but also correctly assign parts to objects.

A telling example of this deficit is provided by the drawings of another patient with integrative agnosia:

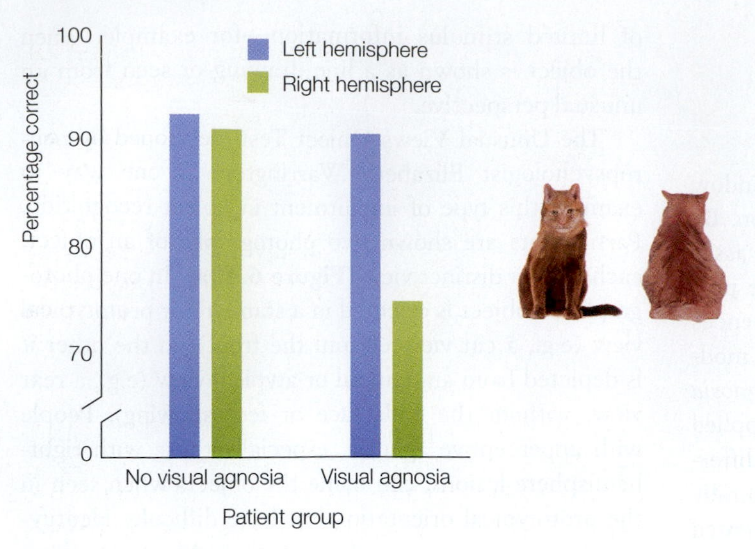

a Unusual-views test

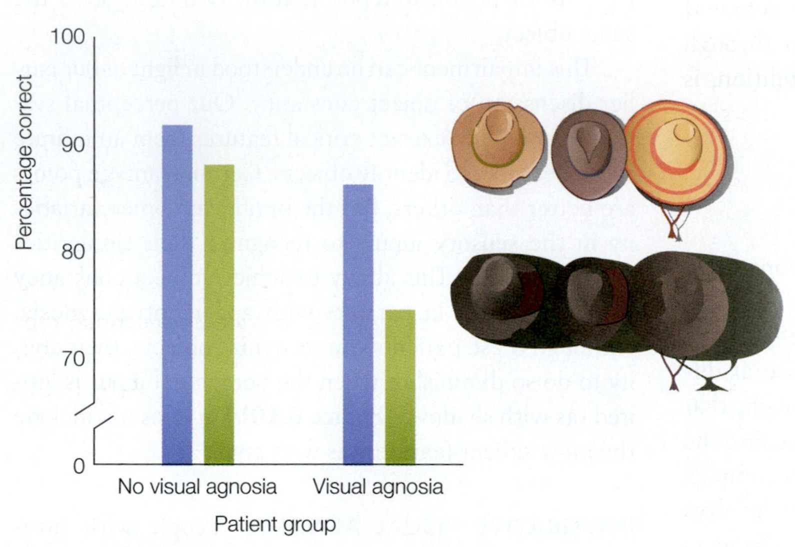

b Shadows test

FIGURE 6.40 Tests used to identify apperceptive agnosia.
(a) In the unusual-views test, participants must judge whether two images seen from different vantage points show the same object. (b) In the shadows test, participants must identify the object(s) when seen under normal or shadowed illumination. In both tests, patients with visual agnosia arising from damage to posterior regions in the right hemisphere performed much worse than either patients with anterior lesions (and no agnosia) or patients with agnosia arising from left-hemisphere lesions.

C.K., a young man who had suffered a head injury in an automobile accident (Behrmann et al., 1994). C.K. was shown a picture consisting of two diamonds and one circle in a particular spatial arrangement (**Figure 6.41a**) and was asked to reproduce the drawing. Glance at the drawing in **Figure 6.41b**. Not bad, right?

But now look at the numbers, indicating the order in which C.K. drew the segments to form the overall picture. After starting with the left-hand segments of the upper diamond, C.K. proceeded to draw the upper left-hand arc of the circle and then branched off to draw the lower diamond before returning to complete the upper diamond and the rest of the circle. For C.K., each intersection defined the segments of different parts. By failing to link these parts into recognizable wholes, he exhibited the defining characteristic of integrative agnosia.

Object recognition typically requires that parts be integrated into whole objects. The patient described at the beginning of this chapter, G.S., exhibited some features of integrative agnosia. He was fixated on the belief that the combination lock was a telephone because of the circular array of numbers, a salient feature (part) on the standard rotary phones of his time. He was unable to integrate this part with the other components of the combination lock. In object recognition, the whole truly is greater than the sum of its parts.

ASSOCIATIVE VISUAL AGNOSIA In **associative visual agnosia**, perception occurs without recognition. First described by Heinrich Lissauer in 1890, associative agnosia is an inability to link a percept with its semantic information, such as its name, properties, and function. A patient with associative agnosia can perceive objects with her visual system but cannot understand them or assign meaning to them. At Legoland she may perceive a house and be able to draw a picture of that house, but still be unable to tell that it is a house or describe what a house is for.

Associative visual agnosia rarely exists in a pure form; patients often perform

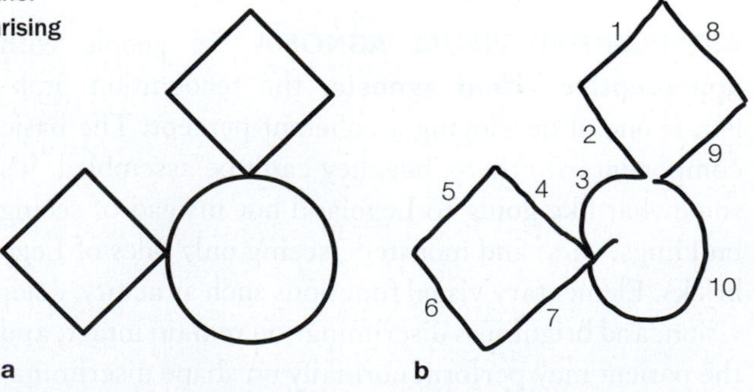

FIGURE 6.41 Patients with integrative agnosia do not see objects holistically.
Patient C.K. was asked to copy the figure shown in (a). His overall performance (b) was quite good; the two diamonds and the circle can be readily identified. As the numbers indicate, however, he produced the segments in an atypical order.

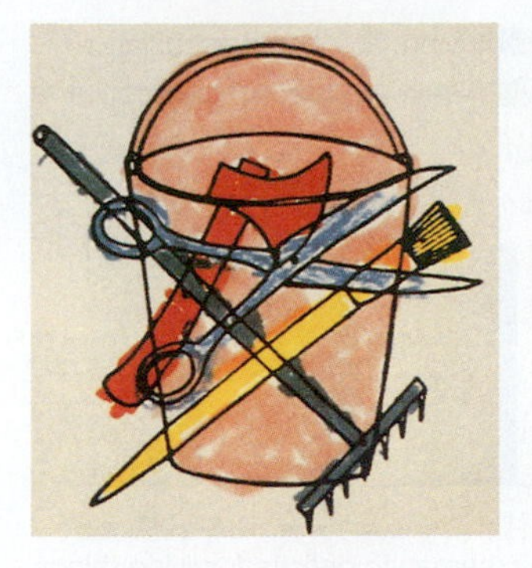

FIGURE 6.42 Associative visual agnosia patient F.R.A.'s drawings.
Despite his inability to name visually presented objects, F.R.A. was quite successful in coloring in the components of these complex drawings. He had clearly succeeded in parsing the stimuli but still was unable to identify the objects.

abnormally on tests of basic perceptual abilities, probably because their lesions are not highly localized. For example, patient G.S.'s problem seems to include both integrative and associative agnosia. Despite his relatively uniform difficulty in identifying visually presented objects, other aspects of his performance—in particular, the twirling fingers—indicate that he has retained knowledge of this object, but access to that information is insufficient to enable him to come up with the name of the object.

Typically, in associative agnosia, perceptual deficiencies are not proportional to the object recognition problem. For instance, one patient, F.R.A., awoke one morning and settled down to his newspaper, only to discover that he could not read (McCarthy & Warrington, 1986). Subsequent tests revealed a more extensive and complex form of agnosia. F.R.A. could copy geometric shapes and could point to objects when they were named. Notably, he could segment a complex drawing into its parts (**Figure 6.42**), something that apperceptive and integrative visual agnosia patients find extremely challenging.

Although F.R.A.'s performance on the segmentation task demonstrated his ability to perceive the objects, he could not name the very same things that he had just colored. When shown line drawings of common objects, he not only had difficulty naming the objects but also fumbled when asked to describe their function. Similarly, when shown images of animals that were depicted to be the same size, such as a mouse and a dog, and asked to point to the one that is physically larger, his performance was barely above chance. Nonetheless, his knowledge of size properties was intact. If the two animal names were said aloud, F.R.A. could do the task perfectly. Thus, his recognition problems reflected an inability to access that knowledge from the visual modality. The term associative visual agnosia is reserved for patients who derive normal visual representations but cannot use this information to recognize things.

While the Unusual Views Object Test requires participants to categorize object information according to perceptual qualities, the Matching-by-Function Test tests conceptual knowledge. In this test, participants are shown three pictures and asked to point to the two that are functionally similar. In **Figure 6.43a**, the correct response is to match the closed umbrella to the open umbrella, even though the former is physically more similar to the cane. In **Figure 6.43b**, the director's chair should be matched with the beach chair, not the more similar-looking wheelchair.

The Matching-by-Function Test requires participants to understand the meaning of the object, regardless of its appearance. Impairment on this test is one of the hallmarks of associative visual agnosia. These patients cannot make the functional connection between the two visual percepts; they lack access to the conceptual representations needed to link the functional association between, for example, the open and closed umbrellas in Figure 6.43a.

Organizational Theories of Category Specificity

Further insight into how perceptual representations are used to recognize objects and link that information to conceptual information has come from seemingly bizarre cases of agnosia in which the patients exhibit object recognition deficits that are selective for specific categories (domains) of objects.

Consider the case of patient J.B.R., who had inflammation of the brain from herpes simplex encephalitis. His illness had left him with a complicated array of deficits, including profound amnesia and word-finding difficulties. His performance on tests of apperceptive agnosia was normal, but he had a severe associative agnosia. Most notably, his agnosia was disproportionately worse for living objects than for nonliving ones. When shown drawings of common objects, such as scissors, clocks, and chairs, and asked to identify them, his success rate was about 90%. Show him a picture of a tiger or a blue jay, however, and he was at a loss. He could correctly identify only 6% of the pictures of living things.

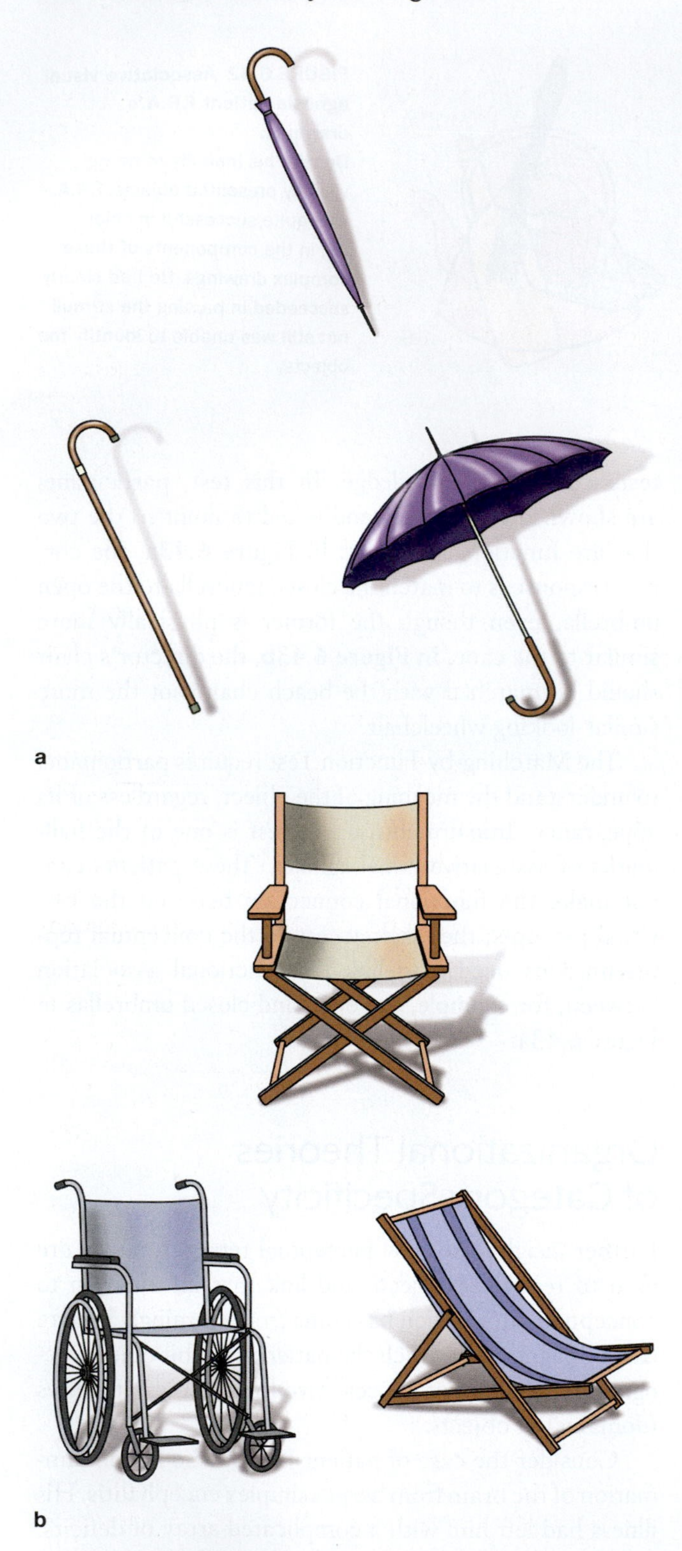

FIGURE 6.43 Matching-by-Function Test.
In each case, participants are asked to view a picture of three objects and choose the two that are most similar in function.

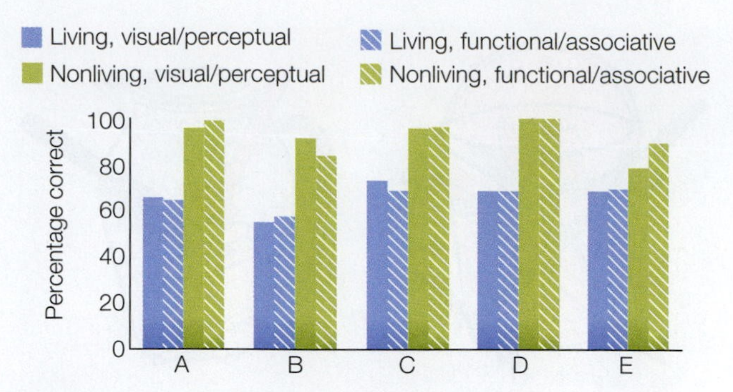

FIGURE 6.44 Category-specific impairments.
Five patients (A–E), who showed a disproportionate agnosia for living things over nonliving things, performed two types of tasks. The solid bars are the results from a visual task in which they had to identify an object or make some sort of visual classification. The hatched bars are the results from questions about object knowledge (e.g., Are dogs domestic animals? Is a plate likely to be found in the kitchen?). The patients' performance was markedly worse when the objects were living things.

Other patients with agnosia have reported a similar dissociation for living and nonliving things (Mahon & Caramazza, 2009; **Figure 6.44**). More puzzling are cases in which the agnosia is even more specific; for example, patients have been described with selective agnosias for fruits and vegetables. These cases have shown that there is more to visual agnosia than meets the eye.

How are we to interpret such puzzling deficits? If associative agnosia represents a loss of knowledge about visual properties, then we might suppose that a category-specific disorder results from a selective loss within, or a disconnection from, this knowledge system. We recognize that birds, dogs, and dinosaurs are animals because they share common features. In a similar way, scissors, saws, and knives share characteristics. Some might be physical (e.g., they all have an elongated shape) and others functional (e.g., they all are used for cutting).

Brain injuries that produce visual agnosia in humans do not completely destroy the connections to semantic knowledge. Even the most severely affected patient will recognize some objects. Because the damage is not total, it seems reasonable that circumscribed lesions might destroy tissue devoted to processing similar types of information. Patients with category-specific deficits support this form of organization.

J.B.R.'s lesion appeared to affect regions associated with processing information about living things. If this interpretation is valid, we should also expect to find patients whose recognition of nonliving things is disproportionately impaired. Reports of agnosia patients exhibiting this pattern, however, are much rarer (Capitani et al., 2003). There could be an anatomical reason for the discrepancy. For instance, regions of the brain that predominantly process or store information about living things could be more susceptible to injury or stroke. Alternatively, the dissociation could be due to differences in how we perceive living and nonliving objects.

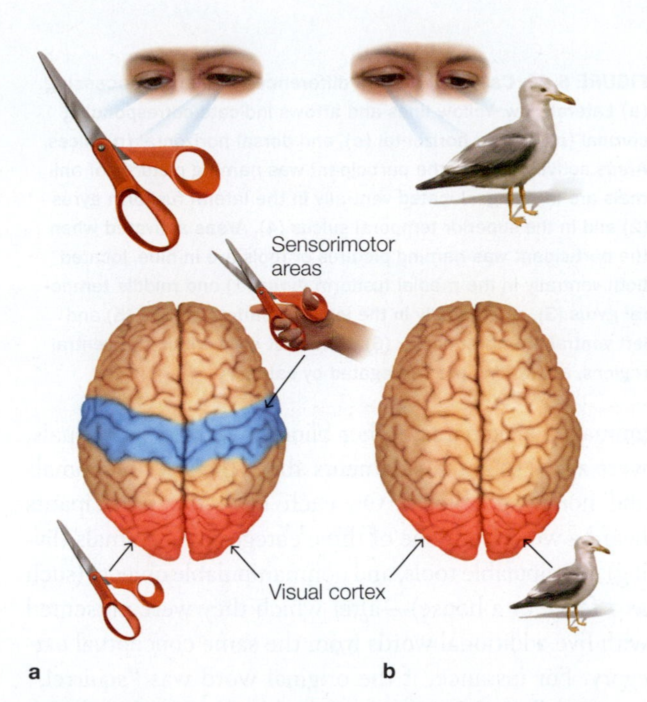

FIGURE 6.45 Sensorimotor areas assist in object recognition. **(a)** Our visual knowledge of many nonliving objects, particularly tools, is supplemented by kinesthetic codes developed through our interactions with these objects. When a picture of scissors is presented to a patient who has an object-specific deficit, the visual code may not be sufficient for recognition. But when the picture is supplemented with priming of kinesthetic codes—for example, the scissors being held in a hand with the blades open as if about to cut something—the person is able to name the object. **(b)** Kinesthetic codes are unlikely to exist for most living things.

One hypothesis is that many nonliving things evoke representations not elicited by living things (A. R. Damasio, 1990). In particular, a feature of many objects is that they can be manipulated. As such, they are associated with kinesthetic and motoric representations. When viewing a nonliving object, we can activate a sense of what the object feels like or of the actions required to manipulate it (**Figure 6.45**). Corresponding representations may not exist for living objects. Although we may have a kinesthetic sense of what a cat's fur feels like, few of us have ever stroked or manipulated an elephant. We certainly have no sense of what it feels like to pounce like a cat or fly like a bird.

According to this hypothesis, nonliving objects such as tools or chairs are easier to recognize because they activate additional forms of representation. Although brain injury can produce a common processing deficit for all categories of stimuli, these extra representations may be sufficient to enable someone to recognize nonliving objects. This hypothesis is supported by patient G.S.'s behavior. Remember that when G.S. was shown the picture of the combination lock, his first response was to call it a telephone. Even when he was verbalizing "telephone," however, his hands began to move as if they were opening a combination lock. Indeed, he was able to name the object after he looked at his hands and realized what they were trying to tell him.

Neuroimaging studies in healthy participants also provide support for this hypothesis. When people view pictures of nonliving objects such as tools, the left ventral premotor cortex, a region associated with action planning, is activated. Moreover, this region is also activated when the stimuli are pictures of natural objects that can be grasped and manipulated, such as a rock (Gerlach et al., 2002; Kellenbach et al., 2003). These results suggest that this area of the brain responds preferentially to action knowledge, or the knowledge of how we interact with objects.

The idea that agnosia patients may have selective problems in recognizing living things relative to nonliving objects is a type of *sensory/functional hypothesis* of conceptual knowledge (Warrington & Shallice, 1984). The core assumption here is that conceptual knowledge is organized primarily around representations of sensory properties (e.g., form, motion, color), as well as motor properties associated with an object, and that these representations depend on modality-specific neural subsystems. Thus, the concept of a hammer draws on visual representations associated with its particular shape, as well as motor representations associated with the actions we employ to use a hammer.

An alternative, *domain-specific hypothesis* (Caramazza & Shelton, 1998) makes a different assumption, positing that conceptual knowledge is organized primarily by categories that are evolutionarily relevant to survival and reproduction. These would include categories such as living animate, living inanimate (e.g., food sources such as plants that don't move on their own), conspecifics, and tools. By this hypothesis, dedicated neural systems evolved because they enhanced survival by more efficiently processing specific categories of objects. Within each domain, functional and neural specializations exist according to the types or modalities of knowledge.

One line of evidence motivating a domain-specific perspective comes from neuroimaging studies that have systematically manipulated different conceptual categories. Such studies have revealed subregions within ventral areas of occipitotemporal cortex that appear to reflect animate–inanimate distinctions. Regions in lateral fusiform gyrus are active when participants are shown pictures of animals or given verbal questions to probe their knowledge of animals. A similar pattern is observed when the stimulus category is tools, but the activation shifts to medial fusiform gyrus (**Figure 6.46**).

Findings such as these provide evidence for an overlap between perceptual and conceptual processing, along with structurally distinct areas for category-specific processing.

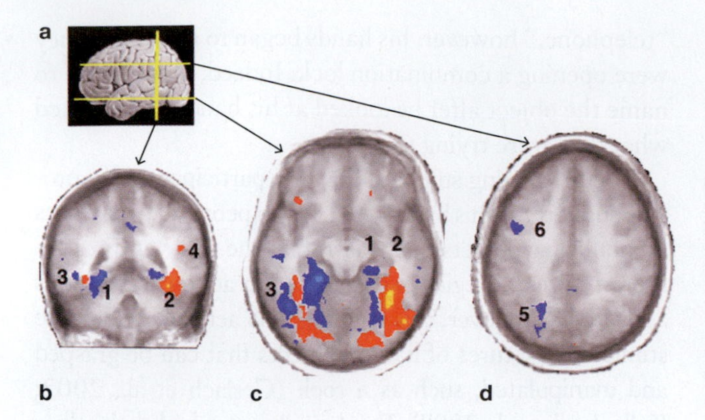

FIGURE 6.46 Category-related differences in neural processing. (a) Lateral view. Yellow lines and arrows indicate corresponding coronal (b), ventral horizontal (c), and dorsal horizontal (d) slices. Areas activated when the participant was naming pictures of animals are in orange, located ventrally in the lateral fusiform gyrus (2) and in the superior temporal sulcus (4). Areas activated when the participant was naming pictures of tools are in blue, located both ventrally in the medial fusiform gyrus (1) and middle temporal gyrus (3), and dorsally in the left intraparietal sulcus (5) and left ventral premotor cortex (6). Note that even within the ventral regions, activations are segregated by category.

Multiple studies have since found that the spatial arrangement of the category-related regions does not vary from person to person (reviewed in A. Martin, 2007).

Advocates of the domain-specific hypothesis have also noted that our knowledge of the function of nonliving objects, such as tools, can be dissociated from our knowledge about the actions required to manipulate the same objects (reviewed in Mahon & Caramazza, 2009). For example, an agnosia patient may be impaired in matching pictures that link objects and the actions required to manipulate them, even though they can exhibit full knowledge of the functional utility of the object (Buxbaum et al., 2000). Thus, even if sensorimotor regions of the brain are engaged when tools are being viewed, this activation may have more to do with the action itself than with functional knowledge of the object (Jeannerod & Jacob, 2005).

Developmental Origins of Category Specificity

Does category specificity within the organization of the visual system emerge from our visual experience, or is the brain hardwired to organize in a category-specific manner? Brian Mahon and his colleagues (2009) addressed this question by investigating whether congenitally blind adults, who obviously have had no visual experience, would show categorical organization in their "visual areas." Rather than having participants look at faces, the researchers focused on the more general categorical distinction between living and nonliving objects. In sighted individuals, nonliving objects produce stronger activation in the medial regions of the ventral stream (the medial fusiform gyrus, lingual gyrus, and parahippocampal cortex), whereas living things produce stronger activation in more lateral regions (the lateral fusiform gyrus and the IT gyrus; reviewed in A. Martin, 2007).

Previous work had shown that these areas were activated in blind individuals for verbal processing (e.g., Amedi et al., 2004). Knowing this, Mahon asked whether a medial–lateral distinction would be apparent when blind participants thought about nonliving objects versus animals. Participants, either blind or sighted individuals, were asked to make judgments about the sizes of animals and nonliving objects. On each trial, the participants heard a word from one of three categories—animals (living), manipulable tools, and nonmanipulable objects (such as a fence or a house)—after which they were presented with five additional words from the same conceptual category. For instance, if the original word was "squirrel," it was followed by "piglet," "rabbit," "skunk," "cat," and "moose," and the participant was asked to indicate whether any of the items were of a vastly different size. The point of the judgment task was to ensure that the participants thought about each stimulus.

The results showed that the regions that exhibited category preferences during the auditory task were the same in sighted and nonsighted groups (**Figure 6.47**). Moreover, these regions showed a similar difference in response to animals or to nonliving objects when the sighted participants repeated the task with pictures instead of words. Thus, visual experience is not necessary for category specificity to develop within the organization of the ventral stream. The difference between animals and nonliving objects must reflect something more fundamental than what can be provided by visual experience. The authors suggest that category-specific regions of the ventral stream are part of larger neural circuits innately prepared to process information about different categories of objects.

TAKE-HOME MESSAGES

- Patients with agnosia are unable to recognize common objects. This deficit is modality specific. Patients with visual agnosia can recognize an object when they touch, smell, taste, or hear it, but not when they see it.
- Apperceptive visual agnosia is a failure in perception that results in the inability to recognize objects.
- Integrative visual agnosia is a failure to recognize objects because of the inability to integrate parts of an object into a coherent whole.
- Associative visual agnosia is the inability to access conceptual knowledge from visual input.

- Visual agnosia can be category specific. Category-specific deficits are deficits of object recognition that are restricted to certain classes of objects.
- There is a debate about how object knowledge is organized in the brain; one theory suggests it is organized by features and motor properties, and the other suggests specific domains relevant to survival and reproduction.

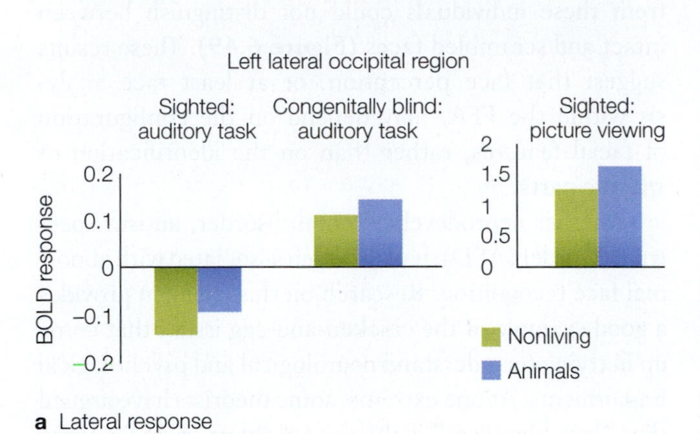

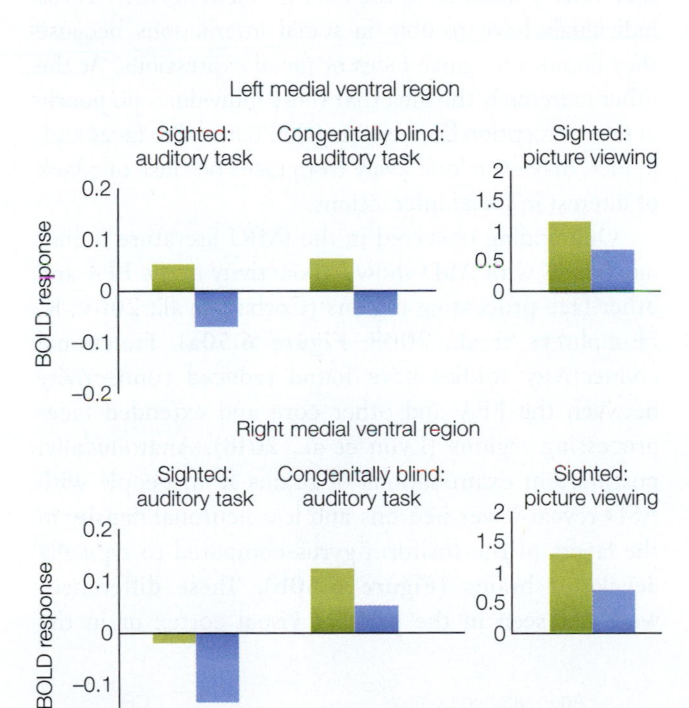

FIGURE 6.47 BOLD response in three regions of interest (ROIs) defined in scans from sighted individuals.
Sighted participants viewed photos of animals or nonliving objects or listened to words naming animals or nonliving objects. Congenitally blind participants listened to the words. (a) The blind participants showed a stronger response to animals compared to nonliving objects in left lateral occipital ROI, similar to that observed in sighted individuals when viewing the pictures. (b) Medial ventral ROIs showed a preference for the nonliving objects in both groups. Note that all three ROIs were deactivated when sighted participants listened to the words.

6.6 Prosopagnosia Is a Failure to Recognize Faces

Prosopagnosia is the term used to describe an impairment in face recognition. Given the importance of face recognition, prosopagnosia is one of the most fascinating and disturbing disorders of object recognition. As with other visual agnosias, prosopagnosia requires that the deficit be specific to the visual modality. Like patient P.T., who was described at the beginning of Chapter 5, people with prosopagnosia are able to recognize someone upon hearing the person's voice.

To give a sense of how bizarre prosopagnosia can be, one widely cited case involved a patient with bilateral occipital lesions who not only was prosopagnosic for friends and family, but also failed to recognize an even more familiar person—himself! (Pallis, 1955). As he reported, "At the club I saw someone strange staring at me, and asked the steward who it was. You'll laugh at me. I'd been looking at myself in the mirror" (Farah, 2004, p. 93). This deficit was particularly striking because in other ways the patient had an excellent memory, recognized common objects without hesitation, and could read and recognize line drawings—all tests that agnosia patients often fail.

Prosopagnosia is usually observed in patients who have lesions in the ventral pathway, especially occipital regions associated with face perception and the fusiform face area. In many cases, the lesions are bilateral, resulting from the unfortunate occurrence of two strokes affecting the territory of the posterior cerebral artery. Or the bilateral damage might be from encephalitis or carbon monoxide poisoning. Prosopagnosia can also occur after unilateral lesions; in these cases, the damage is usually in the right hemisphere.

Developmental Disorders With Face Recognition Deficits

The preceding cases all represent acquired prosopagnosia, an abrupt loss in the ability to recognize faces caused by a neurological incident. However, it has also been noted that people show large individual differences in their ability to recognize faces, leading to the hypothesis that some individuals might have congenital prosopagnosia (CP), defined as a lifetime impairment in face recognition that cannot be attributed to a known neurological condition.

Of course, for any ability or process, there will be individual variation, and by definition, there must be some individuals who score in the bottom tier. This raises the question of whether individuals with CP have some sort of face-specific abnormality or just constitute the tail end of the distribution. Although it is difficult to answer this question, many individuals with CP do not have general recognition problems. For example, problems in discriminating faces or recognizing famous faces can occur despite apparently normal perception for other categories. (You can test your ability to identify faces at http://facememory.psy.uwa.edu.au.)

Surprisingly, CP is estimated to affect about 2% of the U.S. population (Kennerknecht et al., 2006). A familial component has been identified in some cases of CP. Monozygotic twins (they have the same DNA) are more similar than dizygotic twins (50% of their DNA is the same, on average) in their ability to perceive faces. Moreover, this ability is unrelated to general measures of intelligence or attention (Zhu et al., 2009). Genetic analyses suggest that CP may involve a gene mutation with autosomal dominant inheritance. One hypothesis is that during a critical period of development, this gene is abnormally expressed, resulting in a disruption in the development of white matter tracts in the ventral visual pathway.

A few neuroimaging studies have shown that individuals with CP, despite their deficits, show normal activation in the FFA when doing face recognition tasks. In one of these studies, minimal activation was observed in a right anterior temporal region that is associated with face identity (Avidan et al., 2014; **Figure 6.48**), and DTI (diffusion tensor imaging) analyses showed reduced connectivity of this region with the rest of the face-processing network. These results suggest that CP can, at least in this group, arise from impaired information transmission between the FFA and other face-processing regions.

Another study also showed normal overall FFA activation in people with CP. In this case the researchers used multivoxel pattern analysis (MVPA) to classify stimuli by the pattern of activity they evoke across the voxels. For the control participants, MVPA within the right FFA yielded decoding performance that was significantly above chance with the data from two tasks, one that involved determining the presence or type of face parts, and the other in which decoding was based on whether the stimulus was an intact or scrambled face. In the CP participants, by contrast, decoding was successful for only the face parts; the FFA activation patterns from these individuals could not distinguish between intact and scrambled faces (**Figure 6.49**). These results suggest that face perception, or at least face analysis within the FFA, may depend on the configuration of facial features, rather than on the identification of specific parts.

Another neurodevelopmental disorder, autism spectrum disorder (ASD), has also been associated with abnormal face recognition. Research on this problem provides a good example of the chicken-and-egg issues that come up in trying to understand neurological and psychological impairments. At one extreme, some theorists have argued that "face blindness" is the core problem in ASD: These individuals have trouble in social interactions because they do not recognize faces or facial expressions. At the other extreme is the idea that these individuals do poorly at face perception because they don't attend to faces and, in fact, may even look away from faces because of a lack of interest in social interactions.

One finding observed in the fMRI literature is that individuals with ASD show hypoactivity in the FFA and other face-processing regions (Corbett et al., 2009; K. Humphreys et al., 2008; **Figure 6.50a**). Functional connectivity studies have found reduced connectivity between the FFA and other core and extended face-processing regions (Lynn et al., 2018). Anatomically, postmortem examinations of brains from people with ASD reveal fewer neurons and less neuronal density in the layers of the fusiform gyrus compared to typically developed brains (**Figure 6.50b**). These differences were not seen in the primary visual cortex or in the

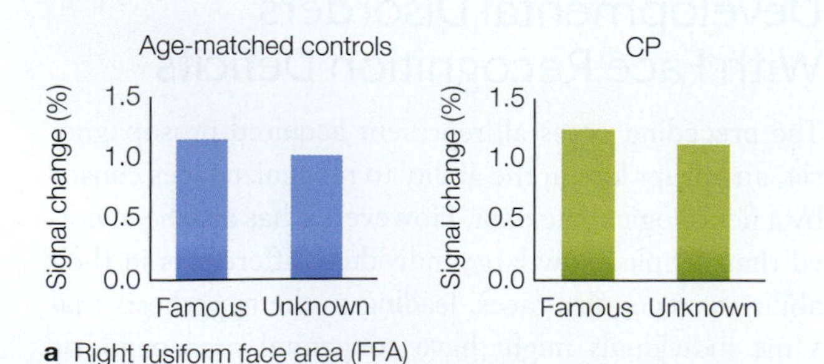

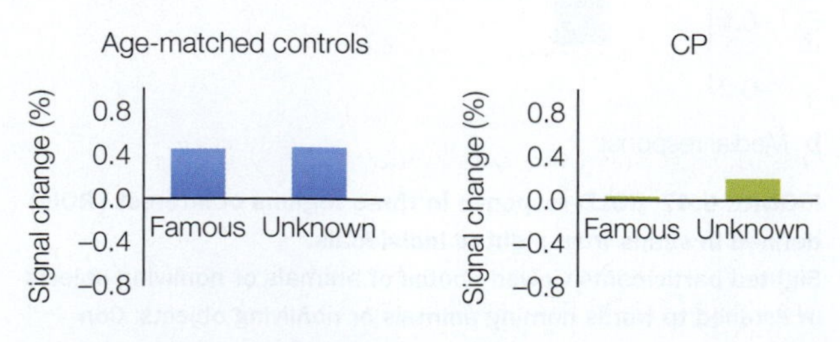

FIGURE 6.48 Comparing activation profiles in congenital prosopagnosia with those in age-matched controls.
(a) The activation profiles in the right FFA were very similar across the control and CP groups. **(b)** Unlike the robust activation in the FFA, there was very weak activation in the right anterior temporal lobe region for the CP group, with only three of the seven CP group members showing any activity in this region.

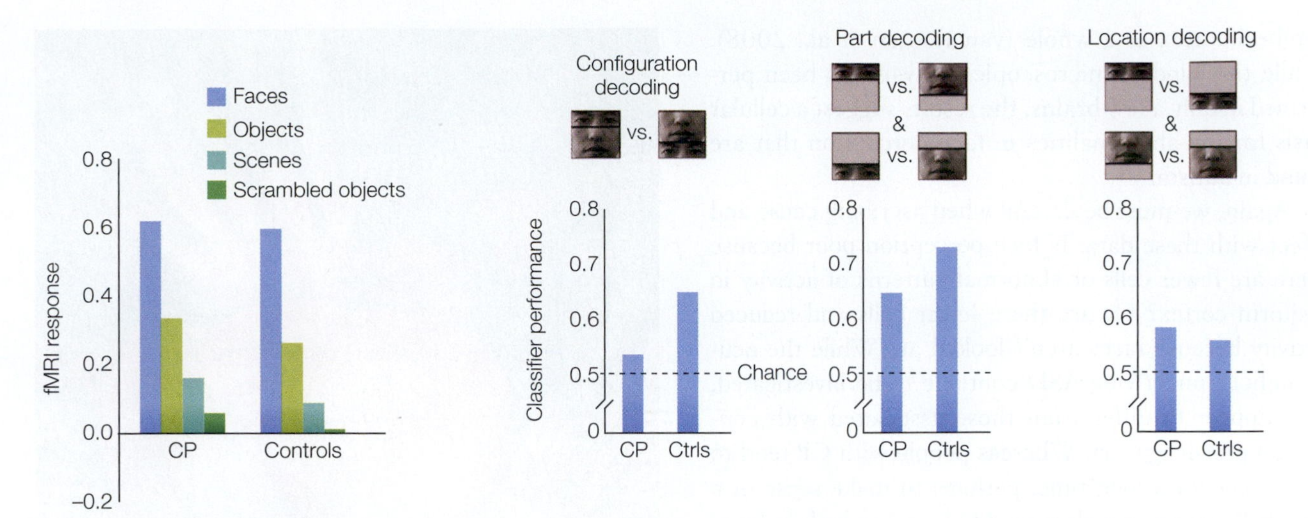

a Normal rFFA activation in CPs and controls

b Impaired configural processing in CPs associated with decreased rFFA activation

FIGURE 6.49 Decoding performance shown by fMRI MVPA reveals processing difference.
(a) CP individuals showed normal activation in fMRI of the right FFA when looking at faces or objects. (b) In the MVPA analysis, the data for the control group could be decoded at better than chance levels to distinguish between normal and scrambled faces (configuration), parts of faces, or the spatial position of face parts. In contrast, decoding based on the configuration of facial parts was at chance levels for those with CP.

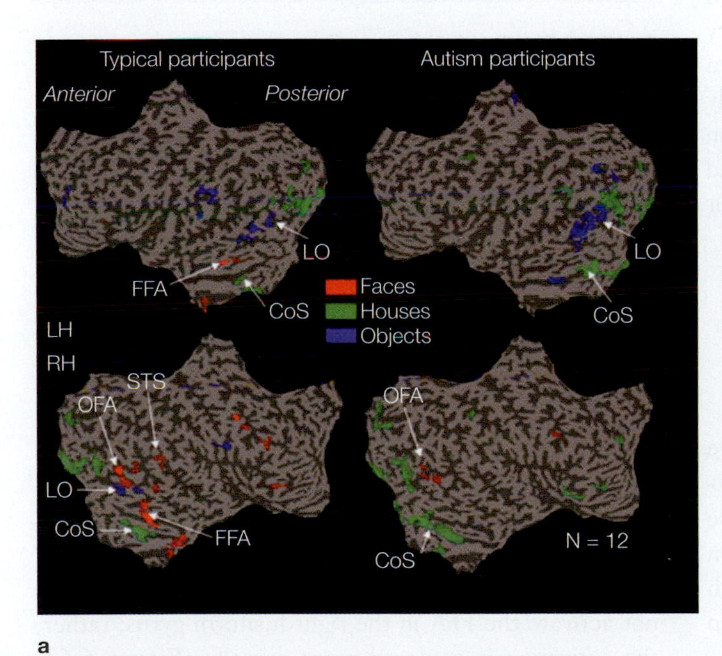

a

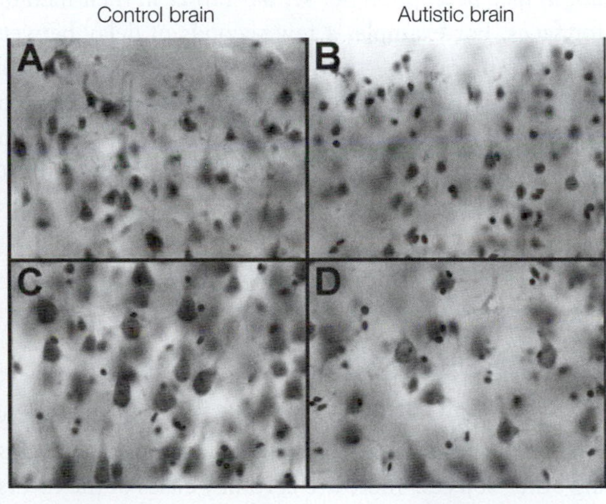

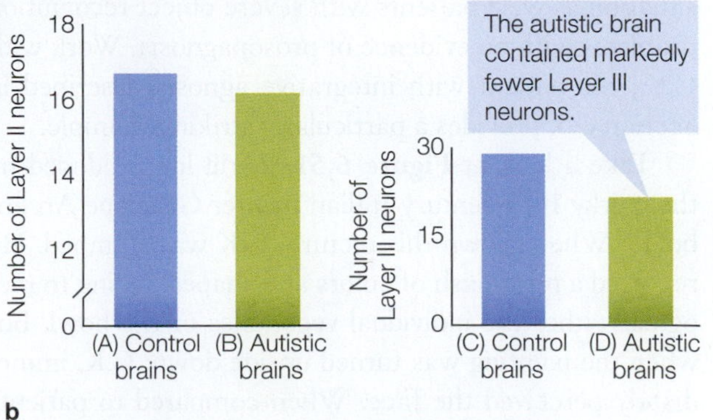

b

FIGURE 6.50 Functional and structural neural correlates of autism.
(a) Flattened cortical maps showing activation in response to faces, houses, and objects from typical developing individuals (left) and individuals with autism (right). The autistic individuals show a marked reduction in areas that are most activated by face stimuli. CoS = collateral sulcus; FFA = fusiform face area; LO = lateral occipital area. (b) Photomicrographs of 200-mm-thick sections showing labeled neurons in cortical layers II (A, B) and III (C, D) of the fusiform gyrus (FG). Samples A and C come from a control brain; samples B and D, from an autistic brain. The number of neurons in the Layer III autistic sample (D) is reduced.

cerebral cortex as a whole (van Kooten et al., 2008). While this kind of microscopic analysis has been performed in only a few brains, the results suggest a cellular basis for the abnormalities in face perception that are found in autism.

Again, we must be careful when ascribing cause and effect with these data. Is face perception poor because there are fewer cells or abnormal patterns of activity in fusiform cortex? Or are there fewer cells and reduced activity because faces aren't looked at? While the neural deficits underlying ASD continue to be investigated, they appear to differ from those associated with congenital prosopagnosia. Whereas people with CP tend to view faces for a long time, perhaps to make sense of a jumbled percept, people with ASD tend to look at faces for a shorter amount of time compared to matched controls (e.g., Klin et al., 2002). Individuals with ASD also score much better when faces are presented in an upright orientation compared to an inverted orientation (Scherf et al., 2008).

As in much of the research on ASD, a simple answer remains elusive even on a question as specific as whether these individuals are impaired in face perception. One intriguing idea is that individuals with ASD are impaired not in face perception per se, but rather in their memory for faces. For example, a few seconds of delay between the presentation of two faces will disproportionately impair ASD individuals on face matching or recognition tasks (Weigelt et al., 2012) compared to controls, and this memory impairment was found to be specific for faces (Weigelt et al., 2013).

FIGURE 6.51 What is this a painting of? The Arcimboldo painting that stumped C.K. when he viewed it right side up became immediately recognizable as something different when he turned it upside down. To see what C.K. saw, keep an eye on the turnip as you turn the image upside down.

Processing Accounts of Prosopagnosia

Multiple case studies describe patients with a selective disorder in face perception but little problem recognizing other objects. There are certainly cases of the reverse situation as well: patients with severe object recognition problems with no evidence of prosopagnosia. Work with C.K., the patient with integrative agnosia described in Section 6.5, provides a particularly striking example.

Take a look at **Figure 6.51**, a still life produced by the quirky 16th-century Italian painter Giuseppe Arcimboldo. When shown this picture, C.K was stumped. He reported a mishmash of colors and shapes, failing to recognize either the individual vegetables or the bowl. But when the painting was turned upside down, C.K. immediately perceived the face. When compared to patients with prosopagnosia, individuals like C.K. provide a double dissociation in support of the hypothesis that the brain has functionally different systems for face and object recognition.

Interestingly, individuals who have agnosia in the absence of prosopagnosia also tend to have acquired **alexia**, a loss of reading ability. What does this tell us about the mechanisms of face recognition and nonfacial object recognition? First, in terms of anatomy, fMRI scans obtained in healthy individuals reveal very different patterns of activation during word perception from those observed in studies of face perception. Letter strings do not activate the FFA in the right fusiform gyrus; rather, the activation is centered more dorsally (**Figure 6.52**; see Chapter 11) and is most prominent in the left hemisphere's fusiform gyrus, in a region called the *visual word form area*, independent of whether the words are presented in the left or right visual field (L. Cohen et al., 2000). Moreover, the magnitude of the activation increases when the letters form familiar words (L. Cohen et al., 2002). Second, the types of errors observed in acquired alexia usually reflect visual confusions. The word *ball* may be misread as *doll*, or *stalk* as *talks*.

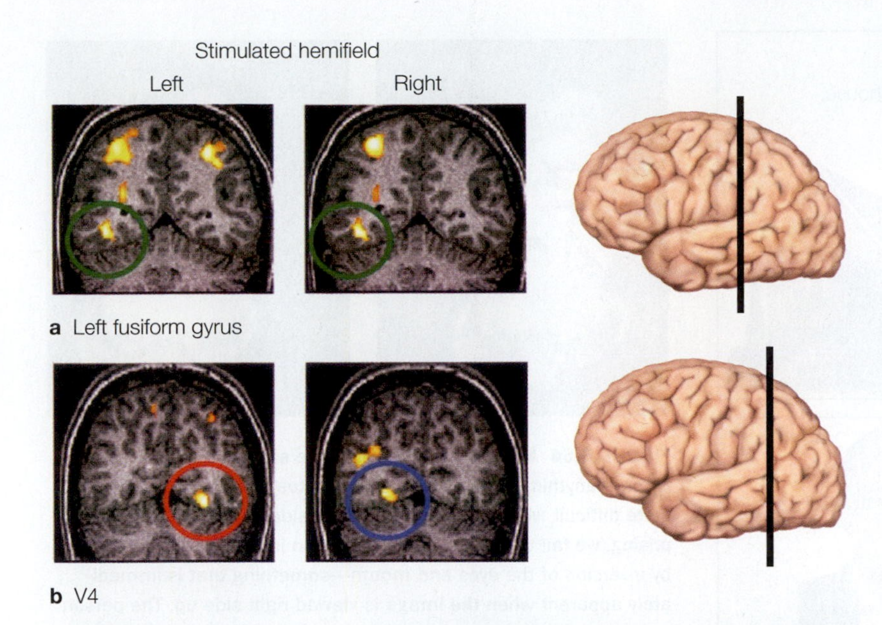

FIGURE 6.52 Activation of the visual word form area in the left hemisphere during reading compared to rest.
In separate blocks of trials, words were presented in either the left visual field **(a)** or the right visual field **(b)**. Independent of the side to which the stimulus was presented, words produced an increase in the BOLD response in the left fusiform gyrus (green circled region in part a), an area referred to as the visual word form area. In contrast, activation in V4 (blue and red circles in part b) was always contralateral to the side of stimulation. The black bars on the lateral views of the brain indicate the anterior–posterior position of the coronal slices shown on the left. V4 is more posterior to the visual word form area.

Whereas object and word recognition may entail the decomposition of a stimulus into its parts (e.g., words into letters), face perception appears to be unique in one special way: It is accomplished by more **holistic processing.** We recognize an individual by the entire facial configuration, the sum of the parts—not by his or her idiosyncratic nose, eyes, or chin structure. According to this hypothesis, if patients with prosopagnosia show a selective deficit in one class of stimuli—faces—it is because they are unable to form the holistic representation necessary for face perception.

Research on healthy people reinforces the notion that face perception requires a representation that is not simply a concatenation of individual parts. Participants in one study were asked to recognize line drawings of faces and houses (J. W. Tanaka & Farah, 1993). Each stimulus was constructed of limited parts. For faces, the parts were eyes, nose, and mouth; for houses, the parts were doors, living room windows, and bedroom windows. In a study phase, participants saw a name and either a face or a house (**Figure 6.53a**, top panel). For the face, participants were instructed to associate the name with the face; for example, "Larry had hooded eyes, a large nose, and full lips." For the house, they were instructed to learn the name of the person who lived in the house; for example, "Larry lived in a house with an arched door, a red brick chimney, and an upstairs bedroom window."

After this learning period, participants were given a recognition memory test (Figure 6.53a, bottom panel). The critical manipulation was whether the probe item was presented in isolation or in context, embedded in the whole object. For example, when asked whether the stimulus matched Larry's nose, the nose was presented either by itself or in the context of Larry's eyes and mouth. As predicted, house perception did not depend on whether the test items were presented in isolation or as an entire object, but face perception did (**Figure 6.53b**). Participants were much better at identifying an individual facial feature of a person when that feature was shown in conjunction with other parts of the person's face.

The idea that faces are generally processed holistically can account for an interesting phenomenon that occurs when the faces being viewed are inverted. Take a look at the photos in **Figure 6.54**. Who do they picture? Are they of the same person or not? Now turn the book upside down. Shocking, eh? One of the images has been "Thatcherized," so called because it was first done to an image of Margaret Thatcher, former prime minister of the United Kingdom (P. Thompson, 1980). For this face, we fail to note that the eyes and mouth have been left in their right-side-up orientation. We tend to see the two faces as identical, largely because the overall configuration of the stimuli is so similar. Rhesus monkeys show the same reaction as humans to distorted, inverted faces: They don't notice the change in features until the images are presented right side up (Adachi et al., 2009).

The relative contributions of the analysis-by-parts and holistic systems depend on the task (**Figure 6.55**). Face perception is at one extreme. Here, the critical information requires a holistic representation to capture the configuration of the defining parts. For these stimuli, discerning the parts is of little importance. Consider how hard it is to notice that a casual acquaintance has shaved his mustache. Rather, recognition requires that we perceive a familiar arrangement of the parts. Faces are special, in the sense that the representation derived from an analysis by parts is not sufficient.

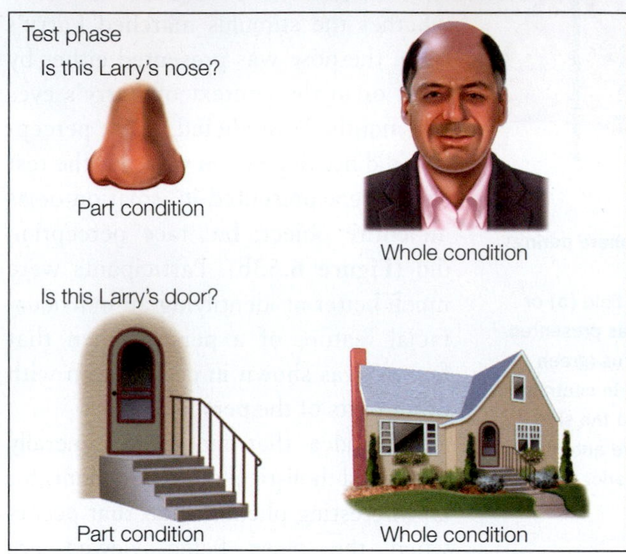

a

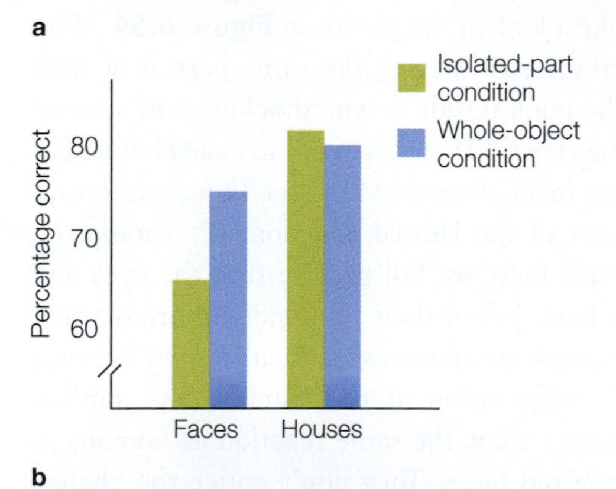

b

FIGURE 6.53 Facial features are poorly recognized in isolation.
(a) In the study phase (top panel), participants learned the names that corresponded with a set of faces and houses. During the recognition test (bottom panel), participants were presented with a face, a house, or a single feature from the face or house. They were asked whether a particular feature belonged to an individual. **(b)** When presented with the entire face, participants were much better at identifying the facial features. Recognition of the house features was the same in both conditions.

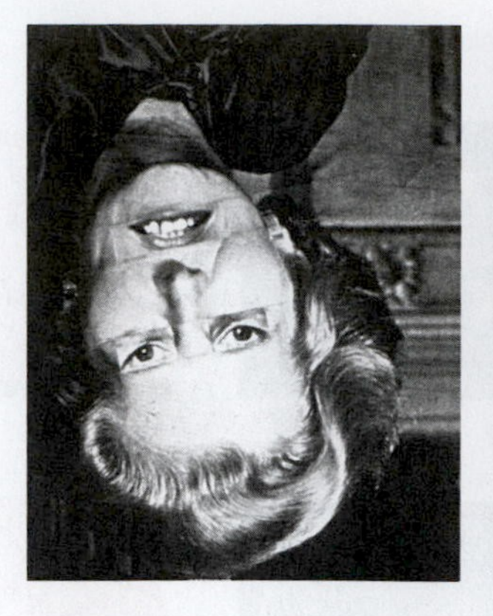
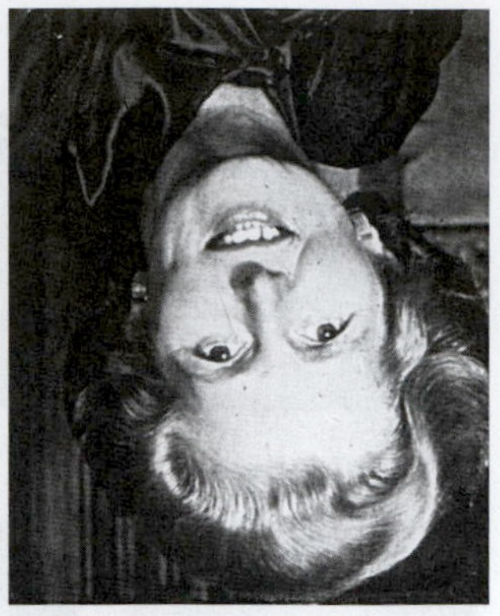

FIGURE 6.54 Are these two photos the same?
Is there anything unusual about the photos? Recognition can be quite difficult when faces are viewed upside down. Even more surprising, we fail to note a severe distortion in the left image created by inversion of the eyes and mouth—something that is immediately apparent when the image is viewed right side up. The person is Margaret Thatcher.

Words represent another special class of objects, but at the other extreme. Reading requires that the letter strings be successfully decomposed into their constituent parts. We benefit little from noting general features such as word length or handwriting. To differentiate one word from another, we have to recognize the individual letters.

In terms of recognition, objects fall somewhere between the two extremes of words and faces. Defining features such as the number pad and receiver can identify a telephone, but recognition is also possible when we perceive the overall shape of this familiar object. If either

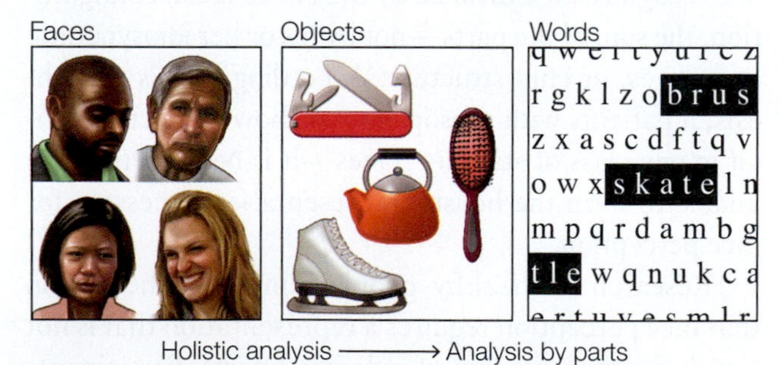

FIGURE 6.55 Recognition can be based on two forms of analysis: holistic analysis and analysis by parts.
The contributions of these two systems vary for different classes of stimuli. Analysis by parts is essential for reading and central for recognizing objects. A unique aspect of face recognition is its dependence on holistic analysis. Holistic analysis also contributes to object recognition.

the analysis-by-parts or the holistic system is damaged, object recognition may still be possible through operation of the intact system. But performance is likely to be suboptimal. Thus, agnosia for objects can co-occur with either alexia or prosopagnosia, but we should expect not to find cases in which face perception and reading are impaired while object perception remains intact. Indeed, a comprehensive review of agnosia failed to reveal any reliable reports of a patient with prosopagnosia and alexia but normal object perception (Farah, 2004).

In normal perception, both holistic and part-based systems are operating to produce fast, reliable recognition. These two processing systems converge on a common percept, although how efficiently they do so will vary for different classes of stimuli. Face perception is based primarily on a holistic analysis of the stimulus. Nonetheless, we are often able to recognize someone by his distinctive nose or eyes. Similarly, with expertise, we may recognize words in a holistic manner, with little evidence of a detailed analysis of the parts.

TAKE-HOME MESSAGES

- Prosopagnosia is an inability to recognize faces that cannot be attributed to deterioration in intellectual function.
- Acquired prosopagnosia results from a neurological incident such as stroke or inflammation. Congenital prosopagnosia is a developmental disorder. CP individuals have had difficulty recognizing faces for their whole lives.
- Holistic processing is a form of perceptual analysis that emphasizes the overall shape of an object. This mode of processing is especially important for face perception; we recognize a face by the overall configuration of its features, and not by the individual features themselves.
- Analysis-by-parts processing is a form of perceptual analysis that emphasizes the component parts of an object. This mode of processing is important for reading, when we decompose the overall shape into its constituent parts.

Summary

This chapter provided an overview of the higher-level processes involved in visual perception and object recognition. Like most mammals, people are visual creatures: Most of us rely on our eyes to identify not only *what* we are looking at, but also *where* to look, to guide our actions. These processes are interactive. To accomplish a skilled behavior, such as catching a thrown object, we have to determine the object's size and shape and track its path through space so that we can anticipate where to place our hands.

Object recognition can be achieved in a multiplicity of ways and involves many levels of representation. It begins with the two-dimensional information that the retina provides. Our visual system must overcome the variability inherent in the sensory input by extracting the critical information that distinguishes one shape from another. For object perception to be useful, the contents of current processing must be connected to our stored knowledge about objects. We do not see a meaningless array of shapes and forms. Rather, visual perception is an efficient avenue for recognizing and interacting with the world (e.g., determining which path to take across a cluttered room, or which tools will make our actions more efficient).

Moreover, vision provides a salient means for one of the most essential goals of perception: recognizing members of our own species. Evolutionary theory suggests that the importance of face perception may have led to the evolution of an alternative form of representation, one that quickly analyzes the global configuration of a stimulus rather than its parts. On the other hand, multiple forms of representation may have evolved, and face perception may be relatively unique in that it is highly dependent on the holistic form of representation.

Our knowledge of how object information is encoded has led to the development of amazing techniques that enable scientists to infer the contents of the mind from the observation of physiological signals, such as the BOLD response. This form of mind reading, or decoding, makes it possible to form inferences about general categories of viewed or imagined objects (e.g., faces versus places). It also can be used to make reasonable estimates of specific images. Brain decoding may offer new avenues for human communication.

Key Terms

agnosia (p. 229)
alexia (p. 268)
apperceptive visual agnosia (p. 259)
associative visual agnosia (p. 260)
dorsal (occipitoparietal) stream (p. 226)
extrastriate body area (EBA) (p. 256)
functional near-infrared spectroscopy (fNIRS) (p. 235)
fusiform body area (FBA) (p. 256)
fusiform face area (FFA) (p. 251)
gnostic unit (p. 237)
holistic processing (p. 269)
integrative visual agnosia (p. 259)
lateral occipital cortex (LOC) (p. 231)
object constancy (p. 225)
optic ataxia (p. 232)
parahippocampal place area (PPA) (p. 255)
prosopagnosia (p. 265)
repetition suppression (RS) effect (p. 235)
ventral (occipitotemporal) stream (p. 226)
visual agnosia (p. 229)

Think About It

1. What are some of the differences between processing in the dorsal and ventral visual pathways? In what ways are these differences useful? In what ways is it misleading to imply a functional dichotomy of two distinct visual pathways?
2. Ms. S. recently suffered a brain injury. She claims to have difficulty in "seeing" as a result of her injury. Her neurologist has made a preliminary diagnosis of agnosia, but nothing more specific is noted. To determine the nature of her perceptual problems, a cognitive neuroscientist is called in. What behavioral and neuroimaging tests should be used to analyze and make a more specific diagnosis? What results would support possible diagnoses? Remember that it is also important to conduct tests to determine whether Ms. S.'s deficit reflects a more general problem in visual perception or memory.
3. Review different hypotheses concerning why brain injury may produce the puzzling symptom of disproportionate impairment in recognizing living things. What sorts of evidence would support one hypothesis over another?
4. As a member of a debate team, you are assigned the task of defending the hypothesis that the brain has evolved a specialized system for perceiving faces. What arguments will you use to make your case? Now change sides. Defend the argument that face perception reflects the operation of a highly experienced system that is good at making fine discriminations.
5. EEG is an appealing alternative to fMRI for mind reading because a patient does not have to be in a scanner for the system to work. Describe what kinds of problems EEG might present for mind reading, and suggest possible solutions.

Suggested Reading

Farah, M. J. (2004). *Visual agnosia* (2nd ed.). Cambridge, MA: MIT Press.

Goodale, M. A., & Milner, A. D. (2004). *Sight unseen: An exploration of conscious and unconscious vision.* Oxford: Oxford University Press.

Kornblith, S., & Tsao, D. Y. (2017). How thoughts arise from sights: Inferotemporal and prefrontal contributions to vision. *Current Opinion in Neurobiology, 46*, 208–218.

Mahon, B. Z., & Caramazza, A. (2011). What drives the organization of object knowledge in the brain? *Trends in Cognitive Sciences, 15*, 97–103.

Martin, A. (2007). The representation of object concepts in the brain. *Annual Review of Psychology, 58*, 25–45.

Naselaris, T., Kay, K. N., Nishimoto, S., & Gallant, J. L. (2011). Encoding and decoding in fMRI. *NeuroImage, 56*(2), 400–410.

Peterson, M. A., & Rhodes, G. (Eds.). (2006). *Perception of faces, objects, and scenes: Analytic and holistic processes.* Oxford: Oxford University Press.

No man is lonely eating spaghetti, for it requires so much attention.

Christopher Morley

CHAPTER

7

Attention

A PATIENT WHO suffered a severe stroke several weeks ago sits with his wife as she talks with his neurologist. At first it seemed that the stroke had left him totally blind, but his wife states that he can sometimes see things, and that they are hoping his vision will improve. The neurologist soon realizes that although her patient does have serious visual problems, he is not completely blind. Taking a comb from her pocket, the doctor holds it in front of her patient and asks him, "What do you see?" (**Figure 7.1a**).

"Well, I'm not sure," he replies, "but . . . oh . . . it's a comb, a pocket comb."

"Good," says the doctor. Next she holds up a spoon and asks the same question (**Figure 7.1b**).

After a moment the patient replies, "I see a spoon."

The doctor nods and then holds up the spoon and the comb together. "What do you see now?" she asks.

He hesitantly replies, "I guess . . . I see a spoon."

"Okay . . . ," she says, as she overlaps the spoon and comb in a crossed fashion so they are both visible in the same location. "What do you see now?" (**Figure 7.1c**). Oddly enough, he sees only the comb. "What about a spoon?" she asks.

"Nope, no spoon," he says, but then suddenly blurts out, "Yes, there it is, I see the spoon now."

"Anything else?"

Shaking his head, the patient replies, "Nope."

Shaking the spoon and the comb vigorously in front of her patient's face, the doctor persists, "You don't see anything else, nothing at all?"

He stares straight ahead, looking intently, and finally says, "Yes . . . yes, I see them now . . . I see some numbers."

"What?" says the puzzled doctor. "Numbers?"

BIG Questions

- Does attention affect perception?
- To what extent does our conscious visual experience capture what we perceive?
- What neural mechanisms are involved in the control of attention?

a

b

c

FIGURE 7.1 Examination of a patient recovering from a cortical stroke.
(a) The doctor holds up a pocket comb and asks the patient what he sees. The patient reports seeing the comb. **(b)** The doctor then holds up a spoon, and the patient reports seeing the spoon too. **(c)** But when the doctor holds up the spoon and the comb at the same time, the patient says he can see only one object at a time. The patient has Bálint's syndrome.

"Yes." He squints and appears to strain his vision, moving his head ever so slightly, and replies, "I see numbers." The doctor then notices that the man's gaze is directed to a point beyond her and not toward the objects she is holding. Turning to glance over her own shoulder, she spots a large clock on the wall behind her!

Even though the doctor is holding both objects in one hand directly in front of her patient, overlapping them in space and in good lighting, he sees only one item at a time. That one item may even be a different item altogether: one that is merely in the direction of his gaze, such as the clock on the wall. The patient can "see" each of the objects presented by the doctor, but he fails to see them all together and cannot accurately describe their locations with respect to each other or to himself. From these symptoms the neurologist diagnoses the patient with Bálint's syndrome, a condition caused by bilateral damage to regions of the posterior parietal and occipital cortex. The result is a severe disturbance of visual attention and awareness, in which only one or a small subset of available objects is perceived at any one time and is mislocalized in space.

Bálint's syndrome is an extreme pathological instance of what we all experience daily: We are consciously aware of only a small bit of the vast amount of information available to our sensory systems from moment to moment. By looking closely at patients with attentional problems, we have come to learn more about how, and on what, the brain focuses attention. The central problem in the study of attention is the question of how the brain is able to select some information at the expense of other information.

Robert Louis Stevenson wrote, "The world is so full of a number of things, I'm sure we should all be as happy as kings." Although those things may make us happy, the sheer number of them presents a problem to our perception system: information overload. We know from experience that we are surrounded by more information than we can handle and comprehend at any given time. The nervous system, therefore, has to make "decisions" about what to process. Our survival may depend on which stimuli are selected and in what order they are prioritized for processing. In this chapter, after describing what is meant by attention and reviewing the anatomical structures involved with it, we consider how damage to the brain changes human attention and gives us insight into how attention is organized in the brain. Then we discuss how attention influences sensation and perception. We conclude with a discussion of the brain networks used for attentional control.

7.1 Selective Attention and the Anatomy of Attention

At the end of the 19th century, the great American psychologist William James (**Figure 7.2**) made an astute observation:

> Everyone knows what attention is. It is the taking possession by the mind, in clear and vivid form, of one out

of what seem several simultaneously possible objects or trains of thought. Focalization, concentration of consciousness are of its essence. It implies withdrawal from some things in order to deal effectively with others, and is a condition which has a real opposite in the confused, dazed, scatterbrain state. (W. James, 1890)

FIGURE 7.2
William James (1842–1910).

James insightfully captured key characteristics of attentional phenomena that are under investigation today. "It is the taking possession by the mind" suggests that we can choose the focus of attention; that is, it can be voluntary. His mention of "one out of what seem several simultaneously possible objects or trains of thought" refers to the inability to attend to many things at once, and hence the selective aspects of attention. James raised the idea of limited capacity in attention by noting that "it implies withdrawal from some things in order to deal effectively with others."

As clear and articulate as James's writings were, little was known about the behavioral, computational, or neural mechanisms of attention during his lifetime. Since then, knowledge about attention has blossomed, and researchers have identified multiple types and levels of attentive behavior. First, let's distinguish selective attention from arousal. **Arousal** refers to the global physiological and psychological state of the organism, and it is best thought of on a continuum ranging from deep sleep to hyperalertness (such as during periods of intense fear). We will discuss this further in Chapter 14.

In contrast, **selective attention** is not a global brain state. Instead, at any level of arousal, it is the allocation of attention among relevant inputs, thoughts, and actions while simultaneously ignoring irrelevant or distracting ones. Selective attention is the ability to prioritize and attend to some things and not others. What determines the priority? Many things. For instance, an optimal strategy in many situations is to attend to stimuli that are relevant to current behavior and goals. For example, to survive this class, you need to attend to this chapter rather than your social media feed.

This is *goal-driven control* (also called *top-down control*), steered by an individual's current behavioral goals and shaped by learned priorities based on personal experience and evolutionary adaptations. Still, if you hear a loud bang, even while dutifully attending to this book, you will reflexively pop up your head and check it out. That is good survival behavior because a loud noise may presage danger.

ANATOMICAL ORIENTATION

Anatomy of Attention

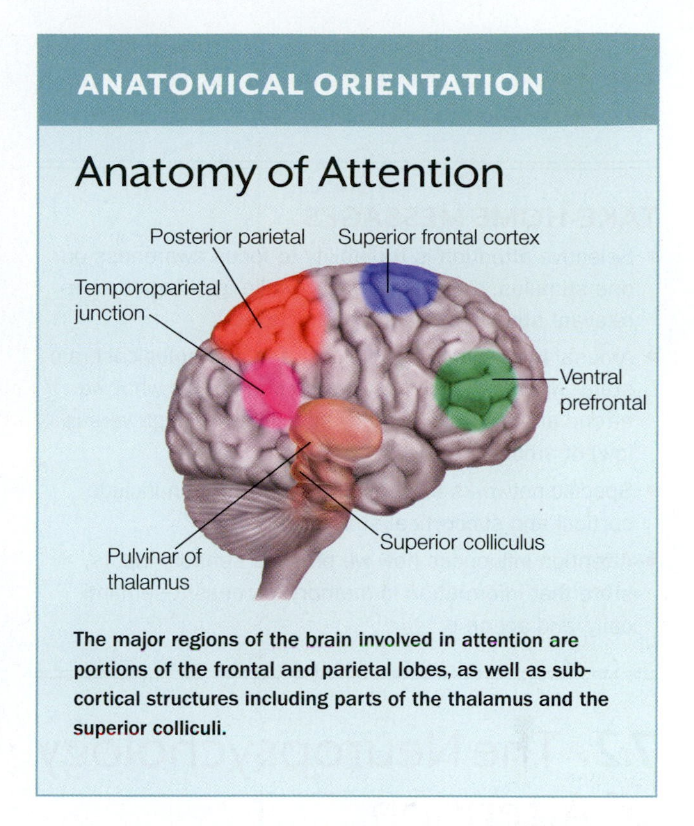

The major regions of the brain involved in attention are portions of the frontal and parietal lobes, as well as subcortical structures including parts of the thalamus and the superior colliculi.

Your reaction is stimulus driven and is therefore termed *stimulus-driven control* (also known as *bottom-up control*), which is much less dependent on current behavioral goals.

The mechanisms that determine where and on what our attention is focused are referred to as attentional control mechanisms, and they involve widespread but highly specific cortical and subcortical networks that interact so that we can selectively process information (see the "Anatomical Orientation" box). Several cortical areas are important in attention: portions of the superior frontal cortex, posterior parietal cortex, and posterior superior temporal cortex, as well as more medial brain structures, including the anterior cingulate cortex. The superior colliculus in the midbrain and the pulvinar nucleus of the thalamus, located between the midbrain and the cortex, are involved in the control of attention.

We know that damage to these structures can lead to deficits in the ability to orient both overt attention (i.e., eye gaze direction) and covert attention (i.e., attention directed without changes in eye, head, or body orientation). Finally, attention acts on sensory systems, and therefore much work on attention investigates the effect of attention on sensory signal processing.

Attentional control mechanisms influence specific stages of information processing, where it is said that "selection" of inputs (or outputs) takes place—hence the term *selective attention.* (As shorthand, we will often just use the term *attention* when referring to the more specific concept of selective attention.) Attention influences how we code sensory inputs, store that information in memory, process it semantically, and act on it to survive in a challenging world. This chapter focuses on the mechanisms of selective attention and its role in perception and awareness.

TAKE-HOME MESSAGES

- Selective attention is the ability to focus awareness on one stimulus, thought, or action while ignoring other, irrelevant stimuli, thoughts, and actions.
- Arousal is a global physiological and psychological brain state, whereas selective attention describes what we attend and ignore within any specific level (high versus low) of arousal.
- Specific networks for the control of attention include cortical and subcortical structures.
- Attention influences how we process sensory inputs, store that information in memory, process it semantically, and act on it.

7.2 The Neuropsychology of Attention

Much of what neuroscientists know about brain attention systems has been gathered from examinations of patients who have brain damage that influences attentional behavior. Many disorders result in deficits in attention, but only a few provide clues to which brain systems are being affected. Though the best-known disorder of attention, attention deficit hyperactivity disorder (ADHD), has heterogeneous genetic and environmental risk factors, it is characterized by disturbances in neural processing that may result from anatomical variations of white matter throughout the attention network. Structural MRI studies of ADHD patients have found decreased white matter volume throughout the brain, especially the prefrontal cortex (see Bush, 2010). The portions of the brain's attention networks affected by ADHD are yet to be fully identified.

In contrast, neuroscientists have derived more information about attentional control mechanisms, and the underlying neuroanatomical systems supporting attention, by investigating classic syndromes like unilateral spatial neglect (described next) and Bálint's syndrome. Because these disorders are the result of focal brain damage (e.g., stroke), they can be mapped in postmortem analyses and localized with brain imaging in the living human. Let's consider how brain damage has helped us understand these mechanisms.

Neglect

A patient with neglect may notice you more easily when you are on her right side, comb her hair only on the right, eat from only the right half of her plate, and read only the right-hand page of a book. What's more, she may deny having any problems. Depending on the extent and location of her lesion, she may show all or a subset of these symptoms.

Unilateral spatial neglect, or simply **neglect**, is quite common. It results when the brain's attention network is damaged in one hemisphere, typically as the result of a stroke. More severe and persistent effects occur when the right hemisphere is damaged. As in the hypothetical patient just described, a right-hemisphere lesion biases attention toward the right, resulting in a neglect of what is going on in the left visual field. The patient behaves as though the left regions of space and the left parts of objects simply do not exist, and has limited or no awareness of her lesion and deficit.

The late German artist Anton Räderscheidt suffered a stroke in the right hemisphere at age 67, resulting in left-sided neglect. In a self-portrait done shortly after his stroke (**Figure 7.3a**), the entire left half of the canvas is largely

a

b

c

d

FIGURE 7.3 Recovering from a stroke.
Self-portraits by the late German artist Anton Räderscheidt, painted at different times following a severe right-hemisphere stroke, which left him with neglect to contralesional space. © 2013 Artists Rights Society (ARS), New York/VG Bild-Kunst, Bonn.

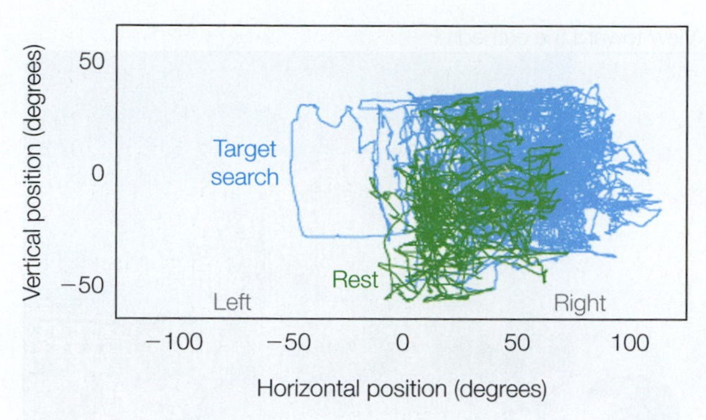

a Neglect

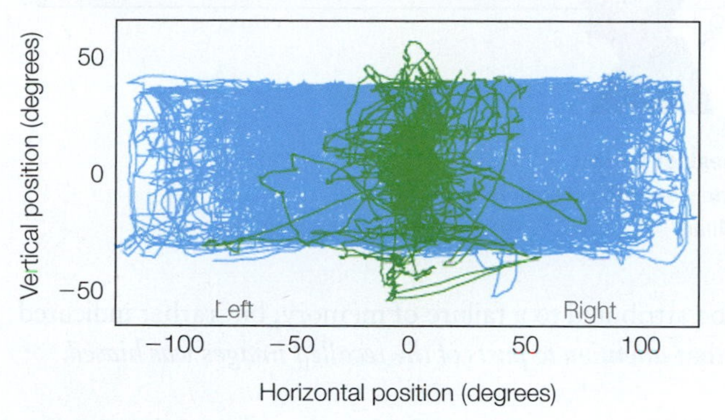

b Control

FIGURE 7.4 Gaze bias in neglect patients.
(a) Neglect patients showed an ipsilesional gaze bias while searching for a target letter in a letter array (blue traces) and at rest (green traces). (b) Non-neglect patients showed no bias.

untouched, and the left half of his face is missing. Over the following several months, Räderscheidt progressively used more of the canvas and included more of his face in his portraits (**Figure 7.3b and c**), until finally (**Figure 7.3d**), he used most of the canvas and had a bilaterally symmetrical face, although some minor asymmetries persisted.

Despite having normal vision, patients with neglect exhibit deficits in attending to and acting in the direction opposite the side of the unilateral brain damage. This phenomenon can be observed in their patterns of eye movements (**Figure 7.4**): These patterns, during rest and during a bilateral visual search in patients with a right-hemisphere lesion and left-sided neglect (Figure 7.4a), can be compared to those of patients with right-hemisphere strokes without neglect (Figure 7.4b). The neglect patients show a pattern of eye movements biased in the direction of the right visual field, while those without neglect search the entire array, moving their eyes equally to the left and right (Corbetta & Shulman, 2011).

NEUROPSYCHOLOGICAL TESTS OF NEGLECT Neuropsychological tests are used to diagnose neglect. In the line cancellation test, patients are given a sheet of paper containing many horizontal lines and are asked to bisect them in the middle. Patients with left-sided neglect tend to bisect the lines to the right of the midline. They may

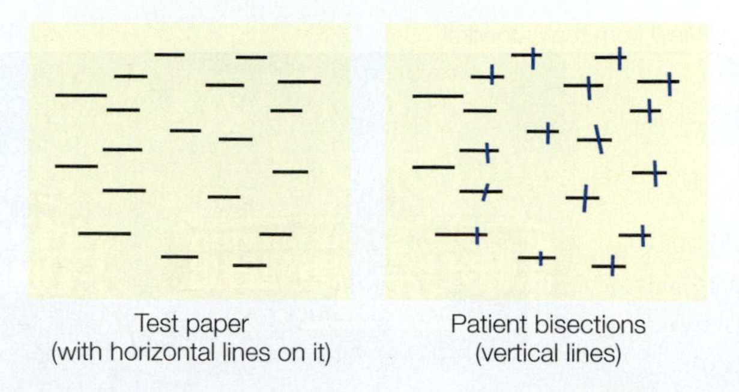

FIGURE 7.5 Patients with neglect are biased in line cancellation tasks.
Patients suffering from neglect are given a sheet of paper containing many horizontal lines and asked under free-viewing conditions to bisect the lines precisely in the middle with a vertical line. They tend to bisect the lines to the right (for a right-hemisphere lesion) of the midline of each page and each line, owing to neglect for contralesional space and the contralesional side of individual objects.

also completely miss lines on the left side of the paper (**Figure 7.5**). The pattern of line cancellation is evidence of neglect at the level of object representations (each line) as well as visual space (the visual scene represented by the test paper).

A related test is to copy objects or scenes. **Figure 7.6** shows an example from a patient with a right-hemisphere stroke who was asked to copy a clock. Like the artist Räderscheidt, the patient showed an inability to draw the entire object and tended to neglect the left side. Even when such patients know and can state that clocks are round and include the numbers 1 to 12, they cannot properly copy the image. Moreover, they cannot draw it from memory.

Neglect can also affect the imagination and memory. In Milan, Italy, Eduardo Bisiach and Claudio Luzzatti (1978) studied patients with neglect caused by unilateral damage to the right hemisphere. They asked the participants to imagine themselves standing on the steps of the Duomo di Milano (the Milan Cathedral) and to describe from memory the piazza from that viewpoint. Amazingly,

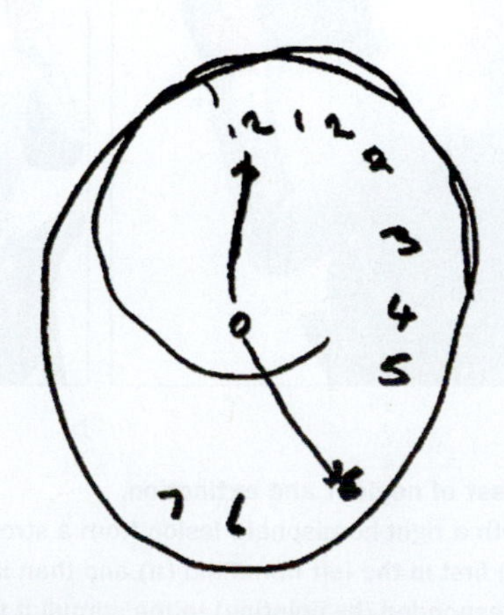

FIGURE 7.6 Image drawn by a right-hemisphere stroke patient who has neglect.
Note that hours are confined to the right side of the dial, as if there were no left side of visual space.

FIGURE 7.7 Visual recollections of two ends of an Italian piazza by a neglect patient.
The neglected side in visual memory (shaded gray) was contralateral to the side with cortical damage. The actual study was performed using the famous Piazza del Duomo in Milan.

the patients neglected things on the side of the piazza contralateral to their lesion, just as if they were actually standing there looking at it. Furthermore, when imagining themselves standing across the piazza, facing *toward* the Duomo, they reported items from visual memory that they had previously neglected, and they neglected the side of the piazza that they had just described (**Figure 7.7**).

Thus, neglect is found for items in visual memory during remembrance of a scene, as well as for items in the external sensory world. The key point in Bisiach and Luzzatti's experiment is that the patients' neglect could not be attributed to a failure of memory, but rather indicated that *attention to parts of the recalled images was biased.*

EXTINCTION Visual field testing shows that neglect patients are not blind in their left visual field: They are able to detect stimuli normally when those stimuli are salient and presented *in isolation*. For example, when simple flashes of light or the wiggling fingers of a neurologist are shown at different single locations within the visual field of a neglect patient, the patient can see each stimulus (**Figure 7.8a and b**). This result tells us

a

b

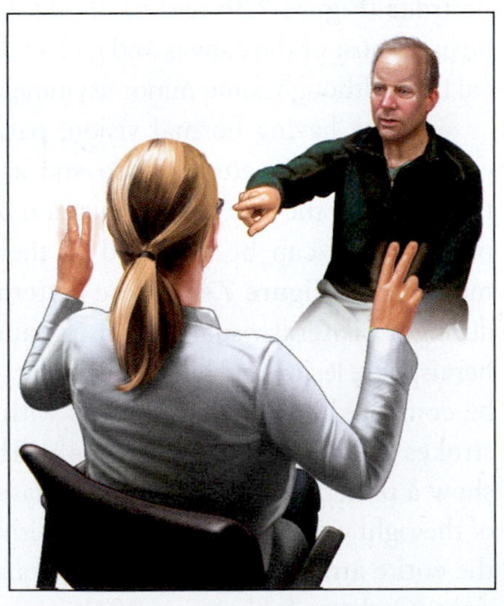

c

FIGURE 7.8 Test of neglect and extinction.
To a patient with a right-hemisphere lesion from a stroke, a neurologist presented a visual stimulus (raised fingers) first in the left hemifield (a) and then in the right hemifield (b). The patient correctly detected and responded (by pointing) to the stimuli if they were presented one at a time, demonstrating an ability to see each stimulus and therefore a lack of major visual field defects. When the stimuli were presented simultaneously in the left and right visual fields (c), however, extinction was observed: The patient reported seeing only the stimulus in the right visual field.

that the patient does not have a primary visual deficit. The patient's neglect becomes obvious, however, when he is presented simultaneously with two stimuli, one in each hemifield. In that case, the patient fails to perceive or act on the contralesional stimulus (**Figure 7.8c**). This result is known as **extinction**, because the presence of the competing stimulus in the ipsilateral hemifield prevents the patient from detecting the contralesional stimulus.

These biases against the contralesional sides of space and objects can be overcome if the patient's attention is directed to the neglected locations of items. This is one reason the condition is described as a bias, rather than a loss of the ability to focus attention contralesionally. One patient's comments help us understand how these deficits might feel subjectively: "It doesn't seem right to me that the word neglect should be used to describe it. I think concentrating is a better word than neglect. It's definitely concentration. If I am walking anywhere and there's something in my way, if I'm concentrating on what I'm doing, I will see it and avoid it. The slightest distraction and I won't see it" (Halligan & Marshall, 1998).

Comparing Neglect and Bálint's Syndrome

Let's compare the pattern of deficits in neglect with those of the patient with Bálint's syndrome described at the beginning of the chapter. In contrast to the patient with neglect, a Bálint's patient demonstrates three main deficits that are characteristic of the disorder:

- *Simultanagnosia* is a difficulty in perceiving the visual field as a whole scene, such as when the patient saw only the comb or the spoon, but not both at the same time (Figure 7.1).
- *Ocular apraxia* is a deficit in making eye movements (saccades) to scan the visual field, resulting in the inability to guide eye movements voluntarily: When the physician overlapped the spoon and comb in space as in Figure 7.1c, the Bálint's patient should have been able, given his direction of gaze, to see both objects, but he could not.
- *Optic ataxia* is a problem in making visually guided hand movements: If the doctor had asked the Bálint's patient to reach out and grasp the comb, the patient would have had a difficult time moving his hand through space toward the object.

The patterns of perceptual deficits in neglect and Bálint's syndrome are quite different, however, because different brain areas are damaged in each disorder. Neglect is the result of unilateral lesions of the parietal, posterior temporal, and frontal cortex, and it can also be due to damage in subcortical areas including the basal ganglia, thalamus, and midbrain. In contrast, Bálint's patients suffer from bilateral occipitoparietal lesions. Neglect shows us that disruption of a network of cortical and subcortical areas, especially in the right hemisphere, results in disturbances of spatial attention. Bálint's syndrome shows us that posterior parietal and occipital damage to both hemispheres leads to an inability to perceive multiple objects in space, which is necessary for creating a scene.

From patients with neglect, we understand that the symptoms involve biases in attention based on spatial coordinates, either with respect to the patient (egocentric reference frame) or with respect to an object in space (allocentric reference frame). This finding tells us that attention can be directed within space and also within objects. Most likely these two types of neglect are guided by different processes. Indeed, the brain mechanisms involved with attending objects can be affected even when no spatial biases are seen. This phenomenon is evident in patients with Bálint's syndrome, who have relatively normal visual fields but cannot attend to more than one or a few objects at a time, even when the objects overlap in space.

The phenomenon of extinction in neglect patients suggests that sensory inputs are competitive, because when two stimuli presented simultaneously compete for attention, the one in the ipsilesional hemifield wins the competition and reaches the patient's awareness. Extinction also demonstrates that after brain damage, patients experience reduced attentional capacity: When two competing stimuli are presented at once, the neglect patient is aware of only one of them.

These observations from brain damage and resultant attentional problems set the stage for us to consider several questions:

- How does attention influence perception?
- Where in the perceptual system does attention influence perception?
- What neural mechanisms control what we attend?

To answer these questions, let's look next at the cognitive and neural mechanisms of attention.

TAKE-HOME MESSAGES

- Unilateral spatial neglect may result from damage to the right parietal, temporal, or frontal cortices, as well as to subcortical structures. This kind of damage leads to reduced attention to and processing of the left-hand side of scenes and objects, not only in external personal hemispace but also in internal memory.
- Neglect is not the result of sensory deficits, because visual field testing shows that these patients have

intact vision. Under the right circumstances, they can easily see objects that are sometimes neglected.

- A prominent feature of neglect is extinction, the failure to perceive or act on stimuli contralateral to the lesion (contralesional stimuli) when presented simultaneously with a stimulus ipsilateral to the lesion (ipsilesional stimulus).
- Patients with Bálint's syndrome have three main deficits characteristic of the disorder: difficulty perceiving the visual field as a whole scene, an inability to guide eye movements voluntarily, and difficulty reaching to grab an object.

7.3 Models of Attention

Attention can be divided into two main forms: voluntary attention and reflexive attention. **Voluntary attention**, also known as **endogenous attention**, is our ability to intentionally attend to something, such as this book. It is a top-down, goal-driven process, meaning that our goals, expectations, and rewards guide what we attend. **Reflexive attention**, also referred to as **exogenous attention**, is a bottom-up, stimulus-driven process in which a sensory event—maybe a loud bang, the sting of a mosquito, a whiff of garlic, a flash of light, or motion—captures our attention.

These two forms of attention can be thought of as opposing systems—one supporting our ability to focus attention to achieve momentary behavioral goals, and the other being driven by the world around us. It is useful to think of these two attention systems as being in balance, so that we are neither so focused on something like a beautiful flower that we miss the tiger sneaking up behind us, nor so distracted by environmental sights and sounds that we attend to flashing billboards when we need to concentrate on driving in heavy traffic. As we will see later in this chapter, these two forms of attention differ in their properties and partly in their neural mechanisms.

Attention orienting also can be either overt or covert. We all know what **overt attention** is: When you turn your head to orient toward a stimulus—whether it is for your eyes to get a better look or your ears to pick up a whisper—you are exhibiting overt attention. However, you could appear to be reading this book while actually paying attention to the two students whispering at the table behind you. This behavior is **covert attention**. Much of attention research focuses on understanding covert attention mechanisms, because these necessarily involve changes in internal neural processing and not merely the aiming of sense organs to better pick up information.

Hermann von Helmholtz and Covert Attention

In 1894, Hermann von Helmholtz was investigating aspects of the visual processing of briefly perceived stimuli. He constructed a screen on which letters were painted at various distances from the center (**Figure 7.9**). He hung the screen at one end of his lab, turned off all the lights to create a completely dark environment, and then used an electrical spark to make a flash of light that briefly illuminated the screen. As often happens in science, he stumbled onto an interesting phenomenon.

Helmholtz noted that the screen was too large to view without moving his eyes. Nonetheless, even when he kept his eyes fixed on the center of the screen, he could decide in advance where he would pay attention using covert attention. As noted earlier, *covert* means that the location toward which he directed his attention could be different from the location toward which he was looking. Through these covert shifts of attention, Helmholtz observed that during the brief period of illumination, he could perceive letters located within the focus of his attention better than letters that fell outside the focus of his attention, even when his eyes remained directed toward the center of the screen.

Try this yourself using Figure 7.9. Hold the textbook 12 inches in front of you and stare at the plus sign in the

FIGURE 7.9 Helmholtz's visual attention experiment. Experimental setup by Helmholtz to study visual attention. Helmholtz observed that, while keeping his eyes fixated in the center of the screen during a very brief illumination of the screen, he could covertly attend to any location on the screen and perceive the letters located within that region but had difficulty perceiving the letters at other locations.

center of Helmholtz's array of letters. Now, without moving your eyes from the plus sign, read out loud the letters closest to the plus sign in a clockwise order. You have covertly focused on the letters around the plus sign. As Helmholtz wrote in his *Treatise on Physiological Optics*,

> These experiments demonstrated, so it seems to me, that by a voluntary kind of intention, even without eye movements, and without changes of accommodation, one can concentrate attention on the sensation from a particular part of our peripheral nervous system and at the same time exclude attention from all other parts. (Helmholtz, 1909–11/1968)

In the mid 20th century, experimental psychologists began to develop methods for quantifying the influence of attention on perception and awareness. Models of how the brain's attention system might work were built from these data and from observations like those of Helmholtz—as well as from everyday experiences, such as attending a crowded party.

The Cocktail Party Effect

Imagine yourself at a Super Bowl party having a conversation with a friend. How can you focus on this single conversation while the TV is blaring and boisterous conversations are going on around you? British psychologist E. C. Cherry (1953) wondered the same thing while attending cocktail parties. His curiosity and subsequent research helped to found the modern era of attention studies with what was dubbed the *cocktail party effect*.

Selective auditory attention enables you to participate in a conversation at a busy restaurant or party while ignoring the rest of the sounds around you. By selectively attending, you can perceive the signal of interest amid the other noises. If, however, the person you are conversing with is boring, then you can give covert attention to a conversation going on behind you while still seeming to focus on the conversation in front of you (**Figure 7.10**).

FIGURE 7.10 Auditory selective attention in a noisy environment. The cocktail party effect of Cherry (1953), illustrating how, in the noisy, confusing environment of a cocktail party, people are able to focus attention on a single conversation, and, as the man in the middle right of the cartoon illustrates, to covertly shift attention to listen to a more interesting conversation than the one in which they continue to pretend to be engaged.

Cherry investigated this ability by designing a cocktail party in the lab—the first use of the dichotic listening task described in Chapter 4. Normal participants, wearing headphones, listened to competing speech inputs to the two ears. Cherry then asked the participants to attend to and verbally "shadow" the speech (i.e., immediately repeat each word) coming into one ear while simultaneously ignoring the input to the other ear. Cherry discovered that under such conditions, for the most part, participants could not report any details of the speech in the unattended ear (**Figure 7.11**). In fact, all they could reliably report from the unattended ear was whether the speaker was male or female. *Attention—in this case voluntary attention—affected what was processed.*

This finding led Cherry and others to propose that attention to one ear results in better encoding of the inputs to the attended ear and loss or degradation of the unattended inputs to the other ear. You experience this effect when the person sitting next to you in lecture whispers a juicy tidbit in your ear. A moment later, you realize that you missed what the lecturer just said, although you could easily have heard him with your other ear.

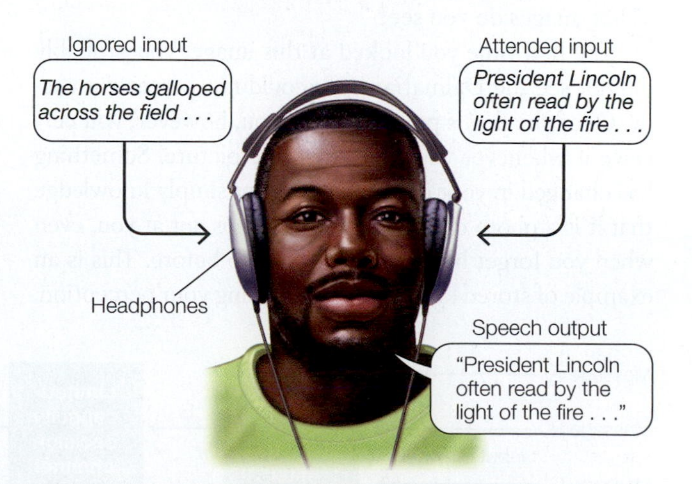

FIGURE 7.11 Dichotic listening study setup. Different auditory information (stories) is presented to each ear of a participant. The participant is asked to "shadow" (immediately repeat) the auditory stimuli from one ear's input (e.g., shadow the left-ear story and ignore the right-ear input).

FIGURE 7.12
What images do you see?

As foreshadowed by William James, **bottlenecks** in information processing—stages through which only a limited amount of information can pass—seem to occur at stages of perceptual analysis that have a limited capacity. There are many stages of processing between the time information enters your eardrum and the time you become aware of what was said. At which stages are there bottlenecks that make attention necessary to favor one signal over another?

This question has led to one of the most debated issues in psychology over the past six decades: Are the effects of selective attention evident *early* in sensory processing or only later, after sensory and perceptual processing are complete? Does the brain faithfully process all incoming sensory inputs to create a representation of the external world, or can processes like attention influence sensory processing? Is your perception of the external world biased by the current goals and stored knowledge of your internal world? Consider the example in **Figure 7.12.** What images do you see?

The first time you looked at this image, you probably did not see the Dalmatian; you could not perceive it easily. Once the dog is pointed out to you, however, you perceive it whenever you are shown the picture. Something has changed in your brain, and it is not simply knowledge that it is a photo of a dog; the dog jumps out at you, even when you forget having seen the photo before. This is an example of stored knowledge influencing your perception. Perhaps it is not either-or; it may be that attention affects processing at many steps along the way from sensory transduction to awareness.

Early-Selection Models Versus Late-Selection Models

Cambridge University psychologist Donald Broadbent (1958) elaborated on the idea that the *information-processing system* (i.e., the totality of neural processing that stimulus inputs or actions undergo in the brain) has processing bottlenecks (**Figure 7.13**). In Broadbent's model, the sensory inputs that can enter higher levels of the brain for processing are screened early in the information-processing stream by a gating mechanism so that only the "most important," or attended, events pass through. **Early selection** is the idea that a stimulus can be selected for further processing or be tossed out as irrelevant *before* perceptual analysis of the stimulus is complete.

In contrast, models of **late selection** hypothesize that the perceptual system first processes all inputs equally, and *then* selection takes place at higher stages of information processing that determine whether the stimuli gain access to awareness, are encoded in memory, or initiate a response. **Figure 7.14** illustrates the differential stages of early versus late selection.

The original all-or-none early-selection models quickly ran into a problem. Cherry observed in his cocktail party experiments that salient information from the *unattended ear* was sometimes consciously perceived—for example, when the listener's own name or something very interesting was included in a nearby conversation. The idea of a simple gating mechanism, which assumed that ignored information was completely lost, could not explain this experimental finding.

Anne Treisman (1969) proposed that information from an unattended channel was not completely blocked from higher analysis but was degraded or attenuated instead—a point that Broadbent agreed with. Thus, early-selection versus late-selection models were modified to make room for the possibility that information in the unattended channel could reach higher stages of analysis, but with greatly reduced signal strength. To test these

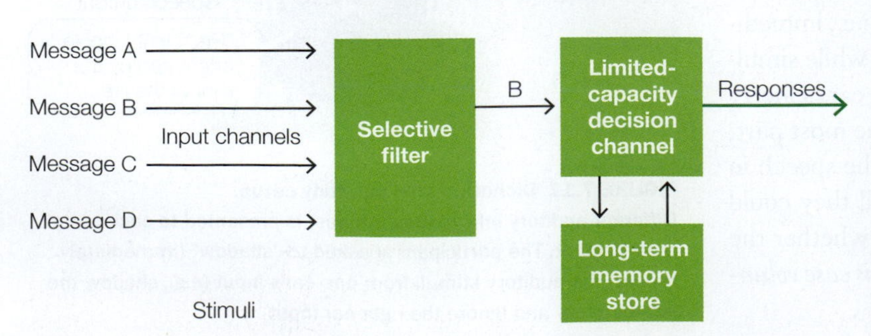

FIGURE 7.13 Broadbent's model of selective attention.
In this model, a gating mechanism determines which limited information is passed on for higher-level analysis. The gating mechanism takes the form of top-down influences on early perceptual processing, under the control of higher-order executive processes. The gating mechanism is needed at stages where processing has limited capacity.

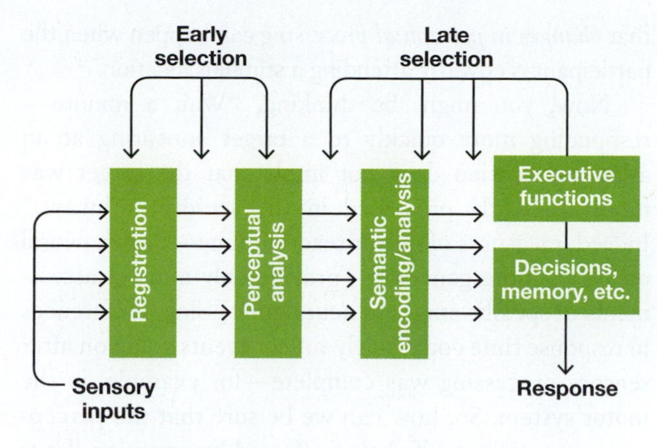

FIGURE 7.14 Early versus late selection of information processing.
Early-selection mechanisms of attention would influence the processing of sensory inputs before the completion of perceptual analysis. In contrast, late-selection mechanisms of attention would act only after complete perceptual processing of the sensory inputs, at stages where the information had been recoded as a semantic or categorical representation (e.g., "chair").

competing models of attention, researchers employed increasingly sensitive methods for quantifying the effects of attention, as described next.

Quantifying the Role of Attention in Perception

One way of measuring the effect of attention on information processing is to examine how participants respond to target stimuli under differing conditions of attention. One popular method is to provide cues that direct the participant's attention to a particular location or target feature before presenting the task-relevant target stimulus. In these so-called *cuing tasks*, the focus of attention is manipulated by the information in the cue.

In cuing studies of voluntary spatial attention, University of Oregon professor Michael Posner and his colleagues presented participants with a cue that directs their attention to one location on a computer screen (**Figure 7.15**). Next, a target stimulus is flashed onto the screen at either the cued location or another location. Participants may be asked to press a button as fast as they can following the presentation of a target stimulus to indicate that it occurred, or they may be asked to respond to a question about the stimulus, such as "Was it red or blue?" The design of this study enables researchers to learn how long it takes to perform the task (reaction time, or response time), how accurately the participant performs the task (accuracy, or error rate), or both.

In one version of this experiment, participants are instructed that although the cue, such as an arrow, will indicate the most likely location of the upcoming stimulus,

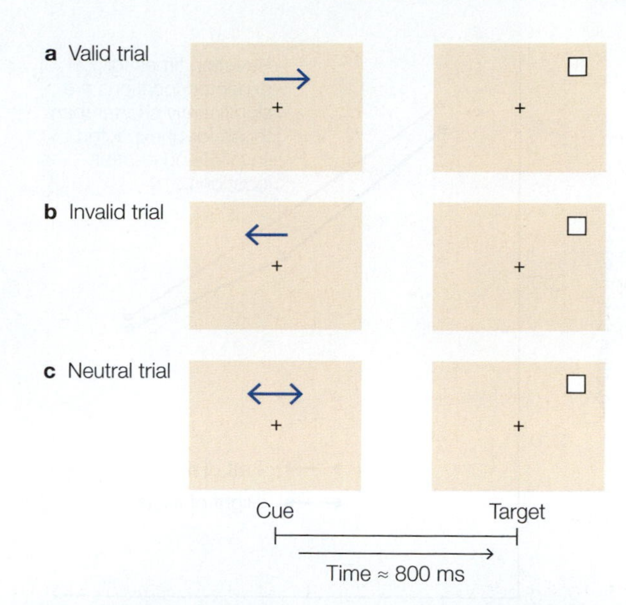

FIGURE 7.15 The spatial cuing paradigm popularized by Michael Posner and colleagues.
A participant sits in front of a computer screen, fixates on the central cross, and is told never to deviate eye fixation from the cross. An arrow cue indicates which visual hemifield the participant should covertly attend to. The cue is then followed by a target (the white box) in either the correctly cued **(a)** or the incorrectly cued **(b)** location. On other trials **(c)**, the cue (e.g., double-headed arrow) tells the participant that it is equally likely that the target will appear in the right or left location.

they are to respond to the target wherever it appears. The cue, therefore, predicts the location of the target on most trials (a trial is one presentation of the cue and subsequent target, along with the required response). This form of cuing is known as **endogenous cuing**, where the orienting of attention to the cue is voluntary and driven by the participant's goals (here, compliance with the instructions) and the meaning of the cue. In contrast, an *exogenous* cue automatically captures attention because of its physical features (e.g., a flash of light; see "Reflexive Visuospatial Attention" in Section 7.4 for this mechanism).

When a cue correctly predicts the location of the subsequent target, it is a *valid trial* (Figure 7.15a). If the relation between cue and target is strong—that is, the cue usually (say, 90% of the time) predicts the target location—then participants learn to use the cue to predict the next target's location. Sometimes, though, because the target may be presented at a location not indicated by the cue, the participant is misled in an *invalid trial* (Figure 7.15b). Finally, the researcher may include some cues that give no information about the most likely location of the impending target—a *neutral trial* (Figure 7.15c).

In cuing studies of voluntary attention, the time between presentation of the cue and the subsequent target is very brief: a few hundred milliseconds, or at most a second or two. When participants are not permitted to move their eyes to the cued location in space but instead

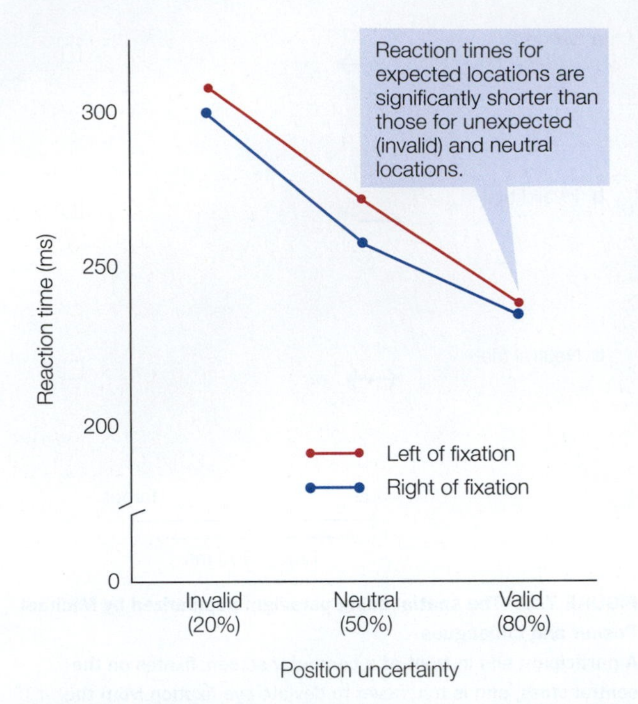

FIGURE 7.16 Quantification of spatial attention using behavioral measures.
Results of the study by Posner and colleagues illustrated in Figure 7.15, as shown by reaction times to unexpected (invalid), neutral, and expected (valid) location targets for the right and left visual hemifields.

must keep them fixed on a central fixation point (covert attention), and the cue correctly predicts the target's location, participants respond faster than when neutral cues are given (**Figure 7.16**). This faster response demonstrates the *benefits* of attention. In contrast, reaction times are longer (i.e., responses are slower) when the stimulus appears at an unexpected location, revealing the *costs* of attention. If participants are asked to discriminate a particular feature of the target, then the benefits and costs of attention can be expressed in terms of accuracy instead of, or in addition to, measures of reaction time.

These benefits and costs have been attributed to the influence of covert attention on the efficiency of information processing. According to most theories, a highly predictive cue induces participants to direct their covert attention internally, shining a sort of mental "spotlight" of attention onto the cued visual field location. The spotlight is a metaphor to describe how the brain may attend *to a spatial location.* Because participants are typically required to keep their eyes on a fixed spot different from the one to be attended, internal or covert mechanisms of attention must be at work.

Posner and his colleagues (1980) have suggested that this attentional spotlight affects reaction times by influencing sensory and perceptual processing; that is, stimuli that appear in an attended location are processed faster during perceptual processing than are stimuli that appear in an unattended location. This enhancement of attended stimuli, a type of early selection, is consistent with the proposal that *changes in perceptual processing* can happen when the participant is covertly attending a stimulus location.

Now, you might be thinking, "Wait a minute—responding more quickly to a target appearing at an attended location does not imply that the target was more efficiently processed in the *sensory* pathways." Indeed, measures of motor reaction time—or behavioral measures more generally—provide only indirect assessments of specific stages of neural processing. Differences in response time could solely reflect events going on after sensory processing was complete—for example, in the motor system. So, how can we be sure that the perceptual system is actually being affected by attention if our measure is the speed or accuracy of motor responses?

Ideally, this question would be resolved by direct measurement of different discrete stages of perceptual and post-perceptual processing, rather than by attempts to infer them from the behavioral responses. In order to determine whether changes in attention truly affect perceptual processing stages in the brain, researchers combined noninvasive recording methods with the experimental methods developed by cognitive psychologists, such as cuing paradigms. This combination of methods yielded the first definitive physiological evidence favoring early selection in humans, which came from studies using event-related potential (ERP) recordings to measure sensory processes during attention.

For example, neural signals elicited by attended sounds were strongly amplified in the auditory cortex starting at 50 ms after sound onset (Hillyard et al., 1973). In the visual modality, attended input signals were similarly enhanced (and unattended inputs suppressed) in extrastriate visual cortex starting at about 80 ms (Van Voorhis and Hillyard, 1977). The early timing of these effects of attention indicated that attentional selection occurs at early levels of sensory processing before the stimulus properties can be fully analyzed. In the next section we will look closely at the effects of attention on visual processing.

TAKE-HOME MESSAGES

- Attention involves both top-down (voluntary), goal-directed processes and bottom-up (reflexive), stimulus-driven mechanisms, and it can be either overt or covert.
- According to early-selection models, a stimulus need not be completely perceptually analyzed before it can be selected for further processing or rejected as irrelevant. Broadbent proposed such a model of attention.
- Late-selection models hypothesize that attended and ignored inputs are processed equivalently by the perceptual system, and that selection can occur only upon reaching a stage of semantic (meaning) encoding and analysis.

- Our perceptual system contains limited-capacity stages at which it can process only a certain amount of information at any given time, resulting in processing bottlenecks. Attention limits the information to only the most relevant, thereby preventing overload.
- Spatial attention is often thought of metaphorically as a "spotlight" of attention that can move around as the person consciously desires or can be reflexively attracted by salient sensory events.

7.4 Neural Mechanisms of Attention and Perceptual Selection

Although most of the experiments discussed in this chapter focus on visual attention, this should not be taken to suggest that attention is only a visual phenomenon. Selective attention operates in all sensory modalities. Nevertheless, in this chapter we focus on the visual system as the model system.

In this section we will explore how attention influences the sensory processing of incoming signals during both goal-directed and stimulus-drawn attention. We will discuss when (time course) and where (functional anatomy) attention influences incoming signal processing, using evidence from human and animal studies and describing both cortical and subcortical mechanisms. Finally, we will consider the neural mechanisms underlying attentional selection of simple stimulus features such as color and location, or higher-order features such as objects, when we are searching for something or someone in a complex scene, like a friend in a busy airport terminal.

Voluntary Visuospatial Attention

Visuospatial attention involves selecting a stimulus on the basis of its spatial location. It can be voluntary, such as when you attend to this page, or it can be reflexive, such as when motion at the door of the classroom attracts your attention and you look up. Effects of visuospatial attention can be seen in both the cortex and the subcortex.

CORTICAL ATTENTION EFFECTS Neural mechanisms of visuospatial attention have been investigated using cuing methods combined with ERP recordings. In a typical experiment, participants are given instructions to covertly attend to stimuli presented at one location (e.g., the right field) and to ignore stimuli presented at another location (e.g., the left field) while ERP recordings are made (**Figure 7.17a**). Recall that ERPs are the brain signals evoked by a stimulus, neural event, or

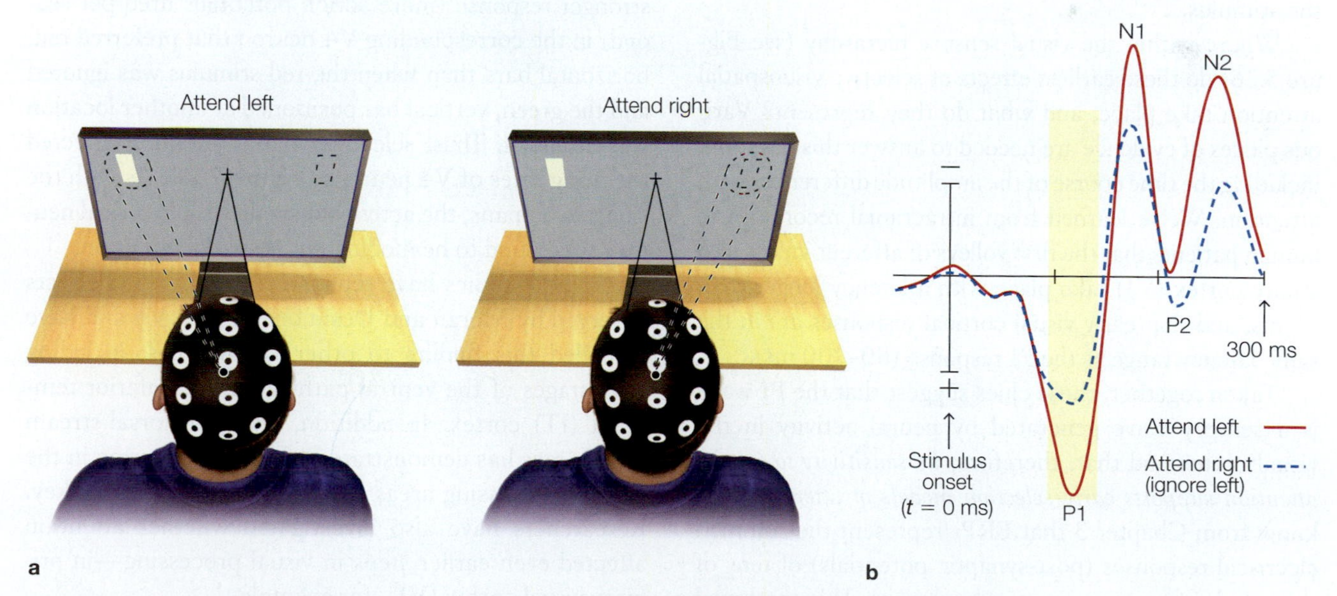

FIGURE 7.17 Stimulus display used to reveal physiological effects of sustained, selective spatial attention.
(a) The participant fixates the eyes on the central crosshairs while stimuli (here, the white rectangle) are flashed to the left (shown in figure) and right fields. At left, the participant is instructed to covertly attend the left stimuli and ignore those on the right. At right, the participant is instructed to attend the stimuli on the right and ignore those on the left. His responses to the stimuli are compared when they are attended and ignored. **(b)** Sensory ERPs recorded from a single right occipital scalp electrode in response to the left-field stimulus. Note that positive voltages are plotted downward. Attended stimuli (red trace) elicit ERPs with greater amplitude than do unattended stimuli (dashed, blue trace). The yellow-shaded area on the ERP shows the difference in amplitude between attended and unattended events in the P1 latency range.

motor response that can be extracted using signal averaging from the ongoing EEG.

A typical sensory-evoked ERP recording from a stimulus in one visual field shows a series of positive and negative voltage deflections in the first couple hundred milliseconds after the onset of the stimulus, whether the stimulus is attended or ignored. These brain responses are evoked by the physical features of the stimulus and represent cortical stimulus processing. The *first* big ERP wave has a *positive* polarity, begins following a latency period of 60 to 70 ms after stimulus onset, and peaks at about 100 ms over the occipital cortex contralateral to the visual hemifield of the stimulus. It is often referred to as the *P1* component (*P* for positive polarity, and *1* because it is the first big wave; **Figure 7.17b**). It is followed by a negative wave that peaks at about 180 ms (N1), and then by a series of positive and negative waves (P2, N2, etc.).

Early studies revealed that attention modulates the amplitudes of these sensory-evoked ERPs, beginning with the P1 wave (Van Voorhis & Hillyard, 1977). When a visual stimulus appears at a location to which a participant is attending, the P1 wave is larger in amplitude (Figure 7.17b, solid red line) than when the same stimulus appears at the same location but attention is focused elsewhere (Figure 7.17b, dashed blue line). The same is true for the attention effects observed in studies of auditory and tactile selective attention, where the auditory and tactile sensory ERPs are larger when participants attend the stimulus.

Where within the visual sensory hierarchy (see Figure 5.26) do these earliest effects of selective visuospatial attention take place, and what do they represent? Various pieces of evidence are needed to answer this question, including the time course of the amplitude differences with attention. We've learned from intracranial recordings in human patients that the first volleys of afferent inputs into striate cortex (V1) take place with a latency longer than 35 ms, and that early visual cortical responses are in the same latency range as the P1 response (60–100 ms).

Taken together, these clues suggest that the P1 wave is a sensory wave generated by neural activity in the visual cortex and that, therefore, *its sensitivity to spatial attention supports early-selection models of attention.* We know from Chapter 3 that ERPs represent the summed electrical responses (post-synaptic potentials) of tens of thousands of neurons, not single neurons. This combined response produces a large enough signal to propagate through the skull to be recorded on the human scalp. But can the effect of attention be detected in the response of single visual neurons in the cortex?

Jeff Moran and Robert Desimone (1985) revealed the answer to this question. They investigated how selective visuospatial attention affected the firing rates of individual neurons in the visual cortex of monkeys. The researchers trained the monkeys to fixate on a central spot on a monitor, to covertly attend to the stimulus at one location in the visual field, and to perform a task related to it while ignoring the other stimulus. Using single-neuron recordings, they first characterized the responses of single neurons in extrastriate visual area V4 to figure out which regions of the visual field were sending them information (i.e., what their receptive field was; see Chapter 5) and which specific stimulus features the neurons responded to most vigorously.

The team found, for example, that neurons in V4 fired robustly in response to one stimulus with a particular color and orientation (e.g., a red, horizontal bar) more than another (e.g., a green, vertical bar). Next, they simultaneously presented the preferred (red, horizontal) and non-preferred (green, vertical) stimuli near each other in space, so that both stimuli were within the neuron's receptive field.

Responses of single neurons were recorded and compared under two conditions: when the monkey *attended* the preferred (red, horizontal bar) stimulus at a specific location, and when it instead attended the non-preferred (green, vertical bar) stimulus that was located a short distance away. Because the two stimuli (attended and ignored) were positioned in different locations, the task can be characterized as a spatial attention task. How did attention affect the firing rate of the neurons?

When the red stimulus was attended, it elicited a stronger response (more action potentials fired per second) in the corresponding V4 neuron that preferred red, horizontal bars than when the red stimulus was ignored and the green, vertical bar positioned at another location was attended. Thus, selective spatial attention affected the firing rates of V4 neurons (**Figure 7.18**). As with the ERPs in humans, the activity of single visual cortical neurons was found to be modulated by spatial attention.

Several studies have replicated the attention effects observed by Moran and Desimone in area V4 and have extended this finding to other visual areas, including later stages of the ventral pathway in the inferior temporal (IT) cortex. In addition, work in dorsal-stream visual areas has demonstrated effects of attention in the motion-processing areas MT and MST of the monkey. Researchers have also investigated whether attention affected even earlier steps in visual processing—in primary visual cortex (V1), for example.

Carrie McAdams and Clay Reid at Harvard Medical School (2005) carried out experiments to determine which level of processing within V1 was influenced by attention. Recall from Chapters 5 and 6 that many stages of neural processing take place within a visual area, and that in V1, different neurons display characteristic receptive-field proper ties; some are called *simple cells*, others

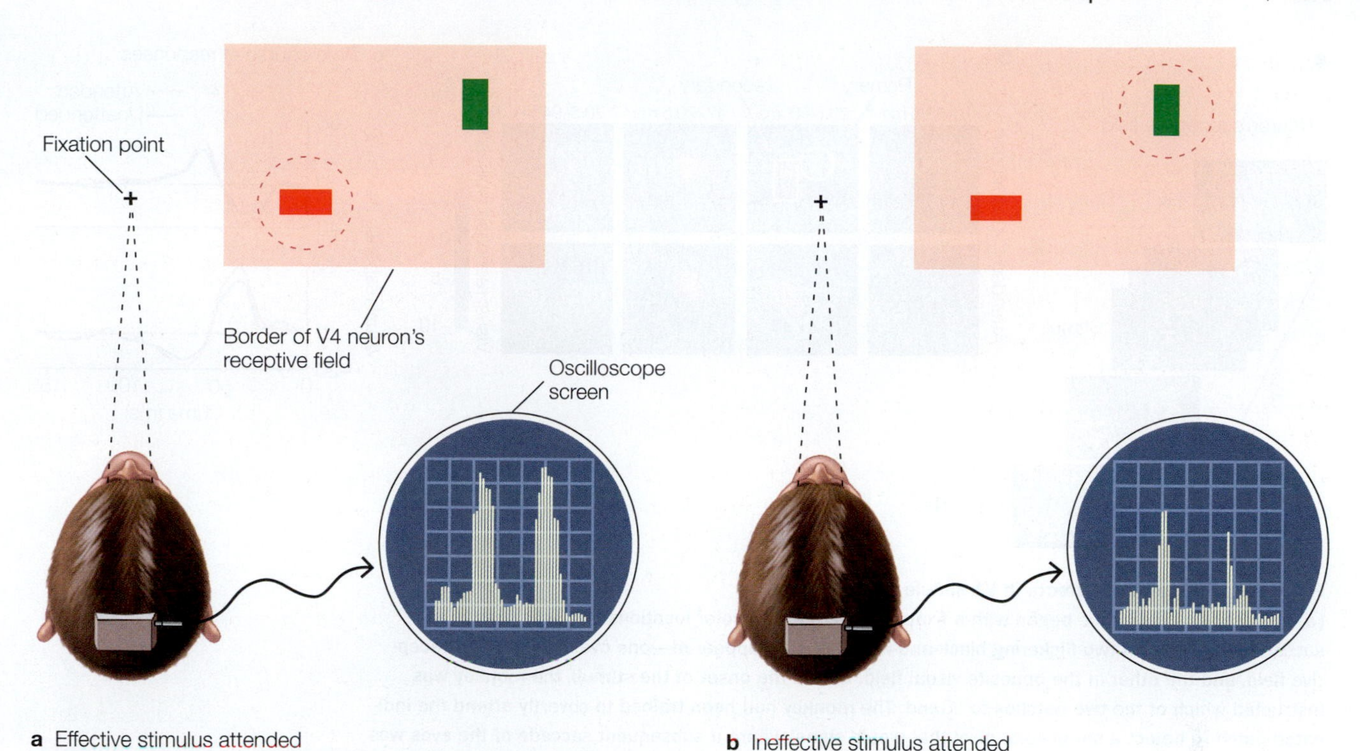

FIGURE 7.18 Spatial attention modulates activity of V4 neurons.
The areas circled by dashed lines indicate the attended locations for each trial. For this neuron a red bar is an effective sensory stimulus, and a green bar is an ineffective sensory stimulus. The neuronal firing rates are shown to the right of each monkey head. The first burst of activity in each image is to the cue; the second is to the target array. **(a)** When the animal attended the red bar, the V4 neuron gave a strong response. **(b)** When the animal attended the green bar, a weak response was generated.

complex cells, and so on. Simple cells exhibit orientation tuning and respond to contrast borders (like those found along the edge of an object). Simple cells are also situated and active relatively early in the hierarchy of neuronal processing in V1—so, if attention were to affect them, this would be further evidence of how early in processing, and by what mechanism, spatial attention acts within V1.

McAdams and Reid trained monkeys to fixate on a central point and covertly attend a black-and-white flickering noise pattern in order to detect a small, colored pixel that could appear anywhere within the pattern (**Figure 7.19a**). The monkeys were to signal when they detected the color by making a rapid eye movement (a saccade) from fixation to the location on the screen that contained that color. The attended location would be positioned either over the receptive field of the V1 neuron being recorded or in the opposite visual field. Thus, the researchers could evaluate responses of the neuron when that region of space was attended and when it was ignored (in different blocks).

They also could use the flickering noise pattern to create a spatiotemporal receptive-field map (**Figure 7.19b**) showing primary or secondary subregions of the receptive field that were either excited or inhibited by light. In this way, the researchers could determine whether the neuron had the properties of simple cells and whether attention affected the firing pattern and receptive-field organization. They found that *spatial attention enhanced the responses of the simple cells* (**Figure 7.19c**) but did not affect the spatial or temporal organization of their receptive fields, which remained unchanged over the trials.

So, from monkey cellular recordings it is clear that attention affects processing at multiple stages in the cortical visual pathways from V1 to IT cortex. Neuroimaging studies of spatial attention in humans show results consistent with the findings in monkeys, and they have the advantage of being able to measure the influence of attention on cortical visual processing in multiple different visual areas at one time. Work in humans also offers the opportunity to compare the information from functional imaging to the ERP findings in humans that were described earlier.

In an early study, Hans-Jochen Heinze and his colleagues (1994) directly related ERP findings to functional brain neuroanatomy by combining positron emission tomography (PET) imaging with ERP recordings. They demonstrated that visuospatial attention modulates the blood flow in visual cortex and that these hemodynamic changes could be related to the ERP effects observed on the P1 wave of the ERP. These findings suggested that the P1 and the attention effects on P1 (see Figure 7.17) took place in early extrastriate cortex. Subsequent studies using functional MRI have permitted a more fine-grained analysis of the effects of spatial attention in humans.

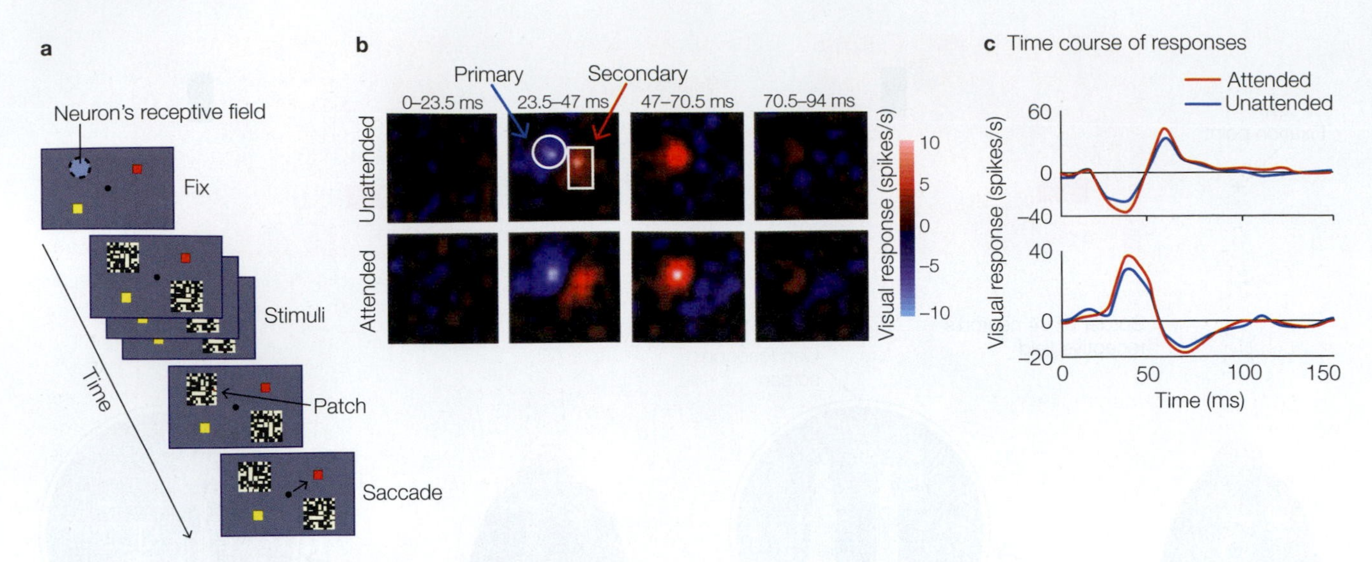

FIGURE 7.19 Attention effects in V1 simple cells.
(a) The stimulus sequence began with a fixation point and two color locations that would serve as saccade targets. Then two flickering black-and-white patches appeared—one over the neuron's receptive field, and the other in the opposite visual field. Before the onset of the stimuli, the monkey was instructed which of the two patches to attend. The monkey had been trained to covertly attend the indicated patch to detect a small color pixel that would signal where a subsequent saccade of the eyes was to be made (to the matching color) for a reward. **(b)** The spatiotemporal receptive field of the neuron when unattended (opposite visual field patch attended; top row) and when attended (bottom row). Each of the eight panels corresponds to the same spatial location as that of the black-and-white stimulus over the neuron's receptive field (RF). Primary and secondary subregions of the RF are indicated. The excitatory (red) and inhibitory (blue) regions of the receptive field are evident (the brighter the color, the more responsive the RF); they are largest from 23.5 to 70.5 ms after stimulus onset (middle two panels). Note that the amplitudes of the responses were larger when attended than when unattended. This difference is summarized as plots in **(c)**.

For example, Joseph Hopfinger and his colleagues (2000) used a modified version of a spatial cuing task combined with event-related fMRI. On each trial, an arrow cue was presented at the center of the display and indicated the side to which participants should direct their attention. Eight seconds later, the bilateral target display (flickering black-and-white checkerboards) appeared for 500 ms. The participants' task was to press a button if some of the checks were gray rather than white, but only if the gray target appeared on the cued side.

The 8-second gap between the arrow and the target display allowed the slow hemodynamic responses linked to the attention-directing cues to be analyzed separately from the hemodynamic responses linked to the detection of and response to the target displays. The results, shown in **Figure 7.20** in coronal sections through the visual cortex of a single participant in the Hopfinger study, indicate that attention to one visual hemifield activated multiple regions of visual cortex in the contralateral hemisphere.

Roger Tootell, Anders Dale, and their colleagues at Massachusetts General Hospital (Tootell et al., 1998) used fMRI to create retinotopic maps to investigate how all of the attention-related activations in visual cortex related to the multiple visual cortical areas in humans. To differentiate and identify one activated visual area from another on the scans, they combined high-resolution mapping of the borders of early visual cortical areas (**Figure 7.21a**) with a spatial attention task. Participants were required to selectively attend to stimuli located in one visual field quadrant while ignoring those in the other quadrants; different quadrants were attended to in different conditions while the participants' brains underwent fMRI scanning.

The researchers were thus able to map the sensory responses to target stimuli (**Figure 7.21b**), and the attention-related modulations of these sensory responses onto flattened computer maps of the visual cortex, thereby directly relating the attention effects to the multiple visual cortical areas (**Figure 7.21c and d**). They found that spatial attention increased activity in multiple visual areas in the cortical regions coding the attended target locations, but not in regions that were ignored. This work provides a high-resolution view of the functional anatomy of multiple areas of visual cortex during sustained spatial attention in humans.

We now understand that visuospatial attention can influence stimulus processing at many stages of cortical visual processing from V1 to IT cortex. Are the effects of attention the same at these different stages of processing, or does attention act at different stages of the visual hierarchy to accomplish different processing goals?

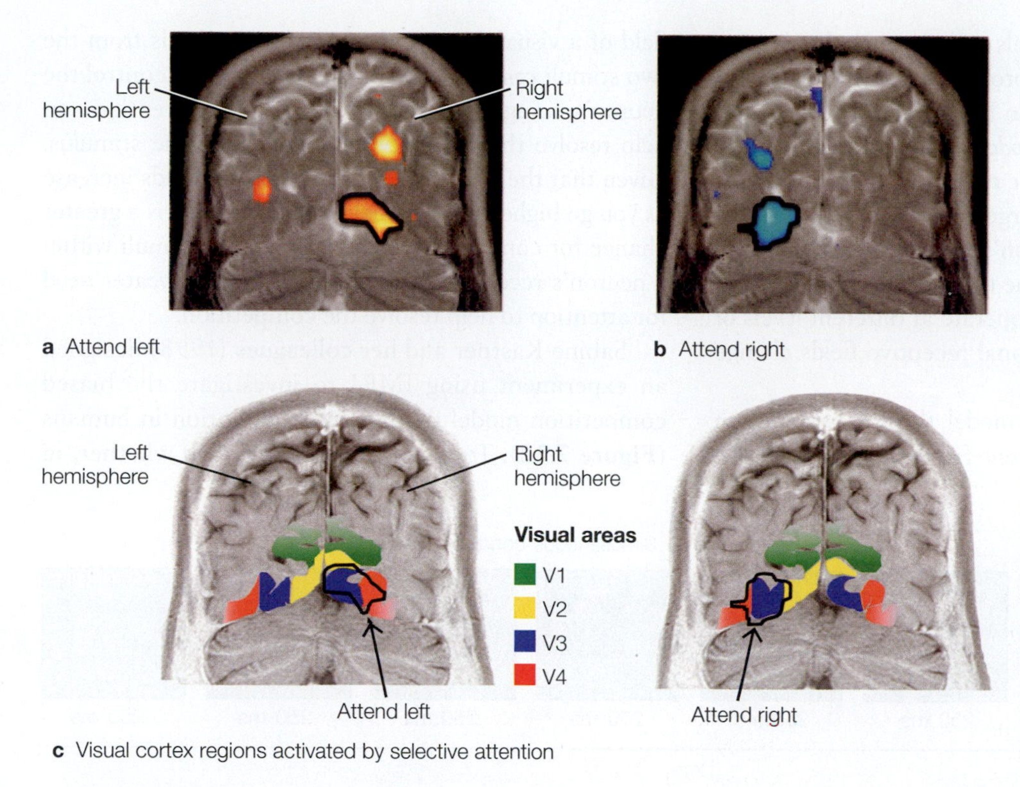

FIGURE 7.20 Selective attention activates specific regions of the visual cortex. Areas of activation in a single participant were overlaid onto a coronal section through the visual cortex obtained by structural MRI. The statistical contrasts reveal **(a)** where attention to the left hemifield produced more activity than attention to the right (reddish to yellow colors) and **(b)** the reverse, where attention to the right hemifield elicited more activity than did attention to the left (bluish colors). As demonstrated in prior studies, the effects of spatial attention were activations in the visual cortex contralateral to the attended hemifield. **(c)** The regions activated by attention (shown in black outline) were found to cross multiple early visual areas (shown as colored regions; refer to key).

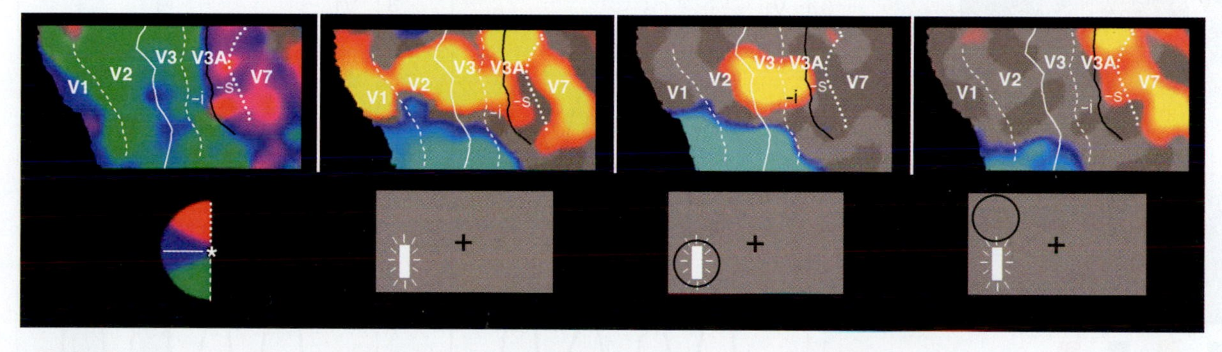

FIGURE 7.21 Spatial attention produces modulation of activity in multiple extrastriate visual areas. Flattened right dorsal (above the calcarine fissure) visual cortex showing the retinotopic mapping of the lower-left visual field quadrant in one participant (top). The lines identifying the borders between visual areas correspond to the vertical (dashed) or horizontal (solid) meridians of the polar angle. Area V3A has representations in two quadrants of the dorsal visual cortex, upper (labeled "s" for superior) and lower (labeled "i" for inferior). The black line in V3A reflects the location of the horizontal meridian between the two. **(a)** A polar-angle retinotopic map (top) was made to define the visual areas. The colors on the map correspond to those in the polar-angle plot (bottom) of the left visual hemifield. In the remaining retinotopic maps (b–d), red-to-yellow colors show relative increases in activity, while blue-to-white colors indicate relative decreases in activity. Regions in the parafoveal/foveal portions of all the cortical maps, away from the locations coding the sensory stimuli, show reductions in activity. **(b)** Pure sensory responses to the target, independent of attention. In this control condition, the participants simply viewed the flashing bar stimuli and performed no attention task. All visual areas from V1 through V7 were activated in a spatially specific manner by the sensory stimulus. **(c)** Attending to the lower-left target activated visual areas V2, V3, and V3A (red-to-yellow). The attention difference was calculated by comparing the response to attending a lower-left target versus attending a target in another quadrant. The circle indicates where attention was directed. **(d)** Ignoring lower-left targets (while attending to upper-left targets) produced this map showing an absence of attention-related activations. Note that there are attention-related increases in activity in the portion of V3A (and adjacent V7) that correspond to the upper visual field. Minor increases in V1 activity with attention, although observed in the study, are not visible in the maps in (c) and (d).

Let's consider some models and evidence that help to answer this question. One prominent model, proposed by Robert Desimone and John Duncan (1995), is known as the *biased competition model* for selective attention. This model may help answer two questions. First, why are the effects of attention larger when multiple competing stimuli fall within a neuron's receptive field, as in the work of Moran and Desimone that we described earlier? Second, how does attention operate at different levels of the visual hierarchy as neuronal receptive fields change their properties?

In the biased competition model, the idea is that when different stimuli in a visual scene fall within the receptive field of a visual neuron, the bottom-up signals from the two stimuli *compete* like two snarling dogs to control the neuron's firing. The model suggests that attention can help resolve this competition by favoring one stimulus. Given that the sizes of neuronal receptive fields increase as you go higher in the visual hierarchy, there is a greater chance for competition between different stimuli within a neuron's receptive field and, therefore, a greater need for attention to help resolve the competition.

Sabine Kastner and her colleagues (1998) designed an experiment using fMRI to investigate the biased competition model during spatial attention in humans (**Figure 7.22**). To do this, they first asked whether, in

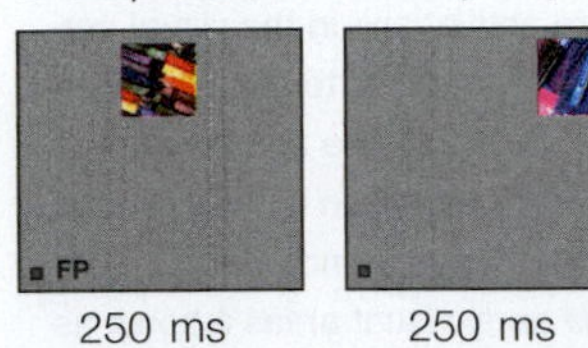
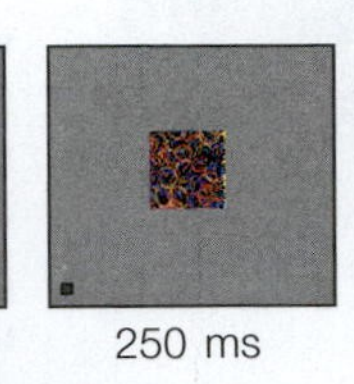
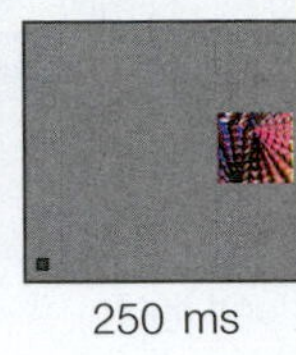
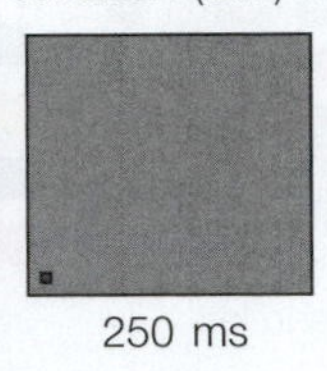
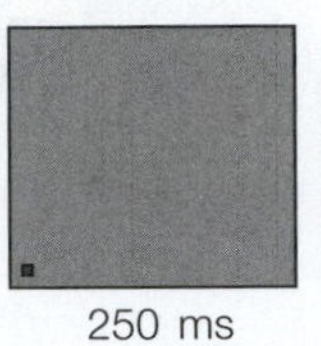
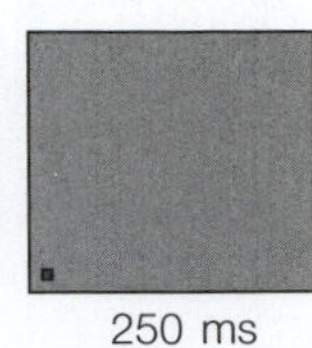

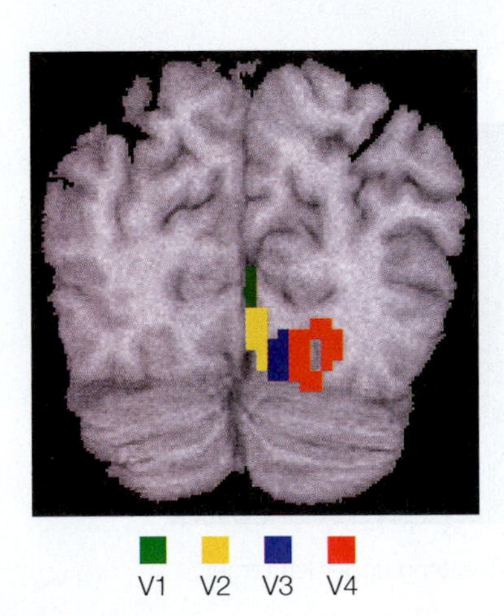
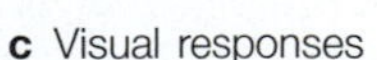

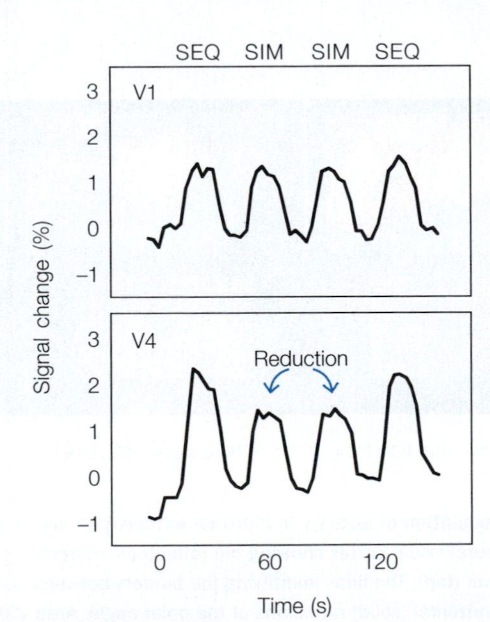
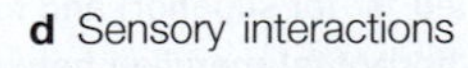

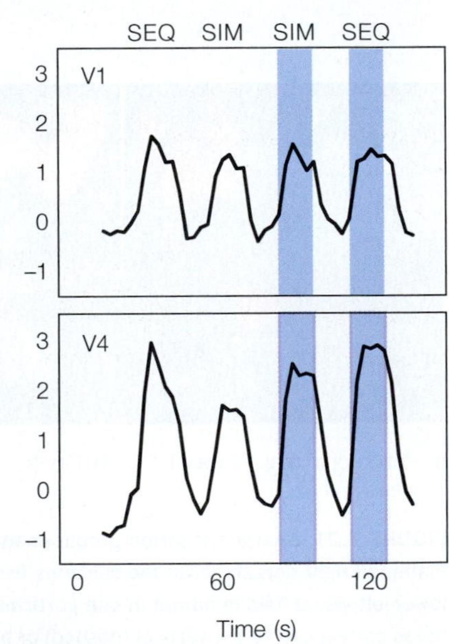

FIGURE 7.22 Investigating the biased competition model of attention.
Competing stimuli were presented either sequentially **(a)** or simultaneously **(b)**, in two different types of experiments each. In the first type, stimuli were presented in the absence of directed attention; in the second, they were presented during directed attention, where covert attention was directed to the stimulus closest to the point of fixation (FP), and the other stimuli were merely distractors. **(c)** Coronal MRI section in one participant (left hemisphere is on the right), where the pure sensory responses in multiple visual areas are mapped. **(d)** Results from experiments lacking directed attention. The percentage of signal changed over time in areas V1 and V4 as a function of whether the stimuli were presented sequentially (SEQ) or simultaneously (SIM). The sequentially presented stimuli evoked activations that were stronger, especially in V4, than the activations evoked by simultaneously presented stimuli. **(e)** Results from experiments with directed attention. The experiments included an unattended condition (not shaded) and one where attention was directed to the target stimulus (shaded blue). In V4 especially, the amplitudes during the SEQ and SIM conditions were more similar when attention was directed to the target stimulus than when it was not.

a

b

FIGURE 7.23 Competition varies between objects, depending on their scale.
The same stimulus can occupy a larger or smaller region of visual space, depending on its distance from the observer. **(a)** Viewed up close (i.e., at large scale), a single flower may occupy all of the receptive field of a V4 neuron (yellow circle), whereas multiple flowers fit within the larger receptive field of high-order inferior temporal (IT) neurons (blue circle). **(b)** Viewed from a greater distance (at small scale), multiple flowers are present within the smaller V4 receptive field and the larger IT receptive field.

the *absence* of focused spatial attention, nearby stimuli could interfere with one another. The answer was yes. They found that when they presented two nearby stimuli simultaneously, the stimuli interfered with each other and the neural response evoked by each stimulus was reduced compared to when one stimulus was presented alone in the sequential condition (Figure 7.22d). If attention was introduced and directed to one stimulus in the display, however, then simultaneous presentation of the competing stimulus no longer interfered (Figure 7.22e). This effect tended to be larger in area V4, where attention appears to have more of an effect than in V1. The attention focused on one stimulus attenuated the influence of the competing stimulus. To return to our analogy, one of the snarling dogs (the competing stimulus) was muzzled.

For a given stimulus, spatial attention appears to operate differently at early (V1) versus later (e.g., V4) stages of the visual cortex. Why? Perhaps because the neuronal receptive fields differ in size from one visual cortical area to the next. Thus, although smaller stimuli might fall within a receptive field of a single V1 neuron, larger stimuli would not; but these larger stimuli would fall within the larger receptive field of a V4 neuron. In addition, exactly the same stimulus can occupy different spatial scales, depending on its distance from the observer. For example, when you view the flowers in **Figure 7.23a** from a greater distance (**Figure 7.23b**), they occupy less of your visual field (compare what you see in the yellow circles, representing a V4 neuron's receptive field). All of the flowers could, though, fall into the receptive field of a single neuron at a later stage of the visual hierarchy (compare what is within the blue circles, representing the larger receptive field of an IT neuron).

In line with the biased competition model, attention could act to select one flower versus another early in the visual cortical hierarchy (i.e., within V4 when the spatial scale of the flowers was small (Figure 7.23b), but not when the spatial scale was large and there was only a single flower in the receptive field (Figure 7.23a); attention could act only at higher levels of the cortical hierarchy in this case (i.e., above V4). This observation suggests that attention should operate at different stages of vision, depending on the spatial scale of the attended and ignored stimuli. Does it? How would you design a study to answer this question?

Max Hopf, Steven Luck, and colleagues (2006) combined recordings of ERPs, magnetoencephalography (MEG), and fMRI. The simple stimuli they used are shown in **Figure 7.24**. In each trial, stimulus arrays consisting of four groups of four squares each, appeared in each visual field quadrant (Figure 7.24a). To create a small-spatial-scale target, a single small square was shifted up or down (Figure 7.24b); for a large-scale pattern, one set of four small squares was shifted (Figure 7.24c). Participants were instructed to attend to the arrays of one color (red or green), as instructed beforehand, and to push one of two buttons, depending on whether the displaced squares shifted up or down, regardless of spatial scale. This task required, therefore, that the participants detect the shifted square and focus attention at the appropriate spatial scale to determine the finer detail of the direction of the shift.

The study revealed that attention acted at earlier levels of the visual system (within visual area V4) for the

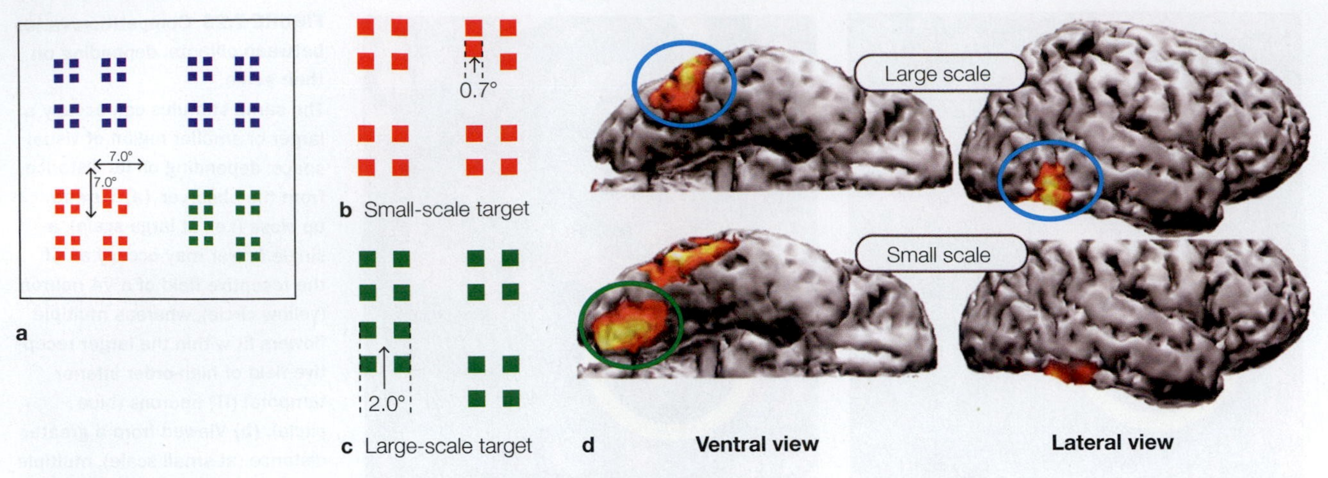

FIGURE 7.24 Study of effects of attention for different stimulus spatial scales.
(a) A sample stimulus array from the spatial-scale experiment. One 16-square array was positioned in each quadrant of the visual field. Two blue arrays were distractors. **(b)** A small-scale target was created by displacing one square up or down. **(c)** A large-scale target was created by displacing a set of four squares up or down. **(d)** MEG measures for the N2pc effect (an ERP reflecting focused attention) from 250 to 300 ms after the onset of the arrays, from a single volunteer. Large-scale trials (top) and small-scale trials (bottom) are shown on a ventral view (left images) and a left lateral view (right images) of the right hemisphere. For the small-scale trials, the activity in the brain is more posterior, reflecting neural responses from earlier stages of the visual system. Areas circled in blue are lateral occipital cortex; those in green are ventral extrastriate cortex.

smaller targets than it did for the larger targets (lateral occipital complex; Figure 7.24d). So, although attention does act at multiple levels of the visual hierarchy, it also optimizes its action to match the spatial scale of the visual task. One may extend this idea to hypothesize that attention to yet other aspects of task-relevant visual stimuli (location, color, motion, form, identity, etc.) would be supported by modulations of processing in visual areas tuned for those stimulus attributes; we will return to this idea later in the chapter, when we discuss feature and object attention.

SUBCORTICAL ATTENTION EFFECTS Could attentional filtering or selection occur even earlier along the visual processing pathways—in the thalamus or in the retina? Unlike the cochlea, the human retina contains no descending neuronal projections that could be used to modulate retinal activity by attention. But massive neuronal projections do extend from the visual cortex (layer VI neurons) back to the thalamus. These projections synapse on neurons in the *perigeniculate nucleus*, which is the portion of the **thalamic reticular nucleus (TRN)** that surrounds the lateral geniculate nucleus (LGN; **Figure 7.25**).

These neurons maintain complex interconnections with neurons in the thalamic relays and could, in principle, modulate information flow from the thalamus to the cortex. Such a process has been shown to take place in cats during intermodal (visual–auditory) attention (Yingling & Skinner, 1976). The TRN was also implicated in a model to select the visual field location for the current spotlight of attention in perception—an idea proposed by Nobel laureate Francis Crick (1992). Is there support for such a mechanism?

Studies on monkeys in which attention affected the metabolic activity of the LGN neurons provided initial hints that attention might influence LGN processing (Vanduffel et al., 2000). Subsequent studies by Sabine Kastner and her colleagues used high-resolution fMRI to assess whether attention had the same influence in the human LGN (reviewed in Kastner et al., 2006). Researchers presented participants with a bilateral array of flickering checkerboard stimuli (**Figure 7.26a**), which activated the LGN and multiple visual cortical areas (**Figure 7.26b**). Participants were cued to attend to either the left or the right half of the array.

The results showed that the amplitude of the activation was greater in the LGN and visual cortex that were contralateral to the attended array (**Figure 7.26c**, red lines in graphs) compared to the activity in response to the unattended array (black lines). So, *highly focused* visuospatial attention can modulate activity in the thalamus. Since fMRI studies do not provide timing information, however, it is hard to know what such effects indicate. Do they reflect attentional gating of the afferent LGN neuron's signals heading to V1? Or, instead, do they reflect reafferent feedback to the thalamus from the cortex that is not the incoming afferent volley of information?

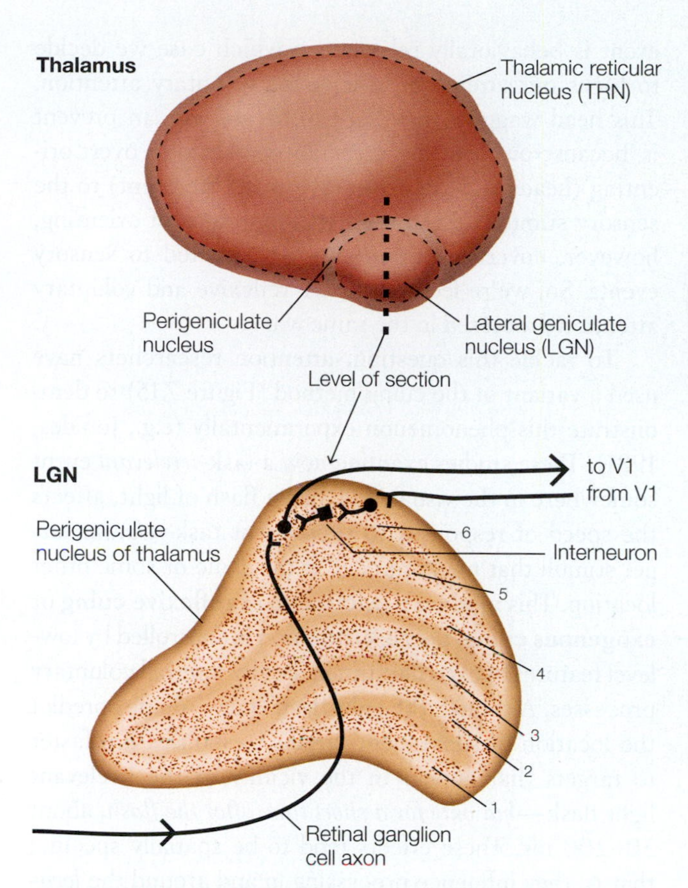

FIGURE 7.25 The thalamus, its perigeniculate nucleus, and projections to and from the thalamus and visual cortex.

Kerry McAlonan and colleagues at the National Eye Institute (2008) recorded from LGN relay neurons and the surrounding TRN neurons of monkeys that had been trained to attend covertly to a target at one location while ignoring other targets. When the monkeys' attention was directed to the location of the stimulus within the LGN neuron's receptive field, the firing rate of the neuron increased (**Figure 7.27a**). In addition, however, the firing rate decreased in the surrounding TRN neurons (which, recall, are not relay neurons, but instead are interneurons that receive input from the visual cortex; **Figure 7.27b**). Why is that? Well, we know from other work that the TRN neurons synapse onto the LGN neurons with *inhibitory* signals.

We can now explain the entire circuit. Attention involves either activating or inhibiting signal transmission from the LGN to visual cortex via the TRN circuitry. Either a descending neural signal from the cortex or a separate signal from subcortical inputs travels to the TRN neurons. These inputs to the TRN can excite the TRN neurons, thereby inhibiting information transmission from LGN to visual cortex; alternatively, the inputs can suppress the TRN neurons, thus increasing transmission from LGN to visual cortex. The latter mechanism is consistent with the increased neuronal responses observed for the neurons in LGN and V1 when coding the location of an attended stimulus.

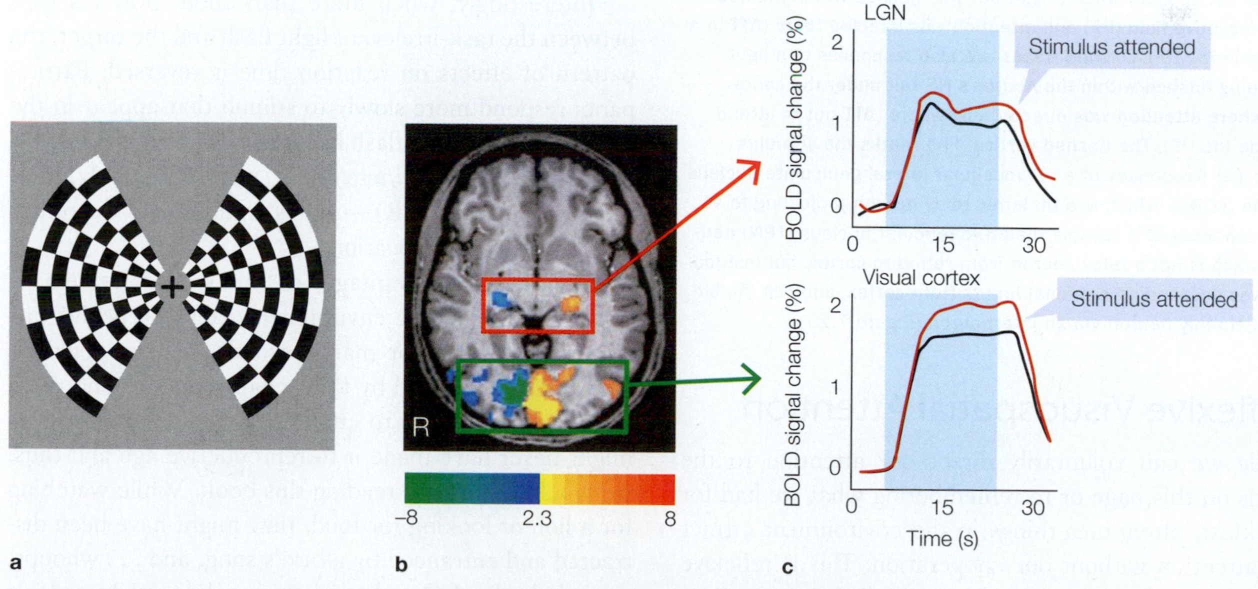

FIGURE 7.26 Functional MRI study of spatial attention effects in the lateral geniculate nucleus. **Before stimulus onset, an arrow cue at fixation instructed the participants which hemifield to attend. Next, a checkerboard stimulus (a) was presented bilaterally for 18 seconds (shown as blue-shaded area in c). The task was to detect randomly occurring luminance changes in the flickering checks in the cued hemifield. (b) Functional MRI activations (increased BOLD responses) were observed in the LGN (red box) and in multiple visual cortical areas (green box). (c) Increased activations were seen when the stimulus in the hemifield contralateral to the brain region being measured was attended. The effect was observed both in the LGN (top) and in multiple visual cortical areas (bottom).**

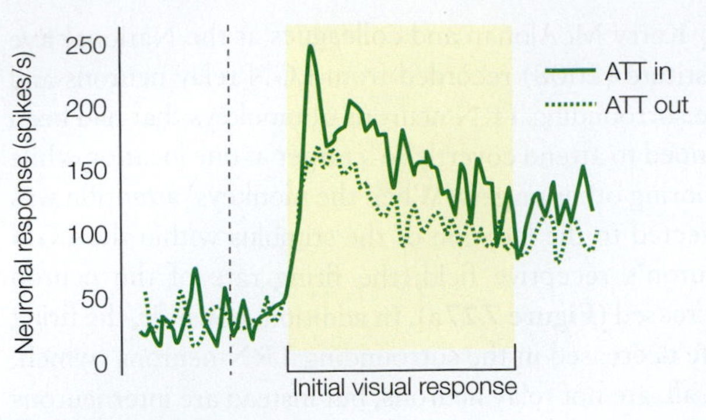

a LGNp responses

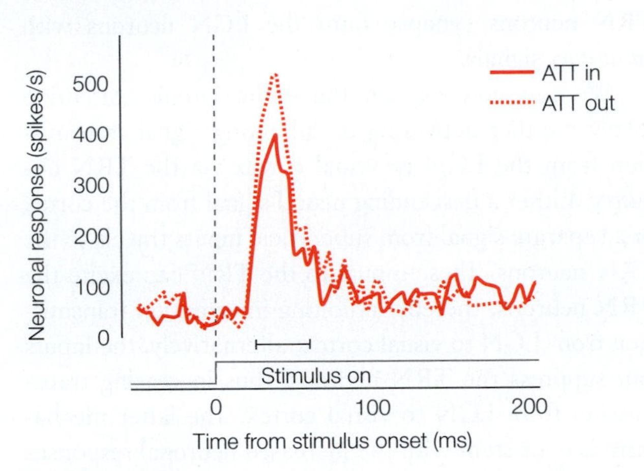

b TRN responses

FIGURE 7.27 Effects of spatial attention on neuronal firing rates in the thalamus.

The solid lines show the amplitude of the neuronal response (spikes per second) when a light bar was flashed within the neuron's receptive field (RF) and attention was directed there (ATT in = attend in the RF). Dashed traces are also responses to a light bar being flashed within the neuron's RF, but under the condition where attention was directed elsewhere (ATT out = attend outside the RF). The dashed vertical line marks the stimulus onset. **(a)** Responses of a parvocellular lateral geniculate nucleus neuron (LGNp), which is a thalamic relay neuron projecting to V1. **(b)** Responses of a sample thalamic reticular nucleus (TRN) neuron, which is not a relay neuron from retina to cortex, but instead receives descending neuronal inputs from cortex, and can inhibit the LGN relay neuron via an interneuron (Figure 7.25).

Reflexive Visuospatial Attention

While we can voluntarily direct our attention to the words on this page or to remembering what we had for breakfast, oftentimes things in the environment attract our attention without our cooperation. This is reflexive attention, and it is activated by stimuli that are salient (conspicuous) in some way. The more salient the stimulus, the more easily our attention is captured: Think of how we respond to rapid movement that we see out of the corner of the eye (eek! a rat!) or the shattering of glass in a restaurant. Heads turn toward the sounds and sights and then wag back a moment or two later, unless the event is behaviorally relevant, in which case we decide to focus our attention on it, using voluntary attention. This head wagging may happen before we can prevent it, because our reflexive attention may lead to overt orienting (heads and eyes turning toward the event) to the sensory stimulus. Even without overt signs of orienting, however, covert attention can be attracted to sensory events. So, we're led to ask, are reflexive and voluntary attention processed in the same way?

To tackle this question, attention researchers have used a variant of the cuing method (Figure 7.15) to demonstrate this phenomenon experimentally (e.g., Jonides, 1981). These studies examine how a task-*irrelevant* event somewhere in the visual field, like a flash of light, affects the speed of responses to subsequent task-*relevant* target stimuli that might appear at the same or some other location. This method is referred to as **reflexive cuing** or **exogenous cuing**, because attention is controlled by low-level features of external stimuli, not by internal voluntary processes. Although the light flash "cues" do not predict the location of subsequent targets, responses are faster to targets that appear in the vicinity of the irrelevant light flash—*but only for a short time after the flash*, about 50–200 ms. These effects tend to be spatially specific; that is, they influence processing in and around the *location* of the reflexive cue only. Therefore, they can also be described by the spotlight metaphor introduced earlier in this chapter. In this case, however, the spotlight is reflexively attracted to a location and is short-lived.

Interestingly, when more than about 300 ms pass between the task-irrelevant light flash and the target, the pattern of effects on reaction time is reversed: Participants respond more slowly to stimuli that appear in the vicinity of where the flash had been. This phenomenon is called the *inhibitory aftereffect* or, more commonly, **inhibition of return (IOR)**—that is, inhibition of the return of attention to that location.

Consider the advantages of this kind of system. If sensory events in the environment caused reflexive orienting that lasted for many seconds, people would be continually distracted by things happening around them and would be unable to attend to a goal. Our ancestors might never have made it to reproductive age and thus, we wouldn't be here reading this book. While watching for a lion or looking for food, they might have been distracted and entranced by a bird's song, and . . . whoops, missed the lion! Or whoops, no meal again! In today's world, imagine the consequences if a driver's attention became reflexively focused on a distraction off to the side of the road and then remained focused on that event for more than an instant.

Our automatic orienting system has built-in mechanisms to prevent reflexively directed attention from becoming stuck at a location for more than a couple hundred milliseconds. The reflexive capturing of attention subsides, and the likelihood that our attention will be drawn back to that location is reduced slightly. If the event is important and salient, however, we can rapidly invoke our voluntary mechanisms to sustain attention longer, thereby overriding the inhibition of return. Thus, the nervous system has evolved clever, complementary mechanisms of voluntary and reflexive attention so that we can function in a cluttered, rapidly changing sensory world.

Responses to endogenous and exogenous cues result in attention shifts that enhance the processing of attended sensory stimuli and decrease the processing of unattended stimuli. In the case of reflexive attention, the cuing effect is quick and short-lived, and processing of stimuli in the neighborhood of the cue is enhanced. With voluntary attention, however, the cuing effect is slower and more sustained. Do these differences in processing represent different neural mechanisms?

We have learned that voluntarily focusing attention at a location in response to visual cues will enhance the visual responses to stimuli occurring at that location. Do these same neural changes occur when our attention is reflexively attracted to a location in the visual field by a sensory event? Joseph Hopfinger and George Mangun (1998, 2001) answered yes to this question. They recorded ERPs in response to target stimuli in a reflexive cuing task like the one described earlier (**Figure 7.28a**). They found that the early occipital P1 wave is larger for targets that quickly follow a sensory cue at the same location, versus trials in which the sensory cue and target occur at different locations. As the time after cuing grows longer, however, this effect reverses and the P1 response diminishes—and may even be inhibited—just as in measurements of reaction time (**Figure 7.28b**).

These data indicate that both reflexive (stimulus-driven) and voluntary (goal-directed) shifts in spatial attention induce similar physiological modulations in early visual processing. Presumably, the neural networks implementing these attentional modulations of sensory analysis are different, reflecting the differing ways in which attentional control is triggered for the two forms of attention.

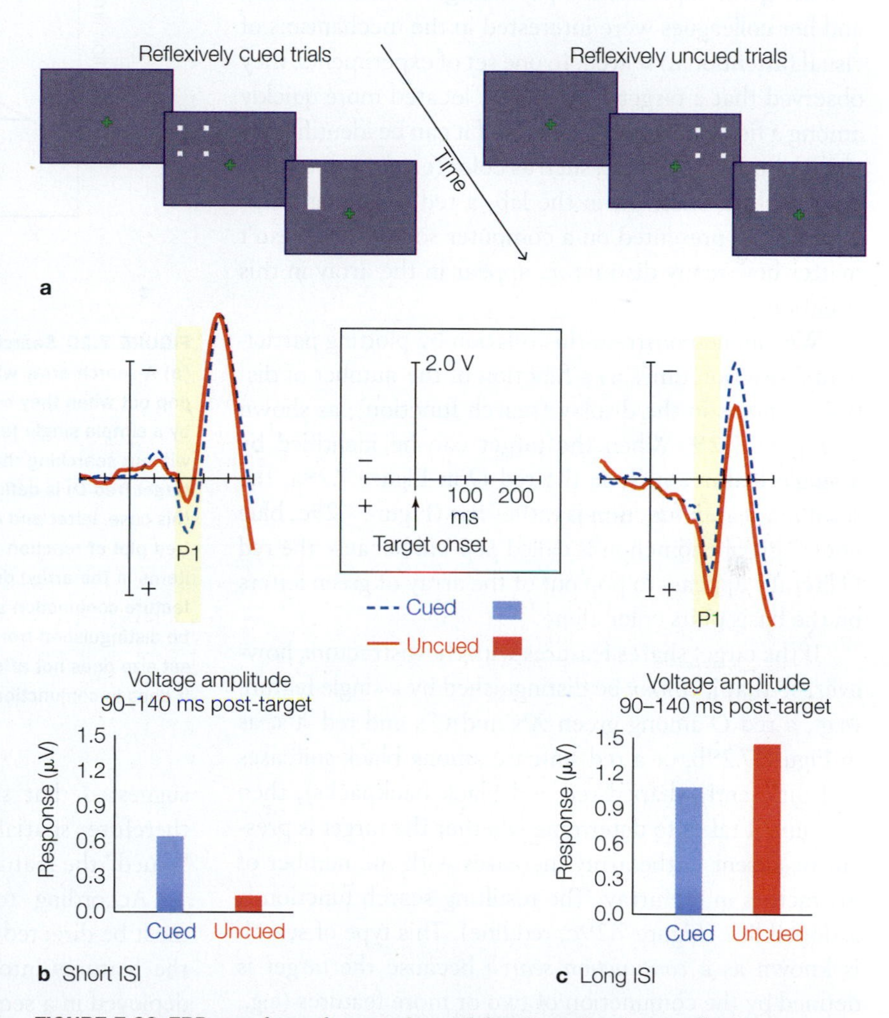

FIGURE 7.28 ERP waveforms from study participants performing a reflexive cuing task.
(a) When attention is reflexively attracted to a location by an irrelevant abrupt onset of a visual stimulus (four dots), reaction times to subsequent targets (vertical rectangle) presented to that same location are facilitated for short periods of time, as described in the text. (b) When ERPs are measured to these targets, the same cortical response (P1 wave; see yellow-shaded time period) that is affected by voluntary spatial attention is enhanced by reflexive attention for short cue-to-target interstimulus intervals (ISIs). The time course of this reflexive attention effect on ERP amplitudes is not the same as that for voluntary cuing, but it is similar to the pattern observed in reaction times during reflexive cuing. (c) The enhanced response is replaced within a few hundred milliseconds by a relative inhibition of the P1 response.

Visual Search

In everyday perception, voluntary attention (driven by our goals) and reflexive attention (driven by stimuli in the world) interact in a push–pull fashion, struggling to control the focus of our attention. For example, we frequently search about for a specific item in a cluttered scene. Perhaps we watch for a friend coming out of class or for our suitcase on the baggage claim carousel of a busy airport. If the suitcase is red and covered with flowered stickers, the search is quite easy. If the suitcase is a medium-sized black bag with rollers, however, the task can be quite challenging.

As you cast your gaze around for that friend or suitcase, you don't keep going back to places that you have just scanned. Instead, you are biased, moving your eyes to new objects in new locations. The last time you stood in baggage claim, you probably didn't wonder what role attentional processes play in this visual search process. How are voluntary and reflexive spatial attention mechanisms related to **visual search**?

The great experimental psychologist Anne Treisman and her colleagues were interested in the mechanisms of visual (attentional) search. In one set of experiments, they observed that a target item can be located more quickly among a field of distractor stimuli if it can be identified by a single stimulus feature, such as color (e.g., a red suitcase among black ones; or, in the lab, a red *O* among green *X*'s and *O*'s presented on a computer screen). It doesn't matter how many distractors appear in the array in this situation.

We can demonstrate this relation by plotting participants' reaction times as a function of the number of distractor items in the display (search function), as shown in **Figure 7.29**. When the target can be identified by a single feature, such as the red *O* in Figure 7.29a, the resulting search function is rather flat (Figure 7.29c, blue line). This phenomenon is called *pop-out* because the red *O* literally appears to pop out of the array of green letters on the basis of its color alone.

If the target shares features with the distractors, however, so that it *cannot* be distinguished by a single feature (e.g., a red *O* among green *X*'s and *O*'s and red *X*'s, as in Figure 7.29b, or a red suitcase among black suitcases and differently shaped red and black backpacks), then the time it takes to determine whether the target is present or absent in the array increases with the number of distractors in the array. The resulting search function is a sloped line (Figure 7.29c, red line). This type of search is known as a *conjunction search* because the target is defined by the conjunction of two or more features (e.g., the color red and the letter's identity as an *O*, or the color and shape of the travel totes).

To explain why conjunction targets take longer to find, Treisman and Gelade (1980) proposed that while elementary stimulus features such as color, motion, shape, and spatial frequency can be analyzed preattentively (without attention) and in parallel within multiple specialized feature maps (located within specialized visual cortical areas), something else is required to bind the disparate feature signals together. The researchers suggested that spatial location was the key, and that therefore spatial attention was the mechanism that "glued" the features together.

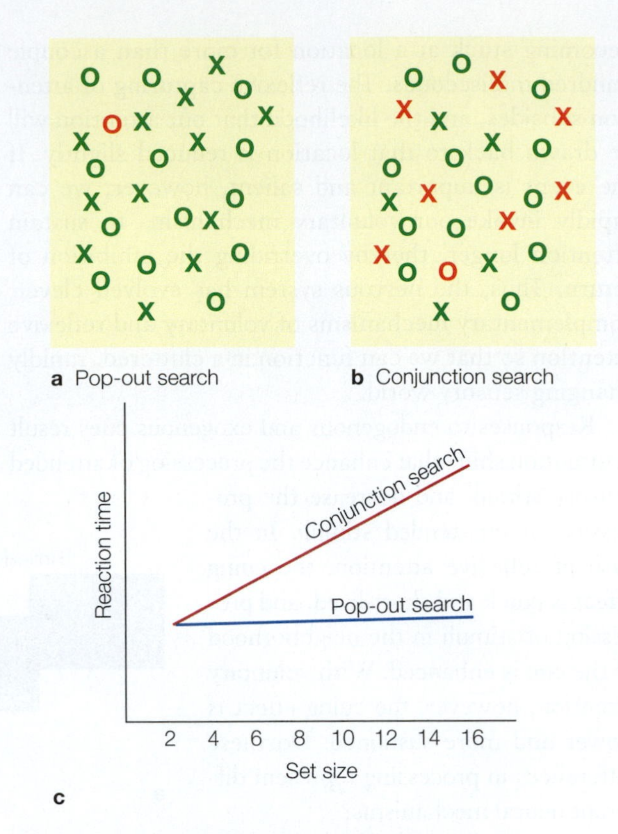

FIGURE 7.29 Searching for targets among distractors.
(a) A search array with a pop-out target (red *O*). Stimuli are said to pop out when they can be identified from among distractor stimuli by a simple single feature and the observer can find the target without searching the entire array. **(b)** A search array in which the target (red O) is defined by a conjunction of separate features (in this case, letter and color) shared with the distractors. **(c)** Idealized plot of reaction times as a function of set size (the number of items in the array) during visual search for pop-out stimuli versus feature conjunction stimuli. In pop-out searches, where an item can be distinguished from distractors by a single feature, increasing the set size does not affect the participants' reaction times as much as it does in conjunction searches.

According to their formulation, spatial attention must be directed to relevant stimuli in order to integrate the features into the perceived object, and it must be deployed in a sequential (serial) manner for each item in the array. This condition is necessary to link the information (in this case, color and letter identity, or travel tote color and shape) in the different feature maps so that the target can be analyzed and identified. This concept is called the **feature integration theory of attention,** and understanding the neural bases of these mechanisms remains of central importance in cognitive neuroscience.

If Treisman was correct, then we might hypothesize that Treisman's "glue" is the same as Posner's "spotlight of attention." Steven Luck and his colleagues (1993) tested this idea using ERP methods. They reasoned that if Posner's spatial spotlight of attention served as the glue for feature integration, then, during visual search for a conjunction target, they should be able to reveal the spatial spotlight using ERPs, just as was done in studies of voluntary and reflexive spatial attention (see Figure 7.17). They presented participants with stimulus arrays that contained a field of upright and inverted blue, green, and red *t* shapes. In each trial, the target they were to detect was a *t* of a particular color (blue or green, which was assigned before each block of trials; **Figure 7.30a**).

In order to measure whether spatial attention was allocated selectively to locations in the arrays, the researchers used an ERP probe method: At brief time intervals after the search array was presented, a solitary task-irrelevant probe stimulus, which had no features in common with the targets or distractors, was flashed either at the location of the designated target item (e.g., the green *t*) or at the location of a distractor item on the opposite side of the array (e.g., the blue *t*). The probe stimulus, which itself elicited an ERP, was the white outline of a square, which appeared around either the blue *t* or the green *t*, but never around a red *t*. The neural responses to the probes could then be used to reveal whether the typical spatial attention effects in visual cortical processing seen with ERPs in cuing tasks were present during visual conjunction search. The researchers found that indeed they were.

The probe elicited larger early visual responses (P1 waves) at the location of the designated conjunction target (where attention was focused), as compared to regions where only distractors were present. This study showed that conjunction search affects the P1 wave in much the same way that cued spatial attention does (compare **Figure 7.30b** with Figure 7.17b), supporting the idea that a kind of spotlight of spatial attention is employed during visual search, and revealing the neural basis of that effect: modulations of early cortical visual processing.

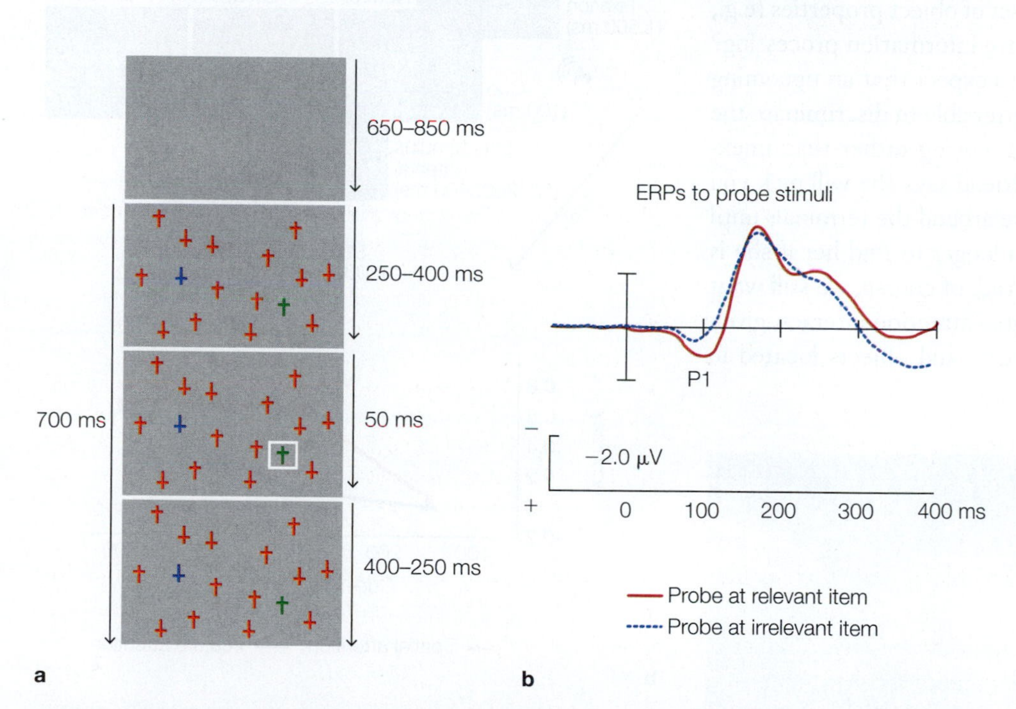

FIGURE 7.30 Visual search trial with probe stimulus.
(a) Stimuli were shown to participants, who were told to search for either a blue or a green *t* on each trial, and to indicate by pushing a button whether that item was upright or inverted. The red *t*'s were always irrelevant distractors. An irrelevant white, outlined square was flashed (for 50 ms) as a probe stimulus around either the blue or the green *t*. Moreover, the white probe could be flashed around the blue or green item when the colored item was the target, or when it was merely an irrelevant distractor. In this way, the amplitude of the probe ERP could be taken as an index of the location and strength of spatial attention just after the onset of the search array, at the point where participants would have located the target and discriminated its form (upright or inverted). The white probe was flashed either 250 ms or 400 ms after the onset search array. The search array remained on the screen for 700 ms. **(b)** The irrelevant white probe elicited a larger sensory-evoked occipital P1 wave when it occurred at the location of a relevant target (e.g., blue *t*) compared to the irrelevant target (e.g., green *t*). These findings support the idea that focal spatial attention is directed to the location of the target in the array during visual search. The corresponding amplitude modulations of sensory-evoked activity in early visual cortex that occur with the focused attention mirror those seen in spatial cuing paradigms.

Feature Attention

As our own experience tells us, we have learned that selectively attending to spatial locations, either voluntarily or reflexively, leads to changes in our ability to detect and respond to stimuli in the sensory world, and our improved detection is promoted by changes in neural activity in the visual cortex. Yet the question remains, Does spatial attention automatically move freely from item to item until the target is located, or does visual information in the array help guide the movements of spatial attention among the array items? As Robert Louis Stevenson pointed out, the world is full of objects of interest; however, some are more interesting than others. For instance, when you gaze across the expanse of Monument Valley (**Figure 7.31**), your attention is drawn to the buttes and mesas, not to a random bush. Why?

Objects are defined by their collection of elementary features, as we discussed in Chapters 5 and 6. Does selectively attending to a specific stimulus feature (e.g., motion, color, shape) or to a set of object properties (e.g., a face versus a house) influence information processing? For instance, if we are cued to expect that an upcoming stimulus is moving, are we better able to discriminate the target stimulus if it is indeed moving rather than unexpectedly stationary? If your friend says she will pick you up at the airport and will drive around the terminals until you spot her, will it take you longer to find her if she is parked at the curb instead? And, of course, we still want to know how feature and spatial attention interact, given that the world is full of features and objects located in specific locations.

FIGURE 7.31 Monument Valley, in northern Arizona.
What draws your attention in this picture? What are the salient objects that jump out?

Marissa Carrasco and her colleagues at New York University performed a set of experiments to address these questions. They compared *spatial attention* and *feature attention* in a voluntary cuing paradigm (Liu et al., 2007). The dependent measure of attention was detection accuracy. In one condition (using spatial attention), arrow cues indicated the location where attention should be directed. In the other condition (the feature attention condition), arrows indicated the direction of motion of the upcoming target (**Figure 7.32a**).

The researchers found that prior knowledge from the cue produced the typical voluntary cuing effect for spatial attention: Participants were more accurate at detecting the presence of the target (a change in the velocity of moving dots) at the cued location compared to when the cue (a double-headed arrow) did not signal one location

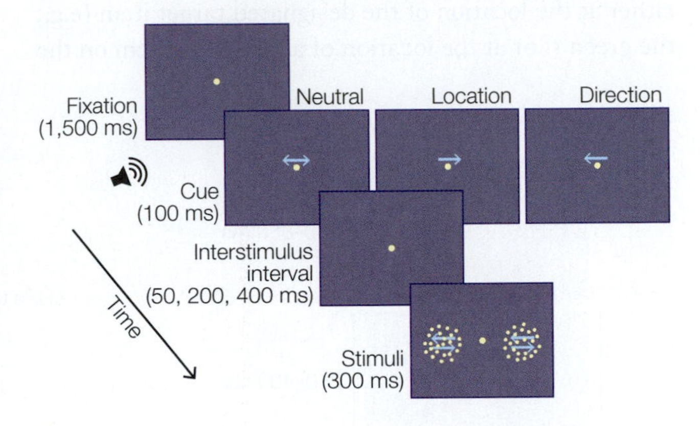

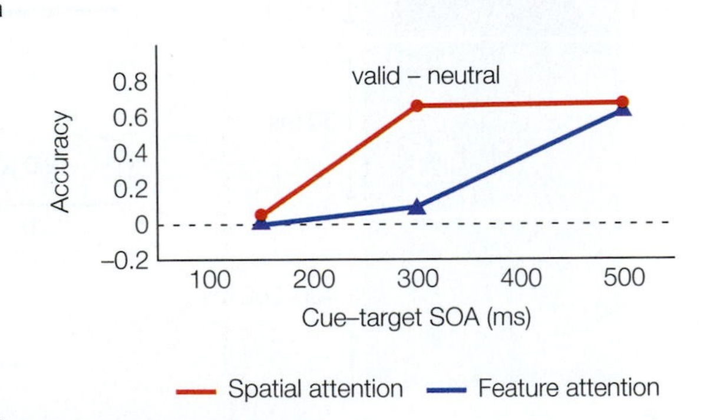

FIGURE 7.32 Pre-cuing attention to visual features improved performance.
(a) Each trial began with a warning tone that was followed by one of three types of cues. The cues indicated either the location or the direction of motion of the subsequent target if present, and the double-headed arrow indicated an equal probability that the location or direction of motion would be left or right. **(b)** The difference in accuracy of detection (valid versus neutral cue) of the moving dots is plotted here as a function of cue-to-target stimulus onset asynchrony (SOA), for both the spatial attention and feature attention conditions. (SOA is the amount of time between the start of one stimulus and the start of another stimulus.) Note that in both cases, the selective-attention effects build up over time, such that at longer SOAs the effects are larger, with the spatial attention effects appearing more rapidly in this study.

over another (**Figure 7.32b**, red line). In a similar vein, during the feature attention condition, cuing the direction of motion of the target also enhanced accuracy independently of whether it appeared in the left- or right-visual-field array (Figure 7.32b, blue line). Thus, precuing attention to a visual feature (in this case, motion direction) can improve performance. This finding tells us that attention can be directed in advance both to spatial locations and to nonspatial features of the target stimuli.

Let's now ferret out the neural bases of selective attention to features and objects, and contrast these mechanisms with those of spatial attention. In the early 1980s, Thomas Münte, a German neurologist working with Steven Hillyard in San Diego, developed a clever experimental paradigm to investigate spatial and feature attention mechanisms (Hillyard & Münte, 1984).

Using ERPs, they isolated the brain responses that are related to selectively attending stimulus color from those related to attending stimulus location. Rather than cuing participants to different stimulus features, they presented participants with blocks of many trials in which small red and blue vertical rectangles, some tall and some short, were flashed in a random sequence in the left and right visual fields. Each block of trials lasted a minute or so. Participants fixated on the central crosshairs on the screen while covertly attending to one color—red or blue—at the attended location, left or right. For example, participants were told, "For the next minute, attend and push the button to the shorter red bars on the right only." Thus, they had to ignore the other color at the attended location, as well as both colors at the unattended location. There were four different attention conditions, and the investigators could compare the ERPs generated under each one.

In this ingenious setup, the comparisons revealed independent processing for spatial attention and feature attention. For example, for a left, red stimulus, spatial attention (attend left versus attend right) could be experimentally uncoupled from feature attention (attend red versus attend blue). The brain responses for each of these conditions are shown in **Figure 7.33**. In Figure 7.33a, the ERPs show the typical spatial attention effects seen in Figure 7.17 (solid versus dashed ERP traces). Figure 7.33b shows the feature attention ERPs. Note the very different patterns that spatial and feature (in this case, color) attention produced in the ERPs. These are especially obvious in the ERP attention difference waves (Figure 7.33c and d), where the waveform elicited by the stimulus when ignored is subtracted from the waveform elicited by the same stimulus when attended. The early P1 attention effect that indexes spatial attention (Figure 7.33c) is absent for feature attention (Figure 7.33d), which shows only longer latency changes in the difference waveform. Also of interest from this work is the fact that the effects of attention to color stimuli were

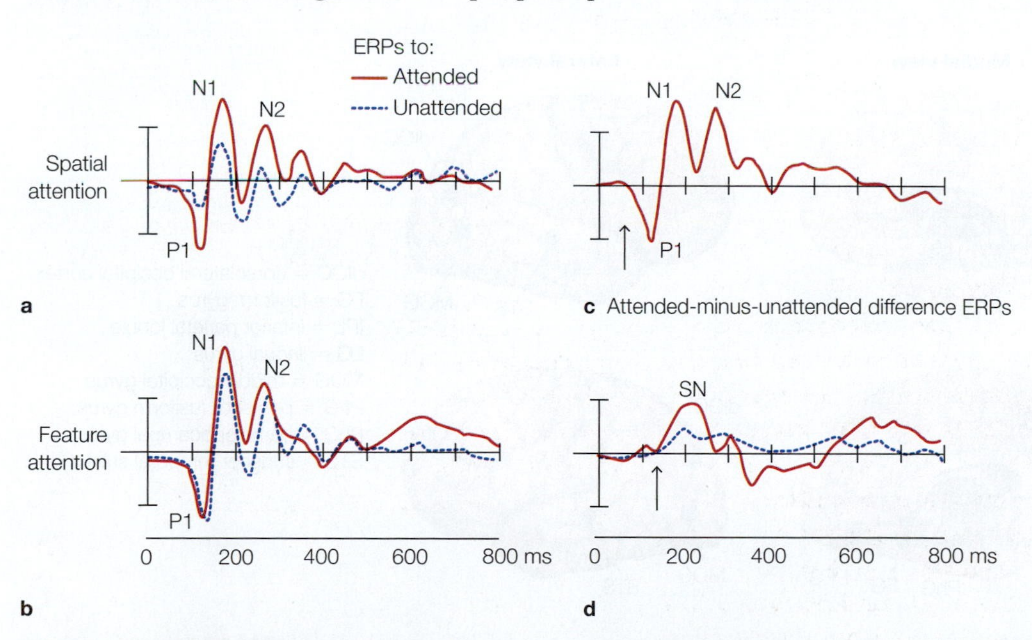

FIGURE 7.33 ERPs to spatial attention and feature attention are uncoupled.
(a) ERPs recorded to right-visual-field stimuli when participants covertly attended right (solid line) or left (dashed line) independently of stimulus color or which color was attended. **(b)** ERPs to right-visual-field stimuli when attending right and the color of the evoking stimulus was attended (solid line) versus when attending right but the unattended color was presented there (dashed line). **(c)** Difference ERPs associated with attended versus unattended spatial locations. **(d)** Difference ERPs associated with attended versus unattended color stimuli at the attended location (solid line) and the unattended location (dashed line). The arrows in (c) and (d) indicate the onset of the attention effects, which was later in the feature attention experiment (d). Positive voltage is plotted downward.

largely absent at the unattended location (Figure 7.33d). This research indicates that both spatial attention and feature attention can produce selective processing of visual stimuli, and that their mechanisms differ.

Where do these feature attention effects take place in the brain? Well, it depends. Maurizio Corbetta and his colleagues at Washington University investigated the neural systems involved in feature discrimination under two different conditions: divided attention and selective attention (Corbetta et al., 1991). In this groundbreaking neuroimaging study of selective attention, the researchers used PET imaging to identify changes that occur in extrastriate cortex and elsewhere when people selectively attend to a single stimulus feature, such as color, shape, or motion, versus when their attention is divided among all three features.

Participants underwent PET scans while being shown pairs of visual displays containing arrays of stimulus elements. The first display of each trial was a reference stimulus, such as a red square; the second was a test stimulus, perhaps a green circle. During the selective-attention condition, participants were instructed to compare the two arrays to determine whether a change had occurred to a *pre-specified* stimulus dimension (color, shape, or motion). During the divided-attention condition, participants were instructed to detect a change in *any of the three* stimulus dimensions.

This experiment design permitted the investigators to contrast brain activity under conditions in which the participants selectively attended a particular stimulus dimension (e.g., only color) with the condition in which they divided their attention among all stimulus dimensions. As you might expect, behavioral sensitivity for discriminating slight changes in a stimulus was higher when participants were judging only one feature (selective attention) rather than multiple features (divided attention).

Compared to divided attention, selective attention to one feature activated distinct, largely nonoverlapping regions of extrastriate cortex (**Figure 7.34**). Extrastriate cortical regions specialized for the perceptual processing of color, shape, or motion were modulated only during visual attention to the corresponding stimulus features. These findings provide additional support for the idea that *selective attention*, in modality-specific cortical areas, alters the perceptual processing of inputs *before the completion of feature analysis.*

Subsequent fMRI studies have identified specialized areas of human visual cortex that process features such as stimulus motion or color. Corresponding areas had been found previously in monkey visual cortex. These specialized feature analysis regions are modulated by selective visual attention, as suggested by the earlier work of Corbetta and colleagues.

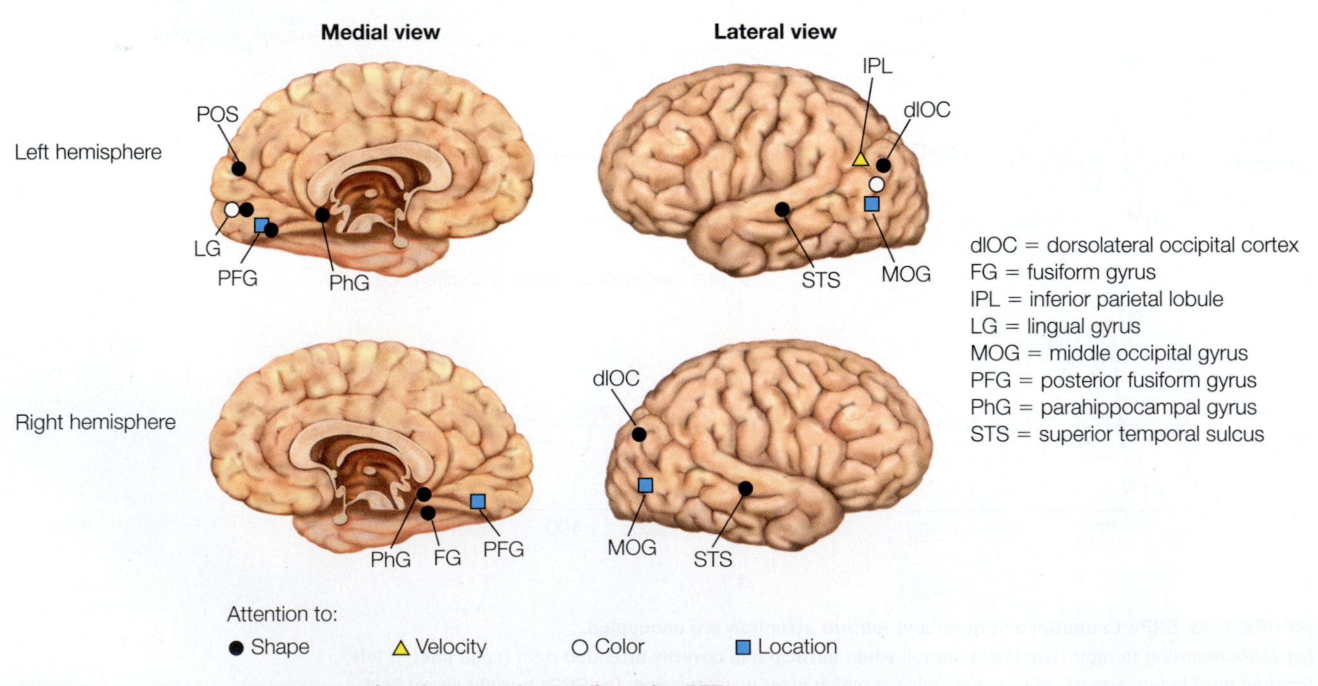

FIGURE 7.34 Summary of early neuroimaging attention studies using PET.
PET studies by Corbetta and colleagues (1991), Heinze and colleagues (1994), and Mangun and colleagues (1997) revealed regions of extrastriate cortex specialized for the processing of color, shape, or motion (from the work of Corbetta) that are selectively modulated during visual attention to these stimulus features (feature selective attention). As described earlier, we now know that spatial attention influences processing in multiple visual cortical areas (Figure 7.21) and in subcortical structures (Figures 7.26 and 7.27).

When do these various attention effects occur during processing? To address this question, one study combined MEG and fMRI to provide temporal and spatial information (Schoenfeld et al., 2007). Participants were cued to attend selectively to either changes in color or changes in motion in an upcoming display (**Figure 7.35a**). The stimulus sequence randomly presented motion and color changes, permitting the measurement of brain activity in response to changes in either feature as a function of attention to motion or color.

By using fMRI to localize brain regions sensitive to selective attention to color or motion, the investigators found (as expected) that attending to motion modulated activity in the visual cortical motion-processing area MT/V5 (in the dorsal stream; **Figure 7.35b**). Similarly, attending to color led to modulations in ventral visual cortex area V4v (in the posterior fusiform gyrus; **Figure 7.35c and d**). Importantly, the team's related MEG recordings demonstrated that attention-related activity in these areas appeared with a latency of 100 ms or less after onset of the change in the stimulus—much sooner than previous studies had reported.

Thus, feature-based selective attention acts at relatively early stages of visual cortical processing with relatively short latencies after stimulus onset. Spatial attention, however, still beats the clock and has an earlier effect. We see that the effects of feature attention occur with longer latencies (100 ms versus 70 ms after stimulus onset) and at later stages of the visual hierarchy (extrastriate cortex rather than striate cortex or the subcortical visual relays in the thalamus) than does spatial attention. This difference does not indicate that spatial attention always drives our attention, because if one does not know where a stimulus will appear but does know which features are relevant, as during visual search, feature attention may provide the first signal that then triggers spatial attention to focus on a location.

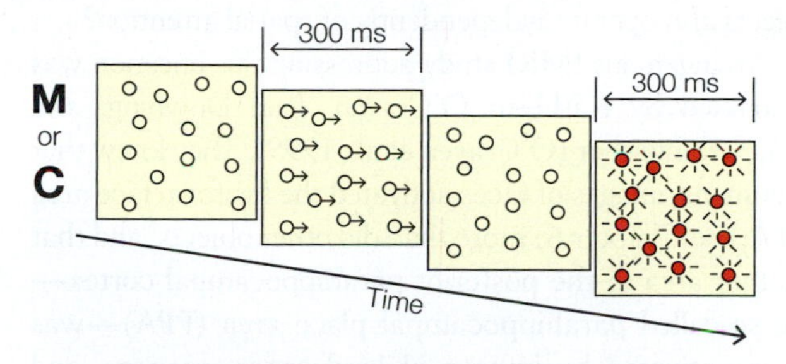

a

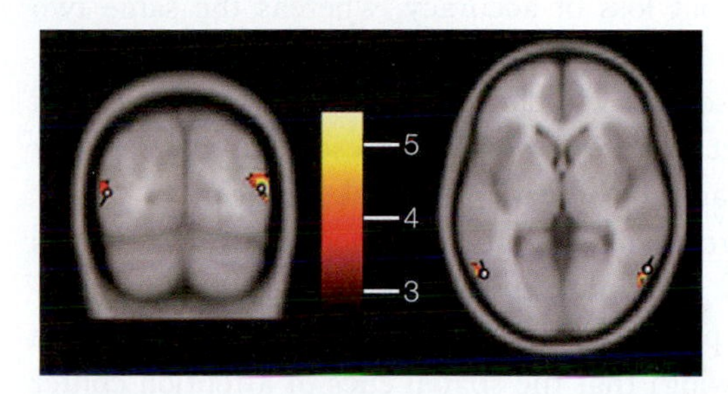

b Attend motion

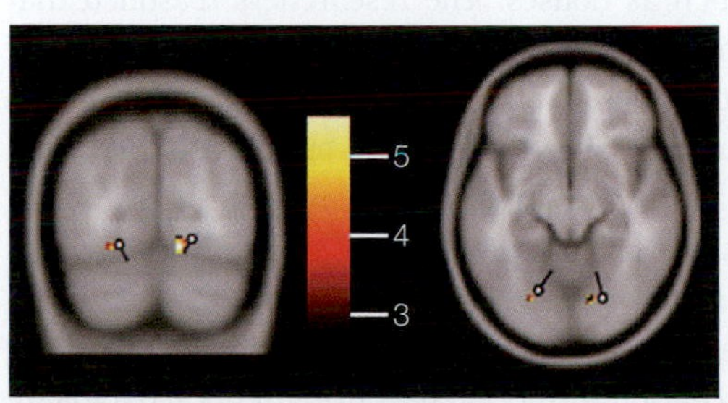

c Attend color

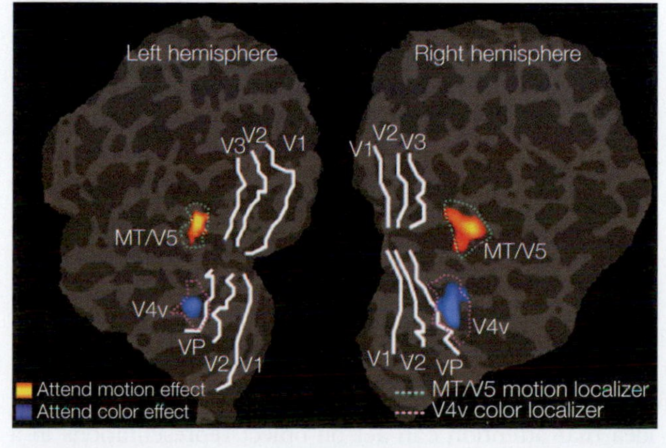

d

FIGURE 7.35 Attention modulates activity in feature-specific visual cortex.
(a) Each block of the experiment began with a letter cue (*M* or *C*) indicating that participants should attend to either motion (fast versus slow) or color (red versus orange), respectively, and press a button representing the specified feature. Dots would appear, and they randomly would either move or change color. In this way, responses to changes in motion (or color) could be contrasted when motion was attended versus when color was attended. **(b)** When motion was attended, activity in lateral occipitotemporal regions (human MT/V5) was modulated. **(c)** When color was attended, ventral area V4 (V4v; in the posterior fusiform gyrus) was modulated. This relation was found for fMRI BOLD responses (shown in red and yellow in b and c) and for MEG measures taken in a separate session (shown as circles with arrows in b and c, overlapping regions of significant BOLD signal change). The high temporal resolution of the MEG measures indicated that the latency of the attention effect after the onset of the moving or color arrays was about 100 ms. **(d)** Retinotopic mapping on a single participant verifies the extrastriate region associated with the motion and color attention effects on flattened cortical representations.

Object Attention

Now that we've described the effects of spatial-based attention and feature-based attention in visual cortex, let's turn to another question: Can attention also act on higher-order stimulus representations—namely, objects? When searching for a friend in a crowd, we don't merely search where we think our friend will be, especially if we haven't agreed on a place to meet. We also don't search for our friend only by hair color (unless it is highly salient, like fluorescent pink). Rather, we look for the conjunction of features that defines the person. For lack of a better word, we can refer to these qualities as *object properties*—elementary stimulus features that, when combined in a particular way, yield an identifiable object or person. Behavioral work has demonstrated evidence for *object-based attention* mechanisms.

In a seminal study, John Duncan (1984) contrasted attention to location (spatial attention) with attention to objects (object-based attention). Holding spatial distance constant, he discovered that two perceptual judgments concerning the same object could be made simultaneously without loss of accuracy, whereas the same two judgments about *different* objects could not. For instance, in a split second you can process that a dog is big and brown, but when two dogs are present, processing that one is big and the other is brown takes longer.

This processing limitation in attending to two objects implicates an object-based attention system in addition to a space-based system. In line with this view, the costs (slowing) that the spatial cues of attention confer on behavioral reaction time are greater than the benefits (speeding) when two objects are being attended as compared to one object (Egly et al., 1994). This result suggests that the spread of attention is facilitated within the confines of an object, or that there is an additional cost to moving attention between objects, or both.

Notger Mueller and Andreas Kleinschmidt (2003) designed an fMRI study to determine what effect objects had on spatial attention. They wondered whether attending to an object had any impact on processing in the early visual processing areas, and if so, what sort of impact? They cued participants on a trial-by-trial basis to expect a target at one location in the visual field (e.g., upper-left quadrant) and then presented targets there on most trials (valid trials). In a minority of trials, they presented the targets to uncued locations (invalid trials). Following the design of Egly and colleagues (1994), Mueller and Kleinschmidt included objects on the screen so that the uncued target could fall either within the same object that was cued (but at another location in that object), or at another location that was not within the bounds of the object. **Figure 7.36a** illustrates their design.

The displayed objects were wrench-like figures, and these figures could be oriented horizontally on the screen or vertically. For example, when the wrenches were oriented horizontally and the upper-left-quadrant location was cued, the upper-right-quadrant location would be spatially uncued (unattended) but be within the *same* object. When the wrenches were vertically oriented, however, that location would be spatially uncued and within a *different* object.

Mueller and Kleinschmidt replicated the behavioral reaction time effects of Egly and colleagues (**Figure 7.36b**). What's more, they found that in visual cortical areas V1 through V4, *increased activity* occurred in uncued locations that were located on the same object (the wrench) as the cued location, compared to when the uncued location was not on the cued object (**Figure 7.36c and d**).

This result is evidence that the presence of objects influences the way spatial attention is allocated in space: In essence, attention spreads within the object, thereby leading to some activity for uncued locations on the object as well. An effect of spatial attention also remains, because, within the object, the cued location still shows greater activity than uncued locations show. Thus, object representations can modulate spatial attention. Can attention to objects also operate independently of spatial attention?

An ingenious fMRI study addressing this question was conducted by Kathleen O'Craven, Paul Downing, and Nancy Kanwisher (O'Craven et al., 1999). They knew that in humans, images of faces activated the fusiform face area (FFA; see Chapter 6) more than did other objects, and that another area in the posterior parahippocampal cortex—the so-called parahippocampal place area (PPA)—was more activated by images of landscapes, scenery, and structures such as houses. The researchers reasoned that selective attention to faces or houses should differentially modulate activity in the FFA and PPA, with attention to faces boosting responses in the FFA but not the PPA, and vice versa. Moreover, attention to motion should affect motion-sensitive brain regions (MT/MST; also known as MT/V5, or MT+) but not the FFA or PPA.

O'Craven's group tested this hypothesis directly using fMRI in a face–house–motion selective-attention paradigm, where superimposed faces and houses (**Figure 7.37a**) that were either moving or static were presented in different attention conditions: attend faces, attend houses, or attend motion. The first experiment used a block design: In separate blocks, participants were instructed to selectively attend the faces, the houses, or the motion direction. Their task was to detect when the same attended item appeared twice in a row (e.g., same person, same house, or same direction of motion). **Figure 7.37b** shows the resulting pattern of brain activity.

As predicted, attention to faces produced the largest signals in the FFA, attention to houses produced the largest signals in the PPA, and attention to motion caused the greatest activity in MT/MST. This pattern of results supports the idea that attention can act on object representations in a highly selective fashion, independent of spatial attention; in

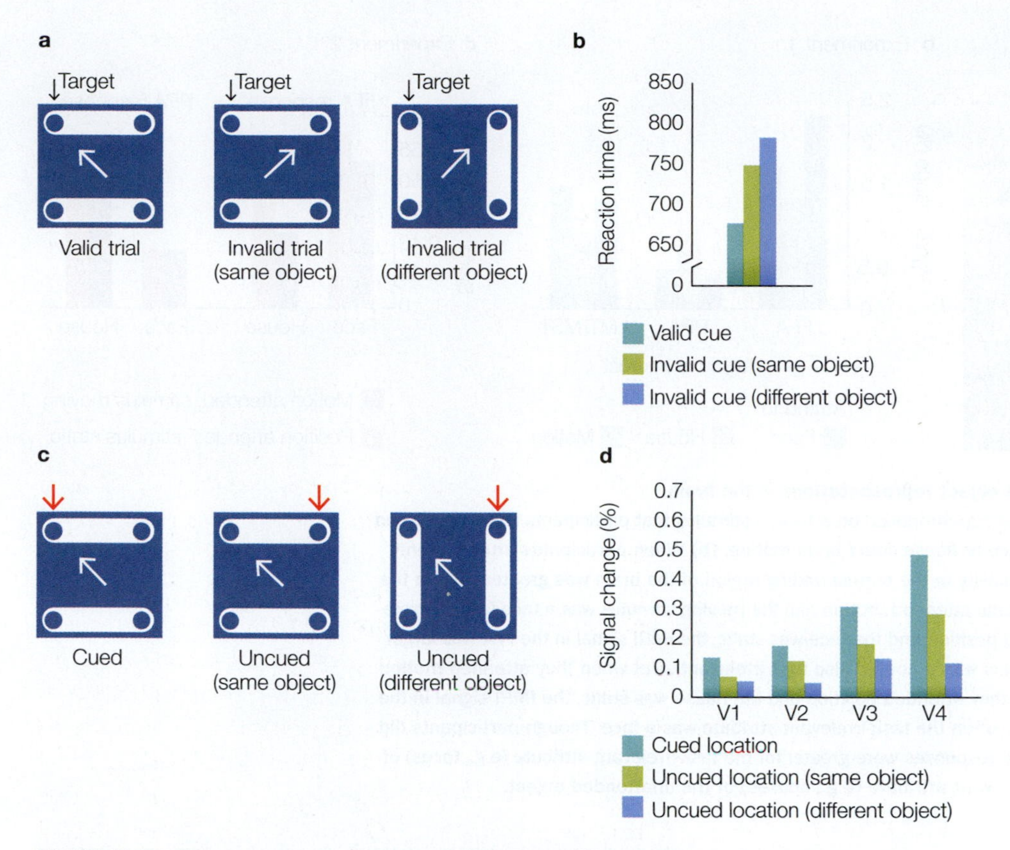

FIGURE 7.36 Object representations can modulate spatial attention.
(a) Wrench-like objects were continually presented on the screen and were oriented horizontally (at left and middle) or vertically (at right). On each trial, a centrally located cue (white arrow) indicated the most likely location of subsequent targets that required a fast response, whether at the cued location (frequent) or elsewhere (infrequent). **(b)** Reaction times to targets were fastest when the cues validly predicted the target location, were slowest to invalid trials when the target appeared on a different object, and were intermediate in speed for invalid trials when the target appeared on the same object. **(c)** In this phase of the experiment, the upper-left location was always cued, and the target appeared in that location on most trials (at left). Uncued locations (e.g., in the upper-right quadrant) could be either on the same object as the cued location (at middle) or on a different object (at right). The red arrows above each panel indicate the visual field locations corresponding to regions of interest in the visual cortex from which hemodynamic responses were extracted. **(d)** Hemodynamic responses (percentage signal change) are shown as bar graphs from regions of interest in visual cortical areas V1 to V4. In each area, the largest response is in the cued location, and smaller responses are obtained from uncued locations (the main effect of spatial attention). Importantly, when the uncued location was on the same object as the cued location, the fMRI activation was larger, demonstrating the effect of object attention.

other words, because the two objects—faces and houses—were overlapping in space, it was not possible simply to use spatial attention to focus on one object and not the other.

In the second experiment, the researchers tested whether task-irrelevant attributes of an attended object would be selected along with the task-relevant attribute, which is a central claim of object-based theories. Using an event-related design, they presented randomly intermixed trials of either moving faces superimposed on stationary houses, or moving houses superimposed on stationary faces. Participants were told either to attend selectively to the direction of motion (regardless of whether the face or house was moving) and detect when two consecutive presentations of the stimuli contained the same direction of motion, or to attend to the position of the static image on the screen (regardless of whether it was the face or the house that was static) and detect when two consecutive presentations of the stimuli had the same position on the screen.

As **Figure 7.37c** shows, even though the task-relevant stimulus attributes were motion and position, independent of the task-irrelevant face–house distinction, attention to the shared irrelevant attribute (face) produced greater activity in the FFA than attention to the task-relevant attributes (motion or position) shared with the house stimulus. The inverse pattern was seen in the PPA, where activity was greater when the attended attributes were shared with the house stimulus.

These results demonstrate how attention acts on object representations and show that objects, being composed of many features, show interesting properties. For

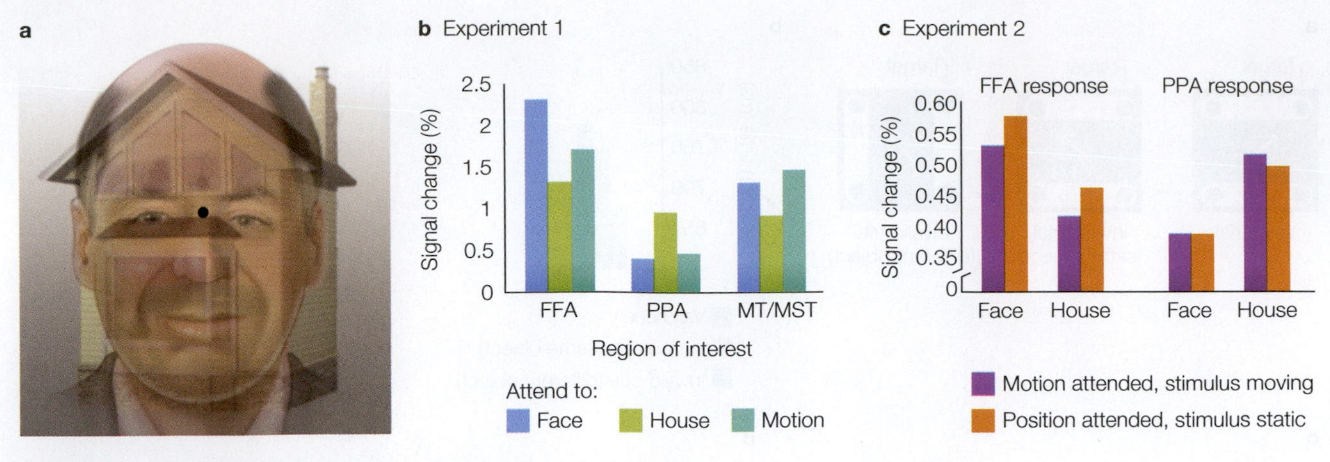

FIGURE 7.37 Attention modulates object representations in the brain.
(a) Example of an image with a house superimposed on a face: a stimulus that participants could not attend to using spatial mechanisms. The face or house could be in motion. **(b)** When participants attended only faces, only houses, or only motion, activity in the corresponding region of the brain was greater than in the other two regions. **(c)** When participants attended motion and the moving stimulus was a face (a task-irrelevant attribute), or when they attended position and the face was static, the fMRI signal in the FFA was larger (leftmost bars) than when the stimulus was a house (also task irrelevant). But when they attended motion and the *house* was moving, or when they attended position and the house was static, the fMRI signal in the PPA was larger (rightmost bars) than when the task-irrelevant attribute was a face. Though participants did not have to attend to faces or houses, responses were greater for the task-irrelevant attribute (e.g., faces) of the attended object than to the irrelevant attribute (e.g., houses) of the unattended object.

example, attention facilitates processing of all the features of the attended object, and attending one feature can facilitate the object representation in object-specific regions such as the FFA. Importantly, these findings show that even when spatial attention is not involved, *object representations can be the level of perceptual analysis affected by goal-directed attentional control.*

SPIKES, SYNCHRONY, AND ATTENTION We now know that when attention is focused on a stimulus, neurons in the visual system that code that stimulus increase their postsynaptic responses and their firing rates. How does this happen in a selective fashion so that attended information is routed appropriately to influence subsequent stages of processing? Although we remain uncertain about the precise mechanisms, various hypotheses have been proposed, and some interesting models are being tested. One such model suggests that at different stages of visual analysis (e.g., V1 and V4), neurons that code the receptive-field location of an attended stimulus show increased synchrony in their activity.

Conrado Bosman, Pascal Fries, and their colleagues (Bosman et al., 2012) used cortical surface grids of more than 250 electrodes in the monkey to test this model. They presented monkeys with two drifting gratings separated in visual space, and they trained the monkeys to keep their eyes fixed on a central crosshair but covertly attend one drifting grating at a time to detect when the shape of the gratings changed slightly. Given the retinotopic organization and small receptive-field size of V1 (about 1° of visual angle), stimuli separated by several degrees activate different populations of neurons in V1. In higher-order visual areas like V4, which have much larger receptive fields (several degrees of visual angle), however, the same stimuli fall within the receptive field of the same V4 neuron (**Figure 7.38a**).

The researchers hypothesized that if spatial attention can alter the flow of information from early stages of the visual hierarchy (V1) to later stages (V4) in a spatially specific manner, then this effect might promote selective synchronization of local field potentials (LFPs) between these early and later stages of visual processing (**Figure 7.38b**). That is precisely what they observed. They measured the cortical surface LFPs oscillating within the gamma-band frequencies of 60–80 Hz and found that coherence increased with spatial attention between the site in V1 that coded the attended stimulus location (e.g., location V1a in the figure) and the V4 site that coded the stimulus location.

So, if the monkey attended location V1a, it showed increased synchronization in gamma-band LFPs with V4 (**Figure 7.38c**, red). At the same time, however, the coherence remained low between the other V1 site that coded the ignored location (e.g., location V1a in the figure) and V4 (Figure 7.38c, blue). Interestingly enough, though, when the animal was cued to switch attention to the other stimulus location (i.e., V1b in the figure), then the V1–V4 coherence went up for that V1 site and V4, and coherence at the first location dropped (**Figure 7.38d**, blue versus red).

These studies suggest that attention alters the effective connectivity between neurons by altering the pattern

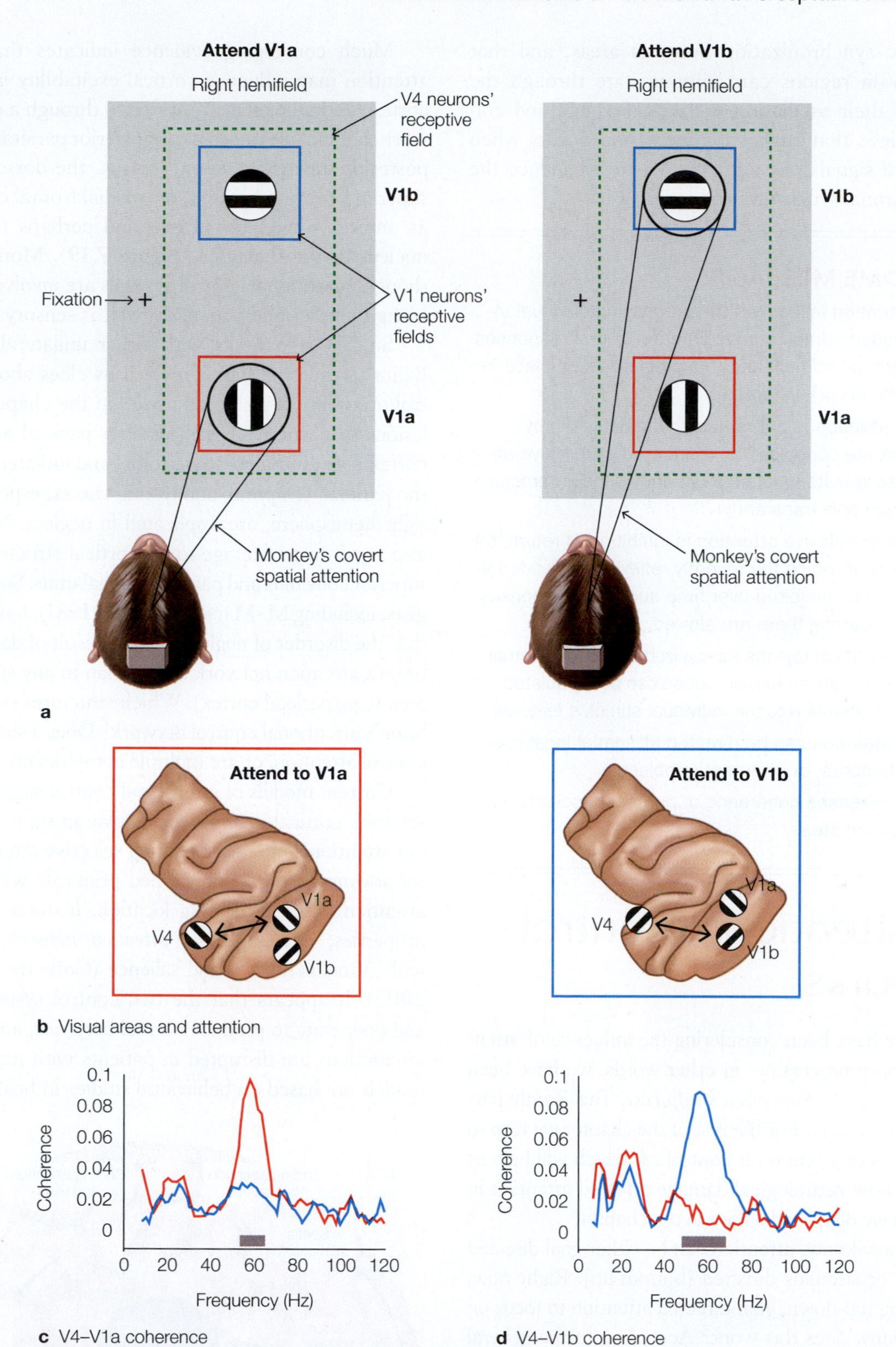

FIGURE 7.38 Neuronal coherence with attention in visual cortex.
(a) Grating stimuli were presented that were in the same V4 receptive field (larger box with dashed, green outline) but were in different receptive fields in area V1 (small boxes outlined in red or blue). (b) Diagram of the left visual cortex of the macaque monkey, showing two regions in V1 (V1a and V1b) that mapped the stimuli shown in (a), as well as how these stimuli were represented in higher-order visual area V4. The arrows indicate hypothesized coherences in attention. (c, d) Neuronal coherence is shown between regions of V1 and V4, depending on which stimulus is attended (see text for more details).

of rhythmic synchronization between areas, and that different brain regions can communicate through the coupling of their oscillation patterns. Bosman and colleagues believe that such communication occurs when the attended signals passing from V1 to V4 induce the gamma neuronal synchronization with V4.

TAKE-HOME MESSAGES

- Spatial attention influences the processing of visual inputs: Attended stimuli produce greater neural responses than do ignored stimuli, and this process takes place in multiple visual cortical areas.
- Reflexive attention is automatic and is activated by stimuli that are conspicuous in some way. Reflexive attention also results in changes in early sensory processing, although only transiently.
- A hallmark of reflexive attention is inhibition of return, the phenomenon in which the recently reflexively attended location becomes inhibited over time such that responses to stimuli occurring there are slowed.
- Extrastriate cortical regions specialized for the perceptual processing of color, shape, or motion can be modulated during visual attention to the individual stimulus features.
- Selective attention can be directed at spatial locations, at object features, or at an entire object.
- Attention increases coherence of neuronal oscillations between visual areas.

7.5 Attentional Control Networks

Thus far, we have been considering the influence of attention on sensory processing; in other words, we have been looking at the *sites of attention's influence.* This is only part of the attention story. For the rest of the chapter we turn to how the focus of attention is controlled, which will help us understand how neurological damage affected attention in the patients we described earlier in the chapter.

As we now know, attention can be either goal directed (top-down) or stimulus directed (bottom-up). Right now, you are using top-down, goal-directed attention to focus on this book. How does this work? According to the general model that has been with us for decades, top-down neuronal projections from attentional control systems (with inputs about goals, information learned by experience, reward mechanisms, etc.) contact neurons in sensory-specific cortical areas to alter their excitability. As a result, the response in the sensory areas to a stimulus may be enhanced if the stimulus is given high priority, or attenuated if it is irrelevant to the current goal. We observe these effects of attention as changes in behavior and neural activity.

Much converging evidence indicates that selective attention may influence cortical excitability in the visual cortex (and other sensory systems) through a control network that includes at least the posterior parietal cortex, the posterior superior temporal cortex, the dorsolateral and superior prefrontal cortex, the medial frontal cortex (such as anterior cingulate cortex), and perhaps the pulvinar nucleus of the thalamus (**Figure 7.39**). More generally, though, attentional control systems are involved in modulating thoughts and actions, as well as sensory processes.

Studies of patients with either unilateral neglect or Bálint's syndrome have provided us clues about the control of attention. As noted earlier in the chapter, bilateral lesions to portions of the posterior parietal and occipital cortex result in Bálint's syndrome, and unilateral lesions of the parietal, temporal, and frontal cortex, especially in the right hemisphere, are implicated in neglect. Neglect may also result from damage to subcortical structures like the superior colliculus and parts of the thalamus. Some neurologists, including M.-Marsel Mesulam (1981), have suggested that the disorder of neglect was the result of damage to the brain's attention network rather than to any specific brain area (e.g., parietal cortex). Which structures constitute the brain's attentional control network? Does a single network control attention, or are multiple networks involved?

Current models of attentional control suggest that two separate cortical systems are at play in supporting different attentional operations during selective attention: a *dorsal attention network*, concerned primarily with voluntary attention based on spatial location, features, and object properties; and a *ventral attention network*, concerned with stimulus novelty and salience (Corbetta & Shulman, 2002). It appears that the two control systems interact and cooperate to produce normal behavior, and that these interactions are disrupted in patients with neglect. These models are based on behavioral studies in healthy persons

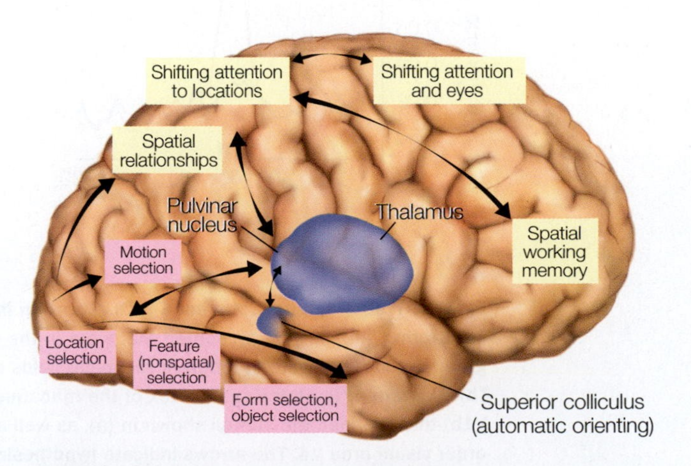

FIGURE 7.39 Sources and sites of attention.
Model of executive control systems, showing how visual cortex processing is affected by the goal-directed control of a network of brain areas.

or in patients with brain lesions, as well as on the results of neuroimaging and electrophysiology experiments.

The Dorsal Attention Network

Joseph Hopfinger and his colleagues (2000) and Maurizio Corbetta and his coworkers (2000) both employed event-related fMRI to study attentional control. We reviewed some of the findings from Hopfinger's study earlier in this chapter, focusing on how spatial attention involves selective processing in visual cortex (the site of attention). Now we return to this research to see what these investigators learned about the brain regions that control attention. Later we will discuss the work of Corbetta and colleagues to complete the story.

FINDING THE SOURCES OF ATTENTIONAL CONTROL OVER SPATIAL ATTENTION Recall that Hopfinger and his coworkers used a modified spatial cuing paradigm like the one shown in Figure 7.15. The participants were presented a cue and were required on some trials to orient attention to one half of the visual field and ignore the other. Then, after a delay, two stimuli were presented simultaneously, one in each visual hemifield, and the participant was to discriminate target features of the stimulus at the pre-cued location and make a response. Earlier we focused on the brain activity triggered by the appearance of the target stimuli, but to investigate attentional control these researchers looked earlier in the trial at the brain activity after the cue but before the targets appeared. Such activity can be ascribed to goal-directed attentional control.

What did the researchers find? When the participant attended and responded to the stimulus, a network of dorsal frontal and parietal cortical regions showed increased activity. These regions together are now called the **dorsal attention network**. None of the regions in this network were primarily involved in sensory processing of the visual features of the cue, which took place in the visual cortex. We now understand that this dorsal frontoparietal network reflects the *sources* of attentional signals in the *goal-directed* control of attention.

Why did the researchers conclude that these regions are involved in attentional control? First, the identified brain regions were found to be active only when the participants were instructed (cued) to covertly attend either right or left locations. Second, when the targets appeared after the cue, a different pattern of activity was observed. Third, when participants only *passively* viewed the presented cues—and didn't attend to them or act on them—then the frontoparietal brain regions that were active in the former condition were not activated during passive viewing, even though the visual cortex was engaged in processing the visual features of the passively viewed cues.

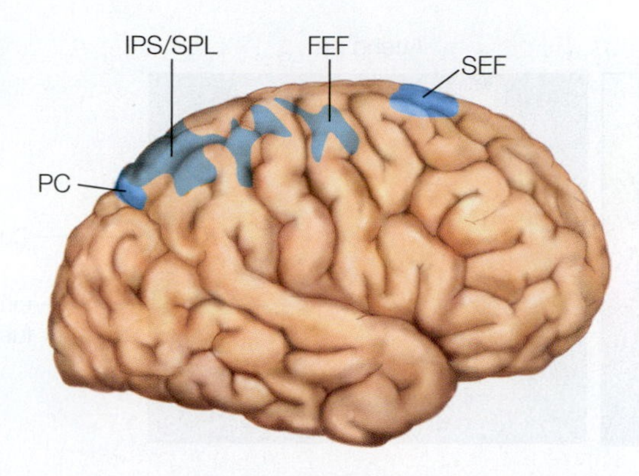

FIGURE 7.40 Cortical regions involved in attentional control. Diagrammatic representation of cortical activity seen during attentional control. In blue are the regions of the dorsal attention network, which includes the intraparietal sulcus (IPS), superior parietal lobule (SPL), precuneus (PC), frontal eye field (FEF), and supplementary eye field (SEF).

The key cortical nodes involved in the dorsal attention network are the frontal eye fields (FEFs, located at the junction of the precentral and superior frontal sulcus in each hemisphere) and the supplementary eye fields (SEFs) in the frontal cortex; the intraparietal sulcus (IPS), superior parietal lobule (SPL), and precuneus (PC) in the posterior parietal lobe; and related regions (**Figure 7.40**). From studies like Hopfinger's, we know that the dorsal attention network is active when voluntary attention is engaged. How does this network function to modulate sensory processing?

LINKING THE CONTROL NETWORK FOR SPATIAL ATTENTION TO ATTENTIONAL CHANGES First let's look at the evidence that activity in the dorsal attention network is actually linked to attention-related changes in sensory processing. In Hopfinger's study, after the cue was presented but *before the target displays appeared*, activations were observed not only in the dorsal attention network, but also in visual cortical regions that would later process the incoming target (**Figure 7.41**).

These activations in visual cortex were spatially specific—dependent on the locus of spatial attention within the visual field. What caused the visual cortex to be selectively activated even before any stimuli were presented? The idea is that these activations reflect a sort of attentional "priming" of the sensory cortex for information coming from a particular location in the visual field. This priming is thought to enable the enhanced neural responses to attended-location stimuli that we detailed earlier in humans and monkeys (see, for example, Figures 7.17, 7.18, and 7.20).

The priming of visual cortex described here from fMRI resembles what has been observed under similar circumstances in neurophysiological studies in monkeys (Luck et al., 1997). Such priming is possible if neurons in the dorsal attention network send signals either directly or indirectly to the visual cortex, producing selective

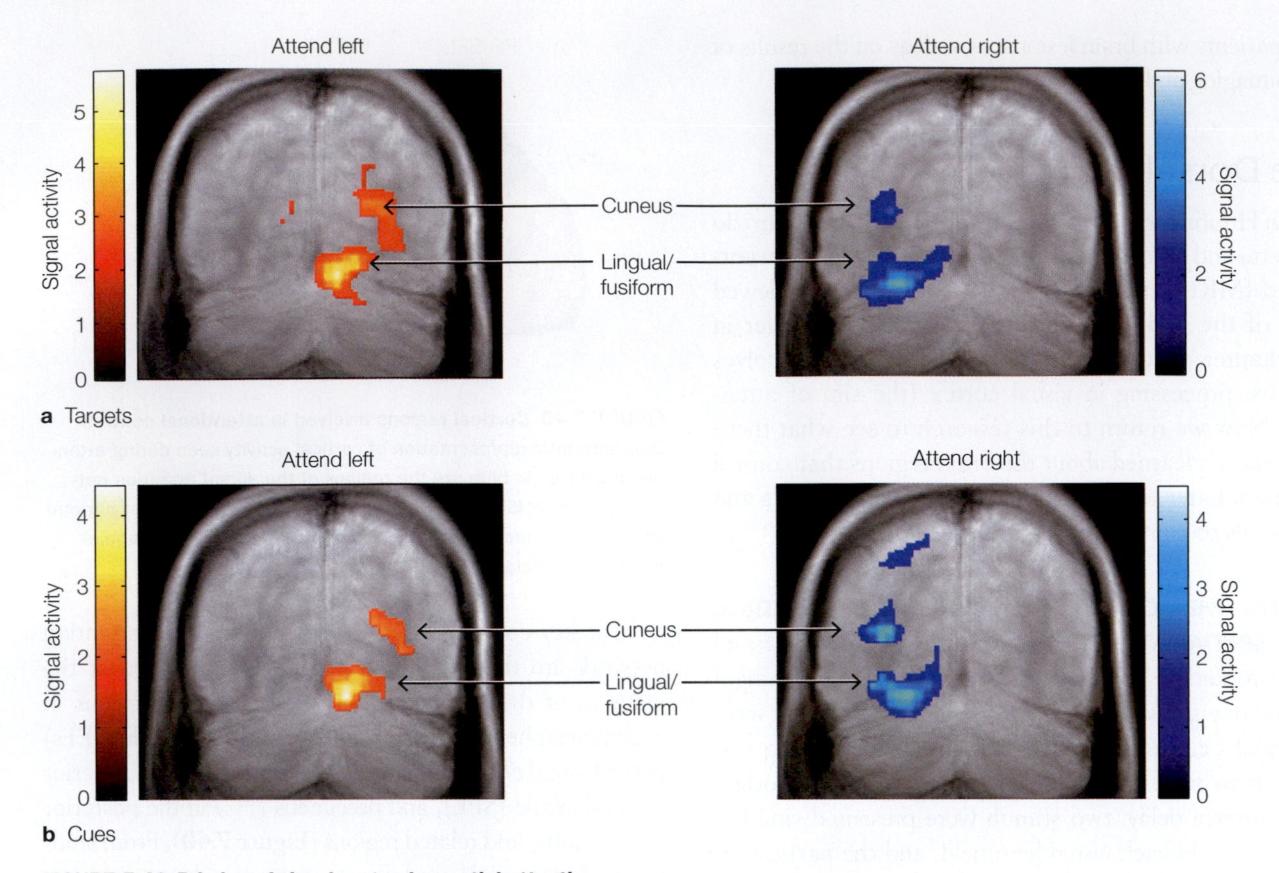

FIGURE 7.41 Priming of visual cortex by spatial attention.
(a) The same visual cortical activation (attended versus unattended) that Figure 7.20a showed is seen here, but collapsed over a group of six participants (from Hopfinger et al., 2000). (b) When these same regions of visual cortex were investigated before the targets actually appeared but after the cue was presented, a preparatory priming of these areas was observed as increased activity. These regions of increased activity closely overlapped with the regions that would later receive the target stimuli shown in (a), but the amplitude of the effects was smaller.

changes in visual processing in those visual neurons (e.g., biasing inputs in favor of one location versus another). Do any data support this biasing effect on the visual cortex?

FRONTAL CORTEX AND ATTENTIONAL CONTROL

Indirect evidence comes from patients with prefrontal cortical lesions. Neurologist Robert T. Knight and his colleagues (Barceló et al., 2000) found that patients with frontal cortex damage due to stroke had "decreased" visually evoked responses in ERP recordings over visual cortex. This evidence suggests that the frontal cortex (source) has a modulatory influence on the visual cortex (site).

More direct evidence comes from intracranial studies in monkeys. As mentioned earlier, a key component of the frontoparietal attention network is the frontal eye fields. The FEFs are located bilaterally in a region around the intersection of the middle frontal gyrus with the precentral gyrus in the dorsal–lateral–posterior portions of the prefrontal cortex (Figure 7.40). They coordinate eye movement and gaze shifts, which are important for orienting and attention. Stimulation of FEF neurons produces topographically mapped saccadic eye movements.

Tirin Moore and his colleagues at Stanford University (Moore & Fallah, 2001) investigated reports suggesting that brain mechanisms for planning eye movements and directing visuospatial attention overlapped. To confirm whether such overlapping existed, they looked at whether altering oculomotor signals within the brain by stimulating them with electrodes would affect spatial attention. Using intracortical electrical stimulation and recording techniques in monkeys, they stimulated FEF neurons with very low currents that were too weak to evoke saccadic eye movements, but strong enough to bias the selection of targets for eye movements.

Was there any effect on attention? Yes! While the monkey was performing a spatial attention task, the weak FEF stimulations resulted in enhanced performance in the attention task, and these effects were spatially specific. Attention was enhanced to attended targets only if the targets were at the right spot—the specific location in space where the saccadic eye movements would have been directed, if the stimulation to the FEF had been strong enough to generate them.

This finding led the researchers to hypothesize that if FEF microstimulation initiates both saccade preparation

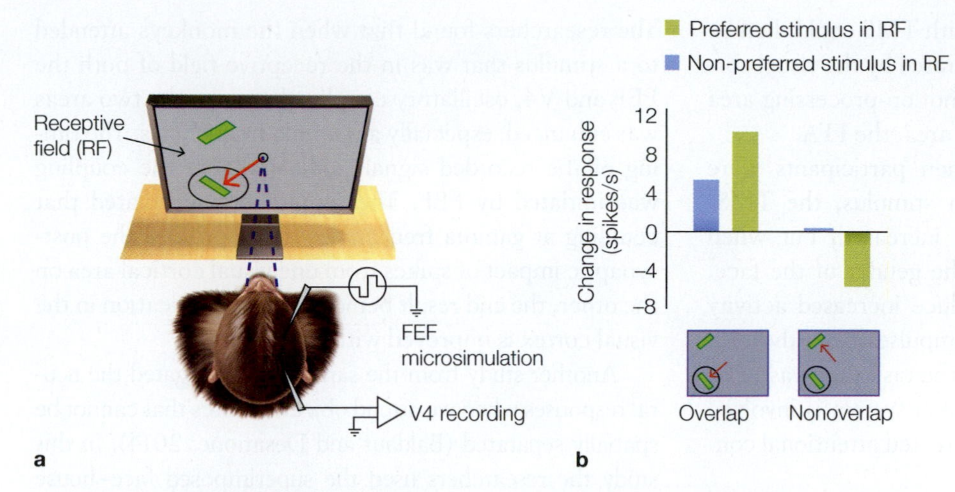

FIGURE 7.42 FEF stimulation participates in attentional control of visual cortex. (a) The experimental setup: stimulus display, and recording and stimulating procedure. The monkey fixated on a central point while stimuli flashed within the receptive field (circled region on the computer screen) of the recorded V4 neuron, or outside the receptive field (RF). Subthreshold stimulation of the FEF was performed either for neurons whose saccade vector (indicated by red arrow) was oriented toward the neuron's RF or for neurons whose vector was oriented away, toward the other stimulus. (b) Under the overlap condition, when the RF and saccade vector overlapped, the responses of the V4 neuron were increased in comparison to the nonoverlap condition. The difference was greater when the flashed stimulus elicited large responses from the neuron (preferred stimulus) compared to when the stimulus did not (non-preferred stimulus). FEF stimulation mimics the effects of visual attention on V4 activity.

and improved attention performance, then it also might induce a spatial-attention-like modulation of the visual cortex (Moore & Armstrong, 2003). To test this hypothesis, they placed a stimulating electrode in FEF that could deliver very weak electrical stimulation. This time, they also recorded from V4 neurons whose receptive fields were located in the visual field where stimulation of the FEF would direct a saccade (**Figure 7.42a**).

First they presented a stimulus to the receptive field of the V4 neuron. The stimulus was one of two types: either preferred or non-preferred for that particular neuron. The neuron's elicited response was always weaker in the case of the non-preferred stimulus. Then stimulation was applied to the FEF site 200 to 500 ms after the appearance of the visual stimulus. This delay enabled the investigators to examine the effects of FEF stimulation on the activity in V4 that was evoked by the visual stimulus, as opposed to any changes in V4 activity that might have been the direct result of FEF stimulation alone.

The FEF stimulation could have had one of three results: It could have amplified the V4 activity, interfered with it, or had no effect on it. What happened? While the monkey was fixating on a central point on the screen, weak stimulation of the FEF-enhanced stimulus evoked V4 activity (i.e., it increased the number of spikes per second) for the preferred over the non-preferred stimulus (**Figure 7.42b**). If the V4 neuron was not activated by the visual stimulus, then stimulation of the FEF did not affect the activity of the V4 cell. This result mimics the ones observed when monkeys attend and ignore stimuli in V4 (Figure 7.18). FEF signals appear to participate in goal-directed attentional control over V4 activity.

The fact that microstimulation of the FEF in monkeys modulated the neuronal responses in the posterior visual fields is evidence that goal-directed signals from the frontal cortex cause modulations of neuronal activity. What is the nature of these signals? Are they task specific? For instance, if your task is to identify a face, will goal-directed signals alert only the fusiform face area? Or are signals more broadly transmitted, such that the motion area would also be alerted? Yosuke Morishima and his colleagues (2009) set their sights on answering these questions.

They designed an attention task in which human participants were cued on a trial-by-trial basis to perform a visual discrimination task for either motion direction or face gender. The cue was followed by either a short interval of 150 ms or a long interval of 1,500 ms before the stimulus was presented. The stimulus was a vertical grating that moved to the right or the left, superimposed on an image of a male or female face. In half of the trials, 134 ms after the cue the FEF was stimulated using transcranial magnetic stimulation (TMS).

Morishima and coworkers used TMS at levels low enough not to affect task performance. The goal here was not to modify attentional-related processing in FEF neurons; instead, TMS was used simply to evoke a signal from the FEF to regions of the visual cortex that were functionally interconnected with it. These evoked changes in visual cortex activity with TMS could then be measured by recording ERPs generated by the visual cortex activity, either in the human motion-processing area MT/V5, or in the face-processing area, the FFA.

The results revealed that when participants were cued to discriminate the motion stimulus, the TMS-induced activity in MT/V5 was increased, but when they were cued to discriminate the gender of the face, the same TMS was found to induce increased activity in the FFA (**Figure 7.43**). Thus, impulses from the FEF actually coded information about the task that was to be performed, indicating that the dorsal system is involved in generating task-specific, goal-directed attentional control signals.

This study neatly demonstrates that the FEF, a component of the dorsal attention network, has an influence on visual cortex. This goal-directed influence is task specific, such that the functional connectivity between FEF and specific visual areas is increased as a function of the specific state of attention (e.g., attend face versus attend motion). Earlier we described the work of Bosman and Fries, and how it revealed the mechanism by which neurons at different levels of the visual hierarchy (i.e., V1 to V4) could interact via neuronal synchrony of oscillatory signals. Does this inter-area synchrony in visual cortex arise from intrinsic properties, or is it biased by top-down control signals? Further, could oscillatory synchrony also support the interactions between frontal cortex and visual cortex? Let's consider some evidence.

Georgia Gregoriou, Robert Desimone, and their colleagues (2009) investigated whether the FEF is a source of enhanced neuronal synchrony effects in area V4 during spatial attention, by simultaneously recording spikes and local field potentials from FEF and V4 in two monkeys while the monkeys performed a covert attention task. The researchers found that when the monkeys attended to a stimulus that was in the receptive field of both the FEF and V4, oscillatory coupling between the two areas was enhanced, especially at gamma frequencies. The timing of the recorded signals indicated that the coupling was initiated by FEF. The researchers speculated that coupling at gamma frequencies may optimize the postsynaptic impact of spikes from one visual cortical area on the other, the end result being that communication in the visual cortex is improved with attention.

Another study from the same lab investigated the neural responses when we attend object features that cannot be spatially separated (Baldauf and Desimone, 2014). In this study the researchers used the superimposed face–house stimuli as in Figure 7.37a. The stimuli phased in and out, and the volunteers were cued to attend to either the face or the house and detect an occasional target. Using MEG and fMRI, the researchers found that a particular region in the prefrontal cortex (PFC)—the inferior frontal junction (IFJ)—played an important role in the top-down control of feature-based attention. As expected, attention to faces enhanced the sensory responses in the FFA, and attention to houses enhanced sensory responses in the PPA.

Of interest to us here, depending on whether a face or a house was attended, the increases in sensory responses in the FFA or PPA were accompanied by induced gamma synchrony between the IFJ and either the FFA or the PPA, and the IFJ appeared to be the driver of the synchrony. The researchers note that these two studies demonstrate striking parallels in neural mechanisms: In both, the PFC seems to be the source of top-down biasing signals, with the FEF providing signals for spatial attention and the IFJ providing signals for object or feature attention. (Could periodic stimulation of the frontal cortex increase our attention and help us concentrate? See **Box 7.1**.)

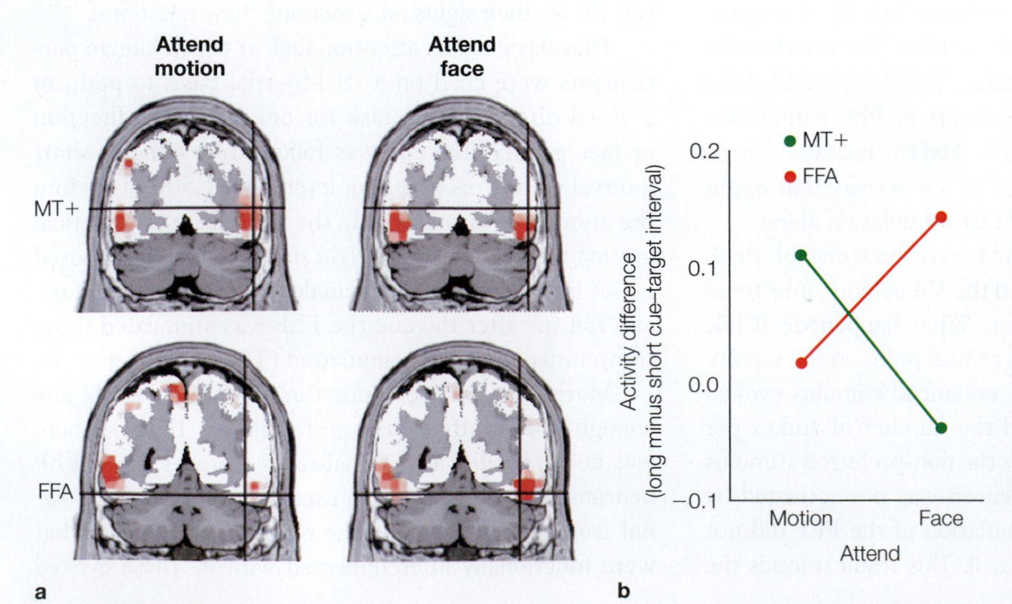

FIGURE 7.43 Impulses from the FEF code information about the task that is to be performed. (a) Coronal sections through a template brain, showing activations in the posterior brain regions (in red) coding motion (MT+; top row at crosshairs) and faces (FFA; bottom row at crosshairs) that were induced by TMS to FEF when participants were attending motion (left) and attending faces (right). The maximum activations are seen in MT+ when attending motion (top left) and in the FFA when attending faces (bottom right). (b) Graph of the differential activity evoked in MT+ and FFA when attending motion and faces.

BOX 7.1 | HOT SCIENCE

A Thinking Cap?

You get to the library early, find an empty table, and begin working on a paper. As the library starts filling up, students walking by or sitting at your table distract you. In order to pursue your goal of finishing a paper, you have to overcome distraction by these variously salient stimuli. Increasing evidence suggests that disorders of attentional control and lapses of attention result from dysfunction in the frontal cortex. In fact, activity in your middle frontal gyrus (MFG) predicts the likelihood that a salient distractor will grab your attention. The more active this region is, the less likely it is that the distractor will hijack it (Leber, 2010). If only you could just put on a "thinking cap" to crank up the activity of this brain region to better focus your attention!

Joshua Cosman, Priyaka Atreya, and Geoff Woodman (2015) thought they might be able to improve attentional ability by using a cheap, portable, and unlikely tool: transcranial direct current stimulation (tDCS; see Chapter 3), which passes a tiny current through the scalp and skull into the brain, akin to a DIY setup using a simple battery and electrodes pasted on the scalp. As if in a scene from *Star Wars: The Last Jedi*, they asked volunteers to wear a device that placed electrodes over the frontal cortex. Then, in different conditions intended to either inhibit or excite neuronal activity in the MFG (compared to a sham, no-stimulation control condition), they stimulated the voluntary participants' brains (**Figure 7.44a**). After the stimulation, the volunteers performed three blocks of an attention capture task (**Figure 7.44b**).

Then, something seemingly magical happened: Excitation of the MFG neurons resulted in the participants being *less* distracted (less slowed in their reaction times to targets) by task-irrelevant stimuli during the task. The effect lasted about 15 minutes, being observed in only the first block of trials of the task, and only when the current was applied in the direction that was designed to excite MFG neurons (**Figure 7.44c**)—but it was real. Though this technology sounds a little like science fiction, perhaps it will someday take the form of a wearable gadget that periodically buzzes you to enhance attention. A "thinking cap" may be available sooner than we think!

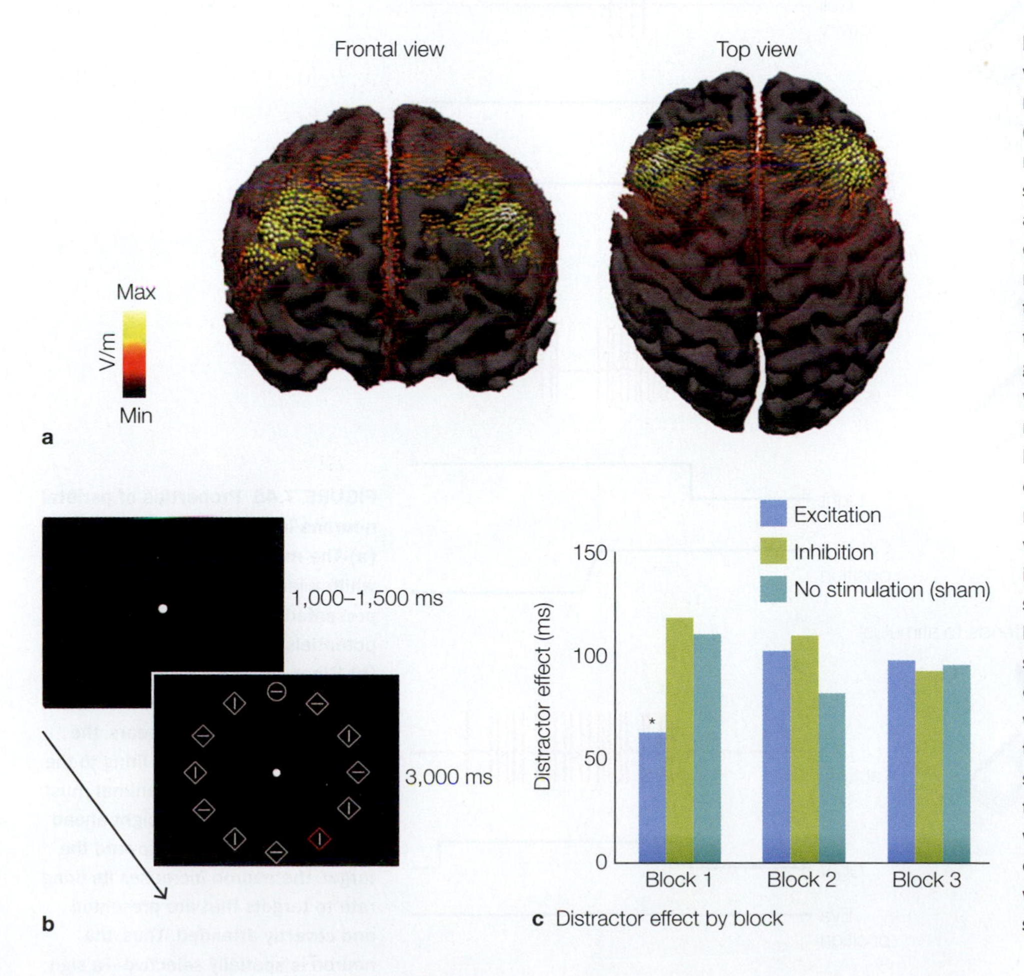

FIGURE 7.44 Brain stimulation with small electrical current reduces visual distraction. (a) Estimated distribution of current flow in the brain during active stimulation. (b) Volunteers were asked to search for the item that differed in shape from all other members of the array and to report the orientation of the line inside that shape. These items were all gray. In half the trials, a distractor was present that differed in color, randomly presenting as red, green, blue, or yellow. (c) The distractor effect is plotted as the difference in reaction time for distractor present versus absent (i.e., degree of slowing) under excitatory, inhibitory, and sham stimulation conditions. The benefit of excitatory stimulation is seen as a reduction in the slowing of reaction time by distractors (bar with asterisk at far left), meaning that the participants were not as slowed in their responses when distractors were present. This benefit was seen only during the first block of trials, which was completed within the first 15 minutes after stimulation.

THE PARIETAL CORTEX AND CONTROL OF ATTENTION

The areas along the intraparietal sulcus (IPS) and the superior parietal lobule (SPL) in the posterior parietal lobe are the other major cortical regions that belong to the dorsal attention network (Figure 7.40). The parietal lobe has extensive connections with subcortical areas like the pulvinar and the frontal cortex, as well as other parts of the visual pathways. It contains multiple representations of space. What is the role of the parietal cortex in attention?

Numerous physiological studies in monkeys have found that attentional shifts are correlated with significant changes in the activity of parietal neurons. Whenever attention is directed to a stimulus, the firing rates of primate parietal neurons increase when using the stimulus as a target for a saccade or a reaching movement (Mountcastle, 1976) and when covertly discriminating its features (Wurtz et al., 1982). When a monkey is merely waiting for the next trial in a sequence of trials, however, the parietal neurons do not usually show an enhanced response to visual stimuli in their receptive fields (**Figure 7.45**).

Most studies of attention using single-neuron recording and functional imaging have focused on the intraparietal area, especially the IPS and a subregion within the IPS, known in monkeys as the lateral intraparietal area, or LIP (**Figure 7.46**). This region is involved in saccadic eye movements and in visuospatial attention. To investigate what role LIP neurons play in visuospatial attention, James Bisley and Michael Goldberg (2006) collected intracranial recordings of LIP neurons from monkeys engaged in a discrimination task. The monkeys were to detect the properties of a stimulus at a covertly attended location to determine whether to execute a planned saccade toward that attended location. While the animal was covertly attending the cued location, occasional distractor stimuli appeared elsewhere. LIP neuronal activity when a distractor was present was compared with activity when there was no distractor. These results were also compared to the monkey's performance (i.e., its contrast detection threshold; **Figure 7.47**).

The best performance was observed when the target feature to be discriminated occurred in the location where

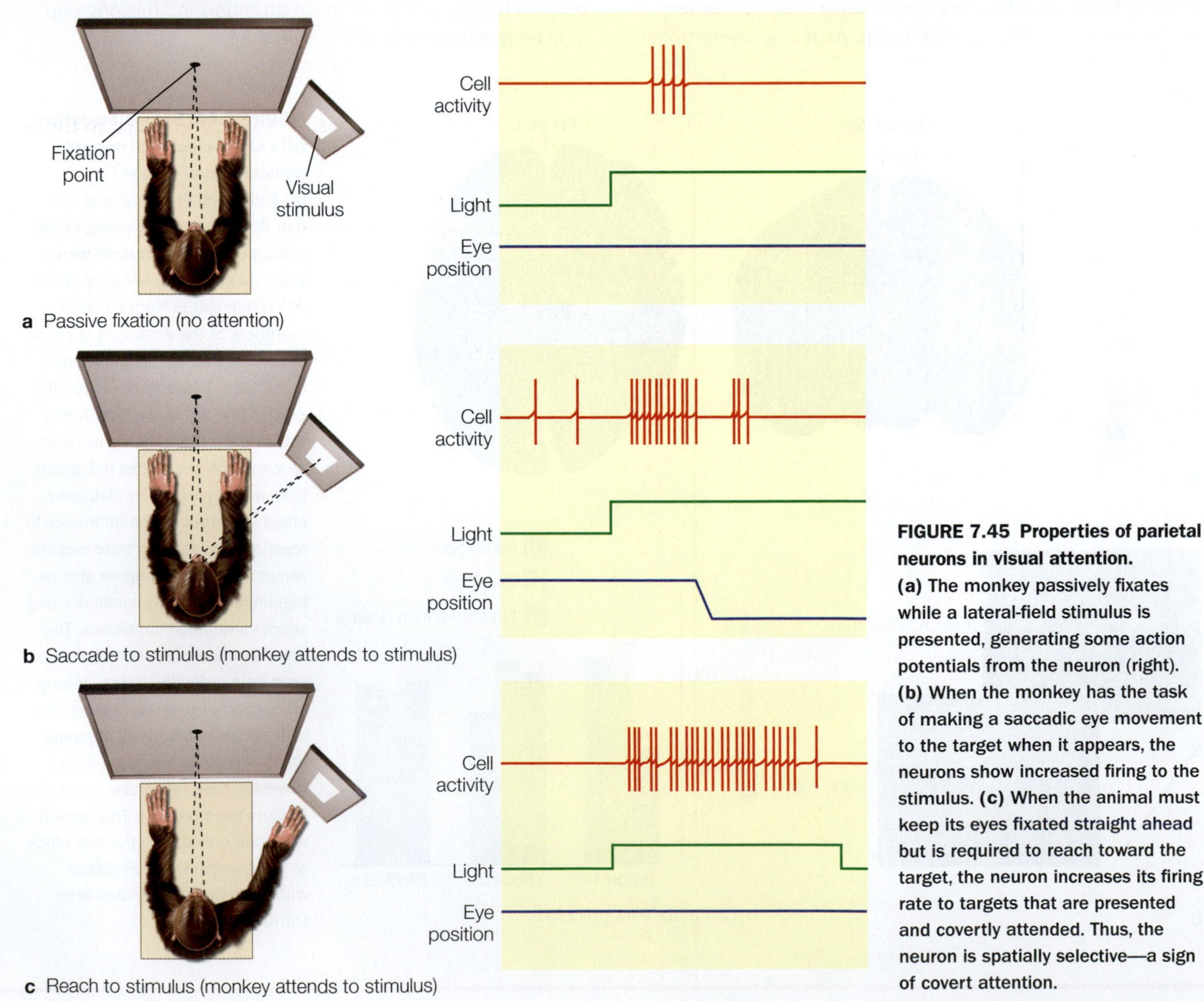

FIGURE 7.45 Properties of parietal neurons in visual attention. **(a)** The monkey passively fixates while a lateral-field stimulus is presented, generating some action potentials from the neuron (right). **(b)** When the monkey has the task of making a saccadic eye movement to the target when it appears, the neurons show increased firing to the stimulus. **(c)** When the animal must keep its eyes fixated straight ahead but is required to reach toward the target, the neuron increases its firing rate to targets that are presented and covertly attended. Thus, the neuron is spatially selective—a sign of covert attention.

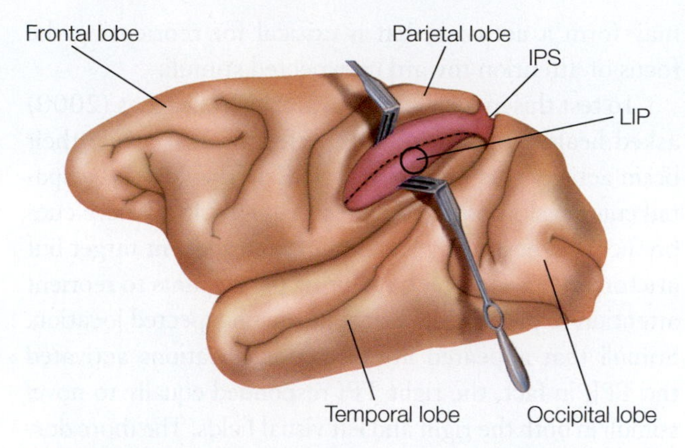

FIGURE 7.46 Location of the intraparietal area involved in visuospatial attention.
Left lateral view of a macaque brain. The intraparietal sulcus (IPS) in the parietal lobe is shown retracted to reveal the depths of the sulcus, which contains several distinct areas. One of these distinct areas is the lateral intraparietal area (LIP). Neurons in the LIP receive inputs from and project to neurons in the frontal eye field and the superior colliculus. In humans, functional imaging data suggest that the functional equivalent of the monkey LIP is also located in the IPS, but along its medial aspect.

LIP neuronal activity was higher. Put another way, if neuronal activity was highest at the attended location, performance was better for targets presented to that attended location. But if a distractor had been presented and neuronal activity had temporarily switched to be higher at another region of the LIP (corresponding to where the distractor was presented), then target discrimination was better at that (supposedly unattended) location.

For example, Figure 7.47 plots the results from one monkey. Right after the distractor appeared, probe performance was better (Figure 7.47a; the red curve is below the blue curve) at the location of the distractor. But at about 400 ms (yellow shading), the curves cross. For the remainder of the plot the performance is better at the saccade target location (the blue curve is now below the red curve). These data tell us that the distractor briefly captured attention to its location (Figure 7.28), but then attention returned to the location of the saccade goal.

What were the neurons doing during this period? In Figure 7.47b, the red curve plots the neuronal responses evoked by the distractor stimulus, and the blue curve shows responses to the earlier saccade goal stimulus at the attended location. When the neuronal response to the distractor is larger than to the saccade goal stimulus, behavioral performance (Figure 7.47a) is better for the probe at the distractor location. But when the neuronal response to the distractor drops below that for the saccade goal stimulus, at about 400 ms, performance crosses back in favor of the attended location for probe discrimination.

Thus, by looking at the pattern of activity over the extent of the LIP, the researchers could actually predict the monkey's performance. By inference, they also could predict the momentary locus of the animal's visual attention. Bisley and Goldberg (2006) interpreted these findings as evidence that activity in the LIP provides a salience or priority map.

A salience map combines the maps of different individual features (color, orientation, movement, etc.) of a stimulus, resulting in an overall topographic map that shows how conspicuous a stimulus is, compared to those surrounding it (Koch & Ullman, 1985). This map is used by the oculomotor system as a saccade goal when a saccade is appropriate (i.e., when the stimulus is highly salient). At the same time, the visual system uses this map to determine the locus of attention. Thus, it appears that the LIP, which is an area of the parietal cortex and a component of the dorsal attention system, is concerned with the location and salience of objects. Let's now turn our attention to the ventral network.

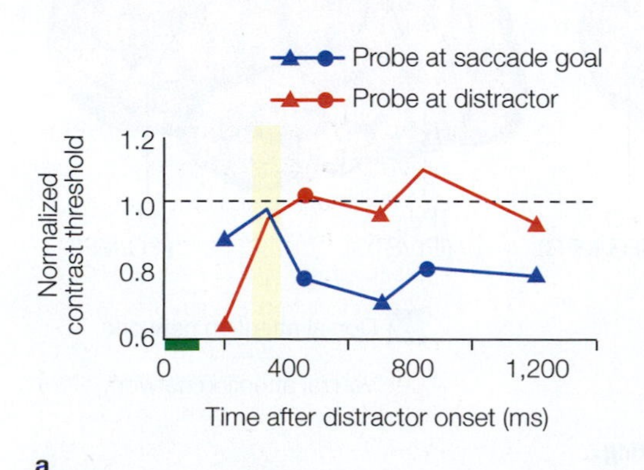

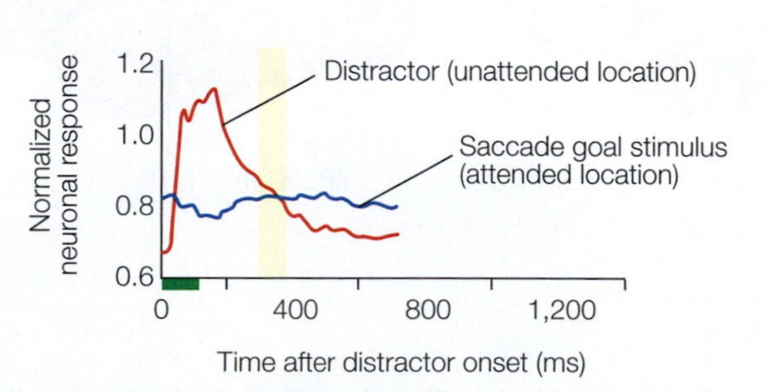

FIGURE 7.47 Behavioral and neuronal attention effects in monkey parietal cortex during visuospatial attention.
(a) Behavioral performance from one monkey. Smaller values on the *y*-axis indicate better performance because they mean that the monkey could detect the probe orientation at a lower stimulus contrast. Red curve: Probe appeared at the unattended location where the distractor had appeared. Blue curve: Probe appeared at the attended location (i.e., the saccade target). **(b)** Neuronal responses from the same monkey.

The Ventral Attention Network

So far, we have learned that the dorsal attention network is involved in focusing attention on items related to our current behavioral goals. Sometimes, however, the events that attract our attention away from a current goal should not be ignored. If a fire alarm goes off while you are intensely focused on reading and understanding this chapter, your attention should certainly shift to the alarm! According to Corbetta and his colleagues, this reaction to salient, unexpected, or novel stimuli is supported by the **ventral attention network.** While the dorsal attention network keeps you focused on this book, the ventral attention network is standing guard, ready to take over if any significant stimuli are detected in any sensory modality.

Corbetta took as a starting point the observation that neglect patients can detect a visual stimulus in the visual hemifield (left hemifield) opposite to their lesion (right hemisphere) when cued to its location, but if their attention is focused on a different location (right hemifield), then they are slow to respond and may even fail to detect an opposite-hemifield target. Structural imaging in patients has shown that in posterior cortex, such lesions are centered on the temporoparietal junction (TPJ), the region at the border of the inferior parietal lobe and the posterior superior temporal lobe. In anterior cortex, lesions are typically located in regions more ventral to those of the dorsal attention network in the inferior and middle frontal gyri (**Figure 7.48a**). These findings suggested that these more ventral right-hemisphere regions may form a network that is critical for reorienting the focus of attention toward unexpected stimuli.

To test this model, Corbetta and his colleagues (2000) asked healthy participants to perform a task while their brain activity was imaged with fMRI. They used the spatial cuing tasks described earlier (Figure 7.15), where cues predict the most likely location of a subsequent target but are sometimes incorrect, requiring participants to reorient attention to process the target at the unexpected location. Stimuli that appeared in unexpected locations activated the TPJ; in fact, the right TPJ responded equally to novel stimuli in both the right and left visual fields. The more dorsal intraparietal sulcus, however, was uniquely active when a cued location was attended and received maintained attention before the target was presented. These findings indicate that distinct parietal regions, and related cortical areas, mediate these different attentional properties.

Additional imaging studies conducted by the group identified what we now refer to as the ventral attention network. It is strongly lateralized to the right hemisphere, and it includes the TPJ and the inferior and middle frontal gyri of the ventral frontal cortex (**Figure 7.48b**). Some have likened the activity of the ventral attention network to a circuit breaker, interrupting the current attentional focus established by the goal-directed dorsal network.

Of course, the dorsal and ventral networks interact with one another (**Figure 7.48c**). Corbetta and colleagues have suggested that the dorsal attention network, with its salience maps in the parietal cortex, provides the TPJ with

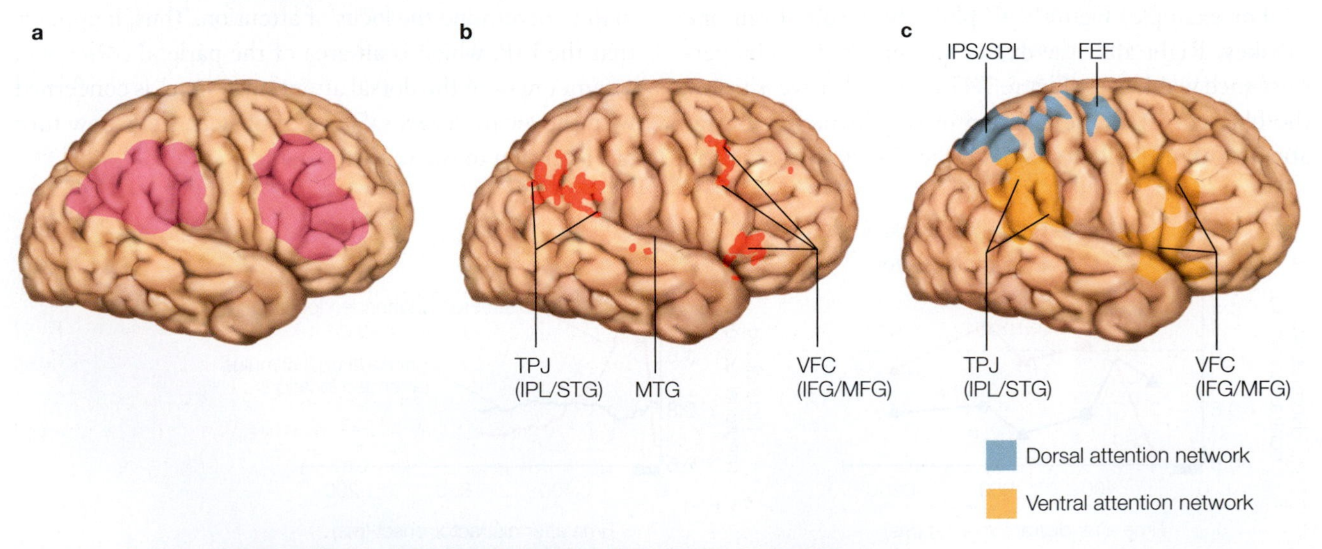

FIGURE 7.48 Brain regions involved in detection of novelty and attentional reorienting.
(a) Regions of cortex known from neurological and neuropsychological studies to result in neglect when lesioned. **(b)** This view of the right hemisphere shows regions of the temporoparietal junction (TPJ), middle temporal gyrus (MTG), and ventral frontal cortex (VFC) that were activated when participants received an invalid trial in which a cue incorrectly predicted the target location. **(c)** Both attention networks shown together, as described by fMRI studies. The dorsal attention network is shown in blue; the right ventral attention network, in yellow. FEF = frontal eye field; IFG = inferior frontal gyrus; IPL = inferior parietal lobule; IPS = intraparietal sulcus; MFG = middle frontal gyrus; SPL = superior parietal lobule; STG = superior temporal gyrus.

behaviorally relevant information about stimuli, such as their visual salience. Together, the dorsal and ventral attention networks cooperate to make sure attention is focused on behaviorally relevant information, with the dorsal attention network focusing attention on relevant locations and potential targets, and the ventral attention network signaling the presence of salient, unexpected, or novel stimuli, enabling us to reorient the focus of our attention.

Subcortical Components of Attentional Control Networks

Our discussion of attentional control of cortical mechanisms has been motivated to a great extent by evidence from patients with brain damage, such as those with neglect. In addition to cortical damage, though, subcortical damage is also well known to produce deficits in attention (Rafal and Posner, 1987) and clinical neglect (Karnath et al., 2004). What subcortical structures play significant roles in attentional control and selection in sensory cortex, and how do they contribute to our attentional abilities?

SUPERIOR COLLICULUS The **superior colliculus** is a midbrain structure made up of many layers of neurons, receiving direct inputs from the retina and other sensory systems, as well as from the basal ganglia and the cerebral cortex. As described in Chapter 2, there is one superior colliculus on each side of the midbrain, each receiving input primarily from the contralateral side of space. The superior colliculus projects multiple outputs to the thalamus and the motor system that, among other things, control the eye movements involved in changing the focus of overt attention. Since overt and covert attention are necessarily related, investigation of the role of the superior colliculus in covert attention has a long history.

In the early 1970s, Robert Wurtz and his colleagues discovered visually responsive neurons in the superior colliculus that were activated depending on *how* monkeys responded to stimuli. The neurons showed increased firing only when the animal was required both to attend to the location of the stimulus and also to prepare to make an eye movement toward the target. This finding led to the proposal that superior colliculus neurons do not participate in voluntary visual selective attention per se, but are merely part of the eye movement system, having a role in preparing to make overt eye movements to a location, but not in covert mechanisms of visual attention. While this is true for some neurons in the superior colliculus, it is not true for all neurons located there.

Desimone and colleagues (1990) investigated the role of the superior colliculus in attention by using deactivation methods in monkeys performing a target discrimination task. They injected a GABA agonist, which inhibits neuronal firing, into small zones of the superior colliculus corresponding to the receptive-field location of a target stimulus. They observed that this local deactivation of superior colliculus neurons reduced the animal's performance in discriminating the designated targets, but only if a distractor stimulus was also present somewhere in the visual field. This pattern led to speculation that the superior colliculus may indeed participate in covert attention (during distraction), as well as in overt eye movement planning.

William Newsome and his colleagues (Müller et al., 2005) performed a more direct test using electrical microstimulation. They trained monkeys to perform a task in which they had to detect and indicate the direction of motion of a small patch of dots in a larger array of flickering dots. The researchers then inserted an electrode to locally stimulate neurons in the superior colliculus. If they used a strong current, above the threshold that evokes an overt eye movement, they could see where the monkey's eyes moved (using eye-tracking methods) and thereby identify the region of visual space that those neurons coded. (Each superior colliculus contains a topographic map of the contralateral visual hemifield.) If they used a weak, subthreshold current, then the neurons were excited but an eye movement was not triggered.

They reasoned that if subthreshold stimulation mimicked the effects of covert attention on the neurons, then they should see improved discrimination of motion targets in the region coded by the neurons compared to other regions of the visual field (or to no stimulation at all). That, indeed, is what they found: The animal's performance at discriminating the direction of motion (left versus right) was improved when stimulated in the superior colliculus region corresponding to the visual field location of the motion target. It was as though the electrical stimulation had caused a shift of spatial attention to that location in space.

Gattass and Desimone (2014) replicated these basic findings in a different task and also showed that the superficial layers of the superior colliculus were more critical for this effect (the deep layers are more involved in saccadic eye movements). In addition, when monkeys were trained to attend a stimulus at one location and to ignore a distractor stimulus elsewhere in the visual field, stimulation of the superior colliculus at a site that corresponded to the distractor that was supposed to be ignored could cause a shift of attention to the distractor.

In humans, functional imaging has shown that the superior colliculus is activated during spatial attention. For example, Jin Fan and his colleagues have shown that the superior colliculus is activated along with structures of the dorsal attention network when participants orient covert spatial attention to an attention-directing cue (Xuan et al., 2016). Experimental studies in patients with damage to the superior colliculus also demonstrate a causal role in covert attention mechanisms.

Patients with degeneration of the superior colliculus (and parts of the basal ganglia) suffer from a disease known as *progressive supranuclear palsy (PSP)*. When tested in cued attention paradigms, these patients have difficulty *shifting* their attention in response to a cue, and are slowed in responding to cued targets (especially in the vertical direction; Rafal et al., 1988). This pattern is different from that of patients with cortical lesions that cause neglect, whose most profound deficit in cued attention tasks is significant slowing in responding to uncued stimuli (invalid targets) when first cued elsewhere (in line with damage to the right ventral attention system).

Finally, the superior colliculus also appears to be involved in inhibitory processes during visual search. This association was demonstrated by a patient with a rare injury to one superior colliculus (Sapir et al., 1999). This patient had a reduced inhibition of return (IOR) for inputs to the lesioned colliculus. However, although the superior colliculus is involved in IOR, it in turn appears to depend on being activated by input from the frontal eye fields and the parietal cortex (parts of the dorsal network) in the hemisphere ipsilateral to the site of IOR (Ro et al., 2003). Taken together, the animal and human findings clearly identify the superior colliculus as a participant in the brain's attentional control mechanisms.

PULVINAR OF THE THALAMUS One of the many outputs from the superior colliculus goes to the inferior pulvinar. Located in a posterior region of the thalamus, the **pulvinar** (**Figure 7.49**) is composed of several cytoarchitectonically distinct subnuclei, each of which has specific inputs and outputs to cortical areas of all the lobes. For example, there are no direct connections to the ventrolateral pulvinar (VLP) from the parietal cortex, but there are with the dorsomedial pulvinar. Also, ventral-stream visual areas V1, V2, V4, and IT project topographically to the VLP, which in turn sends projections back to these visual areas, forming a pulvinar–cortical loop. Each of these subnuclei performs different functions (Petersen et al., 1985), not all of which are understood.

The pulvinar has visually responsive neurons that exhibit selectivity for color, motion, and orientation, but it is not considered part of the classical retinogeniculostriate pathway of the visual hierarchy. That is, unlike the lateral geniculate nucleus of the thalamus, which serves as a relay between the retina and primary visual cortex, the pulvinar does not receive direct inputs from the retina. It does, however, receive visual inputs from the superior colliculus, which receives inputs from the retina, and these same pulvinar neurons project to specific cortical targets directly, such as motion area MT. Pulvinar neurons show enhanced activity when a stimulus is the target of

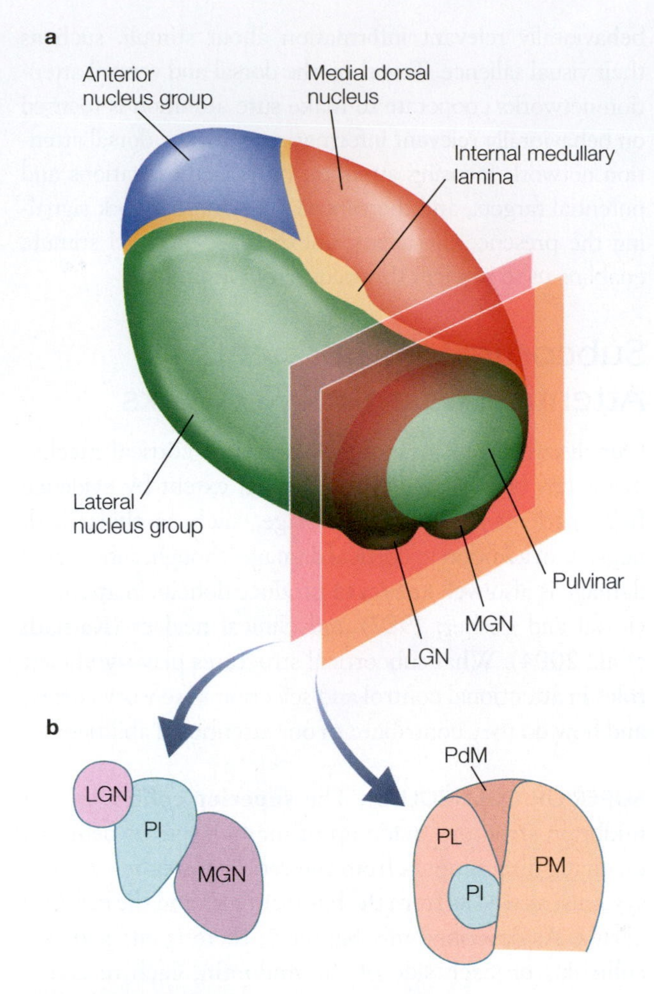

FIGURE 7.49 Anatomical diagram of the thalamus, showing the pulvinar.
(a) This diagram of the entire left thalamus shows the divisions of the major groups of nuclei, and the relationships between the visual lateral geniculate nucleus (LGN) and the pulvinar, and between the auditory medial geniculate nucleus (MGN) and the pulvinar. **(b)** These cross sections through the pulvinar show at anterior levels the LGN and MGN; and at more posterior levels, the lateral (PL), dorsomedial (PdM), medial (PM), and inferior (PI) subdivisions of the pulvinar.

a saccadic eye movement or when a stimulus is attended without eye movements toward the target. Thus, this structure may be involved in both voluntary and reflexive attention.

To figure out whether and how the pulvinar functions in attentional control, Steve Petersen, David Lee Robinson, and their colleagues investigated cells in the *dorsomedial pulvinar*, which has connections with the parietal cortex (Petersen et al., 1987, 1992). They administered microinjections of the GABA agonist *muscimol*, a drug that temporarily inhibits neuronal activity, to the pulvinar of monkeys to investigate how pulvinar inactivation would affect the animals' attentional ability (**Figure 7.50**). The monkeys' sensory processing remained intact, but they had difficulty orienting attention covertly to targets in the visual

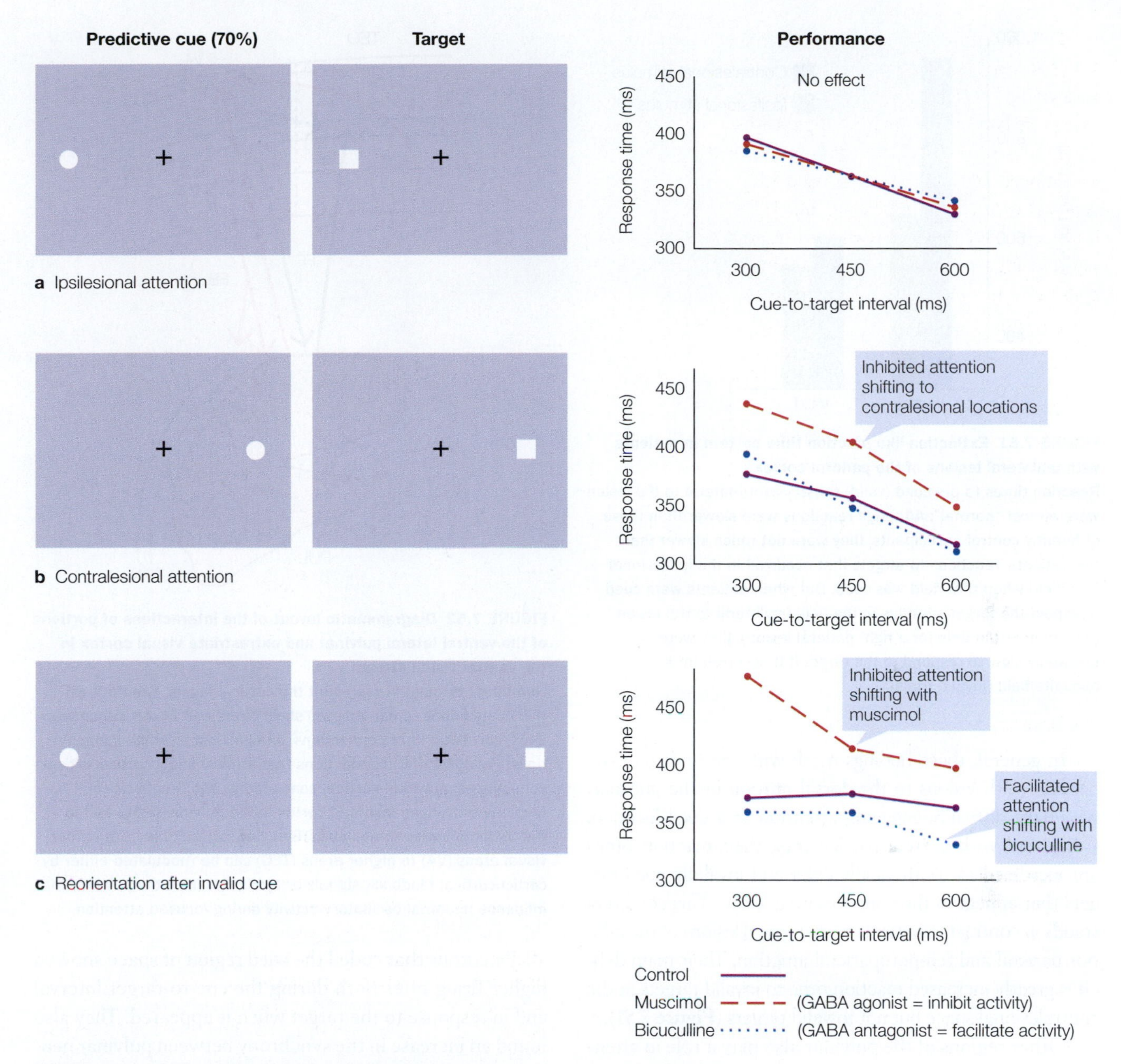

FIGURE 7.50 Effects on behavior when the left dorsomedial region of the pulvinar is injected with GABA agonists and antagonists.
The trial types—predictive peripheral cue (left column) and target (middle column)—correspond to the data presented on the right. The measure is response time to target detection as a function of cue-to-target interval (ms). **(a)** When animals had to direct attention in the direction ipsilesional to the injected pulvinar, the drugs had no effect. **(b)** When they were directing attention contralesionally, deactivation of the pulvinar with muscimol resulted in poorer (slower) behavioral responses. **(c)** Facilitation of neuronal activity with bicuculline resulted in improved (faster) behavioral responses when attention had to be reoriented into the contralesional hemifield following an invalid cue.

field contralateral to the injection, as well as difficulty filtering distracting information. When competing distractors were present in the visual field, they had difficulty discriminating color or form.

These attention impairments are similar to what is seen with parietal cortex deactivation. Petersen and colleagues also showed that when a different drug, the GABA antagonist *bicuculline*, was administered, the monkeys readily directed their attention covertly to contralesional targets. Hence, cells in the dorsomedial pulvinar appear to play a major role in covert spatial attention and the filtering of stimuli, presumably via its interactions with portions of the parietal cortex that are part of the dorsal attentional control network.

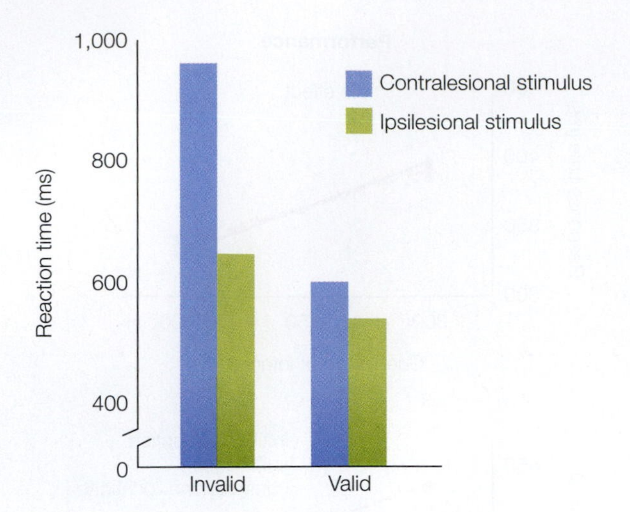

FIGURE 7.51 Extinction-like reaction time pattern in patients with unilateral lesions of the parietal cortex.
Reaction times to pre-cued (valid) targets contralateral to the lesion were almost "normal": Although reactions were slower than those of healthy control participants, they were not much slower than the patients' reactions to targets that occurred in the ipsilesional hemifield when that field was cued. But when patients were cued to expect the target stimulus in the field ipsilateral to the lesion (e.g., right visual field for a right parietal lesion), they were unusually slow to respond to the target if it occurred in the opposite field (invalid trials).

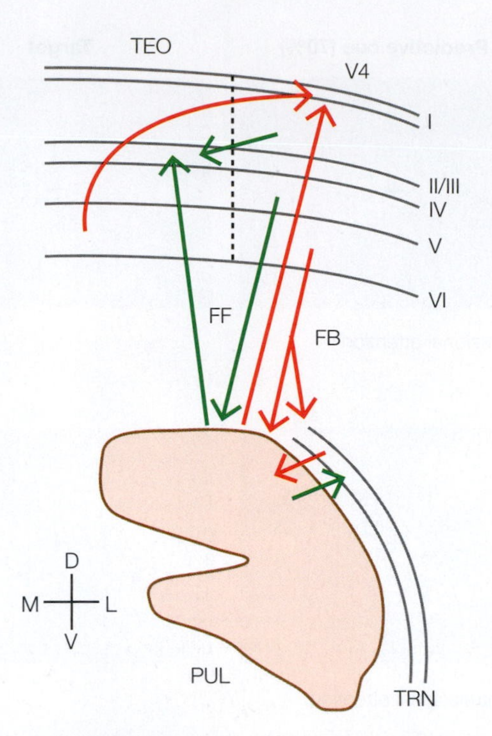

FIGURE 7.52 Diagrammatic layout of the interactions of portions of the ventral lateral pulvinar and extrastriate visual cortex in the ventral visual stream.
Numbers I through VI represent the cortical layers. Feedforward (FF) connections (green arrows) show direct corticocortical connections, corticopulvinar connections, and pulvinar–cortical connections. Feedback (FB) connections (red arrows) show corticocortical connections, pulvinar–cortical connections, and feedback connections from deep layers of cortex to the pulvinar (PUL) and to the thalamic reticular nucleus (TRN). Sensory signals from earlier visual areas (V4) to higher areas (TEO) can be modulated either by corticocortical feedback signals or by signals from the pulvinar that influence neuronal oscillatory activity during focused attention.

In general, these findings mesh with the findings from patients with lesions to the dorsal portion of the pulvinar, who have difficulty engaging attention at a cued location. Compared with normal participants, their reaction times are increased for both validly cued and invalidly cued targets that appear in the contralesional space. This condition stands in contrast to patients with cortical lesions of the inferior parietal and temporoparietal junction. Their main deficit is greatly increased reaction time to invalid targets in the contralesional space but not to valid targets (**Figure 7.51**).

Other regions of the pulvinar also play a role in attention modulation in visual cortex. Yuri Saalmann, Sabine Kastner, and their colleagues (Saalmann et al., 2012) were interested in the VLP and its feedforward and feedback connection loops between higher-order visual cortices V4 and the temporo-occipital area, or TEO, a higher-order visual area located just anterior to V4 in the ventral visual pathway (**Figure 7.52**).

Because of the reciprocal connections with the ventral visual stream, the researchers thought the VLP might play a part in synchronizing processing across the visual cortex during selective attention. They ran a study in monkeys, first using diffusion tensor imaging (DTI) to identify the regions of the pulvinar that were anatomically interconnected with V4 and TEO. Then they recorded neuronal firing and local field potentials simultaneously in the three structures while the animals performed a cued spatial attention task. They found that VLP neurons that coded the cued region of space showed higher firing rates both during the cue-to-target interval and in response to the target when it appeared. They also found an increase in the synchrony between pulvinar neurons during focused attention.

The researchers wondered whether this pulvinar activity was influencing how the visual cortex was processing attended versus ignored information. To investigate this question, they reasoned that because of the pulvinar's interconnections with V4 and TEO, they should record the local field potentials in these regions and then look for evidence that attention influences the V4-to-TEO synchrony. They found it: Synchrony was higher in the alpha (8–15 Hz) frequency range and in the 30- to 60-Hz band of the gamma frequency ranges (**Figure 7.53**). Further analyses provided compelling evidence that the pulvinar modulates the synchronization between cortical areas according to the direction of spatial attention.

Huihui Zhou, Robert Schafer, and Robert Desimone (2016) directly tested the causal influence of the VLP on cortical responses by reversibly deactivating it

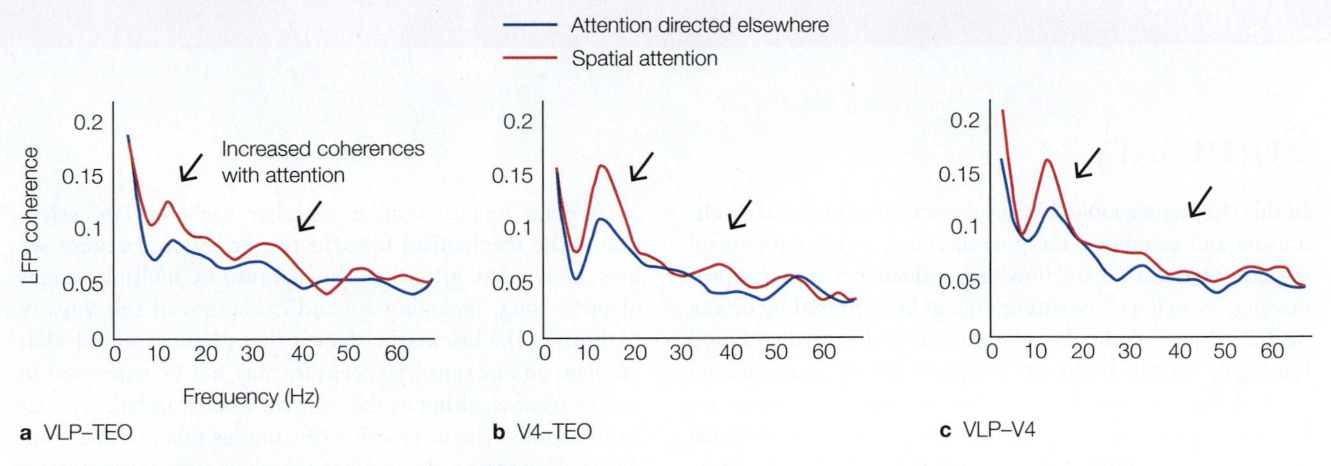

FIGURE 7.53 Synchronization of signals with attention.
Plots of the coherence between local field potentials (LFPs) recorded in a monkey when the receptive-field locations of the neurons were the focus of spatial attention (red) versus when attention was directed elsewhere in the visual field (blue). Plots show the effects of attention on coherences between the VLP and visual area TEO (a), between visual area V4 and the TEO (b), and between the VLP and V4 (c). The coherence of local neuronal field potentials between interconnected brain regions (visual cortex and pulvinar) goes up with spatial attention (red traces) in the low-frequency alpha-band range (8–15 Hz) and higher-frequency gamma-band range (30–60 Hz). Further analysis reveals that the pulvinar is the source of control influences leading to attention-related increases in synchronization in the ventral visual pathways.

with muscimol. Then they recorded from corresponding V4 and IT neurons before and after the inactivation in the affected and nonaffected portions of the visual field to see the effects as monkeys performed a spatial attention task. They found that in the sites not affected by muscimol, no changes were observed in the monkeys' task performance. But in the regions of space affected by the deactivated pulvinar, the animals were profoundly impaired at performing the task. The researchers also found that pulvinar deactivation reduced the effects of attention on neuronal synchronization. This finding provides additional evidence that the pulvinar plays a critical role in attentional control by coordinating the synchronous activity of interconnected brain regions in the ventral visual pathway.

Given what we have learned about the role of the dorsal attention network (frontal and parietal cortex) in top-down attentional control, the work studying the pulvinar suggests that frontal and parietal cortex exerts control over sensory processing via interactions with the pulvinar. However, the precise mechanisms of the interactions between top-down cortical control over attention and the pulvinar remain incompletely understood.

TAKE-HOME MESSAGES

- Current evidence suggests that two separate frontoparietal cortical systems direct different attentional control operations during orienting: a *dorsal attention network*, concerned primarily with orienting attention, and a *ventral attention network*, concerned with the nonspatial aspects of attention and alerting. The two systems interact and cooperate to produce normal behavior.
- The dorsal frontoparietal attention network is bilateral and includes the superior frontal cortex, inferior parietal cortex (located in the posterior parietal lobe), superior temporal cortex, and portions of the posterior cingulate cortex and insula.
- The ventral network is strongly lateralized to the right hemisphere and includes the posterior parietal cortex of the temporoparietal junction (TPJ) and the ventral frontal cortex (VFC) made up of the inferior and middle frontal gyri.
- In addition, there are subcortical networks that include the superior colliculi and the pulvinar of the thalamus.

Summary

In this chapter we looked at key aspects of attentional mechanisms and examined the goal-directed, top-down control systems of attention and how they influence perceptual processing, as well as how attention can be captured by events in the sensory world. The picture we find is of distributed but highly specific brain systems participating in attentional control. The roles and limits of these systems in attention are becoming more clearly defined as we combine attentional theory, experimental and cognitive psychological findings, and neurophysiological approaches in healthy participants and patients with brain damage.

Systems for controlling attention include portions of the parietal lobe, temporal cortex, frontal cortex, and subcortical structures; these constitute the *sources* of attentional control. The result in visual processing—which has been our example system—is that, in the sensory pathways, we observe modulations in the activity of neurons as they analyze and encode perceptual information as a function of their relevance. These areas affected by attention are the *sites* of attentional selection.

We no longer wonder whether early or late selection is the mechanism for selective attention, because we now know that attention can operate at multiple stages of processing, including subcortical stages of the sensory pathways. The fascinating fact is that physical stimuli that impinge on our sensory receptors may not be expressed in our awareness, either at the time they occur or later via our recollections. The interaction of stimulus salience and goal-directed attention determines which inputs reach awareness and which do not.

Attentional phenomena are diverse and entail many brain computations and mechanisms. When these are compromised by damage or disease, the results can be devastating for the individual. Cognitive neuroscience is vigorously carving away at the physiological and computational underpinnings of these phenomena, with the dual goals of providing a complete account of how the healthy brain functions, and shedding light on how to ameliorate attentional deficits in all their forms.

Key Terms

arousal (p. 277)
bottlenecks (p. 284)
covert attention (p. 282)
dorsal attention network (p. 309)
early selection (p. 284)
endogenous attention (p. 282)
endogenous cuing (p. 285)
exogenous attention (p. 282)
exogenous cuing (p. 296)
extinction (p. 281)
feature integration theory of attention (p. 298)
inhibition of return (IOR) (p. 296)
late selection (p. 284)
neglect (p. 278)
overt attention (p. 282)
pulvinar (p. 318)
reflexive attention (p. 282)
reflexive cuing (p. 296)
selective attention (p. 277)
superior colliculus (p. 317)
thalamic reticular nucleus (TRN) (p. 294)
unilateral spatial neglect (p. 278)
ventral attention network (p. 316)
visual search (p. 298)
voluntary attention (p. 282)

Think About It

1. Do we perceive everything that strikes the retina? What might be the fate of stimuli that we do not perceive but that nonetheless stimulate our sensory receptors?
2. Are the same brain mechanisms involved when we focus our intention voluntarily as when our attention is captured by a sensory event, such as a flash of light?
3. Is neglect following brain damage a deficit in perception, attention, or awareness?
4. Compare and contrast the way attention is reflected in the activity of single neurons in visual cortex versus parietal cortex. Can these differences be mapped onto the distinction between attentional control and attentional selection?
5. What brain networks support top-down control over the focus of attention, and how might these top-down influences change the way that interconnected regions of sensory cortex process information with attention?

Suggested Reading

Briggs, F., Mangun, G. R., & Usrey, W. M. (2013). Attention enhances synaptic efficacy and signal-to-noise in neural circuits. *Nature*, *499*, 476–480. doi:10.1038/nature12276

Corbetta, M., & Shulman, G. (2011). Spatial neglect and attention networks. *Annual Review of Neuroscience*, *34*, 569–599.

Hillis, A. E. (2006). Neurobiology of unilateral spatial neglect. *Neuroscientist*, *12*, 153–163.

Luck, S. J., Woodman, G. F., & Vogel, E. K. (2000). Event-related potential studies of attention. *Trends in Cognitive Sciences*, *4*, 432–440.

Mangun, G. R. (Ed.). (2012). *The neuroscience of attention: Attentional control and selection.* New York: Oxford University Press.

Moore, T. (2006). The neurobiology of visual attention: Finding sources. *Current Opinion in Neurobiology*, *16*, 1–7.

Posner, M. (2011). *Attention in a social world.* New York: Oxford University Press.

Posner, M. (2012). *Cognitive neuroscience of attention* (2nd ed.). New York: Guilford.

Rees, G., Kreiman, G., & Koch, C. (2002). Neural correlates of consciousness in humans. *Nature Reviews Neuroscience*, *3*, 261–270.

Wolfe, J. M., & Horowitz, T. S. (2004). What attributes guide the deployment of visual attention and how do they do it? *Nature Reviews Neuroscience*, *5*, 495–501.

Life's aim is an act, not a thought.

Charles Sherrington

CHAPTER

8

Action

IN JULY 1982, emergency room physicians in the San Jose, California, area were puzzled. Four patients, ranging in age from 26 to 42 years, had been seen recently at different hospitals, all presenting a similar picture: Although they were conscious, they were essentially immobile. None of them could speak, their facial expressions seemed frozen, and they showed extreme rigidity in their arms. It was as if they had each peered into Medusa's eyes and been turned into stone statues. The symptoms and their rapid onset resembled no known disease. The physicians knew they had to act fast—but without a diagnosis, they could not prescribe a treatment.

Interviews with the patients' friends and family uncovered an important clue: All four patients were heroin users. Yet their symptoms weren't those associated with a large dose of heroin, a powerful central nervous system depressant that typically causes muscular flaccidity, not rigidity. No one had seen a heroin overdose produce these effects, nor did the symptoms resemble those of other street narcotics. Furthermore, drug-using friends of the patients confirmed that this heroin had unexpectedly produced a burning sensation at the site of injection, rapidly followed by a blurring of vision, a metallic taste in the mouth, and, most troubling, an almost immediate jerking of the limbs.

Stanford University neurologist William Langston (1984) was struck by how similar the patients' symptoms were to those of a patient with advanced Parkinson's disease, a condition marked by muscular rigidity, disorders of posture, and *akinesia*, the inability to produce volitional movement (**Figure 8.1a**). In fact, everything about the patients' conditions matched this disorder except their age and the rapid onset. The onset of Parkinson's disease is gradual and rarely becomes clinically evident until a person is over the age of 45. The heroin users, however, had developed full-blown symptoms of advanced Parkinson's disease within days. Langston suspected that the patients had injected a new synthetic drug being

BIG Questions

- How do we select, plan, and execute movements?
- What cortical and subcortical computations in the sensorimotor network support the production of coordinated movement?
- How is our understanding of the neural representation of movement being used to help people who have lost the ability to use their limbs?
- What is the relationship between the ability to produce movement and the ability to understand the motor intentions of other individuals?

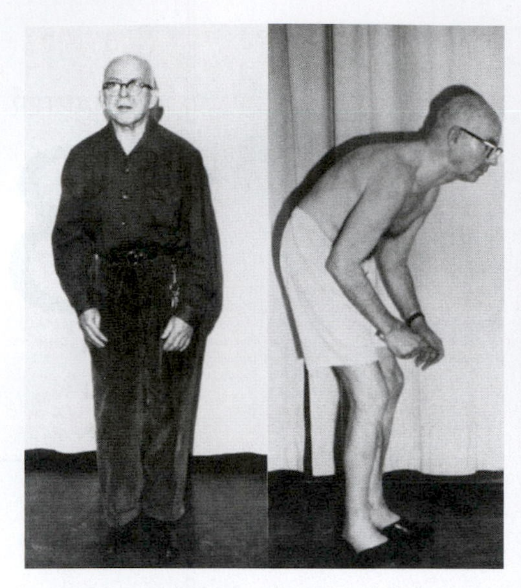

a

b

FIGURE 8.1 Parkinson's disease disrupts posture, as well as the production and flexibility of voluntary movement.
(a) This man has had Parkinson's disease for many years and is no longer able to maintain an upright posture. (b) These people developed symptoms of Parkinson's disease in their 20s and 30s, after ingesting the drug MPTP. Facial expression, including blinking, is frequently absent, giving people with Parkinson's disease the appearance of being frozen.

sold as heroin, and it had triggered the acute onset of Parkinson's disease.

This diagnosis proved to be correct. Parkinson's disease results from cell death in the region of the brain called the substantia nigra. These cells are a primary source of the neurotransmitter dopamine. Langston could not see any structural damage on CT and MRI scans, but subsequent PET studies confirmed hypometabolism of dopamine in the patients. Langston adopted the universal treatment for Parkinson's disease and administered L-dopa, a synthetic cousin of dopamine that is highly effective in compensating for the loss of endogenous dopamine. The patients immediately showed a positive response: Their muscles relaxed, and they could move in a limited way. However, the episode ultimately left them with permanent brain damage and parkinsonian symptoms (**Figure 8.1b**).

Although this incident was tragic for these patients, it triggered a breakthrough in research. The tainted drug turned out to be a previously unknown substance bearing little resemblance to heroin but sharing structural similarity with meperidine, a synthetic opioid that creates the sensations of heroin. On the basis of its chemical structure, it was given the name *MPTP* (1-methyl-4-phenyl-1,2,3,6-tetrahydropyridine).

Laboratory tests demonstrating that MPTP is selectively toxic for dopaminergic cells led to great leaps forward in medical research on the basal ganglia and on treatments for Parkinson's disease. Before the discovery of this drug, it had been difficult to induce parkinsonism in nonhuman species. Other primates do not develop Parkinson's disease naturally, perhaps because their life expectancy is shorter than ours, and the location of the substantia nigra in the brainstem makes it difficult to lesion with traditional methods. By administering MPTP, researchers could now destroy the substantia nigra and create a parkinsonian animal. Over the past 30 years, these findings have helped fuel the development of new treatment methods for Parkinson's disease.

Parkinson's disease is just one of many neurological disorders that affect our ability to produce coordinated movement. The output of the motor system, unlike an internal process such as perception or attention, can be directly observed from our actions; in some ways, this makes it easier for neurologists to make a differential diagnosis of movement disorders. For example, the symptoms of Parkinson's disease are clearly different from those related to strokes of the motor cortex or degeneration of the cerebellum. The many ways in which our motor system can be disrupted also confirm that the control of action involves a distributed network of cortical and subcortical brain structures.

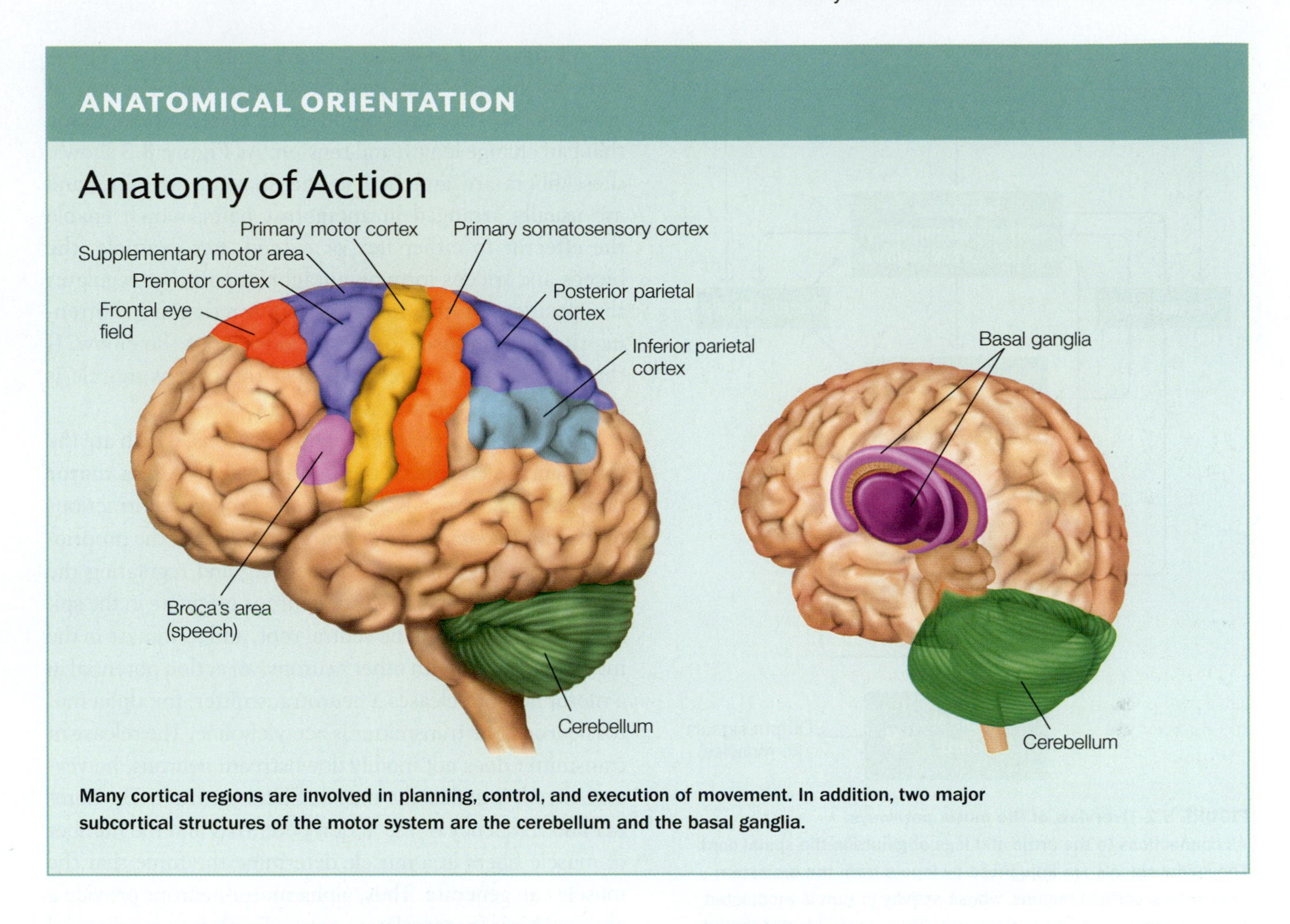

Many cortical regions are involved in planning, control, and execution of movement. In addition, two major subcortical structures of the motor system are the cerebellum and the basal ganglia.

In this chapter we start by reviewing the organization of the motor system, beginning with a look at its anatomy. Then we develop a more detailed picture from a cognitive neuroscience perspective, focusing on the computational problems faced by the motor system: What are motor neurons encoding? How are motor goals represented? How are actions planned and selected? The chapter is peppered with discussions of movement disorders to illustrate what happens when particular regions of the brain no longer function properly; also included is an overview of exciting new treatment methods for some of these disorders. We close with a look at motor learning and expertise.

8.1 The Anatomy and Control of Motor Structures

To understand motor control, we have to consider the organization and function of much of the dorsal territory of the cerebral cortex, as well as much of the subcortex. Indeed, one self-proclaimed motor chauvinist, Daniel Wolpert, claims that the only reason we have a brain is to enable movement (see his entertaining discussion at http://www.ted.com/talks/daniel_wolpert_the_real_reason_for_brains). One can certainly make a case that the association areas of the frontal lobe should also be included in the "anatomy of action" (see the discussion of prefrontal contributions to complex actions in Chapter 12).

As in perception, we can describe a hierarchical organization within the motor system (S. H. Scott, 2004). The lowest level of the hierarchy centers on the spinal cord (**Figure 8.2**). Axons from the spinal cord provide the point of contact between the nervous system and muscles, with incoming sensory signals from the body going to ascending neurons in the spinal cord, and outgoing motor signals to the muscles coming from descending spinal motor neurons. As we will see, the spinal circuitry is capable of producing simple reflexive movements.

At the top of the hierarchy are cortical regions that help translate abstract intentions and goals into movement patterns. Processing within these regions is critical for planning an action to fit with an individual's current goals, perceptual input, and past experience. Between the association areas and the spinal cord sit the primary motor cortex and brainstem structures, which,

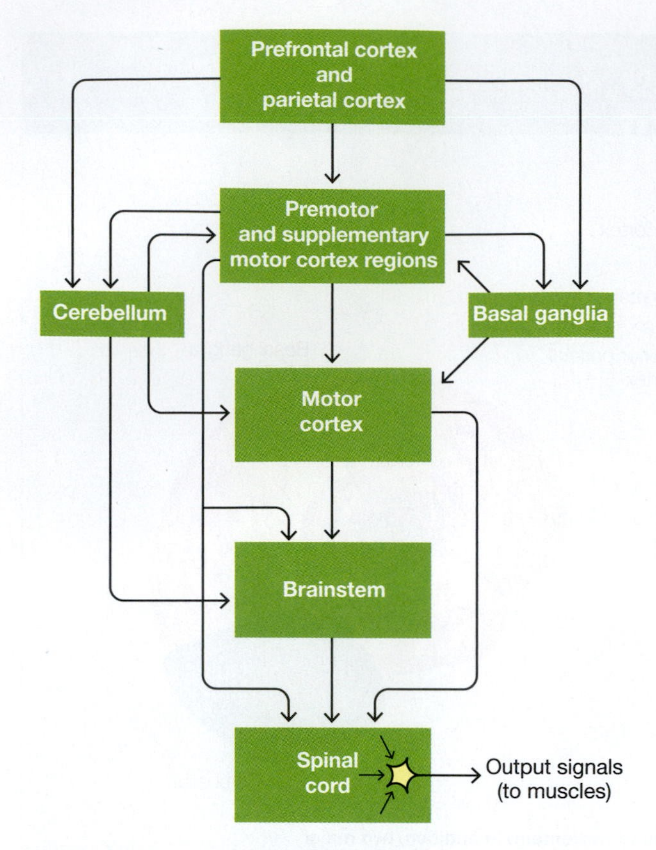

FIGURE 8.2 Overview of the motor pathways.
All connections to the arms and legs originate in the spinal cord. The spinal signals are influenced by inputs from the brainstem and various cortical regions, whose activity in turn is modulated by the cerebellum and basal ganglia. Thus, control is distributed across various levels of a control hierarchy. Sensory information from the muscles (not shown) is transmitted back to the brainstem, cerebellum, and cortex.

with the assistance of the cerebellum and the basal ganglia, convert these patterns into commands to the muscles.

Because of this hierarchical structure, lesions at various levels of the motor system affect movement differently. In this section, along with the anatomy, we discuss the deficits produced by lesions to particular regions. We begin at the bottom of the anatomical hierarchy and make our way to the top.

Muscles, Motor Neurons, and the Spinal Cord

Action, or motor movement, is generated by stimulating skeletal muscle fibers of an effector. An **effector** is a part of the body that can move. For most actions, we think of distal effectors—those far from the body center, such as the arms, hands, and legs. We can also produce movements with more proximal or centrally located effectors, such as the waist, neck, and head. The jaw, tongue, and vocal tract are essential effectors for producing speech; the eyes are effectors for vision.

All forms of movement result from changes in the state of muscles that control an effector or group of effectors. Muscles are composed of elastic fibers, tissue that can change length and tension. As **Figure 8.3** shows, these fibers are attached to the skeleton at joints and are usually arranged in antagonist pairs, which enable the effector to either flex or extend. For example, the biceps and triceps form an antagonist pair that regulates the position of the forearm. Contracting or shortening the biceps muscle causes flexion about the elbow. If the biceps muscle is relaxed, or if the triceps muscle is contracted, the forearm is extended.

Muscles are activated by motor neurons, which are the final neural elements of the motor system. **Alpha motor neurons** innervate muscle fibers and produce contractions of the fibers. *Gamma motor neurons* are part of the proprioceptive system, important for sensing and regulating the length of muscle fibers. Motor neurons originate in the spinal cord, exit through the ventral root, and terminate in the muscle fibers. As with other neurons, an action potential in a motor neuron releases a neurotransmitter; for alpha motor neurons, the transmitter is acetylcholine. The release of transmitter does not modify downstream neurons, however. Instead, it makes the muscle fibers contract. The number and frequency of the action potentials and the number of muscle fibers in a muscle determine the force that the muscle can generate. Thus, alpha motor neurons provide a physical basis for translating nerve signals into mechanical actions, changing the length and tension of muscles.

Input to the alpha motor neurons comes from a variety of sources. Alpha motor neurons receive peripheral input from *muscle spindles*, sensory receptors embedded in the muscles that provide information about how much the muscle is stretched. The axons of the spindles form an afferent nerve that enters the dorsal root of the spinal cord and synapses on **spinal interneurons** that project to alpha motor neurons. If the stretch is unexpected, the alpha motor neurons are activated, causing the muscle to return to its original length; this response is called the stretch reflex (**Figure 8.4**). Reflexes allow postural stability to be maintained without any help from the cortex. They also serve protective functions; for example, reflexes can contract a muscle to avoid a painful stimulus well before pain is consciously perceived.

Spinal interneurons are innervated by afferent sensory nerves from the skin, muscles, and joints, as well as by descending motor fibers (upper motor neurons) that originate in several subcortical and motor cortical structures. Thus, the signals to the muscles involve continual integration of sensory feedback with the motor commands from higher centers. This integration is essential for both postural stability and voluntary movement.

The descending signals can be either excitatory or inhibitory. For example, descending commands that

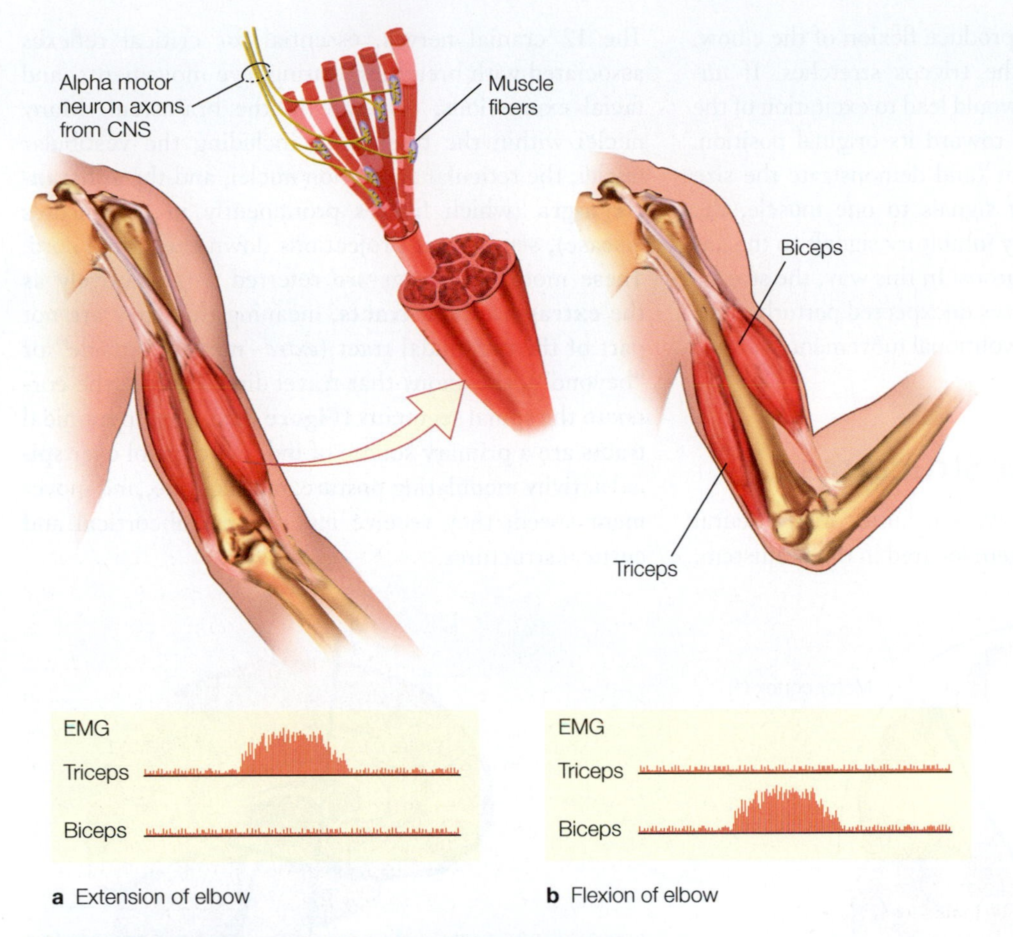

FIGURE 8.3 Muscles are activated by the alpha motor neurons.
An electromyogram (EMG) is recorded from electrodes placed on the skin over the muscle to measure electrical activity produced by the firing of alpha motor neurons. The input from the alpha motor neurons causes the muscle fibers to contract. Antagonist pairs of muscles span many of our joints. Activation of the triceps produces extension of the elbow (a); activation of the biceps produces flexion of the elbow (b).

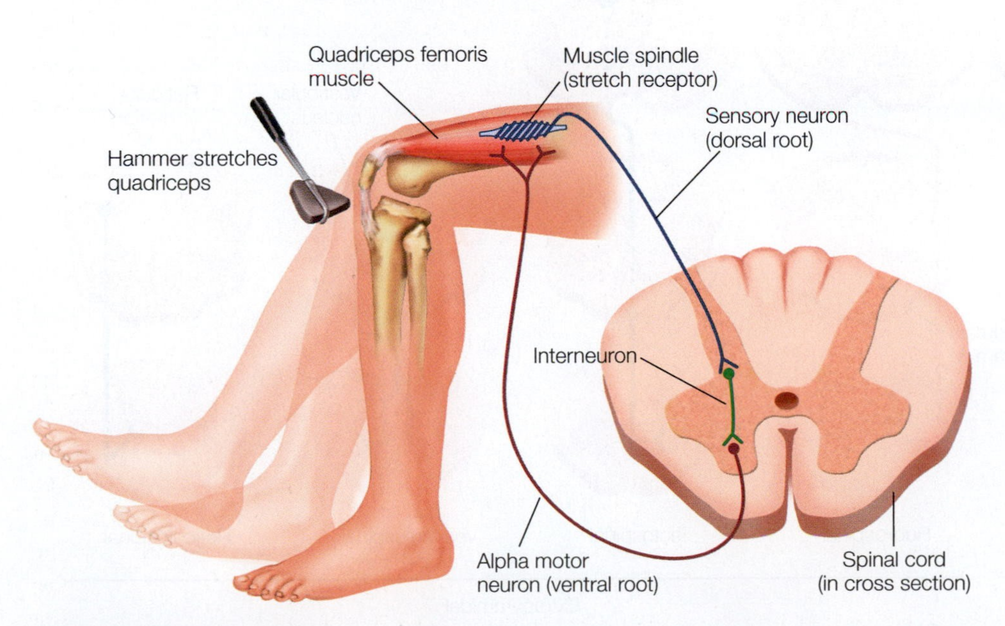

FIGURE 8.4 The stretch reflex.
When the doctor taps your knee, the quadriceps is stretched. This stretch triggers receptors in the muscle spindle to fire. The sensory signal is transmitted through the dorsal root of the spinal cord and, via an interneuron, activates an alpha motor neuron to contract the quadriceps. In this manner, the stretch reflex helps maintain the stability of the limb following an unexpected perturbation.

activate the biceps muscle produce flexion of the elbow. Because of this flexion, the triceps stretches. If unchecked, the stretch reflex would lead to excitation of the triceps and move the limb toward its original position. Thus, to produce movement (and demonstrate the size of your biceps), excitatory signals to one muscle, the agonist, are accompanied by inhibitory signals to the antagonist muscle via interneurons. In this way, the stretch reflex that efficiently stabilizes unexpected perturbations can be overcome to permit volitional movement.

Subcortical Motor Structures

Moving up the hierarchy, we encounter many neural structures of the motor system located in the brainstem. The 12 cranial nerves, essential for critical reflexes associated with breathing, eating, eye movements, and facial expressions, originate in the brainstem. Many nuclei within the brainstem, including the vestibular nuclei, the reticular formation nuclei, and the **substantia nigra** (which figures prominently in Parkinson's disease), send direct projections down the spinal cord. These motor pathways are referred to collectively as the **extrapyramidal tracts**, meaning that they are not part of the pyramidal tract (*extra-* means "outside" or "beyond"), the axons that travel directly from the cortex to the spinal segments (**Figure 8.5**). Extrapyramidal tracts are a primary source of indirect control over spinal activity modulating posture, muscle tone, and movement speed; they receive input from subcortical and cortical structures.

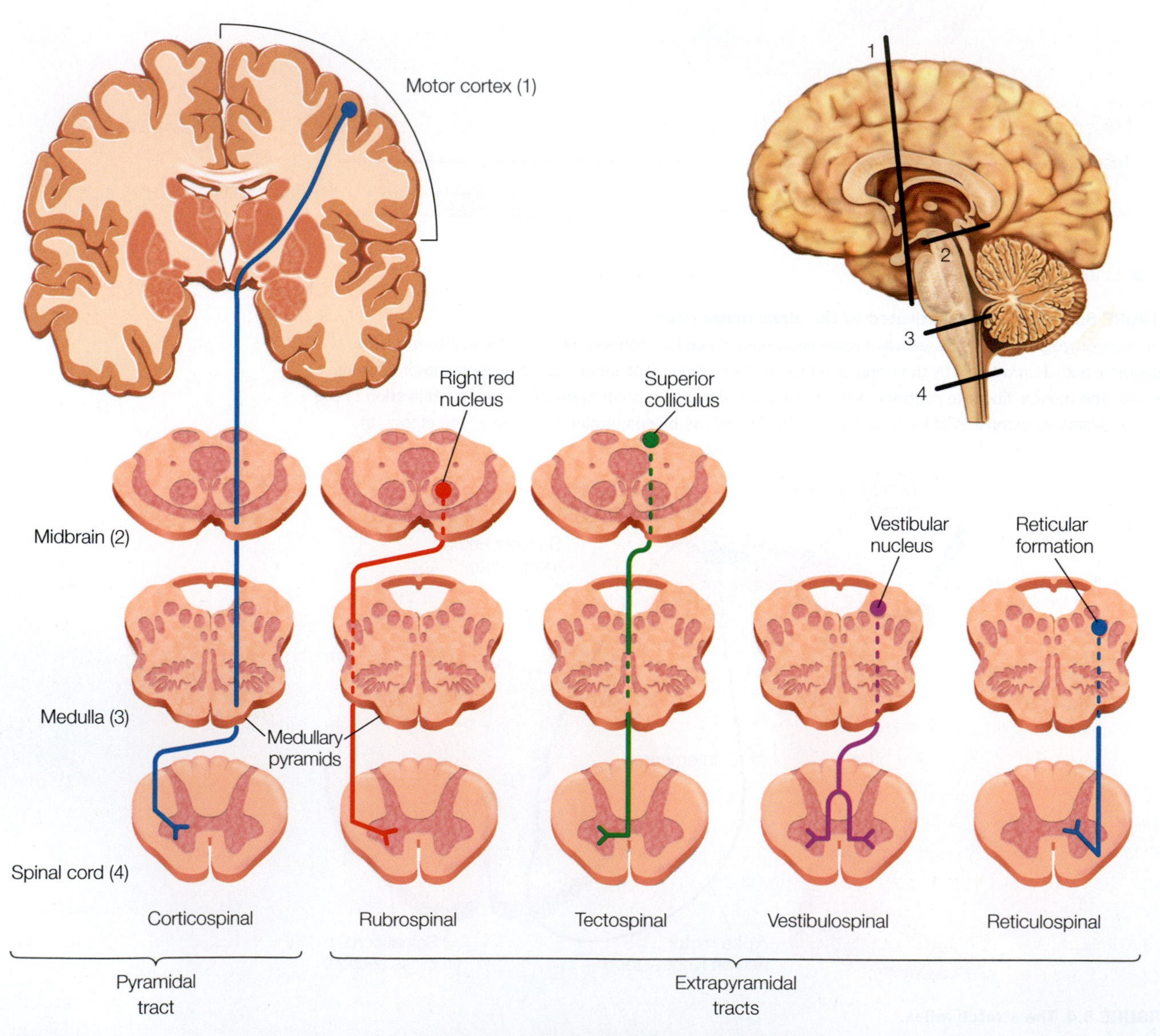

FIGURE 8.5 The brain innervates the spinal cord via the pyramidal and extrapyramidal tracts. **The pyramidal (corticospinal) tract originates in the cortex and terminates in the spinal cord. Almost all of these fibers cross over to the contralateral side at the medullary pyramids. The extrapyramidal tracts originate in various subcortical nuclei and terminate in both contralateral and ipsilateral regions of the spinal cord.**

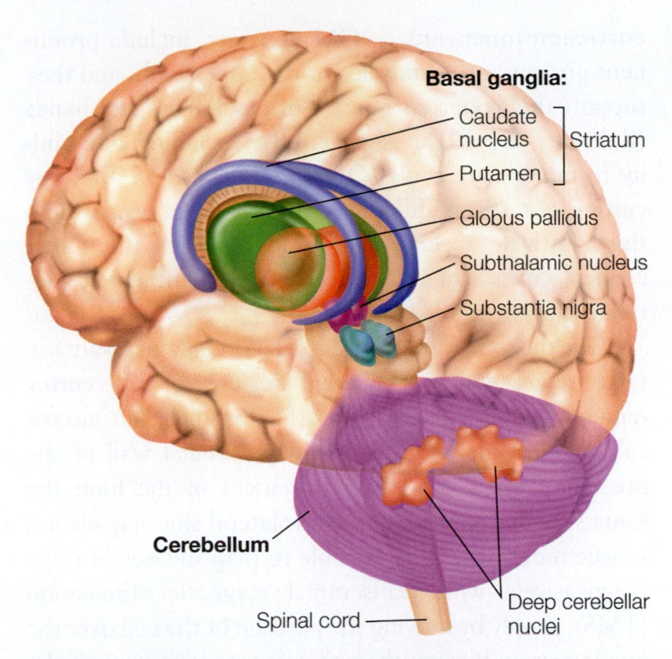

FIGURE 8.6 The basal ganglia and the cerebellum are two prominent subcortical components of the motor pathways. The basal ganglia proper include the caudate, putamen, and globus pallidus, three nuclei that surround the thalamus. Functionally, however, the subthalamic nucleus and substantia nigra are also considered part of the basal ganglia. The cerebellum sits below the posterior portion of the cerebral cortex. All cerebellar output originates in the deep cerebellar nuclei.

Figure 8.6 shows the location of two prominent subcortical structures that play a key role in motor control: the cerebellum and the basal ganglia. The **cerebellum** is a massive, densely packed structure containing over 75% of all of the neurons in the human central nervous system. Inputs to the cerebellum project primarily to the cerebellar cortex, with the output from the deep cerebellar nuclei projecting to brainstem nuclei and the cerebral cortex via the thalamus. Damage to the cerebellum from stroke, tumor, or degenerative processes results in a syndrome known as **ataxia.** Patients with ataxia have difficulty maintaining balance and producing well-coordinated movements.

The other major subcortical motor structure is the **basal ganglia**, a collection of five nuclei: the *caudate nucleus* and the *putamen* (referred to together as the *striatum*), the *globus pallidus*, the *subthalamic nucleus*, and the *substantia nigra* (Figure 8.6). The organization of the basal ganglia bears some similarity to that of the cerebellum: Input is restricted mainly to the two nuclei forming the striatum, and output is almost exclusively by way of the internal segment of the globus pallidus and part of the substantia nigra. The remaining components (the rest of the substantia nigra, the subthalamic nucleus, and the external segment of the globus pallidus) modulate activity within the basal ganglia. Output axons of the globus pallidus terminate in the thalamus, which in turn projects to motor and frontal regions of the cerebral cortex. Later we will see that all the inputs and outputs of the basal ganglia play a critical role in motor control, especially in the selection and initiation of actions.

Cortical Regions Involved in Motor Control

We will use the term *motor areas* to refer to cortical regions involved in voluntary motor functions, including the planning, control, and execution of movement. Motor areas include the primary motor cortex, the premotor cortex, and the supplementary motor area (see the "Anatomical Orientation" box at the beginning of this chapter), and sensory areas include somatosensory cortex. Parietal and prefrontal cortex are also essential in producing movement, with the latter especially important for more complex, goal-oriented behaviors.

The motor cortex regulates the activity of spinal neurons in direct and indirect ways. The **corticospinal tract (CST)** consists of axons that exit the cortex and project directly to the spinal cord (Figure 8.5). The CST is frequently referred to as the *pyramidal tract* because the mass of axons resembles a pyramid as it passes through the medulla oblongata. CST axons terminate either on spinal interneurons or directly (monosynaptically) on alpha motor neurons. These are the longest neurons in the brain; some axons extend for more than a meter. Most corticospinal fibers originate in the primary motor cortex, but some originate in premotor cortex, supplementary motor area, or even somatosensory cortex.

As with the sensory systems, each cerebral hemisphere is devoted primarily to controlling movement on the opposite side of the body. About 80% of the CST axons cross (decussate) at the junction of the medulla and the spinal cord (the most caudal end of the medullary pyramids, the motor tract that runs the length of the medulla, containing the corticobulbar and corticospinal tracts); another 10% cross when they exit the spinal cord. Most extrapyramidal fibers also decussate; the one exception to this crossed arrangement is the cerebellum.

PRIMARY MOTOR CORTEX The **primary motor cortex (M1)**, or Brodmann area 4 (**Figure 8.7**), is located in the most posterior portion of the frontal lobe, spanning the anterior wall of the central sulcus and extending onto the precentral gyrus. M1 receives input from almost all cortical areas implicated in motor control. These areas include the parietal, premotor, supplementary motor, and frontal cortices, as well as subcortical

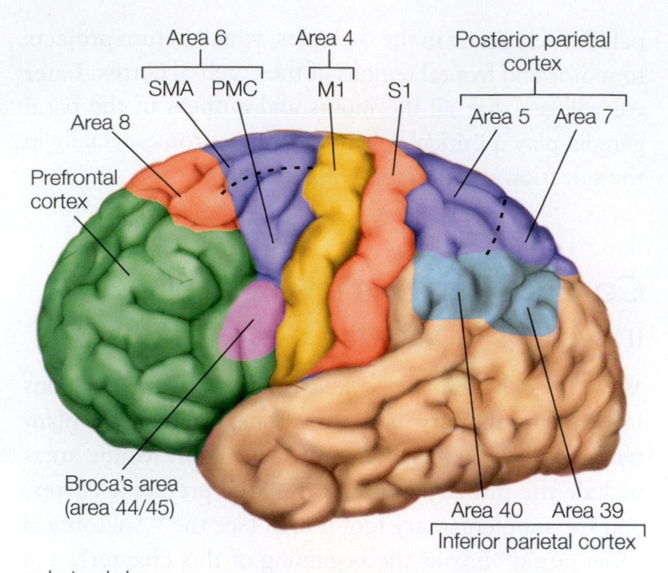

a Lateral view

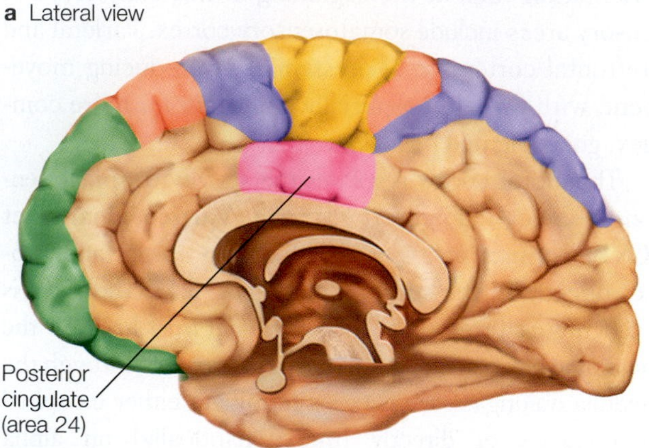

b Medial view

FIGURE 8.7 Motor areas of the cerebral cortex. Brodmann area 4 is the primary motor cortex (M1). Area 6 encompasses the supplementary motor area (SMA) on the medial surface, as well as premotor cortex (PMC) on the lateral surface. Area 8 includes the frontal eye fields. Inferior frontal regions (area 44/45) are involved in speech. Regions of parietal cortex associated with the planning and control of coordinated movement include primary (S1) and secondary somatosensory areas, and posterior and inferior parietal regions.

structures such as the basal ganglia and cerebellum. In turn, the output of the primary motor cortex makes the largest contribution to the corticospinal tract.

M1 includes two anatomical subdivisions: an evolutionarily older rostral region and a more recently evolved caudal region (Rathelot & Strick, 2009). The rostral part appears to be homologous across many species, but the caudal part is thought to be present only in humans and some of our primate cousins (Lemon & Griffiths, 2005). Corticospinal neurons that originate in the rostral region of M1 terminate on spinal interneurons. Corticospinal neurons that originate in the caudal region may terminate on interneurons or directly stimulate alpha motor neurons. The latter, known as **corticomotoneurons** or **CM neurons**, include prominent projections to muscles of the upper limb, and they support the dexterous control of our fingers and hands (Baker et al., 2015; **Figure 8.8**), including our ability to manipulate tools (Quallo et al., 2012). Thus, by cutting out the middlemen (the spinal interneurons), this relatively recent adaptation provides the direct cortical control of effectors that is essential for volitional movement.

Like the somatosensory cortex, M1 contains a somatotopic representation: Different regions of the cortex represent different body parts. For example, an electrical stimulus applied directly to the medial wall of the precentral gyrus can elicit movement of the foot; the same stimulus applied at a ventrolateral site may elicit a tongue movement. It is possible to map this somatotopy noninvasively with transcranial magnetic stimulation (TMS), simply by moving the position of the coil over the motor cortex. Placing the coil a few centimeters off the midline will elicit jerky movements of the upper arm. As the coil is shifted laterally, the twitches shift to the wrist and then to hand movements.

Given the relatively crude spatial resolution of TMS (approximately 1 cm of surface area), the elicited movements are not limited to single muscles. Even with more precise stimulation methods, however, it is apparent that the somatotopic organization in M1 is not nearly as distinct as that seen in the somatosensory cortex. It is as if the map within M1 for a specific effector, such as the arm, was chopped up and thrown back onto the cortex in a mosaic pattern. Moreover, the representation of each effector does not correspond to its actual size, but rather to the importance of that effector for movement and the level of control required for manipulating it. Thus, despite their small size, the fingers span a large portion of the human motor cortex, reflecting their essential role in manual dexterity.

The resolution of fMRI is sufficient to reveal, in vivo, somatotopic maps in the motor cortex and adjacent motor areas. Studies of these maps show that, despite considerable variability between individuals, there are common principles that constrain the organization of the motor cortex. Naveed Ejaz and his colleagues (2015) looked at different ways to account for the organization of finger representations across the motor cortex and observed that the distance between representations was closely correlated with a measure of how often two fingers are used together (**Figure 8.9**). For example, the ring and pinky fingers are functionally quite close, consistent with the fact that these two fingers tend to move together as when we grasp an object. In contrast, the thumb is quite distant from the other fingers, although it is relatively close to the index finger, its partner for holding things

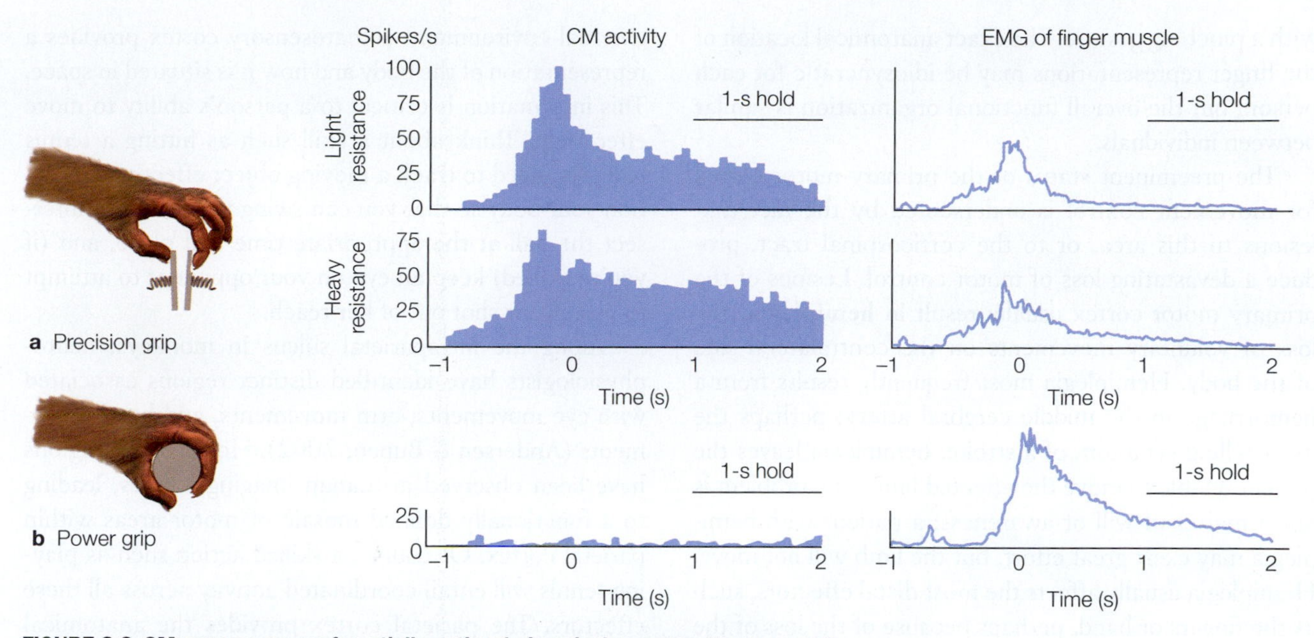

FIGURE 8.8 CM neurons are preferentially active during pinch compared to power grip. Recordings are from a single CM neuron in the primary motor cortex of a monkey that projects to a finger muscle. Peri-event histograms for precision grip with light and heavy resistance for a CM neuron (a) and power grip (b) show that the CM neuron fired more strongly for the precision grip tasks. The EMGs of the finger muscle show that muscle activity was stronger for the power grip. While the muscle was active in both tasks, activation during the power grip came largely from non-CM corticospinal and extrapyramidal neurons, suggesting that CM neurons specialize in fine motor control.

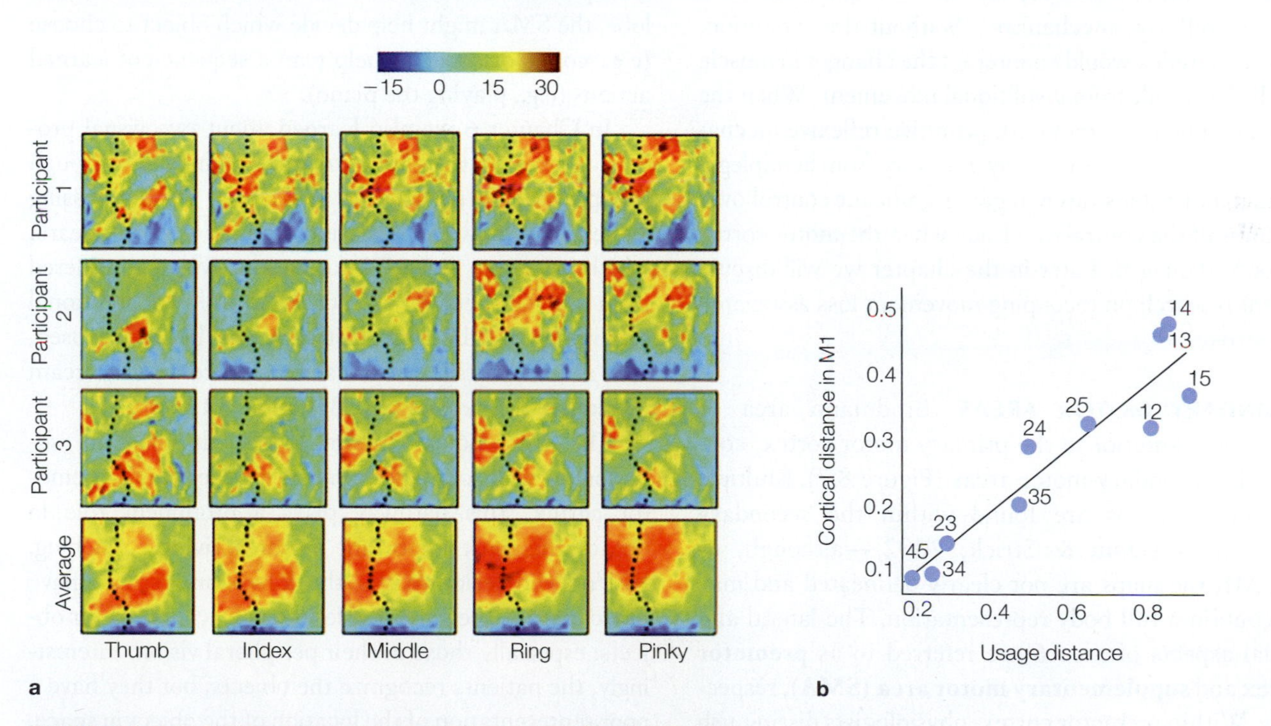

FIGURE 8.9 Organization of finger representations across the motor cortex. (a) 3-T fMRI activity patterns in the right M1 for single-finger presses of the left hand. Color represents the degree of activity from lowest (blue) to highest (red). Each of the top three rows represents a separate individual, and the group average is from six individuals. Though there is quite a bit of variation between the individuals, the group average shows some orderliness. The dotted line indicates the bottom of the central sulcus. (b) Data from a second experiment with different participants using 7-T fMRI to ensure higher spatial resolution. The distance between cortical representations of fingers in M1 showed a very tight correlation with a measure of how often two fingers are used together ("Usage distance" on *x*-axis). The two-digit numbers indicate finger pairs; for example, "35" indicates the middle-and-pinky-finger pair.

with a pinching gesture. The exact anatomical location of the finger representations may be idiosyncratic for each person, but the overall functional organization is similar between individuals.

The preeminent status of the primary motor cortex for movement control is underscored by the fact that lesions to this area, or to the corticospinal tract, produce a devastating loss of motor control. Lesions of the primary motor cortex usually result in **hemiplegia**, the loss of voluntary movements on the contralateral side of the body. Hemiplegia most frequently results from a hemorrhage in the middle cerebral artery; perhaps the most telling symptom of a stroke, hemiplegia leaves the patient unable to move the affected limb. The problem is not a matter of will or awareness; a patient with hemiplegia may exert great effort, but the limb will not move. Hemiplegia usually affects the most distal effectors, such as the fingers or hand, perhaps because of the loss of the corticomotor neurons.

Reflexes are absent immediately after a stroke that produces hemiplegia. Within a couple of weeks, though, the reflexes return and are frequently hyperactive or even spastic (resistant to stretch). These changes result from a shift in control. Voluntary movement requires the inhibition of reflexive mechanisms. Without this inhibition, the stretch reflex would counteract the changes in muscle length that result from a volitional movement. When the cortical influence is removed, primitive reflexive mechanisms take over. Unfortunately, recovery from hemiplegia is minimal. Patients rarely regain significant control over the limbs of the contralateral side when the motor cortex has been damaged. Later in the chapter we will discuss current research on recouping movement loss associated with stroke.

SECONDARY MOTOR AREAS Brodmann area 6, located just anterior to the primary motor cortex, contains the secondary motor areas (Figure 8.7). Multiple somatotopic maps are found within the secondary motor areas (Dum & Strick, 2002)—although, as with M1, the maps are not clearly delineated and may not contain a full body representation. The lateral and medial aspects of area 6 are referred to as **premotor cortex** and **supplementary motor area (SMA)**, respectively. Within premotor cortex, physiologists distinguish between ventral premotor cortex (vPMC) and dorsal premotor cortex (dPMC).

Secondary motor areas are involved with the planning and control of movement, but they do not accomplish this feat alone. The premotor cortex has strong reciprocal connections with the parietal lobe. As we saw in Chapter 6, the parietal cortex is a critical region for the representation of space. And this representation is not limited to the external environment; somatosensory cortex provides a representation of the body and how it is situated in space. This information is critical to a person's ability to move effectively. Think about a skill such as hitting a tennis ball. You need to track a moving object effectively, position your body so that you can swing the racket to intersect the ball at the appropriate time and place, and (if you're skilled) keep an eye on your opponent to attempt to place your shot out of her reach.

Along the intraparietal sulcus in monkeys, neurophysiologists have identified distinct regions associated with eye movements, arm movements, and hand movements (Andersen & Buneo, 2002). Homologous regions have been observed in human imaging studies, leading to a functionally defined mosaic of motor areas within parietal cortex. Of course, a skilled action such as playing tennis will entail coordinated activity across all these effectors. The parietal cortex provides the anatomical substrate for sensory-guided actions, such as grabbing a cup of coffee or catching a ball (see Chapter 6).

The SMA, in contrast, has stronger connections with the medial frontal cortex, areas that are associated with preferences and goals, as we will see in Chapter 12. For example, via its reciprocal connections to the frontal lobe, the SMA might help decide which object to choose (e.g., coffee or soda) or help plan a sequence of learned actions (e.g., playing the piano).

In Chapter 6 we also learned about two visual processing streams: the dorsal stream, which passes through the parietal cortex and is specialized for processing "where" or "how" information, and the ventral stream, which processes "what" information. When considered from the perspective of motor control, an additional subdivision of the dorsal stream has been proposed, into a dorso-dorsal stream and a ventro-dorsal stream (Binkofski & Buxbaum, 2013; **Figure 8.10**).

The dorso-dorsal stream passes through the superior parietal lobe and projects to the dorsal premotor cortex. This pathway plays a prominent role in one of the most important motor activities: reaching. Patients with lesions within the dorso-dorsal stream have **optic ataxia:** They are unable to reach accurately for objects, especially those in their peripheral vision. Interestingly, the patients recognize the objects, but they have a poor representation of the location of the object in space, or more precisely, a poor representation of the location of the object with respect to their own body.

The ventro-dorsal stream passes through the inferior parietal lobe and projects to the ventral premotor cortex. This pathway is associated with producing both transitive gestures (those that involve the manipulation of an object) and intransitive gestures (those that involve movements to signify an intension—e.g.,

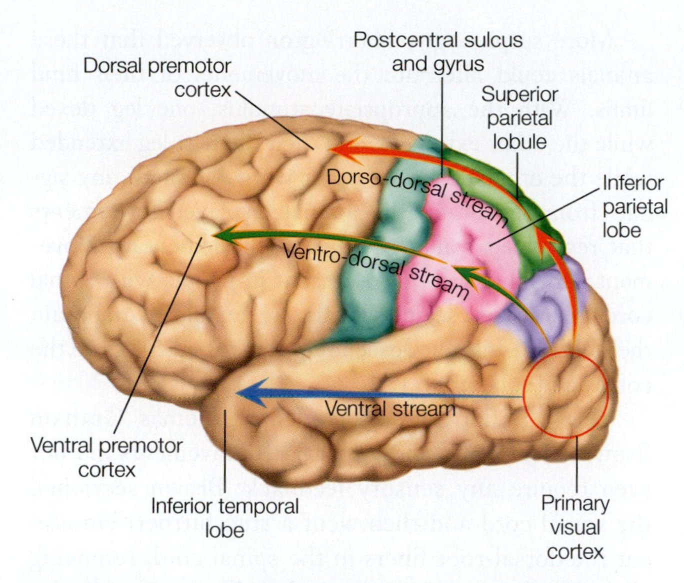

FIGURE 8.10 Proposed dorso-dorsal and ventro-dorsal processing streams, along with the ventral stream. Patients with lesions within the dorso-dorsal stream have optic ataxia, while those with lesions to the ventro-dorsal stream have apraxia.

waving goodbye). Lesions along this processing stream can result in **apraxia**—a loss of *praxis*, or skilled action—a condition that affects motor planning, as well as the knowledge of which actions are possible with a given object.

Apraxia is defined, in part, by exclusionary criteria. Apraxic individuals have normal muscle strength and tone, and they can produce simple gestures like opening and closing their fist or moving each finger individually. Yet they cannot use an object in a coherent manner, and they have difficulty linking a series of gestures into meaningful actions, such as sequencing an arm and wrist gesture to salute. Or they may use a tool in an inappropriate manner. For example, if given a comb and asked to demonstrate its use, a person with apraxia may tap the comb on his forehead. The gesture reveals some general knowledge about the tool—it is applied to the head—but the representation of how the tool is used is lost. Apraxia is most commonly a result of left-sided lesions, yet the problems may be evident in gestures produced by either limb.

Many other association areas of the cortex are implicated in motor function beyond the parietal lobe. Broca's area (located within the posterior aspect of the inferior frontal gyrus in the left hemisphere; Hillis et al., 2004) and the insular cortex (medial to Broca's area) are involved in the production of speech movements. Area 8 includes the frontal eye fields, a region (as the name implies) that contributes to the control of eye movements. The anterior cingulate cortex is also implicated in the selection and control of actions, evaluating the effort or costs required to produce a movement (see Chapter 12).

In summary, the motor cortex has direct access to spinal mechanisms via the corticospinal tract. Movement can also be influenced through many other connections. First, the primary motor cortex and premotor areas receive input from many regions of the cortex by way of corticocortical connections. Second, some cortical axons terminate on brainstem nuclei, thus providing a cortical influence on the extrapyramidal tracts. Third, the cortex sends massive projections to the basal ganglia and cerebellum. Fourth, the *corticobulbar tract* is composed of cortical fibers that terminate on the cranial nerves.

TAKE-HOME MESSAGES

- Alpha motor neurons provide the point of translation between the nervous system and the muscular system, originating in the spinal cord and terminating on muscle fibers. Action potentials in alpha motor neurons cause the muscle fibers to contract.
- The corticospinal or pyramidal tract is made up of descending fibers that originate in the cortex and project monosynaptically to the spinal cord. Extrapyramidal tracts are neural pathways that project from the subcortex to the spinal cord.
- Two prominent subcortical structures involved in motor control are the cerebellum and the basal ganglia.
- The primary motor cortex (M1; Brodmann area 4) spans the anterior bank of the central sulcus and the posterior part of the central gyrus. It is the source of most of the corticospinal tract. Lesions to M1 or the corticospinal tract result in hemiplegia, the loss of the ability to produce voluntary movement. The deficits are present in effectors contralateral to the lesion.
- Brodmann area 6 includes secondary motor areas. The lateral aspect is referred to as premotor cortex; the medial aspect, as supplementary motor area.
- Apraxia is a disorder in which the patient has difficulty producing coordinated, goal-directed movement, despite having normal strength and control of the individual effectors.

8.2 Computational Issues in Motor Control

We have seen the panoramic view of the motor system: how muscles are activated and which spinal, subcortical, and cortical areas shape this activity. Though we have identified the major anatomical components, we have only touched on their function. We now turn to some core computational issues that must be addressed when constructing theories about how the brain choreographs the many signals required to produce actions.

Central Pattern Generators

As described earlier, the spinal cord is capable of producing orderly movement. The stretch reflex provides an elegant mechanism to maintain postural stability even in the absence of higher-level processing. Are these spinal mechanisms a simple means for assembling and generating simple movements into more complicated actions?

In the late 1800s, the British physiologist and Nobel Prize winner Charles Sherrington developed a procedure in which he severed the spinal cord in cats to disconnect the spinal apparatus from the cortex and subcortex (Sherrington, 1947). This procedure enabled Sherrington to observe the kinds of movements that could be produced in the absence of descending commands. As expected, stretch reflexes remained intact; in fact, these reflexes were exaggerated because inhibitory influences were removed from the brain.

More surprisingly, Sherrington observed that these animals could alternate the movements of their hind limbs. With the appropriate stimulus, one leg flexed while the other extended, and then the first leg extended while the other flexed. In other words, without any signals from the brain, the animal displayed movements that resembled walking. While such elementary movement capabilities are also present in people with spinal cord injuries, these individuals are unable to maintain their posture without descending control signals from the cortex and subcortex.

One of Sherrington's students, Thomas Graham Brown, went on to show that such movements did not even require any sensory feedback. Brown sectioned the spinal cord and then went a step further: He also cut the dorsal-root fibers in the spinal cord, removing all feedback information from the effector. Even under these extreme conditions, the cat was able to generate rhythmic walking movements when put on a kitty treadmill (**Figure 8.11**). Thus, neurons in the spinal

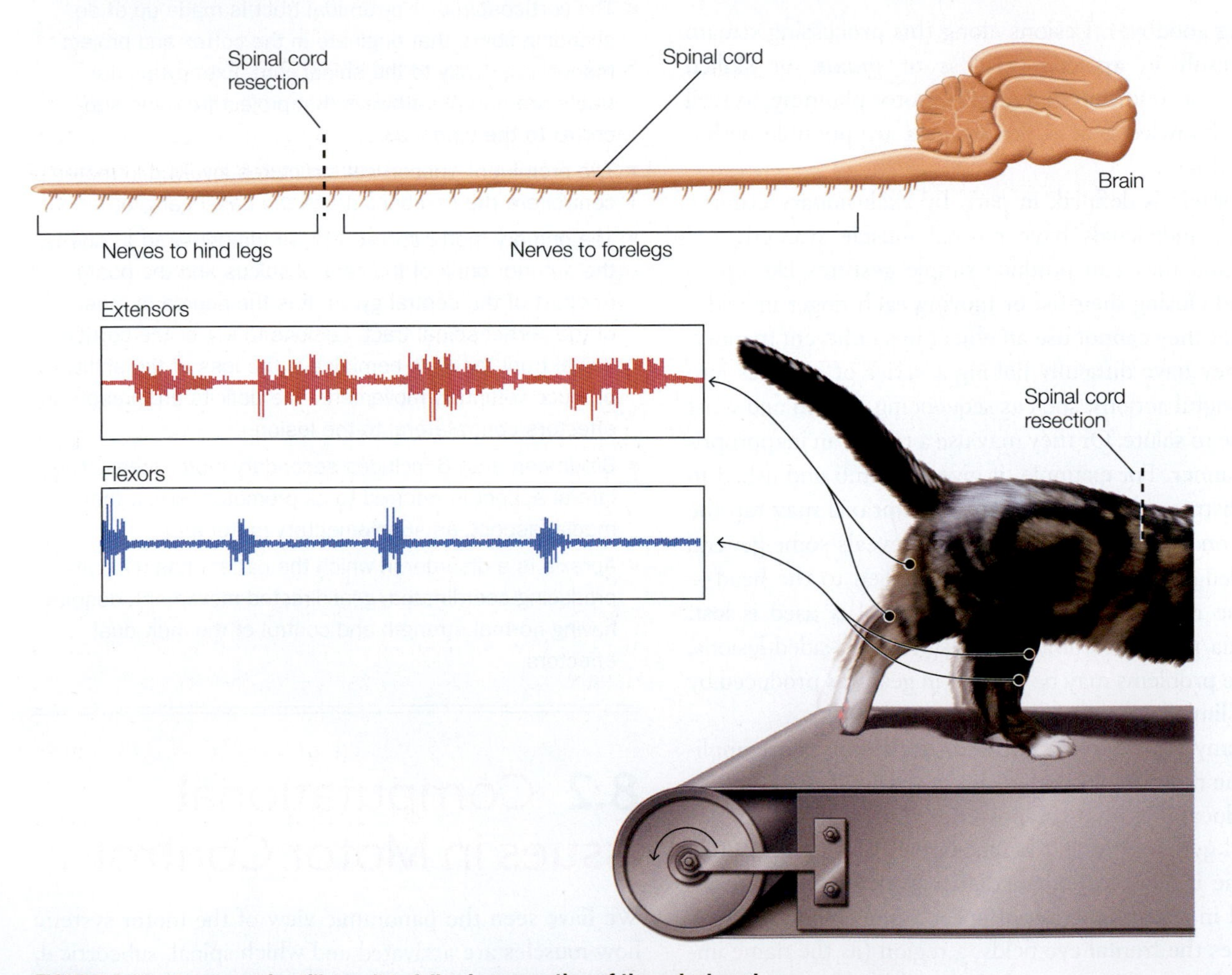

FIGURE 8.11 Movement is still possible following resection of the spinal cord.
In Brown's classic experiment with cats, the spinal cord was severed so that the nerves to the hind legs were isolated from the brain. The cats were able to produce stereotypical rhythmic movements with the hind legs when supported on a moving treadmill. Because all inputs from the brain had been eliminated, the motor commands must have originated in the lower portion of the spinal cord.

cord could produce an entire sequence of actions without any descending commands or external feedback signals.

These neurons have come to be called **central pattern generators.** They offer a powerful mechanism for the hierarchical control of movement. Consider, for instance, how the nervous system might initiate walking. Brain structures would not have to specify patterns of muscle activity. Rather, they would simply activate the appropriate pattern generators in the spinal cord, which in turn would trigger muscle commands. The system is truly hierarchical, because the highest levels are concerned only with issuing commands to achieve an action, whereas lower-level mechanisms translate the commands into a specific neuromuscular pattern to produce the desired movement.

Central pattern generators most likely evolved to trigger actions essential for survival, such as locomotion. The production of other movements may have evolved through elaboration of these mechanisms. When we reach to pick up an object, for example, low-level mechanisms could automatically make the necessary postural adjustments to keep the body from tipping over as the center of gravity shifts.

Central Representation of Movement Plans

If cortical neurons are not coding specific patterns of motor commands, what are they doing? To answer this question, we have to think about how actions are represented (Keele, 1986). Consider this scenario: You are busily typing at the computer and decide to pause and take a sip of coffee. To accomplish this goal, you must move your hand from the keyboard to the coffee cup. How is this action coded in your brain?

It could be represented in at least two ways. First, by comparing the positions of your hand and the cup, you could plan the required movement trajectory—the path that would transport your hand from the keyboard to the cup. Alternatively, your action plan might simply specify the cup's location (on the desk) and the motor commands that correspond to the limb's being at the required position (arm extended at an angle of 75°), not how to get there. Of course, both forms of representations—trajectory based and location based—might exist in motor areas of the cortex and subcortex.

In an early study attempting to understand the neural code for movements, Emilio Bizzi and his colleagues (1984) at the Massachusetts Institute of Technology (MIT) performed an experiment to test whether trajectory and/or location were being coded. The experiments involved monkeys that had, through a surgical procedure, been deprived of all somatosensory, or *afferent*, signals from the limbs. These deafferented monkeys were trained in a simple pointing experiment. On each trial, a light appeared at one of several locations. After the light was turned off, the animal was required to rotate its elbow to bring its arm to the target location—the point where the light had been.

The critical manipulation included trials in which an opposing torque force was applied just when movement started. This force was designed to keep the limb at the starting position for a short time. Because the room was dark and the animals were deafferented, they were unaware that their movements were counteracted by an opposing force. The crucial question was, Where would the movement end once the torque force was removed?

If the animal had learned that a muscular burst would transport its limb a certain distance, applying an opposing force should have resulted in a movement trajectory that fell short of the target. If, however, the animal generated a motor command specifying the desired position, it should have achieved this goal once the opposing force was removed. As **Figure 8.12** shows, the results clearly favor the latter location hypothesis. When the torque motor was on, the limb stayed at the starting location. As soon as it was turned off, the limb rapidly moved to the correct location. This experiment provided dramatic evidence showing that central representations can be based on a location code.

Although this experiment provides impressive evidence of location planning, it doesn't mean that location is the only thing being coded—just that location is one of the things being coded. We know that the form with which a movement is executed can also be controlled. For example, in reaching for your coffee cup you could choose simply to extend your arm. Alternatively, you might rotate your body, reducing the distance the arm has to move. If the coffee cup were tucked behind a book, you could readily adjust the reach to avoid a spill. Indeed, for many tasks, such as dodging a predator or being in a tango competition, the trajectory and type of movement are as important as the final goal. So, although **endpoint control** reveals a fundamental capability of the motor control system, distance and trajectory planning demonstrate additional flexibility in the control processes.

Hierarchical Representation of Action Sequences

We must also take into account that most of our actions are more complex than simply reaching to a location in space. More commonly, an action requires a sequential

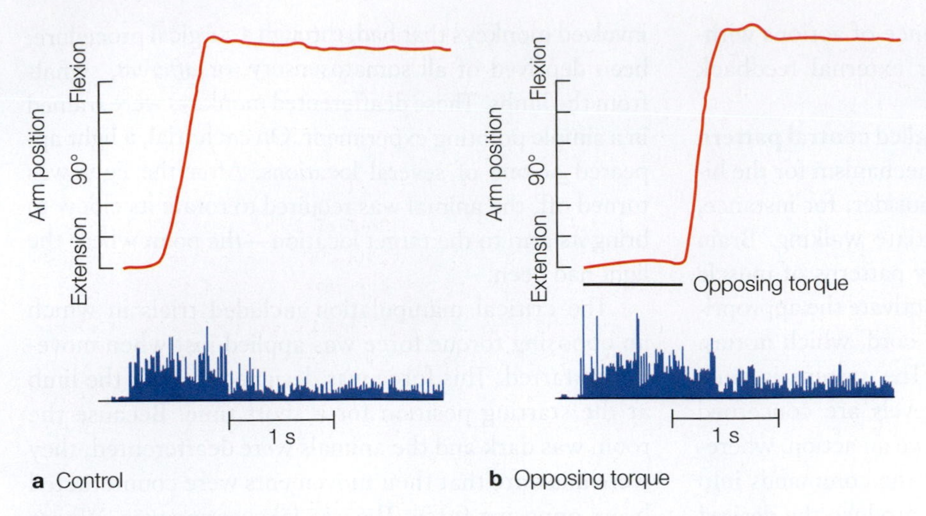

FIGURE 8.12 Endpoint control.
Deafferented monkeys were trained to point in the dark to a target indicated by the brief illumination of a light. The top traces (red) show the position of the arm as it goes from an initial position to the target location. The bottom traces (blue) show the EMG activity in the biceps. (a) In the control condition, the animals were able to make the pointing movements accurately, despite the absence of all sources of feedback. (b) In the experimental condition, an opposing force was applied at the onset of the movement, preventing the arm from moving (bar under the arm position trace). Once this force was removed, the limb rapidly moved to the correct target location. Because the animal could not sense the opposing force, it must have generated a motor command corresponding to the target location.

set of simple movements. In serving a tennis ball, we have to toss the ball with one hand and swing the racket with the other so that it strikes the ball just after the apex of rotation. In playing the piano, we must strike a sequence of keys with appropriate timing and force. Are these actions simply constructed by the linking of independent movements, or are they guided by hierarchical representational structures that govern the entire sequence? The answer is that they are guided. Hierarchical representational structures organize movement elements into integrated chunks. Researchers originally developed the idea of "chunking" when studying memory capacity, but it has also proved relevant to the representation of action.

Donald MacKay (1987) of UCLA developed a behavioral model to illustrate how hierarchical ideas could prove insightful for understanding skilled action. At the top of the hierarchy is the *conceptual level* (**Figure 8.13**), corresponding to a representation of the goal of the action. In this example, the man's intention (goal) is to accept the woman's invitation to dance. At the next level this goal must be translated into an effector system. The man can make a physical gesture or offer a verbal response. Embedded within each of those options are more options. He can nod his head, extend his hand, or, if he has the gift of gab, select one sentence from a large repertoire of potential responses: "I was hoping you would ask," or "You will have to be careful, I have two left feet." Lower levels of the hierarchy then translate these movement plans into patterns of muscular activation. For example, a verbal response entails a pattern of activity across the speech articulators, and extension of the hand requires movements of the arm and fingers.

Viewing the motor system as a hierarchy enables us to recognize that motor control is a distributed process. As in a large corporation where the chief executive, sitting at the top of the organizational hierarchy, is unconcerned with what is going on in the shipping department, so too, the highest levels of the motor hierarchy may not be concerned with the details of a movement.

Hierarchical organization can also be viewed from a phylogenetic perspective. Unlike humans, many animals without a cerebral cortex are capable of complex actions: The fly can land with near-perfect precision, and the frog can flick its tongue at the precise moment to snare its evening meal (watch an example of coordinated yet inflexible behavior at http://www.youtube.com/watch?v=JqpMqS06hk0).

We might consider the cortex as an additional piece of neural machinery superimposed on a more elementary control system. Movement in organisms with primitive motor structures is based primarily on simple reflexive actions. A blast of water against the abdominal cavity of the sea slug automatically elicits a withdrawal response. More highly evolved motor systems, however, have additional layers of control that can shape and control these reflexes. For example,

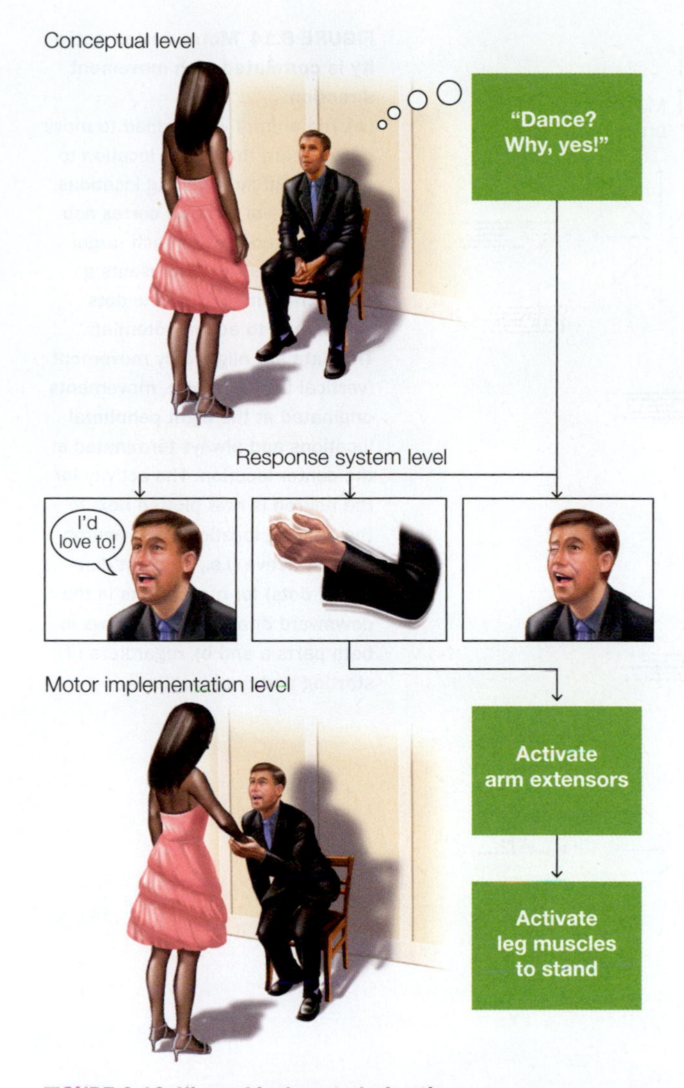

FIGURE 8.13 Hierarchical control of action.
Motor planning and learning can occur at multiple levels. At the lowest level are the actual commands to implement a particular action. At the highest level are abstract representations of the goal for the action. Usually, the same goal can be achieved by multiple different actions.

brainstem nuclei can inhibit spinal neurons so that a change in a muscle's length does not automatically trigger a stretch reflex.

In a similar way, the cortex can provide additional means for regulating the actions of the lower levels of the motor hierarchy, offering an organism even greater flexibility in its actions. We can generate any number of movements in response to a sensory signal. As a ball comes whizzing toward him, a tennis player can choose to hit a crosscourt forehand, go for a drop shot, or pop a defensive lob. Cortical mechanisms also enable us to generate actions that are minimally dependent on external cues. We can sing aloud, wave our hands, or pantomime a gesture. Reflecting this greater flexibility, the fact that the corticospinal tract is one of the latest evolutionary adaptations, appearing only in mammals, is no surprise. It affords a new pathway that the cerebral hemispheres can take to activate ancient motor structures.

TAKE-HOME MESSAGES

- Neurons within the spinal cord can generate an entire sequence of actions without any external feedback signal. These circuits are called central pattern generators.
- Descending motor signals modulate the spinal mechanism to produce voluntary movements.
- The motor system is hierarchically organized. Subcortical and cortical areas represent movement goals at various levels of abstraction.

8.3 Physiological Analysis of Motor Pathways

So far in this chapter we have stressed two critical points on movement: First, as with all complex domains, motor control depends on several distributed anatomical structures. Second, these distributed structures operate in a hierarchical fashion. We have seen that the concept of hierarchical organization also applies at the behavioral level of analysis. The highest levels of planning are best described by how an action achieves an objective; the lower levels of the motor hierarchy are dedicated to translating a goal into a movement. We now turn to the problem of relating structure to behavior: What are the functional roles of the different components of the motor system? In this section we take a closer look at the neurophysiology of motor control to better understand how the brain produces actions.

Neural Coding of Movement

Neurophysiologists have long puzzled over how best to describe cellular activity in the motor structures of the CNS. Stimulation of the primary motor cortex, either during neurosurgery or via TMS, can produce discrete movements about single joints, providing a picture of the somatotopic organization of the motor cortex. This method, however, does not provide insight into the activity of single neurons, nor can it be used to study how and when cells become active during volitional movement. To address these issues, we have to record the activity of single cells and ask which parameters of movement are coded by such cellular activity. For example, is cellular activity correlated with parameters of muscle activity such

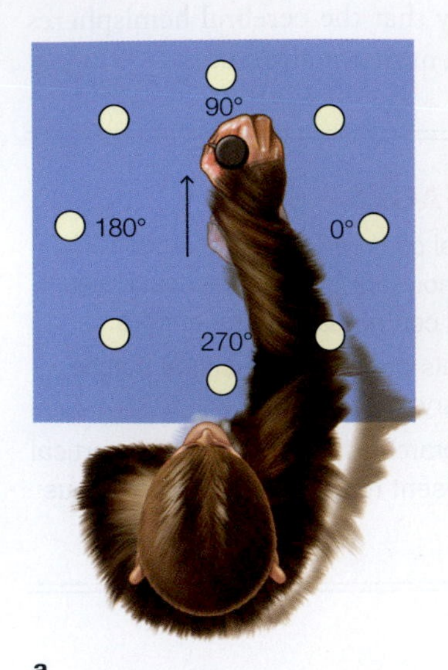

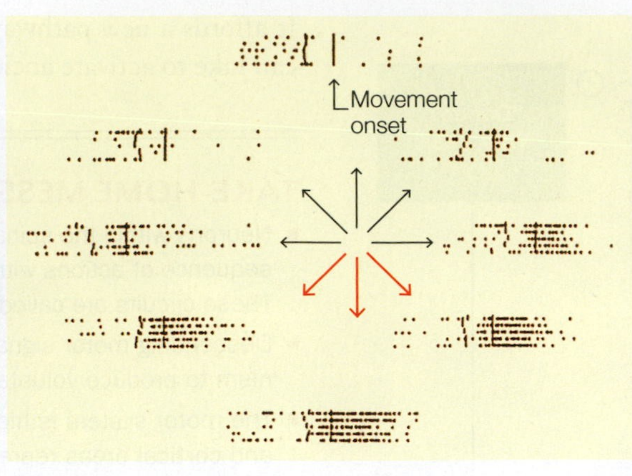

a

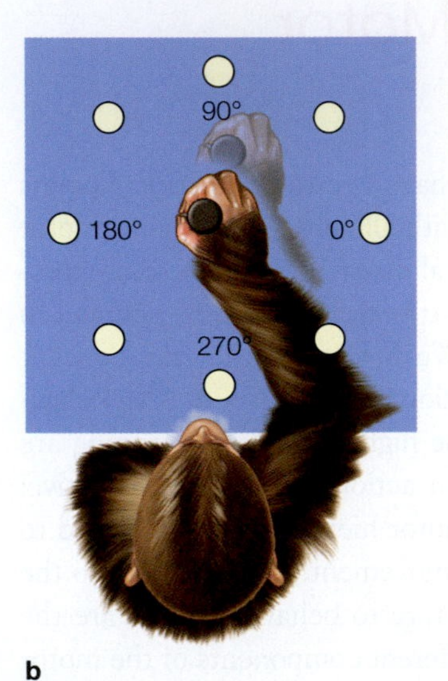

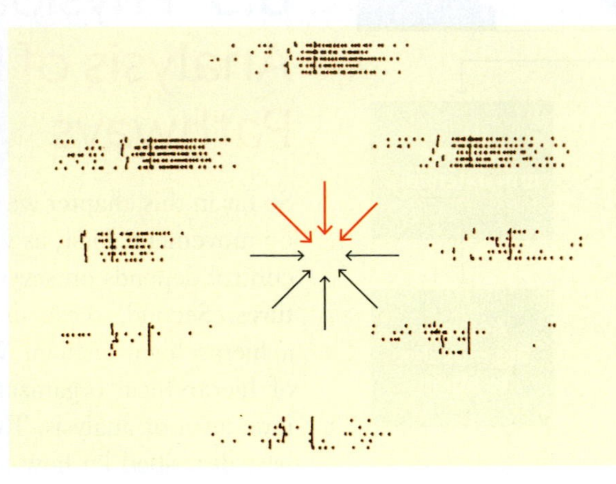

b

FIGURE 8.14 Motor cortex activity is correlated with movement direction.
(a) The animal was trained to move a lever from the center location to one of eight surrounding locations. The activity of a motor cortex neuron is plotted next to each target location. Each row represents a single movement, and the dots correspond to action potentials. The data are aligned by movement (vertical bar). **(b)** Here, movements originated at the eight peripheral locations and always terminated at the center location. The activity for the neuron is now plotted next to the starting locations. The neuron is most active (i.e., greatest density of dots) for movements in the downward direction (red arrows in both parts a and b), regardless of starting and final locations.

as force, or with more abstract entities such as movement direction or desired final location?

In a classic series of experiments, Apostolos Georgopoulos (1995) and his colleagues studied this question by recording from cells in various motor areas of rhesus monkeys. The monkeys were trained with the apparatus shown in **Figure 8.14** on what has come to be called the *center-out task*. The animal initiates the trial by moving the lever to the center of the table. After a brief hold period, a light illuminates one of eight surrounding target positions, and the animal moves the lever to this position to obtain a food reward. This movement is similar to a reaching action and usually involves rotating two joints, the shoulder and the elbow.

The results of these studies convincingly demonstrate that the activity of the cells in the primary motor cortex correlates much better with *movement direction* than with target location. Figure 8.14a shows a neuron's activity when movements were initiated from a center location to eight radial locations. This cell was most strongly activated (red arrows) when the movement was in toward the animal. Figure 8.14b shows results from the same cell when movements were initiated at radial locations and always ended at the center position. In this condition the cell was most active for movements initiated from the most distant position, again in toward the animal.

Many cells in the motor cortex show directional tuning, or exhibit what is referred to as a **preferred direction**. This tuning is relatively broad. For example, the cell shown in Figure 8.14 shows a significant increase in activity for movements in four of the eight directions. Directional tuning is not just observed in the primary motor cortex; similar tuning properties are found in cells

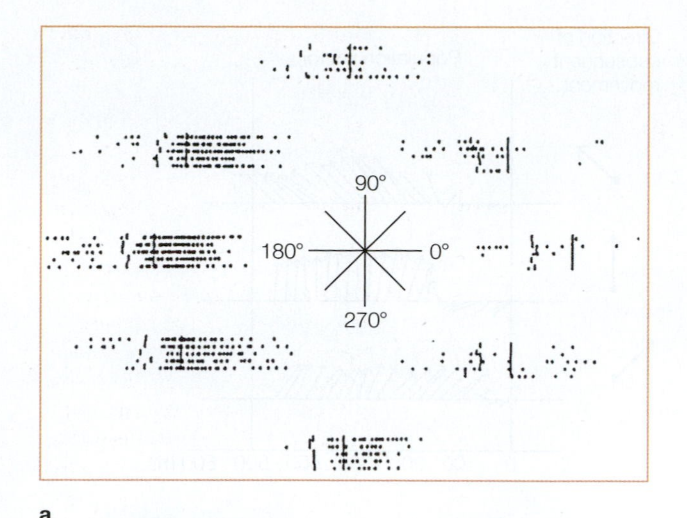

a

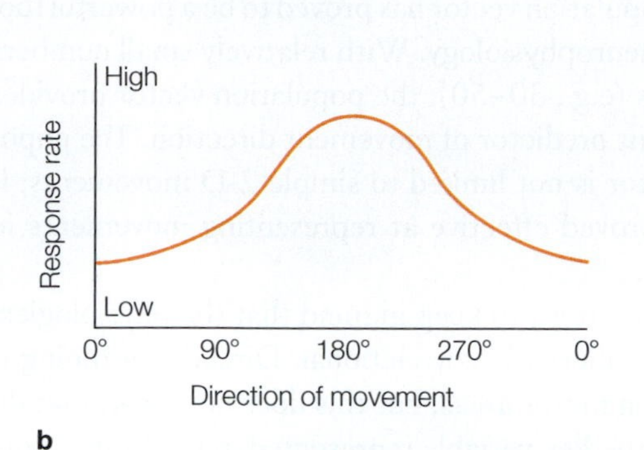

b

High
Response rate
Cell 1
Cell 2
Low
0° 90° 180° 270° 0°
Direction of movement

Movement direction	Direction vector for cell 1		Direction vector for cell 2		Population vector for cells 1 and 2
Left (180°)	←	+	↑	=	
Up (90°)	←	+	↑	=	

c

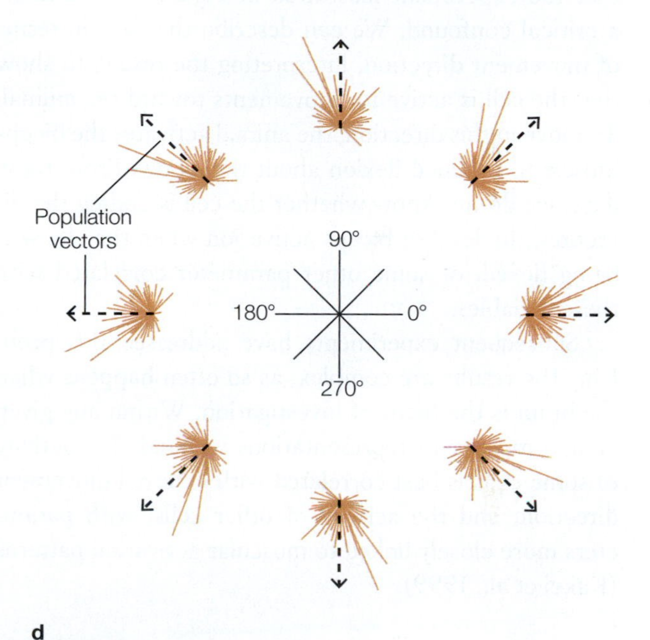

d

FIGURE 8.15 The population vector provides a cortical representation of movement.
The activity of a single neuron in the motor cortex is measured for each of eight movements (a) and plotted as a tuning profile (b). The preferred direction for this neuron is 180°, the leftward movement. (c) Each neuron's contribution to a particular movement can be plotted as a vector. The direction of the vector is always plotted as the neuron's preferred direction, and the length corresponds to its firing rate for the target direction. The population vector (dashed line) is the sum of the individual vectors. (d) For each direction, the solid, brown lines are the individual vectors for each of 241 motor cortex neurons; the dashed, black line is the population vector calculated over the entire set of neurons. Although many neurons are active during each movement, the summed activity closely corresponds to the actual movements.

in premotor and parietal cortical areas, as well as in the cerebellum and basal ganglia.

An experimenter would be hard-pressed to predict the direction of an ongoing movement if observing the activity of only this individual cell. We can assume, however, that activity is distributed across many cells, each with its unique preferred direction. To provide a more global representation, Georgopoulos and his colleagues introduced the concept of the **population vector** (**Figure 8.15**).

The idea is quite simple: Each neuron can be considered to be contributing a "vote" to the overall activity level. The strength of the vote will correspond to how closely the movement matches the cell's preferred direction: If the match is close, the cell will fire strongly; if the match is poor, the cell will fire weakly or even be inhibited.

Thus, the activity of each neuron can be described as a vector, oriented to the cell's preferred direction with a strength equal to its firing rate. The population vector is the sum of all the individual vectors.

The population vector has proved to be a powerful tool in motor neurophysiology. With relatively small numbers of neurons (e.g., 30–50), the population vector provides an excellent predictor of movement direction. The population vector is not limited to simple 2-D movements; it also has proved effective at representing movements in 3-D space.

It is important to keep in mind that the physiological method is inherently correlational. Directional tuning is prevalent in motor areas, but this does not mean that direction is the key variable represented in the brain. Note that the experiment illustrated in Figure 8.14 contains a critical confound. We can describe the data in terms of movement direction, interpreting the results to show that the cell is active for movements toward the animal. To move in this direction, the animal activates the biceps muscle to produce flexion about the elbow. From these data, we do not know whether the cell is coding the direction, the level of biceps activation when the elbow is being flexed, or some other parameter correlated with these variables.

Subsequent experiments have addressed this problem. The results are complex, as so often happens when the brain is the focus of investigation. Within any given area, a mixture of representations is found. The activity of some cells is best correlated with external movement direction, and the activity of other cells, with parameters more closely linked to muscular activation patterns (Kakei et al., 1999).

Alternative Perspectives on Neural Representation of Movement

The population vector is dynamic and can be calculated continuously over time. Indeed, after defining the preferred direction of a set of neurons, we can calculate the population vector from the activation of that set of neurons even before the animal starts to move. To do this, and to provide a way to dissociate planning- and movement-related activity, experimenters frequently impose a delay period. The animal is first given a cue indicating the direction of a forthcoming movement and then required to wait for a "go" signal before initiating the movement (**Figure 8.16**).

This procedure reveals that the population vector shifts in the direction of the upcoming movement well *before the movement is produced*, suggesting that at least some of the cells are involved in planning the movement and not simply recruited once execution of the movement has begun. In this example, the state of the population vector 300 ms *before* movement onset was sufficient to predict the direction of the forthcoming movement.

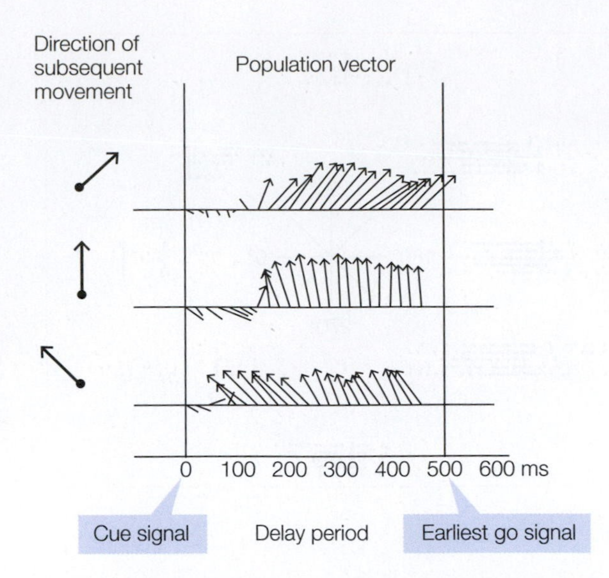

FIGURE 8.16 The direction of the population vector predicts the direction of a forthcoming movement.
At the cue, one of eight targets is illuminated, indicating the direction for a subsequent movement. The animal must refrain from moving until the go signal (500 ms later in this example). The population vector was calculated every 20 ms. The population vector is oriented in the direction for the planned movement, even though EMG activity is silent in the muscles during the delay period.

This result may not sound like such a big deal to you, but it put motor researchers into a frenzy—although not until about 10 years after Georgopolous's initial studies on the population vector. With hindsight, can you see why? As a hint, consider how this finding might be used to help people with spinal cord injuries. It suggested that we could build a decoder that would convert neural signals from motor regions of the brain into control signals to guide prosthetic devices, a brain–machine interface (BMI) system. We will explore this idea in Section 8.6.

Even though directional tuning and population vectors have become cornerstone concepts in motor neurophysiology, it is also important to consider that many cells do not show strong directional tuning. Even more puzzling, the tuning may be inconsistent: The tuning exhibited by a cell before movement begins may shift during the actual movement (**Figure 8.17**). What's more, many cells that exhibit an increase in activity during the delay phase show a brief drop in activity just before movement begins, or different firing patterns during the preparation and execution of a movement. These findings are at odds with the assumption that the planning phase is just a weaker or subthreshold version of the cell's activity during the movement phase.

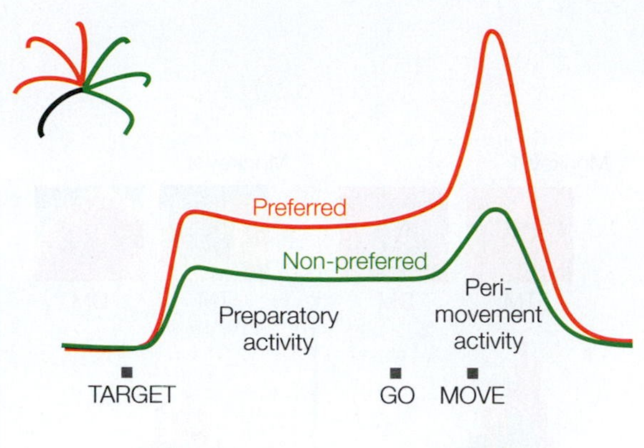

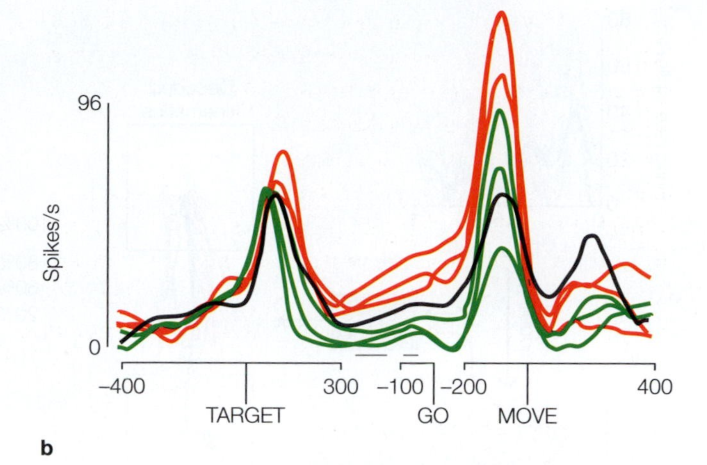

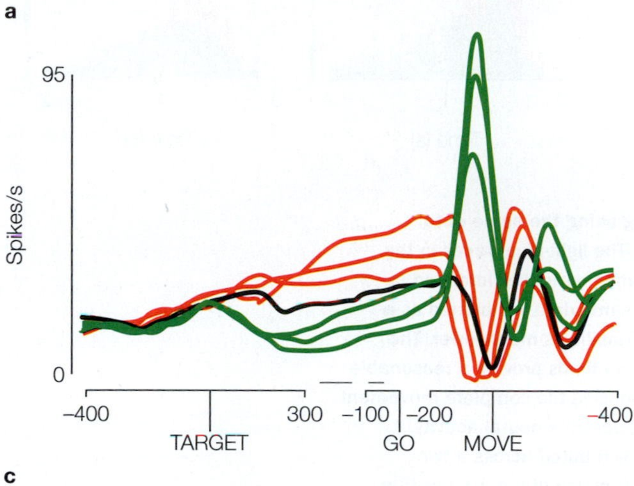

FIGURE 8.17 Planning- and execution-related activity are not always correlated.
(a) Schematic of what would be expected if neural activation during movement execution was an amplified version of the activation observed during movement planning. This neuron is more active when planning movements toward the upper-left region of the workspace (red) compared to when the movement will be to the right (green). This difference observed during planning is maintained after the go signal when the animal executes the movement. **(b)** A neuron in motor cortex showing a firing pattern similar to that of the idealized neuron. **(c)** A different neuron in motor cortex that shows a different preferred direction during the planning phase compared to the execution phase (reversal of red–green pattern at about the time of movement onset).

What are we to make of these unexpected findings, in which the tuning properties change over the course of an action? Mark Churchland and his colleagues (2012) suggest that we need a radically different perspective on motor neurophysiology. Rather than viewing neurons as static representational devices (e.g., with a fixed directional tuning), we should focus on the dynamic properties of neurons, recognizing that movement arises as the neurons move from one state to another.

By this view, we might see that neurons wear many hats, coding different features, depending on time and context. There need not be a simple mapping from behavior to neural activity. Indeed, given the complex biomechanical challenge of using limbs to interact with a wide range of objects and environments, we might expect the nervous system to have evolved to code multiple variables, such as force, velocity, and context. This multidimensional information may be harder for the experimenter to decode, but it is likely the result of an important adaptation that gives the motor system maximum flexibility.

Following this reasoning, Churchland and his colleagues compared the performance of a neural decoder formulated on a classic population vector model with one built according to a dynamic model. The traditional method defined the directional tuning of the neurons to create a population vector using simple linear summation. In contrast, the dynamic model defined the trajectory of the neural activity in abstract, multidimensional space. These two types of representations were compared by the simulation of predicted trajectories in moving a virtual limb to different target locations. Both models were sufficient to move a computer cursor in the direction of the target, but the dynamic model provided a much better prediction of the animals' actual movements (**Figure 8.18**).

Although scientists refer to one part of the brain as motor cortex and another region as sensory cortex, we know that these areas are closely intertwined. People produce movements in anticipation of their sensory consequences: We increase the force used to grip and lift a full cup of coffee in anticipation of the weight we expect to experience. Similarly, we use sensory information to adjust our actions. If the cup is empty, we quickly reduce the grip force to avoid moving the cup upward too quickly. Physiologists observe this interdependence and have recognized for some time that the motor cortex isn't just "motor," and the sensory cortex isn't just "sensory." For example, in rats the neurons that control whisker movements are located predominantly in somatosensory cortex.

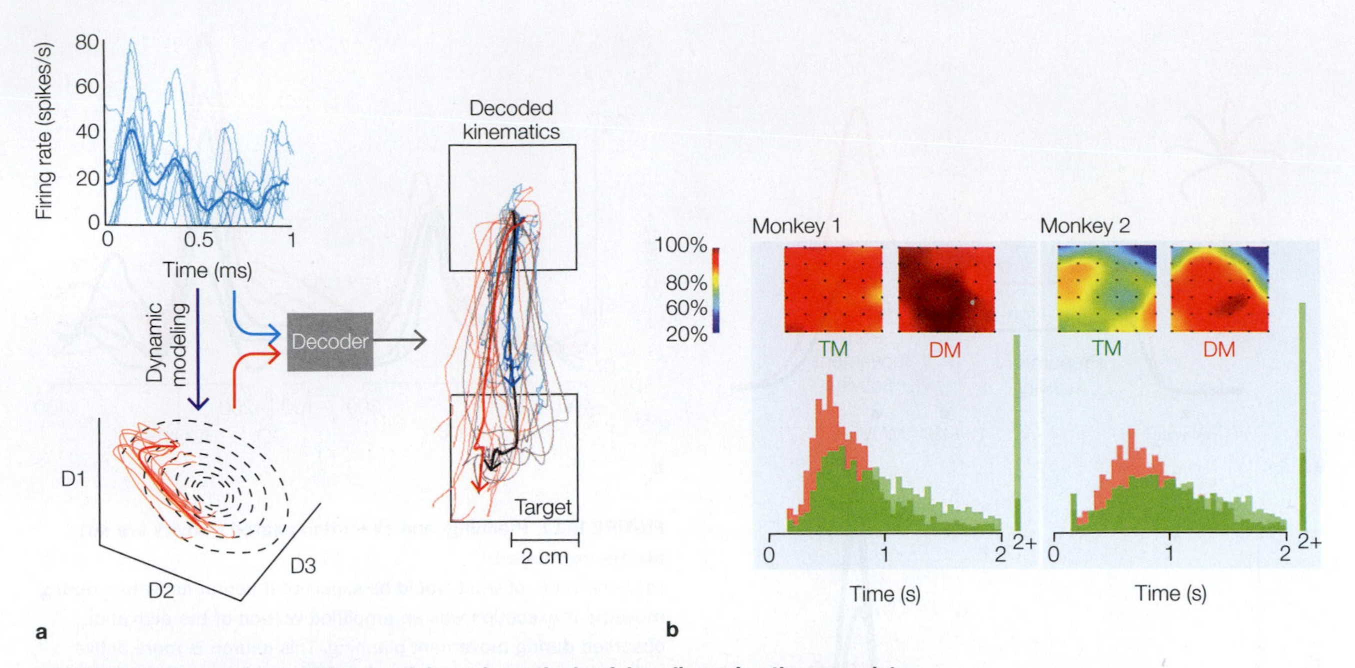

FIGURE 8.18 Comparing traditional and dynamic methods of decoding using the same data. **(a)** A decoding algorithm to translate neural activity into control signals. The light-blue traces in the upper-left panel show the firing of a single neuron across several trials when a monkey intended to reach downward to a target; the average firing rate is in bold. When the same data are plotted as a trajectory in multidimensional space (orange traces at lower left), the variability is much lower. The output from both decoding methods is depicted on the right. While both methods provide a reasonable match to the arm trajectory, the dynamic model does a better job of producing the complete movement (actual movement in gray). D1, D2, and D3 are abstract dimensions that describe neural activity. **(b)** Comparison of two decoders from two monkeys reaching to targets distributed across a two-dimensional workspace. Heat maps show accuracy (in percentage) as a function of the *x–y* position of the targets for the traditional (linear) method (TM) decoder and the dynamic method (DM) decoder. Both decoders were more accurate with data from monkey 1 (left) than from monkey 2 (right), but the DM decoder was superior for both animals. The lower graphs are frequency histograms of the time required to reach target locations with the two decoders (TM in green; DM in red).

In monkeys, sensory inputs rapidly reshape motor activity (reviewed in Hatsopoulos & Suminski, 2011). In fact, some evidence suggests that the directional tuning of some motor cortex neurons is more about "sensory" tuning. Consider the same shoulder movement induced by two different sensory events: one caused by a nudge to the elbow, and the other following a nudge to the shoulder. As early as 50 ms after each nudge, well before the sensory signals in sensory cortex are processed and sent to the motor system, M1 neurons already show differential responses to the two types of nudges. It appears that the sensory information is processed within M1 directly, allowing for a fast adjustment in the motor output based on the feedback (Pruszynski, Kurtzer, Nashed, et al., 2011; Pruszynski, Kurtzer, & Scott, 2011).

Taken together, the neurophysiological evidence points to a more nuanced picture than we might have anticipated from our hierarchical control model. Rather than a linkage of different neural regions with specific levels in a processing hierarchy—one that moves from abstract to more concrete representations—the picture reveals an interactive network of motor areas that represent multiple features. This complexity will become even more apparent in the next section, where we turn our attention to motor planning.

TAKE-HOME MESSAGES

- Neurons in cortical and subcortical motor areas exhibit directional tuning, in which the firing rate is strongest for movements in a limited set of directions.
- The population vector is a representation based on combining the activity of many neurons. Even when the input to the vector comes from a relatively small number of neurons, the population vector provides a good match to the behavior.
- Before movement even begins, the population vector is a reliable signal of the direction of a forthcoming movement. This finding indicates that some cells are involved in both planning and executing movements.

- Neurons have dynamic properties, coding different features depending on time and context. There need not be a simple mapping from behavior to neural activity.
- The heterogeneous responses exhibited by neurons in M1 include both motor and sensory information.

8.4 Goal Selection and Action Planning

We now understand that motor representations are hierarchical and need to encompass the *goals* of an action in addition to the activation patterns required to produce the movement necessary to achieve those goals. Using the current context, including sensory information and feedback, the motor cortex may have more than one option for achieving those goals. In this section we will look at how we select goals and plan motor movements to achieve them.

Consider again the situation where you are at your computer, working on a paper, with a steaming cup of coffee on your desk. You may not realize it, but you are faced with a problem that confronts all animals in their environment: deciding what to do and how to do it. Should you continue typing or sip your coffee? If you choose the coffee, then some intermediate goals must be attained—for example, reaching for the cup, grasping the cup, and bringing it to your mouth—to achieve the overarching goal of a swig of coffee. Every step requires a set of gestures, but in each case there is more than one way to perform them. For example, the cup is closer to your left hand, but your right hand is more trustworthy. Which to use? Decisions must be made at multiple levels. We have to choose a goal, choose an option for achieving the goal, and choose how to perform each intermediate step.

Action Goals and Movement Plans

Paul Cisek of the University of Montreal (2007) offers one hypothesis for how we set goals and plan actions. It incorporates many of the ideas and findings that we are going to look at, providing a general framework for action selection. Cisek's *affordance competition hypothesis* is rooted in an evolutionary perspective. This hypothesis considers that the brain's functional architecture has evolved to mediate real-time interactions with the world. *Affordances* are the opportunities for action defined by the environment (J. J. Gibson, 1979).

Our ancestors, driven by internal needs such as hunger and thirst, evolved in a world where they engaged in interactions with a changing, and sometimes hostile, environment that held a variety of opportunities and demands for action. To survive and reproduce, early humans had to be ever ready, anticipating the next predator or properly positioning themselves to snag available prey or ripe fruit. Many interactions don't allow time for carefully evaluating goals, considering options, and then planning the movements—what's known as *serial processing*.

A better survival strategy is to develop multiple plans in parallel. The affordance competition hypothesis proposes that the processes of action selection (what to do) and specification (how to do it) occur simultaneously within an interactive neural network, and they evolve continuously. Even when performing one action, we are preparing for the next. The brain uses the constant stream of sensory information arriving from the environment through sensorimotor feedback loops to continuously specify and update potential actions and how to carry them out. That's the affordance part. In addition, our internal state, longer-range goals, expected rewards, and anticipated costs provide information that can be used to assess the utility of the different actions. That's the competition part. At some point, one option wins out over the other competitors. An action is selected and executed.

This selection process involves many parts of the motor pathway, where interactions within frontoparietal circuits have a prominent role (**Figure 8.19**).

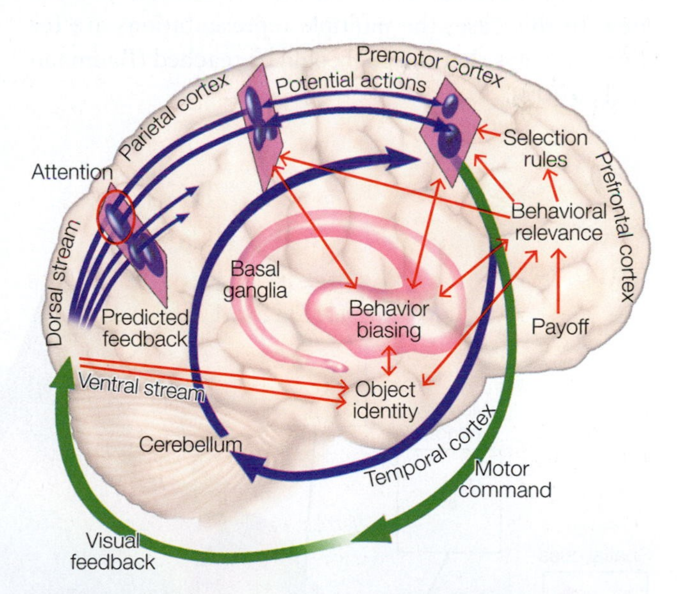

FIGURE 8.19 The affordance competition hypothesis, as applied to visually guided movement.
This schematic shows the processes and pathways involved in choosing to reach for one object among many objects in a display. The multiple pathways from visual cortex across the dorsal stream correspond to action plans for reaching to the different objects. The relative thickness of the blue arrows and circles indicates the strength for each competing plan. Selection is influenced by many sources (red arrows). The movement (green arrows) results in visual feedback of the action, starting the competition anew, but now in a different context.

The affordance competition hypothesis implies that decision-making processes are embedded in the neural systems associated with motor control, not carried out by some sort of detached central control center. Is there any evidence supporting this idea? Let's start with the notion that an action has multiple goals and each goal is linked with the plan to accomplish it.

Cisek based his model on evidence obtained in single-cell recordings from the premotor cortex of monkeys (Cisek & Kalaska, 2005). In each trial of his study, the animal was presented with two targets, either of which it could reach with its right arm. After a delay period, a cue indicated the target location for the current trial. During this delay period, neural signatures for both movements could be observed in the activity of premotor neurons, even though the animal had yet to receive a cue for the required action. These signatures can be viewed as potential action plans.

With the onset of the cue, the decision scales were tipped. Activity associated with movement to that target became stronger, and activity associated with the other movement became suppressed. Thus, after the cue, the initial dual representation consolidated into a single movement (**Figure 8.20**). In a variant of this task, only one target is presented. Even here, though, researchers can observe the simultaneous specifications of multiple potential actions in the anterior intraparietal area. In this case, the multiple representations are for different ways that the goal could be reached (Baumann et al., 2009).

Other cells in premotor cortex have been shown to represent action goals more abstractly. For example, some neurons discharge whenever the monkey grasps an object, regardless of the effector used. It could be the right hand, the left hand, the mouth, or both hand and mouth. Giacomo Rizzolatti of the University of Parma, Italy, proposed that these neurons form a basic vocabulary of motor acts (Rizzolatti et al., 2000). Some cells are preferentially activated when the animal *reaches* for an object with its hand; others become active when the animal makes the same gesture to *hold* the object; and still others are activated when the animal attempts to *tear* the object—a behavior that might find its roots in the wild, where monkeys break off tree leaves. Therefore, cellular activity in this area might reflect not only the trajectory of a movement, but also basic gestural classes of actions such as reaching, holding, and tearing.

In the example illustrated in Figure 8.20, we considered the situation in which the system eventually selects one goal, even if multiple movement plans were activated to achieve that goal. A different situation arises when there are two simultaneous action goals. What if you want to pat your head and rub your stomach at the same time? We all know this is a tough assignment. The two movements compete and can interfere with one another. We end up rubbing, not patting, our head; or patting, not rubbing, our stomach. We fail to map one action for one hand and a different action for the opposite hand. According to the selection hypothesis, this

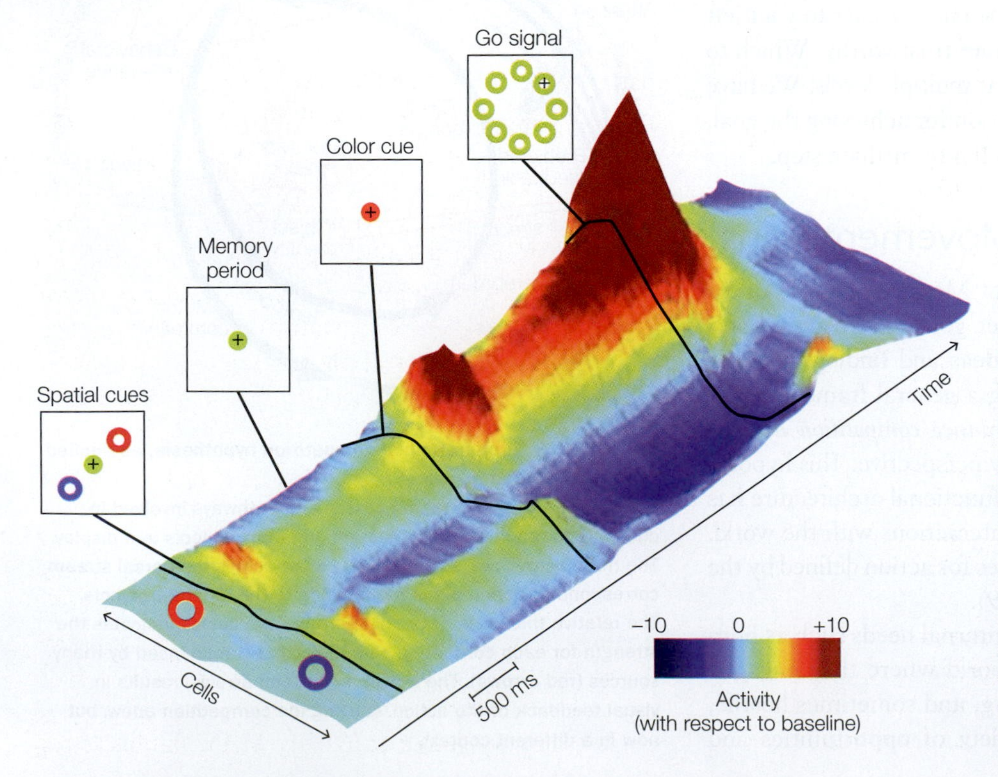

FIGURE 8.20 3-D representation of activity in a population of neurons in the dorsal premotor cortex. The preferred direction of the cells is represented along the bottom left of the figure; time, along the bottom right. When the two spatial cues appear, the firing rate increases in neurons tuned to either target. When the color cue appears, indicating the target, activity increases for cells tuned to this direction and decreases for cells tuned to the other direction. The go signal indicated to the monkey when to initiate movement.

FIGURE 8.21 Bimanual movements following resection of the corpus callosum.
While looking at a central fixation point, participants were briefly shown the two patterns. They were instructed to simultaneously draw the pattern on the left with the left hand and the one on the right with the right hand. **(a)** Normal participants were able to draw the patterns that shared a common axis but had severe difficulty when the orientation of the two figures differed by 90°. **(b)** A split-brain patient performed equally well in both conditions.

bimanual conflict reflects competition between two different movement plans.

Even though the movements are performed by separate hands, there appears to be cross talk between the two hemispheres. This hypothesis was supported by an experiment involving a patient whose corpus callosum had been resected (Franz et al., 1996). Instead of tummy rubbing and head patting, this experiment involved drawing simultaneously with both hands. The stimuli were a pair of U-shaped figures presented in different orientations (**Figure 8.21**). The stimuli were projected briefly—one in the left visual field, the other in the right—and the participant's task was to reproduce the two patterns simultaneously, using the left hand for the pattern projected in the left visual field and the right hand for the pattern in the right visual field.

The key comparison was between conditions in which the open ends of the two U shapes had either the same or different orientations for the two hands. As you can demonstrate to yourself, it is much harder to reproduce the pattern shown in the bottom row of Figure 8.21 than the pattern shown in the top row. But the split-brain patient exhibited no difference between the two conditions, performing both movements quickly and accurately. Indeed, he was even able to draw a square with one hand and a circle with the other—something that people with an intact corpus callosum find incredibly difficult. These results reveal cross talk between the two hemispheres during some stage of motor planning, most likely at the stage when an abstract action goal is being translated into a movement plan.

Representational Variation Across Motor Areas of the Cortex

As described earlier, Brodmann area 6 includes premotor cortex on the lateral surface and the supplementary motor area on the medial surface. Lateral premotor cortex is more heavily connected with parietal cortex—a finding consistent with the hypothesis that this region plays a role in sensory-guided action. The SMA, with its strong connections to medial frontal cortex, is likely biased to influence action selection and planning that are based on internal goals and personal experience (see Chapter 12).

The SMA has also been hypothesized to play an important role in more complex actions, such as those involving sequential movements or those requiring coordinated movements of the two limbs. Unlike the drawing tasks described in Figure 8.21, where the two hands have different goals, most bimanual skills require the precise interplay of both hands. The two hands may work in a similar fashion, as when we push a heavy object or row a boat, or they may take on different, complementary roles, as when we open a jar or tie our shoes.

In both monkeys and humans, damage to the SMA can lead to impaired performance on tasks that require integrated use of the two hands, even though the individual gestures performed by either hand alone are unaffected (Wiesendanger et al., 1996). If a person is asked to pantomime opening a drawer with one hand and retrieving an object from it with the other, both hands may mime the opening gesture. Again, this deficit fits with the idea of a competitive process in which an abstract goal—to retrieve an object from the drawer—is activated and a competition ensues to determine how the required movements are assigned to each hand. When the SMA is damaged, the assignment process is disrupted and execution fails, even though the person is still able to express the general goal.

Lesions of the SMA can also result in *alien hand syndrome*, a condition in which one limb produces a seemingly meaningful action but the person denies responsibility for the action. For example, the person may reach out and grab an object but then be surprised to find the object in her hand. In more bizarre cases, the two hands may work in opposition to one another—a condition that is especially prevalent after lesions or resection of the corpus callosum. One patient described how her left hand would attempt to unbutton her blouse as soon as she finished getting dressed. When she was asked to give the experimenter a favorite book, her left hand reached out and snagged the closest book, whereupon she exclaimed with surprise, "Oh, that's not the one!" These behaviors provide further evidence of motor planning as a competitive process, one that can entail a competition not just between potential targets of an action (e.g., the coffee cup or the computer keyboard), but also between the two limbs.

As we might expect, given its role in spatial representation, planning-related activity is also evident in the parietal lobe. When a spatial target is presented to a monkey, neurons begin to discharge in at least two regions within posterior parietal cortex (PPC): the lateral intraparietal area (LIP) and the medial intraparietal area (MIP; Calton et al., 2002; Cui & Andersen, 2007). When an arm movement is used to point to the target, the activity becomes stronger in the MIP than the LIP. But if the animal simply looks at the target, activity becomes stronger in the LIP than the MIP.

Besides demonstrating effector specificity within the PPC, these findings emphasize that plans for both reaching and eye movements are simultaneously prepared, consistent with the affordance competition hypothesis. Effector specificity within the parietal lobe has also been identified in humans with the aid of fMRI, which shows that different regions of the intraparietal sulcus are activated for eye and arm movements (Tosoni et al., 2008).

Together, these results help reveal how action selection and movement planning evolve within parietofrontal pathways. In general, we see many similarities between posterior parietal cortex and premotor regions. For example, cells in both regions exhibit directional tuning, and population vectors derived from either area provide an excellent match to behavior.

These areas, however, also have some interesting differences. One difference is seen in the *reference frame* for movement. To take our coffee cup example, we need to recognize that reaching requires a transformation from vision-centered coordinates to hand-centered coordinates. Our eyes can inform us of where objects lie in space. To reach an object with our hand, however, we need to define the position of the object with respect to the hand, not the eyes. Moreover, to sense hand position, we don't have to look at our hands. Somatosensory information is sufficient.

You can prove this to yourself by trying to reach for something with the starting position of your hand either visible or occluded. Your accuracy is just as good either way. Physiological studies suggest that representations within parietal cortex tend to be in an eye-centered reference frame, whereas those in premotor cortex are more hand centered (Batista et al., 1999). Thus, parietofrontal processing involves a reference frame transformation.

Another intriguing difference between parietal and premotor motor areas comes from a fascinating study that attempted to identify where intentions are formed and how we become aware of them (Desmurget et al., 2009). The study employed direct brain stimulation during neurosurgery. When the stimulation was over posterior parietal cortex, the patients reported that they experienced the intention or desire to move, making comments such as, "I felt a desire to lick my lips." In fact, if the stimulation level was increased, the intention was replaced with the perception that they had actually performed the movement.

This experience, however, was illusory. The patients did not produce any overt movement, and even careful observation of the muscles showed no activity. In contrast,

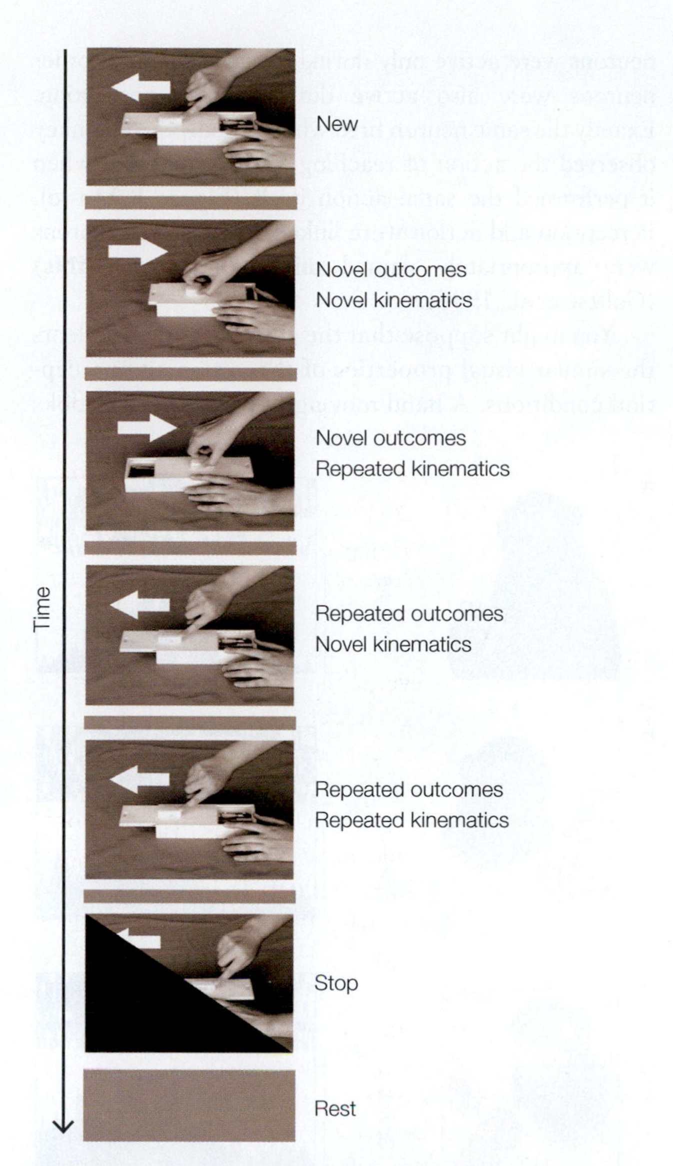

FIGURE 8.22 A set of stimuli for inducing repetition suppression. Participants watched a series of movie clips of a hand opening or closing a box. In this example, the initial clip shows the hand moving forward to open the box. In subsequent clips, the outcome was either repeated or novel, and the kinematics (direction of motion) was either repeated or novel relative to the previous clip. Repetition suppression (RS) effects were measured by comparison of the BOLD response over successive clips.

stimulation of the dorsal premotor cortex triggered complex multi-joint movements such as arm rotation or wrist flexion, but here the patients had no conscious awareness of the action and no sense of movement intention. The researchers suggested that the posterior parietal cortex is more strongly linked to motor intention (i.e., movement goals), and premotor cortex is linked more to movement execution. The signal we are aware of when making a movement emerges not from the movement itself, but rather from the prior conscious intention and predictions that we make about the movement in advance of action.

This idea is further supported by an fMRI study conducted by Antonia Hamilton and Scott Grafton (2007) at UC Santa Barbara. They asked whether motor representations in parietal regions correspond to the nuts and bolts of the movements, or to the grander intentions concerned with the goals and outcome of the action. This study took advantage of the widely studied *repetition suppression (RS) effect* (see Chapter 6).

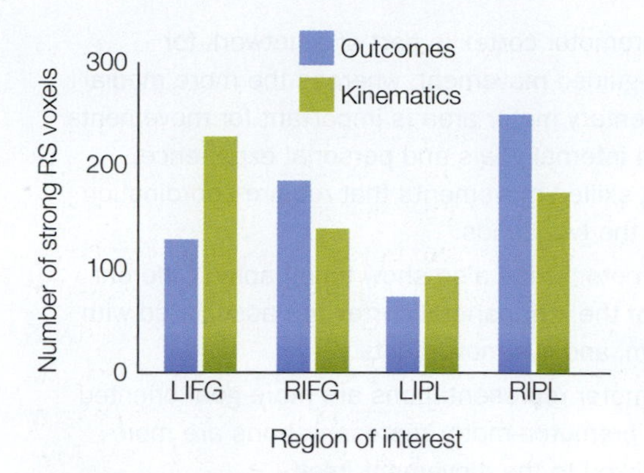

FIGURE 8.23 Brain regions showing repetition suppression effects for repeated outcomes and movements. Voxels showing RS in the inferior frontal gyrus (IFG) and the inferior parietal lobule (IPL) in the right and left hemispheres. RS was strongest in the left IFG when the movement was repeated and strongest in the right IPL when the outcome was repeated.

RS was first described in studies of visual perception: When a stimulus is repeated, the blood oxygen level–dependent (BOLD) response to the second presentation of the stimulus is lower than that to the initial presentation. In applying this fMRI method to action perception, the researchers asked whether the RS effect was linked to the goal of an action, the specific movement, or a combination of these factors (**Figure 8.22**). To test this, participants were shown videos of short action clips. The videos showed a box that could be opened by sliding the cover forward or backward. The researchers could present pairs of video clips in which either the same goal (e.g., closing the cover) was achieved by two different actions (one sliding forward and the other backward), or the same movement was made but had two different results: an open box or a closed box.

The results showed that RS in the right inferior parietal cortex was related to the action goal, whereas RS in left frontal cortex was related to the movement (**Figure 8.23**), providing a slick demonstration of goal-based processing in parietal cortex and movement-based processing in frontal cortex.

TAKE-HOME MESSAGES

- The affordance competition hypothesis proposes that the processes of action selection (what to do) and specification (how to do it) occur simultaneously within an interactive neural network that continuously evolves from planning to execution, with action selection emerging from a competitive process.

- Lateral premotor cortex is part of a network for stimulus-guided movement, whereas the more medial supplementary motor area is important for movements based on internal goals and personal experience, including skilled movements that require coordination between the two hands.
- Parietal motor areas also show topography: Different regions of the intraparietal cortex are associated with hand, arm, and eye movements.
- Parietal motor representations are more goal oriented, whereas premotor–motor representations are more closely linked to the movement itself.
- Conscious awareness of movement appears to be related to the neural processing of action intention rather than the movement itself.

8.5 Links Between Action and Perception

Defining where in the brain perception ends and action starts may be an impossible task. Perceptual systems have evolved to support action; likewise, actions are produced in anticipation of sensory consequences. For a monkey in the wild, seeing a ripe banana on a tree engages the action systems required to retrieve the food, and movement toward the fruit engages perception systems in anticipation of the tasty treat.

As part of their studies on the vocabulary of motor intentions, Rizzolatti's research group was conducting a study of premotor cortex in monkeys, recording from neurons that were involved in the control of hand and mouth actions. The story goes that a graduate student walked into the lab holding a cone of gelato. As he moved the cone to his mouth to lick it, a surge in cellular activity was observed in the monkey's neuron that would be activated if the monkey were grasping and moving something to its mouth, even though, in this instance, the animal was not moving. In fact, the animal seemed distracted, having shifted its focus to the gelato licker.

As can often happen in science, this serendipitous observation became a starting point for a line of work that has provided some of the most compelling evidence of how perception, action, and cognition are linked. Simply observing or imagining an action was all it took to activate some of the same premotor cells involved in the actual movement. For instance, Rizzolatti and his colleagues had monkeys view different objects. On some trials, the monkey produced an action such as reaching for or grasping the object (e.g., a peanut). On other trials, the monkey observed the experimenter performing similar actions (Pellegrino et al., 1992). Although some premotor neurons were active only during production trials, other neurons were also active during action perception. Exactly the same neuron fired when an individual monkey observed the action of reaching for a peanut and when it performed the same action itself (**Figure 8.24a–c**). Perception and action were linked. These latter neurons were appropriately named **mirror neurons (MNs)** (Gallese et al., 1996).

You might suppose that the activity in MNs reflects the similar visual properties of the action and perception conditions. A hand moving toward a peanut looks

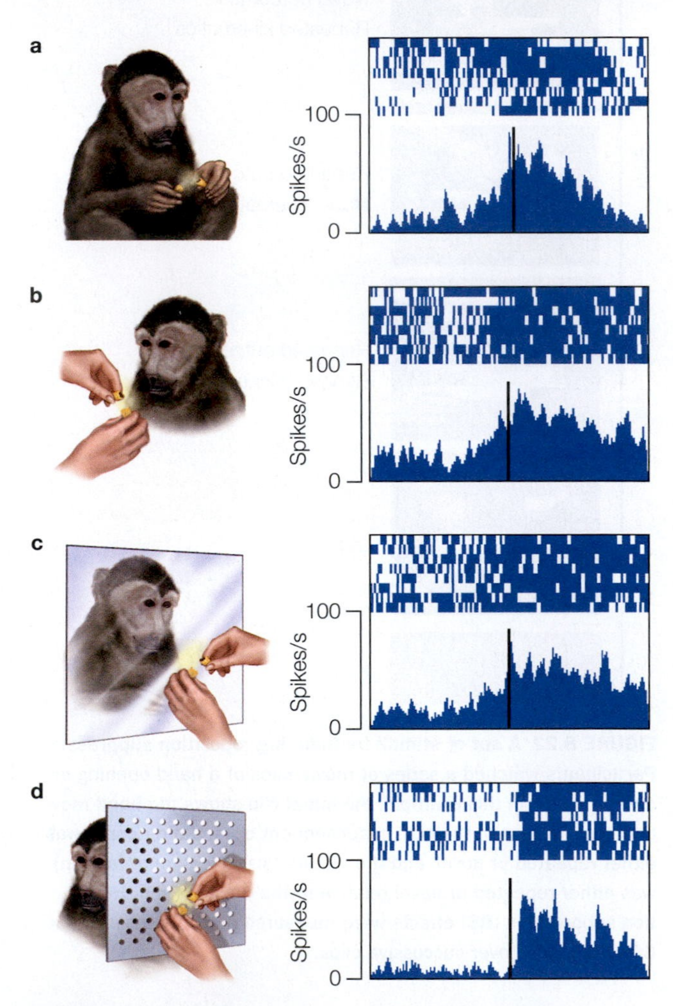

FIGURE 8.24 Identification of a mirror neuron. Responses of a single neuron in a monkey's ventral premotor cortex during the performance or perception of different actions. The bold black line marks the onset of the salient event in each condition: **(a)** when the monkey itself breaks a peanut and views and hears the breaking of the peanut, **(b)** when the monkey watches someone else breaking a peanut and views and hears the breaking of the peanut, **(c)** when the monkey sees someone else breaking a peanut but cannot hear the peanut breaking, and **(d)** when the monkey hears but does not see someone else breaking a peanut. Note that when only heard (d), all activity is after the sound because the animal doesn't see the person moving to break the peanut. This neuron is considered a mirror neuron because it responds not only to actions that are undertaken by the monkey, but also to actions that are viewed or heard by the monkey.

much the same whether the hand is yours or someone else's. Additional experiments, however, ruled out this hypothesis. First, the same MN that is activated when the monkey cracks a peanut itself is activated when the monkey merely *hears* a peanut being cracked (**Figure 8.24d**). Second, MNs are also active when a monkey watches someone reach behind a screen for a peanut but cannot see the grasping of the peanut. In fact, there doesn't even need to be a peanut behind the screen, as long as the monkey thinks there's a hidden nut (Umilta et al., 2001). Thus, the activity of the MN is correlated with a goal-oriented action—retrieving a peanut—independent of how this information is received: by the monkey's own action, by viewing someone else's action, by hearing someone else's action, or by viewing only a portion of someone else's action but believing that the action is taking place.

Neurons in the parietal and temporal lobes also show similar activity patterns during action production and comprehension, suggesting that MNs are widely distributed, rather than located in a single region dedicated to linking perception and action. As discussed earlier in this chapter and in Chapter 6, the dorsal pathway, including parietal and premotor cortex, activates when people make judgments about the use of an object and while they use the object. Interestingly, the extent and intensity of the activation patterns reflect the individual's own particular motor repertoire: Skilled dancers show stronger activation in areas with MNs when watching videos of familiar dance routines as compared to unfamiliar routines (**Figure 8.25**).

The work on mirror neurons—or more appropriately, a **mirror neuron network**—has revealed the

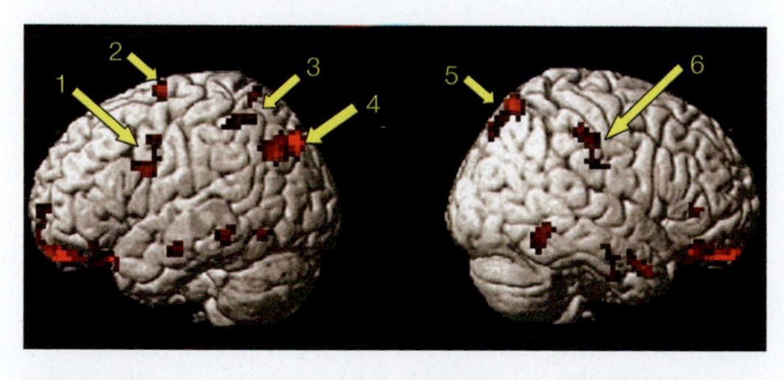

FIGURE 8.25 Activation of mirror neurons is affected by level of expertise.
When skilled dancers observe a dance they know well (versus a dance they don't know at all), an increase in the BOLD response is observed in the premotor cortex (1, 2), intraparietal sulcus (3, 6), posterior superior temporal sulcus (4), and superior parietal lobe (5). These areas make up the neural network of action observation and include regions that are also activated when the person produces skilled movements, constituting what is considered to be the human mirror neuron network.

intimate links between perception and action, suggesting that our ability to understand the actions of others depends on the neural structures that would be engaged if we were to produce the action ourselves. The engagement of the motor system during action comprehension can even be observed in the primary motor cortex. For example, the excitability of neurons in motor cortex is modulated when people observe actions produced by another individual, and this modulation shows a high degree of effector specificity. TMS-elicited motor evoked potentials (MEPs) in hand muscles are larger when people observe video clips of gestures being made with the same hand as compared to videos of the same gestures by the opposite hand. Similar effects are elicited with relatively abstract presentations of the actions, such as the sounds of hands clapping.

The excitability changes within motor cortex also reflect the participants' expertise. One study of action comprehension compared three groups of people: elite basketball players, expert sports journalists (selected because they watched basketball 7–8 hours a week), and a control group who knew nothing about basketball (Aglioti et al., 2008). The participants were shown short video clips, either of a person about to shoot a basketball free throw or of a person about to initiate a free kick in soccer (**Figure 8.26**).

Both the basketball players and the journalists showed an increase in motor cortex excitability of arm muscles while watching the basketball shots, and they actually showed an excitability decrease in these muscles when watching the soccer kicks. In contrast, the novices showed a small and nonspecific effect: an increase in arm MEPs for both basketball and soccer videos. Even more interesting, only the skilled players showed differential responses to video clips depicting a free throw that would be successful versus those depicting a throw that would be inaccurate even before the outcome was known. These results suggest that, with expertise, the motor system has a fine sensitivity to discriminate good and poor performance during action observation, a form of action comprehension. It also suggests that the well-practiced motor system is anticipatory in nature, giving it the ability to predict others' actions in the arena of their expertise.

Coaches and sports psychologists recognize the intimate relationship between action observation and action production. The skier mentally visualizes his movements from one gate to the next as he prepares to run a slalom course. This process is thought to help strengthen perception-action links. For example, in one neuroimaging study, participants learned to associate novel 3-D objects with their sounds, either by manipulating the objects or by watching the experimenter manipulate them. Active manipulation led to a well-known result:

a Static **b** Shooting the basketball **c** Kicking a soccer ball

FIGURE 8.26 Excitation of motor cortex increases during action observation by skilled performers. Examples of photographs shown to elite basketball players, expert observers, and novices while MEPs were recorded from forearm muscles. Relative to the static condition (a), basketball players and expert observers showed an increase in arm muscle MEPs when observing the player shooting a basketball (b), but not when observing him kick a soccer ball (c). Novices showed weaker activations in all conditions.

better learning. More interesting, when participants were viewing the objects that had been actively learned, sensorimotor areas showed greater activation compared to when they were viewing the objects that had been passively learned (Butler & James, 2013), and there was an increased connectivity between motor and visual systems.

Is the activation that is seen in motor areas during observation of action essential for comprehending action? Does the modulation of excitability in motor cortex indicate that understanding the actions of another requires representations in motor cortex? Or are these activation patterns some sort of priming effect, reflecting the subtle and automatic planning of the action when a familiar stimulus is presented? These are difficult questions to answer (see Hickok, 2009). Nonetheless, fMRI and TMS studies are important in demonstrating the degree of overlap between neural systems involved in perception and action. They remind us that dividing the brain into perception and motor regions may be useful for pedagogical reasons (say, for defining chapters in a textbook), but that the brain does not honor such divisions.

TAKE-HOME MESSAGES

- Mirror neurons respond to an action both when that action is produced by an animal itself and when the animal observes a similar action produced by another individual.
- A human sensorimotor mirror network spans frontoparietal cortex, with activation extending into the motor cortex during action observation.
- The mirror neuron network has been hypothesized to be essential for comprehending and anticipating actions produced by other individuals.

8.6 Recouping Motor Loss

Lesions to the primary motor cortex or the spinal motor neurons can result in hemiplegia, as mentioned in Section 8.1, or in *hemiparesis*, a unilateral weakness. Such lesions severely impact the patient's ability to use the affected limbs on the contralesional side; unfortunately, these patients rarely regain significant control over the limbs. Here we will look at how the insights gained from basic research on the motor system are being translated into new interventions, making it possible for people with severe motor disabilities to once again control their interactions with the environment.

Regaining Movement After Loss of Motor Cortex

Two critical questions for the clinician and patient are, What is the patient's potential for recovery? and What is the best strategy for rehabilitation? In a recent report, a panel of experts reviewed the current status of biomarkers for predicting motor recovery from stroke (L. A. Boyd et al., 2017). While somewhat pessimistic overall in tone, the evidence recommended assessing two measures: The integrity of the corticospinal tract as measured with DTI, and the presence of upper-limb MEPs in response to TMS. These biomarkers look especially promising when the assessment is performed after the patient has recovered from the critical initial post-stroke period (the post-acute phase), outperforming the location of the lesion and even the behavioral asymmetry between the affected and unaffected limbs.

Traditionally, the main treatment to regain motor function is physical therapy, a behavioral intervention that seeks to retrain the affected limbs. Unfortunately, physical therapy tends to produce only modest recovery. Intuitively, we might think that more therapy is better, but a recent study challenged this notion (Lang et al., 2016). Eighty-five post-stroke patients with upper-limb hemiparesis were divided into four groups. One group received standard physical therapy with an individualized training program that continued until no further improvements were seen. The other groups participated in an intensive 8-week training program, performing a series of specific limb training exercises and completing 3,200, 6,400, or 9,600 repetitions of the task. Discouragingly, the researchers saw only a modest change in motor function and no real evidence that the degree of benefit was related to the amount of training. In fact, the group that practiced 6,400 repetitions showed no measurable benefit.

A different behavioral method is based on the idea that the brain may favor short-term solutions over long-term gains. For example, a patient with hemiparesis of the right arm and an itch on her right leg is likely to reach across her body to scratch it with her left arm rather than using her weak limb. Indeed, the situation may snowball, exacerbating the difference in functionality of the two limbs. To counteract this pattern, rehabilitation specialists use constraint-induced movement therapy (CIMT), a method that restrains patients from using their unaffected limb. For example, they might wear a thick mitt on the unaffected hand, forcing them to use the affected hand if they need to grasp something. Intensive CIMT can improve both strength and function in the paretic upper limbs, with improvements measurable even 2 years later (S. L. Wolf et al., 2008).

Scientists are currently seeking novel interventions that more directly target specific neural mechanisms. One approach is to look for agents that can directly promote neural recovery in the damaged hemisphere. To develop this idea, researchers induced small strokes in the motor cortex of mice, producing a loss of motor function (**Figure 8.27a**). In a manner similar to the compensatory processes observed in humans, the mice adapt, using the unaffected limb. However, if the tissue surrounding the lesion, the peri-infarct cortex, is intact, the mice begin to show a degree of recovery. Moreover, stimulating the peri-infarct cortex with TMS accelerates this recovery process (reviewed in Carmichael, 2006).

Why is recovery slow or limited? Thomas Carmichael at UCLA has carefully examined this question in the rodent model (Clarkson et al., 2010). His work has shown that, after stroke, there is an increase in GABA in the peri-infarct zone. This inhibitory neurotransmitter reduces the efficacy of sensory inputs and in turn leads to neuronal hypoactivity.

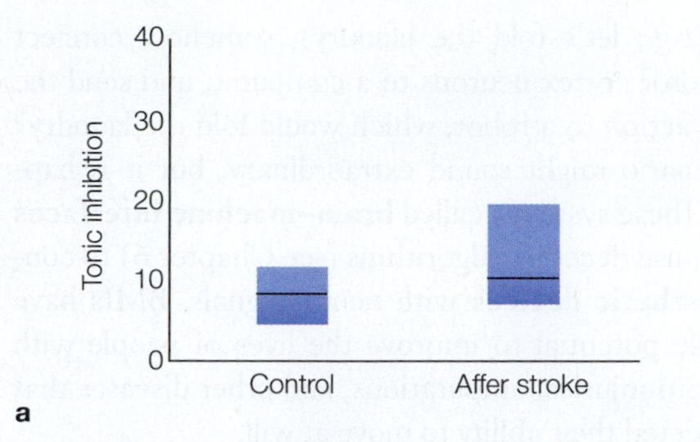

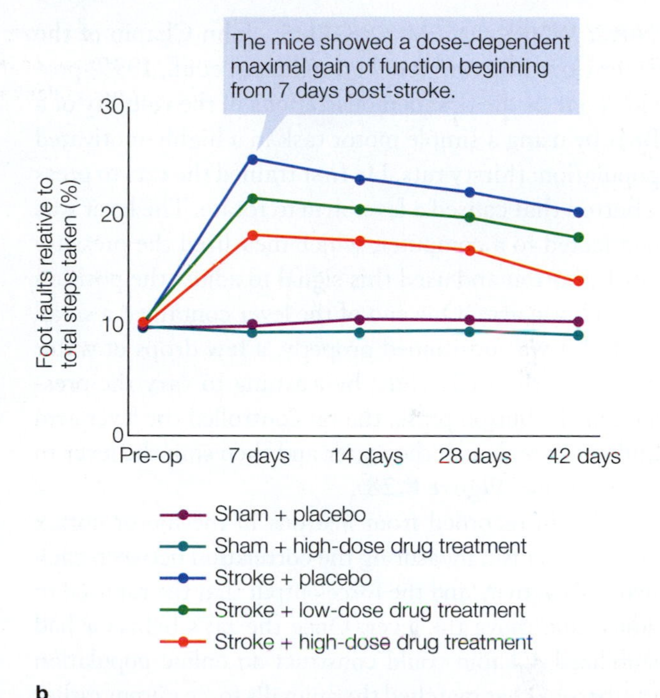

FIGURE 8.27 Inducing and treating cortical strokes in mice. **(a) Tonic inhibition in mouse peri-infarct motor cortex increases following induced stroke. Results are from patch-clamp recordings from slices of motor cortex. (b) Behavioral recovery after reducing tonic inhibition by applying a drug to reduce GABA efficacy. The *y*-axis shows forelimb foot faults as an index to behavior; the *x*-axis shows time since the stroke. Treatment started 3 days post-stroke.**

These observations led Carmichael and his colleagues to use pharmacological interventions to reduce GABA levels. These drug interventions have shown early and robust gain of motor recovery after a stroke in the mouse model (**Figure 8.27b**), and the next step is clinical trials in humans. In the interim, scientists are using other methods to promote neural plasticity in humans, such as repetitive TMS over the lesioned cortex (Kleim et al., 2006).

The Brain–Machine Interface

Can neural signals be used to control a movement directly with the brain, bypassing the intermediate stage of muscles? For instance, could you plan an action in your motor cortex (e.g., let's fold the laundry), somehow connect those motor cortex neurons to a computer, and send the planned action to a robot, which would fold the laundry? This scenario might sound extraordinary, but it is happening. These systems, called **brain–machine interfaces (BMIs)**, use decoding algorithms (see Chapter 6) to control **prosthetic devices** with neural signals. BMIs have incredible potential to improve the lives of people with spinal cord injuries, amputations, and other diseases that have affected their ability to move at will.

EARLY WORK ON BMI SYSTEMS John Chapin of the State University of New York (Chapin et al., 1999) provided one of the first demonstrations of the viability of a BMI by using a simple motor task in a highly motivated population: thirsty rats. He first trained the rats to press a button that caused a lever arm to rotate. The lever was connected to a computer, which measured the pressure on the button and used this signal to adjust the position of a robotic arm. One end of the lever contained a small well; if it was positioned properly, a few drops of water would fill the well. Thus, by learning to vary the pressure of the button press, the rat controlled the lever arm and could replenish the water and then spin the lever to take a drink (**Figure 8.28**).

Chapin recorded from neurons in the motor cortex during this task, measuring the correlation between each neuron's activity and the force output that the rat used to adjust and move the lever. Once the rat's behavior had stabilized, Chapin could construct an online population vector, one that matched the animal's force output rather than movement direction. With as few as 30 neurons or so, the match between the population vector and behavior was excellent.

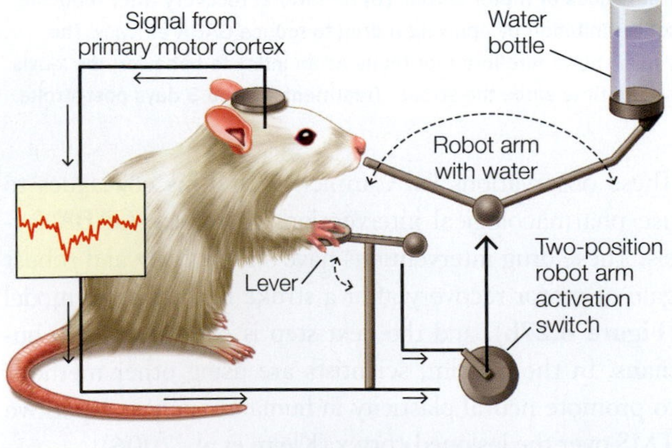

Here is where things get interesting. Chapin then disconnected the input of the button to the computer and instead used the output of the time-varying population vector as input to the computer to control the position of the lever arm. The rats still pushed the button, but the button no longer controlled the lever; the lever was now controlled by their brain activity. If the activity level in the vector was high, the arm swiveled in one direction; if low, it swiveled in the other direction, or even stopped the lever arm entirely. Amazingly, population vectors generated from as few as 25 neurons proved sufficient for the rats to successfully control the robotic arm to obtain water.

As impressive as this result was, Chapin could not, of course, tell the animals about the shift from arm control to brain control. Unaware of the switch to BMI, the rats continued to press and release the button. Over time, though, the animals became sensitive to the lack of a precise correlation between their arm movements and the lever position. Amazingly, they continued to generate the cortical signals necessary to control the lever, but they also stopped moving their limb. They learned they could kick back, relax, and simply think about pushing the button with the precision required to satiate their thirst.

Over the past generation, research on BMI systems has skyrocketed. Three elements are required: a method to record neural activity, a computer with decoding algorithms, and a prosthetic effector. In the first primate studies, monkeys were trained to control the two-dimensional position of a computer cursor. With more sophisticated algorithms, these animals have learned to use BMI systems that control a robotic arm with multiple joints, moving the prosthetic limb through three-dimensional space to grasp food and bring it to the mouth (Velliste et al., 2008; see videos at http://motorlab.neurobio.pitt.edu/multimedia.php).

Current BMI systems now work not only with output from primary motor cortex, but also with cells in premotor, supplementary motor, and parietal cortex (Carmena et al., 2003). The control algorithms have also become more advanced, adopting ideas from work on machine learning. Rather than using a serial process in which the directional tuning of the neurons is fixed during the initial free-movement stage, researchers now use algorithms that allow the tuning to be updated by real-time visual feedback as the animal learns to control the BMI device (D. M. Taylor et al., 2002).

MAKING BMI SYSTEMS STABLE One major challenge facing BMI researchers is how to establish a stable control system, one that can last for years. In a typical experiment, the animal starts each daily session by

FIGURE 8.28 Rats can be trained to use a lever to control a robotic arm that delivers drops of water.
Neurons in the rat's primary motor cortex are recorded while the animal presses the lever. A population vector is constructed, representing the force exerted by the animal. A switch is then activated so that the position of the lever is now based on the population vector. The rat soon learns that it does not have to press the lever to retrieve the water.

performing real movements to enable the researcher to construct the tuning profiles of each neuron. The process is rather like a daily recalibration. Once the neuron profiles are established, the BMI system is implemented. This approach, though, is not practical for BMI use as a clinical treatment. First, it is very difficult to record a fixed set of neurons over a long period of time. Moreover, if BMI is to be useful for paralyzed individuals or people who have lost a limb, construction of neuron profiles using real movements won't be possible.

To address this issue, researchers have looked at both the stability and the flexibility of neural representations. Karunesh Ganguly and Jose Carmena (2009) at UC Berkeley implanted a grid of 128 microelectrodes in the motor cortex of a monkey. This device enabled them to make continuous daily recordings. Although the signal from some electrodes would change from day to day, a substantial number of neurons remained stable for days (**Figure 8.29a**).

Using the output from this stable set, a BMI system successfully performed center-out reaching movements over a 3-week period. The animals achieved close to 100% accuracy in reaching the targets, and the time required to complete each movement became much shorter as the study proceeded (**Figure 8.29b**). This result suggested that with a stable decoder, the motor cortex neurons used a remarkably stable activation pattern for prosthetic control.

The shocker came in the next experiment. Using these well-trained animals, researchers randomly shuffled the decoder. For example, if a neuron had a preferred direction of 90°, the algorithm was altered so that the output of this neuron was now treated as if it had a preferred direction of 130°. This new "stable" decoder, of course,

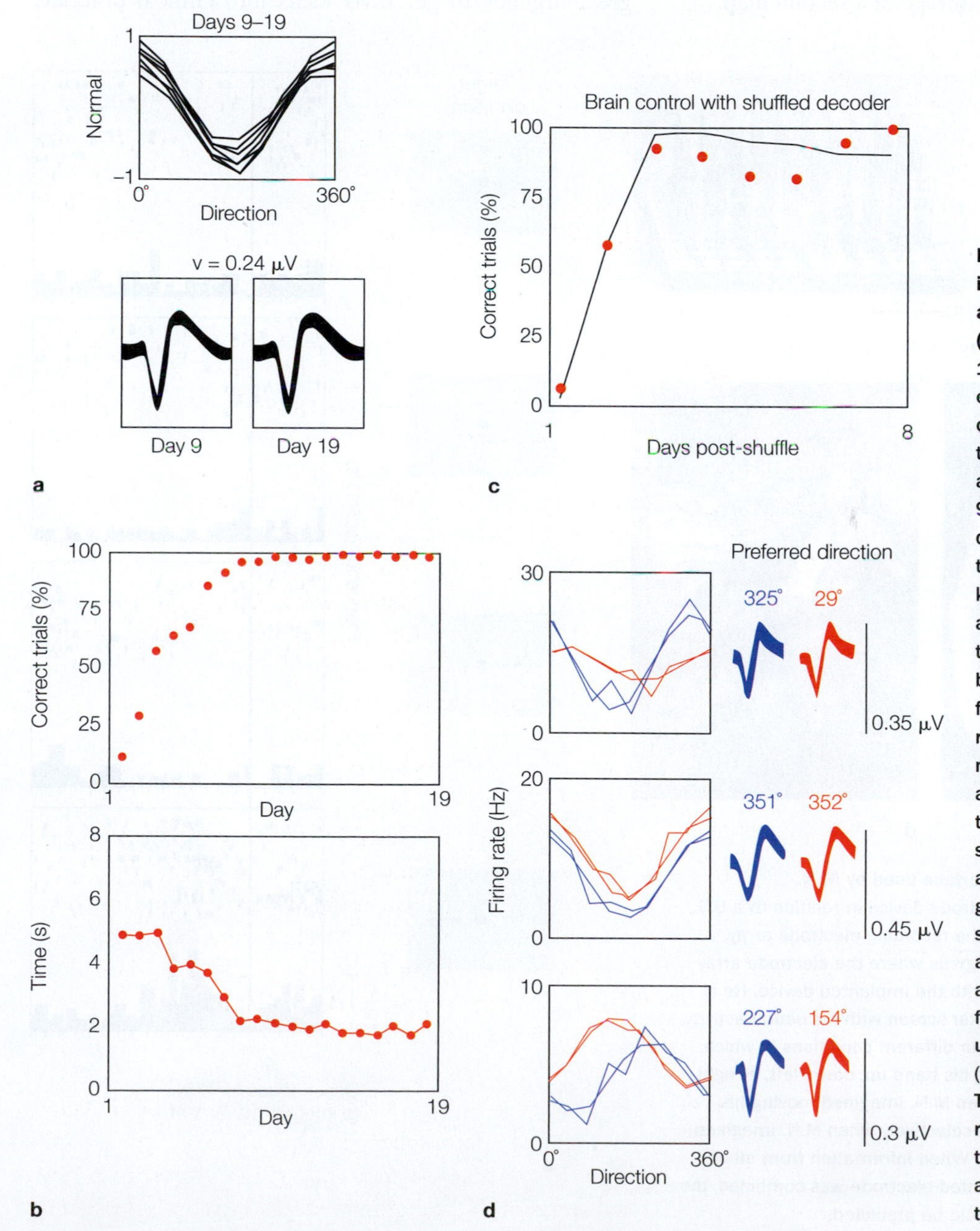

FIGURE 8.29 Stability and flexibility of performance and neural activity during BMI control. **(a)** Recordings were made for 19 consecutive days from an ensemble of neurons in motor cortex. Directional tunings for two neurons show remarkable stability across Sessions 9 through 19. **(b)** Using a fixed decoder based on the output of the neural ensemble, the monkey learns to successfully move a cursor under BMI control in the center-out task. Accuracy becomes near-perfect within a few days, and the amount of time required on each trial drops significantly. **(c)** Performance with a shuffled decoder. The input to the BMI algorithm was randomly shuffled in Session 20, and the animal failed to reach any targets. With continued use of the shuffled decoder, however, the animal quickly became proficient at reaching the target. **(d)** Tuning functions for three neurons when used in the original decoder (blue) or a shuffled decoder (red). Tuning functions for some neurons shifted dramatically for the two contexts. With practice, the animal could successfully control the cursor with either decoder.

played havoc with BMI performance. The monkey would think "move up," and the cursor would move sideways. Over a few days of practice, however, the monkey was able to adapt to the new decoder, again reaching near-perfect performance (**Figure 8.29c**).

With visual feedback, the monkey could learn to use a decoder unrelated to arm movements; as long as the algorithm remained stable, the monkey could actually reshape the decoder. Even more impressive, when the original decoder was reinstated, the animal again quickly adapted. Interestingly, with this adaptive system, the tuning functions of each neuron varied from one context to the next and even deviated from their shape during natural movement (**Figure 8.29d**). It appears, then, that long-term neuroprosthetic control leads to the formation of a remarkably stable cortical map that is readily recalled and resistant to the storage of a second map.

These results hold great promise for the translation of BMI research into the clinic. They demonstrate that the representation of individual neurons can be highly flexible, adapting to the current context. Such flexibility is essential for ensuring that the system will remain stable over time, and it is also essential for using a single BMI system to control a host of devices, such as computer cursors or eating utensils. It is reasonable to assume that a single set of neurons can learn to incorporate the different challenges presented by devices that have no friction or mass (e.g., the position of a mouse on a computer screen) and by devices with large mass and complicated moving parts (e.g., a prosthetic arm or a robot).

MOVING BMI RESEARCH INTO THE CLINIC There is great urgency to get BMI ideas into clinical practice.

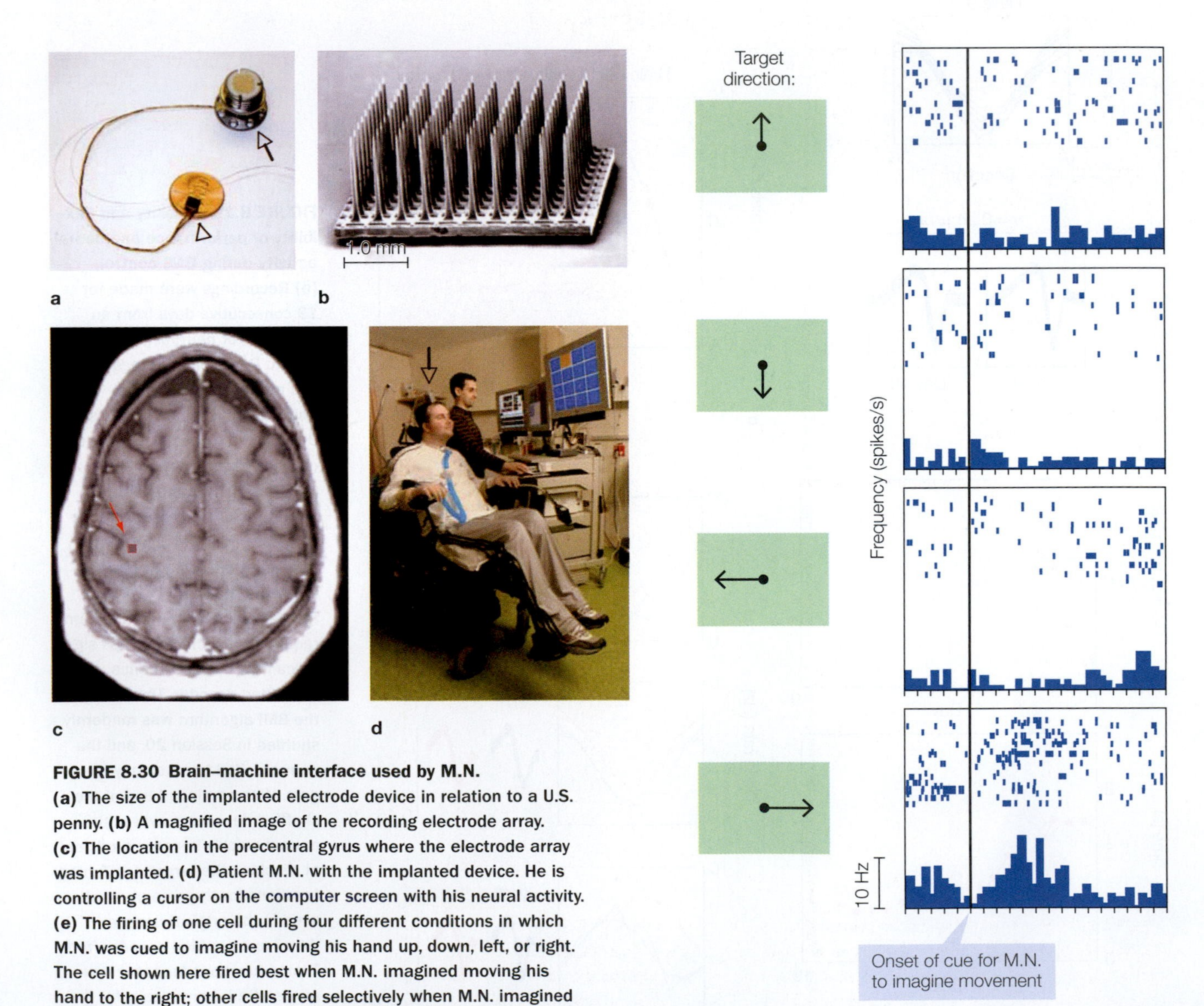

FIGURE 8.30 Brain–machine interface used by M.N.
(a) The size of the implanted electrode device in relation to a U.S. penny. **(b)** A magnified image of the recording electrode array. **(c)** The location in the precentral gyrus where the electrode array was implanted. **(d)** Patient M.N. with the implanted device. He is controlling a cursor on the computer screen with his neural activity. **(e)** The firing of one cell during four different conditions in which M.N. was cued to imagine moving his hand up, down, left, or right. The cell shown here fired best when M.N. imagined moving his hand to the right; other cells fired selectively when M.N. imagined moving his hand left, up, or down. When information from all of the cells recorded from the implanted electrode was combined, the desired direction of movement could be predicted.

The number of patients who would benefit from such systems is huge: In the United States alone, over 5.5 million people suffer some form of paralysis, from either injury or disease, and 1.7 million have limb loss. This need has motivated some scientists to move toward clinical trials in humans.

John Donoghue and his colleagues at Brown University presented the first such trial, working with a patient, M.N., who had become quadriplegic following a stab wound that severed his spinal cord. The researchers implanted an array of microchips in the patient's motor cortex (Hochberg et al., 2006). Despite 3 years of paralysis, the cells were quite active. Moreover, the firing level of the neurons varied as M.N. imagined different types of movements. Some units were active when he imagined making movements that involved the shoulder; others, when he imagined moving his hand. The researchers were also able to determine the directional tuning profiles of each neuron, by asking M.N. to imagine movements over a range of directions.

From these data, they created population vectors and used them as control signals for BMI devices. Using the output of about a hundred neurons, M.N. was able to move a cursor around a computer screen (**Figure 8.30**). His responses were relatively slow, and the path of the cursor was somewhat erratic. Nonetheless, M.N. could control the cursor to open his e-mail, use software programs to make drawings, or play simple computer games, such as Pong. When connected to a prosthetic limb, M.N. could control the opening and closing of the hand—a first step to performing much more complicated tasks. Another patient learned, after months of training, to use a BMI system to control a robotic arm to reach for and grasp objects (Hochberg et al., 2012).

Instead of employing a robotic arm, other researchers are aiming to regain control over actual limb movements by using neural signals from the cortex to stimulate the peripheral muscles and nerves, bypassing the damaged spinal cord (Ajiboye et al., 2017; **Figure 8.31a**). One such system was successfully tested in a patient who had been quadriplegic for 8 years from a high-cervical spinal cord injury. Two recording-electrode arrays, each with 96 channels, were implanted in the hand area of his motor cortex. The output from the cortical recordings was connected to an external device that provided input to 36 stimulating electrodes that penetrated the skin, terminating in the muscles of the upper and lower arm and allowing the restoration of finger, thumb, wrist, elbow, and shoulder movements (**Figure 8.31b**). In future

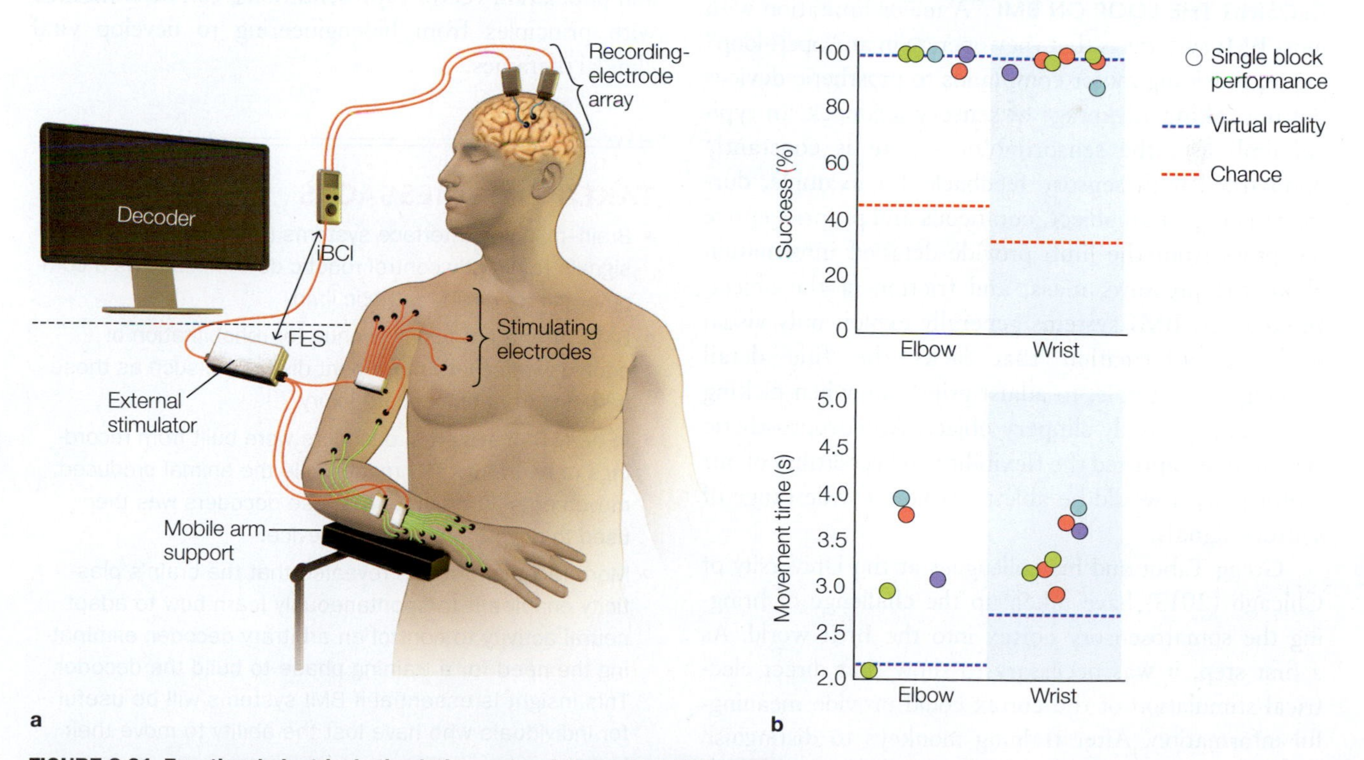

FIGURE 8.31 Functional electrical stimulation and an intracortical BMI system.
(a) Neural signals from the brain are used to drive the functional electrical stimulator (FES), which activates arm (triceps and biceps) and wrist muscles. iBCI = intracortical brain–computer interface.
(b) This graph shows the patient's performance when using the brain decoder to move a virtual arm (dashed blue line) and to move his own arm (colored circles) compared with chance (dashed red line). Different colored circles indicate trials on different days. The top graph tracks success; the bottom graph tracks movement time. Good performance was achieved with either the arm or wrist.

work, these systems will become wireless, removing the need for external connections.

So far, we have focused on BMI systems that use invasive methods, neurosurgically implanting recording devices in the cortex. These approaches have the advantage of obtaining neural signals with great fidelity; however, they not only involve the risk associated with any surgical procedure, but also require repeated surgeries because the recording devices fail over time. An alternative is to use noninvasive methods, recording neural signals at the scalp.

To this end, University of Minnesota researchers are working on a BMI using EEG. Their challenge is to create decoding algorithms from relatively crude EEG signals that can accurately control interface devices. In initial tests with healthy college students, the participants were quite successful at moving a robotic arm in a 2-D plane to hover above an object and then guiding the arm down in the third dimension to grasp the object. This level of control was possible after just a few training sessions and was preserved over the course of several months (Meng et al., 2016; see video at http://images.nature.com/original/nature-assets/srep/2016/161214/srep38565/extref/srep38565-s4.mov.)

CLOSING THE LOOP ON BMI A major limitation with most BMI systems is that they operate in an "open-loop" mode, providing motor commands to prosthetic devices but not taking advantage of sensory feedback. In typical limb use, the sensorimotor system is constantly bombarded with sensory feedback; for example, during grasping of an object, cutaneous and proprioceptive receptors from the limb provide detailed information about the pressure, mass, and friction of the object. In contrast, BMI systems generally exploit only visual feedback—information that lacks the fine detail needed, for example, to adjust grip force when picking up an unexpectedly slippery object. A neuroprosthetic system that captured the flexibility and versatility of our motor system would be able to exploit a wide range of sensory signals.

Gregg Tabot and his colleagues at the University of Chicago (2013) have taken up the challenge of bringing the somatosensory cortex into the BMI world. As a first step, it was necessary to show that direct electrical stimulation of the cortex could provide meaningful information. After training monkeys to distinguish between pressures applied at different skin locations, the researchers identified the regions in somatosensory cortex that were activated during the task. They then positioned stimulating electrodes in those regions, enabling comparison of the animals' discrimination performance on real stimuli (vibratory stimuli applied on the skin) and virtual stimuli (direct cortical stimulation). Performance was nearly as good for the virtual stimuli as for the real stimuli. Presumably, this information could be included in a closed-loop BMI system, providing a better approximation of how we naturally combine information from many sensory sources to achieve the exquisite control we summon when using our hands to manipulate tools.

There are major challenges to closing the loop. When designing a BMI for amputees or for people with spinal injuries, we can't predetermine what the stimulation patterns should be. Once the electrodes are in place, however, we can map the somatotopic organization of the array by systematically delivering pulses through each electrode and recording the participant's subjective reports. Moreover, as we have seen with open-loop BMI systems and cochlear implants (see Chapter 5), the brain exhibits tremendous plasticity in learning from arbitrary input patterns. Thus, it may be sufficient simply to activate the somatosensory cortex in a consistent manner (e.g., depending on limb position) and allow the natural dynamics of neural activity to figure out the meaning of these signals.

BMI research is still in its infancy. This work, though, provides a compelling example of how basic findings in neuroscience, such as the coding of movement direction and population vector representations, can be combined with principles from bioengineering to develop vital clinical therapies.

TAKE-HOME MESSAGES

- Brain–machine interface systems (BMIs) use neural signals to directly control robotic devices such as a computer cursor or a prosthetic limb.
- BMIs offer a promising avenue for rehabilitation of people with severe movement disorders, such as those resulting from spinal cord injury.
- In early BMI systems, decoders were built from recordings of neural activity made while the animal produced movements. The output of these decoders was then used to drive the prosthetic device.
- More recent work has revealed that the brain's plasticity enables it to spontaneously learn how to adapt neural activity to control an arbitrary decoder, eliminating the need for a training phase to build the decoder. This insight is essential if BMI systems will be useful for individuals who have lost the ability to move their limbs.
- Current BMI research is using a wide range of techniques and neural signals, some of which involve invasive procedures and others of which use noninvasive procedures.

8.7 Movement Initiation and the Basal Ganglia

With multiple action plans duking it out in the cortex, how do we decide which movement to execute? We can't use our right arm to simultaneously type on the computer keyboard and reach for a cup of coffee. Parallel processing works fine for planning, but at some point, the system must commit to a particular action.

The basal ganglia play a critical role in movement initiation. To understand this, it is important to examine the neuroanatomical wiring of this subcortical structure, diagrammed in **Figure 8.32**. The afferent fibers to the basal ganglia terminate in the striatum, composed in primates of two nuclei: the caudate and putamen. The basal ganglia have two output nuclei: the *internal segment of the globus pallidus (GP_i)* and the *pars reticularis of the substantia nigra (SN_r)*. Although they receive the same inputs, their outputs are different. SN_r axons project to and terminate primarily in the superior colliculus and provide a crucial signal for the initiation of eye movements. GP_i axons, on the other hand, terminate in thalamic nuclei, which in turn project to the cerebral cortex, including major projections to the motor cortex, supplementary motor area, and prefrontal cortex.

Processing within the basal ganglia takes place along two pathways that originate with GABAergic projection neurons from the striatum (DeLong, 1990). The *direct pathway* involves fast, direct, inhibitory connections from the striatum to the GP_i and SN_r. The *indirect pathway* takes a slower, roundabout route to the GP_i and SN_r. Striatal axons inhibit the *external segment of the globus pallidus (GP_e)*, which in turn inhibits the subthalamic nucleus and GP_i. The output from the basal ganglia via the GP_i and SN_r is also inhibitory. Indeed, these nuclei have high baseline firing rates, producing strong tonic inhibition of the motor system via their inhibitory projection to the thalamus and superior colliculi.

The final internal pathway of note is the projection from the *pars compacta of the substantia nigra (SN_c)* to the striatum, known as the *dopamine pathway*. Interestingly, this pathway has opposite effects on the direct and indirect pathways, even though the transmitter, dopamine, is the same in both pathways. The substantia nigra excites the direct pathway by acting on one type of dopamine receptor (D_1) and inhibits the indirect pathway by acting on a different type of dopamine receptor (D_2).

The Basal Ganglia as a Gatekeeper

Tracing what happens when cortical fibers activate the striatum can help us understand basal ganglia function.

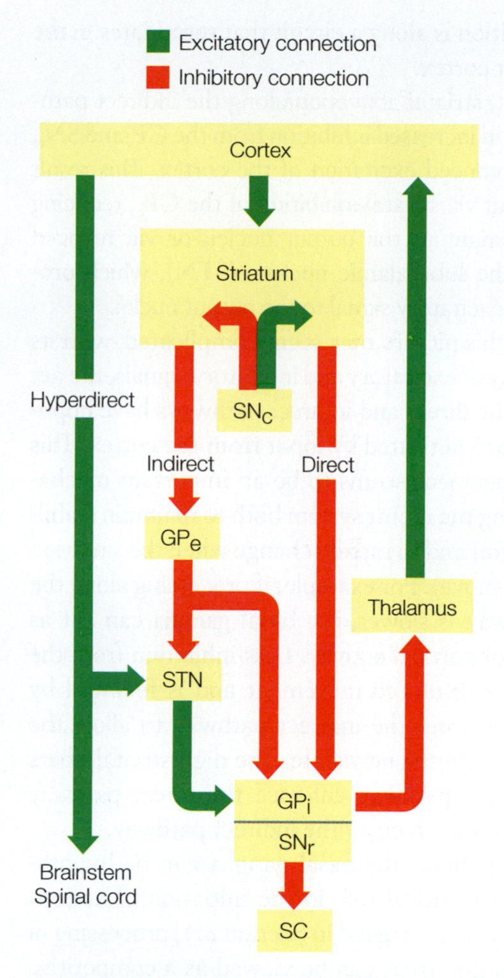

FIGURE 8.32 Wiring of the direct and indirect pathways in the basal ganglia.
Green links indicate excitatory projections, and red links indicate inhibitory projections. Inputs from the cortex project primarily to the striatum. From here, processing flows along two pathways. The direct pathway (center right) goes to the output nuclei: the internal segment of the globus pallidus (GP_i) and the pars reticularis of the substantia nigra (SN_r). SN_r axons project to and terminate primarily in the superior colliculus (SC) and provide a crucial signal for the initiation of eye movements. The indirect pathway (center left) includes a circuit through the external segment of the globus pallidus (GP_e) and the subthalamic nucleus (STN) and then to the output nuclei. The output projections to the thalamus are relayed to the cortex, frequently terminating close to the initial source of input. The dopaminergic projections of the pars compacta of the substantia nigra (SN_c) modulate striatal activity by facilitating the direct pathway via the D_1 receptors and inhibiting the indirect pathway via the D_2 receptors. The output of the basal ganglia also inhibits other subcortical structures, such as the superior colliculus.

When the direct pathway is activated, it sends inhibitory signals to the target neurons in the output nuclei (GP_i and SN_r) of the basal ganglia, which result in the inhibition of inhibiting signals to the thalamus. The sum effect of this double chain of inhibition is disinhibition of the thalamus, resulting in increased excitation of the cortex. In this way, activation of the direct pathway will promote movement if the disinhibition is along a circuit that terminates in the primary motor cortex.

In contrast, striatal activation along the indirect pathway will result in increased inhibition from the GP_i and SN_r, and as such, reduced excitation of the cortex. This result can come about via striatal inhibition of the GP_e, reducing an inhibitory input to the output nuclei, or via reduced inhibition of the subthalamic nucleus (STN), which provides a strong excitatory signal to the output nuclei.

Although this picture may seem complicated, with its confusing array of excitatory and inhibitory signals, the net result is that the direct and indirect pathways have opposite effects when activated by input from the cortex. This puzzling arrangement seems to be an important mechanism for helping the motor system both to maintain stability (e.g., posture) and to rapidly change when the situation changes (e.g., move). For example, if processing along the indirect pathway is slower, the basal ganglia can act as a gatekeeper of cortical activity. Less inhibition from the direct pathway results in movement and is followed by more inhibition from the indirect pathway to allow the system to adjust to the new state. The nigrostriatal fibers of the dopamine pathway enhance the direct pathway while reducing the effects of the indirect pathway.

Seen in this light, the basal ganglia can be hypothesized to play a critical role in the initiation of actions (**Figure 8.33**). As we argued in Section 8.4, processing in the cortical motor areas can be viewed as a competitive process in which candidate actions compete for control of the motor apparatus. The basal ganglia are positioned to help resolve the competition. The strong inhibitory baseline activity keeps the motor system in check, allowing cortical representations of possible movements to become activated without triggering movement. As a specific motor plan gains strength, the inhibitory signal is decreased for selected neurons. This movement representation breaches the gate, thus winning the competition.

Interestingly, computational analyses demonstrate that the physiology of the direct pathway in the basal ganglia is ideally designed to function as a winner-take-all system—a method for committing to one action plan from among the various alternatives. Greg Berns and Terry Sejnowski (1996) evaluated the functional consequences of all possible pairwise connections of two synapses, each of which could be either excitatory or inhibitory. By their analysis, a series of two successive inhibitory links is the most efficient way to make a selected pattern stand out from the background. With this circuit, the disinhibited signal stands out from a quiet background. In contrast, with a pair of excitatory connections the selected pattern has to raise its signal above a loud background. Similarly, a combination of inhibitory and excitatory synapses in either order is not efficient in making the selected pattern distinct from the background.

Berns and Sejnowski noted that the double inhibition of the direct pathway is relatively unique to the basal ganglia. This arrangement is particularly useful for selecting a response in a competitive system. For example, imagine standing on a beach, searching for your friend's kayak on the horizon. If the ocean is filled with all sorts of sailing vessels, your task is challenging. But if the waters happen to be empty when you're looking, it will be easy to detect the kayak as it comes into view. Similarly, a new input pattern from the striatum will stand out much more clearly when the background activity is inhibited.

The Basal Ganglia and Learning

Actions have consequences. These consequences affect the probability that a behavior will or will not be repeated—what we call a *reinforcement contingency*. When a consequence is rewarding, a similar context in the future is likely to result in repetition of the action, just as a dog learns to sit to obtain a treat. A reward, or even the anticipation of a reward, triggers the firing of dopamine neurons (see Chapter 12). And although dopamine has been related to the production of movement (as we will soon see), it is also known to play a critical role in reinforcement behavior

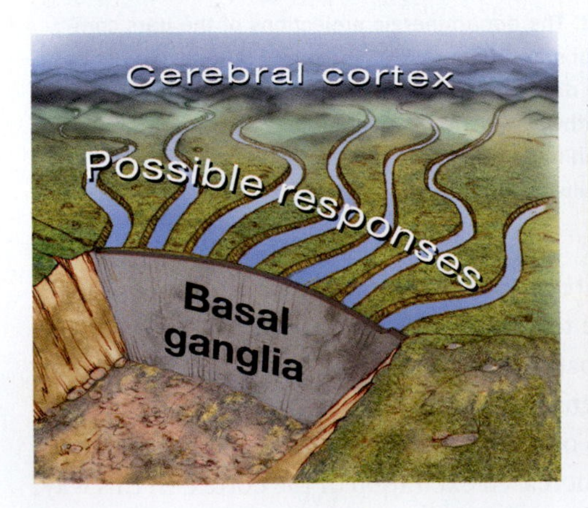

FIGURE 8.33 Computational model of the basal ganglia's role in movement initiation. The inhibitory output of the basal ganglia keeps potential responses in check until activation for one of the options reaches a threshold, resulting in the initiation of that movement. By this model, "selection" occurs even though the basal ganglia do not need to evaluate the possible choices, but rather need only to monitor their activation level.

and learning (Olds & Milner, 1954, a topic described in detail in Chapter 12).

A dual role for dopamine in movement selection and reward learning is adaptive. It is desirable for a system to learn to produce movements that have rewarding consequences. For example, by reinforcing a winning cross-court forehand in tennis with the release of dopamine in the striatum, the likelihood of producing a similar movement in the future is increased. In our gating model, we might suppose that the dopamine lowers the threshold required to trigger a movement given a familiar (and presumably rewarded) context.

Physiologically, scientists have explored how dopamine modifies the input–output channels in the basal ganglia, biasing the system to produce certain responses over others. The D_1 receptors in the direct pathway are excitatory, producing excitatory postsynaptic potentials (EPSPs); the D_2 receptors in the indirect pathway are inhibitory, producing inhibitory postsynaptic potentials (IPSPs). The net result is that dopamine release promotes selected actions represented in the direct pathway and discourages nonselected actions via the indirect pathway. This dual effect makes it more likely that the same response will be initiated when the rewarded input pattern is reactivated in the future. In fact, corticostriatal synaptic plasticity is strongly modulated by dopamine (Reynolds & Wickens, 2000). The next time the tennis ball whizzes by from the same direction, your arm powers back in the previously successful pattern.

Thus, by biasing behavior and making it more likely that an animal will initiate reinforced movements, dopamine neurons facilitate reinforcement learning. The ability to alter responses according to probable outcomes is essential for producing flexible, adaptive movements, as well as for combining patterns of behavior into novel sequences.

Disorders of the Basal Ganglia

A look at the basal ganglia circuits in Figure 8.32 makes it clear that lesions in any part of the basal ganglia can interfere with movement; however, the form of the problem varies considerably, depending on the location of the lesion. For instance, **Huntington's disease** is a hereditary neurodegenerative disorder (see Chapter 3). Patients with the Huntington's gene develop symptoms in the fourth or fifth decade of life, experience a fairly rapid progression, and usually die within 12 years of onset. The onset is subtle, usually a gradual change in mental attitude in which the patient is irritable and absentminded and loses interest in normal activities. Within a year, movement abnormalities are noticed: clumsiness, balance problems, and a general restlessness. Involuntary writhing movements, or *chorea*, gradually dominate normal motor function. The patient may adopt contorted postures, and his arms, legs, trunk, and head may be in constant motion.

We can understand the excessive movements, or **hyperkinesia**, seen with Huntington's disease by considering how the pathology affects information flow through the basal ganglia. The striatal changes occur primarily in inhibitory neurons forming the indirect pathway. As shown in **Figure 8.34a**, these changes lead to increased inhibition of the basal ganglia's output nuclei. Without the basal ganglia providing their inhibitory check on the motor system, the result is hyperkinesia. Later in the disease, many regions of the brain are affected. But atrophy is most prominent in the basal ganglia, where the cell death rate is ultimately as high as 90% in the striatum.

Parkinson's disease, the most common and well-known disorder affecting the basal ganglia, results from the loss of dopamine-producing neurons in the SN_c (**Figure 8.35**). As with most brain tissue, these neurons atrophy with age. Parkinsonian symptoms become manifest when too many of these neurons are lost. Motor symptoms of Parkinson's disease related to the basal ganglia include the disorders of posture and locomotion called **hypokinesia** and **bradykinesia**. Hypokinesia is a reduced ability to initiate voluntary movement; bradykinesia refers to a slowing in the rate of movement. At the extreme end of these symptoms lies **akinesia**, the absence of voluntary movement.

Parkinson's patients often act as if they are stuck in a posture and cannot change it. This problem, which we might think of as a stuck or blocked gate, is especially evident when the patients try to initiate a new movement. Many patients develop small tricks to help them overcome akinesia. For example, one patient walked with a cane, not because he needed help maintaining his balance, but because it was a visual target that helped him to get a jump start. When he wanted to walk, he placed the cane in front of his right foot and kicked it—which caused him to overcome inertia and commence his walking. Once started, the movements tend to be smaller in amplitude and slower in velocity. Walking is accomplished with short steps because the amplitude and speed of the muscular contractions are reduced.

Look at **Figure 8.34b**. Parkinson's disease initially and primarily reduces the inhibitory activity along the way. With no excitatory SN_c input into the striatum, the inhibitory output along the direct pathway decreases, which in turn increases the inhibitory output from the

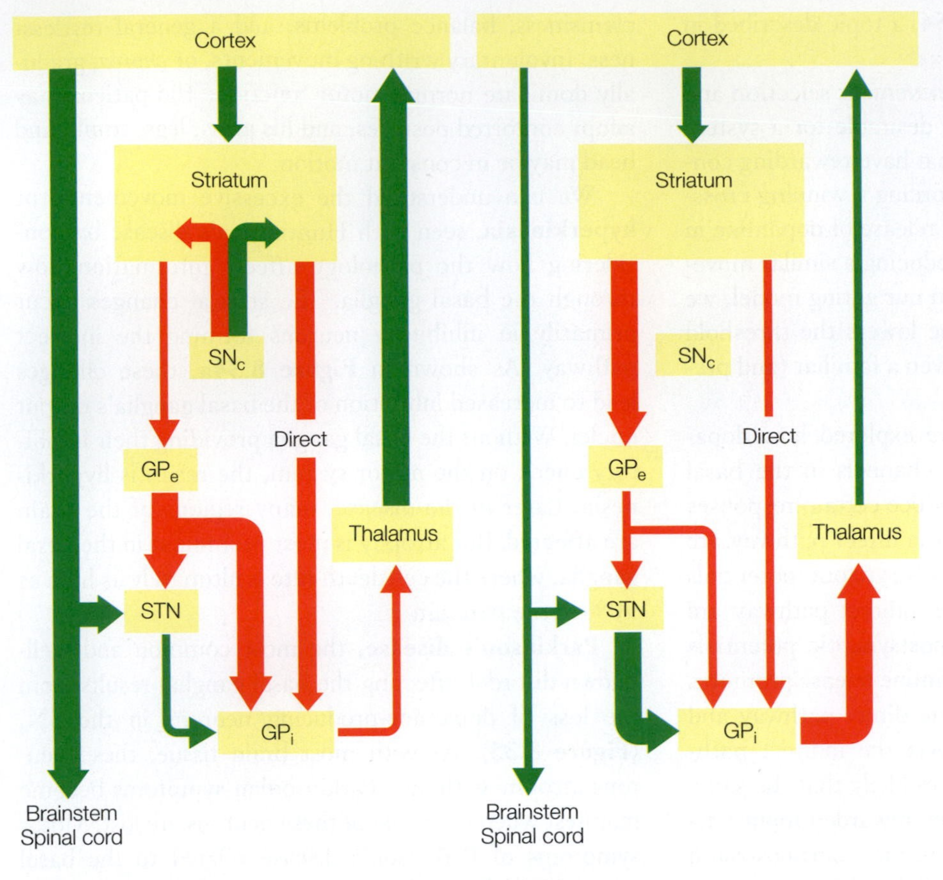

FIGURE 8.34 Differential neurochemical alterations in Huntington's and Parkinson's diseases. As in Figure 8.32, green links indicate excitatory projections, and red links indicate inhibitory projections. (a) In Huntington's disease, the inhibitory projection along the indirect pathway from the striatum to the external segment of the globus pallidus (GP_e) is reduced. The net consequence is reduced inhibitory output from the internal segment of the globus pallidus (GP_i) and thus an increase in cortical excitation and movement. (b) Parkinson's disease reduces inhibitory activity primarily along the direct pathway, resulting in increased inhibition from the GP_i to the thalamus and thus a reduction in cortical activity and movement.

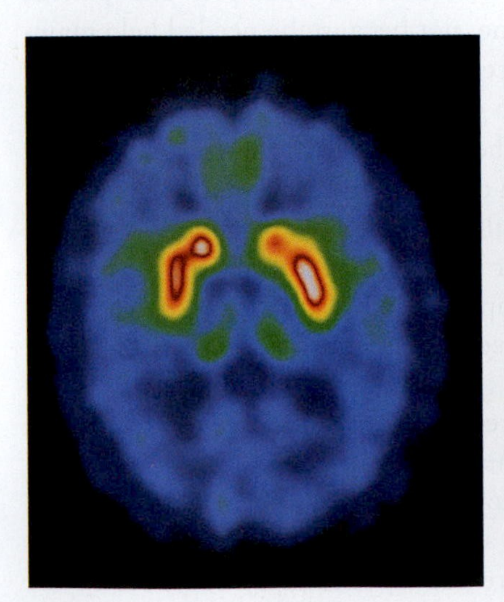

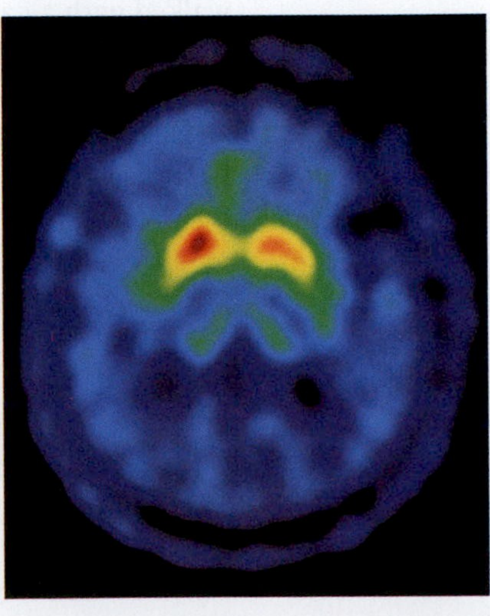

FIGURE 8.35 Radioactive tracers label the distribution of specific neurotransmitters with PET.
Healthy individuals and Parkinson's disease patients were injected with a radioactive tracer, fluorodopa (seen as yellow, orange, and red). This agent is visible in the striatum, reflecting the dopaminergic projections to this structure from the substantia nigra. Compare the greater uptake in the scan from a healthy person (a) to the uptake in a patient's scan (b).

GP_i to the thalamus. At the same time, decreased SN_c input inhibits the indirect pathway. The net physiological effect is increased thalamic inhibition, either because the GP_e produces less inhibition of the GP_i or because the STN increases its excitation of the GP_i. The overall result is reduced excitation of the cortex due to the excessive thalamic inhibition. The cortex may continue to plan movements, but without normally functioning basal ganglia, the ability to quickly initiate a movement is compromised. Once movement is initiated, it is frequently slow.

One of the great breakthroughs in neurology occurred in the 1950s with the development of L-dopa, a synthetic precursor of dopamine. L-Dopa can cross the blood–brain barrier and be metabolized to create dopamine, providing a replacement therapy for the loss of endogenous dopamine. This therapy provided a tremendous benefit to people with Parkinson's disease and continues to do so today. Almost all people who are diagnosed with Parkinson's are put on some form of L-dopa therapy, a simple medication protocol that considerably improves their motor problems.

Over time, however, as the dopamine-producing cells continue to die off (because L-dopa does not prevent their loss) and striatal neurons become sensitized to L-dopa, the amount of required medication tends to increase. With this gradual shift come additional symptoms, some of which may reflect changes in the motor pathways of the basal ganglia—in particular, the appearance of drug-induced hyperkinesias. Other symptoms may result from the impact of L-dopa on other parts of the brain that have relatively intact dopamine receptors. These regions, in effect, become overdosed because the effects of L-dopa are systematic throughout the brain. Excessive activity due to L-dopa therapy in areas of the frontal lobes containing dopamine receptors has been associated with impairments in cognition (reviewed in Cools, 2006).

In addition to the indirect impact that L-dopa therapy can have on cognition, the basal ganglia appear to have a more direct effect on cognition. To understand this, it is important to consider that the basal ganglia contain processing loops not just with the motor system, but also with other cortical areas, such as the parietal lobe, frontal lobe, and limbic system (**Figure 8.36**). That is, these areas send projections to the basal ganglia, that information is processed within the direct and indirect pathways, and the output is then transmitted back to these cortical areas.

This arrangement has led researchers to consider how the computations performed by the basal ganglia may extend beyond motor control. In particular, much as the motor loop of the basal ganglia enables the system to shift from one motor state to another, a similar operation may support how we shift between different mental states. Indeed, Parkinson's patients exhibit a difficulty shifting mental states that is similar to the difficulty they have initiating movements (i.e., changing movement states).

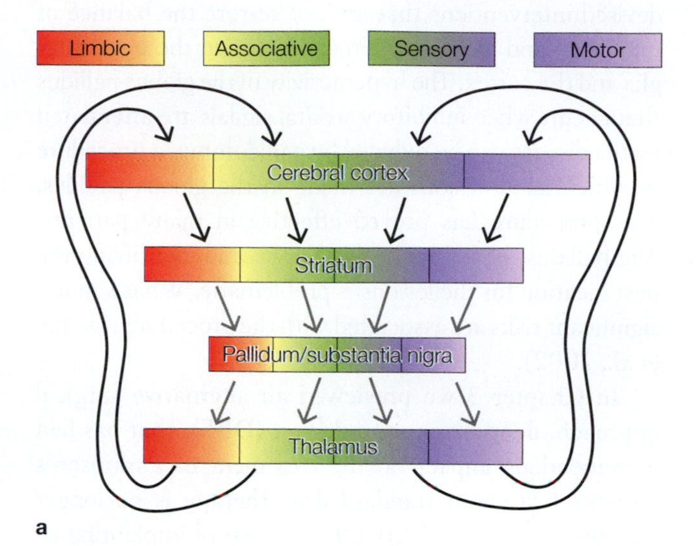

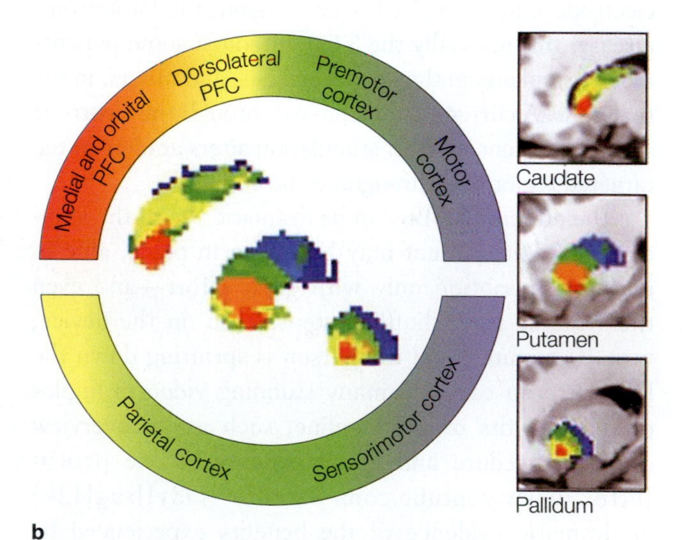

FIGURE 8.36 Connections between the cortex and the basal ganglia.
(a) Different regions of the cortex project to different regions of the basal ganglia in connection loops that are, for the most part, separate. Information is transmitted in separate channels to and from limbic (red), associative (yellow-green), sensory (blue-green), and motor (blue-white) regions of the basal ganglia (mostly caudate and putamen, the two nuclei forming the striatum) and cortex. Black arrows represent glutamatergic projections, and gray arrows represent GABAergic projections. The pallidum is a ventral part of the striatum. **(b)** DTI data show the rostrocaudal gradient of the projections of different cortical areas onto the input regions of the basal ganglia, pictured in the center (rostral on the left, caudal on the right), with the caudate and putamen receiving the lion's share. In the insets, the segmented basal ganglia nuclei are superimposed on structural images. PFC = prefrontal cortex.

Direct Stimulation of the Basal Ganglia

Because of the limitations of drug therapy, clinicians have sought to develop alternative or supplemental treatments for Parkinson's disease. For instance, neurosurgeons have devised interventions that seek to restore the balance of inhibitory and excitatory circuits between the basal ganglia and the cortex. The hyperactivity of the globus pallidus that occurs when inhibitory striatal signals are attenuated by the disease can be reduced by pallidotomy, a procedure in which small lesions are made in the globus pallidus. This procedure has proved effective in many patients. The pallidus, however, is quite large, and identifying the best location for the lesions is problematic. What's more, significant risks are associated with the procedure (De Bie et al., 2002).

In Chapter 3 we previewed an alternative surgical approach, **deep brain stimulation (DBS)**, that has had a tremendous impact on the treatment of Parkinson's patients for whom standard drug therapy is no longer effective (see Figure 3.13). DBS consists of implanting an electrode into a targeted neural region; for Parkinson's disease, this is usually the STN, although some patients receive implants in the globus pallidus, and others, in the thalamus. A current is then passed through the electrode at high frequencies. This stimulation alters activity in the targeted region and throughout the circuit.

The effects of DBS can be dramatic. With the stimulator off, the patient may be frozen in place, able to initiate locomotion only with great effort—and even then, taking tiny, shuffling steps. Turn on the device, wait 10 minutes, and the person is sprinting down the hallway. You can find many stunning video examples of the benefits of DBS online, such as an overview of the procedure and initial benefits in one patient (http://www.youtube.com/watch?v=O3yIJsugH2k) or dramatic evidence of the benefits experienced by a patient who had developed severe tremors over the course of extended L-dopa therapy (http://www.youtube.com/watch?v=uBh2LxTW0s0).

DBS has proved extremely popular: In its first decade of use, the procedure was performed on over 75,000 patients, and the prevalence of the procedure is increasing. The success of DBS as a treatment for Parkinson's disease has led to a surge of interest in using similar invasive methods to treat other neurological and psychiatric conditions. DBS, targeted at other brain structures, is now used for patients with dystonia (involuntary muscle spasms and twisting of the limbs) or obsessive-compulsive disorder. Clinical trials are also under way in the treatment of chronic headache, Alzheimer's disease (Lyons, 2011), and even coma.

Why DBS works in general, and in Parkinson's disease specifically, is still a bit of a mystery (Gradinaru et al., 2009). Indeed, the most common form of DBS involving implants in the STN would seem to be counterproductive. Increased output from the STN should increase the output of the GP_i, and thus result in greater inhibition of the cortex and an exacerbation of parkinsonian symptoms.

The artificial stimulation induced by DBS clearly alters neuronal activity in some way to produce its clinical benefits. What is unclear is which circuit elements are responsible for the therapeutic effects. One hypothesis is that the periodic output of the DBS stimulator normalizes the oscillatory activity that constitutes one way in which the basal ganglia and cortex communicate. At rest, EEG recordings in healthy people show prominent beta oscillations (15–30 Hz) over sensorimotor cortex. This signal drops when movement is initiated. Patients with Parkinson's disease exhibit exaggerated beta oscillations, and the intensity of this signal is correlated with the severity of their bradykinesia. Andrea Kühn and her colleagues (2008) showed that DBS of the STN suppresses beta activity (**Figure 8.37a**). Moreover, the patients' increase in movement was correlated with the degree of suppression.

So, one possible mechanism of DBS treatment is that it disrupts exaggerated beta activity, resulting in improved movement. The disruption may come about from a change in the output of the basal ganglia back to the cortex. Alternatively, animal models suggest that high-frequency stimulation of the STN may directly influence the activity of neurons in the motor cortex (Q. Li et al., 2012). How could this come about? As Figure 8.32 shows, there is a direct projection from the motor cortex to the STN, a so-called **hyperdirect pathway.** When DBS-like stimulation is applied to the STN of the rat, neurons in the motor cortex show latency changes in antidromic activation—that is, action potentials that result from membrane changes that travel in the reverse direction up the axon (**Figure 8.37b**).

The link between beta power and movement led researchers to ask whether people can learn to control this EEG signal with neurofeedback training. In an initial test of this idea, three Parkinson's patients undergoing DBS surgery also had a strip of electrodes placed on the cortical surface over sensorimotor cortex. These electrodes allowed for high-fidelity monitoring of cortical beta activity, with the level of this activity indicated by the position of the cursor on a computer screen. The patients were then trained to alter the position of the cursor—in effect, to figure out how to think in such a way that they could control, in real time, the intensity of the beta oscillations. The patients were able to succeed

a

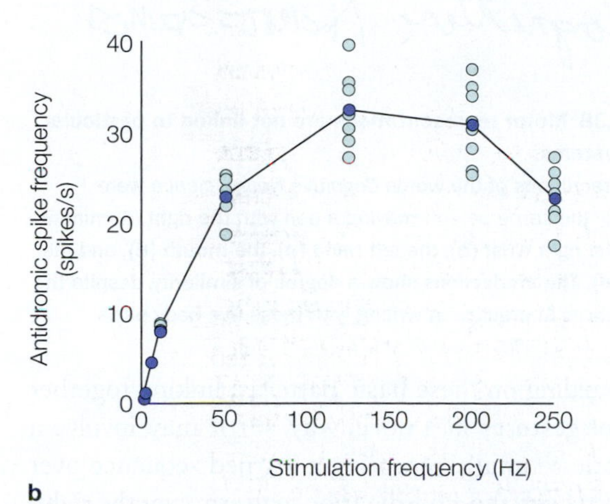

b

FIGURE 8.37 Investigating the origins of parkinsonian symptoms.
(a) In humans, increases in the power of the beta oscillations in the basal ganglia are negatively correlated with movement. (b) In rats with Parkinson's-inducing lesions, the firing rates of neurons in the motor cortex increase as the rate of DBS stimulation increases, at least up to a stimulation frequency of 125 Hz. These changes are due to the DBS signals causing changes to travel up the axons (antidromically). The light blue circles represent data from an individual rat; dark blue circles represent averaged data from several rats.

at this task after only a few hours of training (Khanna et al., 2016), suggesting another way in which a closed-loop system could improve the efficacy of treatments for neurological disorders.

Because of its prevalence in the general population, the known changes in neurochemistry, and the development of excellent animal models, Parkinson's disease has proved to be a model disease for the development of innovative interventions—drugs, stem cell implants (not discussed here), and neurosurgical procedures. Perhaps at some point in the future, we will be able to dispense with the DBS procedure entirely, providing Parkinson's patients with a way to alleviate their symptoms by mentally regulating abnormal physiological signals such as beta oscillations.

TAKE-HOME MESSAGES

- The basal ganglia are a group of subcortical nuclei that form an internal circuit, which in turn forms a processing loop with the cerebral cortex.
- The output signals from the basal ganglia are inhibitory. Thus, in the tonic state, the basal ganglia dampen cortical activity. Movements are initiated when this inhibition is removed.
- Dopamine is produced in the substantia nigra pars compacta, a brainstem nucleus that projects to the striatum. Dopamine modifies synaptic efficacy in the striatum, enabling a form of motor learning that promotes the repetition of actions that have been rewarded.
- Parkinson's disease results from the atrophy of dopamine-producing cells in the substantia nigra. The hallmarks of this disorder are akinesia, the inability to produce voluntary movement; hypokinesia, a reduction in muscle movement; and bradykinesia, a slowing of movement.
- The treatment of Parkinson's disease has spurred major innovations in neurology. The development in the 1950s of L-dopa helped pioneer work on targeting specific transmitter systems to treat neurological and psychiatric disorders. More recently, the success of invasive methods such as pallidotomy and DBS has inspired neurosurgeons to consider similar interventions for other disorders.

8.8 Learning and Performing New Skills

Dick Fosbury was a revolutionary figure in the world of sports. In high school, he was a very good high jumper, though not quite good enough to get the scholarship he desired to go to college and study engineering. One day, however, he had an idea. His school had recently replaced the wood-chip landing pad in the high-jump pit with soft foam rubber. Fosbury realized that he no longer had to land on his feet to avoid injury. Instead of taking off on the inside foot and "scissoring" his legs over the bar, he could rotate his body to go over the bar backward, raising his feet toward the sky, and then land on his back. With this conceptual breakthrough, Fosbury went on to reach new heights, culminating in the gold medal at the 1968 Olympics in Mexico City. High jumpers all over the world adopted the "Fosbury flop." And yes, Fosbury did get his scholarship and did become an engineer.

Shift in Cortical Control With Learning

People frequently attribute motor learning to the lower levels of the hierarchical representation of action sequences. We speak of "muscle memory," of our muscles having learned how to respond in a way that seems automatic—for example, when we maintain balance on a bike, or our fingers type away at a keyboard. The fact that we have great difficulty verbalizing how we perform these skills reinforces the notion that the learning is noncognitive. The Olympic gymnast Peter Vidmar expressed this sentiment when he said, "As I approach the apparatus . . . the only thing I am thinking about is . . . the first trick. . . . Then, my body takes over and hopefully everything becomes automatic" (Schmidt, 1987, p. 85).

On closer study, however, we find that some aspects of motor learning are independent of the muscular system used to perform the actions. Demonstrate this independence to yourself by taking a piece of paper and signing your name. Having done this, repeat the action but use your nondominant hand. Now do it again, holding the pen between your teeth. If you feel especially adventurous, you can take off your shoes and socks and hold the pen between your toes.

Although the atypical productions will not be as smooth as your standard signature, the more dramatic characteristic of this demonstration is the high degree of similarity across all of the productions. **Figure 8.38** shows the results of one such demonstration. This high-level representation of the action is independent of any particular muscle group. The differences in the final product show that some muscle groups simply have more experience in translating an abstract representation into a concrete action.

When people are acquiring a new action, the first effects of learning likely will be at a more abstract level. Fosbury's learning, for example, started in the abstract realm with a simple insight: The new landing material could allow for a different landing position. From this point, he was able to adopt a radically new style of jumping. As Fosbury described it, "I adapted an antiquated style and modernized it to something that was efficient" (Zarkos, 2004). These cognitive abilities no doubt apply to all types of learning, not just learning motor skills. For instance, the same abilities contribute to the makings of a great jazz improviser. She is great not only because of the technical motor expertise of her fingers (though that is important), but because she sees new possibilities for a riff, a new pattern.

Once Fosbury settled on what to do, he had to learn to do it. Learning a skill takes practice, and becoming very skilled at anything requires a lot of practice. Our motor system has some basic movement patterns that can be controlled by subcortical circuits. Learning a new skill can involve building on these basic patterns, linking together a series of gestures in a novel way. Or it may involve a more subtle retuning, repeating a learned sequence over and over to get the coordination pattern exactly right. Gradually, the motor system learns to execute the movement in what feels like an automatic manner, requiring little conscious thought.

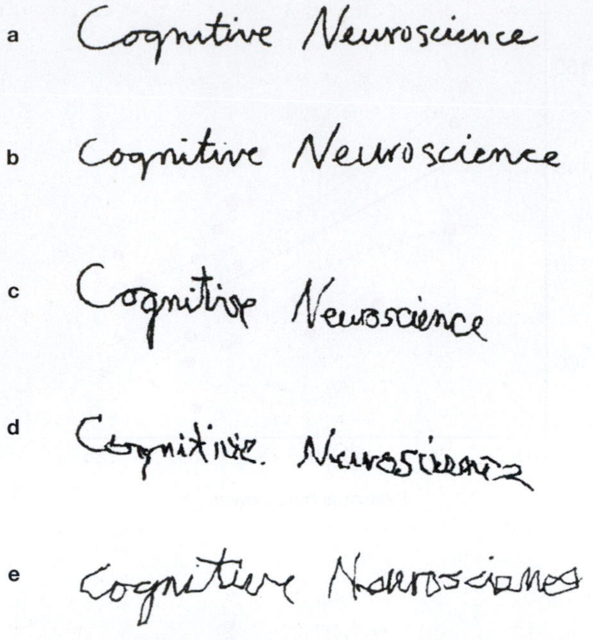

FIGURE 8.38 Motor representations are not linked to particular effector systems.
These five renditions of the words *Cognitive Neuroscience* were produced by the same person moving a pen with the right (dominant) hand **(a)**, the right wrist **(b)**, the left hand **(c)**, the mouth **(d)**, and the right foot **(e)**. The productions show a degree of similarity, despite the vast differences in practice in writing with these five body parts.

Learning how to produce the action in an optimal manner—becoming an expert—takes us to a different level of skill. Becoming an expert fine-tunes the system to make the movement in the most efficient and skillful manner. This result requires other cognitive abilities, such as persistence, attention, and self-control. Motor skill also involves honing perceptual skills. LeBron James's success on the basketball court is due not only to his extraordinary motor skills, but also to his ability to rapidly recognize the position of his teammates and opponents. His pattern recognition abilities enable him to quickly determine whether he should drive to the basket or pull up and pass to one of his open teammates.

Adaptive Learning Through Sensory Feedback

Imagine climbing aboard a boat that is rocking in the waves. At first you feel clumsy, unwilling to let go of the gunwales, but soon you adapt, learning to remain steady despite the boat's motion. Next, you're even willing to venture a few steps across the deck. After a few hours at sea, you're an old salt, not giving a thought to the pitch and roll of the boat. When you come back to shore, you are surprised to find your first few steps are wobbly again. It takes a moment or two to become acclimated to the stability of the dock, and to abandon your rolling gait.

In this example, your sea legs are a form of **sensorimotor adaptation.** Researchers have devised all sorts of novel environments to challenge the motor system and explore the neural mechanisms essential for this form of motor learning. One of the first and most radical tests was performed by George Stratton (1896), the founder of the psychology department at UC Berkeley. He devised a set of eyeglasses that inverted the visual input. After initially donning his new spectacles, Stratton was at a loss, afraid to take a step for fear he would fall over. Reaching was impossible. He would reach for a glass and observe his arm moving in the wrong direction. But with time, Stratton's motor system adapted (just as the monkeys in BMI studies did when the decoder algorithm was shuffled). By the fourth day, he was walking about at a nearly normal speed and his movements were coordinated. With time, observers were hard-pressed to realize from watching Stratton that his world was topsy-turvy. His sensorimotor system had adapted to the new environment.

More modern studies of sensorimotor adaptation use less dramatic environmental distortions. In some, visuomotor rotations are imposed when people perform the center-out task such that the visual feedback of the limb is displaced by 45°, introducing a mismatch between the visual and proprioceptive (felt position of the limb) information (**Figure 8.39**). In others, force fields are imposed that displace the moving limb to the side when a person attempts to reach directly to a target. In either case the motor system is amazingly adept at modifying itself in response to these perturbations. Within a hundred movements or so, people have modified their behavior to make straight movements to the targets.

Although participants are aware that the environment was altered with the introduction of the perturbation, their sensorimotor system nevertheless quickly adapts without any awareness by the participants that they have altered their movement. The automatic nature of the shift becomes obvious when the perturbation is removed and the person has to repeat the adaptation process; this is called *de-adaptation*, just as when you step from a boat back onto the dock. We cannot simply switch back to the normal state, but rather must relearn how to control our limbs in the absence of a visual or force distortion.

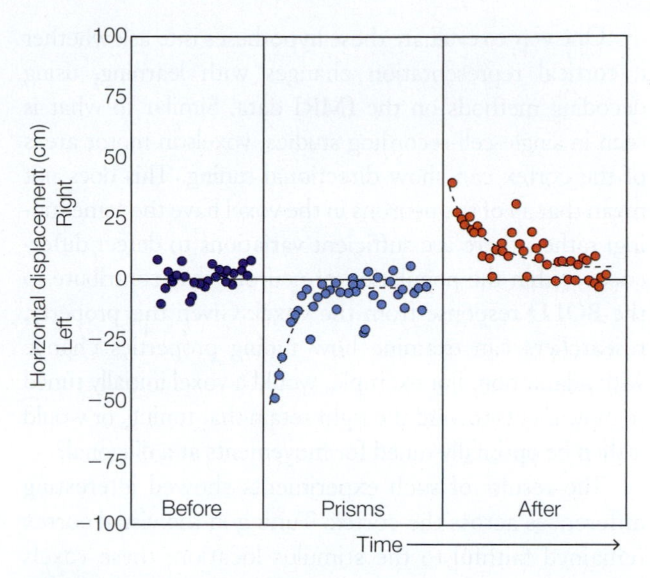

FIGURE 8.39 Prism adaptation.
Control participants throw a ball, attempting to hit a visual target. At baseline ("Before"), the responses are scattered about the target. After they put on the prism glasses, the throws shift to the left. After about 20 throws, a participant becomes adapted to the glasses and is again successful in landing the ball near the target. When the glasses are removed ("After"), the participant makes large errors in the opposite direction. This aftereffect eventually disappears as the person "de-adapts."

Neural Mechanisms of Adaptation

Cognitive neuroscientists have employed many tools to explore the neural systems of **sensorimotor learning**. Imaging studies show that with the introduction of a perturbation, such as the visuomotor rotation discussed in the previous section, there is a large increase in activity in many cortical areas, including prefrontal, premotor, and motor cortex in the frontal lobes, as well as changes in parietal, temporal, and even visual cortex (Seidler, 2006). Increases are also seen subcortically in the cerebellum and basal ganglia. With practice, the activation in these areas is reduced, returning to the state observed before the perturbation.

Knowing exactly how to interpret these activation patterns is difficult: Do they reflect the formation and storage of new motor patterns? Or are the activations indicative of other processes that are engaged when a perturbation is introduced? For example, a visuomotor rotation introduces a violation of a visual expectancy: You expect the cursor to move up, but instead it moves to the side. The activations could be the result of this prediction error, or they might reflect the increased attention needed to adjust to the visual feedback. The changes in the BOLD response in the motor cortex could be the result of adaptation, or they could occur because people tend to make corrective movements when feedback indicates an error. Other activations may be triggered by the participants' awareness that the environment has been distorted.

One way to evaluate these hypotheses is to ask whether a cortical representation changes with learning, using decoding methods on the fMRI data. Similar to what is seen in single-cell-recording studies, voxels in motor areas of the cortex can show directional tuning. This does not mean that all of the neurons in the voxel have the same tuning; rather, there are sufficient variations to detect differences within the population of neurons that contribute to the BOLD response from the voxel. Given this property, researchers can examine how tuning properties change with adaptation. For example, would a voxel initially tuned to movements toward the right retain that tuning, or would it then be optimally tuned for movements at a diagonal?

The results of such experiments showed interesting differences across the cortex. Tuning in the visual cortex remained faithful to the stimulus location; these voxels retained their retinotopic mapping. Directional tuning in the motor cortex also remained unchanged, faithful to movement direction. That is, a voxel that was maximally active for movements to the right showed this same profile, even though the target requiring this movement now appeared along one of the diagonals.

In contrast, the tuning of voxels in the posterior parietal cortex changed during the course of adaptation. In fact, in the early stages of learning, the decoder failed. After adaptation, however, the activity patterns could again be decoded, but the directional tuning was altered (Haar et al., 2015; **Figure 8.40**). This finding suggests that the posterior parietal neurons learned the new sensorimotor map, retaining the new associations between the visual input and the required motor output. This plasticity hypothesis can also explain why the decoder failed during learning: The parietal neurons were in a state of transition.

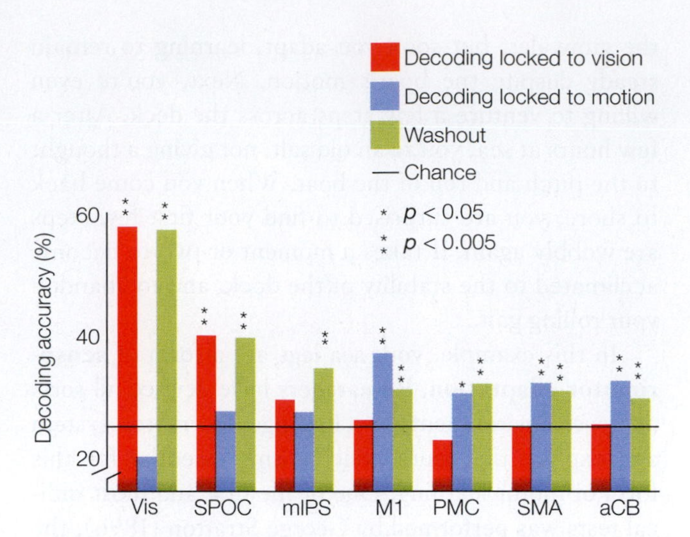

FIGURE 8.40 Decoding accuracies across participants. Red and blue bars represent decoding during adaptation, locked to either vision (red) or movement (blue). Green bars represent decoding after adaptation (washout). Accuracy based either on the visual position of the target (red) or on movement (blue) during adaptation remains similar during washout (green) for the relevant dimension in most cortical areas. The one exception is the IPS (intraparietal sulcus), where decoding based on sensory or motor signals is at chance (black line) during adaptation. Vis = early visual cortex; SPOC = superior parieto-occipital cortex; mIPS = medial intraparietal sulcus; M1 = primary motor cortex; PMC = premotor cortex; SMA = supplementary motor area; aCB = anterior cerebellum.

Researchers have also conducted neuropsychological and brain stimulation studies to gain more insight into the functional contribution of various brain regions in motor learning. For instance, patients who have cerebellar damage due to either degenerative processes or stroke have severe impairments in learning to move in novel environments (T. A. Martin et al., 1996; **Figure 8.41**). Similar

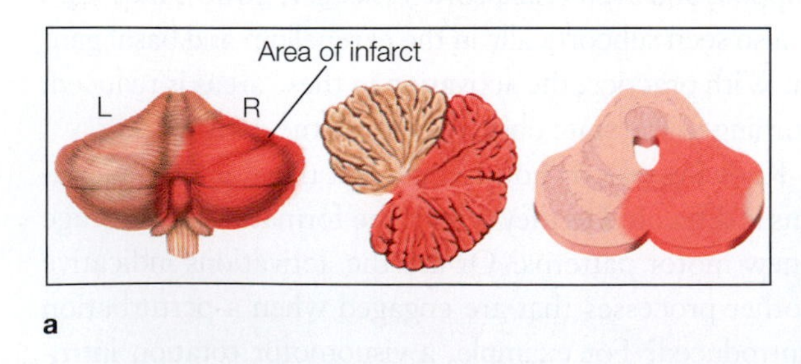

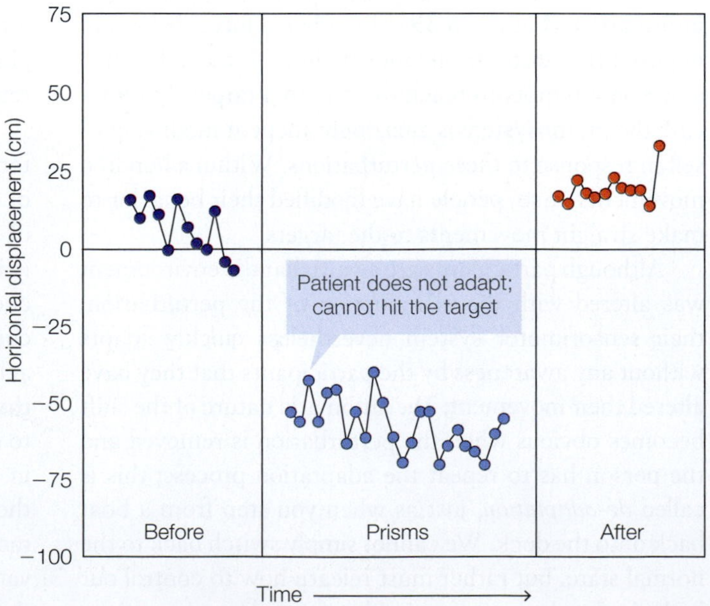

FIGURE 8.41 Impaired prism adaptation in a patient with a large cerebellar lesion.
(a) The regions shaded red show the extent of damage in the inferior cerebellum. The damage is mostly in the right cerebellum, although it extends across the midline. **(b)** There is no evidence of adaptation when the prism glasses are worn. The patient shows a bias to throw the ball slightly to the right before and after adaptation.

problems can be observed in patients with prefrontal or parietal lesions. Thus, even though the decoding results suggest that tuning changes are prominent in the parietal lobe, the capacity to learn requires the contribution of many neural regions.

In an attempt to clarify the contributions of the cerebellum and M1 to motor learning, Joseph Galea and his colleagues (2011) applied transcranial direct current stimulation (tDCS) during a visuomotor adaptation task, targeting either primary motor cortex or the cerebellum. As discussed in Chapter 3, this procedure is thought to increase the excitability of the area under the anodal electrode. Assuming that more excitable neurons are better for learning (i.e., more "plastic"), the researchers considered two hypotheses. First, if an area is involved in using the error information to modify the sensorimotor system, then learning to compensate for the visuomotor perturbation should occur more quickly. Second, if an area is involved in retaining the new behavior, the effects of learning should persist for a longer period of time, even when the perturbation is removed. To look at retention in this study, the feedback was removed and the experimenters measured how long it took for the participant to show normal reaching movements.

The results point to a striking functional dissociation between the cerebellum and motor cortex (**Figure 8.42**). Cerebellar tDCS led to faster learning. Participants receiving stimulation over this region learned to compensate for the visuomotor perturbation faster than those receiving tDCS over M1 or sham stimulation over the cerebellum (in which the stimulator was turned on for only a few seconds). When the perturbation was removed, however, the effects of learning decayed (or were implicitly "forgotten") at the same rate as for the sham group. The opposite pattern was observed for the group receiving M1 tDCS. For these participants, learning occurred at the same rate as those given sham stimulation, but the retention interval was extended.

In sum, results indicate that the cerebellum is essential for learning the new mapping, but M1 is important for consolidating the new mapping (long-term retention). And, to link this finding back to the fMRI study of adaptation, we see that the parietal cortex is important for the storage of the new sensorimotor map.

Error-Based Learning From Forward Models

The brain uses a plethora of signals for learning. Earlier in this chapter we discussed how dopamine can serve as a reward signal, strengthening input–output relationships in the striatum to favor one movement pattern over another (see also Chapter 12 on decision making). Both rewards and errors help us learn. An errant toss of a dart provides information about how to adjust the angle of the throw. A flat musical note informs the pianist that she has struck the wrong key.

Error-based learning is essential for the development of coordinated movement. Importantly, the error not only tells us that a movement was improperly executed, but also provides critical information about how the movement should be adjusted. The dart landed to the right of the target; the piano sound was lower than expected. These examples capture how the brain operates in a predictive mode: Your motor system is issuing commands for movement, and it is also generating predictions of the anticipated sensory consequences of those movements. **Sensory prediction errors** occur when the

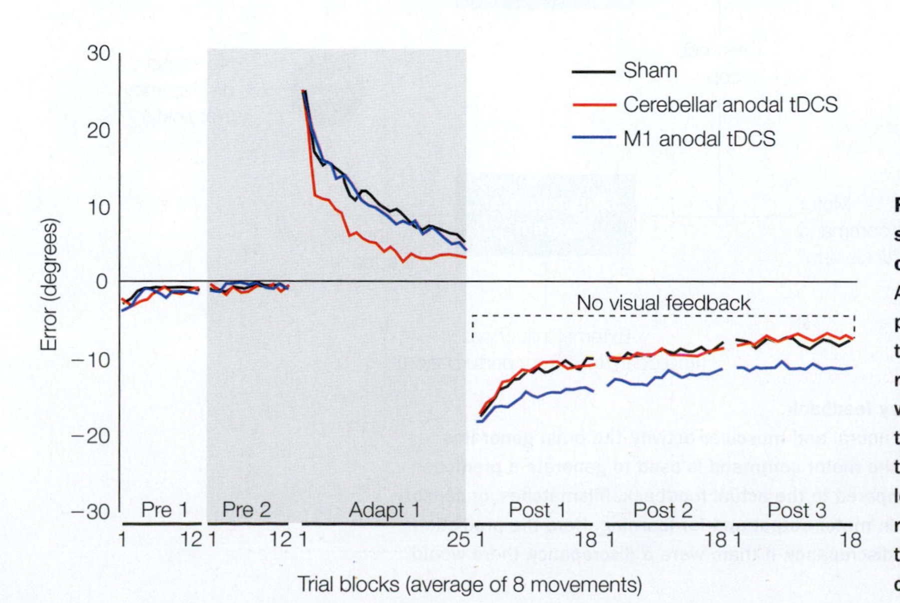

FIGURE 8.42 Double dissociation in sensorimotor adaptation following tDCS of the cerebellum and motor cortex. Anodal tDCS was applied during a baseline phase (Pre 2) and throughout the adaptation phase, in which the visual feedback was rotated. Learning was faster when the tDCS was applied over the cerebellum, compared to the sham and M1 conditions, although all three groups eventually reached comparable levels of adaptation. When the rotation was removed, the aftereffect persisted longer when tDCS was applied over M1, suggesting stronger consolidation in this condition.

actual feedback doesn't match these predictions. The brain uses this information to adjust ongoing movements, as well as for learning.

Prediction is especially important because the brain's motor commands to the muscles and the sensory signals from the limbs take time to travel back and forth. It can take 50 to 150 ms for a motor command to be generated in the cortex and for the sensory consequences of that action to return to the cortex. Such a long delay would make it impossible to rely on feedback from the body to control our movements. To compensate for these delays, we have a system that generates a **forward model:** an expectancy of the sensory consequences of our action.

The cerebellum is a key part of the neural network for the generation of forward models (Wolpert, Miall, et al., 1998). It receives a copy of motor signals being sent to the muscles from the cortex—information that can be used to generate sensory predictions. It also receives massive input from the various receptors of the somatosensory system. By comparing these sources of information, the cerebellum can help ensure that an ongoing movement is produced in a coordinated manner. It can also use a mismatch to aid in sensorimotor learning.

For example, when we put on prism glasses, the visual information is shifted to one side. If we reach to a target, a mismatch will occur between where the hand was directed and our visual (and tactile) feedback of the outcome of the movement. Given sufficient time, we use that error to correct the movement to reach the target. Furthermore, error corrections help make our predictions of the future better suited for the novel environment. Consider again the tDCS results discussed in the previous section. Cerebellar stimulation led to faster learning, presumably because the error signals were amplified. Imaging studies of motor learning support a similar conclusion. In general, activation in the cerebellum decreases with practice, a finding interpreted as reflecting a reduction in error as skill improves.

The concepts of forward models and sensory predictions offer insight into an age-old question: Why is it so hard to tickle yourself? When you attempt to tickle yourself by stroking your forearm, a forward model generates a prediction of the expected sensory input from the skin (**Figure 8.43**). Because of this prediction, the actual sensory information is not surprising: You expected it exactly when and where it happened. The brain, with its passion for detecting change, generates only a weak response to the sensory input. However, even if you are aware that someone else is going to tickle you, the prediction is much cruder when it is not linked to a motor command. You know the sensation is coming, but you can't anticipate the precise timing and location, so the brain produces a more vigorous response as the information arrives.

Prediction is a feature of all brain areas (which all do pattern matching of some sort). What, then, makes cerebellar predictions unique? One hypothesis is that the cerebellum generates predictions that are *temporally* precise. We need to know more than *what* is coming in the future; we also need to predict exactly *when* it is coming. Indeed, the importance of the cerebellum in

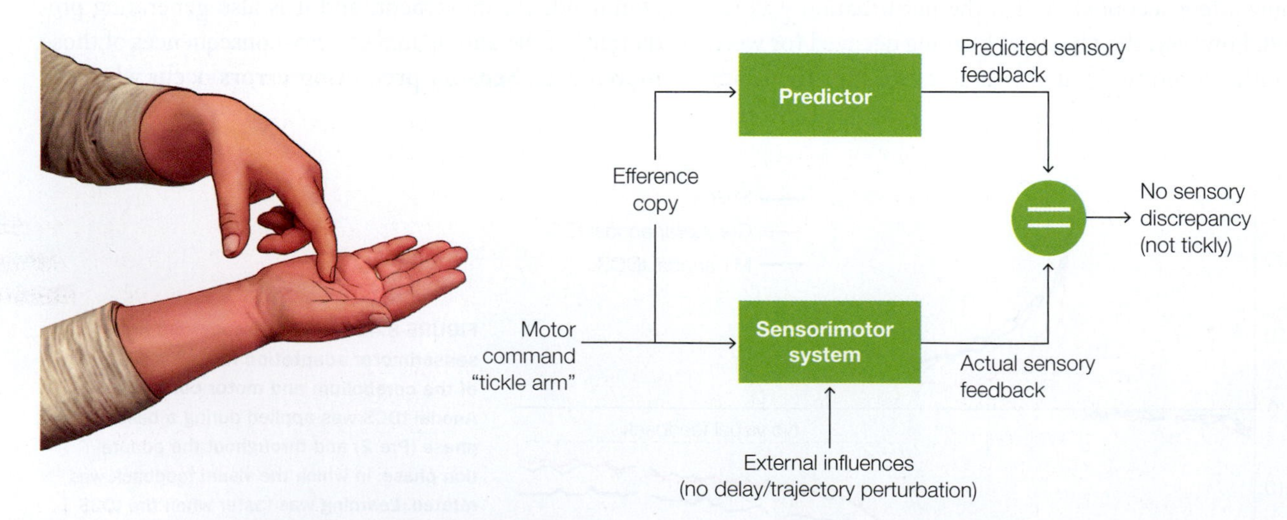

FIGURE 8.43 Forward model to predict sensory feedback.
Because of the processing delays introduced by neural and muscular activity, the brain generates predictions of future sensory signals. A copy of the motor command is used to generate a prediction of the expected feedback. This prediction is compared to the actual feedback. Mismatches, or sensory prediction errors, are used to make corrections in motor output and for learning. Here the prediction equaled the feedback, so there was no sensory discrepancy. If there were a discrepancy, there would be a tickle sensation.

BOX 8.1 | HOT SCIENCE

Snooping Around in the Cerebellum

The 60 billion granule cells that are compactly nestled in the cerebellum account for over 75% of all of the neurons in the brain. Yet, until recently, our understanding of these neurons has been limited to theoretical models. Because of their tiny size, just about 6 μm in diameter, it was impossible for neurophysiologists to record the activity of the granule cells—until now.

To overcome this limitation, researchers at Stanford University (M. J. Wagner et al., 2017) devised new ways to use two-photon calcium imaging to study the granule cells in mice. Calcium imaging takes advantage of the fact that in living cells, depolarization involves the activation of voltage-gated Ca^{2+} channels and, consequently, an influx of Ca^{2+}. The researchers created a special line of transgenic mice whose granule cells had been transfected with genes that encode fluorescent proteins. These proteins bind to the Ca^{2+} ions, causing them to fluoresce. The changes in fluorescence can be visualized and measured with powerful two-photon microscopes.

Using this method, the research team studied activity in the granule cell layer of the cerebellum while the mice pushed a lever in order to obtain sugar water. Since the cells could be tracked over multiple days, the researchers could monitor their activity as the animals mastered the task and came to expect the reward following each lever push. Consistent with classic models of sensorimotor control, many of these cerebellar neurons modulated their activity during the lever press, and the magnitude of the calcium signal even showed a tight correlation with the velocity of the movement.

More surprising, for a small percentage of the granule cells, the activity appeared to be related to the outcome of the trial: Some cells showed a burst of activity right after the sugary reward was delivered, whereas others became active when an expected reward was withheld, which became evident only after training. The activity of these cells when an expectation was violated can be seen as a new example of the predictive capacity of the cerebellum: The granule cell activity indicated the violation of a forward model, one that generated an expectation of a reward subsequent to a movement.

Having the tools to measure granule cell activity opens new opportunities to advance our understanding of the cerebellum. Indeed, the massive computational capacity of the cerebellum, coupled with anatomical results showing that the cerebellum has extensive connectivity with most of the cerebral cortex, has inspired new hypotheses about the importance of this subcortical structure to predictive processing that extends well beyond sensorimotor control.

the production of skilled movement reflects the complex coordination required within the sensorimotor system to integrate motor commands with sensory information. Although the complex processing that occurs in the cerebellum has been notoriously difficult to investigate, a new technique to unravel its processing has recently been developed (see **Box 8.1**).

Expertise

Mastering a motor skill requires extensive practice (**Figure 8.44**). A concert violinist, Olympic gymnast, or professional billiards player trains for years in order to achieve elite performance. To remain at the top of their field, experts have to continue honing their skills, performing their repertoire over and over again to automatize the movement patterns.

A long-standing debate in the motor skill literature has centered on the question of whether learning entails a shift in control from the cortex to the subcortex, or the other way around, from the subcortex to the cortex. The idea that the subcortex comes to dominate skilled performance fits with our understanding that structures like the basal ganglia are essential for habitual behavior; for the billiards player, the opening break has become a habit of sorts. But when we appreciate how versatile experts are, modifying their movements to accommodate the current context, our focus shifts to the cerebral cortex and how its expansion has greatly increased our ability to make fine discriminations and remember past experiences.

Risa Kawai and her colleagues (2015) recently took a fresh look at this problem, asking how lesions of the motor cortex impact the ability to learn a new motor sequence and to perform a well-learned motor sequence. For this experiment, Kawai created a challenging task for rats that went against two aspects of rat behavior. First, rats don't like to wait for rewards: If they expect one, they want it pronto. Second, rats don't like to reach for things: Being quadrupeds, they typically use their forelimbs for locomotion or to hold pellets of food. In this experiment, thirsty rats had to learn to reach to press a

FIGURE 8.44 Humans show an extraordinary ability to develop motor skills.

lever, and then had to wait for 700 ms before pressing it again, to get a drink (**Figure 8.45a**).

The waiting was the hardest part for the rats. You might expect that, with enough practice, they would simply learn to hang out by the lever until 700 ms had passed. But, for these impulsive little guys, a more natural way to let the time pass was to move their arms about in an arm "dance" that lasted 700 ms. The particular pattern learned by each rat was idiosyncratic, but once learned, the rat would produce its unique dance in a very stereotyped manner (**Figure 8.45b**; view the dance in movie S1 of the supplemental information at http://dx.doi.org/10.1016/j.neuron.2015.03.024).

Once the rats had learned these dances, the researchers lesioned their primary motor cortex. Surprisingly, even after bilateral lesions of motor cortex, there was little discernible effect on the acquired skill (**Figure 8.45c**). Thus, once a movement sequence has been learned by a rat, the motor cortex is no longer essential for the precise execution of the movement. In contrast, when the lesions were made before training, the rats were unable to learn a well-timed movement sequence, indicating that motor cortex is necessary for learning to inhibit a response (**Figure 8.45d**). Note that these rats still pressed the lever and, in fact, did so faster than expected, so it wasn't a motor execution problem.

It appears that, at least for rats, the cortex comes in handy for learning new motor skills, but the subcortex can get along fine without cortical input during the execution of well-consolidated skills. The relevance of this work for understanding human motor control remains to be seen; at least some parts of the picture are surely different in humans. For example, bilateral lesions of the motor cortex would produce a profound loss of movement in all affected limbs. Furthermore, as noted earlier, expert performance is not only a matter of the rote repetition of a fixed movement pattern, but also entails the flexibility to modify that pattern in creative ways.

Observations like these have motivated a large body of literature exploring how experts differ from nonexperts. The multitalented Francis Galton, Charles Darwin's cousin, opined that innate ability, zeal, and laborious work were required to become eminent in a

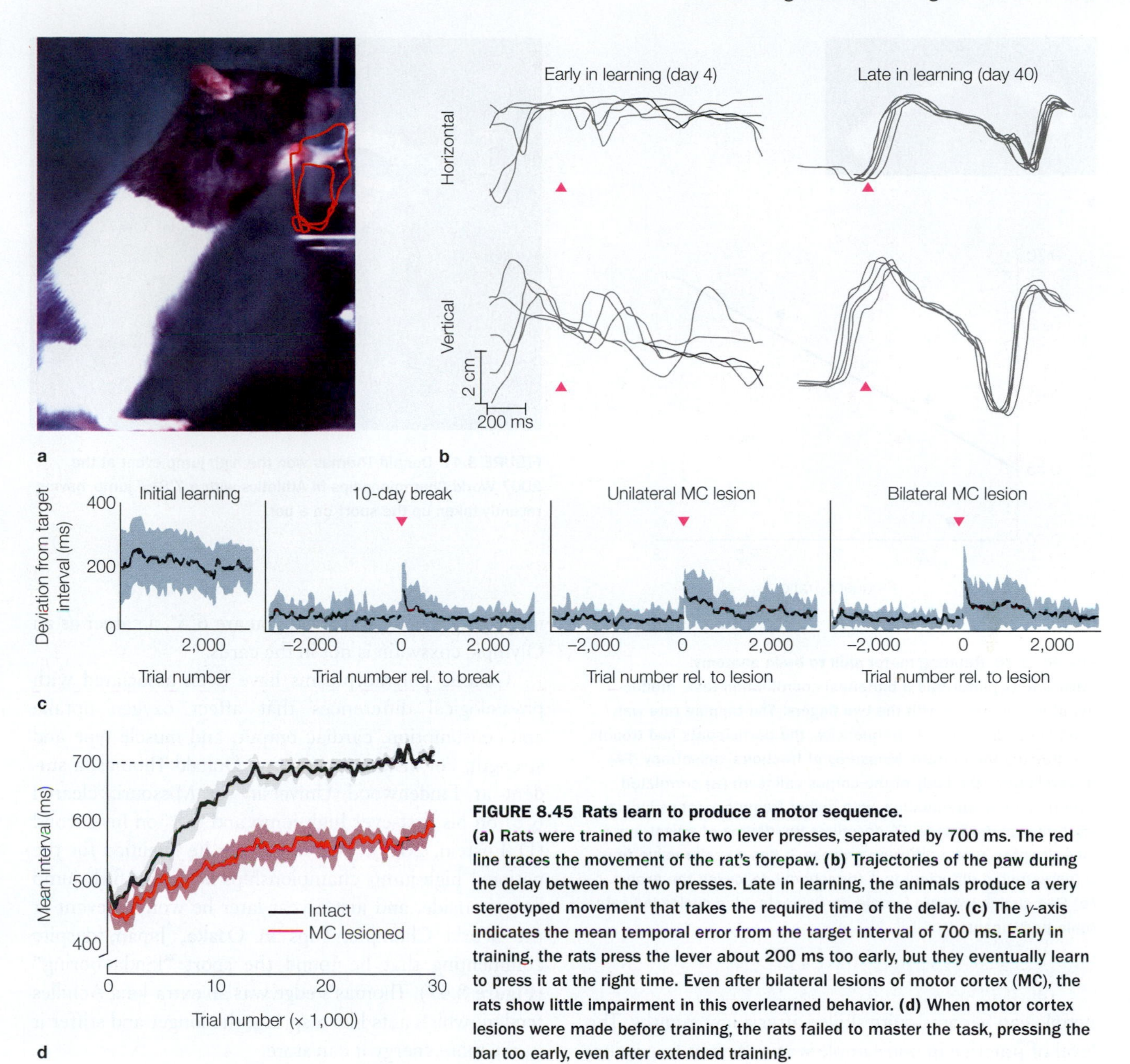

FIGURE 8.45 Rats learn to produce a motor sequence. **(a)** Rats were trained to make two lever presses, separated by 700 ms. The red line traces the movement of the rat's forepaw. **(b)** Trajectories of the paw during the delay between the two presses. Late in learning, the animals produce a very stereotyped movement that takes the required time of the delay. **(c)** The *y*-axis indicates the mean temporal error from the target interval of 700 ms. Early in training, the rats press the lever about 200 ms too early, but they eventually learn to press it at the right time. Even after bilateral lesions of motor cortex (MC), the rats show little impairment in this overlearned behavior. **(d)** When motor cortex lesions were made before training, the rats failed to master the task, pressing the bar too early, even after extended training.

field. Do experts have brains that differ in both structure and function? Are these differences innate, the result of extensive practice, or some combination of nature and nurture?

Neuroanatomists have identified some realms of skilled performance that are associated with structural differences. Studies using diffusion-weighted MRI have found evidence that the connectivity in a specific region of the corpus callosum between the left and right supplementary motor areas varies between individuals. The degree of bimanual coordination that a person exhibits correlates positively with the connectivity between the two regions (Johansen-Berg et al., 2007; **Figure 8.46**). This is certainly an interesting observation, but it tells us nothing about causality. Did the person become more coordinated because of the stronger connectivity, or did this difference in connectivity emerge because she engages in more bimanual activities, perhaps because she finds them more rewarding?

To get at causality, researchers have looked at changes that occur in the brain after extensive practice. Consider juggling, a skill that requires the coordination of the two hands, not to mention the ability to integrate complex spatial patterns created by the motions of the hands and balls. To the novice, juggling may seem impossible, but with just a modest amount of daily practice, most

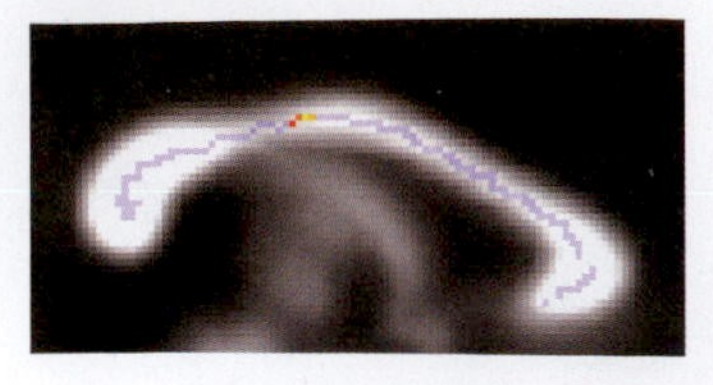

a

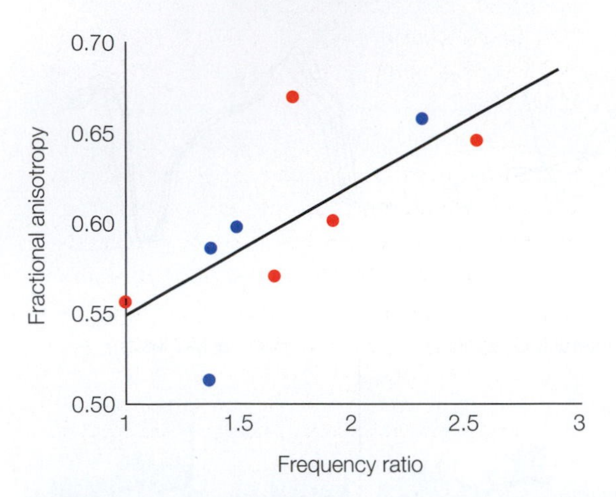

b

FIGURE 8.46 Relating motor skill to brain anatomy. Participants performed a bimanual coordination task, producing alternating taps with the two fingers. The tapping rate was varied such that, at high frequencies, the participants had trouble maintaining the pattern. Measures of fractional anisotropy (FA) in voxels from the body of the corpus callosum **(a)** correlated with bimanual coordination, with higher frequency ratios indicating better performance. FA describes the degree of anisotropy (see Chapter 3) of a diffusion process. It has a scalar value from 0 (unrestricted diffusion) to 1 (directional, following the axons). **(b)** Red circles indicate female participants; blue circles indicate male participants.

FIGURE 8.47 Donald Thomas won the high jump event at the 2007 World Championships in Athletics with a 7′8½″ jump, having recently taken up the sport on a bet.

people can become quite skilled after a few months. This level of practice in one sample was sufficient to produce measurable increases in gray matter in areas V5 and the intraparietal sulcus, temporal and parietal regions associated with motion processing and with movement planning and control (Draganski et al., 2004). When the jugglers stopped practicing, the gray matter volume in these regions of interest shrank, although it remained above the baseline level. Findings like these indicate that practice can readily shape the macroscopic landscape of the brain.

Our parents and teachers may often remind us that practice makes perfect, but it is also hard to argue against the idea that other factors are at play in determining expertise. Some individuals just seem to be more adept at certain skills. Some factors are genetic, or result from gene–environment interactions: For example, anatomical differences can be important for certain motor skills. If you are 5′5″ tall, it is unlikely that you will end up playing pro basketball. If you are 6′5″, a career as an Olympic coxswain is not in the cards.

Genetic polymorphisms have been associated with physiological differences that affect oxygen uptake and consumption, cardiac output, and muscle type and strength. For instance, on a bet, Donald Thomas, a student at Lindenwood University in Missouri, cleared 6′6″ on his first-ever high jump and 6′8″ on his second (D. Epstein, 2013). Two days later he qualified for the national high-jump championships with the fifth jump he ever made, and just a year later he won his event at the World Championships in Osaka, Japan, despite commenting that he found the sport “kinda boring” (**Figure 8.47**). Thomas’s edge was an extra-long Achilles tendon, which acts like a spring; the longer and stiffer it is, the more energy it can store.

We readily consider how genetics might influence muscle size and height, but we often ignore that people also exhibit large individual differences in motivation: Some people are more willing to put in hours of practice than others. Although Galton defined motivation as “zeal,” a more modern notion is that motivation is about the importance we place on action outcomes and their utilities (Niv, 2007). In other words, is it worth the effort? How much do we value the goal and its predicted reward relative to the cost we have to expend? Worth is subjective and has many variables, and in Chapter 12 we will consider this issue in detail.

An interesting study of musical performers revealed that the most elite performers actually found practice less pleasurable than non-elite but skilled performers did (Ericsson et al., 1993). One inference drawn from this work is that expertise requires not just hours of practice, but effortful practice in which the performer is constantly pushing herself to explore new methods or endlessly repeating the selected routine, not for pleasure but for gain.

It is clear that experts, amateurs, and novices have different brains. Researchers find it easier to identify structural differences in experts in a physical activity—compared to, say, experts in theoretical physics—perhaps because we have a good idea of where we might expect to observe such differences. We can look in the hand area of the right motor cortex to see structural differences between violin players and musicians who play instruments that do not place such an emphasis on left-hand fingering skills. Even so, we should be cautious in assuming that such differences are at the heart of expertise. Across domains as diverse as motor skills, mathematics, and the arts, many commonalities are found among the most elite performers. A good explanation of the neural correlates of these commonalities has yet to be articulated.

TAKE-HOME MESSAGES

- Sensorimotor learning is improvement, through practice, in the performance of motor behavior.
- Sensorimotor adaptation entails modifying the relationship between sensory and motor associations. Learning new visuomotor associations engages a broad network of cortical and subcortical areas with the establishment of a new map, producing changes in the posterior parietal cortex.
- The cerebellum is critical for error-based learning. Errors are derived from a comparison of the predicted and observed sensory information and lead to changes in a forward model, a representation that can be used to generate the sensory expectancies for a movement.
- The acquisition of a motor skill involves the formation of new movement patterns that can result in changes in both structure and connectivity.

Summary

Cognitive neuroscience has had a major impact on our conceptualization of how the brain produces skilled action. The selection, planning, and execution of volitional movement involves activity across a distributed network of cortical and subcortical brain regions. These structures entail some degree of hierarchical organization as an abstract action goal is translated into a specific pattern of muscle activity, but the process also includes considerable interaction between different levels of representation as we use our limbs in a flexible manner.

Similar to what we saw in the chapters on perception and object recognition, considerable effort has been made to understand which properties of the world are represented by neurons in the motor pathway. The codes appear to be quite diverse: The activity of neurons in the motor cortex can be closely linked with specific muscles, whereas the activity of neurons in planning-related areas is more closely associated with properties such as movement direction. Recent work suggests that there are even more abstract levels of neural representation and that the tuning properties of these neurons are dynamic, coding different features, depending on time and context. As such, there is not a simple mapping from neural activity to behavior.

The population activity of neurons in the motor pathway can be decoded to predict an ongoing movement. This insight has led to the development of brain–machine interface (BMI) systems in which neural activity is used to control prosthetic devices such as a computer mouse or an artificial limb. This work has tremendous potential to improve the quality of life of people who have lost their ability to control their limbs as the result of neurological disease or injury. Currently, BMI systems are being developed that involve either invasive or noninvasive methods to record neural activity.

As with other processing domains, such as perception and attention, different regions within the motor system show some degree of specialization. Areas in association cortex such as the posterior parietal cortex are crucial for providing spatial representations essential for goal-directed actions. Secondary motor areas, such as premotor and supplementary motor cortices, are involved with movement selection, with the former being guided by information from the environment and the latter more driven by internal goals and personal experience, including previously learned skilled motor movements. The motor cortex provides a prominent descending projection to the spinal cord with its output, the pyramidal tract, providing a critical signal to activate the muscles.

Many parts of the subcortex are also essential for motor control. A number of subcortical nuclei provide a second source of direct input to the spinal cord: the extrapyramidal tract, with this information essential for maintaining postural stability, as well as for supporting volitional movement. Two prominent subcortical structures—the basal ganglia and cerebellum—are key components of the motor system, as evidenced by the prominent movement disorders observed in diseases associated with the degeneration of these structures. The basal ganglia play a critical role in movement initiation, whereas the cerebellum generates predictions to anticipate the sensory consequences of a movement, using errors to fine-tune the system for future movements.

Key Terms

akinesia (p. 361)
alpha motor neurons (p. 328)
apraxia (p. 335)
ataxia (p. 331)
basal ganglia (p. 331)
bradykinesia (p. 361)
brain–machine interfaces (BMIs) (p. 354)
central pattern generators (p. 337)
cerebellum (p. 331)
corticomotoneurons (CM neurons) (p. 332)
corticospinal tract (CST) (p. 331)
deep brain stimulation (DBS) (p. 364)
effector (p. 328)
endpoint control (p. 337)
extrapyramidal tracts (p. 330)
forward model (p. 370)
hemiplegia (p. 334)
Huntington's disease (p. 361)
hyperdirect pathway (p. 364)
hyperkinesia (p. 361)
hypokinesia (p. 361)
mirror neuron network (p. 351)
mirror neurons (MNs) (p. 350)
optic ataxia (p. 334)
Parkinson's disease (p. 361)
population vector (p. 341)
preferred direction (p. 340)
premotor cortex (p. 334)
primary motor cortex (M1) (p. 331)
prosthetic devices (p. 354)
sensorimotor adaptation (p. 367)
sensorimotor learning (p. 367)
sensory prediction errors (p. 369)
spinal interneurons (p. 328)
substantia nigra (p. 330)
supplementary motor area (SMA) (p. 334)

Think About It

1. Viewed both from a functional perspective and from a neuroanatomical/neurophysiological perspective, motor control is organized hierarchically. Outline this hierarchy, starting with the most basic or primitive aspects of motor behavior and progressing to the highest-level or most sophisticated aspects.
2. What is the difference between the pyramidal and extrapyramidal motor pathways? What type of movement disorder would you expect to see if the pyramidal tract were damaged? How would extrapyramidal damage differ?
3. Explain the concept of the population vector. How could it be used to control a prosthetic (artificial) limb?
4. Why do people with Parkinson's disease have difficulty moving? Provide an explanation based on the physiological properties of the basal ganglia. How does dopamine replacement therapy or deep brain stimulation improve their condition?
5. When we first learn a skill such as skiing, it helps to listen to the instructor provide step-by-step guidance to make a turn. With practice, the action becomes effortless. What changes, both psychologically and neurally, do you expect take place as you move from beginner to expert?

Suggested Reading

Chaudhary, U., Birbaumer, N., & Ramos-Murguialday, A. (2016). Brain-computer interfaces for communication and rehabilitation. *Nature Reviews Neurology*, *12*(9), 513–525.

Cisek, P., & Kalaska, J. F. (2010). Neural mechanisms for interacting with a world full of action choices. *Annual Review of Neuroscience*, *33*, 269–298.

Rizzolatti, G., Fogassi, L., & Gallese, V. (2000). Cortical mechanisms subserving object grasping and action recognition: A new view on the cortical motor functions. In M. S. Gazzaniga (Ed.), *The new cognitive neurosciences* (2nd ed., pp. 539–552). Cambridge, MA: MIT Press.

Shadmehr, R., Smith, M. A., & Krakauer, J. W. (2010). Error correction, sensory prediction, and adaptation in motor control. *Annual Review of Neuroscience*, *33*, 89–108.

Shadmehr, R., & Wise, S. P. (2005). *The computational neurobiology of reaching and pointing*. Cambridge, MA: MIT Press.

Yarrow, K., Brown, P., & Krakauer, J. W. (2009). Inside the brain of an elite athlete: The neural processes that support high achievement in sports. *Nature Reviews Neuroscience*, *10*, 585–596.

When I was younger, I could remember anything, whether it had happened or not.

Mark Twain

CHAPTER

9

Memory

FROM THE TIME HE WAS A CHILD, H.M. had suffered from progressively worsening epilepsy, uncontrollable by medication. By the year 1953, at age 27, H.M. was having a hundred minor seizures every day and a major seizure every few days, and he was no longer able to work.

At that time, neurologists knew that many seizures originate in the medial portions of the temporal lobe, and that their electrical impulses can spread across the brain, producing violent seizures and loss of consciousness. It was also becoming increasingly clear that surgically removing the seizure focus, the brain region where seizure activity originates, could help patients with epilepsy. William Beecher Scoville, a neurosurgeon at Hartford Hospital in Connecticut, offered H.M. an experimental surgical therapy: bilateral resection of his medial temporal lobes. Like W.J. from Chapter 4, H.M. was desperate. He agreed to the surgery. H.M.'s temporal lobes, including his amygdalae, entorhinal cortex, and hippocampi, were removed.

Although the surgery succeeded in treating H.M.'s epilepsy, his physicians, family, and friends soon realized that he was now experiencing new problems. H.M. had profound amnesia—but not the kind of amnesia that we usually see depicted in television shows or movies, in which the character loses all personal memories. H.M. knew who he was and remembered his personal history, facts he had learned in school, language, how to do things, social events, people, almost everything—up until a couple of years before his surgery. For those previous couple of years, he drew a blank. More troubling was that when a nurse left the room and returned after a short delay, he could not remember ever having seen or spoken with her before. He could follow a conversation and remember a string of numbers for a while, but he could not repeat them an hour later. So, while his short-term memory was intact, H.M. could not form *new* long-term memories.

BIG Questions

- What is forgotten in amnesia, and are all forms of amnesia the same?
- Are memories about personal events processed in the same way as procedural memories for how to perform a physical task?
- What brain systems have proved to be critical for the formation of long-term memory?
- Where are memories stored in the brain, and by what cellular and molecular mechanisms?

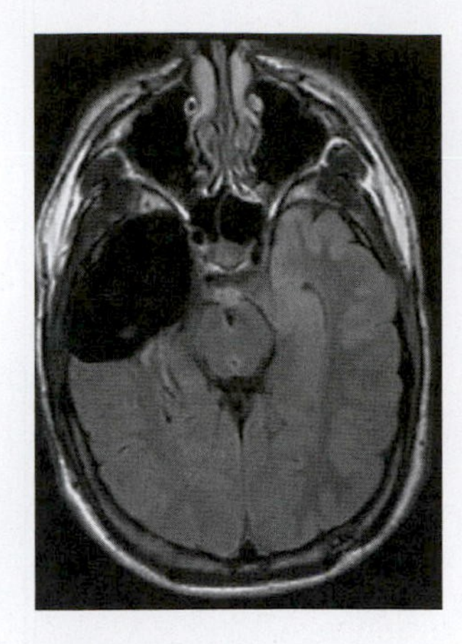

FIGURE 9.1 An anterior temporal lobectomy.
Axial MRI image following removal of the right amygdala, hippocampus, and anterior temporal lobe.

No surgeon had ever removed both of a patient's temporal lobes before, so no one knew that it would lead to severe amnesia. Since then, great care is taken to avoid removing both medial temporal lobes, or even one medial temporal lobe if the other is compromised in any way from prior damage or disease. This adapted form of the surgery, known as *unilateral temporal lobectomy* (**Figure 9.1**), is still used successfully today for certain patients suffering from epilepsy.

While some of our knowledge about the world is hardwired, much of it comes from our experiences and what we remember and learn from them. In order for those past experiences to be useful, certain kinds of information have to be stashed in memory: what happened, where and when, who or what was involved, and the positive or negative outcomes of the experiences. These facts help to guide our actions when we are confronted with the same or similar situations in the future (Nadel & Hardt, 2011). By enabling us to avoid situations that we found dangerous in the past and to seek those that were previously beneficial, the cognitive abilities that allow us to store these types of information provide a survival advantage.

In the mid 20th century, memory was being investigated at the organ and cellular levels. At the organ level, through loss-of-function studies on patients with brain lesions, particularly H.M., particular regions of the brain had come under close scrutiny. Without the medial temporal lobe, new memories could not be formed, and the recall of some stored memories was severely hampered. Following up on these findings, researchers were able to describe distinct memory systems for different types of learning and localize them in different parts of the brain. And at the cellular level, Donald Hebb theorized that synaptic connections were plastic and changed in an activity-dependent manner. Plastic changes in synaptic connections were proposed as the mechanism behind encoding information, though the code itself remained unknown.

In this chapter we explore what cognitive neuroscience has uncovered about learning and memory. After introducing the processes that contribute to memory and discussing how it is categorized, we tour the brain regions involved in memory processing and describe what we have learned about memory from patients with amnesia. Next we discuss the current thinking about the types of memory systems that exist and how they work. At the end of the chapter we will discuss the cellular mechanisms that are thought to mediate memory formation.

9.1 Learning and Memory, and Their Associated Anatomy

Despite the vast stores of information contained in our brains, we continuously acquire new information. **Learning** is the process of acquiring that new information, and the outcome of learning is **memory.** That is, a memory is created when something is learned, and this learning may occur either by a single exposure or by the repetition of information, experiences, or actions.

We retain some forms of information only briefly, while other memories last a lifetime. You may not remember what you had for dinner last Thursday, but your second-grade birthday cake with tigers on it remains vivid. Not only that, you may also remember many of the birthday guests. This latter characteristic of memory led the University of Toronto's Endel Tulving to describe some forms of memory as "mental time travel" (M. A. Wheeler et al., 1997). By this, Tulving meant that the very act of remembering something that happened to us previously is to reexperience the context of the past experience in the present.

Researchers believe that humans and animals have several types of memory mediated by different systems. Models of memory distinguish between very brief *sensory memory*, with a lifetime measured in milliseconds to seconds; *short-term memory* and *working memory*, which persist for seconds to minutes; and memories that may persist for decades, which we call *long-term memory*.

Researchers also make distinctions among the types of information stored. Long-term memory is commonly divided

TABLE 9.1 Types of Memory

	Characteristic of Memory			
Type of Memory	**Time Course**	**Capacity**	**Conscious Awareness?**	**Mechanism of Loss**
Sensory	Milliseconds to seconds	High	No	Primarily decay
Short-term and working	Seconds to minutes	Limited (7 ± 2 items)	Yes	Interference and decay
Long-term nondeclarative	Minutes to years	High	No	Primarily interference
Long-term declarative	Minutes to years	High	Yes	Primarily interference

into *declarative memory*, which consists of our conscious memory for both facts we have learned (semantic memory) and events we have experienced (episodic memory); and *nondeclarative memory*, which is nonconscious memory that cannot be verbally reported, often expressed through the performing of procedures (procedural memory).

While all forms of memory involve cellular and circuitry changes in the nervous system, the nature and location of these changes remain important questions. **Table 9.1** presents an overview of the various types of memory, which we explore in detail in this chapter.

Researchers divide learning and memory into three major processing stages:

1. **Encoding** is the processing of incoming information and experiences, which creates *memory traces*, traditionally thought to be alterations in the synaptic strength and number of neuronal connections. (Research in the last few years, however, has challenged the traditional notion that synaptic strength is the mechanism behind encoding.)

   Encoding has two separate steps, the first of which is **acquisition**. Sensory systems are constantly being bombarded by tons of stimuli, and most produce only a very brief transient sensory response that fades quickly (about 1,000 ms after presentation) without ever reaching short-term memory. During this period, however, the stimuli are available for processing; this state is known as a *sensory buffer*. Only some of these stimuli are sustained and acquired by short-term memory.

   Not all memory traces appear to get past the second step, **consolidation**, in which changes in the brain stabilize a memory over time, resulting in a long-term memory. Consolidation can take days, months, or even years, and it creates a stronger representation over time. There are many theories about what is occurring when a memory is being consolidated, which we discuss in Section 9.6.

2. **Storage** is the retention of memory traces. It is the result of acquisition and consolidation, and it represents the permanent record of the information.

3. **Retrieval** involves accessing stored memory traces, which may aid in decision making and change behavior. We have conscious access to some but not all of the information stored in memory.

The brain has the ability to change through experience—in other words, to learn. At the neuronal level, this means that changes occur in the synaptic connections between neurons, discussed in Section 9.7. It also implies that learning can occur in multiple regions of the brain. Learning can be accomplished in a number of ways, and it appears that different parts of the brain are specialized for different types of learning. For instance, in Chapter 8 we discussed the role of the basal ganglia in reinforcement learning and the involvement of the cerebellum in trial-and-error learning based on prediction error signals. The amygdala is involved with fear learning, which we will read more about in Chapter 10.

The "Anatomical Orientation" box on p. 382 illustrates the components of what has come to be called the medial temporal lobe memory system, first described after H.M.'s surgery. It is made up of the **hippocampus**—an infolding of a portion of the medial temporal lobe that is shaped like a seahorse (*Hippocampus* is the genus name for the fish known as a seahorse)—and various structures interconnected with the hippocampus. These include the surrounding entorhinal cortex, perirhinal cortex, and parahippocampal cortex within the temporal lobe, and subcortical structures including the mammillary bodies and anterior thalamic nuclei.

The hippocampus is reciprocally connected with wide regions of the cortex via the entorhinal cortex and the output projection pathway of the fimbria and fornix to the subcortical portions of the system, which themselves project to the prefrontal cortex. The parietal lobe and other regions of the temporal lobe (not shown here) are also involved in aspects of memory. The amygdala, also located in the temporal lobe, is primarily involved in affective processing, and though it can have an influence on fear learning and memory, it is not involved with memory in general.

ANATOMICAL ORIENTATION

Anatomy of Memory

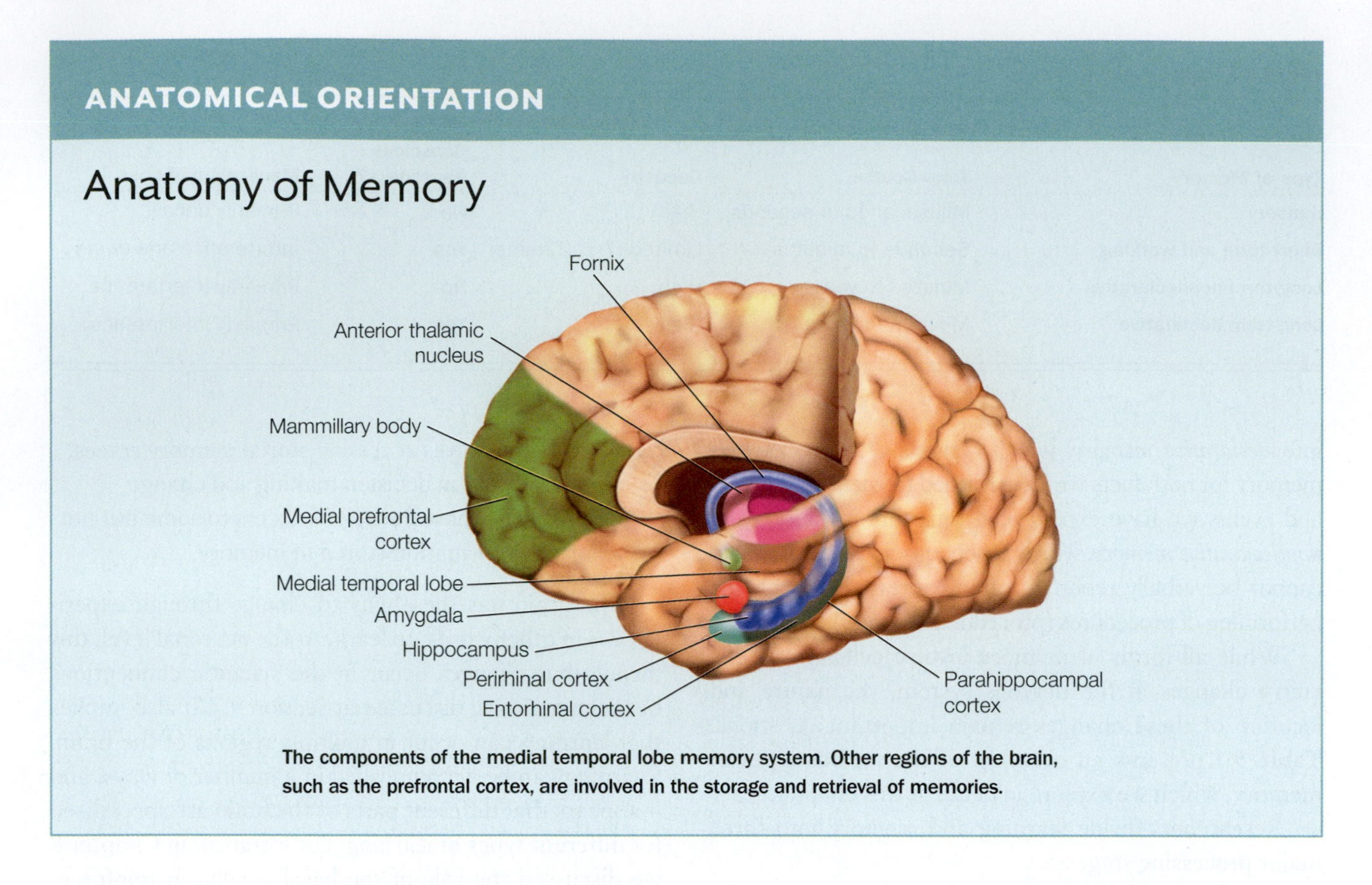

The components of the medial temporal lobe memory system. Other regions of the brain, such as the prefrontal cortex, are involved in the storage and retrieval of memories.

TAKE-HOME MESSAGES

- Learning is the process of acquiring new information, the outcome of which is memory.
- Memories can be short-term or long-term. Long-term memories may be declarative, consisting of either the conscious memory for facts (semantic memory) or the conscious memory of past experiences (episodic memory). Long-term memories may also be nondeclarative memories for how to do things, such as brushing your teeth or skating on ice.
- Learning and memory have three major stages: encoding (acquisition and consolidation), storage, and retrieval.
- The medial temporal lobe memory system is made up of the hippocampus and the surrounding entorhinal cortex, perirhinal cortex, and parahippocampal cortex within the temporal lobes.

9.2 Memory Deficits: Amnesia

Our understanding of memory relies heavily on the study of individuals whose memory is impaired. Memory deficits and loss, known collectively as **amnesia**, can result from brain damage caused by surgery, disease, and physical or psychological trauma. Amnesia is a form of memory impairment that affects all of the senses. Typically, people with amnesia display deficits in specific types of memory or in aspects of memory processing. Each type of functional deficit is associated with a lesion in a different brain region. For instance, left-hemisphere damage can result in selective impairment in verbal memory, whereas right-hemisphere damage may result in nonverbal-memory impairment.

The loss of memory for events that occur after a lesion or other physiological trauma is known as **anterograde amnesia**. It results from the inability to learn *new* things. A loss of memory for events and knowledge that occurred before a lesion or other physiological trauma is called **retrograde amnesia**. Sometimes retrograde amnesia is **temporally limited**, extending back only a few minutes or hours. In severe cases, it is extensive, sometimes encompassing almost the entire previous life span. Retrograde amnesia tends to be greatest for the most recent events. This effect, known as a **temporal gradient** or **Ribot's law**, was first postulated by Théodule-Armand Ribot, a 19th-century French psychologist. Amnesia can differentially affect short-term memory, working memory, or long-term memory abilities.

Brain Surgery and Memory Loss

Because the extent and locations of lesions can be known after a surgery, a lot of the information about the organization of human memory was first derived from patients left accidentally amnesic after surgical treatments. We return now to the story of H.M. In 1954, after the bilateral removal of H.M.'s medial temporal lobes, the neurosurgeon Scoville reported "a very grave, recent memory loss, so severe as to prevent the patient from remembering the locations of the rooms in which he lives, the names of his close associates, or even the way to the toilet" (Scoville, 1954).

To better understand the deficits of H.M. and his other postsurgical patients with medial temporal lobe resections, Scoville teamed up with neuropsychologist Brenda Milner (see Chapter 1). Through neuropsychological examinations, Milner found that the extent of the memory deficit depended on how much of the medial temporal lobe had been removed. The more posterior along the medial temporal lobe the resection had been made, the worse the amnesia was (Scoville & Milner, 1957). Strikingly, however, only *bilateral* resection of the hippocampus resulted in severe amnesia. By comparison, in one patient whose entire right medial temporal lobe (hippocampus and hippocampal gyrus) was removed, no residual memory deficit was reported by Scoville and Milner (although today's more sensitive tests would have revealed some memory deficits).

H.M., whose name was revealed to be Henry Molaison after his death in 2008 at the age of 82, was the most interesting and famous of these patients. Over the years, he unstintingly allowed himself to be tested by over a hundred researchers. His case holds a prominent position in the history of memory research for several reasons, including the fact that although he had a memory deficit, he had no other cognitive deficits. In addition, because his memory loss was the result of surgery, the exact regions of the brain that were affected were thought to be known (Milner et al., 1968; Scoville & Milner, 1957)—although, as we will see later in the chapter, this last point was not quite true.

After the surgery, H.M. knew some of the autobiographical details of his life, and he retained all other knowledge about the world that he had learned in his life up to the 2 years immediately before his surgery. From those 2 years forward, he could remember nothing. He also showed selective memory loss for personal events (episodic memory) as far back as a decade before the surgery. H.M. had normal short-term memory (sensory memory and working memory) and procedural memory (such as how to ride a bicycle, tie his shoes, or play a game).

Like many other people with amnesia, H.M. also had normal digit span abilities (how many numbers a person can hold in memory over a short period of time) and did well at holding strings of digits in working memory. Unlike healthy participants, however, he did poorly on digit span tests that required the acquisition of new long-term memories. It appeared that the transfer of information from short-term storage to long-term memory had been disrupted: He could not form new long-term memories (anterograde amnesia). Surprisingly, H.M. could learn some things: Tasks that involved motor skills, perceptual skills, or procedures became easier over time, though he could not remember practicing the new skills or being asked to learn them. There was a dissociation between remembering the experience of learning how to do one of these things (a type of declarative memory) and the actual learned information (nondeclarative memory).

H.M. changed scientists' understanding of the brain's memory processes. It had previously been thought that memory could not be separated from perceptual and intellectual functions, but these functions remained intact in H.M., implying that memory was distinct from these processes. Researchers also learned that the medial temporal lobes are necessary for the formation of long-term memories but not for the formation and retrieval of short-term memories, or for the formation of new long-term nondeclarative memories that involve the learning of procedures or motor skills.

Studies in H.M. and other patients with amnesia have also shown that they can learn some forms of new information in addition to procedures, motor skills, and perceptual skills. Some can also learn new concepts and world knowledge (semantic memory) with extensive study. But the amnesic patients nonetheless do not remember the *episodes* during which they learned or observed the information previously. Thus, growing evidence suggests that long-term memories for events, facts, and procedures can be partially dissociated from one another, as expressed in their differential sensitivity to brain damage.

Dementias

Memory loss can also be caused by diseases that result in dementia. **Dementia** is an umbrella term for the loss of cognitive function in different domains (including memory) beyond what is expected in normal aging. While the neuronal degeneration that results in dementia is often widespread, some dementias are limited to specific areas of the brain and also aid in our understanding of memory.

The most common types of dementia are irreversible and are the result of neurodegenerative disease, vascular disease, or a combination of the two. Neurodegenerative diseases that cause dementia are commonly associated with the pathological misfolding of particular proteins that are prone to aggregate in the brain. They are classified according to the predominance of the specific type of accumulated abnormal protein (Llorens et al., 2016). The most common of these protein-associated neurodegenerative diseases is *Alzheimer's disease (AD)*, which, according to the World Health Organization, contributes to 60%–70% of dementia cases.

Alzheimer's disease is characterized by the extracellular deposition of aggregated *beta-amyloid proteins*, negatively affecting synapse formation and neuroplasticity, and also by the intracellular accumulation of *neurofibrillary tangles*, which are aggregations of microtubules associated with hyper-phosphorylated tau protein. The medial temporal lobe structures are the first to be affected in AD, and the pathology later extends to lateral temporal, parietal, and frontal neocortices. The progression of the disease is not completely uniform, and a patient's symptoms depend on which tissue has been affected. Currently, the front-runner for the causative mechanism of AD involves reduced cellular responsiveness to insulin in the brain, which appears before the onset of symptoms (Talbot et al., 2012) and is thought to promote or trigger the key pathophysiological events that result in AD.

Vascular dementia is the second most common type of dementia, making up about 15% of cases (O'Brien & Thomas, 2015). It is caused by decreased oxygenation of neural tissue and cell death, resulting from ischemic or hemorrhagic infarcts, rupture of small arterial vessels in the brain associated with diabetes, and rupture of cerebral arteries caused by the accumulation of beta-amyloid plaques in the walls of the vessels, which damages and weakens them. Vascular dementia can affect multiple brain areas, resulting in diverse symptoms, and can co-occur with AD. In fact, 50% of all cases of dementia have been found to have mixed etiologies (Rahimi & Kovacs, 2014).

Less common are the *frontotemporal lobar dementias*, a heterogeneous group of neurodegenerative diseases characterized by accumulations of different proteins in the frontal and temporal lobes but not the parietal and occipital lobes, resulting in language and behavioral changes that may overlap with AD.

TAKE-HOME MESSAGES

- Anterograde (forward-going) amnesia is the loss of the ability to form new memories, as in the case of H.M.
- Retrograde (backward-going) amnesia is the loss of memory for events that happened in the past.
- Retrograde amnesia tends to be greatest for the most recent events—an effect known as a temporal gradient or Ribot's law.
- The most common neurodegenerative cause of dementia is Alzheimer's disease.

9.3 Mechanisms of Memory

Although patients with memory deficits have revealed many key aspects of human memory, models of memory continue to evolve, and different models emphasize different factors in the organization of learning and memory. Various models may focus on how long memories persist, the type of information that is retained, whether memories are conscious or unconscious, and the time it takes to acquire them. In this section we discuss different forms of memory that have been proposed, which are summarized in **Figure 9.2** along with their associated brain areas, and we describe some of the evidence supporting theoretical distinctions among them.

Short-Term Forms of Memory

As mentioned earlier, short-term memories persist for milliseconds, seconds, or minutes. They include the transient retention of sensory information in sensory structures (sensory memory), short-term stores for information about yourself and the world (short-term memory), and memory used in the service of other cognitive functions, such as adding two numbers together in your mind (working memory).

SENSORY MEMORY Imagine watching the final game of the World Cup. The score is tied with seconds to go, when your mother enters the room and begins a soliloquy. Suddenly, you detect an increase in the volume of her voice and hear, "You haven't heard a word I've said!" Wisely, your response is not to admit it. Instead, in the nick of time, you retrieve her previous utterance and you reply, "You said that the neighbor's goat is in our yard again and to get it out."

Almost everyone you ask about this phenomenon knows what you mean. The auditory verbal information just presented to you seems to persist as a sort of echo in your head, even when you are not really paying attention to it. If you try to retrieve it quickly enough, you find it is still there, and you can repeat it out loud to assuage your interrogator. We refer to this type of memory as **sensory memory**, which, for hearing, we call *echoic memory*. For vision, we say *iconic memory*.

The persistence of the auditory sensory memory trace in humans has been measured in different ways, including physiological recording. An event-related potential (ERP) known as the electrical *mismatch negativity (MMN)*, or its magnetic counterpart, the *mismatch field (MMF)*, has proved highly informative about the duration of echoic memory. The MMN and MMF brain

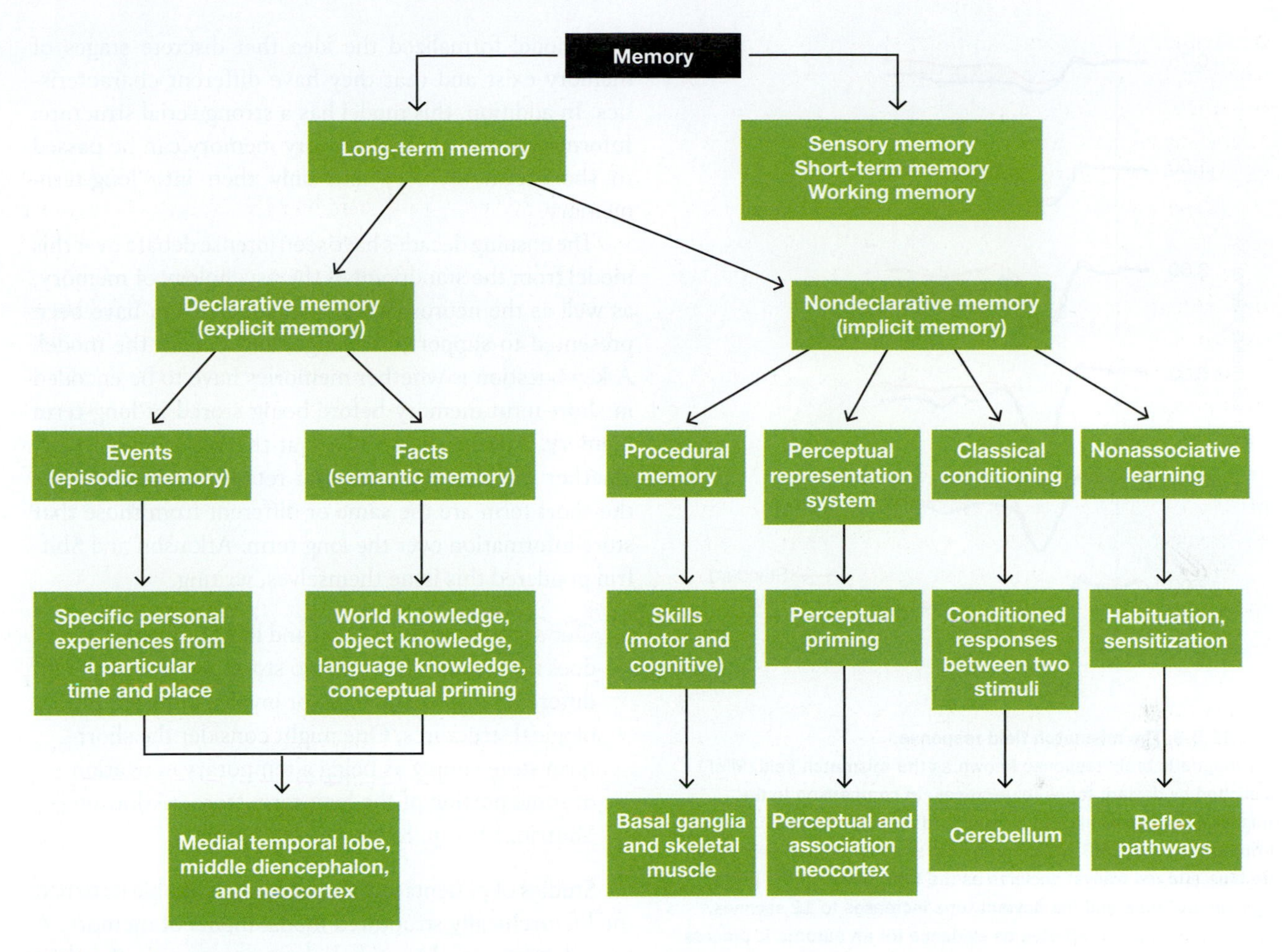

FIGURE 9.2 The hypothesized structure of human memory.
The brain regions that are thought to contribute to different types of memory are indicated.

responses are elicited by the presentation of a rare deviant stimulus, such as a high-frequency tone, presented within a sequence of identical and more commonly presented low-frequency tones.

These mismatch responses are interpreted as representing sensory memory processes that hold recent auditory experience in echoic memory for comparison to new inputs: When the inputs differ (i.e., the rare deviant stimulus is presented), the MMN and MMF are generated. Since sensory memory is defined by its short time course, the amplitudes of these brain responses at different time intervals between the deviant and common tones can be used to index how long the echoic memory trace persists.

Mikko Sams, Ritta Hari, and their colleagues at the Helsinki University of Technology in Finland (1993) did precisely that. They varied the interstimulus intervals between standard and deviant tones and found that the MMF could still be elicited by a deviant tone at interstimulus intervals of 9 to 10 seconds (**Figure 9.3**). After about 10 seconds, the amplitude of the MMF declined to the point where it could no longer be distinguished reliably from the responses to the standard tones. Because the MMF is generated in the auditory cortex, these physiological studies also provide information about where sensory memories are stored: in the sensory structures as a short-lived neural trace.

Compared to an auditory sensory memory, the neural trace for a visual sensory memory does not persist very long. Most estimates suggest that the neural trace for a visual stimulus lasts only 300 to 500 ms. Both echoic and iconic sensory memory, however, have a relatively high capacity: These forms of memory can, in principle, retain a lot of information, but only for short periods of time.

SHORT-TERM MEMORY In contrast to sensory memory, **short-term memory** has a longer time course—seconds to minutes—and a more limited capacity. Early data on short-term memory led to the development of some influential models that proposed discrete stages of information processing during learning and memory.

The *modal model*, developed by Richard Atkinson and Richard Shiffrin (1968), proposes that information is first stored in sensory memory (**Figure 9.4**). From there, items selected by attentional processes can move

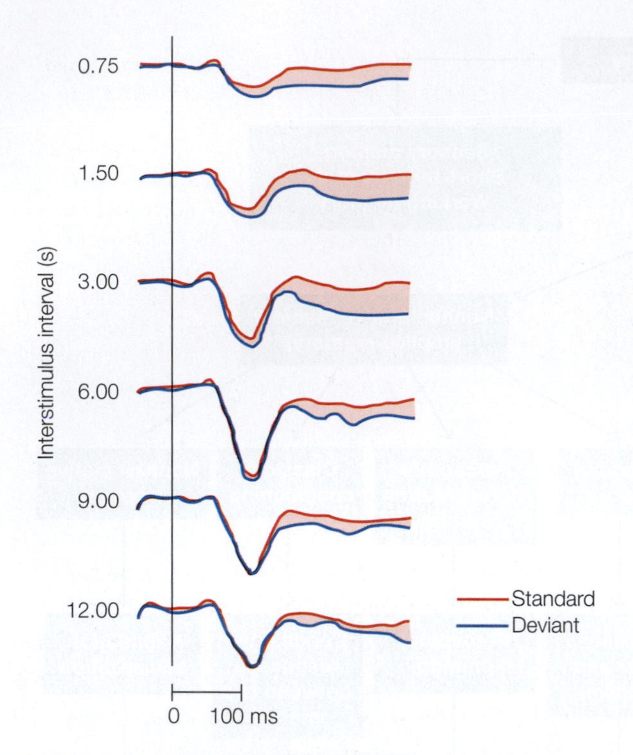

FIGURE 9.3 The mismatch field response.
The magnetic brain response known as the mismatch field (MMF) is elicited by deviant tones (blue traces) in comparison to the magnetic responses elicited by standard tones (red traces). The amplitude of the MMF (indicated by the shaded difference between the blue and red traces) declines as the time between the preceding standard tone and the deviant tone increases to 12 seconds. This result can be interpreted as evidence for an automatic process in auditory sensory (echoic) memory that has a time course on the order of approximately 10 seconds.

into short-term storage. Once in short-term memory, if the item is rehearsed, it can be moved into long-term memory. The modal model suggests that, at each stage, information can be lost by *decay* (information degrades and is lost over time), *interference* (new information displaces old information), or a combination of the two.

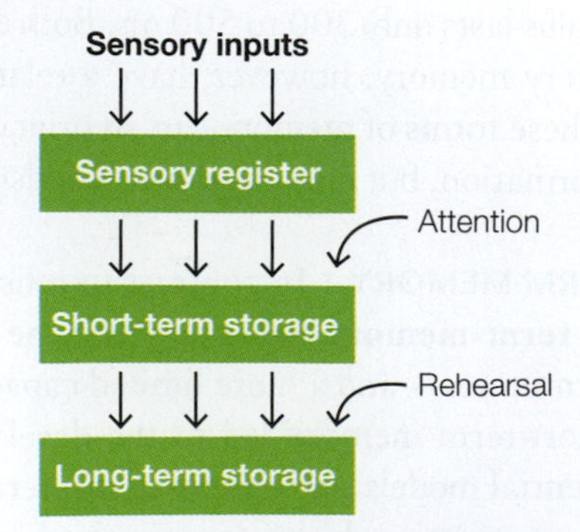

FIGURE 9.4 The Atkinson and Shiffrin modal model of memory.
Sensory information enters the information-processing system and is first stored in a sensory register. Items that are selected via attentional processes are then moved into short-term storage. With rehearsal, the item can move from short-term to long-term storage.

This model formalized the idea that discrete stages of memory exist and that they have different characteristics. In addition, this model has a strong serial structure: Information coming into sensory memory can be passed to short-term memory and only then into long-term memory.

The ensuing decades have seen intense debate over this model from the standpoint of the psychology of memory, as well as the neuroscience of memory. Data have been presented to support, challenge, and extend the model. A key question is whether memories have to be encoded in short-term memory before being stored in long-term memory. Another way to look at this question is to ask whether the brain systems that retain information over the short term are the same or different from those that store information over the long term. Atkinson and Shiffrin pondered this issue themselves, writing,

> Our account of short-term and long-term storage does not require that the two stores necessarily be in different parts of the brain or involve different physiological structures. One might consider the short-term store simply as being a temporary activation of some portion of the long-term store. (Atkinson & Shiffrin, 1971, p. 89)

Studies of patients with brain damage enable us to test the hierarchically structured modal model of memory. A typical test to evaluate short-term memory is the digit span test, which involves reading and remembering a list of digits and, after a delay of a few seconds, repeating the numbers. The lists can be from two to five or more digits long, and the maximum number that a person can recall and report is known as the person's digit span ability.

In 1969, neuropsychologists Elizabeth Warrington and Tim Shallice at University College London reported that patient K.F., with damage to the left perisylvian cortex (the region around the Sylvian fissure), displayed reduced digit span ability (about 2 items, as opposed to 5 to 9 items for healthy persons). Remarkably, however, in a long-term memory test of associative learning, in which words are paired, K.F. retained the ability to form certain types of new long-term memories that could last much longer than a few seconds. Therefore, it seemed that the patient displayed an interesting dissociation between short-term and long-term memory.

If this interpretation of the finding is true, it has important implications for models of memory: Short-term memory might not be required in order to form long-term memory. This conclusion is in contrast to how information flows in the modal model, which requires serial processing. One issue with this view is that the two tests presented to K.F. were different (digit span and word association), so it's hard to pinpoint whether

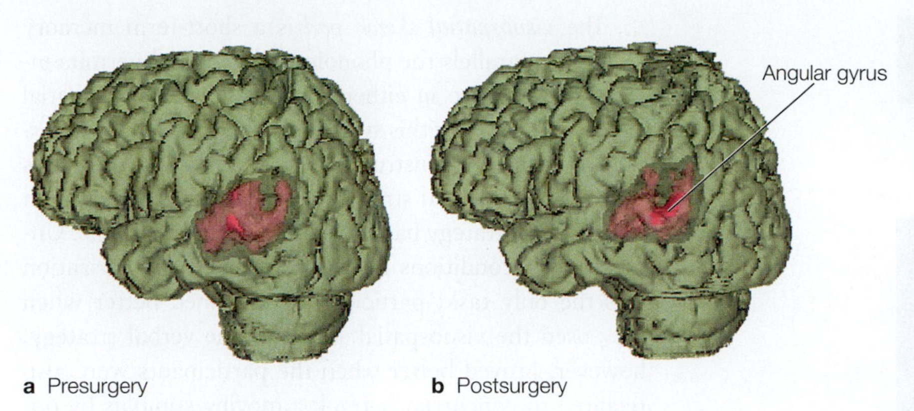

FIGURE 9.5 MRI scans reconstructed to provide a 3-D rendering of patient E.E.'s left hemisphere.
E.E. had selective deficits in short-term memory. **(a)** The reconstructed scan taken before surgery; **(b)** the scan taken after surgery. The area of the tumor is indicated by shading. The physicians used positron emission tomography (PET) with a radiolabeled methionine tracer to identify the tumor according to its increased metabolic profile (red).

the dissociation is attributable to memory processes or to the different nature of the tasks.

Results from a similar patient come from the work of Hans Markowitsch and colleagues at Bielefeld University in Germany (1999). Their patient, E.E., had a tumor centered in the left angular gyrus. The tumor affected the inferior parietal cortex and posterior superior temporal cortex (**Figure 9.5**), regions similar to but slightly different from those affected in patient K.F.

After undergoing surgery to remove the tumor, E.E. showed below-normal short-term memory ability but preserved long-term memory—a pattern similar to K.F.'s. E.E. showed normal speech production, speech comprehension, and reading comprehension. He had poor short-term memory for abstract verbal material, however, as well as deficits in transposing numbers from numerical to verbal and vice versa, even though he could calculate normally. But on tests of his visuospatial short-term memory and both verbal and nonverbal long-term memory, E.E. performed normally.

The pattern of behavior displayed by these patients demonstrates a deficit of short-term memory abilities but a preservation of long-term memory. This pattern suggests that short-term memory is not the gateway to long-term memory in the manner laid out in the modal model. Perhaps information from sensory memory registers can be encoded directly into long-term memory. In contrast, patients like H.M. have preserved short-term memory but deficits in the ability to form new long-term memories. Together, these two different patterns of memory deficits present an apparent double dissociation for short- and long-term retention of information, specifically in relation to both the memory processes and the underlying neuroanatomy (i.e., left perisylvian cortex versus medial temporal lobes).

As described in Chapter 3, a double dissociation is the strongest pattern of effects that can be obtained in attempts to identify and distinguish two mental processes. Investigators disagree, however, on whether these interesting patient case studies demonstrate a true double dissociation. Some have argued that the evidence from these cases does not support a strong double dissociation of short- and long-term memory. Because the short-term memory tests are testing for the retention of overlearned materials such as digits and words, they may not be effective for learning about short-term memory. In fact, when novel materials are used to test short-term memory retention, patients with medial temporal lobe lesions sometimes fail.

WORKING MEMORY The concept of working memory was developed to extend the concept of short-term memory and to elaborate the kinds of mental processes that are involved when information is retained over a period of seconds to minutes. **Working memory** represents a limited-capacity store for retaining information over the short term (*maintenance*) and for performing mental operations on the contents of this store (*manipulation*). For example, we can remember (maintain) a list of numbers, and we can also add (manipulate) them in our head by using working memory.

The contents of working memory could originate from sensory inputs as in the modal model, such as when someone asks you to multiply 55 by 3, or they could be retrieved from long-term memory, such as when you visit the carpet store and recall the dimensions of your living room and multiply them to figure out its square footage. In each case, working memory contains information that can be acted on and processed, not merely maintained by rehearsal.

Psychologists Alan Baddeley and Graham Hitch at the University of York (1974) argued that the idea of a unitary short-term memory was insufficient to explain the maintenance and processing of information over short periods. They proposed a three-part working memory system consisting of a *central executive mechanism* that presides over and coordinates the interactions between two subordinate short-term memory stores (the phonological loop and the visuospatial "sketch pad") and long-term memory (**Figure 9.6**).

The *phonological loop* is a hypothesized mechanism for acoustically coding information in working memory;

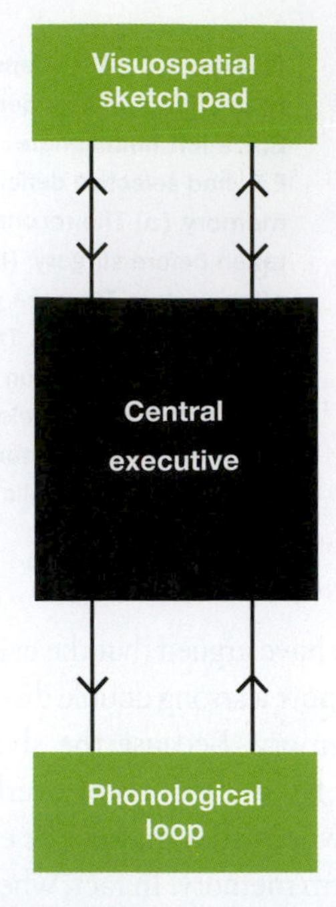

FIGURE 9.6 Simplified representation of the Baddeley and Hitch working memory model.
This three-part working memory system has a central executive system that controls two subordinate systems: the phonological loop, which encodes information phonologically (acoustically) in working memory; and the visuospatial sketch pad, which encodes information visually in working memory. The one-way arrows indicate that the phonological loop involves a rehearsal of information to keep it active. The visuospatial sketch pad has bidirectional arrows because information can be put into it, manipulated, and read out.

thus, it is modality specific. The evidence for modality specificity first came from studies that asked participants to recall strings of consonants. The letters were presented visually, but the pattern of recall errors indicated that perhaps the letters were not coded visually over the short term. The participants were apparently using an acoustic code, because during recall they were more likely to replace a presented letter with an erroneous letter having a similar sound (e.g., *T* for *G*) rather than one with a similar shape (e.g., *Q* for *G*). This was the first insight suggesting that an acoustic code might play a part in rehearsal.

In line with this idea is evidence that immediate recall of lists of words is poorer when many words on the list sound similar than when they sound dissimilar, even when the dissimilar words are semantically related. This finding indicates that an acoustic code rather than a semantic code is used in working memory, because words that sound similar interfere with one another, whereas words related by meaning do not. The phonological loop might have two parts: a short-lived acoustic store for sound inputs, and an articulatory component that plays a part in the subvocal rehearsal of visually presented items to be remembered over the short term.

The *visuospatial sketch pad* is a short-term memory store that parallels the phonological loop and permits information storage in either purely visual or visuospatial codes. Evidence for this system came from studies of participants who were instructed to remember a list of words using either a verbal strategy such as rote rehearsal or a visuospatial strategy based on an imagery mnemonic. Under control conditions in which word list memorization was the only task, participants performed better when they used the visuospatial strategy. The verbal strategy, however, proved better when the participants were also required to concurrently track a moving stimulus by operating a stylus during the retention interval. In contrast, people are impaired on verbal-memory tasks (but not nonverbal-memory tasks) when they are required to repeat nonsense syllables during the retention interval, presumably because the phonological loop is disrupted. A unitary memory system cannot explain dissociations like these.

Deficits in short-term memory abilities, such as remembering items on a digit span test, can be correlated with damage to subcomponents of the working memory system. Each system can be damaged selectively by different brain lesions. Patients with lesions of the left supramarginal gyrus (Brodmann area 40) have deficits in phonological working memory: They cannot hold strings of words in working memory. The rehearsal process of the phonological loop involves a region in the left premotor area (Brodmann area 44). Thus, a left-hemisphere network consisting of the lateral frontal and inferior parietal lobes is involved in phonological working memory (**Figure 9.7**). These deficits for auditory–verbal material (digits, letters, words) are not associated with deficits in speech perception or production.

Damage to the parieto-occipital region of either hemisphere compromises visuospatial short-term memory, but

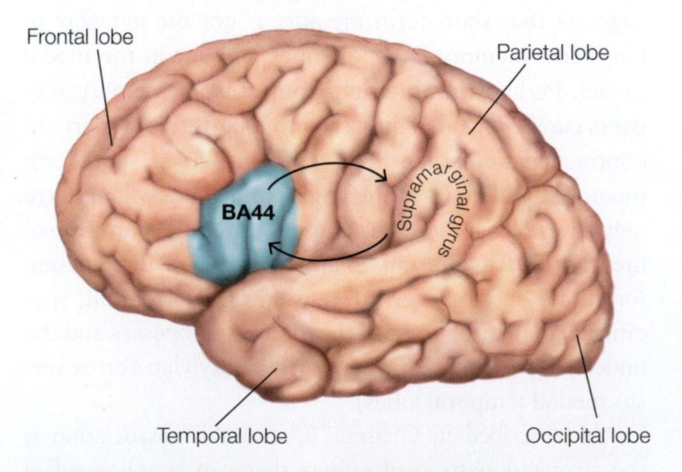

FIGURE 9.7 The phonological working memory loop.
Lateral view of the left hemisphere, indicating that there is an information loop involved in phonological working memory flowing between BA44 and the supramarginal gyrus (BA40).

damage to the right hemisphere produces more severe deficits. Patients with lesions in the right parieto-occipital region have difficulty with nonverbal visuospatial working memory tasks like retaining and repeating the sequence of blocks *touched* by another person. For example, if an investigator touches blocks on a table in sequences that the patient must repeat, and gradually increases the number of blocks touched, patients with parieto-occipital lesions show below-normal performance, even when their vision is otherwise normal. Similar lesions in the left hemisphere can lead to impairments in short-term memory for visually presented *linguistic* material.

Early neuroimaging studies have helped to support this distinction. Using PET imaging in healthy volunteers, Edward Smith and his colleagues at Columbia University (1996) provided evidence for dissociations in the brain regions activated during the performance of spatial versus verbal working memory tasks. Participants were presented with an array of either location markers or letters on a computer screen, and they were asked to remember the locations or the letters during a delay period of 3 seconds. Next the researchers presented either a location marker (spatial location task) or a letter (verbal-memory task) and asked participants whether the location or the letter had been in the original array. For the verbal working memory task, they found activation (increasing blood flow coupled to increased neural activity) in left-hemisphere sites in inferolateral frontal cortex, but for the spatial working memory task, activation was primarily in right-hemisphere regions (inferior frontal, posterior parietal, and extrastriate cortex in the occipital lobe; **Figure 9.8**).

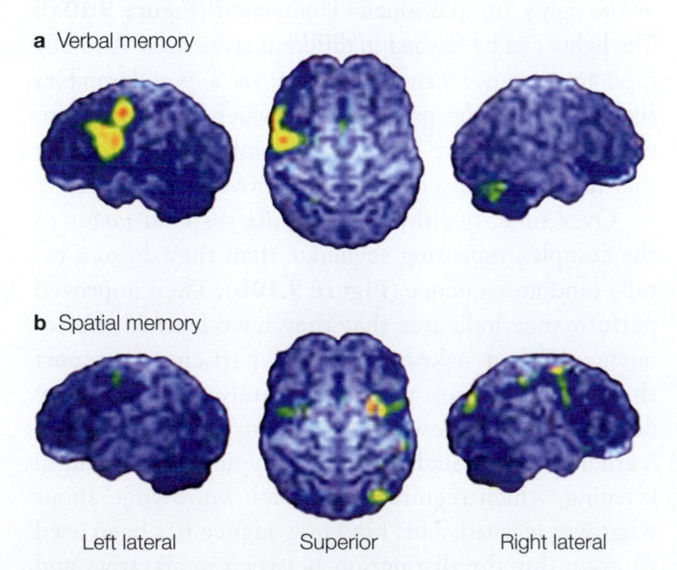

FIGURE 9.8 Changes in local cerebral blood flow on working memory tasks, measured with PET.
Verbal (a) and spatial (b) working memory tasks were tested in healthy volunteers. The verbal task corresponded primarily to activity in the left hemisphere, whereas the spatial task activated mainly the right hemisphere.

Several years later, Smith and colleagues compiled a meta-analysis of 60 PET and fMRI studies (Wager & Smith, 2003). Although their analysis confirmed that activation is found during working memory tasks with verbal stimuli in the left ventrolateral prefrontal cortex, the evidence for spatial working memory showed activation to be not just right-sided, but rather more bilateral in the brain. The left-hemisphere activity during spatial working memory may reflect, at least in some studies, a verbal recoding of the nonverbal stimuli. For example, when asked to remember the locations of a set of stimuli, we might think "upper left" and "lower right." We will discuss working memory further in Chapter 12.

Long-Term Forms of Memory

Information retained for a significant time (days, months, or years) is referred to as **long-term memory**. Theorists have tended to split long-term memory into two major divisions, taking into account the observable fact that people with amnesia may retain one type of long-term memory and not another. The key distinction is between declarative and nondeclarative memories.

DECLARATIVE MEMORY **Declarative memory** is defined as memory for events and for facts, both personal and general, to which we have conscious access, and which we can verbally report. This form of memory is sometimes referred to as *explicit memory*. Because H.M. was impaired in forming new declarative memories, we know that this capacity depends on the medial temporal lobe.

In the 1970s, Endel Tulving introduced the idea that declarative memory can be further broken down into episodic memory and semantic memory. **Episodic memory** comprises memories of events that the person has experienced that include what happened, where it happened, when, and with whom. Episodic memories differ from personal knowledge (**Figure 9.9**). For instance, you have personal knowledge of what day you were born, but you do not remember the experience. Episodic memories also differ from autobiographical memories, which can be a hodgepodge of episodic memory and personal knowledge. Episodic memories always include the self as the agent or recipient of some action. For example, the memory of falling off your new red bicycle (what) on Christmas day (when), badly skinning your elbow on the asphalt driveway (where), and your mother (who) running over to comfort you is an episodic memory.

Episodic memory is the result of rapid associative learning in that the *what*, *where*, *when*, and *who* of a single episode—its *context*—become associated and bound together and can be retrieved from memory as a single

FIGURE 9.9 Tulving and his cat.
According to Endel Tulving, animals like his cat have no episodic memory, although they have knowledge of many things. Tulving argues that they therefore do not remember their experiences the same way we do; they can merely know about such experiences.

personal recollection. More recently, however, evidence has been unearthed that not all memory of experiences is conscious. We will discuss this research in Section 9.5 when we examine relational memory.

Semantic memory, in contrast, is objective knowledge that is factual in nature but does not include the context in which it was learned. For instance, you may know that corn is grown in Iowa, but you most likely don't remember when or where you learned that fact. A fact can be learned after a single episode, or it may take many exposures. Semantic memory reflects knowing facts and concepts such as how to tell time, who the lead guitarist is for the Rolling Stones, and where Lima is located. This kind of world knowledge is fundamentally different from our recollection of events in our own lives.

During human development, episodic and semantic memory appear at different ages. Two-year-old toddlers have been able to demonstrate recall of things they witnessed at age 13 months (Bauer & Wewerka, 1995). Not until children are at least 18 months old, however, do they seem to include themselves as part of the memory, although this ability tends to be more reliably present in 3- to 4-year-olds (Perner & Ruffman, 1995; M. A. Wheeler et al., 1997).

When Tulving introduced the idea of episodic memory versus semantic memory decades ago, the dominant thinking was that there was a unitary memory system. But his formulation, along with results from lesion studies, suggested that different underlying brain systems might support these two different flavors of declarative long-term memory. We will return to this question later in the chapter.

NONDECLARATIVE MEMORY **Nondeclarative memory** is so named because it is not expressed verbally; it cannot be "declared" but is expressed through performance. It is also known as *implicit memory* because it is knowledge that we are not conscious of. Several types of memory fall under this category: priming, simple learned behaviors that derive from conditioning, habituation, sensitization, and procedural memory such as learning a motor or cognitive skill.

Nondeclarative memory is revealed when previous experiences facilitate performance on a task that does not require intentional recollection of the experiences. This type of memory was not impaired in H.M., because it does not depend on the medial temporal lobe. It involves other brain structures, including the basal ganglia, the cerebellum, the amygdala, and the neocortex.

Procedural memory. One form of nondeclarative memory is **procedural memory**, which is required for tasks that include learning motor skills—such as riding a bike, typing, and swimming—and cognitive skills, such as reading. It depends on extensive and repeated experience. The ability to form habits and to learn procedures and rote behaviors depends on procedural memory. Studies of amnesia have revealed some fundamental distinctions between long-term memory for events in your life (such as seeing your first bike under the Christmas tree) and for procedural skills (such as riding a bicycle).

One test of procedural learning is the *serial reaction-time task*. In one experimental setup, participants sit at a console and, placing the fingers of one hand over four buttons, press the button that corresponds to one of four lights as the lights are individually illuminated (**Figure 9.10a**). The lights can be flashed in different sequences: A totally random sequence can be flashed, or a pseudorandom sequence might be presented, in which the participant thinks the lights are flashing randomly, when in reality they are flashing in a complex, repetitive sequence.

Over time, healthy participants respond faster to the complex repeating sequence than they do to a totally random sequence (**Figure 9.10b**). Their improved performance indicates that they have learned the sequence. When asked, however, participants report that the sequences were completely random. They do not seem to know that a pattern existed, yet they learned the skill. Such behavior is typical of procedural learning, which requires no explicit knowledge about what was learned. This kind of evidence has been used to argue for the distinction between declarative and procedural knowledge, because participants appear to acquire one (procedural knowledge) in the absence of the other (declarative knowledge).

Some have challenged the idea that healthy participants learn without having any explicit knowledge of

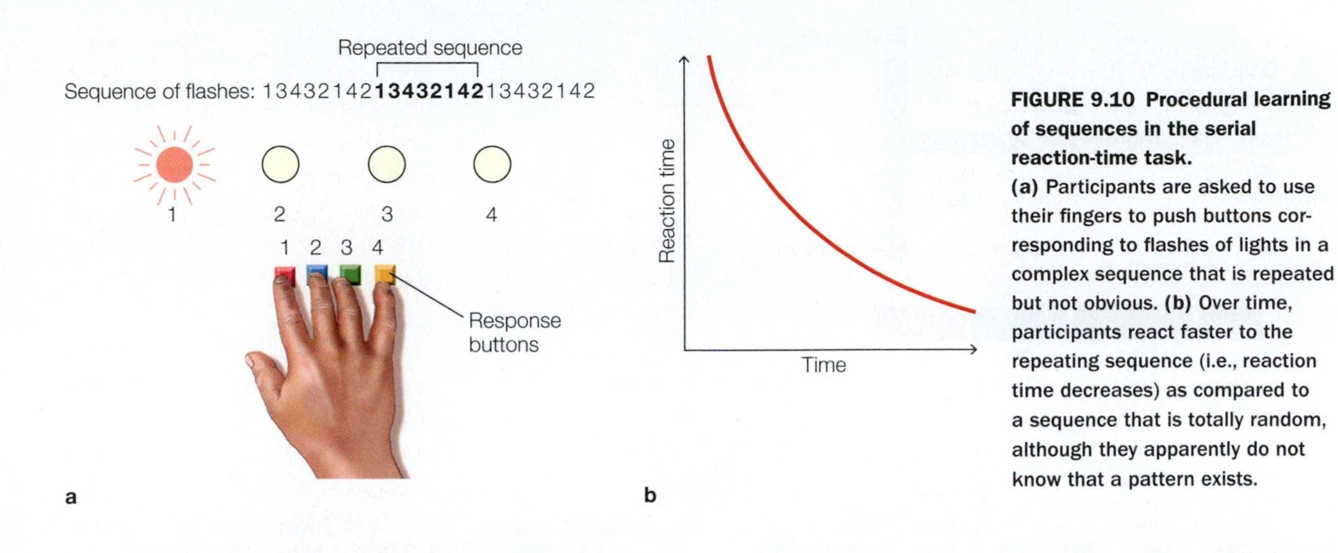

FIGURE 9.10 Procedural learning of sequences in the serial reaction-time task.
(a) Participants are asked to use their fingers to push buttons corresponding to flashes of lights in a complex sequence that is repeated but not obvious. **(b)** Over time, participants react faster to the repeating sequence (i.e., reaction time decreases) as compared to a sequence that is totally random, although they apparently do not know that a pattern exists.

what was learned. For example, sometimes investigators ask volunteers about the sequences and find that the participants can, in fact, explicitly describe the learned material. Perhaps the reason some participants deny any such knowledge is that they have less confidence in it. Given this possibility in healthy participants, if we do not find evidence for explicit knowledge during skill acquisition, how can we be sure it is not there? Perhaps the person merely failed to demonstrate it.

An answer comes from procedural learning studies in persons with anterograde amnesia, like H.M. These people cannot form new declarative (or at least episodic) memories. When tasks like the one in Figure 9.10a were presented to amnesic patients, those with dense anterograde amnesia (with loss of episodic learning) improved their performance for repeated sequences (compared to random ones) over a series of days; their improvement was shown as a decrease in reaction time (as in Figure 9.10b). Even though they stated that they had never performed the task before, these amnesic participants learned the procedure. Therefore, procedural learning can proceed independently of the brain systems required for episodic memory.

Which brain systems support procedural memory? Much evidence suggests that corticobasal ganglia loops are critical for such learning (e.g., Packard & Knowlton, 2002; Yin & Knowlton, 2006). For example, Terra Barnes and her colleagues reasoned that if this is correct, then, as habits and procedures are learned, changes in behavior should be accompanied by changes in activity of the basal ganglia neurons. Furthermore, this activity should also change if a habit is extinguished and then reacquired.

To test for such activity, the researchers recorded neurons from the sensorimotor striatum of rats undergoing acquisition, extinction, and reacquisition training on a conditional T-maze task, set up as shown in **Figure 9.11a** (Barnes et al., 2005). During the acquisition phase, rats learned two auditory cues. Each tone indicated that a reward was either on the left or on the right in a T-maze. Once the rats made the correct choice on 72.5% of the trials in a session, they graduated to the "overtraining" stage and continued to participate in training sessions.

After being overtrained, the rats entered into extinction sessions during which the reward was either withheld or placed randomly. Then, in reacquisition sessions, the original training setup was reinstated. The researchers found that spike distributions, response tuning, and task selectivity were dynamically reconfigured as the procedural behavior was acquired, extinguished, and reacquired. As **Figure 9.11b** shows, early in training (rows 1–5 at the top, the acquisition phase) all the task-responsive neurons remained active throughout the task time. Even the neurons that later did not respond during the task were active in the early acquisition trials (**Figure 9.11c**).

These observations suggested to the researchers that all task events were salient early in training, as a type of neuronal exploration was occurring. But as training progressed to the overtrained stage, firing at the start and end of the learned procedure strengthened in the task-responsive neurons, whereas activity in the task-unresponsive neurons fell silent—suggesting that sharply tuned responses of "expert neurons" appeared and responded near the start and end of the learned procedure. A reversal of this pattern was seen in the extinction stage, and it was once again instigated during reacquisition.

More evidence comes from patients with disorders of the basal ganglia or of inputs to these subcortical structures. They show poor performance on a variety of procedural learning tasks. As we learned in Chapter 8, these individuals include patients with Parkinson's disease, in which cell death in the substantia nigra disrupts dopaminergic projections into the basal ganglia, and patients

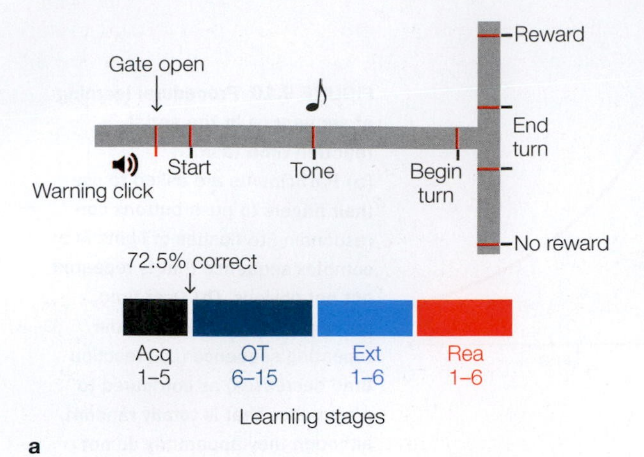

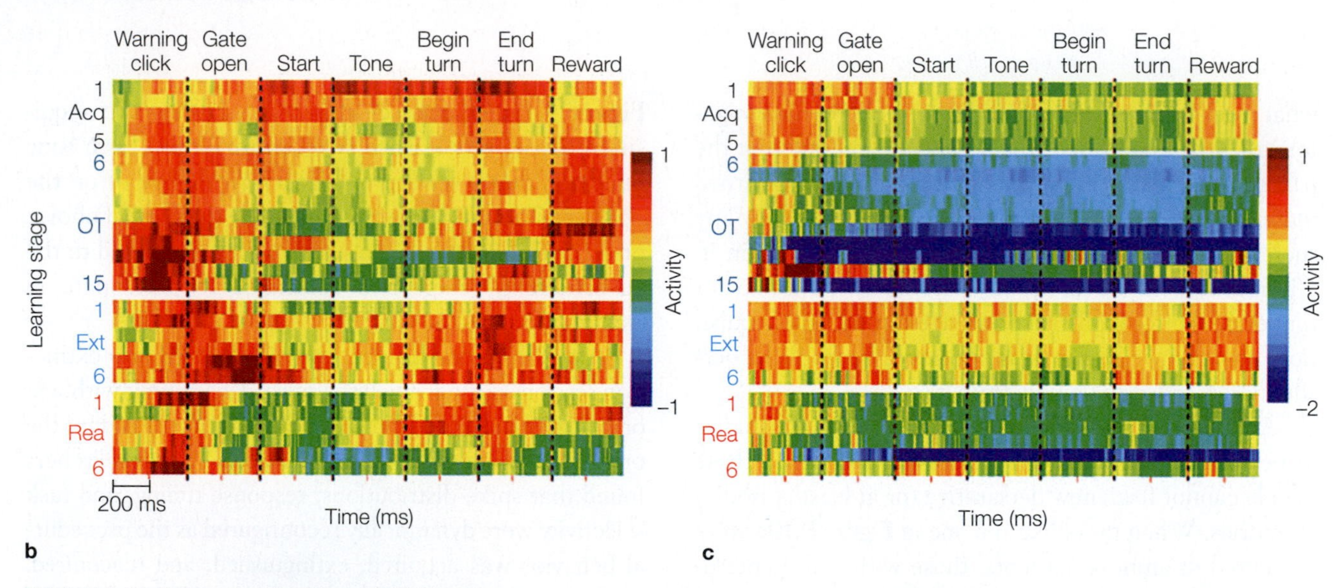

FIGURE 9.11 T-maze task and behavioral learning.
(a) Rats learned to navigate a T-maze for a reward and were given an auditory cue ("Tone") that indicated whether they were to learn to turn left or right for a piece of chocolate. The training stages were acquisition (Acq), overtraining (OT), extinction (Ext), and reacquisition (Rea); the acquisition stage ended when the rat made the correct run 72.5% of the time. Numbers indicate the number of sessions in each stage required for the different rats. **(b)** Average activity of task-responsive neurons, with red being the most active. Notice that with more training, peak activity becomes concentrated at the beginning and end of the task. **(c)** Average activity of task-unresponsive neurons. Notice that they become silent (dark blue) as training progresses.

with Huntington's disease, which is characterized by degeneration of neurons in the basal ganglia.

These patients, who are not amnesic per se, have impairments in acquisition and retention of motor skills as assessed by a variety of tests involving motor skill learning. For example, patients with Huntington's disease have difficulty with the prism adaptation task that we discussed in Section 8.8, in which wearing prism goggles shifts the visual world. Both controls and people with Alzheimer's disease initially make reaching errors but, with practice, reduce the error and adapt, whereas patients with Huntington's disease do not adapt as well. Their decreased ability to adapt suggests that motor behavior based on perceptual input depends on the basal ganglia (the neostriatum in particular), and not on the cortical and medial temporal lobe regions that are affected in Alzheimer's disease (Paulsen et al., 1993).

Priming. Another form of nondeclarative memory is priming. **Priming** refers to a change in the response to a stimulus, or in the ability to identify a stimulus, following prior exposure to that stimulus. For instance, if you were to see a picture of a bicycle's handlebars from an odd angle, you would more quickly recognize them as part of a bike if you had just seen a typical picture of a bike. If you had not, you might find them more difficult to identify. Priming can be perceptual, conceptual, or semantic.

Multiple studies support the theory that perceptual priming and declarative memory are mediated by different systems. Perceptual priming acts within the **perceptual representation system (PRS)** (Schacter, 1990). In the PRS, the structure and form of objects and words can be primed by prior experience; depending on the stimulus, the effects persist for a few hours to months.

For example, participants can be presented with lists of words, and their memory of the lists can be evaluated using a word-fragment completion task. In such a task, during the later test phase participants are shown only some letters from real words—for example, "t_ou_h_s" for *thoughts*. These fragments can be from either new words (not present in the original list) or old words (originally present). The participants are asked to simply complete the fragments. Participants are significantly better and faster at correctly completing fragments for words that were also presented in the initial list; they show priming. The important idea is that participants benefit from having seen the words before, even if they are not told and do not realize that the words were in the previous list.

This priming for fragment completion is specific for the sensory modality of the learning and test phases. To put this another way, if the word lists are presented auditorily and the word-fragment completion is done visually (or vice versa), then the priming is reduced, suggesting that priming reflects a PRS that subserves structural, visual, and auditory representations of word form. Finally, perceptual priming can also be seen with nonword stimuli such as pictures, shapes, and faces.

How long after exposure to a stimulus can it influence later performance? The answer appears to depend on the stimulus. In several early studies, word-priming effects disappeared within 2 hours (e.g., Graf et al., 1984), while others found effects lasting a few days to a week or a few weeks (Gabrieli et al., 1995; McAndrews et al., 1987; Squire et al., 1987). Much-longer-lasting priming effects, seen when pictures are the stimulus, have been reliably found at 48 weeks (Cave, 1997).

This type of priming is also found in amnesic patients like H.M., who showed evidence of priming even when he could not remember ever having seen the word list or ever having done a fragment completion task before. This behavior tells us that the PRS does not rely on the medial temporal lobe. Further evidence comes from a study using a picture-naming paradigm to test the effects of priming on 11 people with amnesia who had known or suspected hippocampal damage (Cave & Squire, 1992).

In this task, researchers measured how quickly participants named a previously seen picture (dog, toaster, etc.) compared to a newly seen one. They found that the participants with amnesia were faster at naming previously seen pictures than new ones, and that their scores were similar to those of controls. The priming effect, moreover, was still present after a week. Next, the participants' explicit memory was tested using a picture recognition task, where half the pictures they were presented had been shown in the previous session and half were new. The participants merely had to indicate whether they had seen the picture before. In this test the participants with amnesia were severely impaired, scoring well below controls—evidence for a dissociation between implicit and explicit memory. But this is merely a single dissociation. Is there any evidence that brain lesions can affect the PRS while leaving long-term memory intact?

There is. John Gabrieli and his colleagues at Stanford University (1995) tested a patient, M.S., who had a right occipital lobe lesion. M.S. had experienced intractable epileptic seizures as a child and at age 14 underwent surgery to treat them. The surgery removed most of Brodmann areas 17, 18, and 19 of his right occipital lobe, leaving him blind in the left visual field (**Figure 9.12a**).

Tests of explicit memory (recognition and cued recall) and implicit memory (perceptual priming) were administered to M.S., who had demonstrated above-average intelligence and memory, and his performance was compared to that of controls and that of patients who had anterograde amnesia for episodic memory (similar to H.M.). The different tests were done in separate sessions at least 2 weeks apart. Initially, the participants were briefly shown a list of words to read out loud (the perceptual identification test), indicating that they could perceive them.

For the implicit memory task, new words and those previously seen in the perception test were first shown very briefly (16.7 ms), followed by a mask. The participants had to identify the word. If they couldn't, the word was presented at increasing durations until they could identify it. If less time was required to identify the word after it had been seen previously, then there would be evidence for implicit perceptual priming. In the recognition test, which was done 2 weeks later, half the presented words were words that the participants had read in the perceptual identification test, and half were new. Here they were to reply "yes" or "no," depending on whether they had seen the word before.

As in the picture priming experiment, amnesic patients did not show impairment in the implicit perceptual priming test but displayed the expected impairments in explicit word recognition. In contrast, M.S. showed the opposite pattern: impairment in the implicit perceptual priming test (**Figure 9.12b**) but normal performance on

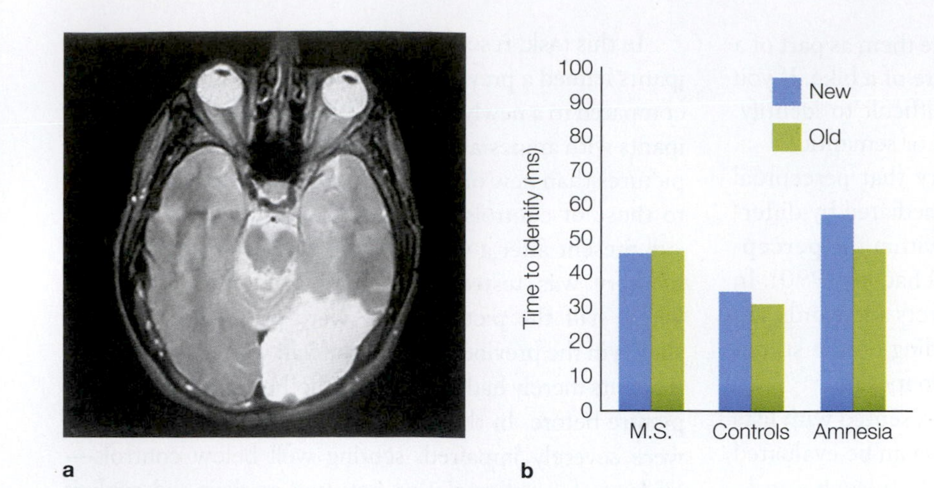

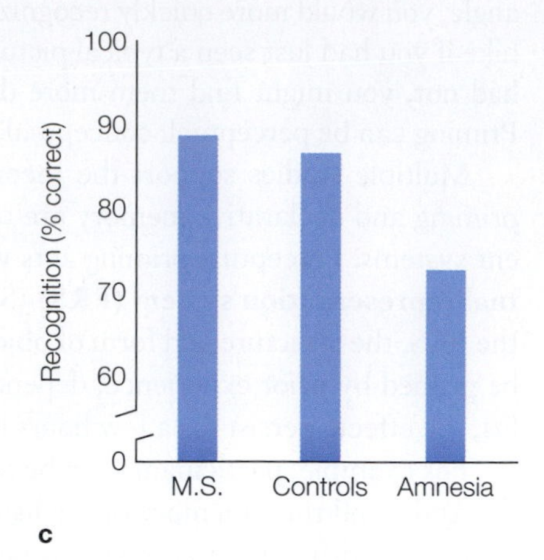

FIGURE 9.12 Double dissociation of declarative and nondeclarative memory in patient M.S. (a) Axial MRI showing the region that was resected from M.S.'s right occipital area. (b) The average time it took to identify words in the implicit memory test. "Old" words were previously presented words. M.S. showed no priming effect, whereas both controls and participants with amnesia showed a timing difference between the new and old words. (c) Accuracy of the recognition test of explicit memory. M.S. had no problem recognizing words in this test of explicit memory, in contrast to patients with anterograde amnesia.

explicit recognition (**Figure 9.12c**). These data show that perceptual priming can be damaged even when explicit memory is not impaired, thereby completing a double dissociation for declarative and nondeclarative memory systems. The anatomical data indicate that perceptual priming depends on the perceptual system, because M.S. had lesions to the visual cortex leading to deficits in perceptual priming.

Priming also occurs for *conceptual features* (as opposed to perceptual features), though it doesn't last nearly as long. Here, participants are quicker at answering general-knowledge questions when the concept was presented earlier. For example, if we had been talking about pasta and its different shapes, and then you were asked to name an Italian food, most likely you would say pasta, rather than pizza or veal parmigiana.

Conceptual priming differs from declarative memory in that it is nonconscious and is not affected by lesions to the medial temporal lobe, but rather by lesions to the lateral temporal and prefrontal regions. These regions were initially suspected when some patients with late-stage Alzheimer's disease had unimpaired perceptual priming but did show impairments in conceptual priming. Early in the progression of Alzheimer's, the pathology is most pronounced in medial temporal lobe structures. As the disease progresses, however, conceptual priming may be lost as the pathology extends beyond medial temporal structures to lateral temporal, parietal, and frontal neocortices (reviewed in Fleischman & Gabrieli, 1998). Functional MRI studies have provided further evidence that the anterior portion of the left inferior frontal gyrus is involved with conceptual priming (e.g., A. D. Wagner et al., 2000).

Another proposed form of priming is *semantic priming*, in which the prime and target are different words from the same semantic category. For instance, the prime may be the word *dog*, but the target word is *bone*. The typical effect of semantic priming is a shorter reaction time or increased accuracy in identifying the target or categorizing it. Semantic priming is brief, lasting only a few seconds, and the theory of how it works is based on the assumption that semantic memory is organized in associative networks. However, a meta-analysis of 26 studies (Lucas, 2000) found strong evidence of a semantic priming effect but no evidence of priming based purely on association. It is controversial whether semantic priming and conceptual priming are fundamentally different. For instance, the prime word *dog* could have the target word *wolf*, which would share conceptual properties.

Is the way the brain codes relationships between words that share conceptual properties (e.g., *dog* and *wolf*) different from the way it represents associative links between dissimilar words that co-occur in particular contexts (e.g., *dog* and *bone*)? Rebecca Jackson and her colleagues (2015) investigated both types of semantic relationships in an fMRI study and found that the same core semantic network (anterior temporal lobe, superior temporal sulcus, ventral prefrontal cortex) was equivalently engaged.

Classical conditioning and nonassociative learning. Two other domains of nondeclarative memory are *classical conditioning* (a type of associative learning) and *nonassociative learning*. In **classical conditioning**, sometimes

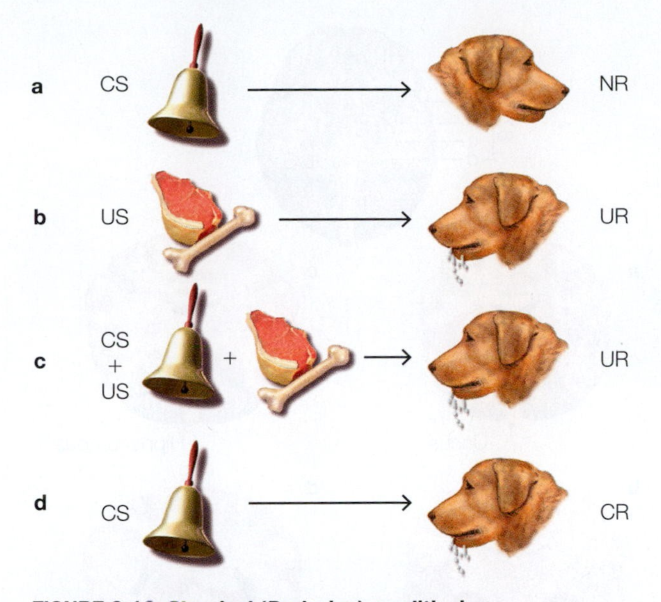

FIGURE 9.13 Classical (Pavlovian) conditioning.
(a) When a stimulus is presented that has no meaning to an animal, such as the sound of a bell (CS), there is no response (NR). **(b)** In contrast, presentation of a meaningful stimulus like food (US) generates an unconditioned response (UR). **(c)** When the sound is paired with the food, the animal learns the association. **(d)** Later, the newly conditioned stimulus (CS) alone can elicit the response, which is now called a conditioned response (CR).

referred to as *Pavlovian conditioning*, a conditioned stimulus (CS, an otherwise neutral stimulus to the organism) is paired with an unconditioned stimulus (US, one that elicits an established response from the organism) and becomes associated with it. The conditioned stimulus will then evoke a conditioned response (CR) similar to that typically evoked by the unconditioned stimulus (the unconditioned response, UR).

The Russian physiologist Ivan Pavlov received a Nobel Prize after first demonstrating this type of learning with his dogs, which he conditioned to start salivating at the sound of a bell that he rang before giving them food (**Figure 9.13**). Before conditioning, the bell was not associated with food and did not cause salivation. After conditioning, in which the bell and the food were paired, the bell (CS) caused salivation even in the absence of the food (US). We will discuss conditioning further in Chapters 10 and 12.

Classical conditioning comes in two flavors: delay conditioning and trace conditioning. In *delay conditioning*, the US begins while the CS is still present, but in *trace conditioning* there is a time gap, and thus a memory trace is necessary for an association to be made between the CS and the US. Studies with healthy participants and those with amnesia resulting from hippocampal damage have found that damage to the hippocampus does not impair delay conditioning but does impair trace conditioning (R. E. Clark & Squire, 1998). Thus, some types of associative learning depend on the hippocampus, and others do not.

Nonassociative learning, as its name implies, does not involve the association of two stimuli to elicit a behavioral change. Rather, it consists of forms of simple learning such as *habituation*, where the response to an unchanging stimulus decreases over time. For instance, the first time you use an electric toothbrush, your entire mouth tingles, but after a few uses you no longer feel a response.

Another type of nonassociative learning is *sensitization*, in which a response increases with repeated presentations of the stimulus. The classic example is rubbing your arm. At first it merely creates a feeling of warmth. If you continue, however, it starts to hurt. This is an adaptive response that warns you to stop the rubbing because it may cause injury. Nonassociative learning involves primarily sensory and sensorimotor (reflex) pathways. We do not consider classical conditioning, nonassociative learning, or nonassociative memory further in this chapter. Instead, we focus on the neural substrates of declarative memory (episodic and semantic memory) and nondeclarative memory (procedural memory and the perceptual representation system).

TAKE-HOME MESSAGES

- Memory classified by duration includes sensory memory, lasting only seconds at most; short-term memory, lasting from seconds to minutes; and long-term memory, lasting from days to years.
- Working memory extends the concept of short-term memory: It contains information that can be acted on and processed, not merely maintained by rehearsal.
- Long-term memory is split into two divisions defined by content: declarative and nondeclarative. Declarative memory is knowledge that we can consciously access, including personal and world knowledge. Nondeclarative memory is knowledge that we cannot consciously access, such as motor and cognitive skills, and other behaviors derived from conditioning, habituation, or sensitization.
- Declarative memory can be further broken down into episodic and semantic memory. Episodic memory involves conscious awareness of past events that we have experienced and the context in which those events occurred. Semantic memory is the world knowledge that we remember even without recollecting the specific circumstances surrounding its learning.
- Procedural memory is a form of nondeclarative memory that involves the learning of various motor and cognitive skills. Other forms of nondeclarative memory include perceptual priming, conditioned responses, and nonassociative learning.

9.4 The Medial Temporal Lobe Memory System

The formation of new declarative memories (both episodic and semantic) depends on the medial temporal lobe. Let's explore how this region, which includes the amygdala, the hippocampus, and the surrounding parahippocampal, entorhinal, and perirhinal cortical areas, is involved in long-term memory. We begin with evidence from patients with memory deficits and then look at lesion studies in animals.

Evidence From Amnesia

As we have learned, memory mechanisms can be divided into encoding (acquisition and consolidation), storage, and retrieval. Let's look first at the functions that are lost in amnesic patients like H.M. and ask, Which neural mechanisms and brain structures enable us to acquire new long-term memories?

H.M.'s original surgical reports indicated that his hippocampi were completely removed bilaterally (**Figure 9.14**). Decades later, Suzanne Corkin of the Massachusetts Institute of Technology and journalist-author Philip Hilts (1995) discovered through some detective work that the clips used in H.M.'s surgery were not ferromagnetic—which meant he could have an MRI. So in 1997, more than 40 years after his surgery, H.M.'s surgical lesion was investigated with modern neuroimaging techniques (**Figure 9.15**).

Data gathered by Corkin and her colleagues were analyzed by neuroanatomist David Amaral of UC Davis (Corkin et al., 1997). This analysis revealed that H.M.'s lesion was smaller than originally reported (**Figure 9.16**). Contrary to Scoville's reports, approximately half of the posterior region of H.M.'s hippocampus was intact, and only 5 cm (not 8 cm) of the medial temporal lobe had been removed. Thus, the posterior parahippocampal gyrus was mostly spared, but the anterior portion, the perirhinal and entorhinal cortices, was removed. The remaining portions of H.M.'s hippocampi, however, were atrophied, probably as a result of the loss of inputs from the surrounding perihippocampal cortex that had been removed in the 1953 surgery. Thus, despite the original error in our knowledge about H.M.'s lesion, it's possible that no functional hippocampal tissue remained. Consequently, H.M.'s lesions could not help us determine the role of the hippocampus versus parahippocampal cortex in memory.

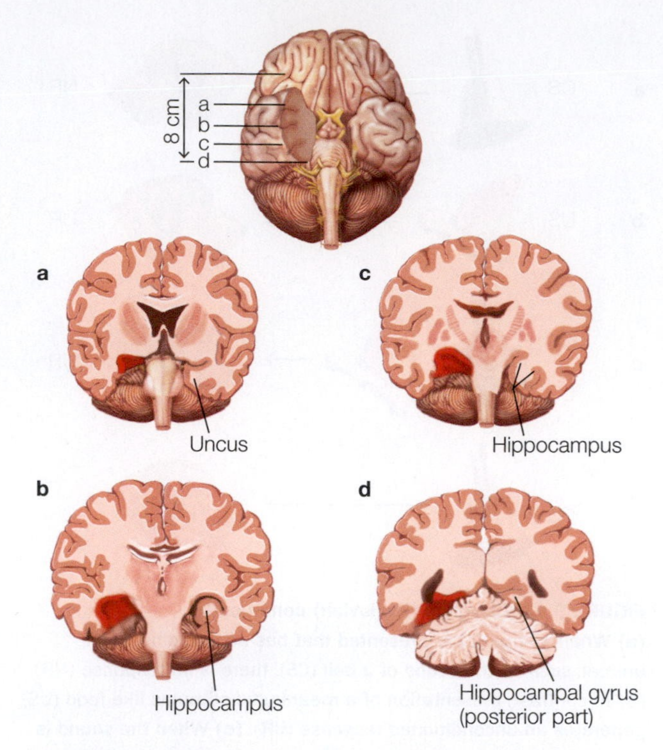

FIGURE 9.14 Region of the medial temporal lobe believed to have been removed from H.M.
As reported by his surgeon, the areas of H.M.'s brain that were removed are shown in red. (The resection is shown here only on the left side to enable comparison with an intact brain, shown on the right side at the same level. H.M.'s actual lesion was bilateral.) At the top is a ventral view of the brain, showing both hemispheres. The four anterior-to-posterior levels (a–d) shown in this ventral view correspond to the four coronal sections in parts **(a)** through **(d)**.

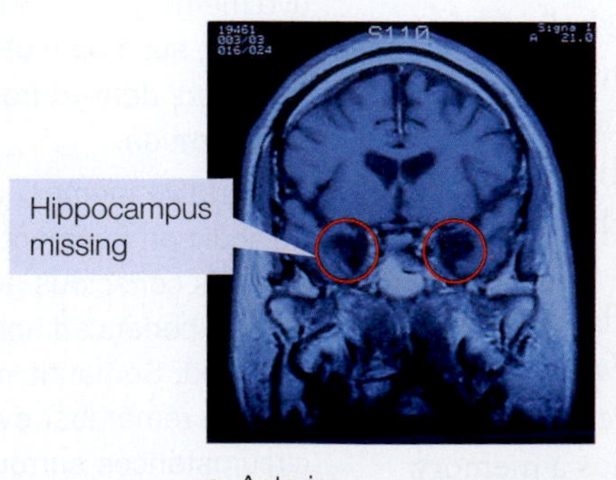

a Anterior

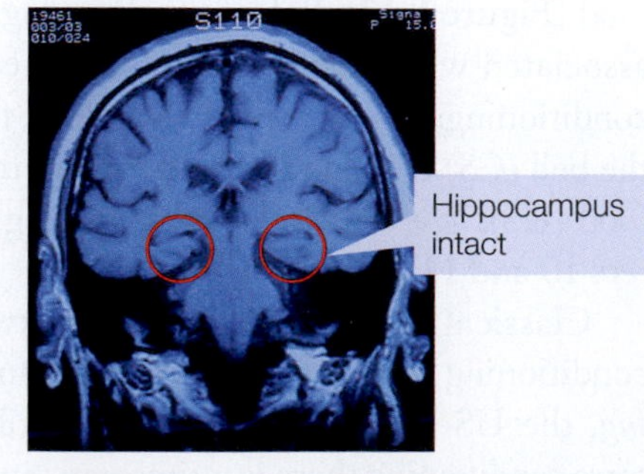

b Posterior

FIGURE 9.15 Coronal MRI scans of H.M.'s brain.
(a) The red circles in this anterior slice indicate where the hippocampus was removed bilaterally. **(b)** This more posterior slice, however, shows that the hippocampus (circled in red) was still intact in both hemispheres! This finding stood in marked contrast to the belief that H.M. had no hippocampus—a view, based on the surgeon's report, that the scientific community had held for 40 years.

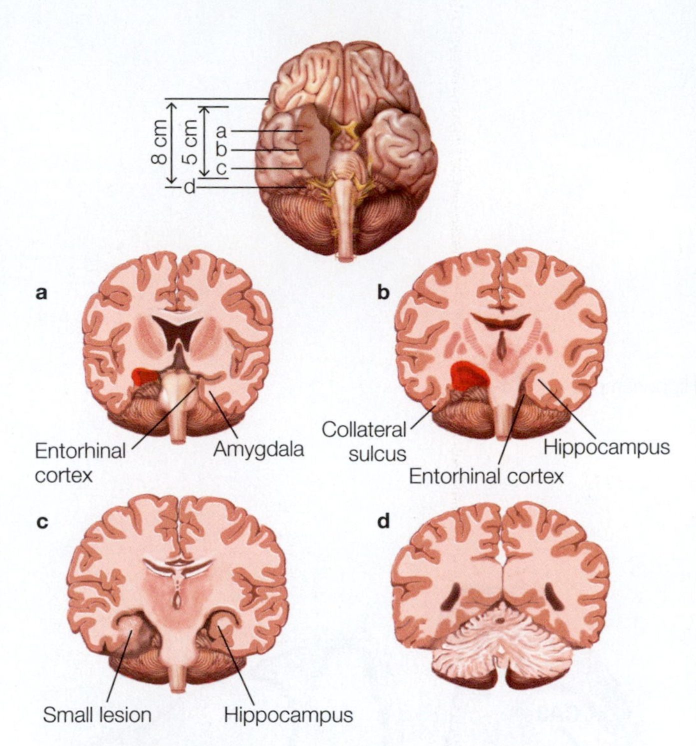

FIGURE 9.16 Region of the medial temporal lobe actually removed from H.M.
Modern reconstruction by David Amaral and colleagues, showing that portions of H.M.'s posterior hippocampus were not removed during surgery. This tissue, however, showed signs of atrophy and might no longer have been functioning normally. Red areas indicate where portions were removed. Compare with Figure 9.14.

Another remarkable patient story revolves around R.B., who in 1978 lost his memory after an ischemic episode (reduction of blood to the brain) during heart bypass surgery. Changes in R.B.'s memory performance were studied in detail by Stuart Zola-Morgan and his colleagues (1986). R.B. developed dense anterograde amnesia similar to H.M.'s: He could not form new long-term memories. He also had a mild temporal retrograde amnesia that went back about one or two years, so R.B.'s amnesia was slightly less severe than H.M.'s retrograde loss. After R.B.'s death, an autopsy revealed that his lesions were restricted to a particular region of the hippocampus only. Although gross examination suggested that the hippocampus was intact (**Figure 9.17a**), histological analysis revealed that, within each hippocampus, he had sustained a specific lesion restricted to the CA1 pyramidal cells. Compare R.B.'s hippocampus (**Figure 9.17c**) with that of a nonamnesic person after death (**Figure 9.17b**).

These findings of specific hippocampal damage in patient R.B. support the idea that the hippocampus is crucial for the formation of new long-term memories. R.B.'s case also supports the distinction between areas that store long-term memories and the role of the hippocampus in forming new memories. Even though retrograde amnesia is associated with damage to the medial temporal lobe, it is temporally limited and does not affect long-term memories of events that happened more than a few years before the amnesia-inducing event. Subsequently, several patients with similar lesions were also identified and studied, and they have shown highly similar patterns of memory loss. Memory must be stored elsewhere.

Further evidence that the hippocampus is involved in long-term memory acquisition comes from patients with **transient global amnesia (TGA)**. This syndrome has a number of causes, but it is triggered most commonly by physical exertion in men over 50 and by emotional stress in women over 50. In this situation, the typical blood flow is disrupted in the brain. In particular, the vertebrobasilar artery system, which supplies blood to the medial temporal lobe and the diencephalon, has been implicated as a critical site. The result is a transient ischemia that later returns to normal.

High-resolution imaging data now suggest that the lesions caused by such an event are located within the CA1 subfield of the hippocampus and that these neurons are selectively vulnerable to metabolic stress (see Bartsch & Deuschl, 2010). This disruption of blood flow results in a sudden transient anterograde amnesia, and retrograde amnesia spanning weeks, months, and sometimes even years. In a typical scenario, a person may wind up in the hospital but not be sure about where he is, or why, or how he got there. He knows his name, birth date, job, and perhaps address, but if he has moved recently, then he will supply his past address and circumstances.

He performs within the standard range on most neuropsychological tests, except for those requiring memory. He has normal short-term memory and thus can repeat lists of words told to him; when asked to remember a list of words, however, he forgets it within a couple of minutes if he is prevented from rehearsing it. He continually asks who the physician is and why she is there. He does show awareness that he *should* know the answer to some questions. He manifests a loss of time sense, and so he responds incorrectly to questions asking how long he has been in the hospital. During the hours following the amnesia-inducing event, distant memories return, and his anterograde memory deficit is resolved. Within 24 to 48 hours, he is essentially back to normal, although mild deficits may persist for days or weeks.

As you may have noticed, patients with transient global amnesia have symptoms similar to those of people with permanent damage to the medial temporal lobe, such as H.M. So far, we do not know whether TGA patients have normal implicit learning or memory, in part because their impairment does not last long enough for researchers to adequately index things like procedural learning.

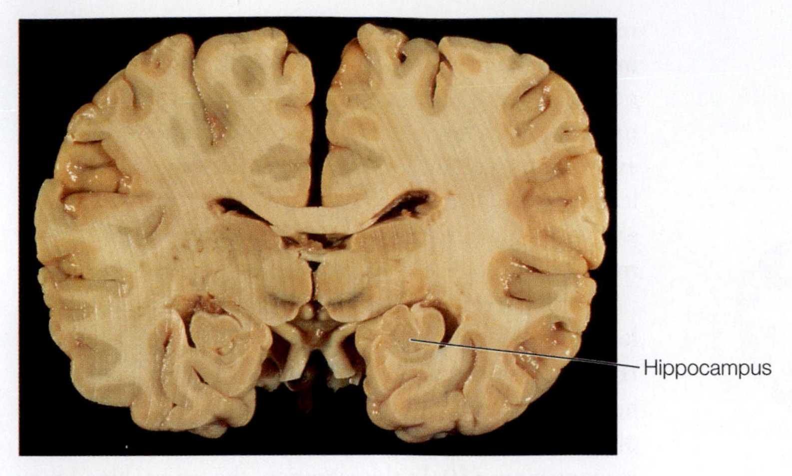

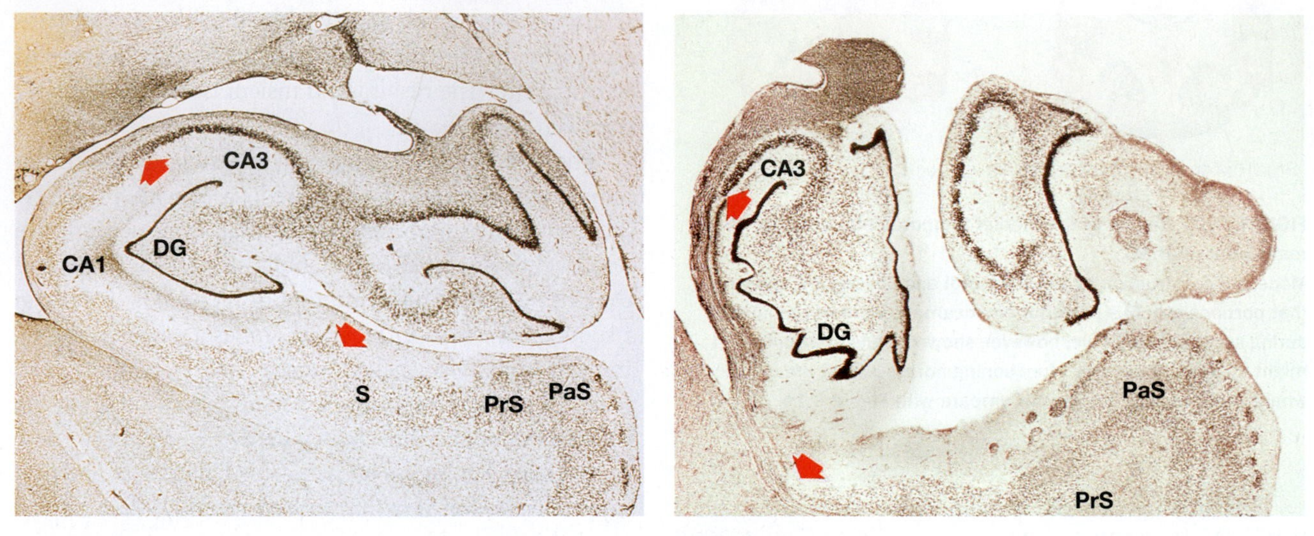

FIGURE 9.17 Comparison of R.B.'s brain with that of a nonamnesic participant.
(a) This section is from R.B.'s brain following his death. In contrast to what the MRI sections from H.M. in Figure 9.16 show—that is, an absence of the anterior and middle portions of the hippocampus—R.B.'s medial temporal lobe appeared intact on gross examination. **(b)** This histological section, obtained at autopsy from the brain of a person who hadn't had amnesia, shows an intact CA1 region (labeled "CA1" and delimited as the region between the arrows). **(c)** Careful histological examination of R.B.'s temporal lobe revealed that cells in the CA1 region of the hippocampus were absent (see the region between the arrows). The absence of cells was the result of an ischemic episode following surgery. Cells of the CA1 region are particularly sensitive to transient ischemia (temporary loss of blood supply to a brain region). DG = dentate gyrus; PaS = parasubiculum; PrS = presubiculum; S = subiculum.

The answer to this question would improve our understanding of human memory and of a form of amnesia that any of us could experience later in life.

Further evidence of hippocampal involvement in long-term memory formation comes from patients with Alzheimer's disease (AD), in whom the hippocampus deteriorates more rapidly than in people undergoing the normal aging process. The amyloid plaques characteristic of AD congregate in this medial temporal area (**Figure 9.18**). MRI measurements of brain volumes have shown that the size of the hippocampus changes with the progression of AD, and that patients who had thicker hippocampi before they developed AD will later display dementia to a lesser extent than the average AD patient displays (Jack et al., 2002; Jobst et al., 1994). Morris Moscovitch and colleagues at the Rotman Research Institute and the University of Toronto have demonstrated that the extent of atrophy in the medial temporal lobe in AD patients is most closely related to their deficits in episodic memory (Gilboa et al., 2005).

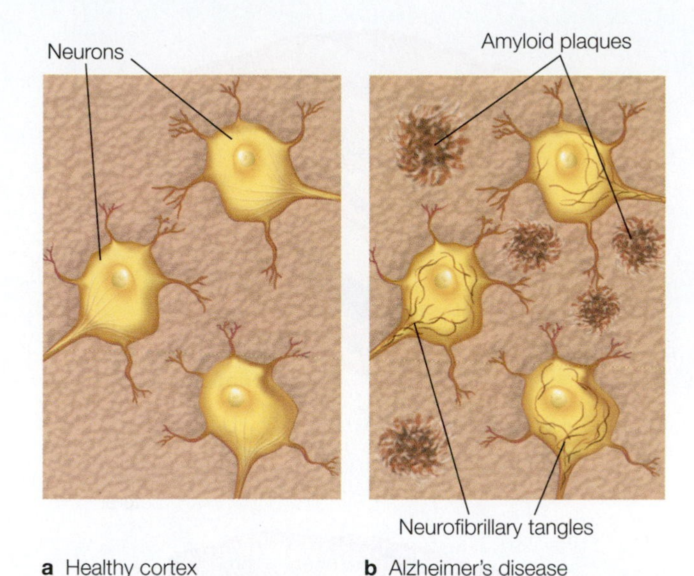

FIGURE 9.18 Comparison of cortex in Alzheimer's patients and healthy participants.
(a) A healthy section of cortex with cortical neurons. (b) A section of cortex in an Alzheimer's patient containing amyloid plaques between neurons and neurofibrillary tangles within neurons.

Lesions that damage the lateral cortex of the anterior temporal lobe but do not extend to the hippocampus, such as those associated with some forms of frontotemporal lobar degeneration and herpes simplex encephalitis, can lead to severe retrograde amnesia for semantic memory but not episodic memory. This memory loss may extend back many decades or may even encompass the patient's entire life. In severe cases, perirhinal atrophy is also observed (Davies et al., 2004).

Some patients with anterior temporal lobe damage and the consequent dense retrograde amnesia, however, can still form new long-term episodic memories. This condition is known as isolated retrograde amnesia. For instance, patients with semantic dementia have progressive loss of previously established semantic knowledge (non-context-specific fact, word, and object knowledge), yet their episodic memory is intact and they are still able to learn new episodic information (Hodges et al., 1992).

If these portions of the temporal lobe are not essential for acquiring new episodic information, then what role do they play? One possibility is that they are sites where long-term semantic memories are stored. Another view is that these regions may be important for the retrieval of information from long-term stores.

Evidence From Animals With Medial Temporal Lobe Lesions

Studies in animals ranging from invertebrates to nonhuman primates with lesions to the hippocampus and surrounding cortex have been invaluable to improving our understanding about the contributions of the medial temporal lobe to memory. A comprehensive review of this field is beyond the scope of this textbook, but a few of the most important findings are essential for understanding memory mechanisms.

A key question has been how much the hippocampus alone, as compared with surrounding structures in the medial temporal lobe, participates in the episodic memory deficits of patients like H.M. For example, does the amygdala influence memory deficits in people with amnesia? Data from amnesic patients indicate that the amygdala is not part of the brain's episodic memory system, although—as we will learn in Chapter 10—it has a role in emotion and emotional memories. Another question is, what kind of memory and learning is impaired with various temporal lobe lesions?

NONHUMAN PRIMATE STUDIES To test whether the amygdala is essential in memory formation, surgical lesions were created in the medial temporal lobe and amygdala of monkeys. In classic work on monkeys conducted by Mortimer Mishkin at the National Institute of Mental Health (1978), either the hippocampus, the amygdala, or both were removed surgically. Mishkin found that the resulting amount of impairment varied according to what had been lesioned.

The brain-lesioned monkeys were tested with a popular behavioral task that Mishkin developed, known as the *delayed nonmatch-to-sample task*: A monkey is placed in a box with a retractable door in the front. While the door is closed so that the monkey cannot see out, a food reward is placed under an object (**Figure 9.19a**). The door is opened, and the monkey is allowed to pick up the object to get the food (**Figure 9.19b**). The door is then closed again, and the same object plus a new object are put in position (**Figure 9.19c**). The new object now covers the food reward, and after a delay that can be varied, the door is reopened and the monkey must pick up the new object to get the food reward. If the monkey picks up the old object, there is no reward (**Figure 9.19d**). With training, the monkey picks the new, or nonmatching, object; hence, learning and memory are measured by observing the monkey's performance.

In his early work, Mishkin found that the monkey's memory was impaired only if the lesion included both the hippocampus and the amygdala. This finding led to the (incorrect) idea that the amygdala is a key structure in memory. That idea, however, does not fit well with data from amnesic people like R.B., who had anterograde amnesia caused by a lesion restricted to CA1 neurons of the hippocampus and no damage to the amygdala.

Stuart Zola-Morgan and colleagues (1993) investigated this dilemma. They distinguished the amygdala,

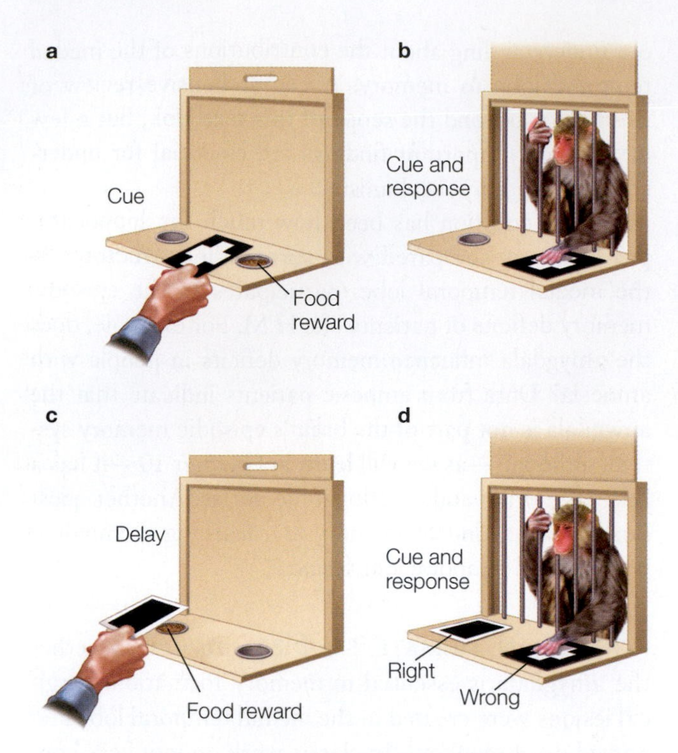

FIGURE 9.19 Delayed nonmatch-to-sample task.
(a) The correct response has a food reward located under it. (b) The monkey is shown the correct response, which will yield a reward for the monkey. (c) The door is closed, and the reward is placed under a second response option. (d) The monkey is then shown two options and must pick the correct response (the one that does *not* match the original sample item) to get the reward. Here the monkey is pictured making an error.

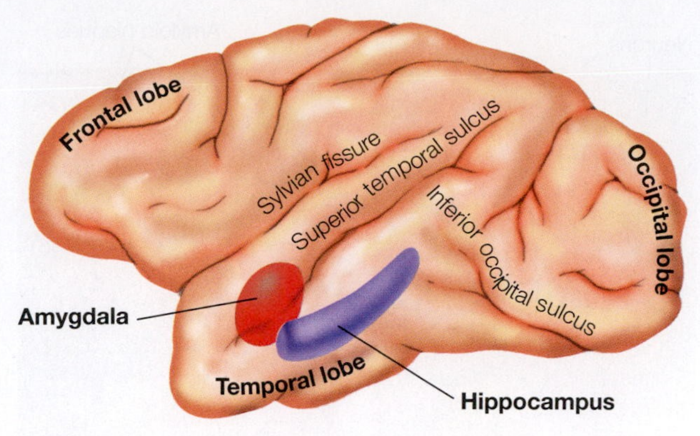

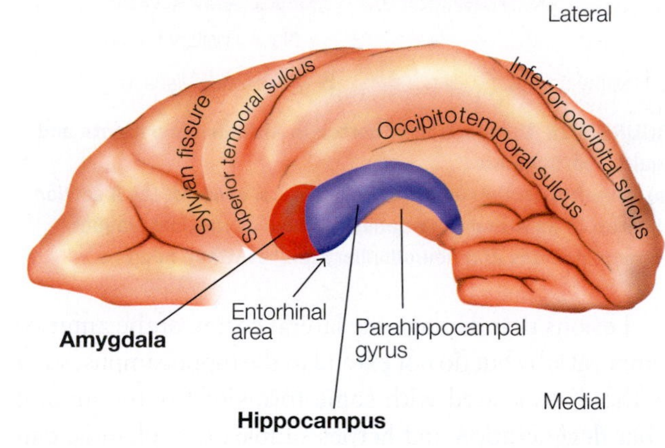

FIGURE 9.20 Gross anatomy of the monkey's medial temporal lobe.
(a) This lateral, see-through view of the left hemisphere shows the amygdala (red) and hippocampus (blue) within the temporal lobe. (b) This view from the ventral surface of the same hemisphere shows the amygdala and hippocampus, and indicates the locations of the parahippocampal gyrus and the entorhinal area (consisting of Brodmann areas 28 and typically also 34, which are located in the most anterior portion of the parahippocampal gyrus).

the hippocampus, and the surrounding cortex near each structure in the monkeys' brains (Brodmann areas 28 and 34; **Figure 9.20**), and they made more surgically selective lesions of the amygdala, the entorhinal cortex, or the surrounding neocortex of the parahippocampal gyrus and the perirhinal cortex (Brodmann areas 35 and 36). They wanted to extend Mishkin's work, which always had involved lesions of the neocortex surrounding the amygdala or hippocampus because of the way the surgery was performed.

The results indicated that lesions of the hippocampus and amygdala produced the most severe memory deficits only when the cortex surrounding these regions was also lesioned. When lesions of the hippocampus and amygdala were made but the surrounding cortex was spared, the presence or absence of the amygdala lesion did not affect the monkey's memory. The amygdala, then, could not be part of the system that supported the acquisition of long-term memory.

In subsequent investigations, Zola-Morgan and his colleagues selectively created lesions of the surrounding cortex in the perirhinal, entorhinal, and parahippocampal regions. These selective lesions worsened memory performance in delayed nonmatch-to-sample tests (**Figure 9.21**). Follow-up work showed that lesions of only the parahippocampal and perirhinal cortices also produced significant memory deficits.

How do we reconcile these results with R.B.'s profound anterograde amnesia, caused by damage limited to the hippocampus and not involving the surrounding parahippocampal or perirhinal cortex? The answer is that the hippocampus cannot function properly if these vital connections are damaged. But more than this, we now know that these regions are involved in a great deal of processing themselves, and hence lesions restricted to the hippocampus do not produce as severe a form of amnesia as do lesions that include surrounding cortex.

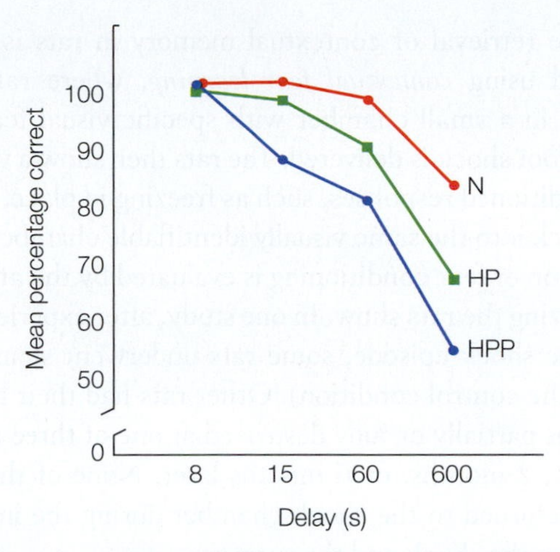

FIGURE 9.21 Selective lesions around the hippocampus worsen memory.
Performance across time intervals on the delayed nonmatch-to-sample task (see Figure 9.19) for normal monkeys (N); monkeys with lesions of the hippocampal formation and the parahippocampal cortex (HP); and monkeys with lesions of the hippocampal formation, parahippocampal cortex, and perirhinal cortex (HPP).

RODENT STUDIES Another key question that animal researchers have addressed involves the kind of memory and learning that is impaired with lesions to the hippocampus. Rodents have a hippocampal memory system that closely corresponds to that of primates (**Figure 9.22**), and early studies in rats found that while hippocampal lesions did not disrupt stimulus–response learning, the lesioned rats did exhibit a bewildering variety of abnormal behaviors. These observations led to the suggestion that the hippocampus was involved with the storage and retrieval of one specific type of memory: contextual memory (Hirsh, 1974).

For instance, when electrodes were implanted in the rat hippocampus, certain cells, later dubbed *place cells*, fired only when the rat was situated in a particular location and facing a particular direction (O'Keefe & Dostrovsky, 1971). A particular place cell might have become silent when the animal moved to a different environment but then assumed a location-specific firing in that new area. As the animal moved about the environment,

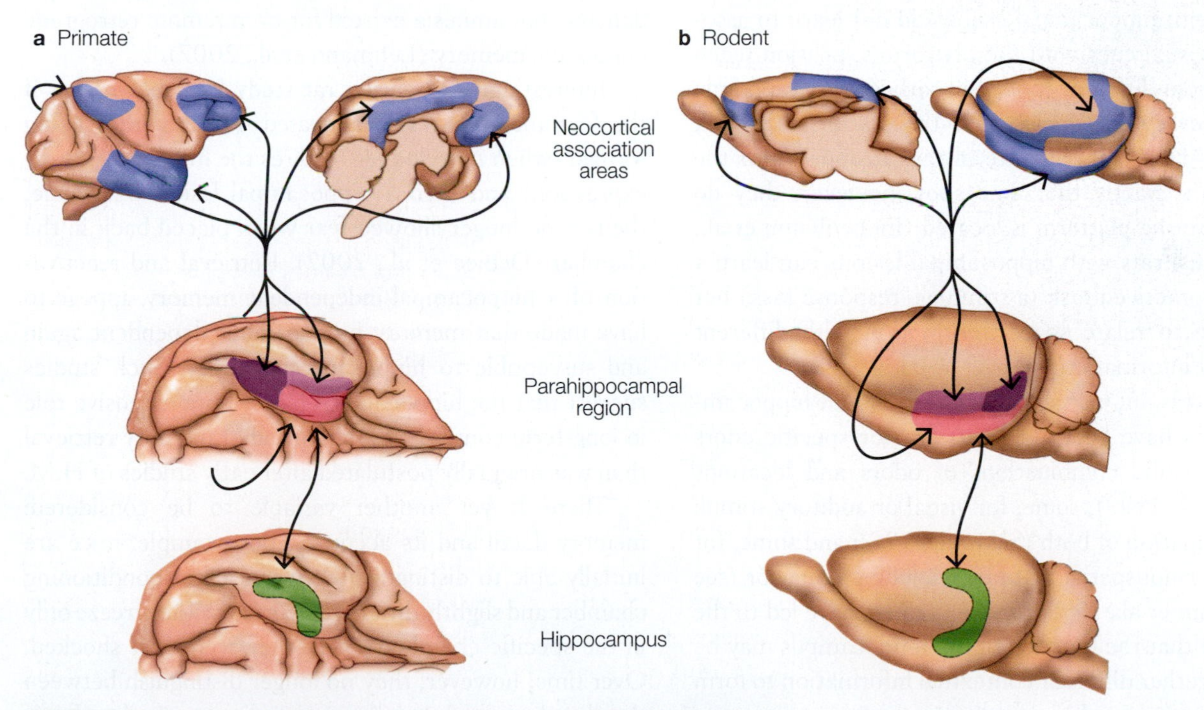

FIGURE 9.22 Anatomy of the hippocampal memory system in monkeys and rats.
Most areas of cortex send information to the hippocampus. Different neocortical zones (blue) project to one or more subdivisions of the parahippocampal region. These subdivisions are the perirhinal cortex (light purple), the parahippocampal cortex (dark purple), and the entorhinal cortex (pink). These latter areas are interconnected and project to different regions of the hippocampus (green), including the dentate gyrus, the CA3 and CA1 fields of the hippocampus, and the subiculum. As a result, various cortical inputs converge within the parahippocampal region. In addition, the parahippocampal region passes this information from the cortex to the hippocampus. Following processing in the hippocampus, information can be fed back via the parahippocampal region to the same areas of the cortex that the original inputs came from.

the activity of specific CA1 and CA3 hippocampal neurons correlated with specific locations.

This study led to the idea that the hippocampus represented spatial contexts (O'Keefe & Nadel, 1978), the *where* in context memory. The hippocampus was soon found to be involved in spatial navigational learning. Subsequently, rudimentary forms of place cells, head direction cells, and grid cells were found to be already active upon the first movements that rat pups made from their nests, demonstrating that three neuronal representations of space were already present before extensive experience. This finding strongly suggests that cognitive maps in the hippocampus representing location are innate (Wills et al., 2010).

In rats, spatial navigational learning is tested using the Morris water maze, a circular tank filled with opaque water (R. G. Morris, 1981). Above the water are different identifiable visual cues, such as windows and doors, and somewhere below the surface of the water is an invisible platform. Rats are dropped into the tank at different points on different trials. The time it takes for them to reach the platform becomes shorter over time, indicating that they learn where the platform is in relation to the visual cues above the water.

Rats with hippocampal lesions do not learn to associate the visual cues with the platform's location when dropped from different spots, but rather swim randomly about on every trial looking for the platform (Schenk & Morris, 1985). If they are always dropped into the water from exactly the same spot, however, they do learn where the platform is located (Eichenbaum et al., 1990). Thus, rats with hippocampal lesions can learn a repeated, practiced task (a stimulus–response task) but are unable to relate space information with different contextual information.

Context is not just about space. Some rat hippocampal neurons have been found to fire for specific odors and for specific combinations of odors and locations (Wood et al., 1999); some, for visual or auditory stimuli or a combination of both (Sakurai, 1996); and some, for many other nonspatial features, including behavior (see Eichenbaum et al., 1999). These findings have led to the suggestion that the function of the hippocampus may be to bind together different contextual information to form a complex contextual memory.

Although initial work in both animals (see Squire, 1992) and humans suggested that the hippocampus was not involved in the retrieval of long-term distant memories and had only a temporary involvement with forming and retrieving new contextual memories, subsequent work has suggested otherwise. For instance, in spatial navigation tasks, both recent and remote memories are equally disrupted after hippocampal lesions (S. J. Martin et al., 2005).

The retrieval of contextual memory in rats is often studied using *contextual fear learning*, where rats are placed in a small chamber with specific visual features and a foot shock is delivered. The rats then show a variety of conditioned responses, such as freezing in place, when put back into the same visually identifiable chamber. The retention of fear conditioning is evaluated by the amount of freezing the rats show. In one study, after experiencing a single shock episode, some rats underwent sham surgery (the control condition). Other rats had their hippocampus partially or fully destroyed at one of three times: 1 week, 2 months, or 6 months later. None of the rats were returned to the shock chamber during the interval between the shock and the surgery.

Two weeks after surgery, all of these groups were tested for fear retention. The control rats froze when put back in the chamber, though the response lessened with longer retention intervals. The rats with a completely destroyed hippocampus did not freeze, no matter the interval, while the rats with partial damage showed some freezing but less than controls, especially at longer intervals. The severity of retrograde amnesia for the contextual fear was related to the extent of hippocampal damage, but amnesia existed for even remote retrograde contextual memory (Lehmann et al., 2007).

Interestingly, an earlier rat study had shown that if the fear memory was reactivated 45 days after being formed (when it no longer requires the hippocampus for expression) and then a hippocampal lesion was made, the rats no longer showed fear when placed back in the chamber (Debiec et al., 2002). Retrieval and reactivation of a hippocampal-independent memory appear to have made that memory hippocampus dependent again and susceptible to hippocampal damage. Such studies suggest that the hippocampus has a more extensive role in long-term contextual (and episodic) memory retrieval than was originally postulated after early studies of H.M.

There is yet another variable to be considered: memory detail and its accuracy. For example, mice are initially able to distinguish between a fear-conditioning chamber and slightly different chambers: They freeze only in the specific chamber where they were first shocked. Over time, however, they no longer distinguish between the chambers, and their fear generalizes to similar chambers (Wiltgen & Silva, 2007). Thus, contextual memories become less detailed and more general with time, allowing the animal to be more adaptable, such that the fear memory is activated in novel but similar contexts.

It has been proposed that *memory quality* may be a critical factor that determines whether the hippocampus is essential for retrieval. The proposal is that it plays a permanent role in retrieving detailed contextual memory but is not necessary for retrieval once detail is lost and memory has generalized. Thus, if testing conditions promote retention of detailed memories, such as spatial navigation in water mazes where the exact location of a platform is required, the hippocampus is needed in the retrieval of both short- and long-term memories. If the conditions result in memory generalization across time, such as in fear conditioning, they will lead to a temporal gradient of hippocampal involvement in memory retrieval, as was seen in Wiltgen and Silva's experiment. In the next sections we see how some of these findings have been mirrored in humans.

TAKE-HOME MESSAGES

- The hippocampus is critical for the formation of long-term memory, and the cortex surrounding the hippocampus is critical for normal hippocampal memory function.
- Evidence from humans and animals with brain damage suggests a degree of independence of procedural memory, perceptual priming, conditioning, and nonassociative learning from the medial temporal lobe memory system.
- Neurons that activate when rats are in a particular place and facing a particular direction have been identified in the hippocampus and are called place cells. They provide evidence that the hippocampus has cells that encode contextual information.
- Damage to the temporal lobe outside of the hippocampus can produce the loss of semantic memory, even while the ability to acquire new episodic memories remains intact.

9.5 Distinguishing Human Memory Systems With Imaging

In 1998, two studies (Brewer et al., 1998; A. D. Wagner et al., 1998) published side by side in *Science* magazine coupled a new analysis technique, event-related fMRI, with an experimental setup called the subsequent-memory paradigm, in which participants are presented with items that they are asked to remember. This method enabled the researchers to isolate activity associated with single events and to directly compare the activity for successfully remembered studied items (hits) to activity for forgotten studied items (misses).

For example, in the Wagner study, which we discussed in Section 3.6, participants were presented with a word and, to enhance encoding, were told to decide whether the word was abstract or concrete while being scanned. Afterward they were shown a series of words

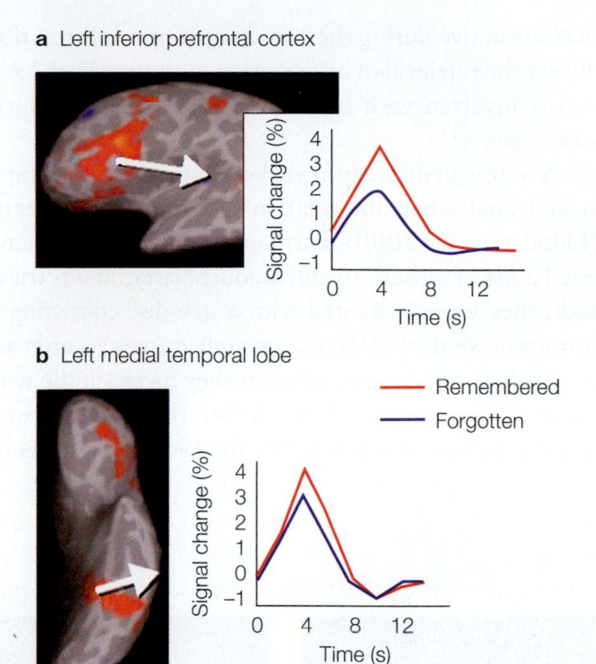

FIGURE 9.23 The subsequent-memory paradigm. The neural responses to each visual event are analyzed according to whether they were remembered or forgotten, revealing activations during memory encoding. The graphs show greater responses for remembered events (red) than for forgotten events (blue) in the left prefrontal (a) and temporal (b) cortices.

(some from the encoding task and some that were new) and were asked to indicate whether it was a word they had just studied (recognition test) and how confident they were about their answer. In this way the researchers were able to determine which words had been subsequently remembered. The event-related design enabled researchers to identify brain regions with differential activation during the encoding of words that were subsequently remembered (the hits) and those subsequently forgotten (the misses; **Figure 9.23**).

Recollection and Recognition: Two Systems

The year after the Wagner and Brewer studies, John Aggleton and Malcolm Brown (1999) proposed that encoding processes that merely identify an item as being familiar (recognition) and encoding processes that correctly identify the item as having been seen before (recollection) depend on different regions of the medial temporal lobes. Many behavioral studies supported the idea that two distinct processes are involved in declarative memory: assessing the item's familiarity, and recollecting the context of when the item was encountered. The key questions involved the hippocampus: Did it become active during the encoding of new information, during the retrieval of information, or during both? And was it involved with both recollection and familiarity assessments?

A subsequent study revealed that the hippocampus is activated when information is correctly recollected (Eldridge et al., 2000). Participants in this task memorized a list of words. Twenty minutes later, in a retrieval task, they were presented with a new list consisting of previously studied (old) and unstudied (new) words and were asked, one by one, whether they had seen the word before. If they answered "yes", then they were asked to make a decision about whether they actually recollected the item (remembered seeing it as an episodic memory with a spatial and temporal context) or it merely seemed familiar to them.

The twist in this study was that neuroimaging data were collected during the *retrieval* phase. The brain responses, measured with fMRI, were sorted according to whether the participants actually recollected the word, were only familiar with the word, were sure they had not seen the word before, or were mistaken about whether they had seen the word. The results were clear: During retrieval, the hippocampus was selectively active only for words that were actually correctly recollected (**Figure 9.24**), thus indicating an episodic memory. The

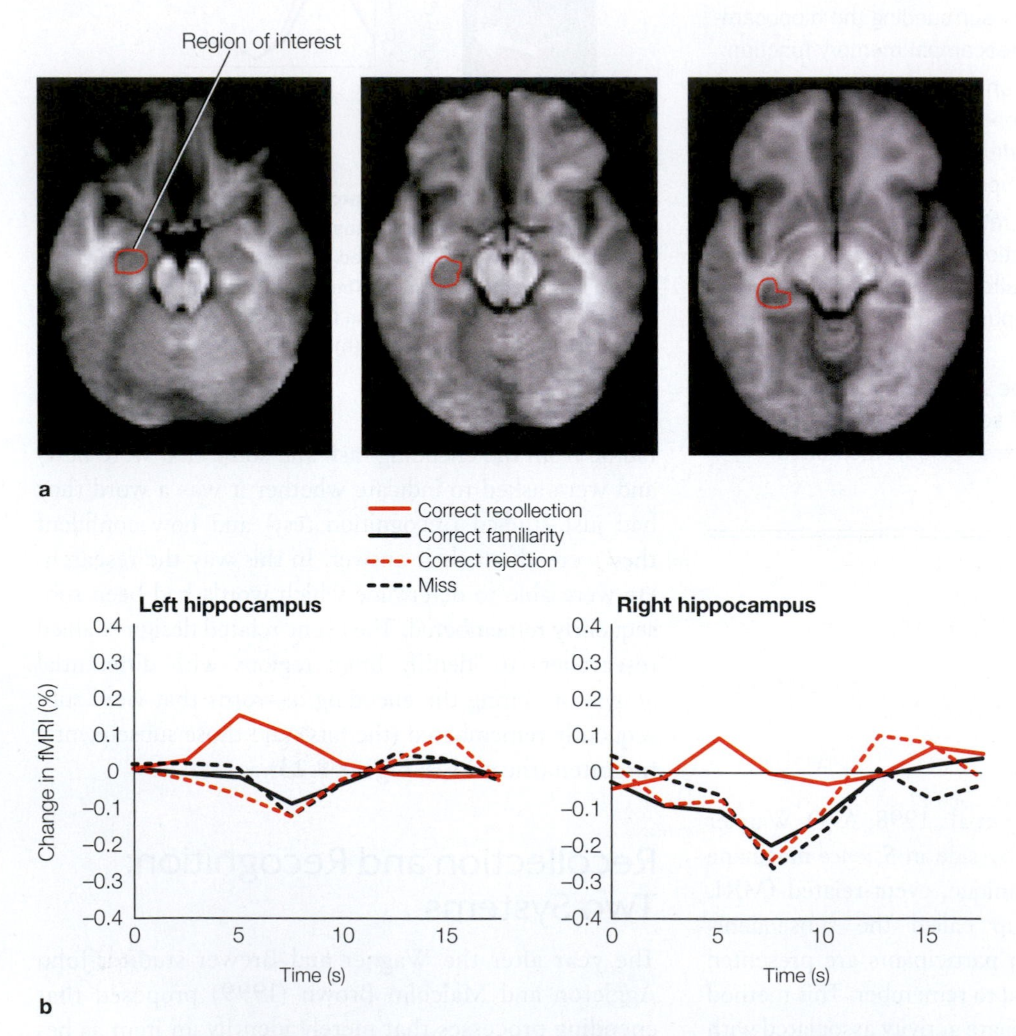

FIGURE 9.24 Retrieval in the hippocampus.
(a) Horizontal sections through the brain at the level of the inferior (left panel), middle (center panel), and superior (right panel) hippocampus. The red outline of the region of interest in the left hippocampus is based on anatomical landmarks. (b) Hemodynamic responses from event-related fMRI measures taken during the retrieval of previously studied words. The hippocampus was activated by correctly recollected words (solid red line) but not by words that the participants had previously seen but could not recollect, indicating that the words merely seemed familiar (solid black line). No hippocampal activity occurred for words that were correctly identified as new (not seen previously; dashed red line) or for errors in which the participant did not remember the words (dashed black line), despite having seen them previously.

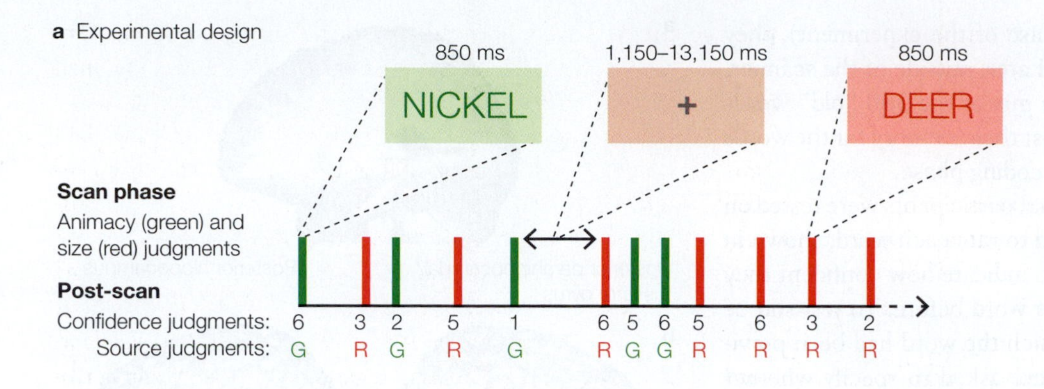

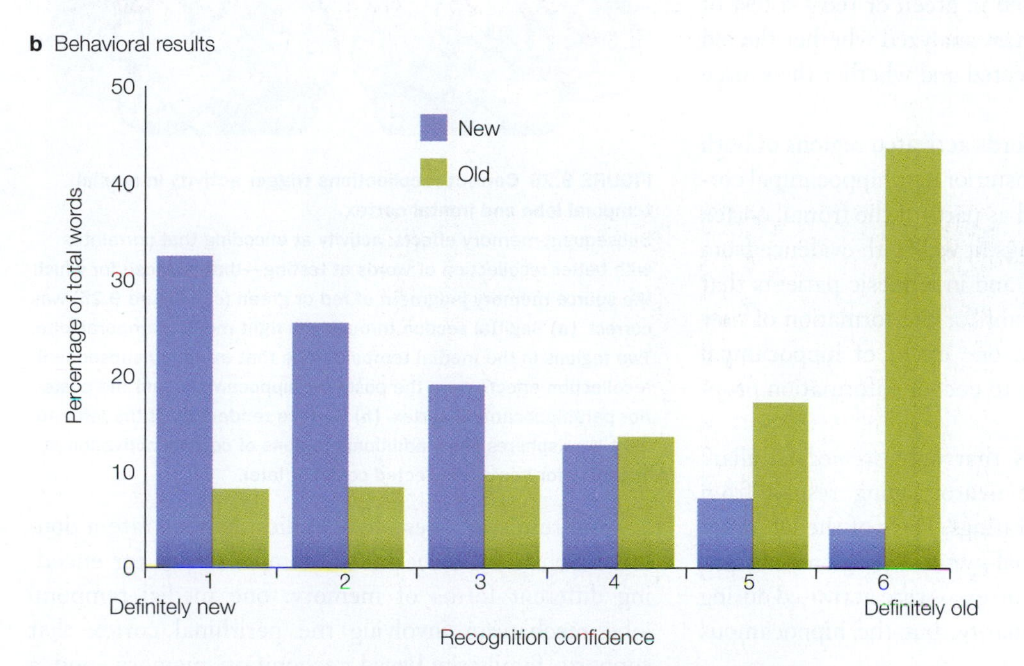

FIGURE 9.25 Testing for involvement of the hippocampus in information encoding.
(a) The sequence of events in one scanning run. During encoding, participants viewed a series of words and made either an animacy judgment (animate versus inanimate) or a size judgment (large versus small) for each word, depending on the color of that word (e.g., green represented a size judgment, so for the word *NICKEL* in green, the correct response would be "small"). Later, participants made two decisions about the items presented, which included the old words and new words not seen before. First, participants were asked to indicate whether and how confidently they recognized the items (e.g., on a scale of 1 to 6, from definitely new to definitely old). Second, they were asked to make a source memory judgment of whether each word had been presented in red or in green. (b) Mean proportions of studied ("old") and unstudied ("new") items endorsed at each confidence level. Performance on the source memory judgment (red or green) is not shown.

hippocampus was not activated for memories that did not contain awareness of the prior event—that is, when the words merely seemed familiar to the participants and were recognized by their familiarity alone. This finding strongly suggests that the hippocampus is involved in both encoding and retrieval of episodic memories, but not of memories based on familiarity.

Such data raised the question of which brain regions are involved in episodic versus nonepisodic (familiarity-based) memory encoding and retrieval. To figure this out, Charan Ranganath and his colleagues (2004) designed another study that combined event-related fMRI with the subsequent-memory paradigm (**Figure 9.25**).

Healthy volunteers were presented with words on a screen at a rate of about one word every 2 seconds. The words (360 in total), printed in either red or green, represented either animate or inanimate items that were either large or small. Depending on the color, the participants were required to make either an animacy judgment or a size judgment for each item to increase the likelihood that they would encode and remember the word. While the participants viewed the words and made their decisions (the encoding phase of the experiment), they were scanned using fMRI. Later, outside of the scanner, they were presented with a mix of the 360 "old" words with 360 "new" words to test their memory for the words they had seen during the encoding phase.

After this recognition test, participants were tested on familiarity: They were asked to rate each word, shown in black, on a scale of 1 to 6 to indicate how confident they were that they had seen the word before. To test source memory (the context in which the word had been previously viewed), they also were asked to specify whether the word had been presented in green or red—a test of episodic memory. Researchers analyzed whether the old words were properly recollected and whether the source was correctly identified.

Correctly recollected words activated regions of both the hippocampus and the posterior parahippocampal cortex during encoding, as well as parts of the frontal cortex (**Figure 9.26**). These findings fit well with evidence from previous studies in animals and in amnesic patients that the hippocampus is important for the formation of new long-term memories. Thus, one effect of hippocampal damage may be an inability to encode information properly in the first place.

What about the words that only *seemed* familiar? **Figure 9.27** presents the neuroimaging results from the analysis of confidence ratings. Parts of the left anterior medial parahippocampal gyrus—a region that corresponds to the perirhinal cortex—were activated during recognition based on familiarity, but the hippocampus itself was not activated.

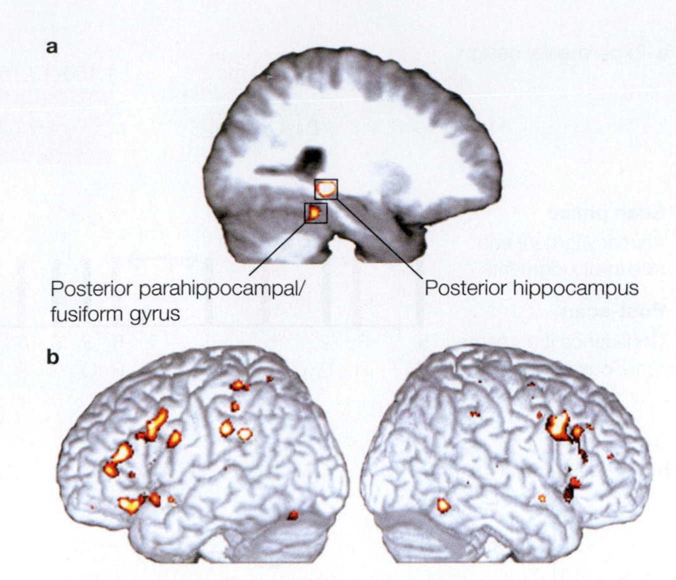

FIGURE 9.26 Correct recollections trigger activity in medial temporal lobe and frontal cortex.
Subsequent-memory effects: activity at encoding that correlates with better recollection of words at testing—that is, those for which the source memory judgment of red or green (see Figure 9.25) was correct. **(a)** Sagittal section through the right medial temporal lobe. Two regions in the medial temporal lobe that exhibited subsequent recollection effects were the posterior hippocampus and the posterior parahippocampal cortex. **(b)** Surface renderings of the left and right hemispheres show additional regions of cortical activation at encoding for items recollected correctly later.

The results of these two studies demonstrate a double dissociation in the medial temporal lobe for encoding different forms of memory: one medial temporal lobe mechanism involving the perirhinal cortex that supports familiarity-based recognition memory, and a

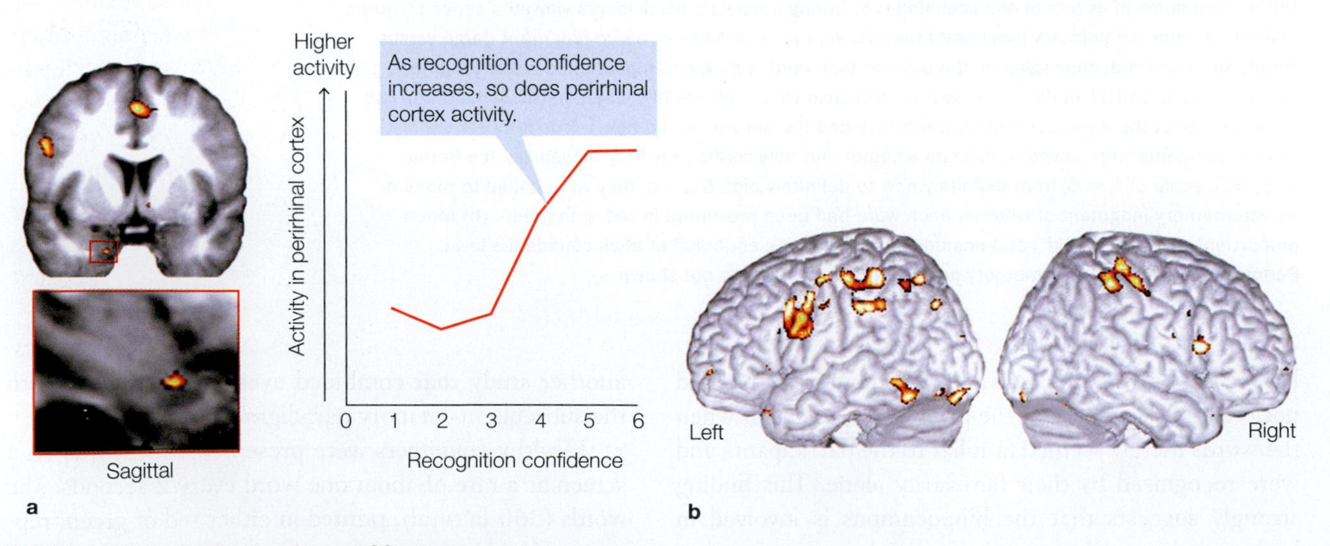

FIGURE 9.27 Familiarity-based recognition memory.
Brain activity during encoding correlates with the confidence of recognizing that an item has been seen before. **(a)** Coronal section through the brain at the level of the anterior medial temporal lobe. Functional MRI activations that correlated with confidence ratings (red box, and expanded sagittal view below the coronal section). The graph shows that as recognition confidence increases, activity in the perirhinal and entorhinal cortex also increases. **(b)** Images of the left and right hemispheres show additional regions of cortical activation.

second system involving the hippocampus and posterior parahippocampal cortex that supports recognition based on the recollection of source (episodic) information.

EPISODIC MEMORY AND THE HIPPOCAMPUS The process of encoding episodic memory involves binding an event to a time and place. When you think back on the first rock concert you ever attended, you probably recall where and when you saw it. As we mentioned for the rodent studies, an early theory proposed that the fundamental role of the hippocampus is to build and maintain spatial maps. The main support for this theory was the discovery of "place cells" identified in the hippocampus. However, you probably also recall who was at the concert with you. Episodic memories involve more than space and time. Furthermore, the memory of your first concert may be distinguished from your memories of other rock concerts, other events held at the same place, and other places you have been with the same friend. The cognitive map theory does not explain how our brain accomplishes these other contextual feats of episodic memory.

How the brain solves the problem of bundling all this information—a question known as the *binding problem*—is central to understanding episodic memory. Anatomy offers some clues: Different types of information from all over the cortex converge on the medial temporal lobe regions surrounding the hippocampus, but not all types pass through the same structures. Information about the features of items ("what" an item is) coming from unimodal sensory regions of neocortex passes through the perirhinal cortex (the anterior portion of the parahippocampus). In contrast, information from multimodal neocortical areas about "where" something is located passes through the more posterior parts of the parahippocampal cortex (**Figure 9.28**).

Both information types project into the entorhinal cortex but do not converge until they are within the hippocampus (Eichenbaum et al., 2007). The *binding-of-items-and-contexts (BIC) model* proposes that the perirhinal cortex represents information about specific items (e.g., who and what), the parahippocampal cortex represents information about the context in which these items were encountered (e.g., where and when), and processing in the hippocampus binds the representations of items with their context (Diana et al., 2007; Ranganath, 2010). As a result, the hippocampus is able to relate the various types of information about something that the individual encounters. This form of memory is referred to as *relational memory*, which we will discuss further. So, in this model perirhinal cortex is sufficient to recognize that something is familiar, but to remember the full episode and everything related to it, the hippocampus is necessary to bind the information into a package.

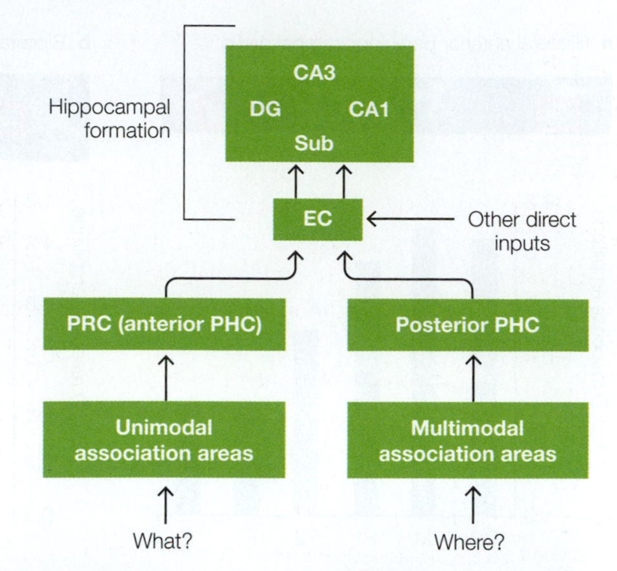

FIGURE 9.28 Flow of information between the neocortex and the hippocampal system.
CA = cornu ammonis neuronal fields (CA1, CA3); DG = dentate gyrus; EC = entorhinal cortex; PHC = parahippocampal cortex; PRC = perirhinal cortex; Sub = subiculum.

A similar distinction has also been found between the recollection and familiarity components of long-term memory *retrieval*. One study that nicely makes this point is the work of Daniela Montaldi and her colleagues at the University of Oxford (2006). During an encoding session, they showed participants pictures of scenes. Two days later, the researchers tested the participants' recognition with a mixed batch of new and old scenes while monitoring their brain activity with fMRI.

The researchers asked the participants to rate the pictures of scenes as new, slightly familiar, moderately familiar, very familiar, or recollected. Their results showed the same activity pattern as in the Ranganath encoding study. The hippocampus was activated only for pictures of scenes that the participants could recollect having seen before. Regions of the medial temporal lobe, like the perirhinal cortex, that are located outside the hippocampus showed activity patterns that correlated with the strength of familiarity for scenes other than recollected ones (**Figure 9.29**).

In sum, evidence from a number of studies indicates that the medial temporal lobe supports different forms of memory and that these different forms of memory (recollection versus familiarity) are supported by different subdivisions of this brain region. The hippocampus is involved in encoding and retrieval of episodic memories (recollection), whereas areas outside the hippocampus, especially the perirhinal cortex, support recognition based on familiarity. These findings also suggest that the nature of the representations should be considered in distinguishing between memory systems (Nadel & Hardt, 2011).

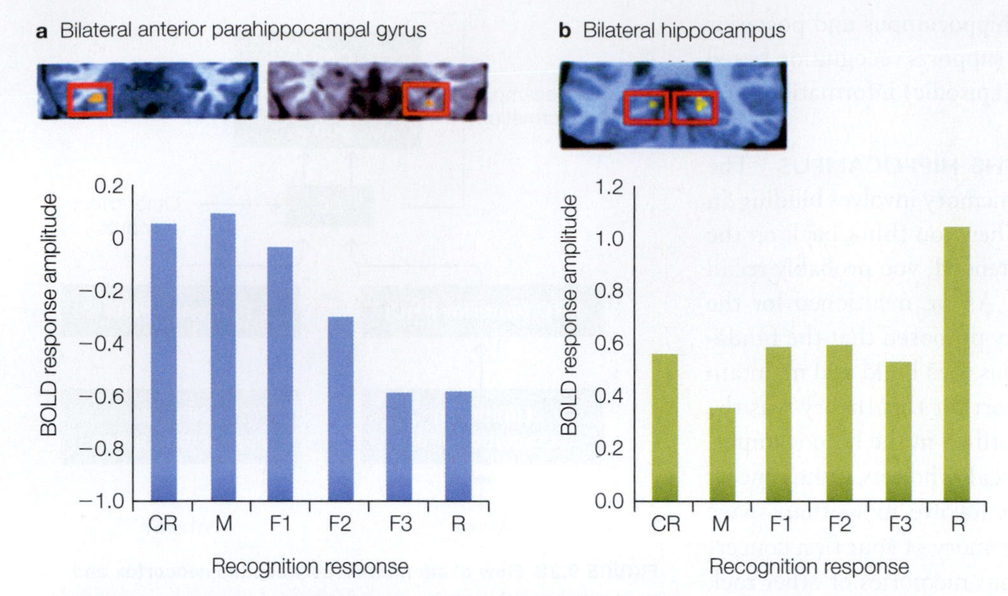

FIGURE 9.29 Recollection and familiarity during retrieval.
Participants studied scenes and were scanned during recognition testing. The partial images of the brain are coronal sections through the hippocampus. (a) Activation in bilateral anterior parahippocampal regions decreased with increasing confidence. (b) In contrast, activations in bilateral hippocampal regions increased for recollected items only, as compared with nonrecollected items. CR = correct rejection (an item that was correctly identified as new); M = miss (an item that was seen before but the participant reported as not having seen previously); F1 = weak familiarity, F2 = moderate familiarity, F3 = strong familiarity; R = recollection.

RELATIONAL MEMORY AND THE HIPPOCAMPUS The memory for relations among the constituent elements of an experience—time, place, person, and so forth—is termed **relational memory.** Relational memory enables us to remember names with faces, the locations of objects or people, or the order in which various events occurred (Konkel & Cohen, 2009). Moreover, we can retrieve the relational context in which someone or something was previously encountered and know that it is different from the present encounter. For instance, if you live in Los Angeles, you may see Tom Hanks drive past in a Porsche and know that you've seen him before—not in a Porsche, but in a movie.

Neal Cohen and his colleagues at the University of Illinois (J. D. Ryan et al., 2000) investigated relational memory by measuring eye fixation in study participants who were watching complex scenes in which the object and spatial relationships were experimentally manipulated. The researchers found that healthy participants were sensitive to changing relationships in the scenes, even when they were unaware of them, as demonstrated by their altered patterns of eye movements (**Figure 9.30**). In contrast, patients with amnesia as a result of hippocampal damage were insensitive to the changes. These researchers have argued, therefore, that the fundamental deficit in medial temporal amnesia is a disorder of relational memory processing in the hippocampus.

Relational memory theory proposes that the hippocampus supports memory for all manner of relations. Cohen and colleagues predicted that memory for all manner of relations would be impaired in patients with hippocampal amnesia (Konkel et al., 2008). These researchers evaluated memory performance for three different types of relational tasks: spatial, associative, and sequential. They also compared recollection of single items by healthy control participants to that of the patients with amnesia, as well as other patients with more extensive medial temporal lobe damage.

Those with hippocampal-only damage were impaired on all of the relational tasks, but not on the single-item recollection task. Patients with more extensive medial temporal lobe damage were impaired on both types of tests. Multiple neuroimaging studies show increased hippocampal activation when the relationship between items is being evaluated; in contrast, when an item is being individually encoded, activity is not observed in the hippocampus but is seen in other medial temporal lobe cortical regions, especially in the perirhinal cortex (Davachi & Wagner, 2002; Davachi et al., 2003).

Long-Term Memory Storage and Retrieval

Where in the brain is the "what" and "where" information stored? The projections of "what" and "where"

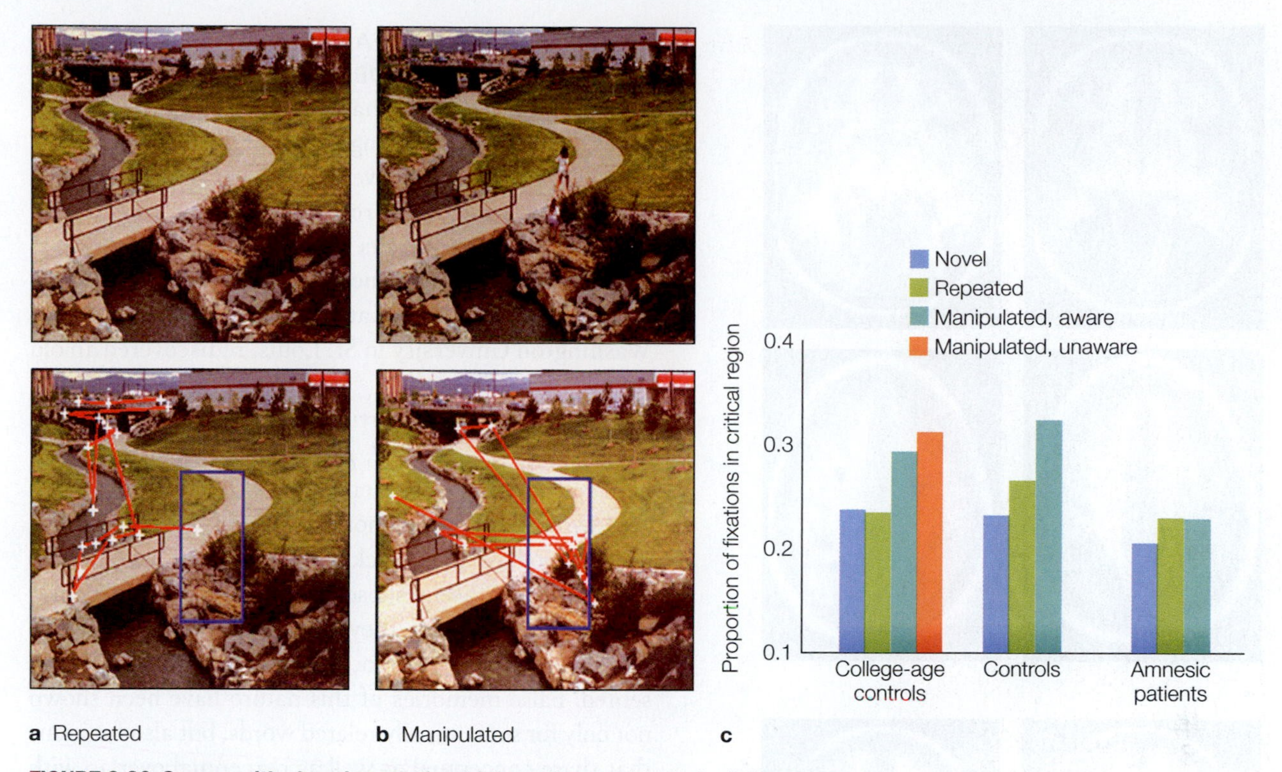

FIGURE 9.30 Scenes with changing relational information used to test relational memory. Eye movements (red lines) and fixations (white crosses), which were recorded as healthy participants viewed either repeated or manipulated scenes at two time points, are shown superimposed on the same scene (bottom panels in parts a and b). The critical area of change is outlined with a blue rectangle. **(a)** When nothing changed in the critical area, the critical area did not attract eye fixations. **(b)** When the scene changed, many eye fixations focused on the critical area that had contained people. Some participants were aware of the change, while others were not. **(c)** Quantification of the proportion of fixations in the critical area in parts (a) and (b) for healthy young controls; age-, education-, and intelligence-matched controls; and six patients with amnesia. Both control groups showed more fixations in the critical region when the scene changed. The amnesic patients failed to show this effect of relational memory.

information from the neocortex into the hippocampus described in the previous section are matched by a similar outflow from the hippocampus that travels back to the entorhinal cortex, then to the perirhinal and parahippocampal cortex, and then to the neocortical areas that provided the inputs to the neocortex in the first place. You may already have guessed the role of this feedback system in memory storage and retrieval, and some findings from neuroimaging studies during retrieval may back up your guess.

Mark Wheeler and his colleagues at Washington University in St. Louis (M. E. Wheeler et al., 2000) investigated brain regions involved in the retrieval of different types of information. They asked participants to learn a set of sounds (auditory stimuli) or pictures (visual stimuli) during a 2-day encoding period. Each sound or picture was paired with a written label describing the item (e.g., the word *BELL*, followed by the sound of a bell). On the third day the participants were given perceptual and memory tests while in an fMRI scanner. In the perceptual test, stimuli (label plus sound or picture) were presented, and brain activity was measured to identify brain regions involved in the perceptual processing of items. In the memory retrieval test, only the written label was presented, and the participant pressed a button to indicate whether the item was associated with a sound or a picture.

Wheeler and coworkers found that during the retrieval of pictures, regions of neocortex that had been activated during perception of the pictures were reactivated. Similarly, during the retrieval of sounds, different areas of the neocortex that had been activated during the perception of sounds were reactivated. In each case during memory retrieval, the modality-specific regions of activity in the neocortex were subsets of the areas activated by presentation of the perceptual information alone, when no memory task was required (**Figure 9.31**). The activated areas of sensory-specific neocortex were not lower-level sensory cortical regions; they were later stages of visual and auditory association cortex, where incoming signals would have been perceptually well processed (e.g., to the point where identity was coded).

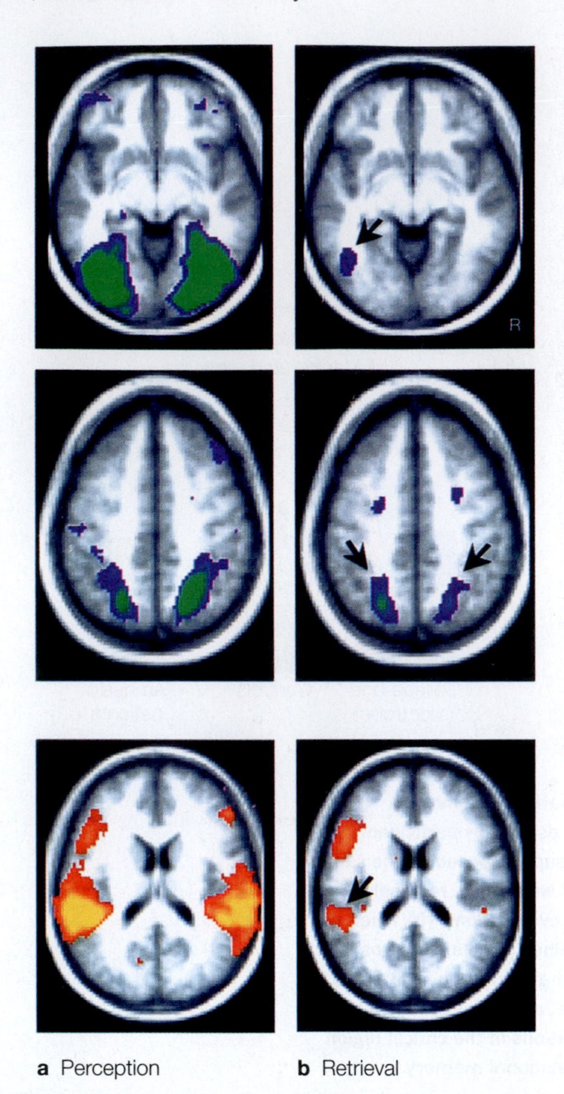

FIGURE 9.31 Reactivation of modality-specific cortex during long-term memory retrieval.
(a) Areas activated by the viewing of pictures (top two panels) and the hearing of sounds (bottom panel). **(b)** Areas activated during the retrieval of pictures (top two panels) or sounds (bottom panel) from memory. Arrows indicate regions of overlap between memory and perceptual activations. The right hemisphere of the brain is on the right of each image.

These results suggest that the specific relational information for items stored in long-term memory may be coded during retrieval by *reactivation* of the neocortical areas that provided input to the hippocampus during the original encoding. In subsequent work, Wheeler and colleagues (M. E. Wheeler et al., 2006) showed that visual processing regions in inferior temporal cortex were involved in the preparation to retrieve visual information, whereas the more dorsal parietal and superior occipital activity was related to the process of searching memory for the relevant item. These findings help refine the role of different brain regions in reactivation during long-term memory retrieval.

RETRIEVAL ERRORS: FALSE MEMORIES AND THE MEDIAL TEMPORAL LOBE When our memory fails, we usually forget events that happened in the past. Sometimes, however, something more surprising occurs: We remember events that never happened. Whereas forgetting has been a topic of research for more than a century, memory researchers did not have a good method to investigate false memories in the laboratory until Henry Roediger and Kathleen McDermott, also at Washington University in St. Louis, rediscovered an old technique in 1995.

In this technique, participants are presented with a list of words (e.g., *thread*, *pin*, *eye*, *sewing*, *sharp*, *point*, *haystack*, *pain*, *injection*, etc.) that are all highly associated with a word that is not presented (in this case, *needle*; did you have to go back and recheck the list?). When participants are asked subsequently to recall or recognize the words in the list, they show a strong tendency to falsely remember the associated word that was not presented. False memories of this nature have been shown not only for semantically related words, but also for items that share conceptual as well as perceptual overlap with studied items. This should not be surprising, since the dominant left hemisphere falsely recognizes new pictures related to the "gist" of a story (see Figure 4.30), while the right hemisphere rarely makes that mistake.

This memory illusion is so powerful that participants often report having a vivid memory of seeing the nonpresented critical item in the study list. For example, in another study, researchers edited childhood photographs of their volunteers into a picture of a hot-air balloon ride (**Figure 9.32**). Although none of the participants had ever actually been in a hot-air balloon, when they were asked to describe their flying experience, 50% of them created false childhood memories (K. A. Wade et al., 2002). During the debriefing session when the participants were told that the picture had been doctored, one of them commented, "That's amazing, 'cause I honestly started to talk myself into believing it! . . . I still feel in my head that I actually was there; I can sort of see images of it, but not distinctly, but yeah. Gosh, that's amazing!"

The vividness of such memories makes it difficult to separate the cognitive and neural basis of true and false memories. Despite this difficulty, when participants are interrogated carefully about the conscious experience associated with remembering true and false items, they tend to rate true items higher than false items in terms of sensory details (Mather et al., 1997; Norman & Schacter, 1997). This difference is often reflected by greater neural activation in the medial temporal lobe and sensory processing regions for true compared to false memories (Dennis et al., 2012; Slotnick & Schacter, 2004).

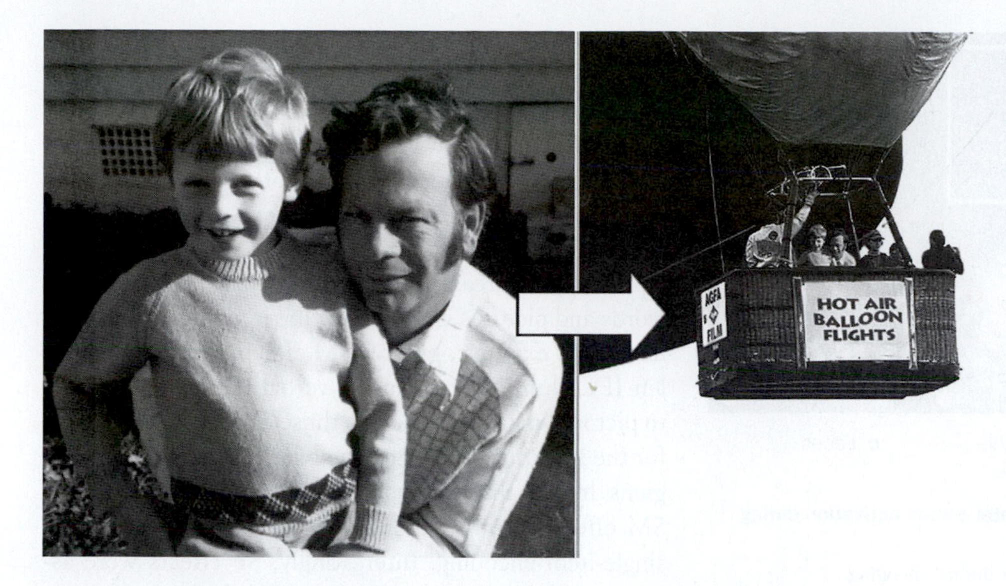

FIGURE 9.32 Planting a false memory.
An actual photograph of the participant as a child was used to create a doctored picture of a hot-air balloon ride.

What makes individuals believe their illusionary recollections? A recent meta-analysis of brain studies attempted to answer this question (Kurkela & Dennis, 2016). Examining many different instances of false memories, the researchers showed that false memories actually do elicit activity in the same retrieval networks that true memories activate. However, there are differences in the degree of brain activity in portions of the retrieval network for true and false memories.

True memories are associated with greater activity in the medial temporal lobe and sensory areas (**Figure 9.33a**), which are activated when a true item is first presented. In contrast, false memories are associated with greater activity in frontal and parietal portions of the retrieval network (**Figure 9.33b**). One way these differences in brain activity can be understood is to appreciate that true memories are for items actually seen and therefore activate both sensory areas and the medial temporal lobe. However, false memories do not activate sensory areas; instead, regions associated with top-down cognitive control are more active for false memories.

The ease with which false memories can be implanted suggests that our episodic memory is naturally malleable. Some researchers argue that our memory systems don't flawlessly preserve our past experiences, but instead flexibly recombine remembered information from multiple sources—an ability that helps solve current problems and anticipates future ones (M. K. Johnson & Sherman, 1990; Schacter et al., 2012), and also enables us to develop rich autobiographical memories of events that may have never happened (Bernstein & Loftus, 2009).

Encoding, Retrieval, and the Frontal Cortex

The earliest neuroimaging studies of amnesic patients consistently found that the frontal cortex was involved in both short-term and long-term memory processes, but its role remains debated. A meta-analysis of the early neuroimaging literature done in 1996 (Nyberg et al., 1996) found that the left frontal cortex was often involved in encoding episodic information, whereas the right

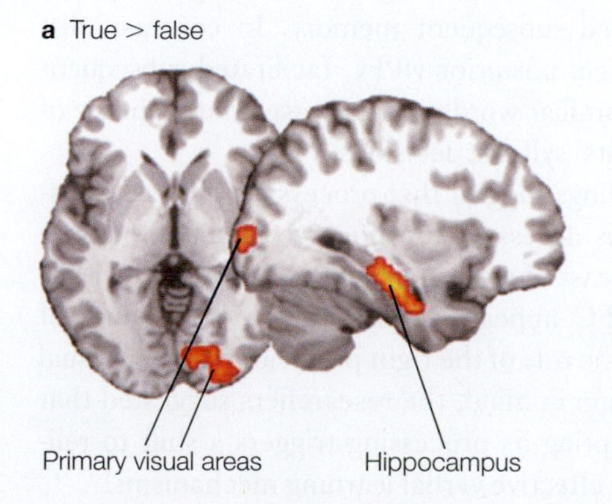

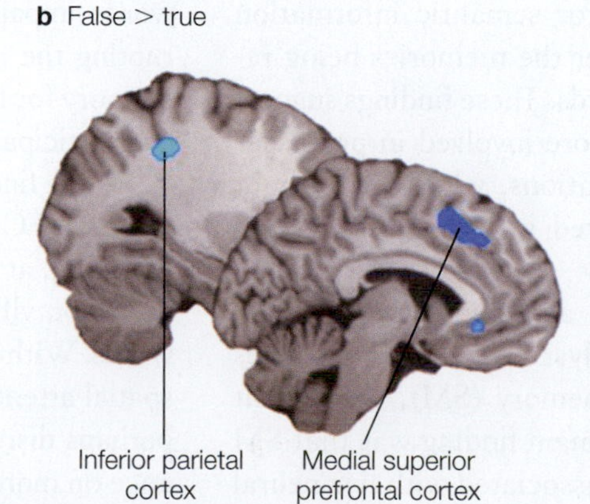

FIGURE 9.33 True and false memories in the brain.
(a) Regions showing greater activation for true compared to false remembering (primary visual cortex and hippocampus). **(b)** Regions showing greater activation for false memories (medial superior prefrontal cortex and inferior parietal cortex).

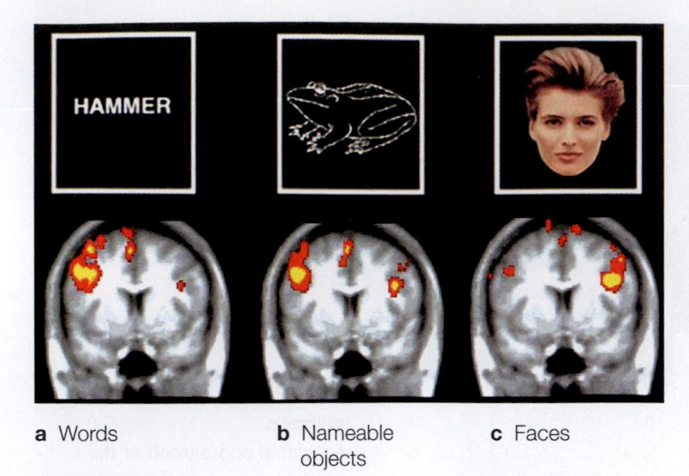

a Words b Nameable objects c Faces

FIGURE 9.34 Material-specific frontal cortex activation during memory encoding.
(a) Words activate left frontal cortex during encoding. (b) Nameable objects activate both left and right frontal cortex during encoding. (c) Encoding of faces activates primarily right frontal cortex.

frontal cortex was often found to be activated in episodic retrieval.

A dominant theory of memory processing that arose from these studies was the hemispheric encoding/retrieval asymmetry, or HERA, model (Tulving et al., 1994), which posited that episodic encoding was predominantly a left-hemisphere process, while episodic retrieval was predominantly a right-hemisphere process. This theory, however, ignored the fact that split-brain patients are not amnesic (M. B. Miller et al., 1997).

Others, including William Kelley at Dartmouth College and his colleagues, argued that lateralization of frontal cortex activity during long-term memory retrieval is related more to the nature of the material being processed than to a distinction between encoding and retrieval (Kelley et al., 1998). **Figure 9.34** shows that both semantic encoding and retrieval involve the left frontal cortex, including Broca's area (Brodmann area 44, extending into area 46) and the ventrolateral region (Brodmann areas 44 and 45). This lateralization to the left hemisphere for semantic information remains, regardless of whether the memories being retrieved are of objects or of words. These findings suggest that the left hemisphere is more involved in processes coded by linguistic representations, whereas the right frontal cortex is more involved in object and spatial memory information.

In 2011, Hongkeun Kim at Daegu University in South Korea did a meta-analysis of 74 fMRI studies involving either subsequent memory (SM), subsequent forgetting (SF), or both. The main finding was that SM effects are most consistently associated with five neural regions: left inferior frontal cortex (IFC), bilateral fusiform cortex, bilateral hippocampal formation, bilateral premotor cortex (PMC), and bilateral posterior parietal cortex (PPC). While all of the studies used visual "events," some used words and others used pictures; some used single-item memory tasks and others used associative memory tasks.

Different areas were preferentially activated for words and pictures, and for specific items and associated items. For example, greater SM effects were seen in the left IFC with the encoding of verbal material compared to pictorial material, whereas those effects were reversed for the fusiform cortex and the bilateral hippocampal regions. In fact, the left hippocampal region showed greater SM effects during pictorial associative versus pictorial single-item encoding. Interestingly, SF effects were associated mostly with activations in default-network regions, which are active during mind wandering (as we will see in Chapter 13). Kim suggests that activation of these regions during encoding may take neural resources away from the processes that lead to effective remembering, resulting in subsequent forgetting.

Is the IFC necessary for episodic memory formation? The first study demonstrating that transient disruption to neural processes localized to part of the inferior frontal gyrus impacts the formation of episodic memory was done by Itamar Kahn and his colleagues (2005). They applied single-pulse transcranial magnetic stimulation (spTMS) to the left and right posterior ventrolateral prefrontal cortex (posterior vlPFC), located on the inferior frontal gyrus, regions that had previously been identified as correlated with episodic memory encoding during a syllable task.

While participants in the study decided how many syllables were in visually presented familiar and unfamiliar (English-appearing but nonsense) words, spTMS was applied over the posterior vlPFC to disrupt processing at different times after the stimulus was presented. Afterward, participants' memory for the words was measured. The researchers found that disrupting the processing of the *left* posterior vlPFC during the encoding of familiar words impaired subsequent memory. In contrast, disrupting the *right* posterior vlPFC facilitated subsequent memory for familiar words and increased the accuracy of the participants' syllable decisions.

These findings suggest that processing in the left posterior vlPFC is necessary for effective episodic memory encoding, at least of words, and that disrupting the right posterior vlPFC appears to facilitate the encoding of words. With the role of the right posterior vlPFC in visual spatial attention in mind, the researchers suggested that perhaps disrupting its processing triggers a shift to reliance on more effective verbal learning mechanisms.

While fMRI studies lack the temporal resolution required to identify the sequence of activations underlying memory encoding, EEG is up to the task. Subsequent-memory analyses are currently being used with intracranial and extracranial EEG recordings. For example, John Burke and his colleagues (2014) recorded intracranial EEG activations from 98 surgical patients. They found that successfully encoding a memory invokes two spatiotemporally distinct activations: Early activations involve the ventral visual pathway and the medial temporal lobe, while later activations involve the left inferior frontal gyrus, left posterior parietal cortex, and left ventrolateral temporal cortex. The researchers speculate that these activity patterns may reflect higher-order visual processing, followed by top-down modulation of attention and semantic information. By looking at shifts in the EEG activations, the researchers were able to predict successful memory formation.

Retrieval and the Parietal Cortex

The advent of fMRI sparked interest not only in the frontal lobe, but also in the parietal lobe. The activation pattern for the contrast between successfully retrieved old items and successfully rejected new items, known as the successful retrieval effect (SRE), spans large regions of the frontal and parietal cortex and has been robust across many studies (see A. D. Wagner et al., 2005). The functional significance of these regions to the retrieval process has been widely studied and debated.

The parietal cortex is well known for its role in attention, but because parietal lobe lesions are not generally associated with memory loss, its role in memory was not considered before the neuroimaging studies of the 1990s. There is one notable exception, however. Lesions in the retrosplenial cortex (RSC) can produce both retrograde and anterograde amnesia. This area, located in the medial aspect of the parietal lobe, is also one of the first regions to undergo pathological changes during the prodromal phase of Alzheimer's disease, known as mild cognitive impairment (Pengas et al., 2010).

Event-related fMRI studies of healthy volunteers revealed greater activation in the RSC when they were correctly identifying previously seen items than when they were correctly making rejections. But other areas of the parietal lobe were also activated, including the inferior and superior parietal lobules, as well as medial structures that extend from the precuneus into the posterior cingulate cortex (PCC).

The anatomical connections of the parietal cortex are suggestive of its involvement in memory. The lateral parietal, retrosplenial, and posterior cingulate cortices are connected to the medial temporal lobe, both directly and indirectly. Notably, the RSC is extensively interconnected with the parahippocampal cortex (PHC), and both the RSC and the PHC interface with similar regions in the posterior hippocampus, subiculum, mammillary bodies, and anterior thalamus, as well as the default network. Meanwhile, the perirhinal cortex displays a completely different connectivity pattern—not with the posterior hippocampus, but with the anterior hippocampus, amygdala, ventral temporopolar cortex (vTPC), and lateral orbitofrontal cortex (Suzuki & Amaral, 1994).

In the past decade we have witnessed an explosion of functional neuroimaging studies, which have revealed that successful *memory retrieval*, especially for contextual information, is consistently associated with activity in lateral PPC, including the RSC. During encoding, however, these areas show less activity than baseline levels (Daselaar et al., 2009), except when the items are encoded in a self-relevant manner (Leshikar & Duarte, 2012) or are likely to evoke self-referential (V. C. Martin et al., 2011) or emotional processing (Ritchey, LaBar, et al., 2011). This encoding preference for self-referential items suggests that the RSC is more attuned to internal information sources: These same parietal regions are active during conscious rest when an individual's mind turns to thinking about self-related past and future scenarios (see Chapter 13).

Many neuroimaging studies claim that the activations seen when remembered items are contrasted with forgotten items are related to memory content, and several hypotheses have been suggested. The working memory maintenance hypothesis (A. D. Wagner et al., 2005) proposes that activation of the parietal cortex is related to the maintenance of information in working memory. The multimodal integration hypothesis (Shimamura, 2011; Vilberg & Rugg, 2008) suggests that parietal activations indicate integration of multiple types of information.

Building on the parietal lobe's anatomy and on the binding-of-items-and-contexts model discussed earlier in relation to the hippocampus, Charan Ranganath and Maureen Ritchey (2012) have proposed a memory model made up of two systems that support different forms of memory-guided behavior. The anterior temporal (AT) system includes the perirhinal cortex and its above-mentioned connections, and the posterior medial (PM) system is composed of the core components of the PHC and RSC, mammillary bodies, anterior thalamic nuclei, subiculum, and default network (**Figure 9.35**).

In their model (**Figure 9.36**), the PRC in the AT system supports memory for items and is involved in familiarity-based recognition, associating features of objects and making fine-grained perceptual or semantic discriminations. Ranganath and Ritchey suggest that the

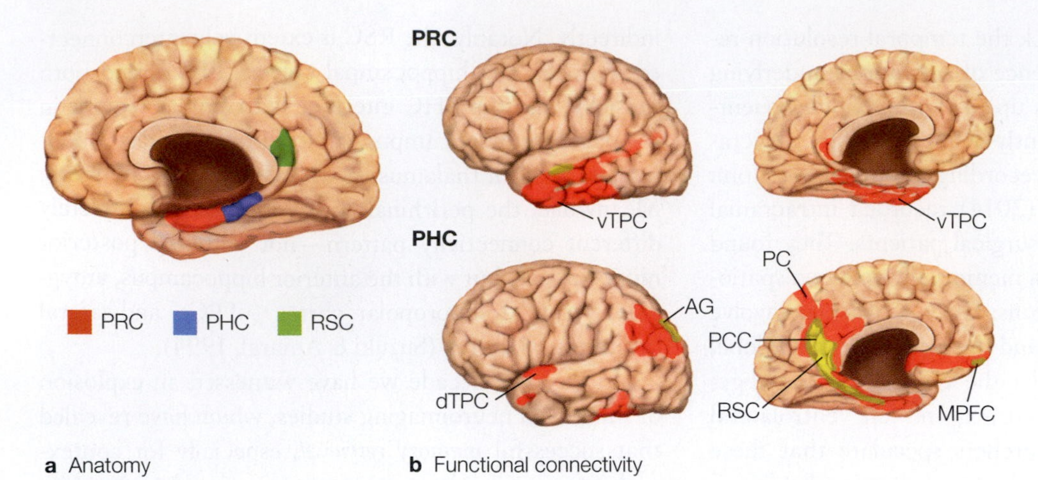

FIGURE 9.35 Anatomy of the perirhinal, parahippocampal, and retrosplenial cortices. (a) The perirhinal cortex (PRC), parahippocampal cortex (PHC), and retrosplenial cortex (RSC) regions are shown. (b) Functional connectivity profiles of the PRC (top) and PHC (bottom), showing regions that were significantly correlated with the PRC and PHC during resting-state scans. Resting-state fMRI scans evaluate covariations in spontaneous fluctuations in the BOLD signal across the brain while the participant performs no task, and they are taken as evidence of intrinsic functional connectivity between brain regions that covary. The PRC was found to be functionally connected to ventral temporopolar cortex (vTPC), where higher-order visual areas are located. In contrast, the PHC is functionally connected to the dorsal temporopolar cortex (dTPC), the retrosplenial cortex (RSC), the posterior cingulate cortex (PCC), the precuneus (PC), the medial prefrontal cortex (MPFC), and the angular gyrus (AG).

overall cognitive job of the anterior system (in collaboration with the amygdala, vTPC, and lateral orbital frontal cortex) may be to assess the significance of entities. The PHC and RSC in the PM system support recollection-based memories, such as memory for scenes, spatial layouts, and contexts. These researchers also propose that this system, together with the other PM system structures, may construct mental representations of the relationships among entities, actions, and outcomes.

Some support for this theory comes from neurological patients. Recall that along with hippocampal damage, Alzheimer's disease, with its episodic memory

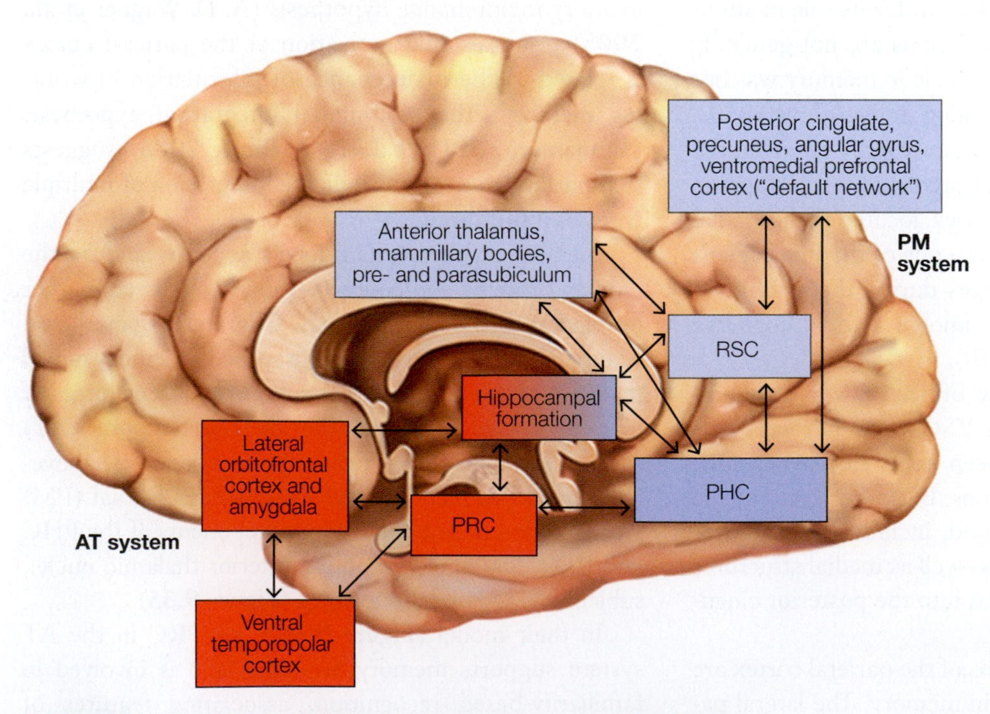

FIGURE 9.36 Model of two neocortical systems for memory-guided behavior. The components of the anterior temporal (AT) system are shown in red. The posterior medial (PM) system is shown in blue. Arrows indicate strong anatomical connections between regions.

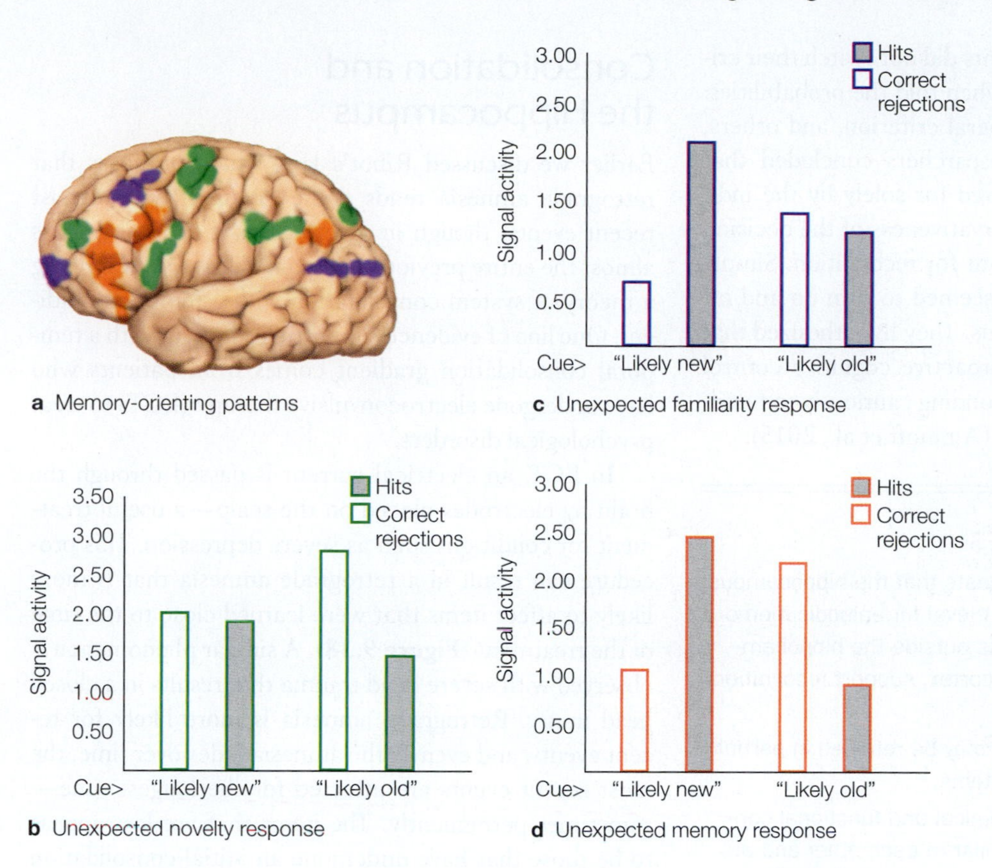

FIGURE 9.37 Three different response patterns were isolated in the left lateral parietal cortex. (a) The colors indicating activation in the brain correspond to the colors of the bar plots in parts (b)–(d), illustrating the response pattern across cue conditions and item types. **(b)** The region of the left anterior intraparietal sulcus (IPS) and postcentral gyrus (green) illustrated an unexpected novelty response pattern. **(c)** The posterior aspect of the anterior angular gyrus region (blue) demonstrated an unexpected familiarity response. **(d)** The mid IPS region (orange) demonstrated a general unexpected memory response.

impairment, is associated with severe disruptions in the RSC, PCC, precuneus, and angular gyrus, which are all components of the proposed PM system. In contrast, patients with semantic dementia, which is characterized by a loss of knowledge about objects, have extensive damage to the anterior temporal lobes.

While recognition clearly entails the retrieval of memory content, some nonmemory processes may also track with successful retrieval (see M. B. Miller & Dobbins, 2014). Roberto Cabeza and colleagues (2008) have proposed a functional parallel between parietal activations during recognition and visuospatial attention. Their *attention-to-memory model* argues that the dorsal regions of the superior parietal lobule are necessary for top-down search of episodic memory for specific content, and that the ventral regions of the inferior parietal lobule are critical to capturing attention once the salient content is identified.

Another hypothesis suggests that cognitive control processes involved in decision making are also in play during memory retrieval. For example, to probe the functional significance of parietal responses during recognition judgment, Ian Dobbins and his colleagues performed fMRI scans while participants did the syllable decision task and the follow-up recognition task. The new twist in the Dobbins experiment was that before each recognition trial, they cued participants (sometimes falsely) that the upcoming test item was likely to be new or likely to be old (Jaeger et al., 2013; O'Connor et al., 2010).

The researchers found that a network of brain regions associated with the successful retrieval effect (SRE) was more active in the "likely new" condition when the test item was actually old versus when the test item was actually new (i.e., there were more hits than correct rejections; **Figure 9.37**). They also found that another network of brain regions was more active in the "likely old" condition when the test item was actually new versus when the test item was actually old (i.e., there were more correct rejections than hits). In their framework, activity associated with the SRE occurs because of reactive cognitive control processes when an event violates expectations.

Michael Miller and Ian Dobbins (2014) examined a specific aspect of the recognition decision process: the decision criterion. To investigate whether the decision criterion modulated the SRE, they manipulated the criterion used to make recognition judgments of words and faces. Before each recognition judgment, the participants were told whether the stimulus had a high probability (70%, liberal criterion) of having been previously seen or a low probability (30%, conservative criterion).

The researchers found that robust SRE activity occurred in recognition conditions in which participants strategically utilized a conservative criterion but not in situations in which they utilized a liberal criterion. They also found that some participants did not switch their criterion from one to the other when told the probabilities: Some continued to use the liberal criterion, and others, the conservative one. The researchers concluded that SRE activity could be accounted for solely by the individual differences in the conservativeness of the decision criterion used by the participant for recognition. Simply changing a decision criterion seemed to turn on and off the SRE activity in these regions. They hypothesized that SRE activity represents the proactive cognitive control processes associated with responding cautiously to familiar items on a recognition test (Aminoff et al., 2015).

TAKE-HOME MESSAGES

- Functional MRI evidence suggests that the hippocampus is involved in encoding and retrieval for episodic memories that are recollected. Areas outside the hippocampus, especially the perirhinal cortex, support recognition based on familiarity.
- Different types of information may be retained in partially or wholly distinct memory systems.
- The PHC and RSC have anatomical and functional connectivity patterns that are similar to each other and are very different from the PRC. The RSC, located in the parietal lobe, appears also to be crucial for memory.
- Both the IFC and the parietal lobe are involved in retrieving memories, but their roles have not been clearly defined.

9.6 Memory Consolidation

Consolidation is the process that stabilizes a memory over time after it is first acquired. It was first proposed by Marcus Fabius Quintilianus, a first-century Roman teacher of rhetoric, who stated,

> [It] is a curious fact, of which the reason is not obvious, that the interval of a single night will greatly increase the strength of the memory. . . . Whatever the cause, things which could not be recalled on the spot are easily coordinated the next day, and time itself, which is generally accounted one of the causes of forgetfulness, actually serves to strengthen the memory. (quoted in Walker, 2009)

Consolidation processes occur at the cellular level, as well as at the system level. We discuss cellular consolidation, also known as synaptic consolidation, in Section 9.7. Here we discuss the two main system consolidation theories, which differ in the role of the hippocampus.

Consolidation and the Hippocampus

Earlier we discussed Ribot's law, which proposes that retrograde amnesia tends to be greatest for the most recent events, though in severe cases it can encompass almost the entire previous life span. Ribot was describing a theory of system consolidation with a temporal gradient. One line of evidence supporting a system with a temporal consolidation gradient comes from patients who have undergone electroconvulsive therapy (ECT) to treat psychological disorders.

In ECT, an electrical current is passed through the brain by electrodes placed on the scalp—a useful treatment for conditions such as severe depression. This procedure can result in a retrograde amnesia that is more likely to affect items that were learned close to the time of the treatment (**Figure 9.38**). A similar phenomenon is observed with severe head trauma that results in a closed head injury. Retrograde amnesia is more likely for recent events, and even as the amnesia fades over time, the most recent events are affected for the longest time—sometimes permanently. The items that are lost appear to be those that have undergone an initial consolidation process but have not yet completed a slower permanent consolidation process. Those that have undergone the latter are more likely to be remembered.

As we learned from H.M., the medial temporal lobes, particularly the hippocampi, are essential for the early consolidation and initial storage of information for episodic and semantic memories. The mechanisms of the slower consolidation process, however, remain more controversial. There are two main theories. The *standard consolidation theory*, proposed by Larry Squire and his colleagues, considers the neocortex to be crucial for the storage of fully consolidated long-term memories, whereas the hippocampus plays only a temporary role.

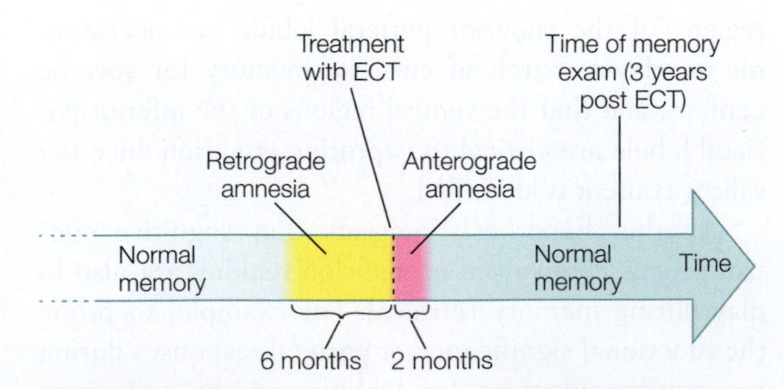

FIGURE 9.38 Effects of electroconvulsive therapy (ECT) on memory performance.
After electroconvulsive therapy, patients show a temporally graded retrograde memory loss, suggesting that memory changes for a long time after initial learning. Some material is forgotten, and the material that remains becomes more resistant to disruption.

In this view, to form a memory, the representations of an event that are distributed throughout the cortex come together in the medial temporal lobe, where the hippocampus binds them. Then, through some sort of interaction between the medial temporal lobe and the neocortex, the ability to retrieve the bound information is slowly transferred to the neocortex. Consolidation occurs after repeated reactivation of the memory creates direct connections within the cortex itself between the various representations so that it no longer requires the hippocampus as the middleman to bind them.

This process takes place when an individual is either awake or asleep, and it eventually makes the memory independent of the hippocampus. The standard consolidation theory proposes that the same process is involved for both episodic and semantic memories. Although it can explain why retrograde amnesia has a temporal gradient (some memories just hadn't completed the consolidation process before damage occurred), it doesn't explain why some people who have amnesia due to hippocampal damage have good long-term memory and others have severe loss.

An alternative model, the *multiple trace theory*, proposed by Lynn Nadel and Morris Moscovitch (1997), suggests that the long-term stores for semantic information rely solely on the neocortex, while episodic memory, consolidated or not, continues to rely on the hippocampus for retrieval. In this formulation, a new memory trace, composed of a combination of attributes, is set down in the hippocampus every time an episodic memory is retrieved: The more times a memory is retrieved, the more traces are set down. Remote events that have been retrieved more often have more hippocampal traces and are more resistant to partial hippocampal damage simply because of their number. The traces are not exactly alike; they may differ in attributes. Slowly, the common elements of the traces are extracted into "gist" information and then stored as semantic memory elsewhere in the cortex.

This theory suggests that episodic memories degrade over time and are slowly converted into semantic memory. It predicts that partial hippocampal damage would partially affect episodic memory, but complete damage would completely destroy it. Both models have some supporting evidence, advocates, and critics.

Sleep and Memory Consolidation

Evidence suggests that sleep plays a crucial role in memory consolidation after learning. Researchers studying the relationship between sleep and memory in the rat used multi-electrode methods to record from place cells in the rat hippocampus, which fire when an animal is in a specific place in its environment in relation to a landmark cue (see Section 9.4). They found that the place cells that fired together during the learning of spatial behavioral tasks were more likely to fire together during postlearning sleep than they had been before the task was learned, indicating that the neurons might be "replaying" the learned tasks during sleep (M. A. Wilson & McNaughton, 1994).

Further studies of a similar nature have shown that during NREM (non–rapid eye movement) sleep (discussed in Chapter 14), hippocampal cells tended not only to replay the spatial sequence that had been activated during learning, but to do so in the same temporal sequence of neuronal firing as during learning. These studies suggest that the hippocampus helps consolidate memory by "replaying" the neuronal firing of the spatial and temporal patterns that were first activated during awake learning. Replay activity has also been found in the prefrontal cortex and ventral striatum, possibly indicating the integration of new memories in the cortex (Pennartz et al., 2004; Peyrache et al., 2009). Replay of this type is not, however, limited to sleep.

Foster and Wilson (2006) reported that sequential replay also takes place in the rat hippocampus when the animal is awake, just after the rat experiences a pattern of spatial activity (e.g., running in a maze). Interestingly, replay during awake periods has the unusual property of taking place in the reverse temporal order of the original experience. One hypothesis is that this sort of awake replay of neural activity represents a basic mechanism for learning and memory.

Thus, two mechanisms are involved in replaying an activity: the reverse-order awake replay of neural activity, and the sleep-related replay in which activity is replayed in the same temporal order as it was experienced. Something about the forward replay during sleep is apparently related to memory consolidation. But the reverse-order awake replay must be doing something different. Foster and Wilson propose that it reflects a mechanism that permits recently experienced events to be compared to their "memory trace" and may, potentially, reinforce learning.

Is it possible to learn while sleeping? John Rudoy, Ken Paller, and their colleagues at Northwestern University (2009) asked whether playing sounds during sleep that were related to the context of awake learning might facilitate the learning and consolidation of individual memories. They first presented volunteers with 50 pictures of objects at different locations on a computer screen matched with a related sound (e.g., a picture of a cat and the sound of meowing). Later, during a testing phase, the participants were presented with sounds and were asked where the associated picture had been located on the screen. Then they took a nap, and as they slept, their EEGs and ERPs were recorded. When it was determined by EEG that they were in slow-wave sleep, they were presented with sounds, half of which they had previously heard and half not. After waking, their recall of the locations of the 50 learned pictures was again tested.

The researchers found that even though the volunteers did not remember hearing the sounds, they showed potentiated learning for the locations of pictures that had been accompanied by sounds presented during sleep, compared to pictures that had not been presented with sound playback during sleep. Further studies have found that auditory cuing during sleep activates hippocampal neurons, enhances skill learning and explicit knowledge of a motor task, and improves consolidation of emotional memories (reviewed in Schreiner & Rasch, 2017). These effects depend on the hippocampus and are not seen in patients with hippocampal sclerosis (Fuentemilla et al., 2013).

Does this mean you can learn Chinese, French, or Dutch while sleeping? Swiss scientists Thomas Schreiner and Björn Rasch (2014) think so. They showed that native German-language speakers who studied German–Dutch word pairs learned them better if they slept while hearing the word pairs replayed during NREM sleep, as compared to being awake for the replay. This learning effect during sleep was found to be associated with great power in the theta band (5- to 7-Hz oscillations) of the EEG during sleep for the replayed word pairs. The researchers suggest that the slow-wave EEG signals seen after replayed word pairs reflect brain processes involved in consolidation, and that these signals are signs of the coordination of brain areas to solidify memories.

Stress and Memory Consolidation

Stress, both physical and psychological, triggers the release of adrenaline and cortisol. In acute situations, when coupled with adrenaline, cortisol can enhance initial encoding and consolidation of information perceived around the time of the stressor. (We discuss the effect of acutely elevated levels of cortisol and enhanced consolidation of emotional memories in Chapter 10.) Chronic high stress, however, has detrimental effects on memory and other cognitive functions. The receptors in the brain that are activated by cortisol, called glucocorticoid receptors, are found at concentrated levels in the hippocampus (especially in the dentate gyrus and CA1 region; Figure 9.17b).

The CA1 region of the hippocampus is the origin of connections from the hippocampus to the neocortex that are important in the consolidation of episodic memory. The functions of this circuitry can be disrupted by high levels of cortisol, perhaps by the impairment of long-term potentiation (LTP; see Section 9.7). Episodic memory is impaired by high levels of cortisol (Kirschbaum et al., 1996): A single 10-mg dose of hydrocortisone detrimentally affects verbal episodic memory. Over the last 20 years, evidence has accumulated that stress effects on memory retrieval are far broader than was originally conceived and affect multiple memory systems, from striatal-based stimulus–response systems to prefrontal-cortex-based extinction memory (reviewed in O. T. Wolf, 2017).

Clinical evidence shows impaired memory function in all disorders that are characterized by chronic high levels of cortisol, including Cushing's syndrome, major depression, and asthma treated with the glucocorticoid prednisone (Payne & Nadel, 2004). Furthermore, Sonia Lupien of McGill University and her colleagues (2005) found that elderly individuals who have experienced chronic stress and have prolonged high levels of cortisol have a 14% reduction in hippocampal volume as compared to age-matched individuals without chronic stress and with normal levels of cortisol. These individuals also show marked impairment of episodic memory. These results indicate a long-term deleterious effect of cortisol on the hippocampus.

TAKE-HOME MESSAGES

- Two prominent theories of long-term memory consolidation are the standard consolidation theory and the multiple trace theory.
- Sleep supports memory consolidation, perhaps when hippocampal neurons replay patterns of firing that were experienced during learning.
- Stress affects episodic memory consolidation when high levels of cortisol influence hippocampal function.

9.7 Cellular Basis of Learning and Memory

Researchers have long believed the synapse, with its dynamic connections, to be a likely structure involved in the mechanics of memory. Most models of the cellular bases of memory hold that memory is the result of changes in the strength of synaptic interactions among neurons in neural networks. How would synaptic strength be altered to enable learning and memory?

In 1949, Donald Hebb, the father of neural network theory, proposed that synaptic connections between coactivated cells change in a manner dependent on their activity. This theory, known as Hebb's law, is commonly summarized as "Cells that fire together wire together." Hebb proposed that the mechanism underlying learning was the strengthening of synaptic connections that results when a weak input and a strong input act on a cell at the same time. This learning theory has been dubbed **Hebbian learning.**

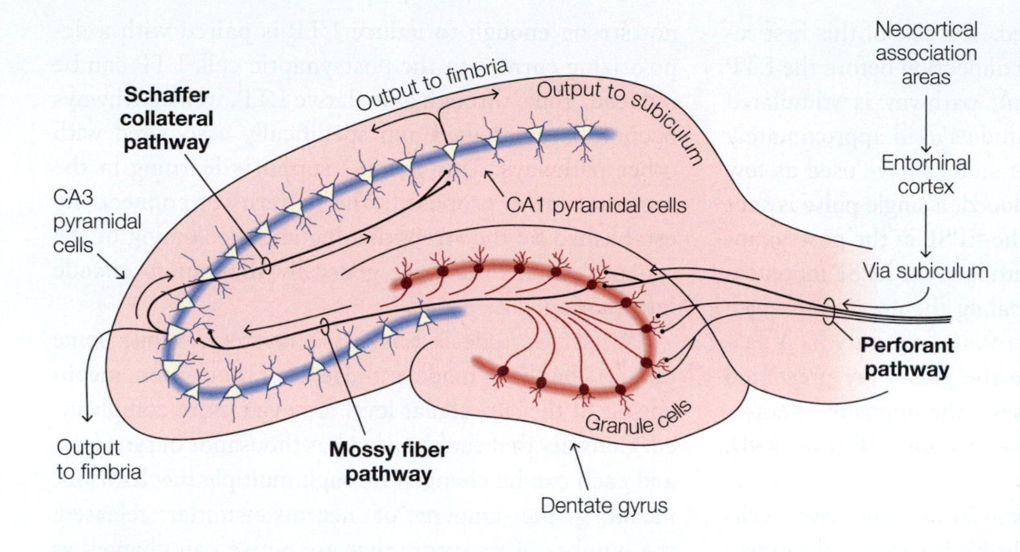

FIGURE 9.39 Synaptic organization of the rat hippocampus. The major projection pathways of the rat hippocampus are analogous to those in humans.

Long-Term Potentiation and the Hippocampus

Because of the role that the hippocampal formation plays in memory, it has long been hypothesized that neurons in the hippocampus must be plastic—that is, able to change their synaptic interactions. Although it is now clear that storage itself does not reside in the hippocampus, this fact does not invalidate the hippocampal models that we will examine, because the same cellular mechanisms can operate in various cortical and subcortical areas.

First let's establish the three major excitatory neural pathways of the hippocampus that extend from the subiculum to the CA1 cells: the perforant pathway, the mossy fibers, and the Schaffer collaterals (**Figure 9.39**). Neocortical association areas project via the parahippocampal cortex or perirhinal cortex to the entorhinal cortex. Neurons from the entorhinal cortex travel via the subiculum along the *perforant pathway* to synapse with granule cells of the dentate gyrus with excitatory inputs. The granule cells have distinctive-looking unmyelinated axons, known as *mossy fibers*, which connect the dentate gyrus to the dendritic spines of the hippocampal CA3 pyramidal cells. The CA3 pyramidal cells are connected to the CA1 pyramidal cells by axon collaterals, known as the *Schaffer collaterals*. This hippocampal system is used to examine synaptic plasticity as the mechanism of learning at the cellular level.

Physiological studies in rabbits done by Timothy Bliss and Terje Lømo (1973) provided evidence for Hebb's law. Bliss and Lømo found that stimulating the axons of the perforant pathway resulted in a long-term increase in the magnitude of excitatory postsynaptic potentials (EPSPs). That is, stimulation led to greater synaptic strength in the perforant pathway so that, when the axons were stimulated again later, larger postsynaptic responses resulted in the granule cells of the dentate gyrus. This phenomenon is known as **long-term potentiation (LTP)** (*potentiate* means "to strengthen or make more potent"), and its discovery confirmed Hebb's law.

LTP can be recorded by the combination of a stimulating electrode placed on the perforant pathway and a recording electrode placed in a granule cell of the dentate gyrus (**Figure 9.40**). A single pulse is presented, and

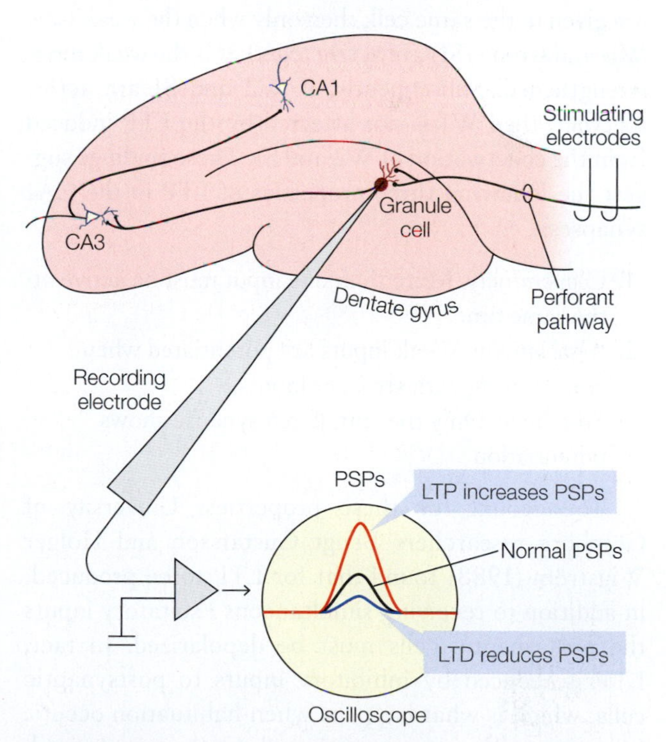

FIGURE 9.40 Stimulus and recording setup for the study of LTP in perforant pathways. The pattern of responses (in millivolts) before and after the induction of long-term potentiation (LTP) is shown as the red curve in the oscilloscope reading. The pattern of responses in long-term depression (LTD) is shown as the blue curve. PSPs = postsynaptic potentials.

the resulting EPSP is measured. The size of this first recording is the strength of the connection before the LTP is induced. Then the perforant pathway is stimulated with a burst of pulses; early studies used approximately 100 pulses/s, but more recent studies have used as few as 5 pulses/s. After LTP is induced, a single pulse is sent again, and the magnitude of the EPSP in the postsynaptic cell is measured. The magnitude of the EPSP increases after the LTP is induced, signaling the greater strength of the synaptic effect (Figure 9.40, red curve). A fascinating finding is that, when the pulses are presented slowly (as low-frequency pulses), the opposite effect—long-term depression (LTD)—develops (Figure 9.40, blue curve).

LTP was also found to occur in the other two excitatory projection pathways of the hippocampus: the mossy fibers and the Schaffer collaterals. The changes could last for hours in isolated slices of hippocampal tissue placed in dishes, and for weeks in living animals. LTP also takes place in other brain regions, including the amygdala, basal ganglia, cerebellum, and cortex—all involved with learning.

HEBBIAN LEARNING By manipulating LTP in the CA1 neurons of the hippocampus, Bliss and Lømo found that if two weak inputs (W1 and W2) and a strong input (S1) are given to the same cell, then only when the weak (say, W1) and strong (S1) are active together is the weak input strengthened. Subsequently, if W2 and S1 are active together, then W1 is not affected by the LTP induced from the coactivation of W2 and S1. These findings suggest the following three properties of LTP in the CA1 synapses:

1. *Cooperativity.* More than one input must be active at the same time.
2. *Associativity.* Weak inputs are potentiated when co-occurring with stronger inputs.
3. *Specificity.* Only the stimulated synapse shows potentiation.

To account for these properties, University of Göteborg researchers Bengt Gustafsson and Holger Wigström (1988) found that for LTP to be produced, in addition to receiving simultaneous excitatory inputs the postsynaptic cells must be depolarized. In fact, LTP is reduced by inhibitory inputs to postsynaptic cells, which is what happens when habituation occurs. Moreover, when postsynaptic cells are hyperpolarized, LTP is prevented.

Conversely, when postsynaptic inhibition is prevented, LTP is facilitated. If an input that is normally not strong enough to induce LTP is paired with a depolarizing current to the postsynaptic cell, LTP can be induced. Thus, through associative LTP, weak pathways become strengthened and specifically associated with other pathways. This process supports learning in the way that Hebb proposed. The patterns of connectivity established by the strengthening and weakening of the synaptic connections are generally thought to encode information.

What the code is remains a mystery. While some progress has been made at the level of the neuron, mechanisms at the subcellular level are even more complicated. Consider that each neuron has thousands of synapses, and each can be changed through multiple mechanisms, including the amount of neurotransmitter released; the number of receptors that are active can change, as can their properties, and new synapses can be formed. Whether any of these mechanisms contribute to memory is unknown.

What has been known since the 1960s is that long-term memory formation requires the expression of new genes. When a protein synthesis inhibitor (which inhibits the expression of new genes) is given to mice right after a training session, they are amnesic for the training experience. Yet recent research has shown that the memory remained in their brains! The implications of this finding are rocking the foundations of current theories about the cellular basis of learning (see **Box 9.1**).

THE NMDA RECEPTOR The molecular mechanism that mediates LTP is fascinating. It depends on the neurotransmitter glutamate, the major excitatory transmitter in the hippocampus. Glutamate binds to two types of glutamate receptors. Normal synaptic transmissions are mediated by the AMPA (α-amino-3-hydroxyl-5-methyl-4-isoxazole propionate) receptor. LTP is initially mediated by the NMDA (*N*-methyl-D-aspartate) receptors (**Figure 9.41**), located on the dendritic spines of postsynaptic neurons. When the NMDA receptors of CA1 neurons are blocked with the chemical AP5 (2-amino-5-phosphonopentanoate), then LTP induction is prevented. Once LTP is established in these cells, however, AP5 treatment has no effect. Therefore, NMDA receptors are central to producing LTP, but not maintaining it. Maintenance of LTP probably depends on the AMPA receptors, although the mechanisms are not fully understood.

NMDA receptors are also blocked by magnesium ions (Mg^{2+}), which prevent other ions from entering the postsynaptic cell. The Mg^{2+} ions can be ejected from the

BOX 9.1 | HOT SCIENCE

I Know You're in There!

Early in the 20th century, Richard Semon, a German evolutionary biologist, came up with the term *engram* to mean the enduring modification to the nervous system produced by an experience. The memory engram is the learned information stored in the brain—the chunk of neural tissue that must be reactivated in order to recall that information.

Researchers have recently been able to isolate memory engram–bearing cells in the hippocampus. Tomás Ryan and his colleagues (2015) compared the physiological properties of engram cells with non-engram cells in the hippocampus of mice while they were learning the response to a stimulus. The researchers identified an increase of synaptic strength and dendritic spine density specifically in consolidated-memory engram cells. Next they used a recently developed technique to interfere with memory consolidation: They gave a protein synthesis inhibitor to the mice right after a training session, resulting in amnesia for the training. At the level of the cells, they found that the treatment that induced amnesia also abolished the increases of synaptic strength and dendritic spine density in the engram.

Next, to test whether amnesia is caused by a consolidation failure, as many studies suggest, they optogenetically activated labeled CA3 engram cells in the two groups of trained mice: those that had been induced with amnesia for their training and those that had not. This is when they stumbled onto something unexpected: Directly activating the engram cells optogenetically produced the same behavior in both groups of mice; both groups demonstrated the trained response! The amnesic mice were able to perform the trained task even when their engram cells showed no increases in synaptic strength. The memory was not abolished even when the enhanced synaptic strength between the engram cells was!

This finding confirms that synaptic strength appears to be necessary for memory retrieval. That is, no matter how memory is stored, when synapses are not operational, information cannot be extracted from cells (Queenan et al., 2017). Shockingly, however, synaptic strength, which has been the top contender as the mechanism for memory *storage*, has to be scrubbed (T. J. Ryan et al., 2015). So, how is memory stored if not by the synaptic changes? The search is on!

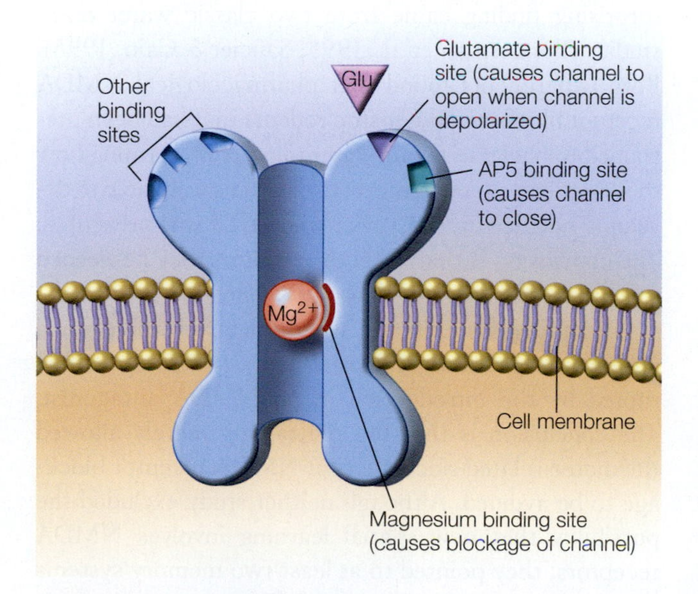

FIGURE 9.41 The NMDA receptor.
As this simplified cross-sectional schematic shows, the NMDA receptor is naturally blocked by Mg^{2+} ions. Unblocking (channel opening) occurs when the proteins that form the channel shift after glutamate binds to the glutamate binding site.

NMDA receptors only when the cell is depolarized. Thus, the ion channel opens only when two conditions are met: (a) the neurotransmitter glutamate binds to the receptors, and (b) the membrane is depolarized. These two conditions are another way of saying that the NMDA receptors are transmitter- and voltage-dependent (also called *gated*; **Figure 9.42**).

The open ion channel allows Ca^{2+} ions to enter the postsynaptic cell. The effect of Ca^{2+} influx via the NMDA receptor is critical in the formation of LTP. The Ca^{2+} acts as an intracellular messenger conveying the signal, which changes enzyme activities that influence synaptic strength. Despite rapid advances in understanding the mechanisms of LTP at physiological and biochemical levels, the molecular mechanisms of synaptic strengthening in LTP are still the subject of extensive debate.

The synaptic changes that create a stronger synapse after LTP induction likely include presynaptic and postsynaptic mechanisms. One hypothesis is that LTP raises the sensitivity of postsynaptic AMPA glutamate

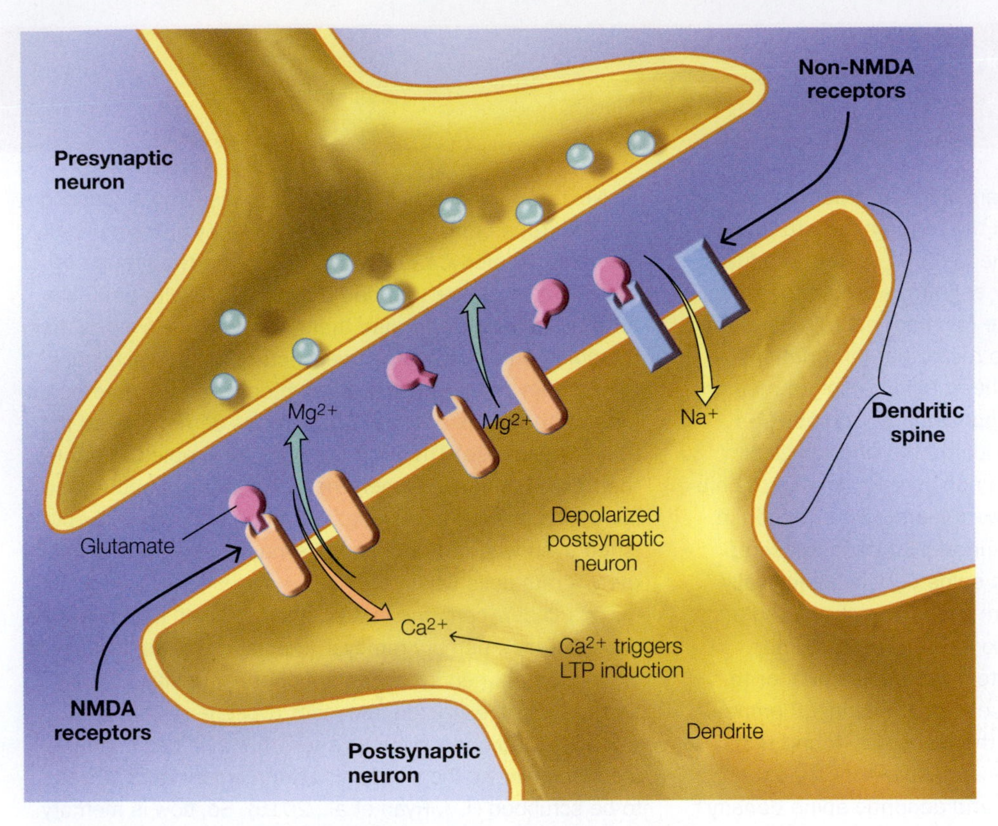

FIGURE 9.42 The role of Mg^{2+} and Ca^{2+} in the functioning of the NMDA receptor.
See text for details.

receptors and prompts more glutamate to be released presynaptically. Or perhaps changes in the physical characteristics of the dendritic spines transmit EPSPs more effectively to the dendrites. Finally, via a message from the postsynaptic cell to the presynaptic cell, the efficiency of presynaptic neurotransmitter release is increased.

Long-Term Potentiation and Memory Performance

With a candidate cellular mechanism for long-term plastic changes in synaptic strength identified, it should be possible to produce deficits in learning and memory, which can be demonstrated behaviorally by the elimination of LTP. Chemically blocking LTP in the hippocampus of normal mice impairs their ability to demonstrate normal place learning; thus, blocking LTP prevents normal spatial memory. In a similar way, genetic manipulations that block the cascade of molecular triggers for LTP also impair spatial learning. These experiments provide strong evidence that blocking NMDA receptors and thus preventing LTP impairs spatial learning.

NMDA receptors in the CA1 region of the hippocampus are necessary for most forms of synaptic plasticity, and their activation is required for spatial and contextual learning. Once learning has occurred, however, new memories can be formed without their activation. This surprising finding came from two classic water maze studies (Bannerman et al., 1995; Saucier & Cain, 1995). Both experiments found that pharmacological NMDA receptor blockers did not stop rodents that had been pretrained to navigate in one water maze from learning how to navigate in a second maze; the animals were able to develop a new spatial map even when LTP was prevented. The conclusion is that NMDA receptors may be needed to learn a spatial strategy but not to encode a new map.

In another experiment, when mice were pretrained with a nonspatial task, spatial memory was not interrupted by the introduction of an NMDA antagonist. The conclusion is that the pretraining merely allowed the motor-related side effects of NMDA receptor blockage to be avoided. Although neither study excluded the possibility that new spatial learning involves NMDA receptors, they pointed to at least two memory systems that could use NMDA receptors. These systems participate in the water maze task, but they might be consolidated by pretraining.

On the cellular and behavioral levels, the role of LTP in memory is still being unraveled. Whether the maintenance of LTP is located presynaptically or postsynaptically, and even whether LTP is necessary for spatial memory, is the subject of much debate. Daniel Zamanillo and his colleagues at the Max Planck Institute in Heidelberg, Germany (1999), used gene knockout protocols to study mice that could not produce LTP in the synapses of neurons between the CA3 and CA1 regions of the hippocampus. Behaviorally, however, these mice could learn spatial tasks just as easily as normal control mice could.

David Bannerman and his colleagues (2012) found that genetically modified mice, which lacked NMDA receptor function in hippocampal CA1 and dentate gyrus granule cells, could not produce LTP in the neurons in these two regions. These mice performed as well as controls in a water maze learning and memory task. Where the mice showed impairment was in the radial arm maze—a circular arena, rather like the hub of a wagon wheel, with six identical arms radiating from it.

Like the water maze, the radial arm maze has physical identifiers in the larger environment in which the maze sits. Food rewards are put at the end of three of the corridors. In this type of maze, the NMDA knockout mice showed little improvement in identifying the corridors with the food. By contrast, controls were able to learn to pick the right corridor and rarely erred. Why the difference in learning success? The researchers suggested that the problem lies in choosing between ambiguous local cues—that is, the six identical corridors—and more distant predictive cues.

To test this idea, they used a modified water maze that added ambiguous local cues. A small local cue was put above the platform, and the same cue, a faux cue, was placed at the opposite end of the tank. The mice were dropped into the water at different positions in the maze. Although both the controls and the genetically modified mice could find the platform, when they were dropped near the faux cue the knockout mice were more likely to swim to the faux cue. The control mice (using their spatial memory) were not influenced by the faux cue, and instead swam to the platform. It appears, then, that the mice lacking the NMDA receptor function are able to form spatial memories, but they don't use them when confronted with ambiguous local cues, suggesting that the NMDA receptor function is more subtle than previously thought (Mayford, 2012). Martine Migaud and colleagues at the University of Edinburgh (1998) studied mice with enhanced LTP and found that they exhibited severe impairments in spatial learning.

Although much remains to be understood about the cellular and molecular basis of learning, two points of agreement are that (a) LTP does exist at the cellular level, and (b) NMDA receptors play a crucial role in LTP induction in many pathways of the brain. Because LTP is also found in brain areas outside of the hippocampal system, the possibility that LTP forms the basis for long-term modification within synaptic networks remains promising.

TAKE-HOME MESSAGES

- In Hebbian learning, if a synapse is active when a postsynaptic neuron is active, the synapse will be strengthened. Long-term potentiation is the long-term strengthening of a synapse.
- NMDA receptors are central to producing LTP but not to maintaining it.

Summary

The ability to acquire new information and the ability to retain it over time define learning and memory, respectively. Cognitive theory and neuroscientific evidence argue that memory is supported by multiple cognitive and neural systems. These systems support different aspects of memory, and their distinctions in quality can be readily identified. Sensory registration, perceptual representation, short-term and working memory, procedural memory, semantic memory, and episodic memory all represent systems or subsystems for learning and memory. The brain structures that support various memory processes differ, depending on the type of information to be retained and how it is encoded and retrieved.

The biological memory system includes (a) the medial temporal lobe, which forms and consolidates new episodic and perhaps semantic memories, and which contains the hippocampus, involved in binding together the relationships among different types of information (Figure 9.2); (b) the parietal cortex, which is involved in the encoding and retrieving of episodic or contextual memory; (c) the prefrontal cortex, which is involved in encoding and retrieving information on the basis of, perhaps, the nature of the material being processed; (d) the temporal cortex, which stores episodic and semantic knowledge; and (e) the association sensory cortices for the effects of perceptual priming. Other cortical and subcortical structures participate in the learning of skills and habits, especially those that require implicit motor learning.

Not all areas of the brain have the same potential for storing information, and although widespread brain areas cooperate in learning and memory, the individual structures form systems that support and enable rather specific memory processes. At the cellular level, although changes in synaptic strength between neurons in neural networks in the medial temporal lobe, neocortex, cerebellum, and elsewhere have traditionally been considered the most likely mechanisms for learning and memory storage, recent evidence indicates that while synaptic strength may mediate memory retrieval, other mechanisms are involved in memory storage. Bit by bit, we are developing a better understanding of the molecular processes that support synaptic plasticity, and thus learning and memory, in the brain.

Key Terms

Think About It

1. Compare and contrast the different forms of memory in terms of their time course. Does the fact that some memories last seconds while others last a lifetime necessarily imply that different neural systems mediate the two forms of memory?
2. Patient H.M. and others with damage to the medial temporal lobe develop amnesia. What form of amnesia do they develop? For example, is it like the amnesia most often shown in Hollywood movies? What information can these amnesic patients retain, what can they learn, and what do the answers to these questions tell us about how memories are encoded in the brain?
3. Can you ride a bike? Do you remember learning to ride it? Can you describe to others the principles of riding a bike? Do you think that, if you gave a detailed set of instructions to another person who had never ridden a bike, she could carefully study your instructions and then hop on a bike and happily ride off into the sunset? If not, why not?
4. Describe the subdivisions of the medial temporal lobe and how they contribute to long-term memory. Consider both encoding and retrieval.
5. Relate models of long-term potentiation (LTP) to changing weights in connectionist networks. What constraints do cognitive neuroscience findings place on connectionist models of memory?

Suggested Reading

Aggleton, J. P., & Brown, M. W. (2006). Interleaving brain systems for episodic and recognition memory. *Trends in Cognitive Sciences*, *10*, 455–463.

Collingridge, G. L., & Bliss, T. V. P. (1995). Memories of NMDA receptors and LTP. *Trends in Neurosciences*, *18*, 54–56.

Corkin, S. (2002). What's new with the amnesic patient H.M.? *Nature Reviews Neuroscience*, *3*, 153–160.

Eichenbaum, H., Yonelinas, A. P., & Ranganath, C. (2007). The medial temporal lobe and recognition memory. *Annual Review of Neuroscience*, *30*, 123–152.

McClelland, J. L. (2000). Connectionist models of memory. In E. Tulving & F. I. M. Craik (Eds.), *The Oxford handbook of memory* (pp. 583–596). New York: Oxford University Press.

Moser, E. I., Moser, M. B., & McNaughton, B. L. (2017). Spatial representation in the hippocampal formation: A history. *Nature Neuroscience*, *20*, 1448–1464.

Nadel, L., & Hardt, O. (2011). Update on memory systems and processes. *Neuropsychopharmacology*, *36*, 251–273.

Queenan, B. N., Ryan, T. J., Gazzaniga, M. S., & Gallistel, C. R. (2017). On the research of time past: The hunt for the substrate of memory. *Annals of the New York Academy of Sciences*, *1396*(1), 108–125.

Ranganath, C., & Blumenfeld, R. S. (2005). Doubts about double dissociations between short- and long-term memory. *Trends in Cognitive Sciences*, *9*, 374–380.

Ranganath, C., & Ritchey, M. (2012). Two cortical systems for memory-guided behaviour. *Nature Reviews Neuroscience*, *13*, 713–726.

Ryan, T. J., Roy, D. S., Pignatelli, M., Arons, A., & Tonegawa, S. (2015). Engram cells retain memory under retrograde amnesia. *Science*, *348*(6238), 1007–1013.

Schreiner, T., & Rasch, B. (2017). The beneficial role of memory reactivation for language learning during sleep: A review. *Brain and Language*, *167*, 94–105.

Squire, L. (2006). Lost forever or temporarily misplaced? The long debate about the nature of memory impairment. *Learning and Memory*, *13*, 522–529.

Squire, L. (2008). The legacy of H.M. *Neuron*, *61*, 6–9.

Any emotion, if it is sincere, is involuntary.

Mark Twain

When dealing with people, remember you are not dealing with creatures of logic, but creatures of emotion.

Dale Carnegie

CHAPTER

10

Emotion

WHEN SHE WAS 42 YEARS OLD, S.M. couldn't remember actually having felt scared since she was 10. This is not because she has not been in frightening circumstances since then; she has been in plenty. She has been held at both knife- and gunpoint, physically accosted by a woman twice her size, and nearly killed in a domestic-violence attack, among multiple other frightening experiences.

S.M. has a rare autosomal recessive genetic disorder, Urbach–Wiethe disease, that leads to degeneration of the amygdalae, typically with an onset at about 10 years of age. Because S.M. doesn't notice that things don't frighten her, she didn't realize anything was wrong until she was 20, when she started having seizures. A CT scan and an MRI revealed highly specific lesions: Both of her amygdalae were severely atrophied, yet the surrounding white matter showed minimal damage.

Standard neuropsychological tests on S.M. revealed normal intelligence, perception, and motor ability, but something curious popped up during tests of her emotion processing: When asked to judge the emotion being expressed on the faces in a series of photographs, she accurately identified expressions conveying sadness, anger, disgust, happiness, and surprise, but one expression stumped her. Although she knew that an emotion was being expressed on those faces and she was capable of recognizing the facial identities, she could not recognize fear. S.M. also had a related deficit: When asked to draw pictures depicting different emotions, she was able to provide reasonable cartoons of a range of states, but not fear. When prodded to try, she eventually drew a picture of a crawling baby but couldn't say why (**Figure 10.1**).

S.M. was able to process the concept of fear. She was able to describe situations that would elicit fear, could describe fear properly, and had no trouble labeling fearful tones in voices. She even stated that she "hated" snakes and spiders and tried to avoid them. Yet, contrary to her declarations, when taken to an exotic

BIG Questions

- What is an emotion?
- What role do emotions play in behavior?
- How are emotions generated?
- Is emotion processing localized, generalized, or a combination of the two?
- What effect does emotion have on the cognitive processes of perception, attention, learning, memory, and decision making, and on our behavior? What effect do these cognitive processes exert over our emotions?

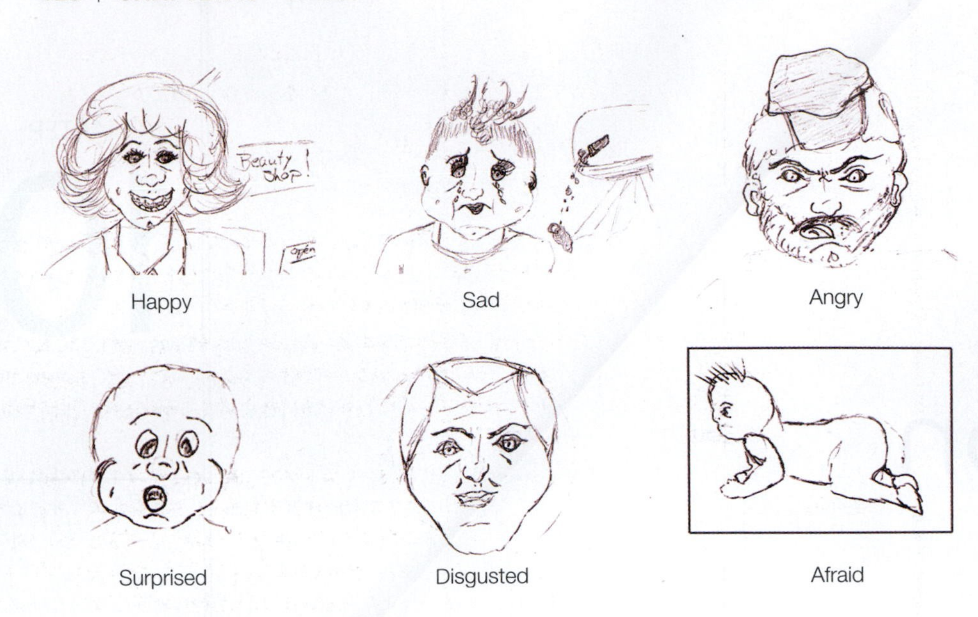

FIGURE 10.1 S.M.'s deficit in comprehending fear is also observed on a production task.
S.M. was asked to draw faces that depicted basic emotions. When prompted to draw a person who was afraid, she hesitated and then produced a picture of a baby. She was, however, not happy with her drawing of "afraid."

pet store, she spontaneously went to the snakes and readily held one, rubbed its scales, and touched its tongue, commenting, "This is so cool!" Was her inability to experience fear due to a lack of experience with it? No, she described being cornered by a growling Doberman pinscher when she was a child (before her disease manifested itself), screaming for her mother, and crying, along with all the accompanying visceral fear reactions. Perhaps this is why she drew a toddler when asked to depict fear.

Even though S.M. understands the concept of fear and has been studied extensively since 1990, she continues to have no insight into her deficit and is unaware that she still becomes involved in precarious situations. It seems that because she cannot experience fear, she does not avoid dangerous situations. What part does the amygdala play in the emotion of fear? Does it have a role in other emotions?

We begin this chapter with some attempts to define emotion. Then we review the areas of the brain that are thought to mediate emotion processing. We also survey the theories about emotions and discuss whether some emotions are universal, whether they have specific circuits, and how they are generated. A good deal of research on emotion has concentrated on the workings of the amygdala, so we examine this part of the brain in some detail. We also look at how emotions affect the cognitive processes of perception, attention, learning, memory, and decision making, and thus behavior. Finally, we take a quick look at other areas of the brain involved in emotions other than fear, and we consider whether cognitive processes exert any control over our emotions.

10.1 What Is an Emotion?

People have been struggling to define emotion for several thousand years. While the layperson can easily identify an emotion, and emotion has been an actively researched topic for the past 40 years, there is still no consensus on its definition. In the *Handbook of Emotions* (3rd ed.), the late philosopher Robert Solomon (2008) devoted an entire chapter to discussing why emotion is so difficult to define.

As a psychological state, emotion has some unique qualities that have to be taken into account. Emotions are embodied; that is, you feel them. They are uniquely recognizable; that is, they are associated with characteristic facial expressions and behavioral patterns of comportment and arousal. They are triggered by emotionally salient stimuli, which are highly relevant for the well-being and survival of the observer—and they can be triggered without warning. Emotions are less susceptible to our intentions than other states are, and they have global effects on virtually all other aspects of cognition (Dolan, 2002).

Evolutionary principles might suggest a general, though vague, definition: Emotions are neurological processes that have evolved to guide behavior in such a manner as to increase survival and reproduction; for example, they improve our ability to learn from the environment and the past. But while this helps us understand their effect, it does not tell us what they are.

How would you define emotion? Maybe your definition starts, "An emotion is a feeling you get when . . ." In that case, we already have a problem, because many researchers claim that a **feeling** is the subjective experience of the emotion, not the emotion itself. These two events are dissociable and they use separate neural systems. Another problem is that researchers do not yet agree on the components of emotions. They also dispute whether the entire constellation of the components and associated behaviors is the emotion, or whether emotion is a state that puts the others in play. Finally, it is debated whether there are specific circuits for specific emotions, and to what extent cognition is involved. As all this makes plain, the study of emotion is a messy and contentious business with plenty of job security.

In 2010, research psychologist Carroll Izard was concerned that researchers attributed different meanings to the word *emotion*, contributing to the oft-expressed notion that there are as many theories of emotions as there are emotion theorists, so he decided to seek a consensus on its definition (Izard, 2010). After querying 35 distinguished scientists in the various disciplines and specialties concerned with emotions, he couldn't quite come up with a definition, but he at least put together a description that contained many aspects of "emotion":

> Emotion consists of neural circuits (that are at least partially dedicated), response systems, and a feeling state/process that motivates and organizes cognition and action. Emotion also provides information to the person experiencing it, and may include antecedent cognitive appraisals and ongoing cognition including an interpretation of its feeling state, expressions or social-communicative signals, and may motivate approach or avoidant behavior, exercise control/regulation of responses, and be social or relational in nature. (Izard, 2010)

Most current models posit that **emotions** are valenced responses (positive or negative) to external stimuli and/or internal mental representations that

- Involve changes across multiple response systems (e.g., experiential, behavioral, peripheral, physiological)
- Are distinct from moods, in that they often have identifiable objects or triggers
- Can be either unlearned responses to stimuli with intrinsic affective properties (e.g., smiling after your very first taste of sugar), or learned responses to stimuli with acquired emotional value (e.g., fear when you see a dog that previously bit you)
- Can involve multiple types of appraisal processes that assess the significance of stimuli to current goals
- Depend on different neural systems (Oschner & Gross, 2005)

Most who study emotion in nonhuman animals do not fully agree with this model. For example, an opposing model that suggests something quite different comes from California Institute of Technology researchers David Anderson and Ralph Adolphs (2014). While they agree that emotions involve highly coordinated behavior, body, and brain effects, they disagree that these various effects are part of the emotion state. They view them as the result or consequence of the emotion state. They argue the following:

- An "emotion" constitutes an internal, central (as in central nervous system) state.
- This state is triggered by specific stimuli (extrinsic or intrinsic to the organism).
- This state is encoded by the activity of particular neural circuits.
- Activation of these specific circuits gives rise, in a causal sense, to externally observable behaviors, and to separately (but simultaneously) associated cognitive, somatic, and physiological responses (**Figure 10.2**).

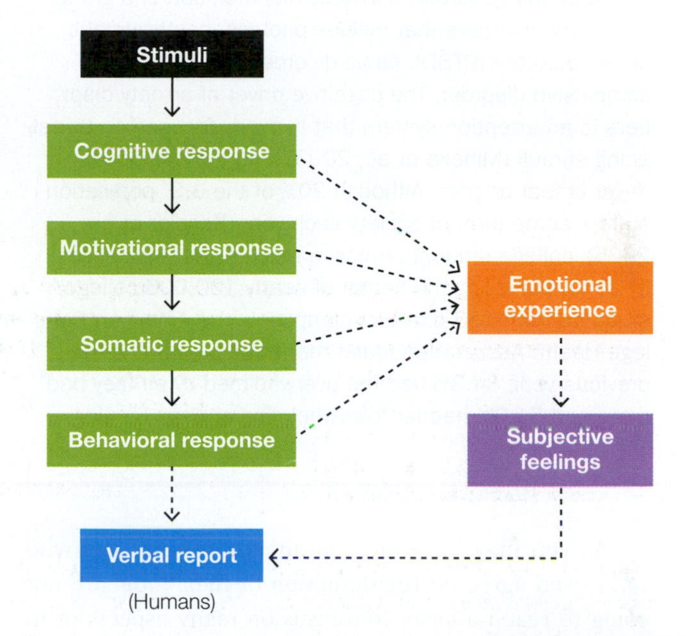

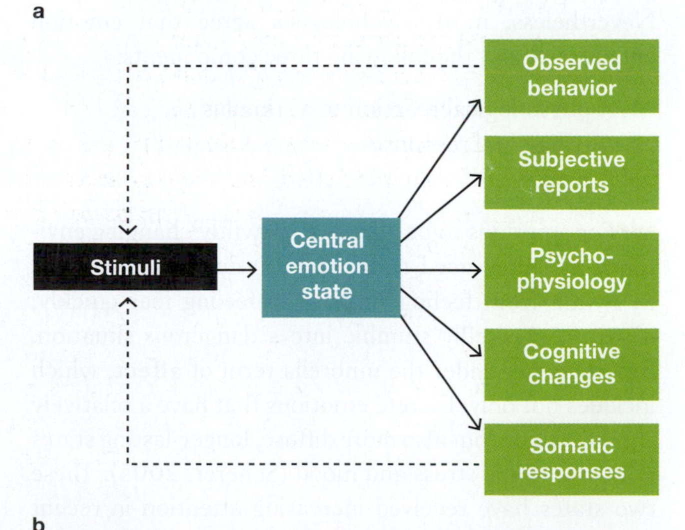

FIGURE 10.2 The causal flow of emotion postulated by Anderson and Adolphs.
(a) The conventional view of emotion reflects theories in which emotions have multiple components that need to be coordinated. (b) Anderson and Adolphs propose that a central emotion state causes multiple parallel responses.

BOX 10.1 | HOT SCIENCE
Tech Stress

Elena, a sophomore in college, feels overwhelmed by her classes and constantly worries about losing her scholarship or not getting into graduate school if her grades fall short. She did well in high school, but since moving away to college, she has found it difficult to manage her study time and social life. She feels nervous all the time, has a hard time getting to sleep, and finds it difficult to concentrate both during lectures and while studying, making her feel even more anxious. Occasionally her heart races and her palms get sweaty.

Elena has generalized anxiety disorder, one of a group of anxiety disorders that include phobias, posttraumatic stress disorder (PTSD), panic disorder, and obsessive-compulsive disorder. The cognitive driver of anxiety disorders is an attention system that is overly focused on threatening stimuli (Mineka et al., 2003), and the emotional driver is fear or grief. Although 20% of the U.S. population suffers some form of anxiety each year (Kessler et al., 2005), college students report a much higher incidence. In 2013, surveying the health of nearly 100,000 college students from 153 different campuses, the American College Health Association found that at some point in the previous year, 84.3% had felt overwhelmed by all they had to do and 51.3% had felt overwhelming anxiety. Similar statistics were reported in 2016, though the sample size was smaller.

Why the increased incidence of anxiety in college students? Theories abound. One points the finger at "helicopter" parents who, though well-intentioned, push their children academically and micromanage their lives. A study found that when these children are in college, they are more likely to be medicated for anxiety and depression (LeMoyne & Buchanan, 2011). Some researchers speculate that because these students never had to solve problems on their own, they are unable to do so in college, becoming anxious when facing difficult situations such as a problem roommate, or when needing to prioritize activities.

Evidence for this idea comes from researchers who found that children who spend more time in less structured activities develop better executive functioning than those who spend more time in structured activities (Barker et al., 2014). *Executive function* (see Chapter 12) refers to cognitive control processes that support goal-directed behavior, such as attention; planning and decision making; maintenance and manipulation of information in memory; inhibition of unwanted thoughts, feelings, and actions; and flexible shifting from one task to another.

As you may have intuited already, researchers who can't even agree on the definition of their topic are not going to reach a clear consensus on many aspects of it. Nevertheless, most psychologists agree that emotion entails (at least) the following three components:

1. A physiological reaction to a stimulus
2. A behavioral response
3. A feeling

For emotions to be adaptive in swiftly changing environments, they need to be short in duration. We need to switch from feeling surprise to feeling fear quickly, if we unexpectedly stumble into a dangerous situation. Emotions fall under the umbrella term of **affect**, which includes not only discrete emotions that have a relatively short duration, but also more diffuse, longer-lasting states such as chronic stress and mood (Scherer, 2005). These two states have received increasing attention in recent years, so we will take a moment to define them here.

Encountering a stimulus or event that threatens us in some way—whether a snarling dog, public speaking, or a gravely ill relative—triggers **stress**, a fixed pattern of physiological and neurohormonal changes (Ulrich-Lai & Herman, 2009). These changes disrupt homeostasis, leading to immediate activation of the sympathetic nervous system's fight-or-flight responses, but also to activation of the hypothalamic-pituitary-adrenal (HPA) axis and release of stress hormones, such as cortisol. Cortisol has many effects on the body, including increasing blood glucose levels and decreasing inflammatory responses, which are adaptive for an acute situation. These changes can lead to a state that can last for many minutes, or even hours (Dickerson & Kemeny, 2004).

If the stress system is in fine fettle, the cortisol feeds back an inhibitory signal to the hypothalamus that shuts down the HPA response, marking the end of the acute episode and restoring homeostasis. With frequent or chronic stress, however, another picture emerges. While the acute stress response is adaptive, chronic levels of stress may lead to changes in HPA axis functioning and sustained release of cortisol and other stress hormones. The chronically elevated level of cortisol can lead to medical disorders such as insulin resistance and weight gain, decreased immunity, and high blood pressure, as well as to mood and anxiety disorders (McEwen, 1998, 2003; see **Box 10.1**). A great deal of recent research has focused on how stress impacts cognitive functions, such as memory and decision making.

A **mood** is a long-lasting diffuse affective state that is characterized by primarily a predominance of enduring

Others wonder how much of the increase in anxiety can be attributed to the increased use of electronic technology. Nearly half of individuals born since 1980 feel moderately to highly anxious if they can't check their text messages every 15 minutes (L. D. Rosen et al., 2013). If heavy smartphone users have their phones confiscated or merely placed out of sight, they exhibit measurable levels of anxiety within 10 minutes, which increase as time passes or if the users are prevented from answering a call (Cheever et al., 2014). An Australian study found that students studying in a computer lab spent an average of only 2.3 minutes on a study task before switching tasks—usually to checking e-mail, looking at social media, or texting (Judd, 2014).

Some studies (see Chapter 12) have found that people who switch tasks frequently between electronic media are less able to ignore distracting stimuli (Cain & Mitroff, 2011; Moisala et al., 2016; Ophir et al., 2009), report frequent mind wandering and attention failures in everyday life (Ralph et al., 2014), and exhibit a generalized reduction in coding and retrieving of information in working and long-term memory (Uncapher et al., 2016). Using fMRI, University of Helsinki researchers reported that in the presence of distracting stimuli, frequent media multitaskers performed worse on cognitive tasks and had increased brain activity in the right prefrontal regions, brain areas involved with attentional and inhibitory control, suggesting that frequent media multitaskers require more effort or top-down attentional control to perform tasks when any distractions are present (Moisala et al., 2016).

Currently we don't know the direction of causality: Frequent multitasking behaviors may lead to reduced cognitive control, or people who have decreased cognitive control may indulge in more frequent media multitasking activity. Adam Gazzaley and Larry Rosen (2016) suggest that the ability to socially connect at any time via technology has pressured us to expect more social interactions, resulting in increased anxiety when communication with the social network is decreased or cut—the fear of missing out. And fear of poor performance is not unreasonable when we consider the effects on learning that increased distractibility, less time spent on task, and less effective working and long-term memory have. With fear being the emotional driver of anxiety, the case can be made that technology has contributed to the increased anxiety in both the social and academic lives of college students like Elena.

subjective feelings without an identifiable object or trigger. While moods generally are of low intensity, they may last hours or days and can affect a person's experience and behavior. Unlike stress, moods do not have a well-defined neurohormonal or physiological substrate, and the neural correlates of different moods are still poorly understood. We can induce moods in the lab by having people watch film clips (e.g., a scene from the movie *The Champ* might bring on a sad mood; Lerner et al., 2004), or by asking them to write about personal events (see, for example, DeSteno et al., 2014).

TAKE-HOME MESSAGES

- The word *emotion* has eluded a consensus definition.
- Three commonly agreed-upon components of emotion are a physiological reaction to a stimulus, a behavioral response, and a feeling.
- The acute stress response is adaptive, but chronic stress can result in medical, mood, and anxiety disorders.
- Moods are diffuse, long-lasting emotional states that do not have an identifiable object or trigger.

10.2 Neural Systems Involved in Emotion Processing

Since there is no set agreement on what an emotion is, identifying the neural systems involved in emotion processing is difficult. Other problems contribute to this haziness: technical issues with the various methods used to study emotion; controversies over whether emotional feelings, which are subjective, can be studied in animals or only in humans, who can report them (LeDoux, 2012); and the various interpretations of research findings. An ever-growing number of imaging studies have found that emotional processes, at least in humans, are intertwined with many other mental functions. Accordingly, our emotions involve many parts of the nervous system, including both subcortical and cortical structures, depending on one's definition.

When emotions are triggered by an external event or stimulus (e.g., a crying baby), our sensory systems play a role; with an internal stimulus, such as an episodic memory (e.g., remembering your first kiss), our memory systems are involved. The physiological components of emotion that produce physical feelings (e.g., the shiver up the spine and the dry mouth that people experience with fear) involve the autonomic nervous system (ANS), a division of the peripheral nervous system.

Recall from Chapter 2 that the ANS, with all its subcortical circuits, is made up of the sympathetic and parasympathetic nervous systems (see Figure 2.18), and that its motor and sensory neurons extend to the heart, lungs, gut, bladder, and sexual organs. The two systems work in combination to achieve homeostasis. As a rule of thumb, the sympathetic system promotes the fight-or-flight response (which uses the motor system), and the parasympathetic system promotes the rest-and-digest response.

The ANS is regulated by the hypothalamus, which also controls the release of multiple hormones through the HPA axis, made up of the paraventricular nucleus (PVN) of the hypothalamus, the anterior lobe of the pituitary gland, and the cortex of the adrenal glands, which sit above the kidneys. For example, the PVN contains neurons that make corticotropin-releasing factor (CRF). Descending from the PVN, axonal projections stretch to the anterior pituitary gland. If the PVN is activated by a stressor, CRF is released and, in a domino effect, causes the pituitary gland to release adrenocorticotropic hormone (ACTH) into the bloodstream, which carries it to the adrenal glands (and other locations throughout the body). In the adrenal glands, ACTH triggers the adrenal cortex to release stress hormones, such as cortisol. Through negative feedback to the PVN, elevated levels of cortisol inhibit the release of CRF, turning off the response.

Arousal is a critical part of many theories on emotion. The arousal system is regulated by the reticular activating system, which is composed of sets of neurons running from the brainstem to the cortex via the rostral intralaminar and thalamic nuclei. All of the neural systems mentioned so far are important in triggering an emotion or in generating physiological and behavioral responses. But can we be more specific about where emotions are produced in the brain? We turn to that question next.

Early Concepts: The Limbic System as the Emotional Brain

The notion that emotion is separate from cognition and has its own network of brain structures that underlie emotional behavior is not new. As we mentioned in Chapter 2, James Papez proposed a circuit theory of the brain and emotion in 1937, suggesting that emotional responses involve a network of brain regions made up of the hypothalamus, anterior thalamus, cingulate gyrus, and hippocampus.

Paul MacLean (1949, 1952), a physician and neuroscientist, hypothesized that the human brain had three regions that had developed gradually and sequentially over the course of evolution. His studies suggested that evolution had left its footprints on the brain's anatomy, histology, structure, and function, with the conserved ancient systems located medially and caudally, and more recent systems situated to the side and rostrally. He became convinced that conserved ancient systems exist in humans just as they do in other mammals, are comparable, and are responsible for the primary social emotions.

MacLean used the term *limbic system* (from the Latin *limbus*, meaning "rim") to describe the complex neural circuits involved with the processing of emotion. The structures of the limbic system roughly form a rim around the corpus callosum (see the "Anatomical Orientation" box on p. 433; also see Figure 2.32). In addition to the Papez circuit, MacLean extended the emotional network to include what he called the visceral brain: most of the medial surface of the cortex, some subcortical nuclei, and portions of the basal ganglia, the amygdala, and the orbitofrontal cortex.

MacLean's work identifying the limbic system as the "emotional" brain was influential. To this day, studies on the neural basis of emotion include references to the "limbic system" or "limbic" structures, and his work continues to influence those who seek to understand the evolved nature of emotions (Panksepp, 2002). The limbic system structures as strictly outlined by MacLean, however, had some errors (Brodal, 1982; Kotter & Meyer, 1992; LeDoux, 1991; Swanson, 1983).

We now know that many brainstem nuclei that are connected to the hypothalamus are not part of the limbic system, and that some brainstem nuclei that are involved in autonomic reactions were not included in MacLean's model. At the same time, a few classic limbic areas have been shown to be more important for other, nonemotional processes, as with the hippocampus and memory, although the hippocampus does play an important part in emotional learning as well. For some researchers, MacLean's concept has proved to be more descriptive and historical than functional, while for others it is foundational to their approach, depending on their concepts of emotion.

Early attempts to identify neural circuits of emotion viewed emotion as a unitary concept that could be localized to one specific circuit or circuits, such as the limbic system. Viewing the "emotional brain" as separate from the rest of the brain spawned a locationist view of emotions. The locationist account hypothesizes that all mental states belonging to the same emotion category, such as fear, are produced by activity that is recurrently associated with specific neural circuits—and that these circuits, when activated, produce behavior that has been evolutionarily successful, is an inherited trait, and exhibits homologies that are seen in other mammalian species (Panksepp, 1998).

ANATOMICAL ORIENTATION

Anatomy of Emotion

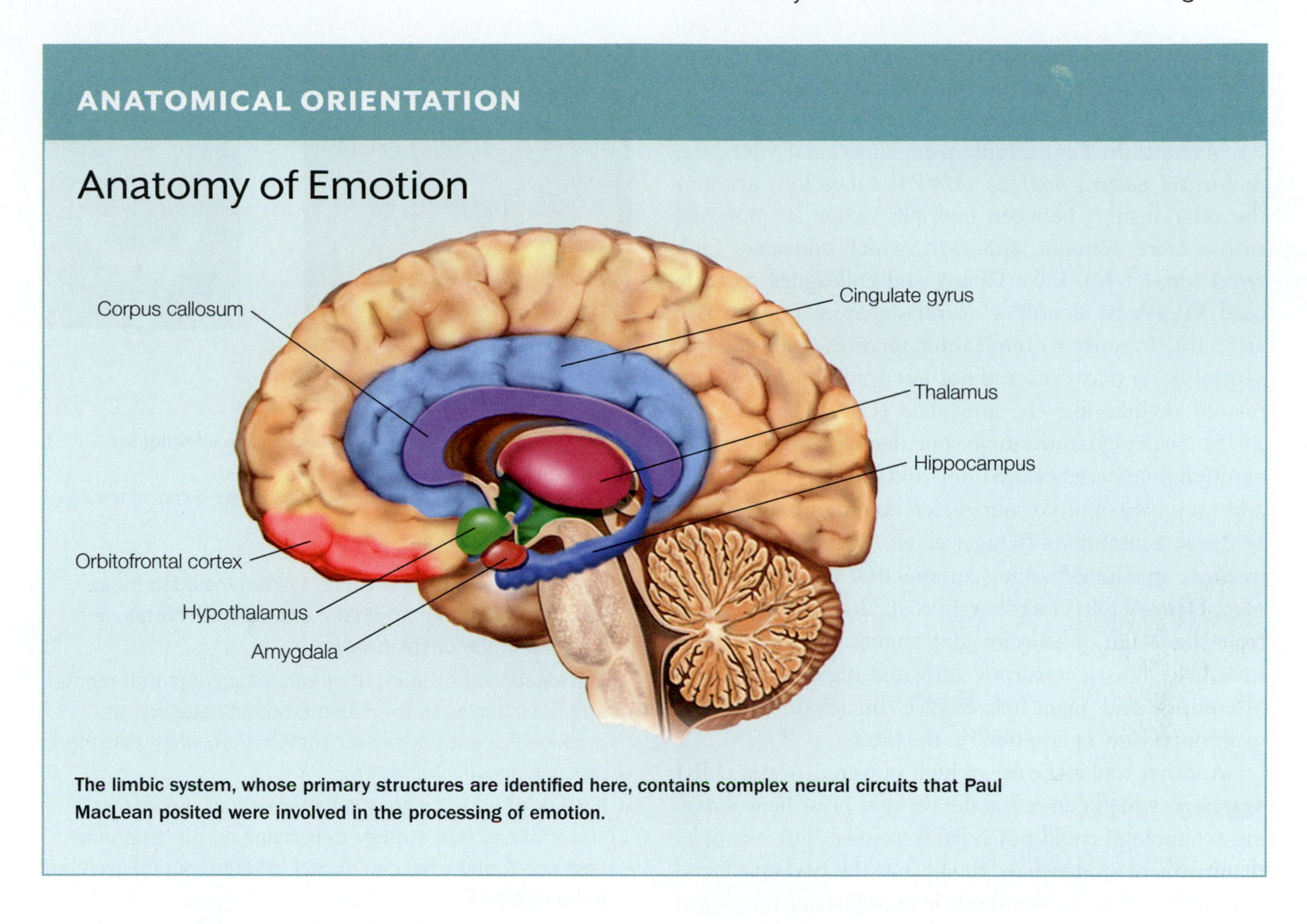

The limbic system, whose primary structures are identified here, contains complex neural circuits that Paul MacLean posited were involved in the processing of emotion.

Emerging Concepts of Emotional Networks

Over the last several decades, scientific investigations of emotion have focused more on human emotion specifically and have become more detailed and complex. By measuring brain responses to emotionally salient stimuli, researchers have revealed a complex interconnected network involved in the *analysis* of emotional stimuli. This network includes the thalamus, the somatosensory cortex, higher-order sensory cortices, the amygdala, the insular cortex (also called the insula), the ventral striatum, and the medial prefrontal cortex, including the orbitofrontal cortex and anterior cingulate cortex (ACC).

Those who study emotion acknowledge that it is a multifaceted concept that may vary along a spectrum from basic to more complex. Indeed, S.M.'s isolated emotional deficit in fear recognition after bilateral amygdala damage (Adolphs et al., 1994, 1995; Tranel & Hyman, 1990; **Figure 10.3**) supports the idea that there is no single emotional circuit. Emotion research now focuses on specific types of emotional tasks and on identifying the neural systems that underlie specific emotional behaviors. Depending on the emotional task or situation, we can expect different neural systems to be involved.

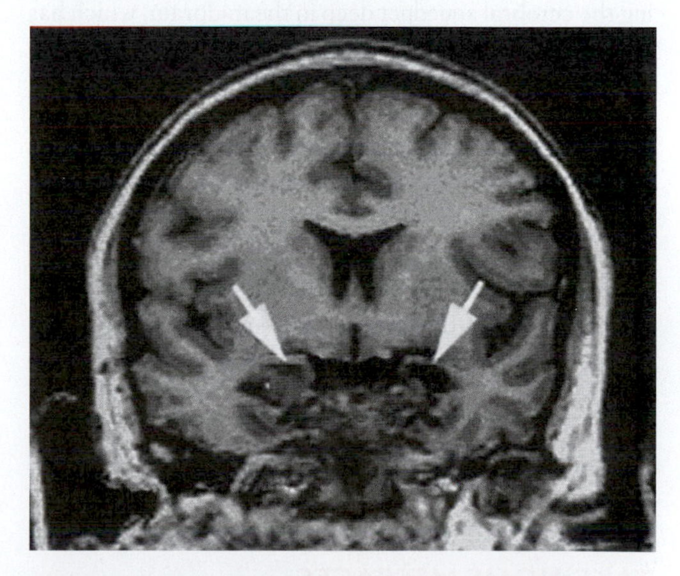

FIGURE 10.3 Bilateral amygdala damage in patient S.M. The white arrows indicate where the amygdalae are located in the right and left hemispheres. Patient S.M. has severe atrophy of the amygdalae, and the brain tissue is now replaced by cerebrospinal fluid (black).

One promising research direction in cognitive neuroscience is the use of machine-learning approaches to recognize patterns and identify neural "signatures" of different emotions. For example, using functional MRI data, *multivoxel pattern analysis (MVPA)* takes into account the relationships between multiple voxels (as opposed to the more common approach, which considers each voxel separately). Luke Chang and colleagues recently used MVPA to identify a neural signature for negative affect in response to unpleasant pictures that spanned several brain networks and not just traditional emotion-related regions like the amygdala (L. J. Chang et al., 2015). Such signatures might one day be used to predict emotional experiences within and across individuals, and may contribute to our understanding of the nature of discrete emotions (Kragel et al., 2016). In addition to these machine-learning approaches, large databases (e.g., NeuroVault; Gorgolewski et al., 2015), storing data from thousands of neuroimaging studies on emotion, can reveal the most *consistently* activated regions in studies of emotion and might help resolve the debate about the locationist view of emotions in the brain.

Another tool is the use of high-powered 7-tesla fMRI scanners, which can reveal details that prior neuroimaging technology could not reliably resolve. For example, many animal studies have found that the periaqueductal gray (PAG) plays a critical role in coordinating emotional responses. The human PAG shares its general architecture not only with other mammals, but with most vertebrates, suggesting that this conserved bit of gray matter has an important emotional function. Yet it is a tiny tube-shaped structure (with an external diameter of 6 mm, an internal diameter of 2 to 3 mm, and a height of 10 mm) surrounding the cerebral aqueduct deep in the midbrain, which has been inaccessible to researchers in live humans.

The PAG was just too small for reliable localization. In 2013, however, with high-powered 7-tesla fMRI, precise localizations of activations in the PAG from emotional stimuli were identified. In fact, discrete activations of its subregions were seen (Satpute et al., 2013; **Figure 10.4**). The subcortical PAG is now recognized to be a hub of emotion processing in humans also.

Finally, researchers who study emotion in other animals are using optogenetic techniques to manipulate neuronal circuits in order to identify the specific behaviors that result from the activation of those circuits (Johansen et al., 2012; Lin et al., 2011).

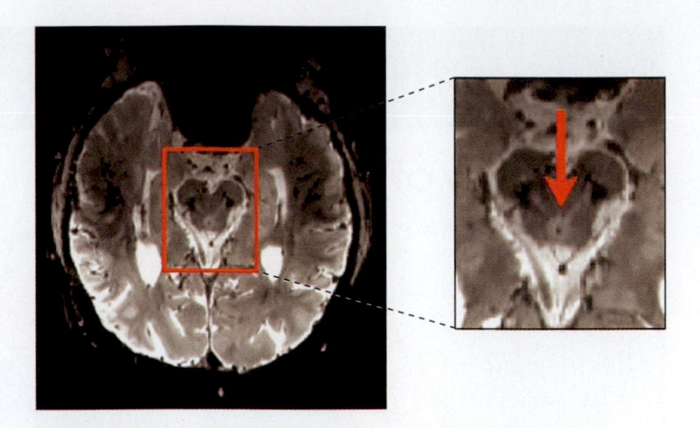

FIGURE 10.4 7-Tesla scan of transaxial slice showing the periaqueductal gray.
The arrow in the enlarged high-resolution image points to the PAG.

TAKE-HOME MESSAGES

- The Papez circuit describes the brain areas that James Papez believed were involved in emotion. They include the hypothalamus, anterior thalamus, cingulate gyrus, and hippocampus. The limbic system includes these structures and the amygdala, orbitofrontal cortex, and portions of the basal ganglia.
- The locationist account of emotion suggests that mental states belonging to the same emotion category are produced by specific neural circuits that, when activated, produce specific behavior.
- Investigators no longer think there is only one neural circuit of emotion. Rather, depending on the emotional task or situation, we can expect different neural systems to be involved.
- Neuroimaging approaches based on machine learning reveal that specific emotional states activate several brain networks.

10.3 Categorizing Emotions

At the core of emotion research is the issue of whether emotions are specific, biologically fundamental, and hard-wired with dedicated brain mechanisms as Darwin supposed, or are states of mind that are assembled from more basic, general causes, as William James suggested. James was of the opinion that emotions are not basic, nor are they found in dedicated neural structures, but are the melding of a mélange of psychological ingredients honed by evolution. As we will soon see, this debate is still ongoing.

In this section we discuss the basic versus dimensional categorization of emotion. *Fearful*, *sad*, *anxious*, *elated*, *disappointed*, *angry*, *shameful*, *disgusted*, *happy*, *pleased*, *excited*, and *infatuated* are some of the terms we use to describe our emotional lives. Unfortunately, our rich language of emotion is difficult to translate into discrete states and variables that can be studied in the laboratory. In an effort to apply some order and uniformity to a definition of emotion, researchers have focused on three primary categories:

1. **Basic emotions**, a closed set of emotions, each with unique characteristics, carved by evolution and reflected through facial expressions
2. **Complex emotions**, combinations of basic emotions, some of which may be socially or culturally learned, that can be identified as evolved, long-lasting feelings
3. **Dimensional theories of emotion** describe emotions that are fundamentally the same but that differ along one or more dimensions, such as valence (pleasant to unpleasant, positive to negative) and arousal (very intense to very mild), in reaction to events or stimuli

Basic Emotions

We may use *delighted*, *joyful*, and *gleeful* to describe how we feel, but most people would agree that all of these words represent a variation of feeling happy. Central to the hypothesis that basic emotions exist is the idea that emotions reflect an inborn instinct. If a relevant stimulus is present, it *will* trigger an evolved brain mechanism in the same way, every time. Thus, we often describe basic emotions as being innate and similar in all humans and many animals. As such, basic emotions exist as entities independent of our perception of them. In this view, each emotion produces predictable changes in sensory, perceptual, motor, and physiological functions that can be measured and thus provide evidence that the emotion exists.

BASIC EMOTIONS IN NONHUMAN ANIMALS Jaak Panksepp defined affects as ancient brain processes for encoding value—that is, as heuristics that the brain uses for making snap judgments about what will enhance or detract from survival (Panksepp & Biven, 2012). He experimentally attempted to study what most cognitive neuroscience researchers shied away from: affective feelings in animals. Disagreeing with researchers who believe that we can gain access to subjective feelings only from verbal reports, he believed that feelings are accompanied by objectively measurable states, if approached indirectly.

Using a learning task, Panksepp found that in all the animal species he tested, electrical stimulation of specific locations within specific subcortical brain structures produced very specific emotional behavioral patterns. The animal reacted as if the generated emotional state was rewarding or punishing, which could be objectively monitored by whether the animal approached or withdrew (Panksepp & Biven, 2012). Panksepp selectively activated rage, fear, separation distress, and generalized seeking patterns of behavior with the flip of a switch. He found that if an electrode stimulated the correct neuroanatomical location, essentially identical emotional tendencies could be evoked in different animal species.

He concluded that there are seven *primary-process emotional systems*, or **core emotional systems**, produced by ancient *subcortical* (unfettered by cognition) neural circuits common to all higher animals, which generate both emotional actions and specific autonomic changes that support those actions. He capitalized the name of each system to indicate that real physical and distinct networks exist for the various emotions in mammalian brains, and he added an elaborating term, calling these systems the *SEEKING/desire* system, *RAGE/anger* system, *FEAR/anxiety* system, *LUST/sex* system, *CARE/maternal nurturance* system, *GRIEF/separation distress* system, and *PLAY/physical social engagement* system. He suggested that humans have the same set of core emotional systems.

Anderson and Adolphs, whose definition of emotion we presented earlier, are not worried about the fact that animals cannot report feelings. One reason for their lack of concern is that they don't much trust humans' reports of their feelings in the first place. Another is that their research suggests that a central emotion state is the causal mechanism engendering feelings along with observed behavior, a psychophysiological reaction, cognitive changes, and somatic responses. It doesn't matter to them that they can't evaluate an animal's feelings, because they can objectively measure these other effects (D. J. Anderson & Adolphs, 2014).

FACIAL EXPRESSIONS AND BASIC EMOTIONS IN HUMANS Darwin argued in *The Expression of the Emotions in Man and Animals* (1872) that human expressions of emotion resembled those of lower animals (**Figure 10.5**). For the past 150 years, many investigators of human emotions have considered **facial expressions** to be one of those predictable changes sparked by an emotional stimulus. Accordingly, research on facial expressions is believed to open an extraordinary window into these basic emotions. This belief is based on the assumption that facial expressions are observable, automatic manifestations that correspond to a person's inner feelings. These investigations into human emotion through facial expression have produced a list of basic emotions somewhat similar to Panksepp's, but more broadly acknowledged.

The earliest research on facial expressions was carried out by Guillaume-Benjamin-Amand Duchenne de Boulogne, a 19th-century French neurologist. One of his patients was an elderly man who suffered from near-total

a

b

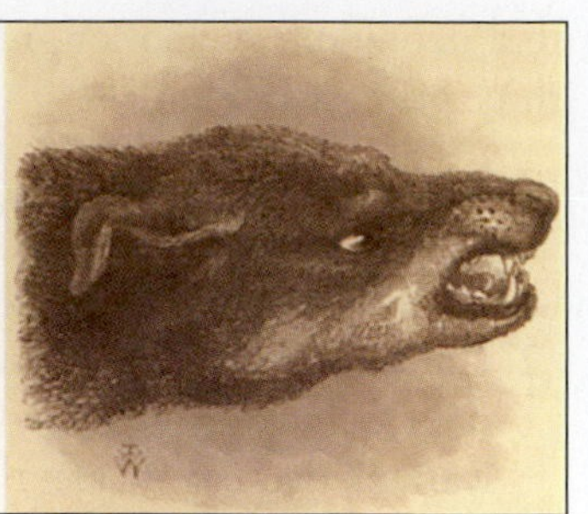

c

FIGURE 10.5 Examples of emotional expressions given by Charles Darwin.
(a) Terror in a human. (b) Disappointment in a chimpanzee. (c) Hostility in a cat and a dog.

facial anesthesia. Duchenne developed a technique to electrically stimulate the man's facial muscles and methodically trigger muscle contractions. He recorded the results with the newly invented camera (**Figure 10.6**) and published his findings in *The Mechanism of Human Facial Expression* (1862).

Duchenne believed that facial expressions revealed underlying emotions, and his studies influenced Darwin's work on the evolutionary basis of human emotional behavior. Darwin had questioned individuals familiar with different cultures about the emotional lives of their members. From these discussions, Darwin determined that humans have evolved to have a finite set of basic emotional states, and that each state is unique in its adaptive significance and physiological expression. The idea that humans have a finite set of universal, basic emotions was born, and this was the idea that William James later protested.

The study of facial expressions was not taken up again until the 1960s, when Paul Ekman, also disagreeing with Darwin, sought evidence for his hypothesis that (a) emotions varied only along a pleasant-to-unpleasant scale; (b) the relationship between a facial expression and what it signified was learned socially; and (c) the meaning of a particular facial expression varied among cultures. He set to work studying cultures from around the world and discovered that, completely counter to all points of his hypothesis, the facial expressions humans use to convey emotion do not vary much from culture to culture. Whether people are from the Bronx, Beijing, or Papua New Guinea, the facial expressions we use to show that we are happy, sad, fearful, disgusted, angry, or surprised are pretty much the same (Ekman & Friesen, 1971; **Figure 10.7**). From this work, Ekman and others suggested that *anger*, *fear*, *sadness*, *disgust*, *happiness*, and *surprise* are the six basic human facial expressions and that each expression represents a basic emotional state (**Table 10.1**). Since then, other emotions have been added as potential candidate basic emotions.

Jessica Tracy and David Matsumoto (2008) provided evidence that might elevate pride and shame to the rank of basic emotions. They looked at the nonverbal expressions of pride or shame in reaction to winning or losing a judo match at the 2004 Olympic and Paralympic Games in contestants from 37 nations. Among the contestants, some were congenitally blind. The researchers assumed that in congenitally blind participants, the body language of their behavioral response was not learned culturally.

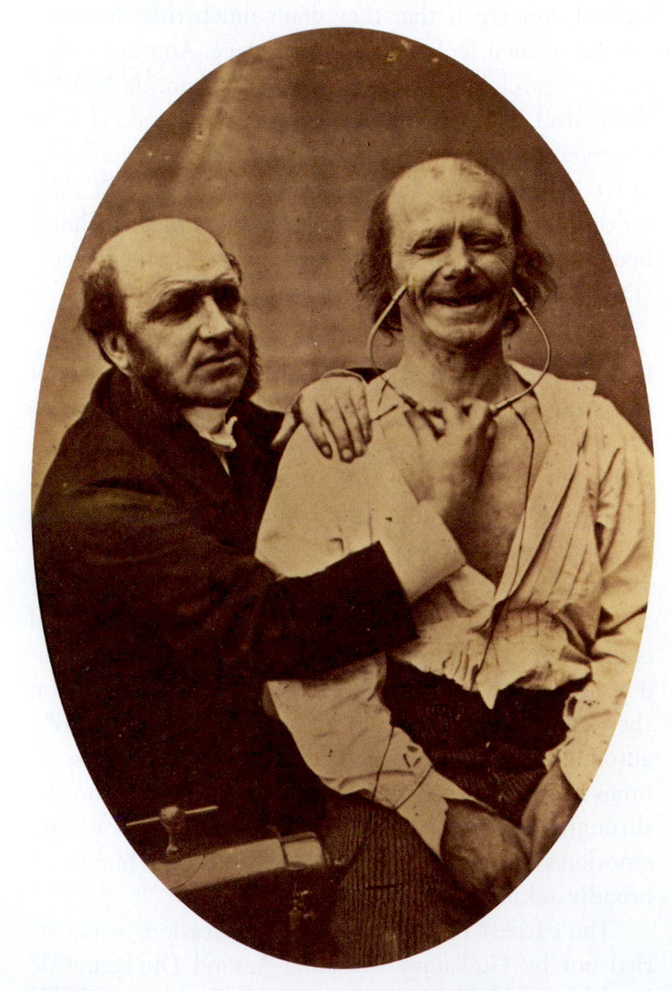

FIGURE 10.6 Duchenne triggering muscle contractions in a patient who had facial anesthesia.

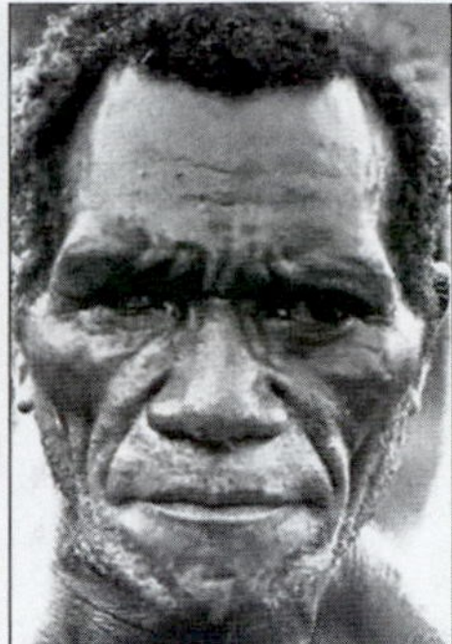
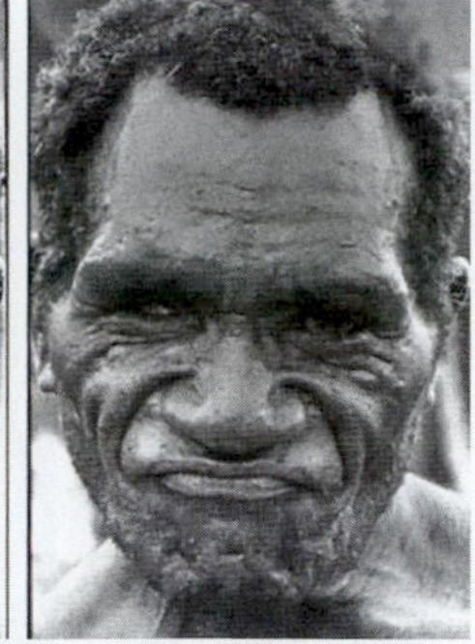

FIGURE 10.7 The universal emotional expressions. The meaning of these facial expressions is similar across all cultures. Can you match the faces to the emotional states of anger, disgust, happiness, and sadness?

TABLE 10.1 Well-Established and Possible Basic Emotions, According to Ekman

Well-Established Basic Emotions	Candidate Basic Emotions
Anger	Contempt
Fear	Shame
Sadness	Guilt
Disgust	Embarrassment
Happiness	Awe
Surprise	Amusement
	Excitement
	Pride in achievement
	Relief
	Satisfaction
	Sensory pleasure
	Enjoyment

SOURCE: Ekman, 1999.

TABLE 10.2 Ekman's Criteria for Basic Emotions

- Distinctive universal signals
- Presence in other primates
- Distinctive physiology
- Distinctive universals in antecedent events
- Rapid onset
- Brief duration
- Automatic appraisal
- Unbidden occurrence

SOURCE: Ekman, 1994.

NOTE: In 1999, Ekman developed three additional criteria: (a) distinctive appearance developmentally; (b) distinctive thoughts, memories, and images; and (c) distinctive subjective experience.

All of the contestants displayed prototypical expressions of pride upon winning (**Figure 10.8**). Most cultures displayed behaviors associated with shame upon losing, though the response was less pronounced in athletes from highly individualistic cultures. This finding suggested to these researchers that behavior associated with pride and shame is innate. Nevertheless, cultural "rules" and developmental factors can shape the experience of pride and shame as well.

Although considerable debate continues as to whether any single list is adequate to capture the full range of human emotional experiences, most scientists accept the idea that all basic emotions share three main characteristics: They are innate, universal, and short-lasting. **Table 10.2** gives a set of criteria that some emotion researchers, such as Ekman, believe are common to all basic emotions.

Some basic emotions, such as fear and anger, have been confirmed in nonhuman mammals, which show dedicated subcortical circuitry for such emotions, as mentioned already. The search for specific physiological reactions for each emotion in humans has been checkered and less fruitful. While Ekman found that humans have specific physiological reactions for anger, fear, and disgust (see Ekman, 1992, for a review), subsequent meta-analyses have not (J. T. Cacioppo et al., 2000; Kreibig, 2010). Although there is a clear relation between emotions and physiological reactions produced by the ANS, the physiological patterns don't always seem to be specific enough to distinguish them in humans. It may be that emotions range on a continuum from discrete to more generalized.

Complex Emotions

Even if we accept that basic emotions exist, we are still faced with identifying which emotions are basic and which are complex (Ekman, 1992; Ortigue, Bianchi-Demicheli, et al., 2010). Some commonly recognized emotions, such as jealousy and parental love, are absent from Ekman's list (see Table 10.1; Ortigue & Bianchi-Demicheli, 2011; Ortigue, Bianchi-Demicheli, et al., 2010). Ekman did not exclude these intense feelings from his list of emotions, but he called them "emotion complexes," differentiating them from basic emotions by their extended duration, from months to a lifetime (Darwin et al., 1998).

Jealousy is one of the most interesting of the complex emotions (Ortigue & Bianchi-Demicheli, 2011). A review of the clinical literature of patients who experienced

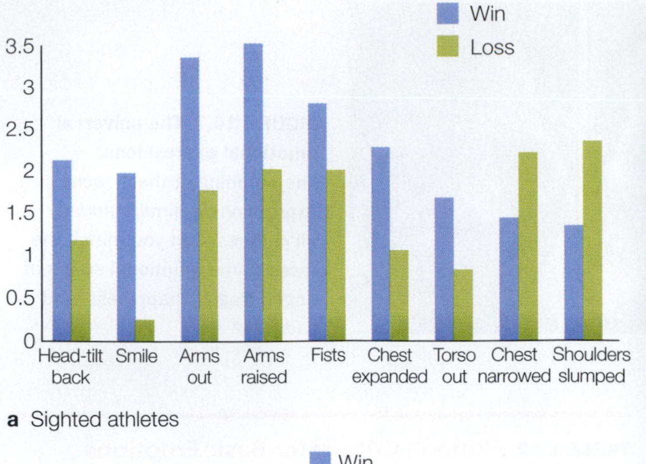

a Sighted athletes

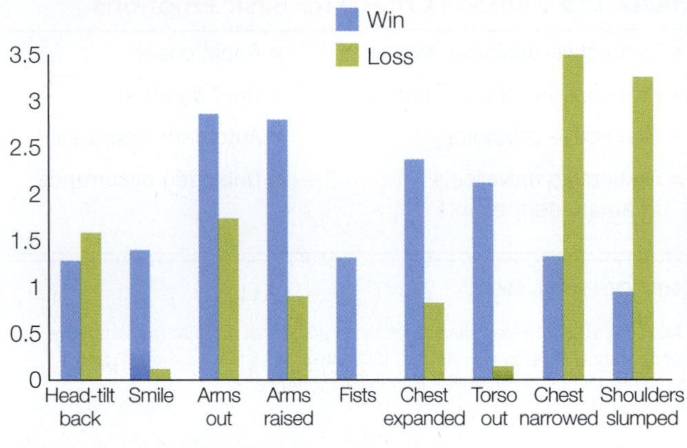

b Congenitally blind athletes

FIGURE 10.8 Athletes from 37 countries exhibit spontaneous pride and shame behaviors. The graphs compare the mean levels of nonverbal behaviors spontaneously displayed in response to wins and losses by sighted athletes (a) and congenitally blind athletes (b).

delusional jealousy following a brain infarct or a traumatic brain injury revealed that a broad network of regions within the brain, including higher-order cortical areas involved with social cognition and theory of mind (see Chapter 13) and interpretation of actions performed by others (see Chapter 8), are involved in jealousy (Ortigue & Bianchi-Demicheli, 2011). Clearly, jealousy is a complex emotion.

Similarly, romantic love is far more complicated than researchers initially thought (Ortigue, Bianchi-Demicheli, et al., 2010). (We do have to wonder who ever thought love was not complicated!) Ekman differentiates love from the basic emotions because no universal facial expressions exist for romantic love (see Table 10.1; Sabini & Silver, 2005). While we can observe behavioral signs of love, such as kissing and hand-holding (Bianchi-Demicheli et al., 2006; Ortigue, Patel, et al., 2010), we all know that these visible behaviors are not love itself, nor are they reliable signs (Ortigue & Bianchi-Demicheli, 2008; Ortigue, Patel, et al., 2010): They can be faked. While love itself may be invisible, its circuits have been localized in the human brain—within subcortical reward, motivation, and emotion systems, as well as higher-order cortical brain networks involved in complex cognitive functions and social cognition—reinforcing the assumption that love is a complex, goal-directed emotion rather than a basic one (Ortigue, Bianchi-Demicheli, et al., 2010; Bianchi-Demicheli et al., 2006).

Dimensional Theories of Emotion

Ekman was convinced by his data that basic emotions exist. However, other researchers instead categorize emotions as reactions that vary along a continuum rather than as discrete states. That is, some hypothesize that a better understanding of emotions comes from studying how arousing or pleasant they may be, or how motivated they make a person feel about approaching or withdrawing from an emotional stimulus.

VALENCE AND AROUSAL Most researchers agree that emotional reactions to stimuli and events can be characterized by two factors: *valence* (pleasant–unpleasant or positive–negative) and *arousal* (the intensity of the internal emotional response, high–low; Osgood et al., 1957; Russell, 1979). For instance, most of us would agree that being happy is a pleasant feeling (positive valence) and being angry is an unpleasant feeling (negative valence). If we found a quarter on the sidewalk, however, we would be happy but not really all that aroused. If we were to win $10 million in a lottery, we would be intensely happy (ecstatic) and intensely aroused. Although in both situations we experience something that is pleasant, the intensity of that feeling is certainly different. By using this dimensional approach—tracking valence and arousal—researchers can more concretely assess the emotional reactions elicited by stimuli. Instead of looking for neural correlates of specific emotions, these researchers look for the neural correlates of the dimensions—arousal and valence—of those emotions.

Yet a person can experience two emotions with opposite valences at the same time (Larsen & McGraw, 2014; Larsen et al., 2001). We can be both scared and amused on a roller coaster, or we can find ourselves in the bittersweet condition of being both happy to be graduating and sad that our tight group of friends is dispersing to the four winds. In these situations, mixed feelings suggest that positive and negative affect have different underlying mechanisms, as is supported by neurochemical evidence. Positive activation states are correlated with an increase in dopamine, whereas an increase in norepinephrine is associated with negative states (reviewed in Watson et al., 1999). The simultaneous presence of opposing emotions is not just a bit of odd trivia; it disputes the suggestion that emotion is primarily a valence of positive or negative feeling.

APPROACH OR WITHDRAW A second dimensional approach characterizes emotions by the actions and goals that they motivate. Richard Davidson and colleagues at the University of Wisconsin–Madison (1990) suggest that different emotional reactions or states can motivate us to either approach or withdraw from a situation. Some stimuli, such as predators or dangerous situations, may be threats; others may offer opportunities for betterment, such as food or potential mates. For example, the positive emotion of happiness may excite a tendency to *approach* or engage in the eliciting situations, whereas the negative emotions of fear and disgust may motivate us to *withdraw* from the eliciting situations.

Motivation, however, involves more than just valence. Anger, a negative emotion, can motivate approach. Sometimes the motivating stimuli can excite both approach and withdrawal: It is 110 degrees outside, and after traveling hours across the Australian outback with no air conditioning, you reach your destination: a campground by the Katherine River. You spot a rope swing suspended above the water and trot toward it, ready to jump in for a refreshing dunk. As you get closer, you glimpse a typically Australian sign: "Watch out for crocs." Hmm . . . you want to go in, yet . . .

Categorizing emotions as basic, complex, or dimensional can serve as a framework for our scientific investigations of emotion. Essential to these investigations, though, is understanding how emotion is defined in each study, so that as we examine them, we can piece together a meaningful consensus, where possible. Next we examine some of the many theories of how emotions are generated.

TAKE-HOME MESSAGES

- Emotions have been categorized as basic, complex, or varying along dimensional lines.
- According to Ekman, six human facial expressions represent basic emotional states: anger, fear, disgust, happiness, sadness, and surprise.
- Complex emotions are produced by a broad network of regions within the brain. In jealousy, for example, these regions include higher-order cortical areas involved with social cognition, theory of mind, and interpretation of actions performed by others.
- The dimensional approach, instead of describing discrete states of emotion, describes emotions as reactions that vary along a continuum.

10.4 Theories of Emotion Generation

As we noted earlier in the chapter, most emotion researchers agree that the response to emotional stimuli is adaptive and that it can be separated into three components. Every theory of **emotion generation** is an attempt to explain

- The physiological reaction (for instance, the racing heart)
- The behavioral reaction (such as the fight-or-flight response)
- The subjective experiential feeling ("I'm scared!")

What the theories don't agree on are the underlying mechanisms, and what causes what. The crux of the disagreement involves the timing of these three components and whether cognition is required to generate an emotional response and subjective feeling or, alternatively, whether an emotional stimulus leads directly to quick automatic processing that results in a characteristic response and feeling. In the discussion that follows, we outline some of the theories.

James–Lange Theory of Emotion

William James, who rejected the idea of basic emotions, proposed that emotions were the perceptual results of somatovisceral feedback from bodily responses to an emotion-provoking stimulus. He thought a sense organ relayed information about that stimulus to the cortex, which then sent this information to the muscles and viscera. The muscles and viscera responded by sending information back to the cortex (feedback), and the stimulus that had simply been apprehended was now emotionally felt. James used the example of fear associated with spotting a bear:

> Our natural way of thinking about these standard emotions is that the mental perception of some fact excites the mental affection called the emotion, and that this latter state of mind gives rise to the bodily expression. My thesis on the contrary is that *the bodily changes follow directly the* PERCEPTION *of the exciting fact, and that our feeling of the same changes as they occur* IS *the emotion.* Common sense says, . . . we meet a bear, are frightened and run. . . . The hypothesis here to be defended says that this order of sequence is incorrect, that the one mental state is not immediately induced by the other, that the bodily manifestations must first be interposed between, and that the more rational statement is that we feel . . . afraid because we tremble, and not that we . . . tremble, because we are . . . fearful, as the case may be. Without the bodily states following on the perception, the latter would be purely cognitive in form, pale, colourless, destitute of emotional warmth. We might then see the bear, and judge it best to run . . . but we could not actually *feel* afraid. (W. James, 1884, p. 189)

Thus, in James's view, you don't run because you are afraid; you run first and are afraid later, because you become aware of your body's physiological changes when you run, and then you cognitively interpret your physical reactions and conclude that what you're feeling is fright. According to this theory, your emotional reaction depends on how you interpret those physical reactions. A similar proposition was suggested by a contemporary of James, Carl Lange, and the theory was dubbed the James–Lange theory.

James and Lange theorized this sequence:

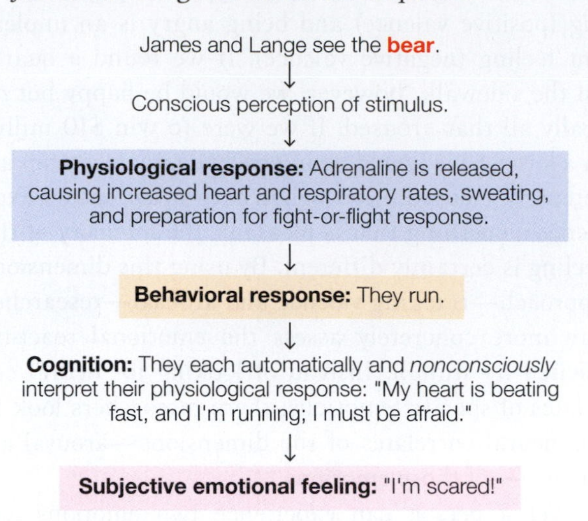

Thus, James and Lange believed that people could not feel an emotion without first having a bodily reaction and informational feedback from the body to the cortex about it. It followed, then, that if there were no physiological sensations, there would be no emotional experience. While this remains an acknowledged theory, problems soon popped up.

Cannon–Bard Theory of Emotion

James's proposal caused quite an uproar. A counterproposal was offered several years later by a pair of experimental physiologists from Harvard: Walter Cannon (who was the first person to describe the fight-or-flight response) and Philip Bard. They believed that physiological responses were not distinct enough to distinguish among fear, anger, and sexual attraction, for example.

Cannon and Bard tested James and Lange's prediction that there would be no emotional experience if physiological sensations were not fed to the cortex. Upon severing the cortex of a cat from the brainstem above the hypothalamus and thalamus, they found just the opposite: The cat still had an emotional reaction when provoked by the presence of a dog. It would growl and bare its teeth, and its hair would stand on end. The cat had the emotional reaction without cognition and without any physiological feedback to the cortex. The same results have been replicated in other species since then (Panksepp et al., 1994).

These researchers proposed that we simultaneously experience emotions and physiological reactions: The thalamus processes the emotional stimulus and sends this information simultaneously to the neocortex and to the hypothalamus, which produces the peripheral response. They thought the neocortex generated the emotional feeling, while the periphery carried out the emotional reaction: One does not cause the other. Returning to the bear-in-the-woods scenario, the Cannon–Bard theory says this:

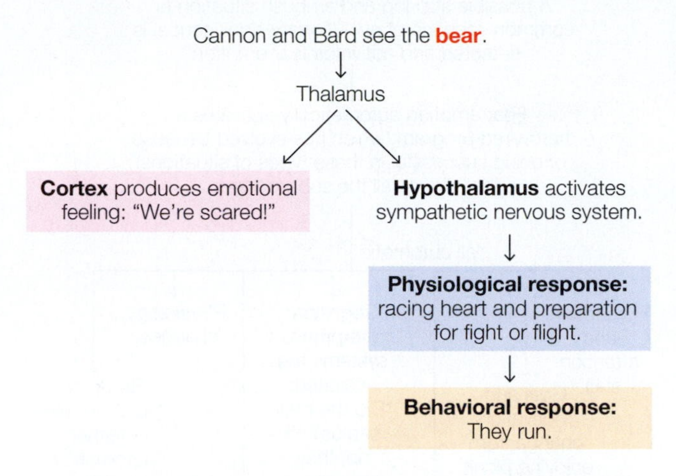

The Cannon–Bard theory remains important because it introduced into emotion research the model of parallel processing and showed that reactions to emotional stimuli could occur without the cortex, at least in nonhuman animals.

Appraisal Theory of Emotion

Appraisal theory is a group of theories in which emotion processing depends on an interaction between the stimulus properties and their interpretation. The theories differ about what is appraised and the criteria used for this appraisal. Since appraisal is a subjective step, it can account for the differences in how people react.

Richard Lazarus proposed a version of appraisal theory in which emotions are a response to the reckoning of the ratio of harm versus benefit in a person's encounter with something. In this appraisal step, each of us considers personal and environmental variables when deciding the significance of the stimulus for our well-being. Thus, the cause of the emotion is both the stimulus and its significance. In this theory, cognitive appraisal comes before emotional response or feeling. This appraisal step may be automatic and unconscious.

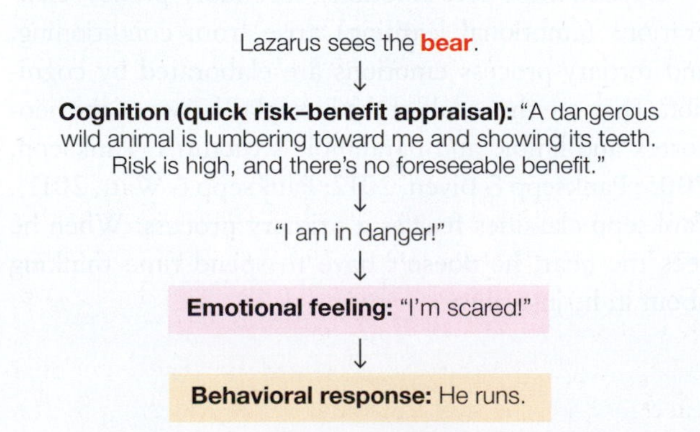

Singer–Schachter Theory: Cognitive Interpretation of Arousal

Jerome Singer and Stanley Schachter agreed with James and Lange that the perception of the body's reaction was the emotion, but they also agreed with Cannon and Bard that there were too many emotions for there to be a specific and unique autonomic pattern for each. In a famous experiment, Singer and Schachter gave two different groups of participants an injection of adrenaline (Schachter & Singer, 1962). The control group was told that they would experience the symptoms associated with adrenaline, such as a racing heart. The other group was told that they had been injected with vitamins and should not experience any side effects. Each of the participants was then placed with a confederate, who was acting in either a euphoric or an angry manner.

When later asked how they had felt during the experiment and why, the participants who had knowingly received an adrenaline injection attributed their physiological responses to the drug, but those who did not know they had been given adrenaline attributed their symptoms to the environment (the happy or angry confederate) and interpreted their emotion accordingly. These findings led to the Singer–Schachter theory, a blend of all three of the preceding theories. It proposes that emotional arousal and then reasoning are required to appraise a stimulus before the emotion can be identified.

At the time the adrenaline study was done, it was assumed that the injected drug would produce equivalent autonomic states independent of the psychological context. We now know that the autonomic and cognitive effects of drugs depend on the context, limiting what we can infer from the findings of this experiment.

LeDoux's Fast and Slow Roads to Emotion

Joseph LeDoux of New York University has proposed that humans have two emotion systems operating in parallel. One is a neural system for our emotional responses that bypasses the cortex and was hardwired by evolution to produce fast responses that increase our chances of survival and reproduction. The other system, which includes cognition, is slower and more accurate; LeDoux proposes that this system generates the conscious feeling of emotion. He suggests that conscious feelings are not hardwired, but rather are learned by experience and are irrelevant to emotional responses.

To more easily distinguish between these two pathways, and to emphasize that mechanisms that detect and respond to threats are not the same as those that give rise to the conscious feeling of fear, LeDoux suggests that the use of mental-state terms like *fear* and *anxiety* should be reserved only for *subjective feelings* of fear and anxiety. Brain circuits that detect and respond to threats should be referred to as *defensive circuits*, and behaviors that occur in response to threats should be referred to as *defensive behaviors* (LeDoux, 2014).

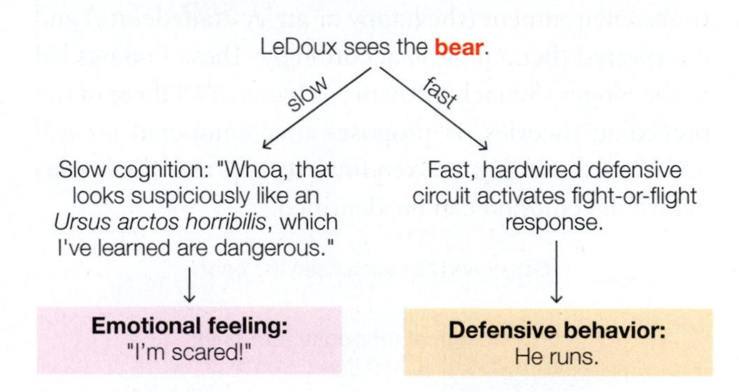

Evolutionary Psychology Approach to Emotion

Evolutionary psychologists Leda Cosmides and John Tooby propose that emotions are conductors of an orchestra of cognitive programs that need to be coordinated to produce successful behavior (Cosmides & Tooby, 2000). They suggest that the emotions are an overarching program that directs the cognitive subprograms and their interactions.

From this viewpoint, an emotion is not reducible to its effects on physiology, behavioral inclinations, cognitive appraisals, or feeling states, because it involves coordinated, evolved instructions for all of these aspects together. An emotion also involves instructions for other mechanisms distributed throughout the human mental and physical architecture.

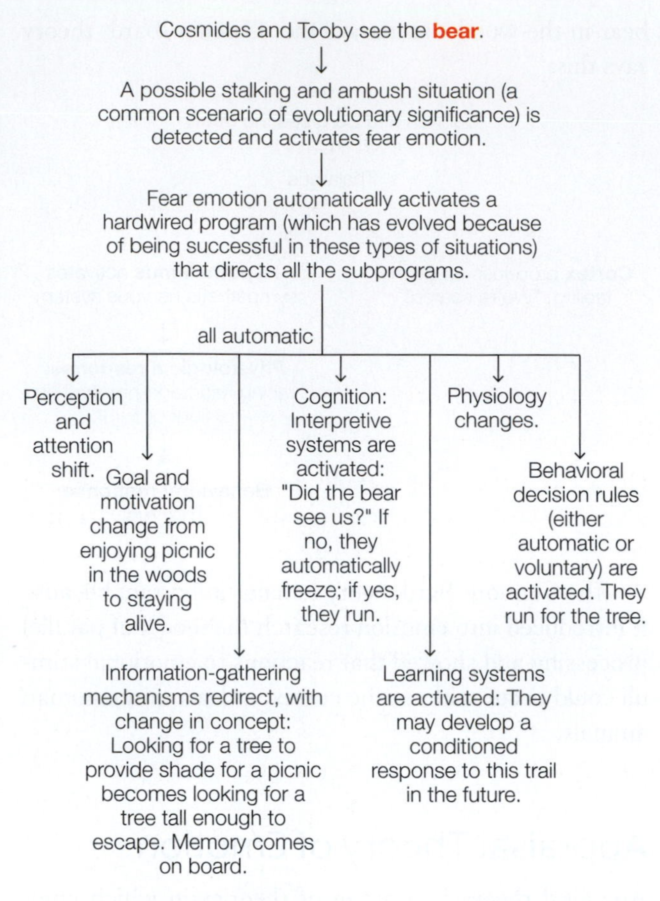

Panksepp's Hierarchical-Processing Theory of Emotion

Jaak Panksepp hypothesized that emotions are subject to a control system with hierarchical processing. His theory posits that emotion is processed in one of three ways, depending on which emotion it is. The most basic are primary-process or core emotions, which provide our most powerful emotional feelings and arise straight from the ancient neural networks in the subcortex. The theory argues that cognition plays no role when it comes to feeling these emotions.

Beyond these core emotions, secondary-process elaborations (emotional learning) arise from conditioning, and tertiary-process emotions are elaborated by cognition. They are the result of the interplay between the neocortex and limbic and paralimbic structures (Panksepp, 2005; Panksepp & Biven, 2012; Panksepp & Watt, 2011). Panksepp classifies fear as a primary process: When he sees the bear, he doesn't have to spend time thinking about it; he just runs:

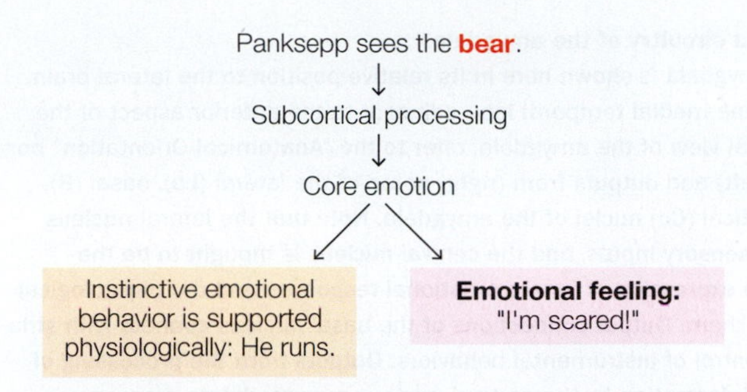

Anderson and Adolphs: Emotions as Central Causative States

David Anderson and Ralph Adolphs, whose emotion definition we presented earlier, argue that an emotional stimulus activates a central nervous system state that, in turn, simultaneously activates multiple systems producing separate responses: feelings, a behavior, a psychophysiological reaction, and cognitive changes.

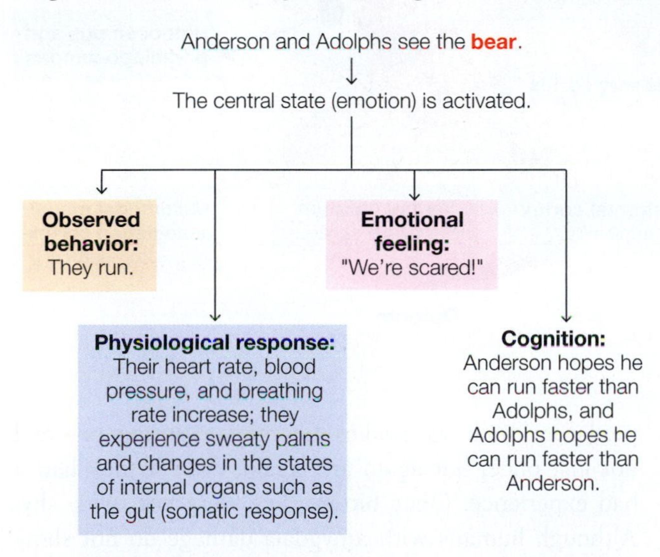

TAKE-HOME MESSAGES

- Emotions are made up of three psychological components—a physiological response, a behavioral response, and a subjective feeling—that have evolved in animals, including humans, enabling responses to significant stimuli that have promoted survival. The underlying mechanisms and timing of the components are disputed.
- Researchers do not agree on when and if cognition plays a part in producing or processing emotions.
- Researchers do not agree on how emotions are generated, and many theories exist.

10.5 The Amygdala

Joseph LeDoux was one of the first in the field of cognitive neuroscience to study emotions. He got the ball rolling with his research on the role of the amygdala in fear conditioning, and he has shown that the amygdala plays a major role in emotion processing in general, not just fear. Because researchers first focused their attention on the amygdala, we know more about its role in emotion than about the roles of other brain regions.

The **amygdalae** (singular **amygdala**) are small, almond-shaped structures in the medial temporal lobe adjacent to the anterior portion of the hippocampus (see the "Anatomical Orientation" box on p. 433, and **Figure 10.9a**). Each amygdala is an intriguing and very complex structure that, in primates, is a collection of 13 nuclei that can be grouped into three main amygdaloid complexes.

1. The largest area is the *basolateral nuclear complex*, consisting of the *lateral* and *basal nuclei*, pictured in **Figure 10.9b**, and *accessory basal nuclei* that are not seen in this view. The lateral nucleus (La) receives sensory inputs. Connections from the lateral nucleus to the basal nucleus (B), and from there to the ventral striatum, control the performance of actions in the face of threat (e.g., escape and avoidance; LeDoux & Gorman, 2001; Ramirez et al., 2015).
2. The centromedial complex (Ce), which consists of the *medial nucleus* and the *central nucleus*, receives information that has been processed in basal nuclei and forms a response. It is connected to regions of the brainstem controlling innate emotional (or defensive) behaviors and their associated physiological (both autonomic and endocrine) responses. Figure 10.9b depicts some of the inputs and outputs of the lateral (La), basal (B), and centromedial (Ce) nuclei.
3. The smallest complex is the *cortical nucleus* (Co), also known as the "olfactory part of the amygdala" because its primary input comes from the olfactory bulb and olfactory cortex. It outputs processing to the medial nucleus, as well as directly to the hippocampus and parahippocampus, and it may, in emotionally arousing situations involving olfaction, modulate memory formation (Kemppainen et al., 2002).

There has been some controversy about the concept of "the amygdala" as a single entity, and some neurobiologists consider the amygdala to be neither a structural nor a functional unit, but rather a bundle of nuclear extensions from other regions (Swanson & Petrovich, 1998).

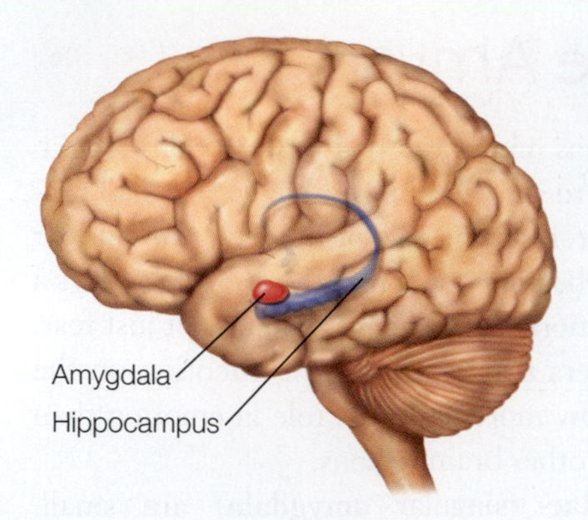

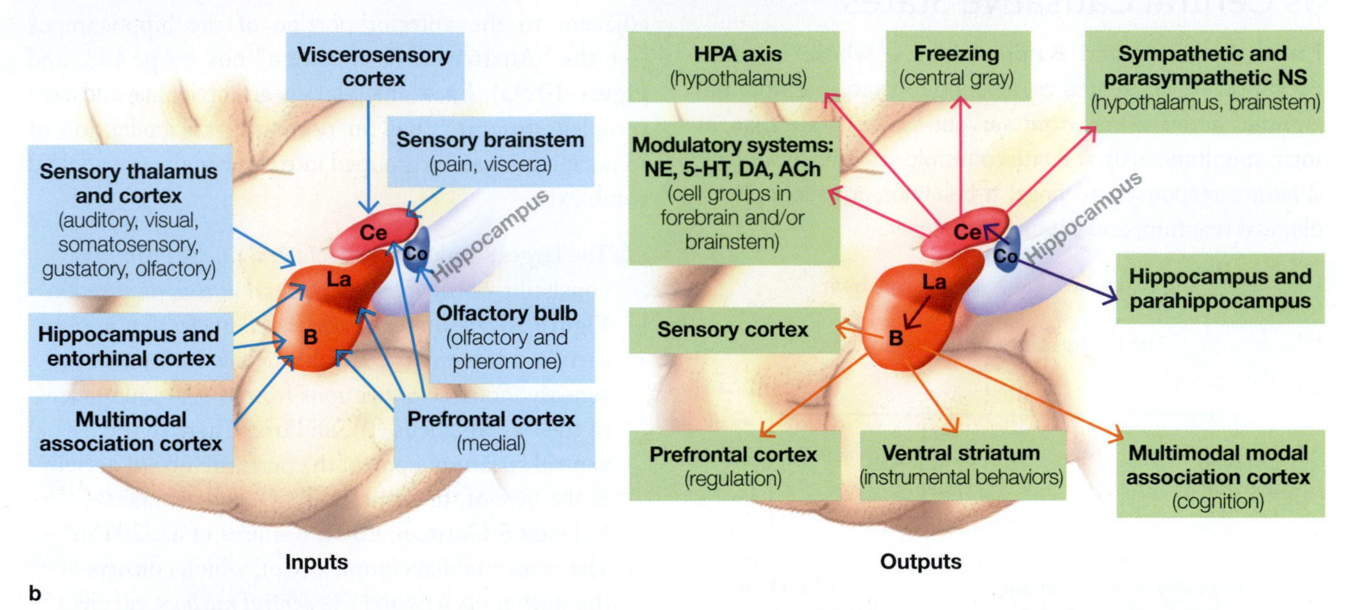

FIGURE 10.9 Location and circuitry of the amygdala.
(a) The left-hemisphere amygdala is shown here in its relative position to the lateral brain aspect. It lies deep within the medial temporal lobe adjacent to the anterior aspect of the hippocampus. (For a sagittal view of the amygdala, refer to the "Anatomical Orientation" box on p. 433.) **(b)** Inputs to (left) and outputs from (right) some of the lateral (La), basal (B), centromedial (Ce), and cortical (Co) nuclei of the amygdala. Note that the lateral nucleus is the major site receiving sensory inputs, and the central nucleus is thought to be the major output region for the expression of innate emotional responses and the physiological responses associated with them. Output connections of the basal nucleus connect with striatal areas involved in the control of instrumental behaviors. Outputs from the processing of olfactory and pheromonal information by the cortical nucleus may modulate memory formation in emotionally arousing situations. 5-HT = 5-hydroxytryptamine (serotonin); ACh = acetylcholine; DA = dopamine; NE = norepinephrine.

For example, the lateral and basal nuclei can be considered extensions of the neocortex, the central and medial nuclei extensions of the striatum, and the cortical nucleus an extension of the olfactory system.

Structures in the medial temporal lobe were first proposed to be important for emotion in the early 20th century, when Heinrich Klüver and Paul Bucy at the University of Chicago (1939) documented unusual emotional responses in monkeys following damage to this region. One of the prominent characteristics of what later came to be known as *Klüver–Bucy syndrome* (Weiskrantz, 1956) was a lack of fear manifested by a tendency to approach objects that would normally elicit a fear response. The observed deficit was called *psychic blindness* because of an inability to recognize the emotional importance of events or objects.

In the 1950s, the amygdala was identified as the primary structure underlying these fear-related deficits. Monkeys whose amygdalae had been more selectively lesioned behaved as if they had Klüver–Bucy syndrome: They were incautious and overly trusting, dauntlessly approaching novel or frightening objects or potential predators such as snakes or human strangers—and not just once, but again and again, even if they had a bad experience. Once bitten, they were not twice shy. Although humans with amygdala damage do not show all of the classic signs of Klüver–Bucy syndrome, they do exhibit deficits in fear processing, as S.M., the woman we met at the beginning of this chapter, demonstrated (Adolphs et al., 1994, 1995; Tranel & Hyman, 1990). She exhibited a lack of cautiousness and distrust and did not learn to avoid what others would term fearful experiences (Feinstein et al., 2011).

While studying the amygdala's role in fear processing, investigators realized that, because of its vast connections to many other brain regions, it might be important for emotion processing in general. In fact, the amygdala is the forebrain's most connected structure. The extensive connections to and from the amygdala suggest that it plays a critical role in learning, memory, and attention in response to emotionally significant stimuli. The amygdala contains receptors for the neurotransmitters glutamate, dopamine, norepinephrine, serotonin, and acetylcholine. It also contains hormone receptors for glucocorticoids and estrogen, and peptide receptors for opioids, oxytocin, vasopressin, corticotropin-releasing factor, and neuropeptide Y.

There are many ideas concerning what role the amygdala plays. One hypothesis is that the amygdala functions as a protection device, to detect and avoid danger (Amaral, 2002). Another more generally suggests that the amygdala is involved in determining what a stimulus is and what is to be done about it (Pessoa, 2011). In either case, it would be involved with attention, perception, value representation, and decision making. In this vein, Kristen Lindquist and colleagues (2012) proposed that the amygdala is active when the rest of the brain cannot easily predict what sensations mean, what to do about them, or what value they hold in a given context. The amygdala signals other parts of the brain to keep working until these issues have been figured out (Whalen, 2007). Lindquist's proposal has been questioned, however, by people who have extensively studied patient S.M. (Feinstein et al., 2011).

Let's look at what we can surmise about the amygdala and emotion processing from S.M.'s story:

1. The amygdala must play a critical role in the identification of facial expressions of fear.
2. S.M. fails to experience the emotion of fear.
3. S.M. appears to have no deficit in any emotion other than fear.
4. S.M.'s inability to feel fear seems to have contributed to her inability to avoid dangerous situations. That is, she doesn't seem to be able to learn from past frightening experiences.

Even without her amygdala, S.M. correctly understands the salience of emotional stimuli, but she has a specific impairment in the induction and experience of fear across a wide range of situations. People who have studied S.M. suggest that the amygdala is a critical brain region for triggering a state of fear in response to encounters with threatening stimuli in the external environment. They hypothesize that the amygdala furnishes connections between sensory and association cortex that are required to represent external fearful stimuli, as well as connections between the brainstem and hypothalamic circuitry, which are necessary for orchestrating the action program of fear. We will see later in this chapter that damage to the lateral amygdala prevents fear conditioning. Without the amygdala, the evolutionary value of fear is lost.

For much of the remainder of this chapter, we will look at the involvement of the amygdala with emotions and cognitive processes such as learning, attention, and perception. Casting the amygdala as a vigilant watchdog looking out for motivationally relevant stimuli (A. K. Anderson & Phelps, 2001; Whalen, 1998) may prove true, but just what is it watching out for? The answer to that question still eludes investigators. Obviously, the amygdala remains enigmatic. Although we cannot yet settle the debate, we will get a feel for how emotion is involved in various cognitive domains as we learn about the amygdala's role in emotion processing.

TAKE-HOME MESSAGES

- The amygdala is the most connected structure in the forebrain.
- The amygdala contains receptors for many different neurotransmitters and for various hormones.
- The amygdala's role is still enigmatic, but it may function as a danger detection device.

10.6 The Influence of Emotion on Learning

Although evolution has given us a limited repertoire of innate fears, we were not born with an extensive list of things to steer clear of. Those need to be learned. Humans are good at this: We don't even have to experience things to be afraid of them. In fact, we may be a little too good at this. Unlike other animals, we can fear things that we have conjured up in our minds—including things that do not even exist, such as ghosts, vampires, and monsters under the bed.

In previous chapters we did not address how emotion affects the various cognitive processes that we discussed, yet we all know from personal experience that it does have an effect. For instance, if we are sad, we may find it difficult to make decisions, think about the future, or carry out any physical activities. If we are anxious, we may hear every household creak that would usually go unnoticed. In the following two sections we will look at how emotion modulates cognitive functions, beginning with how it affects learning, which has been studied most extensively. As you read the following, recall that S.M. was unable to learn to avoid dangerous situations.

Implicit Emotional Learning

One day, early in the 20th century, Swiss neurologist and psychologist Édouard Claparède greeted his patient and introduced himself. In turn, she introduced herself and shook his hand. Not such a great story, until you know that Claparède had done the same thing with this patient every day for the previous 5 years and she never remembered him.

She had Korsakoff's syndrome, characterized by an absence of any long-term declarative memory. One day, Claparède concealed a pin in his palm that pricked his patient when they shook hands. The next day, once again, she did not remember him, but when he extended his hand to greet her, she hesitated for the first time. Claparède was the first to provide evidence that two types of learning, implicit and explicit, are apparently associated with two different pathways (Kihlstrom, 1995).

As first noted by Claparède, implicit learning is a type of Pavlovian learning in which a neutral stimulus (the handshake) acquires aversive properties when paired with an aversive event (the pinprick). This process is a classic example of **fear conditioning**, a primary paradigm used to investigate the amygdala's role in emotional learning. Fear conditioning is a form of classical conditioning in which the unconditioned stimulus is aversive. One advantage of using the fear-conditioning paradigm to investigate emotional learning is that it works in essentially the same way across a wide range of species, from fruit flies to humans.

One laboratory version of fear conditioning is illustrated in **Figure 10.10**. The light is the *conditioned stimulus (CS)*. In this example, we are going to condition a rat to associate this neutral stimulus with an aversive stimulus. Before training (Figure 10.10a), however, the light is solely a neutral stimulus and does not evoke a response from the rat. In this pretraining stage, the rat responds with a normal startle response to any innately aversive stimulus, known as the *unconditioned stimulus (US)*—for example, a foot shock or a loud noise—that invokes an innate fear response. During training (Figure 10.10b), we pair the light with a shock, which we deliver immediately before the light turns off. The rat has a natural fear response to the shock (usually it startles or jumps), called the *unconditioned response (UR)*. We refer to this stage as *acquisition*. After a few pairings of the light (CS) and the shock (US), the rat learns that the light predicts the shock, and soon the rat exhibits a fear response to the light alone (Figure 10.10c). This anticipatory fear response is the *conditioned response (CR)*.

We can enhance the CR by adding another fear-evoking stimulus or by preemptively placing the rat in an anxious state. For example, if the rat sees the light (CS) at the same time that it hears a loud noise, it will have a greater startle reflex, known as a potentiated CR. We can unpair the CS

Light alone (CS): no response

Foot shock alone (US_1): normal startle (UR)

Loud noise alone (US_2): normal startle (UR)

a Before training

Light and foot shock: normal startle (UR)

Light alone: normal startle (CR)

Light and noise but no foot shock: potentiated startle (potentiated CR)

b During training

c After training

FIGURE 10.10 Fear conditioning.
(a) Before training, three different stimuli—light (CS), foot shock (US_1), and loud noise (US_2)—are presented alone, and both the foot shock and the noise elicit a normal startle response in rats. (b) During training, light (CS) and foot shock (US_1) are paired to elicit a normal startle response (UR). (c) In tests following training, presentation of light alone now elicits a response (CR), and presentation of the light together with a loud noise but no foot shock elicits a potentiated startle (potentiated CR) because the rat is startled by the loud noise and has associated the light (CS) with the startling foot shock (US).

and resulting CR by presenting the light (CS) alone, without the shock, but it takes many trials. Because at this point the CR is extinguished, we call the phenomenon **extinction.** Importantly, extinction represents *new* learning about the CS that inhibits expression of the original memory. Because it does not overwrite the original memory, though, the fear response can return after a certain period of time (spontaneous recovery), in a different context (contextual renewal), or upon reexposure to the US (reinstatement). There is ongoing research into techniques that can lead to longer-lasting regulation of unwanted defensive responses (Dunsmoor, Niv, et al., 2015).

In this type of fear-learning paradigm, regardless of the stimulus used or the response evoked, one consistent finding has emerged in rats (and we will soon see that it also holds true in humans): Damage to the amygdala impairs conditioned fear responses. Amygdala lesions block the ability to acquire and express a CR to a neutral CS that is paired with an aversive US.

TWO PATHWAYS: THE HIGH AND LOW ROADS Using the fear-conditioning paradigm, researchers such as Joseph LeDoux (1996), Mike Davis of Emory University (1992), and Bruce Kapp and his colleagues of the University of Vermont (1984) have mapped out the neural circuits of fear learning, from stimulus perception to emotional response. As **Figure 10.11** shows, the lateral nucleus of the amygdala serves as a region of convergence for information from multiple brain regions, allowing for the formation of associations that underlie fear conditioning.

Results from single-unit-recording studies have shown that cells in the superior dorsolateral amygdala have the ability to rapidly undergo changes, pairing the CS to the US. After several trials, these cells reset to their starting point; by then, however, cells in the inferior dorsolateral region have undergone a change that maintains the adverse association. This may be why fear that seemed eliminated can return under stress—because cells of the inferior dorsolateral region retain the memory (LeDoux, 2007). The lateral nucleus sends projections to the central nucleus of the amygdala, which analyzes and places a stimulus in the appropriate context. If it determines that the stimulus is threatening or potentially dangerous, it will initiate an emotional response.

An important aspect of this fear-conditioning circuitry is that information about the fear-inducing stimulus reaches the amygdala through *two separate but simultaneous pathways* (**Figure 10.12**; LeDoux, 1996). One goes directly from the thalamus to the amygdala without being filtered by cognition or conscious control. Signals sent via this pathway, sometimes called the *low road* because the cortex is bypassed, reach the amygdala rapidly (15 ms in a rat), though the information is crude. At the same time, sensory information about the stimulus is being projected to the amygdala via a cortical pathway, sometimes referred to as the *high road*. The high road is significantly slower, taking 300 ms in a rat, but the cognitive analysis of the stimulus is more thorough. In this pathway, the sensory information projects to the thalamus, which then sends the information to the sensory cortex for a finer analysis. The sensory cortex projects the results of this analysis to the amygdala.

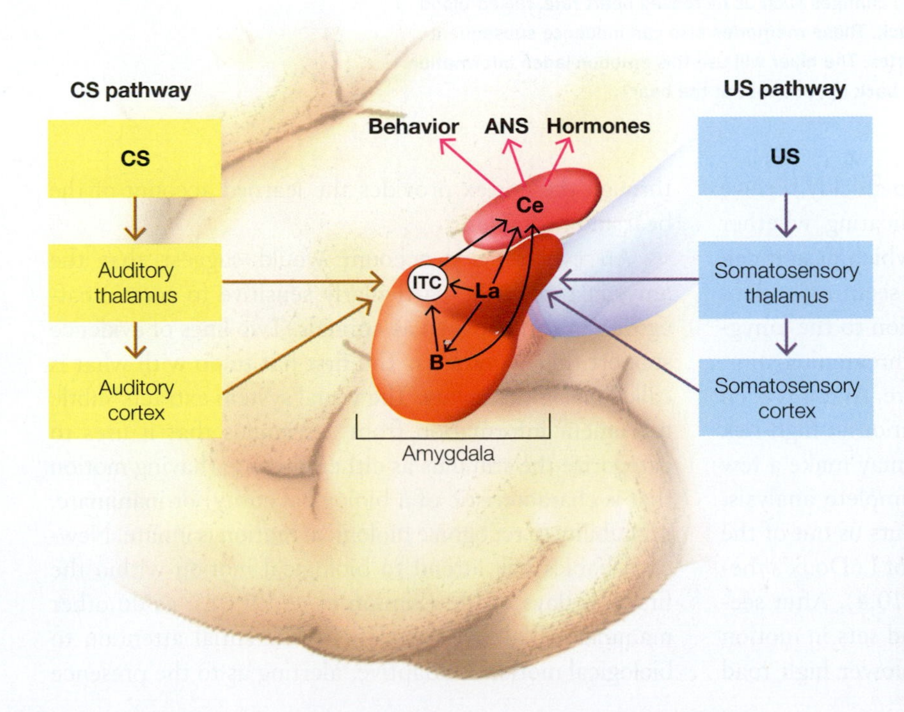

FIGURE 10.11 Amygdala pathways and fear conditioning.
Sensory information from both the CS and the US enters the amygdala through cortical sensory inputs and thalamic inputs to the lateral nucleus. The convergence of this information in the lateral nucleus induces synaptic plasticity, such that after conditioning, the CS information flows through the lateral nucleus and intra-amygdalar connections to the central nucleus just as the US information does. Intercalated cells (ITC) connect the lateral (La) and basal (B) nuclei with the central nucleus in the centromedial complex (Ce).

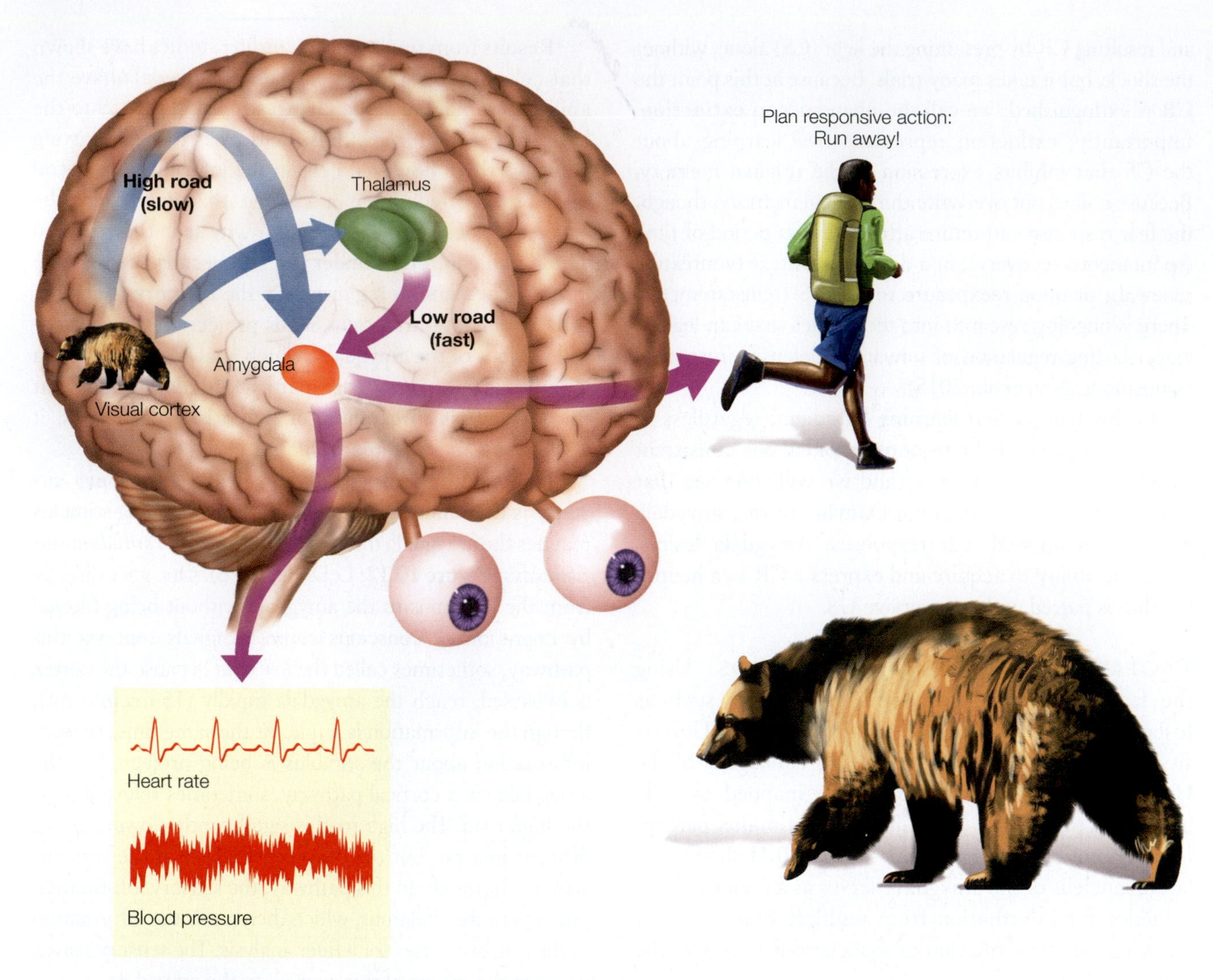

FIGURE 10.12 The amygdala receives sensory input along two pathways.
When a hiker chances upon a bear, the sensory input activates affective memories through the cortical "high road" and subcortical "low road" projections to the amygdala. Even before these memories reach consciousness, however, they produce autonomic changes such as increased heart rate, raised blood pressure, and a startle response like jumping back. These memories also can influence subsequent actions through the projections to the frontal cortex. The hiker will use this emotion-laden information in choosing his next action: Turn and run, slowly back up, or shout at the bear?

The low road allows the amygdala to quickly receive a crude signal from the thalamus indicating whether the stimulus is roughly like the CS, in which case it can immediately respond. Although it may seem redundant to have two pathways to send information to the amygdala, when it comes to responding to a threatening stimulus, it is adaptive to be both fast and sure. And it is even more adaptive to err on the side of caution in high-risk circumstances. By reacting quickly, we may make a few low-risk errors. But if we wait for a complete analysis, we may make one high-risk error that cuts us out of the game completely. Now we see the basis of LeDoux's theory of emotion generation (see Section 10.4). After seeing the bear, the person's faster low road sets in motion the fight-or-flight response, while the slower high road through the cortex provides the learned account of the bear and its foibles.

An evolutionary account would suggest that the amygdala might be particularly sensitive to certain categories of stimuli, such as animals. Two lines of evidence support this hypothesis. The first has to do with what is called *biological motion*. The visual system extracts subtle movement information from a stimulus that it uses to categorize the stimulus as either animate (having motion that is characteristic of a biological entity) or inanimate. This ability to recognize biological motion is innate. Newborn babies will attend to biological motion within the first few days of life (Simion et al., 2008), as do other mammals (Blake, 1993). This preferential attention to biological motion is adaptive, alerting us to the presence of other living things. Interestingly, PET studies have shown that the right amygdala activates when an individual perceives a stimulus exhibiting biological motion (Bonda et al., 1996).

The second line of evidence comes from neuroscientists making single-cell recordings from the amygdala, hippocampus, and entorhinal cortex while patients looked at images of persons, animals, landmarks, or objects. The researchers found neurons in the right amygdala, but not the left, that responded preferentially to pictures of animals but not to pictures of other stimulus categories. There was no difference between the amygdala's responses to threatening animals and cute animals. This categorical selectivity provides evidence of a domain-specific mechanism for processing this biologically important class of stimuli that includes predators or prey (Mormann et al., 2011).

THE AMYGDALA'S EFFECT ON IMPLICIT LEARNING

The amygdala's role in learning to respond to stimuli that represent aversive events through fear conditioning is said to be *implicit*. We use this term because we express the learning indirectly through our behavioral response (e.g., potentiated startle) or physiological response (i.e., autonomic nervous system arousal). When studying nonhuman animals, we can assess the CR only through indirect, or implicit, means of expression: The rat startles when the light goes on.

In humans, however, we can also assess the response directly, by asking the participants to report whether they know that the CS represents a potential aversive consequence (the US). Patients with amygdala damage fail to demonstrate an indirect CR; for instance, they would not shirk Claparède's handshake. When asked to report the parameters of fear conditioning explicitly or consciously, however, these patients demonstrate no deficit, and they might respond with "Oh, the handshake; sure, it will hurt a bit." Thus, we know they learned that the stimulus is associated with an aversive event. Damage to the amygdala appears to leave this latter ability intact (A. K. Anderson & Phelps, 2001; Bechara et al., 1995; LaBar et al., 1995; Phelps et al., 1998).

This concept is illustrated by a fear-conditioning study done with a patient, S.P., who is very much like S.M. Patient S.P. also has bilateral amygdala damage (**Figure 10.13**). To relieve epilepsy, at age 48 S.P. underwent a lobectomy that removed her right amygdala. MRI at that time revealed that her left amygdala was already damaged, most likely from mesial temporal sclerosis, a syndrome that causes neuronal loss in the medial temporal regions of the brain (A. K. Anderson & Phelps, 2001; Phelps et al., 1998). Like S.M., S.P. is unable to recognize fear in the faces of others (Adolphs et al., 1999).

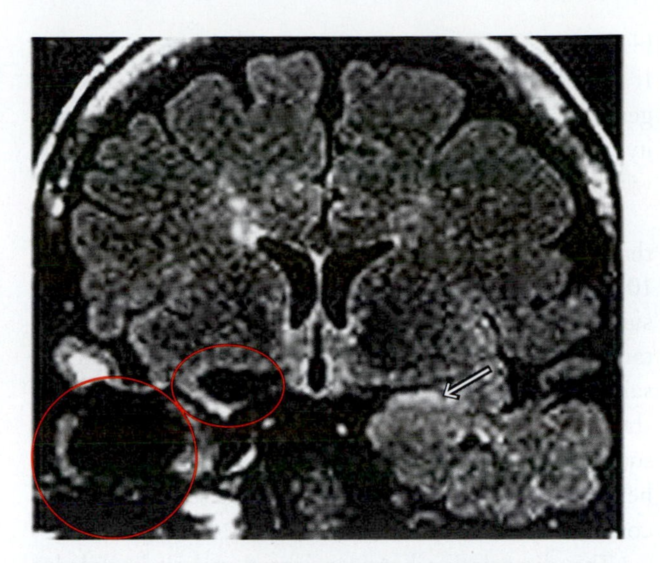

FIGURE 10.13 Bilateral amygdala lesions in patient S.P.
During a surgical procedure to reduce epileptic seizures, the right amygdala and a large section of the right temporal lobe, including the hippocampus, were removed (circled regions). Pathology in the left amygdala is visible in the white band (arrow), indicating regions where cells were damaged by neural disease.

S.P. was shown a picture of a blue square (the CS), which the experimenters periodically presented for 10 seconds. During the acquisition phase, S.P. received a mild electrical shock to the wrist (the US) at the end of the 10-second presentation of the blue square (the CS). In measures of skin conductance response (**Figure 10.14**), S.P.'s performance was as predicted: She had a normal fear response to the shock (the UR), but she had no change in response when she saw the blue square (the CS), even after several acquisition trials. This lack of change in the skin conductance response to the

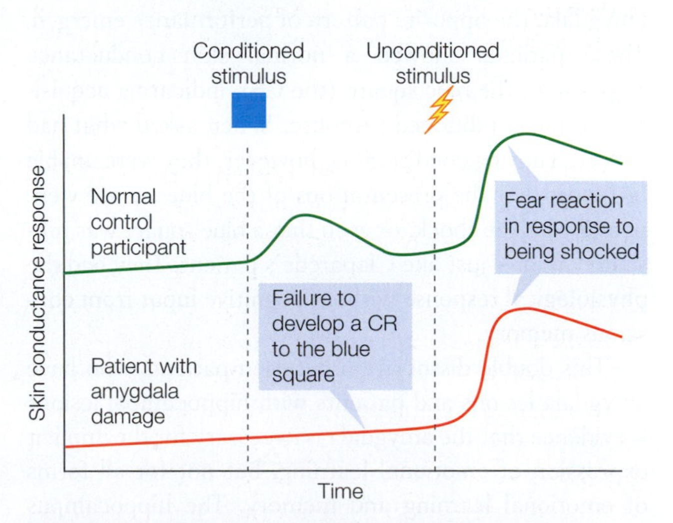

FIGURE 10.14 S.P. showed no skin conductance response to conditioned stimuli.
Unlike control participants, S.P. (red line) showed no response to the blue square (CS) after training but did respond to the shock (the US).

blue square demonstrates that S.P. failed to acquire a CR. It also shows that the amygdala is not necessary for the generation of physiological changes (electrodermal activity), but is necessary for the coupling of sensory stimuli with affect (Bechara et al., 1995).

After the experiment, S.P. was shown her data and that of a control participant, as illustrated in Figure 10.14, and she was asked what she thought. She was surprised that she had shown no change in skin conductance response (CR) to the blue square (CS), and she said she knew after the very first acquisition trial that she was going to get a shock whenever she saw the blue square. She was not sure what to make of the fact that her skin conductance response did not reflect what she consciously knew to be true.

This dissociation between intact explicit knowledge of the events that occurred during fear conditioning and impaired conditioned responses has been observed in other patients with amygdala damage (Bechara et al., 1995; LaBar et al., 1995). These findings suggest that the cortex, with its conscious knowledge of an upcoming shock, cannot generate the physiological changes normally associated with fear if there is no link to the amygdala and its midbrain connections. Although S.P. expected a shock, without those physiological changes she felt no fear. This result presents a serious challenge to theories of emotion generation that require cognition.

As discussed in Chapter 9, explicit or declarative memory for events depends on another medial temporal lobe structure: the hippocampus, which, when damaged, impairs the ability to explicitly report memory for an event. When researchers conducted the conditioning paradigm that we described for S.P. with patients who had bilateral damage to the hippocampus but an intact amygdala, the opposite pattern of performance emerged. These patients showed a normal skin conductance response to the blue square (the CS), indicating acquisition of the conditioned response. When asked what had occurred during conditioning, however, they were unable to report that the presentations of the blue square were paired with the shock, or even that a blue square was presented at all—just like Claparède's patient. They had the physiological response without cognitive input from conscious memory.

This double dissociation between patients who have amygdala lesions and patients with hippocampal lesions is evidence that the amygdala is necessary for the implicit expression of emotional learning, but not for all forms of emotional learning and memory. The hippocampus is necessary for the acquisition of explicit or declarative knowledge of the emotional properties of a stimulus, whereas the amygdala is critical for the acquisition and expression of an implicitly conditioned fear response.

Explicit Emotional Learning

The double dissociation just described clearly indicates that the amygdala is necessary for implicit emotional learning, but not for explicit emotional learning. Does the amygdala have a role in explicit learning and memory also?

Liz is walking down the street in her neighborhood and sees a neighbor's dog, Fang, on the sidewalk. Even though she is a dog owner herself and likes dogs in general, Fang scares her. When she encounters him, she becomes nervous and fearful, so she decides to walk on the other side of the street. Why might Liz, who likes dogs, be afraid of this particular dog? There are a few possible reasons: For example, perhaps Fang bit her once. In this case, her fear response to Fang was acquired through fear conditioning. Fang (the CS) was paired with the dog bite (the US), resulting in pain and fear (the UR) and an acquired fear response to Fang in particular (the CR).

Liz may fear Fang for another reason, however. Perhaps she has heard from her neighbor that Fang is an aggressive dog that *might* bite her. In this case she has no aversive experience linked to this particular dog. Instead, she learned about the aversive properties of the dog explicitly. Her ability to learn and remember this type of information depends on her hippocampal memory system. She likely did not experience a fear response when she heard this information from her neighbor, but did when she actually encountered Fang. Thus, her reaction is not based on actual experience; rather, it is anticipatory, based on her explicit knowledge of Fang's potential aversive properties. Explicit learning—learning to fear a stimulus because of something we're told—is common in humans.

THE AMYGDALA'S EFFECT ON EXPLICIT LEARNING

Does the amygdala play a role in the indirect expression of the fear response in *instructed* fear? From what we know about patient S.M., what would you guess? Elizabeth Phelps of New York University and her colleagues (Funayama et al., 2001; Phelps et al., 2001) addressed this question using an *instructed-fear paradigm*. They told the participants that a blue square might be paired with a shock, but none of the participants actually received a shock: There was no direct reinforcement. They found that patients with amygdala damage *learned and explicitly reported* that some presentations of the blue square might come with a shock to the wrist; however, the patients *did not show a startle response when they saw a blue square*: They knew consciously that they would receive a shock but had no emotional response. In contrast, normal control participants showed an increase in skin conductance response to

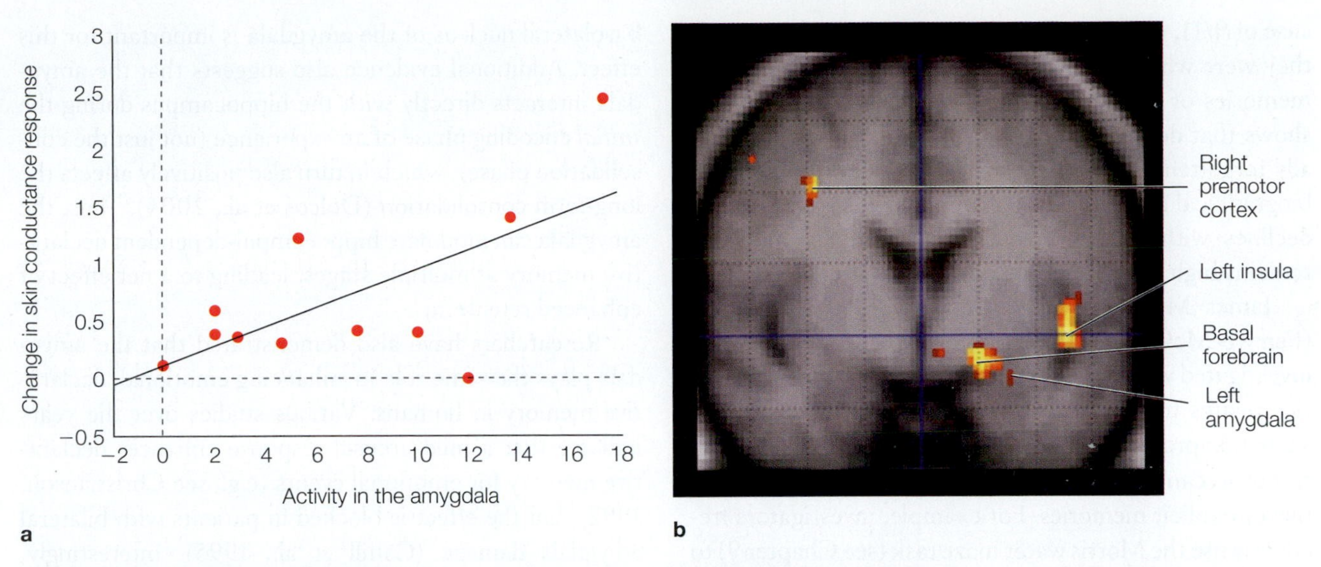

FIGURE 10.15 Responses to instructed fear.
(a) While performing a task in the instructed fear protocol, participants showed an arousal response (measured by skin conductance response) consistent with fear to the blue square, which they were told might be linked to a shock. There is a correlation between the strength of the skin conductance response indicating arousal and the activation of the amygdala. **(b)** Averaged BOLD signal across 12 participants. The presentation of the blue square compared with safe squares led to significantly active regions in the left dorsal amygdala extending into the basal forebrain, the left insula, and the right premotor cortex.

the blue square that correlated with amygdala activity (**Figure 10.15a**). Thus, even though explicit learning of the emotional properties of the blue square depends on the hippocampal memory system, the amygdala is critical for the *expression* of a fear response to the blue square (**Figure 10.15b**).

Similar deficits in fear responses have been observed when patients with amygdala lesions respond to emotional scenes (Angrilli et al., 1996; Funayama et al., 2001). Importantly, there was no direct reinforcement (e.g., shock) in these studies. More recent reports suggest that when researchers decouple instructions and reinforcement, as in this study, the amygdala preferentially attunes to changes in reinforcement over time rather than to explicit instructions (Atlas et al., 2016; Tabbert et al., 2006). In other words, after walking past Fang many times and only seeing him wag his tail, Liz may lose her fear of him.

Although animal models of emotional learning highlight the role of the amygdala in fear conditioning and the indirect expression of the conditioned fear response, human emotional learning can be much more complex. We can learn that stimuli in the world link to potentially aversive consequences in a variety of ways, including instruction, observation, and experience. In whatever way we learn the aversive or threatening nature of stimuli—whether explicit and declarative, implicit, or both—the amygdala may play a role in the indirect expression of the fear response to those stimuli.

THE AMYGDALA, AROUSAL, AND MODULATION OF MEMORY The instructed-fear studies indicate that when an individual is taught that a stimulus is dangerous, hippocampal-dependent memory about the emotional properties of that stimulus (the dog is mean) can influence amygdala activity. The amygdala activity subsequently modulates some indirect emotional responses. But is it possible for the reverse to occur? Can the amygdala modulate the activity of the hippocampus? Put another way, can the amygdala influence what you learn and remember about an emotional event?

The types of things we recollect every day are things like where we left the keys or what we said to a friend the night before. When we look back on our lives, however, we do not remember these mundane events. We remember a first kiss, opening our college acceptance letter, or hearing about a horrible accident. The memories that last over time are those of emotional (not just fearful) or important (i.e., arousing) events. These memories seem to have a persistent vividness that other memories lack.

One type of persistent memory with an emotional flavor is called a "flashbulb" memory (R. Brown & Kulik, 1977; Hirst & Phelps, 2016). Flashbulb memories are autobiographical memories for the circumstances in which a public event became known (e.g., where you were and what you were doing when you saw or heard about the fall of the Berlin Wall, or the terrorist attacks on September 11, 2001). Event memories, on the other hand, are memories of the public event itself. For example, in the case of 9/11, people possess flashbulb memories of where they were when they learned about the attack and event memories of there being four planes involved. Research shows that details of these flashbulb memories are actually forgotten at a normal rate, but unlike ordinary autobiographical memories, where confidence in the memory declines with time, confidence in flashbulb memories remains high, even many years later (Hirst et al., 2015).

James McGaugh and his colleagues at UC Irvine (Ferry & McGaugh, 2000; McGaugh et al., 1992, 1996) investigated whether the persistence of emotional memories relates to action of the amygdala on memory consolidation processes during emotional arousal. An arousal response can influence people's ability to store declarative or explicit memories. For example, investigators frequently use the Morris water maze task (see Chapter 9) to test a rat's spatial abilities and memory. McGaugh found that a lesion to the amygdala does not impair a rat's ability to learn this task under ordinary circumstances. If a rat with a normal amygdala is aroused immediately after training, by either a physical stressor or the administration of drugs that mimic an arousal response, then the rat will show improved retention of this task. The memory is *enhanced* by arousal. A lesion to the rat's amygdala blocks this arousal-induced enhancement of memory, not memory acquisition itself (McGaugh et al., 1996). Using pharmacological lesions to temporarily disable the amygdala immediately after learning also eliminates any arousal-enhanced memory effect (Teather et al., 1998).

Two important aspects of this work help us understand the mechanism underlying the role of the amygdala in enhancing declarative memory observed with arousal. The first is that the *amygdala's role is modulatory*. The tasks used in these studies depend on the hippocampus for acquisition. In other words, the amygdala is not necessary for learning this hippocampal-dependent task, but it is necessary for the arousal-dependent modulation of memory for this task.

The second important facet of this work is that this arousal-dependent modulation of memory can occur *after* initial encoding of the task, *during the retention interval*. All of these studies point to the conclusion that the amygdala modulates hippocampal, declarative memory by *enhancing retention*, rather than by altering the initial encoding of the stimulus. Because this effect occurs during retention, researchers think the amygdala enhances hippocampal consolidation.

As described in Chapter 9, *consolidation* occurs over time, after initial encoding, and leads to memories becoming more or less stable. Thus, when there is an arousal response, the amygdala alters hippocampal processing by strengthening the consolidation of memories. McGaugh and colleagues (1996) showed that the basolateral nucleus of the amygdala is important for this effect. Additional evidence also suggests that the amygdala interacts directly with the hippocampus during the *initial* encoding phase of an experience (not just the consolidation phase), which in turn also positively affects the long-term consolidation (Dolcos et al., 2004). Thus, the amygdala can modulate hippocampal-dependent declarative memory at multiple stages, leading to a net effect of enhanced retention.

Researchers have also demonstrated that the amygdala plays the same role in enhancing emotional, declarative memory in humans. Various studies over the years indicate that a mild arousal response enhances declarative memory for emotional events (e.g., see Christianson, 1992), but the effect is blocked in patients with bilateral amygdala damage (Cahill et al., 1995). Interestingly, we have learned from patients with unilateral amygdala damage that the right amygdala is most important for the retrieval of autobiographical emotional memories with negative valence and high arousal (Buchanan et al., 2006). In addition, fMRI studies show that when perceiving emotional stimuli, amygdala activity correlates with an enhanced recollection of these stimuli: The more active the amygdala, the stronger the memory (Cahill et al., 1996; Hamann et al., 1999). There is also increased bidirectional connectivity between the amygdala and hippocampus during the recalling of emotional information relevant to one's current behavior (A. P. R. Smith et al., 2006). These studies indicate that when aroused, the human amygdala plays a role in the enhancing of declarative memory.

The mechanism for enhancing memory appears related to the amygdala's role in modifying the rate of forgetting. In other words, *arousal may alter how quickly we forget*. This is consistent with the theory that the amygdala, by enhancing hippocampal storage or consolidation, has a post-encoding effect on memory. Although the ability to recollect arousing and nonarousing events may be similar immediately after they occur, arousing events are not forgotten as quickly as nonarousing events are (Kleinsmith & Kaplan, 1963). While normal control participants show less forgetting over time for arousing compared to nonarousing stimuli, patients with amygdala lesions forget both at the same rate (LaBar & Phelps, 1998). Studies on both animal models and human populations converge on the conclusion that the amygdala acts to *modulate hippocampal consolidation* for arousing events.

This mechanism, however, does not underlie all the effects of emotion on human declarative memory. Emotional events are more distinctive and unusual than are everyday life events. They also form a specific class of events. These and other factors may enhance declarative or explicit memory for emotional events in ways that do not depend on the amygdala (Phelps et al., 1998).

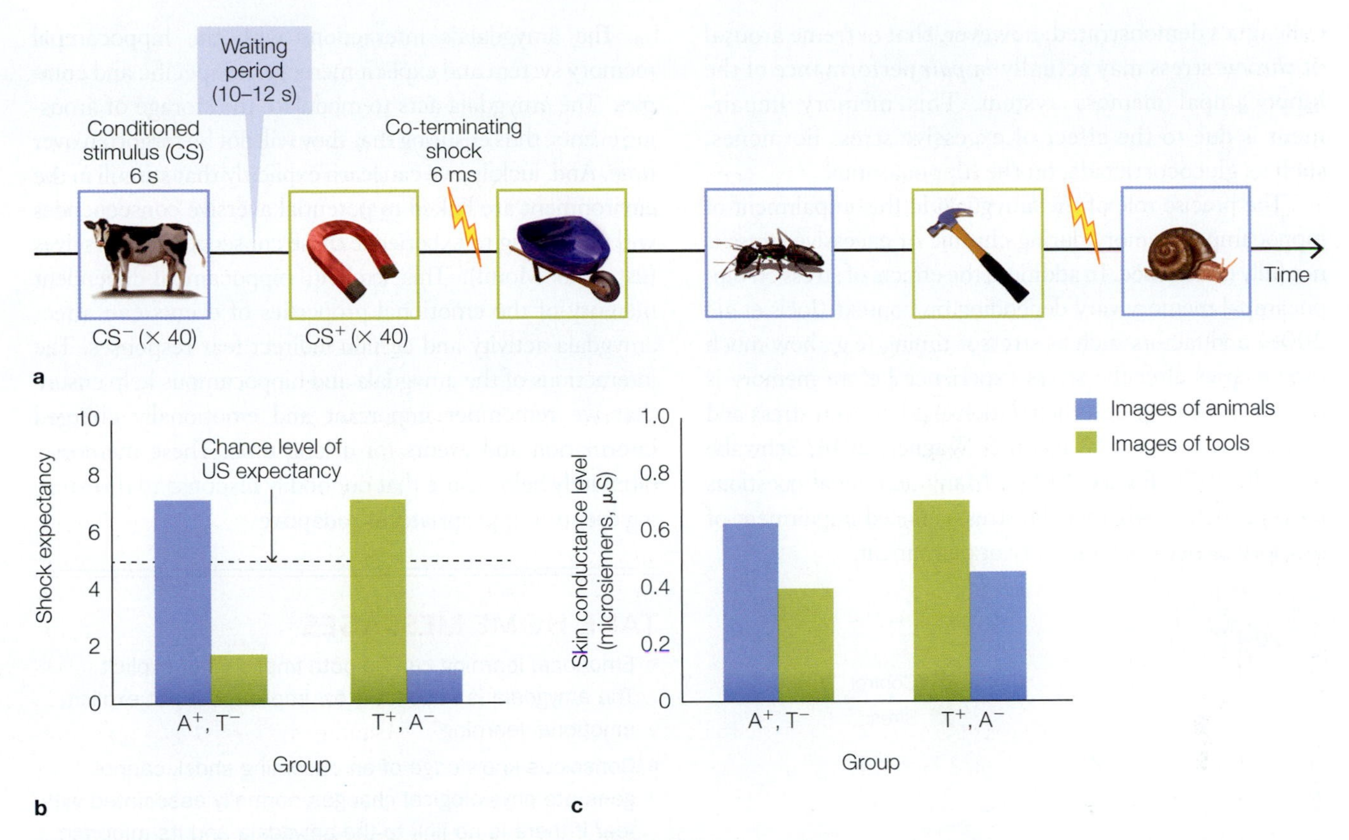

FIGURE 10.16 Fear-conditioning task demonstrating memory tagging.
(a) Example of the two categories of images—tools and animals—in which shocks were given with presentation of half the tool images. **(b)** Expectancy ratings indicate that the participants linked the CS (A^+ and later T^+) with the US (shock). **(c)** Skin conductance responses were greater for the "shock category" images (A^+ and T^+) compared to the "safe category" (A^- and T^-) images. The four scenarios are coded as follows: A^+ = images of animals predicted shock; T^+ = images of tools predicted shock; A^- = images of animals were safe; T^- = images of tools were safe.

Since memories of emotional events are usually relevant to guiding future behavior, we are motivated to recall them. Yet we often recall *insignificant* events that happened *before* an emotional event. For example, a woman may remember what her partner said to her early on the day of her engagement, even if the proposal was a complete surprise. This finding suggests that consolidation might "tag" as important for long-term retention not only emotional events, but also weak memories related to emotional events. A neurobiological account of memory consolidation has proposed a "synaptic tag-and-capture" mechanism whereby new memories that are initially weak and unstable are tagged for later stabilization (Frey & Morris, 1997). This mechanism was proposed to explain findings in rats, where initially weak behavioral training, which would otherwise be forgotten, endured in memory following a novel behavioral experience (Moncada & Viola, 2007).

Researchers have also demonstrated this sort of "behavioral tagging" in humans. Joseph Dunsmoor and colleagues (Dunsmoor, Murty, et al., 2015) showed people pictures from two distinct categories: animals and tools. After this preconditioning phase, they paired one of the categories with a shock in the conditioning phase (**Figure 10.16**). After a period of consolidation, the participants' memory was better not only for the images that were associated with shock in the conditioning phase, but also for images from that same category that were shown only in the preconditioning phase and not associated with the shock. Thus, inconsequential information (here, pictures that were not associated with a shock) can be retroactively credited as relevant to an event and, therefore, selectively remembered if related information is later associated with an emotional response. This behavioral tagging phenomenon has also been demonstrated in humans in the reward-learning domain (Patil et al., 2017).

STRESS AND MEMORY *Acute* stress may facilitate memory. Kevin LaBar and his colleagues at Duke University (Zorawski et al., 2006) found that the amount of endogenous stress hormone (cortisol) released during the acquisition of a conditioned fear accurately predicts how well fear memories are retained one day later in humans. Robert Sapolsky of Stanford University (1992) and his colleagues demonstrated, however, that extreme arousal or *chronic* stress may actually *impair* performance of the hippocampal memory system. This memory impairment is due to the effect of excessive stress hormones, such as glucocorticoids, on the hippocampus.

The precise role of the amygdala in this impairment of hippocampal memory during chronic or excessive stress is not fully understood. In addition, the effects of stress on hippocampal memory vary depending on context (Joëls et al., 2006) and factors such as stressor timing (e.g., how much time elapses after the stress experience before memory is tested), indicating that the relationship between stress and memory is complex (Gagnon & Wagner, 2016; Schwabe & Wolf, 2014; **Figure 10.17**). Many additional questions remain, such as whether the stress-induced impairment of memory retrieval is temporary or permanent.

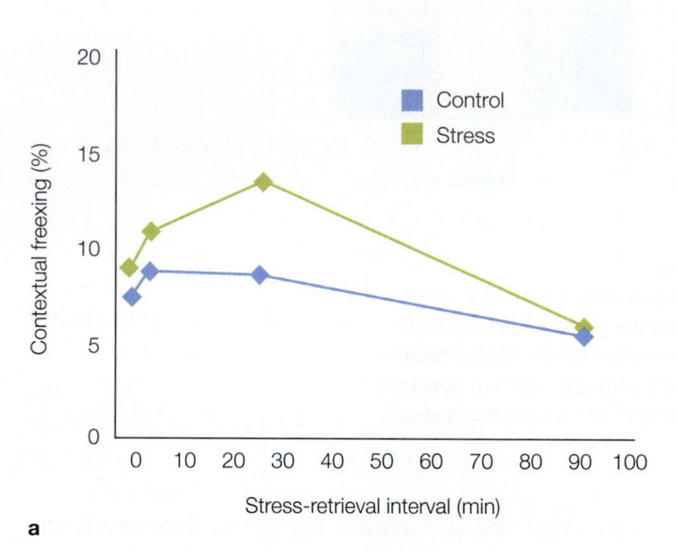

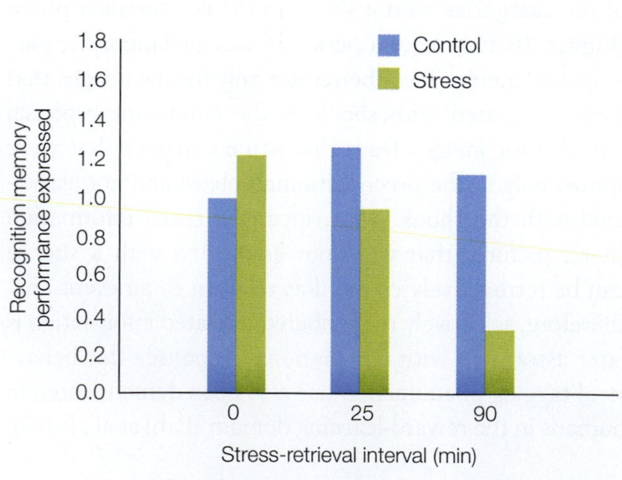

FIGURE 10.17 Recognition memory performance and acute stress.
(a) Participants in one group experienced a stressor, and the control group did not. Cortisol levels in the stressed group rose higher and continued to rise longer than in the nonstressed group. **(b)** A stressful event did not immediately affect memory performance, but it did as time passed and cortisol levels rose.

The amygdala's interactions with the hippocampal memory system and explicit memory are specific and complex. The amygdala acts to modulate the storage of arousing events, thus ensuring that they will not be forgotten over time. And, luckily, we can learn explicitly that stimuli in the environment are linked to potential aversive consequences without having to experience these consequences ourselves (listen to Mom!). This explicit, hippocampal-dependent memory of the emotional properties of events can affect amygdala activity and certain indirect fear responses. The interactions of the amygdala and hippocampus help ensure that we remember important and emotionally charged information and events for a long time. These memories ultimately help ensure that our bodily response to threatening events is appropriate and adaptive.

TAKE-HOME MESSAGES

- Emotional learning can be both implicit and explicit. The amygdala is necessary for implicit, but not explicit, emotional learning.
- Conscious knowledge of an upcoming shock cannot generate physiological changes normally associated with fear if there is no link to the amygdala and its midbrain connections.
- Information can reach the amygdala via two separate pathways: The "low road" goes directly from the thalamus to the amygdala; the "high road" goes from the cortex to the amygdala.
- The hippocampus is necessary for the acquisition of a memory, but if arousal accompanies memory acquisition, the strength and duration of that memory is modulated by amygdala activity.

10.7 Interactions Between Emotion and Other Cognitive Processes

While much research has focused on the effects of emotion on learning and memory, its effects on other cognitive processes are also being unraveled. In this section we will look at how emotion affects perception, attention, and decision making.

The Influence of Emotion on Perception and Attention

No doubt you have had the experience of being in the midst of a conversation, hearing your name mentioned behind you, and immediately turning to see who said it.

We exhibit an increased awareness for and pay attention to emotionally salient stimuli. To study this phenomenon, attention researchers often use the *attentional blink paradigm*, in which stimuli are presented so quickly in succession that an individual stimulus is difficult to identify. Yet when participants are told that they can ignore most of the stimuli—say, disregard all the words printed in green and attend to only the few targets printed in blue—they are able to identify the targets. This ability is limited, however, by the amount of time between the target (blue) stimuli. If a second target stimulus is presented immediately after the first, during an interval known as the early lag period, participants will often miss this second target. This impaired perceptual report reflects the temporal limitations of attention and is known as the **attentional blink**.

Yet, if that second word is emotionally significant, people tend to notice it after all (A. K. Anderson, 2005). An emotionally significant word is distinctive, arousing, and has either a positive or negative valence. In this experiment, arousal value (how reactive the participant is to a stimulus), not the valence of the word or its distinctiveness, overcame the attentional blink. Studies have shown that when the left amygdala is damaged, patients don't recognize the second target, even if it is an arousing word (A. K. Anderson & Phelps, 2001). So, it appears that when attentional resources are limited, arousing emotional stimuli are what reach awareness. Once again, the amygdala plays a critical role by enhancing our attention when emotional stimuli are present.

There are reciprocal connections between the amygdala and the sensory cortical processing regions, as well as the emotional inputs that the amygdala receives even before awareness takes place. Studies indicate that attention and awareness have little impact on the amygdala's response to fearful stimuli (A. K. Anderson et al., 2003; Vuilleumier et al., 2001), consistent with the finding that the emotional qualities of stimuli are processed automatically (Zajonc, 1984). Thus, although your attention may be focused on your upcoming lunch while hiking up the trail, you will still be startled by a movement in the grass. You have just experienced a rapid and automatic change in attention spurred by emotional stimuli.

The proposed mechanism for this attentional change is that early in the perceptual processing of the stimulus, the amygdala receives input about its emotional significance and, through projections to sensory cortical regions, modulates the attentional and perceptual processes (A. K. Anderson & Phelps, 2001; Vuilleumier et al., 2004). This idea is based first on the finding that there is enhanced activation of visual cortical regions to novel emotional stimuli (Kosslyn et al., 1996), combined with imaging studies that show a correlation between visual cortex activation and amygdala activation in response to these same stimuli (J. S. Morris et al., 1998). The correlation between these regions is more pronounced when emotional stimuli are presented subliminally rather than processed consciously, which is consistent with the idea that this pathway is important for "preattentive" processing (L. M. Williams et al., 2006).

Fearful stimuli are not the only stimuli processed in the amygdala. A meta-analysis of 385 imaging studies found that while negative stimuli, especially fearful and disgusting ones, tend to have priority processing, positive stimuli also may activate the amygdala (Costafreda et al., 2008; **Figure 10.18**). It also found external stimuli receiving priority over internally generated stimuli.

Some evidence suggests that *novelty* is a characteristic of a stimulus that engages the amygdala independently of other affective properties, such as valence and arousal. An fMRI study that examined valence, arousal, and novelty of emotional photo images found that the amygdala

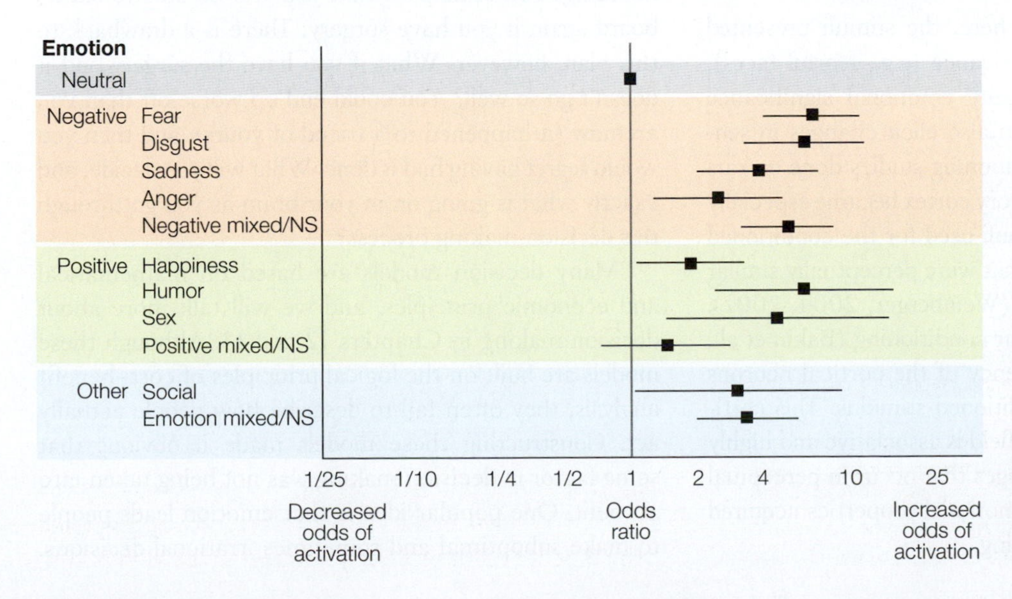

FIGURE 10.18 The odds of amygdala activation with different types of emotion. Results of a meta-analysis employing a meta-regression technique that took into account the impact of multiple experimental factors on the probability of detecting amygdala activation in each study. NS = nonspecified.

had higher peak responses and was activated longer for novel stimuli versus familiar stimuli, and that the effect was independent of both valence and arousal (Weierich et al., 2010). The investigators also observed increased activity in early visual areas V1 and V2 when participants viewed novel emotional stimuli. This activation was differentiated from the activation seen in later visual areas that occurred for valence and arousal.

What's more, fMRI studies show that patients with damage to the amygdala do not show significant activation for fearful versus neutral faces in the visual cortex, whereas controls and patients with hippocampal damage do (Vuilleumier et al., 2004). Taken together, these findings suggest that when emotional stimuli are present, the amygdala has a leading role in mediating the transient changes in visual cortical processing.

Clearly, the amygdala is critical in bringing an unattended but emotional stimulus into the realm of conscious awareness by providing some feedback to the primary sensory cortices, thus affecting perceptual processing. This function was demonstrated by Phelps and her colleagues (2006). They examined the effect of fearful face cues on contrast sensitivity—an aspect of visual processing that occurs early in the primary visual cortex and is enhanced by covert attention—and found that when a face cue directed covert attention, contrast sensitivity was enhanced. This was an expected result.

The interesting finding was that a fearful face enhanced contrast sensitivity, whether or not covert attention was directed to the face: The emotion-laden stimulus enhanced perception without the aid of attention. The team also found that if the fearful face did cue attention, contrast sensitivity was enhanced even more than would have been predicted for the independent effects of a fearful face and covert attention. Thus, emotion-laden stimuli receive greater attention and priority in perceptual processing.

In the studies described here, the stimuli presented had inherent emotional significance (e.g., fearful faces), but neutral stimuli that acquire emotional significance through fear conditioning can also elicit changes in sensory processing. In fear-conditioning studies done on rats (Weinberger, 1995), the auditory cortex became especially sensitive not only to the stimuli used for the conditioned stimulus, but also to stimuli that were perceptually similar to that conditioned stimulus (Weinberger, 2004, 2007). Classical conditioning and fear conditioning (Bakin et al., 1996) shift the tuning frequency of the cortical neurons to the frequency of the conditioned stimulus. This cortical plasticity of the receptive field is associative and highly specific. The idea is that changes that occur in perceptual processing for stimuli with emotional properties acquired through learning are long-lasting.

In a fear-conditioning study in humans that used subliminally exposed face stimuli as the CS and an aversive loud noise as the US, imaging showed an *increasing* responsiveness to the CS in both the amygdala and the visual cortex over a series of trials (J. S. Morris et al., 2001). This response was also found for conditioning with odors (W. Li et al., 2008) and tones (D. C. Knight et al., 2005). The parallel occurrence of a learning response in the amygdala and the visual cortex supports the idea that feedback efferents from the amygdala to the visual cortex act to modulate visual processing of emotionally salient stimuli. Fear conditioning modulates activity in and connectivity between the amygdala and cortical areas coding for the sensory qualities of the CS.

How about *conceptual information* about the CS? Some visual cortex areas are selective to images of particular categories, even when the images are perceptually not that similar (e.g., faces, animals, tools). A learned fear of images from a particular category is reflected in activity in the amygdala and the area of cortex selective to that category (Dunsmoor et al., 2014). Thus, emotional learning can modulate category-level representations of object concepts, resulting in the expression of fear to a range of related stimuli. For example, a bad experience with one dog could lead to a generalized fear of all dogs. Whether emotional learning involves an enduring change in sensory cortical tuning or the change is shorter-lived remains a matter of debate.

Emotion and Decision Making

Suppose you have a big decision to make, and it has an uncertain outcome. You are considering elective knee surgery. You don't need the surgery to survive; you get around okay, and you have no trouble body surfing. The problem is that you can't do your favorite sport, snowboarding. You anticipate that you will be able to snowboard again if you have surgery. There is a drawback to this plan, however. What if you have the surgery and it doesn't go so well? You could end up worse off than you are now (it happened to a friend of yours), and then you would regret having had it done. What will you decide, and exactly what is going on in your brain as you go through this decision-making process?

Many decision models are based on mathematical and economic principles, and we will talk more about decision making in Chapters 12 and 13. Although these models are built on the logical principles of cost–benefit analysis, they often fail to describe how people actually act. Constructing these models made it obvious that some factor in decision making was not being taken into account. One popular idea is that emotion leads people to make suboptimal and sometimes irrational decisions.

The hypothesis that emotion and reason are separable in the brain and compete for control of behavior is often called "dual-systems theory," and it has dominated Western thought since the time of Plato.

Although the notion that emotion is disruptive to decision making is intuitive and is even reflected in our everyday language (e.g., smart decisions are made with the "head," and impulsive decisions are made with the "heart"), dual-systems theory has not been substantiated. First, as we have seen in this chapter, there is no unified system in the brain that drives emotion, so emotion and reason are not clearly separable. Instead, we have seen that emotion often plays a modulatory role in cognitive processes such as memory and attention. Second, some of our most adaptive decisions are driven by emotional reactions.

In the early 1990s, Antonio Damasio and his colleagues at the University of Iowa made a surprising discovery while working with patient E.V.R., who had orbitofrontal cortex (OFC) damage. When faced with social reasoning tasks, E.V.R. could generate solutions to problems, but he could not prioritize his solutions by their effectiveness. In the real world, he made poor decisions about his professional and social life (Saver & Damasio, 1991).

In a group of patients with similar lesions, researchers found that the patients had difficulty anticipating the consequences of their actions and did not learn from their mistakes (Bechara et al., 1994). At the time, researchers believed that the OFC handled emotional functions. Their belief was based on the many connections of the OFC to the insular cortex and the cingulate cortex, the amygdala, and the hypothalamus—all areas involved with emotion processing. Because emotion was considered a disruptive force in decision making, it was surprising that impairing a region involved in emotion would result in impaired decision making. Seemingly, an individual's decision-making ability should have improved with such a lesion. Damasio wondered whether damage to the OFC impaired decision making because emotion was actually needed to optimize it. At the time, this was a shocking suggestion.

To test this idea, Damasio and his colleagues devised the Iowa Gambling Task, in which skin conductance response is measured while participants continually draw cards from their choice of four decks. The cards indicate monetary amounts resulting in either a gain or a loss. What participants don't know is that two of the decks are associated with net winnings; although they have small payoffs, they have even smaller losses. The other two decks are associated with net losses, because although they have large payoffs, they have even larger losses. The cards are stacked in a particular order designed to drive an initial preference for the riskier decks (early big wins) that must then be overcome as losses begin to accrue. Participants must figure out as they play that they can earn the most money by choosing the decks associated with small payoffs.

Healthy adults and patients with damage outside the orbitofrontal cortex gamble in a manner that maximizes winnings. In contrast, patients with orbitofrontal damage fail to favor the decks that result in net winnings. These results led Damasio to propose the *somatic marker hypothesis*, which states that emotional information, in the form of physiological arousal, is needed to guide decision making. When presented with a situation that requires us to make a decision, we may react emotionally to the situation around us. This emotional reaction is manifest in our bodies as **somatic markers**—changes in physiological arousal.

It is theorized that the orbitofrontal structures support our ability to learn to associate a complex situation with the somatic changes that usually accompany that particular situation. The OFC and other brain regions then consider previous situations that elicited similar patterns of somatic change. Once these situations have been identified, the OFC can use these experiences to rapidly evaluate possible behavioral responses to the present situation and estimate their likelihood for reward.

Several studies have since questioned the somatic marker hypothesis and the specific interpretation of these results (Maia & McClelland, 2004). Nevertheless, Damasio's study was one of the first to link emotional responses and brain systems to decision patterns. It also emphasized that emotional responses could contribute to optimal decision making.

Our current understanding (Lerner et al., 2015; Phelps et al., 2014) suggests that there are two primary ways by which emotion influences decision making:

1. *Incidental affect.* Current emotional state, unrelated to the decision at hand, *incidentally* influences the decision.
2. *Integral emotion.* Emotions elicited by the choice options are incorporated into the decision. This process may include emotions that you anticipate feeling after you have made the decision, which humans are notoriously bad at predicting (Gilbert, 2006).

INCIDENTAL AFFECT The emotion that you are currently feeling can influence your decision. For example, say you're leafing through a term paper that took you an entire weekend to write, which your professor has just returned. As you flip it over to see your grade, a friend comes up to you and asks you to head up the fund drive for your soccer club. What you see on that paper will produce an emotion in you—such as elation, frustration, satisfaction, or anger—that may affect the response you give to your friend.

What function is served by having emotions play such a role in decision making? Ellen Peters and her colleagues (2006) suggest that the feelings we experience about a stimulus and the feelings that are independent of the stimulus, such as mood states, have four roles in decision making:

1. They can act as information.
2. They can act as "common currency" between disparate inputs and options (you can feel slightly aroused by a book and very aroused by a swimming pool).
3. They can focus attention on new information, which can then guide the decision.
4. They can motivate decisions to engage in approach or avoidance behavior.

A specific hypothesis about how moods influence decision making is the appraisal tendency framework (ATF; Lerner & Keltner, 2000). The ATF assumes that specific affective states give rise to specific cognitive and motivational properties and thus yield certain action tendencies (Frijda, 1986). These tendencies depend on arousal level and the valence of the mood, but they may differ for different moods of the same valence.

For example, Jennifer Lerner and colleagues (2004) induced a sad, disgusted, or neutral mood and explored its impact on the endowment effect—the phenomenon in which the price one is willing to accept to sell an owned item is greater than the price one would pay to buy the same item. They found that a sad mood reversed the endowment effect (i.e., it resulted in higher buying prices than selling prices), whereas a disgusted mood led to a reduction in both buying and selling prices (**Figure 10.19**). The researchers suggested that sadness is an indication that the current situation is unfavorable, which enhances the value of options that change the situation. Disgust, however, is linked to a tendency to move away from or expel what is disgusting, which carries over to a tendency to reduce the value of *all* items.

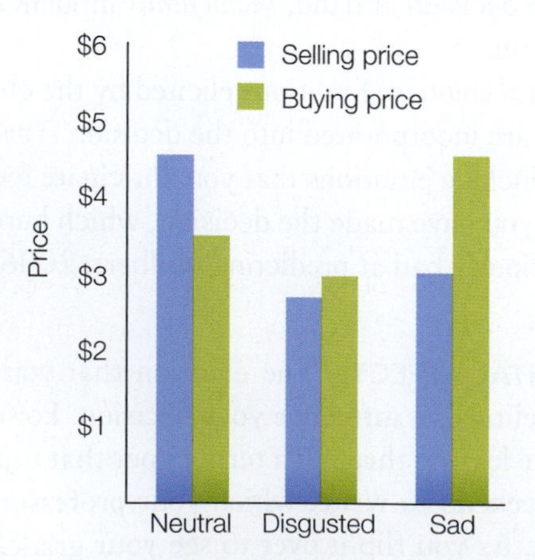

FIGURE 10.19 The effect of emotions on prices for selling and buying.
Differing emotions of the same valence can have opposite effects on economic decisions. Selling price = how much money a person was willing to accept in exchange for an item. Buying price = how much a person was willing to pay for the item.

Another incidental affective state that might influence later decisions is stress. As with its effects on memory, the effects of stress on decision making can vary. One general theme that has emerged, however, is that acute stress leads to an increased reliance on *default* or *habitual* responses (Lempert & Phelps, 2016). Acute stress interferes with functioning of the prefrontal cortex (PFC), a region that is necessary for the flexible control of behavior (Arnsten, 2009), but it enhances performance on tasks that rely on the striatum (Packard & Goodman, 2012). The PFC is proposed to play a role in goal-directed decisions, whereas the striatum is generally linked to choices based on habits (Balleine & O'Doherty, 2010).

To explore the trade-off between PFC- and striatum-mediated choices with stress, Dias-Ferreira and colleagues (2009) examined how stress impacted later performance on a *devaluation task* in rodents. Devaluation tasks alter the value of the reward to assess whether choices are habitual or are directed toward a reinforcement goal. If reducing the value of the reward changes behavior, the task is said to be goal directed. And if devaluing the reward does not alter behavior, the behavior is habitual.

After rats were trained to press a lever to receive a food reward, they were fed to satiety, thus devaluing the reward. Rats that had not been previously stressed reduced their response rate, reflecting the devalued reward outcome. In contrast, stressed rats failed to modify their behavior following devaluation: They kept eating, consistent with habitual responding. In humans, using a devaluation paradigm similar to that described here, Schwabe and Wolf (2009) found that acute stress led to a similar shift from goal-directed to habitual choices in humans, suggesting an explanation for why we often revert to bad habits, such as eating junk food or smoking, when stressed.

INTEGRAL EMOTION Because emotional reactions modulate a range of cognitive functions, it is not surprising that we also take into account the emotional response elicited by potential outcomes in order to make decisions. One domain in which emotion plays a large role is the making of risky decisions that have the possibility of monetary loss. People tend to be loss averse, meaning that we weigh losses more heavily than gains when considering choices.

Using a gambling task, Sokol-Hessner and colleagues (2009) found that higher levels of skin conductance in response to losses relative to gains were linked to greater loss aversion. A greater BOLD signal in the amygdala for losses relative to gains also correlated with loss aversion (Sokol-Hessner et al., 2012). Consistent with these imaging results, patients with amygdala lesions showed reduced loss aversion overall (De Martino et al., 2010), and administering a beta-adrenergic blocker (propranolol), which had previously been shown to diminish the amygdala's modulation of memory (Phelps, 2006), also reduced loss aversion (Sokol-Hessner, Lackovic, et al., 2015). This series of studies provides strong evidence that the amygdala plays a critical role in mediating aversion to losses—a finding that is consistent with the amygdala's role in threat detection, since the possibility of monetary loss is perceived as a threat, prompting avoidance of that option.

Emotions have an impact on our choices, but choices can also impact our emotions. First of all, we like outcomes that we have chosen more than outcomes that have been selected for us. In one study, in half of the trials participants had the opportunity to press a button of their choosing before winning a reward. In the other half of the trials, participants were told which button to press before the reward appeared. Even though the button presses had no effect on the outcomes in the study, people reported liking choice trials more, and this preference was reflected in increased striatal reward signals on those trials (Leotti & Delgado, 2011).

In addition, certain specific emotions are elicited by choice, such as regret and disappointment. Regret is the feeling you get when you compare the voluntary choice you made with rejected alternatives that might have turned out better. You feel regret because you are able to think counterfactually. You can say, "If I had done this instead of that, then things would have been better." We dislike feeling regret, and so, as we learn from experience, we take steps to minimize feeling regret by making choices to avoid it. In contrast, disappointment is an emotion related to an unexpected negative outcome without the sense of personal responsibility or control. "I won teacher of the year, but because I was the last one hired, I was the first one fired."

In a fascinating study (Kishida et al., 2016), patients with Parkinson's disease who were undergoing surgical implantation of a deep brain stimulator consented to having an additional research-exclusive probe placed in their ventral striatum and to playing a simple gambling game during surgery. As the participants placed bets and experienced monetary gains or losses, the probe measured dopamine release in the ventral striatum. Previous studies in animal models had predicted that the ventral striatum encodes reward prediction error (RPE). This is not what the researchers found. Unexpectedly, subsecond dopamine fluctuations appeared to encode an integration of RPEs with counterfactual prediction errors (i.e., how much better or worse the experienced outcome could have been).

These researchers suggest that the [illegible] also captures the qualitative aspec[illegible] (dopamine increase accompanyin[illegible] decrease with a bad one), given one [illegible] ple, one should feel good with a better-t[illegible] outcome, but if alternative outcomes could have [illegible] even better, then the integration of the two scenarios would result in decreased dopamine, in which case one should feel bad, consistent with the feelings of regret at a missed opportunity.

TAKE-HOME MESSAGES

- The amygdala is activated by novel stimuli independent of valence and arousal.
- The amygdala mediates transient changes in visual cortical processing that enhance perception of the emotion-laden stimulus without the aid of attention.
- Both one's current emotional state and the emotions elicited by choice options can influence decision making.
- Acute stress interferes with prefrontal cortex activity, necessary for the flexible control of behavior, and enhances striatal activity, generally linked to choices based on habits.

10.8 Emotion and Social Stimuli

In this section we discuss the involvement of the amygdala in some of the processes that come into play with social interactions. In Chapter 13 we cover the topic of social cognition, which centers on how people and other animals process and encode social information, store and retrieve it, and apply it to social situations.

Facial Expressions

Studies have shown that there is a dissociation between identifying an individual's face and recognizing the emotional expression on that face. Our patient S.M. had no trouble identifying faces; she just couldn't recognize the expression of fear on a face (Adolphs et al., 1994). People with amygdalar damage do not have a problem recognizing nonemotional facial features. In addition, they are able to recognize the similarity between facial expressions whose emotional content they label incorrectly. What's more, their deficit appears to be restricted to the *recognition* of facial expressions. Some of them are able to generate and communicate a full range of facial expressions themselves (A. K. Anderson & Phelps, 2000).

[D]epending on the specific facial expression, it appears [t]hat different neural mechanisms and regions of the brain are at work, not for processing specific facial expressions per se, but more generally for processing different emotions.

Neuroimaging experiments in normal participants and in patients with anxiety disorders have reported increased amygdala activation in response to brief presentations of faces with fearful expressions compared to faces with neutral expressions (Breiter et al., 1996; Cahill et al., 1996; Irwin et al., 1996; J. S. Morris et al., 1998). Although the amygdala is also activated in response to expressions of other emotions, such as happiness or anger, the activation response to fear is significantly greater.

One interesting aspect of the amygdala's response to fearful facial expressions is that the participant does not have to be aware of seeing the fearful face for the amygdala to respond. When fearful facial expressions are presented subliminally and then masked with neutral expressions, the amygdala activates as strongly as when the participant is aware of seeing the faces (Whalen et al., 1998). Conscious cognition is not involved.

This critical role for the amygdala in explicitly evaluating fearful faces also extends to other social judgments about faces, such as indicating from a picture of a face whether the person appears trustworthy or approachable (Adolphs et al., 2000; Said et al., 2010). This finding supports the idea that the amygdala is a danger detector, and it is consistent with the behavior of patients with amygdala damage, who rated pictures of individuals whose faces were deemed untrustworthy by normal controls as both more trustworthy and more approachable (Adolphs et al., 1998).

After nearly a decade of testing S.M., Ralph Adolphs and his colleagues (Adolphs et al., 2005; Kennedy & Adolphs, 2010) discovered an explanation for her inability to recognize fearful faces. Using computer software that exposed only parts of either a fearful or a happy facial expression, the researchers were able to figure out which regions of the face participants relied on to discriminate between expressions. They found that control participants consistently relied on eyes to make decisions about expression. S.M., on the other hand, did not derive information from eyes. Confirming this finding using eye-tracking technology, the researchers found that S.M. did not look at the eyes of *any* face, regardless of the emotion it conveyed (**Figure 10.20a**). So, if S.M. did not automatically use eyes to derive information from any faces, why was fear the only emotion she had trouble identifying?

Most emotional expressions contain other cues that can be used to identify them. For instance, an expression of happiness reliably contains a smile, and disgust usually includes a snarl of sorts. The identifying feature of a fearful expression, however, is the increase in size

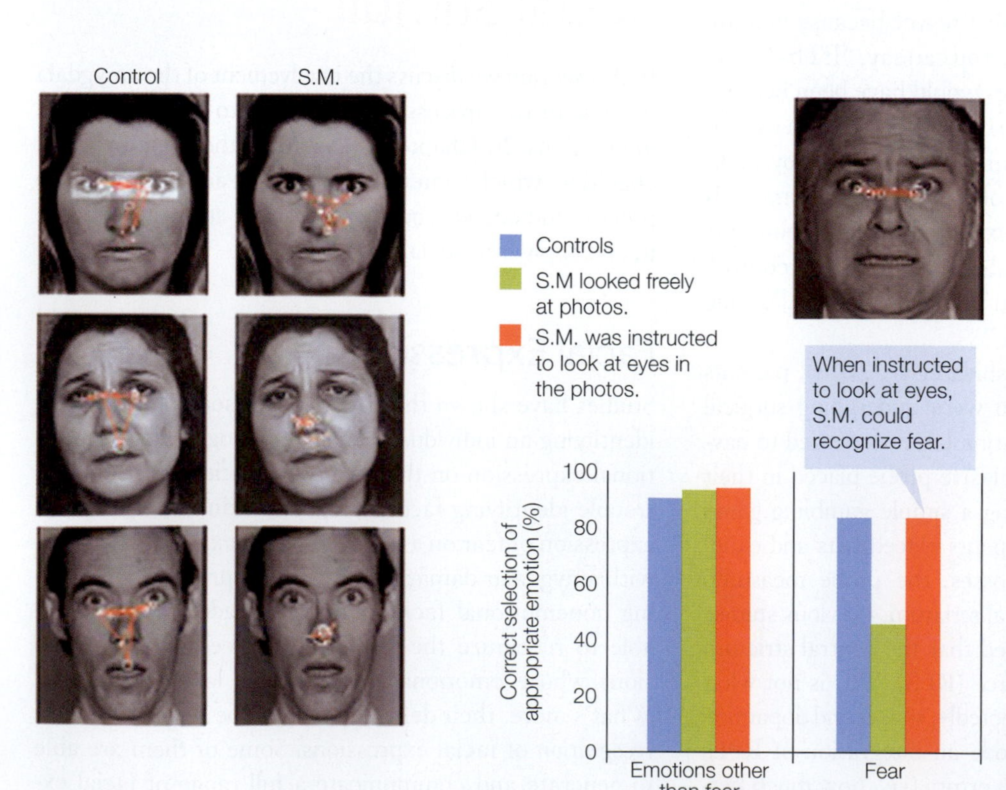

FIGURE 10.20 Abnormal eye movement patterns during face perception following amygdala lesions.
(a) Unlike the eye movements measured in control participants, S.M.'s eye movements do not target the eyes of other faces. (Red lines indicate eye movements, and white circles indicate points of fixation.) **(b)** When instructed to focus on the eyes, however, S.M. is able to identify fearful expressions with the same degree of success that controls do. The photo at top right tracking S.M.'s eye movements shows that, when so instructed, she is able to look at the eyes.

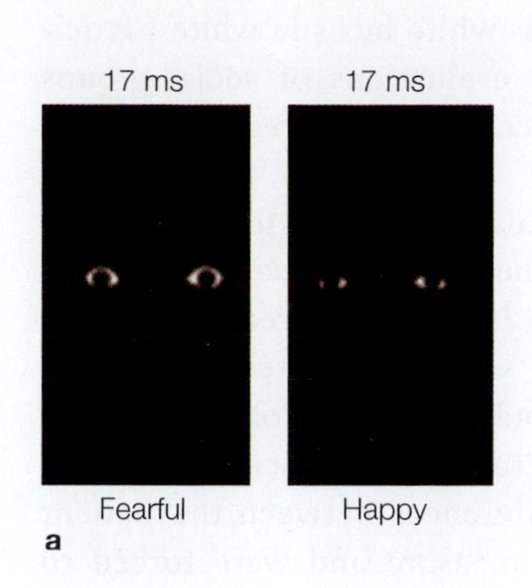

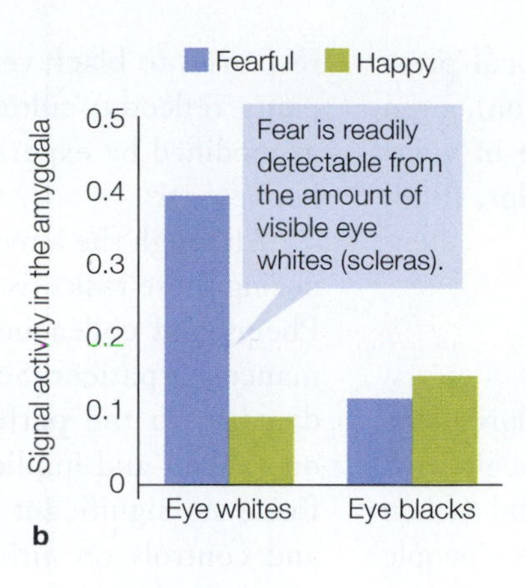

FIGURE 10.21 Size of eye whites alone is sufficient to induce differential amygdala response to fearful expressions.
(a) The area of eye whites is greater in fearful expressions than in happy expressions. **(b)** Activity in the left ventral amygdala in response to eye whites and eye blacks relative to fixation demonstrates that fearful eye whites alone induce an increased response above baseline. Eye blacks were control stimuli, which were identical in shape to the stimuli in (a) but had inverted colors, such that the eye whites were actually black on a white screen.

of the white region (sclera) of the eyes (**Figure 10.21**). Viewing the scleras in a fearful face without any other accompanying facial information is sufficient to increase amygdala activity in normal participants (relative to scleras from facial expressions of happiness; Whalen et al., 2004).

In another study, investigators masked expressions of happiness or sadness in order to find brain areas associated with automatic, implicit analysis of these emotions (Killgore & Yurgelun-Todd, 2004). They found amygdala activity associated with analysis of happy but not sad faces. Although a smile is part of a happy expression, a smile can be faked. First observed by Duchenne and known as the Duchenne smile, the telling part of a truly happy facial expression is the contraction of the orbicularis oculi muscle, which most people cannot voluntarily control (Ekman, 2003). This contraction causes the lateral eye margins to crinkle, the cheeks to be pulled up, and the lateral portion of the brow to drop. Perhaps amygdala activation when looking at happy faces is due to our attention being drawn to the eyes and identifying this aspect of the happy facial expression.

Stunningly, Adolphs and his colleagues could induce S.M. to overcome her deficit by providing her with a simple instruction: "Focus on the eyes." If told to do this, she no longer had any difficulty identifying fearful faces (**Figure 10.20b**). She would focus on the eyes only when reminded, however. Consequently, the amygdala appears to be an integral part of a bottom-up system that automatically directs visual attention to the eyes when encountering any facial expression. With an impaired amygdala, eye gaze is under top-down control. Impaired eye gaze is also a main characteristic of several psychiatric illnesses and social disorders in which the amygdala may be dysfunctional (e.g., autism spectrum disorder).

The finding by Adolphs and colleagues that looking at the eyes is important to recognizing facial expressions, along with their experimental manipulations that promote eye gaze, may point toward promising interventions in such populations (Gamer & Buchel, 2009; Kennedy & Adolphs, 2010). Researchers at the California Institute for Telecommunications and Information Technology at UC San Diego extended these findings by identifying all the physical characteristics (eyebrow angle, pupil dilation, etc.) that make facial expressions of fear and the other basic emotions unique. They have developed an "Einstein" robot that can identify and then imitate facial expressions of others. (You can watch Einstein at http://www.youtube.com/watch?v=pkpWCu1k0ZI.)

Beyond the Face

You may be familiar with the study in which participants were shown a film of various geometric shapes moving around a box. The movement was such that the participants described the shapes as if they were animate, with personalities and motives, moving about in a complex social situation; that is, participants anthropomorphized the shapes (Heider & Simmel, 1944). Patients with either amygdala damage or autism do not do this. They describe the shapes as geometric figures, and their description of the movement is devoid of social or emotional aspirations (Heberlein & Adolphs, 2004). Thus, the amygdala seems to have a role in perceiving and interpreting emotion and sociability in a wide range of stimuli, even inanimate objects. It may play a role in our ability to anthropomorphize.

The amygdala, however, does not appear to be critical for all types of social communication. Unlike patients with damage to the orbitofrontal cortex (which we will discuss in Chapter 13), patients with amygdala lesions, as we saw with S.M., do not show gross impairment in their ability to respond to social stimuli. They can interpret descriptions of emotional situations correctly, and they can give normal ratings to emotional prosody (the speech sounds that indicate emotion), even when a person is speaking in a fearful tone of voice (Adolphs et al., 1999; A. K. Anderson & Phelps, 1998; S. K. Scott et al., 1997).

Social Group Evaluation

The amygdala also appears to be activated during the categorization of people into groups. Although such implicit behavior might sometimes be helpful (when separating people within a social group from people outside of the group, or identifying the trustworthiness of a person), it can also lead to behaviors such as racial stereotyping. A variety of research has looked at racial stereotyping from both a behavioral and a functional imaging perspective.

Behavioral research has gone beyond simple, explicit measures of racial bias, as obtained through self-reporting, to implicit measures examining indirect behavioral responses that demonstrate a preference for one group over another. One common indirect measure for examining bias is the Implicit Association Test (IAT). Devised by Greenwald and colleagues (1998), the IAT measures the degree to which social groups (black versus white, old versus young, etc.) are automatically associated with positive and negative evaluations. (See https://implicit.harvard.edu/implicit to take the test yourself.) Participants are asked to categorize faces from each group while simultaneously categorizing words as either good or bad. For example, for one set of trials the participant responds to "good" words and black faces with one hand, and to "bad" words and white faces with the other hand. In another set of trials, the pairings are switched. The measure of bias is computed by the difference in the response latency between the black-and-good/white-and-bad trials versus the black-and-bad/white-and-good trials.

To study the neural basis of this racial bias, Elizabeth Phelps and her colleagues (2000) used fMRI to examine amygdala activation in white participants viewing black and white faces. They found that the amygdala was activated when white Americans viewed unfamiliar black faces (but not faces of familiar, positively regarded blacks like Michael Jordan, Will Smith, and Martin Luther King Jr.). More important, the magnitude of the amygdala activation was significantly correlated with indirect measures of racial bias as determined by the IAT. Participants who showed more racial bias as measured by the IAT showed greater amygdala activity during the presentation of black faces. The researchers concluded that the amygdala responses and behavioral responses to black versus white faces in white participants reflected cultural evaluations of social groups as modified by experience. But is this really what was happening?

Although the amygdala does appear to be activated during these tasks, is it necessary for such evaluation? Phelps and colleagues (2003) compared the performance of patient S.P., who had bilateral amygdala damage, to the performance of control participants on explicit and implicit measures of racial bias. They found no significant differences between the patient and controls on either measure and were forced to conclude that the amygdala is not a critical structure for the indirect evaluation of race, suggesting instead that it might be important for differences in the perceptual processing of faces belonging to "same" or "other" races.

Expanding on these findings, William Cunningham and colleagues (2004) used fMRI to compare areas of brain activation in white participants when presented with the faces of both black and white males either briefly or for a prolonged amount of time. The results led the researchers to posit two separate systems for social evaluation (**Figure 10.22**). For brief presentations, where the evaluation must be made quickly and automatically, the amygdala was activated, and the activation was greater for black faces than for white faces. With longer presentations, when controlled processing can take place, amygdala activation was not significantly different between races. Instead, significantly more activity occurred in the right ventrolateral prefrontal cortex during viewing of black faces than of white faces. Cunningham's team proposed that there are distinct neural differences between automatic and more controlled processing of social groups, and that the controlled processing may modulate the automatic evaluation—LeDoux's low-road processing being updated by the high-road processing.

We must be careful in drawing sweeping conclusions about racial stereotypes from these data. It may appear that certain processes in the brain make it likely that people will categorize others on the basis of race, but is that what they actually do? This suggestion does not make sense to evolutionary psychologists, who point out that our human ancestors did not travel very great distances, so it would have been highly unusual for them to come across humans of other races. Therefore, it makes no sense that humans should have evolved a neural process to categorize race. It would make evolutionary sense, however, to be able to recognize whether other humans belong to one's own social or family group (and hence whether they can be trusted), and also whether they are male or female.

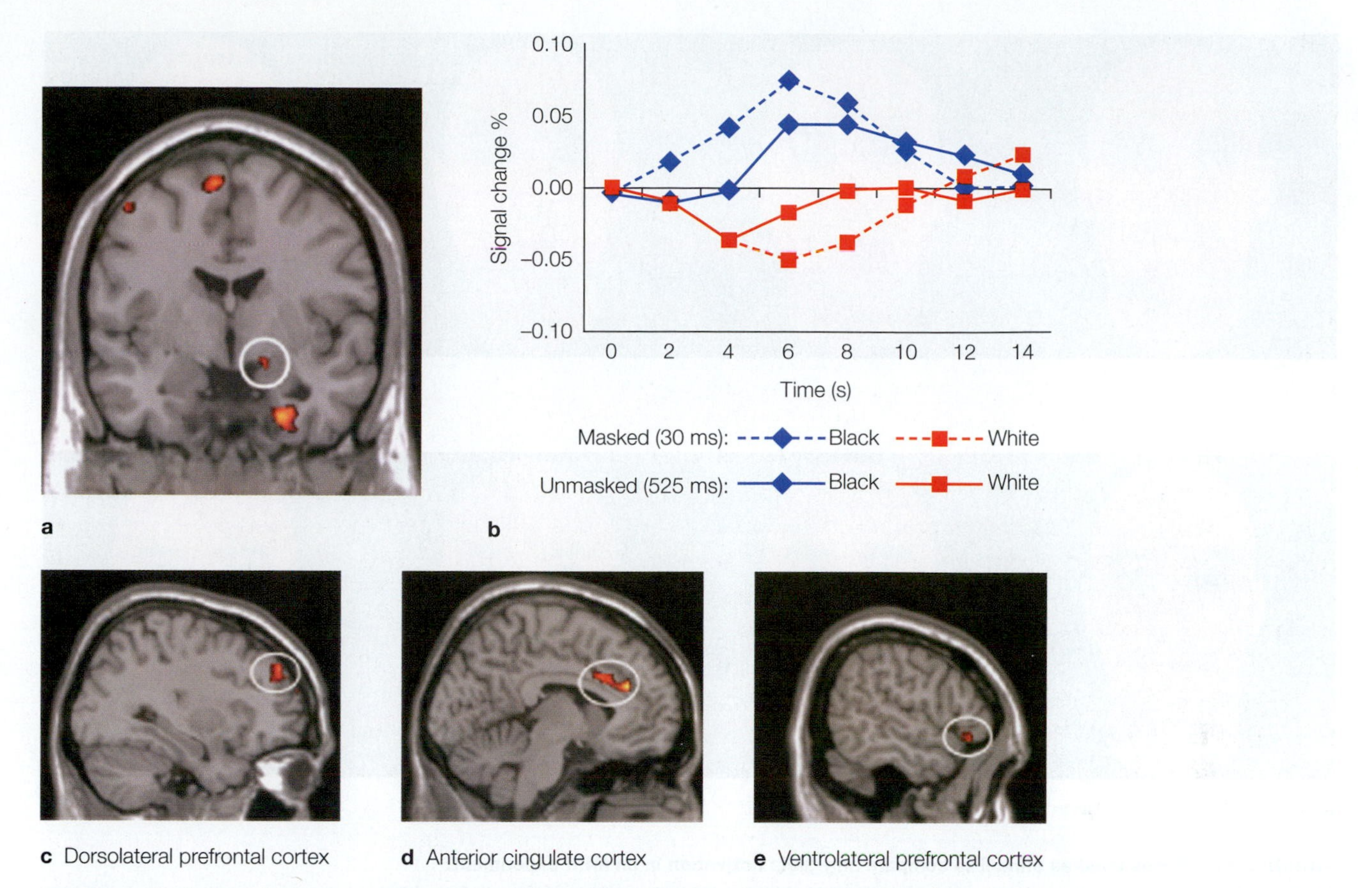

FIGURE 10.22 Differential neural responses in white participants to masked and unmasked black and white faces.
Black and white faces were presented for either 30 ms (masked) or 525 ms (unmasked). **(a)** The right amygdala is more active for black versus white faces when faces are presented for 30 ms. **(b)** The pattern of amygdala activity is similar at 525 ms, though the effect is attenuated. Also during the longer stimulus presentation, activity in the dorsolateral prefrontal cortex **(c)**, anterior cingulate cortex **(d)**, and ventrolateral prefrontal cortex **(e)** was greater for black faces relative to white faces. Activity in one or more of these areas may be responsible for the attenuation of amygdala activity at 525 ms.

Guided by this evolutionary perspective, Robert Kurzban and his colleagues (2001) found that when categorization cues stronger than race were present (e.g., one's own group is a team wearing green shirts, and the opposing group wears red shirts), the categorization based on race disappeared. They also found that sex was always encoded more strongly than race. Their data suggest that coalition affiliation and sex are the categories that our brain evaluates, whereas race is not.

Another study may help explain what is going on here. Researchers compared the amygdala's response to a set of faces that varied along two dimensions centered on an average face (**Figure 10.23**). The faces differed in social content along one dimension (trustworthiness), and along the other dimension they were socially neutral. In both the amygdala and much of the posterior face network, a similar response to both dimensions was seen, and responses were stronger as the difference from an average face grew along the dimension in question. These findings suggest that what may be activating these regions is the degree of difference from a categorically average face (Said et al., 2010). If you are from an Asian culture, your average face would be Asian, and thus, your amygdala would be activated for any non-Asian face. This response is not the same thing as determining whether someone is a racist. Such a categorization strategy could lead to racism, but it does not do so necessarily.

TAKE-HOME MESSAGES

- People with extensive damage to their amygdalae do not recognize fearful or untrustworthy facial expressions.
- The amygdala appears to be an integral part of a system that automatically directs our visual attention to the eyes when we encounter any facial expressions.
- When we look at faces, the activity of the amygdala increases with the degree of difference from a categorically average face.

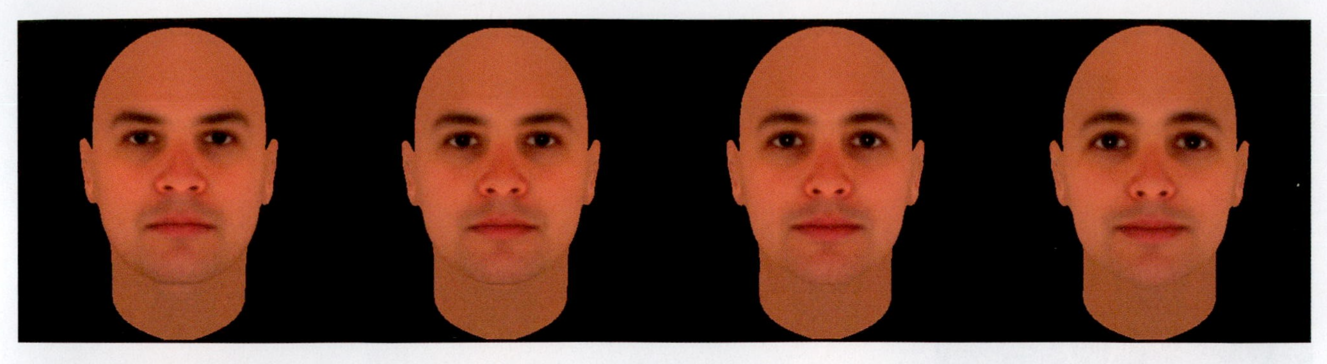

a

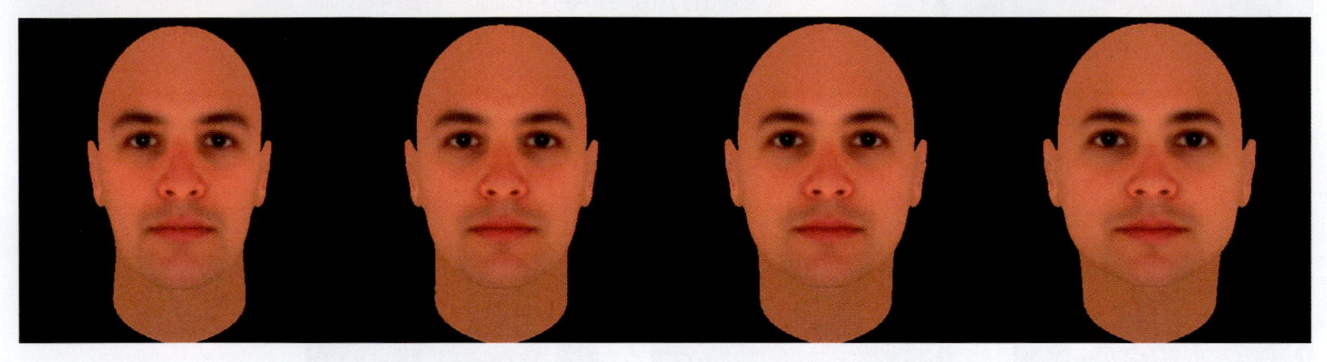

b

FIGURE 10.23 Faces used as stimuli to compare amygdala activation in an fMRI experiment. **(a)** These faces vary along the valence dimension (trustworthiness), taking on values of (from left to right) −3, −1, 1, and 3 standard deviations away from the average face. Trustworthy judgments are highly correlated with valence. **(b)** These socially neutral faces were used in the control condition. Their shape varies (from left to right) from values of −5, −1.67, 1.67, and 5 standard deviations away from the average face. Amygdala responses were stronger for faces with dimensions farther away from an average face.

10.9 Other Areas, Other Emotions

We have seen that the amygdala is involved in a variety of emotional tasks ranging from fear conditioning to social responses. But the amygdala is not the only area of the brain necessary for emotions. We consider the other areas next.

The Insular Cortex

The insular cortex (or **insula**) is tucked between the frontal and temporal lobes in the Sylvian fissure (**Figure 10.24**). The insula has extensive reciprocal connections with areas associated with emotion, such as the amygdala, medial prefrontal cortex, and anterior cingulate gyrus (Augustine, 1996; Craig, 2009). It also has reciprocal connections with frontal, parietal, and temporal cortical areas involved with attention, memory, and cognition (Augustine, 1996).

There is a significant correlation between insular activity and the perception of internal bodily states (Critchley, 2009; Pollatos et al., 2007); this function is known as **interoception.** Various interoceptive stimuli that activate

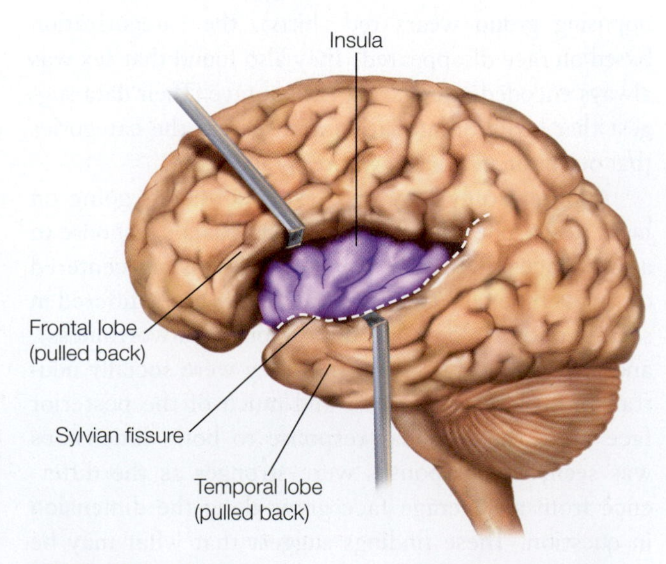

FIGURE 10.24 The insula.

the anterior insula include thirst, sensual touch, itch, distention of the bladder and intestinal tract, exercise, and heartbeat. The connections and activation profile of the insula suggest that it integrates all of the visceral and somatic input and forms a representation of the state of the body (see Chapter 13; Craig, 2009; Saper, 2002). Interestingly, people with a bigger right insula are better at detecting their heartbeats than are people with a smaller right insula (Critchley et al., 2004), and those bigger-right-insula people are also more aware of their emotions (L. F. Barrett et al., 2004) and are more likely to make decisions based on emotional reactions (e.g., choosing to avoid potential loss; Sokol-Hessner, Hartley, et al., 2015).

Several models of emotion speculate that direct access to bodily states is necessary to experience emotion. We should note that a difference exists between experiencing an emotion and knowing that we are experiencing it. Studies indicate that the anterior insula plays a key role in this latter process, but some researchers argue that the anterior cingulate and prefrontal cortices are also involved (Gu et al., 2013). Results from fMRI studies suggest that the anterior insula and anterior cingulate cortex are jointly active in participants experiencing emotional feelings, including maternal and romantic love, anger, fear, sadness, happiness, disgust, and trust. The posterior insula is activated by feelings of sexual desire (S. Cacioppo et al., 2012).

The insula appears to be active with both the physical feelings generated by the body (e.g., abdominal cramps) and the feelings associated with emotional states, suggesting that it may be the junction where cognitive information and emotional information are integrated. The role of the insula as "body information central" is also indicated by its connections to networks across the cortex and to the amygdala (Craig, 2009; Critchley, 2009).

Insular activity also has been reported as associated with evaluative processing—for instance, when people make risk-averse decisions. The riskier the decision, the more active is the insula (Xue et al., 2010). Its activity is also associated with the perception of positive emotions in other people (Jabbi et al., 2007). Gary Berntson and his colleagues (2011) investigated the role of the insula in evaluative processing by examining valence and arousal ratings in response to picture stimuli. They compared the behavioral performance of three groups of participants: a group of patients with lesions of the insula, a control-lesion group, and an amygdala-lesion group. All patients were asked to rate the positivity/negativity (valence) of each presented picture (from *very unpleasant* to *very pleasant*) and how emotionally arousing they found the pictures to be.

Compared with the control-lesion group, the patients with insular lesions reported both *reduced arousal* (to both unpleasant and pleasant stimuli) and *reduced valence* ratings. In contrast, the patients with amygdala lesions had decreased arousal for unpleasant stimuli, but they had the same positive and negative valence ratings as the control-lesion group. These findings are in line with an earlier study (Berntson et al., 2007), which found that patients with amygdala damage showed a complete *lack of an arousal gradient across negative stimuli*, although they displayed a *typical arousal gradient to positive stimuli*.

These results could not be attributed to the inability of amygdala patients to process the hostile nature of the stimuli, because the patients with amygdala damage accurately recognized and categorized both positive and negative features of the stimuli. Taken together, these results support the view that the insula may play a broad role in integrating affective and cognitive processes, whereas the amygdala may have a more selective role in affective arousal, especially for negative stimuli (Berntson et al., 2011).

Disgust

Disgust is one emotion that has been linked directly to the insula. This finding should be no surprise, given the insula's role as the great perceiver of bodily states. Imaging studies have led many cognitive neuroscientists to conclude that the anterior insula is essential for detecting and experiencing disgust (Phillips et al., 1997, 1998). This conclusion is consistent with a report of a patient who had insula damage and was unable to detect disgust conveyed in various modalities (Calder et al., 2000).

Some have taken this evidence and data from other studies (e.g., Wicker et al., 2003) to mean that the anterior insula is the region of the brain that is essential for disgust. A large meta-analysis of fMRI studies done by Katherine Vytal and Stephan Hamann (2010) found that disgust consistently activated the inferior frontal gyrus and the anterior insula, and that these regions reliably differentiated disgust from all other emotion states. In fact, in their analysis these researchers found evidence for the localization of anger, fear, sadness, and happiness in the brain.

In contrast, Kristen Lindquist and her colleagues (2012), in another large meta-analysis of multiple fMRI studies analyzed by a different method, did not find the insula to be consistently and specifically activated by the emotion of disgust. They found that although the anterior insula is more active during instances of disgust perception, anterior insula activation is observed in a number of tasks that involve awareness of bodily states, such as gastric distention, body movement, and orgasm. They also found that activation of the left anterior insula was more likely during incidents of anger than of any other emotion.

Lindquist and colleagues suggest that the anterior insula plays a key but more general role in representing core affective feelings in awareness. This interpretation was problematic, however, when a patient was encountered who continued to have affective feelings after complete bilateral destruction of the insula from herpes encephalitis (A. R. Damasio et al., 2012). The researchers who studied this patient concluded that the insula was instrumental in the utilization of feeling experiences in complex cognitive processes, but was not involved in the generation of those feelings (A. R. Damasio & Damasio, 2016). That is, it allows communication between the subcortical feeling system and different cognitive- and motor-related cortices.

When it comes to mapping emotion in the brain, fMRI is limited. Its spatiotemporal resolution makes it unlikely that a single voxel will demonstrate emotion-specific activation. The newer machine-learning technique of MVPA is better suited to the task. In contrast to Lindquist's meta-analysis, a review of recent functional neuroimaging studies that used MVPA to explore how emotions are manifested in distributed patterns of brain activity found that the brain representations of emotions are better characterized as discrete categories rather than points along a valence continuum (Kragel & LaBar, 2016).

Happiness

Over the last several years, a small but growing body of research has reported on the neural bases of happiness. It's not easy to define what makes us happy, so it is a challenging emotion to study. Researchers have tried to induce a happy mood by various methods, such as having participants view smiling faces or watch amusing films, but these methods have not been consistently reliable, valid, or comparable across studies. Because of these difficulties, only a few neuroimaging studies have focused on happiness (Habel et al., 2005). One group contrasted participants' brain activity in response to smiling faces versus sad faces (Lane et al., 1997).

In a separate fMRI study, 26 healthy male participants were scanned during sad and happy mood induction, as well as while performing a cognitive task that functioned as the experimental control (Habel et al., 2005). Sad and happy moods produced similar activations in the amygdala–hippocampal area extending into the parahippocampal gyrus, prefrontal and temporal cortex, anterior cingulate, and precuneus. Happiness produced stronger activations in the dorsolateral prefrontal cortex, cingulate gyrus, inferior temporal gyrus, and cerebellum (**Figure 10.25**). The study of happiness remains extremely challenging. For example, happiness is not necessarily the opposite of sadness. What's more, happiness is not automatically induced by looking at smiling faces.

Sigmund Freud equated happiness with pleasure, but others have suggested that it also requires achievement, whether cognitive, aesthetic, or moral. Psychologist Mihaly Csikszentmihalyi suggests that people are really happy when totally immersed in a challenging task that closely matches their abilities (Csikszentmihalyi, 1990). He came to this conclusion following an experiment in which he had participants carry beepers that randomly beeped several times a day. On that signal, they would whisk a notebook from their pockets and jot down what they were doing and how much they were enjoying it. Csikszentmihalyi found that there were two types of pleasure: bodily pleasures such as eating and sex, and, even more enjoyable, the state of being "in the zone"—what he called **flow**.

Csikszentmihalyi described flow as the process of having an optimal experience. Flow occurs when you are so into what you're doing that you forget about everything else. It could be riding the top of a wave, working out a theorem, or tangoing across the dance floor. It involves a challenge that you are equal to, that fully engages your attention, and that offers immediate feedback at each step that you are on the right track and pulling it off. When both challenges and skills are high, you are not only enjoying the moment, but also stretching your capabilities. Stretching your capabilities improves the likelihood of learning new skills, and increasing both self-esteem and personal complexity (Csikszentmihalyi & LeFevre, 1989). The concept of flow and what it means suggests that the circuits involved in pleasure, reward, and motivation are essential in the emotion of happiness.

Love

Unlike the studies of happiness, love experiments cannot use facial expressions as either a stimulus or a variable of interest. Indeed, as we noted previously, love is not characterized by any specific facial expressions. Love scientists use stimuli that evoke the concept of the emotion, such as names of loved ones, rather than a facial expression. Subjective feelings of love that participants have for their beloved are usually evaluated with standard self-report questionnaires, such as the Passionate Love Scale (Hatfield & Rapson, 1987).

Stephanie Cacioppo (née Ortigue) and her colleagues (Ortigue, Bianchi-Demicheli, et al., 2010) reviewed fMRI studies of love to identify the brain network(s) commonly activated when participants watch love-related stimuli, independent of whether the love being felt is maternal, passionate, or unconditional (**Figure 10.26**). Overall, love recruits a distributed subcortico-cortical reward, motivational, emotional, and cognitive system that includes dopamine-rich brain areas such as the insula, caudate nucleus and putamen, ventral tegmental area, anterior cingulate cortex, bilateral posterior hippocampus, left inferior frontal gyrus, left middle temporal gyrus, and parietal lobe. This finding reinforces the assumption that love is more complex than a basic emotion. No activation of the amygdala has been reported in fMRI studies of love, whereas amygdala activation has been noted for lust (Cacioppo et al., 2012).

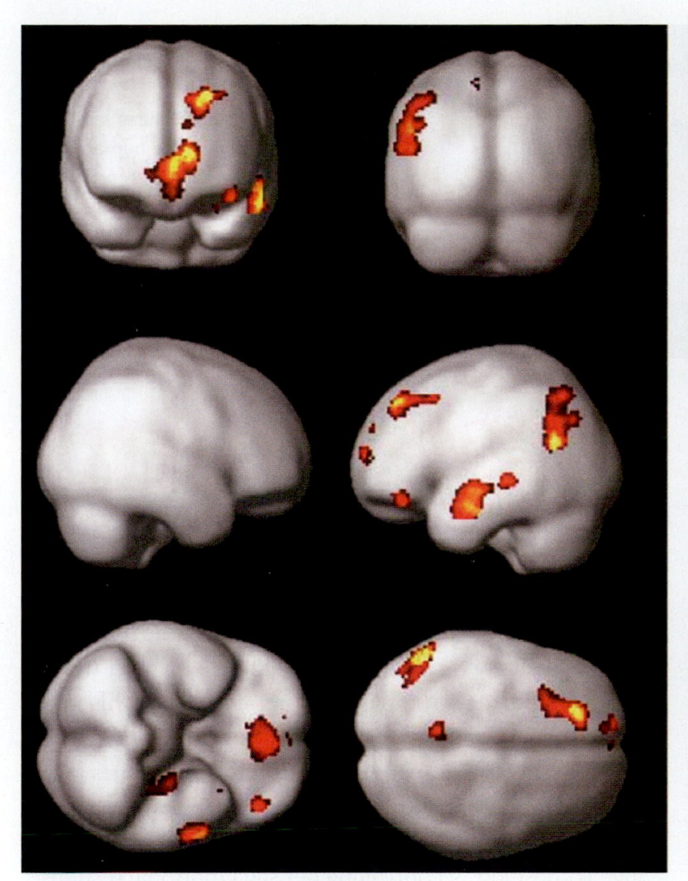

a Sadness minus cognition

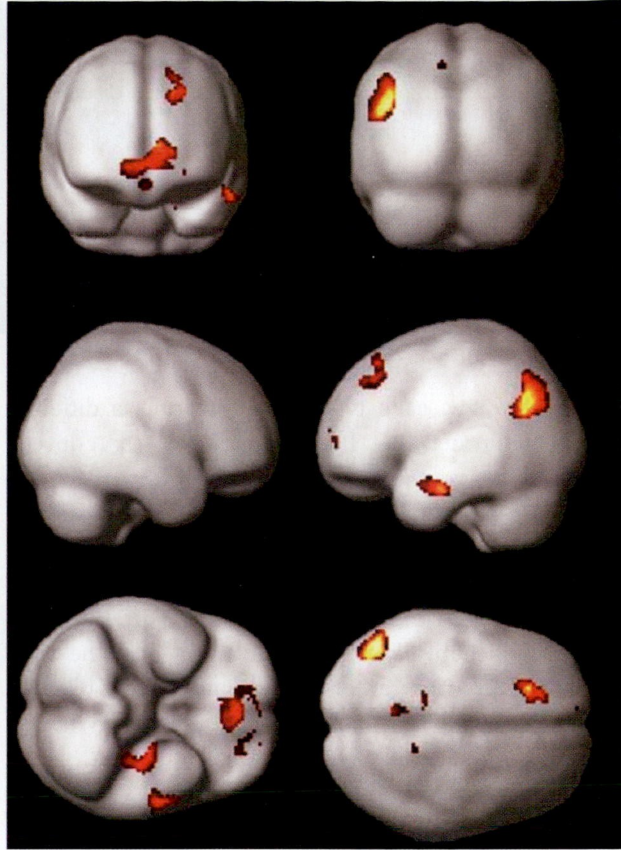

b Happiness minus cognition

FIGURE 10.25 Common and different brain regions are activated with sadness and happiness. Sad and happy moods produced similar activations, but differences emerged. **(a)** In the sadness condition, there was greater activation in the left transverse temporal gyrus and bilaterally in the ventrolateral prefrontal cortex, the left anterior cingulate cortex, and the superior temporal gyrus. **(b)** In the happiness condition, higher activation was seen in the right dorsolateral prefrontal cortex, the left medial and posterior cingulate gyrus, and the right inferior temporal gyrus. It appears that negative and positive moods have distinct activations within a common network.

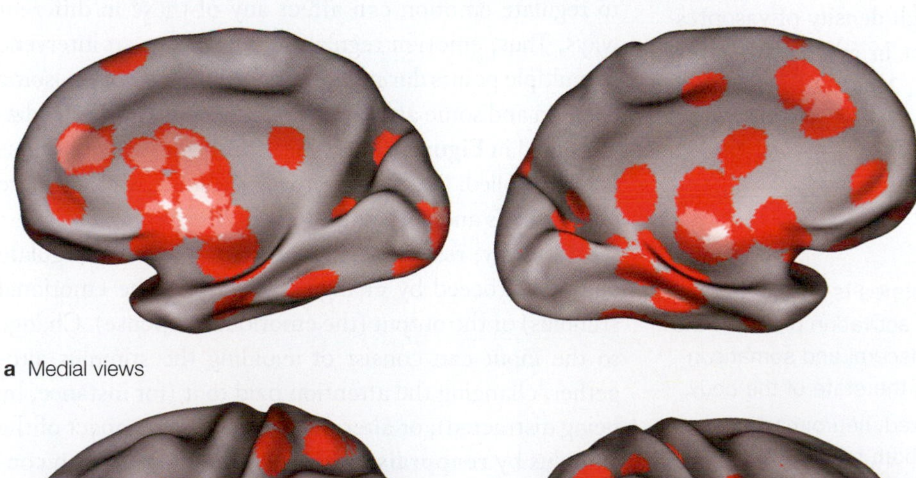

a Medial views

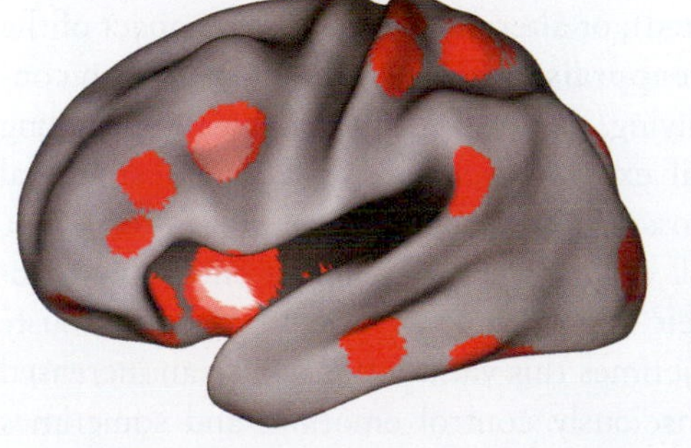

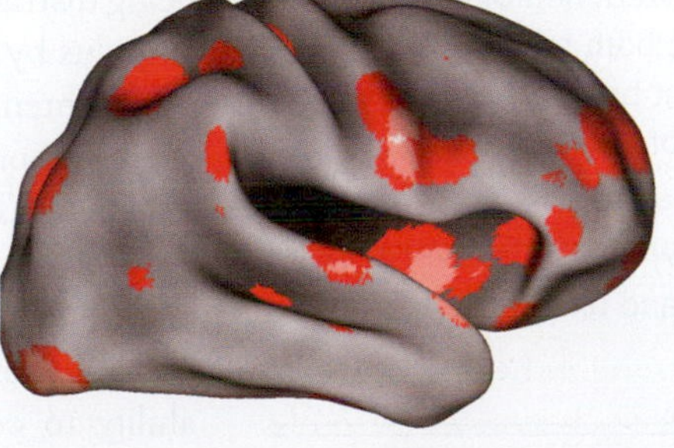

b Lateral views

FIGURE 10.26 Love activations encompass multiple brain regions. Composite meta-analysis map of fMRI studies related to love (including passionate love, maternal love, and unconditional love). Activation results are superimposed on left and right medial views **(a)** and lateral views **(b)** of an average human cortical surface model.

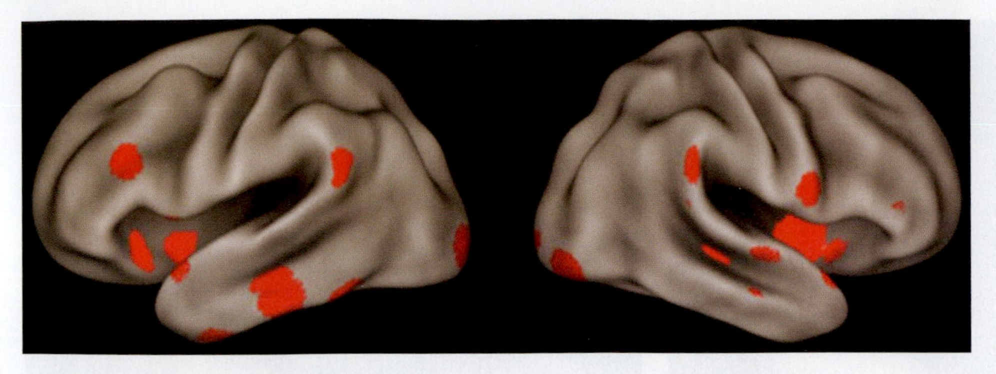

FIGURE 10.27 Passionate love network.
Superimposed on these lateral views of an average human cortical surface model are cortical networks specifically related to passionate love. The recruited brain areas are known to mediate emotion, motivation, reward, social cognition, attention, and self-representation.

Interestingly, each type of love recruits a different specific brain network. For instance, passionate love is mediated by a specific network localized within subcortical areas and also within higher-order brain areas sustaining cognitive functions, such as self-representation, attention, and social cognition (**Figure 10.27**). Furthermore, the reported length of time in love correlates with the cerebral activation in particular regions: the right insular cortex, right anterior cingulate cortex, bilateral posterior cingulate cortices, left inferior frontal gyrus, left ventral putamen/pallidum, left middle temporal gyrus, and right parietal lobe (A. Aron et al., 2005).

The maternal love circuit also involves cortical and subcortical structures that overlap (the area of activity observed with passionate love), but there is one activation that is not shared with passionate love: the subcortical periaqueductal (central) gray matter (PAG). As far as love goes, activations in this region were observed mostly in maternal love, suggesting that PAG activation might be specific to maternal love. This conclusion makes sense because the PAG receives direct connections from the emotion system and contains a high density of vasopressin receptors, which are important in maternal bonding (Ortigue, Bianchi-Demicheli, et al., 2010). Love is a complicated business, and it appears to light up much of the brain—but you didn't need an fMRI study to tell you that!

TAKE-HOME MESSAGES

- The perception of internal bodily states is known as interoception. The connections and activation profile of the insula suggest that it integrates visceral and somatic input and forms a representation of the state of the body.
- Depending on how they are analyzed, neuroimaging studies have been interpreted to both support and refute the theory that there are different brain areas or circuits associated with the processing of different emotions.
- The insula appears to play a broad role in integrating subcortical affective processes and cognitive processes.
- Maternal love, passionate love, and unconditional love recruit different brain networks.

10.10 Get a Grip! Cognitive Control of Emotion

The offensive lineman who yells at the referee for a holding penalty may be considered a "bad sport." But what is really happening? The player is not controlling his negative emotional response to having his goal—blocking the tackle—thwarted. In contrast, the wife who smiles at her husband as he goes off on a dangerous endeavor "so that he will remember me with a smile on my face and not crying" is consciously controlling her sad emotional response.

Emotion regulation refers to the processes that influence the types of emotions we have, when we have them, and how we express and experience them. Recall that brain systems that appraise the significance of a stimulus with respect to our goals and needs contribute to emotion. That appraisal involves attentional processes, evaluation processes, and response processes. Strategies to regulate emotion can affect any of these in different ways. Thus, emotion regulation processes can intervene at multiple points during the generation of emotion, some early on and some after the fact, as seen in the model diagrammed in **Figure 10.28**. Some processes are conscious and controlled, like the wife forcing a smile, and some are unconscious and automatic (Gross, 1998a).

Typically, researchers investigating how we regulate emotion proceed by changing the input (the emotional stimulus) or the output (the emotional response). Change to the input can consist of avoiding the stimulus altogether, changing the attention paid to it (for instance, by being distracted), or altering the emotional impact of the stimulus by **reappraisal**. Change to the output can consist of intensifying, diminishing, prolonging, or curtailing the emotional experience, expression, or physiological response (Gross, 1998b).

We are all well aware that people's emotional reactions and their ability to control them are notoriously variable. Sometimes this variation is due to an increased ability to consciously control emotion, and sometimes

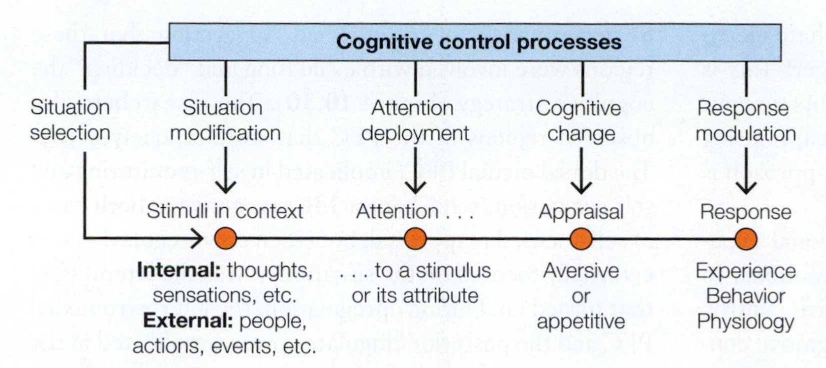

FIGURE 10.28 Kevin Ochsner's proposed model for emotion generation and control.
The arrows pointing down from the cognitive control processes indicate the effects of different emotion regulation strategies and which emotion generation stage they influence.

it is due to an increased ability to automatically control emotion. Characteristic patterns in neural activity in the prefrontal and emotional appraisal systems have been found, both at rest and when under emotional stimulation, that correlate with regulatory ability and with gender, personality, and negative affect.

The capacity to control emotions is important for functioning in the world, especially the social world. We are so adept at controlling our emotions that we tend to notice only when someone does not: the angry customer yelling at the cashier, the giggler during a wedding ceremony, or a depressed friend overwhelmed with sadness. Indeed, disruptions in emotion regulation are thought to underlie mood and anxiety disorders.

Research into emotion regulation over the past couple of decades has concentrated on how and when regulation takes place. In 1998, James Gross at Stanford University proposed the model in **Figure 10.29** to account for seemingly divergent ideas between the psychological and physical literature on emotion regulation. The psychological literature indicated that it was healthier to control and regulate your emotions, while the literature on physical health advanced the idea that chronically suppressing emotions, such as anger, resulted in hypertension and other physical ailments. Gross hypothesized that "shutting down" an emotion at different points in the process of emotion generation would have different consequences and thus could explain the divergent conclusions.

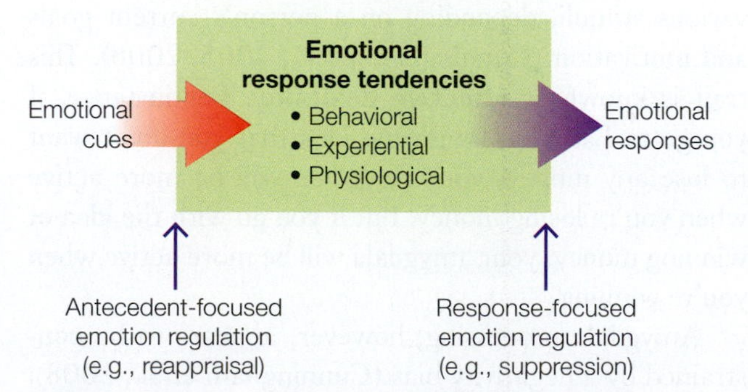

FIGURE 10.29 James Gross's proposed model of emotion regulation.
Gross proposed a model in which emotions may be regulated by manipulating either the input to the system (antecedent-focused emotion regulation) or the system's output (response-focused emotion regulation).

To test his theory, Gross compared reappraisal, a form of antecedent-focused emotion regulation, with emotion **suppression**, a response-focused form. Reappraisal is a cognitive-linguistic strategy that reinterprets an emotion-laden stimulus in nonemotional terms. For instance, a woman wiping the tears from her eyes could be crying because she is sad; or, on reappraisal, she may simply have something in her eye that she's trying to remove. Suppression is a strategy of inhibiting an emotion-expressive behavior during an emotionally arousing situation (for instance, smiling when upset).

In the experiment, Gross showed participants a disgust-eliciting film under one of three conditions. In the reappraisal condition, he asked them to adopt a detached and unemotional attitude; in the suppression condition, to behave such that an observer could not tell they were feeling disgusted; in the third condition, to simply watch the film. He videotaped the participants watching the film while also monitoring their physiological responses. Afterward, they completed an emotion rating form.

Whereas both reappraisal and suppression reduced emotion-expressive behavior, only reappraisal actually reduced the disgust experience. Suppression, on the other hand, actually increased sympathetic activation, causing participants to be more aroused, and this activation lasted for a while after the film ended (Gross, 1998b). Continued research on emotion regulation has provided fMRI data that support Gross's hypothesis about the timing of reappraisal and suppression strategies (Goldin et al., 2008).

How does this behavior apply in the real world? Suppose you come home to find that your friend has dropped in and cleaned your house. You start thinking, "How dare she! She should have asked," and you feel yourself getting madder than a hornet. You now have three choices: You could wallow in your anger; you could suppress it by putting on a false front; or you could reappraise the situation.

Opting for the latter, you think, "Hmmm, I hate cleaning. Now it's spotless and I didn't lift a finger! This is great." You start to feel good, and a smile lights up your face. You have just done a little cognitive reappraising and reduced your physiological arousal. This approach is better for your overall health.

Conscious reappraisal reduces the emotional experience; this finding supports the idea that emotions, to some extent, are subject to conscious cognitive control. In an initial fMRI study to investigate the cognitive control of emotion, Kevin Ochsner and his colleagues (2002) found that using reappraisal to decrease a negative emotion increased prefrontal cortex (PFC) activity (implicated in cognitive control; see Chapter 12) and decreased amygdala activity, suggesting that the PFC can modulate emotional activity in subcortical structures, such as the amygdala. A positively slanted reappraisal can mentally make a bad situation better, but a negative reappraisal can mentally make a bad situation worse (or a good situation bad).

Do these two different regulation strategies use the same neural system? Ochsner and his colleagues (2004) hypothesized that cognitive control regions mediating reappraisal (the PFC) would modulate regions involved in appraising the emotional qualities of a stimulus (amygdala). Thus, cognitive upregulation would be associated with greater activation of the amygdala, and downregulation would be associated with less. They did an fMRI study of reappraisal that looked at both making a bad situation better (downregulating negative emotions) and making a bad situation worse (upregulating negative emotions).

Participants in this study looked at negative images. They were divided into two groups: a self-focused group and a situation-focused group. In the self-focused group, participants were instructed to imagine themselves or a loved one in the negative scene (increasing negative emotion); to view the pictures in a detached way (decreasing negative emotion); or, in the control condition, simply to look at the image. In the situation-focused group, participants were told to increase emotion by imagining that the situation was becoming worse, or to decrease emotion by imagining it was getting better, or again just to look at the image. Each participant then had to report how effective and effortful the reappraisal was. All participants reported success in increasing and decreasing their emotions, but indicated that downregulation took more effort.

The team found that whether negative emotions were enhanced or reduced, regions of the left lateral PFC that are involved in working memory and cognitive control (see Chapter 12) and the dorsal anterior cingulate cortex, which is implicated in the online monitoring of performance, were activated, suggesting that these regions were involved with evaluating and "deciding" the cognitive strategy (**Figure 10.30**). The researchers also observed regions of the PFC that were uniquely active. The dorsal medial PFC, implicated in self-monitoring and self-evaluation (see Chapter 13), was active in both cases of self-focused reappraisal, but when downregulation was externally focused on the situation, it was the lateral PFC that turned on. During upregulation, the left rostromedial PFC and the posterior cingulate cortex (implicated in the retrieval of emotion knowledge) were active, but downregulation activated a different region associated with behavioral inhibition: the right lateral and orbital PFC. It appears, then, that different cognitive reappraisal goals and strategies activate some of the same PFC regions, as well as some regions that are different.

What about the amygdala? Amygdala activation was modulated either up or down, depending on the regulatory goal: Activity increased when the goal was to enhance negative emotion and decreased when the goal was to reduce it. The apparent modulation of the amygdala by prefrontal activity suggests that amygdalar activity will be increased if the current processing goals fit with the evaluative aspects of stimuli (in this case, to make a negative stimulus more negative), not the actual valence (positive or negative) of the emotion.

Does cognitive control via reappraisal depend on interactions between the PFC regions that support cognitive control processes and subcortical networks that generate emotional responses, as we have been assuming? More than a decade after this idea was presented, more than 50 imaging studies now support this hypothesis (Buhle et al., 2014; Ochsner et al., 2012).

Although early research suggested that the amygdala was involved exclusively in automatic processing of negative information, Ochsner's study and more recent research suggest otherwise. The amygdala appears to have a more flexible role in processing the relevance of various stimuli, depending on a person's current goals and motivation (Cunningham et al., 2005, 2008). This trait is known as **affective flexibility**. For instance, if you go to Las Vegas with the idea that you don't want to lose any money, your amygdala will be more active when you're losing money. But if you go with the idea of winning money, your amygdala will be more active when you're winning.

Amygdala processing, however, appears to be constrained by a negativity bias (Cunningham et al., 2008). Amygdala modulation is more pronounced for positive than for negative information, so it processes negative information less flexibly. PFC modulation can't completely eradicate the negative stimuli, but—for survival and your wallet—this is a good thing.

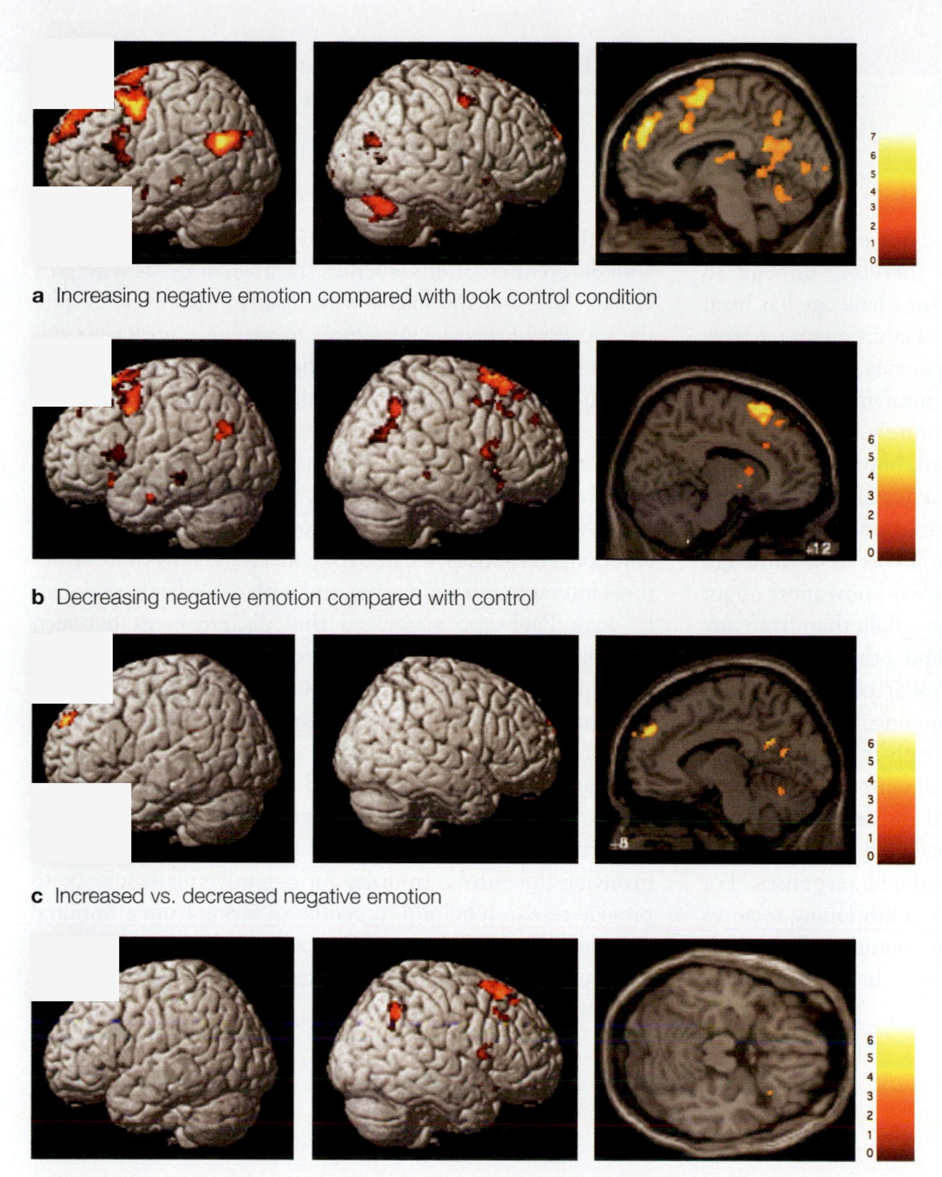

FIGURE 10.30 Unique regions activate when increasing or decreasing negative emotion.
Left and right lateral views are seen in the left and center panels. **(a)** When increasing negative emotions, activations are generally left sided in the dorsolateral prefrontal cortex (PFC) and anterior cingulate cortex. The right panel shows the left medial view. **(b)** When decreasing emotion, some of the same left-hemisphere regions are active, though activations tend to be more bilateral or right sided. The right panel shows the right medial view. **(c)** Regions uniquely activated when increasing negative emotion: the left rostral medial PFC and posterior cingulate, best seen in the medial view of the left hemisphere on the far right. **(d)** Regions uniquely activated when decreasing emotion. The right lateral PFC is seen in the center panel, and right lateral orbitofrontal activation is seen in the axial view in the right panel.

Emotion regulation research is in its adolescence. While much remains to be understood, the use of functional imaging coupled with behavioral studies has been fruitful. Much of the research so far has centered on the two cognitive strategies that we have discussed: reappraisal and suppression. Areas of research that need to be addressed are the deployment of attention (such as ignoring a stimulus or being distracted from it), alternative forms of regulation such as situation selection (avoiding or seeking certain types of stimuli), and situation modification.

Research is also needed to understand when and how people make the decision to regulate their emotions, and how they choose a regulation strategy (Etkin et al., 2015). After all, there are vast individual differences in people's emotional responses to situations and their capacity to regulate their emotions. Achieving a better understanding of emotion regulation will aid in clinical interventions in cases of impaired emotion regulation, which has been implicated in many psychiatric conditions, including depression, borderline personality disorder, social anxiety disorder, and substance abuse disorders (Denny et al., 2009).

TAKE-HOME MESSAGES

- Emotion regulation is complex and involves many processes.
- Emotion regulation depends on the interaction of frontal cortical structures and subcortical brain regions.
- Different emotion regulation strategies have different physiological effects.

Summary

Scientists face many challenges in studying emotion, a state that is often difficult to define and therefore difficult to manipulate and study scientifically. One challenge has been establishing a proper place for studies of emotion in cognitive neuroscience. Earlier research and theories tended to view emotion as separate from cognition, implying that the two could be studied and understood separately. As research in the neuroscience of emotion proceeded, however, it became clear that emotion and cognition influence each other.

Research into the cognitive neuroscience of emotion had to begin somewhere, and the amygdala was first. Although it still remains enigmatic, we nevertheless know more about contributions to emotion from the amygdala than from any other brain area. In both humans and other species, the amygdala plays a critical role in implicit emotional learning, as demonstrated by fear conditioning, and in explicit emotional learning and memory through interactions with the hippocampus. It is also involved with decision making, attention, perception, and social interactions. Recent research has focused on how the amygdala works with other brain areas to produce normal emotional responses. For example, although acquisition of fear conditioning requires the amygdala, normal extinction of a conditioned response involves interactions of the amygdala and the prefrontal cortex (Morgan & LeDoux, 1999).

Other neural structures have been found to be associated with different emotions, such as the angular gyrus with passionate love and the insula with disgust. However, despite the success of relating structures to various emotions, emotion research has shifted from the study of isolated neural structures to the investigation of neural circuits and whether there are specific circuits for specific emotions. The amygdala, orbitofrontal cortex, and insula are critical for different forms of emotion processing, but it is now clear that to understand how the brain produces normal and adaptive emotional responses, we need to understand how these structures interact with each other and with other brain regions.

Jaak Panksepp suggested that disagreement between investigators concerning the existence and specific circuitry of emotional processes may not be resolved until researchers take into account how emotion emerged through the evolution of the brain, building more complex emotions over a foundation of core emotions, and they are clear on whether they're studying a core emotion generated by subcortical structures or secondary- and tertiary-process emotions involving the cortex. In order for cognitive neuroscience to provide research helpful to people suffering from emotional disorders, Panksepp argued that a clearer understanding of the evolutionary origins of their emotional disquiet may lead to more successful treatments.

Key Terms

affect (p. 430)
affective flexibility (p. 470)
amygdala (p. 443)
attentional blink (p. 455)
basic emotion (p. 435)
complex emotions (p. 435)
core emotional systems (p. 435)
dimensional theories of emotion (p. 435)
emotions (p. 429)
emotion generation (p. 439)
emotion regulation (p. 468)
facial expressions (p. 435)
fear conditioning (p. 446)
feeling (p. 428)
flow (p. 466)
insula (p. 464)
interoception (p. 464)
mood (p. 430)
reappraisal (p. 468)
somatic marker (p. 457)
stress (p. 430)
suppression (p. 469)

Think About It

1. Briefly describe the limbic system hypothesis and its historical role in the cognitive neuroscience of emotion. Explain which aspects of the hypothesis have been questioned and which remain valid.
2. Describe the three generally accepted components of emotion and how they apply to the different theories of emotion generation.
3. Explain the role of the amygdala in fear conditioning. Be sure to cover what is known about the neural pathways for emotional learning based on nonhuman animal models. Also explain why the amygdala's role in emotional learning is said to be implicit.
4. What are Paul Ekman's basic emotions, and what is the relationship between them and facial expressions?
5. Describe the effect of emotion on another cognitive process.

Suggested Reading

Adolphs, R., Gosselin, F., Buchanan, T. W., Tranel, D., Schyns, P., & Damasio, A. R. (2005). A mechanism for impaired fear recognition after amygdala damage. *Nature, 433*, 68–72.

Anderson, D. J., & Adolphs, R. (2014). A framework for studying emotions across species. *Cell, 157*(1), 187–200.

Damasio, A. R. (1994). *Descartes' error: Emotion, reason, and the human brain.* New York: Putnam.

LeDoux, J. E. (2012). Rethinking the emotional brain. *Neuron, 73*(4), 653–676.

Ochsner, K. N., Silvers, J. A., & Buhle, J. T. (2012). Functional imaging studies of emotion regulation: A synthetic review and evolving model of the cognitive control of emotion. *Annals of the New York Academy of Sciences, 1251*, E1–E24.

Ortigue, S., Bianchi-Demicheli, F., Patel, N., Frum, C., & Lewis, J. (2010). Neuroimaging of love: fMRI meta-analysis evidence toward new perspectives in sexual medicine. *Journal of Sexual Medicine, 7*(11), 3541–3552.

Panksepp, J., & Biven, L. (2012). *The archaeology of mind: Neuroevolutionary origins of human emotions.* New York: Norton.

Rolls, E. T. (1999). *The brain and emotion.* Oxford: Oxford University Press.

Sapolsky, R. M. (1992). *Stress, the aging brain, and the mechanisms of neuron death.* Cambridge, MA: MIT Press.

Sapolsky, R. M. (2004). *Why zebras don't get ulcers: The acclaimed guide to stress, stress-related diseases, and coping.* New York: Holt Paperbacks.

Vuilleumier, P., & Driver, J. (2007). Modulation of visual processing by attention and emotion: Windows on causal interactions between human brain regions. *Philosophical Transactions of the Royal Society of London. Series B, Biological Sciences, 362*(1481), 837–855.

Whalen, P. J. (1998). Fear, vigilance, and ambiguity: Initial neuroimaging studies of the human amygdala. *Current Directions in Psychological Science, 7*, 177–188.

I personally think we developed language because of our deep inner need to complain.

Jane Wagner

CHAPTER

11

Language

H.W., A WORLD WAR II VETERAN, was 60, robust and physically fit, running his multimillion-dollar business, when he suffered a massive left-hemisphere stroke. After partially recovering, H.W. was left with a slight right-sided hemiparesis (muscle weakness) and a slight deficit in face recognition. His intellectual abilities were less affected, and in a test of visuospatial reasoning, he scored higher than 90% of healthy people his age. When he decided to return to the helm of his company, he enlisted the help of others because he had been left with a difficult language problem. Although he could understand both what was said to him and written language, and he had no problem speaking, he couldn't name most objects, even ones that were familiar to him.

H.W. suffered from a severe *anomia*, an inability to find the words to label things in the world. Testing revealed that H.W. could retrieve adjectives better than verbs, but his retrieval of nouns was the most severely affected. In one test where he was shown 60 common items and asked to name them, H.W. could name only one item, a house. He was impaired in word repetition tests, oral reading of words and phrases, and generating numbers. Yet H.W. was able to compensate for his loss: He could hold complex conversations through a combination of circumlocutions, pointing, pantomiming, and drawing the first letter of the word he wanted to say. For instance, in response to a question about where he grew up, he had the following exchange with researcher Margaret Funnell:

H.W.: It was, uh . . . leave out of here and where's the next legally place down from here (gestures down).

M.F.: Down? Massachusetts.

BIG Questions

- How does the brain derive meaning from language?
- Do the processes that enable speech comprehension differ from those that enable reading comprehension?
- How does the brain produce spoken, signed, and written output to communicate meaning to others?
- What are the brain's structures and networks that support language comprehension?
- What are the evolutionary origins of human language?

H.W.: Next one (gestures down again).

M.F.: Connecticut.

H.W.: Yes. And that's where I was. And at that time, the closest people to me were this far away (holds up five fingers).

M.F.: Five miles?

H.W.: Yes, okay, and, and everybody worked outside but I also, I went to school at a regular school. And when you were in school, you didn't go to school by people brought you to school, you went there by going this way (uses his arms to pantomime walking).

M.F.: By walking.

H.W.: And to go all the way from there to where you where you went to school was actually, was, uh, uh (counts in a whisper) twelve.

H.F.: Twelve miles?

H.W.: Yes, and in those years you went there by going this way (pantomimes walking). When it was warm, I, I found an old one of these (uses his arms to pantomime bicycling).

M.F.: Bicycle.

H.W.: And I, I fixed it so it would work and I would use that when it was warm and when it got cold you just, you do this (pantomimes walking). (Funnell et al., 1996, p. 180)

Though H.W. was unable to produce nouns to describe aspects of his childhood, he did use proper grammatical structures and was able to pantomime the words he wanted. He was acutely aware of his deficits.

H.W.'s problem was not one of object knowledge. He knew what an object was and its use, but he simply could not produce the word for it. He also knew that when he saw the word he wanted, he would recognize it. To demonstrate this, a researcher would give him a description of something and then ask him how sure he was about being able to pick the correct word for it from a list of 10 words. As an example, when asked if he knew the automobile instrument that measures mileage, he said he would recognize the word for it with 100% accuracy; his accuracy was indeed over 90%.

We understand from H.W. that retrieval of object knowledge is not the same as retrieval of the linguistic label, the name of the object. You may have experienced this yourself. Sometimes, when you try to say someone's name, you can't come up with it, but when someone else tries to help you and mentions a bunch of names, you know for sure which ones are not correct. This experience is called the tip-of-the-tongue phenomenon. H.W.'s problems remind us that our apparent ease in communicating has complex underpinnings in the brain.

In this chapter we discuss how the brain derives meaning from both auditory speech input and visual language input, and how it then, in turn, produces spoken and written language output to communicate meaning to others. We begin with a quick anatomical overview and then describe patients with language deficits and the classical model of language that developed from these early findings. Next, with the help of more recent psycholinguistic and cognitive neuroscience methods, we look at what we have learned about language comprehension and production, and we examine some neuroanatomical models that are replacing the classical model of language. Finally, we consider how this miraculous human mental faculty may have arisen through the course of primate evolution.

11.1 The Anatomy of Language and Language Deficits

Of all the higher functions that humans possess, language is perhaps the most specialized and refined, and it may well be what most clearly distinguishes our species. Although some other animals have sophisticated systems for communication, the abilities of even the most prolific of our primate relatives are far inferior to ours. Because there is no animal homologue for human language, the neural bases of language are less well understood than those for sensation, memory, or motor control. This lack of knowledge is not from lack of interest or research. Because language is the means by which we transmit so much information, ranging from grocery lists and cherished memories to scientific innovations and culture, its immense importance to our social selves has made it a hotbed of research. We start with the anatomy of language.

Language input can be auditory or visual, so both of these sensory and perceptual systems are involved with

ANATOMICAL ORIENTATION

Anatomy of Language

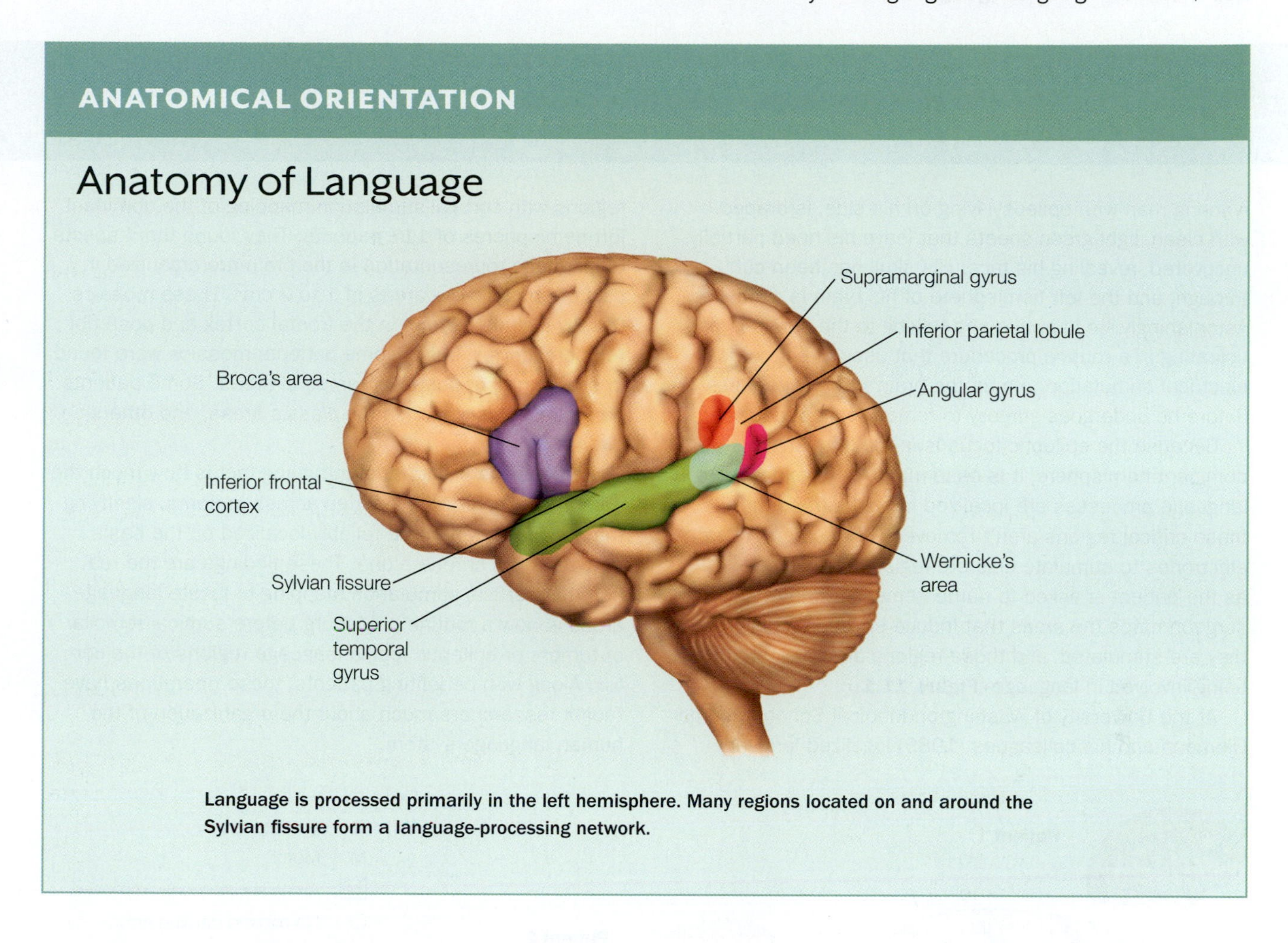

Language is processed primarily in the left hemisphere. Many regions located on and around the Sylvian fissure form a language-processing network.

language comprehension. Language production involves both motor movement and timing. Thus, all the cortical (premotor cortex, motor cortex, and supplementary motor area, or SMA) and subcortical (thalamus, basal ganglia, and cerebellum) structures involved with motor movement and timing, which we discussed in Chapter 8, make key contributions to our ability to communicate (Kotz & Schwartze, 2010).

Split-brain patients, as well as patients with lateralized, focal brain lesions have taught us that a great deal of language processing is lateralized to the left-hemisphere regions surrounding the **Sylvian fissure.** The language areas of the left hemisphere include Wernicke's area in the posterior superior temporal gyrus, portions of the anterior and lateral temporal cortex, the inferior parietal lobe (including the supramarginal gyrus and the angular gyrus), the inferior frontal cortex, which includes Broca's area, and the insular cortex (see the "Anatomical Orientation" box above). Collectively, these brain areas and their interconnections via major white matter tracts form the *left perisylvian language network*; that is, they surround the Sylvian fissure (Hagoort, 2013).

The left hemisphere may handle the lion's share of language processing, but the right hemisphere does make some contributions. The right superior temporal sulcus plays a role in processing the rhythm of language (prosody), and the right prefrontal cortex, middle temporal gyrus, and posterior cingulate activate when sentences have metaphorical meaning.

Brain Damage and Language Deficits

Before the advent of neuroimaging, most of what was discerned about the neural bases of language processing came from studying patients who had brain lesions that resulted in various types of aphasia. **Aphasia** is a broad term referring to the collective deficits in language comprehension and production that accompany neurological damage, even though the articulatory mechanisms are intact. Aphasia may also be accompanied by speech problems caused by the loss of control over articulatory muscles, known as **dysarthria**, and

BOX 11.1 | THE COGNITIVE NEUROSCIENTIST'S TOOLKIT

Stimulation Mapping of the Human Brain

A young man with epilepsy, lying on his side, is draped with clean, light-green sheets that leave his head partially uncovered, revealing his face. His skull has been cut through, and the left hemisphere of his brain is exposed. Astonishingly, he is awake and talking to the surgeon, participating in a routine procedure that uses direct cortical electrical stimulation to map the brain's language areas before he undergoes surgery to remove epileptic tissue.

Because the epileptic focus is in the left, language-dominant hemisphere, it is essential to determine where language processes are localized in his brain so that those critical regions aren't removed. The surgeon uses electrodes to stimulate discrete regions of the cortex as the patient is asked to name items in a photo. The surgeon maps the areas that induce errors in naming when they are stimulated, and those regions are implicated as being involved in language (**Figure 11.1**).

At the University of Washington Medical School, George Ojemann and his colleagues (1989) localized language regions with cortical-stimulation mapping of the dominant left hemispheres of 117 patients. They found that aspects of language representation in the brain are organized in discrete mosaic-like areas of 1 to 2 cm^2. These mosaics usually include regions in the frontal cortex and posterior temporal cortex, but in some patients mosaics were found in only frontal or posterior temporal areas. Some patients had naming disruption in the classic areas, and others did not.

Perhaps the single most intriguing fact is how much the anatomical localizations varied across patients, signifying that language cannot be reliably localized on the basis of anatomical criteria alone. These findings are the reason that cortical-stimulation mapping to locate language areas is now a routine procedure before surgical removal of tumors or epileptic foci in language regions of the cortex. Along with benefiting patients, these operations have taught researchers much about the organization of the human language system.

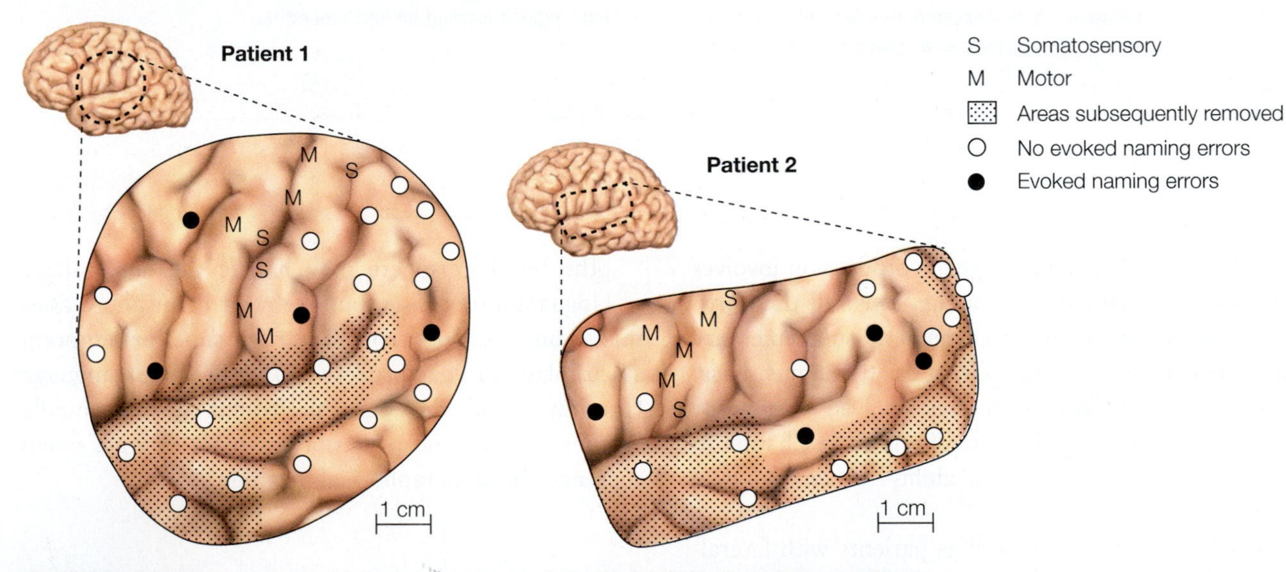

FIGURE 11.1 Regions of the brain of two patients studied with cortical-stimulation mapping. Stimulating the regions of the patients' brains indicated by black dots evoked language errors. These regions implicated as being involved in language were then mapped. Stimulating the regions indicated by white dots did not evoke language errors. The crosshatched areas were later surgically removed.

deficits in the motor planning of articulations, called speech **apraxia**.

Aphasia is extremely common following brain damage: H.W. exhibited **anomia**, a form of aphasia characterized by an inability to name objects. Approximately 40% of all strokes (usually those located in the left hemisphere) produce some aphasia, though it may be transient. In many patients, the aphasic symptoms persist, causing lasting problems in producing or understanding spoken and written language. Developmental dysarthrias can be the result of genetic mutations (see **Box 11.2**).

BROCA'S APHASIA **Broca's aphasia**, also known as *anterior aphasia*, *nonfluent aphasia*, or *expressive aphasia*,

BOX 11.2 | LESSONS FROM THE CLINIC

Genetic Foundations of Language

In 1990, a report was published about the "KE" family in England. Half the family members, spanning three generations, suffered a severe speech and language disorder (Hurst et al., 1990). They were unable to coordinate their speech (developmental dyspraxia) and had multiple linguistic deficits, including impaired grammar, difficulty with word morphology, and inability to repeat heard words.

Researchers sought the neural basis of these deficits by using structural and functional imaging, and they found bilateral abnormalities in several motor-related regions. For instance, affected family members had a 25% reduction in the volume of the caudate nucleus. Abnormally low levels of gray matter were also found in other motor areas, including the inferior frontal gyrus (Broca's area), precentral gyrus, frontal pole, and cerebellum. Meanwhile, abnormally high levels of gray matter were seen in the superior temporal gyrus (Wernicke's area), angular gyrus, and putamen. Functional MRI studies using silent verb generation, spoken verb generation, and word repetition tasks revealed that the affected members had posterior and bilateral activations in regions not generally used for language functions for both tasks (reviewed in Vargha-Khadem et al., 2005).

By looking at the KE family tree, researchers found that the disorder was inherited in a simple fashion: It resulted from a defect in a single autosomal dominant gene (Hurst et al., 1990), meaning that people with the mutation have a 50% chance of passing it to their offspring. The hunt for the gene commenced at the Wellcome Centre for Human Genetics at the University of Oxford. Researchers found a single base-pair mutation in the *FOXP2* gene sequence (adenine for guanine) in the affected members of the KE family (Lai et al., 2001).

This mutation caused the amino acid histidine to be substituted for arginine in the FOXP2 protein. The *FOX* family of genes is large, and this particular arginine is invariant among all of its members, suggesting that it has a crucial functional role. How can one little change do so much damage? *FOX* genes code for proteins that are transcription factors, which act as switches that turn gene expression on or off. Mutations in *FOX* genes may cause phenotypes as varied as cancer, glaucoma, or, as we see here, language disorders.

If the *FOXP2* gene is so important in the development of language, is it unique to humans? This question is complicated, and its complexity speaks to huge differences between talking about genes and talking about the expression of genes. The *FOXP2* gene is present in a broad range of distantly related vertebrates (Scharff & Petri, 2011). Conservation of neural expression patterns has also been found in the development and function of brain circuits relevant to sensorimotor integration and motor-skill learning (cortex, basal ganglia, and cerebellum; reviewed in Fisher, 2017), suggesting that the gene's role is ancient.

The protein encoded by the *FOXP2* gene differs at five amino acids between humans and birds, three amino acids between humans and mice, and only two between humans and chimpanzees or gorillas. The sequencing of both Neanderthal DNA (Krause et al., 2007) and Denisovan DNA (Reich et al., 2010) revealed that these ancient hominins had the same *FOXP2* gene that we have. These researchers also found that the gene changes lie on the common modern-human haplotype (DNA sequences that are next to each other on a chromosome and are transmitted together), which was shown earlier to have been subject to a selective sweep. A selective sweep means what it sounds like: This gene was a hot item that produced a characteristic that gave its owners an obvious competitive advantage. Whoever had it had more offspring, and it became the dominant gene.

Although studies estimate that the selective sweep occurred within the last 200,000 (Enard et al., 2002; Zhang et al., 2002) or 55,000 (Coop et al., 2008) years, the common *FOXP2* genes support the idea that the selective sweep predated the common ancestor of modern human and Neanderthal populations, which existed about 300,000 to 400,000 years ago. Further investigations examining parts of the gene that do not code for protein, however, did reveal human-specific changes that may alter how the gene is regulated (Maricic et al., 2012).

Researchers have tested the hypothesis that the evolutionary changes of the *FOXP2* gene might be linked to the emergence of speech and language. When mice were genetically modified to include the key amino acid sequence, they showed higher levels of synaptic plasticity in corticobasal ganglia circuits (reviewed in Enard, 2011), suggesting that these amino acid changes could have contributed to the evolution of human speech and language by adapting corticobasal ganglia circuits. In contrast, when mice were genetically modified to carry the KE family's *FOXP2* mutation, they showed lower levels of synaptic plasticity in striatal and cerebellar circuits, and significant deficits in species-typical motor-skill learning (Groszer et al., 2008).

Whether the origins of human language rest on a single causative DNA mutation that occurred after a split in the hominin branch or language emerged from multiple genetic changes over the course of evolution remains an unanswered question. With our current ability to sequence both the genomes of living humans and those of ancient hominins from archaeological samples, we now have the ability to empirically evaluate the different hypotheses of the evolutionary origins of language (Fisher, 2017). Stay tuned!

is the oldest and perhaps best-studied form of aphasia. It was first clearly described by the Parisian physician Paul Broca in the 19th century. He performed an autopsy on a patient, Louis Victor Leborgne, who for several years before his death had been able to speak only a single word, "tan." Broca observed that the patient had a brain lesion in the posterior portion of the left inferior frontal gyrus, which is made up of the *pars triangularis* and *pars opercularis*, also referred to as Brodmann areas 44 and 45 (see Chapter 2) and now referred to as **Broca's area** (**Figure 11.2**). When Broca first described this disorder, he related it to damage to this cortical region. After studying many patients with language problems, he also concluded that brain areas that produce speech were localized in the left hemisphere.

In the most severe forms of Broca's aphasia, single-utterance patterns of speech, such as that of Broca's original patient, are often observed. The variability is large, however, and may include unintelligible mutterings, single syllables or words, short simple phrases, sentences that mostly lack function words or grammatical markers, or complete idioms, such as "barking up the wrong tree." Sometimes the ability to sing normally is undisturbed, as might be the ability to recite phrases and prose, or to count. The speech of patients with Broca's aphasia is often telegraphic (containing only content words and leaving out function words that have only grammatical significance, such as prepositions and articles), comes in uneven bursts, and is very effortful (**Figure 11.3a**). Finding the appropriate word or combination of words and then executing the pronunciation is compromised. This condition is often accompanied by apraxia of speech (**Figure 11.3b**). Broca's aphasia patients are aware of their errors and have a low tolerance for frustration.

a

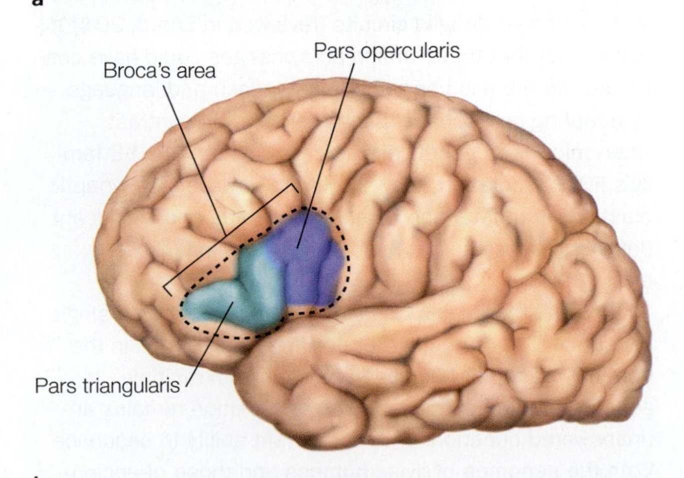

b

FIGURE 11.2 Broca's area.
(a) The preserved brain of Louis Leborgne (Broca's patient "Tan"), which is maintained in a Paris collection. **(b)** The dotted line in this drawing identifies the area in the left hemisphere known as Broca's area.

a Spontaneously speaking

b Repeating

c Listening for comprehension

FIGURE 11.3 Speech problems in Broca's aphasia.
Broca's aphasia patients can have various problems when they speak or when they try to comprehend or repeat the linguistic input provided by the clinician. **(a)** The speech output of this patient is slow and effortful, and it lacks function words. It resembles a telegram. **(b)** Broca's aphasia patients also may have accompanying problems with speech articulation because of deficits in regulation of the articulatory apparatus (e.g., muscles of the tongue). **(c)** Finally, these patients sometimes have a hard time understanding reversible sentences, where a full understanding of the sentence depends on correct syntactic assignment of the thematic roles (e.g., who hit whom).

Broca's notion that these aphasic patients had a disorder only in speech production, however, is not correct. They can also have comprehension deficits related to **syntax**, the rules governing how words are put together in a sentence. Often only the most basic and overlearned grammatical forms are produced and comprehended—a deficit known as **agrammatic aphasia**. For example, consider the following sentences: "The boy hit the girl" and "The boy was hit by the girl." The first sentence can be understood from word order, and patients with Broca's aphasia understand such sentences fairly well. But the second sentence has a more complicated syntax, and in such cases the aphasic patients may misunderstand who did what to whom (**Figure 11.3c**).

Challenges to the idea that Broca's area is responsible for speech deficits seen in aphasia have been raised since Broca's time. For example, aphasiologist Nina Dronkers at UC Davis (1996) reported 22 patients with lesions in Broca's area, as defined by neuroimaging, but only 10 of these patients had the clinical syndrome of Broca's aphasia. It is now recognized that Broca's area is composed of multiple subregions, suggesting that it is involved in more functions than was previously assumed (Amunts et al., 2010). Some of the subregions are involved in language processing, but others may not be.

Broca never dissected the brain of his original patient, Leborgne, and therefore could not determine whether there was damage to structures beneath the brain's surface—but today's imaging techniques can. Leborgne's brain, preserved and housed in Paris (as is Broca's brain), was scanned using high-resolution MRI. His lesions extended into regions underlying the superficial cortical zone of Broca's area, and included the insular cortex and portions of the basal ganglia (Dronkers et al., 2007). This finding suggested that damage to Broca's area may not be solely responsible for the speech production deficits of Leborgne and others suffering from Broca's aphasia.

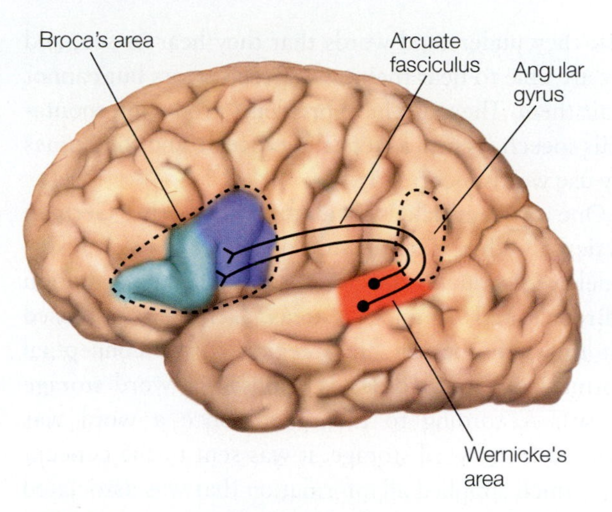

FIGURE 11.4 Lateral view of the classical left-hemisphere language areas and dorsal connections.
Wernicke's area is shown shaded in red. The arcuate fasciculus is the bundle of axons that connects Wernicke's and Broca's areas.

WERNICKE'S APHASIA **Wernicke's aphasia**, also known as *posterior aphasia* or *receptive aphasia*, was first described fully by the German physician Carl Wernicke. It is a disorder primarily of language comprehension: Patients with this syndrome have difficulty understanding spoken or written language and sometimes cannot understand language at all. Although their speech is fluent with normal prosody and grammar, what they say is often nonsensical.

In performing autopsies on his patients who showed language comprehension problems, Wernicke discovered damage in the posterior regions of the superior temporal gyrus, which has since become known as **Wernicke's area** (**Figure 11.4**). As with Broca's aphasia and Broca's area, inconsistencies are seen in the relationship between brain lesion and language deficit in Wernicke's aphasia. Lesions that spare Wernicke's area can also lead to comprehension deficits.

More recent studies have revealed that dense and persistent Wernicke's aphasia is ensured only if there is damage in Wernicke's area *and* in the surrounding cortex of the posterior temporal lobe, or damage to the underlying white matter that connects temporal lobe language areas to other brain regions. Thus, although Wernicke's area remains in the center of a posterior region of the brain whose functioning is required for normal comprehension, lesions confined to Wernicke's area produce only temporary Wernicke's aphasia. It appears that damage to this area does not actually cause the syndrome. Instead, swelling or damage to tissue in surrounding regions contributes to the most severe problems. When swelling around the lesioned cortex goes away, comprehension may improve.

The Wernicke–Lichtheim Model of Brain and Language

Wernicke proposed a model for how the known language areas of the brain were connected. He and others found that a large neural fiber tract, the **arcuate fasciculus** (Figure 11.4), connected Broca's and Wernicke's areas. Wernicke predicted that damage to this fiber tract would disconnect Wernicke's and Broca's areas in a fashion that should result in another form of aphasia, which he termed *Leitungsaphasie* in German, or **conduction aphasia** in English. Patients with conduction aphasia do exist; they understand words that they hear or see, and they are able to hear their own speech errors but cannot repair them. They also have problems producing spontaneous speech, as well as repeating speech, and sometimes they use words incorrectly.

One of Wernicke's contemporaries, the German physician Ludwig Lichtheim, elaborated on Wernicke's model by introducing the idea of a third region in addition to Broca's and Wernicke's areas. Lichtheim proposed that this hypothetical brain region stored conceptual information about words (as opposed to word storage per se). According to Lichtheim, once a word was retrieved from word storage, it was sent to the concept area, which supplied all information that was associated with the word.

Although Lichtheim's idea does not correspond to what we now know of neuroanatomy, it nevertheless led to the *Wernicke–Lichtheim model* (**Figure 11.5**). This classical model proposed that language processing, from sound inputs to motor outputs, involved the interconnection of different key brain regions (Broca's and Wernicke's areas, and Lichtheim's hypothesized concept area) and that damage to different segments of this network would result in the various observed and proposed forms of aphasia.

The Wernicke–Lichtheim model can account for many forms of aphasia, but it does not explain others, and it does not fit with the most current knowledge of

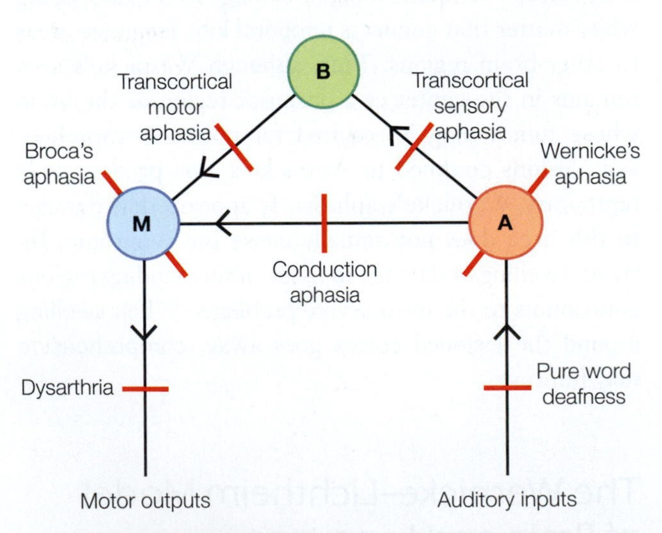

FIGURE 11.5 The historic Wernicke–Lichtheim model of language and aphasia.
The area proposed to store permanent information about word sounds (Wernicke's area) is represented by A (for *auditory*). The speech planning and programming area (Broca's area) is represented by M (for *motor*). Conceptual information was proposed to be stored in area B (for the German word for "concept," *Begriff*). Arrows indicate the direction of information flow. This model formed the basis of predictions that lesions in the three main areas, in the connections between them, or their inputs or outputs could account for various observed and hypothesized aphasic syndromes. The locations of possible lesions are indicated by the red line segments.

the human language system that we will present in this chapter. Though this model has proved to be an oversimplification, its emphasis on the network architecture of language comprehension and production has proven to be both revolutionary and prescient. It remained influential for a century, having been revived by the great American neurologist Norman Geschwind in the 1960s; his research, involving patients with neurological deficits that resulted in various types of aphasia, fit well within the predictions of the Wernicke–Lichtheim model (Geschwind, 1970).

TAKE-HOME MESSAGES

- A left-hemisphere network involving the frontal, parietal, and temporal lobes is especially critical for language production and comprehension. White matter tracts serve as key structures in the left-hemisphere network.
- The right hemisphere does play a role in language, especially in processing the prosody of language.
- Language disorders, generally called aphasia, can include deficits in comprehension or production of language resulting from neurological damage.
- People with Broca's aphasia have problems with speech production, syntax, and grammar, but otherwise comprehend what is said or written fairly well. The lesions that produce Broca's aphasia may not be limited to the classically defined Broca's area in the left inferior frontal cortex.
- People with Wernicke's aphasia have severe comprehension deficits but can produce relatively fluid, but often meaningless speech. Originally linked to damage solely in Wernicke's area (the posterior superior temporal gyrus), Wernicke's aphasia is currently also linked to damage outside the classic area.
- The arcuate fasciculus is a large neural fiber tract connecting Broca's and Wernicke's areas. Damage to this tract of nerve fibers results in conduction aphasia.

11.2 The Fundamentals of Language in the Human Brain

Human language is called a *natural language* because it arises from the abilities of the brain. It can be spoken, gestured, and written. Any natural language has a vocabulary, grammar, and syntactic rules; it uses symbolic coding of information to communicate both concrete and abstract ideas. Language can convey information about the past, the present, and our plans for the future, enabling us to pass information between social partners and to gain information from those who are not present or no longer alive.

Thus, we can learn from the experiences of previous generations (if we are willing to). So, how does the brain cope with spoken, gestured, and written input to derive meaning? And how does the brain produce spoken, signed, and written output to communicate meaning to others?

To answer these questions, we consider several key aspects of language in this chapter. First among these is *storage*: The brain must store representations of words and their associated concepts. A word in a spoken language has two properties: a meaning and a **phonological** (sound-based) **form**. A word in a written language also has an **orthographic** (vision-based) **form**. One of the central ideas in word (lexical) representation is the **mental lexicon**—a mental store of information about words that includes semantic information (the words' meanings), syntactic information (how the words combine to form sentences), and the details of word forms (their spellings and sound patterns). Most theories agree that the mental lexicon plays a central role in language. Some models, however, propose a single mental lexicon for both language comprehension and production, whereas other models distinguish between input and output lexica.

Let's approach the mental lexicon from the standpoint of language comprehension (although these concepts apply to language production as well). Once we have perceptually analyzed words that we heard as sound, read in print or writing, or saw as signed gestures, three general functions involving the mental lexicon are hypothesized:

1. **Lexical access**, the stage(s) of processing in which the output of perceptual analysis activates word-form representations in the mental lexicon, including their semantic and syntactic attributes.
2. **Lexical selection**, the stage in which the representation that best matches the input is identified (i.e., selected).
3. **Lexical integration**, the final stage, in which words are integrated into the full sentence, discourse, or larger context to facilitate understanding of the whole message.

Grammar and syntax are the rules by which lexical items are organized in a particular language to produce the intended meaning. We will begin our exploration of these functions by asking how the mental lexicon might be organized, and how that organization might be represented in the brain.

Organization of the Mental Lexicon

A normal adult speaker has passive knowledge of about 50,000 words, yet can easily recognize and produce about three words per second. Given this speed and the size of the database, the mental lexicon must be organized in a highly efficient manner. For example, it could be organized alphabetically, in which case it might take longer to find words in the middle of the alphabet, such as the ones starting with *K*, *L*, *O*, or *U*, than to find a word starting with an *A* or a *Z*. Instead, however, the mental lexicon is proposed to have other features that help us quickly move from spoken or written input to the representations of words. Linguistic evidence supports the following four organizing principles:

1. The smallest meaningful representational unit in a language is called a **morpheme**; this is also the smallest unit of representation in the mental lexicon. As an example consider the words *frost*, *defrost*, and *defroster*. The root of these words, *frost*, forms one morpheme; the prefix "de" in *defrost* changes the meaning of the word *frost* and is a morpheme as well; and finally, the word *defroster* consists of three morphemes (adding the morpheme "er").
2. More frequently used words are accessed more quickly than less frequently used words; for instance, the word *people* is more readily available than the word *fledgling*.
3. The lexicon is organized in neighborhoods consisting of words that differ from one another by a single letter or phoneme (e.g., *bat*, *cat*, *hat*, *sat*). A **phoneme** is the smallest unit of *sound* that makes a difference to meaning. Words with many overlapping phonemes or letters are thought to cluster in the mental lexicon in such a way that when incoming words access one word representation, other items in its lexical neighborhood are also initially accessed, prompting selection among candidate words, which takes time.
4. Representations in the mental lexicon are organized according to semantic relationships between words. Evidence for this type of organization comes from semantic priming studies that use a lexical decision task. In a semantic priming study, participants are presented with pairs of words. The first member of the word pair is the *prime*, while the second member, the *target*, can be a real word (*truck*), a nonword (like *rtukc*), or a pseudoword (a word that follows the phonological rules of a language but is not a real word, like *trulk*). If the target is a real word, it can be related or unrelated in meaning to the prime word.

   For the task, the participants must decide as quickly and accurately as possible whether the target is a word (i.e., make a lexical decision), pressing a button to indicate their decision. Participants are faster and more accurate at making the lexical decision for a real-word target when it is preceded by a semantically related prime (e.g., the prime *car* for the target *truck*) than by an unrelated prime (e.g., the prime *sunny* for the target *truck*). This pattern of facilitated response speed reveals that words related in meaning must somehow be organized together in the mental lexicon, and therefore also presumably in the brain.

Models of the Mental Lexicon

Several connectionist models have been proposed to explain the effects of semantic priming during word recognition. In an influential model proposed by A. M. Collins and E. F. Loftus (1975), word meanings are represented in a semantic network in which words, depicted as conceptual nodes, are connected with each other. **Figure 11.6** shows an example of a semantic network. The strength of the connection and the distance between the nodes are determined by the semantic or associative relations between the words. For example, the node that represents the word *car* will be close to and have a strong connection with the node that represents the word *truck*. A major component of this model is the assumption that activation spreads from one conceptual node to others, and that nodes that are closer together will benefit more from this spreading activation than will distant nodes.

There are many other connectionist models and ideas of how conceptual knowledge is represented. Some propose that words that co-occur in our language prime each other (e.g., *cottage* and *cheese*), and others suggest that concepts are represented by their semantic features or semantic properties. For example, the word *dog* has several semantic features, such as "is animate," "has four legs," and "barks," and these features are assumed to be represented in the conceptual network.

Such models are confronted with the problem of activation: How many features have to be stored or activated for a person to recognize a dog? For example, we can recognize that a Basenji is a dog even though it does not bark, and we can identify a barking dog that we cannot see. In addition, some words are more "prototypical" examples of a semantic category than others, as reflected in our recognition and production of these words. When we are asked to generate bird names, for example, the word *robin* might come to mind as one of the first examples, whereas a word like *ostrich* might not come up at all, depending on our personal experience.

In sum, it remains a matter of intense investigation how word meanings are represented. No matter how, though, everyone agrees that a mental store of word meanings is crucial to normal language comprehension and production. Evidence from patients with brain damage and from functional brain-imaging studies is still revealing how the mental lexicon and conceptual knowledge may be organized (see **Box 11.3**).

Neural Substrates of the Mental Lexicon

By observing the patterns of deficits in patients with language disabilities, we can infer a number of things about the functional organization of the mental lexicon. Consider that patients with Wernicke's aphasia make errors in speech production that are known as **semantic paraphasias.** For example, they might use the word *horse* when they mean *cow*. Patients with *deep dyslexia* make similar errors in reading: They might read the word *horse* where *cow* is written.

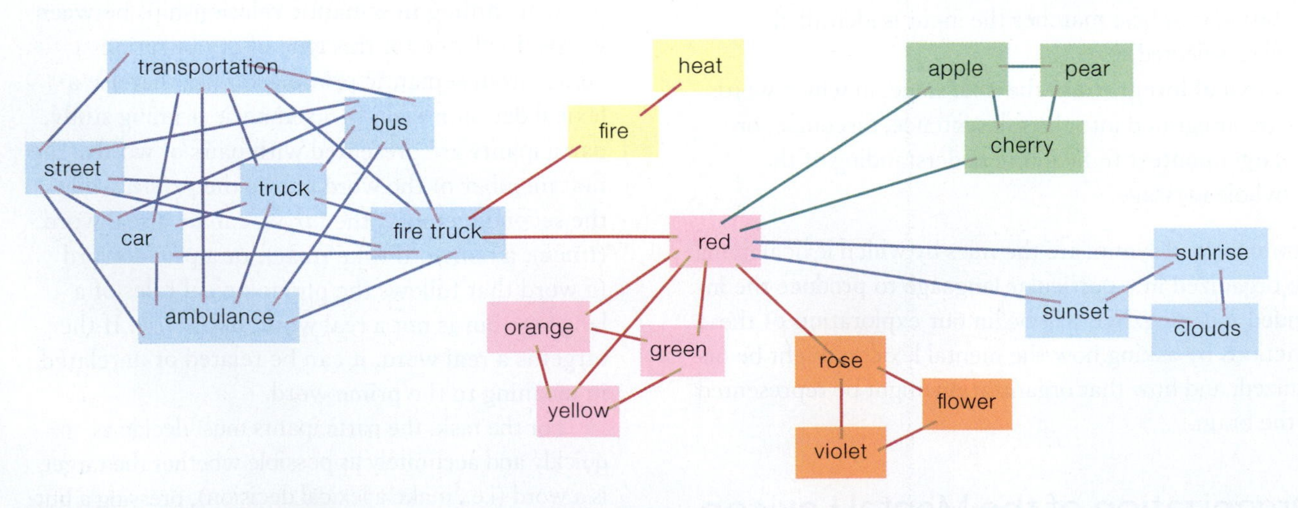

FIGURE 11.6 Semantic network.
Words that have strong associative or semantic relations are closer together in the network (e.g., *car* and *truck*) than are words that have no such relation (e.g., *car* and *clouds*). Semantically related words are colored similarly in the figure, and associatively related terms (e.g., *fire truck* and *fire*) are closely connected.

BOX 11.3 | HOT SCIENCE

Semantic Maps in the Brain

How is the storage of the mental lexicon, which includes the meanings (semantics), usage (syntax), and forms (spelling and sound patterns) of words, organized in the brain? Clues come from a variety of sources. Jack Gallant, Alexander Huth, and their colleagues at UC Berkeley (Huth et al., 2016) adapted their encoding-decoding technique (see Chapter 6) to investigate how the brain represents semantic information. They measured brain activity while student volunteers listened for 2 hours to stories such as those presented by *The Moth Radio Hour*.

To study how the participants' brain activity related to what was happening in the stories over time, the audio stories were first coded by creating a transcript. Then, phonemes and words were aligned from the transcript to their times of occurrence in the audio recordings. The researchers identified the semantic features of each word in the stories and computed their natural co-occurrence with a set of 985 common words in the English language. For example, words from the same semantic domain, such as *month* and *week*, tend to have similar co-occurrence values (correlation 0.74), whereas words from different domains, such as *month* and *tall*, do not (correlation 0.22). Next, the researchers analyzed how the 985 semantic features affected the activity in each voxel of the whole-brain fMRI data obtained while the participants listened to the story.

This method yielded a voxel-wise model describing how words appearing in the stories influenced BOLD signals; from this information, the researchers constructed a semantic map called an *encoding model*, compiled from a group of several participants listening to the same story. To validate the encoding model—that is, to see whether it could be used to predict brain activity—the model was used to predict the related brain activations while one of the students listened to a new story.

The researchers note that this methodology is a data-driven approach: The brain is activated by a large variety of word inputs, and a variety of methods are used to understand how the resulting brain activity clusters. What did this technical tour de force reveal? **Figure 11.7a** shows a color-coded map of major dimensions separating, for example, perceptual and physical categories (tactile, locational in green, turquoise, blue, and brown colors) from human-related categories (social, emotional, violent in red, purple, and pink colors) and a cartoon illustration of words on the surface of the brain (**Figure 11.7b**). For an interactive version of the semantic map, see http://www.gallantlab.org/huth2016.

Several interesting findings came from this study. First, the representation of semantic information in these maps was not restricted to the left perisylvian cortex, nor even to the left hemisphere, but rather was observed throughout both hemispheres, inconsistent with work in patients with focal brain damage, which suggests that semantic representations are lateralized to the left hemisphere. The findings were also quite consistent across individuals, hinting that the anatomical connectivity or cortical cytoarchitectonics constrains the organization of these high-level semantic representations. One of the most fascinating aspects of this work is that if maps such as these are created for a wide variety of information, it may be possible in the future to decode brain activity into meaning or, as we discussed in Chapter 6, to read minds.

Left hemisphere

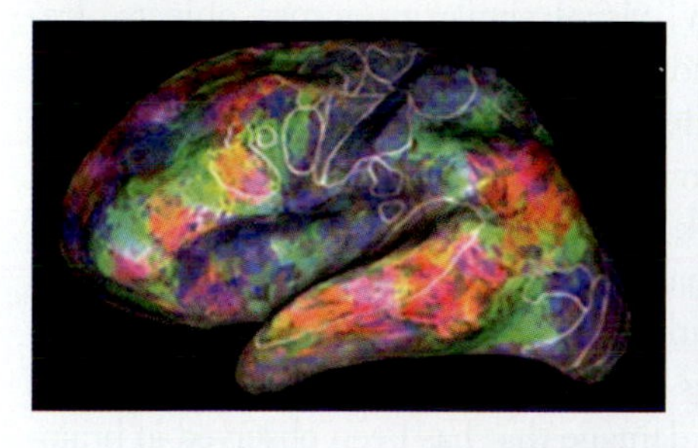

Right hemisphere

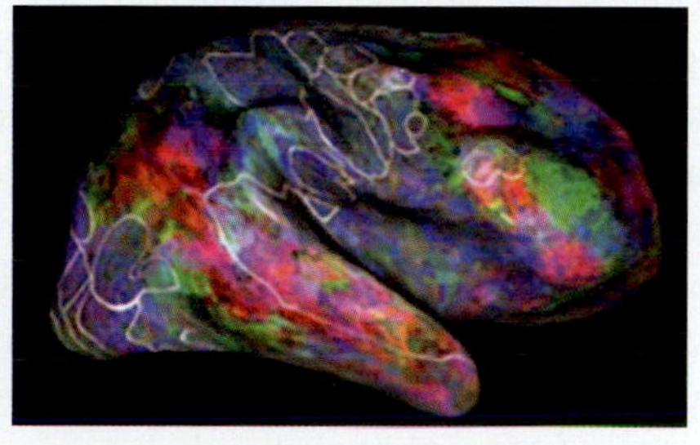

a

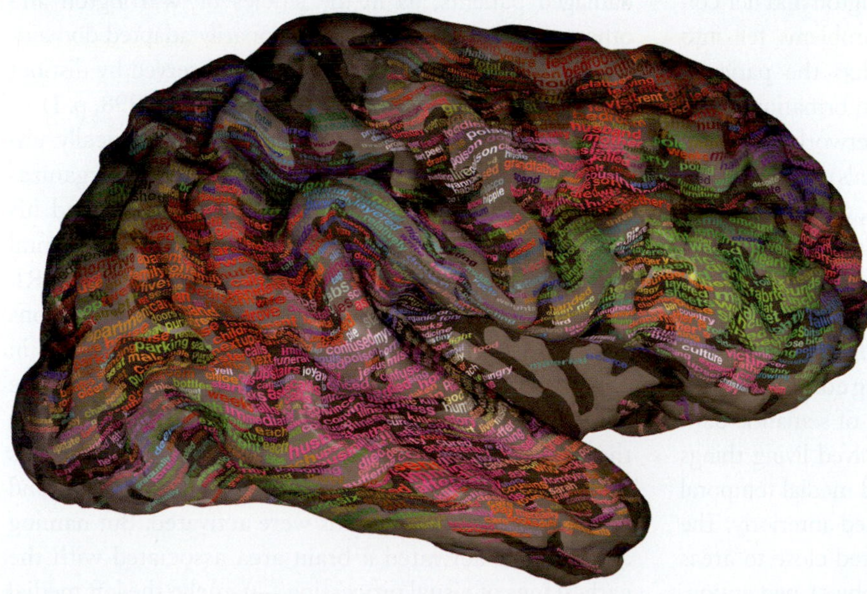

b

FIGURE 11.7 A semantic map compiled from a group of participants.
(a) The representation of semantic information was observed throughout both hemispheres. The 12 different colors represent different word categories. These patterns appear to be relatively consistent across individuals. (b) This cartoon illustration color-codes words by category on the surface of the brain.

Patients with *progressive semantic dementia* initially show impairments in the conceptual system, but other mental and language abilities are spared. For example, these patients can still understand and produce the syntactic structure of sentences. This impairment has been associated with progressive damage to the temporal lobes, mostly on the left side of the brain. But the superior regions of the temporal lobe that are important for hearing and speech processing are spared (we discuss these areas in Section 11.3).

Patients with semantic dementia have difficulty assigning objects to a semantic category. In addition, they often name a category when asked to name a picture; when viewing a picture of a horse, they will say "animal," and a picture of a robin will produce "bird." Neurological evidence from a variety of disorders provides support for the semantic-network idea because related meanings are substituted, confused, or lumped together, as we would predict from the degrading of a system of interconnected nodes that specifies meaning relation.

In the 1970s and early 1980s, Elizabeth Warrington and her colleagues performed groundbreaking studies on the organization of conceptual knowledge in the brain, originating with her studies involving perceptual disabilities in patients possessing unilateral cerebral lesions. Some of these studies were done on patients who would now be classified as suffering from semantic dementia. We discussed these studies in some detail in Chapter 6, so we will only summarize them here.

In Chapter 6 we discussed category-specific agnosias and how they might reflect the organization of semantic-memory (conceptual) knowledge. Warrington and her colleagues found that semantic-memory problems fell into semantic categories. They suggested that the patients' problems were reflections of the types of information stored with different words in the semantic network: Whereas biological categories (fruits, foods, animals) rely more on physical properties or visual features (e.g., what is the color of an apple?), human-made objects are identified by their functional properties (e.g., how do we use a hammer?).

Since these original observations by Warrington, many cases of patients with category-specific deficits have been reported, and there appears to be a striking correspondence between the sites of lesions and the type of semantic deficit. The patients whose impairment involved living things had lesions that included the inferior and medial temporal cortex, and often these lesions were located anteriorly. The anterior inferior temporal cortex is located close to areas of the brain that are crucial for visual object perception, and the medial temporal lobe contains important relay projections from association cortex to the hippocampus, a structure that, as you might remember from Chapter 9, has an important function in the encoding of information in long-term memory. Furthermore, the inferior temporal cortex is the end station for the "what" information, or the object recognition stream, in vision.

Less is known about the localization of lesions in patients who show greater impairment for human-made things, simply because fewer of these patients have been identified and studied. But left frontal and parietal areas appear to be involved in this kind of semantic deficit. These areas are close to or overlap with areas of the brain that are important for sensorimotor functions, so they are likely to be involved in the representation of actions that can be undertaken when human-made artifacts such as tools are being used.

A challenge to Warrington's hypothesis about biological and human-made categories comes from observations by Alfonso Caramazza and others (e.g., Caramazza & Shelton, 1998), who have suggested that Warrington's studies in patients did not always use well-controlled linguistic materials. For example, when comparing living things versus human-made things, some studies did not control the stimulus materials to ensure that the objects tested in each category were matched on qualities like visual complexity, visual similarity across objects, frequency of use, and the familiarity of objects. If these variables differed widely between the categories, then strong conclusions about differences in their representation in a semantic network could not be drawn.

Caramazza has proposed an alternative theory, in which the semantic network is organized along the conceptual categories of animacy and inanimacy. He argues that the selective damage that has been observed in brain-damaged patients, as in the studies of Warrington and others, genuinely reflects "evolutionarily adapted domain-specific knowledge systems that are subserved by distinct neural mechanisms" (Caramazza & Shelton, 1998, p. 1).

In the 1990s, imaging studies in neurologically unimpaired participants looked further into the organization of semantic representations. Alex Martin and his colleagues (1996) at the National Institute of Mental Health (NIMH) conducted studies using PET and fMRI. Their findings reveal how the intriguing dissociations described in impaired patients can also be identified in neurologically normal brains. When participants read the names of or answered questions about animals, or when they named pictures of animals, the more lateral aspects of the fusiform gyrus (on the brain's ventral surface) and the superior temporal sulcus were activated. But naming animals also activated a brain area associated with the early stages of visual processing—namely, the left medial occipital lobe.

In contrast, identifying and naming tools were associated with activation in the more medial aspect of the fusiform gyrus, the left middle temporal gyrus, and the left premotor area, a region that is also activated by imagining hand movements. These findings are consistent with the idea that in our brains, conceptual representations of living things versus human-made tools rely on separable neural circuits engaged in processing of perceptual versus functional information.

Other studies of the representation of conceptual information indicate that there is a network that connects the posterior fusiform gyrus in the inferior temporal lobe to the left anterior temporal lobes. Lorraine Tyler and her colleagues at the University of Cambridge (2011) have studied the representation and processing of concepts of living and nonliving things in patients with brain lesions to the anterior temporal lobes and in unimpaired participants using fMRI, EEG, and MEG measures. In these studies, participants are typically asked to name pictures of living things (e.g., a tiger) and nonliving things (e.g., a knife). Further, the level at which these objects should be named is varied: Participants are asked to name the pictures at either the specific level (e.g., tiger or knife) or the domain-general level (e.g., living or nonliving).

Tyler and colleagues suggest that naming at the specific level requires retrieval and integration of more detailed semantic information than does naming at the domain-general level. For example, whereas naming a picture at a domain-general level requires activation of only a subset of features (e.g., for animals: "has legs," "has fur," "has eyes," etc.), naming at the specific level requires retrieval and integration of additional and more precise features, including size and shape. For example, to distinguish a tiger from a house cat, panther, or zebra, features such as "is large," "has stripes," and "has claws" have to be retrieved and integrated as well.

Interestingly, as can be seen in **Figure 11.8**, whereas nonliving things (e.g., a knife) can be represented by only a few features, living things (e.g., a tiger) are represented by many features. Thus, it may be more difficult to select the feature that distinguishes living things from each other (e.g., a tiger from a zebra) than it is to distinguish nonliving things (e.g., a knife from a spoon). This model suggests that the dissociation between naming

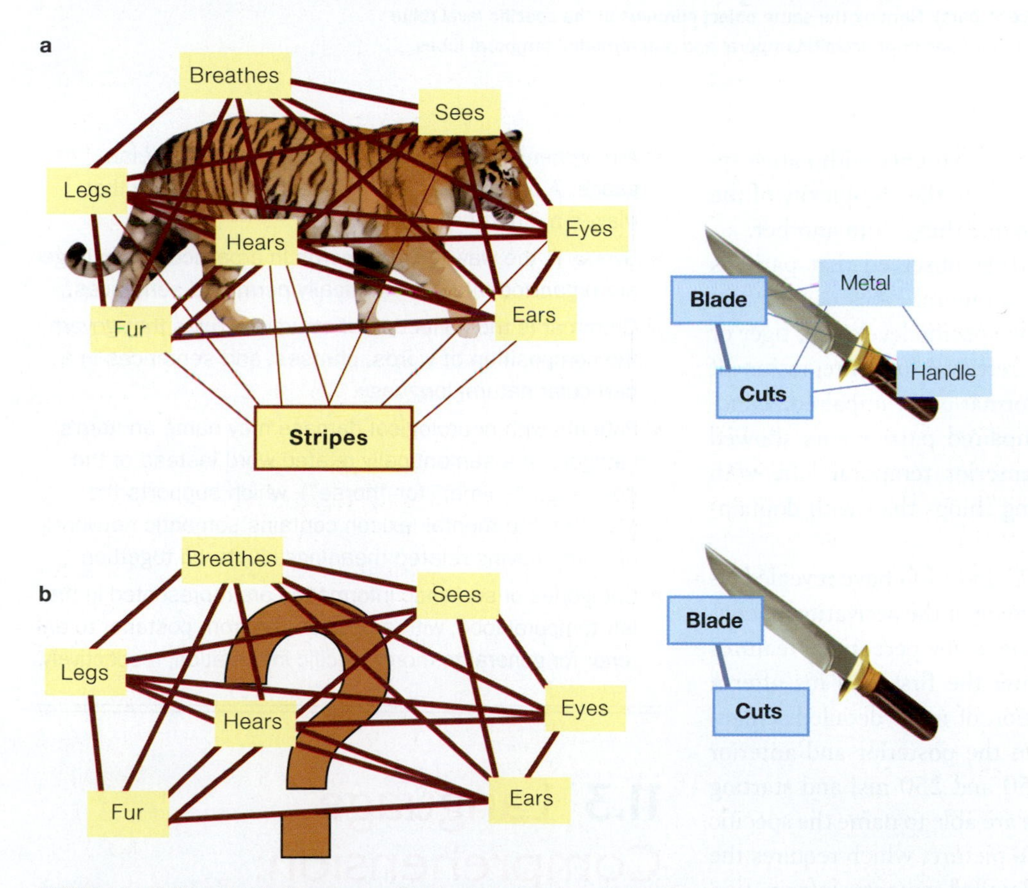

FIGURE 11.8 Hypothetical conceptual structures for tiger and knife.
(a) One model suggests that living things are represented by many features that are not distinct, whereas nonliving things can be represented by only a few features that are distinct. In this hypothetical-concept structure, the thickness of the straight lines correlates with the strength of the features, and the thickness of the boxes' borders correlates with the distinctness of the features. Although the tiger has many features, it has fewer features that distinguish it from other living things, whereas the knife has more distinct features that separate it from other possible objects. **(b)** Following brain damage resulting in aphasia, patients find it harder to identify the distinctive features for living things (left) than for nonliving objects (right).

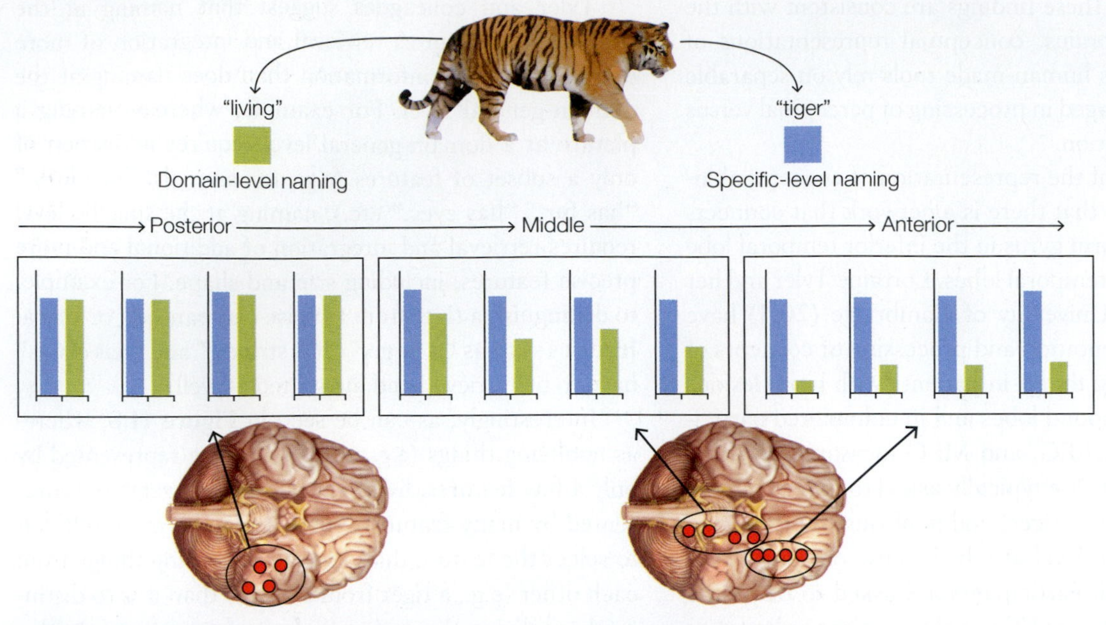

FIGURE 11.9 The anterior temporal lobes are involved in naming living things.
When identifying the tiger at the less complex domain level (living things), activity was restricted to more posterior occipitotemporal sites (green bars). Naming the same object stimulus at the specific level (blue bars) was associated with activity in both posterior occipitotemporal and anteromedial temporal lobes.

of nonliving and living things in patients with category-specific deficits may also be due to the complexity of the features that help distinguish one thing from another.

Tyler and colleagues further observed that patients with lesions to the anterior temporal lobes cannot reliably name living things at the specific level (e.g., tiger or zebra), indicating that the retrieval and integration of more detailed semantic information is impaired. Functional MRI studies in unimpaired participants showed greater activation in the anterior temporal lobe with specific-level naming of living things than with domain-level naming (**Figure 11.9**).

Finally, studies with MEG and EEG have revealed interesting details about the timing of the activation of conceptual knowledge. Activation of the perceptual features occurs in visual cortex within the first 100 ms after a picture is presented; activation of more detailed semantic representations occurs in the posterior and anterior temporal cortex between 150 and 250 ms; and starting around 300 ms, participants are able to name the specific object that is depicted in the picture, which requires the retrieval and integration of detailed semantic information that is unique to the specific object.

TAKE-HOME MESSAGES

- The mental lexicon is a store of information about words that includes semantic information, syntactic information, and the details of word forms.
- A morpheme is the smallest meaningful unit of language. A phoneme is the smallest unit of sound that makes a difference to meaning.
- Syntax is the way in which words in a particular language are organized into grammatically permitted sentences.
- Grammar is the collection of structural rules that govern the composition of words, phrases, and sentences in a particular natural language.
- Patients with neurological damage may name an item's category or a semantically related word instead of the item (e.g., "animal" for "horse"), which supports the idea that the mental lexicon contains semantic networks of words having related meanings clustered together.
- Categories of semantic information are represented in the left temporal lobe, with a progression from posterior to anterior for general to more specific information, respectively.

11.3 Language Comprehension: Early Steps

The brain uses some of the same processes to understand both spoken and written language, but there are also some striking differences in how spoken and written inputs are analyzed. When attempting to understand spoken words (**Figure 11.10**), the listener has to decode

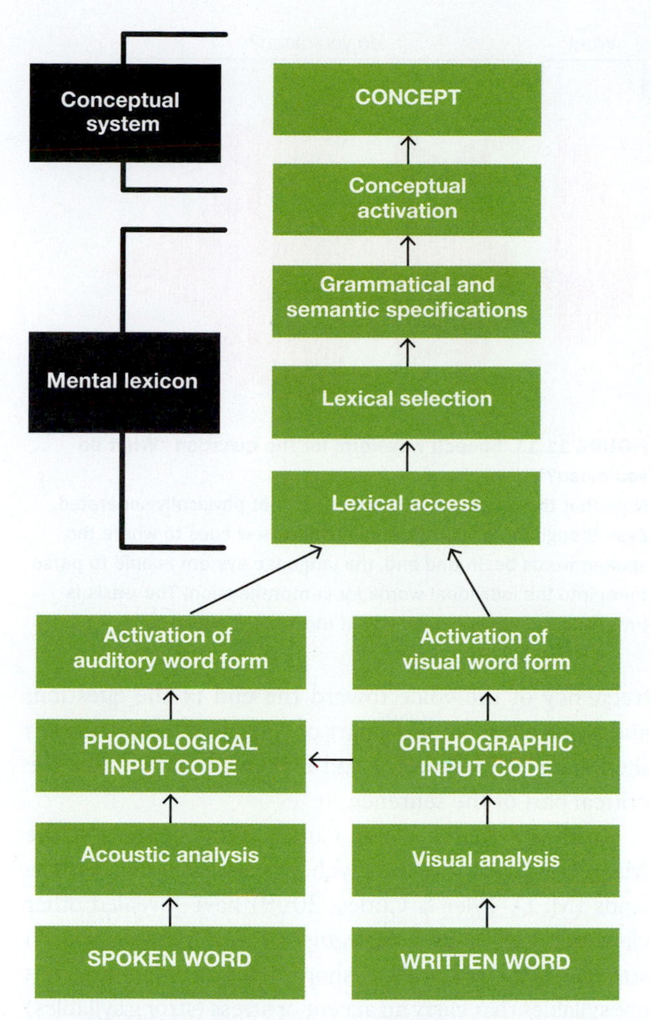

FIGURE 11.10 Schematic representation of the components involved in spoken- and written-language comprehension. Inputs can enter via either auditory (spoken-word; left) or visual (written-word; right) modalities. Notice that the information flows from the bottom up in this figure, from perceptual identification to "higher-level" word and meaning activation. So-called interactive models of language understanding would predict top-down influences to play a role as well. For example, activation at the word-form level would influence earlier perceptual processes. One could introduce this type of feedback into this schematic representation by making the arrows bidirectional.

the acoustic input. The result of this acoustic analysis is translated into a phonological code because, as discussed in the previous section, that is how the lexical representations of auditory word forms are stored in the mental lexicon. The representations in the mental lexicon that match the auditory input can then be accessed (lexical access) and the best match selected (lexical selection). The selected word includes grammatical and semantic information stored with it in the mental lexicon; this information helps to specify how the word can be used in the given language. Finally, the word's meaning (store of the lexical-semantic information) results in activation of the conceptual information.

The process of reading words shares at least the last two steps of linguistic analysis (i.e., lexical and meaning activation) with auditory comprehension, but, because of the different input modality, reading differs at the earlier processing steps, as illustrated in Figure 11.10. Given that the perceptual input is different, what are these earlier stages in reading? The first analysis step requires that the reader identify orthographic units (written symbols that represent the sounds or words of a language) from the visual input. These units may then be directly mapped onto orthographic word forms in the mental lexicon. Alternatively, the identified orthographic units might be translated into phonological units, which in turn activate the phonological word form in the mental lexicon as described for auditory comprehension.

In this section we delve into the early processes involved in the understanding of spoken and written inputs of words. We begin with auditory processing and then turn to the different steps involved in the comprehension of reading, also known as visual language input.

Spoken Input: Understanding Speech

The input signal in spoken language is very different from that in written (or signed) language. Whereas for a reader it is immediately clear that the letters on a page are the physical signals of importance, a listener is confronted with a variety of sounds in the environment and has to identify and distinguish the relevant speech signals from other "noise."

As introduced earlier, the building blocks of spoken language are phonemes. These are the smallest units of sound that make a difference to meaning; in the words *cap* and *tap*, for example, the only difference is the first phoneme (/k/ versus /t/). The English language uses about 40 phonemes (depending on the dialect); other languages may use more or fewer. Perception of phonemes is different for speakers of different languages. For example, in English, the sounds for the letters *L* and *R* are two different phonemes (the words *late* and *rate* mean different things, and we easily hear that difference). But in the Japanese language, *L* and *R* cannot be distinguished by adult native speakers, so these sounds are represented by only one phoneme.

Interestingly, infants have the perceptual ability to distinguish *all* possible phonemes during their first year of life. Patricia Kuhl and her colleagues at the University of Washington found that, initially, infants could distinguish between any phonemes presented to them; but during the first year of life, their perceptual sensitivities became tuned to the phonemes of the language they experienced on a daily basis (Kuhl et al., 1992). So, for example, Japanese infants can distinguish *L* from *R* sounds, but then lose that ability over time. American infants, on the other hand, do not lose that ability, but do lose the ability to distinguish phonemes that are not part of the English language.

The babbling and crying sounds that infants articulate from ages 6 to 12 months grow more and more similar to the phonemes that they most frequently hear. By the time babies are 1 year old, they no longer produce (or perceive) nonnative phonemes. Learning another language often means encountering phonemes that don't occur in a person's native language, such as the guttural sounds of Dutch or the rolling *R* of Spanish. Such nonnative sounds can be difficult to learn, especially when we are older and our native phonemes have become automatic, and they make it challenging or impossible to lose our native accent. Perhaps that was Mark Twain's problem when he quipped, "In Paris they just simply opened their eyes and stared when we spoke to them in French! We never did succeed in making those idiots understand their own language" (from *The Innocents Abroad*).

Recognizing that phonemes are the basic units of spoken language and that we all become experts in the phonemes of our native tongue does not eliminate all challenges for the listener. The listener's brain must resolve additional difficulties involving the variability of the speech signal (e.g., male versus female speakers) and the fact that phonemes often do not appear as separate little chunks of information. Unlike the case for written words, auditory speech signals are not clearly segmented, and it can be difficult to discern where one word begins and another word ends.

When we speak, we usually spew out about 15 phonemes per second, which adds up to about 180 words a minute. The puzzling thing is that we say these phonemes with no gaps or breaks; that is, there are no pauses between words. Thus, the input signal in spoken language is very different from that in written language, where the letters and phonemes are neatly separated into word chunks. Two or more spoken words can be slurred together—speech sounds are often *coarticulated*—and there can be silences within words as well. The question of how we differentiate auditory sounds into separate words is known as the *segmentation problem*. This is illustrated in **Figure 11.11**, which shows the speech signal of the sentence "What do you mean?"

How do we identify the spoken input, given this variability and the segmentation problem? Fortunately, other clues help us divide the speech stream into meaningful segments. One important clue is the *prosodic* information, which is what the listener derives from the speech rhythm and the pitch of the speaker's voice. The speech rhythm comes from variation in the duration of words and the placement of pauses between them. Prosody is apparent in all spoken utterances, but it is perhaps most clearly illustrated when a speaker asks a question or emphasizes something. When asking a question, a speaker raises the

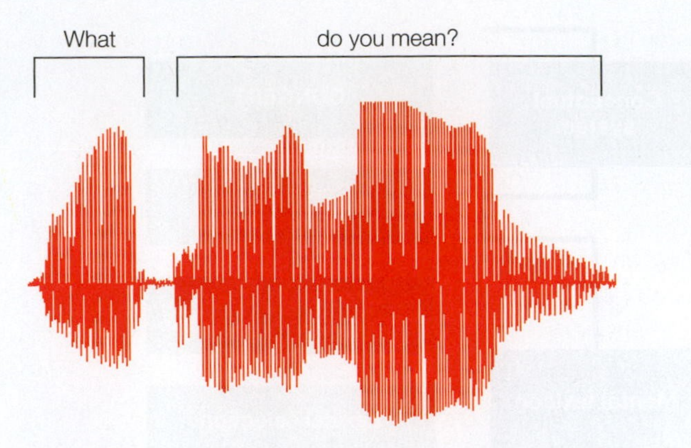

FIGURE 11.11 Speech waveform for the question "What do you mean?"
Note that the words "do you mean" are not physically separated. Even though the physical signal provides few cues to where the spoken words begin and end, the language system is able to parse them into the individual words for comprehension. The *x*-axis is time, and the *y*-axis is intensity of the speech signal.

frequency of the voice toward the end of the question; and when emphasizing a part of speech, a speaker raises the loudness of the voice and includes a pause after the critical part of the sentence.

In their research, Anne Cutler and colleagues at the Max Planck Institute for Psycholinguistics in the Netherlands (M. D. Tyler & Cutler, 2009) have revealed other clues that can be used to segment the continuous speech stream. These researchers showed that English listeners use syllables that carry an accent or stress (strong syllables) to establish word boundaries. For example, a word like *lettuce*, with stress on the first syllable, is usually heard as a single word and not as two words ("let us"). In contrast, words like *invests*, with stress on the last syllable, are usually heard as two words ("in vests") and not as one word.

NEURAL SUBSTRATES OF SPOKEN-WORD PROCESSING Now we turn to the questions of where in the brain the processes of understanding speech signals may take place and which neural circuits and systems support them. From animal studies, studies in patients with brain lesions, and imaging and recording studies in humans (EEG and MEG), we know that the superior temporal cortex is important for sound perception.

At the beginning of the 20th century, it was already well understood that some patients with bilateral lesions restricted to the superior parts of the temporal lobe had specific difficulties recognizing speech sounds, although they could process other sounds relatively normally. Because the patients had no difficulty in other aspects of language processing, their problem seemed to be restricted primarily to auditory or phonemic deficits, and the syndrome was termed *pure word deafness*. Today, with evidence from more recent studies in hand, we can more precisely determine where speech and nonspeech sounds are first distinguished in the brain.

When the speech signal hits the ear, it is first processed by pathways in the brain that are not specialized for speech but are used for hearing in general. Heschl's gyri, which are located on the supratemporal plane, superior and medial to the superior temporal gyrus (STG) in each hemisphere, contain the primary auditory cortex, or the area of cortex that processes the auditory input first (see Chapter 2). The areas that surround Heschl's gyri and extend into the superior temporal sulcus (STS) are collectively known as auditory association cortex.

Imaging and recording studies in humans have shown that Heschl's gyri (see Figure 5.17) of both hemispheres are activated by speech and nonspeech sounds (e.g., tones) alike, but that activation in the STS of each hemisphere is modulated by whether the incoming auditory signal is a speech sound or not. This view is summarized in **Figure 11.12**, showing that there is a hierarchy in the sensitivity to speech in our brain (Peelle et al., 2010; Poeppel et al., 2012).

As we move farther away from Heschl's gyrus, the brain becomes less sensitive to changes in nonspeech sounds but more sensitive to speech sounds. Although more left lateralized, the posterior portions of the STS of both hemispheres seem especially relevant to processing of phonological information. It is clear from many studies, however, that the speech perception network expands beyond the STS.

As described earlier, Wernicke found that patients with lesions in the left temporoparietal region that included the STG (Wernicke's area) had difficulty understanding spoken and written language. This observation led to the now-century-old notion that this area is crucial to word comprehension. Even in Wernicke's original observations, however, the lesions were not restricted to the STG. We can now conclude that the STG alone is probably not the seat of word comprehension.

One contribution to our new understanding of speech perception has come from an fMRI study done by Jeffrey Binder and colleagues at the Medical College of Wisconsin (2000). Participants in the study listened to different types of sounds, both speech and nonspeech. The sounds were of several types: white noise; frequency-modulated tones; reversed speech in which real words were played backward; pseudowords, which were pronounceable strings of nonreal words that contained the same letters as the real word—for example, *sked* from *desk*; and, finally, real words.

These researchers found patterns of consistent activity across the different stimuli that were strongest in the left hemisphere. From their data, along with evidence from other groups, Binder and colleagues (2000) proposed a hierarchical model of word recognition (**Figure 11.13**). First, the stream of auditory information proceeds from auditory cortex in Heschl's gyri to the superior temporal gyrus. In these parts of the brain, no distinction is made between speech and nonspeech sounds, as noted earlier. The first evidence of such a distinction is in the adjacent midportion of the superior temporal sulcus, but still, no lexical-semantic information is processed in this area. Finally, the regions that were more active for words than for nonwords included the middle temporal gyrus, inferior temporal gyrus, angular gyrus, and temporal pole.

Neurophysiological studies, such as those using EEG or MEG recording, now indicate that recognizing whether a speech sound is a word or a pseudoword happens in the first 50 to 80 ms (MacGregor et al., 2012). This processing tends to be lateralized more to the left hemisphere, where the combinations of the different features of speech sounds are analyzed (pattern recognition). From the superior temporal sulcus, the information proceeds to the final processing stage of word recognition in the middle temporal gyrus and the inferior temporal gyrus, and finally to the angular gyrus, posterior to the

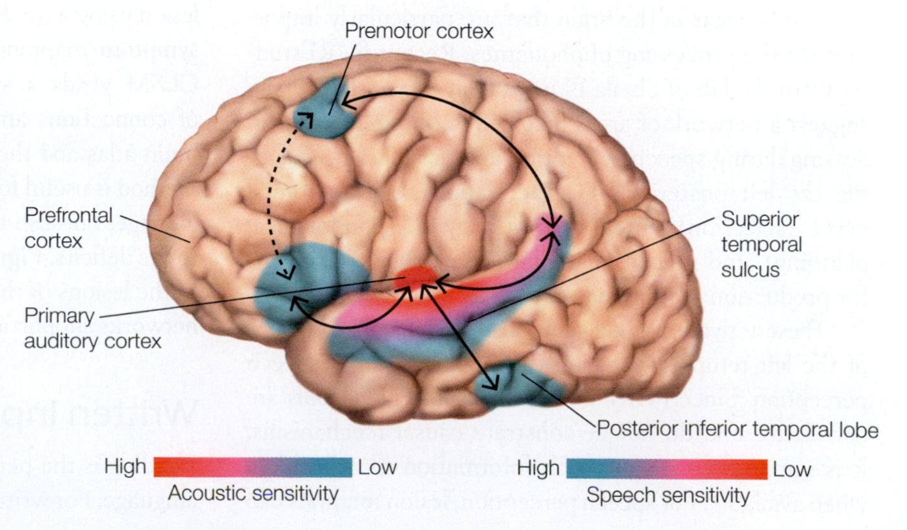

FIGURE 11.12 Hierarchical processing is a key organizational aspect of the human cortical auditory system. Multiple parallel processing pathways radiate outward from primary auditory areas to regions of motor, premotor, and prefrontal cortex. Acoustic sensitivity is highest in primary auditory cortex (Heschl's gyrus; red spot) and is activated by all auditory inputs. Acoustic sensitivity decreases moving anteriorly, inferiorly, and posteriorly away from primary auditory cortex, while intelligibility of the speech increases. Anterior and posterior regions of the superior temporal sulcus are increasingly speech specific. The left posterior inferior temporal cortex is involved in accessing or integrating semantic representations. Areas of the frontal cortex also contribute to speech comprehension.

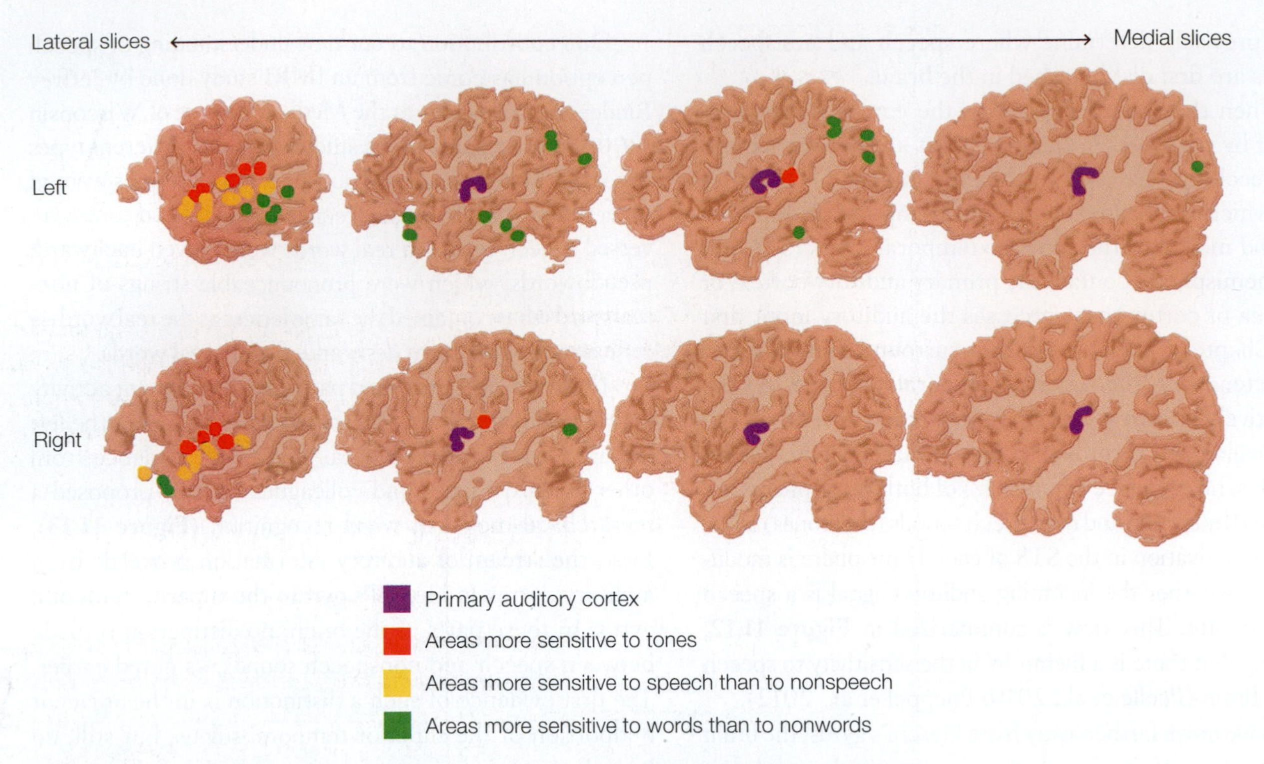

FIGURE 11.13 Regions involved in a hierarchical processing stream for speech processing. Sagittal sections showing Heschl's gyri, which contain the primary auditory cortex, are in purple. Shown in red are areas of the dorsal superior temporal gyri that are activated more by frequency-modulated tones than by random noise. Yellow areas are clustered in the superior temporal sulcus and are speech-sound specific; they show more activation for speech sounds (words, pseudowords, or reversed speech) than for nonspeech sounds. Green areas include regions of the middle temporal gyrus, inferior temporal gyrus, angular gyrus, and temporal pole and are more active for words than for pseudowords or nonwords. Critically, these "word" areas are lateralized mostly to the left hemisphere.

temporal areas just described (see Chapter 2), and in more anterior regions in the temporal pole (Figure 11.12).

During the decade following the Binder study, researchers attempted in multiple studies to localize speech recognition processes. In reviewing 100 fMRI studies, Iain DeWitt and Josef Rauschecker of Georgetown University Medical Center (2012) confirmed the findings that the left mid-anterior STG responds preferentially to phonetic sounds of speech. Researchers also have tried to identify areas in the brain that are particularly important for the processing of phonemes. Recent fMRI studies from the lab of Sheila Blumstein at Brown University suggest a network of areas involved in phonological processing during speech perception and production, including the left posterior STG (activation), supramarginal gyrus (selection), inferior frontal gyrus (phonological planning), and precentral gyrus (generating motor plans for production; Peramunage et al., 2011).

These activation studies demonstrated that wide regions of the left temporal lobe are critical for auditory speech perception. Since fMRI studies in healthy individuals are correlative and do not demonstrate causal mechanisms, it is important to relate such information to other data when available. For speech perception, lesion methods can provide that critical causal information. That is, if a brain region is critical for a given linguistic process, then lesions of that region should result in deficits in patients.

Taking this approach, a group led by neurologist and cognitive neuroscientist Leonardo Bonilha at the University of South Carolina studied a large number of patients with left-hemisphere strokes that had resulted in a variety of aphasic deficits (Bonilha et al., 2017). The researchers then related the patients' aphasic deficits to MRI maps of the lesion using a method known as connectome-based lesion-symptom mapping (CLSM; Gleichgerrcht et al., 2017). CLSM yields a statistical relationship for the strength of connections among all brain regions from a standard brain atlas and the behavioral deficits of the patients. The method is useful for assessing not only cortical gray matter damage, but also the contribution of white matter lesions to the deficits. **Figure 11.14** shows the overlap of the extent of the lesions of the patient group, as well as the identified networks supporting spoken-word comprehension.

Written Input: Reading Words

Reading is the perception and comprehension of written language. For written input, readers must recognize a visual

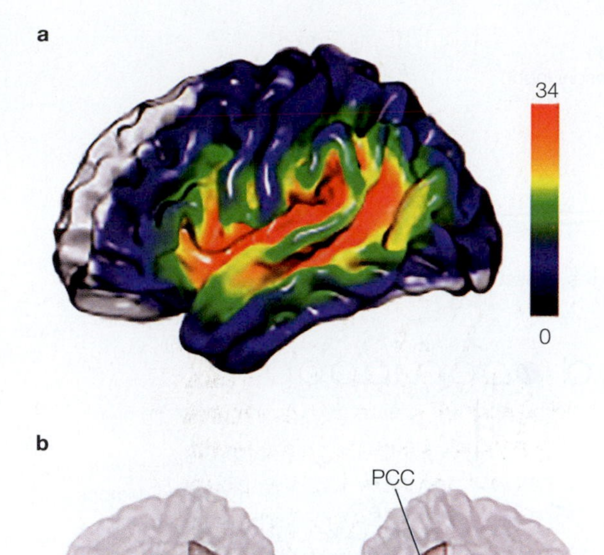

FIGURE 11.14 Networks for spoken-word comprehension. **(a)** Lesion overlap map of the left hemisphere from 34 stroke patients. The greatest overlap of lesions across the patient group is shown in the yellow–red end of the spectrum. **(b)** Regions of the left hemisphere showing the network found to be most involved in the comprehension of spoken words. (Left: lateral view. Right: medial view.) The network is centered on the posterior middle temporal gyrus (PMTG), from which connections link the middle temporal gyrus (MTG), inferior temporal gyrus (ITG), and the posterior cingulate cortex (PCC). The ITG is also directly linked with the PCC.

pattern. Our brain is very good at pattern recognition, but reading is a quite recent invention (about 5,500 years old). Although speech comprehension develops without explicit training, reading requires instruction. Specifically, learning to read requires linking arbitrary visual symbols into meaningful words. The visual symbols that are used vary across different writing systems. Words can be symbolized in writing in three different ways: alphabetic, syllabic, and logographic. For example, many Western languages use an alphabetic system, Japanese uses a syllabic system, and Chinese uses a logographic system.

Regardless of the writing system used, readers must be able to analyze the primitive features, or the shapes of the symbols. In the alphabetic system—our focus here—this process involves the visual analysis of horizontal lines, vertical lines, closed curves, open curves, intersections, and other elementary shapes.

In a 1959 paper that was a landmark contribution to the emerging science of artificial intelligence (i.e., machine learning), Oliver Selfridge proposed a four-stage, biologically plausible model for how visual stimuli were processed. Each stage had specific components that represented discrete substages of information processing and that, taken together, would allow a mechanical or biological visual system to recognize patterns. Selfridge whimsically called the components *demons* and his model the *pandemonium model*. The "demons" in the biological model correspond to specific neurons or neuronal circuits.

Selfridge's demons, working in parallel, record events as they occur; they collectively recognize patterns in those events, and they may trigger subsequent events according to those patterns. In this model, the sensory input is temporarily stored as an iconic memory by the so-called *image demon*. Then a series of *feature demons*, each sensitive to a particular feature, start to decode features like curves, horizontal lines, and so forth in the iconic representation of the sensory input (**Figure 11.15**).

In the next step, each letter is represented by a *cognitive demon* whose activity level depends on how many of the features from the prior feature demon level match those of the letter it represents. Finally, the representation that best matches the input is selected by the *decision demon*. The pandemonium model has been criticized because it consists solely of stimulus-driven (bottom-up) processing and does not allow for feedback (top-down) processing, such as in the word superiority effect (see Chapter 3). It cannot explain, for example, why humans are better at processing letters found in words than letters found in nonsense words or even single letters.

In 1981, James McClelland and David Rumelhart proposed a computational model that has been important for visual letter recognition. This model assumes three levels of representation: a layer for the features of the letters of words, a layer for the letters, and a layer for the representation of words. An important characteristic of this model is that it permits top-down information (i.e., information from the higher cognitive levels, such as the word layer) to influence earlier processes that happen at lower levels of representation (the letter layer and the feature layer).

This model contrasts sharply with Selfridge's model, where the flow of information is strictly bottom-up (from the image demon to the feature demons to the cognitive demons and finally to the decision demon). Another important difference between the two models is that, in the McClelland and Rumelhart model, processes can take place in parallel such that several letters can be processed at the same time, whereas in Selfridge's model, one letter is processed at a time in a serial manner. As **Figure 11.16** shows, the model of McClelland and Rumelhart permits both excitatory and inhibitory links between all the layers.

The empirical validity of a model can be tested on real-life behavioral phenomena or against physiological data. McClelland and Rumelhart's connectionist model does an excellent job of mimicking reality for the word superiority effect. This remarkable result indicates that words are probably not perceived letter by letter. The word

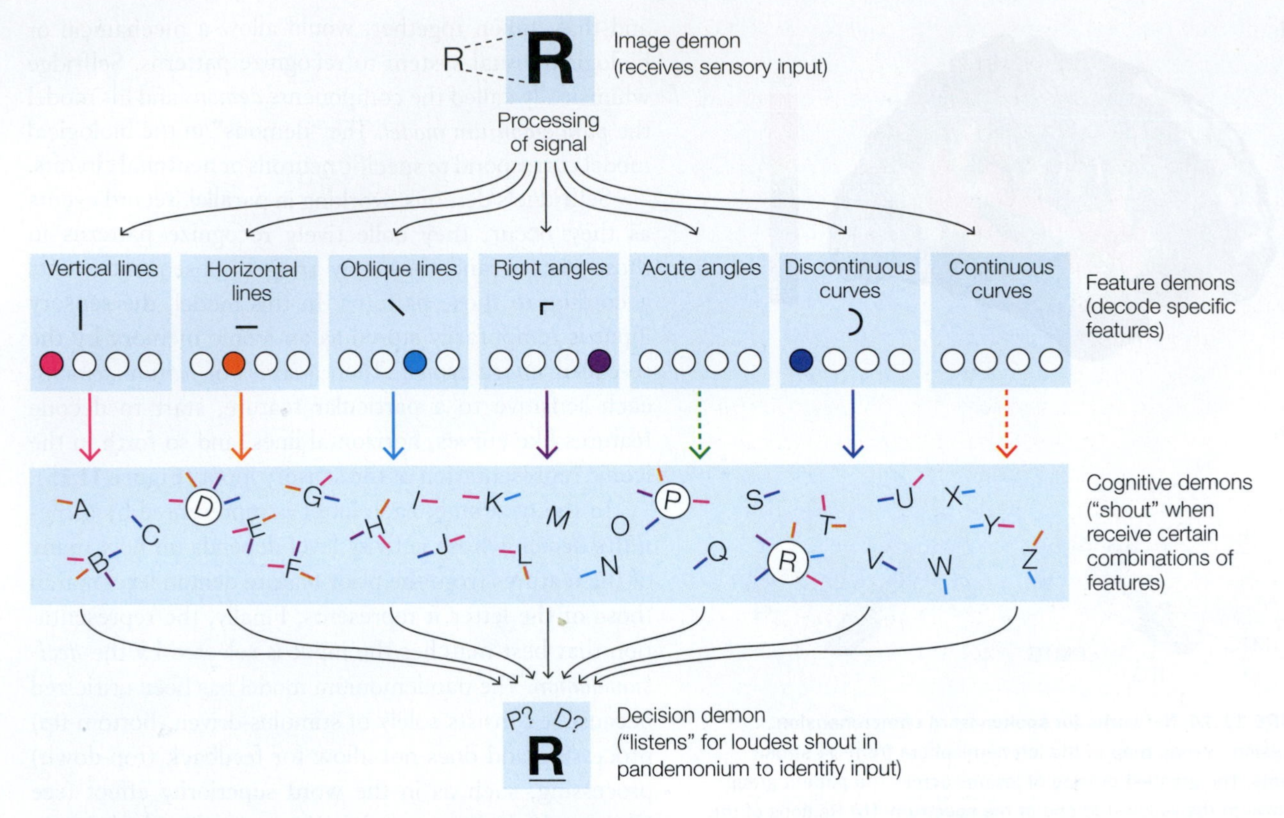

FIGURE 11.15 Selfridge's pandemonium model of letter recognition.
For written input, the reader must recognize a pattern that starts with the analysis of the sensory input (the letter *R*). The sensory input is stored temporarily in iconic memory by the image demon, and a set of feature demons decodes the iconic representations. The cognitive demons are activated by the representations of letters with these decoded features, and the representation that best matches the input is then selected by the decision demon. In this case, the letters *D*, *P*, and *R* share many features with the input letter *R*, and the decision demon chooses the best match among the candidates, which is, of course, the letter *R*.

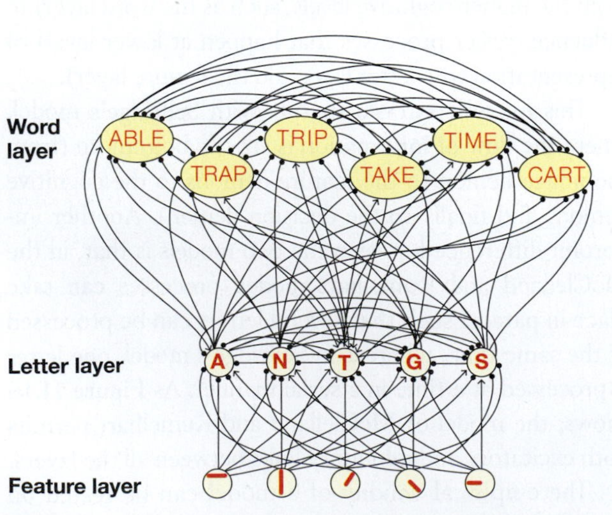

FIGURE 11.16 Fragment of a connectionist network for letter recognition.
Nodes at three different layers represent letter features, letters, and words. Nodes in each layer can influence the activational status of the nodes in the other layers by excitatory (arrows) or inhibitory (lines) connections.

superiority effect can be explained in terms of the McClelland and Rumelhart model, because the model proposes that top-down information of the words can either activate or inhibit letter activations, thereby helping the recognition of letters.

We learned in Chapters 5 and 6 that single-cell-recording techniques have enlightened us about the basics of visual feature analysis and about how the brain analyzes edges, curves, and so on. Unresolved questions remain, however, because letter and word recognition are not really understood at the neuronal level, and recordings in monkeys are not likely to enlighten us about letter and word recognition in humans. Recent studies using PET and fMRI have started to shed some light on where letters are processed in the human brain.

NEURAL SUBSTRATES OF WRITTEN-WORD PROCESSING The actual identification of orthographic units may take place in occipitotemporal regions of the left hemisphere. It has been known for over a hundred years that lesions in this area can give rise to pure **alexia**, a condition in which patients cannot read words, even though other aspects of language are normal. In early PET imaging studies, Steve Petersen and his colleagues (1990) contrasted words with nonwords and found regions of occipital cortex that preferred word strings. They named these regions the *visual word form area (VWFA)*.

In later studies using fMRI in normal participants, Gregory McCarthy at Yale University and his colleagues (Puce et al., 1996) contrasted brain activation in response to letters with activation in response to faces and visual textures. They found that regions of the occipitotemporal cortex were activated preferentially in response to unpronounceable letter strings (**Figure 11.17**). Interestingly, this finding confirmed results from an earlier study by the same group (Nobre et al., 1994), in which intracranial electrical recordings were made from this brain region in patients who later underwent surgery for intractable epilepsy. In this study, the researchers found a large negative-polarity potential at about 200 ms in occipitotemporal regions, in response to the visual presentation of letter strings. This area was not sensitive to other visual stimuli, such as faces, and importantly, it also appeared to be insensitive to lexical or semantic features of words.

The standard model of word reading postulates that visual information is initially processed by the occipitotemporal area contralateral to the stimulated hemifield, and then transferred to the visual word form area in the left hemisphere. If that initial processing occurs in the right hemisphere, it is transferred to the VWFA in the left hemisphere via the posterior corpus callosum.

French scientists Laurent Cohen, Stanislas Dehaene, and their colleagues (2000) investigated the spatial and temporal organization of these processes in a combined ERP and fMRI study that included both healthy persons and patients with lesions to their posterior corpus callosum. While the participants fixated on a central crosshair, a word or a nonword was flashed to either their right or left visual field. Nonwords were consonant strings incompatible with French orthographic principles and were impossible to translate into phonology. When a word flashed on the screen, the participants were to repeat it out loud, and if a nonword flashed, they were to think *rien* (which is French for "nothing").

The fMRI imaging showed that the occipital cortex contralateral to the hemifield of the written input was activated, and the ERPs over contralateral scalp regions indicated that this initial processing took place about 150 ms after stimulus onset in both groups. Then, 30 ms later, a left-lateralized scalp ERP was observed for both right- and left-hemifield written inputs in the healthy patients. This observation was consistent with fMRI activation in part of the VWFA in the left occipitotemporal sulcus (anterior and lateral to area V4)—the region that, when lesioned, causes pure alexia (L. Cohen et al., 2000). This activation was visually elicited only for prelexical forms (before the word form was associated with a meaning; Dehaene et al., 2002), yet was invariant for the location of the stimulus (right or left visual field) and the case of the word stimulus (Dehaene & Cohen, 2001). These findings were in agreement with Nobre's intracranial-recording findings presented earlier.

In the patients with posterior callosal lesions, the VWFA activation and related ERPs were observed only for right-hemifield stimuli, which could directly access the left-hemisphere VWFA. These patients also had

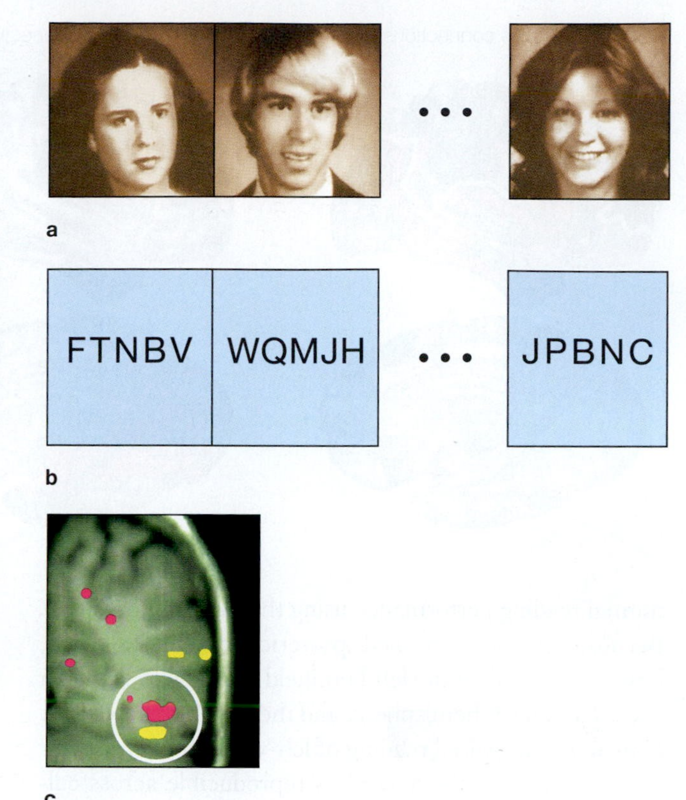

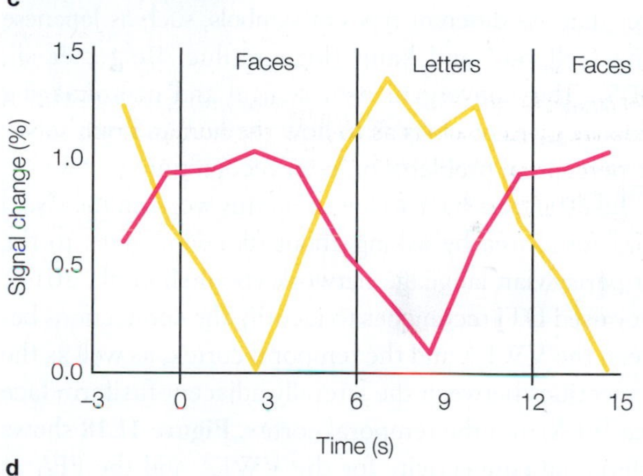

FIGURE 11.17 Regions in occipitotemporal cortex were preferentially activated in response to letter strings.
Stimuli were faces **(a)** or letter strings **(b)**. **(c)** Left-hemisphere coronal slice at the level of the anterior occipital cortex. Faces activated a region of the lateral fusiform gyrus (yellow); letter strings activated a region of the occipitotemporal sulcus (pink). **(d)** The corresponding time course of fMRI activations averaged over all alternation cycles for faces (yellow line) and letter strings (pink line).

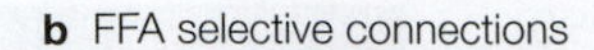

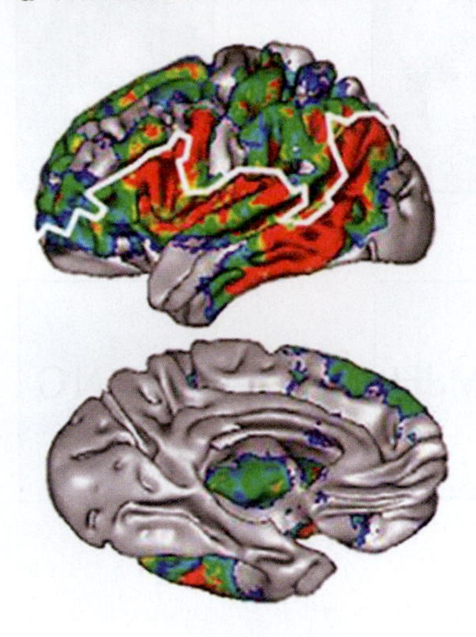

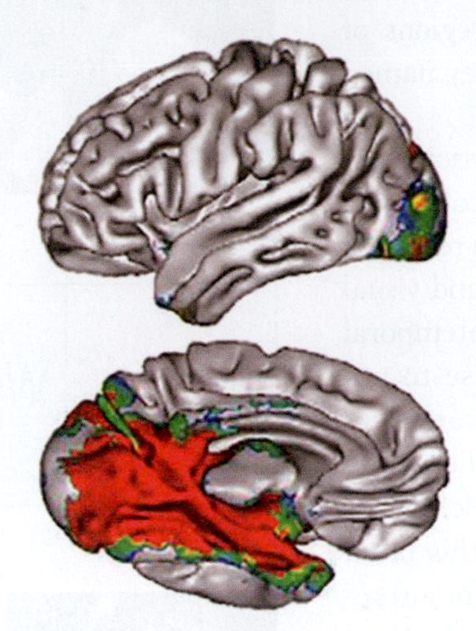

FIGURE 11.18 Connectivity of the VWFA and FFA with language cortex.
The top row shows lateral views of the left hemisphere; the bottom row shows medial views. DTI methods were used to identify the projections of white matter tracts from the visual word form area (VWFA) and fusiform face area (FFA) to other brain areas. **(a)** The VWFA is more strongly connected with areas within the left perisylvian language system. **(b)** The FFA is more connected to medial temporal and occipital areas. Regions shown in red indicate the most selective projections of each of the VWFA and FFA to other cortical areas; regions shown in green and blue are less selective projections. The white line in the top image of part (a) demarcates the regions of the brain that are not strongly connected to the VWFA (above the line) versus those that are (below the line).

normal reading performance using their right visual fields. Because of the sectioned posterior corpus callosum, however, stimuli in the left hemifield could no longer gain access to the left hemisphere, and the patients showed left hemialexia, impaired reading of left-visual-field words.

Activation of the VWFA is reproducible across cultures that use different types of symbols, such as Japanese kana (syllabic) and kanji (logographic; Bolger et al., 2005). This convergent neurological and neuroimaging evidence gives us clues as to how the human brain solves the perceptual problems of letter recognition.

Investigators have followed up this work on the visual word form area by asking about its connections to the left perisylvian language network (Bouhali et al., 2014). They used DTI techniques to identify the connections between the VWFA and the temporal cortex, as well as the connections between the laterally adjacent fusiform face area (FFA) and the temporal cortex. **Figure 11.18** shows differential connectivity for the VWFA and the FFA as statistical maps. The VWFA is better connected with perisylvian language-related areas, including Broca's area and the insula, the superior and lateral temporal lobe, and the posterior inferior parietal lobule; connectivity with the right temporal lobe is minimal. The FFA, however, is better connected to medial occipital and temporal lobe regions, including the hippocampus and parahippocampal gyrus, and regions of the posterior occipital lobe.

TAKE-HOME MESSAGES

- Sound comprehension involves the superior temporal cortex. People with damage to this area may develop pure word deafness.
- Distinguishing speech from nonspeech sounds occurs in the superior temporal sulcus (STS) surrounding early auditory cortex. Distinguishing words from nonwords involves the middle temporal gyrus, inferior temporal gyrus, angular gyrus, and temporal pole and can occur as soon as 50 to 80 ms after word onset.
- Written-word processing takes place in a region in the occipitotemporal cortex of the left hemisphere. Damage to this area can cause pure alexia, a condition in which patients cannot read words, even though other aspects of language are normal.
- Written information from the left visual field first arrives via visual inputs to the contralateral right occipital cortex and is sent to the left-hemisphere visual word form area via the corpus callosum.
- The visual word form area is heavily interconnected with regions of the left perisylvian language system, including inferior frontal, temporal, and inferior parietal cortical regions.

11.4 Language Comprehension: Later Steps

We come now to the point where auditory and visual word comprehension share processing components. Once a phonological or visual representation is identified as a word, then for it to gain any meaning, semantic and syntactic information must be retrieved. Usually, words are not processed in isolation but in the context of other words (sentences, stories, etc.). To understand words in their context, we have to integrate syntactic and semantic properties of the recognized word into a representation of the whole utterance.

The Role of Context in Word Recognition

At what point during language comprehension do linguistic and nonlinguistic contexts (e.g., information seen in pictures) influence word processing? Is it possible to retrieve word meanings before words are heard or seen when the word meanings are highly predictable in the context? More specifically, does context influence word processing before or after lexical access and lexical selection are complete?

Consider the following sentence, which ends with a word that has more than one meaning: "The tall man planted a tree on the bank." *Bank* can mean both "financial institution" and "side of a river." Semantic integration of the meaning of the final word *bank* into the context of the sentence enables us to interpret *bank* as the "side of a river" and not as a "financial institution." The relevant question is, When does the sentence's context influence activation of the multiple meanings of the word *bank*? Do both the contextually appropriate meaning of *bank* (in this case "side of a river") and the contextually inappropriate meaning (in this case "financial institution") become briefly activated, regardless of the context of the sentence? Or does the sentence context immediately constrain activation to the contextually appropriate meaning of the word *bank*?

From this example, we can already see that two types of representations play a role in word processing in the context of other words: lower-level representations, those constructed from sensory input (in our example, the word *bank* itself); and higher-level representations, those constructed from the context preceding the word to be processed (in our example, the sentence preceding the word *bank*). Contextual representations are crucial for determining the proper sense or grammatical form of a word. Without sensory analysis, however, no message representation can take place. The information has to interact at some point, and that point of interaction differs in competing models.

In general, three classes of models attempt to explain word comprehension:

1. *Modular models* (also called autonomous models) claim that normal language comprehension is executed within separate and independent modules. Thus, higher-level representations cannot influence lower-level ones, and therefore the flow is strictly data driven, or bottom-up.
2. *Interactive models* maintain that all types of information can participate in word recognition. In these models, context can have its influence even before the sensory information is available, by changing the activational status of the word-form representations in the mental lexicon. McClelland and colleagues (1989) proposed this type of interactivity model, as noted earlier.
3. *Hybrid models*, which fall between the modular and interactive extremes, are based on the notion that lexical access is autonomous and not influenced by higher-level information, but that lexical selection can be influenced by sensory and higher-level contextual information. In these models, information is provided about word forms that are possible given the preceding context, thereby reducing the number of activated candidates.

An elegant study by Pienie Zwitserlood (1989), involving a lexical decision task, addressed the question of modularity versus interactivity in word processing. She asked participants to listen to short texts such as "With dampened spirits the men stood around the grave. They mourned the loss of their *captain*." At different points during the auditory presentation of the word *captain* (e.g., when only /k/ or only /ka/ or only /kap/, etc., could be heard), a visual target stimulus was presented. This target stimulus could be related to the actual word *captain*, or to an auditory competitor—for example, *capital*. In this example, target words could be words like *ship* (related to *captain*) or *money* (unrelated to *captain*, but related to *capital*). In other cases, a pseudoword would be presented. The task was to decide whether the target stimulus was a word (lexical decision task).

The results of this study showed that participants were faster to decide that *ship* was a word in the context of the story about the men mourning their captain, and slower to decide that *money* was a word, even when only partial sensory information of the stimulus word *captain* was available (i.e., before the whole word was spoken). Apparently, the lexical selection process was influenced by the contextual information that was available from the text that the participants had heard before the whole word *captain* was spoken.

This finding is consistent with the idea that lexical selection can be influenced by sentence context. We do not know for certain which type of model best fits word comprehension, but growing evidence from studies like that of Zwitserlood and others suggests that, at least, lexical selection is influenced by higher-level contextual information. William Marslen-Wilson and colleagues (Zhuang et al., 2011) have performed fMRI studies of word recognition and shown that the processes of lexical access and lexical selection involve a network that includes the middle temporal gyrus (MTG), superior temporal gyrus (STG), and ventral inferior and bilateral dorsal inferior frontal gyri (IFG). They showed that the MTG and STG are important for the translation of speech sounds to word meanings. They also showed that the frontal cortex regions were important in the selection process and that the dorsal IFG became more involved when selection required choosing the actual word from among many lexical candidates (lexical competition).

Integration of Words Into Sentences

Normal language comprehension requires more than just recognizing individual words. To understand the message conveyed by a speaker or a writer, we have to integrate the syntactic and semantic properties of the recognized word into a representation of the whole sentence, utterance, or signed message. Let's consider again the sentence "The tall man planted a tree on the bank." Why do we read *bank* to mean "side of a river" instead of "financial institution"? We do so because the rest of the sentence has created a context that is compatible with one meaning and not the other. This integration process has to be executed quickly, in real time—as soon as we are confronted with the linguistic input. If we come upon a word like *bank* in a sentence, usually we are not aware that this word has an alternative meaning, because the appropriate meaning of this word has been rapidly integrated into the sentence context.

Higher-order semantic processing is important to determine the right sense or meaning of words in the context of a sentence, as with ambiguous words, such as *bank*, that have the same form but more than one meaning. Semantic information in words alone, however, is not enough to understand the message, as made clear in the sentence "The little old lady bites the gigantic dog." Syntactic analysis of this sentence reveals its structure: the actor, the theme or action, and the subject.

The syntax of the sentence demands that we imagine an implausible situation in which an old lady is biting and not being bitten. Syntactic analysis goes on even in the absence of real meaning. In various studies, normal participants can more quickly detect a target word in a sentence when it makes no sense but is grammatically correct than when the grammar is locally disrupted. An example from the famous linguist Noam Chomsky illustrates this: The sentence "Colorless green ideas sleep furiously" is easier to process than "Furiously sleep ideas green colorless." The reason is that the first sentence, even though meaningless, still has an intact syntactic structure, whereas the second sentence lacks both meaning and structure.

How do we process the structure of sentences? As we have learned, when we hear or read sentences, we activate word forms that, in turn, activate the grammatical and semantic information in the mental lexicon. Unlike the representation of words and their syntactic properties that are stored in a mental lexicon, however, representations of whole sentences are not stored in the brain. It is just not feasible for the brain to store the incredible number of different sentences that can be written and produced. Instead, the brain has to assign a syntactic structure to words in sentences, in a process called **syntactic parsing**. Syntactic parsing is, therefore, a building process that does not, and cannot, rely on the retrieval of representations of sentences. To investigate the neural bases of semantic and syntactic analyses in sentence processing, researchers have used cognitive neuroscience tools, such as electrophysiological methods. We review these briefly in the next sections.

Semantic Processing and the N400 Wave

"After pulling the fragrant loaf from the oven, he cut a slice and spread the warm bread with socks." What? You may not realize it, but your brain just had a large N400 response. Marta Kutas and Steven Hillyard at UC San Diego (1980) first described the **N400 response**, an ERP component related to linguistic processes. The name *N400* indicates that it is a negative-polarity voltage peak in brain waves that usually reaches maximum amplitude about 400 ms after the onset of a word stimulus that has evoked it. This brain wave is especially sensitive to semantic aspects of linguistic input. Kutas and Hillyard discovered the wave when they were comparing the processing of the last word of sentences in three conditions:

1. Normal sentences that ended with a word congruent with the preceding context, such as "It was his first day at work."
2. Sentences that ended with a word anomalous to the preceding context, such as "He spread the warm bread with socks."
3. Sentences that ended with a word semantically congruent with the preceding context but physically deviant, such as "She put on her high-heeled SHOES."

The sentences were presented on a computer screen, one word at a time. Participants were asked to read the sentences attentively, knowing that questions about the sentences would be asked at the end of the experiment. Their EEG responses were averaged for the sentences in each condition, and the ERPs were extracted by averaging data for the last word of the sentences separately for each sentence type.

The amplitude of N400 was greater when anomalous words ended the sentence than when the participants read congruent words (**Figure 11.19**). This amplitude difference is called the *N400 effect.* In contrast, words that were semantically congruent with the sentence but were merely physically deviant (e.g., being set in all capital letters) elicited a positive potential rather than an N400. Subsequent experiments showed that nonsemantic deviations like musical or grammatical violations also failed to elicit the N400. Thus, the N400 effect is specific to semantic analysis.

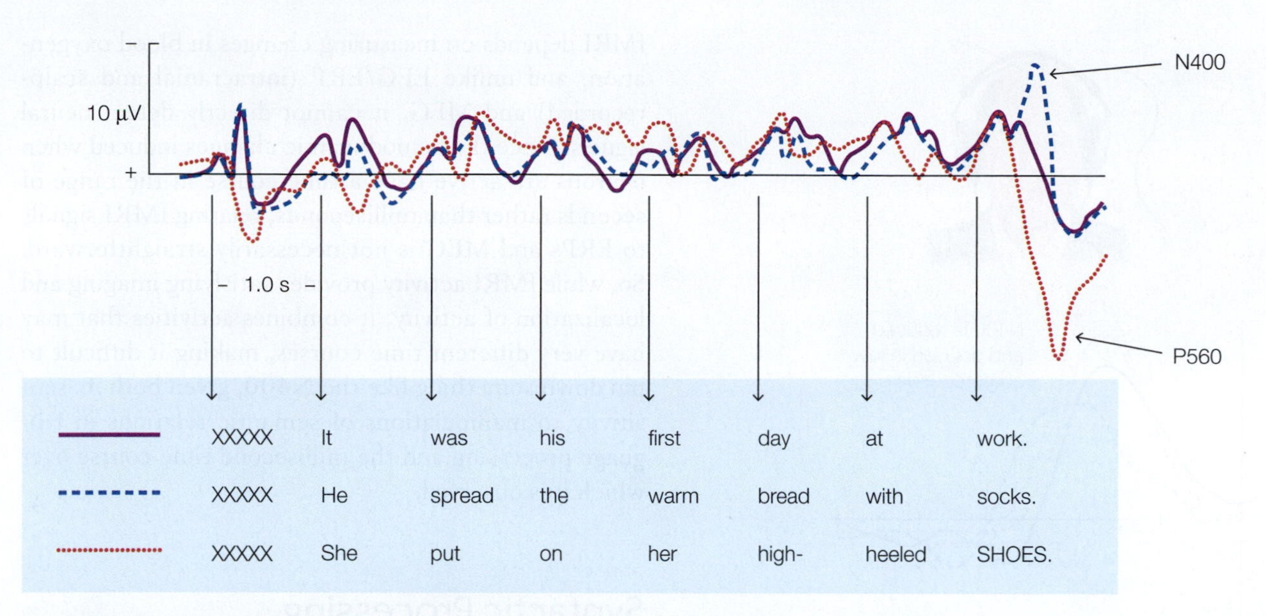

FIGURE 11.19 ERPs reflecting semantic aspects of language.
ERP waveforms differentiate between congruent words at the end of sentences (*work* in the first sentence) and anomalous last words that do not fit the semantic specifications of the preceding context (*socks* in the second sentence). The anomalous words elicit the N400 response. Words that fit into the context but are printed with all capital letters (*SHOES* in the third sentence) elicit a positive wave (P560) and not the N400, indicating that the N400 is not generated simply by surprises at the end of the sentence.

The N400 response is also sensitive to comprehension of language that goes beyond single sentences. In a series of studies, Jos van Berkum and colleagues (van Berkum et al., 1999; Snijders et al., 2008) found an N400 response to words that were inconsistent with the meaning of an entire story. In these studies, participants listened to or read short stories. In the last sentence of these stories, words could be included that were inconsistent with the meaning of the story. For example, in a story about a man who had become a vegetarian, the last sentence could be "He went to a restaurant and ate a steak that was prepared well." Although the word *steak* is fine when this sentence is read by itself, it is inconsistent within the context of the story. The researchers found that participants who read this sentence in this story exhibited an N400 effect.

The N400 response shows a broad scalp distribution in ERP recordings. However, as we learned in Chapter 3, the ERP method is not an imaging tool, but rather an approach that provides exquisite temporal resolution about brain processes. To understand the candidate neural generators of the N400, researchers have turned to functional brain imaging and MEG recording approaches in healthy volunteers, and electrical recording and stimulation methods in patients.

Tamara Swaab, Colin Brown, and Peter Hagoort (1997) recorded the N400 response to semantically anomalous spoken words in sentences from patients with left-hemisphere strokes resulting in severe aphasia (low comprehenders) or mild aphasia (high comprehenders), and they compared the findings to control patients with right-hemisphere strokes and no aphasia, and to healthy age-matched participants. They found that non-aphasic brain-damaged patients (controls with right-hemisphere damage) and aphasic patients with mild comprehension deficits (high comprehenders) had an N400 effect comparable to that of neurologically unimpaired participants (**Figure 11.20**).

In aphasic patients with moderate to severe comprehension deficits (low comprehenders), the N400 effect was reduced and delayed, showing a close relationship between left-hemisphere brain damage resulting in aphasia and the amplitude of the N400 ERP. Their lesions involved primarily the temporal lobe, consistent with their comprehension deficits. This study demonstrates that ERPs can also provide measures of processing in patients whose comprehension is too poor to understand the task instructions.

Intracranial recordings of N400-like ERPs in patients have also pointed to the temporal lobe as a likely site of neural generation of this response. For example, Anna Nobre and colleagues (1994) recorded ERPs from cortical surface electrodes located on the temporal lobes of epilepsy patients. They observed large negative-polarity responses from the ventral-anterior temporal lobe to visually presented, semantically anomalous words

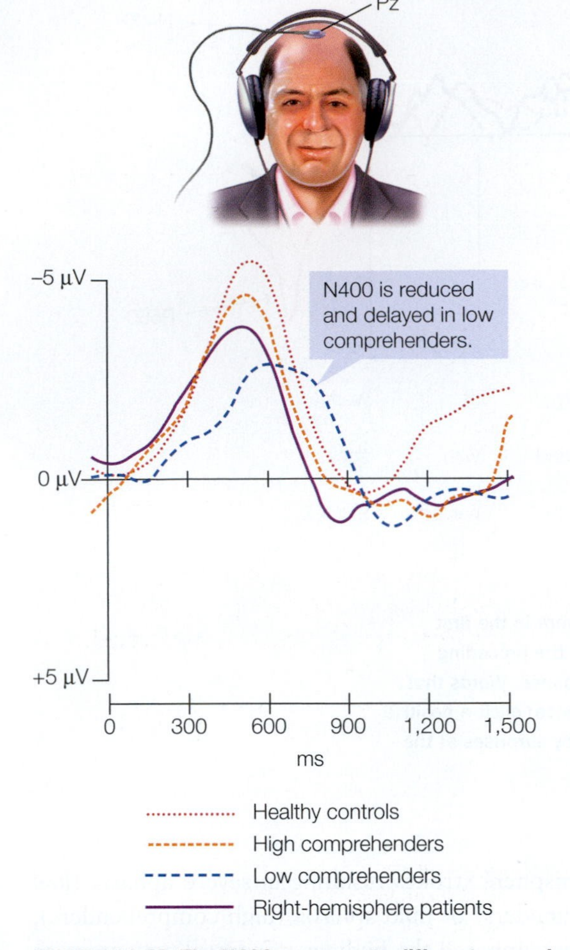

FIGURE 11.20 The N400 response to different anomalous words at the end of a sentence.
The recording is from a single electrode, located at a site along the parietal scalp's midline in elderly healthy control participants, aphasic patients with high comprehension scores, aphasic patients with low comprehension scores, and patients with right-hemisphere lesions (control patients). The waveform for the low comprehenders is clearly delayed and somewhat reduced compared to that for the other groups. The waveforms for the normal control participants, the high comprehenders, and the patients with right-hemisphere lesions are comparable in size and do not differ in latency. This pattern implies a delay in time course of language processing in the patients with low comprehension.

in sentences. These N400-like ERPs had time courses similar to that of the scalp-recorded N400 and were generated by the same type of task.

Recordings of neuromagnetic signals using MEG in healthy participants have supported the evidence from patients that the N400 is likely generated in the left temporal lobe. Work using MEG (Helenius et al., 1998; Simos et al., 1997) has localized sources for N400-like magnetic responses in the left temporal lobe and surrounding areas.

Finally, fMRI studies have also pointed to the left temporal cortex as the source of N400-like activity (e.g., Kuperberg, Holcomb, et al., 2003). However, fMRI depends on measuring changes in blood oxygenation, and unlike EEG/ERP (intracranial and scalp-recorded) and MEG, it cannot directly detect neural signals. Since the hemodynamic changes induced when neurons are active have a time course in the range of seconds rather than milliseconds, relating fMRI signals to ERPs and MEG is not necessarily straightforward. So, while fMRI activity provides satisfying imaging and localization of activity, it combines activities that may have very different time courses, making it difficult to pin down something like the N400, given both its sensitivity to manipulations of semantic relations in language processing and the millisecond time course over which it is observed.

Syntactic Processing and the P600 Wave

The **P600 response**, also known as the *syntactic positive shift (SPS)*, was first reported by Lee Osterhout at the University of Washington and Phil Holcomb at Tufts (1992), and by Peter Hagoort, Colin Brown, and their colleagues in the Netherlands (1993). Osterhout and Holcomb observed it at about 600 ms after the onset of words that were incongruous with the expected syntactic structure. It is evoked by the type of phrase that headline writers love: DRUNK GETS NINE MONTHS IN VIOLIN CASE or ENRAGED COW INJURES FARMER WITH AX. Known as garden path phrases or sentences, they are temporarily ambiguous because they contain a word group that appears to be compatible with more than one structural analysis: We are "led down the garden path," so to speak.

Hagoort, Brown, and colleagues asked participants to silently read sentences that were presented one word at a time on a video monitor. Brain responses to normal sentences were compared with responses to sentences containing a grammatical violation. As **Figure 11.21** shows, there was a large positive shift to the syntactic violation in the sentence, and the onset of this effect occurred approximately 600 ms after the violating word (*throw* in the example). The P600 shows up in response to a number of other syntactic violations as well, and it occurs both when participants have to read sentences and when they have to listen to them. As with the N400, the P600 response has now been reported for several different languages.

Gina Kuperberg and colleagues (Kuperberg, 2007; Kuperberg, Sitnikova, et al. 2003) demonstrated that the P600 response is also evoked by a semantic violation in the absence of any syntactic violation—for instance, a sentence containing a semantic violation between a

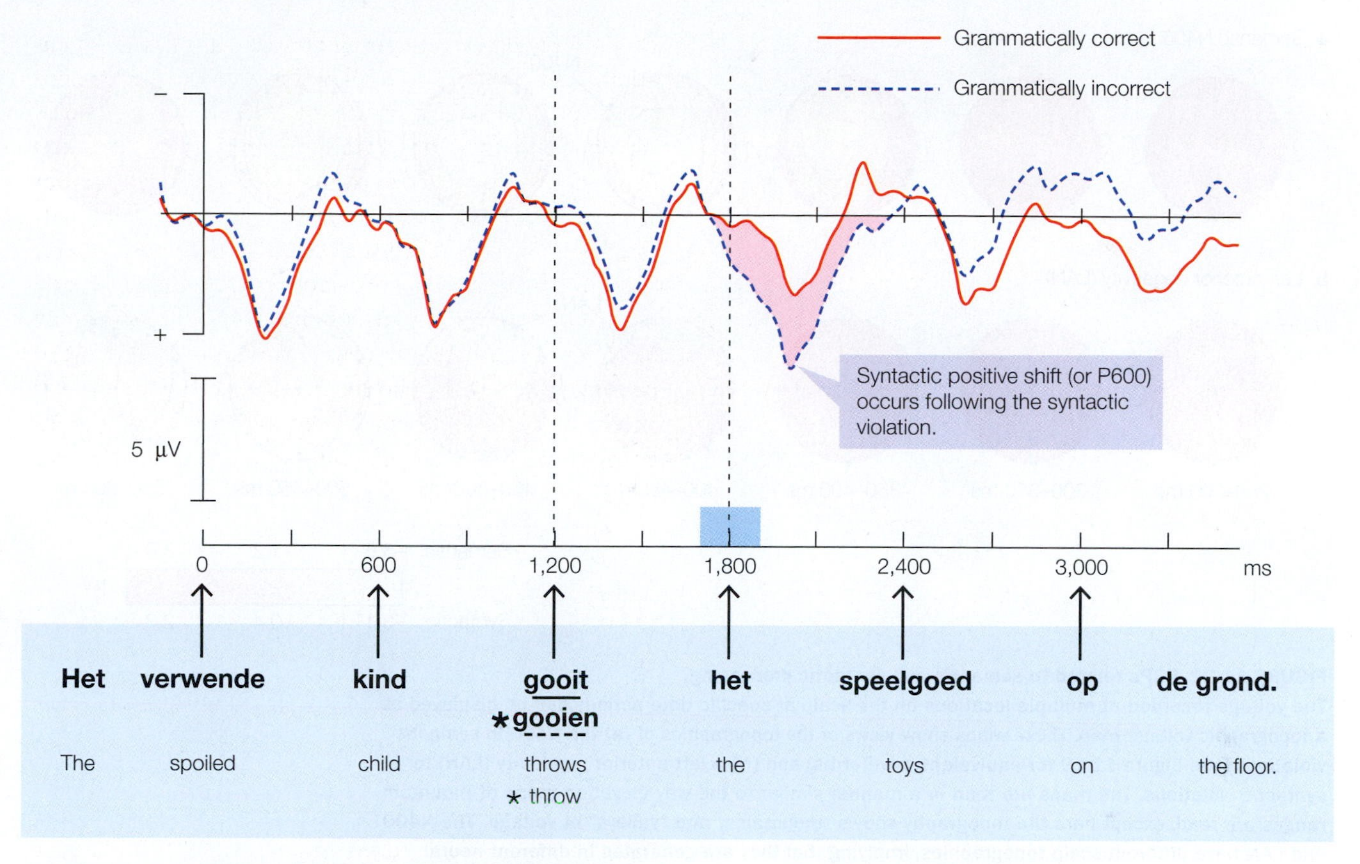

FIGURE 11.21 ERPs reflecting grammatical aspects of language.
ERPs from Pz, a midline parietal scalp site, in response to each word of a sentence that is syntactically anomalous (dashed waveform) versus one that is syntactically correct (solid waveform). In the anomalous sentence, a positive shift (shaded) emerges in the ERP waveform at about 600 ms after the syntactic violation. It is called the syntactic positive shift (SPS), or P600.

verb and its subject but having correct syntax, such as "The eggs would eat toast with jam at breakfast." This sentence is grammatically correct and unambiguous, but it contains a so-called thematic violation (eggs cannot eat). Eggs and eating often occur in the same scenario, however, and are semantically related to each other. The P600 response in these types of sentences is elicited because the syntactic analysis of a sentence's structure (e.g., subject-verb-object) is challenged by strong semantic relations among the words in a sentence.

Syntactic processing is reflected in other types of brain waves as well. Cognitive neuroscientists Thomas Münte and colleagues (1993) and Angela Friederici and colleagues (1993) described a negative wave over the left frontal areas of the brain. This brain wave has been labeled the left anterior negativity (LAN) and has been observed when words violate the required word category in a sentence (as in "the red eats," where noun instead of verb information is required), or when morphosyntactic features are violated (as in "he mow"). The LAN has about the same latency as the N400 but a different voltage distribution over the scalp, as **Figure 11.22** illustrates.

What do we know about the brain circuitry involved in syntactic processing? Some brain-damaged patients have severe difficulty producing sentences and understanding complex sentences. These deficits are apparent in patients with agrammatic aphasia, who generally produce two- or three-word sentences consisting almost exclusively of content words and hardly any function words (*and*, *then*, *the*, *a*, etc.). They also have difficulty understanding complex syntactic structures. So, when they hear the sentence "The gigantic dog was bitten by the little old lady," they will most likely understand it to mean that the lady was bitten by the dog. This problem in assigning syntactic structures to sentences has traditionally been associated with lesions that include Broca's area in the left hemisphere. But not all agrammatic aphasic patients have lesions in Broca's area. Instead, the evidence suggests that the left inferior frontal cortex (in and around the classical Broca's area) has some involvement in syntactic processing.

Neuroimaging evidence from studies by David Caplan and colleagues at Harvard Medical School (2000) provides some additional clues about syntactic processing in the brain. In these studies, PET scans were made while

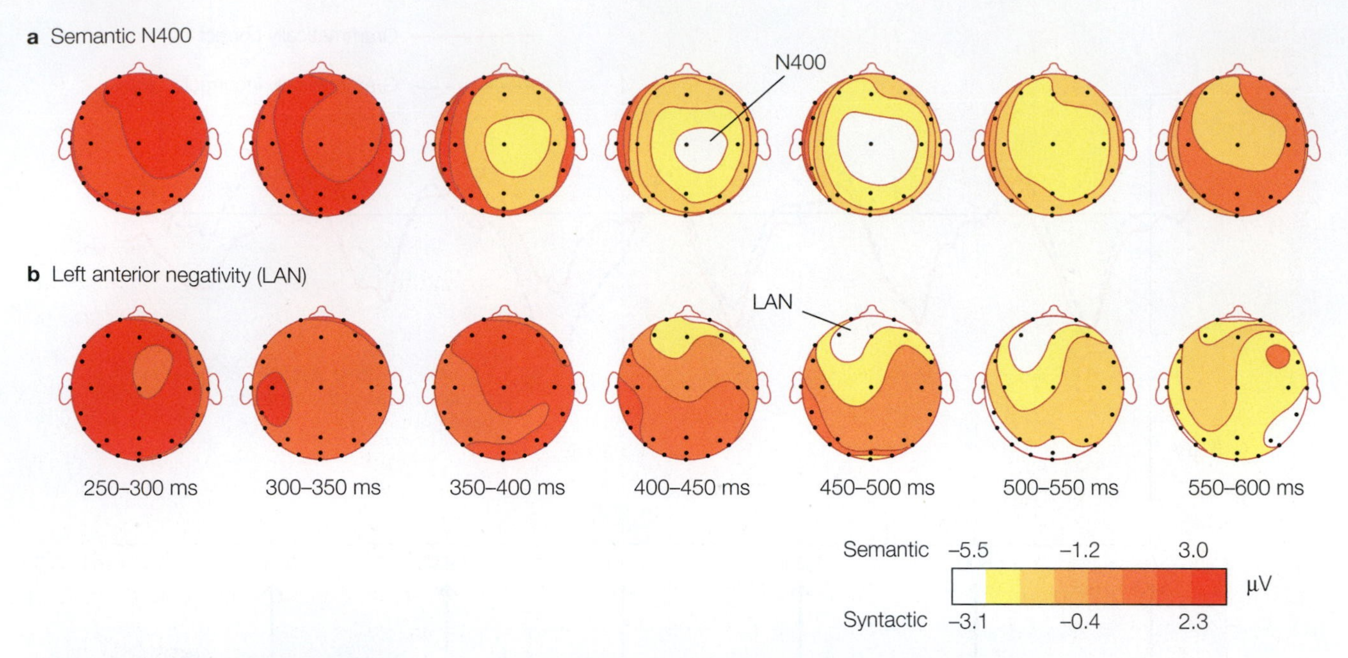

FIGURE 11.22 ERPs related to semantic and syntactic processing.
The voltage recorded at multiple locations on the scalp at specific time periods can be displayed as a topographic voltage map. These maps show views of the topographies of **(a)** the N400 to *semantic* violations (see Figure 11.19 for equivalent waveforms) and **(b)** a left anterior negativity (LAN) to *syntactic* violations. The maps are read in a manner similar to the way elevation maps of mountain ranges are read, except here the topography shows "mountains" and "valleys" of voltage. The N400 and LAN have different scalp topographies, implying that they are generated in different neural structures in the brain.

participants read sentences varying in syntactic complexity. Caplan and colleagues found increased activation in the left inferior frontal cortex for the more complex syntactic structures (**Figure 11.23**).

In other studies, sentence complexity manipulations led to activation of more than just the left inferior frontal cortex. For example, Marcel Just and colleagues (1996) reported activation in Broca's and Wernicke's areas and in the homologous areas in the right hemisphere. PET studies have identified portions of the anterior superior temporal gyrus in the vicinity of Brodmann area 22 (**Figure 11.24a**) as another candidate for syntactic processing. Nina Dronkers at UC Davis and colleagues (1994) also implicated this area in aphasic patients' syntactic processing deficits (**Figure 11.24b**). Thus, a contemporary view is emerging: Syntactic processing takes place in a network of left inferior frontal and superior temporal brain regions that are activated during language processing.

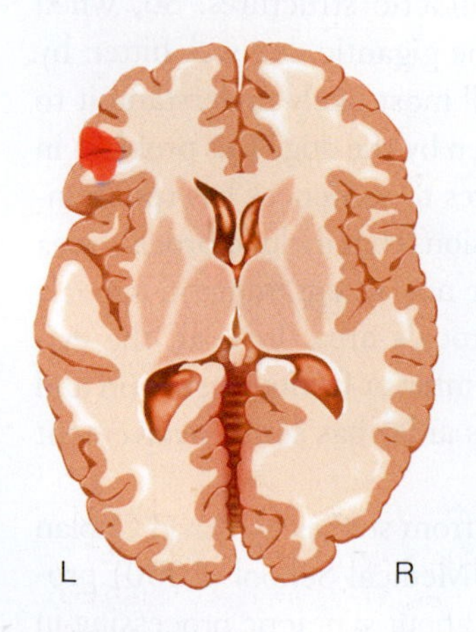

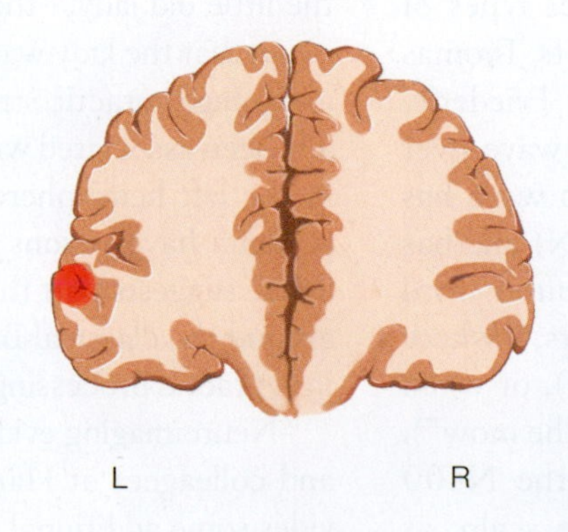

FIGURE 11.23 Frontal cortex activations for complex syntax.
Blood flow increased in left inferior prefrontal cortex (red spots) when participants processed complex syntactic structures relative to simple ones. The change in blood flow was measured using PET imaging.

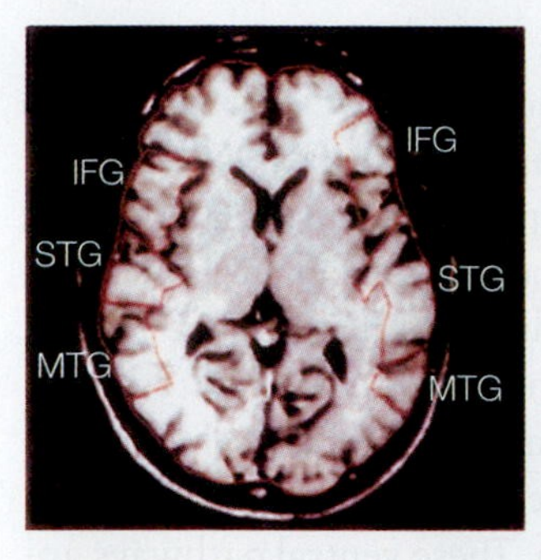

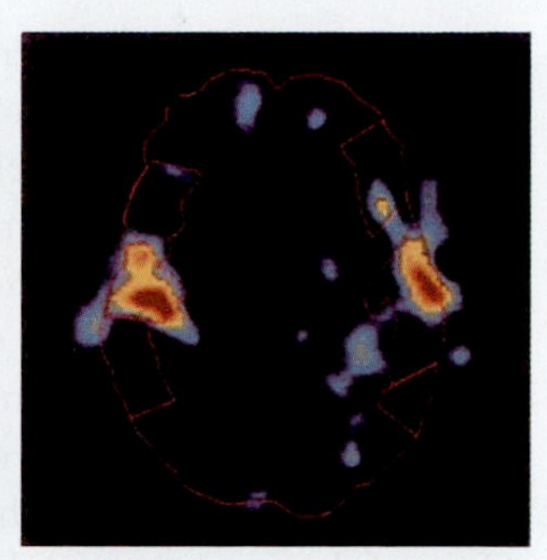
a

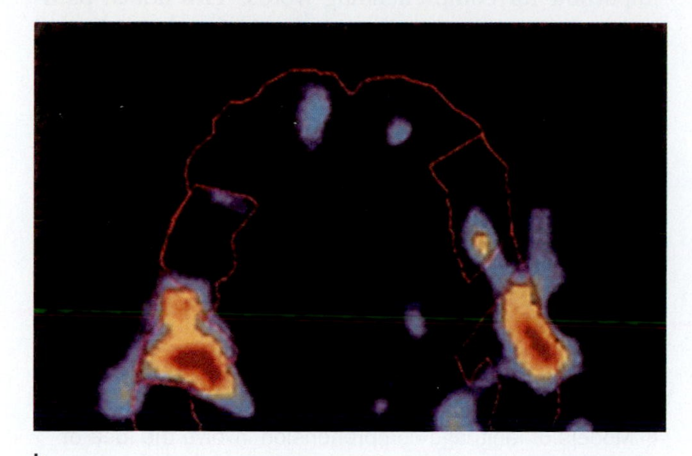
b

FIGURE 11.24 Localization of syntactic processing in the brain. **(a)** PET activations in the anterior portion of the superior temporal gyrus (STG) related to syntactic processing. IFG = inferior frontal gyrus; MTG = middle temporal gyrus. **(b)** Summary of lesions in the anterior superior temporal cortex that lead to deficits in syntactic processing.

TAKE-HOME MESSAGES

- Lexical selection can be influenced by sentence context.
- Lexical access and selection involve a network that includes the middle temporal gyrus (MTG), superior temporal gyrus (STG), and ventral inferior and bilateral dorsal inferior frontal gyri (IFG) of the left hemisphere.
- The left MTG and STG are important for the translation of speech sounds to word meanings.
- Syntactic parsing is the process in which the brain assigns a syntactic structure to words in sentences.
- In the ERP method, the N400 is a negative-polarity brain wave related to semantic processes in language, and the P600/SPS is a large positive component elicited after a syntactic and some semantic violations.
- Syntactic processing takes place in a network of left inferior frontal and superior temporal brain regions that are activated during language processing.

11.5 Neural Models of Language Comprehension

Many new neural models of language have emerged that are different from the classical model initiated by the work of Paul Broca, Carl Wernicke, and others. In the contemporary models, these classical language areas are no longer always considered language specific, nor are their roles in language processing limited to those proposed in the classical model. Moreover, additional areas in the brain have been found to be part of the circuitry that is used for normal language processing.

One neural model of language that combines work in brain and language analysis has been proposed by Peter Hagoort (2005). His model divides language processing into three functional components—memory, unification, and control—and identifies their possible representation in the brain (**Figure 11.25**):

1. *Memory* refers to the linguistic knowledge that, following acquisition, is encoded and consolidated in neocortical memory structures. In this case, memory is language-specific information. Knowledge about the building blocks of language (e.g., phonological, morphological, and syntactic units) is domain specific and coded differently from visual feature or object information.
2. *Unification* refers to the integration of lexically retrieved phonological, semantic, and syntactic information into an overall representation of the whole utterance. In language comprehension, the

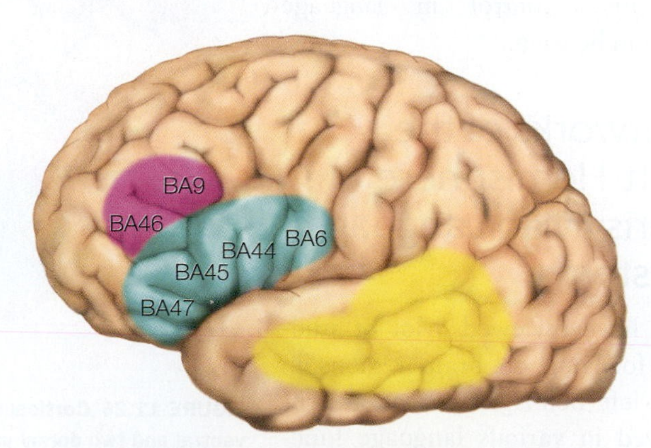

FIGURE 11.25 Memory–unification–control model proposed by Peter Hagoort.
The three components of the model are shown in colors overlaid onto a drawing of the left hemisphere: the memory component (yellow) in the left temporal lobe, the unification component (blue) in the left inferior frontal gyrus, and the control component (purple) in the lateral and medial frontal cortex.

unification processes for phonological, semantic, and syntactic information can operate in parallel (i.e., at the same time), and interaction between these different types of information is possible.

3. *Control* relates language to social interactions and joint action (e.g., in bilingualism and in taking turns during a conversation).

As Figure 11.25 shows, the temporal lobes are especially important for the storage and retrieval of word representations (Hagoort's memory component). Phonological and phonetic properties of words are stored in the central to posterior superior temporal gyrus (STG, which includes Wernicke's area) extending into the superior temporal sulcus (STS), and semantic information is distributed over different parts of the left, middle, and inferior temporal gyri.

The processes that combine and unify (integrate) phonological, lexical-semantic, and syntactic information recruit frontal areas of the brain, including the left inferior frontal gyrus (LIFG), which contains Broca's area. The LIFG now appears to be involved in all three unification processes: semantic unification in Brodmann areas (BA) 47 and 45, syntactic unification in BA45 and BA44, and phonological unification in BA44 and parts of BA6.

The control component of the model becomes important when people are actually involved in communication—for example, when they have to take turns speaking and listening during a conversation. Cognitive control in language comprehension has not been studied very much, but areas that are involved in cognitive control during other tasks, such as the anterior cingulate cortex (ACC) and the dorsolateral prefrontal cortex (dlPFC, BA46/BA9), also play a role during cognitive control in language comprehension.

Networks of the Left-Hemisphere Perisylvian Language System

We have reviewed a lot of studies focusing on brain regions in the left hemisphere that are involved in various language functions. How are these brain regions organized to create a language network in the brain? From recent studies that have considered the functional and structural connectivity in the left hemisphere, several pathways have been identified that connect the representations of words and meanings in the temporal lobes to the unification areas in the frontal lobes.

For spoken-sentence comprehension, Angela Friederici (2012a) has elaborated a model of the language network in which four pathways are distinguished (**Figure 11.26**). Two ventral pathways connect the posterior temporal lobes with the anterior temporal lobe and the frontal operculum. These include the uncinate fasciculus and the fibers of the extreme capsule. These ventral pathways are important for comprehending words. Two dorsal pathways connect the posterior temporal lobes to the frontal lobes. These include the arcuate fasciculus and portions of the superior longitudinal fasciculus. The dorsal pathway that connects to the premotor cortex is involved in speech preparation. The other dorsal pathway connects Broca's area (specifically BA44) with the superior temporal gyrus and superior temporal sulcus. This pathway is important for aspects of syntactic processing.

TAKE-HOME MESSAGES

- Models of language comprehension involve the idea of unifying information from linguistic inputs or from retrieved linguistic representations to create new and more complex linguistic structures and meanings.
- White matter tracts in the left hemisphere connect inferior frontal cortex, inferior parietal cortex, and temporal cortex to create specific circuits for linguistic operations.

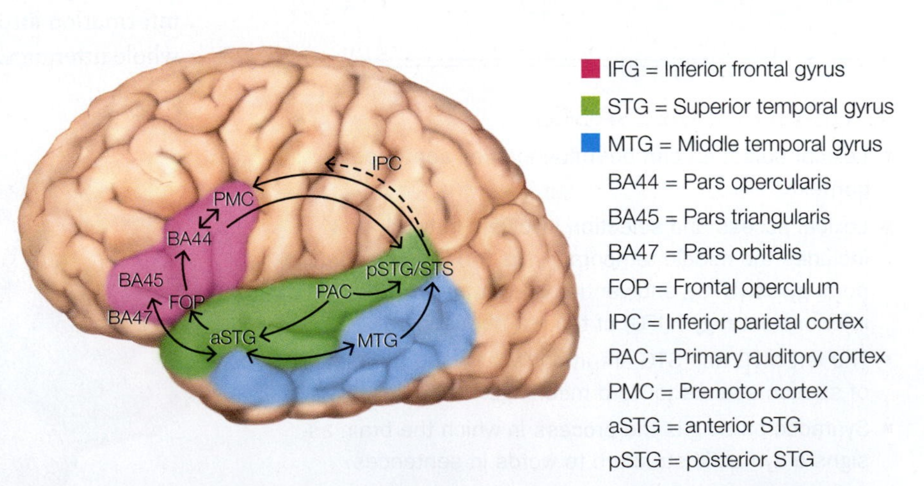

FIGURE 11.26 Cortical language circuit proposed by Angela Friederici, consisting of two ventral and two dorsal pathways.
The black lines indicate direct pathways and the direction of information flow between language-related regions. The broken line suggests an indirect connection between the pSTG/STS and the MTG via the inferior parietal cortex (IPC). The ventral pathways are important for comprehending words. The dorsal pathway that connects to the premotor cortex (PMC) is involved in speech preparation. The other dorsal pathway connects Broca's area (specifically BA44) with the superior temporal gyrus (STG) and superior temporal sulcus (STS) and is involved in syntactic processing.

11.6 Neural Models of Speech Production

So far, we have focused mainly on language comprehension; we now turn our attention to language production. A seemingly trivial but nonetheless important difference between comprehension and production is our starting point. Whereas language comprehension starts with spoken or written input that has to be transformed into a concept, language production starts with a concept for which we have to find the appropriate words.

Speech production has traditionally been studied at two different levels of analysis. Motor control scientists, who are interested in kinematic forces, movement trajectories, and feedback control of orofacial muscles, tend to focus on lower-level articulatory control processes, whereas psycholinguists work at a more abstract level of phonemes, morphemes, and phrases. Not until recently have the two approaches begun to be integrated to form a neuroanatomically grounded model of speech production with hierarchical state feedback controls (Hickok, 2012).

Motor Control and Language Production

In Chapter 8 we learned that motor control involves creating internal forward models, which enable the motor circuit to make predictions about the position and trajectory of a movement and its sensory consequences, and sensory feedback, which measures the actual sensory consequences of an action. Internal forward models provide online control of movement, as the effects of a movement command can be assessed and possibly adjusted on the fly before sensory feedback is given. Meanwhile, sensory feedback has three functions. It enables the circuit to learn the relationship between a motor command and the sensory result; if persistent mismatches occur between the predicted and measured states, it enables updating of the internal model; and it enables the detection of and correction for sudden perturbations.

Feedback control has been documented in the production of speech. Researchers have altered sensory feedback and found that people adjust their speech to correct for sensory feedback "errors" (Houde & Jordan, 1998). To identify the neural circuit underlying auditory feedback control of speech movements, Jason Tourville and his colleagues (2008) performed an experiment that combined fMRI with computational modeling. They measured the neural responses while participants spoke single-syllable words under two conditions: normal auditory feedback and auditory feedback where the frequency of their speech was unexpectedly shifted. The participants responded by shifting their vocal output in a direction opposite to the shift. Acoustic measurements showed compensation to the shift within approximately 135 ms of onset.

During shifted feedback, increased activity was seen in bilateral superior temporal cortex, indicative of neurons coding mismatches between expected and actual auditory signals. Increased activity was also seen in the right prefrontal and motor cortex. Computational modeling was used to assess changes in connectivity between regions during normal feedback versus shifted feedback. The results revealed that during shifted speech, bilateral auditory cortex had an increased influence on right frontal areas. This influence indicated that the auditory feedback control of speech is mediated by projections from auditory error cells in posterior superior temporal cortex that travel to motor correction cells in right frontal cortex.

We learned in Chapter 6 that evidence from vision research suggests that the feedback control for visuomotor pathways is hierarchically organized. The same notion for the organization of feedback control of speech production has been proposed. Since this hierarchical organization overlaps with some aspects of the hierarchical linguistic models of speech production, we will look at these next.

Psycholinguistic Models of Speech Production

An influential cognitive model for language production was proposed by Willem Levelt (1989) of the Max Planck Institute for Psycholinguistics in the Netherlands (**Figure 11.27**). The first step in speech production is to prepare the message. Levelt maintains that there are two crucial aspects to message preparation: macroplanning, in which the speaker determines *what* she wants to express, and microplanning, in which she plans *how* to express it.

The intention of the communication (the *what*) is represented by goals and subgoals, expressed in an order that best serves the communicative plan. Microplanning *how* the information is expressed involves adopting a perspective. If we describe a scene in which a house and a park are situated side by side, we must decide whether to say, "The park is next to the house" or "The house is next to the park." The microplan determines word choice and the grammatical roles that the words play (e.g., subject and object).

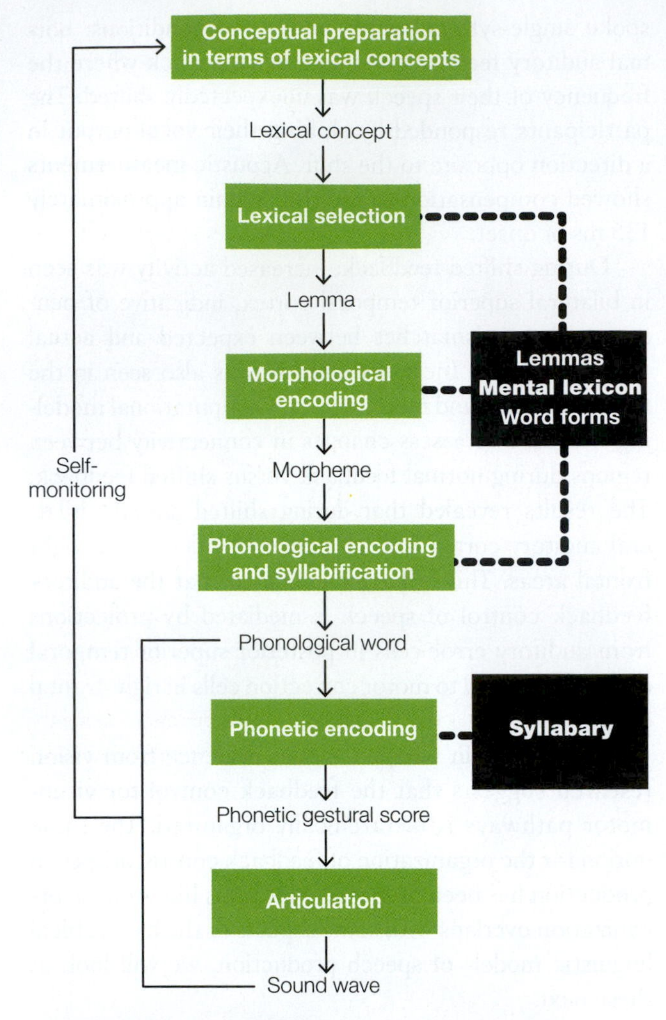

FIGURE 11.27 Outline of Willem Levelt's theory of speech production.
The processing components in language production are displayed schematically. Word production proceeds through stages of conceptual preparation, lexical selection, morphological and phonological encoding, phonetic encoding, and articulation. Speakers monitor their own speech by making use of their comprehension system.

The output of planning is a conceptual message that constitutes the input for the hypothetical processing component, the *formulator*, which puts the message in a grammatically and phonologically correct form. During grammatical encoding, a message's syntactic representation is computed, including information such as "is subject of," "is object of," the grammatically correct word order, and so on. The lowest-level syntactic elements, known as lemmas, specify a word's syntactic properties (e.g., whether the word is a noun or a verb, gender information, and other grammatical features), its semantic features, and the conceptual conditions where it is appropriate to use a certain word. These types of information in the mental lexicon are organized in a network that links lemmas by meaning.

Levelt's model predicts the following result when someone is presented with a picture of a flock of goats and is asked to name the subject of the picture. First the concept that represents a goat is activated, but concepts related to the meaning of *goat* are also activated—for example, *sheep, cheese, farm.* Activated concepts, in turn, activate representations in the mental lexicon, starting with "nodes" at the lemma level to access syntactic information such as word class (in our example, *goat* is a noun, not a verb). At this point, lexical selection occurs when the syntactic properties of the word appropriate to the presented picture must be retrieved. The selected information (in our example, *goat*) activates the word form.

Next the word form undergoes morphological encoding when the pluralizing morpheme "s" is added: *goats*. The modified word form contains both phonological information and *metrical information*, which is information about the number of syllables in the word and the stress pattern (in our example, *goats* consists of one syllable that is stressed). The process of phonological encoding ensures that the phonological information is mapped onto the metrical information.

In contrast to the modular view in Levelt's model, interactive models such as the one proposed by Gary Dell at the University of Illinois (1986) suggest that phonological activation begins shortly after the semantic and syntactic information of words has been activated. Unlike modular models, interactive models permit feedback from the phonological activation to the semantic and syntactic properties of the word, thereby enhancing the activation of certain syntactic and semantic information.

Neural Substrates of Language Production

Ned Sahin and his colleagues (2009) had the rare opportunity to shed some light on this question of how different forms of linguistic information are combined during speech production. They recorded local field potentials from multiple electrodes implanted in and around Broca's area during presurgical screening of three epilepsy patients. To investigate word production in the brain, the patients were engaged in a task involving three conditions that distinguished lexical, grammatical, and phonological linguistic processes.

Most of the electrodes in Broca's area yielded strong responses correlated with distinct linguistic processing stages. The first wave recorded by the cortical electrodes occurred at about 200 ms and appeared to reflect lexical identification. The second wave occurred at about 320 ms and was modulated by inflectional demands. It was not, however, modulated by phonological programming. This was seen in the third wave, which appeared at about

450 ms and reflected phonological encoding. In naming tasks, speech typically occurs at 600 ms.

Sahin and his coworkers could also see that motor neuron commands occur 50 to 100 ms before speech, putting them just after the phonological wave. These apparent processing steps were separated not only temporally, but also spatially by a few millimeters (below the resolution of standard fMRI or MEG), and all were located in Broca's area. These findings provide support for serial processing initially during speech production. Inflectional processing did not occur before the word was identified, and phonological processing did not occur until inflected phonemes were selected. The results are also consistent with the idea that Broca's area has distinct circuits that process lexical, grammatical, and phonological information.

Imaging studies of the brain during picture naming and word generation found activation in the inferior temporal regions of the left hemisphere and in the left frontal operculum (Broca's area). The activation in the frontal operculum might be specific to phonological encoding in speech production. The articulation of words likely involves the posterior parts of Broca's area (BA44), but studies have also shown bilateral activation of motor cortex, the supplementary motor area (SMA), and the insula. PET and fMRI studies of the motor aspects of speech have shown that they involve the SMA, the opercular parts of the precentral gyrus, the posterior parts of the inferior frontal gyrus (Broca's area), the insula, the mouth region of the primary sensorimotor cortex, the basal ganglia, the thalamus, and the cerebellum (reviewed in Ackermann & Riecker, 2010). It is clear that a widespread network of brain regions, predominantly in the left hemisphere in most people, is involved in producing speech.

One model that begins to integrate current knowledge of both motor control and psycholinguistics is the *hierarchical state feedback control (HSFC)* model proposed by Gregory Hickok from UC Irvine (2012; **Figure 11.28**). As in psycholinguistic models, the input to the HSFC model begins with activation of a conceptual representation that in turn excites a corresponding word representation.

At this point, parallel processing begins in the sensory and motor systems associated with two levels of hierarchical control. The higher level codes speech information at the syllable level (i.e., vocal-tract opening and closing cycles). It contains a sensorimotor loop with sensory targets in auditory cortex and motor programs coded in BA44 (in Broca's area), BA6, and area Spt, a region involved with sensorimotor integration in the left planum temporale (see Chapter 4) located in the posterior Sylvian

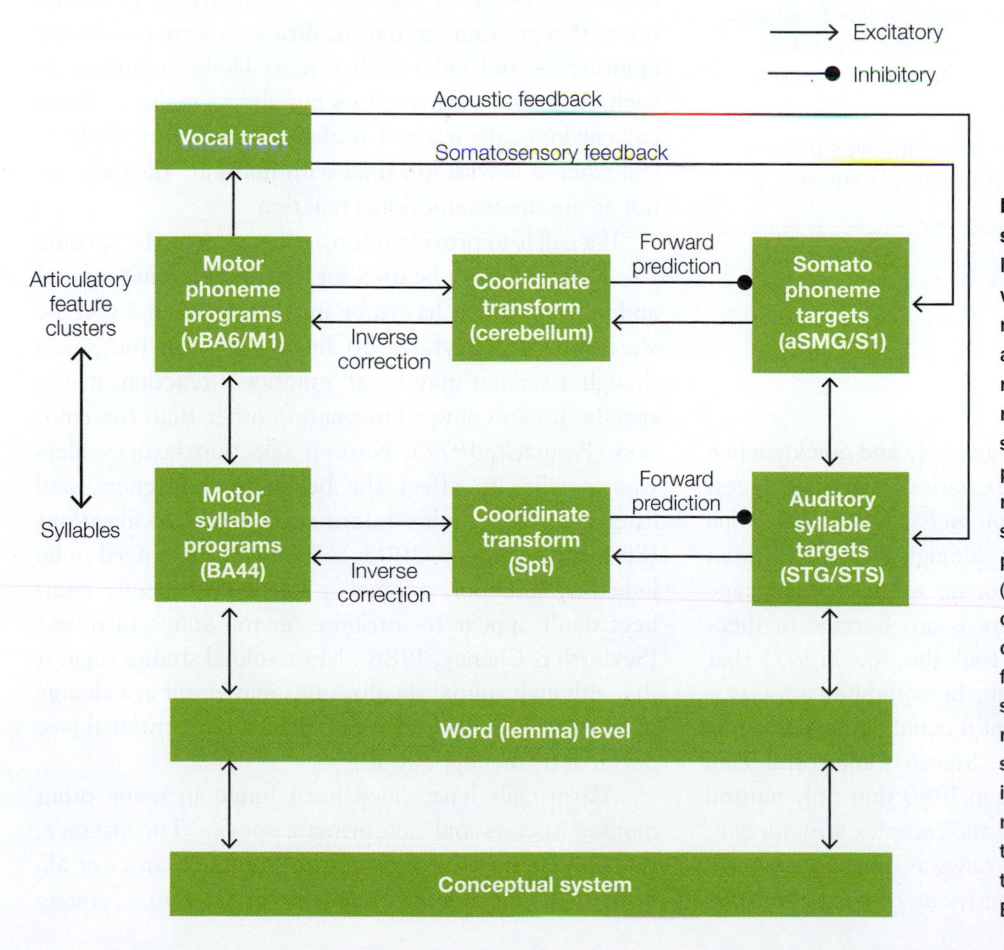

FIGURE 11.28 The hierarchical state feedback control model. Input to the HSFC model begins with the activation of a conceptual representation that in turn excites a corresponding word (lemma) representation, just as in linguistic models. Unlike the situation in some psycholinguistic models, the phonological level is split into a motor and a sensory phonological system. The word level projects in parallel to sensory (right) and motor (left) sides of two hierarchical levels of feedback control, each with its own internal and external sensory feedback loops. aSMG = anterior supramarginal gyrus; M1 = primary motor cortex; S1 = primary somatosensory cortex; Spt = sensorimotor integration region of the left planum temporale; STG = superior temporal gyrus; STS = superior temporal sulcus; vBA6 = ventral Brodmann area 6.

fissure. The lower level codes speech information at the level of articulatory features that roughly correspond to phonemes and involve a sensorimotor loop that includes sensory targets coded primarily in somatosensory cortex, motor programs coded in primary motor cortex (M1), and a cerebellar circuit mediating the two. Though acknowledging that this model is an oversimplification, Hickok suggests that attempting to integrate motor control approaches and psycholinguistics will produce testable hypotheses and further our understanding of speech production.

TAKE-HOME MESSAGES

- Speech production involves the use of orofacial muscles that are controlled by processes using internal forward models and sensory feedback.
- Models of language production must account for the processes of selecting the information to be contained in the message; retrieving words from the lexicon; planning sentences and encoding grammar using semantic and syntactic properties of the word; using morphological and phonological properties for syllabification and prosody; and preparing articulatory gestures for each syllable.
- Each stage in Levelt's model for language production occurs serially, and its output representation is used for input to the next stage. The model avoids feedback, loops, parallel processing, and cascades. The early stages of this model fit well with the findings of ERPs recorded intracranially.
- Hickok's model of speech production involves parallel processing and two levels of hierarchical control.

11.7 Evolution of Language

Young children acquire language easily and quickly when exposed to it. This behavior led Charles Darwin to suggest in his book *The Descent of Man, and Selection in Relation to Sex* that humans have a biological predisposition toward language. The evolutionary origins of language remain unknown, though there is no shortage of theories. Indeed, Noam Chomsky took the view in 1975 that language was so different from the communication systems used by other animals that it could not be explained in terms of natural selection. Steven Pinker and Paul Bloom suggested in an article in 1990 that only natural selection could have produced the complex structures of language. There are divergent views as to when language emerged, whether the question trying to be explained is an underlying cognitive mechanism specific to language or a cooperative social behavior, and what crucial evolutionary problems had to be solved before language could emerge (Sterelny, 2012).

Shared Intentionality

Communication is the transfer of information by speech, signals, writing, or behavior. The function of human language is to influence the behavior of others by changing what they know, think, believe, or desire (Grice, 1957), and we tend to think communication is intentional. When we are looking for the origins of language, however, we cannot assume that communication sprang up in this form. Animal communication is more generally defined as any behavior by one animal that affects the current or future behavior of another animal, intentional or otherwise.

A well-known series of studies in animal communication was conducted by Robert Seyfarth and Dorothy Cheney on vervet monkeys in Kenya (Seyfarth et al., 1980). These monkeys have different alarm calls for snakes, leopards, and predatory birds. Monkeys that hear an alarm call for a snake will stand up and look down. But with a leopard call, they scamper into the trees; and with a bird call, they run from the exposed ends of the branches and huddle by the trunk. Formerly, it was thought that animal vocalizations were exclusively emotional—and indeed, they most likely originated as such. A vervet, however, does not always make an alarm call, seldom calls when it is alone, and is more likely to call when it is with kin than with non-kin. The calls are not an automatic emotional reaction.

If a call is to provide information, it has to be specific (the same call can't be used for several different reasons) and informative (it has to be made only when a specific situation arises; Seyfarth & Cheney, 2003b). Thus, even though a scream may be an emotional reaction, if it is specific it can convey information other than the emotion (Premack, 1972). Natural selection favors callers who vocalize to affect the behavior of listeners, and listeners who acquire information from vocalizations (Seyfarth & Cheney, 2003a). The two do not need to be linked by intention originally, and indeed, vervet monkeys don't appear to attribute mental states to others (Seyfarth & Cheney, 1986). Most animal studies suggest that although animal vocalizations may result in a change of another's behavior, this outcome is unintentional (see Seyfarth & Cheney, 2003b).

Alarm calls have since been found in many other monkey species and non-primate species. For instance, they have been observed with meerkats (Manser et al., 2001) and chickadees (Templeton et al., 2005), among others. The Diana monkeys of West Africa comprehend the alarm calls of another species that resides in the area, the Campbell's monkey (Zuberbühler, 2001). They also understand that if the alarm call is preceded by a "boom" call, the threat is not as urgent.

Campbell's monkeys themselves utilize a rudimentary syntax, sometimes referred to as protosyntax (Ouattara et al., 2009). Adult males have six loud calls that they combine in different, highly context-specific ways. But, as was concluded in other studies, whether these combined calls are used for intentional communication is not known. The communication skills of monkeys are impressive, and more complex than previously thought, but it remains clear that such communication is quite different from human language.

Gesture and Communication

Vocalization is not the only place to look for clues about the evolution of human language. New Zealand psychologist Michael Corballis suggests that human language began with gestures. He has proposed that generative language evolved, perhaps from *Homo habilis* on, as a system of manual gestures, but switched to a predominantly vocal system with *H. sapiens sapiens* (Corballis 1991, 2009). A logical question to ask is whether nonhuman primates use gestures to communicate.

Michael Tomasello, a researcher at the Max Planck Institute for Evolutionary Anthropology in Germany, points out that among primates, especially the great apes, gestures are more important than vocalizations for communication, and that the *function* of communication differs, depending on whether it is vocal or gestural (Tomasello, 2007). In general, vocal calls in the great apes tend to be involuntary signals, associated with a specific emotional state, produced in response to specific stimuli, and broadcast to the surrounding group. They are inflexible.

By contrast, gestures are flexible; they are used in non-urgent contexts to initiate such things as playing and grooming with a specific individual, and some are learned socially by gorillas (Pika et al., 2003), chimps (Liebal et al., 2004), and bonobos (Pika et al., 2005). Tomasello emphasizes that unlike vocalizations, gestures require knowing the attentional state of the communicating partner. It's no good making a gesture if no one is paying attention to you. He concludes that primate gestures are more like human language than like either primate vocalizations or human gestural communication (Tomasello and Call, 2018). He suggests, therefore, that the roots of human language may be found in the gestural communication of the great apes.

Monkeys and the great apes have little cortical control over vocalization but excellent cortical control over the hands and fingers (Ploog, 2002). From these findings and what we know about primate anatomy, it is not surprising that attempts to teach nonhuman primates to speak have failed. Teaching them to communicate manually has been more successful. For instance, Washoe, a chimpanzee, learned a form of manual sign language, and knew approximately 350 signs (Gardner & Gardner, 1969).

Kanzi, a bonobo, has learned to point to abstract visual symbols, or lexigrams, on a keyboard and to use that information to communicate (Savage-Rumbaugh & Lewin, 1994; **Figure 11.29**). Work with Kanzi that

FIGURE 11.29 Sue Savage-Rumbaugh, Kanzi the bonobo, and the lexigrams he has learned to use for communication.
Kanzi is able to match 378 lexigrams with the objects, places, and spoken words they represent. He is able to combine the lexigrams into a protosyntax, and he freely uses the keyboard to ask for objects he wants. He can generalize a specific reference; for instance, he uses the lexigram for bread to mean all breads, including tortillas. Thus, Kanzi is able to understand signs in a symbolic way.

was done over the years by Sue Savage-Rumbaugh and her colleagues has also shown that he possesses a protosyntax. For example, relying on word order, he understands the difference between "Make the doggie bite the snake" and "Make the snake bite the doggie," and he demonstrates his understanding by using stuffed animals.

Another line of evidence comes from Giacomo Rizzolatti and Michael Arbib (1998), who suggested that language arose from a combination of gestures and facial movements, speculating that mirror neurons are a piece of the language puzzle. Mirror neurons were first discovered in area F5 in the monkey, a region in the ventral, rostral premotor cortex (see Chapter 8). The dorsal portion of F5 is involved with hand movements, and the ventral portion, with movement of the mouth and larynx. Area F5 is adjacent to the homologue of human Brodmann area 44, a portion of Broca's area (Petrides et al., 2005). In the monkey, this region is involved in high-level control of orofacial musculature, including muscles involved in communication. Thus, mirror neurons may help us understand the evolution of language.

Initially, this close association of hand and mouth may have been related to eating, but it later could have expanded to gestures and vocal language. There is some evidence for this proposal. In macaque monkeys, neurons in the lateral part of F5 have been found to activate with conditioned vocalizations—that is, voluntary coo calls that the monkeys were trained to make (Coudé et al., 2011).

We know that the left hemisphere controls the motor movements of the right side of the body, in both humans and the great apes. Chimpanzees exhibit preferential use of the right hand in gestural communication both with other chimps and with humans (Meguerditchian et al., 2010), but not when making noncommunicative gestures. This behavior is also seen in captive baboons (Meguerditchian & Vauclair, 2006; Meguerditchian et al., 2010), suggesting that the emergence of language and its typical left lateralization may have arisen from a left-lateralized gestural communication system in the common ancestor of baboons, chimps, and humans.

At present, the proposal that gesturing may have given rise during the course of evolution to human language ability remains interesting, but not universally accepted, and much of the evidence offered in support of this idea has been challenged. Anthropologist and gesture scientist Adam Kendon has argued that oral and gestural communication skills may have evolved in primates in parallel (Kendon, 2017). Moreover, the most dramatic differences between humans and nonhuman primates in the left perisylvian region are those involving the rise of left-hemisphere specializations in humans, the representation of linguistic information in the temporal lobe, and the increased connectivity of the temporal lobe with the networks of the left perisylvian region of the brain.

Left-Hemisphere Dominance and Specialization

Human language is clearly a left-hemisphere-dominant ability. But what is it about the left hemisphere that is different in humans, and how did this specialization arise over the course of evolution? We have some clues. The first question we might ask is whether communication is left-hemisphere dominant in nonhuman primates.

A PET imaging study in chimpanzees found that when they made a communicative gesture or an atypical novel sound while begging for food, the left inferior frontal gyrus, a region considered to be homologous to Broca's area, was activated (Taglialatela et al., 2008). What is an atypical sound? First described in 1991 (Marshall et al., 1991), atypical sounds are produced only by some captive chimps. Three have been identified: a "raspberry," an "extended grunt," and a "kiss." The sounds have been observed to be socially learned and selectively produced to gain the attention of an inattentive human (Hopkins, Taglialatela, et al., 2007).

The left-hemisphere dominance for communication may also be present in the chimpanzee. In humans, the left lateralization of speech is actually visible: The right side of the mouth opens first and wider. In contrast, the left side gears up first with emotional expressions. In two large colonies of captive chimps, the same thing was found: left-hemisphere dominance for the production of learned attention-getting sounds, and right-hemisphere dominance for the production of species-typical vocalizations (Losin et al., 2008; Wallez & Vauclair, 2011). These studies all suggest that the left hemisphere's voluntary control of hand gestures (area F5) and vocalizations may have evolved into an integrative system. But the story is more complicated than this.

The advent of functional and structural brain imaging revolutionized the study of the organization not only of the human brain, but also of the brains of animals. These methods have enabled a comparative structural and functional neuroanatomy to be pursued, which has revealed a remarkable story about the evolution of the left-hemisphere perisylvian language system within primates.

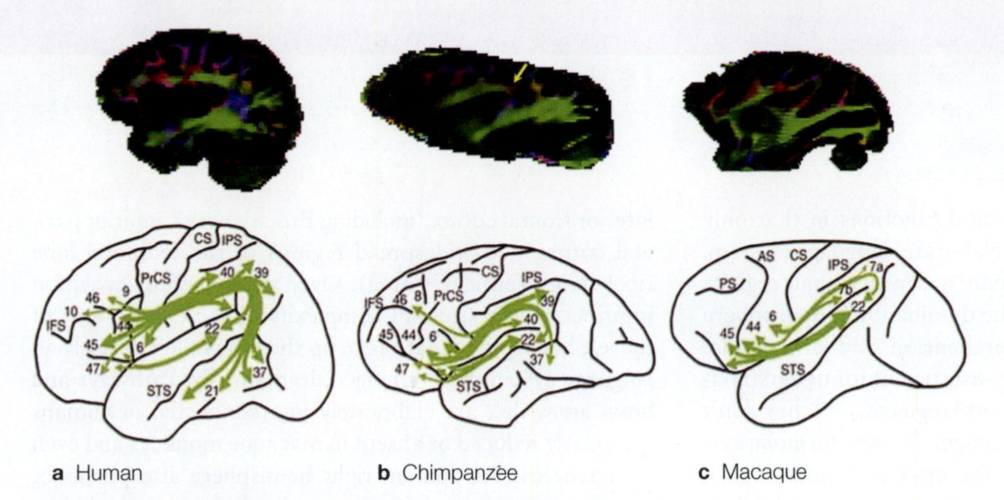

FIGURE 11.30 Neuroanatomy of the human left-hemisphere perisylvian language system compared to chimpanzees and macaques.
DTI images (top) and network models (bottom). (a) Humans have robust interconnectivity of the inferior frontal cortex, inferior parietal cortex, and temporal cortex, especially lateral and inferior temporal cortex by massive projections of the arcuate fasciculus. (b–c) The white matter tracts of the chimpanzee and the macaque monkey show greatly reduced or absent projections into lateral and inferior temporal cortex. CS = central sulcus; IFS = inferior frontal sulcus; IPS = intraparietal sulcus; PrCS = precentral sulcus; STS = superior temporal sulcus.

In humans, the left perisylvian language cortex is defined by its extensive connectivity among key brain regions in the inferior frontal, inferior parietal, and temporal lobes.

As Wernicke had glimpsed in his hypothesis about connections between Wernicke's area and Broca's area, elaborate white matter pathways connect key nodes of the system. Today, though, we know the connectivity to be much richer than Wernicke ever guessed. Was this elaborate system of connections present in our ancestors, perhaps serving another function and later co-opted for human language? Studies of our nonhuman primate relatives tell us a fascinating tale.

James Rilling and his colleagues at Emory University, the Yerkes Primate Center, and Oxford University used modern DTI with MRI in humans, chimpanzees, and macaque monkeys (Rilling et al., 2008). They found a remarkable clue to the evolution of the left perisylvian language system. As we have seen, there are major dorsal and ventral projection pathways in humans that interconnect the temporal lobe with parietal and inferior frontal cortex (**Figure 11.30a**). The large fiber tracts have a rich microstructure. These subprojections interconnect brain areas in a fashion that helps us to understand the complexity of human language and how damage to this system can result in a variety of language disorders (Fridriksson et al., 2018).

In the chimpanzee and macaque monkey (**Figure 11.30b, c**), however, the projections among inferior frontal, parietal, and temporal lobes are greatly reduced, with major differences visible in how the system projects into the lateral and inferior temporal lobe. Indeed, the regions of the temporal lobe that we now know have rich representations of words, meanings, and concepts in humans correspond primarily to high-level extrastriate visual cortical areas in the macaque. These findings fit well with the idea that during human evolution, dramatic changes in connectivity and likely in the cortical areas themselves took place, supporting the rise of human language in all its rich and detailed complexity.

TAKE-HOME MESSAGES

- Nonhuman primates' vocalizations can carry meaning and show evidence of rudimentary syntax. In general, however, animal calls tend to be inflexible, associated with a specific emotional state, and linked to a specific stimulus.
- Some researchers suggest that human speech and language evolved from hand gestures, or a combination of hand gestures and facial movement.
- The greatest evolutionary brain changes we know of involve the size and function of the left temporal cortex and, importantly, how this cortex is interconnected with inferior frontal and parietal cortex.

Summary

Language is unique among mental functions in that only humans possess a true and elaborate language system. We have known for more than a century that regions around the Sylvian fissure of the dominant left hemisphere participate in language comprehension and production. Classical models, however, are insufficient for understanding the computations that support language, and they don't fully explain disorders of language. Newer formulations based on detailed analysis of the effects of neurological lesions, supported by improvements in structural imaging, functional neuroimaging, human electrophysiology, and computational modeling, now provide some surprising modifications of older models.

What has emerged is the left perisylvian language system, which has elaborate white matter connections between inferior frontal cortex (including Broca's area), inferior parietal cortex, and widespread regions of the temporal lobe (including Wernicke's area). Over the course of evolution in primates, the size and complexity of the connections of the left hemisphere that make up the human left perisylvian language system have changed dramatically. Pathways and brain areas that are elaborately interconnected in humans are greatly reduced or absent in macaque monkeys and even chimpanzees. The human right hemisphere also possesses significant linguistic ability, but studies in patients, including split-brain patients, show these abilities to be limited. The human language system is complex, and much remains to be learned about how the biology of the brain enables the rich speech and language comprehension that characterize our daily lives.

Key Terms

agrammatic aphasia (p. 481)
alexia (p. 494)
anomia (p. 478)
aphasia (p. 477)
apraxia (p. 478)
arcuate fasciculus (p. 481)
Broca's aphasia (p. 478)
Broca's area (p. 480)
conduction aphasia (p. 481)
dysarthria (p. 477)
lexical access (p. 483)
lexical integration (p. 483)
lexical selection (p. 483)
mental lexicon (p. 483)
morpheme (p. 483)
N400 response (p. 498)
orthographic form (p. 483)
P600 response (p. 500)
phoneme (p. 483)
phonological form (p. 483)
semantic paraphasia (p. 484)
Sylvian fissure (p. 477)
syntactic parsing (p. 498)
syntax (p. 481)
Wernicke's aphasia (p. 481)
Wernicke's area (p. 481)

Think About It

1. How might the mental lexicon be organized in the brain? Would we expect to find it localized in a particular region in cortex? If so, where, and what evidence supports this view?
2. At what stage of input processing are the comprehension of spoken language and the comprehension of written language the same, and where must they be different? Are there any exceptions to this rule?
3. Describe the route that an auditory speech signal might take in the cortex, from perceptual analysis to comprehension.
4. What evidence exists for the role of the right hemisphere in language processing? If the right hemisphere has a role in language, what might that role be?
5. Can knowledge of the world around you affect the way you process and understand words?
6. Describe the anatomy and circuitry of the left perisylvian language system, and how it has changed over the course of primate evolution.

Suggested Reading

Fridriksson, J., den Ouden, D. B., Hillis, A. E., Hickok, G., Rorden, C., Basilakos, A., et al. (2018). Anatomy of aphasia revisited. *Brain*, *141*(3), 848–862. doi:10.1093/brain/awx363 [Epub ahead of print]

Friederici, A. D. (2012). The cortical language circuit: From auditory perception to sentence comprehension. *Trends in Cognitive Science*, *16*(5), 262–268.

Hagoort, P. (2013). MUC (Memory, Unification, Control) and beyond. *Frontiers in Psychology*, *4*, 416.

Kaan, E., & Swaab, T. (2002). The brain circuitry of syntactic comprehension. *Trends in Cognitive Sciences*, *6*, 350–356.

Lau, E., Phillips, C., & Poeppel, D. (2008). A cortical network for semantics: (De)constructing the N400. *Nature Reviews Neuroscience*, *9*(12), 920–933.

Levelt, W. J. M. (2001). Spoken word production: A theory of lexical access. *Proceedings of the National Academy of Sciences, USA*, *98*, 13464–13471.

Poeppel, D., Emmorey, K., Hickok, G., & Pylkkänen, L. (2012). Towards a new neurobiology of language. *Journal of Neuroscience*, *32*(41), 14125–14131.

Price, C. J. (2012). A review and synthesis of the first 20 years of PET and fMRI studies of heard speech, spoken language and reading. *NeuroImage*, *62*, 816–847.

Rilling, J. K. (2014). Comparative primate neurobiology and the evolution of brain language systems. *Current Opinion in Neurobiology*, *28*, 10–14. doi:10.1016/j.conb.2014.04.002 [Epub, May 14]

If everything seems under control, you're just not going fast enough.

Mario Andretti

CHAPTER

12

Cognitive Control

A SEASONED NEUROLOGIST was caught by surprise when his new patient, W.R., reported his main symptom quite simply: "I have lost my ego." (R. T. Knight & Grabowecky, 1995).

A driven child, W.R. decided at an early age that he wanted to become a lawyer. Focused on this plan, he completed college with an excellent GPA and took the right classes for a prelaw student. He was accepted to his first-choice law school and graduated with a solid, if not stellar, academic record. But then his life derailed: Suddenly, he seemed to have forgotten his plan to work at a top law firm. Four years later, he had yet to look for a job in the legal profession and, in fact, had not taken the bar exam. Instead, he was an instructor at a tennis club.

Accompanying W.R. at the neurologist's office was his brother, who reported that the family had found W.R.'s behavior odd but not atypical of the times, perhaps indicative of an early, antimaterialist midlife crisis. Maybe he would find satisfaction in teaching tennis, his favorite hobby, or perhaps this was just a temporary diversion before he embarked on a career in law after all. But no: W.R. eventually gave up on his job and even lost interest in playing tennis. His nonchalant attitude frustrated his opponents, as he forgot to keep track of the score and whose turn it was to serve. Unable to support himself financially, W.R. hit up his brother with increasingly frequent requests for "temporary" loans.

Clearly a highly intelligent man, W.R. was cognizant that something was amiss. Though he expressed repeatedly that he wished he could pull things together, he simply could not take the necessary steps to find a job or get a place to live. He had little regard for his own future, for his successes, even for his own happiness. His brother noted another radical change in W.R.: He had not been on a date for a number of years and seemed to have lost all interest in romantic pursuits. W.R. sheepishly agreed.

BIG Questions

- What are the computational requirements that enable organisms to plan and execute complex behaviors?
- What are the neural mechanisms that support working memory, and how is task-relevant information selected?
- How does the brain represent the value associated with different sensory events and experiences, and how does it use this information to make decisions when faced with multiple options for taking action?
- How do we monitor ongoing performance to help ensure the success of complex behaviors?

If this had been the whole story, the neurologist might have thought that a psychiatrist was a better option to treat a "lost ego." However, during his last year in law school, W.R. had suffered a seizure. An extensive neurological examination at the time failed to identify the cause of the seizure, so it was diagnosed as an isolated event, perhaps related to the fact that on the night before the seizure, W.R. had been drinking coffee all night while preparing for an exam. After hearing about the events of the previous 4 years, the neurologist decided it was time to reconsider the cause of the seizure.

A CT scan confirmed the neurologist's worst fears. W.R.'s brain had an extremely large astrocytoma that had traversed along the fibers of the corpus callosum, extensively invading the lateral prefrontal cortex in the left hemisphere and a considerable portion of the right frontal lobe. This tumor had very likely caused the initial seizure and over the previous 4 years had slowly grown. The prognosis was now poor, with a life expectancy of about a year.

W.R.'s brother was devastated on hearing the news. W.R., on the other hand, remained relatively passive and detached. Though he understood that the tumor was the culprit behind the dramatic life changes he had experienced, he was not angry or upset. Instead, he appeared unconcerned. He understood the seriousness of his condition, but the news, as with so many of his recent life events, failed to evoke a clear response or any resolve to take some action. W.R.'s self-diagnosis seemed to be right on target: He had lost his ego and, with it, the ability to take command of his own life.

In this chapter our focus turns to cognitive control processes, which are essential for the kind of behavior that is uniquely human, be it going to law school, playing tennis, or recognizing that something is amiss in one's actions or those of a loved one. Cognitive control processes give us the ability to override automatic thoughts and behavior and step out of the realm of habitual responses. They also give us cognitive flexibility, letting us think and act in novel and creative ways.

To facilitate discussion of these functions, we first review the anatomy of the frontal lobe and the behavioral problems that are observed when this region of the brain is damaged. We then focus on goal-oriented behavior and decision making, two complicated processes that rely on cognitive control mechanisms to work properly. And deciding on a goal is only the first step toward attaining it. Planning how to attain it and then sticking with the plan are also complicated affairs involving different cognitive control processes, which we examine in the final sections of this chapter.

12.1 The Anatomy Behind Cognitive Control

Cognitive control, sometimes referred to as *executive function*, refers to the set of psychological processes that enable us to use our perceptions, knowledge, and goals to bias the selection of action and thoughts from a multitude of possibilities. Collectively, the behaviors thus enabled can be described as **goal-oriented behavior**, frequently requiring the coordination of a complex set of actions that may unfold over an extended period of time. The successful completion of goal-oriented behavior faces many challenges, and cognitive control is necessary to meet them.

All of us must develop a plan of action that draws on our personal experiences, yet is tailored to the current environment. Such actions must be flexible and adaptive to accommodate unforeseen changes and events. We must monitor our actions to stay on target and attain our goal, and we may need to inhibit a habitual response in order to do so. Although you might want to stop at the doughnut shop when heading to work in the morning, cognitive control mechanisms can override that sugary urge.

As might be suspected of any complex process, cognitive control requires the integrated function of many different parts of the brain. This chapter highlights the frontal lobes. As we learned in Chapter 8, the most posterior part of the frontal lobe is the *primary motor cortex* (see the "Anatomical Orientation" box on p. 517). Anterior and ventral to the motor cortex are the *secondary motor areas*, made up of the *lateral premotor cortex* and the *supplementary motor area*. The remainder of the frontal lobe is termed the **prefrontal cortex (PFC)**. We will refer to four regions of prefrontal cortex in this chapter: the **lateral prefrontal cortex (LPFC)**, the **frontal pole (FP)**, the **orbitofrontal cortex (OFC)** (sometimes referred to as the ventromedial zone), and the **medial frontal cortex (MFC)**.

In this chapter we concentrate on two prefrontal control systems. The first system, which includes the LPFC, OFC, and FP, supports goal-oriented behavior. This control system works in concert with more posterior regions of the cortex to constitute a working memory system that recruits and selects task-relevant information. This system is involved with planning; simulating consequences; and initiating, inhibiting, and shifting behavior.

ANATOMICAL ORIENTATION

Anatomy of Cognitive Control

Central sulcus
Lateral prefrontal cortex
Frontal pole
Orbitofrontal cortex
Secondary motor areas
Primary motor cortex
Frontal pole
Orbitofrontal cortex
Medial frontal cortex

The prefrontal cortex includes all of the areas in front of the primary motor cortex and secondary motor areas. The four subdivisions of prefrontal cortex are the lateral prefrontal cortex, the frontal pole, the orbitofrontal cortex (which lies above the bony orbits of the eyes), and the medial frontal cortex.

The second control system, which includes the MFC, plays an essential role in guiding and monitoring behavior. It works in tandem with the rest of the prefrontal cortex, monitoring ongoing activity to modulate the degree of cognitive control needed to keep behavior in line with current goals.

The frontal cortex is present in all mammalian species. Evolutionarily speaking, this part of the brain has become much larger in primates relative to other mammals (**Figure 12.1**). Interestingly, when compared to other primate species, the expansion of prefrontal cortex in the human brain is more pronounced in the white matter (the axonal tracts) than in the gray matter (the cell bodies; Schoenemann et al., 2005). This finding suggests that the cognitive capabilities that are uniquely human may be due to how our brains are connected rather than an increase in the number of neurons.

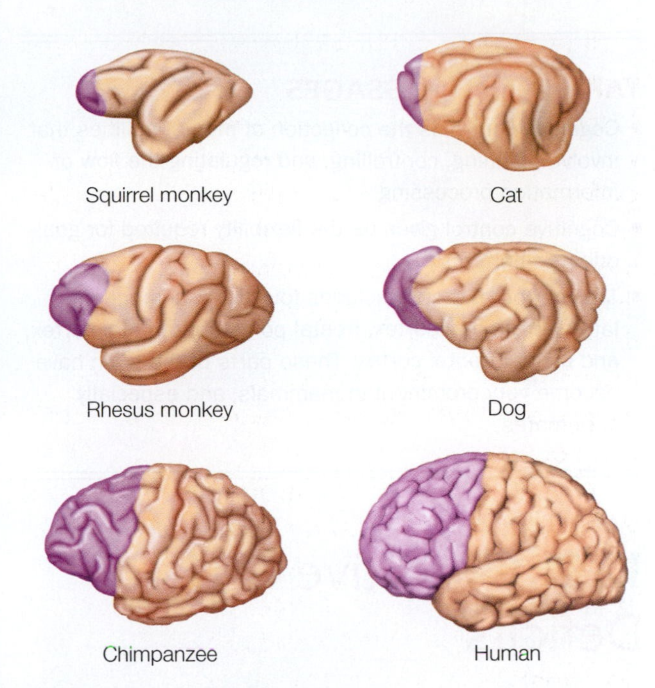

FIGURE 12.1 A comparison of prefrontal cortex in different species. The purple region indicates the PFC in six mammalian species. Although the brains are not drawn to scale, the figure makes clear that the PFC spans a much larger percentage of the overall cortex in the chimpanzee and human.

Because the development of functional capabilities parallels phylogenetic trends, the frontal lobe's expansion is related to the emergence of the complex cognitive capabilities that are especially pronounced in humans. What's more, as investigators frequently note, "Ontogeny recapitulates phylogeny." Compared to the rest of the brain, prefrontal cortex matures late, in terms of the development of neural density patterns and white matter tracts. Correspondingly, cognitive control processes appear relatively late in development, as is evident in the "me-oriented" behavior of infants and teenagers.

The prefrontal cortex coordinates processing across wide regions of the central nervous system (CNS). It contains a massively connected network that links the brain's motor, perceptual, and limbic regions (Goldman-Rakic, 1995; Passingham, 1993). Extensive, reciprocal projections connect the prefrontal cortex to almost all regions of the parietal and temporal cortex, and to prestriate regions of the occipital cortex. The PFC also receives a huge input from the thalamus, relaying information from the basal ganglia, cerebellum, and various brainstem nuclei. Indeed, almost all cortical and subcortical areas influence the prefrontal cortex either through direct projections or indirectly via a few synapses. The prefrontal cortex has many projections to the contralateral hemisphere—projections to homologous prefrontal areas via the corpus callosum, as well as bilateral projections to premotor and subcortical regions.

TAKE-HOME MESSAGES

- Cognitive control is the collection of mental abilities that involve planning, controlling, and regulating the flow of information processing.
- Cognitive control gives us the flexibility required for goal-oriented behavior.
- The prefrontal cortex includes four major components: lateral prefrontal cortex, frontal pole, orbitofrontal cortex, and medial frontal cortex. These parts of the brain have become very prominent in mammals, and especially in primates.

12.2 Cognitive Control Deficits

People with frontal lobe lesions—like W.R., the wayward lawyer—present a paradox. From a superficial look at their everyday behavior, it is frequently difficult to detect a neurological disorder: They do not display obvious deficits in any of their perceptual abilities, they can execute motor actions, and their speech is fluent and coherent. They are unimpaired on conventional neuropsychological tests of intelligence and knowledge. They generally score within the normal range on IQ tests. Their memory for previously learned facts is fine, and they do well on most tests of long-term memory. With more sensitive and specific tests, however, it becomes clear that frontal lesions can disrupt different aspects of normal cognition and memory, producing an array of problems.

Such patients may persist in a response even after being told that it is incorrect; this behavior is known as **perseveration**. They may be apathetic, distractible, or impulsive. They may be unable to make decisions, plan actions, understand the consequences of their actions, organize and segregate the timing of events in memory, remember the source of their memories, and follow rules. They may disregard social conventions (discussed in Chapter 13). Ironically, patients with frontal lobe lesions are aware of their deteriorating social situation, have the intellectual capabilities to generate ideas that may alleviate their problems, and may be able to tell you the pros and cons of each idea. Yet their efforts to prioritize and organize these ideas into a plan and put them into play are haphazard at best. Similarly, although they are not amnesic and can list rules from memory, they may not be able to follow them.

To demonstrate how seemingly subtle deficits in cognition may snowball into severe limitations in real-world situations, Tim Shallice of University College London (Shallice & Burgess, 1991) took three patients with frontal lesions to a shopping center, assigning each a short shopping list. Obtaining all the items on the list presented a real problem for the patients. One patient failed to purchase soap because the store she visited did not carry her favorite brand; another wandered outside the designated shopping center in pursuit of an item that could easily be found within the designated region. All became embroiled in social complications. One succeeded in obtaining a newspaper but was pursued by the merchant for failing to pay!

Studies in animals with lesions to their prefrontal cortex revealed behaviors similar to those exhibited by these patients who were unable to complete a plan and were socially inappropriate. Unilateral lesions of prefrontal cortex tend to produce relatively mild deficits in these animals, but dramatic changes can be observed when PFC lesions are extended bilaterally. Consider the observations of Leonardo Bianchi (1922), an Italian psychiatrist of the early 20th century:

> The monkey which used to jump on to the window-ledge, to call out to his companions, after the operation jumps to the ledge again, but does not call out. The sight of the window determines the reflex of the jump, but the purpose is now lacking, for it is no longer represented in the focal point of consciousness. . . . Another monkey sees the handle of the door and grasps it, but the mental process stops at the sight of the bright colour of the handle. The animal does not attempt to turn it so as to open the door. . . . Evidently there are lacking all those other images that are necessary for the determination of a series of movements coordinated towards one end.

As with W.R., the monkeys demonstrate a loss of goal-oriented behavior. Indeed, the behavior of these monkeys has become *stimulus driven*. The animal sees the ledge and jumps up; another sees the door and grasps the handle, but that is the end of it. They no longer appear to have a purpose for their actions. The sight of the door is no longer a sufficient cue to remind the animal of the food and other animals that can be found beyond it.

A classic demonstration of this tendency for humans with frontal lobe injuries to exhibit stimulus-driven behavior is evident from the clinical observations of François Lhermitte of the Pitié-Salpêtrière Hospital in Paris (Lhermitte, 1983; Lhermitte et al., 1986). Lhermitte invited a patient to meet him in his office. At the entrance to the room, he had placed a hammer, a nail, and a picture. Upon entering the room and seeing these objects, the patient spontaneously used the hammer and nail to hang the picture on the wall. In a more extreme example, Lhermitte put a hypodermic needle on his desk, dropped his trousers, and turned his back to his patient. Whereas most people in this situation would consider filing ethical charges, the patient was unfazed. He simply picked up the needle and gave his doctor a healthy jab in the buttocks!

Lhermitte coined the term **utilization behavior** to characterize this extreme dependency on prototypical responses for guiding behavior. The patients with frontal lobe damage retained knowledge about prototypical uses of objects such as a hammer or needle, saw the stimulus, and responded. They were not able to inhibit their response or flexibly change it to fit the context in which they found themselves. Their cognitive control mechanisms were out of whack.

Deficits in cognitive control are also considered a hallmark of many psychiatric conditions, including depression, schizophrenia, obsessive-compulsive disorder (OCD), and attention deficit hyperactivity disorder (ADHD; De Zeeuw & Durston, 2017), as well as antisocial personality disorder and psychopathy (Zeier et al., 2012). Even in individuals who do not have clinically defined conditions, impairments in cognitive control become manifest when people experience stress, sadness, loneliness, or poor health (reviewed in Diamond & Ling, 2016).

A hallmark of drug or alcohol addiction is the sense of a loss of control. One model of drug addiction suggests that disruption of PFC function underlies the characteristic problems addicts have in inhibiting destructive behaviors and appropriately evaluating the relevance of behavioral cues (Goldstein & Volkow, 2011). Hugh Garavan and colleagues at Trinity College in Ireland conducted a series of studies to ask whether the cognitive control changes that occur in cocaine users would also manifest in the lab (Kaufman et al., 2003). In one task, the participants viewed a stream of stimuli that alternated between two letters and were instructed to quickly press a button with the presentation of each letter. In rare instances, however, the same letter was repeated on successive trials. For these "no-go" trials, participants were instructed to withhold their response.

Chronic cocaine users, none of whom had used cocaine for 18 hours before testing, were more likely to respond on the no-go trials than were matched controls—a result that was interpreted as evidence of a general problem with response inhibition. The cocaine users also showed lower activation in the medial frontal cortex when they produced these erroneous responses. As we will see later in this chapter, this pattern suggests that they had difficulty monitoring their performance. Thus, even when the drug users were not under the influence of cocaine and were not making choices related to their addiction, changes in cognitive control persisted.

TAKE-HOME MESSAGES

- Patients with frontal lobe lesions have difficulty executing a plan and may exhibit stimulus-driven behavior.
- Deficits in cognitive control are found in numerous psychiatric disorders, as well as when mental health is compromised by situational factors such as stress or loneliness.

12.3 Goal-Oriented Behavior

Our actions are not aimless, nor are they entirely automatic—dictated by events and stimuli immediately at hand. We choose to act because we want to accomplish a goal or gratify a personal need.

Researchers distinguish between two fundamental types of actions. **Goal-oriented actions** are based on the assessment of an expected reward or value and the knowledge that there is a causal link between the action and the reward (an action–outcome relationship). Most of our actions are of this type. We turn on the radio when getting in the car so that we can catch the news on the drive home. We put money in the soda machine to purchase a favorite beverage. We resist going to the movies the night before an exam so that we can get in some extra studying, with the hope that this effort will lead to the desired grade.

In contrast to goal-oriented actions stand habitual actions. A **habit** is defined as an action that is no longer under the control of a reward, but is stimulus driven; as such, we can consider it automatic. The habitual commuter might find herself flipping on the car radio without even thinking about the expected outcome. The action is triggered simply by the context. Its habitual nature becomes obvious when our commuter reaches to switch on the radio, even though she knows it is broken. Habit-driven actions occur in the presence of certain stimuli that trigger the retrieval of well-learned associations. These associations can be useful, enabling us to rapidly select a response, such as stopping quickly at a red light (S. A. Bunge, 2004). They can also develop into persistent bad habits, however, such as eating something every time you walk through the kitchen or lighting up a cigarette when anxious. Habitual responses make addictions difficult to break.

The distinction between goal-oriented actions and habits is graded. Though the current context is likely to dictate our choice of action and may even be sufficient to trigger a habit-like response, we are also capable of being flexible. The soda machine might beckon invitingly, but if we are on a health kick, we might just walk past it or choose to purchase a bottle of water. These are situations in which cognitive control comes into play. Of course, if we make the water purchase enough times, a new habit can develop.

Cognitive control provides the interface through which goals influence behavior. Goal-oriented actions require processes that enable us to maintain our goal, focus on the information that is relevant to achieving that goal, ignore or inhibit irrelevant information, monitor our progress toward the goal, and shift flexibly from one subgoal to another in a coordinated way.

Cognitive Control Requires Working Memory

As we learned in Chapter 9, working memory, a type of short-term memory, is the transient representation of task-relevant information—what Patricia Goldman-Rakic (1992, 1996) called the "blackboard of the mind." These representations may be from the distant past, or they may be closely related to something that is currently in the environment or has been experienced recently. The term *working memory* refers to the temporary maintenance of this information, providing an interface that links perception, long-term memory, and action, thus enabling goal-oriented behavior and decision making.

Working memory is critical when behavior is not exclusively stimulus driven. What is immediately in front of us surely influences our behavior, but we are not automatons. We can (usually) hold off eating until all the guests sitting around the table have been served. This capacity demonstrates that we can represent information that is not immediately evident (in this case, social rules), in addition to reacting to stimuli that currently dominate our perceptual pathways (the fragrant food and conversation). We can mind our dinner manners (stored knowledge) by choosing to respond to some stimuli (the conversation) while ignoring other stimuli (the food). This process requires integrating current perceptual information with stored knowledge from long-term memory.

Prefrontal Cortex Is Necessary for Working Memory but Not Associative Memory

The prefrontal cortex appears to be an important interface between current perceptual information and stored knowledge, and thus constitutes a major component of the working memory system. Its importance in working memory was first demonstrated in studies where animals with prefrontal lesions performed a variety of **delayed-response tasks.**

In a test of spatial working memory (**Figure 12.2a**), a monkey is situated within reach of two food wells. At the start of each trial, the monkey observes the experimenter

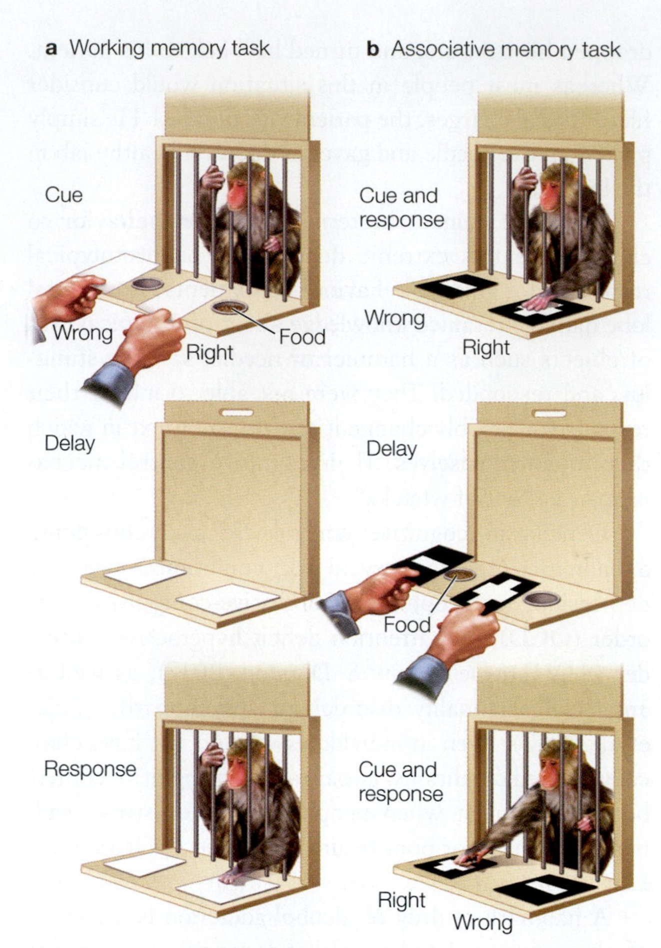

FIGURE 12.2 Working memory versus associative memory. Two delayed-response tasks. **(a)** In the working memory task, the monkey observes one well being baited with food. The location of the food is determined randomly. After a delay period, the animal retrieves the food. **(b)** In the associative memory task, the food reward is always hidden under the same visual cue, and the locations of the two cues are determined randomly. Working memory is required in the first task because, at the time the animal responds, no external cues indicate the location of the food. Long-term memory is required in the second task because the animal must remember which visual cue is associated with the reward.

placing a food morsel in one of the two wells (perception). Then the two wells are covered, and a curtain is lowered to prevent the monkey from reaching toward either well. After a delay period, the curtain is raised and the monkey is allowed to choose one of the two wells to try to recover the food. Although this appears to be a simple task, it demands one critical cognitive capability: The animal must continue to retain the location of the unseen food during the delay period (working memory). Monkeys with prefrontal lesions do poorly on the task.

Do the animals fail this task because of a general deficit in forming associations or because of a deficit in working memory? To answer this question, a second task is used to test associative memory by pairing the food with a distinctive visual cue. The well with the food has a plus sign, and the empty well has a minus sign (**Figure 12.2b**).

In this condition, the researcher may shift the food morsel's location during the delay period, but the associated visual cue—the food cover—will be relocated with the food. Prefrontal lesions do not disrupt performance in this task.

These two tasks clarify the concept of working memory (Goldman-Rakic, 1992). In the working memory task, the animal must remember the currently baited location during the delay period, which it fails to do. In contrast, in the associative learning condition in which it succeeds, the visual cue only needs to reactivate a long-term association of which cue (the plus or minus sign) is associated with the reward. The food's location does not need to be kept in working memory. The reappearance of the two visual cues can trigger the association and guide the animal's performance.

Another, albeit indirect, demonstration of the importance of prefrontal cortex in working memory comes from developmental studies. Adele Diamond of the University of Pennsylvania (1990) pointed out that a common indicator of conceptual intelligence, Piaget's Object Permanence Test, is logically similar to the delayed-response task. In this task, a child observes the experimenter hiding a reward in one of two locations. After a delay of a few seconds, the child is encouraged to find the reward.

Children younger than a year are unable to accomplish this task. At this age, the frontal lobes are still maturing. Diamond maintained that the ability to succeed in tasks such as the Object Permanence Test parallels the development of the frontal lobes. Before this development takes place, the child acts as though the object is "out of sight, out of mind." As the frontal lobes mature, the child can be guided by representations of objects and no longer requires their presence.

It seems likely that many species must have some ability to recognize object permanence. A species would not survive for long if its members did not understand that a predator that had stepped behind a particular bush was still there when no longer visible. Evolutionarily significant differences between species may be found in the capacity of the working memory, how long information can be maintained in working memory, and the ability to maintain attention.

Physiological Correlates of Working Memory

A working memory system requires a mechanism to access stored information and keep that information active. The prefrontal cortex can perform both operations. In delayed-response studies, neurons in the prefrontal cortex of monkeys show sustained activity throughout the delay period (Fuster & Alexander, 1971; **Figure 12.3**). For some cells, activation doesn't commence until after the delay begins and can be maintained for up to a minute. These cells provide a neural correlate for keeping a representation active after the triggering stimulus is no longer visible.

Prefrontal cortex (PFC) cells could simply be providing a generic signal that supports representations in other cortical areas. Alternatively, they could be coding specific stimulus features. To differentiate between these possibilities, Earl Miller and his colleagues (Rao et al., 1997) focused on the lateral prefrontal cortex (LPFC). They trained monkeys on a working memory task that required successive coding of two stimulus attributes: identity and location. **Figure 12.4a** depicts the sequence of events in each trial. A sample stimulus

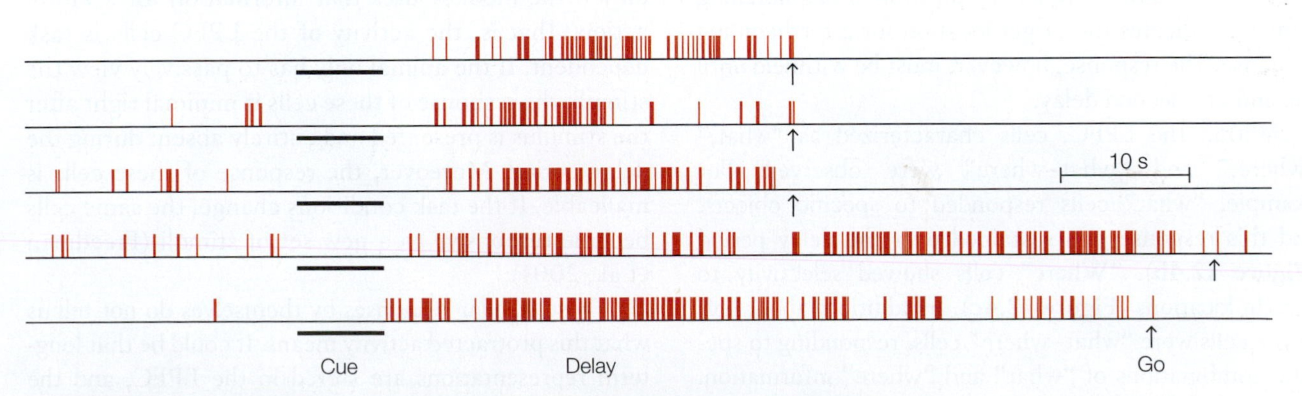

FIGURE 12.3 Prefrontal neurons can show sustained activity during delayed-response tasks.
Each row represents a single trial. During the cue interval, a cue was turned on, indicating the location for a forthcoming response. The monkey was trained to withhold its response until a go signal (arrows) appeared. Each vertical tick represents an action potential. This cell did not respond during the cue interval. Rather, its activity increased when the cue was turned off, and the activity persisted until the response occurred.

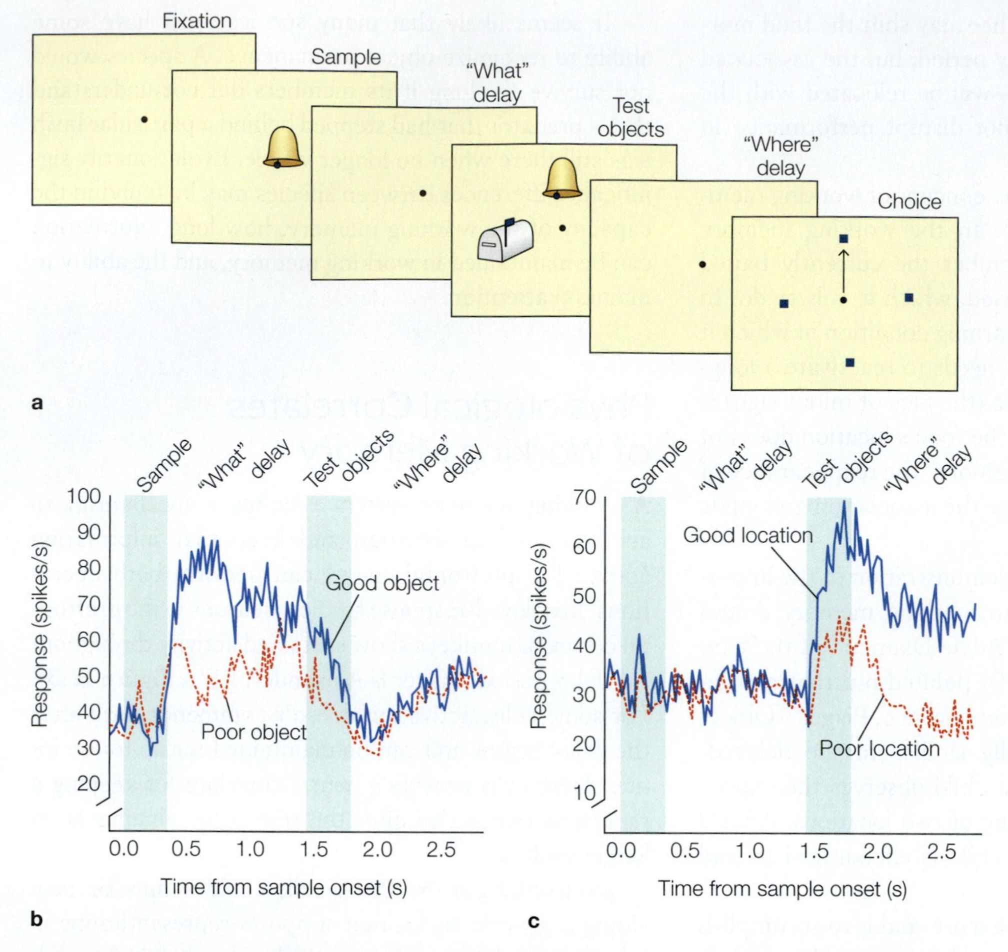

FIGURE 12.4 Coding of "what" and "where" information in single neurons of the LPFC in the macaque. **(a)** Sequence of events in a single trial. See text for details. **(b)** Firing profile of a neuron that shows a preference for one object over another during the "what" delay. The neuronal activity is low once the response location is cued. **(c)** Firing profile of a neuron that shows a preference for one location during the "where" delay. This neuron was not activated during the "what" delay.

is presented, and the animal must remember the identity of this object for a 1-second delay period during which the screen is blank. Then, two objects are shown, one of which matches the sample. The position of the matching stimulus indicates the target location for a forthcoming response. The response, however, must be withheld until the end of a second delay.

Within the LPFC, cells characterized as "what," "where," and "what–where" were observed. For example, "what" cells responded to specific objects, and this response was sustained over the delay period (**Figure 12.4b**). "Where" cells showed selectivity to certain locations (**Figure 12.4c**). In addition, about half of the cells were "what–where" cells, responding to specific combinations of "what" and "where" information. A cell of this type exhibited an increase in firing rate during the first delay period when the target was the preferred stimulus, and the same cell continued to fire during the second delay period if the response was directed to a specific location.

These results indicate that, in terms of stimulus attributes, cells in the LPFC exhibit task-specific selectivity. What's more, these LPFC cells remain active only if the monkey uses that information for a future action. That is, the activity of the LPFC cells is task dependent. If the animal only has to passively view the stimuli, the response of these cells is minimal right after the stimulus is presented and entirely absent during the delay period. Moreover, the response of these cells is malleable. If the task conditions change, the same cells become responsive to a new set of stimuli (Freedman et al., 2001).

These cellular responses by themselves do not tell us what this protracted activity means. It could be that long-term representations are stored in the LPFC, and the activity reflects the need to keep these representations active during the delay. However, patients with frontal lobe lesions do not have deficits in long-term memory. An alternative hypothesis is that LPFC activation reflects a representation of the task goal and, as such, serves as an

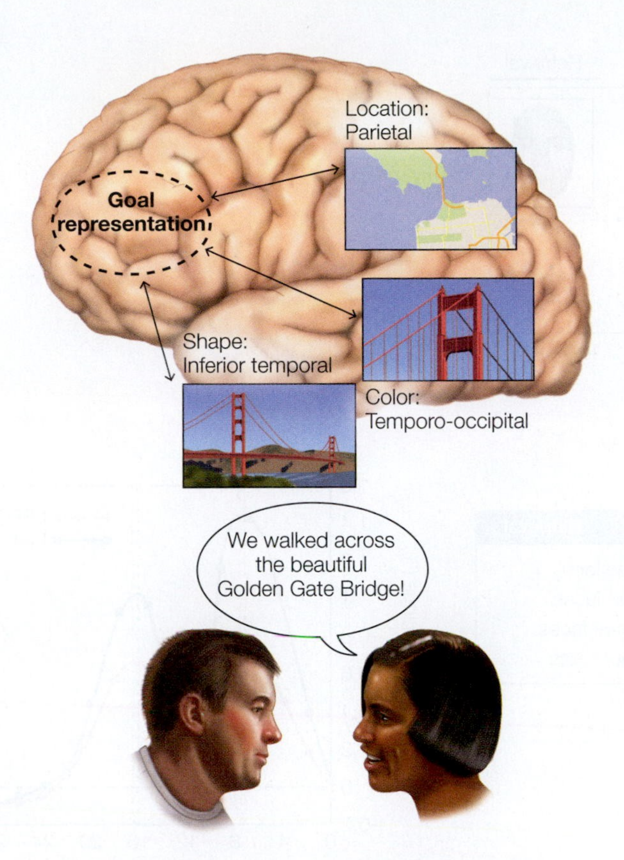

FIGURE 12.5 Working memory arises from the interaction of goal representations and the activation and maintenance of long-term knowledge.
In this example, the woman's goal is to tell her friend about the highlights of her recent trip to San Francisco. Her knowledge of the Golden Gate Bridge requires activation of a distributed network of cortical regions that underlie the representation of long-term memory.

interface with task-relevant long-term representations in other neural regions (**Figure 12.5**).

This goal representation hypothesis jibes nicely with the fact that the prefrontal cortex is extensively connected with postsensory regions of the temporal and parietal cortex. By this view, we can conceptualize working memory as the interaction between a prefrontal representation of the task goal and other parts of the brain that contain perceptual and long-term knowledge relevant to that goal. This sustained interaction between prefrontal cortex and other brain regions facilitates goal-oriented behavior.

This hypothesis is supported by many functional imaging studies. In one representative study, researchers used a variant of a delayed-response task (**Figure 12.6a**). On each trial, four stimuli were presented successively for 1 second each during an encoding interval. The stimuli were either intact faces or scrambled faces. The participants were instructed to remember only the intact faces. Thus, by varying the number of intact faces presented during the encoding interval, the researchers manipulated the processing demands on working memory. After an 8-second delay, a face stimulus—the probe—was presented, and the participant had to decide whether the probe matched one of the faces presented during the encoding period.

The BOLD response in the LPFC bilaterally began to rise with the onset of the encoding period, and this response was maintained across the delay period, even though the screen was blank (**Figure 12.6b**). This lateral prefrontal response was sensitive to the demands on working memory. The sustained response during the delay period was greater when the participant had to remember three or four intact faces as compared to just one or two intact faces.

By using faces, the experimenters could also compare activation in the LPFC with that observed in the fusiform face area (FFA), the inferior temporal lobe region that was discussed in Chapter 6. The BOLD responses for these two regions are shown in **Figure 12.6c**, where the data are combined over the different memory loads. When the stimuli were presented, either during the encoding phase or for the memory probe, the BOLD response was much stronger in the FFA than in the LPFC. During the delay period, as noted already, the LPFC response remained high.

Note, however, that although a substantial drop in the FFA BOLD response occurred during the delay period, the response did not drop to baseline, thus suggesting that the FFA continued to be active during the delay period. In fact, the BOLD response in other perceptual areas of the inferior temporal cortex (not shown) actually went below baseline—the so-called rebound effect. Thus, although the sustained response was small in the FFA, it was considerably higher than what would have been observed with nonfacial stimuli.

The timing of the peak activation in the LPFC and the FFA is also intriguing. During encoding, the peak response was slightly earlier in the FFA as compared to the prefrontal cortex. In contrast, during memory retrieval, the peak response was slightly earlier in the prefrontal cortex. Although this study does not allow us to make causal inferences, the results are consistent with the general tenets of the model sketched in Figure 12.5. The LPFC is critical for working memory because it sustains a representation of the task goal (to remember faces) and works in concert with inferior temporal cortex to sustain information that is relevant for achieving that goal across the delay period.

Working memory, by definition, is a dynamic process. Not only must task-relevant information be maintained, but it is also usually important to manipulate that information. A favorite experimental task for studying

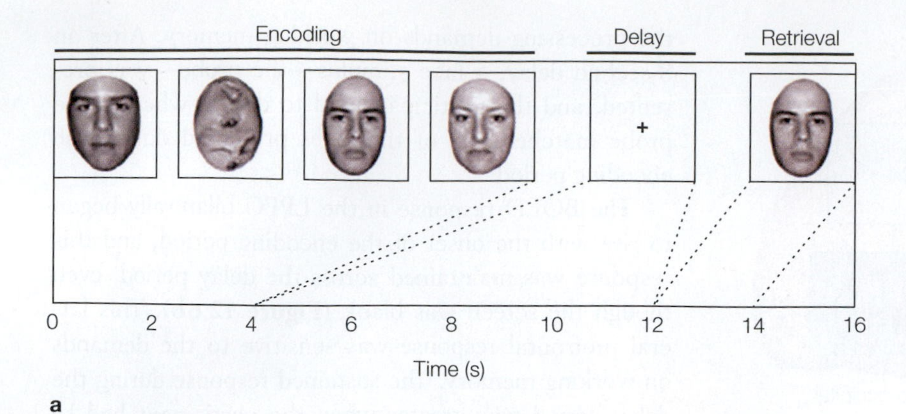

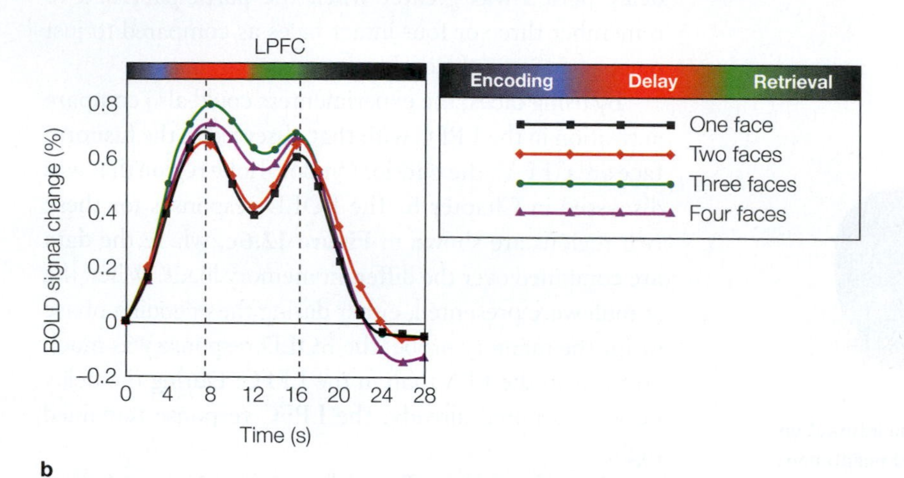

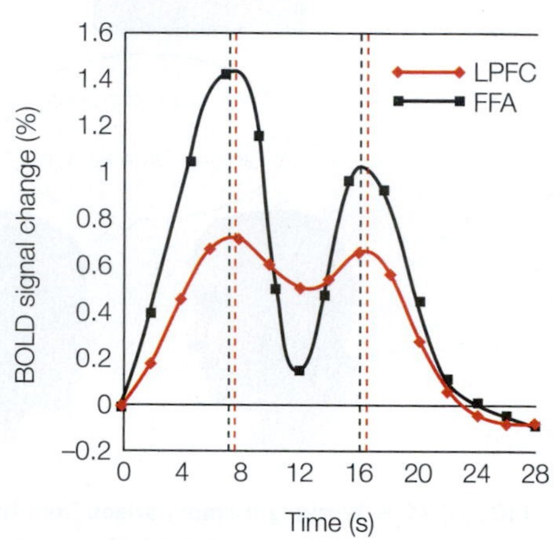

FIGURE 12.6 Functional MRI study of working memory.
(a) In a delayed-response task, a set of intact faces and scrambled faces is presented during an encoding period. After a delay period, a probe stimulus is presented, and the participant indicates whether that face was part of the memory set. **(b)** The BOLD response in the lateral prefrontal cortex (LPFC) rises during the encoding phase and remains high during the delay period. The magnitude of this effect is related to the number of faces that must be maintained in working memory. Dotted lines indicate peaks in hemodynamic responses for encoding and retrieval. **(c)** The BOLD response in the LPFC and the fusiform face area (FFA) rises during the encoding and retrieval periods. The black and red dashed lines indicate the peaks of activation in the FFA and LPFC. During encoding, the peak is earlier in the FFA; during retrieval, the peak is earlier in the LPFC.

the manipulation of information in working memory is the *n*-back task (**Figure 12.7**). In an *n*-back task, the display consists of a continuous stream of stimuli. Participants are instructed to push a button when they detect a repeated stimulus. In the simplest version ($n = 1$), responses are made when the same stimulus is presented on two successive trials. In more complicated versions, n can equal 2 or more.

With *n*-back tasks, it is not sufficient simply to maintain a representation of recently presented items; the working memory buffer must be updated continually to keep track of what the current stimulus must be compared to. Tasks such as *n*-back tasks require both the maintenance and the manipulation of information in working memory. Activation in the LPFC increases as *n*-back task difficulty is increased—a response consistent with the idea that this region is critical for the manipulation operation.

Organizational Principles of Prefrontal Cortex

The prefrontal cortex covers a lot of brain territory. Whereas much of the posterior cortex can be organized in terms of sensory specializations (e.g., auditory versus visual regions), understanding the functional organization of the prefrontal cortex has proved to be more challenging. One hypothesis is that the anterior–posterior gradient across the PFC follows a crude hierarchy: For the simplest of working memory tasks, activity may be limited to more posterior prefrontal regions or even secondary motor areas.

For example, if the task requires the participant to press one key upon seeing a flower and another upon seeing an automobile, then these relatively simple stimulus–response rules can be sustained by the ventral prefrontal cortex and lateral premotor cortex. If the

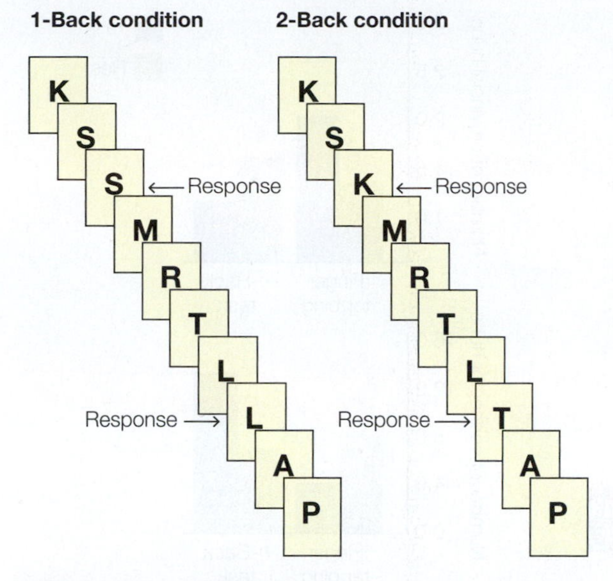

FIGURE 12.7 *n*-Back tasks.
In *n*-back tasks, responses are required only when a stimulus matches one that was shown *n* trials earlier. The contents of working memory must be manipulated constantly in this task because the target is updated on each trial.

stimulus–response rule, however, is defined not by the objects themselves, but by a color surrounding the object, then the more anterior frontal regions are also recruited (S. A. Bunge, 2004). When such contingencies are made even more challenging by changes in the rules from one block of trials to the next, activation extends even more anterior into the frontal pole (**Figure 12.8**). These complex experiments demonstrate how goal-oriented behavior can require the integration of multiple pieces of information.

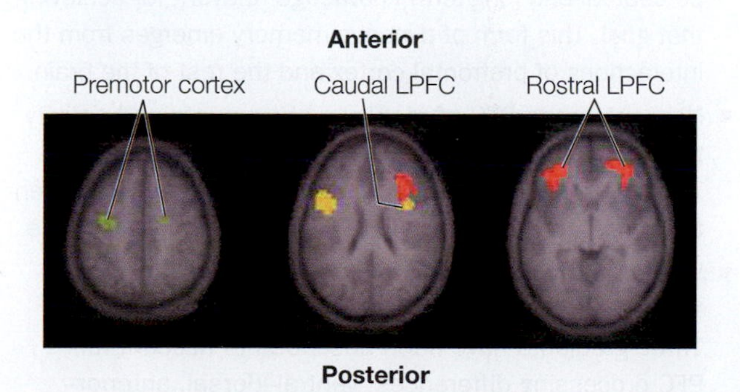

FIGURE 12.8 Hierarchical organization of the prefrontal cortex.
Prefrontal activation in an fMRI study began in the more posterior premotor cortex and moved anteriorly as the experimental task became more complex. Activation in the premotor cortex (shown in green) was related to the number of stimulus–response mappings that had to be maintained. Activation in caudal LPFC (shown in yellow) was related to the contextual demands of the task. For example, a response to a letter might be made if the color of the letter were green, but not if it were white. Activation in rostral LPFC (shown in red) was related to variation in the instructions from one scanning run to the next. For example, the rules in one run might be reversed in the next run.

As a heuristic, we can think of PFC function as organized along three separate axes (see O'Reilly, 2010):

1. A ventral–dorsal gradient organized in terms of maintenance and manipulation, as well as in a manner that reflects general organizational principles observed in more posterior cortex, such as the ventral and dorsal visual pathways for "what" versus "how."
2. An anterior–posterior gradient that varies in abstraction, where the more abstract representations engage the more anterior regions (e.g., frontal pole), and the less abstract engage more posterior regions of the frontal lobes. In the extreme, we might think of the most posterior part of the frontal lobe, the primary motor cortex, as the point where abstract intentions are translated into concrete movement.
3. A lateral–medial gradient related to the degree to which working memory is influenced by information in the environment (more lateral) or information related to personal history and emotional states (more medial). In this view, lateral regions of the PFC integrate external information that is relevant for current goal-oriented behavior, whereas more medial regions allow information related to motivation and potential reward to influence goal-oriented behavior.

For example, suppose it is the hottest day of summer and you are at the lake. You think, "It would be great to have a frosty, cold drink." This idea starts off as an abstract desire but then is transformed into a concrete idea as you remember root beer floats from summer days past. This transformation entails a spread in activation from the most anterior regions of PFC to medial regions, as orbitofrontal cortex helps in recalling the high value you associate with previous root beer float encounters.

More posterior regions become active as you begin to develop an action plan. You become committed to the root beer float, and that goal becomes the center of working memory and thus engages the LPFC. You think about how good these drinks are at A&W restaurants, drawing on links from more ventral regions of the PFC to long-term memories associated with A&W floats. You also draw on dorsal regions that will be essential for forming a plan of action to drive to the A&W. It's a complicated plan, one that no other species would come close to accomplishing. Luckily for you, however, your PFC network is buzzing along now, highly motivated, with the ability to establish the sequence of actions required to accomplish your goal. Reward is just down the road.

Network analyses have also been employed to depict organizational principles of brain connectivity. Jessica Cohen and Mark D'Esposito constructed connectivity

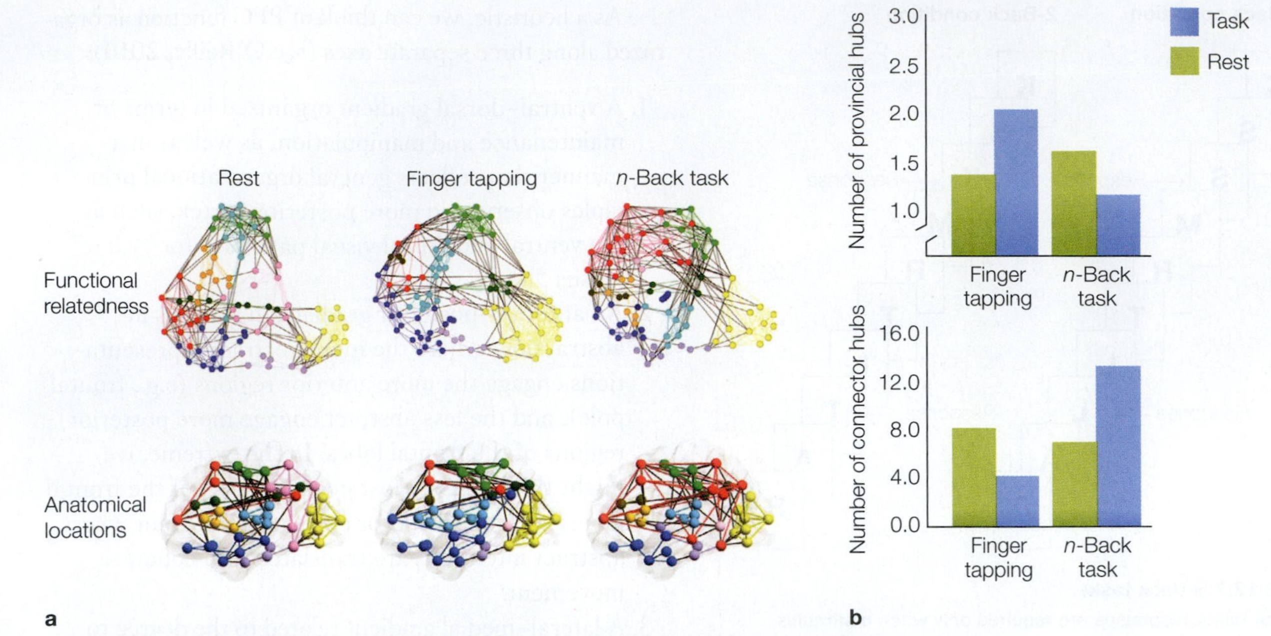

FIGURE 12.9 Changes in functional connectivity during different task states.
(a) Each color represents a network of regions in which the BOLD response was correlated between nodes during rest (left), finger tapping (middle), or performance of an *n*-back task (right). Black lines indicate between-network edges. The top row shows the nodes in a functional space, with distances indicating the similarity between networks. The same nodes are replotted in the bottom row to depict the anatomical location of each node. A cognitive control network (red), spanning prefrontal, parietal, and temporal cortex, is much more pronounced in the *n*-back task. (b) Within-network connections (provincial hubs, top) and between-network connections (connector hubs, bottom) are shown for each task relative to its associated rest condition. Finger tapping is associated with an increase in provincial hubs, whereas the *n*-back task is associated with an increase in connector hubs.

maps to show the cortical networks at work during rest, during a simple motor task (finger tapping), and during an *n*-back task (J. R. Cohen & D'Esposito, 2016). **Figure 12.9a** shows the organization of nine anatomical networks in each of the three conditions (recall from Chapter 3 that the number of networks varies with the criteria used to select them).

While the overall structure persists across the three tasks, there are some systematic differences. In particular, during the demanding *n*-back task, the dorsolateral PFC network expands, showing marked connectivity with parietal regions and areas in the ventral visual pathway. Not only does the cognitive control network become more expansive during the *n*-back task, but the connection strength between networks increases, with more voxels now classified as connector hubs (**Figure 12.9b**). The working memory demands of the *n*-back task require maintaining the goal, staying on task (attention), and keeping track of the visual stimuli. A very different pattern is seen in the finger-tapping task: Here, connection strength becomes greater within a network (provincial hubs). Thus, with the motor task, segregation of distinct networks is increased; in contrast, the more cognitively demanding *n*-back task requires integration across networks.

TAKE-HOME MESSAGES

- Working memory can be conceptualized as the information formed by the combination of a task goal and the perceptual and long-term knowledge relevant for achieving that goal. This form of dynamic memory emerges from the interactions of prefrontal cortex and the rest of the brain.
- Neurons in the PFC of monkeys show sustained activity throughout the delay period in delayed-response tasks. These cells provide a neural correlate for keeping a representation active after the triggering stimulus is no longer visible.
- Various frameworks have been proposed to uncover functional specialization within the prefrontal cortex. Three gradients have been described to account for PFC processing differences: ventral–dorsal, anterior–posterior, and lateral–medial.

12.4 Decision Making

Go back to the hot summer day when you thought, "Hmm . . . that frosty, cold drink is worth looking for. I'm going to get one." That type of goal-oriented behavior begins with a decision to pursue the goal. We might think of the brain as a decision-making device in which our perceptual and memory systems evolved to support decisions that determine our actions. Our brains start making decisions as soon as our eyes flutter open in the morning: Do I get up now or snooze a bit longer? Do I wear shorts or jeans? Do I skip class to study for an exam? Though humans tend to focus on complex decisions such as who will get their vote in the next election, all animals need to make decisions. Even an earthworm decides when to leave a patch of lawn and move on to greener pastures.

Rational observers, such as economists and mathematicians, tend to be puzzled when they consider human behavior. To them, our behavior frequently appears inconsistent or irrational, not based on what seems to be a sensible evaluation of the circumstances and options. For instance, why would someone who is concerned about eating healthy food consume a jelly doughnut? Why would someone who is paying so much money for tuition skip classes? And why are people willing to spend large sums of money to insure themselves against low-risk events (e.g., buying fire insurance even though the odds are overwhelmingly small that they will ever use it), yet equally willing to engage in high-risk behaviors (e.g., texting while driving)?

The field of neuroeconomics has emerged as an interdisciplinary enterprise with the goal of explaining the neural mechanisms underlying decision making. Economists want to understand how and why we make the choices we do. Many of their ideas can be tested both with behavioral studies and, as in all of cognitive neuroscience, with data from cellular activity, neuroimaging, or lesion studies. This work also helps us understand the functional organization of the brain.

Theories about our decision-making processes are either normative or descriptive. **Normative decision theories** define how people *ought* to make decisions that yield the optimal choice. Very often, however, such theories fail to predict what people actually choose. **Descriptive decision theories** attempt to describe what people actually do, not what they should do.

Our inconsistent, sometimes suboptimal choices present less of a mystery to evolutionary psychologists. Our modular brain has been sculpted by evolution to optimize reproduction and survival in a world that differed quite a bit from the one we currently occupy. In that world, you would never have passed up the easy pickings of a jelly doughnut, something that is sweet and full of fat, or engaged in exercise solely for the sake of burning off valuable fat stores; conserving energy would have been a much more powerful factor. Our current brains reflect this past, drawing on the mechanisms that were essential for survival in a world before readily available food.

Many of these mechanisms, as with all brain functions, putter along below our consciousness. We are unaware that we often make decisions by following simple, efficient rules (heuristics) that were sculpted and hard-coded by evolution. The results of these decisions may not seem rational, at least within the context of our current, highly mechanized world. But they may seem more rational if looked at from an evolutionary perspective.

Consistent with this point of view, the evidence indicates that we reach decisions in many different ways. As we touched on earlier, decisions can be goal oriented or habitual. The distinction is that goal-oriented decisions are based on the assessment of expected reward, whereas habits, by definition, are actions taken that are no longer under the control of reward: We simply execute them because the context triggers the action. A somewhat similar way of classifying decisions is to divide them into **action–outcome decisions** or **stimulus–response decisions.** With an action–outcome decision, the decision involves some form of evaluation (not necessarily conscious) of the expected outcomes. After we repeat that action, and if the outcome is consistent, the process becomes habitual; that is, it becomes a stimulus–response decision.

Another distinction can be made between decisions that are model-free or model-based. *Model-based* means that the agent has an internal representation of some aspect of the world and uses this model to evaluate different actions. For example, a cognitive map would be a model of the spatial layout of the world, enabling you to choose an alternative path if you found the road blocked as you set off for the A&W restaurant. *Model-free* means that you have only an input–output mapping, similar to stimulus–response decisions. Here you know that to get to the A&W, you simply look for the tall tower at the center of town, which is right next to the A&W.

Decisions that involve other people are known as *social decisions.* Dealing with other individuals tends to make things much more complicated—a topic we will return to in Chapters 13 and 14.

Is It Worth It? Value and Decision Making

A cornerstone idea in economic models of decision making is that before we make a decision, we first compute the value of each option and then compare the different values in some way (Padoa-Schioppa, 2011). Decision making in this framework is about making choices that will maximize value. For example, we want to obtain the highest possible reward or payoff (**Figure 12.10**). It is not enough, however, to think only about the possible reward level. We also have to consider the likelihood of receiving the reward, as well as the costs required to obtain

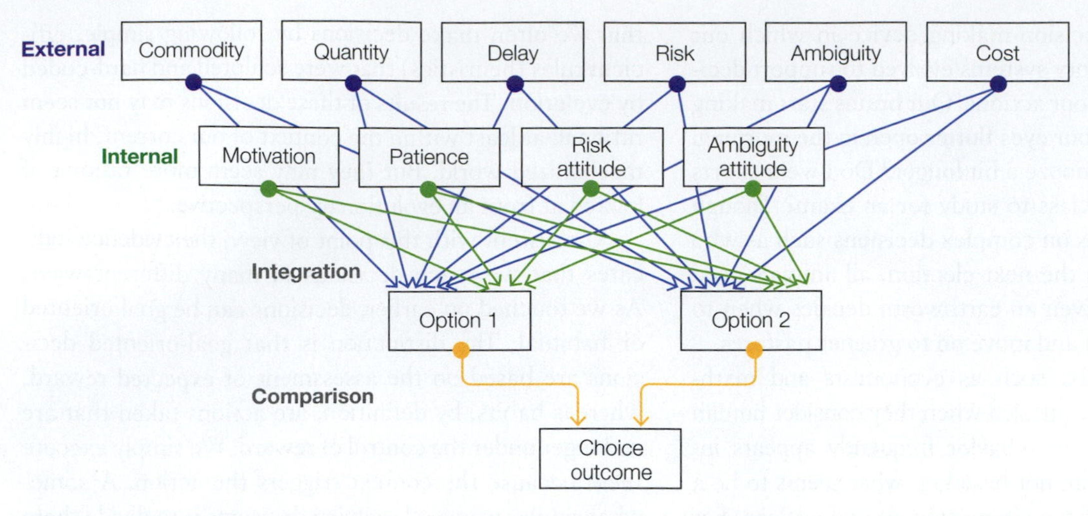

FIGURE 12.10 Decisions require the integration and evaluation of multiple factors.
In this example, the person is asked to choose between two options, each of which has an inferred value. The values are determined by a weighted combination of multiple sources of information. Some sources are external to the agent— for example, will I gain (commodity), how much reward will be obtained (quantity), will I get the reward right away (delay), and how certain am I to obtain the reward (risk)? Other factors are internal to the agent—for example, am I feeling motivated (motivation), am I willing to wait for the reward (patience), is the risk worth it (risk attitude)?

that reward. Although many lottery players dream of winning the million-dollar prize, some may forgo a chance at the big money and buy a ticket with a maximum payoff of a hundred dollars, knowing that their odds of winning are much higher.

COMPONENTS OF VALUE To figure out the neural processes involved in decision making, we need to understand how the brain computes value and processes rewards. Some rewards, such as food, water, or sex, are **primary reinforcers**: They have a direct benefit for survival fitness. Their value, or our response to these reinforcers, is, to some extent, hardwired in our genetic code. But reward value is also flexible and shaped by experience. If you are truly starving, an item of disgust—say, a dead mouse—suddenly takes on reinforcing properties. **Secondary reinforcers**, such as money and status, are rewards that have no intrinsic value themselves, but become rewarding through their association with other forms of reinforcement.

Reward value is not a simple calculation. Value has various components, both external and internal, that are integrated to form an overall subjective worth. Consider this scenario: You are out fishing along the shoreline and thinking about whether to walk around the lake to an out-of-the-way fishing hole. Do you stay put or pack up your gear? Establishing the value of these options requires considering several factors, all of which contribute to the representation of **value**:

Payoff. What kind of reward do the options offer, and how large is the reward? At the current spot, you might land a small trout or perhaps a bream. At the other spot, you've caught a few largemouth bass.

Probability. How likely are you to attain the reward? You might remember that the current spot almost always yields a few catches, whereas you've most often come back empty-handed from the secret hole.

Effort or cost. If you stay put, you can start casting right away. Getting to the fishing hole on the other side of the lake will take an hour of scrambling up and down the hillside. One form of cost that has been widely studied is *temporal discounting*. How long are you willing to wait for a reward? You may not catch large fish at the current spot, but you could feel that satisfying tug 60 minutes sooner if you stayed where you are.

Context. This factor involves external things, like the time of day, as well as internal things, such as whether you are hungry or tired, or looking forward to an afternoon outing with some friends. Context also includes novelty—you might be the type who values an adventure and the possibility of finding an even better fishing hole on your way to the other side of the lake, or you might be feeling cautious, eager to go with a proven winner.

Preference. You may just like one fishing spot better than another for its aesthetics or a fond memory.

As you can see, many factors contribute to subjective value, and they can change immensely from person to person and hour to hour. Given such variation, it is not so surprising that people are highly inconsistent in their decision-making behavior. What seems irrational thinking by another individual might not be, if we could peek into that person's up-to-date value representation of the current choices.

REPRESENTATION OF VALUE How and where is value represented in the brain? Jon Wallis and his colleagues (Kennerley et al., 2009) looked at value representation in the frontal lobes of monkey brains, targeting regions associated with decision making and goal-oriented behavior. While the monkey performed decision-making tasks, the investigators used multiple electrodes to record from cells in three regions: the anterior cingulate cortex (ACC), the lateral prefrontal cortex (LPFC), and the orbitofrontal cortex (OFC). Besides comparing cellular activity in different locations, the experimenters manipulated *cost*, *probability*, and *payoff*. The key question was whether the different areas would show selectivity to particular dimensions. For instance, would OFC be selective to payoff, LPFC to probability, and ACC to cost? Or, would there be an area that coded overall "value" independent of the variable?

As is often observed in neurophysiology studies, the results were quite nuanced. Each of the three regions included cells that responded selectively to a particular dimension, as well as cells that responded to multiple dimensions. Many cells, especially in the ACC, responded to all three dimensions (**Figure 12.11**). A pattern like this suggests that these cells represent an overall measure of value. In contrast, LPFC cells usually encoded just a single decision variable, with a preference for probability. This pattern might reflect the role of this area in working memory, since probability judgments require integrating the consequences of actions over time. In contrast, OFC neurons had a bias to be tuned to payoff, reflecting the amount of reward associated with each stimulus item.

Similar studies with human participants have been conducted with fMRI. Here the emphasis has been on how different dimensions preferentially activate different neural regions. For example, in one study, OFC activation was closely tied to variation in payoff, whereas activation in the striatum of the basal ganglia was related to effort (Croxson et al., 2009). In another study, LPFC activation was associated with the probability of reward, whereas the delay between the time of the action and the payoff was correlated with activity in the medial PFC and lateral parietal lobe (J. Peters & Buchel, 2009).

A classic finding in behavioral economics, **temporal discounting**, is the observation that the value of a reward is reduced when we have to wait to receive that reward. For example, if given a choice, most people would prefer to immediately receive a $10 reward rather than wait a month for $12 (even though the second option translates into an annual interest rate of 240%). But make people choose between $10 now or $50 in a month, and almost everyone is willing to wait. For a given delay, there is some crossover reward level where the subjective value of an immediate reward is the same as that of a larger amount to be paid off in the future. What would that number be for you?

Given the association of the OFC with value representation, researchers at the University of Bologna tested people with lesions encompassing this region on temporal discounting tasks (Sellitto et al., 2010). For both food and monetary rewards, the OFC patients showed abnormal temporal discounting in comparison to patients with lesions outside the OFC or healthy control participants (**Figure 12.12**). Extrapolating from the graph in Figure 12.12c, we can see that a control participant is willing to

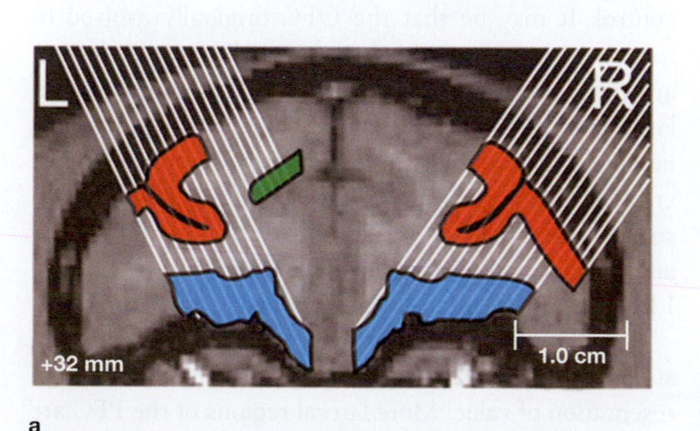

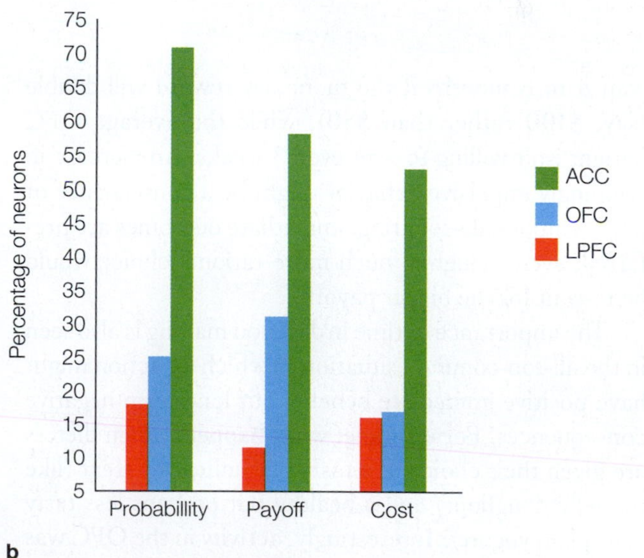

a b

FIGURE 12.11 Cellular representation of value in the prefrontal cortex.
(a) Simultaneous recordings were made from multiple electrodes that were positioned in lateral prefrontal cortex (red), orbitofrontal cortex (blue), or anterior cingulate cortex (green). **(b)** Cellular correlates were found for all three dimensions in each of the three regions, although the number of task-relevant neurons is different between regions. The dimensional preference varies between regions, with the LPFC preferring probability over payoff, and the OFC preferring payoff over probability.

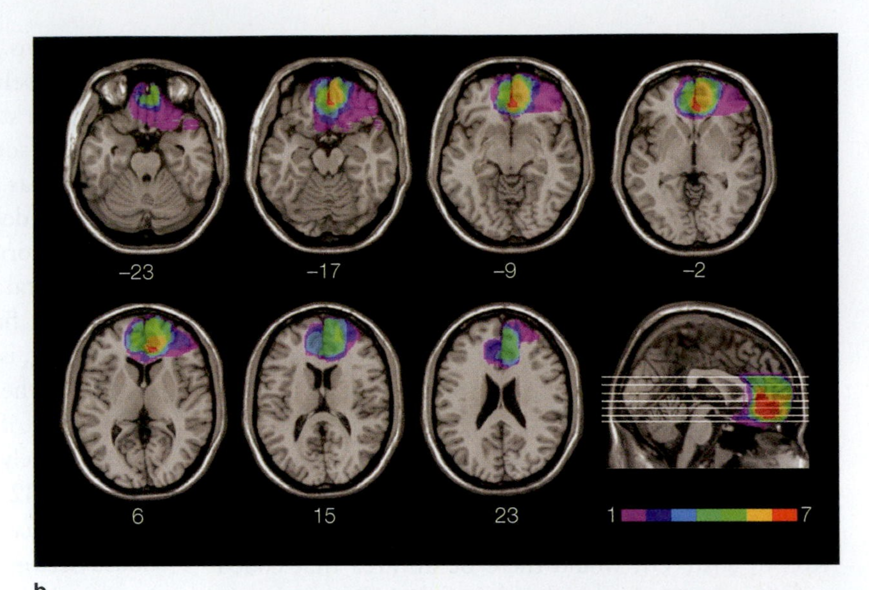

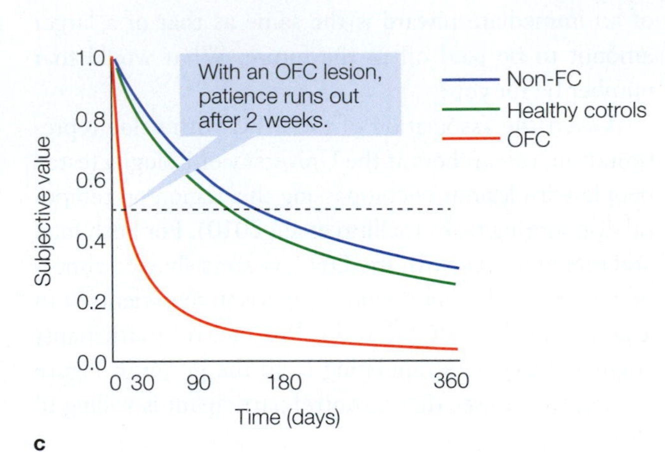

FIGURE 12.12 Patients with OFC lesions strongly prefer immediate rewards over delayed rewards.
(a) The participant must choose either to receive an immediate reward of modest value or to wait for a specified delay period in order to receive a larger reward. **(b)** The locations of orbitofrontal lesions in seven individuals are all projected here onto each of seven different horizontal slices. The color bar indicates the number of lesions affecting each brain region. The white horizontal lines on the sagittal view (bottom right) indicate the level of the horizontal slices, where 23 is the most dorsal. **(c)** Temporal discounting function. The curve indicates how much a delayed reward is discounted, relative to an immediate reward. The dashed line indicates when the delayed option is discounted by 50%. For example, the healthy controls (green) and patients with lesions outside the frontal cortex (non-FC, blue) are willing to wait 4 to 6 months to receive $100 rather than receiving an immediate payoff of $50. The patients with OFC lesions (red) are willing to wait only about 2 weeks for the larger payoff. Similar behavior is observed if the reward is food or vouchers to attend museums.

wait 4 to 6 months if the monetary reward will double (say, $100 rather than $50), while the average OFC patient isn't willing to wait even 3 weeks. An increase in seemingly impulsive behavior might be a consequence of poor temporal discounting; immediate outcomes are preferred, even though a much more rational choice would be to wait for the bigger payoff.

The importance of time in decision making is also seen in the all-too-common situation in which an action might have positive immediate benefits but long-term negative consequences. For example, what happens when dieters are given their choice of a tasty but unhealthy treat (like the jelly doughnut) and a healthy but perhaps less tasty one (plain yogurt)? Interestingly, activity in the OFC was correlated with taste preference, regardless of whether the item was healthy (**Figure 12.13**).

In contrast, the LPFC area was associated with the degree of control (Hare et al., 2009): Activity here was greater on trials in which a preferred but unhealthy item was refused, as compared to trials in which that item was selected. Moreover, this difference was much greater in people who were judged to be better at exhibiting self-control. It may be that the OFC originally evolved to forecast the short-term value of stimuli. Over evolutionary time, structures such as the LPFC began to modulate more primitive, or primary, value signals, providing humans with the ability to incorporate long-term considerations into value representations. These findings also suggest that a fundamental difference between successful and failed self-control might be the extent to which the LPFC can modulate the value signal encoded in the OFC.

Overall, the neurophysiological and neuroimaging studies indicate that the OFC plays a key role in the representation of value. More lateral regions of the PFC are important for some form of modulatory control of these representations or the actions associated with them. We have seen one difference between the neurophysiological and neuroimaging results: The former emphasize a distributed picture of value representation, and the latter emphasize specialization within components

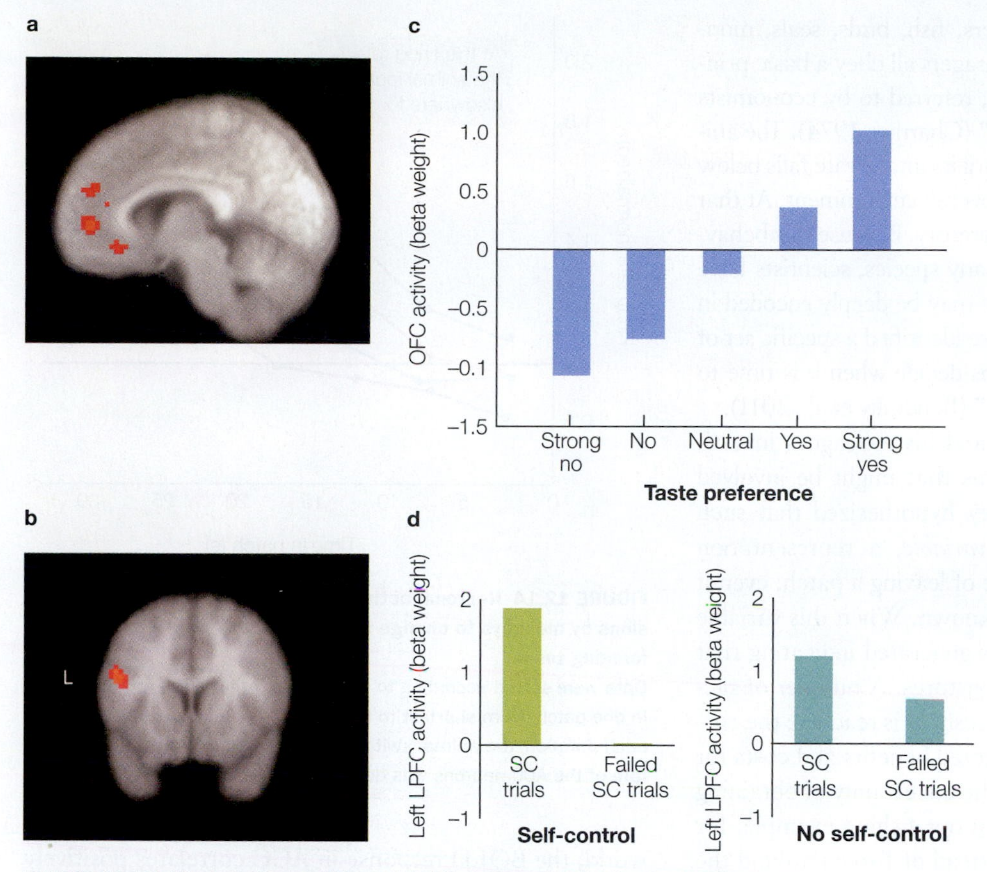

FIGURE 12.13 Dissociation of OFC and LPFC during a food selection task. (a) OFC regions that showed a positive relationship between the BOLD response and food preference. This signal provides a representation of value. (b) LPFC region in which the BOLD response was related to self-control. The signal was stronger on trials in which participants exhibited self-control (did not choose a highly rated but nutritionally poor food) compared to trials in which they failed to exhibit self-control. The difference was especially pronounced in participants who, according to survey data, were rated as having good self-control. (c) Activity in the OFC increased with preference. (d) The left LPFC showed greater activity in successful self-control trials in the self-control group (left) than in the no-self-control group (right). Both groups showed greater activity in the LPFC for successful versus failed self-control (SC) tasks.

of a decision-making network. The discrepancy, though, is probably due to the differential sensitivity of the two methods. The fine-grained spatial resolution of neurophysiology enables us to ask whether individual cells are sensitive to particular dimensions. In contrast, fMRI studies generally provide relative answers, asking whether an area is more responsive to variation in one dimension compared to another dimension.

More Than One Type of Decision System?

The laboratory is an artificial environment. Many of the experimental paradigms used to study decision making involve conditions in which the participant has ready access to the different choices and at least some information about the potential rewards and costs. Thus, participants are able to calculate and compare values. In the natural environment, especially the one our ancestors roamed about in, this situation is the exception, not the norm. More frequently, we must choose between an option with a known value and one or more options of unknown value (Rushworth et al., 2012).

The classic example is foraging: Animals have to make decisions about where to seek food and water, precious commodities that tend to occur in restricted locations and for only a short time. Foraging brings up questions that require decisions—such as, Do I keep eating/hunting/fishing here or move on to (what may or may not be) greener pastures, birdier bushes, or fishier water holes? In other words, do I continue to *exploit* the resources at hand or set out to *explore* in hopes of finding a richer niche? To make the decision, the animal must calculate the value of the current option, the richness of the overall environment, and the costs of exploration.

Worms, bees, wasps, spiders, fish, birds, seals, monkeys, and human subsistence foragers all obey a basic principle in their foraging behavior, referred to by economists as the "marginal value theorem" (Charnov, 1974). The animal exploits a foraging patch until its intake rate falls below the average intake rate for the overall environment. At that point, the animal becomes exploratory. Because this behavior is so consistent across so many species, scientists have hypothesized that this tendency may be deeply encoded in our genes. Indeed, biologists have identified a specific set of genes that influence how worms decide when it is time to start looking for "greener lawns" (Bendesky et al., 2011).

Benjamin Hayden (2011) and his colleagues investigated the neuronal mechanisms that might be involved in foraging-like decisions. They hypothesized that such decisions require a *decision variable*, a representation that specifies the current value of leaving a patch, even if the alternative is relatively unknown. When this variable reaches a threshold, a signal is generated indicating that it is time to look for greener pastures. A number of factors influence how soon this threshold is reached: the current expected payoff, the expected benefits and costs for traveling to a new patch, and the uncertainty of obtaining reward at the next location. In our fishing example, for instance, if it takes 2 hours instead of 1 to go around the lake to a better fishing spot, you are less likely to move.

Hayden recorded from cells in the ACC (part of the medial PFC) of monkeys, choosing this region because it has been linked to the monitoring of actions and their outcomes (which we discuss later in the chapter). The animals were presented with a virtual foraging task in which they chose one of two targets. One stimulus (S1) was followed by a reward after a short delay, but the amount decreased with each successive trial (equivalent to remaining in a patch and reducing the food supply by eating it). The other stimulus (S2) allowed the animals to change the outcome contingencies. They received no reward on that trial, but after a variable period of time (the cost of exploration), the choices were presented again and the payoff for S1 was reset to its original value (a greener patch).

Consistent with the marginal value theorem, the animals became less likely to choose S1 as the waiting time increased or the amount of reward decreased. What's more, cellular activity in the ACC was highly predictive of the amount of time the animal would continue to "forage" by choosing S1. Most interesting, the cells showed the property of a threshold: When the firing rate was greater than 20 spikes per second, the animal left the patch (**Figure 12.14**).

The hypothesis that the ACC plays a critical role in foraging-like decisions is further supported by fMRI studies with humans (Kolling et al., 2012). When the person is making choices about where to sample in a virtual world, the BOLD response in ACC correlates positively with the search value (explore) and negatively with the encounter value (exploit), regardless of which choice participants made. In this condition, ventromedial regions of the PFC did not signal overall value. If, however, experimenters modified the task so that the participants were engaged in a comparison decision, activation in the OFC reflected the chosen option value. Taken together, these studies suggest that ACC signals exert a type of control by promoting a particular behavior: exploring the environment for better alternatives compared to the current course of action (Rushworth et al., 2012).

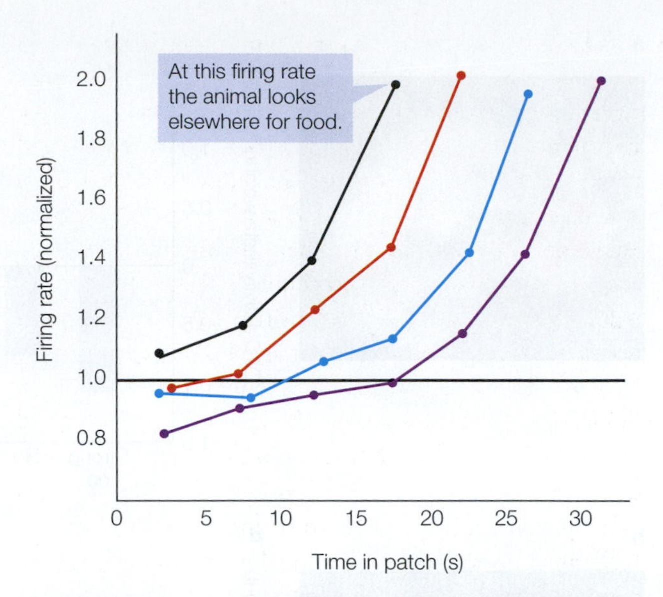

FIGURE 12.14 Neuronal activity in ACC is correlated with decisions by monkeys to change to a new "patch" in a sequential foraging task.
Data were sorted according to the amount of time the animal stayed in one patch (from shortest to longest: black, red, blue, purple). For each duration, the animal switched to a new patch when the firing of the ACC neurons was double the normal level of activity.

It is obvious that people prefer to have a choice between two high-valued rewards rather than two low-valued rewards. For example, you would probably rather choose between two great job offers than two bad job offers. But what if the choice is between a high-valued reward and a low-valued reward? Logically, it would seem that this option should be less preferable to the choice between two high-valued rewards—you are giving up an option to consider a desired outcome for an undesired outcome. However, "preference" is based on multiple factors. Although we like to face "win–win" options, having to choose between them creates anxiety. This anxiety is not present when the choice is simply a good option over a bad option.

Harvard University researchers explored the brain systems involved with the simultaneous, though paradoxical, experiences of feeling both good and anxious.

While undergoing fMRI, participants chose between two low-valued products, a low- and a high-valued product, or two high-valued products in pairs of products that they had an actual chance of winning (in a lottery, conducted at the end of the experiment). The participants were also asked to rate how positive and anxious they felt about each choice (Shenhav & Buckner, 2014; **Figure 12.15a**).

As predicted, win–win choices (high value/high value) generated the most positive feelings but were also associated with the highest levels of anxiety (**Figure 12.15b**). You have great choices, but you are conflicted: Which is better? Conversely, the low/low choice ranked low on both scales. With bad options to choose from, you don't really care which one you select: No conflict, no anxiety. Low/high choices led to high levels of positive feelings and low anxiety. You feel good and there is no conflict: The choice is a slam dunk.

The fMRI data revealed two dissociable neural circuits that correlated with these different variables influencing decision making (**Figure 12.15c**). The OFC tracked how positive the participant felt about the choices, consistent with the hypothesis that this region is important in the representation of the anticipated payoff or reward. In contrast, the BOLD response in the ACC value tracked anxiety, with the highest level of activity on the difficult win–win (high/high) choices. Similar to what we saw in the discussion of foraging, ACC activation is predictive when there is conflict between one option or another—a hypothesis we will return to later in this chapter.

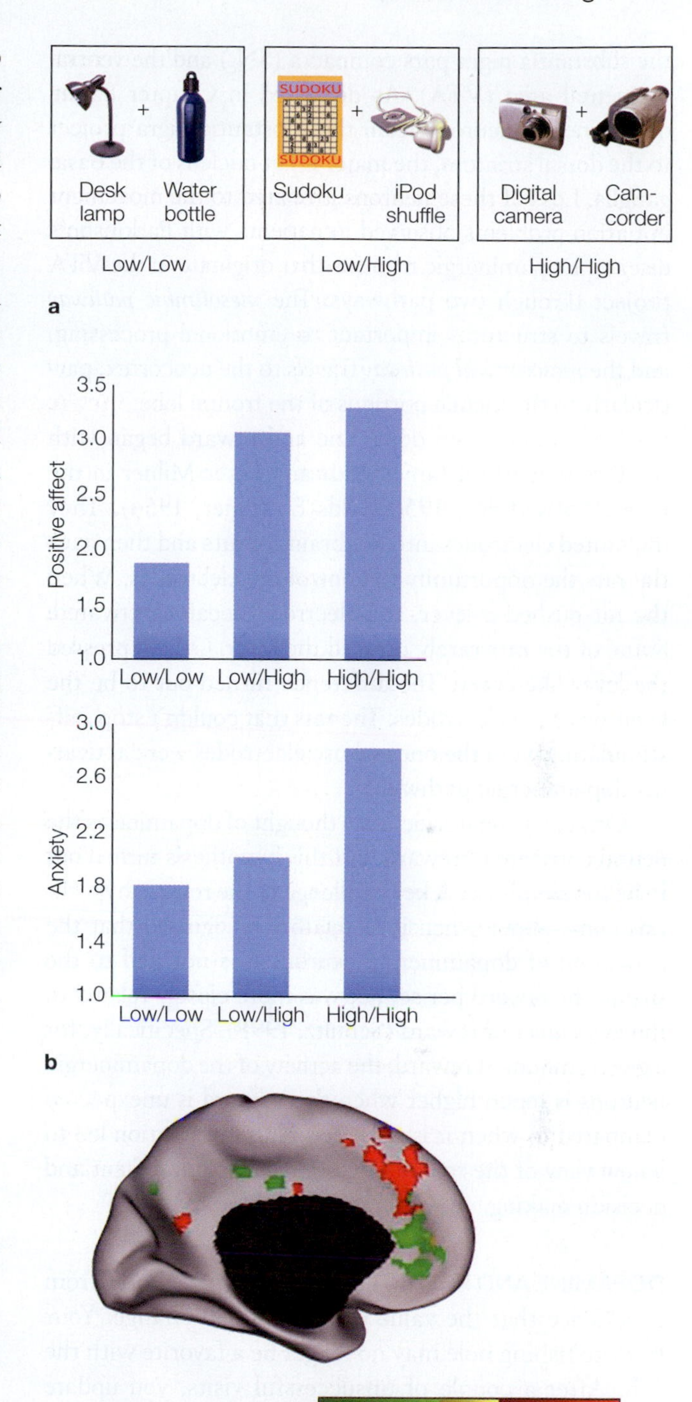

FIGURE 12.15 Neural correlates of decision making under stress.
(a) On each trial, participants indicated their preferred choice between a pair of items, each of which could be of either low or high value. The selected items were entered in a lottery, and one was chosen at random as the reward for participating in the experiment. **(b)** Ratings of desirability (positive affect, top) and anxiety (bottom) for the three conditions. **(c)** Brain regions in which the BOLD response was correlated with higher levels of positive affect (green) or higher levels of anxiety (red). The former was most evident in OFC; the latter was most evident in ACC, part of the medial frontal cortex.

Dopamine Activity and Reward Processing

We have seen that rewards, especially those associated with primary reinforcers like food and sex, are fundamental to the behavior of all animals. It follows that the processing of such signals might involve phylogenetically older neural structures. Indeed, converging lines of evidence indicate that many subcortical areas represent reward information, including the basal ganglia, hypothalamus, amygdala, and lateral habenula (for a review, see O. Hikosaka et al., 2008). Much of the work on reward has focused on the neurotransmitter **dopamine (DA)**. We should keep in mind, however, that reinforcement likely involves the interplay of many transmitters. For instance, evidence suggests that serotonin is important for the temporal discounting of reward value (S. C. Tanaka et al., 2007).

Dopaminergic (dopamine-activated) cells are scattered throughout the midbrain, sending axonal projections to many cortical and subcortical areas. Two of the primary loci of dopaminergic neurons are two brainstem nuclei, the substantia nigra pars compacta (SN_c) and the ventral tegmental area (VTA). As discussed in Chapter 8, the dopaminergic neurons from the substantia nigra project to the dorsal striatum, the major input nucleus of the basal ganglia. Loss of these neurons is related to the movement initiation problems observed in patients with Parkinson's disease. Dopaminergic neurons that originate in the VTA project through two pathways: The *mesolimbic pathway* travels to structures important to emotional processing, and the *mesocortical pathway* travels to the neocortex, particularly to the medial portions of the frontal lobe.

The link between dopamine and reward began with the classic work of James Olds and Peter Milner in the early 1950s (Olds, 1958; Olds & Milner, 1954). They implanted electrodes into the brains of rats and then gave the rats the opportunity to control the electrodes. When the rat pushed a lever, the electrode became activated. Some of the rats rarely pressed the lever. Others pressed the lever like crazy. The difference turned out to be the location of the electrodes. The rats that couldn't stop self-stimulating were the ones whose electrodes were activating dopaminergic pathways.

Originally, neuroscientists thought of dopamine as the neural correlate of reward, but this hypothesis turned out to be too simplistic. A key challenge to the reward hypothesis came about when investigators recognized that the activation of dopaminergic neurons was not tied to the size of the reward per se, but was more closely related to the *expectancy* of reward (Schultz, 1998). Specifically, for a given amount of reward, the activity of the dopaminergic neurons is much higher when that reward is unexpected compared to when it is expected. This observation led to a new view of the role of dopamine in reinforcement and decision making.

DOPAMINE AND PREDICTION ERROR We know from experience that the value of an item can change. Your favorite fishing hole may no longer be a favorite with the fish. After a couple of unsuccessful visits, you update your value (now that fishing hole is not your favorite either) and you look for a new spot. How do we learn and update the values associated with different stimuli and actions? An updating process is essential, because the environment may change. Updating is also essential because our own preferences change over time. Think about that root beer float. Would you be so eager to drink one if you had just downed a couple of ice cream cones?

Wolfram Schultz (1998) and his colleagues conducted a series of revealing experiments using a simple Pavlovian conditioning task with monkeys (see Chapter 9). The animals were trained such that a light, the conditioned stimulus (CS), was followed after a few seconds by an unconditioned stimulus (US), a sip of juice. To study the role of dopamine, Schultz recorded from dopaminergic cells in the VTA. As expected, when the training procedure started, the cells showed a large burst of activity after the US was presented (**Figure 12.16a**). Such a response could be viewed as representing the reward. When the CS–US events were repeatedly presented, however, two interesting things occurred. First, the dopamine response to the juice, the US, decreased over time. Second, the cells started to fire when the light, the CS, was presented. That is, the dopamine response gradually shifted from the US to the CS (**Figure 12.16b**).

A reinforcement account of the reduced response to the US might emphasize that the value of the reward drops over time as the animal feels less hungry. Still, this hypothesis could not account for why the CS now triggers a dopamine response. The response here seems to suggest that the CS has now become rewarding.

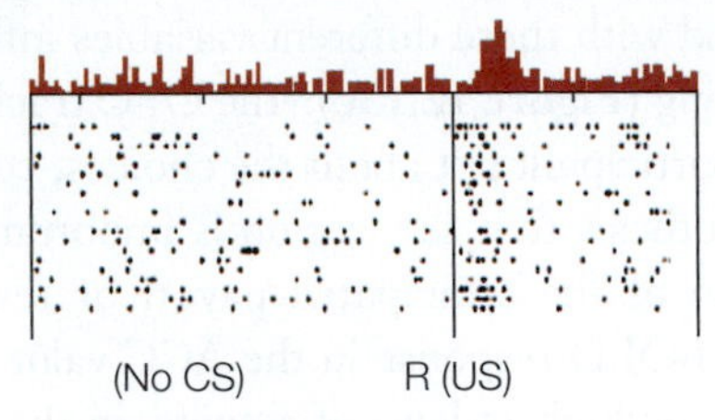

a No predictions; reward occurs

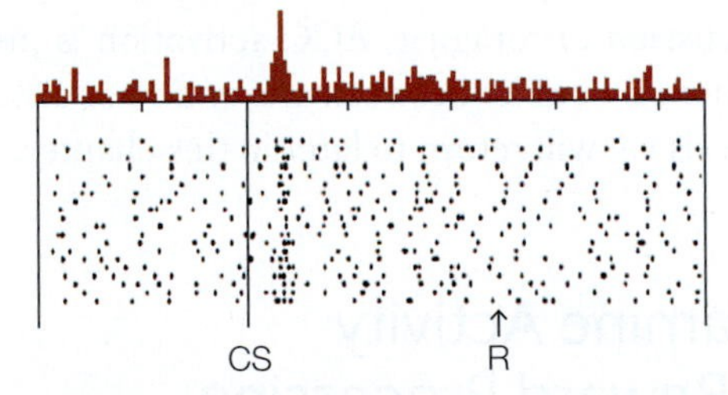

b Reward predicted; reward occurs

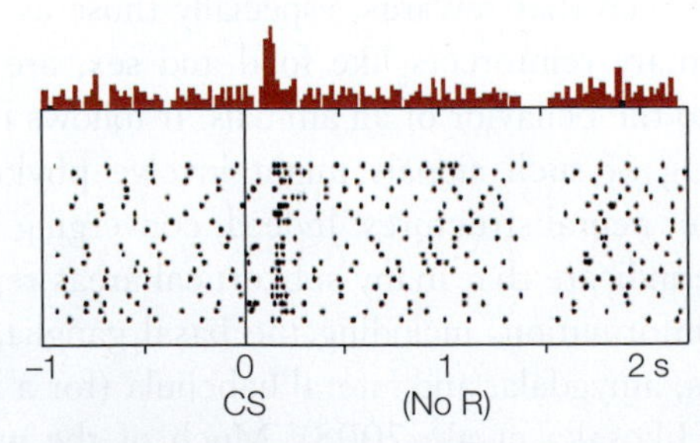

c Reward predicted; no reward occurs

FIGURE 12.16 Dopamine neurons respond to an error in prediction. These raster plots show spikes in a midbrain dopamine neuron on single trials, with the data across trials summarized in the histograms at the top of each panel. **(a)** In the absence of a conditioned stimulus (CS), the DA neuron shows a burst of activity when the unpredicted reward (R), a drop of juice, is given. **(b)** When the CS is repeatedly paired with the reward, the DA neuron shows a temporal shift, now firing when the CS is presented because this is the unexpected, positive event. **(c)** On trials in which the predicted reward is not given, the neuron shows a positive prediction error after the CS (as in b) and a negative prediction error around the time of expected reward.

Schultz proposed a new hypothesis to account for the role of dopamine in reward-based learning. Rather than thinking of the spike in DA neuron activity as representing the reward, he suggested it should be viewed as a **reward prediction error (RPE)**, a signal that represents the difference between the obtained reward and the expected reward. First, consider the *reduction* in the dopaminergic response to the juice. On the first trial, the animal has not learned that the light is always followed by the juice. Thus, the animal does not expect to receive a reward following the light, but a reward is given. This event results in a positive RPE, because the obtained reward is greater than the expected reward: DA is released. With repeated presentation of the light–juice pairing, however, the animal comes to expect a reward when the light is presented. As the expected and obtained values become more similar, the size of the positive RPE is reduced and the dopaminergic response becomes attenuated.

Now consider the *increase* in the dopaminergic response to the light. When the animal is sitting in the test apparatus between trials, it has no expectancy of reward and does not associate the light with a reward. Thus, when the light flashes, the animal has no expectation (it is just hanging out), so there is no RPE. Expectation is low, and the reward is associated with the juice (yippee!), not the light (Figure 12.16a). As the animal experiences rewards after a light flash, however, it begins to associate the light with the juice, and the onset of the light results in a positive RPE (Figure 12.16b). This positive RPE is represented by the dopaminergic response to the light.

To calculate an RPE, a neuron must have two inputs: one corresponding to the predicted reward and one indicating the actual reward. Naoshige Uchida's lab has been investigating this problem, asking whether DA neurons actually do the calculation of reward prediction errors or if this information is instead calculated upstream and then passed on to the DA neurons.

In an ingenious series of experiments, these researchers provided evidence in favor of the former hypothesis. Their first step was to determine whether DA neurons received input of the actual reward. To answer this question, they injected special retroactive tracers into the VTA, which were taken up by axons terminating on DA neurons. This procedure enabled the researchers to identify all of the inputs to the DA neurons. From a combination of cellular recording and optogenetics (discussed in Chapter 3), they characterized the inputs from a broadly distributed set of subcortical areas, such as the hypothalamus (Tian & Uchida, 2015). Some of these had the signature of a reward signal; namely, the activity level scaled with the amount of reward.

These researchers then examined the neuronal mechanisms of reward predictions, focusing on the input to DA neurons from neighboring GABA neurons (Eshel et al., 2015). They developed an optogenetic label in mice that enabled them to specifically control the activity of these GABA neurons while simultaneously recording from DA neurons. The mice were then trained on a task in which an odor signaled the likelihood of reward: Odor A had a 10% chance of reward, and Odor B had a 90% chance of reward.

First let's consider the response of the GABA and DA neurons in the absence of optogenetic stimulation (**Figure 12.17a**). At the time of the actual reward, the

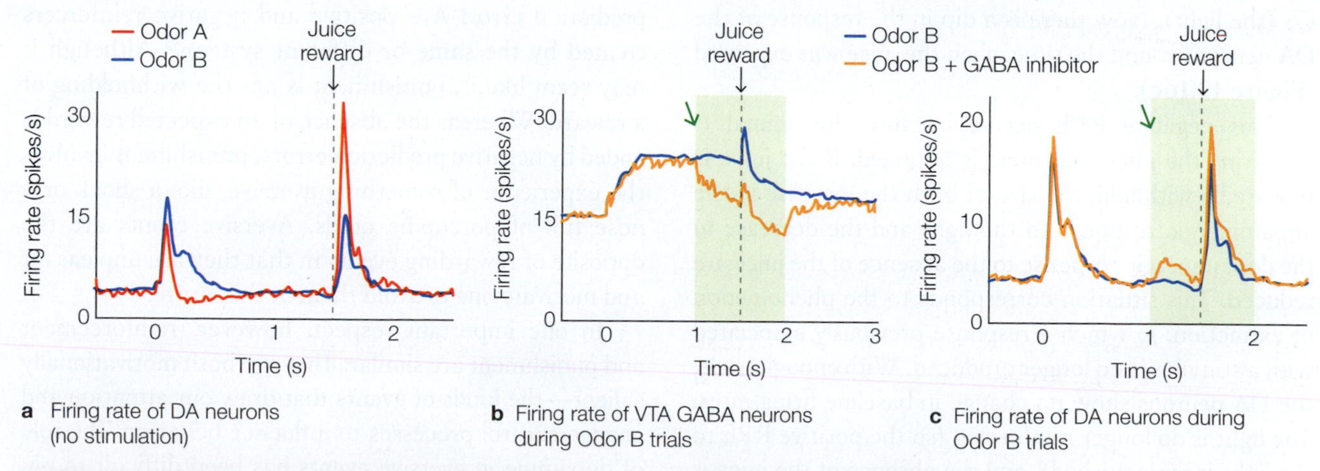

FIGURE 12.17 GABA input to dopamine neurons provides a neuronal signal of reward prediction.
(a) Firing rate of DA neurons to onset of cue (time = 0 s) and juice reward (dashed line). Reward occurs on 10% of the trials for Odor A and 90% of the trials for Odor B. Because Odor B has a higher reward prediction, the positive RPE response of the DA neuron is lower to Odor B at the time of the juice reward. (b) Activity of GABA neurons to Odor B either without optogenetic stimulation (blue) or with optogenetic stimulation (orange). The green arrow indicates onset of stimulation. The results confirm that the optogenetic tag was effective in decreasing activity in GABA neurons. (c) Optogenetic inhibition of the GABA neurons led to an increase in the DA response to Odor B, confirming that the GABA input to DA neurons can signal a predicted reward.

DA neurons have a much stronger response to Odor A than to Odor B: Because the reward is not expected with Odor A, there is a stronger positive RPE. The reduced DA response to Odor A initially is associated with an increase in the firing rate of the inhibitory GABA interneurons (not shown) at the onset of the odor—an effect that persists until the reward delivery.

Now consider what happens on trials in which Odor B is presented along with the optogenetic silencing of the GABA neurons. Confirming that the manipulation is successful, the GABA neurons' firing rate drops off as soon as the light is turned on (green region in **Figure 12.17b**). More interesting, removing this inhibitory input to the DA neurons produces an increase in the response of the DA neuron (**Figure 12.17c**). In contrast, when the GABA neurons are inhibited, the DA response to Odor A is minimally affected (not shown).

These results indicate that GABA neurons provide a signal of reward expectancy to DA neurons. In combination with the evidence showing that the DA neurons receive inputs about the actual reward, we see that the DA neurons are ideally positioned to calculate reward prediction errors.

The prediction error model has proved to be an important idea for thinking about how dopamine is related to both reinforcement and learning. We have described the case in which the obtained reward is greater than the expected reward, resulting in a positive RPE. We can also consider situations with negative RPEs, cases in which the obtained reward is less than the expected reward. This situation happens during a trial when the experimenter meanly withholds the reward (the juice, returning to the example of Figure 12.16) after presenting the CS (the light). Now there is a dip in the response of the DA neuron around the time when the juice was expected (**Figure 12.16c**).

This negative RPE occurs because the animal is expecting the juice, but none is obtained. If the juice is repeatedly withheld, the size of both the increase in the dopaminergic response to the light and the decrease in the dopaminergic response to the absence of the juice are reduced. This situation corresponds to the phenomenon of extinction, in which a response previously associated with a stimulus is no longer produced. With enough trials, the DA neurons show no change in baseline firing rates. The light is no longer reinforcing (so the positive RPE to the light is extinguished), and the absence of the juice is no longer a violation of an expectancy (so the negative RPE when the juice was anticipated is also abolished).

As we have seen in this example, the dopaminergic response changes with learning. Indeed, scientists have recognized that the prediction error signal itself can be useful for reinforcement learning, serving as a teaching signal. As discussed earlier, models of decision making assume that events in the world (or internal states) have associated values. Juice is a valued commodity, especially to a thirsty monkey. Over time, the light also becomes a valued stimulus, signaling the upcoming reward. The RPE signal can be used to update representations of value. Computationally, this process can be described as taking the current value representation and multiplying it by some weighted factor (gain) of the RPE (Dayan & Niv, 2008). If the RPE is positive, the net result is an increase in value. If the RPE is negative, the net result is a decrease in value.

This elegant yet simple model not only predicts how values are updated, but also accounts for changes in the amount that is learned from one trial to the next. Early in training, the value of the light is low. The large RPE that occurs when it is followed by the juice will lead to an increase in the value associated with the light. With repeated trials, though, the size of the RPE decreases, so subsequent changes in the value of the light will also increase more slowly.

This process, in which learning is initially rapid and then occurs in much smaller increments over time, is characteristic of almost all learning functions. Although this effect might occur for many reasons (e.g., the benefits of practice diminish over time), the impressive thing is that it is predicted by a simple model in which value representations are updated by a simple mechanism based on the difference between the predicted and obtained reward.

REWARD AND PUNISHMENT Not all options are rewarding; just consider your dog's response after he has tried to nudge a porcupine out of a rotting tree. Talk about prediction error! Are positive and negative reinforcers treated by the same or different systems? Although it may seem like it, punishment is not the withholding of a reward. Whereas the absence of an expected reward is coded by negative prediction errors, punishment involves the experience of something aversive, like a shock or a nose full of porcupine quills. Aversive events are the opposite of rewarding events in that they are unpleasant and motivate one to avoid them in the future.

In one important respect, however, reinforcement and punishment are similar: They are both motivationally salient—the kinds of events that draw our attention and engage control processes to influence behavior. The role of dopamine in aversive events has been difficult to pin down. Some studies show increases in dopamine activity, others find decreases, and some find both within the same study. Can these findings be reconciled?

The *habenula*, a structure located within the dorsal thalamus, is in a good position to represent emotional and motivational events because it receives inputs from the forebrain limbic regions and sends inhibitory projections to dopamine neurons in the substantia nigra pars compacta. Masayuki Matsumoto and Okihide Hikosaka (2007) recorded from neurons in the lateral habenula and dopaminergic neurons in the SN_c while monkeys made saccadic eye movements to a target that was either to the left or to the right of a fixation point. A saccade to one target was associated with a juice reward, and a saccade to the other target resulted in non-reinforcement.

Habenula neurons became active when the saccade was to the *no-reward* side and were suppressed if the saccade was to the reward side. DA neurons showed the opposite profile: They were excited by the *reward-predicting* targets and suppressed by the targets predicting no reward. Even weak electrical stimulation of the habenula elicited strong inhibition in DA neurons, suggesting that reward-related activity of the DA neurons may be regulated by input from the lateral habenula.

Value is in one sense relative. If given a 50–50 chance to win $100 or $10, we would be disappointed to get only $10. If the game were changed, however, so that we stood to win either $10 or $1, we'd be thrilled to get the $10. Habenula neurons show a similar context dependency. If two actions result in either juice or nothing, the habenula is active when the nothing choice is made. But if the two actions result in either nothing or an aversive puff of air to the eye, the habenula is active only when the animal makes the response that results in the puff.

This context dependency is also seen in DA responses. In our hypothetical game, we might imagine that the expected reward in the first pairing is $55 (the average of $100 and $10), whereas in the second pairing it is only $5.50. The $10 outcome results in a positive RPE in one case and a negative RPE in the other. In sum, there are many computational similarities between how we respond to rewards and punishments, and this finding may reflect the interaction between the habenula and the dopamine system.

In general, fMRI studies lack the spatial resolution to measure activity in small brainstem regions such as the VTA or lateral habenula. Nonetheless, researchers can ask similar questions about the similarity of neural regions in coding positive and negative outcomes. In one study, Ben Seymour and his colleagues (2007) paired different cues with possible financial outcomes that signaled a gain versus nothing, a loss versus nothing, or a gain versus a loss (**Figure 12.18a**). Study participants did not make choices in this experiment; they simply viewed the choices, and the computer determined the outcome. Positive and negative RPEs of gains and losses were both correlated with activity in the ventral striatum, but the specific ventral striatal region differed for the two conditions. Gains were encoded in the more anterior regions, and losses in the more posterior regions (**Figure 12.18b**). A region in the insula also responded to prediction error, but only when the choice resulted in a loss.

Alternative Views of Dopamine Activity

The RPE story elegantly accounts for the role of dopaminergic cells in reinforcement and learning, but there remain viable alternative hypotheses. Kent Berridge (2007) argues that dopamine release is the result, not the cause, of learning. He points out a couple of problems with the notion that dopamine acts as a learning signal. First, mice that are genetically unable to

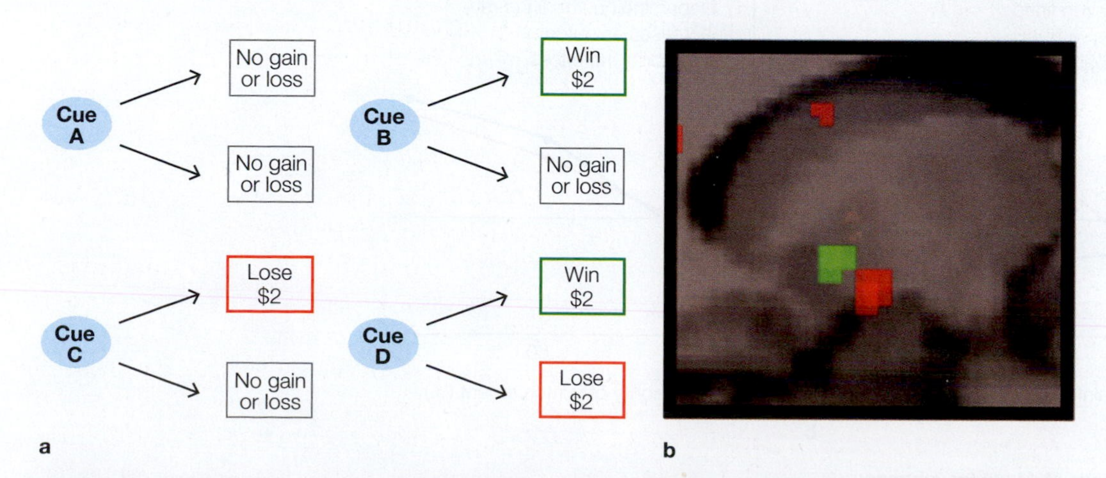

FIGURE 12.18 Coding of gain and loss in the ventral striatum with fMRI.
(a) People were presented with one of four cues: A, B, C, or D. Over time, they learned that each cue was associated with one of two possible outcomes (or, for Cue A, the same neutral outcome).
(b) Prediction errors reliably predicted the BOLD response in the ventral striatum, with the center of the positive RPE response (green) slightly anterior to the center of the negative RPE response (red).

synthesize dopamine can still learn (Cannon & Bseikri, 2004; Cannon & Palmiter, 2003). Second, genetically mutant mice with high dopamine levels do not learn any faster, nor do they maintain habits longer, than mice with normal levels of dopamine.

Given these puzzles, Berridge suggests that dopamine neurons do not cause learning by encoding RPEs. Instead, they code the informational consequences of prediction and learning (generated elsewhere in the brain) and then do something with the information. He proposes that dopamine activity is indicative of the salience of a stimulus or an event.

Berridge describes a reward as made up of three dissociable components: wanting, learning, and liking. His view is that dopamine mediates only the "wanting" component. Dopamine activity indicates that something is worth paying attention to, and when these things are associated with reward, the dopamine activity reflects how desirable the object is. The distinction between wanting and liking may seem subtle, but it can have serious implications when we consider things like drug abuse.

In one experiment, cocaine users were given a drug that lowered their dopamine levels (Leyton et al., 2005). In the lowered dopamine state, cues indicating the availability of cocaine were rated as less desirable. However, the users' feelings of euphoria in response to cocaine and their rate of self-administration were unaffected. That is, with reduced dopamine, study participants still liked cocaine in the same way (reinforcement was unchanged), even though they didn't particularly want it.

It is reasonable to suppose that dopamine serves multiple functions. Indeed, neurophysiologists have described two classes of responses when recording from DA neurons in the brainstem (Matsumoto & Hikosaka, 2009). One subset of DA neurons responded in terms of *valence*. These cells increased their firing rate to stimuli that were predictive of reward and decreased their firing rate to aversive stimuli (**Figure 12.19a**). A greater number of DA neurons, however, were excited by *salience*—the increased likelihood of *any* reinforcement, independent of whether it was a reward or a punishment, and especially when it was unpredictable (**Figure 12.19b**).

The first response class is similar to what would be expected of neurons coding prediction errors; the second, to what would be expected of neurons signaling things that require attention. Interestingly, the valence neurons were located more ventromedially in the substantia nigra and VTA, in areas that project to the ventral striatum and are part of a network involving orbitofrontal cortex. In contrast, the neurons excited by salience were located more dorsolaterally in the substantia nigra, in regions with projections to the dorsal striatum and a network of cortical areas associated with the control of action and orientation.

We can see that when damage occurs within the dopamine system, or when downstream structures in the cortex are compromised, control problems will be reflected in behavioral changes related to motivation, learning, reward valuation, and emotion. These observations bring us back to how frontal lobe control systems are at work in both decision-making and goal-oriented behavior.

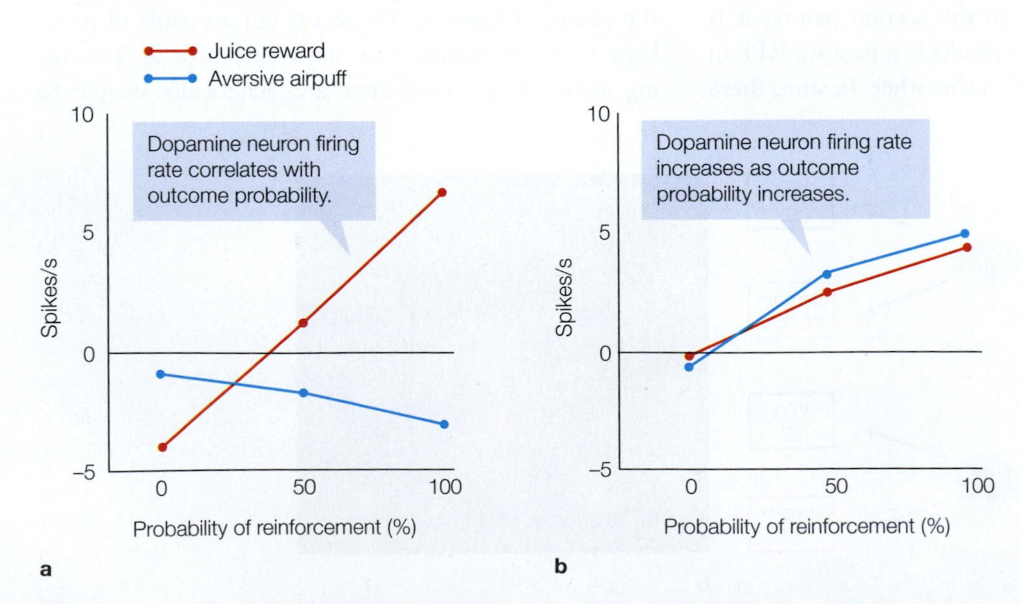

FIGURE 12.19 Two classes of dopamine neurons.
(a) Response profile of DA neurons that code valence. These neurons increase their firing rate as the probability of a positive outcome increases and decrease their firing rate as the probability of a negative outcome increases. **(b)** Response profile of DA neurons coding salience. These neurons increase their firing rate as reinforcement probability increases, independent of whether the reinforcement is positive or negative, signaling that the stimulus is important (or predictive).

TAKE-HOME MESSAGES

- A decision involves the selection of one option among several. It typically involves an evaluation of the expected outcome (reward) associated with each option.
- The subjective value of an item is made up of multiple variables that include payoff amount, context, probability, effort/cost, temporal discounting, novelty, and preference.
- Single-cell recordings in monkeys and fMRI studies in humans have implicated frontal regions, including the orbitofrontal cortex, in value representation.
- Reward prediction error (RPE) is the difference between the expected reward and what is actually obtained. The RPE is used as a learning signal to update value information as expectancies and the valence of rewards change. The activity of some DA neurons provides a neuronal code of prediction errors.
- DA neurons also appear to code other variables that may be important for goal-oriented behavior and decision making, such as signaling the salience of information in the environment.

12.5 Goal Planning: Staying on Task

Once humans choose a goal, we have to figure out how to accomplish it. We usually make a plan in which we organize and prioritize our actions. Patients with prefrontal lesions, like W.R., often exhibit poor planning and prioritizing skills. Three components are essential for successfully developing and executing an action plan (Duncan, 1995).

1. The goal must be identified and subgoals developed. For instance, in preparing for an exam, a conscientious student develops an action plan like the one in **Figure 12.20**. This plan can be represented as a hierarchy of subgoals, each requiring actions to achieve the goal: Reading must be completed, lecture notes reviewed, and material integrated to identify themes and facts.
2. In choosing among goals and subgoals, consequences must be anticipated. Would the information be remembered better if the student set aside an hour a day to study during the week preceding the exam, or would it be better to cram intensively the night before?
3. Requirements for achieving the subgoals must be determined. The student must find a place to study. The coffee supply must be adequately stocked.

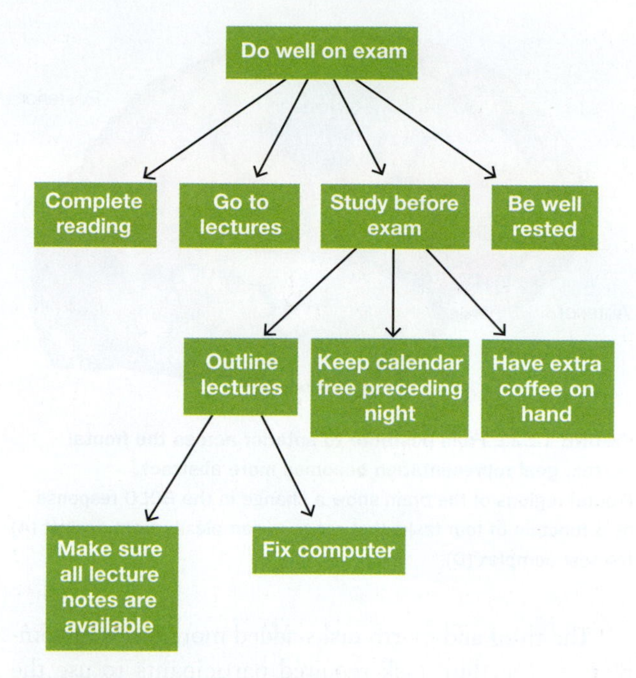

FIGURE 12.20 Action hierarchy.
Successfully achieving a complex goal such as doing well on an exam requires planning and organization at multiple levels of behavior.

It is easy to see that these components are not entirely separate. Purchasing coffee, for example, can be an action and a goal.

When an action plan is viewed as a hierarchical representation, it is easy to see that failure to achieve a goal can happen in many ways. In the example illustrated in Figure 12.20, if reading is not completed, the student may lack knowledge essential for an exam. If a friend arrives unannounced the weekend before the exam, critical study time can be lost. Likewise, the failures of goal-oriented behavior in patients with prefrontal lesions can be traced to many potential sources. Problems can arise because of deficits in filtering irrelevant information, making it difficult to stay focused on the prize. Or the challenge may come in prioritizing information to help select the best way to achieve a particular goal or subgoal.

As discussed earlier, processing differences along the anterior–posterior gradient of the PFC can be described in terms of the level of abstraction of action goals. Consider an fMRI study in which participants completed a series of nested tasks that increased in complexity (Badre & D'Esposito, 2007). The simplest task manipulated *response competition* by varying the number of possible finger responses to a series of colored squares presented one at a time; the response was based on the color of the square, and there could be one, two, or four different responses (Level A). The feature task added another layer of complexity because the response was based on texture, and the colors indicated which response was associated with which texture (Level B).

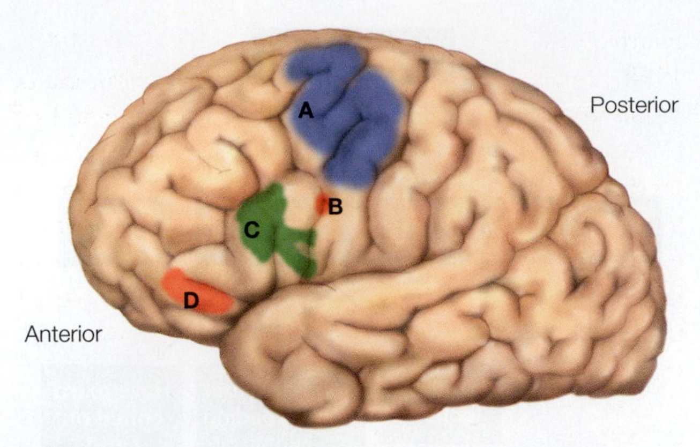

FIGURE 12.21 From posterior to anterior across the frontal cortex, goal representation becomes more abstract. Frontal regions of the brain show a change in the BOLD response as a function of four tasks that range in complexity from easiest (A) to most complex (D).

The third and fourth tasks added more levels of complexity. The third task required participants to use the colors to determine the relevant dimension on which to judge whether two stimuli matched—for example, red meant to judge the shape, and blue meant to judge the size (Level C). The fourth task was similar to the third, except the mapping between the colors and dimensions varied from block to block (Level D).

Consistent with the hierarchical gradient hypothesis, more anterior regions of the PFC were recruited as the task became more complex (**Figure 12.21**). Frontal activation was restricted to premotor regions for the two simplest tasks: where the response was based on just color (Level A), or when the color cued the participant to evaluate a single stimulus (Level B). When the participant had to use color to select the appropriate dimension to compare two stimuli, the activation center shifted to more anterior regions of the prefrontal cortex (Level C), and it extended to the frontal pole if the color dimension mapping varied across blocks (Level D).

It might be supposed that, rather than reflecting a hierarchy, the different activation patterns show that different subregions of the PFC are required for things like response selection or rule specification. A key idea of hierarchy, however, is that processing deficits will be asymmetrical. Individuals who fail at operations required for performance at the lower levels of a hierarchy will also fail when given more challenging tasks. In contrast, individuals who fail at tasks that require the highest levels should still be able to perform tasks that depend only on lower levels. This behavior is indeed what is observed in patients with PFC damage (Badre et al., 2009). Patients whose lesions were restricted to the most anterior regions performed similarly to controls on the first and second task conditions. Patients with more posterior lesions, those centered in premotor cortex, were impaired on all of the tasks.

A clever demonstration of the importance of the frontal lobes in this hierarchical evaluation process captured the real-world problems faced by patients with penetrating head injuries (Goel et al., 1997). The patients were asked to help plan the family budget for a couple having trouble living within their means. The patients understood the overriding need to identify places where savings could be achieved, and they could appreciate the need to budget. Their solutions did not always seem reasonable, however. For instance, instead of eliminating optional expenditures, one patient focused on the family's rent. Noting that the $10,800 yearly expense for rent was by far the biggest expense in the family budget, he proposed that it be eliminated. When the experimenter pointed out that the family would need a place to live, the patient didn't waver from his assessment and was quick with an answer: "Yes. Course I know a place that sells tents cheap. You can buy one of those."

By focusing on the housing costs, the patient also demonstrated some inflexibility in his decision. The large price tag assigned to rent was a particularly salient piece of information, and the patient's budgeting efforts were focused on the potential savings to be found here. From a strictly monetary perspective, this decision made sense. But at a practical level, we realize the inappropriateness of this choice.

Making wise decisions with complex matters, such as long-term financial goals, requires keeping an eye on the overall picture. To succeed in this kind of activity, we must monitor and evaluate the different subgoals. An essential feature of cognitive control is the ability to shift our focus from one subgoal to another. Complex actions require that we maintain our current goal, focus on the information that is relevant to achieving that goal, ignore irrelevant information, and, when appropriate, shift from one subgoal to another in a coordinated manner.

Retrieval and Selection of Task-Relevant Information

Goal-oriented behavior requires selecting task-relevant information and filtering out task-irrelevant information. Here, *selection* refers to the ability to focus attention on perceptual features or information in memory. This selection process is a cardinal feature of tasks associated with the lateral prefrontal cortex, highlighting its role in working memory and attention.

Suppose you are telling a friend about walking across the Golden Gate Bridge during a recent trip to San Francisco (**Figure 12.22**). The conversation will

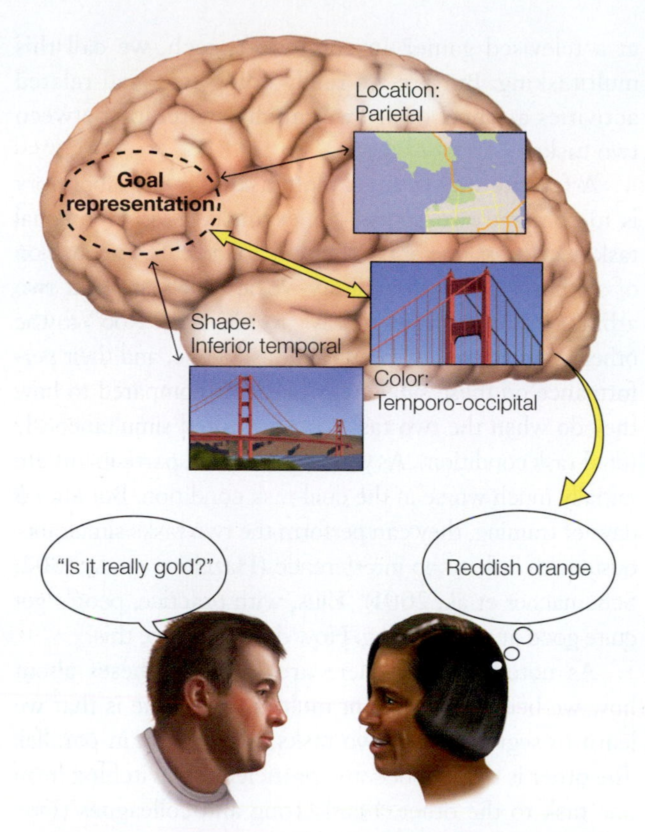

FIGURE 12.22 Prefrontal cortex as a filtering mechanism in the retrieval and maintenance of task-relevant information.
When the person is asked about the color of the Golden Gate Bridge (the task goal), links to memory of the color of the bridge are amplified, while links to memory of the location and shape of the bridge are inhibited.

have activated semantic information from your long-term memory about the location, shape, and color of the bridge, as well as episodic information related to your trip. These representations constitute the contents of working memory. If your friend then asks you about the color of the bridge, you must be able to focus on your memory of its color.

This example demonstrates that working memory is more than the passive sustaining of representations. It also requires an attentional component in which the participant's goals modify the salience of different sources of information. To capture this idea, the PFC has been conceptualized as a **dynamic filtering** mechanism (Shimamura, 2000). Reciprocal projections between the PFC and posterior cortex provide a way for goals, represented in the PFC, to maintain task-relevant information that requires long-term knowledge stored in posterior cortex. As the goals shift—say, from recalling the walk across the bridge to remembering the color of the bridge—the filtering process will make salient links to representations associated with the color.

The contribution of the prefrontal cortex to selection is evident in a series of elegant experiments conducted by Sharon Thompson-Schill (Thompson-Schill et al., 1997, 1998). In early PET studies on language, experimenters found that when participants were given a noun and had to generate a semantically associated word, a prominent increase in activation was observed in the inferior frontal gyrus of the left hemisphere. Thompson-Schill hypothesized that this prefrontal activation reflected filtering of the transient representations (the semantic associates of the target item) as they were being retrieved from long-term memory.

To test this hypothesis, the researchers conducted an fMRI study in which they varied the demands on a filtering process during a verb generation task. In the low-filtering condition, each noun was associated with a single verb. For example, when asked to name the action that goes with scissors, almost everyone will respond "cut," and thus there is no need to filter out competing alternative responses. In the high-filtering condition, however, each noun had several possible associates. For example, for the noun *rope*, multiple answers are reasonable, including *tie*, *lasso*, and *twirl*. Here, a filtering process is required to ensure that one answer is selected.

Note that, in both the low- and high-filtering conditions, the demands on semantic memory are similar. The participant must comprehend the target noun and retrieve semantic information associated with that noun. If a region is involved in the active retrieval of goal-related information, however, then activation should be greater in the high-filtering condition. This pattern was observed in the left inferior frontal cortex (**Figure 12.23**).

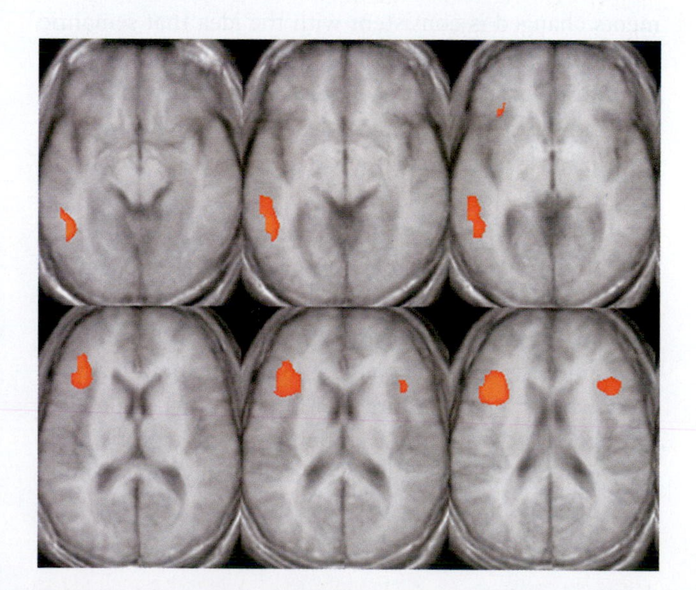

FIGURE 12.23 Involvement of inferior frontal cortex in memory retrieval and response selection.
These scans are a series of axial slices through the inferior frontal cortex. The red areas show higher activity during the high-filtering condition of a verb generation task.

The demanding version of the verb generation task also was associated with an increased BOLD response in the left temporal lobe. As we learned in Chapter 9, this area is hypothesized to be an important component of semantic memory. Indeed, the results of a follow-up study support this hypothesis (Thompson-Schill et al., 1999). Participants were trained to make two types of generation response—one based on naming an action associated with the noun, and another based on naming the color associated with the noun. The initial scanning run revealed a replication of the prefrontal and temporal cortical engagement during the generation tasks, demonstrating that the same inferior frontal region was recruited for both types of semantic associations.

Of special interest, however, was what happened in later scanning runs. The list of nouns was repeated. In one condition, participants performed the same generation task as in the first run; in the other, they were required to perform the alternative generation task of naming a color. This manipulation led to an interesting dissociation between the BOLD response in the prefrontal and temporal cortices. Prefrontal activation increased in scanning runs in which the generation requirements changed. Selection and filtering likely would be high under such conditions.

A different pattern was seen in the temporal lobe. Here the activation decreased on the second run for both the same and the different generation conditions. Such decreases with repetition have been seen in many imaging studies of priming (see Chapter 9). The fact that the decrease was observed even when the generation requirements changed is consistent with the idea that semantic attributes, whether relevant or irrelevant to the task at hand, are automatically activated upon presentation of the nouns. The prefrontal cortex applies a dynamic filter to help retrieve and select information that is relevant to the current task requirements.

The loss of dynamic filtering captures an essential feature of prefrontal damage. The patients' basic cognitive capabilities are generally spared, their intelligence shows little evidence of change, and they can perform normally on many tests of psychological function. In an environment where multiple sources of information compete for attention, however, these patients are in a particularly vulnerable condition: They have difficulty maintaining their focus on a goal.

Multitasking

While you are reading this chapter, are you occasionally shifting your attention to reading e-mail, texting friends, surfing the Web, listening to music, or glancing at a televised game? In common speech, we call this multitasking. But are we really doing two goal-related activities at once, or are we rapidly switching between two tasks?

A favorite way to study multitasking in the laboratory is to combine two tasks—for example, a visual–manual task (e.g., press one of two buttons to indicate the position of a stimulus) and an auditory–vocal task (e.g., hear two arbitrary sounds and say "Tay" to one and "Koo" to the other). People are tested on each task alone, and their performance on these single-task blocks is compared to how they do when the two tasks are presented simultaneously (dual-task condition). As you might expect, participants are initially much worse in the dual-task condition. But after 5 days of training, they can perform the two tasks simultaneously with little to no interference (Hazeltine et al., 2002; Schumacher et al., 2001). Thus, with practice, people get quite good at multitasking. How do we achieve this?

As noted already, there are two hypotheses about how we become proficient multitaskers. One is that we learn to segregate the two tasks, doing each in parallel. The other is that we become proficient in switching from one task to the other. Frank Tong and colleagues (Dux et al., 2009) conducted an innovative fMRI study, scanning participants repeatedly over a 2-week period as they practiced simultaneously performing the visual–manual and auditory–vocal tasks. As expected, the participants become much faster with training, reaching reaction time levels similar to those of single-task conditions, with no loss in accuracy.

At the same time, the BOLD response in the inferior, lateral aspect of prefrontal cortex became weaker over the scanning sessions. However, the connectivity data revealed a different picture. This region remained strongly connected with both auditory cortex and visual cortex, and it showed increased connectivity with two regions of motor cortex—one associated with manual responses, and the other with vocal responses (**Figure 12.24**). Moreover, as training continued, the peak of the frontal response came earlier and was of shorter duration—evidence that the participants were becoming more efficient in switching.

This study suggests that the term *multitasking* may be a misnomer: What we really do is alternate between tasks, and with practice we can become quite proficient in task switching (or so we tell ourselves).

The Benefits and Costs of Goal-Based Selection

You are given a candle, a box of matches, and some thumbtacks. Your task is to fix the candle to the wall and light it. How would you do it?

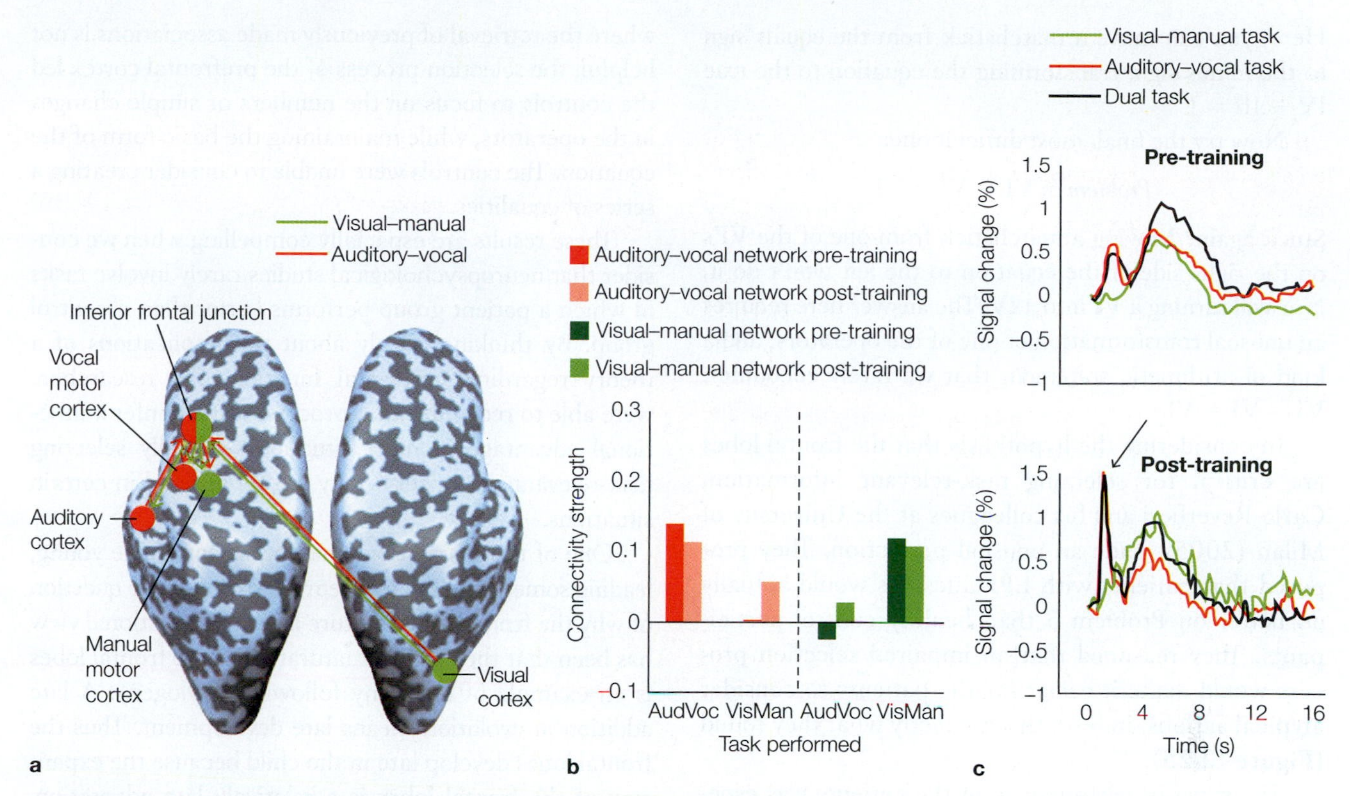

FIGURE 12.24 Functional connectivity of control network with practice in multitasking.
(a) Functional connectivity between prefrontal cortex and perceptual-motor areas for a visual–manual task (green) or an auditory–vocal task (red). (b) Connectivity strength before and after 2 weeks of multitasking training. Connectivity was strong in a task-specific manner and showed little change, even though the participants became extremely proficient in performing the two tasks simultaneously. (c) Activity in the prefrontal cortex remained high and shifted to an earlier latency after training in the dual-task condition (arrow), suggesting persistent cognitive control.

Perhaps you solved this rather quickly: Simply take a thumbtack, stick it through the candle and into the wall, and then light the candle. Not so fast! The diameter of the candle is much thicker than the length of the thumbtack. Take another shot.

Stumped? Don't be discouraged—thousands of students have been mystified by this brainteaser since Rainer Dunker introduced it in his monograph on problem solving in 1945 (cited in Wickelgren, 1974). Here's a hint: Suppose there is only one match, and it sits on the table outside the matchbox. Now give it another go.

When the problem is presented in this format, many people experience an "aha" moment. They suddenly realize that the matchbox can serve more than one purpose. In addition to providing a striker for the matches, it can be used as a crude candlestick. Tack the box to the wall with the thumbtacks, light the candle and let some wax drip into the box, and then set the candle in the melted wax so that when the drippings cool, the candle will be secure in an upright position.

Problems like this one are challenging because the stimuli trigger the retrieval of previously made associations. Thus, in developing an action plan, our experience can lead us to think narrowly about the possible uses of an object. We immediately think of the matchbox's common use—to light matches—and then, having made use of it, mull over how those thumbtacks can be applied to the candle. By emptying the box of matches, we might realize new possibilities; but even here, many people continue to be unable to see novel uses, because of the strong association between the stimulus, the match, and a particular action, striking.

Try loosening up your associations with another brainteaser: Here is a false arithmetic statement in Roman numerals, represented by matchsticks (think of each straight line—vertical, horizontal, or diagonal—as a single matchstick):

Problem 1: VI = VII + I

Provide a correct solution by moving only one stick. Not too hard. Moving one of the I's from the VII to the VI renders a true statement: VII = VI + I.

Now try a problem that, with the one-move rule, is a bit more difficult:

Problem 2: IV = III − I

Here, you can move a matchstick from the equals sign to the minus sign, transforming the equation to the true IV − III = I.

Now try the final, most difficult one:

Problem 3: VI = VI + VI

Stuck again? Moving a matchstick from one of the VI's on the right side of the equation to the left won't do it. Nor will turning a VI into a IV. The answer here requires an unusual transformation of one of the operators, and a kind of arithmetic statement that we rarely encounter: VI = VI = VI.

In considering the hypothesis that the frontal lobes are critical for selecting task-relevant information, Carlo Reverberi and his colleagues at the University of Milan (2005) made an unusual prediction. They proposed that patients with LPFC lesions would actually do better on Problem 3 than healthy control participants. They reasoned that an impaired selection process would make it easier for the patients to consider atypical actions. Indeed, this is exactly what they found (**Figure 12.25**).

The superior performance of the patients was especially striking, given that these individuals were worse than the controls when presented with equations like those in Problem 2, which required standard operator transformations such as swapping the equals and minus signs with the movement of one matchstick. Here the patients' impairment became greater as the number of possible moves increased, consistent with the idea that the LPFC is especially critical when the response space must be narrowed. But for equations like Problem 3, where the retrieval of previously made associations is not helpful, the selection process of the prefrontal cortex led the controls to focus on the numbers or simple changes in the operators, while maintaining the basic form of the equation. The controls were unable to consider creating a series of equalities.

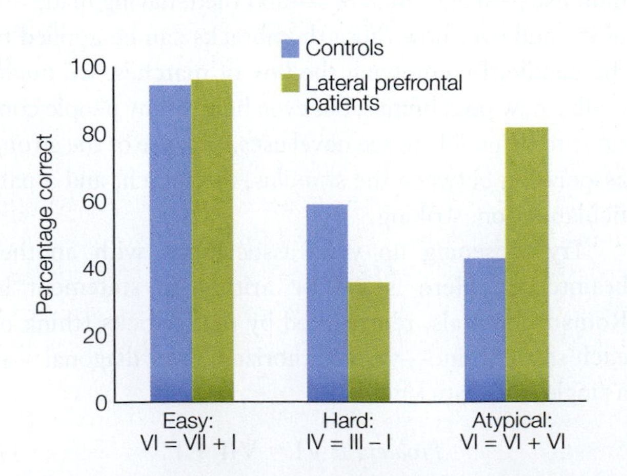

FIGURE 12.25 Patients with lateral prefrontal lesions do better than healthy control participants on a problem-solving task that requires unusual solutions.
For the easy and hard conditions, the solution requires moving a matchstick from one side of the equation to the other to transform a numeral or the operators. For the atypical condition, the solution requires rotating a matchstick to create a three-part equality.

These results are especially compelling when we consider that neuropsychological studies rarely involve tasks in which a patient group performs better than a control group. By thinking deeply about the implications of a theory regarding prefrontal function, the researchers were able to recognize that processes that confer a functional advantage in most situations—rapidly selecting task-relevant responses—may not be optimal in certain situations.

One of those situations may be when we are young, leading some evolutionary theorists to revisit the question of why the frontal lobes mature late. The traditional view has been that the delayed maturation of the frontal lobes is an example of ontogeny following phylogeny: A late addition in evolution means late development. Thus the frontal lobes develop late in the child because the expansion of the frontal lobes is a relatively late adaptation. This point of view leads one to focus on the costs of not having a mature frontal lobe. Children have a hard time engaging in delayed gratification, maintaining focus, and inhibiting behavior.

Yet we can also ask whether there are advantages to this "delay" in development. One hypothesis is that an immature frontal lobe might make people more open-minded, perhaps because they don't have strong response associations to environmental cues or well-established value representations. Such properties are good for learning: The child does not respond to a situation in a predictable manner, but rather is open to recognizing new contingencies. Linda Wilbrecht and her colleagues looked at this idea in mice (C. Johnson & Wilbrecht, 2011). They trained juvenile and adult mice to discriminate among four odors, learning that one of the odors was associated with a reward. After a number of trials, the odor–reward pairs were changed. The juvenile mice learned more quickly than the adult mice—a result reminiscent of the novel problem-solving abilities of patients with frontal lobe damage.

TAKE-HOME MESSAGES

- Successful execution of an action plan involves three components: (1) identifying the goal and developing subgoals, (2) anticipating consequences when choosing among goals, and (3) determining what is required to achieve the goals.

- Goal-oriented behavior requires the retrieval and selection of task-relevant information. The prefrontal cortex can be conceptualized as a dynamic filtering mechanism through which the task-relevant information is activated and maintained in working memory.
- Cognitive control is also essential when we need to maintain multiple goals at the same time, especially when those goals are unrelated. With practice, the brain develops connectivity patterns that enable people to efficiently shift between different goals.
- Through the selection of task-relevant information, the prefrontal cortex helps make action selection more efficient. This benefit of using experience to guide action selection may also come at a cost in terms of considering novel ways to act, given a specific situation.

12.6 Mechanisms of Goal-Based Selection

Dynamic filtering could influence the contents of information processing in at least two distinct ways. One is to accentuate the attended information. For example, when we attend to a location, our sensitivity to detect a stimulus at that location is enhanced. Alternatively, we can selectively attend by excluding information from other locations. Similarly, when multiple sources of information come from the same location, we might selectively enhance the task-relevant information (color in the Stroop test) or inhibit the irrelevant information (the word in the Stroop test).

In behavioral tasks, it is often difficult to distinguish between facilitatory and inhibitory modes of control. Moreover, as seen in times of budgetary crises, the hypotheses are not mutually exclusive. If we have fixed resources, allocating resources to one thing places a limit on what is available for others; thus, the form of goal-based control may vary as a function of task demands.

Evidence for a loss of **inhibitory control** with frontal lobe dysfunction comes from electrophysiological studies. Robert Knight and colleagues recorded the evoked potentials in groups of patients with localized neurological disorders (reviewed in R. T. Knight & Grabowecky, 1995). In the simplest experiment, participants were presented with tones, and no response was required. As might be expected, the evoked responses were attenuated in patients with lesions in the temporoparietal cortex in comparison to control participants (**Figure 12.26a**, middle). This difference was apparent about 30 ms after stimulus onset, the time when stimuli would be expected to reach the primary auditory cortex. The attenuation presumably reflects tissue loss in the region that generates the evoked signal.

A more curious aspect is shown in the bottom panel of Figure 12.26a: Patients with frontal lobe lesions have *enhanced* evoked responses. This enhancement was not seen in the evoked responses at subcortical levels. The effect did not reflect a generalized increase in sensory responsiveness, but was limited to the cortex.

The failure to inhibit irrelevant information was more apparent when the participants were instructed to attend to auditory signals in one ear and ignore similar sounds in the opposite ear, when signals in the attended ear varied between blocks (**Figure 12.26b**). This experimental design enabled researchers to assess the evoked response to identical stimuli under different attentional sets (e.g., response to left-ear sounds when they are attended or ignored).

With healthy participants, these responses diverged at about 100 ms; the evoked response to the attended signal became greater. This difference was *absent* in patients with prefrontal lesions, especially for stimuli presented to the ear contralateral to the lesion (e.g., the left ear for a patient with a lesion in right-hemisphere prefrontal cortex). What happens is that the unattended stimulus produces a heightened response. This result is consistent with the hypothesis that the frontal lobes modulate the salience of perceptual signals by inhibiting unattended information.

In the study just described, we can see inhibition operating to minimize the impact of irrelevant perceptual information. This same mechanism can be applied to memory tasks for which information must be internally maintained. Consider the monkey attempting to perform the spatial delayed-response task we saw in Figure 12.2. After the monkey views the target being placed in one of the food wells, the blind is closed during the delay period. The monkey's mind does not just shut down; the animal sees and hears the blind being drawn, looks about the room during the delay interval, and perhaps contemplates its hunger. These intervening events likely distract the animal and cause it to lose track of which location was baited.

We have all experienced failures in similar situations. We put our keys down, but we forget where. The problem is not that we fail to encode the location, but that something else captures our attention and we fail to block out the distraction. This point is underscored by the finding that primates with prefrontal lesions perform better on delayed-response tasks when the room is darkened during the delay (Malmo, 1942) or when they are given drugs that decrease distractibility.

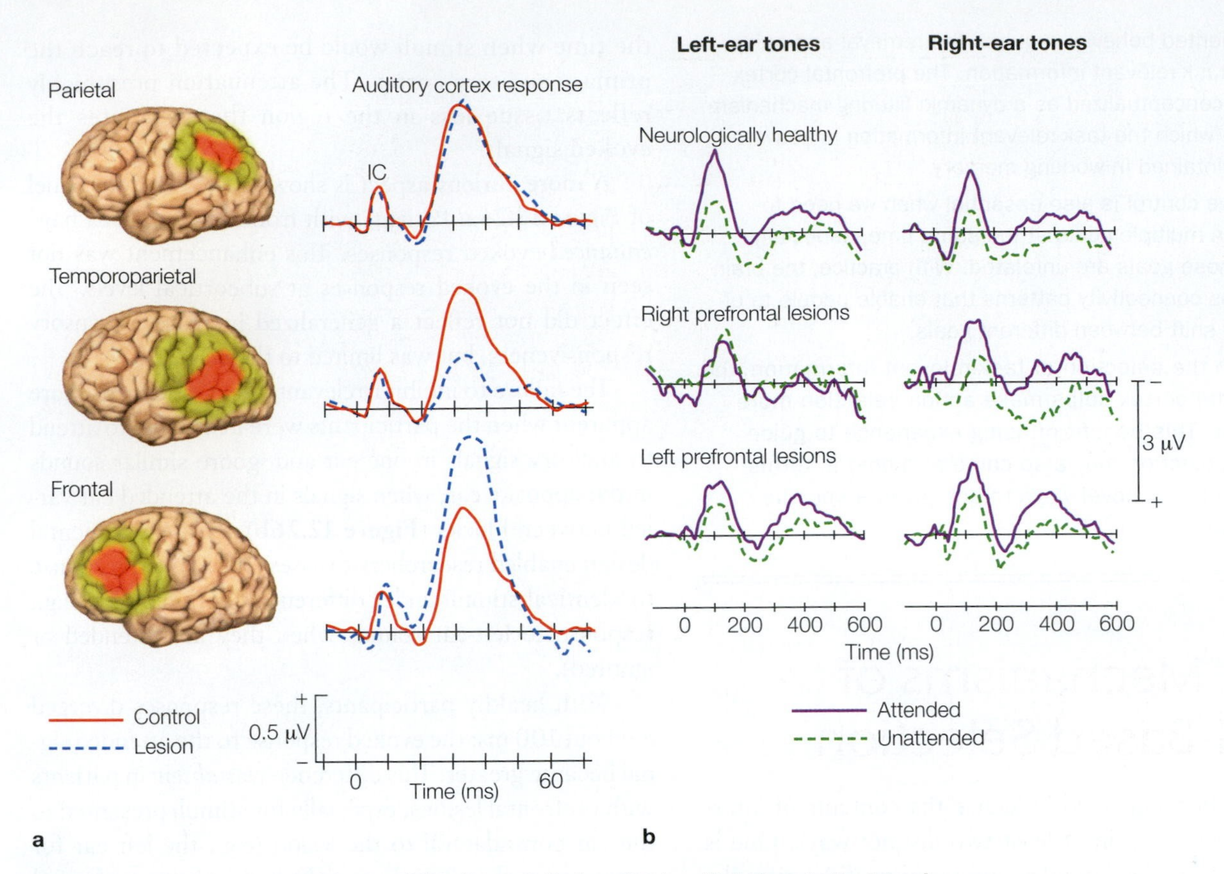

FIGURE 12.26 Evoked potentials reveal filtering deficits in patients with lesions in the lateral prefrontal cortex.
(a) Evoked responses to auditory clicks in three groups of neurological patients. The participants were not required to respond to the clicks. Note that in these ERPs, the positive voltage is above the x-axis. The first positive peak occurs at about 8 ms and reflects neural activity in the inferior colliculus (IC). The second positive peak occurs at about 30 ms (the P30), reflecting neural responses in the primary auditory cortex. Both responses are normal in patients with parietal damage (top). The second peak is reduced in patients with temporoparietal damage (middle), reflecting the loss of neurons in the primary auditory cortex. The auditory cortex response is amplified in patients with frontal damage (bottom), suggesting a loss of inhibition from frontal lobe to temporal lobe. For clarity, the evoked response for control participants is repeated in each panel. **(b)** Difference waves for attended and unattended auditory signals. Participants were instructed to monitor tones in either the left or the right ear. The evoked response to the unattended tones is subtracted from the evoked response to the attended tones. In healthy individuals, the effects of attention are seen at approximately 100 ms, marked by a larger negativity (N100). Patients with right prefrontal lesions show no attention effect for contralesional tones presented in the left ear but show a normal effect for ipsilesional tones. Patients with left prefrontal lesions show reduced attention effects for both contralateral and ipsilateral tones.

The preceding discussion emphasizes how goal-based control might be achieved by the inhibition of task-irrelevant information. Mark D'Esposito and his colleagues (Druzgal & D'Esposito, 2003) used fMRI to further explore interactions between prefrontal cortex and posterior cortex. In a series of experiments, they exploited the fact that regions in the inferior temporal lobe are preferentially activated by face and place stimuli—the so-called FFA (fusiform face area) and PPA (parahippocampal place area), respectively (see Chapter 6).

The researchers asked whether activation in these regions is modulated when people are given the task goal of remembering either faces or places for a subsequent memory test (**Figure 12.27a**). At the start of each trial, an instruction cue indicated the current task. Then a set of four pictures was presented that included two faces and two scenes. As expected, a subsequent memory test verified that the participants had selectively attended to the relevant dimension.

More interesting was the finding that activation in the FFA and PPA was modulated in different ways by the

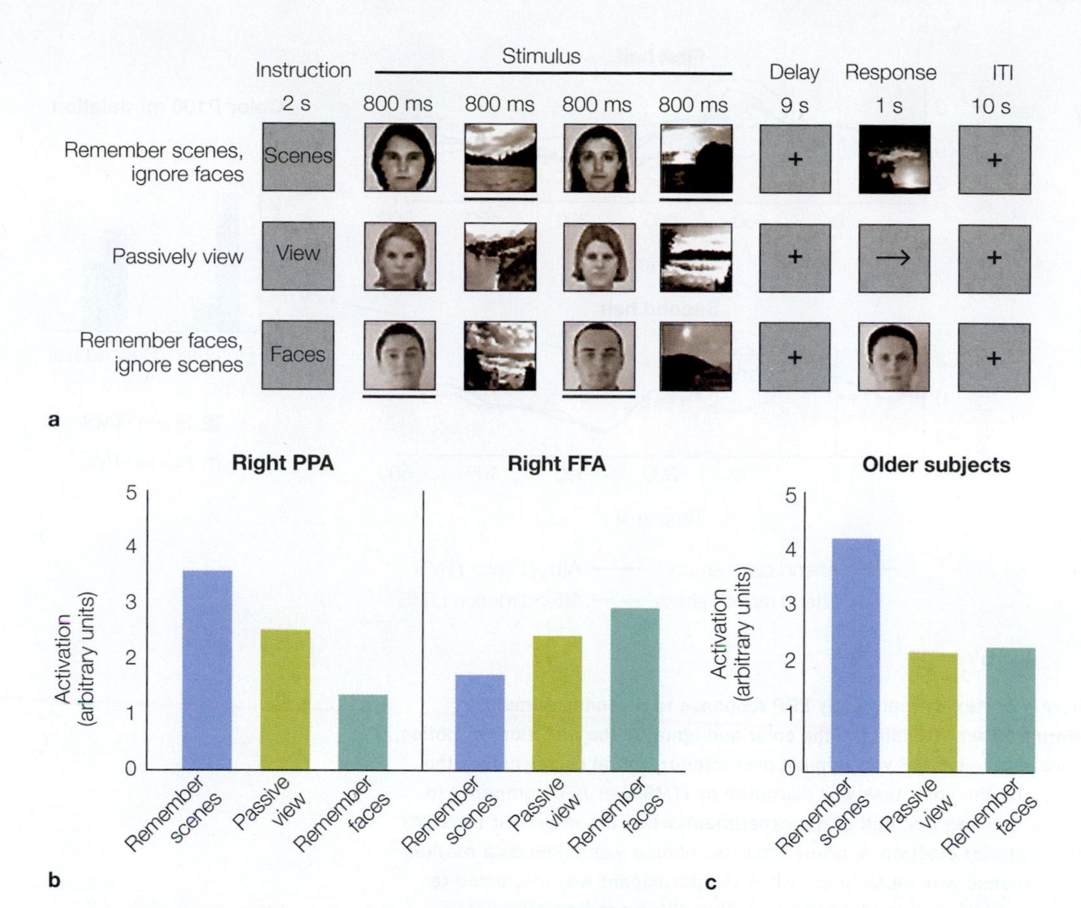

FIGURE 12.27 Modulation in posterior cortex as a function of task goals.
(a) In a delayed-response task, participants had to remember either faces or scenes. **(b)** Compared to a passive-viewing control condition, activation in the parahippocampal place area (PPA) was greater when participants attended to scenes and reduced when participants attended to faces. The reverse effect was observed in the fusiform face area (FFA). **(c)** Within the PPA region of interest, older participants also showed an increase in the BOLD response when attending to scenes. This response was not suppressed in the attend-faces condition, however, suggesting a selective age-related decline in inhibition.

instruction cues (**Figure 12.27b**), showing both enhancement and suppression effects. Compared to the passive-viewing condition (control), the response in the FFA of the right hemisphere was greater when the participants were instructed to remember the faces and smaller when the participants were instructed to remember the scenes. The reverse pattern was evident in the PPA, and here the effect was seen in both hemispheres. This study reveals that the task goal, specified by the instruction, can modulate perceptual processing by either amplifying task-relevant information or inhibiting task-irrelevant information.

In an interesting extension, the experiment was repeated, but this time the participants were older, neurologically healthy individuals (Gazzaley, Cooney, Rissman, et al., 2005). Unlike college-age participants, the older participants showed only an enhancement effect; they did not show the suppression effect in either FFA or PPA when results were compared to the passive-viewing condition (**Figure 12.27c**).

These findings are intriguing for two reasons. First, they suggest that enhancement (i.e., amplification) and suppression (i.e., inhibition) involve different neural mechanisms, and that inhibition is more sensitive to the effects of aging. Second, given that aging is thought to disproportionately affect prefrontal function, perhaps inhibitory goal-based control is more dependent on prefrontal cortex than are the attentional mechanisms that underlie the amplification of task-relevant information.

Prefrontal Cortex and Modulation of Processing

The work just described reveals that the task goal, specified by the instruction, can modulate perceptual processing by either amplifying task-relevant information or inhibiting task-irrelevant information. The data do not reveal, however, whether this modulation is the result of prefrontal activation. To explore this question, researchers applied TMS over prefrontal cortex and then asked how this perturbation affects processing in posterior perceptual areas. In one study, repetitive TMS (rTMS)

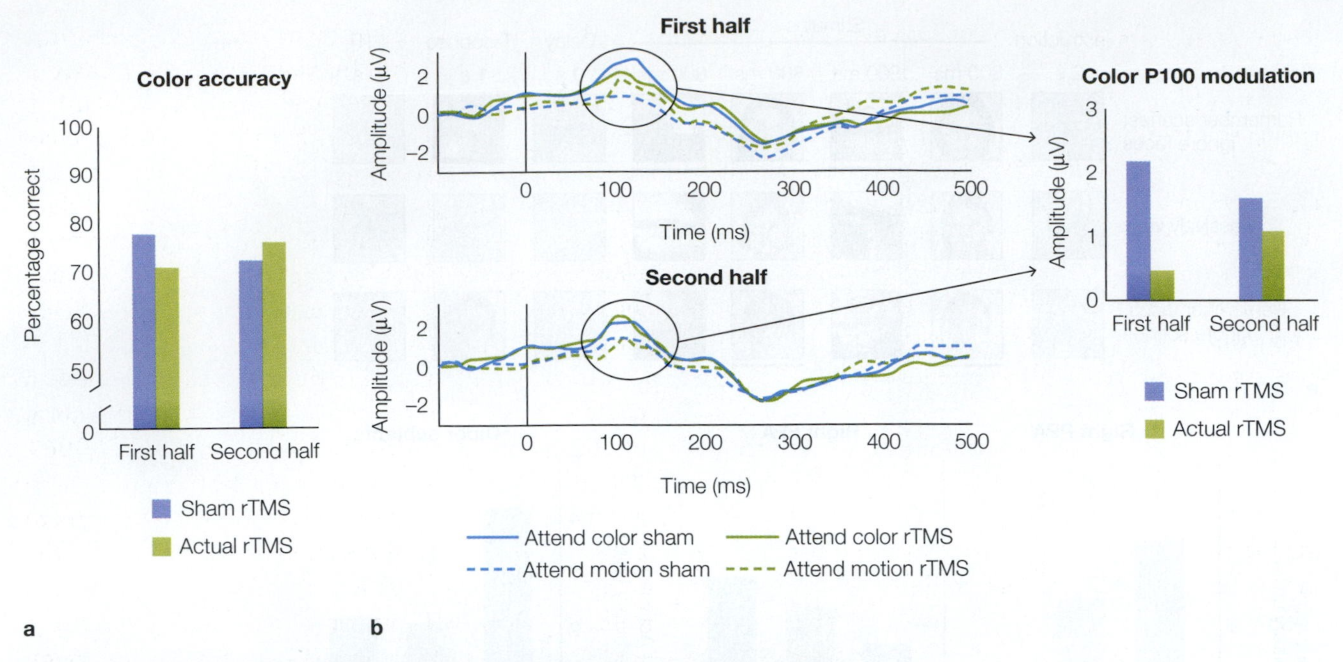

FIGURE 12.28 rTMS of prefrontal cortex disrupts early ERP response to attended stimuli. Participants viewed visual stimuli, either attending to the color and ignoring the direction of motion, or vice versa. Through an offline method, rTMS was applied over inferior frontal cortex before the experiment started. **(a)** Accuracy on the color task was disrupted by rTMS over PFC compared to sham rTMS. This effect lasted for only the first half of the experiment, when the effects of the rTMS were strongest. **(b)** ERPs from posterior electrodes, where P100 amplitude was taken as a marker of color processing. The P100 response was much larger when the participant was instructed to attend to color (solid lines) compared to motion (dashed lines). This difference was attenuated following rTMS, especially in the first half of the test session. Bar graphs indicate the magnitude of attentional modulation.

was applied over inferior frontal cortex while participants were instructed to attend to either the color or the motion of a visual stimulus (Zanto et al., 2011). Not only was performance poorer after rTMS, but the difference between the P100 to the attended and the P100 to the ignored stimuli was reduced (**Figure 12.28**). This reduction occurred because after rTMS, the P100 was larger for the ignored stimuli.

In another study (Higo et al., 2011), participants received either low-frequency rTMS or sham stimulation over prefrontal cortex. Following this, fMRI scans were obtained while performing a task to attend to places, faces, or body parts. Depending on which stimulus was being attended, rTMS attenuated the modulation of category-specific responses in the posterior cortex. Moreover, the results indicated that the effects of frontal rTMS primarily disrupted the participants' ability to ignore irrelevant stimuli but had little effect on their ability to attend to relevant stimuli—a dissociation similar to the one we described for older participants (see Figure 12.27c).

In a related study, Eva Feredoes and Jon Driver (Feredoes et al., 2011) combined event-related TMS and fMRI during a working memory task, targeting dorsal prefrontal cortex. Unlike what has been reported for inferior frontal stimulation, TMS over dorsal PFC led to an increased BOLD response in task-relevant areas (e.g., increased FFA response when responding to faces) when distractors were present.

Let's take a moment to put together these different results. TMS over frontal cortex led to a change in processing within posterior cortex, consistent with the general idea that goal-based representations in prefrontal cortex are used to modulate how perceptual information is selectively filtered. Moreover, the results might be taken to suggest that inferior frontal cortex is important for inhibiting task-irrelevant information, and dorsal frontal cortex is important for enhancing task-relevant information.

This hypothesis, however, has a problem: It requires assuming that the effect of TMS in these studies was to disrupt processing when applied over inferior frontal cortex and to enhance processing when applied over dorsal frontal cortex. Although this effect is possible, especially since the TMS protocols were not identical in the different studies, it is also possible that disrupting one part of prefrontal cortex with TMS produces changes in other prefrontal regions. Perhaps TMS over dorsal PFC has a side effect of improving processing within inferior PFC.

If this hypothesis is correct, then the task-relevant enhancement observed in the Feredoes study is similar to what the other studies have shown. That is, TMS over inferior frontal cortex directly disrupts goal-based selection, while TMS over dorsal frontal cortex produces an indirect benefit in goal-based selection by increasing reliance on inferior frontal cortex. It may be that, neurally, competitive processes operate across our frontal gradients (e.g., dorsal–ventral). At present, we can only speculate on such hypotheses.

Inhibition of Action

Inhibitory control can take many forms. We have seen that failures of inhibition lead to greater distractibility, a hallmark of prefrontal dysfunction. Inhibition is useful for cognitive control in another circumstance: when we are about to take an action and something makes us change our mind. For instance, you are about to swing at a baseball when you see it is curving out of your reach. You suddenly realize that your selected response is not appropriate. In baseball parlance, a quick decision might enable you to "lay off the pitch" and abort the swing; if you've already committed to the action, you might quickly shut it down, hoping to "check the swing" before the bat crosses the plate.

This form of inhibition—the cancellation or rapid termination of a planned action—is actually quite common, even for those of us who never play baseball. At a party, we often find ourselves ready to jump in with a scintillating comment, only to find that the loudmouthed bore (who apparently is not so good at inhibition) has once again commandeered the conversation. Politely, we hold back, waiting for another opportunity.

Inhibition of this form can be seen as the opposite of selecting an action. Are the neural mechanisms the same? That is, to inhibit an action, do we *deselect* that action by generating some sort of negative image of the brain activation? Even if we could do this, it might not be enough to inhibit the unwanted action. The commands to produce the planned action have already been sent to the motor system, and simply deactivating the plan would not be enough to stop an initiated movement.

This form of inhibitory control has been studied with the *stop-signal task*. In the standard form of this experiment, participants are tested in a reaction time task in which they have to choose between two alternatives. For example, if an arrow points to the left, press one button; if to the right, another button. The twist is that, on some of the trials, a signal pops up indicating that the response should be aborted.

This stop signal might be a change in color or the presentation of a sound. The time between the onset of the initial stimulus and the stop signal can be adjusted, creating a situation in which the participant sometimes succeeds in aborting the planned response and sometimes fails to abort the response. Three conditions result: trials without a stop signal (go trials), trials in which the person is able to stop (successful stop trials), and trials in which the person fails to stop (failed stop trials; **Figure 12.29a**).

Adam Aron has employed a multimethod approach to describe the neural network underlying this form of cognitive control (A. R. Aron & Poldrack, 2006). Patients with lesions of the frontal lobe are slow to abort a planned response. This impairment appears to be specific to lesions of the inferior frontal gyrus on the right side, since the deficit is not present in patients with left frontal lesions or in patients with damage restricted to more dorsal parts of the right prefrontal cortex.

The association of the right prefrontal cortex with this form of inhibitory control is also supported by fMRI data obtained in young adults. Here the BOLD response can be plotted for each of the three trial types (**Figure 12.29b**, top). Successful stop trials and failed stop trials both produce a strong response in the right inferior frontal gyrus. In contrast, this area is silent on go trials. The fact that the BOLD signal is very similar for both types of stop trials suggests that an inhibitory process is recruited in both situations, even though the control signal to abort the response is effective on only some trials.

Why would both successful and failed stop trials produce similar activation of the inferior frontal cortex? The BOLD response in motor cortex is revealing (**Figure 12.29b**, bottom). Here we see strong activation on both go trials and failed stop trials. The activation in motor cortex on the failed stop trials is already high, however, when the initial stimulus is presented (time = 0). Note that the participants are under a lot of pressure in these experiments to go as fast as possible. This prestimulus activation likely reflects a high state of anticipation. Even though the right prefrontal cortex generates a stop command, the initial level of activation in motor cortex has led to a fast response, and the person is unable to abort the movement. For an antsy baseball player initially fooled by a curveball, it's strike three.

The right inferior frontal gyrus pattern of activation was also present in the subthalamic nucleus (STN) of the basal ganglia. As we saw in Chapter 8, the basal ganglia are implicated in response initiation. Within this subcortical system, the STN provides a strong excitatory signal to the globus pallidus, helping to maintain inhibition of the cortex. The stop-signal work

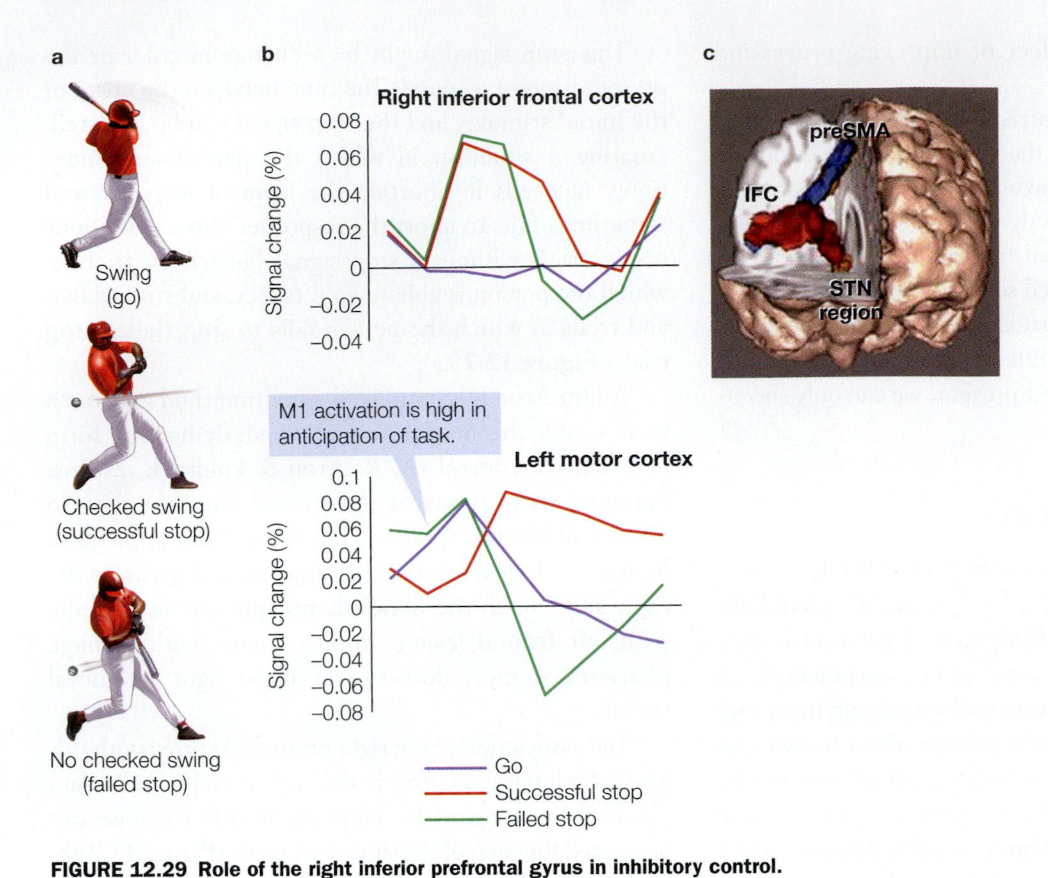

FIGURE 12.29 Role of the right inferior prefrontal gyrus in inhibitory control.
(a) Successful actions sometimes require the ability to abort a planned response. (b) BOLD response in motor cortex (M1) and right inferior frontal cortex (IFC) on trials in which a required response is performed (go), a planned response is successfully aborted (successful stop), or a planned response that should be aborted is erroneously executed (failed stop). The IFC responds on all stop trials, regardless of whether the person is able to abort the response. In M1, activation is high at the start of the trial on failed stop trials, likely reflecting a high state of anticipation in the motor system. (c) DTI reveals an anatomical network linking the IFC with presupplementary motor area (preSMA) and the subthalamic nucleus (STN) of the basal ganglia.

suggests how this inhibition might be recruited within the context of cognitive control. Activation of the right prefrontal cortex generates the command to abort a response, and this command is carried out through recruitment of the STN.

This hypothesis led Aron and his colleagues to predict the existence of an anatomical connection between the right prefrontal cortex and the STN (A. R. Aron et al., 2007). Using diffusion tensor imaging (DTI), the researchers confirmed this prediction (**Figure 12.29c**). With an elegant design motivated by behavioral and fMRI results, they uncovered an anatomical pathway that had never been described in the literature. This anatomical pathway includes the presupplementary motor area, a part of the medial frontal cortex. As we will see shortly, this region is activated in functional imaging studies when response conflict occurs—something that obviously happens in the stop-signal task.

Recall from Chapter 8 that deep brain stimulation (DBS) in the STN is used to treat Parkinson's disease, improving the patient's ability to initiate movement. Michael Frank and colleagues at Brown University (Frank et al., 2007) suggest that this procedure comes with a cost, one in which the person may become too impulsive because the stimulation disrupts a system for inhibitory control. To show this, they compared a group of control participants to Parkinson's disease patients who had DBS implants. The participants were initially trained with a limited set of stimulus pairs. Within each pair, the stimuli had a particular probability of winning a reward. For instance, as seen in **Figure 12.30**, Symbol A was associated with a reward 80% of the time and Symbol B with a reward 20% of the time. Thus, some stimuli had a high probability; others, a low probability.

During the test trials, the experimenter introduced new combinations of the stimuli. Some of these new pairs presented little conflict, because one item was much more likely than the other to lead to reward (e.g., if the pair included a stimulus with an 80% win probability and a stimulus with a 30% win probability). Other pairs entailed high conflict, either because both items

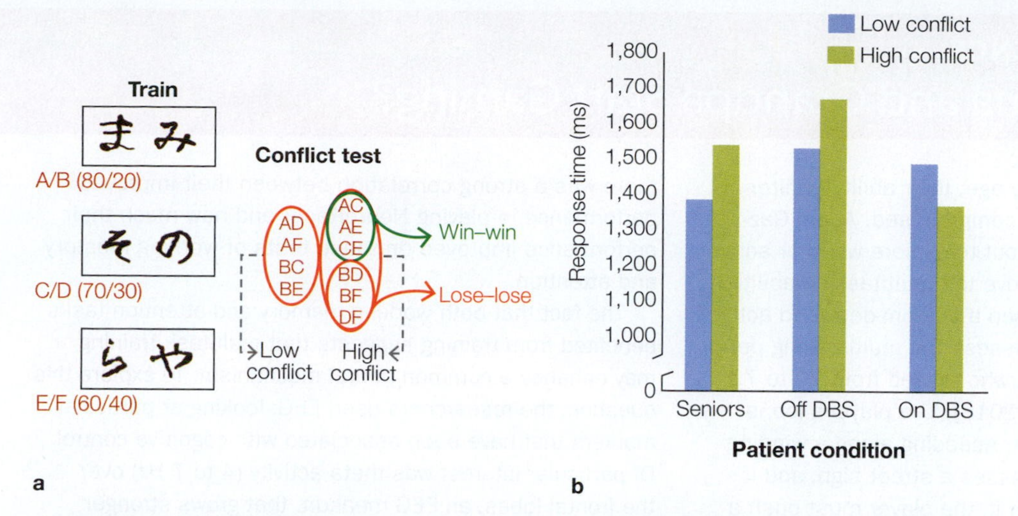

FIGURE 12.30 Loss of inhibitory control in Parkinson's patients following deep brain stimulation. (a) The participant selected one of two symbols on each trial. Feedback was provided after the response. Each symbol had a specific probability of reward (e.g., Symbol A had an 80% probability of reward, while Symbol B had only a 20% probability). During training, there were only three pairs (A and B, C and D, E and F). During the generalization test, untrained pairs were presented. The stimuli could be classified into low- and high-conflict pairs. Low-conflict pairs were defined as trials in which one member had a >50% chance of reward and the other had a <50% chance of reward. For high-conflict pairs, both stimuli had either >50% chance of reward (win–win) or <50% chance of reward (lose–lose). (b) Response times for older controls and Parkinson's patients, tested both off and on DBS. DBS not only reduced response times, but made the patients insensitive to the level of conflict.

were associated with high reward probabilities (70% and 60%), or both were associated with low reward probabilities (30% and 20%).

As expected, control participants were faster to respond on the low-conflict trials. The same pattern was observed for the patients with Parkinson's disease when tested with the stimulator turned off, even though their reaction times were slower. When the stimulator was turned on, the patients responded faster, but they were no longer sensitive to the conflict: They responded faster to the high-conflict trials, especially when they made the wrong choice. Thus, although DBS can help alleviate the motor symptoms of Parkinson's disease, it comes at the cost of increasing impulsivity.

Improving Cognitive Control Through Brain Training

Do older people fret when they catch you playing an action video game instead of reading your history assignment? If so, maybe they shouldn't. A growing body of evidence suggests that playing action video games may improve some aspects of cognitive function—in particular, tasks involving cognitive control and attention such as visual search, *n*-back tasks, and response inhibition (Dye, Green, et al., 2009). **Figure 12.31** summarizes the results over a number of studies, comparing

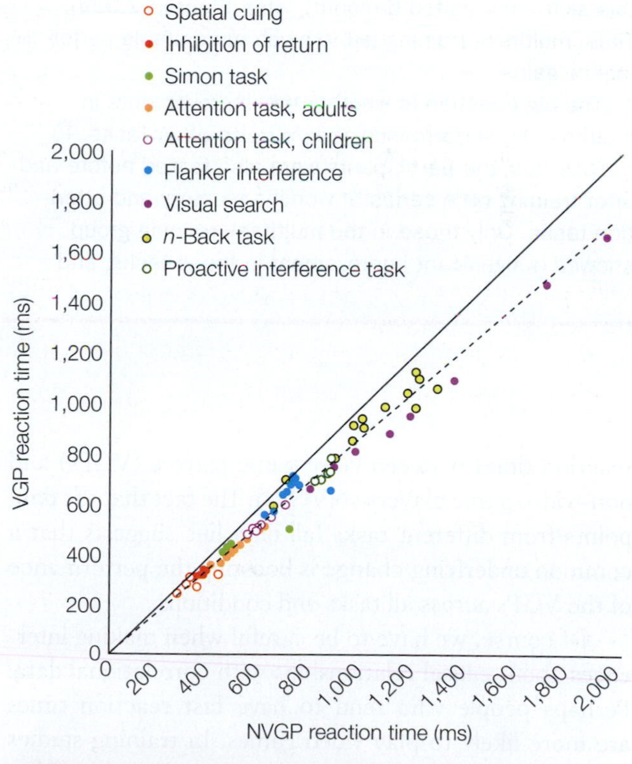

FIGURE 12.31 Expert video game players are faster than non-players on a range of cognitive tasks. This meta-analysis displays data from 89 different experimental conditions (taken from many studies) in which reaction time data were available for both experts (VGPs) and nonexperts (NVGPs). The solid black line shows where the data would be plotted if there were no difference in reaction time between the groups. Nearly all data fall below this line, indicating that video game players are faster on all tasks.

BOX 12.1 | HOT SCIENCE

Should Grandma and Grandpa Start Gaming?

We saw earlier that as people age, their ability to filter out task-irrelevant information is compromised. Adam Gazzaley and his lab have set about to explore whether active video game training can improve the multitasking abilities of older people. First, they used a custom-designed active video game, NeuroRacer, to assess the multitasking performance of the participants, who ranged from 20 to 79 years of age (Anguera et al., 2013). The player's job is to use a joystick to keep a car speeding along a winding road. On occasion, the car passes a street sign, and if the sign has a green circle on it, the player must push a button. As **Figure 12.32a** shows, performance declines with age.

Next, in a training study, older participants (aged 60–85) were assigned to three different conditions: no training, training on a single task (either driving alone or detecting green circles on signs alone), or multitask training. The training was limited to 1-hour sessions 3 days a week for a month. While the single-task and multitask training groups both showed improvement on NeuroRacer at the end of training, only the multitask group retained this skill when tested 6 months later (**Figure 12.32b**). Thus, multitask training led to much more stable performance gains.

The big question is whether the improvements in multitasking performance generalize to other tasks. To assess this, the participants were also tested before and after training on a series of working memory and attention tasks. Only those in the multitask training group showed a significant improvement in these tasks, and there was a strong correlation between their improved performance in playing NeuroRacer and how much their performance improved on these tests of working memory and attention.

The fact that both working memory and attention tasks benefited from training suggests that multitask training may enhance a common neural mechanism. To explore this question, the researchers used EEG, looking at particular markers that have been associated with cognitive control. Of particular interest was theta activity (4 to 7 Hz) over the frontal lobes, an EEG measure that grows stronger as people become engaged in a task. After training, the multitask training group showed a boost in the magnitude of frontal theta power, as well as in the correlation between frontal and posterior theta power, a measure of functional connectivity (**Figure 12.32c**). The size of this change was predictive of long-term gains on NeuroRacer and on the attention task.

Studies such as these have led to the emergence of many technology companies seeking to develop research-based video games that could enhance cognition. These low-cost tools could have great utility in clinical settings, offering new interventions for stroke recovery or to delay the onset of dementia. Even more futuristic, some people are eager to see whether technology can boost mental capacity, perhaps providing a way to compensate for dysfunctional schools, overcome limited educational opportunities, or just produce a generation of young Einsteins—efforts that raise a number of important ethical considerations.

reaction times between video game players (VGPs) and non–video game players (NVGPs). The fact that the data points from different tasks fall on a line suggests that a common underlying change is boosting the performance of the VGPs across all tasks and conditions.

Of course, we have to be careful when making inferences about causal relationships with correlational data. Perhaps people who tend to have fast reaction times are more likely to play video games. In training studies where participants are randomly assigned to play either an action video game or a control-condition game (e.g., a static video game such as Words With Friends), results show that action video game training leads to performance gains. One hypothesis suggests that the training results in faster processing of visual information, and another posits that attentional control is improved.

The critical question for any training program is whether the benefits of practicing in a limited context (e.g., a single video game) will generalize to new tasks and situations, especially those outside the lab. Can playing Grand Theft Auto make you better at remembering the grocery list or meeting a deadline at work? At present, the longitudinal data required to address these real-world tests are lacking (Simons et al., 2016), but there are indications that it might (see **Box 12.1**).

Instead, researchers have focused on asking how active video game training impacts specific components of cognitive control. One study showed that VGPs were faster than NVGPs in dual-task conditions that require switching from one task to another, even if there was no difference between the groups when either task was tested separately (Strobach et al., 2012;

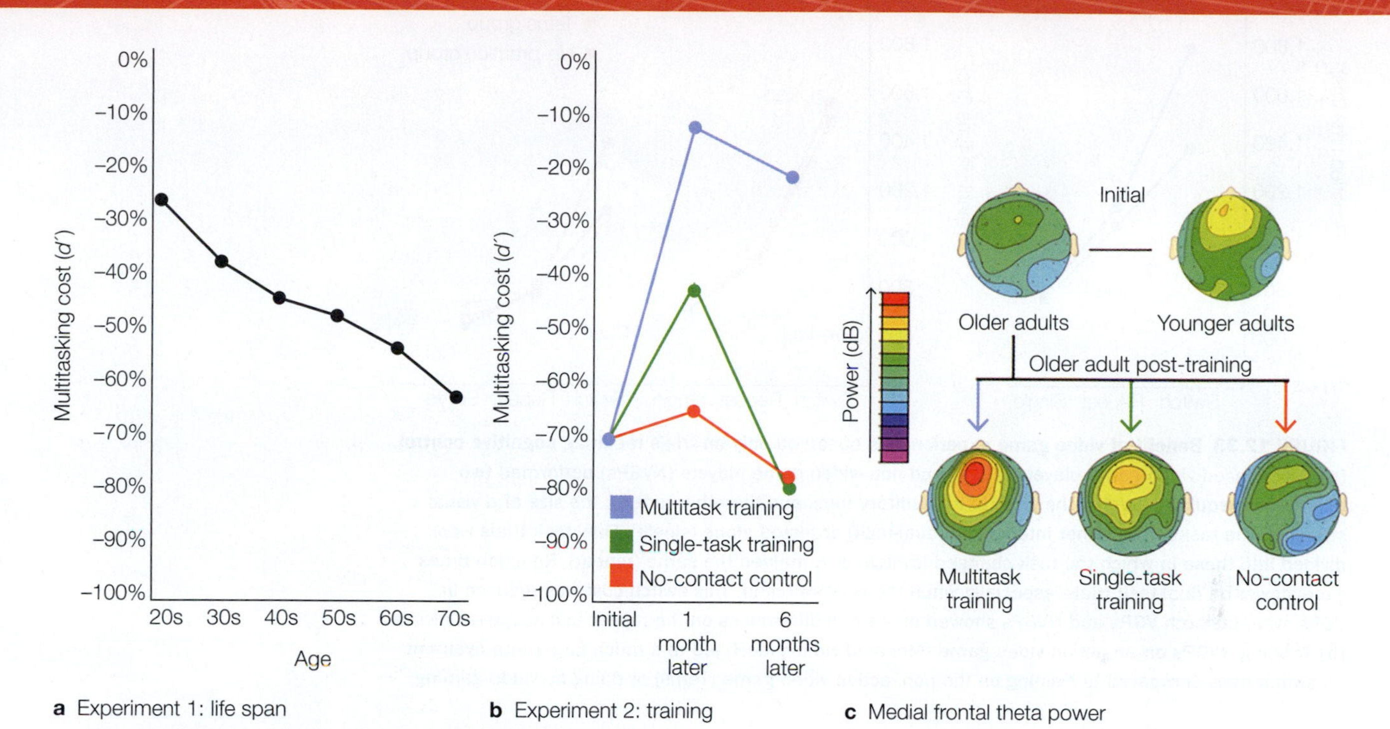

FIGURE 12.32 Training cognitive control.
(a) The cost of multitasking is defined as a change in accuracy on the detection task. In untrained participants, this cost increases with age. Multitask and single-task training for 1 month led to improvements at the end of training, with the effect much larger in the former group. (b) The multitasking group also showed strong retention when retested 6 months after that. (c) Medial frontal theta power (amplitude) during video game playing. Before training on the video game, this signal is much lower in older participants compared to younger participants. After training (multitasking), the older participants show much stronger theta activity.

Figure 12.33a). The researchers then divided the NVGP participants into three groups. One trained on an active video game (Medal of Honor) for 15 hours, another trained on a passive video game (Tetris) for 15 hours, and the third group did not do any training. Only those who did the active video game training showed an improvement on the generalization test, and there, too, the improvements were evident only on switch trials (**Figure 12.33b**).

TAKE-HOME MESSAGES

- Goal-oriented behavior involves the amplification of task-relevant information and the inhibition of task-irrelevant information. Amplification and inhibition may entail separate processes, given that aging selectively affects the ability to inhibit task-irrelevant information.
- Patients with prefrontal cortex damage lose inhibitory control. For example, they cannot inhibit task-irrelevant information.
- A network spanning prefrontal cortex and posterior cortex provides the neural substrates for interactions between goal representations and perceptual information.
- The inhibition of action constitutes another form of cognitive control. The right inferior frontal gyrus and the subthalamic nucleus are important for this form of control.
- Active video game playing has been hypothesized to improve some aspects of cognitive function, such as task switching, perhaps because the games require coordinating multiple subgoals.

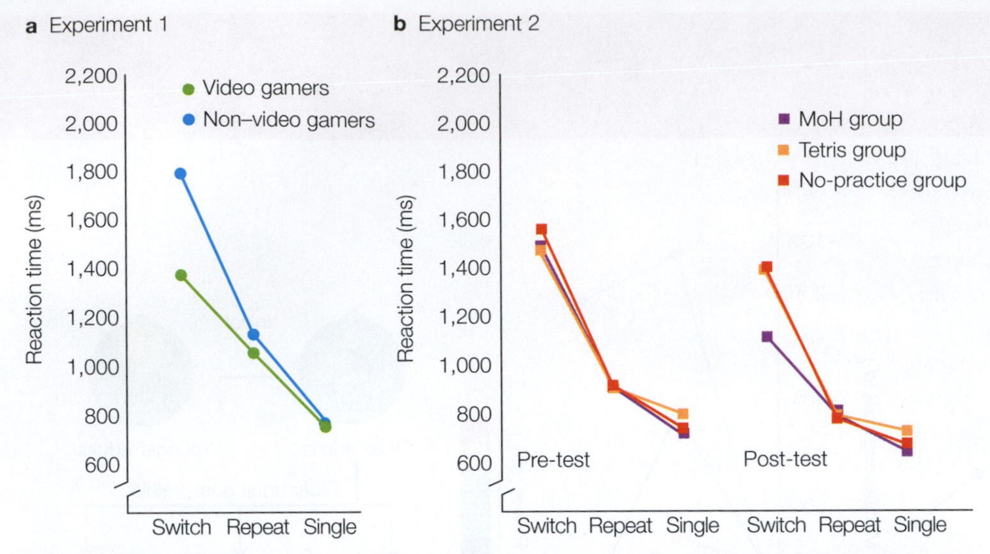

FIGURE 12.33 Benefit of video game experience is observed only on trials requiring cognitive control. **(a)** Experienced video game players (VGPs) and non–video game players (NVGPs) performed two tasks—one requiring judging the pitch of an auditory tone, and the other judging the size of a visual stimulus. The tasks were either interleaved (dual-task) or tested alone (single). Dual-task trials were divided into those in which the task changed (switch) or remained the same (repeat). Reaction times were slower on dual-task trials, especially when the task switched. This switch cost was reduced in VGPs, whereas both VGPs and NVGPs showed only small differences on the repeat and single-task trials. **(b)** Training NVGPs on an action video game (Medal of Honor, MoH) led to a much larger improvement on switch trials compared to training on the non–action video game (Tetris) or doing no video gaming.

12.7 Ensuring That Goal-Oriented Behaviors Succeed

Tim Shallice and Donald Norman proposed a psychological model of cognitive control, outlining the conditions under which the selection of an action might require the operation of a high-level control system, or what they referred to as a supervisory attentional system (SAS). These include any of the following situations:

- Planning or decision making is required.
- Responses are novel or not well learned.
- The required response competes with a strong, habitual response.
- Error correction or troubleshooting is required.
- The situation is difficult or dangerous.

The last four situations share one aspect of cognitive control that has not been discussed in detail to this point. For a person engaged in goal-oriented behavior, especially a behavior that includes subgoals, it is important to have a way to monitor moment-to-moment progress. If this is a well-learned process, there should be a means for signaling deviations from the expected course of events.

The Medial Frontal Cortex as a Monitoring System

One might expect the task of a **monitoring** system to be like that of a supervisor, keeping an eye on the overall flow of activity, ready to step in whenever a problem arises. For a neural monitoring system, however, there is a problem with this analogy: It has the feel of a homunculus. The supervisor has to have knowledge of the entire process and understand how the parts work together. A goal for any physiological model of cognitive control is, in one sense, the opposite: How can the kinds of simple operations that characterize neurons lead to cognitive control operations such as monitoring?

The last 30 years have witnessed burgeoning interest in the *medial frontal cortex (MFC)*, and in particular the **anterior cingulate cortex (ACC)**, as a critical component of a monitoring system. Indeed, the story of the MFC is an interesting chapter in the history of cognitive neuroscience. Buried in the depths of the frontal lobes and characterized by a primitive cytoarchitectonics, the cingulate cortex had historically been considered a component of the limbic system, helping to modulate arousal and autonomic responses during painful or threatening situations. The functional roles ascribed to most cortical regions were inspired by behavioral problems associated with neurological disorders; damage to the cingulate, either in animal models or in the few clinical reports with humans, was associated with *akinetic mutism*, a disorder characterized by minimal movement (akinesia), including the absence of speech (mutism). All of this fit in with ideas treating the cingulate as part of an arousal system. The idea that the anterior cingulate might play a more central role in cognitive control, however, was sparked when serendipitous activations were observed in this region during many of the initial neuroimaging studies.

Subsequent studies have revealed that the medial frontal cortex is consistently engaged whenever a task becomes more difficult—the type of situation in which monitoring demands are likely to be high. One meta-analysis highlighted the center of activation in 38 fMRI studies that included conditions in which monitoring demands were high. The activations were clustered in the anterior cingulate regions (BA24 and BA32) but also extended into BA8 and BA6; thus, we refer to this entire region as medial frontal cortex.

How Does the Medial Frontal Cortex Monitor Processing in Cognitive Control Networks?

As with much of the frontal cortex, the medial frontal cortex exhibits extensive connectivity with much of the brain. For example, DTI studies suggest that the ACC alone has at least 11 subregions (**Figure 12.34**). These subregions are defined by their distinct patterns of white matter connectivity with other brain regions. One region shows strong connectivity with OFC, another with ventral striatum, another with premotor cortex, and so on. This anatomy is consistent with the hypothesis that the MFC is in a key position to influence decision making, goal-oriented behavior, and motor control. Making sense of the functional role of this region has proved to be an area of ongoing and lively debate. We will now review some hypotheses that have been proposed to account for the functional role of the medial frontal cortex in cognitive control.

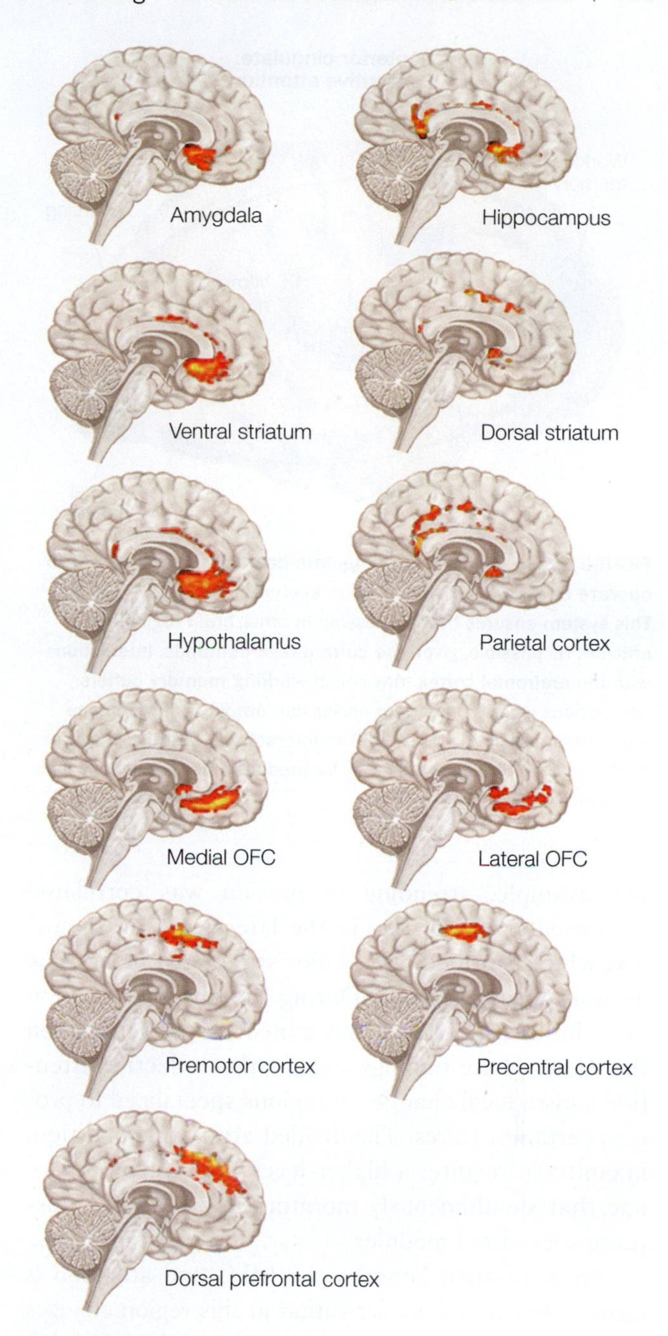

FIGURE 12.34 DTI to identify anatomical connections between the cingulate cortex and other brain regions.
Each of 11 subregions of the cingulate cortex (highlighted separately here) showed significant connectivity with a separate specific brain area. OFC = orbitofrontal cortex.

ATTENTIONAL HIERARCHY HYPOTHESIS An early hypothesis centered on the idea that the medial frontal cortex should be conceptualized as part of an attentional hierarchy. In this view, the MFC occupies an upper rung on the hierarchy, playing a critical role in coordinating activity across attention systems (**Figure 12.35**). Consider a PET study of visual attention in which participants must selectively attend to a single visual dimension (color, motion, shape) or monitor changes in all three dimensions simultaneously. In the latter condition, attentional resources must be divided among the perceptual dimensions (Corbetta et al., 1991).

Compared to control conditions in which stimuli were viewed passively, the selective-attention conditions were associated with enhanced activity in feature-specific regions of visual association areas.

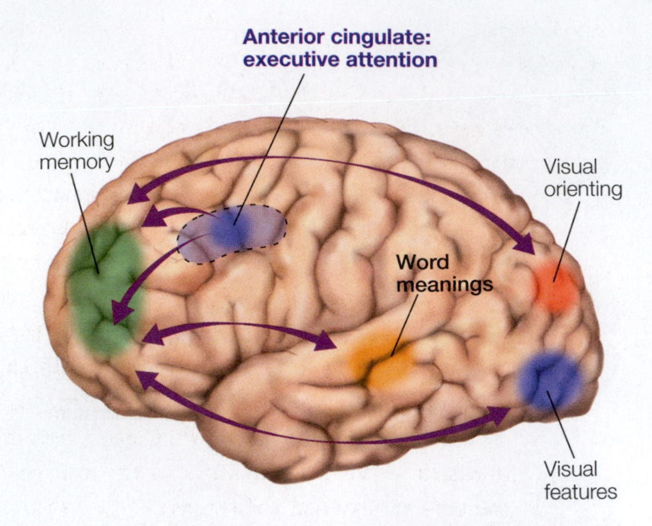

FIGURE 12.35 The anterior cingulate has been hypothesized to operate as an executive attention system.
This system ensures that processing in other brain regions is as efficient as possible, given the current task demands. Interactions with the prefrontal cortex may select working memory buffers; interactions with the posterior cortex can amplify activity in one perceptual module over others. The interactions with the posterior cortex may be direct, or they may be mediated by connections with the prefrontal cortex.

For example, attending to motion was correlated with greater blood flow in the lateral prestriate cortex, whereas attending to color stimulated blood flow in more medial regions. During the divided-attention task, however, the most prominent activation was in the ACC. These findings suggest that selective attention causes local changes in regions specialized to process certain features. The divided-attention condition, in contrast, requires a higher-level attention system—one that simultaneously monitors information across these specialized modules.

An association between the MFC and attention is further shown by how activation in this region changes as attentional demands decrease. If a verb generation task (Figure 12.23) is repeated over successive blocks, the primary activation shifts from the cingulate and prefrontal regions to the insular cortex of the temporal lobe (Raichle et al., 1994). This shift indicates that the task has changed. In the initial trial, participants have to choose between alternative semantic associates. If the target noun is *apple*, then possible responses are "eat," "throw," "peel," or "juggle," and the participant must select among these alternatives. On subsequent trials, however, the task demands change from semantic generation to memory retrieval, since the same semantic associate is almost always reported. For example, a participant who reports "peel" on the first trial will invariably make the same choice on subsequent trials.

Activation of the ACC during the first trial can be related to two of the functions of a supervisory attentional system (SAS): responding both under novel conditions and with more difficult tasks. The generation condition is more difficult than the repeat condition because the response is not constrained. But over subsequent trials, the generation condition becomes easier (as evidenced by markedly reduced response times), and the items are no longer novel. Meanwhile, the elevated activation of the cingulate dissipates, reflecting a reduced need for the SAS. That this shift indicates the loss of novelty rather than a general decrease in MFC activity with practice is shown by the finding that, when a new list of nouns is used, the cingulate activation returns.

One concern with the hierarchy model is that it is descriptive rather than mechanistic. The model recognizes that the MFC is recruited when attentional demands are high, but it does not specify how this recruitment occurs, nor does it specify the kinds of representations supported by the MFC. We might suppose that the representation includes the current goal, as well as all the suboperations required to achieve that goal. This type of representation, however, is quite complex. What's more, even if all of this information were represented in the MFC, we would still not be able to explain how the MFC uses this information to implement cognitive control. In a sense, the hierarchical attention model is reminiscent of the homunculus problem: To explain control, we postulate a controller without describing how the controller is controlled.

ERROR DETECTION HYPOTHESIS Concern about the attentional hierarchy hypothesis inspired researchers to consider other models of how medial frontal cortex might be involved in monitoring behavior. The starting point for one model comes from evidence implicating the MFC in the detection of errors. Evoked-potential studies have shown that the MFC provides an electrophysiological signal correlated with the occurrence of errors. When people make an incorrect response, a large evoked response sweeps over the prefrontal cortex just after the movement is initiated (**Figure 12.36**). This signal, referred to as the **error-related negativity (ERN)** when time-locked to the response, and the **feedback-related negativity (FRN)** when time-locked to feedback, has been localized to the anterior cingulate (Dehaene et al., 1994). Perhaps a monitoring system would detect when an error has occurred, and this information would be used to increase cognitive control.

This hypothesis provides a different perspective on the co-occurrence of activation in medial and lateral

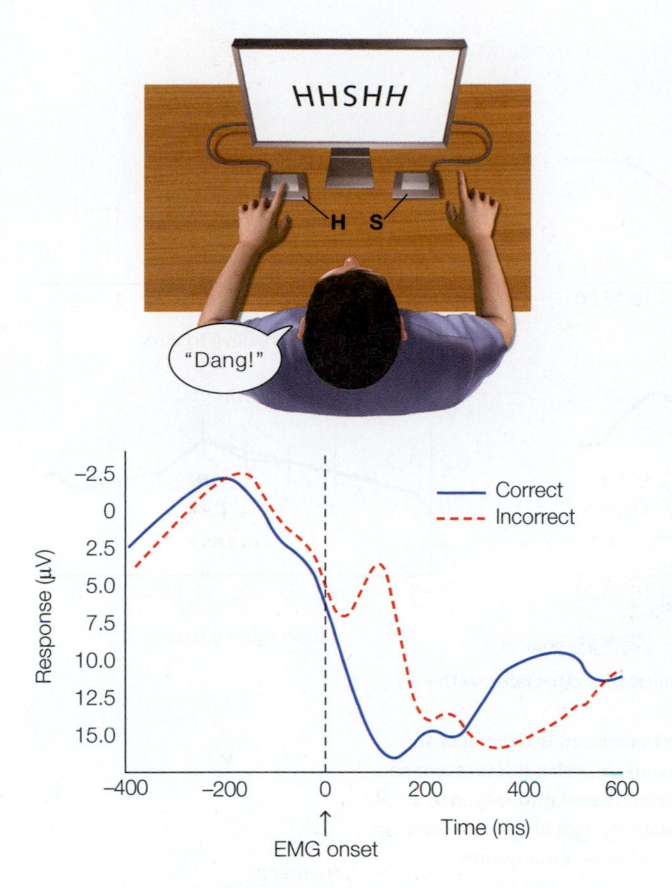

FIGURE 12.36 Errors in a two-choice letter discrimination task spark an error detection signal from the MFC.
Participants made errors when speed was emphasized and when targets were flanked by irrelevant distractors. Evoked potentials for incorrect responses deviated from those obtained on trials with correct responses just after the onset of peripheral motor activity. This error detection signal is maximal over a central electrode positioned above the prefrontal cortex, and it has been hypothesized to originate in the anterior cingulate. The zero position on the *x*-axis indicates the onset of electromyographic (EMG) activity. Actual movement would be observed about 50 to 100 ms later.

prefrontal cortex—one that captures many of the functional benefits of an attention system. Typically, we make errors when we are not paying much attention to the task at hand. Consider being asked to perform the task shown in Figure 12.36 for an hour, during which the stimulus appeared only once every 6 seconds. Pretty boring, right? At some point, your mind would start to wander. You might think about your evening plans. This new goal would begin to occupy your working memory, displacing the experimentally defined (boring) goal to respond to the letter in the center and not the letters on the side. Oops—you suddenly find yourself pressing the wrong key. Physiological responses such as the ERN could be used to reactivate the experimental goal in working memory.

One group of researchers (Eichele et al., 2008) used fMRI to see whether they could predict when people were likely to make an error. They looked at the event-related response over successive trials, asking how the signals changed in advance of an error. Two changes were especially notable. First, before an error was made, the researchers observed a steady decrease in activity within a network spanning the medial frontal cortex and right inferior frontal cortex—a decrease that could be detected up to 30 seconds before the error (**Figure 12.37**).

Second, activity increased over a similar time period in the precuneus and retrosplenial cortex. These two regions are key components of the default network, which is postulated to be associated with self-referential processing (e.g., when you start to think about something other than the task at hand; see Chapter 13). Thus, we can see a shift in activity from the monitoring system to the mind-wandering system, which builds until a person makes an error.

The ERN and FRN are especially salient signals of a monitoring system. The engagement of medial frontal cortex, however, is not limited to conditions in which people make errors. MFC activation is also prominent in many tasks in which errors rarely occur. The Stroop task is one such example. The difficulty that people have when words and colors are incongruent is typically detected in the reaction time data and only minimally, if at all, in measures of accuracy. That is, people take longer, but they don't make mistakes. Still, activation of the MFC is much higher on incongruent trials compared to when the words and colors are congruent (Bush et al., 2000). Similarly, activation is higher when people are asked to generate semantic associates of words compared to when they just repeat the words, even though errors rarely occur.

Moreover, recent work suggests that the FRN may not be an electrophysiological marker of errors per se, but rather may occur whenever an outcome is unexpected. Nicola Ferdinand and her colleagues (2012) devised an experiment to test whether the FRN was modulated by an event's valence (negative, positive, or neutral outcome) or surprise value (expected or unexpected outcome). To do this, they recorded EEGs while participants performed a time estimation task in which they had to press a button 2.5 seconds after a stimulus was presented.

Each trial resulted in one of three types of feedback: negative feedback if the button press was way off the mark (too early or too late), positive feedback if the button press was close to 2.5 seconds, and neutral feedback on trials in which the button press was close to the target time, but not quite at the level required for

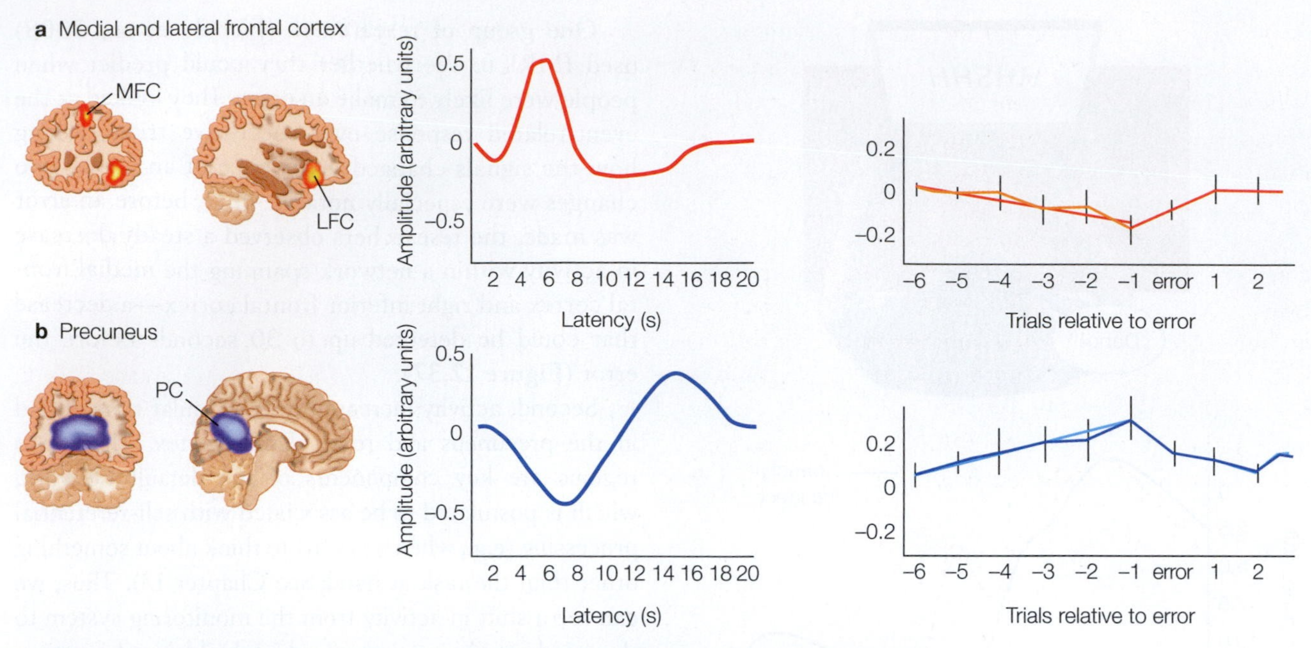

FIGURE 12.37 Balance of activity between monitoring and default networks correlates with likelihood of making an error.
(a) Areas in medial and lateral frontal cortex (MFC and LFC) that exhibit increased BOLD response after stimulus onset. (b) Precuneus (PC) area, a part of the default network, in which BOLD response decreases after stimulus onset. Far-right graphs in both (a) and (b) indicate the relative response across trials. Activation in the MFC is relatively low just before an error, and relatively high in the PC before an error. Note the dramatic change in relative activation in both areas right after an error occurs.

positive feedback. Importantly, the criteria were adjusted such that the neutral feedback was experienced on 60% of the trials, with the remaining trials evenly divided between negative and positive feedback trials. In this way, the participants developed an expectancy for neutral feedback, and each of the high-valence outcomes was unexpected. The results showed similar FRNs on negative and positive feedback trials (**Figure 12.38**).

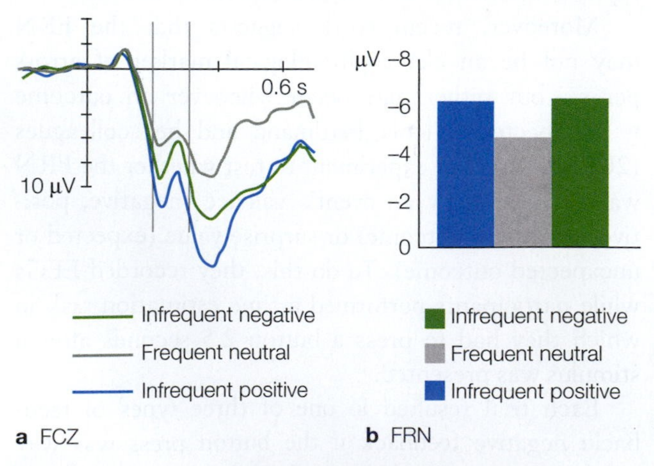

FIGURE 12.38 ERPs elicited by three types of feedback.
(a) ERPs recorded from a medial frontal electrode (FCZ) following frequent (neutral) feedback or two types of infrequent feedback (negative and positive). (b) Both the positive and negative unexpected feedback generated larger negative FRN ERPs at frontocentral sites compared to expected feedback.

This study implies that the FRN is not really about signaling errors, but rather about unexpected feedback. In combination with the observation that the MFC is active in many situations in which errors do not occur, these results underscore that an error detection hypothesis is unlikely to provide an encompassing computational account of MFC function. The fact that the ERN has often been linked to errors reflects the fact that people tend to be overly confident: We, especially the college students who serve as "typical" research participants, expect to come up with the correct answer. In most situations, we are surprised when we make errors.

RESPONSE CONFLICT HYPOTHESIS Jonathan Cohen and his colleagues have hypothesized that a key function of the medial frontal cortex is to evaluate **response conflict** (J. D. Cohen et al., 2000). This hypothesis is intended to provide an umbrella account of the monitoring role of this region, encompassing earlier models that focused on attentional hierarchies or error detection. Difficult and novel situations should engender high response conflict. In semantic generation tasks, there is a conflict between acceptable alternative responses. Errors, by definition, are also situations in which conflict exists. Similarly, tasks such as the Stroop task entail conflict in that the required response is in conflict with a more habitual response.

In Cohen's view, conflict monitoring is a computationally appealing way to allocate attentional resources. When the monitoring system detects that conflict is high, there is a need to increase attentional vigilance. Increases in anterior cingulate activity can then be used to modulate activity in other cortical areas.

Event-related fMRI has been used to pit the error detection hypothesis against the response conflict hypothesis. One study used the flanker task, similar to that shown in Figure 12.36, except that the letters were replaced by a row of five arrows (Botvinick et al., 1999). Participants responded to the direction of the central arrow, pressing a button on the right side if this arrow pointed to the right and a button on the left side if it pointed to the left. On compatible trials, the flanking arrows pointed in the same direction; on incompatible trials, the flanking arrows pointed in opposite directions. Neural activity in the medial frontal cortex was higher on the incompatible trials compared to the compatible trials. Importantly, this increase was observed even when participants responded correctly. These results strongly suggest that the monitoring demands, and not the occurrence of an error, engage the MFC.

Subsequent work has sought to clarify how a conflict-monitoring process might be part of a network for cognitive control. Consider a variant of the Stroop task in which a cue is presented at the beginning of each trial to indicate whether the participant should read the word or name the color (**Figure 12.39a**). After a delay, the cue

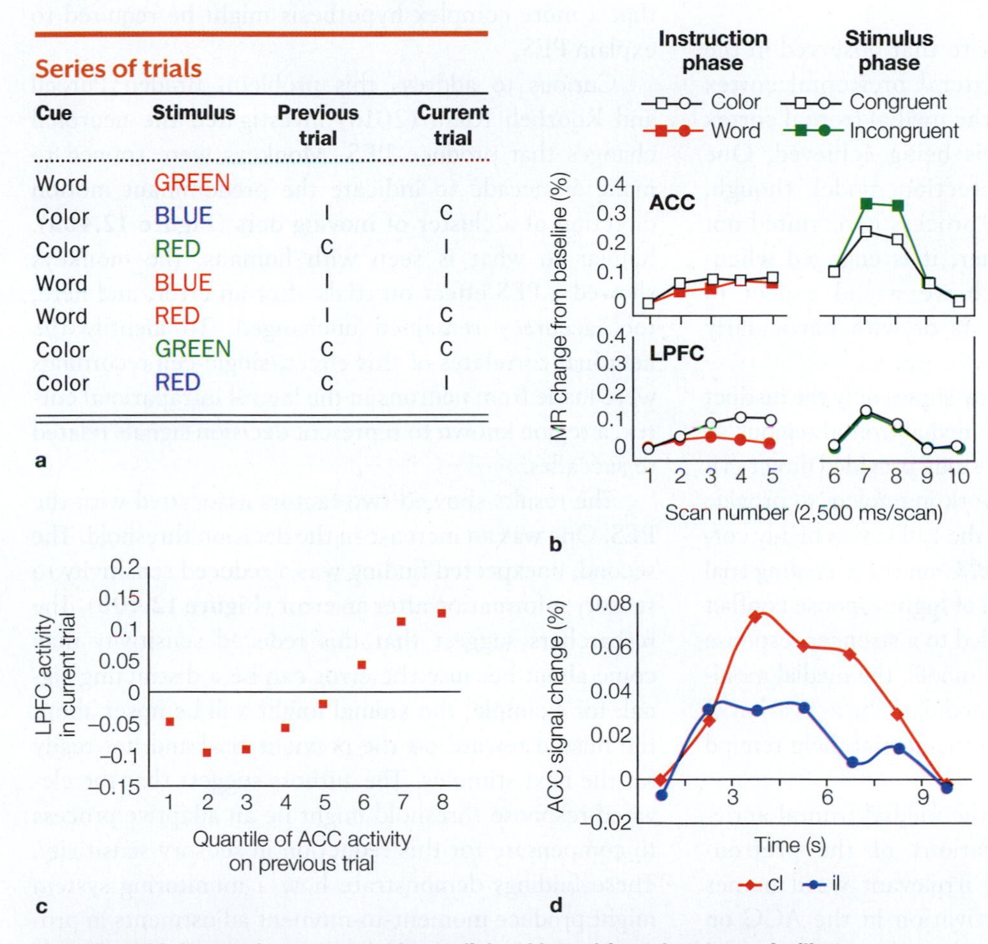

FIGURE 12.39 Interactions between the medial and lateral frontal cortex to facilitate goal-oriented behavior.
(a) Participants performed a series of Stroop trials, responding to either the word or the color as indicated by a cue. C = congruent; I = incongruent. (b) Functional MRI showing a double dissociation between the lateral prefrontal cortex (LPFC) and the anterior cingulate cortex (ACC). LPFC activation in the instruction phase differs between conditions in which the cue indicates that the task will be easy (word) or hard (color). ACC activation varies in the stimulus phase as a function of response conflict (incongruent is greater than congruent). (c) Correlation between ACC and LPFC activation across successive trials. The LPFC representation of the task goal is enhanced following the detection of a conflict by the ACC monitoring system. (d) The ACC signal is lower on incongruent trials preceded by an incongruent trial (iI) as compared to those preceded by a congruent trial (cI). This reduction is hypothesized to occur because the goal representation in LPFC is stronger, and thus there is less conflict.

is replaced by a Stroop stimulus. By using a long delay between the cue and the stimulus, researchers can separately examine the neural responses related to goal selection and the neural responses related to response conflict. Moreover, using a cue enables the experimenters to manipulate two factors: goal difficulty, given the assumption that it is easier to read words than to name their ink color; and color–word congruency.

The results showed distinct neural correlates of these two factors (**Figure 12.39b**). The degree of difficulty for goal selection was evident in the activation of the lateral prefrontal cortex. When the task was made more difficult, the BOLD response in this region increased even before the actual stimulus was presented. In contrast, activation in the ACC was sensitive to the degree of response conflict, being greater when the word and stimulus color were different.

The picture here is similar to that observed in the ERN–FRN literature. The lateral prefrontal cortex represents the task goal, and the medial frontal cortex monitors whether that goal is being achieved. One difference from the error detection model, though, is that the medial monitoring process is recruited not just when errors occur. Rather, it is engaged whenever there is conflict—which we would expect to be quite high in novel contexts or with particularly demanding tasks.

Note that the preceding study shows only the distinct contributions of the lateral and medial frontal regions. A subsequent event-related fMRI study provided direct evidence that these two regions work in tandem to provide cognitive control. Activation in the LPFC was highly correlated with activation in the ACC on the *preceding* trial (**Figure 12.39c**). Thus, a signal of high response conflict on an incongruent Stroop trial led to a stronger response in the LPFC. As with the error model, the medial monitoring function can be used to modulate the activation of the goal in working memory. Difficult trials help remind the person to stay on task.

We can hypothesize that the medial frontal activity modulates filtering operations of the prefrontal cortex, ensuring that the irrelevant word names are ignored. Interestingly, activation in the ACC on incongruent trials was lower when the previous trial was also incongruent (**Figure 12.39d**). Assuming that an incongruent trial leads to a stronger activation of the task goal in working memory and that, as a result, there is better filtering of irrelevant information on the next trial, the degree of conflict generated on that trial will decrease.

The essence of the response conflict hypothesis is that the presence of a conflict signal might influence subsequent performance. For example, after making an error on a reaction time task, participants slow down—an effect known as post-error slowing (PES). As noted already, the error provides a signal that we need to be more vigilant (e.g., use more cognitive control) and perhaps a bit more cautious.

In models of decision making, being more cautious is thought to correspond to a change in a decision threshold; more information must be sampled from the environment before a response is selected. However, the literature on PES shows that the increase in response time is rarely accompanied by an increase in accuracy. This is contrary to the prediction of the decision threshold hypothesis, since requiring more information should also make responses more accurate. As such, the absence of a change in accuracy indicates that a more complex hypothesis might be required to explain PES.

Curious to address this problem, Braden Purcell and Roozbeh Kiani (2016) investigated the neuronal changes that produce PES. Monkeys were trained to make a saccade to indicate the predominant motion direction of a cluster of moving dots (**Figure 12.40a**). Similar to what is seen with humans, the monkeys showed a PES effect on trials after an error, and here, too, accuracy remained unchanged. To identify the neuronal correlates of this effect, single-cell recordings were made from neurons in the lateral intraparietal cortex, a region known to represent decision signals related to saccades.

The results showed two factors associated with the PES. One was an increase in the decision threshold. The second, unexpected finding was a reduced sensitivity to sensory information after an error (**Figure 12.40b**). The researchers suggest that this reduced sensitivity may come about because the error can be a distracting signal; for example, the animal might still be upset about the missed reward on the previous trial and not ready for the next stimulus. The authors suggest that the elevated response threshold might be an adaptive process to compensate for this reduction in sensory sensitivity. These findings demonstrate how a monitoring system might produce moment-to-moment adjustments in processing at the neuronal level to support goal-oriented behavior.

ACC FUNCTION IS STILL UP IN THE AIR The response conflict hypothesis remains a work in progress, and the literature suggests some problems that need to be addressed. Activation in the anterior cingulate is more closely linked with the participant's anticipation of

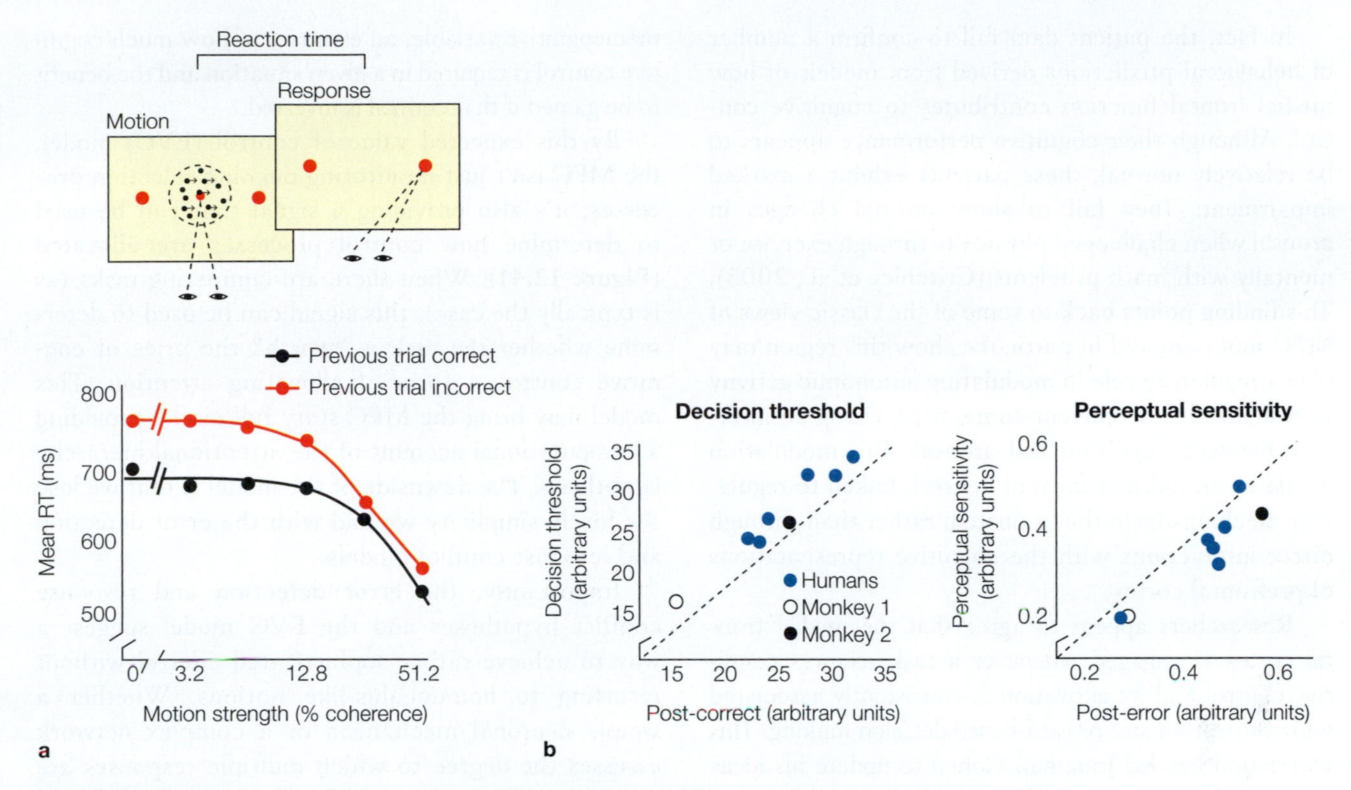

FIGURE 12.40 Neural mechanisms associated with post-error slowing.
(a) Monkeys viewed a cluster of moving dots and moved their eyes to indicate the direction of greatest coherent motion. Reaction times decreased as the amount of coherence increased, but were always slower on trials following an incorrect response. (b) Using a computational model, researchers estimated two parameters: one representing the decision threshold (left), and the other, perceptual sensitivity (right) for post-error versus post-correct trials. Both changed following errors, with the threshold becoming higher (falling above the equality line) and sensitivity lower (falling below the equality line). The lower sensitivity is a surprising result. Contrary to what we would predict, making an error seems to cause a brief reduction in sensitivity of the perceptual system.

possible errors than with the degree of conflict (J. W. Brown & Braver, 2005). This finding suggests that the medial frontal cortex may be doing more than simply monitoring the level of conflict presented by the current environment. It may also be anticipating the likelihood of conflict, in which case it may play a risk prediction and error avoidance role.

Another issue relates back to our earlier discussion of decision making, where we noted that the ACC has been linked to evaluating the effort associated with a behavioral choice, helping to perform a cost–benefit analysis. This hypothesis has led to a reinterpretation of the prevalent activation of MFC observed on difficult tasks. Jack Grinband and his colleagues (2008) observed that the response times tend to be longer in such conditions. They suggested that the activation here may simply reflect the amount of time spent on the task, a variant of effort.

To test this idea, they had participants view a checkerboard that flashed on and off for a variable duration of time, and then simply press a button when the checkerboard disappeared. In this task, the stimulus is unambiguous, only one response is possible, and no decision is required. Thus, there were no errors, nor was there any conflict. Even so, MFC activation was modulated by task duration and was similar to that observed when the participants performed a Stroop task. It is, of course, hard to make inferences about a null result (similar activation in these two tasks), but the results provide an alternative view of why MFC activation is correlated with task difficulty.

More perplexing are the results of studies involving patients with lesions of the medial frontal cortex. These patients show little evidence of impairment on various tasks that would appear to require cognitive control—one reason why the cingulate had not been identified as having a role until fMRI came along. For example, these patients are as sensitive to the effects of an error on the Stroop task as control participants are (Fellows & Farah, 2005).

In fact, the patient data fail to confirm a number of behavioral predictions derived from models of how medial frontal function contributes to cognitive control. Although their cognitive performance appears to be relatively normal, these patients exhibit a marked impairment: They fail to show normal changes in arousal when challenged physically through exercise or mentally with math problems (Critchley et al., 2003). This finding points back to some of the classic views of MFC function, and in particular, how this region may play a regulatory role in modulating autonomic activity in response to the current context, providing an interface between cognition and arousal. This modulation would be an indirect form of control, linked to regulatory mechanisms in the brainstem rather than through direct interactions with the cognitive representations of prefrontal cortex.

Researchers appear to agree that the medial frontal cortex is engaged whenever a task requires cognitive control and its activation is consistently associated with motivation and reward-based decision making. This correlation has led Jonathan Cohen to update his ideas about conflict monitoring (Shenhav et al., 2016), proposing a new model in which the MFC represents more of a metacognitive variable, an estimate of how much cognitive control is required in a given situation and the benefit to be gained if that control is invested.

By this expected value of control (EVC) model, the MFC isn't just monitoring ongoing selection processes; it's also providing a signal that can be used to determine how control processes are allocated (**Figure 12.41**). When there are competing tasks (as is typically the case), this signal can be used to determine whether the task is "worth" the price of cognitive control, a form of allocating attention. This model may bring the MFC story full circle, providing a computational account of the attentional hierarchy hypothesis. The downside of the model is that we lose the lovely simplicity we had with the error detection and response conflict models.

Importantly, the error detection and response conflict hypotheses and the EVC model suggest a way to achieve rather sophisticated control without resorting to homunculus-like notions. Whether a simple neuronal mechanism or a complex network assesses the degree to which multiple responses are concurrently active is still to be seen, and future experiments will determine whether these ideas have

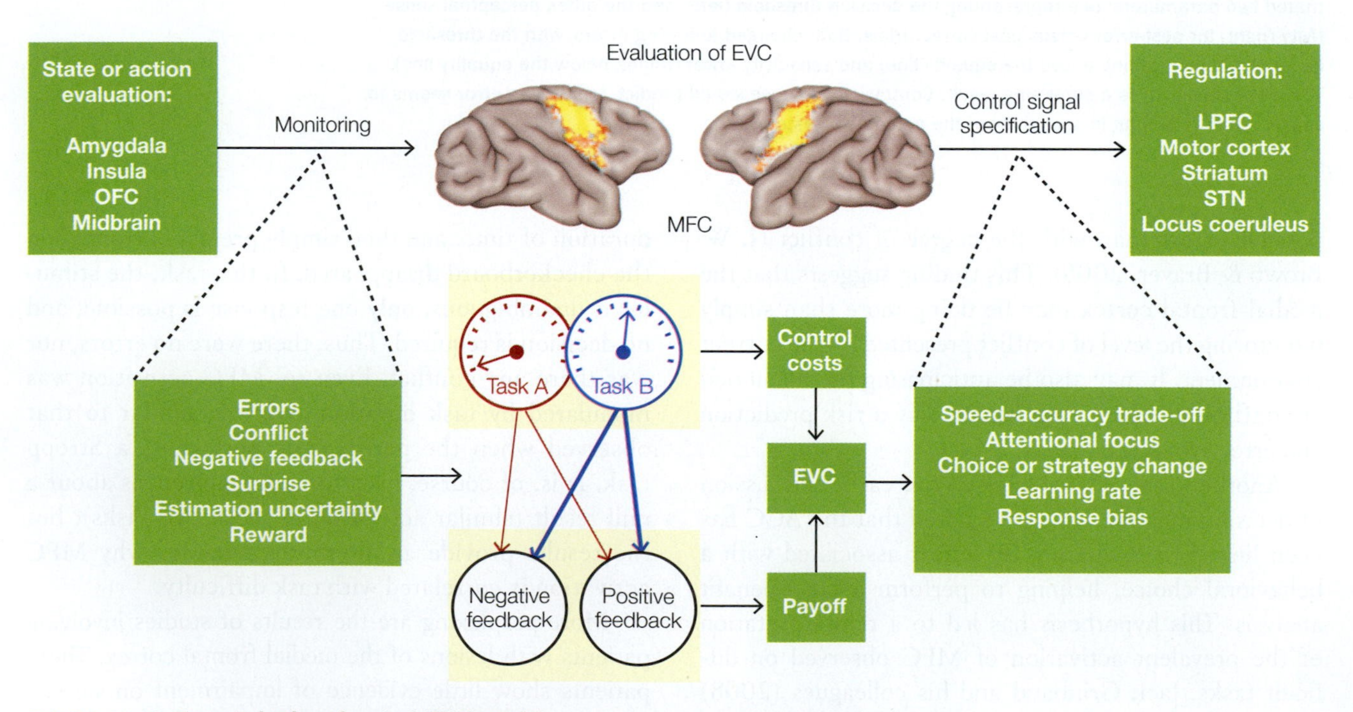

FIGURE 12.41 Expected value of control (EVC) model.
The medial frontal cortex receives inputs indicating the current state of ongoing actions or expected outcomes from potential actions. It uses these inputs to establish a cost–benefit analysis of possible rewards relative to the costs of control. The output is then used to regulate systems involved in planning and executing actions. In this example, Task A has a low EVC, leading to relatively weak control, whereas Task B has a high EVC, leading to relatively strong control.

lasting value. Nonetheless, they offer an encouraging example of how even the most advanced of our cognitive competencies can be subject to rigorous experimental investigation, given the many tools of cognitive neuroscience.

TAKE-HOME MESSAGES

- The medial frontal cortex (MFC), including the anterior cingulate cortex (ACC), is thought to be a critical part of a monitoring system, identifying situations in which cognitive control is required.
- Error-related or feedback-related negativity (ERN or FRN) signals are event-related potentials that occur when unexpected feedback is produced. This response is generated by the medial frontal cortex.
- The medial frontal cortex is engaged when response conflict is high. Through its interactions with lateral regions of the prefrontal cortex, a monitoring system can regulate the level of cognitive control.

Summary

The prefrontal cortex plays a crucial role in cognitive control functions that are critical for goal-oriented behavior and decision making. Cognitive control systems enable us to be flexible in our actions, not driven solely by automatic behavior. The prefrontal cortex contains a massively connected network linking the brain's motor, perceptual, and limbic regions and is in an excellent position to coordinate processing across wide regions of the central nervous system.

Goal-oriented behavior and decision making involve planning, evaluating options, and calculating the value of rewards and consequences. These behaviors require that we represent information that is not always immediately present in the environment. Working memory is essential for this function. It allows for the interaction of current goals with perceptual information and knowledge accumulated from personal experience. Not only must we be able to represent our goals, but these representations must persist for an extended period of time. Working memory must be dynamic. It requires the retrieval, amplification, and manipulation of representations that are useful for the task at hand, as well as the ability to ignore potential distractions. Yet we must also be flexible. If our goals change, or if the context demands an alternative course of action, we must be able to switch from one plan to another. These operations require a system that can monitor ongoing behavior, signaling when we fail or when there are potential sources of conflict.

This chapter emphasized two functional systems: (a) The lateral prefrontal cortex, orbitofrontal cortex, and frontal pole support goal-oriented behavior, providing a working memory system that recruits and selects task-relevant information stored in the more posterior regions of the cortex. (b) The medial frontal cortex is hypothesized to work in tandem with the rest of the prefrontal cortex, monitoring ongoing activity so that it can modulate the degree of cognitive control.

As we pointed out in this chapter and in Chapter 8, the control of action has a hierarchical nature. Just as control in the motor system is distributed across many functional systems, an analogous organization characterizes prefrontal function. With control distributed in this manner, the need for an all-powerful controller, a homunculus, is minimized.

Key Terms

action–outcome decisions (p. 527)
anterior cingulate cortex (ACC) (p. 554)
cognitive control (p. 516)
delayed-response tasks (p. 520)
descriptive decision theories (p. 527)
dopamine (DA) (p. 533)
dynamic filtering (p. 541)
error-related negativity (ERN) (p. 556)
feedback-related negativity (FRN) (p. 556)
frontal pole (FP) (p. 516)
goal-oriented actions (p. 519)
goal-oriented behavior (p. 516)
habit (p. 519)
inhibitory control (p. 545)
lateral prefrontal cortex (LPFC) (p. 516)
medial frontal cortex (MFC) (p. 516)
monitoring (p. 554)
normative decision theories (p. 527)
orbitofrontal cortex (OFC) (p. 516)
perseveration (p. 518)
prefrontal cortex (PFC) (p. 516)
primary reinforcers (p. 528)
response conflict (p. 558)
reward prediction error (RPE) (p. 535)
secondary reinforcers (p. 528)
stimulus–response decisions (p. 527)
temporal discounting (p. 529)
utilization behavior (p. 519)
value (p. 528)

Think About It

1. Describe three examples from your daily activities that demonstrate how actions involve the interplay of habit-like behaviors and goal-oriented behaviors.
2. What are some of the current hypotheses concerning functional specialization across the three gradients on the frontal cortex (dorsal–ventral, anterior–posterior, and lateral–medial)?
3. A cardinal feature of human cognition is that we exhibit great flexibility in our behavior. Flexibility implies choice, and choice entails decision making. Describe some of the neural systems involved in decision making.
4. Review and contrast some of the ways in which the prefrontal cortex and the medial frontal cortex are involved in monitoring and controlling processing.
5. The notion of a supervisory attentional system does not sit well with some researchers, because it seems like a homuncular concept. Is such a system a necessary part of a cognitive control network? Explain your answer.

Suggested Reading

Badre, D., & D'Esposito, M. (2009). Is the rostro-caudal axis of the frontal lobe hierarchical? *Nature Reviews Neuroscience*, *10*, 659–669.

Botvinick, M. M., & Cohen, J. D. (2014). The computational and neural basis of cognitive control: Charted territory and new frontiers. *Cognitive Science*, *38*, 1249–1285.

Braver, T. (2012). The variable nature of cognitive control: A dual mechanisms framework. *Trends in Cognitive Science*, *16*(2), 106–113.

Fuster, J. M. (1989). *The prefrontal cortex: Anatomy, physiology, and neuropsychology of the frontal lobe* (2nd ed.). New York: Raven.

Lee, D., Seo, H., & Jung, M. W. (2012). Neural basis of reinforcement learning and decision making. *Annual Review of Neuroscience*, *35*, 287–308.

Miller, E. K., & Cohen, J. D. (2001). An integrative theory of prefrontal cortex function. *Annual Review of Neuroscience*, *24*, 167–202.

The one thing that unites all human beings, regardless of age, gender, religion, economic status, or ethnic background, is that, deep down inside, we all believe that we are above-average drivers.

Dave Barry

CHAPTER

13

Social Cognition

WHEN CONFRONTED WITH the perfect storm of high speed and an immovable solid object, the skull's armor can protect the brain to a limited degree. Unfortunately, this set of circumstances befell patient M.R. when he crashed his motorcycle. The result was a coup–contrecoup injury: The impact caused his brain first to bounce against the back of the skull and then to rebound into the jagged bony ridges surrounding the eyeball, which sliced away at his brain tissue like knives. The injury left M.R. with extensive damage to the orbitofrontal cortex (OFC), the portion of the frontal lobes that rests behind the eye orbits.

Despite his extensive brain damage, M.R. does well on standard neuropsychological tests of memory, motor, and language skills. Yet, if you were to have a casual conversation with him, you would at once notice something amiss. He might greet you, a stranger, with a too familiar hug, sit too close, or gaze at you just a bit too long while discussing deeply personal topics or endlessly describing every cut he recently made to a bonsai tree, even though it's a topic that clearly bores you. Such socially inappropriate behavior is a common result of orbitofrontal damage like M.R.'s (Beer et al., 2003).

OFC damage does not require fast cars or motorcycles. The most famous case of OFC damage, familiar to neuroscience students, was Phineas Gage, the foreman of a Vermont railroad construction crew, in 1848. He was setting up controlled explosions to blast through rock and, by mistake, tamped down on some exposed gunpowder with an iron rod, creating a spark that ignited it. The resulting explosion blasted the 3-foot-long tamping rod through Gage's skull like a rocket, which entered just below his left eye and exited at the top of his head, creating a large hole in the OFC (**Figure 13.1**). Amazingly, Gage remained conscious and alert throughout the incident.

Over the course of a few months, Gage's physical wounds healed, but his personality and behavior had changed for good. He had been a respected citizen,

BIG Questions

- Where am "I" in my brain?
- Do we process information about others and ourselves in the same way?
- Is social information processing the same for everyone, or is it affected by individual and cultural differences?
- To what extent is emotion involved in social cognition?

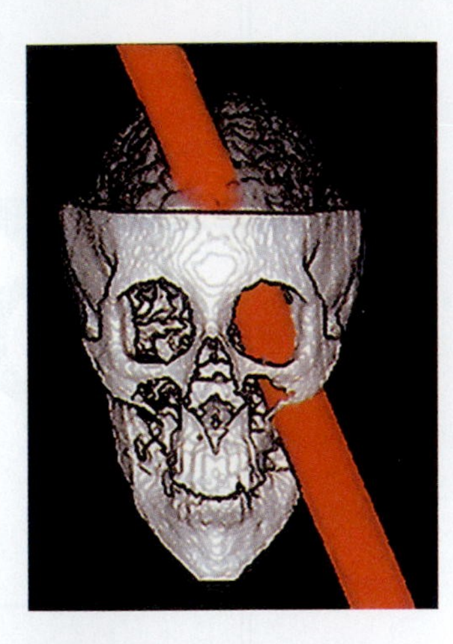

FIGURE 13.1 Computer reconstruction of Phineas Gage's injury.
The tamping iron entered Gage's brain just below the left eye and exited from the top of the head. It destroyed much of the medial region of the prefrontal cortex.

exemplary worker, and well-liked man, but after his injury his friends said he was "no longer Gage" (MacMillan, 2000, p. 13). His physician described the postinjury Gage as "irreverent, indulging in the grossest profanity (which was not previously his custom), manifesting little deference to his fellows, impatient of restraint or advice when it conflicts with his desires" (MacMillan, 1986). Gage was fired from the railroad and spent most of his postinjury life as a stagecoach driver; though his preinjury life had been filled with promise, he never again held a job as prestigious as railroad foreman. Twelve years after his injury, he started to suffer epileptic seizures, finally succumbing during a prolonged seizure in 1860.

Both M.R. and Gage suffered lesions to their frontal lobes that resulted in a change in their social behavior, suggesting that this brain region is involved with social cognition. Social cognitive neuroscience aims to tackle the problem of understanding how brain function supports the cognitive processes underlying human social behavior. It differs from cognitive neuroscience in that it emphasizes that how we think or act may vary with social contexts (Ochsner, 2007b). For example, when we run across a stranger, we have neural systems that have evolved to help us identify friend from foe and trustworthy from untrustworthy, which are crucial for survival and reproductive success (J. T. Cacioppo et al., 2011). Through interactions involving family, friends, not-so-friendly acquaintances, romantic partners, and coworkers—and even, quite frequently, strangers—we form a sense of self and also develop impressions of other people.

Obviously, for a social interaction it takes at least two to tango, and for us to get the tango straight we have to understand both partners. In this chapter we discuss research concerning the neural representation of self, other people, and social knowledge and procedures. We will address these topics with a focus on the ventromedial prefrontal cortex. By recognizing the intimate connections between the regions of prefrontal cortex, we can start to appreciate how a mind emerges from the architecture of the human brain.

We begin with a bit about the anatomical structures that are involved in self/other processing. We then explore how social interactions affect neuronal development, and we discuss the social deficits associated with orbitofrontal damage and developmental disorders. Next we turn to you—or rather, your sense of self and how you get to know yourself. Then we investigate how you get to know others. We consider whether learning about others and learning about ourselves are similar processes, and whether they involve the same neural substrates.

Understanding ourselves and other people, however, is only part of successfully navigating our social worlds. We want to know what the brain can tell us about how we learn social rules and use them to guide our behavior and decisions. Note that social responses, including making facial expressions, evaluating social groups, categorizing coalitions, and stereotyping—which are all considered to be social cognitive neuroscience topics—were covered in Chapter 10, which focused on emotion.

13.1 Anatomical Substrates of Social Cognition

Up to this point in the book we have focused on relatively impersonal goals: naming words, attending to colors, remembering locations. But we humans are party animals. Most of our actions are socially oriented. This intense sociality appears to stem from distinctive social cognitive abilities that set humans apart from other animals.

For example, when Esther Herrmann and colleagues (2007) compared the performance of 2½-year-old human children with some of our closest primate relatives (e.g., chimpanzees) on a wide variety of cognitive tests, they found that chimpanzees and human children performed roughly equivalently on tasks pertaining to the physical world (e.g., tracking, remembering, and reasoning about the location of rewards; understanding causality in chains of events; understanding the functions of tools; quantitative reasoning). However, when it came to tasks tapping their social cognitive abilities—many of which you will learn about in this chapter, such as monitoring the focus of other people's attention by tracking their gaze, or understanding unobserved causal forces like the mental states of others—the human toddlers far outperformed any of the nonhuman primates tested. Compared to the brains of other animals, something is different about ours that enables us to be so social.

Let's begin with the "self" part of the social dyad. While each of us has information about ourselves that includes our personal traits, beliefs, desires, past, location in space, and the very knowledge that our body is our own, there is no single brain region we can point to and say, "This is where the self and all processing related to the self is located." You already know this. Recall from Chapter 4 that severing the corpus callosum results in two conscious hemispheres with separate and different cortical processing: two selves in one body.

Increasingly, the self appears to be a pastiche: It is made up of separable processes, full of separable content from a vast supply of sources coming from within and without the brain and the body. Lose a process, and you lose a part of your old self and turn into a new one, who, like Gage, may be quite different. (We will discuss a different aspect of the self, the subjective experience of being you, in the next chapter.) When we step into the social world and mix the self with others, we activate the "social brain," which also appears to be made up of interconnected systems, some of which may be specifically dedicated to social interactions.

Regions of the **prefrontal cortex (PFC)** are a primary focus in this chapter. The PFC is the anterior aspect of the frontal lobe (see the "Anatomical Orientation" box on p. 570) and evolution's latest addition to the brain. The lateral aspect of the PFC is divided into the dorsolateral prefrontal cortex (dlPFC) and the ventrolateral prefrontal cortex (vlPFC). The medial regions that we are concerned with are the **orbitofrontal cortex (OFC)** and the ventromedial prefrontal cortex (vmPFC). The regions that have been implicated in self-referential processing are the dlPFC and vmPFC, posterior cingulate cortex (PCC), and medial and lateral parietal cortex.

Subjective feelings also contribute to our sense of self and are mediated by all the regions we outlined in Chapter 10, including the OFC, anterior cingulate cortex (ACC), and insula, as well as the autonomic nervous system (ANS), hypothalamic-pituitary-adrenal (HPA) axis, and endocrine systems that regulate bodily states, emotion, and reactivity. Because memory is also part of self-referential processing, the temporal lobe is involved.

When we try to understand other individuals, various brain networks are activated that, depending on the task, can include the amygdala and its interconnections with the superior temporal sulcus (STS), the medial PFC, and the OFC, along with the ACC, the fusiform face area (FFA), regions associated with mirror neurons, the insula, the temporal poles, the temporoparietal junction (TPJ), and the medial parietal cortex.

TAKE-HOME MESSAGES

- There is no single region in the brain where the self is located.
- The prefrontal cortex houses processing that is critical for successful social behavior.

13.2 Social Interactions and Development

The prefrontal cortex, necessary for cognitive control, impulse control, and decision making, continues to develop throughout childhood and adolescence. This period of maturation is accompanied by parallel developmental changes in social behavior, such as an increase in peer–peer interactions that are characterized by an abundance of social play behavior (Blakemore, 2008; Crone & Dahl, 2012; Spear, 2000). Developing brain regions are more likely than fully developed regions to be negatively impacted by adverse events and to benefit from positive ones. During childhood and adolescence, adverse social events such as neglect or abuse increase the risk for mental illnesses later in life, such as depression, anxiety, schizophrenia, or drug abuse (A. R. Burke et al., 2017).

To study the impact of adverse social experience on neurodevelopment, researchers frequently use rats, which are highly social animals with neuronal and behavioral development similar to that of humans. Researchers have found that socially isolating rats (depriving them of social contact but allowing visual, auditory, and olfactory contact with other rats) during a time period equivalent to childhood and adolescence in humans greatly impedes the rats' social development. Findings include changes in PFC function, disrupted synaptic plasticity, decreases in dopamine and increases in serotonin signaling in the PFC, and social behavioral deficits, such as increased aggression, anxiety, and fear (Lukkes et al., 2009), which last into adulthood (reviewed in Fone & Porkess, 2008). Even if resocialized, the adult rats continue to have decreased social functioning.

However, it is not just social isolation that has an impact. Even if reared by a nonplayful or an atypically playful rat, young rats show social deficits and neuronal changes (Schneider et al., 2016), suggesting that the experience of play itself is important and not just social

ANATOMICAL ORIENTATION

Anatomy of Social Cognition

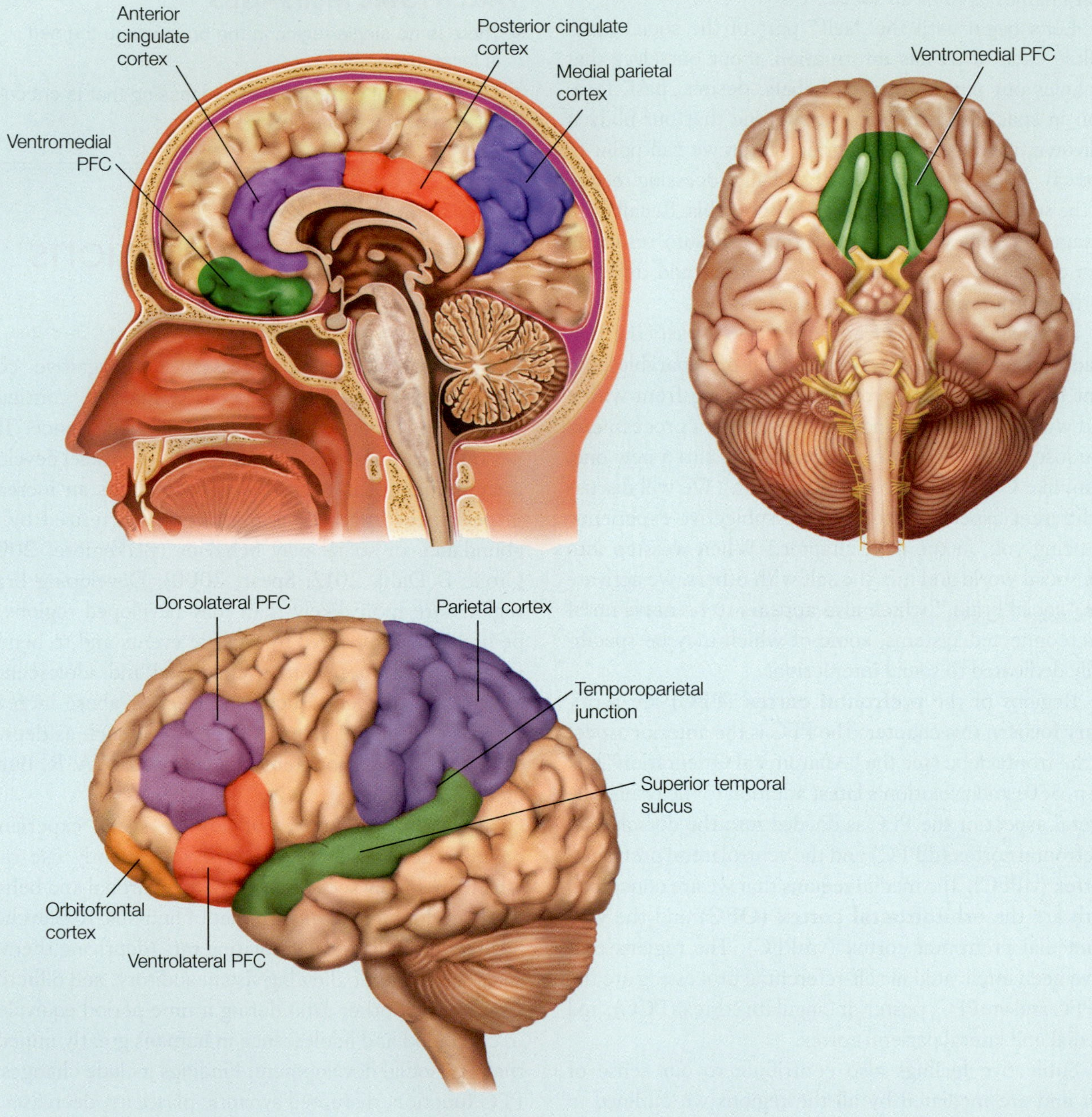

contact. One study focused on the time period during which social play behavior peaks in rats (postnatal Days 21–42; Baarendse et al., 2013). The researchers socially isolated rats during this period and afterward resocialized them.

After these rats had grown to adulthood, their impulsivity and decision making were tested under various conditions and compared to the behavior of rats that had engaged in social play during their youth. The adult rats that had been isolated demonstrated impaired decision making and acted more impulsively under novel or challenging circumstances. Later, whole-cell recordings from their PFC pyramidal neurons showed that the isolated rats were less sensitive to dopamine than the rats that had participated in social play as youths. Other studies have found that socially reared rats exhibit a pruned dendritic arbor and decreased neuronal density in the medial PFC (Bell et al., 2010; Himmler et al., 2013).

Another study compared corticosterone responses between prepubertal and adult male rats following acute stress, repeated stress, and novel stress. The paraventricular nucleus of the hypothalamus (which activates the HPA stress response; see Chapter 10) showed activation under each stress paradigm; in the prepubertal group, however, the activations were greater and more prolonged than in the adult group (Lui et al., 2012). This difference was not due to differences in cell density or volume (Romeo et al., 2007). It appears that experiencing stress early in life results in greater and prolonged activation of the HPA, leading to the neural and physiological repercussions of prolonged elevated cortisol levels (Lui et al., 2012).

Humans, as both children and adults, can have a perception of social isolation—a sense of loneliness—even though they may not be objectively alone. People who perceive isolation have higher morbidity and mortality rates, increased vascular resistance and higher blood pressure, increased incidence of metabolic syndrome, increased HPA activity, increased morning cortisol levels, fragmented sleep, sedentary lifestyles, underexpression of anti-inflammatory genes and overexpression of inflammatory genes, decreased immunity, and diminished impulse control. Perceived isolation is a predictor of cognitive decline, lifetime change in IQ, worsening of depression symptoms, and risk for Alzheimer's disease, even when researchers control for marital status, depression, social group size, and social activity (reviewed in J. T. Cacioppo & Cacioppo, 2014).

The central nervous system appears to be vulnerable to social stress during childhood and adolescence, resulting in high concentrations of glucocorticoids that can impact brain development. Even the perception of social isolation impacts the brain and contributes to cognitive decline and overall morbidity and mortality throughout life.

TAKE-HOME MESSAGES

- The prefrontal cortex continues to develop through adolescence.
- Social isolation and lack of social play during childhood and adolescence have negative impacts on the neuronal development of areas that support social behavior, resulting in social behavioral deficits that last into adulthood.
- Social stress during childhood affects the neuronal development of the brain.
- Social stress in adults contributes to neural degeneration.

13.3 Social Behavioral Deficits in Acquired and Neurodevelopmental Disorders

Social behavioral deficits can be the result of both acquired lesions to the frontal cortex and neurodevelopmental disorders that affect the frontal cortex. Functional deficits in these individuals provide clues to the neural underpinnings of social behavior.

Changes in social functioning are common in patients with acquired lesions to their orbitofrontal cortex, which include trauma, tumors, stroke or surgery, and neurodegenerative disorders such as Parkinson's, Huntington's, and Alzheimer's diseases. Typical findings include blunted affect, impaired autonomic response to emotional pictures and emotional memories (A. R. Damasio, 1990), and diminished regret, all of which suggest deficits in emotional processing. People with orbitofrontal damage may also demonstrate cognitive control deficits that affect social behavior: They may be less inhibited; tolerate frustration poorly and anger easily; and show increased aggression, immaturity, and impaired goal-directed behavior. They also lack insight into these changes and their inappropriate social conduct (Barrash et al., 2000).

Several neurodevelopmental disorders are associated with deficits in social behavior, including antisocial personality disorder (APD), schizophrenia, and autism spectrum disorder (ASD). People with APD are aware of social norms (the roles, rules, expectations, and goals that govern social situations) but fail to conform to them. These individuals may appear friendly yet act deceitfully and show indifference to the welfare of others; they understand that others have mental states—desires, beliefs, goals, and intentions—but they lack empathy. They may also have low impulse control, exhibit reckless and aggressive behavior, and fail to plan ahead, demonstrating problems of cognitive control.

Both schizophrenia and ASD are heterogeneous disorders with varying symptoms, including deficits in social perception (perceiving social cues from facial expressions, eye gaze, and body motion), in social knowledge (being aware of social norms), and in the theory of mind (understanding the mental states of others; see Section 13.5 and also Chapter 4). These impairments cause difficulties in interpreting the speech and action of others in order to understand their intentions, knowledge, and beliefs.

Individuals with ASD share three main symptoms: social deficits, communication deficits, and restricted, repetitive patterns of behavior, interests, or activities. They tend to show little interest in others and may prefer to engage with objects or in repetitive behavior, such as rocking their bodies or twisting their hands and fingers. They may become upset if routine patterns are interrupted, such as having their dinner table set in an unusual way or being assigned a new school bus driver.

Simon Baron-Cohen of Cambridge University and his colleagues (1985) have proposed that individuals with ASD direct their attention away from other people because of deficits in their theory of mind, which he calls mindblindness (Baron-Cohen, 1995). The lack of this intuitive knowledge makes social interactions difficult. ASD research has found impairments on a variety of tasks that require the use of facial perception for social judgments (e.g., Baron-Cohen, 1995; Klin et al., 1999; Weeks & Hobson, 1987). We will return to autism later in the chapter.

TAKE-HOME MESSAGES

- Deficits in social cognition are observed in people with some neurodevelopmental disorders and with acquired damage to the orbitofrontal cortex.
- Social deficits seen in autism spectrum disorder and schizophrenia may be the result of deficits in the ability to understand that others have mental states.
- Some social deficits seen in antisocial personality disorder are associated with deficits in cognitive control and a lack of empathy.

13.4 Socrates's Imperative: Know Thyself

Socrates emphasized the importance of "knowing thyself." How exactly do we do that? We develop our self-knowledge (i.e., information about our characteristics, desires, and thoughts) through self-perception processes designed to gather information about the self. Because the self is simultaneously the perceiver and the perceived, self-perception is a unique social cognitive process. Knowing oneself involves the physical you (Is that my arm?) as well as the unobservable essence of you: your traits, memories, experiences, and so forth (Am I loyal? Who taught me to swim? Where have I swum?).

In addition, we must distinguish ourselves from others: Our sense of self relies partially on seeing the difference between our self-knowledge and the knowledge we have about other people's characteristics, desires, and thoughts. For example, you might be one of those unusual individuals who prefers a snake for a pet, but you can readily acknowledge that most people would prefer a dog. Your individual preferences help define what makes you unique compared to other people. The big questions in **social cognitive neuroscience** center on which neural and psychological mechanisms support the processing of information about the self and about other people, whether these mechanisms are the same or different, how the brain differentiates between self and other, and how social contexts affect these processes.

In this section we look at how people represent and gather information about themselves, and at what the brain can tell us about the nature of self-perception.

Self-Referential Processing

Where were you born? Where was Napoleon born? We remember some information better than other information. It is a safe bet that you know where you were born, but when it comes to Napoleon, perhaps not. According to Fergus Craik and Robert Lockhart's levels-of-processing model of memory (1972), the depth of processing profoundly affects the storage of information. They found that information processed in a more meaningful way is remembered better than superficially processed information. For example, test participants were much more likely to remember a list of words when they considered their meaning than when they considered their font.

Other research groups have found that people remember significantly more information when they process it in relation to themselves (Markus, 1977; T. B. Rogers et al., 1977). For example, people are more likely to remember the adjective *happy* if they have to judge how well it describes themselves than if they have to judge how well it describes the president of the United States (**Figure 13.2**). The enhanced memory for information processed in relation to the self is known as the **self-reference effect**. So, if you have been to Corsica and have visited Napoleon's birthplace in Ajaccio, or if you were born there yourself, you are more likely to remember his birthplace than if you had never been there.

Two hypotheses have been considered about why memory is better for information processed in relation to the self. One suggests that the self is a unique cognitive structure with unique mnemonic or organizational elements that promote processing that is distinct from the processing that all other cognitive structures promote (T. B. Rogers et al., 1977). The other hypothesis bursts the bubble on a special self and suggests that we simply have more knowledge about the self, which encourages more elaborate coding of information that relates to the self (Klein & Kihlstrom, 1986).

From this latter perspective, the greater depth of processing might result from participants considering the

FIGURE 13.2 A typical self-referential processing experiment.
(a) Participants answer a series of questions about their own personality traits, as well as the personality traits of someone else. (b) Then they are asked which of the trait words they can remember.

adjective in relation to their wealth of stored information about the self. In contrast, their more superficial judgment of whether the word *happy* has two syllables exists only in relation to a single dimension that they may have stored about that word. While numerous behavioral studies have been conducted to examine these hypotheses, it was several imaging studies that revealed the neural systems underlying the self-reference effect.

If the self is a special cognitive structure characterized by unique information processing, then distinct neural regions should be activated in relation to the self-reference effect. William Kelley and his colleagues at Dartmouth College (2002) conducted one of the first fMRI studies to test this hypothesis. Participants judged personality adjectives in one of three experimental conditions: in relation to the self ("Does this trait describe you?"), in relation to another person ("Does this trait describe George Bush?"—the president at the time the study was conducted), or in relation to its printed format ("Is this word presented in uppercase letters?"). As found in numerous other studies of the self-reference effect, participants were most likely to remember words from the self condition and least likely to remember words from the printed-format condition.

Was there unique brain activity, then, when participants were making judgments in the self condition? The medial prefrontal cortex (MPFC) was differentially activated in the self condition compared to the other two conditions (**Figure 13.3**). Later studies found that the level of activity in the MPFC predicted which items would be remembered on a surprise memory test (Macrae et al., 2004). The relation between the MPFC and self-reference also extends to instances in which participants have to view themselves through another person's eyes.

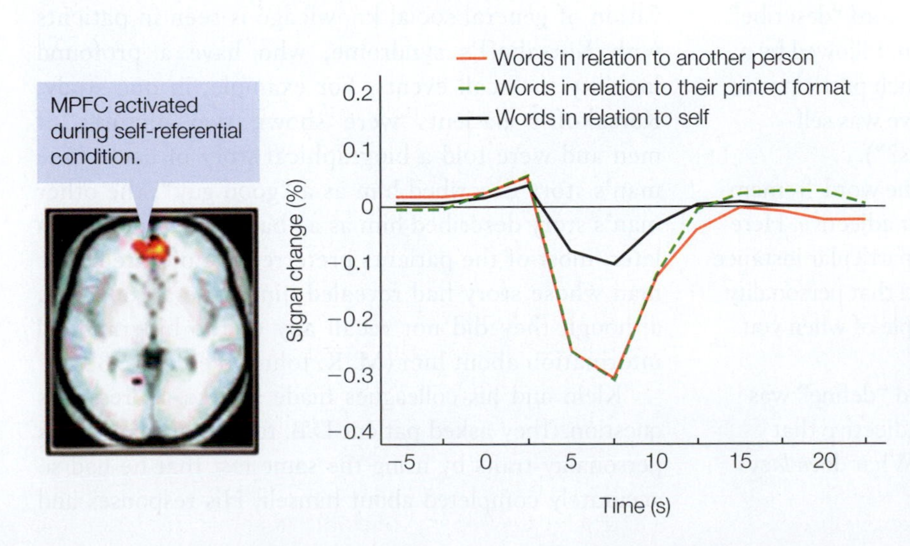

FIGURE 13.3 MPFC activity increases with self-referential processing.
Greater activity of the medial prefrontal cortex (MPFC) is associated with self-referential processing when compared to processing words in relation to another person ("other") or in relation to the printed format of the words.

A similar MPFC region is activated when people are asked to judge whether another individual would use particular adjectives to describe them (Ochsner et al., 2005).

Although much of this research has been conducted with fMRI, ERP studies provide convergent results. Self-referential processing produces positive-moving shifts in ERPs that emerge from a midline location consistent with the location of the MPFC (Magno & Allan, 2007). These studies suggest that self-referential processing is more strongly associated with MPFC function than is the processing of information about people we do not know personally.

Self-Descriptive Personality Traits

In addition to having a uniquely strong memory for traits that we judge in relation to ourselves, we have a unique way of deciding whether the trait is self-descriptive. For instance, when you attempt to describe yourself (Am I stingy?), you draw on a different source of information than when you try to describe someone else (Is Antonio stingy?). In other words, not only do we have a uniquely strong memory for traits that we judge in relation to ourselves, but we also have a unique way of deciding whether the traits are self-descriptive. Specifically, when we decide whether an adjective is self-descriptive, we rely on self-perceptions that are summaries of our personality traits rather than considering various episodes in our lives. In contrast, when making judgments of other individuals, we often focus on specific instances in which the person might have exhibited behaviors associated with the adjective.

Stanley Klein and his colleagues at UC Santa Barbara (1992) arrived at this finding when they asked whether self-descriptive judgments rely on recall of specific autobiographical episodes. How did they figure this out? Participants were randomly subjected to three conditions.

- In the *self-judgment* condition, the word "describe" was flashed on the computer screen, followed by a personality trait adjective, after which participants were to decide whether the adjective was self-descriptive (e.g., "Are you generous?").
- In the *autobiographical* condition, the word "remember" was flashed, followed by a trait adjective. Here participants were asked to recall a particular instance from their lives when they exhibited that personality characteristic (e.g., "Give an example of when you were stubborn").
- In the *definition* condition, the word "define" was flashed, followed by a personality adjective that participants were to define (e.g., "What does *lazy* mean?").

In a second session 2 weeks later, participants performed the same tasks, but half of the adjectives were traits that they had seen in the previous session, and the other half were traits that they had not been asked about before.

If self-descriptions rely on searching episodic memory for examples, then participants should answer faster when asked about a personality characteristic that they had lately considered in relation to themselves, having recently cruised through their episodic memory bank to make the self-descriptive judgment. What were the results? When asked whether a trait was self-descriptive, having previously performed an autobiographical task with that trait was no more effective at prompting recall than was having previously defined the trait. Similarly, on the autobiographical task, a trait adjective that had previously been judged as self-descriptive was no more effective than one that the participant had defined. These findings suggest that our judgments about self-descriptions are not linked to recall of specific past behaviors.

If this conclusion is correct, then we should be able to maintain a sense of self even if we are robbed of our autobiographical memories. Case studies of patients with dense amnesia (Klein et al., 2002; Tulving, 1993) support this conclusion. Consider two patients, one who developed retrograde amnesia, and one who developed anterograde amnesia (see Chapter 9): D.B.'s memory problems developed after a heart attack as a result of the transient loss of oxygen to the brain—a condition known as *hypoxia*; K.C. was in a motorcycle accident and sustained brain damage that resulted in amnesia. Neither of these patients could recall a single thing they had done or experienced in their entire life, yet both could accurately describe their own personality. For example, D.B. and K.C.'s personality judgments were consistent with judgments provided by their family members.

Possibly, however, their behavior reflected the preservation of more general social knowledge rather than the preservation of trait self-knowledge. Preservation of general social knowledge is seen in patients with Korsakoff's syndrome, who have a profound inability to recall events. For example, in one study, Korsakoff's patients were shown two pictures of men and were told a biographical story of each. One man's story described him as a "good guy"; the other man's story described him as a "bad guy." One month later, most of the patients preferred the picture of the man whose story had revealed him to be a good guy, although they did not recall any of the biographical information about him (M. K. Johnson et al., 1985).

Klein and his colleagues made sure to address this question. They asked patient D.B. to rate his daughter's personality traits by using the same test that he had so accurately completed about himself. His responses and those of his daughter varied wildly, while those of control patients and their children did not. Although D.B. was unable to retrieve accurate trait information about his daughter, he had no trouble recalling information about himself (Klein et al., 2002). These results provide additional support for the suggestion that trait-based semantic knowledge about the self exists outside of general semantic knowledge. They also suggest that at least some of the mechanisms of self-referential processing rely on neural systems distinct from the neural systems used to process information about other people.

Trait-based semantic knowledge about the self is remarkably robust against a host of neural insults and damage (Klein & Lax, 2010). In this regard it is unlike other types of semantic knowledge, even other types of semantic knowledge about the self; for example, you may not know your birthday or recognize yourself in the mirror, but you still know that you are stubborn. This robustness suggests that semantic trait knowledge about oneself is a special type of self-knowledge. The fact that this special self-knowledge is separate from other knowledge about the self also suggests that the self is not a single unified entity.

These findings lead to the conclusion that rather than being centered in one unique cognitive structure, the self is distributed across multiple systems. In fact, several different systems for self-knowledge have been identified, and they can be isolated functionally from each other. For example, there is one system for episodic memories of your own life (I had a great time hiking in South Dakota), another for semantic knowledge of the facts of your life (I am half Norwegian), another for a sense of personal agency (I am the agent that causes my arm to lift up), another for the ability to recognize your body in the mirror, in photos, and just looking down at your feet (That's me, all right!), and there are many more systems mediating other types of self-knowledge.

These different systems for self-knowledge are at least partially anatomically separable as well. For example, Michel Desmurget and colleagues (2009) were able to artificially give individuals the sense that they had moved or spoken (without their having *actually* moved or spoken) by electrically stimulating regions of the posterior parietal cortex in patients undergoing awake brain surgery. Thus, activity in the posterior parietal cortex appears to play a causal role in generating the sense of personal agency—one of the core systems of self-knowledge just described.

On the other hand, damage to medial temporal lobe regions (e.g., resection of the left and right medial temporal lobe in patient H.M., described in Chapter 9) can profoundly impair the ability to form and access episodic memories about one's own life without impacting other systems for self-knowledge (e.g., the sense of personal agency). Thus, invasive methods and lesion studies confirm that self-knowledge appears to be both fundamentally distributed and reliant on multiple distinct brain systems. Although these systems interact a great deal in day-to-day life, they can be dissociated from one another through the use of carefully designed psychological and neuroscientific paradigms.

Self-Reference as a Baseline Mode of Brain Function

As we have seen in many previous chapters, during fMRI studies participants are given a task to perform. Typically, they are asked to rest between tasks. Imagine yourself lying in a "magnet" with nothing to do and being told to rest. Does your mind turn off like a TV screen? No; you start thinking about the weekend, summer break, your friends, the paper you have to write—something. And usually that something is all about you, or about something or someone connected to you in some way.

Can studying the brain tell us anything about why self-referential processing is so prevalent? Some research suggests that the medial prefrontal cortex (MPFC), the region associated with self-referential processing, has unique physiological properties that may permit self-referential processing to occur even when we are not actively trying to think about ourselves; that is, it is our brain's default processing mode.

This notion emerged as it gradually dawned on researchers that although participants inside the MRI machine were supposedly at rest, activity in specific brain regions was noticeably increasing. In fact, this activity was as vigorous as the activity detected in other regions during mental tasks such as math problems. The brain at rest apparently was not "off." When participants were quizzed about what they were thinking during their "rest periods," the typical answer related to self-referential processing (Gusnard & Raichle, 2001; Gusnard et al., 2001).

Obviously, even when you are resting quietly, blood continues to circulate to your brain as it uses oxygen. In fact, a network of brain regions that includes the MPFC has metabolic rates that are higher "at rest." These circulatory and metabolic demands are costly because they take blood and oxygen away from other organs. Why would the brain consume so much of the body's energy when it is not engaged in a specific cognitive task?

Raichle, Gusnard, and their colleagues argue that when we are at rest, cognitively speaking, our brains continue to engage but revert to a number of psychological processes that describe a default mode of brain function

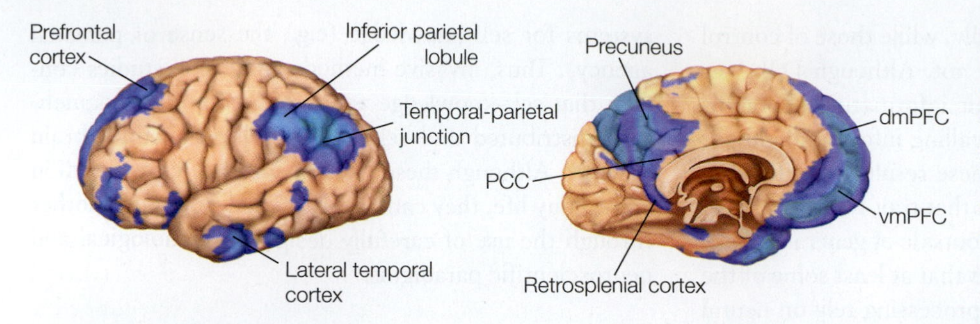

FIGURE 13.4 The default network. Combined data from nine positron emission tomography (PET) studies showing the regions that were most active during passive tasks (in blue). The lateral (left) and medial (right) surfaces of the left hemisphere are shown. The medial temporal lobe (see the "Anatomical Orientation" box in Chapter 9) is not shown in this projection.

(Gusnard & Raichle, 2001). The researchers named the brain regions that support these processes the **default network** (Raichle et al., 2001). The default network consists of the MPFC (made up of the dmPFC and vmPFC), precuneus, posterior cingulate cortex, retrosplenial cortex, TPJ, medial temporal lobe, and inferior parietal lobule (**Figure 13.4**). The researchers hypothesized that the higher metabolic rate in the MPFC reflects self-referential processing, such as thinking about what we might be getting ready to do or evaluating our current condition. Thus, they concluded, the default network is there to ensure that we always have some idea of what is going on around us. This is called the *sentinel hypothesis*.

The default network is most active when tasks direct our attention away from external stimuli and we are inwardly focused, engaged in self-reflective thought and judgment assessments that depend on social and emotional content. The default network is connected to the medial temporal lobe memory system, which explains why we often consider the past in these ramblings. However, no primary sensory or motor regions are connected to the default network, and it is deactivated during active tasks (**Figure 13.5**).

Thus, when you want to detach yourself from ruminating about your own plight, you can do so by performing an active task such as reading, practicing your guitar chords, or rotating your tires. The great Antarctic explorer Sir Ernest Shackleton knew this instinctively. In his book, *South*, he describes the ordeal that he and his men went through when their ship was sunk and they were stranded on the pack ice just off the Antarctic coast in 1915. At one point he relates,

> Then I took out to replace the cook [with] one of the men who had expressed a desire to lie down and die. The task of keeping the galley fire alight was both difficult and strenuous, and it took his thoughts away from the chances of immediate dissolution. In fact, I found him a little later gravely concerned over the drying of a naturally not over-clean pair of socks which were hung up in close proximity to our evening milk. Occupation had brought his thoughts back to the ordinary cares of life. (Shackleton, 1919/2004, p. 136)

Interestingly, however, while performing active tasks that involve self-referential judgments, the MPFC

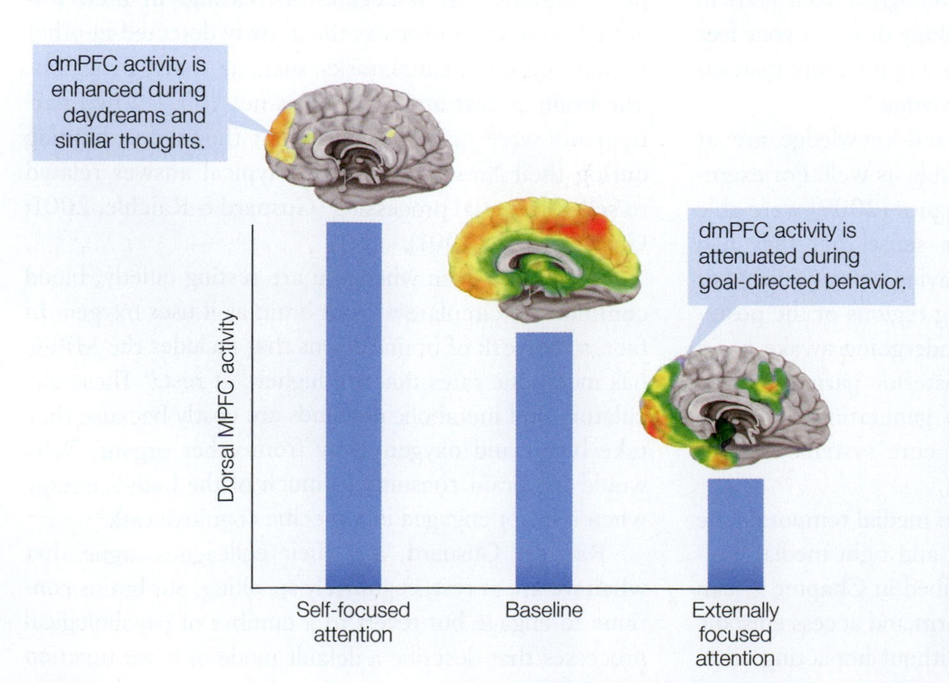

FIGURE 13.5 Focus inward is accompanied by increased dmPFC activity. Activity in the dorsomedial prefrontal cortex (dmPFC) increases during tasks that involve self-referential mental activity or self-focused attention and decreases during tasks that involve externally focused attention. This finding is consistent with the observation that during goal-directed behaviors, self-focused attention decreases, and it also indicates that at baseline, some degree of self-referential mental activity should be engaging this region—a suggestion that has been supported by functional imaging data.

deactivates less than it does for other types of tasks. The fact that we generally think about ourselves when left to daydream would suggest that when we're given a self-referential task, our MPFC would not show a significant change in activation, because it chronically engages in self-referential thinking, even during the rest or baseline condition. In the self-reference studies described alongside Figure 13.2, for example, the president and printed-format conditions directed cognitive resources away from self-referential thinking, and the MPFC showed a strong deactivation relative to baseline under those conditions.

Since the default network was first described, however, multiple studies have found that various tasks activate a set of regions remarkably similar to the default network. These include autobiographical memory tasks, tasks that require envisioning the self in the future or navigating to a different location, and tasks that evaluate personal moral dilemmas (e.g., is it morally acceptable to push one person off a sinking boat to save five others?). Furthermore, similar regions of the brain are activated when we think about the beliefs and intentions of other people—that is, their mental states. Thus, the default network appears to do more than solely self-referential processing. Can you spot a common thread, or common cognitive process, running through all of these tasks?

Although they differ in content and goal, each task requires the participants to envision themselves in conditional situations, situations other than the here and now—that is, to adopt an alternative, counterfactual perspective (Buckner & Carroll, 2007; J. P. Mitchell, 2009). For example, imagine what you might think and feel if you had to change a flat tire in a rainstorm, without a raincoat, on the way to an important interview. Alternatively, how would you feel if you won a trip to the Seychelles? Each scenario requires you to focus on thoughts that (most likely) have no relation to the stimuli in your current environment. This type of cognitive process is exactly what we need so that we can infer the mental states of others, such as trying to imagine how your friend felt after catching a seemingly impossible touchdown pass in the Rose Bowl game. As this account suggests, the processes that give rise to our understanding of other people's minds overlap with the processes that support speculations about our own activities.

Recent evidence is consistent with a key role for the default network in understanding other people's minds and suggests that high levels of activity in the default network during periods of rest may prepare us for effective social cognition. Robert Spunt and colleagues at UCLA used fMRI to measure activity in areas of the default network in participants during brief (20-second) rest periods preceding trials of three different cognitive tasks: evaluating whether a sentence matched the mental state of an individual depicted in a photograph, evaluating whether a sentence matched the individual's physical description, or solving a mathematical problem (Spunt et al., 2015).

Strikingly, these researchers found that increased activity in the default network during the 20-second rest period predicted the ease and efficiency with which participants performed the mental-state matching task, but similar increased default network activity before the physical-description matching task or the mathematical task had no effect on performance. These researchers suggest that evolution has honed our neural processes such that when no immediate task is at hand, our brains prepare us for the difficult task of making sense of other minds. The next time someone tells you to enjoy the moment instead of daydreaming, you can reply, "Dude, I'm in prep mode to mind-read."

Self-Perception as a Motivated Process

Even though we have the richest possible set of data against which to judge ourselves, this process is often inaccurate. A wide range of behavioral studies have shown that people often have unrealistically positive self-perceptions (S. E. Taylor & Brown, 1988). Among high school students, 70% rank themselves as above average in leadership ability, while 93% of college professors believe that they are above average at their work (reviewed in Gilovich, 1991). More than 50% of people believe they are above average in intelligence, physical attractiveness, and a host of other positive characteristics. This view through rose-colored glasses extends to our expectations in life. People tend to believe they are more likely than others to experience positive future events, such as winning the lottery, and less likely than others to experience negative future events, such as getting a divorce.

How does the brain enable us to maintain these positive illusions about ourselves? Studies suggest that the most ventral portion of the anterior cingulate cortex is responsible for focusing attention on positive information about the self. Joseph Moran and his colleagues at Dartmouth College (2006) did an fMRI study asking participants to make a series of self-descriptive judgments just like those in the self-reference studies. As expected from research on positive biases in self-perception, the participants tended to select more positive adjectives and fewer negative adjectives as self-descriptive. Differences in activity in the ventral anterior cingulate cortex were associated with making judgments about positive adjectives compared to

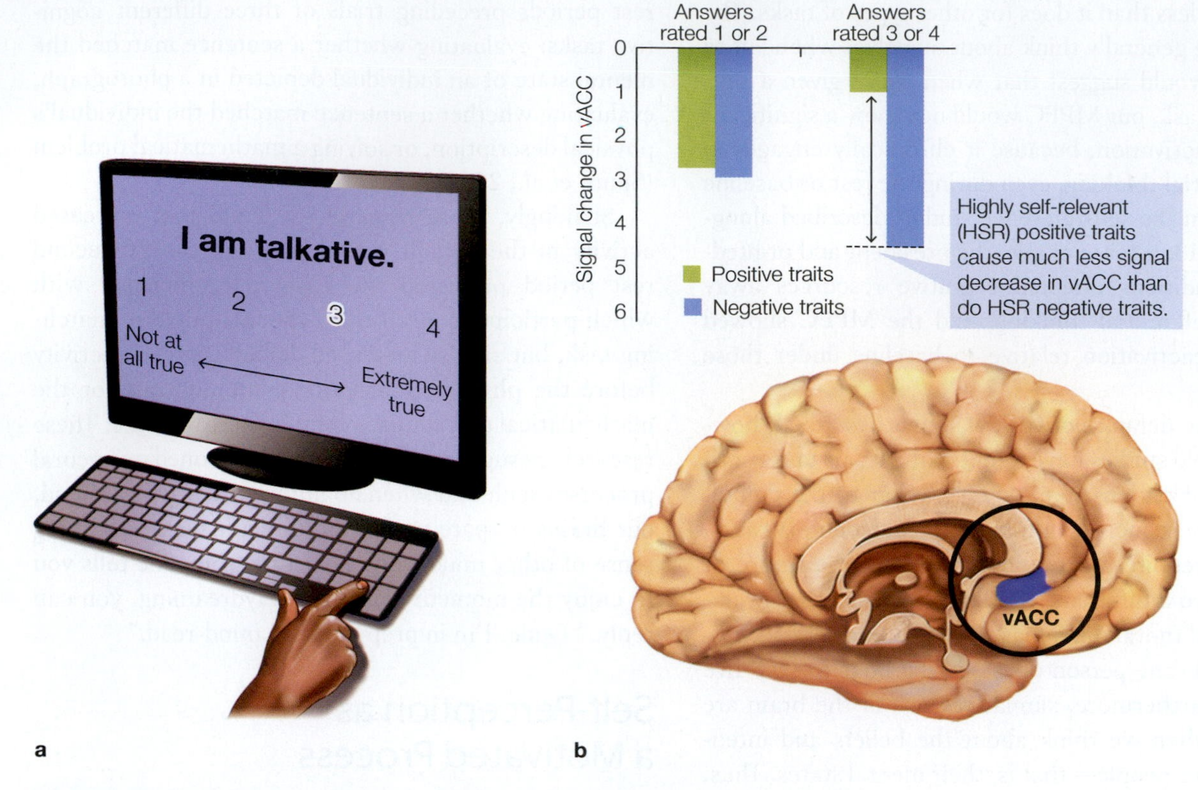

FIGURE 13.6 Neural activity in relation to judging positive information about the self.
(a) Participants rated the self-descriptiveness of a variety of personality traits. (b) Less deactivation in the anterior cingulate was associated with rating positive personality traits in comparison to negative personality traits. vACC = ventral anterior cingulate cortex.

negative adjectives—particularly for adjectives considered to be self-descriptive (**Figure 13.6**).

Another fMRI study found that a similar region of the anterior cingulate cortex was activated differentially when participants imagined experiencing a positive event in the future as compared to a negative event (Sharot et al., 2007). These studies suggest that the anterior cingulate cortex is important for distinguishing positive self-relevant information from negative self-relevant information. Marking information as positive versus negative may permit people to focus more on the positive.

Although self-perceptions are sometimes biased in a positive direction, on average, self-perceptions are not delusional or completely detached from reality. Accurate self-perception is essential for appropriate social behavior. For example, people must have some insight into their behavior to make sure they are following social rules and norms and avoiding social mistakes. Patients with damage to the orbitofrontal cortex (like M.R. in the chapter-opening story) tend to have unrealistically positive self-views, along with inappropriate social behavior.

Jennifer Beer wondered whether patients' behavior was inappropriate because they lacked insight into their own behavior or because they were unaware of the social norms. To explore this question, she videotaped healthy control participants, patients who had damage to the orbitofrontal cortex, and patients with lateral prefrontal cortex damage while they engaged in a structured social interaction with a stranger (Beer et al., 2006). In this interaction, the stranger made conversation with the participants by asking them a series of questions. Unlike the other two groups, patients with orbitofrontal damage tended to bring up impolite conversation topics.

After the interview, the participants rated how appropriate their answers had been, considering that they had been talking to a stranger. Patients with orbitofrontal damage believed they had performed very well on the social interaction task. When they were shown the videotaped interview, however, these patients become embarrassed by their social mistakes (**Figure 13.7**). This study suggests that the orbitofrontal cortex is important for spontaneous, accurate self-perceptions, and that, rather than being unaware of social norms, patients with orbitofrontal damage demonstrate lack of insight.

a

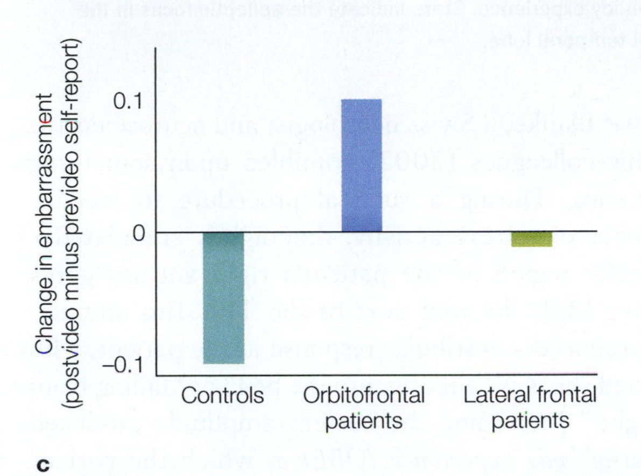

c

b

FIGURE 13.7 Study of self-insight in patients with orbitofrontal damage.
(a) Participants first performed a social skills task that required them to make conversation with an experimenter they did not know well. (b) After performing the task and reporting on their perceptions of their own social appropriateness and emotions, participants watched a videotape of their task performance. (c) In contrast to the other brain-damaged participants and the healthy control participants, patients with orbitofrontal damage became embarrassed after viewing their social mistakes on videotape.

Predicting Our Future Mental State

When we predict our future mental state, do we consider actual experiences and extrapolate, or do we generate an output from a set of rules? What if we were asked to choose between spending a year alone in a space station on Mars or alone in a submarine under the polar ice cap? This is a choice between scenarios that no one has experienced, so memory offers no help; nor are there general rules about how to choose.

When participants had to make predictions about their mental states in novel scenarios, fMRI revealed that the ventral region of the MPFC (the vmPFC)—a region involved with simulating other people's minds, other times, and other places—was consistently engaged. It has also been found that people's preferences for one novel situation over another are stable over time: Ask them 9 months later and they make the same choice. Taking these two findings together, Jason Mitchell speculates that when we make these types of predictions, we begin by simulating the experience, just as we would when we simulate the experience of another, and then calculate our preference from those simulations (J. P. Mitchell, 2009).

Studies of patients with damage to the vmPFC support the notion that it contributes to predictions about an individual's own likes and dislikes. In one study (Fellows & Farah, 2007), three groups were examined: patients with damage principally involving the orbitofrontal and/or the ventral portion of the medial wall of the frontal lobe, patients with damage to the dorsolateral PFC, and healthy controls. Each participant was asked which of two actors, foods, or colors they preferred. For instance, "Do you prefer Ben Affleck or Matthew Broderick?" When controls or patients with dlPFC damage chose Ben over Matthew, but Matthew over Tom Cruise, their preferences remained stable; they also said they liked Ben more than Tom. Not so with patients who had damage to their vmPFC. Their preferences were inconsistent: They might choose Ben over Matthew and Matthew over Tom, but then choose Tom over Ben.

If you were offered either $20 today or a guaranteed $23 next week, which would you pick? Oddly enough, most people pick the $20. In general, people tend to make shortsighted decisions, even when they can foresee the consequences and understand that they would be better off with a different choice. Why do we do this? Brain regions associated with introspective self-reference (such as the vmPFC) are more engaged when we're judging how much a person would enjoy an event in the present than when predicting future events (J. P. Mitchell et al., 2011).

Furthermore, vmPFC activity is an indicator of shortsightedness. By looking at the magnitude of vmPFC reduction, researchers could predict the extent to which participants would make shortsighted monetary decisions several weeks later. The more the vmPFC was activated when predicting future events, the fewer shortsighted decisions were made. If you happen to be one of the few people who can delay the payoff, most likely your vmPFC engages better than most when thinking about the future. Considering the previous finding that the vmPFC contributes to the ability to simulate future events from a first-person perspective, Mitchell proposes that an individual's shortsighted decisions may result in part from a failure to fully imagine the subjective experience of a future self.

Body Ownership and Embodiment

All the information you know about the world is received through sense organs mounted on a moving target—your body. This happens without you having the slightest doubt that the body is yours (body ownership), that all its parts belong to you, and that you and your body are in the same place at the same time. Most of us take for granted the feeling of body ownership, complete with all its parts, and the feeling of spatial unity between the "self" and the body, referred to as **embodiment**—yet these certainties arise from complex and specific brain mechanisms that integrate sensory and motor information.

One region of the brain that has been implicated in this processing is the extrastriate body area located in the lateral occipitotemporal cortex, which responds selectively to human bodies and body parts and to imagined and executed movements of one's own body (Astafiev et al., 2004; Downing et al., 2001). Here we will focus on another relevant cortical region: the temporoparietal junction (TPJ). The TPJ is involved in self processing and integrating multisensory body-related information, which plays a key role in the feeling of embodiment.

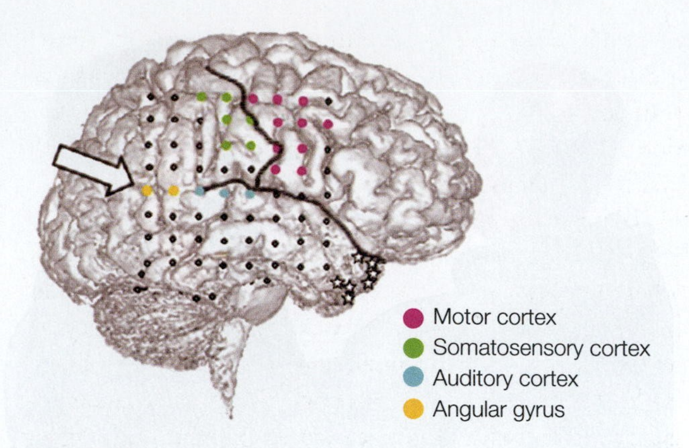

FIGURE 13.8 Location of the angular gyrus. Three-dimensional surface reconstruction of the right hemisphere from MRI. Colored spots indicate the location of subdural electrodes where focal electrical stimulation evoked behavioral responses. Stimulation (arrow) at the angular gyrus produced an out-of-body experience. Stars indicate the epileptic focus in the medial temporal lobe.

Olaf Blanke, a Swiss neurologist and neuroscientist, and his colleagues (2002) stumbled upon something fascinating. During a surgical procedure to localize the focus of seizure activity, they lightly stimulated a particular region of the patient's right angular gyrus (**Figure 13.8**), located next to the TPJ. This stimulation produced a vestibular response in the patient, who reported she was "sinking into the bed" or "falling from a height." Increasing the current amplitude produced an *out-of-body experience (OBE)* in which the patient reported, "I see myself lying in bed, from above, but I only see my legs and lower trunk."

An OBE, or disembodiment phenomenon, occurs when a person seems to be awake yet sees his body and the world from a location outside his physical body (Blanke et al., 2005). During an OBE, you experience a threefold deviation from the normal self: You feel that you are not residing in your own body (abnormal sense of spatial unity between self and body); you feel as if you are inhabiting another body, usually hovering above the physical body (abnormal self-location); and you see your own body and a view of the world from that location (abnormal egocentric visuospatial perspective; Blanke et al., 2005).

A few years before Blanke's observation, researchers had performed an fMRI study in which participants changed their egocentric perspective. They were shown a picture of a figure and were asked to make judgments about the scene from the figure's viewpoint; that is, they had to imagine a perspective other than their own. The study implicated areas near the TPJ as the location of this processing, but only when the participants transformed their egocentric perspective. The TPJ was not active when they attempted a different imagination task: the mental rotation of objects. The researchers hypothesized a dissociation between imagined egocentric perspective transformations and object-based spatial transformations (Zacks et al., 1999), the former involving the TPJ and the latter not.

Blanke's group pursued its observations in a study (Blanke et al., 2005) seeking to answer the question of whether spontaneous OBEs relied on the same or similar mechanisms involved when participants *imagined* having an OBE, since areas around the TPJ had been implicated in both. In the study, healthy participants undergoing continuous EEG were asked to imagine themselves to be experiencing an OBE. Their ERP responses were enhanced over the TPJ.

The researchers then used TMS to determine whether activity in the TPJ was required for transforming one's body location and visual perspective, or whether it was a general mechanism for transforming anything. When TMS was applied over the TPJ, it interrupted the imagined transformations of body location but not the imagined rotation of other objects. The final participant in the study was an epileptic patient for whom intracranial recordings had shown spontaneous OBEs originating from the TPJ. When she imagined an OBE that mimicked the perceptions she had had during a spontaneous OBE, the seizure focus showed partial activation. This combination of results suggested to the researchers that the TPJ is a crucial structure for mediating spatial unity of self and body and for the conscious experience of the normal self. If the processing in the TPJ is disordered, errors can occur and our brains can misinterpret our location.

Out-of-body experiences are one of three types of visual body illusions known as **autoscopic phenomena (APs)** that affect the entire body (as opposed to body part illusions, such as phantom limbs). (Derived from the Greek words for "self" and "watcher," *autoscopy* is the experience of perceiving the surroundings from a position outside of one's own body.) The second AP type is *autoscopic hallucination*. In this case, people do not feel as if they have left their body, but they see a double of themselves in extrapersonal space. The third type of AP is *heautoscopy*, which is the experience of seeing a double of oneself in extrapersonal space but being unsure of whether one feels disembodied or not (Blanke et al., 2004).

The different APs are associated with damage to different regions of the temporoparietal cortex. Neuroanatomical studies have shown that out-of-body experiences are caused by damage to right temporoparietal cortex, autoscopic hallucinations tend to be caused by damage to right parieto-occipital or right temporo-occipital cortex, and heautoscopy results from left temporoparietal lesions (Blanke & Metzinger, 2009; **Figure 13.9**).

Blanke has proposed that autoscopic phenomena result from two disintegrations: one within personal space, and a second one between personal and extrapersonal space. The first disintegration occurs as a result of conflicting sensory input—that is, the failure of two or more sources of tactile, proprioceptive, kinesthetic, and visual information to match up. For instance, imagine seeing yourself touch a part of your body, but feeling the sensation a tad later than you expected to. The second disintegration occurs when there is conflicting visual and vestibular information, such as when your vestibular system senses that you are moving in one direction but your visual information doesn't correspond.

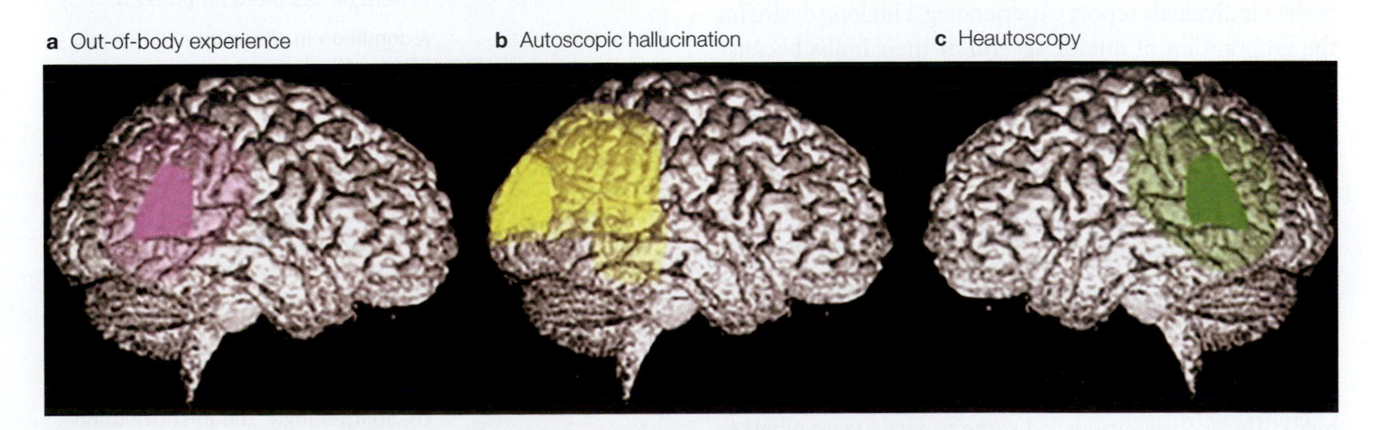

FIGURE 13.9 Location of brain damage for each of the three autoscopic phenomena.
(a) Purple indicates the area of damage associated with out-of-body experiences, localized primarily in the right temporoparietal cortex, in 12 patients. Although single cases of each AP type have been reported after damage to the right or left hemisphere, the hemispheres of predominant involvement are shown here. (b) Yellow indicates the center of damage for autoscopic hallucinations in the right parieto-occipital or right temporo-occipital cortex, based on 7 patients. (c) Green indicates damage in the left temporoparietal cortex associated with heautoscopy in 10 patients.

BOX 13.1 | LESSONS FROM THE CLINIC

An Unwanted Limb

Since the age of 4, Patrick hadn't felt as though his left leg belonged to him. The leg appeared perfectly normal to others—including doctors. But to Patrick it was a foreign body, and an increasingly bothersome one. He wanted it removed.

As a teenager living in a small, rural American town in the 1960s, Patrick became obsessed with amputees, searching the library for pictures of them. He realized that he wasn't the only person with such an obsession when he found that most of the pictures of amputees had been cut and stolen from the library books. But he wasn't going to learn more than that from any book, because the first modern case description of a desire to be an amputee wasn't published until 1977, where it was defined as a deviant sexual desire.

Patrick kept his wish to be rid of his leg a secret for 40 years, until, in the early 1990s, he met another "wannabe amputee" through a classified ad in a local newspaper, which led him to meeting others, including some who had performed do-it-yourself amputations. By now Patrick was becoming desperate to lose his leg. One DIY amputee suggested to him that if he was serious, he should practice first—which he did, cutting off one of his fingers above the first joint.

A decade later, in his 50s and still hauling around his unwanted appendage, Patrick met a psychologist online who suffered from body integrity identity disorder and was involved with an underground movement for a radical BIID treatment: voluntary amputation, which was not legal. Anywhere. This psychologist was the gatekeeper for a sympathetic surgeon in China who performed secret, illegal voluntary amputations. After meeting and screening Patrick, the psychologist connected him with the surgeon. Patrick traveled halfway around the world to have the operation done. When he awoke from anesthesia and looked down, he couldn't believe that the leg was finally gone. He later commented, "I wouldn't want my leg back for all the money in the world, that's how happy I am" (Ananthaswamy, 2015). Although he was never formally diagnosed, Patrick had been suffering nearly all his life from the neurological disorder xenomelia.

While aberrant processing in the TPJ produces autoscopic phenomena that involve the whole body, aberrant processing in other brain regions produces another group of disorders that involve only parts of the body; a partial list is provided in **Table 13.1.** One such disorder is **xenomelia** (from the Greek words for "foreign" and "limb"; McGeoch et al., 2011), also known as *body integrity identity disorder (BIID)*, a rare condition in which able-bodied individuals report experiencing a lifelong desire for the amputation of one or several of their limbs because they do not feel that the limb belongs to their body. In fact, they say they would feel "more complete" after its removal (see **Box 13.1**; Blanke et al., 2009).

Many people with xenomelia have tried to amputate their limbs themselves, unable to find a willing surgeon. Although xenomelia was originally thought to be a psychosis, observers noted that the offending limb was most often the left leg (similar to how hemineglect most often presents on the left side; see Chapter 7) and that the condition most often affected males (90% of people with this syndrome are men). These observations led some to investigate whether the problem was neurological rather than psychological, and indeed, extensive psychiatric examinations revealed the absence of any psychotic disorder (First, 2005).

V. S. Ramachandran (of phantom limb fame; see Chapter 5) and his colleagues found empirical evidence that xenomelia has a neurological basis (Brang et al., 2008).

TABLE 13.1 Partial List of Anomalies in Bodily Experience

Disorder	Description
Alien limb syndrome	The feeling that the problem limb displays a will of its own.
Asomatognosia	The feeling that the body, or only one lateral half, or one limb, seems absent or has been amputated.
Asymbolia	A condition in which pain is felt but it is not unpleasant.
Feeling of presence	The feeling that a ghostly companion is following one's every move.
Hemineglect	Denial or ignorance of the contralesional side of the body.
Misoplegia	Hatred of the body or limb(s), which may be the target of abusive and self-destructive behavior.
Somatoparaphrenia	The feeling that the body or parts of it belong to another person, always on the side opposite to the lesion. Or, contrastingly, the misattribution of someone else's hand as one's own when that hand is in the other person's contralesional hemispace.
Xenomelia	The feeling that one or more limbs do not belong to one's body, and the lifelong desire to amputate them.

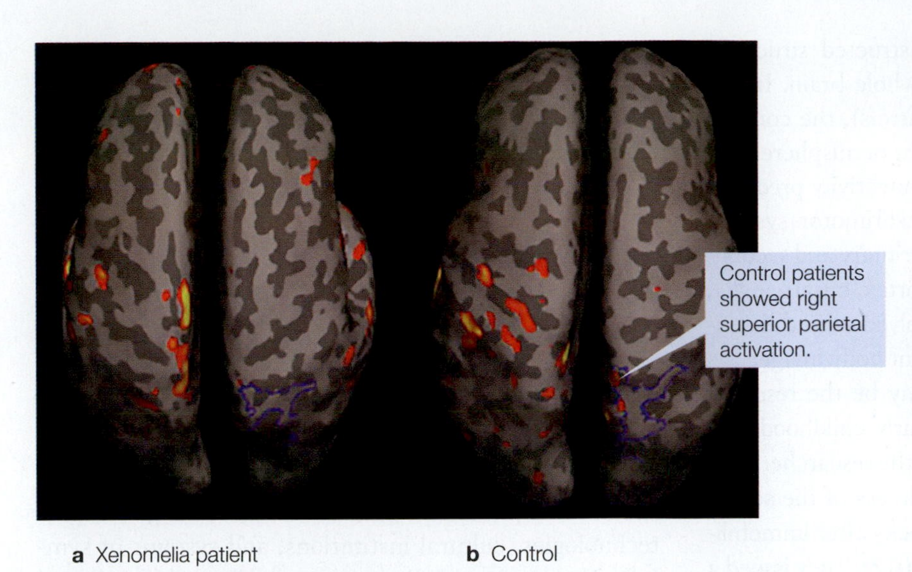

FIGURE 13.10 MEG activation to a tactile stimulus in xenomelia and control participants.
A stimulus was applied to the right foot of **(a)** a patient with xenomelia who wanted a midthigh amputation of his right leg and **(b)** a control participant. The MEG response is overlaid on the inflated left and right hemispheres of each patient's brain. The right superior parietal lobule (SPL), outlined in blue, revealed significantly reduced activation in the leg that the participants with xenomelia desired amputated, compared to their other leg and to the controls' legs. The pointer indicates activation in the right SPL of the control individual. The SPL is critical for sensorimotor integration, and the absence of activation in (a) suggests that the limb has not been incorporated into the body image of the xenomelia patient.

They recorded magnetoencephalography (MEG) signals in response to tactile stimulation below and above the line of a desired amputation in four patients with xenomelia (McGeoch et al., 2011). Compared to touch on accepted body parts and in controls, touch on the undesired limb elicited no cortical response in one particular brain area: the right superior parietal lobule (SPL) (**Figure 13.10**).

The SPL is where somatosensory, visual, and vestibular signals converge and is critical for sensorimotor integration (Wolpert, Goodbody, et al., 1998). The absence of activation of the right SPL in these individuals suggests that the limb has not been incorporated into their body image. The result is the seemingly bizarre situation in which the individual can feel sensation in the limb in question but has no sense of ownership. Since it isn't his, it feels foreign and he doesn't want it.

These findings were backed up by researchers at the University of Zurich who performed a structural imaging study in which 10 men, each of whom intensely desired to have either one or both legs amputated, were compared with a carefully matched control group (Hilti et al., 2013). In the xenomelia group, the researchers found neuroarchitectural abnormalities in exactly those cortical areas implicated by Ramachandran's group: decreased cortical surface area in the right anterior insular cortex (Brang et al., 2008) and decreased cortical thickness in the SPL (McGeoch et al., 2011). Furthermore, the cortical surface area of the right primary somatosensory cortex involved in representation of the left leg was decreased, as was the surface area of the right secondary somatosensory cortex (**Figure 13.11**).

Next, using diffusion tensor imaging (DTI) combined with fiber tractography (a 3D modeling method)

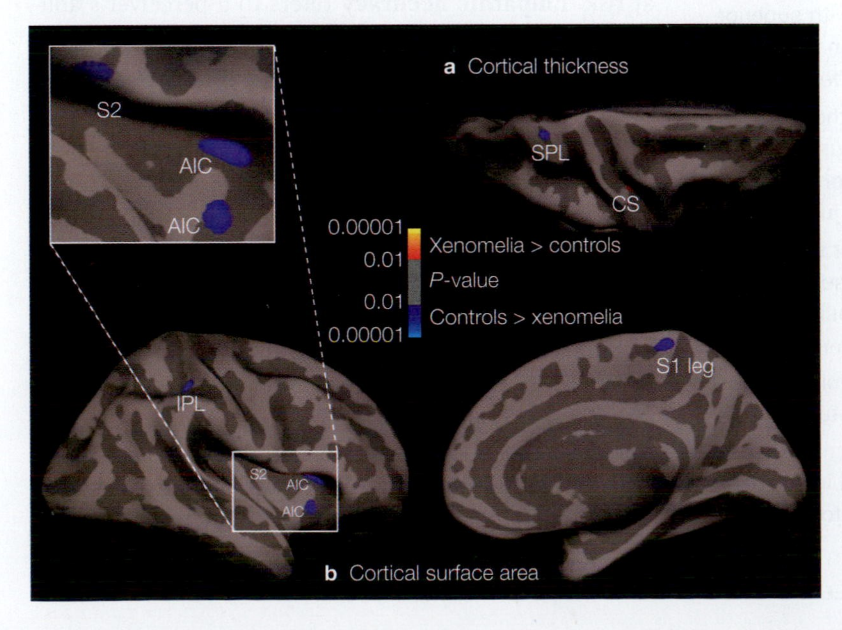

FIGURE 13.11 Alteration of right-hemisphere neuroarchitecture in xenomelia.
The maps are overlaid on the mean right-hemisphere inflated surface model of 26 participants (13 with xenomelia and 13 controls). **(a)** Cortical thickness is decreased (blue) in the superior parietal lobule (SPL) and increased (red) in the central sulcus (CS) in participants with xenomelia compared with control participants. **(b)** Cortical surface area is decreased in the anterior insular cortex (AIC), primary somatosensory leg representation (S1 leg), secondary somatosensory cortex (S2), and inferior parietal lobule (IPL) of participants with xenomelia. The magnified inset is tilted to show the entire extent of the S2 cluster.

and rs-fMRI, the research team constructed structural and functional connectomes for the whole brain. In the xenomelia group (as compared to controls), the connectome revealed a subnetwork in the right hemisphere with increased structural and functional connectivity predominantly in nodes belonging to the sensorimotor system, including the superior parietal lobule, primary and secondary somatosensory cortex, premotor cortex, basal ganglia, thalamus, and insula—all regions involved with the construction and maintenance of a coherent body image.

Although aberrant connectivity may be the result of a failure in neuronal pruning during early childhood or a response to focal neurological damage, the researchers had previously found that the cortical thickness of the sensorimotor cortex changed in a mere 2 weeks after immobilization of the right arm (Langer et al., 2012). They issued a word of warning concerning the interpretation of the data and the direction of causality: If 2 weeks of immobilization induces rapid reorganization of the sensorimotor system, it would not be surprising if years of attentional fixation and continuous rejection of a body part could induce relatively circumscribed neuroarchitectural changes (Hilti et al., 2013). Research continues in this area.

The feelings of body ownership and embodiment are not trivial; rather, they are necessary for successful interaction with the world and other people. Research involving individuals who suffer disorders of embodiment and body ownership is revealing more about the complex neural processes that contribute to these most basic feelings of self.

TAKE-HOME MESSAGES

- The default network is strongly active when we are engaged in self-reflective thought and judgment assessments that depend on social and emotional content.
- The medial prefrontal cortex is associated with superior memory for information processed in relation to the self. This ability is known as the self-reference effect.
- It is possible to maintain a sense of self in the absence of specific autobiographical memories, because a distinct neural system supports the summaries of personality traits typically used to make self-descriptive judgments.
- The anterior cingulate cortex is important for selectively attending to positive information about the self, but orbitofrontal cortex function ensures that positively biased self-views do not deviate too far from reality.
- The vmPFC is key to predicting our state of mind: The more activated it is when we consider the future, the less shortsighted our decisions will be.
- Embodiment is the feeling of being localized in one's own body, and the TPJ is a crucial structure for mediating the feeling of spatial unity of self and body.

13.5 Understanding the Mental States of Others

Though we may spend much of our time thinking about ourselves, we are also eager to interact with others. Just as the brain mechanisms that support self-perception and awareness are important features of human cognition, so are the mechanisms that support our abilities to interact and cooperate with others. When engaging in complex social interactions, it is critical for us to understand the mental states of others and to accurately anticipate their behavior. These cognitive skills are necessary for the cooperation involved with creating complex technologies, cultural institutions, and systems of symbols. These unique skills of understanding others' mental states may have been driven by social cooperation (Moll & Tomasello, 2007).

In contrast to our self-perceptions (which have privileged access to our rich autobiographical memories, unexpressed mental states, and internal physiological signals), our perceptions of other people are made without direct access to their mental and physiological states. Instead, our social perceptions are based on what is externally seen or heard: facial expressions, body movements, clothes, actions, and words. From these cues we infer what others are thinking and how they feel. Our inferences may not always be right, but we are pretty good at making them.

How good are we? William Ickes made a study of this feature and concluded that we are as good as it is good for us to be. Evolutionary pressures have calibrated our accuracy at a level high enough to enable us to deal well with others, but not so high that we weigh everyone else's interest equal to our own, thus putting our genetic future at risk. **Empathic accuracy** refers to a perceiver's ability to correctly infer a target person's thoughts and feelings. Total strangers achieve an empathic accuracy score of about 20%, whereas close friends are accurate about 30% of the time. Even the empathic accuracy between spouses is only 30%–35% (see Ickes's commentary in Zaki & Ochsner, 2011), so don't always expect your spouse to understand your thoughts and desires!

To infer the thoughts of others, the perceiver must translate what is observable (others' behavior, facial expressions, etc.) into an inference about what is unobservable—their psychological state. There are two dominant theories about how we accomplish this feat, and the most likely proposition is that we use a combination of both. The first of these, **mental state attribution theory** (Zaki & Ochsner, 2011)—originally called **theory theory** (Gopnik & Wellman, 1992)—proposes that we acquire a commonsense "folk psychology" and use it, somewhat like a scientific theory, to infer the thoughts of others (or, more poetically, to "mind-read"). Thus, from our theories of what we know about other people's past, current situation, family, culture, eye gaze direction, body language, and so forth, we infer their mental state.

While there is no doubt that we have the ability to explain the behavior of others by using the cognitive processes that mental state attribution theory posits, for the most part we don't. In social situations, our understanding of others is immediate and automatic. We don't need to invoke folk psychology to infer the thoughts of a child whose ice cream has slid off a cone and into the dirt. While various forms of theory theory were being batted around, an alternative theory was suggested: **simulation theory**, which has since, with a few adornments, morphed into **experience sharing theory** (Zaki & Ochsner, 2011).

Experience sharing theory proposes that we do not need to have an elaborate theory about the mind of others in order to infer their thoughts or predict their actions. We simply observe someone else's behavior, simulate it, and use our own mental state produced by that simulation to predict the mental state of the other. We are so good at simulation that we can do it without even seeing the other person. When merely told of another's situation, we can infer their inner thoughts, desires, and feelings just by imagining ourselves in their situation.

As is often true in the evaluation of hypotheses about complex processes, the evidence suggests that both experience sharing theory and mental state attribution theory are at work—and that each is associated with its own network of brain regions and developmental timescale. Before we explore these two hypotheses in more detail, let's take a closer look at theory of mind.

Theory of Mind

The ability to impute mental states to oneself and to other people (regardless of the processes involved) is known as **theory of mind (ToM)**, a term coined by David Premack and Guy Woodruff of the University of Pennsylvania (1978). After working with chimpanzees for several years, they began to speculate about what might account for differences in cognition across species. They suggested that chimpanzees might be capable of inferring information about the mental states of other chimpanzees. This idea initiated an avalanche of research looking for evidence to support it.

Although considerable debate continues on the competence of social cognition in nonhuman species (Call & Tomasello, 2008; E. Herrmann et al., 2007), the work of Premack and Woodruff sparked a deep interest in theory-of-mind research in humans. They speculated that humans most often impute purpose or intention to others, with imputing beliefs and thoughts running a close second. For example, when you see a woman rummaging around in her purse as she walks toward her car, you are more likely to think about her intention—to find her keys—than to imagine her thoughts as she rummages. Theory of mind, also known as *mentalizing*, has received a considerable amount of attention in the developmental psychology literature and in cognitive neuroscience studies.

DEVELOPMENTAL MILESTONES For a helpless newborn, as psychologist Andrew Meltzoff points out, connecting with others is a matter of life or death. What can a baby do to connect to others? From the get-go, an infant prefers to look at a human face rather than at other objects, and when a face comes into view, she doesn't lie there like a lump of lead. Instead, she has a social interaction through **imitative behavior**. Stick your tongue out and she will stick her tongue out.

Meltzoff found that from the age of 42 minutes to 72 hours old, newborns will accurately imitate facial expressions (Meltzoff & Moore, 1983), and he suggests that this innate ability to automatically imitate others is the foundation, a first step, that leads to our theory of mind (Meltzoff, 2002) and the growth of social cognition. In fact, automatic imitation and how it is accomplished have provided the first hints about the location of the mechanisms underlying experience sharing (simulation) theory.

Research using ERP has found that even 4-month-old infants exhibit early evoked gamma activity at occipital channels and a late gamma burst over right prefrontal cortex channels in response to direct eye contact. These findings suggest that infants are quick to process information about faces and use neural structures similar to those found in adults (Grossmann et al., 2007). In adulthood, we continue to focus on the social aspects of our environment. Numerous studies have shown that humans spend, on average, 80% of their waking time in the company of others, and that 80%–90% of conversations are spent talking about ourselves and gossiping about other people (Emler, 1994).

Much of the behavioral work on theory of mind has examined how this ability develops over a person's life span. Researchers have created many tasks to understand how theory of mind works. For several years, the Sally–Anne **false-belief task** was the essential test in determining the presence or absence of theory of mind. In one version of this task, participants view a series of drawings that depict scenarios involving the characters

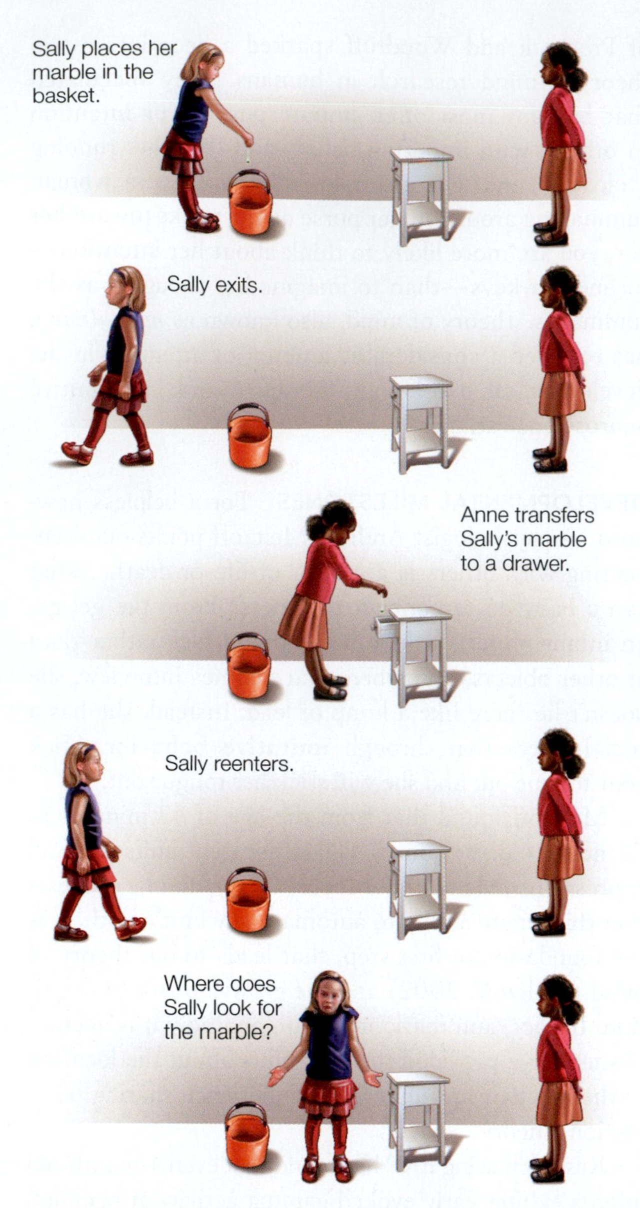

FIGURE 13.12 The Sally–Anne false-belief task for investigating theory of mind.
This task is used with children to determine whether they can interpret what Sally is thinking about the location of the marble. Because Sally does not see Anne move the marble from the basket to the drawer, Sally should be expected to look for the marble in the basket.

Sally and Anne (**Figure 13.12**). The pictures begin with Sally placing a marble in a basket and then leaving the room. After Sally is gone, Anne moves the marble into a drawer. Sally then comes back into the room. The key question here is, Where will Sally look for the marble?

To answer the question correctly, participants have to ignore their own knowledge about the location of the marble and answer from Sally's perspective. Sally is unaware of Anne's devious behavior, so she expects the marble to be in the basket where she left it. Participants who are unable to recognize that Sally does not share their knowledge predict that she will look in the drawer. To solve the Sally–Anne task, participants must understand that Sally and Anne can have different beliefs about the world. In other words, they must understand that people have different perspectives.

Children don't reliably pass this test until they are about 4 years old. It eventually dawned on researchers, however, that this task was too difficult for younger children and that it was more than just a false-belief task. It could be that later-developing cognitive control abilities, such as inhibition and problem solving, were confounding the results, and that theory of mind might develop earlier than age 4 or even be innate. Changing the task revealed that infants younger than 4 years demonstrate the ability.

When an adult is looking for an object but doesn't know where it is, 12-month-old babies who know the object's location will point to where it is. When the adult does know the location, however, the babies do not point to it (Liszkowski et al., 2008), demonstrating not only that they understand the goals and intentions of the adult, but also that they share **joint attention**; that is, the two individuals share their focus on the same object. Fifteen-month-old babies show "surprise" when someone searches in a container for a toy that was placed in the container in their absence (Onishi & Baillargeon, 2005), suggesting that they understand that the person should have had a false belief and are surprised when that person doesn't.

Once children reach the age of 3 or 4, they recognize that their physical vantage point gives them an individual perspective on the world that is different from the physical vantage point of other people. This is the moment in time when, Jamil Zaki and Kevin Ochsner (2011) suggest, the processes underlying mental state attribution theory begin to come online. By 5 or 6 years of age, children are aware that two people can have different beliefs about the state of the world. At about 6 or 7 years of age, children can appreciate that the literal meanings of words sometimes communicate only part of the speaker's intention, or that the actual intention may be quite different from the literal meaning of what is said. They are ready to tell jokes. At about 9 to 11 years of age, children are able to simultaneously represent more than one person's mental state, and to discern when one person hurts another person's feelings. They are ready to be teenagers.

This is how things stood until Hungarian developmental psychologists Agnes Kovacs, Erno Teglas, and Ansgar Endress (2010) came up with a new task and a radical hypothesis. David Premack happily pointed out that "their ideas constitute the first significant novelty in ToM in at least ten years" (personal communication).

The researchers proposed that theory of mind is innate and automatic. They reasoned that if this is so, then computing the mental states of others should be spontaneous, and the mere presence of another should automatically trigger the computation of their beliefs, even when performing a task in which those beliefs are irrelevant. They designed a visual detection task to test this idea.

The participants in the study by Kovacs and colleagues were adults. They were shown several animated movie scenarios that started with an agent placing a ball on a table in front of an opaque screen. The ball then rolled behind the screen. Next followed one of four possible scenarios:

1. The ball stayed behind the screen while the agent was watching, and after the agent left, the ball stayed put.
2. The ball rolled out from behind the screen while the agent was watching, and after the agent left, the ball stayed put.
3. The ball stayed behind the screen while the agent was watching, but after the agent left, the ball rolled away.
4. The ball rolled out from behind the screen while the agent was watching, but after the agent left, the ball returned to its position behind the screen.

In the first two instances, the returning agent had a true belief about the location of the ball. In the latter two examples, the returning agent had a false belief about the ball's location.

At the end of the film, the screen was removed, and either the ball was there or it was not (independent of what the film had shown). The participants' task was to press a button as soon as they detected the ball. The time it took for them to push the button—their reaction time (RT)—was measured. Notice that the agent's beliefs were irrelevant to the task. The researchers predicted, however, that the participant would take the agent's belief into account, and thus the RT should be faster when both the participant and the agent thought the ball was behind the screen and it was (scenario 1), compared to a baseline condition when neither the participant nor the agent thought the ball was there but it was (scenario 2). The baseline scenario should produce the slowest RT.

Indeed, when both the participant and the agent thought the ball was there and it was, the participant's RT was faster compared to the baseline condition. It was also faster when the participant alone believed it was there (scenario 4). What do you think happened when the participant did not believe it was there but the agent did and it was (scenario 3)? This RT was also faster than

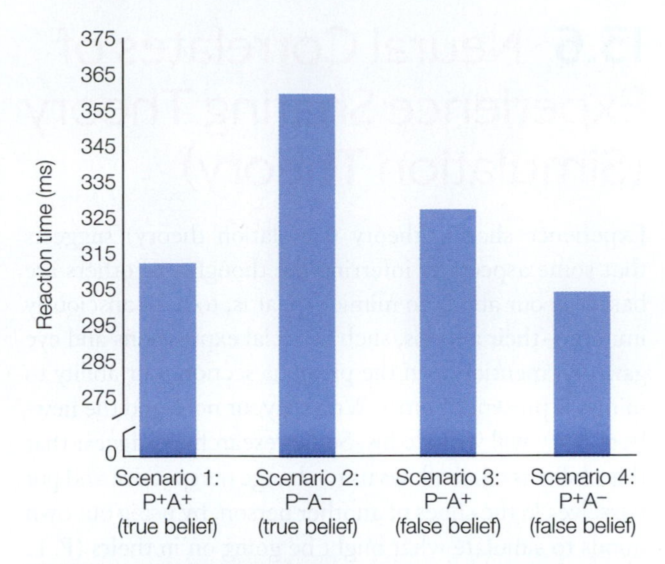

FIGURE 13.13 False-belief task.
The participant's reaction time is influenced by the agent's belief, even though the agent's belief is irrelevant. P = participant; A = agent; + indicates belief that the ball was there; − indicates belief that the ball was absent.

the baseline condition. The agent's belief, though inconsistent with the participant's belief, influenced the participant's RT as much as the participant's own belief did (**Figure 13.13**).

Thus, it appears that adults track the beliefs of others automatically—but is this behavior acquired or innate? Do young infants also do this? The experiment was redesigned for 7-month-olds, this time using a violation-of-expectation task. The same results were found, suggesting that theory of mind is innate and that the mere presence of another person automatically triggers belief computations. In addition, the researchers proposed that the mechanisms for computing someone else's beliefs might be part of a core human-specific "social sense" that was essential for the evolution of human societies. In the next two sections we will look at those mechanisms.

TAKE-HOME MESSAGES

- Theory of mind is the ability to impute mental states to oneself and other people.
- Theory of mind is important for social development and interactions. It underlies the capacity to cooperate, empathize, and accurately anticipate the behavior of others.
- Theory of mind appears to be innate and automatic.
- Two theories have been proposed regarding how we read the thoughts and intentions of others: experience sharing theory (simulation theory) and mental state attribution theory (theory theory).

13.6 Neural Correlates of Experience Sharing Theory (Simulation Theory)

Experience sharing theory (simulation theory) suggests that some aspects of inferring the thoughts of others are based on our ability to mimic—that is, to nonconsciously imitate—their actions, such as facial expressions and eye gaze. As mentioned in the previous section, our ability to mimic is present at birth. Wrinkle your nose and the newborn baby will wrinkle his. Some researchers suggest that this ability is what allows us to change perspective and put ourselves in the shoes of another person, by using our own minds to simulate what might be going on in theirs (P. L. Harris, 1992; **Figure 13.14**).

Recall that within the default network, MPFC activation is associated with the perception of both the self and other people. Experience sharing theory suggests that the MPFC is involved in both types of perception because the perception of self is sometimes used in the perception of others. For example, in one fMRI study, scientists hypothesized that a similar region would be engaged when one was thinking about oneself and a similar person, but would not be activated when one was thinking about a dissimilar person (J. P. Mitchell et al., 2006).

The researchers had participants read descriptions of two people: One person shared similar political views with the participants, and the other held the opposite political views. Next the researchers measured the participants' brain activity while the participants were answering questions about their own preferences, as well as when they were speculating about the preferences of the people with similar and dissimilar views. A ventral subregion of the MPFC was found to increase its activity for self-perceptions and for perceptions of the similar people, whereas a different, more dorsal region of the MPFC was significantly activated for perceptions of the dissimilar people. These activation patterns in the MPFC have been held up as evidence that participants may have reasoned that their own preferences would predict the preferences of someone like them but would not be informative for speculating about the preferences of someone dissimilar.

Other studies have since shown a variable pattern of activation between the ventral and dorsal regions: It is dependent not on similarity per se, but on the level of relatedness between the two people based on characteristics like familiarity, closeness, emotional importance, warmth, competence, and knowledge. For instance, Kevin Ochsner and Jennifer Beer showed that a similar region of the MPFC was activated for both self-perception and the perception of a current romantic partner (Ochsner et al., 2005). This effect was not driven by perceived similarities between the self and the romantic partner. The researchers suggest that this activation likely represents commonalities in the complexity or the emotional nature of the information we store about ourselves and our romantic partners.

FIGURE 13.14 Experience sharing theory.
Experience sharing theory proposes that people make inferences about the actions of others by using their own expectations based on experiences from their own lives. The woman on the right imagines herself in her friend's situation and infers her friend's mental state from how she would feel in the same situation.

Studies like this one suggest that the MPFC is important for thinking about the self and other people when a common psychological process underlies the thought processes. Sometimes we may use ourselves as a way of understanding someone whom we do not know well but who appears to be related to us in some way. A big-wave surfer who sees a guy in a wet suit checking out waves with a board under his arm is more likely to engage his MPFC than if he glances over and sees a guy in an Italian business suit smoking a cigar while gazing at the surf. At other times, these processes may be linked because we create incredibly rich stores of information about ourselves, as well as about others we are close to.

Mirror Neurons

Many researchers invoke mirror neurons (MNs; see Chapter 8)—which activate both while one is observing another's action and when one is performing it oneself—as the neural basis of shared representation, and they suggest that through this mutual activation, the observer's action can be understood. Using imaging, researchers have identified networks of anatomically connected cortical areas that are active both during one's performance of an action and during observation of another person performing the same action.

Numerous neuroimaging studies report activation during action observation and action execution in brain regions consistent with the proposal of a human mirror neuron network, and they have been summarized in recent meta-analyses (Caspers et al., 2010; Molenberghs et al., 2012). These regions include the rostral inferior parietal lobule (rIPL), dorsal premotor cortex (dPMC), medial frontal cortex (MFC), ventrolateral prefrontal cortex (vlPFC), and anterior cingulate gyrus (ACG; see Bonini, 2017). Each of these areas has anatomical pathways that convey visual information (processed mainly in the STS) about the actions of others. Some researchers have proposed that the mirror neuron network is causal in action understanding, with action production and action understanding having overlapping mechanisms (e.g., Gallese et al., 2004; Gazzola & Keysers, 2009), but findings from imaging techniques have all been correlational, and the claims remain controversial (Lamm & Majdandžić, 2015).

John Michael and his colleagues (2014) investigated the effects of offline TMS on regions of the premotor cortex that are well known to activate during action observation. They applied continuous theta burst stimulation (cTBS) over the hand area of the PMC in one session and over the lip area in a separate session. During each session, their participants performed three tasks that were designed to probe three different components of action understanding: the motion (simple task), the proximal goal (intermediate task), and the distal goal (complex task; **Figure 13.15**).

They found a double dissociation. After cTBS was applied over the hand area, recognition of hand movement decreased, but not recognition of lip movement. And after cTBS was given over the lip area, recognition of lip movement decreased, but not recognition of hand movement. These findings provide some support for the notion that somatotopic regions of the PMC play a causal role in action understanding and that there is an overlap of the mechanisms supporting action understanding and action performance.

As we mentioned in Chapter 8, it appears, then, that MNs activate both while we're perceiving another's action and, when enough contextual clues are around, while we're predicting another's action. Being able to predict the actions of others during social interactions is relevant for the preparation of our own appropriate reaction: Should we reach out to shake a new acquaintance's hand or merely smile?

Luca Bonini and his colleagues (2014), using single-neuron studies in monkeys, have found that MNs become more active earlier when the action of another occurs in the monkey's extrapersonal space as opposed to its peripersonal space. In fact, some of the MNs switched back and forth from a predictive firing pattern to a reactive firing pattern, depending on where the observed action was taking place. This finding suggests to Bonini that motor prediction may play different roles, depending on context, in preparing our own reactions in a social situation (Bonini, 2017).

Empathy

Empathy, our capacity to understand and respond to the unique affective experiences of another person (Decety & Jackson, 2004), epitomizes the strong relation between self-perception and the perception of others. Though the details regarding the process of empathy are debatable, it is generally agreed that the first step is to take the other person's perspective.

The perception–action model of empathy assumes that during perception of another's emotional state of mind, the same affective state is activated in the observer, triggering somatic and autonomic responses; thus, by experiencing it, the observer understands it. Given the role of mirror neurons in imitation and action recognition, it has been proposed that MNs may mediate a critical physiological mechanism that enables us to represent another's internal state within our own bodies. This mechanism is sometimes referred to as *embodied simulation*. For it to occur, some connection needs to be made with the

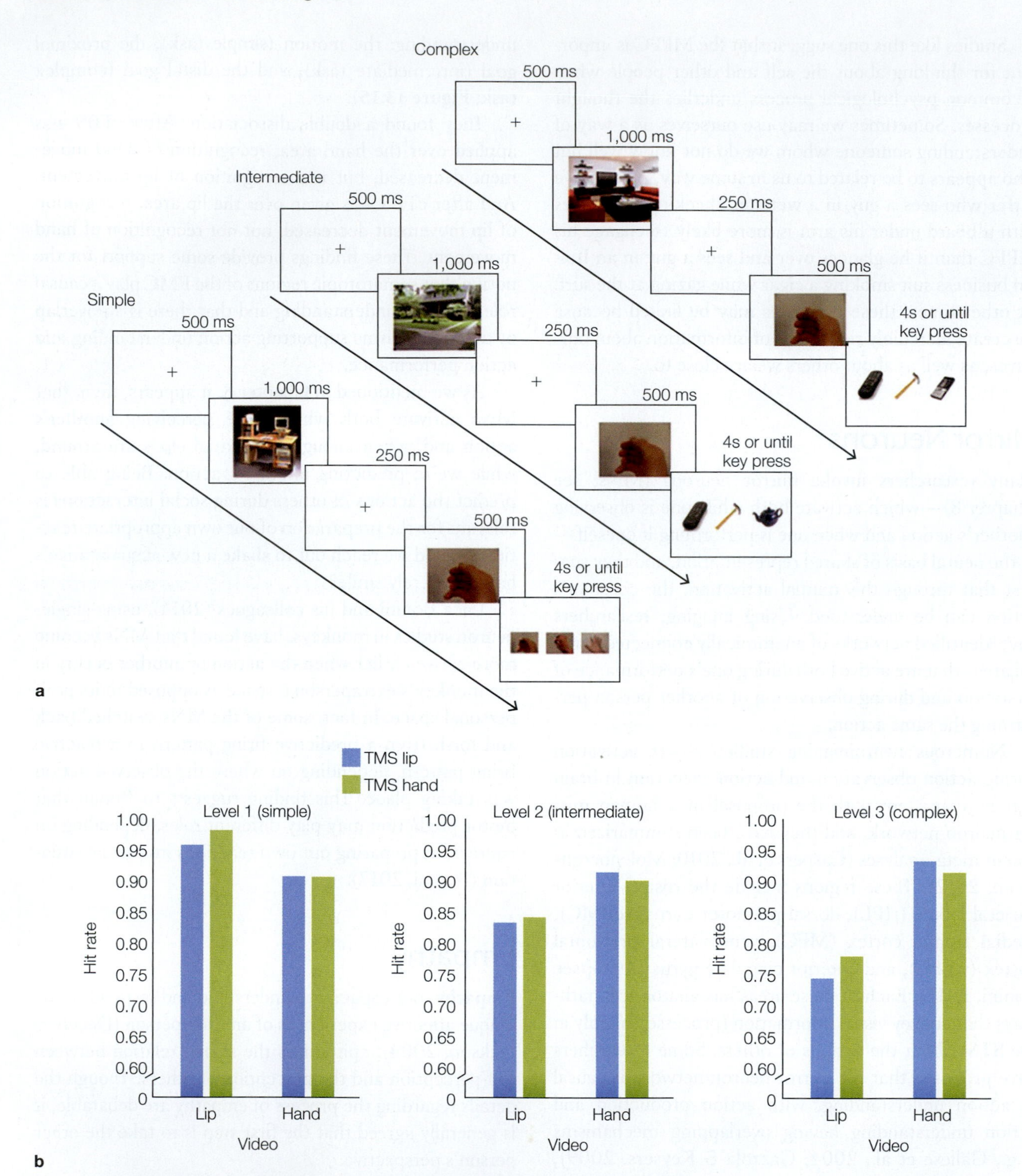

FIGURE 13.15 cTBS of lip and hand regions of the premotor homunculus.
(a) Example of a trial sequence testing three levels of action understanding. On each trial an image was first presented, depicting the context of an action. Then a short video of a pantomimed action was shown, followed by a screen with three possible responses from which the participant had to choose. In the simplest block, the participant had to choose the image that was in the video. In the intermediate block, the participant had to choose the image that best complemented the action seen in the video. In the most complex task, the participant had to choose the object that complemented both the action and the context. While two of the objects complemented the action, only one of them complemented both the action and the context. (b) As complexity of the task increased, hit rates decreased. The type of video had an effect: Rates were lower for lip actions than for hand actions. An interaction between the type of video and the complexity of the task was found: As the task became more complex, the hit rates for lip actions decreased more than those for hand actions.

structures for emotional processing. Evidence for such a connection was found in the primate brain, where the mirror neuron network and the limbic system are anatomically connected by the insula, suggesting that a large-scale network could be at the heart of the ability to empathize.

In humans, an emotion that can reliably be aroused experimentally is disgust, and it has been used in the search for the mechanisms of recognizing emotions in others. For example, a series of experiments found that the experience of disgust and the perception of facial expressions of disgust activate similar regions within the anterior insula. In fact, the magnitude of insula activation when observing facial expressions of disgust increases with the intensity of the other person's facial expression of disgust (Phillips et al., 1997; **Figure 13.16**). A subsequent fMRI study found that when people inhaled odorants that produce a feeling of disgust, the same sites in the anterior insula (and to a lesser extent the anterior cingulate cortex) were engaged as when they observed facial expressions of disgust (Wicker et al., 2003).

Consistent with these fMRI findings were those found in a study using depth electrodes that had been implanted in the insula of several patients during a presurgical evaluation for temporal lobe epilepsy. When these patients viewed emotional facial expressions, neurons in the ventral anterior insula fired only when they were viewing expressions of disgust (Krolak-Salmon et al., 2003). Electrical stimulation of this region of the insula also elicits nausea (Penfield & Faulk, 1955) and visceromotor activity (Calder et al., 2000), both of which are associated with conscious subjective feeling states.

Finally, additional support comes from one case study: A patient with anterior insula damage who lost his ability to recognize disgust from facial expressions, nonverbal emotional sounds, or emotional prosody felt less disgust than did controls when presented with disgust-inducing scenarios (Calder et al., 2000). Together, these studies suggest that the insula is important for experiencing disgust, as well as for perceiving it in others, and some researchers suggest that mirror neurons may be the means by which we recognize this emotion (Bastiaansen et al., 2009).

Pain, while not exactly an emotion, is another state of strong feeling that can be reliably activated. In a pain study conducted by Tania Singer and her colleagues at University College London, fMRI revealed that the insula and anterior cingulate are activated when one is experiencing physical pain in oneself, as well as during the perception of physical pain in others (Singer et al., 2004).

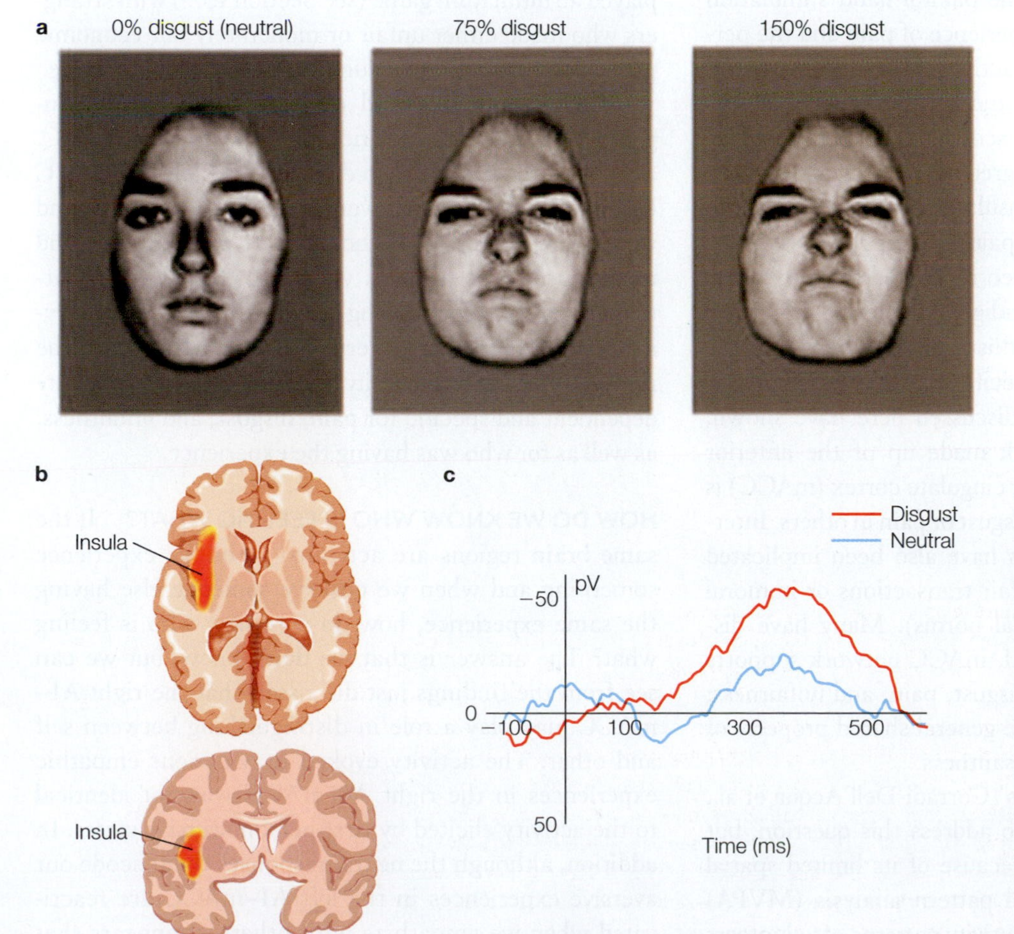

FIGURE 13.16 Exploring the neural regions responsive to disgust.
(a) Computer morphing methods were used to generate a range of disgusted faces. A value of 100% (not shown) corresponds to a photo of someone showing actual disgust, 75% to a morphed version showing moderate disgust, and 150% to a morphed version showing extreme disgust.
(b, c) As the expressions of disgust became more intense, the BOLD response in the insula increased. pV = picovolts.

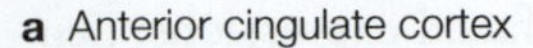

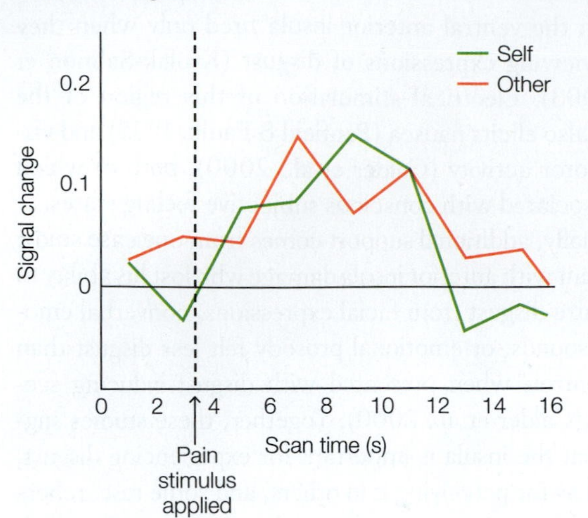

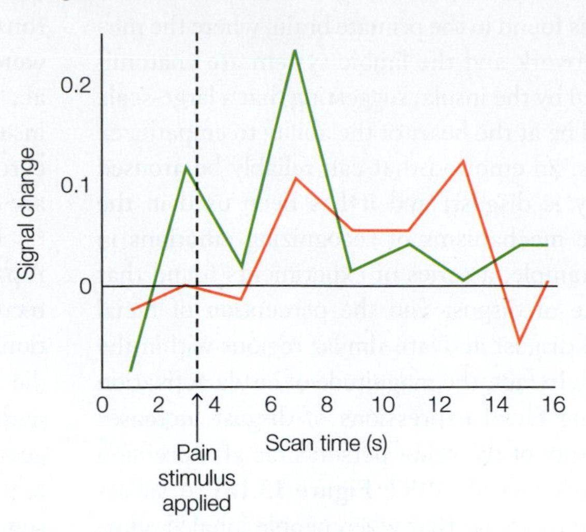

FIGURE 13.17 Study of empathy for pain.
When a painful stimulus was applied to a participant (self) or the participant's romantic partner (other), fMRI revealed that shared networks were activated. Here the time course of pain-related activation is shown for peak activations in the ACC (a) and the right anterior insula (b). The *y*-axis represents the estimated degree of perceived pain.

The researchers examined brain activity when participants either received painful stimulation through an electrode on their hand or saw a computer signal indicating that their romantic partner, who was in the same room, was receiving the same painful hand stimulation (**Figure 13.17**). Both the experience of pain and the perception of a loved one's pain activated the anterior insula, adjacent frontal operculum, and anterior cingulate. Furthermore, participants who scored high on a questionnaire that measured their degree of empathy showed the greatest activation in the insula and anterior cingulate when they were perceiving pain in their romantic partners. These findings have been replicated in many other studies, using different paradigms (reviewed in Singer & Lamm, 2009). Whether this overlap implies that the shared responses are pain specific is controversial.

The studies that we've discussed here have shown, using fMRI, that a network made up of the anterior insula (AI) and mid–anterior cingulate cortex (mACC) is recruited when we witness disgust or pain in others. Interestingly, these same regions have also been implicated during the witnessing of unfair transactions or immoral acts (transgressions of social norms). Many have disputed the notion that the AI–mACC network supports processing specifically for disgust, pain, and unfairness; instead, they propose a more general shared property of these stimuli, such as unpleasantness.

Singer and her colleagues (Corradi-Dell'Acqua et al., 2016) went back to work to address this question, but they could not use fMRI, because of its limited spatial resolution. Using multivoxel pattern analysis (MVPA) instead, they compared the activity patterns of volunteers being subjected to an electrical stimulus that was either painful or not, or tasting a gustatory stimulus that was either disgusting or not, or watching a befriended confederate undergo these experiences. Finally, the participants played an ultimatum game (see Section 13.9) with strangers who made either unfair or moderately fair economic proposals, either to the volunteers or to the confederate.

The researchers found evidence for both domain-general and domain-specific coding in the AI–mACC, as is often the case in such disputes. The left AI–mACC had activity patterns that were modality independent and were shared across the modalities of pain, disgust, and unfairness. These patterns were also shared when participants were experiencing aversive stimuli or observing others experiencing aversive stimuli. Meanwhile, the right AI–mACC had activity patterns that were modality dependent and specific for pain, disgust, and unfairness, as well as for who was having the experience.

HOW DO WE KNOW WHO IS FEELING WHAT? If the same brain regions are activated when we experience something and when we observe someone else having the same experience, how do we know who is feeling what? The answer is that we don't know, but we can see from the findings just discussed that the right AI–mACC may play a role in distinguishing between self and other: The activity evoked by vicarious empathic experiences in the right AI–mACC was not identical to the activity elicited by first-person aversive states. In addition, although the neural responses that encode our aversive experiences in the left AI–mACC are reactivated when we empathize with others, it appears that modality-specific pain or taste information is not part of the package of information that is shared. So, although we may feel a generalized unpleasantness while watching others receive aversive stimuli, we do not actually feel the sensations that they feel.

Ryan Murray and his colleagues (2012) performed a meta-analysis of 23 fMRI and 2 PET studies that compared self-relevant processing against processing of close others and of public figures. The objective of the meta-analysis was to identify self-specific activations, as well as activations that might permit differentiation between our evaluation of close others and our evaluation of people with whom we have no connection. They found that the anterior insula is activated when one is appraising and processing information about the self and close others but not about public figures. This finding led the researchers to suggest that when we appraise ourselves and close others, we share a conscious mental representation that is internal, visceral, and actually felt physiologically, known as *embodied awareness*.

Self-specific processing, however, was found in the ventral and dorsal anterior cingulate cortex (vACC and dACC), which were not active during the appraisal of close others and public figures (**Figure 13.18**). The dACC not only triages attention, allocating and regulating it during goal-directed activity, but also responds to self-related stimuli and is active during self-reflection and action monitoring (Schmitz & Johnson, 2007).

The researchers also found differential activations within the MPFC for the self, close others, and public figures. Activation for the self was clustered primarily in the right vmPFC, whereas activation for close others was clustered primarily in the left vmPFC, including some shared activation differentially engaging the vmPFC according to the level of relatedness. Activation for public figures was significantly dissociated from both these regions; public figures instead activated the dmPFC in the left superior frontal gyrus. Thus, it appears that activations across different regions of the brain differentiate who is feeling what.

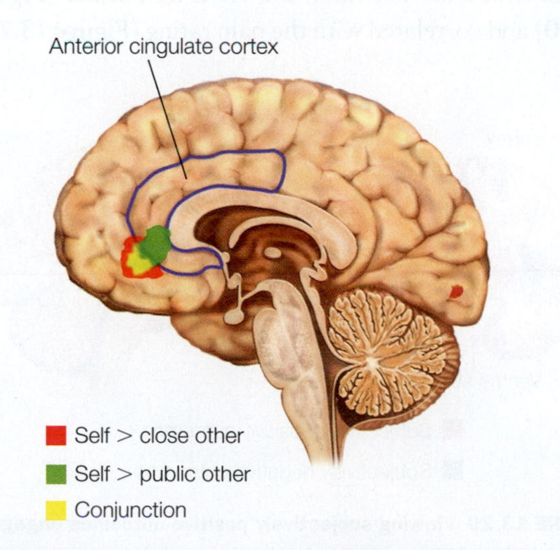

FIGURE 13.18 Differential activations distinguish between self and others.
Regions activated during performance of a task relevant to public figures were more dorsal than, and significantly dissociated from, activations associated with the monitoring of both close others and self. Activation for public figures appeared mostly in the left superior frontal gyrus, while activation for close others centered in the left vmPFC. Activation for self was found in the right vmPFC.

MODULATION OF EMPATHIC RESPONSES After recognizing the distinction between ourselves and other people, we somehow need to monitor our responses. For instance, a doctor needs to understand when a patient is in pain, but the patient wants the doctor to relieve the pain, not share it. Jean Decety (reviewed in Decety, 2011) and his colleagues have proposed a model for empathy in which automatic perception–action coupling and emotion sharing come first, followed by the uncoupling of self from other, and then by other processes that influence the extent of the empathic experience, as well as the likelihood of behavior that benefits others: the perceiver's motivation, intentions, and emotional self-regulation.

One example of evidence for goal-directed regulation was an inventive experiment conducted by Decety and his colleagues in Taiwan. They hypothesized that regions typically associated with perceptions of physical pain would not be activated in acupuncturists, whose jobs require them to detach themselves from the painful aspect of administering acupuncture and instead focus on the long-term benefit to the patient (Cheng et al., 2007).

To investigate this hypothesis, the researchers observed the brain activity of professional acupuncturists versus that of laypeople while they watched video clips depicting body parts receiving nonpainful stimulation (touch with cotton swab) or painful stimulation (sting of acupuncture needles). Consistent with previous research, the study found that regions associated with the experience of pain, including the insula, anterior cingulate, and somatosensory cortex, were activated in nonexperts. In the acupuncturists, by contrast, these regions were not significantly activated—but regions associated with mental state attribution about others, such as the MPFC and right TPJ, were activated. Regions underpinning self-regulation (dlPFC and MPFC) and attention (precentral gyrus, superior parietal lobule, and TPJ) also were activated. These findings suggest that activation of the mirror neuron network can be modulated by a goal-directed process that enhances flexible responses.

The researchers went on to study these acupuncturists by using ERPs (Decety et al., 2010), looking for the point where information processing is regulated. Control participants had an early N100 differentiation between pain and no-pain conditions over the frontal area, and a late-positive potential at about 300–800 ms over the centroparietal regions. Neither of these effects were detected in the physicians. It appears that in these acupuncturists, emotional regulation occurs very early in the stimulus-driven processing of the perception of pain in others.

Tania Singer has studied whether fairness in social relations also affects empathy. That is, if you perceived someone as unfair, would you feel less empathy for them? For instance, would you feel the same when seeing a stranger trip and fall as when seeing the mugger who just grabbed your wallet trip and fall? In Singer's study (Singer et al., 2006), male and female participants played a card game (involving cash) with two confederates: one who cheated and one who did not. Then, Singer used fMRI to measure the participants' brain activity while they watched the confederates experiencing pain. Although both sexes had activation in the empathy-associated brain regions (frontoinsular cortex and ACC) when watching the fair confederate receive pain, the male participants had no empathy-induced activations when they saw the cheater in pain, while the women showed only a small decrease in empathy.

Instead, the males had increased activation in the ventral striatum and nucleus accumbens, which are reward-associated areas. In other words, the males actually enjoyed seeing the cheater in pain. The degree of activation in the reward area correlated with an expressed desire for revenge, as indicated on a questionnaire that participants completed after the experiment. Singer suggests that this activation of reward areas may be a neural foundation for theories proposing that people (at least men) value another's gain positively if it was won fairly, but negatively if it was won unfairly, implying that they like cooperating with fair opponents but punishing unfair ones. Don't get too attached to fairness being the motivation for punishment, however. We will return to this later.

What about sports rivalries? Mina Cikara wondered whether the modulation of empathy seen on a personal level also applied at the group level (Cikara et al., 2011). For instance, when you watch a game between your favorite team and a rival, how do you feel when you see the opposing team fail? How about when they score?

For her study, Cikara recruited avid fans of rival baseball teams: the Boston Red Sox and New York Yankees. While undergoing fMRI, participants viewed simulated figures representing the Red Sox or Yankees making baseball plays. In some plays the favored player was successful, and in others the rival was successful. Participants also viewed some control scenarios in which a player from a neutral team made plays against either

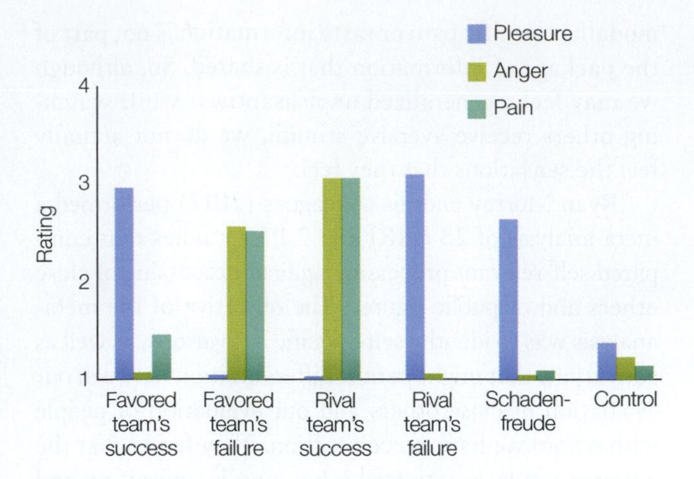

FIGURE 13.19 Empathy is modulated by group membership.
The bars indicate the average ratings for pleasure, anger, and pain for the success or failure of favored or rival teams.

the Red Sox or the Yankees, or against another neutral team. After each play, participants rated the feelings of anger, pain, or pleasure that they had experienced while watching that play (**Figure 13.19**). Two weeks later, the participants filled out a questionnaire asking them to rate the likelihood that they would heckle, insult, throw food at, threaten, shove, or hit a rival fan (i.e., either a Yankees fan or a Red Sox fan) or a fan of a neutral team (e.g., the Baltimore Orioles).

Viewing subjectively positive plays (when the rival team failed) increased the response in the ventral striatum, whereas failure of the favored team and success of the rival team activated the ACC and insula (**Figure 13.20**) and correlated with the pain rating (**Figure 13.21**).

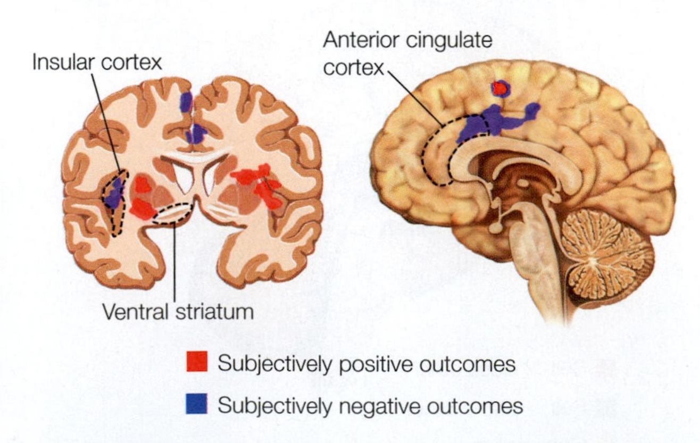

FIGURE 13.20 Viewing subjectively positive outcomes engaged the ventral system.
A subjectively positive outcome was one in which a favored team was successful or a rival team failed against a favored team. In this case, activations were seen in the ventral striatum, along with the left middle frontal and superior frontal gyrus, left insula, bilateral caudate, and supplementary motor area (SMA). A subjectively negative outcome was the opposite and activated the ACC, SMA, and right insula.

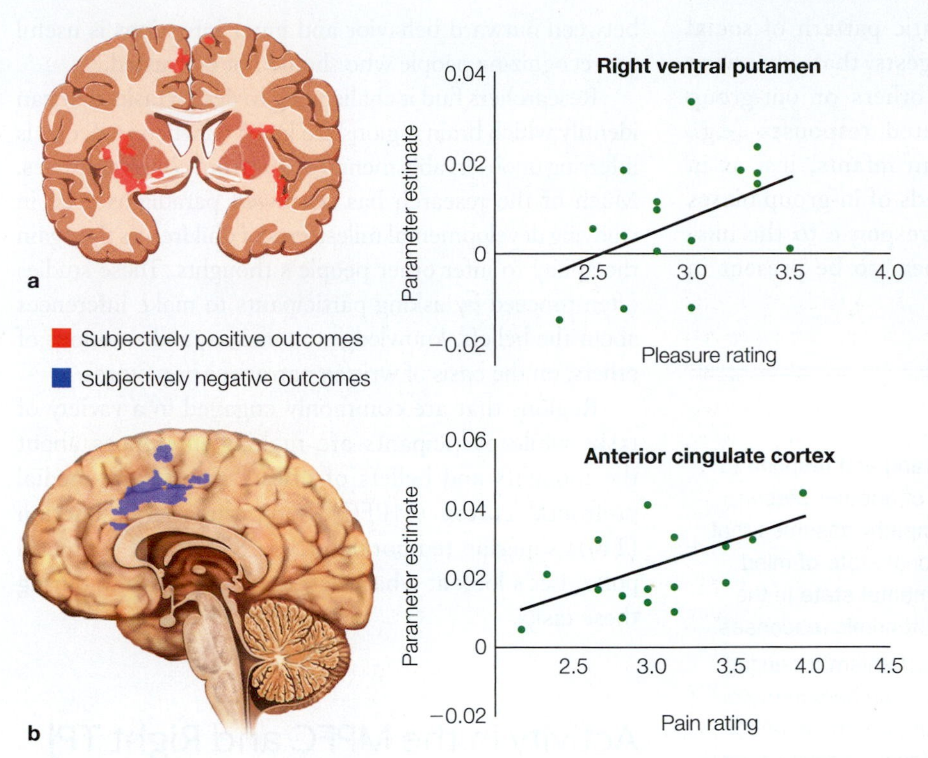

FIGURE 13.21 Brain activity correlated with pleasure and pain ratings. **(a)** In the positive-outcome plays, only the activations in the right ventral putamen (ventral striatum) correlated with pleasure ratings. The participants' self-reported pleasure ratings while viewing positive plays are plotted against the activations in right ventral putamen in the scatter plot on the right. **(b)** Only the ACC activations correlated with the participants' pain ratings. The self-reported pain in response to subjectively negative plays is plotted against activations in the ACC in the scatter plot on the right.

Note that seeing an animated hypothetical baseball play elicited the same pain response in a diehard baseball fan as did (in previous studies) watching a close other undergo a painful experience! As in the Singer study discussed earlier, the ventral striatum reward effect correlated with the self-reported likelihood of aggression against the fan of the rival team. Thus, the response to a rival group's misfortune is neural activation associated with pleasure (i.e., schadenfreude—enjoyment of others' troubles), which is correlated with endorsing harm against those groups.

Strikingly, a series of studies by Karen Wynn and colleagues at Yale University suggests that the tendencies to prefer others who are similar to ourselves and to tolerate or even enjoy the maltreatment of individuals who are dissimilar to ourselves emerge very early in life. Wynn and her team implemented multiple variations of a paradigm in which prelinguistic infants were first given a choice between two snack foods (e.g., Cheerios and graham crackers) and then saw two different puppets approaching bowls of each food, making eating noises, and expressing either a negative ("Ewww, yuck! I don't like that!") or a positive ("Mmmm, yum, I like that!") response.

In one study, the infants were then given a choice between two puppets: one that had expressed a food preference similar to their own, and another that had expressed a dissimilar preference. Nearly all infants chose to play with the puppet that evinced food preferences similar to their own (Mahajan & Wynn, 2012), suggesting that even before our first birthdays, we prefer others who appear similar to ourselves, even when such similarities are trivial (e.g., preferring Cheerios over graham crackers as infants; rooting for the Red Sox rather than the Yankees as adults).

In a later study, Wynn and her team added another step to the paradigm: After indicating their own food preferences and observing the food preferences expressed by two rabbit puppets (one similar and one dissimilar to themselves), the infants observed a second set of brief puppet shows that starred either the similar or the dissimilar rabbit puppet. Each show started with one of the rabbit puppets (the similar or dissimilar puppet, depending on the experimental condition) bouncing and catching a ball before accidentally dropping it. Next, on alternating events, either a "helper" dog puppet would appear and return the ball to the puppet that had dropped it, or a "harmer" dog puppet would appear that would take the ball and abscond with it. The infants were then given the choice of engaging with either of the two dog puppets.

As you might expect, the infants preferred the dog puppet that had helped rather than harmed the rabbit puppet similar to themselves. But the results from the dissimilar rabbit puppet condition were most remarkable: Infants as young as 9 months of age exhibited a strong preference for the dog puppet that had harmed the dissimilar rabbit puppet over the puppet that had helped the dissimilar rabbit puppet (Hamlin et al., 2013).

Although pragmatic concerns make it difficult to carry out task-based fMRI studies in human infants

(Deen et al., 2017), the systematic pattern of social preferences described here suggests that observing misfortunes befalling dissimilar others or out-group members may elicit reward-related responses (e.g., in the ventral striatum) in human infants, just as in adults. From an early age, the seeds of in-group biases and of experiencing pleasure in response to the misfortunes of dissimilar others appear to be present in the human mind.

TAKE-HOME MESSAGES

- Empathy is our capacity to understand and respond to the unique emotional experiences of another person. The perception–action model of empathy assumes that perceiving another person's emotional state of mind automatically activates the same mental state in the observer, triggering somatic and autonomic responses.
- Mirror neurons provide a neural mechanism for engaging in mental simulation. Just as researchers in motor control emphasize the role of mirror neurons in understanding the actions of other individuals, social cognitive neuroscientists have argued that mirror neurons could be essential for understanding the intentions and emotions of other individuals.
- The left AI–mACC has modality-independent activity patterns, whereas the right AI–ACC has modality-dependent activity patterns that are specific for pain, disgust, and unfairness, as well as for who (self or other) is having the experience.
- Social preferences for similar others emerge in infants before 1 year of age.

13.7 Neural Correlates of Mental State Attribution Theory (Theory Theory)

Sometimes mental states don't match their observable cues. Consider a situation in which you ask someone out on a date. She declines, smiles, and tells you that she has a prior engagement. Now what do you do? How do you know whether she truly has other plans or whether she doesn't want to go out with you? Did she smile because she really wants to go but can't, in which case you can venture another request? Or was she merely being polite, in which case she would be annoyed if you pursued her further? Our daily lives are filled with instances in which people hide their true thoughts and feelings. In more extreme cases, our ability to recognize the mismatch between outward behavior and inner intentions is useful for recognizing people who should not be trusted.

Researchers find it challenging to design tasks that can identify which brain regions are involved when someone is inferring unobservable mental states from observable cues. Much of the research has borrowed paradigms used in studying developmental milestones of children as they gain the ability to infer other people's thoughts. These studies often proceed by asking participants to make inferences about the beliefs, knowledge, intentions, and emotions of others, on the basis of written narratives or pictures.

Regions that are commonly engaged in a variety of tasks while participants are making inferences about the thoughts and beliefs of others include the medial prefrontal cortex (MPFC), temporoparietal junction (TPJ), superior temporal sulcus (STS), and temporal poles. Let's look at what these regions are up to during these tasks.

Activity in the MPFC and Right TPJ

One study compared brain activity of participants engaged in two conditions: forming an impression of another person and performing a sequencing task (J. P. Mitchell et al., 2004). Participants viewed pictures of people paired with statements about their personality, such as, "At the party, he was the first to start dancing on the table" (**Figure 13.22a**). A cue indicated whether participants were to make an inference about the personality of the person in the picture (impression formation task) or to remember the order in which specific statements were presented in relation to a particular face (sequencing task). Both conditions required participants to think about other people, but only the impression formation task required them to think about the internal states of those people. The impression formation task engaged the MPFC much more than the sequencing task did (**Figure 13.22b**).

The results of this study suggest that MPFC activation plays a strong role in forming impressions about the internal states of other people, but not in thinking about other types of information regarding another person. Thus, they suggest that social cognition relies on a distinct set of mental processes. Subsequent studies have shown that the relation between the MPFC and impression formation is specific to animate beings, but it is not present when individuals form impressions of inanimate objects (J. P. Mitchell et al., 2005). Together, these studies indicate that the MPFC is important for reasoning about the intangible mental states of other beings, including animals. As discussed earlier, evidence suggests that the MPFC supports the ability to change perspective.

a

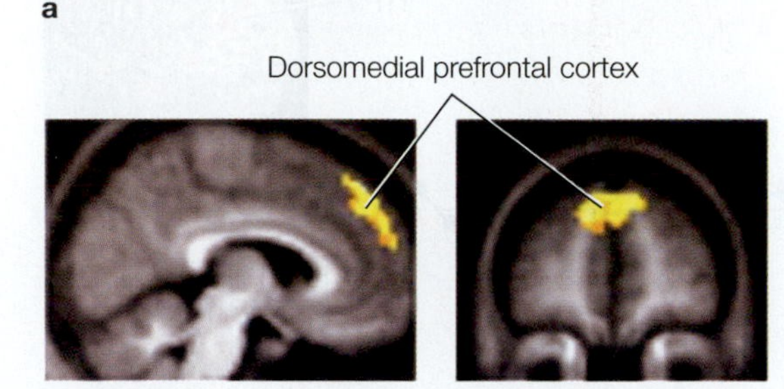

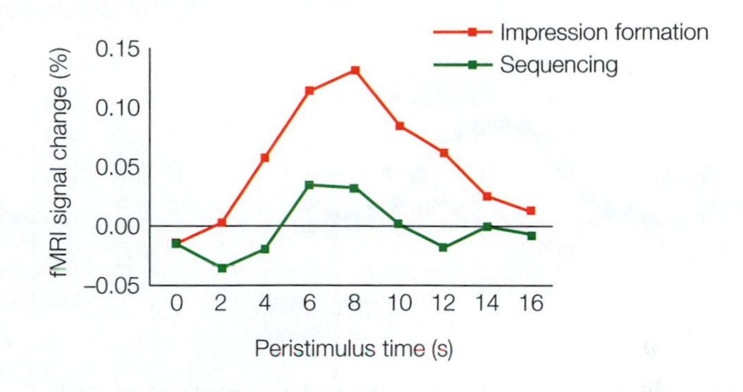

b

FIGURE 13.22 A study of personality inference.
(a) Participants were presented with a series of pictures that paired faces with statements about personality, and instructed either to make an inference about the person's personality or to pay attention to the order in which the statements were presented. (b) MPFC activity was associated with forming impressions of personality in comparison to remembering the sequence of the statements.

Another brain region that has been associated with making inferences about other people's mental states is the right hemisphere's temporoparietal junction (rTPJ). Rebecca Saxe at the Massachusetts Institute of Technology conducted a series of studies to examine the specificity of this region (Saxe & Powell, 2006; Saxe & Wexler, 2005; Saxe et al., 2009). First she localized the TPJ by adapting a process developed in fMRI studies of face perception. Recall from Chapter 6 that investigators explore the response characteristics of the fusiform face area (FFA) by using a localizer task to identify the FFA on an individual basis. For example, a participant might view faces or places, and the difference between the two conditions is used to specify the location of that person's FFA. After identifying the FFA, researchers can perform further manipulations to ask how the FFA's activity varies as a function of other experimental manipulations (see Chapter 12).

Saxe developed a similar method to identify which rTPJ region is engaged during theory-of-mind judgments (Saxe & Powell, 2006). Her localizer task, based on the Sally–Anne false-belief task (Figure 13.12), presented a series of false-belief stories, as well as control scenarios involving falsehoods that had nothing to do with the mental states of other people. When these conditions were compared, a region of the rTPJ was consistently more active in the theory-of-mind condition. For each study participant, researchers defined the exact location of activity within the rTPJ. Activity in this region was then examined for differential activity in relation to a series of other tasks that measure person perception (**Figure 13.23**).

Activity in the rTPJ is associated with reasoning about other people's mental states, but it does not respond to just any condition involving socially relevant information about other people. In one study, participants were presented with three kinds of information about a person: social background, mental state, and a life event. For example, participants might learn about Lisa, a fictional person. Lisa lives in New York City with her parents (social background) but wants to move to her own apartment (mental state), and she finds out that the apartment she wants is available (life event). The study found that the rTPJ was significantly activated when participants were presented with the information about a mental state compared to information about a social background or a life event (Saxe & Wexler, 2005).

As you learned in earlier chapters, neuroscientists favor a network approach to the relation between brain regions and psychological function, rather than a strict

a **False belief sample story**

John told Emily that he had a Porsche. Actually, his car is a Ford. Emily doesn't know anything about cars, though, so she believed John.

When Emily sees John's car, she thinks it is a

_____ Porsche

_____ Ford

False photograph sample story

A photograph was taken of an apple hanging on a tree branch. The film took half an hour to develop. In the meantime, a strong wind blew the apple to the ground.

The developed photograph shows the apple on the

_____ ground

_____ branch

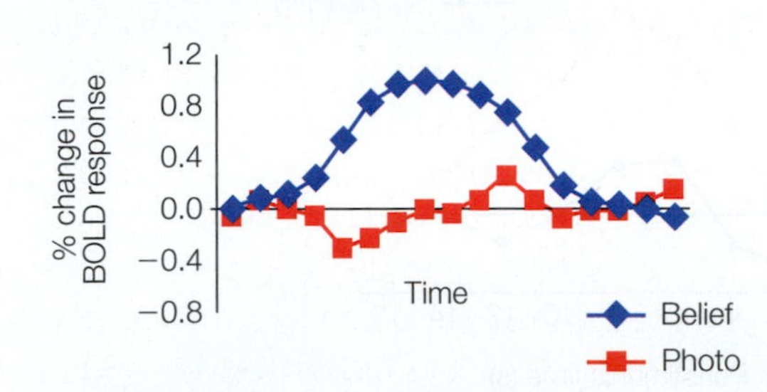

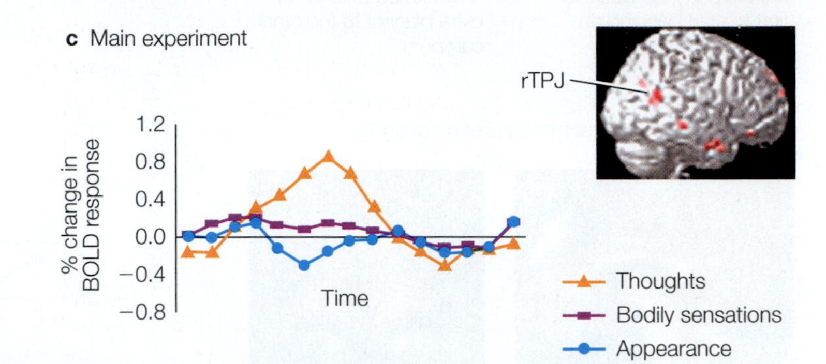

FIGURE 13.23 The localizer procedure for theory of mind and the rTPJ.
(a) Participants complete false-belief tasks that involve either false beliefs about other people (as illustrated, for example, in the sample stories), or false photos that have nothing to do with the mental states of other people (such as a photo of an apple hanging from a branch). (b) Researchers identify a specific region in the brain that activates more strongly to false beliefs of people than to false photographs. (c) They then examine this region of the brain for differential activity in relation to forming impressions about different aspects of people, such as their thoughts, bodily sensations, or physical appearance.

localization approach. A single brain region is unlikely to support a psychological process as complicated as thinking about another person's mental states. Although the rTPJ is theorized to be specialized for reasoning about the mental states of other people, we have learned in this chapter that the MPFC is also involved in this process. What roles do the rTPJ and MPFC play in reasoning about mental states of others?

Currently, two different hypotheses have been suggested. One is that the rTPJ is specialized for reasoning about the mental states of other people, and the MPFC supports broader reasoning about other people, including—but not limited to—their mental states. A second hypothesis suggests that the MPFC supports reasoning about social tasks, and the rTPJ is important for redirecting attention in both social and nonsocial tasks.

Let's look at the evidence for the first hypothesis. Participants' brain activity was examined in relation to processing information about a person's physical appearance ("Alfredo was a heavyset man"), internal physiology ("Sheila was starving because she had skipped breakfast"), or mental states ("Nicky knew his sister would be angry because her flight was delayed by 10 hours"). The study found that the MPFC was activated in relation to information about physical appearance and internal physiology. In contrast, the rTPJ was selectively activated for the information about mental states (Figure 13.23c; Saxe & Powell, 2006).

What about evidence for the second hypothesis? Chapter 7 described the attentional cuing procedure popularized by Michael Posner and his colleagues (Posner et al., 1980). In that procedure, participants are presented with cues that provide either valid or invalid information about where to direct their attention to successfully identify a target object (see Figure 7.15). Many of the studies that have found activation of the rTPJ in relation to mental states use false-belief tasks that require participants to direct their attention away from invalid information to answer questions about a person's mental states.

Consider again the Sally–Anne false-belief task. We know that participants' most current representation of the marble is in the drawer, where Anne put it. Therefore, they have to redirect their attention to other information to correctly answer that Sally will think the marble is in the basket. Although this task is specifically about mental states rather than someone's physical appearance or other socially relevant information, it is also unique in its requirement that participants redirect their attention.

A later study found that the same region of rTPJ is significantly activated in relation to the false-belief localizer task used by Saxe and her colleagues and in relation to redirecting attention away from nonsocial cues that signaled invalid information in the attentional cuing procedure (J. P. Mitchell, 2008). This finding suggests that the same region of rTPJ supports the control of attention for social and nonsocial stimuli. But does it? Saxe and her colleagues took a second look, this time using a higher-resolution protocol. They found that the rTPJ actually has two distinct regions: One population of neurons engages for mentalizing, and the other engages for reorienting attention (Scholz et al., 2009).

Currently, there is no definitive answer about the differential roles of the rTPJ and MPFC in person perception. But research continues on this question and promises to deepen our understanding of how we accomplish the difficult task of understanding the minds of other people.

The Superior Temporal Sulcus: Integrating Nonverbal Cues and Mental States

The studies described in the preceding discussion first provide information about someone's mental states and then examine the brain systems that are recruited for reasoning about mental states versus reasoning about other kinds of information. In the real world, however, we are not given a paragraph about what someone is thinking, nor can we count on people telling us exactly what they are thinking. In fact, in the real world, paying attention to nonverbal cues rather than verbal cues may be your best strategy when people try to hide their mental state from you. We know this is a good strategy, because patients with language comprehension deficits are better at detecting when someone is lying than are either patients with right-hemisphere lesions who have no language deficits or control participants (Etcoff et al., 2000).

Nonverbal cues such as body language, posture, facial expression, and eye gaze play a powerful role in person perception. You have already learned about the neuroscience of facial perception, which involves regions such as the fusiform face area (Chapter 6) and the role of the amygdala in using the face to make social judgments (Chapter 10). Research has also shown that attention to the direction of eye gaze is an important source of nonverbal information about another person's attentional state.

Within their first year of life, children develop joint attention, the ability to monitor another person's attention. One of the most typical ways that children monitor where other people are directing their attention is by noting the direction of their eye gaze. Humans are the only primates that follow eye gaze rather than the direction where the head is pointing. We humans can tell where the eye is gazing because of our large scleras, the whites of our eyes, an anatomical feature that no other primate possesses (Kobayashi & Kohshima, 2001).

Michael Tomasello and his colleagues (2007) suggest that eyes enabled a new social function in human evolution: supporting cooperative (mutualistic) social interactions. Eye gaze may also be helpful for understanding when people's words don't match their mental states. For example, when a prospective date declines your invitation, does she make eye contact while turning you down or avoid your gaze? What neural systems support the ability to attend to other people's eye gaze and use this information to reason about their mental state?

One of the earliest lines of research examining this question comes from single-cell-recording studies in monkeys. David Perrett and his colleagues at the University of St. Andrews in Scotland (1985) discovered that cells in the superior temporal sulcus (STS) are helpful for identifying head position and gaze direction. Amazingly, some cells responded to head position, while others responded to gaze direction. Although head position and direction of eye gaze are often consistent, the ability to distinguish head position from eye gaze direction opens the door for using these cues to make inferences about mental states. Individuals who turn their head in the same direction as their gaze may be thinking something very different from individuals who keep their head facing forward but point their gaze in a different direction.

Converging evidence showing that the STS is important for interpreting eye gaze in relation to mental states comes from human neuroimaging studies. Kevin Pelphrey and his colleagues at Duke University (2003) examined whether activity in the STS depended on the mental states indicated by shifts of eye gaze in another person. Participants watched an animated woman who directed her attention either toward or away from a checkerboard that appeared and flickered in her left or right visual field (**Figure 13.24**). Randomly, the figure took either 1 or 3 seconds to shift her gaze.

If the STS were involved solely in tracking shifts in eye gaze, then it would be activated to the same degree in relation to any shift in eye gaze. If, however, the STS were involved in integrating shifts in eye gaze with mental states, then activation of the STS should be related to where the character directs her attention, because eye gaze shifted toward the checkerboard and eye gaze shifted away from the checkerboard would indicate two different mental states.

a Congruent

b Incongruent

STS, right hemisphere

c

FIGURE 13.24 Interpreting intention from eye gaze direction.
Participants viewed a virtual-reality character whose eye gaze moved either in a congruent manner toward a flashing checkerboard (a) or in an incongruent manner away from a flashing checkerboard (b). (c) The STS tracked the *intention* behind shifts in eye gaze rather than simply shifts in eye gaze.

Consistent with the latter prediction, activity in a posterior region of the STS varied in relation to shifts in eye gaze direction (Pelphrey et al., 2003). Gaze shifts to empty space evoked longer activation of the STS compared to when the gaze shifted to the checkerboard; that is, the context of the gaze had an effect. The researchers conjectured that when the figure unexpectedly did not look at the target, observers were flummoxed and had to reformulate their expectation. This process takes longer, so STS activity was prolonged.

The researchers found unexpectedly that STS activation was also related to the timing of the gaze. If the gaze shift occurred at 1 second after the checkerboard appeared, the context effect was seen, but if it took 3 seconds for the figure's gaze to shift, the effect was not seen. They proposed that when the time between the presentation of the checkerboard and the gaze shift was too long, the gaze shift was more ambiguous. The observer did not necessarily link it to the appearance of the checkerboard, and no expectations were violated when the gaze direction varied.

In a related study, a similar region in the STS was more strongly activated when a virtual-reality character made eye contact with the participant versus when the character averted his gaze from the participant (Pelphrey et al., 2004). Thus, the STS appears to signal the focus of attention of another individual, as well as to provide important social signals: That individual may be trying to direct our attention away from a novel object or may be wishing to engage in a social interaction. Interestingly, these studies also demonstrate that the activity in a visual processing region is sensitive to the context of the observed action.

TAKE-HOME MESSAGES

- The medial prefrontal cortex is involved in the perception of others when we use ourselves to understand others, or when we represent information about the other person in a manner that is as complex as the way we store information about ourselves.
- The right temporoparietal junction is important for reasoning about other people's mental states.
- Humans are the only primates that follow eye gaze direction rather than head direction.
- Processing that occurs in the superior temporal sulcus is important for inferring mental states from eye gaze direction.

13.8 Autism Spectrum Disorder and the Mental States of Others

Autism spectrum disorder (ASD) refers to a group of neurodevelopmental disorders that include autism, Asperger's syndrome, childhood disintegrative disorder, and pervasive developmental disorders not otherwise specified. They are heterogeneous etiologically at the biological level and symptomatically at the behavioral level, with an individual's deficits landing anywhere on a spectrum ranging from mild to severe. Manuel Casanova, who has done extensive work in pediatric neuropathology, hypothesizes that a combination of genetic susceptibility and exposure to exogenous risk at neurodevelopmentally critical times can explain the heterogeneity of ASD (Casanova, 2007, 2014). He suggests that the underlying pathology in ASD is abnormal stem cell proliferation followed by abnormal neuronal migration, which in turn sets off a cascade of obligatory events that will lead to the variety of signs and symptoms seen in ASD (Casanova, 2014; for review, see Packer, 2016).

The study of ASD provides a fascinating window into the important roles of both mental state attribution abilities and imitation abilities in navigating our social worlds. If these impairments are a central feature of ASD, then we should see differences between autistic people and controls in the neural regions and neural connectivity involved in person perception and social cognition. Is this the case?

Anatomical and Connectivity Differences in ASD

Autism spectrum disorders are associated with a number of anatomical differences that arise during neuronal development. These include alterations to the structure of cortical minicolumns, alterations to synaptic spines on individual cortical units, and alterations within the cortical subplate, a region involved with proper cortical development and later with regulating interregional communication (reviewed in Hutsler & Casanova, 2016). These changes at the level of the neuron affect the future organization of cortical circuits and connectivity.

Changes in anatomy are accompanied by changes in connectivity: Hyperconnectivity within the frontal lobe regions is characteristic, as are decreased long-range connectivity and decreased reciprocal interactions with other cortical regions (e.g., Courchesne & Pierce, 2005). Such connectivity differences emerge early. Using diffusion tensor imaging (DTI), Jason Wolff and his colleagues (2012) determined the structural brain connectivity of 92 infants who had a high risk of ASD (i.e., they had siblings with a confirmed diagnosis of ASD), examining them at 6 months old and again at 2 years old. At 2 years of age, 28 of these infants had a confirmed diagnosis of ASD. These 28 infants showed perturbations in the development of cortical white matter already present at 6 months, in comparison with the infants who did not have ASD.

Several studies have reported regional structural abnormalities in white matter and a partial disconnection between the higher-order association areas of the brain during development. These changes to cortical circuitry are thought to be the basis of the behavioral phenotype seen in ASD and to contribute to changes in cortical functioning (see Belmonte et al., 2004; Frith, 2004; and Hutsler & Casanova, 2016).

Disconnection between the higher-order association areas implies differences in interhemispheric connectivity. Evidence for this conclusion was uncovered by researchers in Taiwan (Lo et al., 2011). Using DTI, they found a loss of leftward asymmetry and reduction of interhemispheric connections in adolescents with autism compared to neurotypical controls, suggesting that some of the cognitive and behavioral deficits observed in ASD may be the result of alterations in long-range connectivity in the corpus callosum (CC) involved in social cognition and language processing. It appears that atypical lateralization is already present in young children, and a recent study in toddlers using MRI and DTI found that decreased lateralization correlated with increased ASD severity (Conti et al., 2016).

These findings are not surprising in light of various MRI studies that have found a reduction in size of the anterior (Hardan et al., 2000), splenum, and genu (Vidal et al., 2006) portions of the CC in individuals with ASD compared to neurotypical controls, as well as abnormal myelin development (necessary for fast communication in long-range neurons) in the CC (Gozzi et al., 2012). Recall from Chapter 4 that the CC is organized topographically from anterior to posterior. Alterations in the anterior callosum may indicate that interhemispheric communication between the frontal lobes is impaired in individuals with ASD (Courchesne et al., 2004; Hutsler & Avino, 2015), resulting in deficits in working memory, cognitive control, and theory of mind, as well as the inability to suppress inappropriate responses. Decreased posterior connectivity may affect processing for human faces.

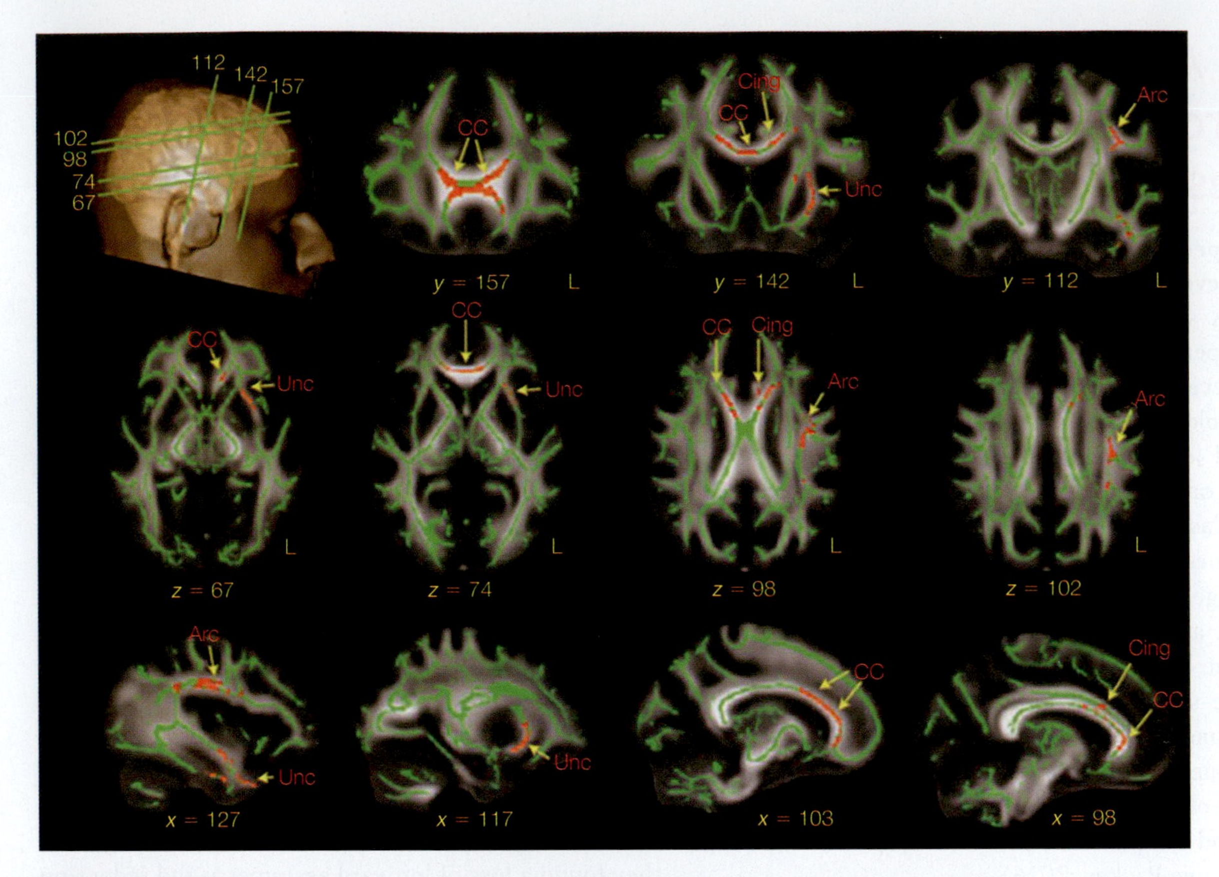

FIGURE 13.25 Fractional anisotropy reveals differences in white matter connectivity between individuals with ASD and neurotypical controls.
Researchers compared the white matter networks of 61 adult ASD males with 61 neurotypical controls discerned from diffusion tensor MRI data, tractography, and tract-based spatial statistics (an automated, operator-independent, whole-brain, voxel-by-voxel analysis of white matter integrity). Compared to controls, the ASD group had significantly lower fractional anisotropy (the relative degree of anisotropy in a voxel) in the left arcuate fasciculus (Arc), external capsule, anterior and posterior cingulum (Cing), anterior corpus callosum (CC), and uncinate fasciculus (Unc). There were no increases in fractional anisotropy in the ASD group compared to controls. Numbered green lines on the head at upper left indicate the location of the same numbered scan. The red regions indicate reduced fractional anisotropy values in the ASD group. There were no increases in fractional anisotropy in the ASD group compared with controls.

A recent large study of adult men with ASD confirmed that white matter differences that persist into adulthood are localized to major association and commissural tracts of the frontal lobe (**Figure 13.25**) and that white matter differences within particular networks are associated with specific childhood behaviors (Catani et al., 2016). For example, connectivity abnormalities of the left arcuate fasciculus, important for language and social function, were associated with stereotyped utterances and delayed echolalia (repetition of vocalizations made by someone else) in childhood. The study also confirmed that white matter differences were greater in the left hemisphere.

Autism spectrum disorders have also been associated with abnormal function in a number of regions associated with person perception, including the MPFC, amygdala, FFA (discussed in Chapter 6), STS, anterior insula, and TPJ. It has become apparent that no single brain region or even a single system is responsible for the behaviors of autistic individuals. Although different brain regions support our ability to make sense of other people's minds and visible cues, the connectivity changes and resulting behavioral changes seen in ASD suggests that they function as a network.

Theory of Mind in ASD

False-belief tasks are particularly challenging for children with ASD. Even when they are well past the age when most children are able to solve these problems, autistic individuals perform these tasks as if the characters have access to all the information in the story. In the Sally–Anne false-belief task (Figure 13.12), although they understand that Sally initially put the marble in the basket, they also act as if Sally knows that Anne moved the marble to the drawer. Therefore, they report that Sally will look for the marble in the drawer.

Michael Lombardo and his colleagues (2011) designed an experiment to look for the specific neural systems responsible for the impairments in representing mental-state information in ASD. They compared activations between ASD individuals and controls during a mentalizing task or a physical judgment task about themselves or another. During these tasks, the rTPJ was the only mentalizing region that responded atypically in ASD individuals: In typically-developing individuals, the rTPJ was selectively more responsive to mentalizing than to physical judgments (both in the self and in other conditions), but in ASD individuals the rTPJ was less responsive, and specialization was completely absent. This lack of selectivity correlated with the degree of social impairment: The less selective the rTPJ response, the more impaired that individual was in representing the mental states of others.

Several neuroimaging studies show that, when performing theory-of-mind tasks, autistic individuals exhibit significantly less activation in the STS (important for interpreting eye gaze in relation to mental states; reviewed in Frith, 2003). Instead, they exhibit activation in this region for a broader range of conditions. For example, in the checkerboard task illustrated in Figure 13.24, they show increased STS activation to any shift in eye gaze, rather than specifically in response to shifts in eye gaze toward unexpected locations.

False-belief tasks often give participants information about other people's mental states, but, as mentioned earlier, in real life we are often left to infer these states from nonverbal cues such as facial expression and eye gaze direction. While some previous studies suggested that individuals with ASD tend to look at the mouth and not the eyes, two more-recent reviews of eye-tracking studies don't support those findings (Falck-Ytter & von Hofsten, 2011; Guillon et al., 2014). Instead, Quintin Guillon and his colleagues found that decreased attention to social stimuli, such as faces and gaze direction, occurs when the social content of an encounter increases. For example, when speech is directed specifically to a child with ASD, or if the number of people in the social context increases, the child is less likely to attend to social stimuli. This finding suggests that the deficit in attention to faces that individuals with ASD show is not generalized, but rather context dependent (Chawarska et al., 2012).

Indeed, functional imaging has shown normal early visual processing for faces in ASD (Hadjikhani et al., 2004), suggesting that the differences in the visual capacities of individuals with ASD are the result of top-down processes. Interestingly, higher processing in the fusiform face area and occipital face area in ASD individuals does not show the right-sided asymmetry during processing of human faces that is seen in neurotypical individuals. Yet individuals with ASD do have typical lateralization responses when they're looking at animal faces (Whyte et al., 2016) and robot faces (Jung et al., 2016), suggesting that processing may not be abnormal in ASD individuals for all types of face stimuli and that specific interhemispheric connections may be affected in ASD.

Eye gaze research has focused on the attention paid to the object that the other person is gazing toward. This response is used as a measure of understanding that the object of another's gaze direction has a social value compared to objects not gazed at. So far, studies show that ASD individuals take longer to follow another's gaze and spend less time than controls do looking at objects gazed at by someone else, providing evidence that people with ASD don't automatically understand the referential nature of gaze direction (reviewed in Guillon et al., 2014). Altogether, these studies suggest that in the brains of ASD individuals, the neural regions associated with person perception and theory of mind are not activated in the same way as in typically-developing brains.

The Default Network in ASD

It has been suggested that, because the default network is engaged during social, emotional, and introspective processing, dysfunction in the default network may be at the root of some difficulties in these domains (Kennedy & Courchesne, 2008b). Indeed, several studies have found abnormalities in the function of the default network in ASD individuals. When healthy participants engage in non-self-referential thinking (thus turning off the default network), they experience deactivation in the MPFC. In participants with ASD, however, there is no change in MPFC activity when they're switching from a resting state or doing an active task (Kennedy et al., 2006; **Figure 13.26**). Is this lack of change because the default network is always on or always off? PET studies are consistent with the always-off conclusion.

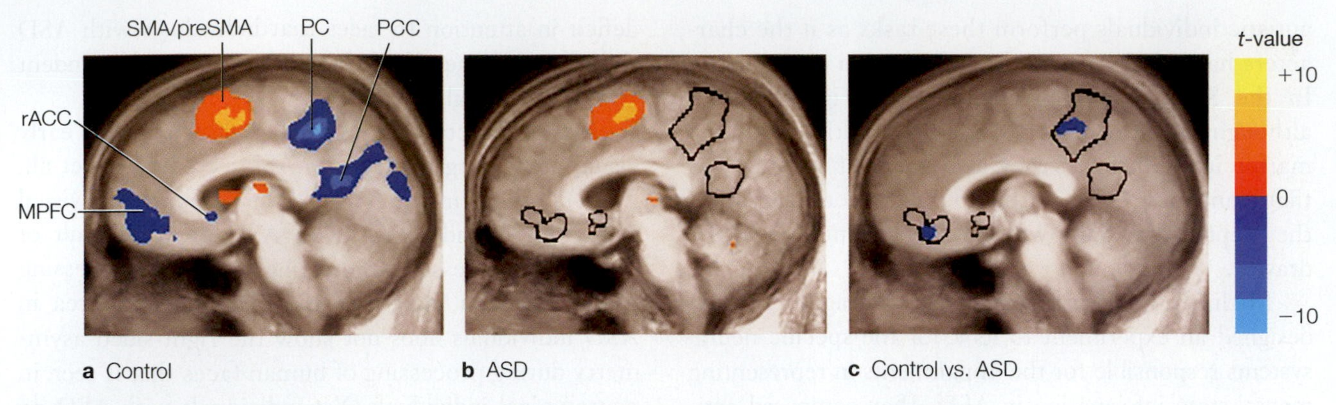

FIGURE 13.26 Group whole-brain analysis of functional activity between control and ASD individuals. The color bar at right indicates activations (positive *t*-values) and deactivations (negative *t*-values). **(a)** For control participants, large regions of deactivation in the MPFC and right anterior cingulate cortex (rACC) and in the posterior cingulate cortex (PCC) and precuneus (PC) occurred during a number task. **(b)** No deactivation, however, occurred in individuals with ASD. The black outlines correspond to areas of deactivation in controls, which were active during the rest condition. **(c)** A direct group comparison between control and ASD participants revealed a significant deactivation difference between groups in the MPFC and rACC and in the precuneus. The right superior temporal sulcus and bilateral angular gyrus also deactivated in control participants but not in ASD participants, although these regions were not significantly different in the direct group comparison.

Interestingly, participants with ASD reported very different types of thoughts from those reported by neurotypical individuals when their mind was at rest. All of the ASD individuals had difficulty reporting at all, since they had never thought about their inner experience. Two out of three reported seeing only images with no internal speech, feelings, or bodily sensations. The third appeared to have no inner thoughts at all, but merely described what his current actions were (Hurlburt et al., 1994). Was the difference in functional activity due to different cognitive processes used by ASD individuals while resting; that is, was it task dependent? Or was there pervasive dysfunction in the region; was it task independent? Daniel Kennedy and his colleagues speculated that an absence of this resting activity in ASD individuals may be directly related to their differences in internal thought (Kennedy & Courchesne, 2008b).

To pursue this idea, these researchers asked typically-developing participants and ASD individuals to read particular statements about themselves or about a close other person (e.g., their mother) and to judge whether the statements were true or false while undergoing fMRI (Kennedy & Courchesne, 2008a). The self/other statements described either a personality trait (internal condition) or an observable external behavior or characteristic (external condition). All person judgment conditions were compared to a baseline task, which was a cognitively demanding math problem. Finally, a resting-state scan was performed.

The researchers found reduced activity in the vmPFC and vACC in the autism group during all judgment conditions, as well as in the resting condition, suggesting that dysfunction of these regions was independent of the task. The activity in the dmPFC, and retrosplenial cortex and PCC, however, was task specific: Individuals with ASD had reduced activity during the internal condition but similar or slightly increased activity during the external condition, suggesting specific deficits with judgments that rely on inference but not those that rely on external observation. Yet functional similarities were also present: In the self/other judgments, with the exception of the vmPFC and vACC, the rest of the network's activation was indistinguishable between the two groups, suggestive of task-specific dysfunction (Kennedy & Courchesne, 2008a; **Figure 13.27**).

These findings suggest that the social deficits seen in autistic individuals are due partially to the fact that their brains not being constantly prepared for the type of social thought that marks typical cognition. Some evidence does support this notion. In an fMRI study, when children with ASD were given explicit instructions to perform a social task (e.g., "pay attention to the faces"), they showed significant activity in regions recruited by typically-developing children who were not given the explicit directions—specifically, the MPFC and inferior frontal gyrus—but they did not have activity in the same regions when given vague instructions (e.g., "pay attention"; Wang et al., 2007). The children with ASD failed to instinctively engage in social processing, although

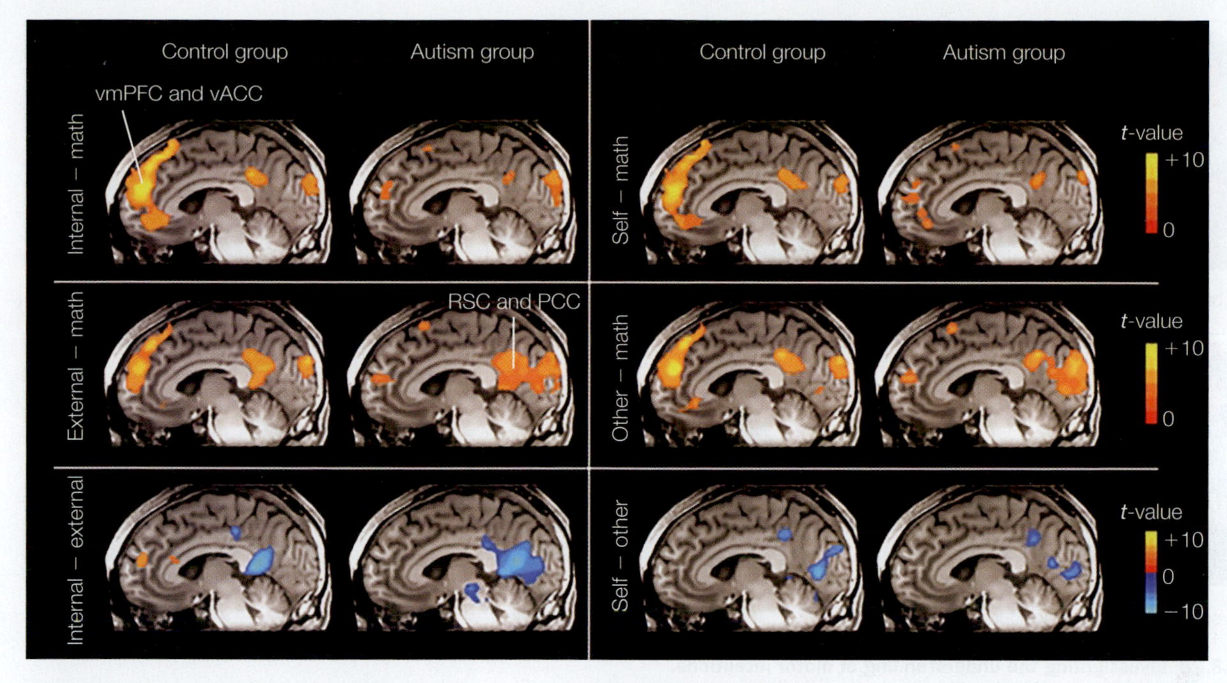

a Internal/external condition   b Self/other condition

FIGURE 13.27 Functional activity in control and autism groups.
The top two rows show regions with greater activity during internal/external (a) and self/other (b) judgments as compared to a math judgment. In all conditions, ASD individuals had reduced activity in the vmPFC and vACC, suggesting that dysfunction of these regions was independent of the task. Otherwise, both groups recruited largely similar regions during internal/external and self/other judgments. Note in the bottom row that the activity in the dmPFC and in the retrosplenial cortex and PCC was task specific. Specific regions of the RSC and PCC in both groups were more active (blue) for external and other judgments (compared to internal and self judgments).The researchers suggest that this distinction may indicate variations in the extent to which mental imagery is associated with these different types of judgments.

they could engage when explicitly instructed to do so. It may be that they do not experience the constant impulse to view most events through a social lens (Kennedy & Courchesne, 2008a).

Many people with ASD show an unusual proficiency in a visuospatial or other nonsocial domain, such as exceptional musical or drawing talent, extraordinary puzzle-solving aptitude, or the capacity to perform complex mathematical or calendrical calculations mentally. Although only about 10% of autistic individuals demonstrate such a skill at the savant level, most have at least one enhanced nonsocial ability (Happé, 1999; Mottron & Belleville, 1993; Rimland & Fein, 1988). Freed from the constant demands of social cognition, their minds may engage more intensely in nonsocial processing.

The Mirror Neuron Network in ASD

You may wonder whether anyone has proposed that deficits in the mirror neuron network contribute to the difficulties that ASD individuals exhibit with mimicry and imitation. For instance, ASD individuals do not exhibit the degree of yawn contagion that typically-developing children do (Senju et al., 2007), and although they can voluntarily mimic pictures of faces, they do not show automatic mimicry (McIntosh et al., 2006). For ASD individuals, some types of imitation are more difficult, such as imitating nonmeaningful or novel actions (for a review, see Williams et al., 2004), and some are easier, such as when the goal is clear or the person being copied is familiar (Oberman et al., 2008). It seems, then, that sometimes children with ASD understand the goal of observed motor acts (a function of mirror neurons), and sometimes they don't. This behavior suggests that several factors play a role in imitation and that if a mirror neuron network is involved, its role is not fully understood.

Luigi Cattaneo at the University of Parma suggested that in individuals with ASD, the primary deficit in the mirror neuron network lies in how it links the initial motor acts into action chains, rather than in how responsive the mirror neurons are to the observation of other people's actions. The idea is that mirror neurons respond

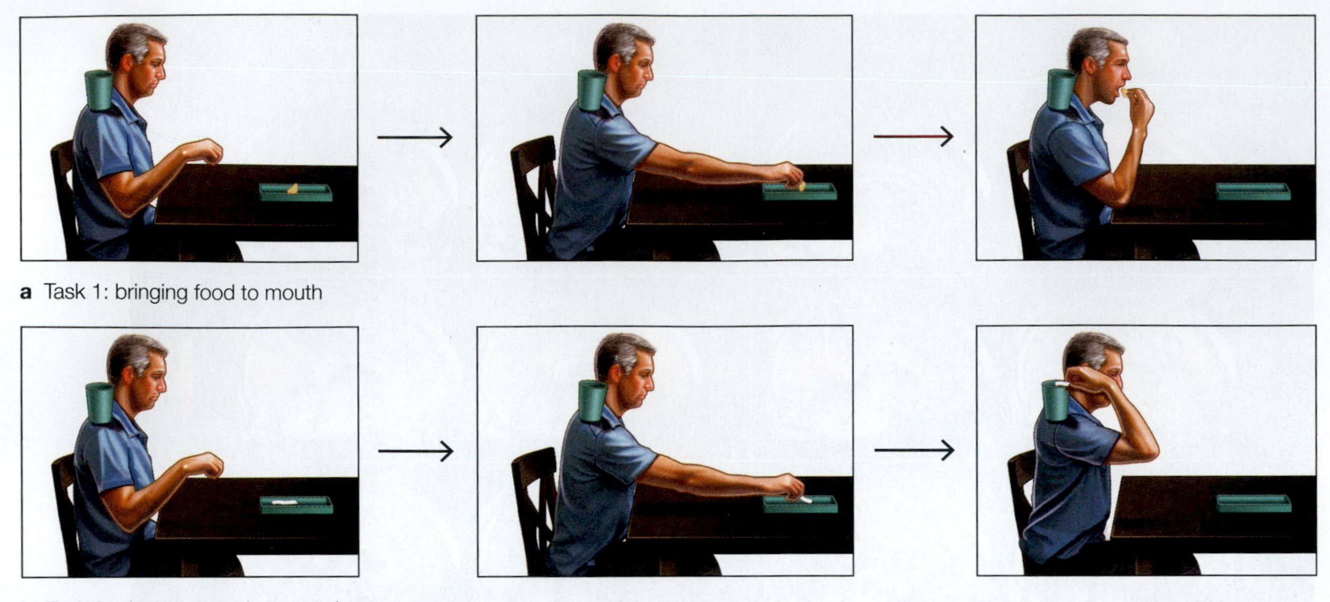

FIGURE 13.28 Investigating the understanding of motor intentions.
(a) In one task, either the participant or the experimenter reaches for a piece of food, grasps it, and puts it in his mouth. (b) In a second task, the participant or experimenter reaches for a piece of paper, grasps it, and puts it in a container on his shoulder.

to the initial motor action (such as reaching for food) by firing a specific action chain (reach, grasp, place in mouth) based on the initial motor movement. Thus, the observer of the action has an internal copy of the action before it occurs, enabling her to gain an understanding of the other person's intentions.

Cattaneo suspected something was awry in this network. To test this hypothesis, he designed a clever experiment using electromyography to record the activity of the mylohyoid muscle involved in mouth opening (Cattaneo et al., 2007). In one condition, children with ASD and typically-developing children were asked either to reach for a piece of food, grasp it, and eat it, or to reach for a piece of paper, grasp it, and place it in a container. In a second condition, the children observed an experimenter performing these tasks (**Figure 13.28**).

Each task was subdivided into three movement phases: reaching, grasping, and bringing the object to the mouth or to the container. Cattaneo reasoned that if an action chain had been activated by the initial reaching movement, then the mouth muscle would be activated as soon as a person started for the food; if not, then the muscle would be activated only as the food approached the mouth.

In typically-developing children, the mylohyoid (MH) was activated early in the reaching and grasping phases of both carrying out a grasping-for-eating task (**Figure 13.29a**) and observing a grasping-for-eating task (**Figure 13.29c**). This early activation of the muscle involved in the final stage of the task indicates an early understanding of the final goal of the task.

Not so for children with ASD, however. The MH was activated only during the last movement phase, the bringing-to-the-mouth action (**Figure 13.29b**), and no MH activation occurred during observation of the task (**Figure 13.29d**). This evidence suggests that individual motor acts are not integrated into an action chain in ASD children, so they lack full comprehension of the intention of others.

Intention can be broken down into what a person is doing and why. These authors point out that the *what* of a motor act can be understood in two ways. One way is through a direct matching mechanism (i.e., mirror neurons). The what could also be predicted, however, by the semantic cues of the object itself. Just knowing what an object is can suggest the motor action that will follow. So even if a person's mirror neuron network were impaired, she could still predict the what goal of a motor act through external cues. In other words, sometimes the what process doesn't actually depend on the person's mental state, because recognizing the object is all the information that is needed to predict the goal.

How about the *why* goal of the motor act, especially when it is not related to an object? For example, when parents of children with ASD extend their arms to hug

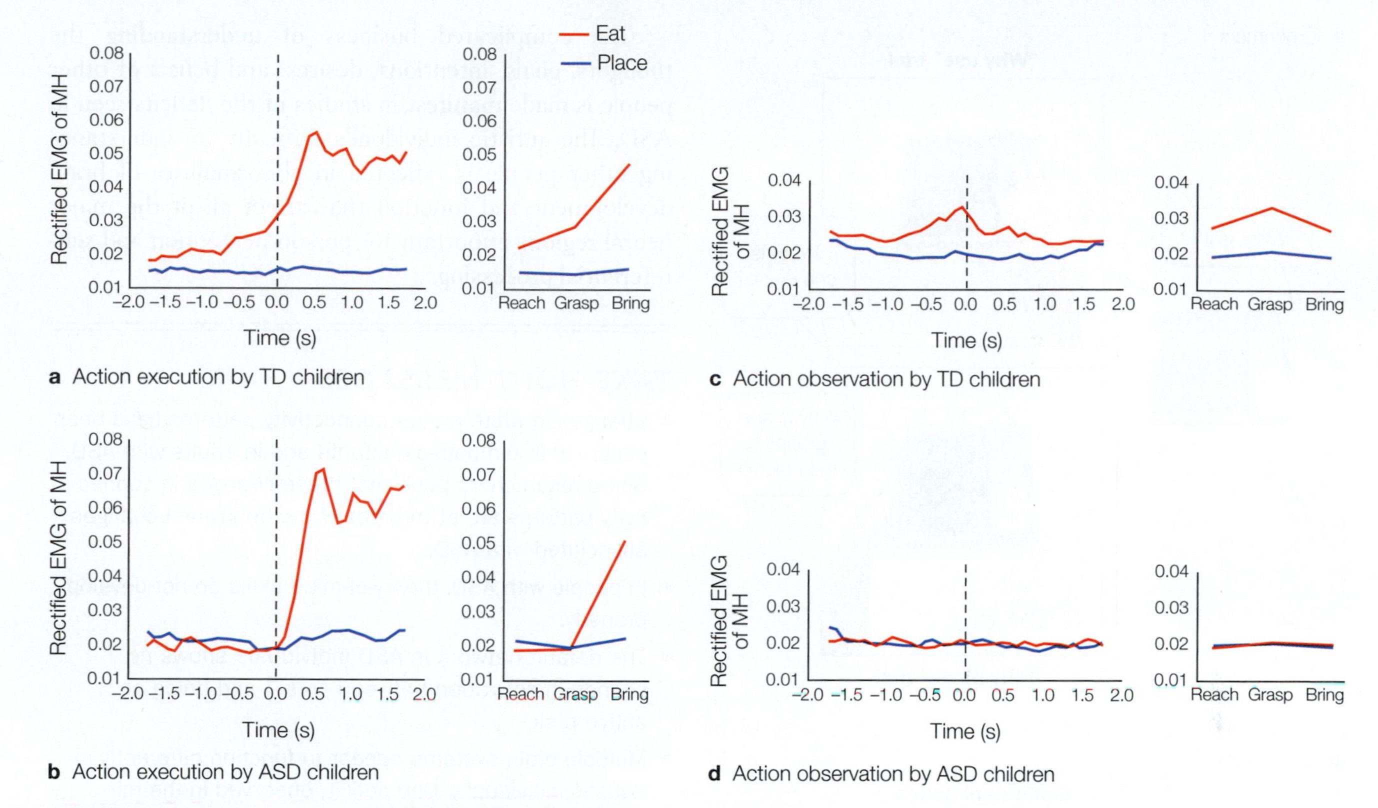

FIGURE 13.29 The time course of mylohyoid muscle activity.
Reach action begins at time 0. (a) In typically-developing (TD) children, the activity of the MH muscle differs depending on the action. During *execution* of the bringing-to-the-mouth action (red), the EMG indicates that the MH muscle's activity increased several hundred milliseconds before the hand actually grasped the food. When the activity was a placing action (blue) with no eating involved, the muscle remained inactive. (b) In children with ASD, there is no activation of the MH muscle during the execution of either reaching or grasping. (c) Similar results are seen during *observation* of the bringing-to-the-mouth task (red) and the placing task (blue) in typically-developing children. (d) In ASD children, however, observing a hand grasping food and bringing it to the mouth elicits no MH action.

their children, the children fail to extend their arms in return. To analyze this kind of behavior, Sonia Boria and her colleagues at the University of Parma (2009) looked at whether autistic children understood both the what and the why of an action.

They conducted two experiments. In the first, children with ASD and typically-developing children were presented pictures depicting hand–object interactions (**Figure 13.30a**). In half of the why trials, the hand grip shown was congruent with the function of the object ("why use" trials); in the other half, the grip corresponded to the position typically used to move that object ("why place" trials). Then the children were asked what the individual was doing and why she was doing it. Both sets of children could accurately report the what, or the goal, of the motor acts (i.e., she is grabbing the object). The children with ASD, however, made several errors in the why task, and all of these errors occurred in the "why place" trials.

In the second experiment, the children saw pictures of a hand grip that was compatible with the object's use (**Figure 13.30b**). The object was placed in a context suggesting either that it was going to be used (congruent with the grasp) or that it was about to be placed into a container (incongruent with the grasp). Here, both groups of children performed equally, correctly reporting the agent's intention.

The researchers concluded that we can understand the intentions of others in two different ways: by relying on motor information derived from the hand–object interaction, and by using semantic information derived from the object's standard use or the context in which it is being used. Children with ASD have no deficit in the second type of understanding, but they have difficulties in understanding the intentions of others when they have to rely exclusively on motor cues. In other words, they understand the intentions from external cues, not internal ones, thus providing additional support for the notion

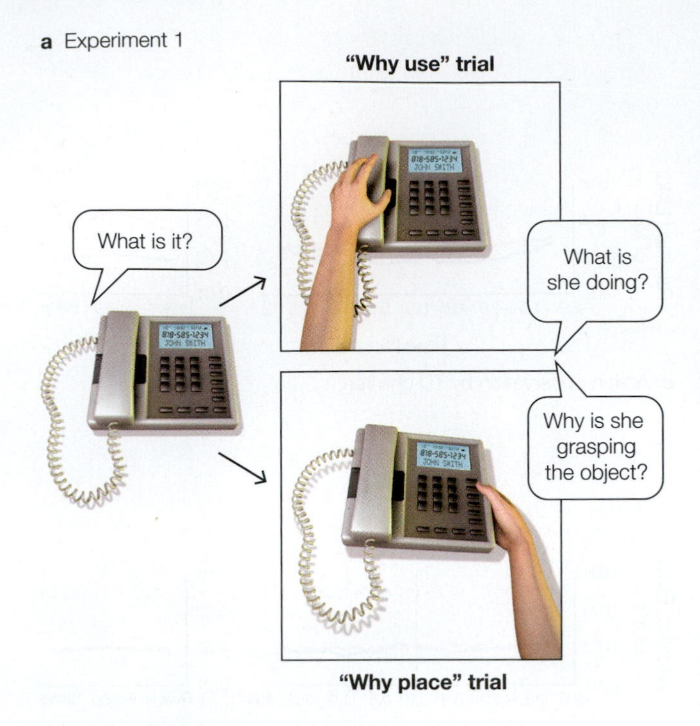

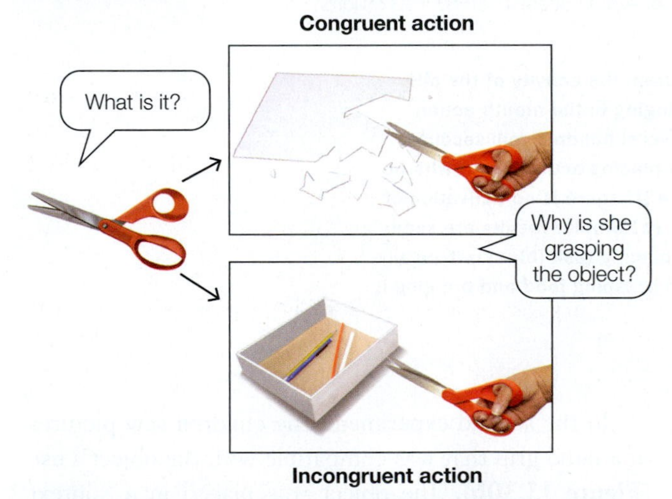

FIGURE 13.30 The what and the why of an action inferred by motor and object cues.
(a) In Experiment 1, participants saw hand grips that were congruent with either the function of the object ("why use" trials) or the position typically used to move that object ("why place" trials). **(b)** In Experiment 2, the hand grip was always congruent with the function of the object, but only one situation was congruent with the inferred action of cutting. Autistic children infer intention through object cues.

that ASD involves a deficit in the mechanics of the mirror neuron network.

This evidence, in turn, suggests that the mirror neuron network is highly interconnected. These studies and many others suggest that the imitation deficits and some of the other cognitive differences seen in ASD may be a result of underconnectivity in the mirror neuron network and the involvement of alternative communication pathways (Kana et al., 2011).

The complicated business of understanding the thoughts, goals, intentions, desires, and beliefs of other people is made manifest in studies of the deficits seen in ASD. The autistic individual's difficulty in understanding other people is reflected in abnormalities of brain development and function that affect all of the major neural regions important for person perception and self-referential processing.

TAKE-HOME MESSAGES

- Changes in white matter connectivity patterns have been observed in 6-month-old infants and in adults with ASD. Some researchers posit that these changes in connectivity patterns are at the root of the behavioral changes associated with ASD.
- In people with ASD, theory-of-mind skills do not develop properly.
- The default network in ASD individuals shows no change in activation between "rest" and doing an active task.
- Multiple brain systems appear to function differently in autistic individuals. One deficit, observed in the mirror neuron network, results in a failure of linking motor acts into action chains that allow motor intentions to be understood.

13.9 Social Knowledge

In 1985, Simon Yates and Joe Simpson were the first mountaineers ever to reach the summit of Siula Grande, a remote peak in the Peruvian Andes. In his book *Touching the Void*, Simpson explained that the climb was made with no support or backup team. It would be remembered as much for these accomplishments as it was for the moral dilemma faced by the climbers. Early in the descent, Joe fell and broke his leg. He later told an interviewer (Lloyd-Pierce, 1997) that Simon should have said to him,

> "I'll go off and get some help," which would have been a euphemism for, "You've had it." Instead, he chose to try and save my life by lowering me thousands of feet down the mountain on a rope, at great risk to himself. It was an incredible feat of mountaineering and we descended about 3,000ft in this way.

The two men developed a system in which Simon would brace himself with his climbing axes and then lower Joe down using a 300-meter rope. After being lowered as far as the rope would permit, often out of Simon's view, Joe used his climbing axes to brace himself on the mountain and then tugged on the rope. Simon would then make his way down to meet Joe and repeat the process. Late in the day a storm hit, and the icy mountain temperatures dropped even further. With only one more stretch to go before they could rest for the night in a sheltered spot, disaster struck a second time.

In the dark, Simon inadvertently lowered Joe down over what turned out to be an ice overhang. Simon suddenly felt all of Joe's weight tugging him and he knew Joe was dangling in the air. Unfortunately, Joe's hands were so frostbitten that he was unable to tie the knots required to climb back up the rope. They were in this position for about an hour. Joe tried to yell to Simon, but he could not be heard over the storm. Joe said,

> I was dragging him down with me. In order to stop himself plummeting over the edge, the only thing he could do was cut the rope and let me go—to prevent us both being dragged to our deaths. He obviously knew that this could kill me, but he had no choice.

Simon's hands were also numb, and he no longer had his strength and grip. He could not pull Joe back. Simon recalled,

> I was being pulled towards the edge of the cliff, too. Cutting the rope was the only choice I had, even though it was obvious that it was likely to kill Joe. There wasn't much time to think; it was just something which had to be done quickly or I'd have been dragged to my death.

He cut the rope.

The biggest taboo in the mountaineering community is to cut the rope attaching you to your partner. Ironically, Simon's decision to violate the moral code of mountaineering may have been the only reason they both survived. The result, however, does not stop others from moralizing. Simon noted,

> Sometimes someone who thinks what I did was unacceptable will come up and verbally assault me. The rope between two climbers is symbolic of trust and to cut it is viewed as a selfish act. What's important is that Joe didn't think that, and the first thing he did when he crawled back into camp was to thank me for trying to get him down.

Although Joe wrote that Simon did what Joe himself would have done in the same situation, Simon was ostracized by much of the mountaineering community.

Yates and Simpson's story is certainly an extreme case, but it illustrates the reality that social behavior is shaped by multiple influences. To negotiate our social worlds successfully, we must not only understand the rules for appropriate behavior, but also make choices consistent with those rules. In this section we consider questions about social knowledge and its use in decision making. How do we know which aspects of knowledge to apply to a particular situation? If our own interests conflict with societal norms, deciding how to proceed can be difficult. What can the brain systems used to make these sorts of decisions tell us about this psychological process?

Representations of Social Knowledge

One of the most complicated aspects of social behavior is the lack of straightforward rules. The very same behavior that is appropriate in one context may be wildly inappropriate in another. For example, handshake etiquette varies from country to country. In Australia, shake firm and fast, and never use both hands. In Turkey, shake long and lightly. In Thailand, never shake hands at all! Or consider hugging.

In the United States, greeting a close friend with a hug is OK, but greeting a stranger with a hug is not. Should you hug someone you know who is not a close friend? When is it appropriate to greet a person with a hug? Social cognitive neuroscientists are just beginning to research the neural systems that help us make these decisions. Current findings suggest that the orbitofrontal cortex (OFC) is important for taking a particular situation into account in order to apply the appropriate rules.

Patients with OFC damage have the most difficulty when they need to draw on their social knowledge to make sense of social interactions. In one fascinating task developed to measure this ability, Valerie Stone and her colleagues presented participants with a series of scenarios in which a character commits a social faux pas by accidentally saying something impolite. One scenario tells the story of Jeanette and Anne. Anne receives a vase as a wedding gift from Jeanette. A year later, Anne has forgotten that the vase was from Jeanette. Jeanette accidentally breaks the vase while at Anne's house. Anne tells Jeanette not to worry, because it was a wedding gift that she never liked anyway.

The researchers measured social reasoning by asking participants to identify whether someone in the scenario had made a social mistake, and if so, why. Stone and her colleagues gave this test to patients with OFC damage, patients with lateral prefrontal cortex damage, and healthy control participants (Stone et al., 1998).

In comparison to all other participants, patients with OFC damage did not perform as well on the test, thus demonstrating a decreased ability to apply their social knowledge to the scenarios.

Patients with OFC damage understood that a character like Jeanette would feel bad about breaking the vase, but they did not understand that Anne's comment about not liking the vase actually was intended to reassure Jeanette. Instead, they often believed that Anne had intended to hurt Jeanette's feelings. The patients with OFC damage were not as able to take context into account when reasoning about social mistakes. It has since been demonstrated that only lesions to the frontal pole of the OFC lead to deficits in the faux pas test (Roca et al., 2010, 2011). These results suggest that damage to specific regions of the OFC impairs the ability to use social knowledge to reason about social interactions.

Earlier in this chapter we saw that although patients with OFC damage knew that certain topics of conversation were impolite, they introduced them anyway and were unaware that they had violated any social rules. This lack of awareness may be especially problematic because it makes it difficult for people with OFC damage to feel embarrassment that might motivate them to behave differently in the future.

In another study, patients with OFC damage and healthy control participants took part in a teasing task that required them to make up nicknames for an experimenter they did not know well (Beer et al., 2003). Healthy control participants used flattering nicknames and later apologized for having to tease someone they did not know well. In contrast, patients with OFC damage offered unflattering nicknames, often in a singsong voice usually reserved for teasing someone you know well. The OFC patients were not embarrassed by their inappropriate teasing and reported feeling especially proud of their social behavior.

Without awareness of their social mistakes, patients with OFC damage never generate the emotional feedback they need to change their future behavior. When we do something that makes us feel embarrassed, we don't like that feeling and are strongly motivated to avoid feeling that way again. When we do something that makes us feel proud, however, we are likely to repeat the action in order to continue the good feeling. These findings suggest that even though patients with OFC damage report an understanding of social rules, they do not apply this knowledge to their own social interactions (**Figure 13.31**).

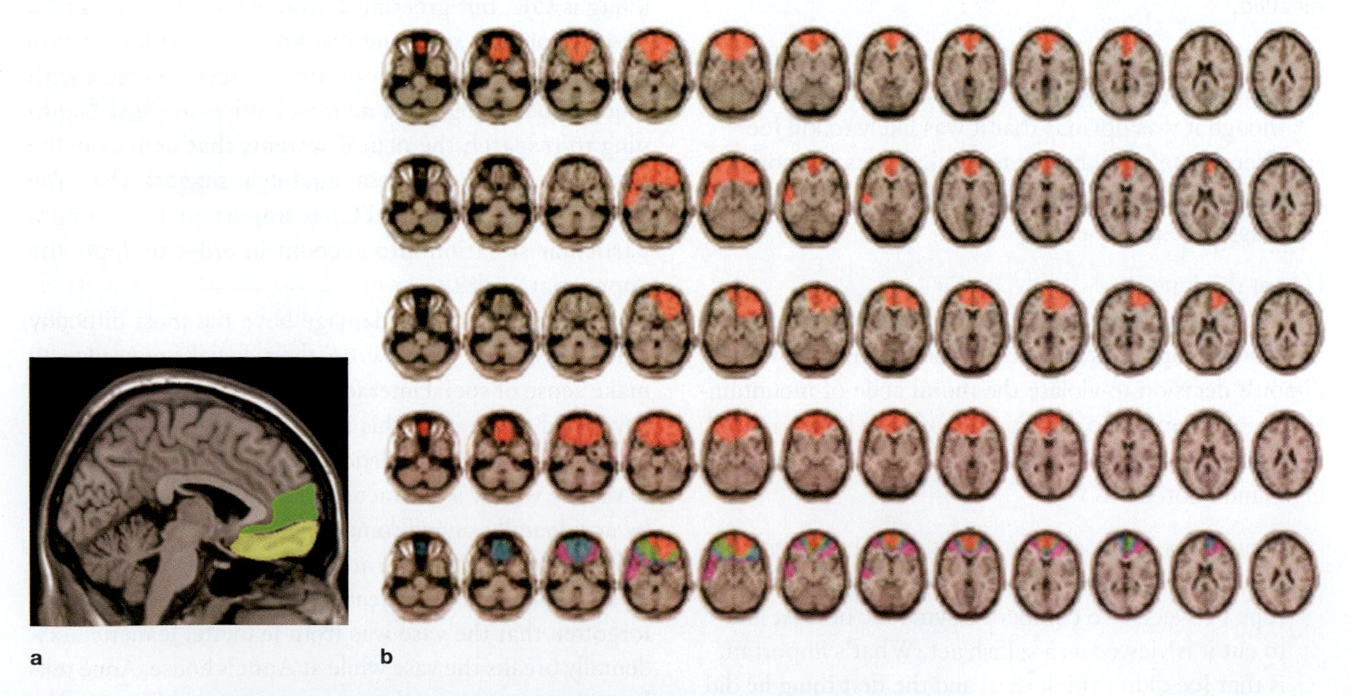

FIGURE 13.31 Reconstruction of the orbitofrontal lesions in patients with socially inappropriate behavior.
Patients with OFC damage may lack insight into their behavior at a particular moment, while maintaining accurate summaries of their traits. **(a)** The orbitofrontal cortex (yellow) lies just beneath the medial prefrontal cortex region (green) associated with the summaries of personality traits. **(b)** Typical OFC damage. Damage is indicated in red. Each of the first four rows represents brain slices of a single patient in ascending order from the left, with the most superior slice at far right. The fifth (bottom) row is a composite of the findings from all the patients, indicating the extent of overlap in the location of lesions. Red indicates 75%–100% overlap; green, 50%–75%; blue, 25%–50%; pink, 0%–25%.

Adult patients who have sustained OFC damage and behave inappropriately can retain intact social knowledge about what is proper—that is, social rules—but they appear to have trouble learning new social knowledge. This view is supported by case studies of OFC damage sustained in childhood. These patients also show inappropriate social behavior, but in contrast to patients who incur this damage in adulthood, they do not understand social rules. They did not learn the rules before being injured and could not learn them afterward (S. W. Anderson et al., 1999). This finding suggests that the orbitofrontal cortex is important for learning social knowledge, as well as for applying it to specific social interactions.

Using Social Knowledge to Make Decisions

The research described in the preceding discussion suggests that the orbitofrontal cortex is important for both learning social knowledge and using it in relevant situations. Even if we know the rules for a given social situation, we still have to decide what to do to ensure that we abide by the rules. For example, if you are at a dinner party at a stranger's house, you know that there are certain rules for being a polite guest, but they do not always point to one specific behavioral choice. For example, should you mention that you are a vegetarian? The answer depends on the particular situation. How do we make decisions about our social behavior? Which brain mechanisms support decision making that is based on social knowledge?

Patients with vmPFC damage are notoriously poor at making social decisions. (Here the ventromedial prefrontal cortex includes the medial OFC.) Early research attempting to identify and understand the function of the brain regions involved with social decision making assigned gambling tasks to vmPFC patients. These patients had a difficult time making decisions when the outcome was uncertain. Lesley Fellows and Martha Farah (2007) wondered, however, whether this difficulty was specific to decisions involving uncertainty, or reflected a general difficulty in assessing the relative value of options. In their experiment (discussed in Section 13.4), where the task was a simple preference judgment between two options of colors, actors, or food, they showed that vmPFC damage impairs value-based decision making even when no uncertainty exists.

In Chapter 10, we learned that people with OFC damage are unable to respond to changing patterns of reward and punishment (Iowa Gambling Task). That is, they can learn that a stimulus is rewarding (it has value), but when it becomes punishing (the value changes), they still choose it. Thus **reversal learning** does not take place, and individuals with OFC damage don't learn from a negative experience.

To learn from experience, we must be able to change behavior as a result of unexpected negative feedback. Thus, in a social situation, sometimes hugging someone is appropriate and you get a hug back—positive feedback that your behavior was okay. Sometimes, however, the hug is not appropriate and the person stands frozen in your embrace. If your behavior unexpectedly receives the cold shoulder, you feel embarrassed, and you are guided by that negative feedback to change your behavior.

When we consider that the vmPFC is involved in coding stimulus value, it seems odd that patients with vmPFC lesions can selectively learn a stimulus value initially, but not when the stimulus value is reversed. Geoffrey Schoenbaum and his colleagues found in rats that, although the OFC may be critical in reversal learning, its importance is not because it flexibly represents positive and negative value. They found that the better the reversal learning, the less flexible the OFC value coding was. It appeared to them that the OFC does not code stimulus value, but signals the amygdala when the value expectation is violated (Schoenbaum et al., 2007).

Following this idea, Elizabeth Wheeler and Lesley Fellows (2008) investigated whether feedback (positive or negative) regarding the expectation of stimulus value influences behavior through separate and distinct neural mechanisms. The study participants were divided into three groups: patients with damage to the ventromedial frontal lobe (vmFL, as the researchers called the region encompassing both the medial OFC and the adjacent ventromedial PFC), healthy controls, and patients with damage to the dorsolateral frontal cortex (dlFC). The researchers asked the participants to perform a probabilistic learning task with positive and negative feedback while undergoing fMRI. They found that vmFL damage selectively disrupted the ability to learn from negative feedback, but not from positive feedback. The controls and patients with dlFC damage performed equally and were able to learn from both positive and negative feedback. These findings suggest two distinct neural mechanisms.

Wheeler and Fellows point out that the results of this experiment are consistent with much of the literature that implicates the vmFL in reversal learning, extinction, fear conditioning, regret, and envy. But the findings are hard to reconcile with the previous study by Fellows and Farah, which suggests (as do findings in neuroeconomics) that this region represents relative reward value and preferences. Perhaps, as the researchers propose, the vmFL carries representations of the expected (relative) reward value not to guide choice per se, but to serve as a benchmark against which outcomes can be compared.

When the outcomes are negative and unexpectedly fail to match expectations, the vmFL enables avoidance learning. Geoffrey Schoenbaum and his colleagues (2007) suggest that this process may take place indirectly, by signaling to the amygdala and other regions to form new associative representations that may flexibly change their behavior. This proposal implies that in patients where the vmFL is not functioning, it provides no benchmark, compares no outcomes, and generates no negative feedback, so no reversal learning can take place. A bad social experience has no effect. The positive feedback system is intact, however, and learning can take place through positive feedback.

Can we apply this finding to social judgments? For instance, when you expect a hug back and don't get one, is your OFC activated? Penn State researchers specifically addressed the role of vmPFC in the interpretation of negatively valenced feedback during social decision making (Grossman et al., 2010). They matched healthy controls with patients who had vmPFC degeneration due to frontotemporal lobar degeneration (FTLD), a neurodegenerative disease. These patients make socially inappropriate comments, engage in socially unacceptable behavior, and often show little insight into the effects of these behaviors, despite the social (and sometimes legal) consequences of the behaviors.

The participants first judged 20 social situations (e.g., cutting into the ticket line at a movie theater) or minor infractions of the law (such as rolling through a red light at 2:00 a.m.) on a scale of 1 to 5 for social acceptability. These scenarios were then given contingencies that were either negatively biased (e.g., rolling through a red light at 2:00 a.m. *when a police car is at the intersection*) or positively biased (e.g., rolling through a red light at 2:00 a.m. *when rushing a sick child to the emergency room*). This time, participants were asked to judge according to two randomly presented instructions: "Should everyone do this all of the time?" (rule-based condition) or "Is this generally okay?" (similarity-based condition). This manipulation was intended to ferret out differences that could be due to insensitivity to perceived legal and social rules; none were noted in the performance of the FTLD patients.

Although both the FTLD patients and the healthy adults rated the positively biased scenarios as equally acceptable, they rated the negatively biased scenarios differently. The FTLD patients judged negative scenarios to be more acceptable than the healthy adults judged them to be. When healthy adults judged these negative social scenarios, significantly greater activation was observed in their vmPFC (the very region of cortical atrophy in FTLD patients) than when they judged the positive social scenarios (**Figure 13.32**). These studies support the hypothesis that the vmPFC plays a crucial role in evaluating the negative consequences of social decision making.

As suggested in the previous section, the orbitofrontal cortex plays a strong role in applying social knowledge to our decisions in social settings. This region likely helps us choose the correct behaviors by supporting reversal learning through evaluation of the negative consequences of social decisions. As the case of patient M.R. from the chapter-opening story suggests, the OFC is helpful for recognizing when a hug is appropriate and when it is not.

Identifying Violators of Social Contracts

Consider this conditional logic problem: There are four cards on a table. Each card has a letter on one side and a number on the other. Currently you can see R, Q, 4, 9. Turn over only the cards needed to prove whether the following rule is false: "If a card has an R on one side, then it has a 4 on the other." What's your answer?

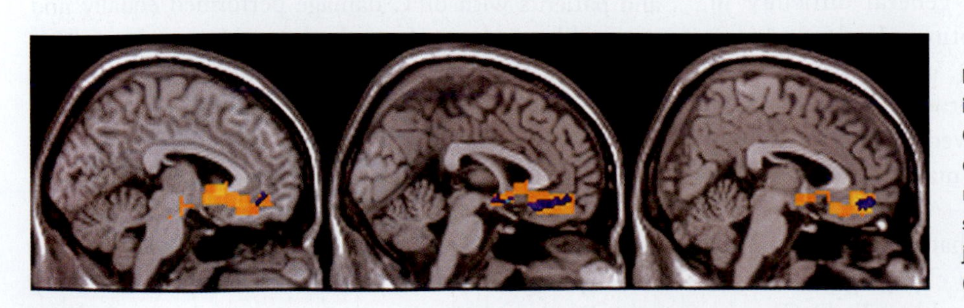

FIGURE 13.32 The role of the vmPFC in making social judgments. Cortical atrophy in the FTLD with social disorder (blue) overlaps with brain regions that are seen to activate in fMRI studies of healthy adults undertaking judgments of negative social scenarios (orange).

Now try this situation, which involves a social contract: There are four cards representing people sitting at a table. One side of each card reveals the person's age, and the other side shows what the person is drinking. You see 16, 21, soda, beer. Turn over only the cards needed to prove whether anyone is violating the following rule: "If you are younger than 21, you may not drink beer."

Which question was easier for you? The evolutionary psychologist Leda Cosmides found that people have a harder time with the logic question; only 5%–30% of people get it right (the answer is R and 9; most people say only R). It is a different story, however, when it comes to identifying violators of a social contract: When asked a version of the second question, 65%–80% of people get it right (the answer is 16 and beer). This result holds for people from Stanford University, France, and the Ecuadorian Amazon, not just for adults but for 3-year-olds as well. People of all ages from all over the world find it simple to spot cheaters in a social exchange situation, but they have trouble with logic problems of the same form (if *P*, then *Q*; Cosmides & Tooby, 2004).

Cosmides and John Tooby propose that humans have a specific adaptive algorithm in the brain—innate, not learned—that automatically activates in social contract situations when violations are likely to reveal the presence of someone who intends to cheat. They have found that the algorithm does not activate in situations where violations to social exchange rules are accidental, cheating is too difficult, or a cheater would not profit from cheating (Cosmides et al., 2010).

Jens Van Lier and his colleagues (2013) investigated this proposal and verified that these performance results were independent of cognitive capacity or age. They also established that increasing cognitive load had no impact on social contract performance, whereas performance on nonsocial contracts did depend on available cognitive capacity. These findings support the idea that the brain has specific cognitive processes devoted to detecting cheaters in social contract situations, and that detecting cheaters is not a domain-general learning ability.

Additional neuroanatomical support comes from patient R.M., who had extensive bilateral damage affecting his orbitofrontal cortex, temporal pole, and amygdala. Cosmides and her colleagues compared his performance in two contexts: (a) social contract problems of the form "If you take the benefit B, then you must satisfy the requirement R," giving the example "If you borrow my car, then you have to fill up the tank with gas"; and (b) precautionary rules of the form "If you engage in hazardous activity H, then you must take precaution P," with the example "If you do a trapeze act, you must use a safety net." On the precautionary tasks, R.M. performed as well as control participants and two other patients with similar but nonoverlapping brain lesions—but he was 31 percentage points worse than they were on social contract reasoning. His dissociation in reasoning performance supplies additional evidence that reasoning about social exchange is a specialized and separable component of human social intelligence (Stone et al., 2002).

When violators of social contracts are detected, what happens next? Social exchange can evolve only if cheaters (also known as free riders) are identified and punished or ostracized. If cheating carries no penalty, then cheaters, who benefit without contributing, will eventually take over. With a majority of cheaters, reciprocal exchange can't sustain itself.

Financial games are often used to understand social decision making, such as the decision to punish. For example, in the ultimatum game one player (P1) must split a sum of money with another player (P2). P1 offers a portion of the sum to P2, and P2 must either accept or reject the offer. The offer may be fair (e.g., very close to 50% for each person) or unfair (e.g., 80% for P1 and 20% for P2). If P2 rejects the offer, however, then neither player gets any money.

In one study using the ultimatum game, the consideration of unfair offers was associated with activity in the dorsolateral prefrontal cortex and the insula (Sanfey et al., 2003). As we have seen, insula activity is often associated with negative emotions such as disgust, anger, pain, and distress, suggesting that participants in the ultimatum game experienced these emotions while considering the offer. What's more, increased insula activity during consideration of an unfair offer predicted a likelihood that the offer would be rejected.

From a rational economic perspective, participants should not let negative emotional reactions lead them to reject the unfair offer. Even if it is unfair, they will still gain some money instead of no money. From a broader perspective, however, the negative emotional reaction leads participants to reject unfair offers that might otherwise compromise their reputation. If you continually accept less than your share, word gets around and you lose social status, with the loss in status entailing other consequences, including negative effects on economic, physical, and mental health. For example, men who lose social status are four times more likely to suffer depression (Tiffin et al., 2005).

By rejecting the offer and incurring a small loss, however, you can punish the other player for violating the social contract. In financial games with repeated encounters, players who punish their opponents by rejecting unfair offers gain trust and respect, and are thought of as being group focused and altruistic (Barclay, 2006). The benefits of this increase in social status can offset the costs of being a punisher. So, are punishers being altruistic?

Recall Tania Singer's study (discussed in Section 3.6), which found that people enjoy punishing cheaters and suggested that the motivation to punish was driven by fairness. A recent study by Max Krasnow and his colleagues (2016) disputes fairness as the motivation for punishment. If the ultimatum game is varied a bit, such that P2 has to accept whatever offer P1 makes (the dictator game), behaviors change. P1 is less generous and no longer offers half the money. In addition, if the player's identity is masked, P1 offers even less—and when anonymous in single-encounter games, P1 may offer nothing at all.

Tweaking the game further, you can add a third party, the punisher, who can spend money to reduce the dictator's earnings. The researchers found that in their modified version of the dictator game with multiple encounters, punishers acted differently, depending on their personal treatment by the dictator. When punishers didn't know how they would be treated by the dictator, they inferred that the dictator's mistreatment of other people predicted mistreatment of themselves, and this inference predicted the amount of punishment they doled out. However, if they themselves had been treated well by the dictator, even though they knew others had been treated poorly, they punished less. These findings suggest to the researchers that instead of unfairness being the grounds for punishment, humans' punitive psychology evolved to defend personal interests.

Moral Decisions

How do we resolve moral dilemmas like the one that Simon Yates faced on the Siula Grande climb? Simon's problem was a real-life example of the classic trolley dilemma in philosophy. In this thought experiment, a conductor loses control of his trolley car. As a witness to this event, you can see that, if nothing is done, five people are likely to be killed because they are directly in the path of the speeding trolley.

You are offered two different scenarios. In the first scenario (**Figure 13.33a**), you can throw a switch and divert the trolley onto another track. This option, however, ensures the death of a single construction worker who is on the alternate track. Do you throw the switch or not? In the second scenario (**Figure 13.33b**), you are standing next to a stranger on a footbridge that crosses over the trolley tracks when you see the out-of-control trolley car speeding toward five people. This time, the only way to stop the trolley is to push the person next to you off the footbridge onto the tracks to impede the trolley's movement. Do you push the stranger onto the tracks in order to save the other five people?

Most people agree that throwing the switch is acceptable but pushing the person off the footbridge is not. In both cases, one person's life is sacrificed to save five others, so why is one option acceptable and not the other?

a

b

FIGURE 13.33 The trolley car dilemma.
Would you be willing to sacrifice one life to save five lives? Would your decision be different if saving the five lives meant that you had to (a) pull a switch to direct a trolley toward one person or (b) physically push a person off a footbridge into the path of a trolley car? Research suggests that the strong emotional response to actually pushing someone would make you decide differently in these two scenarios.

Simon's dilemma on Siula Grande draws on aspects of both scenarios in the trolley car dilemma. We know already that Simon could not simply walk away from Joe and was willing to put his life at great risk to try to save Joe's. When both their lives were more immediately threatened, Simon cut the rope, with the intent of saving at least one life instead of losing two. Did Simon solve his moral dilemma by using emotion or by using logic? Joe was going to fall no matter what Simon did: cut the rope, lose his grip because of exhaustion, or be pulled off the cliff. Put yourself in Simon's shoes. What would you have done?

Joshua Greene and his colleagues at Princeton University (2004) argue that we make different choices in the switch-throwing and stranger-pushing scenarios of the trolley car dilemma because the level of personal involvement in causing the single death differentially engages emotional decision making. If you throw a switch, you still maintain some distance from the death of the construction worker. When you actually push the stranger off the bridge, you perceive yourself as more directly causing the death.

Greene and colleagues conducted a series of fMRI studies that contrasted moral dilemmas involving high levels of personal engagement with dilemmas involving low levels of personal engagement (Greene et al., 2001, 2004). As predicted, personal dilemmas and impersonal dilemmas were associated with distinct patterns of activation. Across the studies, impersonal decisions were associated with greater activation in the right lateral prefrontal cortex and bilateral parietal lobe, areas associated with working memory (see Chapter 9). In contrast, when participants chose options that required more personal effort, regions such as the medial frontal cortex, the posterior cingulate gyrus, and the amygdala were significantly activated—regions that we have learned are associated with emotional and social cognitive processes. Together, these studies suggest that the differences in our moral decisions are related to the extent that we permit emotions to influence our decisions about what is morally acceptable.

TAKE-HOME MESSAGES

- Current models of the role of the orbitofrontal cortex in social decision making propose that this region helps individuals identify which social rules are appropriate for a given situation so that they may flexibly change their behavior.
- Damage to the ventromedial frontal lobe disrupts the ability to learn from negative feedback but not from positive feedback.
- The orbitofrontal cortex is important both for learning social knowledge and for using that knowledge in relevant situations.
- Humans appear to have an innate ability to spot violators of social contracts.

Summary

In the more than 100 years separating the cases of Phineas Gage and the patient M.R., researchers have learned very little about the relation between brain function and social cognition. With the development of new research tools and new theories, however, the field of social cognitive neuroscience has blossomed. Exciting insights into how the brain supports our ability to know ourselves, to know other people, and to make decisions about our social worlds have already resulted, though we still have a long way to go.

We know from behavioral research that self-perception is unique in many regards, even at the neural level. We store incredibly elaborate information about ourselves, and the medial prefrontal cortex supports the particularly deep processes by which we encode this information. The increased baseline metabolism in this region may indicate that we chronically engage in self-referential thought, and many other processes represent momentary diversions of our cognitive resources from self-referential thought. Although the orbitofrontal cortex helps us consider contextual information so that we remain relatively accurate in our self-perceptions, the anterior cingulate may help us view ourselves through rose-colored glasses by marking positive information about the self.

When we attempt to understand other people, we are faced with the difficult task of trying to reason about their mental states, which are not directly accessible to us. This process heavily relies on our ability to use nonverbal cues such as facial expression and eye gaze direction to gather information about possible mental states. Then we have to represent this abstract information and use it to form an impression of what the person might be thinking. A number of structures support our ability to make inferences about other people's minds: the medial prefrontal cortex, right temporoparietal junction, superior temporal sulcus, fusiform face area, and amygdala. The widespread impairment of these regions in autism spectrum disorder, a developmental disorder marked by deficits in person perception and social behavior, reinforces the theory that these regions work together to support theory-of-mind abilities.

Although we often contrast self-perception and the perception of other people, the processes are not always completely distinct. The intrinsic relation between these two types of perception is illustrated by their neural commonalities. The medial prefrontal cortex may support the perception of both self and others when we draw on properties of self-perception to make sense of other people. In addition, the mirror neuron network appears to support our ability to empathize with other people.

Along with understanding ourselves and other people, we need to understand the rules for social interactions and how to make decisions to satisfy the multitude of rules that govern a particular social interaction. The process of making social decisions engages a large network of neural structures, including the orbitofrontal cortex, the dorsolateral prefrontal cortex, the amygdala, the anterior cingulate, the medial prefrontal cortex, the caudate, and the insula.

Some of the same brain regions are activated in relation to the three main processes of social cognition: self-perception, person perception, and social knowledge. It may be tempting to describe these regions as the "social brain." It is important to keep in mind, however, that almost every brain function has been adapted for social functions, even if they are not uniquely social. Although social interaction may influence how we select motor movements or where we direct our attention, motor movement and vision are also useful for finding food and other nonsocial functions. Disorders like ASD suggest, however, that abnormal function in certain brain regions most powerfully affects social function.

Key Terms

autism spectrum disorder (ASD) (p. 601)
autoscopic phenomena (APs) (p. 581)
default network (p. 576)
embodiment (p. 580)
empathic accuracy (p. 584)
empathy (p. 589)
experience sharing theory (p. 585)
false-belief task (p. 585)
imitative behavior (p. 585)
joint attention (p. 586)
mental state attribution theory (p. 584)
orbitofrontal cortex (OFC) (p. 569)
prefrontal cortex (PFC) (p. 569)
reversal learning (p. 611)
self-reference effect (p. 572)
simulation theory (p. 585)
social cognitive neuroscience (p. 572)
theory of mind (ToM) (p. 585)
theory theory (p. 584)
xenomelia (p. 582)

Think About It

1. Why do we have regions in the brain dedicated to processing information about the self? Why is it important to distinguish the self?
2. Are humans born with a theory of mind, or does it develop over time?
3. What kinds of social and emotional behaviors might be accounted for by the concept of mirror neurons? Would these behaviors be possible without some sort of mirrorlike network?
4. What might have been the evolutionary advantage for the development of empathy and theory of mind?

Suggested Reading

Adolphs, R. (2003). Cognitive neuroscience of human social behaviour. *Nature Reviews Neuroscience*, *3*, 165–178.

Ananthaswamy, A. (2015). *The man who wasn't there: Investigations into the strange new science of the self.* New York: Penguin.

Baron-Cohen, S., & Belmonte, M. K. (2005). Autism: A window onto the development of the social and the analytic brain. *Annual Review of Neuroscience*, *28*, 109–126.

Gazzaniga, M. S. (2005). *The ethical brain.* New York: Dana.

Gazzaniga, M. S. (2008). *Human: The science behind what makes us unique.* New York: Ecco.

Hutsler, J. J., & Avino, T. (2015). The relevance of subplate modifications to connectivity in the cerebral cortex of individuals with autism spectrum disorders. In M. F. Casanova & I. Opris (Eds.), *Recent advances on the modular organization of the cortex* (pp. 201–224). Dordrecht, Netherlands: Springer.

Hutsler, J. J., & Casanova, M. F. (2016). Cortical construction in autism spectrum disorder: Columns, connectivity and the subplate. *Neuropathology and Applied Neurobiology*, *42*(2), 115–134.

Lieberman, M. D. (2007). Social cognitive neuroscience: A review of core processes. *Annual Review of Psychology*, *58*, 259–289.

Macmillan, M. (2002). *An odd kind of fame: Stories of Phineas Gage* (reprint ed.). Cambridge, MA: MIT Press.

Schurz, M., Radua, J., Aichhorn, M., Richlan, F., & Perner, J. (2014). Fractionating theory of mind: A meta-analysis of functional brain imaging studies. *Neuroscience & Biobehavioral Reviews*, *42*, 9–34.

If evolution is to work smoothly, consciousness in some shape must have been present at the very origin of things.

William James

CHAPTER

14

The Consciousness Problem

ON THE MORNING OF MAY 24, 1987, K.P., obviously confused and upset, stumbled out of his car and into a Canadian police station with bloody hands, reporting, "I think I have killed some people . . . my hands." K.P. recalled falling asleep at about 1:30 a.m. while watching *Saturday Night Live*, anxious about his plan to confess his gambling debts to his parents-in-law and grandmother later that day. The next thing he remembered was looking down at his mother-in-law, a woman with whom he had a close mother–son relationship, and seeing a "frightened 'help-me' look" on her face. With only patches of recall of the following events, he remembered realizing in the car that he had a knife in his hands, and he remembered giving his shocking report to the police. It was only then, in the station, that he became aware that his hands were painful and that he had multiple severed flexor tendons.

Later the police filled in the gaps of K.P.'s memory. He had gotten up from his couch, put on his shoes and jacket, left his house (uncharacteristically, without locking the door), driven 23 km to his parents-in-law's house, gone in, strangled his father-in-law unconscious, repeatedly and fatally stabbed his mother-in-law, and finally driven himself to the police station.

K.P.'s medical and psychological evaluations revealed no evidence of recent drug use, epilepsy, organic brain lesions, or other medical problems. Four expert psychiatrists evaluated his mental state and found no evidence of depression, anxiety, dissociative features, thought disorders, delusions, hallucinations, paranoid ideation, or other suggestions of psychosis. No suggestion of motivation or personal gain could be found. K.P. denied any homicidal intention or plans, and he appeared horrified and remorseful to the police who first saw him. What he did have was a recent history of sleep deprivation provoked by anxiety and a history of sleepwalking since childhood, confirmed by an evaluation at a sleep disorder clinic.

Given the facts of K.P.'s case—no identifiable motive, no attempt to hide the body or weapon, no memory of the event, an obvious grief and affection for the victims,

BIG Questions

- Can the firing of neurons explain your subjective experience?
- How are complex systems organized?
- What distinguishes a living hunk of matter from a nonliving one if both are made of the same chemicals?
- What evidence suggests there is a consciousness circuit?

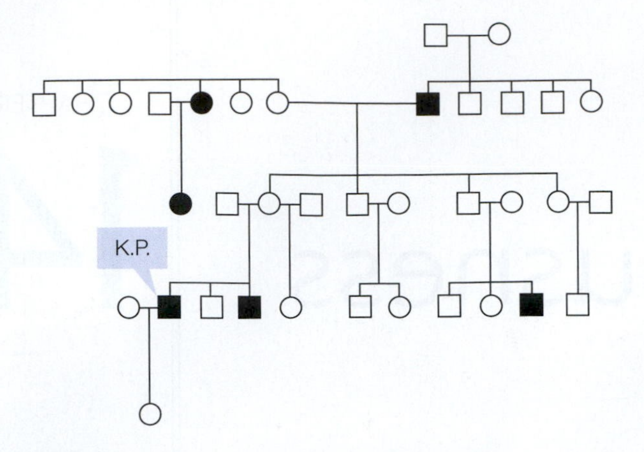

FIGURE 14.1 K.P.'s family pedigree for sleepwalking. Males are indicated by squares and females by circles. Individuals with a history of sleepwalking are shaded in black.

the lack of medical causes, a family history of sleepwalking (**Figure 14.1**), and sleep laboratory evidence of somnambulism—a jury concluded that the assault and homicide had occurred during an episode of sleepwalking (Broughton et al., 1994).

This case and others similar to it, in which violence was committed during a state of sleepwalking, raise the question of what the person was conscious of at the time. It is likely that K.P. consciously experienced aspects of the episode, but very differently from how his awake self would have experienced them. Can this episode tell us something about how the brain produces conscious experience?

The questions of what consciousness is, what sort of neural processing produces it, and where those processes are located in the brain remain a mystery, and the holy grail of neuroscience. This chapter is written from the perspective that there is not a consciousness circuit per se; if there were a specific location in the brain where consciousness processing was generated, it would have been found by now. We will set out on an odyssey in search of answers to questions about consciousness. It will involve learning about the organizational architecture of the brain, observing multiple clinical cases, and grasping what changed physicists' view of the world early in the 20th century. It is a lesson that many in biology have ignored. Our travels will lead to some surprising conclusions.

14.1 The Mind–Brain Problem

The problem of consciousness, otherwise known as the mind–brain problem, was originally the realm of philosophers. The basic question is, How can a purely physical system (the body and brain) construct conscious intelligence (the thoughts of the mind)? In seemingly typical human fashion, philosophers have adopted dichotomous perspectives: dualism and materialism. **Dualism**, famously expounded by René Descartes, states that mind and brain are two distinct and separate phenomena, and that conscious experience is nonphysical and beyond the scope of the physical sciences. **Materialism** asserts that both mind and body are physical mediums, and that understanding the physical workings of the body and brain well enough will lead to an understanding of the mind.

The underlying question is whether there is an unbridgeable gap between the subjective mind and the objective workings of the material brain, or if it is a gap in understanding how one produces the other. Philosopher Joseph Levine (2001) was the first to dub this the *explanatory gap*. He suggests that if we can't explain how "the experience of pain = the firing of neurons," then "it must be that the terms flanking the identity sign themselves represent distinct things."

Levine was not joining the dualist camp; rather, he thought the problem lay in our understanding of how to bridge the gap. Within these two philosophies, views differ on the specifics, but each side ignores an inconvenient problem: Dualism tends to ignore biological findings, and materialism overlooks the reality of subjective experience. The problem is that if you ignore one side of the gap or the other, you will miss the link between the two. And the link is the hardest problem of all. In this chapter we tackle this problem from a new angle, with help from systems engineering and physics.

Notice that we have been throwing the word *consciousness* around without having defined it. This common problem has led to much confusion in the literature. Harvard psychologist Steven Pinker was so frustrated by the different uses of the word—with some people defining consciousness as the ability to recognize oneself in a mirror, some claiming that only humans are conscious, and others saying that consciousness is a recent invention or is learned from one's culture—that he was driven to comment,

> Something about the topic of consciousness makes people, like the White Queen in *Through the Looking Glass*, believe six impossible things before breakfast. Could most animals really be *unconscious*—sleepwalkers, zombies, automata, out cold? Hath not a dog senses, affections, passions? If you prick them, do they not feel pain? And was Moses really unable to taste salt or see red or enjoy sex? Do children learn to become conscious in the same way that they learn to wear baseball caps turned around? People who write about consciousness are not crazy, so they must have something different in mind when they use the word. (Pinker, 1997, p. 133)

In both the 1986 and 1995 editions of the *International Dictionary of Psychology*, the psychologist Stuart Sutherland pulled out all the stops in his definition of **consciousness**:

> **Consciousness** The having of perceptions, thoughts, and feelings; awareness. The term is impossible to define

> except in terms that are unintelligible without a grasp of what consciousness means. Many fall into the trap of equating consciousness with self-consciousness—to be conscious it is only necessary to be aware of the external world. Consciousness is a fascinating but elusive phenomenon: it is impossible to specify what it is, what it does, or why it evolved. Nothing worth reading has been written on it. (Sutherland, 1995)

That last sentence is excellent. It will save us a lot of time!

Sutherland's first point is that the conscious state has a lot of possible contents. It can consist of perceptions: sounds, sights, tastes, touches, and fragrances. It can have highfalutin thoughts of differential equations or mundane worries about whether you left the oven on. And these thoughts are accompanied by feelings. Sutherland also wants us to be clear on the fact that while we are aware of these contents, we don't have to have awareness that we are aware—that is, meta-awareness—to be conscious.

The knowledge you have about yourself, self-consciousness, is just one type of data stored in the cortex, like data about your siblings, parents, friends, and, of course, your dog. Self-consciousness is no more mysterious than perception or memory. As we learned in Chapter 13, we have all sorts of information about ourselves that is processed separately by different modules. The more interesting question that we will address later in this chapter is why, when all this processing about the self is separate, do we feel unified—a single entity calling the shots?

We also have what is known as access awareness, the ability to report on the contents of mental experience, but we don't have access to how the contents were built up by all the neurons, neurotransmitters, and so forth in the nervous system. The nervous system has two modes of information processing: conscious processing and nonconscious processing (we will reserve the term *unconscious* in this chapter to refer to an arousal state). Conscious processing can be accessed by the systems underlying verbal reports, rational thought, and deliberate decision making, and it includes the product of visual processing and the contents of short-term memory. Nonconscious processing, which cannot be accessed, includes autonomic (gut-level) responses; the internal operations of vision, language, and motor control; and repressed desires or memories (if there are any).

Sutherland also tips his hat to the mind–brain problem of consciousness when he describes consciousness as something you just have to experience in order to define. Subjective experience, phenomenal awareness, raw feelings, the first-person viewpoint of an experience, what it feels like to be or do something—these are all on one side of Levine's equation. The difference between subjective and objective experience is the difference between "I am feeling nauseated" and "A student has the stomach flu." Try to explain nausea to someone who has never felt it.

These sentient experiences are called **qualia** by philosophers. For instance, philosophers are always wondering what another person's experience is like when they both look at the same color, same sunset, same anything. In a paper that spotlighted qualia, philosopher Thomas Nagel famously asked, "What is it like to be a bat?" (1974)—not in the sense of "Is it like a bird?" but "What would it feel like for me to be a bat?" which makes Sutherland's point that if you have to ask, you will never know.

Explaining how the firing of neurons (the other side of Levine's equation) generates sentience is known as the "hard problem" of consciousness. Some think it will never be explained. Some philosophers handle the problem by denying it is there. Daniel Dennett (1991) suggests that consciousness is an illusion, a good one, and, like some optical illusions, one we fall for every time. Owen Flanagan (1991) doesn't think that the phenomenal side of conscious mental states is at all mysterious, but just part of the coding. As for Sutherland's final quip, even with all the palaver about the mind and brain over the last 2,500 years, no one has figured it out, but many continue to try.

For example, Francis Crick teamed up with computational neuroscientist Cristof Koch to discover the *neural correlates of consciousness*, stressing that any change in a subjective state must be associated with a change in a neuronal state. Koch (2004) emphasized that "the converse need not necessarily be true; two different neuronal states of the brain may be mentally indistinguishable." Crick hoped that revealing the neural correlates would do for consciousness studies what discovering the structure of DNA had done for genetics. Focusing on the visual system, Crick and Koch sought to discover the minimal set of neuronal events and mechanisms for a specific conscious percept. They both knew that this endeavor would not solve the mystery of consciousness but instead would provide constraints for possible models.

Others have assumed that there is a neural circuit that enables consciousness. Gerard Edelman and Giulio Tononi (2000) proposed that the brain's interactive, reciprocal, and self-propagating feedback, especially in the thalamocortical system, gives rise to consciousness. As for access to consciousness, Bernard Baars introduced the *global workspace theory* (1988, 1997, 2002), which suggests that consciousness enables multiple networks to cooperate and compete in solving problems, such as the retrieval of specific items from immediate memory. Baars conceives targeted retrieval to be somewhat like working memory, but much more fleeting.

Stanislas Dehaene elaborates on this model, suggesting that information becomes conscious if the neural population that represents it is the focus of top-down attention. Attention amplifies the neural firings into a state of coherent activity involving many neurons distributed throughout the brain. Dehaene (2014) suggests that this global availability of information through the "global workspace" is what we subjectively experience as a conscious state.

Meanwhile, Michael Graziano and his colleagues have developed the *attention schema theory* of subjective awareness from the perspective that the brain is an information-processing machine that builds internal modes, and that cognition has partial access to these models. One of the models is of attention itself (Webb & Graziano, 2015). They propose that what we are conscious of is the content of the model, which leads the brain to conclude that it has subjective experience. While some of these theories have features in common, none explain all aspects of consciousness.

Cognitive neuroscience can be brought to bear on the topic of consciousness by breaking the problem down into three categories: the contents of conscious experience, access to this information, and sentience (the subjective experience). While the field has much to say about the contents of our conscious experience—such as self-knowledge, memory, perception, and so forth—and about the information to which we have access, we will find that bridging the gap between the firing of neurons and phenomenal awareness continues to be elusive. Before we take a look at these different aspects of consciousness, however, we need to differentiate wakefulness from consciousness and introduce an important aspect of the brain: its organizational architecture, which neuroscientists have not yet taken into full account. It is a framework that will help us in our quest.

TAKE-HOME MESSAGES

- Consciousness is the having of perceptions, thoughts, and feelings; awareness.
- Self-knowledge is one type of information that makes up the contents of our conscious experience.
- We are able to report on only the contents of mental experience, known as access awareness, and not the processing that produces them.
- Explaining how the chemical interactions of the body produce our subjective conscious experience is the hard problem that cognitive neuroscience faces.

14.2 The Anatomy of Consciousness

When we look at the multiple anatomical regions that contribute to aspects of consciousness (see the "Anatomical Orientation" box on p. 623), it is helpful to distinguish between states of arousal that range from deep unconscious sleep to full wakefulness, including simple awareness and more complex conscious states.

The neurologist Antonio Damasio separates consciousness into two categories: core consciousness and extended consciousness (A. R. Damasio, 1998). *Core consciousness* (or awareness) is what results when the consciousness "switch" is "flipped on": The organism is alive, awake, alert, and aware of one moment, now, and of one place, here. It is not concerned with the future or the past. Core consciousness is the foundation on which to build *extended consciousness*, the increasingly complex contents of conscious experience, provided by input from the cortex.

The brain regions needed to turn on the consciousness switch and to modulate wakefulness are located in the evolutionarily oldest part of the brain, the brainstem. As we have learned, the brainstem's primary job is homeostatic regulation of the body and brain, performed mainly by nuclei in the *medulla oblongata*, along with some input from the *pons*. Disconnect this portion of the brainstem, and the body dies (and the brain and consciousness along with it). This is true for all mammals.

Above the medulla are the nuclei of the pons and the mesencephalon (midbrain). Within the pons is the *reticular formation*, a heterogeneous collection of nuclei, some of which compose the neural circuits of the *reticular activating system (RAS)*, involved with arousal, regulating sleep–wake cycles, and mediating attention. Depending on the location, damage to the pons may result in locked-in syndrome, unresponsive wakefulness syndrome, coma, or death. The RAS has extensive connections to the cortex via two pathways. The dorsal pathway courses through the *intralaminar nucleus of the thalamus* to the cortex. People with lesions of the thalamus are usually awake but unresponsive. The ventral pathway passes through the *hypothalamus* and the *basal forebrain* and on to the cortex. People with an injury to the ventral pathway find it difficult to stay awake and tend to sleep more than the usual amount.

The brainstem receives information via the spinal cord from afferent neurons involved with pain, interoception, and somatosensory, proprioceptive, and vestibular information. It also receives afferent signals from the thalamus, hypothalamus, amygdala, cingulate gyrus, insula, and prefrontal cortex. Thus, information about the state of the organism in its current milieu—along with ongoing changes in the organism's state as it interacts with objects and the environment—is mediated by the brainstem. In concert with the brainstem and thalamus, the cerebral cortex maintains wakefulness and contributes to selective attention.

The information provided by the cortex expands the contents of what the organism is conscious of, but we will see that the cortex may not be necessary for conscious experience. The contents of that experience, which are provided by the cortex, depend on the species and the information that its cortex is capable of supplying. In humans, some of the information stored in the cortex provides us with an elaborate sense of self. It places the self in individual historical time, and it depends on the gradual buildup of an

ANATOMICAL ORIENTATION

Anatomy of Consciousness

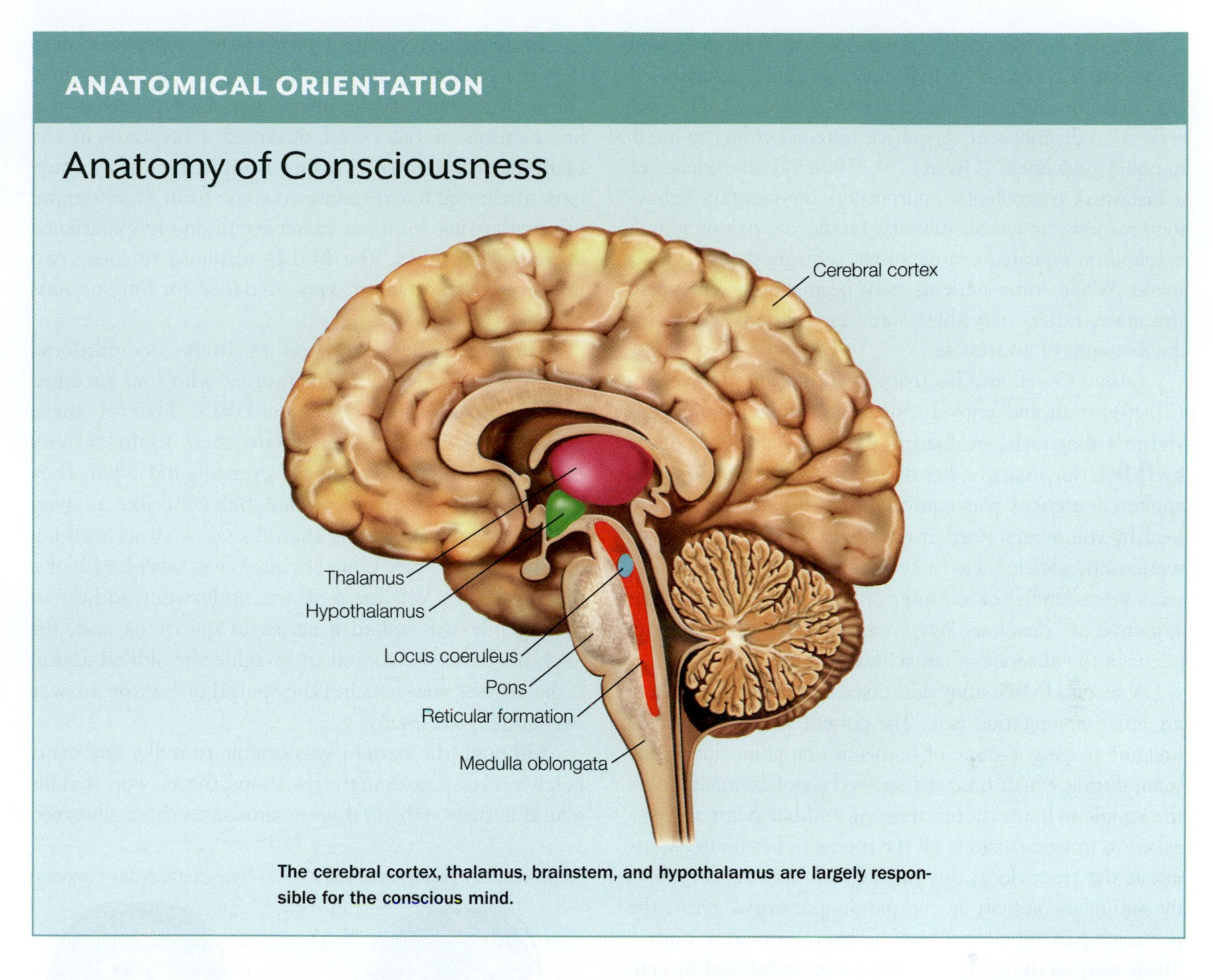

The cerebral cortex, thalamus, brainstem, and hypothalamus are largely responsible for the conscious mind.

autobiographical self from memories of past experiences and expectations of future experiences.

TAKE-HOME MESSAGES

- Processing in the brainstem and thalamus is sufficient for an organism to be alive, awake, alert, and aware of the current moment and place.
- The reticular activating system is involved with arousal, regulating sleep–wake cycles, and mediating attention.
- The contents of our conscious experience are expanded by processing in the cerebral cortex.

14.3 Levels of Arousal and Consciousness

While a level of wakefulness is necessary for consciousness, consciousness is not necessary for wakefulness. For example, patients with *unresponsive wakefulness syndrome (UWS)*, formerly known as vegetative state (Laureys et al., 2010), "awaken" from a coma—that is, open their eyes—but show only reflex behavior. They are not conscious, in contrast with *minimally conscious state (MCS)* patients, who show localization to pain and nonreflex movement. For example, they will visually fixate on or pursue a stimulus, or will follow simple commands like "squeeze my hand" (Bruno et al., 2011; Giacino et al., 2002).

Complicating the diagnosis is **locked-in syndrome (LIS)**, a condition in which one is unable to move any muscle but is fully conscious and has normal sleep–wake cycles. Some LIS patients have the ability to voluntarily blink an eyelid or make very small vertical eye movements, alerting only the very watchful observer that they are conscious. Others cannot even do this and exhibit no external signs.

LIS is caused by a lesion to the ventral part of the pons in the brainstem, where neurons connect the cerebellum with the cortex. Patients with LIS may retain their full cognitive ability and have sensation, and months or years may pass before a caregiver realizes that the patient is conscious. During that interval, some patients have had medical procedures without anesthesia and have heard conversations about their own fate in which they could not participate.

For example, in 2005, 5 months after a traffic accident that resulted in a severe traumatic brain injury (TBI), a

23-year-old woman remained unresponsive with preserved sleep–wake cycles. A multidisciplinary team had assessed her condition and concluded that she "fulfilled all of the criteria for a diagnosis of vegetative state according to international guidelines" (Owen et al., 2006). If no evidence of a sustained, reproducible, purposeful, or voluntary behavioral response to visual, auditory, tactile, or noxious stimuli is found on repeated examinations, a diagnosis of UWS is made. While some patients may permanently remain in this state, others may show some inconsistent but reproducible signs of awareness.

Adrian Owen and his team at Cambridge University (2006) attempted a novel approach to aid in the accident victim's diagnosis, evaluating her for neural responses by fMRI. Surprisingly, her brain's activity in response to spoken sentences was equivalent to the activity seen in healthy volunteers. Furthermore, when ambiguous words were used, additional activity similar to that of the volunteers was seen in her left inferior frontal region. Was this evidence of conscious awareness, or could such activity occur in the absence of conscious awareness?

A second fMRI study addressed this question by using an active imagination task. The patient was instructed to imagine playing a game of tennis at one point during the scan, during which time she showed significant activity in the supplementary motor area. At another point she was asked to imagine visiting all the rooms of her house, starting at the front door; this mental task was accompanied by significant activity in the parahippocampal gyrus, the posterior parietal cortex, and the lateral premotor cortex. These were all the same activations seen in the healthy controls doing the same task (Owen et al., 2006; **Figure 14.2**).

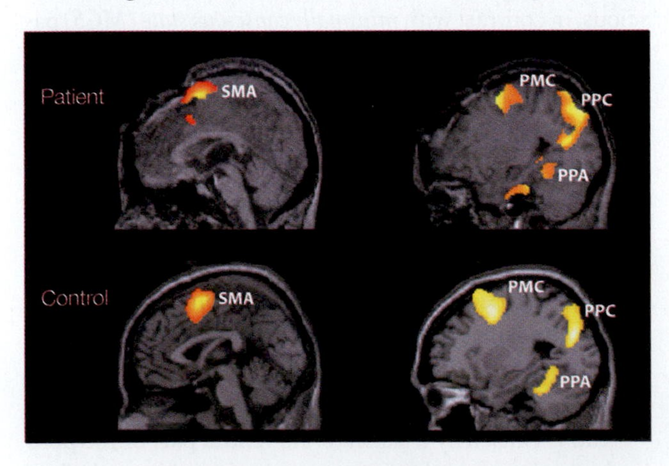

a Tennis imagery **b** Spatial navigation imagery

FIGURE 14.2 Activation sites in UWS patient and controls while imagining playing tennis or walking through their house.
The same regions were active in both the patient diagnosed with UWS and the controls when they were imagining the same situation. **(a)** When they imagined playing tennis, the supplementary motor area (SMA) was active. **(b)** When they imagined walking around their house, the parahippocampal place area (PPA), posterior parietal cortex (PPC), and lateral premotor cortex (PMC) were active.

The especially striking part of this experiment was that the patient seemed to have been responding in a volitional manner. If the researchers had merely shown her pictures of faces and observed a response in the fusiform face area (FFA), for example, then they could have attributed her response to some form of automatic priming arising from her extensive preinjury experience in perceiving faces. The BOLD response to these two imagery tasks, however, was sustained for long periods of time.

The researchers went on to study 54 additional patients with severe brain injuries who had received diagnoses of either MCS or UWS. Five of these patients were able to modulate their brain activity in the same way that normal controls did when they imagined performing a skilled behavior like playing tennis, or undertaking a spatial task such as walking around their home. One of these five, who had had a diagnosis of UWS for 5 years, underwent additional testing. He was asked a series of questions and, for each one, was instructed to imagine the skilled action if the answer was yes, and the spatial task if the answer was no (**Figure 14.3**).

Although the patient was unable to make any overt behavioral responses to the questions, the answers that his neural activity indicated were similar to those observed

"Is your father's name Alexander?"

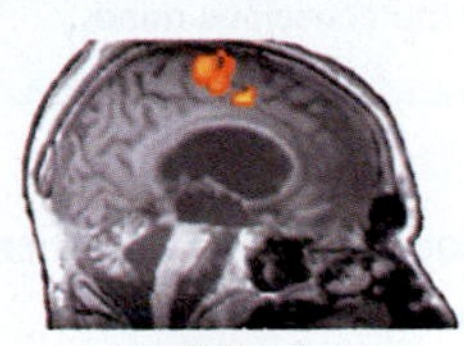

Patient

"Do you have any brothers?"

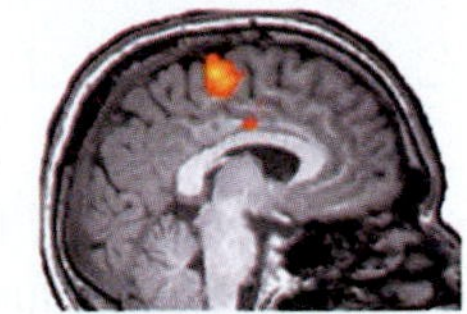

Control

a "Yes" response via motor imagery

"Is your father's name Thomas?"

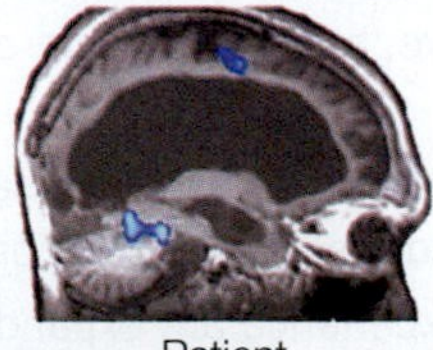

Patient

"Do you have any sisters?"

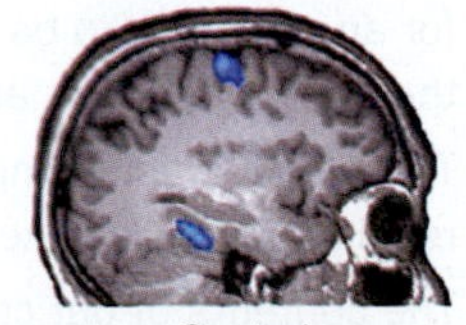

Control

b "No" response via spatial imagery

FIGURE 14.3 Communication fMRI scans from a patient diagnosed with UWS and controls.
One patient who had been diagnosed with UWS was asked **(a)** to imagine a motor task if the answer to a question was yes, and **(b)** to imagine a spatial imagery task if the answer was no. His scans were compared to scans of controls without brain injury performing either task. The patient correctly answered five of six questions, and he did not get the sixth question wrong; he simply had no response. When he answered "yes" by imagining a motor task, his SMA was active, and when he answered "no" by imagining the spatial task, his lateral PMC, PPA, and PPC were active.

BOX 14.1 | LESSONS FROM THE CLINIC

A Life Worth Living

We may imagine that having locked-in syndrome (LIS) is a fate worse than death, but those who suffer it do not appear to agree. Their self-scored perception of mental health, personal and general health, and bodily pain is close to that of controls (Lulé et al., 2009). Our best glimpse into their world was supplied by the editor in chief of the French magazine *Elle*, Jean-Dominique Bauby, who suffered a stroke at the age of 43. Several weeks later he awoke from a coma; although he was fully conscious with no cognitive loss, he was only able to move his left eyelid.

After it was recognized that Bauby was conscious, arrangements were made for an amanuensis to work with him. Each day before she arrived, he would construct and memorize sentences. Sitting at his bedside and using a frequency-ordered French alphabet, she would go through the alphabet until Bauby blinked at the correct letter, which she wrote down. It took 200,000 blinks to write *The Diving Bell and the Butterfly*, a book describing his conscious experience as he lay paralyzed (**Figure 14.4**). Though he described feeling stiffness and pain, and dearly missing playful and spontaneous interactions with his children, Bauby continued,

> My mind takes flight like a butterfly. There is so much to do. You can wander off in space or in time, set out for Tierra del Fuego or for King Midas's court. You can visit the woman you love, slide down beside her and stroke her still-sleeping face. You can build castles in Spain, steal the Golden Fleece, discover Atlantis, realize your childhood dreams and adult ambitions. (Bauby, 1997, p. 5)

a

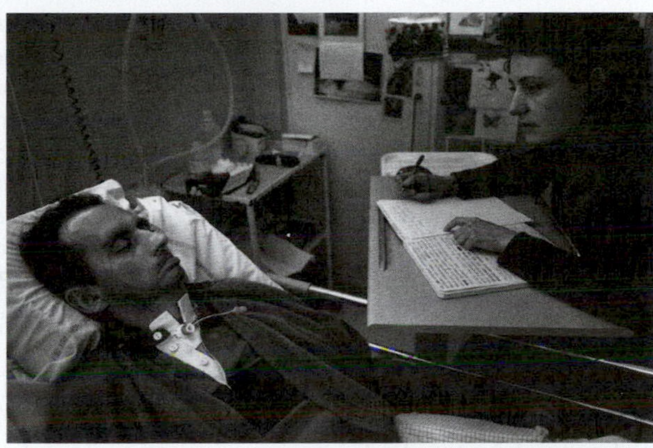

b

FIGURE 14.4 Jean-Dominique Bauby, (a) before stroke and (b) afterward with LIS, while describing his experience to an amanuensis.

in control participants without brain injury, representing clear evidence that the patient was consciously aware and able to communicate by modulating his brain activity (Monti et al., 2010). The ethical necessity of differentiating among UWS, MCS, and LIS is obvious, but it can be difficult (see **Box 14.1**).

Arousal Regulation

Sleep and wakefulness are regulated by a complex interplay of neurotransmitters, neuropeptides, and hormones released by structures located in the basal forebrain, hypothalamus, and brainstem. The overarching controller is our biological clock, the grand circadian pacemaker: the **suprachiasmatic nucleus (SCN)** in the hypothalamus. The SCN receives light inputs directly from the retina, allowing its neurons to synchronize to the day–night cycle. Thus, through diverse neurochemical and hormonal pathways, the SCN synchronizes the cells throughout the brain and body.

As seen in **Figure 14.5**, arousal is modulated by neurotransmitters released by neurochemically distinct systems that produce norepinephrine (NE), acetylcholine (ACh), serotonin, dopamine, or histamine, which innervate and increase arousal in multiple regions, including the cerebral cortex, basal forebrain, and lateral hypothalamus. For example, the photoactivated SCN stimulates the neurons of the locus coeruleus (LC) to release high

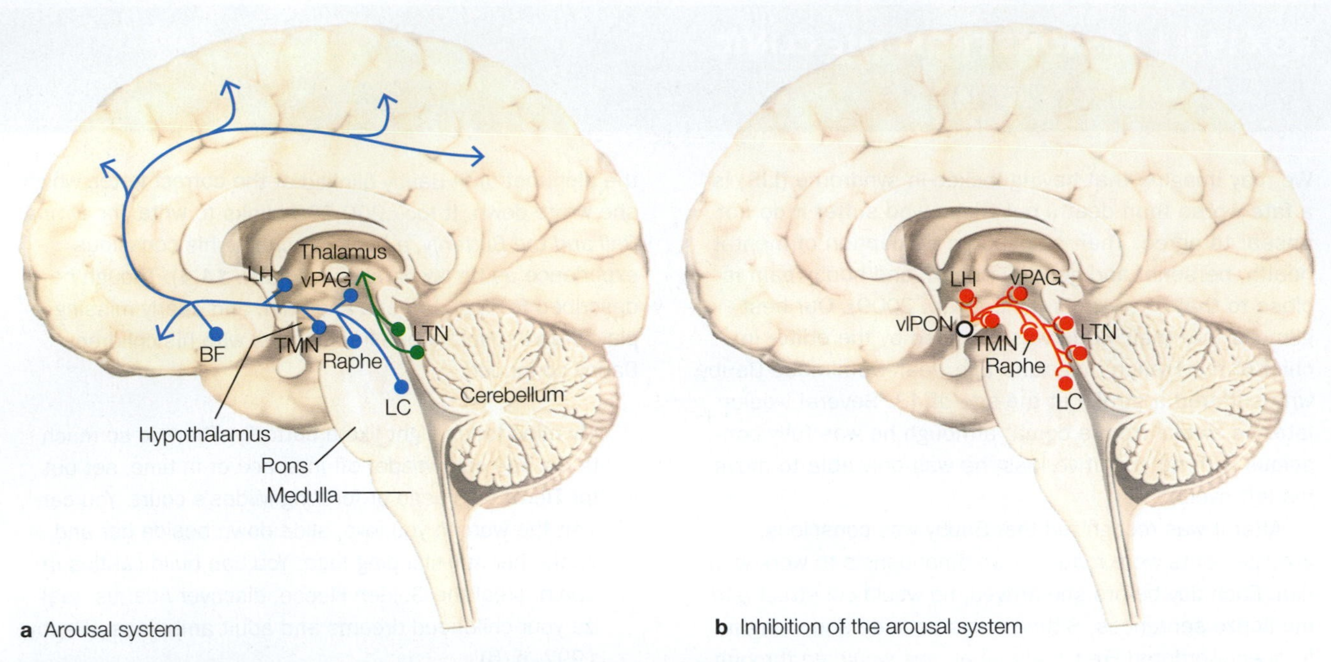

FIGURE 14.5 The neuroanatomy and neurotransmitters of arousal and sleep.
(a) The arousal system has two pathways that produce cortical arousal. The dorsal pathway (green) through the thalamus has cholinergic neurons from the laterodorsal tegmental nuclei (LTN). The ventral pathway (blue) through the hypothalamus and basal forebrain (BF) has noradrenergic neurons in the locus coeruleus (LC, another of the RAS nuclei), serotonergic neurons in the dorsal raphe nucleus, dopaminergic neurons in the ventral periaqueductal gray (vPAG), and histaminergic neurons in the tuberomammillary nucleus (TMN) of the hypothalamus. Antihistamines can cause drowsiness because they inhibit the histaminergic neurons. The lateral hypothalamus (LH) has neurons that secrete orexin during wakefulness, and neurons containing melanin-concentrating hormone that are active during REM sleep and are thought to inhibit the arousal system. Studies show that taking melatonin promotes sleep onset and length. (b) Neurons projecting from the ventrolateral preoptic nucleus (vlPON, indicated by the open circle) contain the inhibitory neurotransmitters GABA and galanin and are active during sleep, inhibiting the arousal circuits.

levels of NE, which spread across the brain to increase wakefulness. LC activity increases with stress, or with the presence of novel or salient stimuli indicating reward or threat, making it difficult to fall asleep.

We all know this. Who can easily fall asleep when they know they have an early plane to catch? How many Christmas Eves do children spend tossing and turning? How long does it take to fall asleep after hearing a strange noise in the house? ACh from the laterodorsal tegmental nuclei, serotonin from the raphe nucleus of the RAS, and dopamine from the periaqueductal gray also contribute to arousal. The neuropeptides orexin-A and orexin-B, produced in the lateral hypothalamus, are also essential for regulating wakefulness, especially long periods of wakefulness (the all-nighter before an exam), and for suppressing REM sleep. Loss of orexin-producing neurons causes the sleep disorder narcolepsy, characterized by overwhelming drowsiness.

Homeostatic mechanisms kick in after periods of prolonged wakefulness, mediated by sleep-producing substances called somnogens. One such substance is adenosine, formed intracellularly or extracellularly by the breakdown of adenine nucleotides. Levels of adenosine increase as wakefulness is prolonged and decrease during sleep. Coffee is ubiquitous at exam time because it is an adenosine receptor antagonist, promoting wakefulness. The sleep-inducing system is made up primarily of the neurons from the *preoptic area* of the hypothalamus and adjacent basal forebrain neurons. These neurons project to the brainstem and to hypothalamic areas involved in the promotion of wakefulness, where they secrete the neurotransmitter GABA and a neuropeptide, galanin, to inhibit arousal.

When we fall asleep, the brain passes through distinct brain states with typical patterns of EEG activity. We quickly pass through three increasingly deep levels of sleep until we reach the deepest sleep, Stage 4 **non–rapid eye movement (NREM) sleep**, where our brain waves are less frequent and have a higher amplitude (**Table 14.1**). Then, throughout the night, we cycle between **rapid eye movement (REM) sleep**, which has low-amplitude, more frequent brain waves, and NREM sleep with

TABLE 14.1 Characteristics of Sleep Stages

Sleep Stage	Psychological State	EEG Pattern
Awake	Variable states of arousal	
NREM (deep sleep)	Nonconscious thoughts	
REM	Vivid dreams	

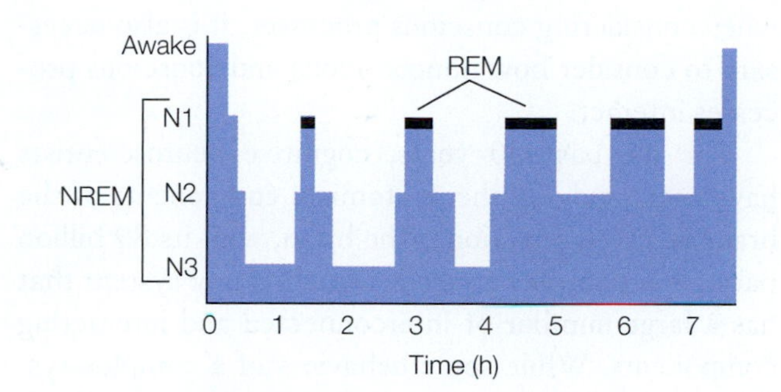

FIGURE 14.6 Stages of sleep.
Cycling sleep patterns seen over the course of a night's sleep. Notice that early in sleep, NREM sleep is deeper and more prolonged.

high-amplitude waves of low frequency (**Figure 14.6**). NREM sleep cycles become progressively less deep the longer we sleep. Normally, when NREM sleep shifts into REM sleep, there is a loss of muscle tone, preventing motor movement during REM sleep.

We are now ready to revisit K.P. from the beginning of the chapter. Sleepwalking, also known as somnambulism, is a *parasomnia*, a sleep disorder that may involve abnormal movements, behaviors, emotions, perceptions, and dreams. While up to 17% of children may sleepwalk, only 2% to 4% of adults continue to do so (Mahowald & Schenck, 2005). Sleepwalking can be triggered by anxiety and emotional distress, fatigue, fever, and medications, including alcohol. It usually occurs after an abrupt, spontaneous, and incomplete arousal from NREM sleep in the first third of the sleep period (**Figure 14.7**).

Sleepwalkers engage in automatic behaviors and lack conscious awareness or memory of the event. Their actions tend to be relatively harmless, such as moving objects or walking around the room, but sleepwalkers may also engage in very complex behaviors such as cooking or repairing things, or even more dangerous ones, such as riding a bike or driving a car. Such behaviors make it difficult to believe that sleepwalkers are not consciously aware of their actions, but the behaviors are never recalled upon awakening. Sleepwalkers cannot be awoken, and it can be dangerous to try: The sleepwalker may feel threatened by physical contact, triggering a fight-or-flight response—that is, automatic violent behavior. Sleepwalking violence includes incidents of assault, rape, and murder.

While it is commonly believed that sleep happens only at the level of the entire organism, new lines of evidence suggest that sleep can occur locally in subsets of neural circuitry, which may be awake only when their processing is required (Ray & Reddy, 2016; Vyazovskiy et al., 2011). Neuroimaging (Bassetti et al., 2000) and EEG (Terzaghi et al., 2009) have enabled researchers to see what is happening in the brain during sleepwalking episodes (**Figure 14.8**). It appears that half the brain is awake—the cerebellum, posterior cingulate cortex (important for monitoring functions), and brainstem—while the cortex, anterior cingulate cortex (important for cognitive control and emotional regulation), and cerebrum are asleep.

So, while the regions involved with control of complex motor behavior and emotion generation are active, those

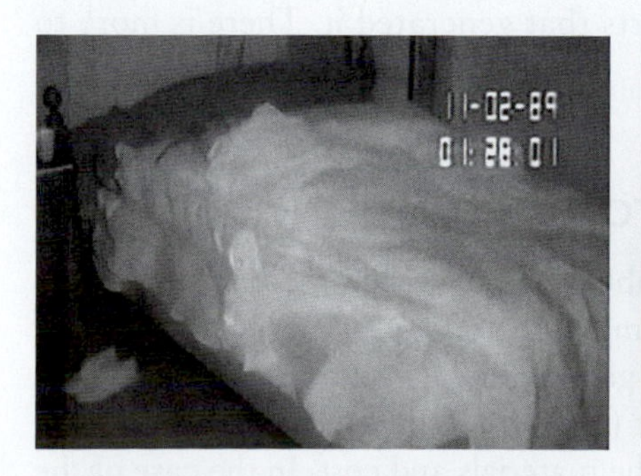

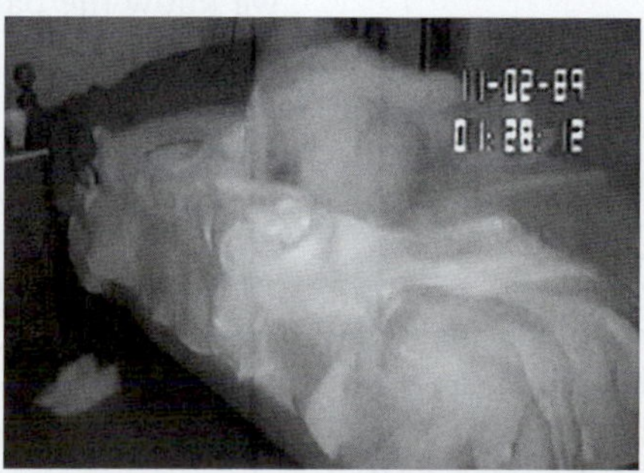

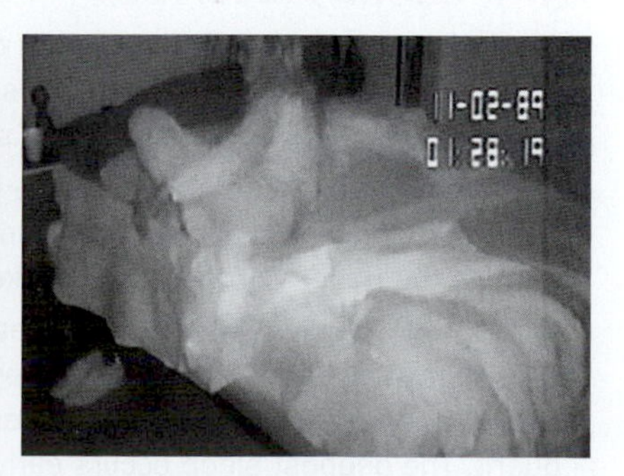

FIGURE 14.7 A sleepwalking episode.
A patient with a history of sleepwalking shows a very rapid progression (18 seconds) from lying in her bed in deep sleep (slow-wave NREM sleep) to having an abrupt spontaneous arousal, immediately followed by standing up and sleepwalking.

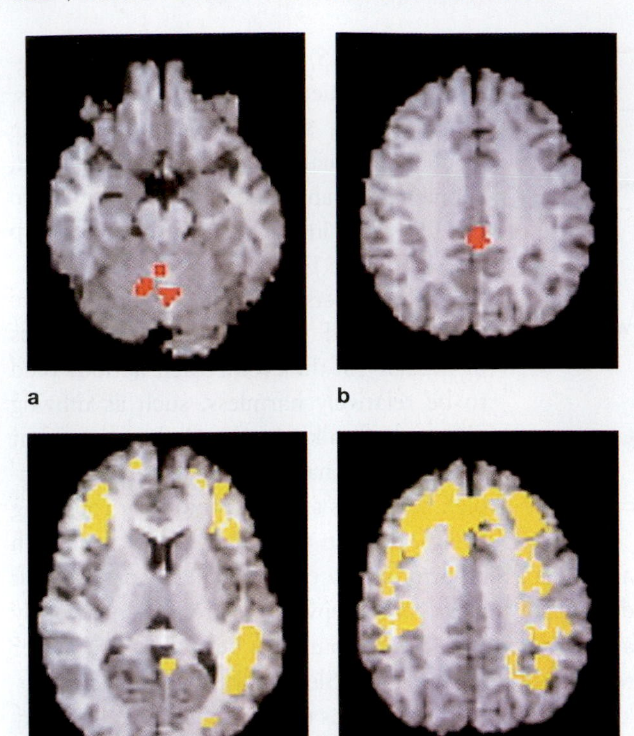

FIGURE 14.8 Neuroimaging findings during sleepwalking. Areas in red indicate 25% more blood flow during a sleepwalking episode than in quiet Stages 3 to 4 NREM sleep in cerebellum (a) and posterior cingulate cortex (b). (c, d) Areas in yellow are deactivated during sleepwalking compared to normal wakeful volunteers. Large areas of frontal and parietal association cortices remain deactivated during sleepwalking.

in the frontal lobe that are involved in planning, attention, judgment, inhibition of automatic responses, recognition of emotional expressions, and emotion regulation are asleep, along with the parietal association cortex. Whatever K.P. was aware of during his sleepwalking episode—whatever enabled him to drive a car and navigate—was not provided by or regulated by cortical processing.

TAKE-HOME MESSAGES

- Sleep and arousal are regulated by a complex interplay of excitatory and inhibitory neurotransmitters, neuropeptides, and hormones released by structures located in the basal forebrain, hypothalamus, and brainstem.
- The suprachiasmatic nucleus (SCN) in the hypothalamus acts as the body's circadian pacemaker.
- Throughout the night, sleep cycles between REM sleep with short-amplitude and more frequent brain waves and NREM sleep with high-amplitude waves that are less frequent. The deepest sleep occurs early in the sleep cycle.
- During sleepwalking, the brain areas that mediate cognitive control and emotional regulation are asleep.

14.4 The Organizational Architecture of Complex Systems

We have seen throughout this book that the vast majority of mental processes happen outside of our conscious awareness. An enormous amount of research in cognitive science clearly shows that we are conscious of only the contents of our mental life, not what generates the contents. For instance, you are conscious of the letters and words on this page and understand what they mean, but are not conscious of the processes that produced your perceptions and comprehension. Thus, when considering conscious processes, it is also necessary to consider how nonconscious and conscious processes interact.

For the past 50 years, cognitive neuroscientists have been studying the anatomical components of the brain and their functions. The brain, with its 89 billion parts, is a **complex system**, which is any system that has a large number of interconnected and interacting components. While some behaviors of a complex system may be predictable, many are not. Yet any engineer of complex systems could tell us that there is something missing from cognitive neuroscience's approach to understanding the brain: Learning about the parts gets you only so far.

Understanding the *organization* of the parts is also necessary in order to relate the system's structure to its function. The organization of the system, also known as its **architecture**, affects the interactions between the parts. For example, a Harley-Davidson motorcycle has a place to sit, wheels, a windshield, an engine, and a place to store stuff. So does a train. But a Harley is not a train. They may have the same parts, but they have different architectures and functions. Moreover, simply looking at a part in isolation tells us nothing of its function, nor by looking solely at a function can we know the parts that generated it. There is more to the story.

Layered Architecture

Architecture is about design within the bounds of constraints. For example, the design of a bridge must take into account the geology and geography of its site; what will be crossing it (pedestrians or semis), how many, and how often; and the materials and cost. In the case of the brain's architecture, the constraints include energy costs, brain and skull size, and processing speeds. The components of a complex system—whether it is biological (such as the brain) or technological (such as a jumbo jet)—are arranged in a specific manner that enables their functionality and robustness; that is, they have a highly organized architecture.

John Doyle, a professor of control and dynamical systems, electrical engineering, and bioengineering at the California Institute of Technology, makes the point that complexity does not come about by accident in highly organized systems. It arises from design strategies to build things that work efficiently, effectively, and reliably. Such strategies have evolved in biological systems and have been created in technological systems that produce *robustness* (or, using Darwin's term, fitness). Doyle notes that "A [property] of a [system] is robust if it is [invariant] with respect to a [set of perturbations]" (Alderson & Doyle, 2010), with the brackets indicating that each of these aspects must be specified. Doyle uses clothing as an example of an easily understood complex system (Doyle & Csete, 2011).

Let's say you are going camping where the temperature is cold at night and warm during the day. The complex system that we will consider is your camping outfit. It is a layered system consisting of an underwear layer, a comfort layer, and a warmth layer. Each layer has a specific function. Each piece of clothing itself is made from materials with a layered architecture: the fiber layer, spun into the thread or yarn layer, woven into the cloth layer. The materials have physical and chemical properties at the microscopic level that affect their weave, elasticity, water resistance, breathability, UV protection, and even insect repulsion that you take into account as you assemble your layered outfit.

What would be a robust choice for the warmth layer? How about a down jacket? Down [property] clothing [system] is a robust choice because it will keep you warm [invariant] when the temperature is cold [the perturbation]. However, if it rains [an unspecified perturbation], down loses its warmth. While down may be robust to cold, it is not robust (hence fragile) to wetness. To make your system robust to wetness, you add another layer, a nylon rain jacket.

When we add a feature that protects the system from a particular challenge, we add robustness, but also complexity and a new fragility. That rain jacket keeps you dry from rain [an external wetness perturbation] but, while blocking rain, it also traps internal wetness from perspiration [internal wetness perturbation]. It is robust to rain but fragile to sweat. No added feature is robust for all events, and each brings its own fragility. Systems add layers to combat fragilities. The failure of one layer is the condition under which a new one may arise. Robust yet fragile features are a characteristic of highly evolved complex systems.

The fundamental design strategy that evolved in biological systems to increase fitness—a modular, layered architecture—has been adopted by designers of technical systems because it promises robustness and functionality. Understanding how the brain is organized into layers will help us understand consciousness. With a modular, layered architecture, multiple types of processing go on simultaneously—that is, "in parallel." For example, your olfactory system runs independently of the motor system: You don't have to be standing still to smell bread baking. It is also robust to single-system failures: You can lose your olfactory system, but your motor and visual systems still work, just as you can lose your soft comfort layer, but your underwear layer still works. They run independently in parallel.

The complex system of your brain is a system of systems. Your olfactory, visual, and motor systems are each made up of layers. A layer can be a single module or groups of modules. In a layered architecture, each layer acts independently because it has its own specific **protocol**—that is, rules that stipulate the allowed interactions, both within a layer and between adjacent layers. Processing can proceed up a "stack" of layers, with the output from the layer below being passed to the one above. The layer above, in turn, processes the information it receives according to its own specific protocol, which may be similar to or completely different from that of the previous layer, and passes its output up to the next layer in the stack. No layer "knows" what the input to the previous layer was, or what processing occurred, or what the output of the next layer will be. Processing cannot skip a layer in the stack, because the higher layer's protocol "knows" how to process only input that comes from an adjacent layer.

The processing of each layer is hidden from the next. This phenomenon is called *abstraction*. Each layer works on a spartan need-to-know basis, and all it needs to know is its own specific protocol. Consider making marinara sauce. Your recipe is the protocol. It tells you how to make the sauce from olive oil, onions, garlic, and tomatoes, but there is nothing in the recipe about growing the vegetables and fruit, picking them, packing them, shipping them, or displaying them in a store, nor anything about making olive oil and so forth. You don't need to know anything about those processes to make the sauce.

Now think of the beauty of this aspect of complex systems. The user of a complex system interacts with only the top layer, which in technical systems is known as the *application layer*. You can use your smartphone without having any idea of how the processing layers work or even that there are processing layers. You can make the marinara sauce without knowing how to grow

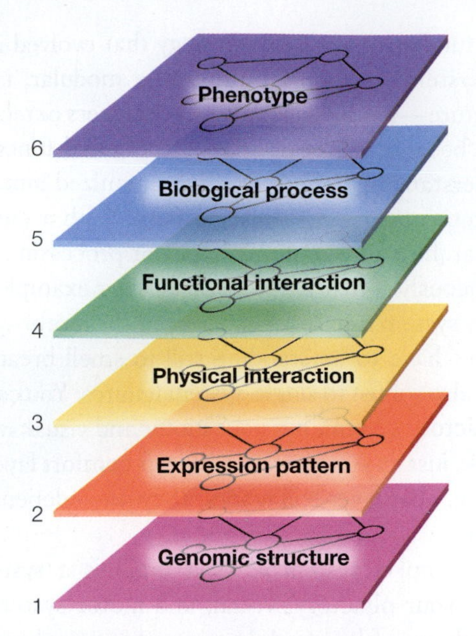

FIGURE 14.9 Six levels of abstraction within DNA replication in a biological system.
We can follow a gene from one abstraction level to another, resulting in the phenotype. Layer 1, the lowest layer of this scheme (though there are multiple lower layers extending down to subatomic structures), contains genes (coding sequences) and their organization within the chromosome. Layer 2 contains the expression of the genes into the physical components of RNA and proteins. Layer 3 handles protein–protein interactions and protein-DNA interactions, while layer 4 takes on the functional interactions between the physical elements in layer 3—for example, gastro-intestinal networks or signaling and metabolic pathways. Layer 5 handles the networks involved with a specific biological process. The highest layer, 6, represents phenotypes and relations between them. The relationships described by the protocols that link one layer with its neighbors are different at each level.

the ingredients. If we consider your body as an application layer, you can eat the sauce without knowing how to digest it.

Likewise, you don't have to know how your brain works to use its application layer. In fact, for thousands of years people used their brain's application layer without knowing they had a brain! While it is understood that complex biological systems have a layered architecture (Boucher & Jenna, 2013; **Figure 14.9**), with compositional, interaction, and control layers, not all of their functions and dynamics have been identified yet or appreciated by many in neuroscience.

When it comes to understanding the layered architecture of the brain, our most difficult assignment is figuring out the protocols that allow one layer to talk to the next. The protocol is the main constraint on the layer's processing, but it also allows flexibility. One way the flexibility of these architectural layers has been visualized is as a bow tie with the protocol as the knot, with input funneling into it and output fanning out from it (Friedlander et al., 2015; **Figure 14.10**).

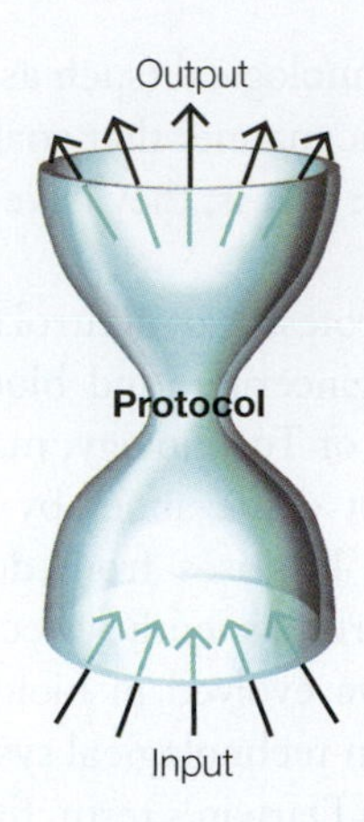

FIGURE 14.10 Bow tie in a multilayered network.
The layer's inputs are processed according to the specifications of that layer's protocol. The processing results are the layer's output.

For example, when you are considering the warmth layer of your complex outfit system, its protocol is "must trap body heat." The input is huge: everything in your wardrobe. With all those inputs, there are multiple possible outputs satisfying the protocol's constraint: a sheepskin coat, fleece pants, an alpaca poncho, a down jacket, fiberfill skiing overalls, skydiving coveralls, a faux rabbit-fur jacket with leopard-skin pants, or even a wet suit.

The protocol could be more specific and add "practical" or "fashionable" as constraints, eliminating some choices. Notice, however, that while the protocol limits the number of outcomes, it does not cause the outcome; there are many possible outcomes. Doyle calls a protocol "a constraint that deconstrains" (Doyle & Csete, 2011). The important thing about a protocol is that it enables selection from variation. Because it allows a layer to evolve and develop robustness to perturbations, this flexibility may be the most important aspect of a layered architecture.

Multiple Realizability

Understanding that a protocol doesn't dictate an outcome is important. Neuroscientists who are unaware that they are dealing with a layered system containing protocols assume that they can look at a behavior and predict the neuronal firing pattern—that is, which brain state produced it. But this is not the case, as has been shown by neuroscientist Eve Marder and her colleagues (Prinz et al., 2004).

The spiny lobster has a simple nervous system. Marder has spent her career studying the neural underpinnings of the motility patterns of the lobster's gut (**Figure 14.11**). She isolated the entire neural network, mapped out every single neuron and synapse,

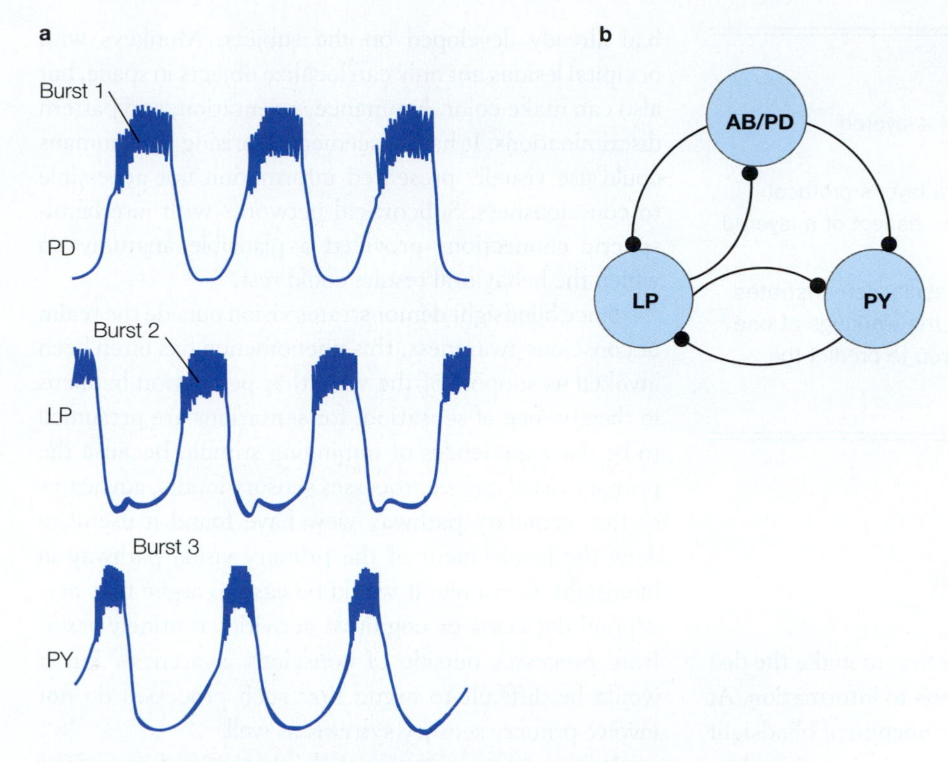

FIGURE 14.11 The pyloric rhythm and pyloric circuit architecture of the spiny lobster.
(a) In the spiny lobster, the stomatogastric ganglion, which has a small number of neurons and a stereotyped motor pattern, produces the pyloric rhythm. The pyloric rhythm has a triphasic motor pattern with bursts occurring first from the anterior burster (AB) neuron electronically coupled to two pyloric dilator (PD) neurons. The next burst is from a lateral pyloric (LP) neuron, followed by a pyloric (PY) neuron. The recordings are done intracellularly from neurons in the stomatogastric ganglion. **(b)** This schematic presents a simplified version of the underlying circuit. All synapses in the circuit are inhibitory. To generate the 20 million model circuits, the strengths of the seven synapses were varied, and five or six different versions of the neurons in the circuit were used.

and modeled the synapse dynamics to the level of neurotransmitter effects. From a neural reductionist perspective, which ignores the idea that a layered system has protocol constraints that deconstrain, it should be possible to piece together all of Marder's input information and describe the exact neuronal output pattern of synapses and neurotransmitters that results in the function of the lobster gut.

Marder's laboratory simulated the more than 20 million possible network combinations of synapse strengths and neuron properties for this relatively simple gut nervous system. After modeling all those timing combinations, Marder found that about 1% to 2% of them could lead to the motility pattern observed in nature. Yet even this small number of combinations yields 100,000 to 200,000 different tunings of the nervous system that will result in exactly the same gut behavior at any given moment. That is, the lobster's normal pyloric rhythms can be generated by networks with very different cellular and synaptic properties (**Figure 14.12**).

The idea that there are many ways to implement a system to produce one behavior is known as **multiple realizability**. In a hugely complex system such as the human brain, how many possible tunings might there be for a single behavior? Can single-unit recordings and molecular approaches alone ever reveal what is going on to produce human behavior? This is a profound problem for the reductionist neuroscientist, because Marder's work shows that while analysis of nerve circuits might be able to explain how the brain could work, such analysis on its own cannot tell the whole story. Neuroscientists will have to figure out how, and at what layer, to approach the nervous system to learn the rules for understanding it.

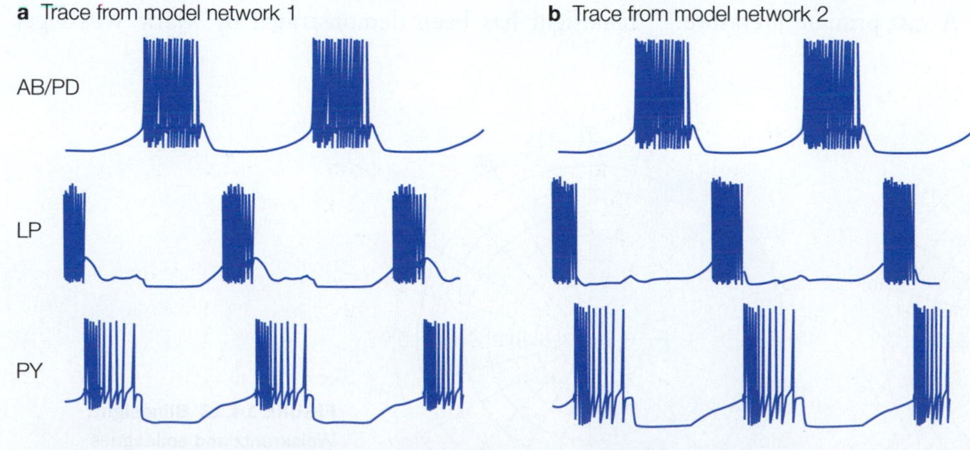

FIGURE 14.12 Networks with very different cellular and synaptic properties can generate the typical pyloric rhythm.
(a, b) The voltage traces from two model pyloric networks are very similar, even though they are produced by circuits with very different membranes and synaptic properties. The permeabilities and conductances for various ions differ among the circuits.

TAKE-HOME MESSAGES

- The brain is a complex system with a layered architecture.
- The flexibility and adaptability that a layer's protocol provides may be the most important aspect of a layered system.
- The phenomenon of multiple realizability demonstrates that in a complex system, knowing the workings at one level of organization will not allow you to predict the actual functioning at another level.

14.5 Access to Information

The philosopher Ned Block was the first to make the distinction between sentience and access to information. At the time, he suggested that the phenomenon of blindsight might provide an example where one (access to visual information) existed without the other ("I cannot see the object"). **Blindsight**, a term coined by Larry Weiskrantz at Oxford University (1974, 1986), refers to the phenomenon in which some patients suffering a lesion in their visual cortex can respond to visual stimuli presented in the blind part of their visual field (**Figure 14.13**).

Most interestingly, these activities happen outside the realm of consciousness. Patients will deny that they can do a visual task, yet their performance is clearly above that of chance when forced to answer. Such patients have access to information but do not experience it, though some say they have a "feeling" that guides their choice and the stronger that feeling is, the more accurate their guesses are.

Weiskrantz believed that subcortical pathways supported some visual processing. A vast primate literature had already developed on the subject. Monkeys with occipital lesions not only can localize objects in space, but also can make color, luminance, orientation, and pattern discriminations. It hardly seemed surprising that humans could use visually presented information not accessible to consciousness. Subcortical networks with interhemispheric connections provided a plausible anatomy on which the behavioral results could rest.

Since blindsight demonstrates vision outside the realm of conscious awareness, this phenomenon has often been invoked as support of the view that perception happens in the absence of sensation, for sensations are presumed to be our experiences of impinging stimuli. Because the primary visual cortex processes sensory inputs, advocates of the secondary pathway view have found it useful to deny the involvement of the primary visual pathway in blindsight. Certainly, it would be easy to argue that perceptual decisions or cognitive activities routinely result from processes outside of conscious awareness. But it would be difficult to argue that such processes do not involve primary sensory systems as well.

It is premature to conclude that this phenomenon reflects processing solely in subcortical pathways. Information may reach extrastriate visual areas in the cortex, either through direct geniculate projections or via projections from other subcortical structures. Using positron emission tomography (PET), researchers have shown that extrastriate regions such as human area MT can be activated by moving stimuli, even when the ipsilateral striate cortex is completely destroyed (Barbur et al., 1993). Another possibility is that the lesions in the primary visual cortex are incomplete and that blindsight results from residual function in the spared tissue. The representations in the damaged region may be sufficient to guide eye movements, even though they fail to achieve awareness.

Involvement of the damaged primary pathway in blindsight has been demonstrated by Mark Wessinger

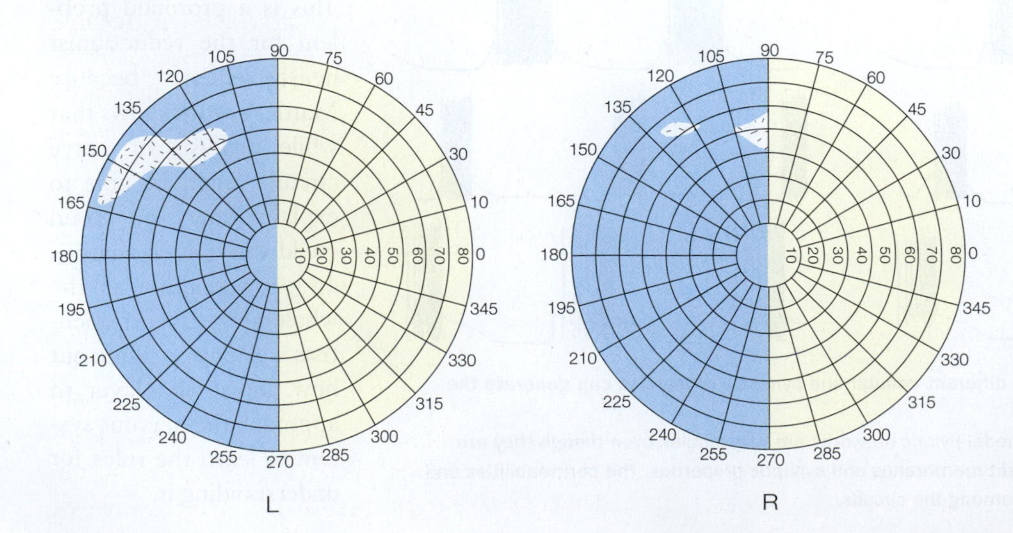

FIGURE 14.13 Blindsight. Weiskrantz and colleagues reported the first case of blindsight in a patient with a lesion in the visual cortex. The hatched areas indicate preserved areas of vision for the patient's left and right eyes.

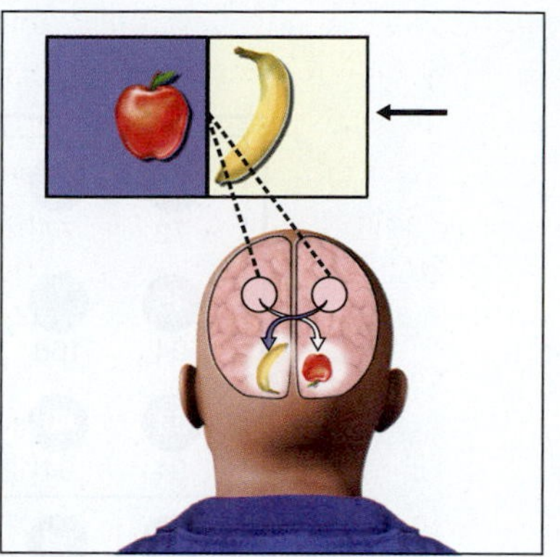

FIGURE 14.14 The Dual-Purkinje-Image Eyetracker.
The eye tracker compensates for a participant's eye movements by moving the image in the visual field in the same direction as the eyes, thus stabilizing the image on the retina.

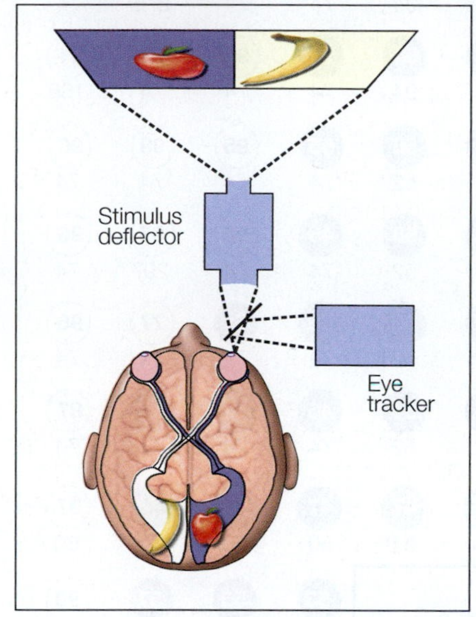

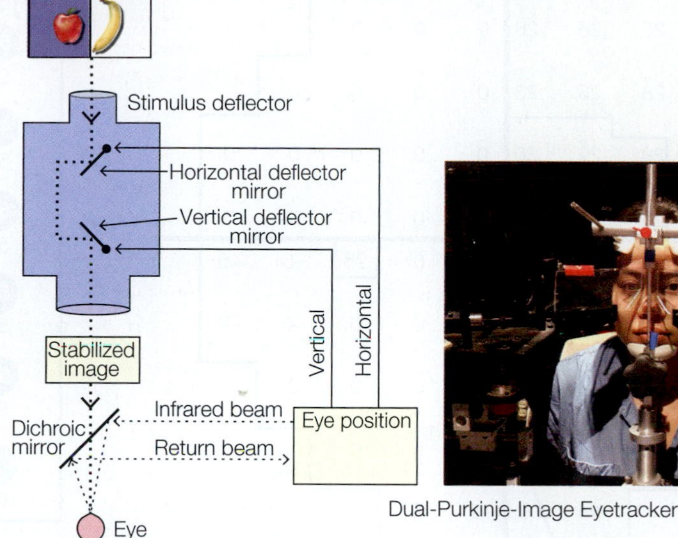

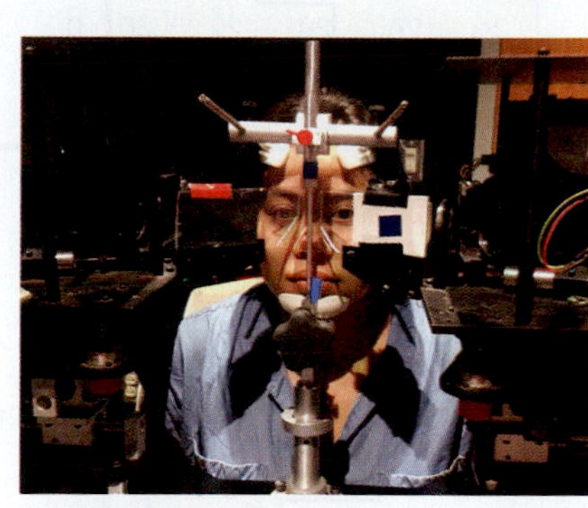

Dual-Purkinje-Image Eyetracker

and Robert Fendrich at Dartmouth College (Fendrich et al., 1992). They investigated this fascinating phenomenon using a Dual-Purkinje-Image Eyetracker that was augmented with an image stabilizer, enabling the sustained presentation of information in discrete parts of the visual field (**Figure 14.14**). Armed with this piece of equipment and with the cooperation of C.L.T., a robust 55-year-old outdoorsman who had suffered a right occipital stroke 6 years before his examination, they began to tease apart the various explanations for blindsight.

Standard field-of-vision measurements (perimetry) indicated that C.L.T. had a left homonymous hemianopsia with lower-quadrant macular sparing (**Figure 14.15a**). This blind region within the left visual field was explored carefully with the eye tracker, which presents a high-contrast, retinally stabilized stimulus, and an interval, two-alternative, forced-choice procedure. This procedure requires that a stimulus be presented on every trial and that the participant respond on every trial, even though he denies having seen a stimulus. Such a design is more sensitive to subtle influences of the stimulus on the participant's responses. C.L.T. also indicated his confidence on every trial. The investigators found regions of above-chance performance surrounded by regions of chance performance within C.L.T.'s blind field (**Figure 14.15b**). Simply stated, they found islands of blindsight.

MRI reconstructions revealed a lesion that had damaged the calcarine cortex, which was consistent with C.L.T.'s clinical blindness. But the imaging also demonstrated some spared tissue in the region of the calcarine fissure. Assuming that this tissue mediated C.L.T.'s central vision with awareness, it seemed reasonable that similar tissue mediated C.L.T.'s islands of blindsight. More important, both PET and fMRI conclusively demonstrated that these regions were metabolically active—alive and processing information! Thus, the most parsimonious explanation for C.L.T.'s blindsight was that it was directed by spared, albeit severely dysfunctional, remnants of the primary visual pathway rather than by a more general secondary visual system.

Before we can assert that blindsight is due to subcortical or extrastriate structures, we must be extremely careful to rule out the possibility of spared striate cortex. With careful perimetric mapping, it is possible to discover regions of vision within a scotoma that would go undetected with conventional perimetry. Although

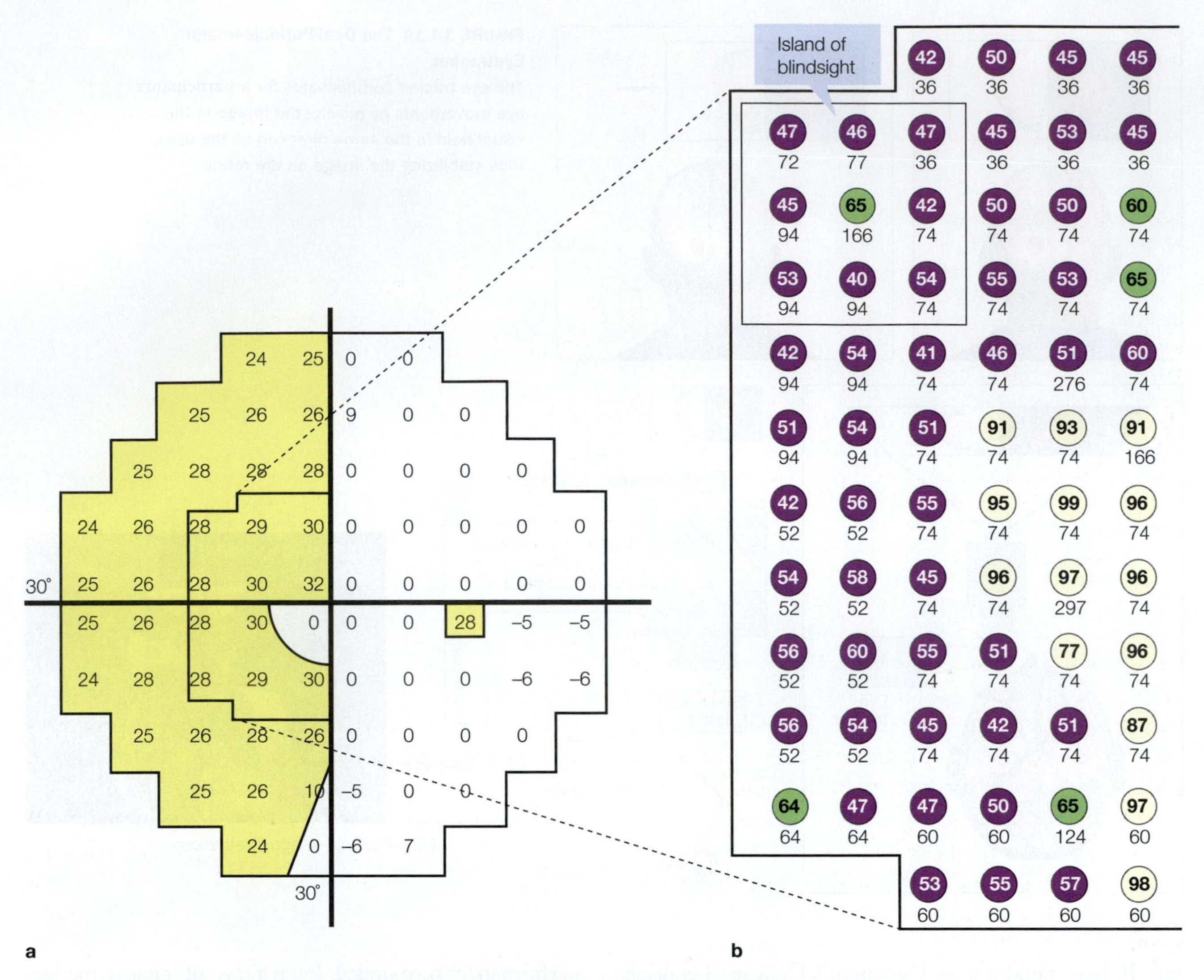

FIGURE 14.15 Results of standard and stabilized image perimetry in left visual hemifield.
(a) The results of standard perimetry from C.L.T.'s right eye. Shading indicates regions diagnosed as clinically blind. The patient has sparing in the macular region of the left lower quadrant. **(b)** The results of stabilized perimetry testing of the region within the inner border in part (a). Each test location is represented by a circle. The number in a circle represents the percentage of correct detections. The number under the circle indicates the number of trials at that location. Cream circles show unimpaired detection, green circles show impaired detection that was above the level of chance, and purple circles indicate detection that was no better than chance.

the blindsight phenomenon has been reported in many other patients, the interpretation of the effect remains controversial.

We do not have to resort to blindsight, however, for evidence of access to information without sentience. It is commonplace to design demanding perceptual tasks for which both participants with neurological deficits and controls with no neurological problems routinely report low confidence in their visual awareness—yet they perform at a level above chance. In these populations it is unnecessary to propose secondary visual systems to account for such reports, since the primary visual system is intact and fully functional.

For example, patients with unilateral neglect as a result of right-hemisphere damage are unable to name stimuli entering their left visual field (see Chapter 7). The conscious brain cannot access this information. When asked to judge whether two lateralized visual stimuli, one in each visual field, are the same or different, however, these same patients can do so (**Figure 14.16**; Volpe et al., 1979). When they are questioned on the nature of the stimuli after a trial, they easily name the stimulus in the right visual field but deny having seen the stimulus in the neglected left field.

In short, patients with parietal lobe damage but spared visual cortex can make perceptual judgments outside of

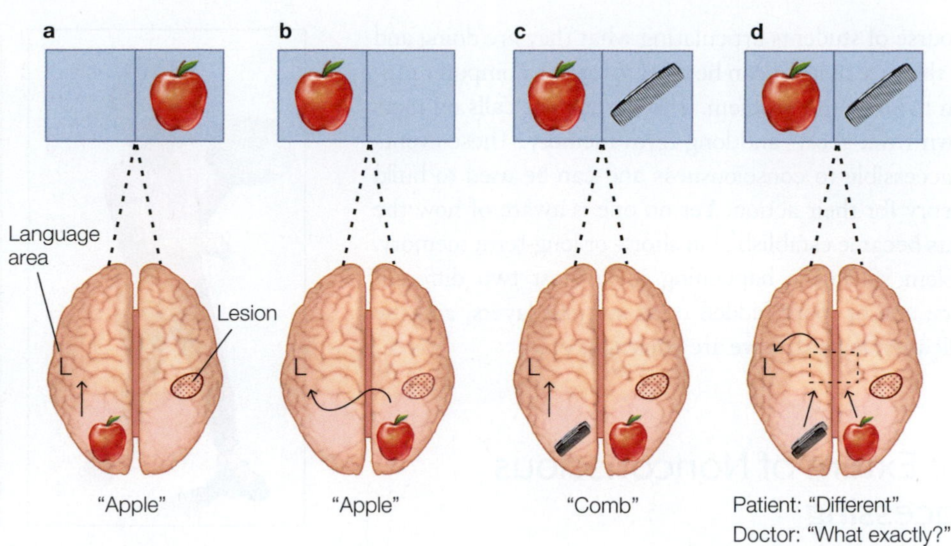

FIGURE 14.16 The same–different paradigm presented to patients with neglect.
(a, b) A patient with unilateral neglect is presented with a single image, first to one hemifield, then to the other. The patient subsequently is asked to judge whether the images are the same or different—a task that he is able to perform. **(c, d)** When the images are presented simultaneously to both hemifields, the patient is able to determine whether the images are the same or different but cannot verbalize which image he saw in the extinguished hemifield that enabled him to make the correct comparison and decision.

conscious awareness. Their failure to consciously access information for comparing the stimuli should not be attributed to processing within a secondary visual system, because their geniculostriate pathway is still intact. They have lost the function of a chunk of parietal cortex, and because of that damage they have lost a chunk of the contents that make up their conscious awareness.

Recall that spatial neglect can also affect the imagination and memory, as demonstrated by the patients who were able to describe from memory the piazza in Milan (see Figure 7.7). They neglected things on the side of the piazza contralateral to their lesion, just as if they were actually standing there looking at it, but they were able to describe those same items when they imagined viewing the piazza from the opposite side. We are now prepared to make sense of these findings if we think about a layered architecture.

The pattern of loss reveals that there are two different layers. The modules and layers that generate the mental images remain functional. We know this because all the information is present. The final layer of this processing stack outputs its information to a control layer that evaluates which side of space the image will be reported from, and this layer is malfunctioning. It is allowing only information from the right side of space into conscious awareness.

To elucidate how conscious and nonconscious processing layers interact within the cortex, it is necessary to investigate them in the intact, healthy brain. Richard Nisbett and Lee Ross at the University of Michigan (1980) clearly made this point. In a clever experiment, using the tried-and-true technique of learning word pairs, they first exposed participants to word associations like *ocean–moon*. The idea is that participants might subsequently say "tide" when asked to free-associate in response to the word *detergent*. That is exactly what they do, but they do not know why. When asked, they might say, "Oh, my mother always used Tide to do the laundry." As we know from Chapter 4, that's their left-brain interpreter system coming up with an explanation using only the information that was available to it, which was the word *detergent* and the response, "tide."

Any student will commonly and quickly declare that she is fully aware of how she solves a problem even when she really does not know. Students solve the famous Tower of Hanoi problem (**Figure 14.17**) all the time. The running

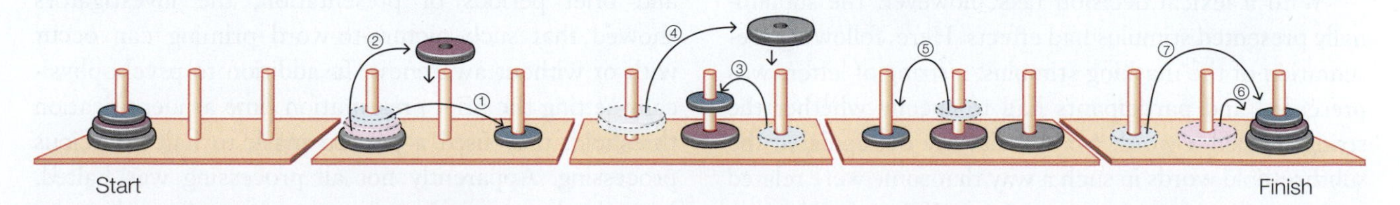

FIGURE 14.17 The Tower of Hanoi problem.
The task is to rebuild the rings on another tower in as few steps as possible without ever putting a larger ring on top of a smaller ring. It can be done in seven steps, and after much practice, students learn the task. After they have solved it, however, their explanations for how they solved it can be quite bizarre.

discourse of students articulating what they are doing and why they are doing it can be used to write a computer program to solve the problem. The participant calls on facts known from short- and long-term memory. These events are accessible to consciousness and can be used to build a theory for their action. Yet no one is aware of how the events became established in short- or long-term memory. Problem solving is happening in at least two different layers: one or more hidden nonconscious layers, and the application layer that we are conscious of.

The Extent of Nonconscious Processing

Cognitive psychologists have examined the extent and kind of information that can be processed nonconsciously. The classic approach is to use the technique of **subliminal perception**, in which the stimulus is presented below the threshold of sensation or awareness. In one experiment, a picture of a girl either throwing a cake at someone or simply presenting the cake in a friendly manner is flashed so quickly that the viewer denies seeing it. A neutral picture of the girl is presented subsequently, and the participant's judgment of the girl's personality proves to be biased by the subliminal exposures presented earlier (**Figure 14.18**). Hundreds of such demonstrations have been recounted, although they are not easy to replicate. Many psychologists maintain that elements of the picture are captured nonconsciously and that this result is sufficient to bias judgment.

a

b

FIGURE 14.18 Testing subliminal perception.
(a) A participant is quickly shown just one picture of a girl, similar to these images, in such a way that the participant is not consciously aware of the picture's content. The participant is then shown a neutral picture (b) and is asked to describe the girl's character. Judgments of the girl's character have been found to be biased by the previous subthreshold presentation.

Cognitive psychologists have sought to reaffirm the role of nonconscious processing through various experimental paradigms. A leader in this effort has been Tony Marcel of Cambridge University (1983a, 1983b). Marcel used a masking paradigm in which the brief presentation of either a blank screen or a word was followed quickly by a masking stimulus of a crosshatch of letters. One of two tasks followed presentation of the masking stimulus. In a detection task, participants merely had to choose whether a word had been presented. Participants responded at a level of chance on this task. They simply could not tell whether a word had been presented.

With a lexical decision task, however, the subliminally presented stimulus had effects. Here, following presentation of the masking stimulus, a string of letters was presented and participants had to specify whether the string formed a word. Marcel cleverly manipulated the subthreshold words in such a way that some were related to the word string and some were not. If there had been at least lexical processing of the subthreshold word, related words should have elicited faster responses, and this is exactly what Marcel found.

Since then, investigations of conscious and nonconscious processing of pictures and words have been combined successfully into a single cross-form priming paradigm. In this paradigm, both pictures and word stems are presented (**Figure 14.19**). Using both extended and brief periods of presentation, the investigators showed that such picture-to-word priming can occur with or without awareness. In addition to psychophysically setting the brief presentation time at identification threshold, they used a pattern mask to halt conscious processing. Apparently not all processing was halted, however, because priming occurred equally well under both conditions.

Given that participants denied seeing the briefly presented stimuli, nonconscious processing must have

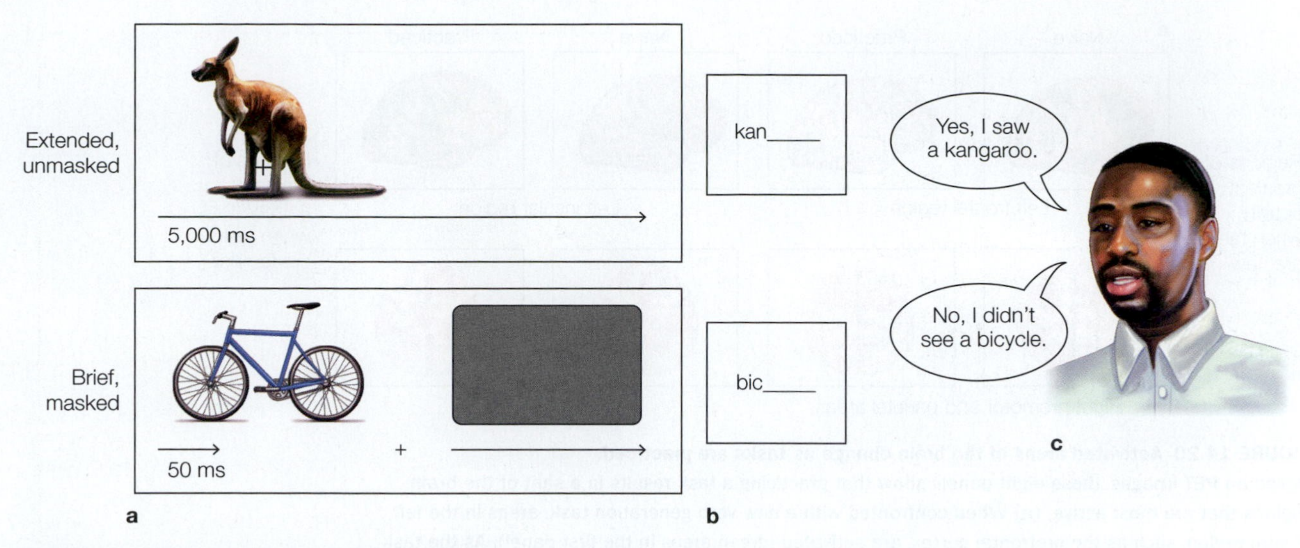

FIGURE 14.19 Picture-to-word priming paradigm.
(a) During the study, either extended and unmasked (top) or brief and masked (bottom) presentations were used. (b) During the test, participants were asked to complete word stems ("kan" and "bic" in this example). Priming performance was identical between extended and brief presentations. (c) Afterward, participants were asked whether they remembered seeing the words as pictures. Here, performance differed: Participants usually remembered seeing the extended presentations but regularly denied having seen the brief presentations.

allowed them to complete the word stems (primes). In other words, they were extracting conceptual information from the pictures, even without consciously seeing them. In a layered system this apparent disconnect presents no conundrum; we would say that the output of a nonconscious layer was the input to the application layer.

How often does this happen in everyday life? Considering the complexity of the visual world and how rapidly our eyes look around, briefly fixating from object to object (about 100–200 ms), this situation probably happens quite often! These data further underscore the need to consider both conscious and nonconscious processes, along with the framework of a layered architecture, when developing a theory of consciousness.

Shifting Processing from Conscious to Nonconscious Layers

An often overlooked aspect of consciousness is the abil[illegible], controlled processing to nonconscious, automatic processing. Such "movement" from conscious to nonconscious is necessary when we are learning complex motor tasks such as riding a bike or driving a car, as well as for complex cognitive tasks such as verb generation and reading.

At Washington University in St. Louis, Marcus Raichle and Steven Petersen, two pioneers in the brain-imaging field, proposed a "scaffolding to storage" framework to account for this movement (Petersen et al., 1998). Initially, according to their framework, we must use conscious processing during practice while developing complex skills (or memories); this activity can be considered the scaffolding process. During this time, the memory is being consolidated, or the skill is being developed and honed. Once the task is learned, brain activity and brain involvement change. This change can be likened to the removal of the scaffolding, or the disinvolvement of support structures and the involvement of more permanent structures as the tasks are "stored" for use.

Using PET techniques, Petersen and Raichle demonstrated this scaffolding-to-storage movement in the awake-behaving human brain. Participants performed either a verb generation task, which was compared to simply reading verbs, or a maze-tracing task, which was compared to tracing a square. The study clearly demonstrated that early, unlearned, conscious processing uses a much different network of brain regions than does later, learned, nonconscious processing (**Figure 14.20**). The researchers hypothesized that during learning, a scaffolding set of regions is used to handle novel task demands. After learning, a different set of regions is involved, perhaps regions specific to the storage or representation of the particular skill or memory. In terms of a layered architecture, the processing has moved to a lower layer and has been abstracted.

Dynamic network analysis has since identified changes in functional connectivity between brain regions

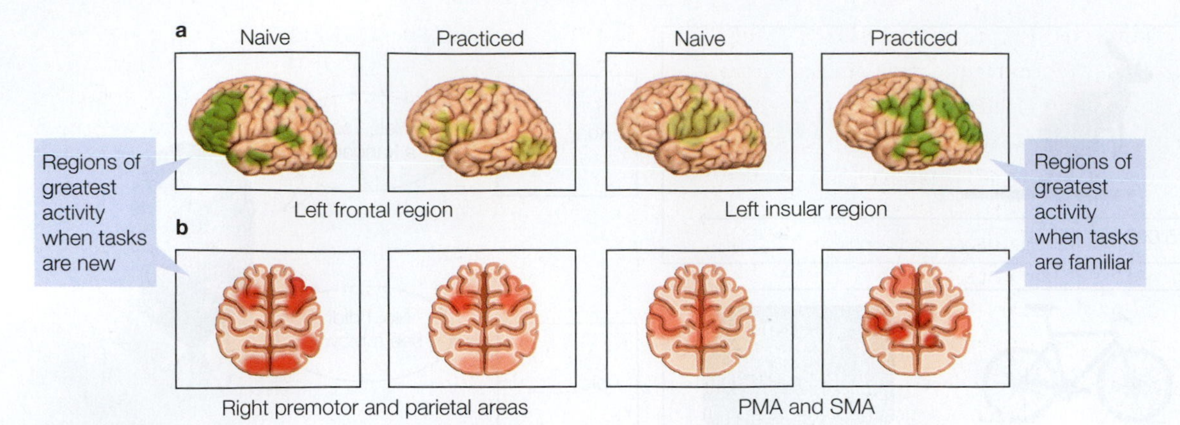

FIGURE 14.20 Activated areas of the brain change as tasks are practiced.
Based on PET images, these eight panels show that practicing a task results in a shift of the brain regions that are most active. (a) When confronted with a new verb generation task, areas in the left frontal region, such as the prefrontal cortex, are activated (green areas in the first panel). As the task is practiced, blood flow to these areas decreases (as depicted by the fainter color in the second panel). In contrast, the insula is less active during naive verb generation. With practice, however, activation in the insula increases, suggesting that practice causes activity in the insula to replace activity previously observed in the frontal regions. (b) An analogous shift in activity is observed elsewhere in the brain during a motor-learning maze-tracing task. Activity in the premotor and parietal areas seen early in the maze task (red areas in the first panel) subsides with practice (fainter red in the second panel), while increases in blood flow are then seen in the primary and supplementary motor areas (PMA and SMA) as a result of practice.

over the course of learning a motor task as it becomes automatic (see Section 3.7). Further, once this movement from conscious to nonconscious has occurred, it is sometimes difficult to reinitiate conscious processing. A classic example is learning to drive with a clutch. Early on, you have to consciously practice the steps of releasing the gas pedal while depressing the clutch, moving the shift lever, and slowly releasing the clutch while applying pressure to the gas pedal again—all without stalling the car. After a few jerky attempts, you know the procedures well; they become automatic and you no longer think about them. The process has been stored, but it is rather difficult to separate the steps.

Similar processes occur in learning other complex skills. Chris Chabris, a cognitive psychologist at Harvard University, studied chess players as they progressed from the novice to the master level (Chabris & Hamilton, 1992). During lightning chess, masters play many games simultaneously and very fast. Their play seems intuitive as they make move after move after move, and in essence they *are* playing by intuition—*learned* intuition, that is. They know, without really knowing how they know, what the next best move is.

For novices, such lightning play is not possible. They have to painstakingly examine the pieces and moves one by one. ("OK, if I move my knight over there, she will take my bishop; no, that won't work. Let's see, if I move the rook—no, then she will move her bishop and then I can take her knight . . . whoops, that will put me in check . . . hmm.") But after many hours of practice and hard work, as the novices develop into chess masters, they see and react to the chessboard differently. They now begin to view and play it as a series of groups of pieces and moves, as opposed to separate pieces with serial moves. Chabris's research showed that during early stages of learning, the talking, language-based left brain is consciously controlling the game. With experience, however, as the different moves and possible groupings are learned, the perceptual, feature-based right brain takes over.

For example, International Grandmaster chess player and two-time U.S. chess champion Patrick Wolff, who at age 20 defeated the world chess champion Garry Kasparov in 25 moves, was given 5 seconds to look at a picture of a chessboard with all the pieces set in a pattern that made chess sense. He was then asked to reproduce it, and he quickly and accurately did so, getting 25 out of 27 pieces in the correct position. Even a good player would place only about 5 pieces correctly (Chabris, 1999).

In a different trial, however, with the same board and the same number of pieces, but with the pieces in positions that didn't make chess sense, he got only a few pieces right, as would a person who doesn't play chess. Wolff's original accuracy was due to his right brain automatically matching up patterns that it had learned from years of playing chess. You can watch this test at http://www.youtube.com/watch?v=PBoiARwlGyY.

Although neuroscientists may know that Wolff's right-brain pattern perception mechanism is the source of this capacity, Wolff himself did not. When he was asked about his ability, his left-brain interpreter struggled for an explanation: "You sort of get it by trying to, to understand what's going on quickly and of course you chunk things, right? . . . I mean obviously, these pawns, just, but, but it, I mean, you chunk things in a normal way, like I mean one person might think this is sort of a structure, but actually I would think this is more, all the pawns like this" (Gazzaniga, 2011). When asked, the speaking left brain of the master chess player can assure us that it can explain how the moves are made, but it fails miserably to do so—as often happens when you try, for example, to explain how to use a clutch to someone who doesn't drive a standard-transmission car.

The transition from controlled, conscious processing to automatic, nonconscious processing requires multiple interactions among many brain processes, including consciousness, as the neural circuit is compiled, tested, recompiled, retested, and so on. Eventually, as the cognitive control regions disengage, nonconscious processing begins to take over. We can think of this as processing being moved to a lower layer hidden from view.

This theory seems to imply that once conscious processing has effectively enabled us to move a task to a lower layer (the realm of the nonconscious), we no longer need conscious processing. This transition would enable us to perform that task nonconsciously and allow our limited conscious processing to turn to another task. We could nonconsciously ride our bikes and think about quantum mechanics at the same time. Consciousness may have evolved to improve the efficiency of nonconscious processing. The ability to relegate learned tasks and memories to nonconscious processing enables us to devote our limited consciousness resources to recognizing and adapting to changes and novel situations in the environment, thus increasing our chances of survival.

TAKE-HOME MESSAGES

- Most of the processing that goes on in the brain is nonconscious.
- We have conscious access to only a limited amount of information processed by the brain.
- Subliminal processing is defined as brain activity evoked by a stimulus that is below the threshold for awareness. When processing is subliminal, the information is inaccessible to awareness.
- Early, unlearned, conscious processing uses a much different network of brain regions than does later, learned, nonconscious processing.
- The ability to relegate learned tasks and memories to nonconscious processing enables us to devote our limited consciousness resources to recognizing and adapting to changes and novel situations in the environment, thus increasing our chances of survival.

14.6 The Contents of Conscious Experience

One notable way to differentiate the contents of conscious experience from sentience is by studying brains of people who are missing some contents but continue to be sentient. The contents of our conscious experience are made up of perceptions, thoughts, memories, and feelings. We may know some people personally who have lost some contents to their conscious perceptual experience—who may be blind, be deaf, or have lost their sense of smell. We have already met many people in this book who have lost some of the contents of their thoughts. For example, H.M. (see Chapter 9) could no longer access some of his long-term memory, so it was no longer part of the contents of his conscious experience—yet he remained sentient.

In contrast, the principal early symptom of Alzheimer's disease is the loss of the contents of short-term memory, which results from the loss of neurons in the entorhinal cortex and the hippocampus. Neuronal loss then progresses to other regions, becoming widespread and resulting in the slow destruction of the brain. The conscious experience of people with Alzheimer's changes as cortical function is lost and depends on whatever neural circuitry continues to function or malfunction. The contents of their conscious experience are more restricted and very different from what they were before the illness. As a result, drastic changes in personality and odd behavior may be observed, but even with widespread neurodegeneration, patients remain conscious and sentient. They may get confused about where they are, but they still feel fear when lost and feel happy while recounting a favorite long-term memory.

We have also learned about patients with lesions in Wernicke's area who can no longer comprehend speech and who speak nonsense, having lost language as a means of communication, yet they still understand a smile and can read the intentions of others. We have met people with frontal lobe damage who can no longer make or institute plans or whose personality has markedly changed; people whose basal ganglia are malfunctioning, restricting their movement and thus restricting the contents of their conscious experience; and people with a lesion to the pons, no longer able to move or communicate effortlessly.

These people all remain conscious and sentient, even with these severe lesions in various areas throughout the brain. What has changed is the contents of their conscious experience, which have become extremely restricted.

The Brain's Interpreter and the Unified Feeling of Self

Even after learning that the brain's modular organization has been well established, that we have functioning modules that have some kind of physical instantiation, that these networks operate mainly outside the realm of awareness, providing specialized bits of information, and that many of our cognitive capacities appear to be automatic domain-specific operations, we still feel we are a single entity in charge of our thoughts and body. Despite knowing that these modular systems are beyond our control and fully capable of producing behaviors, mood changes, and cognitive activity, part of the contents of our conscious experience is that we are a unified conscious agent—an "I" with a past, a present, and a future. With all of this apparently independent activity running in parallel, what allows for the sense of conscious unity that we possess?

A private narrative appears to take place inside us all the time. It consists partly of the effort to tie together into a coherent whole the diverse activities of thousands of specialized systems that we have inherited through evolution to handle the challenges presented to us each day by both environmental and social situations. Years of research have confirmed that humans have a specialized process to carry out this interpretive synthesis, and, as we discussed in Chapter 4, it is located in the brain's left hemisphere. This system, called the *interpreter*, is most likely cortically based and works largely outside of conscious awareness.

The interpreter makes sense of all the internal and external information that bombards the brain. Asking how one thing relates to another and looking for causes and effects, it offers up hypotheses and makes order out of the chaos of information. The interpreter is the glue that binds together the thousands of bits of information from all over the cortex into a cause-and-effect, "makes sense" running narrative: our personal story, which then becomes part of the contents of our memory. It explains why we do the things we do, and why we feel the way we do. Our dispositions, emotional reactions, and past learned behavior are all fodder for the interpreter. If some action, thought, or emotion doesn't fit in with the rest of the story, the interpreter will rationalize it ("I am a really cool, macho guy with tattoos and a Harley, and I got a poodle because . . . ah, um . . . my great-grandmother was French").

Looking at the past decades of split-brain research, we find one unalterable fact: Disconnecting the two cerebral hemispheres, an event that finds one half of the cortex no longer interacting in a direct way with the other half, does not typically disrupt the cognitive intelligence and verbal ability of these patients. The left, dominant hemisphere remains the major force in their conscious experience, and that force is sustained, it would appear, not by the whole cortex, but by specialized circuits within the left hemisphere. In short, the inordinately large human brain does not render its unique contributions simply by being a bigger brain, but by accumulating specialized circuits.

The interpreter is a system of primary importance to the human brain. Interpreting the cause and effect of both internal and external events enables the formation of beliefs. Can a mental state, a belief, free us from simply responding to stimulus–response aspects of everyday life? When a stimulus such as a pork roast is placed in front of your dog, she will have no "issues" about scarfing it down. But you might. Faced with such a stimulus, even if you were hungry, you might not partake, if you have a belief that you should not eat animal products or your religious beliefs forbid it. It seems that your behavior can hinge on a belief. Oddly, though, most neuroscientists will deny that a mental state can affect the physical processing of the brain.

TAKE-HOME MESSAGES

- The cortex can sustain massive injury, yet consciousness persists.
- The contents of our conscious experience appear to be the result of local processing in modules.
- The human interpretive system is in the left hemisphere, most likely cortically based, and works outside of conscious awareness. It distills all the internal and external information bombarding the brain into a cohesive narrative, which becomes our personal story.
- The interpreter looks for causes and effects of internal and external events and, in so doing, enables the formation of beliefs, which enable us to engage in goal-directed behavior and free us from reflexive, stimulus-driven behavior.

14.7 Can Mental States Affect Brain Processing?

Any theories about consciousness must consider the question of whether a conscious thought has any control over the brain that processes it. The brain is a decision-making device, guided by experience, that gathers and

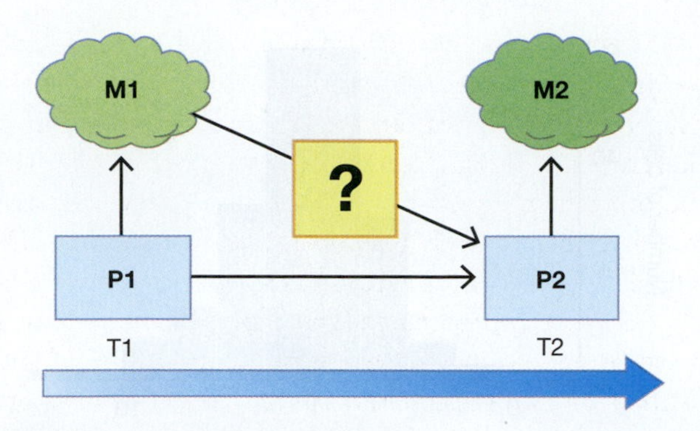

FIGURE 14.21 Rethinking causality.
Any explanation of causality in the brain must relate the mental states M1 and M2 to the change in their corresponding physical states, P1 and P2.

computes information in real time to inform its decisions. If the brain gathers information to inform decisions, can a mental state such as a belief, which is the result of an experience or a social interaction, affect or constrain the brain and, by so doing, influence its future mental states and behaviors? Can a thought or belief, the end product of processing across the whole brain, constrain the very brain that produced it? That is, does the whole constrain its parts?

The classic puzzle is usually put this way: There is a physical state, P1, at time 1 (T1), which produces a mental state, M1 (**Figure 14.21**). Then after a bit of time, now time 2 (T2), there is another physical state, P2, which produces another mental state, M2. How do we get from M1 to M2? This is the conundrum. We know that mental states are produced by processes in the brain, so M1 does not directly generate M2 without involving the brain. If we just go from P1 to P2 and then to M2, then our mental life is doing no work and we are truly just along for the ride. No one really likes that notion, but that is the belief of most materialists. The tough question is this: Does M1, in some downward-constraining process, guide P2 and thus affect M2?

Theoretical biologist David Krakauer at the University of Wisconsin helps us think about this by pointing out that when we program a computer,

> we interface with a complex physical system that performs computational work. W[illegible] program at the level of electrons, Micro B, but at a level of a higher effective theory, Macro A (for example, Lisp programming) that is then compiled down, without loss of information, into the microscopic physics. Thus, A causes B. Of course, A is physically made from B, and all the steps of the compilation are just B with B physics. But from our perspective, we can view some collective B behavior in terms of A processes. . . . The deeper point is that without these higher levels, there would be no possibility of communication, as we would have to specify every particle we wish to move in the utterance, rather than have the mind-compiler do the work. (Gazzaniga, 2011)

Psychology professors Kathleen Vohs (Carlson School of Management in Minnesota) and Jonathan Schooler (UC Santa Barbara) showed in a clever experiment that people behave more ethically when they believe they have free will. An earlier survey of people in 36 countries had reported that more than 70% agreed that their life was in their own hands. Other studies had shown that invoking a sense of personal accountability could change behavior (Harmon-Jones & Mills, 1999; C. M. Mueller & Dweek, 1998).

Vohs and Schooler set about to see empirically whether people's behavior is affected by the belief that they are free to function. In their study, college students, before taking a test, were given either a series of sentences that had a deterministic bias, such as "Ultimately, we are biological computers—designed by evolution, built through genetics, and programmed by the environment," or a passage about free will, such as "I am able to override the genetic and environmental factors that sometimes influence my behavior." After thinking about what they had read, the students were given a computerized test. They were then told that because of a glitch in the software, the answer to each question would pop up automatically. To prevent this from happening, they were asked to press a particular computer key; thus, it took extra effort not to cheat.

What happened? The students who read the deterministic sentences were more likely to cheat than those who had read the sentences about free will. In essence, a mental state affected behavior. Vohs and Schooler (2008) suggested that disbelief in free will produces a subtle cue that exerting effort is futile, thus granting permission not to bother. People prefer not to bother because bothering, in the form of self-control, requires exertion and depletes energy (Gailliot et al., 2007).

Florida State University social psychologists Roy Baumeister and colleagues (2009) found that reading deterministic passages also resulted in more aggressive and less helpful behavior toward others. They suggest that a belief in free will may be crucial for motivating people to control their automatic impulses to act selfishly, and a significant amount of self-control and mental energy are required to override selfish impulses and restrain aggressive impulses. The mental state supporting the idea of voluntary actions had an effect on the subsequent action decision. Not only do we seem to believe that we control our actions, but also society seems to benefit if everyone believes that.

Baumeister and his colleagues also found that, compared with people who do not believe in free will, those who do believe in free will enjoy greater self-efficacy and less of a sense of helplessness (Baumeister & Brewer, 2012), are more autonomous and proactive (Alquist et al., 2013), perform better academically (Feldman et al., 2016) and in the workplace (Stillman et al., 2010), are more positive, and perceive their capacity for decision making as greater (Feldman et al., 2014).

Although the notion that a belief affects behavior seems elementary to ordinary people, it is firmly denied by most neuroscientists. Why? This view implies top-down causation, and in a neural reductionist world, a mental state cannot affect the physical neurons, the nuts and bolts of a determinist brain. We will return to the philosophically thorny subject of determinism in Section 14.9.

Neurons, Neuronal Groups, and the Contents of Consciousness

Neuroscientists have been extraordinarily innovative in analyzing how neurons enable perceptual activities. Recording from single neurons in the visual system, they have tracked the flow of visual information and how it becomes encoded and decoded (see Chapter 5). William Newsome at Stanford University, for instance, studied how neuronal events in area MT of the monkey cortex, which is actively involved in motion detection, correlate with the actual perceptual event (Newsome et al., 1989). One of his first findings was striking: The animal's psychophysical performance capacity to discriminate motion could be predicted by the response pattern of a single neuron (**Figure 14.22**). In other words, a single neuron in area MT was as sensitive as the whole monkey to changes in the visual display.

This finding stirred the research community because it raised a fundamental question about how the brain does its job. Newsome's observation challenged the common view that the signal averaging that surely goes on in the nervous system eliminated the noise carried by individual neurons and that the decision-making capacity of pooled neurons should be superior to the sensitivity of single neurons. Yet Newsome did not side with those who believe that a single neuron is the source for any one behavioral act. It is well known that killing a single neuron, or even hundreds of them, will not impair an animal's ability to

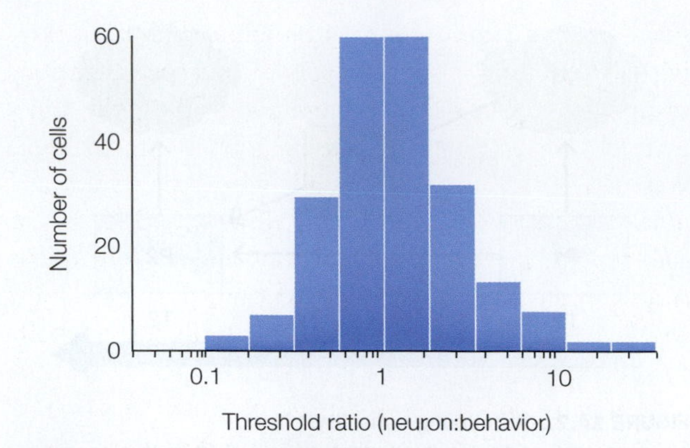

FIGURE 14.22 Motion discrimination can be predicted by the response pattern of a single neuron.
Motion stimuli, with varying levels of coherent motion, were presented to rhesus monkeys trained in a task to discriminate the direction of motion. The monkey's decision regarding the direction of apparent motion and the responses of 60 single middle temporal visual area (MT) cells, which are selective for direction of motion, were recorded and compared on each trial. In this histogram comparing the monkey's performance with the neuron's performance, a value less than 1 represents trials in which the neuron's threshold was lower than the monkey's (i.e., the neuron's performance was better than the monkey's), and a value greater than 1, trials in which the monkey's performance was better than the neuron's. In most cases (values near 1) the neuron's threshold and the behavior's threshold were similar. On average, individual cells in MT were as sensitive as the entire monkey. In subsequent work, the firing rate of single cells predicted (albeit weakly) the monkey's choice on a trial-by-trial basis.

perform a task, so a single neuron's behavior must be redundant.

Fueling deterministic views of the brain, Newsome found that he could directly manipulate the visual information and influence an animal's decision processes: Altering the response rate of these same neurons by careful microstimulation can tilt the animal toward making the right decision on a perceptual task. Maximum effects are seen during the interval when the animal is thinking about the task. Newsome and his colleagues (Celebrini & Newsome, 1995; Salzman et al., 1990), in effect, inserted an artificial signal into the monkey's nervous system and influenced how the animal thought.

Does this discovery mean that the microstimulation site can be considered as the place where the decision is made? Researchers are not convinced that this is the way to think about the problem. Instead, they believe they have tapped into part of a neuronal loop involved with this particular perceptual discrimination. They argue that stimulation at different sites in the loop creates different perceptual subjective experiences.

For example, suppose that a bouncing ball was moving upward and that you, under microstimulation, responded as if it were moving downward. If the stimulation occurred early in the relevant neuronal loop, you might think you had actually witnessed downward motion. If, however, the stimulation occurred late in the loop and merely found you choosing the downward response instead of the upward one, your sensation would be quite different. Why, you might ask yourself, did I do that?

This question raises the issue of when we become conscious of our thoughts, intentions, and actions. Do we consciously choose to act, and then consciously initiate an act? Or is an act initiated nonconsciously, and only afterward do we consciously think we initiated it?

Benjamin Libet (1996), an eminent neuroscientist-philosopher, researched this question for nearly 35 years. In a groundbreaking and often controversial series of experiments, he investigated the neural time factors in conscious and nonconscious processing. These experiments are the basis for his backward referral hypothesis. Libet and colleagues (1979) concluded that awareness of a neural event is delayed approximately 500 ms after the onset of the stimulating event and, more important, that this awareness is referred back in time to the onset of the stimulating event.

To put it another way, you think that you were aware of the stimulus from the onset of the stimulus and are unaware of the time gap. Surprisingly, according to participant reports, brain activity related to an action increased as early as 350 ms before the conscious intention to act (**Figure 14.23**). Using more sophisticated fMRI techniques, John-Dylan Haynes (Soon et al., 2008) showed that the outcome of a decision can be encoded in brain activity up to 10 seconds before it enters awareness.

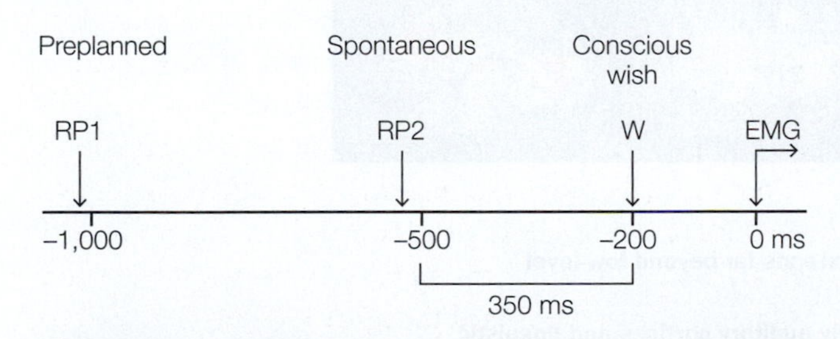

FIGURE 14.23 Sequence of events preceding a fully self-initiated voluntary act in Libet's studies.
Time 0 is the point at which muscle movement was detected by electromyography. When voluntary acts were spontaneous with no preplanning of when to act, the onset of the readiness potential (RP) averaged 550 ms before the muscle was activated (RP2) and 350 ms before the participant was aware of the wish (W) to act. The conscious wish to act preceded the act by 200 ms, whether the act was preplanned or spontaneous.

Interpreting Confusing Findings From the Perspective of Layered Architecture

When the brain is viewed as a layered system (see Doyle & Csete, 2011), we realize the reasoning trap we can easily fall into when we consider Libet's findings that neural events associated with a physical response occur before a person is consciously aware of even wanting to will an act. We are mixing up two organization levels: Micro B and Macro A. We are applying macro-level organization principles to the micro level of neuron interactions. It is like trying to apply Newton's laws to the quantum world.

What difference does it make if brain activity goes on before we are consciously aware of something? Consciousness is a different layer of organization on its own timescale, different from that of neural events, and the timescale of consciousness is current with respect to conscious processes. There is no question that we humans enjoy mental states arising from our underlying neuronal, cell-to-cell interactions. Mental states do not exist without those interactions but, as argued earlier, they cannot be defined or understood solely by knowing the cellular interactions. These mental states that emerge from our neural actions, such as beliefs, thoughts, and desires, in turn constrain the very brain activity that gave rise to them. Mental states can and do influence our decisions to act one way or another.

Physicists have already dealt with this question, and they issue a warning. McGill University physicist Mario Bunge reminds us to take a more holistic approach: "[We] should supplement every bottom-up analysis with a top-down analysis, because the whole constrains the parts: just think of the strains in a component of a metallic structure, or the stress in a member of a social system, by virtue of their interactions with other constituents of the same system" (M. Bunge, 2010, p. 74). From this perspective, to control the teeming, seething nonconscious system, a control layer is necessary. The overall idea is that there is a hierarchy of layers, from particle physics to atomic physics to chemistry to biochemistry to cell biology to physiology, emerging into nonconscious and conscious mental processes. The deep challenge of science is to understand the different layers' protocols and how they enable the layers to interact.

Howard Pattee, professor emeritus at SUNY Binghamton and a physicist and theoretical biologist, found a good biological example of upward and downward causation in the genotype–phenotype mapping of gene replication. Genotype–phenotype mapping requires the gene to describe the sequence of parts forming enzymes, and that description, in turn, requires enzymes to read the description. "In its simplest logical form, the parts represented by symbols (codons) are, in part, controlling the construction of the whole (enzymes), but the whole is, in part, controlling the identification of the parts (translation) and the construction itself (protein synthesis)" (Pattee, 2001).

The Social Layer

Viewing the mind–brain system as layered enables us to begin to understand how the system works, and how beliefs and mental states play their role and stay part of our determined system. With that understanding comes the insight that layers exist both below the mind–brain layers and above them. Indeed, there is a *social* layer; and in the context of interactions with that layer, we can begin to understand concepts such as personal responsibility and freedom. Bunge tells us that "we must place the thing of interest in its context instead of treating it as a solitary individual" (M. Bunge, 2010, pp. 73–74).

The realization that we can't look at the behavior of just one brain has come slowly to neuroscience and psychology. Asif Ghazanfar at Princeton University, who studies vocalization in both macaques and humans, makes the point that during vocalization, a dynamic relationship is going on that involves different parts of the brain, and another dynamic relationship is going on with the other animal that is listening. The vocalizations of one monkey modulate the brain processes going on in the other monkey (Ghazanfar et al., 2008).

This behavior is true for humans also. Uri Hasson and his colleagues at Princeton (Stephens et al., 2010) used fMRI to measure the brain activity of a pair of conversing participants. They found that the listener's brain activity mirrored the speaker's (**Figure 14.24**) and that sometimes some areas of the brain even showed anticipatory responses. When there were such anticipatory responses, greater understanding resulted; the behavior of one person affected another person's behavior. Hasson and Ghazanfar make the point that we have to look at the whole picture, not just one brain in isolation (Hasson et al., 2012).

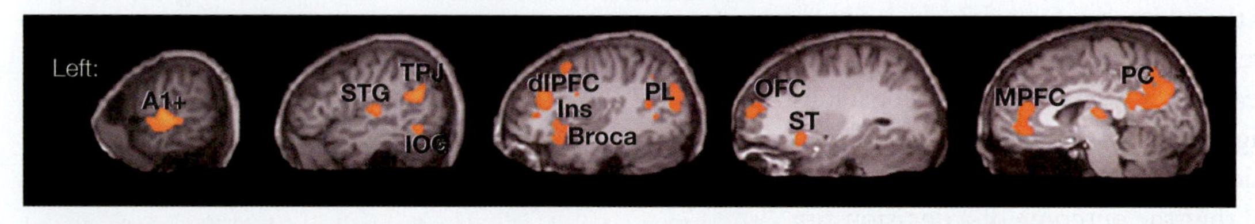

a Speaker–listener neural coupling

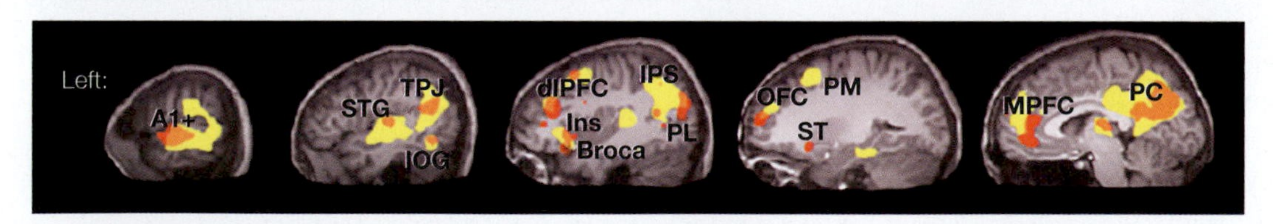

b Overlap of speaker–listener and listener–listener neural coupling

FIGURE 14.24 The neural coupling between speaker and listener extends far beyond low-level auditory areas.
(a) Sagittal slices of the left hemisphere show regions, including early auditory cortices and linguistic and extralinguistic brain areas, in which the activity during speech production is coupled to the activity during speech comprehension. (b) Listener–listener couplings are yellow, and speaker–listener couplings are red. Orange coloring indicates the overlap between areas that reliably activate across all listeners. There is a large overlap between brain areas that listeners use to process incoming verbal information (comprehension activity) and areas with similar time-locked activity in the speaker's brain (production–comprehension coupling). A1+ = early auditory cortices; Broca = Broca's area; dlPFC = dorsolateral prefrontal cortex; Ins = insula; IOG = inferior occipital gyrus; IPS = intraparietal sulcus; MPFC = medial prefrontal cortex; OFC = orbitofrontal cortex; PC = precuneus; PL = parietal lobule; PM = premotor cortex; ST = striatum; STG = superior temporal gyrus; TPJ = temporoparietal junction.

When it comes to the interplay between brains, having a deterministic brain is a moot point. At this social level of analysis we are a couple layers of organization beyond basic brain function, and this social layer is where we should place such concepts as following rules and personal responsibility. Being personally responsible is a social concept, not a brain mechanism, and it is found in the space between human brains, in the interactions between people. Accountability makes no sense in a world made up of one brain. When more than one human brain interacts, a new protocol comes into play with new properties, such as personal responsibility.

Just as a mental state can constrain the brain that produces it, a social group can constrain the individuals that shape it. For example, among the pigtail macaque monkeys, Jessica Flack found that a few powerful individuals police the activity of the group members (Flack et al., 2005). The presence of such individuals can prevent conflicts from occurring, but if that tactic is not fully successful, those individuals can reduce the intensity of conflicts or terminate them and prevent them from spreading. When the policing macaques are temporarily removed, conflict increases.

The presence of the policing macaques also facilitates active socio-positive interactions among group members. A group of macaques could foster either a harmonious, productive society or a divided, insecure grouping of cliques, depending on the organization of its individuals. A police presence "influences large-scale social organization and facilitates levels of social cohesion and integration that might otherwise be impossible." Flack concludes, "This means that power structure, by making effective conflict management possible, influences social network structure and therefore feeds back down to the individual level to *constrain individual behaviour* [italics added]" (Flack et al., 2005). The same thing happens when, in the rearview mirror, you see a highway patrol car coming down the on-ramp: You check your speedometer and slow down. Individual behavior is not solely the product of an isolated deterministic brain, but is affected by the social group.

TAKE-HOME MESSAGES

- Multiple studies have shown that people who believe in free will behave differently from those who do not, suggesting that a mental state can affect behavior.
- Brain activity related to an action may increase as early as 350 ms before the conscious intention to act.
- The mind–brain system is layered, and each layer works within its own time frame.
- In a conversation, a listener's brain activity can mirror that of the speaker. One person's behavior can affect the brain behavior of another person.
- Individual behavior is affected by the social group.

14.8 The Contents of Animal Consciousness

Multiple studies using diverse methods have provided evidence that structural and functional modules exist in the brain networks across multiple animal species that include insects (Carruthers, 2006), nematodes (Sporns & Betzel, 2016), and arthropods (Sztarker & Tomsic, 2011), and that share many of the same properties. If we share modular brains with other species, do we share similar cognition and consciousness? Descartes denied that animals were conscious, but Darwin was not so rash. Darwin wrote, "The difference in mind between man and the higher animals, great as it is, is certainly one of degree and not of kind" (1871, p. 105). Researchers searching for evidence of early conscious states in animals have focused primarily on behavior in birds and mammals, which may reflect the contents of what an animal is conscious of, not sentience.

One behavior that is considered to indicate complex cognition is tool use. All sorts of animals use tools, including some birds, especially those of the Corvidae family: ravens, crows, magpies, jays, nutcrackers, and rooks. For example, New Caledonian crows make two types of tools, each used for different jobs, which they carry with them to search for food. Researchers have observed them using one tool to obtain a second tool necessary to retrieve food—known as a metatool problem (A. H. Taylor et al., 2010; to watch one of these crows, go to http://www.youtube.com/watch?v=zk5LzdNQMAQ).

Crows from different parts of the main island of Caledonia, Grande Terre, have different tool designs (**Figure 14.25**), which is evidence of cultural variation and transmission (Holzhaider et al., 2010b), although hand-raised crows make basic stick tools without social learning (Hunt et al., 2007). These behaviors suggest that crows are conscious in the sense that they are alive, alert, and experiencing the moment, and that conscious experience appears to be enhanced by specialized modules providing content that other birds do not have.

Other researchers have looked for evidence of self-awareness in animals, but designing a test to demonstrate it has proved difficult. They have approached the

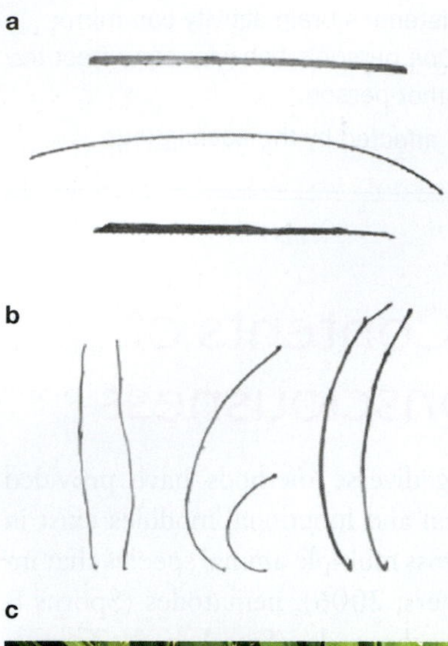

FIGURE 14.25 Barbed and hooked-stick tools manufactured by New Caledonian crows to extract food.
(a) From top to bottom: Barbed tools with wide, narrow, and two-stepped designs made from pandanus palms. (b) From left to right: Pairs of hooked tools made from fern stolons, a thorny vine, and forked twigs. The length of the fern stolon at far left is 13.9 cm. (c) Spiny leaves of the pandanus palm.

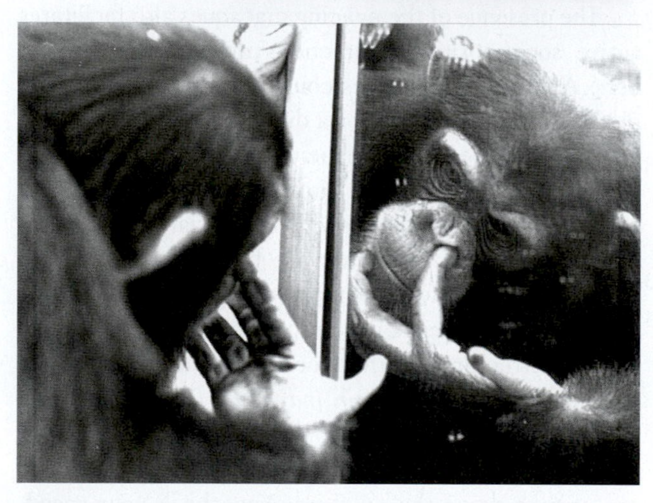

FIGURE 14.26 Evidence for self-awareness in chimpanzees.
When initially presented with a mirror, chimpanzees react to it as if they are confronting another animal. After 5 to 30 minutes, however, chimpanzees will engage in self-exploratory behaviors, indicating that they know they are indeed viewing themselves.

challenge from two angles: through testing whether nonhuman animals recognize themselves in a mirror, and through imitation. In the **mirror self-recognition (MSR)** test, an animal is anesthetized and a sticker or paint is applied to an area of the body that the animal cannot normally see. Later, when it is awake, the animal is placed where there is a mirror. Gordon Gallup (1970), who designed the MSR test, proposed that if the animal then started to investigate the sticker or paint mark after seeing it in the mirror, such behavior would imply self-recognition and the presence of a self-concept and self-awareness (Gallup, 1982).

Only a few members of a few species can pass the test. MSR develops in some chimps around puberty, and it is present to a lesser degree in older chimps (Povinelli et al., 1993; **Figure 14.26**). Orangutans also may show MSR, but only the rare gorilla possesses it (Suarez & Gallup, 1981; Swartz, 1997). Although there have been reports that dolphins, one Asian elephant, magpies, and pigeons have passed the test, those results have not yet been replicated. Children reliably develop MSR by the age of 2 (Amsterdam, 1972).

Gallup's suggestion that mirror self-recognition implies the presence of a self-concept and self-awareness has come under attack. For instance, Robert Mitchell

(1997), a psychologist at Eastern Kentucky University, questioned the degree of self-awareness that is demonstrated by recognizing oneself in the mirror. He pointed out that MSR requires only an awareness of the body, not an abstract concept of self; there is no need to invoke more than the matching of sensation to visual perception. Even people do not require attitudes, values, intentions, emotion, or episodic memory to recognize their own bodies in the mirror.

Another problem with the MSR test is that some patients with prosopagnosia, although they have a sense of self, are unable to recognize themselves in a mirror. They think they are seeing someone else. So, although the MSR test can indicate a degree of self-awareness, it is of limited value in evaluating just how self-aware an animal is. It does not answer the question of whether an animal is aware of only its visible self, or of unobservable features as well.

Imitation provides another approach. If we can imitate another's actions, then we are capable of distinguishing between our own actions and the other person's. The ability to imitate is used as evidence for self-recognition in developmental studies of children. Although it has been searched for extensively, scant evidence has been found that other animals imitate. Most of the evidence in primates points to the ability to reproduce the result of an action, not to imitate the action itself (Tennie et al., 2006, 2010).

Another avenue exploring the contents of conscious experience was opened in 1978 when David Premack and Guy Woodruff posed this question: Does a chimpanzee have a theory of mind? Josep Call and Michael Tomasello, at the Max Planck Institute for Evolutionary Anthropology, reviewed 30 years of research in 2008 and concluded,

> There is solid evidence from several different experimental paradigms that chimpanzees understand the goals and intentions of others, as well as the perception and knowledge of others. Nevertheless, despite several seemingly valid attempts, there is currently no evidence that chimpanzees understand false beliefs. Our conclusion for the moment is, thus, that chimpanzees understand others in terms of a perception–goal psychology, as opposed to a full-fledged, human-like belief–desire psychology.

That position changed in 2016, when Christopher Krupenye and his colleagues in Tomasello's lab adapted the Sally–Anne false-belief task developed for 2-year-old children (see Figure 13.12; Krupenye et al., 2016) to test where the apes' eyes looked (using eye tracking) when anticipating the action of an actor. They tested chimpanzees, bonobos, and orangutans and found that apes indeed accurately anticipated the goal-directed behavior of an agent who held a false belief. When an actor returned to look for an object that had been moved while he was away (and hence had a false belief about its location), the apes looked in anticipation to where the actor had last seen the object, even though the apes knew it was no longer there. This result shows that apes may understand that others' behavior may be guided by beliefs, even when those beliefs are false.

If you have ever been to a sheepdog trial, you have witnessed dogs' impressive ability to use communicative cues from humans. Researchers have also taken note, and early studies indicate that dogs possess some aspects of theory of mind. Not surprisingly, because humans and dogs have evolved together, dogs excel in social interactions with humans. For example, they can find and fetch hidden objects or food (in such experiments, the food is fragrance-free) by following social cues, such as pointing.

In doing this, the dog must first infer that the pointer wants it to check out what is being pointed at and then also infer why it should do that: Does the pointer want me to fetch the item for her, or is she just giving me information about its location? Tomasello suggests that this ability involves understanding both what to do and why to do it—two levels of intention (Kirchhofer et al., 2012; Tomasello, 2008). Chimps don't seem to be able to do this. They can follow the pointing, but they can't figure out the why.

When it comes to nonsocial domains, however, dogs aren't flexible. For example, when presented with two strings, one tied to food and one not, they can't figure out that they should grab the one tied to the food. Chimps can. In fact, dogs can't figure out strings at all, including how to untangle themselves from a rope that has become wrapped around a tree. The differing cognitive abilities of dogs, chimps, crows, and humans—some shared and some not—suggest that we possess specific, yet different, modules that have evolved in response to different environmental pressures. These modules contribute different contents to our conscious experience.

TAKE-HOME MESSAGES

- Researchers have looked for evidence of consciousness by studying animal behavior such as tool use and conducting mirror self-recognition tests.
- Evidence has recently been found that chimpanzees understand that others' behavior is guided by beliefs.

- Different species of animals have different contents to their conscious experience, depending on the neural processing that they possess, which in turn is a product of evolution.

14.9 Sentience

As mentioned earlier, **sentience** encompasses the subjective qualia, phenomenal awareness, raw feelings, and first-person viewpoint of an experience—what it is like to be or do something. Explaining how the objective physical matter that makes up neurons—the same physical matter found in rocks, carbon, oxygen, calcium, and so forth—produces subjective experience is the hard problem of consciousness. It doesn't matter whether the mechanism for consciousness is local modules or a central brain circuit; we still have to explain the gap between the subjective and objective. To do this, we need to take a look at what physicists discovered early in the last century, which eventually resulted in the great physicist Niels Bohr's principle of complementarity—and in physicists distancing themselves from a deterministic view of the world.

The Unexpected, Unpredictable Quantum World

Physics class may not have put you into an existential crisis, but that's what happened to people in 17th-century England when Isaac Newton wrote down Galileo's laws of motion as algebraic equations and realized something that Galileo hadn't spotted: The equations also described Johannes Kepler's observations about planetary motion. Newton surmised that all the physical matter of the universe—everything from your chair to the moon—operates according to a set of fixed, knowable laws.

If the universe and everything in it follow a set of determined laws, then, it was inferred, everything must be determined, including people's behavior and, in fact, their entire lives. **Determinism** is the philosophical belief that all current and future events and actions, including human cognition, decisions, and behavior, are caused by preceding events combined with the laws of nature. The corollary, then, is that every event and action can, in principle, be predicted in advance, if all parameters are known. Furthermore, Newton's laws also work in reverse, which means that time does not have a direction, and that everything about something's past can be known by looking at its present state.

Determinists believe that the universe and everything in it are completely governed by causal laws and are predictable, that you have no control over your actions and everything was preordained at the big bang. This state of affairs was well accepted by scientists for about 200 years, though cracks had begun to appear right away in 1698, with the invention of the first practical steam engine. The problem was that it was terribly inefficient. Too much energy was dissipated or lost. This didn't make sense in Newton's deterministic world where energy couldn't just get lost, so the physicists had a problem on their hands.

The upshot was the creation of a new field of physics, thermodynamics, concerned with heat, energy, and work. By 1850, the first two laws of thermodynamics were formulated. The first law, also known as the conservation of energy, would have pleased Newton: The energy of an isolated system is constant. The second law was where the problem for Newton's universal laws crept in: When a hot object and a cold object are in contact, heat flows from the hot object (cooling it off) to the cold object (warming it) until an equilibrium is reached (**Figure 14.27a**). If the two are then separated, they do not return to their original temperature. The process is irreversible. A melted ice cube doesn't spontaneously re-form.

Another problem is that, even though we can imagine it happening, "heat" never flows from the cold object to the hot object and cools it, even though this would be consistent with the first law of conservation of energy (**Figure 14.27b**). The second law of thermodynamics proposed a new variable state, *entropy* (the disorder of a system), to explain these observations. The second law says that heat does not spontaneously flow from a

a

b

FIGURE 14.27 The second law of thermodynamics.
(a) A hot cup of coffee will melt a pile of snow until the two objects are in thermodynamic equilibrium. (b) "Heat" never flows from the snow to the hot cup, cooling it off. The entropy of an isolated system always increases.

cold object to a hot one and that, in an isolated system, entropy will increase over time.

To explain these laws of thermodynamics, physicists were required to accept something that chemists already had: atomic theory, which states that matter is made up of tiny particles called atoms. The physicist Ludwig Boltzmann further recognized that the particles in a gas (which may be atoms or molecules) are constantly moving, hitting and bouncing off each other and the walls of whatever contains them. The result: random chaotic motion.

Boltzmann's great insight was that the entropy, the disorder of a system, was the collective result of all the molecular motion. He realized that the second law of thermodynamics was valid only in a statistical sense, not in a predictable deterministic sense. For example, even that little bit of water that was the ice cube is made up of millions and millions of particles moving freely around each other. There is an inconceivably tiny possibility that even with no energy (e.g., a freezer) added to the system, those particles will randomly return to the exact configuration they were in when they were an ice cube, thus re-forming it. It has never happened, but statistically it could.

Boltzmann shook the foundations of determinism with his theory, but physicists fought back, attacking it for years. One of them, the physicist Max Planck, was trying to predict the thermal electromagnetic radiation of an opaque and nonreflective body, known as black-body radiation, which had stumped physicists. After multiple unsuccessful attempts using Newton's laws, Planck resorted to the statistical notion of energy and the idea that energy came in discrete packets. With that tweak to his equations, he was able to accurately predict black-body radiation. What Planck didn't realize at the time was that he had pulled what some consider to be the final stone from the foundation of the physicist's deterministic world. He had unwittingly stumbled into the quantum world, where microscopic objects behave differently from macroscopic objects. They do not obey Newton's laws.

Quantum theory was developed to explain not just black-body radiation, but also the emission of electrons from the surface of a metal in response to light (a phenomenon called the photoelectric effect), as well as why, when an electron loses energy, it stays in orbit and doesn't crash into the nucleus. None of these observations could be explained by either Newton's laws or James Clerk Maxwell's laws of classical electromagnetism.

The realization that atoms didn't obey Newton's so-called universal laws of motion put physicists in a dither. How could Newton's laws be fundamental universal laws if atoms—the stuff objects are made of—didn't obey the same laws as the objects themselves? As the brilliant and entertaining California Institute of Technology physicist Richard Feynman (1998) once pointed out, exceptions prove the rule . . . wrong. Newton's laws must not be universal. The rug was pulled out from under those who thought that a single explanation could cover everything in the universe—the original dream of physicists. Physicists found themselves jerked out of the macro layer that we inhabit (the physical world's application layer where Newton's laws are the protocol) into the micro layer hidden from view: the nonintuitive, statistical, and indeterminate quantum world, which has a different protocol.

Albert Einstein, another physicist reluctant to abandon the world of determinism, was about to discover some of the quantum world's secrets. One of them was that light could be both a wave and a particle. When explaining the photoelectric effect in 1905, Einstein described light as a particle, which we now call a *photon.* That same year, writing about special relativity, Einstein treated light as a continuous wave. Light had a dual nature, and depending on the problem he was working on, Einstein invoked one or the other. The problem was that neither the classical concept of "particle" nor that of "wave" could fully describe the behavior of quantum-scale objects at any one point in time.

Another physicist trying to maintain the deterministic world of causality was Erwin Schrödinger. His famous Schrödinger equation mathematically described how a quantum mechanical wave changes over time. The equation is reversible and deterministic, but it ignores the particle nature of the electron, and it cannot determine the electron's exact location at a given moment. The best guess is merely a probability.

In order to know the exact location of the electron, a measurement has to be made, and this requirement presents what, for a number of reasons, has come to be known as the measurement problem. To begin, a measurement is subjective, not objective. The measurer decides what, when, and where to measure. And a measurement is not reversible: Once it is made, the quantum state of the system collapses; that is, all possible states of the system reduce to one, and all other possibilities have been extinguished. The measurement actually affects the state of the system. Furthermore, the electron's paired properties—momentum and position—cannot both be known at the same time: Measuring one affects the value of the other.

The Principle of Complementarity

Niels Bohr, pondering the behavior of electrons and photons, realized that all quantum systems have a dual nature: Both wave behavior and particle behavior are inherent to them. That is, all matter can exist in two different states at the same time. Only a measurement forces the system to reveal one or the other at any one moment. Bohr's contemplations led him to formulate the *principle of complementarity*, stating that in a complementary system, which has two simultaneous modes of description, one is not reducible to the other. The system is both at the same time.

Bohr argued that whether we see light as a particle or a wave is not inherent in light but depends on how we measure and observe it; the light and the measuring apparatus are part of the system. Theoretical biologist Robert Rosen (1996) wrote that Bohr changed the concept of objectivity itself from what is inherent solely in a material system to what is inherent in a system–observer pair. Consider the question of whether a tree falling in a forest makes a sound if no one is there. The sound waves are generated by the tree falling, whether or not anyone is there, but the eardrum is the measuring device that records them; the sound waves and the eardrum are a system–observer pair.

Einstein was very unhappy with the dual description and predictions no better than probabilities, but Bohr was able to counter all of Einstein's objections by using quantum theory (**Figure 14.28**). Accepting that two descriptions were necessary to explain a single system pushed the boundaries of physics and the imaginations of physicists. Feynman (1998) quipped, "I think I can safely say that nobody understands quantum mechanics."

FIGURE 14.28 Albert Einstein and Niels Bohr.
This photograph was taken at the 1930 Solvay Conference in Brussels, where Einstein had first heard Bohr present his principle of complementarity 3 years earlier.

In formulating the principle of complementarity, Bohr accepted both subjective measurement and objective causal laws as fundamental to the explanation for phenomena. He emphasized, however, that the system itself is unified, not a duality. It is two sides of the same coin. When he first presented these ideas, Bohr suggested that the distinction between subject and object in the quantum world was analogous to the distinction between the subjective mind and the objective brain.

Since the bridge between the mind and brain continues to be a puzzle with no clear solution, we now enter into the realm of speculation. Here we present a novel view, not well known outside the world of biosemiotics (the study of the production and interpretation of signs and codes in biological systems), founded on the work of Howard Pattee, who sees more than an analogy. He argues that complementarity (two modes of description) is an epistemic necessity and a prerequisite for life.

Pattee (1972) argues that the difference between living matter and nonliving matter, which are made of the same chemical building blocks, is that living matter can replicate and evolve over the course of time. Pattee built on the work of Princeton's great mathematical genius John von Neumann, who described, before the discovery of DNA, that a self-replicating, evolving system requires two things: the writing and reading of hereditary records in symbol form (i.e., information) and a separate construction process to build what that information specifies (von Neumann & Burks, 1966). In addition, to self-replicate, the boundaries of the self must be specified. So, what is needed to make another self is to describe, translate, and construct the parts that describe, translate, and construct. For example, DNA has the hereditary information, coded in a set of symbols, to make proteins, but proteins split the DNA molecule to begin the replication process.

This self-referential loop is what Pattee calls *semiotic closure*, and semiotic closure must be present in all cells that self-replicate. Do you see where Pattee went with this? He points out that records, whether hereditary or any other type, are irreversible measurements and, by their very nature, subjective. The construction process is not. "What physicists agree on is that measurement and observation, in both classical and quantum models, require a clear distinction between the objective event and subjective records of events" (Pattee & Rączaszek-Leonardi, 2012, p. vii).

Inherent in any living hunk of matter is a complementary system that has two simultaneous modes of description—the subjective information (a genotype, in the form of DNA) and the objective construction from that information (a phenotype)—and one is not reducible to the other. Because the process involves a self-referential loop, the gap between subjective information recorded in symbolic code and physical construction has been bridged.

Pattee does not see any ghosts in the machinery. Both the records and the constructors are made of physical structures. When von Neumann had his realization about what was required for self-replication, he wrote that he had avoided answering the "most intriguing, exciting, and important question of why the molecules or aggregates that in nature really occur . . . are the sorts of things they are, why they are essentially very large molecules in some cases but large aggregations in other cases" (von Neumann & Burks, 1966, p. 77)

Pattee speculates that it is the very size of the molecules that bridges the gap and ties the quantum and classical worlds: "Enzymes are small enough to take advantage of quantum coherence [subatomic particles that synchronize together] to attain the enormous catalytic power on which life depends, but large enough to attain high specificity and arbitrariness in producing effectively decoherent products [particles that do not have quantum properties] that can function as classical structures" (Pattee and Rączaszek-Leonardi, 2012, p. 13).

Pattee suggests a mind-warping idea: The source of the gap between the immaterial mind and the material brain, the subjective and objective, the measurer and the measured, was there long before the brain. It resulted from a process equivalent to quantum measurement (done in order to make that hereditary record) that began with self-replication at the origin of life. The gap between subject and object was already there with the very first live cell: Two complementary modes of description are inherent in life itself, have been conserved by evolution, and continue to be necessary for differentiating subjective experience from the event itself.

> This is a universal and irreducible complementarity. Neither model can derive the other or be reduced to the other. By the same logic that a detailed objective model of a measuring device cannot produce a subject's measurement, so a detailed objective model of a material brain cannot produce a subject's thought. (Pattee & Rączaszek-Leonardi, 2012, p. 18)

The implication is that the gap between subjective conscious experience and the objective neural firings of our physical brains may be bridged by a similar set of processes, which could be occurring inside cells. Though little known, this is a humdinger of an idea.

Sentience in Animals

Along with Pattee, Jaak Panksepp, whose studies of emotion in animals we encountered in Chapter 10, also thought that we had been looking much too high in the evolutionary tree for how neural systems produce subjective affective experience. Panksepp agreed with Steven Pinker that to deny animals sentience is to believe the impossible. He placed the responsibility for this wacky idea at Descartes's feet and thought that when Descartes asked, "What is this 'I' that 'I' know?" had he just replied, "I feel, therefore I am," leaving cognition out of the subjective-experience equation, we would not have been distracted (or attracted) by his assumption (Panksepp & Biven, 2012).

Panksepp argued that subjective experience arose when the evolutionarily old emotion system linked up with a "body map," which only requires sensations from inside and outside the organism to be tacked onto related neurons in the brain. This information about the state of the agent, along with the construction of a neural simulation of the agent in space, built from the firing of neurons, was all that was necessary for subjective experience. Again we have information and construction, the same complementarity that Pattee sees as necessary for the replication of DNA and life itself.

From their studies of insects, biologist Andrew Barron and neuroscience philosopher Colin Klein at Australia's Macquarie University (2016) suggest that phenomenal awareness has a long evolutionary past. From honeybees and crickets to butterflies and fruit flies, Barron and Klein have found structures in insect brains that generate a unified spatial model of the insect's state and location as it moves around its environment, just as is constructed in the vertebrate midbrain. These researchers suggest that the animal's egocentric representation of the world, its awareness of its body in space (which enables it to duck your flyswatter), is sufficient for subjective experience and was present in some form in the common ancestor of vertebrates and invertebrates 550 million years ago (see **Box 14.2**).

BOX 14.2 | HOT SCIENCE
Bug Brains

The geneticist and evolutionary biologist Theodosius Dobzhansky once commented, "Nothing in biology makes sense except in the light of evolution." The University of Arizona's Nicholas Strausfeld, a neurobiologist who studies arthropods, laments, "This dictum should resonate in the laboratories of brain researchers everywhere, but it rarely does" (http://neurosci.arizona.edu/faculty/strausfeld/lab).

Current research shows that the brains of arthropods (of which insects are a branch) are much more complex than they were originally thought to be. Strausfeld, along with King's College London neurobiologist Frank Hirth, reviewed the anatomical, developmental, behavioral, and genetic characteristics of the central complex of arthropods, an area critical in the selection of motor actions and the control of multijoint movement, and they compared it with the basal ganglia of vertebrates (Strausfeld & Hirth, 2013; **Figure 14.29**). The multitude of similarities they found suggests that the arthropod central complex and vertebrate basal ganglia circuitries, which underlie the selection and maintenance of behavioral actions, are deeply homologous.

For example, developmental errors that disrupt central complex circuitry in insects can cause parkinsonism-like defects, such as ataxia, tripping, and hesitancy. Within both the central complex and the basal ganglia, control mechanisms with both inhibitory (GABAergic) and modulatory (dopaminergic) circuits aid in the regulation of adaptive behaviors. In fact, the researchers found that these circuitries are not examples of convergent evolution, as many had previously assumed, but rather have a common ancestry and were derived from an evolutionarily conserved genetic program. That is, the ancestor that vertebrates share with arthropods was cruising around processing information about its location and sensations to guide its actions. Pushing the evolutionary time frame back even earlier, these researchers suggest that the common ancestor we share with arthropods had brain gear sufficient to support phenomenal experience.

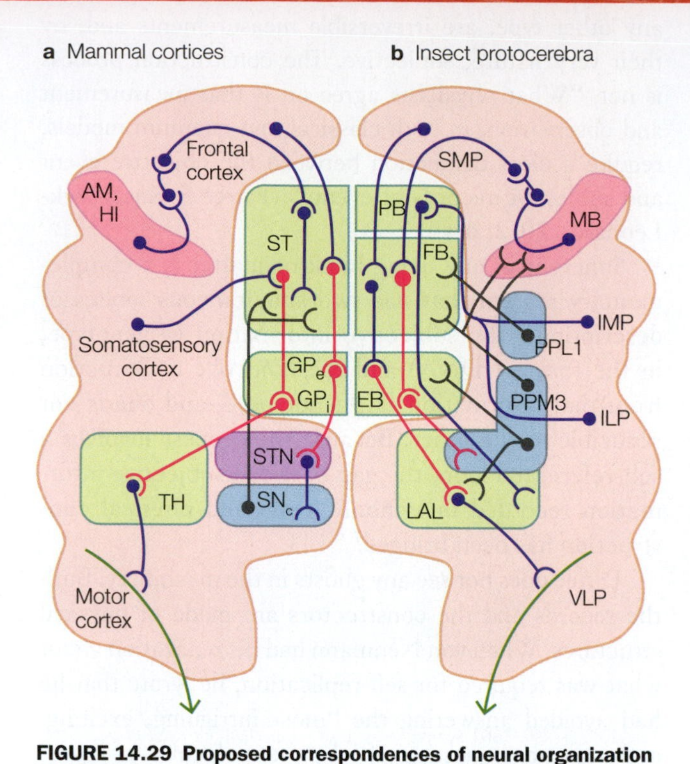

FIGURE 14.29 Proposed correspondences of neural organization of the mammalian basal ganglia and insect central complex. The mammal's striatum (ST) corresponds to the insect's fan-shaped body (FB) and protocerebral bridge (PB); similarly, the mammal's external and internal globus pallidus (GP$_e$ and GP$_i$) correspond to the insect's ellipsoid body (EB). (a) In mammals, inputs to the striatum derive from sensory and association cortices (beige), from the hippocampus (HI) and amygdala (AM), and from the limbic system (not shown) via the frontal cortex. (b) In insects, inputs to the FB and PB derive from sensory intermediate and inferolateral protocerebra (IMP and ILP) and associative superior medial protocerebrum (SMP), which receives learned visual cues and outputs from the mushroom bodies (MB), which correspond to the mammalian hippocampus. The lateral accessory lobes (LAL) equate to the vertebrate thalamus (TH) supplied from the globus pallidus. Both the TH and the LAL supply motor centers (motor cortex in mammals and the inferolateral and ventrolateral protocerebra, ILP and VLP, in insects). Inhibitory pathways are shown in red, dopaminergic pathways in gray, and excitatory or modulatory pathways in blue. Descending motor pathways are in green. PPL1 and PPM3 are dopamine-containing neurons. SN$_c$ = pars compacta of the substantia nigra; STN = subthalamic nucleus.

Sentience Without a Cortex

Perhaps the most severe restriction of conscious experience is found in children who are born without a cerebral cortex—a condition known as *anencephaly*—either because of genetic or developmental malfunction or because of prenatal vascular, toxic, or infectious trauma. A related condition is *hydranencephaly*, in which very minimal cerebral cortex is present (**Figure 14.30**), often as the result of fetal trauma or disease.

The medical and scientific community has neglected to study the subjective experiences of these children, on the assumption that the cortex is necessary for sentience. Many are treated as if they have persistent UWS

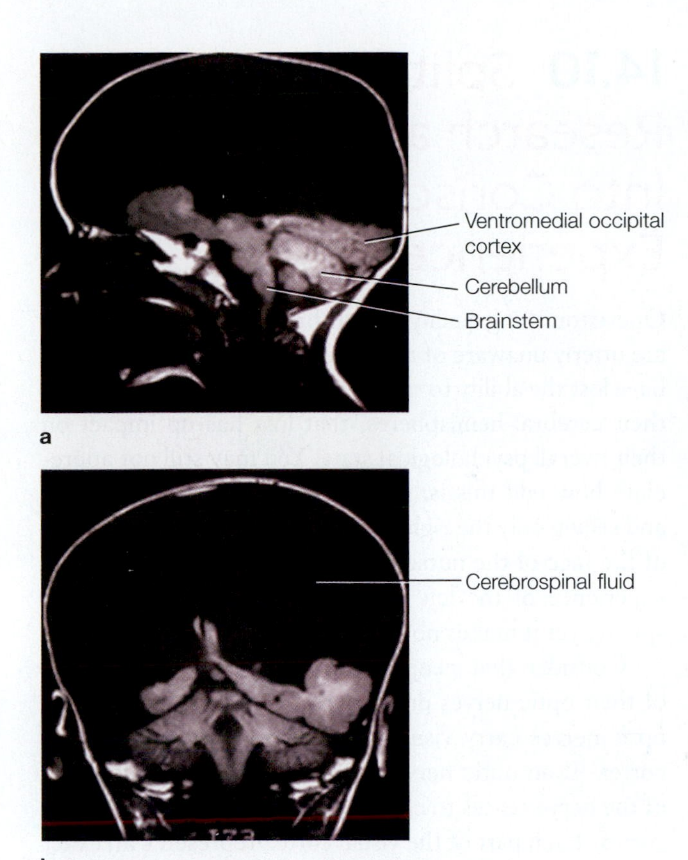

FIGURE 14.30 MRI scans of a child with hydranencephaly.
As these sagittal (a) and frontal (b) views show, some ventromedial occipital and midline cortical matter is spared. The cerebellum and brainstem are intact. The rest of the cranium is filled with cerebrospinal fluid.

without conscious awareness of any kind, feeling neither emotions nor pain. Medical personnel are often surprised when asked by the parents of these children to administer pain medications because the children are crying during invasive procedures. From what neuroscientist Björn Merker, who has spent much of his career studying the subcortex, has learned about subcortical processing, he is neither confident in the UWS assessment nor happy about the medical treatment spawned by the assumption that these patients have no conscious awareness.

Merker met up with five families at Walt Disney World and spent a week following and observing their children (aged 10 months to 5 years) with hydranencephaly to supplement the limited information currently available in the scientific literature about their behavior. He observed,

> [The children] are not only awake and often alert, but show responsiveness to their surroundings in the form of emotional or orienting reactions to environmental events. . . . They express pleasure by smiling and laughter, and aversion by "fussing," arching of the back and crying (in many gradations), their faces being animated by these emotional states. A familiar adult can employ this responsiveness to build up play sequences predictably progressing from smiling, through giggling, to laughter and great excitement on the part of the child. The children respond differentially to the voice and initiatives of familiars, and show preferences for certain situations and stimuli over others, such as a specific familiar toy, tune, or video program, and apparently can even come to expect their regular presence in the course of recurrent daily routines. (Merker, 2007, p. 79)

From his observations and interactions with these children, Merker concluded that even without a cerebral cortex or the cognition it supplies, they were feeling emotions, were having subjective experiences, and were conscious (**Figure 14.31**). While the contents of their subjective experience are severely restricted, they contain raw emotional feelings and an awareness of their environment that results in emotional responses appropriate to the stimuli presented.

Many have the opinion that these children are experiencing the world not through their subcortical structures, but through the bits of spared cerebral cortex. Countering this argument is that even though the very limited intact and questionably functional cortical regions vary widely from child to child, their behavior is fairly consistent. In addition, their behavior does not match up with the cortical tissue that is present. For example, their hearing is usually preserved even though the auditory tissue is not (as we would expect from what we learned in Chapter 5); however, while some visual cortex is commonly spared, vision tends to be compromised.

Observations of children with hydranencephaly suggest that only subcortical structures are necessary to transform raw neural input into something resembling core emotional feelings. Merker has concluded, along with Panksepp, that consciousness does not require cortical processing. There is no question that cortical processes elaborate and enhance the contents of that subjective experience, but just to have subjective experience, no cortical circuit is necessary.

FIGURE 14.31 Reaction of a child with hydranencephaly to a social situation.
Parents attentively faced their 3-year-old girl with hydranencephaly and placed her baby brother in her arms, helping to support him while photographing.

Over the years, neurologist Antonio Damasio has changed his mind about the necessity for cortical processing in relation to feelings. He and neuroanatomist Hanna Damasio now conclude, "We do not see any evidence in favor of the idea that the engendering of feelings in humans would be confined to the cerebral cortex. On the contrary, based on anatomical and physiological evidence, subcortical structures and even the peripheral and enteric nervous systems appear to make important contributions to the experience of feelings" (A. R. Damasio & Damasio, 2016, p. 3). With a grasp of the contribution of subcortical processing to consciousness, it is easier for us to realize why it is so hard to get rid of the persistent sensation of feelings.

We mentioned in Chapter 10 that subcortical brain areas arose early in the evolutionary process and are anatomically, neurochemically, and functionally homologous in all mammals that have been studied (Panksepp, 2005). If we think of the brain as a layered system, a more primitive form of consciousness would consist of raw emotional feelings and the motivations they engender, unfettered by cortical processing. As brains evolved to become more complex, additional contents and layers of control were added. A layered brain can accommodate this description. This view suggests that although the contents of each species' conscious experience vary, all animals are sentient.

TAKE-HOME MESSAGES

- The physical matter in the macroscopic world that we inhabit operates under a set of fixed, knowable laws. Microscopic objects behave differently from macroscopic objects: They obey quantum mechanical laws, not Newton's laws of classical mechanics.
- Albert Einstein described electrons and photons as both waves and particles. Niels Bohr formulated the principle of complementarity, which argues that quantum objects have complementary properties that cannot both be measured and known at the same time. A single system has two modes of description, and one is not reducible to the other.
- Complementarity, when applied to the mind–brain problem, indicates that we cannot understand the gap between phenomenal experience and the firing of neurons by studying only the latter.
- Howard Pattee argues that complementarity, with its two modes of description, is a prerequisite for all matter that can replicate and evolve; that is, it is an epistemic necessity for life.
- Several lines of evidence suggest that although the cortex provides contents to conscious experience, it is not necessary for sentience.

14.10 Split-Brain Research as a Window Into Conscious Experience

One astonishing quality of split-brain patients is that they are utterly unaware of their special status. Although they have lost the ability to transfer most information between their cerebral hemispheres, that loss has no impact on their overall psychological state. You may still not appreciate how odd this is. Imagine waking up from surgery and seeing only the right half of space, only the right half of the face of the nurse asking how you feel. That is the experience of the left hemisphere, the speaking hemisphere, yet it makes no complaint. Why not?

Consider that people with damage to one or both of their optic nerves do complain about vision loss. The optic nerves carry visual field information to the visual cortex. If an optic nerve is damaged, the damaged part of the nerve ceases to carry that information to the visual cortex. Each part of the visual cortex represents an exact part of the visual world (see Chapter 5). Any portion of the visual cortex that is not receiving input sends a signal reporting the problem, and this signal is experienced consciously by the person, who then complains of a blind spot in the visual field.

If, instead, the visual cortex is damaged, the results are very different. There will still be a blind spot in the visual field, but the patient doesn't complain about it. Why not? When the visual cortex itself is lesioned, it stops functioning. It does not put out a signal that it is not getting information; it puts out no signals at all. Since it was solely responsible for representing visual information from a particular part of space, no other part of the visual cortex signals that information is missing. That part of space ceases to exist for that person's conscious experience. People in this situation do not complain about holes in their visual field, because they do not know they have them. No neurons are signaling that they do.

Similarly, following callosotomy, patients aren't bothered that they have lost the ability to verbalize what is in their left visual field. It is not that they have been warned that such a loss will occur; they do not even comment that it is occurring. No reports at all are coming from the visual cortex in the right hemisphere to the talking left hemisphere. Without information that there even is a left visual field, it ceases to exist for the left hemisphere. Not only does the left hemisphere not miss the right hemisphere and all that it does, but it acts as if the right hemisphere were never there. Meanwhile, the whole conscious experience of the left visual field is now perceived and enjoyed by only the less communicative right hemisphere.

These findings that the loss of huge regions of cortex does not disrupt consciousness have major implications for understanding the role of the brain in conscious experience. They argue against the notion that there is a single consciousness circuit, instead suggesting that any part of the cortex, when supported by subcortical processing, can produce consciousness. And, as suggested by Merker, Panksepp, and Damasio, subcortical processing alone appears to be enough to produce conscious experience with limited contents.

A Proposal: Bubbles, Not a Network

The idea presented here is that consciousness may be a product of hundreds or thousands of specialized systems—that is, modules (Gazzaniga, 2011, 2018). Each of these specialized neural circuits enables the processing and mental representation of specific aspects of conscious experience. For instance, the neural circuits responsible for the itch on your back, your memory of Friday night's date, and your plans for the afternoon are fighting for entry to your consciousness. From moment to moment, different modules win the competition, and the results of this processing bubble into your conscious awareness.

This dynamic, moment-to-moment cacophony of systems constitutes your consciousness. Yet what emerges is not complete chaos. Control layers manage the plethora of independent stimuli and resultant behavior, enhancing some signals and quashing others. You end up with a unified experience in which your consciousness flows smoothly from one thought to the next, linked together by time into a single unified narrative, just as the single frames of a film smoothly join together to tell a story. The interpreter is crafting this narrative. This specialized neural system continually interprets and rationalizes your behavior, emotions, and thoughts after they occur.

Remarkably, this view of consciousness is completely dependent on the existence of the specialized modules. If a particular module is impaired or loses its inputs, it alerts the whole system that something is wrong. In the case when the optic nerve is severed, the patient immediately notices being blinded. But if the module itself is removed, as in the case of cortical blindness, then no warning signal is sent and the specific information usually processed by that specialized system is no longer acknowledged (out of sight, out of mind—so to speak).

Summary

How the physical brain enables our subjective conscious experience remains a great mystery, and we looked at several aspects of consciousness in this chapter. We saw that a level of wakefulness is necessary for consciousness, but consciousness is not necessary for wakefulness. Sleep and wakefulness are regulated by a complex interplay of several neurotransmitters, neuropeptides, and hormones released by subcortical structures. We differentiated our ability to access information from the contents of that information. We can lose all sorts of function throughout the brain, resulting in lost contents or lost access to the contents of our conscious experience, but we remain conscious in the sense that we are sentient. We can even split the brain in half and create two conscious entities with different conscious experiences.

As we learn more and more about neural processing, we are coming to understand that all that we think and do is the result of interactions of cells, matter that is subject to physical laws and interactions. This knowledge has led many to take a deterministic stance and infer that we are along for the ride and have no conscious control over our behavior. Yet the idea that a particular behavior is produced by a particular neuronal circuit was challenged by researchers after Eve Marder found that many different neural tunings can produce the same behavior—a phenomenon known as multiple realizability.

The brain should be viewed as a complex system with multiple levels of organization, ranging from neurons to mental states to brains interacting with other brains. Determinists frequently mix up their organizational layers and reason that the laws governing the behavior of neurons are the same as those governing the higher layers. Meanwhile, out of the quantum world came Niels Bohr's principle of complementarity, the idea that a system may have two simultaneous descriptions, one not reducible to the other.

We entertained Howard Pattee's speculation that the gap between our subjective experience and the physical mechanisms of the brain is intrinsic to life itself. He argues that at the very origin of biology, the very first living hunk of matter was a system with two irreducible descriptions made up of hereditary records (genotype) and objective physical constructions of what those records described (phenotype). Pattee suggests that this early gap has been conserved throughout evolution and is present in the gap between the subjective mind and the physical brain. Whether Pattee is correct or not, the physical mechanisms involved in closing this gap are the challenge for future neuroscientists. If we don't start trying to understand the different layers of brain organization and how they interact, we may never get a handle on consciousness.

Key Terms

Think About It

1. What are the implications of the findings that mental states can affect neural states?
2. In what way does the principle of complementarity apply to the great philosophical debates: random versus predictable, experience versus observation, individual versus group, nurture versus nature, and mind versus brain?
3. Does knowing the structure of the brain tell us anything about how it functions? Explain.
4. Because individuals with blindsight have deficits in visual awareness, they are often held up as archetypal cases for consciousness investigations. What is wrong with this approach? Can studying nonconscious processing in the damaged brain really tell us anything about consciousness in the intact, healthy brain? Explain your answer.

Suggested Reading

Churchland, P. (1988). *Matter and consciousness.* Cambridge, MA: MIT Press.

Damasio, A. R. (2010). *Self comes to mind: Constructing the conscious brain.* New York: Pantheon.

Dennett, D. C. (1991). *Consciousness explained.* Boston: Little, Brown.

Feynman, R. (1964, November 18). *Probability and uncertainty: The quantum mechanical view of nature* [The character of physical law, No. 6]. Lecture, Cornell University, Ithaca, NY. Retrieved from http://www.cornell.edu/video/richard-feynman-messenger-lecture-6-probability-uncertainty-quantum-mechanical-view-nature

Gazzaniga, M. S. (2018). *The consciousness instinct: Unraveling the mystery of how the brain makes the mind.* New York: Farrar, Straus and Giroux.

Koch, C. (2004). *The quest for consciousness: A neurobiological approach.* Englewood, CO: Roberts.

Koch, C. (2012). *Consciousness: Confessions of a romantic reductionist.* Cambridge, MA: MIT Press.

Makari, G. (2015) *Soul machine: The invention of the modern mind.* New York: Norton.

Pattee, H. H., & Rączaszek-Leonardi, J. (2012). *Laws, language and life.* Dordrecht, Netherlands: Springer.

Premack, D., and Woodruff, G. (1978). Does the chimpanzee have a theory of mind? *Behavioral and Brain Sciences, 1,* 515–526.

Glossary

A

A1 See *primary auditory cortex.* (Ch. 5)

ACC See *anterior cingulate cortex.* (Ch. 12)

achromatopsia A selective disorder of color perception resulting from a lesion or lesions of the central nervous system, typically in the ventral pathway of the visual cortex. In achromatopsia, the deficit in color perception is disproportionately greater than that associated with form perception. Colors, if perceived at all, tend to be muted. (Ch. 5)

acquired alexia See *alexia.* (Ch. 6, 11)

acquisition The first step of memory encoding in which sensory stimuli are acquired by short-term memory. (Ch. 9)

action–outcome decision A decision that involves some form of evaluation (not necessarily conscious) of the expected outcomes. Compare *stimulus–response decision.* (Ch. 12)

action potential The active or regenerative electrical signal that is required for synaptic communication. Action potentials are propagated along the axon and result in the release of neurotransmitters. (Ch. 2)

acuity The capacity to accurately discriminate fine detail. (Ch. 5)

adaptation In perception, adjustments to the sensitivity of a sensory system to the current environment and to important changes in the environment. In physiology, the reduction in firing rate that typically occurs in the sensory system when a stimulus is continuously present. (Ch. 5)

affect Either a discrete emotion that has a relatively short duration or a more diffuse, longer-lasting state such as stress or mood. (Ch. 10)

affective flexibility The ability to process the relevance of various emotional stimuli, depending on one's current goals and motivation. (Ch. 10)

aggregate field theory The theory that all individual mental functions are performed by the brain as a whole, not by discrete parts. (Ch. 1)

agnosia A neurological syndrome in which disturbances of perceptual recognition cannot be attributed to impairments in basic sensory processes. Agnosia can be restricted to a single modality, such as vision or audition. (Ch. 6)

agrammatic aphasia Difficulty producing and/or understanding the structure of sentences. Agrammatic aphasia is seen in brain-damaged patients who may speak using only content words, leaving out function words such as *the* and *a.* (Ch. 11)

akinesia The absence of voluntary movement. Compare *bradykinesia*, *hyperkinesia*, and *hypokinesia.* (Ch. 8)

akinetopsia A selective disorder of motion perception resulting from a lesion or lesions of the central nervous system. Patients with akinetopsia fail to perceive stimulus movement, created by either a moving object or their own motion, in a smooth manner. In severe cases, the patient may only infer motion by noting that the position of objects in the environment has changed over time, as if the patient were constructing dynamics through a series of successive static snapshots. (Ch. 5)

alexia A neurological syndrome in which the ability to read is disrupted. Alexia is frequently referred to as *acquired alexia* to indicate that it results from a neurological disturbance such as a stroke, usually including the occipitoparietal region of the left hemisphere. In contrast, *developmental alexia* (dyslexia) refers to problems in reading that are apparent during childhood development. The phrases *acquired alexia* and *developmental alexia* are commonly used to indicate that reading is abnormal, either from a neurological disturbance or as part of development. (Ch. 6, 11)

alpha motor neurons The neurons that terminate on muscle fibers, causing contractions that produce movements. Alpha motor neurons originate in the spinal cord and exit through the ventral root of the cord. (Ch. 8)

amnesia Deficits in learning and memory ability following brain damage or disease. (Ch. 9)

amygdala (pl. amygdalae) A collection of neurons anterior to the hippocampus in the medial temporal lobe that is involved in emotional processing. (Ch. 2, 10)

anomia A type of aphasia in which the person has difficulty generating the words used to label things in the world. (Ch. 11)

anterior aphasia See *Broca's aphasia.* (Ch. 11)

anterior cingulate cortex (ACC) The anterior portion of the cingulate cortex, located below the frontal lobe along the medial surface. This region is characterized by a primitive cellular architecture (three-layered cortex) and is part of the interface between the frontal lobe and the limbic system. The ACC is implicated in various types of cognitive control, such as response monitoring, error detection, and attention. (Ch. 12)

anterior commissure The nerve bundle connecting the left and right cerebral hemispheres that is located anterior to the corpus callosum. Compare *posterior commissure.* (Ch. 4)

anterograde amnesia The loss of the ability to form new memories. Compare *retrograde amnesia.* (Ch. 9)

AP See *autoscopic phenomenon.* (Ch. 13)

aphasia A language deficit following brain damage or disease. (Ch. 11)

apperceptive visual agnosia A form of agnosia associated with deficits in the operation of higher-level perceptual analyses. A patient with apperceptive agnosia may recognize an object when seen from a typical viewpoint. But if the orientation is unusual, or the object is occluded by shadows, recognition deteriorates. Compare *associative visual agnosia* and *integrative visual agnosia.* (Ch. 6)

apraxia 1. A neurological syndrome characterized by loss of skilled or purposeful movement that cannot be attributed to weakness or an inability to innervate the muscles. Apraxia results from lesions of the cerebral cortex, usually in the left hemisphere. (Ch. 8) 2. Difficulty pronouncing words. (Ch. 11)

architecture The organizational structure of a system. (Ch. 14)

arcuate fasciculus A white matter tract that connects the posterior temporal region with frontal brain regions and is believed to transmit language-related information between the posterior and anterior brain regions. (Ch. 11)

area MT Also *area V5.* A region in the visual cortex containing cells that are highly responsive to motion. Area MT is part of the dorsal pathway, thought to play a role not only in motion perception but also in representing spatial information. (Ch. 5)

area V4 A region in the visual cortex containing cells that are thought to process color information. (Ch. 5)

area V5 See *area MT.* (Ch. 5)

arousal The global physiological and psychological state of an organism, ranging from deep sleep to hyperalertness. Compare *selective attention.* (Ch. 7)

ASD See *autism spectrum disorder.* (Ch. 13)

association cortex The volume of the neocortex that is not strictly sensory or motor, but receives inputs from multiple sensorimotor modalities. (Ch. 2)

associationism The theory that the aggregate of a person's experience determines the course of mental development. (Ch. 1)

associative visual agnosia A form of agnosia associated with deficits in the ability to link perceptual representations with long-term knowledge of the percepts. For example, the patient may be able to identify that two pictures are of the same object, yet fail to demonstrate an understanding of what the object is used for or where it is likely to be found. Compare *apperceptive visual agnosia* and *integrative visual agnosia.* (Ch. 6)

ataxia A movement disorder associated with lesions or atrophy of the cerebellum. Ataxic movements are clumsy and erratic, even though muscle strength is normal. (Ch. 8)

attentional blink A phenomenon often observed during rapid serial presentations of visual stimuli, in which a second salient target that is presented between 150 and 450 ms after the first one goes undetected. (Ch. 10)

auditory nerve See *cochlear nerve.* (Ch. 5)

autism spectrum disorder (ASD) A group of neurodevelopmental disorders that include autism, Asperger's syndrome, childhood disintegrative disorder, and pervasive developmental disorders not otherwise specified. These disorders are characterized by deficits in social cognition and social communication often associated with an increase in repetitive behavior or obsessive interests. (Ch. 13)

autonomic motor system See *autonomic nervous system.* (Ch. 2)

autonomic nervous system Also *autonomic motor system* or *visceral motor system.* The body system that regulates heart rate, breathing, and glandular secretions and may become activated during emotional arousal, initiating a fight-or-flight behavioral response to a stimulus. It has two subdivisions, the sympathetic and parasympathetic branches. (Ch. 2)

autoscopic phenomenon (AP) A visual body illusion that affects the entire body. Out-of-body experiences, autoscopic hallucinations, and heautoscopy are three times of APs. (Ch. 13)

axon The process extending away from a neuron down which action potentials travel. The terminals of axons contact other neurons at synapses. (Ch. 2)

axon collaterals Branches off an axon that can transmit signals to more than one cell. (Ch. 2)

axon hillock A part of the cell body of a neuron where the membrane potentials are summed before being transmitted down the axon. (Ch. 2)

B

basal ganglia A collection of five subcortical nuclei: the caudate, putamen, globus pallidus, subthalamic nucleus, and substantia nigra. The basal ganglia are involved in motor control and learning. Reciprocal neuronal loops project from cortical areas to the basal ganglia and back to the cortex. Two prominent basal ganglia disorders are Parkinson's disease and Huntington's disease. (Ch. 2, 8)

basic emotion An emotion with unique characteristics, carved by evolution, and reflected through facial expressions. Compare *complex emotion.* (Ch. 10)

BBB See *blood–brain barrier.* (Ch. 2)

behaviorism The theory that environment and learning are the primary factors in mental development, and that people should be studied by outside observation. (Ch. 1)

BIID See *xenomelia.* (Ch. 13)

binocular rivalry A phenomenon that occurs when each eye sees a different image simultaneously. A single image is perceived and then, after a few seconds, perception switches to the other image. The neural inputs to each eye appear to vie for dominance, presumably entailing a competition between excitatory and inhibitory processes in the visual cortex. (Ch. 3)

blindsight Residual visual abilities within a field defect in the absence of awareness. Blindsight can be observed when there is damage in the primary visual cortex. The residual function is usually observed with indirect measures such as by prodding the patient to look at or point to the location of a stimulus, even if the patient denies having seen the stimulus. (Ch. 14)

block design An experimental design used in PET and less commonly with fMRI studies. A block consists of multiple trials of the same type. The activity across the block is averaged and can be compared to activity in another block of a different type of trial. Compare *event-related design.* (Ch. 3)

blood–brain barrier (BBB) A physical barrier formed by the end feet of astrocytes between the blood vessels in the brain and the tissues of the brain. The BBB limits which materials in the blood can gain access to neurons in the nervous system. (Ch. 2)

blood oxygen level–dependent (BOLD) Referring to a change in the magnetic resonance (MR) signal intensity of the hydrogen ion concentration in the brain, which results from changes in the local tissue oxygenation state. Increased neural activity triggers an increase in the amount of oxygenated blood entering local capillaries in the tissue, thus altering the ratio of oxygenated to deoxygenated hemoglobin in the tissue. Because deoxygenated hemoglobin is paramagnetic, it disrupts the local magnetic properties of the tissue, and the MR signal intensity drops. Conversely, when oxygenated blood increases in response to local neuron activity, the MR signal intensity increases, and this is known as the BOLD response. The BOLD signal is an indirect measure of neural activity and is delayed with respect to the neural activity that leads to the BOLD signal, taking about 2–3 seconds to begin, and about 5–6 seconds after the onset of neural activity to peak. (Ch. 3)

BMI See *brain–machine interface.* (Ch. 8)

body integrity identity disorder (BIID) See *xenomelia.* (Ch. 13)

BOLD See *blood oxygen level–dependent.* (Ch. 3)

bottleneck A stage of information processing where not all of the inputs can gain access or pass through. (Ch. 7)

bradykinesia Slowness in the initiation and execution of movements. Bradykinesia is a prominent symptom in Parkinson's disease. Compare *akinesia*, *hyperkinesia*, and *hypokinesia.* (Ch. 8)

brain–machine interface (BMI) A device that uses the interpretation of neuronal signals to perform desired operations with a mechanical device outside the body. For instance, signals recorded from neurons or EEG can be used to move a prosthetic arm. (Ch. 8)

brainstem The region of the nervous system that contains groups of motor and sensory nuclei, nuclei of widespread modulatory neurotransmitter systems, and white matter tracts of ascending sensory information and descending motor signals. (Ch. 2)

Broca's aphasia Also *anterior aphasia*, *expressive aphasia*, and *nonfluent aphasia.* The oldest and perhaps best-studied form of aphasia, characterized by speech difficulties in the absence of severe comprehension problems. However, Broca's aphasics may also suffer from problems in fully comprehending grammatically complex sentences. Compare *Wernicke's aphasia.* (Ch. 11)

Broca's area An area located in the left hemisphere of the frontal cortex, identified by Paul Broca in the 19th century, that is important to language production. Compare *Wernicke's area.* (Ch. 11)

C

CAT See *computerized tomography.* (Ch. 3)

cellular architecture See *cytoarchitectonics.* (Ch. 1, 2)

central nervous system (CNS) The brain and spinal cord. Compare *peripheral nervous system.* (Ch. 2)

central pattern generator A neural network limited to the spinal cord that produces patterned motor outputs without descending commands from the cerebral cortex or sensory feedback. (Ch. 8)

central sulcus The deep fold or fissure between the frontal and parietal lobes that separates the primary motor cortex from the primary somatosensory cortex. (Ch. 2)

cerebellum Literally, "small cerebrum" or "little brain." A large, highly convoluted (infolded) structure located dorsal to the brainstem at the level of the pons. The cerebellum maintains (directly or indirectly) interconnectivity with widespread cortical, subcortical, brainstem, and spinal cord structures, and plays a role in various aspects of coordination ranging from locomotion to skilled, volitional movement. (Ch. 2, 8)

cerebral cortex The layered sheet of neurons that overlies the forebrain. The cerebral cortex consists of neuronal subdivisions (areas) interconnected with other cortical areas, subcortical structures, and the cerebellum and spinal cortex. (Ch. 2)

cerebral specialization The adaptation of the activity in a particular brain region to subserve a given cognitive function or behavior. (Ch. 4)

cerebral vascular accident Stroke, a sudden loss of blood supply to the brain caused by an arterial occlusion or rupture, resulting in cell death and loss of brain function. (Ch. 3)

chemical senses The two senses that depend on environmental molecules for stimulation: taste and smell. (Ch. 5)

classical conditioning Also *Pavlovian conditioning.* A type of associative learning in which a conditioned stimulus (an otherwise neutral stimulus to the organism) is paired with an unconditioned stimulus (one that elicits an established response from the organism) and becomes associated with it. The conditioned stimulus will then evoke a conditioned response similar to that typically evoked by the unconditioned stimulus (the unconditioned response). Compare *nonassociative learning.* (Ch. 9)

CM neurons See *corticomotoneurons.* (Ch. 8)

CNS See *central nervous system.* (Ch. 2)

cochlear nerve Also *auditory nerve.* A branch of the vestibulocochlear nerve (8th cranial nerve) that carries auditory information from synapses with hair cells of the cochlea to the cochlear nucleus in the brainstem. (Ch. 5)

cochlear nuclei Nuclei in the medulla where the cochlear nerve synapses. (Ch. 5)

cognitive control Also *executive function.* Processes that facilitate information processing. Control operations are thought to help coordinate activity across different neural regions; for example, the representation of a current goal in the prefrontal cortex can help control the retrieval of information in long-term memory. (Ch. 12)

cognitive neuroscience The study of how the brain enables the mind. (Ch. 1)

cognitive psychology The branch of psychology that studies how the mind internally represents the external world and performs the mental computations required for all aspects of thinking. Cognitive psychologists study the vast set of mental operations associated with such things as perception, attention, memory, language, and problem solving. (Ch. 3)

commissures White matter tracts that cross from the left to the right side, or vice versa, of the central nervous system. The corpus callosum is the largest commissure in the brain. See also *anterior commissure* and *posterior commissure.* (Ch. 2, 4)

complex emotion A combination of basic emotions that can be identified as an evolved, long-lasting feeling. Some complex emotions may be socially or culturally learned. Compare *basic emotion.* (Ch. 10)

complex system Any system that has a large number of interconnected and interacting components. (Ch. 14)

computerized tomography (CT or CAT) A noninvasive neuroimaging method that provides images of internal structures such as the brain. CT is an advanced version of the conventional X-ray. Whereas conventional X-rays compress three-dimensional objects into two dimensions, CT allows for the reconstruction of three-dimensional space from compressed two-dimensional images through computer algorithms. (Ch. 3)

conduction aphasia A form of aphasia that is considered a disconnection syndrome. Conduction aphasia may occur when the arcuate fasciculus, the pathway from Wernicke's area to Broca's area, is damaged, thereby disconnecting the posterior and anterior language areas. (Ch. 11)

cones Photoreceptors that are concentrated in the fovea, providing high acuity but requiring higher levels of light than *rods* require to activate. Cones can replenish their pigments more quickly than rods can, and thus provide better daylight vision. There are three types of cones, each type sensitive to light of specific wavelengths, mediating color vision. (Ch. 5)

connectivity map Also *connectome.* A visualization of structural or functional connections within the brain. (Ch. 3)

connectome See *connectivity map.* (Ch. 3)

consciousness The ability to be aware of some of the contents of mental activity. (Ch. 14)

consolidation The process by which memory representations become stronger over time. Consolidation is believed to include changes in the brain system participating in the storage of information. (Ch. 9)

core emotional system Also *primary process.* Any of seven circuits, proposed by Jaak Panksepp, common to all higher animals, that generate both emotional actions and specific autonomic changes that support those actions. (Ch. 10)

corpus callosum A fiber system composed of axons that connect the cortex of the two cerebral hemispheres. It is the largest white matter structure in the brain. (Ch. 2, 4)

cortical plasticity The capacity of the brain to reorganize itself anatomically and functionally. (Ch. 5)

cortical visual areas Regions of visual cortex that are identified on the basis of their distinct retinotopic maps. The areas are specialized to represent certain types of stimulus information, and through their integrated activity they provide the neural basis for visually based behavior. See also *extrastriate visual areas.* (Ch. 5)

corticomotoneurons (CM neurons) Specialized corticospinal neurons with axons that terminate directly on spinal motor neurons. Most are located in the primary motor cortex. (Ch. 8)

corticospinal tract (CST) Also *pyramidal tract.* A bundle of axons that originate in the cortex and terminate monosynaptically on alpha motor neurons and spinal interneurons in the spinal cord. Many of these fibers originate in the primary motor cortex, although some come from secondary motor areas. The corticospinal tract is important for the control of voluntary movements. Compare *extrapyramidal tracts.* (Ch. 8)

covert attention Directing attention without overtly changing sensory receptors—for example, attending to a conversation without turning the eyes and head toward the speakers. Compare *overt attention.* (Ch. 7)

CST See *corticospinal tract.* (Ch. 8)

CT See *computerized tomography.* (Ch. 3)

cytoarchitectonics Also *cellular architecture.* The study of the cellular composition of structures in the body. (Ch. 1, 2)

D

DA See *dopamine.* (Ch. 12)

DBS See *deep brain stimulation.* (Ch. 3, 8)

declarative memory Also *explicit memory.* Knowledge to which we have conscious access, including personal and world knowledge (events and facts). The term *declarative* signals the idea that declarations can be made about this knowledge and that, for the most part, we are aware that we possess the information. Compare *nondeclarative memory.* (Ch. 9)

decremental conduction See *electrotonic conduction.* (Ch. 2)

deep brain stimulation (DBS) The electrical stimulation of brain structures via an implanted electrode. Stimulation of the subthalamic nucleus, one of the nuclei of the basal ganglia, is used as a treatment for Parkinson's disease. (Ch. 3, 8)

default network A network of brain areas that is active when a person is at wakeful rest and not engaged with the outside world. (Ch. 13)

degenerative disorder A disorder or disease, either genetic or environmental, in which the function or structure of the affected tissues will continue to deteriorate over time. (Ch. 3)

delayed-response task A task in which the correct response must be produced after a delay period of several seconds. Such tasks require the operation of working memory because the animal or person must maintain a record of the stimulus information during the delay period. (Ch. 12)

dementia A loss of cognitive function in different domains (including memory) beyond what is expected in normal aging. (Ch. 9)

dendrites Large treelike processes of neurons that receive inputs from other neurons at locations called synapses. (Ch. 2)

dependent variable The variable in an experiment that is being evaluated by the researcher. Compare *independent variable.* (Ch. 3)

depolarization A change in the membrane potential in which the electrical current inside the cell becomes less negative. With respect to the resting potential, a depolarized membrane potential is closer to the firing threshold. Compare *hyperpolarization.* (Ch. 2)

descriptive decision theory A theory that attempts to describe what people actually do, not what they should do. Compare *normative decision theory.* (Ch. 12)

determinism The philosophical belief that all current and future events and actions, including human cognition, decisions, and behavior, are caused by preceding events combined with the laws of nature. (Ch. 14)

developmental alexia See *alexia.* (Ch. 6, 11)

dichotic listening task An auditory task in which two competing messages are presented simultaneously, one to each ear, while the participant tries to report only one or both messages. The ipsilateral projections from each ear are presumably suppressed when a message comes over the contralateral pathway from the other ear. (Ch. 4)

diffusion tensor imaging (DTI) A neuroimaging technique employed using an MRI scanner that allows white matter pathways in the brain to be imaged. (Ch. 3)

dimensional theories of emotion Theories that describe emotions that are fundamentally the same but differ along one or more dimensions, such as valence (pleasant to unpleasant, positive to negative) and arousal (very intense to very mild). (Ch. 10)

dopamine (DA) An organic chemical amine that in the brain functions as a neurotransmitter. It is formed from L-dopa by removal of a carboxyl group. (Ch. 12)

dorsal attention network A proposed attention control network, involving dorsal frontal and parietal cortical regions, that mediates voluntary attention. Compare *ventral attention network.* (Ch. 7)

dorsal stream Also *occipitoparietal stream.* A processing pathway for visual stimuli that is specialized for spatial perception (for determining where an object is) and for analyzing the spatial configuration between different objects in a scene. Compare *ventral stream.* (Ch. 6)

double dissociation A method used to develop functional models of mental and/or neural processes. Evidence of a double dissociation requires a minimum of two groups and two tasks. In neuropsychological research, a double dissociation is present when one group is impaired on one task and the other group is impaired on the other task. In imaging research, a double dissociation is present when one experimental manipulation produces changes in activation in one neural region and a different manipulation produces changes in activation in a different neural region. Double dissociations provide a strong argument that the observed differences in performance reflect functional differences between the groups, rather than unequal sensitivity of the two tasks. Compare *single dissociation.* (Ch. 3)

DTI See *diffusion tensor imaging.* (Ch. 3)

dualism A major philosophical approach to describing consciousness, which holds that the mind and brain are two separate phenomena. (Ch. 14)

dynamic filtering The hypothesis that a key component of working memory involves the selection of information that is most relevant, given current task demands. This selection is thought to be accomplished through the filtering of, or exclusion of, potentially interfering and irrelevant information. (Ch. 12)

dysarthria Difficulty saying words. (Ch. 11)

dyslexia See *alexia.* (Ch. 6, 11)

E

early selection The theoretical model positing that attention can attenuate or filter out sensory input at early stages of processing before perceptual analysis is complete and the information has been encoded. Compare *late selection.* (Ch. 7)

EBA See *extrastriate body area.* (Ch. 6)

echoic memory See *sensory memory.* (Ch. 9)

ECoG See *electrocorticography.* (Ch. 3)

EEG See *electroencephalography.* (Ch. 3)

effector Any part of the body that can move, such as an arm, finger, or leg. (Ch. 8)

electrical gradient A force that develops when a charge distribution across the neuronal membrane develops such that the charge inside is more positive or negative than the one outside. Electrical gradients result from asymmetrical distributions of ions across the membrane. (Ch. 2)

electrocorticography (ECoG) A technique to measure the electrical activity of the cerebral cortex. In ECoG, electrodes are placed directly on the surface of the brain, either outside the dura or beneath it. Compare *electroencephalography.* (Ch. 3)

electroencephalography (EEG) A technique to measure the electrical activity of the brain. In EEG, surface recordings are made from electrodes placed on the scalp. The EEG signal includes endogenous changes in electrical activity (e.g., due to changes in arousal), as well as changes triggered by specific events (e.g., stimuli or movements). Compare *electrocorticography.* (Ch. 3)

electrotonic conduction Also *decremental conduction.* Ionic current that flows passively through the cytoplasm and across the membrane of an activated neuron that diminishes with distance from the site of generation. (Ch. 2)

embodiment The feeling of spatial unity between the "self" and the body. (Ch. 13)

emotion An affective (positive or negative) mental response to a stimulus that is composed of a physiological response, a behavioral response, and a feeling (e.g., change in heart rate, jumping back, and feeling scared). (Ch. 10)

emotion generation An unagreed-upon set of processes that may or may not combine an automatic bottom-up response with a top-down response, which involves memory and/or linguistic representations. (Ch. 10)

emotion regulation Voluntary and involuntary processes deployed to manage and respond to emotions. (Ch. 10)

empathic accuracy The ability to accurately infer the thoughts, feelings, and/or emotional state of another person. (Ch. 13)

empathy The ability to experience and understand what others feel while still knowing the difference between oneself and others. Empathy is often described as the ability to "put oneself in another person's shoes." (Ch. 13)

empiricism The idea that all knowledge comes from sensory experience. Compare *rationalism.* (Ch. 1)

encoding The processing of incoming information to be stored. Encoding consists of two stages: acquisition and consolidation. Compare *retrieval.* (Ch. 9)

endogenous attention See *voluntary attention.* (Ch. 7)

endogenous cuing An experimental method that uses a symbolic cue (e.g., arrow) to induce or instruct participants to voluntarily (i.e., endogenously) direct attention according to task requirements. Compare *reflexive cuing.* (Ch. 7)

endpoint control A hypothesis concerning how movements are planned in terms of the desired final location. Endpoint control models emphasize that the motor representation is based on the final position required of the limbs to achieve the movement goal. (Ch. 8)

episodic memory A form of declarative memory that stores autobiographical information about events in one's life, including contextual information about those with whom they happened, and when, where, and why they happened. Compare *semantic memory.* (Ch. 9)

equilibrium potential The membrane potential at which a given ion (e.g., K^+) has no net flux across the membrane—that is, the point where the numbers of ions moving outward and inward across the membrane are the same. (Ch. 2)

ERN See *error-related negativity.* (Ch. 12)

ERP See *event-related potential.* (Ch. 3)

error-related negativity (ERN) An electrophysiological signal correlated with the occurrence of errors. It is derived from the EEG record following an erroneous response and is seen as a prominent negative deflection in the ERP that is time-locked to the response. It is hypothesized to originate in the anterior cingulate. Compare *feedback-related negativity.* (Ch. 12)

event-related design An experimental design, used in fMRI studies, in which different types of trials may occur randomly. The BOLD response to particular stimuli or responses can be extracted from signal data. Compare *block design.* (Ch. 3)

event-related potential (ERP) A change in electrical activity that is time-locked to specific events, such as the presentation of a stimulus or the onset of a response, embedded within an EEG recording. When the events are repeated many times, averaging the EEG signals reveals the relatively small changes in neural activity triggered by these events. In this manner, the background fluctuations in the EEG signal are removed, revealing the event-related signal with great temporal resolution. (Ch. 3)

executive function See *cognitive control.* (Ch. 12)

exogenous attention See *reflexive attention.* (Ch. 7)

exogenous cuing See *reflexive cuing.* (Ch. 7)

experience sharing theory Originally called *simulation theory.* A theory proposing that we do not need to have an elaborate theory about the mind of others in order to infer their thoughts or predict their actions. We simply observe someone else's behavior, simulate it, and use our own mental state produced by that simulation to predict the mental state of the other. Compare *mental state attribution theory.* (Ch. 13)

explicit memory See *declarative memory.* (Ch. 9)

expressive aphasia See *Broca's aphasia.* (Ch. 11)

extinction 1. In a patient with neglect, the failure to perceive or respond to a stimulus contralateral to a lesion when presented with a simultaneous stimulus ipsilateral to the lesion (ipsilesional). (Ch. 7) 2. The disappearance of a conditioned response when it is no longer rewarded. (Ch. 10)

extrapyramidal tracts A collection of motor tracts that originate in various subcortical structures, including the vestibular nucleus and the red nucleus. These tracts are especially important for maintaining posture and balance. Compare *corticospinal tract.* (Ch. 8)

extrastriate body area (EBA) A functionally defined area in the lateral occipitotemporal cortex that shows a stronger response to images containing body parts relative to other animate and inanimate stimulus categories. Compare *fusiform body area.* (Ch. 6)

extrastriate visual areas A subdivision of cortical visual areas that lie outside the striate cortex (Brodmann area 17, the primary visual cortex) and are considered secondary visual areas because they receive input either directly or indirectly from the primary visual cortex. (Ch. 5)

F

facial expression The nonverbal communication of emotion by the manipulation of particular groups of facial muscles. Research findings suggest that six basic human facial expressions represent the emotional states anger, fear, disgust, happiness, sadness, and surprise. (Ch. 10)

false-belief task A task that measures the ability to attribute false beliefs to others. (Ch. 13)

FBA See *fusiform body area.* (Ch. 6)

fear conditioning Learning in which a neutral stimulus acquires aversive properties by virtue of being paired with an aversive event. (Ch. 10)

feature integration theory of attention A psychological theory of visual perception based on the idea that the visual system can process in parallel elementary features such as color, shape, and motion, but requires spatial attention to bind the features that define an object. (Ch. 7)

feedback-related negativity (FRN) An electrophysiological signal correlated with the occurrence of errors. It is derived from the EEG record following an erroneous response and is seen as a prominent negative deflection in the ERP that is time-locked to feedback. It is hypothesized to originate in the anterior cingulate. Compare *error-related negativity.* (Ch. 12)

feeling Either the sensation of touch or the conscious sensation of an emotion. (Ch. 10)

FFA See *fusiform face area.* (Ch. 6)

fissure See *sulcus.* (Ch. 2)

flow As described by psychologist Mihaly Csikszentmihalyi, the enjoyable state of being "in the zone." He suggests that people are really happy when totally immersed in a challenging task that closely matches their abilities. (Ch. 10)

fMRI See *functional magnetic resonance imaging.* (Ch. 3)

fNIRS See *functional near-infrared spectroscopy.* (Ch. 6)

forward model The idea that the brain generates predictions of expected events. In motor control, the prediction of the expected sensory consequences of a movement. (Ch. 8)

fovea The central region of the retina that is densely packed with cone cells and provides high-resolution visual information. (Ch. 5)

FP See *frontal pole.* (Ch. 12)

free nerve endings See *nociceptors.* (Ch. 5)

FRN See *feedback-related negativity.* (Ch. 12)

frontal lobe The mass of cortex anterior to the central sulcus and dorsal to the Sylvian fissure. The frontal lobe contains two principal regions—the motor cortex and the prefrontal cortex—each of which can be further subdivided into specific areas both architectonically and functionally. (Ch. 2)

frontal pole (FP) The most anterior part of the prefrontal cortex, including area 10 and parts of area 9. This region is hypothesized to play a critical role in the hierarchical representation of action goals. (Ch. 12)

functional asymmetries Differences in the functions that each hemisphere subserves. (Ch. 4)

functional magnetic resonance imaging (fMRI) A neuroimaging method that utilizes MRI to track blood flow changes in the brain that are thought to be correlated with local changes in neural activity. (Ch. 3)

functional near-infrared spectroscopy (fNIRS) A noninvasive neuroimaging technique that measures near-infrared light absorbance in oxygenated and deoxygenated hemoglobin, providing information about ongoing brain activity similar to functional MRI studies. (Ch. 6)

fusiform body area (FBA) A functionally defined area in the lateral occipitotemporal cortex, adjacent to and partially overlapping the fusiform face area, that shows a stronger response to images containing body parts relative to other animate and inanimate stimulus categories. Compare *extrastriate body area.* (Ch. 6)

fusiform face area (FFA) A functionally defined area of the brain, located in the ventral surface of the temporal lobe in the fusiform gyrus, that responds to selective stimuli, such as faces. Compare *parahippocampal place area.* (Ch. 6)

G

ganglion cell A type of neuron in the retina. Ganglion cells receive input from the photoreceptors (rods and cones) and intermediate cells of the retina and send axons to the thalamus and other subcortical structures. (Ch. 5)

glial cell One of two cell types (along with the *neuron*) in the nervous system. Glial cells are more numerous than neurons, by perhaps a factor of 10, and may account for more than half of the brain's volume. They typically do not conduct signals themselves; but without them, the functionality of neurons would be severely diminished. Tissue made of glial cells is termed *glia.* (Ch. 2)

glomeruli (s. glomerulus) The neurons of the olfactory bulb. (Ch. 5)

gnostic unit A neuron or small set of neurons tuned for a specific percept (e.g., an apple). The concept of the gnostic unit is based on the idea that hierarchical models of perception imply that, at higher levels in the system, neurons become much more selective in terms of what they respond to. (Ch. 6)

goal-oriented action An action that is planned and produced to achieve a particular result. Goal-oriented actions stand in contrast to more habitually or stimulus driven behavior and are strongly under the control of reinforcement. Compare *habit.* (Ch. 12)

goal-oriented behavior Behavior that enables us to interact in the world in a purposeful manner. Goals reflect the intersection of our internal desires and drives, coupled with the current environmental context. (Ch. 12)

gray matter Regions of the nervous system that contain primarily neuronal cell bodies. Gray matter includes the cerebral cortex, the basal ganglia, and the nuclei of the thalamus. Gray matter is so called because, in preservative solution, these structures look gray in comparison to the *white matter* where myelinated axons are found (which look more white). (Ch. 2)

gyrus (pl. gyri) A protruding rounded surface of the cerebral cortex that one can see upon gross anatomical viewing of the intact brain. Compare *sulcus.* (Ch. 2)

H

habit A response that is under stimulus control. Habits are formally defined as behaviors that occur independently of reinforcement. For example, if the reward is no longer given to a stimulus, the persistent response is referred to as a habit. Compare *goal-oriented action.* (Ch. 12)

handedness The tendency to perform the majority of one's manual actions with either the right or left hand. (Ch. 4)

Hebbian learning Donald Hebb's theory of learning, which proposes that the mechanism underlying learning is the strengthening of synaptic connections that results when a weak input and a strong input act on a cell at the same time. (Ch. 9)

hemiplegia A neurological condition characterized by the loss of voluntary movements on one side of the body. Hemiplegia typically results from damage to the corticospinal tract, either from lesions to the motor cortex or from white matter lesions that destroy the descending fibers. (Ch. 8)

hemodynamic response A change in blood flow to neural tissues. Hemodynamic responses can be detected by PET and fMRI. (Ch. 3)

heterotopic areas Noncorresponding areas of the brain. Usually such areas are referred to as *heterotopic* because of their connections with one another. For instance, a connection between M1 on the left side and V2 on the right side joins heterotopic areas. Compare *homotopic areas.* (Ch. 4)

heterotopic connections Connections from one region that travel within the corpus callosum to a different region in the opposite hemisphere. Compare *homotopic connections.* (Ch. 4)

hierarchical structure A configuration that may be described at multiple levels, from global features to local features; the finer components are embedded within the higher-level components. (Ch. 4)

hippocampus (pl. hippocampi) A layered structure in the medial temporal lobe that receives inputs from wide regions of the cortex via inputs from the surrounding regions of the temporal lobe, and sends projections out to subcortical targets. The hippocampus is involved in learning and memory, particularly memory for spatial locations in mammals and episodic memory in humans. (Ch. 2, 9)

holistic processing Perceptual analysis that emphasizes the overall shape of an object. Face perception has been hypothesized to be the best example of holistic processing, in that the recognition of an individual appears to reflect the composition of the person's facial features rather than being based on the recognition of the individual features. (Ch. 6)

homotopic areas Areas in corresponding locations in the two hemispheres. A connection between M1 on the right side and M1 on the left side joins homotopic areas. Compare *heterotopic areas.* (Ch. 4)

homotopic connections Connections from one region that travel within the corpus callosum to a corresponding region in the opposite hemisphere. Compare *heterotopic connections.* (Ch. 4)

homunculus See *primary somatosensory cortex.* (Ch. 5)

Huntington's disease A genetic degenerative disorder in which the primary pathology, at least in the early stages of the disease, is observed in the striatum (caudate and putamen) of the basal ganglia. Prominent symptoms include clumsiness and involuntary movements of the head and trunk. Cognitive impairments are also seen and become pronounced over time. Compare *Parkinson's disease.* (Ch. 8)

hyperdirect pathway Direct connections from the motor cortex to the subthalamic nucleus (STN) that bypass the striatum and convey excitatory input directly to the STN and pallidum. (Ch. 8)

hyperkinesia A movement disorder characterized by excessive movement. Hyperkinesia is a prominent symptom of Huntington's disease. Compare *hypokinesia*, *akinesia*, and *bradykinesia.* (Ch. 8)

hyperpolarization A change in the membrane potential in which the electrical current inside of the cell becomes more negative. With respect to the resting potential, a hyperpolarized membrane potential is farther from the firing threshold. Compare *depolarization.* (Ch. 2)

hypokinesia A movement disorder characterized by the absence of movement or a reduction in the production of movement. Hypokinesia is a prominent symptom of Parkinson's disease. Compare *hyperkinesia*, *akinesia*, and *bradykinesia.* (Ch. 8)

hypothalamus A small collection of nuclei that form the floor of the third ventricle. The hypothalamus is important for the autonomic nervous system and the endocrine system, and it controls functions necessary for the maintenance of homeostasis. (Ch. 2)

I

iconic memory See *sensory memory.* (Ch. 9)

imitative behavior The spontaneous and uncontrolled mimicking of another person's behavior that is sometimes exhibited by patients with frontal lobe damage. (Ch. 13)

implicit memory See *nondeclarative memory.* (Ch. 9)

independent variable The variable in an experiment that is manipulated by the researcher. Compare *dependent variable.* (Ch. 3)

inferior colliculus A part of the midbrain that is involved in auditory processing. Compare *superior colliculus.* (Ch. 5)

inhibition of return (IOR) Also *inhibitory aftereffect.* The phenomenon, observed in an exogenously cued spatial attention task, where after the attention is reflexively attracted to a location by the exogenous cue, there is a slower behavioral response to stimuli in that location that are presented later than 300 ms after the exogenous cue. (Ch. 7)

inhibitory aftereffect See *inhibition of return.* (Ch. 7)

inhibitory control The hypothesis that one aspect of cognitive control is the regulation of habitual responses or environmentally dictated actions by active inhibition. A loss of inhibitory control is assumed to underlie the tendency of some patients with prefrontal lesions to produce socially inappropriate behavior. (Ch. 12)

insula Also *insular cortex.* A part of cortex hidden in the Sylvian fissure. The insula also has extensive reciprocal connections with areas associated with emotion, such as the amygdala, medial prefrontal cortex, and anterior cingulate gyrus; as well as with frontal, parietal, and temporal cortical areas involved with attention, memory, and cognition. (Ch. 2, 10)

integrative visual agnosia A form of agnosia associated with deficits in the recognition of objects due to a failure to group and integrate the component parts into a coherent whole. Patients with this deficit can faithfully reproduce drawings of objects; however, their percept is of isolated, unconnected parts or contours. Compare *apperceptive visual agnosia* and *associative visual agnosia.* (Ch. 6)

interaural time The difference in time between when a sound reaches each of the two ears. This information is represented at various stages in the auditory pathway and provides an important cue for sound localization. (Ch. 5)

interoception Physical sensations arising from inside the body, such as pain, temperature, hunger, and so on. (Ch. 10)

interpreter A left-hemisphere mechanism that seeks explanations for internal and external events in order to produce appropriate response behaviors. (Ch. 4)

ion channel A passageway in the cell membrane, formed by a transmembrane protein that creates a pore, through which ions of a particular size and/or charge are allowed to pass. (Ch. 2)

ion pump A protein in the cell membrane of a neuron that is capable of transporting ions against their concentration gradient. The sodium–potassium pump transports sodium ions (Na^+) out of the neuron and potassium ions (K^+) into the neuron. (Ch. 2)

IOR See *inhibition of return.* (Ch. 7)

J

joint attention The ability to monitor someone else's attention by observing that person's gaze or actions and directing one's own attention similarly. (Ch. 13)

L

late selection The theoretical model positing that all inputs are equally processed perceptually, but attention acts to differentially filter these inputs at later stages of information processing. Compare *early selection.* (Ch. 7)

lateral fissure See *Sylvian fissure.* (Ch. 2, 4, 11)

lateral geniculate nucleus (LGN) The thalamic nucleus that is the main target of axons of the optic tract. Output from the LGN is directed primarily to the primary visual cortex (Brodmann area 17). (Ch. 5)

lateral occipital cortex (LOC) A region of extrastriate cortex that is part of the ventral pathway. Processing in the LOC is essential for shape perception and recognition. (Ch. 6)

lateral prefrontal cortex (LPFC) The region of the cerebral cortex that lies anterior to Brodmann area 6, along the lateral surface. This region has been implicated in various executive functions, such as working memory and response selection. (Ch. 12)

layer A common organizational cluster of neurons in the central nervous system. (Ch. 2)

learning The process of acquiring new information. (Ch. 9)

lexical access The process by which perceptual inputs activate word information in the mental lexicon, including semantic and syntactic information about the word. (Ch. 11)

lexical integration The function of words being integrated into a full sentence, discourse, or large current context to discern the message. (Ch. 11)

lexical selection The process of selecting from a collection of representations the activated word that best matches the sensory input. (Ch. 11)

LGN See *lateral geniculate nucleus.* (Ch. 5)

limbic system Several structures that form a border (*limbus* in Latin) around the brainstem, named the *grand lobe limbique* ("limbic lobe") by Paul Broca, which now include the amygdala, orbitofrontal cortex, and portions of the basal ganglia. (Ch. 2)

LIS See *locked-in syndrome.* (Ch. 14)

LOC See *lateral occipital cortex.* (Ch. 6)

locked-in syndrome (LIS) A condition in which one is unable to move any muscle (although sometimes an eye muscle is spared) but is fully conscious and has normal sleep–wake cycles. (Ch. 14)

long-term memory The retention of information over the long term, from hours to days and years. Compare *sensory memory* and *short-term memory.* (Ch. 9)

long-term potentiation (LTP) A process by which synaptic connections are strengthened when certain types of synaptic stimulation, such as prolonged high-frequency input, result in a long-lasting increase in the strength of synaptic transmission. (Ch. 9)

LPFC See *lateral prefrontal cortex.* (Ch. 12)

LTP See *long-term potentiation.* (Ch. 9)

M

M1 See *primary motor cortex.* (Ch. 8)

magnetic resonance imaging (MRI) A neuroimaging technique that exploits the magnetic properties of organic tissue. Certain atoms are especially sensitized to magnetic forces because of the number of protons and neutrons in their nuclei. The orientation of these atoms can be altered by the presence of a strong magnetic field. A radio frequency signal can be used to knock these aligned atoms from their orientation in the magnetic field. The atoms will then realign with the magnetic field and give off a radio frequency signal that can be measured by sensitive detectors. Structural MRI studies usually measure variations in the density of hydrogen ions in the tissue being scanned. Functional MRI measures changes over time in the signal intensity of the targeted atom. (Ch. 3)

magnetic resonance spectroscopy (MRS) A technique to analyze data from MRI that uses signals from hydrogen protons in localized regions of the brain to determine the relative concentrations of different biochemicals. (Ch. 3)

magnetoencephalography (MEG) A technique that measures magnetic signals generated by the brain. The electrical activity of neurons produces small magnetic fields that can be measured by sensitive magnetic detectors placed along the scalp, similar to the way EEG measures surface electrical activity. MEG can be used in an event-related manner similar to ERP studies, with similar temporal resolution. The spatial resolution, in theory, can be superior with MEG because magnetic signals are minimally distorted by organic tissue such as the brain or skull. (Ch. 3)

materialism A major philosophical approach to describing consciousness, based on the theory that the mind and brain are both physical mediums. (Ch. 14)

medial frontal cortex (MFC) The medial region of the frontal cortex that includes parts of areas 24, 32, and inferior aspects of 6 and 8. The MFC is associated with cognitive control—in particular, monitoring functions for error detection and resolving conflict. (Ch. 12)

medulla The brainstem's most caudal portion. The medulla is continuous with the spinal cord and contains the prominent, dorsally positioned nuclear groups known as the *gracile* and *cuneate nuclei* (which relay somatosensory information from the spinal cord to the brain) and the ventral pyramidal tracts (which contain descending projection axons from the brain to the spinal cord). Various sensory and motor nuclei are found in the medulla. (Ch. 2)

MEG See *magnetoencephalography.* (Ch. 3)

memory The persistence of learning in a state that can be revealed later. (Ch. 9)

mental lexicon A mental store of information about words, including semantic information (meanings of the words), syntactic information (rules for using the words), and the details of word forms (spellings and sound patterns). (Ch. 11)

mental state attribution theory Originally called *theory theory.* A theory proposing that we acquire a commonsense "folk psychology" and use it, somewhat like a scientific theory, to infer the thoughts of others ("mind-read"). Compare *experience sharing theory.* (Ch. 13)

mentalizing See *theory of mind.* (Ch. 13)

MFC See *medial frontal cortex.* (Ch. 12)

microcircuit A small network of localized interconnected neurons that together process specific kinds of information and contribute to information-processing tasks such as sensation, action, and thought. Compare *neural network.* (Ch. 2)

midbrain The mesencephalon; the part of the brain consisting of the *tectum* (meaning "roof," and representing the dorsal portion), *tegmentum* (the main portion), and ventral regions occupied by large fiber tracts (*crus cerebri*) from the forebrain to the spinal cord (corticospinal tract), cerebellum, and brainstem (corticobulbar tract). The midbrain contains neurons that participate in visuomotor functions (e.g., superior colliculus, oculomotor nucleus, trochlear nucleus), visual reflexes (e.g., pretectal region), auditory relays (inferior colliculus), and the mesencephalic tegmental nuclei involved in motor coordination (red nucleus). It is bordered anteriorly by the diencephalon, and caudally by the pons. (Ch. 2)

mirror neuron (MN) A neuron that shows similar responses when an animal is either performing an action or observing that action produced by another organism. For instance, a mirror neuron responds when you pick up a pencil and when you watch someone else pick up a pencil. Mirror neurons are hypothesized to provide a strong link between perception and action, perhaps providing an important basis for the development of conceptual knowledge. (Ch. 8)

mirror neuron network A distributed network of neurons that respond not only to one's own actions but also to perceived actions. (Ch. 8)

mirror self-recognition (MSR) The ability to recognize that the image one sees in a mirror is oneself. Gordon Gallop proposed being able to recognize oneself in a mirror implies that one is self-aware. (Ch. 14)

MN See *mirror neuron.* (Ch. 8)

module A specialized, independent, and frequently localized network of neurons that serve a specific function. (Ch. 4)

monitoring The cognitive control associated with evaluating whether current representations and/or actions are conducive to the achievement of current goals. Errors can be avoided or corrected by a monitoring system. Monitoring is one of the hypothesized operations of a supervisory attentional system. (Ch. 12)

Montreal procedure A surgical procedure to treat epilepsy, originally developed by Wilder Penfield and Herbert Jasper, in which the neurons that produced seizures were surgically destroyed. (Ch. 1)

mood A long-lasting diffuse affective state that is characterized primarily by a predominance of enduring subjective feelings without an identifiable object or trigger. (Ch. 10)

morpheme The smallest grammatical unit of a language that carries bits of meaning. Morphemes may or may not be whole words; for example, "dog," "spit," "un-," and "-ly" are all morphemes. Compare *phoneme.* (Ch. 11)

MRI See *magnetic resonance imaging.* (Ch. 3)

MRS See *magnetic resonance spectroscopy.* (Ch. 3)

MSR See *mirror self-recognition.* (Ch. 14)

multiple realizability The idea that there are many ways to implement a system to produce one behavior. (Ch. 14)

multisensory integration The integration of information from more than one sensory modality. Watching someone speak requires the integration of auditory and visual information. (Ch. 5)

multiunit recording A neurophysiological method in which an array of electrodes is inserted in the brain such that the activity of many cells can be recorded simultaneously. Compare *single-cell recording.* (Ch. 3)

multivoxel pattern analysis (MVPA) A pattern classification algorithm in which the researcher identifies the distributed patterns of neural activity consistently present for a particular event, task, stimulus, and so forth. These activation patterns can provide information about the functional role not just of brain areas, but of networks within and beyond them. (Ch. 3)

MVPA See *multivoxel pattern analysis.* (Ch. 3)

myelin A fatty substance that surrounds the axons of many neurons and increases the effective membrane resistance, helping to speed the conduction of action potentials. (Ch. 2)

N

N400 response Also simply *the N400.* A negative-polarity event-related potential that is elicited by words and that is larger in amplitude for words that do not fit well into the sentence context. Compare *P600 response.* (Ch. 11)

neglect See *unilateral spatial neglect.* (Ch. 7)

neocortex The portion of the cortex that typically contains six main cortical layers (with sublayers) and has a high degree of specialization of neuronal organization. The neocortex is composed of areas like the primary sensory and motor cortex and association cortex and, as its name suggests, is the most modern (evolved) type of cortex. (Ch. 2)

neural network A complex network made up of long-distance connections between various brain regions. Neural networks are macrocircuits composed of multiple embedded *microcircuits*, and they support more complex analyses, integrating information processing from many microcircuits. (Ch. 2, 3)

neuron One of two cell types (along with the *glial cell*) in the nervous system. Neurons are responsible for processing sensory, motor, cognitive, and affective information. (Ch. 2)

neuron doctrine The concept, proposed by Santiago Ramón y Cajal in the 19th century, that the neuron is the fundamental unit of the nervous system, and that the nervous system is composed of billions of these units (neurons) connected to process information. (Ch. 1)

neurotransmitter A chemical substance that transmits the signal between neurons at chemical synapses. (Ch. 2)

nociceptors Also *free nerve endings.* The somatosensory receptors that convey pain information. (Ch. 5)

node of Ranvier A location at which myelin is interrupted between successive patches of axon, and where an action potential can be generated. (Ch. 2)

nonassociative learning A type of learning that does not involve the association of two stimuli to elicit a behavioral change. It consists of simple forms of learning such as habituation and sensitization. Compare *classical conditioning.* (Ch. 9)

nondeclarative memory Also *implicit memory.* Knowledge to which we typically have no conscious access, such as motor and cognitive skills (procedural knowledge). For example, the ability to ride a bicycle is a nondeclarative form of knowledge. Although we can describe the action itself, the actual information one needs to ride a bicycle is not easy to describe. Compare *declarative memory.* (Ch. 9)

nonfluent aphasia See *Broca's aphasia.* (Ch. 11)

non–rapid eye movement (NREM) sleep Sleep that is characterized by high-amplitude brain waves that are less frequent than in *rapid eye movement sleep.* (Ch. 14)

normative decision theory A theory that defines how people *ought* to make decisions that yield the optimal choice. Compare *descriptive decision theory.* (Ch. 12)

NREM sleep See *non–rapid eye movement sleep.* (Ch. 14)

nucleus (pl. nuclei) 1. In neuroanatomy, a collection of cell bodies in the central nervous system—for example, the lateral geniculate nucleus. (Ch. 2) 2. In biology, a cellular organelle where DNA is stored. (Ch. 2)

O

object constancy The ability to recognize invariant properties of an object across a wide range of viewing positions, illumination, and contexts. For example, although the size of the retinal image changes dramatically when a car recedes in the distance, our percept is that the car remains the same size. Similarly, we are able to recognize that an object is the same when seen from different perspectives. (Ch. 6)

occipital lobe A cortical lobe located at the posterior of the cerebral cortex that primarily contains neurons involved in visual information processing. (Ch. 2)

occipitoparietal stream See *dorsal stream.* (Ch. 6)

occipitotemporal stream See *ventral stream.* (Ch. 6)

odorant A molecule conducted through the air that leads to activation of the olfactory receptors and may be perceived as having a fragrance when processed through the olfactory system. Compare *tastant.* (Ch. 5)

OFC See *orbitofrontal cortex.* (Ch. 12, 13)

olivary nucleus A collection of nuclei in the medulla and pons that is the first site where auditory information from the right and left ears converges. (Ch. 5)

optic ataxia A neurological syndrome in which the patient has great difficulty using visual information to guide her actions, even though she is unimpaired in her ability to recognize objects. Optic ataxia is associated with lesions of the parietal lobe. (Ch. 6, 8)

optogenetics A procedure in which genes are manipulated so that they express a photosensitive protein that, when exposed to light, will activate the neuron. The genetic manipulation can be modified such that the protein expression is limited to particular neural regions. (Ch. 3)

orbitofrontal cortex (OFC) Also *ventromedial zone.* A region of the frontal lobe, located above the orbits of the eyes, that is implicated in a range of functions, including perceptual processes associated with olfaction and taste, as well as those associated with monitoring whether one's behavior is appropriate. (Ch. 12, 13)

orthographic form The vision-based form of a word in written language. Compare *phonological form.* (Ch. 11)

overt attention Turning the head to orient toward a visual, auditory, olfactory, or other sensory stimulus. Compare *covert attention.* (Ch. 7)

P

P600 response Also *syntactic positive shift (SPS).* A positive-polarity event-related potential elicited when words violate syntactic rules in sentences. It is also seen in some cases of semantic violations with correct syntax. Compare *N400 response.* (Ch. 11)

parahippocampal place area (PPA) A functionally defined area of the brain, located in the parahippocampal region of the temporal lobe, that shows a preferential response to stimuli depicting scenes or places. Compare *fusiform face area.* (Ch. 6)

parietal lobe A cortical lobe located posterior to the central sulcus, anterior to the occipital lobe, and superior to the posterior temporal cortex. This cortical region contains a variety of neurons, including the somatosensory cortex, gustatory cortex, and parietal association cortex, which includes regions involved in visuomotor orienting, attention, and representation of space. (Ch. 2)

Parkinson's disease A degenerative disorder of the basal ganglia in which the pathology results from the loss of dopaminergic cells in the substantia nigra. Primary symptoms include difficulty in initiating movement, slowness of movement, poorly articulated speech, and, in some cases, resting tremor. Compare *Huntington's disease.* (Ch. 8)

Pavlovian conditioning See *classical conditioning.* (Ch. 9)

perceptual representation system (PRS) A form of nondeclarative memory, acting within the perceptual system, in which the structure and form of objects and words can be primed by prior experience and can be revealed later through implicit memory tests. (Ch. 9)

peripheral nervous system (PNS) A courier network that delivers sensory information to the CNS and then conducts the motor commands of the CNS to control muscles of the body; the parts of the nervous system outside the brain and spinal cord. Compare *central nervous system.* (Ch. 2)

permeability The extent to which ions can cross a neuronal membrane. (Ch. 2)

perseveration The tendency to produce a particular response on successive trials, even when the context has changed such that the response is no longer appropriate. Commonly observed in patients with prefrontal damage, perseveration is thought to reflect a loss of inhibitory control. (Ch. 12)

PET See *positron emission tomography.* (Ch. 3)

PFC See *prefrontal cortex.* (Ch. 2, 12, 13)

pharmacological study An experimental method in which the independent variable is the administration of a chemical agent or drug. In one example, participants are given drugs that act as dopamine agonists and then observed as they perform decision-making tasks. (Ch. 3)

phoneme The smallest perceived unit of sound in a language. In English, there are 40 phonemes. Compare *morpheme.* (Ch. 11)

phonological form The sound-based form of a word in spoken language. Compare *orthographic form.* (Ch. 11)

photoreceptors Specialized cells in the retina that transduce light energy into changes in membrane potential. The photoreceptors are the interface for the visual system between the external world and the nervous system. The human eye has two types of photoreceptors: rods and cones. (Ch. 5)

phrenology The study of the physical shape of the human head, based on the belief that variations in the skull's surface can reveal specific intellectual and personality traits. Today phrenology is understood to lack validity. (Ch. 1)

pituitary gland An endocrine gland that synthesizes and secretes hormones that aid in the regulation of multiple processes to maintain the normal state of the body (homeostasis). It is under the control of the hypothalamus. (Ch. 2)

planum temporale The surface area of the temporal lobe that includes Wernicke's area. The planum temporale has long been believed to be larger in the left hemisphere because of the lateralization of language function, although this theory is currently controversial. (Ch. 4)

PNS See *peripheral nervous system.* (Ch. 2)

pons A region in the brain that includes the pontine tegmental regions on the floor of the fourth ventricle, and the pons itself, a vast system of fiber tracts interspersed with pontine nuclei. The fibers are continuations of the cortical projections to the spinal cord, brainstem, and cerebellar regions. The pons also includes the primary sensory nuclear groups for auditory and vestibular inputs, and somatosensory inputs from, and motor nuclei projecting to, the face and mouth. Neurons of the reticular formation can also be found in the anterior regions of the pons. (Ch. 2)

population vector The sum of the preferred directions of individual neurons within a group that represents the activity across that group. Population vectors reflect the aggregate activity across the cells, providing a better correlation with behavior than that obtained from the analysis of individual neurons. For example, the population vector calculated from neurons in the motor cortex can predict the direction of a limb movement. (Ch. 8)

positron emission tomography (PET) A neuroimaging method that measures metabolic activity or blood flow changes in the brain by monitoring the distribution of a radioactive tracer. The PET scanner measures the photons that are produced during the decay of a tracer. A popular tracer for cognitive neuroscience studies is O15 because its decay time is rapid and the distribution of oxygen increases to neural regions that are active. (Ch. 3)

posterior aphasia See *Wernicke's aphasia.* (Ch. 11)

posterior commissure The nerve bundle connecting the left and right cerebral hemispheres that is located posterior to the corpus callosum. It contains fibers that contribute to the pupillary light reflex. Compare *anterior commissure.* (Ch. 4)

postsynaptic Referring to the neuron located after the synapse with respect to information flow. Compare *presynaptic.* (Ch. 2)

PPA See *parahippocampal place area.* (Ch. 6)

preferred direction A property of cells in the motor pathway, referring to the direction of movement that results in the highest firing rate of the neuron. Voxels have also been shown to have preferred directions in fMRI studies, indicating that such preferences can even be measured at the cell population level of analysis. (Ch. 8)

prefrontal cortex (PFC) A region of cortex that takes part in the higher aspects of motor control and the planning and execution of behavior, perhaps especially tasks that require the integration of information over time and thus mandate the involvement of working memory mechanisms. The prefrontal cortex has three or more main areas that are commonly referred to in descriptions of the gross anatomy of the frontal lobe: the dorsolateral prefrontal cortex, the anterior cingulate and medial frontal regions, and the orbitofrontal cortex. (Ch. 2, 12, 13)

premotor cortex A secondary motor area that includes the lateral aspect of Brodmann area 6, just anterior to the primary motor cortex. Although some neurons in the premotor cortex project to the corticospinal tract, many terminate on neurons in the primary motor cortex and help shape the forthcoming movement. (Ch. 8)

presynaptic Referring to the neuron located before the synapse with respect to information flow. Compare *postsynaptic.* (Ch. 2)

primary auditory cortex (A1) The initial cortical processing area of the auditory system. (Ch. 5)

primary gustatory cortex The initial cortical processing area for gustation (the sense of taste), located in the insula and operculum. (Ch. 5)

primary motor cortex (M1) A region of the cerebral cortex that lies along the anterior bank of the central sulcus and precentral gyrus, forming Brodmann area 4. Some axons originating in the primary motor cortex form the majority of the corticospinal tract; others project to cortical and subcortical regions involved in motor control. The primary motor cortex contains a prominent somatotopic representation of the body. (Ch. 8)

primary olfactory cortex Also *pyriform cortex*. The initial cortical processing area for olfaction, located at the ventral junction of the frontal and temporal cortices, near the limbic cortex. (Ch. 5)

primary process See *core emotional system*. (Ch. 10)

primary reinforcer A reward or outcome that has a direct benefit for survival. The classic examples are food, water, and sex, since without these, the individual or the species would not survive. Compare *secondary reinforcer*. (Ch. 12)

primary somatosensory cortex (S1) The initial cortical processing area for somatosensation, including Brodmann areas 1, 2, and 3. This area of the brain contains a somatotopic representation of the body called the sensory *homunculus*. Compare *secondary somatosensory cortex*. (Ch. 5)

primary visual cortex (V1) The initial cortical processing area for vision, located in the most posterior portion of the occipital lobe, known as Brodmann area 17. (Ch. 5)

priming A form of learning in which behavior or a physiological response is altered because of a recent stimulus or state. Priming usually refers to changes that occur over a short timescale; for example, hearing the word "river" primes the word "water." (Ch. 9)

procedural memory A form of nondeclarative memory that involves the learning of a variety of motor skills (e.g., knowledge of how to ride a bike) and cognitive skills (e.g., knowledge of how to read). (Ch. 9)

proprioception The awareness of the position of one's own body parts, such as limbs. This awareness arises from the information provided by specialized nerve cells at the linkage of the muscles and tendons. (Ch. 5)

prosopagnosia A neurological syndrome characterized by a deficit in the ability to recognize faces. Some patients will show a selective deficit in face perception, a type of category-specific deficit. In others, the prosopagnosia is one part of a more general agnosia. Prosopagnosia is frequently associated with bilateral lesions in the ventral pathway, although it can also occur with unilateral lesions of the right hemisphere. (Ch. 6)

prosthetic device Also *prosthesis* (Greek for "addition, application, attachment"). An artificial device that functions as a replacement for a missing body part. (Ch. 8)

protocol In a layered architecture, the set of rules, or specifications, that stipulate the allowed interfaces, or interactions, either within a layer or between layers. (Ch. 14)

PRS See *perceptual representation system*. (Ch. 9)

pruning See *synapse elimination*. (Ch. 2)

pulvinar A large region of the posterior thalamus comprising many nuclei having interconnections with specific regions of the cortex. (Ch. 7)

pyramidal tract See *corticospinal tract*. (Ch. 8)

pyriform cortex See *primary olfactory cortex*. (Ch. 5)

Q

qualia (s. quale) In philosophy, an individual's personal perceptions or experiences of something. (Ch. 14)

quantum theory A fundamental theory of physics that describes the nature and behavior of atoms and subatomic particles. (Ch. 14)

R

rapid eye movement (REM) sleep Sleep that is characterized by low-amplitude brain waves that are more frequent than in *non–rapid eye movement sleep*. (Ch. 14)

rationalism The idea that, through right thinking and rejection of unsupportable or superstitious beliefs, true beliefs can be determined. Compare *empiricism*. (Ch. 1)

rCBF See *regional cerebral blood flow*. (Ch. 3)

reappraisal A cognitive strategy to reassess an emotion. (Ch. 10)

receptive aphasia See *Wernicke's aphasia*. (Ch. 11)

receptive field The area of external space within which a stimulus must be presented in order to activate a cell. For example, cells in the visual cortex respond to stimuli that appear within a restricted region of space. In addition to spatial position, the cells may be selective to other stimulus features, such as color or shape. Cells in the auditory cortex also have receptive fields. The cell's firing rate increases when the sound comes from the region of space that defines its receptive field. (Ch. 3, 5)

reflexive attention Also *exogenous attention*. The automatic orienting of attention induced by bottom-up, or stimulus-driven, effects, such as when a flash of light in the periphery captures one's attention. Compare *voluntary attention*. (Ch. 7)

reflexive cuing Also *exogenous cuing*. An experimental method that uses an external (i.e., exogenous) sensory stimulus (e.g., flash of light) to automatically attract attention without voluntary control. Compare *endogenous cuing*. (Ch. 7)

refractory period The short period of time following an action potential during which the neuron may not be able to generate action potentials or may be able to do so only with larger-than-normal depolarizing currents. (Ch. 2)

regional cerebral blood flow (rCBF) The distribution of the brain's blood supply, which can be measured with various imaging techniques. In PET scanning, rCBF is used as a measure of metabolic changes following increased neural activity in restricted regions of the brain. (Ch. 3)

relational memory Memory that relates the individual pieces of information relevant to a particular memory and that supports episodic memories. (Ch. 9)

REM sleep See *rapid eye movement sleep*. (Ch. 14)

repetition suppression (RS) effect The phenomenon seen during functional MRI in which the BOLD response to a stimulus decreases with each subsequent stimulus repetition. (Ch. 6)

response conflict A situation in which more than one response is activated, usually because of some ambiguity in the stimulus information. It has been hypothesized that the anterior cingulate monitors the level of response conflict and modulates processing in active systems when conflict is high. (Ch. 12)

resting membrane potential The difference in voltage across the neuronal membrane at rest, when the neuron is not signaling. (Ch. 2)

retina A layer of neurons along the back surface of the eye. The retina contains a variety of cells, including photoreceptors (the cells that respond to light) and ganglion cells (the cells whose axons form the optic nerve). (Ch. 5)

retinotopic map A topographic representation in the brain in which some sort of orderly spatial relationship is maintained that reflects spatial properties of the environment in an eye-based reference frame. For example, primary visual cortex contains a retinotopic map of the contralateral side of space, relative to the center of gaze. Multiple retinotopic maps have been identified in the cortex and subcortex. (Ch. 3, 5)

retrieval The utilization of stored information to create a conscious representation or to execute a learned behavior like a motor act. Compare *encoding*. (Ch. 9)

retrograde amnesia The loss of memory for events that happened in the past. Compare *anterograde amnesia*. (Ch. 9)

reversal learning An attempt to teach someone to respond in the opposite way from what they were previously taught. (Ch. 13)

reward prediction error (RPE) A theoretical construct in theories of reinforcement learning that is defined as the difference between an expected and actual outcome or reward. A greater-than-expected reward yields a positive prediction, which can be used to increase the likelihood of the behavior. A less-than-expected reward yields a negative prediction, which can be used to decrease the likelihood of the behavior. (Ch. 12)

Ribot's law See *temporal gradient*. (Ch. 9)

rods Photoreceptors that have a lower threshold for light stimuli than *cones* have, and thus enable vision in low-light conditions. Rods are found in the periphery of the retina and not in the fovea. Many rods connect to one ganglion cell. (Ch. 5)

RPE See *reward prediction error*. (Ch. 12)

RS effect See *repetition suppression effect*. (Ch. 6)

S

S1 See *primary somatosensory cortex*. (Ch. 5)

S2 See *secondary somatosensory cortex*. (Ch. 5)

saccades The rapid eye movements that are made to change fixation from one point to another. A saccade lasts 20 to 100 ms. (Ch. 5)

saltatory conduction The mode of conduction in myelinated neurons, in which action potentials are generated down the axon only at nodes of Ranvier. Measurement of the propagation of the action potential gives it the appearance of jumping from node to node—hence the term *saltatory*, which comes from the Latin *saltare*, meaning "to jump." (Ch. 2)

SCN See *suprachiasmatic nucleus*. (Ch. 14)

secondary reinforcer Rewards that do not have intrinsic, or direct, value, but have acquired their desirability as part of social and cultural norms. Money and social status are important secondary reinforcers. Compare *primary reinforcer*. (Ch. 12)

secondary somatosensory cortex (S2) The area of the brain that receives inputs from *primary somatosensory cortex* and processes higher-level somatosensory information. (Ch. 5)

selective attention The ability to focus one's concentration on a subset of sensory inputs, trains of thought, or actions, while simultaneously ignoring others. Selective attention can be distinguished from nonselective attention, which includes simple behavioral arousal (i.e., being generally more versus less attentive). Compare *arousal*. (Ch. 7)

self-reference effect An effect rooted in the theoretical perspective that the recall of information is related to how deeply the information was initially processed. Specifically, the self-reference effect is the superior memory for information that is encoded in relation to oneself. (Ch. 13)

semantic memory A form of declarative memory that stores knowledge that is based on facts one has learned, but not knowledge of the context in which the learning occurred. Compare *episodic memory*. (Ch. 9)

semantic paraphasia The production of a word related in meaning to the intended word (e.g., *horse* for *cow*) instead of the intended word itself. Wernicke's aphasia patients often produce semantic paraphasias. (Ch. 11)

sensorimotor adaptation A form of motor learning in which a learned skill is modified because of a change in the environment or agent. For example, a soccer player who adjusts her shot to compensate for a strong crosswind is exhibiting a form of motor adaptation. (Ch. 8)

sensorimotor learning The improvement, through practice, in the performance of sensory-guided motor behavior. (Ch. 8)

sensory memory The short-lived retention of sensory information, measurable in milliseconds to seconds, as when we recover what was said to us a moment earlier when we were not paying close attention to the speaker. Sensory memory for audition is called *echoic memory*; sensory memory for vision is called *iconic memory*. Compare *short-term memory* and *long-term memory*. (Ch. 9)

sensory prediction error The discrepancy between the motor system's predicted outcome of a particular movement and the sensory feedback of the movement's actual outcome. (Ch. 8)

sentience The ability to be conscious and experience subjectivity. (Ch. 14)

short-term memory The retention of information over seconds to minutes. See also *working memory*. Compare *sensory memory* and *long-term memory*. (Ch. 9)

simulation A method used in computer modeling to mimic a certain behavior or process. Simulations require a program that explicitly specifies the manner in which information is represented and processed. The resulting model can be tested to see whether its output matches the simulated behavior or process. The program can then be used to generate new predictions. (Ch. 3)

simulation theory See *experience sharing theory*. (Ch. 13)

single-cell recording A neurophysiological method used to monitor the activity of individual neurons. The procedure requires positioning a small recording electrode either inside a cell or, more typically, near the outer membrane of a neuron. The electrode measures changes in the membrane potential and can be used to determine the conditions that cause the cell to respond. Compare *multiunit recording.* (Ch. 3)

single dissociation A method used to develop functional models of mental and/or neural processes. Evidence of a single dissociation requires a minimum of two groups and two tasks. A single dissociation is present when the groups differ in their performance on one task but not the other. Single dissociations provide weak evidence of functional specialization, since it is possible that the two tasks differ in terms of their sensitivity to detect group differences. Compare *double dissociation.* (Ch. 3)

SMA See *supplementary motor area.* (Ch. 8)

social cognitive neuroscience An emerging field of brain science that combines social-personality psychology and cognitive neuroscience with the goal of understanding the neural mechanisms involved in social interaction in humans. (Ch. 13)

soma (pl. somata) The cell body of a neuron. (Ch. 2)

somatic marker A physiological-emotional mechanism that was once theorized to help people sort through possible options and make a decision. Somatic markers were thought to provide a common metric for evaluating options with respect to their potential benefit. (Ch. 10)

somatotopy A point-for-point representation of the body surface in the nervous system. In the somatosensory cortex, regions of the body near one another (e.g., the index and middle fingers) are represented by neurons located near one another. Regions that are farther apart on the body surface (e.g., the nose and the big toe) are coded by neurons located farther apart in the somatosensory cortex. (Ch. 2)

spike-triggering zone The location, at the juncture of the soma and the axon of a neuron, where currents from synaptic inputs on the soma and distant dendrites are summed and where voltage-gated Na^+ channels are located that can be triggered to generate action potentials that can propagate down the axon. (Ch. 2)

spinal interneurons Neurons found in the spinal cord. Many descending axons from the pyramidal and extrapyramidal tracts synapse on interneurons, which, in turn, synapse on other interneurons or alpha motor neurons. (Ch. 8)

spine A little knob attached by a small neck to the surface of a dendrite. Synapses are located on spines. (Ch. 2)

splenium (pl. splenia) The posterior portion of the corpus callosum. It interconnects the occipital lobe. (Ch. 4)

SPS See *P600 response.* (Ch. 11)

stimulus–response decision An *action–outcome decision* that has become habitual through repetition. (Ch. 12)

storage The permanent record resulting from the acquisition (creation) and consolidation (maintenance) of information. (Ch. 9)

stress A fixed pattern of physiological and neurohormonal changes that occurs when we encounter a stimulus, event, or thought that threatens us (or we expect will threaten us) in some way. (Ch. 10)

stroke See *cerebral vascular accident.* (Ch. 3)

subliminal perception The phenomenon by which a stimulus that is not consciously perceived nevertheless influences one's conscious state. (Ch. 14)

substantia nigra One of the nuclei that form the basal ganglia. The substantia nigra is composed of two parts: The axons of the substantia nigra *pars compacta* provide the primary source of the neurotransmitter dopamine and terminate in the striatum (caudate and putamen). The substantia nigra *pars reticularis* is one of the output nuclei from the basal ganglia. (Ch. 8)

sulcus (pl. sulci) Also *fissure.* An invaginated region that appears as a cut or crease of the surface of the cerebral cortex. Compare *gyrus.* (Ch. 2)

superior colliculus A subcortical visual structure located in the midbrain. The superior colliculus receives input from the retinal system and is interconnected with the subcortical and cortical systems. It plays a key role in visuomotor processes and may be involved in the inhibitory component of reflexive attentional orienting. Compare *inferior colliculus.* (Ch. 5, 7)

supplementary motor area (SMA) A secondary motor area that includes the medial aspect of Brodmann area 6, just anterior to the primary motor cortex. The SMA plays an important role in the production of sequential movements, especially those that have been well learned. (Ch. 8)

suppression Intentionally excluding a thought or feeling from conscious awareness. A strategy for inhibiting an emotion-expressive behavior during an emotionally arousing situation. (Ch. 10)

suprachiasmatic nucleus (SCN) Either of a pair of nuclei, located in the hypothalamus above the optic chiasm, that are involved with the regulation of circadian rhythms. (Ch. 14)

Sylvian fissure Also *lateral fissure.* A large fissure (sulcus) on the lateral surface of the cerebral cortex first described by the anatomist Franciscus Sylvius. The Sylvian fissure separates the frontal cortex from the temporal lobe below. (Ch. 2, 4, 11)

synapse The specialized site on the neural membrane where a neuron comes close to another neuron to transmit information. Synapses include both presynaptic (e.g., synaptic vesicles with neurotransmitter) and postsynaptic (e.g., receptors) specializations in the neurons that are involved in chemical transmission. Electrical synapses involve special structures called gap junctions that make direct cytoplasmic connections between neurons. (Ch. 2)

synapse elimination Also *pruning.* The elimination of some synaptic contacts between neurons during development, including postnatally. (Ch. 2)

synaptic cleft The gap between neurons at synapses. (Ch. 2)

synaptogenesis The formation of synaptic connections between neurons in the developing nervous system. (Ch. 2)

syncytium (pl. syncytia) A continuous mass of tissue that shares a common cytoplasm. (Ch. 1)

synesthesia A mixing of the senses whereby stimulation of one sense (e.g., touch) automatically causes an illusory perceptual experience in the same or another sense (e.g., vision). (Ch. 5)

syntactic parsing The assignment of a syntactic structure to a word in a sentence (e.g., this word is the object of the sentence, and this word is the action). (Ch. 11)

syntactic positive shift (SPS) See *P600 response.* (Ch. 11)

syntax The rules that constrain word combinations and sequences in a sentence. (Ch. 11)

T

tACS See *transcranial alternating current stimulation.* (Ch. 3)

tastant A food molecule that stimulates a receptor in a taste cell to initiate the sensory transduction of gustation. Compare *odorant.* (Ch. 5)

TBI See *traumatic brain injury.* (Ch. 3)

tDCS See *transcranial direct current stimulation.* (Ch. 3)

temporal discounting The observation that people tend to value immediate outcomes more highly than delayed outcomes, and that the subjective value of a reward decreases as the time to its receipt increases. (Ch. 12)

temporal gradient Also *Ribot's law.* The effect in which some cases of retrograde amnesia tend to be greatest for the most recent events. (Ch. 9)

temporal lobe Lateral ventral portions of the cerebral cortex bounded superiorly by the Sylvian fissure and posteriorly by the anterior edge of the occipital lobe and ventral portion of the parietal lobe. The ventromedial portions contain the hippocampal complex and amygdala. The lateral neocortical regions are involved in higher-order vision (object analysis), the representation of conceptual information about the visual world, and linguistic representations. The superior portions within the depths of the Sylvian fissure contain auditory cortex. (Ch. 2)

temporally limited amnesia Retrograde amnesia following brain damage that extends backward from the time of the damage but does not include the entire life of the individual. (Ch. 9)

tFUS See *transcranial focused ultrasound.* (Ch. 3)

TGA See *transient global amnesia.* (Ch. 9)

thalamic reticular nucleus (TRN) A thin layer of neurons surrounding the nuclei of the thalamus, which receives inputs from the cortex and subcortical structures and sends projections to the thalamic relay nuclei. (Ch. 7)

thalamus A group of nuclei, primarily major sensory relay nuclei for somatosensory, gustatory, auditory, visual, and vestibular inputs to the cerebral cortex. The thalamus also contains nuclei involved in basal ganglia–cortical loops, and other specialized nuclear groups. It is a part of the diencephalon, a subcortical region, located in the center of the mass of the forebrain. Each hemisphere contains one thalamus, and they are connected at the midline in most humans by the massa intermedia. (Ch. 2)

theory of mind (ToM) Also *mentalizing.* The ability to attribute mental states such as beliefs, desires, thoughts, and intentions to others and to understand that they may be different from one's own. (Ch. 13)

theory theory See *mental state attribution theory.* (Ch. 13)

threshold The membrane potential value to which the membrane must be depolarized for an action potential to be initiated. (Ch. 2)

TMS See *transcranial magnetic stimulation.* (Ch. 3)

ToM See *theory of mind.* (Ch. 13)

tonotopic map A mapping of different frequencies onto the hair cells along the cochlear canal and also the auditory cortex, with neighboring frequencies represented in neighboring spatial locations. (Ch. 5)

tract A bundle of axons in the central nervous system. (Ch. 2)

transcranial alternating current stimulation (tACS) A noninvasive method in which an oscillating low-voltage electrical current is delivered to the brain via electrodes placed on the scalp. By inducing oscillations at specific frequencies, experimenters can causally link brain oscillations of a specific frequency range to specific cognitive processes. Compare *transcranial direct current stimulation.* (Ch. 3)

transcranial direct current stimulation (tDCS) A noninvasive method in which a constant low-voltage electrical current is delivered to the brain via electrodes placed on the scalp. This method is hypothesized to potentiate neurons near the anodal electrode and to hyperpolarize neurons near the cathodal electrode. Compare *transcranial alternating current stimulation.* (Ch. 3)

transcranial focused ultrasound (tFUS) A noninvasive method to stimulate the brain that focuses low-intensity, low-frequency ultrasound extracranially. This method can produce focal effects limited to a 5-mm area. (Ch. 3)

transcranial magnetic stimulation (TMS) A noninvasive method used to stimulate neurons in the intact human brain. A strong electrical current is rapidly generated in a coil placed over the targeted region. This current generates a magnetic field that causes the neurons in the underlying region to discharge. TMS is used in clinical settings to evaluate motor function by direct stimulation of the motor cortex. Experimentally, the procedure is used to transiently disrupt neural processing, thus creating brief, reversible lesions. (Ch. 3)

transcranial static magnetic stimulation (tSMS) A noninvasive method that uses strong magnets to create magnetic fields that perturb electrical activity and temporarily alters cortical function. (Ch. 3)

transient global amnesia (TGA) A sudden, dramatic, but transient (lasting only hours) amnesia that is both anterograde and retrograde. (Ch. 9)

traumatic brain injury (TBI) A form of brain injury resulting from an accident such as a diving accident, bullet wound, or blast injury. The damage in TBI is usually diffuse, with both gray matter and white matter tracts affected by the accelerative forces experienced at the time of the injury. (Ch. 3)

TRN See *thalamic reticular nucleus.* (Ch. 7)

tSMS See *transcranial static magnetic stimulation.* (Ch. 3)

U

unilateral spatial neglect Also simply *neglect.* A behavioral pattern exhibited by neurological patients with lesions to the forebrain, in which they fail at or are slowed in acknowledging that objects or events exist in the hemispace opposite their lesion. Neglect is most closely associated with damage to the right parietal cortex. (Ch. 7)

utilization behavior An extreme dependency on the prototypical use of an object without regard for its use in a particular context. (Ch. 12)

V

V1 See *primary visual cortex.* (Ch. 5)

value An abstract entity referring to the overall preference given to a stimulus or action. The value is assumed to reflect the combination of a number of different attributes, such as how much reward will be received, the likelihood of that reward, and the efforts and costs required to achieve the reward. (Ch. 12)

ventral attention network A proposed attention control network, involving ventral frontal cortex and the temporoparietal junction of the right hemisphere, that mediates reflexive attention on the basis of stimulus novelty and salience. Compare *dorsal attention network.* (Ch. 7)

ventral stream Also *occipitotemporal stream.* The visual pathway that traverses the occipital and temporal lobes. This pathway is associated with object recognition and visual memory. Compare *dorsal stream.* (Ch. 6)

ventricle Any of four large, interconnected cavities of the brain. (Ch. 2)

ventromedial zone See *orbitofrontal cortex.* (Ch. 12, 13)

vesicle A small intracellular organelle, located in the presynaptic terminals at synapses, that contains neurotransmitter. (Ch. 2)

visceral motor system See *autonomic nervous system.* (Ch. 2)

visual agnosia A failure of perception that is limited to the visual modality. In visual agnosia, the patient is relatively good at perceiving properties such as color, shape, or motion, yet cannot recognize objects or identify their uses. (Ch. 6)

visual search The visual task of finding a specific stimulus in a display or scene with multiple stimuli. (Ch. 7)

voltage-gated ion channel A transmembrane ion channel that changes molecular conformation when the membrane potential changes, altering the conductance of the channel for specific ions such as sodium, potassium, or chloride. (Ch. 2)

voluntary attention Also *endogenous attention.* The volitional, or intentional, focusing of attention on a source of input, train of thought, or action. Compare *reflexive attention.* (Ch. 7)

voxel The smallest unit of three-dimensional data that can be represented in an MRI. (Ch. 3)

W

Wada test A clinical procedure in which amobarbital is injected to temporarily disrupt function in one of the cerebral hemispheres. This procedure, used to identify the source of epileptic seizures, provided important initial insights into hemispheric specialization. (Ch. 4)

Wernicke's aphasia Also *posterior aphasia* or *receptive aphasia.* A language deficit usually caused by brain lesions in the posterior parts of the left hemisphere, resulting in the inability to link words with the objects or concepts that they represent—that is, comprehension deficits. Compare *Broca's aphasia.* (Ch. 11)

Wernicke's area An area of human left posterior superior temporal gyrus, identified by Carl Wernicke in the 19th century, that is important to language comprehension. Compare *Broca's area.* (Ch. 11)

white matter Regions of the nervous system composed of millions of individual axons, each surrounded by myelin. The myelin is what gives the fibers their whitish color—hence the name *white matter.* Compare *gray matter.* (Ch. 2)

working memory A limited-capacity store for retaining information over the short term (maintenance) and for performing mental operations on the contents of this store (manipulation). See also *short-term memory.* (Ch. 9)

X

xenomelia Also *body integrity identity disorder (BIID).* A rare condition in which able-bodied individuals report experiencing a lifelong desire for the amputation of one or several of their limbs because they do not feel that the limb belongs to their body. (Ch. 13)

References

Aboitiz F., Scheibel, A. B., Fisher, R. S., & Zaidel, E. (1992). Fiber composition of the human corpus callosum. *Brain Research, 598,* 143–153.

Ackermann, H., & Riecker, A. (2010). Cerebral control of motor aspects of speech production: Neurophysiological and functional imaging data. In B. Maassen & P. H. H. M. van Lieshout (Eds.), *Speech motor control: New developments in basic and applied research* (pp. 117–134). Oxford: Oxford University Press.

Adachi, I., Chou, D., & Hampton, R. (2009). Thatcher effect in monkeys demonstrates conservation of face perception across primates. *Current Biology, 19,* 1270–1273.

Addante, R. J., Watrous, A. J., Yonelinas, A. P., Ekstrom, A. D., & Ranganath, C. (2011). Prestimulus theta activity predicts correct source memory retrieval. *Proceedings of the National Academy of Sciences, USA, 108,* 10702–10707.

Adolphs, R., Gosselin, F., Buchanan, T. W., Tranel, D., Schyns, P., & Damasio, A. R. (2005). A mechanism for impaired fear recognition after amygdala damage. *Nature, 433,* 68–72.

Adolphs, R., Tranel, D., & Damasio, A. R. (1998). The human amygdala in social judgment. *Nature, 393,* 470–474.

Adolphs, R. A., Tranel, D., Damasio, H., & Damasio, A. R. (1994). Impaired recognition of emotion in facial expressions following bilateral amygdala damage to the human amygdala. *Nature, 372,* 669–672.

Adolphs, R., Tranel, D., Damasio, H., & Damasio, A. R. (1995). Fear and the human amygdala. *Journal of Neuroscience, 75,* 5879–5891.

Adolphs, R., Tranel, D., & Denburg, N. (2000). Impaired emotional declarative memory following unilateral amygdala damage. *Learning & Memory, 7,* 180–186.

Adolphs, R., Tranel, D., Hamann, S., Young, A. W., Calder, A. J., Phelps, E. A., et al. (1999). Recognition of facial emotion in nine individuals with bilateral amygdala damage. *Neuropsychologia, 37,* 1111–1117.

Afraz, S., Kiani, R., & Esteky, H. (2006). Microstimulation of inferotemporal cortex influences face categorization. *Nature, 442,* 692–695.

Aggleton, J. P., & Brown, M. W. (1999). Episodic memory amnesia and the hippocampal-anterior thalamic axis. *Behavioral and Brain Sciences, 22,* 425–444.

Aglioti, S. M., Cesari, P., Romani, M., & Urgesi, C. (2008). Action anticipation and motor resonance in elite basketball players. *Nature Neuroscience, 11,* 1109–1116.

Aguirre, G. K., & D'Esposito, M. E. (1999). Topographical disorientation: A synthesis and taxonomy. *Brain, 122,* 1613–1628.

Ahn, Y. Y., Jeong, H., & Kim, B. J. (2006). Wiring cost in the organization of a biological neuronal network. *Physica A: Statistical Mechanics and Its Applications, 367,* 531–537.

Airan, R. D., Thompson, K. R., Fenno, L. E., Bernstein, H., & Deisseroth, K. (2009). Temporally precise *in vivo* control of intracellular signaling. *Nature, 458,* 1025–1029.

Ajiboye, A. B., Willett, F. R., Young, D. R., Memberg, W. D., Murphy, B. A., Miller, J. P., et al. (2017). Restoration of reaching and grasping movements through brain-controlled muscle stimulation in a person with tetraplegia: A proof-of-concept demonstration. *Lancet, 389*(10081), 1821–1830.

Akelaitis, A. J. (1941). Studies on the corpus callosum: Higher visual functions in each homonymous visual field following complete section of corpus callosum. *Archives of Neurology and Psychiatry, 45,* 788.

Akelaitis, A. J. (1943). Studies on the corpus callosum. *Journal of Neuropathology & Experimental Neurology, 2*(3), 226–262.

Alderson, D. L., & Doyle, J. C. (2010). Contrasting views of complexity and their implications for network-centric infrastructures. *IEEE Transactions on Systems, Man, and Cybernetics. Part A: Systems and Humans, 40*(4), 839–852.

Allen, G., Buxton, R. B., Wong, E. C., & Courchesne, E. (1997). Attentional activation of the cerebellum independent of motor involvement. *Science, 275,* 1940–1943.

Allen, M. (1983). Models of hemisphere specialization. *Psychological Bulletin, 93,* 73–104.

Alquist, J. L., Ainsworth, S. E., & Baumeister, R. F. (2013). Determined to conform: Disbelief in free will increases conformity. *Journal of Experimental Social Psychology, 49*(1), 80–86.

Amaral, D. G. (2002). The primate amygdala and the neurobiology of social behavior: Implications for understanding social anxiety. *Biological Psychiatry, 51,* 11–17.

Amedi, A., Floel, A., Knecht, S., Zohary, E., & Cohen, L. G. (2004). Transcranial magnetic stimulation of the occipital pole interferes with verbal processing in blind subjects. *Nature Neuroscience, 7,* 1266–1270.

American College Health Association. (2013). *American college health association—National college health assessment II survey: Undergraduate reference group executive summary spring 2013.* Hanover, MD: American College Health Association. Retrieved from http://www.acha-ncha.org/reports_ACHA-NCHAIIb.html

American College Health Association. (2017). *American college health association—National college health assessment II survey: Undergraduate reference group executive summary fall 2016.* Hanover, MD: American College Health Association. Retrieved from http://www.acha-ncha.org/reports_ACHA-NCHAIIc.html

Aminoff, E. M., Freeman, S., Clewett, D., Tipper, C., Frithsen, A., Johnson, A., et al. (2015). Maintaining a cautious state of mind during a recognition test: A large-scale fMRI study. *Neuropsychologia, 67,* 132–147.

Amsterdam, B. K. (1972). Mirror self-image reactions before age two. *Developmental Psychobiology, 5,* 297–305.

Amunts, K., Lenzen, M., Friederici, A.D., Schleicher, A., Morosan, P., Palomero-Gallagher, N., et al. (2010). Broca's region: Novel organizational principles and multiple receptor mapping. *PLoS Biology, 8,* e1000489.

Ananthaswamy, A. (2015). *The man who wasn't there: Investigations into the strange new science of the self.* New York: Penguin.

Andersen, R. A., & Buneo, C. A. (2002). Intentional maps in posterior parietal cortex. *Annual Review of Neuroscience, 25,* 189–220. [Epub, March 27]

Anderson, A. K. (2005). Affective influences on the attentional dynamics supporting awareness. *Journal of Experimental Psychology. General, 134*(2), 258–281.

Anderson, A. K., Christoff, K., Panitz, D., De Rosa, E., & Gabrieli, J. D. (2003). Neural correlates of the automatic processing of threat facial signals. *Journal of Neuroscience, 23*(13), 5627–5633.

Anderson, A. K., & Phelps, E. A. (1998). Intact recognition of vocal expressions of fear following bilateral lesions of the human amygdala. *Neuroreport, 9*, 3607–3613.

Anderson, A. K., & Phelps, E. A. (2000). Expression without recognition: Contributions of the human amygdala to emotional communication. *Psychological Science, 11*, 106–111.

Anderson, A. K., & Phelps, E. A. (2001). Lesions of the human amygdala impair enhanced perception of emotionally salient events. *Nature, 411*, 305–309.

Anderson, D. J., & Adolphs, R. (2014). A framework for studying emotions across species. *Cell, 157*(1), 187–200.

Anderson, S. W., Bechara, A., Damasio, H., Tranel, D., & Damasio, A. R. (1999). Impairment of social and moral behavior related to early damage in human prefrontal cortex. *Nature Neuroscience, 2*, 1032–1037.

Andino, S. L. G., & Menendez, R. G. de P. (2012). Coding of saliency by ensemble bursting in the amygdala of primates. *Frontiers in Behavioral Neuroscience, 6*(38), 1–16.

Angrilli, A., Marui, A., Palomba, D., Flor, H., Birbaumer, N., Sartori, G., et al. (1996). Startle reflex and emotion modulation impairment after a right amygdala lesion. *Brain, 119*, 1991–2000.

Anguera, J. A., Boccanfuso, J., Rintoul, J. L., Al-Hashimi, O., Faraji, F., Janowich, J., et al. (2013). Video game training enhances cognitive control in older adults. *Nature, 501*(7465), 97–101.

Annett, M. (2002). *Handedness and brain asymmetry: The right shift theory.* Hove, England: Psychology Press.

Aravanis, A. M., Wang, L. P., Zhang, F., Meltzer, L. A., Mogri, Z. M., Schneider, M. B., et al. (2007). An optical neural interface: In vivo control of rodent motor cortex with integrated fiberoptic and optogenetic technology. *Journal of Neural Engineering, 4*(3), S143–S156.

Ardekani, B. A., Figarsky, K., & Sidtis, J. J. (2013). Sexual dimorphism in the human corpus callosum: An MRI study using the OASIS brain database. *Cerebral Cortex, 23*(10), 2514–2520.

Arevalo, M. A., Azcoitia, I., & Garcia-Segura, L. M. (2015). The neuroprotective actions of oestradiol and oestrogen receptors. *Nature Reviews Neuroscience, 16*(1), 17–29.

Armstrong, K. M., Schafer, R. J., Chang, M. H., & Moore, T. (2012). Attention and action in the frontal eye field. In R. Mangun (Ed.), *The neuroscience of attention* (pp. 151–166). Oxford: Oxford University Press.

Arnsten, A. F. (2009). Stress signalling pathways that impair prefrontal cortex structure and function. *Nature Reviews Neuroscience, 10*(6), 410–422.

Aron, A., Fisher, H., Mashek, D., Strong, G., Li, H., & Brown, L. L. (2005). Reward, motivation and emotion systems associated with early-stage intense romantic love. *Journal of Neurophysiology, 94*, 327–337.

Aron, A. R., Behrens, T. E., Smith, S., Frank, M. J., & Poldrack, R. A. (2007). Triangulating a cognitive control network using diffusion-weighted magnetic resonance imaging (MRI) and functional MRI. *Journal of Neuroscience, 27*, 3743–3752.

Aron, A. R., & Poldrack, R. A. (2006). Cortical and subcortical contributions to Stop signal response inhibition: Role of the subthalamic nucleus. *Journal of Neuroscience, 26*, 2424–2433.

Astafiev, S. V., Stanley, C. M., Shulman, G. L., & Corbetta, M. (2004). Extrastriate body area in human occipital cortex responds to the performance of motor actions. *Nature Neuroscience, 7*(5), 542–548.

Atkinson, R. C., & Shiffrin, R. M. (1968). Human memory: A proposed system and its control processes. In K. W. Spence & J. T. Spence (Eds.), *The psychology of learning and motivation* (Vol. 2, pp. 89–195). New York: Academic Press.

Atkinson, R. C., & Shiffrin, R. M. (1971). The control of short-term memory. *Scientific American, 225*(2), 82–90.

Atlas, L. Y., Doll, B. B., Li, J., Daw, N. D., & Phelps, E. A. (2016). Instructed knowledge shapes feedback-driven aversive learning in striatum and orbitofrontal cortex, but not the amygdala. *eLife, 5*, e15192.

Augustine, J. R. (1996). Circuitry and functional aspects of the insular lobe in primates including humans. *Brain Research Reviews, 22*, 229–244.

Avidan, G., Tanzer, M., Hadj-Bouziane, F., Liu, N., Ungerleider, L. G., & Behrmann, M. (2014). Selective dissociation between core and extended regions of the face processing network in congenital prosopagnosia. *Cerebral Cortex, 24*(6), 1565–1578.

Azevedo, F. A., Carvalho, L. R., Grinberg, L. T., Farfel, J. M., Ferretti, R. E., Leite, R. E., et al. (2009). Equal numbers of neuronal and nonneuronal cells make the human brain an isometrically scaled-up primate brain. *Journal of Comparative Neurology, 513*(5), 532–541.

Baarendse, P. J., Counotte, D. S., O'donnell, P., & Vanderschuren, L. J. (2013). Early social experience is critical for the development of cognitive control and dopamine modulation of prefrontal cortex function. *Neuropsychopharmacology, 38*(8), 1485.

Baars, B. J. (1988). *A cognitive theory of consciousness.* Cambridge: Cambridge University Press.

Baars, B. J. (1997). *In the theater of consciousness.* New York: Oxford University Press.

Baars, B. J. (2002). The conscious access hypothesis: Origins and recent evidence. *Trends in Cognitive Sciences, 6*(1), 47–52.

Baddeley, A., & Hitch, G. (1974). Working memory. In G. H. Bower (Ed.), *The psychology of learning and motivation* (Vol. 8, pp. 47–89). New York: Academic Press.

Badre, D., & D'Esposito, M. (2007). Functional magnetic resonance imaging evidence for a hierarchical organization of the prefrontal cortex. *Journal of Cognitive Neuroscience, 19*(12), 2082–2099.

Badre, D., Hoffman, J., Cooney, J. W., & D'Esposito, M. (2009). Hierarchical cognitive control deficits following damage to the human frontal lobe. *Nature Neuroscience, 12*(4), 515–522.

Baird, A. A., Colvin, M. K., Vanhorn, J. D., Inati, S., & Gazzaniga, M. S. (2005). Functional connectivity: Integrating behavioral, diffusion tensor imaging, and functional magnetic resonance imaging data sets. *Journal of Cognitive Neuroscience, 17*, 687–693.

Baker, S. N., Zaaimi, B., Fisher, K. M., Edgley, S. A., & Soteropoulos, D. S. (2015). Pathways mediating functional recovery. *Progress in Brain Research, 218*, 389–412.

Bakin, J. S., South, D. A., & Weinberger, N. M. (1996). Induction of receptive field plasticity in the auditory cortex of the guinea pig during instrumental avoidance conditioning. *Behavioral Neuroscience, 110*, 905–913.

Baldauf, D., & Desimone, R. (2014). Neural mechanisms of object-based attention. *Science, 344*(6182), 424–427.

Balleine, B. W., & O'Doherty, J. P. (2010). Human and rodent homologies in action control: Corticostriatal determinants of goal-directed and habitual action. *Neuropsychopharmacology, 35*(1), 48–69.

Bandyopadhyay, S., Shamma, S. A., & Kanold, P. O. (2010). Dichotomy of functional organization in the mouse auditory cortex. *Nature Neuroscience, 13*, 361–368.

Banissy, M. J., Walsh, V., & Ward, J. (2009). Enhanced sensory perception in synaesthesia. *Experimental Brain Research, 196*(4), 565–571.

Bannerman, D. M., Bus, T., Taylor, A., Sanderson, D. J., Schwarz, I., Jensen, V., et al. (2012). Dissecting spatial knowledge from spatial choice by hippocampal NMDA receptor deletion. *Nature Neuroscience, 15*, 1153–1159.

Bannerman, D. M., Good, M. A., Butcher, S. P., Ramsay, M., & Morris, R. G. M. (1995). Distinct components of spatial learning revealed by prior training and NMDA receptor blockade. *Nature, 378*, 182–186.

Barbur, J. L., Watson, J. D. G., Frackowiak, R. S. J., & Zeki, S. (1993). Conscious visual perception without V1. *Brain, 116*, 1293–1302.

Barceló, F., Suwazono, S., & Knight, R. T. (2000). Prefrontal modulation of visual processing in humans. *Nature Neuroscience, 3*(4), 399–403.

Barclay, P. (2006). Reputational benefits for altruistic behavior. *Evolution and Human Behavior, 27*, 325–344.

Barker, J. E., Semenov, A. D., Michaelson, L., Provan, L. S., Snyder, H. R., & Munakata, Y. (2014). Less-structured time in children's daily lives predicts self-directed executive functioning. *Frontiers in Psychology, 5*, 593.

Barnes, T. D., Kubota, Y., Hu, D., Jin, D. Z., & Graybiel, A. M. (2005). Activity of striatal neurons reflects dynamic encoding and recoding of procedural memories. *Nature, 437*(7062), 1158–1161.

Baron-Cohen, S. (1995). *Mindblindness: An essay on autism and theory of mind*. Cambridge, MA: MIT Press.

Baron-Cohen, S., Burt, L., Smith-Laittan, F., Harrison, J., & Bolton, P. (1996). Synaesthesia: Prevalence and familiality. *Perception, 25*, 1073–1079.

Baron-Cohen, S., Leslie, A. M., & Frith, U. (1985). Does the autistic child have a "theory of mind"? *Cognition, 21*, 37–46.

Barrash, J., Tranel, D., & Anderson, S. W. (2000). Acquired personality disturbances associated with bilateral damage to the ventromedial prefrontal region. *Developmental Neuropsychology, 18*, 355–381.

Barrett, A. M., Crucian, G. P., Raymer, A. M., & Heilman, K. M. (1999). Spared comprehension of emotional prosody in a patient with global aphasia. *Neuropsychiatry, Neuropsychology, and Behavioral Neurology, 12*, 117–120.

Barrett, L. F., Quigley, K. S., Bliss-Moreau, E., & Aronson, K. R. (2004). Interoceptive sensitivity and self-reports of emotional experience. *Journal of Personality and Social Psychology, 87*, 684–697.

Barron, A. B., & Klein, C. (2016). What insects can tell us about the origins of consciousness. *Proceedings of the National Academy of Sciences, USA, 113*(18), 4900–4908.

Bartholomeus, B. (1974). Effects of task requirements on ear superiority for sung speech. *Cortex, 10*, 215–223.

Bartoshuk, L. M., Duffy, V. B., & Miller, I. J. (1994). PTC/PROP tasting: Anatomy, psychophysics and sex effects. *Physiology and Behavior, 56*, 1165–1171.

Bartsch, T., & Deuschl, G. (2010). Transient global amnesia: Functional anatomy and clinical implications. *Lancet Neurology, 9*, 205–214.

Başar, E., Başar-Eroglu, C., Karakaş, S., & Schürmann, M. (2001). Gamma, alpha, delta, and theta oscillations govern cognitive processes. *International Journal of Psychophysiology, 39*, 241–248.

Bassett, D. S., Bullmore, E., Meyer-Lindenberg, A., Weinberger, D. R., & Coppola, R. (2009). Cognitive fitness of cost efficient brain functional networks. *Proceedings of the National Academy of Sciences, USA, 106*, 11747–11752.

Bassett, D. S., & Gazzaniga, M. S. (2011). Understanding complexity in the human brain. *Trends in Cognitive Sciences, 15*(5), 200–209.

Bassett, D. S., Greenfield, D. L., Meyer-Lindenberg, A., Weinberger, D. R., Moore, S.W., & Bullmore, E. T. (2010). Efficient physical embedding of topologically complex information processing networks in brains and computer circuits. *PLoS Computational Biology, 6(4)*, e1000748.

Bassett, D. S., Yang, M., Wymbs, N. F., & Grafton, S. T. (2015). Learning-induced autonomy of sensorimotor systems. *Nature Neuroscience, 18*(5), 744–751.

Bassetti, C., Vella, S., Donati, F., Wielepp, P., & Weder, B. (2000). SPECT during sleepwalking. *Lancet, 356*(9228), 484–485.

Bastiaansen, J. A., Thioux, M., & Keysers, C. (2009). Evidence for mirror systems in emotions. *Philosophical Transactions of the Royal Society of London. Series B, Biological Sciences, 364*(1528), 2391–2404.

Batista, A. P., Buneo, C. A., Snyder, L. H., & Anderson, R. A. (1999). Reach plans in eye-centered coordinates. *Science, 285*, 257–260.

Bauby, J. D. (1997). *The diving bell and the butterfly*. New York: Knopf.

Bauer, P. J., & Wewerka, S. S. (1995). One- to two-year-olds' recall of events: The more expressed, the more impressed. *Journal of Experimental Child Psychology, 59*, 475–496.

Baumann, M. A., Fluet, M. C., & Scherberger, H. (2009). Context-specific grasp movement representation in the macaque anterior intraparietal area. *Journal of Neuroscience, 29*(20), 6436–6448.

Baumeister, R. F., & Brewer, L. E. (2012). Believing versus disbelieving in free will: Correlates and consequences. *Social and Personality Psychology Compass, 6*(10), 736–745.

Baumeister, R. F., Masicampo, E. J., & DeWall, C. N. (2009). Prosocial benefits of feeling free: Disbelief in free will increases aggression and reduces helpfulness. *Personality and Social Psychology Bulletin, 35*(2), 260–268.

Baumgart, F., Gaschler-Markefski, B., Woldorff, M. G., Heinze, H. J., & Scheich, H. (1999). A movement-sensitive area in auditory cortex. *Nature, 400*, 724–726.

Baylis, G. C., Rolls, E. T., & Leonard, C. M. (1985). Selectivity between faces in the responses of a population of neurons in the cortex in the superior temporal sulcus of the monkey. *Brain Research, 342*, 91–102.

Bear, M. F., Connors, B. W., & Paradiso, M. A. (1996). *Neuroscience: Exploring the brain*. Baltimore: Williams & Wilkins.

Bechara, A., Damasio, A. R., Damasio, H., & Anderson, S. W. (1994). Insensitivity to future consequences following damage to human prefrontal cortex. *Cognition, 50*, 7–12.

Bechara, A., Tranel, D., Damasio, H., Adolphs, R., Rockland, C., & Damasio, A. R. (1995). Double dissociation of conditioning and declarative knowledge relative to the amygdala and hippocampus in human. *Science, 269*, 1115–1118.

Bechara, A., Tranel, D., Damasio, H., & Damasio, A. R. (1996). Failure to respond autonomically to anticipated future outcomes following damage to prefrontal cortex. *Cerebral Cortex, 6*, 215–225.

Beckmann, M., Johansen-Berg, H., & Rushworth, M. F. S. (2009). Connectivity-based parcellation of human cingulate cortex and its relation to functional specialization. *Journal of Neuroscience, 29*(4), 1175–1190.

Bedford, R., Elsabbagh, M., Gliga, T., Pickles, A., Senju, A., Charman, T., et al. (2012). Precursors to social and communication difficulties in infants at-risk for autism: Gaze following and attentional engagement. *Journal of Autism and Developmental Disorders, 42*(10), 2208–2218.

Bedny, M. (2017). Evidence from blindness for a cognitively pluripotent cortex. *Trends in Cognitive Sciences, 21*(9), 637–648.

Bedny, M., Konkle, T., Pelphrey, K., Saxe, R., & Pascual-Leone, A. (2010). Sensitive period for a multimodal response in human visual motion area MT/MST. *Current Biology, 20*(21), 1900–1906.

Bedny, M., Pascual-Leone, A., Dodell-Feder, D., Fedorenko, E., & Saxe, R. (2011). Language processing in the occipital cortex of congenitally blind adults. *Proceedings of the National Academy of Sciences, USA, 108*(11), 4429–4434.

Bedny, M., Richardson, H., & Saxe, R. (2015). "Visual" cortex responds to spoken language in blind children. *Journal of Neuroscience, 35*(33), 11674–11681.

Beer, J. S., Heerey, E. H., Keltner, D., Scabini, D., & Knight, R. T. (2003). The regulatory function of self-conscious emotion: Insights from patients with orbitofrontal damage. *Journal of Personality and Social Psychology, 85*, 594–604.

Beer, J. S., John, O. P., Scabini, D., & Knight, R. T. (2006). Orbitofrontal cortex and social behavior: Integrating self-monitoring and emotion-cognition interactions. *Journal of Cognitive Neuroscience, 18*, 871–880.

Behrens, T. E., Woolrich, M. W., Jenkinson, M., Johansen-Berq, H., Nunes, R. G., Clare, S., et al. (2003). Characterization and propagation of uncertainty in diffusion-weighted MR imaging. *Magnetic Resonance in Medicine, 50*, 1077–1088.

Behrmann, M., Moscovitch, M., & Winocur, G. (1994). Intact visual imagery and impaired visual perception in a patient with visual agnosia. *Journal of Experimental Psychology. Human Perception and Performance, 20*, 1068–1087.

Bell, H. C., Pellis, S. M., & Kolb, B. (2010). Juvenile peer play experience and the development of the orbitofrontal and medial prefrontal cortices. *Behavioural Brain Research, 207*(1), 7–13.

Belliveau, J. W., Rosen, B. R., Kantor, H. L., Rzedzian, R. R., Kennedy, D. N., McKinstry, R. C., et al. (1990). Functional cerebral imaging by susceptibility-contrast NMR. *Magnetic Resonance in Medicine, 14*, 538–546.

Belmonte, M. K., Allen, G., Beckel-Mitchener, A., Boulanger, L. M., Carper, R. A., & Webb, S. J. (2004). Autism and abnormal development of brain connectivity. *Journal of Neuroscience, 24*(42), 9228–9231.

Bendesky, A., Tsunozaki, M., Rockman, M. V., Kruglyak, L., & Bargmann, C. I. (2011). Catecholamine receptor polymorphisms affect decision making in *C. elegans*. *Nature, 472*, 313–318.

Berger, H. (1929). Über das Elektrenkephalogramm des Menschen. *European Archives of Psychiatry and Clinical Neuroscience, 87*(1), 527–570.

Bernard, C. (1957.) *An introduction to the study of experimental medicine* (Dover ed.). (H. C. Greene, Trans.). New York: Dover. (Original work published 1865)

Berns, G. S., & Sejnowski, T. (1996). How the basal ganglia makes decisions. In A. Damasio, H. Damasio, & Y. Christen (Eds.), *The neurobiology of decision making* (pp. 101–113). Cambridge, MA: MIT Press.

Bernstein, D., & Loftus, E. F. (2009). How to tell if a particular memory is true or false. *Perspectives on Psychological Science, 4*, 370–374.

Berntson, G. G., Bechara, A., Damasio, H., Tranel, D., & Cacioppo, J. T. (2007). Amygdala contribution to selective dimensions of emotion. *Social Cognitive Affective Neuroscience, 2*(2), 123–129.

Berntson, G. G., Norman, G. J., Bechara, A., Bruss, J., Tranel, D., & Cacioppo, J. T. (2011). The insula and evaluative processes. *Psychological Science, 22*, 80–86.

Berridge, K. C. (2007). The debate over dopamine's role in reward: The case for incentive salience. *Psychopharmacology, 191*, 391–431.

Bertolino, A., Caforio, G., Blasi, G., De Candia, M., Latorre, V., Petruzzella, V., et al. (2004). Interaction of COMT (Val(108/158)Met) genotype and olanzapine treatment on prefrontal cortical function in patients with schizophrenia. *American Journal of Psychiatry, 161*, 1798–1805.

Bianchi, L. (1922). *The mechanism of the brain.* (J. H. MacDonald, Trans.). Edinburgh, Scotland: E. & S. Livingstone.

Bianchi-Demicheli, F., Grafton, S. T., & Ortigue, S. (2006). The power of love on the human brain. *Social Neuroscience, 1*(2), 90–103.

Binder, J., & Price, C. J. (2001). Functional neuroimaging of language. In R. Cabeza & A. Kingstone (Eds.), *Handbook of functional neuroimaging of cognition* (pp. 187–251). Cambridge, MA: MIT Press.

Binder, J. R., Frost, J. A., Hammeke, T. A., Bellgowan, P. S. F., Rao, S. M., & Cox, J. A. (1999). Conceptual processing during the conscious resting state: A functional MRI study. *Journal of Cognitive Neuroscience, 11*, 80–93.

Binder, J. R., Frost, J. A., Hammeke, T. A., Bellgowan, P. S. F., Springer, J. A., Kaufman, J. N., et al. (2000). Human temporal lobe activation by speech and non-speech sounds. *Cerebral Cortex, 10*, 512–528.

Binkofski, F., & Buxbaum, L. J. (2013). Two action systems in the human brain. *Brain and Language, 127*(2), 222–229.

Bisiach, E., & Luzzatti, C. (1978). Unilateral neglect of representational space. *Cortex, 14*, 129–133.

Bisley, J. W., & Goldberg, M. E. (2006). Neural correlates of attention and distractibility in the lateral intraparietal area. *Journal of Neurophysiology, 95*, 1696–1717.

Bitterman, Y., Mukamel, R., Malach, T., Fried, I., & Nelken, I. (2008). Ultra-fine frequency tuning revealed in single neurons of human auditory cortex. *Nature, 451*(7175), 197–201.

Bizley, J. K., & Cohen, Y. E. (2013). The what, where and how of auditory-object perception. *Nature Reviews Neuroscience, 14*(10), 693–707.

Bizzi, E., Accornero, N., Chapple, W., & Hogan, N. (1984). Posture control and trajectory formation during arm movement. *Journal of Neuroscience, 4*, 2738–2744.

Blake, R. (1993). Cats perceive biological motion. *Psychological Science, 4*, 54–57.

Blakemore, S. J. (2008). The social brain in adolescence. *Nature Reviews Neuroscience, 9*, 267–277.

Blakemore, S. J., Frith, C. D., & Wolpert, D. M. (1999). Spatiotemporal prediction modulates the perception of self-produced stimuli. *Journal of Cognitive Neuroscience, 11*(5), 551–559.

Blanke, O., Landis, T., Spinelli, L., & Seeck, M. (2004). Out-of-body experience and autoscopy of neurological origin. *Brain, 127*(2), 243–258.

Blanke, O., & Metzinger, T. (2009). Full-body illusions and minimal phenomenal selfhood. *Trends in Cognitive Sciences, 13*(1), 7–13.

Blanke, O., Mohr, C., Michel, C. M., Pascual-Leone, A., Brugger, P., Seeck, M., et al. (2005). Linking out-of-body experience and self processing to mental own-body imagery at the temporoparietal junction. *Journal of Neuroscience, 25*(3), 550–557.

Blanke, O., Morgenthaler, F. D., Brugger, P., & Overney, L. S. (2009). Preliminary evidence for a fronto-parietal dysfunction in able-bodied participants with a desire for limb amputation. *Journal of Neuropsychology, 3*(2), 181–200.

Blanke O., Ortigue, S., Landis, T., & Seeck, M. (2002). Neuropsychology: Stimulating illusory own-body perceptions. *Nature, 419*, 269–270.

Bleuler, E. (1911). *Dementia praecox: Oder die Gruppe der Schizofrenien* (Handbuch der Psychiatrie. Spezieller Teil, Abt. 4, Hälfte 1). Leipzig, Germany: Deuticke.

BLISS, T. V. P., & LØMO, T. (1973). Long-lasting potentiation of synaptic transmission in the dentate area of the anaesthetized rabbit following stimulation of the perforant pathway. *Journal of Physiology, 232*, 331–356.

BLOCK, J. R., & YUKER, H. E. (1992). *Can you believe your eyes? Over 250 illusions and other visual oddities.* Mattituck, NY: Amereon.

BOCK, A. S., BINDA, P., BENSON, N. C., BRIDGE, H., WATKINS, K. E., & FINE, I. (2015). Resting-state retinotopic organization in the absence of retinal input and visual experience. *Journal of Neuroscience, 35*(36), 12366–12382.

BOGGIO, P. S., NUNES, A., RIGONATTI, S. P., NITSCHE, M. A., PASCUAL-LEONE, A., & FREGNI, F. (2007). Repeated sessions of noninvasive brain DC stimulation is associated with motor function improvement in stroke patients. *Restorative Neurology and Neuroscience, 25*(2), 123–129.

BOLGER, D. J., PERFETTI, C. A., & SCHNEIDER, W. (2005). Cross-cultural effect on the brain revisited: Universal structures plus writing system variation. *Human Brain Mapping, 25*, 92–104.

BOLLIMUNTA, A., MO, J., SCHROEDER, C. E., & DING, M. (2011). Neuronal mechanisms and attentional modulation of corticothalamic alpha oscillations. *Journal of Neuroscience, 31*(13), 4935–4943.

BONDA, E., PETRIDES, M., OSTRY, D., & EVANS, A. (1996). Specific involvement of human parietal systems and the amygdala in the perception of biological motion. *Journal of Neuroscience, 16*, 3737–3744.

BONILHA, L., HILLIS, A. E., HICKOK, G., DEN OUDEN, D. B., RORDEN, C., & FRIDRIKSSON, J. (2017). Temporal lobe networks supporting the comprehension of spoken words. *Brain, 140*(9), 2370–2380.

BONINI, L. (2017). The extended mirror neuron network: Anatomy, origin, and functions. *Neuroscientist, 23*(1), 56–67.

BONINI, L., MARANESI, M., LIVI, A., FOGASSI, L., & RIZZOLATTI, G. (2014). Space-dependent representation of objects and other's action in monkey ventral premotor grasping neurons. *Journal of Neuroscience, 34*(11), 4108–4119.

BORIA, S., FABBRI-DESTRO, M., CATTANEO, L., SPARACI, L., SINIGAGLIA, C., SANTELLI, E., ET AL. (2009). Intention understanding in autism. *PLoS One, 4*(5), e5596. doi:10.1371/journal.pone.0005596

BOSMAN, C. A., SCHOFFELEN, J. M., BRUNET, N., OOSTENVELD, R., BASTOS, A. M., WOMELSDORF, T., ET AL. (2012). Attentional stimulus selection through selective synchronization between monkey visual areas. *Neuron, 75*(5), 875–888.

BOTVINICK, M., NYSTROM, L. E., FISSELL, K., CARTER, C. S., & COHEN, J. D. (1999). Conflict monitoring versus selection-for-action in anterior cingulate cortex. *Nature, 402*, 179–181.

BOUCHER, B., & JENNA, S. (2013). Genetic interaction networks: Better understand to better predict. *Frontiers in Genetics, 4*, art. 290.

BOUHALI, F., THIEBAUT DE SCHOTTEN, M., PINEL, P., POUPON, C., MANGIN, J. F., DEHAENE, S., ET AL. (2014). Anatomical connections of the visual word form area. *Journal of Neuroscience, 34*(46), 15402–15414.

BOYD, L. A., HAYWARD, K. S., WARD, N. S., STINEAR, C. M., ROSSO, C., FISHER, R. J., ET AL. (2017). Biomarkers of stroke recovery: Consensus-based core recommendations from the Stroke Recovery and Rehabilitation Roundtable. *International Journal of Stroke, 12*(5), 480–493.

BOYD, R., GINTIS, H., BOWLES, S., & RICHERSON, P. J. (2003). The evolution of altruistic punishment. *Proceedings of the National Academy of Sciences, USA, 100*, 3531–3535.

BOYDEN, E. S., ZHANG, F., BAMBERG, E., NAGEL, G., & DEISSEROTH, K. (2005). Millisecond-timescale, genetically targeted optical control of neural activity. *Nature Neuroscience, 8*, 1263–1268.

BRADSHAW, J. L., & NETTLETON, N. C. (1981). The nature of hemispheric specialization in man. *Behavioral and Brain Sciences, 4*, 51–91.

BRADSHAW, J. L., & ROGERS, L. J. (1993). *The evolution of lateral asymmetries, language, tool use, and intellect.* San Diego, CA: Academic Press.

BRAITENBERG, V. (1984). *Vehicles: Experiments in synthetic psychology.* Cambridge, MA: MIT Press.

BRANG, D., MCGEOCH, P. D., & RAMACHANDRAN, V. S. (2008). Apotemnophilia: A neurological disorder. *Neuroreport, 19*, 1305–1306.

BRAVER, T. (2012). The variable nature of cognitive control: A dual mechanisms framework. *Trends in Cognitive Science, 16*(2), 106–113.

BREITER, H. C., ETCOFF, H. L., WHALAN, P. J., KENNEDY, W. A., RAUCH, S. L., BUCKNER, R. L., ET AL. (1996). Response and habituation of the human amygdala during visual processing of facial expression. *Neuron, 17*, 875–887.

BREMNER, J. D., RANDALL, P., VERMETTEN, E., STAIB, L., BRONEN, R. A., MAZURE, C., ET AL. (1997). Magnetic resonance imaging-based measurement of hippocampal volume in posttraumatic stress disorder to childhood physical and sexual abuse: A preliminary report. *Biological Psychiatry, 41*, 23–32.

BREWER, J. B., ZHAO, Z., DESMOND, J. E., GLOVER, G. H., & GABRIELI, J. D. (1998). Making memories: Brain activity that predicts how well visual experience will be remembered. *Science, 281*(5380), 1185–1187.

BRIDGE, H., THOMAS, O. M., MININI, L., CAVINA-PRATESI, C., MILNER, A. D., & PARKER, A. J. (2013). Structural and functional changes across the visual cortex of a patient with visual form agnosia. *Journal of Neuroscience, 33*(31), 12779–12791.

BROADBENT, D. A. (1958). *Perception and communication.* New York: Pergamon.

BROCA, P. (1861). Remarks on the seat of the faculty of articulated language, following an observation of aphemia (loss of speech). *Bulletin de la Société Anatomique, 6*, 330–357.

BRODAL, A. (1982). *Neurological anatomy.* New York: Oxford University Press.

BRODMANN, K. (1909). *Vergleichende Lokalisationslehre der Grosshirnrinde in ihren Prinzipien dargestellt auf Grund des Zellenbaues.* Leipzig, Germany: J. A. Barth.

BROMBERG-MARTIN, E. S., MATSUMOTO, M., & HIKOSAKA, O. (2010). Dopamine in motivational control: Rewarding, aversive, and alerting. *Neuron, 68*, 815–834.

BROTCHIE, P., IANSEK, R., & HORNE, M. K. (1991). Motor function of the monkey globus pallidus. *Brain, 114*, 1685–1702.

BROUGHTON, R., BILLINGS, R., CARTWRIGHT, R., DOUCETTE, D., EDMEADS, J., EDWARDH, M., ET AL. (1994). Homicidal somnambulism: A case report. *Sleep, 17*(3), 253–264.

BROWN, J. W., & BRAVER, T. S. (2005). Learned predictions of error likelihood in the anterior cingulate cortex. *Science, 307*, 1118–1121.

BROWN, R., & KULIK, J. (1977). Flashbulb memories. *Cognition, 5*(1), 73–99.

BROWN, T. (1911). The intrinsic factors in the act of progression in the mammal. *Proceedings of the Royal Society of London, Series B, 84*, 308–319.

BRUNO, M. A., VANHAUDENHUYSE, A., THIBAUT, A., MOONEN, G., & LAUREYS, S. (2011). From unresponsive wakefulness to minimally conscious PLUS and functional locked-in syndromes: Recent advances in our understanding of disorders of consciousness. *Journal of Neurology, 258*(7), 1373–1384.

BRYDEN, M. P. (1982). *Laterality: Functional asymmetry in the intact human brain.* New York: Academic Press.

Buchanan, T. W., Tranel, D., & Adolphs, R. (2006). Memories for emotional autobiographical events following unilateral damage to medial temporal lobe. *Brain, 129,* 115–127.

Buckner, R. L., & Carroll, D. C. (2007). Self-projection and the brain. *Trends in Cognitive Science, 11,* 49–57.

Budge, J. (1862). *Lehrbuch der speciellen Physiologie des Menschen.* Leipzig, Germany: Voigt & Günther.

Buhle, J. T., Silvers, J. A., Wager, T. D., Lopez, R., Onyemekwu, C., Kober, H., et al. (2014). Cognitive reappraisal of emotion: A meta-analysis of human neuroimaging studies. *Cerebral Cortex, 24*(11), 2981–2990.

Bullmore, E. T., & Bassett, D. S. (2011). Brain graphs: Graphical models of the human brain connectome. *Annual Review of Clinical Psychology, 7,* 113–140.

Bunge, M. (2010). *Matter and mind.* Berlin: Springer.

Bunge, S. A. (2004). How we use rules to select actions: A review of evidence from cognitive neuroscience. *Cognitive, Affective & Behavioral Neuroscience, 4,* 564–579.

Burke, A. R., McCormick, C. M., Pellis, S. M., & Lukkes, J. L. (2017). Impact of adolescent social experiences on behavior and neural circuits implicated in mental illnesses. *Neuroscience and Biobehavioral Reviews, 76,* 280–300.

Burke, J. F., Long, N. M., Zaghloul, K. A., Sharan, A. D., Sperling, M. R., & Kahana, M. J. (2014). Human intracranial high-frequency activity maps episodic memory formation in space and time. *NeuroImage, 85,* 834–843.

Bush, G. (2010). Attention-deficit/hyperactivity disorder and attention networks. *Neuropsychopharmacology, 35*(1), 278–300.

Bush, G., Luu, P., & Posner, M. I. (2000). Cognitive and emotional influences in anterior cingulate cortex. *Trends in Cognitive Sciences, 4,* 215–222.

Butler, A. J., & James, K. H. (2013). Active learning of novel sound-producing objects: Motor reactivation and enhancement of visuo-motor connectivity. *Journal of Cognitive Neuroscience, 25*(2), 203–218.

Buxbaum, L. J., Veramontil, T., & Schwartz, M. F. (2000). Function and manipulation tool knowledge in apraxia: Knowing "what for" but not "how." *Neurocase, 6*(2), 83–97.

Cabeza, R., Ciaramelli, E., Olson, I. R., & Moscovitch, M. (2008). The parietal cortex and episodic memory: An attentional account. *Nature Reviews Neuroscience, 9*(8), 613–625.

Cacioppo, J. T., Berntson, G. G., Larsen, J. T., Poehlmann, K. M., & Ito, T. A. (2000). The psychophysiology of emotion. In R. J. Lewis & J. M. Haviland-Jones (Eds.), *The handbook of emotions* (2nd ed., pp. 173–191). New York: Guilford.

Cacioppo, J. T., & Cacioppo, S. (2014). Social relationships and health: The toxic effects of perceived social isolation. *Social and Personality Psychology Compass, 8*(2), 58–72.

Cacioppo, J. T., Hawkley, L. C., Norman, G. J., & Berntson, G. G. (2011). Social isolation. *Annals of the New York Academy of Sciences, 1231,* 17–22.

Cacioppo, S., Bianchi-Demicheli, F., Frum, C., Pfaus, J. G., & Lewis, J. W. (2012). The common neural bases between sexual desire and love: A multilevel kernel density fMRI analysis. *Journal of Sexual Medicine, 9*(4), 1048–1054.

Cahill, L., Babinsky, R., Markowitsch, H. J., & McGaugh, J. L. (1995). The amygdala and emotional memory. *Science, 377,* 295–296.

Cahill, L., Haier, R. J., Fallon, J., Alkire, M. T., Tang, C., Keator, D., et al. (1996). Amygdala activity at encoding correlated with long-term, free recall of emotional information. *Proceedings of the National Academy of Sciences, USA, 93,* 8016–8021.

Cain, M. S., & Mitroff, S. R. (2011). Distractor filtering in media multitaskers. *Perception, 40*(10), 1183–1192.

Calder, A. J., Keane, J., Manes, F., Antoun, N., & Young, A. W. (2000). Impaired recognition and experience of disgust following brain injury. *Nature Neuroscience, 3,* 1077–1078.

Call, J., & Tomasello, M. (2008). Does the chimpanzee have a theory of mind? 30 years later. *Trends in Cognitive Science, 12,* 187–192.

Calton, J. L., Dickinson, A. R., & Snyder, L. H. (2002). Non-spatial, motor-specific activation in posterior parietal cortex. *Nature Neuroscience, 5,* 580–588.

Calvert, G. A., Bullmore, E. T., Brammer, M. J., Campbell, R., Williams, S. C., McGuire, P. K., et al. (1997). Activation of auditory cortex during silent lipreading. *Science, 276,* 593–596.

Cameron, I. G., Coe, B., Watanabe, M., Stroman, P. W., & Munoz, D. P. (2009). Role of the basal ganglia in switching a planned response. *European Journal of Neuroscience, 29*(12), 2413–2425.

Cannon, C. M., & Bseikri, M. R. (2004). Is dopamine required for natural reward? *Physiology and Behavior, 81,* 741–748.

Cannon, C. M., & Palmiter, R. D. (2003). Reward without dopamine. *Journal of Neuroscience, 23,* 10827–10831.

Canolty, R. T., Soltani, M., Dalal, S. S., Edwards, E., Dronkers, M. F., Nagarajan, S. S., et al. (2007). Spatiotemporal dynamics of word processing in the human brain. *Frontiers in Neuroscience, 1*(1), 185–196.

Capitani, E., Laiacona, M., Mahon, B., & Caramazza, A. (2003). What are the facts of semantic category-specific deficits? A critical review of the clinical evidence. *Cognitive Neuropsychology, 20*(3–6), 213–261.

Caplan, D., Alpert, N., Waters, G., & Olivieri, A. (2000). Activation of Broca's area by syntactic processing under conditions of concurrent articulation. *Human Brain Mapping, 9,* 65–71.

Caramazza, A., & Shelton, J. (1998). Domain-specific knowledge systems in the brain: The animate-inanimate distinction. *Journal of Cognitive Neuroscience, 10,* 1–34.

Cardinale, R., Shih, P., Fishman, I., Ford, L., & Muller, R.-A. (2013). Pervasive rightward asymmetry shifts of functional networks in autism spectrum disorder. *JAMA Psychiatry, 70*(9), 975–982.

Carmel, D., & Bentin, S. (2002). Domain specificity versus expertise: Factors influencing distinct processing of faces. *Cognition, 83,* 1–29.

Carmena, J. M., Lebedev, M. A., Crist, R. E., O'Doherty, J. E., Santucci, D. M., Dimitrov, D. F., et al. (2003). Learning to control a brain–machine interface for reaching and grasping by primates. *PLoS Biology, 1*(2), E42. [Epub, October 13]

Carmichael, S. T. (2006). Cellular and molecular mechanisms of neural repair after stroke: Making waves. *Annals of Neurology, 59*(5), 735–742.

Carpenter, M. (1976). *Human neuroanatomy* (7th ed.). Baltimore: Williams & Wilkins.

Carper, R. A., Treiber, J. M., Yandall DeJesus, S., & Muller, R.-A. (2016). Reduced hemispheric asymmetry of white matter microstructure in autism spectrum disorder. *Journal of the American Academy of Child and Adolescent Psychiatry, 55*(12), 1073–1080.

Carruthers, P. (2006). *The architecture of the mind: Massive modularity and the flexibility of thought.* Oxford: Oxford University Press.

Casanova, M. F. (2007). The neuropathology of autism. *Brain Pathology, 17,* 422–433.

Casanova, M. F. (2014). Autism as a sequence: From heterochronic germinal cell divisions to abnormalities of cell migration and cortical dysplasias. *Medical Hypotheses, 83,* 32–38.

Casanova, M. F., Buxhoeveden, D., Switala, A., & Roy, E. (2002). Minicolumnar pathology in autism. *Neurology, 58*, 428–432.

Casanova, M. F., & Tillquist, C. R. (2008). Encephalization, emergent properties, and psychiatry: A minicolumnar perspective. *Neuroscientist, 14*, 101–118.

Casanova, M. F., van Kooten, I. A. J., Switala, A. E., van Engeland, H., Heinsen, H., Steinbusch, H. W. M., et al. (2006). Minicolumnar abnormalities in autism. *Acta Neuropathologica, 112*(3), 287–303.

Caspers, S., Zilles, K., Laird, A. R., & Eickhoff, S. B. (2010). ALE meta-analysis of action observation and imitation in the human brain. *NeuroImage, 50*(3), 1148–1167.

Catani, M., Dell'Acqua, F., Budisavljevic, S., Howells, H., Thiebaut de Schotten, M., Froudist-Walsh, S., et al. (2016). Frontal networks in adults with autism spectrum disorder. *Brain, 139*(2), 616–630.

Cattaneo, L., Fabbri-Destro, M., Boria, S., Pieraccini, C., Monti, A., Cossu, G., et al. (2007). Impairment of actions chains in autism and its possible role in intention understanding. *Proceedings of the National Academy of Sciences, USA, 104*, 17825–17830.

Cave, C. B. (1997). Very long-lasting priming in picture naming. *Psychological Science, 8*, 322–325.

Cave, C. B., & Squire, L. R. (1992). Intact and long-lasting repetition priming in amnesia. *Journal of Experimental Psychology. Learning, Memory, and Cognition, 18*(3), 509–520.

Celebrini, S., & Newsome, W. T. (1995). Microstimulation of extrastriate area MST influences performance on a direction discrimination task. *Journal of Neurophysiology, 73*, 437–448.

Centers for Disease Control and Prevention. (2014). *Report to Congress on traumatic brain injury in the United States: Epidemiology and rehabilitation.* National Center for Injury Prevention and Control.

Cerf, M., Thiruvengadam, M., Mormann, F., Kraskov, A., Quiroga, R. Q., Koch, C., et al. (2010). On-line, voluntary control of human temporal lobe neurons. *Nature, 467*, 1104–1110.

Chabris, C. F. (1999). *Cognitive and neuropsychological mechanisms of expertise: Studies with chess masters.* Unpublished doctoral dissertation, Harvard University, Cambridge, MA.

Chabris, C. F., & Hamilton, S. E. (1992). Hemispheric specialization for skilled perceptual organization by chess masters. *Neuropsychologia, 30*, 4–57.

Chakravarthy, V. S., Joseph, D., & Bapi, R. S. (2009). What do the basal ganglia do? A modeling perspective. *Biological Cybernetics, 103*, 237–253.

Chang, L., & Tsao, D. Y. (2017). The code for facial identity in the primate brain. *Cell, 169*(6), 1013–1028.

Chang, L. J., Gianaros, P. J., Manuck, S. B., Krishnan, A., & Wager, T. D. (2015). A sensitive and specific neural signature for picture-induced negative affect. *PLoS Biology, 13*(6), e1002180.

Chao, L. L., & Martin, A. (2000). Representation of manipulable man-made objects in the dorsal stream. *NeuroImage, 12*, 478–484.

Chapin, J. K., Moxon, K. A., Markowitz, R. S., & Nicolelis, M. A. (1999). Real-time control of a robot arm using simultaneously recorded neurons in the motor cortex. *Nature Neuroscience, 2*, 664–670.

Chappell, M. H., Ulug, A. M., Zhang, L., Heitger, M. H., Jordan, B. D., Zimmerman, R. D., et al. (2006). Distribution of microstructural damage in the brains of professional boxers: A diffusion MRI study. *Journal of Magnetic Resonance Imaging, 24*, 537–542.

Charnov, E. (1974). Optimal foraging: The marginal value theorem. *Theoretical Population Biology, 9*(2), 129–136.

Chawarska, K., Macari, S., & Shic, F. (2012). Context modulates attention to social scenes in toddlers with autism. *Journal of Child Psychology and Psychiatry, 53*(8), 903–913.

Chawla, D., Lumer, E. D., & Friston, K. J. (1999). The relationship between synchronization among neuronal populations and their mean activity levels. *Neural Computation, 11*, 1389–1411.

Cheever, N. A., Rosen, L. D., Carrier, L. M., & Chavez, A. (2014). Out of sight is not out of mind: The impact of restricting wireless mobile device use on anxiety levels among low, moderate and high users. *Computers in Human Behavior, 37*, 290–297.

Chen, B. L., Hall, D. H., & Chklovskii, D. B. (2006). Wiring optimization can relate neuronal structure and function. *Proceedings of the National Academy of Sciences, USA, 103*(12), 4723–4728.

Chen, X., Gabitto, M., Peng, Y., Ryba, N. J., & Zuker, C. S. (2011). A gustotopic map of taste qualities in the mammalian brain. *Science, 333*(6047), 1262–1266.

Cheng, Y., Lin, C. P., Liu, H. L., Hsu, Y. Y., Lim, K. E., Hung, D., et al. (2007). Expertise modulates the perception of pain in others. *Current Biology, 17*, 1708–1713.

Cherniak, C., Mokhtarzada, Z., Rodriguez-Esteban, R., & Changizi, K. (2004). Global optimization of cerebral cortex layout. *Proceedings of the National Academy of Sciences, USA, 101*(4), 1081–1086.

Cherry, E. C. (1953). Some experiments on the recognition of speech, with one and two ears. *Journal of the Acoustical Society of America, 25*, 975–979.

Chomsky, N. (1956). Three models for the description of language. *IEEE Transactions on Information Theory, 2*(3), 113–124.

Chomsky, N. (1975). *Reflections on language.* New York: Pantheon.

Chomsky, N. (2006). *Language and mind* (3rd ed.). Cambridge: Cambridge University Press.

Christianson, S. A. (1992). *The handbook of emotion and memory: Research and theory.* Hillsdale, NJ: Erlbaum.

Chura, L. R., Lombardo, M. V., Ashwin, E., Auyeung, B., Chakrabarti, B., Bullmore, E. T., et al. (2010). Organizational effects of fetal testosterone on human corpus callosum size and asymmetry. *Psychoneuroendocrinology, 35*, 122–132.

Churchland, M. M., Cunningham, J. P., Kaufman, M. T., Foster, J. D., Nuyujukian, P., Ryi, S. I., et al. (2012). Neural population dynamics during reaching. *Nature, 487*, 51–56. doi:10.1038/nature11129

Churchland, M. M., Cunningham, J. P., Kaufman, M. T., Ryu, S. I., & Shenoy, K. V. (2010). Cortical preparatory activity: Representation of movement or first cog in a dynamical machine? *Neuron, 68*, 387–400.

Cikara, M., Botvinick, M. M., & Fiske, S. T. (2011). Us versus them: Social identity shapes neural responses to intergroup competition and harm. *Psychological Science, 22*(3), 306–313.

Cisek, P. (2007). Cortical mechanisms of action selection: The affordance competition hypothesis. *Philosophical Transactions of the Royal Society of London. Series B, Biological Sciences, 362*(1485), 1585–1599.

Cisek, P., & Kalaska, J. F. (2005). Neural correlates of reaching decisions in dorsal premotor cortex: Specification of multiple direction choices and final selection of action. *Neuron, 45*(5), 801–814.

Clark, D. D., & Sokoloff, L. (1999). Circulation and energy metabolism of the brain. In G. J. Siegel, B. W. Agranoff, R. W. Albers, S. K. Fisher, & M. D. Uhler (Eds.), *Basic neurochemistry: Molecular, cellular and medical aspects* (6th ed., pp. 637–670). Philadelphia: Lippincott-Raven.

Clark, R. E., & Squire, L. R. (1998). Classical conditioning and brain systems: The role of awareness. *Science, 280*, 77–81.

Clarkson, A. N., Huang, B. S., MacIsaac, S., Mody, I., & Carmichael, S. T. (2010). Reducing excessive GABA-mediated tonic inhibition promotes functional recovery after stroke. *Nature, 468*(7321), 305–309.

Clune, J., Mouret, J.-B., & Lipson, H. (2013, March). The evolutionary origins of modularity. *Proceedings of the Royal Society of London, Series B, 280*(1755), 20122863.

Cohen, J. D., Botvinick, M., & Carter, C. S. (2000). Anterior cingulate and prefrontal cortex: Who's in control? *Nature Neuroscience, 3*, 421–423.

Cohen, J. R., & D'Esposito, M. (2016). The segregation and integration of distinct brain networks and their relationship to cognition. *Journal of Neuroscience, 36*(48), 12083–12094.

Cohen, J. Y., Haesler, S., Vong, L., Lowell, B. B., & Uchida, N. (2012). Neuron-type specific signals for reward and punishment in the ventral tegmental area. *Nature, 482*(7383), 85.

Cohen, L., Dehaene, S., Naccache, L., Lehéricy, S., Dehaene-Lambertz, G., Hénaff, M. A., et al. (2000). The visual word form area: Spatial and temporal characterization of an initial stage of reading in normal subjects and posterior split-brain patients. *Brain, 123*, 291–307.

Cohen, L., Lehéricy, S., Chochon, F., Lemer, C., Rivaud, S., & Dehaene, S. (2002). Language-specific tuning of visual cortex? Functional properties of the visual word form area. *Brain, 125*(Pt. 5), 1054–1069.

Collins, A. M., & Loftus, E. F. (1975). A spreading-activation theory of semantic processing. *Psychological Review, 82*, 407–428.

Collins, K. L., Guterstam, A., Cronin, J., Olson, J. D., Ehrsson, H. H., & Ojemann, J. G. (2017). Ownership of an artificial limb induced by electrical brain stimulation. *Proceedings of the National Academy of Sciences, USA, 114*(1), 166–171.

Conti, E., Calderoni, S., Gaglianese, A., Pannek, K., Mazzotti, S., Rose, S., et al. (2016). Lateralization of brain networks and clinical severity in toddlers with autism spectrum disorder: A HARDI diffusion MRI study. *Autism Research, 9*(3), 382–392.

Cools, R. (2006). Dopaminergic modulation of cognitive function: Implications for L-DOPA treatment in Parkinson's disease. *Neuroscience and Biobehavioral Reviews, 30*(1), 1–23.

Coop, G., Wen, X., Ober, C., Pritchard, J. K., & Przeworski, M. (2008). High-resolution mapping of crossovers reveals extensive variation in fine-scale recombination patterns among humans. *Science, 319*(5868), 1395–1398.

Corballis, M. C. (1991). *The lopsided ape: Evolution of the generative mind.* New York: Oxford University Press.

Corballis, M. C. (2009). The evolution of language. *Annals of the New York Academy of Sciences, 1156*(1), 19–43.

Corballis, P. M., Fendrich, R., Shapley, R. M., & Gazzaniga, M. S. (1999). Illusory contour perception and amodal boundary completion: Evidence of a dissociation following callosotomy. *Journal of Cognitive Neuroscience, 11*, 459–466.

Corbett, B. A., Carmean, V., Ravizza, S., Wendelken, G., Henry, M. L., Carter, C., et al. (2009). A functional and structural study of emotion and face processing in children with autism. *Psychiatry Research: Neuroimaging, 173*, 196–205.

Corbetta, M., Kincade, J. M., Lewis, C., Snyder, A. Z., & Sapir, A. (2005). Neural basis and recovery of spatial attention deficits in spatial neglect. *Nature Neuroscience, 8*, 1603–1610.

Corbetta, M., Kincade, J. M., Ollinger, J. M., McAvoy, M. P., & Shulman, G. L. (2000). Voluntary orienting is dissociated from target detection in human posterior parietal cortex. *Nature Neuroscience, 3*, 292–297.

Corbetta, M., Miezin, F. M., Dobmeyer, S., Shulman, G. L., & Petersen, S. E. (1991). Selective and divided attention during visual discriminations of shape, color and speed: Functional anatomy by positron emission tomography. *Journal of Neuroscience, 11*, 2383–2402.

Corbetta, M., & Shulman, G. (2002). Control of goal-directed and stimulus-driven attention in the brain. *Nature Reviews Neuroscience, 3*, 201–215.

Corbetta, M., & Shulman, G. (2011). Spatial neglect and attention networks. *Annual Review of Neuroscience, 34*, 569–599.

Coren, S., Ward, L. M., & Enns, J. T. (1994). *Sensation and perception* (4th ed.). Ft. Worth, TX: Harcourt Brace.

Corkin, S., Amaral, D., Gonzalez, R., Johnson, K., & Hyman, B. T. (1997). H.M.'s medial temporal lobe lesion: Findings from magnetic resonance imaging. *Journal of Neuroscience, 17*, 3964–3979.

Corradi-Dell'Acqua, C., Tusche, A., Vuilleumier, P., & Singer, T. (2016). Cross-modal representations of first-hand and vicarious pain, disgust and fairness in insular and cingulate cortex. *Nature Communications, 7*, 10904.

Corthout, E., Uttl, B., Ziemann, U., Cowey, A., & Hallett, M. (1999). Two periods of processing in the (circum)striate visual cortex as revealed by transcranial magnetic stimulation. *Neuropsychologia, 37*, 137–145.

Cosman, J. D., Atreya, P. V., & Woodman, G. F. (2015). Transient reduction of visual distraction following electrical stimulation of the prefrontal cortex. *Cognition, 145*, 73–76.

Cosmides, L., Barrett, H. C., & Tooby, J. (2010). Adaptive specializations, social exchange, and the evolution of human intelligence. *Proceedings of the National Academy of Sciences, USA, 107*(Suppl. 2), 9007–9014.

Cosmides, L., & Tooby, J. (2000). Evolutionary psychology and the emotions. In M. Lewis & J. M. Haviland-Jones (Eds.), *Handbook of emotions* (2nd ed., pp. 91–115). New York: Guilford.

Cosmides, L., & Tooby, J. (2004). Social exchange: The evolutionary design of a neurocognitive system. In M. S. Gazzaniga (Ed.), *Cognitive neurosciences* (3rd ed., pp. 1295–1308). Cambridge, MA: MIT Press.

Costafreda, S. G., Brammer, M. J., David, A. S., & Fu, C. H. (2008). Predictors of amygdala activation during the processing of emotional stimuli: A meta-analysis of 385 PET and fMRI studies. *Brain Research Reviews, 58*(1), 57–70.

Coudé, G., Ferrari, P. F., Rodà, F., Maranesi, M., Borelli, E., Veroni, B., et al. (2011). Neurons controlling voluntary vocalization in the macaque ventral premotor cortex. *PLoS One, 6*(11), e26822.

Courchesne, E., & Pierce, K. (2005). Why the frontal cortex in autism might be talking only to itself: Local over-connectivity but long-distance disconnection. *Current Opinions in Neurobiology, 15*(2), 225–230.

Courchesne, E., Redcay, E., & Kennedy, D. P. (2004). The autistic brain: Birth through adulthood. *Current Opinion in Neurology, 17*(4), 489–496.

Craig, A. D. (2009). How do you feel—now? The anterior insula and human awareness. *Nature Reviews Neuroscience, 10*, 59–70.

Craik, F. I. M., & Lockhart, R. S. (1972). Levels of processing: A framework for memory research. *Journal of Verbal Learning and Verbal Behavior, 11*, 671–684.

Crick, F. (1992). Function of the thalamic reticular complex: The searchlight hypothesis. In S. M. Kosslyn & R. A. Andersen (Eds.), *Frontiers in cognitive neuroscience* (pp. 366–372). Cambridge, MA: MIT Press.

Crick, F. (1999). The impact of molecular biology on neuroscience. *Philosophical Transactions of the Royal Society of London. Series B, Biological Sciences, 354*(1392), 2021–2025.

Critchley, H. D. (2009). Psychophysiology of neural, cognitive and affective integration: fMRI and autonomic indicants. *International Journal of Psychophysiology, 73*, 88–94.

Critchley, H. D., Mathias, C. J., Josephs, O., O'Doherty, J., Zanini, S., Dewar, B. K., et al. (2003). Human cingulate cortex and autonomic control: Converging neuroimaging and clinical evidence. *Brain, 126*, 2139–2152.

Critchley, H. D., Wiens, S., Rothstein, P., Öhman, A., & Dolan, R. J. (2004). Neural systems supporting interoceptive awareness. *Nature Neuroscience, 7*, 189–195.

Crone, E. A., & Dahl, R. E. (2012). Understanding adolescence as a period of social-affective engagement and goal flexibility. *Nature Reviews Neuroscience, 13*(9), 636.

Croxson, P. L., Walton, M. E., O'Reilly, J. X., Behrens, T. E. J., & Rushworth, M. F. S. (2009). Effort based cost-benefit valuation and the human brain. *Journal of Neuroscience, 29*, 4531–4541.

Csikszentmihalyi, M. (1990). *Flow: The psychology of optimal experience*. New York: Harper & Row.

Csikszentmihalyi, M., & LeFevre, J. (1989). Optimal experience in work and leisure. *Journal of Personality and Social Psychology, 56*, 815–822.

Cui, H., & Andersen, R. A. (2007). Posterior parietal cortex encodes autonomously selected motor plans. *Neuron, 56*, 552–559.

Culham, J. C., Danckert, S. L., DeSouza, J. F., Gati, J. S., Menon, R. S., & Goodale, M. A. (2003). Visually guided grasping produces fMRI activation in dorsal but not ventral stream brain areas. *Experimental Brain Research, 153*, 180–189.

Cunningham, W. A., Johnson, M. K., Raye, C. L., Gatenby, J. C., Gore, J. C., & Banaji, M. R. (2004). Separable neural components in the processing of black and white faces. *Psychological Science, 15*, 806–813.

Cunningham, W. A., Raye, C. L., & Johnson, M. K. (2005). Neural correlates of evaluation associated with promotion and prevention regulatory focus. *Cognitive, Affective & Behavioral Neuroscience, 5*(2), 202–211.

Cunningham, W. A., Van Bavel, J. J., & Johnsen, I. R. (2008). Affective flexibility: Evaluative processing goals shape amygdala activity. *Psychological Science, 19*(2), 152–160.

Damasio, A. R. (1990). Category-related recognition defects as a clue to the neural substrates of knowledge. *Trends in Neurosciences, 13*, 95–98.

Damasio, A. R. (1998). Investigating the biology of consciousness. *Philosophical Transactions of the Royal Society of London. Series B, Biological Sciences, 353*, 1879–1882.

Damasio, A. [R.], & Damasio, H. (2016). Pain and other feelings in humans and animals. *Animal Sentience, 1*(3), 33.

Damasio, A. [R.], Damasio, H., & Tranel, D. (2012). Persistence of feelings and sentience after bilateral damage of the insula. *Cerebral Cortex, 23*(4), 833–846.

Damasio, A. R., Tranel, D., & Damasio, H. (1990). Individuals with sociopathic behavior caused by frontal damage fail to respond autonomically to social stimuli. *Behavioral Brain Research, 41*, 81–94.

Damasio, H., Grabowski, T., Frank, R., Galaburda, A. M., & Damasio, A. R. (1994). The return of Phineas Gage: Clues about the brain from the skull of a famous patient. *Science, 264*, 1102–1105.

Damasio, H., Tranel, D., Grabowski, T., Adolphs, R., & Damasio, A. (2004). Neural systems behind word and concept retrieval. *Cognition, 92*, 179–229.

Darwin, C. (1871). *The descent of man and selection in relation to sex*. London: Murray.

Darwin, C. (1873). *The expression of the emotions in man and animals*. Oxford: Oxford University Press.

Darwin, C., Ekman, P., & Prodger, P. (1998). *The expression of the emotions in man and animals* (3rd ed.). Oxford: Oxford University Press.

Daselaar, S. M., Prince, S. E., Dennis, N. A., Hayes, S. M., Kim, H., & Cabeza R. (2009). Posterior midline and ventral parietal activity is associated with retrieval success and encoding failure. *Frontiers in Human Neuroscience, 3*, 13.

DaSilva, A. F., Tuch, D. S., Wiegell, M. R., & Hadjikhani, N. (2003). A primer on diffusion tensor imaging of anatomical substructures. *Neurosurgical Focus, 15*, E4.

Davachi, L., Mitchell, J. P., & Wagner, A. D. (2003). Multiple routes to memory: Distinct medial temporal lobe processes build item and source memories. *Proceedings of the National Academy of Sciences, USA, 100*, 2157–2162.

Davachi, L., & Wagner, A. D. (2002). Hippocampal contributions to episodic encoding: Insights from relational and item-based learning. *Journal of Neurophysiology, 88*, 982–990.

Davidson, R. J., Ekman, P., Saron, C., Senulis, J., & Friesen, W. V. (1990). Approach-withdrawal and cerebral asymmetry: Emotional expression and brain physiology. *Journal of Personality and Social Psychology, 58*, 330–341.

Davies, R. R., Graham, K. S., Xuereb, J. H., Williams, G. B., & Hodges, J. R. (2004). The human perirhinal cortex and semantic memory. *European Journal of Neuroscience, 20*, 2441–2446.

Davis, M. (1992). The role of the amygdala in conditioned fear. In J. P. Aggleton (Ed.), *The amygdala: Neurobiological aspects of emotion, memory and mental dysfunction* (pp. 255–306). New York: Wiley-Liss.

Daw, N. D., O'Doherty, J. P., Dayan, P., Seymour, B., & Dolan, R. J. (2006). Cortical substrates for exploratory decisions in humans. *Nature, 441*, 876–879.

Dayan, P., & Niv, Y. (2008). Reinforcement learning: The good, the bad and the ugly. *Current Opinion in Neurobiology, 18*, 185–196.

DeArmond, S., Fusco, M., & Dewey, M. (1976). *A photographic atlas: Structure of the human brain* (2nd ed.). New York: Oxford University Press.

De Bie, R. M., de Haan, R. J., Schuurman, P. R., Esselink, R. A., Bosch, D. A., & Speelman, J. D. (2002). Morbidity and mortality following pallidotomy in Parkinson's disease: A systematic review. *Neurology, 58*, 1008–1012.

Debiec, J., LeDoux, J. E., & Nader, K. (2002). Cellular and systems reconsolidation in the hippocampus. *Neuron, 36*, 527–538.

Decety, J. (2011). The neuroevolution of empathy. *Annals of the New York Academy of Sciences, 1231*, 35–45.

Decety, J., & Grezes, J. (1999). Neural mechanisms subserving the perception of human actions. *Trends in Cognitive Sciences, 3*, 172–178.

Decety, J., & Jackson, P. L. (2004). The functional architecture of human empathy. *Behavioral and Cognitive Neuroscience Reviews, 3*, 71–100.

Decety, J., Yang, C.-Y., & Cheng, Y. (2010). Physicians down-regulate their pain empathy response: An event–related brain potential study. *NeuroImage, 50*, 1676–1682.

Deen, B., Richardson, H., Dilks, D. D., Takahashi, A., Keil, B., Wald, L. L., et al. (2017). Organization of high-level visual cortex in human infants. *Nature Communications, 8*, 13995.

De Fockert, J. W., Rees, G., Frith, C. D., & Lavie, N. (2001). The role of working memory in visual selective attention. *Science, 291*, 1803–1806.

Dehaene, S. (2014). *Consciousness and the brain: Deciphering how the brain codes our thoughts.* New York: Penguin.

Dehaene, S., & Cohen, L. (2011). The unique role of the visual word form area in reading. *Trends in Cognitive Sciences, 15*(6), 254–261.

Dehaene, S., Le Clec'H, G., Poline, J.-B., Le Bihan, D., & Cohen, L. (2002). The visual word form area: A prelexical representation of visual words in the fusiform gyrus. *Neuroreport, 13,* 321–325.

Dehaene, S., Posner, M. I., & Tucker, D. M. (1994). Localization of a neural system for error detection and compensation. *Psychological Science, 5,* 303–305.

Deibert, E., Kraut, M., Kremen, S., & Hart, J., Jr. (1999). Neural pathways in tactile object recognition. *Neurology, 52,* 1413–1417.

Delis, D., Robertson, L., & Efron, R. (1986). Hemispheric specialization of memory for visual hierarchical stimuli. *Neuropsychologia, 24,* 205–214.

Dell, G. S. (1986). A spreading activation theory of retrieval in sentence production. *Psychological Review, 93,* 283–321.

DeLong, M. R. (1990). Primate models of movement disorders of basal ganglia origin. *Trends in Neurosciences, 13,* 281–285.

De Martino, B., Camerer, C. F., & Adolphs, R. (2010). Amygdala damage eliminates monetary loss aversion. *Proceedings of the National Academy of Sciences, USA, 107*(8), 3788–3792.

Dennett, D. (1991). *Consciousness explained.* Boston: Little, Brown.

Dennis, N. A., Bowman, C. R., & Vandekar, S. N. (2012). True and phantom recollection: An fMRI investigation of similar and distinct neural correlates and connectivity. *NeuroImage, 59*(3), 2982–2993.

Denny, B. T., Silvers, J. A., & Ochsner, K. N. (2009). How we heal what we don't want to feel: The functional neural architecture of emotion regulation. In A. M. Kring & D. M. Sloan (Eds.), *Emotion regulation and psychopathology: A transdiagnostic approach to etiology and treatment* (pp. 59–87). New York: Guilford.

Desimone, R. (1991). Face-selective cells in the temporal cortex of monkeys. *Journal of Cognitive Neuroscience, 3,* 1–8.

Desimone, R., Albright, T. D., Gross, C. G., & Bruce, C. (1984). Stimulus-selective properties of inferior temporal neurons in the macaque. *Journal of Neuroscience, 4,* 2051–2062.

Desimone, R., & Duncan, J. (1995). Neural mechanisms of selective visual attention. *Annual Review of Neuroscience, 18*(1), 193–222.

Desimone, R., Wessinger, M., Thomas, L., & Schneider, W. (1990). Attentional control of visual perception: Cortical and subcortical mechanisms. *Cold Spring Harbor Symposia on Quantitative Biology, 55,* 963–971.

Desmurget, M., Epstein, C. M., Turner, R. S., Prablanc, C., Alexander, G. E., & Grafton, S. T. (1999). Role of the posterior parietal cortex in updating reaching movements to a visual target. *Nature Neuroscience, 2,* 563–567.

Desmurget, M., Reilly, K. T., Richard, N., Szathmari, A., Mottolese, C., & Sirigu, A. (2009). Movement intention after parietal cortex stimulation in humans. *Science, 324,* 811–813.

DeSteno, D., Li, Y., Dickens, L., & Lerner, J. S. (2014). Gratitude: A tool for reducing economic impatience. *Psychological Science, 25*(6), 1262–1267.

Dettman, S. J., Dowell, R. C., Choo, D., Arnott, W., Abrahams, Y., Davis, A., et al. (2016). Long-term communication outcomes for children receiving cochlear implants younger than 12 months: A multicenter study. *Otology & Neurotology, 37*(2), e82–e95.

DeWitt, I., & Rauschecker, J. P. (2012). Phoneme and word recognition in the auditory ventral stream. *Proceedings of the National Academy of Sciences, USA, 109*(8), E505–E514.

De Zeeuw, P., & Durston, S. (2017). Cognitive control in attention deficit hyperactivity disorder. In T. Egner (Ed.), *Wiley handbook of cognitive control* (pp. 602–618). Chichester, England: Wiley.

Diamond, A. (1990). The development and neural bases of memory functions as indexed by the A(not)B and delayed response tasks in human infants and infant monkeys. In A. Diamond (Ed.), *The development and neural bases of higher cognitive functions* (pp. 267–317). New York: New York Academy of Sciences.

Diamond, A., & Ling, D. S. (2016). Conclusions about interventions, programs, and approaches for improving executive functions that appear justified and those that, despite much hype, do not. *Developmental Cognitive Neuroscience, 18,* 34–48.

Diana, R. A., Yonelinas, A. P., & Ranganath, C. (2007). Imaging recollection and familiarity in the medial temporal lobe: A three-component model. *Trends in Cognitive Sciences, 11,* 379–386.

Dias-Ferreira, E., Sousa, J. C., Melo, I., Morgado, P., Mesquita, A. R., Cerqueira, J. J., et al. (2009). Chronic stress causes frontostriatal reorganization and affects decision-making. *Science, 325*(5940), 621–625.

Dickerson, S. S., & Kemeny, M. E. (2004). Acute stressors and cortisol responses: A theoretical integration and synthesis of laboratory research. *Psychological Bulletin, 130*(3), 355.

Ditterich, J., Mazurek, M. E., & Shadlen, M. N. (2003). Microstimulation of visual cortex affects the speed of perceptual decisions. *Nature Neuroscience, 6*(8), 891–898.

Dolan, R. J. (2002). Emotion, cognition, and behavior. *Science, 298*(5596), 1191–1194.

Dolcos, F., LaBar, K. S., & Cabeza, R. (2004). Interaction between the amygdala and the medial temporal lobe memory system predicts better memory for emotional events. *Neuron, 42,* 855–863.

Donders, F. C. (1969). On the speed of mental processes. *Acta Psychologica, 30,* 412–431. (Translation of *Die Schnelligkeit psychischer Processe,* originally published 1868)

Do Rego, J. L., Seong, J. Y., Burel, D., Leprince, J., Luu-The, V., Tsutsui, K., et al. (2009). Neurosteroid biosynthesis: Enzymatic pathways and neuroendocrine regulation by neurotransmitters and neuropeptides. *Frontiers in Neuroendocrinology, 30*(3), 259–301.

Downar, J., Crawley, A. P., Mikulis, D. J., & Davis, K. D. (2000). A multimodal cortical network for the detection of changes in the sensory environment. *Nature Neuroscience, 3*(3), 277–283.

Downing, P., Jiang, Y., Shuman, M., & Kanwisher, N. (2001). A cortical area selective for visual processing of the human body. *Science, 293,* 2470–2473.

Doyle, J., & Csete, M. (2011). Architecture, constraints, and behavior. *Proceedings of the National Academy of Sciences, USA, 108*(Suppl. 3), 15624–15630.

Drachman, D. A. (2014). The amyloid hypothesis, time to move on: Amyloid is the downstream result, not cause, of Alzheimer's disease. *Alzheimer's & Dementia, 10*(3), 372–380.

Draganski, B., Gaser, C., Busch, V., Schuierer, G., Bogdahn, U., & May, A. (2004). Neuroplasticity: Changes in grey matter induced by training. *Nature, 427*(6972), 311–312.

Driver, J., & Noesselt, T. (2007). Multisensory interplay reveals crossmodal influences on "sensory-specific" brain regions, neural responses, and judgments. *Neuron, 57,* 11–23.

Dronkers, N. F. (1996). A new brain region for coordinating speech articulation. *Nature, 384,* 159–161.

Dronkers, N. F., Plaisant, O., Iba-Zizen, M. T., & Cabanis, E. A. (2007). Paul Broca's historic cases: High-resolution MR imaging of the brains of Leborgne and Lelong. *Brain, 130*(5), 1432–1441.

Dronkers, N. F., Wilkins, D. P., Van Valin, R. D., Redfern, B. B., & Jaeger, J. J. (1994). A reconsideration of the brain areas involved in the disruption of morphosyntactic comprehension. *Brain and Language, 47,* 461–462.

Druzgal, T. J., & D'Esposito, M. (2003). Dissecting contributions of prefrontal cortex and fusiform face area to face working memory. *Journal of Cognitive Neuroscience, 15*, 771–784.

Duchenne de Bologne, G. B. (1862). *The mechanism of human facial expression.* (R. A. Cuthbertson, Trans.). Paris: Jules Renard.

Dum, R. P., & Strick, P. L. (2002). Motor areas in the frontal lobe of the primate. *Physiology & Behavior, 77*, 677–682.

Duncan, J. (1984). Selective attention and the organization of visual information. *Journal of Experimental Psychology. General, 113*, 501–517.

Duncan, J. (1995). Attention, intelligence, and the frontal lobes. In M. S. Gazzaniga (Ed.), *The cognitive neurosciences* (pp. 721–733). Cambridge, MA: MIT Press.

Duncan, J., & Humphreys, G. W. (1989). Visual search and stimulus similarity. *Psychological Review, 96*(3), 433.

Dunsmoor, J. E., Kragel, P. A., Martin, A., & LaBar, K. S. (2014). Aversive learning modulates cortical representations of object categories. *Cerebral Cortex, 24*(11), 2859–2872.

Dunsmoor, J. E., Murty, V. P., Davachi, L., & Phelps, E. A. (2015). Emotional learning selectively and retroactively strengthens memories for related events. *Nature, 520*(7547), 345–348.

Dunsmoor, J. E., Niv, Y., Daw, N., & Phelps, E. A. (2015). Rethinking extinction. *Neuron, 88*(1), 47–63.

Duong, T. Q., Kim, D. S., Ugurbil, K., & Kim, S. G. (2000). Spatiotemporal dynamics of the BOLD fMRI signals: Toward mapping submillimeter cortical columns using the early negative response. *Magnetic Resonance in Medicine, 44*, 231–242.

Dux, P. E., Tombu, M. N., Harrison, S., Rogers, B. P., Tong, F., & Marois, R. (2009). Training improves multitasking performance by increasing the speed of information processing in human prefrontal cortex. *Neuron, 63*, 127–138.

Dye, M. W., Green, C. S., & Bavelier, D. (2009). Increasing speed of processing with action video games. *Current Directions in Psychological Science, 18*(6), 321–326.

Dye, M. W., Hauser, P. C., & Bavelier, D. (2009). Is visual selective attention in deaf individuals enhanced or deficient? The case of the useful field of view. *PLoS One, 4*(5), e5640.

Edelman, G., & Tononi, G. (2000). *A universe of consciousness: How matter becomes imagination.* New York: Basic Books.

Efron, R. (1990). *The decline and fall of hemispheric specialization.* Hillsdale, NJ: Erlbaum.

Egly, R., Driver, J., & Rafal, R. D. (1994). Shifting visual attention between objects and locations—Evidence from normal and parietal lesion subjects. *Journal of Experimental Psychology. General, 123*, 161–177.

Eichele, T., Debener, S., Calhoun, V. D., Specht, K., Engel, A. K., Hugdah, K., et al. (2008). Prediction of human errors by maladaptive changes in event-related brain networks. *Proceedings of the National Academy of Sciences, USA, 105*, 6173–6178.

Eichenbaum, H. (2000). A cortical-hippocampal system for declarative memory. *Nature Reviews Neuroscience, 1*, 41–50.

Eichenbaum, H., Dudchenko, P., Wood, E., Shapiro, M., & Tanila, H. (1999). The hippocampus, memory, and place cells: Is it spatial memory or a memory space? *Neuron, 23*, 209–226.

Eichenbaum, H., Stewart, C., & Morris, R. G. M. (1990). Hippocampal representation in spatial learning. *Journal of Neuroscience, 10*, 331–339.

Eichenbaum, H., Yonelinas, A. P., & Ranganath, C. (2007). The medial temporal lobe and recognition memory. *Annual Review of Neuroscience, 30*, 123–152.

Eisenberg, J. F. (1981). *The mammalian radiations: An analysis of trends in evolution, adaptation and behavior.* Chicago: University of Chicago Press.

Ejaz, N., Hamada, M., & Diedrichsen, J. (2015). Hand use predicts the structure of representations in sensorimotor cortex. *Nature Neuroscience, 18*(7), 1034–1040.

Ekman, P. (1973). Cross-cultural studies in facial expression. In P. Ekman (Ed.), *Darwin and facial expression: A century of research in review.* New York: Academic Press.

Ekman, P. (1992). An argument for basic emotions. *Cognition & Emotion, 6*, 169–200.

Ekman, P. (1994). All emotions are basic. In P. Ekman and R. J. Davidson (Eds.), *The nature of emotion: Fundamental questions* (pp. 15–19). New York: Oxford Univeristy Press.

Ekman, P. (1999). Basic emotions. In T. Dalgleish & M. Power (Eds.), *Handbook of cognition and emotion* (pp. 45–66). New York: Wiley.

Ekman, P. (2003). Darwin, deception and facial expressions. *Annals of the New York Academy of Sciences, 1000*, 205–221.

Ekman, P., & Friesen, W. V. (1971). Constants across cultures in the face and emotion. *Journal of Personality and Social Psychology, 17*, 124–129.

Elbert, T., Pantev, C., Wienbruch, C., Rockstroh, B., & Taub, E. (1995). Increased cortical representation of the fingers of the left hand in string players. *Science, 270*, 305–307.

Eldridge, L. L., Knowlton, B. J., Furmanski, C. S., Bookheimer, S. Y., & Engel, S. A. (2000). Remembering episodes: A selective role for the hippocampus during retrieval. *Nature Neuroscience, 3*, 1149–1152.

Emberson, L. L., Crosswhite, S. L., Richards, J. E., & Aslin, R. N. (2017). The lateral occipital cortex is selective for object shape, not texture/color, at six months. *Journal of Neuroscience, 37*(13), 3698–3703.

Emler, N. (1994). Gossip, reputation and adaptation. In R. F. Goodman & A. Ben-Ze'ev (Eds.). *Good gossip* (pp. 117–138). Lawrence: University of Kansas Press.

Enard, W. (2011). FOXP2 and the role of cortico-basal ganglia circuits in speech and language evolution. *Current Opinion in Neurobiology, 21*(3), 415–424.

Enard, W., Przeworski, M., Fisher, S. E., Lai, C. S., Wiebe, V., Kitano, T., et al. (2002). Molecular evolution of FOXP2, a gene involved in speech and language. *Nature, 418*, 869–872.

Engel, A. K., Fries, P., & Singer, W. (2001). Dynamic predictions: Oscillations and synchrony in top-down processing. *Nature Reviews Neuroscience, 2*, 704–716.

Engel, A. K., Kreiter, A. K., Konig, P., & Singer, W. (1991). Synchronization of oscillatory neuronal responses between striate and extrastriate visual cortical areas of the cat. *Proceedings of the National Academy of Sciences, USA, 88*, 6048–6052.

Epstein, D. (2013). *The sports gene: Inside the science of extraordinary athletic performance.* New York: Penguin.

Epstein, R., & Kanwisher, N. (1998). A cortical representation of the local visual environment. *Nature, 392*, 598–601.

Ericsson, K. A., Krampe, R. T., & Tesch-Romer, C. (1993). The role of deliberate practice in the acquisition of expert performance. *Psychology Review, 100*, 363–406.

Eriksen, C. W., & Eriksen, B. (1971). Visual perceptual processing rates and backward and forward masking. *Journal of Experimental Psychology, 89*, 306–313.

Eriksson, P. S., Perfilieva, E., Björk-Eriksson, T., Alborn, A., Nordborg, C., Peterson, D., et al. (1998). Neurogenesis in the adult human hippocampus. *Nature Medicine, 4*, 1313–1317.

Eshel, N., Bukwich, M., Rao, V., Hemmelder, V., Tian, J., & Uchida, N. (2015). Arithmetic and local circuitry underlying dopamine prediction errors. *Nature, 525*(7568), 243.

Etcoff, N. L., Ekman, P., Magee, J. J., & Frank, M. G. (2000). Lie detection and language comprehension. *Nature, 405*, 139.

Etkin, A., Büchel, C., & Gross, J. J. (2015). The neural bases of emotion regulation. *Nature Reviews Neuroscience, 16*(11), 693–700.

Eyler, L. T., Pierce, K., & Courchesne, E. (2012). A failure of left temporal cortex to specialize for language is an early emerging and fundamental property of autism. *Brain, 135*(3), 949–960.

Falck-Ytter, T., & von Hofsten, C. (2011). How special is social looking in ASD: A review. *Progress in Brain Research, 189*, 209–222.

Faraday, M. (1933). *Faraday's diary. Being the various philosophical notes of experiment investigation during the years 1820–1862.* London: Bell.

Farah, M. J. (2004). *Visual agnosia* (2nd ed.). Cambridge, MA: MIT Press.

Feinstein, J. S., Adolphs, R., Damasio, A., & Tranel, D. (2011). The human amygdala and the induction and experience of fear. *Current Biology, 21*, 34–38.

Feldman, G., Baumeister, R. F., & Wong, K. F. E. (2014). Free will is about choosing: The link between choice and the belief in free will. *Journal of Experimental Social Psychology, 55*, 239–245.

Feldman, G., Chandrashekar, S. P., & Wong, K. F. E. (2016). The freedom to excel: Belief in free will predicts better academic performance. *Personality and Individual Differences, 90*, 377–383.

Fellows, L. K., & Farah, M. J. (2005). Is anterior cingulate cortex necessary for cognitive control? *Brain, 128*, 788–796.

Fellows, L. K., & Farah, M. J. (2007). The role of ventromedial prefrontal cortex in decision making: Judgment under uncertainty or judgment per se? *Cerebral Cortex, 17*, 2669–2674.

Fendrich, R., Wessinger, C. M., & Gazzaniga, M. S. (1992). Residual vision in a scotoma: Implications for blindsight. *Science, 258*, 1489–1491.

Ferdinand, N. K., Mecklinger, A., Kray, J., & Gehring, W. J. (2012). The processing of unexpected positive response outcomes in the mediofrontal cortex. *Journal of Neuroscience, 32*(35), 12087–12092.

Feredoes, E., Heinen, K., Weiskopf, N., Ruff, C., & Driver, J. (2011). Causal evidence for frontal involvement in memory target maintenance by posterior brain areas during distracter interference of visual working memory. *Proceedings of the National Academy of Sciences, USA, 108*, 17510–17515.

Ferry, B., & McGaugh, J. L. (2000). Role of amygdala norepinephrine in mediating stress hormone regulation of memory storage. *Acta Pharmacologica Sinica, 21*, 481–493.

Ferstl, E. C., Guthke, T., & von Cramon, D. Y. (2002). Text comprehension after brain injury: Left prefrontal lesions affect inference processes. *Neuropsychology, 16*(3), 292–308.

Feynman, R. P. (1998). *The meaning of it all.* New York: Perseus.

Finger, S. (1994). *Origins of neuroscience.* New York: Oxford University Press.

Finn, E. S., Shen, X., Scheinost, D., Rosenberg, M. D., Huang, J., Chun, M. M., et al. (2015). Functional connectome fingerprinting: Identifying individuals using patterns of brain connectivity. *Nature Neuroscience, 18*(11), 1664–1671.

First, M. B. (2005). Desire for amputation of a limb: Paraphilia, psychosis, or a new type of identity disorder. *Psychological Medicine, 35*, 919–928.

Fisher, S. E. (2017). Evolution of language: Lessons from the genome. *Psychonomic Bulletin & Review, 24*(1), 34–40.

Flack, J. C., Krakauer, D. C., & de Waal, F. B. M. (2005). Robustness mechanisms in primate societies: A perturbation study. *Proceedings of the Royal Society of London, Series B, 272*(1568), 1091–1099.

Flanagan, O. J. (1991). *The science of the mind.* Cambridge, MA: MIT Press.

Fleischman, D. A., & Gabrieli, J. D. (1998). Repetition priming in normal aging and Alzheimer's disease: A review of findings and theories. *Psychology and Aging, 13*(1), 88.

Florence, S. L., & Kaas, J. H. (1995). Large-scale reorganization at multiple levels of the somatosensory pathway follows therapeutic amputation of the hand in monkeys. *Journal of Neuroscience, 15*, 8083–8095.

Flourens, M.-J.-P. (1824). *Recherches expérimentales sur les proprieties et les functiones du systeme nerveux dans le animaux vertébrés.* Paris: Ballière.

Fone, K. C., & Porkess, M. V. (2008). Behavioural and neurochemical effects of post-weaning social isolation in rodents—Relevance to developmental neuropsychiatric disorders. *Neuroscience and Biobehavioral Reviews, 32*(6), 1087–1102.

Fornito, A., & Bullmore, E. T. (2010). What can spontaneous fluctuations of the blood oxygenation-level-dependent signal tell us about psychiatric disorders? *Current Opinion in Psychiatry, 23*(3), 239–249.

Foster, D., & Wilson, M. (2006). Reverse replay of behavioral sequences in hippocampal place cells during the awake state. *Nature, 440*, 680–683.

Fox, P. T., Miezin, F. M., Allman, J. M., Van Essen, D. C., & Raichle, M. E. (1987). Retinotopic organization of human visual cortex mapped with positron-emission tomography. *Journal of Neuroscience, 7*, 913–922.

Fox, P. T., Mintun, M. A., Reiman, E. M., & Raichle, M. E. (1988). Enhanced detection of focal brain responses using intersubject average and change-distribution subtracted PET images. *Journal of Cerebral Blood Flow and Metabolism, 8*, 642–653.

Fox, P. T., & Raichle, M. E. (1986). Focal physiological uncoupling of cerebral blood flow and oxidative metabolism during somatosensory stimulation in human subjects. *Proceedings of the National Academy of Sciences, USA, 83*, 1140–1144.

Fox, P. T., Raichle, M. E., Mintun, M. A., & Dence, C. (1988). Nonoxidative glucose consumption during focal physiologic neural activity. *Science, 241*, 462–464.

Franco, M. I., Turin, L., Mershin, A., & Skoulakis, E. M. C. (2011). Molecular vibration-sensing component in *Drosophila melanogaster* olfaction. *Proceedings of the National Academy of Sciences, USA, 108*(9), 3797–3802.

Frank, M. J., & Fossella, J. A. (2011). Neurogenetics and pharmacology of learning, motivation and cognition. *Neuropsychopharmacology, 36*, 133–152.

Frank, M. J., Samanta, J., Moustafa, A. A., & Sherman, S. J. (2007). Hold your horses: Impulsivity, deep brain stimulation, and medication in parkinsonism. *Science, 318*, 1309–1312.

Frankfort, H., Frankfort, H. A., Wilson, J. A., & Jacobsen, T. (1977). *The intellectual adventure of ancient man: An essay of speculative thought in the ancient Near East* (first Phoenix ed.). Chicago: University of Chicago Press.

Franz, E., Eliassen, J., Ivry, R., & Gazzaniga, M. (1996). Dissociation of spatial and temporal coupling in the bimanual movements of callosotomy patients. *Psychological Science, 7*, 306–310.

Frasnelli, E., Vallortigara, G., & Rogers, L. J. (2012). Left–right asymmetries of behaviour and nervous system in invertebrates. *Neuroscience and Biobehavioral Reviews, 36*(4), 1273–1291.

Frazier, L. (1987). Structure in auditory word recognition. *Cognition, 25*, 157–187.

Frazier, T. W., Keshavan, M. S., Minshew, N. J., & Hardan, A. Y. (2012). A two-year longitudinal MRI study of the corpus callosum in autism. *Journal of Autism and Developmental Disorders, 42*(11), 2312–2322.

FREEDMAN, D. J., RIESENHUBER, M., POGGIO, T., & MILLER, E. K. (2001). Categorical representations of visual stimuli in the primate prefrontal cortex. *Science, 291*, 312–316.

FREGNI, F., BOGGIO, P., MANSUR, C., WAGNER, T., FERREIRA, M., LIMA, M. C., ET AL. (2005). Transcranial direct current stimulation of the unaffected hemisphere in stroke patients. *Neuroreport, 16*(14), 1551–1555.

FREIHERR, J., HALLSCHMID, M., FREY, W. H., III, BRÜNNER, Y. F., CHAPMAN, C. D., HÖLSCHER, C., ET AL. (2013). Intranasal insulin as a treatment for Alzheimer's disease: A review of basic research and clinical evidence. *CNS Drugs, 27*(7), 505–514.

FREUD, S. (1882) Über den Bau der Nervenfasern und Nervenzellen beim Flusskrebs (Sitzungsberichte der Kaiserliche Akademie der Wissenschaften, Mathematisch-Naturwissenschaftliche Classe, Vol. 85). [Vienna: K. K. Hof- und Staatsdruckerei].

FREY, U., & MORRIS, R. G. (1997). Synaptic tagging and long-term potentiation. *Nature, 385*, 533–536.

FRICKER-GATES, R. A., SHIN, J. J., TAI, C. C., CATAPANO, L. A., & MACKLIS, J. D. (2002). Late-stage immature neocortical neurons reconstruct interhemispheric connections and form synaptic contacts with increased efficiency in adult mouse cortex undergoing targeted neurodegeneration. *Journal of Neuroscience, 22*, 4045–4056.

FRIDRIKSSON, J., DEN OUDEN, D. B., HILLIS, A. E., HICKOK, G., RORDEN, C., BASILAKOS, A., ET AL. (2018). Anatomy of aphasia revisited. *Brain, 141*(3), 848–862. doi:10.1093/brain/awx363. [Epub ahead of print, January 17]

FRIEDERICI, A. D. (2012). The cortical language circuit: From auditory perception to sentence comprehension. *Trends in Cognitive Science, 16*(5), 262–268.

FRIEDERICI, A. D., PFEIFER, E., & HAHNE, A. (1993). Event-related brain potentials during natural speech processing: Effects of semantic, morphological and syntactic violations. *Cognitive Brain Research, 1*, 183–192.

FRIEDLANDER, T., MAYO, A. E., TLUSTY, T., & ALON, U. (2015). Evolution of bow-tie architectures in biology. *PLoS Computational Biology, 11*(3), e1004055.

FRIEDRICH, F. J., EGLY, R., RAFAL, R. D., & BECK, D. (1998). Spatial attention deficits in humans: A comparison of superior parietal and temporal-parietal junction lesions. *Neuropsychology, 12*, 193–207.

FRIJDA, N. H. (1986). *The emotions: Studies in emotion and social interaction.* Cambridge: Cambridge University Press.

FRITH, C. D. (2000). The role of the dorsolateral prefrontal cortex in the selection of action as revealed by functional imaging. In S. Monsell & J. Driver (Eds.), *Attention and performance: Vol. 18. Control of cognitive processes* (pp. 549–565). Cambridge, MA: MIT Press.

FRITH, C. D. (2003). What do imaging studies tell us about the neural basis of autism? *Novartis Foundation Symposium, 251*, 149–166.

FRITH, C. [D.] (2004). Is autism a disconnection disorder? *Lancet Neurology, 3*, 577.

FRITSCH, G., & HITZIG, E. (1870). Ueber die elektrische Erregbarkeit des Grosshirns (On the electrical excitability of the cerebrum). *Archiv für Anatomie, Physiologie und wissenschaftliche Medizin, 37*, 300–332.

FRUHMANN, B. M., JOHANNSEN, L., & KARNATH, H. O. (2008). Time course of eye and head deviation in spatial neglect. *Neuropsychology, 22*, 697–702.

FUENTEMILLA, L., MIRÓ, J., RIPOLLÉS, P., VILÀ-BALLÓ, A., JUNCADELLA, M., CASTAÑER, S., ET AL. (2013). Hippocampus-dependent strengthening of targeted memories via reactivation during sleep in humans. *Current Biology, 23*(18), 1769–1775.

FUKUDA, K., AWH, E., & VOGEL, E. K. (2010). Discrete capacity limits in visual working memory. *Current Opinions in Neurobiology, 20*(2), 177–182.

FULTON, J. F. (1928). Observations upon the vascularity of the human occipital lobe during visual activity. *Brain, 51*, 310–320.

FUNAYAMA, E. S., GRILLON, C. G., DAVIS, M., & PHELPS, E. A. (2001). A double dissociation in the affective modulation of startle in humans: Effects of unilateral temporal lobectomy. *Journal of Cognitive Neuroscience, 13*, 721–729.

FUNNELL, M., METCALFE, J., & TSAPKINI, K. (1996) In the mind but not on the tongue: Feeling of knowing in an anomic patient. In Lynne M. Reder (Ed.), *Implicit memory and metacognition* (pp. 171–194). Mahwah, NJ: Erlbaum.

FUSTER, J. M. (1989). *The prefrontal cortex: Anatomy, physiology, and neuropsychology of the frontal lobe* (2nd ed.). New York: Raven.

FUSTER, J. M., & ALEXANDER, G. E. (1971). Neuron activity related to short-term memory. *Science, 173*(3997), 652–654.

GABRIELI, J. D. E., FLEISCHMAN, D. A., KEANE, M. M., REMINGER, S. L., & MORRELL, F. (1995). Double dissociation between memory systems underlying explicit and implicit memory in the human brain. *Psychological Science, 6*, 76–82.

GAFFAN, D., & HARRISON, S. (1987). Amygdalectomy and disconnection in visual learning for auditory secondary reinforcement by monkeys. *Journal of Neuroscience, 7*, 2285–2292.

GAFFAN, D., & HORNAK , J. (1997). Visual neglect in the monkey. Representation and disconnection. *Brain, 120*(Pt. 9), 1647–1657.

GAGNON, S. A., & WAGNER, A. D. (2016). Acute stress and episodic memory retrieval: Neurobiological mechanisms and behavioral consequences. *Annals of the New York Academy of Sciences, 1369*, 55–75.

GAILLIOT, M. T., BAUMEISTER, R. F., DEWALL, C. N., MANER, J. K., PLANT, E. A., TICE, D. M., ET AL. (2007). Self-control relies on glucose as a limited energy source: Willpower is more than a metaphor. *Journal of Personality and Social Psychology, 92*, 325–336.

GALEA, J. M., ALBERT, N. B., DITYE, T., & MIALL, R. C. (2010). Disruption of the dorsolateral prefrontal cortex facilitates the consolidation of procedural skills. *Journal of Cognitive Neuroscience, 22*(6), 1158–1164.

GALEA, J. M., VAZQUEZ, A., PASRICHA, N., DE XIVRY, J. J. O., & CELNIK, P. (2011). Dissociating the roles of the cerebellum and motor cortex during adaptive learning: The motor cortex retains what the cerebellum learns. *Cerebral Cortex, 21*(8), 1761–1770.

GALL, F. J., & SPURZHEIM, J. (1810–1819). *Anatomie et physiologie du système nerveux en général, et du cerveau en particulier.* Paris: Schoell.

GALLAGHER, M., & HOLLAND, P. C. (1992). Understanding the function of the central nucleus: Is simple conditioning enough? In J. P. Aggleton (Ed.), *The amygdala: Neurobiological aspects of emotion, memory, and mental dysfunction* (pp. 307–321). New York: Wiley-Liss.

GALLANT, J. L., SHOUP, R. E., & MAZER, J. A. (2000). A human extrastriate area functionally homologous to macaque V4. *Neuron, 27*, 227–235.

GALLESE, V., FADIGA, L., FOGASSI, L., & RIZZOLATTI, G. (1996). Action recognition in the premotor cortex. *Brain, 119*(2), 593–609.

GALLESE, V., KEYSERS, C., & RIZZOLATTI, G. (2004). A unifying view of the basis of social cognition. *Trends in Cognitive Sciences, 8*, 396–403.

GALLUP, G. G., JR. (1970). Chimpanzees: Self-recognition. *Science, 2*, 86–87.

GALLUP, G. G., JR. (1982). Self-awareness and the emergence of mind in primates. *American Journal of Primatology, 2*, 237–248.

GALUSKE, R. A., SCHLOTE, W., BRATZKE, H., & SINGER, W. (2000). Interhemispheric asymmetries of the modular structure in human temporal cortex. *Science, 289*, 1946–1949.

GAMER, M., & BUCHEL, C. (2009). Amygdala activation predicts gaze toward fearful eyes. *Journal of Neuroscience, 29*, 9123–9126.

Ganguly, K., & Carmena, J. M. (2009). Emergence of a stable cortical map for neuroprosthetic control. *PLoS Biology, 7*(7), e1000153. doi:10.1371/journal.pbio.1000153

Gardner, R. A., & Gardner, B. T. (1969). Teaching sign language to a chimpanzee. *Science, 165*, 664–672.

Gattass, R., & Desimone, R. (2014). Effect of microstimulation of the superior colliculus on visual space attention. *Journal of Cognitive Neuroscience, 26*(6), 1208–1219.

Gaub, B. M., Berry, M. H., Holt, A. E., Isacoff, E. Y., & Flannery, J. G. (2015). Optogenetic vision restoration using rhodopsin for enhanced sensitivity. *Molecular Therapy, 23*(10), 1562–1571.

Gauthier, I., Skudlarski, P., Gore, J. C., & Anderson, A. W. (2000). Expertise for cars and birds recruits brain areas involved in face recognition. *Nature Neuroscience, 3*, 191–197.

Gauthier, I., Tarr, M. J., Anderson, A. W., Skudlarski, P., & Gore, J. C. (1999). Activation of the middle fusiform "face area" increases with expertise in recognizing novel objects. *Nature Neuroscience, 2*, 568–573.

Gazzaley, A., Cooney, J. W., McEvoy, K., Knight, R. T., & D'Esposito, M. (2005). Top-down enhancement and suppression of the magnitude and speed of neural activity. *Journal of Cognitive Neuroscience, 17*, 507–517.

Gazzaley, A., Cooney, J. W., Rissman, J., & D'Esposito, M. (2005). Top-down suppression deficit underlies working memory impairment in normal aging. *Nature Neuroscience, 8*, 1298–1300.

Gazzaley, A., & Rosen, L. D. (2016). *The distracted mind: Ancient brains in a high-tech world.* Cambridge: MIT Press.

Gazzaniga, M. S. (1985). *The social brain.* New York: Basic Books.

Gazzaniga, M. S. (2000). Cerebral specialization and interhemispheric communication: Does the corpus callosum enable the human condition? *Brain, 123*, 1293–1326.

Gazzaniga, M. S. (2011). *Who's in charge?* New York: Harper Collins.

Gazzaniga, M. S. (2015). *Tales from both sides of the brain.* New York: Harper Collins.

Gazzaniga, M. S. (2018). *The consciousness instinct: Unraveling the mystery of how the brain makes the mind.* New York: Farrar, Straus and Giroux.

Gazzaniga, M. S., Bogen, J. E., & Sperry, R. (1962). Some functional effects of sectioning the cerebral commissures in man. *Proceedings of the National Academy of Sciences, USA, 48*, 1756–1769.

Gazzaniga, M. S., & LeDoux, J. E. (1978). *The integrated mind.* New York: Plenum.

Gazzaniga, M. S., & Smylie, C. S. (1983). Facial recognition and brain asymmetries: Clues to underlying mechanisms. *Annals of Neurology, 13*, 536–540.

Gazzaniga, M. S., & Smylie, C. S. (1984). Dissociation of language and cognition: A psychological profile of two disconnected right hemispheres. *Brain, 107*, 145–153.

Gazzaniga, M. S., & Smylie, C. S. (1990). Hemispheric mechanisms controlling voluntary and spontaneous facial expressions. *Journal of Cognitive Neuroscience, 2*, 239–245.

Gazzola, V., & Keysers, C. (2009). The observation and execution of actions share motor and somatosensory voxels in all tested subjects: Single-subject analyses of unsmoothed fMRI data. *Cerebral Cortex, 19*, 1239–1255.

Gehring, W. J., Goss, B., Coles, M. G. H., Meyer, D. E., & Donchin, E. (1993). A neural system for error detection and compensation. *Psychological Science, 4*, 385–390.

Gelstein, S., Yeshurun, Y., Rozenkrantz, L., Shushan, S., Frumin, I., Roth, Y., et al. (2011). Human tears contain a chemosignal. *Science, 331*(6014), 226–230.

Georgopoulos, A. P. (1990). Neurophysiology of reaching. In M. Jeannerod (Ed.), *Attention and performance XIII: Motor representation and control* (pp. 227–263). Hillsdale, NJ: Erlbaum.

Georgopoulos, A. P. (1995). Motor cortex and cognitive processing. In M. S. Gazzaniga (Ed.), *The cognitive neurosciences* (pp. 507–517). Cambridge, MA: MIT Press.

Gerhart, J., & Kirschner, M. (2007). The theory of facilitated variation. *Proceedings of the National Academy of Sciences, USA, 104*(Suppl. 1), 8582–8589.

Gerlach, C., Law, I., & Paulson, O. B. (2002). When action turns into words. Activation of motor-based knowledge during categorization of manipulable objects. *Journal of Cognitive Neuroscience, 14*, 1230–1239.

Geschwind, N. (1970). The organization of language and the brain. *Science, 170*, 940–944.

Geschwind, N., & Levitsky, W. (1968). Human brain: Left-right asymmetries in temporal speech region. *Science, 161*, 186–187.

Ghazanfar, A. A., Chandrasekaran, C., & Logothetis, N. K. (2008). Interactions between the superior temporal sulcus and auditory cortex mediate dynamic face/voice integration in rhesus monkeys. *Journal of Neuroscience, 28*, 4457–4469.

Giacino, J. T., Ashwal, S., Childs, N., Cranford, R., Jennett, B., Katz, D. I., et al. (2002). The minimally conscious state definition and diagnostic criteria. *Neurology, 58*(3), 349–353.

Giard, M.-H., Fort, A., Mouchetant-Rostaing, Y., & Pernier, J. (2000). Neurophysiological mechanisms of auditory selective attention in humans. *Frontiers in Bioscience, 5*, D84–D94.

Gibson, J. J. (1979). *The ecological approach to visual perception.* Boston: Houghton Mifflin.

Gibson, J. R., Beierlein, M., & Connors, B. W. (1999). Two networks of electrically coupled inhibitory neurons in neocortex. *Nature, 402*, 75–79.

Giedd, J. N., Blumenthal, J., Jeffries, N. O., Castellanos, F. X., Liu, H., Zijdenbos, A., et al. (1999). Brain development during childhood and adolescence: A longitudinal MRI study. *Nature Neuroscience, 2*, 861–863.

Gilbert, D. (2006). *Stumbling on happiness.* New York: Random House.

Gilbertson, M. W., Shenton, M. E., Ciszewski, A., Kasai, K., Lasko, N. B., Orr, S. P., et al. (2002). Smaller hippocampal volume predicts pathologic vulnerability to psychological trauma. *Nature Neuroscience, 5*, 1242–1247.

Gilboa, A., Ramirez, J., Köhler, S., Westmacott, R., Black, S. E., & Moscovitch, M. (2005). Retrieval of autobiographical memory in Alzheimer's disease: Relation to volumes of medial temporal lobe and other structures. *Hippocampus, 15*, 535–550.

Gilovich, T. (1991). *How we know what isn't so.* New York: Macmillan.

Gleichgerrcht, E., Fridriksson, J., Rorden, C., & Bonilha, L. (2017). Connectome-based lesion-symptom mapping (CLSM): A novel approach to map neurological function? *NeuroImage. Clinical, 16*, 461–467.

Glisky, E. L., Polster, M. R., & Routhuieaux, B. C. (1995). Double dissociation between item and source memory. *Neuropsychology, 9*, 229–235.

Goel, V., Grafman, J., Tajik, J., Gana, S., & Danto, D. (1997). A study of the performance of patients with frontal lobe lesions in a financial planning task. *Brain, 120*, 1805–1822.

Goel, V., Tierney, M., Sheesley, L., Bartolo, A., Vartanian, O., & Grafman, J. (2007). Hemispheric specialization in human prefrontal cortex for resolving certain and uncertain inferences. *Cerebral Cortex, 17*, 2245–2250.

Goldin, P. R., McRae, K., Ramel, W., & Gross, J. J. (2008). The neural bases of emotion regulation: Reappraisal and suppression of negative emotion. *Biological Psychiatry, 63*, 577–586.

Goldman-Rakic, P. S. (1987). Circuitry of primate prefrontal cortex and regulation of behavior by representational memory. In *Handbook of physiology: Vol. 5. The nervous system* (pp. 373–417). Bethesda, MD: American Physiological Society.

Goldman-Rakic, P. S. (1992). Working memory and the mind. *Scientific American, 267*(3), 111–117.

Goldman-Rakic, P. S. (1995). Architecture of the prefrontal cortex and the central executive. In J. Grafman, K. J. Holyoak, & F. Boller (Eds.), *Structure and functions of the human prefrontal cortex* (pp. 71–83). New York: New York Academy of Sciences.

Goldman-Rakic, P. S. (1996). Regional and cellular fractionation of working memory. *Proceedings of the National Academy of Sciences, USA, 93*(24), 13473–13480.

Goldsby, R. A. (1976). *Basic biology*. New York: Harper and Row.

Goldstein, R. Z., & Volkow, N. D. (2011). Dysfunction of the prefrontal cortex in addiction: Neuroimaging findings and clinical implications. *Nature Reviews Neuroscience, 12*(11), 652–669.

Golgi, C. (1894). *Untersuchungen über den feineren Bau des centralen und peripherischen Nervensystems*. Jena, Germany: Fischer.

Goodale, M. A., & Milner, A. D. (1992). Separate visual pathways for perception and action. *Trends in Neurosciences, 15*, 22–25.

Goodale, M. A., & Milner, A. D. (2004). *Sight unseen: An exploration of conscious and unconscious vision*. Oxford: Oxford University Press.

Gopnik, A., & Wellman, H. (1992). Why the child's theory of mind really is a theory. *Mind and Language, 7*(1–2), 145–171.

Gorgolewski, K. J., Varoquaux, G., Rivera, G., Schwarz, Y., Ghosh, S. S., Maumet, C., et al. (2015). NeuroVault.org: A web-based repository for collecting and sharing unthresholded statistical maps of the human brain. *Frontiers in Neuroinformatics, 9*(8).

Gotts, S. J., Jo, H. J., Wallace, G. L., Saad, Z. S., Cox, R. W., & Martin, A. (2013). Two distinct forms of functional lateralization in the human brain. *Proceedings of the National Academy of Sciences, USA, 110*(36), E3435–E3444.

Gozzi, M., Nielson, D. M., Lenroot, R. K., Ostuni, J. L., Luckenbaugh, D. A., Thurm, A. E., et al. (2012). A magnetization transfer imaging study of corpus callosum myelination in young children with autism. *Biological Psychiatry, 72*(3), 215–220.

Grabowecky, M., Robertson, L. C., & Treisman, A. (1993). Preattentive processes guide visual search. *Journal of Cognitive Neuroscience, 5*, 288–302.

Gradinaru, V., Mogri, M., Thompson, K. R., Henderson, J. M., & Deisseroth, K. (2009). Optical deconstruction of parkinsonian neural circuitry. *Science, 324*, 354–359.

Graef, S., Biele, G., Krugel, L. K., Marzinzik, F., Wahl, M., Wotka, J., et al. (2010). Differential influence of levodopa on reward-base learning in Parkinson's disease. *Frontiers in Human Neuroscience, 4*, 169.

Graf, P., Squire, L. R., & Mandler, G. (1984). The information that amnesic patients do not forget. *Journal of Experimental Psychology. Learning, Memory, and Cognition, 10*(1), 164.

Grafton, S. T., Fadiga, L., Arbib, M. A., & Rizzolatti, G. (1997). Premotor cortex activation during observation and naming of familiar tools. *NeuroImage, 6*, 231–236.

Graham, J., Carlson, G. R., & Gerard, R. W. (1942). Membrane and injury potentials of single muscle fibers. *Federation Proceedings, 1*, 31.

Gratton, C., Lee, T. G., Nomura, E. M., & D'Esposito, M. (2013). The effect of theta-burst TMS on cognitive control networks measured with resting state fMRI. *Frontiers in Systems Neuroscience, 7*, 124.

Gratton, G., & Fabiani, M. (1998). Dynamic brain imaging: Event-related optical signal (EROS) measures of the time course and localization of cognitive-related activity. *Psychonomic Bulletin & Review, 5*, 535–563.

Gray, C. M., Konig, P., Engel, A. K., & Singer, W. (1989). Oscillatory responses in cat visual cortex exhibit inter-columnar synchronization which reflects global stimulus properties. *Nature, 338*, 334–337.

Greenberg, J. O. (1995). *Neuroimaging: A companion to Adams and Victor's Principles of neurology*. New York: McGraw-Hill.

Greene, J. D., Nystrom, L. E., Engell, A. D., Darley, J. M., & Cohen, J. D. (2004). The neural bases of cognitive conflict and control in moral judgment. *Neuron, 44*, 389–400.

Greene, J. D., Sommerville, R. B., Nystrom, L. E., Darley, J. M., & Cohen, J. D. (2001). An fMRI investigation of emotional engagement in moral judgment. *Science, 293*, 2105–2108.

Greenfield, P. M. (1991). Language, tools and brain: The ontogeny and phylogeny of hierarchically organized sequential behavior. *Behavioral and Brain Sciences, 14*(4), 531–551.

Greenwald, A. G., McGhee, J. L., & Schwartz, J. L. (1998). Measuring individual differences in social cognition: The Implicit Association Test. *Journal of Personality and Social Psychology, 74*, 1474–1480.

Grefkes, C., & Fink, G. R. (2005). The functional organization of the intraparietal sulcus in humans and monkeys. *Journal of Anatomy, 207*, 3–17.

Gregoriou, G. G., Gotts, S. J., Zhou, H., & Desimone, R. (2009). High-frequency, long-range coupling between prefrontal and visual cortex during attention. *Science, 324*(5931), 1207–1210.

Grice, H. P. (1957). Meaning. *Philosophical Review, 66*, 377–388.

Grill-Spector, K., Knouf, N., & Kanwisher, N. (2004). The fusiform face area subserves face perception, not generic within-category identification. *Nature Neuroscience, 7*, 555–562.

Grill-Spector, K., Kourtzi, Z., & Kanwisher, N. (2001). The lateral occipital complex and its role in object recognition. *Vision Research, 41*, 1409–1422.

Grinband, J., Savitskaya, J., Wager, T. D., Teichert, T., Ferrera, V. P., & Hirsch, J. (2011a). Conflict, error likelihood, and RT: Response to Brown & Yeung et al. *NeuroImage, 57*, 320–322.

Grinband, J., Savitskaya, J., Wager, T. D., Teichert, T., Ferrera, V. P., & Hirsch, J. (2011b). The dorsal medial frontal cortex is sensitive to time on task, not response conflict or error likelihood. *NeuroImage, 57*, 303–311.

Grinband, J., Wager, T. D., Lindquist, M., Ferrera, V. P., & Hirsch, J. (2008). Detection of time-varying signals in event-related fMRI designs. *NeuroImage, 43*, 509–520.

Gross, J. (1998a). Antecedent- and response-focused emotion regulation: Divergent consequences for experience, expression, and physiology. *Journal of Personality and Social Psychology, 74*, 224–237.

Gross, J. (1998b). The emerging field of emotion regulation: An integrative review. *Review of General Psychology, 2*(3), 271–299.

Grossenbacher, P. G., & Lovelace, C. T. (2001). Mechanisms of synesthesia: Cognitive and physiological constraints. *Trends in Cognitive Sciences, 5*, 36–41.

Grossman, M., Eslinger, P. J., Troiani, V., Anderson, C., Avants, B., Gee, J. C., et al. (2010). The role of ventral medial prefrontal cortex in social decisions: Converging evidence from fMRI and frontotemporal lobar degeneration. *Neuropsychologia, 48*, 3505–3512.

Grossmann, T., Johnson, M. H., Farroni, T., & Csibra, G. (2007). Social perception in the infant brain: Gamma oscillatory activity in response to eye gaze. *Social, Cognitive, and Affective Neuroscience, 2*, 284–291.

Groszer, M., Keays, D. A., Deacon, R. M., De Bono, J. P., Prasad-Mulcare, S., Gaub, S., et al. (2008). Impaired synaptic plasticity and motor learning in mice with a point mutation implicated in human speech deficits. *Current Biology, 18*(5), 354–362.

Grzimek's Encyclopedia of Mammals, Vol. 3. (1990). New York: McGraw-Hill.

Gu, X., Hof, P. R., Friston, K. J., & Fan, J. (2013). Anterior insular cortex and emotional awareness. *Journal of Comparative Neurology, 521*(15), 3371–3388.

Guillin, O., Abi-Dargham, A., & Laruelle, M. (2007). Neurobiology of dopamine in schizophrenia. *International Review Neurobiology, 78*, 1–39.

Guillon, Q., Hadjikhani, N., Baduel, S., & Rogé, B. (2014). Visual social attention in autism spectrum disorder: Insights from eye tracking studies. *Neuroscience and Biobehavioral Reviews, 42*, 279–297.

Gusnard, D. A., Akbudak, R., Shulman, G. L., & Raichle, M. E. (2001). Medial prefrontal cortex and self-referential mental activity: Relation to a default mode of brain function. *Proceedings of the National Academy of Sciences, USA, 98*(7), 4259–4264.

Gusnard, D. A., & Raichle, M. E. (2001). Searching for a baseline: Functional imaging and the resting human brain. *Nature Reviews Neuroscience, 2*, 685–694.

Gustafsson, B., & Wigström, H. (1988). Physiological mechanisms underlying long-term potentiation. *Trends in Neurosciences, 11*(4), 156–162.

Haar, S., Donchin, O., & Dinstein, I. (2015). Dissociating visual and motor directional selectivity using visuomotor adaptation. *Journal of Neuroscience, 35*(17), 6813–6821.

Habel, U., Klein, M., Kellermann, T., Shah, N. J., & Schneider, F. (2005). Same or different? Neural correlates of happy and sad mood in healthy males. *NeuroImage, 26*, 206–214.

Habib, M., & Sirigu, A. (1987). Pure topographical disorientation: A definition and anatomical basis. *Cortex, 23*, 73–85.

Hadamard, J. (1945). *An essay on the psychology of invention in the mathematical field.* Princeton, NJ: Princeton University Press.

Hadjikhani, N., Chabris, C. F., Joseph, R. M., Clark, J., McGrath, L., Aharon, I., et al. (2004). Early visual cortex organization in autism: An fMRI study. *Neuroreport, 15*(2), 267–270.

Haerer, A. F. (1992). *DeJong's the neurologic examination* (5th ed.). Philadelphia: Lippincott.

Hagoort, P. (2005). On Broca, brain, and binding: A new framework. *Trends in Cognitive Neurosciences, 9*, 416–423.

Hagoort, P. (2013). MUC (Memory, Unification, Control) and beyond. *Frontiers in Psychology, 4*, 416.

Hagoort, P., Brown, C., & Groothusen, J. (1993). The syntactic positive shift (SPS) as an ERP measure of syntactic processing. *Language and Cognitive Processes, 8*, 439–483.

Halligan, P. W., & Marshall, J. C. (1998). Neglect of awareness. *Conscious Cognition, 7*, 356–380.

Hamani, C., Neimat, J., & Lozano, A. M. (2006). Deep brain stimulation for the treatment of Parkinson's disease. *Journal of Neural Transmission, 70*(Suppl.), 393–399.

Hamann, S. B., Ely, T. D., Grafton, S. T., & Kilts, C. D. (1999). Amygdala activity related to enhanced memory for pleasant and aversive stimuli. *Nature Neuroscience, 2*, 289–293.

Hamilton, A. F. de C., & Grafton, S. T. (2007). Action outcomes are represented in human inferior frontoparietal cortex. *Cerebral Cortex, 18*, 1160–1168.

Hamlin, J. K., Mahajan, N., Liberman, Z., & Wynn, K. (2013). Not like me = bad: Infants prefer those who harm dissimilar others. *Psychological Science, 24*(4), 589–594.

Happé, F. (1999). Cognitive deficit or cognitive style? *Trends in Cognitive Sciences, 3*(6), 216–222.

Hardan, A. Y., Minshew, N. J., & Keshavan, M. S. (2000). Corpus callosum size in autism. *Neurology, 55*(7), 1033–1036.

Hare, T. A., Camerer, C. F., & Ranger, A. (2009). Self-control in decision making involves modulation of the vmPFC valuation system. *Science, 324*, 646–648.

Harel, N. Y., & Strittmatter, S. M. (2006). Can regenerating axons recapitulate developmental guidance during recovery from spinal cord injury? *Nature Reviews Neuroscience, 7*, 603–616.

Harkness, R. D., & Maroudas, N. G. (1985). Central place foraging by an ant (*Cataglyphis bicolor* Fab.): A model of searching. *Animal Behaviour, 33*, 916–928.

Harmon-Jones, E., & Mills, J. (1999). *Cognitive dissonance: Progress on a pivotal theory in social psychology.* Washington, DC: American Psychological Association.

Harris, L. J. (1989). Footedness in parrots: Three centuries of research, theory, and mere surmise. *Canadian Journal of Psychology, 43*, 369–396.

Harris, P. L. (1992). From simulation to folk psychology: The case for development. *Mind and Language, 7*, 120–144.

Hart, J., Berndt, R. S., & Caramazza, A. (1985). Category-specific naming deficit following cerebral infarction. *Nature, 316*, 439–440.

Hasson, U., Ghazanfar, A. A., Galantucci, B., Garrod, S., & Keysers, C. (2012). Brain-to-brain coupling: A mechanism for creating and sharing a social world. *Trends in Cognitive Sciences, 16*(2), 114–121.

Hatfield, E., & Rapson, R. L. (1987). Passionate love/sexual desire: Can the same paradigm explain both? *Archives of Sexual Behavior, 16*(3), 259–278.

Hatsopoulos, N. G., & Suminski, A. J. (2011). Sensing with the motor cortex. *Neuron, 72*, 477–487.

Hayden, B., Pearson, J. M., & Platt, M. L. (2011). Neuronal basis of sequential foraging decision in a patchy environment. *Nature Neuroscience, 14*(7), 933–939.

Haynes, J.-D., & Rees, G. (2005). Predicting the orientation of invisible stimuli from activity in human primary visual cortex. *Nature Neuroscience, 8*(5), 686–691.

Hazeltine, E., Teague, D., & Ivry, R. B. (2002). Simultaneous dual-task performance reveals parallel response selection after practice. *Journal of Experimental Psychology. Human Perception and Performance, 28*(3), 527–545.

Hebb, D. (1949). *The organization of behavior: A neuropsychological theory.* New York: Wiley.

Heberlein, A. S., & Adolphs, R. (2004). Impaired spontaneous anthropomorphizing despite intact perception and social knowledge. *Proceedings of the National Academy of Sciences, USA, 101*, 7487–7491.

Heider, F., & Simmel, M. (1944). An experimental study of apparent behavior. *American Journal of Psychology, 57*, 243–259.

Heilman, K. M., Scholes, R., & Watson, R. T. (1975). Auditory affective agnosia: Disturbed comprehension of affective speech. *Journal of Neurology, Neurosurgery, and Psychiatry, 38*, 69–72.

Heinze, H. J., Mangun, G. R., Burchert, W., Hinrichs, H., Scholz, M., Münte, T. F., et al. (1994). Combined spatial and temporal imaging of brain activity during visual selective attention in humans. *Nature, 372*, 543–546.

Helenius, P., Salmelin, R., Service, E., & Connolly, J. F. (1998). Distinct time courses of word and context comprehension in the left temporal cortex. *Brain, 121*, 1133–1142.

Helmholtz, H. von. (1968). Treatise on physiological optics. In R. M. Warren and R. P. Warren (Trans.), *Helmholtz on perception, its physiology and development.* New York: Wiley, 1968. (Original work published 1909–11)

Henke, K. (2010). A model for memory systems based on processing modes rather than consciousness. *Nature Reviews Neuroscience, 11*, 523–532.

Henke, K., Mondadori, C. R. A., Treyer, V., M., Nitsch, R. M., Buck, A., & Hock, C. (2003). Nonconscious formation and reactivation of semantic associations by way of the medial temporal lobe. *Neuropsychologia, 41*, 863–876.

Henke, K., Treyer, V., Nagy, E. T., Kneifel, S., Düsteler, M., Nitsch, R.M., et al. (2003). Active hippocampus during nonconscious memories. *Consciousness and Cognition, 12*, 31–48.

Herculano-Houzel, S. (2009). The human brain in numbers: A linearly scaled-up primate brain. *Frontiers in Human Neuroscience, 3*, 31.

Herrmann, C. S., Rach, S., Neuling, T., & Strüber, D. (2013). Transcranial alternating current stimulation: A review of the underlying mechanisms and modulation of cognitive processes. *Frontiers in Human Neuroscience, 7*, 279.

Herrmann, E., Call, J., Hernàndez-Lloreda, M. V., Hare, B., & Tomasello, M. (2007). Humans have evolved specialized skills of social cognition: The cultural intelligence hypothesis. *Science, 317*, 1360–1366.

Hickok, G. (2009). Eight problems for the mirror neuron theory of action understanding in monkeys and humans. *Journal of Cognitive Neuroscience, 21*(7), 1229–1243.

Hickok, G. (2012). Computational neuroanatomy of speech production. *Nature Reviews Neuroscience, 13*(2), 135.

Higo, T., Mars, R. B., Boorman, E. D., Buch, E. R., & Rushworth, M. F. (2011). Distributed and causal influence of frontal operculum in task control. *Proceedings of the National Academy of Sciences, USA, 108*, 4230–4235.

Hikosaka, K., Iwai, E., Saito, H., & Tanaka, K. (1988). Polysensory properties of neurons in the anterior bank of the caudal superior temporal sulcus of the macaque monkey. *Journal of Neurophysiology, 60*, 1615–1637.

Hikosaka, O., Bromberg-Martin, E., Hong, S., & Matsumoto, M. (2008). New insights on the subcortical representation of reward. *Current Opinions in Neurobiology, 18*, 203–208.

Hillis, A. E., Work, M., Barker, P. B., Jacobs, M. A., Breese, E. L., & Maurer, K. (2004). Re-examining the brain regions crucial for orchestrating speech articulation. *Brain, 127*, 1461–1462.

Hillyard, S. A., & Anllo-Vento, L. (1998). Event-related brain potentials in the study of visual selective attention. *Proceedings of the National Academy of Sciences, USA, 95*, 781–787.

Hillyard, S. A., Hink, R. F., Schwent, V. L., & Picton, T. W. (1973). Electrical signs of selective attention in the human brain. *Science, 182*, 177–180.

Hillyard, S. A., & Münte, T. F. (1984). Selective attention to color and location: An analysis with event-related brain potentials. *Perception & Psychophysics, 36*(2), 185–198.

Hilti, L. M., Hänggi, J., Vitacco, D. A., Kraemer, B., Palla, A., Luechinger, R., et al. (2013). The desire for healthy limb amputation: Structural brain correlates and clinical features of xenomelia. *Brain, 136*(1), 318–329.

Hilts, P. J. (1995). *Memory's ghost: The strange tale of Mr. M. and the nature of memory.* New York: Simon & Schuster.

Himmler, B. T., Pellis, S. M., & Kolb, B. (2013). Juvenile play experience primes neurons in the medial prefrontal cortex to be more responsive to later experiences. *Neuroscience Letters, 556*, 42–45.

Hirsh, R. (1974). The hippocampus and contextual retrieval of information from memory: A theory. *Behavioral Biology, 12*, 421–444.

Hirst, W., & Phelps, E. A. (2016). Flashbulb memories. *Current Directions in Psychological Science, 25*(1), 36–41.

Hirst, W., Phelps, E. A., Meksin, R., Vaidya, C. J., Johnson, M. K., Mitchell, K. J., et al. (2015). A ten-year follow-up of a study of memory for the attack of September 11, 2001: Flashbulb memories and memories for flashbulb events. *Journal of Experimental Psychology. General, 144*(3), 604.

Hochberg, L. R., Bacher, D., Jarosiewicz, B., Masse, N. Y., Simeral, J. D., Vogel, J., et al. (2012). Reach and grasp by people with tetraplegia using a neurally controlled robotic arm. *Nature, 485*(7398), 372.

Hochberg, L. R., Serruya, M. D., Friehs, G. M., Mukand, J. A., Saleh, M., Caplan, A. H., et al. (2006). Neuronal ensemble control of prosthetic devices by a human with tetraplegia. *Nature, 442*, 164–171.

Hodges, J. R., Patterson, K., Oxbury, S., & Funnell, E. (1992). Semantic dementia. Progressive fluent aphasia with temporal lobe atrophy. *Brain, 115*, 1783–1806.

Hodgkin, A. L., & Huxley, A. F. (1939). Action potentials recorded from inside a nerve fibre. *Nature, 144*, 710–711.

Hofer, H., & Frahm, J. (2006). Topography of the human corpus callosum revisited—Comprehensive fiber tractography using diffusion tensor magnetic resonance imaging. *NeuroImage, 32*, 989–994.

Holbourn, A. H. S. (1943). Mechanics of head injury. *Lancet, 2*, 438–441.

Holmes, G. (1919). Disturbances of visual orientation. *British Journal of Ophthalmology, 2*, 449–468.

Holmes, N. P., & Spence, C. (2005). Multisensory integration: Space, time and superadditivity. *Current Biology, 15*, R762–R764.

Holtzman, J. D. (1984). Interactions between cortical and subcortical visual areas: Evidence from human commissurotomy patients. *Vision Research, 24*, 801–813.

Holtzman, J. D., & Gazzaniga, M. S. (1982). Dual task interactions due exclusively to limits in processing resources. *Science, 218*, 1325–1327.

Holtzman, J. D., Sidtis, J. J., Volpe, B. T., Wilson, D. H., & Gazzaniga, M. S. (1981). Dissociation of spatial information for stimulus localization and the control of attention. *Brain, 104*, 861–872.

Holzhaider, J. C., Hunt, G. R., & Gray, R. D. (2010). Social learning in New Caledonian crows. *Learning & Behavior, 38*(3), 206–219.

Homae, F., Watanabe, H., Nakano, T., Asakawa, K., & Taga, G. (2006). The right hemisphere of sleeping infant perceives sentential prosody. *Neuroscience Research, 54*, 276–280.

Hopf, J. M., Boehler, C. N., Luck, S. J., Tsotsos, J. K., Heinze, H. J., & Schoenfeld, M. A. (2006). Direct neurophysiological evidence for spatial suppression surrounding the focus of attention in vision. *Proceedings of the National Academy of Sciences, USA, 103*(4), 1053–1058.

Hopf, J. M., Luck, S. J., Boelmans, K., Schoenfeld, M. A., Boehler, C. N., Rieger, J., et al. (2006). The neural site of attention matches the spatial scale of perception. *Journal of Neuroscience, 26*, 3532–3540.

Hopfinger, J. B., Buonocore, M. H., & Mangun, G. R. (2000). The neural mechanisms of top-down attentional control. *Nature Neuroscience, 3*, 284–291.

Hopfinger, J. B., & Mangun, G. R. (1998). Reflexive attention modulates visual processing in human extrastriate cortex. *Psychological Science, 9*, 441–447.

Hopfinger, J. B., & Mangun, G. R. (2001). Tracking the influence of reflexive attention on sensory and cognitive processing. *Cognitive, Affective & Behavioral Neuroscience, 1*, 56–65.

Hopkins, W. D. (2006). Comparative and familial analysis of handedness in great apes. *Psychological Bulletin, 132*, 538–559.

Hopkins, W. D., Cantalupo, C., & Taglialatela, J. (2007). Handedness is associated with asymmetries in gyrification of the cerebral cortex of chimpanzees. *Cerebral Cortex, 17*(8), 1750–1756.

Hopkins, W. D., Taglialatela, J. P., & Leavens, D. A. (2007). Chimpanzees differentially produce novel vocalizations to capture the attention of a human. *Animal Behaviour, 73*(2), 281–286.

Horikawa, T., Tamaki, M., Miyawaki, Y., & Kamitani, Y. (2013). Neural decoding of visual imagery during sleep. *Science, 340*(6132), 639–642.

Houde, J. F., & Jordan, M. I. (1998). Sensorimotor adaptation in speech production. *Science, 279*(5354), 1213–1216.

Huang, V. S., Haith, A., Mazzoni, P., & Krakauer, J. W. (2011). Rethinking motor learning and savings in adaptation paradigms: Model-free memory for successful actions combines with internal models. *Neuron, 70*, 787–801.

Hubel, D. H., & Wiesel, T. N. (1968). Receptive fields and functional architecture of monkey striate cortex. *Journal of Physiology, 195*, 215–243.

Hubel, D. H., & Wiesel, T. N. (1970). The period of susceptibility to the physiological effects of unilateral eye closure in kittens. *Journal of Physiology, 206*(2), 419–436.

Hubel, D. H., & Wiesel, T. N. (1977). Ferrier lecture. Functional architecture of macaque monkey visual cortex. *Proceedings of the Royal Society of London, Series B, 198*, 1–59.

Humphreys, G. W., & Riddoch, M. J. (1987). The fractionation of visual agnosia. In G. W. Humphreys & M. J. Riddoch (Eds.), *Visual object processing: A cognitive neuropsychological approach.* Hove, England: Erlbaum.

Humphreys, G. W., Riddoch, M. J., Donnelly, N., Freeman, T., Boucart, M., & Muller, H. M. (1994). Intermediate visual processing and visual agnosia. In M. J. Farah & G. Ratcliff (Eds.), *The neuropsychology of high-level vision: Collected tutorial essays* (pp. 63–102). Hillsdale, NJ: Erlbaum.

Humphreys, K., Hassan, U., Avidan, G., Minshew, N., & Behrmann, M. (2008). Cortical patterns of category-selective activation for faces, places, and objects in adults with autism. *Autism Research, 1*, 52–83.

Hung, C. C., Yen, C. C., Ciuchta, J. L., Papoti, D., Bock, N. A., Leopold, D. A., et al. (2015). Functional mapping of face-selective regions in the extrastriate visual cortex of the marmoset. *Journal of Neuroscience, 35*(3), 1160–1172.

Hung, J., Driver, J., & Walsh, V. (2005). Visual selection and posterior parietal cortex: Effects of repetitive transcranial magnetic stimulation on partial report analyzed by Bundesen's theory of visual attention. *Journal of Neuroscience, 25*, 9602–9612.

Hunt, G. R., Lambert, C., & Gray, R. D. (2007). Cognitive requirements for tool use by New Caledonian crows (*Corvus moneduloides*). *New Zealand Journal of Zoology, 34*(1), 1–7.

Hupé, J.-M., Bordier, C., & Dojat, M. (2011). The neural bases of grapheme–color synesthesia are not localized in real color-sensitive areas. *Cerebral Cortex, 22*(7), 1622–1633.

Hurlburt, R. T., Happe, F., & Frith, U. (1994). Sampling the form of inner experience in three adults with Asperger syndrome. *Psychological Medicine, 24*, 385–395.

Hurst, J., Baraitser, M., Auger, E., Graham, F., & Norell, S. (1990). An extended family with a dominantly inherited speech disorder. *Developmental Medicine and Child Neurology, 32*, 347–355.

Huth, A. G., de Heer, W. A., Griffiths, T. L., Theunissen, F. E., & Gallant, J. L. (2016). Natural speech reveals the semantic maps that tile human cerebral cortex. *Nature, 532*(7600), 453–458. doi:10.1038/nature17637

Hutsler, J. J., & Avino, T. (2015). The relevance of subplate modifications to connectivity in the cerebral cortex of individuals with autism spectrum disorders. In M. F. Casanova & I. Opris (Eds.), *Recent advances on the modular organization of the cortex* (pp. 201–224). Dordrecht, Netherlands: Springer.

Hutsler, J. J., & Casanova, M. F. (2016). Cortical construction in autism spectrum disorder: Columns, connectivity and the subplate. *Neuropathology and Applied Neurobiology, 42*(2), 115–134.

Hutsler, J., & Galuske, R. A. (2003). Hemispheric asymmetries in cerebral cortical networks. *Trends in Neuroscience, 26*, 429–435.

Hyde, I. H. (1921). A micro-electrode and unicellular stimulation. *Biological Bulletin, 40*, 130–133.

Ido, T., Wan, C. N., Casella, B., Fowler, J. S., Wolf, A. P., Reivich, M., et al. (1978). Labeled 2-deoxy-2-fluoro-D-glucose analogs. ^{18}F-labeled 2-deoxy-2-fluoro-D-glucose, 2-deoxy-2-fluoro-D-mannose and C-14-2-deoxy-2-fluoro-D-glucose. *Journal of Labelled Compounds and Radiopharmaceuticals, 14*, 175–183.

Igaz, L. M., Bekinschtein, P., Vianna, M. M., Izquierdo, I., & Medina, J. H. (2004). Gene expression during memory formation. *Neurotoxicity Research, 6*, 189–204.

Illes, J., & Racine, E. (2005). Imaging or imagining? A neuroethics challenge informed by genetics. *American Journal of Bioethics, 5*, 1–14.

Innocenti, G. M., Aggoun-Zouaoui, D., & Lehmann, P. (1995). Cellular aspects of callosal connections and their development. *Neuropsychologia, 33*, 961–987.

Irwin, W., Davidson, R. J., Lowe, M. J., Mock, B. J., Sorenson, J. A., & Turski, P. A. (1996). Human amygdala activation detected with echo-planar functional magnetic resonance imaging. *Neuroreport, 7*, 1765–1769.

Ito, M., Tamura, H., Fujita, I., & Tanaka, K. (1995). Size and position invariance of neuronal responses in monkey inferotemporal cortex. *Journal of Neurophysiology, 73*, 218–226.

Ivry, R. B., & Hazeltine, E. (1999). Subcortical locus of temporal coupling in the bimanual movements of a callosotomy patient. *Human Movement Science, 18*, 345–375.

Izard, C. E. (2010). The many meanings/aspects of emotion: Definitions, functions, activation, and regulation. *Emotion Review, 2*(4), 363–370.

Jabbi, M., Swart, M., & Keysers, C. (2007). Empathy for positive and negative emotions in the gustatory cortex. *NeuroImage, 34*, 1744–1753.

Jack, C. R., Jr., Dickson, D. W., Parisi, J. E., Xu, Y. C., Cha, R. H., O'Brien, P. C., et al. (2002). Antemortem MRI findings correlate with hippocampal neuropathology in typical aging and dementia. *Neurology, 58*, 750–757.

Jackson, J. H. (1867, December 21). Remarks on the disorderly movements of chorea and convulsion, and on localisation. *Medical Times and Gazette, 2*, 669–670.

Jackson, J. H. (1868). Notes on the physiology and pathology of the nervous system. *Medical Times and Gazette, 2*, 177–179.

Jackson, J. H. (1876). Case of large cerebral tumour without optic neuritis and with left hemiplegia and imperceptions. *Royal Ophthalmological Hospital Reports, 8*, 434–444.

Jackson, R. L., Hoffman, P., Pobric, G., & Lambon Ralph, M. A. (2015). The nature and neural correlates of semantic association versus conceptual similarity. *Cerebral Cortex, 25*(11), 4319–4333.

Jaeger, A., Konkel, A., & Dobbins, I. G. (2013). Unexpected novelty and familiarity orienting responses in lateral parietal cortex during recognition judgment. *Neuropsychologia, 51*(6), 1061–1076.

James, T. W., Culham, J., Humphrey, G. K., Milner, A. D., & Goodale, M. A. (2003). Ventral occipital lesions impair object recognition but not object-directed grasping: An fMRI study. *Brain, 126*(Pt. 11), 2463–2475.

James, W. (1884). What is an emotion? *Mind, 9*(34), 188–205.

James, W. (1890). *Principles of psychology.* New York: Holt.

Jasper, H., & Penfield, W. (1954). *Epilepsy and the functional anatomy of the human brain* (2nd ed.). New York: Little, Brown.

Jeannerod, M., & Jacob, P. (2005). Visual cognition: A new look at the two-visual systems model. *Neuropsychologia, 43*(2), 301–312.

Jensen, J., Willeit, M., Zipursky, R. B., Savina, I., Smith, A. J., Menon, M., et al. (2008). The formation of abnormal associations in schizophrenia: Neural and behavioral evidence. *Neuropsychopharmacology, 33*(3), 473–479.

Jiang, Y., & He, S. (2006). Cortical responses to invisible faces: Dissociating subsystems for facial-information processing. *Current Biology, 16*, 2023–2029.

Jiang, Y., Zhou, K., & He, S. (2007). Human visual cortex responds to invisible chromatic flicker. *Nature Neuroscience, 10*(5), 657–662.

Jobst, K. A., Smith, A. D., Szatmari, M., Esiri, M. M., Jaskowski, A., Hindley, N., et al. (1994). Rapidly progressing atrophy of medial temporal lobe in Alzheimer's disease. *Lancet, 343*, 829–830.

Joëls, M., Pu, Z., Wiegert, O., Oitzl, M. S., & Krugers, H. J. (2006). Learning under stress: How does it work? *Trends in Cognitive Sciences, 10*(4), 152–158.

Johansen, J. P., Wolff, S. B. E., Lüthi, A., & LeDoux, J. E. (2012). Controlling the elements: An optogenetic approach to understanding the neural circuits of fear. *Biological Psychiatry, 71*, 1053–1060.

Johansen-Berg, H., Della-Maggiore, V., Behrens, T. E., Smith, S. M., & Paus, T. (2007). Integrity of white matter in the corpus callosum correlates with bimanual coordination skills. *NeuroImage, 36*(Suppl. 2), T16–T21.

Johnson, C., & Wilbrecht, L. (2011). Juvenile mice show greater flexibility in multiple choice reversal learning than adults. *Developmental Cognitive Neuroscience, 1*(4), 540–551.

Johnson, M. K., Kim, J. K., & Risse, G. (1985). Do alcoholic Korsakoff's syndrome patients acquire affective reactions? *Journal of Experimental Psychology. Learning, Memory, and Cognition, 11*, 22–36.

Johnson, M. K., & Sherman, S. (1990). Constructing and reconstructing the past and the future in the present. In T. E. Higgins & R. M. Sorrentino (Eds.), *Handbook of motivation and cognition: Foundations of social behavior* (Vol. 2, pp. 482–526). New York: Guilford.

Johnson, V. E., Stewart, W., Weber, M. T., Cullen, D. K., Siman, R., & Smith, D. H. (2016). SNTF immunostaining reveals previously undetected axonal pathology in traumatic brain injury. *Acta Neuropathologica, 131*(1), 115–135.

Johnson-Frey, S. H., Newman-Norlund, R., & Grafton, S. T. (2004). A distributed left hemisphere network active during planning of everyday tool use skills. *Cerebral Cortex, 15*, 681–695.

Johnsrude, I. S., Owen, A. M., White, N. M., Zhao, W. V., & Boh-bot, V. (2000). Impaired preference conditioning after anterior temporal lobe resection in humans. *Journal of Neuroscience, 20*, 2649–2656.

Jolly, A. (1966). Lemur social behaviour and primate intelligence. *Science, 153*, 501–506.

Jonides, J. (1981). Voluntary versus automatic control over the mind's eye. In J. Long & A. Baddeley (Eds.), *Attention and performance IX* (pp. 187–203). Hillsdale, NJ: Erlbaum.

Judd, T. (2014). Making sense of multitasking: The role of Facebook. *Computers & Education, 70*, 194–202.

Jung, C. E., Strother, L., Feil-Seifer, D. J., & Hutsler, J. J. (2016). Atypical asymmetry for processing human and robot faces in autism revealed by fNIRS. *PLoS One, 11*(7), e0158804.

Just, M., Carpenter, P., Keller, T., Eddy, W., & Thulborn, K. (1996). Brain activation modulated by sentence comprehension. *Science, 274*, 114–116.

Kaas, J. H. (1995). The reorganization of sensory and motor maps in adult mammals. In M. S. Gazzaniga (Ed.), *The cognitive neurosciences* (pp. 51–71). Cambridge, MA: MIT Press.

Kaas, J. H., Nelson, R. J., Sur, M., Dykes, R. W., & Merzenich, M. M. (1984). The somatotopic organization of the ventroposterior thalamus of the squirrel monkey, *Saimiri sciureus. Journal of Comparative Neurology, 226*, 111–140.

Kahn, A. E., Mattar, M. G., Vettel, J. M., Wymbs, N. F., Grafton, S. T., & Bassett, D. S. (2017). Structural pathways supporting swift acquisition of new visuomotor skills. *Cerebral Cortex, 27*(1), 173–184.

Kahn, I., Pascual-Leone, A., Theoret, H., Fregni, F., Clark, D., & Wagner, A. D. (2005). Transient disruption of ventrolateral prefrontal cortex during verbal encoding affects subsequent memory performance. *Journal of Neurophysiology, 94*(1), 688–698.

Kakei, S., Hoffman, D. S., & Strick, P. L. (1999). Muscle and movement representations in the primary motor cortex. *Science, 285*, 2136–2139.

Kakei, S., Hoffman, D. S., & Strick P. L. (2001). Direction of action is represented in the ventral premotor cortex. *Nature Neuroscience, 4*, 1020–1025.

Kali, S., & Dayan, P. (2004). Off-line replay maintains declarative memories in a model of hippocampal–neocortical interactions. *Nature Neuroscience, 7*, 286–294.

Kana, R. K., Wadsworth, H. M., & Travers, B. G. (2011). A systems level analysis of the mirror neuron hypothesis and imitation impairments in autism spectrum disorders. *Neuroscience and Biobehavioral Reviews, 53*, 894–902.

Kandel, E. R., Schwartz, J. H., & Jessell, T. M. (Eds.). (1991). *Principles of neural science* (3rd ed.). New York: Elsevier.

Kanjlia, S., Lane, C., Feigenson, L., & Bedny, M. (2016). Absence of visual experience modifies the neural basis of numerical thinking. *Proceedings of the National Academy of Sciences, USA, 113*(40), 11172–11177.

Kanwisher, N., Woods, R., Iacoboni, M., & Mazziotta, J. C. (1997). A locus in human extrastriate cortex for visual shape analysis. *Journal of Cognitive Neuroscience, 9*, 133–142.

Kao, J. C., Nuyujukian, P., Ryu, S. I., Churchland, M. M., Cunningham, J. P., & Shenoy, K. V. (2015). Single-trial dynamics of motor cortex and their applications to brain-machine interfaces. *Nature Communications, 6*, art. 7759.

Kapp, B. S., Pascoe, J. P., & Bixler, M. A. (1984). The amygdala: A neuroanatomical systems approach to its contributions to aversive conditioning. In N. Butters & L. R. Squire (Eds.), *Neuropsychology of memory* (pp. 473–488). New York: Guilford.

Karnath, H.-O., Fruhmann Berger, M., Küker, W., & Rorden, C. (2004). The anatomy of spatial neglect based on voxelwise statistical analysis: A study of 140 patients. *Cerebral Cortex, 14*, 1165–1172.

Karnath, H.-O., Himmelbach, M., & Rorden, C. (2002). The subcortical anatomy of human spatial neglect: Putamen, caudate nucleus and pulvinar. *Brain, 125*, 350–360.

Karnath, H.-O., Rennig, J., Johannsen, L., & Rorden, C. (2011). The anatomy underlying acute versus chronic spatial neglect. *Brain, 134*(Pt. 3), 903–912.

Karnath, H.-O., Rüter, J., Mandler, A., & Himmelbach, M. (2009). The anatomy of object recognition—Visual form agnosia caused by medial occipitotemporal stroke. *Journal of Neuroscience, 29*(18), 5854–5862.

Karns, C. M., Dow, M. W., & Neville, H. J. (2012). Altered cross-modal processing in the primary auditory cortex of congenitally deaf adults: A visual-somatosensory fMRI study with a double-flash illusion. *Journal of Neuroscience, 32*(28), 9626–9638.

Kashtan, N., & Alon, U. (2005). Spontaneous evolution of modularity and network motifs. *Proceedings of the National Academy of Sciences, USA, 102*(39), 13773–13778.

Kashtan, N., Noor, E., & Alon, U. (2007). Varying environments can speed up evolution. *Proceedings of the National Academy of Sciences, USA, 104*(34), 13711–13716.

Kastner, S., DeWeerd, P., Desimone, R., & Ungerleider, L. C. (1998). Mechanisms of directed attention in the human extrastriate cortex as revealed by functional MRI. *Science, 282*, 108–111.

Kastner, S., Schneider, K., & Wunderlich, K. (2006). Beyond a relay nucleus: Neuroimaging views on the human LGN. *Progress in Brain Research, 155*, 125–143.

KAUFMAN, J. N., ROSS, T. J., STEIN, E. A., & GARAVAN, H. (2003). Cingulate hypoactivity in cocaine users during a GO-NOGO task as revealed by event-related functional magnetic resonance imaging. *Journal of Neuroscience, 23*, 7839–7843.

KAWAI, R., MARKMAN, T., PODDAR, R., KO, R., FANTANA, A. L., DHAWALE, A. K., ET AL. (2015). Motor cortex is required for learning but not for executing a motor skill. *Neuron, 86*(3), 800–812.

KAY, K. N., NASELARIS, T., PRENGER, R. J., & GALLANT, J. L. (2008). Identifying natural images from human brain activity. *Nature, 452*, 352–356.

KEELE, S. W. (1986). Motor control. In K. R. Boff, L. Kaufman, & J. P. Thomas (Eds.), *Handbook of perception and human performance* (Vol. 2, pp. 1–60). New York: Wiley.

KEELE, S. W., IVRY, R., MAYR, U., HAZELTINE, E., & HEUER, H. (2003). The cognitive and neural architecture of sequence representation. *Psychological Review, 110*, 316–339.

KELLENBACH, M. L., BRETT, M., & PATTERSON, K. (2003). Actions speak louder than functions: The importance of manipulability and action in tool representation. *Journal of Cognitive Neuroscience, 15*, 30–46.

KELLEY, W. M., MACRAE, C. N., WYLAND, C. L., CAGLAR, S., INATI, S., & HEATHERTON, T. F. (2002). Finding the self? An event-related fMRI study. *Journal of Cognitive Neuroscience, 14*, 785–794.

KELLEY, W. M., MIEZIN, F. M., MCDERMOTT, K. B., BUCKNER, R. L., RAICHLE, M. E., COHEN, N. J., ET AL. (1998). Hemispheric specialization in human dorsal frontal cortex and medial temporal lobe for verbal and nonverbal memory encoding. *Neuron, 20*(5), 927–936.

KEMPPAINEN, S., JOLKKONEN, E., & PITKÄNEN, A. (2002). Projections from the posterior cortical nucleus of the amygdala to the hippocampal formation and parahippocampal region in rat. *Hippocampus, 12*(6), 735–755.

KENDON A. (2017). Reflections on the "gesture-first" hypothesis of language origins. *Psychonomic Bulletin & Review, 24*(1), 163–170.

KENNEDY, D. P., & ADOLPHS, R. (2010). Impaired fixation to eyes following amygdala damage arises from abnormal bottom-up attention. *Neuropsychologia, 48*(12), 3392–3398.

KENNEDY, D. P., & COURCHESNE, E. (2008a). Functional abnormalities of the default network during self- and other-reflection in autism. *Social Cognitive and Affective Neuroscience, 3*, 177–190.

KENNEDY, D. P., & COURCHESNE, E. (2008b). The intrinsic functional organization of the brain is altered in autism. *NeuroImage, 39*(4), 1877–1885.

KENNEDY, D. P., REDCAY, E., & COURCHESNE, E. (2006). Failing to deactivate: Resting functional abnormalities in autism. *Proceedings of the National Academy of Sciences, USA, 103*, 8275–8280.

KENNERKNECHT, I., GRUETER, T., WELLING, B., WENTZEK, S., HORST, J., EDWARDS, S., ET AL. (2006). First report of prevalence of non-syndromic hereditary prosopagnosia (HPA). *American Journal of Medical Genetics. Part A, 140*(15), 1617–1622.

KENNERLEY, S. W., DAHMUBED, A. F., LARA, A. H., & WALLIS, J. D. (2009). Neurons in the frontal lobe encode the value of multiple decision variables. *Journal of Cognitive Neuroscience, 21*(6), 1162–1178.

KENNETT, S., EIMER, M., SPENCE, C., & DRIVER, J. (2001). Tactile-visual links in exogenous spatial attention under different postures: Convergent evidence from psychophysics and ERPs. *Journal of Cognitive Neuroscience, 13*, 462–478.

KERNS, J. G., COHEN, J. D., MACDONALD, A. W., CHO, R. Y., STENGER, V. A., & CARTER, C. S. (2004). Anterior cingulate conflict monitoring and adjustments in control. *Science, 303*, 1023–1026.

KESSLER, R. C., BERGLUND, P., DEMLER, O., JIN, R., MERIKANGAS, K. R., & WALTERS, E. E. (2005). Lifetime prevalence and age-of-onset distributions of DSM-IV disorders in the National Comorbidity Survey Replication. *Archives of General Psychiatry, 62*(6), 593–602.

KHANNA, P., SWANN, N., DE HEMPTINNE, C., MIOCINOVIC, S., MILLER, A., STARR, P. A., ET AL. (2016). Neurofeedback control in parkinsonian patients using electrocorticography signals accessed wirelessly with a chronic, fully implanted device. *IEEE Transactions on Neural Systems and Rehabilitation Engineering, 25*(10), 1715–1724. doi:10.1109/TNSRE.2016.2597243

KIHLSTROM, J. (1995). Memory and consciousness: An appreciation of Claparède and recognition et moïtè. *Consciousness and Cognition, 4*(4), 379–386.

KILLGORE, W. D. S., & YURGELUN-TODD, D. A. (2004). Activation of the amygdala and anterior cingulate during nonconscious processing of sad versus happy faces. *NeuroImage, 21*, 1215–1223.

KIM, H. (2011). Neural activity that predicts subsequent memory and forgetting: A meta-analysis of 74 fMRI studies. *NeuroImage, 54*(3), 2446–2461.

KIM, S.-G., UGURBIL, K., & STRICK, P. L. (1994). Activation of a cerebellar output nucleus during cognitive processing. *Science, 265*, 949–951.

KIMBURG, D. Y., & FARAH, M. (1993). A unified account of cognitive impairments following frontal lobe damage: The role of working memory in complex, organized behavior. *Journal of Experimental Psychology, 122*(4), 411–428.

KIMURA, D. (1973). The asymmetry of the human brain. *Scientific American, 228*(3), 70–78.

KINGSTONE, A., ENNS, J., MANGUN, G. R., & GAZZANIGA, M. S. (1995). Guided visual search is a left hemisphere process in split-brain patients. *Psychological Science, 6*, 118–121.

KINGSTONE, A., FRIESEN, C. K., & GAZZANIGA, M. S. (2000). Reflexive joint attention depends on lateralized cortical connections. *Psychological Science, 11*, 159–166.

KINGSTONE, A., & GAZZANIGA, M. S. (1995). Subcortical transfer of higher order information: More illusory than real? *Neuropsychology, 9*, 321–328.

KINSBOURNE, M. (1982). Hemispheric specialization and the growth of human understanding. *American Psychologist, 37*, 411–420.

KIRCHER, T. T., SENIOR, C., PHILLIPS, M. L., RABE-HESKETH, S., BENSON, P. J., BULLMORE, E. T., ET AL. (2001). Recognizing one's own face. *Cognition, 78*, B1–B15.

KIRCHHOFER, K. C., ZIMMERMANN, F., KAMINSKI, J., & TOMASELLO, M. (2012). Dogs (*Canis familiaris*), but not chimpanzees (*Pan troglodytes*), understand imperative pointing. *PLoS One, 7*(2), e30913.

KIRSCHBAUM, C., WOLF, O. T., MAY, M., WIPPICH, W., & HELLHAMMER, D. H. (1996). Stress- and treatment-induced elevations of cortisol levels associated with impaired declarative memory in healthy adults. *Life Sciences, 58*, 1475–1483.

KIRSCHNER, M., & GERHART, J. (1998). Evolvability. *Proceedings of the National Academy of Sciences, USA, 95*, 8420–8427.

KISHIDA, K. T., SAEZ, I., LOHRENZ, T., WITCHER, M. R., LAXTON, A. W., TATTER, S. B., ET AL. (2016). Subsecond dopamine fluctuations in human striatum encode superposed error signals about actual and counterfactual reward. *Proceedings of the National Academy of Sciences, USA, 113*(1), 200–205.

KITTERLE, F., CHRISTMAN, S., & HELLIGE, J. (1990). Hemispheric differences are found in identification, but not detection of low versus high spatial frequencies. *Perception & Psychophysics, 48*, 297–306.

KLATT, D. H. (1989). Review of selected models of speech perception. In W. Marslen-Wilson (Ed.), *Lexical representation and process* (pp. 169–226). Cambridge, MA: MIT Press.

KLEIM, J. A., CHAN, S., PRINGLE, E., SCHALLERT, K., PROCACCIO, V., JIMENEZ, R., ET AL. (2006). BDNF val66met polymorphism is associated with modified experience-dependent plasticity in human motor cortex. *Nature Neuroscience, 9*, 735–737.

KLEIN, S. B., & KIHLSTROM, J. F. (1986). Elaboration, organization, and the self-reference effect in memory. *Journal of Experimental Psychology. General, 115*, 26–38.

KLEIN, S. B., & LAX, M. L. (2010). The unanticipated resilience of trait self-knowledge in the face of neural damage. *Memory, 18*, 918–948.

KLEIN, S. B., LOFTUS, J., & KIHLSTROM, J. F. (2002). Memory and temporal experience: The effects of episodic memory loss on an amnesic patient's ability to remember the past and imagine the future. *Social Cognition, 20*, 353–379.

KLEIN, S. B., LOFTUS, J., & PLOG, A. E. (1992). Trait judgments about the self: Evidence from the encoding specificity paradigm. *Personality and Social Psychology Bulletin, 18*, 730–735.

KLEINSMITH, L. J., & KAPLAN, S. (1963). Paired-associate learning as a function of arousal and interpolated interval. *Journal of Experimental Psychology, 65*, 190–193.

KLIN, A., JONES, W., SCHULTZ, R., VOLKMAR, F., & COHEN, D. (2002). Visual fixation patterns during viewing of naturalistic social situations as predictors of social competence in individuals with autism. *Archives of General Psychiatry, 59*, 809–816.

KLIN, A., SPARROW, S. S., DE BILDT, A., CICCHETTI, D. V., COHEN, D. J., & VOLKMAR F. R. (1999). A normed study of face recognition in autism and related disorders. *Journal of Autism and Developmental Disorders, 29*, 499–508.

KLINGBERG, T., HEDEHUS, M., TEMPLE, E., SALZ, T., GABRIELI, J. D., MOSELEY, M. E., ET AL. (2000). Microstructure of temporo-parietal white matter as a basis for reading ability: Evidence from diffusion tensor magnetic resonance imaging. *Neuron, 25*, 493–500.

KLUNK, W. E., ENGLER, H., NORDBERG, A., WANG, Y., BLOMQVIST, G., HOLT, D. P., ET AL. (2004). Imaging brain amyloid in Alzheimer's disease with Pittsburgh Compound-B. *Annals of Neurology, 55*(3), 306–319.

KLÜVER, H., & BUCY, P. C. (1939). Preliminary analysis of functions of the temporal lobes in monkeys. *Archives of Neurology, 42*, 979–1000.

KNIGHT, D. C., NGUYEN, H. T., & BANDETTINI, P. A. (2005). The role of the human amygdala in the production of conditioned fear responses. *NeuroImage, 26*(4), 1193–1200.

KNIGHT, R. T., & GRABOWECKY, M. (1995). Escape from linear time: Prefrontal cortex and conscious experience. In M. S. Gazzaniga (Ed.), *The cognitive neurosciences* (pp. 1357–1371). Cambridge, MA: MIT Press.

KNOWLTON, B. J., SQUIRE, L. R., PAULSEN, J. S., SWERDLOW, N. R., & SWENSON, M. (1996). Dissociations within nondeclarative memory in Huntington's disease. *Neuropsychology, 10*(4), 538–548.

KOBAYASHI, H., & KOHSHIMA, S. (2001). Unique morphology of the human eye and its adaptive meaning: Comparative studies on external morphology of the primate eye. *Journal of Human Evolution, 40*, 419–435.

KOCH, C. (2004). *The quest for consciousness: A neurobiological approach*. Englewood, CO: Roberts.

KOCH, C., & ULLMAN, S. (1985). Shifts in selective visual attention: Towards the underlying neural circuitry. *Human Neurobiology, 4*, 219–227.

KOECHLIN, E., ODY, C., & KONNEIHER, F. (2003). The architecture of cognitive control in the human prefrontal cortex. *Science, 302*, 1181–1185.

KOHLER, E., KEYSERS, C., UMILTA, A., FOGASSI, L., GALLESE, V., & RIZOLATT, G. (2002). Hearing sounds, understanding actions: Action representation in mirror neurons. *Science, 297*, 846–848.

KOLASINSKI, J., MAKIN, T. R., LOGAN, J. P., JBABDI, S., CLARE, S., STAGG, C. J., ET AL. (2016). Perceptually relevant remapping of human somatotopy in 24 hours. *eLife, 5*.

KOLB, B., & WHISHAW, I. Q. (1996). *Fundamentals of human neuropsychology* (4th ed.). New York: Freeman.

KOLLING, N., BEHRENS, T., MARS, R., & RUSHWORTH, M. (2012). Neural mechanisms of foraging. *Science, 336*(6077), 95–98.

KÖLMEL, H. W. (1985). Complex visual hallucinations in the hemianopic field. *Journal of Neurology, Neurosurgery, and Psychiatry, 48*(1), 29–38.

KONISHI, M. (1993). Listening with two ears. *Scientific American, 268*(4), 66–73.

KONISHI, S., NAKAJIMA, K., UCHIDA, I., KAMEYAMA, M., NAKAHARA, K., SEKIHARA, K., ET AL. (1998). Transient activation of inferior prefrontal cortex during cognitive set shifting. *Nature Neuroscience, 1*, 80–84.

KONKEL, A., & COHEN, N. J. (2009). Relational memory and the hippocampus: Representations and methods. *Frontiers in Neuroscience, 3*(2), 166.

KONKEL, A., WARREN, D. E., DUFF, M. C., TRANEL, D. N., & COHEN, N. J. (2008). Hippocampal amnesia impairs all manner of relational memory. *Frontiers of Human Neuroscience, 2*, 15.

KOSSLYN, S. M., SHIN, L. M., THOMPSON, W. L., MCNALLY, R. J., RAUCH, S. L., PITMAN, R. K., ET AL. (1996). Neural effects of visualizing and perceiving aversive stimuli: A PET investigation. *Neuroreport, 7*, 1569–1576.

KOTTER, R., & MEYER, N. (1992). The limbic system: A review of its empirical foundation. *Behavioural Brain Research, 52*, 105–127.

KOTZ, S. M., & SCHWARTZE, M. (2010). Cortical speech processing unplugged: A timely subcortico-cortical framework. *Trends in Cognitive Sciences, 14*, 392–399.

KOUNEIHER, F., CHARRON, S., & KOECHLIN, E. (2008). Motivation and cognitive control in the human prefrontal cortex. *Nature Neuroscience, 12*(7), 939–947.

KOVACS, A., TEGLAS, E., & ENDRESS, A. (2010). The social sense: Susceptibility to others' beliefs in human infants and adults. *Science, 330*, 1830–1834.

KRACK, P., POLLAK, P., LIMOUSIN, P., HOFFMANN, D., XIE, J., BENAZZOUZ, A., ET AL. (1998). Subthalamic nucleus or internal pallidal stimulation in young onset Parkinson's disease. *Brain, 121*, 451–457.

KRAGEL, P. A., & LABAR, K. S. (2016). Decoding the nature of emotion in the brain. *Trends in Cognitive Sciences, 20*(6), 444–455.

KRASNOW, M. M., DELTON, A. W., COSMIDES, L., & TOOBY, J. (2016). Looking under the hood of third-party punishment reveals design for personal benefit. *Psychological Science, 27*(3), 405–418.

KRAUSE, J., LALUEZA-FOX, C., ORLANDO, L., ENARD, W., GREEN, R. E., BURBANO, H. A., ET AL. (2007). The derived FOXP2 variant of modern humans was shared with Neandertals. *Current Biology, 17*, 1908–1912.

KRAVITZ, A. V., FREEZE, B. S., PARKER, P. R., KAY, K., THWIN, M. T., DEISSEROTH, K., ET AL. (2010). Regulation of parkinsonian motor behaviours by optogenetic control of basal ganglia circuitry. *Nature, 466*(7306), 622–626.

KREIBIG, S. D. (2010). Autonomic nervous system activity in emotion: A review. *Biological Psychology, 84*(3), 394–421.

KROLAK-SALMON, P., HÉNAFF, M. A., ISNARD, J., TALLON-BAUDRY, C., GUÉNOT, M., VIGHETTO, A., ET AL. (2003). An attention modulated response to disgust in human ventral anterior insula. *Annals of Neurology, 53*, 446–453.

KRUPENYE, C., KANO, F., HIRATA, S., CALL, J., & TOMASELLO, M. (2016). Great apes anticipate that other individuals will act according to false beliefs. *Science, 354*(6308), 110–114.

KUFFLER, S., & NICHOLLS, J. (1976). *From neuron to brain*. Sunderland, MA: Sinauer.

KUHL, P. K., WILLIAMS, K. A., LACERDA, F., STEVENS, K. N., & LINDBLOM, B. (1992). Linguistic experience alters phonetic perception in infants by 6 months of age. *Science, 255*(5044), 606–608.

Kühn, A. A., Kempf, F., Brücke, C., Doyle, L. G., Martinez-Torres, I., Pogosyan, A., et al. (2008). High-frequency stimulation of the subthalamic nucleus suppresses oscillatory β activity in patients with Parkinson's disease in parallel with improvement in motor performance. *Journal of Neuroscience, 28*(24), 6165–6173.

Kuperberg, G. R. (2007). Neural mechanisms of language comprehension: Challenges to syntax. *Brain Research, 1146*, 23–49.

Kuperberg, G. R., Holcomb, P. J., Sitnikova, T., & Greve, D. (2003). Distinct patterns of neural modulation during the processing of conceptual and syntactic anomalies. *Journal of Cognitive Neuroscience, 15*, 272–293.

Kuperberg, G. R., Sitnikova, T., Caplan, D., & Holcomb, P. (2003). Electrophysiological distinctions in processing conceptual relationships within simple sentences. *Cognitive Brain Research, 17*, 117–129.

Kurkela, K. A., & Dennis, N. A. (2016). Event-related fMRI studies of false memory: An Activation Likelihood Estimation meta-analysis. *Neuropsychologia, 81*, 149–167.

Kurzban, R., Tooby, J., & Cosmides, L. (2001). Can race be erased? Coalitional computation and social categorization. *Proceedings of the National Academy of Sciences, USA, 98*, 15387–15392.

Kutas, M., & Federmeier, K. D. (2000). Electrophysiology reveals semantic memory use in language comprehension. *Trends in Cognitive Sciences, 4*, 463–470.

Kutas, M., & Hillyard, S. A. (1980). Reading senseless sentences: Brain potentials reflect semantic incongruity. *Science, 207*, 203–205.

Kwong, K. K., Belliveau, J. W., Chesler, D. A., Goldberg, I. E., Weisskoff, R. M., Poncelet, B. P., et al. (1992). Dynamic magnetic resonance imaging of human brain activity during primary sensory stimulation. *Proceedings of the National Academy of Sciences, USA, 89*(12), 5675–5679.

LaBar, K. S., LeDoux, J. E., Spencer, D. D., & Phelps, E. A. (1995). Impaired fear conditioning following unilateral temporal lobectomy in humans. *Journal of Neuroscience, 15*, 6846–6855.

LaBar, K. S., & Phelps, E. A. (1998). Role of the human amygdala in arousal mediated memory consolidation. *Psychological Science, 9*, 490–493.

Ladavas, E., Paladini, R., & Cubelli, R. (1993). Implicit associative priming in a patient with left visual neglect. *Neuropsychologia, 31*, 1307–1320.

Lai, C. S., Fisher, S. E., Hurst, J. A., Vargha-Khaderm, F., & Monaco, A. P. (2001). A novel forkhead-domain gene is mutated in a severe speech and language disorder. *Nature, 413*, 519–523.

Lamantia, A. S., & Rakic, P. (1990). Cytological and quantitative characteristics of four cerebral commissures in the rhesus monkey. *Journal of Comparative Neurology, 291*, 520–537.

Lamm, C., & Majdandžić, J. (2015). The role of shared neural activations, mirror neurons, and morality in empathy–A critical comment. *Neuroscience Research, 90*, 15–24.

Lamme, V. (2003). Why visual attention and awareness are different. *Trends in Cognitive Sciences, 17*, 12–18.

Landau, W. M., Freygang, W. H., Roland, L. P., Sokoloff, L., & Dety, S. S. (1955). The local circulation of the living brain: Values in the unanesthetized and anesthetized cat. *Transactions of the American Neurological Association, 80*, 125–129.

Lane, R. D., Reiman, E. M., Ahern, G. L., Schwartz, G. E., & Davidson, R. J. (1997). Neuroanatomical correlates of happiness, sadness, and disgust. *American Journal of Psychiatry, 154*, 926–933.

Lang, C. E., Strube, M. J., Bland, M. D., Waddell, K. J., Cherry-Allen, K. M., Nudo, R. J., et al. (2016). Dose response of task-specific upper limb training in people at least 6 months poststroke: A phase II, single-blind, randomized, controlled trial. *Annals of Neurology, 80*(3), 342–354.

Langer, N., Hänggi, J., Müller, N. A., Simmen, H. P., & Jäncke, L. (2012). Effects of limb immobilization on brain plasticity. *Neurology, 78*(3), 182–188.

Langston, W. J. (1984). I. MPTP neurotoxicity: An overview and characterization of phases of toxicity. *Life Sciences, 36*, 201–206.

Larsen, J. T., & McGraw, A. P. (2014). The case for mixed emotions. *Social and Personality Psychology Compass, 8*(6), 263–274.

Larsen, J. T., McGraw, A. P., & Cacioppo, J. T. (2001). Can people feel happy and sad at the same time? *Journal of Personality and Social Psychology, 81*(4), 684.

Larsson, J., & Heeger, D. J. (2006). Two retinotopic visual areas in human lateral occipital cortex. *Journal of Neuroscience, 26*(51), 13128–13142.

Laruelle, M. (1998). Imaging dopamine transmission in schizophrenia. A review and meta-analysis. *Quarterly Journal of Nuclear Medicine, 42*, 211–221.

Lashley, K. S. (1929). *Brain mechanisms and intelligence: A quantitative study of injuries to the brain.* Chicago: University of Chicago Press.

Lassen, N. A., Ingvar, D. H., & Skinhøj, E. (1978). Brain function and blood flow. *Scientific American, 239*, 62–71.

Lau, Y., Hinkley, L., Bukshpun, P., Strominger, Z., Wakahiro, M., Baron-Cohen, S., et al. (2013). Autism traits in individuals with agenesis of the corpus callosum. *Journal of Autism and Developmental Disorders, 43*(5), 1106–1118.

Laureys, S., Celesia, G. G., Cohadon, F., Lavrijsen, J., León-Carrión, J., Sannita, W. G., et al. (2010). Unresponsive wakefulness syndrome: A new name for the vegetative state or apallic syndrome. *BMC Medicine, 8*(1), 68.

Lauterbur, P. (1973). Image formation by induced local interactions: Examples employing nuclear magnetic resonance. *Nature, 242*, 190–191.

Lebedev, M. A., & Nicolelis, M. A. (2006). Brain-machine interfaces: Past, present and future. *Trends in Neurosciences, 29*, 536–546.

Leber, A. B. (2010). Neural predictors of within-subject fluctuations in attentional control. *Journal of Neuroscience, 30*, 11458–11465.

LeDoux, J. E. (1991). Emotion and the limbic system concept. *Concepts in Neuroscience, 2*, 169–199.

LeDoux, J. E. (1994). Emotion, memory and the brain. *Scientific American, 270*(6), 50–57.

LeDoux, J. E. (1996). *The emotional brain: The mysterious underpinnings of emotional life.* New York: Simon & Schuster.

LeDoux, J. E. (2007). The amygdala. *Current Biology, 17*(20), R868–R874.

LeDoux, J. E. (2012). Rethinking the emotional brain. *Neuron, 73*(4), 653–676.

LeDoux, J. E. (2014). Coming to terms with fear. *Proceedings of the National Academy of Sciences, USA, 111*(8), 2871–2878.

LeDoux, J. E., & Gorman, J. (2001). A call to action: Overcoming anxiety through active coping. *American Journal of Psychiatry, 158*(12), 1953–1955.

Lehmann, H., Lacanilao, S., & Sutherland, R. J. (2007). Complete or partial hippocampal damage produces equivalent retrograde amnesia for remote contextual fear memories. *European Journal of Neuroscience, 25*, 1278–1286.

Lemon, R. N., & Griffiths, J. (2005). Comparing the function of the corticospinal system in different species: Organizational differences for motor specialization? *Muscle & Nerve, 32*(3), 261–279.

LeMoyne, T., & Buchanan, T. (2011). Does "hovering" matter? Helicopter parenting and its effect on well-being. *Sociological Spectrum, 31*(4), 399–418.

Lempert, K. M. & Phelps, E. A. (2016). Affect in economic decision making. In L. F. Barrett, M. Lewis, & J. M. Haviland-Jones (Eds.), *Handbook of emotions* (4th ed., pp. 98–112). New York: Guilford.

Leotti, L. A., & Delgado, M. R. (2011). The inherent reward of choice. *Psychological Science, 22*(10), 1310–1318.

Lerner, J. S., & Keltner, D. (2000). Beyond valence: Toward a model of emotion-specific influences on judgement and choice. *Cognition & Emotion, 14*(4), 473–493.

Lerner, J. S., Li, Y., Valdesolo, P., & Kassam, K. S. (2015). Emotion and decision making. *Annual Review of Psychology, 66*, 799–823.

Lerner, J. S., Small, D. A., & Loewenstein, G. (2004). Heart strings and purse strings: Carryover effects of emotions on economic decisions. *Psychological Science, 15*(5), 337–341.

Leshikar, E. D., & Duarte, A. (2012). Medial prefrontal cortex supports source memory accuracy for self-referenced items. *Social Neuroscience, 7*(2), 126–145.

Levelt, W. J. M. (1989). *Speaking: From intention to articulation.* Cambridge, MA: MIT Press.

Levine, J. (2001). *Purple haze: The puzzle of consciousness.* Oxford: Oxford University Press.

Leyton, M., Casey, K. F., Delaney, J. S., Kolivakis, T., & Benkelfat, C. (2005). Cocaine craving, euphoria, and self-administration: A preliminary study of the effect of catecholamine precursor depletion. *Behavioral Neuroscience, 119*, 1619–1627.

Lhermitte, F. (1983). "Utilization behaviour" and its relation to lesions of the frontal lobes. *Brain, 106*, 237–255.

Lhermitte, F., Pillon, B., & Serdaru, M. (1986). Human autonomy and the frontal lobes. Part I: Imitation and utilization behavior: A neuropsychological study of 75 patients. *Annals of Neurology, 19*, 326–334.

Li, Q., Ke, Y., Chan, D. C., Qian, Z. M., Yung, K. K., Ko, H., et al. (2012). Therapeutic deep brain stimulation in parkinsonian rats directly influences motor cortex. *Neuron, 76*(5), 1030–1041.

Li, W., Howard, J. D., Parrish, T. B., & Gottfried, J. A. (2008). Aversive learning enhances perceptual and cortical discrimination of indiscriminable odor cues. *Science, 319*(5871), 1842–1845.

Li, Y., Liu, Y., Li, J., Qin, W., Li, K., Yu, C., et al. (2009). Brain anatomical networks and intelligence. *PLoS Computational Biology, 5*(5), e1000395.

Libet, B. (1996). Neuronal processes in the production of conscious experience. In M. Velmans (Ed.), *The science of consciousness* (pp. 96–117). London: Routledge.

Libet, B., Gleason, C. A., Wright, E. W., & Pearl, D. K. (1983). Time of conscious intention to act in relation to onset of cerebral activity (readiness potential): The unconscious initiation of a freely voluntary act. *Brain, 106*(3), 623–642.

Libet, B., Wright, E. W., Feinstein, B., & Pearl, D. K. (1979). Subjective referral of the timing for a conscious sensory experience: A functional role for the somatosensory specific projection system in man. *Brain, 102*(1), 193–224.

Liebal, K., Call, J., & Tomasello, M. (2004). Use of gesture sequences in chimpanzees. *American Journal of Primatology, 64*, 377–396.

Lin, D., Boyle, M. P., Dollar, P., Lee, H., Lein, E. S., Perona, P., et al. (2011). Functional identification of an aggression locus in the mouse hypothalamus. *Nature, 470*(7333), 221–226.

Lindquist, K. A., Wager, T. D., Kober, H., Bliss-Moreau, E., & Barrett, L. F. (2012). The brain basis of emotion: A meta-analytic review. *Behavioral and Brain Sciences, 35*, 121–143.

Lipson, H., Pollack, J. B., & Suh, N. P. (2002). On the origin of modular variation. *Evolution, 56*(8), 1549–1556.

Lissauer, H. (1890). Ein Fall von Seelenblindheit nebst einem Beitrage zur Theorie derselben. *Archiv für Psychiatrie, 21*, 222–270.

Liszkowski, U., Carpenter, M., & Tomasello, M. (2008). Twelve-month-olds communicate helpfully and appropriately for knowledgeable and ignorant partners. *Cognition, 108*, 732–739.

Liu, T., Stevens, S. T., & Carrasco, M. (2007). Comparing the time course and efficacy of spatial and feature-based attention. *Vision Research, 47*, 108–113.

Llorens, F., Schmitz, M., Ferrer, I., & Zerr, I. (2016). CSF biomarkers in neurodegenerative and vascular dementias. *Progress in Neurobiology, 138*, 36–53.

Lloyd-Pierce, N. (1997, February 23). How we met Joe Simpson and Simon Yates. *Independent.* Retrieved from http://www.independent.co.uk/arts-entertainment/how-we-met-joe-simpson-and-simon-yates-1280331.html

Lo, Y. C., Soong, W. T., Gau, S. S. F., Wu, Y. Y., Lai, M. C., Yeh, F. C., et al. (2011). The loss of asymmetry and reduced interhemispheric connectivity in adolescents with autism: A study using diffusion spectrum imaging tractography. *Psychiatry Research. Neuroimaging, 192*(1), 60–66.

Lockhart, D. J., & Barlow, C. (2001). Expressing what's on your mind: DNA arrays and the brain. *Nature Reviews Neuroscience, 2*, 63–68.

Loftus, W. C., Tramo, M. J., Thomas, C. E., Green, R. L., Nordgren, R. A., & Gazzaniga, M. S. (1993). Three-dimensional quantitative analysis of hemispheric asymmetry in the human superior temporal region. *Cerebral Cortex, 3*, 348–355.

Logothetis, M. K., Pauls, J., Augath, M., Trinath, T., & Oeltermann, A. (2001). Neurophysiological investigation of the basis of the fMRI signal. *Nature, 412*, 150–157.

Lombardo, M. V., Chakrabarti, B., Bullmore, E. T., & Baron-Cohen, S. (2011). Specialization of right temporo-parietal junction for mentalizing and its association with social impairments in autism. *NeuroImage, 56*, 1832–1838.

Lomber, S. G., & Malhotra, S. (2008). Double dissociation of "what" and "where" processing in auditory cortex. *Nature Neuroscience, 11*(5), 609–616.

Losin, E. A., Russell, J. L., Freeman, H., Meguerditchian, A., & Hopkins, W. D. (2008). Left hemisphere specialization for orofacial movements of learned vocal signals by captive chimpanzees. *PLoS One, 3*(6), e2529.

Lucas, M. (2000). Semantic priming without association: A meta-analytic review. *Psychonomic Bulletin & Review, 7*(4), 618–630.

Luciani, L. (1901–1911). *Fisiologia del Homo.* Firenze, Italy: Le Monnier.

Luck, S. J., Chelazzi, L., Hillyard, S. A., & Desimone, R. (1997). Mechanisms of spatial selective attention in areas V1, V2, and V4 of macaque visual cortex. *Journal of Neurophysiology, 77*, 24–42.

Luck, S. J., Fan, S., & Hillyard, S. A. (1993). Attention-related modulation of sensory-evoked brain activity in a visual search task. *Journal of Cognitive Neuroscience, 5*, 188–195.

Luck, S. J., Hillyard, S. A., Mangun, G. R., & Gazzaniga, M. S. (1989). Independent hemispheric attentional systems mediate visual search in split-brain patients. *Nature, 342*, 543–545.

Luders, E., Narr, K. L., Zaidel, E., Thompson, P. M., Jancke, L., & Toga, A. W. (2006). Parasagittal asymmetries of the corpus callosum. *Cerebral Cortex, 16*, 346–354.

Luders, E., Toga, A. W., & Thompson, P. M. (2014). Why size matters: Differences in brain volume account for apparent sex differences in callosal anatomy. The sexual dimorphism of the corpus callosum. *NeuroImage, 84*, 820–824.

Lui, P., Padow, V. A., Franco, D., Hall, B. S., Park, B., Klein, Z. A., et al. (2012). Divergent stress-induced neuroendocrine and behavioral responses prior to puberty. *Physiology & Behavior, 107*(1), 104–111.

Lukkes, J. L., Mokin, M. V., Scholl, J. L., & Forster, G. L. (2009). Adult rats exposed to early-life social isolation exhibit increased anxiety and conditioned fear behavior, and altered hormonal stress responses. *Hormones and Behavior, 55*(1), 248–256.

Lulé, D., Zickler, C., Häcker, S., Bruno, M. A., Demertzi, A., Pellas, F., et al. (2009). Life can be worth living in locked-in syndrome. *Progress in Brain Research, 177,* 339–351.

Luo, Y. H. L., & da Cruz, L. (2016). The Argus(®) II retinal prosthesis system. *Progress in Retinal and Eye Research, 50,* 89–107.

Lupien, S. J., Fiocco, A., Wan, N., Maheu, F., Lord, C., Schramek, T., et al. (2005). Stress hormones and human memory function across the life span. *Psychoneuroendocrinology, 30,* 225–242.

Lynn, A. C., Padmanabhan, A., Simmonds, D., Foran, W., Hallquist, M. N., Luna, B., et al. (2018). Functional connectivity differences in autism during face and car recognition: Underconnectivity and atypical age-related changes. *Developmental Science, 21*(1).

Lyons, M. K. (2011). Deep brain stimulation: Current and future clinical applications. *Mayo Clinic Proceedings, 86*(7), 662–672.

MacDonald, A. W., Cohen, J. D., Stenger, V. A., & Carter, C. S. (2000). Dissociating the role of the dorsolateral prefrontal and anterior cingulate cortex in cognitive control. *Science, 288,* 1835–1838.

MacGregor, L. J., Pulvermuller, F., van Casteren, M., & Shtyrov, Y. (2012). Ultra-rapid access to words in the brain. *Nature Communications, 3*(711). doi:10.1038/ncomms1715

MacKay, D. G. (1987). *The organization of perception and action: A theory for language and other cognitive skills.* New York: Springer.

MacLean, P. D. (1949). Psychosomatic disease and the "visceral brain": Recent developments bearing on the Papez theory of emotion. *Psychosomatic Medicine, 11,* 338–353.

MacLean, P. D. (1952). Some psychiatric implications of physiological studies on frontotemporal portion of limbic system (visceral brain). *Electroencephalography and Clinical Neurophysiology, 4,* 407–418.

MacLeod, C. (1991). Half a century of research on the Stroop effect: An integrative review. *Psychological Bulletin, 109,* 163–203.

MacMillan, M. B. (1986). A wonderful journey through skull and brains: The travels of Mr. Gage's tamping iron. *Brain and Cognition, 5,* 67–107.

MacMillan, M. (2000). *An odd kind of fame: Stories of Phineas Gage.* Cambridge, MA: MIT Press.

Macrae, C. N., Moran, J. M., Heatherton, T. F., Banfield, J. F., & Kelley, W. M. (2004). Medial prefrontal activity predicts memory for self. *Cerebral Cortex, 14,* 647–654.

Magno, E., & Allan, K. (2007). Self-reference during explicit memory retrieval: An event-related potential analysis. *Psychological Science, 18,* 672–677.

Mahajan, N., & Wynn, K. (2012). Origins of "us" versus "them": Prelinguistic infants prefer similar others. *Cognition, 124*(2), 227–233.

Mahon, B., Anzellotti, S., Schwarzbach, J., Zampini, M., & Caramazza, A. (2009). Category-specific organization in the human brain does not require visual experience. *Neuron, 63,* 397–405.

Mahon, B. Z., & Caramazza, A. (2009). Concepts and categories: A cognitive neuropsychological perspective. *Annual Review of Psychology, 60,* 27–51.

Mahowald, M. W., & Schenck, C. H. (2005). Insights from studying human sleep disorders. *Nature, 437*(7063), 1279.

Maia, T. V., & McClelland, J. L. (2004). A reexamination of the evidence for the somatic marker hypothesis: What participants really know in the Iowa gambling task. *Proceedings of the National Academy of Sciences, USA, 101*(45), 16075–16080.

Mainland, J., & Sobel, N. (2006). The sniff is part of the olfactory percept. *Chemical Senses, 31,* 181–196. [Epub, December 8, 2005]

Malhotra, P., Coulthard, E. J., & Husain, M. (2009). Role of right posterior parietal cortex in maintaining attention to spatial locations over time. *Brain, 132,* 645–660.

Malmo, R. (1942). Interference factors in delayed response in monkeys after removal of frontal lobes. *Journal of Neurophysiology, 5,* 295–308.

Mampe, B., Friederici, A. D., Christophe, A., & Wermke, K. (2009). Newborns' cry melody is shaped by their native language. *Current Biology, 19,* 1994–1997.

Mangun, G. R., & Hillyard, S. A. (1991). Modulations of sensory-evoked brain potentials indicate changes in perceptual processing during visual-spatial priming. *Journal of Experimental Psychology. Human Perception and Performance, 17,* 1057–1074.

Mangun, G. R., Hopfinger, J., Kussmaul, C., Fletcher, E., & Heinze, H. J. (1997). Covariations in PET and ERP measures of spatial selective attention in human extrastriate visual cortex. *Human Brain Mapping, 5,* 273–279.

Manser, M. B., Bell, M. B., & Fletcher, L. B. (2001). The information that receivers extract form alarm calls in suricates. *Proceedings of the Royal Society of London, Series B, 268,* 2485–2491.

Marcel, A. (1983a). Conscious and unconscious perception: Experiments on visual masking and word recognition. *Cognitive Psychology, 15,* 197–237.

Marcel, A. (1983b). Conscious and unconscious perception: An approach to the relations between phenomenal experience and perceptual process. *Cognitive Psychology, 15,* 238–300.

Maricic, T., Günther, V., Georgiev, O., Gehre, S., Ćurlin, M., Schreiweis, C., et al. (2012). A recent evolutionary change affects a regulatory element in the human FOXP2 gene. *Molecular Biology and Evolution, 30*(4), 844–852.

Markowitsch, H. J., Kalbe, E., Kessler, J., von Stockhausen, H. M., Ghaemi, M., & Heiss, W. D. (1999). Short-term memory deficit after focal parietal damage. *Journal of Clinical and Experimental Neuropsychology, 21,* 784–797.

Markus, H. (1977). Self-schemata processing information about the self. *Journal of Personality and Social Research, 35,* 63–78.

Marois, R., Yi, D. J., & Chun, M. M. (2004). The neural fate of consciously perceived and missed events in the attentional blink. *Neuron, 41,* 465–472.

Marshall, A. J., Wrangham, R. W., & Arcadi, A. C. (1991). Does learning affect the structure of vocalizations in chimpanzees? *Animal Behaviour, 58*(4), 825–830.

Marslen-Wilson, W., & Tyler, L. K. (1980). The temporal structure of spoken language understanding. *Cognition, 8,* 1–71.

Martin, A. (2007). The representation of object concepts in the brain. *Annual Review of Psychology, 58,* 25–45.

Martin, A., Wiggs, C. L., Ungerleider, L. G., & Haxby, J. V. (1996). Neural correlates of category specific behavior. *Nature, 379,* 649–652.

Martin, S. J., De Hoz, L., & Morris, R. G. (2005). Retrograde amnesia: Neither partial nor complete hippocampal lesions in rats result in preferential sparing of remote spatial memory, even after reminding. *Neuropsychologia, 43,* 609–624.

Martin, T. A., Keating, J. G., Goodkin, H. P., Bastian, A. J., & Thach, W. T. (1996). Throwing while looking through prisms. I. Focal olivocerebellar lesions impair adaptation. *Brain, 119,* 1183–1198.

Martin, V. C., Schacter, D. L., Corballis, M. C., & Addis, D. R. (2011). A role for the hippocampus in encoding simulations of future events. *Proceedings of the National Academy of Sciences, USA, 108,* 13858–13863.

Martinez, A., Anllo-Vento, L., Sereno, M. I., Frank, L. R., Buxton, R. B., Dubowitz, D. J., et al. (1999). Involvement of striate and extrastriate visual cortical areas in spatial attention. *Nature Neuroscience, 2*, 364–369.

Mather, M., Henkel, L. A., & Johnson, M. K. (1997). Evaluating characteristics of false memories: Remember/know judgments and memory characteristics questionnaire compared. *Memory and Cognition, 25*, 826–837.

Matsumoto, M., & Hikosaka, O. (2007). Lateral habenula as a source of negative reward signals in dopamine neurons. *Nature, 447*, 1111–1117.

Matsumoto, M., & Hikosaka, O. (2009). Two types of dopamine neuron distinctly convey positive and negative motivational signals. *Nature, 459*, 837–841.

Mattar, M., Wymbs, N. F., Bock, A. S., Aguirre, G. K., Grafton, S. T., & Bassett, D. S. (2018). Predicting future learning from baseline network architecture. *NeuroImage, 172*, 107–117.

Mattingley, J. B., Rich, A. N., Yelland, G., & Bradshaw, J. L. (2001). Unconscious priming eliminates automatic binding of colour and alphanumeric form in synaesthesia. *Nature, 410*, 580–582.

Matyas, F., Sreenivasan, V., Marbach, F., Wacongne, C., Barsy, B., Mateo, C., et al. (2010). Motor control by sensory cortex. *Science, 330*, 1240–1243.

Maunsell, J. H. R., & Van Essen, D. C. (1983). Functional properties of neurons in middle temporal visual area of the macaque monkey. I. Selectivity for stimulus direction, speed, and orientation. *Journal of Neurophysiology, 49*, 1127–1147.

Mayford, M. (2012). Navigating uncertain waters. *Nature Neuroscience, 15*, 1056–1057.

Mazoyer, B., Tzourio, N., Frak, V., Syrota, A., Murayama, N., Levier, O., et al. (1993). The cortical representation of speech. *Journal of Cognitive Neuroscience, 5*, 467–479.

McAdams, C. J., & Reid, R. C. (2005). Attention modulates the responses of simple cells in monkey primary visual cortex. *Journal of Neuroscience, 25*, 11023–11033.

McAlonan, K., Cavanaugh, J., & Wurtz, R. H. (2008). Guarding the gateway to cortex with attention in visual thalamus. *Nature, 456*, 391–394.

McAndrews, M. P., Glisky, E. L., & Schacter, D. L. (1987). When priming persists: Long-lasting implicit memory for a single episode in amnesic patients. *Neuropsychologia, 25*(3), 497–506.

McCarthy, R., & Warrington, E. K. (1986). Visual associative agnosia: A clinico-anatomical study of a single case. *Journal of Neurology, Neurosurgery, and Psychiatry, 49*, 1233–1240.

McClelland, J. L., & Rumelhart, D. E. (1981). An interactive activation model of context effects in letter perception: Part 1. An account of the basic findings. *Psychological Review, 88*, 375–407.

McClelland, J. L., St. John, M., & Taraban, R. (1989). Sentence comprehension: A parallel distributed processing approach. *Language and Cognitive Processes, 4*, 287–335.

McEwen, B. S. (1998). Stress, adaptation, and disease: Allostasis and allostatic load. *Annals of the New York Academy of Sciences, 840*(1), 33–44.

McEwen, B. S. (2003). Mood disorders and allostatic load. *Biological Psychiatry, 54*(3), 200–207.

McGaugh, J. L., Cahill, L., & Roozendaal, B. (1996). Involvement of the amygdala in memory storage: Interaction with other brain systems. *Proceedings of the National Academy of Sciences, USA, 93*, 13508–13514.

McGaugh, J. L., Introini-Collision, I. B., Cahill, L., Munsoo, K., & Liang, K. C. (1992). Involvement of the amygdala in neuromodulatory influences on memory storage. In J. P. Aggleton (Ed.), *The amygdala: Neurobiological aspects of emotion, memory, and mental dysfunction* (pp. 431–451). New York: Wiley-Liss.

McGeoch, P. D., Brang, D., Song, T., Lee, R. R., Huang, M., & Ramachandran, V. S. (2011). Xenomelia: A new right parietal lobe syndrome. *Journal of Neurology, Neurosurgery, and Psychiatry, 82*(12), 1314–1319.

McHenry, L. C., Jr. (1969). *Garrison's history of neurology*. Springfield, IL: Thomas.

McIntosh, D. N., Reichmann-Decker, A., Winkielman, P., & Wilbarger, J. (2006). When the social mirror breaks: Deficits in automatic, but not voluntary, mimicry of emotional facial expressions in autism. *Developmental Science, 9*(3), 295–302.

McManus, C. (1999). Handedness, cerebral lateralization, and the evolution of handedness. In M. C. Corballis & S. E. G. Lea (Eds.), *The descent of mind* (pp. 194–217). Oxford: Oxford University Press.

Meadows, J. C. (1974). Disturbed perception of colours associated with localized cerebral lesions. *Brain, 97*, 615–632.

Meguerditchian, A., Molesti, S., & Vauclair, J. (2011). Right-handedness predominance in 162 baboons for gestural communication: Consistency across time and groups. *Behavioral Neuroscience, 125*(4), 653–660.

Meguerditchian, A., & Vauclair, J. (2006). Baboons communicate with their right hand. *Behavioural Brain Research, 171*, 170–174.

Meguerditchian, A., Vauclair, J., & Hopkins, W. D. (2010). Captive chimpanzees use their right hand to communicate with each other: Implications for the origin of the cerebral substrate for language. *Cortex, 46*(1), 40–48.

Meintzschel, F., & Ziemann, U. (2005). Modification of practice-dependent plasticity in human motor cortex by neuromodulators. *Cerebral Cortex, 16*(8), 1106–1115.

Meltzoff, A. N. (2002). Imitation as a mechanism of social cognition: Origins of empathy, theory of mind, and the representation of action. In U. Goswami (Ed.), *Blackwell handbook of childhood cognitive development* (pp. 6–25). Malden, MA: Blackwell.

Meltzoff, A. N., & Moore, M. K. (1983). Newborn infants imitate adult facial gestures. *Child Development, 54*, 702–709.

Meng, J., Zhang, S., Bekyo, A., Olsoe, J., Baxter, B., & He, B. (2016). Noninvasive electroencephalogram based control of a robotic arm for reach and grasp tasks. *Scientific Reports, 6*, 38565.

Merabet, L. B., Hamilton, R., Schlaug, G., Swisher, J. D., Kiriakopoulos, E. T., Pitskel, N. B., et al. (2008). Rapid and reversible recruitment of early visual cortex for touch. *PLoS One, 3*(8), e3046.

Merker, B. (2007). Consciousness without a cerebral cortex. *Behavioural and Brain Sciences, 30*(1), 63–134.

Merzenich, M. M., & Jenkins, W. M. (1995). Cortical plasticity, learning and learning dysfunction. In B. Julesz & I. Kovacs (Eds.), *Maturational windows and adult cortical plasticity* (pp. 1–24). Reading, MA: Addison-Wesley.

Merzenich, M. M., Kaas, J. H., Sur, M., & Lin, C. S. (1978). Double representation of the body surface within cytoarchitectonic areas 3b and 1 in "SI" in the owl monkey (*Aotus trivirgatus*). *Journal of Comparative Neurology, 181*, 41–73.

Merzenich, M. M., Recanzone, G., Jenkins, W. M., Allard, T. T., & Nudo, R. J. (1988). Cortical representational plasticity. In P. Rakic & W. Singer (Eds.), *Neurobiology of neocortex* (pp. 41–67). New York: Wiley.

Mesulam, M.-M. (1981). A cortical network for directed attention and unilateral neglect. *Annals of Neurology, 10*, 309–325.

Mesulam, M.-M. (1998). From sensation to cognition. *Brain, 121*, 1013–1052.

Mesulam, M.-M. (2000). *Principles of behavioral and cognitive neurology*. New York: Oxford University Press.

Metcalfe, J., Funnell, M., & Gazzaniga, M. S. (1995). Right hemisphere superiority: Studies of a split-brain patient. *Psychological Science, 6*, 157–164.

Meunier, D., Lambiotte, R., & Bullmore, E. T. (2010). Modular and hierarchically modular organization of brain networks. *Frontiers in Neuroscience, 4*, 200.

Meyer-Lindenberg, A., Buckholtz, J. W., Kolachana, B. R., Hariri, A., Pezawas, L., Blasi, G., et al. (2006). Neural mechanisms of genetic risk for impulsivity and violence in humans. *Proceedings of the National Academy of Sciences, USA, 103*, 6269–6274.

Michael, J., Sandberg, K., Skewes, J., Wolf, T., Blicher, J., Overgaard, M., et al. (2014). Continuous theta-burst stimulation demonstrates a causal role of premotor homunculus in action understanding. *Psychological Science, 25*(4), 963–972.

Migaud, M., Charlesworth, P., Dempster, M., Webster, L. C., Watabe, A. M., Makhinson, M., et al. (1998). Enhanced long-term potentiation and impaired learning in mice with mutant post-synaptic density-95 protein. *Nature, 396*, 433–439.

Miller, G. (1951). *Language and communication*. New York: McGraw-Hill.

Miller, G. (1956). The magical number seven, plus-or-minus two: Some limits on our capacity for processing information. *Psychological Review, 101*, 343–352.

Miller, G. (1962). *Psychology, the science of mental life*. New York: Harper & Row.

Miller, M. B., & Dobbins, I. G. (2014). Memory as decision making. In M. S. Gazzaniga & G. R. Mangun (Eds.), *The cognitive neurosciences* (5th ed., pp. 577–590). Cambridge, MA: MIT Press.

Miller, M. B., Kingstone, A., & Gazzaniga, M. S. (1997). HERA and the split-brain. *Society of Neuroscience Abstract, 23*, 1579.

Miller, M. B., Sinnott-Armstrong, W., Young, L., King, D., Paggi, A., Fabri, M., et al. (2010). Abnormal moral reasoning in complete and partial callosotomy patients. *Neuropsychologia, 48*(7), 2215–2220.

Miller, M. B., van Horn, J. D., Wolford, G. L., Handy, T. C., Valsangkar-Smyth, M., Inati, S., et al. (2002). Extensive individual differences in brain activations associated with episodic retrieval are reliable over time. *Journal of Cognitive Neuroscience, 14*(8), 1200–1214.

Milner, B., Corkin, S., & Teuber, H. (1968). Further analysis of the hippocampal amnesic syndrome: 14-year follow-up study of HM. *Neuropsychologia, 6*, 215–234.

Milner, B., Corsi, P., & Leonard, G. (1991). Frontal-lobe contributions to recency judgements. *Neuropsychologia, 29*, 601–618.

Mineka, S., Rafaeli, E., & Yovel, I. (2003). Cognitive biases in emotional disorders: Information processing and social-cognitive perspectives. In R. J. Davidson, K. R. Scherer, & H. H. Goldsmith (Eds.), *Handbook of affective science* (pp. 976–1009). Oxford: Oxford University Press.

Mishkin, M. (1978). Memory in monkeys severely impaired by combined but not by separate removal of amygdala and hippocampus. *Nature, 273*, 297–298.

Mitchell, J. P. (2008). Activity in right temporo-parietal junction is not selective for theory-of-mind. *Cerebral Cortex, 18*, 262–271.

Mitchell, J. P. (2009). Inferences about mental states. *Philosophical Transactions of the Royal Society of London. Series B, Biological Sciences, 364*(1521), 1309–1316.

Mitchell, J. P., Banaji, M. R., & Macrae, C. N. (2005). General and specific contributions of the medial prefrontal cortex to knowledge about mental states. *NeuroImage, 28*, 757–762.

Mitchell, J. P., Macrae, C. N., & Banaji, M.R. (2004). Encoding-specific effects of social cognition on the neural correlates of subsequent memory. *Journal of Neuroscience, 24*, 4912–4917.

Mitchell, J. P., Macrae, C. N., & Banaji, M. R. (2006). Dissociable medial prefrontal contributions to judgments of similar and dissimilar others. *Neuron, 50*, 655–663.

Mitchell, J. P., Schirmer, J., Ames, D. L., & Gilbert, D. T. (2011). Medial prefrontal cortex predicts intertemporal choice. *Journal of Cognitive Neuroscience, 23*(4), 1–10.

Mitchell, R. W. (1994). Multiplicities of self. In S. T. Parker, R. W. Mitchell, & M. L. Boccia (Eds.), *Self-awareness in animals and humans*. Cambridge: Cambridge University Press.

Mitchell, R. W. (1997). Kinesthetic-visual matching and the self-concept as explanations of mirror-self-recognition. *Journal for the Theory of Social Behavior, 27*, 101–123.

Moeller, S., Crapse, T., Chang, L., & Tsao, D. Y. (2017). The effect of face patch microstimulation on perception of faces and objects. *Nature Neuroscience, 20*(5), 743.

Moerel, M., De Martino, F., Santoro, R., Ugurbil, K., Goebel, R., Yacoub, E., et al. (2013). Processing of natural sounds: Characterization of multipeak spectral tuning in human auditory cortex. *Journal of Neuroscience, 33*(29), 11888–11898.

Moisala, M., Salmela, V., Hietajärvi, L., Salo, E., Carlson, S., Salonen, O., et al. (2016). Media multitasking is associated with distractibility and increased prefrontal activity in adolescents and young adults. *NeuroImage, 134*, 113–121.

Molenberghs, P., Cunnington, R., & Mattingley, J. B. (2012). Brain regions with mirror properties: A meta-analysis of 125 human fMRI studies. *Neuroscience and Biobehavioral Reviews, 36*(1), 341–349.

Moll, H., & Tomasello, M. (2007). Cooperation and human cognition: The Vygotskian intelligence hypothesis. *Philosophical Transactions of the Royal Society of London. Series B, Biological Sciences, 362*(1480), 639–648.

Molnar, Z. (2004). Thomas Willis (1621–1645), the founder of clinical neuroscience. *Nature Reviews Neuroscience, 5*, 329–335.

Moncada, D., & Viola, H. (2007). Induction of long-term memory by exposure to novelty requires protein synthesis: Evidence for a behavioral tagging. *Journal of Neuroscience, 27*(28), 7476–7481.

Monchi, O., Petrides, M., Petre, V., Worsley, K., & Dagher, A. (2001). Wisconsin card sorting revisited: Distinct neural circuits participating in different stages of the task identified by event-related functional magnetic resonance imaging. *Journal of Neuroscience, 21*, 7733–7741.

Montaldi, D., Spencer, T. J., Roberts, N., & Mayes, A. R. (2006). The neural system that mediates familiarity memory. *Hippocampus, 16*, 504–520.

Monti, M. M., Vanhaudenhuyse, A., Coleman, M. R., Boly, M., Pickard, J. D., Tshibanda, L., et al. (2010). Willful modulation of brain activity in disorders of consciousness. *New England Journal of Medicine, 362*, 579–589.

Moore, T., & Armstrong, K. M. (2003). Selective gating of visual signals by microstimulation of frontal cortex. *Nature, 421*, 370–373.

Moore, T., & Fallah, M. (2001). Control of eye movements and spatial attention. *Proceedings of the National Academy of Sciences, USA, 98*, 1273–1276.

Moran, J., & Desimone, R. (1985). Selective attention gates visual processing in extrastriate cortex. *Science, 229*, 782–784.

Moran, J. M., Macrae, C. N., Heatherton, T. F., Wyland, C. L., & Kelley, W. M. (2006). Neuroanatomical evidence for distinct cognitive and affective components of self. *Journal of Cognitive Neuroscience, 18*, 1586–1594.

Moray, N. (1959). Attention in dichotic listening: Effective cues and the influence of instructions. *Quarterly Journal of Experimental Psychology, 9*, 56–60.

Morgan, M. A., & LeDoux, J. E. (1999). Contribution of ventrolateral prefrontal cortex to the acquisition and extinction of conditioned fear in rats. *Neurobiology of Learning and Memory, 72*, 244–251.

Morishima, Y., Akaishi, R., Yamada, Y., Okuda, J., Toma, K., & Sakai, K. (2009). Task-specific signal transmission from prefrontal cortex in visual selective attention. *Nature Neuroscience, 12*, 85–91.

Mormann, F., Dubois, J., Kornblith, S., Milosavljevic, M., Cerf, M., Ison, M., et al. (2011). A category-specific response to animals in the right human amygdala. *Nature Neuroscience, 14*, 1247–1249. Retrieved from http://www.nature.com.proxy.library.ucsb.edu:2048/neuro/journal/vaop/ncurrent/full/nn.2899.html

Morris, J. S., Buchel, C., & Dolan, R. J. (2001). Parallel neural responses in amygdala subregions and sensory cortex during implicit fear conditioning. *NeuroImage, 13*, 1044–1052.

Morris, J. S., Friston, K. J., Büchel, C., Frith, C. D., Young, A. W., Calder, A. J., et al. (1998). A neuromodulatory role for the human amygdala in processing emotional facial expressions. *Brain, 121*, 47–57.

Morris, R. G. (1981). Spatial localization does not require the presence of local cues. *Learning and Motivation, 12*, 239–260.

Moruzzi, G., & Magoun, H. W. (1949). Brainstem reticular formation and activation of the EEG. *Electroencephalography and Clinical Neurophysiology, 1*, 455–473.

Moscovitch, M., Winocur, G., & Behrmann, M. (1997). What is special about face recognition? Nineteen experiments on a person with visual object agnosia and dyslexia but normal face recognition. *Journal of Cognitive Neuroscience, 9*, 555–604.

Mottron, L., & Bellevile, S. (1993). A study of perceptual analysis in a high-level autistic subject with exceptional graphic abilities. *Brain and Cognition, 23*(2), 279–309.

Mountcastle, V. B. (1976). The world around us: Neural command functions for selective attention. *Neurosciences Research Program Bulletin, 14*(Suppl.), 1–47.

Mueller, C. M., & Dweek, C. S. (1998). Intelligence praise can undermine motivation and performance. *Journal of Personality and Social Psychology, 75*, 33–52.

Mueller, N. G., & Kleinschmidt, A. (2003). Dynamic interaction of object- and space-based attention in retinotopic visual areas. *Journal of Neuroscience, 23*, 9812–9816.

Müller, J. R., Philiastides, M. G., & Newsome, W. T. (2005). Microstimulation of the superior colliculus focuses attention without moving the eyes. *Proceedings of the National Academy of Sciences, USA, 102*(3), 524–529.

Münte, T. F., Heinze, H.-J., & Mangun, G. R. (1993). Dissociation of brain activity related to semantic and syntactic aspects of language. *Journal of Cognitive Neuroscience, 5*, 335–344.

Münte, T. F., Schilz, K., & Kutas, M. (1998). When temporal terms belie conceptual order. *Nature, 395*, 71–73.

Murphey, D. K., Yoshor, D., & Beauchamp, M. S. (2008). Perception matches selectivity in the human anterior color center. *Current Biology, 18*, 216–220.

Murray, R. J., Schaer, M., & Debbane, M. (2012). Degrees of separation: A quantitative neuroimaging meta-analysis investigating self-specificity and shared neural activation between self- and other-reflection. *Neuroscience and Biobehavioral Reviews, 36*, 1043–1059.

Nadel, L., & Hardt, O. (2011). Update on memory systems and processes. *Neuropsychopharmacology, 36*, 251–273.

Nadel, L., & Moscovitch, M. (1997). Memory consolidation, retrograde amnesia and the hippocampal complex. *Current Opinion in Neurobiology, 7*(2), 217–227.

Naeser, M. A., Palumbo, C. L., Helm-Estabrooks, N., Stiassny-Eder, D., & Albert, M. L. (1989). Severe non-fluency in aphasia: Role of the medial subcallosal fasciculus plus other white matter pathways in recovery of spontaneous speech. *Brain, 112*, 1–38.

Nagel, G., Ollig, D., Fuhrmann, M., Kateriya, S., Musti, A. M., Bambaer, E., et al. (2002). Channelrhodopsin-1: A light-gated proton channel in green algae. *Science, 296*(5577), 2395–2398.

Nagel, T. (1974). What is it like to be a bat? *Philosophical Review, 83*(4), 435–450.

Narain, C., Scott, S. K., Wise, R. J., Rosen, S., Leff, A., Iversen, S. D., et al. (2003). Defining a left-lateralized response specific to intelligible speech using fMRI. *Cerebral Cortex, 13*, 1362–1368.

Naselaris, T., Olman, C. A., Stansbury, D. E., Ugurbil, K., & Gallant, J. L. (2015). A voxel-wise encoding model for early visual areas decodes mental images of remembered scenes. *NeuroImage, 105*, 215–228.

Navon, D. (1977). Forest before trees: The precedence of global features in visual perception. *Cognitive Psychology, 9*, 353–383.

Netter, F. H. (1983). *The CIBA collection of medical illustrations: Vol. 1. Nervous system, Part 1: Anatomy and physiology.* Summit, NJ: CIBA Pharmaceutical.

Newsome, W. T., Britten, K. H., & Movshon, J. A. (1989). Neuronal correlates of a perceptual decision. *Nature, 341*, 52–54.

Newsome, W. T., & Pare, E. B. (1988). A selective impairment of motion perception following lesions of the middle temporal visual area (MT). *Journal of Neuroscience, 8*, 2201–2211.

Nieuwland, M., & Van Berkum, J. (2005). Testing the limits of the semantic illusion phenomenon: ERPs reveal temporary semantic change deafness in discourse comprehension. *Cognitive Brain Research, 24*, 691–701.

Nisbett, R., & Ross, L. L. (1980). *Human inference: Strategies and shortcomings of social judgment.* Englewood Cliffs, NJ: Prentice-Hall.

Nishimoto, S., Vu, A. T., Naselaris, T., Benjamini, Y., Yu, B., & Gallant, J. L. (2011). Reconstructing visual experiences from brain activity evoked by natural movies. *Current Biology, 21*, 1–6.

Nissen, M. J., Knopman, D. S., & Schacter, D. L. (1987). Neurochemical dissociation of memory systems. *Neurology, 37*, 789–794.

Niv, Y. (2007). Cost, benefit, tonic, phasic: What do response rates tell us about dopamine and motivation? *Annals of the New York Academy of Sciences, 1104*, 357–376.

Nobre, A. C. (2001). The attentive homunculus: Now you see it, now you don't. *Neuroscience and Biobehavioral Reviews, 25*, 477–496.

Nobre, A. C., Allison, T., & McCarthy, G. (1994). Word recognition in the human inferior temporal lobe. *Nature, 372*, 260–263.

Norman, K. A., & Schacter, D. L. (1997). False recognition in younger and older adults: Exploring the characteristics of illusory memories. *Memory and Cognition, 25*, 838–848.

Nottebohm, F. (1980). Brain pathways for vocal learning in birds: A review of the first 10 years. *Progress in Psychobiology and Physiological Psychology, 9*, 85–124.

Nunn, J. A., Gregory, L. J., Brammer, M., Williams, S. C., Parslow, D. M., Morgan, M. J., et al. (2002). Functional magnetic resonance imaging of synesthesia: Activation of V4/V8 by spoken words. *Nature Neuroscience, 5*, 371–375.

Nyberg, L., Cabeza, R., & Tulving, E. (1996). PET studies of encoding and retrieval: The HERA model. *Psychonomic Bulletin & Review, 3*, 134–147.

Oberauer, K. (2002). Access to information in working memory: Exploring the focus of attention. *Journal of Experimental Psychology. Learning, Memory, and Cognition, 28*, 411–421.

Oberman, L. M., Ramachandran, V. S., & Pineda, J. A. (2008). Modulation of mu suppression in children with autism spectrum disorders in response to familiar or unfamiliar stimuli: The mirror neuron hypothesis. *Neuropsychologia, 46*(5), 1558–1565.

O'Brien, J. T., & Thomas, A. (2015). Vascular dementia. *Lancet, 386*(10004), 1698–1706.

Ochsner, K. N. (2007a). How thinking controls feeling: A social cognitive neuroscience approach. In E. Harmon-Jones & P. Winkielman (Eds.), *Social neuroscience: Integrating biological and psychological explanations of social behavior* (pp. 106–133). New York: Guilford.

Ochsner, K. N. (2007b). Social cognitive neuroscience: Historical development, core principles, and future promise. In A. Kruglanski & E. Higgins (Eds.), *Social psychology: A handbook of basic principles.* New York: Guilford.

Ochsner, K. N., Beer, J. S., Robertson, E. A., Cooper, J., Gabrieli, J. D. E., Kihlstrom, J. F., et al. (2005). The neural correlates of direct and reflected self-knowledge. *NeuroImage, 28*, 797–814.

Ochsner, K. N., Bunge, S. A., Gross, J. J., & Gabrieli, J. D. (2002). Rethinking feelings: An FMRI study of the cognitive regulation of emotion. *Journal of Cognitive Neuroscience, 14*(8), 1215–1229.

Ochsner, K., & Gross, J. (2005). The cognitive control of emotion. *Trends in Cognitive Sciences, 9*(5), 242–249.

Ochsner, K. N., Ray, R. D., Cooper, J. C., Robertson, E. R., Chopra, S., Gabrieli, J. D. E., et al. (2004). For better or for worse: Neural systems supporting the cognitive down- and up-regulation of negative emotion. *NeuroImage, 23*, 483–499.

Ochsner, K. N., Silvers, J. A., & Buhle, J. T. (2012). Functional imaging studies of emotion regulation: A synthetic review and evolving model of the cognitive control of emotion. *Annals of the New York Academy of Sciences, 1251*, E1–E24.

O'Connor, A. R., Han, S., & Dobbins, I. G. (2010). The inferior parietal lobule and recognition memory: Expectancy violation or successful retrieval? *Journal of Neuroscience, 30*(8), 2924–2934.

O'Connor, D. H., Fukui, M. M., Pinsk, M. A., & Kastner, S. (2002). Attention modulates responses in the human lateral geniculate nucleus. *Nature Neuroscience, 5*, 1203–1209.

O'Craven, K. M., Downing, P. E., & Kanwisher, N. (1999). fMRI evidence for objects as the units of attentional selection. *Nature, 401*, 584–587.

O'Doherty, J., Dayan, P., Schultz, J., Deichmann, R., Friston, K., & Dolan, R. J. (2004). Dissociable roles of ventral and dorsal striatum in instrumental conditioning. *Science, 304*, 452–454.

Oertel-Knöchel, V., & Linden, D. E. J. (2011). Cerebral asymmetry in schizophrenia. *Neuroscientist, 17*(5), 456–467.

Oesterhelt, D., & Stoeckenius, W. (1971). Rhodopsin-like protein from the purple membrane of *Halobacterium halobium. Nature New Biology, 233*, 149–152.

Ogawa, S., Lee, T. M., Kay, A. R., & Tank, D. W. (1990). Brain magnetic resonance imaging with contrast dependent on blood oxygenation. *Proceedings of the National Academy of Sciences, USA, 87*, 9868–9872.

Ojemann, G., Ojemann, J., Lettich, E., & Berger, M. (1989). Cortical language localization in left, dominant hemisphere. *Journal of Neurosurgery, 71*, 316–326.

O'Keefe, J., & Dostrovsky, J. (1971). The hippocampus as a spatial map. Preliminary evidence from unit activity in the freely-moving rat. *Brain Research, 1*, 171–175.

O'Keefe, J., & Nadel, L. (1978). *The hippocampus as a cognitive map.* Oxford: Oxford University Press.

Oldendorf, W. H. (1961). Isolated flying spot detection of radio-density discontinuities—displaying the internal structural pattern of a complex object. *IRE Transactions on Bio-medical Electronics, 8*, 68–72.

Olds, J. (1958). Self-stimulation of the brain: Its use to study local effects of hunger, sex, and drugs. *Science, 127*(3294), 315–324.

Olds, J., & Milner, P. M. (1954). Positive reinforcement produced by electrical stimulation of septal area and other regions of rat brain. *Journal of Comparative Physiology and Psychology, 47*, 419–427.

Oliveira, F. T., Diedrichsen, J., Verstynen, T., Duque, J., & Ivry, R. B. (2010). Transcranial magnetic stimulation of posterior parietal cortex affects decisions of hand choice. *Proceedings of the National Academy of Sciences, USA, 107*, 17751–17756.

Onishi, K. H., & Baillargeon, R. (2005). Do 15-month-old infants understand false beliefs? *Science, 308*(5719), 255–258.

Ophir, E., Nass, C., & Wagner, A. D. (2009). Cognitive control in media multitaskers. *Proceedings of the National Academy of Sciences, USA, 106*(37), 15583–15587.

O'Reilly, R. (2010). The what and how of prefrontal cortical organization. *Trends in Neurosciences, 33*, 355–361.

Ortigue, S., & Bianchi-Demicheli, F. (2008). The chrono-architecture of human sexual desire: A high-density electrical mapping study. *NeuroImage, 43*(2), 337–345.

Ortigue, S., & Bianchi-Demicheli, F. (2011). Intention, false beliefs, and delusional jealousy: Insights into the right hemisphere from neurological patients and neuroimaging studies. *Medical Science Monitor, 17*, RA1–RA11.

Ortigue, S., Bianchi-Demicheli, F., Patel, N., Frum, C., & Lewis, J. (2010). Neuroimaging of love: fMRI meta-analysis evidence toward new perspectives in sexual medicine. *Journal of Sexual Medicine, 7*(11), 3541–3552.

Ortigue, S., Patel, N., Bianchi-Demicheli, F., & Grafton, S.T. (2010). Implicit priming of embodied cognition on human motor intention understanding in dyads in love. *Journal of Social and Personal Relationships, 27*(7), 1001–1015.

Osborn, A. G., Blaser, S., & Salzman, K. L. (2004). *Diagnostic imaging. Brain.* Salt Lake City, UT: Amirsys.

Osgood, C. E., Suci, G. J., & Tannengaum, P. H. (1957). *The measurement of meaning.* Urbana: University of Illinois Press.

Osterhout, L., & Holcomb, P. J. (1992). Event-related brain potentials elicited by syntactic anomaly. *Journal of Memory and Language, 31*, 785–806.

Ouattara, K., Lemasson, A., & Zuberbühler, K. (2009). Campbell's monkeys concatenate vocalizations into context-specific call sequences. *Proceedings of the National Academy of Sciences, USA, 106*(51), 22026–22031.

Oudiette, D., Dealberto, M. J., Uguccioni, G., Golmard, J. L., Merino-Andreu, M., Tafti, M., et al. (2012). Dreaming without REM sleep. *Consciousness and Cognition, 21*(3), 1129–1140.

Owen, A. M., Coleman, M. R., Boly, M., Davis, M. H., Laureys, S., & Pickard, J. (2006). Detecting awareness in the vegetative state. *Science, 313*, 1402.

Packard, M. G., & Goodman, J. (2012). Emotional arousal and multiple memory systems in the mammalian brain. *Frontiers in Behavioral Neuroscience, 6*, 14.

Packard, M. G., & Knowlton, B. J. (2002). Learning and memory functions of the basal ganglia. *Annual Review of Neuroscience, 25*(1), 563–593.

PACKER, A. (2016). Neocortical neurogenesis and the etiology of autism spectrum disorder. *Neuroscience and Biobehavioral Reviews, 64*, 185–195.

PADOA-SCHIOPPA, C. (2011). Neurobiology of economic choice: A good-based model. *Annual Review of Neuroscience, 34*, 333–359.

PALLIS, C. A. (1955). Impaired identification of faces and places with agnosia for colors. *Journal of Neurology, Neurosurgery, and Psychiatry, 18*, 218–224.

PANKSEPP, J. (1998). *Affective neuroscience: The foundations of human and animal emotions.* New York: Oxford University Press.

PANKSEPP, J. (2002). Foreword: The MacLean legacy and some modern trends in emotion research. In G. Cory & R. Gardner (Eds.), *The evolutionary neuroethology of Paul MacLean: Convergences and frontiers* (pp. ix–xxvii). Westport, CT: Greenwood/Praeger.

PANKSEPP, J. (2005). Affective consciousness: Core emotional feelings in animals and humans. *Consciousness and Cognition, 14*, 30–80.

PANKSEPP, J., & BIVEN, L. (2012). *The archaeology of mind: Neuroevolutionary origins of human emotions.* New York: Norton.

PANKSEPP, J., NORMANSELL, L., COX, J. F., & SIVIY, S. M. (1994). Effects of neonatal decortication on the social play of juvenile rats. *Physiology & Behavior, 56*(3), 429–443.

PANKSEPP, J., & WATT, D. (2011). What is basic about basic emotions? Lasting lessons from affective neuroscience. *Emotion Review, 3*(4), 387–396.

PAPADOURAKIS, V., & RAOS, V. (2013). Cue-dependent action-observation elicited responses in the ventral premotor cortex (area F5) of the macaque monkey. *Society for Neuroscience Abstracts*, program no. 263.08, p. 2.

PAPEZ, J. W. (1937). A proposed mechanism of emotion. *Archives of Neurology and Psychiatry, 79*, 217–224.

PARVIZI, J., JACQUES, C., FOSTER, B. L., WITHOFT, N., RANGARAJAN, V., WEINER, K. S., ET AL. (2012). Electrical stimulation of human fusiform face-selective regions distorts face perception. *Journal of Neuroscience, 32*(43), 14915–14920.

PASCUAL-LEONE, A., BARTRES-FAZ, D., & KEENAN, J. P. (1999). Transcranial magnetic stimulation: Studying the brain-behaviour relationship by induction of "virtual lesions." *Philosophical Transactions of the Royal Society of London. Series B, Biological Sciences, 354*, 1229–1238.

PASSINGHAM, R. E. (1993). *The frontal lobes and voluntary action.* New York: Oxford University Press.

PATIL, A., MURTY, V. P., DUNSMOOR, J. E., PHELPS, E. A., & DAVACHI, L. (2017). Reward retroactively enhances memory consolidation for related items. *Learning & Memory, 24*(1), 65–69.

PATTEE, H. H. (1972). Physical problems of decision-making constraints. *International Journal of Neuroscience, 3*(3), 99–105.

PATTEE, H. H. (2001). Causation, control, and the evolution of complexity. In P. B. Andersen, P. V. Christiansen, C. Emmeche, & M. O. Finnermann (Eds.), *Downward causation: Minds, bodies and matter* (pp. 63–77). Copenhagen: Aarhus University Press.

PATTEE, H. H., & RĄCZASZEK-LEONARDI, J. (2012). *Laws, language and life.* Dordrecht, Netherlands: Springer.

PAUL, L. K., CORSELLO, C., KENNEDY, D. P., & ADOLPHS, R. (2014). Agenesis of the corpus callosum and autism: A comprehensive comparison. *Brain, 137*, 1813–1829.

PAULING, L., & CORYELL, C. D. (1936). The magnetic properties and structure of hemoglobin, oxyhemoglobin and carbonmonoxyhemoglobin. *Proceedings of the National Academy of Sciences, USA, 22*, 210–216.

PAULSEN, J. S., BUTTERS, N., SALMON, D. P., HEINDEL, W. C., & SWENSON, M. R. (1993). Prism adaptation in Alzheimer's and Huntington's disease. *Neuropsychology, 7*(1), 73–81.

PAYNE, J., & NADEL, L. (2004). Sleep, dreams, and memory consolidation: The role of the stress hormone cortisol. *Learning and Memory, 11*, 671–678.

PEELLE, J. E., JOHNSRUDE, I., & DAVIS, M. H. (2010). Hierarchical processing for speech in human auditory cortex and beyond. *Frontiers in Human Neuroscience, 4*, 51.

PELLEGRINO, G. D., FADIGA, L., FOGASSI, L., GALLESE, V., & RIZZOLATTI, G. (1992). Understanding motor events: A neurophysiological study. *Experimental Brain Research, 91*(1), 176–180.

PELPHREY, K. A., SINGERMAN, J. D., ALLISON, T., & MCCARTHY, G. (2003). Brain activation evoked by perception of gaze shifts: The influence of context. *Neuropsychologia, 41*, 156–170.

PELPHREY, K. A., VIOLA, R. J., & MCCARTHY, G. (2004). When strangers pass: Processing of mutual and averted social gaze in the superior temporal sulcus. *Psychological Science, 15*, 598–603.

PENFIELD, W., & FAULK, M. E., JR. (1955). The insula; further observations on its function. *Brain, 78*, 445–470.

PENFIELD, W., & JASPER, H. (1954). *Epilepsy and the functional anatomy of the human brain.* Boston: Little, Brown.

PENG, Y., GILLIS-SMITH, S., JIN, H., TRÄNKNER, D., RYBA, N. J., & ZUKER, C. S. (2015). Sweet and bitter taste in the brain of awake behaving animals. *Nature, 527*(7579), 512–515.

PENGAS, G., HODGES, J. R., WATSON, P., & NESTOR, P. J. (2010). Focal posterior cingulate atrophy in incipient Alzheimer's disease. *Neurobiology of Aging, 31*(1), 25–33.

PENNARTZ, C. M. A., LEE, E., VERHEUL, J., LIPA, P., BARNES, C. A., & MCNAUGHTON, B. L. (2004). The ventral striatum in off-line processing: Ensemble reactivation during sleep and modulation by hippocampal ripples. *Journal of Neuroscience, 24*(29), 6446–6456.

PERAMUNAGE, D., BLUMSTEIN, S. E., MYERS, E. B., GOLDRICK, M., & BAESE-BERK, M. (2011). Phonological neighborhood effects in spoken word production: An fMRI study. *Journal of Cognitive Neuroscience, 23*(3), 593–603.

PERANI, D., DEHAENE, S., GRASS, F., COHEN, L., CAPP, S. F., DUPOUX, E., ET AL. (1996). Brain processes of native and foreign languages. *Neuroreport, 7*, 2439–2444.

PERETZ, I., KOLINSKY, R., TRAMO, M., LABRECQUE, R., HUBLET, C., DEMEURISSE, G., ET AL. (1994). Functional dissociations following bilateral lesions of auditory cortex. *Brain, 117*, 1283–1301.

PERLMUTTER, J. S., & MINK, J. W. (2006). Deep brain stimulation. *Annual Review of Neuroscience, 29*, 229–257.

PERNER, J., & RUFFMAN, T. (1995). Episodic memory and autonoetic consciousness: Developmental evidence and a theory of childhood amnesia. *Journal of Experimental Child Psychology, 59*, 516–548.

PERRETT, D. I., SMITH, P. A. J., POTTER, D. D., MISTLIN, A. J., HEAD, A. S., MILNER, A. D., ET AL. (1985). Visual cells in the temporal cortex sensitive to face view and gaze direction. *Proceedings of the Royal Society of London, Series B, 223*(1232), 293–317.

PESSIGLIONE, M., SEYMOUR, B., FLANDIN, G., DOLAN, R. J., & FRITH, C. D. (2006). Dopamine-dependent prediction errors underpin reward-seeking behaviour in humans. *Nature, 442*(31), 1042–1045.

PESSOA, L. (2011). Emotion and cognition and the amygdala: From "What is it?" to "What's to be done?" *Neuropsychologia, 49*(4), 3416–3429.

PETERS, B. L., & STRINGHAM, E. (2006). No booze? You may lose: Why drinkers earn more money than nondrinkers. *Journal of Labor Research, 27*, 411–422.

PETERS, E., VÄSTFJÄLL, D., GÄRLING, T., & SLOVIC, P. (2006). Affect and decision making: A "hot" topic. *Journal of Behavioral and Decision Making, 19*, 79–85.

PETERS, J., & BUCHEL, C. (2009). Overlapping and distinct neural systems code for subjective value during intertemporal and risky decision making. *Journal of Neuroscience, 29*, 15727–15734.

PETERSEN, S. E., FIEZ, J. A., & CORBETTA, M. (1992). Neuroimaging. *Current Opinion in Neurobiology, 2*, 217–222.

PETERSEN, S. E., FOX, P. T., SNYDER, A. Z., & RAICHLE, M. E. (1990). Activation of extrastriate and frontal cortical areas by visual words and word-like stimuli. *Science, 249*(4972), 1041–1044.

PETERSEN, S. E., ROBINSON, D. L., & KEYS, W. (1985). Pulvinar nuclei of the behaving rhesus monkey: Visual responses and their modulation. *Journal of Neurophysiology, 54*(4), 867–886.

PETERSEN, S. E., ROBINSON, D. L., & MORRIS, J. D. (1987). Contributions of the pulvinar to visual spatial attention. *Neuropsychologia, 25*, 97–105.

PETERSEN, S. E., VAN MIER, H., FIEZ, J. A., & RAICHLE, M. E. (1998). The effects of practice on the functional anatomy of task performance. *Proceedings of the National Academy of Sciences USA, 95*, 853–860.

PETRIDES, M., CADORET, G., & MACKEY, S. (2005). Orofacial somatomotor responses in the macaque monkey homologue of Broca's area. *Nature, 435*(7046): 1235–1238.

PEYRACHE, A., KHAMASSI, M., BENCHENANE, K., WIENER, S. I., & BATTAGLIA, F. P. (2009). Replay of rule-learning related neural patterns in the prefrontal cortex during sleep. *Nature Neuroscience, 12*(7), 919–926.

PHELPS, E. A. (2006). Emotion and cognition: Insights from studies of the human amygdala. *Annual Review of Psychology, 57*, 27–53.

PHELPS, E. A., CANNISTRACI, C. J., & CUNNINGHAM, W. A. (2003). Intact performance on an indirect measure of race bias following amygdala damage. *Neuropsychologia, 41*, 203–208.

PHELPS, E. A., & GAZZANIGA, M. S. (1992). Hemispheric differences in mnemonic processing: The effects of left hemisphere interpretation. *Neuropsychologia, 30*, 293–297.

PHELPS, E. A., LABAR, D. S., ANDERSON, A. K., O'CONNOR, K. J., FULBRIGHT, R. K., & SPENCER, D. S. (1998). Specifying the contributions of the human amygdala to emotional memory: A case study. *Neurocase, 4*, 527–540.

PHELPS, E. A., LEMPERT, K. M., & SOKOL-HESSNER, P. (2014). Emotion and decision making: Multiple modulatory neural circuits. *Annual Review of Neuroscience, 37*, 263–287.

PHELPS, E. A., LING, S., & CARRASCO, M. (2006). Emotion facilitates perception and potentiates the perceptual benefit of attention. *Psychological Science, 17*, 292–299.

PHELPS, E. A., O'CONNOR, K. J., CUNNINGHAM, W. A., FUNAYMA, E. S., GATENBY, J. C., GORE, J. C., ET AL. (2000). Performance on indirect measures of race evaluation predicts amygdala activity. *Journal of Cognitive Neuroscience, 12*, 729–738.

PHELPS, E. A., O'CONNOR, K. J., GATENBY, J. C., GRILLON, C., GORE, J. C., & DAVIS, M. (2001). Activation of the human amygdala to a cognitive representation of fear. *Nature Neuroscience, 4*, 437–441.

PHILLIPS, M. L., YOUNG, A. W., SCOTT, S. K., CALDER, A. J., ANDREW, C., GIAMPIETRO, V., ET AL. (1998). Neural responses to facial and vocal expressions of fear and disgust. *Proceedings of the Royal Society of London, Series B, 265*, 1809–1817.

PHILLIPS, M. L., YOUNG, A. W., SENIOR, C., BRAMMER, M., ANDREW, C., CALDER, A. J., ET AL. (1997). A specific neural substrate for perceiving facial expressions of disgust. *Nature, 389*, 495–498.

PIKA, S., LIEBAL, K., & TOMASELLO, M. (2003). Gestural communication in young gorillas (*Gorilla gorilla*): Gestural repertoire, and use. *American Journal of Primatology, 60*, 95–111.

PIKA, S., LIEBAL, K., & TOMASELLO, M. (2005). Gestural communication in subadult bonobos (*Pan paniscus*): Repertoire and use. *American Journal of Primatology, 65*, 39–61.

PINKER, S. (1997). *How the mind works.* New York: Norton.

PINKER, S., & BLOOM, P. (1990). Natural language and natural selection. *Behavioral and Brain Sciences, 13*, 707–726.

PITCHER, D., CHARLES, L., DEVLIN, J. T., WALSH, V., & DUCHAINE, B. (2009). Triple dissociation of faces, bodies, and objects in extrastriate cortex. *Current Biology, 19*, 1–6.

PITCHER, D., DILKS, D. D., SAXE, R. R., TRIANTAFYLLOU, C., & KANWISHER, N. (2011). Differential selectivity for dynamic versus static information in face-selective cortical regions. *NeuroImage, 56*(4), 2356–2363.

PLANT, G. T., LAXER, K. D., BARBARO, N. M., SCHIFFMAN, J. S., & NAKAYAMA, K. (1993). Impaired visual motion perception in the contralateral hemifield following unilateral posterior cerebral lesions in humans. *Brain, 116*, 1303–1335.

PLOMIN, R., CORLEY, R., DEFRIES, J. C., & FULKER, D. W. (1990). Individual differences in television viewing in early childhood: Nature as well as nurture. *Psychological Science, 1*, 371–377.

PLOOG, D. (2002). Is the neural basis of vocalisation different in nonhuman primates and *Homo sapiens*? In T. J. Crow (Ed.), *The speciation of modern* Homo sapiens (pp. 121–135). Oxford: Oxford University Press.

POEPPEL, D., EMMOREY, K., HICKOK, G., & PYLKKÄNEN, L. (2012). Towards new neurobiology of language. *Journal of Neuroscience, 32*(41), 14125–14131.

POHL, W. (1973). Dissociation of spatial discrimination deficits following frontal and parietal lesions in monkeys. *Journal of Comparative and Physiological Psychology, 82*, 227–239.

POLANÍA, R., NITSCHE, M. A., KORMAN, C., BATSIKADZE, G., & PAULUS, W. (2012). The importance of timing in segregated theta phase-coupling for cognitive performance. *Current Biology, 22*, 1314–1318.

POLLATOS, O., GRAMANN, K., & SCHANDRY, R. (2007). Neural systems connecting interoceptive awareness and feelings. *Human Brain Mapping, 28*, 9–18.

POSNER, M. I. (1986). *Chronometric explorations of mind.* New York: Oxford University Press.

POSNER, M. I., & RAICHLE, M. E. (1994). *Images of mind.* New York: Freeman.

POSNER, M. I., SNYDER, C. R. R., & DAVIDSON, J. (1980). Attention and the detection of signals. *Journal of Experimental Psychology. General, 109*, 160–174.

POSNER, M. I., WALKER, J. A., FRIEDRICH, F. J., & RAFAL, B. D. (1984). Effects of parietal injury on covert orienting of attention. *Journal of Neuroscience, 4*, 1863–1874.

POVINELLI, D. J., RULF, A. R., LANDAU, K., & BIERSCHWALE, D. T. (1993). Self-recognition in chimpanzees (*Pan troglodytes*): Distribution, ontogeny, and patterns of emergence. *Journal of Comparative Psychology, 107*, 347–372.

PRABHAKARAN, V., NARAYANAN, K., ZHAO, Z., & GABRIELI, J. D. (2000). Integration of diverse information in working memory within the frontal lobe. *Nature Neuroscience, 3*, 85–90.

PREMACK, D. (1972). Concordant preferences as a precondition for affective but not for symbolic communication (or how to do experimental anthropology). *Cognition, 1*, 251–264.

PREMACK, D., & WOODRUFF, G. (1978). Does the chimpanzee have a theory of mind? *Behavioral and Brain Sciences, 1*, 515–526.

PREUSS, T. M., & COLEMAN, G. Q. (2002). Human-specific organization of primary visual cortex: Alternating compartments of dense Cat-301 and calbindin immunoreactivity in layer 4A. *Cerebral Cortex, 12*, 671–691.

Price, C. J. (2012). A review and synthesis of the first 20 years of PET and fMRI studies of heard speech, spoken language and reading. *NeuroImage, 62*, 816–847.

Prigge, M. B., Lange, N., Bigler, E. D., Merkley, T. L., Neeley, E. S., Abildskov, T. J., et al. (2013). Corpus callosum area in children and adults with autism. *Research in Autism Spectrum Disorders, 7*(2), 221–234.

Prinz, A. A., Bucher, D., & Marder, E. (2004). Similar network activity from disparate circuit parameters. *Nature Reviews Neuroscience, 7*(12), 1345–1352.

Pruszynski, J. A., Kurtzer, I., Nashed, J. Y., Omrani, M., Brouwer, B., & Scott, S. H. (2011). Primary motor cortex underlies multi-joint integration for fast feedback control. *Nature, 478*, 387–391.

Pruszynski, J. A., Kurtzer, I., & Scott, S. H. (2011). The long-latency reflex is composed of at least two functionally independent processes. *Journal of Neurophysiology, 106*, 449–459.

Puce, A., Allison, T., Asgari, M., Gore, J. C., & McCarthy, G. (1996). Differential sensitivity of human visual cortex to faces, letterstrings, and textures: A functional magnetic resonance imaging study. *Journal of Neuroscience, 16*, 5205–5215.

Purcell, B. A., & Kiani, R. (2016). Neural mechanisms of post-error adjustments of decision policy in parietal cortex. *Neuron, 89*(3), 658–671.

Purves, D., Augustine, G., & Fitzpatrick, D. (2001). *Neuroscience* (2nd ed.). Sunderland, MA: Sinauer.

Putman, M. C., Steven, M. S., Doron, C., Riggall, A. C., & Gazzaniga, M. S. (2010). Cortical projection topography of the human splenium: Hemispheric asymmetry and individual difference. *Journal of Cognitive Neuroscience, 22*(8), 1662–1669.

Quallo, M. M., Kraskov, A., & Lemon, R. N. (2012). The activity of primary motor cortex corticospinal neurons during tool use by macaque monkeys. *Journal of Neuroscience, 32*(48), 17351–17364.

Quaranta, A., Siniscalchi, M., Frate, A., & Vallortigara, G. (2004). Paw preference in dogs: Relations between lateralised behaviour and immunity. *Behavioural Brain Research, 153*(2), 521–525.

Queenan, B. N., Ryan, T. J., Gazzaniga, M. S., & Gallistel, C. R. (2017). On the research of time past: The hunt for the substrate of memory. *Annals of the New York Academy of Sciences, 1396*(1), 108–125.

Quiroga, R. Q., Reddy, L., Keriman, G., Koch, C., & Fried, I. (2005). Invariant visual representation by single neurons in the human brain. *Nature, 435*, 1102–1107.

Rafal, R. D., & Posner, M. I. (1987). Deficits in human visual spatial attention following thalamic lesions. *Proceedings of the National Academy of Sciences, USA, 84*, 7349–7353.

Rafal, R. D., Posner, M. I., Friedman, J. H., Inhoff, A. W., & Bernstein, E. (1988). Orienting of visual attention in progressive supranuclear palsy. *Brain, 111*(Pt. 2), 267–280.

Rahimi, J., & Kovacs, G. G. (2014). Prevalence of mixed pathologies in the aging brain. *Alzheimers Research Therapy, 6*, 82.

Raichle, M. E. (1994). Visualizing the mind. *Scientific American, 270*(4), 58–64.

Raichle, M. E. (2008). A brief history of human brain mapping. *Trends in Neuroscience, 32*, 118–126.

Raichle, M. E., Fiez, J. A., Videen, T. O., MacLeod, A. K., Pardo, J. V., Fox, P. T., et al. (1994). Practice-related changes in human brain functional anatomy during nonmotor learning. *Cerebral Cortex, 4*, 8–26.

Raichle, M. E., MacLeod, A. M., Snyder, A. Z., Powers, W. J., Gusnard, D. A., & Shulman, G. L. (2001). A default mode of brain function. *Proceedings of the National Academy of Sciences, USA, 98*, 676–682.

Ralph, B. C., Thomson, D. R., Cheyne, J. A., & Smilek, D. (2014). Media multitasking and failures of attention in everyday life. *Psychological Research, 78*(5), 661–669.

Ramachandran, V. S., Stewart, M., & Rogers-Ramachandran, D. C. (1992). Perceptual correlates of massive cortical reorganization. *Neuroreport, 3*(7), 583–586.

Ramirez, F., Moscarello, J. M., LeDoux, J. E., & Sears, R. M. (2015). Active avoidance requires a serial basal amygdala to nucleus accumbens shell circuit. *Journal of Neuroscience, 35*(8), 3470–3477.

Ramirez-Amaya, V., Marrone, D. F., Gage, F. H., Worley, P. F., & Barnes, C. A. (2006). Integration of new neurons into functional neural networks. *Journal of Neuroscience, 26*, 12237–12241.

Ramón y Cajal, S. (1909–1911). *Histologie du système nerveaux de l'homme et de vertébrés.* Paris: Maloine.

Rampon, C., Tang, Y. P., Goodhouse, J., Shimizu, E., Kyin, M., & Tsien, J. Z. (2000). Enrichment induces structural changes and recovery from nonspatial memory deficits in CA1 NMDAR1-knockout mice. *Nature Neuroscience, 3*, 238–244.

Ranganath, C. (2010). Binding items and contexts: The cognitive neuroscience of episodic memory. *Current Directions in Psychological Science, 19*(3), 131–137.

Ranganath, C., & Ritchey, M. (2012). Two cortical systems for memory guided behaviour. *Nature Reviews Neuroscience, 13*, 713–726.

Ranganath, C., Yonelinas, A. P., Cohen, M. X., Dy, C. J., Tom, S. M., & D'Esposito, M. (2004). Dissociable correlates of recollection and familiarity within the medial temporal lobes. *Neuropsychologia, 42*, 2–13.

Rao, S. C., Rainer, G., & Miller, E. K. (1997). Integration of what and where in the primate prefrontal cortex. *Science, 276*, 821–824.

Rathelot, J.-A., & Strick, P. L. (2009). Subdivisions of primary motor cortex based on cortico-motoneuronal cells. *Proceedings of the National Academy of Sciences, USA, 106*(3), 918–923.

Ray, S., & Reddy, A. B. (2016). Cross-talk between circadian clocks, sleep-wake cycles, and metabolic networks: Dispelling the darkness. *BioEssays, 38*(4), 394–405.

Redcay, E., & Courchesne, E. (2005). When is the brain enlarged in autism? A meta-analysis of all brain size reports. *Biological Psychiatry, 58*(1), 1–9.

Reddy, L., Tsuchiya, N., & Serre, T. (2010). Reading the mind's eye: Decoding category information during mental imagery. *NeuroImage, 50*(2), 818–825.

Reich, D., Green, R. E., Kircher, M., Krause, J., Patterson, N., Durand, E. Y., et al. (2010). Genetic history of an archaic hominin group from Denisova Cave in Siberia. *Nature, 468*(7327), 1053.

Reicher, G. M. (1969). Perceptual recognition as a function of meaningfulness of stimulus material. *Journal of Experimental Psychology, 81*, 275–280.

Reichert, H., & Boyan, G. (1997). Building a brain: Developmental insights in insects. *Trends in Neuroscience, 20*, 258–264.

Reinholz, J., & Pollmann, S. (2005). Differential activation of object-selective visual areas by passive viewing of pictures and words. *Brain Research. Cognitive Brain Research, 24*, 702–714.

Reuter-Lorenz, P. A., & Fendrich, R. (1990). Orienting attention across the vertical meridian: Evidence from callosotomy patients. *Journal of Cognitive Neuroscience, 2*, 232–238.

Reverberi, C., Toraldo, A., d'Agostini, S., & Skrap, M. (2005). Better without (lateral) frontal cortex? Insight problems solved by frontal patients. *Brain, 128*, 2882–2890.

Reynolds, J. N. J., & Wickens, J. R. (2000). Substantia nigra dopamine regulates synaptic plasticity and membrane potential fluctuations in the rat neostriatum, in vivo. *Neuroscience, 99*, 199–203.

Rhodes, G., Byatt, G., Michie, P. T., & Puce, A. (2004). Is the fusiform face area specialized for faces, individuation, or expert individuation? *Journal of Cognitive Neuroscience, 16*, 189–203.

Riddoch, M. J., Humphreys, G. W., Gannon, T., Bott, W., & Jones, V. (1999). Memories are made of this: The effects of time on stored visual knowledge in a case of visual agnosia. *Brain, 122*(Pt. 3), 537–559.

Rilling, J. K. (2014). Comparative primate neurobiology and the evolution of brain language systems. *Current Opinion in Neurobiology, 28*, 10–14. doi:10.1016/j.conb.2014.04.002 [Epub, May 14]

Rilling, J. K., Glasser, M. F., Preuss, T. M., Ma, X., Zhao, T., Hu, X., et al. (2008). The evolution of the arcuate fasciculus revealed with comparative DTI. *Nature Neuroscience, 11*(4), 426–428.

Rimland, B., & Fein, D. (1988). Special talents of autistic savants. In L. K. Obler & D. Fein (Eds.), *The exceptional brain: Neuropsychology of talent and special abilities* (pp. 474–492). New York: Guilford.

Ringo, J. L., Doty, R. W., Demeter, S., & Simard, P. Y. (1994). Time is of the essence: A conjecture that hemispheric specialization arises from interhemispheric conduction delays. *Cerebral Cortex, 4*, 331–343.

Risse, G. L., Gates, J. R., & Fangman, M. C. (1997). A reconsideration of bilateral language representation based on the intracarotid amobarbital procedure. *Brain and Cognition, 33*, 118–132.

Ritchey, M., Dolcos, F., Eddington, K. M., Strauman, T. J., & Cabeza, R. (2011). Neural correlates of emotional processing in depression: Changes with cognitive behavioral therapy and predictors of treatment response. *Journal of Psychiatric Research, 45*(5), 577–587.

Ritchey, M., LaBar, K. S., & Cabeza, R. (2011). Level of processing modulates the neural correlates of emotional memory formation. *Journal of Cognitive Neuroscience, 23*, 757–771.

Rivolta, D., Castellanos, N. P., Stawowsky, C., Helbling, S., Wibral, M., Grützner, C., et al. (2014). Source-reconstruction of event-related fields reveals hyperfunction and hypofunction of cortical circuits in antipsychotic-naive, first-episode schizophrenia patients during Mooney face processing. *Journal of Neuroscience, 34*(17), 5909–5917.

Rizzolatti, G., & Arbib, M. A. (1998). Language within our grasp. *Trends in Neurosciences, 21*, 188–194.

Rizzolatti, G., Fogassi, L., & Gallese, V. (2000). Cortical mechanisms subserving object grasping and action recognition: A new view on the cortical motor functions. In M. S. Gazzaniga (Ed.), *The cognitive neurosciences* (2nd ed., pp. 539–552). Cambridge, MA: MIT Press.

Rizzolatti, G., Gentilucci, M., Fogassi, L., Luppino, G., Matelli, M., & Camarda, R. (1988). Functional organization of inferior area 6 in the macaque monkey. *Experimental Brain Research, 71*, 465–490.

Ro, T., Farnè, A., & Chang, E. (2003). Inhibition of return and the human frontal eye fields. *Experimental Brain Research, 150*, 290–296.

Roberts, D. C., Loh, E. A., & Vickers, G. (1989). Self-administration of cocaine on a progressive ratio schedule in rats: Dose-response relationship and effect of haloperidol pretreatment. *Psychopharmacology, 97*, 535–538.

Roberts, T. P. L., Poeppel, D., & Rowley, H. A. (1998). Magnetoencephalography and magnetic source imaging. *Neuropsychiatry, Neuropsychology, and Behavioral Neurology, 11*, 49–64.

Robertson, C. E., Ratai, E. M., & Kanwisher, N. (2016). Reduced GABAergic action in the autistic brain. *Current Biology, 26*(1), 80–85.

Robertson, I. H., Manly, T., Beschin, N., Daini, R., Haeske-Dewick, H., Hömberg, V., et al. (1997). Auditory sustained attention is a marker of unilateral spatial neglect. *Neuropsychologia, 35*, 1527–1532.

Robertson, L. C., Lamb, M. R., & Knight, R. T. (1988). Effects of lesions of temporal–parietal junction on perceptual and attentional processing in humans. *Journal of Neuroscience, 8*, 3757–3769.

Robertson, L. C., Lamb, M. R., & Zaidel, E. (1993). Interhemispheric relations in processing hierarchical patterns: Evidence from normal and commissurotomized subjects. *Neuropsychology, 7*, 325–342.

Robinson, D. L., Goldberg, M. E., & Stanton, G. B. (1978). Parietal association cortex in the primate: Sensory mechanisms and behavioral modulation. *Journal of Neurophysiology, 41*, 910–932.

Robinson, D. L., & Petersen, S. (1992). The pulvinar and visual salience. *Trends in Neurosciences, 15*, 127–132.

Roca, M., Parr, A., Thompson, R., Woolgar, A., Torralva, T., Antoun, N., et al. (2010). Executive function and fluid intelligence after frontal lobe lesions. *Brain, 133*(1), 234–247.

Roca, M., Torralva, T., Gleichgerrcht, E., Woolgar, A., Thompson, R., Duncan, J., et al. (2011). The role of Area 10 (BA10) in human multitasking and in social cognition: A lesion study. *Neuropsychologia, 49*(13), 3525–3531.

Rodrigues, S. M., Le Doux, J. E., & Sapolsky, R. M. (2009). The influence of stress hormones on fear circuitry. *Annual Review of Neuroscience, 32*, 289–313.

Roediger, H. L., & McDermott, K. B. (1995). Creating false memories: Remembering words not presented in lists. *Journal of Experimental Psychology. Learning, Memory, and Cognition, 21*, 803–814.

Rogers, L. J., & Workman, L. (1993). Footedness in birds. *Animal Behaviour, 45*, 409–411.

Rogers, R. D., Sahakian, R. A., Hodges, J. R., Polkey, C. E., Kennard, C., & Robbins, T. W. (1998). Dissociating executive mechanisms of task control following frontal lobe damage and Parkinson's disease. *Brain, 121*, 815–842.

Rogers, T. B., Kuiper, N. A., & Kirker, W. S. (1977). Self-reference and the encoding of personal information. *Journal of Personality and Social Psychology, 35*, 677–688.

Roiser, J. P., Stephan, K. E., den Ouden, H. E. M., Barnes, T. R. E., Friston, K. J., & Joyce, E. M. (2009). Do patients with schizophrenia exhibit aberrant salience? *Psychological Medicine, 39*(2), 199–209.

Rolheiser, T., Stamatakis, E. A., & Tyler, L. K. (2011). Dynamic processing in the human language system: Synergy between the arcuate fascicle and extreme capsule. *Journal of Neuroscience, 31*(47), 16949–16957.

Romei, V., Murray, M., Merabet, L. B., & Thut, G. (2007). Occipital transcranial magnetic stimulation has opposing effects on visual and auditory stimulus detection: Implications for multisensory interactions. *Journal of Neuroscience, 27*(43), 11465–11472.

Romeo, R. D., Karatsoreos, I. N., Jasnow, A. M., & McEwen, B. S. (2007). Age- and stress-induced changes in corticotropin-releasing hormone mRNA expression in the paraventricular nucleus of the hypothalamus. *Neuroendocrinology, 85*(4), 199–206.

Ronemus, M., Iossifov, I., Levy, D., & Wigler, M. (2014). The role of de novo mutations in the genetics of autism spectrum disorders. *Nature Reviews Genetics, 15*(2), 133–141.

Rose, J. E., Hind, J. E., Anderson, D. J., & Brugge, J. F. (1971). Some effects of stimulus intensity on response of auditory nerve fibers in the squirrel monkey. *Journal of Neurophysiology, 24*, 685–699.

Rosen, L. D., Whaling, K., Rab, S., Carrier, L. M., & Cheever, N. A. (2013). Is Facebook creating "iDisorders"? The link between clinical symptoms of psychiatric disorders and technology use, attitudes and anxiety. *Computers in Human Behavior, 29*(3), 1243–1254.

Rosen, R. (1996). On the limitations of scientific knowledge. In J. L. Casti & A. Karlqvist (Eds.), *Boundaries and barriers: On the limits to scientific knowledge* (pp. 199–214). Reading, MA: Perseus.

Rosenbaum, R. S., Kohler, S., Schacter, D. L., Moscovitch, M., Westmacott, R., Black, S. E., et al. (2005). The case of K.C.: Contributions of a memory-impaired person to memory theory. *Neuropsychologia, 43*, 989–1021.

Roser, M. E., Fugelsang, J. A., Dunbar, K. N., Corballis, P. M., & Gazzaniga, M. S. (2005). Dissociating processes supporting causal perception and causal inference in the brain. *Neuropsychology, 19*, 591–602.

Rossi, S., Hallett, M., Rossini, P. M., Pascual-Leone, A., & Safety of TMS Consensus Group. (2009). Safety, ethical considerations, and application guidelines for the use of transcranial magnetic stimulation in clinical practice and research. *Clinical Neurophysiology, 120*(12), 2008–2039.

Rossit, S., Harvey, M., Butler, S. H., Szymanek, L., Morand, S., Monaco, S., et al. (2018). Impaired peripheral reaching and on-line corrections in patient DF: Optic ataxia with visual form agnosia. *Cortex, 98*, 84–101.

Rothschild, G., Nelken, I., & Mizrahi, A. (2010). Functional organization and population dynamics in the mouse primary auditory cortex. *Nature Neuroscience, 13*, 353–360.

Rouw, R., & Scholte, H. S. (2007). Increased structural connectivity in grapheme-color synesthesia. *Nature Neuroscience, 10*(6), 792–797.

Rowland, L. P. (Ed.). (1989). *Merritt's textbook of neurology* (8th ed.). Philadelphia: Lea & Febiger.

Rudoy, J. D., Voss, J. L., Westerberg, C. E., & Paller, K. A. (2009). Strengthening individual memories by reactivating them during sleep. *Science, 326*(5956), 1079.

Rushworth, M. F. S., Kolling, N., Sallet, J., & Mars, R. B. (2012). Valuation and decision-making in frontal cortex: One or many serial or parallel systems? *Current Opinion in Neurobiology, 22*, 1–10.

Rushworth, M. F. S., Walton, M. E., Kennerley, S. W., & Bannerman, D. M. (2004). Action sets and decisions in the medial frontal cortex. *Trends in Cognitive Sciences, 8*(9), 410–417.

Russell, J. A. (1979). Affective space is bipolar. *Journal of Personality and Social Psychology, 37*, 345–356.

Russell, J. A. (2003). Core affect and the psychological construction of emotion. *Psychological Review, 110*, 145–172.

Ryan, J. D., Althoff, R. R., Whitlow, S., & Cohen, N. J. (2000). Amnesia is a deficit in relational memory. *Psychological Science, 11*, 454–461.

Ryan, T. J., Roy, D. S., Pignatelli, M., Arons, A., & Tonegawa, S. (2015). Engram cells retain memory under retrograde amnesia. *Science, 348*(6238), 1007–1013.

Saalmann, Y. B., Pinsk, M. A., Wang, L., Li, X., & Kastner, S. (2012). The pulvinar regulates information transmission between cortical areas based on attention demands. *Science, 337*(6095), 753–756.

Sabbah, N., Authié, C. N., Sanda, N., Mohand-Saïd, S., Sahel, J. A., Safran, A. B., et al. (2016). Increased functional connectivity between language and visually deprived areas in late and partial blindness. *NeuroImage, 136*, 162–173.

Sabini, J., & Silver, M. (2005). Ekman's basic emotions: Why not love and jealousy? *Cognition & Emotion, 19*(5), 693–712.

Sacco, R., Gabriele, S., & Persico, A. M. (2015). Head circumference and brain size in autism spectrum disorder: A systematic review and meta-analysis. *Psychiatry Research. Neuroimaging, 234*(2), 239–251.

Sadato, N., Pascual-Leone, A., Grafman, J., Deiber, M. P., Ibanez, V., & Hallett, M. (1998). Neural networks for Braille reading by the blind. *Brain, 121*(7), 1213–1229.

Sadato, N., Pascual-Leone, A., Grafman, J., Ibanez, V., Deiber, M.-P., Dold, G., et al. (1996). Activation of the primary visual cortex by Braille reading in blind subjects. *Nature, 380*, 526–528.

Sagiv, N., & Bentin, S. (2001). Structural encoding of human and schematic faces: Holistic and part-based processes. *Journal of Cognitive Neuroscience, 13*, 937–951.

Sahin, N. T., Pinker, S., Cash, S. S., Schomer, D., & Halgren, E. (2009). Sequential processing of lexical, grammatical, and phonological information within Broca's area. *Science, 326*, 445–449.

Said, C. P., Dotsch, R., & Todorov, A. (2010). The amygdala and FFA track both social and non-social face dimensions. *Neuropsychologia, 48*, 3596–3605.

Sakai, K., & Passingham, R. E. (2003). Prefrontal interactions reflect future task operations. *Nature Neuroscience, 6*, 75–81.

Sakurai, Y. (1996). Hippocampal and neocortical cell assemblies encode processes for different types of stimuli in the rat. *Journal of Neuroscience, 16*(8), 2809–2819.

Salzman, C. D., Britten, K. H., & Newsome, W. T. (1990). Cortical microstimulation influences perceptual judgments of motion direction. *Nature, 346*, 174–177.

Sams, M., Hari, R., Rif, J., & Knuutila, J. (1993). The human auditory sensory memory trace persists about 10 sec: Neuromagnetic evidence. *Journal of Cognitive Neuroscience, 5*, 363–370.

Sanbonmatsu, D. M., Strayer, D. L., Medeiros-Ward, N., & Watson, J. M. (2013). Who multi-tasks and why? Multi-tasking ability, perceived multi-tasking ability, impulsivity, and sensation seeking. *PLoS One, 8*(1), e54402.

Sanfey, A. G., Rilling, J. K., Aronson, J. A., Nystrom, L. E., & Cohen, J. D. (2003). The neural basis of economic decision-making in the ultimatum game. *Science, 300*, 1755–1758.

Saper, C. B. (2002). The central autonomic nervous system: Conscious visceral perception and autonomic pattern generation. *Annual Review of Neuroscience, 25*, 433–469.

Sapir, A., Soroker, N., Berger, A., & Henik, A. (1999). Inhibition of return in spatial attention: Direct evidence for collicular generation. *Nature Neuroscience, 2*, 1053–1054.

Sapolsky, R. M. (1992). *Stress, the aging brain, and the mechanisms of neuron death.* Cambridge, MA: MIT Press.

Sapolsky, R. M., Uno, H., Rebert, C. S., & Finch, C. E. (1990). Hippocampal damage associated with prolonged glucocorticoid exposure in primates. *Journal of Neuroscience, 10*, 2897–2902.

Satpute, A. B., Wager, T. D., Cohen-Adad, J., Bianciardi, M., Choi, J. K., Buhle, J. T., et al. (2013). Identification of discrete functional subregions of the human periaqueductal gray. *Proceedings of the National Academy of Sciences, USA, 110*(42), 17101–17106.

Saucier, D., & Cain, D. P. (1995). Spatial learning without NMDA receptor-dependent long-term potentiation. *Nature, 378*, 186–189.

Savage-Rumbaugh, S., & Lewin, R. (1994). *Kanzi: The ape at the brink of the human mind.* New York: Wiley.

Saver, J. L., & Damasio, A. R. (1991). Preserved access and processing of social knowledge in a patient with acquired sociopathy due to ventromedial frontal damage. *Neuropsychologia, 29*, 1241–1249.

Savla, G. N., Vella, L., Armstrong, C. C., Penn, D. L., & Twamley, E. W. (2012). Deficits in domains of social cognition in schizophrenia: A meta-analysis of the empirical evidence. *Schizophrenia Bulletin, 39*(5), 979–992.

SAXE, R., & POWELL, L. J. (2006). It's the thought that counts: Specific brain regions for one component of theory of mind. *Psychological Science, 17*, 692–699.

SAXE, R., & WEXLER, A. (2005). Making sense of another mind: The role of the right temporo-parietal junction. *Neuropsychologia, 43*, 1391–1399.

SAXE, R. R., WHITFIELD-GABRIELI, S., SCHOLZ, J., & PELPHREY, K. A. (2009). Brain regions for perceiving and reasoning about other people in school-aged children. *Child Development, 80*, 1197–1209.

SCHACTER, D. L. (1990). Perceptual representation systems and implicit memory: Toward a resolution of the multiple memory systems debate. *Annals of the New York Academy of Sciences, 608*, 543–571.

SCHACTER, D. L., CHAMBERLAIN, J., GAESSER, B., & GERLACH, K. D. (2012). Neuroimaging of true, false, and imaginary memories: Findings and implications. In L. Nadel & W. Sinnott-Armstrong (Eds.), *Memory and law: Perspectives from cognitive neuroscience.* New York: Oxford University Press.

SCHACTER, D. L., GILBERT, D. T., & WEGNER, D. M. (2007). *Psychology.* New York: Worth.

SCHACHTER, S., & SINGER, J. (1962). Cognitive, social and physiological determinants of emotional state. *Psychological Review, 69*, 379–399.

SCHALK, G., KAPELLER, C., GUGER, C., OGAWA, H., HIROSHIMA, S., LAFER-SOUSA, R., ET AL. (2017). Facephenes and rainbows: Causal evidence for functional and anatomical specificity of face and color processing in the human brain. *Proceedings of the National Academy of Sciences, USA, 114*(46), 201713447.

SCHARFF, C., & PETRI, J. (2011). Evo-devo, deep homology and FoxP2: Implications for the evolution of speech and language. *Philosophical Transactions of the Royal Society of London. Series B, Biological Sciences, 366*(1574), 2124–2140.

SCHEIBEL, A. B., PAUL, L. A., FRIED, I., FORSYTHE, A. B., TOMIYASU, U., WECHSLER, A., ET AL. (1985). Dendritic organization of the anterior speech area. *Experimental Neurology, 87*(1), 109–117.

SCHENK, F., & MORRIS, R. G. M. (1985). Dissociation between components of a spatial memory in rats after recovery from the effects of retrohippocampal lesion. *Experimental Brain Research, 58*, 11–28.

SCHENKER, N. M., BUXHOEVEDEN, D. P., BLACKMON, W. L., AMUNTS, K., ZILLES, K., & SEMENDEFERI, K. (2008). A comparative quantitative analysis of cytoarchitecture and minicolumnar organization in Broca's area in humans and great apes. *Journal of Comparative Neurology, 510*, 117–128.

SCHERER, K. R. (2005). What are emotions? And how can they be measured? *Social Science Information, 44*(4), 695–729.

SCHERF, S. K., BEHRMANN, M., MINSHEW, N., & LUNA, B. (2008). Atypical development of face and greeble recognition in autism. *Journal of Child Psychology and Psychiatry, 49*(8), 838–847.

SCHINDLER, I., RICE, N. J., MCINTOSH, R. D., ROSSETTI, Y., VIGHETTO, A., & MILNER, A. D. (2004). Automatic avoidance of obstacles is a dorsal stream function: Evidence from optic ataxia. *Nature Neuroscience, 7*, 779–784.

SCHIRBER, M. (2005, February 18). Monkey's brain runs robotic arm. *LiveScience.* Retrieved from http://www.livescience.com/technology/050218_monkey_arm.html

SCHMIDT, R. A. (1987). The acquisition of skill: Some modifications to the perception–action relationship through practice. In H. Heuer & A. F. Sanders (Eds.), *Perspectives on perception and action* (pp. 77–103). Hillsdale, NJ: Erlbaum.

SCHMITZ, W., & JOHNSON, S. C. (2007). Relevance to self: A brief review and framework of neural systems underlying appraisal. *Neuroscience and Biobehavioral Reviews, 31*(4), 585–596.

SCHNEIDER, P., BINDILA, L., SCHMAHL, C., BOHUS, M., MEYER-LINDENBERG, A., LUTZ, B., ET AL. (2016). Adverse social experiences in adolescent rats result in enduring effects on social competence, pain sensitivity and endocannabinoid signaling. *Frontiers in Behavioral Neuroscience, 10*, 203.

SCHOENBAUM, G., SADDORIS, M. P., & STALNAKER, T. A. (2007). Reconciling the roles of orbitofrontal cortex in reversal learning and the encoding of outcome expectancies. *Annals of the New York Academy of Sciences, 1121*, 320–335.

SCHOENEMANN, P. T., SHEEHAN, M. J., & GLOTZER, L. D. (2005). Prefrontal white matter volume is disproportionately larger in humans than in other primates. *Nature Neuroscience, 8*, 242–252.

SCHOENFELD, M., HOPF, J. M., MARTINEZ, A., MAI, H., SATTLER, C., GASDE, A., ET AL. (2007). Spatio-temporal analysis of feature-based attention. *Cerebral Cortex, 17*(10), 2468–2477.

SCHOLZ, J., TRIANTAFYLLOU, C., WHITFIELD-GABRIELI, S., BROWN, E. N., & SAXE, R. (2009). Distinct regions of right temporo-parietal junction are selective for theory of mind and exogenous attention. *PLoS One, 4*(3), e4869.

SCHREINER, T., & RASCH, B. (2014). Boosting vocabulary learning by verbal cueing during sleep. *Cerebral Cortex, 25*(11), 4169–4179.

SCHREINER, T., & RASCH, B. (2017). The beneficial role of memory reactivation for language learning during sleep: A review. *Brain and Language, 167*, 94–105.

SCHULTZ, W. (1998). Predictive reward signal of dopamine neurons. *Journal of Neurophysiology, 80*(1), 1–27.

SCHULTZ, W., DAYAN, P., & MONTAGUE, P. R. (1997). A neural substrate of prediction and reward. *Science, 275*, 1593–1599.

SCHUMACHER, E. H., SEYMOUR, T. L., GLASS, J. M., FENCSIK, D. E., LAUBER, E. J., KIERAS, D. E., ET AL. (2001). Virtually perfect time sharing in dual-task performance: Uncorking the central cognitive bottleneck. *Psychological Science, 12*(2), 101–108.

SCHUMMERS, J., YU, H., & SUR, M. (2008). Tuned responses of astrocytes and their influence on hemodynamic signals in the visual cortex. *Science, 320*, 1638–1643.

SCHWABE, L., & WOLF, O. T. (2009). Stress prompts habit behavior in humans. *Journal of Neuroscience, 29*(22), 7191–7198.

SCHWABE, L., & WOLF, O. T. (2014). Timing matters: Temporal dynamics of stress effects on memory retrieval. *Cognitive, Affective & Behavioral Neuroscience, 14*(3), 1041–1048.

SCHWARZKOPF, D. S., SONG, C., & REES, G. (2011). The surface area of human V1 predicts the subjective experience of object size. *Nature Neuroscience, 14*(1), 28–30.

SCHWARZLOSE, R., BAKER, C., & KANWISHER, N. (2005). Separate face and body selectivity on the fusiform gyrus. *Journal of Neuroscience, 25*(47), 11055–11059.

SCHWEIMER, J., & HAUBER, W. (2006). Dopamine D1 receptors in the anterior cingulate cortex regulate effort-based decision making. *Learning and Memory, 13*, 777–782.

SCHWEIMER, J., SAFT, S., & HAUBER, W. (2005). Involvement of catecholamine neurotransmission in the rat anterior cingulate in effort-related decision making. *Behavioral Neuroscience, 119*, 1687–1692.

SCOTT, S. H. (2004). Optimal feedback control and the neural basis of volitional motor control. *Nature Reviews Neuroscience, 5*, 534–546.

SCOTT, S. K., YOUNG, A. W., CALDER, A. J., HELLAWELL, D. J., AGGLETON, J. P., & JOHNSON, M. (1997). Impaired auditory recognition of fear and anger following bilateral amygdala lesions. *Nature, 385*, 254–257.

SCOVILLE, W. B. (1954). The limbic lobe in man. *Journal of Neurosurgery, 11*, 64–66.

SCOVILLE, W. B., & MILNER, B. (1957). Loss of recent memory after bilateral hippocampal lesions. *Journal of Neurology, Neurosurgery, and Psychiatry, 20*, 11–21.

Seidler, R. D., Noll, D. C., & Chintalapati, P. (2006). Bilateral basal ganglia activation associated with sensorimotor adaptation. *Experimental Brain Research, 175*, 544–555.

Sekuler, R., & Blake, R. (1990). *Perception* (2nd ed.). New York: McGraw-Hill.

Selfridge, O. G. (1959). Pandemonium: A paradigm for learning. In *Proceedings of a symposium on the mechanisation of thought processes* (pp. 511–526). London: H.M. Stationary Office.

Sellitto, M., Ciaramelli, E., & di Pellegrino, G. (2010). Myopic discounting of future rewards after medial orbitofrontal damage in humans. *Journal of Neuroscience, 30*(49), 16429–16436.

Senju, A., Maeda, M., Kikuchi, Y., Hasegawa, T., Tojo, Y., & Osanai, H. (2007). Absence of contagious yawning in children with autism spectrum disorder. *Biology Letters, 3*(6), 706–708.

Seyfarth, R. M., & Cheney, D. L. (1986.) Vocal development in vervet monkeys. *Animal Behaviour, 34*, 1640–1658.

Seyfarth, R. M., & Cheney, D. L. (2003a). Meaning and emotion in animal vocalizations. *Annals of the New York Academy of Sciences, 1000*, 32–55.

Seyfarth, R. M., & Cheney, D. L. (2003b). Signalers and receivers in animal communication. *Annual Review of Psychology, 54*, 145–173.

Seyfarth, R. M., Cheney, D. L., & Marler, P. (1980). Vervet monkey alarm calls: Semantic communication in a free-ranging primate. *Animal Behaviour, 28*, 1070–1094.

Seymour, B., Daw, N., Dayan, P., Singer, T., & Dolan, R. (2007). Differential encoding of losses and gains in the human striatum. *Journal of Neuroscience, 27*, 4826–4831.

Seymour, S. E., Reuter-Lorenz, P. A., & Gazzaniga, M. S. (1994). The disconnection syndrome. *Brain, 117*(1), 105–115.

Shackleton, E. H. (2004). *South: The* Endurance *expedition*. New York: Penguin. (Original work published 1919)

Shah, N., & Nakamura, Y. (2010). Case report: Schizophrenia discovered during the patient interview in a man with shoulder pain referred for physical therapy. *Physiotherapy Canada, 62*(4), 308–315.

Shallice, T., & Burgess, P. W. (1991). Deficits in strategy application following frontal lobe damage in man. *Brain, 114*, 727–741.

Shallice, T., Burgess, P. W., Schon, F., & Baxter, D. M. (1989). The origins of utilization behaviour. *Brain, 112*, 1587–1598.

Shallice, T., & Warrington, E. (1970). Independent functioning of verbal memory stores: A neuropsychological study. *Quarterly Journal of Experimental Psychology, 22*, 261–273.

Shams, L., Kamitani, Y., & Shimojo, S. (2000). Illusions. What you see is what you hear. *Nature, 408*, 788.

Sharot, T., Riccardi, A. M., Raio, C. M., & Phelps, E. A. (2007). Neural mechanisms mediating optimism bias. *Nature, 450*, 102–105.

Shaw, P., Greenstein, D., Lerch, J., Clasen, L., Lenroot, R., Gogtay, N., et al. (2006). Intellectual ability and cortical development in children and adolescents. *Nature, 440*, 676–679.

Sheinberg, D. L., & Logothetis, N. K. (1997). The role of temporal cortical areas in perceptual organization. *Proceedings of the National Academy of Sciences, USA, 94*, 3408–3413.

Shenhav, A., & Buckner, R. L. (2014). Neural correlates of dueling affective reactions to win–win choices. *Proceedings of the National Academy of Sciences, USA, 111*(30), 10978–10983.

Shenhav, A., Cohen, J. D., & Botvinick, M. M. (2016). Dorsal anterior cingulate cortex and the value of control. *Nature Neuroscience, 19*(10), 1286–1291.

Shepherd, G. M. (1991). *Foundations of the neuron doctrine*. New York: Oxford University Press.

Sherrington, C. S. (1947). *The integrative action of the nervous system* (2nd ed.). New Haven, CT: Yale University Press.

Sherwood, C. C., Wahl, E., Erwin, J. M., Hof, P. R., & Hopkins, W. D. (2007). Histological asymmetries of primary motor cortex predict handedness in chimpanzees (*Pan troglodytes*). *Journal of Comparative Neurology, 503*(4), 525–537.

Shi, R., Werker, J. F., & Morgan, J. L. (1999). Newborn infants' sensitivity to perceptual cues to lexical and grammatical words. *Cognition, 72*(2), B11–21.

Shiell, M. M., Champoux, F., & Zatorre, R. J. (2014). Enhancement of visual motion detection thresholds in early deaf people. *PLoS One, 9*(2), e90498.

Shiell, M. M., Champoux, F., & Zatorre, R. J. (2016). The right hemisphere planum temporale supports enhanced visual motion detection ability in deaf people: Evidence from cortical thickness. *Neural Plasticity*, art. 7217630.

Shimamura, A. P. (2000). The role of the prefrontal cortex in dynamic filtering. *Psychobiology, 28*, 207–218.

Shimamura, A. P. (2011). Episodic retrieval and the cortical binding of relational activity. *Cognitive Affective Behavioral Neuroscience, 11*, 277–291.

Shmuelop, L., & Zohary, E. (2006). Dissociation between ventral and dorsal fMRI activation during object and action recognition. *Neuron, 47*, 457–470.

Shors, T. J. (2004). Memory traces of trace memories: Neurogenesis, synaptogenesis and awareness. *Trends in Neurosciences, 27*, 250–256.

Sidtis, J. J., Volpe, B. T., Holtzman, J. D., Wilson, D. H., & Gazzaniga, M. S. (1981). Cognitive interaction after staged callosal section: Evidence for transfer of semantic activation. *Science, 212*, 344–346.

Siegel, J. S., Ramsey, L. E., Snyder, A. Z., Metcalf, N. V., Chacko, R. V., Weinberger, K., et al. (2016). Disruptions of network connectivity predict impairment in multiple behavioral domains after stroke. *Proceedings of the National Academy of Sciences, USA, 113*(30), E4367–E4376.

Simion, F., Regolin, L., & Bulf, H. (2008). A predisposition for biological motion in the newborn baby. *Proceedings of the National Academy of Sciences, USA, 105*, 809–813.

Simons, D. J., Boot, W. R., Charness, N., Gathercole, S. E., Chabris, C. F., Hambrick, D. Z., et al. (2016). Do "brain-training" programs work? *Psychological Science in the Public Interest, 17*(3), 103–186.

Simos, P. G., Basile, L. F., & Papanicolaou, A. C. (1997). Source localization of the N400 response in a sentence-reading paradigm using evoked magnetic fields and magnetic resonance imaging. *Brain Research, 762*, 29–39.

Simpson, J. (1988). *Touching the void*. New York: HarperCollins.

Singer, T., & Lamm, C. (2009). The social neuroscience of empathy. *Annals of the New York Academy of Sciences, 1156*(1), 81–96.

Singer, T., Seymour, B., O'Doherty, J., Kaube, H., Dolan, R. J., & Frith, C. D. (2004). Empathy for pain involves the affective but not sensory components of pain. *Science, 303*, 1157–1162.

Singer, T., Seymour, B., O'Doherty, J., Stefan, K. E., Dolan, R. J., & Frith, C. D. (2006). Empathic neural responses are modulated by the perceived fairness of others. *Nature, 439*(7075), 466–469.

Slotnick, S. D., & Schacter, D. L. (2004). A sensory signature that distinguishes true from false memories. *Nature Neuroscience, 7*(6), 664.

Smilek, D., Dixon, M. J., & Merikle, P. M. (2005). Synaesthesia: Discordant male monozygotic twins. *Neurocase, 11*, 363–370.

SMITH, A. P. R., STEPHAN, K. E., RUGG, M. D., & DOLAN, R. J. (2006). Task and content modulate amygdala–hippocampal connectivity in emotional retrieval. *Neuron, 49*, 631–638.

SMITH, E. E., JONIDES, J., & KOEPPE, R. A. (1996). Dissociating verbal and spatial working memory using PET. *Cerebral Cortex, 6*, 11–20.

SNIJDERS, T. M., VOSSE, T., KEMPEN, G., VAN BERKUM, J. J., PETERSSON, K. M., & HAGOORT, P. (2008). Retrieval and unification of syntactic structure in sentence comprehension: An fMRI study using word-category ambiguity. *Cerebral Cortex, 19*(7), 1493–1503.

SNODGRASS, J. G., & VANDERWART, M. (1980). A standardized set of 260 pictures: Norms for name agreement, image agreement, familiarity, and visual complexity. *Journal of Experimental Psychology. Human Learning and Memory, 6*, 174–215.

SOBEL, N., PRABHAKARAN, V., DESMOND, J. E., GLOVER, G. H., GOODE, R. L., SULLIVAN, E. V., ET AL. (1998). Sniffing and smelling: Separate subsystems in the human olfactory cortex. *Nature, 392*, 282–286.

SOKOL-HESSNER, P., CAMERER, C. F., & PHELPS, E. A. (2012). Emotion regulation reduces loss aversion and decreases amygdala responses to losses. *Social Cognitive and Affective Neuroscience, 8*(e), 341–350.

SOKOL-HESSNER, P., HARTLEY, C. A., HAMILTON, J. R., & PHELPS, E. A. (2015). Interoceptive ability predicts aversion to losses. *Cognition & Emotion, 29*(4), 695–701.

SOKOL-HESSNER, P., HSU, M., CURLEY, N. G., DELGADO, M. R., CAMERER, C. F., & PHELPS, E. A. (2009). Thinking like a trader selectively reduces individuals' loss aversion. *Proceedings of the National Academy of Sciences, USA, 106*(13), 5035–5040.

SOKOL-HESSNER, P., LACKOVIC, S. F., TOBE, R. H., CAMERER, C. F., LEVENTHAL, B. L., & PHELPS, E. A. (2015). Determinants of propranolol's selective effect on loss aversion. *Psychological Science, 26*(7), 1123–1130.

SOLOMON, R. C. (2008). The philosophy of emotions. In M. Lewis, J. M. Haviland-Jones, & L. F. Barrett (Eds.), *The handbook of emotions* (3rd ed., pp. 1–16). New York: Guilford.

SOON, C. S., BRASS, M., HEINZE, H.-J., & HAYNES, J.-D. (2008). Unconscious determinants of free decision in the human brain. *Nature Neuroscience, 11*(5), 543–545.

SPEAR, L. P. (2000). The adolescent brain and age-related behavioral manifestations. *Neuroscience and Biobehavioral Reviews, 24*(4), 417–463.

SPERRY, R. W. (1984). Consciousness, personal identity and the divided brain. *Neuropsychologia, 22*(6), 661–673.

SPERRY, R. W., GAZZANIGA, M. S., & BOGEN, J. E. (1969). Interhemispheric re[illegible]ships: The neocortical commissures; syndromes of hemisphere disconnection. In P. J. Vinken & G. W. Bruyn (Eds.), *Handbook of clinical neurology* (Vol. 4, pp. 273–290). Amsterdam: North-Holland.

SPINOZZI, G., CASTORINA, M. G., & TRUPPA, V. (1998). Hand preferences in unimanual and coordinated-bimanual tasks by tufted capuchin monkeys (*Cebus apella*). *Journal of Comparative Psychology, 112*(2), 183.

SPORNS, O., & BETZEL, R. F. (2016). Modular brain networks. *Annual Review of Psychology, 67*, 613–640.

SPUNT, R. P., MEYER, M. L., & LIEBERMAN, M. D. (2015). The default mode of human brain function primes the intentional stance. *Journal of Cognitive Neuroscience, 27*(6), 1116–1124.

SQUIRE, L. R. (1992). Memory and the hippocampus: A synthesis from findings with rats, monkeys, and humans. *Psychological Review, 99*, 195–231.

SQUIRE, L. R., BLOOM, F. E., MCCONNELL, S. K., ROBERTS, J. L., SPITZER, N. C., & ZIGMOND, M. J. (EDS.). (2003). *Fundamental neuroscience* (2nd ed.). Amsterdam: Academic Press.

SQUIRE, L. R., SHIMAMURA, A. P., & GRAFT, P. (1987). Strength and duration of priming effects in normal subjects and amnesic patients. *Neuropsychologia, 25*(1), 195–210.

SQUIRE, L. R., & SLATER, P. (1983). Electroconvulsive therapy and complaints of memory dysfunction: A prospective three-year follow-up study. *British Journal of Psychiatry, 142*, 1–8.

STAGG, C. J., & NITSCHE, M. A. (2011). Physiological basis of transcranial direct current stimulation. *Neuroscientist, 17*(1), 37–53.

STEIN, B. E., & MEREDITH, M. A. (1993). *The merging of the senses.* Cambridge, MA: MIT Press.

STEIN, B. E., STANFORD, T. R., WALLACE, M. T., VAUGHAN, J. W., & JIANG, W. (2004). Crossmodal spatial interactions in subcortical and cortical circuits. In C. Spence & J. Driver (Eds.), *Crossmodal space and crossmodal attention* (pp. 25–50). Oxford: Oxford University Press.

STEIN, M. B., KOVEROLA, C., HANNA, C., TORCHIA, M. G., & MCCLARTY, B. (1997). Hippocampal volume in woman victimized by childhood sexual abuse. *Psychological Medicine, 27*, 951–959.

STEPHENS, G. J., SILBERT, L. J., & HASSON, U. (2010). Speaker-listener neural coupling underlies successful communication. *Proceedings of the National Academy of Sciences, USA, 107*(32), 14425–14430.

STERELNY, K. (2012). Language, gesture, skill: The co-evolutionary foundations of language. *Philosophical Transactions of the Royal Society of London. Series B, Biological Sciences, 367*(1599), 2141–2151.

STERNBERG, S. (1966). High speed scanning in human memory. *Science, 153*, 652–654.

STERNBERG, S. (1975). Memory scanning: New findings and current controversies. *Quarterly Journal of Experimental Psychology, 27*, 1–32.

STEVEN, M. S., & PASCUAL-LEONE, A. (2006). Transcranial magnetic stimulation and the human brain: An ethical evaluation. In J. Illes (Ed.), *Neuroethics: Defining the issues in theory, practice, and policy* (pp. 201–212). Oxford: Oxford University Press.

STEVENS, L. K., MCGRAW, P. V., LEDGEWY, T., & SCHLUPPECK, D. (2009). Temporal characteristics of global motion processing revealed by transcranial magnetic stimulation. *European Journal of Neuroscience, 30*, 2415–2426.

STILLMAN, T. F., BAUMEISTER, R. F., VOHS, K. D., LAMBERT, N. M., FINCHAM, F. D., & BREWER, L. E. (2010). Personal philosophy and personnel achievement: Belief in free will predicts better job performance. *Social Psychological and Personality Science, 1*(1), 43–50.

STONE, V. E., BARON-COHEN, S., & KNIGHT, R. T. (1998). Frontal lobe contributions to theory of mind. *Journal of Cognitive Neuroscience, 10*, 640–656.

STONE, V. E., COSMIDES, L., TOOBY, J., KROLL, N., & KNIGHT, R. T. (2002). Selective impairment of reasoning about social exchange in a patient with bilateral limbic system damage. *Proceedings of the National Academy of Sciences, USA, 99*(17), 11531–11536.

STRATTON, G. M. (1896). Some preliminary experiments on vision without inversion of the retinal image. *Psychological Review, 3*(6), 611–617.

STRAUSFELD, N. J., & HIRTH, F. (2013). Deep homology of arthropod central complex and vertebrate basal ganglia. *Science, 340*(6129), 157–161.

STRIEDTER, G. F. (2005). *Principles of brain evolution.* Sunderland, MA: Sinauer.

STRNAD, L., PEELEN, M. V., BEDNY, M., & CARAMAZZA, A. (2013). Multivoxel pattern analysis reveals auditory motion information in MT+ of both congenitally blind and sighted individuals. *PLoS One, 8*(4), e63198.

Strobach, T., Frensch, P. A., & Schubert, T. (2012). Video game practice optimizes executive control skills in dual-task and task switching situations. *Acta Psychologica, 140*(1), 13–24.

Stromswold, K., Caplan, D., Alpert, N., & Rauch S. (1996). Localization of syntactic comprehension by positron emission tomography. *Brain and Language, 52*, 452–473.

Stroop, J. (1935). Studies of interference in serial verbal reaction. *Journal of Experimental Psychology, 18*, 643–662.

Suarez, S. D., & Gallup, G. G., Jr. (1981). Self-recognition in chimpanzees and orangutans, but not gorillas. *Journal of Human Evolution, 10*, 175–188.

Sutherland, S. (1995). Consciousness. In *The international dictionary of psychology* (2nd ed.). London: Macmillan.

Suzuki, W. A., & Amaral, D. G. (1994). Perirhinal and parahippocampal cortices of the macaque monkey: Cortical afferents. *Journal of Comparative Neurology, 350*, 497–533.

Swaab, T. Y., Brown, C. M., & Hagoort, P. (1997). Spoken sentence comprehension in aphasia: Event-related potential evidence for a lexical integration deficit. *Journal of Cognitive Neuroscience, 9*, 39–66.

Swanson, L. W. (1983). The hippocampus and the concept of the limbic system. In W. Seifert (Ed.), *Neurobiology of the hippocampus* (pp. 3–19). London: Academic Press.

Swanson, L. W., & Petrovich, G. D. (1998). What is the amygdala? *Trends in Neurosciences, 21*, 323–331.

Swartz, K. B. (1997). What is mirror self-recognition in nonhuman primates, and what is it not? *Annals of the New York Academy of Sciences, 818*, 64–71.

Sweet, W. H., & Brownell, G. L. (1953). Localization of brain tumors with positron emitters. *Nucleonics, 11*, 40–45.

Sztarker, J., & Tomsic, D. (2011). Brain modularity in arthropods: Individual neurons that support "what" but not "where" memories. *Journal of Neuroscience, 31*(22), 8175–8180.

Tabbert, K., Stark, R., Kirsch, P., & Vaitl, D. (2006). Dissociation of neural responses and skin conductance reactions during fear conditioning with and without awareness of stimulus contingencies. *NeuroImage, 32*(2), 761–770.

Tabot, G. A., Dammann, J. F., Berg, J. A., Tenore, F. V., Boback, J. L., Vogelstein, R. J., et al. (2013). Restoring the sense of touch with a prosthetic hand through a brain interface. *Proceedings of the National Academy of Sciences, USA, 110*(45), 18279–18284.

Taglialatela, J. P., Russell, J. L., Schaeffer, J. A., & Hopkins, W. D. (2008). Communicative signaling activates "Broca's" homolog in chimpanzees. *Current Biology, 18*(5), 343–348.

Talairach, J., & Tournoux, P. (1988). *Co-planar stereotaxic atlas of the human brain: 3-dimensional proportional system—an approach to cerebral imaging.* New York: Thieme.

Talbot, K., Wang, H. Y., Kazi, H., Han, L. Y., Bakshi, K. P., Stucky, A., et al. (2012). Demonstrated brain insulin resistance in Alzheimer's disease patients is associated with IGF-1 resistance, IRS-1 dysregulation, and cognitive decline. *Journal of Clinical Investigation, 122*(4), 1316.

Taleb, N. (2014). *Antifragile.* New York: Random House.

Tambini, A., & Davachi, L. (2013). Persistence of hippocampal multivoxel patterns into postencoding rest is related to memory. *Proceedings of the National Academy of Sciences, USA, 110*(48), 19591–19596.

Tanaka, J. W., & Farah, M. J. (1993). Parts and wholes in face recognition. *Quarterly Journal of Experimental Psychology. A, Human Experimental Psychology, 46*, 225–245.

Tanaka, S. C., Schweighofer, N., Asahi, S., Shishida, K., Okamoto, Y., Yamawaki, S., et al. (2007). Serotonin differentially regulates short- and long-term prediction of rewards in the ventral and dorsal striatum. *PLoS One, 2*, e1333.

Taub, E., & Berman, A. J. (1968). Movement and learning in the absence of sensory feedback. In S. J. Freedman (Ed.), *The neuropsychology of spatially oriented behavior* (pp. 173–191). Homewood, IL: Dorsey.

Taylor, A. H., Elliffe, D., Hunt, G. R., & Gray, R. D. (2010). Complex cognition and behavioural innovation in New Caledonian crows. *Proceedings of the Royal Society of London, Series B, 277*(1694), 2637–2643.

Taylor, C. T., Wiggett, A. J., & Downing, P. E. (2007). Functional MRI analysis of body and body part representations in the extrastriate and fusiform body areas. *Journal of Neurophysiology, 98*, 1626–1633.

Taylor, D. M., Tillery, S. I., & Schwartz, A. B. (2002). Direct cortical control of 3D neuroprosthetic devices. *Science, 296*, 1829–1832.

Taylor, S. E., & Brown, J. D. (1988). Illusion and well-being: A social psychological perspective on mental health. *Psychological Bulletin, 103*, 193–210.

Teather, L. A., Packard, M. G., & Bazan, N. G. (1998). Effects of posttraining intrahippocampal injections of platelet-activating factor and PAF antagonists on memory. *Neurobiology of Learning and Memory, 70*, 349–363.

Templeton, C. N., Greene, E., & Davis, K. (2005). Allometry of alarm calls: Black-capped chickadees encode information about predator size. *Science, 308*, 1934–1937.

Tennie, C., Call, J., & Tomasello, M. (2006). Push or pull: Imitation versus emulation in human children and great apes. *Ethology, 112*, 1159–1169.

Tennie, C., Call, J., & Tomasello, M. (2010). Evidence for emulation in chimpanzees in social settings using the floating peanut task. *PLoS One, 5*(5), e10544. doi:10.1371/journal.pone.0010544

Ter-Pogossian, M. M., Phelps, M. E., & Hoffman, E. J. (1975). A positron emission transaxial tomograph for nuclear medicine imaging (PETT). *Radiology, 114*, 89–98.

Ter-Pogossian, M. M., & Powers, W. E. (1958). The use of radioactive oxygen-15 in the determination of oxygen content in malignant neoplasms. In *Radioisotopes in scientific research: Vol. 3. Proceedings of the 1st UNESCO International Conference, Paris.* New York: Pergamon.

Terzaghi, M., Sartori, I., Tassi, L., Didato, G., Rustioni, V., LoRusso, G., et al. (2009). Evidence of dissociated arousal states during NREM parasomnia from an intracerebral neurophysiological study. *Sleep, 32*(3), 409–412.

Thibault, C., Lai, C., Wilke, N., Duong, B., Olive, M. F., Rahman, S., et al. (2000). Expression profiling of neural cells reveals specific patterns of ethanol-responsive gene expression. *Molecular Pharmacology, 58*, 1593–1600.

Thiebaut de Schotten, M., Dell'Acqua, F., Forkel, S. J., Simmons, A., Vergani, F., Murphy, D. G. M., et al. (2011). A lateralized brain network for visuospatial attention. *Nature Neuroscience, 14*(10), 1245–1247.

Thiebaut de Schotten, M., Dell'Acqua, F., Valabregue, R., & Catani, M. (2012). Monkey to human comparative anatomy of the frontal lobe association tracts. *Cortex, 48*(1), 8212.

Thomason, M. E., Dassanayake, M. T., Shen, S., Katkuri, Y., Alexis, M., Anderson, A. L., et al. (2013). Cross-hemispheric functional connectivity in the human fetal brain. *Science Translational Medicine, 5*(173), 173ra24.

Thompson, P. (1980). Margaret Thatcher: A new illusion. *Perception, 9*, 483–484.

THOMPSON, R. F. (2000). *The brain: A neuroscience primer* (3rd ed.). New York: Freeman.

THOMPSON-SCHILL, S. L., D'ESPOSITO, M., AGUIRRE, G. K., & FARAH, M. J. (1997). Role of left inferior prefrontal cortex in retrieval of semantic knowledge: A reevaluation. *Proceedings of the National Academy of Sciences, USA, 94*, 14792–14797.

THOMPSON-SCHILL, S. L., D'ESPOSITO, M., & KAN, I. P. (1999). Effects of repetition and competition on activity in left prefrontal cortex during word generation. *Neuron, 23*, 513–522.

THOMPSON-SCHILL, S. L., SWICK, D., FARAH, M. J., D'ESPOSITO, M., KAN, I. P., & KNIGHT, R. T. (1998). Verb generation in patients with focal frontal lesions: A neuropsychological test of neuroimaging findings. *Proceedings of the National Academy of Sciences, USA, 95*, 15855–15860.

THORNDIKE, E. (1911). *Animal intelligence: An experimental study of the associative processes in animals.* New York: Macmillan.

THULBORN, K. R., WATERTON, J. C., MATTHEWS, P. M., & RADDA, G. K. (1982). Oxygenation dependence of the transverse relaxation time of water protons in whole blood at high field. *Biochimica et Biophysica Acta, 714*, 265–270.

THUT, G., NIETZEL, A., & PASCUAL-LEONE, A. (2005). Dorsal posterior parietal rTMS affects voluntary orienting of visual-spatial attention. *Cerebral Cortex, 15*(5), 628–638.

TIAN, J., HUANG, R., COHEN, J. Y., OSAKADA, F., KOBAK, D., MACHENS, C. K., ET AL. (2016). Distributed and mixed information in monosynaptic inputs to dopamine neurons. *Neuron, 91*(6), 1374–1389.

TIAN, J., & UCHIDA, N. (2015). Habenula lesions reveal that multiple mechanisms underlie dopamine prediction errors. *Neuron, 87*(6), 1304–1316.

TIFFIN, P. A., PEARCE, M. S., & PARKER, L. (2005). Social mobility over the lifecourse and self reported mental health at age 50: Prospective cohort study. *Journal of Epidemiology and Community Health, 59*(10), 870–872.

TIGNOR, R. L. (2008). *Worlds together, worlds apart: A history of the world from the beginnings of humankind to the present* (2nd ed.). New York: Norton.

TOMASELLO, M. (2007). If they are so good at grammar, then why don't they talk? Hints from apes and humans' use of gestures. *Language Learning and Development, 3*, 1–24.

TOMASELLO, M. (2008). *Origins of human communication.* Cambridge, MA: MIT Press.

TOMASELLO, M., & CALL, J. (2018). Thirty years of great ape gestures. *Animal Cognition.* doi:10.1007/s10071-018-1167-1 [Epub ahead of print, February 21]

TOMASELLO, M., HARE, B., LEHMANN, H., & CALL, J. (2007). Reliance on head versus eyes in the gaze following of great apes and human infants: The cooperative eye hypothesis. *Journal of Human Evolution, 52*, 314–320.

TOOTELL, R. B., HADJIKHANI, N., HALL, E. K., MARRETT, S., VANDUFFEL, W., VAUGHAN, J. T., ET AL. (1998). The retinotopy of visual spatial attention. *Neuron, 21*, 1409–1422.

TOSONI, A., GALATI, G., ROMANI, G. L., & CORBETTA, M. (2008). Sensory-motor mechanisms in human parietal cortex underlie arbitrary visual decisions. *Nature Neuroscience, 11*, 1446–1453.

TOURVILLE, J. A., REILLY, K. J., & GUENTHER, F. H. (2008). Neural mechanisms underlying auditory feedback control of speech. *NeuroImage, 39*(3), 1429–1443.

TRACY, J., & MATSUMOTO, D. (2008). The spontaneous expression of pride and shame: Evidence for biologically innate nonverbal displays. *Proceedings of the National Academy of Sciences, USA, 105*, 11655–11660.

TRANEL, D., & HYMAN, B. T. (1990). Neuropsychological correlates of bilateral amygdala damage. *Archives of Neurology, 47*, 349–355.

TREISMAN, A. M. (1969). Strategies and models of selective attention. *Psychological Review, 76*, 282–299.

TREISMAN, A. M., & GELADE, G. (1980). A feature-integration theory of attention. *Cognitive Psychology, 12*, 97–136.

TRITSCH, N. X., GRANGER, A. J., & SABATINI, B. L. (2016). Mechanisms and functions of GABA co-release. *Nature Reviews Neuroscience, 17*(3), 139.

TSAO, D. Y., FREIWALD, W. A., TOOTELL, R. B., & LIVINGSTONE, M. S. (2006). A cortical region consisting entirely of face-selective cells. *Science, 311*, 670–674.

TULVING, E. (1993). Self-knowledge of an amnesiac individual is represented abstractly. In T. K. Srull & R. S. Wyer (Eds.), *The mental representation of trait and autobiographical knowledge about the self* (pp. 147–156). Hillsdale, NJ: Erlbaum.

TULVING, E., KAPUR, S., CRAIK, F. I. M., MOSCOVITCH, M., & HOULE, S. (1994). Hemispheric encoding/retrieval asymmetry in episodic memory: Positron emission tomography findings. *Proceedings of the National Academy of Sciences, USA, 91*, 2016–2020.

TURIN, L. (1996). A spectroscopic mechanism for primary olfactory reception. *Chemical Senses, 21*, 773–791.

TURK, D. J., HEATHERTON, T. F., KELLEY, W. M., FUNNELL, M. G., GAZZANIGA, M. S., & MACRAE, C. N. (2002). Mike or me? Self-recognition in a split-brain patient. *Nature Neuroscience, 5*(9), 841–842.

TYE, K. M., PRAKASH, R., KIM, S.-Y., FENNO, L. E., GROSENICK, L., ZARABI, H., ET AL. (2011). Amygdala circuitry mediating reversible and bidirectional control of anxiety. *Nature, 471*(7338), 358–362.

TYLER, L. K., MARSLEN-WILSON, W. D., RANDALL, B., WRIGHT, P., DEVEREUX, B. J., ZHUANG, J., ET AL. (2011). Left inferior frontal cortex and syntax: Function, structure and behaviour in patients with left hemisphere damage. *Brain, 134*, 415–431.

TYLER, M. D., & CUTLER, A. (2009). Cross-language differences in cue use for speech segmentation. *Journal of the Acoustical Society of America, 126*(1), 367–376.

ULRICH-LAI, Y. M., & HERMAN, J. P. (2009). Neural regulation of endocrine and autonomic stress responses. *Nature Reviews Neuroscience, 10*(6), 397–409.

UMILTA, M. A., KOHLER, E., GALLESE, V., FOGASSI, L., FADIGA, L., KEYSERS, C., ET AL. (2001). I know what you are doing: A neurophysiological study. *Neuron, 31*, 155–165.

UNCAPHER, M. R., THIEU, M. K., & WAGNER, A. D. (2016). Media multitasking and memory: Differences in working memory and long-term memory. *Psychonomic Bulletin & Review, 23*(2), 483–490.

UNGERLEIDER, L. G., & MISHKIN, M. (1982). Two cortical visual systems. In D. J. Engle, M. A. Goodale, & R. J. Mansfield (Eds.), *Analysis of visual behavior* (pp. 549–586). Cambridge, MA: MIT Press.

VALLORTIGARA, G., CHIANDETTI, C., & SOVRANO, V. A. (2011). Brain asymmetry (animal). *Wiley Interdisciplinary Reviews: Cognitive Science, 2*(2), 146–157.

VAN BERKUM, J. J., HAGOORT, P., & BROWN, C. M. (1999). Semantic integration in sentences and discourse: Evidence from the N400. *Journal of Cognitive Neuroscience, 11*(6), 657–671.

VAN DEN HEUVEL, M. P., STAM, C. J., KAHN, R. S., & HULSHOFF POL, H. E. (2009). Efficiency of functional brain networks and intellectual performance. *Journal of Neuroscience, 29*, 7619–7624.

VANDER, A., SHERMAN, J., & LUCIANO, D. (2001). *Human physiology: The mechanisms of body function* (8th ed.). Boston: McGraw-Hill.

Vanderauwera, J., Altarelli, I., Vandermosten, M., De Vos, A., Wouters, J., & Ghesquière, P. (2016). Atypical structural asymmetry of the planum temporale in relation is related to family history of dyslexia. *Cerebral Cortex, 28*(1), 1–10.

Vanduffel, W., Tootell, R. B. H., & Orban, G. G. (2000). Attention-dependent suppression of metabolic activity in the early stages of the macaque visual system. *Cerebral Cortex, 10*(2), 109–126.

van Kooten, I. A., Palmen, S. J., von Cappeln, P., Steinbusch, H. W., Korr, H., Heinsen, H., et al. (2008). Neurons in the fusiform gyrus are fewer and smaller in autism. *Brain, 131*, 987–999.

Van Lier, J., Revlin, R., & De Neys, W. (2013). Detecting cheaters without thinking: Testing the automaticity of the cheater detection module. *PLoS One, 8*(1), e53827.

Van Voorhis, S., & Hillyard, S. A. (1977). Visual evoked potentials and selective attention to points in space. *Perception & Psychophysics, 22*(1), 54–62.

Van Wagenen, W. P., & Herren, R. Y. (1940). Surgical division of commissural pathways in the corpus callosum: Relation to spread of an epileptic seizure. *Archives of Neurology and Psychiatry, 44*, 740–759.

Vargha-Khadem, F., Gadian, D. G., Copp, A., & Mishkin, M. (2005). FOXP2 and the neuroanatomy of speech and language. *Nature Reviews Neuroscience, 6*, 131–138.

Velliste, M., Perel, S., Spalding, M. C., Whitford, A. S., & Schwartz, A. B. (2008). Cortical control of a prosthetic arm for self-feeding. *Nature, 453*, 1098–1101.

Verdon, V., Schwartz, S., Lovblad, K. O., Hauert, C. A., & Vuilleumier, P. (2010). Neuroanatomy of hemispatial neglect and its functional components: A study using voxel-based lesion-symptom mapping. *Brain, 133*, 880–894.

Vidal, C. N., Nicolson, R., DeVito, T. J., Hayashi, K. M., Geaga, J. A., Drost, D. J., et al. (2006). Mapping corpus callosum deficits in autism: An index of aberrant cortical connectivity. *Biological Psychiatry, 60*(3), 218–225.

Vigneau, M., Beaucousin, V., Hervé, P. Y., Jobard, G., Petit, L., Crivello, F., et al. (2011). What is right-hemisphere contribution to phonological, lexico-semantic, and sentence processing? Insights from a meta-analysis. *NeuroImage, 54*(1), 577–593.

Vilberg, K. L., & Rugg, M. D. (2008). Memory retrieval and the parietal cortex: A review of evidence from a dual-process perspective. *Neuropsychologia, 46*, 1787–1799.

Vitali, P., Migliaccio, R., Agosta, F., Rosen, H. J., & Geschwind, M. D. (2008). Neuroimaging in dementia. *Seminars in Neurology, 28*(4), 467–483.

Vohs, K. D., & Schooler, J. W. (2008). The value in believing in free will: Encouraging a belief in determinism increases cheating. *Psychological Science, 19*(1), 49–54.

Volfovsky, N., Parnas, H., Segal, M., & Korkotian, E. (1999). Geometry of dendritic spines affects calcium dynamics in hippocampal neurons: Theory and experiments. *Journal of Neurophysiology, 82*, 450–462.

Volpe, B. T., LeDoux, J. E., & Gazzaniga, M. S. (1979). Information processing of visual field stimuli in an "extinguished" field. *Nature, 282*, 722–724.

Volpe, B. T., Sidtis, J. J., Holtzman, J. D., Wilson, D. H., & Gazzaniga, M. S. (1982). Cortical mechanisms involved in praxis: Observations following partial and complete section of the corpus callosum in man. *Neurology, 32*(6), 645–650.

Von Neumann, J., & Burks, A. W. (1966). Theory of self-reproducing automata. *IEEE Transactions on Neural Networks, 5*(1), 3–14.

Von Neumann, J., & Burks, A. W. (1996). *Theory of self-reproducing automata*. Urbana: University of Illinois Press.

Vuilleumier, P., Armony, J. L., Driver, J., & Dolan, R. J. (2001). Effects of attention and emotion on face processing in the human brain: An event-related fMRI study. *Neuron, 30*, 829–841.

Vuilleumier, P., Richardson, M. P., Armony, J. L., Driver, J., & Dolan, R. J. (2004). Distant influences of the amygdala lesion on visual cortical activation during emotional face processing. *Nature Neuroscience, 7*, 1271–1278.

Vyazovskiy, V. V., Olcese, U., Hanlon, E. C., Nir, Y., Cirelli, C., & Tononi, G. (2011). Local sleep in awake rats. *Nature, 472*(7344), 443–447.

Vytal, K., & Hamann, S. (2010). Neuroimaging support for discrete neural correlates of basic emotions: A voxel-based meta-analysis. *Journal of Cognitive Neuroscience, 22*(12), 2864–2885.

Wada, J., & Rasmussen, T. (1960). Intracarotid injection of sodium amytal for the lateralization of cerebral speech dominance: Experimental and clinical observations. *Journal of Neurosurgery, 17*(2), 266–282.

Wade, K. A., Garry, M., Read, J. D., & Lindsay, D. S. (2002). A picture is worth a thousand lies: Using false photographs to create false childhood memories. *Psychonomic Bulletin & Review, 9*(3), 597–603.

Wade, N. (2003, October 7). American and Briton win Nobel for using chemists' test for M.R.I.'s. *New York Times*.

Wager, T. D., & Smith, E. E. (2003). Neuroimaging studies of working memory: A meta-analysis. *Cognitive, Affective & Behavioral Neuroscience, 3*, 255–274.

Wagner, A. D., Koutstaal, W., Maril, A., Schacter, D. L., & Buckner, R. L. (2000). Task-specific repetition priming in left inferior prefrontal cortex. *Cerebral Cortex, 10*(12), 1176–1184.

Wagner, A. D., Schacter, D. L., Rotte, M., Koutstaal, W., Maril, A., Dale, A. M., et al. (1998). Building memories: Remembering and forgetting of verbal experiences as predicted by brain activity. *Science, 281*, 1188–1191.

Wagner, A. D., Shannon, B. J., Kahn, I., & Buckner, R. L. (2005). Parietal lobe contributions to episodic memory retrieval. *Trends in Cognitive Sciences, 9*(9), 445–453.

Wagner, G. P., Pavlicev, M., & Cheverud, J. M. (2007). The road to modularity. *Nature Reviews Genetics, 8*, 921–931.

Wagner, M. J., Kim, T. H., Savall, J., Schnitzer, M. J., & Luo, L. (2017). Cerebellar granule cells encode the expectation of reward. *Nature, 544*, 96.

Walker, M. P. (2009). The role of slow wave sleep in memory processing. *Journal of Clinical Sleep Medicine, 5*(2 Suppl.), S20.

Wallez, C., & Vauclair, J. (2011). Right hemisphere dominance for emotion processing in baboons. *Brain and Cognition, 75*(2), 164–169.

Wallrabenstein, I., Gerber, J., Rasche, S., Croy, I., Kurtenbach, S., Hummel, T., et al. (2015). The smelling of Hedione results in sex-differentiated human brain activity. *NeuroImage, 113*, 365–373.

Wang, A. T., Lee, S. S., Sigman, M., & Dapretto, M. (2007). Reading affect in the face and voice: Neural correlates of interpreting communicative intent in children and adolescents with autism spectrum disorders. *Archives of General Psychiatry, 64*, 698–708.

Wapner, W., Judd, T., & Gardner, H. (1978). Visual agnosia in an artist. *Cortex, 14*, 343–364.

Warrington, E. K. (1982). Neuropsychological studies of object recognition. *Philosophical Transactions of the Royal Society of London. Series B, Biological Sciences, 298*, 13–33.

Warrington, E. K., & Shallice, T. (1969). The selective impairment of auditory verbal short-term memory. *Brain, 92*(4), 885–896.

Warrington, E. K., & Shallice, T. (1984). Category specific semantic impairments. *Brain, 107*, 829–854.

Watson, D., Wiese, D., Vaidya, J., & Tellegen, A. (1999). The two general activation systems of affect: Structural findings, evolutionary considerations, and psychobiological evidence. *Journal of Personality and Social Psychology, 76*(5), 820.

Watts, D. J., & Strogatz, S. H. (1998). Collective dynamics of "small-world" networks. *Nature, 393*, 440–442.

Webb, T. W., & Graziano, M. S. A. (2015, April 23). The attention schema theory: A mechanistic account of subjective awareness. *Frontiers in Psychology, 6*.

Weeks, S. J., & Hobson., R. P. (1987). The salience of facial expression for autistic children. *Journal of Child Psychology and Psychiatry, 28*(1), 137–152.

Weickert, T. W., Goldberg, T. E., Mishara, A., Apud, J. A., Kolachana, B. S., Egan, M. F., et al. (2004). Catechol-O-methyltransferase val108/158met genotype predicts working memory response to antipsychotic medications. *Biological Psychiatry, 56*, 677–682.

Weierich, M. R., Wright, C. I., Negreira, A., Dickerson, B. C., & Barrett, L. F. (2010). Novelty as a dimension in the affective brain. *NeuroImage, 49*, 2871–2878.

Weigelt, S., Koldewyn, K., & Kanwisher, N. (2012). Face identity recognition in autism spectrum disorders: A review of behavioral studies. *Neuroscience and Biobehavioral Reviews, 36*(3), 1060–1084.

Weigelt, S., Koldewyn, K., & Kanwisher, N. (2013). Face recognition deficits in autism spectrum disorders are both domain specific and process specific. *PLoS One, 8*(9), e74541.

Weinberger, N. M. (1995). Retuning the brain by fear conditioning. In M. S. Gazzaniga (Ed.), *The cognitive neurosciences* (pp. 1071–1089). Cambridge, MA: MIT Press.

Weinberger, N. M. (2004). Specific long-term memory traces in primary auditory cortex. *Nature Reviews Neuroscience, 5*(4), 279–290.

Weinberger, N. M. (2007). Associative representational plasticity in the auditory cortex: A synthesis of two disciplines. *Learning & Memory, 14*(1–2), 1–16.

Weiner, K. S., & Grill-Spector, K. (2015). The evolution of face processing networks. *Trends in Cognitive Sciences, 19*(5), 240–241.

Weiskrantz, L. (1956). Behavioral changes associated with ablation of the amygdaloid complex in monkeys. *Journal of Comparative and Physiological Psychology, 49*, 381–391.

Weiskrantz, L. (1974). Visual capacity in the hemianopic field following a restricted occipital ablation. *Brain, 97*, 709–728.

Weiskrantz, L. (1986). *Blindsight: A case study and implications.* Oxford: Oxford University Press.

Wells, D. L., & Millsopp, S. (2009). Lateralized behaviour in the domestic cat, *Felis silvestris catus. Animal Behaviour, 78*(2), 537–541.

Werker, J. F., & Hensch, T. K. (2015). Critical period in speech production: New directions. *Annual Review of Psychology, 66*, 173–196.

Wernicke, C. (1876). Das Urwindungssystem des menschlichen Gehirns. *Archiv für Psychiatrie und Nervenkrankheiten, 6*, 298–326.

Wessinger, C. M., Buonocore, M. H., Kussmaul, C. L., & Mangun, G. R. (1997). Tonotopy in human auditory cortex examined with functional magnetic resonance imaging. *Human Brain Mapping, 5*, 18–25.

Whalen, P. J. (1998). Fear, vigilance, and ambiguity: Initial neuroimaging studies of the human amygdala. *Current Directions in Psychological Science, 7*(6), 177–188.

Whalen, P. J. (2007). The uncertainty of it all. *Trends in Cognitive Sciences, 11*, 499–500.

Whalen, P. J., Kagan, J., Cook, R. G., Davis, F. C., Kim, H., Polis, S., et al. (2004). Human amygdala responsivity to masked fearful eye whites. *Science, 306*, 2061.

Whalen, P. J., Rauch, S. L., Etcoff, N. L., McInerney, S. C., Lee, M. B., & Jenike, M. A. (1998). Masked presentations of emotional facial expressions modulate amygdala activity without explicit knowledge. *Journal of Neuroscience, 18*, 411–418.

Wheeler, E. Z., & Fellows, L. K. (2008). The human ventromedial frontal lobe is critical for learning from negative feedback. *Brain, 131*(5), 1323–1331.

Wheeler, M. A., Stussl, D. T., & Tulving, E. (1997). Toward a theory of episodic memory: The frontal lobes and autonoetic consciousness. *Psychological Bulletin, 121*(3), 331–354.

Wheeler, M. E., & Buckner, R. L. (2004). Functional-anatomic correlates of remembering and knowing. *NeuroImage, 21*(4), 1337–1349.

Wheeler, M. E., Petersen, S. E., & Buckner, R. L. (2000). Memory's echo: Vivid remembering reactivates sensory-specific cortex. *Proceedings of the National Academy of Sciences, USA, 97*, 11125–11129.

Wheeler, M. E., Shulman, G. L., Buckner, R. L., Miezin, F. M., Velanova, K., & Petersen, S. E. (2006). Evidence for separate perceptual reactivation and search processes during remembering. *Cerebral Cortex, 16*, 949–959.

Whyte, E. M., Behrmann, M., Minshew, N. J., Garcia, N. V., & Scherf, K. S. (2016). Animal, but not human, faces engage the distributed face network in adolescents with autism. *Developmental Science, 19*(2), 306–317.

Wichmann, T., & DeLong, M. R. (1996). Functional and pathophysiological models of the basal ganglia. *Current Opinion in Neurobiology, 6*, 751–758.

Wickelgren, W. A. (1974). *How to solve problems.* San Francisco: Freeman.

Wicker, B., Keysers, C., Plailly, J., Royet, J.-P., Gallese, V., & Rizzolatti, G. (2003). Both of us disgusted in my insula: The common neural basis of seeing and feeling disgust. *Neuron, 40*, 655–664.

Wiesendanger, M., Rouiller, E. M., Kazennikov, O., & Perrig, S. (1996). Is the supplementary motor area a bilaterally organized system? *Advances in Neurology, 70*, 85–93.

Williams, J. H., Whiten, A., & Singh, T. (2004). A systematic review of action imitation in autistic spectrum disorder. *Journal of Autism and Developmental Disorders, 34*, 285–299.

Williams, L. M., Das, P., Liddell, B. J., Kemp, A. H., Rennie, C. J., & Gordon, E. (2006). Mode of functional connectivity in amygdala pathways dissociates level of awareness for signals of fear. *Journal of Neuroscience, 26*(36), 9264–9271.

Willis, J., & Todorov, A. (2006). First impressions: Making up your mind after a 100-ms exposure to a face. *Psychological Science, 17*, 592–598.

Wills, T. J., Cacucci, F., Burgess, N., & O'Keefe, J. (2010). Development of the hippocampal cognitive map in preweanling rats. *Science, 328*(5985), 1573–1576.

Wilson, F. A., Scalaidhe, S. P., & Goldman-Rakic, P. S. (1993). Dissociation of object and spatial processing domains in primate prefrontal cortex. *Science, 260*, 1955–1958.

Wilson, M. A., & McNaughton, B. L. (1994). Reactivation of hippocampal ensemble memories during sleep. *Science, 265*, 676–679.

Wilson, M. A., & Tonegawa, S. (1997). Synaptic plasticity, place cells, and spatial memory: Study with second generation knockouts. *Trends in Neurosciences, 20*, 102–106.

Wiltgen, B. J., & Silva, A. J. (2007). Memory for context becomes less specific with time. *Learning and Memory, 14*, 313–317.

Wise, R. J. (2003). Language systems in normal and aphasic human subjects: Functional imaging studies and inferences from animal studies. *British Medical Bulletin, 65*, 95–119.

Withers, G. S., George, J. M., Banker, G. A., & Clayton, D. F. (1997). Delayed localization of synelfin (synuclein, NACP) to presynaptic terminals in cultured rat hippocampal neurons. *Brain Research. Developmental Brain Research, 99*, 87–94.

Woldorff, M. G., Hazlett, C. J., Fichtenholtz, H. M., Weissman, D. H., Dale, A. M., & Song, A. W. (2004). Functional parcellation of attentional control regions of the brain. *Journal of Cognitive Neuroscience, 16*(1), 149–165.

Wolf, O. T. (2017). Stress and memory retrieval: Mechanisms and consequences. *Current Opinion in Behavioral Sciences, 14*, 40–46.

Wolf, S. L., Winstein, C. J., Miller, J. M., Thompson, P. A., Taub, E., Uswatte, G., et al. (2008). Retention of upper limb function in stroke survivors who have received constraint-induced movement therapy: The EXCITE randomised trial. *Lancet Neurology, 7*, 33–40.

Wolfe, J. M., Cave, K. R., & Franzel, S. L. (1989). Guided search: An alternative to the feature integration model for visual search. *Journal of Experimental Psychology. Human Perception and Performance, 15*(3), 419.

Wolff, J. J., Gu, H., Gerig, G., Elison, J. T., Styner, M., Gouttard, S., et al. (2012). Differences in white matter fiber tract development present from 6 to 24 months in infants with autism. *American Journal of Psychiatry, 169*(6), 589–600.

Wolford, G., Miller, M. B., & Gazzaniga, M. (2000). The left hemisphere's role in hypothesis formation. *Journal of Neuroscience, 20*(6), RC64. Retrieved from http://www.jneurosci.org/cgi/content/full/20/6/RC64

Wolpert, D. M., Goodbody, S. J., & Husain, M. (1998). Maintaining internal representations: The role of the human superior parietal lobe. *Nature Neuroscience, 1*(6), 529–533.

Wolpert, D. M., Miall, R. C., & Kawato, M. (1998). Internal models in the cerebellum. *Trends in Cognitive Science, 2*, 338–347.

Wood, E. R., Dudchenko, P. A., & Eichenbaum, H. (1999). The global record of memory in hippocampal neuronal activity. *Nature, 397*, 613–616.

Woodard, J. S. (1973). *Histologic neuropathology: A color slide set.* Orange: California Medical Publications.

World Health Organization. (2015, March). Dementia [Fact sheet no. 362]. [Retrieved January 14, 2018, from https://web.archive.org/web/20150318030901/http://www.who.int/mediacentre/factsheets/fs362/en]

Wurtz, R. H., Goldberg, M. E., & Robinson, D. L. (1982). Brain mechanisms of visual attention. *Scientific American, 246*(6), 124–135.

Xuan, B., Mackie, M. A., Spagna, A., Wu, T., Tian, Y., Hof, P. R., et al. (2016). The activation of interactive attentional networks. *NeuroImage, 129*, 308–319.

Xue, G., Lu, Z., Levin, I. P., & Bechara, A. (2010). The impact of prior risk experiences on subsequent risky decision-making: The role of the insula. *NeuroImage, 50*, 709–716.

Yacoub, E., Harel, N., & Uğurbil, K. (2008). High-field fMRI unveils orientation columns in humans. *Proceedings of the National Academy of Sciences, USA, 105*(30), 10607–10612.

Yamins, D. L., Hong, H., Cadieu, C. F., Solomon, E. A., Seibert, D., & DiCarlo, J. J. (2014). Performance-optimized hierarchical models predict neural responses in higher visual cortex. *Proceedings of the National Academy of Sciences, USA, 111*(23), 8619–8624.

Yeo, B. T., Krienen, F. M., Sepulcre, J., Sabuncu, M. R., Lashkari, D., Hollinshead, M., et al. (2011). The organization of the human cerebral cortex estimated by intrinsic functional connectivity. *Journal of Neurophysiology, 106*(3), 1125–1165.

Yin, H. H., & Knowlton, B. J. (2006). The role of the basal ganglia in habit formation. *Nature, 7*, 464–476.

Yingling, C. D., & Skinner, J. E. (1976). Selective regulation of thalamic sensory relay nuclei by nucleus reticularis thalami. *Electroencephalography and Clinical Neurophysiology, 41*, 476–482.

York, G. K., & Steinberg, D. A. (2006). *An introduction to the life and work of John Hughlings Jackson with a catalogue raisonné of his writings.* London: Wellcome Trust Centre for the History of Medicine at UCL.

Zacks, J., Rypma, B., Gabrieli, J. D. E., Tversky, B., & Glover, G. H. (1999). Imagined transformations of bodies: An fMRI investigation. *Neuropsychologia, 37*(9), 1029–1040.

Zajonc, R. B. (1984). On the primacy of affect. *American Psychologist, 39*, 117–123.

Zaki, J., & Ochsner, K. (2011). Reintegrating the study of accuracy into social cognition research. *Psychological Inquiry, 22*, 159–182.

Zamanillo, D., Sprengel, R., Hvalby, O., Jensen, V., Burnashev, N., Rozov, A., et al. (1999). Importance of AMPA receptors for hippocampal synaptic plasticity but not for spatial learning. *Science, 284*, 1805–1811.

Zangaladze, A., Epstein, C. M., Grafton, S. T., & Sathian, K. (1999). Involvement of visual cortex in tactile discrimination of orientation. *Nature, 401*, 587–590.

Zanto, T. P., Rubens, M. T., Thangavel, A., & Gazzaley, A. (2011). Causal role of the prefrontal cortex in top-down modulation of visual processing and working memory. *Nature Neuroscience, 14*(5), 656–663.

Zarei, M., Johansen-Berg, H., Smith, S., Ciccarelli, O., Thompson, A. J., & Matthews, P. M. (2006). Functional anatomy of interhemispheric cortical connections in the human brain. *Journal of Anatomy, 209*(3), 311–320.

Zarkos, J. (2004). Raising the bar: A man, the "Flop" and an Olympic gold medal. *Sun Valley Guide.* Retrieved from http://www.svguide.com/s04/s04_fosburyflop.htm

Zeier, J. D., Baskin-Sommers, A. R., Hiatt Racer, K. D., & Newman, J. P. (2012). Cognitive control deficits associated with antisocial personality disorder and psychopathy. *Personality Disorders, 3*(3), 283.

Zeki, S. (1993a). The mystery of Louis Verrey. *Gesnerus, 50*, 96–112.

Zeki, S. (1993b). *A vision of the brain.* Oxford, England: Blackwell.

Zemelman, B. V., Lee, G. A., Ng, M., & Miesenböck, G. (2002). Selective photostimulation of genetically chARGed neurons. *Neuron, 33*(1), 15–22.

Zhang, J., Webb, D. M., & Podlaha, O. (2002). Accelerated protein evolution and origins of human-specific features: Foxp2 as an example. *Genetics, 162*, 1825–1835.

Zhao, J., Thiebaut de Schotten, M., Altarelli, I., Dubois, J., & Ramus, F. (2016). Altered hemispheric lateralization of white matter pathways in developmental dyslexia: Evidence from spherical deconvolution tractography. *Cortex, 76*, 51–62.

Zhou, H., Schafer, R. J., & Desimone, R. (2016). Pulvinar-cortex interactions in vision and attention. *Neuron, 89*(1), 209–220.

Zhu, Q., Song, Y., Hu, S., Li, X., Tian, M., Zhen, Z., et al. (2010). Heritability of the specific cognitive ability of face perception. *Current Biology, 20*(2), 137–142.

Zhuang, J., Randall, B., Stamatakis, E. A., Marslen-Wilson, W. D., & Tyler, L. K. (2011). The interaction of lexical semantics and cohort competition in spoken word recognition: An fMRI study. *Journal of Cognitive Neuroscience, 23*(12), 3778–3790.

Ziemann, U., Muellbacher, W., Hallett, M., & Cohen, L. G. (2001). Full text modulation of practice-dependent plasticity in human motor cortex. *Brain, 124*, 1171–1181.

Zihl, J., von Cramon, D., & Mai, N. (1983). Selective disturbance of movement vision after bilateral brain damage. *Brain, 106,* 313–340.

Zimmer, C. (2004). *Soul made flesh: The discovery of the brain—and how it changed the world.* New York: Free Press.

Zola-Morgan, S., Squire, L. R., & Amaral, D. G. (1986). Human amnesia and the medial temporal region: Enduring memory impairment following a bilateral lesion limited to field CA1 of the hippocampus. *Journal of Neuroscience, 6*(10), 2950–2967.

Zola-Morgan, S., Squire, L. R., Clower, R. P., & Rempel, N. L. (1993). Damage to the perirhinal cortex exacerbates memory impairment following lesions to the hippocampal formation. *Journal of Neuroscience, 13,* 251–265.

Zorawski, M., Blanding, N. Q., Kuhn, C. M., & LaBar, K. S. (2006). Effects of sex and stress on acquisition and consolidation of human fear conditioning. *Learning & Memory, 13,* 441–450.

Zuberbühler, K. (2001). A syntactic rule in forest monkey communication. *Animal Behaviour, 63*(2), 293–299.

Zwitserlood, P. (1989). The locus of the effects of sentential-semantic context in spoken-word processing. *Cognition, 32,* 25–64.

Credits

FRONT MATTER

Photos: Michael Gazzaniga: Office of Public Affairs and Communications/UCSB; **Richard Ivry:** Kelly Davidson Studio/eLife; **George R. Mangun:** Tamara Swaab.

CHAPTER 1

Photos: 2 Alfred Pasieka/Science Photo Library/Getty Images **4 top left** Reproduced with the permission of the Bodleian Library, University of Oxford **4 right** Reproduced with the permission of the Bodleian Library, University of Oxford **4 bottom left** The Print Collector/Alamy **5** Erich Lessing/Art Resource, NY **6** US National Library of Medicine **7 bottom center** From Luciani, Luigi. Fisologia del Homo. Le Monnier, Firenze, 1901–1911 **7 top left** General Research Division, New York Public Library, Astor, Lenox and Tilden Foundations **7 top center** General Research Division, New York Public Library, Astor, Lenox and Tilden Foundations **7 top right** General Research Division, New York Public Library, Astor, Lenox and Tilden Foundations **7 bottom left** Mary Evans Picture Library **7 bottom right** Mary Evans Picture Library/Sigmund Freud Copyrights **8** New York Academy of Medicine **9 left** akg-images/Interfoto **9 right** From Golgi, Camillo, Untersuchungenber den Flineren des Centralen und Peripherischen Nerven Systems. Fisher, Jena, 1894 **10 top right** Bibliothéque Nationale de France **10 top left** Everett Collection Historical/Alamy **10 bottom** Science Source **11 left** Everett Collection Historical/Alamy **11 right** From Budge, Julius, Lehrbuch der Speciallen Physiologie des Menschen, vol. 8 (1862) **12 bottom right** Benjamin Harris/University of New Hampshire **12 top** Courtesy of the National Library of Medicine **12 bottom left** George Rinhart/Getty Images **13 center right** Courtesy of the late George A. Miller **13 left** Hipix/Alamy **13 center left** McGill University Archives, PR050904 **13 center right** Photo by Owen Egan, Courtesy of The Montreal Neurological Institute, McGill University **14 left** Bettmann/Getty Images **14 right** Robert A. Lisak **15 left** From La Fatica, by Angelo Mosso (1891) **15 center** Fulton, J.F. Observations upon the vascularity of the human occipital lobe during visual activity. Brain (1928) 51 (3): 310–320. © Oxford University Press. **15 right** Sokoloff (2000) Seymour S. Kety, M.D. Journal of Cerebral Blood Flow & Metabolism. © 2000, Rights Managed by Nature Publishing Group. **16 right** Becker Medical Library, Washington University School of Medicine **16 left** DIZ Muenchen GmbH, Sueddeutsche Zeitung Photo/Alamy **17 right** AP Photo **17 left** Courtesy UCLA Health Sciences Media Relations **18 (both)** Seiji Ogawa, et al., (1990), Oxygenation-sensitive contrast in magnetic resonance image of rodent brain at high magnetic fields, Magn. Reson. Med., Vol. 14, Issue 1, 68, 78 ©Wiley-Liss, Inc. **19** Kwong et al. © (1992) Dynamic magnetic resonance imaging of human brain activity during primary sensory stimulation. PNAS. Courtesy of K.K. Kwong.

Drawn art: Figure 1.32 b: Reprinted from *Brain Mapping: The* Systems, Marcus E. Raichle, "Chapter 2: A Brief History of Functional Brain Mapping," pp. 33–75, Copyright © Academic Press (2000), with permission from Elsevier.

CHAPTER 2

Photos: 22 Dr. Thomas Deerinck/Visuals Unlimited, Inc. **24** Manuscripts and Archives, Yale University **25 top left** C.J. Guerin, Ph.D. MRC Toxicology Unit/Science Source **25 bottom right** CNRI/Getty Images **25 bottom center** Deco Images II/Alamy **25 bottom left** Rick Stahl/Nikon Small World **25 top center** Robert S. McNeil/Baylor College of Medicine/Science Source **25 top right** Science Source/Getty Images **26** Thomas Deerinck/Visuals Unlimited **27 bottom** CNRI/Science Source/Science Source **27 center** Courtesy Dr. S. Halpain, University of California San Diego **27 top right** docstock/Visuals Unlimited **46** Courtesy of Allen Song, Duke University **51** Courtesy of Allen Song, Duke University **53** Courtesy of Allen Song, Duke University **54 (all)** The Brain: A Neuroscience Primer by Richard F. Thompson. © 1985, 1993, 2000 by Worth Publishers. Used with permission **56** The Brain: A Neuroscience Primer by Richard F. Thompson. © 1985, 1993, 2000 by Worth Publishers. Used with permission. **65 bottom** Carolina Biological/Medical Images/DIOMEDIA **65 top** Joo Lee/Getty Images **68 (all)** Erikson et al., Neurogenesis in the adult hippocampus, Nature Medicine 4 (1998): 1312–1317. © Nature Publishing Group. **69 (all)** Erikson et al., Neurogenesis in the adult hippocampus, Nature Medicine 4 (1998): 1312–1317. © Nature Publishing Group.

CHAPTER 3

Photos: 72 Anthony Rakusen/Getty Images **80 (both)** Woodward, J.S., Histologic Neuropathology: A Color Slide Set. Orange, CA: California Medical Publications, 1973 **81 top (all)** de Leeuw et al. Progression of cerebral white matter lesions in Alzheimers disease: a new window for therapy? Journal of Neurology, Neurosurgery and Psychiatry. Sep 1, 2005;76:1286–1288. ©2005 BMJ Publishing Group **81 bottom (both)** Woodward, J.S., Histologic Neuropathology: A Color Slide Set. Orange, CA: California Medical Publications, 1973 **82 top** Holbourn, A.H.S., Mechanics of head injury, The Lancet 2: 177, 180. Copyright © 1943 Elsevier. **88 both** Rampon et al. (2000). Enrichment induces structural changes and recovery from nonspatial memory deficits in CA1 NMDAR1-knockout mice, Nature Neuroscience 3: 238–244. Copyright © 2000, Rights Managed by Nature Publishing Group. **90 top** Synthetic Neurobiology Group, MIT **90 bottom** From chapter, Transcranial magnetic stimulation & the human brain, by Megan Steven & Alvaro Pascual-Leone. Neuroethics: Defining the Issues in Theory, Practice & Policy, edited by Illes, Judith, (2005). By permission of Oxford University Press **94 (all)** Greenberg, J.O., and Adams, R.D. (Eds.), Neuroimaging: A Companion to Adams and Victor, Principles of Neurology. New York: McGraw-Hill, Inc., 1995. Reprinted by permission of McGraw-Hill, Inc. **95 (both)** Images courtesy of Dr. Megan S. Steven, Karl Doron, and Adam Riggall. Darmouth Brain Imaging Center at Darmouth College **98 all** Quiroga et al. 2005. Invariant visual representation by single neurons in the human brain, Nature 435:23 1102–1107. © 2005 Nature Publishing Group. **99 top right** Canolty et al. 2007. Frontiers in Neuroscience 1:1 185–196. Image courtesy of the authors. **99 bottom** Canolty et al., 2007 **99 top left** From Brain Electricity and the Mind, Jon Lieff, M.D. 2012 **100** Ramare/AgeFotostock **103 bottom right** James King-Holmes/Science Source **103 bottom left** Rivolta, D., Castellanos, N. P., Stawowsky, C., Helbling, S., Wibral, M., Grützner, C., & Singer, W. (2014). Source-reconstruction of event-related fields reveals hyperfunction and hypofunction of cortical circuits in antipsychotic-naive, first-episode schizophrenia patients during Mooney face processing. Journal of Neuroscience, 34(17), 5909–5917. **105** Courtesy of Marcus Raichle,

M.D./Becker Medical Library, Washington University **106 both** Vital et al. (2008). Neuroimaging in dementia. 2008. Seminars in Neurology 28(4): 467, 483. Images courtesy Gil Rabinovici, UC San Francisco and William Jagust, UC Berkeley. **109 both** Wagner et al. (1998). Building memories: Remembering and forgetting of verbal experiences as predicted by brain activity, Science 281 (1998): 1188–1191. Copyright © 1998, AAAS. **110 both** Robertson, C. E., Ratai, E. M., & Kanwisher, N. (2016). Reduced GABAergic action in the autistic brain. Current Biology, 26(1), 80–85 **112 all** Bullmore, E. T., & Bassett, D. S. (2011). Brain graphs: graphical models of the human brain connectome. Annual review of clinical psychology, 7, 113–140 **113 all** Yeo, B. T., Krienen, F. M., Sepulcre, J., Sabuncu, M. R., Lashkari, D., Hollinshead, M., & Fischl, B. (2011). The organization of the human cerebral cortex estimated by intrinsic functional connectivity. Journal of neurophysiology, 106(3), 1125–1165. **114 both** Finn, E. S., Shen, X., Scheinost, D., Rosenberg, M. D., Huang, J., Chun, M. M., Papademetris, X., & Constable, R. T. (2015). Functional connectome fingerprinting: identifying individuals using patterns of brain connectivity. Nature neuroscience, 18(11), 1664–1671. **119** Deibert et al. (1999). Neural pathways in tactile object recognition. Neurology 52 (9): 1413–1417. Lippincott Williams & Wilkins, Inc. Journals. **120** Frank et al. (2011). Neurogenetics and Pharmacology of Learning, Motivation, and Cognition. Neuropsychopharmacology 6, 133–152. Copyright © 2010, Rights Managed by Nature Publishing **121 all** Gratton, C., Lee, T. G., Nomura, E. M., & D'Esposito, M. (2013). The effect of theta-burst TMS on cognitive control networks measured with resting state fMRI. Frontiers in systems neuroscience, 7, 124.

Drawn art: Figure 3.10 a–b: Pessiglione et al., Figure 1 from "Dopamine-dependent prediction errors underpin reward-seeking behavior in humans." *Nature*, *442*(31), 1042–1045. Copyright © 2006 Nature Publishing Group. Reprinted with permission. **Figure 3.34 b:** Reprinted from *Current Biology*, *26*(1), Robertson, C.E., Ratai, E., Kanwisher, N., "Reduced GABAergic action in the autistic brain," 80–85, Copyright © Elsevier Inc. (2016), with permission from Elsevier. **Figure 3.38:** Kahn, A.E., et al., "Structural pathways supporting swift acquisition of new visuomotor skills," *Cerebral Cortex*, *26*(1), 173–184, by permission of Oxford University Press. **Figure 3.43:** Sarfaty Siegel, J., et al., Figure 3 from "Disruptions of network connectivity predict impairment in multiple behavioral domains after stroke," *PNAS*, *113*(30), E4367–E4376. Copyright © 2016 National Academy of Sciences. **Figure 3.44 b:** Gratton C, Lee TG, Nomura EM and D'Esposito M (2013). Modified from Figure 4 from The effect of theta-burst TMS on cognitive control networks measured with resting state fMRI. Front. Syst. Neurosci. *7*(124). Copyright © 2013 Gratton, Lee, Nomura and D'Esposito. Distributed under the terms of the Creative Commons Attribution License (CC BY). https://creativecommons.org/licenses/by/3.0/.

CHAPTER 4

Photos: 124 Roger Harris/Science Photo Library/Getty Images **127 left** From Brain Games® Puzzles, by Publications International, Ltd., 2016 **127 center** From Drawing on the Right Side of the Brain, 4 edition, Betty Edwards TarcherPerigee, 2012 **127 right** The Photo Works/Alamy Stock Photo **129** Arthur Toga and Paul M. Thompson (2003). Mapping Brain Asymmetry, Nature Reviews Neuroscience 4, 37–48. © 2003 Rights managed by Nature Publishing Group. Photo Courtesy Dr. Arthur W. Toga and Dr. Paul M. Thompson, Laboratory of Neuro Imaging at UCLA **130 both** Hutsler (2003). The specialized structure of human language cortex. Brain and Language. August 2003. Copyright © Elsevier. **132 all** Sabine Hofer & Jens Frahm. (September 2006). Topography of the human corpus callosum revisited-Comprehensive fiber tractography using diffusion tensor magnetic resonance imaging. NeuroImage, 32, 989–994. 2006 Elsevier **133** Courtesy of Pietro Gobbi and Daniele Di Motta, Atlas of Anatomy Central Nervous System http://www.biocfarm.unibo.it/aunsnc/Default.htm **133 both** Courtesy of Pietro Gobbi and Daniele Di Motta, Atlas of Anatomy Central Nervous System http://www.biocfarm.unibo.it/aunsnc/Default.htm **137** Michael Gazzaniga **138** Michael Gazzaniga **143 all** David J. Turk, Todd F. Heatherton, William M. Kelley, Margaret G. Funnell, Michael S. Gazzaniga, and C. Neil Macreae, Mike or me? Self-recognition in a split-brain patient. Sept. 2002. Nature Neuroscience, vol. 5, no. 9, pp. 841–2. ©2002 Nature Publishing Group. **144 all** DeJong, The Neurologic Examination, 5th edition. Philadelphia, Pennsylvania: J.B. Lippincott Company; 1992 **153 all** Phelps, E. A., and Gazzaniga, M. S. (1992). Hemispheric differences in mnemonic processing: The effects of left hemisphere interpretation. Neuropsychologia, 30, 293, 297. © 2012 Elsevier Ltd. All rights reserved. **155 all** Gazzaniga, M.S. 2000. Cerebral specialization and interhemispheric communication. Does the corpus callosum enable the human condition? Brain 123: 1293,1326. © 2000 Oxford University Press.

Drawn art: Figure 4.24: Republished with permission of SAGE Publications, Inc. Journals, from "Guided visual search is a left-hemisphere process in split-brain patients," Kingstone, et al., *Psychological Science*, *6*(2), 1995; permission conveyed through Copyright Clearance Center, Inc. **Figure 4.27:** Reprinted from *Neuropsychologia*, *24*(2), Efron, Robertson, & Delis, "Hemispheric specialization of memory for visual hierarchical stimuli," 205–214, Copyright © Elsevier Ltd. (1985), with permission from Elsevier.

CHAPTER 5

Photos: 168 Nick Norman/Getty Images **172 top** Seymour/Photo Researchers/Science Source **172 bottom (both)** Science Photo Library/Science Source **175 (all)** Sobel et al. (1998) Sniffing and smelling: separate subsystems in the human olfactory cortex. *Nature* 92: 282–286. © (1998) Rights Managed by Nature Publishing Group **176 (all)** Gelstein, S., et al. (2011) Human tears contain a chemo-signal. Science, 331(6014), 226–230 **179 (all)** Chen, X., et al. (2011) A gusto-topic map of taste qualities in the mammalian brain. *Science*, 333(6047), 1262–1266 **180 (all)** Peng, Y., et al. (2015) Sweet and bitter taste in the brain of awake behaving animals. *Nature*, 527(7579), 512–515 **183 left** BrazilPhotos.com/Alamy **183 right** Paul Chmielowiec/Getty Images **187** Moerel, M., et al. (2013) Processing of natural sounds: characterization of multi-peak spectral tuning in human auditory cortex. *Journal of Neuroscience*, 33(29), 11888–11898 **189 left** Roy Lawe/Alamy **189 right** All Canada Photos/Alamy Stock Photo **197 (all top)** © David Somers **197 (all bottom)** Yacoub et al. July 29, (2008) PNAS, vol. 105, no. 30, pp. 10607–10612. © 2008 National Academy of Sciences of the USA **203** © manu/Fotolia.com **204 (all)** Gallant et al. (2000). A human extra-striate area functionally homologous to macaque V4, *Neuron* 27 2000: 227–235. © (2000) Elsevier **205 (all top)** Gallant et al. (2000). A human extra-striate area functionally homologous to macaque V4, *Neuron* 27 2000: 227–235. © (2000) Elsevier **205 (bottom left)** Musée d'Orsay, Paris. Photo: Giraudon/Art Resource **205 (bottom right)** © 2018 Estate of Pablo Picasso/Artists Rights Society (ARS), New York, NY. Photo: TPX/age fotostock. All rights reserved **208** Jon Driver and Toemme Noesselt, (January 10, 2008). Multisensory interplay reveals cross-modal influences on sensory-specific brain regions, neural responses, and judgments. *Neuron*, Vol. 57, Issue 1 11–23. doi.1016/j.neuron.2007.12.013. © 2008 Elsevier Inc. **210** Romke Rouw and H. Steven Scholte, University of Amsterdam. Increased structural connectivity in grapheme-color synesthesia. *Nature Neuroscience* 10, 792–797 (2007); Published online: 21 May 2007 | doi:10.1038/nn1906. © (2007) Rights Managed by Nature Publishing Group **212 (all)** Bedny, M., et al. (2015) Visual cortex responds to spoken language in blind children. *Journal of Neuroscience*, 35(33), 11674–11681 **214** Merabet, L.B., et al. (2008) Rapid and Reversible Recruitment of Early Visual Cortex for Touch. PLoS ONE 3(8): e3046. doi:10.1371/journal.pone.0003046 **215 left** Kolasinski, J., Makin, T. R., Logan, J. P., Jbabdi, S., Clare, S., Stagg, C. J., & Johansen-Berg, H. (2016). Perceptually relevant remapping of human somatotopy in 24 hours. eLife **215 right** Kolasinski, J., et al. (2016).

Perceptually relevant remapping of human somatotopy in 24 hours eLife **218 both** Falabella, P., et al. (2017). Argus II Retinal Prosthesis System In Artificial Vision (pp. 49–63). Springer International Publishing.

Drawn art: Figure 5.5 a–b: Chandrashekar, J., et al. Figure 1a from "The receptors and cells for mammalian cells, buds and papillae," *Nature, 444*(7117), 288. Reprinted by permission from Macmillan Publishers Ltd., Copyright © 2006, Nature Publishing Group. **Figure 5.7 b–c:** Peng, Y., Gillis-Smith, S., Jin, H., Tränkner, D., Ryba, N. J., & Zuker, C. S. Figure 1 from "Sweet and bitter taste in the brain of awake behaving animals," *Nature, 527*(7579), 512–515. Reprinted by permission from Macmillan Publishers Ltd., Copyright © 2015, Nature Publishing Group. **Figure 5.40:** Republished with permission of Society for Neuroscience, from "Occipital transcranial magnetic stimulation has opposing effects on visual and auditory stimulus detection: implications for multisensory interactions," Romei, V., Murray, M. M., Merabet, L. B. & Thut, G., *Journal of Neuroscience, 27*(43), 2007; permission conveyed through Copyright Clearance Center, Inc. **Figure 5.45 b:** Kolasinski, J., Makin, T. R., Logan, J. P., Jbabdi, S., Clare, S., Stagg, C. J., & Johansen-Berg, H. Adapted from Figure 1B from "Perceptually relevant remapping of human somatotopy in 24 hours," eLife, *5*(17280). Copyright © 2016 Kolasinski et al. Distributed under the terms of the Creative Commons Attribution License (CC BY). https://creativecommons.org/licenses/by/4.0/. **Figure 5.46:** Reprinted with permission from Cochlear Americas. **Figure 5.47 a:** Zrenner et al., Figure 2a-c from "Subretinal electronic chips allow blind patients to read letters and combine them to words." *Proceedings of the Royal Society B, 278*, 1489–1497. Copyright © The Royal Society. Distributed under the terms of the Creative Commons Attribution License (CC BY 4.0). https://creativecommons.org/licenses/by/4.0/.

CHAPTER 6

Photos: 222 Stephanie Keith/Getty Images **225 top left** Adelrepeng/Dreamstime.com **225 center left** Carl & Ann Purcell/Getty Images **226** Michael Doolittle/Alamy Stock Photo **227** Courtesy of the Laboratory of Neuro Imaging at UCLA and Martinos Center for Biomedical Imaging at MGH, Consortium of the Human Connectome Project www.humanconnectomeproject.org **231 both bottom** Culham et. al. Ventral occipital lesions impair object guarantors brain. Brain, 2003, 126, 2463–2475, by permission of Oxford University Press **233 right** Adam Eastland Art + Architecture/Alamy Stock Photo **233 left** Denys Kuvaiev/Alamy Stock Photo **233 center** Konstantin Labunskiy/Alamy Stock Photo **234** Kanwisher et al. A locus in human extrastriate cortex for visual shape analysis, Journal of Cognitive Neuroscience 9 (1997): 133–142. Copyright © 1997, Massachusetts Institute of Technology **235 bottom left** Emberson, L. L., Crosswhite, S. L., Richards, J. E., & Aslin, R. N. (2017). The lateral occipital cortex is selective for object shape, not texture/color, at six months. Journal of Neuroscience, 37(13), 3698–3703. **237** Kyodo/AP **239 all top** Cohen et al. The visual word form area Spatial and temporal characterization of an initial stage of reading in normal subjects and posterior split-brain patients. 2000, Brain, Vol. 123, Issue 2, pp. 291–307. © 2000 Oxford University Press. **240 all** Kriegeskorte, N. (2015). Deep neural networks: a new framework for modeling biological vision and brain information processing. Annual review of vision science, 1, 417–446. **241 all top, center** Yamins, D. L., et al. (2014). Performance-optimized hierarchical models predict neural responses in higher visual cortex. Proceedings of the National Academy of Sciences, 111(23), 8619–8624. **242 right** Bar, M., Kassam, K. S., Ghuman, A. S., Boshyan, J., Schmid, A. M., Dale, A. M. & Halgren, E. (2006). Top-down facilitation of visual recognition. PNAS, 103(2), 449–454. **243 all** Wikimedia Commons **244 all** Kay et al. (2008). Identifying natural images from human brain activity. Nature 452, 352–355. © Nature Publishing Group **245** Kay et al. (2008). Identifying natural images from human brain activity. Nature 452, 352–355. © Nature Publishing Group **246 all top** Courtesy Jack Gallant **246 all bottom** Naselaris et al. (2009). Bayesian Reconstruction of natural Images from Human brain Activity. Neuron 63(6), 902–915, September 24, 2009 © 2009 Elsevier. **247 all** Horikawa, T., Tamaki, M., Miyawaki, Y., & Kamitani, Y. (2013). Neural decoding of visual imagery during sleep. Science, 340(6132), 639–642. **249 all** Baylis et al. (1985) Selectivity between faces in the responses of a population of neurons in the cortex in the superior temporal sulcus of the monkey, Brain Research pp. 91–102. Copyright © 1985, Elsevier. **250 all** Tsao, et al, A Cortical Region Consisting Entirely of Face-Selective Cells, Science 311: 670–674 (2006). Reprinted with permission from AAAS. **251 all** McCarthy et al. (1997) Face-specific processing in the human fusiform gyrus, Journal of Cognitive Neuroscience p. 605, 610. Copyright © 1997 Massachusetts Institute of Technology. **252** Weiner, K. S., & Grill-Spector, K. (2015). The evolution of face processing networks. Trends in cognitive sciences, 19(5), 240–241. **254 all** Chang, L., & Tsao, D. Y. (2017). The code for facial identity in the primate brain. Cell, 169(6), 1013–1028. **255 all** Chang, L., & Tsao, D. Y. (2017). The code for facial identity in the primate brain. Cell, 169(6), 1013–1028. **256** Taylor et al. (2007) Functional MRI Analysis of Body and Body part Representations in the Extrasite and Fusiform Body Areas. J. Neurophysiol. Sept. 2007 98 no. 3:1626–1633. © 2007 American Physiological Society **257 top all** Moeller, S., Crapse, T., Chang, L., & Tsao, D. Y. (2017). The effect of face patch microstimulation on perception of faces and objects. Nature neuroscience, 20(5), 743. **257 bottom all** Schalk, G., et al. (2017). Facephenes and rainbows: Causal evidence for functional and anatomical specificity of face and color processing in the human brain. PNAS, 201713447. **258 all** Pitcher et al. (2009) Triple Dissociation of Faces, Bodies, and Objects in Extrastriate Cortex. Current Biology, Feb.24, 2009, 19(4) pp. 319, 324. © 2009 Elsevier **261 all** McCarthy, G., and Warrington, E.K., Visual associative agnosia: A Clinico-anatomical study of a single case, Journal of Neurology, Neurosurgery and Psychiatry 49 (1986): 1233, 1240. Copyright © 1986, British Medical Journal Publishing Group. **264 all** Martin, A. (2007). The representation of object concepts in the brain. Annu. Rev. Psychol., 58, 25–45. **267 bottom** van Kooten et al. (2008). Neurons in the fusiform gyrus are fewer and smaller in autism. Brain Copyright © 2008, Oxford University Press. **268** Scala/Art Resource, NY **269 all** Cohen et al. The visual word form area Spatial and temporal characterization of an initial stage of reading in normal subjects and posterior split-brain patients. 2000, Brain, Vol. 123, Issue 2, pp. 291–307. © 2000 Oxford University Press. **270 both** Thompson, P. (1980) Margaret Thatcher: A new illusion. Perception 9 (4) 483–484. Copyright © Pion Ltd, London. www.envplan.com.

Drawn art: Figure 6.18 a–b: Kriegeskorte, N., Figures 1B and 1C from "Deep neural networks: a new framework for modelling biological vision and brain information processing," *Annual Review of Vision Science, 1*(1), 417–446. Reprinted with permission. **Figure 6.21:** Bar, M., Kassam, K. S., Ghuman, A. S., Boshyan, J., Schmid, A. M., Dale, A. M., et al, Figure 1 from "Top-down facilitation of visual recognition," *PNAS* 2006, *103*(2), 449–454. Copyright © 2006 National Academy of Sciences. **Figure 6.22 a–b:** Bar, M., Kassam, K. S., Ghuman, A. S., Boshyan, J., Schmid, A. M., Dale, A. M., et al, Figure 1 from "Top-down facilitation of visual recognition," *PNAS* 2006, *103*(2), 449–454. Copyright © 2006 National Academy of Sciences. **Figure 6.28 a–b:** From Horikawa, T., Tamaki, M., Miyawaki, Y., & Kamitani, Y., Figures 1A and 3E from "Neural decoding of visual imagery during sleep," *Science, 340*(6132), 639–642. Reprinted with permission from AAAS. **Figure 6.33:** Reprinted from *Cognition, 83*(1), Bentin & Carmel, "Domain specificity versus expertise: Factors influencing distinct processing of faces", 1–29, Copyright © Elsevier B.V. (2002), with permission from Elsevier. **Figures 6.34 d and 6.35 b:** Reprinted from *Cell, 169*(6), Chang, L. & Tsao, D. Y., "The code for facial identity in the primate brain," 1013–1028, Copyright © Elsevier Inc. (2017), with permission from Elsevier. **Figure 6.37 b:** Moeller, S., Crapse, T., Chang, L., & Tsao, D. Y., Figure 2A from "The effect of face patch microstimulation on perception of faces and objects," *Nature Neuroscience, 20*(5), 743–752. Reprinted by permission from Macmillan Publishers Ltd., Copyright © 2017, Nature Publishing Group. **Figure 6.41 a–b:** Behrmann, M., et al., Figure from "Intact visual imagery and impaired visual perception in a patient with visual agnosia," *Journal of Experimental Psychology: Human Perception and Performance, 20.* Copyright © 1994 by the American Psychological Association. Reprinted by permission. **Figure 6.44:** Mahon, B. Z., & Caramazza, A., Figure 2 from "Concepts and categories: A cognitive neuropsychological perspective," *Annual Review of Psychology, 60,* 27–51. Reprinted with permission.

CHAPTER 7

Photos: 274 Alan Poulson Photography/Shutterstock **277** Courtesy National Library of Medicine, Bethesda, Maryland **278 all** © 2018 Artists Rights Society (ARS), New York/VG Bild-Kunst, Bonn **279 bottom** Institute of Neurology and Institute of Cognitive Neuroscience, University College London, London, UK **284** Ronald C. James **290** McAdams et al. (2005) Attention Modulates the Responses of Simple Cells in Monkey Primary Visual Cortex, Journal of Neuroscience, Vol. 25, No. 47, pp. 11023–33. Copyright © 2005 by the Society for Neuroscience. **291 top all** Tootell et al., 1998, Neuron **292 all** Kastner, S., et al. (1998). Mechanisms of directed attention in the human extrastriate cortex as revealed by functional MRI. Science, 282(5386), 108–111. **293 both** Hopf et al. (2006). The neural site of attention matches the spatial scale of perception. Journal of Neuroscience, 26, 3532–3540. © Society for Neuroscience. **295 bottom center** O'Connor et al. (2002) Attention modulates responses in the human lateral geniculate nucleus. Nature Neuroscience, Nov 5 (11): 1203–9. Copyright © 2002, Rights Managed by Nature Publishing Group. **300** DavorLovincic/iStockphoto **303 all** Schoenfeld et al. (2007). Spatio-temporal Analysis of Feature-Based Attention, Cerebral Cortex, 17:10. Copyright 2007 by Oxford University Press. **310 all** Hopfinger et al. (2000) The neural mechanism of top-down attentional control, Nature Neuroscience 3 (2000): 284–291. Copyright © 2000, Rights Managed by Nature Publishing Group. **313 all** Cosman, J. D., et al. (2015). Transient reduction of visual distraction following electrical stimulation of the prefrontal cortex. Cognition, 145, 73–76.

Drawn art: Figure 7.4: Fruhmann, B.M., Johannsen, L. & Karnath, H.O., Figure 1 from "Time course of eye and head deviation in spatial neglect," *Neuropsychology* 22(6), 697–702. Copyright © 2008 by the American Psychological Association. Reprinted by permission. **Figure 7.19:** Republished with permission of Society for Neuroscience, from "Attention Modulates the Responses of Simple Cells in Monkey Primary Visual Cortex," McAdams & Reid, *Journal of Neuroscience, 25*(47), 2005; permission conveyed through Copyright Clearance Center, Inc. **Figure 7.22 d–e:** From Kastner, S., De Weerd, P., Desimone, R., & Ungerleider, L. G. (1998), "Mechanisms of directed attention in the human extrastriate cortex as revealed by functional MRI," *Science, 282*(5386), 108–111. Reprinted with permission from AAAS. **Figure 7.24 a–d:** Republished with permission of Society for Neuroscience, from "The neural site of attention matches the spatial scale of perception," Hopf, J.M., Luck, S.J., Boelmans, K., Schoenfeld, M.A., Boehler, C.N., Rieger, J., & Heinz, H. J., *Journal of Neuroscience, 26,* 2009; permission conveyed through Copyright Clearance Center, Inc. **Figure 7.27 a–b:** McAlonan, K., Cavanaugh, J., & Wurtz, R.H., Adapted from figure 1b,c of "Guarding the gateway to cortex with attention in visual thalamus." *Nature, 456,* 391–394. Copyright © 2008 Nature Publishing Group. Reprinted with permission. **Figure 7.30 a–b:** Republished with permission of MIT Press, from "Attention-related modulation of sensory-evoked brain activity in a visual search task," Luck, S.J., Fan, S. & Hillyard, S. A., *Journal of Cognitive Neuroscience, 5*(2), 188–195, 1993; permission conveyed through Copyright Clearance Center, Inc. **Figure 7.32 a–b:** Reprinted from *Vision Research, 47*(1), Liu, et al., "Comparing the time course and efficacy of spatial and feature-based attention," 108–113, Copyright © Elsevier Ltd. (2007), with permission from Elsevier. **Figure 7.33 a–b:** Hillard, S. & Munte, T. F., Adapted from figures 3 and 4 of "Selective attention to color and location: An analysis with event-related brain potentials." *Perception & Psychophysics,* Vol. 36, No. 2, 185–198. Reprinted by permission of Springer Science + Business Media. **Figure 7.35:** M. Schoenfeld, JM Hopf, A. Martinez, H. Mai, C. Sattler, A. Gasde, HJ Heinze, S. Hillyard, "Spatio-temporal analysis of feature-based attention," *Cerebral Cortex,* 2007, *17*(10), 2468–2477, by permission of Oxford University Press. **Figure 7.36 a–d:** Republished with permission of Society for Neuroscience, from "Dynamic Interaction of Object- and Space-Based Attention in Retinotopic Visual Areas," Mueller & Kleinschmidt, *Journal of Neuroscience,* 23(30), 2003; permission conveyed through Copyright Clearance Center, Inc. **Figure 7.42 a–b:** Armstrong, K. M., Schafer, R. J., Chang, M. H. & Moore, T., Figure 7.3 from "Attention and action in the frontal eye field." In R. Mangun (Ed.), *The Neuroscience of Attention* (pp. 151–166). Oxford, England: Oxford University Press. Reprinted with permission. **Figure 7.43 a–b:** Morishima, Y., Akaishi, R., Yamada, Y., Okuda, J., Toma, K., & Sakai, K. Figure 4 a & b from "Task-specific signal transmission from prefrontal cortex in visual selective attention." *Nature Neuroscience, 12,* 85–91. Reprinted by permission from Macmillan Publishers Ltd, Copyright © 2009, Nature Publishing Group. **Figure 7.44 c:** Reprinted from *Cognition,* 145, Cosman, J. D., Atreya, P. V., & Woodman, G. F., "Transient reduction of visual distraction following electrical stimulation of the prefrontal cortex," pp. 73–76, Copyright © Elsevier Ltd. (2015), with permission from Elsevier. **Figure 7.47 a–b:** From Bisley & Goldberg (2003), "Neuronal activity in the lateral intraparietal area and spatial attention," *Science, 299*(5603), 81–86. Reprinted with permission from AAAS. **Figure 7.53 a–c:** From Saalmann, Y. B., Pinsk, M. A., Wang, L., Li, X., & Kastner, S. (2012), "The pulvinar regulates information transmission between cortical areas based on attention demands," *Science,* 337(6095), pp. 753–756. Reprinted with permission from AAAS.

CHAPTER 8

Photos: 324 Damon Winter/The New York Times/Redux **326 (both)** Lewis P. Rowland (Ed.), Merritt, *Textbook of Neurology, 8th edition.* Philadelphia: Lea & Febiger, 1989, p. 661. Copyright © 1989 by Lea & Febiger **333** Ejaz, N., Hamada, M., & Diedrichsen, J. (2015). Hand use predicts the structure of representations in sensorimotor cortex. *Nature neuroscience,* 18(7), 1034–1040. **344** Kao, J. C., et al. (2015). Single-trial dynamics of motor cortex and their applications to brain-machine interfaces. *Nature Communications,* 6. **349** Hamilton, A. F. & Grafton, S.T. 2007. Action outcomes are represented in human inferior frontoparietal cortex. Cerebral Cortex, 18, 1160–1168 **351** Calvo-Merino et al. (2005) *Cerebral Cortex,* Vol. 15 Action Observation and Acquired Motor Skills: an fMRI Study with Expert Dancers, 1243, 1249. Copyright Elsevier 2005. **352** Agliot, et al. 2008. Action anticipation and motor resonance in elite basketball players. Copyright © 2006, Nature Neuroscience, vol. 11, 1109–1116 **356** Hochberg et al. (2006) Neuronal ensemble control of prosthetic devices by a human with tetraplegia. *Nature* July 13; 442:164,171. Copyright © 2006, Rights Managed by Nature Publishing Group. **362 (both)** Greenberg, J.O., and Adams, R.D. (Eds.), *Neuroimaging: A Companion to Adams and Victor, Principles of Neurology.* New York: MacGraw-Hill, Inc., 1995. Reprinted by permission of McGraw-Hill, Inc. **363 (all)** Redgrave, P., et al. (2010). Goal-directed and habitual control in the basal ganglia: implications for Parkinson, disease. *Nature Reviews Neuroscience,* 11(11), 760. **372 top left** Scott Markewitz/Getty Images **372 top right** ZUMA Press, Inc./Alamy Stock Photo **372 bottom left** triloks/Getty Images **372 bottom right** Lebrecht Music and Arts Photo Library/Alamy Stock Photo **373** Kawai, R., et al. (2015). Motor cortex is required for learning but not for executing a motor skill. Neuron, 86(3), 800–812. **374** Michael Steele/Getty Images.

Drawn art: Figure 8.8 a–b: Reprinted from *Progress in brain research*, *218*, Baker, S. N., Zaaimi, B., Fisher, K. M., Edgley, S. A., & Soteropoulos, D. S., "Pathways mediating functional recovery," 389–412. Copyright © Elsevier B. V. (2015), with permission from Elsevier. **Figure 8.9 b:** Ejaz, N., Hamada, M., & Diedrichsen, J. Figure 4d from "Hand use predicts the structure of representations in sensorimotor cortex," *Nature neuroscience*, 2015, *18*(7), 1034–1040. Reprinted by permission from Macmillan Publishers Ltd, Copyright © 2015, Nature Publishing Group. **Figure 8.10:** Reprinted from *Brain and language*, *127*(2), Binkofski, F., & Buxbaum, L. J., "Two action systems in the human brain," 222–229, Copyright © Elsevier Inc. (2013), with permission from Elsevier. **Figure 8.17 a–c:** Churchland, M. M., Cunningham, J. P., Kaufman, M.T. Ryu, S.I. & Shenoy, K.V., Figure 2 from "Cortical preparatory activity: representation of movement or first cog in a dynamical machine?" *Neuron*, *68*, 387–400. Copyright © 2010 by Elsevier Science & Technology Journals. Reproduced with permission of Elsevier Science & Technology Journals. **Figure 8.18 a–b:** Kao, J. C., Nuyujukian, P., Ryu, S. I., Churchland, M. M., Cunningham, J. P., & Shenoy, K. V. Figures 4 and 6 from "Single-trial dynamics of motor cortex and their applications to brain-machine interfaces," *Nature Communications*, *6* (2015). Reprinted by permission from Macmillan Publishers Ltd, Copyright © 2015, Nature Publishing Group. **Figure 8.19:** Cisek, P. & Kalasca, J. F., Figure 1 from "Neural mechanisms for interacting with a world full of action choices." *Annual Review of Neuroscience*, *33*, 269–298. Reprinted with permission. **Figure 8.20:** Cisek, P. & Kalasca, J. F., Figure 2 from "Neural mechanisms for interacting with a world full of action choices." *Annual Review of Neuroscience*, *33*, 269–298. Reprinted with permission. **Figure 8.23:** Hamilton & Grafton, "Action outcomes are represented in human inferior frontoparietal cortex," *Cerebral Cortex*, 2007, *18*(5), 1160–1168, by permission of Oxford University Press. **Figure 8.27 a:** Clarkson, A.N., Huang, B.S., MacIsaac, S., Mody, I., & Carmichael, S.T. Figure 1b from "Reducing excessive GABA-mediated tonic inhibition promotes functional recovery after stroke," *Nature*, 2010, *468*(7321), 305–309. Reprinted by permission from Macmillan Publishers Ltd, Copyright © 2010, Nature Publishing Group. **Figure 8.29 a–d:** Ganguly, K. & Carmena, J. M., (2009) Figure 2 and 3 from "Emergence of a stable cortical map for neuroprosthetic control." *PLoS Biology* *7*(7): e1000153. doi:10.1371/ journal.pbio.1000153. Copyright © 2009 Ganguly, Carmena. Distributed under the terms of the Creative Commons Attribution License (CC BY 4.0). https://creativecommons.org/licenses/by/4.0/. **Figure 8.30 e:** Hochberg et al., Figure 4 from "Neuronal ensemble control of prosthetic devices by a human with tetraplegia," *Nature*, 2006, *442*, 164–171. Reprinted by permission from Macmillan Publishers Ltd, Copyright © 2006, Nature Publishing Group. **Figure 8.31 a:** Reprinted from *The Lancet*, *389*(10081), Ajiboye, A. B., Willett, F. R., Young, D. R., Memberg, W. D., Murphy, B. A., Miller, J. P., "Restoration of reaching and grasping movements through brain-controlled muscle stimulation in a person with tetraplegia: a proof-of-concept demonstration," 1821–1830, Copyright © Elsevier Ltd. (2017), with permission from Elsevier. **Figure 8.37 a:** Republished with permission of Society for Neuroscience, from "High-frequency stimulation of the subthalamic nucleus suppresses oscillatory ß activity in patients with Parkinson's disease in parallel with improvement in motor performance," Kühn, A. A., Kempf, F., Brücke, C., Doyle, L. G., Martinez-Torres, I., Pogosyan, A., *Journal of Neuroscience*, *28*(24), 2008; permission conveyed through Copyright Clearance Center, Inc. **Figure 8.37 b:** Reprinted from *Neuron*, *76*(5), Li, Q., Ke, Y., Chan, D. C., Qian, Z. M., Yung, K. K., Ko, H., & Yung, W. H., "Therapeutic deep brain stimulation in Parkinsonian rats directly influences motor cortex," 1030–1041, Copyright © Elsevier Inc. (2012), with permission from Elsevier. **Figure 8.39:** Martin et al., "Throwing while looking through prisms. I. Focal olivocerebellar lesions impair adaptation." *Brain*, 1996, *119*, 1183–1198, by permission of Oxford University Press. **Figure 8.40:** Republished with permission of Society for Neuroscience, from "Dissociating visual and motor directional selectivity using visuomotor adaptation," Haar, S., Donchin, O., & Dinstein, I., *Journal of Neuroscience*, 35(17), 2015; permission conveyed through Copyright Clearance Center, Inc. **Figure 8.41 a–b:** Martin et al., "Throwing while looking through prisms. I. Focal olivocerebellar lesions impair adaptation." *Brain*, 1996, *119*, 1183–1198, by permission of Oxford University Press. **Figure 8.42:** Galea, J. M., Vazquez, A., Pasricha, N., Dexivry J. J. O. & Celnik, P., "Dissociating the roles of the cerebellum and motor cortex during adaptive learning: The motor cortex retains what the cerebellum learns. *Cerebral Cortex*, 2010, *21*(8), 1761–1770, by permission of Oxford University Press. **Figure 8.43:** Republished with permission of MIT Press, from "Spatiotemporal prediction modulates the perception of self-produced stimuli," Blakemore, S. J., Frith, C. D., & Wolpert, D. M., *Journal of Cognitive Neuroscience*, *11*(5), 551–559, 1999; permission conveyed through Copyright Clearance Center, Inc. **Figure 8.45 b–d:** Reprinted from *Neuron*, 2015, *86*(3), Kawai, R., Markman, T., Poddar, R., Ko, R., Fantana, A.L., Dhawale, A.K., Kampff, A.R. and Ölveczky, "Motor cortex is required for learning but not for executing a motor skill,» 800–812. Copyright © Elsevier Inc. (2015), with permission from Elsevier. **Figure 8.46:** Reprinted from *Neuroimage*, *36* (Suppl. 2), Johansen-Berg, H., Della-Maggiore, V., Behrens, T. E., Smith, S. M. & Paus, T., "Integrity of white matter in the corpus callosum correlates with bimanual co-ordination skills," T16–T21, Copyright © Elsevier Inc. (2007), with permission from Elsevier.

CHAPTER 9

Photos: 378 Blend Images/Alamy **380** H. Urbach (ed.), MRI in Epilepsy, Medical Radiology. Diagnostic Imaging, DOI: 10.1007/174_2012_775, Springer-Verlag Berlin Heidelberg 2013 **387 both** Markowitsch et al. (1999) Short-term memory deficit after focal parietal damage, Journal of Clinical & Experimental Neuropsychology 21 (1999): 784–797. Copyright © 1999 Routledge. **389 all** Jonides et al. (1998) Inhibition in verbal working memory revealed by brain activation. PNAS. Vol. 95 no. 14. Copyright © 1998, The National Academy of Science. **390** Drawing © Ruth Tulving, Courtesy the artist. **392 both** Barnes, T. D., Kubota, Y., Hu, D., Jin, D. Z., & Graybiel, A. M. (2005). Activity of striatal neurons reflects dynamic encoding and recoding of procedural memories. Nature, 437(7062), 1158–1161. **394** Gabrieli, J.D.E., Fleischman, D. A., Keane, M. M., Reminger, S.L., & Morrell, F. (1995). Double dissociation between memory systems underlying explicit and implicit memory in the human brain. Psychological Science, 6, 76,82 **396 both** Corkin et al., H.M.'s medial temporal lobe lesion: Findings from magnetic resonance imaging, The Journal of Neuroscience 17: 3964–3979, Copyright © 1997 Society of Neuroscience. **398 all** Courtesy of Professor David Amaral **403 all** Paller, K. A., & Wagner, A. D. (2002) Observing the transformation of experience into memory. Trends in cognitive sciences, 6(2), 93–102. **404 all** Eldridge et al. (2000) Remembering episode: a selective role for the hippocampus during retrieval. Nature Neuroscience, (3) 11:1149–52. Copyright © 2000, Rights Managed by Nature Publishing Group. **406 all top** Ranganath et. al. (2004) Dissociable correlates of recollection and familiarity within the medial temporal lobes Neuropsychologia, Vol. 42, 2,13. Copyright © 2004, Elsevier 2004. **408 all** Eichenbaum et al. (2007) The Medial Temporal Lobe and Recognition Memory. Vol. 30 CoAnnual Review of Neuroscience, Volume 30 © 2007 by Annual Reviews. **409 all** Hannula et al. Worth a glance: using eye movements to investigate the cognitive neuroscience of memory. Frontiers in Human Neuroscience. 4: 1–16. © 2010 Hannula, Althoff, Warren, Riggs, Cohen and Ryan. **410 all** Wheeler et al. Memory's echo: Vivid remembering reactivates sensory-specific cortex, Proceedings of the National Academy of Sciences, © September 26, © (2000) vol. 97, no. 20, 11125–11129 **411 both top** Wade, K. A., Garry, M., Read, J. D., & Lindsay, D. S. (2002). A picture is worth a thousand lies: Using false photographs to create false childhood memories. Psychonomic Bulletin & Review, 9(3), 597–603. **412 all** Kelley, W. M., Miezin, F. M., McDermott, K. B., Buckner, R. L., Raichle, M. E.,

Cohen, N. J., & Petersen, S. E. (1998). Hemispheric specialization in human dorsal frontal cortex and medial temporal lobe for verbal and nonverbal memory encoding. Neuron, 20(5), 927–936. **426 bottom all** Ranganath et. al. (2004) Dissociable correlates of recollection and familiarity within the medial temporal lobes Neuropsychologia, Vol. 42, 2,13. Copyright © 2004, Elsevier.

Drawn art: Figure 9.11 a–b: Barnes, T. D., Kubota, Y., Hu, D., Jin, D. Z., & Graybiel, A. M., Figure 1 b-c from "Activity of striatal neurons reflects dynamic encoding and recoding of procedural memories," *Nature*, 2005, *437*(7062), 1158–1161. Reprinted by permission from Macmillan Publishers Ltd, Copyright © 2005, Nature Publishing Group. **Figure 9.12 b–c:** Gabrieli, J. D. E., et al., Figure 2 from "Double dissociation between memory systems underlying explicit and implicit memory in the human brain," *Psychological Science*, *6*, 76–82. Copyright 1995 Sage Publications. Reprinted by permission of Association for Psychological Science. **Figure 9.23:** Reprinted from *Trends in Cognitive Sciences*, *6*(2), Paller, K. A., & Wagner, A. D., "Observing the transformation of experience into memory," 93–102, Copyright © Elsevier Ltd. (2018), with permission from Elsevier. **Figure 9.24 b:** Eldridge, L. L.; Knowlton, B. J.; Furmanski, C. S.; Bookheimer, S. Y.; and Engel, S. A., Figure 1b from "Remembering episodes: a selective role for the hippocampus during retrieval," *Nature neuroscience*, 2000, *3*(11), 1149–1152. Reprinted by permission from Macmillan Publishers Ltd, Copyright © 2000, Nature Publishing Group. **Figure 9.25 a–b:** Reprinted from *Neuropsychologia*, *42*(1), Ranganath, et al., "Dissociable correlates of recollection and familiarity within the medial temporal lobes," 2–13. Copyright © Elsevier Ltd. (2003), with permission from Elsevier. **Figure 9.33 a:** Reprinted from *Neuroimage*, *59*(3), Dennis, N. A., Bowman, C. R., & Vandekar, S. N., "True and phantom recollection: an fMRI investigation of similar and distinct neural correlates and connectivity," 2982–2993, Copyright © Elsevier Inc. (2012), with permission from Elsevier. **Figure 9.33 b:** Reprinted from *Neuropsychologia*, *81*, Kurkela, K. A., & Dennis, N. A., "Event-related fMRI studies of false memory: An Activation Likelihood Estimation meta-analysis," 149–167, Copyright © Elsevier Ltd. (2015), with permission from Elsevier. **Figure 9.37 a–d:** Reprinted from *Neuropsychologia*, *51*(6), Jaeger, A., Konkel, A., & Dobbins, I. G., "Unexpected novelty and familiarity orienting responses in lateral parietal cortex during recognition judgment," 1061–1076, Copyright © Elsevier Ltd. (2013), with permission from Elsevier.

CHAPTER 10

Photos: 426 Tim Shaffer/Reuters **428 all** Adolphs et. al. (1995) Fear and the Human Amygdala. The Journal of Neuroscience, 15 (9):5878–5891. Copyright © Society for Neuroscience **433** Adolphs et. al. (1995) Fear and the Human Amygdala. The Journal of Neuroscience, 15 (9):5878–5891. Copyright © Society for Neuroscience **434 both** Satpute, A. B., et al. (2013). Identification of discrete functional subregions of the human periaqueductal gray. PNAS, 110(42), 17101–17106. **436 top all** Anderson, D. J., & Adolphs, R. (2014). A Framework for Studying Emotions across Species. Cell, 157, 187–200. **436 bottom** Wikimedia Commons **437 all** Copyright 2017 Paul Ekman Group LLC. All rights reserved. **438 both** Photos reproduced with permission © 2004, Bob Willingham. Tracy JL and Matsumoto D. 2008. The spontaneous expression of pride and shame: Evidence for biologically innate nonverbal displays. PNAS 105:11655–1660. **449** Anderson et al. (2001) Lesions of the human amygdala impair enhanced perception of emotionally salient events. Nature; May 17; 41:305–309; Copyright © 2001, Rights Managed by Nature Publishing Group. **451** Phelps et al. (2001). Activation of the left amygdala to a cognitive representation of fear. Nature Neuroscience, 4, 437–41. © 2001 Rights Managed by Nature Publishing Group. **460 all** Adolphs et al. (2005). A mechanism for impaired fear recognition after amygdala damage. Nature; January 6; 433:68–72; Copyright © 2005, Rights Managed by Nature Publishing Group. **461 both** Whalen, et. al. 2004 Human Amygdala Responsivity to Masked Fearful Eye Whites. Science Vol. 306, p. 2061. Copyright © 2004, AAAS. **463 all** Cunningham et al., (2004). Separable neural components in the processing of Black and White Faces. Psychological Science, 15, 806–813. Copyright © 2004, Association for Psychological Science **464 all** Said et al. (2010). The amygdala and FFA track both social and non-social face dimensions. Neuropsychologia, 48, 3596–3605. © 2010 Elsevier. **467 top all** Habel et al. May 2005. Same or different? Neural correlates of happy and sad mood in healthy males. NeuroImage 26(1):206–214. © 2005 Elsevier. **467 bottom all** Ortigue et al. (2010a). Neuroimaging of Love: fMRI Meta-analysis Evidence toward New Perspectives in Sexual Medicine. Journal of Sexual Medicine, 7 (11), 3541–3552. doi: 10.1111/j.1743-6109.2010.01999.x. © 2010 International Society for Sexual Medicine **468 both** Ortigue et al. (2010a). Neuroimaging of Love: fMRI Meta-analysis Evidence toward New Perspectives in Sexual Medicine. Journal of Sexual Medicine, 7 (11), 3541–3552. DOI: 10.1111/j.1743-6109.2010.01999.x. © 2010 International Society for Sexual Medicine **471 all** Ochsner et al. (2004). For better or for worse: Neural systems supporting the cognitive down- and up-regulation of negative emotion. NeuroImage, 23, 483–499. © 2004 Elsevier, Inc. All rights reserved.

Drawn art: Figure 10.8: Tracy, J. & Matsumoto, D. (2008), Figures 1 and 2 from "The spontaneous expression of pride and shame: Evidence for biologically innate nonverbal displays." *Proceedings of the National Academy of Science USA*, *105*, 11655–11660. Reprinted with permission. **Figure 10.16 a–c:** Dunsmoor, J. E., Kragel, P. A., Martin, A., & LaBar, K. S., "Aversive learning modulates cortical representations of object categories," *Cerebral Cortex*, 2013, *24*(11), 2859–2872, by permission of Oxford University Press. **Figure 10.17 a:** Schwabe, L., & Wolf, O. T., Figure 1 from "Timing matters: temporal dynamics of stress effects on memory retrieval." *Cognitive, Affective, & Behavioral Neuroscience*, 2014, *14*(3), 1041–1048. Reprinted by permission of Springer Science + Business Media. **Figure 10.19:** Lerner, J. S., Small, D. A., & Loewenstein, G., Figure 2 from "Heart strings and purse strings carryover effects of emotions on economic decision," *Psychological Science*, *15*(5), 337–341. Copyright 2004 Sage Publications. Reprinted by permission of Association for Psychological Science. **Figure 10.28:** Ochsner, K., Silvers, J., & Buhle, J. T. (2012). Figure 2a from "Functional imaging studies of emotion regulation: a synthetic review and evolving model of the cognitive control of emotion." *Annals of the New York Academy of Sciences*, *1251*(1), E1–E24, March. Copyright © 2012 The New York Academy of Sciences. Reprinted with permission of The New York Academy of Sciences. **Figure 10.29:** Gross, J., Figure 1 from "Antecedent- and response-focused emotion regulation: Divergent consequences for experience, expression, and physiology." *Journal of Personality and Social Psychology*, *74*, 224–237. Reprinted by permission of the American Psychological Association.

CHAPTER 11

Photos: 474 Colin Hawkins/cultura/Corbis **480** Courtesy Musée Depuytren, Paris **485 all** Huth, A. G., de Heer, W. A., Griffiths, T. L., Theunissen, F. E., & Gallant, J. L. (2016). Natural speech reveals the semantic maps that tile human cerebral cortex. Nature, 532(7600), 453–458. **493** Bonilha, L., Hillis, A. E., Hickok, G., den Ouden, D. B., Rorden, C., & Fridriksson, J. (2017). Temporal lobe networks supporting the comprehension of spoken words. Brain, 140(9), 2370–2380. **495 bottom** Caplan et al, 2000. Activation of Broca's area by syntactic processing under conditions of concurrent articulation, Human Brain Mapping. Copyright © 2000 Wiley-Liss, Inc. **495 top all** Puce et al. Differential sensitivity of human visual cortex to faces, letterstrings, and textures: A functional magnetic resonance imaging study, Journal of Neuroscience 16 (1996) Copyright © 2013 by the Society for Neuroscience **496 all** Bouhali, F., de Schotten, M. T.,

Pinel, P., Poupon, C., Mangin, J. F., Dehaene, S., & Cohen, L. (2014). Anatomical connections of the visual word form area. Journal of Neuroscience, 34(46), 15402–15414. **503 all** Courtesy of Nina Dronkers **509 left** Great Ape Trust of Iowa **509 right** Great Ape Trust of Iowa **511 all** Rilling, J. K., Glasser, M. F., Preuss, T. M., Ma, X., Zhao, T., Hu, X., & Behrens, T. E. (2008). The evolution of the arcuate fasciculus revealed with comparative DTI. Nature neuroscience, 11(4), 426.

Drawn art: Figure 11.8 a–b: "Conceptual structure: Towards an integrated neurocognitive account," Kirsten I. Taylor, Barry J. Devereux & Lorraine K. Tyler, *Language and Cognitive Processes*, 26 July 2011, *26*(9), 1368–1401, reprinted by permission of the publisher (Taylor & Francis Ltd., http://www.tandfonline.com/). **Figure 11.9:** Taylor, K. I., Moss, H. E. & Tyler, L. K. (2007). Figure from "The conceptual structure account: A cognitive model of semantic memory and its neural instantiation." J. Hart & M. Kraut (eds.), *The Neural Basis of Semantic Memory*. Cambridge: Cambridge University Press. pp. 265–301. Reprinted with permission. **Figure 11.16:** McClelland, James L., David E. Rumelhart, and PDP Research Group, *Parallel Distributed Processing, Volume 2: Explorations in the Microstructure of Cognition: Psychological and Biological Models*, figure: "Fragment of a Connectionist Network for Letter Recognition," © 1986 Massachusetts Institute of Technology, by permission of The MIT Press. **Figure 11.22 a–b:** Republished with permission of MIT Press, from "Dissociation of Brain Activity Related to Syntactic and Semantic Aspects of Language," Munte, Heinze and Mangun, *Journal of Cognitive Neuroscience*, 5(3), 1993; permission conveyed through Copyright Clearance Center, Inc. **Figure 11.26:** Reprinted from *Trends in Cognitive Science*, *16*(5), Robert C. Berwick, Angela D. Friederici, Noam Chomsky, Johan J. Bolhuis, "Evolution, brain, and the nature of language," 262–268. Copyright © Elsevier Ltd. (2012), with permission from Elsevier. **Figure 11.28:** Hickok, G. (2012). Figure 4 from "Computational neuroanatomy of speech production," *Nature Reviews Neuroscience*, *13*(2), 135–145. Reprinted by permission from Macmillan Publishers Ltd, Copyright © 2011, Nature Publishing Group. **Figure 11.30 a–c:** Rilling, J. K., Glasser, M. F., Preuss, T. M., Ma, X., Zhao, T., Hu, X., & Behrens, T. E. (2008). Figures 1 and 2b from "The evolution of the arcuate fasciculus revealed with comparative DTI," *Nature neuroscience*, *11*(4), 426. Reprinted by permission from Macmillan Publishers Ltd, Copyright © 2008, Nature Publishing Group.

CHAPTER 12

Photos: 514 Randy Faris/Getty Images **524 all** Druzgal et al. (2003) Dissecting Contributions of Prefrontal Cortex and Fusiform Face, Journal of Cognitive Neuroscience, Vol. 15, No. 6. Copyright © 2003, Massachusetts Institute of Technology. **525 bottom all** Koechlin et al. (2003) The Architecture of Cognitive Control in the Human Prefrontal Cortex, Science, Vol. 302. no. 5648, pp. 1181–1185. Copyright © 2003 AAAS. **526 left all** Cohen, J. R., & D'Esposito, M. (2016). The segregation and integration of distinct brain networks and their relationship to cognition. Journal of Neuroscience, 36(48), 12083–12094. **529** Kennerley et al. (2009). Neurons in the frontal lobe encode the value of multiple decision variables. Journal of Cognitive Neuroscience, 21(6): 1162–1178. © 2009, Massachusetts Institute of Technology **530** Sellitto, M., Ciaramelli, E., & di Pellegrino, G. (2010). Myopic discounting of future rewards after medial orbitofrontal damage in humans. Journal of Neuroscience, 30(49), 16429–16436. **531 both** Hare et al. (2009) Self-control in decision-making involves modulation of the vmPFC valuation system. Science, 324, 646–648. © 2009, American Association for the Advancement of Science **533** Shenhav, A., & Buckner, R. L. (2014). Neural correlates of dueling affective reactions to win-win choices. PNAS, 111(30), 10978–10983. **537** Seymour et al. (2007). Differential encoding of losses and gains in the human striatum. Journal of Neuroscience 27(18) 4826–4831. © Society for Neuroscience. **541** Thompson-Schill et al., (1997) Role of left interior prefrontal cortex in retrieval of semantic knowledge: A reevaluation, PNAS. 94: 14792–14797. **547 top all** Adam Gazzaley, et al. Age-related top-down suppression deficit in the early stages of cortical visual memory processing. PNAS September 2, 2008. 105 (35) 13122–13126 **550** Courtesy David Flitney, Oxford University **553** Anguera, J. A., Boccanfuso, J., Rintoul, J. L., Al-Hashimi, O., Faraji, F., Janowich, J., & Gazzaley, A. (2013). Video game training enhances cognitive control in older adults. Nature, 501(7465), 97–101.

Drawn art: Figure 12.6 b–c: Republished with permission of MIT Press, from "Dissecting contributions of prefrontal cortex and fusiform face area to face working memory," Druzgal, T. J., & D'Esposito, M., *Journal of Cognitive Neuroscience*, *15*(6), 2003; permission conveyed through Copyright Clearance Center, Inc. **Figure 12.15 a–b:** Shenhav, A., & Buckner, R. L., Figures 1 and 2 from "Neural correlates of dueling affective reactions to win–win choices," *Proceedings of the National Academy of Sciences*, *111*(30), 10978–10983. Reprinted with permission. **Figure 12.16 a–c:** From Schultz, W.; Dayan, P.; Read Montague, P. (2003), "A Neural Substrate of Prediction and Reward," *Science*, *275*(5306), 1593–1599. Reprinted with permission from AAAS. **Figure 12.17 a–c:** Eshel, N., Bukwich, M., Rao, V., Hemmelder, V., Tian, J., & Uchida, N. (2008). Figure 3 b-d from "Arithmetic and local circuitry underlying dopamine prediction errors," *Nature*, *525*(7568), 243. Reprinted by permission from Macmillan Publishers Ltd, Copyright © 2008, Nature Publishing Group. **Figure 12.24 a–c:** Reprinted from *Neuron*, *63*, Dux, P.E., Tombu, M.N., Harrison, S., Rogers, B.P., Tong, F., & Marois, R., "Training improves multitasking performance by increasing the speed of information processing in human prefrontal cortex," 127–138, Copyright © Elsevier Inc. (2009), with permission from Elsevier. **Figure 12.28 a–b:** Zanto, T. P., Rubens, M. T., Thangavel, A., & Gazzaley, A. (2011). Figure 3a and 4 a and b from "Causal role of the prefrontal cortex in goal-based modulation of visual processing and working." *Nature Neuroscience*, 14(5) 656–663. Reprinted by permission from Macmillan Publishers Ltd, Copyright © 2011, Nature Publishing Group. **Figure 12.30 a–b:** From Frank, M. J., Samanta, J., Moustafa, A. A., & Sherman, S. J. (2007). "Hold your horses: Impulsivity, deep brain stimulation, and medication in parkinsonism," *Science*, *318*, 1309–1312. Reprinted with permission from AAAS. **Figure 12.31:** Dye, M. W., Green, C. S., & Bavelier, D., Figure 1 from "Increasing speed of processing with action video games," *Current Directions in Psychological Science*, *18*(6), 321–326. Copyright 2009 Sage Publications. Reprinted by permission of Association for Psychological Science. **Figure 12.32 a–b:** Anguera, J. A., Boccanfuso, J., Rintoul, J. L., Al-Hashimi, O., Faraji, F., Janowich, J., et al. (2013). Figure 2 from "Video game training enhances cognitive control in older adults," *Nature*, *501*(7465), 97–101. Reprinted by permission from Macmillan Publishers Ltd, Copyright © 2013, Nature Publishing Group. **Figure 12.33 a–b:** Reprinted from *Acta psychologica*, *140*(1), Strobach, T., Frensch, P. A., & Schubert, T., "Video game practice optimizes executive control skills in dual-task and task switching situations," 13–24, Copyright © Elsevier B. V. (2012), with permission from Elsevier. **Figure 12.38 a–b:** Republished with permission of Society for Neuroscience, from "The processing of unexpected positive response outcomes in the mediofrontal cortex," Ferdinand, N. K., Mecklinger, A., Kray, J., & Gehring, W. J., *Journal of Neuroscience*, *32*(35), 2012; permission conveyed through Copyright Clearance Center, Inc. **Figure 12.40 a:** Reprinted from *Neuron*, *89*(3), Purcell, B. A., & Kiani, R., "Neural mechanisms of post-error adjustments of decision policy in parietal cortex," 658–671, Copyright © Elsevier Inc. (2016), with permission from Elsevier. **Figure 12.41:** Shenhav, A., Cohen, J. D., & Botvinick, M. M. (2016). Figure 1 from "Dorsal anterior cingulate cortex and the value of control," *Nature neuroscience*, *19*(10), 1286–1291. Reprinted by permission from Macmillan Publishers Ltd. Copyright © 2016 Nature Publishing Group.

CHAPTER 13

Photos: 566 Caiaimage/Paul Bradbury/Getty Images **568** Damasio et. al. (1994). The Return of Phineas Gage: Clues about the brain from the skull of a famous patient. Science Vol. 264. No. 5162, pp. 1102–1105. Copyright © 1994, AAAS. **573** Kelley et al. (2002). Finding the self? An event-related fMRI study. Journal of Cognitive Neuroscience, 14, 785, 794. Copyright © 2002, Massachusetts Institute of Technology. **576 bottom all** Debra A. Gusnard, and Marcus E. Raichle, (2001). Searching for a baseline: functional imaging and the resting human brain. National Reviews Neuroscience. 2(10):685, 694. © 2001 Rights Managed by Nature Publishing Group. **580** Blanke O., et al. (2002) Neuropsychology: Stimulating illusory own-body perceptions. Nature, 419, 269–270. **581 all** Blanke, O., & Metzinger, T. (2009). Full-body illusions and minimal phenomenal selfhood. Trends in cognitive sciences, 13(1), 7–13. **583 bottom all** Hilti, L. M., et al. (2013). The desire for healthy limb amputation: structural brain correlates and clinical features of xenomelia. Brain, 136(1), 318–329. **583 top both** McGeoch, P. D., et al. (2011). Xenomelia: a new right parietal lobe syndrome. Journal of Neurology, Neurosurgery & Psychiatry. **590 top all** Michael, J., et al. (2014). Continuous theta-burst stimulation demonstrates a causal role of premotor homunculus in action understanding. Psychological Science, 25(4), 963–972 **591 all** Phillips et al. (1997) A specific neural substrate for perceiving facial expressions of disgust. Nature; October 2; 389:495, 498. Copyright © 1997, Rights Managed by Nature Publishing Group. **597 both** Mitchell et al. (2004) Encoding-Specific Effects of Social Cognition on the Neural Correlates of Subsequent Memory. The Journal of Neuroscience, 24(21): 4912, 4917. Copyright © 2004, Society for Neuroscience **598** Saxe et al. (2006). It's the Thought That Counts: Specific Brain Regions for One Component of Theory of Mind, Psychological Science 17 (8), 692, 699. Copyright © 2006, Association for Psychological Science **600 all** Pelphrey et al. (2006). Brain Mechanisms for interpreting the actions of others from Biological-Motion Cues. Current Directions in Psychological Science. June vol. 15 no. 3 136–140. Copyright © 2006, APS. **602** Catani, M., et al. (2016). Frontal networks in adults with autism spectrum disorder. Brain, 139(2), 616 630. **604 all** Kennedy, D. P., et al. (2006). Failing to deactivate: Resting functional abnormalities in autism. Proceedings of the National Academy of Sciences, 103, 8275–8280. Fig 1 **605 all** Kennedy, D. P., & Courchesne, E. (2008). Functional abnormalities of the default network during self-and other-reflection in autism. Social Cognitive and Affective Neuroscience, 3, 177–190. **610 right, all** Beer et al., (2003) The Regulatory Function of Self-Conscious Emotion: Insights From Patients With Orbitofrontal Damage. Journal of Personality and Social Psychology, 85, (4) 594–604. Copyright © 2003 by the APA. **610 left** Jennifer S. Beer (2007). The default self: feeling good or being right? Trends in Cognitive Sciences, Volume 11, Issue 5, Pages 187–189. Copyright © 2007, Elsevier 2007. **612 all** Grossman et al. (2010). The role of ventral medial prefrontal cortex in social decisions: Converging evidence from fMRI and frontotemporal lobar degeneration. Neuropsychologia, 48, 3505–3512. Copyright © 2010, Elsevier.

Drawn art: Figure 13.15 b: Michael, J., Sandberg, K., Skewes, J., Wolf, T., Blicher, J., Overgaard, M., & Frith, C. D., (2014). Figure 3 from "Continuous theta-burst stimulation demonstrates a causal role of premotor homunculus in action understanding," *Psychological Science, 25*(4), 963–972. https://doi.org/10.1177%2F0956797613520608. Copyright © 2014 Sage Publications. Distributed under the terms of the Creative Commons Attribution License (CC BY 3.0). https://creativecommons.org/licenses/by/3.0/. **Figure 13.19:** Cikara, M., Botvinick, M.M., & Fiske, S.T. (2011). Figure 2 from "Us Versus Them: Social Identity Shapes Neural Responses to Intergroup Competition and Harm." *Psychological Science*, 22 (3), 306–313. Copyright © 2011 by Association for Psychological Science. Reprinted with permission. **Figure 13.21 a–b:** Cikara, M., Botvinick, M.M., & Fiske, S.T. (2011). Figure 4 from "Us Versus Them: Social Identity Shapes Neural Responses to Intergroup Competition and Harm." *Psychological Science*, 22 (3), 306–313. Copyright © 2011 by Association for Psychological Science. Reprinted with permission. **Figure 13.28:** Cattaneo, et al., Figure 1 from "Impairment of actions chains in autism and its possible role in intention understanding." *Proceedings of the National Academy of Science USA., 104*, 17825–17830. Reprinted with permission.

CHAPTER 14

Photos: 618 Eric Tam/Getty Images **624 right, all** Monti, M. M., et al. (2010). Willful modulation of brain activity in disorders of consciousness. New England Journal of Medicine, 362, 579–589 **624 left, all** Owen, A. M., et al. (2006). Detecting awareness in the vegetative state. Science, 313, 1402. **625 right** © Estate Jeanloup Sieff **625 left** Paul Cooper/REX/Shutterstock **627 all** Mahowald, M. W., & Schenck, C. H. (2005). Insights from studying human sleep disorders. Nature, 437(7063), 1279. **627 top right** T. E., Arrigoni, E., & Lipton, J. O. (2017). Neural circuitry of wakefulness and sleep. Neuron, 93(4), 747–765. **628 all** Bassetti, C., Vella, S., Donati, F., Wielepp, P., & Weder, B. (2000). SPECT during sleepwalking. The Lancet, 356(9228), 484–485. **633** Michele Rucci/Active Perception Lab **644 all** Stephens, G. J., Silbert, L. J., & Hasson, U. (2010). Speaker-listener neural coupling underlies successful communication. Proceedings of the National Academy of Sciences, 107(32), 14425–14430. **646 bottom left** Fahroni/Getty Images **646 top left** Hunt, G. R., Lambert, C., & Gray, R. D. (2007). Cognitive requirements for tool use by New Caledonian crows (Corvus moneduloides). New Zealand Journal of Zoology, 34(1), 1–7. **646 right, all** Povinelli, D.J., et al. (1993) Self-recognition ion chimpanzees (Pan troglodytes): Distribution, ontogeny, and patterns of emergence. Journal of Comparative Psychology. 107:347–372. Photo © Daniel Povinelli **650** Paul Ehrenfest/Wikimedia Commons **653 bottom, both** Merker, B. (2007). Consciousness without a cerebral cortex. Behavioural and brain sciences, (30)1, 63–134. **653 top left, both** Strausfeld, N. J., & Hirth, F. (2013). Deep homology of arthropod central complex and vertebrate basal ganglia. Science, 340(6129), 157–161.

Drawn art: Figure 14.6: Reprinted from *Frontiers in Genetics, 93*(4), Scammell, T. E., Arrigoni, E., & Lipton, J. O., "Neural circuitry of wakefulness and sleep," 747–765, Copyright © Elsevier Ltd. (2017), reprinted with permission from Elsevier. **Figure 14.9:** Boucher, B. & Jenna, S. (2013). Figure 2 from "Genetic interaction networks: better understand to better predict," *Frontiers in genetics*, 17 December 2013. https://doi.org/10.3389/fgene.2013.00290. Copyright © 2013 Boucher and Jenna. Distributed under the terms of the Creative Commons Attribution License (CC BY 3.0). https://creativecommons.org/licenses/by/3.0/. **Figure 14.12 a–b:** Prinz, A.A., Bucher, D., & Marder, E. (2004). Figure 5 from "Similar network activity from disparate circuit parameters." *Nature Neuroscience*, 7(12), 1345–1352. Reprinted by permission from Macmillan Publishers Ltd, Copyright © 2011, Nature Publishing Group. **Figure 14.15 a:** From Fendrich, R., Wessinger, C. M., & Gazzaniga, M.S. (1992). "Residual vision in a scotoma: implications for blindsight," *Science, 258*(5087), 1489–91. Reprinted with permission from AAAS. **Figure 14.23:** Libet, B. (1999). Figure 1.3 from "Do we have free will?" *Journal of Consciousness Studies, 6*(8–9), 47–57. Copyright © 1999 Imprint Academic. Reprinted with permission. **Figure 14.29:** From Strausfeld, N. J., & Hirth, F. (2013). Figure 2 from "Deep homology of arthropod central complex and vertebrate basal ganglia," *Science, 340*(6129), 157–161. Reprinted with permission from AAAS.

Index

B

D

F

G

H

M

Q

R

S

T

W

X

Y

Z